National Employment Screening Services

TULSA, OKLAHOMA

The Guide
To Background Investigations

A comprehensive source directory
for employee screening.

FIFTH EDITION

National Employment Screening Services makes no representation that the contents of this publication are absolutely accurate or complete. Errors and omissions, whether typographical, clerical or otherwise, do sometimes occur and may occur anywhere within the body of this publication. National Employment Screening Services does not assume and hereby disclaims any liability to any party for any loss or damage arising in any way from errors or omissions herein, whether such errors or omissions result from negligence, accident or any other cause.

The dissemination and use of some information available through sources described in the publication are subject to state and/or federal regulation. This publication is sold subject to the condition that the contents hereof shall be used by the purchaser in accordance with applicable state and federal laws and requirements. National Employment Screening Services cannot guarantee that readers will be able to obtain any particular record from any source listed herein or that such records may be lawfully used for employment screening, background investigations or any other purpose. National Employment Screening Services cannot assume and hereby disclaims any liability to any party for any loss or damage arising in any way from the use of this publication or any information obtained from any source contained herein.

ISSN 0897-3156
ISBN 0-941233-52-9

Printed in the United States of America by National Employment Screening Services.

All correspondence and inquiries should be directed to National Employment Screening Services, 8801 S. Yale, Tulsa, Oklahoma 74137.

CONTENTS

PREFACE TO THE FIFTH EDITION

The GUIDE TO BACKGROUND INVESTIGATIONS has undergone quite a transformation since the inaugural edition appeared in 1987.

Originally entitled the NATIONAL EMPLOYMENT SCREENING DIRECTORY, the first slim volume contained only 320 pages. Readers were given four sub-directories covering, respectively, worker's compensation records, driving records, state criminal records and educational records.

This fairly modest amount of information actually represented a huge advance in the field of employment screening. For the first time, employers had a resource that pointed them to inexpensive public records that could significantly enhance their employment screening efforts.

PROGRESS.

What that first edition did, it did well. However, it quickly became apparent that a few basic changes could make the publication even more valuable.

In the years since 1987, entirely new record sources have been added. Vital statistics, federal criminal, civil and bankruptcy repositories made their way into the *Second Edition*. Misdemeanor criminal record repositories and the eleven regional Federal Record Centers were made a part of the *Third Edition*. Medical licensing boards, teacher certifications and incorporations enhanced the *Fourth Edition*. And, with this edition civil court record repositories, bar associations, accountancy boards, securities commissions, state maps with county borders, airmen certificates, aircraft registry and Canadian driving records have been included.

Some sources that were in the original volume have been so improved as to constitute essentially a new reservoir of information. The educational records section, for example, which began as essentially a list of the name, address and telephone number for some 3000 U.S. post-secondary programs has expanded dramatically. Readers are now given the specific procedures which each institution uses to verify degrees and/or attendance for employers.

And, organizational changes have also been made to enhance the utility of the GUIDE. Beginning with the *Second Edition*, records were grouped geographically, rather than by subject. No longer did an investigator have to flip back and forth between various sections of the book to find sources on a given individual. Everything for a given state was in one place. This format continues in the present volume.

ADDITIONS.

The *Fifth Edition* continues to build on the foundation laid by its four predecessors. Seven new record sources have been added:

State bar associations. Investigators wanting to confirm that an individual is authorized to practice law can do so in all fifty states. While the demand for this type of record by GUIDE users is not enormous, it warrants importance in the legal industry.

Accountancy board. Employers wanting to verify that an individual is actually registered as a Certified Public Accountant or merely wanting to see if their license has been revoked or suspended can contact the Accountancy board within each state.

Securities commission. This commission holds records pertaining to several types of licenses for selling securities, stocks and bonds. While at a glance this record's offering seems small, it actually offers additional clarifying information. The State

Records Directory explains in more detail how professionals can benefit by accessing this type of record.

Civil court records. Civil claims are easily accessible at the county level within each state. Employers may want to incorporate this type of record in their pre-employment screening process.

State maps. A separate maps section has been included showing each state's county borders. This section will be helpful for all GUIDE users.

Federal Aviation Adminisration. This nation-wide repository holds airmen certification and aircraft registry records for the entire United States.

Canada driving records. Companies with branch offices in Canada can tap into a valuable source of information. Employers can check driving records in all ten provinces and two territories.

Each edition of the GUIDE also seeks to cut back on information which has proved to not be widely used. Thus, the *Fourth Edition* dropped the Legislative Update section included in the *Third Edition.* Ongoing research has shown that the record repositories appear to be the real attraction to users.

OUR MISSION.

National Employment Screening Services is committed to providing publications and products that will enable security and personnel professionals to do their job more effectively, for less money, in less time. Whether you are new to the GUIDE or are a long time customer we believe you will find the *Fifth Edition* to be another significant step toward that goal.

We value and solicit users' thoughts and suggestions. For your convenience, at the end of the GUIDE, you will find a postage prepaid reply card which you can use to jot down your comments for NESS. If you or your associates need additional copies of the GUIDE, order cards are also available on this page. If you have questions about the GUIDE or would like information about volume purchase discounts, feel free to contact NESS at 1-800-247-8713.

INTRODUCTION

The process of selecting a particular individual for a particular job cannot be reduced to a formula. It requires the unique skill and judgment of a professional who knows and utilizes the appropriate resources.

THE GUIDE TO BACKGROUND INVESTIGATIONS is one of these resources. Since its inception, the GUIDE has tried to show the value and insure the availability of public and quasi-public records as an employment screening tool. The *Fifth Edition* continues to pursue this goal.

WHY BACKGROUND INVESTIGATIONS?

It is no secret that many, if not most, employers give little attention to pre-employment background investigations. The focus, instead, is placed on applications, interviews, resumes, skills tests and other "traditional" screening techniques.

However, there are at least five separate reasons why background investigations should be added to the professional's standard practices:

1. Input.
We are all products of our past. The collection of experiences—good and bad—that define our past doesn't necessarily determine our future. But background does clearly influence what a person can and will become.

Thus, an employer who is interviewing applicants for employment has an obvious need to know fundamental facts in the individuals' background that may play a role in their future. The professional's goal is to find the persons who will be best suited emotionally, temperamentally and skill-wise for the jobs the company offers. That takes input from a variety of sources, including background investigations.

2. "Negligent Hiring."
The second reason employee screening is so important is the real threat of liability employers now face under the legal doctrine of "negligent hiring."

Courts are now accepting the premise that some facts in an employees' background should disqualify them for a given position. A driver with a long history of recklessness behind the wheel, a salesperson with a background of violent assault, a bookkeeper with a record of theft, for example.

If the employee causes a foreseeable injury to a third party and the court determines that the employer's failure to detect or heed the warning signs was unreasonable, the company may well be held liable for damages. Since this risk cannot easily be quantified, employers are well advised to exercise the utmost care in the investigation and selection of all employees.

3. Demise of "Employment at Will."
The formerly universal notion that employers could hire and fire whomever they wanted whenever they wanted is slowly eroding.

Different states are proceeding down this path at varying rates of speed. Some have drawn their exceptions to "employment at will" fairly narrowly—for example, prohibiting dismissals when an employee misses work to serve on a jury.

More protective states go much further. The most restrictive states actually require that a worker cannot be dismissed without a showing of clear and just cause. The employer must document the reasons behind all dismissals to show that there was an adequate basis for the action.

Employee-initiated lawsuits for "wrongful discharge" are even more common than those for negligent hiring. And one study showed that claimants win two thirds of the cases that go to trial, with an average jury award of over $600,000. Careful pre-employment screening will reduce the risk of many wrongful discharge problems later.

4. Technology.

Explosive technological advances in the workplace increase the dangers of unqualified or unethical workers. With personal computers now as powerful as mainframes of a few years ago and networks linking their memories and databases together, those who are inclined to steal have the potential to do more damage than ever before.

Sound background investigations will ferret out many high risk candidates.

5. Exaggerated Credentials.

Many observers say that falsification or exaggeration of credentials on resumes and employment applications is at an all-time high.

An employee who comes into a job under false pretenses is the wrong person in the wrong job. The falsification suggests a dangerous character defect that could resurface in another context later on. The lack of appropriate qualifications may also mean that the individual is not objectively competent for the task. Neither is a problem the company can or should ignore.

THE NEED TO KNOW.

These and other facts have led to an inescapable conclusion – employers simply have to know who they are hiring before they hire them. The risks otherwise are just too great.

Possible Solutions.

How can pre-employment background screening be handled? There are only two basic alternatives.

Some companies retain an outside service bureau to conduct background checks on a fee basis. The employer submits required identifiers on the applicants and the service bureau searches specified source materials.

A variety of tools may be utilized, depending on the quality of the bureau, the needs of the employer and the fee that is being paid. Previous places of employment, educational records, references and criminal records are usually at the top of the list.

The service bureau approach is not without problems. The quality of these investigations varies widely, from highly professional and complete to amateurish and unreliable. Just as important from the employer's perspective, climbing rates have made many of the best bureaus prohibitively expensive.

The alternative, of course, is "do-it-yourself" screening. Here, too, however, employers encounter various practical problems. A sharp increase in defamation of character lawsuits has essentially stopped the flow of information from previous employers about an applicant's tenure and performance. Resumes and interviews are successful as employment screening devices only to the extent the applicant is both truthful and candid.

The Missing Link.

The dilemma is real. Security and human resource professionals have encountered an ever-increasing need for reliable sources of background data but a steadily dwindling ability to get it.

What has been needed is a mechanism that economically provides reliable and objective evidence that will help employers shape their assessments of applicants' background and potential. Ideally, the solution should give information on both character and competence.

ANSWERS THROUGH PUBLIC RECORDS.

Good service bureaus know that there is one additional source that can supply much of the data that employers need. This resource is the vast reservoir of governmentally created and held public records.

Hard facts in the public domain – criminal convictions, histories of alcohol or drug abuse and potentially threatening work-related injuries, among others – can dramatically increase the efficiency and effectiveness of any employer's background checks. And, best of all, public records are a truly independent source of information. Their use guarantees that an employer's success will not be solely dependent on the veracity of its applicants or the willingness of previous employers to talk.

Ironically, however, while professional service bureaus regularly tap these records, employers seldom do. Public records have in the past been little used in the course of most companies' employment screening efforts.

Utility vs. Availability.

Why the pervasive unwillingness of employers to use publicly held records as part of their standard investigative procedures? The problem has not been the utility of the records themselves. Few would argue that public records contain a wealth of potentially relevant information about employees and job applicants.

The impediments have been more practical than theoretical.

Simply determining the whereabouts of the records needed in a given case is the first hurdle. There is no national repository for worker's compensation claim histories, for example. Each state keeps its own records, each at a different location. Criminal records are an even more revealing example. Most of these files are maintained at the county level. Over 3000 different locations, each setting its own procedures on the release of information for employment or other purposes.

The mobility of our society, the maze of procedures and the sheer number of offices involved have made a systematic method of access nearly impossible. As a result, important records, purportedly "public" in nature, have not really been readily available at all.

The GUIDE is designed to eliminate many of the practical roadblocks to the use of public records. Human resource and security professionals will find in these pages over 10,000 sources nationwide for the types of records than can most aid their work.

The GUIDE is more than just a list of addresses and phone numbers. Users will see not only how to contact a given office but also the procedures, fees and logistics required for access in each of these offices.

SUMMARY OF CONTENTS.

If you used the *Fourth Edition* of the GUIDE, you will find the format of the *Fifth Edition* familiar. Four main sub-directories form the bulk of the *Fifth Edition*:
*The State Records Directory
*The State Maps Directory
*The Federal Records Directory
*The Educational Records Directory
While this organizational scheme corresponds to the format used in the past editions, the content within each of these sections has been greatly enhanced and expanded.

1. State Records Directory.

This first of the major sub-directories in the GUIDE covers helpful records. Included are sources for criminal records, worker's compensation claim histories, driving records, vital statistics, departments of education, medical licensing boards and secretary of state. A handy city-county cross reference lets you locate the county that handles records for various municipalities in the state.

Each state section begins with a short narrative generally including statistical information on record accessibility in the state.

The narrative will also provide the state's information hot line number to enable users to quickly locate other offices or answer questions in unusual situations.

In addition, the *Fifth Edition* adds several new features to this section:

State Bar Association. GUIDE users who are interested in verifying the credentials of attorneys will find this addition of particular value. Each state listing shows what procedures must be followed to do so.

In some states membership into the bar association is automatic upon passing the bar exam, while in other states an attorney must decide whether or not to join the association.

Accountancy Boards. The procedures to verify CPA licenses in each of the states are another enhancement that will be helpful to particular users.

Securities Commission. Employers and investigators will find it easier to check the status of a licensed agent with this addition to the GUIDE. For each of the 50 states, the State Records Directory shows how to verify the qualifications for agents.

Civil Records. Following the criminal record information is civil court records. The GUIDE makes it simple to obtain civil court record information. Procedures for each county's civil division is explained in the GUIDE.

As is the case with all the GUIDE's sources, the repositories for these new records were directly contacted in each state.

2. State Maps Directory.

An entire section has been added for this new resource. The State Maps section groups all 50 states alphabetically and outlines every county border within the state.

An employer or investigator residing in the state of Nevada, for example, may need to perform a criminal or civil record check in Chelsea, Alabama. Using the city-county cross reference the investigator already knows that Chelsea is in Shelby county. After locating Shelby county on the map in Alabama, an investigator can quickly see the surrounding counties and may choose to contact those counties near Shelby.

This enhanceent of the GUIDE will give employers and others the option to perform a more thorough criminal or civil record check.

3. Federal Records Directory.

Data generated and maintained at the national level can also aid background checks. The *Federal Records Directory*, originally introduced in the *Second Edition* of the GUIDE, details record availability for the nation's ninety-three federal district courts. Also included are the eleven regional Federal Record Centers.

The *Federal Records Directory* shows how to obtain federal criminal conviction data, civil litigation records and bankruptcy filings in each of the districts. Each court's entry begins with a listing of the counties under its jurisdiction. Thus, when you know the locations with which an individual has had significant contacts, you can quickly determine which federal courts should be contacted during your investigation.

All of the over 300 offices included in this section have again been personally contacted to obtain accurate, current information on their procedures and policies.

4. Federal Aviation Administration.

This edition of the GUIDE contains data for confirming airmen certification and aircraft registry. Surprisingly, each has its own nation-wide repository.

The FAA will confirm airmen license, type of license, rating and more. The GUIDE lists the procedures.

The FAA also will confirm aircraft registry, date of registration, ownership and other vital information. Aircraft registered in the United States are assigned the letter "N" which precedes the registration number. This country code signifies that the aircraft is registered in the United States.

5. Canada Driving Records.

Recognized as a valuable tool, the GUIDE now gives information for obtaining driving records in Canada. Directions for each of Canada's ten provinces and two territories are detailed.

The cost for Canadian driving records is slightly higher than those in the United States. On the lower end of the scale a record check in Manitoba will cost CND$4 and on the higher end of the scale both Saskatchewan and Nova Scotia will charge CND$10.

Each of the provinces and territories' Motor Vehicle Division was contacted by phone to gather this information.

6. Educational Records Directory.

Education can reveal much about a person's initiative and abilities. With a minimum of interpretation, educational credentials can help an employer assess the suitability of an applicant for a given position.

Unfortunately, falsification and exaggeration of educational credentials are becoming disturbingly common. Resume "padding" has become epidemic in a number of professions and industries.

As a consequence, educational verification should be an important element in all background investigations. The *Educational Records Directory* includes procedures for confirming attendance and degrees as well as transcript release requirements at over 3000 institutions and programs.

All this information, of course, has been updated and amended for the *Fifth Edition*. Human resource and security professionals will find an extremely high level of cooperation from these institutions. Since the schools have a strong interest in helping their students and graduates attain employment, they will almost always release the necessary information to an employer. In fact, over 97% of the schools and programs reported to our interviewers that they will verify a student's degree and/or attendance for employers.

KEEPING CURRENT.

Updating information on the thousands of separate sources contained in the *State Records Directory* is no small task. But it is absolutely necessary. Without current data on the record repositories, background checks will suffer in terms of both efficiency and completeness.

An office that honored only mail requests last year may have added phone accessibility this year. An employer who is unaware of the new streamlined procedure, however, and continues to mail in search requests would lose valuable time. The opportunity to convert a week or ten days turnaround time into minutes would be missed.

A fee change could create similar problems. That $2 check you sent last year to another office may be returned with the record request unprocessed – because the office has upped its search fees to $3.

The listings in this edition represent the most up-to-date compilation of procedures and requirements available for each of the repositories. The updating process is a lengthy one. Each record repository which had previously appeared in the GUIDE was mailed a form to verify or correct its listing. Some 80% of the offices returned their responses by the deadline.

Those repositories which did not return their form in time were personally contacted on the phone by an NESS interviewer to verify or correct our information. Any questionable or unclear statements obtained either by mail or on the phone was flagged for a follow-up clarification call.

New offices making their first appearance in the GUIDE were all personally contacted by phone to insure that complete and accurate information was obtained for the initial listing.

As has been the case with each edition, the *Fifth Edition* includes literally thousands of changes in office locations, procedures, fees and record availability. More and more offices and colleges are adding FAX capabilities as a convenience to the public.

LIMITATIONS OF THE GUIDE.

During the lengthy data gathering process, controls and contacts were organized so that the information published for each office would be as current and accurate as possible.

As a result, users can expect that most of the data they find will be reliable. However, keep in mind the fact that the GUIDE is reporting not first-hand, but second-hand information. Each listing simply reflects what we were told. It is certain that in some limited number of cases we were given incomplete, misleading or even incorrect summaries of a given office's procedures.

Users should remember another fact as well. The information reported in the GUIDE is itself inherently changeable. During the life span of this edition, many offices can be expected to make minor or even major modifications to their procedures for record access.

That is the reason updated editions of the GUIDE are published. The frequent publication schedule will keep the information reasonably fresh. However, as time passes and offices change locations or policies, some percentage of the data that was correct when published will become inaccurate, incomplete or out of date.

Thus, while the thoroughness of the data gathering process ensures that the contents of the GUIDE will be generally reliable, no user should expect 100% accuracy of the contents. National Employment Screening Services cannot vouch independently for the accuracy of the entries or any parts thereof.

SUGGESTED PRECAUTIONS.

Another warning is also in order. A variety of local, state and national laws and regulations will impact the right of an employer or prospective employer to secure and utilize the data covered by the GUIDE. The fact that a source is included in the GUIDE is no guarantee that every reader will be able to obtain or use the records it maintains.

The Minimum.

Readers are accordingly urged to seek the advice of an attorney concerning the use, verification and disclosure of information secured through these sources. In general, we believe that the screening procedure should include the following elements:

1. A thorough understanding of and compliance with the state and federal laws and regulations governing background investigations in the jurisdiction in which a search is being conducted.

2. Full disclosure to the applicant of the nature of the information to be gathered and the purpose for which it will be used.

3. Written authorization from the applicant acknowledging that he or she has been fully informed of the records search and consents to the conduct of the search.

4. Strict procedures to maintain the confidentiality of the information obtained.

Readers are also cautioned that National Employment Screening Services cannot assume or be responsible for any loss or damage arising in any way from the use of this GUIDE or any information obtained from any source contained herein.

IDENTIFIERS.

Every records repository will require certain identifiers to process a search request. For example, the office may ask for the name, social security number, birthdate, and last known address of the person to be checked. Identifiers serve two different, but related purposes.

First, these keys ensure that the repository will be able to access its records to conduct a search. The files may be indexed, for example, by name or social security number. Thus, if you do not have one or the other of these identifiers, the office simply may not be able to process a records request.

Second, the identifiers act as an important safeguard for both the requesting party and the person on whom the search is being conducted. There is always the chance that the "Harold Johnson" on whom a given

repository has a record is not the same "Harold Johnson" on whom a check has been requested. The possibility of a misidentification can be decreased substantially, however, if other identifiers also match on the individuals.

More Than The Minimum.

Each record repository listed in the GUIDE will include the identifiers that office requires to process a search. These are the minimum, the data you have to supply before the office can proceed with your search.

As a general rule, you should go beyond the minimum whenever possible. Supply the office with every piece of information you have that might aid their search. For example, always include maiden or other previous names, if applicable. Although no repository can be expected to give a 100% positive identification, the more pointers you can match, the smaller the chance of a mistake.

GETTING STARTED.

Remember that THE GUIDE TO BACKGROUND INVESTIGATIONS is intended to make your background investigations both more economical and more efficient. Organization plays a big part in both of these goals.

We suggest that the best place to start when beginning to use the GUIDE is with the section immediately following this *Introduction*. Called *Using The Guide to Background Investigations*, it offers a simple step-by-step method that will help you realize the maximum benefit from the GUIDE's sources.

USING THE GUIDE TO BACKGROUND INVESTIGATIONS

The *Fifth Edition* of THE GUIDE TO BACKGROUND INVESTIGATIONS is designed for one purpose—to make your job easier.

It is not a book to be read. It is a resource to be used. By unlocking a variety of potentially job relevant public and educational records, the GUIDE means both new information and new efficiencies for the human resource or security professional.

This section will help you see how the GUIDE can best be applied in your employment screening processes.

LEARNING BY DOING.

As you begin to use the GUIDE TO BACKGROUND INVESTIGATIONS, be aware that familiarity itself is the key to realizing its potential. An independent survey of over 400 GUIDE users has shown that those who use the book the most are the most satisfied with its performance. Conversely, those who do not employ the GUIDE in a significant way will most likely fail to realize its true benefits.

General Organization.
There are four sections in the *Fifth Edition* of the GUIDE:

The State Records Directory, detailing procedures for accessing state conviction data, worker's compensation claim histories, driving records, vital statistics, incorporations, medical licenses and other state-held data.

State Maps Directory, showing each state's county borders.

The Federal Records Directory, explaining how to check criminal, civil and bankruptcy records in each of the nation's ninety three federal judicial districts and eleven Federal Record Centers.

The Educational Records Directory, offering concise instructions for verifying educational credentials at over 3000 post-secondary institutions and programs.

Required Reading.
Each of the three source directories begins with a short introduction. These brief narratives will explain what specific sources the directory includes, the overall availability of those records and how this information can be used in the investigative process.

These introductions should not be taken as "optional" reading. A few minutes with the text will alert you to problems and potentials you may not have considered on your own. They may clarify why a record search you have been omitting should be added to your background checks.

Abbreviations.
For simplicity, NESS has abbreviated a handful of often-used terms in the search requirements for the various record repositories.

When used in the GUIDE, the following abbreviations have the indicated meaning:

DOB	Date of birth
FAX	Facsimile phone number
NCES	National Center for Education Statistics
PO	Post Office
SASE	Self addressed, stamped envelope
SSN	Social security number
US	United States

GETTING STARTED.

If you are currently evaluating one or more job applicants, now is a perfect time to put the GUIDE to work.

Gather the applicant's biographical data from the resume or the application. Use the GUIDE to research public and educational records on the applicant in the places he or she has lived or worked. You'll become familiar with the process at the same time as you gather helpful information you can immediately use.

If no applicant reviews are currently in progress, don't just put the GUIDE on a shelf. Do a background check for practice on one of your current employees or, better yet, yourself. A little experience now will increase your confidence and efficiency on subsequent searches that really do count.

After just a few uses, you'll see how the GUIDE can make you more organized, more efficient and more skillful in your background checks. As you explore the many applications of the GUIDE, the following steps and suggestions may prove helpful:

1. Location Is Critical.

The key to effective use of public records on a given applicant is knowing the locations which need to be checked.

Start with the employment application. It should point you to the basic location(s) with which the applicant has had significant contacts. Additional sources such as the applicant's "motor vehicle report" and social security number may reveal others.

2. Social Security Numbers.

The social security number a job applicant gives you tells much more than many investigators realize.

When you understand the numbering system, you will be able to spot the state in which an applicant's number was issued, perhaps thereby uncovering another location to check in your search. You will also often be able to spot unlikely or impossible numbers that suggest a falsified application.

To explain more about what social security numbers can mean in employment screening, NESS regularly produces a short booklet entitled the *"Social Security Number Guide."* If you do not already have a copy of this publication, contact NESS at 1-800-247-8713 for more information.

3. State Records.

The *State Records Directory* provides access information on several classes of records maintained at the state or county level.

The utility of some – for example, worker's compensation claim histories and criminal records – will be quite obvious. The purpose of others may be a bit less clear until you read the introductory text in the *State Records Directory*.

Pay special attention to the possibilities for using motor vehicle reports (MVRs) in your screening program. Completely apart from the traffic violations it will reveal, the MVR will supply or confirm a host of identifying data about an individual, including the applicant's full name, date of birth, current address, previous address and perhaps previous state of residence. This inexpensive report can help you catch falsified applications or supply missing information to an incomplete investigation file.

The city-county cross references located at the end of each state's section provide the necessary link to find data maintained at the county level.

4. Federal Records.

Each federal district court in the *Federal Records Directory* contains a list of the counties within its jurisdiction. You'll be able to see at a glance where federal records for a given location are held. The districts themselves are listed alphabetically by state, with separate instructions for accessing federal civil, criminal and bankruptcy records in each location. To help locate the Federal Records Directory, the *Fifth Edition* of the GUIDE has tabbed pages for this section.

Also included are instructions for the nation's eleven federal archive centers, the primary storage facilities for certain closed files no longer physically housed in the district courts themselves.

5. Educational Credentials.

The *Educational Records Directory* lists in alphabetical order over 3000 colleges and universities, with the specific procedures each institution follows for confirming attendance and degrees.

Some 97% of these institutions will cooperate with employers in background investigations, with over 84% verifying degree and/or attendance over the phone.

6. Action.

Remember, you don't have to review thousands of applicants to get your money's worth out of the GUIDE.

If you are able to detect only one falsified employment application or save one expensive outside background investigation you will easily recoup the cost of your investment in this resource.

Put the GUIDE to the test. See what you can learn. See how it can help.

THE STATE RECORDS DIRECTORY

INTRODUCTION

For any company interested in employee screening, state-held public records constitute a resource of exceptional versatility. Through these records, an employer can learn a host of job-relevant facts about employees or applicants—whether they have been convicted of a crime, whether there is a documented history of drug or alcohol abuse, how often they have filed worker's compensation claims and much more.

The billions of records that are on file in various state repositories are especially valuable because they are independent, objective sources of information. The *State Records Directory*, used in conjunction with your telephone and mailbox, will bring both the sources and the records they maintain within easy reach.

Substantial thought has been given to compiling the record types which are of greatest value in an employment context. Only the most broadly applicable sources and certain specialized records which have a particular importance in society are included in the *Directory*.

The various source materials are grouped by state for easy use. The listings for each state (and the District of Columbia) contain twelve separate elements:

1. A short introduction, describing the basic availability of records within the state.
2. Driving records.
3. Worker's compensation records.
4. Vital statistics.
5. Teacher certifications.
6. Medical licensing boards.
7. Bar associations.
8. Accountancy boards.
9. Securities commision.
10. Incorporations.
11. State criminal records.
12. A city-county cross reference.

To maximize the potential of the *State Records Directory* in your work, you should understand why and how these particular contents were chosen for inclusion.

UTILITY AND AVAILABILITY.

A background investigation is designed not so much to determine who a person was as to help decipher who the person is. In this process, no single past action or experience can serve as a foolproof indicator of character or competence. But, by drawing from a variety of sources, an employer can begin to get the answers needed to make reasoned personnel decisions.

Some state-held records can play an obvious role in this process.

Criminal conviction data, for example, may be relevant as an employer both selects and manages a staff. Through use of these records, a day care center could help ensure that its employees have no history of child abuse. Another manager could avert trouble by increasing supervision of an employee who is discovered to have a history of theft. Or workers with a documented substance abuse problem could be targeted for special counseling.

Other record types included in the *State Records Directory* serve an equally significant, though perhaps not as obvious function. The driving record (MVR) is the classic example.

Historically used only by those in the transportation and insurance industries, the MVR can actually help in almost any employment context by reliably and inexpensively supplying or confirming much of the vital identifying information needed on a job applicant (date of birth, address, full name, social security number, etc.).

Additional types of licensing boards (bar association, accountancy board and securities commission) have been included because of their unique and significant importance for particular classes of employers.

In short, all the records can make a significant contribution to employment screening efforts. The following paragraphs will summarize the nature, general availability and uses of the various records and other source materials contained in the *State Records Directory*:

1. CRIMINAL RECORDS.

Among the resources available to background investigators, criminal records have, for years, both been hailed for their utility and assailed for their danger. A quick review will delineate the basic outlines of the controversy.

Common Complaints.

Complaints about the use of criminal records for pre-employment screening have taken several different approaches.

There was, first, some question whether the release and use of conviction history would somehow violate an individual's constitutional right of privacy.

The United States Supreme Court, with the groundbreaking decision in *Paul v. Davis*, 424 U.S. 693 (1976), answered this question in the negative. The Court found that criminal records are not within the scope of the privacy protection.

Since then, other state and federal courts have almost unanimously adopted this reasoning. In rejecting the privacy argument, the courts generally will not go so far as to say that the Constitution *requires* that criminal records be available to the public. They instead say that the states are not constitutionally *prohibited* from doing so. There may not be a constitutional requirement of access, but neither is there a constitutional block.

In recent years, the privacy argument has been replaced by a fundamentally different objection. The argument is that fairness, not the Constitution, should bar access to criminal records. Criminal records may occasionally be helpful to investigators and employers, but in far more cases they are unduly prejudicial, the argument goes. Whatever benefit the records may bring employers is easily outweighed by the very real and potentially unfair harm their use may cause other parties.

Clearly, criminal records can be misapplied. An extremely old conviction record could be used to unfairly discriminate against a job applicant. An arrest which was never followed by a conviction might be given undue probative value rather than being rightfully dismissed as immaterial. Or another person's ability to earn a livelihood might be shattered if a state mistakenly reports to his employer that he was convicted of a serious offense when in fact another person with the same name was actually involved.

A more subtle policy argument against the use of criminal records has also been made. Society has an interest in rehabilitating ex-convicts. Everyone benefits when these individuals are put in a position to reenter the mainstream, earn a living, and become contributing members of their community. Release of conviction data to employers may cause some deserving and rehabilitated ex-convicts to be passed over as too risky for employment.

States, EEOC and the Courts.

The dangers inherent in releasing criminal histories to employers and their agents for employment screening purposes are real. Yet in spite of these hazards, most states have reached the conclusion that completely restricting access would subject society to even greater dangers.

The states have determined that the best course is to make the records available, but at the same time place solid safeguards around their use. These protections include both legal remedies to protect those unfairly discriminated against and better controls on the state's data keeping system to minimize the chance of misidentification or other error.

At the federal level, the Equal Employment Opportunity Commission (EEOC) adopts a similar view. The EEOC has mandated that an applicant cannot be denied employment solely because of a prior criminal record that is not relevant to the performance of the job. However, the EEOC has also recognized that a plainly job-relevant criminal record may be a bar to employment.

The trend toward greater availability of criminal records for employers is also supported by a developing line of judicial decisions. Employers are increasingly being held liable when an employee with a clear history of a certain type of criminal activity commits a crime of that nature during the course of employment.

This so-called doctrine of "negligent hiring," in effect, imposes on employers a duty to exercise reasonable care in selecting the workers they thrust into the marketplace. To be sure, this duty is not absolute. Any claim of negligent hiring must meet the normal tests of negligence—an unreasonable action, proof that the action caused injury and a duty of care toward the injured party. The different states have reached various conclusions about how far the duty extends.

However, employer access to criminal records is necessary whenever the judicial branch of a state's government recognizes a legal cause of action for negligent hiring. Otherwise, the state would be imposing a requirement on one hand without giving the means to meet it on the other.

Suggested Safeguards.

While the present pattern is clearly one of increasing access to state-held criminal records, employers who incorporate conviction checks into their background investigations should still take special safeguards.

Title VII of the Civil Rights Act of 1964 has been interpreted to prohibit apparently neutral employment practices that have the effect of working to the detriment of a disproportionate number of minority group members. Employers should, accordingly, consider whether use of conviction data in their particular situation falls into this trap.

Some experts also believe that an employer who denies employment or promotion in whole or in part on the basis of information obtained through a criminal record search is subject to the disclosure requirements of the federal Fair Credit Reporting Act (FCRA).

This is the same statute under which consumer credit and lending institutions operate when they use credit reports. If the FCRA also applies to employers' use of criminal records, the job applicant would need to be furnished the name, address and telephone number of the reporting agency and given an opportunity to inspect his or her file for errors.

In light of these concerns and because of the sensitive nature of conviction data, *Directory* users are urged to consult their attorney concerning local, state and national laws which might affect their particular gathering, use and disclosure of criminal record histories.

The Two Options.

Within a given state, there are generally two possible ways to access criminal records.

First, every state (except Nevada) has a central repository containing certain of its criminal justice case histories. Second, individual counties (and sometimes metropolitan areas) in the state maintain a separate set of records on cases involving their authorities and courts.

Thus, the first question the investigator must answer is whether to use the records of the central repository or to conduct the search at the county level. Making a reasoned decision requires an understanding of the strengths and limitations of each approach.

Central State Repositories.

The Strengths. The central repository has the advantage of convenience. Instead of having to search in every county with which a subject may have had contact, an interested party has only to contact one state office. If the individual has lived, worked or had other associations in several locations throughout the state, this can mean significant savings of both time and money.

The ability of the central repository to cover the entire state brings another benefit as well. In a county-by-county search, employers sometimes miss locations which should be checked. Whether these omissions are due to the applicant's deception, the employer's oversight or some other factor, the result is the same. Any criminal convictions in these locations will escape detection.

In contrast, the central repository will, in theory, hold records from throughout the state, even those localities of which the employer may not have been aware. Thus, failure to have a complete history of an individual's residences, places of employment and other associations within a state is less of an impediment to a thorough investigation. In fact, the central repository search may be helpful in simply revealing locales with which the individual has had a past connection.

The Disadvantages. Despite these seemingly big pluses, employers should also be aware that the state repository approach has significant limitations. The reality of a central state repository is often something less than its promise.

No central repository has a database which is 100% accurate and complete. One problem is that the repository has to depend almost entirely upon the cooperation of others. The state's courts and law enforcement officials are charged with funnelling their records to the repository, but the repository rarely has enforcement powers to insure that this is done.

Local staff shortages may prevent the criminal justice agencies from forwarding complete records to the central office. In other states, the central repository may have authority to maintain only certain classes of records – serious felonies, for example, or convictions occurring after a certain date. Others contain only cases with a final disposition – an employer wouldn't be informed of any pending or open matters.

In addition, there is legitimate concern about the accuracy of those records that are held in central repositories. While many states have solid, well maintained systems, others may release information that can be misleading. A good system will purge or, at least, not release records of arrests that are never prosecuted or ultimately lead to acquittal rather than conviction. Some states, unfortunately, are slow to remove any record once it makes its way into the system. Duplicate entries and data entry errors present another danger.

Users should also expect a time lag between the entry of a record by a court or other criminal justice agency and its appearance in the central repository. It may take weeks, months or even years before a conviction shows up in the central files.

Perhaps the biggest stumbling block, however, is that in many states the central repository is only open to selected groups. A state might, for example, open the central

files only to government agencies, school districts, banks, trucking firms and day care agencies. All employers and interested parties not falling into one of these classifications would be denied access.

While there is no "typical" state, the *State Records Directory* has noted major access restrictions imposed by the central repositories whenever possible. The offices themselves can give more information about their particular requirements.

The County-by-County Approach.

To avoid some of the problems discussed above, many background investigators will want to adopt a county-by-county approach for some or all of their screening. Though far from flawless, this method also has some significant strengths.

The Strengths. Taken individually, no single county or parish will have the breadth of data contained at the state level. A given county will be able to report only cases and adjudications from its own courts. However, as to its particular records, the individual county often offers more complete data than is available through the state repository.

The reasons for the discrepancies between the actual records on file at the counties and the statewide compilation in the central repository are discussed above – staff shortages which prevent all the files from being sent up, legislative restrictions on the central repository's authority, and the lag time between entry of a decision and transmission to the state office.

The net effect is that in some states, the counties are the sole source of certain conviction records.

It is also safe to say that county courthouses usually offer quicker turnaround on conviction searches than do centralized state repositories. To illustrate, no state repository will currently process phone requests. Yet, over 1500 counties across the country will do phone searches. Mail response times may also be shortened by going through a county courthouse. The county clerk will be handling fewer requests than will the state office and can, thus, process individual requests more expeditiously.

The Weaknesses. The central repository's greatest strength suggests the county-by-county method's biggest weakness. County records are, by definition, completely decentralized. To do a thorough check, each county which may have had jurisdiction over the person should be searched.

Calling or writing these multiple offices will require additional time (and, to some extent, expense). Each additional contact increases the potential for error. And, as suggested earlier, to the extent a less-than-complete history of the locations with which the individual has had contact is known, use of the county-by-county method risks gaps in the record.

Conclusions?

The state repository and county-by-county methods are not true alternatives. Each has strengths the other cannot duplicate. Each has weaknesses only the other can solve.

To be as accurate and complete as possible, both methods should be used whenever feasible. The *State Records Directory* shows how.

2. DRIVING RECORDS.

The transportation industry has long been required by federal law to check driving records (also called "motor vehicle reports" or MVRs) on commercial operators. Auto insurers also make use of the reports in setting premiums for the drivers they are asked to insure. Those individuals with poor driving histories generally have to pay substantially higher premiums than those with good records.

Few employers in other industries and professions appreciate the MVR's value as a standard employment screening device. However, the fact is it can be an extremely valuable tool in almost any hiring context. Detailing basic information about an individual, these reports are quickly accessible and can supply surprisingly helpful information.

A little background may dispel some of the misunderstanding about what driving records are and what they can do.

What Does an MVR Show?

Each state has a department of motor vehicles or similar office charged with a number of responsibilities relating to the licensing and oversight of its drivers. This department maintains records of all traffic violations and driving-related offenses committed by its drivers. Just as important for employment screening purposes, other identifying information on the drivers is kept on file and updated periodically.

A typical MVR pulled on a job applicant will reveal such basic personal data as full name, date of birth, address at the time the license was issued or renewed, physical description, the type of license granted and any restrictions on its use. Some states will also list whether another state's license was surrendered at the time of application, thereby pointing you to other localities with which the individual has had significant contacts.

On top of all of this, of course, the MVR will also list violations of traffic and safety laws committed by the subject while the license has been in effect, as well as any suspensions or revocations.

Due primarily to the requirements of transportation and insurance companies, every state has in place an efficient mail-in, mail-back method for processing MVR requests. State fees range from a low of $1 per subject to a high of about $10. The average charge is toward the lower end of this spectrum, around $3.

Why Use MVRs?

If the typical MVR cost $25 per job applicant or if the records were difficult to obtain, employers would have a hard time assessing its cost effectiveness. But that simply isn't the case. With an average state fee of about $3 for a full report, an MVR can more than pay for itself if it reveals or confirms only one significant fact about an applicant.

Employers who begin to use these records will quickly find multiple ways in which the MVR can demonstrate its utility. Cross-checking the personal data on the MVR with that supplied by the applicant may reveal an incorrect or falsified employment application. Past addresses included in the driving record may uncover other states in which the applicant has lived or worked.

The MVR might verify data required for access to other records. An employer, for example, might be stymied from obtaining an applicant's criminal record without his correct date of birth. The MVR can either supply this date or confirm that the one given by the applicant is correct.

Finally, the usefulness of the driving record itself should not be discounted. No, an employer may not care that a job applicant was stopped once for speeding years ago. But, a suspended or expired license may warrant a question about how the applicant would get to and from work. A pattern of alcohol or drug abuse documented by a series of driving-while-intoxicated convictions could cause future performance problems. Repeated recklessness behind the wheel may carry over into other areas as well.

Electronic Access.

One additional note—with increasing computerization of driving histories, a few states now allow employers to access records directly via their own computer terminal. But be forewarned. A substantial volume of record searches is usually required to make this approach economical. If you are interested in electronic access in a given state, contact the appropriate office at the address or phone number shown in the *State Records Directory* for more information.

3. WORKER'S COMPENSATION RECORDS.

A majority of states impose relatively few restrictions on release of worker's compensation records and organize their files in such a way as to make access a fairly easy matter. Past claims are generally filed alphabetically by the name of the claimant. To process a record request, the name index is consulted to see if the subject has ever filed a claim.

To minimize the possibility of mismatches, the state also typically insists that other identifiers line up as well – date of birth and social security number, for example. A signed release from the person to be searched may or may not be required.

In states fitting this pattern, worker's compensation records can be an immensely useful screening tool, particularly on applicants for physically demanding jobs. Everything an employer needs to conduct a search can probably be obtained from the job application form. Through the search, employers can easily learn something about

the individuals' susceptibility to injury and frequency of claims filing.

Restrictions on Access.

Not all the states, however, are so kind to employers. Whether consciously or not, these states have adopted policies and procedures which create significant obstacles to the use of worker's compensation claim histories in the employment screening process. A couple of common situations are illustrative.

In a few states, claim records are indexed by the employer's name. To check a job applicant's claim history, a company would have to search under each of the individual's previous employers. Missing even one – through an applicant's failure to supply complete references or a conflict between a company's trade and legal names, for example – would lead to an incomplete history.

Even more troubling are the states that index their records by date of injury. To check the state's records on a claim, a prospective employer would have to already know about the claim. The state's files could not be used to uncover previously undisclosed work-related injuries or compensation. They could only serve the lesser purpose of confirming the details of claims that were disclosed by the applicant – type of injury, severity, payments, etc.

The *State Records Directory* shows each state's specific policies and procedures for the release of worker's compensation records.

4. VITAL STATISTICS.

The *Fifth Edition* of the GUIDE again includes information on how to access so-called "vital statistics" within each state. These histories of births, deaths, marriages and divorces can serve several purposes.

The records may be used to confirm identifying information given on an employment application or reveal new locations where records should be checked or aid in locating an individual whose whereabouts are unknown.

Most states have a central office that can be used to obtain at least some vital statistics. The *Directory* includes both the location and phone number of these central offices and the procedures they follow in releasing information to employers. For records that are not in a central state file, the *Directory* will point users to the usual local office which can help.

5. INCORPORATIONS.

Occasionally, the investigator needs to check the status of not just an individual, but also an individual's company. Two examples will illustrate.

Perhaps a job applicant for a professional or managerial position claims ownership in a small corporation. The interviewer might want to determine if that business is still a going concern.

An even more common circumstance is when an applicant's resume lists employment at an unfamiliar local or out-of-state company. The applicant has provided a phone number to call but the interviewer wants proof that he/she will be calling a real business, not just an accomplice in a scam.

Fortunately, it is easy to verify a corporation's status. A corporation is a creature of the state and certain facts about the corporation's existence are public information. Among other pieces of data, a human resource or security professional may be able to obtain the date when the business was incorporated, whether it is in good standing with the taxing authorities, who its officers and directors are and whether it is operating under any trade names.

Since a single office generally controls the corporate records for an entire state (often a state "corporation commission" or "secretary of state"), corporate verifications are fairly easy. The *Fifth Edition* includes the appropriate office for each of the fifty states. You will find how to contact the office, what procedures you should follow and what information the office will release.

6. LICENSING BOARDS.

Also new to this edition of the GUIDE are three other record types which play a particularly important role in the professional arena – bar associations, accountancy boards and securities commission.

Confirming licenses for attorneys and CPAs is an easy task. Each state's bar association can confirm membership and license.

CPAs are required to renew their registration on a regular basis. Each state determines their own regulations and decides the requirements for continuing education.

The Securities Commission holds a wealth of information for employment purposes. The commission's records will reveal the number of years the individual has been licensed, former education – both high school and college – where and when the licensee graduated, and employment history.

Medical licenses should be verified by all employers in the health care field. The welfare of patients allows no less. Teaching and educational verifications are equally important for employers who have the well being of students in their hands.

Health care and educational institutions may know how to check credentials in their own backyard. They may be less certain how to proceed when an applicant from another state or region of the country surfaces.

The *State Records Directory* clearly spells out the accessibility of these licensing boards throughout the country.

7. CIVIL COURT RECORDS.

The *Fifth Edition* includes information for Civil Court records in each of the nation's 3,178 counties. Civil records are generally divided between the higher and lower courts based on the monetary amount of the claim. In the state of Texas, for example, claims for $50,000 and more are filed in District Court, and claims for less than $50,000 are filed in County Court. However, in Vermont, the monetary split is $2,000. The GUIDE outlines this information within each state's introduction.

Civil records in some states may have more value than discovering law suits and torts. For example, in Tennessee, workman's compensation records are first filed in Civil Court, then forwarded to the Department of Labor. Oklahoma, on the other hand, bypasses Civil Court and files directly with Worker's Compensation Court.

Incorporating civil records for background checks may prove to be valuable.

8. CITY-COUNTY CROSS REFERENCES.

The "city-county cross reference" included at the end of each state's listing has proven to be one of the most popular and most used features in the GUIDE. Alphabetically, by state, over 30,000 U.S. cities cross-referenced to the courthouses that control their criminal records. Hundreds of cities have been added in this edition.

The cross references are important because most employment applications capture only the cities in which applicants have lived or worked. Although vitally necessary for gathering public records, the corresponding county names are usually not compiled. The cross references eliminate the need to either amend your standard application form or consult some other source.

USING THE STATE RECORDS DIRECTORY.

Before your first background check in a given state, look at the short narrative that appears at the start of the state's listing.

The state introduction's primary purpose is to provide brief statistics and information on the accessibility of public records in the state – for example, the percentage of counties in the state that release criminal records by phone and mail.

Each state summary includes the state's "information hot line" number. Use this number when unexpected questions or complications arise during use of the *State Records Directory* or as you have other dealings with the state.

Following the short introduction, each state section will present the ten central state offices that maintain driving records, worker's compensation claims, vital statistics, teaching certificates, medical licenses, bar associations, CPA verifications, securities licenses, corporations, criminal and civil records, respectively. Next are separate entries for the county or parish criminal record repositories throughout the state. Last is the state's city-county cross reference, matching each municipality in the state to the county (or parish) courthouse that controls its records.

For more on how to incorporate public records into your background investigations, see *Using The Guide to Background Investigations*, beginning on page 15.

Alabama

The Alabama Department of Public Safety, which serves as the state criminal record repository, limits dissemination of criminal record information to those persons, agencies, corporations and other entities that have either a "need to know" or "right to know" as defined by state law. In contrast, all sixty seven (67) Alabama counties reported that they make criminal conviction information available as a matter of public record. Twelve (12) counties require requests to be made in person, with the remaining fifty five (55) accepting mail and/or phone requests.

For more information or for offices not listed, contact the state's information hot line at (205) 261-2500.

Driving Records

Department of Public Safety
Driver License Division
PO Box 1471
Montgomery, AL 36102-1471
(205) 242-4400

Driving records are available by mail. $5.75 fee per request. Turnaround time is 7 working days. Written request must include job applicant's full name, date of birth and license number. Make money order payable to the Alabama Department of Public Safety.

Worker's Compensation Records

Worker's Compensation Division
Department of Industrial Relations Building
Montgomery, AL 36130
(205) 242-2868
Fax (205) 240-3267

Worker's compensation records are currently not of public record; however, if the request for information is accompanied by a signed release, date of inquiry and the name and address of the insurance carrier involved can be obtained. The records are filed by name, SSN and date of accident. Records are computerized since January 1, 1986. A search for computerized records can be done for a $4.00 fee. Prior to January 1, 1986 records are on microfilm. Research time is charged at the rate of $25.00 per hour, with a minimum 1/2 hour charge.

Vital Statistics

Bureau of Vital Statistics
State Department of Public Health
434 Monroe Street
MRoom 215
Montgomery, AL 36130
(205) 261-5033

Birth and death records since January 1908 are available for $5.00 each. Additional copies are obtainable for $2.00 each. Fee for special searches is $5.00 per hour. Make certified check or money order payable to Bureau of Vital Statistics.

Marriage records are available for $5.00 fee. Check or money order. Request must include name, marriage date, spouse's name, and county where license was purchased. Divorce records available in city court where divorce occurred.

Department of Education

Teacher Certification Office
State Dept. Of Education
Gordon Persons Building
50 N. Ripley St.
Montgomery, AL 36130
(205) 242-9977
Fax (205) 242-9708

Field of certification is available by phone or mail. Include name and SSN.

Medical Licensing

Medical Licensure Commission
P.O. Box 887
Montgomery, AL 36101-0887
(205) 242-4153
Fax (205) 242-4155

Will confirm licenses for MDs and DOs by phone or mail. No search fee. $10.00 fee for Board grades. For licenses not mentioned, contact the above office.

Alabama Board of Nursing
State of Alabama
RSA Plaza, Suite 250
770 Washington Ave.
Montgomery, AL 36130
(205) 242-4060

Will confirm license by phone. No fee. Include name or license number.

Bar Association

Alabama Bar Association
PO Box 671
Montgomery, AL 36101
(205) 269-1515

Will confirm licenses by phone. No fee. Include name.

Accountancy Board

Board of Accountancy
RSA Plaza Suite 236
770 Washington Ave.
Montgomery, AL 36130
(205) 242-5700

Will confirm licenses by phone. No fee. Include name.

Securities Commission

Securities Commission
770 Washington Ave.
Montgomery, AL 36130
(205) 242-2377

Will confirm licenses by phone. No fee. Include name and SSN.

Secretary of State

Secretary of State
Corporation Section
PO Box 5616
Montgomery, AL 36103-5616
(205) 242-5324
Fax (205) 240-3138
Trade Names (205) 242-5325
Corporations (205) 240-5324

Service agent, president and secretary's address and date incorporated are available by phone or mail. Contact the above office for additional information. For standing with tax commission contact the Franchise Tax Division, State Department of Revenue, 50 Ripley Street, Montgomery, AL 36130. Telephone (205) 242-9800.

Criminal Records

Central Repository

Alabama Department of Public Safety
Attention: A.B.I.
PO Box 1511
Montgomery, AL 36192
(205) 242-4244

Access to criminal records by non-criminal justice agencies through the central repository is limited to those entities that are specifically authorized access by Alabama law. However, pending legislation may allow access with a signed release. Contact the above office or the counties listed below for additional information and instructions.

Autauga County

Circuit Clerk, Criminal Records
PO Box 126
Pratville, AL 36067
(205) 361-3737

Felony and misdemeanor records are available by mail. No release necessary. No search fee. Search information required: name, date of birth, SSN, years to search.

Civil records are available by mail. No release necessary. No search fee. Search information required: name, years to search. Specify plantiff or defendant.

Baldwin County

Circuit Clerk, Criminal Records
PO Box 1149
Bayminette, AL 36507
(205) 937-0280

Felony and misdemeanor records from 1977 forward are available by mail. Turnaround time is 3 weeks. No release necessary. $3.00 search fee. Certified check only, payable to Circuit Clerk. Search information required: name, date of birth, social security number, race.

Civil records are available by mail. No release necessary. $3.00 search fee. Search information required: name, years to search. Specify plantiff or defendant.

Barbour County

Clerk of Circuit Court, Criminal Records
PO Box 237
Clayton, AL 36016
(205) 775-8366
Fax (205) 775-8366

Felony and misdemeanor records are available by mail or fax. No release necessary. $5.00 search fee. Search information required: name, date of birth, years to search, SASE. Additional records are available from Barbour County Courthouse, Eufala Div., Broad & Orange St., Eufala, AL 36027, (205) 687-7631.

Civil records are available by mail or fax. No release necessary. $5.00 search fee. Search information required: name, date of birth, years to search. Specify plantiff or defendant.

Bibb County

Circuit Clerk, Criminal Records
Bibb County Courthouse
Centerville, AL 35042
(205) 926-3103

Felony records are available by mail or phone. No release necessary. No search fee. Search information required: name, date of birth.

Civil records are available by mail. No release necessary. No search fee. Search information required: name, years to search. Specify plantiff or defendant.

Blount County

Circuit Clerk's Office, Criminal Records
PO Box 69
Oneonta, AL 35121
(205) 274-9111 Ext. 202
Fax (205) 274-9111

Felony and misdemeanor records are available by mail or fax. No release necessary. No search fee. Search information required: name, years to search.

Civil records are available by mail. No release necessary. No search fee. $.25 fee per copy. Search information required: name, years to search. Specify plantiff or defendant.

Bullock County

Clerk of Circuit Court, Criminal Records
PO Box 230
Union Springs, AL 36089
(205) 738-2280

Felony and misdemeanor records are available by mail. No release necessary. No search fee. Search information required: name, years to search, SASE.

Civil records are available by mail. No release necessary. No search fee. Search information required: name, years to search. Specify plantiff or defendant.

Butler County

Clerk of Circuit Court, Criminal Records
PO Box 134
Greenville, AL 36037
(205) 382-3521

Felony and misdemeanor records are available by mail. No release necessary. $5.00 search fee. Certified check or money order, payable to Circuit Court Clerk. Search information required: name, SSN, date of birth, previous address, years to search.

Civil records are available by mail. No release necessary. $5.00 search fee. Search information required: name, years to search. Specify plantiff or defendant.

Calhoun County

Felony records
Clerk of the Circuit Court, Criminal Records
County Courthouse
2nd Floor
Anniston, AL 36201
(205) 231-1750

Felony records are available in person only. See Alabama state repository for additional information.

Civil records
Clerk of the Circuit Court
County Courthouse
2nd Floor
Anniston, AL 36201
(205) 231-1750

Civil records are available n persopn only. See Alabama state repository for additional information.

Misdemeanor records
District Court
1106 Gurenee Ave.
Anniston, AL 36201
(205) 236-2558

Misdemeanor records are available by mail. No release necessary. No search fee. $1.25 fee for certification. Search information required: name, date of birth, SSN, years to search, sex, race, address, SASE.

Civil records
District Court
1106 Gurenee Ave.
Anniston, AL 36201
(205) 236-2558

Civil records are available by mail. No release necessary. No search fee. $1.25 fee for certification. Search information required: name, years to search, SASE. Specify plantiff or defendant.

Chambers County

Clerk of Circuit Court, Criminal Records
Chambers County Courthouse
La Fayette, AL 36862
(205) 864-4348

Felony and misdemeanor records are available by mail. No release necessary. No search fee. Search information required: name, date of birth, SASE.

Civil records are available by mail. No release necessary. No search fee. $1.00 for certification. Search information required: name, years to search, SASE. Specify plantiff or defendant.

Cherokee County

Clerk of Circuit Court, Criminal Records
Cherokee County Courthouse
Centre, AL 35960
(205) 927-3340 or 927-3637

Felony and misdemeanor records are available by mail or phone. No release necessary. No search fee. Search information required: name, date of birth, sex, race, years to search, SSN.

Civil records are available by mail. No release necessary. No search fee. $.25 fee per copy. $1.00 for certification. Search information required: name, date of birth, years to search. Specify plantiff or defendant.

Chilton County

Clerk of Circuit Court, Criminal Records
PO Box 1946
Clanton, AL 35045
(205) 755-4275

Felony and misdemeanor records are available by mail. No release necessary. No search fee. Search information required: name, date of birth, SSN, years to search.

Civil records are available by mail. No release necessary. No search fee. Search information required: name, SSN, years to search. Specify plantiff or defendant.

Choctaw County

Clerk of District Court, Criminal Records
Choctaw County Courthouse
Butler, AL 36904
(205) 459-2155

Felony and misdemeanor records are available in person only. See Alabama state repository for additional information.

Civil records are available by mail. No release necessary. No search fee. Search information required: name, years to search. Specify plantiff or defendant.

Clarke County

Clerk of District Court, Criminal Records
PO Box 921
Grove Hill, AL 36451
(205) 275-3363

Felony and misdemeanor records are available by mail from 1977 forward. No release necessary. $5.00 fee. Search information required: name, SSN, date of birth, previous address.

Civil records are available by mail. No release necessary. $5.00 search fee. Search information required: name, years to search. Specify plantiff or defendant.

Clay County

Circuit Court Clerk, Criminal Records
PO Box 816
Ashland, AL 36251
(205) 354-7926
Fax (205) 354-7926

Felony and misdemeanor records are available by mail, phone or fax. No release necessary. No search fee. Search information required: name, years to search.

Civil records are available by mail or fax. No release necessary. $10.00 search fee. Search information required: name, date of birth, years to search. Specify plantiff or defendant.

Cleburne County

Clerk of District Court, Criminal Records
Courthouse
406 Vickery Street
Heflin, AL 36264
(205) 463-2651

Felony and misdemeanor records are available by mail or phone. No release necessary. No search fee. Search information required: name, date of birth, SSN.

Civil records are available by mail. No release necessary. No search fee. Search information required: name, date of birth, SSN, years to search. Specify plantiff or defendant.

Coffee County

Clerk of Circuit Court, Criminal Records
PO Box 402
Elba, AL 36323
(205) 897-2954

Felony and misdemeanor records are available by mail. No release necessary. No search fee. Search information required: name, date of birth, years to search.

Civil records are available by mail. No release necessary. No search fee. Search information required: name, years to search. Specify plantiff or defendant.

Colbert County

Clerk of District Court, District Criminal Division
Colbert County Courthouse
Tuscumbia, AL 35674
(205) 386-8516 Extension 10

Felony and misdemeanor records are available in person only. See Alabama state repository for additional information.

Civil records are available in person only. See Alabama state repository for additional information.

Conecuh County

Clerk of District Court, Criminal Records
PO Box 107
Conecuh County Courthouse
Evergreen, AL 36401
(205) 578-2066

Felony and misdemeanor records are available by mail. No release necessary. No search fee. Search information required: name, SSN, date of birth, previous address, SASE.

Civil records are available in person only. See Alabama state repository for additional information.

Coosa County

Clerk of District Court, Criminal Records
PO Box 98
Rockford, AL 35136
(205) 377-4988

Felony and misdemeanor records are available by maile. No release necessary. $1.00 search fee. $2.00 for certification. Search information required: name, date of birth, SASE.

Civil records are available by mail. No release necessary. No search fee. Search information required: name, years to search. Specify plantiff or defendant.

Covington County

Clerk of Circuit Court, Criminal Records
Covington County Courthouse
Andalusia, AL 36420
(205) 222-4313

Felony and misdemeanor records are available by mail. No release necessary. No search fee. $.25 per copy. $1.00 for certification. Search information required: name, years to search.

Civil records are available by mail. No release necessary. $.25 per copy. $1.00 for certification. Search information required: name, years to search. Specify plantiff or defendant.

Crenshaw County

Felony and misdemeanor records
Clerk of Circuit Court, Criminal Records
PO Box 167
Luverne, AL 36049
(205) 335-6568 Extension 55

Felony and misdemeanor records are available by mail. No release necessary. No search fee. Search information required: name, date of birth, years to search.

Civil records
Clerk of Circuit Court
PO Box 167
Luverne, AL 36049
(205) 335-6568 Extension 32

Civil records are available by mail. No release necessary. No search fee. Search information required: name, date of birth, years to search, case number if available. Specify plantiff or defendant.

Cullman County

Felony records
Clerk of Circuit Court, Criminal Records
Room 303
Cullman County Courthouse
Cullman, AL 35055
(205) 739-3530
Fax (205) 732-0876

Felony records are available by mail or fax. A release is required. No search fee. Search information required: name, date of birth.

Civil records
Clerk of Circuit Court
Room 303
Cullman County Courthouse
Cullman, AL 35055
(205) 739-3530
Fax (205) 732-0876

Civil records are available by mail or fax. No release necessary. No search fee. Search information required: name, date of birth, years to search. Specify plantiff or defendant.

Misdemeanor records
District Court
Cullman County Courthouse, Room 211
Cullman, AL 35055
(205) 739-3530 Ext. 207

Misdemeanor records are available by mail. No release necessary. No search fee. $.25 per copy. $1.25 for first certified copy, $.25 for each additional page. Search information required: name, date of birth, address, SSN.

Civil records
District Court
Cullman County Courthouse, Room 211
Cullman, AL 35055
(205) 739-3530 Ext. 207

Civil records are available by mail. No release necessary. No search fee. $.25 per copy. $1.25 for first certified copy, $.25 for each additional page. Search information required: name, years to search. Specify plantiff or defendant.

Dale County

Clerk of Circuit Court, Criminal
Records
PO Box 1350
Ozark, AL 36361
(205) 774-5003

Felony and misdemeanor records are available in person only. See Alabama state repository for additional information.

Civil records are available in person only. See Alabama state repository for additional information.

Dallas County

Felony records
Clerk of Circuit Court, Criminal
Records
PO Box 1158
Selma, AL 36701
(205) 874-2523

Felony records are available in person only. See Alabama state repository for additional information.

Civil records
Clerk of Circuit Court
PO Box 1158
Selma, AL 36701
(205) 874-2523

Civil records are available by mail. No release necessary. No search fee. Search information required: name, years to search. Specify plantiff or defendant.

Misdemeanor records
District Court
PO Box 1158
Selma, AL 36701
(205) 874-2527

Misdemeanor records are available in person only. See Alabama state repository for additional information.

Civil records
District Court
PO Box 1158
Selma, AL 36701
(205) 874-2527

Civil records are available by mail. No release necessary. No search fee. Search information required: name, years to search. Specify plantiff or defendant.

De Kalb County

Clerk of Circuit Court, Criminal
Records
PO Box 1149
De Kalb County Courthouse
Fort Payne, AL 35967
(205) 845-0541

Felony and misdemeanor records are available by mail or phone. No release necessary. No search fee. Copies are $.25 per page, $1.00 for certification. Checks payable to Circuit Clerk. Search information required: name, date of birth, years to search.

Civil records are available by mail or phone. No release necessary. No search fee. Copies are $.25 per page, $1.00 for certification. Search information required: name, years to search. Specify plantiff or defendant.

Elmore County

Clerk of Circuit Court
PO Box 320
Wetumpka, AL 36092
(205) 567-1123

Felony and misdemeanor records are available in person only. See Alabama state repository for additional information.

Civil records are available in person only. See Alabama state repository for additional information.

Escambia County

Felony and misdemeanor records
Clerk of Circuit Court, Criminal
Records
PO Box 856
Brewton, AL 36427
(205) 867-6261

Felony and misdemeanor records are available by mail or phone. No release necessary. No fee. search $.25 fee per copy, $1.00 fee for certification. Search information required: name, date of birth, years to search.

Civil records
Clerk of Circuit Court
PO Box 856
Brewton, AL 36427
(205) 867-0220

Civil records are available by mail or phone. No release necessary. No fee. search $.25 fee per copy, $1.00 fee for certification. Search information required: name, years to search. Specify plantiff or defendant.

Etowah County

Felony and misdemeanor records
Clerk of Circuit Court, Criminal
Records
PO Box 798
Gadsden, AL 35999
(205) 549-5437 or 549-5430

Felony and misdemeanor records are available by mail. No release necessary. No search fee. $.25 per copy. $1.25 for certification. Search information required: name, date of birth, race and sex.

Civil records
Clerk of Circuit Court
PO Box 798
Gadsden, AL 35999
(205) 549-5491

Civil records are available by mail. No release necessary. No search fee. $.25 per copy. $1.25 for certification. Search information required: name, years to search. Specify plantiff or defendant.

Fayette County

Clerk of Circuit Court, Criminal
Records
PO Box 206
Fayette, AL 35555
(205) 932-4617

Felony and misdemeanor records are available by mail or phone. No release necessary. No search fee. $.25 per copy. $1.00 for certification. Make check payable to Circuit Clerk. Cashier's check or money order accepted. Search information required: name, date of birth, previous address.

Civil records are available by mail. No release necessary. No search fee. or phone. No release necessary. No search fee. $.25 per copy. $1.00 for certification. Search information required: name, years to search. Specify plantiff or defendant.

Franklin County

Felony and misdemeanor records
Clerk of Circuit Court, Criminal
Records
PO Box 143
Russellville, AL 35653
(205) 332-8862

Felony and misdemeanor records are available by mail. No release necessary. $5.00 fee to search 5 years. Certified check or money order payable to Clerk of Court. Search information required: name, SSN, date of birth, previous address, years to search.

Civil records
Clerk of Circuit Court
PO Box 143
Russellville, AL 35653
(205) 332-8866

Civil records are available by mail. No release necessary. $5.00 fee to search 5 years. Search information required: name, date of birth, SSN, previous address, years to search. Specify plantiff or defendant.

Geneva County

Clerk of Circuit Court, Criminal
Records
PO Box 86
Geneva, AL 36340
(205) 684-2494

Felony and misdemeanor records are available by mail. No release necessary. $5.00 search fee. $.25 per copy. $1.00 for certification. Search information required: name, date of birth, years to search.

Civil records are available by mail. No release necessary. $5.00 search fee. $.25 per copy. $1.00 for certification. Search information required: name, date of birth, years to search. Specify plantiff or defendant.

Greene County

Clerk of Circuit Court, Criminal
Records
PO Box 307
Eutaw, AL 35462
(205) 372-3598
Fax (205) 372-4027

Felony and misdemeanor records are available by mail, phone or fax. No release necessary. No search fee. Search information required: name, date of birth.

Civil records are available by mail, phone or fax. No release necessary. No search fee. Search information required: name, date of birth, years to search. Specify plantiff or defendant.

Hale County

Clerk of District Court, Criminal
Records
Hale County Courthouse
Room 8
Greensboro, AL 36744
(205) 624-4334

Felony and misdemeanor records are available by mail. No release necessary. No search fee. Search information required: name, date of birth.

Civil records are available by mail. No release necessary. No search fee. Search information required: name, date of birth, years to search. Specify plantiff or defendant.

Henry County

Clerk of Circuit Court, Criminal Records
PO Box 337
Abbeville, AL 36310
(205) 585-2753

Felony and misdemeanor records are available by mail. No release necessary. $3.00 search fee. Search information required: name, date of birth, years to search.

Civil records are available by mail. No release necessary. $3.00 search fee. Search information required: name, years to search. Specify plantiff or defendant.

Houston County

Felony and misdemeanor records
Clerk of Circuit Court, Criminal Records
PO Drawer 6406
Dothan, AL 36302
(205) 677-4858

Felony and misdemeanor records are available by mail. No release necessary. No search fee. $.25 fee per copy. $1.25 for certification. Search information required: name, date of birth, SASE.

Civil records
Clerk of Circuit Court
PO Drawer 6406
Dothan, AL 36302
(205) 677-4859

Civil records are available by mail. No release necessary. No search fee. $.25 fee per copy. $1.25 for certification. Search information required: name, date of birth, years to search. Specify plantiff or defendant.

Jackson County

Clerk of Circuit Court, Criminal Records
PO Box 397
Scottsboro, AL 35768
(205) 574-9320

Felony and misdemeanor records are available by mail. A release is required. No search fee. Search information required: name, date of birth, race, previous address, years to search.

Civil records are available by mail. A release is required. No search fee. Search information required: name, years to search. Specify plantiff or defendant.

Jefferson County

Felony and misdemeanor records
Criminal Justice Building
801 N. 21st, Room 207
Birmingham, AL 35263
(205) 325-5309

Felony and misdemeanor records are available by mail or phone. No release necessary. No search fee. $.25 fee per copy. $1.50 for certification. Search information required: name, date of birth, sex, years to search, SASE. For additional records contact: Criminal Justice Building, 606 Courthouse Annex, Bessemer, AL 35020, (205) 481-4165.

Civil records
Criminal Justice Building
801 N. 21st, Room 207
Birmingham, AL 35263
(205) 325-5309

Civil records are available by mail. No release necessary. No search fee. $.25 fee per copy. $1.50 for certification. Search information required: name, date of birth, sex, years to search, SASE. Specify plantiff or defendant.

Lamar County

Clerk of Circuit Court, Criminal Records
PO Box 434
Vernon, AL 35592
(205) 695-7193

Felony and misdemeanor records are available by mail. No release necessary. No search fee. $.25 fee per copy, $1.25 for certification. Search information required: name, date of birth. Will do search over phone, but prefers mail inquiries.

Civil records are available by mail. No release necessary. No search fee. $.25 fee per copy. $1.25 for certification. Search information required: name, years to search. Specify plantiff or defendant.

Lauderdale County

Clerk of Circuit Court, Criminal Records
PO Box 795
Florence, AL 35631
(205) 760-5710

Records are available in person. See Alabama state repository for additional information.

Civil records are available in person. See Alabama state repository for additional information.

Lawrence County

Clerk of Circuit Court
PO Box 265
Moulton, AL 35650
(205) 974-2432

Records are available in person. See Alabama state repository for additional information.

Civil records are available in person. See Alabama state repository for additional information.

Lee County

Clerk of Circuit Court, Criminal Records
PO Box 2524
Opelika, AL 36803
(205) 749-7141 Extension 244

Felony and misdemeanor records are available by mail or phone. No release necessary. No search fee. Search information required: name, date of birth.

Civil records are available by mail. No release necessary. No search fee. Search information required: name, date of birth, years to search. Specify plantiff or defendant.

Limestone County

Clerk of Circuit Court
PO Box 964
Athens, AL 35611
(205) 233-6406

Felony and misdemeanor records are available in person only. See Alabama state repository for additional information.

Civil records are available in person only. See Alabama state repository for additional information.

Lowndes County

Clerk of Circuit Court, Criminal Records
PO Box 876
Hayneville, AL 36040
(205) 548-2252

Felony and misdemeanor records are available by mail. No release necessary. No search fee. Search information required: name, date of birth, race.

Civil records are available by mail. No release necessary. No search fee. Search information required: name, date of birth, years to search. Specify plantiff or defendant.

Macon County

Clerk of Circuit Court, Criminal Records
PO Box 723
Tuskegee, AL 36083
(205) 727-3650

Felony and misdemeanor records are available by mail. $2.50 search fee. Certified check only, payable to Circuit Court. Search information required: name, date of birth, SSN, years to search.

Civil records are available by mail. No release necessary. $2.50 search fee. Search information required: name, date of birth, SSN, years to search. Specify plantiff or defendant.

Madison County

Felony records
Clerk of Circuit Court
Madison County Courthouse
Room 217
Huntsville, AL 35801
(205) 532-3386

Felony records are available in person only. See Alabama state repository for additional information.

Civil records
Clerk of Circuit Court
Madison County Courthouse
Room 217
Huntsville, AL 35801
(205) 532-3386

Civil records are available in person only. See Alabama state repository for additional information.

Misdemeanor records
District Court
Madison County Courthouse
Room 231
Huntsville, AL 35801
(205) 532-3375

Misdemeanor records are available in person at the above office.

Civil records
District Court
Madison County Courthouse
Room 231
Huntsville, AL 35801
(205) 532-3375

Civil records are available in person only. See Alabama state repository for additional information.

Marengo County

Clerk of Circuit Court, Criminal Records
PO Box 566
Linden, AL 36748
(205) 295-2223

Felony and misdemeanor records are available by mail or phone. No release necessary. No search fee. Search information required: name, date of birth.

Civil records are available by mail. No release necessary. No search fee. Search information required: name, years to search. Specify plantiff or defendant.

Marion County

Clerk of Circuit Court, Criminal Records
PO Box 1595
Hamilton, AL 35570
(205) 921-7451

Felony and misdemeanor records are available by mail or phone. No release necessary. No fee for first 5 years searched. Search information required: name, date of birth, social security number.

Civil records are available by mail. No release necessary. No fee for first 5 years searched. Search information required: name, years to search. Specify plantiff or defendant.

Marshall County

Felony and misdemeanor records
Clerk of Circuit Court, Criminal Records
PO Box 248
Guntersville, AL 35976
(205) 571-7791

Felony and misdemeanor records are available by mail or phone. No release necessary. No search fee. Search information required: name, date of birth, race, years to search. Additional records are available from Marshall County Courthouse, 200 W. Main, Albertville, AL 35950.

Civil records
Clerk of Circuit Court
PO Box 248
Guntersville, AL 35976
(205) 571-7789

Civil records are available by mail. No release necessary. No search fee. $.25 fee per copy. $1.00 for certification. Search information required: name, years to search. Specify plantiff or defendant.

Mobile County

Felony records
Clerk of Circuit Court, Criminal Records
PO Box 298
Mobile, AL 36601
(205) 690-8430

Felony records are available by mail or phone. No release necessary. No search fee. $.25 fee per copy, $1.00 for certification. Search information required: name, date of birth.

Civil records
Clerk of Circuit Court
PO Box 298
Mobile, AL 36601
(205) 690-8430 Ext. 8420

Civil records are available by phone. No release necessary. No search fee. Search information required: name, years to search. Specify plantiff or defendant.

Misdemeanor records
District Court
PO Box 829
Mobile, AL 36601
(205) 690-8518
Fax (205) 690-8511

Misdemeanor records are available by mail or fax. Records computerized from 1985 forward. No release necessary. No search fee. $.25 fee per copy. $1.25 for certification. Search information required: name, date of birth, sex, race.

Civil records
District Court
PO Box 829
Mobile, AL 36601
(205) 690-8518
Fax (205) 690-8511

Civil records are available by mail. No release necessary. No search fee. $.25 fee per copy. $1.25 for certification. Search information required: name, date of birth, case number, years to search. Specify plantiff or defendant.

Monroe County

Clerk of Circuit Court
County Courthouse
Monroeville, AL 36460
(205) 743-2283

Felony and misdemeanor records are available by mail or phone. No release necessary. No search fee. Search information required: name, date of birth, and previous Alabama address.

Civil records are available by mail or phone. No release necessary. No search fee. Search information required: name, date of birth, years to search. Specify plantiff or defendant.

Montgomery County

Clerk of Circuit Court, Criminal Records
PO Box 1667
Montgomery, AL 36192-2501
(205) 832-1260

Felony and misdemeanor records are available by mail. A release is required. No search fee. Search information required: name, date of birth, sex, race. Records easily accessible from 1966.

Civil records are available by mail. No release necessary. No search fee. Search information required: name, case number, if known, years to search. Specify plantiff or defendant.

Morgan County

Clerk of Circuit Court, Criminal Records
PO Box 668
Decatur, AL 35602
(205) 351-4790

Felony and misdemeanor records are available in person. For additional information, see Alabama state repository.

Civil records are available n person. For additional information, see Alabama state repository.

Perry County

Clerk of Circuit Court, Criminal Records
PO Box 505
Marion, AL 36756
(205) 683-6106

Felony and misdemeanor records are available by mail or phone. No release necessary. No search fee. Search information required: name, date of birth, sex, race, years to search.

Civil records are available by mail. No release necessary. No search fee. Search information required: name, years to search. Specify plantiff or defendant.

Pickens County

Clerk of Circuit Court, Criminal Records
PO Box 418
Carrollton, AL 35447
(205) 367-2050

Felony and misdemeanor records are available by mail or phone. No release necessary. No search fee. Search information required: name, date of birth, previous address, SASE.

Civil records are available by mail. No release necessary. No search fee. Search information required: name, years to search, SASE. Specify plantiff or defendant.

Pike County

Clerk of Circuit Court, Criminal Records
POBox 948
Pike County Courthouse
Troy, AL 36081
(205) 566-4622

Felony and misdemeanor records are available by mail. No release necessary. No search fee. Search information required: name, date of birth, SSN.

Civil records are available by mail. No release necessary. No search fee. Search information required: name, years to search. Specify plantiff or defendant.

Randolph County

Clerk of Circuit Court, Criminal
Records
PO Box 328
Wedowee, AL 36278
(205) 357-4551

Felony and misdemeanor records are available in person only. See Alabama state repository for additional information.

Civil records are available by mail. No release necessary. No search fee. Search information required: name, date of birth, case number, if known, years to search. Specify plantiff or defendant.

Russell County

Clerk of Circuit Court, Criminal
Records
PO Box 518
Phenix City, AL 36867
(205) 298-0516

Felony and misdemeanor records are available by mail. No search fee. Search information required: full name, date of birth, years to search.

Civil records are available by mail. No release necessary. No search fee. Search information required: name, date of birth, years to search. Specify plantiff or defendant.

Shelby County

Clerk of Circuit Court, Criminal
Records
PO Box 1810
Columbiana, AL 35051
(205) 669-3774

Felony and misdemeanor records are available by mail. No release necessary. $4.00 search fee. Checks payable to Jeane Jurgens, Clerk. Turnaround time is 1 week. Search information required: name, date of birth, sex, race, years to search, SASE.

Civil records are available in person only. See Alabama state repository for additional information.

St. Clair County

Clerk of Circuit Court, Criminal
Records
Courthouse
PO Box 476
Ashville, AL 35953
(205) 594-7921

Felony and misdemeanor records are available by mail. No release necessary. No search fee. Turnaround time is 2 weeks. Search information required: name, SSN, date of birth, sex, race, years to search.

Civil records are available in person only. See Alabama state repository for additional information.

Sumter County

Clerk of Circuit Court, Criminal
Records
PO Box 936
Livingston, AL 35470
(205) 652-2291

Felony and misdemeanor records are available by mail. No release necessary. No search fee. Turnaround time is 2 weeks. Search information required: name, SSN, date of birth, sex, race, years to search.

Civil records are available by mail. No release necessary. No search fee. Turnaround time is 2 weeks. Search information required: name, SSN, date of birth, sex, race, years to search. Specify plantiff or defendant.

Talladega County

Clerk of Circuit Court
PO Box 512
Judicial Bldg.
Talladega, AL 35160-0755
(205) 761-2102

Felony records are available by mail. No release necessary. No search fee. $.25 fee per copy. $1.25 for certification. Search information required: name, years to search.

Civil records are available by mail. No release necessary. No search fee. $.25 fee per copy. $1.25 for certification. Search information required: name, years to search. Specify plantiff or defendant.

Tallapoosa County

Clerk of Circuit Court, Criminal
Records
Tallapoosa County Courthouse
Dadeville, AL 36853
(205) 825-1098

Felony and misdemeanor records are available by mail. No release necessary. No search fee. Turnaround time is 2 weeks. Search information required: name, date of birth, previous address.

Civil records are available by mail. No release necessary. No search fee. Turnaround time is 2 weeks. Search information required: name, date of birth, previous address, years to search. Specify plantiff or defendant.

Tuscaloosa County

Felony records
Clerk of Circuit Court
Criminal Records, 3rd Floor,
Courthouse
714 Greensboro Ave.
Tuscaloosa, AL 35401
(205) 349-3870 Ext. 326

Felony records are available by mail. No release necessary. No search fee. $1.25 for certification. Search information required: name, SSN, date of birth, sex, race.

Civil records
Clerk of Circuit Court
Courthouse
714 Greensboro Ave.
Tuscaloosa, AL 35401
(205) 349-3870 Ext. 326

Civil records are available by mail. No release necessary. No search fee. $1.25 for certification. Search information required: name, years to search. Specify plantiff or defendant.

Misdemeanor records
District Court
PO Box 1687
Tuscaloosa, AL 35403
(205) 349-3870 Ext. 357

Misdemeanor records are available by mail or phone. No release necessary. No search fee. Search information required: name, date of birth, sex, race.

Civil records
District Court
PO Box 1687
Tuscaloosa, AL 35403
(205) 349-3870 Ext. 357

Civil records are available by mail. No release necessary. No search fee. $1.25 for certification. Search information required: name, years to search. Specify plantiff or defendant.

Walker County

Clerk of Circuit Court, Criminal
Records
PO Box 749
Jasper, AL 35501
(205) 384-7268 or 3405

Felony and misdemeanor records are available by mail. No release necessary. $2.00 search fee. $1.00 fee for certification. Search information required: name, date of birth, race, years to search.

Civil records are available by mail. No release necessary. No search fee. $1.00 fro certification. Search information required: name, years to search. Specify plantiff or defendant.

Washington County

Clerk of Circuit Court, Criminal
Records
PO Box 548
Chatom, AL 36518
(205) 847-2239

Felony and misdemeanor records are available by mail. No release is necessary. No search fee. $.25 fee per copy. $2.50 for certification. Search information required: full name, years to search.

Civil records are available by mail. No release necessary. No search fee. $.25 fee per copy. $2.50 for certification. Search information required: name, date of birth, years to search. Specify plantiff or defendant.

Wilcox County

Clerk of Circuit Court, Criminal
Records
PO Box 656
Camden, AL 36726
(205) 682-4126

Felony and misdemeanor records are available by mail or phone. No release necessary. No search fee. Search information required: name, date of birth.

Civil records are available by mail or phone. No release necessary. No search fee. Search information required: name, date of birth, years to search. Specify plantiff or defendant.

Winston County

Clerk of Circuit Court, Criminal
Records
PO Box 309
Double Springs, AL 35553
(205) 489-5533

Felony and misdemeanor records are available by mail. No release necessary. $5.00 search fee. Search information required: name, SASE.

Civil records are available by mail. No release necessary. No search fee. Search information required: name, years to search. Specify plantiff or defendant.

City-County Cross Reference

Abbeville *Henry*
Abernant *Tuscaloosa*
Acmar *Saint Clair*
Adamsville *Jefferson*
Addison *Winston*
Adger *Jefferson*
Akron *Hale*
Alabaster *Shelby*
Alberta *Wilcox*
Albertville *Marshall*
Aldrich *Shelby*
Alexander City *Tallapoosa*
Alexandria *Calhoun*
Aliceville *Pickens*
Allgood *Blount*
Alpine *Talladega*
Alton *Jefferson*
Altoona *Etowah*
Andalusia *Covington*
Anderson *Lauderdale*
Annemanie *Wilcox*
Anniston *Calhoun*
Arab *Marshall*
Ariton *Dale*
Ardmore *Limestone*
Arley *Winston*
Arlington *Wilcox*
Armstrong *Macon*
Ashford *Houston*
Ashland *Clay*
Ashville *Saint Clair*
Athens *Limestone*
Atmore *Escambia*
Attalla *Etowah*
Auburn *Lee*
Autaugaville *Autauga*
Avon *Houston*
Axis *Mobile*
Babbie *Covington*
Baileyton *Cullman*
Baker Hill *Barbour*
Banks *Pike*
Bankston *Fayette*
Bay Minette *Baldwin*
Bayou LaBatre *Mobile*
Bayview *Jefferson*
Bear Creek *Marion*
Beatrice *Monroe*
Beaverton *Lamar*
Belk *Fayette*
Bellamy *Sumter*
Belle Mina *Limestone*
Bellwood *Geneva*
Berry *Fayette*
Bessemer *Jefferson*
Bigbee *Washington*
Billingsley *Autauga*
Birmingham *Jefferson*
Black *Geneva*
Blountsville *Blount*
Bluff Park *Jefferson*
Boaz *Marshall*
Boligee *Greene*
Bolinger *Choctaw*
Bon Air *Talladega*
Bon Secour *Baldwin*
Booth *Autauga*
Boykin *Wilcox*
Brantley *Crenshaw*
Bremen *Cullman*
Brent *Bibb*
Brewton *Escambia*
Bridgeport *Jackson*

Brierfield *Bibb*
Brilliant *Marion*
Brooklyn *Conecuh*
Brookside *Jefferson*
Brookwood *Tuscaloosa*
Brownsboro *Madison*
Brundidge *Pike*
Bryant *Jackson*
Bucks *Mobile*
Buhl *Tuscaloosa*
Burkville *Lowndes*
Burnt Corn *Monroe*
Burnwell *Walker*
Butler *Choctaw*
Bynum *Calhoun*
Cahaba *Jefferson*
Calera *Shelby*
Calvert *Washington*
Camden *Wilcox*
Campbell *Clarke*
Camp Hill *Tallapoosa*
Capshaw *Limestone*
Carbon Hill *Walker*
Cardiff *Jefferson*
Carrollton *Pickens*
Castleberry *Conecuh*
Catherine *Wilcox*
Cecil *Montgomery*
Cedar Bluff *Cherokee*
Center Point *Jefferson*
Central *Elmore*
Centre *Cherokee*
Centreville *Bibb*
Chalkville *Jefferson*
Chancellor *Geneva*
Chapman *Butler*
Chatom *Washington*
Chelsea *Shelby*
Cherokee *Colbert*
Chickasaw *Mobile*
Childersburg *Talladega*
Choccolocco *Calhoun*
Chunchula *Mobile*
Citronelle *Mobile*
Clanton *Chilton*
Clay *Jefferson*
Clayhatchee *Dale*
Claysville *Marshall*
Clayton *Barbour*
Cleveland *Blount*
Clinton *Greene*
Clio *Barbour*
Clopton *Dale*
Cloverdale *Lauderdale*
Coalburg *Jefferson*
Coaling *Tuscaloosa*
Coden *Mobile*
Coffee Springs *Geneva*
Coffeeville *Clarke*
Coker *Tuscaloosa*
Colbert Heights *Colbert*
Coldwater *Calhoun*
Collinsville *DeKalb*
Columbia *Houston*
Columbiana *Shelby*
Concord *Jefferson*
Cook Springs *Saint Clair*
Coosada *Elmore*
Cordova *Walker*
Cottondale *Tuscaloosa*
Cottonton *Russell*
Cottonwood *Houston*
Courtland *Lawrence*

Cowarts *Houston*
Coy *Wilcox*
Cragford *Clay*
Crane Hill *Cullman*
Creola *Mobile*
Cropwell *Saint Clair*
Crossville *DeKalb*
Cuba *Sumter*
Cullman *Cullman*
Cusseta *Chambers*
Dadeville *Tallapoosa*
Daleville *Dale*
Danville *Morgan*
Daphne *Baldwin*
Dauphin Island *Mobile*
Daviston *Tallapoosa*
Dawson *DeKalb*
Dayton *Marengo*
DeArmanville *Calhoun*
Deatsville *Elmore*
Decatur *Morgan*
Deer Park *Washington*
Delmar *Winston*
Delta *Clay*
Demopolis *Marengo*
Detroit *Lamar*
Dickinson *Clarke*
Dixiana *Jefferson*
Dixons Mills *Marengo*
Docena *Jefferson*
Dolomite *Jefferson*
Dora *Walker*
Dothan *Houston*
Double Springs *Winston*
Douglas *Marshall*
Dozier *Crenshaw*
Duncanville *Tuscaloosa*
Dutton *Jackson*
Eastaboga *Calhoun*
East Brewton *Escambia*
Echola *Tuscaloosa*
Eclectic *Elmore*
Edgewater *Jefferson*
Edwardsville *Cleburne*
Elba *Coffee*
Elberta *Baldwin*
Eldridge *Walker*
Elkmont *Limestone*
Elmore *Elmore*
Elrod *Tuscaloosa*
Emelle *Sumter*
Empire *Walker*
Enterprise *Coffee*
Epes *Sumter*
Equality *Coosa*
Estillfork *Jackson*
Ethelsville *Pickens*
Eufaula *Barbour*
Eutaw *Greene*
Eva *Morgan*
Evergreen *Conecuh*
Excel *Monroe*
Fabius *Jackson*
Fackler *Jackson*
Fairfield *Jefferson*
Fairhope *Baldwin*
Fairview *Cullman*
Falkville *Morgan*
Farmersville *Lowndes*
Faunsdale *Marengo*
Fayette *Fayette*
Fitzpatrick *Bullock*
Five Points *Chambers*

Flat Rock *Jackson*
Flint City *Morgan*
Flomaton *Escambia*
Florala *Covington*
Florence *Lauderdale*
Foley *Baldwin*
Forestdale *Jefferson*
Forest Home *Butler*
Forkland *Greene*
Fort Davis *Macon*
Fort Deposit *Lowndes*
Fort Mitchell *Russell*
Fort Payne *DeKalb*
Fosters *Tuscaloosa*
Franklin *Monroe*
Frankville *Washington*
Frisco City *Monroe*
Fruitdale *Washington*
Fruithurst *Cleburne*
Fulton *Clarke*
Fultondale *Jefferson*
Furman *Wilcox*
Fyffe *DeKalb*
Gadsden *Etowah*
Gainestown *Clarke*
Gainesville *Sumter*
Gallant *Etowah*
Gallion *Hale*
Gantt *Covington*
Garden City *Cullman*
Gardendale *Jefferson*
Gaylesville *Cherokee*
Geneva *Geneva*
Georgiana *Butler*
Geraldine *DeKalb*
Gilbertown *Choctaw*
Glen Allen *Fayette*
Glencoe *Etowah*
Glenwood *Crenshaw*
Good Hope *Cullman*
Goodsprings *Walker*
Goodwater *Coosa*
Goodway *Monroe*
Gordo *Pickens*
Gordon *Houston*
Goshen *Pike*
Grady *Montgomery*
Graham *Randolph*
Grand Bay *Mobile*
Grant *Marshall*
Graysville *Jefferson*
Greenhill *Lauderdale*
Green Pond *Bibb*
Greensboro *Hale*
Greenville *Butler*
Grove Hill *Clarke*
Groveoak *DeKalb*
Guin *Marion*
Gulf Shores *Baldwin*
Guntersville *Marshall*
Gurley *Madison*
Hackleburg *Marion*
Haleyville *Winston*
Hamilton *Marion*
Hammondville *De Kalb*
Hanceville *Cullman*
Hardaway *Macon*
Harpersville *Shelby*
Hartford *Geneva*
Hartselle *Morgan*
Harvest *Madison*
Hatchechubbee *Russell*
Hayden *Blount*

Hayneville *Lowndes*
Hazel Green *Madison*
Headland *Henry*
Heflin *Cleburne*
Helena *Shelby*
Henagar *DeKalb*
Higdon *Jackson*
Highland Home *Crenshaw*
Hillsboro *Lawrence*
Hillview *Jefferson*
Hissop *Coosa*
Hobson City *Calhoun*
Hodges *Franklin*
Hokes Bluff *Etowah*
Hollins *Clay*
Holly Pond *Cullman*
Hollytree *Jackson*
Hollywood *Jackson*
Holt *Tuscaloosa*
Homewood *Jefferson*
Honoraville *Crenshaw*
Hoover *Jefferson*
Hope Hull *Montgomery*
Horton *Marshall*
Houston *Winston*
Hueytown *Jefferson*
Huntsville *Madison*
Hurtsboro *Russell*
Huxford *Escambia*
Ider *DeKalb*
Irondale *Jefferson*
Irvington *Mobile*
Jachin *Choctaw*
Jack *Coffee*
Jackson *Clarke*
Jacksons Gap *Tallapoosa*
Jacksonville *Calhoun*
Jasper *Walker*
Jefferson *Marengo*
Jemison *Chilton*
Jones *Autauga*
Joppa *Cullman*
Kansas *Walker*
Kellerman *Tuscaloosa*
Kellyton *Coosa*
Kennedy *Lamar*
Kent *Elmore*
Killen *Lauderdale*
Kimberly *Jefferson*
Kinston *Coffee*
Knoxville *Greene*
Laceys Spring *Morgan*
Ladonia *Russell*
Lafayette *Chambers*
Lakeview *De Kalb*
Lamison *Wilcox*
Lanett *Chambers*
Langston *Jackson*
Lapine *Montgomery*
Lavaca *Choctaw*
Lawley *Bibb*
Leeds *Jefferson*
Leesburg *Cherokee*
Leighton *Colbert*
Lenox *Conecuh*
Leroy *Washington*
Lester *Limestone*
Letohatchee *Lowndes*
Level Plains *Dale*
Lexington *Lauderdale*
Lillian *Baldwin*
Lincoln *Talladega*
Linden *Marengo*
Lineville *Clay*
Lipscomb *Jefferson*
Lisman *Choctaw*

Little River *Baldwin*
Littleville *Colbert*
Livingston *Sumter*
Loachapoka *Lee*
Lockhart *Covington*
Locust Fork *Blount*
Logan *Cullman*
Louisville *Barbour*
Lower Peach Tree *Wilcox*
Lowndesboro *Lowndes*
Loxley *Baldwin*
Luverne *Crenshaw*
Lynn *Winston*
McCalla *Jefferson*
McCullough *Escambia*
McIntosh *Washington*
McKenzie *Butler*
McShan *Pickens*
McWilliams *Wilcox*
Madison *Madison*
Magazine *Mobile*
Magnolia *Marengo*
Magnolia Springs *Baldwin*
Malcolm *Washington*
Malvern *Geneva*
Mantua *Greene*
Maplesville *Chilton*
Marbury *Autauga*
Margaret *Saint Clair*
Marion *Perry*
Marion Junction *Dallas*
Mathews *Montgomery*
Maylene *Shelby*
Megargel *Monroe*
Melvin *Choctaw*
Mentone *DeKalb*
Meridianville *Madison*
Mexia *Monroe*
Midland City *Dale*
Midway *Bullock*
Millbrook *Elmore*
Millers Ferry *Wilcox*
Millerville *Clay*
Millport *Lamar*
Millry *Washington*
Minor *Jefferson*
Minter *Dallas*
Mobile *Mobile*
Monroeville *Monroe*
Montevallo *Shelby*
Montgomery *Montgomery*
Montrose *Baldwin*
Moody *St. Clair*
Mooresville *Limestone*
Morris *Jefferson*
Morvin *Clarke*
Moulton *Lawrence*
Moundville *Hale*
Mount Hope *Lawrence*
Mount Meigs *Montgomery*
Mount Olive *Jefferson*
Mount Vernon *Mobile*
Mountain Brook *Jefferson*
Mulga *Jefferson*
Munford *Talladega*
Muscadine *Cleburne*
Muscle Shoals *Colbert*
Myrtlewood *Marengo*
Nanafalia *Marengo*
Natural Bridge *Winston*
Nauvoo *Walker*
Needham *Choctaw*
Newbern *Hale*
New Brockton *Coffee*
New Castle *Jefferson*
Newell *Randolph*

New Hope *Madison*
New Market *Madison*
Newton *Dale*
Newville *Henry*
Normal *Madison*
Northport *Tuscaloosa*
Notasulga *Macon*
Oak Grove *Talladega*
Oak Hill *Wilcox*
Oakman *Walker*
Odenville *Saint Clair*
Ohatchee *Calhoun*
Oneonta *Blount*
Opelika *Lee*
Opp *Covington*
Orange Beach *Baldwin*
Orrville *Dallas*
Overton *Jefferson*
Owens Cross Roads
 Madison
Oxford *Calhoun*
Ozark *Dale*
Paint Rock *Jackson*
Palmerdale *Jefferson*
Panola *Sumter*
Pansey *Houston*
Parrish *Walker*
Paul *Conecuh*
Pea Ridge *Shelby*
Pelham *Shelby*
Pell City *Saint Clair*
Pennington *Choctaw*
Perdido *Baldwin*
Perdue Hill *Monroe*
Perote *Bullock*
Peterman *Monroe*
Peterson *Tuscaloosa*
Petrey *Crenshaw*
Phenix City *Russell*
Phil Campbell *Franklin*
Piedmont *Calhoun*
Pike Road *Montgomery*
Pinckard *Dale*
Pine Apple *Wilcox*
Pine Hill *Wilcox*
Pine Level *Montgomery*
Pinedale Shores *St. Claire*
Pinson *Jefferson*
Pisgah *Jackson*
Pittsview *Russell*
Plantersville *Dallas*
Pleasant Grove *Jefferson*
Point Clear *Baldwin*
Port Birmingnam *Jefferson*
Prairie *Wilcox*
Prattville *Autauga*
Priceville *Morgan*
Prichard *Mobile*
Princeton *Jackson*
Quinton *Walker*
Ragland *Saint Clair*
Rainbow City *Etowah*
Rainsville *DeKalb*
Ralph *Tuscaloosa*
Ramer *Montgomery*
Ranburne *Cleburne*
Randolph *Bibb*
Red Bay *Franklin*
Red Level *Covington*
Reece City *Etowah*
Reform *Pickens*
Remlap *Blount*
Repton *Conecuh*
River Falls *Covington*
Riverside *Saint Clair*
Roanoke *Randolph*

Robertsdale *Baldwin*
Robinwood *Jefferson*
Rockford *Coosa*
Rock Mills *Randolph*
Rocky Ridge *Jefferson*
Rogersville *Lauderdale*
Russellville *Franklin*
Rutledge *Crenshaw*
Ryland *Madison*
Safford *Dallas*
Saginaw *Shelby*
Saint Elmo *Mobile*
Saint Stephens *Washington*
Salem *Lee*
Salitpa *Clarke*
Samantha *Tuscaloosa*
Samson *Geneva*
Saraland *Mobile*
Sardis *Dallas*
Sardis City *Etowah*
Satsuma *Mobile*
Sawyerville *Hale*
Sayre *Jefferson*
Scottsboro *Jackson*
Seale *Russell*
Section *Jackson*
Selma *Dallas*
Semmes *Mobile*
Shannon *Jefferson*
Sheffield *Colbert*
Shelby *Shelby*
Shorter *Macon*
Shorterville *Henry*
Silas *Choctaw*
Silverhill *Baldwin*
Sipsey *Walker*
Skipperville *Dale*
Skyline *Jackson*
Slocomb *Geneva*
Smiths *Lee*
Snead *Blount*
Snow Hill *Wilcox*
Somerville *Morgan*
Southside *Etowah*
Spanish Fort *Baldwin*
Spring Garden *Cherokee*
Springville *Saint Clair*
Sprott *Perry*
Spruce Pine *Franklin*
Stanton *Chilton*
Stapleton *Baldwin*
Steele *Saint Clair*
Sterrett *Shelby*
Stevenson *Jackson*
Stewart *Hale*
Stockton *Baldwin*
Sulligent *Lamar*
Sumiton *Walker*
Summerdale *Baldwin*
Sunflower *Washington*
Sunny South *Wilcox*
Sweet Water *Marengo*
Sycamore *Talladega*
Sylacauga *Talladega*
Sylvania *DeKalb*
Talladega *Talladega*
Tallassee *Elmore*
Tanner *Limestone*
Tarrant City *Jefferson*
Taylor *Houston*
Theodore *Mobile*
Thomaston *Marengo*
Thomasville *Clarke*
Thorsby *Chilton*
Tibbie *Washington*
Tillmans Corner *Mobile*

Titus *Elmore*
Toney *Madison*
Town Creek *Lawrence*
Townley *Walker*
Toxey *Choctaw*
Trafford *Jefferson*
Trenton *Jackson*
Trinity *Morgan*
Troy *Pike*
Trussville *Jefferson*
Tuscaloosa *Tuscaloosa*
Tuscumbia *Colbert*
Tuskegee *Macon*
Tuskegee Institute *Macon*
Tyler *Dallas*
Union Grove *Marshall*
Union Springs *Bullock*
Uniontown *Perry*
Uriah *Monroe*
Valhermoso Springs
  Morgan
Valley *Chambers*
Valley Head *DeKalb*
Vance *Tuscaloosa*
Vandiver *Shelby*
Verbena *Chilton*
Vernon *Lamar*
Vestavia Hills *Jefferson*
Vina *Franklin*
Vincent *Shelby*
Vinegar Bend *Washington*
Vinemont *Cullman*
Vredenburgh *Monroe*
Wadley *Randolph*
Wagarville *Washington*
Walker Springs *Clarke*
Walnut Grove *Etowah*
Ward *Sumter*
Warrior *Jefferson*
Waterloo *Lauderdale*
Watson *Jefferson*
Wattsville *Saint Clair*
Waverly *Lee*
Weaver *Calhoun*
Webb *Houston*
Wedowee *Randolph*
Wellington *Calhoun*
Weogufka *Coosa*
West Blocton *Bibb*
West Greene *Greene*
Westover *Shelby*
Westwood *Jefferson*
Wetumpka *Elmore*
Whatley *Clarke*
Wilmer *Mobile*
Wilsonville *Shelby*
Wilton *Shelby*
Winfield *Marion*
Wing *Covington*
Woodland *Randolph*
Woodstock *Bibb*
Woodville *Jackson*
York *Sumter*

Alaska

While criminal conviction data is widely available at the borough level in Alaska, access through the central state repository is limited to select groups specifically authorized by state law to receive it. Civil court records at the Superior Court are for claims $5,000 and greater.

For more information or for offices not listed, contact the state's information hot line at (907) 465-2111.

Driving Records

Motor Vehicle/Driver Services
Driving Records
PO Box 20020
Juneau, AK 99802
(907) 465-4335
Fax (907) 463-5860

Driving records are available by mail or fax. $5.00 fee per request. Turnaround time is 7 working days. Written request must include job applicants full name, date of birth, license number and signed driver release. Make check payable to State of Alaska.

Worker's Compensation Records

Worker's Compensation Division
Department of Labor
PO Box 25512
Juneau, AK 99802-5512
(907) 465-2797

Records are available by mail only. Written request must include job applicant's full name, SSN and, if available, date of injury. There is no search fee. Records are computerized from 1982 forward. $.50 fee per screen copy. $.75 fee per copy for records prior to 1982. A signed release is not required. Requests must include claimant's address.

Vital Statistics

Department of Health and Social Services
Bureau of Vital Statistics
P. O. Box H
Juneau, AK 99811-0675
(907) 465-3392

Birth and death records from 1913 are available for $7.00 each. Make certified check or money order payable to Bureau of Vital Statistics. Employee must request copy.

Marriage records are available for $7.00. Include name, marriage date, spouse's name and place where marriage took place. Turnaround time is 3 weeks. Divorce records are available for $7.00. Include name, divorce date, spouse's name, place divorce granted. Turnaround time is 3 weeks. A signed release is required. Visa and Mastercard accepted. $10.00 service charge.

Department of Education

Teacher Certification
801 W. 10th, Suite 200
Juneau, AK 99811-1894
(907) 465-2831

Field of certification, effective date, expiration date are available by phone or mail. Include name and SSN.

Medical Licensing

State of Alaska
Department of Commerce
Division of Occupational Licensing
PO Box 110806
Juneau, AK 99811-0806
(907) 465-2541

Will confirm licenses for MDs and DOs by phone or mail. $5.00 fee. For licenses not mentioned, contact the above office.

Alaska Board of Nursing
Department of Commerce and Economic Development
Division of Occupational Licensing
3601 "C" Street, Suite 722
Anchorage, AK 99503
(907) 465-2544

Will confirm license by phone. No fee. Include name, license number, if available.

Bar Association

Alaska Bar Association
PO Box 100279
Anchorage, AK 99510
(907) 465-2544

Will confirm licenses by phone. No fee. Include name.

Accountancy Board

Occupational Licensing Division
Board of Accountancy
PO Box 110806
Juneau, AK 99811-0806
(907) 465-2580

Will confirm licenses by phone. No fee. Include name.

Securities Commission

Securities and Corporations
Department of Commerce and Economic Develoment
PO Box 110807-0807
(907) 465-2521

Will confirm licenses by phone. No fee. Include name and SSN.

Secretary of State

Department of Commerce
Corporation Section
PO Box D
Juneau, AK 99811
(907) 465-2350

Service agent and address, date incorporated, standing with tax commission, trade names are available by phone or mail. Contact the above office for additional information.

Criminal Records

Central Repository

Dept. of Public Safety
Records and Identification
5700 E. Tudor Road
Anchorage, AK 99507
(907) 269-5659

Access to criminal records by non-criminal justice agencies through the central repository is primarily limited to criminal justice agencies. Contact the above office or see listings below for additional information and instructions.

Aleutian Islands Borough

See Anchorage Borough.

Anchorage Borough

3rd Judicial District, Criminal Records
Clerk of Court, Criminal Records
303 K. Street
Anchorage, AK 99501
(907) 264-0444
Fax (907) 278-4272

Felony and misdemeanor records are available by mail. No release necessary. $15.00 fee. Check payable to Clerk of Court. Search information required: name, date of birth, SSN, years to search.

Civil records are available by mail. No release necessary. $15.00 search fee. Search information required: name, years to search. Specify plantiff or defendant.

Bethel Borough

Clerk of Court
Bethel Courthouse
PO Box 130
Bethel, AK 99559
(907) 543-2196
Fax (907) 543-4419

Felony and misdemeanor records are available by mail, fax or phone. No release necessary. No search fee. $.25 fee per copy. $5.00 fee for certification. Make money order payable to Alaska Court System. Search information required: name, date of birth, SASE.

Civil records are available by mail. A release is required. No search fee. $.25 fee per copy. $5.00 fee for certification. Search information required: name, date of birth, SSN, years to search. Specify plantiff or defendant.

Bristol Bay Borough

See Naknek District Court

Dillingham Borough

District Court
PO Box 909
Dillingham, AK 99576
(907) 842-5215

Misdemeanor records are available by mail or phone. No release necessary. No search fee. $.25 fee per copy and $7.00 fee for certification, prepaid. Search information required: name, date of birth. See Anchorage Borough for felony records.

Civil records are available by mail or phone. No release necessary. No search fee. $.25 fee per copy and $7.00 fee for certification, prepaid. Search information required: name, years to search. Specify plantiff or defendant.

Fairbanks North Star Borough

Clerk of Trial Court, Records Dept.
Room 342
604 Barnette Street
Fairbanks, AK 99701
(907) 452-9280
Fax (907) 452-6554

Felony and misdemeanor records are available by mail or fax. No release necessary. $15.00 search fee. Search information required: name, date of birth, years to search, SASE.

Clerk of Trial Court, Records Dept.
Room 342
604 Barnette Street
Fairbanks, AK 99701
(907) 452-9282
Fax (907) 452-6554

Civil records are available by mail. No release necessary. Fax requests are accepted. $15.00 search fee. Search information required: name, date of birth, years to search. Specify plantiff or defendant.

Haines Borough

Clerk of Court, Criminal Records
PO Box 169
Haines, AK 99827
(907) 766-2801
Fax (907) 766-3148

Felony and misdemeanor records are available by fax or mail. A release is required. No search fee. $7.00 fee for certification. Search information required: name, date of birth, years to search. Also see Juneau Borough.

Civil records are available by mail or fax. A release is required. No search fee. $7.00 fee for certification. Search information required: name, date of birth, years to search. Also see Juneau Borough. Specify plantiff or defendant.

Juneau Borough

Juneau Trial Court
Diamond Court Bldg.
PO Box 114100
Juneau, AK 99811-4100
(907) 463-4700
Fax (907) 463-3788

Felony and misdemeanor records are available by fax or mail. No release necessary. No search fee. $.25 fee per copy, prepaid, $7.00 for certified copy. Search information required: name, SASE, date of birth, years to search.

Civil records are available by mail or fax. No release necessary. No search fee. $.25 fee per copy, prepaid, $7.00 for certified copy. Search information required: name, SASE, date of birth, years to search. Specify plantiff or defendant.

Kenai Peninsula Borough

Clerk of Court, Criminal Records
3670 Lake Street
Homer, AK 99603
(907) 235-8171
Fax (907) 235-4257

Felony and misdemeanor records are available by fax or mail. No release necessary. No search fee. $.25 fee per copy, $7.00 fee for certification. $2.00 fee for additional copies of same document. Make check payable to Alaska Court System. Search information required: name, date of birth, years to search.

Civil records are available by mail or fax. No release necessary. No search fee. $.25 fee per copy, $7.00 fee for certification. $2.00 fee for additional copies of same document. Search information required: name, date of birth, years to search. Specify plantiff or defendant.

Kenai Peninsula Borough

Clerk of Court, Criminal Records
Room 106
145 Main Street Loop
Kenai, AK 99611
(907) 283-3110

Felony and misdemeanor records are available by mail. No release necessary. $15.00 search fee. $.25 fee per copy, $5.00 fee for certification, $2.00 fee for additional copies of same document. Search information required: name, date of birth, sex, race, years to search.

Civil records are available by mail. No release necessary. $15.00 search fee. $.25 fee per copy, $5.00 fee for certification, $2.00 fee for additional copies of same document. Search information required: name, years to search. Specify plantiff or defendant.

Ketchikan Gateway Borough

Clerk of Court, Criminal Records
Room 400
415 Main Street
Ketchikan, AK 99901
(907) 225-3195

Felony and misdemeanor records since 1958 are available by mail or phone. No release necessary. $15.00 search fee. $.25 fee per copy, $5.00 fee for certification. Search information required: name, date of birth, years to search.

Civil records are available by mail or phone. No release necessary. $15.00 search fee. $.25 fee per copy, $5.00 fee for certification. Search information required: name, years to search. Specify plantiff or defendant.

Kobuk Borough

See Fairbanks North Star Borough.

Kodiak Island Borough

Alaska Court System
Trial Court
202 Marine Way
Kodiak, AK 99615
(907) 486-5765

Felony and misdemeanor records are available by mail. No release necessary. $15.00 search fee. $.25 fee per copy, $5.00 fee for certification. Make check payable to State of Alaska. Search information required: name, date of birth, years to search.

Civil records are available by mail. No release necessary. $15.00 search fee. $.25 fee per copy, $5.00 fee for certification. Search information required: name, years to search. Specify plantiff or defendant.

Matanuska–Susitna Borough

Trial Court, Criminal Records
435 S Denali Street
Palmer, AK 99645
(907) 745-4282

Felony and misdemeanor records are available by mail. No release necessary. $15.00 search fee. $.25 fee per copy, $7.00 fee for certification. Search information required: name, date of birth, years to search.

Civil records are available by mail. No release necessary. $15.00 search fee. $.25 fee per copy, $7.00 fee for certification. Search information required: name, years to search. Specify plantiff or defendant.

Naknek District Court

Clerk of Court, Criminal Records
PO Box 229
Naknek, AK 99633
(907) 246-4240

Felony and misdemeanor records are available by mail. No search fee. $.25 fee per copy, $7.00 fee for certification. No release necessary. Search information required: name, date of birth.

Civil records are available by mail. No release necessary. No search fee. $.25 fee per copy, $7.00 fee for certification. Search information required: name, years to search. Specify plantiff or defendant.

Nome Borough

Nome Trial Courts
PO Box 100
Nome, Alaska 99762
(907) 443-5216
Fax (907) 443-2192

Felony and misdemeanor records are available by mail. No release necessary. $15.00 search fee. $.25 fee per copy, $5.00 fee for certification. Search information required: name, date of birth, SSN.

Civil records are available by mail. No release necessary. $15.00 search fee. $.25 fee per copy, $5.00 fee for certification. Search information required: name, years to search. Specify plantiff or defendant.

North Slope Borough

Clerk of Court
Pouch 2700
Barrow, AK 99723
(907) 852-4800

Records are available by mail. $15.00 search fee. $.25 fee per copy. Make company check payable to Alaska Court System. Search information required: name, date of birth, SSN, years to search.

Civil records are available by mail. No release necessary. 15.00 search fee. $.25 fee per copy. Search information required: name, years to search. Specify plantiff or defendant.

Prince of Wales Borough

See Ketchikan Gateway Borough.

Sitka Borough

Trial Court Clerk, Criminal Records
Room 203
304 Lake Street
Sitka, AK 99835
(907) 747-3291
Fax (907) 747-6690

Felony and misdemeanor records are available by mail or fax. No release necessary. $15.00 fee paid in advance. Make check payable to Trial Court Clerk. Search information required: name, date of birth.

Civil records are available by mail. No release necessary. $15.00 search fee. Search information required: name, years to search. Specify plantiff or defendant.

Skagway-Yakutat-Angoon Boroughs

See Ketchikan Gateway Borough.

Southeast Fairbanks Borough

See Fairbanks North Star Borough

Valdez-Cordova Boroughs

See Anchorage Borough.

Wade Hampton Borough

See Anchorage Borough.

Wrangell-Petersburg Boroughs

See Ketchikan Gateway Borough.

Yukon-Koyukuk Boroughs

See Anchorage Borough.

City-County Cross Reference

Akiachak *Bethel*
Akiak *Bethel*
Akutan *Aleutian Islands*
Alakanuk *Wade Hampton*
Aleknagik *Dillingham*
Allakaket *Yukon-Koyukuk*
Ambler *Kobuk*
Anaktuvuk Pass *North Slope*
Anchor Point *Kenai Peninsula*
Anchorage *Anchorage*
Anderson *Southeast Fairbanks*
Angoon *Skagway-Yakutat-Angoon*
Aniak *Bethel*
Anvik *Yukon-Koyukuk*
Arctic Village *Yukon-Koyukuk*
Barrow *North Slope*
Beaver *Yukon-Koyukuk*
Bethel *Bethel*
Bettles Field *Yukon-Koyukuk*
Brevig Mission *Nome*
Buckland *Kobuk*
Cantwell *Yukon-Koyukuk*
Central *Yukon-Koyukuk*
Chefornak *Bethel*
Chevak *Wade Hampton*
Chicken *Southeast Fairbanks*
Chignik *Dillingham*
Chignik Lagoon *Dillingham*
Chitina *Valdez-Cordova*
Chugiak *Anchorage*

Circle *Yukon-Koyukuk*
Clam Gulch *Kenai Peninsula*
Clarks Point *Dillingham*
Cold Bay *Aleutian Islands*
College *Fairbanks North Star*
Cooper Landing *Kenai Peninsula*
Copper Center *Valdez-Cordova*
Cordova *Valdez-Cordova*
Craig *Prince of Wales*
Crooked Creek *Bethel*
Deering *Kobuk*
Delta Junction *Southeast Fairbanks*
Dillingham *Dillingham*
Eagle *Southeast Fairbanks*
Eagle River *Anchorage*
Eek *Bethel*
Egegik *Dillingham*
Ekwok *Dillingham*
Elfin Cove *Skagway-Yakutat-Angoon*
Elim *Nome*
Emmonak *Wade Hampton*
Ester *Fairbanks North Star*
Fairbanks *Fairbanks North Star*
False Pass *Aleutian Islands*
Flat *Yukon-Koyukuk*
Fort Yukon *Yukon-Koyukuk*
Fortuna Ledge *Wade Hampton*
Gakona *Valdez-Cordova*
Galena *Yukon-Koyukuk*

Gambell *Nome*
Girdwood *Anchorage*
Glennallen *Valdez-Cordova*
Goodnews Bay *Bethel*
Grayling *Yukon-Koyukuk*
Gustavus *Skagway-Yakutat-Angoon*
Haines *Haines*
Healy *Yukon-Koyukuk*
Holy Cross *Yukon-Koyukuk*
Homer *Kenai Peninsula*
Hoonah *Skagway-Yakutat-Angoon*
Hooper Bay *Wade Hampton*
Hope *Kenai Peninsula*
Hughes *Yukon-Koyukuk*
Huslia *Yukon-Koyukuk*
Hydaburg *Prince of Wales*
Hyder *Prince of Wales*
Iliamna *Dillingham*
Juneau *Juneau*
Kake *Wrangell-Petersburg*
Kaktovik *North Slope*
Kalskag *Bethel*
Kaltag *Yukon-Koyukuk*
Karluk *Kodiak Island*
Kasigluk *Bethel*
Kasilof *Kenai Peninsula*
Kenai *Kenai Peninsula*
Ketchikan *Ketchikan Gateway*
Kiana *Kobuk*
King Cove *Aleutian Islands*
King Salmon *Bristol Bay*
Kipnuk *Bethel*

Kivalina *Kobuk*
Klawock *Prince of Wales*
Kobuk *Kobuk*
Kodiak *Kodiak Island*
Kotlik *Wade Hampton*
Kotzebue *Kobuk*
Koyuk *Nome*
Koyukuk *Yukon-Koyukuk*
Kwethluk *Bethel*
Kwigillingok *Bethel*
Lake Minchumina *Yukon-Koyukuk*
Larsen Bay *Kodiak Island*
Levelock *Dillingham*
Lower Kalskag *Bethel*
Manley Hot Springs *Yukon-Koyukuk*
Manokotak *Dillingham*
McGrath *Yukon-Koyukuk*
Mekoryuk *Bethel*
Metlakatla *Prince of Wales*
Minto *Yukon-Koyukuk*
Moose Pass *Kenai Peninsula*
Mountain Village *Wade Hampton*
Naknek *Bristol Bay*
Napakiak *Bethel*
Nenana *Yukon-Koyukuk*
New Stuyahok *Dillingham*
Nikolski *Aleutian Islands*
Ninilchik *Kenai Peninsula*
Noatak *Kobuk*
Nome *Nome*
Nondalton *Dillingham*
Noorvik *Kobuk*
North Pole *Fairbanks North Star*

Northway *Southeast Fairbanks*
Nulato *Yukon-Koyukuk*
Nunapitchuk *Bethel*
Old Harbor *Kodiak Island*
Ouzinkie *Kodiak Island*
Palmer *Matanuska-Susitna*
Pelican *Skagway-Yakutat-Angoon*
Perryville *Dillingham*
Petersburg *Wrangell-Petersburg*
Pilot Point *Dillingham*
Pilot Station *Wade Hampton*
Platinum *Bethel*
Point Baker *Prince of Wales*
Point Hope *North Slope*
Port Alsworth *Dillingham*
Port Lions *Kodiak Island*
Quinhagak *Bethel*
Red Devil *Bethel*
Ruby *Yukon-Koyukuk*
Russian Mission *Wade Hampton*
Saint Marys *Wade Hampton*
Saint Michael *Nome*
Saint Paul Island *Aleutian Islands*
Sand Point *Aleutian Islands*
Savoonga *Nome*
Scammon Bay *Wade Hampton*
Selawik *Kobuk*
Seldovia *Kenai Peninsula*
Seward *Kenai Peninsula*
Shageluk *Yukon-Koyukuk*
Shaktoolik *Yukon-Koyukuk*
Shishmaref *Nome*
Shungnak *Kobuk*
Sitka *Sitka*
Skagway *Skagway-Yakutat-Angoon*
Skwentna *Matanuska-Susitna*
Sleetmute *Bethel*
Soldotna *Kenai Peninsula*
South Naknek *Bristol Bay*
Stebbins *Nome*
Sterling *Kenai Peninsula*
Stevens Village *Yukon-Koyukuk*
Sutton *Matanuska-Susitna*
Talkeetna *Matanuska-Susitna*
Tanana *Yukon-Koyukuk*
Teller *Nome*
Tenakee Springs *Skagway-Yakutat-Angoon*
Togiak *Dillingham*
Tok *Southeast Fairbanks*
Tununak *Bethel*
Tyonek *Kenai Peninsula*
Unalakleet *Nome*
Unalaska *Aleutian Islands*
Valdez *Valdez-Cordova*
Venetie *Yukon-Koyukuk*
Wainwright *North Slope*
Wales *Nome*
Ward Cove *Ketchikan Gateway*
Wasilla *Matanuska-Susitna*
White Mountain *Nome*

Willow *Matanuska-Susitna*
Wrangell *Wrangell-Petersburg*
Yakutat *Skagway-Yakutat-Angoon*

Arizona

All fifteen (15) Arizona counties reported that their criminal records are available by mail and/or phone. Access to criminal history information through the central state repository is limited to those persons, businesses and associations specifically authorized by state law to receive it. Civil suits for $5,000 and more are filed in Superior Court.

For more information or for offices not listed, contact the state's information hot line at (602) 542-4900.

Driving Records

Department of Transportation
Room 504M
1801 West Jefferson
Phoenix, AZ 85007
(602) 255-8357

Driving records are available by mail. $3.00 fee for 39 months searched, $5.00 fee for 5 years searched. Turnaround time is 4-6 weeks. Written request must include job applicant's full name, date of birth and license number, requester's notarized signature and state reason. Make check payable to the Arizona Department of Transportation.

Worker's Compensation Records

Industrial Commission of Arizona
Compliance Department
PO Box 19070
Phoenix, AZ 85005-9070
(602) 542-4661

Requests for record searches may be made to the Mail-Room Department by mail. Request must include, subject's name, date of birth and social security number on Arizona's "Public Records Request Form". Fee based on record's purpose. $.25 fee per copy. A signed release is required.

Vital Statistics

Vital Records Section
Arizona Department of Health Services
PO Box 3887
Phoenix, AZ 85030
(602) 258-6381

Birth records are available on either the "long form" for $8.00 or the "short form" for $5.00. Death records are available for $5.00. Make certified check or money order payable to Vital Records.

Marriage records available at county level where marriage took place. Divorce records available at Superior Court where divorce granted.

Department of Education

Department of Education
Teacher Certification Division
1535 W. Jefferson
Phoenix, AZ 85007
(602) 542-4368

Field of certification is available by phone or mail. Include full name and SSN.

Medical Licensing

Board of Medical Examiners
2001 W. Camelback
Suite 300
Phoenix, AZ 85115
(602) 255-3751

Will confirm licenses for MDs by phone or mail. Board Action requests must be in writing. $2.00 fee. For licenses not mentioned, contact the above office.

Arizona State Board of Nursing
2001 W. Camelback Road, Suite 350
Phoenix, AR 85015
(602) 255-5092

Will confirm license by phone. No fee. Include name, license number, if available. For mail requests, include $25.00. Money order or certified check.

Bar Association

Arizona Bar Association Membership
363 North 1sr Ave.
Phoenix, AZ 85003
(602) 252-4804

Will confirm licenses by phone. No fee. Include name.

Accountancy Board

Arizona Board of Accountancy
3110 Notrh 19th Ave., Suite 140
Phoenix, AZ 85015
(602) 255-3648

Will confirm licenses by mail or phone. $10.00 fee for mail response. Include name.

Securities Commission

Securities Division
Corporation Commission
1200 West Washington Ave.
Suite 201
Phoenix, AZ 85007
(602) 542-4242

Will confirm licenses by phone. No fee. Include name and SSN.

Secretary of State

Arizona Corporation Commission
P.O. Box 6019
Phoenix, AZ 85005
(602) 542-3026

Service agent and address, date incorporated, standing with tax commission, trade names are available by phone or mail. Contact the above office for additional information.

Criminal Records

Central Repository

Department of Public Safety
Attention: Criminal Records
PO Box 6638
Phoenix, AZ 85005
(602) 223-2229
Fax (602) 223-2915

Access to criminal records by non-criminal justice agencies through the central repository is limited to those entities that are specifically authorized access by Arizona law. Statutes prohibit out-of-state non-criminal justice agency access. Contact the above office and counties listed below for additional information and instructions. Due to pending legislation, the above information may change.

Apache County

Clerk of Superior Court, Criminal Records
PO Box 365
St. Johns, AZ 85936
(602) 337-4364 Extension 265

Felony records are available by mail. No release necessary. $11.50 search fee. Search information required: name, SSN.

Clerk of Superior Court
PO Box 667
St. Johns, AZ 85936
(602) 337-4364 Extension 265

Civil records are available by mail. No release necessary. $11.50 search fee. $1.25
fee per copy. $11.50 for certification.
Search information required: name, years to
search. Specify plantiff or defendant.

Cochise County

Felony Records

Clerk of Superior Court, Criminal
Records
Drawer CK
Bisbee, AZ 85603
(602) 432-5471 Extension 350

Felony records are available by mail.
Turnaround time is 1 week. No release necessary. $11.50 fee for each year searched.
Check payable to Clerk of Superior Court.
Search information required: name, years to
search, and the type of information requested.

Civil records

Clerk of Superior Court
Drawer CK
Bisbee, AZ 85603
(602) 432-9364

Civil records are available by mail. No release necessary. $11.50 search fee. Search
information required: name, years to
search. Specify plantiff or defendant.

Coconino County

Felony records

Clerk of Superior Court, Criminal
Records
Coconino County Courthouse
Flagstaff, AZ 86001
(602) 779-6535

Felony records are available by mail.
Turnaround time is 1 weeks. No release
necessary. $11.50 fee per year searched.
Check payable to Clerk of Superior Court.
Search information required: name, years to
search. Turnaround time is 1 to 2 weeks.

Civil records

Clerk of Superior Court
Coconino County Courthouse
Flagstaff, AZ 86001
(602) 779-6535

Civil records are available by mail. No release necessary. $11.50 fee per year
searched. $1.15 fee per copy. $11.00 for
certification. Search information required:
name, years to search, type of case to
search. Specify plantiff or defendant.

Misdemeanor records

Flagstaff Justice Court
Coconino County Courthouse
Flagstaff, AZ 86001
(602) 779-6806

Misdemeanor records from 1987 to present
are available by mail. No release necessary.
No search fee. $.50 fee per copy. $8.75 fee
for certification. Search information required: name. For later records, contact
county attorney.

Civil records

Flagstaff Justice Court
Coconino County Courthouse
Flagstaff, AZ 86001
(602) 779-6806

Civil records are available by mail. No release necessary. No search fee. $.50 fee per

copy. $8.75 fee for certification. Search in-
formation required: name, years to search.
Specify plantiff or defendant.

Gila County

Clerk of Superior Court, Criminal
Records
1400 E. Ash Street
Globe, AZ 85501
(602) 425-3231 Extension 246
Fax (602) 425-7802

Felony and misdemeanor records are available by mail. No release necessary. $11.50
search fee. $1.15 fee per copy. $11.50 for
certification. Certified check or money order, payable to Clerk of Superior Court.
Search information required: name, date of
birth, years to search.

Civil records are available by mail. No release necessary. $11.50 search fee. $1.15
fee per copy. $11.50 for certification.
Search information required: name, years to
search. Specify plantiff or defendant.

Graham County

Clerk of Superior Court
800 Main Street
Safford, AZ 85546
(602) 428-3100

Felony records are available by mail. No release necessary. $11.50 fee per year
searched. Make check payable to Clerk of
Court. Search information required: name,
years to search.

Greenlee County

Clerk of Superior Court, Criminal
Records
PO Box 1027
Clifton, AZ 85533
(602) 865-4242

Felony records are available by mail. No release necessary. $11.50 fee for each year
searched. $1.15 fee per copy. $11.50 for
certification. Company checks only,
payable to Clerk of Superior Court. Search
information required: name.

Civil records are available by mail. No release necessary. $11.50 search fee for each
year searched. $1.15 fee per copy. $11.50
for certification. Search information required: name, years to search. Specify plantiff or defendant.

La Paz County

Superior Court Clerk
PO Box 730
Parker, AZ 85344
(602) 669-6131

Felony records are available by mail. No release necessary. $11.50 search fee for each
year searched. $1.15 fee per copy. $11.50
for certification. Make check payable to
Superior Court Clerk. Search information
required: name, date of birth, years to
search. Records available from 1983 to present.

Civil records are available by mail. No release necessary. $11.50 search fee for each
year searched. $1.15 fee per copy. $11.50
for certification. Search information required: name, years to search. Specify plantiff or defendant.

Maricopa County

Superior Court Clerk, Correspondence
Clerk's Office
201 W. Jefferson
Phoenix, AZ 85003
(602) 506-8575 or 506-3860
Fax (602) 506-7619

Felony records are available by mail from
1968 or by phone from 1987 forward. No
release necessary. $11.50 fee for each year
searched. Make check payable to Clerk of
Superior Court. Search information required: name, date of birth, years to search,
SASE.

Mohave County

Clerk of Superior Court, Criminal
Records
PO Box 7000
Kingman, AZ 86402-7000
(602) 753-0713

Felony records are available by mail. No release necessary. $11.50 fee for each year
searched. $1.15 fee per copy. $11.50 for
certification. Make check payable to Clerk
of Superior Court. Search information required: name, SSN, date of birth, years to
search.

Civil records are available by mail. No release necessary. $11.50 search fee per year
searched. $1.15 fee per copy. $11.50 for
certification. Search information required:
name, years to search, SASE. Specify plantiff or defendant.

Navajo County

Clerk of Superior Court, Criminal
Records
PO Box 668
Holbrook, AZ 86025
(602) 524-6161 Extension 389

Felony records are available by mail. No release necessary. $11.50 search fee for each
year searched. $1.15 fee per copy. $11.50
for certification. Certified check only,
payable to Clerk of Superior Court. Search
information required: name, SSN, date of
birth if available, years to search, SASE.

Civil records are available by mail. No release necessary. $11.50 search fee for each
year searched. $1.15 fee per copy. $11.50
for certification. Search information required: full name, years to search, SASE.
Specify plantiff or defendant.

Pima County

Clerk of Superior Court, Legal
Records
110 W. Congress
Tucson, AZ 85701
(602) 740-3240

Felony records are available by mail. No release necessary. $11.50 search fee from
1983 forward. Prior to 1983, $11.50 for
each year searched. Make money order or
certified check payable to Clerk of Superior
Court. Search information required: name,
date of birth, years to search, SASE.

Civil records are available by mail. No release necessary. $11.50 search fee. $1.25
fee per copy. $11.50 for certification.
Search information required: name, years to
search, SASE. Specify plantiff or defendant.

Pinal County

Clerk of Superior Court, Front Counter
PO Box 889
Florence, AZ 85232
(602) 868-5801 Extension 296

Felony records are available by mail or by-phone for a three year period. No release necessary. $11.50 fee per year searched. $1.15 per copy. $11.50 for certification. Search information required: name, years to search.

Civil records are available by mail. No release necessary. No search fee for first 3 years searched. $11.50 search fee thereafter. $1.15 fee per copy. $11.50 for certification. Search information required: name, years to search. Specify plantiff or defendant.

Santa Cruz County

Clerk of Superior Court, Criminal Records
PO Box 1265
Nogales, AZ 85628
(602) 281-2047

Felony records are available by mail or phone. No release necessary. No search fee. Search information required: name.

Civil records are available by mail. No release necessary. $11.50 search fee per year searched. $1.25 fee per copy. $11.50 for certification. Search information required: name, years to search. Specify plantiff or defendant.

Yavapai County

Clerk of Superior Court
Yavapai County Courthouse
Prescott, AZ 86301
(602) 771-3312
Fax (602) 445-9182

Felony and misdemeanor records are available by mail. No release necessary. $11.50 search fee per year searched. $1.15 per copy. $11.50 fee for certification. Make check payable to Clerk of Superior Court. Search information required: name, years to search.

Civil records are available by mail. No release necessary. $11.50 search fee. $1.15 fee per copy. $11.50 for certification. Search information required: name, years to search. Specify plantiff or defendant.

Yuma County

Clerk of Superior Court, Criminal Records
168 2nd Ave.
Yuma, AZ 85364
(602) 329-2164

Felony records are available by mail. No release necessary. $11.50 search fee for each year searched. $1.15 fee per copy. $11.50 for certification. Certified check only, payable to Clerk of Superior Court. Search information required: name, years to search, SASE.

Civil records are available by mail. No release necessary. $11.50 search fee for each year searched. $1.15 fee per copy. $11.50 for certification. Search information required: name, years to search, SASE. Specify plantiff or defendant.

City-County Cross Reference

Aguila *Maricopa*
Ajo *Pima*
Alpine *Apache*
Apache Junction *Pinal*
Arivaca *Pima*
Arizona City *Pinal*
Arlington *Maricopa*
Ash Fork *Yavapai*
Avondale-Goodyear
  Maricopa
Bagdad *Yavapai*
Bapchule *Pinal*
Benson *Cochise*
Bisbee *Cochise*
Black Canyon City
  Yavapai
Blue *Greenlee*
Bouse *LaPaz*
Bowie *Cochise*
Buckeye *Maricopa*
Bullhead City *Mohave*
Bylas *Graham*
Cameron *Coconino*
Camp Verde *Yavapai*
Carefree *Maricopa*
Casa Grande *Pinal*
Casas Adobes *Pima*
Cashion *Maricopa*
Catalina *Pima*
Cave Creek *Maricopa*
Central *Graham*
Central Heights *Gila*
Chambers *Apache*
Chandler *Maricopa*
Chinle *Apache*
Chino Valley *Yavapai*
Chloride *Mohave*
Chuichu *Pinal*
Cibecue *Navajo*
Clarkdale *Yavapai*

Claypool *Gila*
Clay Springs *Navajo*
Clifton *Greenlee*
Cochise *Cochise*
Colorado City *Mohave*
Concho *Apache*
Congress *Yavapai*
Coolidge *Pinal*
Cornville *Yavapai*
Cortaro *Pima*
Cottonwood *Yavapai*
Crane *Yuma*
Dennehotso *Apache*
Dewey *Yavapai*
Dilkon *Navajo*
Dolan Springs *Mohave*
Douglas *Cochise*
Dragoon *Cochise*
Dudleyville *Pinal*
Duncan *Greenlee*
Eagar *Apache*
Ehrenberg *LaPaz*
Elfrida *Cochise*
Elgin *Santa Cruz*
El Mirage *Maricopa*
Eloy *Pinal*
Flagstaff *Coconino*
Florence *Pinal*
Fort Apache *Navajo*
Fort Defiance *Apache*
Fort Thomas *Graham*
Fredonia *Coconino*
Gadsden *Yuma*
Ganado *Apache*
Gila Bend *Maricopa*
Gilbert *Maricopa*
Glendale *Maricopa*
Globe *Gila*
Goodyear *Maricopa*
Grand Canyon *Coconino*

Greasewood *Navajo*
Green Valley *Pima*
Greer *Apache*
Gu Achi *Pima*
Guadalupe *Maricopa*
Hayden *Gila*
Heber *Navajo*
Hereford *Cochise*
Higley *Maricopa*
Holbrook *Navajo*
Hotevilla *Navajo*
Houck *Apache*
Huachuca City *Cochise*
Humboldt *Yavapai*
Jerome *Yavapai*
Joseph City *Navajo*
Kayenta *Navajo*
Keams Canyon *Navajo*
Kearny *Pinal*
Kingman *Mohave*
Kirkland *Yavapai*
Kykotsmovi Village
  Navajo
Lake Havasu City *Mohave*
Lake Montezuma *Yavapai*
Lakeside *Navajo*
Laveen *Maricopa*
Leupp *Coconino*
Litchfield Park *Maricopa*
Littlefield *Mohave*
Lukachukai *Apache*
Lukeville *Pima*
McNary *Apache*
McNeal *Cochise*
Mammoth *Pinal*
Marana *Pima*
Maricopa *Pinal*
Mayer *Yavapai*
Mesa *Maricopa*
Miami *Gila*

Moenkopi *Coconino*
Morenci *Greenlee*
Morristown *Maricopa*
Mountainaire *Coconino*
Mount Lemmon *Pima*
Naco *Cochise*
Nazlini *Apache*
New River *Maricopa*
Nogales *Santa Cruz*
Nutrioso *Apache*
Oatman *Mohave*
Oracle *Pinal*
Oro Valley *Pima*
Overgaard *Navajo*
Page *Coconino*
Palominas *Cochise*
Palo Verde *Maricopa*
Parker *LaPaz*
Patagonia *Santa Cruz*
Paulden *Yavapai*
Payson *Gila*
Peach Springs *Mohave*
Pearce *Cochise*
Peoria *Maricopa*
Peridot *Gila*
Phoenix *Maricopa*
Picacho *Pinal*
Pima *Graham*
Pine *Gila*
Pinedale *Navajo*
Pinetop *Navajo*
Pinetop Lakeside *Navajo*
Pinon *Navajo*
Pirtleville *Cochise*
Plantsite *Greenlee*
Polacca *Navajo*
Pomerene *Cochise*
Prescott *Yavapai*
Prescott Valley *Yavapai*
Quartzsite *LaPaz*

Queen Creek *Maricopa*
Red Rock *Pinal*
Rillito *Pima*
Rimrock *Yavapai*
Riviera *Mohave*
Roll *Yuma*
Roosevelt *Gila*
Rough Rock *Apache*
Round Rock *Apache*
Sacaton *Pinal*
Safford *Graham*
Sahuarita *Pima*
Saint David *Cochise*
Saint Johns *Apache*
Saint Michaels *Apache*
Salome *LaPaz*
San Carlos *Gila*
Sanders *Apache*
San Luis *Yuma*
San Manuel *Pinal*
San Simon *Cochise*
Santa Maria *Maricopa*
Sasabe *Pima*
Sawmill *Apache*
Scottsdale *Maricopa*
Second Mesa *Navajo*
Sedona *Coconino*
Seligman *Yavapai*
Sells *Pima*
Shonto *Navajo*
Show Low *Navajo*
Sierra Vista *Cochise*
Skull Valley *Yavapai*
Snowflake *Navajo*
Solomon *Graham*
Somerton *Yuma*
Sonoita *Santa Cruz*
South Tuscon *Pima*
Springerville *Apache*
Stanfield *Pinal*
Steamboat Canyon *Apache*
Sun City *Maricopa*
Sun City West *Maricopa*
Sunlakes *Maricopa*
Sunsites *Cochise*
Supai *Coconino*
Superior *Pinal*
Suprise *Maricopa*
Tacna *Yuma*
Taylor *Navajo*
Teec Nos Pos *Apache*
Tempe *Maricopa*
Thatcher *Graham*
Tolleson *Maricopa*
Tombstone *Cochise*
Tonalea *Coconino*
Tonopah *Maricopa*
Tonto Basin *Gila*
Topawa *Pima*
Topock *Mohave*
Tuba City *Coconino*
Tucson *Pima*
Tumacacori *Santa Cruz*
Vail *Pima*
Valley Farms *Pinal*
Vernon *Apache*
Waddell *Maricopa*
Wellton *Yuma*
Wenden *LaPaz*
Whiteriver *Navajo*
Wickenburg *Maricopa*
Wikieup *Mohave*
Wilhoit *Yavapai*
Willcox *Cochise*
Williams *Coconino*
Window Rock *Apache*

Winkelman *Gila*
Winslow *Navajo*
Wittmann *Maricopa*
Woodruff *Navajo*
Yarnell *Yavapai*
Young *Gila*
Youngtown *Maricopa*
Yucca *Mohave*
Yuma *Yuma*

Arkansas

Both the Arkansas central repository and all seventy five (75) individual counties in the state make criminal conviction information available for employment screening purposes. Sixty six counties reported that records are available by phone or mail and a twenty three will allow fax requests.

For more information or for offices not listed, contact the state's information hot line at (501) 371-3000.

Driving Records

Traffic Violation Records
PO Box 1272, Room 123
Little Rock, AR 72203
(501) 682-7207
(800) 662-8247

Driving records are available by mail. $7.00 fee per request. $10.00 fee for commercial driving record. Turnaround time is 24 hours. Written request must include job applicant's full name, date of birth, license number, reason for request and a signed driver release. Make check payable to Department of Finance.

Worker's Compensation Records

Data Processing Department
Worker's Compensation Commission
625 Marshall Street
Little Rock, AR 72201
(501) 682-3930

To obtain worker's compensation records, send written request with the job applicant's complete name and SSN. Specify the years to be checked. There is a $5.00 fee for an electronic record search July 1, 1979 forward. An additional charge of $1.00 per year searched prior to July 1, 1979. A signed release is not required.

Vital Statistics

Division of Vital Records
Arkansas Department of Health
4815 West Markham Street
Little Rock, AR 72205
(501) 661-2134

Birth records are available for $5.00 each. Death records are available for $4.00 each. Duplicate copies of death records at the same time are $1.00 each. Make certified check or money order payable to Arkansas Department of Health.

Marriage records and divorce records are available for $5.00 each.

Department of Education

Teacher Education and Licensure
Department of Education
Room 106 & 107B
No. 4 State Capital Mall
Little Rock, AR 72201-1071
(501) 682-4342

Field of certification, effective date, expiration date are available by phone or mail. Include name and SSN.

Medical Licensing

State Medical Board
2100 Riverfront Dr., Suite 200
Little Rock, AR 72202
(501) 324-9410

Will confirm licenses for MDs and DOs by phone or mail. No fee. For licenses not mentioned, contact the above office.

Arkansas State Board of Nursing
1123 S. University
Little Rock, AR 72204
(501) 686-2700

Will confirm license by phone. No fee. Include name, license number.

Bar Association

Arkansas Bar Association
400 West Markham
Little Rock, AR 72201
(501) 375-4605

Will confirm licenses by phone. No fee. Include name.

Accountancy Board

Arkansas Board of Accountancy
101 East Capitol, Suite 430
Little Rock, AR 72201
(501) 682-1520

Will confirm licenses by phone. No fee. Include name.

Securities Commission

Securities Department
Heritage West Building
Third Floor
201 East Markham, Suite 300
Little Rock, AR 72201
(501) 324-9260

Will confirm licenses by phone. No fee. Include name and SSN.

Secretary of State

Secretary of State
Corporation Division
State Capitol Building
Room 058
Little Rock, AR 72201-1094
(501) 682-5151

Service agent and address, date incorporated, standing with tax commission, trade names are available by phone or mail. Contact the above office for additional information.

Criminal Records

State Repository

Identification Bureau
PO Box 5901
3 Natural Resources Drive
Little Rock, AR 72215
(501) 221-8233

Criminal records are available by mail only. Results of searches include both conviction and arrest information. Written request must include applicant's full name, date of birth, race, sex and a signed release. Also include a self-addressed, stamped envelope. Place each request on a separate page. At this time there is no fee for the service. Requests are processed in 3-4 days from receipt.

Arkansas County

Circuit Clerk's Office, Criminal Records
PO Box 719
Stuttgart, AR 72160
(501) 673-2056
Fax (501) 673-7311

Felony and misdemeanor records are available by mail. No release necessary. $6.00 search fee. $1.00 fee per copy. Search information required: name, maiden name, date of birth, years to search.

Civil records are available by mail. No release necessary. $6.00 search fee. $1.00 fee per copy. Search information required: name, date of birth, years to search. Specify plaintiff or defendant.

Ashley County

Felony records
Circuit Clerk, Criminal Records
Ashley County Courthouse
Hamburg, AR 71646
(501) 853-5113

Felony records are available in person only. See Arkansas state repository for additional information.

Civil records
Circuit Clerk
Ashley County Courthouse
Hamburg, AR 71646
(501) 853-5113

Civil records are available in person only. See Arkansas state repository for additional information.

Misdemeanor records
Municipal Court
PO Box 558
Hamburg, AR 71646
(501) 853-8326

Misdemeanor records since 1978 are available by mail or phone. No release necessary. No search fee. Search information required: name, date of birth, years to search, sex, race, date of offense.

Baxter County

Circuit Clerk, Criminal Records
Courthouse
Mountain Home, AR 72653
(501) 425-3475
Fax (501) 424-5105

Felony records are available by mail or fax. No release necessary. No search fee. Copies are $.25 per page. Make company check or money order payable to Baxter County Clerk. Search information required: name, date of birth, SSN.

Civil records are available by mail or fax. No release necessary. No search fee. Search information required: name, years to search. Specify plaintiff or defendant.

Benton County

Circuit Clerk, Criminal Records
PO Box 699
Bentonville, AR 72712
(501) 271-1015
Fax (501) 271-1019

Felony records are available by mail. No release necessary. No search fee. Search information required: name, SASE, years to search.

Civil records are available by mail. No release necessary. $15.00 search fee. Search information required: name, years to search, SASE. Specify plaintiff or defendant.

Boone County

Felony records
Circuit Clerk, Criminal Records
PO Box 957
Harrison, AR 72601
(501) 741-5560

Felony records are available by mail or phone. No release necessary. No search fee. Search information required: name, years to search.

Civil records
Circuit Clerk
PO Box 957
Harrison, AR 72601
(501) 741-5560

Civil records are available by mail or phone. No release necessary. No search fee. Search information required: name, years to search. Specify plaintiff or defendant.

Misdemeanor records
Municipal Court
PO Box 446
Harrison, AR 72601
(501) 741-2788

Misdemeanor records are available by mail. No release necessary. No search fee. Search information required: name, date of birth, address, years to search.

Bradley County

Felony records
Bradley County Courthouse, Criminal Records
PO Box 984
Warren, AR 71671
(501) 226-2272

Felony records are available by mail. No release necessary. $6.00 search fee. Make check payable to Circuit Clerk. Search information required: name, date of birth, years to search.

Civil records
Bradley County Courthouse
PO Box 984
Warren, AR 71671
(501) 226-2272

Civil records are available by mail. No release necessary. $6.00 search fee. Search information required: name, years to search. Specify plaintiff or defendant.

Misdemeanor records
Municipal Court
PO Box 352
Warren, AR 71671
(501) 226-2567

Misdemeanor records are available by mail or phone. No search fee. No release necessary. Search information required: name, date of birth, years to search.

Calhoun County

Circuit Clerk, Criminal Records
PO Box 626
Hampton, AR 71744
(501) 798-2517

Felony and misdemeanor records are available by mail or phone. No release necessary. $3.00 search fee, $.50 for each record found. Make company check payable to Calhoun County Clerk. Search information required: name, date of birth, SASE, years to search.

Civil records are available by mail. No release necessary. $3.00 search fee, $.50 for each record found. Search information required: name, years to search. Specify plaintiff or defendant.

Carroll County

Circuit Clerk, Criminal Records
44 S. Main
Eureka Springs, AR 72632
(501) 253-8646

Felony and misdemeanor records are available by mail or by phone from 1985 forward. No release necessary. $6.00 search fee. $.25 fee per copy. $2.00 for certification. Search information required: name, years to search.

Civil records are available by mail or phone. No release necessary. $6.00 search fee. $.25 fee per copy. $2.00 for certification. Search information required: name, years to search. Specify plaintiff or defendant.

Chicot County

County Courthouse, Criminal Records
Circuit Clerk
Lake Village, AR 71653
(501) 265-2366
Fax (501) 265-5856

Felony and misdemeanor records are available by mail or phone. A release is required. $6.00 search fee. Search information required: name, date of birth.

Civil records are available by mail. A release is required. $6.00 search fee. Search information required: name, date of birth, years to search. Specify plaintiff or defendant.

Clark County

Circuit Clerk, Criminal Records
PO Box 576
Arkadelphia, AR 71923
(501) 246-4281

Felony records are available by mail. No release necessary. $5.00 search fee. $.50 per copy. $5.00 for certification. Search information required: name, years to search.

Civil records are available by mail. No release necessary. $5.00 search fee. $.50 fee per copy. $5.00 for certification. Search information required: name, date of birth, years to search. Specify plaintiff or defendant.

Clay County

Circuit Clerk, Criminal Records
PO Box 29
Piggott, AR 72454
(501) 598-2524

Felony records are available by mail or phone. No release necessary. No search fee. Search information required: name, date of birth.

Civil records are available by mail or phone. No release necessary. No search fee. Search information required: name, date of birth, years to search. Specify plaintiff or defendant.

Cleburne County

Felony records
Circuit Clerk, Criminal Records
PO Box 543
Heber Springs, AR 72543
(501) 362-8149
Fax (501) 362-3500

Felony records are available by mail or phone. No release necessary. No search fee. $.25 fee per copy. Search information required: name, years to search.

Civil records
Circuit Clerk, Criminal Records
PO Box 543
Heber Springs, AR 72543
(501) 362-8149
Fax (501) 362-3500

Civil records are available by mail. No release necessary. No search fee. $.25 fee per copy. Search information required: name, years to search. Specify plaintiff or defendant.

Misdemeanor records
Municipal Court
Clevern County Courthouse
Heber Springs, AR 72543
(501) 362-6585

Misdemeanor records are available by mail or phone from 1989 forward. No release necessary. No search fee. $.25 fee per copy. Search information required: name, years to search, SASE.

Cleveland County

Felony records
Circuit Clerk, Criminal Records
PO Box 368
Rison, AR 71665
(501) 325-6902

Felony records are available by mail. A release is required. No search fee. Search information required: name, date of birth, years to search.

Civil records
Circuit Clerk
PO Box 368
Rison, AR 71665
(501) 325-6902

Civil records are available by mail. A release is required. No search fee. Search information required: name, years to search. Specify plaintiff or defendant.

Misdemeanor records
Municipal Court
PO Box 405
Rison, AR 71665
(501) 325-7382

Misdemeanor records are available by mail from 1987 forward. A release is required. No search fee. Search information required: name, date of birth, years to search, SASE.

Civil records
Municipal Court
PO Box 405
Rison, AR 71665
(501) 325-7382

Civil records are available by mail. A release is required. No search fee. Search information required: name, years to search. Specify plaintiff or defendant.

Columbia County

Circuit Clerk, Criminal Records
PO Box 327
Magnolia, AR 71753
(501) 234-4001

Felony records are available by mail or phone. No release necessary. $10.00 search fee. Search information required: name, date of birth, SASE.

Civil records are available by mail. No release necessary. $10.00 search fee. Search information required: name, years to search, SASE. Specify plaintiff or defendant.

Conway County

Felony records
Circuit Clerk, Criminal Records
Conway County Courthouse
115 Moose Street, Room 206
Morrilton, AR 72110
(501) 354-9617

Felony records are available by mail or phone. No release necessary. $6.00 search fee. $.50 fee per copy. Search information required: name, date of birth, years to search.

Civil records
Circuit Clerk
Conway County Courthouse
115 Moose Street, Room 206
Morrilton, AR 72110
(501) 354-9617

Civil records are available by mail. No release necessary. $6.00 search fee. $.50 fee per copy. Search information required: name, date of birth, years to search. Specify plaintiff or defendant.

Misdemeanor records
Municipal Clerk
Room 2, Conway County Courthouse
Morrilton, AR 72110
(501) 354-9615

Misdemeanor records since 1975 are available by mail. No release necessary. No search fee. Search information required: name, years to search, date of offense.

Craighead County

Felony records
Circuit Clerk, Criminal Records
PO Box 120
Jonesboro, AR 72403
(501) 932-3181
Fax (501) 933-4534

Felony records are available by mail or phone. No release necessary. $6.00 search fee. Search information required: name, years to search.

Civil records
Circuit Clerk
PO Box 120
Jonesboro, AR 72403
(501) 932-3181
Fax (501) 933-4534

Civil records are available in person only. See Arkansas state repository for additional information.

Misdemeanor records
Municipal Court
524 S. Church
Jonesboro, AR 72401
(501) 933-4580
Fax (501) 933-4582

Misdemeanor records are available by mail, phone or fax. No release necessary. Search information required: name, date of birth, years to search, SASE.

Civil records
Municipal Court
524 S. Church
Jonesboro, AR 72401
(501) 933-4580

Civil records are available by mail. No release necessary. $2.00 search fee per year searched. $.25 fee per copy. $2.00 for certification. Search information required: name, years to search. Specify plaintiff or defendant.

Crawford County

Circuit Clerk, Criminal Records
Crawford County Courthouse
Van Buren, AR 72956
(501) 474-1821

Felony and misdemeanor records are available by mail. No release necessary. $6.00 search fee. $1.00 fee per copy. Search information required: name, date of birth, years to search.

Civil records are available by mail or phone. No release necessary. No search fee. Search information required: name, date of birth, years to search. Specify plaintiff or defendant.

Crittenden County

Circuit Clerk, Criminal Records
Marion, AR 72364
(501) 739-3248

Felony and misdemeanor records are available by mail. No release necessary. $5.00 fee. Company checks only, payable to Circuit Clerk. Search information required: name, date of birth, years to search.

Civil records are available by mail. No release necessary. $5.00 search fee. Search information required: name, date of birth, years to search, SASE. Specify plaintiff or defendant.

Cross County

Felony records
Circuit Clerk
County Courthouse
Wynne, AR 72396
(501) 238-2241

Felony records are available by mail. No release necessary. $6.00 fee. Search information required: name, years to search, case number (if available).

Civil records
Circuit Clerk
County Courthouse
Wynne, AR 72396
(501) 238-2241

Civil records are available in person only. See Arkansas state repository for additional information.

Misdemeanor records
Municipal Court
206 S. Falls Blvd.
Wynne, AR 72396
(501) 238-9171

Misdemeanor records are available by mail. No release necessary. No search fee. Search information required: name, date of birth, years to search, case number (if available).

Dallas County

Circuit Clerk, Criminal Records
Dallas County Courthouse
202 3rd Street West
Fordyce, AR 71742-3299
(501) 352-2307

Felony records are available by mail. No release necessary. $6.00 search fee. $.25 fee per copy. Search information required: name, SASE.

Civil records are available by mail. No release necessary. $6.00 search fee. $.25 fee per copy. Search information required: name, years to search, SASE. Specify plaintiff or defendant.

Desha County

Circuit Clerk, Criminal Records
PO Box 398
Arkansas City, AR 71630
(501) 877-2411

Felony records are available by mail or phone. No release necessary. $6.00 fee for each 5 years searched. Search information required: name, SSN, date of birth, sex, race, previous address.

Civil records are available by mail or phone. No release necessary. No search fee. $.50 fee per copy. Search information required: name, date of birth, years to search, SASE. Specify plaintiff or defendant.

Drew County

Circuit Clerk, Criminal Records
210 S. Main
Courthouse
Monticello, AR 71655
(501) 367-2446
Fax (501) 367-7291

Felony and misdemeanor records are available by mail, phone or fax. No release necessary. $6.00 fee. Make check payable to Circuit Clerk. Search information required: name, previous address, years to search.

Civil records are available by mail, phone or fax. No release necessary. $6.00 search fee. Search information required: name, years to search. Specify plaintiff or defendant.

Faulkner County

Circuit Clerk,
801 Locust, Room 15
Faulkner County Courthouse
Conway, AR 72032
(501) 450-4911
Fax (501) 450-4948

Felony records are available by mail or fax. No release necessary. $6.00 search fee for any seven years searched. Search information required: name, date of birth.

Civil records are available by mail or fax. No release necessary. $6.00 search fee. Search information required: name, years to search. Specify plaintiff or defendant.

Franklin County

Circuit Clerk, Criminal Records
Franklin County Courthouse
Ozark, AR 72949
(501) 667-3818
Fax (501) 667-2234

Felony records are available by mail, phone or fax. No release necessary. No search fee. Search information required: name.

Civil records are available by mail, phone or fax. A release is required. No search fee. Search information required: name, date of birth, years to search. Specify plaintiff or defendant.

Fulton County

Felony records
Fulton County Circuit Clerk, Criminal Records
PO Box 485
Salem, AR 72576
(501) 895-3310

Felony records are available by mail or phone. No release necessary. No search fee. $.10 fee per copy. Search information required: name, years to search.

Civil records
Fulton County Circuit Clerk
PO Box 485
Salem, AR 72576
(501) 895-3310

Civil records are available by mail. No release necessary. No search fee. $.10 fee per copy. Search information required: name, years to search, SASE. Specify plaintiff or defendant.

Misdemeanor records
Municipal Court
PO Box 928
Salem, AR 72576
(501) 895-4136

Misdemeanor records are available by mail or phone. No release necessary. No search fee. Search information required: name, years to search, date of birth.

Garland County

Felony records
Circuit Clerk, Criminal Records
Garland County Courthouse
Hot Springs, AR 71901
(501) 321-1650
Fax (501) 321-6832

Felony records are available by mail. No release necessary. No search fee. Search information required: name, date of birth, sex, race, years to search.

Civil records
Circuit Clerk
Garland County Courthouse
Hot Springs, AR 71901
(501) 321-1650

Civil records are available by phone. No release necessary. No search fee. Search information required: name, years to search. Specify plaintiff or defendant.

Misdemeanor records
Municipal Court
PO Box 700
Hot Springs, AR 71902
(501) 321-6765
Fax (501) 321-6832

Misdemeanor records since 1972 are available by mail. Turnaround time is 1 week. No release necessary. No search fee. Search information required: name, date of birth, years to search, SASE.

Grant County

Felony records
Courthouse, Grant County Circuit Clerk
Sheridan, AR 72150
(501) 942-2631
Fax (501) 942-2442

Felony records are available by mail, phone or fax. No release necessary. $6.00 fee. $.20 fee per copy. Make check payable to Circuit Clerk. Search information required: name, date of birth.

Civil records
Courthouse, Grant County Circuit Clerk
Sheridan, AR 72150
(501) 942-2631
Fax (501) 942-2442

Civil records are available by mail. No release necessary. $6.00 search fee. $.20 fee per copy. Search information required: name, years to search. Specify plaintiff or defendant.

Misdemeanor records
Municipal Court Clerk's Office
Sheridan, AR 72150
(501) 942-3464

Misdemeanor records since 1980 are available by mail or phone. A release is required. No search fee. Make check payable to Circuit Clerk. Search information required: name, date of birth, SSN, previous address, SASE.

Greene County

Circuit Clerk, Criminal Records
PO Box 1028
Paragould, AR 72450
(501) 239-6330
Fax (501) 239-3550

Felony records are available by mail or fax. Turnaround time is 1 week. No release necessary. $6.00 search fee. $.25 per copy, $3.00 for certification. Search information required: name, SSN, date of birth, sex, race, SASE.

Civil records are available by mail or fax. No release necessary. $6.00 search fee. $.25 fee per copy. $3.00 for certification. Search information required: name, date of birth, years to search. Specify plaintiff or defendant.

Hempstead County

Felony records
Circuit Clerk, Criminal Records
PO Box 1420
Hope, AR 71801
(501) 777-2384

Felony records are available by mail. No release necessary. Search information required: name, years to search.

Civil records
Circuit Clerk
PO Box 1420
Hope, AR 71801
(501) 777-2384

Civil records are available by mail. No release necessary. $6.00 search fee. Search information required: name, years to search. Specify plaintiff or defendant.

Misdemeanor records
Municipal Court
PO Box 1420
Hope, AR 71801
(501) 777-2525

Misdemeanor records since April 1987 are available by mail. No release necessary. $5.00 search fee. Make check or money order payable to Municipal Clerk. Search information required: name, date of birth, years to search, SASE.

Hot Spring County

Circuit Clerk, Criminal Records
200 Locust Street
Malvern, AR 72104
(501) 332-2281
Fax (501) 332-2281

Felony and misdemeanor records are available by mail. No release necessary. $3.00 fee. Company checks only, payable to Circuit Clerk. Search information required: name.

Civil records are available in person only. See Arkansas state repository for additional information.

Howard County

Felony records
Circuit Clerk, Criminal Records
Room 7
421 N. Main
Nashville, AR 71852
(501) 845-7506 or 845-7507

Felony records are available by mail or phone. Release, if available. $6.00 search fee. Company checks only, payable to Circuit Clerk. Search information required: name, date of birth, years to search.

Civil records
Circuit Clerk
Room 7
421 N. Main
Nashville, AR 71852
(501) 845-7506 or 845-7507

Civil records are available by mail. A release is required. $6.00 search fee. Search information required: name, date of birth, years to search. Specify plaintiff or defendant.

Misdemeanor records
Howard County Municipal Court
421 N. Main, Rm. 21
Nashville, AR 71852
(501) 845-7522 Extension 29
Fax (501) 845-3705

Misdemeanor records since 1981 are available by mail, phone or fax. No release necessary. No search fee. Search information required: name, date of birth, years to search.

Independence County

Felony records
Circuit Clerk, Criminal Records
Independence County Courthouse
Main and Broad Street
Batesville, AR 72501
(501) 793-8833

Felony records are available by mail. No release necessary. No search fee. Search information required: name, date of birth, SASE.

Civil records are available by mail. No release necessary. No search fee. Search information required: name, date of birth, years to search, SASE. Specify plaintiff or defendant.

Misdemeanor records
Municipal Court
368 E. Main
Batesville, AR 72501
(501) 793-8817

Misdemeanor records are available by mail. No release necessary. No search fee. Search information required: name, date of birth, SASE.

Izard County

Circuit Clerk, Criminal Records
PO Box 95
Melbourne, AR 72556
(501) 368-4316
Fax (501) 368-5042

Felony and misdemeanor records are available by mail or fax. No release necessary. $6.00 fee. Make check payable to Circuit Clerk. Search information required: name.

Civil records are available by mail or fax. No release necessary. $6.00 search fee. Search information required: name, years to search. Specify plaintiff or defendant.

Jackson County

Circuit Clerk, Criminal Records
Jackson County Courthouse
Newport, AR 72112
(501) 523-3826

Felony records are available by mail. No release necessary. $10.00 fee. Make check payable to Circuit Clerk. Search information required: name, years to search.

Civil records are available in person only. See Arkansas state repository for additional information.

Jefferson County

Circuit Clerk, Criminal Records
PO Box 7433
Pine Bluff, AR 71611
(501) 541-5307

Felony records are available in person only. See Arkansas state repository for additional information.

Civil records are available in person only. See Arkansas state repository for additional information.

Johnson County

Felony records
Circuit Clerk, Criminal Records
PO Box 217
Clarksville, AR 72830
(501) 754-2977

Felony records are available by mail or phone. No release necessary. No search fee. Search information required: name, date of birth.

Civil records
Circuit Clerk
PO Box 217
Clarksville, AR 72830
(501) 754-2977

Civil records are available by mail or phone. No release necessary. No search fee. Search information required: name, years to search. Specify plaintiff or defendant.

Misdemeanor records
Municipal Court
PO Box 581
Clarksville, AR 72830
(501) 754-8533

Misdemeanor records are available by mail. No release necessary. No search fee. Search information required: name, date of birth, driver's license (if available).

Lafayette County

Circuit Clerk, Criminal Records
PO Box 986
Lewisville, AR 71845
(501) 921-4878

Felony and misdemeanor records are available in person only. See Arkansas state repository for additional information.

Civil records are available in person only. See Arkansas state repository for additional information.

Lawrence County

Circuit Clerk, Criminal Records
PO Box 581
Walnut Ridge, AR 72476
(501) 886-3421
Fax (501) 886-3421

Felony records are available by mail, phone or fax. No release necessary. No search fee. Search information required: name, years to search.

Civil records are available by mail, phone or fax. No release necessary. No search fee. Search information required: name, years to search. Specify plaintiff or defendant.

Lee County

Courthouse, Criminal Records
Circuit Clerk
Marianna, AR 72360
(501) 295-7710

Felony records are available in person only. See Arkansas state repository for additional information.

Civil records are available by mail. No release necessary. No search fee. Search information required: name, years to search. Specify plaintiff or defendant.

Lincoln County

Courthouse, Criminal Records
Circuit Clerk
Star City, AR 71667
(501) 628-3154

Felony records are available by mail. No release necessary. $6.00 fee. Company checks only, payable to Lincoln County Circuit Clerk. Search information required: name, date of birth, previous address.

Civil records are available by mail. No release necessary. $6.00 search fee. Search information required: name, date of birth, years to search. Specify plaintiff or defendant.

Little River County

Circuit Clerk, Criminal Records
PO Box 575
Ashdown, AR 71822
(501) 898-7211

Felony records are available by mail. No release necessary. $6.00 search fee. Make check payable to Circuit Clerk. Search information required: name, date of birth, years to search.

Civil records are available by mail. No release necessary. $6.00 search fee. Search information required: name, years to search. Specify plaintiff or defendant.

Logan County

Circuit Clerk, Criminal Records
Courthouse
Booneville, AR 72927
(501) 675-2894
Fax (510) 675-2894

Felony records are available by mail or fax. No release necessary. $6.00 search fee. Make check payable to Circuit Clerk. Search information required: name, date of birth, years to search.

Civil records are available by mail or fax. No release necessary. $6.00 search fee. Search information required: name, date of birth, years to search. Specify plaintiff or defendant.

Lonoke County

Circuit Clerk, Criminal Records
PO Box 231
Lonoke, AR 72086
(501) 676-2316

Felony and misdemeanor records are available by mail. A release is required. $6.00 fee. Make company check payable to Circuit Clerk. Search information required: name, SASE.

Civil records are available by mail. A release is required. $6.00 search fee. Search information required: name, years to search, SASE. Specify plaintiff or defendant.

Madison County

Felony records
Circuit Clerk, Criminal Records
PO Box 416
Huntsville, AR 72740
(501) 738-2215
Fax (501) 738-2735

Felony records are available in person only. See Arkansas state repository for additional information.

Civil records
Circuit Clerk
PO Box 416
Huntsville, AR 72740
(501) 738-2215
Fax (501) 738-2735

Civil records are available in person only. See Arkansas state repository for additional information.

Misdemeanor records
Municipal Court
PO Box 549
Huntsville, AR 72740
(501) 738-2911

Misdemeanor records ar available by mail. No release necessary. No search fee. Search information required: name. years to search.

Marion County

Marion County Clerk, Criminal Records
PO Box 385
Yellville, AR 72687
(501) 449-6226

Felony records are available by mail. No release necessary. $6.00 fee. Make company check payable to Circuit Clerk. Search information required: name, date of birth.

Civil records are available in person only. See Arkansas state repository for additional information.

Miller County

Felony records
Circuit Clerk, Criminal Records
Miller County Courthouse
412 Laurel, Room 109
Texarkana, AR 75502
(501) 774-4501

Felony records are available by mail. No release necessary. $6.00 fee. $1.00 fee per copy. Make company check payable to Circuit Clerk. Search information required: name, date of birth, sex, race.

Civil records
Circuit Clerk
Miller County Courthouse
412 Laurel, Room 109
Texarkana, AR 75502
(501) 774-4501

Civil records are available by mail. No release necessary. No search fee. $1.00 fee per copy. Search information required: name, date suit was filed. Specify plaintiff or defendant.

Misdemeanor records
Municipal Court
100 North State Line
Box 2
Texarkana, AR 75501
(903) 798-3181

Misdemeanor records since 1980 are available by mail. $10.00 search fee. A notorized release is required. Search information required: name, date of birth, race, sex, years to search, SASE.

Civil records
Municipal Court
100 North State Line
Box 2
Texarkana, AR 75501
(903) 798-3181

Civil records are available by mail. A release is required. $5.00 search fee. $.08 fee per copy. Search information required: name, date suit was filed, years to search. Specify plaintiff or defendant.

Mississippi County

Circuit Clerk, Criminal Records
PO Box 1496
Blytheville, AR 72316
(501) 762-2332
Fax (501) 763-0150

Felony records are available by mail or fax. No release necessary. $3.00 fee. Search information required: name, SSN, date of birth, sex, race, previous address. Additional records are available from Circuit Clerk, PO Box 471, Osceola, AR 72370.

Civil records are available by mail or fax. No release necessary. $3.00 search fee. Search information required: name, date of birth, SSN, years to search. Specify plaintiff or defendant.

Monroe County

Circuit Clerk, Criminal Records
123 Madison Street
Clarendon, AR 72029
(501) 747-3615

Felony and misdemeanor records are available by mail or phone. No release necessary. No search fee. $.25 fee per copy. Search information required: name, date of birth, previous address.

Civil records are available by mail or phone. No release necessary. No search fee. $.25 fee per copy. Search information required: name, date of birth, previous address, years to search. Specify plaintiff or defendant.

Montgomery County

Felony records
Circuit Clerk, Criminal Records
PO Box 37
Mount Ida, AR 71957
(501) 867-3521

Felony records are available by mail. No release necessary. $3.00 fee. Make check payable to Circuit Clerk. Search information required: name.

Civil records
Circuit Clerk
PO Box 37
Mount Ida, AR 71957
(501) 867-3521

Civil records are available by mail. No release necessary. $3.00 search fee. Search information required: name, years to search. Specify plaintiff or defendant.

Misdemeanor records
Montgomery County Municipal Court
PO Box 558
Mount Ida, AR 71957
(501) 867-2221
Fax (501) 867-4354

Misdemeanor records since 1979 are available by mail, phone or fax. No release necessary. No search fee. Search information required: name, date of offense.

Civil records
Montgomery County Municipal Court
PO Box 558
Mount Ida, AR 71957
(501) 867-2221
Fax (501) 867-4354

Civil records are available by mail, phone or fax. No release necessary. No search fee. Search information required: name, date of birth, years to search. Specify plaintiff or defendant.

Nevada County

Felony records
Circuit Clerk, Criminal Records
PO Box 552
Prescott, AR 71857
(501) 887-2511

Felony records are available by mail or phone. No release necessary. $6.00 search fee. $.25 fee per copy. Make company check payable to Circuit Clerk. Search information required: name.

Civil records
Circuit Clerk
PO Box 552
Prescott, AR 71857
(501) 887-2511

Civil records are available by mail. No release necessary. $6.00 search fee. $.25 fee per copy. Search information required: name, years to search. Specify plaintiff or defendant.

Misdemeanor records
Municipal Court
PO Box 22
Prescott, AR 71857
(501) 887-6016

Misdemeanor records since 1980 are available by mail. No release necessary. No search fee. Search information required: name.

Civil records
Municipal Court
PO Box 22
Prescott, AR 71857
(501) 887-6016

Civil records are available by mail. No release necessary. No search fee. Search information required: name, years to search. Specify plaintiff or defendant.

Newton County

Felony records
Circuit Clerk, Criminal Records
PO Box 410
Jasper, AR 72641
(501) 446-5125

Felony records are available in person only. See Arkansas state repository for additional information.

Civil records
Circuit Clerk
PO Box 410
Jasper, AR 72641
(501) 446-5125

Civil records are available in person only. See Arkansas state repository for additional information.

Misdemeanor records
Municipal Court
PO Box 550
Jasper, AR 72641
(501) 446-5335

Misdemeanor records since 1976 are available by mail or phone. No release necessary. No search fee. $.25 fee per copy. $3.00 for certification. Make company check payable to Newton County Municipal Court. Search information required: name, date of birth, SASE.

Civil records
Municipal Court
PO Box 550
Jasper, AR 72641
(501) 446-5335

Civil records are available by mail or phone. No release necessary. No search fee. $.25 fee per copy. $3.00 for cerification. Search information required: name, date of birth, years to search, SASE. Specify plaintiff or defendant.

Ouachita County

Felony records
Circuit Clerk, Criminal Records
PO Box 667
Camden, AR 71701
(501) 836-7357

Felony records are available by mail. No release necesary. $6.00 flat fee plus $1.00 fee per year searched. $.50 fee per copy. $2.50 for certification. Search information required: name, years to search.

Civil records
Circuit Clerk
PO Box 667
Camden, AR 71701
(501) 836-7357

Civil records are available in person only. See Arkansas state repository for additional information.

Misdemeanor records
Municipal Clerk
Ouachita County Court
145 Jefferson St.
Camden, AR 71701
(501) 836-0331

Misdemeanor records since 1975 are available by mail. A release is required. $5.00 search fee. Search information required: name, years to search.

Civil records
Municipal Clerk
Ouachita County Court
145 Jefferson St.
Camden, AR 71701
(501) 836-0331

Civil records are available in person only. See Arkansas state repository for additional information.

Perry County

Felony records
Circuit Clerk, Criminal Records
Perry County Courthouse
PO Box 358
Perryville, AR 72126
(501) 889-5126

Felony records are available by phone. No release necessary. No search fee. Copies are $1.00 per page. Search information required: name, date of birth.

Civil records
Circuit Clerk
Perry County Courthouse
PO Box 358
Perryville, AR 72126
(501) 889-5126

Civil records are available in person only. See Arkansas state repository for additional information.

Misdemeanor records
Municipal Court
PO Box 186
Perryville, AR 72126
(501) 889-5296

Misdemeanor records since 1985 are available by mail. No release necessary. No search fee. Search information required: name, date of birth, years to search.

Civil records
Municipal Court
PO Box 186
Perryville, AR 72126
(501) 889-5296

Civil records are available by mail. No release necessary. No search fee. Search information required: name, date of birth, years to search. Specify plaintiff or defendant.

Phillips County

Circuit Clerk, Criminal Records
Phillips County Courthouse
Helena, AR 72342
(501) 338-8251

Felony and misdemeanor records are available by mail. No release necessary. $6.00 search fee. Certified check only, payable to Circuit Clerk. Search information required: name, SSN, date of birth, race, years to search.

Civil records are available by mail. No release necessary. $6.00 search fee. Search information required: name, date of birth, years to search. Specify plaintiff or defendant.

Pike County

Felony records
Circuit Clerk, Criminal Records
PO Box 219
Murfreesboro, AR 71958
(501) 285-2231

Felony records are available by mail. No release necessary. $6.00 fee. Company checks only, payable to Pike County Clerk. Search information required: name, years to search.

Civil records
Circuit Clerk
PO Box 219
Murfreesboro, AR 71958
(501) 285-2231

Civil records are available by mail. No release necessary. $6.00 search fee. $.50 fee per copy. $3.00 for certification. Search information required: name, years to search. Specify plaintiff or defendant.

Misdemeanor records
Municipal Court
(501) 285-3865

Misdemeanor records since 1981 are available in person only. No fee. Open Tuesday and Thursday.

Civil records
Municipal Court
(501) 285-3865

Civil records are available by mail. A release is required. No search fee. $.25 fee per copy. $1.75 for certification. Search information required: name, years to search. Specify plaintiff or defendant.

Poinsett County

Circuit Clerk, Criminal Records
PO Box 46
Harrisburg, AR 72432
(501) 578-2244
Fax (501) 578-2244

Felony and misdemeanor records are available by mail or fax. No release necessary. $6.00 search fee. Search information required: name, date of birth, years to search.

Civil records are available by mail or fax. No release necessary. $6.00 search fee. Search information required: name, date of birth, years to search. Specify plaintiff or defendant.

Polk County

Felony records
Circuit Clerk, Criminal Records
507 Church Street
Mena, AR 71953
(501) 394-6010 Extension 13
Felony records are available by mail. No release necessary. $6.00 search fee. Search information required: name, years to search.

Civil records are available by mail. No release necessary. $6.00 search fee. $.50 fee per legal copy. $.25 fee for regular copy. Search information required: name, years to search. Specify plaintiff or defendant.

Misdemeanor records
Municipal Court
507 Church Street
Mena, AR 71953
(501) 394-3271
Fax (501) 394-1975

Misdemeanor records are available by mail, phone or fax. No release necessary. No search fee. Search information required: name, years to search.

Civil records
Municipal Court
507 Church Street
Mena, AR 71953
(501) 394-3271
Fax (501) 394-3271

Civil records are available by mail, phone or fax. No release necessary. No search fee. Search information required: name, years to search. Specify plaintiff or defendant.

Pope County

Circuit Clerk, Criminal Records
PO Box 926
Russellville, AR 72801
(501) 968-7499

Felony records are available in person. See Arkansas state repository for additional information.

Civil records are available in person. See Arkansas state repository for additional information.

Prairie County

Circuit Clerk, Criminal Records-Northern District
PO Box 1011
Des Arc, AR 72040
(501) 256-4434

Felony and misdemeanor records are available by mail or phone. No release necessary. No search fee. Search information required: name, date of birth, years to search. Additional records are available from Southern District-DeValls Courthouse, PO Box 325, DeValls Bluff, AR 72041.

Civil records are available by phone. No release necessary. No search fee. Search information required: name, years to search. Specify plaintiff or defendant.

Pulaski County

Circuit Clerk, Criminal Records
Room 200
Pulaski County Courthouse
Little Rock, AR 72201
(501) 372-8430

Felony and misdemeanor records are available in person only. For further information and instructions, contact the above office.

Civil records are available in person. See Arkansas state repository for additional information.

Randolph County

Felony records
Circuit Clerk
Randolph County Courthouse
Pocahontas, AR 72455
(501) 892-5522
Fax (501) 892-8794

Felony records are available by mail, phone, or fax. No release necessary. No search fee. Search information required: name.

Civil records
Circuit Clerk
Randolph County Courthouse
Pocahontas, AR 72455
(501) 892-5522
Fax (501) 892-8794

Civil records are available by mail. No release necessary. No search fee. Search information required: name, years to search. Specify plaintiff or defendant.

Misdemeanor records
Municipal Clerk
PO Box 896
Pocahontas, AR 72455
(501) 892-4033

Misdemeanor records since 1975 are available by mail or phone. No release necessary. No search fee. Search information required: name, date of birth, SSN.

Civil records
Municipal Clerk
PO Box 896
Pocahontas, AR 72455
(501) 892-9661

Civil records are available by mail. A release is required. No search fee. Search information required: name, years to search. Specify plaintiff or defendant.

Saline County

Circuit Clerk, Criminal Records
Saline County Courthouse
PO Box 1560
Benton, AR 72015
(501) 776-5615

Felony records are available by mail or phone. No release necessary. No fee. Search information required: name.

Civil records are available by mail. No release necessary. No search fee. Search information required: name, years to search. Specify plaintiff or defendant.

Scott County

Circuit Clerk, Criminal Records
PO Box 464
Waldron, AR 72958
(501) 637-2642

Felony and misdemeanor records are available by mail. A release is required. No search fee. Search information required: name, date of birth, SSN, years to search.

Civil records are available by mail. A release is required. No search fee. Search information required: name, date of birth, SSN, years to search. Specify plaintiff or defendant.

Searcy County

Felony records
Circuit Clerk, Criminal Records
PO Box 813
Marshall, AR 72650
(501) 448-3807

Felony records are available by mail or phone. No release necessary. No search fee. $3.00 fee for certified copy. Company checks only, payable to Searcy County Circuit Clerk. Search information required: name.

Civil records
Circuit Clerk
PO Box 813
Marshall, AR 72650
(501) 448-3807

Civil records are available by mail or phone. No release necessary. $6.00 search fee. $.10 fee per copy. Search information required: name, years to search. Specify plaintiff or defendant.

Misdemeanor records
Marshall Municipal Court
General Delivery
PO Box 837
Marshall, AR 72650
(501) 448-5411

Misdemeanor records since 1980 are available by mail or phone. No release necessary. No search fee. Search information required: name, date of birth, years to search, SASE, date of offense.

Civil records
Marshall Municipal Court
General Delivery
PO Box 837
Marshall, AR 72650
(501) 448-5411

Civil records are available by mail. No release necessary. No search fee. $.25 fee per copy. $1.75 for certification. Search information required: name, years to search, SASE. Specify plaintiff or defendant.

Sebastian County

Circuit Clerk, Criminal Records
PO Box 1179
Fort Smith, AR 72902
(501) 782-1046

Felony records are available by mail. No release necessary. $6.00 search fee. Checks payable to Circuit Clerk. Search information required: name, years to search. Office has access to Fort Smith city limits only. Additional records are available from Circuit Clerk in Greenwood District, PO Box 310, Greenwood, AR 72936, (501) 996-4175.

Civil records are available by mail. No release necessary. $6.00 search fee. Search information required: name, years to search. Specify plaintiff or defendant.

Sevier County

Circuit Clerk, Criminal Records
Sevier County Courthouse
115 N. 3rd
DeQueen, AR 71832
(501) 584-3055

Felony records are available by mail. No release necessary. $6.00 search fee. Copies are $.50 per page. Search information required: name, years to search.

Civil records are available by mail. No release necessary. $6.00 search fee. $.50 fee per copy. Search information required: name, years to search. Specify plaintiff or defendant.

Sharp County

Felony records
Circuit Clerk, Criminal Records
PO Box 307
Ashflat, AR 72513
(501) 994-7361

Felony records are available by mail or phone. No release necessary. $6.00 search fee. Make check payable to Circuit Clerk. Search information required: name, years to search.

Civil records
Circuit Clerk
PO Box 307
Ashflat, AR 72513
(501) 994-7361

Civil records are available by mail. No release necessary. $6.00 search fee. $.15 fee per copy. $3.00 for certification. Search information required: name, years to search. Specify plaintiff or defendant.

Misdemeanor records
Municipal Court Clerk
PO Box 2
Ashflat, AR 72513
(501) 994-2745
Fax (501) 994-7901

Misdemeanor records since 1985 are available by mail or fax. A release is required. No search fee. $3.00 for certification. Search information required: name, years to search.

Civil records
Municipal Court Clerk
PO Box 2
Ashflat, AR 72513
(501) 994-2745
Fax (501) 994-7901

Civil records are available by mail or fax. A release is required. No search fee. $.25 fee per copy. $2.00 for certification. Search information required: name, date of birth, SSN, years to search, SASE. Specify plaintiff or defendant.

Stone County

Felony records
Circuit Clerk, Criminal Records
PO Drawer 120
Mountain View, AR 72560
(501) 269-3271
Fax (501) 269-2299

Felony records are available by mail, phone or fax. No release necessary. No search fee. Search information required: name.

Civil records
Circuit Clerk
PO Drawer 120
Mountain View, AR 72560
(501) 269-3271
Fax (501) 269-2299

Civil records are available by mail, phone or fax. No release necessary. No search fee. $.25 fee per copy. $2.50 for certification. Search information required: name, years to search. Specify plaintiff or defendant.

Misdemeanor records
Municipal Court Clerk
PO Box 1284
Mountain View, AR 72560
(501) 269-3465

Misdemeanor records since 1979 are available by mail. A release is required. No fee. Search information required: name, date of birth, date of offense.

Civil records
Municipal Court Clerk
PO Box 1284
Mountain View, AR 72560
(501) 269-3465

Civil records are available by mail or phone. No release necessary. No search fee. Search information required: name, years to search. Specify plaintiff or defendant.

St. Francis County

Felony records
Circuit Clerk, Criminal Records
PO Box 1775
Forrest City, AR 72335
(501) 633-8365

Felony records are available in person only. See Arkansas state repository for additional information.

Civil records
Circuit Clerk
PO Box 1775
Forrest City, AR 72335
(501) 633-8365

Civil records are available in person only. See Arkansas state repository for additional information.

Misdemeanor records
Forest City Municipal Court
Courthouse
Forrest City, AR 72335
(501) 633-8369
Fax (501) 633-8831

Misdemeanor records since 1960 are available by mail, phone or fax. No release necessary. No search fee. Search information required: name, date of birth, SASE, years to search.

Civil records
Forest City Municipal Court
Courthouse
Forrest City, AR 72335
(501) 633-8369
Fax (501) 633-8831

Civil records are available by mail, phone or fax. A release is required. No search fee. $.25 fee per copy. Search information required: name, years to search, SASE. Specify plaintiff or defendant.

Union County

Felony records
Circuit Clerk, Criminal Records
Union County Courthouse
El Dorado, AR 71730
(501) 864-1940

Felony records are available by mail. No release necessary. $6.00 search fee per name, per seven years searched. Search information required: name, SASE.

Civil records
Circuit Clerk
Union County Courthouse
El Dorado, AR 71730
(501) 864-1940

Civil records are available by mail. No release necessary. $6.00 search fee. Search information required: name, years to search, SASE. Specify plaintiff or defendant.

Misdemeanor records
Union County Courthouse
Municipal Clerk's Office, 2nd Floor
El Dorado, AR 71730
(501) 864-1950

Misdemeanor records since 1987 are available by mail. A release is required. No search fee. Search information required: name, SASE, years to search.

Civil records
Union County Courthouse
Municipal Clerk's Office, 2nd Floor
El Dorado, AR 71730
(501) 864-1950

Civil records are available by mail. No release necessary. No search fee. Search information required: name, years to search. Specify plaintiff or defendant.

Van Buren County

Felony records
Van Buren Circuit Clerk, Criminal Records
PO Box 80
Clinton, AR 72031
(501) 745-4140

Felony records are available by mail. No release necessary. $5.00 search fee. Search information required: name.

Civil records
Van Buren Circuit Clerk
PO Box 80
Clinton, AR 72031
(501) 745-4140

Civil records are available by mail. No release necessary. $5.00 search fee. Search information required: name, years to search, SASE. Specify plaintiff or defendant.

Misdemeanor records
Van Buren County Municipal Court
PO Box 368
Clinton, AR 72031
(501) 745-8894
Fax (501) 745-5444

Misdemeanor records since 1987 are available by mail or fax. No release necessary. No search fee. $5.00 fee for certification. Search information required: name, date of birth, SASE.

Civil records
Van Buren County Municipal Court
PO Box 368
Clinton, AR 72031
(501) 745-8894
Fax (501) 745-5444

Civil records are available by mail or phone. No release necessary. No search fee. $.25 fee per copy. $5.00 for certification. Search information required: name, years to search, SASE. Specify plaintiff or defendant.

Washington County

Felony and misdemeanor records
Washington County
Courthouse Annex
Fayetteville, AR 72701
(501) 444-1538
Fax (501) 444-1537

Felony and misdemeanor records are available by mail or fax. No release necessary. No search fee. $.50 fee per copy, $2.00 for certified copy. $5.00 fee for fax response. Company checks only, payable to Circuit Clerk's Office. Search information required: name, SSN, date of birth.

Civil records
Curcuit Clerks Office
Washington County
2 North College
Fayetteville, AR 72701
(501) 444-1538
Fax (501) 444-1537

Civil records are available by mail or fax. No release necessary. $6.00 search fee. $.50 fee per copy. $2.00 for certification. Search information required: name, years to search. Specify plaintiff or defendant.

White County

Circuit Clerk, Criminal Records
301 W. Arch
Searcy, AR 72143
(501) 279-6223

Felony records are available by mail or phone. No release necessary. No search fee. $.50 fee per copy. Search information required: name, years to search, SASE.

Civil records are available by mail. No release necessary. No search fee. $.50 fee per copy. Search information required: name, years to search, SASE. Specify plaintiff or defendant.

Woodruff County

Felony records
Circuit Clerk, Criminal Records
PO Box 492
Augusta, AR 72006
(501) 347-2391

Felony records are available by mail or phone. No release necessary. No search fee. Search information required: name.

Civil records
Circuit Clerk
PO Box 492
Augusta, AR 72006
(501) 347-2391

Civil records are available by phone. No release necessary. No search fee. Search information required: name, years to search. Specify plaintiff or defendant.

Misdemeanor records
Municipal Court
PO Box 381
Augusta, AR 72006
(501) 347-2790
Fax (501) 347-2436

Misdemeanor records are available by mail, phone or fax. No release necessary. No search fee. Search information required: name, years to search.

Civil records
Municipal Court
PO Box 381
Augusta, AR 72006
(501) 347-2790
Fax (501) 347-2436

Civil records are available by mail, phone or fax. No release necessary. No search fee. Search information required: name, years to search. Specify plaintiff or defendant.

Yell County

Felony records
Circuit Clerk, Criminal Records
PO Box 219
Danville, AR 72833
(501) 495-2630
Fax (501) 495-2630

Felony records are available by mail or fax. No release necessary. $6.00 fee. Company checks only, payable to Circuit Clerk. Search information required: name, years to search.

Civil records
Circuit Clerk
PO Box 219
Danville, AR 72833
(501) 495-2630
Fax (501) 495-2630

Civil records are available by mail or fax. No release necessary. No search fee. $.25 fee per copy. $6.00 for certification. Search information required: name, years to search. Specify plaintiff or defendant.

Misdemeanor records
Yell Municipal Court
Courthouse
Danville, AR 72834
(501) 229-1389

Misdemeanor records since 1978 are available by mail or phone. A release is required. No search fee. Search information required: name, date of birth, years to search.

Civil records
Yell Municipal Court
Courthouse
Danville, AR 72834
(501) 229-1389

Civil records are available by mail. No release necessary. No search fee. $.25 fee per copy. $2.00 for certification. Search information required: name, years to search. Specify plaintiff or defendant.

City-County Cross Reference

Adona *Perry*
Alco *Stone*
Alexander *Pulaski*
Alicia *Lawrence*
Alix *Franklin*
Alleene *Little River*
Alma *Crawford*
Almyra *Arkansas*
Alpena *Boone*
Altheimer *Jefferson*
Altus *Franklin*
Amagon *Jackson*
Amity *Clark*
Antoine *Pike*
Arkadelphia *Clark*
Arkansas City *Desha*

Armorel *Mississippi*
Ashdown *Little River*
Ash Flat *Sharp*
Atkins *Pope*
Aubrey *Lee*
Augusta *Woodruff*
Austin *Lonoke*
Avoca *Benton*
Balch *Jackson*
Bald Knob *White*
Banks *Bradley*
Barling *Sebastian*
Barton *Phillips*
Bass *Newton*
Bassett *Mississippi*
Batesville *Independence*

Bauxite *Saline*
Bay *Craighead*
Bearden *Ouachita*
Beaver *Carroll*
Beebe *White*
Bee Branch *Van Buren*
Beech Grove *Greene*
Beedeville *Jackson*
Beirne *Clark*
Bella Vista *Benton*
Belleville *Yell*
Ben Lomond *Sevier*
Benton *Saline*
Bentonville *Benton*
Bergman *Boone*
Berryville *Carroll*

Bexar *Fulton*
Bigelow *Perry*
Biggers *Randolph*
Birdeye *Cross*
Biscoe *Prairie*
Bismarck *Hot Spring*
Black Oak *Craighead*
Black Rock *Lawrence*
Blackwell *Conway*
Blakely *Garland*
Blevins *Hempstead*
Blue Mountain *Logan*
Bluff City *Nevada*
Bluffton *Yell*
Blytheville *Mississippi*
Board Camp *Polk*

Boles *Scott*
Bonanza *Sebastian*
Bonnerdale *Hot Spring*
Bono *Craighead*
Booneville *Logan*
Boswell *Izard*
Bradford *White*
Bradley *Lafayette*
Branch *Franklin*
Brickeys *Lee*
Brinkley *Monroe*
Brockwell *Izard*
Brookland *Craighead*
Bruno *Marion*
Bryant *Saline*
Buckner *Lafayette*
Bull Shoals *Marion*
Burdette *Mississippi*
Cabot *Lonoke*
Caddo Gap *Montgomery*
Caldwell *Saint Francis*
Cale *Nevada*
Calico Rock *Izard*
Calion *Union*
Camden *Ouachita*
Cammack Village *Pulaski*
Camp *Fulton*
Canehill *Washington*
Caraway *Craighead*
Carlisle *Lonoke*
Carthage *Dallas*
Casa *Perry*
Cash *Craighead*
Casscoe *Arkansas*
Cave City *Sharp*
Cave Springs *Benton*
Cecil *Franklin*
Cedarville *Crawford*
Center Ridge *Conway*
Centerton *Benton*
Centerville *Yell*
Charleston *Franklin*
Chatfield *Crittenden*
Cherokee Village *Sharp*
Cherry Valley *Cross*
Chester *Crawford*
Chidester *Ouachita*
Choctaw *Van Buren*
Clarendon *Monroe*
Clarkedale *Crittenden*
Clarkridge *Baxter*
Clarksville *Johnson*
Cleveland *Conway*
Clinton *Van Buren*
Coal Hill *Johnson*
College Station *Pulaski*
Colt *Saint Francis*
Columbus *Hempstead*
Combs *Madison*
Compton *Newton*
Concord *Cleburne*
Conway *Faulkner*
Cord *Independence*
Corning *Clay*
Cotter *Baxter*
Cotton Plant *Woodruff*
Cove *Polk*
Coy *Lonoke*
Cozahome *Searcy*
Crawfordsville *Crittenden*
Crocketts Bluff *Arkansas*
Crossett *Ashley*
Crumrod *Phillips*
Curtis *Clark*
Cushman *Independence*
Damascus *Faulkner*

Danville *Yell*
Dardanelle *Yell*
Datto *Clay*
Decatur *Benton*
Deer *Newton*
Delaplaine *Greene*
Delaware *Logan*
Delight *Pike*
Dell *Mississippi*
Dennard *Van Buren*
DeQueen *Sevier*
Dermott *Chicot*
Des Arc *Prairie*
Desha *Independence*
DeValls Bluff *Prairie*
DeWitt *Arkansas*
Diamond City *Boone*
Diaz *Jackson*
Dierks *Howard*
Doddridge *Miller*
Dogpatch *Newton*
Dolph *Izard*
Donaldson *Hot Spring*
Dover *Pope*
Drasco *Cleburne*
Driver *Mississippi*
Dumas *Desha*
Dyer *Crawford*
Dyess *Mississippi*
Earle *Crittenden*
Edgemont *Cleburne*
Edmondson *Crittenden*
Egypt *Craighead*
Elaine *Phillips*
El Dorado *Union*
Elizabeth *Fulton*
Elkins *Washington*
Elm Springs *Washington*
El Paso *White*
Emerson *Columbia*
Emmet *Nevada*
England *Lonoke*
Enola *Faulkner*
Ethel *Arkansas*
Etowah *Mississippi*
Eudora *Chicot*
Eureka Springs *Carroll*
Evansville *Washington*
Evening Shade *Sharp*
Everton *Boone*
Fairfield Bay *Van Buren*
Farmington *Washington*
Fayetteville *Washington*
Fisher *Poinsett*
Flippin *Marion*
Floral *Independence*
Fordyce *Dallas*
Foreman *Little River*
Forrest City *Saint Francis*
Fort Smith *Sebastian*
Fouke *Miller*
Fountain Hill *Ashley*
Fox *Stone*
Franklin *Izard*
Frenchmans Bayou
   Mississippi
Friendship *Hot Spring*
Fulton *Hempstead*
Gamaliel *Baxter*
Garfield *Benton*
Garland City *Miller*
Garner *White*
Gassville *Baxter*
Gateway *Benton*
Genoa *Miller*
Gentry *Benton*

Gepp *Fulton*
Gilbert *Searcy*
Gillett *Arkansas*
Gillham *Sevier*
Gilmore *Crittenden*
Glencoe *Fulton*
Glenwood *Pike*
Goodwin *Saint Francis*
Goshen *Washington*
Gould *Lincoln*
Grady *Lincoln*
Grannis *Polk*
Grapevine *Grant*
Gravelly *Yell*
Gravette *Benton*
Greenbrier *Faulkner*
Green Forest *Carroll*
Greenland *Washington*
Greenway *Clay*
Greenwood *Sebastian*
Greers Ferry *Cleburne*
Gregory *Woodruff*
Griffithville *White*
Grubbs *Jackson*
Guion *Izard*
Gurdon *Clark*
Guy *Faulkner*
Hackett *Sebastian*
Hagarville *Johnson*
Hamburg *Ashley*
Hampton *Calhoun*
Hanover *Stone*
Hardy *Sharp*
Harrell *Calhoun*
Harriet *Searcy*
Harrisburg *Poinsett*
Harrison *Boone*
Hartford *Sebastian*
Hartman *Johnson*
Harvey *Scott*
Haskell *Saline*
Hasty *Newton*
Hatfield *Polk*
Hattieville *Conway*
Hatton *Polk*
Havana *Yell*
Haynes *Lee*
Hazen *Prairie*
Heber Springs *Cleburne*
Hector *Pope*
Helena *Phillips*
Henderson *Baxter*
Hensley *Pulaski*
Hermitage *Bradley*
Heth *Saint Francis*
Hickory Plains *Prairie*
Hickory Ridge *Cross*
Higden *Cleburne*
Higginson *White*
Hindsville *Madison*
Hiwasse *Benton*
Holly Grove *Monroe*
Hope *Hempstead*
Horatio *Sevier*
Horseshoe Bend *Izard*
Hot Springs National Park
   Garland
Hotsprings Village
   Garland
Houston *Perry*
Howell *Woodruff*
Hoxie *Lawrence*
Hughes *Saint Francis*
Humnoke *Lonoke*
Humphrey *Arkansas*
Hunt *Johnson*

Hunter *Woodruff*
Huntington *Sebastian*
Huntsville *Madison*
Huttig *Union*
Ida *Cleburne*
Imboden *Lawrence*
Ivan *Dallas*
Jacksonport *Jackson*
Jacksonville *Pulaski*
Jasper *Newton*
Jefferson *Jefferson*
Jennie *Chicot*
Jersey *Bradley*
Jerusalem *Conway*
Jessieville *Garland*
Joiner *Mississippi*
Jonesboro *Craighead*
Judsonia *White*
Junction City *Union*
Keiser *Mississippi*
Kensett *White*
Keo *Lonoke*
Kibler *Crawford*
Kingsland *Cleveland*
Kingston *Madison*
Kirby *Pike*
Knobel *Clay*
Knoxville *Johnson*
LaCrosse *Izard*
LaGrange *Lee*
Lake City *Craighead*
Lake Hamilton *Garland*
Lakeview *Baxter*
Lake View *Phillips*
Lake Village *Chicot*
Lamar *Johnson*
Lambrook *Phillips*
Laneburg *Nevada*
Langley *Pike*
Lavaca *Sebastian*
Lawson *Union*
Leachville *Mississippi*
Lead Hill *Boone*
Leola *Grant*
Lepanto *Poinsett*
Leslie *Searcy*
Letona *White*
Lewisville *Lafayette*
Lexa *Phillips*
Lincoln *Washington*
Little Rock *Pulaski*
Lockesburg *Sevier*
Locust Grove
   Independence
London *Pope*
Lonoke *Lonoke*
Lonsdale *Garland*
Louann *Ouachita*
Lowell *Benton*
Luxora *Mississippi*
Lynn *Lawrence*
McAlmont *Pulaski*
McCaskill *Hempstead*
McCrory *Woodruff*
McDougal *Clay*
McGehee *Desha*
McNeil *Columbia*
McRae *White*
Mabelvale *Pulaski*
Macon *Pulaski*
Madison *Saint Francis*
Magazine *Logan*
Magness *Independence*
Magnolia *Columbia*
Malvern *Hot Spring*
Mammoth Spring *Fulton*

Mandeville *Miller*
Manila *Mississippi*
Mansfield *Scott*
Marcella *Stone*
Marianna *Lee*
Marion *Crittenden*
Marked Tree *Poinsett*
Marmaduke *Greene*
Marshall *Searcy*
Marvell *Phillips*
Maumelle *Pulaski*
Mayflower *Faulkner*
Maynard *Randolph*
Maysville *Benton*
Melbourne *Izard*
Mellwood *Phillips*
Mena *Polk*
Menifee *Conway*
Midland *Sebastian*
Midway *Baxter*
Mineral Springs *Howard*
Minturn *Lawrence*
Moko *Fulton*
Monette *Craighead*
Monroe *Monroe*
Monticello *Drew*
Montrose *Ashley*
Moro *Lee*
Morrilton *Conway*
Morrow *Washington*
Moscow *Jefferson*
Mountainburg *Crawford*
Mountain Home *Baxter*
Mountain Pine *Garland*
Mountain View *Stone*
Mount Holly *Union*
Mount Ida *Montgomery*
Mount Judea *Newton*
Mount Pleasant *Izard*
Mount Vernon *Faulkner*
Mulberry *Crawford*
Murfreesboro *Pike*
Nail *Newton*
Nashville *Howard*
Natural Dam *Crawford*
Newark *Independence*
New Blaine *Logan*
New Edinburg *Cleveland*
Newhope *Pike*
Newport *Jackson*
Norfork *Baxter*
Norman *Montgomery*
Norphlet *Union*
North Crossett *Ashley*
North Little Rock *Pulaski*
Oak Grove *Carroll*
Oakland *Marion*
Oark *Johnson*
Oden *Montgomery*
Ogden *Little River*
Oil Trough *Independence*
O'Kean *Randolph*
Okolona *Clark*
Ola *Yell*
Omaha *Boone*
Oneida *Phillips*
Onia *Stone*
Osceola *Mississippi*
Oxford *Izard*
Ozan *Hempstead*
Ozark *Franklin*
Ozone *Johnson*
Palestine *Saint Francis*
Pangburn *White*
Paragould *Greene*
Paris *Logan*

Parkdale *Ashley*
Parkin *Cross*
Parks *Scott*
Paron *Saline*
Parthenon *Newton*
Patterson *Woodruff*
Peach Orchard *Clay*
Pearcy *Garland*
Pea Ridge *Benton*
Peel *Marion*
Pelsor *Pope*
Pencil Bluff *Montgomery*
Perry *Perry*
Perryville *Perry*
Pettigrew *Madison*
Pickens *Desha*
Piggott *Clay*
Pindall *Searcy*
Pine Bluff *Jefferson*
Pineville *Izard*
Plainview *Yell*
Pleasant Grove *Stone*
Pleasant Plains
  Independence
Plumerville *Conway*
Pocahontas *Randolph*
Pollard *Clay*
Ponca *Newton*
Poplar Grove *Phillips*
Portia *Lawrence*
Portland *Ashley*
Pottsville *Pope*
Poughkeepsie *Sharp*
Powhatan *Lawrence*
Poyen *Grant*
Prairie Grove *Washington*
Prattsville *Grant*
Prescott *Nevada*
Prim *Cleburne*
Proctor *Crittenden*
Pyatt *Marion*
Quitman *Cleburne*
Ratcliff *Logan*
Ravenden *Lawrence*
Ravenden Springs
  Randolph
Rector *Clay*
Redfield *Jefferson*
Reydell *Jefferson*
Reyno *Randolph*
Rison *Cleveland*
Rivervale *Poinsett*
Roe *Monroe*
Rogers *Benton*
Roland *Pulaski*
Romance *White*
Rondo *Lee*
Rose Bud *White*
Rosie *Independence*
Rosston *Nevada*
Round Pond *Saint Francis*
Rover *Yell*
Royal *Garland*
Rudy *Crawford*
Russell *White*
Russellville *Pope*
Saffell *Lawrence*
Sage *Izard*
Saint Charles *Arkansas*
Saint Francis *Clay*
Saint Joe *Searcy*
Saint Paul *Madison*
Salado *Independence*
Salem *Fulton*
Salesville *Baxter*
Saratoga *Howard*

Scotland *Van Buren*
Scott *Pulaski*
Scranton *Logan*
Searcy *White*
Sedgwick *Lawrence*
Sheridan *Grant*
Sherrill *Jefferson*
Sherwood *Pulaski*
Shirley *Van Buren*
Sidney *Sharp*
Siloam Springs *Benton*
Sims *Montgomery*
Smackover *Union*
Smithville *Lawrence*
Snow Lake *Desha*
Solgohachia *Conway*
Sparkman *Dallas*
Springdale *Washington*
Springfield *Conway*
Springtown *Benton*
Stamps *Lafayette*
Star City *Lincoln*
State University *Craighead*
Stephens *Ouachita*
Steprock *White*
Story *Montgomery*
Strawberry *Lawrence*
Strong *Union*
Sturkie *Fulton*
Stuttgart *Arkansas*
Subiaco *Logan*
Success *Clay*
Sulphur Rock
  Independence
Sulphur Springs *Benton*
Summers *Washington*
Summit *Marion*
Sweet Home *Pulaski*
Swifton *Jackson*
Taylor *Columbia*
Texarkana *Bowie, Tx*
Thida *Independence*
Thornton *Calhoun*
Tichnor *Arkansas*
Tillar *Drew*
Tilly *Pope*
Timbo *Stone*
Tollette *Howard*
Tomato *Mississippi*
Tontitown *Washington*
Traskwood *Saline*
Trumann *Poinsett*
Tucker *Jefferson*
Tuckerman *Jackson*
Tumbling Shoals *Cleburne*
Tupelo *Jackson*
Turner *Phillips*
Turrell *Crittenden*
Twist *Cross*
Tyronza *Poinsett*
Ulm *Prairie*
Umpire *Howard*
Uniontown *Crawford*
Valley Springs *Boone*
Van Buren *Crawford*
Vandervoort *Polk*
Vanndale *Cross*
Vendor *Newton*
Village *Columbia*
Vilonia *Faulkner*
Viola *Fulton*
Violet Hill *Izard*
Wabash *Phillips*
Wabbaseka *Jefferson*
Walcott *Greene*
Waldenburg *Poinsett*

Waldo *Columbia*
Waldron *Scott*
Walnut Ridge *Lawrence*
Ward *Lonoke*
Warren *Bradley*
Washington *Hempstead*
Watson *Desha*
Waveland *Yell*
Weiner *Poinsett*
Wesley *Madison*
West Crossett *Ashley*
Western Grove *Newton*
West Fork *Washington*
West Helena *Phillips*
West Memphis *Crittenden*
West Point *White*
West Ridge *Mississippi*
Wheatley *Saint Francis*
Wheeler *Washington*
Whelen Springs *Clark*
White Hall *Ashley*
Wickes *Polk*
Wideman *Izard*
Widener *Saint Francis*
Wilburn *Cleburne*
Williford *Sharp*
Willisville *Nevada*
Wilmar *Drew*
Wilmot *Ashley*
Wilson *Mississippi*
Wilton *Little River*
Winchester *Drew*
Winslow *Washington*
Winthrop *Little River*
Wiseman *Izard*
Witter *Madison*
Witts Springs *Searcy*
Wolf Bayou *Cleburne*
Woodson *Pulaski*
Wooster *Faulkner*
Wright *Jefferson*
Wrightsville *Pulaski*
Wynne *Cross*
Yellville *Marion*
Yorktown *Lincoln*

California

Access to criminal record histories through the California Department of Justice, which serves as the state's central repository, is limited to those persons specifically authorized by state law to receive it. However, fifty seven (57) of the state's fifty eight (58) counties reported that conviction data was generally available for employment screening purposes by phone or mail and a few by fax. Civil records for $25,00 and larger are filed at the Superior Court level.

For more information or for offices not listed, contact the state's information hot line at (916) 322-9900.

Driving Records

Department of Motor Vehicles
Bond and Control Department
PO Box 944231
Sacramento, CA 94244-2310
(916) 657-6557

Driving records are available by mail. $5.00 fee per request. Turnaround time is 10 days. Written request must include job applicant's full name, date of birth and license number. Contact the above office for Form INF70. Make check payable to Department of Motor Vehicles.

Worker's Compensation Records

Department of Industrial Relations
525 Golden Gate Avenue
San Francisco, CA 94102
(415) 557-1954

Currently worker's compensation records are decentralized at 22 district offices. Although records are public, staff shortages have required the state to limit access to parties making in person requests. The state is in the process of developing an automated record retrieval system that may allow for the centralized access of records. Fee varies. Search information required: name, SSN, date of injury.

Vital Statistics

Vital Statistics Section
Department of Health Services
410 North Street
Sacramento, CA 95814
(916) 445-2684

Birth records are available for $11.00, and death records for $7.00. Some birth records are accessible by computer. Turnaround time is 4-6 weeks. Employers can obtain records with a written release. Make check or money order payable to Vital Statistics. Search information required: name, date of birth, father's name, mother's maiden name, city of birth.

Marriage certificates available from this office prior to 1985. Marriage certificates after 1985 available at county where license was purchased. Divorce records available at county level, county clerk's office where divorce was filed.

Department of Education

Department of Education
Teacher Certification
Attn: Licensing Division
1812 9th Street
Sacramento, CA 95814
(916) 445-7256

Field of certification, effective date, expiration date are available by phone or mail. Include name, DOB and SSN.

Medical Licensing

Medical Board of California
1426 Howe Ave.
Suite 54
Sacramento, CA 95825-3236
(916) 920-6343

Will confirm licenses for MDs, DOs and PODs by phone or mail. No fee. For licenses not mentioned, contact the above office.

California Board of Registered Nursing
PO Box 944210
Sacramento, CA 94244-2100
(916) 322-3350

Will confirm license by phone. No fee. Include name, license number, if available. For mail requests, include $2.00 for each name.

Bar Association

California Bar Association
555 Franklin
San Francisco, CA 94102
(415) 561-8200

Will confirm licenses by phone. No fee. Include name.

Accountancy Board

Department of Consumer Affairs
Board of Accountancy
2135 Butano Drive
Sacramento, CA 95825
(916) 920-7121

Will confirm licenses by phone. No fee. Include name.

Securities Commission

Broker-Dealer/Investment
3700 Wilshire Blvd., Suite 600
Loa Angeles, CA 90010
(213) 736-2505

Will confirm licenses by phone. No fee. Include name and SSN.

Secretary of State

Secretary of State
1230 J Street
Sacramento, CA 95814
(916) 445-0620

Service agent and address, date incorporated, standing with tax commission, trade names are available by phone or mail. Contact the above office for additional information.

Criminal Records

State Repository

State Department of Justice
Record Control Section
Division of Law Enforcement
PO Box 903417
Sacramento, CA 94203-4170
(916) 739-5496

Access to criminal records by non-criminal justice agencies through the state's central repository is limited to those entities that are specifically authorized access by law or court order. California will consider access by out-of-state, non-criminal justice agencies if appropriate statutes exist. There is a $27.00 fee for fingerprint checks. Contact the above office for additional information and instructions.

Alameda County

Alameda County Courthouse
Room 107
1225 Fallon Street
Oakland, CA 94612
(510) 272-6777

Felony records are available by mail. No release necessary. $5.00 search fee. $.75 fee per copy. $1.75 for certification. Company checks only, payable to County of Alameda. Search information required: name, date of birth.

Civil records are available by mail. No release necessary. $5.00 search fee. $.75 fee per copy. $1.75 for certification. Search information required: name, years to search. Specify plaintiff or defendant.

Alpine County

Superior Court, Criminal Records
PO Box 276
Markleeville, CA 96120
(916) 694-2281
Fax (916) 694-2491

Felony and misdemeanor records are available by mail or fax. No release necessary. $2.75 search fee for each year searched. Make check payable to Superior Court Clerk. Search information required: name, date of birth.

Civil records are available by mail or fax. No release necessary. $5.00 search fee. $.50 fee per copy. $1.75 for certification. Search information required: name, years to search. Specify plaintiff or defendant.

Amador County

Felony records
County Clerk, Criminal Records
108 Court Street
Jackson, CA 95642
(209) 223-6463

Felony records are available by mail or phone. No release necessary. $1.75 fee for each year searched. Make money order payable to Amador County Clerk. Search information required: name.

Civil records
County Clerk
108 Court Street
Jackson, CA 95642
(209) 223-6463

Civil records are available by mail. No release necessary. $1.75 search fee. $.50 fee per copy. $1.75 for certification. Search information required: name, years to search, SASE. Specify plaintiff or defendant.

Misdemeanor records
Justice Court
108 Court Street
Jackson, CA 95642
(209) 223-6358

Misdemeanor records are available from 1986 forward by mail or phone. No release necessary. No search fee. $1.00 fee for first copy, $.25 each additional copy. Search information required: name, date of birth, driver's license, SASE.

Civil records
Justice Court
108 Court Street
Jackson, CA 95642
(209) 223-6358

Civil records are available by mail. No release necessary. No search fee. $1.00 fee per copy. $2.75 for certification. Search information required: name, years to search. Specify plaintiff or defendant.

Butte County

County Clerk, Criminal Records
25 County Center Drive
Oroville, CA 95965
(916) 538-7551

Felony records are available by mail or phone. Phone searches limited to 1-2 years. No release necessary. $2.25 fee for each year searched. Make money order payable to Butte County Clerk. Search information required: name, SASE, years to search.

Civil records are available by mail. No release necessary. $3.00 search fee. $.50 fee per copy. $1.75 for certification. Search information required: name, years to search, SASE. Specify plaintiff or defendant.

Calaveras County

Felony records
Superior Court, Criminal Records
Government Center
San Andreas, CA 95249
(209) 754-6311

Felony records are available by mail. No release necessary. $1.75 fee for each year searched. $.50 fee per copy. $1.75 for certification. Make check payable to County Clerk. Search information required: name, years to search.

Civil records
Superior Court
Government Center
San Andreas, CA 95249
(209) 754-6311

Civil records are available by mail. No release necessary. $1.75 fee for each year searched. $.50 fee per copy. $1.75 for certification. Search information required: name, years to search. Specify plaintiff or defendant.

Misdemeanor records
Justice Court
Government Center
San Andreas, CA 95249
(209) 754-6336
Fax (209) 754-6689

Misdemeanor records since 1980 are available by mail or fax. No release necessary. $5.00 fee for each year searched. $.50 fee per copy, $1.75 fee for certified copy. Make check payable to Justice Court. Search information required: name, SSN, date of birth, years to search, driver's license number.

Civil records
Justice Court
Government Center
San Andreas, CA 95249
(209) 754-6336
Fax (209) 754-6689

Civil records are available by mail or fax. No release necessary. $5.00 fee for each year searched. $.50 fee per copy, $1.75 fee for certified copy. Search information required: name, years to search. Specify plaintiff or defendant.

Colusa County

Felony records
County Clerk, Criminal Records
546 Jay Street
Colusa, CA 95932
(916) 458-4660

Felony records are available by mail. No release necessary. $5.00 search fee. $.50 fee per copy. Make check payable to Colusa County Clerk. Search information required: name, SASE.

Civil records
County Clerk
546 Jay Street
Colusa, CA 95932
(916) 458-4660

Civil records are available by mail. No release necessary. $5.00 search fee. $.50 fee per copy. $1.75 for certification. Search information required: name, years to search. Specify plaintiff or defendant.

Misdemeanor records
Colusa Justice Court
547 Market St.
Colusa, CA 95932
(916) 458-5149

Misdemeanor records are available by mail. No release necessary. $1.75 fee per year searched. $.50 fee per copy. $1.75 for certification. Search information required: name, date of birth, years to search.

Civil records
Colusa Justice Court
547 Market St.
Colusa, CA 95932
(916) 458-5149

Civil records are available by mail. No release necessary. $1.75 fee per year searched. $.50 fee per copy. $2.25 for certification. Search information required: name, years to search. Specify plaintiff or defendant.

Contra Costa County

Contra Costa County Superior Court, Criminal Bureau
PO Box 911
725 Court Street
Martinez, CA 94553
(510) 372-2048 or 646-2048

Felony records are available by mail. No release necessary. $5.00 search fee. $.50 fee per copy. $1.75 for certification. Company check or money order, payable to County Clerk. Search information required: name, date of birth, SASE.

Civil records are available by mail. No release necessary. $5.00 search fee. $.50 fee per copy. $1.75 for certification. Search information required: name, years to search. Specify plaintiff or defendant.

Del Norte County

Felony records
County Clerk, Criminal Records
450 H. Street
Cresent City, CA 95531
(707) 464-7205

Felony records are available by mail or phone. No release necessary. No search fee. Search information required: name, years to search.

Civil records
County Clerk
450 H. Street
Cresent City, CA 95531
(707) 464-7205

Civil records are available by mail. No release necessary. No search fee. Search information required: name, years to search. Specify plaintiff or defendant.

Misdemeanor records
Justice Court
680 5th St.
Cresent City, CA 95531
(707) 464-7240

Misdemeanor records are available by mail. No release necessary. $1.75 fee per year searched. $.50 fee per copy. Search information required: name, years to search, date of offense, offense, date of birth.

Civil records
Justice Court
680 5th St.
Cresent City, CA 95531
(707) 464-7240

Civil records are available by mail or phone. No release necessary. No search fee. Search information required: name, years to search. Specify plaintiff or defendant.

El Dorado County

County Clerk, Criminal Records
495 Main Street
Placerville, CA 95667
(916) 621-6426

Felony records are available by mail. No release necessary. $5.00 search fee. $.50 fee per copy. $1.75 for certification. Search information required: name, date of birth, SASE.

Civil records are available by mail or by phone from 1989 forward. No release necessary. $5.00 search fee prior to 1989. $.50 fee per copy. $1.75 for certification. Search information required: name, years to search. Specify plaintiff or defendant.

Fresno County

Fresno County Clerk's Office
PO Box 1628
Fresno, CA 93717
(209) 488-3352

Felony records are available by mail. No release necessary. $1.75 fee for each year searched. $.50 fee per copy. $1.75 for certification. Make check payable to Fresno County Clerk. Search information required: name, date of birth, years to search.

Civil records are available by mail. No release necessary. $1.75 fee for each year searched. $.50 fee per copy. $1.75 for certification. Search information required: name, date of birth, years to search. Specify plaintiff or defendant.

Glenn County

Glenn County Clerk, Criminal Records
PO Box 391
526 W. Sycamore
Willows, CA 95988
(916) 934-6407

Felony records are available by mail. No release necessary. $1.75 fee for each year searched. Certified check only, payable to Glenn County Clerk. Search information required: name, years to search, SASE.

Civil records are available by mail or phone. No release necessary. No search fee. $.50 fee per copy. $1.75 for certification. Search information required: name, years to search. Specify plaintiff or defendant.

Humboldt County

Courthouse, Criminal Records
County Clerk
825 5th St.
Eureka, CA 95501
(707) 445-7257

Felony records are available by mail. No release necessary. $5.00 search fee. Make check payable to Humboldt County Clerk. Search information required: name, SSN, previous address, years to search. This office begins answering phones at 8:30 am Pacific Time.

Civil records are available by mail. No release necessary. $5.00 search fee. $.50 fee per copy. $1.75 for certification. Search information required: name, years to search. Specify plaintiff or defendant.

Imperial County

County Clerk, Criminal Records
939 Main Street
El Centro, CA 92243
(619) 339-4217

Felony records are available by mail or phone. No release necessary. $2.50 fee for each year searched. Company checks only, payable to County Clerk. Search information required: name, SASE, years to search.

Civil records are available by mail. No release necessary. $2.50 search fee. $1.00 fee for first copy, $.50 fee each additional copy. $1.75 for certification. Search information required: name, years to search. Specify plaintiff or defendant.

Inyo County

County Clerk, Criminal Records
PO Drawer F
Independence, CA 93526
(619) 878-2411

Felony records are available by mail or phone. No release necessary. $1.75 fee for each year searched. Search information required: name, years to search.

Civil records are available by mail. No release necessary. $1.75 fee for each year searched. $.50 fee per copy. $1.75 for certification. Search information required: name, years to search, SASE. Specify plaintiff or defendant.

Kern County

County Clerk, Criminal Records
1415 Truxtun Ave.
Bakersfield, CA 93301
(805) 861-2621

Felony records are available by mail. No release necessary. $4.00 fee per year searched. $.75 fee per copy. $1.75 for certification. Search information required: name, date of birth.

Civil records are available by mail. No release necessary. $5.00 search fee. $.75 fee per copy. $1.75 for certification. Search information required: name, years to search. Specify plaintiff or defendant.

Kings County

Kings County Government Bldg., Criminal
County Clerk
Government Center
1400 W. Lacey Blvd.
Hanford, CA 93230
(209) 582-3211

Felony and misdemeanor records are available by mail. No release necessary. $5.00 search fee. Search information required: name, date of birth, alias, SASE.

Civil records are available by mail. No release necessary. No search fee. $.50 fee per copy. $1.75 for certification. Search information required: name, years to search. Specify plaintiff or defendant.

Lake County

Superior Court Clerk, Criminal Records
255 N. Forbes
Lakeport, CA 95453
(707) 263-2374

Felony records are available by mail. No release necessary. $1.75 fee for each year searched. $.50 fee per copy. $1.75 for certification. Make check payable to Superior Court Clerk. Search information required: name, years to search.

Civil records are available by mail. No release necessary. $1.75 fee for each year searched. $.50 fee per copy. $1.75 for certification. Search information required: name, years to search. Specify plaintiff or defendant.

Lassen County

Felony records
Lassen County Clerk, Criminal Records
Courthouse
220 South Lassen Street
Susanville, CA 96130
(916) 257-8311 Extension 124

Felony records are available by mail or phone. No release necessary. $1.75 fee for each year searched. Company check or money order, payable to Lassen County Clerk. Search information required: name.

Civil records
Lassen County Clerk
Courthouse
220 South Lassen Street
Susanville, CA 96130
(916) 257-8311 Extension 124

Civil records are available by mail or phone. No release necessary. No search fee. $.50 fee per copy. Search information required: name, years to search. Specify plaintiff or defendant.

Misdemeanor records
Lassen County Justice Court
220 S. Lassen Street
Susanville, CA 96130
(916) 257-8311 Extension 205

Misdemeanor records since 1983 are available by mail. No release necessary. No search fee. $.75 fee per copy, $1.75 fee for certified copy. Company check or money order, payable to Justice Court. Search information required: name, years to search, date of offense, case number (if available).

Civil records
Lassen County Justice Court
220 S. Lassen Street
Susanville, CA 96130
(916) 257-8311 Extension 205

Civil records are available by mail. No release necessary. No search fee. $.75 fee per copy, $1.75 for certification. Search information required: name, years to search. Specify plaintiff or defendant.

Los Angeles County

Criminal Courts Bldg., Certification Desk
210 W. Temple Street
Room M-6
Los Angeles, CA 90012
(213) 974-5171

Felony records are available by mail. No release necessary. $5.00 search fee. Make check payable to Los Angeles Superior Court Clerk. Search information required: name, date of birth, years to search, SASE.

Civil records are available by phone. No release necessary. No search fee. Search information required: name, years to search. Specify plaintiff or defendant.

Madera County

County Clerk's Office
209 W. Yosemite
Madera, CA 93637
(209) 675-7721
Fax (209) 673-3302

Felony records are available by mail or fax. $1.75 fee per year searched. Make checks payable to County Clerk. Search information required: name, years to search, SASE. See California state repository for additional information.

Civil records are available by mail. No release necessary. $1.75 fee for each year searched. $.50 fee per copy. $1.75 for certification. Search information required: name, years to search, SASE. Specify plaintiff or defendant.

Marin County

Felony records
Marin County Clerk, Criminal Desk
PO Box E
San Rafael, CA 94913-3904
(415) 499-6427

Felony records are available by mail. No release necessary. $1.75 fee per year searched. Make cashier's check or money order payable to Marin County Clerk. Search information required: name, years to search.

Civil records
Marin County Clerk
PO Box E
San Rafael, CA 94913-3904
(415) 499-6427

Civil records are available by mail. No release necessary. $5.00 search fee. $.75 fee per copy. $1.75 for certification. Search information required: name, years to search. Specify plaintiff or defendant.

Misdemeanor records
Municipal Court
Marin County Hall of Justice
Civic Center, Rm. 195A
San Rafael, CA 94901
(415) 499-6225

Misdemeanor records since 1984 are available by mail. A release is required. No search fee. $.50 fee per copy. $2.25 for certification. Make check payable to Municipal Court. Search information required: name, date of birth, driver's license number, case number (if available), date of offense.

Civil records
Municipal Court
Marin County Hall of Justice
Civic Center, Rm. 195A
San Rafael, CA 94901
(415) 499-6225

Civil records are available by mail. No release necessary. $1.75 fee per year searched. $.50 fee per copy. $1.75 for certification. Search information required: name, years to search. Specify plaintiff or defendant.

Mariposa County

Felony records
Mariposa County Clerk, Criminal Records
PO Box 247
Mariposa, CA 95338
(209) 966-2005

Felony records are available by mail. No release necessary. $1.75 fee for each year searched. Make check payable to Mariposa County Clerk. Search information required: full name, years to search, SASE.

Civil records
Mariposa County Clerk
PO Box 247
Mariposa, CA 95338
(209) 966-2005

Civil records are available by mail. No release necessary. $1.75 fee for each year searched. $.30 fee per copy. $1.75 for certification. Search information required: name, years to search. Specify plaintiff or defendant.

Misdemeanor records
Justice Court
PO Box 316
Mariposa, CA 95338
(209) 966-5711

Misdemeanor records are available by mail or phone. No release necessary. $1.75 fee for each year searched. $.30 fee for first copy, $.20 each additional copy. $1.75 for certification. Make check payable to Mariposa Justice Court. Search information required: name, years to search, SASE, date of offense, offense, case number.

Civil records
Justice Court
PO Box 316
Mariposa, CA 95338
(209) 966-5711

Civil records are available by mail or phone. No release necessary. No search fee. $.30 fee for first copy, $.20 each additional copy. $1.75 for certification. Search information required: name, years to search. Specify plaintiff or defendant.

Mendocino County

County Clerk, Criminal Records
PO Box 148
Ukiah, CA 95482
(707) 463-4379

Felony records are available by mail. No release necessary. $1.75 fee for each year searched. $.50 fee per copy. $1.75 for certification. Check payable to Mendocino County Clerk. Search information required: name, years to search.

Civil records are available by mail. No release necessary. $1.75 fee for each year searched. $.50 fee per copy. $1.75 for certification. Search information required: name, years to search. Specify plaintiff or defendant.

Merced County

Merced County Clerk, Criminal Records
2222 M Street
Merced, CA 95340
(209) 385-7501

Felony records are available by mail. No release necessary. $1.75 fee for each year searched. Certified check only, payable to Merced County Clerk. Search information required: name, date of birth, years to search, SASE.

Civil records are available by mail. No release necessary. $1.75 fee for each year searched. $.50 fee per copy. $1.75 for certification. Search information required: name, years to search, SASE. Specify plaintiff or defendant.

Modoc County

Felony records
County Clerk, Criminal Records
PO Box 131
Alturas, CA 96101
(916) 233-3939 Extension 200

Felony records are available by mail. No release necessary. $1.75 fee for each year searched. $.50 fee per copy. $1.75 for certification. Certified check only, payable to Modoc County Clerk. Search information required: name, years to search, SASE.

Civil records
County Clerk
PO Box 131
Alturas, CA 96101
(916) 233-3939 Extension 200

Civil records are available by mail. No release necessary. $1.75 fee for each year searched. $.50 fee per copy. $1.75 for certification. Search information required: name, years to search. Specify plaintiff or defendant.

Misdemeanor records
Modoc Justice Court
Courthouse Annex
Alturas, CA 96101
(916) 233-3939 Ext. 518

Misdemeanor records since 1980 are available by mail or phone. No release necessary. No search fee. $.50 fee per copy, $3.50 per certified copy. Certified check or money order, payable to Modoc Justice Court. Search information required: name, years to search, SASE, date of birth, offense.

Civil records
Modoc Justice Court
Courthouse Annex
Alturas, CA 96101
(916) 233-3939 Ext. 518

Civil records are available by mail. No release necessary. No search fee. $.50 fee per copy. $6.00 for certification. Search information required: name, years to search. Specify plaintiff or defendant.

Mono County

County Clerk's Office
PO Box 537
Bridgeport, CA 93517
(619) 932-5241 Extension 240
Fax (619) 932-7520

Felony records are available by mail, phone or fax. No release necessary. $2.00 fee for each year searched. Make company check payable to County Clerk. Search information required: name, date of birth, years to search, SASE .

Civil records are available by mail. No release necessary. $2.00 fee for each year searched. $.25 fee per copy. $1.75 for certification. Search information required: name, years to search. Specify plaintiff or defendant.

Monterey County

Monterey County Clerk,
PO Box 1819
Salinas, CA 93902
(408) 755-5030

Felony records are available by mail. No release necessary. $1.75 fee for each year searched. $.75 fee per copy, $1.75 fee for certified copy. Company checks only, payable to Monterey County Clerk. Search information required: name, years to search, SASE.

Civil records are available by mail. No release necessary. $1.75 fee for each year searched. $.75 fee per copy. $1.75 for certification. Search information required: name, years to search. Specify plaintiff or defendant.

Napa County

Clerk of Superior Court, Criminal Records
PO Box 880
Napa, CA 94559-0880
(707) 253-4481
Fax (707) 253-4229

Felony and misdemeanor records are available by mail or fax. No release necessary. $1.75 fee for each year searched. Certified check only, payable to Napa Superior Court. Search information required: name, SASE, years to search.

Civil records are available by mail or fax. No release necessary. $1.75 fee for each year searched. $.50 fee per copy. $1.75 for certification. Search information required: name, years to search. Specify plaintiff or defendant, SASE.

Nevada County

Felony records
County Clerk, Criminal Records
PO Box 6126
201 Church Street
Nevada City, CA 95959-6126
(916) 265-1293

Felony records are available by mail. No release necessary. $1.75 fee for each year searched. Make check or money order, payable to County Clerk. Search information required: name, years to search, SASE.

Civil records
County Clerk
PO Box 6126
201 Church Street
Nevada City, CA 95959-6126
(916) 265-1293

Civil records are available by mail. No release necessary. No search fee. $.50 fee per copy. $1.75 for certification. Search information required: name, years to search, SASE. Specify plaintiff or defendant.

Misdemeanor records
Municipal Court
201 Church Street
Nevada City, CA 95959
(916) 265-1311

Misdemeanor records are available by mail. Confirm by phone first. No release necessary. No search fee. $.50 fee per copy, $1.75 fee for certified copy. Make check or money order, payable to Justice Court. Search information required: name, years to search, SASE, date of birth, docket number (if available).

Civil records
Municipal Court
201 Church Street
Nevada City, CA 95959
(916) 265-1311

Civil records are available by mail. No release necessary. $5.00 fee for each year searched. $.50 fee per copy. $2.25 for certification. Search information required: name, years to search, SASE. Specify plaintiff or defendant.

Orange County

Orange County Clerk, Criminal Section
Superior Court
PO Box 838
Santa Ana, CA 92702-0838
(714) 834-2200

Felony records are available by mail. No release necessary. $4.00 fee for each year searched. Make check payable to Orange County Clerk. Search information required: name, date of birth, years to search.

Civil records are available by mail. No release necessary. $4.50 search fee per year. $.80 fee per copy. $1.75 for certification. Search information required: name, years to search. Specify plaintiff or defendant.

Placer County

Placer County Clerk, Criminal Records
101 Maple Street
Auburn, CA 95603
(916) 889-6550

Felony records are available by mail. No release necessary. $1.75 search fee per name from 1974 to present. $1.75 fee for each year searched prior to 1974. $.50 fee per copy, $1.75 for certification. Make check payable to Placer County Clerk. Search information required: name, SASE, years to search.

Civil records are available by mail. No release necessary. $1.75 search fee. $.50 fee for first copy, $.25 each additional. $1.75 for certification. Search information required: name, years to search. Specify plaintiff or defendant.

Plumas County

Felony records
Plumas County Clerk, Criminal Records
PO Box 10207
Quincy, CA 95971
(916) 283-6305
Fax (916) 283-6415

Felony records are available by mail, phone or fax. No release necessary. No search fee. Search information required: name, date of birth, years to search, SASE.

Civil records
Plumas County Clerk
PO Box 10207
Quincy, CA 95971
(916) 283-6305
Fax (916) 283-6415

Civil records are available by mail. No release necessary. No search fee. $.50 fee per copy. $1.75 for certification. $12.00 for certification of judgement document. Search information required: name, years to search. Specify plaintiff or defendant.

Misdemeanor records
Justice Court
PO Box 10628
Quincy, CA 95971
(916) 283-1245
Fax (916) 283-6415

Misdemeanor records since 1980 are available by mail only. A release is required. No search fee. Search information required: name, date of birth, years to search, SASE.

Civil records
Justice Court
PO Box 10628
Quincy, CA 95971
(916) 283-1245
Fax (916) 283-6415

Civil records are available by mail or fax. No release necessary. No search fee. $.50 fee per copy. $1.75 for certification. Search information required: name, years to search. Specify plaintiff or defendant.

Riverside County

Riverside County
Superior Court Clerk
Criminal Section
PO Box 431
Riverside, CA 92502
(714) 275-1433

Felony records are available by mail. No release necessary. $1.75 fee for each year searched. Certified check or money order payable to Superior Court Clerk. Search information required: name, SSN, date of birth, SASE.

Civil records are available by mail. No release necessary. No search fee. $.50 fee per copy. $1.75 for certification. Search information required: name, years to search. Specify plaintiff or defendant.

Sacramento County

Sacramento County Clerk,
Correspondence
720 9th Street
Sacramento, CA 95814
(916) 440-5522

Felony records are available by mail. No release necessary. $1.75 fee per year searched. Company checks only, payable to Sacramento County Clerk. Search information required: name, date of birth, SSN, SASE.

Civil records are available by mail. No release necessary. $3.50 fee per year searched. $.50 fee per copy. $1.75 for certification. Search information required: name, years to search. Specify plaintiff or defendant.

San Benito County

Felony records
San Benito County Superior Court
440 5th Street
Courthouse, Room 206
Hollister, CA 95023
(408) 637-3786
Fax (408) 637-9095

Felony records are available by mail, phone or fax. No release necessary. No search fee. Fax requests must have cover sheet stating "Telephone Superior Court that a fax is at your facility for pickup". Search information required: name, date of birth, SASE. Specify "criminal records."

Civil records
San Benito County Superior Court
440 5th Street
Courthouse, Room 206
Hollister, CA 95023
(408) 637-3786
Fax (408) 637-9095

Civil records are available by mail or fax. No release necessary. $5.00 search fee. $.50 fee per copy. $1.75 for certification. Search information required: name, years to search. Specify plaintiff or defendant.

Misdemeanor records
Justice Court
440 5th Street
Courthouse, Room 103
Hollister, CA 95023
(408) 637-3741

Misdemeanor records since 1978 are available by mail only. Turnaround time is 2 weeks. No release necessary. No search fee. Search information required: name, date of birth, SASE, date of offense, years to search. Specify "criminal records."

Civil records
Justice Court
440 5th Street
Courthouse, Room 103
Hollister, CA 95023
(408) 637-3741

Civil records are available by mail. No release necessary. $1.75 fee per year searched. $.50 fee per copy. $2.25 for certification. Search information required: name, years to search. Specify plaintiff or defendant.

San Bernardino County

County Clerk, Felony check
Research Department
351 N. Arrowhead
San Bernardino, CA 92415
(714) 387-3965

Felony records are available by mail. No release necessary. $5.00 search fee. $.50 fee per copy. $1.75 for certification. Company checks only, payable to County Clerk. Search information required: name, date of birth, SASE.

Civil records are available by mail. No release necessary. $5.00 search fee. $.50 fee per copy. $1.75 for certification. Search information required: name, date of birth, years to search. Specify plaintiff or defendant, SASE.

San Diego County

San Diego County Clerk, Criminal Division
PO Box 128
San Diego, CA 92112-4104
(619) 531-3151

Felony records are available by mail. No release necessary. $1.75 fee for each year searched. Certified check only, payable to Clerk of the Superior Court. Search information required: name, years to search, SASE.

Civil records are available by mail. No release necessary. $1.75 fee per year searched. $.60 fee per copy. $1.75 for certification. Search information required: name, years to search, SASE. Specify plaintiff or defendant.

San Francisco County

Felony records
San Francisco County Clerk
Room 306, Hall of Justice
850 Bryant Street
San Francisco, CA 94103
(415) 553-1896

Felony records are available by mail. No release necessary. $5.00 search fee. $.50 fee per copy, $1.75 fee for certified copy. Company checks only, payable to County Clerk. Search information required: name, date of birth, years to search, SASE.

Civil records
San Francisco Superior Court
County Clerk
City Hall, Room 317
400 Venice Street
San Francisco, CA 94102
(415) 553-1896

Civil records are available by mail. No release necessary. $1.75 fee per year searched. $.50 fee per copy. $2.25 fee for certification. Search information required: name, years to search. Specify plaintiff or defendant.

Misdemeanor records
San Francisco Municipal Court
Room 201, Hall of Justice
850 Bryant Street
San Francisco, CA 94103
(415) 553-1665

Misdemeanor records since 1978 are available by mail. No release necessary. $1.75 fee per year searched, not to exceed $10.00. $.50 fee per copy, $1.75 fee for certified copy. Checks payable to Clerk of Municipal Court. Search information required: name, date of birth, SSN, years to search, SASE.

Civil records
San Francisco Municipal Court
City Hall, Room 300
850 Bryant Street
San Francisco, CA 94102
(415) 554-4532

Civil records are available by mail. No release necessary. $1.75 fee per year searched. $.50 fee per copy. $1.75 for certification. Search information required: name, years to search. Specify plaintiff or defendant.

San Joaquin County

San Joaquin County Clerk, Criminal Department
222 East Weber Street
Room 303
Stockton, CA 95202
(209) 468-2945

Felony records are available by mail or phone. No release necessary. No search fee. $.50 fee per copy, $1.75 fee for certified copy. Search information required: name, date of birth, years to search.

San Joaquin Superior Court
222 East Weber Street
Room 303
Stockton, CA 95202
(209) 468-2355

Civil records are available by mail. No release necessary. $5.00 search fee. $.50 fee per copy. $1.75 for certification. Search information required: name, years to search. Specify plaintiff or defendant.

San Luis Obispo County

Felony records
San Luis Obispo County Clerk
Room 385
County Government Center
San Luis Obispo, CA 93408
(805) 549-5241

Felony records are available by mail or phone. No release necessary. No fee. Search information required: name, date of birth, years to search, SASE.

Civil records
San Luis Obispo County Clerk
Room 385
County Government Center
San Luis Obispo, CA 93408
(805) 549-5241

Civil records are available by mail or phone. No release necessary. No search fee. $.50 fee per copy. $1.75 for certification. Search information required: name, years to search. Specify plaintiff or defendant.

Misdemeanor records
San Luis Obispo Municipal Court
1050 Monteray, Rm 220
San Luis Obispo, CA 93408
(805) 549-5670

Misdemeanor records since 1975 are available by mail or phone. No release necessary. No search fee. $.90 fee per copy, $2.65 fee for certified copy. Make checks payable to San Luis Obispo Municipal Court. Search information required: name, date of birth, SASE.

Civil records
San Luis Obispo Municipal Court
1050 Monteray, Rm 220
San Luis Obispo, CA 93408
(805) 549-5670

Civil records are available by mail or phone. No release necessary. No search fee. $.50 fee per copy. $1.75 for certification. Search information required: name, years to search. Specify plaintiff or defendant.

San Mateo County

San Mateo County Clerk
Hall of Justice and Records
401 Marshall Street
Redwood City, CA 94063
(415) 363-4711 Extension 1213
Fax (415) 363-4914

Felony records are available by mail or fax. No release necessary. $1.75 fee for each year searched. Make check payable to San Mateo County Clerk. Search information required: name, date of birth, SASE.

Civil records are available by mail. No release necessary. $5.00 search fee. $.50 fee per copy. $1.75 for certification. Search information required: name, years to search. Specify plaintiff or defendant.

Santa Barbara County

Santa Barbara Superior Court,
Criminal Records
PO Box 159
Santa Barbara, CA 93102-0159
(805) 568-2237

Felony records are available by mail or phone. No release necessary. Record checks for years prior to 1975 will be charged $1.75 per year. Search information required: name.

Civil records are available by mail or phone. No release necessary. No search fee. $.50 fee per copy. $1.75 for certification. Search information required: name, years to search. Specify plaintiff or defendant.

Santa Clara County

Felony and misdemeanor records
Santa Clara County Clerk
Criminal Division
190 W. Hedding Street
San Jose, CA 95110
(408) 299-2974

Felony records are available by mail. No release necessary. $4.00 fee for each year searched. $.50 fee per copy, $1.75 fee for certification. Make check payable to County Clerk. Search information required: name, date of birth, years to search.

Civil records
Santa Clara County Clerk
191 N. 1st Street
San Jose, CA 95113
(408) 299-2964

Civil records are available by mail. No release necessary. $4.00 search fee. $.50 fee per copy. $2.00 for certification. Search information required: name, years to search. Specify plaintiff or defendant.

Santa Cruz County

Santa Cruz County Clerk
Room 110
701 Ocean Street
Santa Cruz, CA 95060
(408) 425-2171

Felony records are available by mail or phone. No release necessary. $5.00 search fee. $.50 fee per copy, $2.25 fee for certified copy. Make check payable to County Clerk. Search information required: name, date of birth, years to search.

Civil records are available by mail or phone. No release necessary. No search fee. $.50 fee per copy. $1.75 for certification. Search information required: name, years to search. Specify plaintiff or defendant.

Shasta County

Shasta County Clerk, Criminal
Records
PO Box 880
Redding, CA 96099
(916) 225-5631

Felony records are available by mail. No release necessary. $5.00 search fee. $.50 fee per copy. $1.75 for certification. Company checks or money order, payable to Shasta County Clerk. Search information required: name, SASE, years to search.

Civil records are available by mail. No release necessary. $5.00 search fee. $.50 fee per copy. $1.75 for certification. $6.00 marital decree certification. Search information required: name, years to search. Specify plaintiff or defendant.

Sierra County

Felony records
County Clerk, Criminal Records
PO Drawer D
Downieville, CA 95936
(916) 289-3698
Fax (916) 289-3318

Felony records are available by mail, phone or fax. No release necessary. $1.75 fee for each year searched. Make check payable to County Clerk. Search information required: name, years to search, SASE.

Civil records
County Clerk
PO Drawer D
Downieville, CA 95936
(916) 289-3698
Fax (916) 289-3318

Civil records are available by mail, phone or fax. No release necessary. $1.75 fee per year searched. $.50 fee per copy. $1.75 for certification. Search information required: name, years to search. Specify plaintiff or defendant.

Misdemeanor records
Justice Court
PO Box 401
Downieville, CA 95936
(916) 289-3215

Misdemeanor records are available by mail or phone. No release necessary. $1.75 fee for each year searched. $.50 fee per copy, $.50 fee for certified copy. Make check payable to Justice Court. Search information required: name, years to search, SASE.

Civil records
Justice Court
PO Box 401
Downieville, CA 95936
(916) 289-3215

Civil records are available by mail. No release necessary. No search fee. $.50 fee per copy. $1.75 for certification. Search information required: name, years to search. Specify plaintiff or defendant.

Siskiyou County

Superior Court, Criminal Records
PO Box 338
Yreka, CA 96097
(916) 842-8084

Felony records are available by mail or phone. No release necessary. $1.75 fee per year searched. Checks payable to County Clerk. Search information required: name, years to search.

Civil records are available by mail. No release necessary. $1.75 fee per year searched. $.50 fee per copy. $1.75 for certification. Search information required: name, years to search. Specify plaintiff or defendant.

Solano County

Solano County Clerk, Criminal
Records
600 Union Ave.
Fairfield, CA 94533
(707) 421-6470

Felony records are available by mail. No release necessary. $5.00 search fee. Certified check only, payable to Solano County Clerk. Search information required: name, SSN, date of birth, sex, race, SASE.

Civil records are available by mail. No release necessary. $5.00 search fee. $.50 fee per copy. $1.75 for certification. Search information required: name, years to search. Specify plaintiff or defendant.

Sonoma County

Felony records
County Clerk, Criminal Records
PO Box 11187
Santa Rosa, CA 95406
(707) 527-2611

Felony records are available by mail. No release necessary. $1.75 fee for each year searched. $.50 fee per copy. Certified check only, payable to Sonoma County Clerk. Search information required: full name, date of birth, years to search, SASE.

Civil records
County Clerk
PO Box 11187
Santa Rosa, CA 95406
(707) 527-2611

Civil records are available by mail. No release necessary. $1.75 fee for each year searched. $.50 fee per copy. $1.75 for certification. Search information required: name, years to search, SASE. Specify plaintiff or defendant.

Misdemeanor records
Municipal Court, Criminal Division
600 Administration Dr., Rm. 102
Santa Rosa, CA 95403
(707) 527-2094

Misdemeanor records since 1983 are available by mail. No release necessary. $1.75 fee for each year searched. $.50 fee per copy. Certified check only, payable to Sonoma County Municipal Court. Search information required: name, date of birth, years to search, SASE.

Civil records
Sonoma County Municipal Court
600 Administration Dr., Rm. 107J
Santa Rosa, CA 95403
(707) 527-1840

Civil records are available by mail. No release necessary. $1.75 fee for each year searched. $.50 fee per copy. $3.50 for certification. Search information required: name, years to search. Specify plaintiff or defendant.

Stanislaus County

Stanislaus Superior Court, Criminal Records
PO Box 1098
Modesto, CA 95353
(209) 525-6416

Felony records are available by mail. No release necessary. $5.00 search fee. Make check payable to Stanislaus Superior Court. Search information required: name, date of birth, years to search, SASE.

Civil records are available by mail. No release necessary. $5.00 search fee. $.50 fee per copy. $1.75 for certification. Search information required: name, date of birth, SSN, years to search, SASE. Specify plaintiff or defendant.

Sutter County

Felony records
Sutter County Clerk, Criminal Records
433 2nd Street
Yuba City, CA 95991
(916) 741-7120

Felony records are available by mail. No release necessary. $5.00 search fee. $.50 fee per copy. Search information required: name, years to search, SASE.

Civil records
Sutter County Clerk
433 2nd Street
Yuba City, CA 95991
(916) 741-7120

Civil records are available by mail. No release necessary. $5.00 search fee. $.50 fee per copy. $2.25 for first certification, $.50 each additional certification. Search information required: name, years to search, SASE. Specify plaintiff or defendant.

Misdemeanor records
Municipal Court
PO Box 1580
Yuba City, CA 95992
(916) 741-7352

Misdemeanor records since 1976 are available by mail. No release necessary. No search fee. $.50 fee per copy, $1.25 fee for certification. Search information required: name, years to search.

Civil records
Municipal Court
PO Box 1580
Yuba City, CA 95992
(916) 741-7351

Civil records are available by mail. No release necessary. No search fee. $.50 fee per copy. $2.25 for first certification. Search information required: name, years to search. Specify plaintiff or defendant.

Tehama County

Criminal Court Check, Criminal Records
PO Box 250
Red Bluff, CA 96080
(916) 527-6441

Felony records are available by mail. No release necessary. No search fee. $.50 fee per copy, $1.75 fee for certified copy. Search information required: name, years to search, SASE.

Civil records are available by mail. No release necessary. No search fee. $.50 fee per copy. $1.75 for certification. Search information required: name, years to search, SASE. Specify plaintiff or defendant.

Trinity County

County Clerk
PO Box 1258
Weaverville, CA 96093
(916) 623-1222
Fax (916) 623-3762

Records are available in person only. See California state repository for additional information.

Civil records are available by mail. No release necessary. $1.75 fee per year searched. $.50 fee per copy. $2.25 for certification. Search information required: name, years to search. Specify plaintiff or defendant.

Tulare County

Tulare County Clerk, Criminal Records
Courthouse, Room 201
Visalia, CA 93291
(209) 733-6374

Felony records are available by mail. No release necessary. $5.00 search fee. $.50 fee per copy. Make check payable to Tulare County Clerk. Search information required: name, date of birth, sex, SASE.

Civil records are available by mail or phone. No release necessary. No search fee. $.50 fee per copy. $1.75 for certification. Search information required: name, years to search. Specify plaintiff or defendant.

Tuolumne County

County Clerk of Superior Court, Criminal Records
2 South Green Street
Sonora, CA 95370
(209) 533-5555

Felony records are available by mail or phone. No release necessary. No fee. Search information required: name.

Civil records are available by mail. No release necessary. $5.00 search fee. $.50 fee for first copy, $.25 each additional copy. $1.75 for certification. Search information required: name, years to search. Specify plaintiff or defendant.

Ventura County

Felony records
Ventura Superior Court, Criminal Records
800 S. Victoria Ave.
Ventura, CA 93009
(805) 654-2240

Felony records are available by mail. $5.00 search fee. Records are available by phone from 1989 to present. No release necessary. Search information required: name, date of birth, SASE.

Civil records
Ventura Superior Court
800 S. Victoria Ave.
Ventura, CA 93009
(805) 654-2265

Civil records are available by mail. No release necessary. $5.00 search fee. $.50 fee per copy. $2.25 for certification. Search information required: name, years to search, SASE. Specify plaintiff or defendant.

Misdemeanor records
Ventura County Municipal Court
PO Box 6489
Ventura, CA 93006-6489
(805) 654-2611

Misdemeanor records since 1978 are available by mail or phone. No release necessary. $5.00 search fee. $.50 fee per copy. $1.75 for certification. Make checks only, payable to Ventura County Municipal Court. Search information required: name, SASE.

Civil records
Ventura County Municipal Court
PO Box 6489
Ventura, CA 93006-6489
(805) 654-2611

Civil records are available by mail. No release necessary. $5.00 search fee. $.50 fee per copy. $1.75 for certification. Search information required: name, years to search. Specify plaintiff or defendant.

Yolo County

Clerk of the Superior Court
County of Yolo
PO Box 459
Woodland, CA 95695
(916) 666-8170

Felony records are available by mail. No release necessary. $5.00 search fee. $.50 fee per copy. $2.25 for certification. Search information required: name, years to search, SASE.

Civil records are available by mail. No release necessary. $5.00 search fee. $.50 fee per copy. $1.75 for certification. Search information required: name, years to search, SASE. Specify plaintiff or defendant.

Yuba County

Yuba County Clerk, Criminal Records
215 5th Street
Marysville, CA 95901
(916) 741-6258

Felony records are available by mail. No release necessary. $1.75 fee per year searched. $.50 fee per copy. Search information required: name, date of birth, years to search.

Civil records are available by mail. No release necessary. $1.75 fee per year searched. $.50 fee per copy. Search information required: name, date of birth, years to search. Specify plaintiff or defendant.

City-County Cross Reference

Acampo *San Joaquin*
Acton *Los Angeles*
Adelanto *San Bernardino*
Adin *Modoc*
Agoura Hills *Los Angeles*
Aguanga *Riverside*
Ahwahnee *Madera*
Alameda *Alameda*
Alamo *Contra Costa*
Albany *Alameda*
Albion *Mendocino*
Alderpoint *Humboldt*
Alhambra *Los Angeles*
Alleghany *Sierra*
Almanor *Plumas*
Alpaugh *Tulare*
Alpine *San Diego*
Alta *Placer*
Altadena *Los Angeles*
Alta Loma *San Bernardino*
Alturas *Modoc*
Alviso *Santa Clara*
Amador City *Amador*
Amboy *San Bernardino*
Anaheim *Orange*
Anderson *Shasta*
Angels Camp *Calaveras*
Angelus Oaks *San Bernardino*
Angwin *Napa*
Annapolis *Sonoma*
Antioch *Contra Costa*
Anza *Riverside*
Applegate *Placer*
Apple Valley *San Bernardino*
Aptos *Santa Cruz*
Arbuckle *Colusa*
Arcadia *Los Angeles*
Arcata *Humboldt*
Armona *Kings*
Arnold *Calaveras*
Aromas *Monterey*
Arroyo Grande *San Luis Obispo*
Artesia *Los Angeles*
Artois *Glenn*
Arvin *Kern*
Atascadero *San Luis Obispo*

Atherton *San Mateo*
Atwater *Merced*
Atwood *Orange*
Auberry *Fresno*
Auburn *Placer*
Avalon *Los Angeles*
Avenal *Kings*
Avery *Calaveras*
Avila Beach *San Luis Obispo*
Azusa *Los Angeles*
Baker *San Bernardino*
Bakersfield *Kern*
Baldwin Park *Los Angeles*
Ballico *Merced*
Bangor *Butte*
Banning *Riverside*
Bard *Imperial*
Barstow *San Bernardino*
Bass Lake *Madera*
Bayside *Humboldt*
Bayview *Humbolt*
Baywood Park *San Luis Obispo*
Beaumont *Riverside*
Bell *Los Angeles*
Bella Vista *Shasta*
Bellflower *Los Angeles*
Bell Gardens *Los Angeles*
Belmont *San Mateo*
Belvedere-Tiburon *Marin*
Benicia *Solano*
Ben Lomond *Santa Cruz*
Berkeley *Alameda*
Berry Creek *Butte*
Bertsch Ter *Del Norte*
Bethel Island *Contra Costa*
Beverly Hills *Los Angeles*
Bieber *Lassen*
Big Bar *Trinity*
Big Bear City *San Bernardino*
Big Bear Lake *San Bernardino*
Big Bend *Shasta*
Big Creek *Fresno*
Biggs *Butte*
Big Oak Flat *Tuolumne*
Big Pine *Inyo*
Big River *San Bernardino*

Big Sur *Monterey*
Biola *Fresno*
Birds Landing *Solano*
Bishop *Inyo*
Blairsden *Plumas*
Blocksburg *Humboldt*
Bloomington *San Bernardino*
Blue Jay *San Bernardino*
Blue Lake *Humboldt*
Blythe *Riverside*
Bodega *Sonoma*
Bodega Bay *Sonoma*
Bodfish *Kern*
Bolinas *Marin*
Bonita *San Diego*
Bonsall *San Diego*
Boonville *Mendocino*
Boron *Kern*
Borrego Springs *San Diego*
Boulder Creek *Santa Cruz*
Boulevard *San Diego*
Boyes Hot Springs *Sonoma*
Bradbury *Los Angeles*
Bradley *Monterey*
Brawley *Imperial*
Brea *Orange*
Brentwood *Contra Costa*
Bridgeport *Mono*
Bridgeville *Humboldt*
Brisbane *San Mateo*
Broadmoor *San Mateo*
Broderick *Yolo*
Brookdale *Santa Cruz*
Brooks *Yolo*
Browns Valley *Yuba*
Brownsville *Yuba*
Bryn Mawr *San Bernardino*
Buellton *Santa Barbara*
Buena Park *Orange*
Burbank *Los Angeles*
Burlingame *San Mateo*
Burney *Shasta*
Burnt Ranch *Trinity*
Burson *Calaveras*
Butte City *Glenn*
Buttonwillow *Kern*
Byron *Contra Costa*
Cabazon *Riverside*

Cadiz *San Bernardino*
Calexico *Imperial*
Caliente *Kern*
California City *Kern*
California Hot Springs *Tulare*
Calimesa *Riverside*
Calipatria *Imperial*
Calistoga *Napa*
Callahan *Siskiyou*
Calwa *Fresno*
Camarillo *Ventura*
Cambria *San Luis Obispo*
Cambrian Park *Santa Clara*
Camino *El Dorado*
Campbell *Santa Clara*
Camp Meeker *Sonoma*
Campo *San Diego*
Camptonville *Yuba*
Canby *Modoc*
Canoga Park *Los Angeles*
Cantua Creek *Fresno*
Canyon *Contra Costa*
Canyondam *Plumas*
Capitola *Santa Cruz*
Cardiff By The Sea *San Diego*
Carlotta *Humboldt*
Carlsbad *San Diego*
Carmel *Monterey*
Carmel Highlands *Monterey*
Carmel Valley *Monterey*
Carmichael *Sacramento*
Carnelian Bay *Placer*
Carpinteria *Santa Barbara*
Carson *Los Angeles*
Caruthers *Fresno*
Casmalia *Santa Barbara*
Cassel *Shasta*
Castella *Shasta*
Castroville *Monterey*
Catheys Valley *Mariposa*
Cathedral City *Riverside*
Cayucos *San Luis Obispo*
Cazadero *Sonoma*
Cedar Glen *San Bernardino*
Cedar Ridge *Nevada*

Cedarville *Modoc*
Central Valley *Shasta*
Ceres *Stanislaus*
Cerritos *Los Angeles*
Challenge *Yuba*
Chatsworth *Los Angeles*
Cherry Valley *Riverside*
Chester *Plumas*
Chicago Park *Nevada*
Chico *Butte*
Chilcoot *Plumas*
Chinese Camp *Tuolumne*
Chino *San Bernardino*
Cholame *San Luis Obispo*
Chowchilla *Madera*
Chualar *Monterey*
Chula Vista *San Diego*
Cima *San Bernardino*
Citrus Heights *Sacramento*
Claremont *Los Angeles*
Clarksburg *Yolo*
Clayton *Contra Costa*
Clearlake *Lake*
Clearlake Oaks *Lake*
Clearlake Park *Lake*
Clements *San Joaquin*
Clio *Plumas*
Clipper Mills *Butte*
Cloverdale *Sonoma*
Clovis *Fresno*
Coachella *Riverside*
Coalinga *Fresno*
Coarsegold *Madera*
Cobb *Lake*
Coleville *Mono*
Colfax *Placer*
College City *Colusa*
Coloma *El Dorado*
Colton *San Bernardino*
Columbia *Tuolumne*
Colusa *Colusa*
Comptche *Mendocino*
Compton *Los Angeles*
Concord *Contra Costa*
Cool *El Dorado*
Copperopolis *Calaveras*
Corcoran *Kings*
Corning *Tehama*
Corona *Riverside*
Corona Del Mar *Orange*
Coronado *San Diego*
Corte Madera *Marin*
Costa Mesa *Orange*
Cotati *Sonoma*
Cottonwood *Shasta*
Coulterville *Mariposa*
Courtland *Sacramento*
Cowan Heights *Orange*
Covelo *Mendocino*
Covina *Los Angeles*
Crescent City *Del Norte*
Crescent Mills *Plumas*
Cressey *Merced*
Crestline *San Bernardino*
Creston *San Luis Obispo*
Crest Park *San Bernardino*
Crockett *Contra Costa*
Crows Landing *Stanislaus*
Cudahy *Los Angeles*
Rancho Cucamonga *San Bernardino*
Culver City *Los Angeles*
Cupertino *Santa Clara*
Cutler *Tulare*
Cuyama *Santa Barbara*
Cypress *Orange*

Daggett *San Bernardino*
Daly City *San Mateo*
Dana Point *Orange*
Danville *Contra Costa*
Darwin *Inyo*
Davenport *Santa Cruz*
Davis *Yolo*
Davis Creek *Modoc*
Death Valley *Inyo*
Delano *Kern*
Delhi *Merced*
Del Mar *San Diego*
Del Rey *Fresno*
Del Ray Oaks *Monterey*
Denair *Stanislaus*
Descanso *San Diego*
Desert Center *Riverside*
Desert Hot Springs *Riverside*
Divore *San Bernadino*
Diablo *Contra Costa*
Diamond Bar *Los Angeles*
Diamond Springs *El Dorado*
Di Giorgio *Kern*
Dillon Beach *Marin*
Dinuba *Tulare*
Dixon *Solano*
Dobbins *Yuba*
Dorris *Siskiyou*
Dos Palos *Merced*
Douglas City *Trinity*
Downey *Los Angeles*
Downieville *Sierra*
Doyle *Lassen*
Duarte *Los Angeles*
Dublin *Alameda*
Ducor *Tulare*
Dulzura *San Diego*
Duncans Mills *Sonoma*
Dunlap *Fresno*
Dunnigan *Yolo*
Dunsmuir *Siskiyou*
Durham *Butte*
Dutch Flat *Placer*
Eagle Mountain *Riverside*
Eagleville *Modoc*
Earlimart *Tulare*
Earp *San Bernardino*
East Blythe *Riverside*
East Los Angeles *Los Angeles*
East Nicolaus *Sutter*
Easton *Fresno*
East Palo Alto *San Mateo*
East Quincy *Plumas*
East Richmond *Contra Costa*
Edison *Kern*
Edwards *Kern*
El Cajon *San Diego*
El Centro *Imperial*
El Cerrito *Contra Costa*
El Dorado *El Dorado*
El Dorado Hills *El Dorado*
Eldridge *Sonoma*
El Granada *San Mateo*
Elk *Mendocino*
Elk Creek *Glenn*
Elk Grove *Sacramento*
Elmira *Solano*
El Monte *Los Angeles*
El Nido *Merced*
El Portal *Mariposa*
El Rio *Ventura*
El Segundo *Los Angeles*

El Sobrante *Contra Costa*
El Toro *Orange*
El Verano *Sonoma*
Elverta *Sacramento*
Emerald Bay *Orange*
Emeryville *Alamede*
Empire *Stanislaus*
Encinitas *San Diego*
Escalon *San Joaquin*
Escondido *San Diego*
Esparto *Yolo*
Essex *San Bernardino*
Etiwanda *San Bernardino*
Etna *Siskiyou*
Eureka *Humboldt*
Exeter *Tulare*
Fairfax *Marin*
Fairfield *Solano*
Fair Oaks *Sacramento*
Fallbrook *San Diego*
Fall River Mills *Shasta*
Farmersville *Tulare*
Farmington *San Joaquin*
Fawnskin *San Bernardino*
Fellows *Kern*
Felton *Santa Cruz*
Ferndale *Humboldt*
Fiddletown *Amador*
Fields Landing *Humboldt*
Fillmore *Ventura*
Finley *Lake*
Firebaugh *Fresno*
Fish Camp *Mariposa*
Five Points *Fresno*
Florence *Los Angeles*
Florin *Sacramento*
Floriston *Nevada*
Folsom *Sacramento*
Fontana *San Bernardino*
Forbestown *Butte*
Ford City *Kern*
Forest Falls *San Bernardino*
Foresthill *Placer*
Forest Knolls *Marin*
Forest Ranch *Butte*
Forestville *Sonoma*
Forks Of Salmon *Siskiyou*
Fort Bidwell *Modoc*
Fort Bragg *Mendocino*
Fort Jones *Siskiyou*
Fortuna *Humboldt*
Foster City *San Mateo*
Fountain Valley *Orange*
Fowler *Fresno*
Frazier Park *Kern*
Freedom *Santa Cruz*
Fremont *Alameda*
French Camp *San Joaquin*
French Gulch *Shasta*
Fresno *Fresno*
Friant *Fresno*
Fullerton *Orange*
Fulton *Sonoma*
Galt *Sacramento*
Garberville *Humboldt*
Gardena *Los Angeles*
Garden Grove *Orange*
Garden Valley *El Dorado*
Gasquet *Del Norte*
Gazelle *Siskiyou*
Georgetown *El Dorado*
Gerber *Tehama*
Geyserville *Sonoma*
Gilroy *Santa Clara*
Glen Avon *Riverside*

Glencoe *Calaveras*
Glendale *Los Angeles*
Glendora *Los Angeles*
Glen Ellen *Sonoma*
Glenhaven *Lake*
Glenn *Glenn*
Glennville *Kern*
Gold Run *Placer*
Goleta *Santa Barbara*
Gonzales *Monterey*
Goodyears Bar *Sierra*
Goshen *Tulare*
Grand Terrace *San Bernardino*
Grass Valley *Nevada*
Graton *Sonoma*
Greenacres *Kern*
Greenbrae *Marin*
Greenfield *Monterey*
Green Valley Lake *San Bernardino*
Greenview *Siskiyou*
Greenville *Plumas*
Greenwood *El Dorado*
Grenada *Siskiyou*
Gridley *Butte*
Grimes *Colusa*
Grizzly Flats *El Dorado*
Groveland *Tuolumne*
Grover City *San Luis Obispo*
Guadalupe *Santa Barbara*
Gualala *Mendocino*
Guasti *San Bernardino*
Guatay *San Diego*
Guerneville *Sonoma*
Guinda *Yolo*
Gustine *Merced*
Hacienda Heights *Los Angeles*
Half Moon Bay *San Mateo*
Hamilton City *Glenn*
Hanford *Kings*
Happy Camp *Siskiyou*
Harbor City *Los Angeles*
Harmony *San Luis Obispo*
Hat Creek *Shasta*
Hathaway Pines *Calaveras*
Hawaiin Gardens *Los Angeles*
Hawthorne *Los Angeles*
Hayfork *Trinity*
Hayward *Alameda*
Healdsburg *Sonoma*
Heber *Imperial*
Helendale *San Bernardino*
Helm *Fresno*
Hemet *Riverside*
Herald *Sacramento*
Hercules *Contra Costa*
Herlong *Lassen*
Hermosa Beach *Los Angeles*
Hesperia *San Bernardino*
Hickman *Stanislaus*
Hidden Hills *Los Angeles*
Highgrove *Riverside*
Highland *San Bernardino*
Highway City *Fresno*
Hillsborough *San Mateo*
Hilmar *Merced*
Hinkley *San Bernardino*
Hollister *San Benito*
Holt *San Joaquin*
Holtville *Imperial*
Homeland *Riverside*

Home Gardens *Riverside*
Homestead Valley *Marin*
Homewood *Placer*
Honeydew *Humboldt*
Hood *Sacramento*
Hoopa *Humboldt*
Hopland *Mendocino*
Hornbrook *Siskiyou*
Hornitos *Mariposa*
Horse Creek *Siskiyou*
Hughson *Stanislaus*
Huntington Beach *Orange*
Huntington Park *Los Angeles*
Huron *Fresno*
Hyampom *Trinity*
Hydesville *Humboldt*
Idyllwild *Riverside*
Igo *Shasta*
Imperial *Imperial*
Imperial Beach *San Diego*
Independence *Inyo*
Indio *Riverside*
Inglewood *Los Angeles*
Inverness *Marin*
Inyokern *Kern*
Ione *Amador*
Irvine *Orange*
Irwindale *Los Angeles*
Isleton *Sacramento*
Ivanhoe *Tulare*
Jackson *Amador*
Jacumba *San Diego*
Jamestown *Tuolumne*
Jamul *San Diego*
Janesville *Lassen*
Jenner *Sonoma*
Johannesburg *Kern*
Jolon *Monterey*
Joshua Tree *San Bernardino*
Julian *San Diego*
Junction City *Trinity*
June Lake *Mono*
Keeler *Inyo*
Keene *Kern*
Kelseyville *Lake*
Kelso *San Bernardino*
Kensington *Contra Costa*
Kentfield *Marin*
Kenwood *Sonoma*
Kerman *Fresno*
Kernville *Kern*
Kettleman City *Kings*
Keyes *Stanislaus*
King City *Monterey*
Kings Beach *Placer*
Kingsburg *Fresno*
Klamath *Del Norte*
Klamath River *Siskiyou*
Kneeland *Humboldt*
Knightsen *Contra Costa*
Knights Landing *Yolo*
Korbel *Humboldt*
Kyburz *El Dorado*
LaCanada-Flintridge *Los Angeles*
La Crescenta *Los Angeles*
Ladera *San Mateo*
Lafayette *Contra Costa*
LaGrange *Stanislaus*
Laguna Beach *Orange*
Laguna Hills *Orange*
Laguna Niguel *Orange*
Lagunitas *Marin*
LaHabra *Orange*

La Habra Heights *Los Angeles*
LaHonda *San Mateo*
LaJolla *San Diego*
La Palma *Orange*
Lake Arrowhead *San Bernardino*
Lake City *Modoc*
Lake Elsinore *Riverside*
Lakehead *Shasta*
Lake Hughes *Los Angeles*
Lake Isabella *Kern*
Lakeport *Lake*
Lakeside *San Diego*
Lakeview *Riverside*
Lakewood *Los Angeles*
LaMesa *San Diego*
LaMirada *Los Angeles*
Lamont *Kern*
Lancaster *Los Angeles*
LaPuente *Los Angeles*
LaQuinta *Riverside*
Larkspur *Marin*
Lathrop *San Joaquin*
Laton *Fresno*
LaVerne *Los Angeles*
Lawndale *Los Angeles*
Laytonville *Mendocino*
Lebec *Kern*
Lee Vining *Mono*
Leggett *Mendocino*
Le Grand *Merced*
Lemoncove *Tulare*
Lemon Grove *San Diego*
Lemoore *Kings*
Lenwood *San Bernadino*
Leucadia *San Diego*
Lewiston *Trinity*
Likely *Modoc*
Lincoln *Placer*
Lincoln Acres *San Diego*
Linden *San Joaquin*
Lindsay *Tulare*
Litchfield *Lassen*
Little Norway *El Dorado*
Littleriver *Mendocino*
Littlerock *Los Angeles*
Live Oak *Sutter*
Livermore *Alameda*
Livingston *Merced*
Llano *Los Angeles*
Lockeford *San Joaquin*
Lockwood *Monterey*
Lodi *San Joaquin*
Loleta *Humboldt*
Loma Linda *San Bernardino*
Loma Mar *San Mateo*
Lomita *Los Angeles*
Lompoc *Santa Barbara*
Lone Pine *Inyo*
Long Barn *Tuolumne*
Long Beach *Los Angeles*
Lookout *Modoc*
Loomis *Placer*
Los Alamitos *Orange*
Los Alamos *Santa Barbara*
Los Altos *Santa Clara*
Los Angeles *Los Angeles*
Los Banos *Merced*
Los Gatos *Santa Clara*
Los Molinos *Tehama*
Los Nietos *Los Angeles*
Los Olivos *Santa Barbara*
Los Osos *San Luis Obispo*
Los Serranos *San*

Bernadino
Lost Hills *Kern*
Lotus *El Dorado*
Lower Lake *Lake*
Loyalton *Sierra*
Lucerne *Lake*
Lucerne Valley *San Bernardino*
Lynwood *Los Angeles*
Lytle Creek *San Bernardino*
McArthur *Shasta*
McCloud *Siskiyou*
McFarland *Kern*
McKinleyville *Humboldt*
McKittrick *Kern*
Macdoel *Siskiyou*
Madeline *Lassen*
Madera *Madera*
Madison *Yolo*
Mad River *Trinity*
Magalia *Butte*
Malibu *Los Angeles*
Mammoth Lakes *Mono*
Manchester *Mendocino*
Manhattan Beach *Los Angeles*
Manteca *San Joaquin*
Manton *Tehama*
Maricopa *Kern*
Marina *Monterey*
Marin City *Marin*
Mariposa *Mariposa*
Markleeville *Alpine*
Marshall *Marin*
Martinez *Contra Costa*
Marysville *Yuba*
Maxwell *Colusa*
Meadow Valley *Plumas*
Meadow Vista *Placer*
Mecca *Riverside*
Meiners Oaks *Ventura*
Mendocino *Mendocino*
Mendota *Fresno*
Menlo Park *San Mateo*
Mentone *San Bernardino*
Merced *Merced*
Meridian *Sutter*
Middletown *Lake*
Midpines *Mariposa*
Midway City *Orange*
Milford *Lassen*
Millbrae *San Mateo*
Mill Valley *Marin*
Millville *Shasta*
Milpitas *Santa Clara*
Mineral *Tehama*
Mira Loma *Riverside*
Miramonte *Fresno*
Miranda *Humboldt*
Mission Viejo *Orange*
Mi-Wuk Village *Tuolumne*
Moccasin *Tuolumne*
Modesto *Stanislaus*
Mojave *Kern*
Mokelumne Hill *Calaveras*
Monrovia *Los Angeles*
Montague *Siskiyou*
Montara *San Mateo*
Montclair *San Bernardino*
Montebello *Los Angeles*
Montecito *Santa Barbara*
Monterey *Monterey*
Monterey Park *Los Angeles*
Monte Rio *Sonoma*
Montgomery Creek *Shasta*

Montrose *Los Angeles*
Moonridge *San Bernadino*
Moorpark *Ventura*
Moraga *Contra Costa*
Moreno Valley *Riverside*
Morgan Hill *Santa Clara*
Morongo Valley *San Bernardino*
Morro Bay *San Luis Obispo*
Moss Beach *San Mateo*
Moss Landing *Monterey*
Mountain Center *Riverside*
Mountain Ranch *Calaveras*
Mountain View *Santa Clara*
Mount Hermon *Santa Cruz*
Mount Laguna *San Diego*
Mount Shasta *Siskiyou*
Mt. Aukum *El Dorado*
Mt Baldy *San Bernardino*
Murphys *Calaveras*
Murrieta *Riverside*
Muscoy *San Bernadino*
Myers Flat *Humboldt*
Napa *Napa*
National City *San Diego*
Needles *San Bernardino*
Nestor *San Diego*
Nevada City *Nevada*
New Almaden *Santa Clara*
Newark *Alameda*
Newberry Springs *San Bernardino*
Newcastle *Placer*
New Cuyama *Santa Barbara*
Newman *Stanislaus*
Newport Beach *Orange*
Nicasio *Marin*
Nice *Lake*
Nicolaus *Sutter*
Niland *Imperial*
Nipomo *San Luis Obispo*
Norco *Riverside*
Norden *Nevada*
North Edwards *Kern*
North Fairoaks *San Mateao*
North Fork *Madera*
North Highlands *Sacramento*
North Hollywood *Los Angeles*
North Palm Springs *Riverside*
North Richmond *Contra Costa*
Northridge *Los Angeles*
North San Juan *Nevada*
Norwalk *Los Angeles*
Novato *Marin*
Nubieber *Lassen*
Nuevo *Riverside*
Oakdale *Stanislaus*
Oakhurst *Madera*
Oakland *Alameda*
Oakley *Contra Costa*
Oak Run *Shasta*
Oak View *Ventura*
Oakville *Napa*
Occidental *Sonoma*
Oceano *San Luis Obispo*
Oceanside *San Diego*
Ocotillo *Imperial*
Oildale *Kern*
Ojai *Ventura*

Olancha *Inyo*
Old Station *Shasta*
Olema *Marin*
Olivehurst *Yuba*
O'Neals *Madera*
Ontario *San Bernardino*
Onyx *Kern*
Orange *Orange*
Orange Cove *Fresno*
Orangevale *Sacramento*
Orcuit *Santa Barbara*
Oregon House *Yuba*
Orick *Humboldt*
Orinda *Contra Costa*
Orland *Glenn*
Orleans *Humboldt*
Oro Grande *San Bernardino*
Orosi *Tulare*
Oroville *Butte*
Otay *San Diego*
Oxnard *Ventura*
Pacifica *San Mateo*
Pacific Grove *Monterey*
Pacific House *El Dorado*
Pacific Palisades *Los Angeles*
Pacoima *Los Angeles*
Paicines *San Benito*
Pajaro *Santa Cruz*
Pala *San Diego*
Palermo *Butte*
Palmdale *Los Angeles*
Palm Desert *Riverside*
Palm Springs *Riverside*
Palo Alto *Santa Clara*
Palo Cedro *Shasta*
Palomar Mountain *San Diego*
Palomar Park *San Mateo*
Palos Verdes Peninsula *Los Angeles*
Palo Verde *Imperial*
Paradise *Butte*
Paramount *Los Angeles*
Parker Dam *San Bernardino*
Parkway *Sacramento*
Parlier *Fresno*
Pasadena *Los Angeles*
Paskenta *Tehama*
Paso Robles *San Luis Obispo*
Patterson *Stanislaus*
Patton *San Bernardino*
Pauma Valley *San Diego*
Pearblossom *Los Angeles*
Pebble Beach *Monterey*
Pedley *Riverside*
Penngrove *Sonoma*
Penryn *Placer*
Perris *Riverside*
Pescadero *San Mateo*
Petaluma *Sonoma*
Petrolia *Humboldt*
Phelan *San Bernardino*
Phillipsville *Humboldt*
Philo *Mendocino*
Pico Rivera *Los Angeles*
Piedmont *Alameda*
Piedra *Fresno*
Piercy *Mendocino*
Pilot Hill *El Dorado*
Pinecrest *Tuolumne*
Pine Grove *Amador*
Pine Valley *San Diego*

Pinole *Contra Costa*
Pinon Hills *San Bernardino*
Pioneer *Amador*
Pioneer Point *San Bernadino*
Pioneertown *San Bernardino*
Piru *Ventura*
Pismo Beach *San Luis Obispo*
Pittsburg *Contra Costa*
Pixley *Tulare*
Placentia *Orange*
Placerville *El Dorado*
Planada *Merced*
Platina *Shasta*
Pleasant Hill *Contra Costa*
Pleasant Grove *Sutter*
Pleasanton *Alameda*
Plymouth *Amador*
Point Arena *Mendocino*
Point Reyes Station *Marin*
Pollock Pines *El Dorado*
Pomona *Los Angeles*
Pope Valley *Napa*
Poplar *Tulare*
Port Costa *Contra Costa*
Porterville *Tulare*
Port Hueneme *Ventura*
Portola *Plumas*
Posey *Tulare*
Potrero *San Diego*
Potter Valley *Mendocino*
Poway *San Diego*
Prather *Fresno*
Princeton *Colusa*
Proberta *Tehama*
Project City *Shasta*
Quarte Hill *Los Angeles*
Quincy *Plumas*
Rackerby *Yuba*
Rail Road Flat *Calaveras*
Raisin *Fresno*
Ramona *San Diego*
Rancho Cordova *Sacramento*
Rancho Palos Verdes *Los Angeles*
Rancho Mirage *Riverside*
Rancho Santa Fe *San Diego*
Ravendale *Lassen*
Raymond *Madera*
Red Bluff *Tehama*
Redcrest *Humboldt*
Redding *Shasta*
Red Hill *Orange*
Redlands *San Bernardino*
Redondo Beach *Los Angeles*
Redway *Humboldt*
Redwood City *San Mateo*
Redwood Estates *Santa Clara*
Redwood Valley *Mendocino*
Reedley *Fresno*
Rescue *El Dorado*
Reseda *Los Angeles*
Rialto *San Bernardino*
Richgrove *Tulare*
Richmond *Contra Costa*
Richvale *Butte*
Ridgecrest *Kern*
Rimforest *San Bernardino*

Rio Dell *Humboldt*
Rio Linda *Sacramento*
Rio Oso *Sutter*
Rio Vista *Solano*
Ripley *Riverside*
Ripon *San Joaquin*
Riverbank *Stanislaus*
Riverdale *Fresno*
River Pines *Amador*
Riverside *Riverside*
Robbins *Sutter*
Rocklin *Placer*
Rodeo *Contra Costa*
Rohnert Park *Sonoma*
Rolling Hills *Los Angeles*
Rosamond *Kern*
Rosemead *Los Angeles*
Roseville *Placer*
Ross *Marin*
Rough And Ready *Nevada*
Round Mountain *Shasta*
Rowland Heights *Los Angeles*
Rubidoux *Riverside*
Running Springs *San Bernardino*
Rutherford *Napa*
Ryde *Sacramento*
Sacramento *Sacramento*
Saint Helena *Napa*
Salida *Stanislaus*
Salinas *Monterey*
Salton City *Imperial*
Salyer *Trinity*
Samoa *Humboldt*
San Andreas *Calaveras*
San Anselmo *Marin*
San Antonio Heights *San Bernadino*
San Ardo *Monterey*
San Bernardino *San Bernardino*
San Bruno *San Mateo*
San Carlos *San Mateo*
San Clemente *Orange*
San Diego *San Diego*
San Dimas *Los Angeles*
San Fernando *Los Angeles*
San Francisco *San Francisco*
San Gabriel *Los Angeles*
Sanger *Fresno*
San Geronimo *Marin*
San Gregorio *San Mateo*
San Jacinto *Riverside*
San Joaquin *Fresno*
San Jose *Santa Clara*
San Juan Bautista *San Benito*
San Juan Capistrano *Orange*
San Leandro *Alameda*
San Lorenzo *Alameda*
San Lucas *Monterey*
San Luis Obispo *San Luis Obispo*
San Luis Rey *San Diego*
San Marcos *San Diego*
San Martin *Santa Clara*
San Mateo *San Mateo*
San Miguel *San Luis Obispo*
San Marino *Los Angeles*
San Pablo *Contra Costa*
San Pedro *Los Angeles*
San Quentin *Marin*

San Rafael *Marin*
San Ramon *Contra Costa*
San Simeon *San Luis Obispo*
Santa Ana *Orange*
Santa Barbara *Santa Barbara*
Santa Clara *Santa Clara*
Santa Clarita *Los Angeles*
Santa Cruz *Santa Cruz*
Santa Fe Springs *Los Angeles*
Santa Margarita *San Luis Obispo*
Santa Maria *Santa Barbara*
Santa Monica *Los Angeles*
Santa Paula *Ventura*
Santa Rita Park *Merced*
Santa Rosa *Sonoma*
Santa Venetia *Marin*
Santa Ynez *Santa Barbara*
Santa Ysabel *San Diego*
Santee *San Diego*
Saratoga *Santa Clara*
Sattley *Sierra*
Saugus *Los Angeles*
Sausalito *Marin*
Scotia *Humboldt*
Scott Bar *Siskiyou*
Scotts Valley *Santa Cruz*
Seal Beach *Orange*
Seaside *Monterey*
Sebastopol *Sonoma*
Seeley *Imperial*
Seiad Valley *Siskiyou*
Selma *Fresno*
Sequoia National Park *Tulare*
Shafter *Kern*
Shandon *San Luis Obispo*
Shasta *Shasta*
Shaver Lake *Fresno*
Sheridan *Placer*
Sherwood Forest *Contra Costa*
Shingle Springs *El Dorado*
Shingletown *Shasta*
Short Acres *Kings*
Shoshone *Inyo*
Sierra City *Sierra*
Sierra Madre *Los Angeles*
Sierraville *Sierra*
Signal Hill *Los Angeles*
Silverado *Orange*
Simi Valley *Ventura*
Skyforest *San Bernardino*
Sloughhouse *Sacramento*
Smartville *Yuba*
Smith River *Del Norte*
Snelling *Merced*
Soda Springs *Nevada*
Solana Beach *San Diego*
Soledad *Monterey*
Solvang *Santa Barbara*
Somerset *El Dorado*
Somis *Ventura*
Sonoma *Sonoma*
Sonora *Tuolumne*
Soquel *Santa Cruz*
Soulsbyville *Tuolumne*
South Dos Palos *Merced*
South El Monte *Los Angeles*
South Gate *Los Angeles*
South Lake Tahoe *El Dorado*

South Pasadena *Los Angeles*
South San Francisco *San Mateo*
South Taft *Kern*
South Whittier *Los Angeles*
Spring Valley *San Diego*
Springville *Tulare*
Squaw Valley *Fresno*
Standish *Lassen*
Stanford *Santa Clara*
Stanton *Orange*
Stevinson *Merced*
Stewarts Point *Sonoma*
Stinson Beach *Marin*
Stirling City *Butte*
Stockton *San Joaquin*
Stonyford *Colusa*
Stratford *Kings*
Strathmore *Tulare*
Strawberry Point *Marin*
Strawberry Valley *Yuba*
Suisun City *Solano*
Sultana *Tulare*
Summerland *Santa Barbara*
Summit City *Shasta*
Sun City *Riverside*
Sunland *Los Angeles*
Sunnyslope *Riverside*
Sunnyvale *Santa Clara*
Sunol *Alameda*
Sunset Beach *Orange*
Sun Valley *Los Angeles*
Surfside *Orange*
Susanville *Lassen*
Sutter *Sutter*
Sutter Creek *Amador*
Taft *Kern*
Tahoe City *Placer*
Tahoe Vista *Placer*
Talmage *Mendocino*
Tamalphis Valley *Marin*
Tarzana *Los Angeles*
Taylorsville *Plumas*
Tecate *San Diego*
Tecopa *Inyo*
Tehachapi *Kern*
Tehama *Tehama*
Temecula *Riverside*
Temple City *Los Angeles*
Templeton *San Luis Obispo*
Termo *Lassen*
Terra Bella *Tulare*
Thermal *Riverside*
Thermalito *Butte*
Thornton *San Joaquin*
Thousand Oaks *Ventura*
Thousand Palms *Riverside*
Three Rivers *Tulare*
Tiburon *Contra Costa*
Tipton *Tulare*
Tollhouse *Fresno*
Tomales *Marin*
Topanga *Los Angeles*
Topaz *Mono*
Torrance *Los Angeles*
Trabuco Canyon *Orange*
Tracy *San Joaquin*
Tranquillity *Fresno*
Traver *Tulare*
Tres Pinos *San Benito*
Trinidad *Humboldt*
Trinity Center *Trinity*

Trona *San Bernardino*
Truckee *Nevada*
Tujunga *Los Angeles*
Tulare *Tulare*
Tulelake *Siskiyou*
Tuolumne *Tuolumne*
Tupman *Kern*
Turlock *Stanislaus*
Tustin *Orange*
Twain *Plumas*
Twain Harte *Tuolumne*
Twentynine Palms *San Bernardino*
Twin Bridges *El Dorado*
Twin Peaks *San Bernardino*
Ukiah *Mendocino*
Union City *Alameda*
University Heights *San Mateo*
Upland *San Bernardino*
Upper Lake *Lake*
Vacaville *Solano*
Vallecito *Calaveras*
Vallejo *Solano*
Valle Vista *Riverside*
Valley Center *San Diego*
Valley Ford *Sonoma*
Valley Home *Stanislaus*
Valley Springs *Calaveras*
Van Nuys *Los Angeles*
Venice *Los Angeles*
Ventura *Ventura*
Verdugo City *Los Angeles*
Victor *San Joaquin*
Victorville *San Bernardino*
Villa Grande *Sonoma*
Villa Park *Orange*
Vina *Tehama*
Vineburg *Sonoma*
Vinton *Plumas*
Visalia *Tulare*
Vista *San Diego*
Volcano *Amador*
Wallace *Calaveras*
Walnut *Los Angeles*
Walnut Creek *Contra Costa*
Walnut Grove *Sacramento*
Walnut Park *Los Angeles*
Warner Springs *San Diego*
Wasco *Kern*
Washington *Nevada*
Waterford *Stanislaus*
Watsonville *Santa Cruz*
Weaverville *Trinity*
Weed *Siskiyou*
Weed Patch *Kern*
Weimar *Placer*
Weldon *Kern*
Weott *Humboldt*
West Covina *Los Angeles*
Westhaven *Humboldt*
Westlake Village *Los Angeles*
Westley *Stanislaus*
Westminster *Orange*
Westmorland *Imperial*
West Point *Calaveras*
West Sacramento *Yolo*
Westwood *Lassen*
Wheatland *Yuba*
Whiskeytown *Shasta*
Whitethorn *Humboldt*
White Water *Riverside*

Whitmore *Shasta*
Whittier *Los Angeles*
Wildomar *Riverside*
Williams *Colusa*
Willits *Mendocino*
Willow Brook *Los Angeles*
Willow Creek *Humboldt*
Willows *Glenn*
Wilmington *Los Angeles*
Wilseyville *Calaveras*
Wilton *Sacramento*
Winchester *Riverside*
Windsor *Sonoma*
Winterhaven *Imperial*
Winters *Yolo*
Winton *Merced*
Wofford Heights *Kern*
Woodacre *Marin*
Woodbridge *San Joaquin*
Woodcrest *Riverside*
Woodlake *Tulare*
Woodland *Yolo*
Woodland Hills *Los Angeles*
Woodside *San Mateo*
Woodville *Tulare*
Woody *Kern*
Wrightwood *San Bernardino*
Yermo *San Bernardino*
Yettem *Tulare*
Yolo *Yolo*
Yorba Linda *Orange*
Yorkville *Mendocino*
Yosemite National Park *Mariposa*
Yountville *Napa*
Yreka *Siskiyou*
Yuba City *Sutter*
Yucaipa *San Bernardino*
Yucca Valley *San Bernardino*
Zamora *Yolo*
Zenia *Trinity*

Colorado

Records of convictions by Colorado courts are specifically authorized to be open for inspection. Both the Colorado Bureau of Investigation (the state criminal record repository) and sixty two of the state's sixty three (63) counties reported that criminal records are available for employment screening purposes by phone or mail. Twenty three (23) counties honor facsimile requests. Civil suits for $10,000 and greater are filed in District Court.

For more information or for offices not listed, contact the state's information hot line at (303) 866-5000.

Driving Records

Motor Vehicle Division
Traffic Records
140 West 6th Avenue
Denver, CO 80204
(303) 572-5611

Driving records are available by mail. $2.20 fee per request. Turnaround time is 2 weeks. Written request must include job applicant's full name, date of birth, SASE sent with fee and, if available, license number. Make check payable to Department of Revenue.

Worker's Compensation Records

Division of Labor
Worker's Compensation Section
1120 Lincoln, Suite 1400
Denver, CO 80203
(303) 764-2929

Records are available by phone or mail. Written requests must include applicant's full name, date of birth and SSN. There is no fee. A signed release is not required for records prior to July, 1989.

Vital Statistics

Vital Records Section
Colorado Department of Health
4210 East 11th Avenue, Rm. 100
Denver, CO 80220
(303) 320-8474
Fax (800) 423-1108

Birth and death records are available $12.00 each. $4.00 additional fee with Visa or Mastercard. Charge card requests may be made via fax (800-423-1108), phone (303-331-4890) or mail. Turnaround time for fax request is next day. Turnaround time for phone and mail requests is five working days. State office has death records from 1900 and birth records from 1910. State office also has birth records for some counties for years before 1910. Turnaround time is 3-5 weeks. Make certified check or money order payable to Vital Statistics. Search information required for birth records: name, date of birth, place of birth, father's name, mother's maiden name; for death records: name, date of death, place of death, self-addressed legal envelope. Birth and death records are confidential and are only issued to the registrant or immediate family. $16.50 fee for Visa or Mastercard charges.

Marriage records available at county level through County Clerk, Recorder's Office in county where marriage took place. Divorce records available at county office where decree was granted.

Department of Education

Department of Education
Teacher Certification
201 E. Colfax Ave.
Denver, CO 80203
(303) 866-6620

Field of certification is available by phone or mail. Include full name and SSN.

Medical Licensing

Board of Medical Examiners
1560 Broadway
Suite 775
Denver, CO 80202-5140
(303) 894-7690

Will confirm licenses for MDs and DOs by phone or mail. No fee. For licenses not mentioned, contact the above office.

Colorado Board of Nursing
1560 Broadway, Suite 670
Denver, CO 80202
(303) 894-2430

Will confirm license by phone. No fee. Include name, license number, if available.

Bar Association

Colorado Bar Association
1900 Grant #950
Denver, CO 80203

Will confirm licenses by phone. No fee. Include name.

Accountancy Board

Colorado State Public Accountancy Board
1560 Broadway, Suite 1370
Denver, CO 80202
(303) 866-5000

Will confirm licenses by phone. No fee. Include name.

Securities Commission

Department of Regulatory Agencies
Division of Securities
1580 Lincoln Street, No. 420
Denver, CO 80203-1506
(303) 894-2320

Will confirm licenses by phone. No fee. Include name and SSN.

Secretary of State

Secretary of State
Corporation Division
1560 Broadway
Suite 200
Denver, CO 80202
(303) 894-2251
Fax (303) 894-2242

Service agent and address, date incorporated, standing with tax commission, trade names are available by phone or mail. $3.00 fee for first 3 names, $1.00 for each additional name. Contact the above office for additional information.

Criminal Records

State Repository

Colorado Bureau of Investigation
Attention: Identification Unit
690 Kipling Street, Suite 3000
Denver, CO 80215
(303) 239-4201

Criminal records are available by mail only. All requests should include the applicant's full name, date of birth and if available, SSN. There is a $3.50 fee per name searched. $13.00 fee for fingerprint search. Make company check or money order payable to Colorado Bureau of Investigation. All inquiries will receive a response (printout of record summary or confirmation that no records were found).

Adams County

Felony records
Clerk of District Court, Criminal Records
1931 E. Bridge Street
Brighton, CO 80601
(303) 659-1161

Felony records are available by mail. No release necessary. $4.00 search fee for records from 1976 forward. $8.00 search fee for records prior to 1976. $.75 fee per copy. $5.75 for certified copy. Search information required: name, date of birth, SASE, case number if available.

Civil records
Clerk of District Court
1931 E. Bridge Street
Brighton, CO 80601
(303) 659-1161

Civil records are available by mail. No release necessary. $3.10 search fee. Copies are $.75 per page, $5.75 for certification. Search information required: name, years to search. Specify plaintiff or defendant.

Misdemeanor records
County Clerk
1931 E. Bridge Street
Brighton, CO 80601
(303) 659-1161

Misdemeanor records since 1985 are available by mail. A release is required. $3.10 search fee. Copies are $.75 per page, $5.00 for certified copy. Search information required: name, date of birth, SASE, case number if available, years to search. Requester's name, address and day phone must be included.

Alamosa County

Felony records
Clerk of the District Court, Criminal Records
Alamosa County Courthouse
702 4th Street
Alamosa, CO 81101
(719) 589-4996

Felony records are available by mail or phone. No release necessary. $12.50 search fee. Copies are $.75 per page, $1.00 for microfilm, $5.00 for certified copy. Search information required: name, date of birth, SASE, years to search

Civil records
Clerk of the District Court
Alamosa County Courthouse
702 4th Street
Alamosa, CO 81101
(719) 589-4996

Civil records are available by mail. No release necessary.$12.00 search fee. $.75 fee per copy. $5.00 for certification. Search information required: name, date of birth, years to search,SASE. Specify plaintiff or defendant. .

Misdemeanor records
Alamosa County Court
Courthouse
4th and San Juan
Alamosa, CO 81101
(719) 589-6213

Misdemeanor records are available by mail. No release necessary. No search fee. Copies are $.75 per page. Search information required: name, date of birth, SASE, years to search.

Arapahoe County

Clerk of the District Court, Criminal Records
7325 South Potomac
Englewood, CO 80112
(303) 649-6355

Felony records are available by mail. No release necessary. $5.00 fee. No charge for searches from 1985 to present. Make check payable to Clerk of District Court. Search information required: name, SASE.

Civil records are available by mail. No release necessary. $5.00 search fee. Search information required: name, years to search, SASE.

Archuleta County

Clerk of the Combined Courts, Criminal Records
PO Box 148
Pagosa Springs, CO 81147
(303) 264-2400

Felony and misdemeanor records are available by mail. No release necessary. No search fee. $.75 fee per copy. $5.00 for certification. Search information required: name, SASE.

Civil records are available by mail. No release necessary. No search fee. $.75 fee per copy. $5.00 for certification. Search information required: name, years to search. Specify plaintiff or defendant.

Baca County

Clerk of the District Court, Criminal Records
Baca County Courthouse
741 Main Street
Springfield, CO 81073
(719) 523-4555

Felony records are available by mail or phone. No release necessary. No search fee. Copies are $.75 per page, $5.00 for certification. Company checks only, payable to Baca County Combined Clerk. Search information required: name, SASE.

Civil records are available by mail. No release necessary. No search fee. $.75 fee per copy. $5.00 for certification. Search information required: name, years to search. Specify plaintiff or defendant.

Bent County

Clerk of the District Court, Criminal Records
Bent County Combined Courts
Las Animas, CO 81054
(719) 456-1353

Felony and misdemeanor records are available by mail. A release is required. $8.00 search fee. $.75 fee per copy. $5.00 for certification. Search information required: name, date of birth, SASE.

Civil records are available by mail. No release necessary. $8.00 search fee. $.75 fee per copy. $5.00 for certification. Search information required: name, years to search. Specify plaintiff or defendant.

Boulder County

Clerk's Office, Criminal Records
Boulder Justice Center
PO Box 4249
Boulder, CO 80306
(303) 441-3750

Felony and misdemeanor records are available by mail or phone. No release necessary. No search fee. Copies are $.75 per page, $5.00 for certified copy. Search information required: name, date of birth, years to search.

Civil records are available by mail from 1983 forward. No release necessary. No search fee. $.75 fee per copy. $5.00 for certification. Search information required: name, years to search. Specify plaintiff or defendant.

Chaffee County

Clerk of District Court, Criminal Records
PO Box 279
Salida, CO 81201
(719) 539-2561
Fax (719) 539-6281

Felony and misdemeanor records are available by mail, fax or phone. No release necessary. No search fee. $.75 fee per copy. $5.00 for certification. Search information required: name, date of birth, years to search.

Civil records are available by mail, fax or phone. No release necessary. No search fee. $.75 fee per copy. $5.00 for certification. Search information required: name, years to search. Specify plaintiff or defendant.

Cheyenne County

Clerk of Combined Courts, Criminal Records
PO Box 696
Cheyenne Wells, CO 80810
(719) 767-5649

Felony and misdemeanor records are available by mail. A release is required. No search fee. $.75 fee per copy. $5.00 for certification. Search information required: name, date of birth, previous address, years to search, case number, if available, SASE.

Civil records are available by mail. A release is required. No search fee. $.75 fee per copy. $5.00 for certification. Search information required: name, date of birth, years to search, SASE. Specify plaintiff or defendant.

Clear Creek County

Clerk of the District Court, Criminal Records
PO Box 367
Georgetown, CO 80444
(303) 569-3273

Felony and misdemeanor records are available by mail. No release necessary. No search fee. $.75 fee per copy. $5.00 for certification. Search information required: name, date of birth, SASE, years to search.

Civil records are available by mail. No release necessary. No search fee. $.75 fee per copy. $5.00 for certification. Search information required: name, date of birth, years to search, SASE. Specify plaintiff or defendant.

Conejos County

Clerk of Combined Courts, Criminal Records
PO Box 128
Conejos, CO 81129
(719) 376-5466
Fax (719) 376-5466

Felony and misdemeanor records are available by mail or fax. A release is required. $5.00 search fee. Copies are $.75 fee per page. $1.00 for certified copy. Company checks only, payable to Clerk of the Combined Courts. Search information required: name, date of birth.

Civil records are available by mail or fax. Call prior to sending fax. A release is required. $5.00 search fee. $.75 fee per copy. $5.00 for certification. Search information required: name, date of birth, years to search. Specify plaintiff or defendant.

Costilla County

Clerk of Combined Courts, Criminal Records
PO Box 301
401 Church Place
San Luis, CO 81152
(719) 672-3681
Fax (719) 672-3681

Felony and misdemeanor records are available by mail or fax. Call prior to sending fax. No release necessary. No search fee. $1.00 fee per copy. $1.00 for certification. Search information required: name, date of birth.

Civil records are available by mail or fax. Call prior to sending fax. No release necessary. No search fee. $1.00 fee per copy. $1.00 for certification. Search information required: name, date of birth, years to search. Specify plaintiff or defendant.

Crowley County

Clerk of District Court
6th and Main, Courthouse
Ordway, CO 81063
(719) 267-4468

Felony and misdemeanor records are available by mail or phone. A release is required. No search fee. $.50 fee per copy. $5.00 for certification. Search information required: name, date of birth, years to search, SASE.

Civil records are available by mail or phone. A release is required. No search fee. $.50 fee per copy. $5.00 for certification. Search information required: name, date of birth, years to search, SASE. Specify plaintiff or defendant.

Custer County

Clerk of the Combined Courts, Criminal Records
PO Box 60
Westcliffe, CO 81252
(719) 783-2274

Felony and misdemeanor records are available for physical inspection at the above office. For additional information, see Colorado state repository.

Civil records are available by mail. A release is required. No search fee. $.75 fee per copy. $5.00 for certification. Search information required: name, years to search. Specify plaintiff or defendant.

Delta County

Delta Combined Courts, Criminal Records
501 Palmer, Room 338
Delta, CO 81416
(303) 874-4416
Fax (303) 874-4306

Felony and misdemeanor records are available by mail or fax. No release necessary. No search fee. $.75 fee per copy. Search information required: name, date of birth, SASE.

Civil records are available by mail or fax. No release necessary. No search fee. $.75 fee per copy. Search information required: name, date of birth, years to search, SASE. Specify plaintiff or defendant.

Denver County

Felony records
Denver District Court, Criminal
1437 Bannock, Room 426
Denver, CO 80202
(303) 640-2876

Felony records are available by mail or phone. No release necessary. No search fee. $.75 fee per copy. $5.00 for certification. Search information required: name, date of birth, SASE.

Civil records
Denver District Court
1437 Bannock, Room 426
Denver, CO 80202
(303) 640-2876

Civil records are available by mail. No release necessary. No search fee. $.75 fee per copy. $5.00 for certification. Search information required: name, years to search. Specify plaintiff or defendant.

Misdemeanor records
Denver County Court
1437 Bannock, Room 111
Denver, CO 80253
(303) 640-5911
Fax (303) 460-5920

Misdemeanor records are available by mail, fax or phone. No release necessary. No fee. Search information required: name, date of birth, SASE.

Dolores County

Clerk of Combined Courts, Criminal Records
PO Box 511
Dove Creek, CO 81324
(303) 677-2258

Felony and misdemeanor records are available by mail or phone. No release necessary. No search fee. $.75 fee per copy. $5.00 for certification. Search information required: name, date of birth, SASE.

Civil records are available by mail or phone. No release necessary. No search fee. $.75 fee per copy. $5.00 for certification. Search information required: name, date pof birth, years to search SASE. Specify plaintiff or defendant.

Douglas County

Felony records
Clerk of District Court, Criminal Records
355 S. Wilcox
Castle Rock, CO 80104
(303) 688-9698

Felony records are available by mail or by phone with a maximum of two names. No release necessary. No search fee. Copies are $.75 per page, $5.00 for certified copy. One name per search request. Search information required: name, SASE.

Civil records
Clerk of District Court
355 S. Wilcox
Castle Rock, CO 80104
(303) 688-9698

Civil records are available by mail or by phone with a maximum of two names. No release necessary. No search fee. $.75 fee per copy. $5.00 for certification. Search information required: name, years to search, SASE. Specify plaintiff or defendant.

Misdemeanor records
Douglas County Court
355 S. Wilcox
Castle Rock, CO 80104
(303) 688-5159

Misdemeanor records since 1978 are available by mail. No release necessary. No search fee. Copies are $.75 per page, $5.75 for certified copy. Search information required: name, SASE, date of birth.

Eagle County

Eagle Combined Courts, Criminal Records
PO Box 597
Eagle, CO 81631
(303) 328-6373

Felony and misdemeanor records are available by mail. No release necessary. No search fee. $.75 fee per copy. $5.00 for certification. Search information required: name, date of birth, years to search, SASE.

Civil records are available by mail. No release necessary. No search fee. $.75 fee per copy. $5.00 for certification. Search information required: name, date of birth, years to search, SASE. Specify plaintiff or defendant.

El Paso County

Felony records
Clerk of District Court, Criminal Division
Judicial Bldg.
20 E. Vermijo
Colorado Springs, CO 80903
(719) 630-2837 or 2838

Felony records are available by mail. No release necessary. $8.00 search fee. Copies are $.75 fee per page, $5.00 for certified copy. Make check or money order payable to Clerk of District Court. Search information required: name, date of birth, SASE.

Civil records
Clerk of District Court
Judicial Bldg.
20 E. Vermijo
Colorado Springs, CO 80903
(719) 630-2837 or 2838

Civil records are available by mail. A release is required. $8.00 search fee.$.75 fee per copy. $5.00 for certification. Search information required: name, date of birth, years to search, SASE. Specify plaintiff or defendant.

Misdemeanor records
El Paso County Court
Judicial Bldg.
20 E. Vermijo
Colorado Springs, CO 80903
(719) 630-2810

Misdemeanor records since 1985 are available by mail. Turnaround time is 1-2 weeks. A release is required. $8.00 fee. Copies are $.75 fee per page, $5.75 for certified copy. Make checks payable to El Paso County Court. Search information required: name, date of birth, SASE.

Elbert County

Clerk of the District Court, Criminal Records
PO Box 232
Kiowa, CO 80117
(303) 621-2131

Felony and misdemeanor records are available by phone only. No release necessary. No search fee. Copies are $.75 per page, $1.75 for certified copy. Search information required: name, date of birth, sex, SASE.

Civil records are available by mail. No release necessary. No search fee. $.75 fee per copy. $1.75 for certification. Search information required: name, years to search. Specify plaintiff or defendant.

Fremont County

Clerk of Combined Courts, Criminal Records
615 Macon, Room 204
Canon City, CO 81212
(719) 275-7522
Fax (719) 275-2359

Felony and misdemeanor records are available by mail or fax. No release necessary. No search fee. $.75 fee per copy. $5.00 for certification. Turnaround time is 10 working days. Search information required: name, SASE.

Civil records are available by mail or fax. No release necessary. No search fee. $.75 fee per copy. $5.00 for certification. Search information required: name, years to search, SASE. Specify plaintiff or defendant.

Garfield County

Combined Court of Garfield County, Criminal Records
109 8th Street
Suite 104
Glenwood Springs, CO 81601
(303) 945-5075
Fax (303) 945-8756

Felony and misdemeanor records are available by mail or fax. No release necessary. No search fee. $.75 fee per copy. $5.00 for certification. Search information required: name, date of birth, years to search, SASE.

Civil records are available by mail or fax. No release necessary. No search fee. $.75 fee per copy. $5.00 for certification. Search information required: name, years to search, SASE. Specify plaintiff or defendant.

Gilpin County

Clerk of District Court, Criminal Records
PO Box 426
Central City, CO 80427
(303) 582-5323
Fax (303) 572-9050

Felony and misdemeanor records are available by mail or fax. Turnaround time is 1 week. No release necessary. No search fee. Copies are $.75 per page, $5.00 for certified copy. Search information required: name, date of birth.

Civil records are available by mail. No release necessary. No search fee. $.75 fee per copy. $5.00 for certification. Search information required: name, date of birth, years to search. Specify plaintiff or defendant.

Grand County

Clerk of District Court, Criminal Records
PO Box 192
Hot Sulphur Springs, CO 80451
(303) 725-3357

Felony and misdemeanor records are available by mail. Turnaround time is 1 week. No release necessary for files without limited access. No search fee. $.75 fee per copy. $5.00 for certification. Search information required: name, date of birth, years to search, SASE.

Civil records are available by mail. No release necessary. No search fee. $.75 fee per copy. $5.00 for certification. Search information required: name, date of birth, years to search. Specify plaintiff or defendant.

Gunnison County

Clerk of Combined Courts, Criminal Records
200 E. Virginia Ave.
Gunnison, CO 81230
(303) 641-3500
Fax (303) 641-6876

Felony and misdemeanor records are available by mail, phone or fax. No release necessary. No search fee. Search information required: name.

Civil records are available by mail, phone or fax. No release necessary. No search fee. Search information required: name, years to search. Specify plaintiff or defendant.

Hinsdale County

Clerk of the Combined Courts, Criminal Records
PO Box 245
Lake City, CO 81235
(303) 944-2227
Fax (303) 944-2289

Felony and misdemeanor records are available by mail, phone or fax. No release necessary. No search fee. Search information required: name, years to search.

Civil records are available by mail or fax. No release necessary. No search fee. Search information required: name, years to search. Specify plaintiff or defendant.

Huerfano County

Huerfano Combined Courts, Criminal Records
401 Main Street
Walsenburg, CO 81089
(719) 738-1040
Fax (719) 738-3113-11

Felony and misdemeanor records are available by mail. Turnaround time is 1 week. A release is required. No fee. Search information required: name, SSN, date of birth, sex, race, years to search.

Civil records are available by mail. No release necessary. No search fee. Search information required: name, years to search. Specify plaintiff or defendant.

Jackson County

Clerk of Combined Courts, Criminal Records
PO Box 308
Walden, CO 80480
(303) 723-4363

Felony and misdemeanor records are available by mail. Turnaround time is 1 week. No release necessary. No search fee. Search information required: name, SASE.

Civil records are available by mail. No release necessary. No search fee. Search information required: name, years to search. Specify plaintiff or defendant.

Jefferson County

Felony records
Clerk of District Court, Criminal Records
1701 Arapahoe
Golden, CO 80401-6199
(303) 278-6145

Felony records from 1985 are available by mail. No release necessary. $5.00 search fee. $.75 fee per copy. $5.00 for certification. Search information required: full name, SSN, date of birth, years to search, SASE.

Civil records
Clerk of District Court
1701 Arapahoe
Golden, CO 80401-6199
(303) 278-6145

Civil records are available by mail. No release necessary. $5.00 search fee. $.75 fee per copy. $5.00 for certification. Search information required: name, years to search, SASE. Specify plaintiff or defendant.

Misdemeanor records
Clerk of County Court
1701 Arapahoe
Golden, CO 804019
(303) 278-6237

Misdemeanor records since 1975 are available by mail. Records since 1986 are available by phone. No release necessary. $5.00 search fee. $.75 fee per copy. $5.00 for certification. Search information required: name, SSN, date of birth, years to search, SASE.

Civil records
Clerk of County Court
1701 Arapahoe
Golden, CO 804019
(303) 278-6237

Civil records are available by mail. No release necessary. $5.00 search fee. $.75 fee per copy. $5.00 for certification. Search information required: name, years to search. Specify plaintiff or defendant.

Kiowa County

Clerk of Combined Courts, Criminal
Records
PO Box 353
Eads, CO 81036
(719) 438-5558

Felony and misdemeanor records are available by mail or phone. Turnaround time is 1 week. A release is required. No search fee. $.75 fee per copy. $5.00 for certification. Search information required: name, SSN, date of birth, sex, race.

Civil records are available by mail. No release necessary. No search fee. $.75 fee per copy. $5.00 for certification. Search information required: name, years to search. Specify plaintiff or defendant.

Kit Carson County

Clerk of District Court, Criminal
Records
PO Box 547
Burlington, CO 80807
(719) 346-5524

Felony and misdemeanor records are available by mail. No release necessary. No search fee. $.75 fee per copy. $5.00 for certification. Search information required: name, date of birth, years to search.

Civil records are available by mail. No release necessary. No search fee. $.75 fee per copy. $5.00 for certification. Search information required: name, years to search. Specify plaintiff or defendant.

La Plata County

Felony records
Clerk of District Court, Criminal
Records
PO Box 3340
Durango, CO 81302-3340
(303) 247-2304

Felony records are available by mail or phone. No release necessary. No search fee. $.75 fee per copy. $5.00 for certification. Search information required: name, date of birth, SASE.

Civil records
Clerk of District Court
PO Box 3340
Durango, CO 81302-3340
(303) 247-2304

Civil records are available by mail or phone. No release necessary. No search fee. $.75 fee per copy. $5.00 for certification. Search information required: name, years to search. Specify plaintiff or defendant.

Misdemeanor records
La Plata County Court
Box 498
Durango, CO 81302
(303) 247-2004

Misdemeanor records since 1978 are available by mail only. Turnaround time is 1 week. A release is required. No search fee. $.75 fee per copy. $5.00 for certification. Search information required: name, date of birth, SASE, offense.

Civil records
La Plata County Court
Box 498
Durango, CO 81302
(303) 247-2004

Civil records are available by mail. No release necessary. No search fee. $.75 fee per copy. $5.00 for certification. Search information required: name, years to search. Specify plaintiff or defendant.

Lake County

Clerk of Combined Courts
PO Box 55
Leadville, CO 80461
(719) 486-0535 or 0334

Felony and misdemeanor records are available by mail or phone. No release necessary. No search fee. Copies are $.75 per page, $5.00 for certified copy. Search information required: name, date of birth, years to search.

Civil records are available by mail. No release necessary. No search fee. $.75 fee per copy. $5.00 for certification. Search information required: name, date of birth, years to search. Specify plaintiff or defendant.

Larimer County

Clerk of District Court, Criminal
Records
PO Box 2066
Ft. Collins, CO 80522
(303) 498-7918

Felony and misdemeanor records are available by mail or phone. No release necessary. No search fee. $.75 fee per copy. $5.00 for certification. Search information required: name, date of birth, SASE.

Civil records are available by mail or phone. No release necessary. No search fee. $.75 fee per copy. $5.00 for certification. Search information required: name, years to search. Specify plaintiff or defendant.

Las Animas County

Las Animas County Courthouse
200 E. 1st St., Rm 301
Trinidad, CO 81082
(719) 846-2221
Fax (719) 846-9367

Felony records are available by mail or fax. No release necessary. No search fee. Copies are $.75 per page, $5.00 for certified copy. Search information required: name, date of birth, years to search, SASE.

Civil records are available by mail or fax. No release necessary. No search fee. $.75 fee per copy. $5.00 for certification. Search information required: name, years to search. Specify plaintiff or defendant.

Lincoln County

Combined Courts of Lincoln County,
Criminal Records
PO Box 128
Hugo, CO 80821
(719) 743-2455

Felony and misdemeanor records are available by mail or phone. No release necessary. No search fee. $.75 fee per copy. $5.00 for certification. Search information required: name, date of birth, SASE.

Civil records are available by mail or phone. No release necessary. No search fee. $.75 fee per copy. $5.00 for certification. Search information required: name, years to search. Specify plaintiff or defendant.

Logan County

Felony records
Clerk of the District Court, Criminal
Records
PO Box 71
Sterling, CO 80751
(303) 522-6565

Felony records are available by mail or phone. Turnaround time is 2-3 weeks. No release necessary. No search fee. $.75 fee per copy. $5.00 for certification. Search information required: name, date of birth, SASE.

Civil records
Clerk of the District Court
PO Box 71
Sterling, CO 80751
(303) 522-6565

Civil records are available by mail. No release necessary. No search fee. $.75 fee per copy. $5.00 for certification. Search information required: name, date of birth, years to search, SASE. Specify plaintiff or defendant.

Misdemeanor records
Logan County Court
Courthouse Annex
PO Box 1907
Sterling, CO 80751
(303) 522-1572

Misdemeanor records are available by mail or phone. Turnaround time is 1 week. A release, if available. No search fee. Copies are $.75 per page, $5.00 for certified copy. Search information required: name, date of birth, years to search.

Civil records
Logan County Court
Courthouse Annex
PO Box 1907
Sterling, CO 80751
(303) 522-1572Civil records are available by mail. No release necessary. No search fee. $.75 fee per copy. $5.00 for certification. Search information required: name, date of birth, years to search. Specify plaintiff or defendant.

Mesa County

Felony records
Clerk of District Court, Criminal
Records
PO Box 20000
Grand Junction, CO 81502-5032
(303) 242-4761

Felony records are available by mail only. Turnaround time is 1-4 days. No release necessary. No search fee. $.75 fee per copy. $5.00 for certification. Search information required: name. date of birth, years to search, SASE.

Civil records
Clerk of District Court
PO Box 20000
Grand Junction, CO 81502-5032
(303) 242-4761

Civil records are available by mail. No release necessary. No search fee. $.75 fee per copy. $5.00 for certification. Search information required: name, years to search. Specify plaintiff or defendant.

Misdemeanor records
Mesa County Court
PO Box 20000-5030
Grand Junction, CO 81502-5032
(303) 243-1136

Misdemeanor records since 1983 are available by mail. Turnaround time is 1-2 weeks. No release necessary. No search fee. $.75 fee per copy. $5.00 for certification. Search information required: name, date of birth, SASE.

Civil records
Mesa County Court
PO Box 20000-5030
Grand Junction, CO 81502-5032
(303) 243-1136

Civil records are available by mail. No release necessary. No search fee. $.75 fee per copy. $5.00 for certification. Search information required: name, years to search, SASE. Specify plaintiff or defendant.

Mineral County

Mineral County Courthouse, Criminal Records
PO Box 337
Creede, CO 81130
(719) 658-2575

Felony records are available by mail. $5.00 search fee. $.75 fee per copy. $5.00 for certification. Search information required: name, date of birth.

Civil records are available by mail. $5.00 search fee. $.75 fee per copy. $5.00 for certification. Search information required: name, years to search. Specify plaintiff or defendant.

Moffat County

Clerk of the Combined Courts, Criminal Records
221 W. Victory Way
Craig, CO 81625
(303) 824-8254
Fax (303) 824-8923

Felony and misdemeanor records are available by mail, phone or fax. Turnaround time is 2-3 weeks. A release is required. No search fee. Copies are $.75 per page, $5.00 for certified copy. Search information required: name, SSN, date of birth, sex, race, years to search. No juvenile information given out.

Civil records are available by mail, phone or fax. No release necessary. No search fee. $.75 fee per copy. $5.00 for certification. Search information required: name, years to search. Specify plaintiff or defendant.

Montezuma County

Felony records
Clerk of District Court
109 W. Main
Montezuma County Courthouse
Cortez, CO 81321
(303) 565-1111

Felony records are available by mail or phone. Turnaround time is 1 week. A release is required. No search fee. $.75 fee per copy. $5.00 for certification. Search information required: name, date of birth, years to search.

Civil records
Clerk of District Court
109 W. Main
Montezuma County Courthouse
Cortez, CO 81321
(303) 565-1111

Civil records are available by mail or phone. No release necessary. No search fee. $.75 fee per copy. $5.00 for certification. Search information required: name, years to search. Specify plaintiff or defendant.

Misdemeanor records
Montezuma County Court
Justice Building
601 N. Mildred Rd.
Cortez, CO 81321
(303) 565-7580

Misdemeanor records since 1980 are available by mail. Turnaround time is 1 week. A release is required for acquittals. No search fee. Copies are $5.00 for certified copy. Search information required: name, date of birth.

Civil records
Montezuma County Court
Justice Building
601 N. Mildred Rd.
Cortez, CO 81321
(303) 565-7580

Civil records are available by mail. No release necessary. No search fee. $5.00 for certification. Search information required: name, years to search. Specify plaintiff or defendant.

Montrose County

Clerk of District Court, Criminal Records
PO Box 368
Montrose, CO 81402
(303) 249-4364
Fax (303) 249-8546

Felony and misdemeanor records are available by mail. Turnaround time is 1 week. A release is required. No search fee. Search information required: name, date of birth, sex, race, years to search, SASE.

Civil records are available by mail. No release necessary. No search fee. Search information required: name, date of birth, years to search, SASE. Specify plaintiff or defendant.

Morgan County

Felony records
Clerk of District Court, Criminal Records
PO Box 130
Ft. Morgan, CO 80701
(303) 867-8266

Felony records are available by mail. A release is required. No search fee. $.75 fee per copy. Search information required: name, date of birth, years to search.

Civil records
Clerk of District Court
PO Box 130
Ft. Morgan, CO 80701
(303) 867-8266

Civil records are available by mail. A release is required. No search fee. $.75 fee per copy. Search information required: name, years to search. Specify plaintiff or defendant.

Misdemeanor records
Morgan County Court
PO Box 695
Ft. Morgan, CO 80701
(303) 867-8244
Fax (303) 867-8244

Misdemeanor records since 1970 are available by mail, phone or fax. No release necessary. No search fee. Copies are $.75 per page, $5.00 for certified copy. Search information required: name, date of birth, years to search.

Civil records
Morgan County Court
PO Box 695
Ft. Morgan, CO 80701
(303) 867-8244
Fax (303) 867-8244

Civil records are available by mail, phone or fax. No release necessary. No search fee. $.75 fee per copy. $5.00 for certification. Search information required: name, date of birth, years to search. Specify plaintiff or defendant.

Otero County

Clerk of District Court, Criminal Records
Otero County Courthouse
Room 201
La Junta, CO 81050
(719) 384-4951
Fax (719) 384-4991

Felony and misdemeanor records are available by mail or fax. Turnaround time is 1 week. A release is required. No search fee. Copies are $.75 per page, $5.00 for certified copy. Search information required: name, date of birth, sex, SASE.

Civil records are available by mail. No release necessary. No search fee. $.75 fee per copy. $5.00 for certification. Search information required: name, date of birth, years to search, SASE. Specify plaintiff or defendant.

Ouray County

Ouray County Court, Criminal Records
PO Box 643
Ouray, CO 81427
(303) 325-4405
Fax (303) 325-7364

Felony and misdemeanor records are available by mail or fax. Turnaround time is 1 week. A release is required. No search fee. $2.00 fee for fax plus $.75 per incoming or outgoing page. Search information required: name, date of birth, years to search.

Civil records are available by mail or fax. No release necessary. No search fee. Search information required: name, date of birth, years to search. Specify plaintiff or defendant.

Park County

Clerk of Combined Courts, Criminal Records
PO Box 190
Fair Play, CO 80440
(719) 836-2940
Fax (719) 836-2892

Felony and misdemeanor records are available by mail or fax. Turnaround time is 1 week. No release necessary. No search fee. $.75 fee per copy. $5.00 for certification. Search information required: name, date of birth, SASE.

Civil records are available by mail or fax. No release necessary. No search fee. $.75 fee per copy. $5.00 for certification. Search information required: name, years to search, SASE. Specify plaintiff or defendant.

Phillips County

Courthouse, Criminal Records
Holyoke, CO 80734
(303) 854-3279

Felony and misdemeanor records are available by mail or phone. No release necessary. No search fee. Copies are $.75 per page. $5.00 for certified copy. Search information required: name, date of birth, years to search.

Civil records are available by mail or phone. No release necessary. No search fee. $.75 fee per copy. $5.00 for certification. Search information required: name, date of birth, years to search. Specify plaintiff or defendant.

Pitkin County

Clerk of Combined Courts, Criminal Records
506 E. Main Street
Aspen, CO 81611
(303) 925-7635
Fax (303) 925-6349

Felony and misdemeanor records are available by mail or fax. No release necessary. $5.00 search fee. $1.00 fee for fax. $.75 fee per copy. $5.00 fee for Visa or Mastercard charges. Search information required: name, SSN, date of birth, years to search.

Civil records are available by mail or fax. No release necessary. $5.00 search fee. $1.00 fee for fax. $.75 fee per copy. $5.00 for certification. $5.00 fee for Visa or Mastercard charges. Search information required: name, years to search. Specify plaintiff or defendant.

Prowers County

Clerk of District Court, Criminal Records
PO Box 1178
Lamar, CO 81052
(719) 336-7424
Fax (719) 336-9757

Felony and misdemeanor records are available by mail or fax. Turnaround time is 1 week. No release necessary. No search fee. $.75 fee per copy, $5.00 fee for certification. Search information required: name, years to search, SASE.

Civil records are available by mail or fax. No release necessary. No search fee. $.75 fee per copy. $5.00 for certification. Search information required: name, years to search, SASE. Specify plaintiff or defendant.

Pueblo County

Clerk of District Court, Criminal Records
Pueblo County Judicial Bldg.
320 West 10th
Pueblo, CO 81003
(719) 546-1791

Felony and misdemeanor records are available by mail or phone. Turnaround time is 1 week. A release is required. $8.00 search fee. $.75 fee per copy. $5.00 for certification. Search information required: name, date of birth, years to search.

Civil records are available by mail or phone. No release necessary. $8.00 search fee. $.75 fee per copy. $5.00 for certification. Search information required: name, years to search. Specify plaintiff or defendant.

Rio Blanco County

Clerk of Combined Courts
PO Box 1150
Meeker, CO 81641
(303) 878-5622
Fax (303) 878-4295

Felony records are available by mail or fax. Turnaround time is 1 week. No release necessary. No search fee. $.75 fee per copy. $5.00 for certification. $1.00 fee per fax copy. Visa or Mastercard required. Search information required: name, date of birth, years to search, SASE.

Civil records are available by mail or fax. No release necessary. No search fee. $.75 fee per copy. $5.00 for certification. $1.00 fee per fax copy. Visa or Mastercard required. Search information required: name, years to search. Specify plaintiff or defendant.

Rio Grande County

Rio Grande Combined Courts, Criminal Records
PO Box W
Del Norte, CO 81132
(719) 657-3394
Fax (719) 657-2636

Felony and misdemeanor records are available by mail, phone or fax. Turnaround time is 1-2 weeks. No release necessary. No search fee. $10.00 fee for fax. Copies are $.75 per page, $5.00 for certified copy. Search information required: name, date of birth, SASE.

Civil records are available by mail, phone or fax. No release necessary. No search fee. $10.00 fee for fax. $.75 fee per copy. $5.00 for certification. Search information required: name, date of birth, years to search. Specify plaintiff or defendant.

Routt County

Clerk of the Combined Courts, Criminal Records
PO Box 773117
Steamboat Springs, CO 80477
(303) 879-5020
Fax (303) 879-3531

Felony and misdemeanor records are available by mail or fax. No release necessary. No search fee. Search information required: name, SSN, date of birth, SASE.

Civil records are available by mail or phone. No release necessary. No search fee. Search information required: name, years to search. Specify plaintiff or defendant.

Saguache County

Clerk of Combined Courts, Criminal Records
PO Box 164
Saguache, CO 81149
(719) 655-2522
Fax (719) 655-2523

Felony and misdemeanor records are available by mail. No release necessary. No search fee. $.75 fee per copy, $5.00 fee for certification. Search information required: name, date of birth, SASE.

Civil records are available by mail. No release necessary. No search fee. $.75 fee per copy. $5.00 for certification. Search information required: name, address if available, years to search. Specify plaintiff or defendant.

San Juan County

Clerk of Combined Courts, Criminal Records
PO Box 441
Silverton, CO 81433
(303) 387-5790

Felony and misdemeanor records are available by mail. A release is required. No search fee. $.25 fee per copy. $5.00 for certification. Search information required: name, date of birth, SASE.

Civil records are available by mail. A release is required. No search fee. $.25 fee per copy. $5.00 for certification. Search information required: name, years to search. Specify plaintiff or defendant.

San Miguel County

Clerk of Combined Courts, Criminal Records
PO Box 919
Telluride, CO 81435
(303) 728-3891
Fax (303) 728-6347

Felony and misdemeanor records are available by mail. No release necessary. No search fee. $.75 fee per copy. $5.00 for certification. Search information required: name, date of birth, SASE.

Civil records are available by mail. No release necessary. No search fee. $.75 fee per copy. $5.00 for certification. Search information required: name, years to search, SASE. Specify plaintiff or defendant.

Sedgwick County

Clerk of Combined Courts, Criminal Records
3rd and Pine
Julesburg, CO 80737
(303) 474-3627

Felony and misdemeanor records are available by mail. No release necessary. No search fee. $.75 fee per copy. $5.00 for certification. Search information required: name, date of birth, SASE.

Civil records are available by mail. No release necessary. No search fee. $.75 fee per copy. $5.00 for certification. Search information required: name, years to search, SASE. Specify plaintiff or defendant.

Summit County

Felony records
Clerk of District Court, Criminal Records
Criminal Division
PO Box 269
Breckenridge, CO 80424
(303) 453-2241

Felony records are available by mail. No release necessary. No search fee. $.75 fee per copy. $5.00 for certification. Search information required: name, date of birth, years to search, SASE.

Civil records
Clerk of District Court
Criminal Division
PO Box 269
Breckenridge, CO 80424
(303) 453-2241

Civil records are available by mail. No release necessary. No search fee. $.75 fee per copy. $5.00 for certification. Search information required: name, date of birth, years to search, SASE. Specify plaintiff or defendant.

Misdemeanor records
Summit County Court
PO Box 185
Breckenridge, CO 80424
(303) 453-2272
Fax (303) 453-6479

Misdemeanor records are available by mail. No release necessary. No search fee. $.75 fee per copy, $5.00 fee for certification. Search information required: name, years to search, SASE.

Civil records
Summit County Court
PO Box 185
Breckenridge, CO 80424
(303) 453-2272
Fax (303) 453-6479

Civil records are available by mail. No release necessary. No search fee. $.75 fee per copy. $5.00 for certification. Search information required: name, years to search. Specify plaintiff or defendant.

Teller County

Clerk of the District Court, Criminal Records
PO Box 997
Cripple Creek, CO 80813
(719) 689-2543

Felony and misdemeanor records are available by mail. No release necessary. $8.00 search fee. $.75 fee per copy. $5.00 for certification. Search information required: name, date of birth.

Civil records are available by mail. No release necessary. $8.00 search fee. $.75 fee per copy. $5.00 for certification. Search information required: name, years to search. Specify plaintiff or defendant.

Washington County

Washington County Combined Courts, Criminal Records
PO Box 455
Akron, CO 80720
(303) 345-2756

Felony and misdemeanor records are available by mail or phone. No release necessary. No search fee. $.75 fee per copy. $5.00 for certification. Search information required: name, date of birth, SASE.

Civil records are available by mail. No release necessary. No search fee. $.75 fee per copy. $5.00 for certification. Search information required: name, years to search, SASE. Specify plaintiff or defendant.

Weld County

Felony records
Clerk of District Court, Criminal Records
PO Box C
Greeley, CO 80632
(303) 356-4000 Extension 4521

Felony records are available by mail. Release, if available. $8.00 search fee. $.75 fee per copy. $5.00 for certification. Search information required: name, date of birth, SASE, years to search, SSN.

Civil records
Clerk of District Court
PO Box C
Greeley, CO 80632
(303) 356-4000 Extension 4521

Civil records are available by mail. No release necessary. $8.00 search fee. $.75 fee per copy. $5.00 for certification. Search information required: name, date of birth, years to search, SASE. Specify plaintiff or defendant.

Misdemeanor records
Clerk of County Court
PO Box C
Greeley, CO 80632
(303) 356-4000 Extension 4563

Misdemeanor records are available by mail or phone. No release necessary. $8.00 search fee. $.75 fee per copy. $5.00 for certification. Search information required: name, date of birth, SASE.

Yuma County

Yuma County Combined Courts, Criminal Records
PO Box 347
Wray, CO 80758
(303) 332-4118

Felony and misdemeanor records are available by mail. A release is required. No search fee. Copies are $.75 per page, $5.00 for certification. Search information required: name, date of birth, date offense.

Civil records are available by mail. No release necessary. No search fee. $.75 fee per copy. $5.00 for certification. Search information required: name, years to search. Specify plaintiff or defendant.

City-County Cross Reference

Agate *Elbert*
Aguilar *Las Animas*
Akron *Washington*
Alamosa *Alamosa*
Allenspark *Boulder*
Alma *Park*
Almont *Gunnison*
Amherst *Phillips*
Anton *Washington*
Antonito *Conejos*
Arapahoe *Cheyenne*
Arboles *Archuleta*
Arlington *Kiowa*
Arriba *Lincoln*
Arvada *Jefferson*
Aspen *Pitkin*
Atwood *Logan*
Ault *Weld*
Aurora *Adams*
Austin *Delta*
Avon *Eagle*
Avondale *Pueblo*
Bailey *Park*
Basalt *Eagle*
Bayfield *LaPlata*

Bedrock *Montrose*
Bellvue *Larimer*
Bennett *Adams*
Berthoud *Larimer*
Bethune *Kit Carson*
Beulah *Pueblo*
Black Forest *El Paso*
Black Hawk *Gilpin*
Blanca *Costilla*
Blende *Pueblo*
Boncarbo *Las Animas*
Bond *Eagle*
Boone *Pueblo*
Boulder *Boulder*
Bow Mar *Arapahoe*
Branson *Las Animas*
Breckenridge *Summit*
Briggsdale *Weld*
Brighton *Adams*
Bristol *Prowers*
Broomfield *Boulder*
Brush *Morgan*
Buena Vista *Chaffee*
Burlington *Kit Carson*
Burns *Eagle*

Byers *Arapahoe*
Cahone *Dolores*
Calhan *El Paso*
Campion *Larimer*
Campo *Baca*
Canon City *Fremont*
Capulin *Conejos*
Carbondale *Garfield*
Carr *Weld*
Cascade *El Paso*
Castle Rock *Douglas*
Cedaredge *Delta*
Center *Saguache*
Central City *Gilpin*
Chama *Costilla*
Cheraw *Otero*
Cherry Hills Village
    Arapahoe
Cherry Knolls *Arapahoe*
Cheyenne Wells *Cheyenne*
Chivington *Kiowa*
Chromo *Archuleta*
Cimarron *Montrose*
Clark *Routt*
Clifton *Mesa*

Coal Creek *Fremont*
Coaldale *Fremont*
Cokedale *Las Animas*
Collbran *Mesa*
Colorado Springs *El Paso*
Columbine Valley
    Arapahoe
Commerce City *Adams*
Conejos *Conejos*
Conifer *Jefferson*
Cope *Washington*
Cortez *Montezuma*
Cory *Delta*
Cotopaxi *Fremont*
Cowdrey *Jackson*
Craig *Moffat*
Crawford *Delta*
Creede *Mineral*
Crested Butte *Gunnison*
Crestone *Saguache*
Cripple Creek *Teller*
Crook *Logan*
Crowley *Crowley*
Dacono *Weld*
DeBeque *Mesa*

Deer Trail *Arapahoe*
Del Norte *Rio Grande*
Delta *Delta*
Denver *Denver*
Dillon *Summit*
Dinosaur *Moffat*
Divide *Teller*
Dolores *Montezuma*
Dove Creek *Dolores*
Drake *Larimer*
Dumont *Clear Creek*
Dupont *Adams*
Durango *LaPlata*
Eads *Kiowa*
Eagle *Eagle*
Eastlake *Adams*
Eaton *Weld*
Eckert *Delta*
Eckley *Yuma*
Edgewater *Jefferson*
Edwards *Eagle*
Egnar *San Miguel*
Elbert *Elbert*
Eldorado Springs *Boulder*
Elizabeth *Elbert*
El Jebel *Eagle*
Empire *Clear Creek*
Englewood *Arapahoe*
Erie *Weld*
Estes Park *Larimer*
Evans *Weld*
Evergreen *Jefferson*
Fairplay *Park*
Farisita *Huerfano*
Federal Heights *Adams*
Firestone *Weld*
Flagler *Kit Carson*
Fleming *Logan*
Florence *Fremont*
Florissant *Teller*
Fort Collins *Larimer*
Fort Garland *Costilla*
Fort Lupton *Weld*
Fort Lyon *Bent*
Fort Morgan *Morgan*
Fountain *El Paso*
Fowler *Otero*
Foxton *Jefferson*
Franktown *Douglas*
Fraser *Grand*
Frederick *Weld*
Frisco *Summit*
Fruita *Mesa*
Fruitvale *Mesa*
Galeton *Weld*
Gardner *Huerfano*
Gateway *Mesa*
Genoa *Lincoln*
Georgetown *Clear Creek*
Gilcrest *Weld*
Gill *Weld*
Glade Park *Mesa*
Glendale *Denver*
Glen Haven *Larimer*
Glenwood Springs *Garfield*
Golden *Jefferson*
Granada *Prowers*
Granby *Grand*
Grand Junction *Mesa*
Grand Lake *Grand*
Grant *Park*
Greeley *Weld*
Green Mountain Falls *El Paso*
Greenwood Village *Arapahoe*

Grover *Weld*
Guffey *Park*
Gulnare *Las Animas*
Gunnison *Gunnison*
Gypsum *Eagle*
Hamilton *Moffat*
Hartman *Prowers*
Hartsel *Park*
Hasty *Bent*
Haswell *Kiowa*
Haxtun *Phillips*
Hayden *Routt*
Henderson *Adams*
Hereford *Weld*
Hesperus *LaPlata*
Hillrose *Morgan*
Hoehne *Las Animas*
Holly *Prowers*
Holyoke *Phillips*
Hooper *Alamosa*
Hotchkiss *Delta*
Hot Sulphur Springs *Grand*
Howard *Fremont*
Hoyt *Morgan*
Hudson *Weld*
Hugo *Lincoln*
Hygiene *Boulder*
Idaho Springs *Clear Creek*
Idalia *Yuma*
Idledale *Jefferson*
Ignacio *LaPlata*
Iliff *Logan*
Indian Hills *Jefferson*
Irondale *Adams*
Jamestown *Boulder*
Jansen *Las Animas*
Jaroso *Costilla*
Jefferson *Park*
Joes *Yuma*
Johnstown *Weld*
Julesburg *Sedgwick*
Karval *Lincoln*
Keenesburg *Weld*
Kersey *Weld*
Kim *Las Animas*
Kiowa *Elbert*
Kirk *Yuma*
Kit Carson *Cheyenne*
Kittredge *Jefferson*
Kremmling *Grand*
Lafayette *Boulder*
Laird *Yuma*
LaJara *Conejos*
LaJunta *Otero*
Lake City *Hinsdale*
Lake George *Park*
Lakewood *Jefferson*
Lamar *Prowers*
Laporte *Larimer*
Larkspur *Douglas*
LaSalle *Weld*
Las Animas *Bent*
LaVeta *Huerfano*
Lazear *Delta*
Leadville *Lake*
Lewis *Montezuma*
Limon *Lincoln*
Lincoln Park *Fremont*
Lindon *Washington*
Littleton *Arapahoe*
Livermore *Larimer*
Log Lane Village *Morgan*
Loma *Mesa*
Lombard Village *Pueblo*
Longmont *Boulder*
Louisville *Boulder*
Louviers *Douglas*

Loveland *Larimer*
Lucerne *Weld*
Lyons *Boulder*
McClave *Bent*
McCoy *Eagle*
Mack *Mesa*
Maher *Montrose*
Manassa *Conejos*
Mancos *Montezuma*
Manitou Springs *El Paso*
Manzanola *Otero*
Marvel *LaPlata*
Masonville *Larimer*
Matheson *Elbert*
Maybell *Moffat*
Mead *Weld*
Meeker *Rio Blanco*
Meredith *Pitkin*
Merino *Logan*
Mesa *Mesa*
Mesa Verde National Park *Montezuma*
Mesita *Costilla*
Milliken *Weld*
Minturn *Eagle*
Model *Las Animas*
Moffat *Saguache*
Molina *Mesa*
Monte Vista *Rio Grande*
Montrose *Montrose*
Monument *El Paso*
Morrison *Jefferson*
Mosca *Alamosa*
Mountain View *Jefferson*
Nathrop *Chaffee*
Naturita *Montrose*
Nederland *Boulder*
New Castle *Garfield*
New Raymer *Weld*
Niwot *Boulder*
Nob Hill *El Paso*
North La Junta *Otero*
Norwood *San Miguel*
Nucla *Montrose*
Nunn *Weld*
Oak Creek *Routt*
Olathe *Montrose*
Olney Springs *Crowley*
Ophir *San Miguel*
Orchard *Morgan*
Orchard City *Delta*
Orchard Mesa *Mesa*
Ordway *Crowley*
Otis *Washington*
Ouray *Ouray*
Ovid *Sedgwick*
Padroni *Logan*
Pagosa Springs *Archuleta*
Palisade *Mesa*
Palmer Lake *El Paso*
Paoli *Phillips*
Paonia *Delta*
Parachute *Garfield*
Paradox *Montrose*
Parker *Douglas*
Parlin *Gunnison*
Parshall *Grand*
Peetz *Logan*
Penrose *Fremont*
Perl-Mack *Adams*
Peyton *El Paso*
Phippsburg *Routt*
Pierce *Weld*
Pine *Jefferson*
Pinecliffe *Boulder*
Pitkin *Gunnison*
Placerville *San Miguel*

Platteville *Weld*
Pleasant View *Montezuma*
Poncha Springs *Chaffee*
Powderhorn *Gunnison*
Pritchett *Baca*
Pryor *Huerfano*
Pueblo *Pueblo*
Pueblo West *Pueblo*
Ramah *El Paso*
Rand *Jackson*
Rangely *Rio Blanco*
Red Cliff *Eagle*
Red Feather Lakes *Larimer*
Redvale *Montrose*
Rico *Dolores*
Ridgway *Ouray*
Rifle *Garfield*
Rockvale *Fremont*
Rocky Ford *Otero*
Roggen *Weld*
Rollinsville *Gilpin*
Romeo *Conejos*
Rush *El Paso*
Rye *Pueblo*
Saguache *Saguache*
Salida *Chaffee*
San Acacio *Costilla*
Sanford *Conejos*
San Luis *Costilla*
San Pablo *Costilla*
Sargents *Saguache*
Security *El Paso*
Sedalia *Douglas*
Sedgwick *Sedgwick*
Segundo *Las Animas*
Seibert *Kit Carson*
Severance *Weld*
Shawnee *Park*
Sheridan Lake *Kiowa*
Sherrelwood *Adams*
Silt *Garfield*
Silver Cliff *Custer*
Silver Plume *Clear Creek*
Silverthorne *Summit*
Silverton *San Juan*
Simla *Elbert*
Slater *Moffat*
Slick Rock *San Miguel*
Snowmass *Pitkin*
Snyder *Morgan*
Somerset *Gunnison*
South Fork *Rio Grande*
Southwood *Arapahoe*
Springfield *Baca*
Steamboat Springs *Routt*
Sterling *Logan*
Stoneham *Weld*
Stonington *Baca*
Strasburg *Adams*
Stratmoor Hills *El Paso*
Stratton *Kit Carson*
Sugar City *Crowley*
Swink *Otero*
Tabernash *Grand*
Telluride *San Miguel*
Texas Creek *Fremont*
Thornton *Adams*
Timnath *Larimer*
Toponas *Routt*
Towaoc *Montezuma*
Towner *Kiowa*
Trinchera *Las Animas*
Trinidad *Las Animas*
Two Buttes *Baca*
U S A F Academy *El Paso*
Uravan *Montrose*
Vail *Eagle*

Vernon *Yuma*
Victor *Teller*
Vilas *Baca*
Villa Grove *Saguache*
Vona *Kit Carson*
Walden *Jackson*
Walsenburg *Huerfano*
Walsh *Baca*
Ward *Boulder*
Watkins *Adams*
Wattenberg *Weld*
Weldona *Morgan*
Wellington *Larimer*
Westcliffe *Custer*
Western Hills *Adams*
Westminster *Adams*
Weston *Las Animas*
Wetmore *Custer*
Wheat Ridge *Jefferson*
Whitewater *Mesa*
Widefield *El Paso*
Wiggins *Morgan*
Wild Horse *Cheyenne*
Wiley *Prowers*
Windsor *Weld*
Winter Park *Grand*
Wolcott *Eagle*
Woodland Park *Teller*
Woodrow *Washington*
Woody Creek *Pitkin*
Wray *Yuma*
Yampa *Routt*
Yellow Jacket *Montezuma*
Yoder *El Paso*
Yuma *Yuma*

Connecticut

All eight (8) counties reported that conviction data was available for employment screening purposes by phone and/or by mail.

Worker's Compensation records are now available by mail or phone.

For more information or for offices not listed, contact the state's information hot line at (203) 566-2750.

Driving Records

Motor Vehicle Department
Copy Records Unit
60 State Street
Weathersfield, CT 06109-1896
(203) 566-2240 Extension 3720

Driving records are available by mail. $5 fee per request. Turnaround time is 2 to 4 days. Written request must include job applicant's full name, date of birth and license number. Make check payable to Motor Vehicle Department.

Worker's Compensation Records

State of Connecticut
Worker's Compensation Commission
255 Main Street, 2nd Floor
Hartford, CT 06106
(203) 566-4154

Records available by mail or phone. Written requests must include applicant's full name, date of birth, and SSN. No search fee. No release necessary.

Vital Statistics

City Hall
Vital Records Section
550 Main Street
Hartford, CT 06103
(203) 566-1124

Birth and death records are available for $5.00. $5.00 for certification. A release is required. State office has had records since July 1897. For earlier records, write to Registrar of Vital Statistics in town or city where event occurred. Make certified check or money order payable to Connecticut Department of Health Services. Four weeks turnaround.

Marriage records are available for $5.00. Turnaround time is 6 weeks. Include husband's name, wife's maiden name, marriage date, and town where event occurred, if known. Divorce records available through Superior Court where divorce granted. No release needed.

Department of Education

State Department of Education
Bureau of Certification
POBox 2219
Hartford,CT 06145
(203) 566-4183 or 566-3825

Field of certification, effective date, expiration date are available by mail. Include name and SSN.

Medical Licensing

Connecticut Department of Health Services
Licensing and Registration
150 Washington Street
Hartford, CT 06106
(203) 566-5296

Will confirm licenses for MDs and PODs by phone or mail. No fee. For licenses not mentioned, contact the above office.

Examinations and Licensure
Division of Medical Quality Assurance
Connecticut Dept. of Health Services
150 Washington Street
Hartford, CT 06106
(203) 566-4979

Will confirm license by phone. No fee. Include name, license number.

Bar Association

Connecticut Bar Association
101 Corporate Place
Rocky Hill, CT 06067
(203) 721-0025

Will confirm licenses by phone. No fee. Include name.

Accountancy Board

Secretary of State Board of 30 Trinity Street
Hartford, CT 06106
(203) 566-7835

Will confirm licenses by phone. No fee. Include name.

Securities Commission

Department of Banking
Securities Division
44 Capitol Ave. Hartford, CT 06106
(203) 566-4560

Will confirm licenses by phone. No fee. Include name and SSN.

Secretary of State

Secretary of State
Corporation Division
30 Trenty St.
Hartford, CT 06106
(203) 566-8570

Service agent, President and Secretary's address and date incorporated are available by mail. Contact the above office for additional

Criminal Records

State Repository

State Police
Bureau of Identification
294 Colony Street, Building 3
Meriden, CT 06450
(203) 238-6151

The dissemination of criminal records by the central state repository is limited to authorized criminal justice agencies and other non-criminal justice entities where a statute or executive order specifically provides such authorization. Contact the state at the above mailing address for additional information and instructions.

Fairfield County

Felony records
Clerk of Superior Court - A, Criminal Records
1061 Main Street
Bridgeport, CT 06601
(203) 579-6527

Felony records are available by mail. No release necessary. No search fee. $.50 fee per copy. $2.00 for certification. Search information required: name, date of birth, years to search.

Civil records
Clerk of Superior Court
1061 Main Street
Bridgeport, CT 06601
(203) 579-6527

Civil records are available by mail. No release necessary. No search fee. $.50 fee per copy. $2.00 for certification. Search information required: name, years to search. Specify plaintiff or defendant.

Misdemeanor records
Superior Court-6A 2
172 Golden Hill St.
Bridgeport, CT 06604
(203) 579-6560

Misdemeanor records are available by mail or phone. No release necessary. No search fee. $.50 fee per copy. $2.00 for certification. Search information required: name, date of birth, years to search.

Civil records
Superior Court-6A 2
172 Golden Hill St.
Bridgeport, CT 06604
(203) 579-6560

Civil records are available by mail. No release necessary. No search fee. $.50 fee per copy. $2.00 for certification. Search information required: name, years to search. Specify plaintiff or defendant.

Hartford County

Felony records
Clerk of Criminal Court, Part A,
Criminal Records
95 Washington Street
Hartford, CT 06106
(203) 566-1634

Felony records are available by mail. No release necessary. No search fee. Copies are $.50 per page, $2.00 for certified copy. Make money order payable to Clerk of Superior Court. Search information required: name, date of birth, SASE.

Civil records
Clerk of Court
95 Washington Street
Hartford, CT 06106
(203) 566-3170

Civil records are available by mail. No release necessary. No search fee. $.50 fee per copy. $2.00 for certification. Search information required: name, years to search. Specify plaintiff or defendant.

Litchfield County

Felony records
Superior Court, Criminal Records
PO Box 247
Litchfield, CT 06759
(203) 567-0885
Fax (203) 567-4779

Felony records are available by mail, phone or fax. No release necessary. No search fee. Copies are $.50 per page, $2.00 for certified copy. Make check payable to Clerk of Superior Court. Search information required: name or maiden name, date of birth, SASE.

Civil records
Superior Court
PO Box 247
Litchfield, CT 06759
(203) 567-0885
Fax (203) 567-4779

Civil records are available by mail. No release necessary. No search fee. $.50 fee per copy. $2.00 for certification. Search information required: name, years to search. Specify plaintiff or defendant.

Misdemeanor records
Superior Court GA 18
Box 779
Winsted, CT 06098
(203) 379-8537

Misdemeanor records are available by mail or phone. No release necessary. No search fee. Copies are $.50 fee per page, $2.50 for certified copy. Make check payable to Clerk of Superior Court. Search information required: name or maiden name, date of birth, SASE.

Civil records
Superior Court GA 18
Box 779
Winsted, CT 06098
(203) 379-8537

Civil records are available by mail. No release necessary. No search fee. $.50 fee per copy. $2.50 for certification. Search information required: name, years to search. Specify plaintiff or defendant.

Middlesex County

Felony records
Clerk of Superior Court - Judicial Division
265 DeKoven Drive
Middletown, CT 06457
(203) 344-2966

Felony records are available by mail or phone. No release necessary. No search fee. Copies are $.50 fee per page, $2.00 for certified copy. Search information required: name, date of birth, previous address, date of birth, SASE.

Civil records
Clerk of Superior Court
265 DeKoven Drive
Middletown, CT 06457
(203) 344-2966

Civil records are available by mail or phone. No release necessary. No search fee. $.50 fee per copy. $2.00 for certification. Search information required: name, years to search. Specify plaintiff or defendant.

Misdemeanor records
Superior Court GA 9
90 Court St.
Middletown, CT 06457
(203) 344-3091

Misdemeanor records are available by mail. A release is required. No search fee. Search information required: name, previous address, date of birth, SASE.

Civil records
Superior Court GA 9
90 Court St.
Middletown, CT 06457
(203) 344-3091

Civil records are available by mail. A release is required. No search fee. Search information required: name, years to search. Specify plaintiff or defendant.

New Haven County

Felony records
County Court House
235 Church Street
New Haven, CT 06510
(203) 789-7908

Felony records are available by mail. No release necessary. No search fee. $.50 fee per copy. $2.00 for certification. Search information required: name, date of birth, years to search.

Civil records
County Court House
235 Church Street
New Haven, CT 06510
(203) 789-7908

Civil records are available by mail. No release necessary. No search fee. $.50 fee per copy. $2.00 for certification. Search information required: name, date of birth, years to search. Specify plaintiff or defendant.

Misdemeanor records
Superior Court
121 Elm Street
New Haven, CT 06510
(203) 789-7462

Misdemeanor records are available by mail. No release necessary. No search fee. $.50 fee per copy. $2.00 for certification. Search information required: name, date of birth, years to search.

New London County

Pre 1978 Felony part A records
Clerk of Court
70 Huntington Street
New London, CT 06320
(203) 447-0893

Felony records prior to 1978 are available by mail. No release necessary. No search fee. $.50 fee per copy. Search information required: name, date of birth, SASE.

Civil records
Clerk of Court
70 Huntington Street
New London, CT 06320
(203) 447-0893

Civil records are available by mail. No release necessary. No search fee. $.50 fee per copy. Search information required: name, date of birth, years to search SASE. Specify plaintiff or defendant.

Misdemeanor and Post 1978 felony records
Superior Court GA 10
112 Broadstreet
New London, CT 06320
(203) 443-8343

Felony and misdemeanor records since 1978 are available by mail. Records are computerized from 1990 forward. No release necessary. No search fee. Search information required: name, date of birth, SASE.

Civil records
Superior Court GA 10
112 Broadstreet
New London, CT 06320
(203) 443-8343

Civil records are available by mail. No release necessary. No search fee. Search information required: name, date of birth, years to search, SASE. Specify plaintiff or defendant.

Tolland County

Felony records
Tolland County Superior Court - JD,
Criminal Records
69 Brooklyn Street
Rockville, CT 06066
(203) 875-6294

Felony records are available by mail. No release necessary. No search fee. Copies are $.50 per page, $2.00 for certified copy. Search information required: name, date of birth, years to search.

Civil records
Tolland County Superior Court
69 Brooklyn Street
Rockville, CT 06066
(203) 875-6294

Civil records from 1990 forward are available by mail. No release necessary. $.50 fee per copy. $2.00 for certification. No search fee. Search information required: name, date of birth, years to search. Specify plaintiff or defendant.

Misdemeanor records
Superior Court GA 19
55 W. Main St.
Rockville, CT 06066
(203) 875-2527

Misdemeanor records are available by mail from 1974 forward. No release necessary. No search fee. Search information required: name, date of birth, SSN if available, years to search.

Civil records
Superior Court GA 19
55 W. Main St.
Rockville, CT 06066
(203) 875-2527

Civil records are available by mail. No release necessary. No search fee. Search information required: name, years to search. Specify plaintiff or defendant.

Windham County

Felony records
Clerk of Superior Court
155 Church Street
Putnam, CT 06260
(203) 928-7749

Felony records are available by mail or phone. No release necessary. No search fee. Search information required: name, date of birth.

Civil records
Clerk of Superior Court
155 Church Street
Putnam, CT 06260
(203) 928-7749

Civil records are available by mail. No release necessary. No search fee. Search information required: name, years to search. Specify plaintiff or defendant.

Misdemeanor records
Superior Court
172 Main St.
PO Box 688
Danielson, CT 06239
(203) 774-8516

Misdemeanor records are available by mail or phone. No release necessary. No search fee. Search information required: name, date of birth.

Civil records
Superior Court
172 Main St.
PO Box 688
Danielson, CT 06239
(203) 774-8516

Civil records are available by mail. No release necessary. No search fee. Search information required: name, years to search. Specify plaintiff or defendant.

City-County Cross Reference

Abington *Windham*
Addison *Hartford*
Amston *Tolland*
Andover *Tolland*
Ansonia *New Haven*
Ashford *Windham*
Avon *Hartford*
Ballouville *Windham*
Baltic *New London*
Bantam *Litchfield*
Beacon Falls *New Haven*
Berlin *Hartford*
Bethany *New Haven*
Blue Hills *Hartford*
Bethel *Fairfield*
Bethlehem *Litchfield*
Bloomfield *Hartford*
Botsford *Fairfield*
Branford *New Haven*
Bridgeport *Fairfield*
Bridgewater *Litchfield*
Bristol *Hartford*
Broad Brook *Hartford*
Brookfield *Fairfield*
Brookfield Center *Fairfield*
Brooklyn *Windham*
Canaan *Litchfield*
Candlewood Shores
　Fairfield
Cannondale *Fairfield*
Canterbury *Windham*
Canton *Hartford*
Canton Center *Hartford*
Centerbrook *Middlesex*
Central Village *Windham*
Chaplin *Windham*
Cheshire *New Haven*
Chester *Middlesex*

Clinton *Middlesex*
Cobalt *Middlesex*
Colchester *New London*
Colebrook *Litchfield*
Collinsville *Hartford*
Columbia *Tolland*
Cornwall *Litchfield*
Cornwall Bridge *Litchfield*
Cos Cob *Fairfield*
Coventry *Tolland*
Cromwell *Middlesex*
Danbury *Fairfield*
Danielson *Windham*
Darien *Fairfield*
Dayville *Windham*
Deep River *Middlesex*
Derby *New Haven*
Durham *Middlesex*
East Berlin *Hartford*
East Brooklyn *Windham*
East Canaan *Litchfield*
Eastford *Windham*
East Glastonbury *Hartford*
East Granby *Hartford*
East Haddam *Middlesex*
East Hampton *Middlesex*
East Hartford *Hartford*
East Hartland *Hartford*
East Haven *New Haven*
East Killingly *Windham*
East Lyme *New London*
East River *New Haven*
East Windsor *Hartford*
East Windsor Hill *Hartford*
East Woodstock *Windham*
Ellington *Tolland*
Enfield *Hartford*
Essex *Middlesex*

Fabyan *Windham*
Fairfield *Fairfield*
Falls Village *Litchfield*
Farmington *Hartford*
Bozrah *New London*
Gales Ferry *New London*
Gaylordsville *Litchfield*
Georgetown *Fairfield*
Giants Neck *New Haven*
Gilman *New London*
Glasgo *New London*
Glastonbury *Hartford*
Goshen *Litchfield*
Granby *Hartford*
Greens Farms *Fairfield*
Greenwich *Fairfield*
Grosvenor Dale *Windham*
Groton *New London*
Guilford *New Haven*
Haddam *Middlesex*
Hadlyme *New London*
Hamden *New Haven*
Hampton *Windham*
Hanover *New London*
Harwinton *Litchfield*
Hartford *Hartford*
Hawleyville *Fairfield*
Hazardville *Hartford*
Hebron *Tolland*
Higganum *Middlesex*
Honeypot Glen *New Haven*
Indian Neck *New Haven*
Ivoryton *Middlesex*
Jewett City *New London*
Kensington *Hartford*
Kent *Litchfield*
Lakeside *Litchfield*
Lakeville *Litchfield*

Lebanon *New London*
Litchfield *Litchfield*
Madison *New Haven*
Manchester *Hartford*
Mansfield Center *Tolland*
Mansfield Depot *Tolland*
Marion *Hartford*
Melrose *Hartford*
Meriden *New Haven*
Middlebury *New Haven*
Middlefield *Middlesex*
Middle Haddam *Middlesex*
Middletown *Middlesex*
Milford *New Haven*
Milldale *Hartford*
Mixville *New Haven*
Monroe *Fairfield*
Montville *New London*
Moodus *Middlesex*
Moosup *Windham*
Morris *Litchfield*
Mystic *New London*
Naugatuck *New Haven*
New Britain *Hartford*
New Canaan *Fairfield*
New Fairfield *Fairfield*
New Hartford *Litchfield*
New Haven *New Haven*
New London *New London*
New Milford *Litchfield*
New Preston *Litchfield*
Newington *Hartford*
Newtown *Fairfield*
Niantic *New London*
Norfolk *Litchfield*
North Branford *New Haven*
North Canton *Hartford*
Northford *New Haven*

North Franklin *New London*
North Granby *Hartford*
North Grosvenordale *Windham*
North Haven *New Haven*
North Stonington *New London*
North Westchester *New London*
North Windham *Windham*
Norwalk *Fairfield*
Norwich *New London*
Oakdale *New London*
Oakville *Litchfield*
Old Greenwich *Fairfield*
Old Lyme *New London*
Old Mystic *New London*
Old Saybrook *Middlesex*
Oneco *Windham*
Orange *New Haven*
Oxford *New Haven*
Pawcatuk *New London*
Pequabuck *Litchfield*
Pine Bridge *New Haven*
Pine Meadow *Litchfield*
Pine Orchard *New Haven*
Plainfield *Windham*
Plainville *Hartford*
Plantsville *Hartford*
Pleasant Valley *Litchfield*
Pleasure Beach *New London*
Plymouth *Litchfield*
Pomfret *Windham*
Pomfret Center *Windham*
Poquonock *Hartford*
Portland *Middlesex*
Prospect *New Haven*
Putnam *Windham*
Quaker Hill *New London*
Quinebaug *Windham*
Redding *Fairfield*
Redding Ridge *Fairfield*
Ridgefield *Fairfield*
Riverside *Fairfield*
Riverton *Litchfield*
Rockfall *Middlesex*
Rocky Hill *Hartford*
Rogers *Windham*
Roxbury *Litchfield*
Salisbury *Litchfield*
Sandy Hook *Fairfield*
Scotland *Windham*
Seymour *New Haven*
Sharon *Litchfield*
Shelton *Fairfield*
Sherman *Fairfield*
Short Beach *New Haven*
Simsbury *Hartford*
Somers *Tolland*
Somersville *Tolland*
South Britain *New Haven*
Southbury *New Haven*
South Glastonbury *Hartford*
Southington *Hartford*
South Kent *Litchfield*
South Lyme *New London*
Southport *Fairfield*
South Willington *Tolland*
South Windham *Windham*
South Windsor *Hartford*
South Woodstock *Windham*
Stafford *Tolland*

Stafford Springs *Tolland*
Staffordville *Tolland*
Stamford *Fairfield*
Sterling *Windham*
Stevenson *Fairfield*
Stonington *New London*
Storrs *Tolland*
Stratford *Fairfield*
Suffield *Hartford*
Taconic *Litchfield*
Taftville *New London*
Tariffville *Hartford*
Terryville *Litchfield*
Thomaston *Litchfield*
Thompson *Windham*
Tolland *Tolland*
Torrington *Litchfield*
Trumbull *Fairfield*
Uncasville *New London*
Unionville *Hartford*
Upper Stepney *Fairfield*
Vernon-Rockville *Tolland*
Versailles *New London*
Voluntown *New London*
Wallingford *New Haven*
Washington Depot *Litchfield*
Waterbury *New Haven*
Waterford *New London*
Watertown *Litchfield*
Wauregan *Windham*
Weatogue *Hartford*
Wequetequock *New London*
Westbrook *Middlesex*
West Cornwall *Litchfield*
West Granby *Hartford*
West Hartford *Hartford*
West Haven *New Haven*
West Mystic *New London*
Weston *Fairfield*
West Hartland *Hartford*
Westport *Fairfield*
West Redding *Fairfield*
West Simsbury *Hartford*
West Suffield *Hartford*
West Willington *Tolland*
Wethersfield *Hartford*
Willimantic *Windham*
Wilton *Fairfield*
Windham *Windham*
Windsor *Hartford*
Windsor Locks *Hartford*
Winsted *Litchfield*
Wolcot *New Haven*
Woodbridge *New Haven*
Woodbury *Litchfield*
Woodmont *New Haven*
Woodstock *Windham*
Woodstock Valley *Windham*
Yantic *New London*

Delaware

Worker's compensation and driving records are readily available at the state level in Delaware. While the state criminal record repository's procedures are somewhat cumbersome and expensive, three (3) counties present even more problems with records being available in person only.

For more information or for offices not listed, contact the state's information hot line at (302) 736-4000.

Driving Records

Division of Motor Vehicles
PO Box 698
Dover, DE 19903
(302) 739-4461

Driving records are available by mail. $4 fee per request. Turnaround time is 5 working days. Written request must include job applicant's full name date of birth, driver's license number and SASE. Make check payable to Division of Motor Vehicle Department.

Worker's Compensation Records

Industrial Accident Board
820 N. French Street
Carval Building
Wilmington, DE 19801
(302) 571-2884

Telephone inquiries are accepted for confirmation of record, date or accident, nature of injury and employer involved. For more detailed information, requests must be made in writing with a release signed by the applicant. There is no fee.

Vital Statistics

Bureau of Vital Statistics
Division of Public Health
PO Box 637
Dover, DE 19903
(302) 739-4721

Birth and death records are available for $5.00 each. Additional copies at the time of initial request are $3.00. Employers can obtain records with a written release. Make any type of check or money order payable to Office of Vital Statistics.

Marriage records are available. $5.00 for first copy and $3.00 for each additional copy. Request must include full name, marriage date, full spouse's name, and town married in. Divorce records available at county level through Family Courts.

Department of Education

Certification Division
Departmment of Public Instruction
PO Box 1402
Townsend Building
Dover, DE 19903
(302) 739-4686

Information is currently not considered public.

Medical Licensing

Medical Board Office
P.O. Box 1401
Oneal Building
Dover, DE 19903
(302) 739-4522

Will confirm licenses for MDs and PODs by phone or mail. No fee. For licenses not mentioned, contact the above office.

Delaware Board of Nursing
Margaret O'Neill Building
PO Box 1401
Dover, DE 19901
(302) 739-4522

Will confirm license by phone. No fee. Include name, license number.

Bar Association

Delaware Bar Association
1225 King Street
Wilmington, DE 19899
(302) 739-5278

Will confirm licenses by phone. No fee. Include name.

Accountancy Board

State Board of Accountancy
O'Niell Building
PO Box 1401
Dover, DE 19903
(302) 739-4522

Will confirm licenses by phone. No fee. Include name.

Securities Commission

Department of Justice
Division of Securities
8th Floor, State Office Building
820 North French Street
Wilmington, DE 19801
(302) 577-2515

Will confirm licenses by phone. No fee. Include name and SSN.

Secretary of State

Secretary of State
Department of Corporation
PO Box 898
Dover, DE 19903
(302) 739-3073

Service agent and address, date incorporated, standing with tax commission, trade names are available by phone or mail. $1.00 fee per copy, $20.00 fee for certification. Contact the above office for additional information.

Criminal Records

State Repository

Delaware State Police Headquarters
Attention: Criminal Records Section
PO Box 430
Dover, DE 19903-0430
(302) 739-5882 or 739-5883

Criminal record checks are available by mail only. Each request must include a signed release, a set of fingerprints and a separate $25.00 certified check or money order made payable to the Delaware State Police. Information supplied includes both conviction and arrest records. There is a 5 day turnaround plus mail time.

Kent County

Kent County Prothonotary
Courthouse
The Green
Dover, DE 19901
(302) 739-5328

Records are available in person only. See Delaware state repository for additional information.

Civil records are available in person only. See Delaware state repository for additional information.

New Castle County

Courthouse
Office of Prothonotary
11th and King
Wilmington, DE 19801
(302) 577-6480

Records are available in person only. See Delaware state repository for additional information.

Civil records are available in person only. See Delaware state repository for additional information.

Sussex County

Office of Prothonotary, Criminal Records
PO Box 31
Georgetown, DE 19947
(302) 856-5740

Felony records are available in person only. See Delaware State Repository for additional information.

Civil records are available in person only. See Delaware state repository for additional information.

City-County Cross Reference

Arden *New Castle*
Bear *New Castle*
Bellefonte *New Castle*
Belvidere *New Castle*
Bethany Beach *Sussex*
Bethel *Sussex*
Birchwood Park *New Castle*
Blades *Sussex*
Brandywood *New Castle*
Bridgeville *Sussex*
Camden-Wyoming *Kent*
Carrcroft *New Castle*
Castle Hills *New Castle*
Chalfonte *New Castle*
Cheswold *Kent*
Clarksville *Sussex*
Claymont *New Castle*
Clayton *Kent*
Coventry *New Castle*
Dagsboro *Sussex*
Darley Woods *New Castle*

Delaware City *New Castle*
Delmar *Sussex*
Devonshire New Castle
Dover *Kent*
Dunleith *New Castle*
Edgemoor *New Castle*
Eismere *New Castle*
Ellendale *Sussex*
Fairfax *New Castle*
Farmington *Kent*
Felton *Kent*
Frankford *Sussex*
Frederica *Kent*
Georgetown *Sussex*
Greenwood *Sussex*
Gwinhurst *New Castle*
Harbeson *Sussex*
Harrington *Kent*
Hartly *Kent*
Hockessin *New Castle*
Houston *Kent*
Kenton *Kent*

Kirkwood *New Castle*
Lancaster Village *New Castle*
Laurel *Sussex*
Lewes *Sussex*
Lincoln *Sussex*
Little Creek *Kent*
Magnolia *Kent*
Marshallton *New Castle*
Meadowood *New Castle*
Middletown *New Castle*
Milford *Sussex*
Millsboro *Sussex*
Millville *Sussex*
Milton *Sussex*
Minquadale *New Castle*
Montchanin *New Castle*
Nassau *Sussex*
Newark *New Castle*
Newport *New Castle*
New Castle *New Castle*
Ocean View *Sussex*

Odessa *New Castle*
Port Penn *New Castle*
Rehoboth Beach *Sussex*
Rising Sun *Kent*
Rockland *New Castle*
Rodney Village *Kent*
Saint Georges *New Castle*
Seaford *Sussex*
Selbyville *Sussex*
Sharpley *New Castle*
Silview *New Castle*
Smyrna *Kent*
Stanton *NewCastle*
Stratford *New Castle*
Talleyville *New Castle*
Townsend *New Castle*
Viola *Kent*
Wilmington *New Castle*
Woodside *Kent*
Wyoming *Kent*
Yorklyn *New Castle*

District of Columbia

Worker's compensation, driving and criminal records are all readily available in the District.

For more information or for offices not listed, contact the District of Columbia's information hot line at (202) 727-1000.

Driving Records

Bureau of Motor Vehicles
Driving Records
301 C Street NW, Room 1157
Washington, DC 20001
(202) 727-6761

Driving records are available by mail. $5.00 fee per request. $3.00 for certification. Turnaround time is 7-10 days. Written request must include job applicant's full name, license number, SSN, and date of birth if applicant no longer has a D.C. permit. Make check payable to the D.C. Treasurer.

Worker's Compensation Records

Department of Employment Services
PO Box 56700
Washington, DC 20011
(202) 576-7091

Worker's Compensation Records are available by mail only. A signed release is required. $.20 fee per copy. Search information required: name, date of birth, SSN, date of injury, SASE.

Vital Statistics

Birth and Death Records

Vital Records Branch
425 I Street Northwest, Room 3009
Washington, DC 20001
(202) 727-5314

Birth and death records are available. Records are also accessible by computer. For birth records include persons full name, date and place of birth, father's name, mother's maiden name, name of hospital, SSN, release. Birth certificate fee: $12.00 fee per computer copy, $18.00 fee per copy of origninal. All copies are certified. For death certificate, include full name, $12.00 fee. Make any type of check or money order payable to D.C. Treasurer.

Marriage Records

Marriage Bureau
Superior Court House
500 Indiana Ave. N.W.
Room 4485
Washington DC 20001
(202) 879-4843
Fax (202) 879-4848

Marriage records are available by mail or fax. $10.00 fee for each copy. Money order only. $10.00 charge for each year searched. Money order payable to Clerk of Superior Court. Turnaround time varies according to mail back-up. Include name, marriage date, spouse's name, and maiden name.

Divorce Records

Domestic Relations
Superior Court House
500 Indiana Ave. N.W.
Room 4230
Washington, DC 20001
(202) 879-1410

Divorce records are available by mail. Fee is $10.00. $.50 fee per copy. $5.00 for certification. Check or money order, payable to Court of District of Columbia. Turnaround time is one week. Include name, spouse's (maiden) name, and where married.

Department of Education

Board of Education
Teacher Certification Office Rm. 1013
415 12th St. Northwest
Washington, DC 20004
(202) 724-4249

Field of certification is available by mail. A written release is required. Include name.

Medical Licensing

Board of Medicine
605 G Street Northwest Rm. LL202
Washington, DC 20001
(202) 727-5365

Will confirm licenses for MDs by phone or mail. $20.00 fee. Make check payable to DC Treasury. For licenses not mentioned, contact the above office.

District of Columbia Board of Nursing
614 "H" Street, NW
Room 910
Washington, DC 20001
(202) 727-7823

Will confirm license by phone. No fee. Include name, license number, if available. For mail requests, include $20.00.

Bar Association

District of Columbia Bar Association
Membership Department
1707 L Northwest
Washington, DC 20036
(202) 331-3883

Will confirm licenses by phone. No fee. Include name.

Accountancy Board

District of Columbia Board of Accountancy
License & Certification Division
614 H Northwest, ARoom 910
Washington, DC 20001

Will confirm licenses by phone. No fee. Include name, license number if available.

Securities Commission

Public Service Commission
Division of Securities
450 5th St., NW, Suite 821
Washington, DC 20001
(202) 626-5105

Will confirm licenses by phone. No fee. Include name and SSN.

Secretary of State

Department of Consumer and
Regulatory Affairs
614 H St. Northwest Rm. 407
Washington, DC 20001
(202) 727-7278

Service agent and address, date incorporated, standing with the department, corporate names are available by phone or mail. No fee. $5.00 fee per copy. Contact the above office for additional information.

Criminal Records

Central Repository

Criminal Records
500 Indian Avenue Northwest
Criminal Division, Room 4001
Washington, DC 20001
(202) 879-1373

Felony and misdemeanor records are available by mail or phone. Will only confirm conviction from Superior Court. Phone inquiries are limited to records entered into the computer since 1973. No release necessary. No fee. Search information required: name, date of birth, years to search.

Florida

All sixty seven (67) Florida counties reported that conviction records are generally available for employment screening purposes by phone and/or mail. Thirty one (31) counties reported that records are available by fax. Circuit court holds civil records for $10,000 and more.

For more information or for offices not listed, contact the state's information hot line at (904) 488-1234.

Driving Records

Department of Highway Safety & Motor Vehicles
Attn: Record Dept.
2900 Apalachee Pkwy.
Tallahassee, FL 32399-0575
(904) 487-2370

Driving records are available by mail. $2 fee for 3 year record, $3 fee for 7 year record. Turnaround time is 2-3 weeks. Written request must include job applicant's full name, date of birth, and license number, if available. Also specify the number of years to be searched (3 or 7). Make check payable to Division of Driver Licenses.

Worker's Compensation Records

State of Florida
Department of Labor
Division of Worker's Compensation
Ashley Bldg., Rm. 108
1321 Executive Center Drive, East
Tallahassee, FL 32399-0681
(904) 488-3030

Due to a cut in personnel, the state of Florida no longer supplies worker's compensation records directly to employers. To obtain a list of the service bureaus currently processing records for employment purposes, contact the state of Florida using the above telephone number.

Vital Statistics

Office of Vital Statistics
PO Box 210
Jacksonville, FL 32231-0042
(904) 359-6000

Birth records are available for $9.00, and death records for $5.00 if date of event is known. Turnaround time is 2-3 weeks. If the exact date is unknown, the fee is $2.00 for each year up to a maximum of $55.00 for death records and $50.00. Fee includes one copy of record found. Some records are accessible by computer. Make any type check or money order payable to Office of Vital Statistics.

Marriage certificate is available for $5.00. Check or Money Order. Include husband's name, wife's maiden name, marriage date, and city where married. Turn-around time is 2 weeks. Divorce records available for $5.00. Include name, divorce date, spouse's name, and city where divorced.

Turnaround time is 2 to 3 weeks. Master Card or Visa is accepted. $4.50 service fee.

Department of Education

Teacher Certification
325 W. Gaines St., Suite 201
Tallahasse, FL 32399-0400
(904) 488-2319

Field of certification, effective date, and expiration date are available by phone. Include name and SSN.

Medical Licensing

Department of Professional Regulation
1940 N. Monroe St.
Tallahasse, FL 32399
(904) 487-1395

Will confirm licenses for MDs by phone or mail. No fee. For licenses not mentioned, contact the above office. Send inquiries to the attention of the Board Granting Certification.

Florida Board of Nursing
111 Coastline Drive, East
Suite 516
Jacksonville, FL 32202
(904) 487-1395

Will confirm license by phone. No fee. Include full name or license number.

Bar Association

State Bar Association
650 Apalachee Parkway
Tallahassee, FL 32399-3230
(904) 561-5600

Will confirm licenses by phone. No fee. Include name.

Accountancy Board

Board of Accountancy
4001 Northwest 43rd Street
Suite 16
Gainseville, FL 32606
(904) 336-2165

Will confirm licenses by phone. No fee. Include name.

Securities Commission

Department of Banking and Finance
Division of Securities
Office of Controller
LL-22
Tallahassee, FL 32399-0350
(904) 488-9805

Will confirm licenses by phone. No fee. Include name and SSN.

Secretary of State

Department of State
Division of Corporation
POBox 6327
Tallahassee, FL 32314
(904) 488-9000

Service agent and address, date incorporated, trade names are available by phone or mail. No search fee. $1.00 fee per copy. Contact the above office for additional information.

Criminal Records

State Repository

Florida Department of Law Enforcement
Attention: Crime Information Bureau
PO Box 1489
Tallahassee, FL 32302
(904) 488-6236

Criminal record checks available by mail only. Information returned includes both arrest and conviction data. Each request must include the full name, date of birth, race, sex, SSN, previous address, SASE. All requests must also include a $10.00 check made payable to the Florida Department of Law Enforcement.

Special instructions: If more than one name is submitted on a single request form, leave a 2" space between each applicant and write only on left side of page. State will place results of inquiries on right side. Turnaround time is 8-12 working days.

Alachua County

Clerk of Circuit Court, Criminal
Records
PO Box 600
Gainesville, FL 32602
(904) 374-3612
Fax (904) 338-3201

Felony and misdemeanor records are available by mail or fax. No release necessary.
$1.00 search fee for each year searched.
Certified check only, payable to Circuit
Clerk. Search information required: name,
date of birth, SASE.

Civil records are available by mail or fax.
No release necessary. $1.00 fee for each
year searched. Search information required:
name, date of birth, SASE, years to search.
Specify plaintiff or defendant.

Baker County

Clerk of Circuit Court, Criminal
Records
339 E. MacClenny Ave.
MacClenny, FL 32063
(904) 259-3121
Fax (904) 259-2799

Felony and misdemeanor records are available by mail or fax. No release necessary.
$1.00 fee for each year searched. Company
checks only, payable to Clerk of Circuit
Court. Search information required: name,
date of birth, sex, race, years to search,
SASE.

Civil records are available by mail or fax.
No release necessary. $1.00 fee for each
year searched. Search information required:
name, date of birth, years to search. Specify
plaintiff or defendant.

Bay County

Clerk of the Circuit Court, Criminal
Records
PO Box 2269
Panama City, FL 32402
(904) 763-9061
Fax (904) 763-5736

Felony and misdemeanor records are available by mail or fax. No release necessary.
$1.00 fee for each year searched. $2.00 fee
per page for fax request, prepaid. Make
check payable to Clerk of Court. Search information required: name, date of birth.

Civil records are available by mail or fax.
No release necessary. No search fee for first
year searched. $1.00 fee for each year
searched thereafter. $2.00 fee per page for
fax request prepaid. Search information required: name, date of birth, years to search.
Specify plaintiff or defendant.

Bradford County

Felony records
Clerk of the Circuit Court, Criminal
Records
PO Drawer B
Starke, FL 32091
(904) 964-6280 Ext. 255

Felony records are available by mail. No release necessary. $1.00 fee for each year
searched. Make check payable to Circuit
Clerk. Search information required: name,
date of birth, years to search, SASE.

Civil records
Clerk of the Circuit Court
PO Drawer B
Starke, FL 32091
(904) 964-6280 Ext. 255

Civil records are available by mail. No release necessary. $1.00 fee for each year
searched. $1.00 fee per copy. $1.00 for certification. Search information required:
name, date of birth, years to search. Specify
plaintiff or defendant.

Misdemeanor records
Clerk of the Circuit Court, Criminal
Records
PO Drawer B
Starke, FL 32091
(904) 964-6280 Ext. 206

Misdemeanor records are available by mail.
No release necessary. $1.00 fee for each
year searched. Make check payable to
Circuit Clerk. Search information required:
name, date of birth, years to search, SASE.

Civil records
Clerk of the Circuit Court
PO Drawer B
Starke, FL 32091
(904) 964-6280 Ext. 206

Civil records are available by mail. No release necessary. $1.00 fee for each year
searched. $1.00 fee per copy. $1.00 for certification. Search information required:
name, date of birth, years to search, SASE.
Specify plaintiff or defendant.

Brevard County

Felony records
Clerk of the Circuit Court, Criminal
Law Department
PO Drawer H
Titusville, FL 32781-0239
(407) 264-5259
Fax (407) 264-5269

Felony and misdemeanor records are available by mail or fax. No release necessary.
$1.00 fee for each year searched. $1.00 fee
per copy. $1.00 for certification. Check
payable to Clerk of Court. Search information required: name, date of birth, alias,
maiden name, years to search, SASE.

Civil records
Clerk of the Circuit Court,
PO Drawer H
Titusville, FL 32781-0239
(407) 264-5840
Fax (407) 264-5269

Civil records are available by mail or fax.
No release necessary. $1.00 fee for each
year searched. $1.00 fee per copy. $1.00 for
certification. Search information required:
name, date of birth, years to search, SASE.
Specify plaintiff or defendant.

Broward County

Correspondence Clerk
Room 349
201 Southeast 6th St.
Ft. Lauderdale, FL 33301
(305) 765-4573

Felony and misdemeanor records are available by mail or phone. No release necessary. $1.00 fee for each year searched.
Certified check or money order payable to
Clerk of Circuit Court. Search information
required: name, date of birth, sex, race,
SASE.

Civil records are available by mail. No release necessary. $1.00 fee for each year
searched. $1.00 fee per copy. $2.00 for certification. Search information required:
name, date of birth, years to search, SASE.
Specify plaintiff or defendant.

Calhoun County

Clerk of Circuit Court, Criminal
Records
425 E. Central Ave.
Blountstown, FL 32424
(904) 674-4545
Fax (904) 674-5553

Felony and misdemeanor records are available by mail, phone or fax. No release necessary. No search fee. Search information
required: name, date of birth, years to
search.

Civil records are available by mail, phone
or fax. No release necessary. No search fee.
Search information required: name, date of
birth, years to search. Specify plaintiff or
defendant.

Charlotte County

Clerk of Court
Felony Division
PO Box 1687
Punta Gorda, FL 33951
(813) 637-2114

Felony and misdemeanor records are available by mail. Turnaround time is 1 week.
No release necessary. $1.00 fee for each
year searched. $.15 fee per copy, $1.00 fee
for certified copy. Certified check only,
payable to Clerk of Court. Search information required: name, date of birth.

Civil records are available by mail. No release necessary. $1.00 fee for each year
searched. $.15 fee per copy, $1.00 fee for
certified copy. Search information required:
name, date of birth, years to search. Specify
plaintiff or defendant

Citrus County

Felony records
Clerk of Court, Criminal Records
110 N. Apopka
Room 101, Courthouse
Inverness, FL 32650
(904) 637-9440

Felony records are available by mail.
Turnaround time is 2 weeks. No release
necessary. No search fee for current year.
$1.00 fee for each year searched prior to
current year. Company checks only,
payable to Clerk of Court. Search information required: name, date of birth, years to
search, SASE.

Civil records
Clerk of Court
110 N. Apopka
Room 101, Courthouse
Inverness, FL 32650
(904) 637-9440

Civil records are available by mail. No release necessary. $1.00 search fee for each
year searched. $1.00 fee per copy. $2.00 for
certification. Search information required:
name, date of birth, SASE, years to search.
Specify plaintiff or defendant.

Misdemeanor records
Citrus County Clerk's Office
Courthouse
110 N. Apopica
Inverness, FL 32650
(904) 637-9435
Fax (904) 637-9413

Misdemeanor records are available by mail. Turnaround time is 2 weeks. No release necessary. $1.00 fee for each year searched. Company checks only, payable to Clerk of Court. Search information required: name, date of birth, years to search, SASE.

Civil records
Citrus County Clerk's Office
Courthouse
110 N. Apopica
Inverness, FL 32650
(904) 637-9452
Fax (904) 637-9413

Civil records are available by mail. No release necessary. $1.00 fee for each year searched prepaid. Search information required: name, date of birth, years to search. Specify plaintiff or defendant.

Clay County

Clerk of Court, Criminal Records
PO Box 698
Green Cove Springs, FL 32043
(904) 284-6300 Extension 349
Fax (904) 284-6390

Felony and misdemeanor records are available by mail or fax. Turnaround time is 1 week. No release necessary. $1.00 fee for each year searched. Certified check only, payable to Clerk of Court. Search information required: name, date of birth, years to search, SASE.

Civil records are available by mail or fax. No release necessary. $1.00 fee for each year searched. Search information required: name, date of birth, years to search. Specify plaintiff or defendant.

Collier County

Clerk of Court, Criminal Records
PO Box 413044
Naples, FL 33941-3044
(813) 732-2645

Felony and misdemeanor records are available by mail. Turnaround time is 1 week. No release necessary. $1.00 fee per year searched. $1.00 for certification. Make check payable to Clerk of Court. Search information required: name, SSN, date of birth, sex, race, SASE. Contact the book-keeping department at (813) 732-2725 to set up a deposit account.

Civil records are available by mail. No release necessary. $1.00 fee per year searched. $1.00 for certification. Search information required: name, date of birth, years to search, SASE. Specify plaintiff or defendant.

Columbia County

Clerk of Court, Criminal Records
PO Drawer 2069
Lake City, FL 32056-2069
(904) 758-1056
Fax (904) 758-1056

Felony records are available by mail. Turnaround time is 2 weeks. No release necessary. $1.00 fee for each year searched. $.15 fee per copy. Make check payable to Court Clerk. Search information required: name, SSN, date of birth, sex, race, years to search, SASE.

Civil records are available by mail. No release necessary. $1.00 fee for each year searched. $.15 fee per copy. Search information required: name, date of birth, years to search. Specify plaintiff or defendant.

Dade County

Felony and misdemeanor records
Dade County Metro-Justice Bldg.
Criminal Records
1351 N.W. 12th Street
Miami, FL 33125
(305) 547-7168

Felony and misdemeanor records are available by mail. No release necessary. $1.00 fee per year. $1.00 fee per copy, $1.00 fee for certified copy. Make check payable to Clerk of Circuit Court. Search information required: name, SSN, date of birth, sex, race, years to search. Address request to: Felony (room 702) or Misdemeanor (room 702).

Civil records
Dade County Metro-Justice Bldg.
1351 N.W. 12th Street
Miami, FL 33125
(305) 547-4888

Civil records are available by mail. No release necessary. $1.00 fee per year. $1.00 fee per copy, $1.00 fee for certified copy. Search information required: name, date of birth, years to search. Specify plaintiff or defendant.

De Soto County

Clerk of Court, Criminal Records
PO Box 591
Arcadia, FL 33821
(813) 993-4876

Felony and misdemeanor records are available by mail. No release necessary. $1.00 fee for each year searched. $1.00 fee per copy. $1.00 for certification. Make check payable to Clerk of Court. Search information required: name, SSN, date of birth, sex, race, years to search, SASE.

Civil records are available by mail. No release necessary. $1.00 fee for each year searched. $1.00 fee per copy. $1.00 for certification. Search information required: name, date of birth, years to search, SASE. Specify plaintiff or defendant.

Dixie County

Clerk of Court, Criminal Records
PO Box 1206
Cross City, FL 32628
(904) 498-7021

Felony records are available by mail. No release necessary. $1.00 fee for each year searched. $1.00 fee per copy. $1.00 for certification. Certified check only, payable to Clerk of Court. Search information required: name, SSN, date of birth, sex, race, years to search.

Civil records are available by mail. No release necessary. $1.00 fee for each year searched. $1.00 fee per copy. $1.00 for certification. Search information required: name, date of birth, years to search. Specify plaintiff or defendant.

Duval County

Jacksonville Sheriff's Department,
Criminal Records
501 E. Bay Street
Jacksonville, FL 32202
(904) 630-2216

Felony records are available by mail. Turnaround time is 1 week. No release necessary. $5.00 search fee. Certified check only, payable to City of Jacksonville. Search information required: name, SSN, date of birth, sex, race.

Civil records are available by mail. No release necessary. $5.00 search fee. Search information required: name, date of birth, years to search. Specify plaintiff or defendant.

Escambia County

Felony records
Clerk of Court, Criminal Records
190 Governmental Center
Pensacola, FL 32501-5796
(904) 436-5160

Felony records are available by mail. No release necessary. $1.00 fee for first 10 years searched. $10.00 fee for additional years searched. $1.00 fee per copy. $1.00 for certification. $4.00 fee for written response. Include additional page for request to be returned. Certified check only, payable to Clerk of Court. Search information required: name, date of birth, if available, race, sex. Turnaround time is 1 week.

Civil records
Clerk of Court
190 Governmental Center
Pensacola, FL 32501-5796
(904) 436-5260

Civil records are available by mail. No release necessary. $1.00 fee for first 10 years searched. $10.00 additional fee for additional years searched. $1.00 fee per copy. $1.00 for certification. $4.00 fee for written response. Search information required: name, date of birth, years to search. Specify plaintiff or defendant.

Misdemeanor records
County Criminal
190 Governmental Center
Pensacola, FL 32501
(904) 436-5200
Fax (904) 436-5610

Misdemeanor records since 1973 are available by mail, fax or phone. No release necessary. $1.00 fee for each year searched, $4.00 additional fee to receive information in writing. $1.00 for each additional year. Certified check only, payable to Clerk of Court. Search information required: name, date of birth, race, sex..

Civil records
County Criminal
190 Governmental Center
Pensacola, FL 32501
(904) 436-5200
Fax (904) 436-5610

Civil records are available by mail, fax or phone. No release necessary. $1.00 fee for each year searched, $4.00 additional fee to receive information in writing. $1.00 for each additional year. Search information required: name, date of birth, years to search. Specify plaintiff or defendant.

Flagler County

Clerk of the Circuit Court, Criminal Records
PO Box 787
Bunnell, FL 32110
(904) 437-7430

Felony and misdemeanor records are available by mail. No release necessary. $1.00 fee for each year searched. Or $2.00 fee for each year for both felony and misdemeanor. Certified check or money order payable to Clerk of Court. Search information required: name, alias, SASE, years to search.

Civil records are available by mail. No release necessary. $1.00 fee for each year searched. Search information required: name, date of birth, years to search, SASE. Specify plaintiff or defendant.

Franklin County

Clerk of Court, Criminal Records
PO Box 340
Apalachicola, FL 32320
(904) 653-8861
Fax (904) 653-2261

Felony and misdemeanor records are available by mail, fax or phone. No release necessary. No search fee. Search information required: name, years to search.

Civil records are available by mail, fax or phone. No release necessary. No search fee. Search information required: name, date of birth, years to search. Specify plaintiff or defendant.

Gadsden County

Felony and misdemeanor records
Clerk of Court, Criminal Records
PO Box 1649
Quincy, FL 32353-1649
(904) 875-8610
Fax (904) 875-8612

Felony and misdemeanor records are available by mail, fax or phone. $1.00 fee from 1984 forward, $1.00 fee per year prior to 1984. No release necessary. Check payable to Clerk of Court. Search information required: name, SSN, date of birth, sex, race, years to search.

Civil records
Clerk of Court
PO Box 1649
Quincy, FL 32353-1649
(904) 875-8621
Fax (904) 875-8612

Civil records are available by mail or fax. No release necessary. $1.00 fee per year searched. $1.00 fee per copy. $2.00 for certification. Search information required: name, date of birth, years to search. Specify plaintiff or defendant.

Gilchrist County

Clerk of Court, Criminal Records
PO Box 37
Trenton, FL 32693
(904) 463-2345
Fax (904) 463-2934

Felony and misdemeanor records are available by mail. No release necessary. $1.00 fee for each year searched. $1.00 fee per copy. Certified check only, payable to Clerk of Court. Search information required: name, date of birth, SSN, years to search, SASE.

Civil records are available by mail. No release necessary. $1.00 fee for each year searched. $1.00 fee per copy. Search information required: name, date of birth, years to search, SASE. Specify plaintiff or defendant.

Glades County

Clerk of Court, Criminal Records
PO Box 10
Moore Haven, FL 33471
(813) 946-0113
Fax (813) 946-0560

Felony and misdemeanor records are available by mail or fax. Turnaround time is 1 week. No release necessary. $1.00 fee for each year searched. $1.00 fee per copy, $1.00 fee for certification. Certified check only, payable to Clerk of Court. Search information required: name, years to search.

Civil records are available by mail or fax. No release necessary. $1.00 fee for each year searched. $1.00 fee per copy, $1.00 fee for certification. Search information required: name, years to search. Specify plaintiff or defendant.

Gulf County

Clerk of Court, Criminal Records
1000 5th Street
Port St. Joe, FL 32456
(904) 229-6113
Fax (904) 229-6174

Felony and misdemeanor records are available by mail or fax. No release necessary. $1.00 fee for each year searched. $.15 fee per copy, $1.00 fee for certification. Certified check only, payable to Circuit Clerk. Search information required: name, SSN, date of birth, sex, race, SASE.

Civil records are available by mail. No release necessary. $1.00 fee for each year searched. $.15 fee per copy, $1.00 fee for certification. Search information required: name, date of birth, years to search, SASE. Specify plaintiff or defendant.

Hamilton County

Clerk of Court, Criminal Records
PO Box 312
Jasper, FL 32052
(904) 792-1288
Fax (904) 792-3524

Felony and misdemeanor records are available by mail, fax or phone. Turnaround time is 1 week. A release is required. $1.00 fee per year searched. Search information required: name, date of birth, years to search, SASE.

Civil records are available by mail, fax or phone. No release necessary. A release is required. $1.00 fee per year searched. Search information required: name, date of birth, years to search. Specify plaintiff or defendant.

Hardee County

Clerk of Court, Criminal Records
PO Drawer 1749
Wauchula, FL 33873
(813) 773-4174
Fax (813) 773-0958

Felony and misdemeanor records are available by mail. Turnaround time is 1 week. No release necessary. $1.00 fee for each year searched. $.15 fee per copy. $1.00 for certification. Make company check payable to Clerk of Court. Search information required: name, date of birth, SSN, race, SASE.

Civil records are available by mail. No release necessary. $1.00 fee for each year searched. $.15 fee per copy. $1.00 for certification. Search information required: name, date of birth, years to search. Specify plaintiff or defendant.

Hendry County

Clerk of Circuit Court
Felony Division
PO Box 1760
La Belle, FL 33935
(813) 675-5217

Felony and misdemeanor records are available by mail or phone. No release necessary. $2.00 fee for each year searched. Search fee includes copies. $2.00 fee for certification. Make check payable to Clerk of Circuit Court. Search information required: name, SSN, date of birth, SASE.

Civil records are available by mail. No release necessary. $2.00 fee for each year searched. Search fee includes copies. $2.00 fee for certification. Search information required: name, date of birth, years to search, SASE. Specify plaintiff or defendant.

Hernando County

Clerk of Court
20 N. Main Street, Room 248
Brooksville, FL 34601
(904) 754-4201 Ext. 152 (Felony)
(904) 754-4201 Ext. 122 (Misdemeanor)

Felony and misdemeanor records are available by mail. No release necessary. $1.00 fee from 1982 forward. $1.00 fee per year searched prior to 1982. $1.00 fee per copy, $1.00 fee for certification. Search information required: name, date of birth.

Civil records are available by mail. No release necessary. $1.00 fee per year searched. $1.00 fee per copy. $2.00 for certification. Search information required: name, date of birth, years to search. Specify plaintiff or defendant.

Highlands County

Highlands County Clerk of Court, Criminal Records
PO Box 1827
Sebring, FL 33871
(813) 385-2581 Extension 255
Fax (813) 385-3895

Felony and misdemeanor records are available by mail or fax. Call before faxing. Turnaround time is 1 week. No release necessary. $1.00 fee for each year searched. $2.00 for certification. Make check payable to Clerk of Court. Search information required: name, date of birth, sex, race, years to search, SASE.

Civil records are available by mail or fax. Call before faxing. No release necessary. $1.00 fee for each year searched. $2.00 for certification. Search information required: name, date of birth, years to search, SASE. Specify plaintiff or defendant.

Hillsborough County

Felony records
Clerk of the Circuit Court, Criminal Records
Hillsborough County
PO Box 1110
Tampa, FL 33601
(813) 223-7811 Extension 802

Felony records are available by mail. Turnaround time is 2-3 weeks. No release necessary. $1.00 fee for each year searched. $.15 fee for a single-sided copy, $.20 fee for double-sided copy. $1.00 for certification. Company checks only, payable to Clerk of Circuit Court. Search information required: name, SSN, date of birth, SASE.

Civil records
Clerk of the Circuit Court
Hillsborough County
PO Box 1110
Tampa, FL 33601
(813) 223-7811 Extension 252

Civil records are available by mail. No release necessary. $.50 fee for each year searched. $.50 fee per copy. $1.50 for certification. Search information required: name, date of birth, years to search. Specify plaintiff or defendant.

Misdemeanor records
County Court
County Criminal #238
PO Box 1110
Tampa, FL 33601-8089
(813) 223-7811 Extension 802

Misdemeanor records are available by mail. Turnaround time is 2-3 weeks. No release necessary. $1.00 fee for each year searched. $.15 fee per copy, $1.00 fee for certification. Company checks only, payable to Clerk of Circuit Court. Search information required: name, SSN, date of birth, SASE.

Civil records
County Court
PO Box 1110
Tampa, FL 33601-8089
(813) 223-7811 Extension 803

Civil records are available by mail. No release necessary. $1.00 fee for each year searched. $.15 fee per copy, $115. fee for certification. Search information required: name, date of birth, years to search. Specify plaintiff or defendant.

Holmes County

Clerk of Court, Criminal Records
201 N. Oklahoma Street
Bonifay, FL 32425
(904) 547-1100
Fax (904) 547-6630

Felony and misdemeanor records are available by mail or fax. Turnaround time is 1 week. No release necessary. $1.00 fee for each year searched. $1.00 fee per copy. $1.00 for certification. Company checks only, payable to Clerk of Court. Search information required: name, SSN, date of birth, sex, race, years to search.

Civil records are available by mail or fax. No release necessary. $1.00 fee for each year searched. $1.00 fee per copy. $1.00 for certification. Search information required: name, date of birth, years to search. Specify plaintiff or defendant.

Indian River County

Clerk of Court, Criminal Division
PO Box 1028
Vero Beach, FL 32961
(407) 567-8000

Felony and misdemeanor records are available by mail. Turnaround time is 1 week. No release necessary. $1.00 fee for each year searched. $2.00 for certification. Certified check only, payable to Clerk of Court. Search information required: name, SSN, date of birth, sex, race, years to search.

Civil records are available by mail. No release necessary. $1.00 fee for each year searched. $2.00 for certification. Search information required: name, date of birth, years to search. Specify plaintiff or defendant.

Jackson County

Clerk of Court, Criminal Records
PO Drawer 510
Marianna, FL 32446
(904) 482-9552

Felony and misdemeanor records are available by mail or phone. A release is required. $1.00 fee per year searched. $1.00 fee per copy, $1.00 fee for certification. Search information required: name, SSN, date of birth, sex, race, SASE.

Civil records are available by mail. No release necessary. A release is required. $1.00 fee per year searched. $1.00 fee per copy, $1.00 fee for certification. Search information required: name, date of birth, years to search. Specify plaintiff or defendant.

Jefferson County

Jefferson County Courthouse,
Criminal Records
Room 10
Monticello, FL 32344
(904) 997-3596
Fax (904) 997-4885

Felony records are available by mail, fax or phone. A release is required. $1.00 fee for each year searched. $1.00 fee per copy. $1.00 for certification. Company checks only, payable to Clerk of Court. Search information required: name, date of birth, sex, race.

Civil records are available by mail, fax or phone. A release is required. $1.00 fee for each year searched. $1.00 fee per copy. $1.00 for certification. Search information required: name, date of birth, years to search. Specify plaintiff or defendant.

Lafayette County

Clerk of Court, Criminal Records
PO Box 88
Mayo, FL 32066
(904) 294-1600
Fax (904) 294-1377

Felony and misdemeanor records are available by mail, fax or phone. Turnaround time is 1 week. No release necessary. $1.00 fee for each year searched. $.15 fee per copy. $2.00 fee for certification. Company checks only, payable to Clerk of Court. Search information required: name, date of birth, years to search, SASE.

Civil records are available by mail, fax or phone. No release necessary. $1.00 fee for each year searched. $.15 fee per copy. $2.00 fee for certification. Search information required: name, date of birth, years to search, SASE. Specify plaintiff or defendant.

Lake County

Clerk of Court, Felony Division, Criminal Records
315 W. Main Street
Tavares, FL 32778-3887
(904) 343-9815
Fax (904) 343-9638

Felony and misdemeanor records are available by mail or fax. No release necessary. $1.00 fee for each year searched. $1.00 fee for certification. Search information required: name, date of birth, SASE.

Civil records are available by mail or fax. No release necessary. $1.00 fee for each year searched. $1.00 fee for certification. Search information required: name, date of birth, years to search. Specify plaintiff or defendant.

Lee County

Felony and misdemeanor records
Clerk of Court, Criminal Division
PO Box 2469
Ft. Myers, FL 33902
(813) 335-2372

Felony and misdemeanor records are available by mail. No release necessary. $1.00 fee for each year searched. $1.00 fee for each year searched. $1.00 fee for certification. Make check payable to Clerk of Court. Search information required: name, SSN, date of birth, sex, race, years to search, SASE.

Civil records
Clerk of Court
PO Box 310
Ft. Myers, FL 33902
(813) 335-2372

Civil records are available by mail. No release necessary. $1.00 fee for each year searched. $1.00 fee for each year searched. $1.00 fee for certification. Search information required: name, date of birth, years to search, SASE. Specify plaintiff or defendant.

Leon County

Felony and misdemeanor records
Clerk of Court, Criminal Division
PO Box 726
Tallahassee, FL 32302
(904) 488-2131 (Felony)
Fax (904) 488-8863
(904) 488-7160 (Misdemeanor)
Fax (904) 922-5452

Felony and misdemeanor records are available by mail or fax. No release necessary. No search fee. Search information required: name, SSN, date of birth, sex, race, SASE.

Civil records
Clerk of Court
PO Box 726
Tallahassee, FL 32302
(904) 488-7539
Fax (904) 922-5452

Civil records are available by mail or fax. No release necessary. No search fee. Search information required: name, date of birth, years to search, SASE. Specify plaintiff or defendant.

Levy County

Clerk of Court, Criminal Division
PO Box 610
Bronson, FL 32621
(904) 486-4311

Felony and misdemeanor records are available by mail. Turnaround time is 1 week. A release is required. $1.00 fee for each year searched. $1.00 fee per copy. $1.00 fee for certification. Company checks only, payable to Clerk of Court. Search information required: name, date of birth, sex, race, years to search, SASE.

Civil records are available by mail. No release necessary. $1.00 fee for each year searched. $1.00 fee per copy. $1.00 fee for certification. Search information required: name, date of birth, years to search. Specify plaintiff or defendant.

Liberty County

Clerk of Court, Criminal Records
PO Box 399
Bristol, FL 32321
(904) 643-2215

Felony and misdemeanor records are available by mail. No release necessary. $1.00 fee per year searched. $1.00 for certification. Search information required: name, date of birth, sex, race, years to search, SASE.

Civil records are available by mail. No release necessary. $1.00 fee per year searched. $1.00 for certification. Search information required: name, date of birth, years to search, SASE. Specify plaintiff or defendant.

Madison County

Clerk of Court, Criminal Records
PO Box 237
Madison, FL 32340
(904) 973-4176
Fax (904) 973-3780

Felony and misdemeanor records are available by mail, fax or phone. No release necessary. No search fee. $1.00 fee per copy. $1.00 for certification. Search information required: name, date of birth, race, SASE.

Civil records are available by mail, fax or phone. No release necessary. No search fee. $1.00 fee per copy. $1.00 for certification. Search information required: name, date of birth, years to search. Specify plaintiff or defendant.

Manatee County

Felony and misdemeanor records
Clerk of Court
PO Box 1000
Bradenton, FL 34206
(813) 749-1800 Extension 4254

Felony and misdemeanor records are available by mail or phone. No release necessary. No fee for phone requests. $5.00 fee for mail requests plus $1.00 fee for each year searched. $1.00 for certification. Certified check only, payable to Clerk of Court. Search information required: name, date of birth, SASE.

Civil records
Clerk of Court
PO Box 1000
Bradenton, FL 34206
(813) 749-1800 Extension 4206

Civil records are available by mail or phone. No release necessary. No release necessary. No fee for phone requests. $5.00 fee for mail requests plus $1.00 fee for each year searched. $1.00 for certification. Search information required: name, date of birth, years to search, SASE. Specify plaintiff or defendant.

Marion County

Clerk of Court, Criminal Division
PO Box 1030
Ocala, FL 32678-1030
(904) 620-3861

Felony and misdemeanor records are available by mail. Turnaround time is 1 week. No release necessary. $1.00 fee for each year searched. $.15 fee per copy. $1.00 for certification. Make company check payable to Clerk of Court. Search information required: name, SSN, date of birth, sex, race, years to search.

Civil records are available by mail. No release necessary. $1.00 fee for each year searched. $.15 fee per copy. $1.00 for certification. Search information required: name, date of birth, years to search. Specify plaintiff or defendant.

Martin County

Clerk of Court, Criminal Division
PO Box 9016
Stuart, FL 34995
(407) 288-5400

Felony and misdemeanor records are available by mail. Turnaround time is 1-2 weeks. No release necessary. No fee for first year searched. $1.00 fee for each additional year. $1.00 fee per copy, $2.00 fee for certification. Make check payable to Clerk of Court. Search information required: name, alias, date of birth, years to search, SSN.

Civil records are available by mail. No release necessary. $1.00 fee for each year searched. $1.00 fee per copy, $2.00 fee for certification. Search information required: name, date of birth, years to search. Specify plaintiff or defendant.

Monroe County

Felony and misdemeanor records
Clerk of Court, Criminal Division
500 Whitehead Street
Key West, FL 33040
(305) 294-4641 Extension 322

Felony and misdemeanor records are available by mail. No release necessary. $1.00 fee for each year searched. $.15 fee per copy, $1.00 fee for certification. Certified check only, payable to Clerk of Court. Search information required: name, date of birth, years to search, SASE.

Civil records
Clerk of Court
500 Whitehead Street
Key West, FL 33040
(305) 294-4641 Extension 3361

Civil records are available by mail. No release necessary. $1.00 fee for each year searched. $.15 fee per copy, $1.00 fee for certification. Search information required: name, date of birth, years to search, SASE. Specify plaintiff or defendant.

Nassau County

Clerk of Court, Criminal Records
PO Box 456
Fernandina Beach, FL 32034
(904) 261-6127
Fax (904) 879-1029

Felony and misdemeanor records before 1985 are available by mail, fax or phone. For fax request, call first. Turnaround time is 1-2 weeks. No release necessary. $1.00 fee for each year searched prior to 1992. $1.00 fee per copy. $1.00 for certification. Company checks only, payable to Clerk of Court. Search information required: name, SSN, date of birth, sex, race. Provide approximate arrest date, if available.

Civil records are available by mail, fax or phone. For fax request, call first. No release necessary. $1.00 fee per year searched. $1.00 fee per copy. $1.00 for certification. Search information required: name, date of birth, years to search. Specify plaintiff or defendant.

Okaloosa County

Clerk of Circuit Court, Criminal Records
Box 1265
Okaloosa County Courthouse
Crestview, FL 32536
(904) 689-5000
Fax (904) 689-5818

Felony and misdemeanor records are available by mail or fax. $2.00 fee for fax response. Turnaround time is 1-2 weeks. No release necessary. $1.00 fee for each year searched. $.15 fee percopy. $1.00 for certification. Make check payable to Clerk of Circuit Court. Search information required: name, SSN, date of birth, sex, race, years to search.

Civil records are available by mail or fax. $2.00 fee for fax response. No release necessary. $1.00 fee for each year searched. $.15 fee per copy. $1.00 for certification. Search information required: name, date of birth, years to search. Specify plaintiff or defendant.

Okeechobee County

Clerk of Court, Criminal Records
304 N.W. 2nd Street, Room 101
Okeechobee, FL 34972
(813) 763-2131

Felony and misdemeanor records are available by mail. Turnaround time is 1-2 weeks. No release necessary. $1.00 fee for each year searched. $1.00 fee per copy, $1.00 fee for certification. Company checks only, payable to Clerk of Court. Search information required: name, SSN, date of birth, sex, race, years to search, SASE.

Civil records are available by mail. No release necessary. $1.00 fee for each year searched. $1.00 fee per copy, $1.00 fee for certification. Search information required: name, date of birth, years to search, SASE. Specify plaintiff or defendant.

Orange County

Felony and misdemeanor records
Clerk of Court, Criminal Records
Room 417 Orange County Courthouse
65 E. Central
Orlando, FL 32801
(407) 836-2056

Felony and misdemeanor records are available by mail or phone. Turnaround time is 1 week. No release necessary. $1.00 fee per year searched. $1.00 fee per copy. $2.00 for certification. Search information required: name, date of birth, SASE.

Civil records
Clerk of Court
Room 417 Orange County Courthouse
65 E. Central
Orlando, FL 32801
(407) 836-2065

Civil records are available by mail. No release necessary. $1.00 fee per year searched. $1.00 fee per copy. $2.00 for certification. Search information required: name, date of birth, years to search, SASE. Specify plaintiff or defendant.

Osceola County

Felony and misdemeanor records
Clerk of Court, Criminal Division
12 S. Vernon Ave.
Kissimmee, FL 32741-5491
(407) 847-1300 Extension 450

Felony and misdemeanor records are available by mail. No release necessary. $1.00 fee per year searched. $1.00 fee per copy. $2.00 for certification. Check payable to Clerk of Court. Search information required: name, date of birth.

Civil records
Clerk of Court
12 S. Vernon Ave.
Kissimmee, FL 32741-5491
(407) 847-1325

Civil records are available by mail. No release necessary. $1.00 fee per year searched. $1.00 fee per copy. $2.00 for certification. Search information required: name, date of birth, years to search. Specify plaintiff or defendant.

Palm Beach County

Criminal Division, Criminal Division
Room 402
PO Box 2906
West Palm Beach, FL 33402-3544
(407) 355-2574

Felony and misdemeanor records are available by mail. Turnaround time is 1-2 weeks. No release necessary. Fee is $5.00 for a 5-year search, $10.00 for searches over 5 years. $.15 fee per copy. $1.00 for certification. Checks payable to Clerk of Court. Search information required: name, alias, date of birth, years to search.

Civil records are available by mail. No release necessary. Fee is $5.00 for a 5-year search, $10.00 for searches over 5 years. $.15 fee per copy. $1.00 for certification. Search information required: name, date of birth, years to search. Specify plaintiff or defendant.

Pasco County

Clerk of Circuit Court
Pasco County
705 East Live Oak Avenue
Dade City, FL 33525
(904) 521-4503

Felony and misdemeanor records are available by mail. Turnaround time is 1 week. No release necessary. $1.00 search fee. $.15 fee per copy. $1.00 for certification. Certified check only, payable to Clerk of Circuit Court. Search information required: name, SSN, date of birth, sex, race.

Civil records are available by mail. No release necessary. $1.00 search fee. $.15 fee per copy. $1.00 for certification. Search information required: name, date of birth, years to search. Specify plaintiff or defendant.

Pinellas County

Clerk of the Circuit Court, Criminal Records
5100 144th Ave. N.
Clearwater, FL 34620
(813) 530-6793

Felony and misdemeanor records are available by mail. Turnaround time is 1-2 weeks. No release necessary. No search fee. $2.00 fee per copy, $1.00 fee for certification. Search information required: name, date of birth, sex, race, SASE.

Civil records are available by mail. No release necessary. No search fee. $1.00 fee per copy, $2.00 fee for certification. Search information required: name, date of birth, years to search, SASE. Specify plaintiff or defendant.

Polk County

Felony and misdemeanor records
Clerk of Court, Criminal Division
PO Box 9000
Drawer CC-9
Bartow, FL 33830-9000
(813) 534-4000 Extension 4462

Felony and misdemeanor records are available by mail. No release necessary. $1.00 fee for each year searched. $1.00 fee per copy, $1.00 fee for certification. Certified check only, payable to Clerk of Court. Search information required: name, SSN, date of birth, sex, race, years to search.

Civil records
Clerk of Court
PO Box 9000
Drawer CC-12
Bartow, FL 33830-9000
(813) 534-4000

Civil records are available by mail. No release necessary. $1.00 fee for each year searched. $1.00 fee per copy, $1.00 fee for certification. Search information required: name, date of birth, years to search. Specify plaintiff or defendant.

Putnam County

Clerk of Court, Criminal Records
PO Box 758
Palatka, FL 32078
(904) 329-0255
Fax (904) 329-0888

Felony and misdemeanor records are available by mail or fax. Turnaround time is 1-2 weeks. No release necessary. $1.00 fee for each year searched. $1.00 fee per copy, $1.00 fee for certification. Make check payable to Clerk of Circuit Court. Search information required: name, date of birth, sex, race, years to search.

Civil records are available by mail. No release necessary. 1.00 fee for each year searched. $1.00 fee per copy, $1.00 fee for certification. Search information required: name, date of birth, years to search. Specify plaintiff or defendant.

Santa Rosa County

Clerk of Court, Criminal Records
PO Box 472
Milton, FL 32572
(904) 623-0135 Ext 2133 (Felony)
(904) 623-0135 Ext 2146 (Misdemeanor)
Fax (904) 626-7248

Felony and misdemeanor records are available by mail or fax. Turnaround time is 1-2 weeks. No release necessary. $1.00 fee for each year searched. $1.00 fee per copy. $1.00 for certification. Make check payable to Clerk of Court. Search information required: name, date of birth, SASE.

Civil records are available by mail or fax. No release necessary. $1.00 fee for each year searched. $1.00 fee per copy. $1.00 for certification. Search information required: name, date of birth, years to search, SASE. Specify plaintiff or defendant.

Sarasota County

Felony and misdemeanor records
Clerk of Circuit Court, Criminal Records
PO Box 3079
Sarasota, FL 34230-3079
(813) 951-5501

Felony and misdemeanor records are available by mail. No release necessary. $5.00 fee for first year searched. $1.00 fee for each additional year. $1.00 fee per copy. $2.00 for certification. Company checks only, payable to Clerk of Court. Search information required: name, SSN, if available, date of birth, sex, race, years to search, SASE.

Civil records
Clerk of Circuit Court
PO Box 3079
Sarasota, FL 34230-3079
(813) 951-5221

Civil records are available by mail. No release necessary. $5.00 fee for first year searched. $1.00 fee for each additional year. $1.00 fee per copy. $2.00 for certification. Search information required: name, date of birth, years to search, SASE. Specify plaintiff or defendant.

Seminole County

Felony and misdemeanor records
Clerk of Court, Criminal Records
PO Drawer C
Sanford, FL 32771
(407) 323-4330 Extension 4356
Fax (407) 330-7193

Felony and misdemeanor records are available by mail. No release necessary. $1.00 fee for each year searched. $1.00 fee per copy. $1.00 for certification. Make check payable to Clerk of Court. Search information required: name, date of birth, SASE.

Civil records
Clerk of Court
PO Drawer C
Sanford, FL 32771
(305) 323-4366
Fax (407) 330-7193

Civil records are available by mail. No release necessary. $1.00 fee for each year searched. $1.00 fee per copy. $1.00 for certification. Search information required: name, date of birth, years to search, SASE. Specify plaintiff or defendant.

St. John County

Felony and misdemeanor records
Clerk of Court, Criminal Records
PO Drawer 300
St. Augustine, FL 32085
(904) 823-2396

Felony and misdemeanor records are available by mail. No release necessary. $2.00 fee for first year searched. $1.00 fee for each additional year searched. $2.00 for certification. Certified check only, payable to Clerk of Court. Search information required: name, SSN, date of birth, sex, race, years to search, SASE.

Civil records
Clerk of Court, Criminal Records
PO Drawer 300
St. Augustine, FL 32085
(904) 823-2335

Civil records are available by mail. No release necessary. $2.00 fee for first year searched. $1.00 fee for each additional year searched. $2.00 for certification. Search information required: name, date of birth, years to search, SASE. Specify plaintiff or defendant.

St. Lucie County

Felony and misdemeanor records
Clerk of Court, Criminal Records
PO Drawer 700
Ft. Pierce, FL 34954
(407) 468-1789
Fax (407) 489-6975

Felony and misdemeanor records are available by mail or fax. A release is required. $1.00 fee for each year searched. $3.00 for certification. Certified check only, payable to Clerk of Court. Search information required: name, years to search, date of birth, SASE.

Civil records
Clerk of Court
PO Drawer 700
Ft. Pierce, FL 34954
(407) 489-6950
Fax (407) 489-6975

Civil records are available by mail or fax. A release is required. $1.00 fee for each year searched. $3.00 for certification. Search information required: name, date of birth, years to search, SASE. Specify plaintiff or defendant.

Sumter County

Clerk of Circuit Court, Criminal Records
209 N. Florida Street
Bushnell, FL 33513
(904) 793-0215 Extension 437

Felony and misdemeanor records are available by mail. No release necessary. $1.00 fee for each year searched. $.15 fee per copy. $1.00 for certification. Make check payable to Clerk of Circuit Court. Search information required: name, date of birth, years to search, SASE.

Civil records are available by mail. No release necessary. $1.00 fee for each year searched. $.15 fee per copy. $1.00 for certification. Search information required: name, date of birth, years to search, SASE. Specify plaintiff or defendant.

Suwannee County

Suwannee County Clerk, Criminal Records
Suwannee County Courthouse
Live Oak, FL 32060
(904) 362-2827 Extension 18&13

Felony and misdemeanor records are available by mail. No release necessary. $1.00 fee for each year searched. $1.00 fee per copy, $1.00 for certification. Make check payable to Clerk of Court. Search information required: name, date of birth, years to search, SASE.

Civil records are available by mail. No release necessary. $1.00 fee for each year searched. $1.00 fee per copy, $1.00 fee for certification. Search information required: name, date of birth, years to search, SASE. Specify plaintiff or defendant.

Taylor County

Clerk of Circuit Court, Criminal Records
PO Box 620
Perry, FL 32347
(904) 584-3531

Felony and misdemeanor records are available by mail or phone. No release necessary. No search fee from 1982 forward. $1.00 search fee per year prior to 1982. $1.00 for certification. Make company check payable to Clerk of Circuit Court. Search information required: name, date of birth, sex, race.

Civil records are available by mail. No release necessary. No search fee from 1982 forward. $1.00 search fee prior to 1982. $1.00 for certification. Search information required: name, date of birth, years to search. Specify plaintiff or defendant.

Union County

Union County Courthouse, Criminal Records
Room 103
Lake Butler, FL 32054
(904) 496-3711

Felony and misdemeanor records are available by mail or phone. No release necessary. No search fee. $1.00 fee for first page of copies, $.15 each additional copy. Search information required: name, years to search, SASE.

Civil records are available by mail or phone. No release necessary. No search fee. 1.00 fee for first page of copies, $.15 each additional copy. Search information required: name, date of birth, years to search, SASE. Specify plaintiff or defendant.

Volusia County

Felony and misdemeanor records
Volusia County Courthouse
PO Box 43
DeLand, FL 32721
(904) 736-5909

Felony and misdemeanor records are available by mail or fax. No release necessary. $1.00 fee for each year searched per department. $1.00 fee per copy. $1.00 for certification. Company checks only, payable to Clerk of Court. Search information required: name, SSN, date of birth, sex, race, years to search. Specify department (felony or misdemeanor).

Civil records
Volusia County Courthouse
PO Box 43
DeLand, FL 32721
(904) 736-5907

Civil records are available by mail. No release necessary. $1.00 fee for each year searched. $1.00 fee per copy. $1.00 for certification. Search information required: name, date of birth, years to search. Specify plaintiff or defendant.

Wakulla County

Clerk of Circuit Court, Criminal Records
PO Box 337
Crawfordville, FL 32327
(904) 926-3341

Felony and misdemeanor records are available by mail. No release necessary. $1.00 fee per year searched. $.15 fee for first page of copies, $1.00 each additional copy. $1.00 for certification. Search information required: name, SSN, date of birth, sex, race.

Civil records are available by mail. No release necessary. $1.00 fee per year searched.. $.15 fee for first page of copies, $1.00 each additional copy. $1.00 for certification. Search information required: name, date of birth, years to search. Specify plaintiff or defendant.

Walton County

Clerk of the Circuit Court, Criminal Records
PO Box 1260
De Funiak Springs, FL 32433
(904) 892-8115
Fax (904) 892-8130

Felony and misdemeanor records are available by mail, fax or phone. No release necessary. $1.00 fee for each year searched. $1.00 fee per copy. $2.00 for certification. Make check payable to Clerk of Court. Search information required: name, date of birth, years to search.

Civil records are available by mail, fax or phone. No release necessary. $1.00 fee for each year searched. $1.00 fee per copy. $2.00 for certification. Search information required: name, date of birth, years to search. Specify plaintiff or defendant.

Washington County

Clerk of Court, Criminal Records
PO Box 647
Chipley, FL 32428
(904) 638-6289

Felony and misdemeanor records are available by mail or phone. No release necessary. $1.00 fee for each year searched. $1.00 fee per copy. $2.00 for certification. Make check payable to Clerk of Court. Search information required: name, SSN, date of birth, sex, race, SASE.

Civil records are available by mail. No release necessary. $1.00 fee for each year searched. $1.00 fee per copy. $2.00 for certification. Search information required: name, date of birth, years to search, SASE. Specify plaintiff or defendant.

City-County Cross Reference

Alachua *Alachua*
Alford *Jackson*
Altamonte Springs
  Seminole
Altha *Calhoun*
Altoona *Lake*
Alturas *Polk*
Alva *Lee*
Anna Maria *Manatee*
Anthony *Marion*
Apalachicola *Franklin*
Apollo Beach
  Hillsborough
Apopka *Orange*
Arcadia *DeSoto*
Archer *Alachua*
Argyle *Walton*
Aripeka *Pasco*
Astatula *Lake*
Astor *Lake*
Atlantic Beach *Duval*
Auburndale *Polk*
Aventura *Dade*
Avon Park *Highlands*
Babson Park *Polk*
Bagdad *Santa Rosa*
Baker *Okaloosa*
Baldwin *Duval*
Balm *Hillsborough*
Barberville *Volusia*
Bartow *Polk*
Bascom *Jackson*
Bay Pines *Pinellas*
Bee Ridge *Sarasota*
Bell *Gilchrist*
Belle Glade *Palm Beach*
Belleair *Pinellas*
Belleview *Marion*
Beverly Hills *Citrus*
Bithlo *Orange*
Blountstown *Calhoun*
Boca Grande *Lee*
Boca Raton *Palm Beach*
Bokeelia *Lee*
Bonifay *Holmes*
Bonita Springs *Lee*
Bostwick *Putnam*
Bowling Green *Hardee*
Boynton Beach *Palm*
  Beach

Bradenton *Manatee*
Bradenton Beach *Manatee*
Bradley *Polk*
Brandon *Hillsborough*
Branford *Suwannee*
Bristol *Liberty*
Bronson *Levy*
Brooker *Bradford*
Brooksville *Hernando*
Bryceville *Nassau*
Bunnell *Flagler*
Bushnell *Sumter*
Callahan *Nassau*
Callaway *Bay*
Campbell *Osceola*
Campbellton *Jackson*
Canal Point *Palm Beach*
Candler *Marion*
Cantonment *Escambia*
Cape Canaveral *Brevard*
Cape Coral *Lee*
Captiva *Lee*
Carol City *Dade*
Carrabelle *Franklin*
Caryville *Washington*
Cassadaga *Volusia*
Casselberry *Seminole*
Cedar Key *Levy*
Center Hill *Sumter*
Century *Escambia*
Chattahoochee *Gadsden*
Chiefland *Levy*
Chipley *Washington*
Chokoloskee *Collier*
Christmas *Orange*
Chuluota *Seminole*
Citra *Marion*
Citrus Springs *Citrus*
Clarcona *Orange*
Clarksville *Calhoun*
Clearwater *Pinellas*
Clermont *Lake*
Clewiston *Hendry*
Cocoa *Brevard*
Cocoa Beach *Brevard*
Coleman *Sumter*
Conway *Orange*
Cooper City *Broward*
Copeland *Collier*
Coral Cove *Sarasota*

Coral Gables *Dade*
Coral Springs *Broward*
Cortez *Manatee*
Cottondale *Jackson*
Crawfordville *Wakulla*
Crescent City *Putnam*
Crestview *Okaloosa*
Cross City *Dixie*
Crystal Beach *Pinellas*
Crystal River *Citrus*
Crystal Springs *Pasco*
Cypress *Jackson*
Dade City *Pasco*
Dania *Broward*
Davenport *Polk*
Davie *Broward*
Day *Lafayette*
Daytona Beach
  Volusia DeBary *Volusia*
Deerfield Beach *Broward*
DeFuniak Springs *Walton*
DeLand *Volusia*
DeLeon Springs *Volusia*
Delray Beach *Palm Beach*
Deltona *Volusia*
Destin *Okaloosa*
Dover *Hillsborough*
Dundee *Polk*
Dunedin *Pinellas*
Dunnellon *Marion*
Durant *Hillsborough*
Eagle Lake *Polk*
Earleton *Alachua*
Eastlake Weir *Marion*
East Palatka *Putnam*
Eastpoint *Franklin*
Eaton Park *Polk*
Ebro *Washington*
Edgewater *Volusia*
Eglin A F B *Okaloosa*
Elfers *Pasco*
Elkton *Saint Johns*
Ellenton *Manatee*
El Portal *Dade*
Englewood *Sarasota*
Ensley *Escambia*
Estero *Lee*
Eustis *Lake*
Everglades City *Collier*
Evinston *Alachua*

Fairfield *Marion*
Felda *Hendry*
Fellsmere *Indian River*
Fernandina Beach *Nassau*
Ferndale *Lake*
Flagler Beach *Flagler*
Florahome *Putnam*
Floral City *Citrus*
Florida City *Dade*
Forest City *Seminole*
Fort Lauderdale *Broward*
Fort McCoy *Marion*
Fort Meade *Polk*
Fort Myers *Lee*
Fort Myers Beach *Lee*
Fort Ogden *DeSoto*
Fort Pierce *Saint Lucie*
Fort Walton Beach
  Okaloosa
Fort White *Columbia*
Fountain *Bay*
Freeport *Walton*
Frostproof *Polk*
Fruitland Park *Lake*
Fruitville *Manatee*
Gainesville *Alachua*
Geneva *Seminole*
Georgetown *Putnam*
Gibsonton *Hillsborough*
Gifford *Indian River*
Glen Saint Mary *Baker*
Golden Gate *Collier*
Goldenrod *Orange*
Gonzalez *Escambia*
Goodland *Collier*
Gotha *Orange*
Goulds *Dade*
Graceville *Jackson*
Graham *Bradford*
Grandin *Putnam*
Grand Island *Lake*
Grand Ridge *Jackson*
Grant *Brevard*
Green Cove Springs *Clay*
Greensboro *Gadsden*
Greenville *Madison*
Greenwood *Jackson*
Gretna *Gadsden*
Grove City *Charlotte*
Groveland *Lake*

Gulf Breeze *Santa Rosa*
Gulf Hammock *Levy*
Gulf Port *Pinellas*
Haines City *Polk*
Hallandale *Broward*
Hampton *Bradford*
Harlem *Henry*
Harold *Santa Rosa*
Hastings *Saint Johns*
Havana *Gadsden*
Hawthorne *Alachua*
Hernando *Citrus*
Hialeah *Dade*
Highland City *Polk*
High Springs *Alachua*
Hiland Park *Bay*
Hilliard *Nassau*
Hillsboro Beach *Broward*
Hobe Sound *Martin*
Holder *Citrus*
Holiday *Pasco*
Hollister *Putnam*
Hollywood *Broward*
Holmes Beach *Manatee*
Holt *Okaloosa*
Homeland *Polk*
Homestead *Dade*
Homosassa *Citrus*
Homosassa Springs *Citrus*
Horseshoe Beach *Dixie*
Hosford *Liberty*
Howey In The Hills *Lake*
Hudson *Pasco*
Immokalee *Collier*
Indialantic *Brevard*
Indian Harbour Beach
  Brevard
Indian Rocks Beach
  Pinellas
Indiantown *Martin*
Inglis *Levy*
Intercession City *Osceola*
Interlachen *Putnam*
Inverness *Citrus*
Inwood *Polk*
Islamorada *Monroe*
Island Grove *Alachua*
Istachatta *Hernando*
Jacksonville *Duval*
Jasper *Hamilton*
Jay *Santa Rosa*
Jennings *Hamilton*
Jensen Beach *Martin*
Juno Beach *Palm Beach*
Jupiter *Palm Beach*
Kathleen *Polk*
Kenansville *Osceola*
Kendall *Dade*
Key Largo *Monroe*
Keystone Heights *Clay*
Key West *Monroe*
Killarney *Orange*
Kissimmee *Osceola*
LaBelle *Hendry*
Lacoochee *Pasco*
LaCrosse *Alachua*
Lady Lake *Lake*
Lake Alfred *Polk*
Lake Butler *Union*
Lake City *Columbia*
Lake Como *Putnam*
Lake Geneva *Clay*
Lake Hamilton *Polk*
Lake Harbor *Palm Beach*
Lake Helen *Volusia*
Lakeland *Polk*

Lake Mary *Seminole*
Lake Monroe *Seminole*
Lake Panasoffkee *Sumter*
Lake Placid *Highlands*
Lake Wales *Polk*
Lake Worth *Palm Beach*
Lamont *Jefferson*
Land O'Lakes *Pasco*
Lantana *Palm Beach*
Largo *Pinellas*
Laurel *Sarasota*
Laurel Hill *Okaloosa*
Lawtey *Bradford*
Lecanto *Citrus*
Lee *Madison*
Leesburg *Lake*
Lehigh Acres *Lee*
Leisure City *Dade*
Lithia *Hillsborough*
Live Oak *Suwannee*
Lloyd *Jefferson*
Lochloosa *Alachua*
Long Key *Monroe*
Longboat Key *Manatee*
Longwood *Seminole*
Lorida *Highlands*
Loughman *Polk*
Lowell *Marion*
Loxahatchee *Palm Beach*
Lutz *Hillsborough*
Lynn Haven *Bay*
McAlpin *Suwannee*
McDavid *Escambia*
McIntosh *Marion*
MacClenny *Baker*
Madeira Beach *Pinellas*
Madison *Madison*
Maitland *Orange*
Malabar *Brevard*
Malone *Jackson*
Mango *Hillsborough*
Marathon *Monroe*
Marco *Collier*
Margate *Broward*
Marianna *Jackson*
Mary Esther *Okaloosa*
Mascotte *Lake*
Matlacha *Lee*
Mayo *Lafayette*
Melbourne *Brevard*
Melrose *Putnam*
Memphis *Manatee*
Merritt Island *Brevard*
Miami *Dade*
Micanopy *Alachua*
Middleburg *Clay*
Midway *Gadsden*
Milton *Santa Rosa*
Mims *Brevard*
Minneola *Lake*
Miramar *Broward*
Molino *Escambia*
Monticello *Jefferson*
Montverde *Lake*
Moore Haven *Glades*
Morriston *Levy*
Mount Dora *Lake*
Mulberry *Polk*
Myakka City *Manatee*
Naples *Collier*
Nalcrest *Polk*
Naranja *Dade*
Neptune Beach *Duval*
Newberry *Alachua*
New Port Richey *Pasco*
New Smyrna Beach

  Volusia
Niceville *Okaloosa*
Nichols *Polk*
Nobleton *Hernando*
Nocatee *DeSoto*
Nokomis *Sarasota*
Noma *Holmes*
Oak Hill *Volusia*
Oakland *Orange*
Oakland Park *Broward*
O'Brien *Suwannee*
Ocala *Marion*
Ocean Ridge *Palm Beach*
Ochopee *Collier*
Ocoee *Orange*
Odessa *Hillsborough*
Ojus *Dade*
Okahumpka *Lake*
Okeechobee *Okeechobee*
Oklawaha *Marion*
Oldsmar *Pinellas*
Old Town *Dixie*
Ona *Hardee*
Oneco *Manatee*
Opa-Locka *Dade*
Orange City *Volusia*
Orange Lake *Marion*
Orange Park *Clay*
Orange Springs *Marion*
Orlando *Orange*
Orlovista *Orange*
Ormond Beach *Volusia*
Osprey *Sarasota*
Osteen *Volusia*
Otter Creek *Levy*
Oviedo *Seminole*
Oxford *Sumter*
Ozona *Pinellas*
Pace *Santa Rosa*
Pahokee *Palm Beach*
Paisley *Lake*
Palatka *Putnam*
Palm Beach *Palm Beach*
Palm City *Martin*
Palma Sola *Manatee*
Palmdale *Glades*
Palmetto *Manatee*
Palm Bay *Brevard*
Palm Harbor *Pinellas*
Palm Springs *Palm Beach*
Panacea *Wakulla*
Panama City *Bay*
Parker *Bay*
Parrish *Manatee*
Penney Farms *Clay*
Pensacola *Escambia*
Perrine *Dade*
Perry *Taylor*
Pierson *Volusia*
Pineland *Lee*
Pinellas Park *Pinellas*
Pinetta *Madison*
Pinewood *Dade*
Placida *Charlotte*
Plant City *Hillsborough*
Plymouth *Orange*
Plantation *Monroe*
Point Washington *Walton*
Polk City *Polk*
Pomona Park *Putnam*
Pompano Beach *Broward*
Ponce DeLeon *Holmes*
Ponte Vedra Beach *Saint
  Johns*
Port Charlotte *Charlotte*
Port Orange *Volusia*

Port Richey *Pasco*
Port Saint Joe *Gulf*
Port Salerno *Martin*
Princeton *Dade*
Punta Gorda *Charlotte*
Putnam Hall *Putnam*
Quincy *Gadsden*
Raiford *Union*
Reddick *Marion*
Riverview *Hillsborough*
Rockledge *Brevard*
Roseland *Indian River*
Ruskin *Hillsborough*
Safety Harbor *Pinellas*
Saint Augustine *Saint
  Johns*
Saint Cloud *Osceola*
Saint James City *Lee*
Saint Leo *Pasco*
Saint Marks *Wakulla*
Saint Petersburg *Pinellas*
Salem *Taylor*
Salt Springs *Marion*
Samoset *Manatee*
San Antonio *Pasco*
Sanderson *Baker*
Sanford *Seminole*
Sanibel *Lee*
San Mateo *Putnam*
Santa Rosa Beach *Walton*
Sarasota *Sarasota*
Satellite Beach *Brevard*
Satsuma *Putnam*
Scottsmoor *Brevard*
Sebastian *Indian River*
Sebring *Highlands*
Seffner *Hillsborough*
Seminole *Pinellas*
Seville *Volusia*
Shady Grove *Taylor*
Shalimar *Okaloosa*
Sharpes *Brevard*
Silver Springs *Marion*
Sneads *Jackson*
Solana *Charoltte*
Sopchoppy *Wakulla*
Sorrento *Lake*
South Bay *Palm Beach*
Sparr *Marion*
Springfield *Bay*
Starke *Bradford*
Steinhatchee *Taylor*
Stock Island *Monroe*
Stuart *Martin*
Summerfield *Marion*
Summerland Key *Monroe*
Sumterville *Sumter*
Sun City *Hillsborough*
Surfside *Dade*
Suwannee *Dixie*
Sweetwater *Dade*
Sydney *Hillsborough*
Taft *Orange*
Tallahassee *Leon*
Tallevast *Manatee*
Tamaral *Broward*
Tampa *Hillsborough*
Tangerine *Orange*
Tarpon Springs *Pinellas*
Tavares *Lake*
Tavernier *Monroe*
Tequesta *Palm Beach*
Telogia *Liberty*
Terra Ceia *Manatee*
Thonotosassa *Hillsborough*
Tice *Lee*

Titusville *Brevard*
Trenton *Gilchrist*
Trilby *Pasco*
Umatilla *Lake*
Valparaiso *Okaloosa*
Valrico *Hillsborough*
Venice *Sarasota*
Venus *Highlands*
Vernon *Washington*
Vero Beach *Indian River*
Wabasso *Indian River*
Wacissa *Jefferson*
Waldo *Alachua*
Warrington *Escambia*
Wauchula *Hardee*
Wausau *Washington*
Waverly *Polk*
Webster *Sumter*
Weirsdale *Marion*
Welaka *Putnam*
Wellington *Palm Beach*
Wellborn *Suwannee*
West Palm Beach *Palm Beach*
Westchester *Dade*
Weston *Broward*
Westville *Holmes*
Wewahitchka *Gulf*
White City *St. Lucie*
White Springs *Hamilton*
Wildwood *Sumter*
Williston *Levy*
Wimauma *Hillsborough*
Windermere *Orange*
Winter Beach *Indian River*
Winter Garden *Orange*
Winter Haven *Polk*
Winter Park *Orange*
Woodville *Leon*
Worthington Springs *Union*
Yalaha *Lake*
Yankeetown *Levy*
Youngstown *Bay*
Yulee *Nassau*
Zellwood *Orange*
Zephyrhills *Pasco*
Zolfo Springs *Hardee*

Georgia

All one hundred fifty nine (159) of Georgia's counties reported that criminal records were generally accessible for employment screening purposes. However, seventy eight (78) of these require records requests to be made in person, leaving only eighty one (81) Georgia counties accepting mail or phone requests from employers.

For more information or for offices not listed, contact the state's information hot line at (404) 656-2000.

Driving Records

Department of Public Safety
Driver Services
PO Box 1456
Atlanta, GA 30371
(404) 624-7487

Driving records available by mail. $5.00 fee for 3 year search, $7.00 fee for 7 year search. Turnaround time is 3-4 weeks. Written request must include job applicant's full name, date of birth, license number and a notarized release signed by job applicant. Also specify the number of years to be searched (3 or 7) and include appropriate fee. Make money order, company or cashier's check payable to Department of Public Safety.

Worker's Compensation Records

State Board of Worker's
Compensation
One CNN Center
Suite 1000
South CNN Center
Atlanta, GA 30303-2705
(404) 656-2937

Worker's compensation records are available only to the employee involved in the case.

Vital Statistics

Georgia Department of Human Resources
Vital Records Unit, Room 217-H
47 Trinity Avenue Southwest
Atlanta, GA 30334
(404) 656-7456

Birth and death records are available for $3.00 each. State office has had records since January 1919. For earlier records in Atlanta or Savannah, write to County Health Department in county where event occurred. Duplicate copies ordered at the same time are $1.00 each. Some records are accessible by computer. Make certified check or money order payable to Georgia Department of Human Resources.

Marriage records are available through county court where marriage took place. Divorce records are available at county court where divorce granted.

Department of Education

Professional Standards Commission
Certification Section
1452 Twin Towers East
Atlanta, GA 30334
(404) 656-2406
Fax (404) 651-9185

Field of certification, effective date, and expiration date are available by phone or mail. Include name and SSN.

Medical Licensing

Medical Board
166 Pryor St.
Atlanta, GA 30303
(404) 656-3913

Will confirm licenses for MDs and DOs by mail. No fee. Include name and license number. For licenses not mentioned, contact the above office.

Georgia Board of Nursing
166 Pryor Street, SW
Atlanta, GA 30303
(404) 656-3943

Will confirm license by mail. No fee. Include name, license number.

Bar Association

State Bar Association
800 Hurt Building
50 Hurt Plaza
Atlanta, GA 30303
(404) 527-8700

Will confirm licenses by phone. No fee. Include name.

Accountancy Board

Georgia State Board of Accountancy
166 Pryor Street Southwest
Atlanta, GA 30303
(404) 656-3941

Will confirm licenses by phone. No fee. Include name.

Securities Commission

Securities Commissioner
315 West Tower
2 Martin Luther King, Jr. Drive
Atlanta, GA 30334-1530
(404) 656-2894

Will confirm licenses by phone. No fee. Include name and SSN.

Secretary of State

Secretary of State
Corporation Division
2 Martin Luther King Drive
Suite 315 West
Atlanta, GA 30334
(404) 656-2817

Service agent and address, date incorporated, standing with tax commission, are available by phone or mail. No fee. Contact the above office for additional information

Criminal Records

State Repository

Georgia Crime Information Center
Identification Division
PO Box 370748
Decatur, GA 30037-0748
(404) 244-2644

Felony and misdemeanor records are available by mail only. Each request must include subject's full name, date of birth, sex, race and SSN. Also, include one set of fingerprints, an affidavit signed by the person to be searched specifically authorizing the "Georgia Crime Information Center" to release the records, and a separate money order for $7.50 payable to the Georgia Bureau of Investigation for each subject. Fee is subject to change. Information supplied includes both arrest and conviction data. There is a 7-10 day turnaround plus mail time.

Appling County

Appling County Courthouse, Criminal Records
Baxley, GA 31513
(912) 367-8126

Records are available in person only. See Georgia state repository for additional information.

Civil records are available in person only. See Georgia state repository for additional information.

Atkinson County

Clerk of Superior Court
PO Box 6
Pearson, GA 31642
(912) 422-3343

Felony and misdemeanor records are available in person only. See Georgia state repository for additional information.

Civil records are available in person only. See Georgia state repository for additional information.

Bacon County

Clerk of Superior Court
PO Box 376
Alma, GA 31510
(912) 632-4915

Felony and misdemeanor records are available by mail. A release is required. No search fee. $.25 fee per copy. $2.50 for certification. Search information required: name, years to search, SASE.

Civil records are available by mail. No release necessary. A release is required. No search fee. $.25 fee per copy. $2.50 for certification. Search information required: name, years to search, SASE. Specify plaintiff or defendant.

Baker County

Clerk of Superior Court
PO Box 10
Newton, GA 31770
(912) 734-3004

Felony and misdemeanor records are available in person only. See Georgia state repository for additional information.

Civil records are available in person only. See Georgia state repository for additional information.

Baldwin County

Clerk of Superior Court
PO Drawer 987
Milledgeville, GA 31061
(912) 453-4007

Felony and misdemeanor records are available in person only. See Georgia state repository for additional information.

Civil records are available in person only. See Georgia state repository for additional information.

Banks County

Clerk of Court
PO Drawer C
Homer, GA 30547
(404) 677-2320 Ext. 240

Felony and misdemeanor records are available by mail. No release necessary. $5.00 search fee. $.25 fee per copy. $3.50 for certification. Search information required: name. Turnaround time is 1-2 weeks.

Civil records are available by mail. No release necessary. $5.00 search fee. $.25 fee per copy. $3.50 for certification. Search information required: name, date of birth, years to search. Specify plaintiff or defendant.

Barrow County

Clerk of Court
PO Box 1280
Winder, GA 30680
(404) 307-3035

Felony and misdemeanor records are available in person only. See Georgia state repository for additional information.

Civil records are available in person only. See Georgia state repository for additional information.

Bartow County

Clerk's Office, Felony check
Superior Court, PO Box 749
Courthouse
Cartersville, GA 30120
(404) 382-2930

Felony and misdemeanor records are available in person only. See Georgia state repository for additional information.

Civil records are available in person only. See Georgia state repository for additional information.

Ben Hill County

Clerk of Superior Court, Felony check
PO Box 1104
Fitzgerald, GA 31750
(912) 423-3736

Felony and misdemeanor records are available by mail or phone. No search fee. $.25 fee per copy, $2.50 fee for certification, $1.00 fee if sealed. Search information required: name, years to search. Turnaround time is 1 week.

Civil records are available by mail. No release necessary. No search fee. $.25 fee per copy, $2.50 fee for certification. Search information required: name, date of birth, years to search. Specify plaintiff or defendant.

Berrien County

Clerk of the Superior Court
Courthouse
Nashville, GA 31639
(912) 686-5506

Felony and misdemeanor records are available in person only. See Georgia state repository for additional information.

Civil records are available in person only. See Georgia state repository for additional information.

Bibb County

Felony records
Clerk of Superior Court
PO Box 1015
Macon, GA 31202-1015
(912) 749-6527 Extension 512

Felony records are available by mail. No release necessary. $10.00 search fee. Search information required: name, SSN, years to search. Make request to the attention of Aline Byrd.

Civil records
Clerk of Superior Court
PO Box 1015
Macon, GA 31202-1015
(912) 749-6527 Extension 512

Civil records are available in person only. See Georgia state repository for additional information.

Misdemeanor records
Bibb County State Court
PO Box 5086
Macon, GA 31213-7199
(912) 749-6676

Misdmeanor records are available in person only. See Georgia state repository for additional information

Civil records
Bibb County State Court
PO Box 5086
Macon, GA 31213-7199
(912) 749-6330

Civil records are available by mail. No release necessary. $5.00 search fee. Search information required: name, date of birth, years to search. Specify plaintiff or defendant.

Bleckley County

Clerk of Superior Court, Criminal Records
Bleckley County Courthouse
Cochran, GA 31014
(912) 934-3210
Fax (912) 934-3205

Felony and misdemeanor records are available in person only. See Georgia state repository for additional information.

Civil records are available in person only. See Georgia state repository for additional information.

Brantley County

Clerk of Superior Court, Felony check
PO Box 1067
Nahunta, GA 31553
(912) 462-5635
Fax (912) 462-5538

Felony and misdemeanor records are available by mail. No release necessary. No search fee. $.25 fee per copy. $3.00 for certification. Search information required: name, date of birth, SSN, years to search, SASE.

Civil records are available by mail. No release necessary. No search fee. $.25 fee per copy. $3.00 for certification. Search information required: name, date of birth, years to search. Specify plaintiff or defendant.

Brooks County

Clerk of Superior Court, Felony Records
PO Box 630
Quitman, GA 31643
(912) 263-4747

Felony and misdemeanor records are available by mail. No release necessary. No search fee. $1.00 fee per copy. Search information required: name, years to search, SASE. Specify reason for requesting information.

Civil records are available by mail. No release necessary. No search fee. $1.00 fee per copy. Search information required: name, years to search, reason for requesting information, SASE. Specify plaintiff or defendant.

Bryan County

Clerk of Superior Court, Felony check
PO Drawer H
Pembroke, GA 31321
(912) 653-4681

Felony and misdemeanor records are available in person only. See Georgia state repository for additional information.

Civil records are available in person only. See Georgia state repository for additional information.

Bulloch County

Clerk of Court, Criminal Records
Bulloch County Courthouse
N. Main Street
Statesboro, GA 30458
(912) 764-9009

Felony and misdemeanor records are available in person only. See Georgia state repository for additional information.

Civil records are available in person only. See Georgia state repository for additional information.

Burke County

Clerk of Superior Court
PO Box 803
Waynesboro, GA 30830
(404) 554-2279

Felony and misdemeanor records are available in person only. See Georgia state repository for additional information.

Civil records are available in person only. See Georgia state repository for additional information.

Butts County

Clerk of Superior Court, Felony check
PO Box 320
Jackson, GA 30233
(404) 775-8215

Felony and misdemeanor records are available by mail. No release necessary. No search fee. $.25 fee per copy. $2.50 for first page certified, $.50 each additional page. Search information required: name, years to search, SASE.

Civil records are available by mail. No release necessary. No search fee. $.25 fee per copy. $2.50 for first certification, $.50 each additional. Search information required: name, years to search, SASE. Specify plaintiff or defendant.

Calhoun County

Clerk of Superior Court, Criminal Records
PO Box 68
Morgan, GA 31766
(912) 849-2715

Felony and misdemeanor records are available by mail. No release necessary. No search fee. $.25 fee per copy. $3.00 for certification. Make check payable to Clerk of Superior Court. Search information required: name, SSN, SASE.

Civil records are available by mail. No release necessary. No search fee. $.25 fee per copy. $3.00 for certification. Search information required: name, years to search., SASE. Specify plaintiff or defendant.

Camden County

Clerk of Superior Court, Criminal Records
PO Box 578
Woodbine, GA 31569
(912) 576-5601 Extension 211

Felony and misdemeanor records are available in person only. See Georgia state repository for additional information.

Civil records are available in person only. See Georgia state repository for additional information.

Candler County

Clerk of Superior Court, Felony check
PO Box 830
Metter, GA 30439
(912) 685-5257

Felony and misdemeanor records are available by mail. A release is required. No search fee. $.25 fee per copy. $3.00 for certification. Search information required: name, years to search, SASE.

Civil records are available by mail. A release is required. No search fee. $.25 fee per copy. $3.00 for certification. Search information required: name, years to search. Specify plaintiff or defendant.

Carroll County

Clerk of Superior Court
PO Box 1620
Carrollton, GA 30117
(404) 830-5830

Felony and misdemeanor records are available by mail. No release necessary. $5.00 search fee. $.25 fee per copy, $2.50 fee for certification. Search information required: name, SSN if available, years to search, SASE.

Civil records are available by mail. No release necessary. $5.00 search fee. $.25 fee per copy, $2.50 fee for certification. Search information required: name, date of birth, years to search. Specify plaintiff or defendant.

Catoosa County

Catoosa County Courthouse, Criminal Records
Ringgold, GA 30736
(404) 935-4231

Records are available in person only. See Georgia state repository for additional information.

Civil records are available in person only. See Georgia state repository for additional information.

Charlton County

Clerk of the Superior Court, Criminal Records
Charlton County Courthouse
Folkston, GA 31537
(912) 496-2354

Felony and misdemeanor records are available by mail. No release necessary. No search fee. $.25 fee per copy, $2.50 fee for certification. Search information required: name, years to search, SASE.

Civil records are available by mail. No release necessary. No search fee. $.25 fee per copy, $2.50 fee for certification. Search information required: name, years to search. Specify plaintiff or defendant.

Chatham County

State Court of Chatham County
Crimial Records
Room 308
Savannah, GA 31401
(912) 652-7227
Fax (912) 652-7229

Felony and misdemeanor records are available by mail. No release necessary. $3.00 search fee. $.25 fee per copy. $1.75 for certification. Search information required: name, date of birth, years to search, SASE.

Civil records are available by mail. No release necessary. $3.00 search fee. $.25 fee per copy. $1.75 for certification. Search information required: name, date of birth, years to search, SASE. Specify plaintiff or defendant.

Chattahoochee County

Clerk of the Superior Court, Criminal Records
PO Box 120
Cusseta, GA 31805
(404) 989-3424

Records are available in person only. See Georgia state repository for additional information.

Civil records are available by mail. No release necessary. No search fee. $.25 fee per copy. $3.00 for certification. Search information required: name, date of birth, years to search, SASE. Specify plaintiff or defendant.

Chattooga County

Clerk of Superior Court, Criminal Records
PO Box 159
Summerville, GA 30747
(404) 857-2594

Felony and misdemeanor records are available in person only. See Georgia state repository for additional information.

Civil records are available in person only. See Georgia state repository for additional information.

Cherokee County

Clerk of Superior Court
100 N. Street, Room 3
Canton, GA 30114
(404) 479-1953 Extension 0538

Records are available in person only. See Georgia state repository for additional information.

Civil records are available in person only. See Georgia state repository for additional information.

Clarke County

Clerk of Superior Court, Criminal Records
PO Box 1805
Athens, GA 30603
(404) 613-3190

Felony and misdemeanor records are available in person only. See Georgia state repository for additional information.

Civil records are available in person only. See Georgia state repository for additional information.

Clay County

Clerk of Superior Court, Felony check
PO Box 550
Ft. Gaines, GA 31751
(912) 768-2631

Felony and misdemeanor records are available by mail. A release is required. $15.00 fee. Company checks only, payable to Clerk of Superior Court. Search information required: name, date of birth, years to search. Turnaround time is 1 week.

Civil records are available by mail. A release isrequired. $10.00 search fee. $.25 fee per copy. $3.00 for certification. Search information required: name, date of birth, years to search. Specify plaintiff or defendant.

Clayton County

Clerk of Superior Court, Criminal Records
Clayton County Courthouse
Jonesboro, GA 30236
(404) 477-3405

Felony records are available by mail or phone. A release is required. No search fee. $.25 fee per copy. $2.50 for first page certified, $.50 for each additional page. Search information required: full name, date of birth, years to search, SASE.

Civil records are available by mail or phone. No release necessary. No search fee. $.25 fee per copy. $2.50 for first page certified, $.50 for each additional page. Search information required: name, date of birth, years to search. Specify plaintiff or defendant.

Clinch County

Clerk of Superior Court, Criminal Records
PO Box 433
Homerville, GA 31634
(912) 487-5854

Felony and misdemeanor records are available by mail. No release necessary. No search fee for first 15 minutes. $4.50 fee per hour therafter. $.25 fee per copy, $3.00 for certification. Search information required: name, SSN, years to search

Civil records are available by mail. No release necessary. No search fee for first 15 minutes. $.25 fee per copy, $3.00 for certification. Search information required: name, date of birth, years to search. Specify plaintiff or defendant.

Cobb County

Clerk of Superior Court, Criminal Records
32 Waddell Street
Marietta, GA 30090-9640
(404) 528-1304

Records are available by mail or by phone from 1982 forward. No release necessary. No search fee. $.25 fee per copy, $2.75 for certification. Search information required: name, SASE.

Civil records are available by mail. No release necessary. No search fee. Search information required: name, date of birth, years to search, SASE. Specify plaintiff or defendant.

Coffee County

Clerk of Court, Criminal Records
Coffee County Courthouse
Douglas, GA 31533
(912) 384-2865

Felony and misdemeanor records are available in person only. See Georgia state repository for additional information.

Civil records are available by mail. A release is required. No search fee. $1.00 fee per copy. $3.00 for certification. Search information required: name, date of birth, years to search. Specify plaintiff or defendant.

Colquitt County

Clerk of Superior Court, Criminal Records
PO Box 886
Moultrie, GA 31776
(912) 985-1324

Felony and misdemeanor (previous five years) records are available by mail only. No release necessary. $2.00 search fee. $1.00 fee per copy. $2.50 for certification. Search information required: name, years to search, SASE.

Civil records are available by mail. A release is required. No search fee. $.25 fee per copy. $2.750 for certification. Search information required: name, date of birth, years to search. Specify plaintiff or defendant.

Columbia County

Clerk of the Superior Court
PO Box 100
Appling, GA 30802
(404) 541-1139

Felony and misdemeanor records are available in person only. See Georgia State Repository for additional information.

Civil records are available in person only. See Georgia state repository for additional information.

Cook County

Clerk of Superior Court, Criminal Records
212 N. Hutchinson Ave.
Adel, GA 31620
(912) 896-7717

Felony and misdemeanor records are available by mail. No release necessary. $5.00 search fee. $.2.50 fee for first copy, $.50 for each additional copy. $2.50 fee for certification. Company checks only, payable to Clerk of Superior Court. Search information required: name, years to search, SASE, date of birth.

Civil records are available by mail. No release necessary. $5.00 search fee. $.2.50 fee for first copy, $.50 for each additional copy. $2.50 fee for certification. Search information required: name, date of birth, years to search. Specify plaintiff or defendant.

Coweta County

Clerk of Superior Court
PO Box 943
Newman, GA 30264
(404) 254-2690

Felony and misdemeanor records are available by mail only. A release is required. No search fee. $.25 fee per copy. $2.50 fee for first certification, $.50 each additional. Make check payable to Clerk of Superior Court. Search information required: name, date of birth, SSN, offense, years to search.

Civil records are available by mail. No release necessary. No search fee. $.25 fee per copy. $2.50 fee for first page certified, $.50 each additional page. Search information required: name, date of birth, years to search. Specify plaintiff or defendant.

Crawford County

Clerk of Superior Court, Felony check
PO Box 419
Knoxville, GA 31050
(912) 836-3328

Felony and misdemeanor records are available by mail. No release necessary. No search fee. $.25 fee per copy, $2.50 fee for certification. Search information required: name, SASE, previous address, years to search.

Civil records are available by mail. No release necessary. No search fee. $.25 fee per copy, $2.50 fee for certification. Search information required: name, date of birth, years to search, SASE. Specify plaintiff or defendant.

Crisp County

Clerk of Superior Court, Criminal Records
PO Box 747
Cordele, GA 31015
(912) 276-2616

Felony and misdemeanor records are available by mail. No release necessary. $5.00 search fee. $.25 fee per copy, $2.50 fee for certification. Search information required: name, date of birth, years to search. See Georgia state repository for additional information.

Civil records are available by mail. No release necessary. $5.00 search fee. $.25 fee per copy, $2.50 fee for certification. Search information required: name, date of birth, years to search. Specify plaintiff or defendant.

Dade County

Clerk of Superior Court, Criminal Records
PO Box 417
Trenton, GA 30752
(404) 657-4778
Fax (404) 398-1616

Felony and misdemeanor records are available by mail. No release necessary. No search fee. Search information required: name, SSN, date of birth, years to search, SASE. Turnaround time is 1 week.

Civil records are available in person only. See Georgia state repository for additional information.

Dawson County

Clerk of Superior Court, Criminal
Records
PO Box 222
Dawsonville, GA 30534
(404) 265-2525

Felony and misdemeanor records are available in person only. See Georgia state repository for additional information.

Civil records are available by mail or phone. No release necessary. No search fee. Search information required: name, years to search. Specify plaintiff or defendant.

De Kalb County

Clerk of Superior Court, Criminal
Division
De Kalb County Courthouse
550 N. McDonoegh
Decatur, GA 30030
(404) 371-2575

Felony and misdemeanor records are available by phone. $10.00 search fee for the past ten years. $15.00 for additional years. No release necessary. Search information required: name.

Civil records are available in person only. See Georgia state repository for additional information.

Decatur County

Clerk of Court, Felony check
PO Box 336
Bainbridge, GA 31717
(912) 248-3025

Felony and misdemeanor records are available in person only. See Georgia State Repository for additional information.

Civil records are available in person only. See Georgia state repository for additional information.

Dodge County

Clerk of Superior Court, Criminal
Records
PO Box 4276
Eastman, GA 31023
(912) 374-2871

Felony and misdemeanor records are available in person only. For additional information, see Georgia state repository.

Civil records are available in person only. See Georgia state repository for additional information.

Dooly County

Dooly County Clerk of Superior Court
PO Box 326
Vienna, GA 31092-0326
(912) 268-4234
Fax (912) 268-6142

Felony and misdemeanor records are available in person only. See Georgia state repository for additional information.

Civil records are available in person only. See Georgia state repository for additional information.

Dougherty County

Clerk of Superior Court, Criminal
Records
PO Box 1827
Albany, GA 31703
(912) 431-2198

Records are available in person only. See Georgia state repository for additional information.

Civil records are available in person only. See Georgia state repository for additional information.

Douglas County

Clerk of the Superior Court
6754 Broad Street
Douglasville, GA 30134
(404) 949-2000

Felony and misdemeanor records are available in person only. See Georgia state repository for additional information.

Civil records are available in person only. See Georgia state repository for additional information.

Early County

Clerk of Superior Court, Criminal
Records
PO Box 525
Blakely, GA 31723
(912) 723-3033

Felony and misdemeanor records are available by mail. No release necessary. $9.00 search fee. $1.00 fee per copy. $3.00 for certification. Search information required: name, date of birth, years to search, SASE.

Civil records are available by mail. No release necessary. $9.00 search fee. $1.00 fee per copy. $3.00 for certification. Search information required: name, date of birth, years to search, SASE. Specify plaintiff or defendant.

Echols County

Clerk of Superior Court, Criminal
Records
PO Box 213
Statenville, GA 31648
(912) 559-5642

Records are available in person only. See Georgia state repository for additional information.

Civil records are available in person only. See Georgia state repository for additional information.

Effingham County

Clerk of Superior Court, Criminal
Records
PO Box 387
Springfield, GA 31329
(912) 754-6071 Extension 118

Felony and misdemeanor records are available by mail. A notorized release required. $5.00 search fee. Records are only for previous five years. $2.50 for certification. Search information required: name, date of birth, race, sex, SSN, years to search.

Civil records are available by mail. No release necessary. $5.00 search fee. $2.50 for certification. Search information required: name, date of birth, years to search. Specify plaintiff or defendant.

Elbert County

Clerk of Superior Court, Criminal
Records
PO Box 619
Elberton, GA 30635
(404) 283-2005

Felony and misdemeanor records are available by mail or phone. No release necessary. No search fee. $.25 fee per copy. $1.50 for certification. Search information required: name, date of birth, SSN, years to search.

Civil records are available by mail or phone. No release necessary. No search fee. $.25 fee per copy. $1.50 for certification. Search information required: name, date of birth, years to search. Specify plaintiff or defendant.

Emanuel County

Emanuel County Clerk, Criminal
Records
PO Box 627
Swainsboro, GA 30401
(912) 237-8911

Felony and misdemeanor records are available in person only. See Georgia state repository for additional information.

Civil records are available by mail. No release necessary. No search fee. $.25 fee per copy. $1.75 for certification. Search information required: name, date of birth, years to search. Specify plaintiff or defendant.

Evans County

Clerk of Superior Court, Criminal
Records
PO Box 845
Claxton, GA 30417
(912) 739-3868

Records are available in person only. See Georgia state repository for additional information.

Civil records are available by mail. No release necessary. No search fee. $.25 fee per copy. $2.50 for first certification, $.50 each additional. Search information required: name, date of birth, years to search. Specify plaintiff or defendant.

Fannin County

Clerk of Superior Court, Criminal
Records
PO Box 1300
Blue Ridge, GA 30513
(404) 632-2039

Felony and misdemeanor records are available in person only. See Georgia state repository for additional information.

Civil records are available in person only. See Georgia state repository for additional information.

Fayette County

Clerk of Superior Court, Criminal
Records
PO Box 130
Fayetteville, GA 30214
(404) 461-4703

Records are available in person only. See Georgia state repository for additional information.

Civil records are available in person only. See Georgia state repository for additional information.

Floyd County

Clerk of Superior Court
Floyd County Courthouse
4th Avenue
Rome, GA 30161
(404) 291-5191

Records are available in person only. See Georgia state repository for additional information.

Civil records are available in person only. See Georgia state repository for additional information.

Forsyth County

Clerk of Superior Court, Criminal Records
Room 110
Forsyth County Courthouse
Cumming, GA 30130
(404) 781-2120

Felony and misdemeanor records are available by mail. No release necessary. No search fee. $.25 fee per copy. $2.50 for certification. Search information required. name, SSN, years to search, SASE.

Civil records are available by mail. No release necessary. No search fee. $.25 fee per copy. $2.50 for certification. Search information required: name, date of birth, years to search. Specify plaintiff or defendant.

Franklin County

Clerk of Superior Court, Felony check
PO Box 70
Carnesville, GA 30521
(404) 384-2514

Records are available by mail. A release is required. $5.00 search fee. $.25 fee per copy. $2.50 for certification. Search information required: name, date of birth, years to search, SASE.

Civil records are available by mail. No release necessary. No search fee. $.25 fee per copy. $2.50 for certification. Search information required: name, date of birth, years to search. Specify plaintiff or defendant.

Fulton County

Clerk of Superior Court, Criminal Records
136 Pryor Street
Room 606
Atlanta, GA 30303
(404) 730-5242

Felony records are available by mail. No release necessary. $15.00 fee. Cashiers or certified check payable to Clerk of Superior Court. Search information required: name, SSN, date of birth, sex, race, SASE. Turnaround time is 2 week.

Civil records are available in person only. See Georgia state repository for additional information.

Gilmer County

Clerk of Superior Court, Criminal Records
No. 1 West Side Square
Gilmer County Courthouse
Ellijay, GA 30540
(404) 635-4462
Fax (404) 635-1462

Felony and misdemeanor records are available by mail, fax or phone. No release necessary. No search fee. $.25 fee per copy. $2.50 for first certification, $.50 each additional. Search information required: name, SASE.

Civil records are available by mail, fax or phone. No release necessary. No search fee. $.25 fee per copy. $2.50 for first certification, $.50 each additional. Search information required: name, date of birth, years to search, SASE. Specify plaintiff or defendant.

Glascock County

Clerk of Superior Court, Criminal Records
PO Box 231
Gibson, GA 30810
(404) 598-2084

Records are available in person only. See Georgia state repository for additional information.

Civil records are available in person only. See Georgia state repository for additional information.

Glynn County

Clerk of Superior Court, Felony Check
PO Box 1355
Brunswick, GA 31521
(912) 267-5610

Felony records are available by mail or by phone from 1987 forward . No release necessary. No search fee. $5.00 search fee for records prior to 1987. Search information required: name, years to search, SASE. Turnaround time is 1 week.

Civil records are available by mail. No release necessary. $5.00 search fee. Search information required: name, date of birth, years to search, SASE. Specify plaintiff or defendant.

Gordon County

Clerk of Superior Court, Criminal Records
PO Box 367
Calhoun, GA 30703
(404) 629-9533 Ext. 120

Felony and misdemeanor records are available by mail. A release is required. No search fee. $.25 fee per copy. $2.50 for certification. Search information required: name, SSN, date of birth, sex, race, SASE. Turnaround time is 1 week.

Civil records are available by mail. No release necessary. No search fee. $.25 fee per copy. $2.50 for certification. Search information required: name, date of birth, years to search, SASE. Specify plaintiff or defendant.

Grady County

Clerk of Superior Court, Criminal Records
250 N. Broad Street
Box 8
Cairo, GA 31728
(912) 377-2912

Felony and misdemeanor records are available in person only. See Georgia state repository for additional information.

Civil records are available in person only. See Georgia state repository for additional information.

Greene County

Courthouse, Criminal Records
Greensboro, GA 30642
(404) 453-3340

Felony and misdemeanor records are available by mail or phone. A release is required. No search fee. Search information required: name, years to search, SASE.

Civil records are available by mail. A release is required. No search fee. $.25 fee per copy. $2.00 for first certification, Search information required: name, date of birth, years to search, SASE. Specify plaintiff or defendant.

Gwinnett County

Clerk of Superior Court, Criminal Records
PO Box 880
Lawrenceville, GA 30246
(404) 962-1409

Records are available in person only. See Georgia state repository for additional information.

Civil records are available in person only. See Georgia state repository for additional information.

Habersham County

Clerk of Superior Court, Criminal Records
PO Box 108
Clarkesville, GA 30523
(404) 754-2923

Felony and misdemeanor records are available by mail. No release necessary. No search fee. $.25 fee per copy. $2.25 for certification. Search information required: name, SSN, date of birth, sex, race, years to search, SASE.

Civil records are available by mail. No release necessary. No search fee. $.25 fee per copy. $2.25 for certification. Search information required: name, date of birth, years to search. Specify plaintiff or defendant.

Hall County

Clerk of Superior Court, Criminal Records
PO Box 1275
Gainesville, GA 30503
(404) 531-7000
Fax (404) 536-0702

Felony and misdemeanor records are available by mail or fax. No release necessary. $5.85 search fee per hour. Search information required: name, date of birth, years to search, SASE.

Civil records are available in person only. See Georgia state repository for additional information.

Hancock County

Clerk of Superior Court, Criminal
Records
PO Box 451
Sparta, GA 31087
(404) 444-6644 Extension 215
Fax (404) 444-6221

Felony and misdemeanor records are available by mail. No release necessary. $20.00 search fee. $.25 fee per copy. $4.50 for certification. Make check payable to Clerk of Superior Court. Search information required: name, SSN, date of birth, years to search, SASE.

Civil records are available by mail. No release necessary. No search fee. $20.00 fee. $.25 fee per copy. $4.50 for certification. Search information required: name, date of birth, years to search. Specify plaintiff or defendant.

Haralson County

Clerk of Superior Court, Criminal
Records
PO Box 373
Buchanan, GA 30113
(404) 646-2005

Felony and misdemeanor records are available by mail. A release is required. No search fee. $.25 fee per copy, $2.50 fee for certification. Search information required: name, SSN, date of birth, sex, race, SASE. Turnaround time is 1 week.

Civil records are available in person only. See Georgia state repository for additional information.

Harris County

Clerk of Superior Court
PO Box 528
Hamilton, GA 31811
(404) 376-7189

Records are available in person only. See Georgia state repository for additional information.

Civil records are available by mail. A release is required. No search fee. $.25 fee per copy. $2.50 for first certification, $.50 each additional. Search information required: name, date of birth, years to search. Specify plaintiff or defendant.

Hart County

Clerk of Superior Court
PO Box 386
Hartwell, GA 30643
(404) 376-7189

Records are available in person only. See Georgia state repository for additional information.

Civil records are available in person only. See Georgia state repository for additional information.

Heard County

Clerk of Superior Court, Criminal
Records
PO Box 240
Franklin, GA 30217
(404) 675-3301

Felony and misdemeanor records are available by mail. No release necessary. No search fee. $.25 fee per copy, $2.50 fee for certification. Search information required: name, years to search, SASE.

Civil records are available by mail. No release necessary. No search fee. $.25 fee per copy, $2.50 fee for certification. Search information required: name, years to search, SASE. Specify plaintiff or defendant

Henry County

Clerk of Superior Court, Criminal
Records
Henry County Courthouse
McDonough, GA 30253
(404) 954-2121

Felony and misdemeanor records are available by mail. A release is required. No search fee. $.25 fee per copy, $2.50 fee for certification. Search information required: name, date of birth, years to search.

Civil records are available in person only. See Georgia state repository for additional information.

Houston County

Felony records
Clerk of Superior Court, Criminal
Records
800 Carroll Street
Perry, GA 31069
(912) 987-2170
Fax (912) 987-3252

Felony records are available by mail. No release necessary. No search fee. $.25 fee per copy, $2.50 for certification, $.50 fee for additional certified copies. Search information required: name, years to search, SASE.

Civil records
Clerk of Superior Court
800 Carroll Street
Perry, GA 31069
(912) 987-2170
Fax (912) 987-3252

Civil records are available by mail. No release necessary. No search fee. $.25 fee per copy, $2.50 for certification, $.50 fee for additional certified copies. Search information required: name, date of birth, years to search, SASE. Specify plaintiff or defendant.

Misdemeanor records
Houston County State Court
202 Carl Vinson Pkwy.
Warner Robins, GA 31088
(912) 542-2105
Fax (912) 542-2077

Misdemeanor records since 1978 are available by mail. No release necessary. No fee. Search information required: name, years to search, SASE.

Irwin County

Clerk of Superior Court
PO Box 186
Ocilla, GA 31774
(912) 468-5356

Records are available in person only. See Georgia state repository for additional information.

Civil records are available in person only. See Georgia state repository for additional information.

Jackson County

Clerk of Superior Court
PO Box 7
Jefferson, GA 30549
(404) 367-1199 Extension 251

Records are available in person only. See Georgia state repository for additional information.

Civil records are available in person only. See Georgia state repository for additional information.

Jasper County

Clerk of Superior Court
Jasper County Courthouse
Monticello, GA 31064
(404) 468-6651

Records are available in person only. See Georgia state repository for additional information.

Civil records are available by mail. No release necessary. No search fee. $.25 fee per copy. $2.50 for certification. Search information required: name, date of birth, years to search. Specify plaintiff or defendant.

Jeff Davis County

Clerk of Superior Court, Criminal
Records
PO Box 248
Hazelhurst, GA 31539
(912) 375-5528
Fax (912) 375-6615

Felony and misdemeanor records are available by mail. A release is required. No search fee. $.25 fee per copy. Search information required: name. Turnaround time is 1 week.

Civil records are available by mail. No release necessary. $3.00 search fee. $.25 fee per copy. $2.50 for certification. Search information required: name, date of birth, years to search. Specify plaintiff or defendant.

Jefferson County

Clerk of Superior Court, Criminal
Records
PO Box 151
Louisville, GA 30434
(912) 625-7922
Fax (912) 625-4004

Felony and misdemeanor records are available by mail or phone. No release necessary. No search fee. Search information required: name, date of birth, SASE.

Civil records are available by mail. No release necessary. No search fee. $.25 fee per copy. $2.50 for first certification, $.50 each additional. Search information required: name, date of birth, years to search. Specify plaintiff or defendant.

Jenkins County

Clerk of Superior Court, Criminal
Records
PO Box 659
Millen, GA 30442
(912) 982-4683

Felony and misdemeanor records are available by mail or phone. No release necessary. No search fee. $.25 fee per copy. $2.50 for certification. Search information required: name, date of birth, years to search.

Civil records are available by mail or phone. No release necessary. No search fee. $.25 fee per copy. $2.50 for certification. Search information required: name, date of birth, years to search. Specify plaintiff or defendant.

Johnson County

Clerk of Superior Court, Criminal Records
PO Box 321
Wrightsville, GA 31096
(912) 864-3484

Felony and misdemeanor records are available by mail or phone. No release necessary. No search fee. $.25 fee per copy. $3.00 for certification. Search information required: name, date of birth, SSN, years to search.

Civil records are available by mail. No release necessary. No search fee. Search information required: name, date of birth, years to search. Specify plaintiff or defendant.

Jones County

Clerk of Superior Court, Criminal Records
PO Box 159
Gray, GA 31032
(912) 986-6671

Felony and misdemeanor records are available in person only. See Georgia state repository for additional information.

Civil records are available in person only. See Georgia state repository for additional information.

Lamar County

Clerk of Superior Court
Lamar County Courthouse
326 Thomaston St.
Barnesville, GA 30204
(404) 358-5145

Records are available in person only. See Georgia state repository for additional information.

Civil records are available in person only. See Georgia state repository for additional information.

Lanier County

Lanier County Courthouse, Criminal Records
Clerk of Superior Court
Lakeland, GA 31635
(912) 482-3594
Fax (912) 482-2413

Felony and misdemeanor records are available by mail or phone. No release necessary. No search fee. Search information required: name, date of birth, SASE.

Civil records are available by mail or phone. No release necessary. No search fee. $.25 fee per copy. $3.00 for certification. Search information required: name, date of birth, years to search. Specify plaintiff or defendant.

Laurens County

Clerk of Superior Court
Board of Commissions
PO Box 2028
Dublin, GA 31040
(912) 272-3210

Felony and misdemeanor records are available by mail. No release necessary. No search fee. $.25 fee per copy. $2.50 for first page certified, $.50 each additional page. Search information required: name, date of birth, SSN, years to search, SASE.

Civil records are available in person only. See Georgia state repository for additional information.

Lee County

Clerk of Superior Court, Criminal Records
PO Box 597
Leesburg, GA 31763
(912) 759-6441

Felony and misdemeanor records are available by mail. No release necessary. $5.00 fee. $.25 fee per copy. $3.00 for certification. Certified check only, payable to Clerk of Superior Court. Search information required: name, date of birth, SASE. Turnaround time is 1 week.

Civil records are available by mail. No release necessary. $5.00 fee. $.25 fee per copy. $3.00 for certification. Search information required: name, date of birth, years to search, SASE. Specify plaintiff or defendant.

Liberty County

Clerk of Superior Court, Felony check
PO Box 50
Hinesville, GA 31313
(912) 876-3625
Fax (912) 369-5463

Felony and misdemeanor records are available by mail or fax. No release necessary. No search fee. $.50 fee per copy. $2.50 for certification. Search information required: name, date of birth, SASE.

Civil records are available by mail. No release necessary. No search fee. $.50 fee per copy. $2.50 for certification. Search information required: name, date of birth, years to search, SASE. Specify plaintiff or defendant.

Lincoln County

Clerk of Superior Court, Criminal Records
PO Box 340
Lincolnton, GA 30817
(404) 359-4444

Felony and misdemeanor records are available in person only. See Georgia state repository for additional information.

Civil records are available in person only. See Georgia state repository for additional information.

Long County

Clerk of Superior Court, Criminal Records
PO Box 458
Ludowici, GA 31316
(912) 545-2123

Felony and misdemeanor records are available by mail. No release necessary. $5.00 search fee. Search information required: name, years to search. Turnaround time is 1 week.

Civil records are available by mail. No release necessary. No search fee. $2.50 for first certification, $.50 each additional. Search information required: name, date of birth, years to search. Specify plaintiff or defendant.

Lowndes County

Clerk of Superior Court
PO Box 1349
Valdosta, GA 31603
(912) 333-5127

Records are available in person only. See Georgia state repository for additional information.

Civil records are available in person only. See Georgia state repository for additional information.

Lumpkin County

Clerk of Superior Court, Criminal Records
279 Courthouse Hill
Dahlonega, GA 30533
(404) 864-3736

Records are available in person only. See Georgia state repository for additional information.

Civil records are available in person only. See Georgia state repository for additional information.

Macon County

Clerk of Superior Court, Criminal Records
PO Box 337
Oglethorpe, GA 31068
(912) 472-7661

Felony and misdemeanor records are available by mail. No release necessary. $5.00 search fee. Search information required: name, years to search.

Civil records are available by mail. No release necessary. No search fee. $.25 fee per copy. $2.25 for certification. Search information required: name, date of birth, years to search. Specify plaintiff or defendant.

Madison County

Clerk of Superior Court
PO Box 247
Danielsville, GA 30633
(404) 795-3351

Felony and misdemeanor records are available in person only. See Georgia State Repository for additional information.

Civil records are available in person only. See Georgia state repository for additional information.

Marion County

Clerk of Superior Court
PO Box 41
Buena Vista, GA 31803
(912) 649-7321

Records are available in person only. See Georgia state repository for additional information.

Civil records are available in person only. See Georgia state repository for additional information.

McDuffie County

Clerk of Superior Court, Criminal Records
PO Box 158
Thomson, GA 30824
(404) 595-2134

Felony and misdemeanor records are available by mail. A release is required. No search fee. Search information required: name, date of birth, SSN, years to search.

Civil records are available in person only. See Georgia state repository for additional information.

McIntosh County

Clerk of Superior Court
PO Box 1661
Darien, GA 31305
(912) 437-6641

Felony and misdemeanor records are available by mail. No release necessary. No search fee. $.25 fee per copy. $3.00 for certification. Search information required: name, years to search.

Civil records are available by mail. No release necessary. No search fee. $.25 fee per copy. $3.00 for certification. Search information required: name, years to search. Specify plaintiff or defendant.

Meriwether County

Clerk of Superior Court, Felony check
PO Box 160
Greenville, GA 30222
(404) 672-4416

Felony and misdemeanor records are available in person only. See Georgia State Repository for additional information.

Civil records are available in person only. See Georgia state repository for additional information.

Miller County

Clerk of Superior Court
PO Box 66
Colquitt, GA 31737
(912) 758-4102

Records are available in person only. See Georgia state repository for additional information.

Civil records are available in person only. See Georgia state repository for additional information.

Mitchell County

Clerk of Superior Court
PO Box 427
Camilla, GA 31730
(912) 336-2022

Records are available in person only. See Georgia state repository for additional information.

Civil records are available in person only. See Georgia state repository for additional information.

Monroe County

Clerk of Superior Court
PO Box 450
Forsyth, GA 31029
(912) 994-7022

Records are available in person only. See Georgia state repository for additional information.

Civil records are available in person only. See Georgia state repository for additional information.

Montgomery County

Clerk of Superior Court, Criminal Records
PO Box 311
Mount Vernon, GA 30445
(912) 583-4401

Records are available in person only. See Georgia state repository for additional information.

Civil records are available in person only. See Georgia state repository for additional information.

Morgan County

Clerk of Superior Court
PO Box 130
Madison, GA 30650
(404) 342-3605

Records are available in person only. See Georgia state repository for additional information.

Civil records are available in person only. See Georgia state repository for additional information.

Murray County

Clerk of Superior Court, Criminal Records
PO Box 1000
Chatsworth, GA 30705
(404) 695-2932

Felony and misdemeanor records are available by mail or phone. No release necessary. No search fee. $.25 fee per copy. $2.50 for certification. Search information required: name, years to search, SASE.

Civil records are available by mail. No release necessary. No search fee. $.25 fee per copy. $2.50 for certification. Search information required: name, years to search, SASE. Specify plaintiff or defendant.

Muscogee County

Clerk of Superior Court, Criminal Records
PO Box 2145
Columbus, GA 31994
(404) 571-4857

Felony and misdemeanor records are available in person only. See Georgia State Repository for additional information.

Civil records are available in person only. See Georgia state repository for additional information.

Newton County

Clerk of Superior Court
1124 Clark Street
Covington, GA 30209
(404) 784-2035

Records are available in person only. See Georgia state repository for additional information.

Civil records are available in person only. See Georgia state repository for additional information.

Oconee County

Clerk of Superior Court, Criminal Records
PO Box 113
Watkinsville, GA 30677
(404) 769-5157
Fax (404) 769-0705

Felony and misdemeanor records are available by mail or fax. A release is required. No search fee. $.25 fee per copy. $2.50 for certification. Search information required: name, date of birth. Turnaround time is 1 week.

Civil records are available by mail. No release necessary. No search fee. $.25 fee per copy. $2.50 for certification. Search information required: name, date of birth, years to search. Specify plaintiff or defendant.

Oglethorpe County

Clerk of Superior Court, Criminal Records
PO Box 68
Lexington, GA 30648
(404) 743-5731

Records are available by mail. A release is required. No search fee. $.25 fee per copy. $2.50 for certification. Search information required: name, years to search.

Civil records are available in person only. See Georgia state repository for additional information.

Paulding County

Clerk of Superior Court, Room G-2
Paulding County Courthouse, Court House Square
Dallas, GA 30132
(404) 445-8871

Felony and misdemeanor records are available in person only. See Georgia state repository for additional information.

Civil records are available in person only. See Georgia state repository for additional information.

Peach County

Clerk of Superior Court, Criminal Records
PO Box 389
Ft. Valley, GA 31030
(912) 825-5331

Felony and misdemeanor records are available by mail. No release necessary. No search fee. $.25 fee per copy. $3.00 for certification. Search information required: name, date of birth, race, SASE. Turnaround time is 1 week.

Civil records are available by mail. No release necessary. No search fee. $.25 fee per copy. $3.00 for certification. Search information required: name, date of birth, years to search, SASE. Specify plaintiff or defendant.

Pickens County

Clerk of Superior Court, Criminal Records
PO Box 130
Jasper, GA 30143
(404) 692-2014

Felony and misdemeanor records are available in person only. See Georgia state repository for additional information.

Civil records are available in person only. See Georgia state repository for additional information.

Pierce County

Clerk of Superior Court, Criminal Records
PO Box 107
Blackshear, GA 31516
(912) 449-2020

Felony and misdemeanor records are available by mail. A release is required. $2.00 fee. Make check payable to Clerk of Superior Court. Search information required: name, date of birth, years to search, SASE.

Civil records are available by mail. No release necessary. $2.00 search fee. $.25 fee per copy. $2.50 for certification. Search information required: name, date of birth, years to search. Specify plaintiff or defendant.

Pike County

Clerk of Superior Court, Criminal Records
PO Box 10
Zebulon, GA 30295
(706) 567-8401

Felony and misdemeanor records are available in person only. See Georgia state repository for additional information.

Civil records are available by mail. No release necessary. No search fee. $.25 fee per copy. $2.50 for certification, $.50 each page thereafter. Search information required: name, date of birth, years to search. Specify plaintiff or defendant.

Polk County

Clerk of Superior Court, Criminal Records
PO Box 948
Cedartown, GA 30125
(404) 749-2114

Felony and misdemeanor records are available by mail. A release is required. No search fee. $.25 fee per copy. $2.50 for certification, $.50 each thereafter. Search information required: name, years to search, SASE. Turnaround time is 1 week.

Civil records are available by mail. No release necessary. No search fee. $.25 fee per copy. $2.50 for certification, $.50 each thereafter. Search information required: name, date of birth, years to search, SASE. Specify plaintiff or defendant.

Pulaski County

Clerk of Superior Court, Criminal Records
PO Box 88
Haskinsville, GA 31036
(912) 783-1911

Felony and misdemeanor records are available by mail. A release is required. No search fee. $.25 fee per copy. $2.50 for certification, $.50 each thereafter. Search information required: name, date of birth, SSN, years to search.

Civil records are available by mail. No release necessary. No search fee. $.25 fee per copy. $2.50 for certification, $.50 each thereafter. Search information required: name, date of birth, years to search. Specify plaintiff or defendant.

Putnam County

Clerk of Superior Court, Criminal Records
Putnam County Courthouse
Eatonton, GA 31024
(404) 485-4501

Felony and misdemeanor records are available in person only. See Georgia state repository for additional information.

Civil records are available in person only. See Georgia state repository for additional information.

Quitman County

Clerk of Superior Court
PO Box 307
Georgetown, GA 31754
(912) 334-2578

Records are available by mail. A release is required. $8.00 search fee. $.25 fee per copy. $3.00 for certification. Search information required: name , date of birth, years to search. Turnaround time is 1 week.

Civil records are available by mail. No release necessary. $10.00 search fee. $.25 fee per copy. $3.00 for certification. Search information required: name, date of birth, years to search. Specify plaintiff or defendant.

Rabun County

Clerk of Superior Court, Criminal Records
PO Box 893
Clayton, GA 30525
(404) 782-3615

Felony and misdemeanor records are available by mail. No release necessary. No search fee. $10.00 fee per copy. $4.00 for certification. Search information required: name, date of birth.

Civil records are available by mail. No release necessary. No search fee. $10.00 fee per copy. $4.00 for certification. Search information required: name, date of birth, years to search. Specify plaintiff or defendant.

Randolph County

Clerk of Superior Court
PO Box 98
Cuthbert, GA 31740
(912) 732-2216

Records are available in person only. See Georgia state repository for additional information.

Civil records are available in person only. See Georgia state repository for additional information.

Richmond County

Clerk of Superior Court
Joint Law Enforcement Center
Suite 259 A 401 Walton Way
Augusta, GA 30911
(404) 821-1231

Records are available in person only. See Georgia state repository for additional information.

Civil records are available in person only. See Georgia state repository for additional information.

Rockdale County

Felony Records
Clerk of Superior Court, Criminal Records
PO Box 937
Conyers, GA 30207
(404) 929-4021

Felony records are available by mail. A release is required. $5.00 search fee. $.50 fee per copy. $2.50 fee for certification. Search information required: name, years to search, SASE.

Civil Records
Clerk of Superior Court
PO Box 937
Conyers, GA 30207
(404) 929-4021

Civil records are available by mail. No release necessary. $5.00 search fee. $.50 fee per copy. $2.50 fee for certification.Search information required: name, date of birth, years to search, SASE. Specify plaintiff or defendant.

Misdemeanor Records
State Court
PO Box 939
Canyers, GA 30207
(404) 929-4036

Misdemeanor records are available by mail. A release is required. $5.00 search fee. $.25 fee per copy. $2.50 for certification. Search information required: name, date of birth.

Civil Records
State Court
PO Box 939
Canyers, GA 30207
(404) 929-4036

Civil records are available in person only. See Georgia state repository for additional information.

Schley County

Clerk of Superior Court, Criminal Records
PO Box 7
Ellaville, GA 31806
(912) 937-5581

Felony and misdemeanor records are available by mail. A notarized release is required. $20.00 search fee. $.35 fee per copy. $2.85 for certification. Company checks only, payable to Clerk of Superior Court. Search information required: name, sex, previous address, years to search, SASE. Turnaround time is 1 week.

Civil records are available by mail. No release necessary. $10.00 search fee. $.35 fee per copy. $2.85 for certification. Search information required: name, date of birth, years to search, SASE. Specify plaintiff or defendant.

Screven County

Clerk of Superior Court
PO Box 156
Sylvania, GA 30467
(912) 564-2614

Records are available in person only. See Georgia state repository for additional information.

Civil records are available in person only. See Georgia state repository for additional information.

Seminole County

Clerk of Superior Court
PO Box 672
Donalsonville, GA 31745
(912) 524-2525
Fax (912) 524-8528

Felony and misdemeanor records are available by mail, fax or phone. $1.00 fee per year searched. $.25 fee per copy, $2.50 fee for first certification, $.50 each additional. A release is required. Search information required: name, years to search, date of birth, SSN, previous address. Turnaround time is 1 week.

Civil records are available by mail, fax or phone. No release necessary. $1.00 fee per year searched. $.25 fee per copy, $2.50 fee for first certification, $.50 each additional.. Search information required: name, date of birth, years to search. Specify plaintiff or defendant.

Spalding County

Clerk of Superior Court, Criminal Records
PO Box 163
Griffin, GA 30224
(404) 228-9900

Felony and misdemeanor records are available in person only. See Georgia state repository for additional information.

Civil records are available in person only. See Georgia state repository for additional information.

Stephens County

Stephens County Courthouse
Clerk of Superior Court
Toccoa, GA 30577
(404) 886-3598

Felony and misdemeanor records are available by mail. A notarized release is required. $7.50 search fee. $.25 fee per copy, $2.50 fee for certification. Search information required: name, date of birth, race, sex, SSN, previous address, years to search. Turnaround time is 1 week.

Civil records are available by mail. No release necessary. $7.50 search fee. $.25 fee per copy, $2.50 fee for certification. Search information required: name, date of birth. Specify plaintiff or defendant.

Stewart County

Clerk of Superior Court
PO Box 910
Lumpkin, GA 31815
(912) 838-6220

Felony and misdemeanor records are not available by mail. A release is required. No search fee. $.25 fee per copy, $3.50 fee for certification, $.50 fee per each additional page. Search information required: name, years to search. Turnaround time is 1 week.

Civil records are available by mail. A release is required. No search fee. $.25 fee per copy, $3.50 fee for certification, $.50 fee per each additional page. Search information required: name, date of birth, years to search. Specify plaintiff or defendant.

Sumter County

Clerk of Superior Court
PO Box 333
Americus, GA 31709
(912) 924-5626

Records are available in person only. See Georgia state repository for additional information.

Civil records are available in person only. See Georgia state repository for additional information.

Talbot County

Clerk of Superior Court
PO Box 325
Talbotton, GA 31827
(404) 665-3239

Records are available in person only. See Georgia state repository for additional information.

Civil records are available in person only. See Georgia state repository for additional information.

Taliaferro County

Clerk of Superior Court
PO Box 182
Crawfordville, GA 30631
(404) 456-2123

Records are available in person only. See Georgia state repository for additional information.

Civil records are available in person only. See Georgia state repository for additional information.

Tattnall County

Clerk of Superior Court
PO Box 56
Reidsville, GA 30453
(912) 557-6716

Felony and misdemeanor records are available by mail. No release necessary. $10.00 fee. Make company check payable to Clerk of Court. Search information required: name, years to search, SASE. Turnaround time is 1 week.

Civil records are available by mail. No release necessary. $5.00 search fee. $.25 fee per copy. $3.00 for certification. Search information required: name, date of birth, years to search, SASE. Specify plaintiff or defendant.

Taylor County

Clerk of Superior Court
PO Box 248
Butler, GA 31006
(912) 862-5594

Felony and misdemeanor records are available in person only. See Georgia state repository for additional information.

Civil records are available in person only. See Georgia state repository for additional information.

Telfair County

Clerk of Superior Court, Criminal Records
Telfair County Courthouse
McRae, GA 31055
(912) 868-6525

Felony and misdemeanor records are available by mail or phone. No release necessary. No search fee. $.25 fee per copy. $3.00 for certification. Search information required: name, date of birth, years to search.

Civil records are available by mail or phone. No release necessary. No search fee. $.25 fee per copy. $3.00 for certification. Search information required: name, date of birth, years to search. Specify plaintiff or defendant.

Terrell County

Clerk of Superior Court, Criminal Records
PO Box 189
Dawson, GA 31742
(912) 995-2631

Felony and misdemeanor records are available in person only. See Georgia state repository for additional information.

Civil records are available in person only. See Georgia state repository for additional information.

Thomas County

Clerk of Superior Court
PO Box 1995
Thomasville, GA 31799
(912) 225-4108

Felony and misdemeanor records are available by mail. No release necessary. No search fee. $.25 fee per copy. $2.50 for certification. Make check payable to Clerk of Superior Court. Search information required: name, years to search. Turnaround time is 1 week.

Civil records are available by mail. No release necessary. No search fee. $.25 fee per copy. $2.50 for certification. Search information required: name, date of birth, years to search. Specify plaintiff or defendant.

Tift County

Clerk of Superior Court
PO Box 354
Tifton, GA 31793
(912) 386-7810

Records are available in person only. See Georgia state repository for additional information.

Civil records are available in person only. See Georgia state repository for additional information.

Toombs County

Clerk of Superior Court, Criminal Records
PO Drawer 530
Lyons, GA 30436
(912) 526-3501

Felony and misdemeanor records are available by mail. A release is required. $3.00 fee per 5 years search. Make check payable to Clerk of Court. Search information required: name, date of birth, SASE. Turnaround time is 1 week.

Civil records are available in person only. See Georgia state repository for additional information.

Towns County

Clerk of Superior Court, Felony check
PO Box 178
Hiawassee, GA 30546
(404) 896-2130

Felony and misdemeanor records are available by mail or phone. No release necessary. No search fee. $.25 fee per copy. $2.50 for certification. Search information required: name, years to search. Turnaround time is 1 week.

Civil records are available by mail or phone. No release necessary. No search fee. $.25 fee per copy. $2.50 for certification. Search information required: name, date of birth, years to search. Specify plaintiff or defendant.

Treutlen County

Clerk of Superior Court, Criminal Records
PO Box 356
Soperton, GA 30457
(912) 529-4215

Felony and misdemeanor records are available in person only. See Georgia State Repository for additional information.

Civil records are available by mail. A release is required. No search fee. $.25 fee per copy. $2.00 for certification. Search information required: name, date of birth, years to search. Specify plaintiff or defendant.

Troup County

Clerk of Superior Court, Criminal Records
PO Box 866
La Grange, GA 30241
(404) 883-1740

Felony and misdemeanor records are available in person only. See Georgia state repository for additional information.

Civil records are available in person only. See Georgia state repository for additional information.

Turner County

Clerk of Superior Court
PO Box 106
Ashburn, GA 31714
(912) 567-2011

Felony and misdemeanor records are available by mail. No release necessary. No fee. Search information required: name, years to search. Turnaround time is 1 week.

Civil records are available in person only. See Georgia state repository for additional information.

Twiggs County

Clerk of Superior Court
PO Box 228
Jeffersonville, GA 31044
(912) 945-3350

Records are available in person only. See Georgia state repository for additional information.

Civil records are available in person only. See Georgia state repository for additional information.

Union County

Clerk of Superior Court, Criminal Records
Route 8 Box 8005
Blairsville, GA 30512
(404) 745-2611
Fax (404) 745-1311

Felony and misdemeanor records are available by mail, phone or fax. No release necessary. No search fee. $.25 fee per copy, $2.50 fee for certification. Search information required: name, date of birth, SASE. Turnaround time is 1 week.

Civil records are available by mail. No release necessary. No search fee. $.25 fee per copy, $2.50 fee for first page certified, $.50 each additional page. Search information required: name, date of birth, years to search. Specify plaintiff or defendant.

Upson County

Clerk of Superior Court, Felony check
PO Box 469
Thomaston, GA 30286-0469
(404) 647-7835 or 5847

Felony and misdemeanor records are available by mail. No release necessary. No search fee. $.25 fee per copy, $2.50 fee for certification. Search information required: name, years to search, SASE. Turnaround time is 1 week.

Civil records are available by mail. No release necessary. No search fee. $.25 fee per copy, $2.50 fee for first certification, $.50 each additional page. Search information required: name, date of birth, years to search. Specify plaintiff or defendant.

Walker County

Clerk of Superior Court
PO Box 448
Lafayette, GA 30728
(404) 638-1742

Records are available in person only. See Georgia state repository for additional information.

Civil records are available in person only. See Georgia state repository for additional information.

Walton County

Clerk of Superior Court, Criminal Records
PO Box 745
Monroe, GA 30655
(404) 267-1307

Felony and misdemeanor records are available in person only. See Georgia state repository for additional information.

Civil records are available in person only. See Georgia state repository for additional information.

Ware County

Clerk of Superior Court
PO Box 776
Waycross, GA 31502
(912) 287-4340

Felony and misdemeanor records are available by mail. A notarized release is required. No search fee. Search information required: name, date of birth, SSN, years to search.

Civil records are available by mail. No release necessary. No search fee. $.25 fee per copy, $2.50 fee for first page certified, $.50 each additional page. Search information required: name, date of birth, years to search. Specify plaintiff or defendant.

Warren County

Clerk of Superior Court
PO Box 346
Warrenton, GA 30828
(404) 465-2262

Records are available in person only. See Georgia state repository for additional information.

Civil records are available in person only. See Georgia state repository for additional information.

Washington County

Clerk of Superior Court
PO Box 231
Sandersville, GA 31082
(912) 552-3186

Records are available in person only. See Georgia state repository for additional information.

Civil records are available in person only. See Georgia state repository for additional information.

Wayne County

Clerk of Superior Court
PO Box 918
Jesup, GA 31545
(912) 427-5930

Felony and misdemeanor records are available by mail or phone. A release is required. $5.00 search fee. $.25 fee per copy, $2.50 fee for first page certified, $.50 each additional page. Search information required: name, SSN, date of birth, sex, race, SASE. Turnaround time is 1 week.

Civil records are available by mail, fax or phone. No release necessary. $5.00 search fee. $.25 fee per copy, $2.50 fee for first page certified, $.50 each additional page. Search information required: name, date of birth, years to search, SASE. Specify plaintiff or defendant.

Webster County

Clerk of Superior Court
PO Box 117
Preston, GA 31824
(912) 828-3525

Felony and misdemeanor records are available by mail. A notarized release is required. No search fee. $.25 fee per copy, $2.00 fee for certification, $.50 fee per page on additional certified copies. Search information required: name. Turnaround time is 1 week.

Civil records are available in person only. See Georgia state repository for additional information.

Wheeler County

Clerk of Superior Court, Criminal Records
PO Box 38
Alamo, GA 30411
(912) 568-7137

Felony and misdemeanor records are available by mail. No release necessary. No search fee. Search information required: name, SSN, date of birth, sex, race, years to search.

Civil records are available by mail or phone. No release necessary. No search fee. Search information required: name, date of birth, years to search. Specify plaintiff or defendant.

White County

Clerk of Superior Court
PO Box 1389
Cleveland, GA 30528
(404) 865-2613

Records are available in person only. See Georgia State Repository for additional information.

Civil records are available in person only. See Georgia State Repository for additional information.

Whitfield County

Clerk of Superior Court, Felony check
PO Box 868
Dalton, GA 30722
(404) 275-7450

Felony and misdemeanor records are available by mail or phone. No release necessary. $3.00 search fee. Search information required: name, years to search. Turnaround time is 1 week.

Civil records are available by mail or phone. No release necessary. No search fee. $.25 fee per copy. $3.00 for certification. Search information required: name, date of birth, years to search. Specify plaintiff or defendant.

Wilcox County

Clerk of Superior Court, Felony check
Wilcox County
Abbeville, GA 31001
(912) 467-2442

Felony and misdemeanor records are available by mail or phone. No release necessary. No search fee. Search information required: name, date of birth, race, SASE. Turnaround time is 1 week.

Civil records are available by mail. No release necessary. No search fee. $.25 fee per copy. $3.00 for certification. Search information required: name, date of birth, years to search. Specify plaintiff or defendant.

Wilkes County

Clerk of Superior Court
23 E. Court St.
Room 205
Washington, GA 30673
(404) 678-2423

Felony and misdemeanor records are available by mail. No release necessary. $5.00 search fee. $1.00 fee per copy, $2.00 fee for certification. Check payable to Chief Deputy Clerk. Search information required: name, offense.

Civil records are available by mail. No release necessary. No search fee. $.25 fee per copy. $2.00 for first certification, $.50 for each additional page. Search information required: name, date of birth, years to search. Specify plaintiff or defendant.

Wilkinson County

Clerk of Superior Court, Criminal Records
PO Box 250
Irwinton, GA 31042
(912) 946-2221

Felony and misdemeanor records are available in person only. See Georgia state repository for additional information.

Civil records are available in person only. See Georgia state repository for additional information.

Worth County

Clerk of Superior Court
201 North Main Street
Room 13 Courthouse
Sylvester, GA 31791
(912) 776-8205

Records are available in person only. See Georgia State Repository for more information.

Civil records are available in person only. See Georgia state repository for additional information.

City-County Cross Reference

Abbeville *Wilcox*
Acworth *Cobb*
Adairsville *Bartow*
Adel *Cook*
Adrian *Emanuel*
Ailey *Montgomery*
Alamo *Wheeler*
Alapaha *Berrien*
Albany *Dougherty*
Allenhurst *Liberty*
Allentown *Wilkinson*
Alma *Bacon*
Alpharetta *Fulton*
Alston *Montgomery*
Alto *Habersham*
Ambrose *Coffee*
Americus *Sumter*
Andersonville *Sumter*
Appling *Columbia*

Arabi *Crisp*
Aragon *Polk*
Argyle *Clinch*
Arlington *Calhoun*
Armuchee *Floyd*
Arnoldsville *Oglethorpe*
Ashburn *Turner*
Athens *Clarke*
Atlanta *Fulton*
Attapulgus *Decatur*
Auburn *Barrow*
Augusta *Richmond*
Austell *Cobb*
Avera *Jefferson*
Avondale Estates *DeKalb*
Axson *Atkinson*
Baconton *Mitchell*
Bainbridge *Decatur*
Baldwin *Banks*

Ball Ground *Cherokee*
Barnesville *Lamar*
Barney *Brooks*
Bartow *Jefferson*
Barwick *Brooks*
Baxley *Appling*
Belvedere Park *DeKalb*
Benevolence *Randolph*
Berlin *Colquitt*
Bethlehem *Barrow*
Bibb City *Muscogee*
Bishop *Oconee*
Blackshear *Pierce*
Blacksville *Henry*
Blackwells *Cobb*
Blairsville *Union*
Blakely *Early*
Bloomingdale *Chatham*
Blue Ridge *Fannin*

Bluffton *Clay*
Blythe *Richmond*
Bogart *Oconee*
Bolingbroke *Monroe*
Bonaire *Houston*
Boneville *McDuffie*
Boston *Thomas*
Bostwick *Morgan*
Bowdon *Carroll*
Bowdon Junction *Carroll*
Bowersville *Hart*
Bowman *Elbert*
Box Springs *Talbot*
Braselton *Jackson*
Bremen *Haralson*
Brinson *Decatur*
Bristol *Pierce*
Bronwood *Terrell*
Brookfield *Tift*

Brookhaven *DeKalb*
Brooklet *Bulloch*
Brooks *Fayette*
Broxton *Coffee*
Brunswick *Glynn*
Buchanan *Haralson*
Buckhead *Morgan*
Buena Vista *Marion*
Buford *Gwinnett*
Butler *Taylor*
Byromville *Dooly*
Byron *Peach*
Cadwell *Laurens*
Cairo *Grady*
Calhoun *Gordon*
Calvary *Grady*
Camak *Warren*
Camilla *Mitchell*
Canon *Franklin*
Canton *Cherokee*
Carlton *Madison*
Carnesville *Franklin*
Carrollton *Carroll*
Cartersville *Bartow*
Cassville *Bartow*
Cataula *Harris*
Cave Spring *Floyd*
Cecil *Cook*
Cedar Grove *DeKalb*
Cedar Springs *Early*
Cedartown *Polk*
Centerville *Houston*
Chamblee *DeKalb*
Chatsworth *Murray*
Chauncey *Dodge*
Cherrylog *Gilmer*
Chester *Dodge*
Chickamauga *Walker*
Chicopee *Hall*
Chula *Tift*
Cisco *Murray*
Clarkdale *Cobb*
Clarkesville *Habersham*
Clarkston *DeKalb*
Claxton *Evans*
Clayton *Rabun*
Clermont *Hall*
Cleveland *White*
Climax *Decatur*
Clinchfield *Houston*
Clyo *Effingham*
Cobb *Sumter*
Cobbtown *Tattnall*
Cochran *Bleckley*
Cohutta *Whitfield*
Colbert *Madison*
Coleman *Randolph*
College Park *Fulton*
Collins *Tattnall*
Colquitt *Miller*
Columbus *Muscogee*
Comer *Madison*
Commerce *Jackson*
Concord *Pike*
Conley *Clayton*
Constitution *DeKalb*
Conyers *Rockdale*
Coolidge *Thomas*
Coosa *Floyd*
Cordele *Crisp*
Cornelia *Habersham*
Cotton *Mitchell*
Covena *Emanuel*
Covington *Newton*
Crandall *Murray*
Crawford *Oglethorpe*

Crawfordville *Taliaferro*
Crescent *McIntosh*
Culloden *Monroe*
Cumming *Forsyth*
Cusseta *Chattahoochee*
Cuthbert *Randolph*
Dacula *Gwinnett*
Dahlonega *Lumpkin*
Daisy *Evans*
Dallas *Paulding*
Dalton *Whitfield*
Damascus *Early*
Danielsville *Madison*
Danville *Twiggs*
Darien *McIntosh*
Dasher *Lowndes*
Davisboro *Washington*
Dawson *Terrell*
Dawsonville *Dawson*
Dearing *McDuffie*
Decatur *DeKalb*
Deenwood *Ware*
Deerwood Park *DeKalb*
Demorest *Habersham*
Denton *Jeff Davis*
DeSoto *Sumter*
Dewy Rose *Elbert*
Dexter *Laurens*
Dillard *Rabun*
Dixie *Brooks*
Dock Junction *Glynn*
Doerun *Colquitt*
Donalsonville *Seminole*
Doraville *DeKalb*
Douglas *Coffee*
Douglasville *Douglas*
Dover *Screven*
Dry Branch *Twiggs*
Dublin *Laurens*
Dudley *Laurens*
Duluth *Gwinnett*
Dunaire *DeKalb*
Dunwoody *DeKalb*
Du Pont *Clinch*
Eastanollee *Stephens*
East Dublin *Laurens*
East Ellijay *Gilmer*
Eastman *Dodge*
East Newnan *Coweta*
Eatonton *Putnam*
Eden *Effingham*
Edison *Calhoun*
Elberta *Houston*
Elberton *Elbert*
Elko *Houston*
Ellabell *Bryan*
Ellaville *Schley*
Ellenton *Colquitt*
Ellenwood *Clayton*
Ellerslie *Harris*
Ellijay *Gilmer*
Emerson *Bartow*
Enigma *Berrien*
Epworth *Fannin*
Esom Hill *Polk*
Eton *Murray*
Evans *Columbia*
Experiment *Spalding*
Fairburn *Fulton*
Fairmount *Gordon*
Fair Oaks *Cobb*
Fargo *Clinch*
Farmington *Oconee*
Fayetteville *Fayette*
Felton *Haralson*
Fitzgerald *Ben Hill*

Five Forks *Gwinnett*
Fleming *Liberty*
Flintstone *Walker*
Flovilla *Butts*
Flowery Branch *Hall*
Folkston *Charlton*
Forest Park *Clayton*
Forsyth *Monroe*
Fort Gaines *Clay*
Fort Oglethorpe *Catoosa*
Fortson *Muscogee*
Fort Valley *Peach*
Fowlstown *Decatur*
Franklin *Heard*
Franklin Springs *Franklin*
Funston *Colquitt*
Gainesville *Hall*
Garfield *Emanuel*
Garden City *Chatham*
Gay *Meriwether*
Geneva *Talbot*
Georgetown *Quitman*
Gibson *Glascock*
Gillsville *Hall*
Girard *Burke*
Glenn *Heard*
Glennville *Tattnall*
Glenwood *Wheeler*
Good Hope *Walton*
Gordon *Wilkinson*
Gracewood *Richmond*
Grantville *Coweta*
Gray *Jones*
Grayson *Gwinnett*
Graysville *Catoosa*
Greensboro *Greene*
Greenville *Meriwether*
Griffin *Spalding*
Grovetown *Columbia*
Guyton *Effingham*
Haddock *Jones*
Hagan *Evans*
Hahira *Lowndes*
Hamilton *Harris*
Hampton *Henry*
Hapeville *Fulton*
Haralson *Coweta*
Hardwick *Baldwin*
Harlem *Columbia*
Harrison *Washington*
Hartsfield *Colquitt*
Hartwell *Hart*
Hawkinsville *Pulaski*
Hazlehurst *Jeff Davis*
Helen *White*
Helena *Telfair*
Hephzibah *Richmond*
Hiawassee *Towns*
High Shoals *Oconee*
Hillsboro *Jasper*
Hiltonia *Screven*
Hinesville *Liberty*
Hiram *Paulding*
Hoboken *Brantley*
Hogansville *Troup*
Holly Springs *Cherokee*
Homeland *Charlton*
Homer *Banks*
Homerville *Clinch*
Hortense *Brantley*
Hoschton *Jackson*
Howard *Taylor*
Hull *Madison*
Ideal *Macon*
Ila *Madison*
Iron City *Seminole*

Irwinton *Wilkinson*
Irwinville *Irwin*
Jackson *Butts*
Jacksonville *Telfair*
Jakin *Early*
Jasper *Pickens*
Jefferson *Jackson*
Jeffersonville *Twiggs*
Jenkinsburg *Butts*
Jersey *Walton*
Jesup *Wayne*
Jewell *Warren*
Jonesboro *Clayton*
Juliette *Monroe*
Junction City *Talbot*
Kathleen *Houston*
Kennesaw *Cobb*
Keysville *Burke*
Kingsland *Camden*
Kingston *Bartow*
Kite *Johnson*
Knoxville *Crawford*
LaFayette *Walker*
LaGrange *Troup*
Lakeland *Lanier*
Lakemont *Rabun*
Lake City *Clayton*
Lake Park *Lowndes*
La Vista *DeKalb*
Lavonia *Franklin*
Lawrenceville *Gwinnett*
Leary *Calhoun*
Lebanon *Cherokee*
Leesburg *Lee*
Lenox *Cook*
Leslie *Sumter*
Lexington *Oglethorpe*
Lilburn *Gwinnett*
Lilly *Dooly*
Lincolnton *Lincoln*
Lindale *Floyd*
Lithia Springs *Douglas*
Lithonia *DeKalb*
Lizella *Bibb*
Locust Grove *Henry*
Loganville *Walton*
Louisville *Jefferson*
Louvale *Stewart*
Lovejoy *Clayton*
Ludowici *Long*
Lula *Hall*
Lumber City *Telfair*
Lumpkin *Stewart*
Luthersville *Meriwether*
Lyerly *Chattooga*
Lyons *Toombs*
McCaysville *Fannin*
McDonough *Henry*
McIntyre *Wilkinson*
McRae *Telfair*
Mableton *Cobb*
Macon *Bibb*
Madison *Morgan*
Manchester *Meriwether*
Manor *Ware*
Mansfield *Newton*
Marble Hill *Pickens*
Marietta *Cobb*
Marshallville *Macon*
Martin *Stephens*
Martinez *Columbia*
Mauk *Taylor*
Maysville *Banks*
Meansville *Pike*
Meigs *Thomas*
Meldrim *Effingham*

Menlo *Chattooga*
Meridian *McIntosh*
Mershon *Pierce*
Mesena *Warren*
Metter *Candler*
Midland *Muscogee*
Midville *Burke*
Midway *Liberty*
Milan *Telfair*
Milledgeville *Baldwin*
Millen *Jenkins*
Millwood *Ware*
Milner *Lamar*
Milstead *Rockdale*
Mineral Bluff *Fannin*
Mitchell *Glascock*
Molena *Pike*
Monroe *Walton*
Montezuma *Macon*
Monticello *Jasper*
Montrose *Laurens*
Moreland *Coweta*
Morgan *Calhoun*
Morganton *Fannin*
Morris *Quitman*
Morrow *Clayton*
Morven *Brooks*
Moultrie *Colquitt*
Mountain City *Rabun*
Mount Airy *Habersham*
Mount Vernon
    Montgomery
Mount Zion *Carroll*
Murrayville *Hall*
Musella *Crawford*
Mystic *Irwin*
Nahunta *Brantley*
Nashville *Berrien*
Naylor *Lowndes*
Nelson *Cherokee*
Newborn *Newton*
New Holland *Hall*
Newington *Screven*
Newnan *Coweta*
Newton *Baker*
Nicholls *Coffee*
Nicholson *Jackson*
Norcross *Gwinnett*
Norman Park *Colquitt*
Norristown *Emanuel*
Norwood *Warren*
Nunez *Emanuel*
Oakdale *Cobb*
Oakfield *Worth*
Oakgrove *DeKalb*
Oakman *Gordon*
Oakwood *Hall*
Ochlocknee *Thomas*
Ocilla *Irwin*
Oconee *Washington*
Odum *Wayne*
Offerman *Pierce*
Oglethorpe *Macon*
Oliver *Screven*
Omaha *Stewart*
Omega *Tift*
Orchard Hill *Spalding*
Oxford *Newton*
Palmetto *Fulton*
Panthersville *DeKalb*
Parrott *Terrell*
Patterson *Pierce*
Pavo *Thomas*
Peachtree City *Fayette*
Pearson *Atkinson*
Pelham *Mitchell*

Pembroke *Bryan*
Pendergrass *Jackson*
Perkins *Jenkins*
Perry *Houston*
Phillipsburg *Tift*
Pinehurst *Dooly*
Pine Lake *DeKalb*
Pine Mountain *Harris*
Pine Mountain Valley
    Harris
Pineview *Wilcox*
Pitts *Wilcox*
Plainfield *Dodge*
Plains *Sumter*
Plainville *Gordon*
Pooler *Chatham*
Portal *Bulloch*
Porterdale *Newton*
Poulan *Worth*
Powder Springs *Cobb*
Preston *Webster*
Pulaski *Candler*
Putney *Dougherty*
Quitman *Brooks*
Rabun Gap *Rabun*
Radium Springs *Doughtery*
Ranger *Gordon*
Ray City *Berrien*
Rayle *Wilkes*
Rebecca *Turner*
Redan *DeKalb*
Red Oak *Fulton*
Register *Bulloch*
Rehoboth *DeKalb*
Reidsville *Tattnall*
Remerton *Lowndes*
Rentz *Laurens*
Resaca *Gordon*
Rex *Clayton*
Reynolds *Taylor*
Rhine *Dodge*
Riceboro *Liberty*
Richland *Stewart*
Richmond Hill *Bryan*
Rincon *Effingham*
Ringgold *Catoosa*
Rising Fawn *Dade*
Riverdale *Clayton*
Roberta *Crawford*
Rochelle *Wilcox*
Rockledge *Laurens*
Rockmart *Polk*
Rock Spring *Walker*
Rocky Face *Whitfield*
Rocky Ford *Screven*
Rome *Floyd*
Roopville *Carroll*
Rossville *Walker*
Roswell *Fulton*
Royston *Franklin*
Rupert *Taylor*
Rutledge *Morgan*
Rydal *Bartow*
Saint George *Charlton*
Saint Marys *Camden*
Sale City *Mitchell*
Sandersville *Washington*
Sandy Springs *Fulton*
Sapelo Island *McIntosh*
Sardis *Burke*
Sargent *Coweta*
Sasser *Terrell*
Sautee-Nacoochee *White*
Savannah *Chatham*
Scotland *Telfair*
Scottdale *DeKalb*

Screven *Wayne*
Senoia *Coweta*
Seville *Wilcox*
Shady Dale *Jasper*
Shannon *Floyd*
Sharon *Taliaferro*
Sharpsburg *Coweta*
Shellman *Randolph*
Shiloh *Harris*
Siloam *Greene*
Silver Creek *Floyd*
Skyland *DeKalb*
Smarr *Monroe*
Smithville *Lee*
Smyrna *Cobb*
Snellville *Gwinnett*
Social Circle *Walton*
Soperton *Treutlen*
Sparks *Cook*
Sparta *Hancock*
Springfield *Effingham*
Stapleton *Jefferson*
Statenville *Echols*
Statesboro *Bulloch*
Statham *Barrow*
Stephens *Oglethorpe*
Stillmore *Emanuel*
Stillwell *Effingham*
Stockbridge *Henry*
Stockton *Lanier*
Stone Mountain *DeKalb*
Stovall *Meriwether*
Suches *Union*
Sugar Valley *Gordon*
Summerville *Chattooga*
Sumner *Worth*
Sunny Side *Spalding*
Surrency *Appling*
Suwanee *Gwinnett*
Swainsboro *Emanuel*
Sycamore *Turner*
Sylvania *Screven*
Sylvester *Worth*
Talbotton *Talbot*
Talking Rock *Pickens*
Tallapoosa *Haralson*
Tallulah Falls *Rabun*
Talmo *Jackson*
Tarrytown *Montgomery*
Tate *Pickens*
Taylorsville *Bartow*
Temple *Carroll*
Tennga *Murray*
Tennille *Washington*
The Rock *Upson*
Thomaston *Upson*
Thomasville *Thomas*
Thomson *McDuffie*
Thunderbolt *Chatham*
Tifton *Tift*
Tiger *Rabun*
Tignall *Wilkes*
Toccoa *Stephens*
Toomsboro *Wilkinson*
Townsend *McIntosh*
Trenton *Dade*
Trion *Chattooga*
Tucker *DeKalb*
Tunnel Hill *Whitfield*
Turin *Coweta*
Turnerville *Habersham*
Twin City *Emanuel*
Tybee Island *Chatham*
Tyrone *Fayette*
Ty Ty *Tift*
Unadilla *Dooly*

Union City *Fulton*
Union Point *Greene*
Unionville *Tift*
Uvalda *Montgomery*
Valdosta *Lowndes*
Vanna *Hart*
Varnell *Whitfield*
Vidalia *Toombs*
Vienna *Dooly*
Villa Rica *Carroll*
Vikings *Cobb*
Waco *Haralson*
Wadley *Jefferson*
Waleska *Cherokee*
Walthourville *Liberty*
Waresboro *Ware*
Warm Springs *Meriwether*
Warner Robins *Houston*
Warrenton *Warren*
Warthen *Washington*
Warwick *Worth*
Washington *Wilkes*
Watkinsville *Oconee*
Waverly *Camden*
Waverly Hall *Harris*
Waycross *Ware*
Waynesboro *Burke*
Waynesville *Brantley*
West Green *Coffee*
Weston *Webster*
West Point *Troup*
Whigham *Grady*
White *Bartow*
White Oak *Camden*
White Plains *Greene*
Whitesburg *Carroll*
Wildwood *Dade*
Wiley *Rabun*
Willacoochee *Atkinson*
Williamson *Pike*
Winder *Barrow*
Winston *Douglas*
Winterville *Clarke*
Woodbine *Camden*
Woodbury *Meriwether*
Woodland *Talbot*
Woodstock *Cherokee*
Wray *Irwin*
Wrens *Jefferson*
Wrightsville *Johnson*
Yatesville *Upson*
Young Harris *Towns*
Zebulon *Pike*

Hawaii

All four of Hawaii's jurisdictions as well as the State Repository reported that they make criminal conviction data available for employment screening purposes. Civil court records for $10,000 and more are filed in circuit court.

For more information or for offices not listed, contact the state's information hot line at (808) 548-6222 or 548-2211.

Driving Records

District Court of 1st Circuit
Violations Bureau
Attn: Abstract Dept.
1111 Alakea Street
Honolulu, HI 96813
(808) 548-5735

Driving records are available by mail. $2 fee per request. Written request must include job applicant's full name, date of birth and license number. If requesting more than one record at a time, requests must in double spaced, alphabetical order. Make cashier's check or money order payable to Violations Bureau.

Worker's Compensation Records

Department of Labor and Industrial Relations
Orlando Watanabe, Administrator
PO Box 3769
Honolulu, HI 96812-3769
(808) 548-4131

Worker's Compensation records are currently unavailable for employee screening purposes.

Vital Statistics

Vital Records
State Department of Health
PO Box 3378
Honolulu, HI 96801
(808) 586-4533 or 586-4539

Birth and death records are available for $2.00 each. State office has records from 1800's. Make certified check or money order payable to State Department of Health. Marriage records are available for $2.00. Check or money order payable to State Department of Health. Turnaround time is 2-3 weeks. Include name, marriage date, spouse's name, maiden name, place of event, reason for request, and relationship to registrant. Turnaround time is 2-3 weeks. Divorce records are available for $2.00. Check or money order payable to State Department of Health. Include name, divorce date, spouse's name, place where divorce granted. Records at state level are from 1951 to present. Records prior to 1951 are available at Surrogate Court level. A release is required.

Department of Education

Department of Education
Office of Personnel Services
POBox 2360
Honolulu, HI 96804
(808) 586-3388

Records currently are not considered public information.

Medical Licensing

Bureau of Medical Examiners
POBox 3469
Honolulu, HI 96801
(808) 586-3000

Will confirm licenses for MDs by phone or mail. No fee. For licenses not mentioned, contact the above office.

Hawaii Board of Nursing
PO Box 3469
Honolulu, HI 96801
(808) 586-3000

Will confirm license by phone. No fee. Include name, license number.

Bar Association

Hawaii Bar Association
1136 Union Mall
Penthouse 1
Honolulu, HI 96813
(808) 537-1868

Will confirm licenses by phone. No fee. Include name.

Accountancy Board

Professional & Vocational License Division
License Branch
PO Box 3469
Honolulu, HI 96801
(808) 586-2694

Will confirm licenses by phone. No fee. Include name.

Securities Commission

Department of Commerce and Consumer Affairs
Business Registration Division
PO Box 40, Honolulu, HI 96810
(808) 586-2722

Will confirm licenses by phone. No fee. Include name and SSN.

Secretary of State

Department of Commerce and Consumer Affairs
Business Registration Division
POBox 40
Honolulu, HI 96810
(808) 586-2727
Fax (808) 586-2733

Service agent and address, date incorporated, trade names are available by phone or mail. No fee. Contact the above office for additional information.

Criminal Records

State Repository

Hawaii Criminal Justice Data Center
465 S. King Street
Room 101
Honolulu, HI 96813
(808) 587-3106

Record checks are available by mail only. No release necessary. No fee. All requests must include name, date of birth, SSN, race, sex, SASE.

Hawaii County

3rd Circuit Court, Criminal Records
PO Box 1007
Hilo, HI 96721-1007
(808) 933-1261

Felony and misdemeanor records are available by mail. No release necessary. $2.00 search fee. $1.00 fee per copy, $.50 each additional page. $1.00 for certification. Certified check only, payable to 3rd Circuit Court Clerk. Search information required: name, SSN, date of birth, years to search.

Civil records are available by mail. No release necessary. $2.00 search fee. $1.00 fee for first copy, $.50 each additional page. $1.00 for certification. Search information required: name, date of birth, years to search. Specify plaintiff or defendant.

Honolulu County

Felony records
First Circuit Court, Criminal Records
PO Box 619
Honolulu, HI 96809
(808) 548-8462

Felony records are available by mail. No release necessary. $2.00 search fee. $1.00 fee for first copy, $.50 each additional page. $1.00 for certification. Certified check only, payable to First Circuit Court. Search information required: name, date of birth, SSN, years to search.

Civil records
First Circuit Court
PO Box 619
Honolulu, HI 96809
(808) 548-8462

Civil records are available by mail. No release necessary. $2.00 search fee. $1.00 fee for first copy, $.50 each additional page. $1.00 for certification. Search information required: name, date of birth, years to search. Specify plaintiff or defendant.

Misdemeanor records
Records and Information
Management Division
District Court of the 1st Circuit
1111 Alakea St.
Honolulu, HI 96813
(808) 548-2420
Fax (808) 523-8451

Misdemeanor records are available by mail. A release is required. $2.00 search fee. $1.00 fee for first copy, $.50 each additional page. $1.00 for certification. Make check payable to District Court of 1st Circuit. Search information required: name, SSN, date of birth, court date, criminal case number.

Civil records
District Court of the 1st Circuit
1111 Alakea St.
Honolulu, HI 96813
(808) 548-2420
Fax (808) 523-8451

Civil records are available by mail. No release necessary. $2.00 search fee. $1.00 fee for first copy, $.50 each additional page. $1.00 for certification. Search information required: name, date of birth, years to search. Specify plaintiff or defendant.

Kauai County

Clerk of Court
5th Circuit Court
3059 Umi Street, Room 101
Lihue, HI 96766
(808) 246-3300

Felony and misdemeanor records are available by mail. No release necessary. $2.00 search fee. $1.00 fee for first copy, $.50 each additional page. $1.00 for certification. Make check payable to Fifth Circuit Court Clerk. Search information required: name, date of birth, if available, years to search.

Civil records are available by mail. No release necessary. $2.00 search fee. $1.00 fee for first copy, $.50 each additional page. $1.00 for certification. Search information required: name, date of birth, years to search. Specify plaintiff or defendant.

Maui County

Felony records
2nd Circuit Court, Criminal Records
2145 Main Street
Wailuku, HI 96793
(808) 244-2210

Felony records are available by mail. No release necessary. $2.00 search fee. $1.00 fee for first copy, $.50 each additional page. $1.00 for certification. Company checks only, payable to 2nd Circuit Court Clerk. Search information required: name, years to search, date of birth, SSN.

Civil records are available by mail. No release necessary. $2.00 search fee. $1.00 fee for first copy, $.50 each additional page. $1.00 for certification. Search information required: name, date of birth, years to search. Specify plaintiff or defendant.

Misdmeanor records
District Court
PO Box DDD
Wailuku, HI 96793

Misdmeanor records are available by mail. No release necessary. $2.00 search fee. $1.00 fee for first copy, $.50 each additional page. $1.00 for certification. Company checks only, payable to 2nd Circuit Court Clerk. Search information required: name, years to search, date of birth, SSN.

Civil records
District Court
PO Box DDD
Wailuku, HI 96793

Civil records are available by mail. No release necessary. $2.00 search fee. $1.00 fee for first copy, $.50 each additional page. $1.00 for certification. Search information required: name, date of birth, years to search. Specify plaintiff or defendant.

City-County Cross Reference

Aiea *Honolulu*
Anahola *Kauai*
Captain Cook *Hawaii*
Eleele *Kauai*
Ewa *Honolulu*
Ewa Beach *Honolulu*
Haiku *Maui*
Hakalau *Hawaii*
Halawa Heights *Honolulu*
Haleiwa *Honolulu*
Halii Maile *Maui*
Hana *Maui*
Hanalei *Kauai*
Hanamaulu *Kauai*
Hanapepe *Kauai*
Hauula *Honolulu*
Hawaii National Park *Hawaii*
Hawi *Hawaii*
Hilo *Hawaii*
Holualoa *Hawaii*
Honaunau *Hawaii*
Honokaa *Hawaii*
Honolulu *Honolulu*
Honomu *Hawaii*
Hoolehua *Maui*
Kaaawa *Honolulu*
Kahuku *Honolulu*
Kahului *Maui*
Kahaluu *Honolulu*

Kailua *Honolulu*
Kailua Kona *Hawaii*
Kalaheo *Kauai*
Kalaupapa *Kalawao*
Kamuela *Hawaii*
Kaneohe *Honolulu*
Kapaa *Kauai*
Kapaau *Hawaii*
Kaumakani *Kauai*
Kaunakakai *Maui*
Keaau *Hawaii*
Kealakekua *Hawaii*
Kealia *Kauai*
Kekaha *Kauai*
Keokea *Maui*
Kihei *Maui*
Kilauea *Kauai*
Koloa *Kauai*
Kualapuu *Maui*
Kula *Maui*
Kunia *Honolulu*
Kurtistown *Hawaii*
Lahaina *Maui*
Laie *Honolulu*
Lanai City *Maui*
Laupahoehoe *Hawaii*
Lawai *Kauai*
Lihue *Kauai*
Lower Paia *Maui*
Maili *Honolulu*

Makaha *Honolulu*
Makakilo City *Honolulu*
Makawao *Maui*
Makaweli *Kauai*
Maunaloa *Maui*
Maunawili *Honolulu*
Mililani Town *Honolulu*
Mountain View *Hawaii*
Naalehu *Hawaii*
Nanakuli *Honolulu*
Ninole *Hawaii*
Ookala *Hawaii*
Paauhau *Hawaii*
Paauilo *Hawaii*
Pahala *Hawaii*
Pahoa *Hawaii*
Paia *Maui*
Papaaloa *Hawaii*
Papaikou *Hawaii*
Pearl City *Honolulu*
Pepeekeo *Hawaii*
Pukalani *Maui*
Puunene *Maui*
Volcano *Hawaii*
Wahiawa *Honolulu*
Waialua *Honolulu*
Waianae *Honolulu*
Wailuku *Maui*
Waimanalo *Honolulu*
Waimea *Kauai*

Waipahu *Honolulu*
Waipio Acres *Honolulu*
Whitmore Village *Honolulu*

Idaho

Idaho's Criminal Identification Bureau, the state's central repository for criminal records, requires a signed release to process records requests for employment purposes. Twenty nine (29) of the state's forty four (44) counties reported that they do not require a release. Only four (4) of the counties charge a fee to process a request. Thirty seven (37) counties will honor a fax request.

For more information or for offices not listed, contact the state's information hot line at (208) 334-2411.

Driving Records

Idaho Transportation Department
Driver Services
PO Box 34
Boise, ID 83731
(208) 334-8735
Fax (208) 334-8739

Driving records are available by mail. $4.00 fee per request. $4.00 fee per copy. $8.00 for certification. Turnaround time is 2 days. Written request must include job applicant's full name, date of birth, license number and signed driver release. Make check payable to Idaho Transportation Department.

Worker's Compensation Records

Idaho Industrial Commission
State House Mail
317 Main Street
Boise, ID 83720
(208) 334-6000
Fax (208) 334-3321

Worker's compensation records are available by mail or fax. Request must include subject's full name, SSN and number of years to be checked. There is no search fee. A signed release is required. Specify search or copies of a file.

Vital Statistics

Vital Statistics
Statehouse
Boise, ID 83720
(208) 334-5988

Birth and death records are available for $8.00 each. State office has records from July, 1911. An employer can obtain records with a notarized release. Make any type of check or money order payable to Vital Statistics. Search information required: name, date of birth, place, father's name, mother's maiden name, relationship to individual.

Marriage and divorce records from 1947 are available for $8.00. Include full name, maiden name, marriage date, spouse's name, and place of marriage. Turnaround time is 4 weeks. Notarized release required for marriage and divorce records.

Department of Education

Teacher Certification Department
650 West State Street
Len B. Jordon Building
Boise, ID 83720
(208) 334-3475

Field of certification is available by phone or mail. Include name and SSN.

Medical Licensing

State Board of Medicine
280 N. 8th
Suite 202, State House Mail
Boise, ID 83720
(208) 334-2822
Fax (208) 334-2801

Will confirm licenses for MDs and DOs by phone, mail or fax. No fee. For licenses not mentioned, contact the above office.

Idaho Board of Nursing
280 North 8th, Suite 210
Boise, ID 83720
(208) 334-3110

Will confirm license by phone. No fee. Include name, license number, if available.

Bar Association

State Bar Association
PO Box 895
Boise, ID 83701
(208) 334-3469

Will confirm licenses by phone. No fee. Include name.

Accountancy Board

Idaho Accountancy Board
State House Mail
Boise, ID 83720
(208) 334-2490

Will confirm licenses by phone. No fee. Include name.

Securities Commission

Department of Finance
Securities Bureau
700 West State Street
Boise, ID 83720
(208) 334-3684

Will confirm licenses by phone. No fee. Include name and SSN.

Secretary of State

Secretary of State
State House
Room 203
Boise, ID 83720
(208) 334-2300

Service agent and address, date incorporated, trade names are available by phone or mail. No fee. Contact the above office for additional information

Criminal Records

State Repository

Criminal Identification Bureau
6064 Corporal Lane
Boise, ID 83704
(208) 327-7130

Felony and misdemeanor records are available by mail only. All requests must include subject's full name, date of birth and, if available, social security number. A signed release from the subject is required. A name check only is $5.00. A fingerprint check is $10.00. Make check payable to Idaho Department of Law Enforcement. Information returned includes both conviction and arrest records. Turnaround time is normally 24 to 48 hours plus mail time.

Ada County

Clerk of Court, Criminal Records
514 W. Jefferson
Boise, ID 83702-5931
(208) 383-1234

Felony records are available by mail. No release necessary. No search fee. Search information required: name, years to search, SASE.

Civil records are available by mail. No release necessary. No search fee. $1.00 fee per copy. $1.00 for certification. Search information required: name, date of birth, years to search, SASE. Specify plaintiff or defendant.

Adams County

Clerk of Court, Criminal Records
PO Box 48
Council, ID 83612
(208) 253-4561
Fax (208) 253-4258

Felony and misdemeanor records are available by mail. A release is required. No search fee. $1.00 fee per copy, $1.00 fee for certification. Search information required: name, SASE. Turnaround time is 1-2 weeks.

Civil records are available by mail. No release necessary. A release is required. No search fee. $1.00 fee per copy, $1.00 fee for certification. Search information required: name, date of birth, years to search. Specify plaintiff or defendant.

Bannock County

Deputy Clerk's Office, Criminal Records
PO Box 4847
Pocatello, ID 83205
(208) 236-7352
Fax (208) 236-7013

Felony records are available by mail or fax. No release necessary. No search fee. $1.00 fee per copy. $1.50 for certification. Search information required: name, date of birth, SSN, SASE.

Civil records are available by mail. No release necessary. mail or fax. No release necessary. No search fee. $1.00 fee per copy. $1.50 for certification. Search information required: name, date of birth, years to search, SASE. Specify plaintiff or defendant.

Bear Lake County

Clerk of Court, Criminal Records
PO Box 190
Paris, ID 83261
(208) 945-2208
Fax (208) 945-2780

Felony and misdemeanor records are available by mail. A release is required. No search fee. $1.00 fee per copy. $1.50 for certification. Search information required: name, SSN, date of birth, previous address, years to search. Turnaround time is 1 week.

Civil records are available by mail. A release is required. No search fee. $1.00 fee per copy. $1.50 for certification. Search information required: name, date of birth, years to search. Specify plaintiff or defendant.

Benewah County

Magistrate Court, Criminal Records
Benewah County Courthouse
701 College
St. Maries, ID 83861
(208) 245-3241
Fax (208) 245-3046

Felony and misdemeanor records are available by mail, phone or fax. $3.00 for first page of fax response, $1.00 each additional page. A release is required. No search fee. $1.00 fee per copy. $1.50 for certification. Search information required: name, SSN, date of birth. Turnaround time is 1-2 weeks.

Civil records are available by mail, phone or fax. $3.00 for first page of fax response, $1.00 each additional page. A release is required. No search fee. $1.00 fee per copy. $1.50 for certification. Search information required: name, date of birth, years to search. Specify plaintiff or defendant.

Bingham County

Felony and misdemeanor records
Magistrate Court, Criminal Records
PO Box 807
Blackfoot, ID 83221
(208) 785-5005 Extension 313
Fax (208) 785-5199

Felony and misdemeanor records are available by mail or fax. A release is required. No search fee. $1.00 fee per copy, $1.00 for certification. Search information required: name, SSN, date of birth, years to search. Turnaround time is 1-2 weeks.

Civil records
Magistrate Court
PO Box 717
Blackfoot, ID 83221
(208) 785-5005 Extension 312
Fax (208) 785-5199

Civil records are available by mail or fax. A release is required. No search fee. $1.00 fee per copy, $1.00 for certification. Search information required: name, date of birth, years to search. Specify plaintiff or defendant.

Blaine County

Magistrate Court, Criminal Records
PO Box 1006
Hailey, ID 83333
(208) 788-5525 5521
Fax (208) 788-5527

Felony and misdemeanor records are available by mail, phone or fax. No release necessary. No search fee. $1.00 fee per copy, $1.00 for certification. Search information required: name, years to search, date of birth, SSN, SASE.

Civil records are available by mail. No release necessary. No search fee. $1.00 fee per copy, $1.00 for certification. Search information required: name, date of birth, years to search, SASE. Specify plaintiff or defendant.

Boise County

Boise County Court, Criminal Records
PO Box 126
Idaho City, ID 83631
(208) 392-4452
Fax (208) 392-4473

Felony and misdemeanor records are available by mail or fax. No release necessary. $10.00 fee. $1.00 fee per copy, $1.50 for certification. Certified check only, payable to Clerk of Court. Search information required: name, SSN, previous address, years to search, SASE. Turnaround time is 2 weeks.

Civil records are available by mail. No release necessary. No search fee. $1.00 fee per copy, $1.50 for certification. Search information required: name, date of birth, years to search, SASE. Specify plaintiff or defendant.

Bonner County

Clerk of Court
215 S. First
Sandpoint, ID 83864
(208) 263-6841, Ext. 205
Fax (208) 265-1447

Felony and misdemeanor records are available by mail or fax. No release necessary. No search fee. $1.00 fee per copy, $1.00 for certification. Search information required: name, SSN, date of birth, SASE.

Civil records are available by mail. No release necessary. No search fee. $1.00 fee per copy, $1.00 for certification. Search information required: name, date of birth, years to search. Specify plaintiff or defendant.

Bonneville County

Felony records
District Court Clerk, Criminal Records
605 N. Capitol
Idaho Falls, ID 83402
(208) 529-1388, Ext. 388
Fax (208) 529-1300

Felony records are available by mail or fax. No release necessary. No search fee. $1.00 for certification. Search information required: name, years to search, date of birth, SASE. Turnaround time is 1-2 weeks.

Civil records
District Court Clerk
605 N. Capitol
Idaho Falls, ID 83402
(208) 529-1388
Fax (208) 529-1300

Civil records are available by mail. No release necessary. No search fee. $1.00 for certification. Search information required: name, date of birth, years to search, SASE. Specify plaintiff or defendant.

Misdemeanor records
Magistrate Court, Criminal Records
605 N. Capitol
Idaho Falls, ID 83402
(208) 529-1388
Fax (208) 529-1300

Misdemeanor records since 1977 are available by mail. No release necessary. No search fee. $1.00 fee per copy, $1.00 for certification, prepaid. Check payable to Clerk of District Court. Search information required: name, years to search, date of birth, SSN, SASE. Turnaround time is 1-2 weeks.

Civil records
Magistrate Court
605 N. Capitol
Idaho Falls, ID 83402
(208) 529-1388
Fax (208) 529-1300

Civil records are available by mail. No release necessary. No search fee. Search information required: name, date of birth, years to search. Specify plaintiff or defendant.

Boundary County

Magistrate Court, Criminal Records
PO Box 419
Bonners Ferry, ID 83805-0419
(208) 267-5504

Felony and misdemeanor records are available in person only. See Idaho state repository for additional information.

Civil records are available in person only. See Idaho state repository for additional information.

Butte County

Court Magistrate, Criminal Records
PO Box 171
Arco, ID 83213
(208) 527-8259
Fax (208) 527-8259

Felony and misdemeanor records are available by mail, fax or phone. A release is required. No search fee. $1.00 fee per copy. $1.00 for certification. Search information required: name, SSN, date of birth, SASE. Turnaround time is 1 week.

Civil records are available by mail, fax or phone. No release necessary. No search fee. $1.00 fee per copy. $1.00 for certification. Search information required: name, date of birth, years to search, SASE. Specify plaintiff or defendant.

Camas County

Magistrate Court, Criminal Records
PO Box 430
Fairfield, ID 83327
(208) 764-2238
Fax (208) 764-2349

Felony and misdemeanor records are available by mail or fax. No release necessary. No search fee. $.10 fee per copy. Search information required: name, years to search.

Civil records are available by mail or fax. No release necessary. No search fee. $.10 fee pre copy. Search information required: name, date of birth, years to search. Specify plaintiff or defendant.

Canyon County

Clerk of District Court, Criminal Dept.
1115 Albany
Caldwell, ID 83605
(208) 454-7569
Fax (208) 454-7525

Felony and misdemeanor records are available by mail. A release is required. No search fee. $1.00 fee per copy, $1.00 fee for certification. Search information required: name, years to search, SASE. Turnaround time is 1-2 weeks.

Civil records are available by phone. A release is required. No search fee. $1.00 fee per copy, $1.00 fee for certification. Search information required: name, date of birth, years to search. Specify plaintiff or defendant.

Caribou County

Magistrate Court, Criminal Records
159 S. Main
Soda Springs, ID 83276
(208) 547-4342
Fax (208) 547-4759

Felony and misdemeanor records are available by mail, phone or fax. No release necessary. No search fee. $1.00 fee per copy. $.50 for certification. Search information required: name, SSN, if available, years to search.

Civil records are available by mail, phone or fax. No release necessary. No search fee. $1.00 fee per copy, $.50 for certification. Search information required: name, date of birth, years to search. Specify plaintiff or defendant.

Cassia County

Magistrate Court, Criminal Records
Cassia County Courthouse
1451 Overland
Burley, ID 83318
(208) 678-7351

Felony and misdemeanor records are available by mail. No release necessary. No search fee. Search information required: name, SSN, date of birth, years to search, SASE.

Civil records are available by mail. No release necessary. No search fee. Search information required: name, date of birth, years to search, SASE. Specify plaintiff or defendant.

Clark County

Magistrate Court, Criminal Records
PO Box 205
Dubois, ID 83423
(208) 374-5402
Fax (208) 374-5609

Felony and misdemeanor records are available by mail or fax. No release necessary. No search fee. $.10 fee per copy. $1.00 for certification. Search information required: name, SSN, date of birth, years to search.

Civil records are available by mail or fax. No release necessary. No search fee. $.10 fee per copy. $1.00 for certification. Search information required: name, date of birth, years to search. Specify plaintiff or defendant.

Clearwater County

Magistrate Court, Criminal Records
PO Box 586
Orofino, ID 83544
(208) 476-5596

Felony and misdemeanor records are available in person only. See Idaho state repository for additional information.

Civil records are available in person only. See Idaho state repository for additional information.

Custer County

Magistrate Court, Criminal Records
PO Box 385
Challis, ID 83226
(208) 879-2359

Felony and misdemeanor records prior to 1985 are available by mail. A release is required. No search fee. $1.00 fee per copy, $1.00 fee for certification. Search information required: name, SSN, date of birth, SASE.

Civil records are available by mail. A release is required. No search fee. $1.00 fee per copy, $1.00 fee for certification. Search information required: name, date of birth, years to search, SASE. Specify plaintiff or defendant.

Elmore County

Magistrate Court, Criminal Records
150 S. 4th E., Suite 5
Mountain Home, ID 83647
(208) 587-2133
Fax (801) 587-2159

Felony and misdemeanor records are available by mail or fax. A notarized release required. No search fee. $1.00 fee per copy, $1.00 for certification. Search information required: name, date of birth, years to search, SASE. Turnaround time is 1 week.

Civil records are available by mail or fax. No release necessary. No search fee. $1.00 fee per copy, $1.00 for certification. Search information required: name, date of birth, years to search, SASE. Specify plaintiff or defendant.

Franklin County

Magistrate District Court, Criminal Records
39 W. Oneida
Preston, ID 83263
(208) 852-0877
Fax (208) 852-2926

Felony and misdemeanor records are available by mail or fax. No release necessary. $2.00 search fee. $1.00 fee per copy, $1.00 fee for certification. Search information required: name, SASE. Turnaround time is 1 week.

Civil records are available by mail or fax. No release necessary. $2.00 search fee. $1.00 fee per copy, $1.00 fee for certification. Search information required: name, date of birth, years to search, SASE. Specify plaintiff or defendant.

Fremont County

Magistrate District Court, Criminal Records
PO Box 42
St. Anthony, ID 83445
(208) 624-7401
Fax (208) 624-4607

Felony and misdemeanor records prior to 1983 are available by mail or fax. Records since 1983 are available by phone. A release is required. No search fee. $1.00 fee per copy, $1.00 fee for certification. Search information required: name, date of birth, SSN, SASE.

Civil records are available by mail. No release necessary. No search fee. $1.00 fee per copy, $1.00 fee for certification. Search information required: name, date of birth, years to search, SASE. Specify plaintiff or defendant.

Gem County

Magistrate Court, Criminal Records
415 E. Main
Room 300, Courthouse
Emmett, ID 83617
(208) 365-4221
Fax (208) 365-6172

Felony and misdemeanor records are available by mail or fax. No release necessary. $5.00 search fee. $1.00 fee per copy, $1.00 fee for certification. Search information required: name, SSN, date of birth, years to search. Turnaround time is 1 week.

Civil records are available by mail or fax. No release necessary. $5.00 search fee. $1.00 fee per copy, $1.00 fee for certification. Search information required: name, date of birth, years to search. Specify plaintiff or defendant.

Gooding County

Magistrate Court, Criminal Records
PO Box 477
Gooding, ID 83330
(208) 934-4261
Fax (208) 934-4408

Felony and misdemeanor records are available by mail or fax. No release necessary. No search fee. $1.00 fee per copy, $1.50 fee for certification. Search information required: name, SSN, date of birth, SASE. Turnaround time is 1 week.

Civil records are available by mail or fax. No release necessary. No search fee. $1.00 fee per copy, $1.50 fee for certification. Search information required: name, date of birth, years to search, SASE. Specify plaintiff or defendant.

Idaho County

District Court, Criminal Records
Idaho County Courthouse
Grangeville, ID 83530
(208) 983-2776
Fax (208) 983-2773

Felony and misdemeanor records are available by mail, fax or phone. No release necessary. No search fee. $1.00 fee per copy, $1.00 fee for certification. Search information required: name, SSN, date of birth, SASE.

Civil records are available by mail, fax or phone. No release necessary. No search fee. $1.00 fee per copy, $1.00 fee for certification. Search information required: name, date of birth, years to search. Specify plaintiff or defendant.

Jefferson County

Magistrate Court, Criminal Records
PO Box 71
Rigby, ID 83442
(208) 745-7736
Fax (208) 745-9212

Felony and misdemeanor records are available by mail, fax or phone. A release is required. No search fee. $1.00 fee per copy, $2.00 fee for certification. Search information required: name, SSN, date of birth, years to search, SASE.

Civil records are available by mail, fax or phone. A release is required. No search fee. $1.00 fee per copy, $2.00 fee for certification. Search information required: name, date of birth, years to search, SASE. Specify plaintiff or defendant.

Jerome County

Clerk of District Court, Criminal Records
PO Box 407
Jerome, ID 83338
(208) 324-8811
Fax (208) 324-2719

Felony and misdemeanor records are available by mail, fax or phone. No release necessary. No search fee. $1.00 fee per copy, $1.50 fee for certification. Search information required: name, SSN, date of birth, SASE.

Civil records are available by mail, fax or phone. No release necessary. No search fee. $1.00 fee per copy, $1.50 fee for certification. Search information required: name, date of birth, years to search, SASE. Specify plaintiff or defendant.

Kootenai County

District Court, Criminal Records
324 W. Garden
Coeur D'Alene, ID 83814
(208) 769-4440

Felony and misdemeanor records are available in person only. See Idaho state repository for additional information.

Civil records are available in person only. See Idaho state repository for additional information.

Latah County

Clerk of District Court, Criminal Records
Latah County
PO Box 8068
Moscow, ID 83843
(208) 883-2255 Extension 356

Felony and misdemeanor records are available by mail. No release necessary. $4.00 search fee. $1.00 fee per copy, $1.00 fee for certification. Certified check only, payable to Clerk of District Court. Search information required: name, SSN, date of birth, years to search, SASE. Turnaround time is 1 week.

Civil records are available by mail. No release necessary. $4.00 search fee. $1.00 fee per copy, $1.00 fee for certification. Search information required: name, date of birth, years to search, SASE. Specify plaintiff or defendant.

Lemhi County

District Court, Criminal Records
206 Courthouse Drive
Salmon, ID 83467
(208) 756-2815
Fax (208) 756-4673

Felony and misdemeanor records are available by mail or fax. A release is required. No search fee. $5.00 fee for fax response. $1.00 fee per copy, $1.00 fee for certification. Search information required: name, SASE. Turnaround time is 1 week.

Civil records are available by mail or fax. A release is required. No search fee. $5.00 fee for fax response. $1.00 fee per copy, $1.00 fee for certification. Search information required: name, date of birth, years to search. Specify plaintiff or defendant.

Lewis County

Magistrate Court, Criminal Records
PO Box 39
Nezperce, ID 83543
(208) 937-2251
Fax (208) 937-2651

Felony and misdemeanor records are available by mail or fax. No release necessary. No search fee. $1.00 fee per copy, $1.00 for certification. Search information required: name, date of birth, SASE, years to search. Turnaround time is 1 week.

Civil records are available by mail or fax. No release necessary. No search fee. $1.00 fee per copy, $1.00 for certification. Search information required: name, date of birth, years to search. Specify plaintiff or defendant.

Lincoln County

District Court, Criminal Records
Drawer A
Shoshone, ID 83352
(208) 886-7641
Fax (208) 886-2851

Felony and misdemeanor records are available by mail. A notarized release is required. No search fee. $1.00 fee per copy, $1.50 fee for certification. Search information required: name, years to search, SASE.

Civil records are available by mail. No release necessary. No search fee. $1.00 fee per copy, $1.50 for certification. Search information required: name, date of birth, years to search, SASE. Specify plaintiff or defendant.

Madison County

Magistrate Court, Criminal Records
PO Box 389
Rexburg, ID 83340
(208) 356-9383
Fax (208) 356-8396

Felony and misdemeanor records are available by mail or fax. No release necessary. No search fee. $1.00 fee per copy, $2.00 fee for certification. Search information required: name, SSN, date of birth, SASE. Turnaround time is 1 week.

Civil records are available by mail or fax. No release necessary. No search fee. $1.00 fee per copy, $2.00 for certification. Search information required: name, date of birth, years to search, SASE. Specify plaintiff or defendant.

Minidoka County

Magistrate District Court, Criminal Records
PO Box 474
Rupert, ID 83350
(208) 436-7186
Fax (208) 436-5272

Felony and misdemeanor records are available by mail, fax or phone. No release necessary. No search fee. $1.00 fee per copy, $.50 for certification. Search information required: name, SSN, date of birth, years to search. Turnaround time is 1 week.

Civil records are available by mail, fax or phone. No release necessary. No search fee. $1.00 fee per copy, $.50 for certification. Search information required: name, date of birth, years to search. Specify plaintiff or defendant.

Nez Perce County

Nez Perce County Courthouse, Criminal Records
PO Box 896
Lewiston, ID 83501
(208) 799-3040
Fax (208) 799-3058

Felony and misdemeanor records from September, 1990 are available by mail or fax. No release necessary. No search fee. $.25 fee per copy, $1.00 fee for certification. Search information required: name, date of birth, SSN, years to search, SASE.

Civil records are available by mail or fax. No release necessary. No search fee. $.25 fee per copy, $1.00 for certification. Search information required: name, date of birth, years to search, SASE. Specify plaintiff or defendant.

Oneida County

District and Magistrate Court,
Criminal Records
10 Court Street
Malad City, ID 83252
(208) 766-4285
Fax (208) 766-4285

Felony and misdemeanor records are available by mail or fax. A release is required. No search fee. $1.00 fee per copy. $1.00 for certification. Search information required: name, SSN, date of birth, SASE.

Civil records are available by mail or fax. No release necessary. No search fee. $1.00 fee per copy, $1.00 for certification. Search information required: name, date of birth, years to search, SASE. Specify plaintiff or defendant.

Owyhee County

Owyhee County Magistrate and District Court, Criminal Records
Owyhee County Courthouse
Murphy, ID 83650
(208) 495-2806
Fax (208) 495-2806

Felony and misdemeanor records are available by mail or fax. No release necessary. No search fee. $1.00 fee per copy, $1.00 for certification. Search information required: name, SSN. Turnaround time is 1 week.

Civil records are available by mail or fax. No release necessary. No search fee. $1.00 fee per copy, $1.00 for certification. Search information required: name, date of birth, years to search. Specify plaintiff or defendant.

Payette County

Payette County Clerk, Criminal Records
1130 3rd Ave. N.
Payette, ID 83661
(208) 642-6000
Fax (208) 642-6011

Felony and misdemeanor records are available by mail or fax. No release necessary. No search fee. $1.00 fee per copy, $1.00 for certification. Search information required: name, SSN, date of birth, SASE. Turnaround time is 1 week.

Civil records are available by mail or fax. No release necessary. No search fee. $1.00 fee per copy, $1.00 for certification. Search information required: name, date of birth, years to search, SASE. Specify plaintiff or defendant.

Power County

Magistrate Court, Criminal Records
Power County Courthouse
543 Bannock Ave.
American Falls, ID 83211
(208) 226-7618
Fax (208) 226-7612

Felony and misdemeanor records are available by mail or fax. A release is required. No search fee. $1.00 fee per copy, $1.00 for certification. Search information required: name, SSN, date of birth. Turnaround time is 1 week.

Civil records are available by mail or fax. A release is required. No search fee. $1.00 fee per copy, $1.00 for certification. Search information required: name, date of birth, years to search. Specify plaintiff or defendant.

Shoshone County

Clerk of Court, Criminal Records
PO Box 1049
Wallace, ID 83873
(208) 752-1266
Fax (208) 753-0921

Felony and misdemeanor records are available in person only. See Idaho state repository for additional information.

Civil records are available in person only. See Idaho state repository for additional information.

Teton County

Magistrate Court, Criminal Records
PO Box 770
Driggs, ID 83422
(208) 354-2239
Fax (208) 354-8410

Felony and misdemeanor records are available by mail or fax. A release is required. No search fee. $1.00 fee per copy, $1.00 for certification. Search information required: name, SASE.

Civil records are available by mail or fax. A release is required. No search fee. $1.00 fee per copy, $1.00 for certification. Search information required: name, date of birth, years to search, SASE. Specify plaintiff or defendant.

Twin Falls County

Clerk of District Court, Criminal Records
PO Box 126
Twin Falls, ID 83301
(208) 736-4024
Fax (208) 736-4002

Felony and misdemeanor records are available by mail, fax or phone. No release necessary. No search fee. $1.00 fee per copy, $1.00 fee for certification. Search information required: name, date of birth, years to search.

Civil records are available by mail, fax or phone. No release necessary. No search fee. $1.00 fee per copy, $1.00 for certification. Search information required: name, date of birth, years to search. Specify plaintiff or defendant.

Valley County

Clerk of Court, Criminal Records
PO Box 650
Cascade, ID 83611
(208) 382-4150

Felony and misdemeanor records are available in person or by mail (if docket number known). No release necessary. No search fee. $1.00 fee per copy, $1.00 for certification. Search information required: name, SSN, date of birth, SASE.

Civil records are available by mail. No release necessary. No search fee. $1.00 fee per copy, $1.00 for certification. Search information required: name, date of birth, years to search, SASE. Specify plaintiff or defendant.

Washington County

Clerk of District Court, Criminal Records
PO Box 670
Weiser, ID 83672
(208) 549-2092
Fax (208) 549-3925

Felony and misdemeanor records are available by mail or fax. No release necessary. No search fee. $1.00 fee per copy, $1.00 fee for certification. Search information required: name. Turnaround time is 1 week.

Civil records are available by phone. No release necessary. No search fee. $1.00 fee per copy, $1.00 for certification. Search information required: name, date of birth, years to search. Specify plaintiff or defendant.

City-County Cross Reference

Aberdeen *Bingham*
Ahsahka *Clearwater*
Albion *Cassia*
Almo *Cassia*
American Falls *Power*
Ammon *Bonneville*
Arbon *Power*
Arco *Butte*
Arimo *Bannock*
Ashton *Fremont*
Athol *Kootenai*
Atlanta *Elmore*
Atomic City *Bingham*
Avery *Shoshone*

Bancroft *Caribou*
Banks *Boise*
Basalt *Bingham*
Bayview *Kootenai*
Bellevue *Blaine*
Bern *Bear Lake*
Blackfoot *Bingham*
Blanchard *Bonner*
Bliss *Gooding*
Bloomington *Bear Lake*
Boise *Ada*
Bonners Ferry *Boundary*
Bovill *Latah*
Bruneau *Owyhee*

Buhl *Twin Falls*
Burley *Cassia*
Calder *Shoshone*
Caldwell *Canyon*
Cambridge *Washington*
Carey *Blaine*
Carmen *Lemhi*
Cascade *Valley*
Castleford *Twin Falls*
Cataldo *Kootenai*
Challis *Custer*
Chester *Fremont*
Chubbuck *Bannock*
Clark Fork *Bonner*

Clarkia *Shoshone*
Clayton *Custer*
Clifton *Franklin*
Cobalt *Lemhi*
Cocolalla *Bonner*
Coeur D' Alene *Kootenai*
Conda *Caribou*
Coolin *Bonner*
Cottonwood *Idaho*
Council *Adams*
Craigmont *Lewis*
Culdesac *Nez Perce*
Dayton *Franklin*
Deary *Latah*

Declo *Cassia*
Desmet *Benewah*
Dingle *Bear Lake*
Donnelly *Valley*
Dover *Bonner*
Downey *Bannock*
Driggs *Teton*
Dubois *Clark*
Eagle *Ada*
Eastport *Boundary*
Eden *Jerome*
Elba *Cassia*
Elk City *Idaho*
Elk River *Clearwater*
Ellis *Custer*
Emmett *Gem*
Fairfield *Camas*
Felt *Teton*
Ferdinand *Idaho*
Fernwood *Benewah*
Filer *Twin Falls*
Firth *Bingham*
Fort Hall *Bingham*
Franklin *Franklin*
Fruitland *Payette*
Fruitvale *Adams*
Garden City *Ada*
Garden Valley *Boise*
Genesee *Latah*
Geneva *Bear Lake*
Georgetown *Bear Lake*
Gibbonsville *Lemhi*
Glenns Ferry *Elmore*
Gooding *Gooding*
Grace *Caribou*
Grand View *Owyhee*
Grangeville *Idaho*
Greenleaf *Canyon*
Hagerman *Gooding*
Hailey *Blaine*
Hamer *Jefferson*
Hammett *Elmore*
Hansen *Twin Falls*
Harrison *Kootenai*
Harvard *Latah*
Hayden *Kootenai*
Hazelton *Jerome*
Headquarters *Clearwater*
Heyburn *Minidoka*
Hill City *Camas*
Homedale *Owyhee*
Hope *Bonner*
Horseshoe Bend *Boise*
Howe *Butte*
Huston *Canyon*
Idaho City *Boise*
Idaho Falls *Bonneville*
Indian Valley *Adams*
Inkom *Bannock*
Iona *Bonneville*
Irwin *Bonneville*
Island Park *Fremont*
Jerome *Jerome*
Juliaetta *Latah*
Kamiah *Lewis*
Kellogg *Shoshone*
Kendrick *Latah*
Ketchum *Blaine*
Kimberly *Twin Falls*
King Hill *Elmore*
Kingston *Shoshone*
Kooskia *Idaho*
Kootenai *Bonner*
Kuna *Ada*
Laclede *Bonner*
Lapwai *Nez Perce*

Lava Hot Springs *Bannock*
Leadore *Lemhi*
Lemhi *Lemhi*
Lenore *Nez Perce*
Letha *Gem*
Lewiston *Nez Perce*
Lewisville *Jefferson*
Lincoln *Bonneville*
Lucile *Idaho*
McCall *Valley*
McCammon *Bannock*
Mackay *Custer*
Macks Inn *Fremont*
Malad City *Oneida*
Malta *Cassia*
Marsing *Owyhee*
Marysville *Fremont*
May *Lemhi*
Melba *Canyon*
Menan *Jefferson*
Meridian *Ada*
Middleton *Canyon*
Midvale *Washington*
Monteview *Jefferson*
Montpelier *Bear Lake*
Moore *Butte*
Moreland *Bingham*
Moscow *Latah*
Mountain Home *Elmore*
Moyie Springs *Boundary*
Mullan *Shoshone*
Murphy *Owyhee*
Murtaugh *Twin Falls*
Nampa *Canyon*
Naples *Boundary*
Newdale *Fremont*
New Meadows *Adams*
New Plymouth *Payette*
Nezperce *Lewis*
Nordman *Bonner*
North Fork *Lemhi*
Notus *Canyon*
Oakley *Cassia*
Ola *Gem*
Orofino *Clearwater*
Osburn *Shoshone*
Ovid *Bear Lake*
Palisades *Bonneville*
Paris *Bear Lake*
Parker *Fremont*
Parma *Canyon*
Paul *Minidoka*
Payette *Payette*
Peck *Nez Perce*
Picabo *Blaine*
Pierce *Clearwater*
Pinehurst *Shoshone*
Pingree *Bingham*
Plummer *Benewah*
Pocatello *Bannock*
Pollock *Idaho*
Ponderay *Bonner*
Porthill *Boundary*
Post Falls *Kootenai*
Potlatch *Latah*
Preston *Franklin*
Priest River *Bonner*
Princeton *Latah*
Rathdrum *Kootenai*
Reubens *Lewis*
Rexburg *Madison*
Richfield *Lincoln*
Rigby *Jefferson*
Riggins *Idaho*
Ririe *Jefferson*
Roberts *Jefferson*

Rockland *Power*
Rupert *Minidoka*
Sagle *Bonner*
Saint Anthony *Fremont*
Saint Charles *Bear Lake*
Saint Maries *Benewah*
Salmon *Lemhi*
Sandpoint *Bonner*
Santa *Benewah*
Shelley *Bingham*
Shoshone *Lincoln*
Silverton *Shoshone*
Smelterville *Shoshone*
Soda Springs *Caribou*
Spalding *Nez Perce*
Spirit Lake *Kootenai*
Stanley *Custer*
Star *Ada*
Stites *Idaho*
Sugar City *Madison*
Sun Valley *Blaine*
Swanlake *Bannock*
Swan Valley *Bonneville*
Tendoy *Lemhi*
Tensed *Benewah*
Terreton *Jefferson*
Teton *Fremont*
Tetonia *Teton*
Troy *Latah*
Twin Falls *Twin Falls*
Ucon *Bonneville*
Victor *Teton*
Viola *Latah*
Wallace *Shoshone*
Wayan *Caribou*
Weippe *Clearwater*
Weiser *Washington*
Wendell *Gooding*
Weston *Franklin*
White Bird *Idaho*
Wilder *Canyon*
Winchester *Lewis*
Worley *Kootenai*
Yellow Pine *Valley*

Illinois

All 102 of the state's counties report that they make conviction records available to employers for employment screening purposes. In 100 of the counties, mail and/or phone requests are accepted. Twenty six (26) counties will allow fax requests. Access through the State Repository for criminal records is now available.

For more information or for offices not listed, contact the state's information hot line at (217) 782-2000.

Driving Records

Motor Vehicle Services
2701 S. Dirksen Parkway
Springfield, IL 62723
(217) 782-2720

Driving records are available by mail. $2 fee per request. Turnaround time is 2 weeks. Written request must include job applicant's full name and license number or full name and date of birth. Make check payable to Secretary of State.

Worker's Compensation Records

Illinois Industrial Commission
Suite 8-200
100 West Randolph
Chicago, IL 60601
(312) 814-6611

Due to personnel shortages, information must be obtained in person at the above address.

Vital Statistics

Office of Vital Records
State Department of Public Health
605 West Jefferson Street
Springfield, IL 62702-5097
(217) 782-6553

Certified copies of birth and death records are available each for $15.00. Certification of birth and death records are available each for $10.00. State office has had records since January 1916. For copies of State records prior to January 1916, write to County Clerk in county where event occurred (The fee for a search of the files is $10.00. If the record is found, one certification is issued at no additional charge. Additional certifications of the same record ordered at the same time are $2.00 each. The fee for a full certified copy is $15.00. Additional certified copies of the same record ordered at the same time are $2.00 each). Employer can obtain records with a written release. Include father's name, mother's maiden name, date of birth, place of birth. Make certified check or money order payable to Illinois Department of Public Health.

Verification of marriage and divorce records prior 1962 available at the above office. Fee is $5.00. Turnaround time is 10 days for verification. Include name, marriage date, date of divorce, and spouse's name for verification. Certified copies of all marriage and divorce records are available from county where event took place.

Department of Education

Illinois State Board of Education
100 N. First Street
Springfield, IL 62777
(217) 782-2805

Field of certification is available by phone or mail. Include full name and SSN.

Medical Licensing

Department of Professional Regulation
320 W. Washington
Springfield, IL 62786
(217) 782-0920

Will confirm licenses for MDs by phone for a maximum of 3 names, or mail. No search fee. $20.00 for certification. For licenses not mentioned, contact the above office.

Illinois Department of Professional Regulation
320 West Washington Street, 3rd Floor
Springfield, IL 62786
(217) 782-0458

Will confirm license by phone. No fee. Include name, license number, if available.

Bar Association

Illinois Bar Association
1 N. Old Capitol Plaza, Suite 3345
Springfield, IL 62786
(217) 522-6838

Will confirm licenses by phone. No fee. Include name.

Accountancy Board

State Board of Accountancy
320 W. Washington, 2nd Floor
Springfield, IL 62786
(217) 782-0458

Will confirm licenses by phone. No fee. Include name.

Securities Commission

Office of Secretary of State
Securities Department
900 South Spring Street
Springfield, IL 62704
(217) 785-4929

Will confirm licenses by phone. No fee. Include name and SSN.

Secretary of State

Secretary of State
Corporation Division
Centenial Bldg. 3rd Floor
Springfield, IL 62756
(217) 782-7880

Service agent and address, date incorporated, standing with tax commission, trade names are available by phone or mail. Contact the above office for additional information.

Criminal Records

State Repository

Department of State Police
Forensic Services and Identification
260 N. Chicago Street
Joliet, IL 60431
(815) 740-5160

Felony and miesdemeanor records are available by mail. No release necessary. $4.00 search fee. Search information required: name, date of birth, race, sex, SASE

Adams County

Circuit Clerk's Office, Criminal
Records
Adams County Courthouse
521 Vermont Street
Quincy, IL 62301
(217) 223-6300 Ext. 411

Felony and misdemeanor records are available by mail or phone. No release necessary. No search fee. $.50 fee per copy, $1.00 for certification. Search information required: name, years to search.

Civil records are available by mail. No release necessary. No search fee. $.50 fee per copy, $1.00 for certification. Search information required: name, date of birth, years to search. Specify plaintiff or defendant.

Alexander County

Circuit Clerk's Office, Criminal
Records
2000 Washington Ave.
Cairo, IL 62914
(618) 734-0107
Fax (618) 734-7003

Felony and misdemeanor records are available by mail, fax or phone. A release is required. $4.00 fee for each year searched. $1.00 fee for first copy, $.25 for each additional copy. Make company check payable to Clerk of Circuit Court. Search information required: name. Turnaround time is 1 week.

Civil records are available by mail, fax or phone. A release is required. $4.00 fee for each year searched. $1.00 fee for first copy, $.25 for each additional copy. Search information required: name, date of birth, years to search. Specify plaintiff or defendant.

Bond County

Circuit Clerk's Office, Criminal
Records
200 W. College
Greenville, IL 62246
(618) 664-3208
Fax (618) 664-4689

Felony and misdemeanor records are available by mail or fax. No release necessary. $4.00 fee for each year searched. Make check payable to Bond County Circuit Clerk. Search information required: name, date of birth, years to search, SASE.

Civil records are available by mail or fax. No release necessary. $4.00 fee per year searched. Search information required: name, date of birth, years to search, SASE. Specify plaintiff or defendant.

Boone County

Circuit Clerk's Office
601 N. Main
Belvidere, IL 61008
(815) 544-0371

Felony and misdemeanor records are available by mail. $4.00 fee for each year searched. Make check or money order, payable to Boone County Circuit Clerk. Search information required: name, SSN, date of birth, years to search, SASE.

Civil records are available by mail. No release necessary. $4.00 search fee. Search information required: name, date of birth, years to search, SASE. Specify plaintiff or defendant.

Brown County

Circuit Clerk's Office, Criminal
Records
Brown County Courthouse
Mount Sterling, IL 62353
(217) 773-2713

Felony and misdemeanor records are available by mail or phone. No release necessary. No search fee. $.35 fee per copy. $2.00 for certification. Search information required: name, date of birth, years to search, SASE. Turnaround time is 1 week.

Civil records are available by mail. No release necessary. No search fee. $.35 fee per copy. $2.00 for certification. Search information required: name, date of birth, years to search, SASE. Specify plaintiff or defendant.

Bureau County

Circuit Clerk's Office, Criminal
Records
PO Box 406
Princeton, IL 61356
(815) 872-2001

Felony and misdemeanor records are available by mail. A release is required. No search fee. Search information required: name, date of birth, years to search, SASE. Turnaround time is 1 week.

Civil records are available by mail. A release is required. No search fee. Search information required: name, date of birth, years to search, SASE. Specify plaintiff or defendant.

Calhoun County

Circuit Clerk's Office, Criminal
Records
Calhoun County Courthouse
PO Box 486
Hardin, IL 62047
(618) 576-2451

Felony and misdemeanor records are available by mail or phone. No release necessary. $4.00 search fee. $.15 fee per copy. $2.00 for certification, plus $1.00 fee for first certified page and $.50 each additional page. Search information required: name, date of birth, SASE. Turnaround time is 1 week.

Civil records are available by mail. No release necessary. $4.00 search fee. $.15 fee per copy. $2.00 for certification, plus $1.00 fee for first certified page and $.50 each additional page. Search information required: name, date of birth, years to search. Specify plaintiff or defendant.

Carroll County

Circuit Clerk's Office, Criminal
Records
PO Box 32
Mount Carroll, IL 61053
(815) 244-9171

Felony and misdemeanor records are available by mail. No release necessary. $4.00 fee for each year searched. $1.00 fee for first copy, $.50 each additional page. $2.00 for certification. Make check payable to Circuit Clerk. Search information required: name, date of birth, years to search, SASE.

Civil records are available by mail. No release necessary. $4.00 fee for each year searched. $1.00 fee for first copy, $.50 each additional page. $2.00 for certification. Search information required: name, date of birth, years to search. Specify plaintiff or defendant.

Cass County

Circuit Clerk's Office
PO Box 203
Cass County Courthouse
Virginia, IL 62691
(217) 452-7225

Felony and misdemeanor records are available by mail. No release necessary. $4.00 fee per year searched. $1.00 fee for first copy, $.50 each additional copy. $1.00 for certification. Search information required: name, date of birth, previous address. Turnaround time is 1 week.

Civil records are available by mail. No release necessary. No search fee. $1.00 fee for first copy, $.50 each additional copy. $1.00 for certification. Search information required: name, date of birth, years to search. Specify plaintiff or defendant.

Champaign County

Felony and misdemeanor records
Circuit Clerk's Office
Attn:Criminal Records
101 E. Main
Urbana, IL 61801
(217) 384-3727
Fax (217) 384-3879

Felony and misdemeanor records are available by mail. No release necessary. $4.00 fee for each year searched. $1.00 fee for first copy, $.50 each additional copy. $2.00 for certification. Make check payable to Circuit Clerk of Champaign County. Search information required: name, SSN, date of birth, years to search, SASE.

Civil records
Circuit Clerk's Office
101 E. Main
Urbana, IL 61801
(217) 384-3727
Fax (217) 384-3725

Civil records are available by mail. No release necessary. No search fee. $1.00 fee for first copy, $.50 each additional copy. $2.00 for certification. Search information required: name, date of birth, years to search. Specify plaintiff or defendant.

Christian County

Circuit Clerk's Office, Criminal
Records
PO Box 617
Taylorville, IL 62568
(217) 824-4966
Fax (217) 824-5105

Felony and misdemeanor records are available by mail or fax. No release necessary. $5.00 search fee. $1.00 fee for first copy, $.50 each additional copy. $2.00 for certification. Search information required: name, date of birth, SASE. Turnaround time is 1 week.

Civil records are available by mail. No release necessary. No search fee. $1.00 fee for first copy, $.50 each additional copy. $2.00 for certification. Search information required: name, date of birth, years to search, SASE. Specify plaintiff or defendant.

Clark County

Circuit Clerk's Office, Criminal
Records
PO Box 187
Marshall, IL 62441
(217) 826-2811

Felony and misdemeanor records are available by mail. A release is required. $4.00 fee per year searched. $2.00 for certification. Make check payable to Circuit Clerk's Office. Search information required: name, date of birth, SASE. Turnaround time is 1 week.

Civil records are available by mail. No release necessary. No search fee. $2.00 for certification. Search information required: name, date of birth, years to search, SASE. Specify plaintiff or defendant.

Clay County

Circuit Clerk's Office
PO Box 100
Louisville, IL 62858
(618) 665-3523

Felony and misdemeanor records are available by mail or phone. No release necessary. No search fee. $1.00 fee for first copy, $.50 each additional copy. $2.00 for certification. Certified check only, payable to Circuit Clerk. Search information required: name, date of birth, SASE. Turnaround time is 1 week.

Civil records are available by mail. No release necessary. No search fee. $1.00 fee for first copy, $.50 each additional copy. $2.00 for certification. Search information required: name, date of birth, years to search, SASE. Specify plaintiff or defendant.

Clinton County

Circuit Clerk's Office
Clinton County Courthouse
PO Box 407
Carlyle, IL 62231
(618) 594-2415

Felony and misdemeanor records are available by mail. No release necessary. $10.00 search fee. $.50 fee per copy. $2.00 for certification. Search information required: name, date of birth, years to search, SASE. Turnaround time is 1 week.

Civil records are available by mail. No release necessary. $10.00 search fee. $.50 fee per copy. $2.00 for certification. Search information required: name, date of birth, years to search, SASE. Specify plaintiff or defendant.

Coles County

Circuit Clerk's Office, Criminal
Records
PO Box 48
Charleston, IL 61920
(217) 348-0516

Felony and misdemeanor records are available by mail. A release is required. $5.00 search fee. $.50 fee per copy. Certified check only, payable to Circuit Clerk's Office. Search information required: name, SSN, date of birth, years to search, SASE. Turnaround time is 1 week.

Civil records are available by mail. A release is required. $5.00 search fee. $.50 fee per copy. Search information required: name, date of birth, years to search, SASE. Specify plaintiff or defendant.

Cook County

Clerk of Circuit Court, Criminal
Division
Room 526
2650 S. California Ave.
Chicago, IL 60608
(312) 890-3140

Felony records are available by mail. No release necessary. $6.00 fee for each year searched. $2.00 fee for first copy, $.50 each additional copy. $6.00 for certification. Certified check only, payable to Clerk of Circuit Court. Search information required: name, date of birth, years to search, SASE. Turnaround time is 1 week.

Civil records are available by mail. No release necessary. $6.00 fee for each year searched. $2.00 fee for first copy, $.50 each additional copy. $6.00 fee for certification. Search information required: name, date of birth, years to search, SASE. Specify plaintiff or defendant.

Crawford County

Circuit Clerk's Office, Criminal
Records
PO Box 222
Robinson, IL 62454
(618) 544-3512
Fax (618) 544-2910

Felony and misdemeanor records are available by mail or fax. For fax request, call first. No release necessary. No search fee. $1.00 fee for first copy, $.50 for each additional copy. $2.00 for certification. Search information required: name, date of birth, years to search, SASE. Turnaround time is 1 week.

Civil records are available by mail or fax. For fax request, call first. No release necessary. No search fee. $1.00 fee for first copy, $.50 for each additional copy. $2.00 for certification. Search information required: name, date of birth, years to search, SASE. Specify plaintiff or defendant.

Cumberland County

Circuit Clerk's Office, Criminal
Records
PO Box 145
Toledo, IL 62468
(217) 849-3601

Felony and misdemeanor records are available by mail. A release is required. $1.00 fee per year searched. $1.00 fee for first copy, $.50 for each additional copy. $2.00 for certification. Search information required: name, date of birth, SASE. Turnaround time is 1 week.

Civil records are available by mail. No release necessary. $1.00 fee per year searched. $1.00 fee for first copy, $.50 for each additional copy. $2.00 for certification. Search information required: name, date of birth, years to search, SASE. Specify plaintiff or defendant.

De Kalb County

Circuit Clerk's Office, Criminal
Records
De Kalb County Courthouse
133 W. State Street
Sycamore, IL 60178
(815) 895-7131

Felony and misdemeanor records are available by mail. No release necessary. $4.00 fee for each year searched. $1.00 fee for first copy, $.50 for each additional copy. $2.00 for certification. Make check payable to Circuit Clerk of De Kalb County. Search information required: name, date of birth, sex, years to search. Turnaround time is 1 week.

Civil records are available by mail. No release necessary. $4.00 fee for each year searched. $1.00 fee for first copy, $.50 for each additional copy. $2.00 for certification. Search information required: name, date of birth, years to search. Specify plaintiff or defendant.

De Witt County

Circuit Clerk's Office
PO Box 439
Clinton, IL 61727
(217) 935-2195
Fax (217) 935-3310

Felony and misdemeanor records are available by mail or fax. No release necessary. $4.00 fee for each year searched. $.25 fee per copy. $2.00 for certification. Make check payable to Circuit Clerk of De Witt County. Search information required: name, date of birth, SASE. Turnaround time is 1 week.

Civil records are available by mail or fax. No release necessary. $4.00 fee for each year searched. $.25 fee per copy. $2.00 for certification. Search information required: name, date of birth, years to search, SASE. Specify plaintiff or defendant.

Douglas County

Circuit Clerk's Office, Criminal
Records
PO Box 50
Tuscola, IL 61953
(217) 253-2353

Felony and misdemeanor records are available by mail. No release necessary. $4.00 fee for each year searched. $1.00 fee for first copy, $.50 for each additional copy. $2.00 for certification. Company checks only, payable to Clerk of Court. Search information required: name, years to search, SASE. Turnaround time is 1 week.

Civil records are available by mail. No release necessary. $4.00 fee for each year searched. $1.00 fee for first copy, $.50 for each additional copy. $2.00 for certification. Search information required: name, date of birth, years to search, SASE. Specify plaintiff or defendant.

Du Page County

Circuit Clerk's Office, Criminal Records
PO Box 707
Wheaton, IL 60189-0707
(708) 682-7000
Fax (708) 682-7086

Felony and misdemeanor records are available by mail or fax. No release necessary. $4.00 fee for each year searched. $2.00 fee for first copy, $.50 for each additional copy. $4.00 for certification. Company check only, payable to Circuit Clerk. Search information required: name, date of birth, sex, SSN, SASE. Turnaround time is 1 week.

Civil records are available by mail. No release necessary. $4.00 fee for each year searched. $2.00 fee for first copy, $.50 for each additional copy. $4.00 for certification. Search information required: name, date of birth, years to search, SASE. Specify plaintiff or defendant.

Edgar County

Circuit Clerk's Office, Criminal Records
Edgar County Courthouse
115 W. Court Street, Room M
Paris, IL 61944
(217) 465-4107

Felony and misdemeanor records are available by mail. A release is required. $4.00 fee for each year searched. $.50 fee per copy. $1.00 for certification. Search information required: name, date of birth, SASE. Turnaround time is 1 week.

Civil records are available by mail. A release is required. $4.00 fee for each year searched. $.50 fee per copy. $1.00 for certification. Search information required: name, date of birth, years to search, SASE. Specify plaintiff or defendant.

Edwards County

Circuit Clerk's Office, Criminal Records
Main Street, Courthouse
50 Main Street
Albion, IL 62806
(618) 445-2016
Fax (618) 445-3414

Felony and misdemeanor records are available by mail or fax. No release necessary. $4.00 fee for each year searched. $.30 fee per copy. $2.00 for certification. Make check payable to Circuit Clerk. Search information required: name, SSN, date of birth, SASE. Turnaround time is 1 week.

Civil records are available by mail or fax. No release necessary.$4.00 fee for each year searched. $.30 fee per copy. $2.00 for certification. Search information required: name, date of birth, years to search, SASE. Specify plaintiff or defendant.

Effingham County

Circuit Clerk's Office, Criminal Records
PO Box 586
Effingham, IL 62401
(217) 342-4065
Fax (217) 342-6183

Felony and misdemeanor records are available by mail or fax. No release necessary. $4.00 fee for each year searched. $.50 fee per copy. $2.00 for certification. Certified check only, payable to Circuit Clerk. Search information required: name, date of birth, years to search. Turnaround time is 1 week.

Civil records are available by mail or fax. No release necessary. $4.00 fee for each year searched. $.50 fee per copy. $2.00 for certification. Search information required: name, date of birth, years to search. Specify plaintiff or defendant.

Fayette County

Circuit Clerk's Office
221 S. 7th
Vandalia, IL 62471
(618) 283-5009

Felony and misdemeanor records are available by mail. No release necessary. $5.00 fee for each year searched. $.50 fee per copy. $1.00 for certification. Search information required: name, date of birth, years to search, SASE. Turnaround time is 1 week.

Civil records are available by mail. No release necessary. $5.00 fee for each year searched. $.50 fee per copy. $1.00 for certification. Search information required: name, date of birth, years to search, SASE. Specify plaintiff or defendant.

Ford County

Circuit Clerk's Office, Criminal Records
PO Box 80
Paxton, IL 60957
(217) 379-2641

Felony and misdemeanor records are available by mail or phone. No release necessary. $4.00 fee for each year searched. $1.00 fee for first copy, $.50 for each additional copy. $2.00 for certification. Search information required: name, date of birth, sex, years to search, SASE. Turnaround time is 1-2 weeks.

Civil records are available by mail. No release necessary. No search fee. Search information required: name, date of birth, years to search. Specify plaintiff or defendant.

Franklin County

Circuit Clerk's Office, Criminal Records
Franklin County Courthouse
Benton, IL 62812
(618) 439-2011
Fax (618) 439-4119

Felony and misdemeanor records are available by mail or fax. No release necessary. $4.00 fee for each year searched. $1.00 fee for first copy, $.50 for each additional copy. $2.00 for certification. Search information required: name, years to search. Turnaround time is 1 week.

Civil records are available by mail or fax. No release necessary. $4.00 fee for each year searched. $1.00 fee for first copy, $.50 for each additional copy. $2.00 for certification. Search information required: name, date of birth, years to search. Specify plaintiff or defendant.

Fulton County

Circuit Clerk's Office, Criminal Records
PO Box 152
Lewistown, IL 61542
(309) 547-3041 Extension 23
Fax (309) 547-3041

Felony and misdemeanor records are available by mail, fax or phone. No release necessary. No search fee. $1.00 fee per fax request. $2.00 for first copy, $.50 for each additional copy. $2.00 for certification. Search information required: name, date of birth, SASE. Turnaround time is 1 week.

Civil records are available by mail, fax or phone. No release necessary. No search fee.$1.00 fee per fax request. $2.00 fee for first copy, $.50 for each additional copy. $2.00 for certification. Search information required: name, date of birth, years to search. Specify plaintiff or defendant.

Gallatin County

Circuit Clerk's Office, Criminal Records
Gallatin County
PO Box 503
Shawneetown, IL 62984
(618) 269-3140

Felony and misdemeanor records are available by mail or phone. No release necessary. $2.00 search fee. $.25 fee per copy. $1.00 for certification. Search information required: name, date of birth, years to search, SASE. Turnaround time is 1 week.

Civil records are available by mail. No release necessary. $2.00 search fee. $.25 fee per copy. $1.00 for certification. Search information required: name, date of birth, years to search, SASE. Specify plaintiff or defendant.

Greene County

Greene County Circuit Clerk
519 N. Main
Public Square
Carrollton, IL 62016
(217) 942-3421

Felony and misdemeanor records are available by mail or phone. No release necessary. No search fee. $.25 fee per copy. $2.00 for certification. Search information required: name, date of birth, SASE. Turnaround time is 1 week.

Civil records are available by mail. No release necessary. No search fee. $.25 fee per copy. $2.00 for certification. Search information required: name, date of birth, years to search, SASE. Specify plaintiff or defendant.

Grundy County

Circuit Clerk's Office, Criminal
Records
PO Box 707
Morris, IL 60450
(815) 941-3256

Felony and misdemeanor records are available by mail. A release is required. $4.00 fee for each year searched. $2.00 for certification. Company checks only, payable to Circuit Clerk's Office. Search information required: name, date of birth, sex, SASE. Turnaround time is 1 week.

Civil records are available by mail. No release necessary. $4.00 fee for each year searched. $2.00 for certification. Search information required: name, date of birth, years to search, SASE. Specify plaintiff or defendant.

Hamilton County

Circuit Clerk's Office, Criminal
Records
Hamilton County Courthouse
McLeansboro, IL 62859
(618) 643-3224

Felony and misdemeanor records are available by mail or phone. No release necessary. $2.00 fee for each year searched. $.30 fee per copy. $1.50 for certification. Make company check payable to Circuit Clerk. Search information required: name, years to search, SASE. Turnaround time is 1 week.

Civil records are available by mail. No release necessary. $2.00 fee for each year searched. $.30 fee per copy. $1.50 for certification. Search information required: name, date of birth, years to search. Specify plaintiff or defendant.

Hancock County

Circuit Clerk's Office, Criminal
Records
PO Box 189
Carthage, IL 62321
(217) 357-2616

Felony records are available by mail. No release necessary. No search fee. $.50 fee per copy. $3.00 for certification. Search information required: name, date of birth, years to search, SASE. Turnaround time is 1 week.

Civil records are available by mail. No release necessary. No search fee. $.50 fee per copy. $3.00 for certification. Search information required: name, date of birth, years to search, SASE. Specify plaintiff or defendant.

Hardin County

Circuit Clerk's Office, Criminal
Records
Hardin County Courthouse
PO Box 308
Elizabethtown, IL 62931
(618) 287-2735

Felony records are available by mail or phone. No release necessary. $4.00 fee from 1970 forward for every 2 years searched. $.25 fee per copy. $1.00 for certification. Search information required: name, years to search. Turnaround time is 1-2 weeks.

Civil records are available by mail. No release necessary. No search fee. Search information required: name, date of birth, years to search. Specify plaintiff or defendant.

Henderson County

Circuit Clerk's Office, Criminal
Records
Henderson County Courthouse
Oquawka, IL 61469
(309) 867-3121
Fax (309) 867-3207

Felony and misdemeanor records are available by mail, fax or phone. A release is required. No search fee. $.25 fee per copy, $2.00 for certification. Search information required: name, date of birth, SASE. Turnaround time is 1 week.

Civil records are available by mail, fax or phone. A release is required. No search fee. $.25 fee per copy, $2.00 for certification. Search information required: name, date of birth, years to search, SASE. Specify plaintiff or defendant.

Henry County

Circuit Clerk's Office, Criminal
Records
Henry County Courthouse
PO Box 9
Cambridge, IL 61238
(309) 937-3305

Felony and misdemeanor records are available by mail. A release is required. No search fee. $.50 fee per copy. $2.00 for certification. Search information required: name, date of birth, SASE. Turnaround time is 1 week.

Civil records are available by mail. A release is required. No search fee. $.50 fee per copy. $2.00 for certification. Search information required: name, date of birth, years to search, SASE. Specify plaintiff or defendant.

Iroquois County

Circuit Clerk's Office, Criminal
Records
Iroquois County Courthouse
550 S. 10th
Watseka, IL 60970
(815) 432-6950
Fax (815) 432-6953

Felony and misdemeanor records are available by mail or fax. A release is required. $4.00 search fee. $.50 fee per copy. Search information required: name, date of birth, years to search.

Civil records are available by mail or fax. A release is required. $4.00 search fee. $.50 fee per copy. Search information required: name, date of birth, years to search. Specify plaintiff or defendant.

Jackson County

Circuit Clerk's Office
Jackson County Courthouse
Murphysboro, IL 62966
(618) 684-2153

Felony and misdemeanor records are available by mail or phone. No release necessary. $3.00 search fee. $1.50 fee per copy. $2.00 for certification. Search information required: name, date of birth, SASE. Requests should be submitted on company letterhead. Turnaround time is 1 week.

Civil records are available by mai or phonel. No release necessary. $3.00 search fee. $1.50 fee per copy. $2.00 for certification. Search information required: name, date of birth, years to search, SASE. Specify plaintiff or defendant.

Jasper County

Circuit Clerk's Office, Criminal
Records
100 W. Jourdan
Newton, IL 62448
(618) 783-2524

Felony and misdemeanor records are available by mail or phone. No release necessary. No search fee. $.50 fee per copy. $2.00 for certification; $1.00 for first page, $.50 each additional page. Search information required: name, date of birth, SASE. Turnaround time is 1 week.

Civil records are available by mail. No release necessary. No search fee. $.50 fee per copy. $2.00 for certification; $1.00 for first page, $.50 each additional page. Search information required: name, date of birth, years to search. Specify plaintiff or defendant.

Jefferson County

Circuit Clerk's Office, Criminal
Records
PO Box 1266
Mount Vernon, IL 62864
(618) 244-8008
Fax (618) 244-8029

Felony and misdemeanor records are available by mail or phone. No release necessary. $4.00 search fee. $.25 fee per copy. Search information required: full name, date of birth, SASE. Turnaround time is 1-2 weeks.

Civil records are available by mail. No release necessary. $4.00 search fee. $.25 fee per copy. Search information required: name, date of birth, years to search, SASE. Specify plaintiff or defendant.

Jersey County

Circuit Clerk's Office, Criminal
Records
201 W. Pearl
Jerseyville, IL 62052
(618) 498-5571, Ext. 119
Fax (618) 498-6128

Felony records are available by mail or fax. No release necessary. No search fee. $.50 fee per copy. $2.00 for certification of first 2 pages, $.50 each additional page. Make company check payable to Circuit Clerk. Search information required: name, years to search, SASE. Turnaround time is 1 week.

Civil records are available by mail or fax. No release necessary. No search fee. $.50 fee per copy. $2.00 for certification of first 2 pages, $.50 each additional page. Search information required: name, date of birth, years to search, SASE. Specify plaintiff or defendant.

Jo Daviess County

Circuit Clerk's Office, Criminal
Records
PO Box 333
Galena, IL 61036
(815) 777-0037

Felony and misdemeanor records are available by mail. No release necessary. $4.00 search fee. Search information required: name, date of birth, years to search. Turnaround time is 1 week.

Civil records are available in person only. See Illinois state repository for additional information.

Johnson County

Circuit Clerk's Office
PO Box 517
Vienna, IL 62995
(618) 658-4751

Felony and misdemeanor records are available by mail. No release necessary. $4.00 search fee. $1.00 fee for first copy; $.50 for next 19 copies, $.25 each additional thereafter. $2.00 for certification. Search information required: name, years to search. Turnaround time is 1 week.

Civil records are available by mail. No release necessary. $4.00 search fee. $1.00 fee for first copy; $.50 for next 19 copies, $.25 each additional thereafter. $2.00 for certification. Search information required: name, date of birth, years to search. Specify plaintiff or defendant.

Kane County

Circuit Clerk's Office
PO Box 112
Geneva, IL 60134
(708) 232-3413
Fax (708) 208-2172

Felony and misdemeanor records are available by mail or fax. No release necessary. $4.00 fee for each year searched. $2.00 fee per copy. $2.00 for certification. Certified check only, payable to Circuit Court Clerk. Search information required: name, date of birth. Will only search past two years.

Civil records are available by mail or fax. No release necessary. $4.00 fee for each year searched. $2.00 fee per copy. $2.00 for certification. Search information required: name, date of birth, years to search. Specify plaintiff or defendant.

Kankakee County

Circuit Clerk's Office, Criminal Records
450 E. Court Street
Kankakee, IL 60901
(815) 937-2905
Fax (815) 937-3903

Felony and misdemeanor records are available by mail or fax. No release necessary. No search fee. $1.00 fee for first copy, $.50 each additional copy. $2.00 for certification. Certified check only, payable to Circuit Court Clerk. Search information required: name, years to search, date of birth, SASE. Turnaround time is 1 week.

Civil records are available by mail or fax. No release necessary. No search fee. $1.00 fee for first copy, $.50 each additional copy. $.50 each additional copy. $2.00 for certification. Search information required: name, date of birth, years to search, SASE. Specify plaintiff or defendant.

Kendall County

Circuit Clerk's Office, Criminal Records
PO Drawer M
Yorkville, IL 60560
(708) 553-4184

Felony and misdemeanor records are available by mail. No release necessary. $4.00 fee for each year searched. $.25 fee per copy. $2.00 for certification. Search information required: name, years to search, date of birth. Turnaround time is 1 week.

Civil records are available by mail. No release necessary. $4.00 fee for each year searched. $.25 fee per copy. $2.00 for certification. Search information required: name, date of birth, years to search. Specify plaintiff or defendant.

Knox County

Circuit Clerk's Office, Criminal Records
Knox County Courthouse
Galesburg, IL 61401
(309) 343-3121, Ext. 436
Fax (309) 343-7002

Felony and misdemeanor records are available by mail or fax. No release necessary. No search fee. Search information required: name, years to search.

Civil records are available in person only. See Illinois state repository for additional information.

La Salle County

Circuit Clerk's Office
Courthouse
Ottawa, IL 61350
(815) 434-8271

Records are available in person only. See Illinois state repository for additional information.

Civil records are available in person only. See Illinois state repository for additional information.

Lake County

Circuit Clerk's Office, Criminal Records
Room C-104
18 N. County Street
Waukegan, IL 60085
(708) 360-6794 or 6796

Felony and misdemeanor records are available by mail. No release necessary. $4.00 fee for each year searched. Make check payable to Clerk of Circuit Court. Search information required: name, date of birth, SSN, years to search. Turnaround time is 1 week.

Civil records are available by mail. No release necessary. No search fee. $4.00 fee for each year searched. Search information required: name, date of birth, years to search. Specify plaintiff or defendant.

Lawrence County

Circuit Clerk's Office, Criminal Records
Lawrence County
Lawrenceville, IL 62439
(618) 943-2815
Fax (618) 943-5205

Felony and misdemeanor records are available by mail or fax. No release necessary. $4.00 fee for each year searched. $1.00 fee first copy, $.50 each additional copy. $2.00 for certification. Certified check only, payable to Circuit Clerk's Office. Search information required: name, SASE, date of birth. Turnaround time is 1 week.

Civil records are available by mail or fax. No release necessary. $4.00 fee for each year searched. $1.00 fee first copy, $.50 each additional copy. $2.00 for certification. Search information required: name, date of birth, years to search, SASE. Specify plaintiff or defendant.

Lee County

Circuit Clerk's Office, Criminal Records
PO Box 325
Dixon, IL 61021
(815) 284-5234

Felony and misdemeanor records are available by mail. No release necessary. $4.00 fee for each year searched. $.50 fee per copy. $2.00 for certification. Certified check only, payable to County Circuit Clerk. Search information required: name, years to search, SASE. Turnaround time is 1 week.

Civil records are available by mail. No release necessary. $4.00 fee for each year searched. $.50 fee per copy. $2.00 for certification. Search information required: name, date of birth, years to search, SASE. Specify plaintiff or defendant.

Livingston County

Circuit Clerk's Office, Criminal Records
Livingston County Courthouse
PO Box 320
Pontiac, IL 61764
(815) 844-5166 Extension 135

Felony and misdemeanor records are available by mail. A release is required. $4.00 fee for each year searched. $.50 fee per copy. $2.00 for certification. Certified check only, payable to Circuit Clerk. Search information required: name, date of birth, years to search, SASE. Turnaround time is 1 week.

Civil records are available by mail. No release necessary. $4.00 fee for each year searched. $.50 fee per copy. $2.00 for certification. Search information required: name, date of birth, years to search, SASE. Specify plaintiff or defendant.

Logan County

Circuit Clerk's Office, Criminal Records
Logan County Courthouse
601 Broadway
Lincoln, IL 62656-0158
(217) 735-2376

Felony and misdemeanor records are available by mail. A release is required. $4.00 fee for each year searched. $1.00 fee first copy, $.50 each additional copy. $2.00 for certification. Certified check only, payable to County Circuit Clerk. Search information required: name, SSN, date of birth, years to search, SASE. Turnaround time is 1 week.

Civil records are available by mail. No release necessary. $4.00 fee for each year searched. $1.00 fee first copy, $.50 each additional copy. $2.00 for certification. Search information required: name, date of birth, years to search. Specify plaintiff or defendant.

Macon County

Circuit Clerk's Office, Criminal
Records
253 E. Wood Street
Decatur, IL 62523
(217) 424-1452, Ext. 461

Felony and misdemeanor records are available by mail or phone. No release necessary. $4.00 search fee. $.30 fee first copy, $.10 each additional copy. $2.00 for certification. Certified check only, payable to Macon County Circuit Clerk. Search information required: name, date of birth, years to search, SASE. Turnaround time is 1 week.

Civil records are available by mail or phone. No release necessary. $4.00 search fee. $.30 fee first copy, $.10 each additional copy. $2.00 for certification. Search information required: name, date of birth, years to search, SASE. Specify plaintiff or defendant.

Macoupin County

Circuit Clerk's Office, Criminal
Records
PO Box 197
Carlinville, IL 62626
(217) 854-3211
Fax (217) 854-3211

Felony and misdemeanor records are available by mail or fax. A release is required. No search fee. $1.00 fee first copy, $.50 each additional copy. $2.00 for certification. Search information required: name, date of birth, SASE. Turnaround time is 1 week.

Civil records are available by mail or fax. A release is required. No search fee. $1.00 fee first copy, $.50 each additional copy. $2.00 for certification. Search information required: name, date of birth, years to search, SASE. Specify plaintiff or defendant.

Madison County

Felony records
Circuit Clerk's Office, Criminal
Records
Madison County Courthouse
155 N. Main
Edwardsville, IL 62025
(618) 692-6240 Ext. 4590

Felony records are available by mail. No release necessary. $4.00 fee for each year searched. Certified check only, payable to Circuit Clerk. Search information required: name, date of birth, years to search.

Civil records
Circuit Clerk's Office
Madison County Courthouse
155 N. Main
Edwardsville, IL 62025
(618) 692-6240 Ext. 4590

Civil records are available by mail. No release necessary. $4.00 fee for each year searched. Search information required: name, date of birth, years to search. Specify plaintiff or defendant.

Misdemeanor records
Madison County Courthouse
155 N. Main
Edwardsville, IL 62025
(618) 692-6240 Ext. 4366

Misdemeanor records are available by mail. A release is required. $4.00 fee for each year searched. Certified check payable to Circuit Clerk. Search information required: name, date of arrest, arresting agency.

Civil records
Madison County Courthouse
155 N. Main
Edwardsville, IL 62025
(618) 692-6240 Ext. 4366

Civil records are available by mail. No release necessary. $4.00 fee for each year searched. Search information required: name, date of birth, years to search. Specify plaintiff or defendant.

Marion County

Circuit Clerk's Office, Criminal
Records
PO Box 130
Salem, IL 62881
(618) 548-3856

Felony and misdemeanor records are available in person only. See Illinois state repository for additional information.

Civil records are available in person only. See Illinois state repository for additional information.

Marshall County

Circuit Clerk's Office, Criminal
Records
122 N. Prairie
Box 98
Lacon, IL 61540
(309) 246-6435

Felony and misdemeanor records are available by mail. A release is required. $4.00 fee for each year searched. $2.00 for certification. Certified check only, payable to Circuit Court Clerk. Search information required: name, date of birth, years to search, SASE. Turnaround time is 1 week.

Civil records are available by mail. No release necessary. $4.00 fee for each year searched. $2.00 for certification. Search information required: name, date of birth, years to search. Specify plaintiff or defendant.

Mason County

Circuit Clerk's Office, Criminal
Records
PO Box 446
Havana, IL 62644
(309) 543-6619

Felony and misdemeanor records are available by mail or phone. No release necessary. No search fee. $.50 fee per copy. $2.00 for certification. Search information required: name, years to search.

Civil records are available by mail. No release necessary. No search fee. $.50 fee per copy. $2.00 for certification. Search information required: name, date of birth, years to search. Specify plaintiff or defendant.

Massac County

Circuit Clerk's Office, Criminal
Records
PO Box 152
Metropolis, IL 62960
(618) 524-5011
Fax (618) 524-4230

Felony and misdemeanor records are available by mail or fax. No release necessary. $4.00 fee for each year searched. $.25 fee per copy. $3.00 for first certification, $.50 for each additional page. Company checks only, payable to Circuit Court Clerk. Search information required: name, date of birth, years to search, SASE. Turnaround time is 1 week.

Civil records are available by mail or fax. No release necessary. $4.00 fee for each year searched. $.25 fee per copy. $3.00 for first certification, $.50 for each additional page. Search information required: name, date of birth, years to search. Specify plaintiff or defendant.

McDonough County

Circuit Clerk's Office
McDonough County Courthouse
Macomb, IL 61455
(309) 837-4889

Felony and misdemeanor records are available by mail or phone. No release necessary. No search fee. $1.00 fee for first copy, $.50 each additional copy. $2.00 fee for certification. Make money order payable to Circuit Clerk. Search information required: name, years to search.

Civil records are available by mail or phone. No release necessary. No search fee. $1.00 fee for first copy, $.50 each additional copy. $2.00 fee for certification. Search information required: name, date of birth, years to search. Specify plaintiff or defendant.

McHenry County

Circuit Clerk's Office, Criminal
Records
Room 302
2200 N. Seminary Ave.
Woodstock, IL 60098
(815) 338-2040 Extension 321

Felony and misdemeanor records are available by mail or phone. No release necessary. $4.00 fee per year searched. $2.00 fee for first copy, $.50 each additional copy. $4.00 fee for certification. Search information required: name, date of birth, SASE.

Civil records are available by mail or phone. No release necessary. $4.00 fee per year searched. $2.00 fee for first copy, $.50 each additional copy. $4.00 fee for certification. Search information required: name, date of birth, years to search, SASE. Specify plaintiff or defendant.

McLean County

Circuit Clerk's Office, Criminal Records
104 W. Front, Room 303
Law Justice Center
Bloomington, IL 61701
(309) 888-5320

Felony and misdemeanor records are available by mail. No release necessary. $4.00 fee for each year searched. Make check payable to McLean County Circuit Clerk. Search information required: name, date of birth, years to search, SASE. Turnaround time is 2 weeks.

Civil records are available by mail. No release necessary. $4.00 fee for each year searched. Search information required: name, date of birth, years to search, SASE. Specify plaintiff or defendant.

Menard County

Circuit Clerk's Office, Criminal Records
PO Box 466
Menard County Courthouse
Petersburg, IL 62675
(217) 632-2615

Felony and misdemeanor records are available by mail. No release necessary. $4.00 fee for each year searched. $1.00 fee for first copy, $.50 each additional copy. $1.00 for first certification, $.50 each additional page. Make money order payable to Menard County Circuit Clerk. Search information required: name, years to search, SASE. Turnaround time is 1 week.

Civil records are available by mail. No release necessary. $4.00 fee for each year searched. $1.00 fee for first copy, $.50 each additional copy. $1.00 for first certification, $.50 each additional page. Search information required: name, date of birth, years to search. Specify plaintiff or defendant.

Mercer County

Circuit Clerk's Office, Criminal Records
PO Box 175
Aledo, IL 61231
(309) 582-7122

Felony and misdemeanor records are available by mail or phone. No release necessary. No search fee. $.50 fee per copy. $3.00 for certification. Search information required: name, date of birth, SASE.

Civil records are available by mail or phone. No release necessary. No search fee. $.50 fee per copy. $3.00 for certification. Search information required: name, date of birth, years to search, SASE. Specify plaintiff or defendant.

Monroe County

Circuit Clerk's Office, Criminal Records
Monroe County Courthouse
Main Street
Waterloo, IL 62298
(618) 939-8681

Felony and misdemeanor records are available by mail or phone. No release necessary. No search fee. $.20 fee per copy. $2.00 for certification, $1.00 for first page, $.50 each additional page. Search information required: name, years to search, SASE.

Civil records are available by mail or phone. No release necessary. No search fee. $.20 fee per copy. $2.00 for certification, $1.00 for first page, $.50 each additional page. Search information required: name, date of birth, years to search, SASE. Specify plaintiff or defendant.

Montgomery County

Circuit Clerk's Office, Criminal Records
Montgomery County Courthouse
PO Box C
Hillsboro, IL 62049
(217) 532-9547

Felony and misdemeanor records are available by mail. A release is required. $4.00 fee for each year searched. $2.00 for certification. Make company check payable to Circuit Clerk. Search information required: name, years to search, SASE. Turnaround time is 1 week.

Civil records are available by mail. A release is required. $4.00 fee for each year searched. $2.00 for certification. Search information required: name, date of birth, years to search, SASE. Specify plaintiff or defendant.

Morgan County

Circuit Clerk's Office, Criminal Records
300 W. State Street
Jacksonville, IL 62650
(217) 243-5419

Felony and misdemeanor records are available by mail. No release necessary. $4.00 fee for each year searched. $.50 fee per copy. $1.00 for certification. Search information required: name, date of birth, years to search, SASE.

Civil records are available by mail. No release necessary. $4.00 fee for each year searched. $.50 fee per copy. $1.00 for certification. Search information required: name, date of birth, years to search, SASE. Specify plaintiff or defendant.

Moultrie County

Circuit Clerk's Office, Criminal Records
Moultrie County Courthouse
Sullivan, IL 61951
(217) 728-4622

Felony and misdemeanor records are available by mail. A release is required. $4.00 fee for each year searched. $.25 fee per copy. $2.00 for certification. Certified check only, payable to Clerk of Court. Search information required: name, date of birth, SASE. Turnaround time is 2 weeks.

Civil records are available by mail. No release necessary. $4.00 fee for each year searched. $.25 fee per copy. $2.00 for certification. Search information required: name, date of birth, years to search. Specify plaintiff or defendant.

Ogle County

Circuit Clerk's Office, Criminal Records
PO Box 337
Oregon, IL 61061
(815) 732-3201

Felony and misdemeanor records are available by mail. No release necessary. $4.00 fee for each year searched. $1.00 fee for first copy, $.50 each additional copy. $2.00 for certification. Make company check payable to Circuit Clerk. Search information required: name, years to search, SASE. Turnaround time is 1 week.

Civil records are available by mail. No release necessary. $4.00 fee for each year searched. $1.00 fee for first copy, $.50 each additional copy. $2.00 for certification. Search information required: name, date of birth, years to search, SASE. Specify plaintiff or defendant.

Peoria County

Circuit Clerk's Office, Criminal Records
324 Main Street, Room G-22
Peoria County Courthouse
Peoria, IL 61602
(309) 672-6953

Felony and misdemeanor records are available by mail or phone. No release necessary. No search fee. $2.00 fee for first copy, $.50 each additional copy. $4.00 for certification. Search information required: name, date of birth, years to search.

Civil records are available by mail or phone. No release necessary. No search fee. $2.00 fee for first copy, $.50 each additional copy. $4.00 for certification. Search information required: name, date of birth, years to search. Specify plaintiff or defendant.

Perry County

Circuit Clerk's Office, Criminal Records
PO 217
Pinckneyville, IL 62274
(618) 357-6726

Felony and misdemeanor records are available in person only. See Illinois state repository for more information.

Civil records are available in person only. See Illinois state repository for more information.

Piatt County

Circuit Clerk's Office, Criminal Records
PO Box 288
Monticello, IL 61856
(217) 762-4966
Fax (217) 762-7563

Felony and misdemeanor records are available by mail, phone or fax. No release necessary. No search fee. $1.00 fee for first copy, $.50 each additional copy. $1.00 for certification. Search information required: name, date of birth, years to search, SASE.

Civil records are available by mail. No release necessary. No search fee. $1.00 fee for first copy, $.50 each additional copy. $1.00 for certification. Search information required: name, date of birth, years to search, SASE. Specify plaintiff or defendant.

Pike County

Circuit Clerk's Office, Criminal
Records
Pike County Courthouse
Pittsfield, IL 62363
(217) 285-6612
Fax (217) 285-6612

Felony and misdemeanor records are available by mail, fax or phone. No release necessary. No search fee. $.25 fee per copy. $1.00 for certification. Search information required: name, date of birth, SASE.

Civil records are available by mail, fax or phone. No release necessary. No search fee. $.25 fee per copy. $1.00 for certification. Search information required: name, date of birth, years to search, SASE. Specify plaintiff or defendant.

Pope County

Circuit Clerk's Office, Criminal
Records
PO Box 502
Golconda, IL 62938
(618) 683-3941

Felony and misdemeanor records are available by mail or phone. No release necessary. No search fee. Search information required: name, years to search.

Civil records are available by mail. No release necessary. No search fee. Search information required: name, date of birth, years to search. Specify plaintiff or defendant.

Pulaski County

Circuit Clerk's Office, Criminal
Records
PO Box 88
Mound City, IL 62963
(618) 748-9300
Fax (618) 748-9338

Felony and misdemeanor records are available by mail, fax or phone. No release necessary. No search fee. $1.00 fee for first copy, $.50 each additional copy. $2.00 for certification. Search information required: name, SSN, date of birth, sex, race, years to search.

Civil records are available by mail. No release necessary. No search fee. $1.00 fee for first copy, $.50 each additional copy. $2.00 for certification. Search information required: name, date of birth, years to search. Specify plaintiff or defendant.

Putnam County

Circuit Clerk's Office, Criminal
Records
PO Box 207
Hennepin, IL 61327
(815) 925-7016

Felony and misdemeanor records are available by mail. No release necessary. $4.00 fee for each 5 years searched. $.50 fee per copy. $2.00 for certification. Make check payable to Putnam County Circuit Clerk. Search information required: name, date of birth, years to search, SASE.

Civil records are available by mail. No release necessary. $4.00 fee for each 5 years searched. $.50 fee per copy. $2.00 for certification. Search information required: name, date of birth, years to search. Specify plaintiff or defendant.

Randolph County

Circuit Clerk's Office, Criminal
Records
1 Taylor St.
Chester, IL 62233
(618) 826-3116
Fax (618) 826-3750

Felony and misdemeanor records are available by mail. No release necessary. $4.00 fee for each year searched. $.25 fee per copy. $2.50 for certification. Make money order payable to Circuit Clerk. Search information required: name, date of birth, years to search, SASE. Turnaround time is 1 week.

Civil records are available by mail. No release necessary. $4.00 fee for each year searched. $.25 fee per copy. $2.50 for certification. Search information required: name, date of birth, years to search, SASE. Specify plaintiff or defendant.

Richland County

Circuit Clerk's Office, Criminal
Records
Richland County Courthouse
103 W. Main, Room 21
Olney, IL 62450
(618) 392-2151

Felony and misdemeanor records are available by mail. A release is required. $4.00 fee for each year searched. $1.00 fee for first copy, $.50 each additional copy. $2.00 for certification. Make check payable to Circuit Clerk. Search information required: name, date of birth, years to search, SASE. Turnaround time is 1 week.

Civil records are available by mail. A release is required. $4.00 fee for each year searched. $1.00 fee for first copy, $.50 each additional copy. $2.00 for certification. Search information required: name, date of birth, years to search, SASE. Specify plaintiff or defendant.

Rock Island County

Circuit Clerk's Office, Criminal
Records
PO Box 5230
Rock Island, IL 61204-5230
(309) 786-4451

Felony records are available by mail. No release necessary. $4.00 fee for each year searched. $1.00 fee for first copy, $.50 each additional copy. $2.00 for certification. Certified check only, payable to County Circuit Clerk. Search information required: name, date of birth, years to search, SASE. Turnaround time is 1 week.

Civil records are available by mail. No release necessary. $4.00 fee for each year searched. $1.00 fee for first copy, $.50 each additional copy. $2.00 for certification. Search information required: name, date of birth, years to search, SASE. Specify plaintiff or defendant.

Saline County

Circuit Clerk's Office, Criminal
Records
Saline County Courthouse
Harrisburg, IL 62946
(618) 253-5096

Felony and misdemeanor records are available by mail. No release necessary. $5.00 fee for each 4 years searched. $.25 fee per copy. $2.00 for certification. Certified check only, payable to Circuit Clerk's Office. Search information required: name, date of birth, years to search, SASE. Turnaround time is 2 weeks.

Civil records are available by mail. No release necessary. 5.00 fee for each 4 years searched. $.25 fee per copy. $2.00 for certification. Search information required: name, date of birth, years to search, SASE. Specify plaintiff or defendant.

Sangamon County

Circuit Clerk's Office, Criminal
Records
Sangamon County Bldg.
200 South Ninth Street, Room 402
Springfield, IL 62701
(217) 753-6674
Fax (217) 753-6665

Felony and misdemeanor records are available by mail or fax. No release necessary. $4.00 fee for each year searched. $.50 fee per copy. $2.00 for certification. Make check payable to Circuit Clerk's Office. Search information required: name, date of birth, years to search. Request for records check prior to 1982 must be by mail. Turnaround time is 2 days.

Civil records are available by mail or fax. No release necessary. $4.00 fee for each year searched. $.50 fee per copy. $2.00 for certification. Search information required: name, date of birth, years to search. Specify plaintiff or defendant.

Schuyler County

Circuit Clerk's Office, Criminal
Records
PO Box 189
Schuyler County Courthouse
Rushville, IL 62681
(217) 322-4633

Felony and misdemeanor records are available by mail. No release necessary. No search fee. $1.00 fee for first copy, $.50 each additional. $2.00 fee for certification. Make money order payable to Circuit Clerk. Search information required: name, date of birth, SASE.

Civil records are available by mail. No release necessary. No search fee. $1.00 fee for first copy, $.50 each additional. $2.00 fee for certification. Search information required: name, date of birth, years to search, SASE. Specify plaintiff or defendant.

Scott County

Circuit Clerk's Office, Criminal
Records
Scott County Courthouse
35 E. Market Street
Winchester, IL 62694
(217) 742-5217

Felony and misdemeanor records are available by mail or phone. No release necessary. No search fee. $1.00 fee for first copy, $.50 each additional. $2.00 fee for certification. Search information required: name, years to search, SASE.

Civil records are available by mail or phone. No release necessary. No search fee. $1.00 fee for first copy, $.50 each additional. $2.00 fee for certification. Search information required: name, date of birth, years to search. Specify plaintiff or defendant.

Shelby County

Circuit Clerk's Office, Criminal
Records
PO Box 469
Shelbyville, IL 62565
(217) 774-4212

Felony and misdemeanor records are available by mail or phone. No release necessary. No search fee. $.25 fee per copy. $2.00 fee for certification. Search information required: name, date of birth, years to search, SASE.

Civil records are available by mail or phone. No release necessary. No search fee. $.25 fee per copy. $2.00 fee for certification. Search information required: name, date of birth, years to search, SASE. Specify plaintiff or defendant.

Stark County

Circuit Clerk's Office, Criminal
Records
Stark County Courthouse
Toulon, IL 61483
(309) 286-5941

Felony and misdemeanor records are available by mail. No release necessary. $4.00 search fee. $.50 fee per copy. $.50 fee for certification. Search information required: name, date of birth, years to search, SASE. Turnaround time is 1 week.

Civil records are available by mail. No release necessary. No search fee. $.50 fee per copy. $.50 fee for certification. Search information required: name, date of birth, years to search, SASE. Specify plaintiff or defendant.

Stephenson County

Circuit Clerk's Office, Criminal
Records
15 N. Galena
Stephenson County Courthouse
Freeport, IL 61032
(815) 235-8266

Felony and misdemeanor records are available by mail. A release is required. $4.00 fee for each year searched. $1.00 fee for first copy, $.50 each additional. $3.00 fee for certification. Certified check only, payable to Circuit Clerk's Office. Search information required: name, date of birth, years to search, SASE. Turnaround time is 2 weeks.

Civil records are available by mail. No release necessary. $4.00 fee for each year searched. $1.00 fee for first copy, $.50 each additional. $3.00 fee for certification. Search information required: name, date of birth, years to search, SASE. Specify plaintiff or defendant.

St. Clair County

Felony records
Circuit Clerk's Office, Criminal
Records
10 Public Square
Belleville, IL 62220
(618) 277-6832

Felony records are available by mail. No release necessary. $4.00 fee per year searched. $2.00 fee for first copy, $.50 each additional. $4.00 fee for certification. Search information required: name, date of birth, years to search, SASE.

Civil records
Circuit Clerk's Office
10 Public Square
Belleville, IL 62220
(618) 277-6832

Civil records are available by mail. No release necessary. $4.00 fee per year searched. $2.00 fee for first copy, $.50 each additional. $4.00 fee for certification. Search information required: name, date of birth, years to search, SASE. Specify plaintiff or defendant.

Misdemeanor records
Circuit Clerk's Office
10 Public Square
Belleville, IL 62222
(618) 277-6600

Misdemeanor records since 1980 are available by mail. A release is required. $4.00 fee for each year searched. $2.00 fee for first copy, $.50 each additional copy. $4.00 for certification. Make company check payable to Circuit Clerk. Search information required: name, date of birth, years to search, SASE.

Civil records
Circuit Clerk's Office
10 Public Square
Belleville, IL 62222
(618) 277-6600

Civil records are available by mail. A release is required. $4.00 fee for each year searched. $2.00 fee for first copy, $.50 each additional copy. $4.00 for certification. Search information required: name, date of birth, years to search. Specify plaintiff or defendant.

Tazewell County

Felony records
Circuit Clerk's Office, Criminal
Records
PO Box 69
Pekin, IL 61554
(309) 477-2214

Felony records are available by mail. No release necessary. $4.00 fee per year searched. Search information required: name, years to search.

Civil records
Circuit Clerk's Office
PO Box 69
Pekin, IL 61554
(309) 477-2214

Civil records are available by mail. No release necessary. $4.00 fee per year searched. Search information required: name, date of birth, years to search. Specify plaintiff or defendant.

Misdemeanor records
Circuit Clerk's Office
PO Box 69
Pekin, IL 61555
(309) 477-2218

Misdemeanor records are available in person only. For more information contact above office.

Misdemeanor records
Circuit Clerk's Office
PO Box 69
Pekin, IL 61555
(309) 477-2218

Civil records are available in person only. See Illinois state repository for additional information.

Union County

Circuit Clerk's Office, Criminal
Records
309 W. Market Street
Jonesboro, IL 62952
(618) 833-5913

Felony and misdemeanor records are available by mail. A release is required. $3.00 fee for each year searched. $.25 fee per copy. $1.00 for first certification, $.50 each additional page. Certified check only, payable to Count Circuit Clerk. Search information required: name, date of birth, years to search. Turnaround time is 1 week.

Civil records are available by mail. No release necessary. $3.00 fee for each year searched. $.25 fee per copy. $1.00 for first certification, $.50 each additional page. Search information required: name, date of birth, years to search. Specify plaintiff or defendant.

Vermilion County

Circuit Clerk's Office, Criminal
Records
7 N. Vermilion Street
Danville, IL 61832
(217) 431-2535

Felony and misdemeanor records are available by mail or phone. No release necessary. $4.00 fee per year searched. $1.00 fee for first copy, $.50 each additional copy. Search information required: name, date of birth, SASE.

Civil records are available by mail or phone. No release necessary. $4.00 fee per year searched. $1.00 fee for first copy, $.50 each additional copy. Search information required: name, date of birth, years to search, SASE. Specify plaintiff or defendant.

Wabash County

Circuit Clerk's Office, Criminal
Records
PO Box 1057
Mt. Carmel, IL 62863
(618) 262-5362

Felony and misdemeanor records are available by mail. No release necessary. $4.00 fee for each year searched. $.50 fee per copy. $1.00 for certification. Certified check only, payable to Circuit Clerk. Search information required: name, date of birth, SASE. Turnaround time is 1 week.

Civil records are available by mail. No release necessary. $4.00 fee for each year searched. $.50 fee per copy. $1.00 for certification. Search information required: name, date of birth, years to search, SASE. Specify plaintiff or defendant.

Warren County

Circuit Clerk's Office, Criminal
Records
Warren County Courthouse
Public Square
Monmouth, IL 61462
(309) 734-5179

Felony and misdemeanor records are available by mail. A release is required. $5.00 search fee. $.50 fee per copy. $2.00 for certification, $.50 each page. Company checks only, payable to Circuit Clerk. Search information required: name, date of birth, years to search. Turnaround time is 1-2 weeks.

Civil records are available by mail. No release necessary. $5.00 search fee. $.50 fee per copy. $2.00 for certification, $.50 each page. Search information required: name, date of birth, years to search,. Specify plaintiff or defendant.

Washington County

Circuit Clerk's Office, Criminal
Records
Washington County Courthouse
Nashville, IL 62263
(618) 327-3383

Felony and misdemeanor records are available by mail. A release is required. $4.00 search fee. $.50 fee per copy. $2.00 for certification. Search information required: name, date of birth.

Civil records are available by mail. No release necessary. $4.00 search fee. $.50 fee per copy. $2.00 for certification. Search information required: name, date of birth, years to search. Specify plaintiff or defendant.

Wayne County

Circuit Clerk's Office, Criminal
Records
PO Box 43
Fairfield, IL 62837
(618) 847-4701
Fax (618) 842-2556

Felony and misdemeanor records are available by mail or fax. No release necessary. $4.00 fee per year searched. $.50 fee per copy. $2.00 for certification. Search information required: name, date of birth, SASE.

Civil records are available by mail or fax. No release necessary. $4.00 search fee. $.50 fee per copy. $2.00 for certification. Search information required: name, date of birth, years to search, SASE. Specify plaintiff or defendant.

White County

Circuit Clerk's Office, Criminal
Records
PO Box 310
Carmi, IL 62821
(618) 382-2321
Fax (618) 382-7212

Felony and misdemeanor records are available by mail or fax. No release necessary. No search fee. $.25 fee per copy. $1.00 for first certification, $.50 each additional page. Search information required: name, date of birth, SASE. Turnaround time is 1 week.

Civil records are available by mail or fax. No release necessary. No search fee. $.25 fee per copy. $1.00 for first certification, $.50 each additional page. Search information required: name, date of birth, years to search, SASE. Specify plaintiff or defendant.

Whiteside County

Circuit Clerk's Office, Criminal
Records
Whiteside County Courthouse
Morrison, IL 61270
(815) 772-5188

Felony and misdemeanor records are available by mail or phone. No release necessary. $4.00 search fee. Search information required: name, date of birth, years to search.

Civil records are available by mail or phone. No release necessary. $4.00 search fee. Search information required: name, date of birth, years to search. Specify plaintiff or defendant.

Will County

Circuit Clerk's Office, Criminal
Records
Will County Courthouse
14 W. Jefferson, Room 212
Joliet, IL 60431
(815) 727-8595
Fax (815) 727-8595

Felony and misdemeanor records are available by mail or fax. A release is required. $4.00 fee for each year searched. $2.00 fee for first copy, $.50 each additional copy. $4.00 for certification. Certified check only, payable to County Circuit Clerk. Search information required: name, date of birth, SASE. Turnaround time is 1 week.

Civil records are available by mail or fax. A release is required.$4.00 fee for each year searched. $2.00 fee for first copy, $.50 each additional copy. $4.00 for certification. Search information required: name, date of birth, years to search, SASE. Specify plaintiff or defendant.

Williamson County

Circuit Clerk's Office, Criminal
Records
200 Jefferson
Marion, IL 62959
(618) 997-1301

Felony and misdemeanor records are available by mail. No release necessary. $4.00 fee for each year searched. $2.00 for certification. Certified check only, payable to Circuit Clerk. Search information required: name, years to search, SASE. Turnaround time is 1 week.

Civil records are available by mail. No release necessary. $4.00 fee for each year searched. $2.00 for certification. Search information required: name, date of birth, years to search, SASE. Specify plaintiff or defendant.

Winnebago County

Circuit Clerk's Office, Criminal
Records
400 W. State Street, Room 236
Rockford, IL 61101
(815) 987-3079

Felony records are available by mail or phone. No release necessary. $4.00 fee for each year searched. $2.00 fee per copy. $2.00 for certification. Certified check only, payable to Clerk of Circuit Court. Search information required: name, date of birth.

Civil records are available by mail. No release necessary. $4.00 fee for each year searched. $2.00 fee per copy. $2.00 for certification. Search information required: name, date of birth, years to search. Specify plaintiff or defendant.

City-County Cross Reference

Abingdon *Knox*
Adair *McDonough*
Addieville *Washington*
Addison *Du Page*
Adrian *Hancock*
Akin *Franklin*
Albany *Whiteside*
Albers *Clinton*
Albion *Edwards*
Aledo *Mercer*
Alexander *Morgan*
Alexis *Warren*
Algonquin *McHenry*
Alhambra *Madison*
Allendale *Wabash*
Allerton *Vermilion*
Alma *Marion*
Alorton *St. Clair*
Alpha *Henry*
Alsey *Scott*
Alsip *Cook*
Altamont *Effingham*
Alton *Madison*
Altona *Knox*
Alto Pass *Union*
Alvin *Vermilion*
Amboy *Lee*
Anchor *McLean*
Andalusia *Rock Island*
Andover *Henry*
Anna *Union*
Annapolis *Crawford*
Annawan *Henry*
Antioch *Lake*
Apple River *Jo Daviess*
Arcola *Douglas*
Arenzville *Cass*
Argenta *Macon*
Arlington *Bureau*
Arlington Heights *Cook*
Armington *Tazewell*
Armstrong *Vermilion*
Aroma Park *Kankakee*
Arrowsmith *McLean*
Arthur *Moultrie*
Ashkum *Iroquois*
Ashland *Cass*
Ashley *Washington*
Ashmore *Coles*
Ashton *Lee*
Assumption *Christian*
Astoria *Fulton*
Athens *Menard*
Atkinson *Henry*
Atlanta *Logan*
Atwater *Macoupin*
Atwood *Piatt*
Auburn *Sangamon*
Augusta *Hancock*
Aurora *Kane*
Ava *Jackson*
Aviston *Clinton*
Avon *Fulton*
Baileyville *Ogle*
Baldwin *Randolph*
Bannockburn *Lake*
Bardolph *McDonough*
Barnhill *Wayne*
Barrington *Lake*
Barry *Pike*
Barstow *Rock Island*
Bartelso *Clinton*

Bartlett *Cook*
Bartonville *Peoria*
Basco *Hancock*
Batavia *Kane*
Batchtown *Calhoun*
Bath *Mason*
Baylis *Pike*
Beardstown *Cass*
Beason *Logan*
Beaverville *Iroquois*
Beckemeyer *Clinton*
Beecher *Will*
Beecher City *Effingham*
Belknap *Johnson*
Belle Rive *Jefferson*
Belleville *Saint Clair*
Bellevue *Peoria*
Bellflower *McLean*
Bellmont *Wabash*
Bellwood *Cook*
Belvidere *Boone*
Bement *Piatt*
Benld *Macoupin*
Bensenville *Du Page*
Benson *Woodford*
Benton *Franklin*
Berkeley *Cook*
Berwick *Warren*
Berwyn *Cook*
Bethalto *Madison*
Bethany *Moultrie*
Bible Grove *Clay*
Biggsville *Henderson*
Big Rock *Kane*
Bingham *Fayette*
Birds *Lawrence*
Bishop Hill *Henry*
Bismarck *Vermilion*
Blackstone *Livingston*
Blandinsville *McDonough*
Bloomingdale *Du Page*
Bloomington *McLean*
Blue Island *Cook*
Blue Mound *Macon*
Bluffs *Scott*
Bluff Springs *Cass*
Bluford *Jefferson*
Boles *Johnson*
Bolingbrook *Will*
Bondville *Champaign*
Bone Gap *Edwards*
Bonfield *Kankakee*
Bonnie *Jefferson*
Boody *Macon*
Bourbonnais *Kankakee*
Bowen *Hancock*
Braceville *Grundy*
Bradford *Stark*
Bradley *Kankakee*
Braidwood *Will*
Brandywine *DuPage*
Breese *Clinton*
Bridgeport *Lawrence*
Bridgeview *Cook*
Brighton *Macoupin*
Brimfield *Peoria*
Bristol *Kendall*
Broadlands *Champaign*
Broadview *Cook*
Broadwell *Logan*
Brocton *Edgar*
Brookfield *Cook*

Brookport *Massac*
Broughton *Hamilton*
Brownfield *Pope*
Browning *Schuyler*
Browns *Edwards*
Brownstown *Fayette*
Brussels *Calhoun*
Bryant *Fulton*
Buckingham *Kankakee*
Buckley *Iroquois*
Buckner *Franklin*
Buda *Bureau*
Buffalo *Sangamon*
Buffalo Grove *Cook*
Buffalo Prairie *Rock Island*
Bulpitt *Christian*
Buncombe *Johnson*
Bunker Hill *Macoupin*
Burbank *Cook*
Bureau *Bureau*
Burlington *Kane*
Burnham *Cook*
Burnside *Hancock*
Burnt Prairie *White*
Burr Ridge *DuPage*
Bushnell *McDonough*
Butler *Montgomery*
Butterfield *DuPage*
Byron *Ogle*
Cabery *Kankakee*
Cache *Alexander*
Cahokia *St. Clair*
Cairo *Alexander*
Caledonia *Boone*
Calhoun *Richland*
Calumet City *Cook*
Calumet Park *Cook*
Camargo *Douglas*
Cambria *Williamson*
Cambridge *Henry*
Camden *Schuyler*
Cameron *Warren*
Campbell Hill *Jackson*
Camp Grove *Marshall*
Camp Point *Adams*
Campus *Livingston*
Canton *Fulton*
Cantrall *Sangamon*
Capron *Boone*
Carbon Cliff *Rock Island*
Carbondale *Jackson*
Carlinville *Macoupin*
Carlock *McLean*
Carlyle *Clinton*
Carman *Henderson*
Carmi *White*
Carpentersville *Kane*
Carrier Mills *Saline*
Carrollton *Greene*
Carterville *Williamson*
Carthage *Hancock*
Cary *McHenry*
Casey *Clark*
Caseyville *Saint Clair*
Castleton *Stark*
Catlin *Vermilion*
Cave In Rock *Hardin*
Cedar Point *LaSalle*
Cedarville *Stephenson*
Centralia *Marion*
Central City *Marion*
Centreville *St. Clair*

Cerro Gordo *Piatt*
Chadwick *Carroll*
Chambersburg *Pike*
Champaign *Champaign*
Chana *Ogle*
Chandlerville *Cass*
Channahon *Will*
Chapin *Morgan*
Charleston *Coles*
Chatham *Sangamon*
Chatsworth *Livingston*
Chebanse *Iroquois*
Chenoa *McLean*
Cherry *Bureau*
Cherry Valley *Winnebago*
Chester *Randolph*
Chesterfield *Macoupin*
Chestnut *Logan*
Chicago *Cook*
Chicago Heights *Cook*
Chicago Ridge *Cook*
Chillicothe *Peoria*
Chrisman *Edgar*
Christopher *Franklin*
Cicero *Cook*
Cisco *Piatt*
Cisne *Wayne*
Cissna Park *Iroquois*
Clare *DeKalb*
Claremont *Richland*
Clarendon Hills *Du Page*
Clay City *Clay*
Clayton *Adams*
Claytonville *Iroquois*
Clifton *Iroquois*
Clinton *DeWitt*
Coal City *Grundy*
Coal Valley *Rock Island*
Coatsburg *Adams*
Cobden *Union*
Coello *Franklin*
Coffeen *Montgomery*
Colchester *McDonough*
Colfax *McLean*
Collinsville *Madison*
Collison *Vermilion*
Colmar *McDonough*
Colona *Henry*
Colp *Williamson*
Columbia *Monroe*
Colusa *Hancock*
Compton *Lee*
Concord *Morgan*
Congerville *Woodford*
Cooksville *McLean*
Cordova *Rock Island*
Cornell *Livingston*
Cornland *Logan*
Cortland *DeKalb*
Cottage Hills *Madison*
Coulterville *Randolph*
Countryside *Cook*
Cowden *Shelby*
Creal Springs *Williamson*
Crescent City *Iroquois*
Crest Hill *Will*
Creston *Ogle*
Crestwood *Cook*
Crete *Will*
Creve Coeur *Tazewell*
Cropsey *McLean*
Crossville *White*

Crystal Lake *McHenry*
Crystal Lawns *Will*
Cuba *Fulton*
Cullom *Livingston*
Custer Park *Will*
Cutler *Perry*
Cypress *Johnson*
Dahinda *Knox*
Dahlgren *Hamilton*
Dakota *Stephenson*
Dale *Hamilton*
Dallas City *Hancock*
Dalton City *Moultrie*
Dalzell *Bureau*
Dana *LaSalle*
Danforth *Iroquois*
Danvers *McLean*
Danville *Vermilion*
Darien *DuPage*
Davis *Stephenson*
Davis Junction *Ogle*
Dawson *Sangamon*
Decatur *Macon*
Deer Creek *Tazewell*
Deerfield *Lake*
Deer Grove *Whiteside*
Deerpark *Lake*
DeKalb *DeKalb*
DeLand *Piatt*
Delavan *Tazewell*
Dennison *Clark*
Depue *Bureau*
DeSoto *Jackson*
Des Plaines *Cook*
Dewey *Champaign*
Dewitt *DeWitt*
Diamond *Will*
Dieterich *Effingham*
Divernon *Sangamon*
Dix *Jefferson*
Dixmoor *Cook*
Dixon *Lee*
Dolton *Cook*
Dongola *Union*
Donnellson *Montgomery*
Donovan *Iroquois*
Dorsey *Madison*
Dover *Bureau*
Dow *Jersey*
Dowell *Jackson*
Downers Grove *Du Page*
Downs *McLean*
Dubois *Washington*
Dundas *Richland*
Dundee *Kane*
Dunfermline *Fulton*
Dunlap *Peoria*
Dupo *Saint Clair*
Du Quoin *Perry*
Durand *Winnebago*
Dwight *Livingston*
Eagarville *Macoupin*
Earlville *LaSalle*
East Alton *Madison*
East Carondelet *Saint Clair*
East Dundee *Kane*
East Dubuque *Jo Daviess*
East Galesburg *Knox*
East Hazel Crest *Cook*
East Lynn *Vermilion*
East Moline *Rock Island*
East Peoria *Tazewell*
Easton *Mason*
East Saint Louis *Saint Clair*
Eddyville *Pope*

Edelstein *Peoria*
Edgewood *Effingham*
Edinburg *Christian*
Edwards *Peoria*
Edwardsville *Madison*
Effingham *Effingham*
Elburn *Kane*
Elco *Alexander*
Eldena *Lee*
Eldorado *Saline*
Eldred *Greene*
Eleroy *Stephenson*
Elgin *Kane*
Elizabeth *Jo Daviess*
Elizabethtown *Hardin*
Elk Grove Village *Cook*
Elkhart *Logan*
Elkville *Jackson*
Ellery *Edwards*
Elliott *Ford*
Ellis Grove *Randolph*
Ellisville *Fulton*
Ellsworth *McLean*
Elmhurst *Du Page*
Elmwood *Peoria*
Elmwood Park *Cook*
El Paso *Woodford*
Elsah *Jersey*
Elvaston *Hancock*
Elwin *Macon*
Elwood *Will*
Emden *Logan*
Emington *Livingston*
Emma *White*
Energy *Williamson*
Enfield *White*
Eola *Du Page*
Equality *Gallatin*
Erie *Whiteside*
Esmond *DeKalb*
Essex *Kankakee*
Eureka *Woodford*
Evanston *Cook*
Evansville *Randolph*
Ewing *Franklin*
Fairbury *Livingston*
Fairfield *Wayne*
Fairmont City *St. Clair*
Fairmount *Vermilion*
Fairview *Fulton*
Farina *Fayette*
Farmer City *DeWitt*
Farmersville *Montgomery*
Farmingdale *DuPage*
Farmington *Fulton*
Fenton *Whiteside*
Ferris *Hancock*
Fiatt *Fulton*
Fidelity *Jersey*
Fieldon *Jersey*
Fillmore *Montgomery*
Findlay *Shelby*
Fisher *Champaign*
Fithian *Vermilion*
Flanagan *Livingston*
Flat Rock *Crawford*
Flora *Clay*
Flossmoor *Cook*
Foosland *Champaign*
Ford Heights *Cook*
Forest City *Mason*
Forest Lake *Lake*
Forest Park *Cook*
Forest View *Cook*
Forrest *Livingston*
Forreston *Ogle*

Forsyth *Macon*
Fowler *Adams*
Fox Lake *Lake*
Fox River Grove *McHenry*
Frankfort *Will*
Frankfort Heights *Franklin*
Franklin *Morgan*
Franklin Grove *Lee*
Franklin Park *Cook*
Frederick *Schuyler*
Freeburg *Saint Clair*
Freeman Spur *Williamson*
Freeport *Stephenson*
Fulton *Whiteside*
Fults *Monroe*
Gages Lake *Lake*
Galatia *Saline*
Galena *Jo Daviess*
Galesburg *Knox*
Galt *Whiteside*
Galva *Henry*
Garden Prairie *Boone*
Gardner *Grundy*
Gays *Moultrie*
Geff *Wayne*
Geneseo *Henry*
Geneva *Kane*
Genoa *DeKalb*
Georgetown *Vermilion*
Gerlaw *Warren*
Germantown *Clinton*
German Valley *Stephenson*
Gibson City *Ford*
Gifford *Champaign*
Gilberts *Kane*
Gillespie *Macoupin*
Gilman *Iroquois*
Gilson *Knox*
Girard *Macoupin*
Gladstone *Henderson*
Glasford *Peoria*
Glenarm *Sangamon*
Glen Carbon *Madison*
Glencoe *Cook*
Glendale Heights *DuPage*
Glen Ellyn *Du Page*
Glenview *Cook*
Glenwood *Cook*
Godfrey *Madison*
Golconda *Pope*
Golden *Adams*
Golden Eagle *Calhoun*
Goldengate *Wayne*
Golf *Cook*
Goodfield *Woodford*
Good Hope *McDonough*
Goodwine *Iroquois*
Goreville *Johnson*
Gorham *Jackson*
Grafton *Jersey*
Grand Chain *Pulaski*
Grand Ridge *LaSalle*
Grand Tower *Jackson*
Grandview *Sangamon*
Granite City *Madison*
Grant Park *Kankakee*
Grantsburg *Johnson*
Granville *Putnam*
Graymont *Livingston*
Grayslake *Lake*
Grayville *White*
Greenfield *Greene*
Green Oaks *Lake*
Green Rock *Henry*
Greenup *Cumberland*
Green Valley *Tazewell*

Greenview *Menard*
Greenville *Bond*
Gridley *McLean*
Griggsville *Pike*
Groveland *Tazewell*
Gurnee *Lake*
Hagarstown *Fayette*
Hamburg *Calhoun*
Hamel *Madison*
Hamilton *Hancock*
Hamletsburg *Pope*
Hammond *Piatt*
Hampshire *Kane*
Hampton *Rock Island*
Hanna City *Peoria*
Hanover *Jo Daviess*
Hanover Park *Cook*
Hardin *Calhoun*
Harmon *Lee*
Harrisburg *Saline*
Harristown *Macon*
Hartford *Madison*
Hartsburg *Logan*
Harvard *McHenry*
Harvel *Montgomery*
Harvey *Cook*
Harwood Heights *Cook*
Havana *Mason*
Hawthorn Woods *Lake*
Hazel Crest *Cook*
Hebron *McHenry*
Hecker *Monroe*
Henderson *Knox*
Hennepin *Putnam*
Henning *Vermilion*
Henry *Marshall*
Herald *White*
Herod *Pope*
Herrick *Shelby*
Herrin *Williamson*
Herscher *Kankakee*
Hettick *Macoupin*
Hewittville *Christian*
Heyworth *McLean*
Hickory Hills *Cook*
Hidalgo *Jasper*
Highland Hills *DuPage*
Highland *Madison*
Highland Park *Lake*
Highwood *Lake*
Hillcrest *Ogle*
Hillsboro *Montgomery*
Hillsdale *Rock Island*
Hillview *Greene*
Hinckley *DeKalb*
Hindsboro *Douglas*
Hines *Cook*
Hinsdale *Du Page*
Hodgkins *Cook*
Hoffman *Clinton*
Hoffman Estates *DuPage*
Holcomb *Ogle*
Holder *McLean*
Holiday Hills *McHenry*
Homer *Champaign*
Hometown *Cook*
Homewood *Cook*
Hoopeston *Vermilion*
Hooppole *Henry*
Hopedale *Tazewell*
Hopkins Park *Kankakee*
Hoyleton *Washington*
Hudson *McLean*
Huey *Clinton*
Hull *Pike*
Humboldt *Coles*

Hume *Edgar*
Huntley *McHenry*
Huntsville *Schuyler*
Hurst *Williamson*
Hutsonville *Crawford*
Illinois City *Rock Island*
Illiopolis *Sangamon*
Ina *Jefferson*
Indian Head Park *Cook*
Indianola *Vermilion*
Industry *McDonough*
Ingalls Park *Will*
Ingleside *Lake*
Ingraham *Clay*
Inverness *Cook*
Iola *Clay*
Ipava *Fulton*
Iroquois *Iroquois*
Irving *Montgomery*
Irvington *Washington*
Island Lake *Lake*
Itasca *Du Page*
Iuka *Marion*
Ivesdale *Champaign*
Jacksonville *Morgan*
Jacob *Jackson*
Janesville *Cumberland*
Jerome *Sangamon*
Jerseyville *Jersey*
Jewett *Cumberland*
Johnsburg *McHenry*
Johnsonville *Wayne*
Johnston City *Williamson*
Joliet *Will*
Jonesboro *Union*
Joppa *Massac*
Joy *Mercer*
Junction *Gallatin*
Justice *Cook*
Kampsville *Calhoun*
Kane *Greene*
Kaneville *Kane*
Kankakee *Kankakee*
Kansas *Edgar*
Karbers Ridge *Hardin*
Karnak *Pulaski*
Kasbeer *Bureau*
Keenes *Wayne*
Keeneyville *DuPage*
Keensburg *Wabash*
Keithsburg *Mercer*
Kell *Marion*
Kempton *Ford*
Kenilworth *Cook*
Kenney *DeWitt*
Kent *Stephenson*
Kewanee *Henry*
Keyesport *Clinton*
Kilbourne *Mason*
Kildeer *Lake*
Kincaid *Christian*
Kinderhook *Pike*
Kingston *DeKalb*
Kingston Mines *Peoria*
Kinmundy *Marion*
Kinsman *Grundy*
Kirkland *DeKalb*
Kirkwood *Warren*
Knollwood *Lake*
Knoxville *Knox*
Lacon *Marshall*
Ladd *Bureau*
LaFayette *Stark*
Lafox *Kane*
LaGrange *Cook*
La Grange Highlands *Cook*

La Grange Park *Cook*
LaHarpe *Hancock*
Lake Barrington *Lake*
Lake Bluff *Lake*
Lake Forest *Lake*
Lake Fork *Logan*
Lake In The Hills
    McHenry
Lake Villa *Lake*
Lakewood *Shelby*
Lake Zurich *Lake*
LaMoille *Bureau*
Lanark *Carroll*
Lancaster *Wabash*
Lane *DeWitt*
Lansing *Cook*
LaPlace *Piatt*
LaPrairie *Adams*
LaRose *Marshall*
LaSalle *LaSalle*
Latham *Logan*
Laura *Peoria*
Lawndale *Logan*
Lawrenceville *Lawrence*
Leaf River *Ogle*
Lebanon *Saint Clair*
Lee *Lee*
Lee Center *Lee*
Leland *LaSalle*
Leland Grove *Sangamon*
Lemont *Cook*
Lena *Stephenson*
Lenzburg *Saint Clair*
Leonore *LaSalle*
Lerna *Coles*
Le Roy *McLean*
Lewistown *Fulton*
Lexington *McLean*
Liberty *Adams*
Libertyville *Lake*
Lima *Adams*
Lincoln *Logan*
Lincolnshire *Lake*
Lincolnwood *Cook*
Lindenwood *Ogle*
Lisle *Du Page*
Litchfield *Montgomery*
Literberry *Morgan*
Littleton *Schuyler*
Little York *Warren*
Liverpool *Fulton*
Livingston *Madison*
Loami *Sangamon*
Lockport *Will*
Loda *Iroquois*
Logan *Franklin*
Lomax *Henderson*
Lombard *Du Page*
London Mills *Fulton*
Long Grove *Lake*
Long Lake *Lake*
Long Point *Livingston*
Longview *Champaign*
Loogootee *Fayette*
Loraine *Adams*
Lostant *LaSalle*
Louisville *Clay*
Lovejoy *Saint Clair*
Lovington *Moultrie*
Lowder *Sangamon*
Lowpoint *Woodford*
Ludlow *Champaign*
Lyndon *Whiteside*
Lynn Center *Henry*
Lynwood *Cook*
Lyons *Cook*

McClure *Alexander*
McConnell *Stephenson*
McCullom Lake *McHenry*
McHenry *McHenry*
McLean *McLean*
McLeansboro *Hamilton*
McNabb *Putnam*
Macedonia *Hamilton*
Machesney Park
    Winnebago
Mackinaw *Tazewell*
Macomb *McDonough*
Macon *Macon*
Madison *Madison*
Maeystown *Monroe*
Magnolia *Putnam*
Mahomet *Champaign*
Makanda *Jackson*
Malden *Bureau*
Malta *DeKalb*
Manchester *Scott*
Manhattan *Will*
Manito *Mason*
Manlius *Bureau*
Mansfield *Piatt*
Manteno *Kankakee*
Manville *Livingston*
Maple Park *Kane*
Mapleton *Peoria*
Maquon *Knox*
Marengo *McHenry*
Marietta *Fulton*
Marine *Madison*
Marion *Williamson*
Marissa *Saint Clair*
Mark *Putnam*
Markham *Cook*
Maroa *Macon*
Marseilles *LaSalle*
Marshall *Clark*
Martinsville *Clark*
Martinton *Iroquois*
Maryville *Madison*
Mascoutah *Saint Clair*
Mason *Effingham*
Mason City *Mason*
Matherville *Mercer*
Matteson *Cook*
Mattoon *Coles*
Maunie *White*
Maywood *Cook*
Mazon *Grundy*
Meadowbrook *Madison*
Mechanicsburg *Sangamon*
Media *Henderson*
Medinah *Du Page*
Medora *Macoupin*
Melrose Park *Cook*
Melvin *Ford*
Menard *Randolph*
Mendon *Adams*
Mendota *LaSalle*
Meppen *Calhoun*
Meredosia *Morgan*
Merionette Park *Cook*
Merna *McLean*
Metamora *Woodford*
Metcalf *Edgar*
Metropolis *Massac*
Michael *Calhoun*
Middletown *Logan*
Midlothian *Cook*
Milan *Rock Island*
Milford *Iroquois*
Millbrook *Kendall*
Millcreek *Union*

Milledgeville *Carroll*
Miller City *Alexander*
Millington *Kendall*
Mill Shoals *White*
Millstadt *Saint Clair*
Milmine *Piatt*
Milton *Pike*
Mineral *Bureau*
Minier *Tazewell*
Minonk *Woodford*
Minooka *Grundy*
Mitchell *Madison*
Moecherville *Kane*
Modesto *Macoupin*
Mokena *Will*
Moline *Rock Island*
Momence *Kankakee*
Monee *Will*
Monmouth *Warren*
Monroe Center *Ogle*
Montgomery *Kane*
Monticello *Piatt*
Montrose *Effingham*
Moro *Madison*
Morris *Grundy*
Morrison *Whiteside*
Morrisonville *Christian*
Morton *Tazewell*
Morton Grove *Cook*
Mossville *Peoria*
Mound City *Pulaski*
Mounds *Pulaski*
Mount Auburn *Christian*
Mount Carmel *Wabash*
Mount Carroll *Carroll*
Mount Erie *Wayne*
Mount Morris *Ogle*
Mount Olive *Macoupin*
Mount Prospect *Cook*
Mount Pulaski *Logan*
Mount Sterling *Brown*
Mount Vernon *Jefferson*
Mount Zion *Macon*
Moweaqua *Shelby*
Mozier *Calhoun*
Muddy *Saline*
Mulberry Grove *Bond*
Mulkeytown *Franklin*
Muncie *Vermilion*
Mundelein *Lake*
Murdock *Douglas*
Murphysboro *Jackson*
Murrayville *Morgan*
Nachusa *Lee*
Naperville *Du Page*
Nashville *Washington*
Nason *Jefferson*
National Stock Yards *Saint
    Clair*
Nauvoo *Hancock*
Nebo *Pike*
Neoga *Cumberland*
Neponset *Bureau*
Newark *Kendall*
New Athens *Saint Clair*
New Baden *Clinton*
New Bedford *Bureau*
New Berlin *Sangamon*
New Boston *Mercer*
New Burnside *Johnson*
New Canton *Pike*
New Douglas *Madison*
New Haven *Gallatin*
New Holland *Logan*
New Lenox *Will*
Newman *Douglas*

New Memphis *Clinton*
New Milford *Winnebago*
New Salem *Pike*
Newton *Jasper*
New Windsor *Mercer*
Niantic *Macon*
Niles *Cook*
Nilwood *Macoupin*
Niota *Hancock*
Noble *Richland*
Nokomis *Montgomery*
Nora *Jo Daviess*
Normal *McLean*
Norris *Fulton*
Norris City *White*
North Aurora *Kane*
North Barrington *Lake*
Northbrook *Cook*
North Chicago *Lake*
Northfield *Cook*
North Glen Ellyn *DuPage*
North Henderson *Mercer*
North Riverside *Cook*
Oakbrook *DuPage*
Oakdale *Washington*
Oakford *Menard*
Oak Forest *Cook*
Oakgrove *Rock Island*
Oakland *Coles*
Oak Lawn *Cook*
Oakley *Macon*
Oak Park *Cook*
Oakwood *Vermilion*
Oakwood Hills *McHenry*
Oblong *Crawford*
Oconee *Shelby*
Odell *Livingston*
Odin *Marion*
O'Fallon *Saint Clair*
Ogden *Champaign*
Oglesby *LaSalle*
Ohio *Bureau*
Ohlman *Montgomery*
Okawville *Washington*
Olive Branch *Alexander*
Olmsted *Pulaski*
Olney *Richland*
Olympia Fields *Cook*
Omaha *Gallatin*
Onarga *Iroquois*
Oneida *Knox*
Opdyke *Jefferson*
Opheim *Henry*
Oquawka *Henderson*
Orangeville *Stephenson*
Oraville *Jackson*
Oreana *Macon*
Oregon *Ogle*
Orient *Franklin*
Orion *Henry*
Orland Hills *Cook*
Orland Park *Cook*
Osco *Henry*
Oswego *Kendall*
Ottawa *LaSalle*
Owaneco *Christian*
Ozark *Johnson*
Palatine *Cook*
Palestine *Crawford*
Palmer *Christian*
Palmyra *Macoupin*
Paloma *Adams*
Palos Heights *Cook*
Palos Hills *Cook*
Palos Park *Cook*
Pana *Christian*

Panama *Montgomery*
Papineau *Iroquois*
Paris *Edgar*
Parkersburg *Richland*
Park City *Lake*
Park Forest *Cook*
Park Ridge *Cook*
Patoka *Marion*
Patterson *Greene*
Pawnee *Sangamon*
Paw Paw *Lee*
Paxton *Ford*
Payson *Adams*
Pearl *Pike*
Pearl City *Stephenson*
Pecatonica *Winnebago*
Pekin *Tazewell*
Penfield *Champaign*
Peoria *Peoria*
Peoria Heights *Peoria*
Peotone *Will*
Percy *Randolph*
Perks *Pulaski*
Perry *Pike*
Peru *LaSalle*
Pesotum *Champaign*
Petersburg *Menard*
Philo *Champaign*
Phoenix *Cook*
Piasa *Macoupin*
Pierron *Bond*
Pinckneyville *Perry*
Piper City *Ford*
Pittsburg *Williamson*
Pittsfield *Pike*
Plainfield *Will*
Plainview *Macoupin*
Plainville *Adams*
Plano *Kendall*
Pleasant Hill *Pike*
Pleasant Plains *Sangamon*
Plymouth *Hancock*
Pocahontas *Bond*
Polo *Ogle*
Pomona *Jackson*
Pontiac *Livingston*
Pontoon Beach *Madison*
Poplar Grove *Boone*
Port Byron *Rock Island*
Posen *Cook*
Potomac *Vermilion*
Prairie City *McDonough*
Prairie Du Rocher
  Randolph
Prairie View *Lake*
Preemption *Mercer*
Preston Heights *Will*
Princeton *Bureau*
Princeville *Peoria*
Prophetstown *Whiteside*
Prospect Heights *Cook*
Pulaski *Pulaski*
Putnam *Putnam*
Quincy *Adams*
Radom *Washington*
Raleigh *Saline*
Ramsey *Fayette*
Rankin *Vermilion*
Ransom *LaSalle*
Rantoul *Champaign*
Rapids City *Rock Island*
Raritan *Henderson*
Raymond *Montgomery*
Red Bud *Randolph*
Reddick *Kankakee*
Redmon *Edgar*

Renault *Monroe*
Reynolds *Rock Island*
Richmond *McHenry*
Richton Park *Cook*
Richview *Washington*
Ridge Farm *Vermilion*
Ridgway *Gallatin*
Ridott *Stephenson*
Rinard *Wayne*
Ringwood *McHenry*
Rio *Knox*
River Grove *Cook*
Riverdale *Cook*
River Forrest *Cook*
Riverside *Cook*
Riverton *Sangamon*
Riverwoods *Lake*
Roanoke *Woodford*
Robbins *Cook*
Roberts *Ford*
Robinson *Crawford*
Rochelle *Ogle*
Rochester *Sangamon*
Rockbridge *Greene*
Rock City *Stephenson*
Rockdale *Will*
Rock Falls *Whiteside*
Rockford *Winnebago*
Rock Island *Rock Island*
Rockport *Pike*
Rockton *Winnebago*
Rockwood *Randolph*
Rolling Meadows *Cook*
Rome *Peoria*
Romeoville *Will*
Roodhouse *Greene*
Rosamond *Christian*
Roscoe *Winnebago*
Roselle *Du Page*
Roseville *Warren*
Rosiclare *Hardin*
Rossville *Vermilion*
Round Lake *Lake*
Round Lake Beach *Lake*
Roxana *Madison*
Royal *Champaign*
Royalton *Franklin*
Rushville *Schuyler*
Russell *Lake*
Rutland *LaSalle*
Sadorus *Champaign*
Sailor Springs *Clay*
Saint Anne *Kankakee*
Saint Augustine *Knox*
Saint Charles *Kane*
Saint David *Fulton*
Saint Elmo *Fayette*
Sainte Marie *Jasper*
Saint Francisville
  Lawrence
Saint Jacob *Madison*
Saint Joseph *Champaign*
Saint Libory *Saint Clair*
Saint Peter *Fayette*
Salem *Marion*
Sandoval *Marion*
Sandwich *DeKalb*
San Jose *Mason*
Sauk Village *Cook*
Saunemin *Livingston*
Savanna *Carroll*
Savoy *Champaign*
Sawyerville *Macoupin*
Saybrook *McLean*
Scales Mound *Jo Daviess*
Schaumburg *Cook*

Scheller *Jefferson*
Schiller Park *Cook*
Schram City *Montgomery*
Scottville *Macoupin*
Seaton *Mercer*
Seatonville *Bureau*
Secor *Woodford*
Seneca *LaSalle*
Serena *LaSalle*
Sesser *Franklin*
Seward *Winnebago*
Seymour *Champaign*
Shabbona *DeKalb*
Shannon *Carroll*
Shattuc *Clinton*
Shawneetown *Gallatin*
Sheffield *Bureau*
Shelbyville *Shelby*
Sheldon *Iroquois*
Sheridan *LaSalle*
Sherman *Sangamon*
Sherrard *Mercer*
Shiloh *St. Clair*
Shipman *Macoupin*
Shirland *Winnebago*
Shirley *McLean*
Shobonier *Fayette*
Shorewood *Will*
Shumway *Effingham*
Sibley *Ford*
Sidell *Vermilion*
Sidney *Champaign*
Sigel *Shelby*
Silvis *Rock Island*
Simpson *Johnson*
Sims *Wayne*
Skokie *Cook*
Sleepy Hollow *Kane*
Smithboro *Bond*
Smithfield *Fulton*
Smithshire *Warren*
Smithton *Saint Clair*
Solon Mills *McHenry*
Somonauk *DeKalb*
Sorento *Bond*
South Barrington *Cook*
South Beloit *Winnebago*
South Chicago Heights
  Cook
South Elgin *Kane*
Southern View *Sangamon*
South Holland *Cook*
South Jacksonville *Morgan*
South Pekin *Tazewell*
South Roxana *Madison*
South Streator *Livingston*
Standard City *Macoupin*
South Wilmington *Grundy*
Sparland *Marshall*
Sparta *Randolph*
Speer *Stark*
Springerton *White*
Springfield *Sangamon*
Spring Grove *McHenry*
Spring Valley *Bureau*
Standard *Putnam*
Stanford *McLean*
State Park Place *Madison*
Staunton *Macoupin*
Steeleville *Randolph*
Steger *Cook*
Sterling *Whiteside*
Steward *Lee*
Stewardson *Shelby*
Stickney *Cook*
Stillman Valley *Ogle*

Stockland *Iroquois*
Stockton *Jo Daviess*
Stonefort *Saline*
Stone Park *Cook*
Stonington *Christian*
Stoy *Crawford*
Strasburg *Shelby*
Strawn *Livingston*
Streamwood *Cook*
Streator *LaSalle*
Stronghurst *Henderson*
Sublette *Lee*
Sugar Grove *Kane*
Sullivan *Moultrie*
Summerfield *Saint Clair*
Summer Hill *Pike*
Summit *Cook*
Summit-Argo *Cook*
Sumner *Lawrence*
Sutter *Hancock*
Swansea *St. Clair*
Swanwick *Perry*
Sycamore *DeKalb*
Table Grove *Fulton*
Tallula *Menard*
Tamaroa *Perry*
Tamms *Alexander*
Tampico *Whiteside*
Taylor Ridge *Rock Island*
Taylor Springs
    Montgomery
Taylorville *Christian*
Techny *Cook*
Tennessee *McDonough*
Teutopolis *Effingham*
Texico *Jefferson*
Thawville *Iroquois*
Thayer *Sangamon*
Thebes *Alexander*
Thomasboro *Champaign*
Thompsonville *Franklin*
Thomson *Carroll*
Thornton *Cook*
Tilden *Randolph*
Tilton *Vermilion*
Timewell *Brown*
Tinley Park *Cook*
Tiskilwa *Bureau*
Toledo *Cumberland*
Tolono *Champaign*
Toluca *Marshall*
Tonica *LaSalle*
Topeka *Mason*
Toulon *Stark*
Tovey *Christian*
Towanda *McLean*
Tower Hill *Shelby*
Tower Lakes *Lake*
Tremont *Tazewell*
Trenton *Clinton*
Trilla *Coles*
Tri State Village *DuPage*
Triumph *LaSalle*
Trivoli *Peoria*
Troy *Madison*
Troy Grove *LaSalle*
Tunnel Hill *Johnson*
Tuscola *Douglas*
Ullin *Pulaski*
Union *McHenry*
Union Hill *Kankakee*
University Park *Cook*
Urbana *Champaign*
Ursa *Adams*
Utica *LaSalle*
Valier *Franklin*

Valley View *Kane*
Valmeyer *Monroe*
Vandalia *Fayette*
Van Orin *Bureau*
Varna *Marshall*
Venice *Madison*
Vergennes *Jackson*
Vermilion *Edgar*
Vermont *Fulton*
Vernon *Marion*
Vernon Hills *Lake*
Verona *Grundy*
Versailles *Brown*
Victoria *Knox*
Vienna *Johnson*
Villa Grove *Douglas*
Villa Hills *Lake*
Villa Park *Du Page*
Villa Ridge *Pulaski*
Viola *Mercer*
Virden *Macoupin*
Virginia *Cass*
Wadsworth *Lake*
Waggoner *Montgomery*
Walnut *Bureau*
Walnut Hill *Marion*
Walsh *Randolph*
Walshville *Montgomery*
Waltonville *Jefferson*
Wamac *Marion*
Wapella *DeWitt*
Warren *Jo Daviess*
Warrensburg *Macon*
Warrenville *Du Page*
Warsaw *Hancock*
Wasco *Kane*
Washburn *Woodford*
Washington *Tazewell*
Washington Park *St. Clair*
Wataga *Knox*
Waterloo *Monroe*
Waterman *DeKalb*
Watseka *Iroquois*
Watson *Effingham*
Wauconda *Lake*
Waukegan *Lake*
Waverly *Morgan*
Wayne *Du Page*
Wayne City *Wayne*
Waynesville *DeWitt*
Wedron *LaSalle*
Weldon *DeWitt*
Wellington *Iroquois*
Wenona *Marshall*
West Brooklyn *Lee*
Westchester *Cook*
West Chicago *Du Page*
West City *Franklin*
Western Springs *Cook*
Westervelt *Shelby*
West Dundee *Kane*
Westfield *Clark*
West Frankfort *Franklin*
West Liberty *Jasper*
Westmont *Du Page*
West Peoria *Peoria*
West Point *Hancock*
West Salem *Edwards*
West Union *Clark*
Westville *Vermilion*
West York *Crawford*
Wheaton *Du Page*
Wheeler *Jasper*
Wheeling *Cook*
White Hall *Greene*
White Heath *Piatt*

Whittington *Franklin*
Wildwood *Lake*
Williamsfield *Knox*
Williamsville *Sangamon*
Willisville *Perry*
Willow Brook *DuPage*
Willow Hill *Jasper*
Willow Springs *Cook*
Wilmette *Cook*
Wilmington *Will*
Wilsonville *Macoupin*
Winchester *Scott*
Windsor *Shelby*
Winfield *Du Page*
Winnebago *Winnebago*
Winnetka *Cook*
Winslow *Stephenson*
Winthrop Harbor *Lake*
Witt *Montgomery*
Wolf Lake *Union*
Wonder Lake *McHenry*
Wood Dale *Du Page*
Woodhull *Henry*
Woodland *Iroquois*
Woodlawn *Jefferson*
Woodridge *DuPage*
Wood River *Madison*
Woodson *Morgan*
Woodstock *McHenry*
Woosung *Ogle*
Worden *Madison*
Worth *Cook*
Wrights *Greene*
Wyanet *Bureau*
Wyoming *Stark*
Xenia *Clay*
Yale *Jasper*
Yates City *Knox*
York Center *DuPage*
Yorkfield *DuPage*
Yorkville *Kendall*
Zeigler *Franklin*
Zion *Lake*

Indiana

Eighty one (81) of Indiana's ninety two (92) counties reported that criminal records are available for employment purposes by phone and/or mail. The remaining eleven (11) counties require that the requests be made in person. Fifteen (15) will honor fax requests.

For more information or for offices not listed, contact the state's information hot line at (317) 232-3140 or 232-1000.

Driving Records

Bureau of Motor Vehicles
State Office Building
Room 416
Indianapolis, IN 46204
(317) 232-2894

Driving records are available by mail. $4 fee per request. Turnaround time is 7 to 10 days. Written request must include job applicant's full name, date of birth and license number. Make check payable to Bureau of Motor Vehicles.

Worker's Compensation Records

Industrial Board
Statistical Department
601 State Office Building
100 N. Senate Avenue
Indianapolis, IN 46204
(317) 232-3818

Worker's compensation records are available by mail. A release is required. Request must include subject's full name, the name of employer involved in claim and the year of the accident. There is no search fee. $.15 fee per copy.

Vital Statistics

Division of Vital Records
State Department of Health
1330 West Michigan Street
PO Box 1964
Indianapolis, IN 46206-1964
(317) 633-0276
Fax (317) 633-0210

Birth records are available for $6.00 and death records are available for $4.00. Duplicate copies are $1.00 each. State office has birth records since October 1907 and death records since 1900. For earlier records, write to Health Officer in city or county where event occurred. An employer can obtain records with a written notarized release. Make any type check or money order payable to State Department of Health.

For marriage verification only, no fee. Include name, marriage date, and location of event. Marriage records are available at county level. Fee of $3.00 for certification. Divorce records available at county level. Include name, spouse's name, and divorce date. Fee is set by each county clerk of court.

Department of Education

Teacher Certification
Room 229, State House
Indianapolis, IN 46204-2798
(317) 232-9010

Field of certification and expiration date are available by phone or mail. Include name and SSN.

Medical Licensing

Health Professions Bureau
402 West Washington Street
Room 041
Indianapolis, IN 46204
(317) 232-2960

Will confirm licenses for MDs by phone or mail. No fee. For licenses not mentioned, contact the above office.

Indiana State Board of Nursing
Health Professions Bureau
One American Square
Suite 1020, Box 82067
Indianapolis, IN 46282-0004
(317) 232-2960

Will confirm license by phone. No fee. Include name, license number.

Bar Association

Indiana Bar Association
230 E. Ohio Street, 4th Floor
Indianapolis, IN 46204
(317) 639-5465

Will confirm licenses by phone. No fee. Include name.

Accountancy Board

State Board of Accountancy
100 N. Senate Ave., Room 121
Indianapolis, IN 46204
(317) 232-2980

Will confirm licenses by phone. No fee. Include name.

Securities Commission

Office of Secretary of State
Securities Department
302 W. Washington St., Room E-111
Indianapolis, IN 46204
(317) 2326681

Will confirm licenses by phone. No fee. Include name and SSN.

Secretary of State

Secretary of State
State House
Corporation Room 155
Indianapolis, IN 46204
(317) 232-6576

Service agent and address, date incorporated, standing with tax commission, trade names are available by phone or mail. Contact the above office for additional information.

Criminal Records

State Repository

Indiana State Police
Central Repository
Room 312, 100 North Senate Avenue
Indianapolis, IN 46204
(317) 232-8262

Record checks are available by mail only. All requests must include subject's full name, date of birth, current address, sex, race, height, weight, color of eyes, color of hair, place of birth and driver's license number. Requests should be submitted on State Form 8053R, "Request For Limited Criminal History Information." There is a $7.00 fee per request. Make check payable to the State of Indiana. Contact the above office for forms. Information supplied is conviction data only, except where arrest record is less than a year old. Turnaround time is normally 7-14 days plus mail time.

Adams County

Clerk's Office, Criminal Records
Courthouse
South 2nd Street
Decatur, IN 46733
(219) 724-2600

Felony and misdemeanor records are available by mail. No release necessary. No search fee. $1.00 fee per copy. $1.00 for certification. Search information required: name, years to search, SASE. Turnaround time is 1 week.

Civil records are available by mail. No release necessary. No search fee. $1.00 fee per copy. $1.00 for certification. Search information required: name, date of birth, years to search, SASE. Specify plaintiff or defendant.

Allen County

Felony and misdemeanor records
Clerk of Allen County
Room 200, Courthouse
Ft. Wayne, IN 46802
(219) 428-7245

Felony and misdemeanor records are available by mail. No release necessary. No search fee. Search information required: name, date of birth, years to search.

Civil records
Clerk of Allen County
102 Courthouse
715 S. Calhoun
Ft. Wayne, IN 46802
(219) 428-7630

Civil records are available by mail. A release is required. $3.00 search fee. Search information required: name, date of birth, years to search. Specify plaintiff or defendant.

Bartholomew County

Clerk's Office, Criminal Records
PO Box 924
Columbus, IN 47202-0924
(812) 379-1600
Fax (812) 379-1675

Felony and misdemeanor records are available by mail or fax. No release necessary. No search fee. $1.00 fee per copy, $1.00 fee for certification. Make company check payable to Bartholomew County Clerk. Search information required: name, SSN, date of birth, sex, race, previous address, years to search. Turnaround time is 1 week.

Civil records are available by mail or fax. No release necessary. No search fee. $1.00 fee per copy, $1.00 fee for certification. Search information required: name, date of birth, years to search. Specify plaintiff or defendant.

Benton County

Clerk's Office, Criminal Records
700 E. 5th Street
Fowler, IN 47944
(317) 884-0930
Fax (317) 884-2013

Felony and misdemeanor records are available by phone or fax. No search fee. $1.00 fee per copy, $1.00 fee for certification. No release necessary. Search information required: name, date of birth.

Civil records are available by phone or fax. No release necessary. No search fee. $1.00 fee per copy, $1.00 fee for certification. Search information required: name, date of birth, years to search. Specify plaintiff or defendant.

Blackford County

Clerk's Office, Criminal Records
110 W. Washington Street
Hartford City, IN 47348
(317) 348-1130

Felony and misdemeanor records are available by mail or phone. No release necessary. No search fee. $.25 fee per copy, $2.00 fee for certification. Search information required: name, SASE, years to search. Turnaround time is 1 week.

Civil records are available by mail or phone. No release necessary. No search fee. $.25 fee per copy, $2.00 fee for certification. Search information required: name, date of birth, years to search, SASE. Specify plaintiff or defendant.

Boone County

Circuit Clerk
1 Courthouse Sq. Room 212
Lebanon, IN 46052
(317) 482-3510

Records are available by mail. No release necessary. $3.50 for 10 year search. $.25 fee per copy. $1.00 for each certified copy. Search information required: name, years to search, SASE.

Civil records are available by mail. No release necessary. $3.50 for 10 year search. $.25 fee per copy. $1.00 for each certified copy. Search information required: name, date of birth, years to search, SASE. Specify plaintiff or defendant.

Brown County

Clerk's Office, Criminal Records
PO Box 85
Nashville, IN 47448
(812) 988-4796
Fax (812) 988-5510

Felony and misdemeanor records are available by phone or fax. No release necessary. No search fee. $1.00 fee per copy. $1.00 for certification. Search information required: name, SASE, years to search, date of birth, SSN.

Civil records are available by mail or fax. No release necessary. No search fee. $1.00 fee per copy. $1.00 for certification. Search information required: name, date of birth, years to search. Specify plaintiff or defendant.

Carroll County

Clerk's Office, Criminal Records
Carroll County
2nd Floor Courthouse
Delphi, IN 46923
(317) 564-4485

Felony and misdemeanor records are available by mail. No release necessary. No search fee. $1.00 fee per copy. $1.00 for certification. Search information required: name, years to search. Turnaround time is 1 week.

Civil records are available by mail. No release necessary. No search fee. $1.00 fee per copy. $1.00 for certification. Search information required: name, date of birth, years to search. Specify plaintiff or defendant.

Cass County

Clerk's Office, Criminal Records
200 Court Park
Logansport, IN 46947
(219) 753-7740

Felony and misdemeanor records are available by mail. No release necessary. $1.00 fee per year searched. $1.00 for certification. Search information required: name, date of birth, years to search, SASE. Turnaround time is 2 weeks.

Civil records are available by mail. No release necessary. $1.00 fee per year searched. $1.00 for certification. Search information required: name, date of birth, years to search, SASE. Specify plaintiff or defendant.

Clark County

Clerk of Circuit Court, Criminal Records
501 E. Court Ave.
Jeffersonville, IN 47130
(812) 285-6308

Felony and misdemeanor records are available by mail. A release is required. $5.00 fee. Search information required: name, date of birth, years to search, SASE. Turnaround time is 1 week.

Civil records are available by mail. A release is required. $5.00 search fee. Search information required: name, date of birth, years to search, SASE. Specify plaintiff or defendant.

Clay County

Clerk's Office, Criminal Records
PO Box 33
Brazil, IN 47834
(812) 442-1442, Ext. 147

Felony and misdemeanor records are available by mail. A release is required. $3.00 search fee. $1.00 fee per copy, $2.00 fee for certification. Certified check only, payable to Court Clerk. Search information required: name, years to search. Turnaround time is 2 weeks.

Civil records are available by mail. A release is required. $3.00 search fee. $1.00 fee per copy, $2.00 fee for certification. Search information required: name, date of birth, years to search. Specify plaintiff or defendant.

Clinton County

Clerk's Office, Criminal Records
Clinton County Courthouse
265 Courthouse Square
Frankfort, IN 46041-1993
(317) 659-6335

Felony and misdemeanor records are available by mail. A release is required. No search fee. $1.00 fee per copy, $2.00 fee for certification. Company checks only, payable to County Clerk's Office. Search information required: name, SSN, date of birth, years to search, SASE. Turnaround time is 1 week.

Civil records are available by mail. A release is required. No search fee. $1.00 fee per copy, $2.00 fee for certification. Search information required: name, date of birth, years to search, SASE. Specify plaintiff or defendant.

Crawford County

Clerk's Office, Criminal Records
PO Box 375
English, IN 47118
(812) 338-2565
Fax (812) 338-2507

Felony and misdemeanor records are available by mail. No release necessary. No search fee. $.50 fee per copy, $2.00 fee for certification. Search information required: name, SASE. Turnaround time is 2 weeks.

Civil records are available by mail. No release necessary. No search fee. $.50 fee per copy, $2.00 fee for certification. Search information required: name, date of birth, years to search, SASE. Specify plaintiff or defendant.

Daviess County

Clerk's Office, Criminal Records
Daviess County Courthouse
Washington, IN 47501
(812) 254-1090

Felony and misdemeanor records are available by mail. No release necessary. No search fee. $1.00 fee per copy, $2.00 fee for certification. Search information required: name, date of birth, years to search. Turnaround time is 2 weeks.

Civil records are available by mail. No release necessary. No search fee. $1.00 fee per copy, $2.00 fee for certification. Search information required: name, date of birth, years to search. Specify plaintiff or defendant.

De Kalb County

Courthouse (Circuit Clerk)
PO Box 230
Auburn, IN 46706
(219) 925-0912
Fax (219) 925-5126

Felony and misdemeanor records are available by mail. No release necessary. $1.00 search fee per name. $1.00 fee per copy, $2.00 fee for certification. Search information required: name, years to search, SASE.

Civil records are available by mail. No release necessary. $1.00 search fee per name. $1.00 fee per copy, $2.00 fee for certification. Search information required: name, date of birth, years to search, SASE. Specify plaintiff or defendant.

Dearborn County

Clerk's Office, Criminal Records
Dearborn County Courthouse
West High Street
Lawrenceburg, IN 47025
(812) 537-8869 Extension 267

Felony records are available by mail. No release necessary. No search fee. $1.00 fee per copy. $1.00 for certification. Search information required: name, date of birth, years to search.

Civil records are available by mail. No release necessary. No search fee. $1.00 fee per copy. $1.00 for certification. Search information required: name, date of birth, years to search. Specify plaintiff or defendant.

Decatur County

Circuit Clerk's Office, Criminal Records
150 Courthouse Square
Suite 1
Greensburg, IN 47240
(812) 663-8223

Felony and misdemeanor records are available in person only. See Indiana state repository for additional information.

Civil records are available in person only. See Indiana state repository for additional information.

Delaware County

County Clerk's Office, Criminal Records
PO Box 1089
100 W. Main
Muncie, IN 47308
(317) 747-7726
Fax (317) 747-7768

Felony and misdemeanor records are available by mail, fax or phone. No release necessary. No search fee. $1.00 fee for each page of fax response. $1.00 fee per copy. $1.00 for certification. Search information required: name, date of birth.

Civil records are available by mail, fax or phone. No release necessary. No search fee. $1.00 fee for each page of fax response. $1.00 fee per copy. $1.00 for certification. Search information required: name, date of birth, years to search. Specify plaintiff or defendant.

Dubois County

Clerk of Dubois Circuit Ct., Criminal Records
Dubois County Courthouse
Jasper, IN 47546
(812) 482-5445

Felony and misdemeanor records are available in person only. See Indiana state repository for additional information.

Civil records are available in person only. See Indiana state repository for additional information.

Elkhart County

Clerk's Office, Criminal Records
315 South 2nd Street
Elkhart County Court
Elkhart, IN 46516
(219) 523-2233

Felony and misdemeanor records are available by mail or phone. No release necessary. No search fee. $1.00 fee per copy. $1.00 for certification. Search information required: name, years to search, SASE.

Civil records are available by mail or phone. No release necessary. No search fee. $1.00 fee per copy. $1.00 for certification. Search information required: name, date of birth, years to search, SASE. Specify plaintiff or defendant.

Fayette County

County & Superior Court Clerk, Criminal Records
PO Box 607
Connersville, IN 47331-0607
(317) 825-1813

Felony and misdemeanor records are available by mail. No release necessary. No search fee. $1.00 fee per copy, $2.00 fee for certification. Search information required: name, years to search, SASE. Turnaround time is 1 week.

Civil records are available by mail. No release necessary. No search fee. No search fee. $1.00 fee per copy. $2.00 for certification. Search information required: name, date of birth, years to search, SASE. Specify plaintiff or defendant.

Floyd County

County Clerk's Office, Criminal Records
Room 244
311 W. 1st Street
New Albany, IN 47150
(812) 948-5414

Felony records are available by mail. No release necessary. $5.00 search fee. Search information required: name, SSN, date of birth, years to search, SASE. Turnaround time is 1 week.

Civil records are available by mail. No release necessary. $5.00 search fee. Search information required: name, date of birth, years to search, SASE. Specify plaintiff or defendant.

Fountain County

Circuit Clerk's Office, Criminal Records
PO Box 183
Covington, IN 47932
(317) 793-2192

Felony and misdemeanor records are available by mail. A release is required. No search fee. $1.00 fee per copy. $1.00 for certification. Search information required: name, years to search, SASE. Turnaround time is 1 week.

Civil records are available by mail. No release necessary. No search fee. $1.00 fee per copy. $1.00 for certification. Search information required: name, date of birth, years to search, SASE. Specify plaintiff or defendant.

Franklin County

Circuit Clerk's Office, Criminal Records
459 Main Street
Brookville, IN 47012
(317) 647-5111

Felony and misdemeanor records are available by mail or phone. No release necessary. No search fee. $1.00 fee per copy. $1.00 for certification. Search information required: name, years to search, SASE. Turnaround time is 1 week.

Civil records are available by mail or phone. No release necessary. No search fee. $1.00 fee per copy. $1.00 for certification. Search information required: name, date of birth, years to search, SASE. Specify plaintiff or defendant.

Fulton County

Clerk's Office, Criminal Records
815 Main Street
Rochester, IN 46975
(219) 223-2911

Felony and misdemeanor records are available by mail. No release necessary. No search fee. $1.00 fee per copy. $2.00 for certification. Search information required: name, years to search, SASE. Turnaround time is 1 week.

Civil records are available by mail. No release necessary. No search fee. $1.00 fee per copy. $2.00 for certification. Search information required: name, date of birth, years to search. Specify plaintiff or defendant.

Gibson County

Clerk of Circuit Court, Criminal Records
Gibson County Courthouse
Princeton, IN 47670
(812) 386-8401

Felony and misdemeanor records are available in person only. See Indiana state repository for additional information.

Civil records are available in person only. See Indiana state repository for additional information.

Grant County

County Clerk's Office, Criminal Records
Grant County Courthouse
101 E. 4th Street
Marion, IN 46952
(317) 668-8121

Felony and misdemeanor records are available by mail. No release necessary. $3.00 search fee. $1.00 fee per copy. $1.00 for certification. Make company check payable to Grant County Clerk. Search information required: name, years to search. Turnaround time is 1 week.

Civil records are available by mail. No release necessary. $3.00 search fee. $1.00 fee per copy. $1.00 for certification.Search information required: name, date of birth, years to search. Specify plaintiff or defendant.

Greene County

Clerk's Office, Criminal Records
PO Box 229
Bloomfield, IN 47424
(812) 384-8532

Records are available in person only. See Indiana state repository for additional information.

Civil records are available in person only. See Indiana state repository for additional information.

Hamilton County

County Clerk's Office, Criminal Records
Hamilton County Courthouse
Noblesville, IN 46060
(317) 773-6110

Felony records are available in person only. See Indiana state repository for additional information.

Civil records are available by mail. No release necessary. No search fee. Search information required: name, date of birth, years to search. Specify plaintiff or defendant.

Hancock County

County Clerk's Office, Criminal Records
9 East Main Street, Room 201
Courthouse Square
Greenfield, IN 46140
(317) 462-1109

Felony and misdemeanor records are available by mail or phone. No release necessary. No search fee. $1.00 fee per copy. $1.00 for certification. Search information required: name, years to search, SASE.

Civil records are available by mail. No release necessary. No search fee. $1.00 fee per copy. $1.00 for certification. Search information required: name, date of birth, years to search, SASE. Specify plaintiff or defendant.

Harrison County

Circuit Clerk's Office, Criminal Records
300 N. Capitol
Corydon, IN 47112
(812) 738-4289

Felony and misdemeanor records are available in person only. See Indiana state repository for additional information.

Civil records are available by mail. No release necessary. No search fee. $.50 fee per copy. $1.00 for certification. Search information required: name, date of birth, years to search, SASE. Specify plaintiff or defendant.

Hendricks County

Hendricks County Clerk's Office, Criminal Records
PO Box 599
Danville, IN 46122
(317) 745-9231

Felony and misdemeanor records are available by mail. No release necessary. $4.00 search fee. $1.00 fee per copy. $1.00 for certification. Search information required: name, years to search, SASE. Turnaround time is 1 week.

Civil records are available by mail. No release necessary. $4.00 search fee. $1.00 fee per copy. $1.00 for certification. Search information required: name, date of birth, years to search, SASE. Specify plaintiff or defendant.

Henry County

Circuit Clerk's Office, Criminal Records
PO Box B
New Castle, IN 47362
(317) 529-3000

Felony records are available by mail. No release necessary. No search fee. $1.00 per copy. $1.00 for certification. Search information required: name, years to search, SASE. Turnaround time is 1 week.

Civil records are available by mail. No release necessary. No search fee. $1.00 fee per copy. $1.00 for certification. Search information required: name, date of birth, years to search, SASE. Specify plaintiff or defendant.

Howard County

County Clerk's Office, Criminal Records
PO Box 9004
Howard County Courthouse
Kokomo, IN 46904
(317) 456-2204
Fax (317) 456-2267

Felony and misdemeanor records are available by mail or fax. No release necessary. No search fee. $1.00 fee per copy. $2.00 for certification. Search information required: name, date of birth, years to search, SSN, SASE.

Civil records are available by mail or fax. No release necessary. No search fee. $1.00 fee per copy. $2.00 for certification. Search information required: name, date of birth, years to search, SASE. Specify plaintiff or defendant.

Huntington County

Clerk's Office, Criminal Records
Room 201
Huntington County Courthouse
Huntington, IN 46750
(219) 356-7618

Felony and misdemeanor records are available by mail or phone. No release necessary. No search fee. $.50 fee per copy. $2.00 for certification. Search information required: name, years to search, SASE.

Civil records are available by mail. No release necessary. No search fee. $.50 fee per copy. $2.00 for certification. Search information required: name, date of birth, years to search, SASE. Specify plaintiff or defendant.

The City of Indianapolis

Indianapolis Police Department
I.D. & Records
50 N. Alabama
Indianapolis, IN 46204
(317) 236-3410

Felony and misdemeanor records are available by mail. No release necessary. $7.00 fee. Certified check only, payable to City Controller's Office. Contact the above office to request form # 4-2-36 R2.

Civil records are available by mail. No release necessary. $7.00 search fee. Search information required: name, date of birth, years to search. Specify plaintiff or defendant.

Jackson County

Clerk's Office, Criminal Records
PO Box 122
Brownstown, IN 47220
(812) 358-6116

Felony and misdemeanor records are available by mail. A release is required. No search fee. $.50 fee per copy. $1.00 for certification. Search information required: name, years to search, SASE. Turnaround time is 1 week.

Civil records are available by mail. No release necessary. No search fee. $.50 fee per copy. $1.00 for certification. Search information required: name, date of birth, years to search, SASE. Specify plaintiff or defendant.

Jasper County

Clerk's Office, Criminal Records
Jasper County Courthouse
PO Box 10
Rensselaer, IN 47978
(219) 866-4926

Felony records are available by mail, fax or phone. No release necessary. No search fee. $.25 fee per copy. $1.00 for certification plus $1.00 for each page certified. Search information required: name, SSN, date of birth, years to search, SASE.

Civil records are available by mail, fax. No release necessary. No search fee. $.25 fee per copy. $1.00 for certification plus $1.00 for each page certified. Search information required: name, date of birth, years to search, SASE. Specify plaintiff or defendant.

Jay County

Clerk's Office, Criminal Records
Jay County Courthouse
Portland, IN 47371
(219) 726-4951

Felony records are available by phone. No release necessary. No search fee. $1.00 fee per copy. $2.00 for certification. Search information required: name.

Civil records are available by mail. No release necessary. No search fee. $1.00 fee per copy. $2.00 for certification. Search information required: name, date of birth, years to search. Specify plaintiff or defendant.

Jefferson County

County Clerk's Office, Criminal Records
Room 203
Jefferson County Courthouse
Madison, IN 47250
(812) 265-8923

Felony records are available by mail. A release required. No search fee. $1.00 fee per copy. $1.00 for certification. Search information required: name, SSN, date of birth, SASE. Turnaround time is 1 week.

Civil records are available by mail. A release required. No search fee. $1.00 fee per copy. $1.00 for certification. Search information required: name, date of birth, years to search, SASE. Specify plaintiff or defendant.

Jennings County

Clerk's Office, Criminal Records
Courthouse
Vernon, IN 47282
(812) 346-5977

Felony records are available by mail. No release necessary. No search fee. $.25 fee per copy. $1.00 for certification. Search information required: name, years to search, SASE. Turnaround time is 1 week.

Civil records are available by mail. No release necessary. No search fee. $.25 fee per copy. $1.00 for certification. Search information required: name, date of birth, years to search, SASE. Specify plaintiff or defendant.

Johnson County

Clerk of Court, Criminal Records
Johnson County Courthouse
PO Box 368
Franklin, IN 46131
(317) 736-3708

Felony and misdemeanor records are available by mail or phone. No release necessary. No search fee. $1.00 fee per copy. $1.00 for certification. Search information required: name, SSN, date of birth, SASE.

Civil records are available by mail or phone. No release necessary. No search fee. $1.00 fee per copy. $1.00 for certification. Search information required: name, date of birth, years to search, SASE. Specify plaintiff or defendant.

Knox County

Circuit and Superior Clerk, Criminal Records
PO Box 906
Vincennes, IN 47591
(812) 885-2521

Felony and misdemeanor records are available in person only. See Indiana state repository for additional information.

Civil records are available by mail or phone. No release necessary. No search fee. $1.00 fee per copy. $1.00 for certification. Search information required: name, date of birth, years to search, SASE. Specify plaintiff or defendant.

Kosciusko County

Felony and misdemeanor records
Clerk's Office, Criminal Records
121 N. Lake
Warsaw, IN 46580
(219) 267-4444
   Ext. 329 (Felony)
   Ext. 452 (Misdemeanor)

Felony and misdemeanor records are available by mail or phone. No release necessary. No search fee. $1.00 fee per copy. $1.00 for certification. Search information required: name, years to search.

Civil records
Clerk's Office
121 N. Lake
Warsaw, IN 46580
(219) 267-4444, Ext. 455

Civil records are available by mail or phone. No release necessary. No search fee. $1.00 fee per copy. $1.00 for certification. Search information required: name, date of birth, years to search. Specify plaintiff or defendant.

La Porte County

Circuit Clerk's Office, Criminal Records
Lincolnway
La Porte, IN 46350
(219) 326-6808

Felony and misdemeanor records are available by mail or phone. No release necessary. No search fee. $.25 fee per copy. $1.00 for certification plus $1.00 for each page certified. Search information required: name, years to search.

Civil records are available by mail. No release necessary. No search fee. Search information required: name, date of birth, years to search. Specify plaintiff or defendant.

LaGrange County

Circuit Clerk's Office, Criminal Records
County Courthouse
105 N. Detroit Street
La Grange, IN 46761
(219) 463-3442

Felony and misdemeanor records are available by mail. A release is required. No search fee. $1.00 fee per copy. $1.00 for certification. Search information required: name, SSN, date of birth, years to search. Turnaround time is 3-4 weeks.

Civil records are available by mail. A release is required. No search fee. $1.00 fee per copy. $1.00 for certification. Search information required: name, date of birth, years to search. Specify plaintiff or defendant.

Lake County

Clerk's Office, Criminal Records
Lake County Courthouse
2293 N. Main Street
Crown Point, IN 46307
(219) 755-3000

Felony and misdemeanor records are available by mail. No release necessary. $7.00 search fee. $1.00 fee per copy. $3.00 for certification. Search information required: name, SSN, date of birth, years to search, SASE. Company check or money order payable to Clerk, Lake Superior Court. Turnaround time is 1 week.

Civil records are available by mail. No release necessary. $7.00 search fee. $1.00 fee per copy. $31.00 for certification. Search information required: name, date of birth, years to search, SASE. Specify plaintiff or defendant.

Lawrence County

Clerk's Office, Criminal Records
Lawrence County Courthouse
Room 31
Bedford, IN 47421
(812) 275-7543

Felony and misdemeanor records are available by mail or phone. No release necessary. No search fee. Search information required: name, years to search.

Civil records are available by mail or phone. No release necessary. No search fee. Search information required: name, date of birth, years to search. Specify plaintiff or defendant.

Madison County

Prosecutor's Office, Criminal Records
PO Box 1279
Anderson, IN 46016
(317) 641-9443

Felony and misdemeanor records are available by mail. A release is required. No search fee. $1.00 fee per copy. $1.00 for certification. Search information required: name, SSN, date of birth, years to search. Turnaround time is 1 week.

Civil records are available by mail. A release is required. No search fee. $1.00 fee per copy. $1.00 for certification. Search information required: name, date of birth, years to search. Specify plaintiff or defendant.

Marion County

Indianapolis Police Department
I.D. & Records
50 N. Alabama
Indianapolis, IN 46204
(317) 236-3410
Fax (317) 236-3468

Felony and misdemeanor records are available by mail or fax. No release necessary. $7.00 search fee. Certified check only, payable to City Controller's Office. Contact the above office to request form # 4-2-36 R2. Search information required: name, date of birth, race, sex, SSN, SASE.

Civil records are available by mail or fax. No release necessary. $7.00 search fee. Search information required: name, date of birth, years to search, SASE. Specify plaintiff or defendant.

Marshall County

Marshall County Clerk's Office,
Criminal Records
211 W. Madison Street
Plymouth, IN 46563
(219) 936-8922

Felony and misdemeanor records are available by mail. A release is required. $10.00 fee. Make company check payable to Marshall County Clerk. Search information required: name, years to search. Turnaround time is 1 week.

Civil records are available in person only. See Indiana state repository for additional information.

Martin County

Clerk's Office, Criminal Records
PO Box 120
Shoals, IN 47581
(812) 247-3651

Felony and misdemeanor records are available by mail. A release is required. No search fee. $1.00 fee per copy, $1.00 fee for certification. Search information required: name, years to search. Turnaround time is 1 week.

Civil records are available by mail. A release is required. No search fee. $1.00 fee per copy, $1.00 fee for certification. Search information required: name, date of birth, years to search. Specify plaintiff or defendant.

Miami County

Clerk's Office, Criminal Records
PO Box 184
Peru, IN 46970
(317) 472-3901
Fax (317) 472-1412

Felony and misdemeanor records are available by mail, fax or phone. No release necessary. $5.00 search fee for each 10 years searched. $.25 fee per copy, $2.00 fee for certification. Search information required: name, SSN, date of birth, years to search.

Civil records are available by mail, fax or phone. No release necessary. $5.00 search fee for each 10 years searched. $.25 fee per copy, $2.00 fee for certification. Search information required: name, date of birth, years to search. Specify plaintiff or defendant.

Monroe County

Clerk's Office, Criminal Records
301 N. College
Bloomington, IN 47402
(812) 333-3600

Felony and misdemeanor records are available by mail. No release necessary. $25.00 search fee. $1.00 fee per copy. $1.00 fee for certification. Make check payable to Monroe County Clerk. Search information required: name, years to search, SASE. Turnaround time is 1 week.

Civil records are available by mail. No release necessary. $25.00 search fee. $1.00 fee per copy. $1.00 fee for certification. Search information required: name, date of birth, years to search, SASE. Specify plaintiff or defendant.

Montgomery County

Clerk's Office, Criminal Records
PO Box 768
Crawfordsville, IN 47933
(317) 364-6430

Felony and misdemeanor records are available by mail. No release necessary. No search fee. $1.00 fee per copy, $2.00 fee for certification. Search information required: name, date of birth, years to search. Turnaround time is 2 weeks.

Civil records are available by mail. No release necessary. No search fee. $1.00 fee per copy, $2.00 fee for certification. Search information required: name, date of birth, years to search. Specify plaintiff or defendant.

Morgan County

Clerk's Office, Criminal Records
PO Box 1556
Martinsville, IN 46151
(317) 342-1025
Fax(317) 342-1026

Felony and misdemeanor records are available by mail. No release necessary. No search fee. Search information required: name, date of birth, SNN, years to search, SASE. Turnaround time is 1 week.

Civil records are available in person only. See Indiana state repository for additional information.

Newton County

Clerk's Office, Criminal Records
Newton County Courthouse Square
Superior Court
PO Box 49
Kentland, IN 47951
(219) 474-6081

Felony and misdemeanor records are available by mail. No release necessary. No search fee. $1.00 fee per copy, $1.00 fee for certification.Make company check payable to Clerk of Newton County Court. Search information required: name, years to search. Turnaround time is 1 week.

Civil records are available by mail. No release necessary. No search fee. $1.00 fee per copy, $1.00 fee for certification. Search information required: name, date of birth, years to search. Specify plaintiff or defendant.

Noble County

Clerk's Office, Criminal Records
101 N. Orange Street
Albion, IN 46701
(219) 636-2736

Felony and misdemeanor records are available by mail or phone. No release necessary. No search fee. $1.00 fee per copy, $1.00 fee for certification. Search information required: name, years to search.

Civil records are available by mail. No release necessary. No search fee. $1.00 fee per copy, $1.00 fee for certification. Search information required: name, date of birth, years to search. Specify plaintiff or defendant.

Ohio County

Clerk's Office, Criminal Records
PO Box 185
Rising Sun, IN 47040
(812) 438-2610

Felony and misdemeanor records are available by mail or phone. No release necessary. No search fee. $1.00 fee per copy, $2.00 fee for certification. Search information required: name, years to search.

Civil records are available by mail or phone. No release necessary. No search fee. $1.00 fee per copy, $2.00 fee for certification. Search information required: name, date of birth, years to search. Specify plaintiff or defendant.

Orange County

Clerk's Office, Criminal Records
Orange County Courthouse
Court Street
Paoli, IN 47454
(812) 723-2649

Felony and misdemeanor records are available by mail or phone. A release is required. No search fee. $1.00 fee per copy, $1.00 fee for certification. Search information required: name, SSN, date of birth, years to search. SASE. Turnaround time is 1 week.

Civil records are available by mail or phone. A release is required. No search fee. $1.00 fee per copy, $1.00 fee for certification. Search information required: name, date of birth, years to search. Specify plaintiff or defendant.

Owen County

Clerk's Office, Criminal Records
Owen County Courthouse
PO Box 146
Spencer, IN 47460
(812) 829-5015 or 829-5016

Felony and misdemeanor records are available by mail. Specify if records need to be searched prior to 1983. No release necessary. $5.00 search fee. $1.00 fee per copy, $1.00 fee for certification. Certified check only, payable to Clerk of Court. Search information required: name, previous address. Turnaround time is 1 week.

Civil records are available by mail. No release necessary. $5.00 search fee. $1.00 fee per copy, $1.00 fee for certification. Search information required: name, date of birth, years to search. Specify plaintiff or defendant.

Parke County

Clerk's Office, Criminal Records
Parke County Courthouse
116 W. Ohio, Room 204
Rockville, IN 47872
(317) 569-5132

Felony and misdemeanor records are available by mail or phone. No release necessary. No search fee. Search information required: name, years to search.

Civil records are available by mail or phone. No release necessary. No search fee. Search information required: name, date of birth, years to search. Specify plaintiff or defendant.

Perry County

Clerk's Office, Criminal Records
Perry County Courthouse
Cannelton, IN 47520
(812) 547-3741

Felony and misdemeanor records are available by mail. No release necessary. No search fee. $1.00 fee per copy, $2.00 fee for certification. Search information required: name, years to search. Turnaround time is 1 week.

Civil records are available by mail. No release necessary. No search fee. $1.00 fee per copy, $2.00 fee for certification. Search information required: name, date of birth, years to search. Specify plaintiff or defendant.

Pike County

Clerk's Office, 2nd Floor
Criminal Records
Pike Circuit Court
Pike County Courthouse
Petersburg, IN 47567
(812) 354-6025

Felony and misdemeanor records are available in person only. See Indiana state repository for additional information.

Civil records are available in person only. See Indiana state repository for additional information.

Porter County

Porter County Clerk, Criminal Records
157 South Franklin
Valparaiso, IN 46383
(219) 465-3450

Felony records are available by mail. A release is required. $3.00 search fee. Make check payable to Porter County Clerk. Search information required: name, date of birth. Additional records are available from County Court I, 157 S. Franklin, Valparaiso, IN 46383 & County Court II, 3560 Willow Creek Rd., Portage, IN 46368.

Civil records are available in person only. See Indiana state repository for additional information.

Posey County

Clerk's Office, Criminal Records
Posey County Courthouse
Mount Vernon, IN 47620
(812) 838-1306

Felony and misdemeanor records are available by mail. No release necessary. $7.00 search fee. $1.00 fee per copy, $1.00 fee for certification. Search information required: name, SASE, years to search, date of birth. Turnaround time is 1 week.

Civil records are available by mail. No release necessary. $7.00o search fee. $1.00 fee per copy, $1.00 fee for certification. Search information required: name, date of birth, years to search. Specify plaintiff or defendant.

Pulaski County

Clerk's Office, Criminal Records
Pulaski County Courthouse, Room 203
Winamac, IN 46996
(219) 946-3313

Felony and misdemeanor records are available in person only. See Indiana state repository for additional information.

Civil records are available in person only. See Indiana state repository for additional information.

Putnam County

Putnam County Clerk's Office, Criminal Records
County Courthouse
PO Box 546
Greencastle, IN 46135
(317) 653-2648

Felony and misdemeanor records are available by mail or phone. No release necessary. No search fee. $1.00 fee per copy. $2.00 for certification. Search information required: name, years to search.

Civil records are available by mail. No release necessary. No search fee. $1.00 fee per copy. $2.00 for certification. Search information required: name, date of birth, years to search. Specify plaintiff or defendant.

Randolph County

Felony and misdemeanor records
Clerk's Office, Criminal Records
Randolph County Courthouse
PO Box 230
Winchester, IN 47394-0230
(317) 584-7070 Ext. 25
Fax (317) 584-2958

Felony and misdemeanor records are available by mail, fax or phone. No release necessary. No search fee. $1.00 fee per copy, $1.00 fee for certification. Search information required: name, years to search.

Civil records
Clerk's Office
Randolph County Courthouse
PO Box 230
Winchester, IN 47394-0230
(317) 584-7070 Ext. 28
Fax (317) 584-2958

Civil records are available by mail. No release necessary. No search fee. $1.00 fee per copy. $1.00 for certification. Search information required: name, date of birth, years to search. Specify plaintiff or defendant.

Ripley County

Clerk of the Ripley Circuit Court, Criminal Records
Ripley County Courthouse
PO Box 177
Versaille, IN 47042
(812) 689-6115

Felony and misdemeanor records are available by mail or phone. No release necessary. No search fee. $1.00 fee per copy, $1.00 fee for certification. Search information required: name, SASE, years to search. Turnaround time is 1-2 weeks.

Civil records are available by mail or phone. No release necessary. No search fee. $1.00 fee per copy, $1.00 fee for certification. Search information required: name, date of birth, years to search, SASE. Specify plaintiff or defendant.

Rush County

Clerk of Court, Criminal Records
PO Box 429
Rushville, IN 46173
(317) 932-2086

Felony and misdemeanor records are available in person only. See Indiana state repository for additional information.

Civil records are available in person only. See Indiana state repository for additional information.

Scott County

Clerk's Office, Criminal Records
Scott Circuit Court
Courthouse
Scottsburg, IN 47170
(812) 752-4769

Felony and misdemeanor records are available by mail. No release necessary. No search fee. $1.00 fee per copy, $2.00 fee for certification. Search information required: name, years to search, SASE. Turnaround time is 1 week.

Civil records are available by mail. No release necessary. No search fee. $1.00 fee per copy, $2.00 fee for certification. Search information required: name, date of birth, years to search, SASE. Specify plaintiff or defendant.

Shelby County

Shelby County Clerk, Criminal Records
PO Box 198
Shelbyville, IN 46176
(317) 392-6320

Felony and misdemeanor records are available in person only. See Indiana state repository for additional information.

Civil records are available in person only. See Indiana state repository for additional information.

Spencer County

Felony records
Spencer County Clerk, Criminal Records
PO Box 12
Rockport, IN 47635
(812) 649-6027

Felony records are available by mail or phone. No release necessary. No search fee. $.50 fee per copy. $2.00 for certification. Search information required: name, years to search.

Civil records
Spencer County Clerk
PO Box 12
Rockport, IN 47635
(812) 649-6027

Civil records are available by mail. No release necessary. No search fee. $.50 fee per copy. $2.00 for certification. Search information required: name, date of birth, years to search. Specify plaintiff or defendant.

Misdemeanor records
Spencer County Clerk
PO Box 12
Rockport, IN 47635
(812) 649-6027

Misdemeanor records are available in person only. See Indiana state repository for additional information.

Civil records
Spencer County Clerk
PO Box 12
Rockport, IN 47635
(812) 649-6027

Civil records are available in person only. See Indiana state repository for additional information.

Starke County

County Clerk's Office, Criminal Records
Courthouse
Knox, IN 46534
(219) 772-9128

Felony and misdemeanor records are available by mail. No release necessary. No search fee. 1.00 fee per copy. $2.00 for certification. Search information required: name, years to search, SASE.

Civil records are available by mail. No release necessary. No search fee. 1.00 fee per copy. $2.00 for certification. Search information required: name, date of birth, years to search, SASE. Specify plaintiff or defendant.

Steuben County

Clerk of Court, Criminal Records
PO Box 327
Angola, IN 46703
(219) 665-2361

Felony and misdemeanor records are available by mail. A release is required. No search fee. Search information required: name, date of birth, years to search, SASE. Turnaround time is 1 week.

Civil records are available in person only. See Indiana state repository for additional information.

St. Joseph County

St. Joseph County Clerk, Criminal Records
101 S. Main Street
South Bend, IN 46601
(219) 284-9635

Felony and misdemeanor records are available by mail. No release necessary. No search fee. Search information required: name, years to search, SASE. Turnaround time is 1 week.

Civil records are available in person only. See Indiana state repository for additional information.

Sullivan County

Clerk of Court
Courthouse
100 Courthouse Square, Room 304
Sullivan, IN 47882
(812) 268-4657

Felony and misdemeanor records are available by mail. No release necessary. No search fee. $1.00 fee per copy, $1.00 fee for certification. Search information required: name, date of birth, SSN, years to search.

Civil records are available by mail. No release necessary. No search fee. $1.00 fee per copy, $1.00 fee for certification. Search information required: name, date of birth, years to search. Specify plaintiff or defendant.

Switzerland County

Clerk's Office, Criminal Records
Courthouse
212 W. Main
Vevay, IN 47043
(812) 427-3175

Felony and misdemeanor records are available by mail or phone. A release, if available. No search fee. $1.00 fee per copy, $2.00 fee for certification. Search information required: name, years to search.

Civil records are available by mail. No release necessary. No search fee. $1.00 fee per copy, $2.00 fee for certification. Search information required: name, date of birth, years to search. Specify plaintiff or defendant.

Tippecanoe County

Courthouse
PO Box 1665
Lafayette, IN 47902
(317) 423-9326
Fax (317) 432-1922

Felony records are available by mail or fax. No release necessary. No search fee. $.25 fee per copy, $1.00 fee for certification plus $1.00 for each page certified. Search information required: name, date of birth, SSN, years to search.

Civil records are available by mail. No release necessary. No search fee. $.25 fee per copy, $1.00 fee for certification plus $1.00 for each page certified. Search information required: name, date of birth, years to search. Specify plaintiff or defendant.

Tipton County

Clerk's Office, Criminal Records
PO Box 244
Tipton, IN 46072
(317) 675-2795

Felony and misdemeanor records are available by mail. No release necessary. No search fee. $1.00 fee per copy, $1.00 fee for certification. Search information required: name, years to search. Turnaround time is 1 week.

Civil records are available by mail. No release necessary. No search fee. $1.00 fee per copy, $1.00 fee for certification. Search information required: name, date of birth, years to search. Specify plaintiff or defendant.

Union County

Clerk's Office, Criminal Records
Room 105
26 W. Union Street
Liberty, IN 47353
(317) 458-6121
Fax (317) 458-5263

Felony and misdemeanor records are available by mail or fax. No release necessary. No search fee. $1.00 fee per copy, $1.00 fee for certification. Search information required: name, SSN, date of birth, years to search. Turnaround time is 1 week.

Civil records are available by mail or fax. No release necessary. No search fee. $1.00 fee per copy, $1.00 fee for certification. Search information required: name, date of birth, years to search. Specify plaintiff or defendant.

Vanderburgh County

Vanderburgh County Clerk, Criminal Records
PO Box 3356
Room 216
Courts Bldg.
Evansville, IN 47732-3356
(812) 426-5171
Fax (812) 426-5849

Felony and misdemeanor records are available by mail. A release is required. $7.00 search fee. $1.00 fee per copy, $1.00 fee for certification. Search information required: name, SSN, date of birth, years to search. Turnaround time is 1 week.

Civil records are available by mail. A release is required. $7.00 search fee. $1.00 fee per copy, $1.00 fee for certification. Search information required: name, date of birth, years to search. Specify plaintiff or defendant.

Vermillion County

County Clerk's Office, Criminal Records
PO Box 8
Newport, IN 47966
(317) 492-3500

Felony and misdemeanor records are available by mail. No release necessary. No search fee. $1.00 fee per copy, $2.00 fee for certification. Search information required: name, SSN, years to search. Turnaround time is 1 week. Contact the above for county form.

Civil records are available by mail. No release necessary. No search fee. $1.00 fee per copy, $2.00 fee for certification. Search information required: name, date of birth, years to search. Specify plaintiff or defendant.

Vigo County

Vigo County Clerk, Criminal Records
Vigo County Courthouse, Room 22
Terre Haute, IN 47807
(812) 238-8211
Fax (812) 462-3211

Felony and misdemeanor records are available by mail or fax. A release is required. No search fee. $1.00 fee per copy. $2.00 fee for certification. Search information required: name, date of birth, SSN, years to search, SASE. Turnaround time is 1 week.

Civil records are available by mail or fax. A release is required. No search fee. $1.00 fee per copy. $2.00 fee for certification. Search information required: name, date of birth, years to search. Specify plaintiff or defendant.

Wabash County

Clerk's Office, Criminal Records
Courthouse
One W. Hill
Wabash, IN 46992
(219) 563-0661 Extension 29

Felony and misdemeanor records are available by mail. No release necessary. No search fee. $1.00 fee per copy, $1.00 fee for certification. Search information required: name, years to search, date of birth, SSN. Turnaround time is 2 to 4 days.

Civil records are available in person only. See Indiana state repository for additional information.

Warren County

Clerk's Office, Criminal Records
Courthouse
125 N. Monroe, #11
Williamsport, IN 47993
(317) 762-3510

Felony and misdemeanor records are available by mail or phone. No release necessary. No search fee. $1.00 fee per copy. $1.00 for certification. Make company check payable to Warren County Clerk. Search information required: name, years to search.

Civil records are available by mail or phone. No release necessary. No search fee. $1.00 fee per copy. $1.00 for certification. Search information required: name, date of birth, years to search. Specify plaintiff or defendant.

Warrick County

Clerk's Office
Room 201
PO Box 666
Warrick County Courthouse
Boonville, IN 47601
(812) 897-6160

Felony and misdemeanor records are available by mail or phone. No release necessary. No search fee. Search information required: name, years to search.

Civil records are available by mail or phone. No release necessary. No search fee. Search information required: name, date of birth, years to search. Specify plaintiff or defendant.

Washington County

Clerk of the Circuit Court, Criminal Records
Courthouse
Salem, IN 47167
(812) 883-5302

Felony and misdemeanor records are available by mail or phone. No release necessary. No search fee. $1.00 fee per copy. $1.00 for certification. Search information required: name, years to search, SASE.

Civil records are available by mail or phone. No release necessary. No search fee. $1.00 fee per copy. $1.00 for certification. Search information required: name, date of birth, years to search, SASE. Specify plaintiff or defendant.

Wayne County

Clerk of Wayne County, Criminal Records
PO Box 1172
Richmond, IN 47375
(317) 973-9200

Felony and misdemeanor records are available by mail or phone. No release necessary. No search fee. $1.00 fee per copy. $1.00 for certification. Search information required: name, years to search, SASE.

Civil records are available by mail. No release necessary. No search fee. $1.00 fee per copy. $1.00 for certification. Search information required: name, date of birth, years to search, SASE. Specify plaintiff or defendant.

Wells County

Courthouse Clerk, Criminal Records
102 Market Street West
Bluffton, IN 46714
(219) 824-6479

Felony and misdemeanor records are available by mail. A release is required. No search fee. $1.00 fee per copy. $1.00 for certification. Search information required: name, date of birth, years to search. Turnaround time is 1-2 days.

Civil records are available by mail. A release is required. No search fee. $1.00 fee per copy. $1.00 for certification. Search information required: name, date of birth, years to search. Specify plaintiff or defendant.

White County

Clerk's Office
Courthouse
PO Box 350
Monticello, IN 47960
(219) 583-7032

Records are available in person only. See Indiana state repository for additional information.

Civil records are available in person only. See Indiana state repository for additional information.

Whitley County

Whitley County Clerk, Criminal Records
Courthouse
101 W. Van Buren, Room 10
Columbia City, IN 46725
(219) 248-3102

Felony and misdemeanor records are available by mail. A release is required. $1.00 search fee. $1.00 fee per copy. 1.00 for certification. Certified check only, payable to Whitley County Clerk. Search information required: name, years to search, SASE. Turnaround time is 1 week.

Civil records are available by mail. A release is required. $1.00 search fee. $1.00 fee per copy. 1.00 for certification. Search information required: name, date of birth, years to search, SASE. Specify plaintiff or defendant.

City-County Cross Reference

Buck Creek *Tippecanoe*
Buckskin *Gibson*
Buffalo *White*
Bunker Hill *Miami*
Burket *Kosciusko*
Burlington *Carroll*
Burnettsville *White*
Burney *Decatur*
Burns Harbour *Porter*
Burrows *Carroll*
Butler *DeKalb*
Butlerville *Jennings*
Cambridge City *Wayne*
Camby *Marion*
Camden *Carroll*
Campbellsburg
   Washington
Canaan *Jefferson*
Cannelburg *Daviess*
Cannelton *Perry*
Carbon *Clay*
Carlisle *Sullivan*
Carmel *Hamilton*
Cartersburg *Hendricks*
Carthage *Rush*
Cayuga *Vermillion*
Cedar Grove *Franklin*
Cedar Lake *Lake*
Cedarville *Allen*
Celestine *Dubois*
Centerpoint *Clay*
Centerville *Wayne*
Central *Harrison*
Chalmers *White*
Chandler *Warrick*
Charlestown *Clark*
Charlottesville *Hancock*
Chesterton *Porter*
Chrisney *Spencer*
Churubusco *Whitley*
Cicero *Hamilton*
Clarksburg *Decatur*
Clarks Hill *Tippecanoe*
Clarksville *Clark*
Clay City *Clay*
Claypool *Kosciusko*
Clayton *Hendricks*
Clear Creek *Monroe*
Clermont
Clifford *Bartholomew*
Clinton *Vermillion*
Cloverdale *Putnam*
Coal City *Owen*
Coalmont *Clay*
Coatesville *Hendricks*
Colburn *Tippecanoe*
Colfax *Clinton*
Collegeville *Jasper*
Columbia City *Whitley*
Columbus *Bartholomew*
Commiskey *Jennings*
Connersville *Fayette*
Converse *Miami*
Cortland *Jackson*
Corunna *DeKalb*
Cory *Clay*
Corydon *Harrison*
Covington *Fountain*
Craigville *Wells*
Crandall *Harrison*
Crane *Martin*
Crawfordsville
   Montgomery
Cromwell *Noble*
Cross Plains *Ripley*
Crothersville *Jackson*

Crown Point *Lake*
Culver *Marshall*
Cumberland *Marion*
Cutler *Carroll*
Cynthiana *Posey*
Dale *Spencer*
Daleville *Delaware*
Dana *Vermillion*
Danville *Hendricks*
Darlington *Montgomery*
Darmstadt *Vanderburgh*
Dayton *Tippecanoe*
Decatur *Adams*
Decker *Knox*
Deedsville *Miami*
Delong *Fulton*
Delphi *Carroll*
Demotte *Jasper*
Denham *Pulaski*
Denver *Miami*
Depauw *Harrison*
Deputy *Jefferson*
Derby *Perry*
Dillsboro *Dearborn*
Donaldson *Marshall*
Dublin *Wayne*
Dubois *Dubois*
Dugger *Sullivan*
Dunkirk *Jay*
Dunlap *Elkhart*
Dunreith *Henry*
Dupont *Jefferson*
Dyer *Lake*
Earl Park *Benton*
East Chicago *Lake*
East Enterprise *Switzerland*
Eaton *Delaware*
Eckerty *Crawford*
Economy *Wayne*
Edgewood *Madison*
Edinburgh *Johnson*
Edwardsport *Knox*
Elberfeld *Warrick*
Elizabeth *Harrison*
Elizabethtown
   Bartholomew
Elkhart *Elkhart*
Ellettsville *Monroe*
Elnora *Daviess*
Elwood *Madison*
Eminence *Morgan*
Emison *Knox*
English *Crawford*
Etna Green *Kosciusko*
Evanston *Spencer*
Evansville *Vanderburgh*
Fairbanks *Sullivan*
Fairland *Shelby*
Fairmount *Grant*
Fair Oaks *Jasper*
Fairview Park *Vermillion*
Falmouth *Rush*
Farmersburg *Sullivan*
Farmland *Randolph*
Ferdinand *Dubois*
Fillmore *Putnam*
Finly *Hancock*
Fishers *Hamilton*
Fish Lake *La Porte*
Flat Rock *Shelby*
Flora *Carroll*
Florence *Switzerland*
Floyds Knobs *Floyd*
Folsomville *Warrick*
Fontanet *Vigo*
Forest *Clinton*

Fort Branch *Gibson*
Fort Ritner *Lawrence*
Fortville *Hancock*
Fort Wayne *Allen*
Fountain City *Wayne*
Fountaintown *Shelby*
Fowler *Benton*
Fowlerton *Grant*
Francesville *Pulaski*
Francisco *Gibson*
Frankfort *Clinton*
Franklin *Johnson*
Frankton *Madison*
Fredericksburg *Washington*
Freedom *Owen*
Freelandville *Knox*
Freetown *Jackson*
Fremont *Steuben*
French Lick *Orange*
Friendship *Ripley*
Fulda *Spencer*
Fulton *Fulton*
Galena *Floyd*
Galveston *Cass*
Garrett *DeKalb*
Gary *Lake*
Gas City *Grant*
Gaston *Delaware*
Geneva *Adams*
Gentryville *Spencer*
Georgetown *Floyd*
Gilmer Park *St. Joseph*
Glenwood *Fayette*
Goldsmith *Tipton*
Goodland *Newton*
Goshen *Elkhart*
Gosport *Owen*
Grabill *Allen*
Grandview *Spencer*
Granger *Saint Joseph*
Grantsburg *Crawford*
Graysville *Sullivan*
Greencastle *Putnam*
Greendale *Deerborn*
Greenfield *Hancock*
Greensboro *Henry*
Greensburg *Decatur*
Greens Fork *Wayne*
Greentown *Howard*
Greenville *Floyd*
Greenwood *Johnson*
Griffin *Posey*
Griffith *Lake*
Grovertown *Starke*
Guilford *Dearborn*
Gwynneville *Shelby*
Hagerstown *Wayne*
Hamilton *Steuben*
Hamlet *Starke*
Hammond *Lake*
Hanna *LaPorte*
Hanover *Jefferson*
Hardinsburg *Washington*
Harlan *Allen*
Harmony *Clay*
Harrodsburg *Monroe*
Hartford City *Blackford*
Hartsville *Bartholomew*
Hatfield *Spencer*
Haubstadt *Gibson*
Hayden *Jennings*
Hazleton *Gibson*
Hebron *Porter*
Helmsburg *Brown*
Heltonville *Lawrence*
Hemlock *Howard*

Henryville *Clark*
Highland *Lake*
Hillisburg *Clinton*
Hillsboro *Fountain*
Hillsdale *Vermillion*
Hoagland *Allen*
Hobart *Lake*
Hobbs *Tipton*
Holland *Dubois*
Holton *Ripley*
Homecroft *Marion*
Home Place *Hamilton*
Homer *Rush*
Hope *Bartholomew*
Howe *Lagrange*
Hudson *Steuben*
Hudson Lake *La Porte*
Huntertown *Allen*
Huntingburg *Dubois*
Huntington *Huntington*
Huron *Lawrence*
Hymera *Sullivan*
Idaville *White*
Indianapolis *Marion*
Indian Springs *Martin*
Ingalls *Madison*
Inglefield *Vanderburgh*
Ireland *Dubois*
Jamestown *Boone*
Jasonville *Greene*
Jasper *Dubois*
Jeffersonville *Clark*
Jewell Village
   Bartholomew
Jonesboro *Grant*
Jonesville *Bartholomew*
Judson *Parke*
Kempton *Tipton*
Kendallville *Noble*
Kennard *Henry*
Kentland *Newton*
Kewanna *Fulton*
Keystone *Wells*
Kimmell *Noble*
Kingman *Fountain*
Kingsbury *LaPorte*
Kingsford Heights *LaPorte*
Kirklin *Clinton*
Knightstown *Henry*
Knightsville *Clay*
Knox *Starke*
Kokomo *Howard*
Koleen *Greene*
Koontz Lake *Starke*
Kouts *Porter*
Kurtz *Jackson*
Laconia *Harrison*
LaCrosse *LaPorte*
Ladoga *Montgomery*
Lafayette *Tippecanoe*
LaFontaine *Wabash*
Lagrange *Lagrange*
Lagro *Wabash*
Lake Cicott *Cass*
Lake Eliza *Porter*
Lake James *Steuben*
Lake Station *Lake*
Laketon *Wabash*
Lake Village *Newton*
Lakeville *Saint Joseph*
Lamar *Spencer*
Landess *Grant*
Lanesville *Harrison*
Laotto *Noble*
Lapaz *Marshall*
Lapel *Madison*

LaPorte *LaPorte*
Larwill *Whitley*
Laurel *Franklin*
Lawrence *Marion*
Lawrenceburg *Dearborn*
Leavenworth *Crawford*
Lebanon *Boone*
Leesburg *Kosciusko*
Leiters Ford *Fulton*
Leo *Allen*
Leopold *Perry*
Leroy *Lake*
Lewis *Vigo*
Lewisville *Henry*
Lexington *Scott*
Liberty *Union*
Liberty Center *Wells*
Liberty Mills *Wabash*
Ligonier *Noble*
Lincoln City *Spencer*
Linden *Montgomery*
Linton *Greene*
Little York *Washington*
Lizton *Hendricks*
Logansport *Cass*
Long Beach *La Porte*
Loogootee *Martin*
Losantville *Randolph*
Lowell *Lake*
Lucerne *Cass*
Lydick *St. Joseph*
Lynn *Randolph*
Lynnville *Warrick*
Lyons *Greene*
McCordsville *Hancock*
Mackey *Gibson*
Macy *Miami*
Madison *Jefferson*
Magnet *Perry*
Manilla *Rush*
Marengo *Crawford*
Mariah Hill *Spencer*
Marion *Grant*
Markle *Huntington*
Markleville *Madison*
Marshall *Parke*
Marshfield *Warren*
Martinsville *Morgan*
Maryland *Vigo*
Marysville *Clark*
Marywood *Vigo*
Matthews *Grant*
Mauckport *Harrison*
Maxwell *Hancock*
Mays *Rush*
Mecca *Parke*
Medaryville *Pulaski*
Medora *Jackson*
Melody Hill *Vanderburgh*
Mellott *Fountain*
Memphis *Clark*
Mentone *Kosciusko*
Merom *Sullivan*
Merrillville *Lake*
Metamora *Franklin*
Mexico *Miami*
Miami *Miami*
Michigan City *LaPorte*
Michigantown *Clinton*
Middlebury *Elkhart*
Middletown *Henry*
Middletown Park
  Delaware
Midland *Greene*
Milan *Ripley*
Milford *Kosciusko*

Mill Creek *LaPorte*
Millersburg *Elkhart*
Millhousen *Decatur*
Milltown *Crawford*
Milroy *Rush*
Milton *Wayne*
Mishawaka *Saint Joseph*
Mitchell *Lawrence*
Modoc *Randolph*
Mongo *Lagrange*
Monon *White*
Monroe *Adams*
Monroe City *Knox*
Monroeville *Allen*
Monrovia *Morgan*
Monterey *Pulaski*
Montezuma *Parke*
Montgomery *Daviess*
Monticello *White*
Montmorenci *Tippecanoe*
Montpelier *Blackford*
Mooreland *Henry*
Moores Hill *Dearborn*
Mooresville *Morgan*
Morgantown *Morgan*
Morocco *Newton*
Morris *Ripley*
Morristown *Shelby*
Mount Ayr *Newton*
Mount Pleasant *Perry*
Mount Saint Francis *Floyd*
Mount Summit *Henry*
Mount Vernon *Posey*
Mulberry *Clinton*
Muncie *Delaware*
Munster *Lake*
Nabb *Clark*
Napoleon *Ripley*
Nappanee *Elkhart*
Nashville *Brown*
Nebraska *Jennings*
Needham *Johnson*
New Albany *Floyd*
Newberry *Greene*
Newburgh *Warrick*
New Carlisle *Saint Joseph*
New Castle *Henry*
New Chicago *Lake*
New Elliott *Lake*
New Goshen *Vigo*
New Harmony *Posey*
New Haven *Allen*
New Lisbon *Henry*
New Market *Montgomery*
New Middletown *Harrison*
New Palestine *Hancock*
New Paris *Elkhart*
New Perkin *Washington*
New Point *Decatur*
New Richmond
  Montgomery
New Ross *Montgomery*
New Salisbury *Harrison*
Newtown *Fountain*
New Trenton *Franklin*
New Washington *Clark*
New Waverly *Cass*
New Whiteland *Johnson*
Nineveh *Johnson*
Noblesville *Hamilton*
Norman *Jackson*
North Judson *Starke*
North Liberty *Saint Joseph*
North Manchester *Wabash*
North Salem *Hendricks*

North Terre Haute *Vigo*
North Vernon *Jennings*
North Webster *Kosciusko*
Norway *White*
Notre Dame *Saint Joseph*
Oakford *Howard*
Oakland City *Gibson*
Oaktown *Knox*
Oakville *Delaware*
Odon *Daviess*
Ogden Dunes *Porter*
Oldenburg *Franklin*
Onward *Cass*
Oolitic *Lawrence*
Ora *Starke*
Orestes *Madison*
Orland *Steuben*
Orleans *Orange*
Osceola *Saint Joseph*
Osgood *Ripley*
Ossian *Wells*
Otisco *Clark*
Otterbein *Benton*
Otwell *Pike*
Owensburg *Greene*
Owensville *Gibson*
Oxford *Benton*
Palmyra *Harrison*
Paoli *Orange*
Paragon *Morgan*
Paris Crossing *Jennings*
Parker City *Randolph*
Patoka *Gibson*
Patricksburg *Owen*
Patriot *Switzerland*
Paxton *Sullivan*
Pekin *Washington*
Pence *Warren*
Pendleton *Madison*
Pennville *Jay*
Perrysville *Vermillion*
Pershing *Wayne*
Peru *Miami*
Petersburg *Pike*
Petroleum *Wells*
Pierceton *Kosciusko*
Pierceville *Ripley*
Pimento *Vigo*
Pine Village *Warren*
Pittsboro *Hendricks*
Plainfield *Hendricks*
Plainville *Daviess*
Pleasant Lake *Steuben*
Pleasant Mills *Adams*
Plymouth *Marshall*
Poland *Clay*
Poneto *Wells*
Portage *Porter*
Porter *Porter*
Portland *Jay*
Poseyville *Posey*
Prairie Creek *Vigo*
Prairieton *Vigo*
Preble *Adams*
Princess Lakes *Johnson*
Princeton *Gibson*
Putnamville *Putnam*
Quincy *Owen*
Ragsdale *Knox*
Ramsey *Harrison*
Redkey *Jay*
Reelsville *Putnam*
Remington *Jasper*
Rensselaer *Jasper*
Reynolds *White*
Richland *Spencer*

Richmond *Wayne*
Ridgeville *Randolph*
Riley *Vigo*
Rising Sun *Ohio*
Riverside *Warren*
Roachdale *Putnam*
Roann *Wabash*
Roanoke *Huntington*
Rochester *Fulton*
Rockfield *Carroll*
Rockport *Spencer*
Rockville *Parke*
Rocky Ripple *Marion*
Rolling Prairie *LaPorte*
Rome *Perry*
Rome City *Noble*
Romney *Tippecanoe*
Rosedale *Parke*
Roselawn *Newton*
Roseland *St. Joseph*
Rossville *Clinton*
Royal Center *Cass*
Royerton *Delaware*
Rushville *Rush*
Russellville *Putnam*
Russiaville *Howard*
Saint Anthony *Dubois*
Saint Bernice *Vermillion*
Saint Croix *Perry*
Saint Joe *DeKalb*
Saint John *Lake*
Saint Leon *Dearborn*
Saint Mary-of-the-Woods
  Vigo
Saint Meinrad *Spencer*
Saint Paul *Decatur*
Saint Wendel
  Vanderburgh/Posey
Salamonia *Jay*
Salem *Washington*
Sandborn *Knox*
Sandford *Vigo*
San Pierre *Starke*
Santa Claus *Spencer*
Saratoga *Randolph*
Schererville *Lake*
Schneider *Lake*
Scipio *Jennings*
Scotland *Greene*
Scottsburg *Scott*
Sedalia *Clinton*
Seelyville *Vigo*
Sellersburg *Clark*
Selma *Delaware*
Servia *Wabash*
Seymour *Jackson*
Shadeland *Tippecanoe*
Sharpsville *Tipton*
Shelburn *Sullivan*
Shelby *Lake*
Shelbyville *Shelby*
Shepardsville *Vigo*
Sheridan *Hamilton*
Shipshewana *Lagrange*
Shirley *Henry*
Shoals *Martin*
Sidney *Kosciusko*
Silver Lake *Kosciusko*
Simonton Lake *Elkhart*
Sims *Grant*
Smith Valley *Johnson*
Smithville *Monroe*
Solsberry *Greene*
Somerset *Wabash*
Somerville *Gibson*
South Bend *Saint Joseph*

South Haven
South Milford *Lagrange*
South Port *Marion*
South Whitley *Whitley*
Speed *Clark*
Speedway *Marion*
Spelterville *Vigo*
Spencer *Owen*
Spencerville *DeKalb*
Spiceland *Henry*
Spring Grove *Wayne*
Springport *Henry*
Springville *Lawrence*
Spurgeon *Pike*
Stanford *Monroe*
Star City *Pulaski*
State Line *Warren*
Staunton *Clay*
Stendal *Pike*
Stewartsville *Posey*
Stilesville *Hendricks*
Stinesville *Monroe*
Stockwell *Tippecanoe*
Straughn *Henry*
Stroh *Lagrange*
Sullivan *Sullivan*
Sulphur *Crawford*
Sulphur Springs *Henry*
Sumava Resorts *Newton*
Summitville *Madison*
Sunman *Ripley*
Swayzee *Grant*
Sweetser *Grant*
Switz City *Greene*
Syracuse *Kosciusko*
Talbot *Benton*
Tangier *Parke*
Taswell *Crawford*
Taylorsville *Bartholomew*
Tefft *Jasper*
Tell City *Perry*
Tennyson *Warrick*
Terre Haute *Vigo*
Thayer *Newton*
Thorntown *Boone*
Tippecanoe *Marshall*
Tipton *Tipton*
Tobinsport *Perry*
Topeka *Lagrange*
Town Of Pines *Porter*
Trafalgar *Johnson*
Trail Creek *La Porte*
Troy *Perry*
Tunnelton *Lawrence*
Twelve Mile *Cass*
Tyner *Marshall*
Union City *Randolph*
Uniondale *Wells*
Union Mills *LaPorte*
Unionville *Monroe*
Universal *Vermillion*
Upland *Grant*
Urbana *Wabash*
Utica *Clark*
Vallonia *Jackson*
Valparaiso *Porter*
Van Buren *Grant*
Veedersburg *Fountain*
Velpen *Pike*
Vernon *Jennings*
Versailles *Ripley*
Vevay *Switzerland*
Vincennes *Knox*
Wabash *Wabash*
Wadesville *Posey*
Wakarusa *Elkhart*

Waldron *Shelby*
Walkerton *Saint Joseph*
Wallace *Fountain*
Wallen *Allen*
Walton *Cass*
Wanatah *LaPorte*
Warren *Huntington*
Warren Park *Marion*
Warsaw *Kosciusko*
Washington *Daviess*
Waterloo *DeKalb*
Waveland *Montgomery*
Wawaka *Noble*
Waynetown *Montgomery*
Webster *Wayne*
West Baden Springs
   Orange
West College Corner
   Union
Westfield *Hamilton*
West Fork *Crawford*
West Lafayette *Tippecanoe*
West Harrison *Dearborn*
West Lebanon *Warren*
West Middleton *Howard*
West Newton *Marion*
Westphalia *Knox*
Westpoint *Tippecanoe*
Westport *Decatur*
West Terre Haute *Vigo*
Westville *LaPorte*
Wheatfield *Jasper*
Wheatland *Knox*
Wheeler *Porter*
Whiteland *Johnson*
Whitestown *Boone*
Whiting *Lake*
Wilkinson *Hancock*
Williams *Lawrence*
Williamsburg *Wayne*
Williamsport *Warren*
Willow Branch *Hancock*
Winamac *Pulaski*
Winchester *Randolph*
Windfall *Tipton*
Wingate *Montgomery*
Winona Lake *Kosciusko*
Winslow *Pike*
Wolcott *White*
Wolcottville *Lagrange*
Wolflake *Noble*
Woodburn *Allen*
Woodland Park *Delaware*
Woodridge *Vigo*
Worthington *Greene*
Wyatt *Saint Joseph*
Yeoman *Carroll*
Yoder *Allen*
Yorktown *Delaware*
Young America *Cass*
Zanesville *Allen*
Zionsville *Boone*

Iowa

Sixty nine (69) of Iowa's ninety nine (99) counties make criminal records available for employment screening purposes by phone and/or mail. The remaining thirty (30) counties require that the request be made in person. Fifty nine (59) counties will do civil record searches. Claims above $2,000 are in District Court.

For more information or for offices not listed, contact the state's information hot line at (515) 281-5011.

Driving Records

Department of Transportation
Office of Driver Services
Parkfair Mall
100 Euclid Avenue
PO Box 9204
Des Moines, IA 50306-9204
(515) 237-3144
Driving records are available by mail. $5 fee per request. Turnaround time is 24 hours. Written request must include job applicant's full name, date of birth and license number. Make check payable to Department of Transportation.

Worker's Compensation Records

Division of Industrial Services
Records Department
1000 East Grand
Des Moines, IA 50319
(515) 281-5934
All telephone and mail inquiries must include the subject's complete name and social security number. If known, include date of injury and previous employer involved in claim. There is no search fee. Copies are $.25 per page. This Office requests that phone requests be limited to two persons at a time. A signed release is not required.

Vital Statistics

Iowa Department of Public Health
Vital Records Section
Lucas State Office Building
Des Moines, IA 50319
(515) 281-4944
FAX (515) 281-4958
Birth and death records are available for $6.00 each. State office has had records since July 1880. For birth records, supply full name, father's name and mother maiden name and county of birth. For death records, supply name, date, place of occurrence, requesting party's relationship to decedent and reason for inquiring. Make any type check or money order payable to Iowa Department of Public Health.

Marriage records are available for $6.00. Turnaround time is 2-3 weeks. Include name, marriage date, spouse's name, place of marriage, and self addressed envelope. Divorce records available at county level only, county clerk's office where divorce took place. Release is required.

Department of Education

Practioner Licensing
Grimes State Office Bldg.
Des Moines, IA 50319-0146
(515) 281-3245
Field of certification and expiration date are available by phone or mail. Include name, DOB and SSN.

Medical Licensing

Board of Medical Examiners
1209 E. Court Ave.
Des Moines, IA 50319
(515) 281-5171
Fax (515) 242-5908
Will confirm licenses for MDs and DOs by phone or mail. No fee. For licenses not mentioned, contact the above office.

Iowa Board of Nursing
Executive Hills East
1223 East Court Avenue
Des Moines, IA 50319
(515) 281-3256
Will confirm license by phone. No fee. Include name, license number, if available.

Bar Association

Iowa State Bar Association
521 East Locust
Des Moines, IA 50309
(515) 243-3179
Will confirm licenses by phone. No fee. Include name.

Accountancy Board

Iowa State Accountancy Board
1918 SE Hurlsizer
Ankeny, IA 50021
(515) 281-4126
Will confirm license by phone. No fee. Include name.

Securities Commission

Office of Commissioner of Insurance
Securities Bureau
Lucas State Office Building
East 12th & Walnut, 2nd Floor
Des Moines, IA 50319
(515) 281-4441
Will confirm license by phone. No fee. Include name and SSN.

Secretary of State

Secretary of State
Hoover Office Bldg.
Des Moines, IA 50319
(515) 281-5204
Fax (515) 242-5953
Service agent and address, date incorporated, standing with tax commission, trade names are available by phone or mail. Contact the above office for additional information.

Criminal Records
State Repository

Mr. Gene Shepard
Commissioner of Iowa D.P. S.
Wallace State Office Building
Third Floor
Des Moines, IA 50319
(515) 281-5138
Access by non-criminal justice agencies to criminal records maintained by the state's central repository is limited to those entities that are specifically authorized access by law. Contact the above office or counties listed below for additional information and instructions. If access is granted there is a $6.00 fee for each name searched.

Adair County

Clerk of Court, Criminal Records
Courthouse
Greenfield, IA 50849
(515) 743-2445
Felony and misdemeanor records are available by mail. No release necessary. No search fee. $.25 fee per copy. $2.00 for certification. Make check payable to Clerk of Court. Search information required: name, years to search.

Civil records are available by mail. No release necessary. No search fee. Search information required: name, years to search. Specify plaintiff or defendant.

Adams County

Clerk of District Court, Criminal Records
Courthouse
Corning, IA 50841
(515) 322-4711
Felony and misdemeanor records are available in person only. See Iowa State Repository for additional information.

Civil records are available in person only. See Iowa state repository for additional information.

Allamakee County

Clerk of District Court, Criminal Records
PO Box 248
Waukon, IA 52172
(319) 568-6351
Fax (319) 568-4720
Felony and misdemeanor records are available by mail, fax or phone. No release necessary. $10.00 search fee per hour. $.25 fee per copy. Make check payable to Clerk of District Court. Search information required: name, date of birth, sex, race.

Civil records are available in person only. See Iowa state repository for additional information.

Appanoose County

Clerk of District Court, Criminal Records
Courthouse
Centerville, IA 52544
(515) 856-6101
Felony and misdemeanor records are available by mail. No release necessary. No search fee. $.25 fee per copy. $2.00 for certification. Search information required: name, date of birth, years to search.

Civil records are available by mail or phone. No release necessary. No search fee. Search information required: name, years to search. Specify plaintiff or defendant.

Audubon County

Clerk of Court, Criminal Records
Courthouse
Audubon, IA 50025
(712) 563-4275
Felony and misdemeanor records are available by mail. A release is required. No search fee. Search information required: name, date of birth, address, years to search.

Civil records are available by mail. A release is required. No search fee. $.30 fee per copy. $2.00 for certification. Search information required: name, years to search. Specify plaintiff or defendant.

Benton County

Felony records
Clerk of Court, Criminal Records
PO Box 719
Vinton, IA 52349
(319) 472-2766
Felony records are available by mail or phone. No release necessary. No search fee. Search information required: name, date of birth, years to search.

Civil records
Clerk of Court
PO Box 719
Vinton, IA 52349
(319) 472-2766
Civil records are available by mail. No release necessary. No search fee. $.50 fee per copy. $2.50 for certification. Search information required: name, years to search. Specify plaintiff or defendant.

Misdemeanor records
Iowa District Court
Magistrate Division
PO Box 719
Benton, IA 52349
(319) 472-4902
Misdemeanor records are available by mail. Records go back to 1973. A release is required. No search fee. $.50 fee per copy. $2.50 for certification. Search information required: name, date of birth, years to search, SSN, SASE.

Civil records
Iowa District Court
Magistrate Division
PO Box 719
Benton, IA 52349
(319) 472-4902
Civil records are available by mail. No release necessary. No search fee. $.50 fee per copy. $2.50 for certification. Search information required: name, years to search. Specify plaintiff or defendant.

Black Hawk County

Felony and misdemeanor records
Black Hawk County Courthouse, Criminal Records
Waterloo, IA 50703
(319) 291-2612
Felony and misdemeanor records are available by mail. No release necessary. $6.00 search fee. Make check payable to Clerk of Court. Search information required: name, date of birth, years to search.

Civil records
Black Hawk County Courthouse, Waterloo, IA 50703
(319) 291-2482
Civil records are available by mail. A release is required. $6.00 search fee. $.50 fee per copy. $4.50 for certification. Search information required: name, SSN, years to search, SASE. Specify plaintiff or defendant.

Boone County

Felony records
Clerk of Courts
Courthouse, Criminal Records
Boone, IA 50036
(515) 432-6291
Felony records are available by mail or phone. No release necessary. No search fee. $.25 for each page copied and $2.00 for certified copy. Search information required: name, date of birth, years to search, SASE.

Civil records
Clerk of Courts
Courthouse,
Boone, IA 50036
(515) 432-6291
Civil records are available in person only. See Iowa state repository for additional information.

Misdemeanor records
Magistrate Court
Courthouse
Boone, IA 50036
(515) 432-6291
Misdemeanor records are available by mail. A release is required. No search fee. $.25 fee per copy. $6.00 for certification. Search information required: name, date of birth, years to search, SASE, date of offense.

Civil records
Magistrate Court
Courthouse
Boone, IA 50036
(515) 432-6291
Civil records are available in person only. See Iowa state repository for additional information.

Bremer County

Clerk of Court, Criminal Records
PO Box 328
415 E. Bremer
Waverly, IA 50677
(319) 352-5661
Fax (319) 352-2708
Felony and misdemeanor records are available by mail. No release necessary. No search fee. Search information required: name, date of birth, sex, years to search.

Civil records are available by mail. A release is required. No search fee. $1.00 fee for first copy, $.25 thereafter. $3.75 for certification. Search information required: name, years to search. Specify plaintiff or defendant.

Buchanan County

Clerk of Court, Criminal Records
PO Box 259
Independence, IA 50644
(319) 334-2196
Felony and misdemeanor records are available by mail or phone. No release necessary. No search fee. Search information required: name, date of birth, years to search.

Civil records are available by mail or phone. No release necessary. No search fee. $.50 fee per copy. $2.50 for certification. Search information required: name, years to search, SSN. Specify plaintiff or defendant.

Buena Vista County

Clerk of Court, Criminal Records
PO Box 1186
Storm Lake, IA 50588
(712) 749-2546
Felony and misdemeanor records are available in person only. See Iowa state repository for additional information.

Civil records are available in person only. See Iowa state repository for additional information.

Butler County

Clerk of Court, Criminal Records
PO Box 307
Allison, IA 50602
(319) 267-2487
Felony and misdemeanor records are available by mail. A release is required. No search fee. Search information required: name, years to search.

Civil records are available by mail. A release is required. No search fee. Search information required: name, years to search. Specify plaintiff or defendant.

Calhoun County

Clerk of Court, Criminal Records
PO Box 273
Rockwell City, IA 50579
(712) 297-8122
Felony and misdemeanor records are available by mail or phone. No release necessary. No search fee. Search information required: name, SSN, date of birth.

Civil records are available in person only. See Iowa state repository for additional information

Carroll County

Courthouse, Criminal Records
Carroll, IA 51401
(712) 792-4393
Felony and misdemeanor records are available by mail. A release is required. No search fee. $.50 fee per copy. $2.50 for certification. Search information required: name, date of birth, years to search, SSN.

Civil records are available by mail. A release is required. No search fee. $.50 fee per copy. $2.50 for certification. Search information required: name, date of birth, years to search, SSN. Specify plaintiff or defendant.

Cass County

Courthouse, Criminal Records
Atlantic, IA 50022
(712) 243-2105
Fax (712) 243-4736
Felony and misdemeanor records are available by mail or fax. A release is required. No search fee. $.25 fee per copy. $2.25 for certification. Search information required: name, SSN, date of birth, years to search.

Civil records are available in person only. See Iowa state repository for additional information.

Cedar County

Clerk of Court, Criminal Records
PO Box 111
Tipton, IA 52772
(319) 886-2101
Felony and misdemeanor records are available by mail. No release necessary. No search fee. $6.00 fee for certified copies. Certified check only, payable to Cedar County Clerk of Court. Search information required: name, years to search, date of birth.

Civil records are available in person only. See Iowa State Repository for additional information.

Cerro Gordo County

Clerk of Court, Criminal Records
Courthouse
220 N. Washington
Mason City, IA 50401
(515) 424-6431
Felony and misdemeanor records are available by mail. A release is required. No search fee. Search information required: name, SSN, date of birth, approximate time of offense.

Civil records are available by mail. A release is required. No search fee. $.50 fee per copy. $2.50 for certification. Search information required: name, years to search. Specify plaintiff or defendant.

Cherokee County

Courthouse, Criminal Records
Drawer F
Cherokee, IA 51012
(712) 225-2706
Felony and misdemeanor records are available by mail. No release necessary. No search fee. $.50 fee per copy. Search information required: name, SSN, date of birth, sex, race.

Civil records are available by mail. A release is required. No search fee. $.50 fee per copy. Will not certify copies. Search information required: name, years to search. Specify plaintiff or defendant.

Chickasaw County

Chickasaw County Courthouse, Clerk of Court
New Hampton, IA 50659
(515) 394-2106
Records are available in person only. See Iowa state repository for additional information.

Civil records are available by mail. No release necessary. No search fee. $.50 fee per copy. $2.00 for certification. Search information required: name, years to search. Specify plaintiff or defendant.

Clarke County

Clarke County Courthouse
Criminal Records
Osceola, IA 50213
(515) 342-2213
Felony and misdemeanor records are available by mail. A release is required. No search fee. Search information required: name, years to search, SASE.

Civil records are available by mail. A release is required. No search fee. $.50 fee per copy. $2.50 for certification. Search information required: name, years to search. Specify plaintiff or defendant.

Clay County

Clay County Clerk
PO Box 4104
Spencer, IA 51301
(712) 262-4335
Felony and misdemeanor records are available in person only. See Iowa State Repository for additional information.

Civil records are available in person only. See Iowa State Repository for additional information.

Clayton County

Clerk of Court, Criminal Records
Clayton County Courthouse
Elkader, IA 52043
(319) 245-2204
Felony and misdemeanor records are available by mail or phone. No release necessary. No search fee. Search information required: name, date of birth, years to search, SASE.

Civil records are available by mail or phone. No release necessary. No search fee. $.50 fee per copy. $2.00 for certification. Search information required: name, date of birth, years to search. Specify plaintiff or defendant.

Clinton County

Clerk of Court, Criminal Records
PO Box 157–Clinton County Courthouse
1st Floor, Clerk's Office
Clinton, IA 52732
(319) 243-6210 Extension 224
Felony and misdemeanor records are available by mail. No release necessary. No search fee. $.50 fee per copy. $2.00 for certification. Search information required: name, SSN, date of birth, SASE.

Civil records are available by mail. No release necessary. No search fee. $.50 fee per copy. $2.00 for certification. Search information required: name, SSN, date of birth, years to search, SASE. Specify plaintiff or defendant.

Crawford County

Clerk of Court
PO Box 546
Denison, IA 51442
(712) 263-2242
Records are available in person only. See Iowa State Repository for additional information.

Civil records are available in person only. See Iowa State Repository for additional information.

Dallas County

Clerk of Court, Criminal Records
801 Court Street
Adel, IA 50003
(515) 993-4789
Felony and misdemeanor records are available in person only. See Iowa State Repository for additional information.

Civil records are available in person only. See Iowa State Repository for additional information.

Davis County

Clerk of District Court, Criminal Records
Davis County Courthouse
Bloomfield, IA 52537
(515) 664-2011
Felony and misdemeanor records are available by mail. No release necessary. No search fee. $.50 fee per copy. $2.00 for certification. Search information required: name, date of birth, years to search.

Civil records are available by mail. No release necessary. No search fee. $.50 fee per copy. $2.00 for certification. Search information required: name, years to search. Specify plaintiff or defendant.

Decatur County

Clerk of Court, Criminal Records
Courthouse
207 N. Main Street
Leon, IA 50144
(515) 446-4331
Fax (515) 446-7159
Felony and misdemeanor records are available by mail or phone. No release necessary. No search fee. Search information required: name, date of birth, years to search.

Civil records are available by mail or phone. A release is required. No search fee. $.25 fee per copy. $2.00 for certification. Search information required: name, SSN, date of birth, years to search. Specify plaintiff or defendant.

Delaware County

Clerk of Court, Criminal Records
Delaware County Courthouse
Manchester, IA 52057
(319) 927-4942
Felony and misdemeanor records are available by mail. No release necessary. No search fee. Search information required: full name, years to search.

Civil records are available by mail or phone. No release necessary. No search fee. $.50 fee per copy. $2.50 for certification. Search information required: name, years to search. Specify plaintiff or defendant.

Des Moines County

Clerk of District Court, Criminal Records
Des Moines County Courthouse
PO Box 158
Burlington, IA 52601
(319) 753-8242 Extension 272
Felony and misdemeanor records are available by mail. No release necessary. $6.00 search fee. $.25 fee per copy. Search information required: name, date of birth, SASE, years to search.

Civil records are available by mail. No release necessary. No search fee. $.25 fee per copy. $2.00 for certification. Search information required: name, SSN, date of birth, years to search, SASE. Specify plaintiff or defendant.

Dickinson County

Courthouse, Criminal Records
PO Drawer O N
Spirit Lake, IA 51360
(712) 336-1138
Felony and misdemeanor records are available by mail or phone. No release necessary. No search fee. Search information required: name, years to search.

Civil records are available by mail. No release necessary. No search fee. $.25 fee per copy. $2.25 for certification. Search information required: name, years to search. Specify plaintiff or defendant.

Dubuque County

Clerk of Court, Criminal Records
720 Central
Dubuque, IA 52001
(319) 589-4418
Records are available in person only. See Iowa state repository for additional information.

Civil records are available in person only. See Iowa state repository for additional information.

Emmet County

Clerk of Court
Emmet County
Estherville, IA 51334
(712) 362-3325
Felony and misdemeanor records are available by mail. No release necessary. No search fee. $.25 fee per copy. $2.00 for certification. Search information required: full name, date of birth, SSN, years to search. Use company letterhead on written requests.

Civil records are available by mail. No release necessary. No search fee. $.25 fee per copy. $2.00 for certification. Search information required: name, date of birth, SSN, years to search. Specify plaintiff or defendant.

Fayette County

Clerk of District Court, Criminal Records
PO Box 458
West Union, IA 52175
(319) 422-6061 Extension 24
Felony and misdemeanor records are available by mail or phone. No release necessary. $6.00 search fee. Search information required: name, years to search.

Civil records are available by mail. A release is required. No search fee. $.25 fee per copy. $6.00 for certification. Search information required: name, years to search. Specify plaintiff or defendant.

Floyd County

Courthouse, Criminal Records
Charles City, IA 50616
(515) 257-6122
Felony and misdemeanor records are available by mail or phone. A release is required. No search fee. Search information required: name, SSN, date of birth, years to search.

Civil records are available by mail. No release necessary. No search fee. $.25 fee per copy. $2.50 for certification. Search information required: name, years to search. Specify plaintiff or defendant.

Franklin County

Clerk of Court, Criminal Records
PO Box 28
Hampton, IA 50441
(515) 456-5626
Felony and misdemeanor records are available by mail. No release necessary. No search fee. $.50 fee per copy. $2.50 for certification. Search information required: name, SSN, date of birth.

Civil records are available by mail. No release necessary. No search fee. $.50 fee per copy. $2.50 for certification. Search information required: name, date of birth, years to search. Specify plaintiff or defendant.

Fremont County

Clerk of District Court, Criminal Records
PO Box 549
Sidney, IA 51652
(712) 374-2232
Felony and misdemeanor records are available by mail. No release necessary. No fee. Search information required: name, date of birth, SASE, years to search.

Civil records are available in person only. See Iowa State Repository for additional information.

Greene County

Greene County Courthouse, Criminal Records
Jefferson, IA 50129
(515) 386-2516
Felony and misdemeanor records are available by mail. No release necessary. No search fee. $.25 fee per copy. $2.00 for certification. Search information required: name, SSN, date of birth, years to search, SASE.

Civil records are available by mail. No release necessary. No search fee. $.25 fee per copy. $2.00 for certification. Search information required: name, SSN, date of birth, years to search, SASE. Specify plaintiff or defendant.

Grundy County

Clerk of Court
Grundy County Courthouse
Grundy Center, IA 50638
(319) 824-5229
Records are available in person only. See Iowa state repository for additional information.

Civil records are available in person only. See Iowa state repository for additional information.

Guthrie County

Courthouse, Clerk of Court
Criminal Records
Guthrie Center, IA 50115
(515) 747-3415
Felony and misdemeanor records are available by mail or phone. No release necessary. No search fee. Search information required: name, date of birth, sex, race, years to search, SASE.

Civil records are available by mail. No release necessary. No search fee. $.25 fee per copy. $2.00 for certification. Search information required: name, date of birth, years to search, SASE. Specify plaintiff or defendant.

Hamilton County

Hamilton County Courthouse, Criminal Records
2500 Superior Street
Webster City, IA 50595
(515) 832-4640
Felony and misdemeanor records are available by mail. A release is required. $6.00 fee. Company checks only, payable to Clerk of Court. Search information required: name, date of birth, SSN, years to search, offense, SASE.

Civil records are available by mail. No release necessary. $6.00 search fee. $.25 fee per copy. $2.00 for certification. Search information required: name, date of birth, years to search. Specify plaintiff or defendant.

Hancock County

Clerk of Court, Criminal Records
855 State Street
Garner, IA 50438
(515) 923-2532
Felony and misdemeanor records are available by mail or phone. No release necessary. No search fee. $.50 fee per copy. $6.00 for certification. Search information required: name, years to search.

Civil records are available by mail. No release necessary. No search fee. $.50 fee per copy. $6.00 for certification. Search information required: name, years to search. Specify plaintiff or defendant.

Hardin County

Hardin County Courthouse, Criminal Records
Clerk Of Court
Box 495
Eldora, IA 50627
(515) 858-2328

Felony and misdemeanor records are available by mail. No release necessary. No fee. Search information required: name, date of birth, years to search.

Civil records are available in person only. See Iowa State Repository for additional information.

Harrison County

Clerk of Court, Criminal Records
Courthouse
Logan, IA 51546
(712) 644-2665

Felony and misdemeanor records are available by mail. No release necessary. No search fee. Search information required: name, date of birth, years to search, SASE.

Civil records are available by mail. No release necessary. No search fee. $.50 fee per copy. $2.50 for certification. Search information required: name, years to search. Specify plaintiff or defendant.

Henry County

Clerk of Court, Criminal Records
PO Box 176
Mount Pleasant, IA 52641
(319) 385-2632
Fax (319) 385-0778

Felony and misdemeanor records are available by mail. No release necessary. No search fee. $1.00 fee for fax response. $.25 fee per copy. $2.25 for certification. Search information required: name, years to search.

Civil records are available by mail. A release required. No search fee. $.25 fee per copy. $2.25 for certification. Search information required: name, years to search. Specify plaintiff or defendant.

Howard County

Clerk of Court, Criminal Records
Howard County Courthouse
Cresco, IA 52136
(319) 547-2661

Felony and misdemeanor records are available by mail. No release necessary. No search fee. Search information required: name, years to search.

Civil records are available by mail. No release necessary. No search fee. $.50 fee per copy. $2.50 for certification. Search information required: name, years to search. Specify plaintiff or defendant.

Humboldt County

Humboldt County Courthouse, Criminal Records
Dakota City, IA 50529
(515) 332-1806

Felony and misdemeanor records are available by mail. No release necessary. $6.00 search fee. Make check payable to Clerk of Court. Search information required: name, SSN, date of birth, sex, race, years to search.

Civil records are available by mail. A release required. $6.00 search fee. $.50 fee per copy. $6.00 for certification. Search information required: name, years to search. Specify plaintiff or defendant.

Ida County

Ida County Courthouse, Criminal Records
Ida Grove, IA 51445
(712) 364-2628

Felony and misdemeanor records are available in person only. See Iowa State Repository for additional information.

Civil records are available in person only. See Iowa State Repository for additional information.

Iowa County

Clerk of Court, Criminal Records
Box 266
Marengo, IA 52301
(319) 642-3914

Felony and misdemeanor records are available by mail. A release if available. No search fee. $1.00 fee per copy. $2.00 for certification. Search information required: name, years to search.

Civil records are available by mail. A release required. No search fee. $1.00 fee per copy. $2.00 for certification. Search information required: name, years to search. Specify plaintiff or defendant.

Jackson County

Clerk of Court, Criminal Records
201 W. Platt
Maquoketa, IA 52060
(319) 652-4946

Felony and misdemeanor records are available by mail. No release necessary. $6.00 search fee. Search information required: name, SSN, date of birth, sex, race, years to search.

Civil records are available in person only. See Iowa State Repository for additonal information.

Jasper County

Clerk of Court, Criminal Records
PO Box 666
Newton, IA 50208
(515) 792-3255

Felony and misdemeanor records are available by mail. No release necessary. No search fee. Search information required: name.

Civil records are available by mail. A release is required. No search fee. $.50 fee per copy. $2.00 for certification. Search information required: name, SSN, years to search, SASE. Specify plaintiff or defendant.

Jefferson County

Clerk of Court, Criminal Records
Box 984
Fairfield, IA 52556
(515) 472-3454

Felony and misdemeanor records are available by mail. A release is required. No search fee. $.25 fee per copy. $2.00 for certification. Search information required: name, date of birth, years to search.

Civil records are available by mail. A release required. No search fee. $.25 fee per copy. $2.00 for certification. Search information required: name, date of birth, years to search. Specify plaintiff or defendant.

Johnson County

Courthouse, Criminal Records
PO Box 2510
Iowa City, IA 52244
(319) 356-6063

Felony and misdemeanor records are available by mail. No release necessary. No search fee. Search information required: name, SSN, date of birth, years to search, SASE.

Civil records are available by mail. No release necessary. No search fee. $.25 fee per copy. $2.00 for certification. Search information required: name, years to search. Specify plaintiff or defendant.

Jones County

Clerk of Court, Criminal Records
Courthouse
Anamosa, IA 52205
(319) 462-4341

Felony and misdemeanor records are available in person only. See Iowa State Repository for additional information.

Civil records are available in person only. See Iowa State Repository for additional information.

Keokuk County

Clerk of Court, Criminal Records
Keokuk County Courthouse
Sigourney, IA 52591
(515) 622-2210

Felony and misdemeanor records are available by mail or phone. No release necessary. No search fee. Search information required: name, SSN, date of birth, years to search.

Civil records are available in person only. See Iowa State Repository for additional information.

Kossuth County

Kossuth County Courthouse
Algona, IA 50511
(515) 295-3240

Felony and misdemeanor records are available in person only. See Iowa State Repository for more information.

Civil records are available in person only. See Iowa State Repository for additional information.

Lee County

Clerk of Court, Criminal Records
PO Box 1443
Ft. Madison, IA 52627
(319) 372-3523
Felony and misdemeanor records are available in person only. See Iowa State Repository for additional information.

Civil records are available in person only. See Iowa State Repository for additional information.

Linn County

Linn County Courthouse, Criminal Records
PO Box 1090
Cedar Rapids, IA 52406
(319) 398-3921
Felony and misdemeanor records are available by mail. No release necessary. No search fee. $1.00 fee per copy. $2.00 for certification. Search information required: name, SSN, date of birth, years to search.

Civil records are available by mail. No release necessary. No search fee. $1.00 fee per copy. $2.00 for certification. Search information required: name, SSN, date of birth, years to search. Specify plaintiff or defendant.

Louisa County

Clerk of District Court, Criminal Records
PO Box 268
Wapello, IA 52653
(319) 523-4541
Felony and misdemeanor records are available by mail or phone. No release necessary. No search fee. Search information required: name.

Civil records are available by mail. A release required. No search fee. $6.00 for certification. Search information required: name, years to search. Specify plaintiff or defendant.

Lucas County

Courthouse
Clerk of District Court
Criminal Records
Chariton, IA 50049
(515) 774-4421
Felony and misdemeanor records are available in person only. See Iowa State Repository for additional information.

Civil records are available in person only. See Iowa State Repository for additional information.

Lyon County

Courthouse, Criminal Records
Rock Rapids, IA 51246
(712) 472-2623
Felony and misdemeanor records are available in person only. See Iowa State Repository for additional information.

Civil records are available in person only. See Iowa State Repository for additional information.

Madison County

Clerk of Court, Criminal Records
PO Box 152
Winterset, IA 50273
(515) 462-4451
Felony and misdemeanor records are available in person only. See Iowa State Repository for additional information.

Civil records are available in person only. See Iowa State Repository for additional information.

Mahaska County

Mahaska County Courthouse, Criminal Records
Oskaloosa, IA 52577
(515) 673-7786
Felony and misdemeanor records are available by mail. A release is required. $6.00 search fee. $.25 fee per copy. $6.00 for certification. Search information required: name, SSN, date of birth, SASE.

Civil records are available by mail. A release required. $6.00 search fee. $.25 fee per copy. $6.00 for certification. Search information required: name, SSN, date of birth, years to search, SASE. Specify plaintiff or defendant.

Marion County

Marion County Courthouse, Criminal Records
PO Box 497
Knoxville, IA 50138
(515) 828-2207; 2208; 2209
Felony and misdemeanor records are available by mail or phone. No release necessary. No search fee. Search information required: name, SSN, date of birth.

Civil records are available by mail or phone. No release necessary. No search fee. $.25 fee per copy. $2.00 for certification. Search information required: name, years to search. Specify plaintiff or defendant.

Marshall County

Clerk of Court, Criminal Records
Marshall County Courthouse
4th Floor
Marshalltown, IA 50158
(515) 754-6373
Felony and misdemeanor records are available by mail. A release is required. $6.00 search fee. $.50 fee per copy. Search information required: name, years to search.

Civil records are available in person only. See Iowa state repository for additional information.

Mills County

Mills County Courthouse
Clerk of District Court
Criminal Records
Glenwood, IA 51534
(712) 527-4880
Felony and misdemeanor records are available by mail. A release is required. $6.00 search fee. $2.00 for certification. Make check payable to Clerk of Court. Search information required: name, date of birth, SSN.

Civil records are available by mail. A release required. $6.00 search fee. $2.00 for certification. Search information required: name, SSN, date of birth, years to search. Specify plaintiff or defendant.

Mitchell County

Clerk of Court, Criminal Records
Mitchell County Courthouse
508 State St.
Osage, IA 50461
(515) 732-3726
Felony and misdemeanor records are available by mail or phone. No release necessary. No search fee. Search information required: name, date of birth, years to search.

Civil records are available by mail. No release necessary. No search fee. $.50 fee per copy. $3.00 for certification. Search information required: name, years to search. Specify plaintiff or defendant.

Monona County

Clerk of Court
610 Iowa Ave.
Onawa, IA 51040
(712) 423-2491
Records are available in person only. See Iowa state repository for additional information.

Civil records are available in person only. See Iowa state repository for additional information.

Monroe County

Monroe County Courthouse, Criminal Records
Albia, IA 52531
(515) 932-5212
Felony and misdemeanor records are available by mail. A release is required. $6.00 search fee. $.25 fee per copy. $2.00 for certification. Search information required: name, years to search.

Civil records are available by mail. A release is required. No search fee. $.25 fee per copy. $2.25 for certification. Search information required: name, date of birth, years to search. Specify plaintiff or defendant.

Montgomery County

Montgomery County Courthouse, Criminal Records
Red Oak, IA 51566
(712) 623-4986
Felony and misdemeanor records are available in person only. See Iowa State Repository for additional information.

Civil records are available in person only. See Iowa state repository for additional information.

Muscatine County

Muscatine County Courthouse
Muscatine, IA 52761
(319) 263-6511
Felony and misdemeanor records are available by mail. A release is required. No search fee. $.50 fee per copy. $2.00 for certification. Search information required: name, years to search.

Civil records are available in person only. See Iowa state repository for additional information.

Osceola County

Courthouse, Criminal Records
Sibley, IA 51249
(712) 754-3595

Felony and misdemeanor records are available in person only. See Iowa state repository for additional information.

Civil records are available in person only. See Iowa state repository for additional information.

O'Brien County

O'Brien Clerk of Court, Criminal Records
Courthouse
Primghar, IA 51245
(712) 757-3255
Fax (712) 757-3255

Felony and misdemeanor records are available in person only. See Iowa state repository for additional information.

Civil records are available in person only. See Iowa state repository for additional information.

Page County

Clerk of District Court, Criminal Records
Courthouse
112 E. Main
Clarinda, IA 51632
(712) 542-3214

Felony and misdemeanor records are available in person only. See Iowa state repository for additional information.

Civil records are available in person only. See Iowa state repository for additional information.

Palo Alto County

Palo Alto County Courthouse
PO Box 387
Emmetsburg, IA 50536
(712) 852-3603

Felony and misdemeanor records are available in person only. See Iowa state repository for additional information.

Civil records are available in person only. See Iowa state repository for additional information.

Plymouth County

Clerk of District Court, Criminal Records
Plymouth County
Le Mars, IA 51031
(712) 546-4215

Records are available in person only. See Iowa state repository for additional information.

Civil records are available in person only. See Iowa state repository for additional information.

Pocahontas County

Courthouse, Clerk of Court Office
Pocahontas, IA 50574
(712) 335-4208

Felony and misdemeanor records are available by mail. A release is required. No search fee. Search information required: name, SSN, date of birth, sex, race.

Civil records are available by mail. A release is required. No search fee. $.50 fee per copy. $2.50 for certification. Search information required: name, years to search, SASE. Specify plaintiff or defendant.

Polk County

Clerk of Court, Criminal Records
Polk County Courthouse
5th and Mulberry
Room # 201
Des Moines, IA 50309
(515) 286-3765

Felony and misdemeanor records are available by mail. No release necessary. No search fee. Search information required: name, SSN, date of birth, offense, years to search.

Civil records are available by mail. No release necessary. No search fee. $.25 fee per copy. $2.25 for certification. Search information required: name, date of birth, SSN, years to search. Specify plaintiff or defendant.

Pottawattamie County

Clerk of Court, Criminal Records
227 S. 6th Street
Council Bluffs, IA 51501
(712) 328-5604

Records are available in person only. See Iowa state repository for additional information.

Civil records are available in person only. See Iowa state repository for additional information.

Poweshiek County

Clerk of Court, Criminal Records
PO Box 218
Montezuma, IA 50171
(515) 623-5644

Felony and misdemeanor records are available in person only. See Iowa state repository for more information.

Civil records are available in person only. See Iowa state repository for additional information.

Ringgold County

Clerk of District Court, Criminal Records
Ringgold County Courthouse
Mount Ayr, IA 50854
(515) 464-3234

Felony and misdemeanor records are available in person only. See Iowa State Repository for additional information.

Civil records are available by mail. A release is required. No search fee. $.50 fee per copy. $2.50 for certification. Search information required: name, years to search. Specify plaintiff or defendant.

Sac County

Clerk of Court, Criminal Records
PO Box 368
Courthouse
Sac City, IA 50583
(712) 662-7791

Felony and misdemeanor records are available by mail. A release is required. No search fee. Search information required: name, years to search.

Civil records are available by mail. A release is required. No search fee. $.50 fee per copy. $2.50 for certification. Search information required: name, date of birth, SSN, years to search, SASE. Specify plaintiff or defendant.

Scott County

Clerk of Court, Criminal Records
416 W. 4th Street
Davenport, IA 52801
(319) 326-8784

Felony and misdemeanor records are available by mail. A release is required. $6.00 search fee. Search information required: name, SSN, date of birth, SASE.

Civil records are available by mail. No release necessary. $6.00 search fee. $.50 fee per copy. Will not certify copies. Search information required: name, date of birth, SSN, years to search. Specify plaintiff or defendant.

Shelby County

Clerk of Court, Criminal Records
PO Box 431
Harlan, IA 51537
(712) 755-5543

Felony and misdemeanor records are available by mail or phone. No release necessary. No search fee. Search information required: name, SSN, date of birth, sex, race, years to search.

Civil records are available by mail. No release necessary. No search fee. $.50 fee per copy. $2.50 for certification. Search information required: name, date of birth, SSN, years to search. Specify plaintiff or defendant.

Sioux County

Clerk of Courts, Criminal Records
Sioux County Courthouse
PO Box 40
Orange City, IA 51041
(712) 737-2286

Felony and misdemeanor records are available by mail. No release necessary. No search fee. $.25 fee per copy. $2.25 for certification. Search information required: name, years to search.

Civil records are available by mail. No release necessary. No search fee. $.25 fee per copy. $2.25 for certification. Search information required: name, years to search. Specify plaintiff or defendant.

Story County

Clerk of Court, Criminal Records
PO Box 408
Nevada, IA 50201
(515) 382-6581

Felony and misdemeanor records are available in person only. See Iowa state repository for additional information.

Civil records are available in person only. See Iowa state repository for additional information.

Tama County

Clerk of Court, Criminal Records
PO Box 306
Toledo, IA 52342
(515) 484-3721
Felony and misdemeanor records are available by mail. No release necessary. No search fee. Search information required: name, years to search, SASE.

Civil records are available by mail or phone. No release necessary. No search fee. $.50 fee per copy. $2.50 for certification. Search information required: name, years to search. Specify plaintiff or defendant.

Taylor County

Courthouse, Criminal Records
Bedford, IA 50833
(712) 523-2095
Felony and misdemeanor records are available in person only. See Iowa State Repository for more information.

Civil records are available in person only. See Iowa State Repository for additional information.

Union County

Clerk of District Court, Criminal Records
Union County Courthouse
Creston, IA 50801
(515) 782-7315
Felony and misdemeanor records are available by mail. No release necessary. No search fee. Search information required: name, date of birth, years to search.

Civil records are available by mail. No release necessary. No search fee. $.50 fee per copy. $2.50 for certification. Search information required: name, date of birth, SSN, years to search. Specify plaintiff or defendant.

Van Buren County

Courthouse
Clerk of District Court
Criminal Records
Keosauqua, IA 52565
(319) 293-3108
Felony and misdemeanor records are available by mail. No release necessary. No search fee. $.25 fee per copy. $2.00 for certification. Search information required: name, date of birth, and years to search.

Civil records are available by mail. No release necessary. No search fee. $.25 fee per copy. $2.00 for certification. Search information required: name, years to search. Specify plaintiff or defendant.

Wapello County

Wapello County Courthouse, Criminal Records
101 W. 4th
Ottumwa, IA 52501
(515) 683-0060
Felony and misdemeanor records are available by mail. A release is required. $6.00 search fee. Certified check only, payable to Clerk of District Court. Search information required: name, SSN, date of birth.

Civil records are available by mail. A release is required. $6.00 search fee. $.25 fee per copy. $2.25 for certification. Search information required: name, years to search. Specify plaintiff or defendant.

Warren County

Clerk of Court, Criminal Records
PO Box 379
Indianola, IA 50125
(515) 961-1033
Felony and misdemeanor records are available by mail or phone. No release necessary. No search fee. Search information required: name, SSN, date of birth, sex, race.

Civil records are available by mail. No release necessary. No search fee. $.25 fee per copy. $2.25 for certification. Search information required: name, years to search. Specify plaintiff or defendant.

Washington County

Clerk of Court, Criminal Records
PO Box 391
Washington, IA 52353
(319) 653-7741
Felony and misdemeanor records are available by mail. A release is required. No search fee. Search information required: name, date of birth.

Civil records are available by mail. A release is required. No search fee. $.25 fee per copy. $6.00 for certification. Search information required: name, years to search. Specify plaintiff or defendant.

Wayne County

Clerk of District Court, Criminal Records
PO Box 424
Corydon, IA 50060
(515) 872-2264
Felony and misdemeanor records are available by mail. No release necessary. No search fee. $.50 fee per copy. $2.50 for certification. Search information required: name, SSN, date of birth, years to search.

Civil records are available by mail. No release necessary. No search fee. $.50 fee per copy. $2.50 for certification. Search information required: name, date of birth, years to search. Specify plaintiff or defendant.

Webster County

Webster County Courthouse, Criminal Records
Webster County Clerk's Office
Ft. Dodge, IA 50501
(515) 576-7115
Felony and misdemeanor records are available by mail. A release is required. $2.00 search fee. $.50 fee per copy. $2.50 for certification. Company checks only, payable to Clerk of Court. Search information required: name, date of birth, years to search. Specify Felony or Misdemeanor.

Civil records are available by mail. A release is required. $2.00 search fee. $.50 fee per copy. $2.50 for certification. Search information required: name, years to search. Specify plaintiff or defendant.

Winnebago County

Clerk of Court, Criminal Records
PO Box 468
126 S. Clark
Forest City, IA 50436
(515) 582-4520
Felony and misdemeanor records are available in person only. See Iowa state repository for additional information.

Civil records are available in person only. See Iowa state repository for additional information.

Winneshiek County

Clerk of Court, Criminal Records
201 W. Main
Decorah, IA 52101
(319) 382-2469
Records are available in person only. See Iowa state repository for additional information.

Civil records are available in person only. See Iowa state repository for additional information.

Woodbury County

Courthouse
7th and Douglas
Room #101
Sioux City, IA 51101
(712) 279-6616
Records are available in person only. See Iowa state repository for additional information.

Civil records are available in person only. See Iowa state repository for additional information.

Worth County

Clerk of Court, Criminal Records
Worth County Courthouse
Northwood, IA 50459
(515) 324-2840
Felony and misdemeanor records are available by mail or phone. No release necessary. No search fee. Search information required: name, previous address, years to search.

Civil records are available in person only. See Iowa state repository for additional information.

Wright County

Clerk of Court, Criminal Records
PO Box 306
Clarion, IA 50525
(515) 532-3113
Felony and misdemeanor records are available in person only. If specific date of offense is known, the record will be looked up. $.25 fee per copy. See Iowa State Repository for additional information.

Civil records are available in person only. See Iowa state repository for additional information.

City-County Cross Reference

Ackley *Hardin*
Ackworth *Warren*
Adair *Adair*
Adel *Dallas*
Afton *Union*
Agency *Wapello*
Ainsworth *Washington*
Akron *Plymouth*
Albert City *Buena Vista*
Albia *Monroe*
Albion *Marshall*
Alburnett *Linn*
Alden *Hardin*
Alexander *Franklin*
Algona *Kossuth*
Alleman *Polk*
Allerton *Wayne*
Allison *Butler*
Alta *Buena Vista*
Alta Vista *Chickasaw*
Alton *Sioux*
Altoona *Polk*
Alvord *Lyon*
Amana *Iowa*
Ames *Story*
Anamosa *Jones*
Andover *Clinton*
Andrew *Jackson*
Anita *Cass*
Ankeny *Polk*
Anthon *Woodbury*
Aplington *Butler*
Arcadia *Carroll*
Archer *Obrien*
Aredale *Butler*
Argyle *Lee*
Arion *Crawford*
Arispe *Union*
Arlington *Fayette*
Armstrong *Emmet*
Arnolds Park *Dickinson*
Arthur *Ida*
Asbury *Dubuque*
Ashton *Osceola*
Atalissa *Muscatine*
Atkins *Benton*
Atlantic *Cass*
Auburn *Sac*
Audubon *Audubon*
Aurelia *Cherokee*
Aurora *Buchanan*
Austinville *Butler*
Avoca *Pottawattamie*
Ayrshire *Palo Alto*
Badger *Webster*
Bagley *Guthrie*
Baldwin *Jackson*
Bancroft *Kossuth*
Barnes City *Mahaska*
Barnum *Webster*
Batavia *Jefferson*
Battle Creek *Ida*
Baxter *Jasper*
Bayard *Guthrie*
Beacon *Mahaska*
Beaconsfield *Ringgold*
Beaman *Grundy*
Beaver *Boone*
Bedford *Taylor*
Belle Plaine *Benton*
Bellevue *Jackson*
Belmond *Wright*

Bennett *Cedar*
Benton *Ringgold*
Bernard *Dubuque*
Berwick *Polk*
Bettendorf *Scott*
Bevington *Madison*
Birmingham *Van Buren*
Blairsburg *Hamilton*
Blairstown *Benton*
Blakesburg *Wapello*
Blanchard *Page*
Blencoe *Monona*
Blockton *Taylor*
Bloomfield *Davis*
Blue Grass *Scott*
Bode *Humboldt*
Bonaparte *Van Buren*
Bondurant *Polk*
Boone *Boone*
Booneville *Dallas*
Bouton *Dallas*
Boxholm *Boone*
Boyden *Sioux*
Braddyville *Page*
Bradford *Franklin*
Bradgate *Humboldt*
Brandon *Buchanan*
Brayton *Audubon*
Breda *Carroll*
Bridgewater *Adair*
Brighton *Washington*
Bristow *Butler*
Britt *Hancock*
Bronson *Woodbury*
Brooklyn *Poweshiek*
Brunsville *Plymouth*
Bryant *Clinton*
Buckingham *Tama*
Buffalo *Scott*
Buffalo Center *Winnebago*
Burlington *Des Moines*
Burnside *Webster*
Burr Oak *Winneshiek*
Burt *Kossuth*
Bussey *Marion*
Calamus *Clinton*
Callender *Webster*
Calmar *Winneshiek*
Calumet *Obrien*
Camanche *Clinton*
Cambridge *Story*
Cantril *Van Buren*
Carbon *Adams*
Carlisle *Warren*
Carnarvon *Sac*
Carpenter *Mitchell*
Carroll *Carroll*
Carson *Pottawattamie*
Carter Lake *Pottawattamie*
Cascade *Dubuque*
Casey *Guthrie*
Castalia *Winneshiek*
Castana *Monona*
Cedar *Mahaska*
Cedar Falls *Black Hawk*
Cedar Rapids *Linn*
Center Junction *Jones*
Center Point *Linn*
Centerville *Appanoose*
Central City *Linn*
Chapin *Franklin*
Chariton *Lucas*

Charles City *Floyd*
Charlotte *Clinton*
Charter Oak *Crawford*
Chelsea *Tama*
Cherokee *Cherokee*
Chester *Howard*
Chillicothe *Wapello*
Churdan *Greene*
Cincinnati *Appanoose*
Clare *Webster*
Clarence *Cedar*
Clarinda *Page*
Clarion *Wright*
Clarksville *Butler*
Clearfield *Taylor*
Clear Lake *Cerro Gordo*
Cleghorn *Cherokee*
Clemons *Marshall*
Clermont *Fayette*
Clinton *Clinton*
Clio *Wayne*
Clutier *Tama*
Coggon *Linn*
Coin *Page*
Colesburg *Delaware*
Colfax *Jasper*
College Springs *Page*
Collins *Story*
Colo *Story*
Columbia *Marion*
Columbus City *Louisa*
Columbus Junction *Louisa*
Conesville *Muscatine*
Conrad *Grundy*
Conroy *Iowa*
Coon Rapids *Carroll*
Cooper *Greene*
Coralville *Johnson*
Corning *Adams*
Correctionville *Woodbury*
Corwith *Hancock*
Corydon *Wayne*
Coulter *Franklin*
Council Bluffs
   Pottawattamie
Crawfordsville *Washington*
Crescent *Pottawattamie*
Cresco *Howard*
Creston *Union*
Cromwell *Union*
Crystal Lake *Hancock*
Cumberland *Cass*
Cumming *Warren*
Curlew *Palo Alto*
Cushing *Woodbury*
Cylinder *Palo Alto*
Dakota City *Humboldt*
Dallas *Marion*
Dallas Center *Dallas*
Dana *Greene*
Danbury *Woodbury*
Danville *Des Moines*
Davenport *Scott*
Davis City *Decatur*
Dawson *Dallas*
Dayton *Webster*
Decatur *Decatur*
Decorah *Winneshiek*
Dedham *Carroll*
Deep River *Poweshiek*
Defiance *Shelby*
Delaware *Delaware*

Delhi *Delaware*
Delmar *Clinton*
Deloit *Crawford*
Delphos *Ringgold*
Delta *Keokuk*
Denison *Crawford*
Denmark *Lee*
Denver *Bremer*
Derby *Lucas*
Des Moines *Polk*
DeSoto *Dallas*
Dewar *Black Hawk*
DeWitt *Clinton*
Dexter *Dallas*
Diagonal *Ringgold*
Dickens *Clay*
Dike *Grundy*
Dixon *Scott*
Dolliver *Emmet*
Donahue *Scott*
Donnellson *Lee*
Doon *Lyon*
Dorchester *Allamakee*
Douds *Van Buren*
Dougherty *Cerro Gordo*
Dow City *Crawford*
Dows *Wright*
Drakesville *Davis*
Dubuque *Dubuque*
Dumont *Butler*
Duncombe *Webster*
Dundee *Delaware*
Dunkerton *Black Hawk*
Dunlap *Harrison*
Durango *Dubuque*
Durant *Cedar*
Dyersville *Dubuque*
Dysart *Tama*
Eagle Grove *Wright*
Earlham *Madison*
Earling *Shelby*
Earlville *Delaware*
Early *Sac*
Eddyville *Wapello*
Edgewood *Clayton*
Elberon *Tama*
Eldon *Wapello*
Eldora *Hardin*
Eldridge *Scott*
Elgin *Fayette*
Elkader *Clayton*
Elkhart *Polk*
Elk Horn *Shelby*
Elk Run Heights *Black*
   Hawk
Elkport *Clayton*
Elliott *Montgomery*
Ellston *Ringgold*
Ellsworth *Hamilton*
Elma *Howard*
Elwood *Clinton*
Ely *Linn*
Emerson *Mills*
Emmetsburg *Palo Alto*
Epworth *Dubuque*
Essex *Page*
Estherville *Emmet*
Evansdale *Black Hawk*
Everly *Clay*
Exira *Audubon*
Exline *Appanoose*
Fairbank *Buchanan*

Fairfax *Linn*
Fairfield *Jefferson*
Farley *Dubuque*
Farmersburg *Clayton*
Farmington *Van Buren*
Farnhamville *Calhoun*
Farragut *Fremont*
Fayette *Fayette*
Fenton *Kossuth*
Ferguson *Marshall*
Fertile *Worth*
Festina *Winneshiek*
Floris *Davis*
Floyd *Floyd*
Fonda *Pocahontas*
Fontanelle *Adair*
Forest City *Winnebago*
Fort Atkinson *Winneshiek*
Fort Dodge *Webster*
Fort Madison *Lee*
Fostoria *Clay*
Fredericksburg *Chickasaw*
Frederika *Bremer*
Fremont *Mahaska*
Fruitland *Muscatine*
Galt *Wright*
Galva *Ida*
Garber *Clayton*
Garden City *Hardin*
Garden Grove *Decatur*
Garnavillo *Clayton*
Garner *Hancock*
Garrison *Benton*
Garwin *Tama*
Geneva *Franklin*
George *Lyon*
Gibson *Keokuk*
Gilbert *Story*
Gilbertville *Black Hawk*
Gillett Grove *Clay*
Gilman *Marshall*
Gilmore City *Pocahontas*
Gladbrook *Tama*
Glenwood *Mills*
Glidden *Carroll*
Goldfield *Wright*
Goodell *Hancock*
Goose Lake *Clinton*
Gowrie *Webster*
Graettinger *Palo Alto*
Grafton *Worth*
Grand Junction *Greene*
Grand Mound *Clinton*
Grand River *Decatur*
Grandview *Louisa*
Granger *Dallas*
Grant *Montgomery*
Granville *Sioux*
Gravity *Taylor*
Gray *Audubon*
Greeley *Delaware*
Greene *Butler*
Greenfield *Adair*
Green Island *Jackson*
Green Mountain *Marshall*
Grimes *Polk*
Grinnell *Poweshiek*
Griswold *Cass*
Grundy Center *Grundy*
Gruver *Emmet*
Guthrie Center *Guthrie*
Guttenberg *Clayton*
Halbur *Fremont*
Hamilton *Marion*
Hamlin *Audubon*

Hamburg *Freemont*
Hampton *Franklin*
Hancock *Pottawattamie*
Hanlontown *Worth*
Hansell *Franklin*
Harcourt *Webster*
Hardy *Humboldt*
Harlan *Shelby*
Harper *Keokuk*
Harpers Ferry *Allamakee*
Harris *Osceola*
Hartford *Warren*
Hartley *Obrien*
Hartwick *Poweshiek*
Harvey *Marion*
Hastings *Mills*
Havelock *Pocahontas*
Haverhill *Marshall*
Hawarden *Sioux*
Hawkeye *Fayette*
Hayesville *Keokuk*
Hazleton *Buchanan*
Hedrick *Keokuk*
Henderson *Mills*
Hiawatha *Linn*
Highlandville *Winneshiek*
Hills *Johnson*
Hillsboro *Henry*
Hinton *Plymouth*
Holland *Grundy*
Holstein *Ida*
Holy Cross *Dubuque*
Homestead *Iowa*
Honey Creek
   Pottawattamie
Hopkinton *Delaware*
Hornick *Woodbury*
Hospers *Sioux*
Houghton *Lee*
Hubbard *Hardin*
Hudson *Black Hawk*
Hull *Sioux*
Humboldt *Humboldt*
Humeston *Wayne*
Huxley *Story*
Ida Grove *Ida*
Imogene *Fremont*
Independence *Buchanan*
Indianola *Warren*
Inwood *Lyon*
Ionia *Chickasaw*
Iowa City *Johnson*
Iowa Falls *Hardin*
Ireton *Sioux*
Irwin *Shelby*
Jackson Junction
   Winneshiek
Jamaica *Guthrie*
Janesville *Bremer*
Jefferson *Greene*
Jesup *Buchanan*
Jewell *Hamilton*
Johnston *Polk*
Joice *Worth*
Jolley *Calhoun*
Kalona *Washington*
Kamrar *Hamilton*
Kanawha *Hancock*
Kellerton *Ringgold*
Kelley *Story*
Kellogg *Jasper*
Kensett *Worth*
Kent *Union*
Keokuk *Lee*
Keosauqua *Van Buren*

Keota *Keokuk*
Kesley *Butler*
Keswick *Keokuk*
Keystone *Benton*
Killduff *Jasper*
Kimballton *Audubon*
Kingsley *Plymouth*
Kinross *Keokuk*
Kirkman *Shelby*
Kirkville *Wapello*
Kiron *Crawford*
Klemme *Hancock*
Knierim *Calhoun*
Knoxville *Marion*
Lacona *Warren*
Ladora *Iowa*
Lake City *Calhoun*
Lake Mills *Winnebago*
Lake Park *Dickinson*
Lake View *Sac*
Lakota *Kossuth*
Lamoni *Decatur*
Lamont *Buchanan*
LaMotte *Jackson*
Lanesboro *Carroll*
Lansing *Allamakee*
LaPorte City *Black Hawk*
Larchwood *Lyon*
Larrabee *Cherokee*
Latimer *Franklin*
Laurel *Marshall*
Laurens *Pocahontas*
Lawler *Chickasaw*
Lawton *Woodbury*
Le Claire *Scott*
Ledyard *Kossuth*
Le Grand *Marshall*
Lehigh *Webster*
Leighton *Mahaska*
Leland *Winnebago*
Le Mars *Plymouth*
Lenox *Taylor*
Leon *Decatur*
Lester *Lyon*
Letts *Louisa*
Lewis *Cass*
Liberty Center *Warren*
Libertyville *Jefferson*
Lidderdale *Carroll*
Lime Springs *Howard*
Lincoln *Tama*
Linden *Dallas*
Lineville *Wayne*
Linn Grove *Buena Vista*
Lisbon *Linn*
Liscomb *Marshall*
Littleport *Clayton*
Little Rock *Lyon*
Little Sioux *Harrison*
Livermore *Humboldt*
Logan *Harrison*
Lohrville *Calhoun*
Lone Rock *Kossuth*
Lone Tree *Johnson*
Long Grove *Scott*
Lorimor *Union*
Lost Nation *Clinton*
Lovilia *Monroe*
Lowden *Cedar*
Low Moor *Clinton*
Luana *Clayton*
Lucas *Lucas*
Luther *Boone*
Lu Verne *Kossuth*

Luxemburg *Dubuque*
Luzerne *Benton*
Lynnville *Jasper*
Lytton *Sac*
McCallsburg *Story*
McCausland *Scott*
McClelland *Pottawattamie*
McGregor *Clayton*
McIntire *Mitchell*
Macedonia *Pottawattamie*
Macksburg *Madison*
Madrid *Boone*
Malcom *Poweshiek*
Mallard *Palo Alto*
Maloy *Ringgold*
Malvern *Mills*
Manchester *Delaware*
Manilla *Crawford*
Manly *Worth*
Manning *Carroll*
Manson *Calhoun*
Mapleton *Monona*
Maquoketa *Jackson*
Marathon *Buena Vista*
Marble Rock *Floyd*
Marcus *Cherokee*
Marengo *Iowa*
Marion *Linn*
Marne *Cass*
Marquette *Clayton*
Marshalltown *Marshall*
Martelle *Jones*
Martensdale *Warren*
Martinsburg *Keokuk*
Mason City *Cerro Gordo*
Masonville *Delaware*
Massena *Cass*
Maurice *Sioux*
Maxwell *Story*
Maynard *Fayette*
Mechanicsville *Cedar*
Mediapolis *Des Moines*
Melbourne *Marshall*
Melcher *Marion*
Melrose *Monroe*
Melvin *Osceola*
Menlo *Guthrie*
Meriden *Cherokee*
Merrill *Plymouth*
Meservey *Cerro Gordo*
Middle *Iowa*
Middletown *Des Moines*
Miles *Jackson*
Milford *Dickinson*
Millersburg *Iowa*
Millerton *Wayne*
Milo *Warren*
Milton *Van Buren*
Minburn *Dallas*
Minden *Pottawattamie*
Mineola *Mills*
Mingo *Jasper*
Missouri Valley *Harrison*
Mitchellville *Polk*
Modale *Harrison*
Mondamin *Harrison*
Monmouth *Jackson*
Monona *Clayton*
Monroe *Jasper*
Montezuma *Poweshiek*
Monticello *Jones*
Montour *Tama*
Montpelier *Muscatine*
Montrose *Lee*
Moorhead *Monona*

Moorland *Webster*
Moravia *Appanoose*
Morley *Jones*
Morning Sun *Louisa*
Morrison *Grundy*
Moscow *Muscatine*
Moulton *Appanoose*
Mount Auburn *Benton*
Mount Ayr *Ringgold*
Mount Etna *Adams*
Mount Pleasant *Henry*
Mount Union *Henry*
Mount Vernon *Linn*
Moville *Woodbury*
Murray *Clarke*
Muscatine *Muscatine*
Mystic *Appanoose*
Nashua *Chickasaw*
Nemaha *Sac*
Neola *Pottawattamie*
Nevada *Story*
New Albin *Allamakee*
Newell *Buena Vista*
Newhall *Benton*
New Hampton *Chickasaw*
New Hartford *Butler*
New Liberty *Scott*
New London *Henry*
New Market *Taylor*
New Providence *Hardin*
New Sharon *Mahaska*
Newton *Jasper*
New Vienna *Dubuque*
New Virginia *Warren*
Nichols *Muscatine*
Nodaway *Adams*
Nora Springs *Floyd*
Northboro *Page*
North Buena Vista *Clayton*
North English *Iowa*
North Liberty *Johnson*
Northwood *Worth*
Norwalk *Warren*
Norway *Benton*
Numa *Appanoose*
Oakdale *Johnson*
Oakland *Pottawattamie*
Oakville *Louisa*
Ocheyedan *Osceola*
Odebolt *Sac*
Oelwein *Fayette*
Ogden *Boone*
Okoboji *Dickinson*
Olds *Henry*
Olin *Jones*
Ollie *Keokuk*
Onawa *Monona*
Onslow *Jones*
Oran *Fayette*
Orange City *Sioux*
Orchard *Mitchell*
Orient *Adair*
Osage *Mitchell*
Osceola *Clarke*
Oskaloosa *Mahaska*
Ossian *Winneshiek*
Otho *Webster*
Otley *Marion*
Oto *Woodbury*
Ottosen *Humboldt*
Ottumwa *Wapello*
Oxford *Johnson*
Oxford Junction *Jones*
Oyens *Plymouth*
Pacific Junction *Mills*

Packwood *Jefferson*
Palmer *Pocahontas*
Palo *Linn*
Panama *Shelby*
Panora *Guthrie*
Parkersburg *Butler*
Park View *Scott*
Parnell *Iowa*
Paton *Greene*
Patterson *Madison*
Paullina *Obrien*
Pella *Marion*
Peosta *Dubuque*
Percival *Fremont*
Perry *Dallas*
Pershing *Marion*
Persia *Harrison*
Peru *Madison*
Peterson *Clay*
Pierson *Woodbury*
Pilot Grove *Lee*
Pilot Mound *Boone*
Pisgah *Harrison*
Plainfield *Bremer*
Plano *Appanoose*
Pleasant Valley *Scott*
Pleasantville *Marion*
Plover *Pocahontas*
Plymouth *Cerro Gordo*
Pocahontas *Pocahontas*
Polk City *Polk*
Pomeroy *Calhoun*
Popejoy *Franklin*
Portsmouth *Shelby*
Postville *Allamakee*
Prairie City *Jasper*
Prescott *Adams*
Preston *Jackson*
Primghar *Obrien*
Princeton *Scott*
Prole *Warren*
Promise City *Wayne*
Protivin *Howard*
Pulaski *Davis*
Quasqueton *Buchanan*
Quimby *Cherokee*
Radcliffe *Hardin*
Rake *Winnebago*
Ralston *Carroll*
Randalia *Fayette*
Randall *Hamilton*
Randolph *Fremont*
Raymond *Black Hawk*
Readlyn *Bremer*
Reasnor *Jasper*
Redding *Ringgold*
Redfield *Dallas*
Red Oak *Montgomery*
Reinbeck *Grundy*
Rembrandt *Buena Vista*
Remsen *Plymouth*
Renwick *Humboldt*
Rhodes *Marshall*
Riceville *Mitchell*
Richland *Keokuk*
Ricketts *Crawford*
Ridgeway *Winneshiek*
Ringsted *Emmet*
Rippey *Greene*
Riverside *Washington*
Riverton *Fremont*
Robins *Linn*
Rockford *Floyd*
Rock Rapids *Lyon*
Rock Valley *Sioux*

Rockwell *Cerro Gordo*
Rockwell City *Calhoun*
Rodman *Palo Alto*
Rodney *Monona*
Roland *Story*
Rolfe *Pocahontas*
Rose Hill *Mahaska*
Rowan *Wright*
Rowley *Buchanan*
Royal *Clay*
Rudd *Floyd*
Runnells *Polk*
Russell *Lucas*
Ruthven *Palo Alto*
Rutland *Humboldt*
Ryan *Delaware*
Sabula *Jackson*
Sac City *Sac*
Saint Ansgar *Mitchell*
Saint Anthony *Marshall*
Saint Charles *Madison*
Saint Donatus *Jackson*
Saint Lucas *Fayette*
Saint Marys *Warren*
Saint Olaf *Clayton*
Salem *Henry*
Salix *Woodbury*
Sanborn *Obrien*
Scarville *Winnebago*
Schaller *Sac*
Schleswig *Crawford*
Scotch Grove *Jones*
Scranton *Greene*
Searsboro *Poweshiek*
Selma *Van Buren*
Sergeant Bluff *Woodbury*
Seymour *Wayne*
Shambaugh *Page*
Shannon City *Union*
Sharpsburg *Taylor*
Sheffield *Franklin*
Shelby *Shelby*
Sheldahl *Polk*
Sheldon *Obrien*
Shell Rock *Butler*
Shellsburg *Benton*
Shenandoah *Page*
Sherrill *Dubuque*
Sibley *Osceola*
Sidney *Fremont*
Sigourney *Keokuk*
Silver City *Mills*
Sioux Center *Sioux*
Sioux City *Woodbury*
Sioux Rapids *Buena Vista*
Slater *Story*
Sloan *Woodbury*
Smithland *Woodbury*
Soldier *Monona*
Solon *Johnson*
Somers *Calhoun*
South Amana *Iowa*
South English *Keokuk*
Spencer *Clay*
Sperry *Des Moines*
Spillville *Winneshiek*
Spirit Lake *Dickinson*
Spragueville *Jackson*
Springbrook *Jackson*
Springville *Linn*
Stacyville *Mitchell*
Stanhope *Hamilton*
Stanley *Buchanan*
Stanton *Montgomery*
Stanwood *Cedar*

State Center *Marshall*
Steamboat Rock *Hardin*
Stockport *Van Buren*
Stockton *Muscatine*
Storm Lake *Buena Vista*
Story City *Story*
Stout *Grundy*
Stratford *Hamilton*
Strawberry Point *Clayton*
Stuart *Guthrie*
Sully *Jasper*
Sumner *Bremer*
Superior *Dickinson*
Sutherland *Obrien*
Swaledale *Cerro Gordo*
Swan *Marion*
Swea City *Kossuth*
Swedesburg *Henry*
Swisher *Johnson*
Tabor *Fremont*
Taintor *Mahaska*
Tama *Tama*
Templeton *Carroll*
Tennant *Shelby*
Terril *Dickinson*
Thayer *Union*
Thompson *Winnebago*
Thor *Humboldt*
Thornburg *Keokuk*
Thornton *Cerro Gordo*
Thurman *Fremont*
Tiffin *Johnson*
Tingley *Ringgold*
Tipton *Cedar*
Titonka *Kossuth*
Toddville *Linn*
Toledo *Tama*
Toronto *Clinton*
Tracy *Marion*
Traer *Tama*
Treynor *Pottawattamie*
Tripoli *Bremer*
Troy Mills *Linn*
Truesdale *Buena Vista*
Truro *Madison*
Turin *Monona*
Udell *Appanoose*
Underwood *Pottawattamie*
Union *Hardin*
Unionville *Appanoose*
University Park *Mahaska*
Urbana *Benton*
Ute *Monona*
Vail *Crawford*
Van Horne *Benton*
Van Meter *Dallas*
Van Wert *Decatur*
Varina *Pocahontas*
Ventura *Cerro Gordo*
Victor *Iowa*
Villisca *Montgomery*
Vincent *Webster*
Vining *Tama*
Vinton *Benton*
Viola *Linn*
Volga *Clayton*
Wadena *Fayette*
Walcott *Scott*
Walford *Benton*
Walker *Linn*
Wallingford *Emmet*
Wall Lake *Sac*
Walnut *Pottawattamie*
Wapello *Louisa*
Washburn *Black Hawk*

Washington *Washington*
Washta *Cherokee*
Waterloo *Black Hawk*
Waterville *Allamakee*
Watkins *Benton*
Waucoma *Fayette*
Waukee *Dallas*
Waukon *Allamakee*
Waverly *Bremer*
Wayland *Henry*
Webb *Clay*
Webster *Keokuk*
Webster City *Hamilton*
Weldon *Decatur*
Wellman *Washington*
Wellsburg *Grundy*
Welton *Clinton*
Wesley *Kossuth*
West *Iowa*
West Bend *Palo Alto*
West Branch *Cedar*
West Burlington *Des Moines*
West Chester *Washington*
Westfield *Plymouth*
Westgate *Fayette*
West Liberty *Muscatine*
Westphalia *Shelby*
West Point *Lee*
Westside *Crawford*
West Union *Fayette*
Wever *Lee*
What Cheer *Keokuk*
Wheatland *Clinton*
Whiting *Monona*
Whittemore *Kossuth*
Whitten *Hardin*
Williams *Hamilton*
Williamsburg *Iowa*
Williamson *Lucas*
Wilton *Muscatine*
Winfield *Henry*
Winterset *Madison*
Winthrop *Buchanan*
Wiota *Cass*
Woden *Hancock*
Woodbine *Harrison*
Woodburn *Clarke*
Woodward *Dallas*
Woolstock *Wright*
Worthington *Dubuque*
Wyoming *Jones*
Yale *Guthrie*
Yarmouth *Des Moines*
Yorktown *Page*
Zearing *Story*
Zwingle *Dubuque*

Kansas

While all of Kansas' 105 counties make criminal records available for employment screening purposes, twenty six (26) of these require records requests to be made in person. Seventy nine (79) of the counties will process mail and/or phone requests. Eighty five (85) counties will do civil record checks by phone or mail.

For more information or for offices not listed, contact the state's information hot line at (913) 296-0111.

Driving Records

Kansas Department of Revenue
Driver Control Bureau
Division of Vehicles
PO Box 12021
Topeka, KS 66616-2021
(913) 296-3671
Driving records are available by mail. $3.50 fee per request. Turnaround time is 2 to 3 days. Written request must include job applicant's full name, date of birth and license number. Make check payable to Kansas Department of Revenue.

Worker's Compensation Records

Division of Worker's Compensation
600 Merchant Bank Tower
800 Southwest Jackson
Topeka, KS 66612-1227
(913) 296-3441
Mail and telephone requests must include subject's complete name and social security number. If known, include previous employers involved in claim with applicant and date of injury. Record searches for "hiring purposes" are limited to records entered into the computers after July 1974. There is no fee. A signed release is not required.

Vital Statistics

Bureau of Vital Statistics
Kansas State Department of Health and Environment
Landon State Office Building
900 Southwest Jackson
Topeka, KS 66612-1290
(913) 296-1400
Birth and death records are available for $7.00 each. For birth record include father's name and mother's maiden. For birth record include birth name, date, city, father's name, and mother's maiden name. For death record include name, date, and place of occurrence. State office has records since July 1911. For earlier records, write to County Clerk in county where event occurred. Additional copies of same record ordered at same time are $4.00 each. Some records are accessible by computer.

An employer can obtain records with a written release. Make certified check or money order payable to State Registrar. Marriage records are available. $7.00 for first copy, and $4.00 for each additional copy. Turnaround time is 2-3 weeks or 24 hours by special mail service. Include name, marriage date, date of birth, spouse's name, city where marriage took place, and county where license issued. Written release is required. Divorce certificates from 1951 forward are available at the state office building or at county level where divorce granted. Written release required by one of the parties.

Department of Education

Department of Education
Teacher Certification
120 SE Tenth Ave.
Topeka, KS 66612
(913) 296-2288
Field of certification and expiration date are available by phone or mail. Include name and SSN.

Medical Licensing

State Board of Healing Art
235 S.W. Topeka Blvd.
Topeka, KS 66603
(913) 296-7413
Will confirm licenses for MDs and DOs by phone or mail. No fee. For licenses not mentioned, contact the above office.

Kansas Board of Nursing
Landon State Office Building
900 SW Jackson, Suite 551 S.
Topeka, KS 66612-1256
(913) 296-4929
Will confirm license by phone. No fee. Include name, license number.

Bar Association

Kansas State Bar Association
PO Box 1037
Topeka, KS 66601
(913) 234-5696
Will confirm licenses by phone. No fee. Include name.

Accountancy Board

Kansas State Board of Accountancy
900 SW Jackson, Suite 556
Topeka, KS 66612
(913) 296-2162
Will confirm license by phone. No fee. Include name.

Securities Commission

Office of Securities Commissioner
618 South Kansas Av., 2nd Floor
Topeka, KS 66603-3804
(913) 296-3307
Will confirm license by phone. No fee. Include name and SSN.

Secretary of State

Secretary of State
2nd Floor Capitol
Topeka, KS 66612
(913) 296-4564
Fax (913) 296-4570
Service agent and address, date incorporated, limited partnership, corporate, names are available by phone or mail. Contact the above office for additional information.

Criminal Records

State Repository

Kansas Bureau of Investigation
1620 Southwest Tyler
Topeka, KS 66612
(913) 232-6000
Fax (913) 296-6781
Limited criminal record information may be accessed by non-criminal justice agencies by mail. However, prior to making requests for criminal record checks, employers must have on file with the Kansas Bureau of Investigation a "Non-disclosure Agreement of Access Request." Copies of this form and additional instructions can be obtained by contacting the above office.
If access is granted, requests may be made as either a "name check" or a "fingerprint check". Name checks are $10.00 and fingerprint checks are $17.00 each. A written release is required for each request. Information supplied is conviction data only.

Allen County

Clerk of District Court
PO Box 660
Iola, KS 66749
(316) 365-5145
Records are available by mail. A release is required. $9.80 fee per hour searched. Search information required: name, years to search, SASE.

Civil records are available by mail or phone. No release necessary. $9.80 fee per hour searched. $.25 fee per copy. $1.00 for certification. Search information required: name, SSN, years to search. Specify plaintiff or defendant.

Anderson County

Clerk of District Court
PO Box 305
Garnett, KS 66032
(913) 448-6886
Records are available in person only. See Kansas state repository for additional information.

Civil records are available by mail. No release necessary. No search fee. $.25 fee per copy. $1.00 for certification. Search information required: name, SSN, years to search. Specify plaintiff or defendant.

Atchison County

Clerk of District Court, Criminal Records
PO Box 408
Atchison, KS 66002
(913) 367-7400
Felony and misdemeanor records are available by mail. No release necessary. No search fee from 1989 forward. $9.00 fee per hour prior to 1989. $.25 fee per copy. Search information required: name, years to search.

Civil records are available by mail. No release necessary. No search fee from 1985 forward. $9.00 fee per hour prior to 1985. $.25 fee per copy. Search information required: name, SSN, years to search. Specify plaintiff or defendant.

Barber County

Clerk of District Court, Criminal Records
PO Box 329
Medicine Lodge, KS 67104
(316) 886-5639
Felony and misdemeanor records are available by mail. No release necessary. No search fee. Search information required: name, years to search, SASE.

Civil records are available by mail or phone. No release necessary. No search fee. Search information required: name, SSN, years to search. Specify plaintiff or defendant.

Barton County

Clerk of District Court, Criminal Records
1400 N. Main, Rm. 306
Great Bend, KS 67530
(316) 793-1856
Fax (316) 793-1860
Felony and misdemeanor records are available by mail or fax. No release necessary. $9.50 fee per hour. $.35 fee per copy. Company check payable to Clerk of District Court. Search information required: name, SSN, date of birth, sex, race, years to search.

Civil records are available by mail. No release necessary. No search fee. Search information required: name, SSN, years to search. Specify plaintiff or defendant.

Bourbon County

Clerk of District Court
Court House
210 S. National
Ft Scott, KS 66701
(316) 223-0780
Records are available in person only. See Kansas state repository for additional information.

Brown County

District Clerk's Office, Criminal Records
Brown County Courthouse
P.O. Box 417
Hiawatha, KS 66434
(913) 742-7481
Felony and misdemeanor records are available by mail or phone. No release necessary. No search fee. $.50 fee for first copy, $.25 for each additional page. Search information required: name, date of birth, years to search.

Civil records are available by mail or phone. No release necessary. No search fee. Search information required: name, SSN, years to search. Specify plaintiff or defendant.

Butler County

Clerk of District Court
PO Box 1367
El Dorado, KS 67042
(316) 321-1200
Records are available in person only. See Kansas state repository for additional information.

Civil records are available by mail or phone. No release necessary. No search fee. $.25 fee per copy. $1.00 for certification. Search information required: name, SSN, years to search. Specify plaintiff or defendant.

Chase County

Clerk of District Court
PO Box 207
Cottonwood Falls, KS 66845
(316) 273-6319
Records are available in person only. See Kansas state repository for additional information.

Civil records are available by mail or phone. No release necessary. No search fee. Search information required: name, SSN, years to search. Specify plaintiff or defendant.

Chautauqua County

Clerk of District Court
215 N. Chautauqua
Sedan, KS 67361
(316) 725-3282
Felony and misdemeanor records are available by mail. $8.40 fee per hour. $.25 fee per copy. Search information required: name and years to search.

Civil records are available by mail or phone. No release necessary. No search fee. $.25 fee per copy. $1.00 for certification. Search information required: name, SSN, years to search. Specify plaintiff or defendant.

Cherokee County

District Court Clerk
PO Box 189
Columbus, KS 66725
(316) 429-3880
Felony and misdemeanor records are available by mail. No search fee. Search information required: name, years to check.

Civil records are available by mail or phone. No release necessary. No search fee. Search information required: name, SSN, years to search.

Cheyenne County

District Court Clerk, Criminal Records
PO Box 646
St. Francis, KS 67756
(913) 332-2351
Fax (913) 332-2940
Felony and misdemeanor records are available by mail or fax. No release necessary. No search fee. $.25 fee per copy. Search information required: name, SSN, date of birth, sex, race.

Civil records are available by mail or phone. No release necessary. No search fee. $.25 fee per copy. $1.00 for certification. Search information required: name, SSN, years to search.

Clark County

Clerk of District Court, Criminal Records
PO Box 790
Ashland, KS 67831
(316) 635-2753
Felony and misdemeanor records are available by mail. A release is required. A minimal search fee is charged only if search is considered extensive. Search information required: name, date of birth, years to search.

Civil records are available by mail or phone. No release necessary. No search fee. $.25 fee per copy. $1.00 for certification. Written request only. Search information required: name, SSN, years to search. Specify plaintiff or defendant.

Clay County

Clerk of District Court, Criminal Records
PO Box 203
Clay Center, KS 67432
(913) 632-3443
Felony and misdemeanor records are available by mail. No release necessary. $9.00 fee per hour. $.25 fee per copy. $1.00 fee for certification. Certified check only, payable to District Court Clerk. Search information required: name, date of birth, years to search.

Civil records are available by mail or phone. No release necessary. $9.00 fee per hour searched. $.25 fee per copy. $1.00 for certification. Search information required: name, SSN, years to search. Specify plaintiff or defendant.

Cloud County

Clerk of District Court, Criminal Records
811 Washington
Concordia, KS 66901
(913) 243-8124

Felony and misdemeanor records are available by mail. No release necessary. $9.00 fee per hour. $.25 fee per copy, $2.00 fee for certification.. Search information required: name, SASE, years to search.

Civil records are available by mail. No release necessary. $2.00 search fee. $.25 fee per copy. $1.00 for certification. Search information required: name, SSN, years to search. Specify plaintiff or defendant.

Coffey County

Clerk of District Court
PO Box 330
Burlington, KS 66839
(316) 364-8628

Records are available in person only. See Kansas state repository for additional information.

Civil records are available by mail. No release necessary. No search fee. $.25 fee per copy. $1.00 for certification. Search information required: name, SSN, years to search. Specify plaintiff or defendant.

Comanche County

Clerk of District Court, Criminal Records
PO Box 722
Coldwater, KS 67029
(316) 582-2182

Felony and misdemeanor records are available by mail. No release necessary. $9.00 fee per hour. $.25 fee per copy. $1.00 for certification. Search information required: name.

Civil records are available by mail or phone. No release necessary. $9.00 fee per hour searched. $.25 fee per copy. $1.00 for certification. Search information required: name, SSN, years to search. Specify plaintiff or defendant.

Cowley County

Clerk of District Court, Criminal Records
311 E. 9th
Winfield, KS 67156
(316) 221-4066 Extension 238
Fax (316) 221-3693

Felony and misdemeanor records are available by mail or fax. A release is required. $9.00 fee per hour. Any check payable to Clerk of District Court. Search information required: name, date of birth, years to search. Additional records are available from Clerk of Court, PO Box 1152, Arkansas City, KS 67005.

Civil records are available by mail. A release is required. $9.00 fee per hour searched. $.50 fee per copy. $2.00 for certification. Search information required: name, SSN, years to search. Specify plaintiff or defendant.

Crawford County

Clerk of District Court, Criminal Records
PO Box 1348
Pittsburg, KS 66762
(316) 231-0380 or 0310

Felony and misdemeanor records are available by mail. A release is required. $9.00 fee per hour, prepaid. Search information required: name, date of birth, if available, years to search, SASE.

Civil records are available by mail or phone. No release necessary. $9.00 fee per hour searched. Search information required: name, SSN, years to search.

Decatur County

Clerk of District Court
PO Box 89
Oberlin, KS 67749
(913) 475-2932

Records are available in person only. See Kansas state repository for additional information.

Civil records are available in person only. See Kansas state repository for additional information.

Dickinson County

Clerk of District Court, Criminal Records
PO Box 127
Abilene, KS 67410
(913) 263-3142

Records are available in person only. See Kansas state repository for additional information.

Civil records are available by mail. A release is required. $9.00 fee per hour searched. $1.00 fee per copy. $1.00 for certification. Search information required: name, SSN, years to search. Specify plaintiff or defendant.

Doniphan County

Clerk of District Court, Criminal Records
PO Box 295
Troy, KS 66087
(913) 985-3582

Felony and misdemeanor records are available by mail or phone. No release necessary. No search fee. Search information required: name.

Civil records are available by mail. No release necessary. No search fee. $.50 for first copy, $.25 for each additional copy. Search information required: name, SSN, years to search, SASE. Specify plaintiff or defendant.

Douglas County

Felony and misdemeanor records
Clerk of District Court, Criminal Records
111 E. 11th
Lawrence, KS 66044
(913) 841-7700

Felony and misdemeanor records are available by mail. No release necessary. Search fee: $9.00 per hour. Any check payable to Clerk of District Court. Search information required: name, date of birth, and years to search.

Civil records
Clerk of District Court
111 E. 11th
Lawrence, KS 66044
(913) 841-7210

Civil records are available by mail. No release necessary. $5.00 search fee. $1.00 fee per copy. Search information required: name, SSN, years to search. Specify plaintiff or defendant.

Edwards County

Clerk of the District Court, Criminal Records
PO Box 232
Kinsley, KS 67547
(316) 659-2442

Felony and misdemeanor records are available by mail. No release necessary. $9.00 fee per hour. Certified check only, payable to Clerk of District Court. Search information required: name, years to search.

Civil records are available by mail. No release necessary. $9.00 fee per hour searched. $.25 fee per copy. $1.00 for certification. Search information required: name, SSN, years to search. Specify plaintiff or defendant.

Elk County

Clerk of the District Court
PO Box 306
Howard, KS 67349
(316) 374-2370

Felony records are available by mail. A release is required. No search fee. Search information required: name, years to search.

Civil records are available by mail or phone. No release necessary. No search fee. Search information required: name, SSN, years to search. Specify plaintiff or defendant.

Ellis County

Clerk of the District Court, Criminal Records
PO Box 8
Hays, KS 67601
(913) 628-9417

Felony and misdemeanor records are available by mail. No release necessary. $9.00 fee per hour. $.25 fee per copy. Any check payable to Clerk of District Court. Search information required: name, years to search, SASE.

Civil records are available by mail. No release necessary. No search fee. $.25 fee per copy. $1.00 for certification. Search information required: name, SSN, years to search. Specify plaintiff or defendant.

Ellsworth County

Clerk of District Court, Criminal Records
210 N. Kansas
Ellsworth, KS 67439-3118
(913) 472-4052

Felony and misdemeanor records are available by mail. No release necessary. No search fee. Search information required: name, years to search.

Civil records are available by mail. No release necessary. No search fee. $.35 fee per copy. $.35 for certification. Search information required: name. Specify plaintiff or defendant.

Finney County

Clerk of District Court, Criminal
Records
PO Box 798
Garden City, KS 67846
(316) 272-3555
Records are available in person only. See
Kansas state repository for additional infor-
mation.

Civil records are available in person only.
See Kansas state repository for additional
information.

Ford County

Clerk of District Court, Criminal
Records
PO Box 197
Dodge City, KS 67801
(316) 227-4600
Felony and misdemeanor records are available by mail. No release necessary. $9.00
fee per hour searched. $.25 fee per copy.
$1.00 fee for certification. Any check
payable to Clerk of District Court. Search
information required: name, SASE, years to
search.

Civil records are available by mail or
phone. No release necessary. $9.00 fee per
hour searched. $.25 fee per copy. $1.00 for
certification. Search information required:
name, SSN, years to search. Specify plaintiff or defendant.

Franklin County

Clerk of District Court
PO Box P
Ottawa, KS 66067
(913) 242-6000
Felony and misdemeanor records are available in person only. See Kansas state repository for additional information.

Civil records are available by mail. No release necessary. $9.00 search fee per hour.
$.25 fee per copy. $1.00 for certification.
Search information required: name, SSN,
years to search. Specify plaintiff or defendant.

Geary County

Clerk of District Court
PO Box 1147
Junction City, KS 66441
(913) 762-5221
Records are available in person only. See
Kansas state repository for additional infor-
mation.

Civil records are available in person only.
See Kansas state repository for additional
information.

Gove County

Clerk of District Court, Criminal
Records
PO Box 97
Gove, KS 67736
(913) 938-2310
Felony and misdemeanor records are available by mail or phone. No release necessary. No search fee. Search information required: name, years to search.

Civil records are available by mail or
phone. No release necessary. No search fee.
$.25 fee per copy. $1.00 for certification.
Search information required: name, SSN,
years to search. Specify plaintiff or defendant.

Graham County

Clerk of District Court, Criminal
Records
410 N. Pomeroy
Hill City, KS 67642
(913) 674-3458
Records are available in person only. See
Kansas state repository for additional infor-
mation.

Civil records are available in person only.
See Kansas state repository for additional
information.

Grant County

Clerk of District Court, Criminal
Records
108 S. Glenn
Ulysses, KS 67880
(316) 356-1526
Records are available in person only. See
Kansas state repository for additional infor-
mation.

Civil records are available by mail. No release necessary. No search fee. $.10 fee per
copy. $1.00 for certification. Search infor-
mation required: name, SSN, years to
search. Specify plaintiff or defendant.

Gray County

Clerk of District Court
PO Box 487
Cimarron, KS 67835
(316) 855-3812
Felony and misdemeanor records are available in person only. See Kansas state repository for additional information.

Civil records are available in person only.
See Kansas state repository for additional
information.

Greeley County

Clerk of District Court, Criminal
Records
PO Box 516
Tribune, KS 67879
(316) 376-4292
Felony and misdemeanor records are avail-
able by mail. No release necessary. $6.50
fee per hour. Any check payable to Clerk of
District Court. Search information required:
name, years to search.

Civil records are available in person only.
See Kansas state repository for additional
information.

Greenwood County

Clerk of District Court, Criminal
Records
Greenwood County Courthouse
311 N. Main
Eureka, KS 67045
(316) 583-6041
Fax (316) 583-6798
Felony and misdemeanor records are available by mail or fax. No release necessary.
$9.00 fee per hour. $.25 fee per copy. $1.00
for certification. Fax fees will vary. Search
information required: name, date of birth,
years to search.

Civil records are available by mail or fax.
No release necessary. $9.00 fee per hour
searched. $.25 fee per copy. $1.00 for certification. Search information required:
name, SSN, years to search. Specify plaintiff or defendant.

Hamilton County

Clerk of District Court
PO Box 745
Syracuse, KS 67878
(316) 384-5159
Records are available in person only. See
Kansas state repository for additional infor-
mation.

Civil records are available by mail. No release necessary. No search fee. $.25 fee per
copy. $1.00 for certification. Search infor-
mation required: name, SSN, years to
search. Specify plaintiff or defendant.

Harper County

Clerk of District Court, Criminal
Records
PO Box 467
Anthony, KS 67003
(316) 842-3721
Fax (316) 842-5937
Felony and misdemeanor records are avail-
able in person only. See Kansas state repos-
itory for additional information.

Civil records are available in person only.
See Kansas state repository for additional
information.

Harvey County

Clerk of District Court, Criminal
Records
PO Box 665
Newton, KS 67114
(316) 284-6890
Felony and misdemeanor records are available by mail or phone. No release necessary. No fee. Search information required:
name, date of birth, years to search, offense, if possible.

Civil records are available by mail or
phone. No release necessary. No search fee.
$.20 fee per copy. $1.00 for certification.
Search information required: name, SSN,
years to search. Specify plaintiff or defendant.

Haskell County

Clerk of District Court
PO Box 146
Sublette, KS 67877
(316) 675-2671
Felony and misdemeanor records are available in person only. See Kansas state repository for additional information.

Civil records are available in person only.
See Kansas state repository for additional
information.

Hodgeman County

Clerk of District Court, Criminal
Records
PO Box 187
Jetmore, KS 67854
(316) 357-6522
Fax (316) 357-8300
Felony and misdemeanor records are avail-
able by mail, phone or fax. No release nec-
essary. No search fee. Search information
required: name, date of birth.

Civil records are available by mail or
phone. No release necessary. No search fee.
$.25 fee per copy. $1.00 for certification.
Search information required: name. Specify
plaintiff or defendant.

Jackson County

Courthouse
Holton, KS 66436
(913) 364-2191
Records are available in person only. See Kansas state repository for additional information.

Civil records are available in person only. See Kansas state repository for additional information.

Jefferson County

Clerk of District Court, Criminal Records
PO Box 312
Oskaloosa, KS 66066
(913) 863-2461
Felony and misdemeanor records are available by mail. A release is required. No search fee. $.25 fee per copy. Search information required: name, address, date of birth, SSN, years to search, SASE.

Civil records are available in person only. See Kansas state repository for additional information.

Jewell County

First Line District Court
Courthouse - Criminal Records
307 N. Commercial
Mankato, KS 66956
(913) 378-3651
Felony and misdemeanor records are available by mail or phone. No release necessary. No search fee. Search information required: name, date of birth.

Civil records are available by mail or phone. No release necessary. No search fee. $.25 fee per copy. $1.00 for certification. Search information required: name, SSN, years to search. Specify plaintiff or defendant.

Johnson County

Clerk of District Court, Criminal Records
PO Box 1600
Olathe, KS 66061
(913) 782-5000 Ext. 5587
Felony records are available in person only. See Kansas state repository for additional information.

Civil records are available in person only. See Kansas state repository for additional information.

Kearny County

Clerk of District Court, Criminal Records
PO Box 64
Lakin, KS 67860
(316) 355-6481
Felony records are available in person only. If specific case is known, copies can be made and mailed. See Kansas state repository for additional information.

Civil records are available by mail. No release necessary. No search fee. $.25 fee per copy. $1.00 for certification. Search information required: name, SSN, years to search. Specify plaintiff or defendant.

Kingman County

Clerk of District Court
PO Box 495
Kingman, KS 67068
(316) 532-5151
Fax (316) 532-2952
Felony and misdemeanor records are available by mail, phone or fax. No release necessary. No search fee. $.25 fee per copy. $1.00 for certification. Search information required: name, SASE, years to search.

Civil records are available by mail or phone. No release necessary. No search fee. $.25 fee per copy. $1.00 for certification. Search information required: name, SSN, years to search. Specify plaintiff or defendant.

Kiowa County

Clerk of District Court, Criminal Records
211 E. Florida
Greensburg, KS 67054
(316) 723-3317
Felony and misdemeanor records are available by mail. No release necessary. Search fee: $1.00 per hour. $.25 fee per copy. $1.00 for certification. Search information required: name, years to search, SASE.

Civil records are available by mail. No release necessary. No search fee. $.25 fee per copy. $1.00 for certification. Search information required: name, SSN, years to search. Specify plaintiff or defendant.

Labette County

Labette County District Court
Courthouse
Oswego, KS 67356
(316) 795-4533
Records are available by mail. A release is required. No search fee. $.25 fee per copy, $1.25 fee for certification. Search information required: name, date of birth, years to search.

Civil records are available by mail. A release is required. No search fee. $.25 fee per copy. $1.00 for certification. Search information required: name, SSN, years to search. Specify plaintiff or defendant.

Lane County

Lane County District Court, Criminal Records
PO Box 188
Dighton, KS 67839
(316) 397-2802
Felony and misdemeanor records are available by mail. No release necessary. $9.00 fee per hour. $.25 fee per copy. $1.00 for certification. Any check payable to District Court Clerk. Search information required: name, previous address, present address, years to search.

Civil records are available by mail. No release necessary. No search fee. Search information required: name, SSN, years to search. Specify plaintiff or defendant.

Leavenworth County

Clerk of District Court, Criminal Records
4th & Walnut
Leavenworth, KS 66048
(913) 684-0704
Records are available in person only. See Kansas state repository for additional information.

Civil records are available in person only. See Kansas state repository for additional information.

Lincoln County

Courthouse, Criminal Records
216 E. Lincoln
Lincoln, KS 67455
(913) 524-4057
Felony and misdemeanor records are available by mail. A release is required. No search fee. $.25 fee per copy. $1.00 for certification. Search information required: name, years to search.

Civil records are available by mail. A release is required. No search fee. $.25 fee per copy. $1.00 for certification. Search information required: name, SSN, years to search. Specify plaintiff or defendant.

Linn County

Clerk of District Court
PO Box B
Mound City, KS 66056
(913) 795-2660
Records are available in person only. See Kansas state repository for additional information.

Civil records are available in person only. See Kansas state repository for additional information.

Logan County

Clerk of District Court
710 W. 2nd Street
Oakley, KS 67748
(913) 672-3654
Felony and misdemeanor records are available by mail. No release required. No search fee. $.25 fee per copy. $1.00 for certification. Search information: name, years to search.

Civil records are available by mail. No release necessary. No search fee. $.25 fee per copy. $1.00 for certification. Search information required: name, SSN, years to search. Specify plaintiff or defendant.

Lyon County

Lyon County Courthouse
402 Commercial
Emporia, KS 66801
(316) 342-4950
Records are available in person only. See Kansas state repository for additional information.

Civil records are available by mail. No release necessary. $9.00 fee per hour searched. $.50 fee per copy. $2.00 for certification. Search information required: name, years to search. Specify plaintiff or defendant.

Marion County

Clerk of District Court
Box 298
Marion, KS 66861
(316) 382-2104
Records are available in person only. See Kansas state repository for additional information.

Civil records are available in person only. See Kansas state repository for additional information.

Marshall County

Clerk of District Court, Criminal Records
PO Box 86
Marysville, KS 66508
(913) 562-5301
Fax (913) 562-5685

Felony and misdemeanor records are available by mail or fax. No release necessary. Search fee: $6.50 per hour. Any check payable to Clerk of District Court. Search information required: name, SSN, date of birth, years to search.

Civil records are available in person only. See Kansas state repository for additional information.

McPherson County

Clerk of District Court, Criminal Records
PO Box 1106
McPherson, KS 67460
(316) 241-3422

Felony and misdemeanor records are available by mail or phone. No release necessary. No search fee. Search information required: name, years to search.

Civil records are available by mail. No release necessary. $9.00 fee per hour searched. $.25 fee per copy. Search information required: name, SSN, years to search. Specify plaintiff or defendant.

Meade County

Clerk of District Court, Criminal Records
PO Box 727
Meade, KS 67864
(316) 873-8750

Felony and misdemeanor records are available by mail. No release necessary. $9.00 search fee per hour. $.50 fee per copy. $1.50 fee for certification. Search information required: name, years to search, case number, if available.

Civil records are available by mail. No release necessary. $9.00 fee per hour searched. $.50 fee per copy. $1.00 for certification. Search information required: name, SSN, years to search. Specify plaintiff or defendant.

Miami County

Clerk of District Court, Criminal Records
PO Box 187
Paola, KS 66071
(913) 294-3326

Felony and misdemeanor records are available by mail. No release necessary. $9.00 fee per hour. $.25 fee per copy. $1.00 fee for certification. Check payable to Clerk of District. Search information required: name, years to search.

Civil records are available by mail or phone. No release necessary. $9.00 fee per hour searched. $.25 fee per copy. $1.00 for certification. Search information required: name, SSN, years to search. Specify plaintiff or defendant.

Mitchell County

Clerk of District Court, Criminal Records
115 S. Hersey
Beloit, KS 67420
(913) 738-3753

Felony and misdemeanor records are available by mail. No release necessary. No search fee. $.25 fee per copy. $1.00 for certification. Search information required: name, date of birth, years to search.

Civil records are available by mail or phone. No release necessary. No search fee. $.25 fee per copy. $1.00 for certification. Search information required: name, SSN, years to search. Specify plaintiff or defendant.

Montgomery County

Clerk of District Court, Criminal Records
PO Box 768
Independence, KS 67301
(316) 331-2550

Felony and misdemeanor records are available by mail. No release necessary. No search fee. Search information required: name and years to search.

Civil records are available by mail. No release necessary. No search fee. $.25 fee per copy. $1.00 for certification. Search information required: name, SSN, years to search. Specify plaintiff or defendant.

Morris County

Morris County Courthouse, Clerk of District Court
Council Grove, KS 66846
(316) 767-6838

Felony and misdemeanor records are available by mail. No release necessary. $9.00 fee per hour. Any check payable to Clerk of District Court. Search information required: name, years to search.

Civil records are available by mail . A release is required. $9.00 fee per hour searched. $1.00 fee per copy. $1.00 for certification. Search information required: name, SSN, years to search. Specify plaintiff or defendant.

Morton County

Clerk of District Court, Criminal Records
PO Box 825
Elkhart, KS 67950
(316) 697-2563

Felony and misdemeanor records are available by mail. A release is required. $6.00 fee per hour. Certified check only, payable to Clerk of District Court. Search information required: name, years to search.

Civil records are available by mail or phone. No release necessary. No search fee. $.10 fee per copy. $1.00 for certification. Search information required: name, SSN, years to search. Specify plaintiff or defendant.

Nemaha County

Clerk of District Court, Criminal Records
PO Box 213
Seneca, KS 66538
(913) 336-2146
Fax (913) 336-3373

Felony and misdemeanor records are available by mail or fax. A release is required. $9.00 fee per hour. $1.00 fee to send fax request, $3.00 fee to receive first page of fax and $2.00 fee for additional pages. Certified check only, payable to Clerk of District Court. Search information required: name, date of birth, years to search.

Civil records are available by mail or fax. No release necessary. No search fee. $.50 for first copy. $.25 each additional copy. $1.00 for certification. Search information required: name, SSN, years to search. Specify plaintiff or defendant.

Neosho County

Clerk of District Court, Criminal Records
101 S. Lincoln
PO Box 889
Chanute, KS 66720
(316) 431-2410

Felony and misdemeanor records are available by mail. A release is required. $9.80 fee per hour. $.25 fee per copy. $1.00 for certification. Make check payable to Clerk of District Court. Search information required: name, date of birth, years to search. Write county for proper form.

Civil records are available by mail. No release necessary. No search fee. $.25 fee per copy. $1.00 for certification. Search information required: name, SSN, years to search. Specify plaintiff or defendant.

Ness County

Clerk of District Court, Criminal Records
PO Box 445
Ness City, KS 67560
(913) 798-3693
Fax (913) 798-3829

Felony and misdemeanor records are available by mail or fax. A release is required. No fee. Certified check only, payable to Clerk of District Court. Search information required: name, SSN, date of birth, sex, race, years to search.

Civil records are available by mail. A release is required. No search fee. $.25 fee per copy. $1.00 for certification. Search information required: name, SSN, years to search. Specify plaintiff or defendant.

Norton County

Clerk of District Court
PO Box 70
Norton, KS 67654
(913) 877-5177

Records are available in person only. See Kansas state repository for additional information.

Civil records are available in person only. See Kansas state repository for additional information.

Osage County

Clerk of District Court
PO Box 549
Lyndon, KS 66451
(913) 828-4713
Fax (913) 828-4896

Felony and misdemeanor records are available by mail or fax. $9.50 fee per hour. $2.50 fee plus $.50 per page for fax request, prepaid. No release necessary. Company check payable to Clerk of District Court. Search information required: name, years to search.

Civil records are available by mail. No release necessary. $9.50 search fee includes copying and certification. Search information required: name, SSN, years to search. Specify plaintiff or defendant.

Osborne County

Clerk of Court, Criminal Records
County Courthouse
Osborne, KS 67473
(913) 346-5911
Fax (913) 346-2442

Felony and misdemeanor records are available by mail, phone or fax. No release necessary. $2.00 search fee. Company check payable to Clerk of Court. Search information required: name, years to search.

Civil records are available by mail. No release necessary. No search fee. Search information required: name, SSN, years to search. Specify plaintiff or defendant.

Ottawa County

Clerk of District Court, Criminal Records
307 N. Concord
Minneapolis, KS 67467
(913) 392-2917

Felony and misdemeanor records are available by mail $9.00 per hour search fee. $.35 fee per copy. $1.00 for certification. Contact the above location for form.

Civil records are available by mail or phone. No release necessary. $9.00 fee per hour searched. $.25 fee per copy. $1.00 for certification. Search information required: name, SSN, years to search. Specify plaintiff or defendant.

Pawnee County

Clerk of District Court, Criminal Records
PO Box 270
Larned, KS 67550
(316) 285-6937
Fax (316) 285-3665

Felony and misdemeanor records are available by mail or fax. No release necessary. No search fee. $.25 fee per copy. $1.00 for certification. Check payable to Clerk of District Court. Search information required: name, years to search.

Civil records are available by mail. No release necessary. No search fee. $.25 fee per copy. $1.00 for certification. Search information required: name, SSN, years to search. Specify plaintiff or defendant.

Phillips County

Courthouse
Phillipsburg, KS 67661
(913) 543-2024
Fax (913) 543-2440

Records are available in person only. See Kansas state repository for additional information.

Civil records are available in person only. See Kansas state repository for additional information.

Pottawatomie County

Clerk of District Court, Criminal Records
PO Box 129
Westmoreland, KS 66549
(913) 457-3392
Fax (913) 457-3507

Felony and misdemeanor records are available by mail or fax. No release necessary. No search fee. $.15 fee per copy. $1.00 for certification. Search information required: name, years to search.

Civil records are available by mail. No release necessary. No search fee. Search information required: name, SSN, years to search. Specify plaintiff or defendant.

Pratt County

Clerk of District Court, Criminal Records
PO box 984
Pratt, KS 67124
(316) 672-5995
Fax (316) 672-2902

Felony and misdemeanor records are available by mail or fax. No release necessary. $9.00 fee per hour searched. $.25 fee per copy. $1.00 for certification. Search information required: name, years to search.

Civil records are available by mail or phone. No release necessary. No search fee. Search information required: name, SSN, years to search. Specify plaintiff or defendant.

Rawlins County

Clerk of District Court
PO Box 257
Atwood, KS 67730
(913) 626-3465

Felony and misdemeanor records are available by mail. No search fee. $.25 fee per copy. $1,.00 for certification. Search information required : name.

Civil records are available by mail or phone. No release necessary. No search fee. Search information required: name, SSN, years to search. Specify plaintiff or defendant.

Reno County

Clerk of District Court, Criminal Records
206 W. 1st
Hutchinson, KS 67501
(316) 665-2956

Felony and misdemeanor records are available by mail. No release necessary. $.75 for each 5 minutes searched. $.25 fee per copy. $1.00 for certification. Search information required: name, years to search, SASE.

Civil records are available by mail or phone. No release necessary. No search fee. Search information required: name, SSN, years to search. Specify plaintiff or defendant.

Republic County

Clerk of District Court, Criminal Records
PO Box 8
Belleville, KS 66935
(913) 527-5691
Fax (913) 527-2717

Felony and misdemeanor records are available by mail or fax. No release necessary. Search fee ranges from $2.00–$9.00 per hour. $3.00 fee for first page of fax response. $1.00 for each additional page. Search information required: name, years to search,

Civil records are available by mail. No release necessary. No search fee. Search information required: name, SSN, years to search. Specify plaintiff or defendant.

Rice County

Clerk of District Court, Criminal Records
101 W. Commercial
Lyons, KS 67554
(316) 257-2383
Fax (316) 257-3826

Felony and misdemeanor records are available by mail or fax. $1.50 fee for fax request. No release necessary. $9.00 search fee per hour. $1.00 fee for first copy, $.25 for each additional copy. Search information required: name, date of birth, years to search, case number.

Civil records are available by mail. No release necessary. No search fee. Search information required: name, SSN, years to search. Specify plaintiff or defendant.

Riley County

Clerk of District Court, Criminal Records
PO Box 158
100 Courthouse Plaza
Manhattan, KS 66502
(913) 537-6364

Felony and misdemeanor records are available by mail. No release necessary. $9.00 fee per hour. $.25 fee per copy. $1.00 fee for certification. Search information required: name, date of birth, years to search, SASE. Turnaround time is 3 days.

Civil records are available by mail or phone. No release necessary. No search fee. Search information required: name, SSN, years to search. Specify plaintiff or defendant.

Rooks County

Clerk of District Court, Criminal Records
PO Box 531
Stockton, KS 67669
(913) 425-6718

Felony and misdemeanor records are available by mail. No release necessary. $9.00 fee per hour. $.25 fee per copy. $1.00 fee for certification. Certified check only, payable to Clerk of Court. Search information required: name.

Civil records are available by mail. No release necessary. No search fee. Search information required: name, SSN, years to search. Specify plaintiff or defendant.

Rush County

Rush County District Court, Criminal Records
PO Box 387
La Crosse, KS 67548
(913) 222-2718
Felony and misdemeanor records are available by mail. No release necessary. $8.50 fee per hour. $.25 fee per copy. $1.00 for certification. Search information required: name, years to search.

Civil records are available by mail or phone. No release necessary. No search fee. Search information required: name, SSN, years to search. Specify plaintiff or defendant.

Russell County

Clerk of District Court, Criminal Records
PO Box 876
Russell, KS 67665
(913) 483-5641
Felony and misdemeanor records are available by mail. No release necessary. $9.00 fee per hour. $.35 fee per copy. Certified check only, payable to Clerk of District Court. Search information required: name, driver's license number, years to search.

Civil records are available by mail. No release necessary. No search fee. Search information required: name, SSN, years to search. Specify plaintiff or defendant.

Saline County

Clerk of District Court
PO Box 1756
300 W. Ash
Salina, KS 67402-1756
(913) 826-6617
Felony and misdemeanor records are available by mail. A release is required. Search fee: $9.00 per hour. $.25 fee per copy. $1.00 for certification. Search information required: name, years to search.

Civil records are available by mail. No release necessary. No search fee. Search information required: name, SSN, years to search. Specify plaintiff or defendant.

Scott County

Clerk of District Court, Criminal Records
303 Court
Scott City, KS 67871
(316) 872-7208
Felony and misdemeanor records are available by mail. No release necessary. $6.00 fee per hour. Certified check only, payable to Clerk of District Court. Search information required: name, SSN, date of birth, years to search.

Civil records are available by mail. No release necessary. No search fee. Search information required: name, SSN, years to search. Specify plaintiff or defendant.

Sedgwick County

Clerk of District Court, Criminal Dept.
Room 714
525 N. Main
Wichita, KS 67203
(316) 383-7302
Fax (316) 383-7560
Felony and misdemeanor records are available by mail or fax. No release necessary. $8.00 fee per hour. $.25 fee per copy. $1.00 for certification. Any check payable to Clerk of District Court. Search information required: name, SSN, date of birth, sex, race.

Civil records are available by mail or phone. No release necessary. No search fee. $.25 fee per copy. $1.00 for certification. Search information required: name, SSN, years to search. Specify plaintiff or defendant.

Seward County

Clerk of District Court
415 N. Washington
Liberal, KS 67901
(316) 626-3238
Fax (316) 626-3211
Felony and misdemeanor records are available in person only. See Kansas state repository for additional information.

Civil records are available by mail. No release necessary. No search fee. $.25 fee per copy. $1.00 for certification. Search information required: name, SSN, years to search. Specify plaintiff or defendant.

Shawnee County

Clerk of District Court
200 SE. 7th
Topeka, KS 66603
(913) 291-4327
Felony records are available by mail. $.50 fee per copy. $9.00 search fee. $1.25 for certification. No release necessary. Search information required: name, years to search, SASE.

Civil records are available by mail. No release necessary. No search fee. Search information required: name, SSN, years to search. Specify plaintiff or defendant.

Sheridan County

Clerk of District Court, Criminal Records
PO Box 753
Hoxie, KS 67740
(913) 675-3451
Fax (913) 675-3050
Felony and misdemeanor records are available by mail or fax. No release necessary. $7.00 fee per hour. $.25 fee per copy. $1.00 for certification. Any check payable to Clerk of District Court. Search information required: name, date of birth, years to search.

Civil records are available in person only. See Kansas state repository for additional information.

Sherman County

Clerk of District Court
813 Broadway
Goodland, KS 67735
(913) 899-5681
Felony records are available by mail. No release necessary. Search fee: $6.50 per hour. Search information required: full name, date and type of offense.

Civil records are available in person only. See Kansas state repository for additional information.

Smith County

Clerk of District Court, Criminal Records
PO Box 273
Smith Center, KS 66967
(913) 282-6871
Fax (913) 282-3291
Felony and misdemeanor records are available by mail or fax. A release is required. No search fee. $.25 fee per copy. $1.00 for certification. Search information required: name, years to search.

Civil records are available by mail. No release necessary. No search fee. Search information required: name, SSN, years to search. Specify plaintiff or defendant.

Stafford County

Clerk of District Court, Criminal Records
PO Box 365
St. John, KS 67576
(316) 549-3295
Fax (316) 549-3298
Felony records are available by mail or fax. $9.00 fee per hour. $.35 fee per copy. $1.50 fee per page for fax request. $2.50 fee per page for fax response. No release necessary. Search information required: name, years to search.

Civil records are available by mail or phone. No release necessary. No search fee. Search information required: name, SSN, years to search. Specify plaintiff or defendant.

Stanton County

Clerk of District Court, Criminal Records
PO Box 543
Johnson, KS 67855
(316) 492-2180
Fax (316) 492-2688
Felony and misdemeanor records are available by mail or fax. No release necessary. $9.00 search fee per hour. $.25 fee per copy. $1.00 fee for certification. Check payable to Stanton County District Court. Search information required: name, years to search, SASE.

Civil records are available by mail or phone. No release necessary. No search fee. Search information required: name, SSN, years to search. Specify plaintiff or defendant.

Stevens County

Clerk of District Court, Criminal Records
200 E. 6th
Hugoton, KS 67951
(316) 544-2484
Fax (316) 544-2528
Felony and misdemeanor records are available by mail or fax. No release necessary. $8.40 search fee per hour. $.10 fee per copy. $1.00 for certification. Search information required: name, date of birth, years to search.

Civil records are available by mail. No release necessary. No search fee. Search information required: name, SSN, years to search. Specify plaintiff or defendant.

Sumner County

Clerk of District Court
PO Box 399
Wellington, KS 67152
(316) 326-5936

Felony and misdemeanor records are available by mail. No release necessary. $9.70 search fee per hour. $.25 fee per copy. $2.00 for certification. Search information required: name, years to search.

Civil records are available by mail or phone. No release necessary. Search information required: name, SSN, years to search. Specify plaintiff or defendant.

Thomas County

Clerk of District Court
PO Box 805
Colby, KS 67701
(913) 462-2462

Records are available in person only. See Kansas state repository for additional information.

Civil records are available in person only. See Kansas state repository for additional information.

Trego County

Clerk of District Court
216 N. Main
Wakeeney, KS 67672
(913) 743-2148
Fax (913) 743-2461

Felony and misdemeanor records are available by mail or fax. No release necessary. $9.00 search fee per hour. $.20 fee per copy. $2.00 for certification. Search information required: name, years to search.

Civil records are available by mail. No release necessary. Search information required: name, SSN, years to search. Specify plaintiff or defendant.

Wabaunsee County

Clerk of District Court
Courthouse
Alma, KS 66401
(913) 765-3622
Fax (913) 765-2339

Felony and misdemeanor records are available by mail or fax. No release necessary. $9.00 search fee per hour. $.25 fee per copy. $1.00 for certification. Search information required: name, years to search, case number.

Civil records are available by mail or phone. No release necessary. Search information required: name, SSN, years to search. Specify plaintiff or defendant.

Wallace County

Clerk of District Court, Criminal Records
PO Box 8
Sharon Springs, KS 67758
(913) 852-4289

Felony and misdemeanor records are available by mail. No release necessary. $9.00 search fee per hour. $.25 fee per copy. $1.00 for certification. Search information required: name, years to search.

Civil records are available by mail. No release necessary. Search information required: name, SSN, years to search. Specify plaintiff or defendant.

Washington County

Courthouse, Criminal Records
Clerk of District Court
Washington, KS 66968
(913) 325-2381 or 2953

Felony and misdemeanor records are available by mail. A release is required. $2.00 search fee. $.25 fee per copy. $1.00 for certification. Search information required: name, years to search, SASE.

Civil records are available by mail. No release necessary. Search information required: name, SSN, years to search. Specify plaintiff or defendant.

Wichita County

Courthouse, Criminal Records
P.O. Box 968
Leoti, KS 67861
(316) 375-4454

Felony and misdemeanor records are available by mail. No release necessary. $9.00 search fee per hour. $.25 fee per copy. $1.00 for certification. Search information required: name, years to search.

Civil records are available by mail. No release necessary. Search information required: name, SSN, years to search. Specify plaintiff or defendant.

Wilson County

Clerk of District Court
PO Box 246
Fredonia, KS 66736
(316) 378-4533

Felony and misdemeanor records are available by mail. No release necessary. No search fee. $.25 fee per copy. $1.00 for certification. Search information required: name, years to search.

Civil records are available by mail. No release necessary. Search information required: name, SSN, years to search. Specify plaintiff or defendant.

Woodson County

Clerk of District Court, Criminal Records
PO Box 228
Yates Center, KS 66783
(316) 625-2187

Felony and misdemeanor records are available by mail. No release necessary. $9.40 search fee per hour. $.25 fee per copy. $1.00 for certification. Search information required: name, years to search.

Civil records are available by mail or phone. No release necessary. Search information required: name, SSN, years to search. Specify plaintiff or defendant.

Wyandotte County

Felony and misdemeanor records
Clerk of District Court, Criminal Records
710 N. 7th
Kansas City, KS 66101
(913) 573-2905

Felony and misdemeanor (since 1977) records are available by mail. No release necessary. No search fee. $1.00 fee for first copy, $.25 fee for each additional copy. Search information required: name, SSN, date of birth.

Civil records
Clerk of District Court, Criminal Records
710 N. 7th
Kansas City, KS 66101
(913) 573-2901

Civil records are available by mail or phone. No release necessary. $.25 fee per copy. $1.00 for certification. Search information required: name, SSN, years to search. Specify plaintiff or defendant.

City-County Cross Reference

Benedict *Wilson*
Bennington *Ottawa*
Bentley *Sedgwick*
Benton *Butler*
Bern *Nemaha*
Berryton *Shawnee*
Beverly *Lincoln*
Bird City *Cheyenne*
Bison *Rush*
Bloom *Ford*
Blue Mound *Linn*
Blue Rapids *Marshall*
Bluff City *Harper*
Bogue *Graham*
Bonner Springs *Wyandotte*
Bremen *Marshall*
Brewster *Thomas*
Bronson *Bourbon*
Brookville *Saline*
Brownell *Ness*
Bucklin *Ford*
Bucyrus *Miami*
Buffalo *Wilson*
Buhler *Reno*
Bunker Hill *Russell*
Burden *Cowley*
Burdett *Pawnee*
Burdick *Morris*
Burlingame *Osage*
Burlington *Coffey*
Burns *Marion*
Burr Oak *Jewell*
Burrton *Harvey*
Bushton *Rice*
Byers *Pratt*
Caldwell *Sumner*
Cambridge *Cowley*
Caney *Montgomery*
Canton *McPherson*
Carbondale *Osage*
Carlton *Dickinson*
Carlyle *Allen*
Carona *Cherokee*
Cassoday *Butler*
Catharine *Ellis*
Cawker City *Mitchell*
Cedar *Smith*
Cedar Point *Chase*
Cedar Vale *Chautauqua*
Centerville *Linn*
Centralia *Nemaha*
Chanute *Neosho*
Chapman *Dickinson*
Chase *Rice*
Chautauqua *Chautauqua*
Cheney *Sedgwick*
Cherokee *Crawford*
Cherryvale *Montgomery*
Chetopa *Labette*
Cimarron *Gray*
Circleville *Jackson*
Claflin *Barton*
Clay Center *Clay*
Clayton *Norton*
Clearwater *Sedgwick*
Clements *Chase*
Clifton *Washington*
Climax *Greenwood*
Clyde *Cloud*
Coats *Pratt*
Codell *Rooks*
Coffeyville *Montgomery*
Colby *Thomas*
Coldwater *Comanche*
Collyer *Trego*

Colony *Anderson*
Columbus *Cherokee*
Colwich *Sedgwick*
Concordia *Cloud*
Conway Springs *Sumner*
Coolidge *Hamilton*
Copeland *Gray*
Corning *Nemaha*
Cottonwood Falls *Chase*
Council Grove *Morris*
Courtland *Republic*
Coyville *Wilson*
Crestline *Cherokee*
Cuba *Republic*
Cummings *Atchison*
Cunningham *Kingman*
Damar *Rooks*
Danville *Harper*
Dearing *Montgomery*
Deerfield *Kearny*
Delavan *Morris*
Delia *Jackson*
Delphos *Ottawa*
Denison *Jackson*
Dennis *Labette*
Densmore *Norton*
Denton *Doniphan*
Derby *Sedgwick*
DeSoto *Johnson*
Devon *Bourbon*
Dexter *Cowley*
Dighton *Lane*
Dodge City *Ford*
Dorrance *Russell*
Douglass *Butler*
Dover *Shawnee*
Downs *Osborne*
Dresden *Decatur*
Dunlap *Morris*
Durham *Marion*
Dwight *Morris*
Eastborough *Sedgwick*
Easton *Leavenworth*
Edgerton *Johnson*
Edmond *Norton*
Edna *Labette*
Edson *Sherman*
Edwardsville *Wyandotte*
Effingham *Atchison*
Elbing *Butler*
El Dorado *Butler*
Elk City *Montgomery*
Elk Falls *Elk*
Elkhart *Morton*
Ellinwood *Barton*
Ellis *Ellis*
Ellsworth *Ellsworth*
Elmdale *Chase*
Elsmore *Allen*
Elwood *Doniphan*
Emmett *Pottawatomie*
Emporia *Lyon*
Englewood *Clark*
Ensign *Gray*
Enterprise *Dickinson*
Erie *Neosho*
Esbon *Jewell*
Eskridge *Wabaunsee*
Eudora *Douglas*
Eureka *Greenwood*
Everest *Brown*
Fairview *Brown*
Fairway *Johnson*
Fall River *Greenwood*
Falun *Saline*

Farlington *Crawford*
Florence *Marion*
Fontana *Miami*
Ford *Ford*
Formoso *Jewell*
Fort Dodge *Ford*
Fort Scott *Bourbon*
Fowler *Meade*
Frankfort *Marshall*
Franklin *Crawford*
Fredonia *Wilson*
Freeport *Harper*
Friend *Finney*
Frontenec *Crawford*
Fulton *Bourbon*
Galena *Cherokee*
Galesburg *Neosho*
Galva *McPherson*
Garden City *Finney*
Garden Plain *Sedgwick*
Gardner *Johnson*
Garfield *Pawnee*
Garland *Bourbon*
Garnett *Anderson*
Gas *Allen*
Gaylord *Smith*
Gem *Thomas*
Geneseo *Rice*
Geuda Springs *Sumner*
Girard *Crawford*
Glade *Phillips*
Glasco *Cloud*
Glen Elder *Mitchell*
Goddard *Sedgwick*
Goessel *Marion*
Goff *Nemaha*
Goodland *Sherman*
Gorham *Russell*
Gove *Gove*
Grainfield *Gove*
Grantville *Jefferson*
Great Bend *Barton*
Greeley *Anderson*
Green *Clay*
Greenleaf *Washington*
Greensburg *Kiowa*
Grenola *Elk*
Greenwich Heights
  Sedgwick
Gridley *Coffey*
Grinnell *Gove*
Gypsum *Saline*
Haddam *Washington*
Hallowell *Cherokee*
Halstead *Harvey*
Hamilton *Greenwood*
Hanover *Washington*
Hanston *Hodgeman*
Hardtner *Barber*
Harlan *Smith*
Harper *Harper*
Hartford *Lyon*
Harveyville *Wabaunsee*
Havana *Montgomery*
Haven *Reno*
Havensville *Pottawatomie*
Haviland *Kiowa*
Hays *Ellis*
Haysville *Sedgwick*
Hazelton *Barber*
Healy *Lane*
Hepler *Crawford*
Herington *Dickinson*
Herndon *Rawlins*
Hesston *Harvey*

Hiattville *Bourbon*
Hiawatha *Brown*
Highland *Doniphan*
Hill City *Graham*
Hillsboro *Marion*
Hillsdale *Miami*
Hoisington *Barton*
Holcomb *Finney*
Hollenberg *Washington*
Holton *Jackson*
Holyrood *Ellsworth*
Home *Marshall*
Hope *Dickinson*
Horton *Brown*
Howard *Elk*
Hoxie *Sheridan*
Hoyt *Jackson*
Hudson *Stafford*
Hugoton *Stevens*
Humboldt *Allen*
Hunter *Mitchell*
Huron *Atchison*
Hutchinson *Reno*
Independence *Montgomery*
Ingalls *Gray*
Inman *McPherson*
Iola *Allen*
Ionia *Jewell*
Isabel *Barber*
Iuka *Pratt*
Jamestown *Cloud*
Jennings *Decatur*
Jetmore *Hodgeman*
Jewell *Jewell*
Johnson *Stanton*
Junction City *Geary*
Kalvesta *Finney*
Kanopolis *Ellsworth*
Kanorado *Sherman*
Kansas City *Wyandotte*
Kechi *Sedgwick*
Kelly *Nemaha*
Kendall *Hamilton*
Kensington *Smith*
Kincaid *Anderson*
Kingman *Kingman*
Kingsdown *Ford*
Kinsley *Edwards*
Kiowa *Barber*
Kirwin *Phillips*
Kismet *Seward*
LaCrosse *Rush*
LaCygne *Linn*
Lafontaine *Wilson*
LaHarpe *Allen*
Lake City *Barber*
Lakeshore *Shawnee*
Lakin *Kearny*
Lancaster *Atchison*
Lane *Franklin*
Langdon *Reno*
Lansing *Leavenworth*
Larned *Pawnee*
Latham *Butler*
Lawrence *Douglas*
Lawton *Cherokee*
Leavenworth *Leavenworth*
Leawood *Johnson*
Lebanon *Smith*
Lebo *Coffey*
Lecompton *Douglas*
Lehigh *Marion*
Lenexa *Johnson*
Lenora *Norton*
Leon *Butler*

Leonardville *Riley*
Leoti *Wichita*
Le Roy *Coffey*
Levant *Thomas*
Lewis *Edwards*
Liberal *Seward*
Liberty *Montgomery*
Liebenthal *Rush*
Lincoln *Lincoln*
Lincolnville *Marion*
Lindsborg *McPherson*
Linn *Washington*
Linwood *Leavenworth*
Little River *Rice*
Logan *Phillips*
Longford *Clay*
Long Island *Phillips*
Longton *Elk*
Lorraine *Ellsworth*
Lost Springs *Marion*
Louisburg *Miami*
Louisville *Pottawatomie*
Lucas *Russell*
Ludell *Rawlins*
Luray *Russell*
Lyndon *Osage*
Lyons *Rice*
McCracken *Rush*
McCune *Crawford*
McDonald *Rawlins*
McLouth *Jefferson*
McPherson *McPherson*
Macksville *Stafford*
Madison *Greenwood*
Mahaska *Washington*
Maize *Sedgwick*
Manchester *Dickinson*
Manhattan *Riley*
Mankato *Jewell*
Manter *Stanton*
Maple City *Cowley*
Maple Hill *Wabaunsee*
Mapleton *Bourbon*
Marienthal *Wichita*
Marion *Marion*
Marquette *McPherson*
Marysville *Marshall*
Matfield Green *Chase*
Mayetta *Jackson*
Mayfield *Sumner*
Meade *Meade*
Medicine Lodge *Barber*
Medora *Reno*
Melvern *Osage*
Menlo *Thomas*
Mentor *Saline*
Meriden *Jefferson*
Merriam *Johnson*
Midland Park *Sedgwick*
Milan *Sumner*
Milford *Geary*
Milton *Sumner*
Miltonvale *Cloud*
Minneapolis *Ottawa*
Minneola *Clark*
Mission *Johnson*
Mission Hills *Johnson*
Modoc *Scott*
Moline *Elk*
Montezuma *Gray*
Monument *Logan*
Moran *Allen*
Morganville *Clay*
Morland *Graham*
Morrill *Brown*

Morrowville *Washington*
Moscow *Stevens*
Mound City *Linn*
Moundridge *McPherson*
Mound Valley *Labette*
Mount Hope *Sedgwick*
Mulberry *Crawford*
Mullinville *Kiowa*
Mulvane *Sumner*
Munden *Republic*
Murdock *Kingman*
Muscotah *Atchison*
Narka *Republic*
Nashville *Kingman*
Natoma *Osborne*
Neal *Greenwood*
Nekoma *Rush*
Neodesha *Wilson*
Neosho Falls *Woodson*
Neosho Rapids *Lyon*
Ness City *Ness*
Netawaka *Jackson*
New Albany *Wilson*
New Almelo *Norton*
New Cambria *Saline*
Newton *Harvey*
Nickerson *Reno*
Niotaze *Chautauqua*
Norcatur *Decatur*
North Newton *Harvey*
Norton *Norton*
Nortonville *Jefferson*
Norway *Republic*
Norwich *Kingman*
Oakhill *Clay*
Oaklawn *Sedgwick*
Oakley *Logan*
Oberlin *Decatur*
Odin *Barton*
Offerle *Edwards*
Ogallah *Trego*
Ogden *Riley*
Oketo *Marshall*
Olathe *Johnson*
Olmitz *Barton*
Olpe *Lyon*
Olsburg *Pottawatomie*
Onaga *Pottawatomie*
Oneida *Nemaha*
Opolis *Crawford*
Osage City *Osage*
Osawatomie *Miami*
Osborne *Osborne*
Oskaloosa *Jefferson*
Oswego *Labette*
Otis *Rush*
Ottawa *Franklin*
Overbrook *Osage*
Overland Park *Johnson*
Oxford *Sumner*
Ozawkie *Jefferson*
Palco *Rooks*
Palmer *Washington*
Paola *Miami*
Paradise *Russell*
Park *Gove*
Parkcity *Sedgwick*
Parker *Linn*
Parsons *Labette*
Partridge *Reno*
Pawnee Rock *Barton*
Paxico *Wabaunsee*
Peabody *Marion*
Peck *Sedgwick*
Penalosa *Kingman*

Penokee *Graham*
Perry *Jefferson*
Peru *Chautauqua*
Pfeifer *Ellis*
Phillipsburg *Phillips*
Piedmont *Greenwood*
Pierceville *Finney*
Piqua *Woodson*
Pittsburg *Crawford*
Plains *Meade*
Plainville *Rooks*
Pleasanton *Linn*
Plevna *Reno*
Pomona *Franklin*
Portis *Osborne*
Potter *Atchison*
Potwin *Butler*
Powhattan *Brown*
Prairie View *Phillips*
Prairie Village *Johnson*
Pratt *Pratt*
Prescott *Linn*
Preston *Pratt*
Pretty Prairie *Reno*
Princeton *Franklin*
Protection *Comanche*
Quenemo *Osage*
Quinter *Gove*
Radium *Stafford*
Radley *Crawford*
Rago *Kingman*
Ramona *Marion*
Randall *Jewell*
Randolph *Riley*
Ransom *Ness*
Rantoul *Franklin*
Raymond *Rice*
Reading *Lyon*
Redfield *Bourbon*
Republic *Republic*
Rexford *Thomas*
Richfield *Morton*
Richmond *Franklin*
Riley *Riley*
River View *Sedgwick*
Riverton *Cherokee*
Robinson *Brown*
Rock *Cowley*
Roeland Park *Johnson*
Rolla *Morton*
Rosalia *Butler*
Rose Hill *Butler*
Rossville *Shawnee*
Roxbury *McPherson*
Rozel *Pawnee*
Rush Center *Rush*
Russell *Russell*
Russell Springs *Logan*
Sabetha *Nemaha*
Saint Francis *Cheyenne*
Saint George *Pottawatomie*
Saint John *Stafford*
Saint Marys *Pottawatomie*
Saint Paul *Neosho*
Salina *Saline*
Satanta *Haskell*
Savonburg *Allen*
Sawyer *Pratt*
Scammon *Cherokee*
Scandia *Republic*
Scott City *Scott*
Scranton *Osage*
Sedan *Chautauqua*
Sedgwick *Harvey*
Selden *Sheridan*

Seneca *Nemaha*
Severance *Doniphan*
Severy *Greenwood*
Seward *Stafford*
Sharon *Barber*
Sharon Springs *Wallace*
Shawnee *Johnson*
Shawnee Mission *Johnson*
Sherwood Estates *Shawnee*
Shields *Lane*
Silver Lake *Shawnee*
Simpson *Mitchell*
Smith Center *Smith*
Smolan *Saline*
Soldier *Jackson*
Solomon *Dickinson*
South Haven *Sumner*
South Hutchinson *Reno*
Spearville *Ford*
Spivey *Kingman*
Spring Hill *Johnson*
Stafford *Stafford*
Stark *Neosho*
Sterling *Rice*
Stilwell *Johnson*
Stockton *Rooks*
Strong City *Chase*
Studley *Sheridan*
Stuttgart *Phillips*
Sublette *Haskell*
Summerfield *Marshall*
Sun City *Barber*
Susank *Barton*
Sycamore *Montgomery*
Sylvan Grove *Lincoln*
Sylvia *Reno*
Syracuse *Hamilton*
Talmage *Dickinson*
Tampa *Marion*
Tecumseh *Shawnee*
Tescott *Ottawa*
Thayer *Neosho*
Timken *Rush*
Tipton *Mitchell*
Tonganoxie *Leavenworth*
Topeka *Shawnee*
Toronto *Woodson*
Towanda *Butler*
Travel Air *Sedgwick*
Treece *Cherokee*
Tribune *Greeley*
Troy *Doniphan*
Turon *Reno*
Tyro *Montgomery*
Udall *Cowley*
Ulysses *Grant*
Uniontown *Bourbon*
Utica *Ness*
Valley Center *Sedgwick*
Valley Falls *Jefferson*
Vassar *Osage*
Vermillion *Marshall*
Victoria *Ellis*
Viola *Sedgwick*
Virgil *Greenwood*
Vliets *Marshall*
Wakarusa *Shawnee*
Wakeeney *Trego*
Wakefield *Clay*
Waldo *Russell*
Waldron *Harper*
Walker *Ellis*
Wallace *Wallace*
Walnut *Crawford*
Walton *Harvey*

Wamego *Pottawatomie*
Washington *Washington*
Waterville *Marshall*
Wathena *Doniphan*
Waverly *Coffey*
Webber *Jewell*
Weir *Cherokee*
Welda *Anderson*
Wellington *Sumner*
Wells *Ottawa*
Wellsville *Franklin*
Weskan *Wallace*
West Mineral *Cherokee*
Westmoreland
    Pottawatomie
Westphalia *Anderson*
Westwood *Johnson*
Wetmore *Nemaha*
Wheaton *Pottawatomie*
Wheeler *Cheyenne*
White City *Morris*
White Cloud *Doniphan*
Whitewater *Butler*
Whiting *Jackson*
Wichita *Sedgwick*
Williamsburg *Franklin*
Wilmore *Comanche*
Wilroads Gardens *Ford*
Wilsey *Morris*
Wilson *Ellsworth*
Winchester *Jefferson*
Windom *McPherson*
Winfield *Cowley*
Winona *Logan*
Woodbine *Dickinson*
Woodston *Rooks*
Wright *Ford*
Yates Center *Woodson*
Yoder *Reno*
Zenda *Kingman*
Zurich *Rooks*

Kentucky

All 120 Kentucky counties reported that conviction data is accessible for employment purposes, with 112 accepting mail and/or phone inquiries and only eight (8) requiring requests to be made in person. One hundred five (105) counties are willing to check for civil records. Claims for $4,000 and greater are filed in circuit court.

For more information or for offices not listed, contact the state's information hot line at (502) 564-2500.

Driving Records

Division of Driver Licensing
State Office Building
2nd Floor
501 High St.
Frankfort, KY 40622
(502) 564-6800
Driving records are available by mail. $3 fee per request. Turnaround time is 5 working days. Written request must include job applicant's full name, date of birth and license number. Make check payable to Kentucky State Treasury.

Worker's Compensation Records

The Department of Worker's Claims
1270 Louisville Road
Perimeter Pk West - Bldg C
Frankfort, KY 40601
(502) 564-5550
Contact the above office for form B-010-1. Telephone or mail requests should include subject's full name and social security number. If available, include the date of injury and name of employer involved in claim. No search fee. $.10 fee for copies, $.50 fee for microfilm. A release is required.

Vital Statistics

Office of Vital Statistics
Department for Human Resources
275 East Main Street
Frankfort, KY 40621
(502) 564-4212
Fax (502) 227-0032
Birth records are available for $6.00. Death records are available for $5.00. State office has records since January 1911 and some records for the cities of Louisville, Lexington, Covington, and Newport before then. Some records are accessible by computer. Inquiry must include full name, date of birth, father's name, mother's name and maiden name, and county. Employers can obtain records with a written release. Make certified check or money order payable to Kentucky State Treasurer.

Marriage records since 1958 are available for $5.00. Include name, marriage date, spouse's name, and where marriage took place. Turnaround time is 2-4 weeks. Divorce records are also available for $5.00. Include name, divorce date, spouse's name, and county where divorce was granted. Turnaround time is 2-4 weeks.

Department of Education

Kentucky Department of Education
Division of Certification
18th Floor – Capital Plaza Tower
500 Mero Street
Frankfort, KY 40601
(502) 564-4606
Field of certification is available by phone or mail. Include name and SSN.

Medical Licensing

Kentucky Board of Medical Licensure
400 Sherbon Lane
Suite 222
Louisville, KT 40207
(502) 896-1516
Will confirm licenses for MDs and DOs by phone or mail. $5.00 fee. For licenses not mentioned, contact the above office.

Kentucky Board of Nursing
4010 Dupont Circle, Suite 430
Louisville, KY 40207
(502) 897-5143
Will confirm license by phone. No fee. Include name, license number or SSN.

Bar Association

Kentucky State Bar Association
514 West Main
Frankfort, KY 40601
(502) 564-3795
Will confirm licenses by phone. No fee. Include name.

Accountancy Board

Kentucky State Board of Accountancy
332 West Broadway, Suite 310
Louisville, KY 40202
(502) 588-3037
Will confirm license by phone. No fee. Include name.

Securities Commission

Department of Financial Institutions
Division of Securities
911 Leawood Drive
Frankfort, KY 40601
(502) 564-3390
Will confirm license by phone. No fee. Include name and SSN.

Secretary of State

Secretary of State Office
Corporation Division
PO Box 718
Frankfort, KY 40602
(502) 564-7330
Fax(502) 564-4075
Service agent and address, date incorporated, trade names are available by phone or mail. Contact the above office for additional information.

Criminal Records

State Repository

Records Section
Kentucky State Police
1250 Louisville Road
Frankfort, KY 40601
(502) 227-8713
Criminal records are available by mail to non criminal justice agencies. Only Kentucky state conviction data in which state police were involved are available. Each request must include the subject's full name, date of birth and SSN. There is a $4.00 fee per request. Make checks payable to the Kentucky State Treasury. Turnaround time is normally 1 week plus mail time.

Adair County

Circuit Clerk
Courthouse Public Square
500 Public Square, Suite 6
Columbia, KY 42728
(502) 384-2626

Felony and misdemeanor records are available by mail or phone. No release necessary. No search fee. $.15 fee per copy. $1.00 for certification. Search information required: name, SASE, years to search, SSN, date of birth.

Civil records are available by mail or phone. No release necessary. No search fee. Search information required: name, SSN, years to search. Specify plaintiff or defendant.

Allen County

Allen Circuit Court Clerk, Criminal Records
PO Box 464
Scottsville, KY 42164
(502) 237-3561

Felony and misdemeanor records are available by mail (one name per mail request). No release necessary. No search fee. $.15 fee per copy. $1.00 for certification. Search information required: name, SSN, date of birth, SASE.

Civil records are available by mail or phone. No release necessary. No search fee. Search information required: name, SSN, years to search. Specify plaintiff or defendant.

Anderson County

Felony records
Anderson Circuit Court, Criminal Records
Anderson County Courthouse
151 Main Street
Lawrenceburg, KY 40342
(502) 839-2508

Felony records are available by mail. A release is required. No search fee. $.15 fee per copy. $1.00 for certification. Search information required: name, SSN, date of birth, SASE.

Civil records
Anderson Circuit Court
Anderson County Courthouse
151 Main Street
Lawrenceburg, KY 40342
(502) 839-2508

Civil records are available by mail or phone. No release necessary. No search fee. Search information required: name, SSN, years to search. Specify plaintiff or defendant.

Misdemeanor records
Anderson District Court
Anderson County Courthouse
151 Main Street
Lawrenceburg, KY 40342
(502) 839-5445

Felony records are available by mail. A release is required. No search fee. $.15 fee per copy. $1.00 for certification. Search information required: name, SSN, date of birth, SASE.

Civil records
Anderson District Court
Anderson County Courthouse
151 Main Street
Lawrenceburg, KY 40342
(502) 839-5445

Civil records are available by mail or phone. No release necessary. No search fee. Search information required: name, SSN, years to search. Specify plaintiff or defendant.

Ballard County

Circuit Clerk, Criminal Records
PO Box 265
Wickliffe, KY 42087
(502) 335-5123

Felony and misdemeanor records are available by mail. No release necessary. No search fee. $.25 fee per copy. $1.50 for certification. Search information required: name, SSN, date of birth.

Civil records are available by mail or phone. No release necessary. No search fee. Search information required: name, SSN, years to search. Specify plaintiff or defendant.

Barren County

Circuit Court Clerk, Criminal Records
1st Level Courthouse
102 N. Public Square
Glasgow, KY 42141
(502) 651-3763

Felony and misdemeanor records are available by mail or phone. No release necessary. No search fee. $.15 fee per copy. $1.00 for certification. Search information required: name, years to search, SASE.

Civil records are available by mail or phone. No release necessary. No search fee. Search information required: name, SSN, years to search. Specify plaintiff or defendant.

Bath County

Circuit Court Clerk, Criminal Records
PO Box 558
Owingsville, KY 40360
(606) 674-2186 or 6821

Felony and misdemeanor records are available by mail or phone. No release necessary. No search fee. $.15 fee per copy. $1.00 for certification. Search information required: name, date of birth, SSN, years to search.

Civil records are available by mail or phone. No release necessary. No search fee. Search information required: name, SSN, years to search. Specify plaintiff or defendant.

Bell County

Felony records
Clerk of Circuit Court, Criminal Records
PO Box 306
Pineville, KY 40977
(606) 337-2942

Felony records are available by mail or phone. No release necessary. No search fee. $.15 fee per copy. $3.00 for certification within state, $5.00 for certification outside state. Search information required: name, SSN, date of birth.

Civil records
Clerk of Circuit Court
PO Box 306
Pineville, KY 40977
(606) 337-2942

Civil records are available by mail or phone. No release necessary. No search fee. Search information required: name, SSN, years to search. Specify plaintiff or defendant.

Misdemeanor records
Bell District Court
PO Box 306
Pineville, KY 40977
(606) 337-9900

Misdemeanor records are available in person only. See Kentucky state repository for additional information.

Civil records
Bell District Court
PO Box 306
Pineville, KY 40977
(606) 337-2942

Civil records are available by mail or phone. No release necessary. No search fee. Search information required: name, SSN, years to search. Specify plaintiff or defendant.

Boone County

Felony records
Clerk of the Circuit Court, Criminal Records
PO Box 480
Burlington, KY 41005
(606) 334-2149
Fax (606) 586-9413

Felony records are available by mail or fax. No release necessary. No search fee. $.15 fee per copy. $1.00 for certification. Search information required: name, SSN, date of birth.

Civil records
Clerk of the Circuit Court
PO Box 480
Burlington, KY 41005
(606) 334-2149
Fax (606) 586-9413

Civil records are available by mail or fax. No release necessary. No search fee. Search information required: name, SSN, years to search. Specify plaintiff or defendant.

Misdemeanor records
Boone District Court
PO Box 480
Burlington, KY 41005
(606) 334-2222
Fax (606) 586-9413

Misdemeanor records are available by mail or fax. A release is required. No fee. Search information required: name, date of birth, SSN.

Civil records
Boone District Court
PO Box 480
Burlington, KY 41005
(606) 334-2222
Fax (606) 586-9413

Civil records are available by mail or fax. No release necessary. No search fee. Search information required: name, SSN, years to search. Specify plaintiff or defendant.

Bourbon County

Courthouse, Criminal Records
PO Box 740
Paris, KY 40361
(606) 987-2624

Felony and misdemeanor records are available by mail. No release necessary. No search fee. $.15 fee per copy. $1.00 for certification. Search information required: name, SSN, date of birth, SASE.

Civil records are available by mail or by phone. No release necessary. No search fee. Search information required: name, SSN, years to search. Specify plaintiff or defendant.

Boyd County

Clerk of the Circuit Court, Criminal Records
PO Box 694
Catlettsburg, KY 41129-0694
(606) 739-4131

Felony and misdemeanor records are available in person only. See Kentucky state repository for additional information.

Civil records are available by mail or by phone. See Kentucky state repository for additional information.

Boyle County

Felony records
Clerk of Circuit Court, Criminal Records
Boyle County Courthouse
321 W. Main Street
Suite 240
Danville, KY 40422
(606) 236-7442

Felony records are available by mail. No release necessary. No search fee. $.15 fee per copy. $1.00 for certification. Search information required: name, date of birth, years to search.

Civil records
Clerk of Circuit Court
Boyle County Courthouse
321 W. Main Street
Suite 240
Danville, KY 40422
(606) 236-7442

Civil records are available by mail or phone. No release necessary. No search fee. Search information required: name, SSN, years to search. Specify plaintiff or defendant.

Misdemeanor records
Boyle District Court
Courthouse, 3rd Floor
4th Main
Danville, KY 40422
(606) 236-8362

Misdemeanor records are available by mail or phone. A release is required. No search fee. $.15 fee per copy. $1.00 for certification. Search information required: name, date of birth, SSN, SASE.

Civil records
Boyle District Court
Courthouse, 3rd Floor
4th Main
Danville, KY 40422
(606) 236-8362

Civil records are available by mail or phone. No release necessary. No search fee. Search information required: name, SSN, years to search. Specify plaintiff or defendant.

Bracken County

Courthouse, Criminal Records
PO Box 132
Brooksville, KY 41004
(606) 735-3328
Fax (606) 735-2925

Felony and misdemeanor records are available by mail, phone or fax. No release necessary. No search fee. $.15 fee per copy. $1.00 for certification. Search information required: name, SSN, date of birth, sex, race.

Civil records are available by mail, phone or fax. No release necessary. No search fee. $.15 fee per copy. $1.00 for certification. Search information required: name. Specify plaintiff or defendant.

Breathitt County

Courthouse, Circuit Clerk Office
1127 Main Street
Jackson, KY 41339
(606) 666-5768

Felony and misdemeanor records are available by mail or phone. Release if available. No search fee. $.25 fee per copy. Search information required: name, SSN, date of birth, sex, race.

Civil records are available by mail or phone. No release necessary. No search fee. Search information required: name, SSN, years to search. Specify plaintiff or defendant.

Breckinridge County

Circuit Court, Criminal Records
PO Box 111
Hardinsburg, KY 40143
(502) 756-2239

Felony and misdemeanor records are available by mail. No release necessary. No search fee. $.15 fee per copy. $1.00 for certification. Search information required: name, SSN, date of birth, SASE.

Civil records are available by mail or phone. No release necessary. No search fee. Search information required: name, SSN, years to search. Specify plaintiff or defendant.

Bullitt County

Clerk of Circuit Court, Criminal Records
PO Box 275
Shepherdsville, KY 40165
(502) 955-7764
Fax (502) 543-7104

Felony records are available by mail or fax. A release is required. No search fee. $.15 fee per copy. $1.00 for certifcation. Search information required: name, SSN, date of birth, case number (if available).

Civil records are available by mail or phone. No release necessary. No search fee. Search information required: name, SSN, years to search. Specify plaintiff or defendant.

Butler County

Butler Circuit Clerk
PO Box 625
Morgantown, KY 42261
(502) 526-5631

Felony and misdemeanor records are available by mail. No release necessary. No search fee. $.25 fee per copy. Search information required: name, date of birth, years to search.

Civil records are available by mail or phone. No release necessary. No search fee. Search information required: name, SSN, years to search. Specify plaintiff or defendant.

Caldwell County

Caldwell Circuit Court Clerk
Courthouse, Criminal Records
Room 4
100 Market St.
Princeton, KY 42445
(502) 365-6884

Felony and misdemeanor records are available by mail or phone. A release is required. No search fee. $.15 fee per copy. $1.50 for certification. Search information required: name, SSN, date of birth, sex, race, name of company requesting search.

Civil records are available by mail or phone. No release necessary. No search fee. Search information required: name, SSN, years to search. Specify plaintiff or defendant.

Calloway County

Clerk of Circuit Court, Criminal Records
201 S. 4th Street
Murray, KY 42071
(502) 753-2714

Felony and misdemeanor records are available by mail. No release necessary. $2.00 search fee. $.20 fee per copy. $1.50 for certification. Search information required: name, SSN, DOB, years to search, SASE.

Civil records are available by mail or phone. No release necessary. No search fee. Search information required: name, SSN, years to search.

Campbell County

Circuit Court, Criminal Records
30 W. 4th Street
Newport, KY 41071
(606) 292-6314

Felony and misdemeanor records are available by mail. No release necessary. $5.00 fee. $.25 fee per copy. $1.50 for certification. Company checks only, payable to Clerk of Circuit Court. Search information required: name, SSN, date of birth, sex, race, years to search, SASE.

Civil records are available by mail or phone. No release necessary. No search fee. Search information required: name, SSN, years to search.

Carlisle County

Circuit Court, Criminal Records
PO Box 337
Bardwell, KY 42023
(502) 628-5425

Felony and misdemeanor records are available by mail or phone. No release necessary. No search fee. $.15 fee per copy. Search information required: name.

Civil records are available by mail or phone. No release necessary. No search fee. Search information required: name, SSN, years to search. Specify plaintiff or defendant.

Carroll County

Clerk of Court, Criminal Records
Courthouse
1302 Highland Avenue
Carrollton, KY 41008
(502) 732-4305
Felony and misdemeanor records are available by mail. No release necessary. No search fee. $.15 fee per copy. $1.00 for certification. Search information required: name, SSN, date of birth.

Civil records are available by mail or phone. No release necessary. No search fee. Search information required: name, SSN, years to search. Specify plaintiff or defendant.

Carter County

Clerk of Court, Criminal Records
308 Courthouse
Grayson, KY 41143
(606) 474-5191
Felony and misdemeanor records are available by mail or phone. No release necessary. No search fee. $.15 fee per copy. $2.00 for certification. Search information required: name, SSN, date of birth, SASE.

Civil records are available by mail or phone. No release necessary. No search fee. Search information required: name, SSN, years to search. Specify plaintiff or defendant.

Casey County

Circuit Court Clerk, Criminal Records
PO Box 147
Liberty, KY 42539
(606) 787-6510
Felony and misdemeanor records are available by mail. A release is required. No search fee. $.15 fee per copy. $2.00 for certification. Search information required: name, date of birth, years to search.

Civil records are available by mail or phone. No release necessary. No search fee. Search information required: name, SSN, years to search. Specify plaintiff or defendant.

Christian County

Circuit Court Clerk, Criminal Records
PO Box 635
Hopkinsville, KY 42240
(502) 887-2539
Felony and misdemeanor records are available by mail. No release necessary. No search fee. $.15 fee per copy. $1.00 for certification. Search information required: name, date of birth.

Civil records are available by mail or phone. No release necessary. No search fee. Search information required: name, SSN, years to search. Specify plaintiff or defendant.

Clark County

Felony records
Circuit Court Clerk, Criminal Records
PO Box 715
Winchester, KY 40391
(606) 744-2264
Felony records are available by mail. A release is required. No search fee. $.25 fee per copy. $1.00 for certification. Search information required: name, SSN, date of birth.

Civil records
Circuit Court Clerk
PO Box 715
Winchester, KY 40391
(606) 744-2264
Civil records are available by mail. No release necessary. No search fee. Search information required: name, SSN, years to search. Specify plaintiff or defendant.

Misdemeanor records
Clerk of District Court
PO Box 715
Winchester, KY 40391
(606) 744-3141
Misdemeanor records are available by mail. A release is required. No search fee. $.25 fee per copy. $1.00 for certification. Search information required: name, date of birth, SSN.

Civil records
Clerk of District Court
PO Box 715
Winchester, KY 40391
(606) 744-3141
Civil records are available by mail. No release necessary. No search fee. Search information required: name, SSN, years to search. Specify plaintiff or defendant.

Clay County

Circuit Court Clerk, Criminal Records
PO Box 463
Manchester, KY 40962
(606) 598-3663
Felony and misdemeanor records are available by mail. No release necessary. No fee. Search information required: name, SASE.

Civil records are available by mail. No release necessary. No search fee. Search information required: name, SSN, years to search. Specify plaintiff or defendant.

Clinton County

Clerk of Court, Criminal Records
Courthouse
2nd Floor
Albany, KY 42602
(606) 387-6424
Felony and misdemeanor records are available by mail. A release is required. No search fee. $.10 fee per copy. $1.00 for certification. Search information required: full name, SSN, company letterhead.

Civil records are available by mail. No release necessary. No search fee. Search information required: name, SSN, years to search. Specify plaintiff or defendant and case number.

Crittenden County

County Courthouse, District Court Office
107 S. Main
Marion, KY 42064
(502) 965-4046
Felony and misdemeanor records are available by mail. No release necessary. No search fee. $.15 fee per copy. $1.00 for certification. Search information required: name.

Civil records are available by mail. No release necessary. No search fee. Search information required: name, SSN, years to search. Specify plaintiff or defendant.

Cumberland County

Circuit Court Clerk, Criminal Records
PO Box 384
Burkesville, KY 42717
(502) 864-2611
Felony and misdemeanor records are available by mail or phone. No release necessary. No search fee. $.25 fee per copy. $1.00 for certification. Search information required: name, SSN, date of birth, sex, race, years to search.

Civil records are available by mail or phone. No release necessary. No search fee. Search information required: name, SSN, years to search. Specify plaintiff or defendant.

Daviess County

Circuit Court Clerk, Criminal Records
PO Box 477
Owensboro, KY 42302
(502) 686-3222
Felony and misdemeanor records are available in person only. See Kentucky state repository for additional information.

Civil records are available by mail. No release necessary. No search fee. Search information required: name, SSN, years to search. Specify plaintiff or defendant.

Edmonson County

Circuit Court Clerk, Criminal Records
PO Box 130
Brownsville, KY 42210
(502) 597-2584
Felony and misdemeanor records are available by mail. A release is required. No search fee. $.15 fee per copy. $1.00 for certification. Search information required: name, SSN, date of birth, sex, race, SASE, years to search.

Civil records are available by mail. No release necessary. No search fee. Search information required: name, SSN, years to search. Specify plaintiff or defendant.

Elliott County

Elliot Circuit Court Clerk, Criminal Records
PO Box 788
Sandy Hook, KY 41171
(606) 738-5238
Felony and misdemeanor records are available by mail. No release necessary. No search fee. $.15 fee per copy. $6.00 for certification. Search information required: name, SSN, date of birth, SASE.

Civil records are available by mail. No release necessary. No search fee. Search information required: name, SSN, years to search. Specify plaintiff or defendant.

Estill County

Courthouse, Criminal Records
2nd Floor
Irvine, KY 40336
(606) 723-3970
Felony and misdemeanor records are available by mail or phone. No release necessary. No search fee. Search information required: name, SSN, date of birth.

Civil records are available by mail or phone. No release necessary. No search fee. $.15 fee per copy. Search information required: name, SSN, date of birth. Specify plaintiff or defendant.

Fayette County

Felony and misdemeanor records
Circuit Court Clerk, Criminal Records
215 W. Main Street
Lexington, KY 40507
(606) 253-1011
Felony and misdemeanor records are available by mail. No search fee. A release is required. $.50 fee per copy. $1.00 for certification. Search information required: name, SSN, years to search.

Civil records
Circuit Court Clerk
215 W. Main Street
Lexington, KY 40507
(606) 254-2567
Civil records are available by mail. No release necessary. No search fee. Search information required: name, SSN, years to search. Specify plaintiff or defendant.

Fleming County

Circuit Clerk's Office, Criminal Records
100 Court Square
Courthouse
Flemingsburg, KY 41041
(606) 845-7011

Felony and misdemeanor records are available by mail or phone. No release necessary. No search fee. $.15 fee per copy. $1.00 for certification. Search information required: name, date of birth, years to search.

Civil records are available by mail or by phone. No release necessary. No search fee. Search information required: name, SSN, years to search. Specify plaintiff or defendant.

Floyd County

Felony records
Circuit Court Clerk, Criminal Records
PO Box 109
Prestonsburg, KY 41653
(606) 886-9114
Fax (606) 886-9075
Felony records are available by mail or fax. No release necessary. No search fee. $.25 fee per copy. $2.50 for certification. Search information required: name, date of birth, SSN, previous address, years to search.

Civil records
Circuit Court Clerk
PO Box 109
Prestonsburg, KY 41653
(606) 886-9114
Fax (606) 886-9075
Civil records are available by mail or fax. No release necessary. No search fee. Search information required: name, SSN, years to search. Specify plaintiff or defendant.

Misdemeanor records
District Court Clerk, Criminal Records
PO Box 109
Prestonsburg, KY 41653
(606) 886-9114
Misdemeanor records are available by mail. No release necessary. No search fee. $.25 fee per copy. $2.50 for certification. Search information required: name, date of birth, years to search, SSN.

Civil records
District Court Clerk
PO Box 109
Prestonsburg, KY 41653
(606) 886-9114
Civil records are available by mail. No release necessary. No search fee. Search information required: name, SSN, years to search. Specify plaintiff or defendant.

Franklin County

Franklin County Courthouse, Criminal Records
PO Box 678
Frankfort, KY 40602
(502) 564-8380
Felony and misdemeanor records are available by mail or phone. No release necessary. No search fee. $.15 fee per copy. $1.00 for certification. Search information required: name, SSN, date of birth, sex, race.

Civil records are available by mail or phone. No release necessary. No search fee. Search information required: name, SSN, years to search. Specify both plaintiff and defendant.

Fulton County

Circuit Court Clerk, Criminal Records
PO Box 198
Hickman, KY 42050
(502) 236-3944
Felony and misdemeanor records are available by mail. No release necessary. No search fee. $.15 fee per copy. $1.00 fee for certification, plus postage. Search information required: name, date of birth, SASE.

Civil records are available by mail. No release necessary. No search fee. Search information required: name, SSN, years to search. Specify plaintiff or defendant.

Gallatin County

Felony records
Circuit Court Clerk, Criminal Records
PO Box 256
Warsaw, KY 41095
(606) 567-5241
Felony records are available by mail or phone. No release necessary. No search fee. $.25 fee per copy. Search information required: name, date of birth, years to search.

Civil records
Circuit Court Clerk
PO Box 256
Warsaw, KY 41095
(606) 567-5241
Civil records are available by mail. No release necessary. No search fee. Search information required: name, SSN, years to search. Specify plaintiff or defendant.

Misdemeanor records
Gallatin District Court
PO Box 256
Warsaw, KY 41095
(606) 567-2388
Misdemeanor records are available by phone. Search information required: name, date of birth, SSN.

Civil records
Gallatin District Court
PO Box 256
Warsaw, KY 41095
(606) 567-2388
Civil records are available by mail or by phone. No release necessary. No search fee. Search information required: name, SSN, years to search. Specify plaintiff or defendant.

Garrard County

Circuit Court Clerk, Criminal Records
Courthouse Public Square
Lancaster, KY 40444
(606) 792-6032
Felony and misdemeanor records are available by mail. No release necessary. $1.00 fee. Company checks only, payable to Circuit Court Clerk. Search information required: name, SSN, date of birth, sex, race, years to search.

Civil records are available by mail. No release necessary. No search fee. Search information required: name, SSN, years to search. Specify plaintiff or defendant.

Grant County

Courthouse, Criminal Records
101 N. Main
Williamstown, KY 41097
(606) 824-4467
Felony and misdemeanor records are available by mail. No release necessary. No search fee. $.15 fee per copy. $1.00 for certification. Search information required: name, date of birth, SSN.

Civil records are available by mail or by phone. No release necessary. No search fee. Search information required: name, SSN, years to search. Specify plaintiff or defendant.

Graves County

Circuit Court Clerk's Office, Criminal Records
Courthouse
114 West Broadway
Mayfield, KY 42066
(502) 247-1733
Fax (502) 562-2941
Felony and misdemeanor records are available by mail or fax. No release necessary. No search fee. $.25 fee per copy. $1.00 for certification. Search information required: name, date of birth, SASE, previous address.

Civil records are available by mail or by phone. No release necessary. No search fee. Search information required: name, SSN, years to search. Specify plaintiff or defendant.

Grayson County

Circuit Court Clerk, Criminal Records
125 E. White Oak
Leitchfield, KY 42754
(502) 259-3040
Felony and misdemeanor records are available by mail or phone. No release necessary. No search fee. $1.50 for certification. Search information required: name, date of birth, SSN, years to search.

Civil records are available by mail or phone. No release necessary. No search fee. Search information required: name, SSN, years to search. Specify plaintiff or defendant.

Green County

Circuit Court Clerk, Criminal Records
203 W. Court Street
Greensburg, KY 42743
(502) 932-5631
Felony and misdemeanor records are available by mail. No release necessary. No search fee. $.15 fee per copy. $2.00 for certification. Search information required: name, date of birth, SSN.

Civil records are available by mail. No release necessary. No search fee. Search information required: name, SSN, years to search. Specify plaintiff or defendant.

Greenup County

Courthouse, Criminal Records
Room 201
Greenup, KY 41144
(606) 473-9860
Fax (606) 473-9869
Felony and misdemeanor records are available by mail, phone or fax. No release necessary. No search fee. $1.00 for certification. Search information required: name, SSN, date of birth, sex, race.

Civil records are available by mail, phone or fax. No release necessary. No search fee. Search information required: name, SSN, years to search. Specify plaintiff or defendant.

Hancock County

Clerk of Circuit Court, Criminal Records
Courthouse
PO Box 267
Hawesville, KY 42348
(502) 927-8144
Felony and misdemeanor records are available by mail or phone. No release necessary. No search fee. $.15 fee per copy. $1.00 for certification. Search information required: name, SSN, date of birth, years to search, SASE.

Civil records are available by mail or phone. No release necessary. No search fee. Search information required: name, SSN, years to search. Specify plaintiff or defendant.

Hardin County

Clerk of Hardin County Court
Courthouse, Criminal Records
Elizabethtown, KY 42701
(502) 765-5181
Fax (502) 765-4372
Felony and misdemeanor records are available by mail, phone or fax. No release necessary. No search fee. $.15 fee per copy. $1.00 for certification. Search information required: name, date of birth, SSN.

Civil records are available in person only. See Kentucky state repository for additional information.

Harlan County

Clerk's Office, Criminal Records
PO Box 190
Harlan, KY 40831
(606) 573-2680
Felony and misdemeanor records are available by mail or phone. No release necessary. No search fee. $.25 fee per copy. $3.50 for certification. Search information required: name, date of birth.

Civil records are available in person only. See Kentucky state repository for additional information.

Harrison County

Courthouse
PO Box 10
Cynthiana, KY 41031
(606) 234-1914
Felony and misdemeanor records are available in person only. See Kentucky state repository for additional information.

Civil records are available in person only. See Kentucky state repository for additional information.

Hart County

Hart County Circuit Court, Criminal Records
P.O. Box 548
Munfordville, KY 42765
(502) 524-5181
Felony and misdemeanor records are available in person only. See Kentucky state repository for additional information.

Civil records are available by mail. No release necessary. No search fee. Search information required: name, SSN, years to search. Specify plaintiff or defendant.

Henderson County

Circuit Court Clerk, Criminal Records
PO Box 675
Henderson, KY 42420
(502) 826-2405
Felony and misdemeanor records are available by mail. No release necessary. No search fee. $.15 fee per copy. $1.00 for certification. Search information required: name, SSN, date of birth, sex, race, SASE.

Civil records are available by mail. No release necessary. No search fee. Search information required: name, SSN, years to search. Specify plaintiff or defendant.

Henry County

Henry County Courthouse, Criminal Records
PO Box 286
New Castle, KY 40050
(502) 845-2868
Felony and misdemeanor records are available by mail. A release is required. No search fee. $.15 fee per copy. $1.00 for certification. Search information required: name, SSN, date of birth.

Civil records are available by mail. No release necessary. No search fee. Search information required: name, SSN, years to search. Specify plaintiff or defendant.

Hickman County

Circuit Court Clerk, Criminal Records
Courthouse
Clinton, KY 42031
(502) 653-3901
Felony and misdemeanor records are available by mail. No release necessary. No search fee. $.15 fee per copy. $1.00 for certification. Search information required: name, date of birth, SASE.

Civil records are available by mail. No release necessary. No search fee. Search information required: name, SSN, years to search. Specify plaintiff or defendant.

Hopkins County

Felony records
Hopkins County Circuit Court, Criminal Records
Courthouse
Madisonville, KY 42431
(502) 825-6502
Felony records are available by mail. No release necessary. No search fee. $.15 fee per copy. $1.50 for certification. Search information required: name, SSN, date of birth, SASE.

Civil records
Hopkins County Circuit Court
30 S. Main
Madisonville, KY 42431
(502) 825-6502
Civil records are available by mail. No release necessary. No search fee. Search information required: name, SSN, years to search. Specify plaintiff or defendant.

Misdemeanor records
District Court Office
Courthouse,
30 S. Main
Madisonville, KY 42431
(502) 825-6507
Misdemeanor records are available by mail or phone. No release necessary. No search fee. $.15 fee per copy. $1.50 for certification. Search information required: name, date of birth, SASE.

Civil records
District Court Office
30 S. Main
Madisonville, KY 42431
(502) 825-6507
Civil records are available by mail. No release necessary. No search fee. Search information required: name, SSN, years to search. Specify plaintiff or defendant.

Jackson County

Felony records
Circuit Court Clerk, Criminal Records
PO Box 84
McKee, KY 40447
(606) 287-7783
Felony records are available by mail or phone. No release necessary. No search fee. $.15 fee per copy. Search information required: name, SSN, date of birth, sex, race.

Civil records
Circuit Court Clerk
PO Box 84
McKee, KY 40447
(606) 287-7783
Civil records are available by mail or phone. No release necessary. No search fee. Search information required: name, SSN, years to search. Specify plaintiff or defendant.

Misdemeanor records
Jackson County District Court
PO Box 84
McKee, KY 40447
(606) 287-8651
Misdemeanor records are available by mail or phone. No release necessary. No search fee. Search information required: name, date of birth.

Civil records
Jackson County District Court
PO Box 84
McKee, KY 40447
(606) 287-8651
Civil records are available by mail or phone. No release necessary. No search fee. Search information required: name, SSN, years to search. Specify plaintiff or defendant.

Jefferson County

Circuit Court Clerk, Criminal Records
600 W. Jefferson
Hall of Justice
Louisville, KY 40202
(502) 588-4320
Records are available in person only. See Kentucky state repository for additional information.

Civil records are available in person only. See Kentucky state repository for additional information.

Jessamine County

Felony records
Circuit Court Clerk
Courthouse, Criminal Records
Main Street
Nicholasville, KY 40356
(606) 885-4531
Felony records are available in person only. See Kentucky state repository for additional information.

Civil records
Circuit Court Clerk
Courthouse
Main Street
Nicholasville, KY 40356
(606) 885-4531
Civil records are available by mail. No release necessary. No search fee. Search information required: name, SSN, years to search. Specify plaintiff or defendant.

Misdemeanor records
Jessamine District Court
Courthouse
Nicholasville, KY 40356
(606) 887-1005
Misdemeanor records are available by mail or phone. A release is required. No search fee. Search information required: name, date of birth, SASE, SSN.

Civil records
Jessamine District Court
Courthouse
Nicholasville, KY 40356
(606) 887-1005
Civil Court records are available by mail or phone. A release is required. No search fee. Search information required: name, date of birth, SASE, SSN. Specify plaintiff or defendant.

Johnson County

Circuit Court Clerk, Criminal Records
PO Box 1405
Paintsville, KY 41240
(606) 789-5181
Felony and misdemeanor records are available by mail. A release is required. No search fee. $.15 fee per copy. Search information required: name, SSN, date of birth, previous address, years to search.

Civil records are available by mail. No release necessary. No search fee. Search information required: name, SSN, years to search. Specify plaintiff or defendant.

Kenton County

Felony records
Circuit Court Clerk, Criminal Records
PO Box 669
Covington, KY 41012
(606) 292-6521
Fax (606) 292-6611
Felony records are available by mail or phone. No release necessary. No search fee. $.15 fee per copy. $1.00 for certification. Search information required: name, SSN, date of birth, sex, race, years to search.

Civil records
Circuit Court Clerk
PO Box 669
Covington, KY 41012
(606) 292-6521
Fax (606) 292-6611
Civil records are available by mail or phone. No release necessary. No search fee. Search information required: name, SSN, years to search. Specify plaintiff or defendant.

Misdemeanor records
Administrative Office of Court
Pre-Trial Service
100 Millcreek Park
Frankfort, KY 40601
(502) 564-2350
Misdemeanor records are available in person only. See Kentucky state repository for additional information.

Civil records
Administrative Office of Court
Pre-Trial Service
100 Millcreek Park
Frankfort, KY 40601
(502) 564-2350
Civil records are available in person only. See Kentucky state repository for additional information.

Knott County

Circuit Court Clerk, Criminal Records
PO Box 515
Hindman, KY 41822
(606) 785-5021
Felony and misdemeanor records are available by mail or phone. No release necessary. No search fee. $.25 fee per copy. $3.50 for certification. Search information required: name, date of birth, SSN.

Civil records are available by mail or phone. No release necessary. No search fee. Search information required: name, SSN, years to search. Specify plaintiff or defendant.

Knox County

Felony records
Circuit Court Clerk, Criminal Records
PO Box 1049
401 Court Square, Ste. 202
Barbourville, KY 40906
(606) 546-3075
Felony records are available by mail. No release necessary. $.25 fee per copy. Search information required: name, date of birth.

Civil records
Circuit Court Clerk
PO Box 1049
401 Court Square, Ste. 202
Barbourville, KY 40906
(606) 546-3075
Civil records are available by mail. No release necessary. No search fee. Search information required: name, SSN, years to search. Specify plaintiff or defendant.

Misdemeanor records
District Court
PO Box 1049
Barbourville, KY 40906
(606) 546-3232
Misdemeanor records are available by mail. No release necessary. $.25 fee per copy. Search information required: name, date of birth.

Civil records
District Court
PO Box 1049
Barbourville, KY 40906
(606) 546-3232
Civil records are available by mail. No release necessary. No search fee. Search information required: name, SSN, years to search. Specify plaintiff or defendant.

Larue County

Circuit Court Clerk
209 W. High Street
Larue County Courthouse, Annex
Hodgenville, KY 42748
(502) 358-3421
Felony and misdemeanor records are available by mail. No release necessary. No search fee. $.15 fee per copy. Search information required: name, SSN, date of birth, SASE.

Civil records are available by mail or by phone. No release necessary. No search fee. Search information required: name, SSN, years to search. Specify plaintiff or defendant.

Laurel County

Laurel County Circuit Clerk, Criminal Records
PO Box 1798
Laurel County Courthouse
London, KY 40743
(606) 864-2863
Felony and misdemeanor records are available by mail. A release is required. No search fee. $.15 fee per copy. $2.00 for certification. Search information required: name, SSN, date of birth, sex, race.

Civil records are available by mail. No release necessary. No search fee. Search information required: name, SSN, years to search. Specify plaintiff or defendant.

Lawrence County

Circuit Court Clerk, Criminal Records
Lawrence County
P.O. Box 212
Louisa, KY 41230
(606) 638-4215
Felony and misdemeanor records are available by mail. No release necessary. No search fee. Search information required: name, date of birth, SASE, years to search.

Civil records are available by mail. No release necessary. No search fee. Search information required: name, SSN, years to search. Specify plaintiff or defendant.

Lee County

Circuit Court Clerk
PO Box E
Beattyville, KY 41311
(606) 464-8400
Felony and misdemeanor records are available in person only. See Kentucky state repository for additional information.

Civil records are available in person only. See Kentucky state repository for additional information.

Leslie County

Circuit Court Clerk, Criminal Records
PO Box 114
Hyden, KY 41749
(606) 672-2505
Felony and misdemeanor records are available by mail. No release necessary. No search fee. $.15 fee per copy. $1.00 for certification. Search information required: name, SSN, date of birth.

Civil records are available by mail. No release necessary. No search fee. Search information required: name, SSN, years to search. Specify plaintiff or defendant.

Letcher County

Clerk of Court, Criminal Records
Courthouse
101 W. Main
Whitesburg, KY 41858
(606) 633-7559
Felony and misdemeanor records are available by mail or phone. No release necessary. No search fee. Search information required: name, SSN, date of birth.

Civil records are available in person only. See Kentucky state repository for additional information.

Lewis County

Circuit Court Clerk, Criminal Records
Courthouse
PO Box 70
Vanceburg, KY 41179
(606) 796-3053 or (606) 796-6002
Felony and misdemeanor records are available by mail or phone. No release necessary. No search fee. $.15 fee per copy. Search information required: name, date of birth.

Civil records are available by mail or phone. No release necessary. No search fee. Search information required: name, SSN, years to search. Specify plaintiff or defendant.

Lincoln County

Courthouse, Criminal Records
102 E. Main
Stanford, KY 40484
(606) 365-2535
Felony and misdemeanor records are available by mail. No release necessary. No search fee. Search information required: name, date of birth.

Civil records are available in person only. See Kentucky state repository for additional information.

Livingston County

Circuit Court Clerk, Criminal Records
PO Box 160
Smithland, KY 42081
(502) 928-2172 or 928-2173
Felony and misdemeanor records are available by mail or phone. No release necessary. No search fee. $.15 fee per copy. $1.15 for certification. Search information required: name, date of birth, years to search.

Civil records are available by mail or phone. No release necessary. No search fee. Search information required: name, SSN, years to search. Specify plaintiff or defendant.

Logan County

Felony records
Circuit Court Clerk, Criminal Records
PO Box 420
Russellville, KY 42276-0420
(502) 726-2424
Felony records are available by mail. No release necessary. No search fee. Search information required: name, SSN, date of birth, sex, race, years to search.

Civil records
Circuit Court Clerk
PO Box 420
Russellville, KY 42276-0420
(502) 726-2424
Civil records are available in person only. See Kentucky state repository for additional information.

Misdemeanor records
Logan District Court
PO Box 304
Russellville, KY 42276
(502) 726-3107
Misdemeanor records are available in person only. Contact the above office for more information.

Civil records
Logan District Court
PO Box 304
Russellville, KY 42276
(502) 726-3107
Civil records are available in person only. See Kentucky state repository for additional information.

Lyon County

Circuit Court Clerk, Criminal Records
PO Box 565
Eddyville, KY 42038
(502) 388-7231
Felony and misdemeanor records are available in person only. See Kentucky state repository for additional information.

Civil records are available in person only. See Kentucky state repository for additional information.

Madison County

Felony records
Madison Circuit Clerk, Criminal Records
Madison County Courthouse
101 W. Main
Richmond, KY 40475
(606) 624-4793
Felony recordsare available in person only. See Kentucky state repository for additional information.

Civil records
Madison Circuit Clerk
Madison County Courthouse
101 W. Main
Richmond, KY 40475
(606) 624-4793
Civil records are available in person only. See Kentucky state repository for additional information.

Misdemeanor records
Madison District Court
Courthouse Annex Bldg.
Richmond, KY 40475
(606) 623-6732
Misdemeanor records are available in peron only. See Kentucky state repository for additional information.

Civil records
Madison District Court
Courthouse Annex Bldg.
Richmond, KY 40475
(606) 623-6732
Civil records are available in person only. See Kentucky state repository for additional information.

Magoffin County

Circuit Court Clerk, Criminal Records
PO Box 147
Salyersville, KY 41465
(606) 349-2215
Fax (606) 349-2215
Felony and misdemeanor records are available by mail or fax. No release necessary. No search fee. $.15 fee per copy. Search information required: name, SSN, date of birth, sex, race, SASE.

Civil records are available in person only. See Kentucky state repository for additional information.

Marion County

Courthouse, Circuit Court Clerk
120 W. Main
Lebanon, KY 40033
(502) 692-2681
Felony and misdemeanor records are available by mail or phone. No release necessary. No search fee. $.15 fee per copy. $1.00 for certification. Search information required: name, SSN, date of birth.

Civil records are available by mail. No release necessary. No search fee. Search information required: name, SSN, years to search. Specify plaintiff or defendant.

Marshall County

Circuit Court Clerk, Criminal Records
Courthouse
101 Main Street
Benton, KY 42025
(502) 527-3883
Felony and misdemeanor records are available by mail or phone. No release necessary. No search fee. $.15 fee per copy. $1.00 for certification. Search information required: name.

Civil records are available by mail or phone. No release necessary. No search fee. Search information required: name, SSN, years to search. Specify plaintiff or defendant.

Martin County

Circuit Court Clerk, Criminal Records
PO Box 430
Inez, KY 41224
(606) 298-3508

Felony and misdemeanor records are available by mail. No release necessary. No search fee. Search information required: name, SSN, date of birth.

Civil records are available by mail. No release necessary. No search fee. $.15 fee per copy. $1.00 for certification. Search information required: name, SSN, years to search. Specify plaintiff or defendant.

Mason County

Clerk of Mason Circuit Court, Criminal Records
Courthouse
27 W. 3rd Street
Maysville, KY 41056
(606) 564-4340

Felony and misdemeanor records are available by mail or phone. No release necessary. No search fee. Search information required: name, date of birth.

Civil records are available by mail or phone. A release is required. No search fee. $.15 fee per copy. $1.00 for certification. Search information required: name, SSN, years to search. Specify plaintiff or defendant.

McCracken County

McCracken County Courthouse, Criminal Records
Paducah, KY 42001
(502) 444-8280

Felony and misdemeanor records are available by mail. No release necessary. No search fee. $.25 fee per copy. $1.00 for certification. Search information required: name, date of birth, SSN.

Civil records are available by mail or phone. No release necessary. No search fee. Search information required: name, SSN, years to search. Specify plaintiff or defendant.

McCreary County

Circuit Court Clerk, Criminal Records
PO Box 40
Whitley City, KY 42653
(606) 376-5041

Felony and misdemeanor records are available by mail. A release is required. No search fee. $.15 fee per copy. $1.00 for certification. Search information required: name, date of birth, SSN.

Civil records are available by mail. No release necessary. No search fee. Search information required: name, SSN, years to search. Specify plaintiff or defendant.

McLean County

Circuit Court Clerk, Criminal Records
PO Box 145
Calhoun, KY 42327
(502) 273-3966

Felony and misdemeanor records are available by mail. No release necessary. No search fee. $.15 fee per copy. Search information required: name, SSN, date of birth, SASE.

Civil records are available by mail or by phone. No release necessary. No search fee. Search information required: name, SSN, years to search. Specify plaintiff or defendant.

Meade County

Meade County
CourthouseBrandenburg, KY 40108
(502) 422-4961

Felony and misdemeanor records are available by mail. A release is required. No search fee. $.15 fee per copy. Search information required: name, SSN, date of birth, SASE.

Civil records are available by mail. No release necessary. No search fee. Search information required: name, SSN, years to search. Specify plaintiff or defendant.

Menifee County

Clerk of Circuit Court, Criminal Records
PO Box 172
Frenchburg, KY 40322
(606) 768-2461

Felony and misdemeanor records (misdemeanor since 1978 only) are available by mail or phone. Misdemeanor records go back to 1978. No release necessary. No search fee. Search information required: name, date of birth, SASE.

Civil records are available by mail. No release necessary. No search fee. $.25 fee per copy. $1.00 for certification. Search information required: name, SSN, years to search. Specify plaintiff or defendant.

Mercer County

Clerk of Mercer Circuit Court, Criminal Records
Courthouse
Harrodsburg, KY 40330
(606) 734-5706

Felony and misdemeanor records are available by mail. No release necessary. No search fee. Search information required: name, SSN, date of birth, sex, race, SASE.

Civil records are available by mail. No release necessary. No search fee. $.25 fee per copy. $1.00 for certification. Search information required: name, SSN, years to search. Specify plaintiff or defendant.

Metcalfe County

Circuit Court Clerk, Criminal Records
PO Box 485
Edmondton, KY 42129
(502) 432-3663

Felony and misdemeanor records are available by mail. No release necessary. No search fee. $.15 fee per copy. $1.00 for certification. Search information required: name, date of birth.

Civil records are available by mail or phone. No release necessary. No search fee. Search information required: name, SSN, years to search. Specify plaintiff or defendant.

Monroe County

Monroe Circuit Court Clerk, Criminal Records
PO Box 245
Tompkinsville, KY 42167
(502) 487-5480

Felony and misdemeanor records are available by mail. No release necessary. No search fee. $.15 fee per copy. $1.00 for certification. Search information required: name, SSN, date of birth, sex, race.

Civil records are available by mail. No release necessary. No search fee. Search information required: name, SSN, years to search. Specify plaintiff or defendant.

Montgomery County

Montgomery Circuit Clerk
Courthouse, Criminal Records
1 Court Street
Mount Sterling, KY 40353
(606) 498-5966

Felony and misdemeanor records are available by mail. No release necessary. No search fee. Search information required: name, SSN, date of birth.

Civil recordsfrom 1978 forward are available by mail. No release necessary. No search fee. $1.00 for certification. Search information required: name, SSN, date of birth, SASE, years to search. Specify plaintiff or defendant.

Morgan County

Morgan County Courthouse, Criminal Records
PO Box 85
West Liberty, KY 41472
(606) 743-3763

Felony and misdemeanor records are available by mail. No release necessary. No search fee. Search information required: name, date of birth, SSN.

Civil records are available by mail. No release necessary. No search fee. $.15 fee per copy. $1.00 for certification. Search information required: name, SSN, years to search. Specify plaintiff or defendant.

Muhlenberg County

Circuit Court Clerk, Criminal Records
Muhlenberg County
PO Box 776
Greenville, KY 42345
(502) 338-4850

Felony and misdemeanor records are available by mail or phone. No release necessary. No search fee. Search information required: name.

Civil records are available by mail or phone. No release necessary. No search fee. $.15 fee per copy. $1.00 for certification. Search information required: name, SSN, years to search. Specify plaintiff or defendant.

Nelson County

Courthouse Square, Criminal Records
Bardstown, KY 40004
(502) 348-3648

Felony and misdemeanor records are available by mail or phone. No release necessary. No search fee. $.15 fee per copy. $1.00 for certification. Search information required: name, SSN, date of birth, SASE.

Civil records are available by mail or phone. No release necessary. No search fee. Search information required: name, SSN, years to search. Specify plaintiff or defendant.

Nicholas County

Courthouse, Criminal Records
PO Box 109
Carlisle, KY 40311
(606) 289-2336

Felony and misdemeanor records are available by mail. No release necessary. No search fee. Search information required: name, SSN, date of birth, SASE.

Civil records are available by mail. No release necessary. No search fee. Search information required: name, SSN, years to search. Specify plaintiff or defendant.

Ohio County

Circuit Court Clerk, Criminal Records
130 Washington St.
Community Center
Hartford, KY 42347
(502) 298-3671

Felony and misdemeanor records are available by mail. No release necessary. No search fee. $.15 fee per copy. $1.00 for certification. Search information required: name, SSN, date of birth, sex, race.

Civil records are available by mail. No release necessary. No search fee. Search information required: name, date of birth, SSN, years to search, SASE. Specify plaintiff or defendant.

Oldham County

Circuit Court Clerk, Criminal Records
105 E. Jefferson
La Grange, KY 40031
(502) 222-9837

Felony and misdemeanor records are available by mail. No release necessary. $1.00 search fee. Make check payable to Circuit Court Clerk. Search information required: name, present address, SSN, date of birth, SASE.

Civil records are available by mail or by phone. A release is required. $1.00 search fee. $1.00 for certification. Search information required: name, date of birth, SSN, years to search. Specify plaintiff or defendant.

Owen County

Circuit Court Clerk, Criminal Records
PO Box 473
Owenton, KY 40359
(502) 484-2232

Felony and misdemeanor records are available by mail. No release necessary. No search fee. $.15 fee per copy. $1.00 for certification. Search information required: name, SSN, date of birth, SASE.

Civil records are available by mail. No release necessary. No search fee. Search information required: name, SSN, years to search, SASE. Specify plaintiff or defendant.

Owsley County

Circuit Court Clerk, Criminal Records
PO Box 146
Booneville, KY 41314
(606) 593-6226

Felony and misdemeanor records are available by mail or phone. A release is required. No search fee. $.15 fee per copy. Search information required: name, date of birth, SSN, SASE.

Civil records are available by mail. No release necessary. No search fee. Search information required: name, SSN, years to search. Specify plaintiff or defendant.

Pendleton County

Pendleton County Circuit Clerk,
Criminal Records
PO Box 69
Courthouse Square
Falmouth, KY 41040
(606) 654-3347

Felony and misdemeanor records are available by mail. A release is required. No fee. Search information required: name, date of birth, SSN, SASE.

Civil records are available in person only. See Kentucky state repository for additional information.

Perry County

Circuit Court Clerk, Criminal Records
PO Box 743
Hazard, KY 41702
(606) 436-4042

Felony and misdemeanor records are available by mail or phone. No release necessary. No search fee. $.15 fee per copy. $1.00 for certification. Search information required: name, SSN, date of birth, sex, race, SASE.

Civil records are available by mail or phone. No release necessary. No search fee. Search information required: name, SSN, years to search. Specify plaintiff or defendant.

Pike County

Pike Circuit Court Clerk, Criminal Records
3rd Floor, Hall of Justice
89 Divisio
Pikeville, KY 41501
(606) 437-5157

Felony and misdemeanor records are available by mail. No release necessary. No search fee. $.15 fee per copy. $1.00 for certification. Search information required: name, address, date of birth, years to search, SASE.

Civil records are available by mail. No release necessary. No search fee. Search information required: name, SSN, years to search. Specify plaintiff or defendant.

Powell County

Circuit Court Clerk, Criminal Records
PO Box 562
Stanton, KY 40380
(606) 663-4141

Felony and misdemeanor records are available by mail. A release is required. No search fee. Search information required: name, date of birth, SASE.

Civil records are available by mail. No release necessary. No search fee. $.15 fee per copy. $5.00 for certification. Search information required: name, SSN, years to search. Specify plaintiff or defendant.

Pulaski County

Circuit Court Clerk, Criminal Records
PO Box 664
Somerset, KY 42502
(606) 678-8981

Felony and misdemeanor records are available by mail. No release necessary. No search fee. $.15 fee per copy. $1.00 for certification. Search information required: name, SSN, date of birth, SASE.

Civil records are available by mail or phone. No release necessary. No search fee. $.15 fee per copy. $1.00 for certification. Search information required: name, SSN, years to search. Specify plaintiff or defendant.

Robertson County

Robertson County Circuit Court,
Criminal Records
PO Box 63
Mount Olivet, KY 41064
(606) 724-5993

Felony and misdemeanor records are available by mail. A release is required. No search fee. $.25 fee per copy, $1.00 fee for certification. Search information required: name, SSN, date of birth, SASE.

Civil records are available by mail or phone. No release necessary. No search fee. Search information required: name, SSN, years to search. Specify plaintiff or defendant.

Rockcastle County

Circuit Court Clerk, Criminal Records
PO Box 750
Mount Vernon, KY 40456
(606) 256-2581

Felony and misdemeanor records are available by mail. No release necessary. No search fee. $.30 fee per copy. Search information required: name, SSN, date of birth, SASE.

Civil records are available by mail. No release necessary. No search fee. Search information required: name, SSN, years to search. Specify plaintiff or defendant.

Rowan County

Circuit Court Clerk, Criminal Records
627 E. Main Street
Morehead, KY 40351
(606) 784-4574

Felony and misdemeanor records are available by mail. A release is required. No search fee. $.15 fee per copy. $1.00 for certification. Search information required: name, SSN, date of birth.

Civil records are available by mail. No release necessary. No search fee. Search information required: name, SSN, date of birth, years to search. Specify plaintiff or defendant.

Russell County

Circuit Court Clerk, Criminal Records
410 Monument Square
#203
Jamestown, KY 42629
(502) 343-2185

Felony and misdemeanor records are available by mail. No release necessary. No search fee. $.25 fee per copy. $2.00 for certification. Search information required: name, SSN, date of birth.

Civil records are available by mail. No release necessary. No search fee. Search information required: name, SSN, years to search. Specify plaintiff or defendant.

Scott County

Circuit Court Clerk, Criminal Records
Scott County Courthouse
119 N. Hamilton
Georgetown, KY 40324
(502) 863-0474

Felony and misdemeanor records are available by mail. No release necessary. No search fee. Search information required: name, date of birth, SASE.

Civil records are available in person only. See Kentucky state repository for additional information.

Shelby County

Shelby Circuit Court Clerk
501 Main St.
Shelbyville, KY 40065
(502) 633-1287

Felony records are available by mail. No search fee. No release necessary. Search information required: name, date of birth, SSN, years to search.

Civil records are available by mail or phone. No release necessary. No search fee. Search information required: name, SSN, years to search. Specify plaintiff or defendant.

Simpson County

Circuit Court Clerk, Criminal Records
PO Box 261
Franklin, KY 42134
(502) 586-8910

Felony and misdemeanor records are available by mail or phone. No release necessary. No search fee. $.25 fee per copy. $1.00 for certification. Search information required: name, date of birth.

Civil records are available by mail or phone. No release necessary. No search fee. Search information required: name, SSN, years to search. Specify plaintiff or defendant.

Spencer County

Circuit Court Clerk, Criminal Records
PO Box 282
Taylorsville, KY 40071
(502) 477-3220

Felony and misdemeanor records are available by mail. A release is required. No search fee. $.25 fee per copy. $1.50 for certification. Search information required: name, date of birth, SSN.

Civil records are available by mail or phone. No release necessary. No search fee. Search information required: name, SSN, years to search. Specify plaintiff or defendant.

Taylor County

Taylor Circuit Court Clerk
Taylor County Courthouse, Criminal Records
203 N. Court Street
Campbellsville, KY 42718
(502) 465-6686

Felony and misdemeanor records are available by mail. A release is required. No search fee. $.25 fee per copy. $1.00 for certification. Search information required: name, SSN, date of birth, SASE.

Civil records are available by mail. A release is required. No search fee. Search information required: name, SSN, years to search. Specify plaintiff or defendant.

Todd County

Circuit Court Clerk, Criminal Records
PO Box 337
Elkton, KY 42220
(502) 265-5631

Felony and misdemeanor records are available by mail. No release necessary. $3.00 search fee. Make check payable to Circuit Court Clerk. Search information required: name, date of birth.

Civil records are available in person only. See Kentucky state repository for additional information.

Trigg County

Circuit Court Clerk, Criminal Records
PO Box 673
Cadiz, KY 42211
(502) 522-6270

Felony and misdemeanor records are available by mail or phone. No release necessary. No search fee. $.15 fee per copy. $1.00 for certification. Search information required: name, SASE.

Civil records are available by mail or phone. No release necessary. No search fee. Search information required: name, SSN, years to search. Specify plaintiff or defendant.

Trimble County

Circuit Court Clerk, Criminal Records
PO Box 248
Bedford, KY 40006
(502) 255-3213

Felony and misdemeanor records are available by mail or phone. A release is required. No search fee. $.15 fee per copy. Search information required: name, SSN, date of birth, SASE.

Civil records are available by mail or phone. A release is required. No search fee. Search information required: name, SSN, years to search. Specify plaintiff or defendant.

Union County

Clerk of Circuit Court, Criminal Records
PO Box 59
Morganfield, KY 42437
(502) 389-1811

Felony and misdemeanor records are available by mail. A release is required. No search fee. $.25 fee per cpy. $1.00 for certification. Search information required: name, date of birth, sex, race, SASE.

Civil records are available by mail. A release is required. No search fee. Search information required: name, SSN, years to search. Specify plaintiff or defendant.

Warren County

Justice Center of Warren County, Criminal Records
925 Center Street
PO Box 2170
Bowling Green, KY 42102
(502) 843-5400
Fax (502) 842-9416

Felony and misdemeanor records are available by mail or fax. No release necessary. No search fee. $.15 fee per copy. $1.00 for certification. Search information required: name, SSN, date of birth, years to search, SASE.

Civil records are available by mail or phone. No release necessary. No search fee. Search information required: name, SSN, years to search. Specify plaintiff or defendant.

Washington County

Circuit Court Clerk, Criminal Records
PO Box 148
Springfield, KY 40069
(606) 336-3761

Felony and misdemeanor records are available by mail or phone. No release necessary. No search fee. $.15 fee per copy. $1.00 for certification. Search information required: name, date of birth, SSN.

Civil records are available by mail or phone. No release necessary. No search fee. Search information required: name, SSN, years to search. Specify plaintiff or defendant.

Wayne County

Circuit Court Clerk, Criminal Records
PO Box 816
Monticello, KY 42633
(606) 348-5841

Felony and misdemeanor records are available by mail. No release necessary. No search fee. $.15 fee per copy. $1.00 for certification. Search information required: name, SASE, date of birth.

Civil records are available by mail. No release necessary. No search fee. Search information required: name, SSN, years to search. Specify plaintiff or defendant.

Webster County

Courthouse, Criminal Records
PO Box 217
Dixon, KY 42409
(502) 639-9160

Felony and misdemeanor records are available by mail. No release necessary. No search fee. $.15 fee per copy. $1.00 for certification. Search information required: name, SSN, SASE.

Civil records are available by mail. No release necessary. No search fee. Search information required: name, address, date of birth, SSN, years to search. Specify plaintiff or defendant.

Whitley County

Felony records
Circuit Court Clerk, Criminal Records
PO Box 329
Williamsburg, KY 40769
(606) 549-2973

Felony records are available by mail. No release necessary. No search fee. $.15 fee per copy. $1.50 for certification. Search information required: name, SSN, date of birth, SASE.

Civil records
Circuit Court Clerk
PO Box 329
Williamsburg, KY 40769
(606) 549-2973

Civil records are available by mail. No release necessary. No search fee. Search information required: name, SSN, years to search. Specify plaintiff or defendant.

Misdemeanor records
District Court
PO Box 329
Williamsburg, KY 40769-0329
(606) 549-5162
Misdemeanor records are available by mail or phone. No release necessary. No search fee. $.15 fee per copy. $5.00 for certification. Search information required: name, date of birth, SSN.

Civil records
District Court
PO Box 329
Williamsburg, KY 40769-0329
(606) 549-5162
Civil records are available by mail or phone. No release necessary. No search fee. Search information required: name, SSN, years to search. Specify plaintiff or defendant.

Wolfe County

Circuit Court Clerk, Criminal Records
PO Box 296
Campton, KY 41301
(606) 668-3736
Felony and misdemeanor records are available by mail. No release necessary. No search fee. Search information required: name, SSN, date of birth.

Civil records are available by mail. No release necessary. No search fee. $.25 fee per copy. $1.00 for certification. Search information required: name, SSN, years to search. Specify plaintiff or defendant.

Woodford County

Woodford County Courthouse, Criminal Records
Room 102
Versailles, KY 40383
(606) 873-3711
Felony and misdemeanor records are available in person only. See Idaho state repository for additional information.

Civil records are available in person only. See Kentucky state repository for additional information.

City-County Cross Reference

Aaron *Clinton*
Aberdeen *Butler*
Acorn *Pulaski*
Adairville *Logan*
Adams *Lawrence*
Adolphus *Allen*
Aflex *Pike*
Ages-Brookside *Harlan*
Airport Gardens *Perry*
Albany *Clinton*
Alcalde *Pulaski*
Alexandria *Campbell*
Allegre *Todd*
Allen *Floyd*
Allensville *Todd*
Allock *Perry*
Almo *Calloway*
Alpha *Clinton*
Altro *Breathitt*
Alvaton *Warren*
Amburgey *Knott*
Anchorage *Jefferson*
Anco *Knott*
Annville *Jackson*
Argillite *Greenup*
Argo *Pike*
Arjay *Bell*
Arlington *Carlisle*
Artemus *Knox*
Ary *Perry*
Ashcamp *Pike*
Asher *Leslie*
Ashland *Boyd*
Athol *Lee*
Auburn *Logan*
Augusta *Bracken*
Austin *Barren*
Auxier *Floyd*
Avawam *Perry*
Axtel *Breckinridge*
Bagdad *Shelby*
Baileys Switch *Knox*
Bakerton *Cumberland*
Bandana *Ballard*
Banner *Floyd*
Barbourmeade *Jefferson*
Barbourville *Knox*
Bardstown *Nelson*
Bardwell *Carlisle*
Barlow *Ballard*

Baskett *Henderson*
Battletown *Meade*
Baxter *Harlan*
Bays *Breathitt*
Bear Branch *Leslie*
Beattyville *Lee*
Beaumont *Metcalfe*
Beauty *Martin*
Beaver *Floyd*
Beaver Dam *Ohio*
Bedford *Trimble*
Beech Circle *Muhlenberg*
Beech Creek *Muhlenberg*
Beech Grove *McLean*
Beechmont *Muhlenberg*
Beechwood Village
   Jefferson
Bee Spring *Edmonson*
Belcher *Pike*
Belfry *Pike*
Bellefonte *Greenup*
Bellemeade *Jefferson*
Bellevue *Campbell*
Bellewood *Jefferson*
Belton *Muhlenberg*
Benham *Harlan*
Benton *Marshall*
Berea *Madison*
Berry *Harrison*
Bethanna *Magoffin*
Bethany *Wolfe*
Bethel *Bath*
Bethelridge *Casey*
Bethlehem *Henry*
Betsy Layne *Floyd*
Beulah Heights *McCreary*
Beverly *Bell*
Bevinsville *Floyd*
Big Clifty *Grayson*
Big Creek *Clay*
Bighill *Madison*
Big Laurel *Harlan*
Big Spring *Breckinridge*
Bimble *Knox*
Blackey *Letcher*
Blackford *Webster*
Blaine *Lawrence*
Blandville *Ballard*
Blaze *Morgan*
Bledsoe *Harlan*

Bloomfield *Nelson*
Bluehole *Clay*
Blue River *Floyd*
Boaz *Graves*
Bond *Jackson*
Bonnieville *Hart*
Bonnyman *Perry*
Boone Heights *Knox*
Booneville *Owsley*
Boons Camp *Johnson*
Boston *Nelson*
Bow *Cumberland*
Bowen *Powell*
Bowling Green *Warren*
Bradfordsville *Marion*
Brandenburg *Meade*
Breeding *Adair*
Bremen *Muhlenberg*
Briarwood *Jefferson*
Brinkley *Knott*
Broadfields *Jefferson*
Brodhead *Rockcastle*
Bromley *Kenton*
Bronston *Pulaski*
Brooklyn *Butler*
Brooks *Bullitt*
Brooksville *Bracken*
Browder *Muhlenberg*
Browns Fork *Perry*
Brownsboro Farm
   Jefferson
BrownsboroVillage
   Jefferson
Brownsville *Edmonson*
Bruin *Elliott*
Bryants Store *Knox*
Bryantsville *Garrard*
Buckhorn *Perry*
Buckner *Oldham*
Buffalo *Larue*
Bulan *Perry*
Burdine *Letcher*
Burgin *Mercer*
Burkesville *Cumberland*
Burkhart *Wolfe*
Burlington *Boone*
Burna *Livingston*
Burning Fork *Magoffin*
Burnside *Pulaski*
Burnwell *Pike*

Bush *Laurel*
Buskirk *Morgan*
Busy *Perry*
Butler *Pendleton*
Bypro *Floyd*
Cadiz *Trigg*
Calhoun *McLean*
California *Campbell*
Calvert City *Marshall*
Calvin *Bell*
Camargo *Montgomery*
Campbellsburg *Henry*
Campbellsville *Taylor*
Camp Dix *Lewis*
Campton *Wolfe*
Canada *Pike*
Cane Valley *Adair*
Caney *Morgan*
Caneyville *Grayson*
Canmer *Hart*
Cannel City *Morgan*
Cannon *Knox*
Cannonsburg *Boyd*
Canoe *Breathitt*
Canton *Trigg*
Carlisle *Nicholas*
Carrie *Knott*
Carrollton *Carroll*
Carter *Carter*
Carver *Magoffin*
Casey Creek *Adair*
Catlettsburg *Boyd*
Cave City *Barren*
Cawood *Harlan*
Cecilia *Hardin*
Center *Metcalfe*
Centertown *Ohio*
Central City *Muhlenberg*
Cerulean *Trigg*
Chaplin *Nelson*
Chappell *Leslie*
Chavies *Perry*
Cherrywood Village
   Jefferson
Chloe *Pike*
Chevrolet *Harlan*
Cinda *Leslie*
Cisco *Magoffin*
Clarkson *Grayson*
Clay *Webster*

Clay City *Powell*
Clayhole *Breathitt*
Clearfield *Rowan*
Cleaton *Muhlenberg*
Clermont *Bullitt*
Clifty *Todd*
Climax *Rockcastle*
Clinton *Hickman*
Closplint *Harlan*
Cloverport *Breckinridge*
Coalgood *Harlan*
Cobhill *Estill*
Cold Spring *Campbell*
Coldiron *Harlan*
Colonial *Jefferson*
Columbia *Adair*
Columbus *Hickman*
Combs *Perry*
Concord *Lewis*
Confluence *Leslie*
Conley *Magoffin*
Constance *Boone*
Constantine *Breckinridge*
Conway *Rockcastle*
Coopersville *Wayne*
Corbin *Whitley*
Corinth *Grant*
Cornettsville *Perry*
Cornishville *Mercer*
Corydon *Henderson*
Cottle *Morgan*
Covington *Kenton*
Coxs Creek *Nelson*
Crab Orchard *Lincoln*
Cranks *Harlan*
Crayne *Crittenden*
Craynor *Floyd*
Crescent Park *Kenton*
Crescent Springs *Kenton*
Crestview *Campbell*
Crestview Hills *Kenton*
Crestwood *Oldham*
Crittenden *Grant*
Crockett *Morgan*
Crofton *Christian*
Cromona *Letcher*
Cromwell *Ohio*
Crown *Letcher*
Crystal *Estill*
Cubage *Bell*
Cub Run *Hart*
Culver *Elliott*
Cumberland *Harlan*
Cundiff *Adair*
Cunningham *Carlisle*
Curdsville *Daviess*
Custer *Breckinridge*
Cutshin *Leslie*
Cutuno *Magoffin*
Cynthiana *Harrison*
Dabolt *Jackson*
Daisy *Perry*
Dana *Floyd*
Danville *Boyle*
David *Floyd*
Dawson Springs *Hopkins*
Dayhoit *Harlan*
Dayton *Campbell*
Deane *Letcher*
Deatsville *Nelson*
Debord *Martin*
Decoy *Knott*
Defoe *Henry*
Delphia *Perry*
Delta *Wayne*

Dema *Knott*
DeMossville *Pendleton*
Denniston *Menifee*
Denton *Carter*
Denver *Johnson*
Depoy *Muhlenberg*
Dewitt *Knox*
Dexter *Calloway*
Diablock *Perry*
Dice *Perry*
Dingus *Morgan*
Dixon *Webster*
Dizney *Harlan*
Dorton *Pike*
Dover *Mason*
Draffin *Pike*
Drake *Warren*
Drakesboro *Muhlenberg*
Dreyfus *Madison*
Drift *Floyd*
Druid Hills *Jefferson*
Dry Creek *Knott*
Dry Ridge *Grant*
Dubre *Cumberland*
Dunbar *Butler*
Dundee *Ohio*
Dunmor *Muhlenberg*
Dunnville *Casey*
Dwale *Floyd*
Dwarf *Perry*
Dycusburg *Crittenden*
Earlington *Hopkins*
East Bernstadt *Laurel*
Eastern *Floyd*
East Point *Johnson*
Eastview *Hardin*
Eastwood *Jefferson*
Echols *Ohio*
Eddyville *Lyon*
Edgewood *Kenton*
Edmonton *Metcalfe*
Edna *Magoffin*
Egypt *Jackson*
Eighty Eight *Barren*
Ekron *Meade*
Elizabethtown *Hardin*
Elizaville *Fleming*
Elkfork *Morgan*
Elk Horn *Taylor*
Elkhorn City *Pike*
Elkton *Todd*
Elliottville *Rowan*
Elsmere *Kenton*
Elmrock *Knott*
Elsie *Magoffin*
Emerson *Lewis*
Eminence *Henry*
Emlyn *Whitley*
Emma *Floyd*
Emmalena *Knott*
Endicott *Floyd*
Eolia *Letcher*
Eriline *Clay*
Erlanger *Kenton*
Ermine *Letcher*
Essie *Leslie*
Estill *Floyd*
Etoile *Barren*
Etty *Pike*
Eubank *Pulaski*
Evarts *Harlan*
Ewing *Fleming*
Ezel *Morgan*
Fairdale *Jefferson*
Fairfield *Nelson*

Fairplay *Adair*
Fairview *Christian*
Falcon *Magoffin*
Fall Rock *Clay*
Falls Of Rough *Grayson*
Falmouth *Pendleton*
Fancy Farm *Graves*
Farler *Perry*
Farmers *Rowan*
Farmington *Graves*
Faubush *Pulaski*
Fedscreek *Pike*
Ferguson *Pulaski*
Fern *Jefferson*
Fillmore *Lee*
Fincastle *Jefferson*
Finchville *Shelby*
Finley *Taylor*
Firebrick *Lewis*
Fisherville *Jefferson*
Fishtrap *Pike*
Fisty *Knott*
Flaherty *Radcliff*
Flat Fork *Magoffin*
Flatgap *Johnson*
Flat Lick *Knox*
Flatwoods *Greenup*
Fleming *Letcher*
Fleming-Neon *Letcher*
Flemingsburg *Fleming*
Florence *Boone*
Fogertown *Clay*
Foraker *Magoffin*
Ford *Clark*
Fords Branch *Pike*
Fordsville *Ohio*
Forest Hills *Pike*
Fort Campbell *Christian*
Fort Knox *Hardin*
Fort Mitchell *Kenton*
Fort Thomas *Campbell*
Foster *Bracken*
Fountain Run *Monroe*
Fourmile *Bell*
Foxtown *Jackson*
Frakes *Bell*
Frankfort *Franklin*
Franklin *Simpson*
Frazer *Wayne*
Fredonia *Caldwell*
Fredville *Magoffin*
Freeburn *Pike*
Frenchburg *Menifee*
Fritz *Magoffin*
Fuget *Johnson*
Fulton *Fulton*
Galveston *Floyd*
Gamaliel *Monroe*
Gapville *Magoffin*
Garfield *Breckinridge*
Garner *Knott*
Garrard *Clay*
Garrett *Floyd*
Garrison *Lewis*
Gays Creek *Perry*
Georgetown *Scott*
Germantown *Bracken*
Ghent *Carroll*
Gifford *Magoffin*
Gilbertsville *Marshall*
Gilley *Letcher*
Gillmore *Wolfe*
Girdler *Knox*
Glasgow *Barren*
Glencoe *Gallatin*

Glendale *Hardin*
Glen Dean *Breckinridge*
Glens Fork *Adair*
Glenview *Jefferson*
Glenview Hills *Jefferson*
Goody *Pike*
Goose Rock *Clay*
Gordon *Letcher*
Goshen *Oldham*
Gracey *Christian*
Gradyville *Adair*
Graham *Muhlenberg*
Grahamville *McCracken*
Grahn *Carter*
Grand Rivers *Livingston*
Grassy Creek *Morgan*
Gratz *Owen*
Gravel Switch *Marion*
Gray *Knox*
Gray Hawk *Jackson*
Grays Knob *Harlan*
Graymoor-Devondale
   Jefferson
Grayson *Carter*
Green Hall *Owsley*
Green Road *Knox*
Greensburg *Green*
Greenup *Greenup*
Greenville *Muhlenberg*
Grethel *Floyd*
Guage *Breathitt*
Guerrant *Breathitt*
Gulston *Harlan*
Gunlock *Magoffin*
Guston *Meade*
Guthrie *Todd*
Gypsy *Magoffin*
Haddix *Breathitt*
Hadley *Warren*
Hager *Magoffin*
Hagerhill *Johnson*
Haldeman *Rowan*
Halfway *Allen*
Hallie *Letcher*
Halo *Floyd*
Hamlin *Calloway*
Hampton *Livingston*
Hanson *Hopkins*
Happy *Perry*
Hardburly *Perry*
Hardin *Marshall*
Hardinsburg *Breckinridge*
Hardy *Pike*
Hardyville *Hart*
Harlan *Harlan*
Harned *Breckinridge*
Harold *Floyd*
Harper *Magoffin*
Harrodsburg *Mercer*
Harrods Creek *Jefferson*
Hartford *Ohio*
Hawesville *Hancock*
Hazard *Perry*
Hazel *Calloway*
Hazel Green *Wolfe*
Hebron *Boone*
Heidelberg *Lee*
Heidrick *Knox*
Helechawa *Wolfe*
Hellier *Pike*
Henderson *Henderson*
Hendricks *Magoffin*
Herd *Jackson*
Herndon *Christian*
Hestand *Monroe*

Hickman *Fulton*
Hickory *Graves*
Highland Heights
    Campbell
Highview *Jefferson*
Hi Hat *Floyd*
Hillcrest *Madison*
Hillsboro *Fleming*
Hillview *Bullitt*
Hima *Clay*
Hindman *Knott*
Hinkle *Knox*
Hippo *Floyd*
Hiseville *Barren*
Hitchins *Carter*
Hode *Martin*
Hodgenville *Larue*
Holland *Allen*
Hollow Creek *Jefferson*
Hollybush *Knott*
Holly Villa *Jefferson*
Holmes Mill *Harlan*
Honaker *Floyd*
Hope *Montgomery*
Hopkinsville *Christian*
Horse Branch *Ohio*
Horse Cave *Hart*
Hoskinston *Leslie*
Houston Acres *Jefferson*
Howardstown *Nelson*
Huddy *Pike*
Hudson *Breckinridge*
Hueysville *Floyd*
Huff *Edmonson*
Hulen *Bell*
Hunter *Floyd*
Huntsville *Butler*
Hurstbourne *Jefferson*
Hustonville *Lincoln*
Hyden *Leslie*
Independence *Kenton*
Inez *Martin*
Ingle *Pulaski*
Ingram *Bell*
Insko *Morgan*
Ironville *Boyd*
Irvine *Estill*
Irvington *Breckinridge*
Island *McLean*
Island City *Owsley*
Isom *Letcher*
Isonville *Elliott*
Ivel *Floyd*
Ivyton *Magoffin*
Jackhorn *Letcher*
Jackson *Breathitt*
Jacobs *Carter*
Jamboree *Pike*
Jamestown *Russell*
Jeff *Perry*
Jeffersontown *Jefferson*
Jeffersonville *Montgomery*
Jenkins *Letcher*
Jeremiah *Letcher*
Jetson *Butler*
Job *Martin*
Johns Run *Carter*
Jonancy *Pike*
Jonesville *Grant*
Junction City *Boyle*
Keaton *Johnson*
Keavy *Laurel*
Keene *Jessamine*
Keith *Harlan*
Kenton *Kenton*
Kenvir *Harlan*

Kerby Knob *Jackson*
Kettle *Cumberland*
Kettle Island *Bell*
Kevil *Ballard*
Kimper *Pike*
Kingsley *Jefferson*
Kings Mountain *Lincoln*
Kirksey *Calloway*
Kite *Knott*
Knifley *Adair*
Knob Lick *Metcalfe*
Knottsville *Daviess*
Kona *Letcher*
Krypton *Perry*
Kuttawa *Lyon*
LaCenter *Ballard*
Lackey *Floyd*
LaFayette *Christian*
LaGrange *Oldham*
Lake City *Livingston*
Lakeside Park *Kenton*
Lamb *Monroe*
Lambric *Breathitt*
Lamero *Rockcastle*
Lancaster *Garrard*
Langley *Floyd*
Laura *Martin*
Lawrenceburg *Anderson*
Lawton *Carter*
Leander *Johnson*
Leatherwood *Perry*
Lebanon *Marion*
Lebanon Junction *Bullitt*
Leburn *Knott*
Ledbetter *Livingston*
Lee City *Wolfe*
Leeco *Lee*
Leitchfield *Grayson*
Lejunior *Harlan*
Lenox *Morgan*
Lerose *Owsley*
Letcher *Letcher*
Levee *Montgomery*
Lewisburg *Logan*
Lewisport *Hancock*
Lexington *Fayette*
Liberty *Casey*
Lick Creek *Pike*
Ligon *Floyd*
Lily *Laurel*
Lindseyville *Edmonson*
Linefork *Letcher*
Littcarr *Knott*
Little *Breathitt*
Livermore *McLean*
Livingston *Rockcastle*
Lloyd *Greenup*
Lockport *Henry*
Lola *Livingston*
London *Laurel*
Lone *Lee*
Lone Oak *McCracken*
Longview *Hardin*
Lookout *Pike*
Loretto *Marion*
Lost Creek *Breathitt*
Lost River *Warren*
Lothair *Perry*
Louellen *Harlan*
Louisa *Lawrence*
Louisville *Jefferson*
Lovelaceville *Ballard*
Lovely *Martin*
Lowes *Graves*
Lowmansville *Lawrence*
Loyall *Harlan*

Lucas *Barren*
Lynch *Harlan*
Lyndon Jefferson
Lynn Grove *Calloway*
Lynnview *Jefferson*
Lynnville *Graves*
Lytten *Elliott*
McAndrews *Pike*
McCarr *Pike*
McCombs *Pike*
McDaniels *Breckinridge*
McDowell *Floyd*
McHenry *Ohio*
McKee *Jackson*
McKinney *Lincoln*
McQuady *Breckinridge*
McRoberts *Letcher*
McVeigh *Pike*
Maceo *Daviess*
Mackville *Washington*
Madisonville *Hopkins*
Maggard *Magoffin*
Magnolia *Larue*
Majestic *Pike*
Mallie *Knott*
Malone *Morgan*
Maloneton *Greenup*
Mammoth Cave *Edmonson*
Manchester *Clay*
Manila *Johnson*
Manitou *Hopkins*
Mannsville *Taylor*
Manton *Floyd*
Maple Mount *Daviess*
Mariba *Menifee*
Marion *Crittenden*
Marrowbone *Cumberland*
Marshallville *Magoffin*
Marshes Siding *McCreary*
Martha *Lawrence*
Martin *Floyd*
Mary Alice *Harlan*
Marydell *Laurel*
Mashfork *Magoffin*
Mason *Grant*
Masonic Home *Jefferson*
Masonville *Daviess*
Mayfield *Graves*
Mayking *Letcher*
Mays Lick *Mason*
Maysville *Mason*
Mazie *Lawrence*
Meally *Johnson*
Means *Menifee*
Melber *McCracken*
Melbourne *Campbell*
Melvin *Floyd*
Middleburg *Casey*
Middlesboro *Bell*
Middletown *Jefferson*
Midway *Woodford*
Milburn *Carlisle*
Milford *Bracken*
Millersburg *Bourbon*
Mills *Knox*
Mill Springs *Wayne*
Millstone *Letcher*
Milltown *Adair*
Millwood *Grayson*
Milton *Trimble*
Mima *Morgan*
Minerva *Mason*
Minnie *Floyd*
Minor Lane Heights
    Jefferson
Miracle *Bell*

Mistletoe *Owsley*
Mitchellsburg *Boyle*
Mize *Morgan*
Monticello *Wayne*
Montpelier *Adair*
Moon *Morgan*
Moorefield *Nicholas*
Moorland *Jefferson*
Moorman *Muhlenberg*
Morehead *Rowan*
Morganfield *Union*
Morgantown *Butler*
Morning View *Kenton*
Morrill *Jackson*
Mortons Gap *Hopkins*
Mount Eden *Spencer*
Mount Hermon *Monroe*
Mount Olivet *Robertson*
Mount Sherman *Larue*
Mount Sterling
    Montgomery
Mount Vernon *Rockcastle*
Mount Washington *Bullitt*
Mousie *Knott*
Mouthcard *Pike*
Mozelle *Leslie*
Muldraugh *Meade*
Munfordville *Hart*
Murray *Calloway*
Muses Mills *Fleming*
Myra *Pike*
Nancy *Pulaski*
Narrows *Ohio*
Nazareth *Nelson*
Neafus *Grayson*
Nebo *Hopkins*
Ned *Breathitt*
Nelse *Pike*
Neon *Letcher*
Nerinx *Marion*
Nevisdale *Whitley*
New Castle *Henry*
New Concord *Calloway*
Newfoundland *Elliott*
New Haven *Nelson*
New Hope *Nelson*
New Liberty *Owen*
Newport *Campbell*
Nicholasville *Jessamine*
Noctor *Breathitt*
North Corbin *Laurel*
Northfield *Jefferson*
North Middletown
    Bourbon
Nortonville *Hopkins*
Oakdale *McCracken*
Oak Grove *Christian*
Oakland *Warren*
Oakton *Hickman*
Oakville *Logan*
Offutt *Johnson*
Oil Springs *Johnson*
Okolona *Jefferson*
Olaton *Ohio*
Old Landing *Lee*
Oldtown *Greenup*
Olive Hill *Carter*
Ollie *Edmonson*
Olmstead *Logan*
Olympia *Bath*
Oneida *Clay*
Ophir *Morgan*
Orlando *Rockcastle*
Oscaloosa *Letcher*
Oven Fork *Letcher*
Owensboro *Daviess*

Owenton *Owen*
Owingsville *Bath*
Paducah *McCracken*
Paint Lick *Garrard*
Paintsville *Johnson*
Paris *Bourbon*
Park City *Barren*
Park Hills *Kenton*
Parkers Lake *McCreary*
Parksville *Boyle*
Parkway Village *Jefferson*
Parrot *Jackson*
Partridge *Letcher*
Pathfork *Harlan*
Paw Paw *Pike*
Payne Gap *Letcher*
Payneville *Meade*
Pebworth *Owsley*
Pellville *Hancock*
Pembroke *Christian*
Pendleton *Henry*
Penrod *Muhlenberg*
Peoples *Jackson*
Perry Park *Owen*
Perryville *Boyle*
Petersburg *Boone*
Pewee Valley *Oldham*
Peytonsburg *Cumberland*
Phelps *Pike*
Philpot *Daviess*
Phyllis *Pike*
Pikeville *Pike*
Pilgrim *Martin*
Pine Knot *McCreary*
Pine Ridge *Wolfe*
Pine Top *Knott*
Pineville *Bell*
Pinsonfork *Pike*
Pippa Passes *Knott*
Pittsburg *Laurel*
Plank *Clay*
Plantation *Jefferson*
Pleasant Ridge *Daviess*
Pleasant View *Whitley*
Pleasure Ridge Park
  Jefferson
Pleasureville *Henry*
Plummers Landing
  Fleming
Pomeroyton *Menifee*
Poole *Webster*
Port Royal *Henry*
Powderly *Muhlenberg*
Prairie Village *Jefferson*
Premium *Letcher*
Preston *Bath*
Prestonsburg *Floyd*
Prestonville *Carroll*
Price *Floyd*
Primrose *Lee*
Princeton *Caldwell*
Printer *Floyd*
Prospect *Jefferson*
Providence *Webster*
Provo *Butler*
Pryse *Estill*
Puncheon *Knott*
Putney *Harlan*
Quality *Butler*
Quicksand *Breathitt*
Quincy *Lewis*
Raccoon *Pike*
Raceland *Greenup*
Radcliff *Hardin*
Ransom *Pike*

Ravenna *Estill*
Raywick *Marion*
Redbush *Johnson*
Redfox *Knott*
Reed *Henderson*
Regina *Pike*
Reidland *McCracken*
Renfro Valley *Rockcastle*
Revelo *McCreary*
Reynolds Station *Ohio*
Rhodelia *Meade*
Ricetown *Owsley*
Richardson *Lawrence*
Richardsville *Warren*
Richelieu *Logan*
Richlawn *Jefferson*
Richmond *Madison*
Rineyville *Hardin*
Ritner *Wayne*
River *Johnson*
Riverside *Warren*
Riverside Gardens
  Jefferson
Riverwood *Jefferson*
Roark *Leslie*
Robards *Henderson*
Robinson Creek *Pike*
Rochester *Butler*
Rockfield *Warren*
Rockholds *Whitley*
Rockhouse *Pike*
Rockport *Ohio*
Rockybranch *Wayne*
Rocky Hill *Edmonson*
Rogers *Wolfe*
Rolling Fields *Jefferson*
Rolling Hills *Jefferson*
Rosine *Ohio*
Rosslyn *Powell*
Roundhill *Edmonson*
Rousseau *Breathitt*
Rowdy *Perry*
Rowletts *Hart*
Roxana *Letcher*
Royalton *Magoffin*
Rumsey *McLean*
Rush *Boyd*
Russell *Greenup*
Russell Springs *Russell*
Russellville *Logan*
Sacramento *McLean*
Sadieville *Scott*
Sadler *Grayson*
Saint Catharine
  Washington
Saint Charles *Hopkins*
Saint Dennis *Jefferson*
Saint Francis *Marion*
Saint Helens *Lee*
Saint Joseph *Daviess*
Saint Mary *Marion*
Saint Matthews *Jefferson*
Saint Paul *Lewis*
Saint Regis Park *Jefferson*
Saldee *Breathitt*
Salem *Livingston*
Salt Gum *Knox*
Salt Lick *Bath*
Salvisa *Mercer*
Salyersville *Magoffin*
Sample *Breckinridge*
Samuels *Nelson*
Sanders *Carroll*
Sandgap *Jackson*
Sandy Hook *Elliott*

Sassafras *Knott*
Saul *Perry*
Sawyer *McCreary*
Scalf *Knox*
Science Hill *Pulaski*
Scottsville *Allen*
Scranton *Menifee*
Scuddy *Perry*
Sebastians Branch
  Breathitt
Sebree *Webster*
Seco *Letcher*
Sedalia *Graves*
Seitz *Magoffin*
Senaca Gardens *Jefferson*
Se Ree *Breckinridge*
Sextons Creek *Clay*
Sharon Grove *Todd*
Sharpsburg *Bath*
Shelbiana *Pike*
Shelby Gap *Pike*
Shelbyville *Shelby*
Shively *Jefferson*
Shepherdsville *Bullitt*
Shopville *Pulaski*
Sibert *Clay*
Sidney *Pike*
Siler *Whitley*
Silver Grove *Campbell*
Silverhill *Morgan*
Simpsonville *Shelby*
Sitka *Johnson*
Skyline *Letcher*
Slade *Powell*
Slaughters *Webster*
Slemp *Perry*
Smilax *Leslie*
Smith *Harlan*
Smithfield *Henry*
Smithland *Livingston*
Smith Mills *Henderson*
Smiths Grove *Warren*
Soldier *Carter*
Somerset *Pulaski*
Sonora *Hardin*
South *Grayson*
South Carrollton
  Muhlenberg
Southgate *Campbell*
South Irvine *Estill*
South Portsmouth *Greenup*
South Shore *Greenup*
South Union *Logan*
South Williamson *Pike*
Sparta *Gallatin*
Speight *Pike*
Spottsville *Henderson*
Springdale *Jefferson*
Springfield *Washington*
Springlee *Jefferson*
Spring Lick *Grayson*
Spurlock *Clay*
Stab *Pulaski*
Staffordsville *Johnson*
Stambaugh *Johnson*
Stamping Ground *Scott*
Stanford *Lincoln*
Stanley *Daviess*
Stanton *Powell*
Stanville *Floyd*
Stark *Elliott*
Stearns *McCreary*
Steele *Pike*
Steff *Grayson*
Stella *Magoffin*

Stephens *Elliott*
Stephensburg *Hardin*
Stephensport *Breckinridge*
Steubenville *Wayne*
Stinnett *Leslie*
Stone *Pike*
Stoney Fork *Bell*
Stopover *Pike*
Strathmoor Village
  Jefferson
Strunk *McCreary*
Sturgis *Union*
Sublimity City *Laurel*
Sudith *Menifee*
Sullivan *Union*
Sulphur *Henry*
Summer Shade *Metcalfe*
Summersville *Green*
Summit *Hardin*
Sunfish *Edmonson*
Sunshine *Harlin*
Swamp Branch *Johnson*
Sweeden *Edmonson*
Symbol *Laurel*
Symsonia *Graves*
Talbert *Breathitt*
Talcum *Knott*
Tallega *Lee*
Tateville *Pulaski*
Taylor Mill *Kenton*
Taylorsville *Spencer*
Teaberry *Floyd*
Thealka *Johnson*
Thelma *Johnson*
Thornton *Letcher*
Thousandsticks *Leslie*
Threeforks *Martin*
Tiline *Livingston*
Tinsley *Bell*
Tollesboro *Lewis*
Tolu *Crittenden*
Tomahawk *Martin*
Tompkinsville *Monroe*
Topmost *Knott*
Totz *Harlan*
Tram *Floyd*
Trenton *Todd*
Trosper *Knox*
Turkey Creek *Pike*
Turners Station *Henry*
Tutor Key *Johnson*
Tyner *Jackson*
Typo *Perry*
Ulvah *Letcher*
Ulysses *Lawrence*
Union *Boone*
Union Star *Breckinridge*
Uniontown *Union*
Upper Tygart *Carter*
Upton *Hardin*
Utica *Daviess*
Vada *Lee*
Valley Station *Jefferson*
Valley Village *Jefferson*
Van *Letcher*
Vanceburg *Lewis*
Vancleve *Breathitt*
Van Lear *Johnson*
Varney *Pike*
Verda *Harlan*
Verona *Boone*
Versailles *Woodford*
Vertrees *Hardin*
Vest *Knott*
Vicco *Perry*

Villa Hills *Kenton*
Vincent *Owsley*
Vine Grove *Hardin*
Viper *Perry*
Virgie *Pike*
Volga *Johnson*
Waco *Madison*
Waddy *Shelby*
Waldo *Magoffin*
Walker *Knox*
Wallingford *Fleming*
Wallins Creek *Harlan*
Walnut Grove *Pulaski*
Walton *Boone*
Waneta *Jackson*
Warbranch *Leslie*
Warfield *Martin*
Warsaw *Gallatin*
Washington *Mason*
Watergap *Floyd*
Water Valley *Graves*
Waterview *Cumberland*
Waverly *Union*
Wax *Grayson*
Wayland *Floyd*
Waynesburg *Lincoln*
Webbville *Lawrence*
Webster *Breckinridge*
Weeksbury *Floyd*
Welchs Creek *Butler*
Wellington *Menifee*
Wendover *Leslie*
Westbend *Powell*
West Buechel *Jefferson*
West Liberty *Morgan*
West Louisville *Daviess*
West Paducah *McCracken*
West Point *Hardin*
Westport *Oldham*
West Van Lear *Johnson*
Westview *Breckinridge*
Westwood *Boyd*
Wheatcroft *Webster*
Wheatley *Owen*
Wheelersburg *Magoffin*
Wheelwright *Floyd*
Whick *Breathitt*
Whitehouse *Johnson*
White Mills *Hardin*
White Oak *Morgan*
White Plains *Hopkins*
Whitesburg *Letcher*
Whitesville *Daviess*
Whitley City *McCreary*
Wiborg *McCreary*
Wickliffe *Ballard*
Widecreek *Breathitt*
Wild Cat *Clay*
Wilder *Campbell*
Wildie *Rockcastle*
Willard *Carter*
Williamsburg *Whitley*
Williamsport *Johnson*
Williamstown *Grant*
Willisburg *Washington*
Willow Shade *Metcalfe*
Wilmore *Jessamine*
Winchester *Clark*
Wind Cave *Jackson*
Windsor *Casey*
Windy *Wayne*
Windy Hills *Jefferson*
Wingo *Graves*
Winston *Estill*
Wittensville *Johnson*

Wolf *Carter*
Wolf Coal *Breathitt*
Wolverine *Breathitt*
Wonnie *Magoffin*
Woodbine *Whitley*
Woodburn *Warren*
Woodbury *Butler*
Woodlawn *Campbell*
Woodlawn Park *Jefferson*
Woodman *Pike*
Woollum *Knox*
Wooton *Leslie*
Worthington *Greenup*
Worthville *Carroll*
Wrigley *Morgan*
Wurtland *Greenup*
Yeaddiss *Leslie*
Yerkes *Perry*
York *Greenup*
Yosemite *Casey*
Zachariah *Lee*
Zebulon *Pike*
Zoe *Lee*

Louisiana

Sixty (60) of Louisiana's sixty four (64) parishes make criminal records available for employment purposes by mail or phone. Of the sixty parishes, twenty three (23) honor fax requests. The remaining four parishes require that the requests be made in person. Sixty two (62) parishes allow civil record checks to be made by mail or phone.

For more information or for offices not listed, contact the state's information hot line at (504) 342-6600.

Driving Records

Louisiana Department of Public Safety
O.D.R.
PO Box 64886
Baton Rouge, LA 70896
(504) 925-6009
Driving records are available by mail. $15 fee per request. Turnaround time is 7 to 10 days. Written request must include job applicant's full name, date of birth and license number. Make company, certified check or money order payable to Department of Public Safety.

Worker's Compensation Records

Worker's Compensation
PO Box 94095
Baton Rouge, LA 70804-9095
(504) 342-8484
Worker's compensation records are not currently accessible for employee screening purposes.

Vital Statistics

Department of Vital Records
PO Box 60630
New Orleans, LA 70160
(504) 568-2561
Fax 568-5391
Fax (504) 568-5160 (Marriage Records)

Long form birth records are available for $8.00. Short form birth records and death records are available for $5.00 each. State office has records since 1911. Birth records for City of New Orleans are available from 1892, and death records from 1943. For birth records, include name at birth, date, place, father's name, and mother's maiden name. For death records include name at death, date, and place. An employer can get records with a written release. Make check or money order payable to Department of Vital Records.

New Orleans marriage records are available from 1936. Fee is $5.00. Turnaround time is 3-4 weeks. Include name, marriage date, spouse's name, where it took place. Marriages that occurred in parishes other than New Orleans are obtained from the Clerk of Court in that parish. Divorce records are obtained from the Civil District Court (504) 592-9100.

Department of Education

Department of Education
Teacher Certification
PO Box 94064
Baton Rouge, LA 70804-9064
(504) 342-3490
Fax (504) 342-3499
Field of certification and expiration date are available by mail, phone or fax. Include name and SSN.

Medical Licensing

LSBME
Verification & Licensing
830 Union St.
New Orleans, LA 70112-1499
(504) 524-6763
Fax (504) 568-8893
Will confirm licenses for MDs and DOs by mail, phone or fax. No fee. For licenses not mentioned, contact the above office.

Louisiana State Board of Nursing
907 Pere Marquette Building
150 Baronne Street
New Orleans, LA 70112
(504) 568-5464
Will confirm license by phone. No fee. Include name, license number.

Bar Association

Louisiana State Bar Association
601 St. Charles Ave.
New Orleans, LA 70130
(504) 566-1600
Will confirm licenses by phone. No fee. Include name.

Accountancy Board

Louisiana State Board of Accountancy
1515 World Trade Center
2 Canal Street
New Orleans, LA 70130
(504) 566-1244
Will confirm license by phone. No fee. Include name.

Securities Commission

Securities Commissioner
1450 Poydras Street
Suite 420
New Orleans, LA 70112
(504) 568-5515
Will confirm license by phone. No fee. Include name and SSN.

Secretary of State

Secretary of State
Corporation Division
PO Box 94125
Baton Rouge, LA 70804-9125
(504) 925-4704
Fax (504) 925-4726
Service agent and address, date incorporated, trade names are available by phone, mail or fax. Contact the above office for additional information.

Criminal Records

State Repository

Louisiana Department of Public Safety
Attention: Bureau of Criminal Identification
PO Box 66614
Baton Rouge, LA 70896
(504) 925-6095
Fax (504) 925-7005
Access by non-criminal justice agencies to criminal records held by state central repository is limited to those entities specifically authorized access by law. Will consider statutes from other states. $10.00 fee for non-criminal agencies that have been approved. Contact the above office for additional information and instructions.

Acadia Parish

Acadia Parish Clerk of Court
Criminal Dept.
PO Box 922
Crowley, LA 70526
(318) 788-8881
Fax (318) 788-1048
Felony and misdemeanor records are available by mail or fax. No release necessary. $2.50 search fee. Search information required: name, date of birth, years to search.

Civil records are available in person only. See Louisiana state repository for additional information.

Allen Parish

Clerk of Court, Criminal Records
PO Box 248
Oberlin, LA 70655
(318) 639-4351
Fax (318) 639-2030
Felony and misdemeanor records are available by mail, phone or fax. $15.00 fee per 10 years search. No release necessary. Search information required: name, date of birth, years to search.

Civil records are available by mail. No release necessary. $10.00 search fee. $1.00 fee per copy. $3.50 for certification. Search information required: name, SSN, years to search. Specify plaintiff or defendant.

Ascension Parish

Clerk of Court, Criminal Records
PO Box 192
Donaldsonville, LA 70346
(504) 473-9866
Fax (504) 473-8641
Felony and misdemeanor records are available by mail or fax. No release necessary. $7.00 search fee. $5.00 fee for fax response. $1.00 fee per copy. $3.00 for certification. Company checks only, payable to Ascension Parish Clerk of Courts. Search information required: name, date of birth, years to search.

Civil records are available by mail. No release necessary. $7.00 search fee. $1.00 fee per copy. $3.00 for certification. Search information required: name, date of birth, SSN, years to search. Specify plaintiff or defendant.

Assumption Parish

Clerk of Court, Criminal Records
PO Drawer 249
Napoleonville, LA 70390
(504) 369-6653
Fax (504) 369-2478
Felony and misdemeanor records are available by mail or fax. No release necessary. $5.00 search fee. Search information required: name, SSN, date of birth.

Civil records are available by mail. No release necessary. $5.00 search fee. $1.00 fee per copy. $4.00 for certification. Search information required: name, SSN, years to search. Specify plaintiff or defendant.

Avoyelles Parish

Avoyelles Parish Clerk of Court, Criminal Records
PO Box 196
Marksville, LA 71351
(318) 253-7523
Fax (318) 253-4614
Felony and misdemeanor records are available by mail or fax. No release necessary. $10.00 search fee. $1.00 fee per copy. $3.00 for certification. Search information required: name, years to search.

Civil records are available by mail. No release necessary. $10.00 search fee. $1.00 fee per copy. $3.00 for certification. Search information required: name, SSN, years to search. Specify plaintiff or defendant.

Beauregard Parish

Clerk of Court, Criminal Records
PO Box 100
De Ridder, LA 70634
(318) 463-8595
Felony and misdemeanor records are available by mail. A release is required. $10.00 search fee. $1.00 fee per copy. $2.25 for certification. Search information required: name, years to search.

Civil records are available by mail. No release necessary. $10.00 search fee. $1.00 fee per copy. $2.25 for certification. Search information required: name, years to search. Specify plaintiff or defendant.

Bienville Parish

Clerk of Court
601 Locust, Room 100
Arcadia, LA 71001
(318) 263-2123
Felony and misdemeanor records are available by mail or phone. No release necessary. No search fee. $.50 fee per copy. Search information required: name, years to search, SASE.

Civil records are available by mail. A release is required. $5.00 search fee. $.50 fee per copy. $2.25 for certification. Search information required: name, years to search. Specify plaintiff or defendant.

Bossier Parish

Clerk of Court, Criminal Records
PO Box 369
Benton, LA 71006
(318) 965-2336
Felony and misdemeanor records are available by mail. No release necessary. $5.00 fee. Make check payable to Clerk of Court. Search information required: name, date of birth, years to search.

Civil records are available by mail. No release necessary. $5.00 search fee. $.50 fee per copy. $2.00 for certification. Search information required: name, years to search. Specify plaintiff or defendant.

Caddo Parish

Clerk of Court, Criminal Section
501 Texas St., Room 103
Courthouse
Shreveport, LA 71101-5408
(318) 226-6786
Felony and misdemeanor records are available by mail. No release necessary. $5.00 search fee. Search information required: name, date of birth, years to search.

Civil records are available by mail. No release necessary. $5.00 search fee. $2.50 for certification. Search information required: name, SSN, years to search. Specify plaintiff or defendant.

Calcasieu Parish

Clerk of Court, Criminal Records
PO Box 1030
Lake Charles, LA 70602
(318) 437-3550
Fax (318) 437-3350
Felony and misdemeanor records are available by mail or fax. No release necessary. $10.00 fee for first 10 years searched, $20.00 fee for additional years to search. Make check payable to Clerk of Court. Search information required: name, date of birth, if available, years to search.

Civil records are available by mail or phone. No release necessary. No search fee. $1.00 fee per copy. $5.00 for certification. Search information required: name, SSN, years to search. Specify plaintiff or defendant.

Caldwell Parish

Clerk of Court, Criminal Records
PO Box 1327
Columbia, LA 71418
(318) 649-2273 or (318) 649-2272
Felony and misdemeanor records are available by mail. No release necessary. $10.00 search fee. Search information required: name, years to search.

Civil records are available by mail or phone. No release necessary. No search fee. $1.00 fee per copy. $3.00 for certification. Search information required: name, years to search. Specify plaintiff or defendant.

Cameron Parish

Clerk of Court, Criminal Records
PO Box 549
Cameron, LA 70631
(318) 775-5316
Fax (318) 775-7172
Felony and misdemeanor records are available by mail or fax. No release necessary. No fee. $1.00 fee per copy. $3.00 for certification. Search information required: name, years to search.

Civil records are available by mail. No release necessary. No search fee. $1.00 fee per copy. $3.00 for certification. Search information required: name, years to search. Specify plaintiff or defendant.

Catahoula Parish

Clerk of Court, Criminal Records
PO Box 198
Harrisonburg, LA 71340
(318) 744-5497
Felony and misdemeanor records are available by mail. No release necessary. $25.00 search fee for ten years searched. Search information required: name, years to search.

Civil records are available by mail. No release necessary. $20.00 search fee. $3.50 for certification. Search information required: name, years to search. Specify plaintiff or defendant.

Claiborne Parish

Clerk of Court, Criminal Records
PO Box 330
Homer, LA 71040
(318) 927-9601
Fax (318) 927-2345
Felony and misdemeanor records are available by mail or fax. A release is required. $10.00 search fee. Search information required: name, years to search.

Civil records are available by mail. A release is required. $10.00 search fee. $1.00 fee per copy. $2.25 for certification. Search information required: name, years to search. Specify plaintiff or defendant.

Concordia Parish

Clerk of Court, Criminal Department
Box 790
Vidalia, LA 71373
(318) 336-4205

Felony and misdemeanor records are available by mail. No release necessary. $3.00 search fee. $1.00 fee per page looked up. $5.50 for certification. Search information required: name, SASE, years to search.

Civil records are available by mail. No release necessary. $25.00 search fee. $1.00 fee per copy. $5.50 for certification. Search information required: name, years to search. Specify plaintiff or defendant.

De Soto Parish

Clerk of Court, Criminal Records
PO Box 1206
Mansfield, LA 71052
(318) 872-3110

Felony and misdemeanor records are available by mail. No release necessary. $10.00 search fee. Make checks payable to: Clerk of Court. Search information required: name, years to search.

Civil records are available by mail. No release necessary. $5.00 search fee. $1.00 fee per copy. $3.50 for certification. Search information required: name, years to search. Specify plaintiff or defendant.

East Baton Rouge Parish

Felony and misdemeanor records
Clerk of Court
19th Judicial District Court, Criminal Records
PO Box 1991
Baton Rouge, LA 70802
(504) 389-3964

Felony and misdemeanor records are available by mail. A release is required. $20.00 fee. Search information required: name, date of birth, years to search, SSN, race, sex.

Civil records
19th Judicial District Court,
PO Box 1991
Baton Rouge, LA 70802
(504) 389-3967

Civil records are available by mail. No release necessary. $23.00 search fee. $.50 fee per copy. $2.70 for certification. Search information required: name, SSN, years to search. Specify plaintiff or defendant.

East Carroll Parish

Clerk of Court
400 1st Street
Lake Providence, LA 71254
(318) 559-2399

Felony and misdemeanor records are available by mail. No release necessary. $10.00 search fee. $1.00 fee per copy. $3.00 for certification. Make check payable to Clerk of Court. Search information required: name, years to search, SASE.

Civil records are available by mail. No release necessary. $10.00 search fee. $1.00 fee per copy. $3.00 for certification. Search information required: name, years to search, SASE. Specify plaintiff or defendant.

East Feliciana Parish

Clerk of Court, Criminal Records
PO Box 595
Clinton, LA 70722
(504) 683-5145
Fax (504) 683-3556

Felony and misdemeanor records are available by mail, phone or fax. A release is required. $5.00 fee for each 10 years searched. Search information required: name, date of birth, years to search.

Civil records are available by mail. No release necessary. $5.00 search fee. $1.00 fee per copy. $4.00 for certification. Search information required: name, years to search. Specify plaintiff or defendant.

Evangeline Parish

Evangeline Parish Clerk of Court, Criminal Records
PO Drawer 347
Ville Platte, LA 70586
(318) 363-5671

Records are available in person only. See Louisiana state repository for additional information.

Civil records are available by mail. No release necessary. $10.00 search fee. $.75 per copy. $2.00 for certification. Search information required: name, years to search. Specify plaintiff or defendant.

Franklin Parish

Clerk of Court, Criminal Records
PO Box 431
Winnsboro, LA 71295
(318) 435-5133

Felony and misdemeanor records are available by mail. No release necessary. $10.00 fee. Search information required: name, years to search.

Civil records are available by mail. No release necessary. $10.00 search fee. $.50 fee per copy. $2.50 for certification. Search information required: name, years to search. Specify plaintiff or defendant.

Grant Parish

Clerk of Court, Criminal Records
PO Box 264
Colfax, LA 71417
(318) 627-3246

Felony and misdemeanor records are available by mail or phone. No release necessary. No search fee. $.75 fee per copy. $5.00 for certification. Search information required: name.

Civil records are available by mail. No release necessary. $10.00 search fee. $.75 fee per copy. $5.00 for certification. Search information required: name, years to search. Specify plaintiff or defendant.

Iberia Parish

Clerk of Court, Criminal Records
PO Drawer 12010
New Iberia, LA 70562-2010
(318) 365-7282 Extension 42
Fax (318) 365-0737

Felony and misdemeanor records are available by mail or fax. No release necessary. No search fee. $.50 fee per copy. $6.00 for certification. Search information required: name, date of birth, years to search.

Civil records are available by mail. No release necessary. No search fee. $.50 fee per copy. $5.50 for certification. Search information required: name, years to search. Specify plaintiff or defendant.

Iberville Parish

Felony and misdemeanor records
Clerk of Court
PO Box 423
Plaquemine, LA 70764
(504) 687-5160
Fax (504) 687-5260

Felony and misdemeanor records are available by mail or fax. No release necessary. $10.00 search fee. Search information required: name, date of birth, and case number if available.

Civil records
Clerk of Court
PO Box 423
Plaquemine, LA 70764
(504) 687-5168
Fax (504) 687-5260

Civil records are available by mail, phone or fax. No release necessary. No search fee. $.75 fee per copy. $3.00 for certification. Search information required: name, years to search. Specify plaintiff or defendant.

Jackson Parish

Clerk of Court, Criminal Records
PO Box 737
Jonesboro, LA 71251
(318) 259-2424

Felony and misdemeanor records are available by mail. No release necessary. $10.00 search fee. Search information required: full name.

Civil records are available by mail. No release necessary. $10.00 search fee. $.55 fee per copy. $2.20 for certification. Search information required: name, years to search. Specify plaintiff or defendant.

Jefferson Davis Parish

Clerk of Court, Criminal Records
PO Box 799
Jennings, LA 70546
(318) 824-1160

Felony and misdemeanor records are available by mail. No release necessary. $10.00 fee. Search information required: name, date of birth, years to search. Indicate type of search, felony or misdemeanor.

Civil records are available by mail. No release necessary. $10.00 search fee. $1.00 fee per copy. $4.00 for certification. Search information required: name, years to search. Specify plaintiff or defendant.

Jefferson Parish

Felony records
Clerk of Court, Criminal Records
PO Box 10
Gretna, LA 70053
(504) 364-2993

Felony records are available by mail. No release necessary. No search fee. Search information required: name, date of birth.

Civil records
Clerk of Court
PO Box 10
Gretna, LA 70053
(504) 364-3740
Civil records are available by mail or phone. No release necessary. No search fee. $.50 fee per copy. $1.50 for certification. Search information required: name, years to search. Specify plaintiff or defendant.

Misdemeanor records
Clerk of Court, Criminal Records
2nd Parish Court
Gretna, LA 70053
(504) 364-2993
Misdemeanor records are available by mail. No release necessary. No search fee. Search information required: name, date of birth.

La Salle Parish

Clerk of Court, Criminal Records
PO Box 1372
Jena, LA 71342
(318) 992-2158
Felony and misdemeanor records are available by mail or phone. No release necessary. $10.00 search fee. Search information required: name, years to search.

Civil records are available by mail. No release necessary. No search fee. $.50 fee per copy. $1.10 for certification. Search information required: name, years to search. Specify plaintiff or defendant.

Lafayette Parish

Clerk of Court, Criminal Records
PO Box 2009
Lafayette, LA 70502
(318) 233-0150 Extension 357
Felony and misdemeanor records are available by mail. No release necessary. $5.00 search fee. Company checks only, payable to Lafayette Parish Clerk of Court. Search information required: name, SSN, date of birth, years to search.

Civil records are available by mail. No release necessary. $5.00 search fee. $.50 fee per copy. $6.00 for certification. Search information required: name, years to search. Specify plaintiff or defendant.

Lafourche Parish

Clerk of Court, Criminal Department
PO Box 818
Thibodaux, LA 70302
(504) 447-5550 Extension 23,28 or 30
Fax (504) 447-5800
Felony and misdemeanor records are available by mail or fax. No release necessary. $15.00 search fee. Make check payable to Clerk of Court. Search information required: name, SSN, date of birth, sex, race.

Civil records are available by mail. No release necessary. $15.00 search fee. $1.00 fee per copy. $5.00 for certification. Search information required: name, years to search. Specify plaintiff or defendant.

Lincoln Parish

Clerk of Court, Criminal Records
PO Box 924
Ruston, LA 71273-0924
(318) 251-5130
Felony and misdemeanor records are available by mail. No release necessary. $10.00 search fee. Make check payable to Clerk of Court. Search information required: name, date of birth if available, years to search.

Civil records are available by mail. No release necessary. $10.00 search fee. $1.00 fee per copy. $2.00 for certification. Search information required: name, date of birth, years to search. Specify plaintiff or defendant.

Livingston Parish

Clerk of Court, Criminal Records
PO Box 1150
Livingston, LA 70754
(504) 686-2216
Felony and misdemeanor records are available by mail. No release necessary. $10.00 search fee. Make check payable to Livingston Clerk of Court. Search information required: name, SSN, date of birth, sex, race.

Civil records are available by mail. No release necessary. $10.00 search fee. $.50 fee per copy. $2.00 for certification. Search information required: name, years to search. Specify plaintiff or defendant.

Madison Parish

Madison Clerk of Court, Criminal Records
100 N. Cedar
Tallulah, LA 71282
(318) 574-0655
Felony and misdemeanor records are available by mail. No release necessary. $5.00 search fee. $1.00 fee per copy. $2.00 for certification. Make check payable to Madison Parish Clerk of Court. Search information required: name, date of birth, years to search.

Civil records are available by mail. No release necessary. $5.00 search fee. $1.00 fee per copy. $2.00 for certification. Search information required: name, date of birth, years to search. Specify plaintiff or defendant.

Morehouse Parish

Clerk of Court
Morehouse Parish Courthouse, Criminal Records
Bastrop, LA 71220
(318) 281-3343
Felony and misdemeanor records are available by mail. No release necessary. $10.00 fee. Search information required: name, years to search.

Civil records are available by mail. No release necessary. $10.00 search fee. $1.00 fee per copy. $3.00 for certification. Search information required: name, years to search. Specify plaintiff or defendant.

Natchitoches Parish

Clerk of Court, Criminal Records
PO Box 476
Natchitoches, LA 71458
(318) 352-8152
Fax (318) 352-9321
Felony and misdemeanor records are available by mail or fax. No release necessary. $10.00 search fee. $.50 fee per copy, $5.00 fee for certification. Search information required: name, years to search.

Civil records are available by mail. No release necessary. $10.00 search fee. $.50 fee per copy. $5.00 for certification. Search information required: name, years to search. Specify plaintiff or defendant.

Orleans Parish

Clerk of Court, Criminal Records
2700 Tulane Ave.
New Orleans, LA 70119
(504) 827-3551
Felony and misdemeanor records are available by mail. No release necessary. $10.00 search fee. Search information required: name, date of birth, SASE, previous address, SSN. Turnaround time is 2 working days.

Civil records are available by mail. No release necessary. $10.00 search fee. $.75 fee per copy. $2.25 for certification. Search information required: name, years to search, SASE. Specify plaintiff or defendant.

Ouachita Parish

Clerk of Court, Criminal Section
PO Box 1862
Monroe, LA 71210-1862
(318) 323-8441
Felony and misdemeanor records are available by mail. A release, if available. $10.00 search fee. Make check payable to Clerk of Court Ouachita Parish. Search information required: name, date of birth, years to search.

Civil records are available by mail or phone. No release necessary. No search fee. $.50 fee per copy. $1.00 for certification. Search information required: name, years to search, SASE. Specify plaintiff or defendant.

Plaquemines Parish

Clerk of Court
PO Box 129
Pointe a LaHache, LA 70082
(504) 333-4377
Felony and misdemeanor records are available in person only. See Louisiana State Repository for additional information.

Civil records are available by mail. No release necessary. No search fee. $.50 fee per copy. $3.00 for certification. Search information required: name, years to search. Specify plaintiff or defendant.

Pointe Coupee Parish

Clerk of Court of Pointe Coupee Parish, Criminal Records
PO Drawer 38
New Roads, LA 70760
(504) 638-9596
Records are available in person only. See Louisiana state repository for additional information.

Civil records are available by mail. No release necessary. $10.00 search fee. $1.00 fee per copy. $3.00 for certification. Search information required: name, years to search. Specify plaintiff or defendant.

Rapides Parish

Clerk of Court, Criminal Records
PO Drawer 952
Alexandria, LA 71301
(318) 473-8153
Fax (318) 473-4667
Felony and misdemeanor records are available by mail or fax. No release necessary. $11.00 search fee. $.50 fee per copy. $2.00 for certification. Make check payable to Rapides Parish Clerk of Court. Search information required: name, years to search.

Civil records are available by mail. No release necessary. $11.00 search fee. $.50 fee per copy. $2.00 for certification. Search information required: name, years to search. Specify plaintiff or defendant.

Red River Parish

Clerk of Court
PO Box 606
Coushatta, LA 71019
(318) 932-6741
Fax (318) 932-3519

Felony and misdemeanor records are available by mail or fax. No release necessary. No search fee. $.50 fee per copy. $1.50 for certification. Make check payable to Clerk of Court. Search information required: name, date of birth, previous address.

Civil records are available by mail. No release necessary. No search fee. $.50 fee per copy. $1.50 for certification. Search information required: name, years to search. Specify plaintiff or defendant.

Richland Parish

Clerk of Court, Criminal Division
PO Box 119
Rayville, LA 71269
(318) 728-4171

Felony and misdemeanor records are available by mail. No release necessary. $10.00 search fee includes copying fees and certification, prepaid. Search information required: name, years to search.

Civil records are available by mail. No release necessary. $10.00 search fee includes copying fees and certification. Search information required: name, years to search. Specify plaintiff or defendant.

Sabine Parish

Clerk of Court, Criminal Records
PO Box 419
Many, LA 71449
(318) 256-6223
Fax (318) 256-6224

Felony and misdemeanor records are available by mail, phone or fax. No release necessary. $5.00 search fee. Make check payable to Clerk of Court. Search information required: name, years to search.

Civil records are available by mail. No release necessary. $10.00 search fee. $.75 fee per copy. $3.50 for certification. Search information required: name, years to search. Specify plaintiff or defendant.

St. Bernard Parish

Clerk of Court, Criminal Records
Parish of St. Bernard
PO Box 1746
Chalmette, LA 70044
(504) 271-3434

Felony and misdemeanor records are available by mail. No release necessary. $5.00 search fee. $3.00 fee for certification. Search information required: name, SSN, date of birth, sex, race, and case number, if available.

Civil records are available by mail. No release necessary. No search fee. $1.00 fee per copy. $3.00 for certification. Search information required: name, years to search. Specify plaintiff or defendant.

St. Charles Parish

Clerk of Court, Criminal Records
PO Box 424
Hahnville, LA 70057
(504) 783-6632

Felony and misdemeanor records are available by mail. No release necessary. $5.00 fee. Make check payable to Clerk of Court. Search information required: name, SSN, date of birth, sex, race, years to search.

Civil records are available by mail. No release necessary. $5.00 search fee. $2.00 for certification. Search information required: name, years to search. Specify plaintiff or defendant.

St. Helena Parish

Clerk of Court, Criminal Records
PO Box 308
Greensburg, LA 70441
(504) 222-4514

Felony and misdemeanor records are available by mail. No release necessary. $5.00 search fee. $1.00 fee per copy. $2.00 for certification. Search information required: name, date of birth, years to search.

Civil records are available by mail. No release necessary. $5.00 search fee. $1.00 fee per copy. $2.00 for certification. Search information required: name, years to search. Specify plaintiff or defendant.

St. James Parish

Clerk of Court, Criminal Records
PO Box 63
Convent, LA 70723
(504) 562-7496
Fax (504) 562-2383

Felony and misdemeanor records are available by mail or fax. No release necessary. $5.00 fee for first 5 years searched, $5.00 for each additional year searched. $.75 fee per copy. Certified check only, payable to St. James Parish Clerk of Court. Search information required: name, years to search.

Civil records are available by mail. No release necessary. $5.00 fee for first 5 years searched, $5.00 each additional year. $.75 fee per copy. $3.00 for certification. Search information required: name, years to search. Specify plaintiff or defendant.

St. John The Baptist Parish

Clerk of Court, Criminal Records
PO Box 280
Edgard, LA 70049
(504) 497-3331

Felony and misdemeanor records are available by mail. No release necessary. $5.00 fee for first 5 years searched, $1.00 fee for each additional year. $1.00 fee per copy. $3.50 for certification. Search information required: name, address, years to search.

Civil records are available by mail. No release necessary. $20.00 search fee. $1.00 fee per copy. $3.50 for certification. Search information required: name, years to search. Specify plaintiff or defendant.

St. Landry Parish

Clerk of Court, Criminal Records
PO Box 750
Opelousas, LA 70571
(318) 942-5606 Extension 33

Felony and misdemeanor records are available by mail. No release necessary. $10.00 fee for first 5 years searched, $1.00 each additional year. $.50 fee per copy. $1.50 for certification. Search information required: full name, years to search.

Civil records are available by mail. No release necessary. $10.00 fee for first 5 years searched, $1.00 each additional year. $.50 fee per copy. $1.50 for certification. Search information required: name, years to search. Specify plaintiff or defendant.

St. Martin Parish

Clerk of Court
PO Box 308
St. Martinville, LA 70582
(318) 394-2210
Fax (318) 394-7772

Felony and misdemeanor records are available by mail, phone or fax. No release necessary. $5.00 search fee. Make check payable to St. Martin Parish Clerk of Court. Search information required: full name, SSN, date of birth, years to search.

Civil records are available by mail or phone. No release necessary. No search fee. $.75 fee per copy. $6.00 for certification. Search information required: name, years to search. Specify plaintiff or defendant.

St. Mary Parish

Clerk of Court, Criminal Records
PO Drawer 1231
Franklin, LA 70538
(318) 828-4100 Extension 200
Fax (318) 828-2509

Felony and misdemeanor records are available by mail or fax. No release necessary. $5.00 search fee. Search information required: name, SSN, date of birth, years to search.

Civil records are available by mail. No release necessary. $5.00 search fee. $1.00 fee per copy. $3.00 for certification. Search information required: name, years to search. Specify plaintiff or defendant.

St. Tammany Parish

Clerk of Court, Criminal Records
PO Box 1090
Covington, LA 70434
(504) 898-2430

Felony and misdemeanor records are available by mail. No release necessary. $10.00 fee for first search, $5.00 fee for each additional search at the same time, prepaid. Search information required: full name.

Civil records are available by mail. No release necessary. $10.00 search fee. $.50 fee per copy. $2.00 for certification. Search information required: name, date of birth, years to search. Specify plaintiff or defendant.

Tangipahoa Parish

Clerk of Court, Criminal Department
PO Box 667
Amite, LA 70422
(504) 748-4146 Extension 23
Fax (504) 748-6503

Felony and misdemeanor records are available by mail or fax. No release necessary. $10.00 search fee, prepaid. Search information required: name, years to search.

Civil records are available by mail or fax. No release necessary. $10.00 search fee. Search information required: name, years to search. Specify plaintiff or defendant.

Tensas Parish

Clerk of Court, J.A. Kitchen
PO Box 78
St. Joseph, LA 71366
(318) 766-3921

Records are available in person only. See Louisiana state repository for additional information.

Civil records are available in person only. See Louisiana state repository for additional information.

Terrebonne Parish

Clerk of Court, Criminal Department
PO Box 1569
Houma, LA 70360
(504) 872-0466

Felony and misdemeanor records are available by mail or phone. No release necessary. No fee. Search information required: name, SSN, date of birth, sex, race.

Civil records are available by mail. No release necessary. $10.00 search fee. $.75 fee per copy. $5.00 for certification. Search information required: name, years to search. Specify plaintiff or defendant.

Union Parish

Courthouse Bldg., Criminal Records
Farmerville, LA 71241
(318) 368-3055

Felony and misdemeanor records are available by mail. No release necessary. $15.00 search fee. $.50 fee per copy. $2.00 for certification. Make check payable to Union Parish Court Clerk. Search information required: name, years to search.

Civil records are available by mail. No release necessary. $15.00 search fee. $.50 fee per copy. $2.00 for certification. Search information required: name, years to search. Specify plaintiff or defendant.

Vermilion Parish

Clerk of Court, Criminal Records
PO Box 790
Abbeville, LA 70511-0790
(318) 898-1992
Fax (318) 898-0404

Felony and misdemeanor records are available by mail, phone or fax. No release necessary. No search fee. Search information required: name, SSN, date of birth, sex, race, years to search.

Civil records are available by mail. No release necessary. $10.00 search fee. $1.00 fee per copy. $5.00 for certification. Search information required: name, years to search. Specify plaintiff or defendant.

Vernon Parish

Clerk of Court, Criminal Records
PO Box 40
Leesville, LA 71496-0040
(318) 238-1384

Felony and misdemeanor records are available by mail. No release necessary. $10.00 search fee. Company checks only, payable to Clerk of Court. Search information required: name, date of birth, years to search.

Civil records are available by mail. No release necessary. $10.00 search fee. $1.00 fee per copy. $3.50 for certification. Search information required: name, years to search. Specify plaintiff or defendant.

Washington Parish

Clerk of Court
PO Box 607
Franklinton, LA 70438
(504) 839-4661

Felony and misdemeanor records are available by mail. No release necessary. $10.00 search fee. Make check payable to Clerk of Court. Search information required: name, years to search.

Civil records are available by mail. No release necessary. $10.00 search fee. $1.00 fee per copy. $3.50 for certification. Search information required: name, date of birth, years to search. Specify plaintiff or defendant.

Webster Parish

Clerk of Court, Criminal Records
PO Drawer 370
Minden, LA 71055
(318) 371-0366

Felony and misdemeanor records are available by mail or phone. No release necessary. No search fee. $1.00 fee per copy. Search information required: name, SASE, years to search.

Civil records are available by mail or phone. No release necessary. No search fee. $.50 fee per copy. $3.50 for certification. Search information required: name, years to search. Specify plaintiff or defendant.

West Baton Rouge Parish

Clerk of Court, Criminal Records
PO Box 107
Port Allen, LA 70767
(504) 383-0378

Felony and misdemeanor records are available by mail. No release necessary. $10.00 search fee. Certified check only, payable to Clerk of Court. Search information required: name, date of birth, years to search.

Civil records are available by mail. No release necessary. $10.00 search fee. $1.00 fee per copy. $2.00 for certification. Search information required: name, years to search. Specify plaintiff or defendant.

West Carroll Parish

Clerk of Court, Criminal Records
West Carroll Parish
PO Box 1078
Oak Grove, LA 71263
(318) 428-3281

Felony and misdemeanor records are available by mail. No release necessary. $1.00 fee per year searched. $.50 fee per copy, $3.00 for certification. Search information required: name, date of birth, years to search.

Civil records are available by mail. No release necessary. $1.00 fee per year searched. $.50 fee per copy. $3.00 for certification. Search information required: name, years to search. Specify plaintiff or defendant.

West Feliciana Parish

Clerk of Court, Criminal Records
PO Box 1843
St. Francisville, LA 70775
(504) 635-3794

Felony and misdemeanor records are available by mail. No release necessary. $10.00 search fee. Company checks only, payable to Clerk of Court. Search information required: name, date of birth.

Civil records are available by mail. No release necessary. $10.00 search fee. $1.00 fee per copy. $2.20 for certification. Search information required: name, date of birth, years to search. Specify plaintiff or defendant.

Winn Parish

Winn Parish Courthouse
Clerk of Court
Winnfield, LA 71483
(318) 628-3515

Felony and misdemeanor records are available by mail. No release necessary. $10.00 fee for ten years searched. Company checks only, payable to Clerk of Court. Search information required: name, years to search.

Civil records are available by mail. No release necessary. $10.00 search fee. $.50 fee per copy. $2.25 for certification. Search information required: name, years to search. Specify plaintiff or defendant.

City-Parish Cross Reference

Abbeville *Vermilion*
Abita Springs *Saint Tammany*
Acme *Concordia*
Addis *West Baton Rouge*
Aimwell *Catahoula*
Akers *Tangipahoa*
Albany *Livingston*
Alexandria *Rapides*
Ama *Saint Charles*
Amelia *Saint Mary*
Amite *Tangipahoa*
Anacoco *Vernon*
Anandale *Rapides*
Angie *Washington*
Angola *West Feliciana*
Arabi *Saint Bernard*
Arcadia *Bienville*
Archibald *Richland*
Arnaudville *Saint Landry*
Ashland *Natchitoches*
Athens *Claiborne*
Atlanta *Winn*
Avery Island *Iberia*
Avondale *Jefferson*
Bains *West Feliciana*
Baker *East Baton Rouge*
Baldwin *Saint Mary*
Ball *Rapides*
Barataria *Jefferson*
Basile *Evangeline*
Baskin *Franklin*
Bastrop *Morehouse*
Batchelor *Pointe Coupee*
Baton Rouge *East Baton Rouge*
Bawcomville *Ouchita*
Bayou Cane *Terrebonne*
Bayou Goula *Iberville*
Belcher *Caddo*
Bell City *Calcasieu*
Belle Chasse *Plaquemines*
Belle Rose *Assumption*
Belmont *Sabine*
Bentley *Grant*
Benton *Bossier*
Bernice *Union*
Berwick *Saint Mary*
Bethany *Caddo*
Bienville *Bienville*
Big Bend *Avoyelles*
Blanchard *Caddo*
Blanks *Pointe Coupee*
Bogalusa *Washington*
Bonita *Morehouse*
Boothville *Plaquemines*
Bordelonville *Avoyelles*
Bossier City *Bossier*
Bourg *Terrebonne*
Boutte *Saint Charles*
Boyce *Rapides*
Braithwaite *Plaquemines*
Branch *Acadia*
Breaux Bridge *Saint Martin*
Bridge City *Jefferson*
Brittany *Ascension*
Broussard *Lafayette*
Brusly *West Baton Rouge*
Bryceland *Bienville*
Buckeye *Rapides*

Bueche *West Baton Rouge*
Bunkie *Avoyelles*
Buras *Plaquemines*
Bush *Saint Tammany*
Cade *Saint Martin*
Calhoun *Ouachita*
Calvin *Winn*
Cameron *Cameron*
Campti *Natchitoches*
Carencro *Lafayette*
Carlisle *Plaquemines*
Carville *Iberville*
Castor *Bienville*
Catahoula *Saint Martin*
Cecilia *Saint Martin*
Center Point *Avoyelles*
Centerville *Saint Mary*
Chalmette *Saint Bernard*
Charenton *Saint Mary*
Chase *Franklin*
Chataignier *Evangeline*
Chatham *Jackson*
Chauvin *Terrebonne*
Cheneyville *Rapides*
Chopin *Natchitoches*
Choudrant *Lincoln*
Church Point *Acadia*
Clarence *Natchitoches*
Clarks *Caldwell*
Clayton *Concordia*
Clinton *East Feliciana*
Cloutierville *Natchitoches*
Colfax *Grant*
Collinston *Morehouse*
Columbia *Caldwell*
Convent *Saint James*
Converse *Sabine*
Cottonport *Avoyelles*
Cotton Valley *Webster*
Coushatta *Red River*
Covington *Saint Tammany*
Creole *Cameron*
Creston *Natchitoches*
Crowley *Acadia*
Crowville *Franklin*
Cullen *Webster*
Cut Off *Lafourche*
Cypress *Natchitoches*
Darrow *Ascension*
Davant *Plaquemines*
Delcambre *Vermilion*
Delhi *Richland*
Delta *Madison*
Denham Springs *Livingston*
DeQuincy *Calcasieu*
DeRidder *Beauregard*
Derry *Natchitoches*
Des Allemands *Saint Charles*
Destrehan *Saint Charles*
Deville *Rapides*
Dodson *Winn*
Donaldsonville *Ascension*
Donner *Terrebonne*
Downsville *Union*
Doyline *Webster*
Dry Creek *Beauregard*
Dry Prong *Grant*
Dubach *Lincoln*
Dubberly *Webster*

Dulac *Terrebonne*
Dunn *Richland*
Duplessis *Ascension*
Dupont *Avoyelles*
Duson *Lafayette*
East Point *Red River*
Echo *Rapides*
Edgard *St John Baptist*
Effie *Avoyelles*
Egan *Acadia*
Elizabeth *Allen*
Elmer *Rapides*
Elm Grove *Bossier*
Elton *Jefferson Davis*
Empire *Plaquemines*
Enterprise *Catahoula*
Epps *West Carroll*
Erath *Vermilion*
Eros *Jackson*
Erwinville *West Baton Rouge*
Estherwood *Acadia*
Ethel *East Feliciana*
Eunice *Saint Landry*
Evangeline *Acadia*
Evans *Vernon*
Evergreen *Avoyelles*
Extension *Franklin*
Fairbanks *Ouachita*
Farmerville *Union*
Fenton *Jefferson Davis*
Ferriday *Concordia*
Fields *Beauregard*
Fisher *Sabine*
Flatwoods *Rapides*
Flora *Natchitoches*
Florien *Sabine*
Fluker *Tangipahoa*
Folsom *Saint Tammany*
Fordoche *Pointe Coupee*
Forest *West Carroll*
Forest Hill *Rapides*
Forest Oaks *East Baton Rouge*
Fort Necessity *Franklin*
Franklin *Saint Mary*
Franklinton *Washington*
French Settlement *Livingston*
Frierson *DeSoto*
Frogmore *Concordia*
Fullerton *Vernon*
Galliano *Lafourche*
Garden City *Saint Mary*
Garyville *St John Baptist*
Geismar *Ascension*
Georgetown *Grant*
Gheens *Lafourche*
Gibsland *Bienville*
Gibson *Terrebonne*
Gilbert *Franklin*
Gilliam *Caddo*
Glenmora *Rapides*
Gloster *DeSoto*
Glynn *Pointe Coupee*
Golden Meadow *Lafourche*
Goldonna *Natchitoches*
Gonzales *Ascension*
Gorum *Natchitoches*
Goudeau *Avoyelles*
Grambling *Lincoln*

Gramercy *Saint James*
Grand Cane *DeSoto*
Grand Chenier *Cameron*
Grand Coteau *Saint Landry*
Grand Isle *Jefferson*
Grant *Allen*
Gray *Terrebonne*
Grayson *Caldwell*
Greensburg *Saint Helena*
Greenwell Springs *East Baton Rouge*
Greenwood *Caddo*
Gretna *Jefferson*
Grosse Tete *Iberville*
Gueydan *Vermilion*
Hackberry *Cameron*
Hahnville *Saint Charles*
Hall Summit *Red River*
Hamburg *Avoyelles*
Hammond *Tangipahoa*
Hanna *Red River*
Harahan *Jefferson*
Hardwood *West Feliciana*
Harmon *Red River*
Harrisonburg *Catahoula*
Harvey *Jefferson*
Haughton *Bossier*
Hayes *Calcasieu*
Haynesville *Claiborne*
Hebert *Caldwell*
Heflin *Webster*
Henderson *Saint Martin*
Hessmer *Avoyelles*
Hester *Saint James*
Hicks *Vernon*
Hineston *Rapides*
Hodge *Jackson*
Holden *Livingston*
Homer *Claiborne*
Hornbeck *Vernon*
Hosston *Caddo*
Houma *Terrebonne*
Husser *Tangipahoa*
Iberville *Iberville*
Ida *Caddo*
Independence *Tangipahoa*
Innis *Pointe Coupee*
Inniswold *East Baton Rouge*
Iota *Acadia*
Iowa *Calcasieu*
Jackson *East Feliciana*
Jamestown *Bienville*
Jarreau *Pointe Coupee*
Jeanerette *Iberia*
Jefferson *Jefferson*
Jena *LaSalle*
Jennings *Jefferson Davis*
Jigger *Franklin*
Jones *Morehouse*
Jonesboro *Jackson*
Jonesville *Catahoula*
Joyce *Winn*
Junction City *Union, Ar*
Kaplan *Vermilion*
Keatchie *DeSoto*
Keithville *Caddo*
Kelly *Caldwell*
Kenner *Jefferson*
Kentwood *Tangipahoa*
Kilbourne *West Carroll*

Killian *Livingston*
Killona *Saint Charles*
Kinder *Allen*
Kraemer *Lafourche*
Krotz Springs *Saint Landry*
Kurthwood *Vernon*
Labadieville *Assumption*
Labarre *Pointe Coupee*
Lacamp *Vernon*
Lacassine *Jefferson Davis*
Lacombe *Saint Tammany*
Lafayette *Lafayette*
Lafitte *Jefferson*
Lake Arthur *Jefferson Davis*
Lake Charles *Calcasieu*
Lakeland *Pointe Coupee*
Lake Providence *East Carroll*
Lakeshore *Ouachita*
Lakeview *Cadd*
LaPlace *St John Baptist*
Larose *Lafourche*
Larto *Catahoula*
Lawtell *Saint Landry*
Leander *Vernon*
Lebeau *Saint Landry*
Le Blanc *Allen*
Lecompte *Rapides*
Leesville *Vernon*
Le Moyen *Saint Landry*
Lena *Rapides*
Leonville *Saint Landry*
Lettsworth *Pointe Coupee*
Libuse *Rapides*
Lillie *Union*
Lisbon *Claiborne*
Live Oak Manor *Jefferson*
Livingston *Livingston*
Livonia *Pointe Coupee*
Lockport *Lafourche*
Logansport *DeSoto*
Longleaf *Rapides*
Longstreet *DeSoto*
Longville *Beauregard*
Loranger *Tangipahoa*
Loreauville *Iberia*
Lottie *Pointe Coupee*
Luling *Saint Charles*
Lutcher *Saint James*
Lydia *Iberia*
Madisonville *Saint Tammany*
Mamou *Evangeline*
Mandeville *Saint Tammany*
Mangham *Richland*
Mansfield *DeSoto*
Mansura *Avoyelles*
Many *Sabine*
Maringouin *Iberville*
Marion *Union*
Marksville *Avoyelles*
Marrero *Jefferson*
Marthaville *Natchitoches*
Martin *Red River*
Mathews *Lafourche*
Maurepas *Livingston*
Maurice *Vermilion*
Melder *Rapides*
Melrose *Natchitoches*
Melville *Saint Landry*
Meraux *Saint Bernard*
Mermentau *Acadia*
Mer Rouge *Morehouse*
Merryville *Beauregard*
Metairie *Jefferson*

Midland *Acadia*
Milton *Lafayette*
Minden *Webster*
Mira *Caddo*
Mittie *Allen*
Modeste *Ascension*
Monroe *Ouachita*
Montegut *Terrebonne*
Monterey *Concordia*
Montgomery *Grant*
Mooringsport *Caddo*
Mora *Natchitoches*
Moreauville *Avoyelles*
Morgan City *Saint Mary*
Morganza *Pointe Coupee*
Morrow *Saint Landry*
Morse *Acadia*
Moss Bluff *Calcasieu*
Mount Hermon *Washington*
Nairn *Plaquemines*
Napoleonville *Assumption*
Natalbany *Tangipahoa*
Natchez *Natchitoches*
Natchitoches *Natchitoches*
Negreet *Sabine*
Newellton *Tensas*
New Iberia *Iberia*
Newllano *Vernon*
New Orleans *Orleans*
New Roads *Pointe Coupee*
New Sarpy *Saint Charles*
Noble *Sabine*
Norco *Saint Charles*
North Merrydale *East Baton Rouge*
Norwood *East Feliciana*
Oakdale *Allen*
Oak Grove *West Carroll*
Oak Manor *East Baton Rouge*
Oak Ridge *Morehouse*
Oberlin *Allen*
Oil City *Caddo*
Olla *LaSalle*
Opelousas *Saint Landry*
Oscar *Pointe Coupee*
Otis *Rapides*
Paincourtville *Assumption*
Palmetto *Saint Landry*
Paradis *Saint Charles*
Patterson *Saint Mary*
Paulina *Saint James*
Pearl River *Saint Tammany*
Pelican *DeSoto*
Perry *Vermilion*
Pierre Part *Assumption*
Pilottown *Plaquemines*
Pine Grove *Saint Helena*
Pine Prairie *Evangeline*
Pineville *Rapides*
Pioneer *West Carroll*
Pitkin *Vernon*
Plain Dealing *Bossier*
Plaquemine *Iberville*
Plattenville *Assumption*
Plaucheville *Avoyelles*
Pleasant Hill *Sabine*
Pointe A LaHache *Plaquemines*
Pollock *Grant*
Ponchatoula *Tangipahoa*
Port Allen *West Baton Rouge*
Port Barre *Saint Landry*
Port Sulphur *Plaquemines*

Powhatan *Natchitoches*
Prairieville *Ascension*
Pride *East Baton Rouge*
Princeton *Bossier*
Provencal *Natchitoches*
Quitman *Jackson*
Raceland *Lafourche*
Ragley *Beauregard*
Rayne *Acadia*
Rayville *Richland*
Reddell *Evangeline*
Red Oaks *East Baton Rouge*
Reeves *Allen*
Reserve *St John Baptist*
Rhinehart *Catahoula*
Richwood *Ouachita*
Ringgold *Bienville*
River Ridge *Jefferson*
Roanoke *Jefferson Davis*
Robeline *Natchitoches*
Robert *Tangipahoa*
Rodessa *Caddo*
Rosa *Saint Landry*
Rosedale *Iberville*
Roseland *Tangipahoa*
Rosepine *Vernon*
Rougon *Pointe Coupee*
Ruby *Rapides*
Ruston *Lincoln*
Saint Amant *Ascension*
Saint Benedict *Saint Tammany*
Saint Bernard *Saint Bernard*
Saint Francisville *West Feliciana*
Saint Gabriel *Iberville*
Saint James *Saint James*
Saint Joseph *Tensas*
Saint Landry *Evangeline*
Saint Martinville *Saint Martin*
Saint Maurice *Winn*
Saint Rose *Saint Charles*
Saline *Bienville*
Samtown *Rapides*
Sarepta *Webster*
Schriever *Terrebonne*
Scotlandville *East Baton Rouge*
Scott *Lafayette*
Shongaloo *Webster*
Shreveport *Caddo*
Sibley *Webster*
Sicily Island *Catahoula*
Sieper *Rapides*
Sikes *Winn*
Simmesport *Avoyelles*
Simpson *Vernon*
Simsboro *Lincoln*
Singer *Beauregard*
Slagle *Vernon*
Slaughter *East Feliciana*
Slidell *Saint Tammany*
Sondheimer *East Carroll*
Sorrento *Ascension*
South Mansfield *Desoto*
Spearsville *Union*
Springfield *Livingston*
Springhill *Webster*
Starks *Calcasieu*
Start *Richland*
Sterlington *Ouachita*
Stonewall *DeSoto*
Sugartown *Beauregard*

Sulphur *Calcasieu*
Summerfield *Claiborne*
Sun *Saint Tammany*
Sunnybrook *East Baton Rouge*
Sunset *Saint Landry*
Sunshine *Iberville*
Swartz *Ouachita*
Talisheek *Saint Tammany*
Tallulah *Madison*
Tangipahoa *Tangipahoa*
Taylor *Bienville*
Theriot *Terrebonne*
Thibodaux *Lafourche*
Tickfaw *Tangipahoa*
Tioga *Rapides*
Torbert *Pointe Coupee*
Transylvania *East Carroll*
Triumph *Plaquemines*
Trout *LaSalle*
Tullos *LaSalle*
Tunica *West Feliciana*
Turkey Creek *Evangeline*
Urania *LaSalle*
Vacherie *Saint James*
Venice *Plaquemines*
Ventress *Pointe Coupee*
Verda *Grant*
Vick *Avoyelles*
Vidalia *Concordia*
Ville Platte *Evangeline*
Vinton *Calcasieu*
Violet *Saint Bernard*
Vivian *Caddo*
Waggaman *Jefferson*
Wakefield *West Feliciana*
Walker *Livingston*
Wardville *Rapides*
Washington *Saint Landry*
Waterproof *Tensas*
Watson *Livingston*
Welsh *Jefferson Davis*
Westlake *Calcasieu*
West Monroe *Ouachita*
Westminister *East Baton Rouge*
Westwego *Jefferson*
Weyanoke *West Feliciana*
White Castle *Iberville*
Wildsville *Concordia*
Wilson *East Feliciana*
Winnfield *Winn*
Winnsboro *Franklin*
Wisner *Franklin*
Woodworth *Rapides*
Wyandotte *Terrebonne*
Youngsville *Lafayette*
Zachary *East Baton Rouge*
Zwolle *Sabine*

Maine

All sixteen (16) of Maine's counties honor phone and/or mail requests from employers for criminal conviction data and civil court records. Records for plaintiffs seeking $30,000 and more are held in Superior court, while District court records are less than $30,000.

For more information or for offices not listed, contact the state's information hot line at (207) 289-1110.

Driving Records

Department of Motor Vehicles
Driving Records
State House Station 29
Augusta, ME 04333
(207) 289-2733
Driving records are available by mail. $4.00 fee per request. Turnaround time is 24 hours. Written request must include job applicant's full name and date of birth. Make check payable to Secretary of State.

Worker's Compensation Records

Worker's Compensation Commission
Records Department
State House Station 27
Augusta, ME 04333
(207) 289-3751
Worker's compensation records are available by phone or mail. Request should include: subject's full name, SSN, date of injury and previous employer involved in claim. If the date of injury or the previous employer is unknown and the claim occurred prior to the automation of the system in 1984, the odds of a "no-hit" are increased. There is no search fee. A signed release is not required.

Vital Statistics

Department of Human Services Office of Vital Records
State House
Station 11
Augusta, ME 04333
(207) 289-3184
Fax (207) 289-3181
Birth and death records are available for $5.00 each. State office has had records since 1923. Records prior to 1923 are located at Maine State Archives, State House Station 184, Augusta, ME 04333 For earlier records, write to the municipality where event occurred. Include name, date of birth, mother's name and maiden name, father's name, requesting party's relationship and reason for request. Make certified check or money order payable to Treasurer, State of Maine. Name and return address required.

Marriage records are available. Fee of $5.00. $2.00 for additional request at same time. Include name, marriage date, spouse's name, where marriage took place, purpose of request. Turnaround time is 3-5 days.

Divorce records are available. Fee of $5.00. Include name, divorce date, spouse's name, where divorce granted. Turnaround time is 3-5 days. VISA and Mastercard accepted. Call (207) 289-3181.

Department of Education

Teacher Certification
State House Station 23
Augusta, ME 04333
(207) 289-5944
Field of certification, effective date and expiration date are available by phone or mail. Include name and SSN.

Medical Licensing

Board of Regulation and Medicine
State House Station 137
Augusta, ME 04333
(207) 289-3601
Will confirm licenses for MDs and PAs by phone or mail. Phone inquiries limited to 3 names per call. $10.00 fee for certified confirmation. For licenses not mentioned, contact the above office in writing.

Maine State Board of Nursing
State House Station 158
Augusta, ME 04333
(207) 624-5275
Will confirm license by phone. No fee. Include name, license number or SSN, DOB or address, if available.

Maine Board of Osteopathic Examination & Registration.
State House Station 142
Augusta, ME 04330
(207) 289-2480
Will confirm licenses for DOs by phone or mail. $10.00 fee for certified confirmation through mail. Include name, license number (if available) or SSN, date of birth, address. For licenses not mentioned, contact the above office in writing.

Bar Association

Maine State Bar Association
PO Box 1820
Augusta, ME 04332
(207)623-1121
Will confirm licenses by mail or phone. No fee. Include name.

Accountancy Board

Maine State Board of Accountancy
State House Station 35
Augusta, ME 04333
(207) 582-8723
Will confirm license by phone. No fee. Include name.

Securities Commission

Securities Division
Department of Professional and Financial Regulation
State House Station 121-0121
Augusta, ME 04333
(207) 582-8760
Will confirm license by phone. No fee. Include name and SSN.

Secretary of State

Secretary of State
Bureau of Corporation
State House Station 101
Augusta, ME 04333-0101
(207) 289-4190
Service agent and address, date incorporated are available by phone or mail. Contact the above office for additional information.

Criminal Records

State Repository

State Bureau of Identification
Maine State Police
36 Hospital Street
Augusta, ME 04330-6514
(207) 624-7000
Criminal records available by mail only to non-criminal justice agencies. Each request must include subject's full name, date of birth, aliases and a self-addressed envelope. There is a $7.00 fee per request. Still a fee if no records are found. Make check payable to Treasurer, State of Maine. If more than one name is to be searched at a time, place in double-spaced, alphabetical order. Turnaround time varies. For "no-hits" it is usually three to four days plus mail time. For "hits" search can take as much as three to four weeks.

Androscoggin County

Androscoggin County Courthouse, Criminal Records
Clerk of Court
PO Box 3660
Auburn, ME 04212
(207) 783-5450

Felony and misdemeanor records are available by mail or phone. No release necessary. No search fee. Copies are $2.00 for first page and $.50 for additional pages (certification included). Search information required: name, date of birth.

Civil records are available by mail or phone. No release necessary. No search fee. Search information required: name, years to search. Specify plaintiff or defendant.

Aroostook County

Clerk of Court, Criminal Records
PO Box 787
Houlton, ME 04730
(207) 532-6563

Felony and misdemeanor records are available by mail or phone. No release necessary. Copies are $2.00 for first page and $.50 for each additional page. $2.00 for certification. Search information required: name, date of birth.

Civil records are available by mail or phone. No release necessary. No search fee. Search information required: name, years to search. Specify plaintiff or defendant.

Cumberland County

Felony and misdemeanor records
Superior Court Clerk, Criminal Records
PO Box 287
Portland, ME 04112
(207) 822-4113

Felony and misdemeanor records are available by mail or phone. A release is required. No search fee. Copies are $2.00 for first page, $.50 fee for additional pages. Search information required: name, date of birth.

Civil records
Superior Court Clerk
PO Box 287
Portland, ME 04112
(207) 822-4105

Civil records are available by mail or phone. No release necessary. No search fee. Copies are $2.00 for first page, $.50 fee for additional pages. Search information required: name, date of birth, years to search. Specify plaintiff or defendant.

Franklin County

Franklin County Courthouse, Criminal Records
38 Main St.
Farmington, ME 04938
(207) 778-3346

Felony and misdemeanor records are available by mail or phone. No release necessary. No search fee. Copies are $2.00 for first page, $.50 thereafter. $2.00 for certification. Search information required: name, date of birth.

Civil records are available by mail or phone. No release necessary. No search fee. Search information required: name, years to search. Specify plaintiff or defendant.

Hancock County

Superior Court, Criminal Records
PO Box 1085
Ellsworth, ME 04605
(207) 667-7176

Felony and misdemeanor records are available by mail or phone. No release necessary. No search fee. $2.00 fee for first copy, $.50 thereafter. $2.00 for certification. Search information required: name, date of birth.

Civil records are available by mail or phone. No release necessary. No search fee. Search information required: name, years to search. Specify plaintiff or defendant.

Kennebec County

Clerk of Court, Criminal Records
95 State St.
Augusta, ME 04330
(207) 622-9357

Felony and misdemeanor records are available by mail or by phone for two requests. No release necessary. No search fee. Copies are $2.00 for first page, $.50 for additional page. Search information required: name, date of birth.

Civil records are available by mail or phone. No release necessary. No search fee. Search information required: name, years to search. Specify plaintiff or defendant.

Knox County

Superior Court, Criminal Records
PO Box 1024
Rockland, ME 04841
(207) 594-2576

Felony and misdemeanor records are available by mail or phone. A release is required. No search fee. $2.00 fee for first copy, $.50 per copy thereafter. $2.00 fee for certification. Search information required: name, date of birth.

Civil records are available by mail or phone. No release necessary. No search fee. Search information required: name, years to search. Specify plaintiff or defendant.

Lincoln County

Clerk of Superior Court, Criminal Records
High St.
Wiscasset, ME 04578
(207) 882-7517

Felony and misdemeanor records are available by mail. No release necessary. No search fee. $2.00 fee per copy. $3.00 for certification. Search information required: name, date of birth.

Civil records are available by mail or phone. No release necessary. No search fee. Search information required: name, years to search. Specify plaintiff or defendant.

Oxford County

Clerk of Superior Court, Criminal Records
Oxford County Courthouse
26 Western Ave.
South Paris, ME 04281
(207) 743-8936

Felony and misdemeanor records are available by mail or phone. No release necessary. No search fee. $2.00 fee for first copy, $.50 thereafter. $2.00 for certification. Search information required: name, date of birth.

Civil records are available by mail or phone. No release necessary. No search fee. Search information required: name, years to search. Specify plaintiff or defendant.

Penobscot County

Clerk of Superior Court, Criminal Records
97 Hammond Street
Bangor, ME 04401
(207) 947-0751

Felony and misdemeanor records are available by mail. No release necessary. No search fee. Copies are $2.00 for first page, $.50 per copy thereafter. $2.00 for certification. Search information required: name, date of birth.

Civil records are available by mail. No release necessary. No search fee. Search information required: name, years to search. Specify plaintiff or defendant.

Piscataquis County

Clerk of Superior Court, Criminal Records
51 E. Main St.
Dover-Foxcroft, ME 04426
(207) 564-8419

Felony and misdemeanor records are available by mail or phone. No release necessary. No search fee. $1.00 fee for first copy, $.50 thereafter. $1.00 for certification. Search information required: name, date of birth.

Civil records are available by mail or phone. No release necessary. No search fee. Search information required: name, years to search. Specify plaintiff or defendant.

Sagadahoc County

Felony records
Clerk of Superior Court, Criminal Records
752 High Street
PO Box 246
Bath, ME 04530
(207) 443-9733

Felony records are available by mail or phone. No release necessary. No fee. Search information required: name, date of birth.

Civil records
Clerk of Superior Court
752 High Street
PO Box 246
Bath, ME 04530
(207) 443-9733

Civil records are available by mail or phone. No release necessary. No search fee. Search information required: name, years to search. Specify plaintiff or defendant.

Misdemeanor records
Maine District Court
Customs House
1 Front St.
Bath, ME 04530
(207) 443-6606

Misdemeanor records are available by mail. No release necessary. No fee. Search information required: name, date of birth.

Civil records
Maine District Court
Customs House
1 Front St.
Bath, ME 04530
(207) 443-6606
Civil records are available in person only. See Maine state repository for additional information.

Somerset County

Clerk of Superior Court, Criminal Records
Somerset County Courthouse
PO Box 725
Skowhegan, ME 04976
(207) 474-5161
Felony and misdemeanor records are available by mail or phone. No release necessary. $5.00 search fee. Copies are $2.00 for first page, $.50 thereafter. $2.00 for certification. Search information required: name, date of birth.

Civil records are available by mail or phone. No release necessary. No search fee. Search information required: name, years to search. Specify plaintiff or defendant.

Waldo County

Felony records
Clerk of Superior Court, Criminal Records
73 Church St.
PO Box 188
Belfast, ME 04915
(207) 338-1940
Felony records are available by mail or phone. No release necessary. No search fee. $2.00 for first copy, $.50 thereafter. $2.00 for certification. Search information required: name, date of birth.

Civil records
Clerk of Superior Court
73 Church St.
PO Box 188
Belfast, ME 04915
(207) 338-1940
Civil records are available by mail or phone. No release necessary. No search fee. Search information required: name, years to search. Specify plaintiff or defendant.

Misdemeanor records
Maine District Court
PO Box 382.
Belfast, ME 04915
(207) 338-3107
Misdemeanor records are available by mail. No release necessary. No search fee. Copies are $2.00 for first page, $.50 thereafter. Search information required: name, date of birth.

Civil records
Maine District Court
PO Box 382
Belfast, ME 04915
(207) 338-3107
Civil records are available by mail or phone. No release necessary. No search fee. Search information required: name, years to search. Specify plaintiff or defendant.

Washington County

Superior Court, Criminal Records
PO Box 526
Machias, ME 04654
(207) 255-3326
Felony and misdemeanor records are available by mail or phone. No release necessary. No search fee. Copies are $2.00 for first page, $.50 thereafter. $2.00 for certification. Search information required: name, date of birth.

Civil records are available by mail or phone. No release necessary. No search fee. Search information required: name, years to search. Specify plaintiff or defendant.

York County

Clerk of Court, Criminal Records
PO Box 160
Alfred, ME 04002
(207) 324-5122
Felony records are available by mail or phone. No release necessary. No search fee. Search information required: name, date of birth.

Civil records are available by mail or phone. No release necessary. No search fee. Search information required: name, years to search. Specify plaintiff or defendant.

City-County Cross Reference

Abbot Village *Piscataquis*
Acton *York*
Addison *Washington*
Albion *Kennebec*
Alfred *York*
Alna *Lincoln*
Andover *Oxford*
Anson *Somerset*
Ashland *Aroostook*
Athens *Somerset*
Atlantic *Hancock*
Auburn *Androscoggin*
Augusta *Kennebec*
Aurora *Hancock*
Bailey Island *Cumberland*
Bangor *Penobscot*
Bar Harbor *Hancock*
Bar Mills *York*
Bass Harbor *Hancock*
Bath *Sagadahoc*
Beals *Washington*
Belfast *Waldo*
Belgrade *Kennebec*
Belgrade Lakes *Kennebec*
Benedicta *Aroostook*
Bernard *Hancock*
Berwick *York*
Bethel *Oxford*
Biddeford *York*
Biddeford Pool *York*

Bingham *Somerset*
Birch Harbor *Hancock*
Blaine *Aroostook*
Blue Hill *Hancock*
Blue Hill Falls *Hancock*
Boothbay *Lincoln*
Boothbay Harbor *Lincoln*
Bowdoinham *Sagadahoc*
Bradford *Penobscot*
Bradley *Penobscot*
Brewer *Penobscot*
Bridgewater *Aroostook*
Bridgton *Cumberland*
Bristol *Lincoln*
Brooklin *Hancock*
Brooks *Waldo*
Brooksville *Hancock*
Brookton *Washington*
Brownfield *Oxford*
Brownville *Piscataquis*
Brownville Junction *Piscataquis*
Brunswick *Cumberland*
Bryant Pond *Oxford*
Buckfield *Oxford*
Bucks Harbor *Washington*
Bucksport *Hancock*
Burkettville *Knox*
Burlington *Penobscot*
Burnham *Waldo*

Calais *Washington*
Cambridge *Somerset*
Camden *Knox*
Canaan *Somerset*
Canton *Oxford*
Cape Elizabeth *Cumberland*
Cape Neddick *York*
Cape Porpoise *York*
Caratunk *Somerset*
Cardville *Penobscot*
Caribou *Aroostook*
Carmel *Penobscot*
Casco *Cumberland*
Castine *Hancock*
Center Lovell *Oxford*
Chamberlain *Lincoln*
Charleston *Penobscot*
Chebeague Island *Cumberland*
Cherryfield *Washington*
China *Kennebec*
Chisholm *Franklin*
Cliff Island *Cumberland*
Clinton *Kennebec*
Columbia Falls *Washington*
Coopers Mills *Lincoln*
Corea *Hancock*
Corinna *Penobscot*

Cornish *York*
Costigan *Penobscot*
Cranberry Isles *Hancock*
Crouseville *Aroostook*
Cumberland Center *Cumberland*
Cushing *Knox*
Cutler *Washington*
Damariscotta *Lincoln*
Danforth *Washington*
Danville *Androscoggin*
Deer Isle *Hancock*
Denmark *Oxford*
Dennysville *Washington*
Detroit *Somerset*
Dexter *Penobscot*
Dixfield *Oxford*
Dixmont *Penobscot*
Dover-Foxcroft *Piscataquis*
Dresden *Lincoln*
Dryden *Franklin*
Eagle Lake *Aroostook*
East Andover *Oxford*
East Baldwin *Cumberland*
East Boothbay *Lincoln*
East Corinth *Penobscot*
East Dixfield *Franklin*
East Eddington *Penobscot*
East Hampden *Penobscot*

East Holden *Penobscot*
East Lebanon *York*
East Livermore
  Androscoggin
East Machias *Washington*
East Millinocket *Penobscot*
East Newport *Penobscot*
Easton *Aroostook*
East Orland *Hancock*
East Parsonfield *York*
East Peru *Oxford*
East Poland *Androscoggin*
Eastport *Washington*
East Sebago *Cumberland*
East Stoneham *Oxford*
East Vassalboro *Kennebec*
East Waterboro *York*
East Waterford *Oxford*
East Wilton *Franklin*
East Winthrop *Kennebec*
Eliot *York*
Ellsworth *Hancock*
Emery Mills *York*
Enfield *Penobscot*
Estcourt Station *Aroostook*
Etna *Penobscot*
Eustis *Franklin*
Exeter *Penobscot*
Fairfield *Somerset*
Falmouth *Cumberland*
Falmouth Foreside
  Cumberland
Farmingdale *Kennebec*
Farmington *Franklin*
Farmington Falls *Franklin*
Five Islands *Sagadahoc*
Fort Fairfield *Aroostook*
Fort Kent *Aroostook*
Fort Kent Mills *Aroostook*
Frankfort *Waldo*
Franklin *Hancock*
Freedom *Waldo*
Freeport *Cumberland*
Frenchboro *Hancock*
Frenchville *Aroostook*
Friendship *Knox*
Frye *Oxford*
Fryeburg *Oxford*
Gardiner *Kennebec*
Garland *Penobscot*
Georgetown *Sagadahoc*
Glen Cove *Knox*
Gorham *Cumberland*
Gouldsboro *Hancock*
Grand Isle *Aroostook*
Gray *Cumberland*
Greene *Androscoggin*
Greenville *Piscataquis*
Greenville Junction
  Piscataquis
Grove *Washington*
Guilford *Piscataquis*
Hallowell *Kennebec*
Hampden *Penobscot*
Hampden Highlands
  Penobscot
Hancock *Hancock*
Hanover *Oxford*
Harborside *Hancock*
Harmony *Somerset*
Harrington *Washington*
Harrison *Cumberland*
Hartland *Somerset*
Haynesville *Aroostook*
Hebron *Oxford*
Hinckley *Somerset*

Hiram *Oxford*
Hollis Center *York*
Houlton *Aroostook*
Howland *Penobscot*
Hudson *Penobscot*
Hulls Cove *Hancock*
Island Falls *Aroostook*
Islesboro *Waldo*
Islesford *Hancock*
Jackman *Somerset*
Jay *Franklin*
Jefferson *Lincoln*
Jonesboro *Washington*
Jonesport *Washington*
Kenduskeag *Penobscot*
Kennebunk *York*
Kennebunkport *York*
Kents Hill *Kennebec*
Kezar Falls *York*
Kingfield *Franklin*
Kingman *Penobscot*
Kittery *York*
Kittery Point *York*
Lagrange *Penobscot*
Lambert Lake *Washington*
Lee *Penobscot*
Leeds *Androscoggin*
Levant *Penobscot*
Lewiston *Androscoggin*
Liberty *Waldo*
Lille *Aroostook*
Limerick *York*
Limestone *Aroostook*
Limington *York*
Lincoln *Penobscot*
Lincoln Center *Penobscot*
Lincolnville *Waldo*
Lincolnville Center *Waldo*
Lisbon *Androscoggin*
Lisbon Center
  Androscoggin
Lisbon Falls *Androscoggin*
Litchfield *Kennebec*
Little Deer Isle *Hancock*
Littleton *Aroostook*
Livermore *Androscoggin*
Livermore Falls
  Androscoggin
Locke Mills *Oxford*
Long Island *Cumberland*
Lovell *Oxford*
Lubec *Washington*
Machias *Washington*
Machiasport *Washington*
Madawaska *Aroostook*
Madison *Somerset*
Manchester *Kennebec*
Mapleton *Aroostook*
Maplewood *York*
Mars Hill *Aroostook*
Matinicus *Knox*
Mattawamkeag *Penobscot*
Mechanic Falls
  Androscoggin
Meddybemps *Washington*
Medomak *Lincoln*
Medway *Penobscot*
Mexico *Oxford*
Milbridge *Washington*
Milford *Penobscot*
Millinocket *Penobscot*
Milo *Piscataquis*
Minot *Androscoggin*
Minturn *Hancock*
Monhegan *Lincoln*
Monmouth *Kennebec*

Monroe *Waldo*
Monson *Piscataquis*
Monticello *Aroostook*
Moody *York*
Morrill *Waldo*
Mount Desert *Hancock*
Mount Vernon *Kennebec*
Naples *Cumberland*
Newagen *Lincoln*
Newcastle *Lincoln*
Newfield *York*
New Gloucester
  Cumberland
New Harbor *Lincoln*
New Limerick *Aroostook*
Newport *Penobscot*
New Portland *Somerset*
Newry *Oxford*
New Sharon *Franklin*
New Sweden *Aroostook*
New Vineyard *Franklin*
Nobleboro *Lincoln*
Norridgewock *Somerset*
North Amity *Aroostook*
North Anson *Somerset*
North Berwick *York*
North Bridgton
  Cumberland
North Brooklin *Hancock*
Northeast Harbor *Hancock*
North Edgecomb *Lincoln*
North Fryeburg *Oxford*
North Haven *Knox*
North Monmouth
  Kennebec
North New Portland
  Somerset
North Shapleigh *York*
North Sullivan *Hancock*
North Turner
  Androscoggin
North Vassalboro
  Kennebec
North Waterboro *York*
North Waterford *Oxford*
North Whitefield *Lincoln*
Windham *Cumberland*
Norway *Oxford*
Oakfield *Aroostook*
Oakland *Kennebec*
Ogunquit *York*
Olamon *Penobscot*
Old Orchard Beach *York*
Old Town *Penobscot*
Oquossoc *Franklin*
Orient *Aroostook*
Orland *Hancock*
Orono *Penobscot*
Orrington *Penobscot*
Orrs Island *Cumberland*
Otter Creek *Hancock*
Owls Head *Knox*
Oxbow *Aroostook*
Oxford *Oxford*
Palermo *Waldo*
Palmyra *Somerset*
Paris *Oxford*
Passadumkeag *Penobscot*
Patten *Penobscot*
Pejepscot *Sagadahoc*
Pemaquid *Lincoln*
Pembroke *Washington*
Penobscot *Hancock*
Perham *Aroostook*
Perry *Washington*
Peru *Oxford*

Phillips *Franklin*
Phippsburg *Sagadahoc*
Pine Point *Cumberland*
Pittsfield *Somerset*
Plaisted *Aroostook*
Plymouth *Penobscot*
Poland *Androscoggin*
Poland Spring
  Androscoggin
Portage *Aroostook*
Port Clyde *Knox*
Porter *Oxford*
Portland *Cumberland*
Pownal *Cumberland*
Presque Isle *Aroostook*
Princeton *Washington*
Prospect Harbor *Hancock*
Quimby *Aroostook*
Randolph *Kennebec*
Rangeley *Franklin*
Raymond *Cumberland*
Readfield *Kennebec*
Richmond *Sagadahoc*
Robbinston *Washington*
Rockland *Knox*
Rockport *Knox*
Rockwood *Somerset*
Round Pond *Lincoln*
Roxbury *Oxford*
Rumford *Oxford*
Rumford Center *Oxford*
Rumford Point *Oxford*
Sabattus *Androscoggin*
Saco *York*
Saint Agatha *Aroostook*
Saint Albans *Somerset*
Saint David *Aroostook*
Saint Francis *Aroostook*
Saint George *Knox*
Salsbury Cove *Hancock*
Sandy Point *Waldo*
Sanford *York*
Sangerville *Piscataquis*
Sargentville *Hancock*
Scarborough *Cumberland*
Seal Cove *Hancock*
Seal Harbor *Hancock*
Searsmont *Waldo*
Searsport *Waldo*
Sebago Lake *Cumberland*
Sebasco Estates *Sagadahoc*
Sebec *Piscataquis*
Seboeis *Penobscot*
Sedgwick *Hancock*
Shapleigh *York*
Shawmut *Somerset*
Sheridan *Aroostook*
Sherman Mills *Aroostook*
Sherman Station *Penobscot*
Shirley Mills *Piscataquis*
Sinclair *Aroostook*
Skowhegan *Somerset*
Smithfield *Somerset*
Smyrna Mills *Aroostook*
Soldier Pond *Aroostook*
Solon *Somerset*
Sorrento *Hancock*
South Berwick *York*
South Bristol *Lincoln*
South Casco *Cumberland*
South China *Kennebec*
South Eliot *York*
South Freeport
  Cumberland
South Gardiner *Kennebec*

South Gouldsboro
  Hancock
South Harpswell
  Cumberland
South Hiram *Oxford*
South Paris *Oxford*
South Portland
  Cumberland
South Thomaston *Knox*
South Waterford *Oxford*
Southwest Harbor *Hancock*
South Windham
  Cumberland
Springfield *Penobscot*
Springvale *York*
Spruce Head *Knox*
Stacyville *Penobscot*
Standish *Cumberland*
Steep Falls *Cumberland*
Stetson *Penobscot*
Steuben *Washington*
Stillwater *Penobscot*
Stockholm *Aroostook*
Stockton Springs *Waldo*
Stonington *Hancock*
Stratton *Franklin*
Strong *Franklin*
Sunset *Hancock*
Surry *Hancock*
Swans Island *Hancock*
Temple *Franklin*
Tenants Harbor *Knox*
Thomaston *Knox*
Thorndike *Waldo*
Topsfield *Washington*
Topsham *Sagadahoc*
Trevett *Lincoln*
Troy *Waldo*
Turner *Androscoggin*
Union *Knox*
Unity *Waldo*
Upper Frenchville
  Aroostook
Van Buren *Aroostook*
Vanceboro *Washington*
Vassalboro *Kennebec*
Veazie *Penobscot*
Vienna *Kennebec*
Vinalhaven *Knox*
Waldoboro *Lincoln*
Walpole *Lincoln*
Warren *Knox*
Washburn *Aroostook*
Washington *Knox*
Waterboro *York*
Waterford *Oxford*
Waterville *Kennebec*
Wayne *Kennebec*
Weeks Mills *Kennebec*
Weld *Franklin*
Wellington *Piscataquis*
Wells *York*
West Baldwin *Cumberland*
West Bethel *Oxford*
West Boothbay Harbor
  Lincoln
West Bowdoin *Sagadahoc*
Westbrook *Cumberland*
West Buxton *York*
West Enfield *Penobscot*
West Farmington *Franklin*
Westfield *Aroostook*
West Forks *Somerset*
West Kennebunk *York*
West Minot *Androscoggin*

West Newfield *York*
West Paris *Oxford*
West Peru *Oxford*
West Poland *Androscoggin*
West Rockport *Knox*
West Scarborough
  Cumberland
West Southport *Lincoln*
West Sullivan *Hancock*
West Sumner *Oxford*
West Tremont *Hancock*
Whitefield *Lincoln*
Whiting *Washington*
Whitneyville *Washington*
Wilsons Mills *Oxford*
Wilton *Franklin*
Windham *Cumberland*
Windsor *Kennebec*
Winn *Penobscot*
Winslow *Kennebec*
Winter Harbor *Hancock*
Winterport *Waldo*
Winterville *Aroostook*
Winthrop *Kennebec*
Wiscasset *Lincoln*
Woodland *Washington*
Woolwich *Sagadahoc*
Wytopitlock *Aroostook*
Yarmouth *Cumberland*
Yeazie *Penobscott*
York *York*
York Beach *York*
York Harbor *York*

Maryland

Twenty one (21) of Maryland's twenty three (23) counties make criminal conviction data available for employment purposes in person only. The remaining two counties honor mail requests. All twenty three counties request civil record searches to be done in person. Plaintiff's cases for $10,000 and more will be filed in circuit court.

For more information or for offices not listed, contact the state's information hot line at (410) 974-2000.

Driving Records

Motor Vehicle Administration
6601 Ritchie Highway
Glen Burnie, MD 21062
(410) 787-7758
Driving records available by mail. $7.00 fee per request. Turnaround time is 7-10 days. Written request must include job applicant's full name, date of birth and license number. Make check payable to Motor Vehicle Administration.

Worker's Compensation Records

Worker's Compensation Commission
Central Files
6 North Liberty Street
Baltimore, MD 21201
(410) 333-8113 or (410) 333-8114
Fax (410) 333-8122
Worker's compensation records are available by mail. Written request must include job applicant's full name, SSN, date of accident, years to search. No release necessary. No search fee. $.25 fee per copy. $.50 fee per copy from microfilm.

Vital Statistics

Division of Vital Records
PO Box 68760
Baltimore, MD 21215
(410) 225-5988
Birth and death records are available for $4.00 per copy. State office has had records since August 1898. Records for City of Baltimore are available from January 1875. For birth records include full name at birth, mother's maiden name, father's name, place of occurrence, date of birth. For death certificate include name, date and place of birth. An employer can obtain records with a written release. Need a SASE. Make certified check or money order payable to Division of Vital Records.

For death records prior to 1969, apply to:
Maryland State Archives
350 Rowe Blvd.
Annapolis, MD 21401
(410) 974-3914.

Marriage records available from 1951. Fee of $4.00. Turnaround time is 3 weeks. Include name, marriage date, spouse's name, place of marriage and county where marriage occurred. A release is required, either a signed statement or notarized letter. Divorce records available from July, 1961 at county level in circuit court where divorce granted.

Department of Education

State Department of Education
Teacher Certification
200 W. Baltimore St.
Baltimore, MD 21201
(410) 333-2142
Field of certification and expiration date are available by phone or mail. Include name and SSN.

Medical Licensing

Building of Physician Quality Insurance
PO Box 2571
Baltimore, MD 21215-0095
(410) 764-4705
Will confirm licenses for MDs and DOs by phone or mail. No fee. For licenses not mentioned, contact the above office.

Maryland Board of Nurses
4201 Patterson Ave.
Baltimore, MD 21215
(410) 764-5939
Will confirm license by phone. No fee. Include name, license number, if available.

Bar Association

Maryland State Bar Association
361 Rowe Blvd.
Annapolis, MD 21401
(410) 974-3341
Will confirm licenses by phone. No fee. Include name.

Accountancy Board

Maryland State Board of Accountancy
501 Saint Paul Place, Room902
Baltimore, MD 21202
(410) 333-6322
Will confirm license by phone. No fee. Include name.

Securities Commission

Office of Attorney General
Division of Securities
200 St. Paul Place, 20th Floor
Baltimore, MD 21202-2020
(410) 576-6360
Will confirm license by phone. No fee. Include name and SSN.

Secretary of State

State Department of Assessment and Taxation
Charter Department
301 W. Preston
Baltimore, MD 21201
(410) 225-1330
Service agent and address, date incorporated, are available by phone or mail. Contact the above office for additional information.

Criminal Records

State Repository

Secretary
Department of Public Safety
6776 Reisterstown Road, Room 310
Baltimore, MD 21215-2341
(410) 764-4000

Central Repository

Maryland State Police
1201 Reisterstown
Pikesville, MD 21208-3899
(410) 764-5665
Call or write Department of Public Safety and request a copy of the "Petition for Criminal Record History Information." In certain cases, residents and non-residents with specific state statutes authorizing access may skip the Petition step. For more information, contact the Petition Administrator; PO Box 5743; Pikesville, MD 21208-0743.

Allegany County

Circuit Court for Allegany County, Criminal Clerk
Courthouse, Washington St.
Cumberland, MD 21502
(410) 777-5922
Felony and misdemeanor records are available in person only. See Maryland state repository for additional information.

Civil records are available in person only. See Maryland State Repository for additional information.

Anne Arundel County

Felony records
Circuit Court of Anne Arundel County, Criminal Records
PO Box 71
Annapolis, MD 21404
(410) 222-1397
Felony records are available in person only. See Maryland State Repository for additional information.

Civil records are available in person only. See Maryland State Repository for additional information.

Misdemeanor records
Clerk of District Court, Criminal Division
580 Taylor Ave.
Annapolis, MD 21401
(410) 974-2678
Misdemeanor records are available in person only. See Maryland State Repository for additional information.

Civil records are available in person only. See Maryland State Repository for additional information.

Baltimore County

County Circuit Clerk
401 Bosley Ave.
Towson, MD 21204
(410) 887-2625
Records are available in person only. See Maryland State Repository for additional information.

Civil records are available in person only. See Maryland State Repository for additional information.

The City of Baltimore

The City of Baltimore
Criminal Division
110 North Calvert, Room 200
Baltimore, MD 21202
(410) 333-3750
Felony and misdemeanor records are available by mail. No release necessary. No search fee. $1.00 fee per copy. $6.00 for certification. Search information required: name, address, date of birth.

Civil records are available in person only. See Maryland State Repository for additional information.

Calvert County

Felony records
Clerk of Circuit Court, Criminal Records
Calvert County Courthouse
175 Main Street
Prince Frederick, MD 20678
(410) 535-1600
Felony records are available in person only. See Maryland State Repository for additional information.

Civil records are available in person only. See Maryland State Repository for additional information.

Misdemeanor records
District Court of Maryland
175 Main Street
Prince Frederick, MD 20678
(410) 535-8800
Misdemeanor records are available by mail. No release necessary. No search fee. Search information required: name date of birth, years to search, SASE.

Civil records
District Court of Maryland
175 Main Street
Prince Frederick, MD 20678
(410) 535-8800
Civil records are available by mail. No release necessary. No search fee. Search information required: name date of birth, years to search, SASE.

Caroline County

Felony records
Circuit Clerk's Office
PO Box 458
Denton, MD 21629
(410) 479-1811
Records are available in person only. See Maryland state repository for additional information.

Civil records are available in person only. See Maryland State Repository for additional information.

Misdemeanor records
District Court of Maryland
3rd St.
Denton, MD 21629
(410) 479-4609
Misdemeanor records are available in person only. For more information, contact the above office.

Civil records are available in person only. See Maryland State Repository for additional information.

Carroll County

Circuit Court, Criminal Records
PO Box 190
55 Court Street
Westminster, MD 21158
(410) 876-2085 Extension 2018
Felony and misdemeanor records are available in person only. See Maryland State Repository for additional information.

Civil records are available in person only. See Maryland State Repository for additional information.

Cecil County

Clerk of Court, Criminal Records
Cecil County
126 E. Main Street
Room 108, Courthouse Bldg.
Elkton, MD 21921
(410) 996-5200
Felony records are available in person only. See Maryland State Repository for additional information.

Civil records are available in person only. See Maryland State Repository for additional information.

Charles County

Circuit Court Clerk
PO Box 970
La Plata, MD 20646
(301) 932-3202
Records are available in person only. See Maryland state repository for additional information.

Civil records are available in person only. See Maryland State Repository for additional information.

Dorchester County

Clerk of Circuit Court
PO Box 150
Cambridge, MD 21613
(410) 228-0481
Records are available in person only. See Maryland state repository for additional information.

Civil records are available in person only. See Maryland State Repository for additional information.

Frederick County

Clerk of Circuit Court, Criminal Records
100 W. Patrick Street
Frederick, MD 21701
(301) 694-1972
Felony and misdemeanor records are available in person only. See Maryland State Repository for additional information.

Civil records are available in person only. See Maryland State Repository for additional information.

Garrett County

Garrett County Circuit Clerk, Criminal Records
Courthouse
203 S. 4th Street, Room 109
Oakland, MD 21550
(410) 334-1937
Felony and misdemeanor records are available by mail. No release necessary. No search fee. Search information required: name, date of birth..

Civil records are available in person only. See Maryland State Repository for additional information.

Harford County

Circuit Court Clerk, Criminal Records
20 W. Courtland Street
Bel Air, MD 21014
(410) 838-6000
Records are available in person only. See Maryland state repository for additional information.

Civil records are available in person only. See Maryland State Repository for additional information.

Howard County

Circuit Court Clerk, Criminal Records
8360 Court Ave.
Ellicott City, MD 21043
(410) 313-2111
Felony and misdemeanor records are available in person only. See Maryland State Repository for additional information.

Civil records are available in person only. See Maryland State Repository for additional information.

Kent County

Circuit Court Clerk, Criminal Records
Chestertown, MD 21620
(410) 778-7460
Records are available in person only. See Maryland state repository for additional information.

Civil records are available in person only. See Maryland State Repository for additional information.

Montgomery County

Montgomery County Circuit Court
50 Courthouse Square
Rockville, MD 20850
(301) 217-7057
Records are available in person only. See Maryland state repository for additional information.

Civil records are available in person only. See Maryland State Repository for additional information.

Prince George's County

Prince George's County Circuit Clerk
Criminal Department
14735 Main Street
Room 116
Upper Marlboro, MD 20772
(301) 952-3344
Felony and misdemeanor records are not available by mail or phone. Contact Maryland central repository for additional information.

Civil records are available in person only. See Maryland State Repository for additional information.

Queen Anne's County

Clerk of Circuit Court
Queen Anne's County
Courthouse
Centreville, MD 21617
(410) 758-1773
Felony and misdemeanor records are available in person only. See Maryland State Repository for additional information.

Civil records are available in person only. See Maryland State Repository for additional information.

Somerset County

Courthouse, Criminal Records
PO Box 99
Princess Anne, MD 21853
(410) 651-1555
Felony and misdemeanor records are available in person only. See Maryland State Repository for additional information.

Civil records are available in person only. See Maryland State Repository for additional information.

St. Mary's County

Felony records
Circuit Court Clerk, Criminal Records
PO Box 308
Leonardtown, MD 20650
(301) 475-5621
Felony and records are available in person only. See Maryland State Repository for additional information.

Civil records
Circuit Court Clerk
PO Box 308
Leonardtown, MD 20650
(301) 475-5621
Civil records are available in person only. See Maryland State Repository for additional information.

Misdemeanor records
District Court
St. Mary's County
Carter Building, Washington St.
Leonardtown, MD 20650
(301) 475-4532
Fax (301) 475-4535
Misdemeanor records are available in person only. For more information, contact the above office.

Civil records
District Court
St. Mary's County
Carter Building, Washington St.
Leonardtown, MD 20650
(301) 475-4532
Fax (301) 475-4535
Civil records are available in person only. See Maryland State Repository for additional information.

Talbot County

Felony records
Circuit Court Clerk, Criminal Records
PO Box 723
Easton, MD 21601
(410) 822-2611
Felony records are available in person only. See Maryland State Repository for additional information.

Civil records
Circuit Court Clerk,
PO Box 723
Easton, MD 21601
(410) 822-2611
Civil records are available in person only. See Maryland State Repository for additional information.

Misdemeanor records
District Court Clerk
South Wing
Easton, MD 21601
(410) 822-2750
Misdemeanor records are available in person only. See Maryland State Repository for additional information.

Civil records
District Court Clerk
South Wing
Easton, MD 21601
(410) 822-2750
Civil records are available in person only. See Maryland State Repository for additional information.

Washington County

Circuit Court Clerk, Criminal Records
PO Box 229
95 W. Washington
Hagerstown, MD 21741
(301) 791-3085
Felony and misdemeanor records are available in person only. See Maryland State Repository for additional information.

Civil records are available in person only. See Maryland State Repository for additional information.

Wicomico County

Wicomico Circuit Court Clerk,
Criminal Records
PO Box 198
Salisbury, MD 21803-0198
(410) 543-6551
Felony and misdemeanor records are available in person only. See Maryland State Repository for additional information.

Civil records are available in person only. See Maryland State Repository for additional information.

Worcester County

Circuit Court
Courthouse, Criminal Records
PO Box 40
Snow Hill, MD 21863
(410) 632-1235
Felony and misdemeanor records are available in person only. See Maryland State Repository for additional information.

Civil records are available in person only. See Maryland State Repository for additional information.

City-County Cross Reference

Abell *Saint Marys*
Aberdeen *Harford*
Aberdeen Proving Ground *Harford*
Abingdon *Harford*
Accident *Garrett*
Accokeek *Prince Georges*
Adamstown *Frederick*
Adelphi Prince *Georges*
Allen *Wicomico*
Annapolis *Anne Arundel*
Annapolis Junction *Howard*
Aquasco *Prince Georges*
Arden On The Severn *Anne Arundel*
Ardmore *Prince Georges*
Arnold *Anne Arundel*
Arundel Gardens *Anne Arundel*
Arundel Village *Anne Arundel*
Ashton *Montgomery*
Aspen Hill *Montgomery*
Avenue *Saint Marys*
Baldwin *Baltimore*
Baltimore *Independent City*
Baltimore Highlands *Baltimore*
Barclay *Queen Annes*
Barnaby Village *Prince Georges*
Barnesville *Montgomery*
Barstow *Calvert*
Barton *Allegany*
Bay Ridge *Anne Arundel*
Bayside Beach *Anne Arundel*
Beallsville *Montgomery*
Bel Air *Harford*
Bel Alton *Charles*
Belcamp *Harford*
Beltsville *Prince Georges*
Belvedere Heights *Anne Arundel*
Benedict *Charles*
Benson *Harford*
Berlin *Worcester*
Berwyn Heights *Prince Georges*
Bethesda *Montgomery*
Bethlehem *Caroline*
Betterton *Kent*
Big Pool *Washington*
Bishops Head *Dorchester*
Bishopville *Worcester*
Bittinger *Garrett*
Bivalve *Wicomico*
Bladensburg *Prince Georges*
Bloomington *Garrett*
Boonsboro *Washington*
Boring *Baltimore*
Bowie *Prince Georges*
Bowling Green *Allegany*
Boyds *Montgomery*
Bozman *Talbot*
Braddock Heights *Frederick*
Bradshaw *Baltimore*
Brandywine *Prince Georges*

Brentwood *Prince Georges*
Bridgeport *Washington*
Brinklow *Montgomery*
Brookeville *Montgomery*
Brooklandville *Baltimore*
Brooklyn Park *Anne Arundel*
Brookmont *Montgomery*
Brookwood *Prince Georges*
Broomes Island *Calvert*
Brownsville *Washington*
Brunswick *Frederick*
Bryans Road *Charles*
Bryantown *Charles*
Buckeystown *Frederick*
Burkittsville *Frederick*
Burtonsville *Montgomery*
Bushwood *Saint Marys*
Butler *Baltimore*
Cabin John *Montgomery*
California *Saint Marys*
Callaway *Saint Marys*
Calverton *Montgomery*
Cambridge *Dorchester*
Camp Springs *Prince Georges*
Cape Isle Of Wright *Worcester*
Capitol Heights *Prince Georges*
Cardiff *Harford*
Carney *Baltimore*
Carroll Highlands *Carroll*
Cascade *Washington*
Catonsville *Baltimore*
Cavetown *Washington*
Cecilton *Cecil*
Cedar Heights *Prince Georges*
Centreville *Queen Annes*
Chance *Somerset*
Chaptico *Saint Marys*
Charlestown *Cecil*
Charlotte Hall *Saint Marys*
Chase *Baltimore*
Chelsea Beach *Anne Arundel*
Cheltenham *Prince Georges*
Chesapeake Beach *Calvert*
Chesapeake City *Cecil*
Chesapeake Heights *Wicomico*
Chester *Queen Annes*
Chestertown *Kent*
Cheverly *Prince Georges*
Chevy Chase *Montgomery*
Chevy Chase View *Montgomery*
Chewsville *Washington*
Childs *Cecil*
Chillum *Prince Georges*
Church Creek *Dorchester*
Church Hill *Queen Annes*
Churchton *Anne Arundel*
Churchville *Harford*
Claiborne *Talbot*
Clarksburg *Montgomery*
Clarksville *Howard*
Clear Spring *Washington*

Clements *Saint Marys*
Clinton *Prince Georges*
Cobb Island *Charles*
Cockeysville *Baltimore*
College Park *Prince Georges*
Colmar Manor *Prince Georges*
Colonial Park *Washington*
Colora *Cecil*
Coltons Point *Saint Marys*
Columbia *Howard*
Columbia Park *Prince Georges*
Compton *Saint Marys*
Conowingo *Cecil*
Cooksville *Howard*
Coral Hills *Prince Georges*
Cordova *Talbot*
Corriganville *Allegany*
Cottage City *Prince Georges*
Crapo *Dorchester*
Cresaptown *Allegany*
Crisfield *Somerset*
Crocheron *Dorchester*
Crofton *Anne Arundel*
Crownsville *Anne Arundel*
Crumpton *Queen Annes*
Cumberland *Allegany*
Damascus *Montgomery*
Dameron *Saint Marys*
Dames Quarter *Somerset*
Darlington *Harford*
Davidsonville *Anne Arundel*
Dayton *Howard*
Deale *Anne Arundel*
Deal Island *Somerset*
Defense Heights *Prince Georges*
Delmar *Wicomico*
Denton *Caroline*
Derwood *Montgomery*
Detour *Carroll*
Dickerson *Montgomery*
District Heights-Forestville *Prince Georges*
Dorsey *Howard*
Dowell *Calvert*
Drayden *Saint Marys*
Drum Point *Calvert*
Dundalk *Baltimore*
Dunkirk *Calvert*
Earleville *Cecil*
East New Market *Dorchester*
Easton *Talbot*
Eckhart Mines *Allegany*
Eden *Somerset*
Edgemere *Baltimore*
Edgewater *Anne Arundel*
Edgewood *Harford*
Edmonston *Prince Georges*
Ednor *Montgomery*
Eldersburg *Carroll*
Elk Mills *Cecil*
Elkton *Cecil*
Ellerslie *Allegany*
Ellicott City *Howard*
Elmwood *Baltimore*

Emmitsburg *Frederick*
Emory Grove *Montgomery*
Essex *Baltimore*
Ewell *Somerset*
Fairmount Heights *Prince Georges*
Fair Play *Washington*
Fallston *Harford*
Faulkner *Charles*
Federalsburg *Caroline*
Ferndale *Anne Arundel*
Finksburg *Carroll*
Fishing Creek *Dorchester*
Flintstone *Allegany*
Forest Heights *Prince Georges*
Forest Hill *Harford*
Forestville *Prince Georges*
Fork *Baltimore*
Fort George G Meade *Anne Arundel*
Fort Howard *Baltimore*
Fort Washington Forest *Prince Georges*
Fountain Green *Hartford*
Fountain Head *Washington*
Foxhall *Montgomery*
Frederick *Frederick*
Freeland *Baltimore*
Friendly *Prince Georges*
Friendship *Anne Arundel*
Friendsville *Garrett*
Frostburg *Allegany*
Fruitland *Wicomico*
Fullerton *Baltimore*
Fulton *Howard*
Funkstown *Washington*
Gaither *Carroll*
Gaithersburg *Montgomery*
Galena *Kent*
Galesville *Anne Arundel*
Gambrills *Anne Arundel*
Gapland *Washington*
Garland *Anne Arundel*
Garrett Park *Montgomery*
Garrison *Baltimore*
Georgetown *Cecil*
Germantown *Montgomery*
Gibson Island *Anne Arundel*
Girdletree *Worcester*
Glassmanor *Prince Georges*
Glenarden *Prince Georges*
Glen Arm *Baltimore*
Glen Burnie *Anne Arundel*
Glen Echo *Montgomery*
Glenelg *Howard*
Glen Hills *Montgomery*
Glenn Dale *Prince Georges*
Glenwood *Howard*
Glyndon *Baltimore*
Golden Beach *Saint Marys*
Goldsboro *Caroline*
Golts *Kent*
Grantsville *Garrett*
Grasonville *Queen Annes*
Great Mills *Saint Marys*
Greenbelt *Prince Georges*
Green Haven *Anne Arundel*
Greensboro *Caroline*

Hagerstown *Washington*
Halethorpe *Baltimore*
Hampstead *Carroll*
Hancock *Washington*
Hanover *Anne Arundel*
Harmans *Anne Arundel*
Harewood Park *Baltimore*
Harwood *Anne Arundel*
Havre DeGrace *Harford*
Hebbville *Baltimore*
Hebron *Wicomico*
Helen *Saint Marys*
Henderson *Caroline*
Henryton *Carroll*
Herald Harbour *Anne Arundel*
Hereford *Baltimore*
Hernwood Heights *Baltimore*
Highland *Howard*
High Point *Anne Arundel*
High Ridge *Howard*
Hillcrest Heights *Prince Georges*
Hillsboro *Caroline*
Hillsmere Shores *Anne Arundel*
Hollywood *Saint Marys*
Hughesville *Charles*
Huntingtown *Calvert*
Huntsville *Prince Georges*
Hurlock *Dorchester*
Hyattsville *Prince Georges*
Hydes *Baltimore*
Ijamsville *Frederick*
Indian Head *Charles*
Ingleside *Queen Annes*
Ironsides *Charles*
Issue *Charles*
Jarrettsville *Harford*
Jefferson *Frederick*
Jefferson Heights *Washington*
Jessup *Anne Arundel*
Joppa *Harford*
Keedysville *Washington*
Kennedyville *Kent*
Kensington *Montgomery*
Kent Village *Prince Georges*
Kenwood *Baltimore*
Kettering *Prince Georges*
Keymar *Carroll*
Kings Town *Queen Annes*
Kingsville *Baltimore*
Kitzmiller *Garrett*
Knollwood *Prince Georges*
Knoxville *Frederick*
Ladiesburg *Frederick*
Lake Shore *Anne Arundel*
Landover *Prince Georges*
Landover Hills *Prince Georges*
Langley Park *Prince Georges*
Lanham *Prince Georges*
Lanham-Seabrook *Prince Georges*
Lansdowne *Baltimore*
LaPlata *Charles*
La Vale *Allegany*
Laurel *Prince Georges*
Lawsonia *Somerset*
Layhill *Montgomery*
Leonardtown *Saint Marys*

Lexington Park *Saint Marys*
Lewisdale *Prince Georges*
Libertytown *Frederick*
Linhigh *Baltimore*
Linkwood *Dorchester*
Linthicum *Anne Arundel*
Linthicum Heights *Anne Arundel*
Linwood *Carroll*
Lisbon *Howard*
Little Orleans *Allegany*
Lochearn *Baltimore*
Loch Lynn Heights *Garrett*
Lonaconing *Allegany*
Londontown *Anne Arundel*
Long Beach *Calvert*
Long Green *Baltimore*
Lothian *Anne Arundel*
Loveville *Saint Marys*
Lusby *Calvert*
Lutherville-Timonium *Baltimore*
Luxmanor *Montgomery*
Lynch *Kent*
McDaniel *Talbot*
McHenry *Garrett*
Madison *Dorchester*
Magnolia *Harford*
Manchester *Carroll*
Manokin *Somerset*
Marbury *Charles*
Mardela Springs *Wicomico*
Margate *Anne Arundel*
Marion Station *Somerset*
Marley *Anne Arundel*
Marydel *Caroline*
Maryland City *Anne Arundel*
Maryland Line *Baltimore*
Massey *Kent*
Maugansville *Washington*
Mayo *Anne Arundel*
Meadowood *Montgomery*
Mechanicsville *Saint Marys*
Middleburg *Carroll*
Middletown *Frederick*
Midland *Allegany*
Midlothian *Allegany*
Milford *Baltimore*
Millers *Carroll*
Millersville *Anne Arundel*
Millington *Kent*
Millwood *Prince Georges*
Monkton *Baltimore*
Monrovia *Frederick*
Montgomery Village *Montgomery*
Montrose *Montgomery*
Morganza *Saint Marys*
Morningside *Prince Georges*
Mount Airy *Carroll*
Mount Hebron *Howard*
Mount Pleasant Beach *Anne Arundel*
Mount Rainier *Prince Georges*
Mount Savage *Allegany*
Mount Victoria *Charles*
Myersville *Frederick*
Nanjemoy *Charles*
Nanticoke *Wicomico*
Neavitt *Talbot*

Newark *Worcester*
Newburg *Charles*
New Carrollton *Prince Georges*
Newcomb *Talbot*
New Market *Frederick*
New Midway *Frederick*
New Windsor *Carroll*
Nikep *Allegany*
North Beach *Calvert*
North East *Cecil*
Oakcrest *Prince Georges*
Oakland *Garrett*
Oaklawn *Prince Georges*
Oak View *Montgomery*
Ocean City *Worcester*
Odenton *Anne Arundel*
Oldtown *Allegany*
Olney *Montgomery*
Orchard Beach *Anne Arundel*
Orchard Hills *Washington*
Overlea *Baltimore*
Owings *Calvert*
Owings Mills *Baltimore*
Oxford *Talbot*
Oxon Hill *Prince Georges*
Palmer Park *Prince Georges*
Palmers Corner *Prince Georges*
Paramount *Washington*
Park Hall *Saint Marys*
Parkton *Baltimore*
Parkville *Baltimore*
Parole *Anne Arundel*
Parsonsburg *Wicomico*
Pasadena *Anne Arundel*
Patuxent River *Saint Marys*
Perry Hall *Baltimore*
Perryman *Harford*
Perry Point *Cecil*
Perryville *Cecil*
Phoenix *Baltimore*
Pikesville *Baltimore*
Pinehurst On The Bay *Anne Arundel*
Piney Point *Saint Marys*
Pinto *Allegany*
Pittsville *Wicomico*
Pleasant Hills *Harford*
Pocomoke City *Worcester*
Point of Rocks *Frederick*
Pomfret *Charles*
Poolesville *Montgomery*
Port Deposit *Cecil*
Port Republic *Calvert*
Port Tobacco *Charles*
Potomac *Montgomery*
Potomac Heights *Charles*
Potomac Park *Allegany*
Powellville *Wicomico*
Powhattan Mill *Baltimore*
Preston *Caroline*
Prince Frederick *Calvert*
Prince Georges Facility *Prince Georges*
Princess Anne *Somerset*
Providence *Baltimore*
Pumphrey *Anne Arundel*
Pylesville *Harford*
Quantico *Wicomico*
Queen Anne *Talbot*
Queenstown *Queen Annes*
Randallstown *Baltimore*

Randolph Hills *Montgomery*
Rawlings *Allegany*
Rehobeth *Somerset*
Reisterstown *Baltimore*
Rhodesdale *Dorchester*
Rhodes Point *Somerset*
Riderwood *Baltimore*
Ridge *Saint Marys*
Ridgely *Caroline*
Rippling Ridge *Anne Arundel*
Rising Sun *Cecil*
Riva *Anne Arundel*
Riverdale *Prince Georges*
Riviera Beach *Anne Arundel*
Rockdale *Baltimore*
Rock Hall *Kent*
Rock Hill Beach *Anne Arundel*
Rock Point *Charles*
Rockville *Montgomery*
Rocky Ridge *Frederick*
Rohrersville *Washington*
Rosedale *Baltimore*
Rossville *Baltimore*
Royal Oak *Talbot*
Sabillasville *Frederick*
Saint Charles *Charles*
Saint Inigoes *Saint Marys*
Saint James *Washington*
Saint Leonard *Calvert*
Saint Marys City *Saint Marys*
Saint Michaels *Talbot*
Salisbury *Wicomico*
Sandy Spring *Montgomery*
Sandyville *Carroll*
Savage *Howard*
Scotland *Saint Marys*
Seabrook *Prince Georges*
Seat Pleasant *Prince Georges*
Secretary *Dorchester*
Selby On The Bay *Anne Arundel*
Severn *Anne Arundel*
Severna Park *Anne Arundel*
Shady Side *Anne Arundel*
Sharpsburg *Washington*
Sharptown *Wicomico*
Sherwood *Talbot*
Showell *Worcester*
Silver Hill *Prince Georges*
Silver Spring *Montgomery*
Simpsonville *Howard*
Smithsburg *Washington*
Snow Hill *Worcester*
Solomons *Calvert*
Somerset *Montgomery*
South Gate *Anne Arundel*
Sparks Glencoe *Baltimore*
Spencerville *Montgomery*
Springbrook *Montgomery*
Spring Gap *Allegany*
Stevenson *Baltimore*
Stevensville *Queen Annes*
Still Pond *Kent*
Stockton *Worcester*
Street *Harford*
Sudlersville *Queen Annes*
Suitland *Prince Georges*
Sunderland *Calvert*
Sunnybrook *Baltimore*

Swanton *Garrett*
Sykesville *Carroll*
Takoma Park *Montgomery*
Tall Timbers *Saint Marys*
Taneytown *Carroll*
Taylors Island *Dorchester*
Temple Hills *Prince
    Georges*
Templeville *Queen Annes*
Thurmont *Frederick*
Tilghman *Talbot*
Toddville *Dorchester*
Towson *Baltimore*
Tracys Landing *Anne
    Arundel*
Trappe *Talbot*
Tuscarora *Frederick*
Tyaskin *Wicomico*
Tylerton *Somerset*
Union Bridge *Carroll*
Unionville *Frederick*
University Park *Prince
    Georges*
Upperco *Baltimore*
Upper Fairmount *Somerset*
Upper Falls *Baltimore*
Upper Hill *Somerset*
Upper Marlboro *Prince
    Georges*
Valley Lee *Saint Marys*
Vienna *Dorchester*
Villa Nova *Baltimore*
Wakefield Meadows
    Harford
Waldorf *Charles*
Walkersville *Frederick*
Warwick *Cecil*
Washington Grove
    Montgomery
Waterloo *Anne Arundel*
Welcome *Charles*
Wenona *Somerset*
West Edmondale
    Baltimore
Westernport *Allegany*
West Friendship *Howard*
Westminster *Carroll*
Westover *Somerset*
West River *Anne Arundel*
Whaleysville *Worcester*
Wheaton *Montgomery*
Whiteford *Harford*
White Hall *Baltimore*
White Marsh *Baltimore*
White Plains *Charles*
Willards *Wicomico*
Williamsport *Washington*
Wingate *Dorchester*
Wittman *Talbot*
Woodbine *Carroll*
Woodlawn *Baltimore*
Woodlawn Heights *Anne
    Arundel*
Woodmoor *Baltimore*
Woodsboro *Frederick*
Woodstock *Howard*
Woolford *Dorchester*
Worthington *Howard*
Worton *Kent*
Wye Mills *Talbot*

Massachusetts

Massachusetts counties are more restrictive than most other states' in the release of criminal conviction data. Only seven (7) of the state's fourteen (14) counties release criminal records for employment purposes by phone and/or mail. Thirteen (13) counties allow civil record checks by phone or mail. Superior court holds records for plaintiffs seeking $25,000 or more.

For more information or for offices not listed, contact the state's information hot line at (617) 727-2121.

Driving Records

Registry of Motor Vehicles
Court Records Section
100 Nashua Street
Boston, MA 02114
(617) 727-3842
Driving records are available by mail. $10.00 fee per request. Turnaround time is 3-5 weeks. Written request must include job applicant's full name, date of birth and license number. Make check payable to Registry of Motor Vehicles.

Worker's Compensation Records

Department of Industrial Accidents
600 Washington, 7th Floor
Boston, MA 02111
(617) 727-4300 or 727-4900 Ext. 301
Written release, signed by the person to be searched, must specifically authorize that the Industrial Accident Board is authorized to release information to the prospective employer. The authorization must include the complete name of the employee applicant, SSN, years to search, the name of the previous employer involved in the claim and the date of injury. $10.00 fee for certification. Make certified check payable to Department of Industrial Accidents. For pending files, contact the above office by phone.

Vital Statistics

Registry of Vital Records and Statistics
150 Tremont Street, Room B-3
Boston, MA 02111
(617) 727-0110
Birth and death records are available for $6.00 each. State office has records since 1901. For earlier records, write to Massachusetts Archives at Columbia Pt., 220 Morrissey Boulevard, Boston, MA 02103, (617) 727-2816. Inquiries must include name at birth, mother's maiden name, father's name, and place of occurrence. An employer can obtain records with a written release. Make certified check or money order payable to Commonwealth of Massachusetts.

Marriage records are available. Fee of $6.00. Check acceptable. Include name, marriage date, spouse's name, and city or town where marriage took place. Divorce records available at county level in probate court where divorce granted. SASE.

Department of Education

Department of Education
Bureau of Teacher Certification
1385 Hancock St.
Quincy, MA 02169
(617) 770-7517
Fax (617) 770-7494
Field of certification, effective date and expiration date are available by phone or mail. Include name and SSN.

Medical Licensing

Board of Registration in Medicine
Third Floor
10 W. Street,
Boston, MA 02111
(617) 727-0386
Will confirm licenses, license numbers, medical school attended and date of graduation for MDs and DOs by phone or mail. For letter of standing, contact the above office for proper waiver form. For licenses not mentioned, contact the above office.

Massachusetts Board of Registration in Nursing
100 Cambridge St., Room 1519
Boston, MA 02202
(617) 727-7393
Will confirm license by phone. No fee. Include name, license number.

Bar Association

Massachusetts State Bar of Overseers
Registration Office
75 Federal Street
Boston, MA 02110
(617) 357-1860
Will confirm licenses by phone. No fee. Include name.

Accountancy Board

Massachusetts Board of Public Accountancy
Room 1609
100 Cambridge Street
Boston, MA 02202
(617) 727-1806
Will confirm license by phone. No fee. Include name.

Securities Commission

Securities Division
Department of State Secretary
John W. McCormack Building
One Ashburton Place, Room 1701
Boston, MA 02108
(617) 727-3548
Will confirm license by phone. No fee. Include name and SSN.

Secretary of State

Secretary of State
Corporation Division
1 Ashburton Place
Boston, MA 02108
(617) 727-2850
Service agent and address, date incorporated, standing with tax commission are available by phone or mail. Contact the above office for additional information.

Criminal Records

State Repository

Criminal History Systems Board
1010 Commonwealth Avenue
Boston, MA 02215
(617) 727-0090
Fax (617) 232-1104
Access by non-criminal justice agencies to criminal records held by central repository is limited to those entities specifically authorized access by law. Contact the above office for a certification application. Complete and return the form. Application process takes 4-6 weeks for board approval. $25.00 search fee.

Probation Central Files

One Ashburton Place
Room 401
Boston, MA 02108
(617) 727-5300

Employers may obtain information upon written request by the job applicant. Requests should be printed or typed, including: full name, maiden name, date of birth, social security number, mother's maiden name, father's name, complete address (for return of results) and signature. No fee.

Barnstable County

Felony and misdemeanor records
District County Courthouse
Barnstable, MA 02630
(508) 362-2511

Records are available in person only. See Massachusetts state repository or probation central files for additional information.

Civil records
Barnstable County Courthouse
PO Box 425
Barnstable, MA 02630
(508) 362-2511

Civil records are available by mail. No release necessary. No search fee. $.50 fee per copy. $1.00 for certification. Search information required: name, SSN, years to search. Specify plaintiff or defendant.

Berkshire County

Felony records
Berkshire County Superior Court House
76 East Street
Pittsfield, MA 01201
(413) 499-7487

Felony records are available by mail. A signed, notarized release is required. No search fee. $.50 fee per copy. $1.50 for certification. Search information required: name, years to search.

Civil records
Berkshire County Superior Court House
76 East Street
Pittsfield, MA 01201
(413) 499-7487

Civil records are available by mail. No release necessary. No search fee. $.50 fee per copy. $1.50 for certification. Search information required: name, years to search. Specify plaintiff or defendant.

Misdemeanor records
District Court
24 Wendell Ave.
Pittsfield, MA 01201
(413) 442-5468

Misdemeanor records are available in person only. See Massachusetts state repository or probation central files for additional information.

Civil records
District Court
24 Wendell Ave.
Pittsfield, MA 01201
(413) 442-5468

Civil records are available by mail. No release necessary. No search fee. $1.00 fee per copy. $1.50 for certification. Search information required: name, years to search. Specify plaintiff or defendant.

Bristol County

Felony records
Bristol County, Superior Court
9 Court Street
Taunton, MA 02780
(508) 824-4032

Felony records are available in person only. See Massachusetts state repository or probation central files for additional information.

Civil records
Bristol County, Superior Court
9 Court Street
Taunton, MA 02780
(508) 823-6588

Civil records are available by mail. No release necessary. No search fee. $.50 fee per copy. $1.50 for certification. Search information required: name, years to search. Specify plaintiff or defendant.

Dukes County

Felony and misdemeanor records
County Courthouse
PO Box 1284
Edgartown, MA 02539
(508) 627-3751

Records are available by mail or phone (for open cases). No release necessary. $.50 fee per copy, $1.50 for certification. Search information required: name, date of birth, docket number if available.

Civil records
County Courthouse
PO Box 1284
Edgartown, MA 02539
(508) 627-4668

Civil records are available by mail or phone. No release necessary. No search fee. $.50 fee per copy. $1.50 for certification. Search information required: name, date of birth, years to search. Specify plaintiff or defendant.

Essex County

Felony records
County Court House, Superior Court
34 Federal Street
Salem, MA 01970
(508) 741-0200

Felony records are available in person only. See Massachusetts state repository or probation central files for additional information.

Civil records
County Court House, Superior Court
34 Federal Street
Salem, MA 01970
(508) 741-0200 Ext. 223

Civil records are available by mail or phone. No release necessary. No search fee. $.50 fee per copy. $1.50 for certification. Search information required: name, date of birth, years to search. Specify plaintiff or defendant.

Misdemeanor records
Salem District Court
65 Washington
Salem, MA 01970
(508) 744-1167

Misdemeanor records are available in person only. See Massachusetts state repository for additional information.

Civil records
Salem District Court
65 Washington
Salem, MA 01970
(508) 744-1167

Civil records are available in person only. See Massachusetts state repository for additional information.

Franklin County

Felony records
County Courthouse, Superior Court
425 Main Street
PO Box 1573
Greenfield, MA 01302
(413) 774-5535 Ext. 49

Felony records are available by phone. No release necessary. No search fee. $.50 fee per copy. $1.50 for certification. Search information required: name, years to search, SASE.

Civil records
County Courthouse, Superior Court
425 Main Street
PO Box 1573
Greenfield, MA 01302
(413) 774-5535 Ext. 49

Civil records are available by phone. No release necessary. No search fee. $.50 fee per copy. $1.50 for certification. Search information required: name, years to search, SASE. Specify plaintiff or defendant.

Misdemeanor records
District Court
425 Main Street
Greenfield, MA 01301
(413) 774-5533

Misdemeanor records are available in person only. See Massachusetts state repository or probation central files for additional information.

Civil records
District Court
425 Main Street
Greenfield, MA 01301
(413) 774-5533

Civil records are available by mail. No release necessary. No search fee. $.50 fee per copy. $1.50 for certification. Search information required: name, date of birth, years to search, SASE. Specify plaintiff or defendant.

Hampden County

Common Wealth of MA.
District Court of Springfield
50 State Street
Springfield, MA 01103
(413) 781-8100 Ext. 2136

Records are available in person only. See Massachusetts state repository or contact probation central files for additional information.

Civil records are available by phone. No release necessary. No search fee. $.50 fee per copy. $1.50 for certification. Search information required: name, years to search. Specify plaintiff or defendant.

Hampshire County

Felony records
County Court House
15 Gothic
PO Box 1119
Northampton, MA 01061
(413) 584-5810
Records are available by phone. No release necessary. No search fee. $.50 fee per copy. $10.00 for certification. Search information required: name, date of birth, years to search.

Civil records
County Court House
15 Gothic
PO Box 1119
Northampton, MA 01061
(413) 584-5810
Civil records are available by phone. No release necessary. No search fee. $.50 fee per copy. $10.00 for certification. Search information required: name, date of birth, years to search. Specify plaintiff or defendant.

Misdemeanor records
District Court
PO Box 1119
Northampton, MA 01061
(413) 584-7400
Misdemeanor records are available by mail. No release necessary. No search fee. $.50 fee per copy. $1.50 for certification. Search information required: name, date of birth, years to search.

Civil records
District Court
PO Box 1119
North Hampton, MA 01061
(413) 584-7400
Civil records are available by mail or phone. No release necessary. No search fee. $.50 fee per copy. $1.50 for certification. Search information required: name, date of birth, years to search.Specify plaintiff or defendant.

Middlesex County

New Superior Courthouse
Thorndike St.
Cambridge, MA 02141
(617) 494-4015
Felony records are available in person only. See Massachusetts state repository or probation central files for additional information.

Civil records are available in person only. See Massachusetts state repository for additional information.

Nantucket County

Superior Court Clerk
Town & County Building
Broad Street
Nantucket, MA 02554
(508) 228-2559
Fax (508) 228-3725
Felony records are available by phone or fax. No search fee. No release necessary. No search fee. Search information required: name.

Civil records
Superior Court Clerk
Town & County Building
Broad Street
Nantucket, MA 02554
(508) 228-2559
Fax (508) 228-3725
Civil records are available by mail, fax or phone. No release necessary. No search fee. $.50 fee per copy. $1.00 for certification. Search information required: name, date of birth, years to search. Specify plaintiff or defendant.

Norfolk County

Superior Court Clerk
650 High Street
Dedham, MA 02026
(617) 326-1600
Felony records are available in person only. See Massachusetts state repository or probation central files for additional information.

Civil records are available by mail or phone. No release necessary. No search fee. $.50 fee per copy. $1.50 for certification. Search information required: name, date of birth, years to search. Specify plaintiff or defendant.

Plymouth County

County Courthouse, Superior Court
Brockton, MA 02401
(508) 583-8250
Felony records are available in person only. See Massachusetts state repository or probation central files for additional information.

Civil records are available by mail. No release necessary. No search fee. $.50 fee per copy. $1.50 for certification. Search information required: name, date of birth, years to search. Specify plaintiff or defendant.

Suffolk County

County Courthouse
Boston, MA 02108
(617) 725-8000
Felony and misdemeanor records are available in person only. See Massachusetts state repository or probation central files for additional information.

Civil records are available by mail. No release necessary. No search fee. $.50 fee per copy. $1.50 for certification. Search information required: name, date of birth, years to search. Specify plaintiff or defendant.

Worcester County

Superior Court
County Courthouse
2 Main Street, Room 21
Worcester, MA 01608
(508) 756-2441
Felony records are available by mail. No release necessary. No search fee. $.50 fee per copy. $1.50 for certification. Search information required: name, years to search.

Civil records are available by mail or phone. No release necessary. No search fee. $.50 fee per copy. $1.50 for certification. Search information required: name, years to search. Specify plaintiff or defendant.

City-County Cross Reference

Abington *Plymouth*
Acton *Middlesex*
Acushnet *Bristol*
Adams *Berkshire*
Agawam *Hampden*
Amesbury *Essex*
Amherst *Hampshire*
Andover *Essex*
Arlington *Middlesex*
Ashburnham *Worcester*
Ashby *Middlesex*
Ashfield *Franklin*
Ashland *Middlesex*
Ashley Falls *Berkshire*
Assinippi *Plymouth*
Assonet *Bristol*

Athol *Worcester*
Attleboro *Bristol*
Auburn *Worcester*
Avon *Norfolk*
Ayer *Middlesex*
Baldwinville *Worcester*
Ballardvale *Essex*
Barnstable *Barnstable*
Barre *Worcester*
Becket *Berkshire*
Bedford *Middlesex*
Belchertown *Hampshire*
Bellingham *Norfolk*
Belmont *Middlesex*
Berkshire *Berkshire*
Berlin *Worcester*

Bernardston *Franklin*
Beverly *Essex*
Billerica *Middlesex*
Blackstone *Worcester*
Blandford *Hampden*
Bolton *Worcester*
Bondsville *Hampden*
Boston *Suffolk*
Bourne *Barnstable*
Boxford *Essex*
Boylston *Worcester*
Braintree *Suffolk*
Brant Rock *Plymouth*
Brewster *Barnstable*
Bridgewater *Plymouth*
Brimfield *Hampden*

Brockton *Plymouth*
Brookfield *Worcester*
Brookline *Norfolk*
Bryantville *Plymouth*
Buckland *Franklin*
Burlington *Middlesex*
Buzzards Bay *Barnstable*
Byfield *Essex*
Cambridge *Middlesex*
Canton *Norfolk*
Carlisle *Middlesex*
Carver *Plymouth*
Cataumet *Barnstable*
Centerville *Barnstable*
Charlemont *Franklin*
Charlton *Worcester*

Charlton City *Worcester*
Charlton Depot *Worcester*
Chartley *Bristol*
Chatham *Barnstable*
Chelmsford *Middlesex*
Chelsea *Middlesex*
Cherry Valley *Worcester*
Cheshire *Berkshire*
Chester *Hampden*
Chesterfield *Hampshire*
Chicopee *Hampden*
Chilmark *Dukes*
Clinton *Worcester*
Cochitvate *Middlesex*
Cohasset *Norfolk*
Colrain *Franklin*
Concord *Middlesex*
Conway *Franklin*
Cordvale *Middlesex*
Cotuit *Barnstable*
Cummaquid *Barnstable*
Cummington *Hampshire*
Cuttyhunk *Dukes*
Dalton *Berkshire*
Dartmouth *Bristol*
Danvers *Essex*
Dedham *Norfolk*
Deerfield *Franklin*
Dennis *Barnstable*
Dennis Port *Barnstable*
Dighton *Bristol*
Dorothy Pond *Worcester*
Dover *Norfolk*
Dracut *Middlesex*
Drury *Berkshire*
Dudley *Worcester*
Dunstable *Middlesex*
Duxbury *Plymouth*
East Billerica *Middlesex*
East Bridgewater *Plymouth*
East Brookfield *Worcester*
East Dennis *Barnstable*
East Douglas *Worcester*
East Falmouth *Barnstable*
East Freetown *Bristol*
Eastham *Barnstable*
Easthampton *Hampshire*
East Longmeadow
   Hampden
East Mansfield *Bristol*
East Millbury *Worcester*
Easton *Bristol*
East Orleans *Barnstable*
East Otis *Berkshire*
East Pepperell *Middlesex*
East Princeton *Worcester*
East Sandwich *Barnstable*
East Taunton *Bristol*
East Templeton *Worcester*
East Walpole *Norfolk*
East Wareham *Plymouth*
Edgartown *Dukes*
Egypt *Plymouth*
Elmwood *Plymouth*
Erving *Franklin*
Essex *Essex*
Everett *Middlesex*
Fairhaven *Bristol*
Fall River *Bristol*
Falmouth *Barnstable*
Fayville *Worcester*
Feeding Hills *Hampden*
Fiskdale *Worcester*
Fitchburg *Worcester*
Forestdale *Barnstable*
Foxboro *Norfolk*
Framingham *Middlesex*

Franklin *Norfolk*
Gardner *Worcester*
Georgetown *Essex*
Gilbertville *Worcester*
Glendale *Berkshire*
Gloucester *Essex*
Goshen *Hampshire*
Grafton *Worcester*
Granby *Hampshire*
Graniteville *Middlesex*
Granville *Hampden*
Great Barrington *Berkshire*
Greenbush *Plymouth*
Greenfield *Franklin*
Green Harbor *Plymouth*
Groton *Middlesex*
Groveland *Essex*
Hadley *Hampshire*
Halifax *Plymouth*
Hamilton *Essex*
Hampden *Hampden*
Hanover *Plymouth*
Hanson *Plymouth*
Hardwick *Worcester*
Harvard *Worcester*
Harwich *Barnstable*
Harwich Port *Barnstable*
Hatfield *Hampshire*
Hathorne *Essex*
Haverhill *Essex*
Haydenville *Hampshire*
Hingham *Plymouth*
Hinsdale *Berkshire*
Holbrook *Norfolk*
Holden *Worcester*
Holliston *Middlesex*
Holyoke *Hampden*
Hopedale *Worcester*
Hopkinton *Middlesex*
Housatonic *Berkshire*
Hubbardston *Worcester*
Hudson *Middlesex*
Hull *Plymouth*
Humarock *Plymouth*
Huntington *Hampshire*
Hyannis *Barnstable*
Hyannis Port *Barnstable*
Ipswich *Essex*
Islington *Norfolk*
Jefferson *Worcester*
Kingston *Plymouth*
Lake Pleasant *Franklin*
Lakeville *Plymouth*
Lancaster *Worcester*
Lanesboro *Berkshire*
Lawrence *Essex*
Lee *Berkshire*
Leeds *Hampshire*
Leicester *Worcester*
Lenox *Berkshire*
Lenox Dale *Berkshire*
Leominster *Worcester*
Leverett *Franklin*
Lexington *Middlesex*
Lincoln *Middlesex*
Linwood *Worcester*
Littleton *Middlesex*
Longmeadow *Hampden*
Lowell *Middlesex*
Ludlow *Hampden*
Lunenburg *Worcester*
Lynn *Essex*
Lynnfield *Essex*
Malden *Middlesex*
Manchaug *Worcester*
Manchester *Essex*
Manomet *Plymouth*

Mansfield *Bristol*
Marblehead *Essex*
Marion *Plymouth*
Marlborough *Middlesex*
Marshfield *Plymouth*
Marshfield Hills *Plymouth*
Marstons Mills *Barnstable*
Mashpee *Barnstable*
Mattapoisett *Plymouth*
Maynard *Middlesex*
Medfield *Norfolk*
Medford *Middlesex*
Medway *Norfolk*
Melrose *Middlesex*
Mendon *Worcester*
Menemsha *Dukes*
Merrimac *Essex*
Methven *Essex*
Middleboro *Plymouth*
Middlefield *Hampshire*
Middleton *Essex*
Milford *Worcester*
Millbury *Worcester*
Millis *Norfolk*
Mill River *Berkshire*
Millers Falls *Franklin*
Millville *Worcester*
Milton *Norfolk*
Minot *Plymouth*
Monponsett *Plymouth*
Monroe Bridge *Franklin*
Monson *Hampden*
Montague *Franklin*
Monterey *Berkshire*
Monument Beach
   Barnstable
Morningdale *Worcester*
Nabnasset *Middlesex*
Nahant *Essex*
Nantucket *Nantucket*
Natick *Middlesex*
Needham *Norfolk*
New Bedford *Bristol*
New Braintree *Worcester*
Newton *Middlesex*
Newburyport *Essex*
Norfolk *Norfolk*
North Adams *Berkshire*
Northampton *Hampshire*
North Amherst *Hamshire*
North Andover *Essex*
North Attleboro *Bristol*
North Billerica *Middlesex*
Northborough *Worcester*
Northbridge *Worcester*
North Brookfield
   Worcester
North Carver *Plymouth*
North Chatham *Barnstable*
North Chelmsford
   Middlesex
North Dartmouth *Bristol*
North Dighton *Bristol*
North Eastham *Barnstable*
North Easton *Bristol*
North Falmouth *Barnstable*
Northfield *Franklin*
North Grafton *Worcester*
North Hatfield *Hampshire*
North Marshfield *Plymouth*
North Oxford *Worcester*
North Pembroke *Plymouth*
North Reading *Middlesex*
North Scituate *Plymouth*
North Sudbury *Middlesex*
North Swansea *Bristol*

North Tewksevry
   Middlesex
North Truro *Barnstable*
North Uxbridge *Worcester*
Norton *Bristol*
Norton Grove *Bristol*
Norwell *Plymouth*
Norwood *Norfolk*
Nutting Lake *Middlesex*
Oak Bluffs *Dukes*
Oakdale *Worcester*
Oakham *Worcester*
Ocean Bluff *Plymouth*
Ocean Grove *Plymouth*
Onset *Plymouth*
Orange *Franklin*
Orleans *Barnstable*
Osterville *Barnstable*
Otis *Berkshire*
Oxford *Worcester*
Palmer *Hampden*
Paxton *Worcester*
Peabody *Essex*
Pembroke *Plymouth*
Pepperell *Middlesex*
Petersham *Worcester*
Pigeon Cove *Essex*
Pinehurst *Middlesex*
Pittsfield *Berkshire*
Plainfield *Hampshire*
Plainville *Norfolk*
Plymouth *Plymouth*
Plympton *Plymouth*
Pocasset *Barnstable*
Prides Crossing *Essex*
Princeton *Worcester*
Provincetown *Barnstable*
Quincy *Norfolk*
Randolph *Norfolk*
Raynham *Bristol*
Raynham Center *Bristol*
Reading *Middlesex*
Rehoboth *Bristol*
Revere *Middlesex*
Richmond *Berkshire*
Rochdale *Worcester*
Rochester *Plymouth*
Rockland *Plymouth*
Rockport *Essex*
Rowe *Franklin*
Rowley *Essex*
Russell *Hampden*
Rutland *Worcester*
Sagamore *Barnstable*
Sagamore Beach
   Barnstable
Salem *Essex*
Salisbury *Essex*
Sandisfield *Berkshire*
Sandwich *Barnstable*
Saugus *Essex*
Savoy *Berkshire*
Scituate *Plymouth*
Seekonk *Bristol*
Sharon *Norfolk*
Shattuckville *Franklin*
Shawsheen Village *Essex*
Sheffield *Berkshire*
Shelburne Falls *Franklin*
Sheldonville *Norfolk*
Sherborn *Middlesex*
Shirley *Middlesex*
Shirley Center *Middlesex*
Shore Acres *Plymouth*
Shrewsbury *Worcester*
Shutesbury *Franklin*
Silver Lake *Middlesex*

Somerville *Middlesex*
South Acton *Middlesex*
South Amhurst *Hampshire*
Southampton *Hampshire*
South Ashburnham
    Worcester
South Barre *Worcester*
South Berlin *Worcester*
Southborough *Worcester*
Southbridge *Worcester*
South Carver *Plymouth*
South Chatham *Barnstable*
South Dartmouth *Bristol*
South Deerfield *Franklin*
South Dennis *Barnstable*
South Duxbury *Plymouth*
South Easton *Bristol*
South Egremont *Berkshire*
Southfield *Berkshire*
South Grafton *Worcester*
South Hadley *Hampshire*
South Hamilton *Essex*
South Hanover *Plymouth*
South Harwich *Barnstable*
South Hingham *Plymouth*
South Lancaster *Worcester*
South Lee *Berkshire*
South Orleans *Barnstable*
South Swansea *Bristol*
South Walpole *Norfolk*
South Wellfleet *Barnstable*
Southwick *Hampden*
South Yarmouth
    Barnstable
Spencer *Worcester*
Springfield *Hampden*
Sterling *Worcester*
Still River *Worcester*
Stockbridge *Berkshire*
Stoneham *Middlesex*
Stoughton *Norfolk*
Stow *Middlesex*
Sturbridge *Worcester*
Sudbury *Middlesex*
Sunderland *Franklin*
Swampscott *Essex*
Swansea *Bristol*
Taunton *Bristol*
Teaticket *Barnstable*
Templeton *Worcester*
Tewksbury *Middlesex*
Thorndike *Hampden*
Three Rivers *Hampden*
Topsfield *Essex*
Touisset *Bristol*
Townsend *Middlesex*
Truro *Barnstable*
Turners Falls *Franklin*
Tyngsboro *Middlesex*
Upton *Worcester*
Uxbridge *Worcester*
Vineyard Haven *Dukes*
Wakefield *Middlesex*
Wales *Hampden*
Walpole *Norfolk*
Waltham *Middlesex*
Ware *Hampshire*
Wareham *Plymouth*
Warren *Worcester*
Watertown *Middlesex*
Wayland *Middlesex*
Webster *Worcester*
Wellesley *Norfolk*
Wellfleet *Barnstable*
Wendell *Franklin*

Wendell Depot *Franklin*
Wenham *Essex*
West Acton *Middlesex*
West Andover *Essex*
West Barnstable
    Barnstable
Westborough *Worcester*
West Boxford *Essex*
West Boylston *Worcester*
West Bridgewater
    Plymouth
West Brookfield *Worcester*
West Chatham *Barnstable*
West Chesterfield
    Hampshire
West Concord *Middlesex*
West Dennis *Barnstable*
West Falmouth *Barnstable*
Westfield *Hampden*
Westford *Middlesex*
West Foxboro *Norfolk*
West Groton *Middlesex*
West Hanover *Plymouth*
West Harwich *Barnstable*
West Hatfield *Hampshire*
West Hyannisport
    Barnstable
West Medway *Norfolk*
Westminster *Worcester*
West Newbury *Essex*
Westport *Bristol*
Westport Point *Bristol*
West Springfield *Hampden*
West Stockbridge
    Berkshire
West Tisbury *Dukes*
West Upton *Worcester*
West Wareham *Plymouth*
West Warren *Worcester*
Westwood *Norfolk*
West Yarmouth *Barnstable*
Weymouth *Norfolk*
Whately *Franklin*
Whalom *Worcester*
Wheelwright *Worcester*
White Horse Beach
    Plymouth
White Island Shores
    Plymouth
Whitinsville *Worcester*
Whitman *Plymouth*
Wilbraham *Hampden*
Wilkinsonville *Worcester*
Williamsburg *Hampshire*
Williamstown *Berkshire*
Wilmington *Middlesex*
Winchendon *Worcester*
Winchendon Springs
    Worcester
Winchester *Middlesex*
Windsor *Berkshire*
Woburn *Middlesex*
Woodville *Middlesex*
Worcester *Worcester*
Woronoco *Hampden*
Worthington *Hampshire*
Wrentham *Norfolk*
Yarmouth Port *Barnstable*

Michigan

All of Michigan's eighty three (83) counties reported that they release conviction records for employment screening purposes, though a handful of counties require records requests to be made in person. Thirty three (33) counties will allow requests to be made by facsimile. Civil suits greater than $10,000 are filed in circuit court.

For more information or for offices not listed, contact the state's information hot line at (517) 373-1837.

Driving Records

Department of State
7064 Crowner Drive
Lansing, MI 48918
(517) 322-1618
Fax (517) 322-1181
Driving records are available by mail. $6 fee per request. Turnaround time is 10 days. Written request must include job applicant's full name, date of birth, license number. Make check payable to State of Michigan.

Worker's Compensation Records

Bureau of Worker's Compensation
Claims Processing
PO Box 30016
Lansing, MI 48909
(517) 322-1884 or
(517) 322-1888 (Computerized No.)
Records are available by mail. Requests must include job applicant's name, social security number and, if available, date of injury or name of previous employer involved in claim. There is no fee. A signed release is not required.

Vital Statistics

Michigan Department of Public Health
Office of The State Registrar
PO Box 30195
Lansing, MI 48909
(517) 335-8656
Birth and death records are available for $10.00 each. Make certified checks or money order payable to State of Michigan. State office has records since 1867. Copies of records since 1867 may also be obtained from County Clerk in county where event occurred. Fees vary from county to county. Detroit records may be obtained from the City of Detroit Health Department for births occurring since 1893 and for deaths since 1897.
Marriage records are available at county and state level. $10.00 fee, $3.00 fee for each additional copy. Include name, spouse's name, marriage date and place. Turnaround time is 2-3 weeks. Divorce records are available at county and state level. $10.00 fee, $3.00 fee for each additional copy. Include name, spouse's name, marriage date and place. Turnaround time is 2-3 weeks.

Department of Education

Department of Education
Teacher Certification
PO Box 30008
Lansing, MI 48909
(517) 373-3310
Field of certification, effective date and expiration date are available by phone or mail. Include name and SSN.

Medical Licensing

Department of Licensing & Regulation
PO Box 30018
Lansing, MI 48909
(900) 740-6111
Will confirm licenses for MDs by phone or mail. $15 fee, payable to the above. For licenses not mentioned, contact the above office.

Michigan Board of Nursing
Dept. of Licensing & Regulation
PO Box 30018
Lansing, MI 48909
(900) 740-6111
Will confirm license by phone. No fee. Include name, license number.

Bar Association

Michigan State Bar Association
306 Townsend
Lansing, MI 48933
(517) 327-9030
Will confirm licenses by phone. No fee. Include name.

Accountancy Board

CPA Registration Occupational Board
Department of Commerce Accounting Board
PO Box 30018
Lansing, MI 48909
(517) 373-0682
(900) 740-6111
Will confirm license by mail or phone. $5.00 fee for written response. Include name.

Securities Commission

Department of Commerce
Corporation and Securities
6546 Mercantile Way
PO Box 30054
Lansing, MI 48909
(517) 334-6206
Will confirm license by phone. No fee. Include name and SSN.

Secretary of State

Michigan Department of Commerce
Corporation and Securities Bureau
Corporation Division
PO Box 30054
Lansing, MI 48909
(900) 740-0031
Service agent and address, date incorporated, trade names are available by phone or mail. Contact the above office for additional information.

Criminal Records
State Repository

Michigan State Police
Central Records Division
7150 Harris Drive
Lansing, MI 48913
(517) 322-1956
Criminal record checks are available to non-criminal agencies by mail only. Each request must include subject's full name, date of birth, SSN and a signed release.

There is a $3.00 fee per individual being checked. Still charge if no records are found. Make check payable to State of Michigan. Only conviction information will be released.

Alcona County

Alcona County Clerk, Criminal Records
Box 308
Harrisville, MI 48740
(517) 724-5374
Felony and misdemeanor records are available by mail or phone. A release is required. No search fee. $.25 fee per copy. $5.00 for certification. Search information required: name, date of birth, years to search.

Civil records are available by mail or phone. A release is required. No search fee. $.25 fee per copy. $5.00 for certification. Search information required: name, date of birth, years to search. Specify plaintiff or defendant.

Alger County

Felony records
Alger County Clerk, Criminal Records
101 Court St.
Munising, MI 49862
(906) 387-2076
Felony records are available by mail or phone. No release necessary. No search fee. Search information required: name, years to search.

Civil records
Alger County Clerk
101 Court St.
Munising, MI 49862
(906) 387-2076
Civil records are available by mail or phone. No release necessary. No search fee. $5.00 for certification. Search information required: name, years to search. Specify plaintiff or defendant.

Misdemeanor records
93rd District Court
101 Court St.
Munising, MI 49862
(906) 387-3879
Fax (906) 387-2118
Misdemeanor records are available by mail, fax or phone. No release necessary. No search fee. Search information required: name, date of birth, years to search.

Civil records
93rd District Court
101 Court St.
Munising, MI 49862
(906) 387-3879
Civil records are available by mail or phone. No release necessary. No search fee. $.25 fee per copy. Search information required: name, years to search. Specify plaintiff or defendant.

Allegan County

Felony records
Allegan County Clerk's Office,
Criminal Records
113 Chestnut St.
Allegan, MI 49010
(616) 673-8471
Fax (616) 673-6094
Felony records are available by mail, phone or fax. No release necessary. No search fee. Search information required: name, date of birth, years to search.

Civil records
Allegan County Clerk's Office
113 Chestnut St.
Allegan, MI 49010
(616) 673-8471
Fax (616) 673-6094
Civil records are available by mail. No release necessary. No search fee. $1.00 fee per copy. Search information required: name, years to search. Specify plaintiff or defendant.

Misdemeanor records
57th District Court
Courthouse, 113 Chestnut Street
Allegan, MI 49010
(616) 673-8471 Ext. 356
Misdemeanor records are available in person only. See Michigan state repository for additional information.

Civil records
57th District Court
Courthouse
Allegan, MI 49010
(616) 673-8471 Ext. 350
Civil records are available in person only. See Michigan state repository for additional information.

Alpena County

Felony records
Courthouse
720 Chism
Alpena, MI 49707
(517) 356-0115
Fax (517) 354-3748
Felony records are available by mail, fax or phone. No release necessary. No search fee. $1.00 fee per copy, $5.00 fee for certification. Search information required: name, years to search.

Civil records
Courthouse
720 Chism
Alpena, MI 49707
(517) 356-0115
Civil records are available by mail. No release necessary. No search fee. $1.00 fee per copy. $10.00 for certification. Search information required: name, years to search. Specify plaintiff or defendant.

Misdemeanor records
88th District Court
Court Clerk
719 Chism
Alpena, MI 49707
(517) 354-3330
Misdemeanor records are available by mail only. No release necessary. No fee. Search information required: name, date of birth, years to search, purpose of request, type of offense.

Civil records
88th District Court
Court Clerk
719 Chism
Alpena, MI 49707
(517) 354-3330
Civil records are available by mail. No release necessary. No search fee. $1.00 fee per copy. Search information required: name, years to search. Specify plaintiff or defendant.

Antrim County

Felony records
Antrim County Clerk's Office,
Criminal Records
PO Box 520
Bellaire, MI 49615
(616) 533-8607
Felony records are available by mail or phone. No release necessary. No search fee. $.25 fee per copy. $5.00 for certification. Search information required: name, years to search, date of birth.

Civil records are available by mail or phone. No release necessary. No search fee. $.25 fee per copy. $5.00 for certification. Search information required: name, date of birth, years to search. Specify plaintiff or defendant.

Misdemeanor records
87th District Court
PO Box 597
Bellaire, MI 49615
(616) 533-6441, Ext. 157
Misdemeanor records are available by mail or phone. No release necessary. No fee. Search information required: name, date of birth, years to search.

Civil records
87th District Court
PO Box 597
Bellaire, MI 49615
(616) 533-6441, Ext. 157
Civil records are available by mail or phone. No release necessary. No search fee. $.25 fee per copy. $3.00 for certification. Search information required: name, years to search. Specify plaintiff or defendant.

Arenac County

Felony records
County Clerk, Criminal Records
PO Box 747
Standish, MI 48658
(517) 846-4626
Felony records are available by mail or phone. No release necessary. No fee. Search information required: name, years to search.

Civil records
County Clerk
PO Box 747
Standish, MI 48658
(517) 846-4626
Civil records are available by mail or phone. A release is required. No search fee. $1.00 fee per copy. $3.00 for certification. Search information required: name, years to search. Specify plaintiff or defendant.

Misdemeanor records
81st District Court
PO Box 129
Standish, MI 48658
(517) 846-9538
Fax (517) 846-2008
Misdemeanor records are available by mail, fax or phone. A release is required. No fee. Search information required: name, date of birth, SASE.

Civil records
81st District Court
PO Box 129
Standish, MI 48658
(517) 846-9538
Civil records are available by mail or phone. No release necessary. No search fee. $.25 fee per copy. Search information required: name, years to search. Specify plaintiff or defendant.

Baraga County

Circuit Court Clerk, Criminal Records
Courthouse
L'Anse, MI 49946
(906) 524-6183
Felony records are available by mail. No release necessary. No search fee. $1.00 fee per copy. $5.00 for certification. Search information required: name, years to search.

Civil records are available by mail or phone. No release necessary. No search fee. $1.00 fee per copy. $5.00 for certification. Search information required: name, years to search. Specify plaintiff or defendant.

Barry County

Felony records
County Clerk, Criminal Records
220 W. State St.
Hastings, MI 49058
(616) 948-4810
Felony records are available by mail. No release necessary. $10.00 fee. Make check payable to Barry Court Clerk. Search information required: name, date of birth.

Civil records
County Clerk
220 W. State St.
Hastings, MI 49058
(616) 948-4810
Civil records are available by mail. No release necessary. $7.00 search fee. $1.00 fee per copy. $10.00 for certification. Search information required: name, years to search. Specify plaintiff or defendant.

Misdemeanor records
56th District Court
220 W. Court St.
Hastings, MI 49058
(616) 948-4835
Fax (616) 948-2711
Misdemeanor records are available by mail or fax. A release is required. No search fee. $.25 fee per copy. Search information required: name, date of birth, driver's license number or case number if available.

Civil records
56th District Court
220 W. Court St.
Hastings, MI 49058
(616) 948-4835
Fax (616) 948-2711
Civil records are available by mail, fax or phone. No release necessary. No search fee. $.25 fee per copy. Search information required: name, years to search. Specify plaintiff or defendant.

Bay County

Felony records
County Clerk, Criminal Records
515 Center
Bay City, MI 48708
(517) 892-3528
Fax (517) 893-3266
Felony records are available by mail, phone or fax. No release necessary. No search fee. $.25 fee per copy. $1.00 for certification. $5.00 fee plus $1.00 per page for fax response in Michigan. $10.00 fee plus $1.00 per page for fax response outside of Michigan. Check payable to District Court. Search information required: name, date of birth, years to search.

Civil records
County Clerk
515 Center
Bay City, MI 48708
(517) 892-3528
Fax (517) 893-3266
Civil records are available by mail, phone or fax. No release necessary. No search fee. $.25 fee per copy. $1.00 for certification. Search information required: name, date of birth, years to search. Specify plaintiff or defendant.

Misdemeanor records
74th District Court
Court Clerk
515 Center
Bay City, MI 48708
(517) 892-5528 or 892-5529
Fax (517) 892-2538
Misdemeanor records are available by mail or fax. No search fee. $2.00 fee for fax response. Search information required: name, date of birth, reason for request.

Civil records
74th District Court
Court Clerk
515 Center
Bay City, MI 48708
(517) 892-5528 or 892-5529
Fax (517) 892-2538
Civil records are available by mail. A release is required. No search fee. $.25 fee per copy. $2.00 for certification. Search information required: name, years to search. Specify plaintiff or defendant.

Benzie County

Felony records
County Clerk, Criminal Records
Government Center
Beulah, MI 49617
(616) 882-9671
Fax (616) 882-4844
Felony records are available by mail, phone or fax. No release necessary. No search fee. $.35 fee per copy. $1.00 for certification. Search information required: name, years to search.

Civil records
County Clerk
Government Center
Beulah, MI 49617
(616) 882-9671
Fax (616) 882-4844
Civil records are available by mail or phone. No release necessary. No search fee. $.35 fee per copy. $1.00 for certification. Search information required: name, years to search. Specify plaintiff or defendant.

Misdemeanor records
85th District Court
Courthouse
Beulah, MI 49617
(616) 882-9671 Ext. 36
Misdemeanor records are available by mail. No release necessary. $5.00 search fee. Search information required: name, date of birth.

Civil records
85th District Court
Courthouse
Beulah, MI 49617
(616) 882-9671 Ext. 36
Civil records are available by mail. No release necessary. $3.00 search fee. $1.00 fee per copy. $2.00 for certification. Search information required: name, years to search. Specify plaintiff or defendant.

Berrien County

Felony records
Berrien County Courthouse, Criminal Records
Circuit Court
Port St.
St. Joseph, MI 49085
(616) 983-7111
Fax (616) 982-8647
Felony records are available by mail. No release necessary. $5.00 search fee. Search information required: name, date of birth, SSN, years to search. Contact above office for Record Check Request Form.

Civil records
Berrien County Courthouse
Circuit Court
Port St.
St. Joseph, MI 49085
(616) 983-7111
Fax (616) 982-8647
Civil records are available by mail, phone. or fax. No release necessary. $5.00 search fee. $1.00 fee per copy. Search information required: name, years to search. Specify plaintiff or defendant.

Misdemeanor records
Attention: Administration
5th District Court
811 Port St.
St. Joseph, MI 49085
(616) 983-1541 Ext. 745
Misdemeanor records are available by mail only. No release necessary. $5.00 search fee. $1.00 fee per copy, $2.00 for certified copy. Make money order only payable to 5th District Court. Search information required: full name, date of birth, SSN.

Civil records
Attention: Administration
5th District Court
811 Port St.
St. Joseph, MI 49085
(616) 983-1541 Ext. 745
Civil records are available by mail. No release necessary. $5.00 search fee. $1.00 fee per copy. $2.00 for certification. Search information required: name, years to search. Specify plaintiff or defendant.

Branch County

Branch County Courthouse, Criminal Records
31 Division St.
Coldwater, MI 49036
(517) 279-8411
Felony and misdemeanor records are available by mail. No release necessary. $25.00 search fee. Search information required: name, date of birth, years to search.

Civil records are available by mail. No release necessary. $25.00 search fee. Search information required: name, years to search. Specify plaintiff or defendant.

Calhoun County

Felony records
Docket Office, Criminal Records
315 W. Green
Marshall, MI 49068
(616) 781-0713
Felony records are available by mail or phone. No release necessary. No fee. Search information required: name, case number. Phone requests can obtain only records since 1984.

Civil records
Docket Office
315 W. Green
Marshall, MI 49068
(616) 781-0713
Civil records are available by mail or phone. No release necessary. $1.00 search fee per year prior to 1984. No search fee from 1984 forward. $.50 fee per copy. $1.00 for certification. Search information required: name, years to search. Specify plaintiff or defendant.

Misdemeanor records
Hall of Justice
80th E. State St.
Battlecreek, MI 49017
(616) 966-1571
Misdemeanor records are available by mail only. No release necessary. No search fee. $.25 fee per copy. Search information required: name, date of birth, years to search.

Civil records
Hall of Justice
80th E. State St.
Battlecreek, MI 49017
(616) 966-1571
Civil records are available by mail. No release necessary. No search fee. $.25 fee per copy. Search information required: name, years to search. Specify plaintiff or defendant.

Cass County

Felony records
Cass County Clerk, Criminal Records
120 N. Broadway
Cassopolis, MI 49031-1398
(616) 445-8621 Extension 201
Fax (616) 445-8978
Felony records are available by mail, phone or fax. No release necessary. No search fee. Search information required: name, date of birth, years to search.

Civil records
Cass County Clerk
120 N. Broadway
Cassopolis, MI 49031-1398
(616) 445-8621 Extension 201
Fax (616) 445-8978
Civil records are available by mail, phone or fax. No release necessary. No search fee. $1.00 fee per copy. $10.00 for certification. Search information required: name, years to search. Specify plaintiff or defendant.

Misdemeanor records
District Court
110 N. Broadway
Cassopolis, MI 49031
(616) 445-8621 Extension 213
Misdemeanor records are available by mail. No release necessary. No search fee. $.50 fee per copy. $2.00 for certification. Search information required: name, date of birth, years to search.

Civil records
District Court
110 N. Broadway
Cassopolis, MI 49031
(616) 445-8621 Extension 213
Civil records are available by mail. No release necessary. No search fee. $.50 fee per copy. $2.00 for certification. Search information required: name, date of birth, years to search. Specify plaintiff or defendant.

Charlevoix County

Felony records
County Clerk, Criminal Records
County Bldg.
301 State Street
Charlevoix, MI 49720
(616) 547-7200
Fax (616) 547-7217
Felony records are available by mail, phone or fax. No release necessary. No search fee. Search information required: name, years to search.

Civil records
County Clerk
County Bldg.
301 State Street
Charlevoix, MI 49720
(616) 547-7200
Fax (616) 547-7217
Civil records are available by mail, phone or fax. No release necessary. No search fee. $1.00 fee per copy. $5.00 for certification. Search information required: name, years to search. Specify plaintiff or defendant.

Misdemeanor records
90th District Court
County Bldg.
Charlevoix, MI 49720
(616) 547-7227
Misdemeanor records are available by mail or phone. No search fee. Search information required: name, date of birth.

Civil records
90th District Court
County Bldg.
Charlevoix, MI 49720
(616) 547-7227
Civil records are available by mail or phone. No release necessary. No search fee. Search information required: name, date of birth, years to search. Specify plaintiff or defendant.

Cheboygan County

Felony records
Cheboygan County Clerk, Criminal Records
PO Box 70
Cheboygan, MI 49721
(616) 627-8808
Fax (616) 627-8444
Felony records are available by mail. No release necessary. No search fee. $1.00 fee per copy. $5.00 for certification. Search information required: name, date of birth.

Civil records
Cheboygan County Clerk
PO Box 70
Cheboygan, MI 49721
(616) 627-8808
Fax (616) 627-8444
Civil records are available by mail. No release necessary. No search fee. $1.00 fee per copy. $5.00 for certification. Search information required: name, years to search. Specify plaintiff or defendant.

Misdemeanor records
89th District Court
PO Box 70
Cheboygan, MI 49721
(616) 627-8853
Misdemeanor records are available by mail only. No release necessary. No search fee. Search information required: name, date of birth, offense, years to search.

Civil records
89th District Court
PO Box 70
Cheboygan, MI 49721
(616) 627-8853
Civil records are available by mail. No release necessary. No search fee. $.25 fee per copy. Search information required: name, years to search. Specify plaintiff or defendant.

Chippewa County

Felony records
Chippewa County Clerk, Criminal Records
Courthouse
319 Court
Sault Ste. Marie, MI 49783
(906) 635-6300
Fax (906) 635-6325
Felony records are available by mail or fax. No release necessary. No search fee. $1.00 fee per copy. Search information required: name, years to search, date of charge, charge.

Civil records
Chippewa County Clerk
Courthouse
319 Court
Sault Ste. Marie, MI 49783
(906) 635-6300
Fax (906) 635-6325
Civil records are available by mail. No release necessary. $5.00 search fee. $.50 fee per copy. $5.00 for certification. Search information required: name, years to search. Specify plaintiff or defendant.

Misdemeanor records
91st District Court
325 Court St.
City-County Bldg.
Sault Ste. Marie, MI 49783
(906) 635-6320
Fax (906) 635-6325
Misdemeanor records are available by mail or phone. A release is required. No search fee. Search information required: name, date of birth.

Civil records
91st District Court
325 Court St.
City-County Bldg.
Sault Ste. Marie, MI 49783
(906) 635-6320
Fax (906) 635-6325
Civil records are available by mail or phone. No release necessary. No search fee. $1.00 fee for first copy, $.25 thereafter. $1.00 for certification. Search information required: name, years to search. Specify plaintiff or defendant.

Clare County

Felony records
Circuit Court Clerk, Criminal Records
PO Box 438
Harrison, MI 48625
(517) 539-7131
Felony records are available by mail or phone. No release necessary. No search fee. Search information required: name.

Civil records
Circuit Court Clerk
PO Box 438
Harrison, MI 48625
(517) 539-7131
Civil records are available by mail or phone. No release necessary. No search fee. $.25 fee per copy. $7.00 for certification. Search information required: name, years to search. Specify plaintiff or defendant.

Misdemeanor records
80th District Court
225 W. Main
Harrison, MI 48625
(517) 539-7173
Misdemeanor records are available by mail or phone. No release necessary. No search fee. Search information required: name, date of birth, years to search.

Civil records
80th District Court
225 W. Main
Harrison, MI 48625
(517) 539-7173
Civil records are available by mail or phone. No release necessary. No search fee. $.75 fee per copy. $2.00 for certification. Search information required: name, years to search. Specify plaintiff or defendant.

Clinton County

Felony records
Clinton County Clerk
PO Box 69
St. Johns, MI 48879-0069
(517) 224-5140
Fax (517) 224-5254
Felony records are available by mail, phone or fax. No release necessary. $5.00 search fee. Search information required: name, years to search.

Civil records
Clinton County Clerk
PO Box 69
St. Johns, MI 48879-0069
(517) 224-5140
Fax (517) 224-5254
Civil records are available by mail, phone or fax. No release necessary. $5.00 search fee. $.50 fee per copy. $1.00 for certification. Search information required: name, years to search. Specify plaintiff or defendant. 24-hour turnaround time.

Misdemeanor records
65th District Court
Criminal Division
409 S. U.S. 27
St. Johns, MI 48879
(517) 224-5150
Misdemeanor records are available by mail or phone. No release necessary. No search fee. Search information required: name, date of birth, years to search, offense, date of offense (if available).

Civil records
65th District Court
409 S. U.S. 27
St. Johns, MI 48879
(517) 224-5150
Civil records are available by mail. A release is required. No search fee. $.25 fee per copy. Search information required: name, years to search. Specify plaintiff or defendant.

Crawford County

Felony records
Circuit Court Clerk, Criminal Records
200 Michigan Ave.
Grayling, MI 49738
(517) 348-2841
Fax (517) 348-7582
Felony records are available by mail, phone or fax. No release necessary. No fee. Search information required: name, SASE.

Civil records
Circuit Court Clerk
200 Michigan Ave.
Grayling, MI 49738
(517) 348-2841
Fax (517) 348-7582
Civil records are available by mail, phone or fax. No release necessary. No search fee. $1.00 fee for first copy, $.25 thereafter. $1.00 for certification. Search information required: name, years to search. Specify plaintiff or defendant.

Misdemeanor records
83rd District Court
County Courthouse
Grayling, MI 49738
(517) 348-2841 Ext. 242
Fax (517) 348-7582
Misdemeanor records are available by mail, phone or fax. A release is required. No search fee. $1.00 fee for first copy, $.25 thereafter. $1.00 for certification. $2.00 fee for fax response. Make check payable to 83rd District Court. Search information required: name, date of birth.

Civil records
83rd District Court
County Courthouse
Grayling, MI 49738
(517) 348-2841 Ext. 242
Fax (517) 348-7582
Civil records are available by mail, phone or fax. A release is required. No search fee. $1.00 fee for first copy, $.25 thereafter. $1.00 for certification. Search information required: name, years to search. Specify plaintiff or defendant.

Delta County

Delta County Clerk, Criminal Records
310 Ludington St.
Escanaba, MI 49829
(906) 786-1763
Felony and misdemeanor records are available by mail or phone. A release is required. No search fee. $1.00 fee per copy. $1.00 for certification. Make check payable to County Clerk. Search information required: name, date of birth.

Civil records are available by mail or phone. A release is required. No search fee. $1.00 fee per copy. $1.00 for certification. Search information required: name, years to search. Specify plaintiff or defendant.

Dickinson County

Felony records
Dickinson County Clerk, Criminal Records
PO Box 609
Iron Mountain, MI 49801
(906) 774-0988
Fax (906) 774-3686
Felony records are available by mail. No release necessary. $5.00 fee for first 10 years searched. $5.00 fee for each additional five years. Company checks only, payable to Dickinson County Clerk. Search information required: name, date of birth, years to search.

Civil records
Dickinson County Clerk
PO Box 609
Iron Mountain, MI 49801
(906) 774-0988
Fax (906) 774-3686
Civil records are available by mail. No release necessary. $15.00 search fee for first 10 years. $5.00 search fee for each additional 5 years searched. $.15 fee per copy. $2.00 for certification. Search information required: name, years to search. Specify plaintiff or defendant.

Misdemeanor records
District Court
Dickinson County Courthouse
95B District Court
Iron Mountain, MI 49801
(906) 774-0506
Misdemeanor records are available by mail. A release is required. $25.00 search fee. $1.00 fee per copy. Search information required: name, years to search.

Civil records
District Court
Dickinson County Courthouse
95B District Court
Iron Mountain, MI 49801
(906) 774-0506
Civil records are available by mail. A release is required. $25.00 search fee. $1.00 fee per copy. Search information required: name, years to search. Specify plaintiff or defendant.

Eaton County

Felony records
Circuit Court Clerk, Criminal Records
1045 Independence Blvd.
Charlotte, MI 48813
(517) 543-7500 Ext. 256
Fax (517) 543-7377
Felony records are available by mail or fax. A release is required. No search fee for first 5 years searched. $5.00 fee for additional years searched. Search information required: name, date of birth, SASE, years to search, SASE.

Civil records
Circuit Court Clerk
1045 Independence Blvd.
Charlotte, MI 48813
(517) 543-7500 Ext. 256
Fax (517) 543-7377
Civil records are available by mail, phone, or fax. No release necessary. $5.00 search fee. $5.00 for certification. Search information required: name, years to search. Specify plaintiff or defendant.

Misdemeanor records
56th District Court
1045 Independence
Charlotte, MI 48813
(517) 543-7500 Ext. 282
Misdemeanor records are available by mail or phone. No release necessary. No search fee. Search information required: name, date of birth, years to search.

Civil records
56th District Court
1045 Independence
Charlotte, MI 48813
(517) 543-7500 Ext. 282
Civil records are available by mail. No release necessary. $5.00 search fee. $.25 fee per copy. $5.00 for certification. Search information required: name, years to search. Specify plaintiff or defendant.

Emmet County

Felony records
Emmet County Clerk, Criminal Records
County Bldg.
200 Division St.
Petoskey, MI 49770
(616) 348-1744
Felony records are available by mail or phone. No release necessary. No search fee. Search information required: name, date of birth.

Civil records
Emmet County Clerk
County Bldg.
200 Division St.
Petoskey, MI 49770
(616) 348-1744
Civil records are available by mail or phone. No release necessary. No search fee. $1.00 fee per copy. $1.00 for certification. Search information required: name, years to search. Specify plaintiff or defendant.

Misdemeanor records
90th District Court
County Bldg., 200 Division Street
Petoskey, MI 49770
(616) 348-1750
Fax (616) 348-0633
Misdemeanor records are available by mail only. No search fee. A release is required for copies of file. Indicate criminal or traffic. Search information required: full name, date of birth, information requested.

Civil records
90th District Court
City-County Bldg.
Petoskey, MI 49770
(616) 348-1750
Fax (616) 348-0633
Civil records are available by mail. No release necessary. No search fee. $1.00 fee per copy. $3.00 for certification. Search information required: name, years to search. Specify plaintiff or defendant.

Genesee County

Felony records
Genesee County Clerk
Legal Division
205 Courthouse
Flint, MI 48502
(313) 257-3220
Felony records are available by mail. No release necessary. No search fee. $1.00 fee per copy, $1.00 fee per page of computer printout. Search information required: name, years to search.

Civil records
Genesee County Clerk
Legal Division
205 Courthouse
Flint, MI 48502
(313) 257-3220
Civil records are available by mail or phone. No release necessary. No search fee. $1.00 fee per copy. $1.00 for certification. Search information required: name, years to search. Specify plaintiff or defendant.

Misdemeanor records
67th District Court
Central District Court
630 S. Saginaw, Suite 124
Flint, MI 48502
(313) 257-3170
Misdemeanor records are available by mail. A release is required. No search fee. $1.00 fee per copy, $3.00 fee per computer printout. Search information required: name, date of birth.

Civil records
67th District Court
Central District Court
630 S. Saginaw, Suite 124
Flint, MI 48502
(313) 257-3170
Civil records are available by in person only. See Michigan state repository for additional information.

Gladwin County

Felony records
Gladwin County Clerk, Criminal Records
401 W. Cedar
Gladwin, MI 48624
(517) 426-7351
Felony records are available by mail or phone. No release necessary. No search fee. $.50 fee per copy. Search information required: name, time to search.

Civil records
Gladwin County Clerk
401 W. Cedar
Gladwin, MI 48624
(517) 426-7351
Civil records are available by mail or phone. No release necessary. No search fee. $.50 fee per copy. $1.00 for certification. Search information required: name, years to search. Specify plaintiff or defendant.

Misdemeanor records
80th District Court
401 W. Cedar
Gladwin, MI 48624
(517) 426-9207
Misdemeanor records are available by mail. A release is required. No search fee. $.50 fee per copy. Search information required: name, date of birth, reason for requesting information.

Civil records
80th District Court
401 W. Cedar
Gladwin, MI 48624
(517) 426-9207
Civil records are available by mail. No release necessary. No search fee. $1.00 fee per copy. Search information required: name, years to search. Specify plaintiff or defendant.

Gogebic County

Felony records
Gogebic County Clerk, Criminal Records
Gogebic County Courthouse
200 N. Moore
Bessemer, MI 49911
(906) 663-4518
Felony records are available by mail or phone. No release necessary. No search fee. Search information required: name, time to search.

Civil records
Gogebic County Clerk
Gogebic County Courthouse
200 N. Moore
Bessemer, MI 49911
(906) 663-4518
Civil records are available by mail or phone. No release necessary. No search fee. $.25 fee per copy. $3.00 for certification. Search information required: name, years to search. Specify plaintiff or defendant.

Misdemeanor records
98th District Court
Courthouse
Bessemer, MI 49911
(906) 663-4611
Misdemeanor records are available by mail. A release is required. No search fee. Search information required: name, date of birth, years to search.

Civil records
98th District Court
Courthouse
Bessemer, MI 49911
(906) 663-4611
Civil records are available by mail. No release necessary. No search fee. $3.00 for certification. Search information required: name, years to search. Specify plaintiff or defendant.

Grand Traverse County

Felony records
Circuit Court Records, Criminal Records
328 Washington Street
Traverse City, MI 49684
(616) 922-4710
Felony records are available by mail or phone. No release necessary. No search fee. Search information required: name, years to search.

Civil records
Circuit Court Records
328 Washington Street
Traverse City, MI 49684
(616) 922-4710
Civil records are available by mail or phone. No release necessary. No search fee. $.25 fee per copy. $1.00 for certification. Search information required: name, years to search. Specify plaintiff or defendant.

Misdemeanor records
86th District Court
Courthouse
PO Box 552
Traverse City, MI 49684
(616) 922-4578
Misdemeanor records are available by mail only. No release necessary. No fee. Search information required: full name, date of birth, SASE.

Civil records
86th District Court
Courthouse
PO Box 552
Traverse City, MI 49684
(616) 922-4578
Civil records are available by mail or phone. No release necessary. No search fee. $.25 fee per copy. $2.00 for certification. Search information required: name, years to search, SASE. Specify plaintiff or defendant.

Gratiot County

Felony records
Gratiot County Clerk, Criminal Records
Courthouse - PO Box 437
Ithaca, MI 48847
(517) 875-5215
Felony records are available by mail. No release necessary. $3.00 fee for each seven years searched. $1.00 fee per copy. $10.00 for certification. Search information required: name, years to search.

Civil records
Gratiot County Clerk
Courthouse - PO Box 437
Ithaca, MI 48847
(517) 875-5215
Civil records are available by mail. No release necessary. $8.00 search fee. $1.00 fee per copy. $10.00 for certification. Search information required: name, years to search. Specify plaintiff or defendant.

Misdemeanor records
65th District Court
245 E. Newark
Ithaca, MI 48847
(517) 875-5240
Misdemeanor records are available in person only. See Michigan state repository for additional information.

Civil records
65th District Court
245 E. Newark
Ithaca, MI 48847
(517) 875-5240
Civil records are available by in person only. See Michigan state repository for additional information.

Hillsdale County

Felony records
Hillsdale County Clerk, Criminal Records
Courthouse
Hillsdale, MI 49242
(517) 437-3391
Felony records are available by mail or phone. No release necessary. No search fee. Search information required: name.

Civil records
Hillsdale County Clerk
Courthouse
Hillsdale, MI 49242
(517) 437-3391
Civil records are available by mail or phone. No release necessary. No search fee. $.50 fee per copy. $7.00 for certification. Search information required: name, years to search. Specify plaintiff or defendant.

Misdemeanor records
2nd District Court
49 N. Howell
Hillsdale, MI 49242
(517) 437-7329
Misdemeanor records are available by mail or phone. No release necessary. No search fee. Search information required: full name, date of birth.

Civil records
2nd District Court
49 N. Howell
Hillsdale, MI 49242
(517) 437-7329
Civil records are available by mail or phone. No release necessary. No search fee. $.50 fee per copy. $3.00 for certification. Search information required: name, years to search. Specify plaintiff or defendant.

Houghton County

Felony records
Houghton County Clerk, Criminal Records
Courthouse
401 E. Houghton Ave.
Houghton, MI 49931
(906) 482-5420
Felony records are available by mail or phone. No release necessary. No search fee. $1.00 fee per copy. $1.00 for certification. Search information required: name, years to search.

Civil records
Houghton County Clerk
Courthouse
401 E. Houghton Ave.
Houghton, MI 49931
(906) 482-5420
Civil records are available by mail or phone. No release necessary. No search fee. $1.00 fee per copy. $1.00 for certification. Search information required: name, years to search. Specify plaintiff or defendant.

Misdemeanor records
97th District Court
Courthouse
Houghton, MI 49931
(906) 482-4980
Misdemeanor records are available in person only. See Michigan state repository for additional information. Copies of misdemeanor records are available if specific case is known.

Civil records
97th District Court
Courthouse
Houghton, MI 49931
(906) 482-4980
Civil records are available by mail. No release necessary. No search fee. $3.00 for certification. Search information required: name, years to search. Specify plaintiff or defendant.

Huron County

Felony records
Huron County Clerk, Criminal Records
250 East Huron Avenue
Bad Axe, MI 48413
(517) 269-9942
Fax (517) 269-7221
Felony records are available by mail or phone. No release necessary. No search fee. $1.00 fee per copy. $10.00 for certification. Search information required: name, years to search.

Civil records
Huron County Clerk
250 East Huron Avenue
Bad Axe, MI 48413
(517) 269-9942
Fax (517) 269-7221
Civil records are available by mail or phone. No release necessary. No search fee. $1.00 fee per copy. $10.00 for certification. Search information required: name, years to search. Specify plaintiff or defendant.

Misdemeanor records
73rd District Court
First Division
Huron County Bldg.
Bad Axe, MI 48413
(517) 269-9987
Misdemeanor records are available by mail. No release necessary. No search fee. $1.00 fee per copy. Search information required: name, date of birth, driver's license number, years to search.

Civil records
73rd District Court
First Division
Huron County Bldg.
Bad Axe, MI 48413
(517) 269-9987
Civil records are available by mail. No release necessary. No search fee. $1.00 fee per copy. Search information required: name, years to search. Specify plaintiff or defendant.

Ingham County

Felony records
Clerk of Court, Criminal Records
333 S. Capitol Ave.
Suite C
Lansing, MI 48933
(517) 483-6500 Ext. 6715
Fax (517) 482-0650
Felony records are available by mail or phone for three names searched. No release necessary. No search fee. Search information required: full name, SASE.

Civil records
Clerk of Court
333 S. Capitol Ave.
Suite C
Lansing, MI 48933
(517) 483-6500 Ext. 6715
Fax (517) 482-0650
Civil records are available by mail. No release necessary. No search fee. $.50 fee per copy. $1.00 for certification. Search information required: name, years to search. Specify plaintiff or defendant.

Misdemeanor records
54A District Court
6th Floor, City Hall
124 W. Michigan Avenue
Lansing, MI 48933
(517) 483-4432
Misdemeanor records are available by mail only. No release necessary. No search fee. $.10 fee per copy. Search information required: name, date of birth, years to search.

Civil records
54A District Court
6th Floor, City Hall
124 W. Michigan Avenue
Lansing, MI 48933
(517) 483-4432
Civil records are available by mail or by phone from 1990 forward. No release necessary. No search fee. $.50 fee per copy. $1.00 for certification. Search information required: name, years to search. Specify plaintiff or defendant.

Ionia County

Felony records
Ionia County Clerk, Criminal Records
Courthouse
Ionia, MI 48846
(616) 527-5322
Felony records are available by mail or phone. No release necessary. No search fee. Search information required: name, years to search.

Civil records
Ionia County Clerk
Courthouse
Ionia, MI 48846
(616) 527-5322
Civil records are available by mail or phone. No release necessary. No search fee. $1.00 fee per copy. Search information required: name, years to search. Specify plaintiff or defendant.

Misdemeanor records
64A District Court
Courthouse
101 W. Main St.
Ionia, MI 48846
(616) 527-5346
Misdemeanor records are available by mail or phone. No release necessary. $3.00 search fee. $.25 fee per copy. $1.00 for certification. Search information required: name, years to search.

Civil records
64A District Court
Courthouse
101 W. Main St.
Ionia, MI 48846
(616) 527-5346
Civil records are available by mail. No release necessary. No search fee. $.50 fee per copy. $1.00 for certification. Search information required: name, years to search. Specify plaintiff or defendant.

Iosco County

Felony records
Iosco County Clerk, Criminal Records
PO Box 838
Tawas City, MI 48764
(517) 362-3497
Felony records are available by mail or phone. No release necessary. No search fee. Search information required: name.

Civil records
Iosco County Clerk
PO Box 838
Tawas City, MI 48764
(517) 362-3497
Civil records are available by mail. No release necessary. No search fee. $.50 fee per copy. $1.00 for certification. Search information required: name, years to search. Specify plaintiff or defendant.

Misdemeanor records
81st District Court
PO Box 388
Tawas City, MI 48764
(517) 362-4441
Misdemeanor records are available by mail only. No release necessary. No search fee. Search information required: name, date of birth, information requested.

Civil records
81st District Court
PO Box 388
Tawas City, MI 48764
(517) 362-4441
Civil records are available by mail. No release necessary. No search fee. $3.00 for certification. Search information required: name, years to search. Specify plaintiff or defendant.

Iron County

Felony records
Iron County Clerk, Criminal Records
2 South 6th Street
Crystal Falls, MI 49920
(906) 875-3221
Fax (906) 875-6370
Felony records are available by mail. No release necessary. No search fee. $.25 fee per copy. $5.00 for certification. Search information required: name.

Civil records
Iron County Clerk
2 South 6th Street
Crystal Falls, MI 49920
(906) 875-3221
Fax (906) 875-6370
Civil records are available by mail or phone. No release necessary. No search fee. $.25 fee per copy. $5.00 for certification. Search information required: name, years to search. Specify plaintiff or defendant.

Misdemeanor records
95B District Court
Courthouse
2 South 6th Street
Crystal Falls, MI 49920
(906) 875-6659
Misdemeanor records are available by mail only. A release is required. No search fee. Search information required: name, date of birth, driver's license number, SSN.

Civil records
95B District Court
Courthouse
2 South 6th Street
Crystal Falls, MI 49920
(906) 875-6659
Civil records are available by mail. No release necessary. No search fee. $.25 fee per copy. $1.25 for certification. Search information required: name, years to search. Specify plaintiff or defendant.

Isabella County

Felony records
Isabella County Clerk
County Bldg.
200 N. Main
Mount Pleasant, MI 48858
(517) 772-0911
Felony records are available by mail or phone. No release necessary. No search fee. $1.00 fee per copy. Search information required: name, years to search.

Civil records
Isabella County Clerk
County Bldg.
200 N. Main
Mount Pleasant, MI 48858
(517) 772-0911
Civil records are available by mail or phone. No release necessary. No search fee. $1.00 fee per copy. $1.00 for certification. Search information required: name, years to search. Specify plaintiff or defendant.

Misdemeanor records
76th District Court
200 N. Main
Mount Pleasant, MI 48858
(517) 772-0911 Ext. 273
Misdemeanor records are available in person only. See Michigan state repository for additional information.

Civil records
76th District Court
200 N. Main
Mount Pleasant, MI 48858
(517) 772-0911 Ext. 273
Civil records are available by mail or phone. No release necessary. No search fee. $1.00 fee per copy. $1.00 for certification. Search information required: name, years to search. Specify plaintiff or defendant.

Jackson County

Felony records
Jackson County Clerk, Criminal Records
312 S. Jackson St.
Court Services
Jackson, MI 49201
(517) 788-4268
Fax (517) 788-4683
Felony records are available by mail. No release necessary. $7.23 search fee per hour. $.25 fee per copy. $1.00 fee for certification. Search information required: name, date of birth, if available, years to search.

Civil records
Jackson County Clerk
312 S. Jackson St.
Court Services
Jackson, MI 49201
(517) 788-4268
Fax (517) 788-4683
Civil records are available by mail or phone. No release necessary. $7.50 search fee per hour by mail. $.25 fee per copy. $1.00 for certification. Search information required: name, years to search. Specify plaintiff or defendant.

Misdemeanor records
12th District Court
312 S. Jackson
Jackson, MI 49201
(517) 788-4260
Misdemeanor records are available by mail only. No release necessary. No search fee. $.25 fee per copy. Search information required: name, date of birth, years to search.

Civil records
12th District Court
312 S. Jackson
Jackson, MI 49201
(517) 788-4260
Civil records are available by mail. No release necessary. No search fee. $.25 fee per copy. Search information required: name, years to search. Specify plaintiff or defendant.

Kalamazoo County

Felony records
9th Judicial Circuit Court, Criminal Records
227 W. Michigan
Kalamazoo, MI 49007
(616) 383-8837

Felony records are available by mail. No release necessary. $1.00 search fee. Search information required: name, date of birth, years to search, SASE.

Civil records
9th Judicial Circuit Court
227 W. Michigan
Kalamazoo, MI 49007
(616) 383-8837

Civil records are available by mail. No release necessary. $1.00 search fee. $1.00 fee per copy. $7.00 for certification. Search information required: name, years to search. Specify plaintiff or defendant.

Misdemeanor records
8th District Court
227 W. Michigan
Kalamazoo, MI 49007
(616) 384-8171

Misdemeanor records are available by mail or phone. No release necessary. No search fee depending length of search. Search information required: name, case number, date of offense. Specific cases only, no general searches.

Civil records
8th District Court
227 W. Michigan
Kalamazoo, MI 49007
(616) 384-6413

Civil records are available by mail. No release necessary. No search fee. $.50 fee per copy. Search information required: name, defendant's name, years to search, SASE.

Kalkaska County

Felony records
Kalkaska County Clerk
PO Box 780
Kalkaska, MI 49646
(616) 258-3300

Felony records are available by mail. A release is required. $5.00 search fee. $.30 fee per copy. $1.00 for certification. Search information required: name, years to search.

Civil records
Kalkaska County Clerk
PO Box 780
Kalkaska, MI 49646
(616) 258-3300

Civil records are available by mail. A release is required. $5.00 search fee. $.30 fee per copy. $1.00 for certification. Search information required: name, years to search. Specify plaintiff or defendant.

Misdemeanor records
87th District Court
PO Box 780
Kalkaska, MI 49646
(616) 258-9031
Fax (616) 258-2424

Misdemeanor records are available by mail or phone. No release necessary. No search fee. Search information required: name, date of birth.

Civil records
87th District Court
PO Box 780
Kalkaska, MI 49646
(616) 258-9031
Fax (616) 258-2424

Civil records are available by mail or phone. No release necessary. No search fee. $.30 fee per copy. $1.00 for certification. Search information required: name, years to search. Specify plaintiff or defendant.

Kent County

Felony records
Kent County Clerk, Criminal Records
Hall of Justice
333 Monroe Ave. NW
Grand Rapids, MI 49503
(616) 774-3679

Felony records are available by mail or phone. No release necessary. No search fee. Search information required: name, date of birth.

Civil records
Kent County Clerk
333 Monroe Ave. NW
Grand Rapids, MI 49503
(616) 774-3679

Civil records are available by mail or phone. No release necessary. No search fee. $1.00 fee per copy. Search information required: name, years to search. Specify plaintiff or defendant.

Misdemeanor records
61st District Court
Attn: Criminal
333 Monroe Ave. NW
Grand Rapids, MI 49503
(616) 456-3370

Misdemeanor records are available by mail. No release necessary. No search fee. $.50 fee per copy. $1.00 for certification. Search information required: name, date of birth, years to search, case number (if available).

Civil records
61st District Court
Attn: Criminal
333 Monroe Ave. NW
Grand Rapids, MI 49503
(616) 456-3370

Civil records are available in person only. See Michigan state repository for additional information.

Keweenaw County

Courthouse, Criminal Records
Eagle River, MI 49924
(906) 337-2229

Felony and misdemeanor records are available by mail or phone. No release necessary. No search fee. Search information required: name.

Civil records are available by mail or phone. No release necessary. No search fee. $.50 fee per copy. $3.00 for certification. Search information required: name, years to search. Specify plaintiff or defendant.

Lake County

Felony records
County Clerk, Criminal Records
PO Drawer B
Baldwin, MI 49304
(616) 745-4641
Fax (616) 745-2241

Felony records are available by mail or phone. No release necessary. No search fee. Search information required: name, date of birth.

Civil records
County Clerk
PO Drawer B
Baldwin, MI 49304
(616) 745-4641
Fax (616) 745-2241

Civil records are available by mail or phone. No release necessary. No search fee. $1.00 fee per copy. Search information required: name, years to search. Specify plaintiff or defendant.

Misdemeanor records
78th District Court
PO Box 73
Baldwin, MI 49304
(616) 745-2738

Misdemeanor records are available by mail or phone. No release necessary. No search fee. Search information required: name, date of birth.

Civil records
78th District Court
PO Box 73
Baldwin, MI 49304
(616) 745-2738

Civil records are available by mail or phone. No release necessary. No search fee. $1.00 fee per copy. Search information required: name, years to search. Specify plaintiff or defendant.

Lapeer County

Felony records
County Clerk, Criminal Records
255 Clay St.
Lapeer, MI 48446
(313) 667-0358

Felony records are available by mail or phone. No release necessary. No search fee. Search information required: name.

Civil records
County Clerk
255 Clay St.
Lapeer, MI 48446
(313) 667-0358

Civil records are available by mail or phone. No release necessary. No search fee. $1.00 fee per copy. $7.00 for certification. Search information required: name, years to search. Specify plaintiff or defendant.

Misdemeanor records
District Court
255 Clay St.
Lapeer, MI 48446
(313) 667-0296

Misdemeanor records are available by mail only. No release necessary. No search fee. $.50 fee per copy. Search information required: full name, date of birth, years to search, SASE.

Civil records are available by mail. No release necessary. No search fee. $.50 fee per copy. Search information required: name, years to search, SASE. Specify plaintiff or defendant.

Leelanau County

Felony records
Leelanau County Clerk, Criminal Records
PO Box 467
Leland, MI 49654
(616) 256-9824
Fax (616) 256-7850
Felony records are available by mail, phone or fax. No release necessary. $3.00 search fee. Make check payable to County Clerk. Search information required: name.

Civil records
Leelanau County Clerk
PO Box 467
Leland, MI 49654
(616) 256-9824
Fax (616) 256-7850
Civil records are available by mail, phone or fax. No release necessary. No search fee. $1.00 fee per copy. Search information required: name, years to search. Specify plaintiff or defendant.

Misdemeanor records
86th District Court
PO Box 486
Leland, MI 49654
(616) 256-9931
Misdemeanor records are available by mail or phone. No release necessary. No search fee. $.50 fee per copy. $2.00 for certification. Search information required: name, date of birth, years to search.

Civil records
86th District Court
PO Box 486
Leland, MI 49654
(616) 256-9931
Civil records are available by mail or phone. No release necessary. No search fee. $.50 fee per copy. $2.00 for certification. Search information required: name, years to search. Specify plaintiff or defendant.

Lenawee County

Felony records
Lenawee County Clerk, Criminal Records
425 N. Main Street
Adrian, MI 49221
(517) 263-8831 Extension 2185
Felony records are available by mail or phone. No release necessary. No search fee. Search information required: name.

Civil records
Lenawee County Clerk
425 N. Main Street
Adrian, MI 49221
(517) 263-8831 Extension 2185
Civil records are available by mail or phone. No release necessary. No search fee. $.25 fee per copy. $1.00 for certification. Search information required: name, years to search. Specify plaintiff or defendant.

Misdemeanor records
2nd District Court
425 N. Main Street
Adrian, MI 49221
(517) 263-8831
Fax (517) 265-5721
Misdemeanor records are available by mail or fax. No release necessary. $3.00 search fee. Make check payable to 2nd District Court. Search information required: name, date of birth, years to search.

Civil records
2nd District Court
425 N. Main Street
Adrian, MI 49221
(517) 265-5721
Civil records are available by mail or phone. No release necessary. No search fee. $.25 fee per copy. $1.00 for certification. Search information required: name, years to search. Specify plaintiff or defendant.

Livingston County

Felony records
Livingston County Clerk, Criminal Records
210 S. Highlander Way
Howell, MI 48843
(517) 546-9816
Felony records are available by mail. No release necessary. No search fee. $1.00 fee per copy. $1.00 for certification. Search information required: name, years to search, SASE.

Civil records
Livingston County Clerk
210 S. Highlander Way
Howell, MI 48843
(517) 546-9816
Civil records are available by mail. No release necessary. No search fee. $1.00 fee per copy. $1.00 for certification. Search information required: name, years to search. Specify plaintiff or defendant.

Misdemeanor records
53rd District Court
300 S. Highlander Way
Howell, MI 48843
(517) 548-1000
Misdemeanor records are available by mail. No release necessary. No search fee. $1.00 fee per copy. Search information required: full name, date of birth, years to search.

Civil records
53rd District Court
300 S. Highlander Way
Howell, MI 48843
(517) 548-1000
Civil records are available by mail. No release necessary. No search fee. $1.00 fee per copy. Search information required: name, years to search. Specify plaintiff or defendant.

Luce County

Felony records
Luce County Clerk, Criminal Records
County Government Bldg.
Newberry, MI 49868
(906) 293-5521
Fax (906) 293-3581
Felony records are available by mail, fax or phone. No release necessary. No search fee. Search information required: name.

Civil records
Luce County Clerk
County Government Bldg.
Newberry, MI 49868
(906) 293-5521
Fax (906) 293-3581
Civil records are available by mail or phone. No release necessary. No search fee. $1.00 fee per copy. $2.00 for first page certified, $1.00 thereafter. Search information required: name, years to search. Specify plaintiff or defendant.

Misdemeanor records
92nd District Court
411 W. Harrie
Newberry, MI 49868
(906) 293-5531
Fax (906) 293-3581
Misdemeanor records are available by mail or phone. No release is necessary. No search fee. Search information required: name, date of birth, years to search.

Civil records
92nd District Court
411 W. Harrie
Newberry, MI 49868
(906) 293-5531
Fax (906) 293-3581
Civil records are available by mail. No release necessary. No search fee. Search information required: name, years to search. Specify plaintiff or defendant.

Mackinac County

Felony records
County Clerk, Criminal Records
100 Marley
St. Ignace, MI 49781
(906) 643-7300
Fax (906) 643-7302
Felony records are available by mail, phone or fax. No release necessary. No search fee. $.50 fee per copy. $2.00 fee for first page of fax response, $1.00 for each additional page thereafter. Search information required: name, approximate date of charge.

Civil records
County Clerk
100 Marley
St. Ignace, MI 49781
(906) 643-7300
Fax (906) 643-7302
Civil records are available by mail, phone or fax. No release necessary. No search fee. $.25 fee per copy. $5.00 for certification. Search information required: name, years to search. Specify plaintiff or defendant.

Misdemeanor records
92nd District Court
100 Marley
St. Ignace, MI 49781
(906) 643-7321
Fax (906) 643-7302
Misdemeanor records are available by mail or fax. No release necessary. No search fee. Search information required: name, date of birth, date of offense.

Civil records
92nd District Court
100 Marley
St. Ignace, MI 49781
(906) 643-7321
Fax (906) 643-7302
Civil records are available by mail, phone or fax. A release is required. Search information required: name, years to search. Specify plaintiff or defendant.

Macomb County

Felony records
Macomb Circuit Court
Circuit Court Records
Macomb County Clerk
40 N. Gratiot
Mount Clemens, MI 48043
(313) 469-5208 or (313) 469-5199
Felony records are available by mail or phone. No release necessary. $1.00 fee. Make check payable to Macomb County Clerk. Search information required: name, SASE.

Civil records are available by mail. No release necessary. $1.00 search fee. $.30 fee per copy. $1.00 for certification. Search information required: name, years to search. Specify plaintiff or defendant.

Manistee County

Felony records
County Clerk's Office, Criminal Records
415 3rd St.
Manistee, MI 49660
(616) 723-3331
Fax (616) 723-1492
Felony records are available by mail or fax (requests only). No release necessary. $3.00 search fee. $.25 fee per copy. Search information required: name, years to search.

Civil records
County Clerk's Office
415 3rd St.
Manistee, MI 49660
(616) 723-3331
Fax (616) 723-1492
Civil records are available by mail. No release necessary. No search fee. $.50 fee per copy. $1.00 for certification. Search information required: name, years to search. Specify plaintiff or defendant.

Misdemeanor records
85th District Court
415 3rd St.
Manistee, MI 49660
(616) 723-5010
Misdemeanor records are available by mail or phone. No release necessary. $1.00 search fee. $.50 fee per copy. $1.00 for certification. Search information required: name, date of birth, SSN, years to search.

Civil records
85th District Court
415 3rd St.
Manistee, MI 49660
(616) 723-5010
Civil records are available by mail or phone. No release necessary. No search fee. $.50 fee per copy. $1.00 for certification. Search information required: name, date of birth, SSN, years to search. Specify plaintiff or defendant.

Marquette County

Felony records
Marquette County Courthouse, Criminal Records
County Clerk's Office
Baraga Ave.
Marquette, MI 49855
(906) 228-1525
Felony records are available by mail or phone. A release is required if by mail. No fee. Search information required: name, years to search.

Civil records
Marquette County Courthouse
County Clerk's Office
Baraga Ave.
Marquette, MI 49855
(906) 228-1525
Civil records are available by mail or phone. No release necessary. No search fee. $.50 fee per copy. $3.00 for certification of documentation. $6.00 for certification of judgement. Search information required: name, years to search. Specify plaintiff or defendant.

Misdemeanor records
96th District Court
County Courthouse
Marquette, MI 49855
(906) 228-1550
Misdemeanor records are available by mail or phone. A release is required. No search fee. $.50 fee per copy. Search information required: name, years to search, date of birth.

Civil records
96th District Court
County Courthouse
Marquette, MI 49855
(906) 228-1550
Civil records are available by mail or phone. No release necessary. No search fee. $.50 fee per copy. Search information required: name, date of birth, years to search. Specify plaintiff or defendant.

Mason County

Felony records
Mason County Clerk
Courthouse, Criminal Records
300 E. Ludington Ave.
Ludington, MI 49431
(616) 843-8202
Felony records are available by mail or phone. A release is required. No search fee. Search information required: name, years to search.

Civil records
Mason County Clerk
Courthouse
300 E. Ludington Ave.
Ludington, MI 49431
(616) 843-8202
Civil records are available by mail or phone. No release necessary. No search fee. $.50 fee per copy. $3.00 for first page certified, $.50 thereafter. Search information required: name, years to search. Specify plaintiff or defendant.

Misdemeanor records
79th District Court
Mason County Courthouse
Ludington, MI 49431
(616) 843-4130
Misdemeanor records are available by mail. No release necessary. No search fee. $.50 fee per copy. $1.00 for certification. Search information required: name, date of birth, years to search.

Civil records
79th District Court
Mason County Courthouse
Ludington, MI 49431
(616) 843-4130
Civil records are available by mail or phone. No release necessary. No search fee. $.50 fee per copy. $1.00 for certification. Search information required: name, date of birth, years to search. Specify plaintiff or defendant.

Mecosta County

Felony records
Mecosta County Clerk, Criminal Records
400 Elm
Big Rapids, MI 49307
(616) 592-0783
Fax (616) 796-5577
Felony records are available by mail, phone or fax. No release necessary. No search fee. $1.00 fee per copy. Search information required: name, date of birth, sex, race, years to search.

Civil records
Mecosta County Clerk
400 Elm
Big Rapids, MI 49307
(616) 592-0783
Fax (616) 796-5577
Civil records are available by mail, phone or fax. A release is required. No search fee. $1.00 fee per copy. Search information required: name, years to search. Specify plaintiff or defendant.

Misdemeanor records
District Court
400 Elm
Big Rapids, MI 49307
(616) 592-0799
Fax (616) 796-2180
Misdemeanor records are available by mail. A release is required. No search fee. Search information required: name, date of birth, offense, date of offense.

Civil records
District Court
400 Elm
Big Rapids, MI 49307
(616) 592-0799
Fax (616) 796-2180
Civil records are available by mail or phone. No release necessary. No search fee. $1.00 fee per copy. Search information required: name, date of birth, years to search. Specify plaintiff or defendant.

Menominee County

Felony records
County Clerk's Office, Criminal Records
Courthouse Bldg.
839 10th Avenue
Menominee, MI 49858
(906) 863-9968
Felony records are available by mail or phone. No release necessary. No search fee. Search information required: name, years to search.

Civil records
County Clerk's Office
Courthouse Bldg.
839 10th Avenue
Menominee, MI 49858
(906) 863-9968
Civil records are available by mail or phone. No release necessary. No search fee. $.25 fee per copy. $5.00 for certification. Search information required: name, years to search. Specify plaintiff or defendant.

Misdemeanor records
95th District Court
Courthouse
Menominee, MI 49858
(906) 863-8532
Misdemeanor records are available by mail or phone. No release necessary. No search fee. $.15 fee per copy. Search information required: full name, date of birth.

Civil records
95th District Court
Courthouse
Menominee, MI 49858
(906) 863-8532
Civil records are available by mail or phone. No release necessary. No search fee. $.15 fee per copy. Search information required: name, years to search. Specify plaintiff or defendant.

Midland County

Felony records
Midland County Circuit Court, Criminal Records
Courthouse
301 W Main
Midland, MI 48640
(517) 832-6735
Felony records are available by mail or phone. No release necessary. No search fee. Search information required: name, SASE, years to search.

Civil records
Midland County Circuit Court, Criminal Records
Courthouse
301 W Main
Midland, MI 48640
(517) 832-6735
Civil records are available by mail or phone. No release necessary. No search fee. $.50 fee per copy. $1.00 for certification. Search information required: name, years to search. Specify plaintiff or defendant.

Misdemeanor records
75th District Court
301 W Main
Midland, MI 48640
(517) 832-6700
Misdemeanor records are available by mail or phone. No release necessary. No search fee. $1.00 fee per copy. Search information required: full name, date of birth, years to search.

Civil records
75th District Court
301 W Main
Midland, MI 48640
(517) 832-6700
Civil records are available in person only. See Michigan state repository for additional information.

Missaukee County

Felony records
Missaukee County Clerk, Criminal Records
Courthouse Bldg.
Lake City, MI 49651
(616) 839-4967
Felony records are available by mail or phone. No release necessary. No search fee. $.25 fee per copy. Search information required: name, years to search.

Civil records
Missaukee County Clerk
Courthouse Bldg.
Lake City, MI 49651
(616) 839-4967
Civil records are available by mail or phone. No release necessary. No search fee. $.50 fee per copy. $1.00 for certification. Search information required: name, years to search. Specify plaintiff or defendant.

Misdemeanor records
84th District Court
Courthouse
Lake City, MI 49651
(616) 839-4590
Misdemeanor records are available by mail or phone. A release is required. No search fee. $.25 fee per copy. $5.00 for certification. Search information required: name, date of birth, years to search.

Civil records
84th District Court
Courthouse
Lake City, MI 49651
(616) 839-4590
Civil records are available by mail or phone. No release necessary. No search fee. $.25 fee per copy. $5.00 for certification. Search information required: name, years to search. Specify plaintiff or defendant.

Monroe County

Felony records
County Clerk, Criminal Records
106 E. 1st St.
Monroe, MI 48161
(313) 243-7081
Felony records are available by mail. A release, if available. $5.00 fee for five years searched. Company checks only, payable to Monroe County Clerk. Search information required: name, date of birth, previous address.

Civil records
County Clerk
106 E. 1st St.
Monroe, MI 48161
(313) 243-7081
Civil records are available by mail or phone. No release necessary. No search fee. $.50 fee per copy. $1.00 for certification. Search information required: name, years to search. Specify plaintiff or defendant.

Misdemeanor records
1st District Court
106 E. 1st St.
Monroe, MI 48161
(313) 243-7030
Misdemeanor records are available by mail. No release necessary. No search fee. $.50 fee per copy. $1.00 for certification. Search information required: name, date of birth, years to search.

Civil records
1st District Court
106 E. 1st St.
Monroe, MI 48161
(313) 243-7030
Civil records are available by mail or phone. No release necessary. No search fee. $.50 fee per copy. $1.00 for certification. Search information required: name, years to search. Specify plaintiff or defendant.

Montcalm County

Felony records
Montcalm County Clerk, Criminal Records
PO Box 368
Stanton, MI 48888
(517) 831-5226
Fax (517) 831-4795
Felony records are available by mail. No release necessary. $3.00 search fee. Make check payable to Montcalm County Clerk. Search information required: name, SSN, date of birth, sex, years to search.

Civil records
Montcalm County Clerk
PO Box 368
Stanton, MI 48888
(517) 831-5226
Fax (517) 831-4795
Civil records are available by mail or phone. No release necessary. No search fee. $.25 fee per copy. $1.00 for certification. Search information required: name, years to search. Specify plaintiff or defendant.

Misdemeanor records
64B District Court
PO Box 608
Stanton, MI 48888
(517) 831-5226 Ext. 244 or 245
Misdemeanor records are available in person only. See Michigan state repository for additional information.

Civil records
64B District Court
PO Box 608
Stanton, MI 48888
(517) 831-5226 Ext. 244 or 245
Civil records are available by mail or phone. No release necessary. No search fee. $.25 fee per copy. $1.00 for certification. Search information required: name, years to search. Specify plaintiff or defendant.

Montmorency County

Felony records
County Clerk, Criminal Records
PO Box 415
Atlanta, MI 49709
(517) 785-4794
Felony records are available by mail or phone. No release necessary. No search fee. $.25 fee per copy, $1.00 for certification. Search information required: name, SSN, date of birth.

Civil records
County Clerk
PO Box 415
Atlanta, MI 49709
(517) 785-4794
Civil records are available by mail or phone. No release necessary. No search fee. $.25 fee per copy. $2.25 for certification. Search information required: name, years to search. Specify plaintiff or defendant.

Misdemeanor records
88th District Court
PO Box 415
Atlanta, MI 49709
(517) 785-3122
Fax (517) 785-2266
Misdemeanor records are available by mail. No release necessary. No search fee. Search information required: full name, date of birth, driver's license number, SSN.

Civil records
88th District Court
PO Box 415
Atlanta, MI 49709
(517) 785-3122
Fax (517) 785-2266
Civil records are available by mail. No release necessary. $1.00 search fee. $1.00 fee per copy. $1.00 for certification. Search information required: name, years to search, SASE. Specify plaintiff or defendant.

Muskegon County

Felony records
Circuit Court Records
6 Floor County Bldg.
990 Terrace
Muskegon, MI 49442
(616) 724-6447
Fax (616) 724-6673
Felony records are available by mail, phone or fax. No release necessary. No search fee. $.25 fee per copy. $1.00 for certification. Search information required: name, date of birth, years to search.

Civil records
Circuit Court Records
6 Floor County Bldg.
990 Terrace
Muskegon, MI 49442
(616) 724-6447
Fax (616) 724-6673
Civil records are available by mail, phone or fax. No release necessary. No search fee. $.25 fee per copy. $1.00 for certification. Search information required: name, date of birth, years to search. Specify plaintiff or defendant.

Misdemeanor records
60th District Court
1st Floor County Bldg.
Muskegon, MI 49442
(616) 724-6250
Misdemeanor records are available by mail. No release necessary. No search fee. Search information required: name, date of birth.

Civil records
60th District Court
1st Floor County Bldg.
Muskegon, MI 49442
(616) 724-6250
Civil records are available by mail. No release necessary. No search fee. $.25 fee per copy. $1.00 for certification. Search information required: name, years to search. Specify plaintiff or defendant.

Newaygo County

Felony records
Circuit Court, Criminal Records
PO Box 885
White Cloud, MI 49349
(616) 689-7269
Felony records are available by mail. No release necessary. No search fee. $1.00 fee per copy. Search information required: name.

Civil records
Circuit Court
PO Box 885
White Cloud, MI 49349
(616) 689-7269
Civil records are available by mail. No release necessary. No search fee. $1.00 fee per copy. $5.00 for certification. Search information required: name, years to search. Specify plaintiff or defendant.

Misdemeanor records
78th District Court
Box 8365
White Cloud, MI 49349
(616) 689-7257
Fax (616) 689-7258
Misdemeanor records are available by mail. No release necessary. No search fee. Search information required: name, date of birth, address.

Civil records
78th District Court
Box 8365
White Cloud, MI 49349
(616) 689-7257
Fax (616) 689-7258
Civil records are available by mail. No release necessary. No search fee. Search information required: name, years to search. Specify plaintiff or defendant.

Oakland County

County Clerk, Circuit Clerk Office
1200 N. Telegraph Road
Pontiac, MI 48341
(313) 858-0581
Felony records are available by mail or phone. No release necessary. No search fee. $.25 fee per copy. $1.00 fee for certification. Search information required: name, SASE.

Civil records are available by mail or phone. No release necessary. No search fee. $.25 fee per copy. $1.00 for certification. Search information required: name, years to search. Specify plaintiff or defendant.

Oceana County

Felony records
Oceana Circuit Court Records
PO Box 189
Hart, MI 49420
(616) 873-3977
Felony records are available by mail. No release necessary. No search fee. $1.00 for certification. Search information required: name, date of birth, years to search, SASE.

Civil records
Oceana Circuit Court Records
PO Box 189
Hart, MI 49420
(616) 873-3977
Civil records are available by mail or phone. No release necessary. No search fee. $1.00 for certification. Search information required: name, date of birth, years to search. Specify plaintiff or defendant.

Misdemeanor records
District Court
County Bldg.
Box 167
Hart, MI 49420
(616) 873-4530
Misdemeanor records are available by mail or phone. No release necessary. No search fee. $1.00 for certification. Search information required: name, years to search.

Civil records
District Court
County Bldg.
Box 167
Hart, MI 49420
(616) 873-4530
Civil records are available by mail or phone. No release necessary. No search fee. $1.00 for certification. Search information required: name, years to search. Specify plaintiff or defendant.

Ogemaw County

Felony records
County Clerk, Criminal Records
806 W. Houghton Ave.
PO Box 8
West Branch, MI 48661
(517) 345-0215
Felony records are available by mail or phone. No release necessary. No search fee. Search information required: name, years to search.

Civil records
County Clerk
806 W. Houghton Ave.
PO Box 8
West Branch, MI 48661
(517) 345-0215
Civil records are available by mail. No release necessary. No search fee. $.50 fee per copy. $5.00 for certification. Search information required: name, years to search. Specify plaintiff or defendant.

Misdemeanor records
82nd District Court
PO Box 365
West Branch, MI 48661
(517) 345-5040
Misdemeanor records are available by mail. No release necessary. No search fee. Search information required: name, date of birth, offense, date of offense.

Civil records
82nd District Court
PO Box 365
West Branch, MI 48661
(517) 345-5040
Civil records are available by mail. No release necessary. No search fee. $.50 fee per copy. $1.00 for certification. Search information required: name, years to search. Specify plaintiff or defendant.

Ontonagon County

Felony records
Circuit Court Clerk, Criminal Records
725 Greenland Road
Ontonagon, MI 49953
(906) 884-4255
Fax (906) 884-4880
Felony records are available by mail or phone. No release necessary. No search fee. Search information required: name.

Civil records
Circuit Court Clerk
725 Greenland Road
Ontonagon, MI 49953
(906) 884-4255
Fax (906) 884-4880
Civil records are available by mail or phone. No release necessary. No search fee. $1.00 fee per copy. $1.00 for certification. Search information required: name, years to search. Specify plaintiff or defendant.

Misdemeanor records
98th District Court
725 Greenland Road
Ontonagon, MI 49953
(906) 884-2865
Misdemeanor records are available by mail or phone. No release necessary. No search fee. Search information required: name, date of birth.

Civil records
98th District Court
725 Greenland Road
Ontonagon, MI 49953
(906) 884-2865
Civil records are available by mail. No release necessary. No search fee. $.50 fee per copy. $1.00 for certification. Search information required: name, years to search. Specify plaintiff or defendant.

Osceola County

Felony records
Osceola County Clerk, Criminal Records
301 W. Upton Street
Reed City, MI 49677
(616) 832-3261
Felony records are available by mail or phone. No release necessary. No search fee. $1.00 fee per copy. Search information required: name, years to search.

Civil records
Osceola County Clerk
Courthouse, 301 W. Upton Street
Reed City, MI 49677
(616) 832-3261
Civil records are available by mail. No release necessary. No search fee. $1.00 fee per copy. Search information required: name, years to search. Specify plaintiff or defendant.

Misdemeanor records
77th District Court
227 E. Lincoln
Reed City, MI 49677
(616) 832-3261
Misdemeanor records are available by mail or phone. No release necessary. No search fee. Search information required: name, date of birth, driver's license number.

Civil records
77th District Court
227 E. Lincoln
Reed City, MI 49677
(616) 832-3261
Civil records are available by mail or phone. No release necessary. No search fee. $1.00 fee per copy. $2.00 for certification. Search information required: name, years to search. Specify plaintiff or defendant.

Oscoda County

Felony records
County Clerk, Criminal Records
PO Box 399
Mio, MI 48647
(517) 826-3241
Fax (517) 826-3657
Felony records are available by mail, phone or fax. No release necessary. $2.00 search fee. Make check payable to Oscoda County Clerk. Search information required: name, SASE.

Civil records
County Clerk
PO Box 399
Mio, MI 48647
(517) 826-3241
Fax (517) 826-3657
Civil records are available by mail, phone or fax. No release necessary. No search fee. $1.00 for certification. Search information required: name, years to search. Specify plaintiff or defendant.

Misdemeanor records
82nd District Court
Mio, MI 48647
(517) 826-3241 Ext. 106
Misdemeanor records are available by mail. No release necessary. No search fee. Search information required: name, date of birth, years to search.

Civil records
82nd District Court
Mio, MI 48647
(517) 826-3241 Ext. 106
Civil records are available by mail or phone. No release necessary. No search fee. $1.00 for certification. Search information required: name, years to search. Specify plaintiff or defendant.

Otsego County

Felony records
Circuit Court Clerk, Criminal Records
225 W Main Street
Room 203
Gaylord, MI 49735
(517) 732-6484 Extension 204
Felony records are available by mail or phone. No release necessary. No search fee. Search information required: name, date of birth.

Civil records
Circuit Court Clerk
225 W Main Street
Room 203
Gaylord, MI 49735
(517) 732-6484 Extension 204
Civil records are available by mail or phone. No release necessary. No search fee. $.25 fee per copy. $1.00 for certification. Search information required: name, years to search. Specify plaintiff or defendant.

Misdemeanor records
87th District Court
PO Box 1218
Gaylord, MI 49735
(517) 732-6486
Fax (517) 732-5130
Misdemeanor records are available by mail or phone. No release necessary. No search fee. Search information required: name, date of birth.

Civil records
87th District Court
PO Box 1218
Gaylord, MI 49735
(517) 732-6486
Fax (517) 732-5130
Civil records are available by mail or phone. No release necessary. No search fee. $.25 fee per copy. $.50 for certification. Search information required: name, years to search. Specify plaintiff or defendant.

Ottawa County

Felony records
Ottawa County Clerk, Criminal Records
414 Washington, Rm 301A
Grand Haven, MI 49417
(616) 846-8315
Fax (616) 846-8138
Felony records are available by mail, fax or phone. No release necessary. No search fee. Search information required: name, date of birth, sex, race, years to search.

Civil records
Ottawa County Clerk
414 Washington, Rm 301A
Grand Haven, MI 49417
(616) 846-8315
Fax (616) 846-8138
Civil records are available by mail, fax or phone. No release necessary. No search fee. $.50 fee per copy. $1.00 for certification. Search information required: name, years to search. Specify plaintiff or defendant.

Misdemeanor records
58th District Court
Ottawa County Bldg.
414 Washington
Grand Haven, MI 49417
(616) 846-8280
Fax (616) 846-8291
Misdemeanor records are available by mail or fax. A release is required. No search fee. Search information required: name, date of birth, years to search.

Civil records
58th District Court
Ottawa County Bldg.
414 Washington
Grand Haven, MI 49417
(616) 846-8280
Fax (616) 846-8291
Civil records are available by mail or fax. A release is required. No search fee. Search information required: name, years to search. Specify plaintiff or defendant.

Presque Isle County

Felony records
26th Judicial Circuit Court, Criminal Records
PO Box 110
Rogers City, MI 49779
(517) 734-3288
Felony records are available by mail or phone. No release necessary. No search fee. Search information required: name, years to search.

Civil records
26th Judicial Circuit Court
PO Box 110
Rogers City, MI 49779
(517) 734-3288
Civil records are available by mail or phone. No release necessary. No search fee. $1.00 fee per copy. $5.00 for certification. Search information required: name, years to search. Specify plaintiff or defendant.

Misdemeanor records
89th District Court
Courthouse
PO Box 110
Rogers City, MI 49779
(517) 734-2411
Misdemeanor records are available by mail or phone. No release necessary. No search fee. Search information required: name, date of birth.

Civil records
89th District Court
Courthouse
PO Box 110
Rogers City, MI 49779
(517) 734-2411
Civil records are available by mail or phone. No release necessary. No search fee. $.25 fee per copy. $3.00 for certification. Search information required: name, years to search. Specify plaintiff or defendant.

Roscommon County

Felony records
County Clerk, Criminal Records
PO Box 98
Roscommon, MI 48653
(517) 275-5923
Fax (517) 275-5923
Felony records are available by mail, phone or fax. No release necessary. No search fee. $.50 fee per copy. $1.00 for certification. Search information required: name, date of birth, years to search, SASE.

Civil records
County Clerk
PO Box 98
Roscommon, MI 48653
(517) 275-5923
Fax (517) 275-5923
Civil records are available by mail, phone or fax. No release necessary. No search fee. $.50 fee per copy. $1.00 for certification. Search information required: name, years to search, SASE. Specify plaintiff or defendant.

Misdemeanor records
83rd District Court
PO Box 189
Roscommon, MI 48653
(517) 275-5312
Fax (517) 275-5675
Misdemeanor records are available by mail, phone or fax. No release necessary. No search fee. $3.00 fee for fax response. Search information required: name, date of birth, years to search.

Civil records
83rd District Court
PO Box 189
Roscommon, MI 48653
(517) 275-5312
Fax (517) 275-5675
Civil records are available by mail, phone or fax. No release necessary. No search fee. $3.00 fee for fax response. Search information required: name, years to search. Specify plaintiff or defendant.

Saginaw County

Felony records
County Clerk, Criminal Records
111 S. Michigan Ave.
Saginaw, MI 48602
(517) 790-5247
Felony records are available by mail. No release necessary. No search fee. $1.00 fee per copy, $1.00 fee for certification. Search information required: name, date of birth, years to search.

Civil records
County Clerk
111 S. Michigan Ave.
Saginaw, MI 48602
(517) 790-5247
Civil records are available by mail. No release necessary. No search fee. $1.00 fee per copy. $1.00 for certification. Search information required: name, date of birth, years to search. Specify plaintiff or defendant.

Misdemeanor records
70th District Court
Attn: Criminal Division
111 S. Michigan Ave.
Saginaw, MI 48602
(517) 790-5385
Misdemeanor records are available by mail. No release necessary. No search fee. Search information required: name, date of birth, address, offense, date of offense.

Civil records
70th District Court
111 S. Michigan Ave.
Saginaw, MI 48602
(517) 790-5385
Civil records are available by mail or phone. No release necessary. No search fee. $1.00 fee per copy. $2.00 for certification. Search information required: name, years to search. Specify plaintiff or defendant.

Sanilac County

Felony records
Sanilac County Clerk, Criminal Records
60 W. Sanilac
Sandusky, MI 48471
(313) 648-3212
Felony records are available by mail. No release necessary. $1.00 fee for each year searched. Make check payable to Sanilac County Clerk. Search information required: name, SSN, date of birth, sex, race.

Civil records
Sanilac County Clerk
60 W. Sanilac
Sandusky, MI 48471
(313) 648-3212
Civil records are available by mail or phone. No release necessary. No search fee. $.50 fee per copy. $1.00 for certification. Search information required: name, years to search. Specify plaintiff or defendant.

Misdemeanor records
73rd District Court
2nd Division
Courthouse
Sandusky, MI 48471
(313) 648-3250
Misdemeanor records are available by mail. No release necessary. No search fee. Search information required: name, date of birth.

Civil records
73rd District Court
2nd Division
Courthouse
Sandusky, MI 48471
(313) 648-3250
Civil records are available by mail or phone. No release necessary. No search fee. Search information required: name, years to search. Specify plaintiff or defendant.

Schoolcraft County

Felony records
County Clerk, Criminal Records
300 Walnut Street
County Bldg. 164
Manistique, MI 49854
(906) 341-5532
Felony records are available by mail or phone. No release necessary. No search fee. Search information required: name.

Civil records
County Clerk
300 Walnut Street
County Bldg. 164
Manistique, MI 49854
(906) 341-5532
Civil records are available by mail or phone. No release necessary. No search fee. $1.00 fee per copy. $2.00 for certification. Search information required: name, years to search. Specify plaintiff or defendant.

Misdemeanor records
93rd District Court
Courthouse, Room 135
Manistique, MI 49854
(906) 341-5650
Fax (906) 341-8006
Misdemeanor records are available by mail or phone. No release necessary. No search fee. Search information required: name, date of birth.

Civil records
93rd District Court
Courthouse, Room 135
Manistique, MI 49854
(906) 341-5650
Fax (906) 341-8006
Civil records are available by mail or phone. No release necessary. No search fee. $.50 fee per copy. $1.00 for certification. Search information required: name, years to search. Specify plaintiff or defendant.

Shiawassee County

Felony records
County Clerk
Courthouse
Corunna, MI 48817
(517) 743-2302
Felony records are available by mail or phone. No release necessary. No search fee. Search information required: name, years to search.

Civil records
County Clerk
Courthouse
Corunna, MI 48817
(517) 743-2302
Civil records are available by mail or phone. No release necessary. No search fee. $1.00 fee per copy. $1.00 for certification. Search information required: name, years to search. Specify plaintiff or defendant.

Misdemeanor records
66th District Court
110 E. Mack
Corunna, MI 48817
(517) 743-2395
Misdemeanor records are available by mail. A release is required. No search fee. Search information required: name, date of birth, years to search.

Civil records
66th District Court
110 E. Mack
Corunna, MI 48817
(517) 743-2395
Civil records are available by mail. A release is required. No search fee. $1.00 fee per copy. $1.00 for certification. Search information required: name, years to search. Specify plaintiff or defendant.

St. Clair County

Felony records
St. Clair County Clerk, Criminal
Records
201 McMorran Blvd.
Port Huron, MI 48060
(313) 985-2200
Felony records are available by mail. No release necessary. $5.00 fee for first five years searched, $3.00 each additional year. Make check payable to County Clerk. Search information required: name, date of birth, years to search.

Civil records
St. Clair County Clerk
201 McMorran Blvd.
Port Huron, MI 48060
(313) 985-2200
Civil records are available by mail. No release necessary. $5.00 fee for every five years searched, each additional year is $3.00. $1.00 for certification. Search information required: name, years to search. Specify plaintiff or defendant.

Misdemeanor records
72nd District Court
County Bldg.
201 McMorran Blvd.
Port Huron, MI 48060
(313) 985-2072
Misdemeanor records are available by mail. A release is required. No search fee. $.25 fee per copy. Search information required: name, date of birth, SSN, years to search.

Civil records
72nd District Court
County Bldg.
201 McMorran Blvd.
Port Huron, MI 48060
(313) 985-2072
Civil records are available by mail. A release is required. No search fee. $.25 fee per copy. Search information required: name, date of birth, SSN, years to search. Specify plaintiff or defendant.

St. Joseph County

Felony records
St. Joseph County Clerk, Criminal
Records
PO Box 189
Centreville, MI 49032
(616) 467-6361
Fax (616) 467-1857
Felony records are available by mail or fax. No release fee per year searched. Company checks or money orders payable to County Clerk. Search information required: name, years to search.

Civil records
St. Joseph County Clerk
PO Box 189
Centreville, MI 49032
(616) 467-6361
Fax (616) 467-1857
Civil records are available by mail or fax. No release necessary. $1.00 search fee per year. $1.00 fee per copy. Search information required: name, years to search. Specify plaintiff or defendant.

Misdemeanor records
District Court
Criminal Division of 3rd District
PO Box 67
Centreville, MI 49032
(616) 467-6361 Ext. 304
Misdemeanor records are available by mail or phone. No release necessary. No search fee. $.50 fee per copy. $1.00 for certification. Search information required: name, date of birth, years to search.

Civil records
District Court
Criminal Division of 3rd District
PO Box 67
Centreville, MI 49032
(616) 467-6361 Ext. 304
Civil records are available by mail or phone. No release necessary. No search fee. $.50 fee per copy. $1.00 for certification. Search information required: name, date of birth, years to search. Specify plaintiff or defendant.

Tuscola County

Felony records
Tuscola County Clerk, Criminal
Records
440 N State Street
Caro, MI 48723
(517) 673-5999
Felony records are available by mail or phone. No release necessary. No search fee. Search information required: name, years to search.

Civil records
Tuscola County Clerk
440 N State Street
Caro, MI 48723
(517) 673-5999
Civil records are available by mail or phone. No release necessary. No search fee. $.50 fee per copy. $10.00 for certification. Search information required: name, years to search. Specify plaintiff or defendant.

Misdemeanor records
71B District Court
440 N State Street
Caro, MI 48723
(517) 673-5999 Ext. 236
Misdemeanor records are available in person only. See Michigan state repository for additional information.

Civil records
71B District Court
440 N State Street
Caro, MI 48723
(517) 673-5999 Ext. 236
Civil records are available in person only. See Michigan state repository for additional information.

Van Buren County

Felony records
Van Buren County Clerk, Criminal
Records
Courthouse
Paw Paw, MI 49079
(616) 657-5581 Ext. 265
Felony records are available by mail. A release is required. $1.00 fee per year searched. Search information required: name, years to search.

Civil records
Van Buren County Clerk
Courthouse
Paw Paw, MI 49079
(616) 657-5581 Ext. 265
Civil records are available by mail. No release necessary. No search fee. $.50 fee per copy. $1.00 for certification. Search information required: name, years to search. Specify plaintiff or defendant.

Misdemeanor records
7th District Court East
County Bldg.
Paw Paw, MI 49079
(616) 637-5258
Fax (616) 657-7573
Misdemeanor records are available by mail. No release necessary. $5.00 search fee. Search information required: name, date of birth, driver's license number (if available), SASE.

Civil records
7th District Court East
County Bldg.
Paw Paw, MI 49079
(616) 637-5258
Fax (616) 657-7573
Civil records are available by mail. No release necessary. $5.00 search fee. $.25 fee per copy. Search information required: name, years to search. Specify plaintiff or defendant.

Washtenaw County

Washtenaw County Clerk
Court Services Division
PO Box 8645
Ann Arbor, MI 48107-8645
(313) 994-2507
Felony records since 1979 are available by mail or phone. No release necessary. No search fee. Search information required: name.

Civil records are available by mail or phone. No release necessary. No search fee. $.50 fee per copy. $1.00 for certification. Search information required: name, years to search. Specify plaintiff or defendant.

Wayne County

Felony and misdemeanor records
Hall of Justice
1441 St. Antoine
Detroit, MI 48226
(313) 224-2500
Felony and misdemeanor records are available by mail. No release necessary. No search fee. Search information required: name, date of birth, SSN, SASE.

Civil records
Hall of Justice
1441 St. Antoine
Detroit, MI 48226
(313) 224-5530
Civil records are available by mail. No release necessary. No search fee. $.50 fee per copy. $1.00 for certification. Search information required: name, years to search, SASE. Specify plaintiff or defendant.

Wexford County

Felony records
Wexford County Clerk, Criminal
Records
PO Box 490
Cadillac, MI 49601
(616) 779-9450
Fax (779-0292
Felony records are available by mail, phone
or fax. A release is required. No search fee.
Search information required: name, date of
birth.

Civil records
Wexford County Clerk
PO Box 490
Cadillac, MI 49601
(616) 779-9450
Fax (779-0292
Civil records are available by mail, phone
or fax. No release necessary. No search fee.
$1.00 fee per copy. $10.00 for certification.
Search information required: name, years to
search. Specify plaintiff or defendant.

Misdemeanor records
84th District Court
501 S. Garfield
Cadillac, MI 49601
(616) 779-9515
Misdemeanor records are available by mail
or phone. No release necessary. No search
fee. Search information required: name,
date of birth, driver's license number.

Civil records are available by phone. No release necessary. No search fee.Search information required: name, years to search.
Specify plaintiff or defendant.

City-County Cross Reference

Acme *Grand Traverse*
Ada *Kent*
Addison *Lenawee*
Adrian *Lenawee*
Afton *Cheboygan*
Ahmeek *Keweenaw*
Akron *Tuscola*
Alanson *Emmet*
Alba *Antrim*
Albion *Calhoun*
Alden *Antrim*
Alger *Arenac*
Algonac *Saint Clair*
Allegan *Allegan*
Allen *Hillsdale*
Allendale *Ottawa*
Allen Park *Wayne*
Allenton *Saint Clair*
Allouez *Keweenaw*
Alma *Gratiot*
Almont *Lapeer*
Alpena *Alpena*
Alpha *Iron*
Alto *Kent*
Amasa *Iron*
Anchorville *Saint Clair*
Ann Arbor *Washtenaw*
Applegate *Sanilac*
Arcadia *Manistee*
Argentine *Genesee*
Argyle *Sanilac*
Armada *Macomb*
Ashley *Gratiot*
Athens *Calhoun*
Atlanta *Montmorency*
Atlantic Mine *Houghton*
Atlas *Genesee*
Attica *Lapeer*
Auburn *Bay*
Auburn Hills *Oakland*
Au Gres *Arenac*
Au Sable *Iosco*
Augusta *Kalamazoo*
Au Train *Alger*
Avoca *Saint Clair*
Azalia *Monroe*
Bad Axe *Huron*
Bailey *Muskegon*
Baldwin *Lake*
Bancroft *Shiawassee*
Bangor *Van Buren*
Bannister *Gratiot*
Baraga *Baraga*
Barbeau *Chippewa*
Bark River *Delta*
Baroda *Berrien*
Barron Lake *Cass*
Barryton *Mecosta*

Barton City *Alcona*
Bath *Clinton*
Battle Creek *Calhoun*
Bay City *Bay*
Bay Port *Huron*
Beadle Lake *Calhoun*
Bear Lake *Manistee*
Beaverton *Gladwin*
Bedford *Calhoun*
Beecher *Genesee*
Belding *Ionia*
Bellaire *Antrim*
Belleville *Wayne*
Bellevue *Eaton*
Belmont *Kent*
Bentley *Bay*
Benton Harbor *Berrien*
Benton Heights *Berrien*
Benzonia *Benzie*
Bergland *Ontonagon*
Berkley *Oakland*
Berrien Center *Berrien*
Berrien Springs *Berrien*
Bertrand *Berrien*
Bessemer *Gogebic*
Beulah *Benzie*
Beverly Hills *Oakland*
Big Bay *Marquette*
Big Rapids *Mecosta*
Birch Run *Saginaw*
Birmingham *Oakland*
Bitely *Newaygo*
Black River *Alcona*
Blanchard *Isabella*
Blissfield *Lenawee*
Bloomfield Hills *Oakland*
Bloomfield Village
     Oakland
Bloomingdale *Van Buren*
Boon *Wexford*
Boyne City *Charlevoix*
Boyne Falls *Charlevoix*
Bradley *Allegan*
Branch *Mason*
Brant *Saginaw*
Breckenridge *Gratiot*
Breedsville *Van Buren*
Brethren *Manistee*
Bridgeport *Saginaw*
Bridgewater *Washtenaw*
Bridgman *Berrien*
Brighton *Livingston*
Brimley *Chippewa*
Britton *Lenawee*
Brohman *Newaygo*
Bronson *Branch*
Brooklyn *Jackson*
Brown City *Sanilac*

Brownlee Park *Calhoun*
Bruce Crossing *Ontonagon*
Bullock Creek *Midland*
Brunswick *Newaygo*
Brutus *Emmet*
Buchanan *Berrien*
Buckley *Wexford*
Burlington *Calhoun*
Burnips *Allegan*
Burr Oak *Saint Joseph*
Burt *Saginaw*
Burt Lake *Cheboygan*
Byron *Shiawassee*
Byron Center *Kent*
Cadillac *Wexford*
Cadmus *Lenawee*
Caledonia *Kent*
Calumet *Houghton*
Camden *Hillsdale*
Cannonsburg *Kent*
Capac *Saint Clair*
Carleton *Monroe*
Carney *Menominee*
Caro *Tuscola*
Carp Lake *Emmet*
Carrollton *Saginaw*
Carson City *Montcalm*
Carsonville *Sanilac*
Cascade *Kent*
Caseville *Huron*
Casnovia *Muskegon*
Caspian *Iron*
Cass City *Tuscola*
Cassopolis *Cass*
Cedar *Leelanau*
Cedar Lake *Montcalm*
Cedar Springs *Kent*
Cedarville *Mackinac*
Cement City *Lenawee*
Center Line *Macomb*
Central Lake *Antrim*
Centreville *Saint Joseph*
Ceresco *Calhoun*
Champion *Marquette*
Channing *Dickinson*
Charlevoix *Charlevoix*
Charlotte *Eaton*
Chase *Lake*
Chassell *Houghton*
Chatham *Alger*
Cheboygan *Cheboygan*
Chelsea *Washtenaw*
Chesaning *Saginaw*
Chippewa Lake *Mecosta*
Clare *Clare*
Clarklake *Jackson*
Clarkston *Oakland*
Clarksville *Ionia*

Clawson *Oakland*
Clayton *Lenawee*
Clifford *Lapeer*
Climax *Kalamazoo*
Clinton *Lenawee*
Clio *Genesee*
Cloverdale *Barry*
Cloverville *Muskegon*
Cohoctah *Livingston*
Coldwater *Branch*
Coleman *Midland*
Coloma *Berrien*
Colon *Saint Joseph*
Columbiaville *Lapeer*
Comins *Oscoda*
Commerce *Oakland*
Comstock *Kalamazoo*
Comstock Park *Kent*
Concord *Jackson*
Conklin *Ottawa*
Constantine *Saint Joseph*
Conway *Emmet*
Cooks *Schoolcraft*
Coopersville *Ottawa*
Copemish *Manistee*
Copper City *Houghton*
Copper Harbor *Keweenaw*
Coral *Montcalm*
Cornell *Delta*
Corunna *Shiawassee*
Covert *Van Buren*
Covington *Baraga*
Crescent Lakes Estates
     Oakland
Cross Village *Emmet*
Croswell *Sanilac*
Crystal *Montcalm*
Crystal Falls *Iron*
Curran *Alcona*
Curtis *Mackinac*
Custer *Mason*
Dafter *Chippewa*
Daggett *Menominee*
Dansville *Ingham*
Davisburg *Oakland*
Davison *Genesee*
Dearborn *Wayne*
Dearborn Heights *Wayne*
Decatur *Van Buren*
Decker *Sanilac*
Deckerville *Sanilac*
Deerfield *Lenawee*
Deerton *Alger*
Deford *Tuscola*
Delton *Barry*
DeTour Village *Chippewa*
Detroit *Wayne*
Detroit Beach *Monroe*

DeWitt *Clinton*
Dexter *Washtenaw*
Dimondale *Eaton*
Dollar Bay *Houghton*
Dorr *Allegan*
Douglas *Allegan*
Dowagiac *Cass*
Dowling *Barry*
Drayton Plains *Oakland*
Drummond Island
    Chippewa
Dryden *Lapeer*
Dundee *Monroe*
Durand *Shiawassee*
Eagle *Clinton*
Eagle River *Keweenaw*
East Detroit *Macomb*
East Grand Rapids *Kent*
East Jordan *Charlevoix*
Eastlake *Manistee*
East Lansing *Ingham*
East Leroy *Calhoun*
Eastport *Antrim*
East Tawas *Iosco*
Eaton Rapids *Eaton*
Eau Claire *Berrien*
Eben Junction *Alger*
Eckerman *Chippewa*
Ecorse *Wayne*
Edenville *Midland*
Edmore *Montcalm*
Edwardsburg *Cass*
Elberta *Benzie*
Elk Rapids *Antrim*
Elkton *Huron*
Ellsworth *Antrim*
Elm Hall *Gratiot*
Elmira *Otsego*
Elsie *Clinton*
Elwell *Gratiot*
Emmett *Saint Clair*
Empire *Leelanau*
Engadine *Mackinac*
Erie *Monroe*
Escanaba *Delta*
Essexville *Bay*
Eureka *Clinton*
Evart *Osceola*
Ewen *Ontonagon*
Fairgrove *Tuscola*
Fair Haven *Saint Clair*
Fairview *Oscoda*
Falmouth *Missaukee*
Farmington *Oakland*
Farmington Hills *Oakland*
Farwell *Clare*
Felch *Dickinson*
Fennville *Allegan*
Fenton *Genesee*
Fenwick *Montcalm*
Ferrysburg *Ottawa*
Fife Lake *Grand Traverse*
Filer City *Manistee*
Filion *Huron*
Flat Rock *Wayne*
Flint *Genesee*
Flushing *Genesee*
Forestville *Sanilac*
Foster City *Dickinson*
Fostoria *Tuscola*
Fountain *Mason*
Fowler *Clinton*
Fowlerville *Livingston*
Frankenmuth *Saginaw*
Frankfort *Benzie*

Franklin *Oakland*
Fraser *Macomb*
Frederic *Crawford*
Freeland *Saginaw*
Freeport *Barry*
Free Soil *Mason*
Fremont *Newaygo*
Frontier *Hillsdale*
Fruitport *Muskegon*
Fulton *Kalamazoo*
Gaastra *Iron*
Gagetown *Tuscola*
Gaines *Genesee*
Galesburg *Kalamazoo*
Galien *Berrien*
Garden *Delta*
Garden City *Wayne*
Gaylord *Otsego*
Genesee *Genesee*
Germfask *Schoolcraft*
Gibraltar *Wayne*
Gilford *Tuscola*
Gladstone *Delta*
Gladwin *Gladwin*
Glen Arbor *Leelanau*
Glenn *Allegan*
Glennie *Alcona*
Gobles *Van Buren*
Goetzville *Chippewa*
Goodells *Saint Clair*
Goodrich *Genesee*
Gould City *Mackinac*
Gowen *Montcalm*
Grand Blanc *Genesee*
Grand Haven *Ottawa*
Grand Junction *Van Buren*
Grand Ledge *Eaton*
Grand Marais *Alger*
Grand Rapids *Kent*
Grandville *Kent*
Grant *Newaygo*
Grass Lake *Jackson*
Grawn *Grand Traverse*
Grayling *Crawford*
Greenbush *Alcona*
Greenland *Ontonagon*
Greenville *Montcalm*
Gregory *Livingston*
Greilickville *Leelanau*
Grosse Ile *Wayne*
Grosse Pointe *Wayne*
Grosse Pointe Farms
    Wayne
Grosse Pointe Park *Wayne*
Grosse Pointe Shores
    Wayne
Grosse Pointe Woods
    Wayne
Gulliver *Schoolcraft*
Gwinn *Marquette*
Hadley *Lapeer*
Hale *Iosco*
Hamburg *Livingston*
Hamilton *Allegan*
Hancock *Houghton*
Hanover *Jackson*
Harbert *Berrien*
Harbor Beach *Huron*
Harbor Springs *Emmet*
Harbor Woods *Wayne*
Harrietta *Wexford*
Harris *Menominee*
Harrison *Clare*
Harrisville *Alcona*
Harsens Island *Saint Clair*

Hart *Oceana*
Hartford *Van Buren*
Hartland *Livingston*
Harvey *Marquette*
Haslett *Ingham*
Hastings *Barry*
Hawks *Presque Isle*
Hazel Park *Oakland*
Hemlock *Saginaw*
Henderson *Shiawassee*
Hermansville *Menominee*
Herron *Alpena*
Hersey *Osceola*
Hesperia *Oceana*
Hessel *Mackinac*
Hickory Corners *Barry*
Higgins Lake *Roscommon*
Highland *Oakland*
Highland Park *Wayne*
Hillman *Montmorency*
Hillsdale *Hillsdale*
Holland *Ottawa*
Holly *Oakland*
Holt *Ingham*
Holton *Muskegon*
Homer *Calhoun*
Honor *Benzie*
Hope *Midland*
Hopkins *Allegan*
Horton *Jackson*
Houghton *Houghton*
Houghton Lake
    Roscommon
Houghton Lake Heights
    Roscommon
Howard City *Montcalm*
Howell *Livingston*
Hoxeyville *Wexford*
Hubbard Lake *Alpena*
Hubbardston *Ionia*
Hubbell *Houghton*
Hudson *Lenawee*
Hudsonville *Ottawa*
Hulbert *Chippewa*
Huntington Woods
    Oakland
Huron Gardens *Oakland*
Ida *Monroe*
Idlewild *Lake*
Imlay City *Lapeer*
Indian Lake *Cass*
Indian River *Cheboygan*
Ingalls *Menominee*
Inkster *Wayne*
Interlochen *Grand
    Traverse*
Ionia *Ionia*
Iron Mountain *Dickinson*
Iron River *Iron*
Irons *Lake*
Ironwood *Gogebic*
Ishpeming *Marquette*
Ithaca *Gratiot*
Jackson *Jackson*
Jamestown *Ottawa*
Jasper *Lenawee*
Jeddo *Saint Clair*
Jenison *Ottawa*
Jerome *Hillsdale*
Johannesburg *Otsego*
Jones *Cass*
Jonesville *Hillsdale*
Kalamazoo *Kalamazoo*
Kaleva *Manistee*
Kalkaska *Kalkaska*

Karlin *Grand Traverse*
Kawkawlin *Bay*
Keego Harbor *Oakland*
Kendall *Van Buren*
Kent City *Kent*
Kentwood *Kent*
Kewadin *Antrim*
Kinde *Huron*
Kingsford *Dickinson*
Kingsley *Grand Traverse*
Kingston *Tuscola*
Kinross *Chippewa*
Lachine *Alpena*
Lacota *Van Buren*
Laingsburg *Shiawassee*
Lake *Clare*
Lake Ann *Benzie*
Lake City *Missaukee*
Lake George *Clare*
Lakeland *Livingston*
Lake Leelanau *Leelanau*
Lake Linden *Houghton*
Lake Odessa *Ionia*
Lake Orion *Oakland*
Lakeside *Berrien*
Lakewood Club *Muskegon*
Lakeview *Montcalm*
Lakeville *Oakland*
Lambertville *Monroe*
Lamont *Ottawa*
L' Anse *Baraga*
Lansing *Ingham*
Lapeer *Lapeer*
La Salle Gardens *Oakland*
Lathrop Village *Oakland*
Laurium *Houghton*
Lawrence *Van Buren*
Lawton *Van Buren*
Leland *Leelanau*
Lennon *Shiawassee*
Leonard *Oakland*
Leonidas *Saint Joseph*
Le Roy *Osceola*
Leslie *Ingham*
Level Park *Calhoun*
Levering *Emmet*
Lewiston *Montmorency*
Lexington *Sanilac*
Liberty *Jackson*
Lincoln *Alcona*
Lincoln Park *Wayne*
Linden *Genesee*
Linwood *Bay*
Litchfield *Hillsdale*
Little Lake *Marquette*
Livonia *Wayne*
Long Lake *Iosco*
Lowell *Kent*
Ludington *Mason*
Luna Pier *Monroe*
Lupton *Ogemaw*
Luther *Lake*
Luzerne *Oscoda*
Lyons *Ionia*
McBain *Missaukee*
McBrides *Montcalm*
McMillan *Luce*
Macatawa *Ottawa*
Mackinac Island *Mackinac*
Mackinaw City *Cheboygan*
Madison Heights *Oakland*
Mancelona *Antrim*
Manchester *Washtenaw*
Manistee *Manistee*
Manistique *Schoolcraft*

Manitou Beach *Lenawee*
Manton *Wexford*
Maple City *Leelanau*
Maple Rapids *Clinton*
Marcellus *Cass*
Marenisco *Gogebic*
Marine City *Saint Clair*
Marion *Osceola*
Marlette *Sanilac*
Marne *Ottawa*
Marquette *Marquette*
Marshall *Calhoun*
Martin *Allegan*
Marysville *Saint Clair*
Mason *Ingham*
Mass City *Ontonagon*
Mattawan *Van Buren*
Mayfield *Grand Traverse*
Mayville *Tuscola*
Mears *Oceana*
Mecosta *Mecosta*
Melvin *Sanilac*
Melvindale *Wayne*
Memphis *Saint Clair*
Mendon *Saint Joseph*
Menominee *Menominee*
Merrill *Saginaw*
Merritt *Missaukee*
Mesick *Wexford*
Metamora *Lapeer*
Michigamme *Marquette*
Michigan Center *Jackson*
Middleton *Gratiot*
Middleville *Barry*
Midland *Midland*
Mikado *Alcona*
Milan *Washtenaw*
Milford *Oakland*
Millbrook *Mecosta*
Millersburg *Presque Isle*
Millett *Ingham*
Millington *Tuscola*
Minden City *Sanilac*
Mio *Oscoda*
Mohawk *Keweenaw*
Moline *Allegan*
Monroe *Monroe*
Montague *Muskegon*
Montgomery *Hillsdale*
Montrose *Genesee*
Moran *Mackinac*
Morenci *Lenawee*
Morley *Mecosta*
Morrice *Shiawassee*
Moscow *Hillsdale*
Mosherville *Hillsdale*
Mount Clemens *Macomb*
Mount Morris *Genesee*
Mount Pleasant *Isabella*
Muir *Ionia*
Mullett Lake *Cheboygan*
Mulliken *Eaton*
Munger *Bay*
Munising *Alger*
Munith *Jackson*
Muskegon *Muskegon*
Muskegon Heights
  Muskegon
Nadeau *Menominee*
Nahma *Delta*
Napoleon *Jackson*
Nashville *Barry*
National City *Iosco*
Naubinway *Mackinac*
Nazareth *Kalamazoo*

Negaunee *Marquette*
Newaygo *Newaygo*
New Baltimore *Macomb*
Newberry *Luce*
New Boston *Wayne*
New Buffalo *Berrien*
New Era *Oceana*
New Haven *Macomb*
New Hudson *Oakland*
New Lothrop *Shiawassee*
Newport *Monroe*
New Richmond *Allegan*
New Troy *Berrien*
Niles *Berrien*
Nisula *Houghton*
North Adams *Hillsdale*
North Branch *Lapeer*
Northland *Marquette*
North Muskegon
  Muskegon
Northport *Leelanau*
North Star *Gratiot*
North Street *Saint Clair*
Northville *Wayne*
Norvell *Jackson*
Nortorn Shores *Muskegon*
Norway *Dickinson*
Nottawa *Saint Joseph*
Novi *Oakland*
Nunica *Ottawa*
Oak Hill *Manistee*
Oakley *Saginaw*
Oak Park *Wayne*
Oden *Emmet*
Okemos *Ingham*
Old Mission *Grand
  Traverse*
Olivet *Eaton*
Omena *Leelanau*
Omer *Arenac*
Onaway *Presque Isle*
Onekama *Manistee*
Onondaga *Ingham*
Orchard Lake Village
  Oakland
Onsted *Lenawee*
Ontonagon *Ontonagon*
Orleans *Ionia*
Ortonville *Oakland*
Oscoda *Iosco*
Oshtemo *Kalamazoo*
Osseo *Hillsdale*
Ossineke *Alpena*
Otisville *Genesee*
Otsego *Allegan*
Ottawa Lake *Monroe*
Otter Lake *Lapeer*
Ovid *Clinton*
Owendale *Huron*
Owosso *Shiawassee*
Oxford *Oakland*
Painesdale *Houghton*
Palmer *Marquette*
Palms *Sanilac*
Palmyra *Lenawee*
Palo *Ionia*
Paradise *Chippewa*
Parchment *Kalamazoo*
Paris *Mecosta*
Parkdale *Manistee*
Parma *Jackson*
Patterson Gardens *Monroe*
Paw Paw *Van Buren*
Pearl Beach *Saint Clair*
Peck *Sanilac*

Pelkie *Baraga*
Pellston *Emmet*
Pentwater *Oceana*
Perkins *Delta*
Perrinton *Gratiot*
Perronville *Menominee*
Perry *Shiawassee*
Petersburg *Monroe*
Petoskey *Emmet*
Pewamo *Ionia*
Pickford *Chippewa*
Pierson *Montcalm*
Pigeon *Huron*
Pinckney *Livingston*
Pinconning *Bay*
Pittsford *Hillsdale*
Plainwell *Allegan*
Pleasant Lake *Jackson*
Pleasant Ridge *Oakland*
Plymouth *Wayne*
Pointe Aux Pins *Mackinac*
Pompeii *Gratiot*
Pontiac *Oakland*
Portage *Kalamazoo*
Port Austin *Huron*
Port Hope *Huron*
Port Huron *Saint Clair*
Portland *Ionia*
Port Sanilac *Sanilac*
Posen *Presque Isle*
Potterville *Eaton*
Powers *Menominee*
Prattville *Hillsdale*
Prescott *Ogemaw*
Presque Isle *Presque Isle*
Prudenville *Roscommon*
Pullman *Allegan*
Quincy *Branch*
Quinnesec *Dickinson*
Raco *Chippewa*
Ramsay *Gogebic*
Rapid City *Kalkaska*
Rapid River *Delta*
Ravenna *Muskegon*
Reading *Hillsdale*
Redford *Oakland*
Reed City *Osceola*
Reese *Tuscola*
Remus *Mecosta*
Republic *Marquette*
Rhodes *Gladwin*
Richland *Kalamazoo*
Richmond *Macomb*
Richville *Tuscola*
Ridgeway *Lenawee*
Riga *Lenawee*
Riverdale *Gratiot*
Riverside *Berrien*
River Rouge *Wayne*
Rives Junction *Jackson*
Rochester *Oakland*
Rochester Hills *Macomb*
Rock *Delta*
Rockford *Kent*
Rockland *Ontonagon*
Rockwood *Wayne*
Rodney *Mecosta*
Rogers City *Presque Isle*
Rollin *Lenawee*
Romeo *Macomb*
Romulus *Wayne*
Roosevelt Park *Muskegon*
Roscommon *Roscommon*
Rosebush *Isabella*
Rose City *Ogemaw*

Roseville *Macomb*
Rothbury *Oceana*
Royal Oak *Oakland*
Rudyard *Chippewa*
Ruth *Huron*
Saginaw *Saginaw*
Sagola *Dickinson*
Saint Charles *Saginaw*
Saint Clair *Saint Clair*
Saint Clair Shores *Macomb*
Saint Helen *Roscommon*
Saint Ignace *Mackinac*
Saint James *Charlevoix*
Saint Johns *Clinton*
Saint Joseph *Berrien*
Saint Louis *Gratiot*
Saline *Washtenaw*
Samaria *Monroe*
Sand Creek *Lenawee*
Sand Lake *Kent*
Sandusky *Sanilac*
Sanford *Midland*
Saranac *Ionia*
Saugatuck *Allegan*
Sault Sainte Marie
  Chippewa
Sawyer *Berrien*
Schoolcraft *Kalamazoo*
Scotts *Kalamazoo*
Scottville *Mason*
Sears *Osceola*
Sebewaing *Huron*
Seneca *Lenawee*
Seney *Schoolcraft*
Shaftsburg *Shiawassee*
Shelby *Oceana*
Shelbyville *Allegan*
Shepherd *Isabella*
Sheridan *Montcalm*
Sherwood *Branch*
Shields *Saginaw*
Shingleton *Alger*
Shoreham *Berrien*
Sidnaw *Houghton*
Sidney *Montcalm*
Silverwood *Tuscola*
Six Lakes *Montcalm*
Skandia *Marquette*
Skanee *Baraga*
Smiths Creek *Saint Clair*
Snover *Sanilac*
Sodus *Berrien*
Somerset *Hillsdale*
Somerset Center *Hillsdale*
South Boardman *Kalkaska*
South Branch *Ogemaw*
Southfield *Oakland*
Southgate *Wayne*
South Haven *Van Buren*
South Lyon *Oakland*
South Monroe *Monroe*
South Range *Houghton*
South Rockwood *Monroe*
Spalding *Menominee*
Sparlingville *Saint Clair*
Sparta *Kent*
Spring Arbor *Jackson*
Springfield *Calhoun*
Spring Lake *Ottawa*
Springport *Jackson*
Spruce *Alcona*
Stalwart *Chippewa*
Stambaugh *Iron*
Standish *Arenac*
Stanton *Montcalm*

Stanwood *Mecosta*
Stephenson *Menominee*
Sterling *Arenac*
Sterling Heights *Macomb*
Stevensville *Berrien*
Stockbridge *Ingham*
Sturgis *Saint Joseph*
Sumner *Gratiot*
Sunfield *Eaton*
Sunrise Heights *Calhoun*
Suttons Bay *Leelanau*
Swartz Creek *Genesee*
Sylvan Lake *Oakland*
Tawas City *Iosco*
Taylor *Wayne*
Tecumseh *Lenawee*
Tekonsha *Calhoun*
Temperance *Monroe*
Thompsonville *Benzie*
Three Oaks *Berrien*
Three Rivers *Saint Joseph*
Tipton *Lenawee*
Toivola *Houghton*
Topinabee *Cheboygan*
Tower *Cheboygan*
Traunik *Alger*
Traverse City *Grand
    Traverse*
Trenary *Alger*
Trenton *Wayne*
Trout Creek *Ontonagon*
Trout Lake *Chippewa*
Trowbridge Park
    Marquette
Troy *Oakland*
Trufant *Montcalm*
Turner *Arenac*
Tustin *Osceola*
Twining *Arenac*
Twin Lake *Muskegon*
Ubly *Huron*
Union City *Branch*
Union Lake *Oakland*
Union Pier *Berrien*
Unionville *Tuscola*
Utica *Macomb*
Vandalia *Cass*
Vanderbilt *Otsego*
Vandercook Lake *Jackson*
Vassar *Tuscola*
Vermontville *Eaton*
Vernon *Shiawassee*
Vestaburg *Montcalm*
Vicksburg *Kalamazoo*
Vulcan *Dickinson*
Wakefield *Gogebic*
Waldron *Hillsdale*
Walhalla *Mason*
Walker *Kent*
Walkerville *Oceana*
Wallace *Menominee*
Walled Lake *Oakland*
Walloon Lake *Charlevoix*
Warren *Macomb*
Washington *Macomb*
Waterford *Oakland*
Waters *Otsego*
Watersmeet *Gogebic*
Watervliet *Berrien*
Watton *Baraga*
Wayland *Allegan*
Wayne *Wayne*
Webberville *Ingham*
Weidman *Isabella*
Wells *Delta*

Wellston *Manistee*
West Branch *Ogemaw*
Westland *Wayne*
West Olive *Ottawa*
Weston *Lenawee*
Westphalia *Clinton*
Wetmore *Alger*
Wheeler *Gratiot*
White Cloud *Newaygo*
Whitehall *Muskegon*
White Pigeon *Saint Joseph*
White Pine *Ontonagon*
Whitmore Lake
    Washtenaw
Whittaker *Washtenaw*
Whittemore *Iosco*
Williamsburg *Grand
    Traverse*
Williamston *Ingham*
Willis *Washtenaw*
Willow Run *Washtenaw*
Wilson *Menominee*
Winn *Isabella*
Wixom *Oakland*
Wolf Lake *Muskegon*
Wolverine *Cheboygan*
Woodhaven *Wayne*
Woodland *Barry*
Woodland Beach *Monroe*
Wyandotte *Wayne*
Wyoming *Kent*
Yale *Saint Clair*
Ypsilanti *Washtenaw*
Zeeland *Ottawa*
Zilwaukee *Saginaw*

Minnesota

All of Minnesota's eighty seven (87) counties make criminal conviction data available for employment screening purposes, seventy eight (78) of them by phone or mail. Forty (40) counties reported that records are available by fax.

For more information or for offices not listed, contact the state's information hot line at (612) 296-6013.

Driving Records

Department of Transportation
Investigations
Drivers License, Room 108
St. Paul, MN 55155
(612) 296-2023
Driving records are available by mail. $4 fee per request. Turnaround time is 24 hours. Written request must include job applicant's full name, date of birth and license number. Make check payable to Department of Public Safety.

Worker's Compensation Records

Worker's Compensation Division
Department of Labor and Industry
443 Lafayette Road
St. Paul, MN 55155-4318
(612) 296-6844
Fax (612) 296-9634
Written request must contain job applicant's full name and SSN. A signed release specifically mentioning the "Minnesota Department of Labor, Worker's Compensation Division" is also required. A $3.50 fee is charged for "hits" only. Additional $.50 per copy plus 6.5% tax and postage if mailed back. State will bill for services.

Vital Statistics

Minnesota Department of Health
Section of Vital Statistics
717 Delaware Street Southeast
PO Box 9441
Minneapolis, MN 55440
(612) 623-5120
Birth records are available for $11.00 and death records for $8.00. $5.00 fee for additional birth records, $2.00 for additional death records. State office has records since January 1908. Copies of earlier records may be obtained from Court Administrator in county where event occurred. Records are public except for births out of wedlock. Employer can obtain records with a written release. Make check or money order payable to Minnesota State Treasurer. Marriage records are available at county level through court administrator where license was issued. Divorce records are available at county level where divorce granted.

Department of Education

Personnel Licensing
613 Capitol Square
550 Cedar St.
St. Paul, MN 55101
(612) 296-2046
Field of certification, effective date and expiration date are available by phone or mail. Include name and SSN.

Medical Licensing

Board of Medical Examiners
2700 University Ave. W.
Suite 106
St. Paul, MN 55114
(612) 642-0538
Will confirm licenses for MDs and DOs by mail. $10.00 fee. Include name license number or DOB. For licenses not mentioned, contact the above office.

Minnesota Board of Nursing
2700 University Ave. West, #108
St. Paul, MN 55114
(612) 642-0571
Will confirm license by phone. No fee. Include name, DOB, license number, if available.

Bar Association

Minnesota State Bar Association
514 Nicolet Mall, Suite 300
Minneapolis, MN 55402
Will confirm licenses by phone. No fee. Include name.

Accountancy Board

Minnesota State Board of Accountancy
133 East Seventh Street
St. Paul, MN 55101
(612) 296-7937
Will confirm license by phone. No fee. Include name.

Securities Commission

Department of Commerce
133 East Seventh Street
St. Paul, MN 55101
(612) 296-4026
Will confirm license by phone. No fee. Include name and SSN.

Secretary of State

Secretary of State
Business Recording Section
1800 State Office Building
St. Paul, MN 55155
(612) 296-2803
Correct legal styling of business or corporate name; registered address; registered agent, if any; date of incorporation or filing; and standing with Office of Secretary of State are available by phone or mail. Contact the above office for additional information.

Criminal Records

State Repository

Bureau of Criminal Apprehension
C.J.I.S. Section
1246 University Avenue
St. Paul, MN 55104
(612) 642-0672
Criminal record checks are available by mail only. Each request must include subject's full name, date of birth and a self-addressed, stamped envelope. Requests must also include a notarized release signed by the subject. For additional information on the specific wording required in the release, contact the above office. There is a $8.00 fee per request. Personal checks and cash are not accepted through the mail. Make company check payable to Bureau of Criminal Apprehension. Both conviction and arrest data available.

Aitkin County

Court Administrator, Criminal Records
Courthouse West Annex
209 Second St. NW
Aitkin, MN 56431
(218) 927-2107
Fax (218) 927-6934
Felony and misdemeanor records are available by mail, phone or fax. No release necessary. No fee. Search information required: name, date of birth.

Civil records are available by mail. No release necessary. $5.00 search fee. $1.50 fee per copy. $5.00 for certification. Search information required: name, years to search. Specify plaintiff or defendant.

Anoka County

Clerk of Court, Felony Clerk
Anoka County Courthouse
325 E Main Street
Anoka, MN 55303
(612) 422-7385
Felony and misdemeanor records are available by mail or phone. No release necessary. No fee. Search information required: name, date of birth.

Civil records are available by mail. No release necessary. $5.00 search fee. $3.50 fee per copy. $5.00 for certification. Search information required: name, years to search. Specify plaintiff or defendant.

Becker County

District Court, Criminal Records
Becker County Courthouse
Detroit Lakes, MN 56501
(218) 846-7305
Fax (218) 847-7620
Felony and misdemeanor records are available by mail, fax or phone. No release necessary. No search fee. $.25 fee per copy. $5.00 for certification. $5.00 fee for first page of fax response, $.25 for each additional page of fax response. Company checks only, payable to District Court. Search information required: name, date of birth, years to search.

Civil records are available by mail, phone or fax. No release necessary. No search fee. $.25 fee per copy. $5.00 for certification. Search information required: name, years to search. Specify plaintiff or defendant.

Beltrami County

Beltrami County Clerk of Court,
Criminal Records
PO Box 1008
Bemidji, MN 56601
(218) 759-4520
Felony and misdemeanor records are available by mail. No release necessary. $3.00 search fee. Search information required: name, date of birth, years to search.

Civil records are available by mail. No release necessary. $5.00 search fee. Search information required: name, years to search. Specify plaintiff or defendant.

Benton County

Court Administrator's Office,
Criminal Records
Benton County Courthouse
Foley, MN 56329
(612) 968-6254 Extension 320
Felony and misdemeanor records are available by mail. No release necessary. $5.00 search fee. Make check payable to Court Administrator. Search information required: name, date of birth, years to search.

Civil records are available by mail. No release necessary. $5.00 search fee. $3.50 fee per copy. $5.00 for certification. Search information required: name, years to search. Specify plaintiff or defendant.

Big Stone County

Court Administrator's Office,
Criminal Records
20 Southeast 2nd Street
Ortonville, MN 56278
(612) 839-2537
Felony and misdemeanor records are available in person only. See Minnesota state repository for additional information.

Civil records are available in person only. See Minnesota state repository for additional information.

Blue Earth County

Court Administrator's Office,
Criminal Records
Blue Earth County Courthouse
204 S 5th Street
Mankato, MN 56001
(507) 389-8302
Felony and misdemeanor records are available by mail. No release necessary. $10.00 search fee. Search information required: full name, date of birth.

Civil records are available by mail or phone. No release necessary. No search fee. $3.50 fee for first copy, $.25 for each additional copy. $5.00 for first page certified, $.25 for each additional page. Search information required: name, years to search. Specify plaintiff or defendant.

Brown County

Courthouse, Criminal Records
New Ulm, MN 56073
(507) 354-8511
Fax (507) 359-9562
Felony and misdemeanor records are available by mail, phone or fax. No release necessary. $8.00 search fee, $5.00 fax fee. Search information required: name, date of birth, years to search.

Civil records are available by mail, phone, or fax. No release necessary. $5.00 search fee. $5.00 fax fee. $3.50 fee for first copy, $.25 for each additional copy. $5.00 for first page certified, $.25 for each additional page. Search information required: name, years to search. Specify plaintiff or defendant.

Carlton County

Court Administrator
Carlton County Court System
PO Box 190
Carlton, MN 55718
(218) 384-4281
Felony and misdemeanor records are available by mail. No release necessary. $5.00 search fee. Make check payable to Court Administrator. Search information required: name, date of birth.

Civil records are available by mail. No release necessary. $5.00 search fee. $3.50 fee for first copy, $.25 for each additional copy. $5.00 for first page certified, $.25 for each additional page. Search information required: name, years to search. Specify plaintiff or defendant.

Carver County

Court Administrator's Office,
Criminal Records
Carver County Courthouse
600 E. 4th Street
Chaska, MN 55318
(612) 448-3435
Felony and misdemeanor records are available in person only. See Minnesota state repository for additional information.

Civil records are available in person only. See Minnesota state repository for additional information.

Cass County

Court Administrator, Criminal
Records
Cass County Courthouse
Walker, MN 56484
(218) 547-3300
Fax (218) 547-2440
Felony and misdemeanor records are available by mail. No release necessary. $5.00 search fee. $3.50 fee for first copy, $.25 each additional copy. $5.00 for first page certified, $.25 each additional page. Search information required: name, date of birth.

Civil records are available by mail. No release necessary. $5.00 search fee. $3.50 fee for first copy, $.25 for each additional copy. $5.00 for first page certified, $.25 for each additional page. Search information required: name, years to search. Specify plaintiff or defendant.

Chippewa County

Court Administrator, Criminal
Records
Chippewa County Courthouse
Montevideo, MN 56265
(612) 269-7774
Fax (612) 269-7733
Felony and misdemeanor records are available by mail. No release necessary. $5.00 search. Search information required: name, date of birth.

Civil records are available by mail. No release necessary. $5.00 search fee. $3.50 fee for first copy, $.25 for each additional copy. $5.00 for first page certified, $.25 for each additional page. Search information required: name, years to search. Specify plaintiff or defendant.

Chisago County

Court Administrator
Chisago Courthouse
PO Box 126
Center City, MN 55012
(612) 257-1300 Extension 130
Felony and misdemeanor records are available by mail. No release necessary. $5.00 search fee. Search information required: name, date of birth.

Civil records are available by mail. No release necessary. $5.00 search fee. $5.00 for first page certified, $.25 for each additional page. Search information required: name, years to search. Specify plaintiff or defendant.

Clay County

Court Administrator, Criminal Records
PO Box 280
Moorhead, MN 56560
(218) 299-5043
Felony and misdemeanor records are available by mail. No release necessary. $5.00 search fee. $3.50 fee for first copy, $.25 for each additional copy. $5.00 for first page certified, $.25 each additionalpage. Company checks only, payable to Court Administrator. Search information required: name, date of birth.

Civil records are available by mail. No release necessary. $5.00 search fee. $3.50 fee for first copy, $.25 for each additional copy. $5.00 for first page certified, $.25 for each additional page. Search information required: name, years to search. Specify plaintiff or defendant.

Clearwater County

Court Administrator, Criminal Records
PO Box 127
Bagley, MN 56621
(218) 694-6177
Fax (218) 694-6244
Felony and misdemeanor records are available by mail or fax. No release necessary. No search fee. Search information required: name, date of birth.

Civil records are available by mail. No release necessary. No search fee. $3.50 fee for first copy, $.25 for each additional copy. $5.00 for first page certified, $.25 for each additional page. Search information required: name, years to search. Specify plaintiff or defendant.

Cook County

Court Administrator, Criminal Records
Grand Marais, MN 55604
(218) 387-2282
Fax (218) 387-2610
Felony and misdemeanor records are available by mail or fax. No release necessary. $10.00 search fee per hour. $3.50 fee for first copy, $.25 for each additional copy. $5.00 for first page certified, $.25 for each additional Page. Company checks only, payable to Court Administrator. Search information required: name, date of birth, years to search.

Civil records are available by mail. No release necessary. $10.00 search fee per hour. $3.50 fee for first copy, $.25 for each additional copy. $5.00 for first page certified, $.25 for each additional page. Search information required: name, years to search. Specify plaintiff or defendant.

Cottonwood County

Court Administrator
900 3rd Avenue
Windom, MN 56101
(507) 831-1356
Records are available by mail. $5.00 search fee. No release necessary. Search information required: name, years to search.

Civil records are available by mail. No release necessary. $5.00 search fee. $3.50 fee for first copy, $.25 for each additional copy. $5.00 for first page certified, $.25 for each additional page. Search information required: name, years to search. Specify plaintiff or defendant.

Crow Wing County

Crow Wing County Courthouse
Brainerd, MN 56401
(218) 828-3959
Records are available by mail. No release necessary. No search fee. $3.00 fee for first copy, $.25 for each additional copy. $5.00 for first page certified, $.25 for each additional page. Search information required: name, years to search.

Civil records are available by mail. No release necessary. $5.00 search fee. $3.00 fee for first copy, $.25 for each additional copy. $5.00 for first page certified, $.25 for each additional page. Search information required: name, years to search. Specify plaintiff or defendant.

Dakota County

Dakota County Government Center
1560 Highway 55
Hastings, MN 55033
(612) 438-4295
Records are available in person only. See Minnesota state repository for additional information.

Civil records are available in person only. See Minnesota state repository for additional information.

Dodge County

Court Administrator, Criminal Records
Dodge County Courthouse
Box 96
Mantorville, MN 55955
(507) 635-6260
Fax (507) 635-6265
Felony and misdemeanor records are available by mail or fax. No release necessary. $5.00 search fee. Make check payable to Court Administrator. Search information required: name, date of birth.

Civil records are available by mail or fax. No release necessary. $5.00 search fee. $3.50 fee for first copy, $.25 for each additional copy. $5.00 for first page certified, $.25 for each additional page. Search information required: name, years to search. Specify plaintiff or defendant.

Douglas County

Court Administrator, Criminal Records
Douglas County Courthouse
305 8th Ave. West
Alexandria, MN 56308
(612) 762-2381 Extension 236
Felony and misdemeanor records are available by mail. No release necessary. $5.00 fee. Certified check only, payable to Court Administrator. Search information required: name, date of birth.

Civil records are available by mail. No release necessary. $5.00 search fee. $3.50 fee for first copy, $.25 for each additional copy. $5.00 for first page certified, $.25 for each additional page. Search information required: name, years to search. Specify plaintiff or defendant.

Faribault County

Courthouse, Criminal Records
Blue Earth, MN 56013
(507) 526-5142
Felony and misdemeanor records are available by mail. No release necessary. No search fee. Search information required: name, date of birth, offense.

Civil records are available by mail. No release necessary. $5.00 search fee. $3.50 fee for first copy, $.25 for each additional copy. $5.00 for first certification, $.25 for each additional certification. Search information required: name, years to search. Specify plaintiff or defendant.

Fillmore County

Fillmore County Courthouse
Preston, MN 55965
(507) 765-4483
Fax (507) 765-4571
Records are available by mail or fax. No release necessary. $5.00 search fee. Search information required: name, date of birth.

Civil records are available by mail. No release necessary. $5.00 search fee. $3.50 fee for first copy, $.25 for each additional copy. $5.00 for first page certified, $.25 for each additional page. Search information required: name, years to search. Specify plaintiff or defendant.

Freeborn County

Freeborn County Courthouse, Criminal Records
Criminal Division
411 S. Broadway
Albert Lea, MN 56007
(507) 377-5153
Fax (507) 377-5160
Felony and misdemeanor records are available by mail or phone. No release necessary. No search fee. Search information required: name, date of birth.

Civil records are available by mail. No release necessary. $5.00 search fee. $3.50 fee for first copy, $.25 for each additional copy. $5.00 for first page certified, $.25 for each additional page. Search information required: name, years to search. Specify plaintiff or defendant.

Goodhue County

Court Administrator, Criminal Records
Room 310, Courthouse
Red Wing, MN 55066
(612) 385-3061 or 385-3060
Fax (612) 385-3065
Felony and misdemeanor records are available in person only. See Minnesota state repository for additional information.

Civil records are available by mail or phone. No release necessary. No search fee. $3.50 fee for first copy, $.25 for each additional copy. $5.00 for first page certified, $.25 for each additional page. Search information required: name, years to search. Specify plaintiff or defendant.

Grant County

Court Administrator
Courthouse
Elbow Lake, MN 56531
(218) 685-4825
Felony and misdemeanor records are available by mail. No release necessary. $5.00 fee. Certified check only, payable to Court Administrator. Search information required: name.

Civil records are available by mail or phone. No release necessary. No search fee. $3.50 fee for first copy, $.25 for each additional copy. $5.00 for first page certified, $.25 for each additional page. Search information required: name, years to search. Specify plaintiff or defendant

Hennepin County

Court Administrator, Criminal
Records
300 S. 6th Street, Room C-1153
Hennepin County Government Center
Minneapolis, MN 55487
(612) 348-2611

Felony and misdemeanor records are available by mail. No release necessary. $7.00 search fee, prepaid. $3.50 fee for first copy, $.25 for each additional copy. $5.00 for first certification, $.25 for each additional certification. Make check payable to Hennepin County Criminal Court. Search information required: full name, date of birth, years to search, SASE.

Civil records are available by mail. No release necessary. $7.00 search fee. $3.50 fee for first copy, $.25 for each additional copy. $5.00 for first page certified, $.25 for each additional page. Search information required: name, years to search. Specify plaintiff or defendant.

Houston County

Court Administrator, Criminal
Records
Courthouse
304 S. Marshall
Caledonia, MN 55921
(507) 724-5211 Extension 231
Fax (507) 724-5550

Felony and misdemeanor records are available by mail, phone or fax. No release necessary. No search fee. Search information required: name, date of birth.

Civil records are available by mail, phone or fax. No release necessary. No search fee. $3.50 fee for first copy, $.25 for each additional copy. $5.00 for firstpage certified, $.25 for each additional page. Search information required: name, years to search. Specify plaintiff or defendant.

Hubbard County

Hubbard County Courthouse, Criminal
Records
PO Box 72
Park Rapids, MN 56470
(218) 732-3573

Felony and misdemeanor records are available by mail or phone. No release necessary. No search fee. $3.00 fee for first copy, $.25 for each additional copy. $5.00 for first page certified, $.25 for each additional page. Search information required: name, date of birth.

Civil records are available by mail or phone. No release necessary. No search fee. $3.00 fee for first copy, $.25 for each additional copy. $5.00 for firstpage certified, $.25 for each additional page. Search information required: name, years to search. Specify plaintiff or defendant.

Isanti County

Isanti County Court Administrator,
Criminal Records
237 S.W. 2nd Avenue
Cambridge, MN 55008
(612) 689-2292

Felony and misdemeanor records are available by mail. No release necessary. $5.00 search fee. Search information required: name, date of birth, years to search.

Civil records are available by mail. No release necessary. $5.00 search fee. $3.50 fee for first copy, $.25 for each additional copy. $5.00 for first page certified, $.25 for each additional page. Search information required: name, years to search. Specify plaintiff or defendant.

Itasca County

Court Administrator, Criminal
Records
Itasca County Courthouse
Grand Rapids, MN 55744
(218) 327-2870

Felony and misdemeanor records are available by mail. No release necessary. No search fee. Search information required: full name, date of birth.

Civil records are available by mail or phone. A release is required. No search fee. $3.00 fee for first copy, $.25 for each additional copy. $5.00 for first page certified, $.25 for each additional page. Search information required: name, years to search. Specify plaintiff or defendant.

Jackson County

Court Administrator, Criminal
Records
Courthouse
Jackson, MN 56143
(507) 847-4400
Fax (507) 847-5433

Felony and misdemeanor records are available by mail, phone or fax. No release necessary. No search fee. Search information required: name, date of birth, sex, race.

Civil records are available by mail, phone or fax. No release necessary. $5.00 search fee. $.25 fee per copy. $3.50 for first page certified, $.25 for each additional page. Search information required: name, years to search. Specify plaintiff or defendant.

Kanabec County

Court Administrator, Criminal
Records
Kanabec County Courthouse
18 N. Vine
Mora, MN 55051
(612) 679-1022

Felony and misdemeanor records are available by mail. No release necessary. $5.00 search fee per name. $3.50 fee for first copy, $.25 for each additional copy. $5.00 for first page certified, $.25 for each additional page. Make check payable to Court Administrator. Search information required: name, date of birth.

Civil records are available by mail. No release necessary. $5.00 search fee. $3.50 fee for first copy, $.25 for each additional copy. $5.00 for first page certified, $.25 for each additional page. Search information required: name, years to search. Specify plaintiff or defendant.

Kandiyohi County

Court Administrator, Criminal
Records
PO Box 1337
Willmar, MN 56201
(612) 231-6206

Felony and misdemeanor records are available by mail or phone. No release necessary. $5.00 search fee. Search information required: name, date of birth, years to search.

Kittson County

Court Administrator's Office,
Criminal Records
Box 39
Kittson County Courthouse
Hallock, MN 56728
(218) 843-3632

Felony and misdemeanor records are available by mail. No release necessary. No search fee. $3.50 fee for first copy, $.25 for each additional copy. $5.00 fee for first page certified, $.25 for each additional page. Search information required: name, date of birth, years to search.

Civil records are available by mail. No release necessary. No search fee. $3.50 fee for first copy, $.25 for each additional copy. $5.00 for first page certified, $.25 for each additional page. Search information required: name, years to search. Specify plaintiff or defendant.

Koochiching County

County Courthouse, Criminal Records
International Falls, MN 56649
(218) 283-6261
Fax (218) 283-6262

Felony records are available by mail. No release necessary. $5.00 search fee. Search information required: name, date of birth.

Civil records are available by mail. No release necessary. $5.00 search fee. $3.50 fee for first copy, $.25 for each additional copy. $5.00 for first page certified, $.25 for each additional page. Search information required: name, years to search. Specify plaintiff or defendant.

Lac Qui Parle County

Court Administrator, Criminal
Records
PO Box 36
Madison, MN 56256
(612) 598-3536
Fax (612) 598-3915

Felony and misdemeanor records are available by mail or fax. No release necessary. $5.00 search fee. $3.50 fee for first copy, $.25 for each additional copy. $5.00 for first page certified, $.25 for each additional page. Search information required: name, SSN, date of birth, years to search.

Civil records are available by mail or fax. No release necessary. $5.00 search fee. $3.50 fee for first copy, $.25 for each additional copy. $5.00 for first page certified, $.25 for each additional page. Search information required: name, years to search. Specify plaintiff or defendant.

Lake County

Court Administrator, Criminal
Records
601 3rd Avenue
Lake County Courthouse
Two Harbors, MN 55616
(218) 834-8330
Fax (218) 834-8397
Felony and misdemeanor records are available by mail or fax. A release is required. No fee. Search information required: name, date of birth.

Civil records are available by mail or fax. No release necessary. $5.00 search fee. $3.50 fee for first copy, $.25 for each additional copy. $5.00 for first page certified, $.25 for each additional page. Search information required: name, years to search. Specify plaintiff or defendant.

Lake of the Woods County

Court Administrator, Criminal
Records
PO Box 808
Baudette, MN 56623
(218) 634-1451
Fax (218) 634-2509
Felony and misdemeanor records are available by mail or fax. No release necessary. $10.00 search fee per hour. Make check payable to Court Administrator. Search information required: name, date of birth, years to search.

Civil records are available by mail or fax. No release necessary. $5.00 search fee. $3.50 fee for first copy, $.25 for each additional copy. $5.00 for first page certified, $.25 for each additional page. Search information required: name, years to search. Specify plaintiff or defendant.

Le Sueur County

Court Administrator, Criminal
Records
Box 10
Le Sueur County Courthouse
Le Center, MN 56057
(612) 357-2251
Felony and misdemeanor records are available by mail from 1980. A release is required. $2.00 search fee. $3.50 fee for first copy, $.25 for each additional copy. $5.00 for first page certified, $.25 for each additional page. Search information required: name, address, years to search.

Civil records are available by mail. No release necessary. $2.00 search fee. $3.50 fee for first copy, $.25 for each additional copy. $5.00 for first page certified, $.25 for each additional page. Search information required: name, years to search. Specify plaintiff or defendant.

Lincoln County

Court Administrator's Office
Lincoln County Courthouse
PO Box 15
Ivanhoe, MN 56142
(507) 694-1505
Fax (507) 694-1717
Felony and misdemeanor records are available by mail or fax. No release necessary. No search fee. $5.00 for first page certified, $.25 for each additional page. $5.00 fee for certification. $5.00 fee per incoming or outgoing fax. Search information required: name, date of birth, years to search.

Civil records are available by mail. No release necessary. No search fee. $3.50 fee for first copy, $.25 for each additional copy. $5.00 for first page certified, $.25 for each additional page. Search information required: name, years to search. Specify plaintiff or defendant.

Lyon County

Court Administrator, Criminal
Records
607 W. Main
Marshall, MN 56258
(507) 537-6734
Felony and misdemeanor records are available by mail. No release necessary. $5.00 search fee. Search information required: name, date of birth, years to search.

Civil records are available by mail. No release necessary. $5.00 search fee. $3.50 fee for first copy, $.25 for each additional copy. $5.00 for first page certified, $.25 for each additional page. Search information required: name, years to search. Specify plaintiff or defendant.

Mahnomen County

Court Administrator, Criminal
Records
Mahnomen County Courthouse
Mahnomen, MN 56557
(218) 935-2251
Fax (218) 935-5946
Felony and misdemeanor records are available by mail, phone or fax. No release necessary. No search fee. Search information required: name, date of birth.

Civil records are available by mail, phone or fax. No release necessary. $5.00 search fee. $3.50 fee for first copy, $.25 for each additional copy. $5.00 for first page certified, $.25 for each additional page. Search information required: name, years to search. Specify plaintiff or defendant.

Marshall County

Court Administrator
Marshall County Courthouse, Criminal
Records
208 E. Colvin
Warren, MN 56762
(218) 745-4921
Felony and misdemeanor records are available by mail. No release necessary. $8.00 search fee per hour. Make check payable to Court Administrator. Search information required: name, date of birth, years to search.

Civil records are available by mail. No release necessary. No search fee. $3.50 fee for first copy, $.25 for each additional copy. $5.00 for first page certified, $.25 for each additional page. Search information required: name, years to search. Specify plaintiff or defendant.

Martin County

Martin County Courthouse
Court Administrator Security Bldg.
201 E. Lake Avenue
Fairmont, MN 56031
(507) 238-3214
Fax (507) 238-1913
Felony and misdemeanor records are available by mail or fax. No release necessary. No search fee. Search information required: name, date of birth.

McLeod County

Court Administrator's Office,
Criminal Division Court Administrator
830 E. 11th
Glencoe, MN 55336
(612) 864-5551 Extension 284
Felony and misdemeanor records are available by mail. A release is required. $10.00 search fee. Search information required: name, date of birth, years to search.

Civil records are available by mail. A release is required. $10.00 search fee. $3.00 fee for first copy, $.25 for each additional copy. $5.00 for first page certified, $.25 for each additional page. Search information required: name, years to search. Specify plaintiff or defendant.

Meeker County

Court Administrator, Criminal
Records
325 N. Sibley Ave.
Litchfield, MN 55355
(612) 693-2458
Fax (612) 693-2450
Felony records are available in person only. See Minnesota state repository for additional information.

Civil records are available by mail. No release necessary. $5.00 search fee. $3.50 fee for first copy, $.25 for each additional copy. $5.00 for first page certified, $.25 for each additional page. Search information required: name, years to search. Specify plaintiff or defendant.

Mille Lacs County

Court Administrator, Criminal
Records
Mille Lacs County Courthouse
Milaca, MN 56353
(612) 983-8313
Felony and misdemeanor records are available by mail. No release necessary. No search fee. $3.00 fee for first copy, $.25 for each additional copy. $5.00 for first certification, $.25 for each additional certification. Search information required: name, date of birth, years to search.

Civil records are available by mail or phone. No release necessary. No search fee. $3.50 fee for first copy, $.25 for each additional copy. $5.00 for first page certified, $.25 for each additional page. Search information required: name, years to search. Specify plaintiff or defendant.

Morrison County

Morrison County Courthouse,
Criminal Records
Criminal Division
Little Falls, MN 56345
(612) 632-2941
Fax (612) 632-2941 Ext. 134
Felony and misdemeanor records are available by mail or fax. No release necessary. $5.00 search fee. Make check payable to Court Administrator. Search information required: name, date of birth, years to search, SASE.

Civil records are available by mail or fax. No release necessary. $5.00 search fee. Make check payable to Court Administrator. Search information required: name, date of birth, years to search, SASE. Specify plaintiff or defendant.

Mower County

Court Administrator, Criminal Records
Mower County Courthouse
201 1st N.E.
Austin, MN 55912
(507) 437-9465
Fax (507) 437-9471

Felony and misdemeanor records are available by mail or fax. A release is required. $3.00 search fee, prepaid. Search information required: name, date of birth, years to search, offense.

Civil records are available by mail or fax. No release necessary. $5.00 search fee. $3.50 fee for first copy, $.25 for each additional copy. $5.00 for first page certified, $.25 for each additional page. Search information required: name, years to search. Specify plaintiff or defendant.

Murray County

Court Administrator, Criminal Records
Murray County Courts Bldg.
Slayton, MN 56172
(507) 836-6148 Ext. 132
Fax (507) 836-8673

Felony and misdemeanor records are available by mail or fax. A release is required. No search fee. $3.50 fee for first copy, $.25 for additional copies. $5.00 fee for first certified copy, $.25 for additional certified copies. Search information required: name, years to search.

Civil records are available by mail. No release necessary. $5.00 search fee. $3.50 fee for first copy, $.25 for each additional copy. $5.00 for first page certified, $.25 for each additional page. Search information required: name, years to search. Specify plaintiff or defendant.

Nicollet County

Court Administrator, Criminal Records
PO Box 496
St. Peter, MN 56082
(507) 931-6800 Extension 376
Fax (507) 931-4278

Felony and misdemeanor records are available by mail or phone. No release necessary. $8.00 search fee. Search information required: name, date of birth, years to search.

Civil records are available by mail. No release necessary. $8.00 search fee. $3.50 fee for first copy, $.25 for each additional copy. $5.00 for first page certified, $.25 for each additional page. Search information required: name, years to search. Specify plaintiff or defendant.

Nobles County

Court Administrator, Criminal Records
PO Box 547
Nobles County Courthouse
Worthington, MN 56187
(507) 372-8263

Felony and misdemeanor records are available by mail or phone. No release necessary. No search fee. $3.50 fee for first copy, $.25 for each additional copy. $5.00 for first page certified, $.25 for each additional page. Search information required: name, date of birth, years to search.

Civil records are available by mail or phone. No release necessary. No search fee. $3.50 fee for first copy, $.25 for each additional copy. $5.00 for first page certified, $.25 for each additional page. Search information required: name, years to search. Specify plaintiff or defendant.

Norman County

Court Administrator, Criminal Records
PO Box 272
Ada, MN 56510
(218) 784-7131
Fax (218) 784-3110

Felony and misdemeanor records are available by mail, phone or fax. No release necessary. No search fee. $3.50 fee for first copy, $.25 for each additional copy. $5.00 for first page certified, $.25 for each additional page. $5.00 fax fee. Search information required: name, date of birth, years to search.

Civil records are available by mail, phone or fax. No release necessary. No search fee. $3.50 fee for first copy, $.25 for each additional copy. $5.00 for first page certified, $.25 for each additional page. $5.00 fax fee. Search information required: name, years to search. Specify plaintiff or defendant.

Olmsted County

Olmsted District Court
Criminal Division
515 S.W. 2nd Street
Rochester, MN 55902
(507) 285-8210

Felony and misdemeanor records are available by mail. No release necessary. $5.00 search fee. Make check payable to Olmsted District Court. Search information required: name, date of birth.

Civil records are available by mail. No release necessary. $5.00 search fee. $3.50 fee for first copy, $.25 for each additional copy. $5.00 for first page certified, $.25 for each additional page. Search information required: name, years to search. Specify plaintiff or defendant.

Otter Tail County

Otter Tail County Courthouse, Criminal Records
PO Box 417
Fergus Falls, MN 56537
(218) 739-2271 Extension 275
Fax (218) 739-4983

Felony and misdemeanor records are available by mail, phone or fax. No release necessary. No search fee. Search information required: name, date of birth.

Civil records are available by mail, phone or fax. No release necessary. No search fee. $3.50 fee for first copy, $.25 for each additional copy. $5.00 for first page certified, $.25 for each additional page. Search information required: name, years to search. Specify plaintiff or defendant.

Pennington County

Court Administrator
Pennington County
PO Box 619
Thief River Falls, MN 56701
(218) 681-2407

Felony and misdemeanor records are available by mail. No release necessary. No search fee. Search information required: name, date of birth.

Civil records are available by mail or phone. No release necessary. $5.00 search fee. $3.50 fee for first copy, $.25 for each additional copy. $5.00 for first page certified, $.25 for each additional page. Search information required: name, years to search. Specify plaintiff or defendant.

Pine County

Court Administrator
Pine County Courthouse
Pine City, MN 55063
(612) 629-6781 Extension 182

Felony and misdemeanor records are available by mail. No release necessary. $5.00 search fee. Search information required: name, date of birth, years to search.

Civil records are available by mail. A release is required. $5.00 search fee. $3.50 fee for first copy, $.25 for each additional copy. $5.00 for first page certified, $.25 for each additional page. Search information required: name, years to search. Specify plaintiff or defendant.

Pipestone County

Court Administrator
PO Box 337
Pipestone, MN 56164
(507) 825-4550

Felony and misdemeanor records are available by mail. No release necessary. $8.00 search fee. $3.50 fee for first copy, $.25 for additional copies. $5.00 fee for first page certified, $.25 for additional page. Search information required: name.

Civil records are available by mail. No release necessary. $5.00 search fee. $3.50 fee for first copy, $.25 for each additional copy. $5.00 for first page certified, $.25 for each additional page. Search information required: name, years to search. Specify plaintiff or defendant.

Polk County

Court Administration
PO Box 438
Crookston, MN 56716
(218) 281-2332

Records are available in person only. See Minnesota state repository for additional information.

Civil records are available by mail. No release necessary. No search fee. $3.50 fee for first copy, $.25 for each additional copy. $5.00 for first page certified, $.25 for each additional page. Search information required: name, years to search. Specify plaintiff or defendant.

Pope County

Court Administrator, Criminal Records
Pope County Courthouse
130 E. Minnesota Ave.
Glenwood, MN 56334
(612) 634-5301
Fax (612) 634-5527

Felony and misdemeanor records are available by mail, phone or fax. No release necessary. $10.00 search fee per hour. Make check payable to Court Administrator. Search information required: name.

Civil records are available by mail. No release necessary. $5.00 search fee. $3.50 fee for first copy, $.25 for each additional copy. $5.00 for first page certified, $.25 for each additional page. Search information required: name, years to search. Specify plaintiff or defendant.

Ramsey County

Ramsey County Court Administrator, Criminal Records
Room 1245
Courthouse
St. Paul, MN 55102
(612) 298-6822

Felony and misdemeanor records are available by mail. No release necessary. $10.00 search fee. $3.50 fee for first copy, $.25 for each additional copy. $5.00 for first page certified, $.25 for each additional page. Make check payable to Ramsey County. Search information required: full name, date of birth, years to search.

Civil records are available by mail. No release necessary. No search fee. $3.50 fee for first copy, $.25 for each additional copy. $5.00 for first page certified, $.25 for each additional page. Search information required: name, years to search. Specify plaintiff or defendant.

Red Lake County

Court Administrator, Criminal Records
Red Lake County Courthouse
Box 339
Red Lake Falls, MN 56750
(218) 253-4281

Felony and misdemeanor records are available by mail or phone. No release necessary. No search fee. $3.50 fee for first copy, $.25 for each additional copy. $5.00 for first page certified, $.25 for each additional page. Make check payable to Court Administrator. Search information required: name, date of birth, years to search.

Civil records are available by mail or phone. No release necessary. No search fee. $3.50 fee for first copy, $.25 for each additional copy. $5.00 for first page certified, $.25 for each additional page. Search information required: name, years to search. Specify plaintiff or defendant.

Redwood County

Court Administrator, Criminal Records
Redwood County Courthouse
PO Box 158
Redwood Falls, MN 56283
(507) 637-8327
Fax 507) 637-2611

Felony and misdemeanor records are available by mail or fax. No release necessary. No search fee. $.15 fee per copy. $5.00 for first page certified, $.25 for each additional page. $5.00 fee for first five pages of fax response, $1.00 fee for each additional page of fax response. Search information required: name, date of birth, years to search.

Civil records are available by mail. No release necessary. $5.00 search fee. $3.50 fee for first copy, $.25 for each additional copy. $5.00 for first page certified, $.25 for each additional page. Search information required: name, years to search. Specify plaintiff or defendant.

Renville County

Court Administrator, Criminal Records
Renville County Courthouse
Olivia, MN 56277
(612) 523-2080
Fax (612) 523-2084

Felony and misdemeanor records are available in person only See Minnesota state repository for additional information.

Civil records are available in person only. See Minnesota state repository for additional information.

Rice County

Court Administrator, Criminal Records
Rice County Courthouse
218 N.W. 3rd Street
Fairbault, MN 55021
(507) 332-6107
Fax (507) 332-6199

Felony and misdemeanor records are available by mail or fax. No release necessary. $5.00 search fee. Turnaround time is 1 week to 10 days. Search information required: name, date of birth.

Civil records are available by mail. No release necessary. $5.00 search fee. $3.50 fee for first copy, $.25 for each additional copy. $5.00 for first page certified, $.25 for each additional page. Search information required: name, years to search. Specify plaintiff or defendant.

Rock County

Court Administrator, Criminal Records
PO Box 245
Luverne, MN 56156
(507) 283-9501

Felony and misdemeanor records are available by mail. No release necessary. $10.00 fee. Search information required: name.

Civil records are available by mail. No release necessary. $10.00 search fee. $3.50 fee for first copy, $.25 for each additional copy. $5.00 for first page certified, $.25 for each additional page. Search information required: name, years to search. Specify plaintiff or defendant.

Roseau County

Clerk of Court, Criminal Records
Courthouse
Roseau, MN 56751
(218) 463-2541

Felony and misdemeanor records are available by mail. No release necessary. No search fee. Search information required: name, date of birth, years to search.

Civil records are available by mail. No release necessary. $5.00 search fee. $3.50 fee for first copy, $.25 for each additional copy. $5.00 for first page certified, $.25 for each additional page. Search information required: name, years to search. Specify plaintiff or defendant.

Scott County

Scott County Courthouse, Criminal Records
Room 212
Shakopee, MN 55379
(612) 445-7750 Extension 203

Felony and misdemeanor records are available by mail or phone. No release necessary. $5.00 search fee. $3.50 fee for first copy, $.25 for each additional copy. $5.00 for first page certified, $.25 for each additional page. Search information required: name, years to search. Only records from 1980 to the present are accessible.

Civil records are available by mail or phone. No release necessary. $5.00 search fee. $3.50 fee for first copy, $.25 for each additional copy. $5.00 for first page certified, $.25 for each additional page. Search information required: name, years to search. Specify plaintiff or defendant.

Sherburne County

Court Administrator, Criminal Records
Sherburne County Courthouse
PO Box 318
Elk River, MN 55330
(612) 241-2800

Felony and misdemeanor records are available by mail or phone. No release necessary. $5.00 search fee. $3.50 fee for first copy, $.25 for each additional copy. $5.00 for first page certified, $.25 for each additional page. Make check payable to Court Administrator. Search information required: full name, date of birth, years to search.

Civil records are available by mail or phone. No release necessary. $5.00 search fee. $3.50 fee for first copy, $.25 for each additional copy. $5.00 for first page certified, $.25 for each additional page. Search information required: name, years to search. Specify plaintiff or defendant.

Sibley County

Sibley County Court Administrator, Criminal Records
PO Box 867
Gaylord, MN 55334
(612) 237-2427

Felony and misdemeanor records are available by mail. No release necessary. $5.00 search fee. Search information required: name, date of birth, years to search.

Civil records are available by mail. No release necessary. $5.00 search fee. $3.50 fee for first copy, $.25 for each additional copy. $5.00 for first page certified, $.25 for each additional page. Search information required: name, years to search. Specify plaintiff or defendant.

Stearns County

Court Administrator, Criminal
Records
Stearns County
PO Box 1378
St. Cloud, MN 56302
(612) 656-3620
Fax (612) 656-3626
Felony and misdemeanor records are available by mail or fax. No release necessary.
$5.00 fee. Make check payable to Court
Adminisrator. Search information required:
name, date of birth, years to search.

Civil records are available by mail or fax.
No release necessary. $5.00 search fee.
$3.50 fee for first copy, $.25 for each additional copy. $5.00 for first page certified,
$.25 for each additional page. Search information required: name, years to search.
Specify plaintiff or defendant.

Steele County

Steele County Courthouse, Criminal
Records
PO Box 487
District Court
Owatonna, MN 55060
(507) 451-8040
Felony and misdemeanor records are available by mail or phone. No release necessary. $5.00 search fee. $3.00 fee for first
copy, $.25 for each additional copy. $5.00
for first page certified, $.25 for each additional page. Search information required:
name, years to search.

Civil records are available by mail. No release necessary. $5.00 search fee. $3.00 fee
for first copy, $.25 for each additional copy.
$5.00 for first page certified, $.25 for each
additional page. Search information required: name, years to search. Specify
plaintiff or defendant.

Stevens County

Court Administrator, Criminal
Records
PO Box 530
Stevens County Courthouse
Morris, MN 56267
(612) 589-4764
Fax (612) 589-4764
Felony and misdemeanor records are available by mail, phone or fax. No release necessary. No search fee. Search information
required: name, date of birth.

Civil records are available by mail. No release necessary. $5.00 search fee. $3.50 fee
for first copy, $.25 for each additional copy.
$5.00 for first page certified, $.25 for each
additional page. Search information required: name, years to search. Specify
plaintiff or defendant.

St. Louis County

Court Administrator, Criminal
Records
100 N. 5th Ave. W. #320
Duluth, MN 55802-1294
(218) 726-2442
Felony and misdemeanor records are available by mail. No release necessary. $5.00
search fee. Make check payable to Court
Adnministrator. Search information required: full name, date of birth.

Civil records are available by mail. No release necessary. $5.00 search fee. $3.50 fee
for first copy, $.25 for each additional copy.
$5.00 for first page certified, $.25 for each
additional page. Search information required: name, years to search. Specify
plaintiff or defendant.

Swift County

Court Administrator, Criminal
Records
PO Box 110
Benson, MN 56215
(612) 843-2744
Felony and misdemeanor records are available in person only. See Minnesota state
repository for additional information.

Civil records are available in person only.
See Minnesota state repository for additional information.

Todd County

District Court, Criminal Records
Todd County Courthouse
215 1st Ave. So.
Long Prairie, MN 56347
(612) 732-4460
Fax (612) 732-2506
Felony and misdemeanor records are available by mail. No release necessary. $5.00
search fee. Search information required:
name, date of birth, years to search.

Civil records are available by mail. No release necessary. $5.00 search fee. $3.50 fee
for first copy, $.25 for each additional copy.
$5.00 for first page certified, $.25 for each
additional page. Search information required: name, years to search. Specify
plaintiff or defendant.

Traverse County

Traverse County Courthouse, Criminal
Records
Wheaton, MN 56296
(612) 563-4343
Fax (612) 563-4311
Felony and misdemeanor records are available in person only. See Minnesota state
repository for additional information.

Civil records are available in person only.
See Minnesota state repository for additional information.

Wabasha County

Wabasha County District Court,
Criminal Records
Wabasha County Courthouse
Wabasha, MN 55981
(612) 565-3579 or 4070
Fax (612) 565-2774
Felony and misdemeanor records are available by mail. No release necessary. $5.00
search fee. $3.50 fee for first copy, $.25 for
each additional copy. $5.00 for first page
certified, $.25 for each additional page.
Search information required: name, date of
birth, years to search.

Civil records are available by mail. No release necessary. $5.00 search fee. $3.50 fee
for first copy, $.25 for each additional copy.
$5.00 for first page certified, $.25 for each
additional page. Search information required: name, years to search. Specify
plaintiff or defendant.

Wadena County

Court Administrator, Criminal
Records
Wadena County Courthouse
Wadena, MN 56482
(218) 631-2895
Felony and misdemeanor records are available by mail. No release necessary. $5.00
search fee. Search information required:
name, date of birth, years to search.

Civil records are available by mail. No release necessary. $5.00 search fee. $5.00 for
first copy, $.25 for each additional
page. Search information required: name,
years to search. Specify plaintiff or defendant.

Waseca County

Court Administrator, Criminal
Records
Courthouse
Waseca, MN 56093
(507) 835-0540
Fax (507) 835-0633
Felony and misdemeanor records are available by mail. No release necessary. $5.00
search fee. $3.50 fee for first copy, $.25 for
each additional copy. $5.00 for first page
certified, $.25 for each additional page.
Search information required: name, date of
birth, SASE, years to search.

Civil records are available by mail. No release necessary. $5.00 search fee. $3.50 fee
for first copy, $.25 for each additional copy.
$5.00 for first page certified, $.25 for each
additional page. Search information required: name, years to search. Specify
plaintiff or defendant.

Washington County

Washington County Government
Center
Court Administrator, Criminal
Division
14900 61st Street North
Stillwater, MN 55082-0006
(612) 439-3220
Felony and misdemeanor records are available by mail. No release necessary. $5.00
search fee. $3.50 fee for first copy, $.25 for
each additional copy. $5.00 for first page
certified, $.25 for each additional page.
Make check payable to Court
Administrator. Search information required:
name, date of birth.

Civil records are available by mail. No release necessary. $5.00 search fee. $3.50 fee
for first copy, $.25 for each additional copy.
$5.00 for first page certified, $.25 for each
additional page. Search information required: name, years to search. Specify
plaintiff or defendant.

Watonwan County

Court Administrator, Criminal
Records
Courthouse
St. James, MN 56081
(507) 375-3341 Extension 238
Fax (507) 375-5010
Felony and misdemeanor records are available by mail. No release necessary. $5.00
search fee. Search information required:
name.

Civil records are available by mail. No release necessary. $10.00 search fee. $3.50 fee for first copy, $.25 for each additional copy. $5.00 for first page certified, $.25 for each additional page. Search information required: name, years to search. Specify plaintiff or defendant.

Wilkin County

Wilkin County Courthouse
Criminal Records, PO Box 219
Breckenridge, MN 56520
(218) 643-4972
Fax (218) 643-5733

Felony and misdemeanor records are available by mail or fax. No release necessary. No search fee. $3.50 fee for first copy, $.25 for each additional copy. $5.00 for first page certified, $.25 for each additional page. Search information required: name, years to search.

Civil records are available by mail or fax. No release necessary. $5.00 search fee. $3.50 fee for first copy, $.25 for each additional copy. $5.00 for first page certified, $.25 for each additional page. Search information required: name, years to search. Specify plaintiff or defendant.

Winona County

Court Administrator, Criminal Records
Winona County Courthouse
Winona, MN 55987
(507) 457-6375

Felony and misdemeanor records are available by mail. No release necessary. $5.00 search fee. Check payable to Court Administrator. Search information required: name, date of birth. Turnaround time 5-7 working days.

Civil records are available by mail. No release necessary. $5.00 search fee. $3.50 fee for first copy, $.25 for each additional copy. $5.00 for first page certified, $.25 for each additional page. Search information required: name, date of birth, years to search. Specify plaintiff or defendant.

Wright County

Court Administrator, Criminal Records
Wright County Government Center
10 NW 2nd Street
Buffalo, MN 55313
(612) 682-7541

Felony and misdemeanor records are avail-
able by mail. No release necessary. $5.00 search fee. Make check payable to Clerk Administrator. Search information required: name, date of birth.

Civil records are available by mail. No release necessary. $5.00 search fee. $3.50 fee for first copy, $.25 for each additional copy. $5.00 for first page certified, $.25 for each additional page. Search information required: name, years to search. Specify plaintiff or defendant.

Yellow Medicine County

Court Administrator, Criminal Records
Yellow Medicine County
Granite Falls, MN 56241
(612) 564-3325
Fax (612) 564-4435

Felony and misdemeanor records are available in person only. See Minnesota state repository for additional information.

Civil records are available by mail. A release is required. $5.00 search fee. $3.50 fee for first copy, $.25 for each additional copy. $5.00 for first page certified, $.25 for each additional page. Search information required: name, years to search. Specify plaintiff or defendant.

City-County Cross Reference

Ada *Norman*
Adams *Mower*
Adolph *Saint Louis*
Adrian *Nobles*
Afton *Washington*
Ah-Gwah-Ching *Cass*
Aitkin *Aitkin*
Akeley *Hubbard*
Albany *Stearns*
Alberta *Stevens*
Albert Lea *Freeborn*
Albertville *Wright*
Alborn *Saint Louis*
Alden *Freeborn*
Aldrich *Wadena*
Alexandria *Douglas*
Alpha *Jackson*
Altura *Winona*
Alvarado *Marshall*
Amboy *Blue Earth*
Amiret *Lyon*
Andover *Anoka*
Angle Inlet *Lake Of The Woods*
Angora *Saint Louis*
Angus *Polk*
Annandale *Wright*
Anoka *Anoka*
Appleton *Swift*
Apple Valley *Dakota*
Arco *Lincoln*
Argyle *Marshall*
Arlington *Sibley*
Arnold *Saint Louis*
Ashby *Grant*
Askov *Pine*
Atwater *Kandiyohi*
Audubon *Becker*
Aurora *Saint Louis*
Austin *Mower*
Avoca *Murray*
Avon *Stearns*

Babbitt *Saint Louis*
Backus *Cass*
Badger *Roseau*
Bagley *Clearwater*
Baker *Clay*
Balaton *Lyon*
Bald Eagle *Ramsey*
Barnesville *Clay*
Barnum *Carlton*
Barrett *Grant*
Battle Lake *Otter Tail*
Baudette *Lake Of The Woods*
Bayport *Washington*
Beardsley *Big Stone*
Beaver Bay *Lake*
Beaver Creek *Rock*
Becker *Sherburne*
Bejou *Mahnomen*
Belgrade *Stearns*
Bellaire *Ramsey*
Belle Plaine *Scott*
Bellingham *Lac Qui Parle*
Beltrami *Polk*
Belview *Redwood*
Bemidji *Beltrami*
Bena *Cass*
Benedict *Hubbard*
Benson *Swift*
Beroun *Pine*
Bertha *Todd*
Bethel *Anoka*
Bigelow *Nobles*
Big Falls *Koochiching*
Bigfork *Itasca*
Big Lake *Sherburne*
Bingham Lake *Cottonwood*
Birchdale *Koochiching*
Birchwood Village *Washington*
Bird Island *Renville*
Biwabik *Saint Louis*

Blackduck *Beltrami*
Blaine *Anoka*
Blomkest *Kandiyohi*
Blooming Prairie *Steele*
Bloomington *Hennepin*
Blue Earth *Faribault*
Bluffton *Otter Tail*
Bock *Mille Lacs*
Borup *Norman*
Bovey *Itasca*
Bowlus *Morrison*
Bowstring *Itasca*
Boyd *Lac Qui Parle*
Boy River *Cass*
Braham *Isanti*
Brainerd *Crow Wing*
Branch *Chisago*
Brandon *Douglas*
Breckenridge *Wilkin*
Brewster *Nobles*
Bricelyn *Faribault*
Brimson *Saint Louis*
Britt *Saint Louis*
Brooklyn Center *Hennepin*
Brooklyn Park *Hennepin*
Brook Park *Pine*
Brooks *Red Lake*
Brookston *Saint Louis*
Brooten *Stearns*
Browerville *Todd*
Brownsdale *Mower*
Browns Valley *Traverse*
Brownsville *Houston*
Brownton *McLeod*
Bruno *Pine*
Buckman *Morrison*
Buffalo *Wright*
Buffalo Lake *Renville*
Buhl *Saint Louis*
Burnsville *Dakota*
Burtrum *Todd*
Butterfield *Watonwan*

Byron *Olmsted*
Caledonia *Houston*
Callaway *Becker*
Calumet *Itasca*
Cambridge *Isanti*
Campbell *Wilkin*
Canby *Yellow Medicine*
Cannon Falls *Goodhue*
Canton *Fillmore*
Canyon *Saint Louis*
Carlos *Douglas*
Carlton *Carlton*
Carver *Carver*
Cass Lake *Cass*
Castle Rock *Dakota*
Cedar *Anoka*
Center City *Chisago*
Centerville *Anoka*
Ceylon *Martin*
Champlin *Hennepin*
Chandler *Murray*
Chanhassen *Carver*
Chaska *Carver*
Chatfield *Fillmore*
Chisago City *Chisago*
Chisholm *Saint Louis*
Chokio *Stevens*
Circle Pines *Anoka*
Clara City *Chippewa*
Claremont *Dodge*
Clarissa *Todd*
Clarkfield *Yellow Medicine*
Clarks Grove *Freeborn*
Clearbrook *Clearwater*
Clear Lake *Sherburne*
Clearwater *Wright*
Clements *Redwood*
Cleveland *Le Sueur*
Climax *Polk*
Clinton *Big Stone*
Clitherall *Otter Tail*
Clontarf *Swift*

Cloquet *Carlton*
Cohasset *Itasca*
Cokato *Wright*
Cold Spring *Stearns*
Coleraine *Itasca*
Collegeville *Stearns*
Cologne *Carver*
Columbia Heights *Anoka*
Comfrey *Brown*
Comstock *Clay*
Conger *Freeborn*
Cook *Saint Louis*
Coon Rapids *Anoka*
Corcoran *Hennepin*
Correll *Big Stone*
Cosmos *Meeker*
Cottage Grove *Washington*
Cotton *Saint Louis*
Cottonwood *Lyon*
Courtland *Nicollet*
Crane Lake *Saint Louis*
Cromwell *Carlton*
Crookston *Polk*
Crosby *Crow Wing*
Crosslake *Crow Wing*
Crystal *Hennepin*
Crystal Bay *Hennepin*
Culver *Saint Louis*
Currie *Murray*
Cushing *Morrison*
Cyrus *Pope*
Dakota *Winona*
Dalbo *Isanti*
Dalton *Otter Tail*
Danube *Renville*
Danvers *Swift*
Darfur *Watonwan*
Darwin *Meeker*
Dassel *Meeker*
Dawson *Lac Qui Parle*
Dayton *Hennepin*
Deephaven *Hennepin*
Deer Creek *Otter Tail*
Deer River *Itasca*
Deerwood *Crow Wing*
DeGraff *Swift*
Delano *Wright*
Delavan *Faribault*
Delft *Cottonwood*
Dellwood *Ramsey*
Dennison *Goodhue*
Dent *Otter Tail*
Detroit Lakes *Becker*
Dexter *Mower*
Dilworth *Clay*
Dodge Center *Dodge*
Donaldson *Kittson*
Donnelly *Stevens*
Doran *Wilkin*
Dover *Olmsted*
Dovray *Murray*
Duluth *Saint Louis*
Dumont *Traverse*
Dundas *Rice*
Dundee *Nobles*
Dunnell *Martin*
Eagan *Dakota*
Eagle Bend *Todd*
Eagle Lake *Blue Earth*
East Bethel *Anoka*
East Grand Forks *Polk*
Easton *Faribault*
Echo *Yellow Medicine*
Eden Prairie *Hennepin*
Eden Valley *Meeker*

Edgerton *Pipestone*
Edina *Hennepin*
Effie *Itasca*
Eitzen *Houston*
Elbow Lake *Grant*
Elgin *Wabasha*
Elko *Scott*
Elk River *Sherburne*
Elkton *Mower*
Ellendale *Steele*
Ellsworth *Nobles*
Elmore *Faribault*
Elrosa *Stearns*
Ely *Saint Louis*
Elysian *Le Sueur*
Embarrass *Saint Louis*
Emily *Crow Wing*
Emmons *Freeborn*
Erhard *Otter Tail*
Erskine *Polk*
Esko *Carlton*
Euclid *Polk*
Evan *Brown*
Evansville *Douglas*
Eveleth *Saint Louis*
Excelsior *Hennepin*
Eyota *Olmsted*
Fairfax *Renville*
Fairmont *Martin*
Falcon Heights *Ramsey*
Faribault *Rice*
Farmington *Dakota*
Farwell *Pope*
Federal Dam *Cass*
Felton *Clay*
Fergus Falls *Otter Tail*
Fertile *Polk*
Fifty Lakes *Crow Wing*
Finland *Lake*
Finlayson *Pine*
Fisher *Polk*
Flensburg *Morrison*
Flom *Norman*
Floodwood *Saint Louis*
Florence *Lyon*
Foley *Benton*
Forbes *Saint Louis*
Forest Lake *Washington*
Foreston *Mille Lacs*
Fort Ripley *Crow Wing*
Fosston *Polk*
Fountain *Fillmore*
Foxhome *Wilkin*
Franklin *Renville*
Frazee *Becker*
Freeborn *Freeborn*
Freeport *Stearns*
Frontenac *Goodhue*
Fridley *Anoka*
Frost *Faribault*
Fulda *Murray*
Garden City *Blue Earth*
Garfield *Douglas*
Garrison *Crow Wing*
Garvin *Lyon*
Gary *Norman*
Gaylord *Sibley*
Geneva *Freeborn*
Georgetown *Clay*
Gheen *Saint Louis*
Ghent *Lyon*
Gibbon *Sibley*
Gilbert *Saint Louis*
Gilman *Benton*
Glencoe *McLeod*

Glenville *Freeborn*
Glenwood *Pope*
Glyndon *Clay*
Golden Valley *Hennepin*
Gonvick *Clearwater*
Goodhue *Goodhue*
Goodland *Itasca*
Goodridge *Pennington*
Good Thunder *Blue Earth*
Goodview *Winona*
Graceville *Big Stone*
Granada *Martin*
Grand Marais *Cook*
Grand Meadow *Mower*
Grand Portage *Cook*
Grand Rapids *Itasca*
Grandy *Isanti*
Granger *Fillmore*
Granite Falls *Yellow Medicine*
Grasston *Kanabec*
Greenbush *Roseau*
Green Isle *Sibley*
Greenwald *Stearns*
Grey Eagle *Todd*
Grove City *Meeker*
Grygla *Marshall*
Gully *Polk*
Hackensack *Cass*
Hadley *Murray*
Hallock *Kittson*
Halma *Kittson*
Halstad *Norman*
Hamburg *Carver*
Hamel *Hennepin*
Hampton *Dakota*
Hancock *Stevens*
Hanley Falls *Yellow Medicine*
Hanover *Wright*
Hanska *Brown*
Hardwick *Rock*
Harmony *Fillmore*
Harris *Chisago*
Hartland *Freeborn*
Hastings *Dakota*
Hatfield *Pipestone*
Hawick *Kandiyohi*
Hawley *Clay*
Hayfield *Dodge*
Hayward *Freeborn*
Hazel Run *Yellow Medicine*
Hector *Renville*
Henderson *Sibley*
Hendricks *Lincoln*
Hendrum *Norman*
Henning *Otter Tail*
Herman *Grant*
Hermantown *Saint Louis*
Heron Lake *Jackson*
Hewitt *Todd*
Hibbing *Saint Louis*
Hill City *Aitkin*
Hillman *Morrison*
Hills *Rock*
Hilltop *Anoka*
Hinckley *Pine*
Hines *Beltrami*
Hitterdal *Clay*
Hoffman *Grant*
Hokah *Houston*
Holdingford *Stearns*
Holland *Pipestone*
Hollandale *Freeborn*

Holloway *Swift*
Holmes City *Douglas*
Holyoke *Carlton*
Hope *Steele*
Hopkins *Hennepin*
Houston *Houston*
Hovland *Cook*
Howard Lake *Wright*
Hoyt Lakes *Saint Louis*
Hugo *Washington*
Humboldt *Kittson*
Huntley *Faribault*
Hutchinson *McLeod*
Independence *Hennepin*
International Falls *Koochiching*
Inver Grove Heights *Dakota*
Iona *Murray*
Iron *Saint Louis*
Ironton *Crow Wing*
Isanti *Isanti*
Isle *Mille Lacs*
Ivanhoe *Lincoln*
Jackson *Jackson*
Jacobson *Aitkin*
Janesville *Waseca*
Jasper *Pipestone*
Jeffers *Cottonwood*
Johnson *Big Stone*
Jordan *Scott*
Kanaranzi *Rock*
Kandiyohi *Kandiyohi*
Karlstad *Kittson*
Kasota *Le Sueur*
Kasson *Dodge*
Keewatin *Itasca*
Kelliher *Beltrami*
Kellogg *Wabasha*
Kelly Lake *Saint Louis*
Kelsey *Saint Louis*
Kennedy *Kittson*
Kenneth *Rock*
Kensington *Douglas*
Kent *Wilkin*
Kenyon *Goodhue*
Kerkhoven *Swift*
Kerrick *Pine*
Kettle River *Carlton*
Kiester *Faribault*
Kilkenny *Le Sueur*
Kimball *Stearns*
Kinney *Saint Louis*
Knife River *Lake*
LaCrescent *Houston*
Lafayette *Nicollet*
Lake Benton *Lincoln*
Lake Bronson *Kittson*
Lake City *Wabasha*
Lake Crystal *Blue Earth*
Lake Elmo *Washington*
Lakefield *Jackson*
Lake George *Hubbard*
Lake Hubert *Crow Wing*
Lake Itasca *Clearwater*
Lakeland *Washington*
Lake Lillian *Kandiyohi*
Lake Park *Becker*
Lakeville *Dakota*
Lake Wilson *Murray*
Lamberton *Redwood*
Lancaster *Kittson*
Landfall Village *Washington*
Lanesboro *Fillmore*

Lansing *Mower*
Laporte *Hubbard*
LaSalle *Watonwan*
Lastrup *Morrison*
Lauderdale *Ramsey*
Le Center *Le Sueur*
Lengby *Polk*
Leonard *Clearwater*
Leota *Nobles*
Le Roy *Mower*
Lester Prairie *McLeod*
Le Sueur *Le Sueur*
Lewiston *Winona*
Lewisville *Watonwan*
Lexington *Anoka*
Lindstrom *Chisago*
Lino Lakes *Anoka*
Lismore *Nobles*
Litchfield *Meeker*
Little Canada *Ramsey*
Little Falls *Morrison*
Littlefork *Koochiching*
Little Sauk *Todd*
Loman *Koochiching*
London *Freeborn*
Long Lake *Hennepin*
Long Prairie *Todd*
Longville *Cass*
Lonsdale *Rice*
Loretto *Hennepin*
Louisburg *Lac Qui Parle*
Lowry *Pope*
Lucan *Redwood*
Lutsen *Cook*
Luverne *Rock*
Lyle *Mower*
Lynd *Lyon*
McGrath *Aitkin*
McGregor *Aitkin*
Mcintosh *Polk*
McKinley *Saint Louis*
Mabel *Fillmore*
Madelia *Watonwan*
Madison *Lac Qui Parle*
Madison Lake *Blue Earth*
Magnolia *Rock*
Mahnomen *Mahnomen*
Mahtomedi *Washington*
Mahtowa *Carlton*
Makinen *Saint Louis*
Manhattan Beach *Crow
 Wing*
Mankato *Blue Earth*
Mantorville *Dodge*
Maple Grove *Hennepin*
Maple Lake *Wright*
Maple Plain *Hennepin*
Mapleton *Blue Earth*
Maplewood *Ramsey*
Marble *Itasca*
Marcell *Itasca*
Marietta *Lac Qui Parle*
Marine On Saint Croix
 Washington
Markville *Pine*
Marshall *Lyon*
Max *Itasca*
Mayer *Carver*
Maynard *Chippewa*
Mazeppa *Wabasha*
Meadowlands *Saint Louis*
Medford *Steele*
Melrose *Stearns*
Menahga *Wadena*
Mendota Heights *Dakota*

Mentor *Polk*
Meriden *Steele*
Merrifield *Crow Wing*
Middle River *Marshall*
Milaca *Mille Lacs*
Milan *Chippewa*
Millville *Wabasha*
Milroy *Redwood*
Miltona *Douglas*
Minneapolis *Hennepin*
Minneota *Lyon*
Minnesota City *Winona*
Minnesota Lake *Faribault*
Minnetonka *Hennepin*
Mizpah *Koochiching*
Montevideo *Chippewa*
Montgomery *Le Sueur*
Monticello *Wright*
Montrose *Wright*
Moorhead *Clay*
Moose Lake *Carlton*
Mora *Kanabec*
Morgan *Redwood*
Morris *Stevens*
Morristown *Rice*
Morton *Renville*
Motley *Morrison*
Mound *Hennepin*
Mounds View *Ramsey*
Mountain Iron *Saint Louis*
Mountain Lake
 Cottonwood
Murdock *Swift*
Myrtle *Freeborn*
Nashwauk *Itasca*
Nassau *Lac Qui Parle*
Naytahwaush *Mahnomen*
Nelson *Douglas*
Nerstrand *Rice*
Nevis *Hubbard*
New Auburn *Sibley*
New Brighton *Ramsey*
Newfolden *Marshall*
New Germany *Carver*
New Hope *Hennepin*
New London *Kandiyohi*
New Market *Scott*
New Munich *Stearns*
Newport *Washington*
New Prague *Le Sueur*
New Richland *Waseca*
New Ulm *Brown*
New York Mills *Otter Tail*
Nicollet *Nicollet*
Nielsville *Polk*
Nisswa *Crow Wing*
Norcross *Grant*
North Branch *Chisago*
Northfield *Rice*
North Mankato *Nicollet*
North Oaks *Ramsey*
Northome *Koochiching*
North Saint Paul *Ramsey*
Norwood *Carver*
Noyes *Kittson*
Oakdale *Ramsey*
Oak Island *Lake Of The
 Woods*
Oakland *Freeborn*
Oklee *Red Lake*
Oak Park *Benton*
Odessa *Big Stone*
Odin *Watonwan*
Ogema *Becker*
Ogilvie *Kanabec*

Okabena *Jackson*
Oklee *Red Lake*
Olivia *Renville*
Onamia *Mille Lacs*
Ormsby *Watonwan*
Oronoco *Olmsted*
Orr *Saint Louis*
Ortonville *Big Stone*
Osage *Becker*
Osakis *Douglas*
Oslo *Marshall*
Osseo *Hennepin*
Ostrander *Fillmore*
Otisco *Waseca*
Ottertail *Otter Tail*
Outing *Cass*
Owatonna *Steele*
Palisade *Aitkin*
Parkers Prairie *Otter Tail*
Park Rapids *Hubbard*
Parkville *Saint Louis*
Paynesville *Stearns*
Pease *Mille Lacs*
Pelican Rapids *Otter Tail*
Pemberton *Blue Earth*
Pengilly *Itasca*
Pennington *Beltrami*
Pennock *Kandiyohi*
Pequot Lakes *Crow Wing*
Perham *Otter Tail*
Perley *Norman*
Peterson *Fillmore*
Pierz *Morrison*
Pillager *Cass*
Pine City *Pine*
Pine Island *Goodhue*
Pine River *Cass*
Pipestone *Pipestone*
Pitt *Lake Of The Woods*
Plainview *Wabasha*
Plato *McLeod*
Plummer *Red Lake*
Plymouth *Hennepin*
Ponemah *Beltrami*
Ponsford *Becker*
Porter *Yellow Medicine*
Preston *Fillmore*
Princeton *Mille Lacs*
Prinsburg *Kandiyohi*
Prior Lake *Scott*
Proctor *Saint Louis*
Puposky *Beltrami*
Racine *Mower*
Ramsey *Anoka*
Randall *Morrison*
Randolph *Dakota*
Ranier *Koochiching*
Ray *Koochiching*
Raymond *Kandiyohi*
Reads Landing *Wabasha*
Redby *Beltrami*
Redlake *Beltrami*
Red Lake Falls *Red Lake*
Red Wing *Goodhue*
Redwood Falls *Redwood*
Remer *Cass*
Renville *Renville*
Revere *Redwood*
Rice *Benton*
Richfield *Hennepin*
Richmond *Stearns*
Richville *Otter Tail*
Robbinsdale *Hennepin*
Rochester *Olmsted*
Rockford *Wright*

Rockville *Stearns*
Rogers *Hennepin*
Rollingstone *Winona*
Roosevelt *Roseau*
Roscoe *Stearns*
Roseau *Roseau*
Rose Creek *Mower*
Rosemount *Dakota*
Roseville *Ramsey*
Rothsay *Wilkin*
Round Lake *Nobles*
Royalton *Morrison*
Rush City *Chisago*
Rushford *Fillmore*
Rushmore *Nobles*
Russell *Lyon*
Ruthton *Pipestone*
Rutledge *Pine*
Sabin *Clay*
Sacred Heart *Renville*
Saginaw *Saint Louis*
Saint Anthony *Hennepin*
Saint Bonifacius *Hennepin*
Saint Charles *Winona*
Saint Clair *Blue Earth*
Saint Cloud *Stearns*
Saint Francis *Anoka*
Saint Hilaire *Pennington*
Saint James *Watonwan*
Saint Joseph *Stearns*
Saint Leo *Yellow Medicine*
Saint Louis Park *Hennepin*
Saint Martin *Stearns*
Saint Michael *Wright*
Saint Paul *Ramsey*
Saint Paul Park
 Washington
Saint Peter *Nicollet*
Saint Vincent *Kittson*
Salol *Roseau*
Sanborn *Redwood*
Sandstone *Pine*
Sargeant *Mower*
Sartell *Stearns*
Sauk Centre *Stearns*
Sauk Rapids *Benton*
Saum *Beltrami*
Savage *Scott*
Sawyer *Carlton*
Scanlon *Carlton*
Scandia *Washington*
Schroeder *Cook*
Seaforth *Redwood*
Sebeka *Wadena*
Sedan *Pope*
Shafer *Chisago*
Shakopee *Scott*
Shelly *Norman*
Sherburn *Martin*
Shevlin *Clearwater*
Shoreview *Ramsey*
Shorewood *Carver*
Side Lake *Saint Louis*
Silver Bay *Lake*
Silver Creek *Wright*
Silver Lake *McLeod*
Slayton *Murray*
Sleepy Eye *Brown*
Solway *Beltrami*
Soudan *Saint Louis*
South Haven *Wright*
South International Falls
 Koochiching
South Saint Paul *Dakota*
Spicer *Kandiyohi*

Springfield *Brown*
Spring Grove *Houston*
Spring Lake *Itasca*
Spring Lake Park *Anoka*
Spring Park *Hennepin*
Spring Valley *Fillmore*
Squaw Lake *Itasca*
Stacy *Chisago*
Stanchfield *Isanti*
Staples *Todd*
Starbuck *Pope*
Steen *Rock*
Stephen *Marshall*
Stewart *McLeod*
Stewartville *Olmsted*
Stillwater *Washington*
Storden *Cottonwood*
Strandquist *Marshall*
Strathcona *Roseau*
Sturgeon Lake *Pine*
Sunburg *Kandiyohi*
Svea *Kandiyohi*
Swan River *Itasca*
Swanville *Morrison*
Swatara *Aitkin*
Taconite *Itasca*
Tamarack *Aitkin*
Taopi *Mower*
Taunton *Lyon*
Taylors Falls *Chisago*
Tenstrike *Beltrami*
Theilman *Wabasha*
Thief River Falls *Pennington*
Tintah *Traverse*
Tofte *Cook*
Tower *Saint Louis*
Tracy *Lyon*
Trail *Polk*
Trimont *Martin*
Trosky *Pipestone*
Truman *Martin*
Twig *Saint Louis*
Twin Lakes *Freeborn*
Twin Valley *Norman*
Two Harbors *Lake*
Tyler *Lincoln*
Ulen *Clay*
Underwood *Otter Tail*
Upsala *Morrison*
Utica *Winona*
Vadnais Heights *Ramsey*
Verdi *Lincoln*
Vergas *Otter Tail*
Vermillion *Dakota*
Verndale *Wadena*
Vernon Center *Blue Earth*
Vesta *Redwood*
Victoria *Carver*
Viking *Marshall*
Villard *Pope*
Vining *Otter Tail*
Virginia *Saint Louis*
Wabasha *Wabasha*
Wabasso *Redwood*
Waconia *Carver*
Wadena *Wadena*
Wahkon *Mille Lacs*
Waite Park *Benton*
Waldorf *Waseca*
Walker *Cass*
Walnut Grove *Redwood*
Walters *Faribault*
Waltham *Mower*
Wanamingo *Goodhue*

Wanda *Redwood*
Wannaska *Roseau*
Warba *Itasca*
Warren *Marshall*
Warroad *Roseau*
Warsaw *Rice*
Waseca *Waseca*
Waskish *Beltrami*
Watertown *Carver*
Waterville *Le Sueur*
Watkins *Meeker*
Watson *Chippewa*
Waubun *Mahnomen*
Waverly *Wright*
Wawina *Itasca*
Wayzata *Hennepin*
Webster *Rice*
Welch *Goodhue*
Welcome *Martin*
Wells *Faribault*
Wendell *Grant*
Westbrook *Cottonwood*
West Concord *Dodge*
West Saint Paul Dakota
Whalan *Fillmore*
Wheaton *Traverse*
Whipholt *Cass*
White Bear Beach *Ramsey*
White Bear Lake *Ramsey*
White Earth *Becker*
Wilder *Jackson*
Willernie *Washington*
Williams *Lake Of The Woods*
Willmar *Kandiyohi*
Willow River *Pine*
Wilmont *Nobles*
Wilton *Beltrami*
Windom *Cottonwood*
Winger *Polk*
Winnebago *Faribault*
Winona *Winona*
Winsted *McLeod*
Winthrop *Sibley*
Winton *Saint Louis*
Wolf Lake *Becker*
Wolverton *Wilkin*
Woodbury *Washington*
Wood Lake *Yellow Medicine*
Woodland *Hennepin*
Woodstock *Pipestone*
Worthington *Nobles*
Wrenshall *Carlton*
Wright *Carlton*
Wykoff *Fillmore*
Wyoming *Chisago*
Young America *Carver*
Zim *Saint Louis*
Zimmerman *Sherburne*
Zumbro Falls *Wabasha*
Zumbrota *Goodhue*

Mississippi

Of Mississippi's eighty two (82) counties, seventy eighty (78) reported that they release conviction records for employment screening purposes by phone or mail.

For more information or for offices not listed, contact the state's information hot line at (601) 359-1000.

Driving Records

Mississippi Highway Patrol
Driver Records
PO Box 958
Jackson, MS 39205
(601) 987-1274
Driving records are available by mail. $7.00 fee per request. Turnaround time is 2 days. Written request must include job applicants full name, license number, and social security number (if different than license number) must include SASE. Make check payable to Mississippi Highway Patrol.

Worker's Compensation Records

Mississippi Worker's Compensation Records Department
PO Box 5300
Jackson, MS 39296-5300
(601) 987-4252
Worker's Compensation records are not available for pre-employment screening purposes. Present claims are only available by either the employee involved or the carrier.

Vital Statistics

Vital Records
State Department of Health
PO Box 1700
Jackson, MS 39215-1700
(601) 960-7981
Long form birth records are available for $12.00. Short form birth records are available each for $7.00. Full copies of birth certificates obtained within 1 year after the event are $ 7.00. Duplicates ordered at same time are $3.00 each. Marriage and divorce records are available at $10.00 for the first copy, $2.00 each for additional copies. An employer can obtain records with a written release. Make company check or money order (which must come from a bank or a post office) payable to Mississippi State Department of Health.

Department of Education

Department of Education
Teacher Certification
PO Box 771
Jackson, MS 39205
(601) 359-3483
Field of certification and expiration date are available by phone or mail. Include name and SSN.

Medical Licensing

Medical Licensing Board
2688 D Insurance Center Drive
Jackson, MS 39216
(601) 354-6645
Fax (601) 987-4159
Will confirm licenses for MDs and DOs by phone or mail. No fee. For licenses not mentioned, contact the above office.

Mississippi Board of Nursing
239 N. Lamar St., Suite 401
Jackson, MS 39201
(601) 359-6170
Will confirm license by phone. No fee. Include name, DOB or license number.

Bar Association

Mississippi State Bar Association
PO Box 2168
Jackson, MS 39225-2168
(601) 948-4471
Will confirm licenses by phone. No fee. Include name.

Accountancy Board

Mississippi State Board of Accountancy
961 Highway 80 East
Clinton, MS 39056-5246
(601) 924-8457
Will confirm license by phone. No fee. Include name.

Securities Commission

Office of Secretary of State
Securities Department
PO Box 136
Jackson, MS 39205
(601) 359-6363
Will confirm license by phone. No fee. Include name and SSN.

Secretary of State

Secretary of State
Corporation Division
202 N. Congress St.
Suite 601
Jackson, MS 39201
(601) 359-1633
Service agent and address, date incorporated, trade names are available by phone or mail. Contact the above office for additional information.

Criminal Records

State Repository

Records Department
PO Box 880
Parchman, MS 38738
(601) 745-6611 Ext. 2321
Criminal record checks are available by mail only. Each request must include subject's full name, date of birth, sex and SSN. There is no fee for searches. Only conviction data available.

Adams County

Circuit Clerk
PO Box 1224
Natchez, MS 39121
(601) 446-6326
Felony and misdemeanor records are available by mail or phone. No release necessary. No search fee. Search information required: name, years to search.

Civil records are available by mail. No release necessary. $5.00 search fee for first 5 years searched. $10.00 search fee for each 5 years searched thereafter. $1.00 fee per copy. $1.00 for certification. Search information required: name, years to search. Specify plaintiff or defendant.

Alcorn County

Felony records
Circuit Clerk, Criminal Records
PO Box 430
Corinth, MS 38834
(601) 286-7740
Fax (601) 286-5713
Felony records are available by mail. No release necessary. No search fee. Search information required: name, years to search.

Civil records
Circuit Clerk
PO Box 430
Corinth, MS 38834
(601) 286-7740
Fax (601) 286-5713
Civil records are available in person only. See Mississippi state repository for additional information.

Misdemeanor records
Justice Court
PO Box 226
Corinth, MS 38834
(601) 286-7776
Misdemeanor records are available in person only. see Mississippi state repository for additional information.

Civil records
Justice Court
PO Box 226
Corinth, MS 38834
(601) 286-7776
Civil records are available in person only. See Mississippi state repository for additional information.

Amite County

Felony records
Circuit Clerk, Criminal Records
PO Box 312
Liberty, MS 39645
(601) 657-8932
Fax (601) 657-8733
Felony records are available by mail, phone or fax. Written request required. No release necessary. $5.00 search fee. Search information required: name, SSN, previous address.

Civil records
Circuit Clerk
PO Box 312
Liberty, MS 39645
(601) 657-8932
Fax (601) 657-8733
Civil records are available by mail, phone or fax. No release necessary. $5.00 search fee. Search information required: name, years to search. Specify plaintiff or defendant.

Misdemeanor records
Justice Court
PO Box 362
Liberty, MS 39645
(601) 657-4527
Misdemeanor records are available by mail or phone. Written request required. Release necessary. Possible fee. Search information required: name, date of birth, driver's license number, years to search.

Civil records
Justice Court
PO Box 362
Liberty, MS 39645
(601) 657-4527
Civil records are available in person only. See Mississippi state repository for additional information.

Attala County

Circuit Clerk, Criminal Records
Attala County Courthouse
118 W. Washington
Kosciusko, MS 39090
(601) 289-1471
Felony records are available by mail or phone. No release necessary. $5.00 search fee. Search information required: name, years to search, date of birth.

Civil records are available by mail. A release is required. $5.00 search fee. $.20 fee per copy. $1.50 for certification. Search information required: name, years to search. Specify plaintiff or defendant.

Benton County

Circuit Clerk, Criminal Records
PO Box 262
Ashland, MS 38603
(601) 224-6310
Felony records are available by mail or phone. No release necessary. $10.00 fee. Certified check or money order, payable to Clerk of Court. Search information required: name, years to search.

Civil records are available by mail. No release necessary. $5.00 search fee. $.50 fee per copy. $1.00 for certification. Search information required: name, years to search. Specify plaintiff or defendant.

Bolivar County

Circuit Clerk, Criminal Records
PO Box 670
Cleveland, MS 38732-0670
(601) 843-2061
Felony and misdemeanor records are available by mail. No release necessary. $5.00 search fee per each 7 years. $.25 fee per copy. $1.50 for certification. Make check payable to Circuit Clerk. Search information required: name, SSN, date of birth, sex, race.

Civil records are available by mail. No release necessary. $5.00 search fee per each 7 years. $.25 fee per copy. $1.50 for certification. Search information required: name, years to search. Specify plaintiff or defendant.

Calhoun County

Circuit Clerk's Office, Debra Dunn
PO Box 25
Pittsboro, MS 38951
(601) 983-3101
Felony and misdemeanor records are available by mail. No release necessary. $10.00 search fee. $.50 fee per copy. Search information required: name, date of birth, SASE.

Civil records are available by mail. No release necessary. $10.00 search fee. $.50 fee per copy. Search information required: name, years to search. Specify plaintiff or defendant.

Carroll County

Felony records
Circuit Clerk, Criminal Records
2nd Judicial District
PO Box 6
Vaiden, MS 39176
(601) 464-5476
Felony records are available by mail. No release necessary. $10.00 search fee. $.50 fee per copy. $1.50 for certification. Make check payable to Circuit Clerk. Search information required: name, years to search.

Civil records
Circuit Clerk
2nd Judicial District
PO Box 6
Vaiden, MS 39176
(601) 464-5476
Civil records are available by mail. No release necessary. $10.00 search fee. $.50 fee per copy. $1.50 for certification. Search information required: name, years to search. Specify plaintiff or defendant.

Misdemeanor records
Justice Court
PO Box 10
Carrollton, MS 38917
(601) 237-9285
Misdemeanor records are available in person only. See Mississippi State Repository for additional information.

Civil records
Justice Court
PO Box 10
Carrollton, MS 38917
(601) 237-9285
Civil records are available in person only. See Mississippi state repository for additional information.

Chickasaw County

Felony records
Circuit Clerk, Criminal Records
PO Box 482
Houston, MS 38851
(601) 456-2331
Felony records are available by mail. No release necessary. Contact the above office to obtain felony record check form. Search information required: name.

Civil records
Circuit Clerk
PO Box 482
Houston, MS 38851
(601) 456-2331
Civil records are available by mail. No release necessary. No search fee. $.50 fee per copy. Search information required: name, years to search. Specify plaintiff or defendant.

Misdemeanor records
Justice Court
Courthouse
Houston, MS 38851
(601) 456-3941
Misdemeanor records are available by mail. No release necessary. No search fee. Search information required: name, offense, years to search.

Civil records
Justice Court
Courthouse
Houston, MS 38851
(601) 456-3941
Civil records are available by mail. No release necessary. No search fee. Search information required: name, years to search. Specify plaintiff or defendant.

Choctaw County

Circuit Clerk, Criminal Records
PO Box 34
Ackerman, MS 39735
(601) 285-6245
Felony and misdemeanor records are available by mail. A release is required. $5.00 search fee. Copying fees range from $.50 - $2.00 per page. Make check payable to Circuit Clerk. Search information required: name, years to search.

Civil records are available by mail. No release necessary. $5.00 search fee. $.50 fee per copy. $1.00 for certification. Search information required: name, years to search. Specify plaintiff or defendant.

Claiborne County

Circuit Clerk, Criminal Records
PO Box 549
Port Gibson, MS 39150
(601) 437-5841
Felony records are available by mail. No release necessary. $3.00 search fee. Make check payable to Circuit Court. Search information required: name, SSN.

Civil records are available by mail. No release necessary. $3.00 search fee. $.50 fee per copy. $2.00 for certification. Search information required: name, years to search. Specify plaintiff or defendant.

Clarke County

Felony records
Circuit Clerk, Criminal Records
PO Box 216
Quitman, MS 39355
(601) 776-3111
Fax (601) 776-1013
Felony records are available by mail, phone or fax. No release necessary. No search fee. Search information required: name, SSN, date of birth, sex, race.

Civil records
Circuit Clerk
PO Box 216
Quitman, MS 39355
(601) 776-3111
Fax (601) 776-1013
Civil records are available by mail, phone or fax. No release necessary. $5.00 search fee. $.50 fee per copy. $2.00 for certification. Search information required: name, years to search. Specify plaintiff or defendant.

Misdemeanor records
Justice Court
PO Box 4
Quitman, MS 39355
(601) 776-5371
Misdemeanor records are available by mail or phone. No release necessary. $5.00 search fee. $.50 fee per copy. $2.00 for certification. Search information required: name, date of charge, driver's license number.

Civil records
Justice Court
PO Box 4
Quitman, MS 39355
(601) 776-5371
Civil records are available by mail. No release necessary. $5.00 search fee. $.50 fee per copy. $2.00 for certification. Search information required: name, years to search. Specify plaintiff or defendant.

Clay County

Felony records
Circuit Clerk, Criminal Records
PO Box 364
West Point, MS 39773
(601) 494-3384
Felony records are available by mail. No release necessary. $5.00 search fee. $.50 fee per copy. $2.00 fee for certification. Search information required: name, phone, years to search.

Civil records
Circuit Clerk
PO Box 364
West Point, MS 39773
(601) 494-3384
Civil records are available by mail. No release necessary. $5.00 search fee. $.50 fee per copy. $2.00 for certification. Search information required: name, years to search. Specify plaintiff or defendant.

Misdemeanor records
Justice Court
PO Box 674
West Point, MS 39773
(601) 494-6140
Misdemeanor records are available by mail or phone. Written request required. No release necessary. No search fee. Search information required: name, SSN, address, race.

Civil records
Justice Court
PO Box 674
West Point, MS 39773
(601) 494-6140
Civil records are available by mail. No release necessary. No search fee. Search information required: name, years to search. Specify plaintiff or defendant.

Coahoma County

Felony records
Circuit Clerk, Criminal Records
PO Box 504
Clarksdale, MS 38614
(601) 624-3014
Felony records are available by mail. No release is necessary. $10.00 search fee. $.25 fee per copy, $1.50 fee for certification. Search information required: name, SSN, date of birth, years to search, SASE.

Civil records
Circuit Clerk
PO Box 504
Clarksdale, MS 38614
(601) 624-3014
Civil records are available by mail. No release necessary. $10.00 search fee. $.25 fee per copy. $1.50 for certification. Search information required: name, years to search. Specify plaintiff or defendant.

Misdemeanor records
Justice Court Clerk
144 Ritch Street
Clarksdale, MS 38614
(601) 624-3060
Misdemeanor records are available by mail. Release necessary. No search fee. Search information required: name, date of birth, SSN, address, years to search.

Civil records
Justice Court Clerk
144 Ritch Street
Clarksdale, MS 38614
(601) 624-3060
Civil records are available in person only. See Mississippi state repository for additional information.

Copiah County

Felony records
Circuit Clerk, Criminal Records
PO Box 467
Hazelhurst, MS 39083
(601) 894-1241
Felony records are available by mail or phone. No release necessary. No search fee. Search information required: name, offense.

Civil records
Circuit Clerk
PO Box 467
Hazelhurst, MS 39083
(601) 894-1241
Civil records are available by mail or phone. A release is required. No search fee. $.25 fee per copy. $5.00 for certification. Search information required: name, years to search. Specify plaintiff or defendant.

Misdemeanor records
Justice Court
PO Box 798
Hazelhurst, MS 39083
(601) 894-3218
Misdemeanor records are available by mail or phone. No release necessary. $10.00 search fee. $.25 fee per copy. $1.25 for certification. Search information required: name, years to search.

Civil records
Justice Court
PO Box 798
Hazelhurst, MS 39083
(601) 894-3218
Civil records are available by mail. No release necessary. $10.00 search fee. $.25 fee per copy. $1.25 for certification. Search information required: name, years to search. Specify plaintiff or defendant.

Covington County

Felony records
Circuit Clerk, Criminal Records
PO Box 667
Collins, MS 39428
(601) 765-6506
Felony records are available by mail or phone. No release necessary. No search fee. Search information required: name, SSN, date of birth, years to search.

Civil records
Circuit Clerk
PO Box 667
Collins, MS 39428
(601) 765-6506
Civil records are available by mail or phone. No release necessary. No search fee. $.25 fee per copy. $2.00 for certification. Search information required: name, years to search. Specify plaintiff or defendant.

Misdemeanor records
Justice Court
PO Box 665
Collins, MS 39428
(601) 765-6581
Misdemeanor records are available by mail or phone. No release necessary. No search fee. Search information required: name, date of birth, driver's license number, SSN.

Civil records
Justice Court
PO Box 665
Collins, MS 39428
(601) 765-6581
Civil records are available in person only. See Mississippi state repository for additional information.

De Soto County

Felony records
Courthouse, Criminal Records
2535 Hwy. 51 South
Hernando, MS 38632
(601) 429-1325
Felony and misdemeanor records are available by mail. A release is required. $10.00 search fee. Check payable to Circuit Clerk. Search information required: full name.

Civil records
Courthouse
Hernando, MS 38632
(601) 429-1325
Civil records are available by mail. No release necessary. $1.00 search fee. $.50 fee per copy. $2.00 for certification. Search information required: name, years to search. Specify plaintiff or defendant.

Misdemeanor records
Justice Court
891 E. Rasco
South Haven, MS 38671
(601) 393-5810
Misdemeanor records are available in person only. See Mississippi state repository for additional information.

Civil records
Justice Court
891 E. Rasco
South Haven, MS 38671
(601) 393-5810
Civil records are available in person only. See Mississippi state repository for additional information.

Forrest County

Circuit Clerk, Criminal Records
PO Box 807
Hattiesburg, MS 39401
(601) 582-3213
Felony and misdemeanor records are available by mail. No release necessary. $10.00 search fee. Certified check only, payable to Circuit Clerk. Search information required: name.

Civil records are available by mail. No release necessary. $10.00 search fee. Search information required: name, years to search. Specify plaintiff or defendant.

Franklin County

Felony records
Circuit Clerk, Criminal Records
PO Box 267
Meadville, MS 39653
(601) 384-2320
Felony records are available by mail. No release necessary. $10.00 fee. $.50 fee per copy. $1.50 for certification. Make check payable to Circuit Clerk. Search information required: name, years to search.

Civil records
Circuit Clerk
PO Box 267
Meadville, MS 39653
(601) 384-2320
Civil records are available by mail. No release necessary. $10.00 search fee. $.50 fee per copy. $1.50 for certification. Search information required: name, years to search. Specify plaintiff or defendant.

Misdemeanor records
Franklin County Justice Court
PO Box 365
Meadville, MS 39653
(601) 384-2002
Misdemeanor records are available by mail. No release necessary. No search fee. Search information required: name, years to search.

Civil records
Franklin County Justice Court
PO Box 365
Meadville, MS 39653
(601) 384-2002
Civil records are available by mail. No release necessary. No search fee. Search information required: name, years to search. Specify plaintiff or defendant.

George County

Felony records
Courthouse Square, Criminal Records
Circuit Clerk's Office
Lucedale, MS 39452
(601) 947-4881
Felony records are available by mail or phone. No release necessary. No search fee. Search information required: name, years to search.

Civil records
Courthouse Square
Circuit Clerk's Office
Lucedale, MS 39452
(601) 947-4881
Civil records are available by mail. A release is required. No search fee. $.50 fee per copy. $1.50 for certification. Search information required: name, years to search. Specify plaintiff or defendant.

Misdemeanor records
George County Justice Court
200 Tox Street
Lucedale, MS 39452
(601) 947-4834
Misdemeanor records are available by mail. A release is required. $20.00 search fee. $.25 fee per copy. $1.50 fee for certification. Search information required: name, date of birth, SSN, driver's license number, years to search.

Civil records
George County Justice Court
200 Tox Street
Lucedale, MS 39452
(601) 947-4834
Civil records are available by mail. No release necessary. $20.00 search fee. $.25 fee per copy. $1.50 for certification. Search information required: name, years to search. Specify plaintiff or defendant.

Greene County

Felony records
Circuit Clerk, Criminal Records
PO Box 111
Leakesville, MS 39451
(601) 394-2379
Felony records are available by mail or phone. No release necessary. No search fee. Search information required: name, years to search.

Civil records
Circuit Clerk
PO Box 111
Leakesville, MS 39451
(601) 394-2379
Civil records are available by mail or phone. No release necessary. No search fee. Search information required: name, years to search. Specify plaintiff or defendant.

Misdemeanor records
Justice Court
PO Box 610
Leakesville, MS 39451
(601) 394-2347
Misdemeanor records are available by mail or phone. No release necessary. No search fee. Search information required: name, case number.

Civil records
Justice Court
PO Box 610
Leakesville, MS 39451
(601) 394-2347
Civil records are available by mail or phone. No release necessary. No search fee. $.25 fee per copy. $1.50 for certification. Search information required: name, years to search. Specify plaintiff or defendant.

Grenada County

Felony records
Circuit Clerk, Criminal Records
Grenada County Courthouse
Grenada, MS 38901
(601) 226-1941
Felony records are available in person only. See Mississippi state repository for additional information.

Civil records
Circuit Clerk
Grenada County Courthouse
Grenada, MS 38901
(601) 226-1941
Civil records are available in person only. See Mississippi state repository for additional information.

Misdemeanor records
Justice Court
59 Green St.
Grenada, MS 38901
(601) 226-3331
Misdemeanor records are available by mail. No release necessary. $20.00 search fee. Search information required: name, offense, date of charge, years to search.

Civil records
Justice Court
59 Green St.
Grenada, MS 38901
(601) 226-3331
Civil records are available by mail. No release necessary. $20.00 search fee. Search information required: name, years to search. Specify plaintiff or defendant.

Hancock County

Felony records
Circuit Clerk, Criminal Records
PO Box 249
Bay St. Louis, MS 39520
(601) 467-5265
Fax (601) 467-2779
Felony records are available by mail or fax. No release necessary. $5.00 fee. Company checks only, payable to Circuit Clerk. Search information required: name, years to search, SSN.

Civil records
Circuit Clerk
PO Box 249
Bay St. Louis, MS 39520
(601) 467-5265
Fax (601) 467-2779
Civil records are available by mail or fax. No release necessary. $5.00 search fee. $.50 fee per copy. $1.00 for certification. Search information required: name, years to search. Specify plaintiff or defendant.

Misdemeanor records
Hancock County Justice Court
PO Box 147
Bay St. Louis, MS 39520
(601) 467-5573
Misdemeanor records are available by mail or phone. No release necessary. $5.00 search fee. $.50 fee per copy. $2.00 for certification. Search information required: name, date of birth, address, driver's license number.

Civil records
Hancock County Justice Court
PO Box 147
Bay St. Louis, MS 39520
(601) 467-5573
Civil records are available by mail. No release necessary. $5.00 search fee. $.50 fee per copy. $2.00 for certification. Search information required: name, years to search. Specify plaintiff or defendant.

Harrison County

Felony records
Circuit Clerk, Criminal Records
PO Box 998
Gulfport, MS 39502
(601) 865-4009
Felony records are available by mail. No release necessary. $5.00 search fee. Company checks only, payable to Circuit Clerk. Search information required: name, date of birth.

Civil records
Circuit Clerk
PO Box 998
Gulfport, MS 39502
(601) 865-4009
Civil records are available by mail. No release necessary. $5.00 search fee. $.50 fee per copy. Search information required: name, years to search. Specify plaintiff or defendant.

Misdemeanor records
Justice Court
1620 23rd Ave.
PO Box 1754
Gulfport, MS 39502
(601) 865-4214
Misdemeanor records are available by mail or phone. No release necessary. No search fee. Search information required: name, date of birth, SSN.

Civil records
Justice Court
1620 23rd Ave.
PO Box 1754
Gulfport, MS 39502
(601) 865-4214
Civil records are available by mail. No release necessary. $5.00 search fee. $.50 fee per copy. $1.00 for certification. Search information required: name, years to search. Specify plaintiff or defendant.

Hinds County

Felony records
Circuit Clerk, Criminal Records
PO Box 327
Jackson, MS 39205-0327
(601) 968-6628
Felony records are available by mail or phone. No release necessary. $10.00 search fee. Search information required: name, date of birth, SSN.

Civil records
Circuit Clerk
PO Box 327
Jackson, MS 39205-0327
(601) 968-6628
Civil records are available by mail. A release is required. No search fee. $10.00 fee per copy. $1.00 for certification. Search information required: name, years to search. Specify plaintiff or defendant.

Misdemeanor records
Justice Court
PO Box 3490
Jackson, MS 39207
(601) 968-6782
Misdemeanor records are available from 1986 forward, by mail. No release necessary. No search fee. Search information required: full name, SSN, date of birth, years to search.

Civil records
Justice Court
PO Box 3490
Jackson, MS 39207
(601) 968-6782
Civil records are available by mail. No release necessary. No search fee. $.25 fee per copy. Search information required: name, years to search. Specify plaintiff or defendant.

Holmes County

Felony records
Circuit Clerk, Criminal Records
PO Box 265
Lexington, MS 39095
(601) 834-2476
Felony records are available by mail or phone. No release necessary. No search fee. Search information required: name.

Civil records
Circuit Clerk
PO Box 265
Lexington, MS 39095
(601) 834-2476
Civil records are available by mail. No release necessary. $5.00 search fee. $.50 fee per copy. $2.00 for certification. Search information required: name, years to search. Specify plaintiff or defendant.

Misdemeanor records
Holmes County Justice Court
Drawer D
Lexington, MS 39095
(601) 834-4565
Misdemeanor records are available by mail or phone. A release is required. No search fee. Search information required: name, offense, date of charge, SASE.

Civil records
Holmes County Justice Court
Drawer D
Lexington, MS 39095
(601) 834-4565
Civil records are available by mail or phone. A release is required. No search fee. Search information required: name, years to search, SASE. Specify plaintiff or defendant.

Humphreys County

Felony records
Circuit Clerk, Criminal Records
PO Box 696
Belzoni, MS 39038
(601) 247-3065
Felony records are available by mail or phone. No release necessary. $5.00 search fee. Search information required: name, SASE, years to search.

Civil records
Circuit Clerk
PO Box 696
Belzoni, MS 39038
(601) 247-3065
Civil records are available by mail. A release is required. $5.00 search fee. $.50 fee per copy. $1.00 for certification. Search information required: name, years to search. Specify plaintiff or defendant.

Misdemeanor records
Justice Court
Courthouse
102 Castleman
Belzoni, MS 39038
(601) 247-4337
Misdemeanor records since Jan. 1984 are available by mail or phone. No release necessary. No search fee. Search information required: name, offense.

Civil records
Justice Court
Courthouse
102 Castleman
Belzoni, MS 39038
(601) 247-4337
Civil records are available by mail or phone. No release necessary. No search fee. Search information required: name, years to search. Specify plaintiff or defendant.

Issaquena County

Circuit Clerk, Criminal Records
PO Box 27
Mayersville, MS 39113
(601) 873-2761
Felony and misdemeanor records are available by mail or phone. A release is required. No search fee. Search information required: name, SSN, date of birth, sex, race.

Civil records are available by mail or phone. No release necessary. No search fee. $.50 fee per copy. $1.00 for certification. Search information required: name, years to search. Specify plaintiff or defendant.

Itawamba County

Felony records
Circuit Clerk, Criminal Records
201 W. Main
Fulton, MS 38843
(601) 862-3511
Fax (601) 862-4006
Felony records are available by mail, phone or fax. No release necessary. No search fee. Search information required: name, SSN, date of birth, years to search.

Civil records
Circuit Clerk
201 W. Main
Fulton, MS 38843
(601) 862-3511
Fax (601) 862-4006
Civil records are available by mail, phone or fax. No release necessary. $5.00 search fee. $.50 fee per copy. $1.00 for certification. Search information required: name, years to search. Specify plaintiff or defendant.

Misdemeanor records
Itawamba County Justice Court
201 W. Main
Fulton, MS 38843
(601) 862-4315
Misdemeanor records are available by mail. No release necessary. $8.75 search fee. $.50 fee per copy. Search information required: name, years to search.

Civil records
Itawamba County Justice Court
201 W. Main
Fulton, MS 38843
(601) 862-4315
Civil records are available by mail. No release necessary. $8.75 search fee. $.50 fee per copy. Search information required: name, years to search. Specify plaintiff or defendant.

Jackson County

Circuit Clerk, Criminal Records
PO Box 998
Pascagoula, MS 39567
(601) 769-3039
Fax (601) 769-3180
Felony and misdemeanor records are available by mail. No release necessary. $10.00 search fee. $.50 fee per copy. $1.50 for certification. Make check payable to Circuit Clerk. Search information required: name, date of birth, years to search. Request both county and circuit courts to be checked.

Civil records are available by mail. No release necessary. $10.00 search fee. $.50 fee per copy. $1.50 for certification. Search information required: name, years to search. Specify plaintiff or defendant.

Jasper County

Felony records
Circuit Clerk, Criminal Records
PO Box 447
Bay Springs, MS 39422
(601) 764-2245
Felony records are available in person only. See Mississippi state repository for additional information.

Civil records
Circuit Clerk
PO Box 447
Bay Springs, MS 39422
(601) 764-2245
Civil records are available in person only. See Mississippi state repository for additional information.

Misdemeanor records
Justice Court
PO Box 1054
Bay Springs, MS 39422
(601) 764-2065
Misdemeanor records are available by mail or phone. No release necessary. $5.00 search fee. $.50 fee per copy. $1.50 for certification. Search information required: name, driver's license number, address, race, sex, years to search.

Civil records
Justice Court
PO Box 1054
Bay Springs, MS 39422
(601) 764-2065
Civil records are available by mail. No release necessary. $5.00 search fee. $.50 fee per copy. $1.50 for certification. Search information required: name, years to search. Specify plaintiff or defendant.

Jefferson County

Circuit Clerk, Criminal Records
PO Box 305
Fayette, MS 39069
(601) 786-3422
Felony and misdemeanor records are available by mail. No release necessary. $3.00 search fee. Search information required: name, date of birth, SSN, years to search.

Civil records are available by mail. No release necessary. $3.00 search fee. $.50 fee per copy. $1.50 for certification. Search information required: name, years to search. Specify plaintiff or defendant.

Jefferson Davis County

Felony records
Circuit Clerk, Criminal Records
PO Box 1082
Prentiss, MS 39474
(601) 792-4231
Felony records are available by mail or phone. No release necessary. No search fee. Search information required: name, SSN, date of birth, sex, race.

Civil records
Circuit Clerk
PO Box 1082
Prentiss, MS 39474
(601) 792-4231
Civil records are available by mail. No release necessary. $3.00 search fee. $.25 fee per copy. $2.00 for certification. Search information required: name, years to search. Specify plaintiff or defendant.

Misdemeanor records
Justice Court
PO Box 1407
Prentiss, MS 39474
(601) 792-5129
Misdemeanor records are available by mail or phone. No release necessary. No search fee. $.25 fee per copy. Search information required: name, SSN, years to search.

Civil records
Justice Court
PO Box 1407
Prentiss, MS 39474
(601) 792-5129
Civil records are available by mail or phone. No release necessary. No search fee. $.25 fee per copy. Search information required: name, years to search. Specify plaintiff or defendant.

Jones County

Felony records
Circuit Clerk, Criminal Records
2nd District
PO Box 1336
Laurel, MS 39440
(601) 425-2556
Felony records are available by mail. No release necessary. $6.00 search fee. $.25 fee per copy. Search information required: name, years to search.

Civil records
Circuit Clerk
2nd District
PO Box 1336
Laurel, MS 39440
(601) 425-2556
Civil records are available by mail. No release necessary. $6.00 search fee. $.25 fee per copy. Search information required: name, years to search. Specify plaintiff or defendant.

Misdemeanor records
Justice Court
317 S. Magnolia
Laurel, MS 39440
(601) 428-6500
Fax (601) 428-6500
Misdemeanor records are available by mail. A release is required. No search fee. Search information required: name, date of birth, SSN, years to search.

Civil records
Justice Court
317 S. Magnolia
Laurel, MS 39440
(601) 428-6500
Fax (601) 428-6500
Civil records are available by mail. No release necessary. No search fee. Search information required: name, years to search. Specify plaintiff or defendant.

Kemper County

Felony records
Circuit Clerk, Criminal Records
PO Box 130
Dekalb, MS 39328
(601) 743-2224
Felony records are available in person only. See Mississippi State Repository for additional information.

Civil records
Circuit Clerk
PO Box 130
Dekalb, MS 39328
(601) 743-2224
Civil records are available by mail. No release necessary. $5.00 search fee. $.50 fee per copy. $3.00 for certification. Search information required: name, years to search. Specify plaintiff or defendant.

Misdemeanor records
Kemper County Justice Court
PO Box 661
Dekalb, MS 39328
(601) 743-2793
Misdemeanor records are available by mail. No release necessary. No search fee. Search information required: name, years to search.

Civil records
Kemper County Justice Court
PO Box 661
Dekalb, MS 39328
(601) 743-2793
Civil records are available by mail. No release necessary. No search fee. Search information required: name, years to search. Specify plaintiff or defendant.

Lafayette County

Felony records
Lafayette County Courthouse
County Courthouse
Oxford, MS 38655
(601) 234-4951
Fax (601) 234-5402
Felony records are available by mail or fax. No release necessary. $10.00 fee for first ten years searched, $1.00 fee for each additional year searched. Search information required: name, SSN, date of birth, sex, race.

Civil records
Lafayette County Courthouse
County Courthouse
Oxford, MS 38655
(601) 234-4951
Fax (601) 234-5402
Civil records are available by mail or fax. No release necessary. $10.00 search fee. Search information required: name, years to search. Specify plaintiff or defendant.

Misdemeanor records
Justice Court
1219 Monroe
Oxford, MS 38655
(601) 234-1545
Misdemeanor records are available by mail or phone. No release necessary. $10.00 search fee. Search information required: full name, address, information wanted.

Civil records
Justice Court
1219 Monroe
Oxford, MS 38655
(601) 234-1545
Civil records are available by mail. No release necessary. $15.00 search fee. $.25 fee per copy. Search information required: name, years to search. Specify plaintiff or defendant.

Lamar County

Felony records
Circuit Clerk, Criminal Records
PO Box 729
Purvis, MS 39475
(601) 794-8504
Felony records are available by mail. No release necessary. $20.00 search fee. Search information required: name, SASE, years to search.

Civil records
Circuit Clerk
PO Box 729
Purvis, MS 39475
(601) 794-8504
Civil records are available by mail. No release necessary. $20.00 search fee. Search information required: name, years to search. Specify plaintiff or defendant.

Misdemeanor records
Justice Court
PO Box 1010
Purvis, MS 39475
(601) 794-8504 Ext. 63
Misdemeanor records since Jan. 1, 1984 are available by mail. No release necessary. $30.00 deposit for searches. $.50 fee per copy. Search information required: name, SSN, race, years to search.

Civil records
Justice Court
PO Box 1010
Purvis, MS 39475
(601) 794-8504 Ext. 62
Civil records are available by mail. No release necessary. $30.00 deposit for searches. $.50 fee per copy. Search information required: name, years to search. Specify plaintiff or defendant.

Lauderdale County

Felony records
Circuit Clerk, Criminal Records
PO Box 1005
Meridian, MS 39302
(601) 482-9738
Fax (601) 484-3970
Felony records are available by mail or phone. No release necessary. No search fee. Search information required: name, date of birth, SSN.

Civil records
Circuit Clerk
PO Box 1005
Meridian, MS 39302
(601) 482-9738
Fax (601) 484-3970
Civil records are available by mail or phone. No release necessary. No search fee. $.25 fee per copy. Search information required: name, years to search. Specify plaintiff or defendant.

Misdemeanor records
Justice Court
PO Box 5126
Meridian, MS 39301
(601) 482-9879
Misdemeanor records are available in person only. See Mississippi state repository for additional information.

Civil records
Justice Court
PO Box 5126
Meridian, MS 39301
(601) 482-9879
Civil records are available by mail. No release necessary. No search fee. $1.00 fee per copy. Search information required: name, years to search. Specify plaintiff or defendant.

Lawrence County

Felony records
Circuit Clerk, Criminal Records
PO Box 1249
Monticello, MS 39654
(601) 587-4791
Felony records are available by mail or phone. No release necessary. $20.00 search fee per hour. Minimum fee is $10.00. Make check payable to Circuit Clerk. Search information required: name, SASE.

Civil records
Circuit Clerk
PO Box 1249
Monticello, MS 39654
(601) 587-4791
Civil records are available by mail. No release necessary. $10.00 search fee. $.25 fee per copy. Search information required: name, years to search. Specify plaintiff or defendant.

Misdemeanor records
Justice Court
PO Box 903
Monticello, MS 39654
(601) 587-7183
Misdemeanor records are available by mail. No release necessary. No search fee. Search information required: name, date of birth, age, driver's license number, address, years to search.

Civil records
Justice Court
PO Box 903
Monticello, MS 39654
(601) 587-7183
Civil records are available by mail. No release necessary. No search fee. Search information required: name, years to search. Specify plaintiff or defendant.

Leake County

Felony records
Leake County Courthouse, Criminal Records
PO Box 67
Carthage, MS 39051
(601) 267-8357
Felony records are available by mail. No release necessary. $3.00 search fee. Check payable to Circuit Clerk. Search information required: name, SSN, date of birth, sex, years to search.

Civil records
Leake County Courthouse
PO Box 67
Carthage, MS 39051
(601) 267-8357
Civil records are available by mail. No release necessary. $3.00 search fee. $1.50 for certification. Search information required: name, years to search. Specify plaintiff or defendant.

Misdemeanor records
Justice Court
PO Box 69
Carthage, MS 39051
(601) 267-5677
Misdemeanor records are available in person only. See Mississippi state repository for additional information.

Civil records
Justice Court
PO Box 69
Carthage, MS 39051
(601) 267-5677
Civil records are available in person only. See Mississippi state repository for additional information.

Lee County

Felony records
Circuit Clerk, Criminal Records
PO Box 762
Tupelo, MS 38802
(601) 841-9024
Felony records are available by mail or phone. No release necessary. $10.00 search fee. Search information required: name, reason.

Civil records
Circuit Clerk
PO Box 762
Tupelo, MS 38802
(601) 841-9024
Civil records are available by mail. No release necessary. $10.00 search fee. $.25 fee per copy. $1.50 for certification. Search information required: name, years to search. Specify plaintiff or defendant.

Misdemeanor records
Justice Court
PO Box 108
Tupelo, MS 38801
(601) 841-9014
Misdemeanor records are available by mail. No release necessary. $25.00 search fee for first hour of search. $5.00 fee for each additional hour. Search information required: name, years to search.

Civil records
Justice Court
PO Box 108
Tupelo, MS 38801
(601) 841-9014
Civil records are available by mail. No release necessary. $25.00 search fee. Search information required: name, years to search. Specify plaintiff or defendant.

Leflore County

Leflore County Circuit Clerk,
Criminal Records
PO Box 1953
Greenwood, MS 38930
(601) 453-1041 Ext. 270
Fax (601) 453-7460
Felony records are available by mail, phone or fax. No release necessary. No fee. Search information required: name, years to search, SSN, date of birth.

Civil records are available by mail, phone or fax. No release necessary. $5.00 search fee. Search information required: name, years to search. Specify plaintiff or defendant.

Lincoln County

Felony records
Circuit Clerk, Criminal Records
PO Box 357
Brookhaven, MS 39601
(601) 835-3435
Felony records are available by mail. A release is required. $10.00 search fee. Search information required: name, years to search, SASE.

Civil records
Circuit Clerk
PO Box 357
Brookhaven, MS 39601
(601) 835-3435
Civil records are available by mail. No release necessary. $10.00 search fee. $.50 fee per copy. $1.50 for certification. Search information required: name, years to search. Specify plaintiff or defendant.

Misdemeanor records
Justice Court
PO Box 767
Brookhaven, MS 39601
(601) 835-3474
Fax (601) 835-3475
Misdemeanor records are available by mail. A release is required. $5.00 search fee. $.50 fee per copy. Search information required: name, date of birth, driver's license number, years to search.

Civil records
Justice Court
PO Box 767
Brookhaven, MS 39601
(601) 835-3474
Fax (601) 835-3475
Civil records are available by mail. No release necessary. $5.00 search fee. $.50 fee per copy. $1.50 for certification. Search information required: name, years to search. Specify plaintiff or defendant.

Lowndes County

Felony records
Circuit Clerk
PO Box 127
Columbus, MS 39703
(601) 329-5900
Records are available in person only. See Mississippi state repository for additional information.

Civil records
Circuit Clerk
PO Box 127
Columbus, MS 39703
(601) 329-5900
Civil records are available in person only. See Mississippi state repository for additional information.

Misdemeanor records
Justice Court
11 Airline Rd.
Columbus, MS 39702
(601) 329-5929
Misdemeanor records are available by mail. No release necessary. $11.00 search fee. $.50 fee per copy. Search information required: name, years to search.

Civil records
Justice Court
11 Airline Rd.
Columbus, MS 39702
(601) 329-5929
Civil records are available by mail. No release necessary. $11.00 search fee. $.50 fee per copy. Search information required: name, years to search. Specify plaintiff or defendant.

Madison County

Felony records
Circuit Clerk, Criminal Records
PO Box 11
Canton, MS 39046
(601) 859-4365
Felony records are available by mail or phone. No release necessary. No search fee. $.25 fee per copy. $1.50 for certification. Search information required: name, years to search.

Civil records
Circuit Clerk
PO Box 11
Canton, MS 39046
(601) 859-4365
Civil records are available in person only. See Mississippi state repository for additional information.

Misdemeanor records
Clerk of Court, Madison County
Justice Court
175 N. Union
Canton, MS 39046
(601) 859-6337
Misdemeanor records are available by mail. No release necessary. $6.00 search fee. $.25 fee per copy. Search information required: name, date of birth, SSN, years to search.

Civil records
Clerk of Court, Madison County
Justice Court
175 N. Union
Canton, MS 39046
(601) 859-6337
Civil records are available by mail. No release necessary. $6.00 search fee. $.25 fee per copy. Search information required: name, years to search. Specify plaintiff or defendant.

Marion County

Felony records
Circuit Clerk, Criminal Records
Marion County Courthouse
Columbia, MS 39429
(601) 736-8246
Felony records are available by mail and phone. No release necessary. No search fee. Search information required: name, years to search.

Civil records
Circuit Clerk
Marion County Courthouse
Columbia, MS 39429
(601) 736-8246
Civil records are available by mail. No release necessary. No search fee. Search information required: name, years to search. Specify plaintiff or defendant.

Misdemeanor records
Justice Court
Courthouse Square, Suite #2
Columbia, MS 39429
(601) 736-2572
Misdemeanor records are available in person only. See Mississippi state repository for additional information.

Civil records
Justice Court
Courthouse Square, Suite #2
Columbia, MS 39429
(601) 736-2572
Civil records are available by mail. No release necessary. $5.00 search fee. Search information required: name, years to search. Specify plaintiff or defendant.

Marshall County

Felony records
Circuit Clerk, Criminal Records
PO Box 459
Holly Springs, MS 38635
(601) 252-3434
Felony records are available by mail. No release necessary. $10.00 search fee. Make check payable to Circuit Clerk. Search information required: name, SSN, date of birth.

Civil records
Circuit Clerk
PO Box 459
Holly Springs, MS 38635
(601) 252-3434
Civil records are available by mail. No release necessary. $10.00 search fee. Search information required: name, years to search. Specify plaintiff or defendant.

Misdemeanor records
Justice Court
PO Box 867
Holly Springs, MS 38635
(601) 252-3585
Misdemeanor records are available by mail or phone. No release necessary. $5.00 search fee. $.50 fee per copy. Search information required: name, years to search.

Civil records
Justice Court
PO Box 867
Holly Springs, MS 38635
(601) 252-3585
Civil records are available by mail. No release necessary. $5.00 search fee. $.50 fee per copy. Search information required: name, years to search. Specify plaintiff or defendant.

Monroe County

Felony records
Circuit Clerk, Criminal Records
PO Box 843
Aberdeen, MS 39730
(601) 369-8695
Felony records are available by mail or phone. No release necessary. No search fee. $.50 fee per copy. $3.00 for certification. Search information required: name, SSN, date of birth, sex, race, years to search.

Civil records
Circuit Clerk
PO Box 843
Aberdeen, MS 39730
(601) 369-8695
Civil records are available by mail or phone. No release necessary. No search fee. $.50 fee per copy. $3.00 for certification. Search information required: name, years to search. Specify plaintiff or defendant.

Misdemeanor records
Justice Court
101 9th St.
Amory, MS 38821
(601) 256-8493
Misdemeanor records are available in person only. See Mississippi state repository for additional information.

Civil records
Justice Court
101 9th St.
Amory, MS 38821
(601) 256-8493
Civil records are available in person only. See Mississippi state repository for additional information.

Montgomery County

Felony records
Circuit Clerk, Criminal Records
PO Box 765
Winona, MS 38967
(601) 283-4161
Felony records are available by mail or phone. No release necessary. No search fee. Search information required: name, years to search.

Civil records
Circuit Clerk
PO Box 765
Winona, MS 38967
(601) 283-4161
Civil records are available by mail or phone. No release necessary. No search fee. .25 fee per copy. $1.50 for certification. Search information required: name, years to search. Specify plaintiff or defendant.

Misdemeanor records
Justice Court
PO Box 229
Winona, MS 38967
(601) 283-2290
Misdemeanor records are available by mail. No release necessary. No search fee. Search information required: name, date of charge, years to search.

Civil records
Justice Court
PO Box 229
Winona, MS 38967
(601) 283-2290
Civil records are available by mail. No release necessary. No search fee. Search information required: name, years to search. Specify plaintiff or defendant.

Neshoba County

Felony records
Circuit Clerk, Criminal Records
Neshoba County Courthouse
401 Beacon St.
Philadelphia, MS 39350
(601) 656-4781
Felony records are available by mail or phone. No release necessary. No search fee. $.50 fee per copy. $1.50 fee for certification. Search information required: name, date of birth, address.

Civil records
Circuit Clerk
Neshoba County Courthouse
401 Beacon St.
Philadelphia, MS 39350
(601) 656-4781
Civil records are available by mail. No release necessary. No search fee. Search information required: name, years to search. Specify plaintiff or defendant.

Misdemeanor records
Justice Court
Neshoba County Courthouse
401 Beacon St.
Philadelphia, MS 39350
(601) 656-4053
Fax (601) 656-3280
Misdemeanor records are available by mail. No release necessary. No search fee. Search information required: name, date of birth, years to search, address, SSN.

Civil records
Justice Court
Neshoba County Courthouse
401 Beacon St.
Philadelphia, MS 39350
(601) 656-4053
Fax (601) 656-3280
Civil records are available by mail. No release necessary. $5.00 search fee. $1.00 fee per copy. $1.00 for certification. Search information required: name, years to search. Specify plaintiff or defendant.

Newton County

Felony records
Circuit Clerk, Criminal Records
PO Box 447
Decatur, MS 39327
(601) 635-2368
Felony records are available by mail. No release necessary. $5.00 search fee. Search information required: full name, years to search.

Civil records
Circuit Clerk
PO Box 447
Decatur, MS 39327
(601) 635-2368
Civil records are available by mail. No release necessary. $5.00 search fee. $.50 fee per copy. $2.00 for certification. Search information required: name, years to search. Specify plaintiff or defendant.

Misdemeanor records
Newton County Justice Court
PO Box 69
Decatur, MS 39327
(601) 635-2740
Misdemeanor records are available by mail or phone. No release necessary. $4.00 search fee per 1/4 hour. $.25 fee per copy. $2.00 for certification. Search information required: name, date of birth, SSN, date of charge, years to search.

Civil records
Newton County Justice Court
PO Box 69
Decatur, MS 39327
(601) 635-2740
Civil records are available by mail. No release necessary. $4.00 search fee per hour. $.25 fee per copy. $2.00 for certification. Search information required: name, years to search, SASE. Specify plaintiff or defendant.

Noxubee County

Felony records
Circuit Clerk, Criminal Records
505 S. Jefferson Street
Macon, MS 39341
(601) 726-5737
Felony records are available by mail or phone. No release necessary. No search fee. $.50 fee per copy. $5.00 for certification. Search information required: name, date of birth, years to search.

Civil records
Circuit Clerk
505 S. Jefferson Street
Macon, MS 39341
(601) 726-5737
Civil records are available by mail. No release necessary. No search fee. $.50 fee per copy. $5.00 for certification. Search information required: name, years to search. Specify plaintiff or defendant.

Misdemeanor records
Justice Court
(601) 726-5834
Misdemeanor records are available in person only. See Mississippi state repository for additional information.

Civil records
Justice Court
(601) 726-5834
Civil records are available in person only. See Mississippi state repository for additional information.

Oktibbeha County

Felony records
Circuit Clerk, Criminal Records
Oktibbeha County Courthouse
Starkville, MS 39759
(601) 323-1356
Felony records are available by mail. No release necessary. $10.00 search fee. $.50 fee per copy. Search information required: name, years to search.

Civil records
Circuit Clerk
Oktibbeha County Courthouse
Starkville, MS 39759
(601) 323-1356
Civil records are available by mail. No release necessary. $10.00 search fee. Search information required: name, years to search. Specify plaintiff or defendant.

Misdemeanor records
Justice Court
509 Hospital Dr.
Starkville, MS 39759
(601) 324-3032
Misdemeanor records since 1984 are available by mail or phone. Written request required. No release necessary. No search fee. Search information required: name, SSN, years to search.

Civil records
Justice Court
509 Hospital Dr.
Starkville, MS 39759
(601) 324-3032
Civil records are available by mail. No release necessary. No search fee. Search information required: name, years to search. Specify plaintiff or defendant.

Panola County

Felony records
Circuit Clerk, Criminal Records
PO Box 346
Batesville, MS 38606
(601) 563-6210
Fax (601) 563-8233
Felony records are available by mail, phone or fax. No release necessary. $5.00 search fee. $.50 fee per copy. Make check payable to Circuit Clerk. Search information required: name, date of birth, years to search, alias, SSN.

Civil records
Circuit Clerk
PO Box 346
Batesville, MS 38606
(601) 563-6210
Fax (601) 563-8233
Civil records are available by mail. No release necessary. No search fee. $.50 fee per copy. $2.00 for certification. Search information required: name, years to search. Specify plaintiff or defendant.

Misdemeanor records
Justice Court
PO Box 249
Sardis, MS 38666
(601) 563-6240
Misdemeanor records are available by mail. No release necessary. $8.00 search fee per hour. Search information required: name, years to search

Civil records
Justice Court
PO Box 249
Sardis, MS 38666
(601) 563-6240
Civil records are available by mail. No release necessary. $8.00 search fee per hour. Search information required: name, years to search. Specify plaintiff or defendant.

Pearl River County

Felony records
Circuit Clerk, Criminal Records
Pearl River County Courthouse
Poplarville, MS 39470
(601) 795-4911
Fax (601) 795-3017
Felony records are available by mail or fax. No release necessary. $10.00 search fee. Make check payable to Circuit Clerk. Search information required: name, years to search.

Civil records
Circuit Clerk, Criminal Records
Pearl River County Courthouse
Poplarville, MS 39470
(601) 795-4911
Fax (601) 795-3017
Civil records are available by mail. No release necessary. $5.00 search fee. $1.00 fee per copy. $1.00 for certification. Search information required: name, years to search. Specify plaintiff or defendant.

Misdemeanor records
Justice Court
204 Julia Street
Poplarville, MS 39470
(601) 795-8018
Misdemeanor records are available by mail or by phone from 1990 forward. No search fee. No release necessary. Search information required: name, address, date of birth, SSN, SASE.

Civl records
Justice Court
206 Julia Street
Poplarville, MS 39470
(601) 795-8018
Civil records are available by mail. No release necessary. No search fee. Search information required: name, date of birth, SSN, years to search. Specify plaintiff or defendant.

Perry County

Felony records
Circuit Clerk, Criminal Records
PO Box 198
New Augusta, MS 39462
(601) 964-8398
Felony records are available by mail. A release is required. No search fee. $2.00 for certification. Search information required: name, SSN, years to search.

Civil records
Circuit Clerk
PO Box 198
New Augusta, MS 39462
(601) 964-8398
Civil records are available by mail. No release necessary. No search fee. $2.00 for certification. Search information required: name, SSN, years to search. Specify plaintiff or defendant.

Misdemeanor records
Justice Court Clerk
PO Box 455
New Augusta, MS 39462
(601) 964-8366
Misdemeanor records since 1984 are available by mail. No release necessary. $7.00 search fee per 1/2 hour. $.25 fee per copy. $1.25 for certification. Search information required: name, date of birth, SSN, address, race, sex.

Civil records
Justice Court Clerk
PO Box 455
New Augusta, MS 39462
(601) 964-8366
Civil records are available by mail. No release necessary. $9.05 search fee per hour. Search information required: name, years to search. Specify plaintiff or defendant.

Pike County

Circuit Clerk's Office, Criminal Records
PO Box 31
Magnolia, MS 39652
(601) 783-2581
Felony records are available by mail. No release necessary. $5.00 fee. Search information required: name, years to search.

Civil records are available by mail. No release necessary. $5.00 search fee. $.50 per copy. $1.50 for certification. Search information required: name, years to search. Specify plaintiff or defendant.

Pontotoc County

Felony records
Circuit Clerk, Criminal Records
PO Box 428
Pontotoc, MS 38863
(601) 489-3908
Felony records are available by mail or
phone. No release necessary. No search fee.
Search information required: name, case
number.

Civil records
Circuit Clerk
PO Box 428
Pontotoc, MS 38863
(601) 489-3908
Civil records are available by mail. No re-
lease necessary. No search fee. $.10 fee per
copy. $1.00 for certification. Search infor-
mation required: name, years to search.
Specify plaintiff or defendant.

Misdemeanor records
Justice Court
PO Box 582
Pontotoc, MS 38863
(601) 489-3921
Misdemeanor records are available in per-
son only. See Mississippi state repository
for additional information.

Civil records
Justice Court
PO Box 582
Pontotoc, MS 38863
(601) 489-3921
Civil records are available in person only.
See Mississippi state repository for addi-
tional information.

Prentiss County

Felony records
Clerk of Circuit Court, Criminal
Records
101 N. Main
Bonneville, MS 38829
(601) 728-4611
Felony records are available by mail or
phone. No release necessary. No search fee.
Search information required: name, years to
search.

Civil records
Clerk of Circuit Court
101 N. Main
Bonneville, MS 38829
(601) 728-4611
Civil records are available by mail. No release necessary. No search fee. $.50 fee per
copy. $2.00 for certification. Search infor-
mation required: name, years to search.
Specify plaintiff or defendant.

Misdemeanor records
Justice Court
101 N. Main
Bonneville, MS 38829
(601) 728-8696
Misdemeanor records are available by mail.
No release necessary. No search fee. Search
information required: name.

Civil records
Justice Court
101 N. Main
Bonneville, MS 38829
(601) 728-8696
Civil records are available by mail. No release necessary. No search fee. Search information required: name, years to search.
Specify plaintiff or defendant.

Quitman County

Felony records
Circuit Clerk, Criminal Records
Courthouse
Marks, MS 38646
(601) 326-8003
Fax (601) 326-2330
Felony records are available by mail, fax or
phone. No release necessary. $5.00 search
fee. No fee for phone searches. Company
checks only, payable to Circuit Clerk.
Search information required: name, SSN,
date of birth, sex, race.

Civil records
Circuit Clerk
Courthouse
Marks, MS 38646
(601) 326-8003
Fax (601) 326-2330
Civil records are available by mail. No re-
lease necessary. $5.00 search fee. $.50 fee
per copy. $1.50 for certification. Search in-
formation required: name, years to search.
Specify plaintiff or defendant.

Misdemeanor records
Justice Court
PO Box 100
Marks, MS 38646
(601) 326-2104
Misdemeanor records since 1984 are available by mail. No release necessary. No
search fee. Search information required:
name, date of birth, race, sex, years to
search, SSN, SASE.

Civil records
Justice Court
PO Box 100
Marks, MS 38646
(601) 326-2104
Civil records are available by mail. No release necessary. No search fee. $.50 fee per
copy. $1.50 for certification. Search infor-
mation required: name, years to search, address (if available). Specify plaintiff or defendant.

Rankin County

Felony records
Circuit Clerk, Criminal Records
PO Drawer 1599
Brandon, MS 39043
(601) 825-1466 or 825-2217
Felony records are available by mail or
phone. No release necessary. $5.00 search
fee. Make check payable to Circuit Clerk.
Search information required: name, years to
search.

Civil records
Circuit Clerk
PO Drawer 1599
Brandon, MS 39043
(601) 825-1466 or 825-2217
Civil records are available by mail. No re-
lease necessary. No search fee. $.50 fee per
copy. $1.00 for certification. Search infor-
mation required: name, years to search.
Specify plaintiff or defendant.

Misdemeanor records
Justice Court
PO Box 5896
Pearle, MS 39208
(601) 939-1885
Misdemeanor records since 1984 are available by mail or phone. No release necessary. No search fee. $.50 fee per copy.
$1.50 for certification. Search information
required: name, date of charge, years to
search.

Civil records
Justice Court
PO Box 5896
Pearle, MS 39208
(601) 939-1885
Civil records are available by mail or
phone. No release necessary. No search fee.
$.50 fee per copy. $1.50 for certification.
Search information required: name, years to
search. Specify plaintiff or defendant.

Scott County

Felony records
Circuit Clerk, Criminal Records
PO Box 371
Forest, MS 39074
(601) 469-3601
Felony records are available by mail or
phone. No release necessary. $3.00 search
fee. Certified check only, payable to Circuit
Clerk. Search information required: name,
SSN, date of birth, years to search.

Civil records
Circuit Clerk
PO Box 371
Forest, MS 39074
(601) 469-3601
Civil records are available by mail or
phone. No release necessary. No search fee.
$.50 fee per copy. $1.50 for certification.
Search information required: name, years to
search. Specify plaintiff or defendant.

Misdemeanor records
Justice Court
PO Box 371
Forest, MS 39074
(601) 469-4555
Misdemeanor records are available by mail.
No release necessary. $5.00 search fee.
Search information required: full name,
date of birth, SSN, years to search.

Civil records
Justice Court
PO Box 371
Forest, MS 39074
(601) 469-4555
Civil records are available by mail. No re-
lease necessary. No search fee. $.50 fee per
copy. $1.50 for certification. Search infor-
mation required: name, years to search.
Specify plaintiff or defendant.

Sharkey County

Circuit Clerk, Criminal Records
PO Box 218
Rolling Fork, MS 39159
(601) 873-2755
Felony records are available by mail. No release necessary. $3.00 search fee. Search
information required: name, years to
search.

Civil records are available by mail. A release is required. No search fee. $.50 fee
per copy. $2.00 for certification. Search in-
formation required: name, years to search.
Specify plaintiff or defendant.

Simpson County

Felony records
Circuit Clerk, Criminal Records
PO Box 307
Mendenhall, MS 39114
(601) 847-2474
Felony records are available by mail or
phone. No release necessary. No search fee.
Search information required: full name,
date of birth, SASE.

Civil records
Circuit Clerk
PO Box 307
Mendenhall, MS 39114
(601) 847-2474
Civil records are available by mail. No release necessary. No search fee. $.50 fee per copy. $1.50 for certification. Search information required: name, years to search. Specify plaintiff or defendant.

Misdemeanor records
Simpson County Justice Court
159 Court Ave.
Mendenhall, MS 39114
(601) 847-5848
Misdemeanor records are available by mail. No release necessary. $10.00 search fee. Search information required: name, date of birth, SSN.

Civil records
Simpson County Justice Court
159 Court Ave.
Mendenhall, MS 39114
(601) 847-5848
Civil records are available by mail. No release necessary. $10.00 search fee. Search information required: name, years to search. Specify plaintiff or defendant.

Smith County

Felony records
Circuit Clerk, Criminal Records
PO Box 517
Raleigh, MS 39153
(601) 782-4751
Felony records are available by mail. No release necessary. $10.00 search fee. $.50 fee per copy. $1.50 for certification. Search information required: name, tears to search, SASE.

Civil records
Circuit Clerk
PO Box 517
Raleigh, MS 39153
(601) 782-4751
Civil records are available by mail. No release necessary. $10.00 search fee. $.50 fee per copy. $1.50 for certification. Search information required: name, years to search. Specify plaintiff or defendant.

Misdemeanor records
Justice Court
PO Box 171
Raleigh, MS 39153
(601) 782-4334
Misdemeanor records are available by mail. A release is required. No search fee. Search information required: name, offense if available, SSN, date of birth, years to search.

Civil records
Justice Court
PO Box 171
Raleigh, MS 39153
(601) 782-4334
Civil records are available by mail. A release is required. No search fee. Search information required: name, years to search. Specify plaintiff or defendant.

Stone County

Felony records
Circuit Clerk, Criminal Records
Stone County Courthouse
Wiggins, MS 39577
(601) 928-5246
Felony records are available by mail. No release necessary. $5.00 search fee. Certified check only, payable to Circuit Clerk. Search information required: name, SASE.

Civil records
Circuit Clerk
Stone County Courthouse
Wiggins, MS 39577
(601) 928-5246
Civil records are available by mail. No release necessary. $5.00 search fee. $.25 fee per copy. $1.50 for certification. Search information required: name, years to search. Specify plaintiff or defendant.

Misdemeanor records
Justice Court
231 3rd St.
Wiggins, MS 39577
(601) 928-4415
Misdemeanor records are available by mail. Written request required. Release necessary. Possible search fee. Search information required: name, date of birth, address, driver's license number.

Civil records
Justice Court
231 3rd St.
Wiggins, MS 39577
(601) 928-4415
Civil records are available by mail. No release necessary. $5.00 search fee. $.50 fee per copy. $2.00 for certification. Search information required: name, years to search. Specify plaintiff or defendant.

Sunflower County

Circuit Clerk, Criminal Records
PO Box 576
Indianola, MS 38751
(601) 887-1252
Felony records are available by mail. No release necessary. $5.00 fee for seven years search. Search information required: name, SSN, date of birth, sex, race, SASE.

Civil records are available by mail. No release necessary. $5.00 search fee. $.50 fee per copy. $2.00 for certification. Search information required: name, years to search. Specify plaintiff or defendant.

Tallahatchie County

Felony records
Circuit Clerk, Criminal Records
PO Box 86
Charleston, MS 38921
(601) 647-8758
Fax (601) 647-8490
Felony records are available by mail, phone or fax. No release necessary. $1.00 search fee. Make check payable to Circuit Clerk. Search information required: name.

Civil records
Circuit Clerk
PO Box 86
Charleston, MS 38921
(601) 647-8758
Fax (601) 647-8490
Civil records are available by mail, phone or fax. No release necessary. No search fee. $.50 fee per copy. $1.50 for certification. Search information required: name, years to search. Specify plaintiff or defendant.

Misdemeanor records
Justice Court
PO Box 440
Charleston, MS 38921
(601) 647-3477
Misdemeanor records are available by mail. No release necessary. $10.00 search fee. $.25 fee per copy. Search information required: name, date of birth, driver's license number, years to search.

Civil records
Justice Court
PO Box 440
Charleston, MS 38921
(601) 647-3477
Civil records are available by mail. No release necessary. $10.00 search fee. $.25 fee per copy. Search information required: name, years to search. Specify plaintiff or defendant.

Tate County

Felony records
Circuit Clerk, Criminal Records
201 Ward Street
Senatobia, MS 38668
(601) 562-5211
Felony records are available by mail. No release necessary. No search fee. Search information required: name, SSN.

Civil records
Circuit Clerk
201 Ward Street
Senatobia, MS 38668
(601) 562-5211
Civil records are available by mail. No release necessary. No search fee. $.50 fee per copy. $1.50 for certification. Search information required: name, years to search. Specify plaintiff or defendant.

Misdemeanor records
Tate County Justice Court
201 Ward Street
Senatobia, MS 38668
(601) 562-7626
Misdemeanor records are available by mail or phone. No release necessary. No search fee. Copies available in person. Search information required: name, date of birth, driver's license number, race, years to search.

Civil records
Tate County Justice Court
201 Ward Street
Senatobia, MS 38668
(601) 562-7626
Civil records are available by mail. No release necessary. No search fee. Copies available in person only. Search information required: name, years to search. Specify plaintiff or defendant.

Tippah County

Circuit Clerk's Office, Criminal Records
Tippah County Courthouse
Ripley, MS 38663
(601) 837-7370
Fax (601) 837-1030

Felony records are available by mail or phone. No release necessary. No search fee. Search information required: name, SSN, date of birth, sex, race.

Civil records are available by mail or phone. No release necessary. No search fee. Search information required: name, years to search. Specify plaintiff or defendant.

Tishomingo County

Tishomingo County Courthouse, Circuit Court
Iuka, MS 38852
(601) 423-7026

Felony and misdemeanor records are available by mail. No release necessary. $5.00 search fee. Search information required: name.

Civil records are available by mail. No release necessary. $5.00 search fee. $.25 fee per copy. Search information required: name, years to search. Specify plaintiff or defendant.

Tunica County

Felony records
Circuit Clerk, Criminal Records
PO Box 184
Tunica, MS 38676
(601) 363-2842

Felony records are available by mail or phone. No release necessary. $1.50 search fee. Make check payable to Circuit Clerk. Search information required: name, SSN, date of birth, sex, race, SASE, years to search.

Civil records
Circuit Clerk
PO Box 184
Tunica, MS 38676
(601) 363-2842

Civil records are available by mail. No release necessary. No search fee. $.50 fee per copy. $1.00 for certification. Search information required: name, years to search. Specify plaintiff or defendant.

Misdemeanor records
Justice Court
PO Box 1225
Tunica, MS 38676
(601) 363-2178

Misdemeanor records are available by mail or phone. Written request required. Release necessary. $6.00 fee. Search information required: full name, date of birth, years to search.

Civil records
Justice Court
PO Box 1225
Tunica, MS 38676
(601) 363-2178

Civil records are available by mail. No release necessary. $6.00 search fee. Search information required: name, years to search. Specify plaintiff or defendant.

Union County

Felony records
Circuit Clerk, Criminal Records
PO Box 298
New Albany, MS 38652
(601) 534-1910

Felony records are available by mail or phone. No release necessary. No search fee. $.50 fee per copy. Search information required: name, SSN, years to search, SASE.

Civil records
Circuit Clerk
PO Box 298
New Albany, MS 38652
(601) 534-1910

Civil records are available by mail. No release necessary. $5.00 search fee. $.50 fee per copy. $1.50 for certification. Search information required: name, years to search. Specify plaintiff or defendant.

Misdemeanor records
Justice Court
(601) 534-2111

Misdemeanor records are available in person only. See Mississippi state repository for additional information.

Civil records
Justice Court
(601) 534-2111

Civil records are available in person only. See Mississippi state repository for additional information.

Walthall County

Felony records
Circuit Clerk, Criminal Records
200 Ball Avenue
Tylertown, MS 39667
(601) 876-5677

Felony records are available by mail or phone. No release necessary. No search fee. $.25 fee per copy, $1.50 fee for certification. Search information required: name, years to search, SASE.

Civil records
Circuit Clerk
200 Ball Avenue
Tylertown, MS 39667
(601) 876-5677

Civil records are available by mail. No release necessary. No search fee. $.25 fee per copy. $1.50 for certification. Search information required: name, years to search. Specify plaintiff or defendant.

Misdemeanor records
Justice Court
PO Box 507
Tylertown, MS 39667
(601) 876-2311

Misdemeanor records are available by mail or phone. No release necessary. No search fee. $.25 fee per copy. $1.50 fee for certification. Search information required: full name, SSN, SASE.

Civil records
Justice Court
PO Box 507
Tylertown, MS 39667
(601) 876-2311

Civil records are available by mail or phone. No release necessary. No search fee. $.25 fee per copy. $1.50 for certification. Search information required: name, years to search. Specify plaintiff or defendant.

Warren County

Circuit Clerk, Criminal Records
PO Box 351
Vicksburg, MS 39180
(601) 636-3961

Felony and misdemeanor records are available by mail. No release necessary. $5.00 fee. Make check payable to Circuit Clerk. Search information required: name, years to search.

Civil records are available by mail. A release is required. $5.00 search fee. $.50 fee per copy. $1.50 for certification. Search information required: name, years to search. Specify plaintiff or defendant.

Washington County

Circuit Clerk, Criminal Records
PO Box 1276
Greenville, MS 38702
(601) 378-2747

Felony and misdemeanor records are available by mail. No release necessary. $10.00 search fee. Search information required: name, previous address, years to search.

Civil records are available by mail. No release necessary. $10.00 search fee. $.75 fee per copy. $3.00 for certification. Search information required: name, years to search. Specify plaintiff or defendant.

Wayne County

Felony records
Circuit Clerk, Criminal Records
PO Box 428
Waynesboro, MS 39367
(601) 735-1171

Felony records are available by mail. No release necessary. No search fee. Search information required: name, SSN, years to search, SASE.

Civil records
Circuit Clerk
PO Box 428
Waynesboro, MS 39367
(601) 735-1171

Civil records are available by mail. No release necessary. No search fee. Search information required: name, years to search. Specify plaintiff or defendant.

Misdemeanor records
Justice Court
Wayne County Courthouse
Waynesboro, MS 39367
(601) 735-3118

Misdemeanor records are available by mail. No release necessary. No fee. Search information required: full name, years to search.

Civil records
Justice Court
Wayne County Courthouse
Waynesboro, MS 39367
(601) 735-3118

Civil records are available by mail. No release necessary. No search fee. Search information required: name, years to search. Specify plaintiff or defendant.

Webster County

Felony records
Circuit Clerk, Criminal Records
PO Box 308
Walthall, MS 39771
(601) 258-6287
Felony records are available by mail. A release is required. $5.00 search fee. $.50 fee per copy, $2.00 fee for certification. Search information required: name, SSN, date of birth, sex, race.

Civil records
Circuit Clerk
PO Box 308
Walthall, MS 39771
(601) 258-6287
Civil records are available by mail. No release necessary. $5.00 search fee. $.50 fee per copy. $1.50 for certification. Search information required: name, years to search. Specify plaintiff or defendant.

Misdemeanor records
Justice Court
County Office Building
114 Highway 9 N.
Europa, MS 39744
(601) 258-2590
Misdemeanor records since 1984 are available by mail. No release necessary. No search fee. Copies are available in person only. Search information required: name, date of birth, SSN, driver's license number, years to search.

Civil records
Justice Court
County Office Building
114 Highway 9 N.
Europa, MS 39744
(601) 258-2590
Civil records are available by mail. No release necessary. No search fee. Copies are available in person only. Search information required: name, years to search. Specify plaintiff or defendant.

Wilkinson County

Circuit Clerk, Criminal Records
PO Box 327
Woodville, MS 39669
(601) 888-6697
Fax (601) 888-6776
Felony and misdemeanor records are available by mail or phone. No release necessary. No search fee. $.50 fee per copy. $5.00 for certification. Search information required: name, years to search.

Civil records are available by mail. No release necessary. No search fee. $.50 fee per copy. $5.00 for certification. Search information required: name, years to search. Specify plaintiff or defendant.

Winston County

Felony records
Circuit Clerk, Criminal Records
PO Box 371
Louisville, MS 39339
(601) 773-3581
Felony records are available by mail. No release necessary. $5.00 fee. Make check payable to Circuit Clerk. Search information required: full name, alias, SASE.

Civil records
Circuit Clerk
PO Box 371
Louisville, MS 39339
(601) 773-3581
Civil records are available by mail. No release necessary. $3.00 search fee. $.50 fee per copy. $1.50 for certification. Search information required: name, years to search. Specify plaintiff or defendant.

Misdemeanor records
Justice Court
PO Box 327
Louisville, MS 39339
(601) 773-6016
Misdemeanor records are available in person only. See Mississippi state respository for additional information.

Civil records
Justice Court
PO Box 327
Louisville, MS 39339
(601) 773-6016
Civil records are available in person only. See Mississippi state respository for additional information.

Yalobusha County

Felony records
Circuit Clerk, Criminal Records
PO Box 431
Water Valley, MS 38965
(601) 473-1341
Fax (601) 473-1341 – (Call first)
Felony records are available by mail or fax. No release necessary. $5.00 search fee. $1.00 fee per copy. Company checks only, payable to Circuit Clerk. Search information required: name, SASE.

Civil records
Circuit Clerk
PO Box 431
Water Valley, MS 38965
(601) 473-1341
Fax (601) 473-1341 – (Call first)
Civil records are available by mail or fax. No release necessary. $5.00 search fee. $1.00 fee per copy. Search information required: name, years to search, SASE. Specify plaintiff or defendant.

Misdemeanor records
Justice Court
PO Box 218
Coffeyville, MS 38922
(601) 675-8115
Misdemeanor records are available by mail. No release necessary. $11.00 search fee. $.25 fee per copy. Search information required: name, years to search.

Civil records
Justice Court
PO Box 218
Coffeyville, MS 38922
(601) 675-8115
Civil records are available by mail. No release necessary. $11.00 search fee. $.25 fee per copy. Search information required: name, years to search. Specify plaintiff or defendant.

Yazoo County

Felony records
Circuit Clerk, Criminal Records
PO Box 108
Yazoo City, MS 39194
(601) 746-1872
Felony records are available by mail or phone. No release necessary. No search fee. Search information required: name.

Civil records
Circuit Clerk
PO Box 108
Yazoo City, MS 39194
(601) 746-1872
Civil records are available by mail. No release necessary. $5.00 search fee. $.50 fee per copy. $1.00 for certification. Search information required: name, years to search. Specify plaintiff or defendant.

Misdemeanor records
Justice Court
PO Box 108
Yazoo City, MS 39194
(601) 746-8181
Misdemeanor records since 1984 are available by mail or phone. No release necessary. No search fee. $.50 fee per copy. $1.00 for certification. Search information required: name, date of birth, SSN, years to search.

Civil records
Justice Court
PO Box 108
Yazoo City, MS 39194
(601) 746-8181
Civil records are available by mail or phone. No release necessary. No search fee. $.50 fee per copy. $1.00 for certification. Search information required: name, years to search. Specify plaintiff or defendant.

City-County Cross Reference

Brandon *Rankin*
Braxton *Simpson*
Brookhaven *Lincoln*
Brooklyn *Forrest*
Brooksville *Noxubee*
Bruce *Calhoun*
Buckatunna *Wayne*
Bude *Franklin*
Burnsville *Tishomingo*
Byhalia *Marshall*
Caledonia *Lowndes*
Calhoun City *Calhoun*
Camden *Madison*
Canton *Madison*
Carriere *Pearl River*
Carrollton *Carroll*
Carson *Jefferson Davis*
Carthage *Leake*
Cary *Sharkey*
Cascilla *Tallahatchie*
Cedarbluff *Clay*
Centreville *Wilkinson*
Charleston *Tallahatchie*
Chatawa *Pike*
Chunky *Newton*
Church Hill *Jefferson*
Clara *Wayne*
Clarksdale *Coahoma*
Clermont Harbor *Hancock*
Cleveland *Bolivar*
Clinton *Hinds*
Coahoma *Coahoma*
Coffeeville *Yalobusha*
Coila *Carroll*
Coldwater *Tate*
Collins *Covington*
Collinsville *Lauderdale*
Columbia *Marion*
Columbus *Lowndes*
Como *Panola*
Conehatta *Newton*
Corinth *Alcorn*
Courtland *Panola*
Crawford *Lowndes*
Crenshaw *Panola*
Crosby *Amite*
Crowder *Quitman*
Cruger *Holmes*
Crystal Springs *Copiah*
Daleville *Lauderdale*
Darling *Quitman*
Decatur *Newton*
DeKalb *Kemper*
DeLisle *Harrison*
Delta City *Sharkey*
Dennis *Tishomingo*
Derma *Calhoun*
D'Iberville *Jackson*
D' Lo *Simpson*
Doddsville *Sunflower*
Drew *Sunflower*
Dublin *Coahoma*
Duck Hill *Montgomery*
Dumas *Tippah*
Duncan *Bolivar*
Dundee *Tunica*
Durant *Holmes*
Eastabuchie *Jones*
Ebenezer *Holmes*
Ecru *Pontotoc*
Edwards *Hinds*
Elliott *Grenada*
Ellisville *Jones*
Enid *Tallahatchie*
Enterprise *Clarke*
Escatawpa *Jackson*

Ethel *Attala*
Etta *Union*
Eupora *Webster*
Falkner *Tippah*
Fayette *Jefferson*
Fernwood *Pike*
Flora *Madison*
Florence *Rankin*
Flowood *Rankin*
Forest *Scott*
Forkville *Scott*
Foxworth *Marion*
French Camp *Choctaw*
Friars Point *Coahoma*
Fulton *Itawamba*
Gallman *Copiah*
Gattman *Monroe*
Gautier *Jackson*
Georgetown *Copiah*
Glen *Alcorn*
Glen Allan *Washington*
Glendora *Tallahatchie*
Gloster *Amite*
Golden *Tishomingo*
Goodman *Holmes*
Gore Springs *Grenada*
Grace *Issaquena*
Greenville *Washington*
Greenwood *Leflore*
Greenwood Springs
   Monroe
Grenada *Grenada*
Gulfport *Harrison*
Gunnison *Bolivar*
Guntown *Lee*
Hamilton *Monroe*
Harperville *Scott*
Harriston *Jefferson*
Harrisville *Simpson*
Hatley *Monroe*
Hattiesburg *Forrest*
Hazlehurst *Copiah*
Heidelberg *Jasper*
Hermanville *Claiborne*
Hernando *DeSoto*
Hickory *Newton*
Hickory Flat *Benton*
Hillsboro *Scott*
Holcomb *Grenada*
Hollandale *Washington*
Holly Bluff *Yazoo*
Holly Springs *Marshall*
Horn Lake *DeSoto*
Houlka *Chickasaw*
Houston *Chickasaw*
Hurley *Jackson*
Independence *Tate*
Indianola *Sunflower*
Inverness *Sunflower*
Isola *Humphreys*
Itta Bena *Leflore*
Iuka *Tishomingo*
Jackson *Hinds*
Jayess *Lawrence*
Jonestown *Coahoma*
Jumpertown *Pretiss*
Kilmichael *Montgomery*
Kiln *Hancock*
Kokomo *Marion*
Kosciusko *Attala*
Lake *Scott*
Lake Cormorant *DeSoto*
Lakeshore *Hancock*
Lamar *Benton*
Lambert *Quitman*
Lauderdale *Lauderdale*

Laurel *Jones*
Lawrence *Newton*
Le Tourneau *Warren*
Leakesville *Greene*
Leland *Washington*
Lena *Leake*
Lexington *Holmes*
Liberty *Amite*
Little Rock *Newton*
Long Beach *Harrison*
Lorman *Jefferson*
Louin *Jasper*
Louise *Humphreys*
Louisville *Winston*
Lucedale *George*
Ludlow *Scott*
Lula *Coahoma*
Lumberton *Lamar*
Lyon *Coahoma*
McAdams *Attala*
McCall Creek *Franklin*
McCarley *Carroll*
McComb *Pike*
McCondy *Chickasaw*
McCool *Attala*
McHenry *Stone*
McLain *Greene*
McNeill *Pearl River*
Maben *Oktibbeha*
Macon *Noxubee*
Madden *Leake*
Madison *Madison*
Magee *Simpson*
Magnolia *Pike*
Mantachie *Itawamba*
Mantee *Webster*
Marietta *Prentiss*
Marion *Lauderdale*
Marks *Quitman*
Mathiston *Webster*
Mayersville *Issaquena*
Mayhew *Lowndes*
Meadville *Franklin*
Mendenhall *Simpson*
Meridian *Lauderdale*
Merigold *Bolivar*
Metcalfe *Washington*
Michigan City *Benton*
Midnight *Humphreys*
Mineral Wells *DeSoto*
Minter City *Leflore*
Mississippi State
   Oktibbeha
Mize *Smith*
Money *Leflore*
Monticello *Lawrence*
Montpelier *Clay*
Mooreville *Lee*
Moorhead *Sunflower*
Morgan City *Leflore*
Morgantown *Marion*
Morton *Scott*
Moselle *Jones*
Moss *Jasper*
Moss Point *Jackson*
Mound Bayou *Bolivar*
Mount Olive *Covington*
Myrtle *Union*
Natchez *Adams*
Neely *Greene*
Nesbit *DeSoto*
Nettleton *Lee*
New Albany *Union*
New Augusta *Perry*
Newhebron *Lawrence*
New Site *Prentiss*

Newton *Newton*
Nicholson *Pearl River*
Nitta Yuma *Sharkey*
North Carrollton *Carroll*
North Tunica *Jackson*
Noxapater *Winston*
Oakland *Yalobusha*
Oak Vale *Lawrence*
Ocean Springs *Jackson*
Okolona *Chickasaw*
Olive Branch *DeSoto*
Orange Grove *Harrison*
Osyka *Pike*
Ovett *Jones*
Oxford *Lafayette*
Pace *Bolivar*
Pachuta *Clarke*
Panther Burn *Sharkey*
Paris *Lafayette*
Pascagoula *Jackson*
Pass Christian *Harrison*
Pattison *Claiborne*
Paulding *Jasper*
Pearl *Rankin*
Pearlington *Hancock*
Pelahatchie *Rankin*
Perkinston *Stone*
Petal *Forrest*
Pheba *Clay*
Philadelphia *Neshoba*
Philipp *Tallahatchie*
Picayune *Pearl River*
Pickens *Holmes*
Piney Woods *Rankin*
Pinola *Simpson*
Pittsboro *Calhoun*
Plantersville *Lee*
Pleasant Grove *Panola*
Pontotoc *Pontotoc*
Pope *Panola*
Poplarville *Pearl River*
Porterville *Kemper*
Port Gibson *Claiborne*
Potts Camp *Marshall*
Prairie *Monroe*
Prairie Point *Noxubee*
Prentiss *Jefferson Davis*
Preston *Kemper*
Puckett *Rankin*
Pulaski *Scott*
Purvis *Lamar*
Quitman *Clarke*
Raleigh *Smith*
Randolph *Pontotoc*
Raymond *Hinds*
Red Banks *Marshall*
Redwood *Warren*
Reform *Choctaw*
Rena Lara *Coahoma*
Rich *Coahoma*
Richton *Perry*
Ridgeland *Madison*
Rienzi *Alcorn*
Ripley *Tippah*
Robinsonville *Tunica*
Rolling Fork *Sharkey*
Rome *Sunflower*
Rosedale *Bolivar*
Rose Hill *Jasper*
Roxie *Franklin*
Ruleville *Sunflower*
Ruth *Lincoln*
Sallis *Attala*
Saltillo *Lee*
Sandersville *Jones*
Sandhill *Rankin*

Sandy Hook *Marion*
Sarah *Tate*
Sardis *Panola*
Sarepta *Calhoun*
Satartia *Yazoo*
Saucier *Harrison*
Savage *Tate*
Schlater *Leflore*
Scobey *Yalobusha*
Scooba *Kemper*
Scott *Bolivar*
Sebastopol *Scott*
Seminary *Covington*
Senatobia *Tate*
Shannon *Lee*
Sharon *Madison*
Shaw *Bolivar*
Shelby *Bolivar*
Sherard *Coahoma*
Sherman *Pontotoc*
Shubuta *Clarke*
Shuqualak *Noxubee*
Sibley *Adams*
Sidon *Leflore*
Silver City *Humphreys*
Silver Creek *Lawrence*
Skene *Bolivar*
Sledge *Quitman*
Smithdale *Amite*
Smithville *Monroe*
Sontag *Lawrence*
Soso *Jones*
Southaven *DeSoto*
Star *Rankin*
Starkville *Oktibbeha*
State Line *Greene*
Steens *Lowndes*
Stewart *Montgomery*
Stoneville *Washington*
Stonewall *Clarke*
Stringer *Jasper*
Sturgis *Oktibbeha*
Summit *Pike*
Sumner *Tallahatchie*
Sumrall *Lamar*
Sunflower *Sunflower*
Swan Lake *Tallahatchie*
Swiftown *Leflore*
Taylor *Lafayette*
Taylorsville *Smith*
Tchula *Holmes*
Terry *Hinds*
Thaxton *Pontotoc*
Thomastown *Leake*
Thornton *Holmes*
Tie Plant *Grenada*
Tillatoba *Yalobusha*
Tinsley *Yazoo*
Tiplersville *Tippah*
Tippo *Tallahatchie*
Tishomingo *Tishomingo*
Toccopola *Pontotoc*
Toomsuba *Lauderdale*
Tougaloo *Hinds*
Trebloc *Chickasaw*
Tremont *Itawamba*
Tunica *Tunica*
Tupelo *Lee*
Tutwiler *Tallahatchie*
Tylertown *Walthall*
Union *Newton*
Union Church *Jefferson*
University *Lafayette*
Utica *Hinds*
Vaiden *Carroll*

Valley Park *Issaquena*
Vance *Quitman*
Van Vleet *Chickasaw*
Vardaman *Calhoun*
Vaughan *Yazoo*
Verona *Lee*
Vicksburg *Warren*
Victoria *Marshall*
Vossburg *Jasper*
Walls *DeSoto*
Walnut *Tippah*
Walnut Grove *Leake*
Walthall *Webster*
Washington *Adams*
Waterford *Marshall*
Water Valley *Yalobusha*
Waveland *Hancock*
Waynesboro *Wayne*
Wayside *Washington*
Webb *Tallahatchie*
Weir *Choctaw*
Wesson *Copiah*
West *Holmes*
West Gulfport *Harrison*
West Point *Clay*
Wheeler *Prentiss*
Whitfield *Rankin*
Wiggins *Stone*
Williamsville *Attala*
Winona *Montgomery*
Winstonville *Bolivar*
Woodland *Chickasaw*
Woodville *Wilkinson*
Yazoo City *Yazoo*

Missouri

Of Missouri's 114 counties, 100 make criminal conviction data available for employment screening purposes by phone and/or mail. Fifty one (51) counties will allow record checks by fax. Circuit court holds civil court records for claims $15,000 and above.

For more information or for offices not listed, contact the state's information hot line at (314) 751-2000.

Driving Records

Driver's License Bureau
PO Box 200
Jefferson City, MO 65105
(314) 751-2730
Driving records are available by mail or in person. $1.50 fee per request. Turnaround time is 4 to 7 days. Written request must include job applicant's full name, date of birth and license number. Make check payable to Department of Revenue.

Worker's Compensation Records

Division of Workers Compensation
PO Box 58
Jefferson City, MO 65102
(314) 751-4231
Worker's compensation records are available by mail only. A notorized release is required. $2.00 search fee from January 1986 forward. For record searches prior to 1986, past employers names are required. Requests must include job applicant's full name, SSN and SASE.

Vital Statistics

Department of Health
Bureau of Vital Records
PO Box 570
Jefferson City, MO 65102
(314) 751-6400
Birth and death records are available for $4.00 each. State office has records since January 1910. If event occurred in the City of St. Louis, St. Louis County, or Kansas City before 1910, write to the City or County Health Department. Copies of these special records are $3.00 each in St. Louis City and $5.00 each for the County. In Kansas City, $6.00 for first copy and $3.00 for each additional copy ordered at same time. An employer can obtain records with a written release. Employee signature must be on application. Make certified check or money order payable to Missouri Department of Health.
Marriage records are available at county level where marriage took place. Divorce records are available at county court where divorce granted.

Department of Education

Department of Education
Teacher Certification
PO Box 480
Jefferson City, MO 65102
(314) 751-3486
Field of certification and expiration date are available by phone or mail. Include name and SSN.

Medical Licensing

State Board of Healing Art
PO Box 4
Jefferson City, MO 65102
(314) 751-0098
Will confirm licenses for MDs and DOs by phone or mail. No fee. For licenses not mentioned, contact the above office.

Missouri State Board of Nursing
PO Box 656
3523 North Ten Mile Drive
Jefferson City, MO 65102
(314) 751-2334 Ext. 141
Will confirm license by phone. No fee. Include name, license number, if available.

Bar Association

Missouri State Bar Association
PO Box 119
Jefferson City, MO 65102
(314) 635-4128
Will confirm licenses by phone. No fee. Include name.

Accountancy Board

Missouri State Board of Accountancy
PO Box 613
Jefferson City, MO 65102
(314) 751-0012
Will confirm license by phone. No fee. Include name.

Securities Commission

Office of the Secretary of State
Securities Division
600 W. Main Street
PO B0x 778
Jefferson City, MO 65101
(314) 751-4136
Will confirm license by phone. No fee. Include name and SSN.

Secretary of State

Secretary of State
Corporation Division
PO Box 778
Jefferson, City, MO 65102
(314) 751-4153
Service agent and address, date incorporated, trade names are available by phone or mail. $5.00 fee for mail response. Contact the above office for additional information.

Criminal Records

State Repository

Missouri State Highway Patrol
Criminal Record Division
PO Box 568
Jefferson City, MO 65102
(314) 751-3313
Written requests must include subject's full name, aliases, date of birth, sex, race and SSN. There is a $5.00 fee. Make certified check or money order payable to Missouri Criminal Record System. There is a $14.00 fee for processing a fingerprint card. Only conviction data released.

Adair County
Felony records
Circuit Clerk
Adair County
PO Box 690
Kirksville, MO 63501
(816) 665-2552
Fax (816) 665-3420
Felony records are available by mail, phone or fax. A release necessary. No search fee. $.10 fee per copy. $1.00 for certification. Search information required: name. Records accessible from 1976.

Civil records
Circuit Clerk
Adair County
PO Box 690
Kirksville, MO 63501
(816) 665-2552
Fax (816) 665-3420
Civil records are available by mail, phone or fax. No release necessary. No search fee. $.10 fee per copy. $1.00 for certification. Search information required: name, years to search. Specify plaintiff or defendant.

Misdemeanor records
Circuit Court, Associate Division
Adair County Courthouse
Kirksville, MO 63501
(816) 665-3877
Fax (816) 665-3420
Misdemeanor records are available by mail or phone. No release necessary. No search fee. $2.50 for certification. Search information required: name.

Civil records
Circuit Court, Associate Division
Adair County Courthouse
Kirksville, MO 63501
(816) 665-3877
Fax (816) 665-3420
Civil records are available by mail or phone. No release necessary. No search fee. $2.50 for certification. Search information required: name, years to search. Specify plaintiff or defendant.

Andrew County

Felony records
Circuit Clerk, Criminal Records
PO Box 208
Savannah, MO 64485
(816) 324-4221
Fax (816) 324-5667
Felony records are available by mail, phone or fax. No release necessary. $4.00 search fee. $.25 fee per copy. $1.00 for certification. $3.00 fee for first page of fax response, $1.00 each additional page. Search information required: name, years to search.

Civil records
Circuit Clerk
PO Box 208
Savannah, MO 64485
(816) 324-4221
Fax (816) 324-5667
Civil records are available by mail, phone or fax. No release necessary. No search fee. $.10 fee per copy. $1.00 for certification. Search information required: name, years to search. Specify plaintiff or defendant.

Misdemeanor records
Associate Circuit Court
Division 2
Andrew County Courthouse
PO Box 49
Savannah, MO 64485
(816) 324-3921
Misdemeanor records are available by mail or phone. No release necessary. No search fee. $.50 fee per copy. $1.50 for certification. Search information required: name, date of birth, years to search.

Civil records
Associate Circuit Court
Division 2
Andrew County Courthouse
PO Box 49
Savannah, MO 64485
(816) 324-3921
Civil records are available by mail or phone. No release necessary. No search fee. $.50 fee per copy. $1.50 for certification. Search information required: name, years to search. Specify plaintiff or defendant.

Atchison County

Felony records
Circuit Clerk, Criminal Records
PO Box J
Rockport, MO 64482
(816) 744-2707
Fax (816) 744-5705
Felony records are available by mail or phone. No release necessary. No search fee. $1.00 fee per copy. $1.00 for certification. $2.00 fee for fax response. Search information required: name.

Civil records
Circuit Clerk
PO Box J
Rockport, MO 64482
(816) 744-2707
Fax (816) 744-5705
Civil records are available by mail or phone. No release necessary. No search fee. $1.00 fee per copy. $1.00 for certification. $2.00 fee for fax response. Search information required: name, years to search. Specify plaintiff or defendant.

Misdemeanor records
Associate Circuit Court
PO Box 187
Rockport, MO 64482
(816) 744-2700
Misdemeanor records are available by mail or phone. No release necessary. No search fee. $1.00 fee per copy. $1.00 for certification. Search information required: name, date of birth, years to search.

Civil records
Associate Circuit Court
PO Box 187
Rockport, MO 64482
(816) 744-2700
Civil records are available by mail or phone. No release necessary. No search fee. $1.00 fee per copy. $1.00 for certification. Search information required: name, years to search. Specify plaintiff or defendant.

Audrain County

Felony records
Circuit Clerk, Criminal Records
Division 1
Audrain County Courthouse
Mexico, MO 65265
(314) 581-3223
Fax (314) 581-3237
Felony records are available in person only. See Missouri state repository for additional information.

Civil records
Circuit Clerk
Division 1
Audrain County Courthouse
Mexico, MO 65265
(314) 581-3223
Fax (314) 581-3237
Civil records are available in person only. See Missouri state repository for additional information.

Misdemeanor records
Audrain County
Division 2
Circuit Court Courthouse
Mexico, MO 65265
(314) 581-3860
Misdemeanor records are available in person only. See Missouri state repository for additional information.

Civil records
Audrain County
Division 2
Circuit Court Courthouse
Mexico, MO 65265
(314) 581-3860
Civil records are available in person only. See Missouri state repository for additional information.

Barry County

Felony records
Dick Sanders, Criminal Records
Barry County Courthouse
Cassville, MO 65625
(417) 847-2361
Felony records are available in person only at the above office.

Civil records
Dick Sanders
Barry County Courthouse
Cassville, MO 65625
(417) 847-2361
Civil records are available in person only. See Missouri state repository for additional information.

Misdemeanor records
Associate Circuit Court
Barry County Courthouse
Cassville, MO 65625
(417) 847-2127
Misdemeanor records are available in person only. See Missouri state repository for additional information.

Civil records
Associate Circuit Court
Barry County Courthouse
Cassville, MO 65625
(417) 847-2127
Civil records are available in person only. See Missouri state repository for additional information.

Barton County

Felony records
Barton County Circuit Clerk, Criminal
Records
Courthouse
1007 Broadway
Lamar, MO 64759-1498
(417) 682-2444
Fax (417) 682-2960
Felony records are available by mail, phone
or fax. No release necessary. No search fee.
$.10 fee per copy, $1.50 fee for certification. $1.00 fee for first page of fax re-
sponse, $.50 for each additional page.
Search information required: name, SSN,
date of birth, sex, race, SASE.

Civil records
Barton County Circuit Clerk
Courthouse
1007 Broadway
Lamar, MO 64759-1498
(417) 682-2444
Fax (417) 682-2960
Civil records are available by mail, phone
or fax. No release necessary. No search fee.
$.10 fee per copy. $1.50 for certification.
$1.00 fee for first page of fax response,
$.50 for each additional page. Search infor-
mation required: name, years to search.
Specify plaintiff or defendant.

Misdemeanor records
Associate Circuit Court
Barton County Courthouse
Lamar, MO 64759
(417) 682-5754
Fax (417) 682-2960
Misdemeanor records are available by mail,
phone or fax. No release necessary. No
search fee. $1.00 fee per copy. $1.50 for
certification. $1.00 fee for fax response.
Search information required: name, years to
search, offense.

Civil records
Associate Circuit Court
Barton County Courthouse
Lamar, MO 64759
(417) 682-5754
Fax (417) 682-2960
Civil records are available by mail, phone
or fax. No release necessary. No search fee.
$1.00 fee per copy. $1.50 for certification.
$1.00 fee for fax response. Search informa-
tion required: name, years to search.
Specify plaintiff or defendant.

Bates County

Felony records
Circuit Clerk, Criminal Records
PO Box 288
Butler, MO 64730
(816) 679-5171
Fax (816) 679-4446
Felony records are available by mail. No release necessary. No search fee. $.25 fee per
copy. $1.00 fee per fax incoming and out-
going. Search information required: name,
years to search, SASE.

Civil records
Circuit Clerk
PO Box 288
Butler, MO 64730
(816) 679-5171
Fax (816) 679-4446
Civil records are available by mail or
phone. No release necessary. No search fee.
$.25 fee per copy. $1.00 fee per fax incom-
ing and outgoing. Search information re-
quired: name, years to search, SASE.
Specify plaintiff or defendant.

Misdemeanor records
Associate Circuit Court
Bates County Courthouse
Butler, MO 64730
(816) 679-3311
Fax (816) 679-4446
Misdemeanor records are available by mail,
phone or fax. No release necessary. No
search fee. $.25 fee per copy. $1.50 for certification. Search information required:
name, years to search, date of birth.

Civil records
Associate Circuit Court
Bates County Courthouse
Butler, MO 64730
(816) 679-3311
Fax (816) 679-4446
Civil records are available by mail, phone
or fax. No release necessary. No search fee.
$.25 fee per copy. $1.50 for certification.
Search information required: name, years to
search. Specify plaintiff or defendant.

Benton County

Felony records
Circuit Clerk, Criminal Records
PO Box 37
Warsaw, MO 65355
(816) 438-7712
Fax (816) 438-5755
Felony records are available by mail or
phone. No release necessary. No search fee.
$.25 fee per copy. $1.50 for certification.
$1.00 fee per fax response. Search informa-
tion required: name.

Civil records
Circuit Clerk
PO Box 37
Warsaw, MO 65355
(816) 438-7712
Civil records are available by mail or
phone. No release necessary. No search fee.
$.25 fee per copy. $1.50 for certification.
$1.00 fee per fax response. Search informa-
tion required: name, years to search.
Specify plaintiff or defendant.

Misdemeanor records
Benton County
Associate Circuit Court
PO Box 666
Warsaw, MO 65355
(816) 438-6231
Fax (816) 438-5755
Misdemeanor records are available by mail,
phone or fax. No release necessary. No
search fee. $1.00 fee per copy. $1.50 for
certification. Search information required:
name, years to search.

Civil records
Benton County
Associate Circuit Court
PO Box 666
Warsaw, MO 65355
(816) 438-6231
Fax (816) 438-5755
Civil records are available by mail or
phone. No release necessary. No search fee.
$1.00 fee per copy. $1.50 for certification.
Search information required: name, years to
search. Specify plaintiff or defendant.

Bollinger County

Felony records
Circuit Clerk, Criminal Records
PO Box 12
Marble Hill, MO 63764
(314) 238-2710
Felony records are available by mail. No release necessary. No search fee. $1.00 fee
for first copy, $.25 for each additional copy.
$2.00 for certification. Search information
required: name, date of birth, years to
search, SASE.

Civil records
Circuit Clerk
PO Box 12
Marble Hill, MO 63764
(314) 238-2710
Civil records are available by mail or
phone. No release necessary. No search fee.
$1.00 fee for first copy, $.25 for each additional copy. $2.00 for certification. Search
information required: name, years to
search, SASE. Specify plaintiff or defendant.

Misdemeanor records
Associate Circuit Court
Clerk of Court
Division 5
PO Box 34
Marble Hill, MO 63764
(314) 238-2730
Misdemeanor records are available in per-
son only. See Missouri State Repository for
additional information.

Civil records
Associate Circuit Court
Clerk of Court
Division 5
PO Box 34
Marble Hill, MO 63764
(314) 238-2730
Civil records are available in person only.
See Missouri state repository for additional
information.

Boone County

Circuit Clerk, Criminal Records
Courthouse
701 E.Walnut
Columbia, MO 65201
(314) 874-7570
Fax (314) 875-3664
Felony and misdemeanor records are available by mail or fax. No release necessary.
No search fee. $.25 fee per copy (includes
certification). $.25 fee for fax request or re-
sponse. Search information required: full
name, maiden name, date of birth, SSN (if
available).

Civil records are available by mail or fax. No release necessary. No search fee. $.25 fee per copy (includes certification). $.25 fee for fax request or response. Search information required: name, years to search. Specify plaintiff or defendant.

Buchanan County

Circuit Clerk, Criminal Records
411 Jules Street
St. Joseph, MO 64501
(816) 271-1462
Fax (816) 271-1538
Felony and misdemeanor records are available by mail. No release necessary. $4.00 search fee. $1.00 fee per copy. $2.50 for certification. $3.50 fee for first page of fax response, $1.00 for each additional page. Search information required: name.

Civil records are available by mail or phone. No release necessary. $4.00 search fee. $1.00 fee per copy. $2.50 for certification. $3.50 fee for first page of fax response, $1.00 for each additional page. Search information required: name, years to search. Specify plaintiff or defendant.

Butler County

Felony records
Circuit Clerk-Division I, Criminal Records
Butler County Courthouse
Poplar Bluff, MO 63901
(314) 686-8082
Fax (314) 686-8094
Felony records are available by mail. No release necessary. $1.00 fee for each year searched. Make check payable to Circuit Clerk. Search information required: name, years to search.

Civil records
Circuit Clerk-Division I
Butler County Courthouse
Poplar Bluff, MO 63901
(314) 686-8082
Fax (314) 686-8094
Civil records are available by mail or phone. No release necessary. $1.00 fee for each year searched. Search information required: name, years to search. Specify plaintiff or defendant.

Misdemeanor records
Circuit Court
Division 2
Butler County Courthouse
Poplar Bluff, MO 63901
(314) 686-8087
Misdemeanor records are available by mail. A release is required. No search fee. $.25 fee per copy. $2.50 for certification. Search information required: name, years to search.

Civil records
Circuit Court
Division 2
Butler County Courthouse
Poplar Bluff, MO 63901
(314) 686-8087
Civil records are available by mail or phone. A release is required. No search fee. $.25 fee per copy. $2.50 for certification. Search information required: name, years to search. Specify plaintiff or defendant.

Caldwell County

Felony records
Circuit Clerk, Criminal Records
Caldwell County Courthouse
PO Box 86
Kingston, MO 64650
(816) 586-2581
Felony records are available by mail or phone. No release necessary. No search fee. $.50 fee per copy. $1.00 for certification. Search information required: name, SSN, date of birth, years to search.

Civil records
Circuit Clerk
Caldwell County Courthouse
PO Box 86
Kingston, MO 64650
(816) 586-2581
Civil records are available by mail or phone. No release necessary. No search fee. $.50 fee per copy. $1.00 for certification. Search information required: name, years to search. Specify plaintiff or defendant.

Misdemeanor records
Circuit Court
Division 3
Caldwell County Courthouse
PO Box 8
Kingston, MO 64650
(816) 586-2771
Misdemeanor records are available by mail only. No release necessary. No search fee. $1.00 per copy. $1.00 for certification. Search information required: name, years to search, SSN, date of birth.

Civil records
Circuit Court
Division 3
Caldwell County Courthouse
PO Box 8
Kingston, MO 64650
(816) 586-2771
Civil records are available by mail or phone. No release necessary. No search fee. $1.00 fee per copy. $1.00 for certification. Search information required: name, years to search. Specify plaintiff or defendant.

Callaway County

Felony records
Circuit Clerk, Criminal Records
Callaway County Courthouse
Fulton, MO 65251
(314) 642-0780
Felony records are available by mail or phone. No release necessary. No search fee. $.25 fee per copy. $1.25 for certification. Search information required: name, date of birth, SSN, address.

Civil records
Circuit Clerk
Callaway County Courthouse
Fulton, MO 65251
(314) 642-0780
Civil records are available by mail or phone. No release necessary. No search fee. $.25 fee per copy. $1.25 for certification. Search information required: name, years to search. Specify plaintiff or defendant.

Misdemeanor records
Circuit Court
Division 7
Callaway County Courthouse
Fulton, MO 65251
(314) 642-0777
Misdemeanor records are available by mail. A release is required. No search fee. $.25 fee per copy. $1.25 for certification. Search information required: name, date of offense.

Civil records
Circuit Court
Division 7
Callaway County Courthouse
Fulton, MO 65251
(314) 642-0777
Civil records are available by mail or phone. No release necessary. No search fee. $.25 fee per copy. $1.25 for certification. Search information required: name, years to search. Specify plaintiff or defendant.

Camden County

Felony records
Circuit Clerk, Criminal Records
PO Box 930
Camdenton, MO 65020
(314) 346-4440 Extension 262
Fax (314) 346-5422
Felony records are available by mail, phone or fax. No release necessary. No search fee. $.50 fee per copy. $.50 for certification. Search information required: name, years to search.

Civil records
Circuit Clerk
PO Box 930
Camdenton, MO 65020
(314) 346-4440 Extension 262
Fax (314) 346-5422
Civil records are available by mail, phone or fax. No release necessary. No search fee. $.50 fee per copy. $.50 for certification. Search information required: name, years to search. Specify plaintiff or defendant.

Misdemeanor records
Associate Circuit Court
PO Box 19
Camdenton, MO 65020
(314) 346-4440 Extension 245
Misdemeanor records are available by mail. A release is required. No search fee. $.10 fee per copy. Search information required: name, SASE.

Civil records
Associate Circuit Court
PO Box 19
Camdenton, MO 65020
(314) 346-4440 Extension 245
Civil records are available by mail or phone. No release necessary. No search fee. $.10 fee per copy. Search information required: name, years to search, SASE. Specify plaintiff or defendant.

Cape Girardeau County

Circuit Court-Division 3, Criminal Records
Courthouse
Jackson, MO 63755
(314) 243-8446
Fax (314) 243-0787
Felony and misdemeanor records are available by mail, phone or fax. No release necessary. No search fee. Search information required: name, SSN, date of birth, years to search.

Civil records are available by mai, phone or fax. No release necessary. No search fee. Search information required: name, years to search. Specify plaintiff or defendant.

Carroll County

Circuit Clerk of Carroll County, Criminal Records
PO Box 245
Carrollton, MO 64633
(816) 542-1466

Felony and misdemeanor records are available by mail. A release is required. There is a $2.00 search fee only if record is found. $1.00 fee per copy (includes certification). Check payable to Circuit Clerk. Search information required: name, SASE.

Civil records are available by mail or phone. No release necessary. No search fee. $1.00 fee per copy (includes certification). Search information required: name, years to search. Specify plaintiff or defendant.

Carter County

Circuit Clerk, Criminal Records
PO Box 578
Van Buren, MO 63965
(314) 323-4513
Fax (314) 323-8577

Felony and misdemeanor records are available by mail, phone or fax. No release necessary. No search fee. $.25 fee per copy. $1.00 for certification. Search information required: name, years to search.

Civil records are available by mail, phone or fax. No release necessary. No search fee. $.25 fee per copy. $1.00 for certification. Search information required: name, years to search. Specify plaintiff or defendant.

Cass County

Felony records
Circuit Clerk, Criminal Records
Cass County Courthouse
100 E. Wall
PO Box 407
Harrisonville, MO 64701
(816) 884-5100 Extension 237
Felony records are available in person only. See Missouri state repository for additional information.

Civil records
Circuit Clerk
Cass County Courthouse
100 E. Wall
PO Box 407
Harrisonville, MO 64701
(816) 884-5100 Extension 237
Civil records are available in person only. See Missouri state repository for additional information.

Misdemeanor records
Associate Circuit Court
PO Box 384
Harrisonville, MO 64701
(816) 884-5100 Extension 229
Misdemeanor records are available in person only. See Missouri state repository for additional information.

Civil records
Associate Circuit Court
PO Box 384
Harrisonville, MO 64701
(816) 884-5100 Extension 229
Civil records are available in person only. See Missouri state repository for additional information.

Cedar County

Felony records
Circuit Clerk and Recorder's Office, Criminal Records
PO Box 96
Stockton, MO 65785
(417) 276-3213
Felony records are available by mail. No release necessary. No search fee. $1.00 fee per copy. $2.00 for certification. Make check payable to Circuit Clerk. Search information required: name, SSN, date of birth, sex, race.

Civil records
Circuit Clerk and Recorder's Office
PO Box 96
Stockton, MO 65785
(417) 276-3213
Civil records are available by mail or phone. No release necessary. No search fee. $1.00 fee per copy. $2.00 for certification. Search information required: name, years to search. Specify plaintiff or defendant.

Misdemeanor records
Associate Circuit Court
PO Box 156
Stockton, MO 65785
(417) 276-4213
Misdemeanor records are available by mail. No release necessary. No search fee. $1.00 fee per copy. $1.50 for certification. Checks payable to Associate Circuit Court. Search information required: name, SASE.

Civil records
Associate Circuit Court
PO Box 156
Stockton, MO 65785
(417) 276-4213
Civil records are available by mail or phone. No release necessary. No search fee. $1.00 fee per copy. $1.50 for certification. Search information required: name, years to search. Specify plaintiff or defendant.

Chariton County

Circuit Clerk, Criminal Records
PO Box 112
Keytesville, MO 65261
(816) 288-3602
Fax (816) 288-3612
Felony and misdemeanor records are available by mail, phone or fax. No release necessary. No search fee. $.50 fee per copy. $2.00 for certification. $1.00 fee for fax response. Make check payable to Circuit Clerk. Search information required: name, SASE.

Civil records are available by mail, phone or fax. No release necessary. No search fee. $.50 fee per copy. $2.00 for certification. $1.00 fee for fax response. Search information required: name, years to search, SASE. Specify plaintiff or defendant.

Christian County

Felony records
Clerk of Circuit Court
PO Box 278
Ozark, MO 65721
(417) 485-6372
Fax (417) 485-0391
Felony records are available by mail or fax. $4.00 search fee. $.25 fee per copy. $1.00 for certification. No release necessary. Search information required: name, date of birth, previous address.

Civil records
Clerk of Circuit Court
PO Box 278
Ozark, MO 65721
(417) 485-6372
Fax (417) 485-0391
Civil records are available by mail or fax. No release necessary. $4.00 search fee. $.25 fee per copy. $1.00 for certification. Search information required: name, years to search. Specify plaintiff or defendant.

Misdemeanor records
Associate Circuit Court
PO Box 296
Ozark, MO 65721
(417) 485-2425
Misdemeanor records are available by mail. No release necessary. No search fee. Search information required: name, date of birth, SASE.

Civil records
Associate Circuit Court
PO Box 296
Ozark, MO 65721
(417) 485-2425
Civil records are available by mail or phone. No release necessary. No search fee. Search information required: name, years to search, SASE. Specify plaintiff or defendant.

Clark County

Felony records
Circuit Clerk and Recorder's Off., Criminal Records
111 East Court
Clark County Courthouse
Kahoka, MO 63445
(816) 727-3292
Felony records are available by mail. No release necessary. No search fee. $.25 fee per copy. $3.00 for certification. Search information required: name, date of birth, years to search.

Civil records
Circuit Clerk and Recorder's Off.
111 East Court
Clark County Courthouse
Kahoka, MO 63445
(816) 727-3292
Civil records are available by mail or phone. No release necessary. No search fee. $.25 fee per copy. $3.00 for certification. Search information required: name, years to search. Specify plaintiff or defendant.

Misdemeanor records
Associate Circuit Court
113 W. Court
Kahoka, MO 63445
(816) 727-3628
Misdemeanor records are available by mail or phone. A release is required. No search fee. $.25 fee per copy. $1.25 for certification. Search information required: name, date of birth, SSN.

Civil records
Associate Circuit Court
113 W. Court
Kahoka, MO 63445
(816) 727-3628
Civil records are available by mail or phone. A release is required. No search fee. $.25 fee per copy. $1.25 for certification. Search information required: name, years to search. Specify plaintiff or defendant.

Clay County

Clay County Courthouse, Criminal Division
PO Box 218
Liberty, MO 64068
(816) 792-7707
Fax (816) 792-7778
Felony and misdemeanor records are available by mail. No release necessary. No search fee. $.15 fee per copy. $5.00 for certification. Search information required: name, date of birth.

Civil records are available by mail or phone. No release necessary. No search fee. $.15 fee per copy. $5.00 for certification. Search information required: name, years to search. Specify plaintiff or defendant.

Clinton County

Felony records
Circuit Clerk
PO Box 275
Plattsburg, MO 64477
(816) 539-3731
Felony records are available in person only. See Missouri state repository for additional information.

Civil records
Circuit Clerk
PO Box 275
Plattsburg, MO 64477
(816) 539-3731
Civil records are available in person only. See Missouri state repository for additional information.

Misdemeanor records
Associate Circuit Court
PO Box 383
Plattsburg, MO 64477
(816) 539-3755
Misdemeanor records are available by mail. No release necessary. No search fee. $1.00 fee per copy. $1.50 for certification. Search information required: name, years to search.

Civil records
Associate Circuit Court
PO Box 383
Plattsburg, MO 64477
(816) 539-3755
Civil records are available by mail. No release necessary. No search fee. $1.00 fee per copy. $1.50 for certification. Search information required: name, years to search. Specify plaintiff or defendant.

Cole County

Felony records
Circuit Clerk of Cole County, Criminal Records
PO Box 1156
Jefferson City, MO 65102-1156
(314) 634-9151
Fax (314) 635-0796
Felony records are available by mail or fax. No release necessary. No search fee. $.25 fee per copy. $1.00 for certification. $3.00 fee for fax response. Search information required: name, date of birth and/or SSN.

Civil records
Circuit Clerk of Cole County
PO Box 1156
Jefferson City, MO 65102-1156
(314) 634-9151
Fax (314) 635-0796
Civil records are available by mail or phone. No release necessary. No search fee. $.25 fee per copy. $1.00 for certification. $3.00 fee for fax response. Search information required: name, years to search. Specify plaintiff or defendant.

Misdemeanor records
Associate Circuit Court, Division 3
PO Box 503
Jefferson City, MO 65102
(314) 634-9171
Misdemeanor records are available in person only. See Missouri state repository for additional information.

Civil records
Associate Circuit Court, Division 3
PO Box 503
Jefferson City, MO 65102
(314) 634-9171
Civil records are available in person only. See Missouri state repository for additional information.

Cooper County

Courthouse, Criminal Records
PO Box 8
200 Main, Room26
Boonville, MO 65233
(816) 882-2232
Fax (816) 882-2043
Felony records are available by mail, phone or fax. No release necessary. No search fee. $.50 fee per copy. $1.50 for certification. $.50 fee for fax response. Search information required: name, years to search.

Civil records are available by mail, phone or fax. No release necessary. No search fee. $.50 fee per copy. $1.50 for certification. $.50 fee for fax response. Search information required: name, years to search. Specify plaintiff or defendant.

Crawford County

Felony records
Circuit Clerk
PO Box 177
Steelville, MO 65565
(314) 775-2866
Fax (314) 775-2452
Felony records are available by mail or fax. No release necessary. $4.00 search fee. $1.00 for certification. $2.00 fee for fax response. Certified check only, payable to Circuit Clerk. Search information required: name, date of birth, years to search.

Civil records
Circuit Clerk
PO Box 177
Steelville, MO 65565
(314) 775-2866
Fax (314) 775-2452
Civil records are available by mail or fax. No release necessary. $4.00 search fee. $1.00 for certification. $2.00 fee for fax response. Search information required: name, years to search. Specify plaintiff or defendant.

Misdemeanor records
Associate Division
PO Box BC
Steelville, MO 65565
(314) 775-2149
Fax (314) 775-2452
Misdemeanor records are available by mail or fax. A release is required. No search fee. $.30 fee per copy. $1.50 for certification. $2.00 fee for fax response. Search information required: name, years to search.

Civil records
Associate Division
PO Box BC
Steelville, MO 65565
(314) 775-2149
Civil records are available by mail or phone. A release is required. No search fee. $.30 fee per copy. $1.50 for certification. $2.00 fee for fax response. Search information required: name, years to search. Specify plaintiff or defendant.

Dade County

Felony records
Dade County Circuit Clerk
Courthouse
Greenfield, MO 65661
(417) 637-2271
Felony records are available by mail. No release necessary. $2.00 search fee. $1.00 fee per copy. $1.50 for certification. Search information required: name, years to search.

Civil records
Dade County Circuit Clerk
Courthouse
Greenfield, MO 65661
(417) 637-2271
Civil records are available by mail. No release necessary. $2.00 search fee. $1.00 fee per copy. $1.50 for certification. Search information required: name, years to search. Specify plaintiff or defendant.

Misdemeanor records
Circuit Court, Division 2
Dade County Courthouse
Greenfield, MO 65661
(417) 637-2741
Misdemeanor records are available by phone only. No release necessary. Fee charged for "lengthy" searches. Copies available in person only. Search information required: name.

Civil records
Circuit Court, Division 2
Dade County Courthouse
Greenfield, MO 65661
(417) 637-2741
Civil records are available by mail or phone. No release necessary. Fee only charged for "lengthy" searches. Copies available in person only. Search information required: name, years to search. Specify plaintiff or defendant.

Dallas County

Felony records
Clerk of Circuit Court, Criminal
Records
PO Box 373
Buffalo, MO 65622
(417) 345-2243
Fax (417) 345-5539
Felony records are available in person only.
See Missouri State Repository for additional information.

Civil records
Clerk of Circuit Court
PO Box 373
Buffalo, MO 65622
(417) 345-2243
Fax (417) 345-5539
Civil records are available in person only.
See Missouri State Repository for additional information.

Misdemeanor records
Associate Court
PO Box 1150
Buffalo, MO 65622
(417) 345-7641
Misdemeanor records are available by mail.
No release necessary. No search fee. $1.00
fee per copy. $1.50 for certification. Search
information required: name, date of birth.

Civil records
Associate Court
PO Box 1150
Buffalo, MO 65622
(417) 345-7641
Civil records are available by mail or
phone. No release necessary. No search fee.
$1.00 fee per copy. $1.50 for certification.
Search information required: name, years to
search. Specify plaintiff or defendant.

Daviess County

Circuit Clerk of Daviess County,
Criminal Records
PO Box 337
Gallatin, MO 64640
(816) 663-2932
Felony and misdemeanor records are available by mail or phone. No release necessary. No search fee. $1.00 fee per copy.
$2.00 for certification. Search information
required: name. date of birth, years to
search.

Civil records are available by mail or
phone. No release necessary. No search fee.
$1.00 fee per copy. $2.00 for certification.
Search information required: name, years to
search. Specify plaintiff or defendant.

De Kalb County

Felony records
Circuit Clerk, Criminal Records
PO Box 248
Maysville, MO 64469
(816) 449-2602
Fax (816) 449-2440
Felony records are available by mail, phone
or fax. No release necessary. No search fee.
$1.00 fee per copy. $1.00 for certification.
$4.00 fee for fax response. Search information required: name, years to search, SASE.

Civil records
Circuit Clerk
PO Box 248
Maysville, MO 64469
(816) 449-2602
Fax (816) 449-2440
Civil records are available by mail, phone
or fax. No release necessary. No search fee.
$1.00 fee per copy. $1.00 for certification.
$4.00 fee for fax response. Search information required: name, years to search.
Specify plaintiff or defendant.

Misdemeanor records
Associate Circuit Court
PO Box 512
Maysville, MO 64469
(816) 449-5400
Fax (816) 449-2440
Misdemeanor records are available by mail
or fax. No release necessary. No search fee.
$1.00 fee per copy. $2.50 for certification.
Search information required: name, offense,
years to search.

Civil records
Associate Circuit Court
PO Box 512
Maysville, MO 64469
(816) 449-5400
Fax (816) 449-2440
Civil records are available by mail or fax.
No release necessary. No search fee. $1.00
fee per copy. $2.50 for certification. Search
information required: name, years to
search. Specify plaintiff or defendant.

Dent County

Felony records
Circuit Clerk, Criminal Records
112 East 5th Street
Salem, MO 65560
(314) 729-3931
Felony records are available by mail or
phone. No release necessary. No search fee.
Make check payable to Circuit Clerk.
Search information required: name, date of
birth, years to search.

Civil records
Circuit Clerk
112 East 5th Street
Salem, MO 65560
(314) 729-3931
Civil records are available by mail or
phone. No release necessary. No search fee.
Search information required: name, years to
search. Specify plaintiff or defendant.

Misdemeanor records
Associate Circuit Court
Dent County Judicial Bldg.
Salem, MO 65560
(314) 729-3134
Misdemeanor records are available by mail
or phone. No release necessary. No search
fee. $.25 fee per copy. $2.50 for certification. Search information required: name,
date of birth.

Civil records
Associate Circuit Court
Dent County Judicial Bldg.
Salem, MO 65560
(314) 729-3134
Civil records are available by mail or
phone. No release necessary. No search fee.
$.25 fee per copy. $2.50 for certification.
Search information required: name, years to
search. Specify plaintiff or defendant.

Douglas County

Felony records
Circuit Clerk and Recorder
PO Box 655
Ava, MO 65608
(417) 683-4713
Felony records are available by mail or
phone. No release necessary. No search fee.
$.25 fee per copy. $2.50 for certification.
Search information required: name, date of
birth, SSN, years to search.

Civil records
Circuit Clerk and Recorder
PO Box 655
Ava, MO 65608
(417) 683-4713
Civil records are available by mail or
phone. No release necessary. No search fee.
$.25 fee per copy. $2.50 for certification.
Search information required: name, years to
search. Specify plaintiff or defendant.

Misdemeanor records
Associate Circuit Court
PO Box 276
Ava, MO 65608
(417) 683-2114
Misdemeanor records are available by mail.
No release necessary. No search fee. $.25
fee per copy. $1.50 for certification. Search
information required: name, offense, years
to search.

Civil records
Associate Circuit Court
PO Box 276
Ava, MO 65608
(417) 683-2114
Civil records are available by mail or
phone. No release necessary. No search fee.
$.25 fee per copy. $1.50 for certification.
Search information required: name, years to
search. Specify plaintiff or defendant.

Dunklin County

Felony records
Circuit Clerk, Criminal Records
PO Box 567
Kennett, MO 63857
(314) 888-2456
Felony records are available by mail or
phone. No release necessary. $2.00 search
fee. Make check payable to Circuit Clerk.
Search information required: name.

Civil records
Circuit Clerk
PO Box 567
Kennett, MO 63857
(314) 888-2456
Civil records are available by mail or
phone. No release necessary. $2.00 search
fee. Search information required: name,
years to search. Specify plaintiff or defendant.

Misdemeanor records
Associate Circuit Court
Division 2
Courthouse, Rm. 103
Kennett, MO 63857
(314) 888-3378
Misdemeanor records are available by mail.
No release necessary. $2.00 search fee.
Checks payable to Associate Circuit Court.
Search information required: name, date of
birth, years to search.

Civil records
Associate Circuit Court
Division 2
Courthouse, Rm. 103
Kennett, MO 63857
(314) 888-3378
Civil records are available by mail. No release necessary. $2.00 search fee. Search information required: name, years to search. Specify plaintiff or defendant.

Franklin County

Circuit Clerk, Bill Dean Miller
PO Box 272
Union, MO 63084
(314) 583-6300
Felony records are available by mail. No release necessary. $2.00 search fee. $.25 fee per copy. $1.00 for certification. Make check payable to Circuit Clerk. Search information required: name, date of birth, sex, race, years to search.

Civil records are available by mail or phone. No release necessary. $2.00 search fee. $.25 fee per copy. $1.00 for certification. Search information required: name, years to search. Specify plaintiff or defendant.

Gasconade County

Felony records
Circuit Clerk, Criminal Records
PO Box 241
Hermann, MO 65041
(314) 486-2632
Fax (314) 486-3693
Felony records are available by mail, phone or fax. No release necessary. No search fee. $1.00 fee per copy. $1.50 for certification. Search information required: name, years to search.

Civil records
Circuit Clerk
PO Box 241
Hermann, MO 65041
(314) 486-2632
Fax (314) 486-3693
Civil records are available by mail, phone or fax. No release necessary. No search fee. $1.00 fee per copy. $1.50 for certification. Search information required: name, years to search. Specify plaintiff or defendant.

Misdemeanor records
Associate Circuit Court
Division4
PO Box 176
Hermann, MO 65041
(314) 486-2321
Misdemeanor records are available by mail or phone. No release necessary. No search fee. $.25 fee per copy. $1.50 for certification. Search information required: name, date of birth, address.

Civil records
Associate Circuit Court
Division4
PO Box 176
Hermann, MO 65041
(314) 486-2321
Civil records are available by mail or phone. No release necessary. No search fee. $.25 fee per copy. $1.50 for certification. Search information required: name, years to search. Specify plaintiff or defendant.

Gentry County

Felony records
Gentry County Courthouse, Criminal Records
PO Box 27
Albany, MO 64402
(816) 726-3618
Felony records are available by mail. No release necessary. No search fee. $.15 fee per copy. $1.00 for certification. Search information required: name, years to search.

Civil records
Gentry County Courthouse
PO Box 27
Albany, MO 64402
(816) 726-3618
Civil records are available by mail or phone. No release necessary. No search fee. $.15 fee per copy. $1.00 for certification. Search information required: name, years to search. Specify plaintiff or defendant.

Misdemeanor records
Associate Circuit Court
Division 2
Gentry County Courthouse
Albany, MO 64402
(816) 726-3411
Misdemeanor records are available by mail. No release necessary. No search fee. $.15 fee per copy. $1.50 for certification. Search information required: name, years to search, date of birth.

Civil records
Associate Circuit Court
Division 2
Gentry County Courthouse
Albany, MO 64402
(816) 726-3411
Civil records are available by mail. No release necessary. No search fee. $.15 fee per copy. $1.50 for certification. Search information required: name, years to search. Specify plaintiff or defendant.

Greene County

Circuit Clerk's Office, Criminal Records
940 Boonville
Room 202
Springfield, MO 65802
(417) 868-4074
Felony records are available by mail. No release necessary. $5.00 search fee. $.20 fee per copy. $5.00 for certification. Search information required: name, years to search.

Civil records are available by mail. No release necessary. $5.00 search fee. $.20 fee per copy. $5.00 for certification. Search information required: name, years to search. Specify plaintiff or defendant.

Grundy County

Felony records
Circuit Clerk, Division 1, Criminal Records
Grundy County Courthouse
800 Main Street
Trenton, MO 64683
(816) 359-6605
Felony records are available by mail. No release necessary. $4.00 search fee. $.25 fee per copy. $2.00 for certification. Make check payable to Circuit Court, Division 1. Search information required: name, years to search.

Civil records
Circuit Clerk, Division 1
Grundy County Courthouse
800 Main Street
Trenton, MO 64683
(816) 359-6605
Civil records are available by mail or phone. No release necessary. $4.00 search fee. $.25 fee per copy. $2.00 for certification. Search information required: name, years to search. Specify plaintiff or defendant.

Misdemeanor records
Grundy County Circuit Court
Division 2
Courthouse
Trenton, MO 64683
(816) 359-6606
Misdemeanor records are available by mail or phone. No release necessary. No search fee. $.25 fee per copy. $1.50 for certification. Search information required: name, years to search, SASE.

Civil records
Grundy County Circuit Court
Division 2
Courthouse
Trenton, MO 64683
(816) 359-6606
Civil records are available by mail or phone. No release necessary. No search fee. $.25 fee per copy. $1.50 for certification. Search information required: name, years to search, SASE. Specify plaintiff or defendant.

Harrison County

Felony records
Circuit Clerk's Office, Criminal Records
PO Box 525
Bethany, MO 64424
(816) 425-6425
Fax (816) 425-3772
Felony records are available by mail or phone. No release necessary. No search fee. $.25 fee per copy. $2.00 for certification. Search information required: name, date of birth, years to search.

Civil records
Circuit Clerk's Office
PO Box 525
Bethany, MO 64424
(816) 425-6425
Fax (816) 425-3772
Civil records are available by mail or phone. No release necessary. No search fee. $.25 fee per copy. $2.00 for certification. Search information required: name, years to search. Specify plaintiff or defendant.

Misdemeanor records
Associate Circuit Court
Division 2
PO Box 525
Bethany, MO 64424
(816) 425-6432
Misdemeanor records are available by mail or phone. No release necessary. No search fee. $.25 fee per copy. $2.00 for certification. Search information required: name, date of birth.

Civil records
Associate Circuit Court
Division 252
PO Box 525
Bethany, MO 64424
(816) 425-6432
Civil records are available by mail or phone. No release necessary. No search fee. $.25 fee per copy. $2.00 for certification. Search information required: name, years to search. Specify plaintiff or defendant.

Henry County

Circuit Clerk, Criminal Records
Courthouse
Clinton, MO 64735
(816) 885-6963 Ext. 209, 211, 212
Fax (816) 885-8456
Felony and misdemeanor records are available by mail, phone or fax. No release necessary. No search fee. Search information required: name, date of birth, years to search, SASE.

Civil records are available by mail, phone or fax. No release necessary. No search fee. $.25 fee per copy. $1.50 for certification. Search information required: name, years to search. Specify plaintiff or defendant.

Hickory County

Felony records
Circuit Clerk and Recorder's Office,
Criminal Records
PO Box 101
Hermitage, MO 65668
(417) 745-6421
Fax (417) 745-6670
Felony records are available by mail, phone or fax. A release is required. No search fee. $.25 fee per copy. $1.00 for certification. $1.00 fee per page for fax response. Search information required: name, years to search.

Civl records
Circuit Clerk and Recorder's Office
PO Box 101
Hermitage, MO 65668
(417) 745-6421
Fax (417) 745-6670
Civil records are available by mail or phone. No release necessary. No search fee. $.25 fee per copy. $1.00 for certification. $1.00 fee per page for fax response. Search information required: name, years to search. Specify plaintiff or defendant.

Misdemeanor records
Associate Circuit Court
PO Box 75
Hermitage, MO 65668
(417) 745-6822
Misdemeanor records are available by mail. A release is required. No search fee. Search information required: name, years to search.

Civil records
Associate Circuit Court
PO Box 75
Hermitage, MO 65668
(417) 745-6822
Civil records are available by mail. A release is required. No search fee. Search information required: name, years to search. Specify plaintiff or defendant.

Holt County

Felony records
Circuit Clerk, Criminal Records
Holt County Courthouse
PO Box 318
Oregon, MO 64473
(816) 446-3301
Fax (816) 446-3328
Felony records are available by mail or fax. No release necessary. $4.00 search fee. $1.00 fee per copy. $1.00 for certification. $2.00 fee for fax response. Search information required: name, date of birth.

Civil records
Circuit Clerk
Holt County Courthouse
PO Box 318
Oregon, MO 64473
(816) 446-3301
Fax (816) 446-3328
Civil records are available by mail or fax. No release necessary. $4.00 search fee. $1.00 fee per copy. $1.00 for certification. $2.00 fee for fax response. Search information required: name, years to search. Specify plaintiff or defendant.

Misdemeanor records
Holt County Associate Circuit Court
Division 2
PO Box 173
Oregon, MO 64473
(816) 446-3380
Fax (816) 446-3328
Misdemeanor records are available by mail or phone. No release necessary. No search fee. $.25 fee per copy. $2.50 for certification. $2.00 fee for fax response. Search information required: name, years to search, date of birth.

Civil records
Holt County Associate Circuit Court
Division 2
PO Box 173
Oregon, MO 64473
(816) 446-3380
Civil records are available by mail or phone. No release necessary. No search fee. $.25 fee per copy. $2.50 for certification. $2.00 fee for fax response. Search information required: name, years to search. Specify plaintiff or defendant.

Howard County

Felony records
Howard County Circuit Clerk,
Criminal Records
Courthouse
Fayette, MO 65248
(816) 248-2194
Felony records are available by mail. A release is required. No search fee. $.25 fee per copy. $2.00 for certification. Search information required: name, date of birth, sex, race, years to search.

Civil records
Howard County Circuit Clerk
Courthouse
Fayette, MO 65248
(816) 248-2194
Civil records are available by mail. A release is required. No search fee. $.25 fee per copy. $2.00 for certification. Search information required: name, years to search. Specify plaintiff or defendant.

Misdemeanor records
Associate Division
PO Box 370
Fayette, MO 65248
(816) 248-3326
Misdemeanor records are available in person only. See Missouri state repository for additional information.

Civil records
Associate Division
PO Box 370
Fayette, MO 65248
(816) 248-3326
Civil records are available in person only. See Missouri state repository for additional information.

Howell County

Felony records
Circuit Clerk, Criminal Records
PO Box 1011
West Plains, MO 65775
(417) 256-3741
Felony records are available by mail or phone. No release necessary. No search fee. $.25 fee per copy. $1.50 for certification. Search information required: name, years to search.

Civil records
Circuit Clerk
PO Box 1011
West Plains, MO 65775
(417) 256-3741
Civil records are available by mail or phone. No release necessary. No search fee. $.25 fee per copy. $1.50 for certification. Search information required: name, years to search. Specify plaintiff or defendant.

Misdemeanor records
Associate Court
Courthouse, Rm. 22
West Plains, MO 65775
(417) 256-4050
Misdemeanor records are available by mail or phone. A release is required. No search fee. $.25 fee per copy. $2.50 for certification. Search information required: name, years to search.

Civil records
Associate Court
Courthouse, Rm. 22
West Plains, MO 65775
(417) 256-4050
Civil records are available by mail or phone. A release is required. No search fee. $.25 fee per copy. $2.50 for certification. Search information required: name, years to search. Specify plaintiff or defendant.

Iron County

Felony records
Circuit Clerk, Criminal Records
PO Box 24
Ironton, MO 63650
(314) 546-2811
Felony records are available in person only. See Missouri state repository for additional information.

Civil records
Circuit Clerk
PO Box 24
Ironton, MO 63650
(314) 546-2811
Civil records are available in person only. See Missouri state repository for additional information.

Misdemeanor records
Iron County Associate Circuit Court
PO Box 325
Ironton, MO 63650
(314) 546-2511
Misdemeanor records are available by mail or phone. No release necessary. No search fee. $.25 fee per copy. $1.00 for certification. Search information required: name, years to search.

Civil records
Iron County Associate Circuit Court
PO Box 325
Ironton, MO 63650
(314) 546-2511
Civil records are available by mail or phone. No release necessary. No search fee. $.25 fee per copy. $1.00 for certification. Search information required: name, years to search. Specify plaintiff or defendant.

Jackson County
Criminal Justice Bldg.
Department of Criminal Records
1315 Locust
Kansas City, MO 64106
(816) 881-4351
Felony records are available in person only. See Missouri state repository for additional information.

Civil records are available in person only. See Missouri state repository for additional information.

Jasper County
Circuit Clerk
Room 303 Courthouse
Carthage, MO 64836
(417) 358-0441
Fax (417) 358-0461
Felony records are available by mail. Request may be made by fax. Results will be sent by mail. No release necessary. Fee for extensive searches only. $.20 fee per copy. $1.50 for certification. Search information required: name, SASE, years to search. Call (417) 625-4310 to check Joplin records.

Civil records are available by mail. Request may be made by fax. Results will be sent by mail. No release necessary. Fee for extensive searches only. $.20 fee per copy. $1.50 for certification. Search information required: name, years to search. Specify plaintiff or defendant.

Jefferson County
Felony records
Circuit Clerk
PO Box 100
Hillsboro, MO 63050
(314) 789-5345
Fax (314) 789-3804
Felony records are available by mail or fax. A release is required. No search fee. $1.00 fee per copy. $.50 for certification. Search information required: name, SASE.

Civil records
Circuit Clerk
PO Box 100
Hillsboro, MO 63050
(314) 789-5345
Fax (314) 789-3804
Civil records are available by mail or fax. No release necessary. No search fee. $1.00 fee per copy. $.50 for certification. Search

information required: name, years to search, SASE. Specify plaintiff or defendant.

Misdemeanor records
Associate Circuit Court
Division 11
PO Box 100
Hillsboro, MO 63050
(314) 789-3911 Extension 364
Misdemeanor records are available by mail or phone. No release necessary. No search fee. $1.00 fee per copy. $.50 for certification. Records are available from 1979.

Civil records
Associate Circuit Court
Division 11
PO Box 100
Hillsboro, MO 63050
(314) 789-3911 Extension 364
Civil records are available by mail or phone. No release necessary. No search fee. $1.00 fee per copy. $.50 for certification. Search information required: name, years to search. Specify plaintiff or defendant.

Johnson County
Felony records
Circuit Clerk, Criminal Records
Johnson County Courthouse
Warrensburg, MO 64093
(816) 747-6331
Felony records are available in person only. See Missouri state repository for additional information.

Civil records
Circuit Clerk
Johnson County Courthouse
Warrensburg, MO 64093
(816) 747-6331
Civil records are available in person only. See Missouri state repository for additional information.

Misdemeanor records
Associate Circuit Court
Johnson County Courthouse
Warrensburg, MO 64093
(816) 747-2227
Misdemeanor records are available by mail or phone. No release necessary. No search fee. $1.00 fee per copy. $1.50 for certification. Search information required: name, years to search.

Civil records
Associate Circuit Court
Johnson County Courthouse
Warrensburg, MO 64093
(816) 747-2227
Civil records are available by mail or phone. No release necessary. No search fee. $1.00 fee per copy. $1.50 for certification. Search information required: name, years to search. Specify plaintiff or defendant.

Knox County
Felony records
Circuit Clerk, Criminal Records
PO Box 116
Edina, MO 63537
(816) 397-2305
Fax (816) 397-3331
Felony records are available by mail or fax. No release necessary. No search fee. $1.00 fee per copy. $2.00 for certification. Search information required: name.

Civil records
Circuit Clerk
PO Box 116
Edina, MO 63537
(816) 397-2305
Fax (816) 397-3331
Civil records are available by mail or fax. No release necessary. No search fee. $1.00 fee per copy. $2.00 for certification. Search information required: name, years to search. Specify plaintiff or defendant.

Misdemeanor records
Associate Circuit Court
Knox County Courthouse
PO Box 126
Edina, MO 63537
(816) 397-3146
Fax (816) 397-3331
Misdemeanor records are available by mail, phone or fax. No release necessary. No search fee. $.25 fee per copy. $1.50 for certification. $1.50 fee for fax response. Search information required: name, date of birth.

Civil records
Associate Circuit Court
Knox County Courthouse
PO Box 126
Edina, MO 63537
(816) 397-3146
Fax (816) 397-3331
Civil records are available by mail or phone. No release necessary. No search fee. $.25 fee per copy. $1.50 for certification. $1.50 fee for fax response. Search information required: name, years to search. Specify plaintiff or defendant.

LaClede County
Felony records
LaClede County Courthouse, Criminal Records
204 N. Adams, Room 207
Adams Street
Lebanon, MO 65536
(417) 532-2471
Fax (417) 532-3140
Felony records are available by mail, phone or fax. No release necessary. No search fee. $.25 fee per copy. $1.50 for certification. Search information required: name.

Civil records
LaClede County Courthouse
204 N. Adams, Room 207
Adams Street
Lebanon, MO 65536
(417) 532-2471
Fax (417) 532-3140
Civil records are available by mail, phone or fax. No release necessary. No search fee. $.25 fee per copy. $1.50 for certification. Search information required: name, years to search. Specify plaintiff or defendant.

Misdemeanor records
Associate Circuit Court
250 N. Adams St.
Lebanon, MO 65536
(417) 532-9196
Misdemeanor records are available by mail or phone. No release necessary. No search fee. $.25 fee per copy. $1.25 for certification. Search information required: name, years to search.

Civil records
Associate Circuit Court
250 N. Adams St.
Lebanon, MO 65536
(417) 532-9196
Civil records are available by mail or phone. No release necessary. No search fee. $.25 fee per copy. $1.25 for certification. Search information required: name, years to search. Specify plaintiff or defendant.

Lafayette County

Felony records
Circuit Clerk, Criminal Records
PO Box 340
Lexington, MO 64067
(816) 259-6101
Fax (816) 259-2918
Felony records are available by mail or fax. No release necessary. No search fee. $.25 fee per copy. $2.50 for certification. $2.00 fee for fax response. Search information required: name, date of birth, SASE.

Civil records
Circuit Clerk
PO Box 340
Lexington, MO 64067
(816) 259-6101
Fax (816) 259-2918
Civil records are available by mail or fax. No release necessary. No search fee. $.25 fee per copy. $2.50 for certification. $2.00 fee for fax response. Search information required: name, years to search. Specify plaintiff or defendant.

Misdemeanor records
Associate Circuit Court
Division 3
PO Box 236
Lexington, MO 64067
(816) 259-6151
Misdemeanor records are available by mail. No release necessary. No search fee. Search information required: name, date of birth, address, SASE.

Civil records
Associate Circuit Court
Division 3
PO Box 236
Lexington, MO 64067
(816) 259-6151
Civil records are available by mail or phone. No release necessary. No search fee. Search information required: name, years to search, SASE. Specify plaintiff or defendant.

Lawrence County

Felony records
Circuit Clerk's Office, Criminal Records
PO Box 488
Mount Vernon, MO 65712
(417) 466-2471
Felony records are available by mail. No release necessary. $2.00 search fee. $.25 fee per copy. $2.00 for certification. Search information required: name, date of birth, years to search.

Civil records
Circuit Clerk's Office
PO Box 488
Mount Vernon, MO 65712
(417) 466-2471
Civil records are available by mail or phone. No release necessary. $2.00 search fee. $.25 fee per copy. $2.00 for certification. Search information required: name, date of birth, years to search. Specify plaintiff or defendant.

Misdemeanor records
Associate Division Circuit Court
Box 390
Mount Vernon, MO 65712
(417) 466-2463
Misdemeanor records are available by mail or phone. No release necessary. No search fee. $.30 fee per copy. Search information required: name.

Civil records
Associate Division Circuit Court
Box 390
Mount Vernon, MO 65712
(417) 466-2463
Civil records are available by mail or phone. No release necessary. No search fee. $.30 fee per copy. Search information required: name, years to search. Specify plaintiff or defendant.

Lewis County

Felony records
Circuit Clerk of Lewis County, Criminal Records
PO Box 97
Monticello, MO 63457
(314) 767-5440
Fax (314) 767-5412
Felony records are available by mail, phone or fax. No release necessary. No search fee. $1.00 fee per copy. $1.50 for certification. Search information required: name, date of birth, sex, race, SASE.

Civil records
Circuit Clerk of Lewis County, Criminal Records
PO Box 97
Monticello, MO 63457
(314) 767-5440
Fax (314) 767-5412
Civil records are available by mail, phone or fax. No release necessary. No search fee. $1.00 fee per copy. $1.50 for certification. Search information required: name, years to search, SASE. Specify plaintiff or defendant.

Misdemeanor records
Associate Circuit Court
Box 36
Monticello, MO 63457
(314) 767-5352
Fax (314) 767-5412
Misdemeanor records are available by mail or fax. No release necessary. No search fee. $.25 fee per copy (includes certification). $2.00 fee for fax response. Search information required: name, date of birth, years to search, SASE.

Civil records
Associate Circuit Court
Box 36
Monticello, MO 63457
(314) 767-5352
Fax (314) 767-5412
Civil records are available by mail or fax. No release necessary. No search fee. $.25 fee per copy (includes certification). $2.00 fee for fax response. Search information required: name, years to search, SASE. Specify plaintiff or defendant.

Lincoln County

Felony records
Circuit Clerk's Office, Criminal Records
201 Main Street
Troy, MO 63379
(314) 528-4418
Felony records are available in person only. See Missouri state repository for additional information.

Civil records
Circuit Clerk's Office
201 Main Street
Troy, MO 63379
(314) 528-4418
Civil records are available in person only. See Missouri state repository for additional information.

Misdemeanor records
Associate Circuit Court
201 Main Street
Troy, MO 63379
(314) 528-4521
Misdemeanor records are available by mail. A release is required. $5.00 search fee. $1.50 for certification. Search information required: name, SSN.

Civil records
Associate Circuit Court
201 Main Street
Troy, MO 63379
(314) 528-4521
Civil records are available by mail. No release necessary. $5.00 search fee. $1.50 for certification. Search information required: name, years to search. Specify plaintiff or defendant.

Linn County

Circuit Clerk, Criminal Records
309 1/2 N. Main
PO Box 435
Brookfield, MO 64628
(816) 258-7062
Fax (816) 258-3982
Felony and misdemeanor records are available by mail or phone. No release necessary. No search fee. $.25 fee per copy. $1.50 for certification. Search information required: name, date of birth, years to search. Records accessible from 1967.

Civil records are available by mail or phone. No release necessary. No search fee. $.25 fee per copy. $1.50 for certification. Search information required: name, years to search. Specify plaintiff or defendant.

Livingston County

Felony records
Circuit Clerk's Office, Criminal
Records
Livingston County Courthouse
Chillicothe, MO 64601
(816) 646-1718
Felony records are available by mail or
phone. No release necessary. No search fee.
$.25 fee per copy. $1.50 for certification.
Search information required: name.

Civil records
Circuit Clerk's Office
Livingston County Courthouse
Chillicothe, MO 64601
(816) 646-1718
Civil records are available by mail or
phone. No release necessary. No search fee.
$.25 fee per copy. $1.50 for certification.
Search information required: name, years to
search. Specify plaintiff or defendant.

Misdemeanor records
Associate Division
Livingston County Courthouse
Chillicothe, MO 64601
(816) 646-3103
Misdemeanor records are available by mail
or phone. No release necessary. No search
fee. $.25 fee per copy. $1.50 for certification. Search information required: name,
years to search.

Civil records
Associate Division
Livingston County Courthouse
Chillicothe, MO 64601
(816) 646-3103
Civil records are available by mail or
phone. No release necessary. No search fee.
$.25 fee per copy. $1.50 for certification.
Search information required: name, years to
search. Specify plaintiff or defendant.

Macon County

Felony records
Circuit Clerk, Criminal Records
Courthouse
Macon, MO 63552
(816) 385-4631
Felony records are available by mail. No release necessary. $1.00 search fee. $.25 fee
per copy. $1.50 for certification. Search in-
formation required: name, SASE, years to
search.

Civil records
Circuit Clerk
Courthouse
Macon, MO 63552
(816) 385-4631
Civil records are available by mail. No re-
lease necessary. $1.00 search fee. $.25 fee
per copy. $1.50 for certification. Search in-
formation required: name, years to search,
SASE. Specify plaintiff or defendant.

Misdemeanor records
Associate Circuit Court
Division 2
PO Box 491
Macon, MO 63552
(816) 385-3531
Misdemeanor records are available by mail
or phone. No release necessary. No search
fee. $.50 fee per copy. $1.50 for certification. Search information required: name,
date of birth, SASE.

Civil records
Associate Circuit Court
Division 2
PO Box 491
Macon, MO 63552
(816) 385-3531
Civil records are available by mail or
phone. No release necessary. No search fee.
$.50 fee per copy. $1.50 for certification.
Search information required: name, years to
search, SASE. Specify plaintiff or defen-
dant.

Madison County

Felony records
Madison County Courthouse
Circuit Clerk's Office
Fredericktown, MO 63645
(314) 783-2102
Records are available in person only. See
Missouri state repository for additional in-
formation.

Civil records
Madison County Courthouse
Circuit Clerk's Office
Fredericktown, MO 63645
(314) 783-2102
Civil records are available in person only.
See Missouri state repository for additional
information

Misdemeanor records
Associate Circuit Court
Division 3
PO Box 521
Fredericktown, MO 63645
(314) 783-3105
Fax (314) 783-5920
Misdemeanor records are available by mail
or fax. No release necessary. No search fee.
$1.00 fee per copy. $1.50 for certification.
Search information required: name, date of
birth.

Misdemeanor records
Associate Circuit Court
Division 3
PO Box 521
Fredericktown, MO 63645
(314) 783-3105
Fax (314) 783-5920
Civil records are available by mail or fax.
No release necessary. No search fee. $1.00
fee per copy. $1.50 for certification. Search
information required: name, years to
search. Specify plaintiff or defendant.

Maries County

Felony records
Circuit Clerk
PO Box 213
Vienna, MO 65582
(314) 422-3338
Felony records are available by mail. No release necessary. No search fee. $.15 fee per
copy. $2.50 for certification. Search infor-
mation required: name, date of birth, years
to search.

Civil records
Circuit Clerk
PO Box 213
Vienna, MO 65582
(314) 422-3338
Civil records are available by mail. No re-
lease necessary. No search fee. $.15 fee per
copy. $2.50 for certification. Search infor-
mation required: name, years to search.
Specify plaintiff or defendant.

Misdemeanor records
Associate Circuit Court
PO Box 140
Vienna, MO 65582
(314) 422-3303
Fax (314) 422-3100
Misdemeanor records are available by mail
or fax. A release is required. No search fee.
$.25 fee per copy. $1.50 for certification.
$5.00 fee for fax response. Search informa-
tion required: name, offense, years to
search, date of birth.

Civil records
Associate Circuit Court
PO Box 140
Vienna, MO 65582
(314) 422-3303
Fax (314) 422-3100
Civil records are available by mail or fax. A
release is required. No search fee. $.25 fee
per copy. $1.50 for certification. $5.00 fee
for fax response. Search information required: name, years to search. Specify
plaintiff or defendant.

Marion County

Felony records
Circuit Clerk, Criminal Records
Courthouse
Palmyra, MO 63461
(314) 769-2550
Felony records are available by mail. No release necessary. No search fee. $2.00 fee
per copy. $22.00 for certification. Search
information required: name.

Civil records
Circuit Clerk
Courthouse
Palmyra, MO 63461
(314) 769-2550
Civil records are available by mail or
phone. No release necessary. No search fee.
$2.00 fee per copy. $22.00 for certification.
Search information required: name, years to
search. Specify plaintiff or defendant.

Misdemeanor records
Clerk of Associate Circuit Court
Marion County
Palmyra, MO 63461
(314) 769-2318
Misdemeanor records are available by mail
or phone. A release is required. No search
fee. $.50 fee per copy. $2.00 for certification. Search information required: name,
years to search, SASE.

Civil records
Clerk of Associate Circuit Court
Marion County
Palmyra, MO 63461
(314) 769-2318
Civil records are available by mail or
phone. A release is required. No search fee.
$.50 fee per copy. $2.00 for certification.
Search information required: name, years to
search. Specify plaintiff or defendant.

McDonald County

Felony records
Circuit Clerk, Criminal Records
PO Box 345
Pineville, MO 64856
(417) 223-4729
Felony records are available by mail or
phone. No release necessary. No search fee.
$.50 fee per copy. $1.00 for certification.
Search information required: name, SASE,
years to search.

Civil records
Circuit Clerk
PO Box 345
Pineville, MO 64856
(417) 223-4729
Civil records are available by mail or phone. No release necessary. No search fee. $.50 fee per copy. $1.00 for certification. Search information required: name, years to search, SASE. Specify plaintiff or defendant.

Misdemeanor records
Associate Circuit Court
Division 2
PO Box 674
Pineville, MO 64856
(417) 223-4467
Misdemeanor records are available by mail or phone. No release necessary. No search fee. $.20 fee per copy (includes certification). Search information required: name, offense, years to search.

Civil records
Associate Circuit Court
Division 2
PO Box 674
Pineville, MO 64856
(417) 223-4467
Civil records are available by mail or phone. No release necessary. No search fee. $.20 fee per copy (includes certification). Search information required: name, years to search. Specify plaintiff or defendant.

Mercer County

Circuit Clerk, Division 1 Criminal Records
East Main
Princeton, MO 64673
(816) 748-4335
Felony and misdemeanor records are available by mail or phone. A release if available. No search fee. $.25 fee per copy. $2.00 for certification. Search information required: name, SASE, previous address, years to search.

Civil records are available by mail or phone. A release if available. No search fee. $.25 fee per copy. $2.00 for certification. Search information required: name, years to search, SASE. Specify plaintiff or defendant.

Miller County

Felony records
Miller County Circuit Clerk, Criminal Records
Miller County Courthouse
PO Box 11
Tuscumbia, MO 65082
(314) 369-2303
Felony records are available by mail or phone. No release necessary. No search fee. $.50 fee per copy. $2.00 for certification. Search information required: name, years to search.

Civil records
Miller County Circuit Clerk
Miller County Courthouse
PO Box 11
Tuscumbia, MO 65082
(314) 369-2303
Civil records are available by mail or phone. No release necessary. No search fee. $.50 fee per copy. $2.00 for certification. Search information required: name, years to search. Specify plaintiff or defendant.

Misdemeanor records
Associate Circuit Court
Miller County Annex
Tuscumbia, MO 65082
(314) 369-2330
Misdemeanor records are available by mail. No release necessary. No search fee. $1.00 fee per copy. $2.50 for certification. Search information required: name, date of birth, years to search, SASE.

Civil records
Associate Circuit Court
Miller County Annex
Tuscumbia, MO 65082
(314) 369-2330
Civil records are available by mail. No release necessary. No search fee. $1.00 fee per copy. $2.50 for certification. Search information required: name, date of birth, years to search, SASE. Specify plaintiff or defendant.

Mississippi County

Circuit Clerk, Criminal Records
Courthouse
Circuit Court Division 1
PO Box 304
Charleston, MO 63834
(314) 683-2104
Fax (314) 683-3904
Felony and misdemeanor records are available by mail, phone or fax. No release necessary. No search fee. $1.00 fee for first copy, $.25 for each additional copy. $.50 for certification. $1.00 fee for first page of fax response, $.25 for each additional page. Search information required: name, SSN, date of birth, sex, race, years to search.

Civil records are available by mail, phone or fax. No release necessary. No search fee. $1.00 fee for first copy, $.25 for each additional copy. $.50 for certification. $1.00 fee for first page of fax response, $.25 for each additional page. Search information required: name, years to search. Specify plaintiff or defendant.

Moniteau County

Felony records
Circuit Clerk, Criminal Records
200 East Main
California, MO 65018
(314) 796-2071
Felony records are available by mail or phone. No release necessary. No search fee. $.30 fee per copy. $1.00 for certification. Search information required: name, SASE.

Civil records
Circuit Clerk
200 East Main
California, MO 65018
(314) 796-2071
Civil records are available by mail or phone. No release necessary. No search fee. $.30 fee per copy. $1.00 for certification. Search information required: name, years to search, SASE. Specify plaintiff or defendant.

Misdemeanor records
Associate Circuit Court
Moniteau County
200 E. Main
California, MO 65018
(314) 796-2814
Misdemeanor records are available by mail or phone. No release necessary. No search fee. Search information required: name, years to search.

Civil records
Associate Circuit Court
Moniteau County
200 E. Main
California, MO 65018
(314) 796-2814
Civil records are available by mail or phone. No release necessary. No search fee. $.25 fee per copy. $2.50 for certification. Search information required: name, years to search. Specify plaintiff or defendant.

Monroe County

Felony records
Circuit Clerk, Criminal Records
PO Box 227
Paris, MO 65275
(816) 327-5204
Fax (816) 327-5781
Felony records are available by mail, phone or fax. No release necessary. No search fee. Search information required: name, address, SASE, years to search.

Civil records
Circuit Clerk
PO Box 227
Paris, MO 65275
(816) 327-5204
Fax (816) 327-5781
Civil records are available by mail, phone or fax. No release necessary. No search fee. Search information required: name, years to search. Specify plaintiff or defendant.

Misdemeanor records
Associate Division
Courthouse
Paris, MO 65275
(816) 327-5220
Fax (816) 327-5781
Misdemeanor records are available by mail or fax. No release necessary. No search fee. $.15 fee per copy. $1.50 for certification. Search information required: name, years to search.

Civil records
Associate Division
Courthouse
Paris, MO 65275
(816) 327-5220
Fax (816) 327-5781
Civil records are available by mail or fax. No release necessary. No search fee. $.15 fee per copy. $1.50 for certification. Search information required: name, years to search. Specify plaintiff or defendant.

Montgomery County

Felony records
Circuit Clerk, Criminal Records
211 E. 3rd
Montgomery City, MO 63361
(314) 564-3341
Felony records are available by mail. No release necessary. No search fee. $.25 fee per copy. $1.25 for certification. Search information required: name.

Civil records
Circuit Clerk
211 E. 3rd
Montgomery City, MO 63361
(314) 564-3341
Civil records are available by mail or phone. No release necessary. No search fee. $.25 fee per copy. $1.25 for certification. Search information required: name, years to search. Specify plaintiff or defendant.

Misdemeanor records
Associate Circuit Court
Division 2
Courthouse
Montgomery City, MO 63361
(314) 564-3348
Misdemeanor records are available by mail or phone. No release necessary. No search fee. $.10 fee per copy. $1.00 for certification. Search information required: name, date of birth.

Civil records
Associate Circuit Court
Division 2
Courthouse
Montgomery City, MO 63361
(314) 564-3348
Civil records are available by mail or phone. No release necessary. No search fee. $.10 fee per copy. $1.00 for certification. Search information required: name, years to search. Specify plaintiff or defendant.

Morgan County

Felony records
Circuit Clerk, Criminal Records
PO Box 68
100 E. Newton
Versailles, MO 65084
(314) 378-4413
Felony records are available by mail. No release necessary. No search fee. $.20 fee per copy. $1.00 for certification. Search information required: name, SASE.

Civil records
Circuit Clerk
PO Box 68
100 E. Newton
Versailles, MO 65084
(314) 378-4413
Civil records are available by mail or phone. No release necessary. No search fee. $.20 fee per copy. $1.00 for certification. Search information required: name, years to search. Specify plaintiff or defendant.

Misdemeanor records
Associate Circuit Court
PO Box 7
102 N. Monroe
Versailles, MO 65084
(314) 378-4235
Misdemeanor records are available by mail or phone. No release necessary. No search fee. $1.00 fee per copy. $.50 for certification. Search information required: name, years to search, date of birth.

Civil records
Associate Circuit Court
PO Box 7
102 N. Monroe
Versailles, MO 65084
(314) 378-4235
Civil records are available by mail or phone. No release necessary. No search fee. $1.00 fee per copy. $.50 for certification. Search information required: name, years to search. Specify plaintiff or defendant.

New Madrid County

Felony records
Courthouse, Criminal Records
Circuit Clerk's Office
New Madrid, MO 63869
(314) 748-2228
Felony records are available by mail or phone. No release necessary. No search fee. $.75 fee per copy, (includes certification). Search information required: name, SASE, years to search.

Civil records
Courthouse
Circuit Clerk's Office
New Madrid, MO 63869
(314) 748-2228
Civil records are available by mail or phone. No release necessary. No search fee. $.75 fee per copy, (includes certification). Search information required: name, years to search, SASE. Specify plaintiff or defendant.

Misdemeanor records
Associate Circuit Court
New Madrid County Courthouse
Main St.
New Madrid, MO 63869
(314) 748-5556
Misdemeanor records are available by mail. No release necessary. No search fee. Search information required: name, years to search.

Civil records
Associate Circuit Court
New Madrid County Courthouse
Main St.
New Madrid, MO 63869
(314) 748-5556
Civil records are available by mail or phone. No release necessary. No search fee. Search information required: name, years to search. Specify plaintiff or defendant.

Newton County

Circuit Clerk, Criminal Records
PO Box 130
Neosho, MO 64850
(417) 451-8257
Felony and misdemeanor records are available by mail or phone. No release necessary. No search fee. $.25 fee per copy. $1.00 for certification. Search information required: name, date of birth, SSN, SASE, years to search.

Civil records are available by mail or phone. No release necessary. No search fee. $.25 fee per copy. $1.00 for certification. Search information required: name, years to search. Specify plaintiff or defendant.

Nodaway County

Circuit Clerk, Criminal Records
PO Box 218
Maryville, MO 64468
(816) 582-5431
Fax (816) 582-5499
Felony and misdemeanor records are available by mail or fax. A release is required. No search fee. $.25 fee per copy. $1.25 for certification. Search information required: name, SSN, date of birth.

Civil records are available by mail or fax. A release is required. No search fee. $.25 fee per copy. $1.25 for certification. Search information required: name, years to search. Specify plaintiff or defendant.

Oregon County

Felony records
Circuit Clerk, Criminal Records
PO Box 406
Alton, MO 65606
(417) 778-7460
Felony records are available by mail or phone. No release necessary. No search fee. $.15 fee per copy. $2.00 for certification. Search information required: name, SASE, years to search.

Civil records
Circuit Clerk
PO Box 406
Alton, MO 65606
(417) 778-7460
Civil records are available by mail or phone. No release necessary. No search fee. $.15 fee per copy. $2.00 for certification. Search information required: name, years to search, SASE. Specify plaintiff or defendant.

Misdemeanor records
Associate Circuit Court
PO Box 211
Alton, MO 65606
(417) 778-7461
Misdemeanor records are available by mail. No release necessary. No search fee. $1.00 fee per copy. $1.50 for certification. Search information required: name, years to search, year of offense.

Civil records
Associate Circuit Court
PO Box 211
Alton, MO 65606
(417) 778-7461
Civil records are available by mail or phone. No release necessary. No search fee. $1.00 fee per copy. $1.50 for certification. Search information required: name, years to search. Specify plaintiff or defendant.

Osage County

Circuit Clerk and Recorder, Criminal Records
Osage County Courthouse
PO Box 825
Linn, MO 65051
(314) 897-3114
Felony and misdemeanor records are available by mail or phone. No release necessary. No search fee. $.25 fee per copy. $2.00 for certification. Search information required: name.

Civil records are available by mail or phone. No release necessary. No search fee. $.25 fee per copy. $2.00 for certification. Search information required: name, years to search. Specify plaintiff or defendant.

Ozark County

Felony records
Circuit Clerk, Division I, Criminal Records
PO Box 36
Gainesville, MO 65655
(417) 679-4232
Fax (417) 679-3201
Felony records are available by mail, phone or fax. No release necessary. No search fee. $.25 fee per copy. $1.50 for certification. Search information required: name, SASE, years to search.

Civil records
Circuit Clerk, Division I
PO Box 36
Gainesville, MO 65655
(417) 679-4232
Fax (417) 679-3201
Civil records are available by mail, phone or fax. No release necessary. No search fee. $.25 fee per copy. $1.50 for certification. Search information required: name, years to search, SASE. Specify plaintiff or defendant.

Misdemeanor records
Associate Circuit Court
PO Box 278
Gainesville, MO 65655
(417) 679-4611
Misdemeanor records for past three years are available by mail. No release necessary. No search fee. Search information required: name, specific dates if available.

Civil records
Associate Circuit Court
PO Box 278
Gainesville, MO 65655
(417) 679-4611
Civil records are available by mail. No release necessary. No search fee. $1.00 fee per copy. $1.50 for certification. Search information required: name, years to search. Specify plaintiff or defendant.

Pemiscot County

Circuit Court, Division ll
Pemiscot County Courthouse
Caruthersville, MO 63830
(314) 333-2784
Felony and misdemeanor records are available by mail or phone. No release necessary. No search fee. Copies available in person only. Search information required: name, SASE, years to search. Records accessible from 1979. Records prior to 1979 available in person.

Civil records are available by mail or phone. No release necessary. No search fee. Copies available in person only. Search information required: name, years to search. Specify plaintiff or defendant.

Perry County

Felony records
Circuit Clerk, Criminal Records
Courthouse
15 West Saint Maries
Suite 7
Perryville, MO 63775-1399
(314) 547-7861
Felony records are available in person only. See Missouri state repository for additional information.

Civil records
Circuit Clerk
Courthouse
15 West Saint Maries
Suite 7
Perryville, MO 63775-1399
(314) 547-7861
Civil records are available by mail or phone. No release necessary. No search fee. $.25 fee per copy. $2.50 for certification. Search information required: name, years to search. Specify plaintiff or defendant.

Misdemeanor records
Associate Circuit Court
Division 6
15 West Saint Maries
Perryville, MO 63775-1399
(314) 547-7861
Misdemeanor records are available by mail. No release necessary. No search fee. $.25 fee per copy. $2.50 for certification. Search information required: name, date of birth, years to search.

Civil records
Associate Circuit Court
Division 6
15 West Saint Maries
Perryville, MO 63775-1399
(314) 547-7861
Civil records are available by mail or phone. No release necessary. No search fee. $.25 fee per copy. $2.50 for certification. Search information required: name, years to search. Specify plaintiff or defendant.

Pettis County

Felony records
Circuit Clerk, Criminal Records
PO Box 804
Sedalia, MO 65301
(816) 826-0617
Fax (816) 826-8637
Felony records are available by mail, phone or fax. No release necessary. No search fee. $.10 fee per copy. $1.50 for certification. $2.50 fee for first page of fax, $1.00 for each additional page. Search information required: name.

Civil records
Circuit Clerk
PO Box 804
Sedalia, MO 65301
(816) 826-0617
Fax (816) 826-8637
Civil records are available by mail, phone or fax. No release necessary. No search fee. $.10 fee per copy. $1.50 for certification. $2.50 fee for first page of fax, $1.00 for each additional page. Search information required: name, years to search. Specify plaintiff or defendant.

Misdemeanor records
Associate Circuit Court
415 S. Ohio
Sedalia, MO 65302
(816) 826-4699
Fax (816) 826-8637
Misdemeanor records are available by mail, phone or fax. No release necessary. No search fee. $1.50 for certification. $2.50 fee for first page of fax, $1.00 for each additional page. Search information required: name, years to search.

Civil records
Associate Circuit Court
415 S. Ohio
Sedalia, MO 65302
(816) 826-4699
Fax (816) 826-8637
Civil records are available by mail, phone or fax. No release necessary. No search fee. $1.50 for certification. $2.50 fee for first page of fax, $1.00 for each additional page. Search information required: name, years to search. Specify plaintiff or defendant.

Phelps County

Felony records
Carol Gaddy, Phelps County Courthouse, Criminal Records
Circuit Court
Rolla, MO 65401
(314) 364-1891 Ext. 25
Fax (314) 364-1419
Felony records are available by mail, phone or fax. No release necessary. No search fee. $.20 fee per copy. $1.00 for certification. Search information required: name, years to search.

Civil records
Carol Gaddy, Phelps County Courthouse
Circuit Court
Rolla, MO 65401
(314) 364-1891 Ext. 25
Fax (314) 364-1419
Civil records are available by mail, phone or fax. No release necessary. No search fee. $.20 fee per copy. $1.00 for certification. Search information required: name, years to search. Specify plaintiff or defendant.

Misdemeanor records
Circuit Court
Associate Division
PO Box 1550
Rolla, MO 65401
(314) 364-1891 Ext. 34
Fax (314) 364-1419
Misdemeanor records are available by mail, phone or fax. No release necessary. No search fee. Search information required: name, date of birth, years to search.

Civil records
Circuit Court
Associate Division
PO Box 1550
Rolla, MO 65401
(314) 364-1891 Ext. 34
Fax (314) 364-1419
Civil records are available by mail, phone or fax. No release necessary. No search fee. Search information required: name, years to search. Specify plaintiff or defendant.

Pike County

Felony records
Pike County Circuit Clerk, Criminal Records
Courthouse
115 W. Main
Bowling Green, MO 63334
(314) 324-3112
Felony records are available by mail. No release necessary. No search fee. $.25 fee per copy. $1.00 for certification. Search information required: name, years to search.

Civil records
Pike County Circuit Clerk, Criminal Records
Courthouse
115 W. Main
Bowling Green, MO 63334
(314) 324-3112
Civil records are available by mail. No release necessary. No search fee. $.25 fee per copy. $1.00 for certification. Search information required: name, years to search. Specify plaintiff or defendant.

Misdemeanor records
Associate Division 4
Pike County Courthouse
115 W. Main
Bowling Green, MO 63334
(314) 324-5582
Misdemeanor records since 1979 are available by mail or phone. No release necessary. No search fee. $.50 fee per copy. $1.50 for certification. Search information required: name, date of birth, SSN, year of offense.

Civil records
Associate Division 4
Pike County Courthouse
115 W. Main
Bowling Green, MO 63334
(314) 324-5582
Civil records are available by mail or phone. No release necessary. No search fee. $.50 fee per copy. $1.50 for certification. Search information required: name, years to search. Specify plaintiff or defendant.

Platte County

Circuit Clerk, Criminal Records
PO Box 5CH
328 Main Street
Platte City, MO 64079
(816) 431-2232 Extension 3483
Felony and misdemeanor records are available by mail. No release necessary. No search fee. $.25 fee per copy. $1.25 for certification. Search information required: name, date of birth, case number, if available.

Civil records are available by mail or phone. No release necessary. No search fee. $.25 fee per copy. $1.25 for certification. Search information required: name, years to search. Specify plaintiff or defendant.

Polk County

Felony records
Circuit Clerk
Courthouse
102 E. Broadway, Room14
Bolivar, MO 65613
(417) 326-4912
Fax (417) 326-4194
Felony records are available by mail, phone or fax. No release necessary. $5.00 search fee. $.25 fee per copy. $2.00 for certification. Search information required: name.

Civil records
Circuit Clerk
Courthouse
102 E. Broadway, Room14
Bolivar, MO 65613
(417) 326-4912
Fax (417) 326-4194
Civil records are available by mail, phone or fax. No release necessary. $5.00 search fee. $.25 fee per copy. $2.00 for certification. Search information required: name, years to search. Specify plaintiff or defendant.

Misdemeanor records
Associate Division
Circuit Court
Courthouse, Rm. 7
Bolivar, MO 65613
(417) 326-4921
Fax (417) 326-8272
Misdemeanor records are available by mail, phone or fax. No release necessary. No search fee. $1.00 fee per copy. $1.50 for certification. Search information required: name, date of birth, SSN, offense, year of offense.

Civil records
Associate Division
Circuit Court
Courthouse, Rm. 7
Bolivar, MO 65613
(417) 326-4921
Fax (417) 326-8272
Civil records are available by mail, phone or fax. No release necessary. No search fee. $1.00 fee per copy. $1.50 for certification. Search information required: name, years to search. Specify plaintiff or defendant.

Pulaski County

Felony records
Circuit Clerk of Pulaski County, Criminal Records
301 US Highway 44, Suite 202
Waynesville, MO 65583
(314) 774-6851
Fax (314) 774-6609
Felony and misdemeanor records are available by mail, phone or fax. No release necessary. No search fee. $.25 fee per copy. $2.00 for certification. Search information required: name, years to search.

Civil records are available by mail, phone or fax. No release necessary. No search fee. $.25 fee per copy. $2.00 for certification. Search information required: name, years to search. Specify plaintiff or defendant.

Putnam County

Felony records
Circuit Clerk, Criminal Records
Room 202, Courthouse
Unionville, MO 63565-1659
(816) 947-2071
Fax (816) 947-3722
Felony records are available by mail, phone or fax. No release necessary. No search fee. $.25 fee per copy. $1.00 for certification. Search information required: name, years to search.

Civil records
Circuit Clerk
Room 202, Courthouse
Unionville, MO 63565-1659
(816) 947-2071
Fax (816) 947-3722
Civil records are available by mail, phone or fax. No release necessary. No search fee. $.25 fee per copy. $1.00 for certification. Search information required: name, years to search. Specify plaintiff or defendant.

Misdemeanor records
Associate Circuit Court
Division 2
Room 101, Courthouse
Unionville, MO 63565
(816) 947-2117
Misdemeanor records are available by mail or phone. No release necessary. No search fee. $1.00 fee per copy. $1.50 for certification. Search information required: name, date of birth, years to search.

Civil records
Associate Circuit Court
Division 2
Room 101, Courthouse
Unionville, MO 63565
(816) 947-2117
Civil records are available by mail or phone. No release necessary. No search fee. $1.00 fee per copy. $1.50 for certification.

Search information required: name, years to search. Specify plaintiff or defendant.

Ralls County

Felony records
Ralls County Courthouse, Criminal Records
PO Box 444
New London, MO 63459
(314) 985-5631
Felony records are available by mail. A release is required. No search fee. Search information required: name, SSN, date of birth, sex, race.

Civil records
Ralls County Courthouse
PO Box 444
New London, MO 63459
(314) 985-5631
Civil records are available by mail or phone. No release necessary. No search fee. Search information required: name, years to search. Specify plaintiff or defendant.

Misdemeanor records
Associate Court
PO Box 466
New London, MO 63459
(314) 985-5641
Misdemeanor records are available by mail. A release is required. No search fee. $1.00 fee per copy. $1.50 for certification. Search information required: name, years to search.

Civil records
Associate Court
PO Box 466
New London, MO 63459
(314) 985-5641
Civil records are available by mail or phone. A release is required. No search fee. $1.00 fee per copy. $1.50 for certification. Search information required: name, years to search. Specify plaintiff or defendant.

Randolph County

Felony records
Circuit Clerk of Records
223 N. Williams
Moberly, MO 65270
(816) 263-4474
Fax (816) 263-2894
Felony records are available by mail or fax. No release necessary. No search fee. $.20 fee per copy. $1.50 for certification. $4.50 fee for first page of fax response, $1.50 for each additional page. Search information required: name, years to search.

Civil records
Circuit Clerk of Records
223 N. Williams
Moberly, MO 65270
(816) 263-4474
Fax (816) 263-2894
Civil records are available by mail or fax. No release necessary. No search fee. $.20 fee per copy. $1.50 for certification. $4.50 fee for first page of fax response, $1.50 for each additional page. Search information required: name, years to search. Specify plaintiff or defendant.

Misdemeanor records
Associate Circuit Court
Courthouse
Moberly, MO 65270
(816) 263-4450
Fax (816) 263-1007
Misdemeanor records are available by mail, phone or fax. No release necessary. No search fee. $.20 fee per copy. $1.50 for certification. Search information required: name.

Civil records
Associate Circuit Court
Courthouse
Moberly, MO 65270
(816) 263-4450
Fax (816) 263-1007
Civil records are available by mail, phone or fax. No release necessary. No search fee. $.20 fee per copy. $1.50 for certification. Search information required: name, years to search. Specify plaintiff or defendant.

Ray County

Felony records
Ray County Circuit Clerk, Criminal Records
PO Box 594
Richmond, MO 64085
(816) 776-3377
Felony records are available by mail or phone. A release is required. No search fee. $.15 fee per copy. $1.50 for certification. Certified check only, payable to Circuit Clerk. Search information required: name.

Civil records
Ray County Circuit Clerk
PO Box 594
Richmond, MO 64085
(816) 776-3377
Civil records are available by mail or phone. No release necessary. No search fee. $.15 fee per copy. $1.50 for certification. Search information required: name, years to search. Specify plaintiff or defendant.

Misdemeanor records
Associate Division
Circuit Court
Ray County Courthouse
Richmond, MO 64085
(816) 776-2335
Misdemeanor records are available by mail or phone. No release necessary. No search fee. $1.00 fee per copy. $2.50 for certification. Search information required: name, date of birth, years to search, case number if available.

Civil records
Associate Division
Circuit Court
Ray County Courthouse
Richmond, MO 64085
(816) 776-2335
Civil records are available by mail or phone. No release necessary. No search fee. $1.00 fee per copy. $2.50 for certification. Search information required: name, years to search. Specify plaintiff or defendant.

Reynolds County

Felony records
Circuit Clerk, Criminal Records
PO Box 76
Centerville, MO 63633
(314) 648-2494 Extension 44
Felony records are available in person only. See Missouri state repository for additional information.

Civil records
Circuit Clerk
PO Box 76
Centerville, MO 63633
(314) 648-2494 Extension 44
Civil records are available in person only. See Missouri state repository for additional information.

Misdemeanor records
Associate Circuit Court
PO Box 39
Centerville, MO 63633
(314) 648-2494 Extension 41
Misdemeanor records are available in person only. See Missouri state repository for additional information.

Civil records
Associate Circuit Court
PO Box 39
Centerville, MO 63633
(314) 648-2494 Extension 41
Civil records are available in person only. See Missouri state repository for additional information.

Ripley County

Felony records
Courthouse, Criminal Records
Doniphan, MO 63935
(314) 996-2818
Felony records are available by mail or phone. No release necessary. $10.00 search fee. Search information required: name, date of birth.

Civil records
Courthouse
Doniphan, MO 63935
(314) 996-2818
Civil records are available by mail or phone. No release necessary. $10.00 search fee. Search information required: name, years to search. Specify plaintiff or defendant.

Misdemeanor records
Associate Circuit Court
Division 2
Courthouse
Doniphan, MO 63935
(314) 996-2013
Misdemeanor records are available by mail. No release necessary. No search fee. $.25 fee per copy. $.25 for certification. Search information required: name, date of birth.

Civil records
Associate Circuit Court
Division 2
Courthouse
Doniphan, MO 63935
(314) 996-2013
Civil records are available by mail or phone. No release necessary. No search fee. $.25 fee per copy. $.25 for certification. Search information required: name, years to search. Specify plaintiff or defendant.

Saline County

Felony records
Circuit Clerk
PO Box 597
Marshall, MO 65340
(816) 886-2300
Felony records are available by mail or phone. No release necessary. No search fee. $.25 fee per copy. $1.50 for certification. Search information required: name, years to search, case number if available.

Civil records
Circuit Clerk
PO Box 597
Marshall, MO 65340
(816) 886-2300
Civil records are available by mail or phone. No release necessary. No search fee. $.25 fee per copy. $1.50 for certification. Search information required: name, years to search. Specify plaintiff or defendant.

Misdemeanor records
Associate Circuit Court
Division 6
PO Box 751
Courthouse, Rm. 301
Marshall, MO 65340
(816) 886-6988
Misdemeanor records are available by mail or phone. No release necessary. No search fee. Search information required: name, years to search.

Civil records
Associate Circuit Court
Division 6
PO Box 751
Courthouse, Rm. 301
Marshall, MO 65340
(816) 886-6988
Civil records are available by mail or phone. No release necessary. No search fee. Search information required: name, years to search. Specify plaintiff or defendant.

Schuyler County

Felony records
Circuit Clerk and Recorder's Off., Criminal Records
PO Box 186
Schuyler County Courthouse
Lancaster, MO 63548
(816) 457-3784
Felony records are available by mail or phone. No release necessary. $8.00 search fee. $22.00 for certification. Search information required: name, years to search.

Civil records
Circuit Clerk and Recorder's Off.
PO Box 186
Schuyler County Courthouse
Lancaster, MO 63548
(816) 457-3784
Civil records are available by mail or phone. No release necessary. $8.00 search fee. $22.00 for certification. Search information required: name, years to search. Specify plaintiff or defendant.

Misdemeanor records
Associate Division
Box 158
Lancaster, MO 63548
(816) 457-3755
Misdemeanor records are available by mail
or phone. No release necessary. $4.00
search fee. $.25 fee per copy. $1.50 for certification. Search information required:
name, current and previous address.

Civil records
Associate Division
Box 158
Lancaster, MO 63548
(816) 457-3755
Civil records are available by mail or
phone. No release necessary. $4.00 search
fee. $.25 fee per copy. $1.50 for certification. Search information required: name,
years to search. Specify plaintiff or defendant.

Scotland County

Felony records
Circuit Clerk, Criminal Records
Scotland County
Courthouse Room 106
Memphis, MO 63555
(816) 465-8605
Felony records are available by mail or
phone. No release necessary. No search fee.
$.25 fee per copy. $2.50 for certification.
Search information required: name, date of
birth.

Civil records
Circuit Clerk
Scotland County
Courthouse Room 106
Memphis, MO 63555
(816) 465-8605
Civil records are available by mail or
phone. No release necessary. No search fee.
$.25 fee per copy. $2.50 for certification.
Search information required: name, years to
search. Specify plaintiff or defendant.

Misdemeanor records
Associate Circuit Court
Rm. 102, Courthouse
Memphis, MO 63555
(816) 465-2404
Misdemeanor records are available by mail
or phone. No release necessary. No search
fee. $.25 fee per copy. $2.50 for certification. Search information required: name,
date of birth, SASE.

Civil records
Associate Circuit Court
Rm. 102, Courthouse
Memphis, MO 63555
(816) 465-2404
Civil records are available by mail or
phone. No release necessary. No search fee.
$.25 fee per copy. $2.50 for certification.
Search information required: name, years to
search, SASE. Specify plaintiff or defendant.

Scott County

Felony records
Circuit Clerk, Criminal Records
PO Box 277
Benton, MO 63736
(314) 545-3596
Felony records are available by mail or
phone. No release necessary. No search fee.
$3.00 fee per copy (includes certification).

Search information required: name, date of
charge (if available), years to search,
SASE.

Civil records
Circuit Clerk
PO Box 277
Benton, MO 63736
(314) 545-3596
Civil records are available by mail or
phone. No release necessary. No search fee.
$3.00 fee per copy (includes certification).
Search information required: name, years to
search, SASE Specify plaintiff or defen-
dant.

Misdemeanor records
Associate Circuit Court
PO Box 249
Benton, MO 63736
(314) 545-3576
Fax (314) 545-4231
Misdemeanor records are available by mail,
phone or fax. No release necessary. No
search fee. Search information required:
name, case number (if available), years to
search.

Civil records
Associate Circuit Court
PO Box 249
Benton, MO 63736
(314) 545-3576
Fax (314) 545-4231
Civil records are available by mail, phone
or fax. No release necessary. No search fee.
Search information required: name, years to
search. Specify plaintiff or defendant.

Shannon County

Felony records
Circuit Clerk, Criminal Records
PO Box 148
Eminence, MO 65466
(314) 226-3315
Felony and misdemeanor records are available by mail. No release necessary. No
search fee. $.25 fee per copy. $2.00 for certification. Search information required:
name, SSN, date of birth.

Civil records
Circuit Clerk
PO Box 148
Eminence, MO 65466
(314) 226-3315
Civil records are available by mail or
phone. No release necessary. No search fee.
$.25 fee per copy. $2.00 for certification.
Search information required: name, years to
search. Specify plaintiff or defendant.

Misdemeanor records
Associate Division
PO Box AB
Eminence, MO 65466
(314) 226-5515
Misdemeanor records are available by mail
or phone. No release necessary. No search
fee. $.25 fee per copy. $1.50 for certification. Search information required: name,
years to search.

Civil records
Associate Division
PO Box AB
Eminence, MO 65466
(314) 226-5515
Civil records are available by mail or
phone. No release necessary. No search fee.
$.25 fee per copy. $1.50 for certification.
Search information required: name, years to
search. Specify plaintiff or defendant.

Shelby County

Felony records
Circuit Clerk, Criminal Records
PO Box 176
Shelbyville, MO 63469
(314) 633-2151
Felony records are available by mail or
phone. No release necessary. No search fee.
$.25 fee per copy. $1.00 for certification.
Search information required: name.

Civil records
Circuit Clerk
PO Box 176
Shelbyville, MO 63469
(314) 633-2151
Civil records are available by mail or
phone. No release necessary. No search fee.
$.25 fee per copy. $1.00 for certification.
Search information required: name, years to
search. Specify plaintiff or defendant.

Misdemeanor records
Associate Circuit Court
PO Box 206
Shelbyville, MO 63469
(314) 633-2251
Misdemeanor records are available by mail
or phone. No release necessary. No search
fee. $.25 fee per copy (includes certifica-
tion). Search information required: name,
years to search, year of offense.

Civil records
Associate Circuit Court
PO Box 206
Shelbyville, MO 63469
(314) 633-2251
Civil records are available by mail or
phone. No release necessary. No search fee.
$.25 fee per copy (includes certification).
Search information required: name, years to
search. Specify plaintiff or defendant.

St. Genevieve County

Felony records
Circuit Clerk, Criminal Records
Courthouse
55 S. 3rd Street
St. Genevieve, MO 63670
(314) 883-2705
Felony records are available by mail. No release necessary. No search fee. $1.00 fee
per copy. $1.50 for certification. Search in-
formation required: name, date of birth,
years to search.

Civil records
Circuit Clerk
Courthouse
55 S. 3rd Street
St. Genevieve, MO 63670
(314) 883-2705
Civil records are available by mail. No release necessary. No search fee. $1.00 fee
per copy. $1.50 for certification. Search in-
formation required: name, years to search.
Specify plaintiff or defendant.

Misdemeanor records
Associate Circuit
Division 3
3rd and Market St.
St. Genevieve, MO 63670
(314) 883-2265
Misdemeanor records are available in person only. See Missouri state repository for
additional information.

Civil records
Associate Circuit
Division 3
3rd and Market St.
St. Genevieve, MO 63670
(314) 883-2265
Civil records are available in person only. See Missouri state repository for additional information.

Stoddard County

Felony records
Circuit Clerk, Division 1
Stoddard County Courthouse
PO Box 30
Bloomfield, MO 63825
(314) 568-4640
Fax (314) 568-2271
Felony records are available by mail, phone or fax. No release necessary. No search fee. $.10 fee per copy. $1.50 for certification. Search information required: name, years to search.

Civil records
Circuit Clerk, Division 1
Stoddard County Courthouse
PO Box 30
Bloomfield, MO 63825
(314) 568-4640
Fax (314) 568-2271
Civil records are available by mail, phone or fax. No release necessary. No search fee. $.10 fee per copy. $1.50 for certification. Search information required: name, years to search. Specify plaintiff or defendant.

Misdemeanor records
Associate Circuit Court
Division 2
PO Box 218
Bloomfield, MO 63825
(314) 568-4671
Misdemeanor records are available in person only. See Missouri state repository for additional information.

Civil records
Associate Circuit Court
Division 2
PO Box 218
Bloomfield, MO 63825
(314) 568-4671
Civil records are available in person only. See Missouri state repository for additional information.

Stone County

Felony records
Circuit Clerk, Criminal Records
PO Box 18
Galena, MO 65656
(417) 357-6114 or 357-6115
Fax (417) 357-6163
Felony and misdemeanor records are available by mail, phone or fax. No release necessary. No search fee. $.25 fee per copy. $1.00 for certification. $3.00 fee per fax response. Search information required: name, date of birth.

Civil records
Circuit Clerk
PO Box 18
Galena, MO 65656
(417) 357-6114 or 357-6115
Fax (417) 357-6163
Civil records are available by mail, phone or fax. No release necessary. No search fee. $.25 fee per copy. $1.00 for certification. $3.00 fee per fax response. Search information required: name, years to search. Specify plaintiff or defendant.

Misdemeanor records
Associate Circuit Court
PO Box 186
Galena, MO 65656
(417) 357-6511
Fax (417) 357-6163
Misdemeanor records are available by mail, phone or fax. No release necessary. No search fee. $.25 fee per copy. $2.50 for certification. $3.00 fee per fax response. Search information required: name, date of birth.

Civil records
Associate Circuit Court
PO Box 186
Galena, MO 65656
(417) 357-6511
Fax (417) 357-6163
Civil records are available by mail, phone or fax. No release necessary. No search fee. $.25 fee per copy. $2.50 for certification. $3.00 fee per fax response. Search information required: name, years to search. Specify plaintiff or defendant.

St. Charles County

Circuit Clerk of St. Charles County, Criminal Records
3rd and Jefferson
St. Charles, MO 63301
(314) 949-3080 Extension 5550
Felony and misdemeanor records are available in person only. See Missouri state repository for additional information.

Civil records are available in person only. See Missouri state repository for additional information.

St. Clair County

Circuit Clerk, Criminal Records
PO Box 334
Osceola, MO 64776
(417) 646-2226
Fax (417) 646-2401
Felony and misdemeanor records are available by mail or fax. No release necessary. No search fee. $.25 fee per copy. $1.00 for certification. $1.00 fee for fax response. Search information required: name, date of birth, years to search.

Civil records are available by mail or fax. No release necessary. No search fee. $.25 fee per copy. $1.00 for certification. $1.00 fee for fax response. Search information required: name, years to search. Specify plaintiff or defendant.

St. Francois County

Felony records
Circuit Clerk, Civil and Criminal Records
Courthouse, 3rd Floor
Farmington, MO 63640
(314) 756-4551
Fax (314) 756-8173
Felony records are available by mail, phone or fax. No release necessary. No search fee. $1.50 for certification. Search information required: name, case number, if available.

Civil records
Circuit Clerk
Courthouse, 3rd Floor
Farmington, MO 63640
(314) 756-4551
Fax (314) 756-8173
Civil records are available by mail, phone or fax. No release necessary. No search fee. $1.50 for certification. Search information required: name, years to search. Specify plaintiff or defendant..

Misdemeanor records
Associate Circuit Court
Division 3
2nd Floor, Courthouse
Farmington, MO 63640
(314) 756-5755
Fax (314) 756-8173
Misdemeanor records are available in person only. See Missouri state repository for additional information.

Civil records
Associate Circuit Court
Division 3
2nd Floor, Courthouse
Farmington, MO 63640
(314) 756-5755
Civil records are available in person only. See Missouri state repository for additional information.

St. Louis County

St. Louis County Police Department
Record Room
7900 Forsyth.
Clayton, MO 63105
(314) 889-2311
Felony and misdemeanor records are available by mail. A release is required. $3.50 search fee. Make check payable to Treasurer St. Louis County. Search information required: full name, date of birth, race, sex, SSN.

Civil records are available by mail. No release necessary. $3.50 search fee. Search information required: name, years to search. Specify plaintiff or defendant.

The City of St. Louis

Felony records
St. Louis Municipal Courts
22nd Judicial Circuit
1320 Market, Room 102
St. Louis, MO 63103
(314) 622-4582
Fax (314) 622-4485 or 622-4486
Felony and misdemeanor records are available in person only. See Missouri state repository for additional information.

Civil records
St. Louis Municipal Courts
22nd Judicial Circuit
1320 Market, Room 102
St. Louis, MO 63103
(314) 622-4582
Fax (314) 622-4485
Civil records are available in person only. See Missouri state repository for additional information.

Misdemeanor records
Chief of Deputy Clerk
1400 Market, Room 300
Kiel Auditorium
St. Louis, MO 63103
(314) 622-4701
Misdemeanor records are available in person only. See Missouri state repository for additional information.

Civil records
Chief of Deputy Clerk
1400 Market, Room 300
Kiel Auditorium
St. Louis, MO 63103
(314) 622-4701
Civil records are available in person only. See Missouri state repository for additional information.

Sullivan County

Felony records
Circuit Clerk, Criminal Records
Courthouse
Milan, MO 63556
(816) 265-4717
Fax (816) 265-4711
Felony records are available by mail or fax. A release is required. No search fee. $.25 fee per copy. $1.50 for certification. Search information required: name, SSN, date of birth, sex, race.

Civil records
Circuit Clerk
Courthouse
Milan, MO 63556
(816) 265-4717
Fax (816) 265-4711
Civil records are available by mail or fax. No release necessary. No search fee. $.25 fee per copy. $1.50 for certification. Search information required: name, years to search. Specify plaintiff or defendant.

Misdemeanor records
Associate Circuit Court
Sullivan County Courthouse
Milan, MO 63556
(816) 265-3303
Fax (816) 265-4711
Misdemeanor records are available by mail or fax. A release is required. $5.00 fee for first five years searched. $.25 fee per copy. $1.50 for certification. Search information required: name, date of birth, years to search, year of offense, SASE.

Civil records
Associate Circuit Court
Sullivan County Courthouse
Milan, MO 63556
(816) 265-3303
Fax (816) 265-4711
Civil records are available by mail or fax. No release necessary. $5.00 fee for first five years searched. $.25 fee per copy. $1.50 for certification. Search information required: name, years to search, SASE. Specify plaintiff or defendant.

Taney County

Felony records
Circuit Clerk, Criminal Records
PO Box 335
Forsyth, MO 65653
(417) 546-6132
Felony records are available by mail or phone. A release is required. $4.00 search fee. $.25 fee per copy. $1.50 for certification. Search information required: name, years to search.

Civil records
Circuit Clerk
PO Box 335
Forsyth, MO 65653
(417) 546-6132
Civil records are available by mail or phone. No release necessary. $4.00 search fee. $.25 fee per copy. $1.50 for certification. Search information required: name, years to search. Specify plaintiff or defendant.

Misdemeanor records
Associate Circuit Court
Division 2
PO Box 129
Forsyth, MO 65653
(417) 546-4716
Misdemeanor records are available by mail or phone. No release necessary. No search fee. $.25 fee per copy. $1.50 for certification. Search information required: name, date of birth, years to search.

Civil records
Associate Circuit Court
Division 2
PO Box 129
Forsyth, MO 65653
(417) 546-4716
Civil records are available by mail or phone. No release necessary. No search fee. $.25 fee per copy. $1.50 for certification. Search information required: name, years to search. Specify plaintiff or defendant.

Texas County

Felony records
Courthouse, Criminal Records
PO Box 237
Houston, MO 65483
(417) 967-3742
Fax (417) 967-4220
Felony records are available by mail or fax. A release is required. No search fee. $1.00 fee per copy. $.50 for certification. Search information required: name, date of birth, years to search.

Civil records
Courthouse
PO Box 237
Houston, MO 65483
(417) 967-3742
Fax (417) 967-4220
Civil records are available by mail or fax. No release necessary. No search fee. $1.00 fee per copy. $.50 for certification. Search information required: name, years to search. Specify plaintiff or defendant.

Misdemeanor records
Associate Clerk Office
County Courthouse
Houston, MO 65483
(417) 967-3663
Fax (417) 967-4220
Misdemeanor records are available by mail, phone or fax. No release necessary. No search fee. $.50 fee per copy. $1.50 for certification. Search information required: name.

Civil records
Associate Clerk Office
County Courthouse
Houston, MO 65483
(417) 967-3663
Fax (417) 967-4220
Civil records are available by mail or phone. No release necessary. No search fee. $.50 fee per copy. $1.50 for certification. Search information required: name, years to search. Specify plaintiff or defendant.

Vernon County

Vernon County Police Department
230 W. Cherry
Nevada, MO 64772
(417) 667-6042
Felony records are available by mail. A release is required. No search fee. Search information required: name, date of birth, SSN, SASE.

Civil records are available by mail or phone. No release necessary. No search fee. Search information required: name, years to search. Specify plaintiff or defendant.

Warren County

Felony records
Circuit Clerk, Criminal Records
104 W. Main
Warrenton, MO 63383
(314) 456-3363
Felony records are available in person only. See Missouri state repository for additional information.

Civil records
Circuit Clerk
104 W. Main
Warrenton, MO 63383
(314) 456-3363
Civil records are available in person only. See Missouri state repository for additional information.

Misdemeanor records
Associate Circuit Court
Division 2
Courthouse
104 W. Main
Warrenton, MO 63383
(314) 456-3375
Fax (314) 456-2422
Misdemeanor records are available by mail or fax. No release necessary. No search fee. $.25 fee per copy. $2.50 for certification. Search information required: name, date of birth, years to search, race, sex.

Civil records
Associate Circuit Court
Division 2
Courthouse
104 W. Main
Warrenton, MO 63383
(314) 456-3375
Fax (314) 456-2422
Civil records are available by mail or
phone. No release necessary. No search fee.
$.25 fee per copy. $2.50 for certification.
Search information required: name, years to
search. Specify plaintiff or defendant.

Washington County

Felony records
Circuit Clerk, Criminal Records
PO Box 216
Potosi, MO 63664
(314) 438-4171
Fax (314) 438-2079
Felony records are available by mail. A no-
tarized release is required. No search fee.
$.50 fee per copy. $.50 for certification.
Search information required: name, years to
search.

Civil records
Circuit Clerk
PO Box 216
Potosi, MO 63664
(314) 438-4171
Fax (314) 438-2079
Civil records are available by mail or
phone. No release necessary. No search fee.
$.50 fee per copy. $.50 for certification.
Search information required: name, years to
search. Specify plaintiff or defendant.

Misdemeanor records
Associate Circuit Court
102 N. Missouri St.
Potosi, MO 63664
(314) 438-3691
Misdemeanor records are available by mail.
No release necessary. No search fee. $1.00
fee per copy. $1.50 for certification. Search
information required: name, years to
search.

Civil records
Associate Circuit Court
102 N. Missouri St.
Potosi, MO 63664
(314) 438-3691
Civil records are available by mail or
phone. No release necessary. No search fee.
$1.00 fee per copy. $1.50 for certification.
Search information required: name, years to
search. Specify plaintiff or defendant.

Wayne County

Circuit Clerk, Criminal Records
Courthouse, Box 187-A
Greenville, MO 63944
(314) 224-3221
Felony and misdemeanor records are available by mail. No release necessary. No
search fee. $.25 fee per copy. $.25 for certification. Search information required:
name, years to search.

Civil records are available by mail or
phone. No release necessary. No search fee.
$.25 fee per copy. $.25 for certification.
Search information required: name, years to
search. Specify plaintiff or defendant.

Webster County

Felony records
Circuit Clerk, Criminal Records
Webster County Courthouse
PO Box 529
Marshfield, MO 65706
(417) 468-2006
Fax (417) 468-3786
Felony records are available by mail, phone
or fax. No release necessary. No search fee.
$.15 fee per copy. $2.00 for certification.
Search information required: name, years to
search.

Civil records
Circuit Clerk
Webster County Courthouse
PO Box 529
Marshfield, MO 65706
(417) 468-2006
Fax (417) 468-3786
Civil records are available by mail, phone
or fax. No release necessary. No search fee.
$.15 fee per copy. $2.00 for certification.
Search information required: name, years to
search. Specify plaintiff or defendant.

Misdemeanor records
Associate Circuit Court
Courthouse
Marshfield, MO 65706
(417) 468-2041
Misdemeanor records are available by mail
or phone. No release necessary. No search
fee. $1.00 fee per copy (includes certifica-
tion). Search information required: name,
date of birth.

Civil records
Associate Circuit Court
Courthouse
Marshfield, MO 65706
(417) 468-2041
Civil records are available by mail or
phone. No release necessary. No search fee.
$1.00 fee per copy (includes certification).
Search information required: name, years to
search. Specify plaintiff or defendant.

Worth County

Felony records
Circuit Clerk, Criminal Records
PO Box H
Grant City, MO 64456
(816) 564-2210
Fax (816) 564-2432
Felony records are available by mail, phone
or fax. No release necessary. $8.00 search
fee. $1.00 fee per copy. $2.50 for certification. $1.00 fee for fax response. Make
check payable to Circuit Clerk. Search information required: name, years to search.

Civil records
Circuit Clerk
PO Box H
Grant City, MO 64456
(816) 564-2210
Fax (816) 564-2432
Civil records are available by mail, phone
or fax. No release necessary. $8.00 search
fee. $1.00 fee per copy. $2.50 for certifica-
tion. $1.00 fee for fax response. Search in-
formation required: name, years to search.
Specify plaintiff or defendant.

Misdemeanor records
Associate Circuit Court
PO Box 428
Grant City, MO 64456
(816) 564-2152
Fax (816) 564-2432
Misdemeanor records are available by mail
or fax. No release necessary. No search
fee. $.25 fee per copy. $2.50 for certification. Search information required: name,
date of birth, years to search, offense.

Civil records
Associate Circuit Court
PO Box 428
Grant City, MO 64456
(816) 564-2152
Fax (816) 564-2432
Civil records are available by mail or fax.
No release necessary. No search fee. $.25
fee per copy. $2.50 for certification. Search
information required: name, years to
search. Specify plaintiff or defendant.

Wright County

Felony records
Circuit Clerk, Criminal Records
PO Box 39
Hartville, MO 65667
(417) 741-7121
Felony records are available by mail or
phone. No release necessary. No search fee.
$2.00 fee per copy. $2.00 for certification.
Search information required: name, years to
search.

Civil records
Circuit Clerk
PO Box 39
Hartville, MO 65667
(417) 741-7121
Civil records are available by mail or
phone. No release necessary. No search fee.
$2.00 fee per copy. $2.00 for certification.
Search information required: name, years to
search. Specify plaintiff or defendant.

Misdemeanor records
Associate Circuit Court
PO Box 58
Hartville, MO 65667
(417) 741-6505
Fax (417) 741-6780
Misdemeanor records are available by mail,
phone or fax. No release necessary. No
search fee. $.10 fee per copy. Search infor-
mation required: name, date of birth, SSN
(if available), years to search, information
requested.

Civil records
Associate Circuit Court
PO Box 58
Hartville, MO 65667
(417) 741-6505
Fax (417) 741-6780
Civil records are available by mail, phone
or fax. No release necessary. No search fee.
$.10 fee per copy. Search information re-
quired: name, years to search. Specify
plaintiff or defendant.

City-County Cross Reference

Adrian *Bates*
Advance *Stoddard*
Afton *Saint Louis*
Agency *Buchanan*
Alba *Jasper*
Albany *Gentry*
Aldrich *Polk*
Alexandria *Clark*
Allendale *Worth*
Allenton *Saint Louis*
Alma *Lafayette*
Altamont *Daviess*
Altenburg *Perry*
Alton *Oregon*
Amazonia *Andrew*
Amity *DeKalb*
Amoret *Bates*
Amsterdam *Bates*
Anabel *Macon*
Anderson *McDonald*
Annada *Pike*
Annapolis *Iron*
Anniston *Mississippi*
Appleton City *Saint Clair*
Arab *Bollinger*
Arbela *Scotland*
Arbyrd *Dunklin*
Arcadia *Iron*
Archie *Cass*
Arcola *Dade*
Argyle *Osage*
Armstrong *Howard*
Arnold *Jefferson*
Arrow Rock *Saline*
Asbury *Jasper*
Ashburn *Pike*
Ash Grove *Greene*
Ashland *Boone*
Atlanta *Macon*
Augusta *Saint Charles*
Aurora *Lawrence*
Auxvasse *Callaway*
Ava *Douglas*
Avilla *Jasper*
Avondale *Clay*
Bakersfield *Ozark*
Ballwin *Saint Louis*
Baring *Knox*
Barnard *Nodaway*
Barnett *Morgan*
Barnhart *Jefferson*
Bates City *Lafayette*
Battlefield *Greene*
Beaufort *Franklin*
Belgrade *Washington*
Bell City *Stoddard*
Bella Villa *Saint Louis*
Belle *Maries*
Belleview *Iron*
Bellefontaine *Saint Louis*
Bellefontaine Neighbors
  Saint Louis
Bellflower *Montgomery*
Bel-Nor *Saint Louis*
Bel-Ridge *Saint Louis*
Belton *Cass*
Bendavis *Texas*
Benton *Scott*
Benton City *Audrain*
Berger *Franklin*
Berkeley *Saint Louis*
Bernie *Stoddard*
Bertrand *Mississippi*
Bethany *Harrison*

Bethel *Shelby*
Beulah *Phelps*
Beverly Hills *Saint Louis*
Bevier *Macon*
Bigelow *Holt*
Billings *Christian*
Birch Tree *Shannon*
Bismarck *Saint Francois*
Bixby *Iron*
Black *Reynolds*
Blackburn *Saline*
Black Jack *Saint Louis*
Blackwater *Cooper*
Blackwell *Saint Francois*
Blairstown *Henry*
Bland *Gasconade*
Blodgett *Scott*
Bloomfield *Stoddard*
Bloomsdale *Sainte
  Genevieve*
Blue Eye *Stone*
Blue Springs *Jackson*
Blythedale *Harrison*
Bogard *Carroll*
Bois D Arc *Greene*
Bolckow *Andrew*
Bolivar *Polk*
Bonne Terre *Saint
  Francois*
Bonnots Mill *Osage*
Boonville *Cooper*
Boss *Dent*
Bosworth *Carroll*
Bourbon *Crawford*
Bowling Green *Pike*
Bradleyville *Taney*
Braggadocio *Pemiscot*
Bragg City *Pemiscot*
Brandsville *Howell*
Branson *Taney*
Brashear *Adair*
Braymer *Caldwell*
Brazeau *Perry*
Breckenridge *Caldwell*
Breckenridge Hills *Saint
  Louis*
Brentwood *Saint Louis*
Briar *Ripley*
Bridgeton *Saint Louis*
Brighton *Polk*
Brinktown *Maries*
Brixey *Ozark*
Bronaugh *Vernon*
Brookfield *Linn*
Brookline Station *Greene*
Broseley *Butler*
Browning *Linn*
Brownwood *Stoddard*
Brumley *Miller*
Bruner *Christian*
Brunswick *Chariton*
Bucklin *Linn*
Buckner *Jackson*
Bucyrus *Texas*
Buffalo *Dallas*
Bunceton *Cooper*
Bunker *Reynolds*
Burfordville *Cape
  Girardeau*
Burlington Junction
  Nodaway
Butler *Bates*
Cabool *Texas*
Cadet *Washington*

Cainsville *Harrison*
Cairo *Randolph*
Caledonia *Washington*
Calhoun *Henry*
California *Moniteau*
Callao *Macon*
Camden *Ray*
Camden Point *Platte*
Camdenton *Camden*
Cameron *Clinton*
Campbell *Dunklin*
Canalou *New Madrid*
Canton *Lewis*
Cape Fair *Stone*
Cape Girardeau *Cape
  Girardeau*
Caplinger Mills *Cedar*
Cardwell *Dunklin*
Carl Junction *Jasper*
Carrollton *Carroll*
Carsonville *Saint Louis*
Carterville *Jasper*
Carthage *Jasper*
Caruthersville *Pemiscot*
Cascade *Wayne*
Cassville *Barry*
Catawissa *Franklin*
Catron *New Madrid*
Caulfield *Howell*
Cedar City *Callaway*
Cedarcreek *Taney*
Cedar Hill *Jefferson*
Center *Ralls*
Centertown *Cole*
Centerview *Johnson*
Centerville *Reynolds*
Centralia *Boone*
Chadwick *Christian*
Chaffee *Scott*
Chamois *Osage*
Charlack *Saint Louis*
Charleston *Mississippi*
Cherryville *Crawford*
Chesterfield *Saint Louis*
Chestnutridge *Christian*
Chilhowee *Johnson*
Chillicothe *Livingston*
Chula *Livingston*
Clarence *Shelby*
Clark *Randolph*
Clarksburg *Moniteau*
Clarksdale *DeKalb*
Clarkson Valley *Saint
  Louis*
Clarksville *Pike*
Clarkton *Dunklin*
Claycomo *Clay*
Clayton *Saint Louis*
Clearmont *Nodaway*
Cleveland *Cass*
Clever *Christian*
Clifton Hill *Randolph*
Climax Springs *Camden*
Clinton *Henry*
Clyde *Nodaway*
Coatsville *Schuyler*
Coffey *Daviess*
Cole Camp *Benton*
Collins *Saint Clair*
Columbia *Boone*
Commerce *Scott*
Conception *Nodaway*
Conception Junction
  Nodaway

Concord *Saint Louis*
Concordia *Lafayette*
Conran *New Madrid*
Conway *Laclede*
Cook Station *Crawford*
Cool Valley *Saint Louis*
Cooter *Pemiscot*
Corder *Lafayette*
Cosby *Andrew*
Cottleville *Saint Charles*
Couch *Oregon*
Country Club Hills *Saint
  Louis*
Courtois *Washington*
Cowgill *Caldwell*
Craig *Holt*
Crane *Stone*
Creighton *Cass*
Crestwood *Saint Louis*
Creve Coeur *Saint Louis*
Crocker *Pulaski*
Cross Timbers *Hickory*
Crystal City *Jefferson*
Cuba *Crawford*
Curryville *Pike*
Dadeville *Dade*
Daisy *Cape Girardeau*
Dalton *Chariton*
Darlington *Gentry*
Davisville *Crawford*
Dawn *Livingston*
Dearborn *Platte*
Deepwater *Henry*
Deerfield *Vernon*
Deering *Pemiscot*
Defiance *Saint Charles*
DeKalb *Buchanan*
Delta *Cape Girardeau*
Dellwood *Saint Louis*
Denver *Worth*
Des Arc *Iron*
Des Peres *Saint Louis*
DeSoto *Jefferson*
Devils Elbow *Pulaski*
DeWitt *Carroll*
Dexter *Stoddard*
Diamond *Newton*
Diggins *Webster*
Dittmer *Jefferson*
Dixon *Pulaski*
Doe Run *Saint Francois*
Doniphan *Ripley*
Doolittle *Phelps*
Dora *Ozark*
Dover *Lafayette*
Downing *Schuyler*
Drexel *Cass*
Drury *Douglas*
Dudley *Stoddard*
Duenweg *Jasper*
Dugginsville *Ozark*
Duke *Phelps*
Dunnegan *Polk*
Duquesne *Jasper*
Durham *Lewis*
Dutchtown *Cape
  Girardeau*
Dutzow *Warren*
Eagle Rock *Barry*
Eagleville *Harrison*
East Lynne *Cass*
Easton *Buchanan*
East Prairie *Mississippi*
Edgar Springs *Phelps*

Edgerton *Platte*
Edina *Knox*
Edmundson *Saint Louis*
Edwards *Benton*
Eldon *Miller*
El Dorado Springs *Cedar*
Eldridge *Laclede*
Elk Creek *Texas*
Elkland *Webster*
Ellington *Reynolds*
Ellisville *Saint Louis*
Ellsinore *Carter*
Elmer *Macon*
Elmo *Nodaway*
Elsberry *Lincoln*
Elvins *Saint Francois*
Emden *Shelby*
Eminence *Shannon*
Emma *Saline*
Eolia *Pike*
Essex *Stoddard*
Ethel *Macon*
Etterville *Miller*
Eugene *Cole*
Eunice *Texas*
Eureka *Saint Louis*
Everton *Dade*
Ewing *Lewis*
Excello *Macon*
Excelsior Springs *Clay*
Exeter *Barry*
Fairdealing *Ripley*
Fairfax *Atchison*
Fair Grove *Greene*
Fair Play *Polk*
Fairview *Newton*
Falcon *Laclede*
Farber *Audrain*
Farley *Platte*
Farmington *Saint Francois*
Farrar *Perry*
Faucett *Buchanan*
Fayette *Howard*
Fenton *Saint Louis*
Ferguson *Saint Louis*
Festus *Jefferson*
Fillmore *Andrew*
Fisk *Butler*
Flat River *Saint Francois*
Flemington *Polk*
Fletcher *Jefferson*
Flinthill *Saint Charles*
Florence *Morgan*
Florissant *Saint Louis*
Foley *Lincoln*
Fordland *Webster*
Forest City *Holt*
Foristell *Saint Charles*
Forsyth *Taney*
Fort Leonard Wood
   Pulaski
Fortuna *Moniteau*
Foster *Bates*
Frankford *Pike*
Franklin *Howard*
Fredericktown *Madison*
Freeburg *Osage*
Freeman *Cass*
Freistatt *Lawrence*
Fremont *Carter*
French Village *Saint
   Francois*
Frohna *Perry*
Frontenac *Saint Louis*
Fulton *Callaway*
Gainesville *Ozark*

Galena *Stone*
Gallatin *Daviess*
Galt *Grundy*
Garden City *Cass*
Garrison *Christian*
Gatewood *Ripley*
Gentry *Gentry*
Gerald *Franklin*
Gibbs *Adair*
Gibson *Dunklin*
Gideon *New Madrid*
Gilliam *Saline*
Gilman City *Harrison*
Gipsy *Bollinger*
Gladstone *Clay*
Glasgow *Howard*
Glasgow Village
   Independent City
Glenaire *Clay*
Glenallen *Bollinger*
Glencoe *Saint Louis*
Glendale *Saint Louis*
Glenwood *Schuyler*
Glover *Iron*
Gobler *Pemiscot*
Golden *Barry*
Golden City *Barton*
Goodman *McDonald*
Goodson *Polk*
Gordonville *Cape
   Girardeau*
Gorin *Scotland*
Gower *Clinton*
Graff *Wright*
Graham *Nodaway*
Grain Valley *Jackson*
Granby *Newton*
Grandin *Carter*
Grandview *Jackson*
Grant City *Worth*
Grantwood *Saint Louis*
Grassy *Bollinger*
Gravois Mills *Morgan*
Grayridge *Stoddard*
Gray Summit *Franklin*
Green Castle *Sullivan*
Green City *Sullivan*
Greendale *Saint Louis*
Greenfield *Dade*
Green Ridge *Pettis*
Greentop *Schuyler*
Greenville *Wayne*
Greenwood *Jackson*
Grover *Saint Louis*
Grovespring *Wright*
Grubville *Jefferson*
Guilford *Nodaway*
Hale *Carroll*
Half Way *Polk*
Hallsville *Boone*
Halltown *Lawrence*
Hamilton *Caldwell*
Hanley Hills *Saint Louis*
Hannibal *Marion*
Hardenville *Ozark*
Hardin *Ray*
Harrisburg *Boone*
Harrisonville *Cass*
Hartsburg *Boone*
Hartshorn *Texas*
Hartville *Wright*
Harviell *Butler*
Harwood *Vernon*
Hawk Point *Lincoln*
Hayti *Pemiscot*
Hazelwood *Saint Louis*

Helena *Andrew*
Hematite *Jefferson*
Henley *Cole*
Henrietta *Ray*
Herculaneum *Jefferson*
Hermann *Gasconade*
Hermitage *Hickory*
Higbee *Randolph*
Higginsville *Lafayette*
High Hill *Montgomery*
Highlandville *Christian*
High Ridge *Jefferson*
Hillsboro *Jefferson*
Hillsdale *Saint Louis*
Hiram *Wayne*
Holcomb *Dunklin*
Holden *Johnson*
Holland *Pemiscot*
Holliday *Monroe*
Hollister *Taney*
Holt *Clay*
Holts Summit *Callaway*
Hopkins *Nodaway*
Horine *Jefferson*
Hornersville *Dunklin*
Horton *Vernon*
House Springs *Jefferson*
Houston *Texas*
Houstonia *Pettis*
Huggins *Texas*
Hughesville *Pettis*
Humansville *Polk*
Hume *Bates*
Humphreys *Sullivan*
Hunnewell *Shelby*
Huntsville *Randolph*
Hurdland *Knox*
Hurley *Stone*
Iberia *Miller*
Imperial *Jefferson*
Independence *Jackson*
Ionia *Benton*
Irondale *Washington*
Ironton *Iron*
Isabella *Ozark*
Jackson *Cape Girardeau*
Jacksonville *Randolph*
Jadwin *Dent*
Jameson *Daviess*
Jamesport *Daviess*
Jamestown *Moniteau*
Jasper *Jasper*
Jefferson City *Cole*
Jennings *Saint Louis*
Jerico Springs *Cedar*
Jerome *Phelps*
Jonesburg *Montgomery*
Joplin *Jasper*
Kahoka *Clark*
Kaiser *Miller*
Kansas City *Jackson*
Kearney *Clay*
Kelso *Scott*
Kennett *Dunklin*
Kewanee *New Madrid*
Keytesville *Chariton*
Kidder *Caldwell*
Kimberling City *Stone*
King City *Gentry*
Kingdom City *Callaway*
Kingston *Caldwell*
Kingsville *Johnson*
Kinloch *Saint Louis*
Kirbyville *Taney*
Kirksville *Adair*
Kirkwood *Saint Louis*

Kissee Mills *Taney*
Knob Lick *Saint Francois*
Knob Noster *Johnson*
Knox City *Knox*
Koeltztown *Osage*
Koshkonong *Oregon*
Labadie *Franklin*
LaBelle *Lewis*
Laclede *Linn*
Laddonia *Audrain*
Ladue *Saint Louis*
LaGrange *Lewis*
Lake Lotawana *Jackson*
Lake Ozark *Miller*
Lake Spring *Dent*
Lake Waukomis *Platte*
Lakeshire *Saint Louis*
Lamar *Barton*
LaMonte *Pettis*
Lampe *Stone*
Lanagan *McDonald*
Lancaster *Schuyler*
LaPlata *Macon*
Laquey *Pulaski*
Laredo *Grundy*
LaRussell *Jasper*
Latham *Moniteau*
Lathrop *Clinton*
Latour *Johnson*
Lawson *Ray*
Leasburg *Crawford*
Leadwood *Saint Francios*
Lebanon *Laclede*
Lecoma *Dent*
Lees Summit *Jackson*
Leeton *Johnson*
Lemay *Saint Louis*
Lenox *Dent*
Lentner *Shelby*
Leonard *Shelby*
Leopold *Bollinger*
Leslie *Franklin*
Lesterville *Reynolds*
Levasy *Jackson*
Lewistown *Lewis*
Lexington *Lafayette*
Liberal *Barton*
Liberty *Clay*
Licking *Texas*
Liguori *Jefferson*
Lilbourn *New Madrid*
Lincoln *Benton*
Linn *Osage*
Linn Creek *Camden*
Linneus *Linn*
Livonia *Putnam*
Lockwood *Dade*
Lodi *Wayne*
Lohman *Cole*
Lonedell *Franklin*
Lone Jack *Jackson*
Long Lane *Dallas*
Loose Creek *Osage*
Louisburg *Dallas*
Louisiana *Pike*
Lowndes *Wayne*
Lowry City *Saint Clair*
Lucerne *Putnam*
Ludlow *Livingston*
Luebbering *Franklin*
Luray *Clark*
Lutesville *Bollinger*
Lynchburg *Laclede*
McClurg *Taney*
McFall *Gentry*
McGee *Wayne*

McGirk *Moniteau*
Macks Creek *Camden*
Macomb *Wright*
Macon *Macon*
Madison *Monroe*
Maitland *Holt*
Malden *Dunklin*
Malta Bend *Saline*
Manchester *Saint Louis*
Mansfield *Wright*
Maplewood *Saint Louis*
Mapaville *Jefferson*
Marble Hill *Bollinger*
Marceline *Linn*
Marionville *Lawrence*
Marlborough *Saint Louis*
Marquand *Madison*
Marshall *Saline*
Marshfield *Webster*
Marston *New Madrid*
Marthasville *Warren*
Martinsburg *Audrain*
Martinsville *Harrison*
Maryland Heights *Saint Louis*
Maryville *Nodaway*
Mattese *Saint Louis*
Matthews *New Madrid*
Maysville *DeKalb*
Mayview *Lafayette*
Maywood *Lewis*
Meadville *Linn*
Memphis *Scotland*
Mendon *Chariton*
Menfro *Perry*
Mercer *Mercer*
Meta *Osage*
Metz *Vernon*
Mexico *Audrain*
Miami *Saline*
Middle Brook *Iron*
Middletown *Montgomery*
Milan *Sullivan*
Miller *Lawrence*
Millersville *Cape Girardeau*
Mill Spring *Wayne*
Milo *Vernon*
Mindenmines *Barton*
Mine LaMotte *Madison*
Mineral Point *Washington*
Missouri City *Clay*
Moberly *Randolph*
Mokane *Callaway*
Moline Acres *Saint Louis*
Monett *Barry*
Monroe City *Monroe*
Montgomery City *Montgomery*
Monticello *Lewis*
Montier *Shannon*
Montreal *Camden*
Montrose *Henry*
Moody *Howell*
Mooresville *Livingston*
Mora *Benton*
Morehouse *New Madrid*
Morley *Scott*
Morrison *Gasconade*
Morrisville *Polk*
Morse Mill *Jefferson*
Mosby *Clay*
Moscow Mills *Lincoln*
Mound City *Holt*
Moundville *Vernon*
Mountain Grove *Wright*

Mountain View *Howell*
Mount Vernon *Lawrence*
Murphy *Jefferson*
Myrtle *Oregon*
Napoleon *Lafayette*
Naylor *Ripley*
Neck City *Jasper*
Neelyville *Butler*
Nelson *Saline*
Neosho *Newton*
Nevada *Vernon*
Newark *Knox*
New Bloomfield *Callaway*
New Boston *Linn*
Newburg *Phelps*
New Cambria *Macon*
New Florence *Montgomery*
New Franklin *Howard*
New Hampton *Harrison*
New Hartford *Pike*
New Haven *Franklin*
New London *Ralls*
New Madrid *New Madrid*
New Melle *Saint Charles*
New Offenburg *Sainte Genevieve*
Newtown *Sullivan*
New Wells *Cape Girardeau*
Niangua *Webster*
Nixa *Christian*
Noble *Ozark*
Noel *McDonald*
Norborne *Carroll*
Normandy *Saint Louis*
North Kansas City *Clay*
Northmoor *Platte*
Northwoods *Saint Louis*
Norwood *Wright*
Nottinghill *Ozark*
Novelty *Knox*
Novinger *Adair*
Oak Grove *Jackson*
Oak Ridge *Cape Girardeau*
Oakland *Saint Louis*
Odessa *Lafayette*
O'Fallon *Saint Charles*
Old Appleton *Cape Girardeau*
Oldfield *Christian*
Old Monroe *Lincoln*
Olean *Miller*
Olivette *Saint Louis*
Olney *Lincoln*
Oran *Scott*
Oregon *Holt*
Oronogo *Jasper*
Orrick *Ray*
Osage Beach *Camden*
Osborn *DeKalb*
Osceola *Saint Clair*
Otterville *Cooper*
Overland *Saint Louis*
Owensville *Gasconade*
Oxly *Ripley*
Ozark *Christian*
Pacific *Franklin*
Painton *Stoddard*
Palmyra *Marion*
Pagedale *Saint Louis*
Paris *Monroe*
Parma *New Madrid*
Parnell *Nodaway*
Pascola *Pemiscot*
Patterson *Wayne*

Patton *Bollinger*
Pattonsburg *Daviess*
Paynesville *Pike*
Peace Valley *Howell*
Peculiar *Cass*
Perkins *Scott*
Perry *Ralls*
Perryville *Perry*
Pevely *Jefferson*
Philadelphia *Marion*
Phillipsburg *Laclede*
Pickering *Nodaway*
Piedmont *Wayne*
Pierce City *Lawrence*
Pilot Grove *Cooper*
Pilot Knob *Iron*
Pine Lawn *Saint Louis*
Pineville *McDonald*
Pittsburg *Hickory*
Plato *Texas*
Platte City *Platte*
Plattsburg *Clinton*
Pleasant Hill *Cass*
Pleasant Hope *Polk*
Pleasant Valley *Clay*
Plevna *Knox*
Pocahontas *Cape Girardeau*
Point Lookout *Taney*
Pollock *Sullivan*
Polo *Caldwell*
Pomona *Howell*
Ponce DeLeon *Stone*
Pontiac *Ozark*
Poplar Bluff *Butler*
Portage Des Sioux *Saint Charles*
Portageville *New Madrid*
Portland *Callaway*
Potosi *Washington*
Pottersville *Howell*
Powell *McDonald*
Powersite *Taney*
Powersville *Putnam*
Poynor *Ripley*
Prairie Home *Cooper*
Preston *Hickory*
Princeton *Mercer*
Protem *Taney*
Purcell *Jasper*
Purdin *Linn*
Purdy *Barry*
Puxico *Stoddard*
Queen City *Schuyler*
Quincy *Hickory*
Quitman *Nodaway*
Qulin *Butler*
Racine *Newton*
Ravenwood *Nodaway*
Raymondville *Texas*
Raymore *Cass*
Raytown *Jackson*
Rayville *Ray*
Rea *Andrew*
Redford *Reynolds*
Reeds *Jasper*
Reeds Spring *Stone*
Renick *Randolph*
Republic *Greene*
Revere *Clark*
Reynolds *Reynolds*
Rhineland *Montgomery*
Richards *Vernon*
Rich Hill *Bates*
Richland *Pulaski*
Richmond *Ray*

Richmond Heights *Saint Louis*
Richwoods *Washington*
Ridgedale *Taney*
Ridgeway *Harrison*
Risco *New Madrid*
Riverside *Platte*
Riverview *Saint Louis*
Rives *Dunklin*
Roach *Camden*
Robertsville *Franklin*
Roby *Texas*
Rocheport *Boone*
Rockaway Beach *Taney*
Rockbridge *Ozark*
Rock Hill *Saint Louis*
Rock Port *Atchison*
Rockville *Bates*
Rocky Comfort *McDonald*
Rogersville *Webster*
Rolla *Phelps*
Rombauer *Butler*
Roscoe *Saint Clair*
Rosebud *Gasconade*
Rosendale *Andrew*
Rothville *Chariton*
Rueter *Taney*
Rush Hill *Audrain*
Rushville *Buchanan*
Russellville *Cole*
Rutledge *Scotland*
Saginaw *Newton*
Saint Albans *Franklin*
Saint Ann *Saint Louis*
Saint Catharine *Linn*
Saint Charles *Saint Charles*
Saint Clair *Franklin*
Sainte Genevieve *Sainte Genevieve*
Saint George *Saint Louis*
Saint Elizabeth *Miller*
Saint James *Phelps*
Saint Johns *Saint Louis*
Saint Joseph *Buchanan*
Saint Louis *Independent City*
Saint Marys *Sainte Genevieve*
Saint Patrick *Clark*
Saint Peters *Saint Charles*
Saint Robert *Pulaski*
Saint Thomas *Cole*
Salem *Dent*
Salisbury *Chariton*
Santa Fe *Monroe*
Sappington *Saint Louis*
Sarcoxie *Jasper*
Savannah *Andrew*
Saverton *Ralls*
Schell City *Vernon*
Scott City *Scott*
Sedalia *Pettis*
Sedgewickville *Bollinger*
Seligman *Barry*
Senath *Dunklin*
Seneca *Newton*
Seymour *Webster*
Shelbina *Shelby*
Shelbyville *Shelby*
Sheldon *Vernon*
Shell Knob *Barry*
Sheridan *Worth*
Shook *Wayne*
Shrewsbury *Saint Louis*
Sibley *Jackson*
Sikeston *Scott*

Silex *Lincoln*
Silva *Wayne*
Skidmore *Nodaway*
Slater *Saline*
Smithton *Pettis*
Smithville *Clay*
Solo *Texas*
Souder *Ozark*
South Greenfield *Dade*
South West City *McDonald*
Spanish Lake *Saint Louis*
Sparta *Christian*
Spickard *Grundy*
Spokane *Christian*
Springfield *Greene*
Squires *Douglas*
Stanberry *Gentry*
Stanton *Franklin*
Stark City *Newton*
Steedman *Callaway*
Steele *Pemiscot*
Steelville *Crawford*
Steffenville *Lewis*
Stella *Newton*
Stewartsville *DeKalb*
Stockton *Cedar*
Stotts City *Lawrence*
Stoutland *Camden*
Stoutsville *Monroe*
Stover *Morgan*
Strafford *Greene*
Strasburg *Cass*
Sturdivant *Bollinger*
Sturgeon *Boone*
Success *Texas*
Sugar Creek *Jackson*
Sullivan *Franklin*
Sulphur Springs *Jefferson*
Summersville *Texas*
Sumner *Chariton*
Sunset Hills *Saint Louis*
Sunrise Beach *Camden*
Swedeborg *Pulaski*
Sweet Springs *Saline*
Syracuse *Morgan*
Tallapoosa *New Madrid*
Taneyville *Taney*
Taos *Cole*
Tarkio *Atchison*
Taylor *Marion*
Tebbetts *Callaway*
Tecumseh *Ozark*
Teresita *Shannon*
Thayer *Oregon*
Theodosia *Ozark*
Thompson *Audrain*
Thornfield *Ozark*
Tiff *Washington*
Tiff City *McDonald*
Tina *Carroll*
Tipton *Moniteau*
Treloar *Warren*
Trenton *Grundy*
Trimble *Clinton*
Triplett *Chariton*
Troy *Lincoln*
Truxton *Lincoln*
Tunas *Dallas*
Turners *Greene*
Turney *Clinton*
Tuscumbia *Miller*
Udall *Ozark*
Ulman *Miller*
Union *Franklin*
Union Star *DeKalb*

Unionville *Putnam*
University City *Saint Louis*
Urbana *Dallas*
Urich *Henry*
Utica *Livingston*
Valles Mines *Jefferson*
Valley Park *Saint Louis*
Van Buren *Carter*
Vandalia *Audrain*
Vanduser *Scott*
Vanzant *Douglas*
Velda Village *Saint Louis*
Velda Village Hills *Saint Louis*
Verona *Lawrence*
Versailles *Morgan*
Vichy *Maries*
Vienna *Maries*
Villa Ridge *Franklin*
Vinita Park *Saint Louis*
Vulcan *Iron*
Waco *Jasper*
Wakenda *Carroll*
Waldron *Platte*
Walker *Vernon*
Walnut Grove *Greene*
Walnut Shade *Taney*
Wappapello *Wayne*
Wardell *Pemiscot*
Warrensburg *Johnson*
Warrenton *Warren*
Warsaw *Benton*
Warson Woods *Saint Louis*
Washburn *Barry*
Washington *Franklin*
Wasola *Ozark*
Waverly *Lafayette*
Wayland *Clark*
Waynesville *Pulaski*
Weatherby *DeKalb*
Weaubleau *Hickory*
Webb City *Jasper*
Weber Hill *Jefferson*
Webster Groves *Saint Louis*
Wellington *Lafayette*
Wellston *Saint Louis*
Wellsville *Montgomery*
Wentworth *Newton*
Wentzville *Saint Charles*
Wesco *Crawford*
West Alton *Saint Charles*
Westboro *Atchison*
Weston *Platte*
Westphalia *Osage*
West Plains *Howell*
Wheatland *Hickory*
Wheaton *Barry*
Wheeling *Livingston*
Whiteoak *Dunklin*
Whiteside *Lincoln*
Whitewater *Cape Girardeau*
Wilbur Park *Saint Louis*
Willard *Greene*
Williamsburg *Callaway*
Williamstown *Lewis*
Williamsville *Wayne*
Willow Springs *Howell*
Winchester *Saint Louis*
Windsor *Henry*
Windyville *Dallas*
Winfield *Lincoln*
Winigan *Sullivan*
Winona *Shannon*
Winston *Daviess*

Wittenberg *Perry*
Wolf Island *Mississippi*
Woodson Terrace *Saint Louis*
Wooldridge *Cooper*
Worth *Worth*
Worthington *Putnam*
Wright City *Warren*
Wyaconda *Clark*
Wyatt *Mississippi*
Yukon *Texas*
Zalma *Bollinger*
Zanoni *Ozark*

Montana

All fifty six (56) of Montana's counties reported that they make conviction data available for employment screening purposes. Twenty three (23) counties reported that record requests are available by fax. District court holds civil court records for $3,000 and more.

For more information or for offices not listed, contact the state's information hot line at (406) 444-2511.

Driving Records

Driver Services
303 N. Roberts
Helena, MT 59620-1420
(406) 444-3275
Driving records are available by mail. $3.00 fee per request. Turnaround time is 24 hours. Written request must include job applicant's full name, date of birth and license number. Make check payable to Driver Records.

Worker's Compensation Records

Worker's Compensation Records Department
PO Box 4759
Helena, MT 59604-4759
(406) 444-6500
Worker's compensation records available by mail only. Written request must include applicant's full name, date of birth, SSN and a signed release authorizing access. No search fee.

Vital Statistics

Bureau of Records and Statistics
State Department of Health and Environmental Sciences
Helena, MT 59620
(406) 444-2614
Birth and death records are available for $5.00 each. State office has records since late 1907. An employer can obtain records with a written release. Make check or money order payable to Department of Health.
Marriage records are available at county level, clerk of court, where license was issued. Divorce records are available at county level, clerk of district court, in county where divorce was granted.

Department of Education

Office of Public Instruction
Certification Services
State Capitol
Helena, MT 59620
(406) 444-3150
Field of certification, effective date and expiration date are available by phone or mail. Include name.

Medical Licensing

Board of Medical Examiners
111 N. Jackson
Helena, MT 59620
(406) 444-4276
Will confirm licenses for MDs and DOs by phone or mail. No search fee at present but a $10.00 fee is being contemplated. For licenses not mentioned, contact the above office.

Montana State Board of Nursing
Department of Commerce
Division of Business and
Professional Licensing
111 N. Jackson
Helena, MT 59620-0407
(406) 444-2071
Will confirm license by phone. $10.00 search fee. Include name, license number, if available.

Bar Association

Clerk of Superior Court
Room 323 Justice Building
215 North Sanders
Helena, MT 59620
(406) 444-3858
Will confirm licenses by phone. No fee. Include name.

Accountancy Board

Montana Board of Public Accountancy
111 North Jackson
Helena, MT 59620-0407
(406) 444-3737
Will confirm licenses by phone. No fee. Include name.

Securities Commission

State Auditor's Office
Securities Department
Box 4009
Helena, MT 59604
(406) 444-2040
Will confirm licenses by phone. No fee. Include name and SSN.

Secretary of State

Secretary of State
Room 225, State Capitol
Helena, MT 59620
(406) 444-3665
Fax (406) 444-3976
Service agent and address, date incorporated, trade names are available by phone or mail. Contact the above office for additional information.

Criminal Records

State Repository

Montana Identification Bureau
Department of Justice
303 North Roberts
Helena, MT 59620-1418
(406) 444-3625
Written requests must include subject's full name, date of birth and if available, aliases and SSN. There is a $5.00 fee for each request. Make check payable to Montana Identification Bureau. Only conviction data released. Turnaround time is 1 week plus mail time.

Beaverhead County

Clerk of District Court, Criminal Records
2 S. Pacific St. Box 5
Dillon, MT 59725
(406) 683-5831
Fax (406) 683-5776
Fax (406) 665-1608
Felony records are available by mail or fax. No release necessary. $.50 fee for each year searched. $.50 fee per copy. $2.50 for certification. Search information required: name, years to search.

Civil records are available by mail. No release necessary. $.50 fee for each year searched. $.50 fee per copy. $2.50 for certification. Search information required: name, years to search. Specify plaintiff or defendant.

Big Horn County

District Clerk, Criminal Records
PO Drawer H
Hardin, MT 59034
(406) 665-1504
Fax (406) 665-1608
Felony and high misdemeanor records are available by mail, fax or phone. No release necessary. No search fee. $.50 fee per copy. $2.00 for certification. Search information required: name, years to search.

Civil records are available by mail or phone. No release necessary. No search fee. $.50 fee per copy. $2.00 for certification. Search information required: name, date of birth, years to search. Specify plaintiff or defendant.

Blaine County

Felony records
Clerk of Court, Criminal Records
PO Box 969
Chinook, MT 59523
(406) 357-3230
Felony records are available by mail or phone. No release necessary. No search fee. $.50 fee per copy. $2.00 for certification. Search information required: name, years to search, SASE.

Civil records
Clerk of Court
PO Box 969
Chinook, MT 59523
(406) 357-3230
Civil records are available by mail. No release necessary. $.50 search fee per year. $.50 fee per copy. $2.00 for certification. Search information required: name, date of birth, years to search. Specify plaintiff or defendant.

Misdemeanor records
Justice Court
PO Box 1266
Chinook, MT 59523
(406) 357-2335
Misdemeanor records are available by mail. A release is required. No search fee. $.50 fee per copy. $2.00 for certification. Search information required: name, date of birth.

Civil records
Justice Court
PO Box 1266
Chinook, MT 59523
(406) 357-2335
Civil records are available by mail. No release necessary. No search fee. $.50 fee per copy. $2.00 for certification. Search information required: name, date of birth, years to search. Specify plaintiff or defendant.

Broadwater County

Felony records
Clerk of Court, Criminal Records
PO Box 1158
Townsend, MT 59644
(406) 266-3418
Felony records are available by mail or phone. No release necessary. $.50 fee per year searched. $.50 fee per copy. $2.50 for certification. Search information required: name, years to search.

Civil records
Clerk of Court
PO Box 1158
Townsend, MT 59644
(406) 266-3418
Civil records are available by mail. No release necessary. $.50 fee per year searched. $.50 fee per copy. $2.50 for certification. Search information required: name, date of birth, years to search. Specify plaintiff or defendant.

Misdemeanor records
Justice and City Court
Box 856
Townsend, MT 59644
(406) 266-3145
Misdemeanor records are available by mail. A release required. No search fee. Search information required: name, date of charge, date of birth, address.

Civil records
Justice and City Court
Box 856
Townsend, MT 59644
(406) 266-3145
Civil records are available by mail. No release necessary. No search fee. $.50 fee per copy. $2.00 for certification. Search information required: name, date of birth, years to search. Specify plaintiff or defendant.

Butte-Silver Bow County

Clerk of the District Court, Criminal Records
155 W. Granite Street
Butte, MT 59701
(406) 723-8262
Fax (406) 782-6637
Felony records are available by mail. No release necessary. $.50 fee per year searched. $.50 fee per copy. $2.50 for certification. Search information required: name, years to search.

Civil records are available by mail. No release necessary. $.50 fee per year searched. $.50 fee per copy. $2.50 for certification. Search information required: name, date of birth, years to search. Specify plaintiff or defendant.

Carbon County

Felony records
Clerk of District Court, Criminal Records
PO Box 948
Red Lodge, MT 59068
(406) 446-1225
Fax (406) 446-2640
Felony records are available by mail, phone or fax. No release necessary. $.50 search fee per year. $.50 fee per copy. $2.50 for certification. Search information required: name, years to search.

Civil records
Clerk of District Court
PO Box 948
Red Lodge, MT 59068
(406) 446-1225
Fax (406) 446-2640
Civil records are available by mail. No release necessary. $.50 search fee per year. $.50 fee per copy. $2.50 for certification. Search information required: name, date of birth, years to search. Specify plaintiff or defendant.

Misdemeanor records
Justice Court
Box 2
Red Lodge, MT 59068
(406) 446-1440
Misdemeanor records are available by mail. No release necessary. $2.00 search fee for the first 3 years. $5.00 each additional year thereafter. Search information required: name, date of birth, date of offense, offense.

Civil records
Justice Court
Box 2
Red Lodge, MT 59068
(406) 446-1440
Civil records are available by mail. No release necessary. $3.00 search fee for the first 3 years. $5.00 each additional year thereafter. Search information required: name, date of birth, years to search. Specify plaintiff or defendant.

Carter County

Clerk of District Court, Criminal Records
PO Box 322
Ekalaka Route
Ekalaka, MT 59324
(406) 775-8714
Felony and misdemeanor records are available by mail. No release necessary. $.50 fee for each year searched. $.25 fee per copy. $2.00 for certification. Search information required: name, years to search.

Civil records are available by mail. No release necessary. $.50 fee for each year searched. $.25 fee per copy. $2.00 for certification. Search information required: name, date of birth, years to search. Specify plaintiff or defendant.

Cascade County

Felony records
Clerk of District Court, Criminal Records
PO Box 2806
Great Falls, MT 59403
(406) 761-6700, Ext. 430
Felony records are available by mail or phone. No release necessary. $.50 fee for each year searched. $2.50 for certification. Search information required: name, years to search.

Civil records
Clerk of District Court
PO Box 2806
Great Falls, MT 59403
(406) 761-6700, Ext. 430
Civil records are available by mail or phone. No release necessary. $.50 fee for each year searched. $2.50 for certification. Search information required: name, date of birth, years to search. Specify plaintiff or defendant.

Misdemeanor records
Justice Court
Cascade County Courthouse
Great Falls, MT 59401
(406) 761-6700, Ext. 481
Misdemeanor records are available by mail. No release necessary. $5.00 search fee. $.25 fee per copy. $1.25 for certification. Search information required: name, years to search, date of birth.

Civil records
Justice Court
Cascade County Courthouse
Great Falls, MT 59401
(406) 761-6700, Ext. 481
Civil records are available by mail. No release necessary. $5.00 search fee. $.25 fee per copy. $1.25 for certification. Search information required: name, date of birth, years to search. Specify plaintiff or defendant.

Chouteau County

Clerk of Court, Criminal Records
PO Box 459
Ft. Benton, MT 59442
(406) 622-5024
Fax (406) 622-3631
Felony and misdemeanor records are available by mail or phone. No release necessary. $.50 search fee per year. $.25 fee per copy. $1.25 for certification. Search information required: name, years to search.

Civil records are available by mail or phone. No release necessary. $.50 search fee per year. $.25 fee per copy. $1.25 for certification. Search information required: name, date of birth, years to search. Specify plaintiff or defendant.

Custer County

Custer County Courthouse, Criminal Records
1010 Main
Miles City, MT 59301
(406) 232-7800 Extension 27
Fax (406) 232-7477
Felony and misdemeanor records are available by mail or phone. No release necessary. $.50 fee per year searched. $.50 per copy. $1.25 for certification. Search information required: name, years to search.

Civil records are available by mail. No release necessary. $.50 fee per year searched. $.50 fee per copy. $2.50 for certification. Search information required: name, date of birth, years to search, SASE. Specify plaintiff or defendant.

Daniels County

Clerk of District Court, Criminal Records
PO Box 67
Scobey, MT 59263
(406) 487-2651
Felony and misdemeanor records are available by mail or phone. A release is required. $.50 fee for each year searched. $.50 fee per copy. $2.50 for certification. Search information required: name, years to search.

Civil records are available by mail or phone. No release necessary. No search fee. $.50 fee per copy. $2.50 for certification. Search information required: name, date of birth, years to search. Specify plaintiff or defendant.

Dawson County

Clerk of Court, Criminal Records
PO Box 1009
Glendive, MT 59330
(406) 365-3967
Fax (406) 365-4568
Felony and misdemeanor records are available by mail, fax or phone. A release is required. $.25 fee for each year searched. $.50 fee per copy. $2.50 for certification. Search information required: name, years to search.

Civil records are available by mail. No release necessary. $.25 fee for each year searched. $.50 fee per copy. $2.50 for certification. Search information required: name, date of birth, years to search. Specify plaintiff or defendant.

Deer Lodge County

Clerk of Court, Criminal Records
Deer Lodge County
800 S. Main
Anaconda, MT 59711
(406) 563-8421
Felony and misdemeanor records are available by mail. No release necessary. No search fee. Copies in person only. Search information required: name, date of birth, years to search.

Civil records are available by mail or phone. No release necessary. No search fee. $.50 fee per copy. $2.50 for certification. Search information required: name, date of birth, years to search. Specify plaintiff or defendant.

Fallon County

Clerk of District Court
Drawer M
Baker, MT 59313
(406) 778-2883 Extension 48
Fax (406) 778-3431
Felony records are available by mail, phone or fax. No release necessary. $2.00 search fee. $.50 fee per year searched. $.25 fee for each year searched. $.25 fee per copy. $2.50 for certification. Search information required: name, years to search.

Civil records are available by mail. No release necessary. $2.00 search fee. $.25 fee per copy. $3.00 for certification. Search information required: name, date of birth, years to search. Specify plaintiff or defendant.

Fergus County

Felony records
Clerk of Court, Criminal Records
PO Box 1074
Lewistown, MT 59457
(406) 538-5026
Felony records are available by mail only. No release necessary. No search fee. $.25 fee per copy. $2.00 for certification. Make check payable to Clerk of Court. Search information required: name, years to search.

Civil records
Clerk of Court
PO Box 1074
Lewistown, MT 59457
(406) 538-5026
Civil records are available by mail only. No release necessary. No search fee. $.25 fee per copy. $2.00 for certification. Search information required: name, date of birth, years to search. Specify plaintiff or defendant.

Misdemeanor records
Justice Court
(406) 538-5418
Misdemeanor records are available in person only. See Montana state repository for additional information.

Civil records
Justice Court
(406) 538-5418
Civil records are available in person only. See Montana state repository for additional information.

Flathead County

Felony records
Clerk of District Court, Criminal Records
PO Box 897
Kalispell, MT 59903
(406) 752-5300
Felony records are available by mail only. No release necessary. $.50 fee for each year searched. $.50 fee per copy. $2.50 for certification. Make check payable to Clerk of Court. Search information required: name, SSN, years to search.

Civil records
Clerk of District Court
PO Box 897
Kalispell, MT 59903
(406) 752-5300
Civil records are available by mail. No release necessary. $.50 fee for each year searched. $.50 fee per copy. $2.50 for certification. Search information required: name, date of birth, years to search. Specify plaintiff or defendant.

Misdemeanor records
Justice Court
800 S. Main
Kalispell, MT 59901
(406) 752-5300 Ext. 616
Misdemeanor records are available by mail or phone. No release necessary. No search fee. $.25 fee per copy. $2.50 for certification. Search information required: name, date of birth, years to search.

Civil records
Justice Court
800 S. Main
Kalispell, MT 59901
(406) 752-5300 Ext.616
Civil records are available by mail. No release necessary. No search fee. $.25 fee per copy. $2.50 for certification. Search information required: name, date of birth, years to search. Specify plaintiff or defendant.

Gallatin County

Felony records
Clerk of District Court, Criminal Records
615 S. 16th, Room 200
Bozeman, MT 59715
(406) 585-1360
Fax (406) 585-1363
Felony records are available by mail. No release necessary. $.50 fee for each year searched. $.50 fee per copy. $2.00 for certification. Search information required: name, years to search.

Civil records
Clerk of District Court
615 S. 16th, Room 200
Bozeman, MT 59715
(406) 585-1360
Fax (406) 585-1363
Civil records are available by mail. No release necessary. $.50 fee for each year searched. $.50 fee per copy. $2.00 for certification. Search information required: name, date of birth, years to search. Specify plaintiff or defendant.

Misdemeanor records
Justice Court
615 S. 16th, Room 35
Bozeman, MT 59715
(406) 585-1370
Misdemeanor records are available by mail.
No release necessary. $5.00 search fee.
Make check payable to Justice Court.
Search information required: name, date of
birth, SSN, offense, years to search.

Civil records
Justice Court
615 S. 16th, Room 35
Bozeman, MT 59715
(406) 585-1370
Civil records are available by mail. No release necessary. $5.00 search fee. Search
information required: name, date of birth,
years to search. Specify plaintiff or defendant.

Garfield County

Clerk of District Court, Criminal
Records
PO Box 8
Jordan, MT 59337
(406) 557-6254
Felony and misdemeanor records are available by mail or phone. No release necessary. No search fee. $.20 fee per copy.
$2.00 for certification. Search information
required: name, years to search.

Civil records are available by mail. No release necessary. No search fee. $.20 fee per
copy. $2.00 for certification. Search infor-
mation required: name, date of birth, years
to search. Specify plaintiff or defendant.

Glacier County

Clerk of Court
512 E. Main ST.
Cut Bank, MT 59427
(406) 873-5063, Ext. 32, 34, 36
Fax (406) 873-4218
Felony and misdemeanor records are available by mail or phone. No release necessary. $.50 fee for each year searched. Make
check payable to Clerk of District Court.
Search information required: name, date of
birth, years to search.

Civil records are available in person only.
See Montana state repository for additional
information.

Golden Valley County

Clerk of District Court
Box 10
Ryegate, MT 59074
(406) 568-2231
Felony and misdemeanor records are available by mail. No release necessary. $.50 fee
for each year searched. $.50 fee for first
copy, $.25 each additional copy. $2.00 for
certification. Search information required:
name, date of birth, years to search.

Civil records are available by mail. No release necessary. $.50 fee for first copy, $.25
each additional copy. $2.00 for certifica-
tion. Search information required: name,
date of birth, years to search. Specify plaintiff or defendant.

Granite County

Clerk of District Court, Criminal
Records
PO Box J
Philipsburg, MT 59858
(406) 859-3712
Felony and some misdemeanor records are
available by mail or phone. No release necessary. $.50 fee for each year searched. $.25
fee per copy. $2.50 for certification. Search
information required: name, previous address, years to search.

Civil records are available by mail. No release necessary. $.50 fee for each year
searched. $.25 fee per copy. $2.50 for certification. Search information required:
name, date of birth, years to search. Specify
plaintiff or defendant.

Hill County

Clerk of Court, Criminal Records
Hill County Courthouse
Havre, MT 59501
(406) 265-5481 Extension 25
Fax (406) 265-5487
Felony and some misdemeanor records are
available by mail or fax. No release necessary. $.50 fee for each year searched. $.50
fee per copy. $2.00 for certification. Search
information required: name, years to
search, offense.

Civil records are available by mail. No release necessary. $.50 fee for each year
searched. $.50 fee per copy. $2.00 for certification. Search information required:
name, date of birth, years to search. Specify
plaintiff or defendant.

Jefferson County

Clerk of District Court, Criminal
Records
PO Box H
Boulder, MT 59632
(406) 225-4251
Fax (406) 225-3327
Felony and some misdemeanor records are
available by mail or fax. No release necessary. $.50 fee for each year searched. $.50
fee per copy. $2.00 for certification. Search
information required: name, date of birth,
years to search.

Civil records are available by mail. No release necessary. $.50 fee for each year
searched. $.50 fee per copy. $2.00 for certification. Search information required:
name, date of birth, years to search. Specify
plaintiff or defendant.

Judith Basin County

Clerk of District Court, Criminal
Records
PO Box 307
Stanford, MT 59479
(406) 566-2491
Felony and misdemeanor records are available by mail. A release is required. $2.00
search fee. $.50 fee for first 5 copies, $.25
for each additional copy $2.00 for certifi-
cation. Search information required: name.
Civil records are available by mail. A release is required. $.50 search fee. $.50 fee
for first 5 copies, $.25 for each additional
copy $2.00 for certification. Search infor-
mation required: name, date of birth, years
to search. Specify plaintiff or defendant.

Lake County

Felony and misdemeanor records
Clerk of the District Court, Criminal
Records
Lake County Courthouse
106 4th Ave. E.
Polson, MT 59860
(406) 883-6211 Ext. 250
Fax (406) 883-6255
Felony and misdemeanor records are avail-
able by mail. No release necessary. $3.00
search fee. $.50 fee per copy. $2.00 for cer-
tification. Make check payable to Clerk of
District Court. Search information required:
name, years to search.

Civil records
Clerk of the District Court
Lake County Courthouse
106 4th Ave. E.
Polson, MT 59860
(406) 883-6211 Ext. 310
Fax (406) 883-6255
Civil records are available by mail. No release necessary. $.50 fee for each year
searched. $.50 fee per copy. $2.00 for certification. Search information required:
name, date of birth, years to search. Specify
plaintiff or defendant.

Lewis and Clark County

Felony records
Clerk of District Court, Criminal
Records
228 Broadway
Helena, MT 59601
(406) 447-8216
Felony records are available by mail. No release necessary. $.50 fee for each year
searched. $.50 fee per copy. $2.00 for certification. Company checks only, payable to
Clerk of Court. Search information required: name, years to search.

Civil records
Clerk of District Court
228 Broadway
Helena, MT 59601
(406) 447-8216
Civil records are available by mail. A release is required. $5.00 search fee. $.50 fee
per copy. $2.00 for certification. Search in-
formation required: name, date of birth,
years to search. Specify plaintiff or defendant.

Misdemeanor records
Support Service Division
221 Breckenridge
Helena, MT 59601
(406) 447-8469
Misdemeanor records are available by mail.
A release is required. $5.00 search fee.
Search information required: name, date of
birth, SSN.

Civil records
Support Service Division
221 Breckenridge
Helena, MT 59601
(406) 447-8469
Civil records are available by mail. No release necessary. $5.00 search fee. $.50 fee
per copy. $2.00 for certification. Search in-
formation required: name, date of birth,
years to search. Specify plaintiff or defendant.

Liberty County

Clerk of Court, Criminal Records
PO Box 549
Chester, MT 59522
(406) 759-5615
Fax (406) 759-5395
Felony and misdemeanor records are available by mail. No release necessary. $7.00 search fee. $.25 fee per copy. Search information required: name, SASE.

Civil records are available by mail. No release necessary. $7.00 search fee. $.50 fee per copy. $2.00 for certification. Search information required: name, date of birth, years to search, SASE. Specify plaintiff or defendant.

Lincoln County

Felony records
Clerk of District Court, Criminal Records
512 California Ave.
Libby, MT 59923
(406) 293-7781 Ext. 224
Fax (406) 293-9816
Felony records are available by mail or fax. No release necessary. $3.00 fee for first ten years searched, $.50 fee for each additional year. $.50 fee per copy. $2.00 for certification. $2.00 fee for fax response plus $.50 for first five pages faxed and $.25 for each additional page. Make money order payable to Clerk of District Court. Search information required: name, date of birth, years to search.

Civil records
Clerk of District Court
512 California Ave.
Libby, MT 59923
(406) 293-7781 Ext. 224
Fax (406) 293-9816
Civil records are available by mail or fax. No release necessary. $3.00 fee for first ten years searched, $.50 fee for each additional year. $.50 fee per copy. $2.00 for certification. $2.00 fee for fax response plus $.50 for first five pages faxed and $.25 for each additional page. Search information required: name, date of birth, years to search. Specify plaintiff or defendant.

Misdemeanor records
Justice Court
418 Mineral Ave.
Libby, MT 59923
(406) 293-7781 Ext. 236
Misdemeanor records are available by mail or phone. No release necessary. No fee. Search information required: name, date of birth, date of offense, offense.

Civil records
Justice Court
418 Mineral Ave.
Libby, MT 59923
(406) 293-7781 Ext. 236
Civil records are available by mail. A release is required. No search fee. Search information required: name, date of birth, years to search. Specify plaintiff or defendant.

Madison County

Felony records
Clerk of Court, Criminal Records
PO Box 185
Virginia City, MT 59755
(406) 843-5392
Fax (406) 843-5517
Felony records are available by mail or fax. No release necessary. $.50 fee for each year searched. $2.00 fee for fax request. $.50 fee per copy. $2.00 for certification. Make check payable to Clerk of Court. Search information required: name, date of birth, years to search.

Civil records
Clerk of Court
PO Box 185
Virginia City, MT 59755
(406) 843-5392
Fax (406) 843-5517
Civil records are available by mail or fax. No release necessary. $.50 fee for each year searched. $2.00 fee for fax request. $.50 fee per copy. $2.00 for certification. Search information required: name, date of birth, years to search. Specify plaintiff or defendant.

Misdemeanor records
Justice Court
PO Box 277
Virginia City, MT 59755
(406) 843-5392 Ext. 28
Misdemeanor records are available by mail or phone. No release necessary. No search fee. $.50 fee per copy. $2.00 for certification. Search information required: name, date of birth, SSN, date of offense, SASE.

Civil records
Justice Court
PO Box 277
Virginia City, MT 59755
(406) 843-5392 Ext. 28
Civil records are available by mail. No release necessary. No search fee. $.50 fee per copy. $2.00 for certification. Search information required: name, date of birth, years to search, SASE. Specify plaintiff or defendant.

McCone County

Clerk of Court, Criminal Records
PO Box 208
Circle, MT 59215
(406) 485-3410
Felony records are available by mail. No release necessary. $.50 fee per year searched. $.50 fee per copy. $2.00 for certification. Search information required: name, years to search.

Civil records are available by mail. No release necessary. $.50 fee per year searched. $.50 fee per copy. $2.00 for certification. Search information required: name, date of birth, years to search. Specify plaintiff or defendant.

Meagher County

Felony records
Clerk of District Court, Criminal Records
PO Box 443
Meagher County
White Sulphur Springs, MT 59645
(406) 547-3941
Felony records are available by mail or phone. No release necessary. No search fee. $.50 fee per copy. $2.00 for certification. Search information required: name, years to search.

Civil records
Clerk of District Court
PO Box 443
Meagher County
White Sulphur Springs, MT 59645
(406) 547-3941
Civil records are available by mail or phone. No release necessary. No search fee. $.50 fee per copy. $2.00 for certification. Search information required: name, date of birth, years to search. Specify plaintiff or defendant.

Misdemeanor records
Justice Court of Meagher County
PO Box 698
Meagher County
White Sulphur Springs, MT 59645
(406) 547-3954
Misdemeanor records are available by mail. No release necessary. No search fee. $.50 fee per copy. $2.00 for certification. Search information required: name, date of birth, date of offense.

Civil records
Justice Court of Meagher County
PO Box 698
Meagher County
White Sulphur Springs, MT 59645
(406) 547-3954
Civil records are available by mail or phone. No release necessary. No search fee. $.50 fee per copy. $2.00 for certification. Search information required: name, date of birth, years to search. Specify plaintiff or defendant.

Mineral County

Felony records
Clerk of District Court, Criminal Records
PO Box 819
Superior, MT 59872
(406) 822-4612
Felony records are available by mail. No release necessary. $.50 fee per year searched. $.50 fee per copy. $2.00 for certification. Company checks only, payable to Clerk of District Court. Search information required: name, date of birth, sex, race, years to search.

Civil records
Clerk of District Court
PO Box 819
Superior, MT 59872
(406) 822-4612
Civil records are available by mail. No release necessary. $.50 fee per year searched. $.50 fee per copy. $2.00 for certification. Search information required: name, date of birth, years to search. Specify plaintiff or defendant.

Misdemeanor records
Mineral County Justice Court
PO Box 658
Superior, MT 59872
(406) 822-4516
Misdemeanor records are available by mail. No release necessary. $5.00 search fee. $.25 fee per copy. $2.00 for certification. Search information required: name, date of birth, offense if available, years to search, address, description.

Civil records
Mineral County Justice Court
PO Box 658
Superior, MT 59872
(406) 822-4516
Civil records are available by mail. No release necessary. $5.00 search fee. $.25 fee per copy. $2.00 for certification. Search information required: name, date of birth, years to search. Specify plaintiff or defendant.

Missoula County

Felony and misdemeanor records
Clerk of District Court, Criminal Records
Missoula County Courthouse
Missoula, MT 59802
(406) 523-4780
Fax (406) 721-4043
Felony and misdemeanor records are available by mail. No release necessary. $.50 fee for each year searched. $.50 fee per copy for first five copies, $.25 fee per copy thereafter. Search information required: name, years to search.

Civil records
Clerk of District Court
Missoula County Courthouse
Missoula, MT 59802
(406) 523-4780
Fax (406) 721-4043
Civil records are available by mail. No release necessary. $.50 fee for each year searched. $.50 fee per copy. $2.00 for certification. Search information required: name, date of birth, years to search. Specify plaintiff or defendant.

Musselshell County

Clerk of Court, Criminal Records
PO Box 357
Roundup, MT 59072
(406) 323-1413
Fax (406) 323-1710
Felony and misdemeanor records are available by mail or phone. No release necessary. No search fee. Search information required: name, years to search.

Civil records are available by mail or phone. No release necessary. No search fee. $.50 fee per copy. $2.00 for certification. Search information required: name, date of birth, years to search. Specify plaintiff or defendant.

Park County

Felony records
Clerk of District Court, Criminal Records
PO Box 437
Livingston, MT 59047
(406) 222-6120 Ext. 235
Fax (406) 222-6726
Felony records are available by mail or fax. A release is required. $.50 fee per year searched. Search information required: name, date of birth, years to search.

Civil records
Clerk of District Cour
PO Box 437
Livingston, MT 59047
(406) 222-6120 Ext. 234
Fax (406) 222-6726
Civil records are available by mail. No release necessary. $.50 fee per year searched. $.50 fee for first copy, $.25 for each additional copy. $2.00 for certification. Search information required: name, date of birth, years to search. Specify plaintiff or defendant.

Petroleum County

Felony records
Clerk of District Court, Criminal Records
PO Box 226
Winnett, MT 59087
(406) 429-5311
Felony records are available by mail or phone. No release necessary. $.50 fee per year searched. Make check payable to Clerk of Court. Search information required: name, date of birth, years to search.

Civil records
Clerk of District Court
PO Box 226
Winnett, MT 59087
(406) 429-5311
Civil records are available by mail or phone. No release necessary. No search fee. $.20 fee per copy. $2.00 for certification. Search information required: name, date of birth, years to search. Specify plaintiff or defendant.

Misdemeanor records
Justice Court
Town of Winnett
Box 223
Winnett, MT 59087
(406) 429-5551
Misdemeanor records are available by mail. No release necessary. No search fee. $.15 fee per copy. $2.00 for certification. Search information required: name, years to search, date of birth, SASE.

Civil records
Justice Court
Town of Winnett
Box 223
Winnett, MT 59087
(406) 429-5551
Civil records are available by mail. No release necessary. No search fee. $.15 fee per copy. $2.00 for certification. Search information required: name, date of birth, years to search, SASE. Specify plaintiff or defendant.

Phillips County

Clerk of District Court, Criminal Records
Box I
Malta, MT 59538
(406) 654-1023
Felony and misdemeanor records are available by mail. No release necessary. $.50 fee for each year searched. $.50 fee per copy. $2.00 for certification. Make check payable to Clerk of Court. Search information required: name, date of birth, years to search.

Civil records are available by mail. No release necessary. $.50 fee for each year searched. $.50 fee per copy. $2.00 for certification. Search information required: name, date of birth, years to search. Specify plaintiff or defendant.

Pondera County

Clerk of District Court, Criminal Records
20 Fourth Ave. SW
Conrad, MT 59425
(406) 278-7681 Extension 36 & 37
Felony and misdemeanor records are available by mail. No release necessary. $.50 fee for each year searched. $.50 fee per copy. $2.00 for certification. Search information required: name, date of birth, years to search, SASE.

Civil records are available by mail. No release necessary. $.50 fee for each year searched. $.50 fee per copy. $2.00 for certification. Search information required: name, date of birth, years to search, SASE. Specify plaintiff or defendant.

Powder River County

Felony records
Clerk of Court, Criminal Records
Box G
Broadus, MT 59317
(406) 436-2320
Fax (406) 436-2866
Felony records are available by mail or fax. No release necessary. $.50 fee for each year searched. $.50 fee per copy. $2.00 for certification. Certified check only, payable to Clerk of Court. Search information required: name, date of birth, years to search.

Civil records
Clerk of Court
Box G
Broadus, MT 59317
(406) 436-2320
Fax (406) 436-2866
Civil records are available by mail or fax. No release necessary. $.50 fee for each year searched. $.50 fee per copy. $2.00 for certification. Search information required: name, date of birth, years to search. Specify plaintiff or defendant.

Misdemeanor records
Justice Court
PO Box 488
Broadus, MT 59317
(406) 436-2503
Misdemeanor records are available by mail. No release necessary. No search fee. $.25 fee per copied page. $2.00 for certification. Search information required: name, date of birth, offense, years to search.

Civil records
Justice Court
PO Box 488
Broadus, MT 59317
(406) 436-2503
Civil records are available by mail. No release necessary. No search fee. Search information required: name, date of birth, years to search. Specify plaintiff or defendant.

Powell County

Felony records
Clerk of Court, Criminal Records
409 Missouri Ave.
Deer Lodge, MT 59722
(406) 846-3680 Extension 36 or 37
Felony records are available by mail. No release necessary. No search fee. $.25 fee per copy. $2.00 for certification. Search information required: name, years to search, SASE.

Civil records
Clerk of Court
409 Missouri Ave.
Deer Lodge, MT 59722
(406) 846-3680 Extension 36 or 37
Civil records are available by mail. No release necessary. No search fee. $.25 fee per copy. $2.00 for certification. Search information required: name, date of birth, years to search, SASE. Specify plaintiff or defendant.

Misdemeanor records
Justice of Peace
313 4th Street
Deer Lodge, MT 59722
(406) 846-3680
Misdemeanor records are available by mail. A release is required. No search fee. $.25 fee per copy. $2.00 for certification. Search information required: name, years to search, date of birth.

Misdemeanor records
Justice of Peace
313 4th Street
Deer Lodge, MT 59722
(406) 846-3680
Civil records are available by mail. No release necessary. No search fee. $.25 fee per copy. $2.00 for certification. Search information required: name, date of birth, years to search. Specify plaintiff or defendant.

Prairie County

Felony records
Prairie County Courthouse, Clerk of Court
PO Box 125
Terry, MT 59349
(406) 637-5575
Felony records are available by mail. No release necessary. No search fee. $.25 fee per copy. $2.00 for certification. Search information required: name, years to search.

Civil records
Prairie County Courthouse, Clerk of Court
PO Box 125
Terry, MT 59349
(406) 637-5575
Civil records are available by mail. No release necessary. No search fee. $.25 fee per copy. $2.00 for certification. Search information required: name, date of birth, years to search. Specify plaintiff or defendant.

Misdemeanor records
Justice Court
Box 495
Terry, MT 59349
(406) 637-5407
Misdemeanor records are available by mail. No release necessary. No search fee. $.25 fee per copy. $2.00 for certification. Search information required: name, date of birth, SSN, SASE.

Civil records
Justice Court
Box 495
Terry, MT 59349
(406) 637-5407
Civil records are available by mail. No release necessary. No search fee. $.25 fee per copy. $2.00 for certification. Search information required: name, date of birth, years to search, SASE. Specify plaintiff or defendant.

Ravalli County

Clerk of District Court, Criminal Records
Courthouse
Box 5014
Hamilton, MT 59840
(406) 363-1900
Fax (406) 363-1833 (*2)

Felony and misdemeanor records are available by mail. No release necessary. $.50 fee per year searched, not to exceed $25.00. $.50 fee for first five copies, $.25 for each additional copy. Search information required: name, years to search.

Civil records are available by mail. No release necessary. $.50 fee per year searched. $.50 fee per copy. $2.00 for certification. Search information required: name, date of birth, years to search. Specify plaintiff or defendant.

Richland County

Felony records
Clerk of District Court, Criminal Records
201 West Main
Sidney, MT 59270
(406) 482-1709
Felony records are available by mail or phone. No release necessary. No search fee. $.50 fee per copy. $2.00 for certification. Search information required: name, years to search.

Civil records
Clerk of District Court
201 West Main
Sidney, MT 59270
(406) 482-1709
Civil records are available by mail. No release necessary. No search fee. $.50 fee per copy. $2.00 for certification. Search information required: name, date of birth, years to search. Specify plaintiff or defendant.

Misdemeanor records
Justice Court
123 W. Main
Sidney, MT 59270
(406) 482-2815
Misdemeanor records are available by mail. No release necessary. No search fee. Search information required: name, date of birth, SASE, date of offense.

Civil records
Justice Court
123 W. Main
Sidney, MT 59270
(406) 482-2815
Civil records are available by mail. No release necessary. No search fee. Search information required: name, date of birth, years to search. Specify plaintiff or defendant.

Roosevelt County

Clerk of Court, Criminal Records
Roosevelt County Courthouse
Wolf Point, MT 59201
(406) 653-1590 Extension 66
Fax (406) 653-3100
Felony records are available by mail. No release necessary. No search fee. $.25 fee per copy. $2.00 for certification. Search information required: name, years to search.
Civil records are available by mail. No release necessary. No search fee. $.25 fee per copy. $2.00 for certification. Search information required: name, date of birth, years to search. Specify plaintiff or defendant.

Rosebud County

Clerk of District Court, Criminal Records
PO Box 48
Forsyth, MT 59327
(406) 356-7322
Felony and misdemeanor records are available by mail. A release is required. $.50 fee per year searched. $.50 fee per copy. $2.00 for certification. Search information required: name, years to search.

Civil records are available by mail. No release necessary. $.50 fee per year searched. $.50 fee per copy. $2.00 for certification. Search information required: name, date of birth, years to search. Specify plaintiff or defendant.

Sanders County

Felony records
Clerk of the District Court, Criminal Records
PO Box 519
Thompson Falls, MT 59873
(406) 827-4316 Extension 106
Felony records are available by mail. No release necessary. $.50 fee per year, not to exceed $25.00. $.50 fee per copy. $2.00 for certification. Search information required: name, years to search.

Civil records
Clerk of the District Court
PO Box 519
Thompson Falls, MT 59873
(406) 827-4316 Extension 106
Civil records are available by mail. No release necessary. $.50 fee per year searched. $.50 fee per copy. $2.00 for certification. Search information required: name, date of birth, years to search. Specify plaintiff or defendant.

Misdemeanor records
Justice Court
Box 519
Thompson Falls, MT 59873
(406) 827-4318
Fax (406) 827-4388
Misdemeanor records are available by mail or fax. No release necessary. No search fee. Search information required: name, offense, years to search, date of birth.

Civil records
Justice Court
Box 519
Thompson Falls, MT 59873
(406) 827-4318
Fax (406) 827-4388
Civil records are available by mail or fax. No release necessary. No search fee. Search information required: name, date of birth, years to search. Specify plaintiff or defendant.

Sheridan County

Felony records
Clerk of the District Court, Criminal Records
100 W. Laurel
Plentywood, MT 59254
(406) 765-2310 Extension 304
Fax (406) 765-2129
Felony records are available by mail or by phone for two names searched. No release necessary. No search fee. $.25 fee per copy, plus postage fee. Search information required: name, years to search, SASE.

Civil records
Clerk of the District Court
100 W. Laurel
Plentywood, MT 59254
(406) 765-2310 Extension 304
Fax (406) 765-2129
Civil records are available by mail. No release necessary. $.50 fee per year searched. $.50 fee per copy. $2.00 for certification. . Search information required: name, date of birth, years to search, SASE. Specify plaintiff or defendant.

Misdemeanor records
Sheridan County Justice Court
100 W. Laurel
Plentywood, MT 59254
(406) 765-2310 Extension 301
Misdemeanor records are available by mail. A signed and notarized release is required. No search fee. $.50 fee per copy. $2.00 for certification. Search information required: name, years to search, any information on case. Use company letterhead when making request.

Civil records
Sheridan County Justice Court
100 W. Laurel
Plentywood, MT 59254
(406) 765-2310 Extension 301
Civil records are available by mail. No release necessary. No search fee. $.50 fee per copy. $2.00 for certification. Search information required: name, date of birth, years to search. Specify plaintiff or defendant.

Stillwater County

Felony records
Clerk of the District Court, Criminal Records
PO Box 367
Columbus, MT 59019
(406) 322-5332
Felony records are available by mail. A release is required. $.50 fee per year searched. $.50 fee per copy. $2.00 for certification. Search information required: name, SASE, years to search.

Civil records
Clerk of the District Court
PO Box 367
Columbus, MT 59019
(406) 322-5332
Civil records are available by mail. A release is required. $.50 fee per year searched. $.50 fee per copy. $2.00 for certification. Search information required: name, date of birth, years to search. Specify plaintiff or defendant.

Misdemeanor records
Justice Court
PO Box 77
Columbus, MT 59019
(406) 322-4577
Misdemeanor records are available by mail or phone. No release necessary. No search fee. $.50 fee per copy. $2.00 for certification. Search information required: name, date of birth, offense, years to search, date of offense, SASE.

Civil records
Justice Court
PO Box 77
Columbus, MT 59019
(406) 322-4577
Civil records are available by mail. No release necessary. No search fee. $.50 fee per copy. $2.00 for certification. Search information required: name, date of birth, years to search, SASE. Specify plaintiff or defendant.

Sweet Grass County

Felony records
Clerk of the District Court, Criminal Records
PO Box 698
Big Timber, MT 59011
(406) 932-5154
Felony records are available by mail. No release necessary. $.50 fee per year searched. $.50 fee per copy. $2.00 for certification. Search information required: name, years to search, SASE.

Civil records
Clerk of the District Court
PO Box 698
Big Timber, MT 59011
(406) 932-5154
Civil records are available by mail. No release necessary. $.50 fee per year searched. $.50 fee per copy. $2.00 for certification. Search information required: name, date of birth, years to search, SASE. Specify plaintiff or defendant.

Misdemeanor records
Justice Court
PO Box 1206
Big Timber, MT 59011
(406) 932-5150
Fax (406) 932-4777
Misdemeanor records since 1987 are available by mail or fax. No release necessary. No search fee. $1.50 fee for first page of fax response, $.75 each additional page. $.50 fee per copy. $2.00 for certification. Search information required: name, date of birth, years to search, docket number (if available).

Civil records
Justice Court
PO Box 1206
Big Timber, MT 59011
(406) 932-5150
Fax (406) 932-4777
Civil records are available by mail or fax. No release necessary. No search fee. $1.50 fee for first page of fax response, $.75 each additional page. $.50 fee per copy. $2.00 for certification. Search information required: name, date of birth, years to search. Specify plaintiff or defendant.

Teton County

Clerk of District Court, Criminal Records
PO Box 487
Choteau, MT 59422
(406) 466-2909
Felony and misdemeanor records are available by mail. A release is required. $.50 fee for each year searched. $.50 fee per copy. $2.00 for certification. Search information required: name, years to search.

Civil records are available by mail. No release necessary. $.50 fee for each year searched. $.50 fee per copy. $2.00 for certification. Search information required: name, date of birth, years to search. Specify plaintiff or defendant.

Toole County

Clerk of Court, Criminal Records
PO Box 850
Shelby, MT 59474
(406) 434-2271
Felony and misdemeanor records are available by mail or phone. A release is required if copies are required. $.25 fee for each year searched. $.50 fee per copy. Search information required: name, years to search.

Civil records are available by mail or phone. A release is required if copies are required. $.25 fee for each year searched. $.50 fee per copy. $2.00 for certification. Search information required: name, date of birth, years to search. Specify plaintiff or defendant.

Treasure County

Felony records
Clerk of the District Court
PO Box 392
Hysham, MT 59038
(406) 342-5547
Felony records are available by mail. No release necessary. No search fee. Search information required: name, years to search.

Civil records
Clerk of the District Court
PO Box 392
Hysham, MT 59038
(406) 342-5547
Civil records are available by mail. No release necessary. No search fee. $.50 fee per copy. $2.00 for certification. Search information required: name, date of birth, years to search. Specify plaintiff or defendant.

Misdemeanor records
Justice Court
PO Box 267
Hysham, MT 59038
(406) 342-5532
Misdemeanor records are available by mail. No release necessary. No search fee. Search information required: name, date of birth, address, years to search, type of offense.

Civil records
Justice Court
PO Box 267
Hysham, MT 59038
(406) 342-5532
Civil records are available by mail. No release necessary. No search fee. $.50 fee per copy. $2.00 for certification. Search information required: name, date of birth, years to search. Specify plaintiff or defendant.

Valley County

Felony records
Clerk of District Court, Criminal Records
Box 632
Glasgow, MT 59230
(406) 228-8221 Ext. 68 or 67
Felony records are available by mail or phone. No release necessary. No search fee. Search information required: name, years to search.

Civil records
Clerk of District Court
Box 632
Glasgow, MT 59230
(406) 228-8221 Ext. 68 or 67
Civil records are available by mail. No release necessary. No search fee. $.50 fee per copy. $2.00 for certification. Search information required: name, date of birth, years to search. Specify plaintiff or defendant.

Misdemeanor records
Justice of Peace
Valley County
PO Box 66
Glasgow, MT 59230
(406) 228-8221
Misdemeanor records are available by mail. A release is required. No search fee. Search information required: name, date of birth, years to search, SSN.

Civil records
Justice of Peace
Valley County
PO Box 66
Glasgow, MT 59230
(406) 228-8221
Civil records are available by mail. No release necessary. No search fee. $.25 fee per copy. $2.00 for certification. Search information required: name, date of birth, years to search. Specify plaintiff or defendant.

Wheatland County

Clerk of Court, Criminal Records
Harlowton, MT 59036
(406) 632-4891
Fax (406) 632-4893
Felony and misdemeanor records are available by mail, fax or phone. No release necessary. No search fee. $.25 fee per copy. $2.50 for certification. Search information required: name, years to search.

Civil records are available by mail, fax or phone. No release necessary. No search fee. $.25 fee per copy. $2.50 for certification. Search information required: name, date of birth, years to search. Specify plaintiff or defendant.

Wibaux County

Clerk of District Court, Criminal Records
PO Box 310
Wibaux, MT 59353
(406) 795-2481
Felony and misdemeanor records are available by mail. No release necessary. $.50 fee for each year searched. $.50 fee per copy. $2.00 for certification. Make check payable to Clerk of District Court. Search information required: name, years to search.

Civil records are available by mail. No release necessary. $.50 fee for each year searched. $.50 fee per copy. $2.00 for certification. Search information required: name, date of birth, years to search. Specify plaintiff or defendant.

Yellowstone County

Felony records
Clerk of the District Court, Criminal Division
PO Box 35030
Billings, MT 59107
(406) 256-2860
Felony records are available by mail. No release necessary. $.50 fee for each year searched. $.50 fee per copy. $2.00 for certification. Make check payable to Clerk of the District Court. Search information required: name, years to search, SASE.

Civil records
Clerk of the District Court
PO Box 35030
Billings, MT 59107
(406) 256-2860
Civil records are available by mail. No release necessary. $.50 fee for each year searched. $.50 fee per copy. $2.00 for certification. Search information required: name, date of birth, years to search. Specify plaintiff or defendant.

Misdemeanor records
Justice Court
PO Box 35032
Billings, MT 59107
(406) 256-2889
Misdemeanor records are available in person only. See Montana state repository for additional information.

Civil records
Justice Court
PO Box 35032
Billings, MT 59107
(406) 256-2889
Civil records are available in person only. See Montana state repository for additional information.

City-County Cross Reference

Absarokee *Stillwater*
Alberton *Mineral*
Alder *Madison*
Alzada *Carter*
Anaconda *Deer Lodge*
Angela *Rosebud*
Antelope *Sheridan*
Arlee *Lake*
Ashland *Rosebud*
Augusta *Lewis And Clark*
Avon *Powell*
Babb *Glacier*
Bainville *Roosevelt*
Baker *Fallon*
Ballantine *Yellowstone*
Basin *Jefferson*
Bearcreek *Carbon*
Belfry *Carbon*
Belgrade *Gallatin*
Belt *Cascade*
Biddle *Powder River*
Big Arm *Lake*
Bigfork *Flathead*
Bighorn *Treasure*
Big Sandy *Chouteau*

Big Sky *Gallatin*
Big Timber *Sweet Grass*
Billings *Yellowstone*
Birney *Rosebud*
Black Eagle *Cascade*
Bloomfield *Dawson*
Bonner *Missoula*
Boulder *Jefferson*
Box Elder *Hill*
Boyes *Carter*
Bozeman *Gallatin*
Brady *Pondera*
Bridger *Carbon*
Broadus *Powder River*
Broadview *Yellowstone*
Brockton *Roosevelt*
Brockway *McCone*
Browning *Glacier*
Brusett *Garfield*
Buffalo *Fergus*
Busby *Big Horn*
Butte *Silver Bow*
Bynum *Teton*
Cameron *Madison*

Canyon Creek *Lewis And Clark*
Capitol *Carter*
Cardwell *Jefferson*
Carlyle *Wibaux*
Carter *Chouteau*
Cascade *Cascade*
Charlo *Lake*
Chester *Liberty*
Chinook *Blaine*
Choteau *Teton*
Christina *Fergus*
Circle *McCone*
Clancy *Jefferson*
Clinton *Missoula*
Clyde Park *Park*
Coffee Creek *Fergus*
Cohagen *Garfield*
Colstrip *Rosebud*
Columbia Falls *Flathead*
Columbus *Stillwater*
Condon *Missoula*
Conner *Ravalli*
Conrad *Pondera*
Cooke City *Park*

Corvallis *Ravalli*
Corwin Springs *Park*
Crane *Richland*
Crow Agency *Big Horn*
Culbertson *Roosevelt*
Custer *Yellowstone*
Cut Bank *Glacier*
Dagmar *Sheridan*
Darby *Ravalli*
Dayton *Lake*
Decker *Big Horn*
Deer Lodge *Powell*
Denton *Fergus*
Dillon *Beaverhead*
Divide *Silver Bow*
Dixon *Sanders*
Dodson *Phillips*
Drummond *Granite*
Dupuyer *Pondera*
Dutton *Teton*
East Glacier Park *Glacier*
East Helena *Lewis And Clark*
East Missoula *Missoula*
Edgar *Carbon*

Ekalaka *Carter*
Elliston *Powell*
Elmo *Lake*
Emigrant *Park*
Ennis *Madison*
Ethridge *Toole*
Eureka *Lincoln*
Evergreen *Flathead*
Fairfield *Teton*
Fairview *Richland*
Fallon *Prairie*
Fishtail *Stillwater*
Flaxville *Daniels*
Florence *Ravalli*
Forest Belnap Agency *Blaine*
Forestgrove *Fergus*
Forest Park *Dawson*
Forsyth *Rosebud*
Fort Belnap Agency *Blaine*
Fort Benton *Chouteau*
Fort Harrison *Lewis And Clark*
Fortine *Lincoln*
Fort Peck *Valley*
Fort Shaw *Cascade*
Frazer *Valley*
Frenchtown *Missoula*
Froid *Roosevelt*
Fromberg *Carbon*
Galata *Toole*
Gallatin Gateway *Gallatin*
Gardiner *Park*
Garryowen *Big Horn*
Geraldine *Chouteau*
Geyser *Judith Basin*
Gildford *Hill*
Glasgow *Valley*
Glendive *Dawson*
Glentana *Valley*
Goldcreek *Powell*
Grantsdale *Ravalli*
Grass Range *Fergus*
Great Falls *Cascade*
Greycliff *Sweet Grass*
Hall *Granite*
Hamilton *Ravalli*
Hammond *Carter*
Hardin *Big Horn*
Harlem *Blaine*
Harlowton *Wheatland*
Harrison *Madison*
Hathaway *Rosebud*
Havre *Hill*
Hays *Blaine*
Heart Butte *Pondera*
Helena *Lewis And Clark*
Helmville *Powell*
Heron *Sanders*
Highwood *Chouteau*
Hilger *Fergus*
Hingham *Hill*
Hinsdale *Valley*
Hobson *Judith Basin*
Hogeland *Blaine*
Homestead *Sheridan*
Hot Springs *Sanders*
Huntley *Yellowstone*
Hysham *Treasure*
Ingomar *Rosebud*
Inverness *Hill*
Ismay *Custer*
Jackson *Beaverhead*
Jefferson City *Jefferson*
Joliet *Carbon*
Joplin *Liberty*

Jordan *Garfield*
Judith Gap *Wheatland*
Kalispell *Flathead*
Kevin *Toole*
Kila *Flathead*
Kinsey *Custer*
Kremlin *Hill*
Lakeside *Flathead*
Lambert *Richland*
Lame Deer *Rosebud*
Larslan *Valley*
Laurel *Yellowstone*
Lavina *Golden Valley*
Ledger *Pondera*
Lewistown *Fergus*
Libby *Lincoln*
Lima *Beaverhead*
Lincoln *Lewis And Clark*
Lindsay *Dawson*
Livingston *Park*
Lloyd *Blaine*
Lockwood *Yellowstone*
Lodge Grass *Big Horn*
Lolo *Missoula*
Loma *Chouteau*
Lonepine *Sanders*
Loring *Phillips*
Lothair *Liberty*
McAllister *Madison*
McCabe *Roosevelt*
McLeod *Sweet Grass*
Malta *Phillips*
Manhattan *Gallatin*
Marion *Flathead*
Martin City *Flathead*
Martinsdale *Meagher*
Marysville *Lewis And Clark*
Medicine Lake *Sheridan*
Melrose *Silver Bow*
Melstone *Musselshell*
Melville *Sweet Grass*
Miles City *Custer*
Mill Iron *Carter*
Milltown *Missoula*
Missoula *Missoula*
Moccasin *Judith Basin*
Molt *Stillwater*
Monarch *Cascade*
Moore *Fergus*
Musselshell *Musselshell*
Nashua *Valley*
Neihart *Cascade*
Niarada *Sanders*
North Havre *Hill*
Norris *Madison*
Noxon *Sanders*
Oilmont *Toole*
Olive *Powder River*
Olney *Flathead*
Opheim *Valley*
Orchard Homes *Missoula*
Otter *Powder River*
Outlook *Sheridan*
Ovando *Powell*
Pablo *Lake*
Paradise *Sanders*
Park City *Stillwater*
Peerless *Daniels*
Pendroy *Teton*
Philipsburg *Granite*
Pinesdale *Ravalli*
Plains *Sanders*
Plentywood *Sheridan*
Plevna *Fallon*
Polaris *Beaverhead*

Polson *Lake*
Pompeys Pillar *Yellowstone*
Pony *Madison*
Poplar *Roosevelt*
Power *Teton*
Pray *Park*
Proctor *Lake*
Pryor *Big Horn*
Ramsay *Silver Bow*
Rapelje *Stillwater*
Raymond *Sheridan*
Raynesford *Judith Basin*
Red Lodge *Carbon*
Redstone *Sheridan*
Reedpoint *Stillwater*
Reserve *Sheridan*
Rexford *Lincoln*
Richey *Dawson*
Richland *Valley*
Ringling *Meagher*
Roberts *Carbon*
Rollins *Lake*
Ronan *Lake*
Roscoe *Carbon*
Rosebud *Rosebud*
Roundup *Musselshell*
Roy *Fergus*
Rudyard *Hill*
Ryegate *Golden Valley*
Saco *Phillips*
Saint Ignatius *Lake*
Saint Regis *Mineral*
Saint Xavier *Big Horn*
Sand Coulee *Cascade*
Sanders *Treasure*
Sand Springs *Garfield*
Savage *Richland*
Scobey *Daniels*
Seeley Lake *Missoula*
Shawmut *Wheatland*
Shelby *Toole*
Shepherd *Yellowstone*
Sheridan *Madison*
Sidney *Richland*
Silver Star *Madison*
Simms *Cascade*
Somers *Flathead*
Springdale *Park*
Stanford *Judith Basin*
Stevensville *Ravalli*
Stockett *Cascade*
Stryker *Lincoln*
Sula *Ravalli*
Sumatra *Rosebud*
Sunburst *Toole*
Sun River *Cascade*
Superior *Mineral*
Sweetgrass *Toole*
Terry *Prairie*
Thompson Falls *Sanders*
Three Forks *Gallatin*
Toston *Broadwater*
Townsend *Broadwater*
Trego *Lincoln*
Trout Creek *Sanders*
Troy *Lincoln*
Turner *Blaine*
Twin Bridges *Madison*
Twodot *Wheatland*
Ulm *Cascade*
Valier *Pondera*
Vandalia *Valley*
Vaughn *Cascade*
Victor *Ravalli*
Vida *McCone*
Virginia City *Madison*

Volborg *Custer*
Wagner *Phillips*
Walkerville *Silver Bow*
Warmsprings *Deer Lodge*
Westby *Sheridan*
West Glacier *Flathead*
West Yellowstone *Gallatin*
Whitefish *Flathead*
Whitehall *Jefferson*
White Sulphur Springs *Meagher*
Whitetail *Daniels*
Whitewater *Phillips*
Whitlash *Liberty*
Wibaux *Wibaux*
Willard *Fallon*
Willow Creek *Gallatin*
Wilsall *Park*
Winifred *Fergus*
Winnett *Petroleum*
Wisdom *Beaverhead*
Wise River *Beaverhead*
Wolf Creek *Lewis And Clark*
Wolf Point *Roosevelt*
Worden *Yellowstone*
Wyola *Big Horn*
Zortman *Phillips*
Zurich *Blaine*

Nebraska

Eighty two (82) of Nebraska's ninety three (93) counties make criminal records available for employment screening purposes by phone and/or mail. Civil court records for $15,000 and more are filed in District court.

For more information or for offices not listed, contact the state's information hot line at (402) 471-2311.

Driving Records

Department of Motor Vehicles
Driver Record Office
PO Box 94789
State Office Building
Lincoln, NE 68509-4789
(402) 471-3887
Driving records are available by mail. $1.75 fee per request. Turnaround time is 1 week. Written request must include job applicant's full name, date of birth, license number and a stamped, self-addressed envelope. Make check payable to Department of Motor Vehicles.

Worker's Compensation Records

Nebraska Worker's Compensation Court
PO Box 98908
Lincoln, NE 68509-8908
(402) 471-2568
Worker's compensation records available by mail only. Written request must include job applicant's full name, SSN and check for $5. Request for records prior to 1972 must include additional $5.00. Make check payable to Nebraska Worker's Compensation Court. A signed release is not required for basic claims information. Medical, hospital, and billing information requires release.

Vital Statistics

Bureau of Vital Statistics
State Department of Health
301 Centennial Mall South
PO Box 95007
Lincoln, NE 68509-5007
(402) 471-2871
Birth records are available for $6.00 and death records for $5.00. State office has records since late 1904. An employer can obtain records with a written release. Make certified check or money order payable to Bureau of Vital Statistics.

Marriage and divorce records areavailable for $5.00 each. State office has records since 1909.

Department of Education

Teacher Certification Division
301 Centenial Mall South
Box 94987
Lincoln, NE 68509
(402) 471-2496
Field of certification, effective date, expiration date are available by mail or phone. Include name and SSN.

Medical Licensing

Bureau of Examining Boards
PO Box 94925
Lincoln, NE 68509
(402) 471-2115
Licensing information is available for MDs by mail or phone. $2.00 fee. For other licenses not mentioned, contact the above office.

Bureau of Examining Boards
Nebraska Department of Health
PO Box 95007
Lincoln, NE 68509
(402) 471-2115
Will confirm license by phone. No fee. Include name, license number, if available.

Bar Association

Nebraska State Bar Association
PO Box 81809
Lincoln, NE 68501
(402) 475-7091
Will confirm license by phone. No fee. Include name.

Accountancy Board

Nebraska State Board of Public Accountancy
PO Box 94725
Lincoln, NE 68509
(402) 471-3595
Will confirm license by phone. No fee. Include name.

Securities Commission

Department of Banking and Finance
Bureau of Securities
PO Box 95006
Lincoln, NE 68509-5006
(402) 471-3445
Will confirm license by phone. No fee. Include name and SSN.

Secretary of State

Secretary of State
State Capitol Bldg.
Lincoln, NE 68509
(402) 471-4079
Service agent and address, date incorporated are available by mail or phone. No fee. Contact the above office for additional information.

Criminal Records

State Repository

Nebraska State Patrol
Attention: C.I.D.
PO Box 94907
Lincoln, NE 68509-4907
(402) 471-4545
Fax (402) 479-4002
Felony and misdemeanor records are available. Written requests must include subject's full name, date of birth, SSN and a signed release. A more complete search is available if a full set of rolled fingerprints is supplied. There is a $10.00 fee for each request. Make check payable to Nebraska State Patrol. Requesting party must also provide name and signature on request. Both conviction and arrest records with a disposition are released. Turnaround time is normally ten to fifteen days plus mail time.

Adams County

Felony records
Clerk of The District Court, Criminal Records
PO Box 9
Hastings, NE 68901
(402) 461-7264
Felony records are available by mail or phone. No release necessary. No search fee. $.10 fee per copy. $1.00 for certification. Search information required: name, years to search, SASE.

Civil records
Clerk of The District Court
PO Box 9
Hastings, NE 68901
(402) 461-7264
Civil records are available by mail or phone. No release necessary. No search fee. $.10 fee per copy. $1.00 for certification. Search information required: name, date of birth, years to search, SASE. Specify plaintiff or defendant.

Misdemeanor records
Adams County Court
PO Box 95
Hastings, NE 68902-0095
(402) 461-7143
Fax (402) 461-7270
Misdemeanor records are available by mail or fax. No release necessary. No search fee. $.25 fee per copy. $1.00 for certification. Search information required: name, years to search.

Civil records
Adams County Court
PO Box 95
Hastings, NE 68902-0095
(402) 461-7143
Fax (402) 461-7270
Civil records are available by mail or fax. No release necessary. No search fee. $.25 fee per copy. $1.00 for certification. Search information required: name, date of birth, years to search. Specify plaintiff or defendant.

Antelope County

Felony records
Clerk of District Court, Criminal Records
Antelope County
PO Box 45
Neligh, NE 68756
(402) 887-4508
Felony records are available in person only. For additional information see Nebraska state repository.

Civil records
Clerk of District Court
Antelope County
PO Box 45
Neligh, NE 68756
(402) 887-4508
Civil records are available in person only. For additional information see Nebraska state repository.

Misdemeanor records
Antelope County Court
Courthouse
501 Main Street
Neligh, NE 68756
(402) 887-4650
Misdemeanor records are available in person only. For additional information see Nebraska state repository.

Civil records
Antelope County Court
Courthouse
501 Main Street
Neligh, NE 68756
(402) 887-4650
Civil records are available by mail only. A release is required. $3.00 search fee. $.25 fee per copy. $1.00 for certification. Search information required: name, date of birth, years to search. Specify plaintiff or defendant.

Arthur County

Felony records
Clerk of District Court, Criminal Records
PO Box 146
Arthur, NE 69121
(308) 764-2203
Fax (308) 764-2216
Felony records are available by mail, fax or phone. No release necessary. No search fee. $.10 fee per copy. $5.00 for certificaiton. Search information required: name, years to search.

Civil records
Clerk of District Court
PO Box 146
Arthur, NE 69121
(308) 764-2203
Fax (308) 764-2216
Civil records are available by mail, fax or phone. No release necessary. No search fee. $.10 fee per copy. $5.00 for certificaiton. Search information required: name, years to search. Specify plaintiff or defendant.

Misdemeanor records
Arthur County Courthouse
PO Box 146
Arthur, NE 69121
(308) 764-2201 or 764-2216
Fax (308) 764-2216
Misdemeanor records are available by mail, fax or phone. No release necessary. No search fee. $.10 fee per copy. $5.00 for certificaiton. Search information required: name.

Civil records
Arthur County Courthouse
PO Box 146
Arthur, NE 69121
(308) 764-2201 or 764-2216
Fax (308) 764-2216
Misdemeanor records are available by mail, fax or phone. No release necessary. No search fee. $.10 fee per copy. $5.00 for certificaiton. Search information required: name. Specify plaintiff or defendant.

Banner County

Clerk of the District Court, Criminal Records
PO Box 67
Harrisburg, NE 69345
(308) 436-5265
Fax (308) 436-4180
Felony and misdemeanor records are available by mail, fax or phone. No release necessary. No search fee. $.25 fee per copy. $1.00 for certification. Search information required: name, years to search.

Civil records are available by mail, fax or phone. No release necessary. No search fee. $.25 fee per copy. $1.00 for certification. Search information required: name, years to search. Specify plaintiff or defendant.

Blaine County

Clerk of the District Court, Criminal Records
Courthouse
PO Box 136
Brewster, NE 68821
(308) 547-2222
Fax (308) 547-2224
Felony and misdemeanor records are available by mail or fax. A release is required. $6.00 search fee. $1.00 fee per copy. $2.50 for certification. $1.00 fee per page for faxed response. Search information required: name, years to search.

Civil records are available by mail or fax. A release is required. $6.00 search fee. $1.00 fee per copy. $2.50 for certification. $1.00 fee per page for faxed response. Search information required: name, years to search. Specify plaintiff or defendant.

Boone County

Boone County Courthouse, Criminal Records
Albion, NE 68620
(402) 395-2057
Fax (402) 395-6592
Felony and misdemeanor records are available by mail, fax or phone. No release necessary. No search fee. $.10 fee per copy. $1.00 for certification. Search information required: name, years to search.

Civil records are available by mail, fax or phone. No release necessary. No search fee. $.10 fee per copy. $1.00 for certification. Search information required: name, years to search. Specify plaintiff or defendant.

Box Butte County

Felony records
Clerk of Court, Criminal Records
PO Box 638
Alliance, NE 69301
(308) 762-6293
Felony records are available by mail. No release necesary. No search fee. $.25 fee per copy. $1.00 for certification. Search inforamtion required: name, years to search.

Civil records
Clerk of Court
PO Box 638
Alliance, NE 69301
(308) 762-6293
Civil records are available by mail. No release necesary. No search fee. $.25 fee per copy. $1.00 for certification. Search inforamtion required: name, years to search. Specify plaintiff or defendant.

Misdemeanor records
Box Butte County Court
PO Box 613
Alliance, NE 69301
(308) 762-6800
Misdemeanor records are available by mail or phone. No release necessary. No search fee. $.25 fee per copy. $1.00 for certification. Search information required: name, date of birth.

Civil records
Box Butte County Court
PO Box 613
Alliance, NE 69301
(308) 762-6800
Misdemeanor records are available by mail or phone. No release necessary. No search fee. $.25 fee per copy. $1.00 for certification. Search information required: name, date of birth. Specify plaintiff or defendant.

Boyd County

Felony records
Clerk of the District Court, Criminal Records
PO Box 26
Butte, NE 68722
(402) 775-2391
Fax (402) 775-2419
Felony records are available by mail, fax or phone. No release necessary. No search fee. $.25 fee per copy. $5.00 for certification. Search information required: name, date of birth, years to search.

Civily records
Clerk of the District Court
PO Box 26
Butte, NE 68722
(402) 775-2391
Fax (402) 775-2419
Civil records are available by mail, fax or phone. No release necessary. No search fee. $.25 fee per copy. $5.00 for certification. Search information required: name, date of birth, years to search. Specify plaintiff or defendant.

Misdemeanor records
Boyd County Court
PO Box 396
Butte, NE 68722
(402) 775-2211
Misdemeanor records are available by mail. Please provide a questionnaire of your own with information you are requesting. No release necessary. No search fee. $.25 fee per copy. $1.00 for certification. Search information required: name, date of birth, years to search, SASE.

Civil records
Boyd County Court
PO Box 396
Butte, NE 68722
(402) 775-2211
Civil records are available by mail. No release necessary. No search fee. $.25 fee per copy. $1.00 for certification. Search information required: name, date of birth, years to search, SASE. Specify plaintiff or defendant.

Brown County

Clerk of District Court, Criminal Records
Courthouse
148 W. 4th
Ainsworth, NE 69210
(402) 387-2705
Felony and misdemeanor records are available by mail. A release is required. No search fee. $.25 fee per copy. $1.00 for certification. Search information required: name.

Civil records are available by mail. A release is required. No search fee. $.25 fee per copy. $1.00 for certification. Search information required: name. Specify plaintiff or defendant.

Buffalo County

Felony records
Clerk of the District Court, Criminal Records
PO Box 520
Kearney, NE 68848
(308) 236-1246
Felony records are available by mail. No release necessary. No search fee. $.25 fee per copy. $1.25 for first certification, $.25 each additional page. Search information required: name, date of birth, case number, if available.

Civil records
Clerk of the District Court
PO Box 520
Kearney, NE 68848
(308) 236-1246
Civil records are available by mail. No release necessary. No search fee. $.25 fee per copy. $1.25 for first certification, $.25 each additional page. Search information required: name, date of birth. Specify plaintiff or defendant.

Misdemeanor records
Buffalo County Court
PO Box 520
Kearney, NE 68848
(308) 236-1231
Misdemeanor records are available by mail. No release necessary. No search fee. $.25 fee per copy. $1.00 for certification. Search information required: name, date of birth.

Civil records
Buffalo County Court
PO Box 520
Kearney, NE 68848
(308) 236-1231
Misdemeanor records are available by mail. No release necessary. No search fee. $.25 fee per copy. $1.00 for certification. Search information required: name, date of birth. Specify plaintiff or defendant.

Burt County

Clerk of the District Court, Criminal Records
Burt County Courthouse
111 N. 13 Street
Tekameh, NE 68061
(402) 374-2605
Felony and misdemeanor records are available in person only. See Nebraska state repository for additional information.

Civil records are available in person only. See Nebraska state repository for additional information.

Butler County

Felony records
Clerk of District Court, Criminal Records
451 N. 5th Street
David City, NE 68632
(402) 367-3091 Extension 44
Fax (402) 367-3329
Felony records are available by mail or fax. No release necessary. No search fee. $.10 fee per copy. $1.50 for certification. Search information required: name.

Civil records
Clerk of District Court
PO Box 187
451 N. 5th STreet
David City, NE 68632
(402) 367-3091 Extension 44
Fax (402) 367-3329
Civil records are available by mail. No release necessary. No search fee. $.10 fee per copy. $1.50 for certification. Search information required: name. Specify plaintiff or defendant.

Misdemeanor records
Butler County Court
PO Box 409
David City, NE 68632
(402) 367-3091 Extension 38
Misdemeanor records are available in person only. See Nebraska state repository for additional information.

Civil records
Butler County Court
PO Box 409
David City, NE 68632
(402) 367-3091 Extension 38
Civil records are available in person only. See Nebraska state repository for additional information.

Cass County

Clerk of the District Court
Cass County Courthouse
346 Main Street
Plattsmouth, NE 68048-1957
(402) 296-3278
Felony and misdemeanor records are available by mail. No release necessary. $5.00 search fee. $.25 fee per copy. $1.25 for certification. Search information required: full name, years to search.

Civil records are available by mail. No release necessary. $5.00 search fee. $.25 fee per copy. $1.25 for certification. Search information required: full name, years to search. Specify plaintiff or defendant.

Cedar County

Felony records
Clerk of County Court, Criminal Records
PO Box 169
Hartington, NE 68739
(402) 254-7441
Felony records are available by mail. No release. No search fee. $.25 fee per copy. $1.00 for certification. Search information required: name, years to search.

Civil records
Clerk of County Court
PO Box 169
Hartington, NE 68739
(402) 254-7441
Civil records are available by mail. No release. No search fee. $.25 fee per copy. $1.00 for certification. Search information required: name, years to search. Specify plaintiff or defendant.

Misdemeanor record
Cedar County Court
Box 695
Hartington, NE 68739
(402) 254-7441
Misdemeanor records are available by mail. No release. No search fee. $.25 fee per copy. $1.00 for certification. Search information required: name, years to search.

Civil record
Cedar County Court
Box 695
Hartington, NE 68739
(402) 254-7441
Civil records are available by mail. No release. No search fee. $.25 fee per copy. $1.00 for certification. Search information required: name, years to search. Specify plaintiff or defendant.

Chase County

Felony records
Chase County Clerk, Criminal Records
PO Box 1299
Imperial, NE 69033
(308) 882-5266
Felony records are available by mail. No release necessary. $3.00 search fee. $.25 fee per copy. $1.50 for certification. Make check payable to County Clerk. Search information required: name, date of birth.

Civil records
Chase County Clerk
PO Box 1299
Imperial, NE 69033
(308) 882-5266
Civil records are available by mail. No release necessary. $3.00 search fee. $.25 fee per copy. $1.50 for certification. Make check payable to County Clerk. Search information required: name, date of birth. Specify plaintiff or defendant.

Misdemeanor records
Chase County
PO Box 1299
Imperial, NE 69033
(308) 882-4690
Misdemeanor records are available by mail or phone. No release necessary. No search fee. $.25 fee per copy. $1.25 for certification. Search information required: name, date of birth.

Civil records
Chase County
PO Box 1299
Imperial, NE 69033
(308) 882-4690
Civil records are available by mail or phone. No release necessary. No search fee. $.25 fee per copy. $1.25 for certification. Search information required: name, date of birth, years to search. Specify plaintiff or defendant.

Cherry County

Felony records
Clerk of the District Court, Criminal Records
Cherry County Courthouse
365 N. Main
Valentine, NE 69201
(402) 376-1840
Felony records are available in person only. See Nebraska state repository for additional information.

Civil records
Clerk of the District Court
Cherry County Courthouse
365 N. Main
Valentine, NE 69201
(402) 376-1840
Civil records are available in person only. See Nebraska state repository for additional information.

Misdemeanor records
Cherry County Courthouse
365 North Main
Valentine, NE 69201
(402) 376-2590
Misdemeanor records are availablein person only. See Nebraska state repository for additional information.

Civil records
Cherry County Courthouse
365 North Main
Valentine, NE 69201
(402) 376-2590
Civil records are availablein person only. See Nebraska state repository for additional information.

Cheyenne County

Felony records
Clerk of the District Court, Criminal Records
PO Box 217
Cheyenne County Courthouse
Sidney, NE 69162
(308) 254-2814
Fax (308) 254-4641
Felony records are available by mail, fax or phone. No release necessary. No search fee. $.25 fee per copy plus postage cost. $1.00 for certification. Search information required: name.

Civil records
Clerk of the District Court
PO Box 217
Cheyenne County Courthouse
Sidney, NE 69162
(308) 254-2814
Fax (308) 254-4641
Civil records are available by mail, fax or phone. No release necessary. No search fee. $.25 fee per copy plus postage cost. $1.00 for certification. Search information required: name, date of birth, years to search. Specify plaintiff or defendant.

Misdemeanor records
Cheyenne County Courthouse
PO Box 217
1000 10th Ave.
Sidney, NE 69162
(308) 254-2929
Misdemeanor records are available by mail or phone. No release necessary. No search fee. $.25 fee per copy. $1.00 for certification. Search information required: name, date of birth, years to search.

Civil records
Cheyenne County Courthouse
PO Box 217
1000 10th Ave.
Sidney, NE 69162
(308) 254-2929
Civil records are available by mail or phone. No release necessary. No search fee. $.25 fee per copy. $1.00 for certification. Search information required: name, date of birth, years to search. Specify plaintiff or defendant.

Clay County

Felony records
Clerk of the District Court, Criminal Records
Clay County Courthouse
111 W. Fairfield Street
Clay Center, NE 68933
(402) 762-3595
Felony records are available in person only. See Nebraska state repository for additional information.

Civil records
Clerk of the District Court
Clay County Courthouse
111 W. Fairfield Street
Clay Center, NE 68933
(402) 762-3595
Civil records are available in person only. See Nebraska state repository for additional information.

Misdemeanor records
Clay County Courthouse
PO Box 147
Clay Center, NE 68933
(402) 762-3651
Misdemeanor records are available by mail. A release is required. No search fee. $.25 fee per copy. $1.00 for certification. Search information required: name, date of birth, date of offense.

Civil records
Clay County Courthouse
PO Box 147
Clay Center, NE 68933
(402) 762-3651
Civil records are available by mail. No release necessary. No search fee. $.25 fee per copy. $1.00 for certification. Search information required: name, date of birth, years to search. Specify plaintiff or defendant.

Colfax County

Felony records
Clerk of the District Court, Criminal Records
PO Box 429
Schuyler, NE 68661
(402) 352-2205
Fax (402) 352-3287
Felony records are available by mail, fax or phone. No release necessary. No search fee. $.25 fee per copy. $2.00 for certification. Search information required: name, years to search.

Civil records
Clerk of the District Court
PO Box 429
Schuyler, NE 68661
(402) 352-2205
Fax (402) 352-3287
Civil records are available by mail, fax or phone. No release necessary. No search fee. $.25 fee per copy. $2.00 for certification. Search information required: name, date of birth, years to search. Specify plaintiff or defendant.

Misdemeanor records
Colfax County Court
PO Box 191
411 East 11 St.
Schuyler, NE 68661
(402) 352-3322
Misdemeanor records are available by mail. No release necessary. No search fee. $.25 fee per copy. $1.00 for certification plus $.25 fee per certified copy. Search information required: name, date of birth, reason for request.

Civil records
Colfax County Court
PO Box 191
411 East 11 St.
Schuyler, NE 68661
(402) 352-3322
Civil records are available by mail. No release necessary. No search fee. $.25 fee per copy. $1.00 for certification plus $.25 fee per certified copy. Search information required: name, date of birth, years to search. Specify plaintiff or defendant.

Cuming County

Cuming County District Court
Cuming County Courthouse
PO Box 35
West Point, NE 68788
(402) 372-3955
Records are not available by mail or phone. See Nebraska state repository for additional information.

Civil records are available in person only. See Nebraska state repository for additional information.

Custer County

Felony records
District Court, Criminal Records
Courthouse
Broken Bow, NE 68822
(308) 872-2121
Felony records are available by mail or phone. No release necessary. No search fee. $.25 fee per copy. $1.00 for certification. Search information required: name, years to search.

Civil records
District Court
Courthouse
Broken Bow, NE 68822
(308) 872-2121
Civil records are available by mail or phone. No release necessary. No search fee. $.25 fee per copy. $1.00 for certification. Search information required: name, date of birth, years to search. Specify plaintiff or defendant.

Misdemeanor records
Custer County Court
Courthouse
431 South 10th St.
Broken Bow, NE 68822
(308) 872-5761
Misdemeanor records are available by mail or phone. No release necessary. No search fee. $.25 fee per copy. $1.00 for certification. Search information required: name, years to search.

Civil records
Custer County Court
Courthouse
431 South 10th St.
Broken Bow, NE 68822
(308) 872-5761
Civil records are available by mail or phone. No release necessary. No search fee. $.25 fee per copy. $1.00 for certification. Search information required: name, date of birth, years to search. Specify plaintiff or defendant.

Dakota County

Felony records
Clerk of the District Court, Criminal Records
PO Box 66
Dakota City, NE 68731
(402) 987-2114
Felony records are available by mail. No release necessary. No search fee. $.25 fee per copy. $1.00 for certification. Search information required: name, years to search, SASE.

Civil records
Clerk of the District Court
PO Box 66
Dakota City, NE 68731
(402) 987-2114
Civil records are available in person only. See Nebraska state repository for additional information.

Misdemeanor records
Dakota County Court
PO Box 385
Dakota City, NE 68731
(402) 987-2145
Misdemeanor records are available in person only. See Nebraska state repository for additional information.

Civil records
Dakota County Court
PO Box 385
Dakota City, NE 68731
(402) 987-2145
Civil records are available in person only. See Nebraska state repository for additional information.

Dawes County

Felony records
Clerk of the District Court, Criminal Records
PO Box 630
Chadron, NE 69337
(308) 432-0109
Fax (308) 432-0115
Felony records are available by mail or phone. No release necessary. No search fee. $.25 fee per copy. $1.00 for certification. Search information required: name, years to search.

Civil records
Clerk of the District Court
PO Box 630
Chadron, NE 69337
(308) 432-0109
Fax (308) 432-0115
Civil records are available by mail, fax or phone. No release necessary. No search fee. $.25 fee per copy. $1.00 for certification. Search information required: name, date of birth, years to search. Specify plaintiff or defendant.

Misdemeanor records
Dawes County Court
PO Box 806
Chadron, NE 69337
(308) 432-0116
Misdemeanor records are available by mail or phone. No release necessary. No search fee. $.25 fee per copy. $1.00 for certification. Search information required: name, date of birth, years to search, offense.

Civil records
Dawes County Court
PO Box 806
Chadron, NE 69337
(308) 432-0116
Civil records are available by mail or phone. No release necessary. No search fee. $.25 fee per copy. $1.00 for certification. Search information required: name, date of birth, years to search. Specify plaintiff or defendant.

Dawson County

Felony records
Clerk of District Court, Criminal Records
Dawson County Courthouse
PO Box 429
Lexington, NE 68850
(308) 324-4261
Fax (308) 324-3374
Felony records are available by mail, or fax. A release is required. $5.00 search fee. Certified check only, payable to Clerk of District Court. Search information required: name.

Civil records
Clerk of District Court
Dawson County Courthouse
PO Box 429
Lexington, NE 68850
(308) 324-4261
Fax (308) 324-3374
Civil records are available in person only. See Nebraska for additional information.

Misdemeanor records
Dawson County Court
700 N. Washington
Lexington, NE 68850
(308) 324-5606
Misdemeanor records from 1979 are available by mail or phone. No release necessary. No search fee. $.25 fee per copy. $1.00 for certification. Search information required: name, address, years to search, date of birth.

Civil records
Dawson County Court
700 N. Washington
Lexington, NE 68850
(308) 324-5606
Civil records are available by mail or phone. No release necessary. No search fee. $.25 fee per copy. $1.00 for certification. Search information required: name, date of birth, years to search. Specify plaintiff or defendant.

Deuel County

Deuel County Clerk, Criminal Records
PO Box 327
Chappell, NE 69129
(308) 874-3308
Felony and misdemeanor records are available by mail or phone. No release necessary. No search fee. $.10 fee per copy. $1.50 for certification. Search information required: name.

Civil records are available by mail or phone. No release necessary. No search fee. $.10 fee per copy. $1.50 for certification. Search information required: name, date of birth, years to search. Specify plaintiff or defendant.

Dixon County

Felony records
Clerk of the District Court, Criminal Records
Dixon County Courthouse
PO Box 395
Ponca, NE 68770
(402) 755-2881
Felony records are available by mail or phone. No release necessary. No search fee. $.25 fee per copy. $1.00 for certification. Search information required: name.

Civil records
Clerk of the District Court
Dixon County Courthouse
PO Box 395
Ponca, NE 68770
(402) 755-2881
Civil records are available by mail or phone. No release necessary. No search fee. $.25 fee per copy. $1.00 for certification. Search information required: name, date of birth, years to search. Specify plaintiff or defendant.

Misdemeanor records
Dixon County Court
PO Box 497
Ponca, NE 68770
(402) 755-2355
Misdemeanor records are available by mail or phone. No release necessary. No search fee. $.25 fee per copy. $1.00 for certification. Search information required: name, date of birth.

Civil records
Dixon County Court
PO Box 497
Ponca, NE 68770
(402) 755-2355
Civil records are available by mail or phone. No release necessary. No search fee. $.25 fee per copy. $1.00 for certification. Search information required: name, date of birth, years to search. Specify plaintiff or defendant.

Dodge County

Felony records
Clerk of the District Court, Criminal Records
PO Box 1237
Fremont, NE 68025
(402) 727-2780
Felony records are available by mail. No release necessary. No search fee. $.25 fee per copy. $1.00 for certification. Search information required: name, SASE.

Civil records
Clerk of the District Court
PO Box 1237
Fremont, NE 68025
(402) 727-2780
Civil records are available by mail. No release necessary. No search fee. $.25 fee per copy. $1.00 for certification. Search information required: name, date of birth, years to search, SASE. Specify plaintiff or defendant.

Misdemeanor records
Dodge County Court
428 North Broad Street
Fremont, NE 68025
(402) 727-2740
Misdemeanor records are open for physical inspection at the above office. No phone or mail searches.

Civil records
Dodge County Court
428 North Broad Street
Fremont, NE 68025
(402) 727-2740
Civil records are available in person only. See Nebraska state repository for additional information.

Douglas County

Clerk of the District Court, Criminal Records
Hall of Justice
Omaha, NE 68183
(402) 444-7018
Felony records are available by mail or phone. No release necessary. No search fee. $1.50 fee per copy. $3.50 for certification. Search information required: name, years to search.

Civil records are available by mail or phone. No release necessary. No search fee. $1.50 fee per copy. $3.50 for certification. Search information required: name, date of birth, years to search. Specify plaintiff or defendant.

Dundy County

Felony records
Clerk of the District Court, Criminal Records
PO Box 506
Benkelman, NE 69021
(308) 423-2058
Felony records are available by mail or phone. No release necessary. No search fee. $.50 fee per copy. $1.50 for certification. Search information required: name, years to search.

Civil records
Clerk of the District Court
PO Box 506
Benkelman, NE 69021
(308) 423-2058
Civil records are available by mail or phone. No release necessary. No search fee. $.50 fee per copy. $1.50 for certification. Search information required: name, date of birth, years to search. Specify plaintiff or defendant.

Misdemeanor records
Dundy County Court
PO Box 377
Benkelman, NE 69021
(308) 423-2374
Misdemeanor records are available in person only. See Nebraska state repository for additional information.

Civil records
Dundy County Court
PO Box 377
Benkelman, NE 69021
(308) 423-2374
Civil records are available in person only. See Nebraska state repository for additional information.

Fillmore County

Felony records
Clerk of the District Court, Criminal Records
PO Box 147
Geneva, NE 68361
(402) 759-3811
Felony records are available by mail. A release is required. No search fee. $.25 fee per copy. $1.00 for certification. Search information required: name, years to search.

Civil records
Clerk of the District Court
PO Box 147
Geneva, NE 68361
(402) 759-3811
Civil records are available by mail. A release is required. No search fee. $.25 fee per copy. $1.00 for certification. Search information required: name, date of birth, years to search. Specify plaintiff or defendant.

Misdemeanor records
Fillmore County Court
PO Box 66
Geneva, NE 68361
(402) 759-3514
Misdemeanor records are available by mail or phone. No release necessary. No search fee. $.25 fee per copy. $1.00 for certification. Search information required: name, date of birth, years to search.

Civil records
Fillmore County Court
PO Box 66
Geneva, NE 68361
(402) 759-3514
Civil records are available by mail or phone. No release necessary. No search fee. $.25 fee per copy. $1.00 for certification. Search information required: name, date of birth, years to search. Specify plaintiff or defendant.

Franklin County

Felony records
Clerk of the District Court, Criminal Records
PO Box 146
Franklin, NE 68939
(308) 425-6202
Felony records are available by mail. No release necessary. No search fee. $.25 fee per copy. $1.50 for certification. Search information required: name, SSN, date of birth.

Civil records
Clerk of the District Court
PO Box 146
Franklin, NE 68939
(308) 425-6202
Civil records are available by mail. No release necessary. No search fee. $.25 fee per copy. $1.50 for certification. Search information required: name, date of birth, years to search. Specify plaintiff or defendant.

Misdemeanor records
Franklin County Court
PO Box 174
Franklin, NE 68939
(308) 425-3159
Misdemeanor records are available by mail. A release is required. No search fee. $.25 fee per copy. $1.50 for certification. Search information required: name, date of birth, address, offense.

Civil records
Franklin County Court
PO Box 174
Franklin, NE 68939
(308) 425-3159
Civil records are available by mail. A release is required. No search fee. $.25 fee per copy. $1.50 for certification. Search information required: name, date of birth, years to search. Specify plaintiff or defendant.

Frontier County

Felony records
Clerk of the District Court, Criminal Records
PO Box 40
Stockville, NE 69042
(308) 367-8641
Felony records are available by mail. A release is required. No search fee. $.25 fee per copy. $1.50 for certification. Search information required: name, date of birth, SASE.

Civil records
Clerk of the District Court
PO Box 40
Stockville, NE 69042
(308) 367-8641
Civil records are available by mail. A release is required. No search fee. $.25 fee per copy. $1.50 for certification. Search information required: name, date of birth, years to search, SASE. Specify plaintiff or defendant.

Misdemeanor records
Frontier County Court
PO Box 38
Stockville, NE 69042
(308) 367-8629
Misdemeanor records are available by mail. No release necessary. No search fee. $.25 fee per copy. $1.50 for certification. Search information required: name, date of birth.

Civil records
Frontier County Court
PO Box 38
Stockville, NE 69042
(308) 367-8629
Civil records are available by mail. No release necessary. No search fee. $.25 fee per copy. $1.50 for certification. Search information required: name, date of birth, years to search. Specify plaintiff or defendant.

Furnas County

Felony records
Clerk of the District Court, Criminal Records
PO Box 413
Beaver City, NE 68926
(308) 268-4015
Felony and misdemeanor records are available by mail or phone. No release necessary. No search fee. $.25 fee per copy. $1.00 for certification. Search information required: name, years to search.

Civil records
Clerk of the District Court
PO Box 413
Beaver City, NE 68926
(308) 268-4015
Civil records are available by mail or phone. No release necessary. No search fee. $.25 fee per copy. $1.00 for certification. Search information required: name, date of birth, years to search. Specify plaintiff or defendant.

Misdemeanor records
Furnas County Court
PO Box 373
Beaver City, NE 68926
(308) 268-4015
Misdemeanor records are available by mail or phone. No release necessary. No search fee. $.25 fee per copy. $1.00 for certification. Search information required: name, years to search.

Civil records
Furnas County Court
PO Box 373
Beaver City, NE 68926
(308) 268-4015
Civil records are available by mail or phone. No release necessary. No search fee. $.25 fee per copy. $1.00 for certification. Search information required: name, date of birth, years to search. Specify plaintiff or defendant.

Gage County

Felony records
Clerk of the District Court, Criminal Records
PO Box 845
Gage County Courthouse
Beatrice, NE 68310
(402) 223-1332
Felony records are available by mail or phone. No release necessary. No search fee. $.25 fee per copy. $1.00 for certification. Search information required: name, date of birth.

Civil records
Clerk of the District Court
PO Box 845
Gage County Courthouse
Beatrice, NE 68310
(402) 223-1332
Civil records are available by mail or phone. No release necessary. No search fee. $.25 fee per copy. $1.00 for certification. Search information required: name, date of birth, years to search. Specify plaintiff or defendant.

Misdemeanor records
Gage County Court
PO Box 219
Beatrice, NE 68310-0219
(402) 223-1323
Misdemeanor records are available by mail. No release necessary. No search fee. $.25 fee per copy. $1.00 for certification. Search information required: name, date of birth.

Civil records
Gage County Court
PO Box 219
Beatrice, NE 68310-0219
(402) 223-1323
Civil records are available by mail. No release necessary. No search fee. $.25 fee per copy. $1.00 for certification. Search information required: name, date of birth, years to search. Specify plaintiff or defendant.

Garden County

Felony records
Clerk of the District Court, Criminal Records
Garden County Courthouse
PO Box 486
Oshkosh, NE 69154
(308) 772-3924
Felony records are available by mail. No release necessary. No search fee. $.25 fee per copy. $3.00 for certification. Search information required: name.

Civil records
Clerk of the District Court
Garden County Courthouse
PO Box 486
Oshkosh, NE 69154
(308) 772-3924
Civil records are available by mail. No release necessary. No search fee. $.25 fee per copy. $3.00 for certification. Search information required: name, date of birth, years to search. Specify plaintiff or defendant.

Misdemeanor records
Garden County Court
PO Box 465
Oshkosh, NE 69154
(308) 772-3696
Misdemeanor records are available in person only. See Nebraska state repository for additional information.

Civil records
Garden County Court
PO Box 465
Oshkosh, NE 69154
(308) 772-3696
Civil records are available in person only. See Nebraska state repository for additional information.

Garfield County

Felony records
Clerk of the District Court, Criminal Records
PO Box 218
Burwell, NE 68823
(308) 346-4161
Felony records are available by mail. No release necessary. No search fee. $.20 fee per copy, $1.50 fee for certification. Search information required: name, years to search, SASE.

Civil records
Clerk of the District Court
PO Box 218
Burwell, NE 68823
(308) 346-4161
Civil records are available by mail. No release necessary. No search fee. $.20 fee per copy, $1.50 fee for certification. Search information required: name, date of birth, years to search, SASE. Specify plaintiff or defendant.

Misdemeanor records
Garfield County Court
PO Box 431
Burwell, NE 68823
(308) 346-4123
Misdemeanor records are available by mail only. No release necessary. No search fee. $1.00 fee per copy. Search information required: name, date of birth.

Civil records
Garfield County Court
PO Box 431
Burwell, NE 68823
(308) 346-4123
Civil records are available by mail. No release necessary.No search fee. $1.00 fee per copy. Search information required: name, date of birth, years to search. Specify plaintiff or defendant.

Gosper County

Felony records
Clerk of the District Court, Criminal Records
PO Box 136
Elwood, NE 68937
(308) 785-2611
Felony records are available by mail or phone. A release is required. No search fee. $.25 fee per copy. $1.00 for certification. Search information required: name, date of birth.

Civil records
Clerk of the District Court
PO Box 136
Elwood, NE 68937
(308) 785-2611
Civil records are available by mail or phone. A release is required. No search fee. $.25 fee per copy. $1.00 for certification. Search information required: name, date of birth, years to search. Specify plaintiff or defendant.

Misdemeanor records
Gosper County Court
PO Box 55
Elwood, NE 68937
(308) 785-2531
Misdemeanor records are available by mail only. A release is required. No search fee. $.25 fee per copy. $1.25 for certification. Search information required: name, date of birth, offense, date of offense, SASE.

Civil records
Gosper County Court
PO Box 55
Elwood, NE 68937
(308) 785-2531
Civil records are available by mail. A release is required. No search fee. $.25 fee per copy. $1.25 for certification. Search information required: name, date of birth, years to search, SASE. Specify plaintiff or defendant.

Grant County

Felony records
Clerk of District Court, Criminal Records
Grant County Courthouse
PO Box 97
Hyannis, NE 69350
(308) 458-2488
Felony records are available by mail or phone. No release necessary. No search fee. $.20 fee per copy. $1.50 for certification. Search information required: name, date of birth, previous address, years to search, SASE.

Civil records
Clerk of District Court
Grant County Courthouse
PO Box 97
Hyannis, NE 69350
(308) 458-2488
Civil records are available by mail. No release necessary. No search fee. $.20 fee per copy. $1.50 for certification. Search information required: name, date of birth, years to search, SASE. Specify plaintiff or defendant.

Misdemeanor records
Grant County Courthouse
PO Box 97
Hyannis, NE 69350
(308) 458-2433
Misdemeanor records are available by mail or phone. No release necessary. No search fee. $.20 fee per copy. $1.50 for certification. Search information required: name, SASE.

Civil records
Grant County Courthouse
PO Box 97
Hyannis, NE 69350
(308) 458-2433
Civil records are available by mail. No release necessary. No search fee. $.20 fee per copy. $1.50 for certification. Search information required: name, date of birth, years to search, SASE. Specify plaintiff or defendant.

Greeley County

Clerk of the District Court, Criminal Records
PO Box 287
Greeley, NE 68842
(308) 428-3625
Felony and misdemeanor records are available by mail. A release is required. No search fee. $.25 fee per copy. $1.00 for certification. Search information required: name, date of birth, previous address, years to search.

Civil records are available by mail. A release is required. No search fee. $.25 fee per copy. $1.00 for certification. Search information required: name, date of birth, years to search. Specify plaintiff or defendant.

Hall County

Felony records
Clerk of the District Court, Criminal Records
PO Box 1926
Grand Island, NE 68802
(308) 381-5144
Fax (308) 381-5110
Felony records are available by mail, fax or phone. No release necessary. No search fee. $3.00 fee per copy. $2.00 for certification. Search information required: name, date of birth, years to search.

Civil records
Clerk of the District Court
PO Box 1926
Grand Island, NE 68802
(308) 381-5144
Fax (308) 381-5110
Civil records are available by mail, fax or phone. No release necessary. No search fee. $3.00 fee per copy. $2.00 for certification. Search information required: name, date of birth, years to search. Specify plaintiff or defendant.

Misdemeanor records
Hall County Court
PO Box 1985
Grand Island, NE 68802
(308) 381-5135
Misdemeanor records are available by mail only. No release necessary. $5.00 search fee. $.25 fee per copy. Search information required: name, date of birth, years to search, address.

Civil records
Hall County Court
PO Box 1985
Grand Island, NE 68802
(308) 381-5135
Civil records are available in person only. See Nebraska state repository for additional information.

Hamilton County

Felony records
Clerk of the District Court, Criminal Records
PO Box 201
Hamilton County Courthouse
Aurora, NE 68818
(402) 694-3533
Felony records are available by mail or phone. No release necessary. No search fee. $.25 fee per copy. $1.00 for certification. Search information required: name, date of birth, years to search, SASE.

Civil records
Clerk of the District Court
PO Box 201
Hamilton County Courthouse
Aurora, NE 68818
(402) 694-3533
Civil records are available by mail or phone. No release necessary. No search fee. $.25 fee per copy. $1.00 for certification. Search information required: name, date of birth, years to search, SASE. Specify plaintiff or defendant.

Misdemeanor records
Hamilton County Court
Courthouse
PO Box 323
Aurora, NE 68818
(402) 694-6188
Misdemeanor records are available for physical inspection at the above office. No phone or mail searches.

Civil records
Hamilton County Court
Courthouse
PO Box 323
Aurora, NE 68818
(402) 694-6188
Civil records are available in person only. See Nebraska state repository for additional information.

Harlan County

Clerk of District Court
PO Box 379
Alma, NE 68920
(308) 928-2173
Felony and misdemeanor records are available by mail. A release is required. $3.00 search fee. $.25 fee per copy. $3.00 for certification. Certified check only, payable to Clerk of District Court. Search information required: name, years to search, SASE.

Civil records are available by mail. A release is required. $3.00 search fee. $.25 fee per copy. $3.00 for certification. Search information required: name, date of birth, years to search, SASE. Specify plaintiff or defendant.

Hayes County

Felony records
Clerk of the District Court, Criminal Records
PO Box 370
Hayes Center, NE 69032
(308) 286-3413
Felony records are available by mail. No release necessary. No search fee. $.25 fee per copy. $4.00 for certification. Search information required: name, SASE.

Civil records
Clerk of the District Court
PO Box 370
Hayes Center, NE 69032
(308) 286-3413
Civil records are available by mail. No release necessary. No search fee. $.25 fee per copy. $4.00 for certification. Search information required: name, date of birth, years to search. Specify plaintiff or defendant.

Misdemeanor records
Hayes County Court
Courthouse
Hayes Center, NE 69032
(308) 286-3315
Misdemeanor records are available by mail or phone. Office is open Monday, Wednesday, and Friday afternoons only. No release necessary. No search fee. $.25 per copy. $1.00 for certification. Search information required: name.

Civil records
Hayes County Court
Courthouse
Hayes Center, NE 69032
(308) 286-3315
Civil records are available by mail or phone. No release necessary. No search fee. $.25 per copy. $1.00 for certification. Search information required: name, date of birth, years to search. Specify plaintiff or defendant.

Hitchcock County

Felony records
Clerk of the District Court, Criminal Records
Courthouse
PO Box 248
Trenton, NE 69044
(308) 334-5646
Felony records are available by mail or phone. No release necessary. No search fee. $.50 fee per copy. $1.00 for certification. Search information required: name.

Civil records
Clerk of the District Court
Courthouse
PO Box 248
Trenton, NE 69044
(308) 334-5646
Civil records are available by mail or phone. No release necessary. No search fee. $.50 fee per copy. $1.00 for certification. Search information required: name, date of birth, years to search. Specify plaintiff or defendant.

Misdemeanor records
Hitchcock County Court
PO Box 366
Trenton, NE 69044
(308) 334-5383
Misdemeanor records are available in person only. See Nebraska state repository for additional information.

Civil records
Hitchcock County Court
PO Box 366
Trenton, NE 69044
(308) 334-5383
Civil records are available by mail. No release necessary. No search fee. $.25 fee per copy. $1.00 for certification. Search information required: name, date of birth, years to search. Specify plaintiff or defendant.

Holt County

Felony records
Clerk of the District Court, Criminal Records
Box 755
O'Neill, NE 68763
(402) 336-2840
Felony records are available by mail. No release necessary. No search fee. $.15 fee per copy. $1.00 for certification. Search information required: name, years to search.

Civil records
Clerk of the District Court
Box 755
O'Neill, NE 68763
(402) 336-2840
Civil records are available by mail. No release necessary. No search fee. $.15 fee per copy. $1.00 for certification. Search information required: name, date of birth, years to search. Specify plaintiff or defendant.

Misdemeanor records
Holt County Court
204 N. 4th St.
O'Neill, NE 68763
(402) 336-1662
Misdemeanor records are available for physical inspection at the above office. No phone or mail searches.

Civil records are available in person only. See Nebraska state repository for additional information.

Hooker County

Felony records
Clerk of the District Court, Criminal Records
PO Box 184
Mullen, NE 69152
(308) 546-2244
Felony records are available by mail or phone. No release necessary. No search fee. $1.00 fee per copy. $1.00 for certification. Search information required: name, years to search.

Civil records
Clerk of the District Court
PO Box 184
Mullen, NE 69152
(308) 546-2244
Civil records are available by mail or phone. No release necessary. No search fee. $1.00 fee per copy. $1.00 for certification. Search information required: name, date of birth, years to search. Specify plaintiff or defendant.

Misdemeanor records
Hooker County Court
PO Box 263
Mullen, NE 69152
(308) 546-2249
Misdemeanor records are available by mail only. No release necessary. No search fee. $1.00 fee per copy. $1.00 for certification. Search information required: name, date of birth.

Civil records
Hooker County Court
PO Box 263
Mullen, NE 69152
(308) 546-2249
Civil records are available by mail. No release necessary. No search fee. $1.00 fee per copy. $1.00 for certification. Search information required: name, date of birth, years to search. Specify plaintiff or defendant.

Howard County

Felony records
Clerk of the District Court, Criminal Records
PO Box 25
St. Paul, NE 68873
(308) 754-4343
Felony records are available by mail. No release necessary. No search fee. $.20 fee per copy. $4.00 for certification. Search information required: name, SSN, date of birth, sex, race.

Civil records
Clerk of the District Court
PO Box 25
St. Paul, NE 68873
(308) 754-4343
Civil records are available by mail. No release necessary. No search fee. $.20 fee per copy. $4.00 for certification. Search information required: name, date of birth, years to search. Specify plaintiff or defendant.

Misdemeanor records
Howard County Court
PO Box 94
St. Paul, NE 68873
(308) 754-4192
Misdemeanor records are available by mail only. A release is required. No search fee. $.25 fee per copy. $1.25 for certification. Search information required: name, date of birth, address, years to search.

Civil records
Howard County Court
PO Box 94
St. Paul, NE 68873
(308) 754-4192
Civil records are available by mail. A release is required. No search fee. $.25 fee per copy. $1.25 for certification. Search information required: name, date of birth, years to search. Specify plaintiff or defendant.

Jefferson County

Felony records
Clerk of the District Court, Criminal Records
Jefferson County Court
Courthouse
Fairbury, NE 68352
(402) 729-2019
Fax (402) 729-2016

Felony records are available by mail or fax. No release necessary. No search fee. $.50 fee per copy. $1.00 for certification. Search information required: name.

Civil records
Clerk of the District Court
Jefferson County Court
Courthouse
Fairbury, NE 68352
(402) 729-2019
Fax (402) 729-2016

Civil records are available by mail or fax. No release necessary. No search fee. $.50 fee per copy. $1.00 for certification. Search information required: name, date of birth, years to search. Specify plaintiff or defendant.

Misdemeanor records
Jefferson County Court
Courthouse
411 4th Street
Fairbury, NE 68352
(402) 729-2312

Misdemeanor records are available by mail only. No release necessary. No search fee. $.25 fee per copy. $1.00 for certification. Search information required: name, date of birth, years to search, SASE.

Civil records
Jefferson County Court
Courthouse
411 4th Street
Fairbury, NE 68352
(402) 729-2312

Civil records are available by mail. No release necessary. No search fee. $.25 fee per copy. $1.00 for certification. Search information required: name, date of birth, years to search. Specify plaintiff or defendant.

Johnson County

Felony records
Clerk of the District Court, Criminal Records
PO Box 285
Tecumseh, NE 68450
(402) 335-3246

Felony records are available by mail or phone. A release is required. No search fee. $.25 fee per copy. $1.00 for certification. Search information required: name, date of birth.

Civil records
Clerk of the District Court
PO Box 285
Tecumseh, NE 68450
(402) 335-3246

Civil records are available by mail or phone. A release is required. No search fee. $.25 fee per copy. $1.00 for certification. Search information required: name, date of birth, years to search. Specify plaintiff or defendant.

Misdemeanor records
Johnson County Court
Courthouse
PO Box 285
Tecumseh, NE 68450
(402) 335-3050

Misdemeanor records are available by mail or phone. A release is required. No search fee. $.25 fee per copy. $1.00 for certification. Search information required: name, date of birth, social security number, address, years to search.

Civil records
Johnson County Court
Courthouse
PO Box 285
Tecumseh, NE 68450
(402) 335-3050

Civil records are available by mail or phone. A release is required. No search fee. $.25 fee per copy. $1.00 for certification. Search information required: name, date of birth, years to search. Specify plaintiff or defendant.

Kearney County

Felony records
Clerk of the District Court
PO Box 208
Minden, NE 68959
(308) 832-1155 Ext. 16

Felony records are available by mail or phone. No release necessary. No search fee. $1.00 fee per copy. $1.00 fee for certification. Search information required: name, years to search.

Civil records
Clerk of the District Court
PO Box 208
Minden, NE 68959
(308) 832-1155 Ext. 16

Civil records are available by mail or phone. No release necessary. No search fee. $1.00 fee per copy. $1.00 fee for certification. Search information required: name, date of birth, years to search. Specify plaintiff or defendant.

Misdemeanor records
Kearney County Court
PO Box 377
Minden, NE 68959
(308) 832-1155 Ext. 42

Misdemeanor records are available by mail. A release is required. No search fee. $.25 fee per copy. $1.00 for certification. Search information required: name, date of birth, date of offense, case number (if known).

Civil records
Kearney County Court
PO Box 377
Minden, NE 68959
(308) 832-1155 Ext. 42

Civil records are available by mail. A release is required. No search fee. $.25 fee per copy. $1.00 for certification. earch information required: name, date of birth, years to search. Specify plaintiff or defendant.

Keith County

Felony records
Clerk of the District Court, Criminal Records
PO Box 686
Ogallala, NE 69153
(308) 284-3849
Fax (308) 284-3978

Felony records are available by mail or fax. No release necessary. No search fee. $.25 fee per copy. $1.00 for certification, plus $.25 for each page certified. Search information required: name, years to search.

Civil records
Clerk of the District Court
PO Box 686
Ogallala, NE 69153
(308) 284-3849
Fax (308) 284-3978

Civil records are available by mail or fax. No release necessary. No search fee. $.25 fee per copy. $1.00 for certification, plus $.25 for each page certified. Search information required: name, date of birth, years to search. Specify plaintiff or defendant.

Misdemeanor records
Keith County Court
PO Box 358
Ogallala, NE 69153
(308) 284-3693

Misdemeanor records are available in person only.

Civil records
Keith County Court
PO Box 358
Ogallala, NE 69153
(308) 284-3693

Civil records are available in person only. See Nebraska state repository for additional information.

Keya Paha County

Felony records
Clerk of the District Court, Criminal Records
PO Box 349
Springview, NE 68778
(402) 497-3791
Fax (402) 497-3203

Felony records are available by mail, fax or phone. No release necessary. No search fee. $.25 fee per copy. $4.00 for certification. Search information required: name, years to search.

Civil records
Clerk of the District Court
PO Box 349
Springview, NE 68778
(402) 497-3791
Fax (402) 497-3203

Civil records are available by mail, fax or phone. No release necessary. No search fee. $.25 fee per copy. $4.00 for certification. Search information required: name, date of birth, years to search. Specify plaintiff or defendant.

Misdemeanor records
Keya Paha County Court
PO Box 311
Springview, NE 68778
(402) 497-3021

Misdemeanor records are available by mail or phone. No release necessary. No search fee. $.25 fee per copy. $4.00 for certification. Search information required: name, date of birth.

Civil records
Keya Paha County Court
PO Box 311
Springview, NE 68778
(402) 497-3021
Civil records are available by mail. No release necessary. No search fee. $.25 fee per copy. $4.00 for certification. Search information required: name, date of birth, years to search. Specify plaintiff or defendant.

Kimball County

Felony records
Clerk of the District Court, Criminal Records
114 E. 3rd St.
Kimball, NE 69145
(308) 235-2241 or 235-3591
Felony records are available by mail. A release is required. No search fee. $.50 fee per copy. $1.50 for certification. Search information required: name, years to search.

Civil records
Clerk of the District Court
114 E. 3rd St.
Kimball, NE 69145
(308) 235-2241 or 235-3591
Civil records are available by mail. No release necessary. No search fee. $.50 fee per copy. $1.50 for certification. Search information required: name, date of birth, years to search. Specify plaintiff or defendant.

Misdemeanor records
Kimball County Court
114 E. 3rd
Kimball, NE 69145
(308) 235-2831
Misdemeanor records are available by mail or phone. No release necessary. No search fee. $.50 fee per copy. $1.00 for certification. Search information required: name, years to search, date of offense, SASE.

Civil records
Kimball County Court
Kimball, NE 69145
(308) 235-2831
Civil records are available by mail. No release necessary. No search fee. $.50 fee per copy. $1.00 for certification. Search information required: name, date of birth, years to search. Specify plaintiff or defendant, SASE.

Knox County

Felony records
Clerk of the District Court, Criminal Records
PO Box 126
Center, NE 68724
(402) 288-4484
Felony records are available in person only. See Nebraska state repository for additional information.

Civil records
Clerk of the District Court
PO Box 126
Center, NE 68724
(402) 288-4484
Civil records are available in person only. See Nebraska state repository for additional information.

Misdemeanor records
Knox County Court
PO Box 125
Center, NE 68724
(402) 288-4277
Misdemeanor records are available for physical inspection at the above office.

Civil records
Knox County Court
PO Box 125
Center, NE 68724
(402) 288-4277
Civil records are available in person only. See Nebraska state repository for additional information.

Lancaster County

Felony records
Clerk of District Court, Criminal Records
County-City Bldg
555 S. 10th Street
Lincoln, NE 68508
(402) 471-7328
Felony records are available by mail or phone. No release necessary. No search fee. $.25 fee per copy. $1.00 for certification. Search information required: name, years to search.

Civil records
Clerk of District Court
County-City Bldg
555 S. 10th Street
Lincoln, NE 68508
(402) 471-7328
Civil records are available by mail or phone. No release necessary. No search fee. $.25 fee per copy. $1.00 for certification. Search information required: name, date of birth, years to search. Specify plaintiff or defendant.

Misdemeanor records
Lancaster County Court
County-City Bldg
555 S. 10th Street
Lincoln, NE 68508
(402) 471-7291
Misdemeanor records are available for physical inspection at the above office. Contact the above office for more information.

Civil records are available in person only. See Nebraska state repository for additional information.

Lincoln County

Clerk of the District Court, Criminal Records
Courthouse
PO Box 381
North Platte, NE 69103
(308) 534-4350 Extension 303
Felony and misdemeanor records are available by mail. No release necessary. No search fee. $.25 fee per copy. $1.25 for certification. Search information required: name, years to search.

Civil records are available by mail. No release necessary. No search fee. $.25 fee per copy. $1.25 for certification. Search information required: name, date of birth, years to search. Specify plaintiff or defendant.

Logan County

Felony records
Clerk of the District Court, Criminal Records
PO Box 8
Stapleton, NE 69163
(308) 636-2311
Felony records are available by mail or phone. No release necessary. No search fee. $.50 fee per copy. $1.25 for certification. Search information required: name, date of birth., SASE

Civil records
Clerk of the District Court
PO Box 8
Stapleton, NE 69163
(308) 636-2311
Civil records are available by mail or phone. No release necessary. No search fee. $.50 fee per copy. $1.25 for certification. Search information required: name, date of birth, years to search, SASE. Specify plaintiff or defendant.

Misdemeanor records
Logan County Court
PO Box 202
Stapleton, NE 69163
(308) 636-2677
Fax (308) 636-2288
Misdemeanor records are available by mail or by fax. A release is required. Call before faxing. No search fee. $.50 fee per copy. $1.25 for certification. Search information required: name, date of birth, address, years to search, SASE.

Civil records
Logan County Court
PO Box 202
Stapleton, NE 69163
(308) 636-2677
Fax (308) 636-2288
Civil records are available by mail or by fax. A release is required. Call before faxing. No search fee. $.50 fee per copy. $1.25 for certification. Search information required: name, date of birth, years to search, SASE. Specify plaintiff or defendant.

Loup County

Clerk of the District Court, Criminal Records
PO Box 146
Taylor, NE 68879
(308) 942-6035
Felony and misdemeanor records are available by mail. A release is required. No search fee. $.25 fee per copy. $1.00 for certification. Search information required: name, date of birth, years to search.

Civil records are available by mail. No release necessary. No search fee. $.25 fee per copy. $1.00 for certification. Search information required: name, date of birth, years to search. Specify plaintiff or defendant.

Madison County

Felony records
Madison County Court, Criminal
Records
PO Box 249
Madison, NE 68748
(402) 454-3311 Extension 141 or 142
Felony records are available by mail. No release necessary. No search fee. $.25 fee per copy. $1.50 for certification. Search information required: name, date of birth, years to search.

Civil records
Madison County Court
PO Box 249
Madison, NE 68748
(402) 454-3311 Extension 141 or 142
Civil records are available by mail. No release necessary. No search fee. $.25 fee per copy. $1.50 for certification. Search information required: name, date of birth, years to search. Specify plaintiff or defendant.

Misdemeanor records
Madison County Court
PO Box 230
Madison, NE 68748
(402) 454-3311 Ext. 141
Misdemeanor records are available by mail only. No release necessary. No search fee. $.25 fee per copy. $1.50 for certification. Search information required: name, date of birth.

Civil records
Madison County Court
PO Box 230
Madison, NE 68748
(402) 454-3311 Ext. 141
Civil records are available by mail. No release necessary. No search fee. $.25 fee per copy. $1.50 for certification. Search information required: name, date of birth, years to search. Specify plaintiff or defendant.

McPherson County

Felony records
Clerk of District Court, Criminal
Records
PO Box 122
Tryon, NE 69167
(308) 587-2363
Felony records are available by mail. No release necessary. No search fee. $.50 fee per copy. $1.50 for certification. Search information required: name, date of birth, years to search.

Civil records
Clerk of District Court
PO Box 122
Tryon, NE 69167
(308) 587-2363
Civil records are available by mail. No release necessary. No search fee. $.50 fee per copy. $1.50 for certification. Search information required: name, date of birth, years to search. Specify plaintiff or defendant.

Misdemeanor records
McPherson County Courthouse
PO Box 122
Tryon, NE 69167
(308) 587-2363
Misdemeanor records are available by mail. A release required. No search fee. $.50 fee per copy. $1.50 for certification. Search information required: name, date of birth.

Civil records
McPherson County Courthouse
PO Box 122
Tryon, NE 69167
(308) 587-2363
Civil records are available by mail. A release required. No search fee. $.50 fee per copy. $1.50 for certification. Search information required: name, date of birth, years to search. Specify plaintiff or defendant.

Merrick County

Felony records
Clerk of the District Court, Criminal
Records
PO Box 27
Merrick County Courthouse
Central City, NE 68826
(308) 946-2461
Felony records are available by mail or phone. A release is required. No search fee. $.25 fee per copy. $1.00 for certification. Search information required: name, SSN, date of birth, sex, race.

Civil records
Clerk of the District Court
PO Box 27
Merrick County Courthouse
Central City, NE 68826
(308) 946-2461
Civil records are available by mail. A release is required. No search fee. $.25 fee per copy. $1.00 for certification. Search information required: name, date of birth, years to search. Specify plaintiff or defendant.

Misdemeanor records
Merrick County Court
Courthouse
PO Box 27
Central City, NE 68826
(308) 946-2812
Misdemeanor records are available in person only. See Nebraska state repository for additional information.

Civil records
Merrick County Court
Courthouse
PO Box 27
Central City, NE 68826
(308) 946-2812
Civil records are available in person only. See Nebraska state repository for additional information.

Morrill County

Felony records
Clerk of the District Court, Criminal
Records
PO Box 824
Bridgeport, NE 69336-0824
(308) 262-1261
Felony records are available by mail. No release necessary. No search fee. $.25 fee per copy. $1.00 for certification. Search information required: name, years to search, SASE.

Civil records
Clerk of the District Court
PO Box 824
Bridgeport, NE 69336-0824
(308) 262-1261
Civil records are available by mail. No release necessary. No search fee. $.25 fee per copy. $1.00 for certification. Search information required: name, date of birth, years to search, SASE. Specify plaintiff or defendant.

Misdemeanor records
Morrill County Court
PO Box 418
Bridgeport, NE 69336
(308) 262-0812
Misdemeanor records are available by mail. A release is required. No search fee. $.25 fee per copy. $1.00 for certification. Search information required: full name, date of birth, SSN, years to search.

Civil records
Morrill County Court
PO Box 418
Bridgeport, NE 69336
(308) 262-0812
Civil records are available by mail. No release necessary. No search fee. $.25 fee per copy. $1.00 for certification. Search information required: name, date of birth, years to search. Specify plaintiff or defendant.

Nance County

Felony records
Clerk of the District Court, Criminal
Records
PO Box 338
Fullerton, NE 68638
(308) 536-2365
Fax (308) 536-2742
Felony records are available by mail or fax. No release necessary. No search fee. $.20 fee per copy. $1.00 for certification. Search information required: name, years to search.

Civil records
Clerk of the District Court
PO Box 338
Fullerton, NE 68638
(308) 536-2365
Fax (308) 536-2742
Civil records are available by mail or fax. No release necessary. No search fee. $.20 fee per copy. $1.00 for certification. Search information required: name, date of birth, years to search. Specify plaintiff or defendant.

Misdemeanor records
Nance County Court
PO Box 837
Fullerton, NE 68638
(308) 536-2675
Misdemeanor records are available by mail only. No release necessary. No search fee. $.25 fee per copy. $1.00 fee for certification. Search information required: name, address, years to search, date of birth, SASE.

Civil records
Nance County Court
PO Box 837
Fullerton, NE 68638
(308) 536-2675
Civil records are available by mail. No release necessary. No search fee. $.25 fee per copy. $1.00 for certification. Search information required: name, date of birth, years to search, SASE. Specify plaintiff or defendant.

Nemaha County

Felony records
Clerk of the District Court, Criminal Records
Nemaha County Courthouse
1824 N Street
Auburn, NE 68305
(402) 274-3616
Felony records are available by mail. A release is required. No search fee. $.25 fee per copy. $1.00 for certification. Search information required: name, SASE.

Civil records
Clerk of the District Court
Nemaha County Courthouse
1824 N Street
Auburn, NE 68305
(402) 274-3616
Civil records are available by mail. A release is required. No search fee. $.25 fee per copy. $1.00 for certification. Search information required: name, date of birth, years to search. Specify plaintiff or defendant.

Misdemeanor records
Nemaha County Court
1824 N Street
Auburn, NE 68305
(402) 274-3008
Misdemeanor records are available by mail. A release is required. No search fee. Search information required: name, date of birth, social security number if available, SASE.

Civil records
Nemaha County Court
1824 N Street
Auburn, NE 68305
(402) 274-3008
Civil records are available by mail. A release is required. No search fee. $.25 fee per copy. $1.00 for certification. Search information required: name, date of birth, years to search, SASE. Specify plaintiff or defendant.

Nuckolls County

Felony records
Clerk of the District Court, Criminal Records
Nuckolls County Courthouse
PO Box 362
Nelson, NE 68961
(402) 225-4341
Felony records are available by mail or phone. No release necessary. No search fee. $.25 fee per copy. $1.00 for certification. Search information required: name, years to search.

Civil records
Clerk of the District Court
Nuckolls County Courthouse
PO Box 362
Nelson, NE 68961
(402) 225-4341
Civil records are available by mail. No release necessary. No search fee. $.25 fee per copy. $1.00 for certification. Search information required: name, date of birth, years to search. Specify plaintiff or defendant.

Misdemeanor records
Nuckolls County Court
PO Box 372
Nelson, NE 68961
(402) 225-2371
Misdemeanor records are available by mail or phone. No release necessary. No search fee. $.25 fee per copy. $1.00 for certification. Search information required: name, date of birth, years to search, SASE.

Civil records
Nuckolls County Court
PO Box 372
Nelson, NE 68961
(402) 225-2371
Civil records are available by mail. No release necessary. No search fee. $.25 fee per copy. $1.00 for certification. Search information required: name, date of birth, years to search, SASE. Specify plaintiff or defendant.

Otoe County

Felony records
Clerk of the District Court, Criminal Records
1021 Central Avenue, Room 209
PO Box 726
Courthouse
Nebraska City, NE 68410
(402) 873-6440
Felony records are available by mail. A release is required. $2.00 search fee. $1.00 fee per copy. $1.00 for certification. Search information required: name, years to search.

Civil records
Clerk of the District Court
1021 Central Avenue, Room 209
PO Box 726
Courthouse
Nebraska City, NE 68410
(402) 873-6440
Civil records are available by mail. A release is required. $2.00 search fee. $1.00 fee per copy. $1.00 for certification. Search information required: name, date of birth, years to search, SASE. Specify plaintiff or defendant.

Misdemeanor records
Otoe County Court
1021 Central Avenue
Courthouse
Nebraska City, NE 68410
(402) 873-5588
Misdemeanor records are available by mail only. No release necessary. No search fee. Search information required: name.

Civil records
Otoe County Court
1021 Central Avenue
Courthouse
Nebraska City, NE 68410
(402) 873-5588
Civil records are available by mail. No release necessary. No search fee. $.25 fee per copy. $1.00 for certification. Search information required: name, date of birth, years to search, SASE. Specify plaintiff or defendant.

Pawnee County

Felony records
Clerk of the District Court, Criminal Records
Courthouse
PO Box 431
Pawnee City, NE 68420
(402) 852-2963
Felony records are available by mail or phone. No release necessary. No search fee. $.50 fee per copy. $1.00 for certification. Search information required: name, date of birth.

Civil records
Clerk of the District Court
Courthouse
PO Box 431
Pawnee City, NE 68420
(402) 852-2963
Civil records are available by mail. No release necessary. No search fee. $.25 fee per copy. $1.00 for certification. Search information required: name, date of birth, years to search, SASE. Specify plaintiff or defendant.

Misdemeanor records
Pawnee County Court
PO Box 471
Pawnee City, NE 68420
(402) 852-2388
Misdemeanor records are available by mail only. Release required. No search fee. $.25 fee per copy. $1.00 for certification. Search information required: name, date of birth, social security number.

Civil records
Pawnee County Court
PO Box 471
Pawnee City, NE 68420
(402) 852-2388
Civil records are available by mail. No release necessary. No search fee. $.25 fee per copy. $1.00 for certification. Search information required: name, date of birth, years to search, SASE. Specify plaintiff or defendant.

Perkins County

Felony records
Clerk of District Court, Criminal Records
PO Box 156
Grant, NE 69140
(308) 352-4643
Felony records are available by mail. A release is required. No search fee. $.20 fee per copy. $1.50 for certification. Search information required: name, SSN, date of birth, years to search.

Civil records
Clerk of District Court
PO Box 156
Grant, NE 69140
(308) 352-4643
Civil records are available by mail. A release is required. No search fee. $.20 fee per copy. $1.50 for certification. Search information required: name, date of birth, years to search. Specify plaintiff or defendant.

Misdemeanor records
Perkins County Court
PO Box 222
Grant, NE 69140
(308) 352-4415
Misdemeanor records are available by mail only. A release is required. No search fee. $.25 fee per copy. $1.25 for certification. Search information required: name, date of birth, address, offense.

Civil records
Perkins County Court
PO Box 222
Grant, NE 69140
(308) 352-4415
Civil records are available by mail. A release is required. No search fee. $.25 fee per copy. $1.25 for certification. Search information required: name, date of birth, years to search, SASE. Specify plaintiff or defendant.

Phelps County

Felony records
Clerk of the District Court, Criminal Records
PO Box 462
Holdrege, NE 68949
(308) 995-2281
Felony records are available by mail. No release necessary. No search fee. $.10 fee per copy. $1.00 for certification. Search information required: name, date of birth.

Civil records
Clerk of the District Court
PO Box 462
Holdrege, NE 68949
(308) 995-2281
Civil records are available by mail or phone. No release necessary. No search fee. $.10 fee per copy. $1.00 for certification. Search information required: name, date of birth, years to search. Specify plaintiff or defendant.

Misdemeanor records
Phelps County Court
PO Box 255
Holdrege, NE 68949
(308) 995-6561
Misdemeanor records are available by mail only. No release necessary. No search fee. $.25 fee per copy. $1.00 for certification. Search information required: name, date of birth, address, years to search.

Civil records
Phelps County Court
PO Box 255
Holdrege, NE 68949
(308) 995-6561
Civil records are available by mail. No release necessary. No search fee. $.25 fee per copy. $1.00 for certification. Search information required: name, date of birth, years to search. Specify plaintiff or defendant.

Pierce County

Felony records
Clerk of Court, Criminal Records
111 W. Court Street, Room 12
Pierce, NE 68767
(402) 329-4335
Felony records are available by mail. No release necessary. No search fee. $.25 fee per copy. $1.00 for certification. Search information required: name.

Civil records
Clerk of Court
111 W. Court Street, Room 12
Pierce, NE 68767
(402) 329-4335
Civil records are available by mail. No release necessary. No search fee. $.25 fee per copy. $1.00 for certification. Search information required: name, date of birth, years to search. Specify plaintiff or defendant.

Misdemeanor records
Pierce County Court
111 W. Court Street, Room 11
Pierce, NE 68767
(402) 329-6245
Misdemeanor records are available by mail only. A release is required. No search fee. $.25 fee per copy. $1.00 for certification. Search information required: name, date of birth, current address.

Civil records
Pierce County Court
111 W. Court Street, Room 11
Pierce, NE 68767
(402) 329-6245
Civil records are available by mail. A release is required. No search fee. $.25 fee per copy. $1.00 for certification. Search information required: name, date of birth, years to search. Specify plaintiff or defendant.

Platte County

Felony records
Clerk of the District Court, Criminal Records
PO Box 1188
Columbus, NE 68602-1188
(402) 563-4906
Fax (402) 563-1715
Felony records are available by mail or fax. No release necessary. No search fee. $.25 fee per copy. $1.00 for certification. Search information required: name, date of birth.

Civil records
Clerk of the District Court
PO Box 1188
Columbus, NE 68602-1188
(402) 563-4906
Fax (402) 563-1715
Civil records are available by mail or fax. No release necessary. No search fee. $.25 fee per copy. $1.00 for certification. Search information required: name, date of birth, years to search. Specify plaintiff or defendant.

Misdemeanor records
Platte County Court
PO Box 426
Columbus, NE 68602-0426
(402) 563-4937
Misdemeanor records are available by mail only. No release necessary. No search fee. $.25 fee per copy. $1.00 for certification. Search information required: name, date of birth, years to search.

Civil records
Platte County Court
PO Box 426
Columbus, NE 68602-0426
(402) 563-4937
Civil records are available by mail. No release necessary. No search fee. $.25 fee per copy. $1.00 for certification. Search information required: name, date of birth, years to search. Specify plaintiff or defendant.

Polk County

Clerk of the District Court, Criminal Records
PO Box 447
Osceola, NE 68651
(402) 747-3487
Records are not available by mail or phone. See Nebraska state repository for additional information.

Civil records are available in person only. See Nebraska state repository for additional information.

Red Willow County

Felony records
Clerk of the District Court, Criminal Records
Red Willow County Courthouse
McCook, NE 69001
(308) 345-4583
Felony records are available by mail or phone. No release necessary. No search fee. $.25 fee per copy. $1.00 for certification. Search information required: name, date of birth, years to search.

Civilrecords
Clerk of the District Court
Red Willow County Courthouse
McCook, NE 69001
(308) 345-4583
Civil records are available by mail. No release necessary. $.25 fee per copy. $1.00 for certification. Search information required: name, date of birth, years to search. Specify plaintiff or defendant.

Misdemeanor records
Red Willow County Court
Courthouse
McCook, NE 69001
(308) 345-1904
Misdemeanor records are available by mail only. No release necessary. No search fee. $.25 fee per copy. $1.00 for certification. Search information required: name, date of birth, years to search.

Civil records
Red Willow County Court
Courthouse
McCook, NE 69001
(308) 345-1904
Civil records are available by mail. No release necessary. No search fee. $.25 fee per copy. $1.00 for certification. Search information required: name, date of birth, years to search. Specify plaintiff or defendant.

Richardson County

Felony records
Clerk of the District Court, Criminal Records
Courthouse
17th and Harlam Street
Falls City, NE 68355
(402) 245-2023
Felony records are available by mail or phone. No release necessary. No search fee. $.20 fee per copy. $1.00 for certification. Search information required: name, years to search, SASE.

Civil records
Clerk of the District Court, Criminal Records
Courthouse
Falls City, NE 68355
(402) 245-2023
Civil records are available by mail or phone. No release necessary. No search fee. $.20 fee per copy. $1.00 for certification. Search information required: name, date of birth, years to search, SASE. Specify plaintiff or defendant.

Misdemeanor records
Richardson County Court
Room 205, County Courthouse
Falls City, NE 68355
(402) 245-2812
Misdemeanor records are available by mail or phone. A release is required. No search fee. $.20 fee per copy. $1.00 for certification. Search information required: name, date of birth, address, social security number, date of offense.

Civil records
Richardson County Court
Room 205, County Courthouse
Falls City, NE 68355
(402) 245-2812
Civil records are available by mail or phone. A release is required. No search fee. $.20 fee per copy. $1.00 for certification. Search information required: name, date of birth, years to search. Specify plaintiff or defendant.

Rock County

Felony records
Clerk of the District Court, Criminal Records
PO Box 367
Bassett, NE 68714
(402) 684-3933
Felony records are available by mail. A release is required. No search fee.$.10 fee per copy. $1.50 for certification. Search information required: name.

Civil records
Clerk of the District Court
PO Box 367
Bassett, NE 68714
(402) 684-3933
Civil records are available by mail. No release necessary. No search fee.$.10 fee per copy. $1.50 for certification. Search information required: name, date of birth, years to search. Specify plaintiff or defendant.

Misdemeanor records
Rock County Court
PO Box 249
Bassett, NE 68714
(402) 684-3601
Misdemeanor records are available in person only. See Nebraska state repository for additional information.

Civil records
Rock County Court
PO Box 249
Bassett, NE 68714
(402) 684-3601
Civil records are available in person only. See Nebraska state repository for additional information.

Saline County

Felony records
Clerk of the District Court, Criminal Records
PO Box 865
Wilber, NE 68465
(402) 821-2823
Felony records are available by mail or phone. A release is required. No search fee. $.25 fee per copy, $1.00 fee for certification. Search information required: name, date of birth.

Civil records
Clerk of the District Court
PO Box 865
Wilber, NE 68465
(402) 821-2823
Civil records are available by mail or phone. A release is required. No search fee. $.25 fee per copy, $1.00 fee for certification. Search information required: name, date of birth, years to search. Specify plaintiff or defendant.

Misdemeanor records
Saline County Court
PO Box 865
Wilber, NE 68465
(402) 821-2131
Fax (402) 821-2532
Misdemeanor records are available by mail or fax. No release necessary. No search fee. $.25 fee per copy. $1.00 for certification. Search information required: name, date of birth, address.

Civil records
Saline County Court
PO Box 865
Wilber, NE 68465
(402) 821-2131
Fax (402) 821-2532
Civil records are available by mail. No release necessary. No search fee. $.25 fee per copy. $1.00 for certification. Search information required: name, date of birth, years to search. Specify plaintiff or defendant.

Sarpy County

Felony records
Clerk of the District Court, Criminal Records
Sarpy County Courthouse
1210 Golden Gate Drive, Suite 3131
Papillion, NE 68046-2887
(402) 593-2267
Fax (402) 593-4403
Felony records are available by mail or fax. A release is required. No search fee. $.75 feefor first copy, $.25 each additional copy. $1.00 for certification. Search information required: name, SSN, date of birth, sex, race, years to search.

Civil records
Clerk of the District Court
Sarpy County Courthouse
1210 Golden Gate Drive, Suite 3131
Papillion, NE 68046-2887
(402) 593-2267
Fax (402) 593-4403
Civil records are available by mail. mail or fax. A release is required. No search fee. $.75 feefor first copy, $.25 each additional copy. $1.00 for certification. Search information required: name, date of birth, years to search. Specify plaintiff or defendant.

Misdemeanor records
Sarpy County Court
Criminal Records Division
1210 Golden Gate
Papillion, NE 68046
(402) 593-2257
Misdemeanor records are available by mail. A release is required. No search fee. $.25 fee per copy, $1.00 fee for certification, prepaid. Search information required: name, date of birth, years to search.

Civil records
Sarpy County Court
1210 Golden Gate
Papillion, NE 68046
(402) 593-2257
Civil records are available by mail. A release is required. No search fee. $.25 fee per copy, $1.00 fee for certification, prepaid. Search information required: name, date of birth, years to search. Specify plaintiff or defendant.

Saunders County

Clerk of the District Court
Saunders County
Wahoo, NE 68066
(402) 443-8113
Felony and misdemeanor records are not available by mail or phone. See Nebraska state repository for additional information.

Civil records are available in person only. See Nebraska state repository for additional information.

Scotts Bluff County

Felony records
Clerk of the District Court, Criminal Records
Scotts Bluff County Courthouse
PO Box 47
Gering, NE 69341-0047
(308) 436-6641
Felony records are available by mail. No release necessary. No search fee. $.25 fee per copy. $1.00 for certification. Search information required: name, years to search, SASE.

Civil records
Clerk of the District Court
Scotts Bluff County Courthouse
PO Box 47
Gering, NE 69341-0047
(308) 436-6641
Civil records are available by mail. No release necessary. No search fee. $.25 fee per copy. $1.00 for certification. Search information required: name, date of birth, years to search, SASE. Specify plaintiff or defendant.

Misdemeanor records
Scotts Bluff County Court
Courthouse
1725 10th
Gering, NE 69341
(308) 436-6648
Misdemeanor records are available by mail. A release is required. No search fee. $.25 fee per copy. $1.00 for certification. Search information required: name, date of birth.

Civil records
Scotts Bluff County Court
Courthouse
1725 10th
Gering, NE 69341
(308) 436-6648
Civil records are available by mail. A release is required. No search fee. $.25 fee per copy. $1.00 for certification. Search information required: name, date of birth, years to search. Specify plaintiff or defendant.

Seward County

Felony records
Clerk of the District Court, Criminal Records
PO Box 36
Seward, NE 68434
(402) 643-4895
Felony records are available in person only. See Nebraska state repository for additional information.

Civil records
Clerk of the District Court
PO Box 36
Seward, NE 68434
(402) 643-4895
Civil records are available in person only. See Nebraska state repository for additional information.

Misdemeanor records
Seward County Court
PO Box 37
Seward, NE 68434
(402) 643-3341
Misdemeanor records are available in person only. See Nebraska state repository for additional information.

Civil records
Seward County Court
PO Box 37
Seward, NE 68434
(402) 643-3341
Civil records are available in person only. See Nebraska state repository for additional information.

Sheridan County

Felony records
Clerk of the District Court, Criminal Records
PO Box 581
Rushville, NE 69360
(308) 327-2123
Felony records are available by mail. A release is required. No search fee. $.15 fee per copy. $1.00 for certification. Search information required: name, years to search.

Civil records
Clerk of the District Court
PO Box 581
Rushville, NE 69360
(308) 327-2123
Civil records are available by mail. A release is required. No search fee. $.15 fee per copy. $1.00 for certification. Search information required: name, date of birth, years to search. Specify plaintiff or defendant.

Misdemeanor records
Sheridan County Court
PO Box 430
Rushville, NE 69360
(308) 327-2692
Misdemeanor records are available by mail. No release necessary. No search fee. $.25 fee per copy. $1.00 for certification. Search information required: name, date of birth, years to search.

Civil records are available by mail. No release necessary. No search fee. $.25 fee per copy. $1.00 for certification. Search information required: name, date of birth, years to search. Specify plaintiff or defendant.

Sherman County

Clerk Magistrate
PO Box 55
Loup City, NE 68853
(308) 745-1510
Felony and misdemeanor records are available by mail. No release necessary. No search fee. $.25 fee per copy. $1.00 for certification. Search information required: name, date of birth, sex, race.

Civil records are available by mail. No release necessary. No search fee. $.25 fee per copy. $1.00 for certification. Search information required: name, date of birth, years to search. Specify plaintiff or defendant.

Sioux County

Felony records
Clerk of the District Court, Criminal Records
PO Box 158
Harrison, NE 69346
(308) 668-2443
Felony records are available by mail. No release necessary. No search fee. No search fee. $.50 fee per copy. $1.00 for certification. Search information required: name, SSN, date of birth, sex, race, previous address, SASE.

Civil records
Clerk of the District Court
PO Box 158
Harrison, NE 69346
(308) 668-2443
Civil records are available by mail. No release necessary. No search fee. $.50 fee per copy. $1.00 for certification. Search information required: name, date of birth, years to search, SASE. Specify plaintiff or defendant.

Misdemeanor records
Sioux County Court
PO Box 477
Harrison, NE 69346
(308) 668-2475
Misdemeanor records are available by mail. No release necessary. No search fee. $.50 fee per copy. $1.00 for certification. Search information required: name, date of birth, offense (if available), years to search, address, offense.

Civil records
Sioux County Court
PO Box 477
Harrison, NE 69346
(308) 668-2475
Civil records are available by mail. No release necessary. No search fee. $.50 fee per copy. $1.00 for certification. Search information required: name, date of birth, years to search. Specify plaintiff or defendant.

Stanton County

Felony records
Clerk of the District Court, Criminal Records
PO Box 347
Stanton, NE 68779
(402) 439-2222
Fax (402) 439-2229
Felony records are available by mail or phone. No release necessary. No search fee. $.25 fee per copy. $1.50 for certification. Search information required: name, date of birth.

Civil records
Clerk of the District Court
PO Box 347
Stanton, NE 68779
(402) 439-2222
Fax (402) 439-2229
Civil records are available by mail or phone. No release necessary. No search fee. $.25 fee per copy. $1.50 for certification. Search information required: name, date of birth, years to search. Specify plaintiff or defendant.

Misdemeanor records
Stanton County Court
Courthouse
PO Box 536
Stanton, NE 68779
(402) 439-2221
Misdemeanor records are available by mail. A release is required. No search fee. $.25 fee per copy. $1.00 for certification. Search information required: name, date of birth.

Civil records
Stanton County Court
Courthouse
PO Box 536
Stanton, NE 68779
(402) 439-2221
Civil records are available by mail. A release is required. No search fee. $.25 fee per copy. $1.00 for certification. Search information required: name, date of birth, years to search. Specify plaintiff or defendant.

Thayer County

Felony records
Clerk of the District Court, Criminal Records
PO Box 297
Hebron, NE 68370
(402) 768-6116
Felony records are available by mail or phone. No release necessary. No search fee. $.25 fee per copy. $1.00 for certification. Search information required: name.

Civil records
Clerk of the District Court
PO Box 297
Hebron, NE 68370
(402) 768-6116
Civil records are available by mail or phone. No release necessary. No search fee. $.25 fee per copy. $1.00 for certification. Search information required: name, date of birth, years to search. Specify plaintiff or defendant.

Misdemeanor records
Thayer County Court
PO Box 94
Hebron, NE 68370
(402) 768-6325
Misdemeanor records are available by mail or phone. A release is required. No search fee. $.25 fee per copy. $1.00 for certification. Search information required: name, date of birth, years to search.

Civil records
Thayer County Court
PO Box 94
Hebron, NE 68370
(402) 768-6325
Civil records are available by mail. A release is required. No search fee. $.25 fee per copy. $1.00 for certification. Search information required: name, date of birth, years to search. Specify plaintiff or defendant.

Thomas County

Felony records
Clerk of the District Court, Criminal Records
PO Box 226
Thedford, NE 69166
(308) 645-2261
Felony records are available by mail. No release necessary. No search fee. $.25 fee per copy. $4.00 for certification. Search information required: name, SSN, date of birth, years to search, SASE.

Civil records
Clerk of the District Court
PO Box 226
Thedford, NE 69166
(308) 645-2261
Civil records are available by mail. No release necessary. No search fee. $.25 fee per copy. $4.00 for certification. Search information required: name, date of birth, years to search, SASE. Specify plaintiff or defendant.

Misdemeanor records
Thomas County Court
PO Box 233
Thedford, NE 69166
(308) 645-2266
Misdemeanor records are available by mail only. A release is required. $3.00 search fee. $.25 fee per copy. $4.00 for certification. Search information required: name, years to search, date of birth.

Civil records
Thomas County Court
PO Box 233
Thedford, NE 69166
(308) 645-2266
Civil records are available by mail. A release is required. $3.00 search fee. $.25 fee per copy. $4.00 for certification. Search information required: name, years to search, date of birth. Specify plaintiff or defendant.

Thurston County

Felony records
Clerk of the District Court, Criminal Records
PO Box 218
Pender, NE 68047
(402) 385-3318
Felony records are available in person only. See Nebraska state repository for additional information.

Civil records
Clerk of the District Court
PO Box 218
Pender, NE 68047
(402) 385-3318
Civil records are available in person only. See Nebraska state repository for additional information.

Misdemeanor records
Thurston County Court
Pender, NE 68047
(402) 385-3136
Misdemeanor records are available in person only. See Nebraska state repository for additional information.

Civil records
Thurston County Court
Pender, NE 68047
(402) 385-3136
Civil records are available in person only. See Nebraska state repository for additional information.

Valley County

Felony records
Clerk of the District Court, Criminal Records
125 S. 15th St.
Ord, NE 68862
(308) 728-3700
Felony records are available by mail or phone. No release necessary. No search fee. $.10 fee per copy. $1.00 for certification. Search information required: name, years to search, SASE.

Civil records
Clerk of the District Court
125 S. 15th St.
Ord, NE 68862
(308) 728-3700
Civil records are available by mail or phone. No release necessary. No search fee. $.10 fee per copy. $1.00 for certification. Search information required: name, date of birth, years to search, SASE. Specify plaintiff or defendant.

Misdemeanor records
Valley County Court
125 S. 15th St.
Ord, NE 68862
(308) 728-3831
Misdemeanor records are available by mail or phone. No release necessary. No search fee. $.25 fee per copy. $1.00 for certification. Search information required: name.

Civil records
Valley County Court
125 S. 15th St.
Ord, NE 68862
(308) 728-3831
Civil records are available by mail. No release necessary. No search fee. $.25 fee per copy. $1.00 for certification. Search information required: name, date of birth, years to search. Specify plaintiff or defendant.

Washington County

Felony records
Clerk of District Court
PO Box 431
Blair, NE 68008
(402) 426-6899
Records are not available by mail or phone. See Nebraska state repository for additional information.

Civil records
Clerk of District Court
PO Box 431
Blair, NE 68008
(402) 426-6899
Civil records are available in person only. See Nebraska state repository for additional information.

Misdemeanor records
Washington County Court
PO Box 615
Blair, NE 68008
(402) 426-6833
Misdemeanor records are available for physical inspection at the above office. No phone or mail searches.

Civil records
Washington County Court
PO Box 615
Blair, NE 68008
(402) 426-6833
Civil records are available in person only. See Nebraska state repository for additional information.

Wayne County

Felony records
Clerk of the District Court, Criminal Records
510 Pearl St.
Wayne, NE 68787
(402) 375-2260
Felony records are available by mail or phone. No release necessary. No search fee. $.25 fee per copy. $1.00 for certification. Search information required: name, SSN, date of birth, sex, race, SASE.

Civil records
Clerk of the District Court
510 Pearl St.
Wayne, NE 68787
(402) 375-2260
Civil records are available by mail or phone. No release necessary. No search fee. $.25 fee per copy. $1.00 for certification. Search information required: name, date of birth, years to search, SASE. Specify plaintiff or defendant.

Misdemeanor records
Wayne County Court
510 Pearl St.
Wayne, NE 68787
(402) 375-1622
Misdemeanor records are available by mail. No release necessary. No search fee. $.25 fee per copy. $1.00 for certification. Search information required: name, date of birth, years to search, type of offense, SASE.

Civil records
Wayne County Court
510 Pearl St.
Wayne, NE 68787
(402) 375-1622
Civil records are available by mail. No release necessary. No search fee. $.25 fee per copy. $1.00 for certification. Search information required: name, date of birth, years to search, SASE. Specify plaintiff or defendant.

Webster County

Felony records
Clerk of the District Court, Criminal Records
Courthouse
Red Cloud, NE 68970
(402) 746-2716
Felony records are available by mail or phone. No release necessary. No search fee. $1.00 fee per copy. $1.50 for certification. Search information required: name, years to search.

Civil records
Clerk of the District Court
Courthouse
Red Cloud, NE 68970
(402) 746-2716
Civil records are available by mail. No release necessary. No search fee. $1.00 fee per copy. $1.50 for certification. Search information required: name, date of birth, years to search. Specify plaintiff or defendant.

Misdemeanor records
Webster County Court
621 North Cedar
Red Cloud, NE 68970
(402) 746-2777
Misdemeanor records are available by mail only. Release required. No search fee. $1.00 fee per copy. $1.50 for certification. Search information required: name, years to search.

Civil records
Webster County Court
621 North Cedar
Red Cloud, NE 68970
(402) 746-2777
Civil records are available by mail. No release necessary. No search fee. $1.00 fee per copy. $1.50 for certification. Search information required: name, date of birth, years to search. Specify plaintiff or defendant.

Wheeler County

Felony records
Wheeler County Courthouse
Bartlett, NE 68622
(308) 654-3235
Felony records are not available by mail or phone. See Nebraska state repository for additional information.

Civil records
Wheeler County Courthouse
Bartlett, NE 68622
(308) 654-3235
Civil records are available by mail. No release necessary. No search fee. $.25 fee per copy. $1.50 for certification. Search information required: name, date of birth, years to search. Specify plaintiff or defendant.

Misdemeanor records
Wheeler County Courthouse
PO Box 127
Bartlett, NE 68622
(308) 654-3376
Misdemeanor records are available by mail or phone. No release necessary. No search fee. $.25 fee per copy. $1.50 for certification. Search information required: name, date of birth.

Civil records
Wheeler County Courthouse
PO Box 127
Bartlett, NE 68622
(308) 654-3376
Civil records are available by mail. No release necessary. No search fee. $.25 fee per copy. $1.50 for certification. Search information required: name, date of birth, years to search. Specify plaintiff or defendant.

York County

Felony records
Clerk of the District Court
Courthouse
York, NE 68467
(402) 362-4038
Felony records are available by mail. No release necessary. No search fee. $.25 fee per copy. $1.00 for certification. Search information required: name, date of birth.

Civil records
Clerk of the District Court
Courthouse
York, NE 68467
(402) 362-4038
Civil records are available by mail. No release necessary. No search fee. $.25 fee per copy. $1.00 for certification. Search information required: name, date of birth, years to search. Specify plaintiff or defendant.

Misdemeanor records
York County Court
PO Box 588
York, NE 68467
(402) 362-4925
Misdemeanor records are available in person only.

Civil records
York County Court
PO Box 588
York, NE 68467
(402) 362-4925
Civil records are available in person only. See Nebraska state repository for additional information.

City-County Cross Reference

Adams *Gage*
Ainsworth *Brown*
Albion *Boone*
Alda *Hall*
Alexandria *Thayer*
Allen *Dixon*
Alliance *Box Butte*
Alma *Harlan*
Alvo *Cass*
Amelia *Holt*
Amherst *Buffalo*
Angora *Morrill*
Anselmo *Custer*
Ansley *Custer*
Arapahoe *Furnas*
Arcadia *Valley*
Archer *Merrick*
Arlington *Washington*
Arnold *Custer*
Arthur *Arthur*
Ashby *Grant*
Ashland *Saunders*

Ashton *Sherman*
Atkinson *Holt*
Atlanta *Phelps*
Auburn *Nemaha*
Aurora *Hamilton*
Avoca *Cass*
Axtell *Kearney*
Ayr *Adams*
Bancroft *Cuming*
Barneston *Gage*
Bartlett *Wheeler*
Bartley *Red Willow*
Bassett *Rock*
Battle Creek *Madison*
Bayard *Morrill*
Beatrice *Gage*
Beaver City *Furnas*
Beaver Crossing *Seward*
Bee *Seward*
Beemer *Cuming*
Belden *Cedar*
Belgrade *Nance*

Bellevue *Sarpy*
Bellwood *Butler*
Belvidere *Thayer*
Benedict *York*
Benkelman *Dundy*
Bennet *Lancaster*
Bennington *Douglas*
Bertrand *Phelps*
Berwyn *Custer*
Big Springs *Deuel*
Bingham *Sheridan*
Bladen *Webster*
Blair *Washington*
Bloomfield *Knox*
Bloomington *Franklin*
Blue Hill *Webster*
Blue Springs *Gage*
Boelus *Howard*
Boone *Boone*
Boys Town *Douglas*
Bradshaw *York*
Brady *Lincoln*

Brainard *Butler*
Brewster *Blaine*
Bridgeport *Morrill*
Bristow *Boyd*
Broadwater *Morrill*
Brock *Nemaha*
Broken Bow *Custer*
Brownlee *Cherry*
Brownville *Nemaha*
Brule *Keith*
Bruning *Thayer*
Bruno *Butler*
Brunswick *Antelope*
Burchard *Pawnee*
Burr *Otoe*
Burwell *Garfield*
Bushnell *Kimball*
Butte *Boyd*
Byron *Thayer*
Cairo *Hall*
Callaway *Custer*
Cambridge *Furnas*

Campbell *Franklin*
Carleton *Thayer*
Carroll *Wayne*
Cedar Bluffs *Saunders*
Cedar Creek *Cass*
Cedar Rapids *Boone*
Center *Knox*
Central City *Merrick*
Ceresco *Saunders*
Chadron *Dawes*
Chambers *Holt*
Champion *Chase*
Chapman *Merrick*
Chappell *Deuel*
Chester *Thayer*
Clarks *Merrick*
Clarkson *Colfax*
Clatonia *Gage*
Clay Center *Clay*
Clearwater *Antelope*
Cody *Cherry*
Coleridge *Cedar*
Colon *Saunders*
Columbus *Platte*
Comstock *Custer*
Concord *Dixon*
Cook *Johnson*
Cordova *Seward*
Cornlea *Platte*
Cortland *Gage*
Cotesfield *Howard*
Cozad *Dawson*
Crab Orchard *Johnson*
Craig *Burt*
Crawford *Dawes*
Creighton *Knox*
Creston *Platte*
Crete *Saline*
Crofton *Knox*
Crookston *Cherry*
Culbertson *Hitchcock*
Curtis *Frontier*
Dakota City *Dakota*
Dalton *Cheyenne*
Danbury *Red Willow*
Dannebrog *Howard*
Davenport *Thayer*
Davey *Lancaster*
David City *Butler*
Dawson *Richardson*
Daykin *Jefferson*
Decatur *Burt*
Denton *Lancaster*
Deshler *Thayer*
Deweese *Clay*
DeWitt *Saline*
Diller *Jefferson*
Dix *Kimball*
Dixon *Dixon*
Dodge *Dodge*
Doniphan *Hall*
Dorchester *Saline*
Douglas *Otoe*
Du Bois *Pawnee*
Dunbar *Otoe*
Duncan *Platte*
Dunning *Blaine*
Dwight *Butler*
Eagle *Cass*
Eddyville *Dawson*
Edgar *Clay*
Edison *Furnas*
Elba *Howard*
Elgin *Antelope*
Elk Creek *Johnson*

Elkhorn *Douglas*
Ellsworth *Sheridan*
Elm Creek *Buffalo*
Elmwood *Cass*
Elsie *Perkins*
Elsmere *Cherry*
Elwood *Gosper*
Emerson *Dakota*
Emmet *Holt*
Enders *Chase*
Endicott *Jefferson*
Ericson *Wheeler*
Eustis *Frontier*
Ewing *Holt*
Exeter *Fillmore*
Fairbury *Jefferson*
Fairfield *Clay*
Fairmont *Fillmore*
Falls City *Richardson*
Farnam *Dawson*
Farwell *Howard*
Filley *Gage*
Firth *Lancaster*
Fordyce *Cedar*
Fort Calhoun *Washington*
Foster *Pierce*
Franklin *Franklin*
Fremont *Dodge*
Friend *Saline*
Fullerton *Nance*
Funk *Phelps*
Garland *Seward*
Geneva *Fillmore*
Genoa *Nance*
Gering *Scotts Bluff*
Gibbon *Buffalo*
Giltner *Hamilton*
Glenvil *Clay*
Goehner *Seward*
Gordon *Sheridan*
Gothenburg *Dawson*
Grafton *Fillmore*
Grand Island *Hall*
Grant *Perkins*
Greeley *Greeley*
Greenwood *Cass*
Gresham *York*
Gretna *Sarpy*
Guide Rock *Webster*
Gurley *Cheyenne*
Haigler *Dundy*
Hallam *Lancaster*
Halsey *Thomas*
Hamlet *Hayes*
Hampton *Hamilton*
Hardy *Nuckolls*
Harrisburg *Banner*
Harrison *Sioux*
Hartington *Cedar*
Harvard *Clay*
Hastings *Adams*
Hayes Center *Hayes*
Hay Springs *Sheridan*
Hazard *Sherman*
Heartwell *Kearney*
Hebron *Thayer*
Hemingford *Box Butte*
Henderson *York*
Herman *Washington*
Hershey *Lincoln*
Hickman *Lancaster*
Hildreth *Franklin*
Holbrook *Furnas*
Holdrege *Phelps*
Holstein *Adams*

Homer *Dakota*
Hooper *Dodge*
Hordville *Hamilton*
Hoskins *Wayne*
Howells *Colfax*
Hubbard *Dakota*
Hubbell *Thayer*
Humboldt *Richardson*
Humphrey *Platte*
Huntley *Harlan*
Hyannis *Grant*
Imperial *Chase*
Inavale *Webster*
Indianola *Red Willow*
Inman *Holt*
Irvington *Douglas*
Ithaca *Saunders*
Jackson *Dakota*
Jansen *Jefferson*
Johnson *Nemaha*
Johnstown *Brown*
Julian *Nemaha*
Juniata *Adams*
Kearney *Buffalo*
Kenesaw *Adams*
Kennard *Washington*
Keystone *Keith*
Kilgore *Cherry*
Kimball *Kimball*
La Vista *Sarpy*
Lakeside *Sheridan*
Lamar *Chase*
Laurel *Cedar*
Lawrence *Nuckolls*
Lebanon *Red Willow*
Leigh *Colfax*
Lemoyne *Keith*
Lewellen *Garden*
Lewiston *Pawnee*
Lexington *Dawson*
Liberty *Gage*
Lincoln *Lancaster*
Lindsay *Platte*
Linwood *Butler*
Lisco *Garden*
Litchfield *Sherman*
Lodgepole *Cheyenne*
Long Pine *Brown*
Loomis *Phelps*
Lorton *Otoe*
Louisville *Cass*
Loup City *Sherman*
Lyman *Scotts Bluff*
Lynch *Boyd*
Lyons *Burt*
McCook *Red Willow*
McCool Junction *York*
McLean *Pierce*
Macy *Thurston*
Madison *Madison*
Madrid *Perkins*
Magnet *Cedar*
Malcolm *Lancaster*
Malmo *Saunders*
Manley *Cass*
Marquette *Hamilton*
Marsland *Dawes*
Martell *Lancaster*
Maskell *Dixon*
Mason City *Custer*
Max *Dundy*
Maxwell *Lincoln*
Maywood *Frontier*
Mead *Saunders*
Meadow Grove *Madison*

Melbeta *Scotts Bluff*
Memphis *Saunders*
Merna *Custer*
Merriman *Cherry*
Milford *Seward*
Miller *Buffalo*
Milligan *Fillmore*
Mills *Keya Paha*
Minatare *Scotts Bluff*
Minden *Kearney*
Mitchell *Scotts Bluff*
Monroe *Platte*
Moorefield *Frontier*
Morrill *Scotts Bluff*
Morse Bluff *Saunders*
Mullen *Hooker*
Murdock *Cass*
Murray *Cass*
Naper *Boyd*
Naponee *Franklin*
Nebraska City *Otoe*
Nehawka *Cass*
Neligh *Antelope*
Nelson *Nuckolls*
Nemaha *Nemaha*
Nenzel *Cherry*
Newcastle *Dixon*
Newman Grove *Madison*
Newport *Rock*
Nickerson *Dodge*
Niobrara *Knox*
Norfolk *Madison*
North Bend *Dodge*
North Loup *Valley*
North Platte *Lincoln*
Oak *Nuckolls*
Oakdale *Antelope*
Oakland *Burt*
Obert *Cedar*
Oconto *Custer*
Octavia *Butler*
Odell *Gage*
Odessa *Buffalo*
Ogallala *Keith*
Ohiowa *Fillmore*
Omaha *Douglas*
O'Neill *Holt*
Orchard *Antelope*
Ord *Valley*
Orleans *Harlan*
Osceola *Polk*
Oshkosh *Garden*
Osmond *Pierce*
Otoe *Otoe*
Overton *Dawson*
Oxford *Furnas*
Page *Holt*
Palisade *Hitchcock*
Palmer *Merrick*
Palmyra *Otoe*
Panama *Lancaster*
Papillion *Sarpy*
Parks *Dundy*
Pawnee City *Pawnee*
Paxton *Keith*
Pender *Thurston*
Peru *Nemaha*
Petersburg *Boone*
Phillips *Hamilton*
Pickrell *Gage*
Pierce *Pierce*
Pilger *Stanton*
Plainview *Pierce*
Platte Center *Platte*
Plattsmouth *Cass*

Pleasant Dale *Seward*
Pleasanton *Buffalo*
Plymouth *Jefferson*
Polk *Polk*
Ponca *Dixon*
Potter *Cheyenne*
Prague *Saunders*
Primrose *Boone*
Prosser *Adams*
Purdum *Blaine*
Ragan *Harlan*
Ralston *Douglas*
Randolph *Cedar*
Ravenna *Buffalo*
Raymond *Lancaster*
Red Cloud *Webster*
Republican City *Harlan*
Reynolds *Jefferson*
Richfield *Sarpy*
Richland *Colfax*
Rising City *Butler*
Riverdale *Buffalo*
Riverton *Franklin*
Roca *Lancaster*
Rockville *Sherman*
Rogers *Colfax*
Rosalie *Thurston*
Roseland *Adams*
Royal *Antelope*
Rulo *Richardson*
Rushville *Sheridan*
Ruskin *Nuckolls*
Saint Edward *Boone*
Saint Helena *Cedar*
Saint Libory *Howard*
Saint Mary *Johnson*
Saint Paul *Howard*
Salem *Richardson*
Sargent *Custer*
Schuyler *Colfax*
Scotia *Greeley*
Scottsbluff *Scotts Bluff*
Scribner *Dodge*
Seneca *Thomas*
Seward *Seward*
Shelby *Polk*
Shelton *Buffalo*
Shickley *Fillmore*
Shubert *Richardson*
Sidney *Cheyenne*
Silver Creek *Merrick*
Snyder *Dodge*
South Bend *Cass*
South Sioux City *Dakota*
Spalding *Greeley*
Sparks *Cherry*
Spencer *Boyd*
Sprague *Lancaster*
Springfield *Sarpy*
Springview *Keya Paha*
Stamford *Harlan*
Stanton *Stanton*
Staplehurst *Seward*
Stapleton *Logan*
Steele City *Jefferson*
Steinauer *Pawnee*
Stella *Richardson*
Sterling *Johnson*
Stockville *Frontier*
Strang *Fillmore*
Stratton *Hitchcock*
Stromsburg *Polk*
Stuart *Holt*
Sumner *Dawson*
Superior *Nuckolls*

Surprise *Butler*
Sutherland *Lincoln*
Sutton *Clay*
Swanton *Saline*
Syracuse *Otoe*
Table Rock *Pawnee*
Talmage *Otoe*
Taylor *Loup*
Tecumseh *Johnson*
Tekamah *Burt*
Terrytown *Scotts Bluff*
Thedford *Thomas*
Thurston *Thurston*
Tilden *Madison*
Tobias *Saline*
Trenton *Hitchcock*
Trumbull *Clay*
Tryon *McPherson*
Uehling *Dodge*
Ulysses *Butler*
Unadilla *Otoe*
Union *Cass*
Upland *Franklin*
Utica *Seward*
Valentine *Cherry*
Valley *Douglas*
Valparaiso *Saunders*
Venango *Perkins*
Verdel *Knox*
Verdigre *Knox*
Verdon *Richardson*
Waco *York*
Wahoo *Saunders*
Wakefield *Dixon*
Wallace *Lincoln*
Walthill *Thurston*
Walton *Lancaster*
Washington *Washington*
Waterbury *Dixon*
Waterloo *Douglas*
Wauneta *Chase*
Wausa *Knox*
Waverly *Lancaster*
Wayne *Wayne*
Weeping Water *Cass*
Weissert *Custer*
Wellfleet *Lincoln*
Western *Saline*
Westerville *Custer*
Weston *Saunders*
West Point *Cuming*
Whiteclay *Sheridan*
Whitman *Grant*
Whitney *Dawes*
Wilber *Saline*
Wilcox *Kearney*
Willow Island *Dawson*
Wilsonville *Furnas*
Winnebago *Thurston*
Winnetoon *Knox*
Winside *Wayne*
Winslow *Dodge*
Wisner *Cuming*
Wolbach *Greeley*
Wood Lake *Cherry*
Wood River *Hall*
Wymore *Gage*
Wynot *Cedar*
York *York*
Yutan *Saunders*

Nevada

Note that Nevada is the only state that does not currently have a central repository for criminal history information. All seventeen (17) of the state's counties reported that they make conviction data available for employment screening purposes by phone and/or mail. A handful of the counties allow requests to be made by fax. Civil records for $5,000 and more are filed in District court.

For more information or for offices not listed, contact the state's information hot line at (702) 885-5000.

Driving Records

Department of Motor Vehicles & Public Safety
Records Section
555 Wright Way
Carson City, NV 89711-0250
(702) 687-5505
Driving records are available by mail. $5.00 fee per request. Turnaround time is 24 hours. Written request must include job applicant's full name, date of birth and license number. Request must also specifically state the request is for a "driving record" and for what reason. Make check payable to Department of Motor Vehicles & Public Safety.

Worker's Compensation Records

State Industrial Insurance
Record Search
515 East Musser St.
Carson City, NV 89714
(702) 687-3480
Worker's compensation records are available by mail only. Request must include subject's full name, date of birth, SSN and signed release authorizing access. There is no fee.

Vital Statistics

Vital Statistics
505 East King Street, Room 102
Carson City, NV 89710
(702) 885-4480
Birth records are available for $11.00. Death records are available for $8.00 each. State office has records since July 1911. For earlier records, write to County Recorder in county where event occurred. Make check or money order payable to Vital Statistics. Marriage records are available at county level, County Recorder's Office, in county where marriage license purchased. Divorce records are available at county level, County Clerk's office, in county where divorce granted.

Department of Education

Teacher Certification Division
2100 West King
State Education Department
Carlson City, NV 89710
(702) 687-3115
Field of certification, effective date and expiration date are available by mail or phone. Include name and SSN.

Medical Licensing

State Board of Medical Examiners
PO Box 7238
Reno, NV 89510
(702) 329-2559
Fax (702) 688-2321
Licencing information is available for MDs and PAs by mail or phone. $10.00 fee.

Nevada State Board of Nursing
1281 Terminal Way, Suite 116
Reno, NV 89502
(702) 786-2778
Will confirm license by phone. No fee. Include name, SSN or license number.

Bar Association

State Bar Association of Nevada
295 Halcomb Ave., Suite 2
Reno, NV 89502
(702) 329-4100
Will confirm licenses by phone. No fee. Include name.

Accountancy Board

Nevada State Board of Accountancy
1 East Liberty Street, Suite 311
Reno, NV 89501
(702) 786-0231
Will confirm licenses by phone. No fee. Include name.

Securities Commission

Department of State
Securities Division
1771 Flamingo Road, Suite 212B
Las Vegas, NV 89158
(702) 486-6440
Will confirm licenses by phone. No fee. Include name and SSN.

Secretary of State

Corporation Division
Capitol Complex
Carson City, NV 89710
(702) 687-5105
Service agent and address, date incorporated, standing with tax commission, trade names are available by mail or phone. No fee. Contact the above office for additional information.

Criminal Records

State Repository

Nevada does not currently have a centralized data base of criminal history information. See individual counties listed below.

Carson City County

Felony records
Court Clerk
198 N Carson Street
Carson City, NV 89701
(702) 887-2082
Felony records are available by mail. No release necessary. $1.00 fee for each year searched. Make check payable to Court Clerk. Search information required: name, years to search.

Civil records
Court Clerk
198 N Carson Street
Carson City, NV 89701
(702) 887-2082
Civil records are available by mail. No release necessary. $1.00 search fee per year. $1.00 fee per copy. $2.00 for certification. Search information required: name, date of birth, years to search. Specify plaintiff or defendant.

Misdemeanor records
Court Clerk
Carson City Justice Court
320 N. Carson Street
Carson City, NV 89703
(702) 887-2121
Misdemeanor records are available by mail. A release is required. $1.00 fee per year searched, prepaid. Make company check payable to Carson City. Search information required: name, years to search.

Civil records
Court Clerk
Carson City Justice Court
320 N. Carson Street
Carson City, NV 89703
(702) 887-2121
Civil records from 1985 forward are available by mail. No release necessary. $2.00 search fee per year. $1.00 fee per copy. $2.00 for certification. Search information required: name, date of birth, years to search. Specify plaintiff or defendant.

Churchill County

Felony records
District Court Clerk, Criminal Records
73 N. Maine St.
Fallon, NV 89406
(702) 423-6080 Extension 3
Felony records are available by mail. No release necessary. $1.00 fee per year searched. Search information required: name, years to search.

Civil records
District Court Clerk
73 N. Maine St.
Fallon, NV 89406
(702) 423-6080 Extension 3
Civil records are available by mail. No release necessary. $1.00 search fee per year. $1.00 fee per copy. $2.00 for certification. Search information required: name, date of birth, years to search. Specify plaintiff or defendant.

Misdemeanor records
Justice Court
73 N. Maine St.
Fallon, NV 89406
(702) 423-2845
Misdemeanor records are available by mail or phone. No release necessary. $1.00 fee per person per year, prepaid. Make company check payable to Fallon Justice Court. Search information required: name, date of birth, SSN. Request type of records to be checked.

Civil records
Justice Court
73 N. Maine St.
Fallon, NV 89406
(702) 423-2845
Civil records are available by mail. No release necessary. $1.00 search fee per year. $.25 fee per copy. $2.00 for certification. Search information required: name, date of birth, SSN, years to search. Specify plaintiff or defendant.

Clark County

Felony records
County Clerk's Office, Certification
200 S. 3rd Street
Las Vegas, NV 89155
(702) 455-3156
Felony records are available by mail. No release necessary. $1.00 fee for each year searched. Company checks only, payable to County Clerk. Search information required: name, years to search, SASE.

Civil records
County Clerk's Office
200 S. 3rd Street
Las Vegas, NV 89155
(702) 455-4411
Civil records are available by mail. No release necessary. $1.00 search fee per year. $1.00 fee per copy. $2.00 for certification. Search information required: name, date of birth, years to search. Specify plaintiff or defendant.

Douglas County

Court Clerk, Criminal Records
PO Box 218
Minden, NV 89423
(702) 782-9820
Felony records are available by mail or phone. No release necessary. No search fee. $1.00 fee per copy. $2.00 for certification. Search information required: name, years to search, case number if known.

Civil records are available by mail or phone. No release necessary. No search fee. $1.00 fee per copy. $2.00 for certification. Search information required: name, date of birth, years to search. Specify plaintiff or defendant.

Elko County

Felony records
Elko County Clerk, Criminal Records
Room 204
Elko County Courthouse
Elko, NV 89801
(702) 738-3044
Fax (702) 753-8535
Felony and misdemeanor records are available by mail, fax or phone. No release necessary. $1.00 search fee per year. $.25 fee per copy. $2.00 for certification. Search information required: name, years to search.

Civil records
Elko County Clerk
Room 204
Elko County Courthouse
Elko, NV 89801
(702) 738-3044
Fax (702) 753-8535
Civil records are available by mail, fax or phone. No release necessary. $1.00 search fee per year. $.25 fee per copy. $2.00 for certification. Search information required: name, date of birth, years to search. Specify plaintiff or defendant.

Misdemeanor records
Justice Court
Elko County Justice Court
Box 176
Elko, NV 89803
(702) 738-8404
Misdemeanor records are available by mail or phone. No release necessary. $1.00 search fee per year. $.25 fee per copy. $2.00 for certification. Search information required: name, date of birth, years to search.

Civil records
Elko County Clerk
Room 204
Elko County Courthouse
Elko, NV 89801
(702) 738-8404
Civil records are available by mail or phone. No release necessary. $1.00 search fee per year. $.25 fee per copy. $2.00 for certification. Search information required: name, date of birth, years to search. Specify plaintiff or defendant.

Esmeralda County

Court Clerk
PO Box 547
Goldfield, NV 89013
(702) 485-6367
Fax (702) 485-3524
Felony records are available by mail. No release necessary. No search fee. $1.00 fee per copy. $2.00 for certification. Search information required: name, date of birth, years to search, SASE.

Civil records are available by mail. No release necessary. No search fee. $1.00 fee per copy. $2.00 for certification. Search information required: name, date of birth, years to search. Specify plaintiff or defendant.

Eureka County

Eureka Court Clerk, Criminal Records
PO Box 677
Eureka, NV 89316
(702) 237-5262
Felony records are available by mail. No release necessary. $1.00 search fee for each year searched. $1.00 fee per copy. $2.00 for certification. Make check payable to Eureka County Court Clerk. Search information required: name, years to search.

Civil records are available by mail. No release necessary. $1.00 search fee. $1.00 fee per copy. $2.00 for certification. Search information required: name, date of birth, years to search. Specify plaintiff or defendant.

Humboldt County

Felony records
Humbolt County Clerk, Criminal Records
50 W. 5th Street
PO Box 352
Winnemucca, NV 89445
(702) 623-6343
Felony records are available by mail. No release necessary. $1.00 fee for each year searched. Make check payable to County Clerk. Search information required: name, years to search.

Civil records
Humbolt County Clerk
50 W. 5th Street
PO Box 352
Winnemucca, NV 89445
(702) 623-6343
Civil records are available by mail. No release necessary. $1.00 search fee. $1.00 fee per copy. $2.00 for certification. Search information required: name, date of birth, years to search. Specify plaintiff or defendant.

Misdemeanor records
Humboldt County Justice Court
PO Box 1218
Winnemucca, NV 89446
(702) 623-6377
Misdemeanor records are available by mail. No release necessary. $1.00 fee per person per year. Make company check payable to Justice Court. Search information required: name, date of birth, SSN, type of records to be checked.

Civil records
Humboldt County Justice Court
PO Box 1218
Winnemucca, NV 89446
(702) 623-6377
Civil records are available by mail. No release necessary. $1.00 search fee per year. $.25 fee per copy. $2.00 for certification. Search information required: name, date of birth, years to search. Specify plaintiff or defendant.

Lander County

Lander County Clerk, Criminal Records
315 South Humboldt
Battle Mountain, NV 89820
(702) 635-5738
Fax (702) 635-0604
Felony and misdemeanor records are available by mail, phone or fax. No release necessary. No search fee. Search information required: name, years to search.

Civil records are available by mail. No release necessary. $1.00 search fee per year. $1.00 fee per copy. $2.00 for certification. Search information required: name, date of birth, years to search. Specify plaintiff or defendant.

Lincoln County

County Clerk, Criminal Records
PO Box 90
Pioche, NV 89043
(702) 962-5390
Fax (702)962-5497
Felony records are available by mail or fax. A release is required. $1.00 fee per year searched. Company checks only, payable to County Clerk. Search information required: name, SSN, years to search.

Civil records are available by mail. No release necessary. $1.00 search fee per year. $1.00 fee per copy. $2.00 for certification. Search information required: name, date of birth, years to search. Specify plaintiff or defendant.

Lyon County

County Clerk, Criminal Records
PO Box 816
Yerington, NV 89447
(702) 463-3341 Extension 203
Felony records are available by mail. No release necessary. No search fee. $2.00 for certification. Search information required: name, years to search.

Civil records are available by mail. No release necessary. $1.00 search fee per year. $1.00 fee per copy. $2.00 for certification. Search information required: name, date of birth, years to search, SASE. Specify plaintiff or defendant.

Mineral County

Mineral County Clerk, Criminal Records
PO Box 1450
Hawthorne, NV 89415
(702) 945-2446
Fax (702) 945-5484
Felony records are available by mail, fax or phone. No release necessary. $1.00 fee for each year searched, prepaid. Make check payable to County Clerk. Search information required: name, years to search.

Civil records are available by mail, fax or phone. No release necessary. $1.00 search fee per year searched. $1.00 fee per copy. $2.00 for certification. Search information required: name, date of birth, years to search. Specify plaintiff or defendant.

Nye County

County Clerk, Criminal Records
PO Box 1031
Tonopah, NV 89049
(702) 482-8130
Felony records are available by mail or phone. No release necessary. $1.00 search fee per year searched. $1.00 fee per copy. $2.00 for certification. Search information required: name, years to search.

Civil records are available by mail or phone. No release necessary. $1.00 search fee per year searched. $1.00 fee per copy. $2.00 for certification. Search information required: name, date of birth, years to search. Specify plaintiff or defendant.

Pershing County

Felony records
County Clerk, Criminal Records
PO Box 820
Lovelock, NV 89419
(702) 273-2208
Felony records are available by mail or phone. No release necessary. $1.00 fee for each year searched. Certified check only, payable to County Clerk. Search information required: name, years to search.

Civil records
County Clerk
PO Box 820
Lovelock, NV 89419
(702) 273-2208
Civil records are available by mail or phone. No release necessary. $1.00 search fee per year searched. $1.00 fee per copy. $2.00 for certification. Search information required: name, date of birth, years to search. Specify plaintiff or defendant.

Misdemeanor records
Pershing County Magistrate Court
PO Box 8
Lovelock, NV 89419
(702) 273-2753
Misdemeanor records are available by mail or phone. No release necessary. No search fee. Search information required: name, date of birth, SSN.

Civil records are available by mail. No release necessary. $1.00 search fee per year. $.25 fee per copy. $2.00 for certification. Search information required: name, date of birth, years to search. Specify plaintiff or defendant.

Storey County

County Clerk, Criminal Records
PO Drawer D
Virginia City, NV 89440
(702) 847-0959
Felony and misdemeanor records are available by mail. No release necessary. $1.00 search fee per year. $1.00 fee per copy. $2.00 for certification. Search information required: name, SSN, date of birth, years to search.

Civil records are available by mail. No release necessary. $1.00 search fee per year. $1.00 fee per copy. $2.00 for certification. Search information required: name, date of birth, years to search. Specify plaintiff or defendant.

Washoe County

Washoe County Clerk, Criminal Records
PO Box 11130
Reno, NV 89520
(702) 328-3110
Felony records are available by mail or by phone to obtain case number. Notarized release required.$1.00 search fee per year. $1.00 fee per copy. $2.00 for certification. Make check payable to Washoe County Clerk. Search information required: name, years to search, SASE.

Civil records are available by mail. No release necessary. $1.00 search fee per year. $1.00 fee per copy. $2.00 for certification. Search information required: name, date of birth, years to search, SASE. Specify plaintiff or defendant.

White Pine County

White Pine County Clerk, Criminal Records
PO Box 659
Ely, NV 89301
(702) 289-2341
Fax (702) 289-8842
Felony records are available by mail. No release necessary. $5.00 fee. Search information required: name, date of birth, years to search.

Civil records are available by mail or phone. No release necessary. $.50 search fee per year. $5.00 for certification. Search information required: name, date of birth, years to search. Specify plaintiff or defendant.

City-County Cross Reference

Alamo *Lincoln*
Amargosa Valley *Nye*
Austin *Lander*
Baker *White Pine*
Battle Mountain *Lander*
Beatty *Nye*
Blue Diamond *Clark*
Boulder City *Clark*
Bunkerville *Clark*
Caliente *Lincoln*
Carlin *Elko*
Carson City *Carson City*
Crystal Bay *Washoe*
Dayton *Lyon*
Deeth *Elko*
Denio *Humboldt*
Dyer *Esmeralda*
Elko *Elko*
Ely *White Pine*
Empire *Washoe*
Eureka *Eureka*
Fallon *Churchill*
Fernley *Lyon*
Gabbs *Nye*
Gardnerville *Douglas*
Genoa *Douglas*
Gerlach *Washoe*
Glenbrook *Douglas*
Golconda *Humboldt*
Goldfield *Esmeralda*
Halleck *Elko*
Hawthorne *Mineral*
Henderson *Clark*
Hiko *Lincoln*
Imlay *Pershing*
Indian Springs *Clark*
Jackpot *Elko*
Jarbidge *Elko*
Jean *Clark*
Las Vegas *Clark*
Logandale *Clark*
Lovelock *Pershing*
Lund *White Pine*
Luning *Mineral*
McDermitt *Humboldt*
McGill *White Pine*
Manhattan *Nye*
Mason *Lyon*
Mercury *Nye*
Mesquite *Clark*
Mina *Mineral*
Minden *Douglas*
Moapa *Clark*
Montello *Elko*
Mountain City *Elko*
Nixon *Washoe*
North Las Vegas *Clark*
Orovada *Humboldt*
Overton *Clark*
Owyhee *Elko*
Pahrump *Nye*
Panaca *Lincoln*
Paradise Valley *Humboldt*
Pioche *Lincoln*
Reno *Washoe*
Round Mountain *Nye*
Ruth *White Pine*
Schurz *Mineral*
Searchlight *Clark*
Silver City *Lyon*
Silverpeak *Esmeralda*
Silver Springs *Lyon*

Smith *Lyon*
Sparks *Washoe*
Tonopah *Nye*
Tuscarora *Elko*
Valmy *Humboldt*
Verdi *Washoe*
Virginia City *Storey*
Walker Lake *Mineral*
Wadsworth *Washoe*
Weed Heights *Lyon*
Wellington *Lyon*
Wells *Elko*
Wendover *Elko*
Winnemucca *Humboldt*
Yerington *Lyon*
Zephyr Cove *Douglas*

New Hampshire

Worker's compensation claim histories are available in New Hampshire for employment screening purposes at no charge.

The New Hampshire State Police serves as the state's central repository for criminal records. The State Police now releases criminal history information. All ten (10) of the state's counties make conviction data available for employment screening purposes. For civil court records $10,000 and more, contact Superior court at each county level.

For more information or for offices not listed, contact the state's information hot line at (603) 271-1110.

Driving Records

Director of Motor Vehicles
Records
10 Hazen Drive
Concord, NH 03305
(603) 271-2322
Driving records are available by mail. $7.00 fee per request. Turnaround time is 2 days. Written request must include applicant's full name and date of birth. Make check payable to State of New Hampshire.

Worker's Compensation Records

New Hampshire Department of Labor
Worker's Compensation Division
95 Pleasant Street
Concord, NH 03301
(603) 271-3174
Fax (603) 271-6149
Worker's compensation records are available by mail only. Written request must include the applicant's complete name, SSN and date of birth. Also include date of injury, if known. There is no fee. A signed release is required.

Vital Statistics

Bureau of Vital Records
6 Hazen Drive
Concord, NH 03301-6527
(603) 271-4650
Birth and death records are available for $10.00 each. State office has some records since 1640. Copies of records may be obtained from State office or from City or Town Clerk in place where event occurred. An employer can obtain records with a written release. Make certified check or money order payable to Treasurer of State of New Hampshire.

Marriage records are available for $10.00. Include name, spouse's name, marriage date, and either location where married or year married. Turnaround time is 3-4 weeks. Divorce records are available at county level. Include name, divorce date, and spouse's name. Turnaround time is 3-4 weeks.

Department of Education

Department of Education
Bureau of Teacher Certification
101 Pleasant Street
Concord, NH 03301
(603) 271-2407
Fax (603) 271-1953
Field of certification, effective date, expiration date are available by mail or phone. Include name, SSN.

Medical Licensing

Board of Registration and Medicine
Health and Welfare
6 Hazen Drive
Concord, NH 03301
(603) 271-1203
Licensing information is available for MDs and DOs by mail or phone. No search fee for phone inquiries. $5.00 for mail requests. Make check payable to Treasurer State of New Hampshire. For other licenses not mentioned, contact the above office.

New Hampshire Board of Nursing
Health and Welfare Building
78 Regional Drive
Concord, NH 03301-6527
(603) 271-2323
Will confirm license by phone. No fee. Include name, license number, if available.

Bar Association

New Hampshire State Bar Association
New Hampshire Supreme Court
Noble Drive
Concord, NH 03301
(603) 271-2646
Will confirm licenses by phone. No fee. Include name.

Accountancy Board

New Hampshire Board of Accounting
57 Regional Drive
Concord, NH 03301
(603) 271-3286
Will confirm licenses by phone. No fee. Include name.

Securities Commision

Department of State, Business Services and Regulation Division
Bureau of Securities
State House, Room 204
107 North Main Street
Concord, NH 03301-4989
(603) 271-1463
Will confirm licenses by phone. No fee. Include name and SSN.

Secretary of State

Secretary of State
Corporation Division
107 North Main Street
Room 204 – State House
Concord, NH 03301
(603) 271-3246
Service agent and address, date incorporated, corporate status, trade names available by mail or phone. No fee. Contact the above office for additional information.

Criminal Records

State Repository

State Police Headquarters
Attention: Criminal Records
10 Hazen Drive
Concord, NH 03305
(603) 271-2535 or 271-2538
Criminal records held are available by mail only. An original notorized waiver is required. $10.00 fee per request. Contact the above office for the Criminal History Record Information form.

Belknap County

Felony records
Belknap County Clerk of Superior Court, Criminal Records
64 Court Street
Laconia, NH 03246
(603) 524-3570
Felony records are available by mail. No release necessary. No search fee. Search information required: name, date of birth, years to search.

Civil records
Belknap County Clerk of Superior Court, Criminal Records
64 Court Street
Laconia, NH 03246
(603) 524-3570
Civil records are available by mail or phone. No release necessary. No search fee. $.50 fee per copy. $5.00 for first page certified, $.50 each additional page. Search information required: name, date of birth, years to search. Specify plaintiff or defendant.

Misdemeanor records
Laconia District Court
PO Box 1010
Laconia, NH 03246
(603) 524-4128
Misdemeanor records are available in person only. See New Hampshire state repository for additional information.

Civil records
Laconia District Court
PO Box 1010
Laconia, NH 03246
(603) 524-4128
Civil records are available by mail or phone. No release necessary. No search fee. $1.50 fee per copy. $1.50 for first certification. Search information required: name, date of birth, years to search. Specify plaintiff or defendant.

Carroll County

Clerk of Superior Court, Criminal Records
PO Box 157
Ossipee, NH 03864
(603) 539-2201
Felony and misdemeanor records are available by mail. No release necessary. No search fee. Search information required: name, date of birth, years to search.

Civil records are available by mail. No release necessary. No search fee. $.50 fee per copy. $5.00 for certification. Search information required: name, date of birth, years to search. Specify plaintiff or defendant.

Cheshire County

Cheshire County Superior Court, Criminal Records
PO Box 444
Keene, NH 03431
(603) 352-6902
Felony and misdemeanor records are available by mail or phone. No release necessary. No search fee. Search information required: name, date of birth, years to search.

Civil records are available by mail or phone. No release necessary. No search fee. $1.00 fee per copy. $2.50 for certification. Search information required: name, date of birth, years to search. Specify plaintiff or defendant.

Coos County

Clerk of Superior Court, Criminal Records
PO Box 309
Lancaster, NH 03584
(603) 788-4900
Felony and misdemeanor records are available by mail or phone. No release necessary. No search fee. Search information required: name, date of birth.

Civil records are available by mail. No release necessary. No search fee. $.50 fee per copy. $5.00 for certification. Search information required: name, date of birth, years to search. Specify plaintiff or defendant.

Grafton County

Clerk of Superior Court, Criminal Records
PO Box 207
Woodsville, NH 03785
(603) 787-6961
Felony records are available by mail. No release necessary. No search fee. $.50 fee per copy. $5.00 for certification. Search information required: name, date of birth.

Civil records are available by mail. No release necessary. No search fee. $.50 fee per copy. $5.00 for certification. Search information required: name, date of birth, years to search. Specify plaintiff or defendant.

Hillsborough County

Clerk of Superior Court, Criminal Records
300 Chestnut Street
Manchester, NH 03101
(603) 424-9951
Felony and misdemeanor records are available by mail. No release necessary. $5.00 search fee. Company checks only, payable to Clerk of Superior Court. Search information required: name, date of birth, years to search, SASE.

Civil records are available by mail. No release necessary. $5.00 search fee. $.50 fee per copy. $2.50 for certification. Search information required: name, date of birth, years to search. Specify plaintiff or defendant.

Merrimack County

Clerk of Superior Court, Criminal Records
PO Box 1417
Concord, NH 03301
(603) 225-5501
Felony and misdemeanor records are available by mail or phone. No release necessary. No search fee. $.50 fee per copy. $5.00 for certification. Search information required: name, date of birth, years to search.

Civil records are available by mail. No release necessary. No search fee. $.50 fee per copy. $5.00 for certification. Search information required: name, date of birth, years to search. Specify plaintiff or defendant.

Rockingham County

Superior Court, Criminal Records
1 Hampton Road
Exeter, NH 03833
(603) 772-3714
Felony and misdemeanor records are available by mail. No release necessary. $1.00 search fee. $.50 fee per copy. $5.00 for certification. Search information required: name, date of birth.

Civil records are available by mail. No release necessary. $1.00 search fee. $.50 fee per copy. $5.00 for certification. Search information required: name, date of birth, years to search. Specify plaintiff or defendant.

Strafford County

Clerk of Superior Court, Criminal Records
PO Box 799
Dover, NH 03820
(603) 742-3065
Felony and misdemeanor records are available by mail or phone. No release necessary. No search fee. Search information required: name, date of birth, years to search.

Civil records are available by mail or phone. No release necessary. No search fee. $.50 fee per copy. $5.00 for certification. Search information required: name, date of birth, years to search. Specify plaintiff or defendant.

Sullivan County

Superior Court
Clerk's Office
PO Box 45
Newport, NH 03773
(603) 863-3450
Felony and misdemeanor records are available by mail. A signed release is required. No search fee. $.50 fee per copy. $5.00 for certification. Search information required: name, date of birth, years to search.

Civil records are available by mail. No release necessary. No search fee. $.50 fee per copy. $5.00 for certification. Search information required: name, date of birth, years to search. Specify plaintiff or defendant.

City-County Cross Reference

Acworth *Sullivan*
Alstead *Cheshire*
Alton *Belknap*
Alton Bay *Belknap*
Amherst *Hillsborough*
Andover *Merrimack*
Antrim *Hillsborough*
Ashland *Grafton*
Ashuelot *Cheshire*
Atkinson *Rockingham*
Auburn *Rockingham*
Barnstead *Belknap*
Barrington *Strafford*
Bartlett *Carroll*
Bath *Grafton*
Bedford *Hillsborough*
Belmont *Belknap*
Bennington *Hillsborough*
Berlin *Coos*
Bethlehem *Grafton*
Bradford *Merrimack*
Bristol *Grafton*
Brookline *Hillsborough*
Campton *Grafton*
Canaan *Grafton*
Candia *Rockingham*
Canobie Lake *Rockingham*
Canterbury *Merrimack*
Center Barnstead *Belknap*
Center Conway *Carroll*
Center Harbor *Belknap*
Center Ossipee *Carroll*
Center Sandwich *Carroll*
Center Strafford *Strafford*
Charlestown *Sullivan*
Chester *Rockingham*
Chesterfield *Cheshire*
Chocorua *Carroll*
Claremont *Sullivan*
Colebrook *Coos*
Concord *Merrimack*
Contoocook *Merrimack*
Conway *Carroll*
Cornish Flat *Sullivan*
Danbury *Merrimack*
Danville *Rockingham*
Deerfield *Rockingham*
Derry *Rockingham*
Dover *Strafford*
Drewsville *Cheshire*
Dublin *Cheshire*
Durham *Strafford*
East Andover *Merrimack*
East Candia *Rockingham*
East Derry *Rockingham*
East Hampstead
  Rockingham
East Hebron *Grafton*
East Kingston *Rockingham*
East Lempster *Sullivan*
East Sullivan *Cheshire*
East Swanzey *Cheshire*
East Wakefield *Carroll*
Elkins *Merrimack*
Enfield *Grafton*
Enfield Center *Grafton*
Epping *Rockingham*
Epsom *Merrimack*
Errol *Coos*
Etna *Grafton*
Exeter *Rockingham*
Farmington *Strafford*

Fitzwilliam *Cheshire*
Francestown *Hillsborough*
Franconia *Grafton*
Franklin *Merrimack*
Freedom *Carroll*
Fremont *Rockingham*
Georges Mills *Sullivan*
Gilmanton *Belknap*
Gilmanton Iron Works
  Belknap
Gilsum *Cheshire*
Glen *Carroll*
Glencliff *Grafton*
Goffstown *Hillsborough*
Gorham *Coos*
Goshen *Sullivan*
Grafton *Grafton*
Grantham *Sullivan*
Greenfield *Hillsborough*
Greenland *Rockingham*
Greenville *Hillsborough*
Groveton *Coos*
Guild *Sullivan*
Hampstead *Rockingham*
Hampton *Rockingham*
Hampton Beach
  Rockingham
Hampton Falls
  Rockingham
Hancock *Hillsborough*
Hanover *Grafton*
Harrisville *Cheshire*
Haverhill *Grafton*
Hebron *Grafton*
Henniker *Merrimack*
Hill *Merrimack*
Hillsboro *Hillsborough*
Hinsdale *Cheshire*
Holderness *Grafton*
Hollis *Hillsborough*
Hooksett *Merrimack*
Hudson *Hillsborough*
Intervale *Carroll*
Jackson *Carroll*
Jaffrey *Cheshire*
Jefferson *Coos*
Kearsarge *Carroll*
Keene *Cheshire*
Kingston *Rockingham*
Laconia *Belknap*
Lancaster *Coos*
Lebanon *Grafton*
Lempster *Sullivan*
Lincoln *Grafton*
Lisbon *Grafton*
Little Boars Head
  Rockingham
Littleton *Grafton*
Lochmere *Belknap*
Londonderry *Rockingham*
Lyme *Grafton*
Lyme Center *Grafton*
Lyndeborough
  Hillsborough
Madison *Carroll*
Manchester *Hillsborough*
Marlborough *Cheshire*
Marlow *Cheshire*
Meadows *Coos*
Melvin Village *Carroll*
Meredith *Belknap*
Meriden *Sullivan*

Merrimack *Hillsborough*
Milan *Coos*
Milford *Hillsborough*
Milton *Strafford*
Milton Mills *Strafford*
Mirror Lake *Carroll*
Monroe *Grafton*
Mont Vernon *Hillsborough*
Moultonboro *Carroll*
Mount Sunapee *Merrimack*
Munsonville *Cheshire*
Nashua *Hillsborough*
New Boston *Hillsborough*
Newbury *Merrimack*
New Castle *Rockingham*
New Durham *Strafford*
Newfields *Rockingham*
New Hampton *Belknap*
New Ipswich *Hillsborough*
New London *Merrimack*
Newmarket *Rockingham*
Newport *Sullivan*
Newton *Rockingham*
Newton Junction
  Rockingham
North Branch *Hillsborough*
North Conway *Carroll*
North Hampton
  Rockingham
North Haverhill *Grafton*
North Salem *Rockingham*
North Sandwich *Carroll*
North Stratford *Coos*
North Sutton *Merrimack*
Northfield *Merrimack*
North Walpole *Cheshire*
Northwood *Rockingham*
North Woodstock *Grafton*
Nottingham *Rockingham*
Orford *Grafton*
Ossipee *Carroll*
Pelham *Hillsborough*
Peterborough *Hillsborough*
Piermont *Grafton*
Pike *Grafton*
Pittsburg *Coos*
Pittsfield *Merrimack*
Plainfield *Sullivan*
Plaistow *Rockingham*
Plymouth *Grafton*
Portsmouth *Rockingham*
Potter Place *Merrimack*
Raymond *Rockingham*
Rindge *Cheshire*
Rochester *Strafford*
Rollinsford *Strafford*
Rumney *Grafton*
Rye *Rockingham*
Rye Beach *Rockingham*
Salem *Rockingham*
Salisbury *Merrimack*
Sanbornton *Belknap*
Sanbornville *Carroll*
Sandown *Rockingham*
Sandwich *Carroll*
Seabrook *Rockingham*
Silver Lake *Carroll*
Somersworth *Strafford*
South Danville
  Rockingham
South Effingham *Carroll*
South Hooksett *Merrimack*

South Newbury *Merrimack*
South Sutton *Merrimack*
South Tamworth *Carroll*
Spofford *Cheshire*
Stoddard *Cheshire*
Strafford *Strafford*
Stratham *Rockingham*
Sunapee *Sullivan*
Suncook *Merrimack*
Tamworth *Carroll*
Temple *Hillsborough*
Tilton *Belknap*
Troy *Cheshire*
Twin Mountain *Coos*
Union *Carroll*
Walpole *Cheshire*
Warner *Merrimack*
Warren *Grafton*
Washington *Sullivan*
Waterville Valley *Grafton*
Weare *Hillsborough*
Wentworth *Grafton*
West Chesterfield *Cheshire*
Westmoreland *Cheshire*
West Nottingham
  Rockingham
West Ossipee *Carroll*
West Peterborough
  Hillsborough
West Springfield *Sullivan*
West Stewartstown *Coos*
West Swanzey *Cheshire*
Westport *Cheshire*
Westville *Rockingham*
Whitefield *Coos*
Wilmot Flat *Merrimack*
Wilton *Hillsborough*
Winchester *Cheshire*
Windham *Rockingham*
Winnisquam *Belknap*
Wolfeboro *Carroll*
Wolfeboro Falls *Carroll*
Wonalancet *Carroll*
Woodsville *Grafton*

New Jersey

All twenty one (21) of New Jersey's counties make criminal records available for employment screening purposes, seventeen (17) by mail and/or phone. Superior court holds civil court records for $5,000 and more.

New Jersey worker's compensation claim histories are available to employers free of charge.

For more information or for offices not listed, contact the state's information hot line at (609) 292-2121.

Driving Records

Motor Vehicle Services
Bureau of Information Management
Abstract Section
CN-142
Trenton, NJ 08666-0142
(609) 292-4557
Driving records are available by mail. $5.00 fee for certified record. $4.00 fee for non-certified record. Turnaround time is 7 to 10 days. Written request must include job applicant's full name, date of birth, eye color, license number. Make check payable to Division of Motor Vehicles.

Worker's Compensation Records

State of New Jersey
Department of Labor
Division of Worker's Compensation,
CN-381
Trenton, NJ 08625-0381
(609) 292-2516
Worker's compensation records are available by mail only. Written request must include the job applicant's SSN, complete name and, if available, the claims petition number. There is no search fee. $.50 fee per copy. A signed release is not required.

Vital Statistics

State Department of Health
Bureau of Vital Statistics, CN-370
Trenton, NJ 08625
(609) 292-4087
Birth, marriage, and death records are available for $4.00 each. State office has some records since June 1878. Duplicate records ordered at same time are $2.00 each. If the exact date is unknown, there is an additional fee of $1.00 per year searched. Make certified check or money order payable to Bureau of Vital Records.

Department of Education

Department of Education
Office of Teacher Certification
C.N. 503
Trenton, NJ 08625-0503
(609) 292-2070
Field of certification, effective date, expiration date are available by mail or phone. Include name and SSN.

Medical Licensing

Board of Medical Examiners
28 West State Street
Trenton, NJ 08608
(609) 292-4843
Licensing information for MDs and DOs are available by mail or phone. No fee. For other licenses not mentioned, contact the above office.

New Jersey Board of Nursing
1100 Raymond Blvd., Room 508
Newark, NJ 07102
(201) 648-3647
Will confirm license by phone. No fee. Include name, license number.

Bar Association

New Jersey State Bar Association
Board of Bar Exams
CN 973
Trenton, NJ 08625
(609) 984-7783
Will confirm licenses by phone. No fee. Include name.

Accountancy Board

New Jersey State Board of Accountancy
PO Box 45000
Newark, NJ 07101
(201) 648-3240
Will confirm licenses by phone. No fee. Include name.

Securities Commission

Department of Law and Public Safety
Division of Consumer Affairs
Bureau of Securities
Two Gateway Center, 8th Floor
Newark, NJ 07102
Will confirm licenses by phone. No fee. Include name and SSN.

Secretary of State

Secretary of State
Corporation Division
820 Bear Tavern Road
West Trenton, NJ 08625
(609) 530-6400
Service agent and address, date incorporated, and trade names are available by mail or phone. No fee. Contact the above for additional information.

Criminal Records

State Repository

Division of State Police
Records and I.D. Section
PO Box 7068
West Trenton, NJ 08628-0068
(609) 882-2000
Access to criminal records maintained by central repository is limited to criminal justice and other governmental agencies. Contact the above office or counties listed below for additional information and instructions.

Atlantic County

Criminal Records Department
Room 204
Atlantic County Superior Court
5909 Main Street
Mays Landing, NJ 08330
(609) 625-7000, Extension 5257
Felony records are available by mail or by phone for two names. A release is required. No search fee. Search information required: name, alias, date of birth.

Civil records are available by mail. No release necessary. No search fee. $.75 fee per copy. Search information required: name, date of birth, years to search. Specify plaintiff or defendant.

Bergen County

Bergen County Clerk
Court House, Rm 119
Criminal Dept.
Hackensack, NJ 07601
(201) 646-2105

Felony records are available by mail. $2.00 search fee. No release necessary. Search information required: name, date of birth, SSN, SASE.

Civil records are available by mail or phone. No release necessary. $1.00 search fee. $1.00 fee per copy. $5.00 for certification. Search information required: name, date of birth, years to search. Specify plaintiff or defendant.

Burlington County

Burlington County Clerk, Criminal Records
49 Rancocas Road
Courthouse
Mount Holly, NJ 08060
(609) 265-5186

Felony records are available by mail. No release necessary. $5.00 search fee. Company checks only, payable to Burlington County Clerk. Search information required: name, date of birth, SASE, years to search.

Civil records are available by mail. No release necessary. No search fee. $1.50 fee per copy. $5.00 for certification. Search information required: name, date of birth, years to search. Specify plaintiff or defendant.

Camden County

Camden County Hall of Justice, Criminal Division
Room 150
5th and Mickel Boulevard
Camden, NJ 08103
(609) 757-8448

Felony records are available by mail only. No release necessary. $7.00 fee. Company checks only, payable to Camden County Clerk. Search information required: name, date of birth, years to search, SASE.

Civil records are available by mail. No release necessary. $7.00 search fee. $1.50 fee per copy. $3.00 for certification. Search information required: name, date of birth, years to search, SASE. Specify plaintiff or defendant.

Cape May County

Criminal Case Management
Central Mail Room DN-209B
Cape May Courthouse, NJ 08210
(609) 889-6520
Fax (609) 889-2745

Felony records are available by mail. No release necessary. No search fee. Search information required: name, SSN, date of birth, sex, race, SASE, years to search.

Civil records are available by mail. No release necessary. No search fee. $.75 fee per copy. $5.00 for certification. Search information required: name, date of birth, years to search. Specify plaintiff or defendant.

Cumberland County

Superior Court
Criminal Case Management Office
PO Box 757
Bridgeton, NJ 08302
(609) 451-8000 Extension 479

Felony records are available by mail only. No release necessary. $4.00 search fee. Search information required: name, SSN, date of birth, sex, race, years to search.

Civil records are available by mail. No release necessary. $1.50 search fee. Search information required: name, date of birth, years to search. Specify plaintiff or defendant.

Essex County

Felony records
Criminal Record's Office
Essex County Courts Bldg.
Room 610
Newark, NJ 07102-6681
(201) 621-4862

Felony records are available by mail. No release necessary. No search fee if no record found. Search information required: name, date of birth, SASE, SSN, current address.

Civil records
Essex County Courts Bldg.
Room 610
Newark, NJ 07102-6681
(201) 621-4850

Civil records are available by mail or phone. No release necessary. No search fee. $1.50 fee per copy. $5.00 for certification. Search information required: name, date of birth, years to search. Specify plaintiff or defendant.

Gloucester County

Criminal Case Manager
PO Box 187
Woodbury, NJ 08096
(609) 853-3531

Felony records are available by mail or phone. No release necessary. $4.00 search fee. Search information required: name, SSN, date of birth.

Civil records are available in person only. See New Jersey state repository for additional information.

Hudson County

Hudson County Clerk, Criminal Section
595 Newark Ave.
Jersey City, NJ 07306
(201) 795-6122

Felony records are available in person only. See New Jersey state repository for additional information.

Civil records are available by mail. No release necessary. No search fee. $1.50 fee per copy. $5.00 for certification. Search information required: name, date of birth, years to search. Specify plaintiff or defendant.

Hunterdon County

Hunterdon County Clerk, Criminal Records
71 Main Street
Flemington, NJ 08822
(908) 788-1225

Felony records are available by mail. No release necessary. No search fee. $1.50 fee per copy. $5.00 for certification. Search information required: name, SASE, years to search.

Civil records are available by mail. No release necessary. No search fee. $.50 fee per copy. $5.00 for certification. Search information required: name, date of birth, years to search. Specify plaintiff or defendant.

Mercer County

Mercer County Clerk, Criminal Records
PO Box 8068
Trenton, NJ 08650
(609) 989-6453
Fax (609) 989-6452

Felony records are available by mail. No release necessary. No search fee. $1.50 fee per copy. $3.00 for certification. Search information required: name, SSN, date of birth, sex, race, years to search.

Civil records are available by mail. No release necessary. No search fee. $1.50 fee per copy. $3.00 for first page certified, $1.50 each additional page. Search information required: name, date of birth, years to search. Specify plaintiff or defendant.

Middlesex County

Felony and misdemeanor records
Middlesex County Clerk, Criminal Records
PO Box 1110
New Brunswick, NJ 08903
(908) 745-3488

Felony and misdemeanor records are available by mail. A release is required. $2.00 search fee. $.75 fee per copy. $5.00 for certification. Search information required: name, date of birth, previous address, years to search.

Civil records
Middlesex County Clerk
PO Box 1110
New Brunswick, NJ 08903
(908) 745-3422

Civil records are available by mail. No release necessary. No search fee. $1.50 fee per copy. $5.00 for certification. Search information required: name, date of birth, years to search. Specify plaintiff or defendant.

Monmouth County

Criminal Assignment Clerk
Courthouse
Freehold, NJ 07728
(908) 431-7880

Felony records are available in person only. See New Jersey state repository for additional information.

Civil records are available in person only. See New Jersey state repository for additional information.

Morris County

Criminal/Family Records Management
CN 900
Court Street
Morristown, NJ 07960-0900
(201) 285-6173

Records are available in person only. See New Jersey state repository.

Civil records are available by mail or phone. No release necessary. No search fee. $.75 fee per copy. $5.00 for certification. Search information required: name, date of birth, years to search. Specify plaintiff or defendant.

Ocean County

Criminal Case Processing
Room 220 Justice Complex
PO Box -2191
Toms River, NJ 08754
(908) 929-2009

Felony records are available by mail. No release necessary. $3.00 search fee. Make check payable to Ocean County Clerk. Search information required: name, SSN, date of birth, years to search.

Civil records are available by mail or phone. No release necessary. No search fee. $.25 fee per copy. $1.00 for certification. Search information required: name, date of birth, years to search. Specify plaintiff or defendant.

Passaic County

Criminal Assignment Clerk's Office
Passaic County Courthouse
77 Hamilton Street
Paterson, NJ 07505
(201) 881-4124

Felony records are available for physical inspection on Monday, Wednesday, and Friday between 3-4 pm eastern time only. No mail or phone searches.

Civil records are available in person only. See New Jersey state repository for additional information.

Salem County

Criminal Case Management Office
92 Market Street
PO Box 78
Salem, NJ 08079
(609) 935-7510

Felony records are available by mail. No release necessary. $4.00 search fee. Make check payable to Salem County Clerk. Search information required: name, SSN, date of birth, years to search.

Civil records are available in person only. See New Jersey state repository for additional information.

Somerset County

Somerset County Clerk, Criminal Records
New Courthouse
PO Box 3000
Somerville, NJ 08876
(908) 231-7000 Extension 7215

Felony records are available by mail. No release necessary. $4.00 search fee. Search information required: full name, date of birth, SASE.

Civil records are available by mail. No release necessary. No search fee. $.50 fee per copy. $3.00 for certification. Search information required: name, date of birth, years to search. Specify plaintiff or defendant.

Sussex County

Hall of Records, Criminal Records
4 Park Place
Newton, NJ 07860
(201) 579-0900

Felony and misdemeanor records are available in person only. See New Jersey state repository for additional information.

Civil records are available by mail or phone. No release necessary. No search fee. $.75 fee per copy. $5.00 for certification. Search information required: name, date of birth, years to search. Specify plaintiff or defendant.

Union County

Union County Courthouse
County Clerk's Office
2 Broad Street
Elizabeth, NJ 07207
(201) 527-4960

Felony records are available by mail or phone. No release necessary. $7.00 search-fee. $1.50 fee per copy. $3.00 for certification. Search information required: name, date of birth, SSN.

Civil records are available by mail. No release necessary. $7.00 searchfee. $1.50 fee per copy. $3.00 for certification. Search information required: name, date of birth, years to search. Specify plaintiff or defendant.

Warren County

Warren County Clerk, Criminal Records
Warren County Courthouse
2nd Street
Belvidere, NJ 07823
(201) 475-5361 Extension 202

Felony records are available by mail or phone. No release necessary. $6.00 search fee. Search information required: name, date of birth, SSN.

Civil records are available by mail. No release necessary. $6.00 search fee. Search information required: name, date of birth, years to search. Specify plaintiff or defendant.

City-County Cross Reference

Absecon *Atlantic*
Adelphia *Monmouth*
Allamuchy *Warren*
Allendale *Bergen*
Allenhurst *Monmouth*
Allentown *Monmouth*
Allenwood *Monmouth*
Alloway *Salem*
Almonesson *Gloucester*
Alpha *Warren*
Alpine *Bergen*
Andover *Sussex*
Annandale *Hunterdon*
Asbury *Warren*
Ashland *Camden*
Asbury Park *Monmouth*
Atco *Camden*
Atlantic City *Atlantic*
Atlantic Highlands
  Monmouth
Audobon *Camden*
Audobon Park *Camden*
Augusta *Sussex*

Avalon *Cape May*
Avenel *Middlesex*
Avon By The Sea
  Monmouth
Baptistown *Hunterdon*
Barnegat *Ocean*
Barnegat Light *Ocean*
Barrington *Camden*
Basking Ridge *Somerset*
Bay Head *Ocean*
Bayonne *Hudson*
Bayville *Ocean*
Beach Haven *Ocean*
Beachwood *Ocean*
Bedminster *Somerset*
Belford *Monmouth*
Belle Mead *Somerset*
Belleville *Essex*
Belmar *Monmouth*
Belvidere *Warren*
Bergenfield *Bergen*
Berkeley Heights *Union*
Berlin *Camden*

Bernardsville *Somerset*
Beverly *Burlington*
Birmingham *Burlington*
Blackwood *Camden*
Blairstown *Warren*
Blawenburg *Somerset*
Blenheim *Camden*
Bloomfield *Essex*
Bloomingdale *Passaic*
Bloomsbury *Hunterdon*
Bogota *Bergen*
Boonton *Morris*
Bordentown *Burlington*
Bound Brook *Somerset*
Bradley Beach *Monmouth*
Branchville *Sussex*
Brick *Ocean*
Bridgeport *Gloucester*
Bridgeton *Cumberland*
Bridgewater *Somerset*
Brielle *Monmouth*
Brigantine *Atlantic*
Broadway *Warren*

Brooklawn *Camden*
Brookside *Morris*
Brookwood *Ocean*
Browns Mills *Burlington*
Browntown *Middlesex*
Budd Lake *Morris*
Buena *Atlantic*
Burlington *Burlington*
Butler *Morris*
Buttzville *Warren*
Caldwell *Essex*
Califon *Hunterdon*
Camden *Camden*
Candlewood *Monmouth*
Cape May *Cape May*
Cape May Court House
  Cape May
Cape May Point *Cape May*
Carlstadt *Bergen*
Carneys Point *Salem*
Carteret *Middlesex*
Cedar Brook *Camden*
Cedar Grove *Essex*

Cedar Knolls *Morris*
Cedarville *Cumberland*
Center City *Gloucester*
Changewater *Warren*
Chatham *Morris*
Chatsworth *Burlington*
Cheese Quake *Middlesex*
Cherry Hill *Camden*
Chesilhurst *Camden*
Chester *Morris*
Cinnaminson *Burlington*
Clark *Union*
Clarksboro *Gloucester*
Clarksburg *Monmouth*
Clayton *Gloucester*
Clementon *Camden*
Cliffside Park *Bergen*
Cliffwood *Monmouth*
Clifton *Passaic*
Clinton *Hunterdon*
Closter *Bergen*
Collingswood *Camden*
Cologne *Atlantic*
Colonia *Union*
Colts Neck *Monmouth*
Columbia *Warren*
Columbus *Burlington*
Cookstown *Burlington*
Cranbury *Middlesex*
Cranford *Union*
Creamridge *Monmouth*
Cresskill *Bergen*
Crestwood Village Ocean
Crosswicks *Burlington*
Dayton *Middlesex*
Deal *Monmouth*
Deepwater *Salem*
Deerfield Street
    Cumberland
Delanco *Burlington*
Delaware *Warren*
Delmont *Cumberland*
Delran *Burlington*
Demarest *Bergen*
Dennisville *Cape May*
Denville *Morris*
Deptford *Gloucester*
Dividing Creek
    Cumberland
Dorchester *Cumberland*
Dorothy *Atlantic*
Dover *Morris*
Dumont *Bergen*
Dunellen *Middlesex*
East Brunswick *Middlesex*
East Hanover *Morris*
East Keansburg *Monmouth*
East Newark *Hudson*
East Orange *Essex*
East Rutherford *Bergen*
East Windsor *Mercer*
Eatontown *Monmouth*
Edgewater *Bergen*
Edgewater Park *Burlington*
Edison *Middlesex*
Egg Harbor City *Atlantic*
Eldridge Park *Mercer*
Elizabeth *Union*
Elmer *Salem*
Elmwood Park *Bergen*
Elwood *Atlantic*
Emerson *Bergen*
Englewood *Bergen*
Englewood Cliffs *Bergen*
Englishtown *Monmouth*
Essex Fells *Essex*

Estell Manor *Atlantic*
Ewan *Gloucester*
Fairfield *Essex*
Fair Haven *Monmouth*
Fair Lawn *Bergen*
Fairton *Cumberland*
Fairview *Bergen*
Fanwood *Union*
Far Hills *Somerset*
Farmingdale *Monmouth*
Fellowship *Burlington*
Finderne *Somerset*
Flagtown *Somerset*
Flanders *Morris*
Flemington *Hunterdon*
Florence *Burlington*
Florham Park *Morris*
Folsom *Atlantic*
Fords *Middlesex*
Forked River *Ocean*
Fortescue *Cumberland*
Fort Lee *Bergen*
Franklin *Sussex*
Franklin Lakes *Bergen*
Franklin Park *Somerset*
Franklinville *Gloucester*
Freehold *Monmouth*
Freewood Acres
    Monmouth
Frenchtown *Hunterdon*
Garfield *Bergen*
Garwood *Union*
Gibbsboro *Camden*
Gibbstown *Gloucester*
Gilford Park *Ocean*
Gillette *Morris*
Gladstone *Somerset*
Glassboro *Gloucester*
Glasser *Sussex*
Glendora *Camden*
Glen Gardner *Hunterdon*
Glen Ridge *Essex*
Glen Rock *Bergen*
Glenwood *Sussex*
Gloucester City *Camden*
Goshen *Cape May*
Great Meadows *Warren*
Green Creek *Cape May*
Greendell *Sussex*
Greenfield Village
    Gloucester
Green Village *Morris*
Greenwich *Cumberland*
Grenloch *Gloucester*
Groveville *Mercer*
Guttenberg *Hudson*
Hackensack *Bergen*
Hackettstown *Warren*
Haddonfield *Camden*
Haddon Heights *Camden*
Haddon Hills *Camden*
Hainesport *Burlington*
Haledon *Passaic*
Hamburg *Sussex*
Hamilton Square *Mercer*
Hammonton *Atlantic*
Hampton *Hunterdon*
Hancocks Bridge *Salem*
Harrington Park *Bergen*
Harrison *Hudson*
Harrisonville *Gloucester*
Hasbrouck Heights *Bergen*
Haskell *Passaic*
Haworth *Bergen*
Hawthorne *Passaic*
Hazlet *Monmouth*

Heislerville *Cumberland*
Helmetta *Middlesex*
Hewitt *Passaic*
Hibernia *Morris*
High Bridge *Hunterdon*
Highland Lakes *Sussex*
Highland Park *Middlesex*
Highlands *Monmouth*
Hightstown *Mercer*
Hillsdale *Bergen*
Hillside *Union*
Hilltop
Hoboken *Hudson*
Ho Ho Kus *Bergen*
Holiday City *Ocean*
Holmdel *Monmouth*
Hopatcong *Sussex*
Hope *Warren*
Hopewell *Mercer*
Howell *Monmouth*
Imlaystown *Monmouth*
Ironia *Morris*
Irvington *Essex*
Iselin *Middlesex*
Island Heights *Ocean*
Jackson *Ocean*
Jamesburg *Middlesex*
Jersey City *Hudson*
Jobstown *Burlington*
Johnsonburg *Warren*
Juliustown *Burlington*
Keansburg *Monmouth*
Kearny *Hudson*
Keasbey *Middlesex*
Kendall Park *Middlesex*
Kenilworth *Union*
Kennelon *Morris*
Kenvil *Morris*
Keyport *Monmouth*
Kingston *Somerset*
Kirkwood Voorhees
    Camden
Lafayette *Sussex*
Lake Hiawatha *Morris*
Lake Hopatcong *Morris*
Lakehurst *Ocean*
Lakewood *Ocean*
Lambertville *Hunterdon*
Landing *Morris*
Landisville *Atlantic*
Lanoka Harbor *Ocean*
Laurel Springs *Camden*
Laurence Harbour
    Middlesex
Lawrenceville *Mercer*
Lavallette *Ocean*
Lawnside *Camden*
Layton *Sussex*
Lebanon *Hunterdon*
Ledgewood *Morris*
Leeds Point *Atlantic*
Leesburg *Cumberland*
Leonardo *Monmouth*
Leonia *Bergen*
Liberty Corner *Somerset*
Lincoln Park *Morris*
Lincroft *Monmouth*
Linden *Union*
Lindenwold *Camden*
Linwood *Atlantic*
Little Falls *Passaic*
Little Ferry *Bergen*
Little Silver *Monmouth*
Little York *Hunterdon*
Livingston *Essex*
Lodi *Bergen*

Long Branch *Monmouth*
Long Valley *Morris*
Longport *Atlantic*
Lumberton *Burlington*
Lyndhurst *Bergen*
McAfee *Sussex*
Madison *Morris*
Magnolia *Camden*
Mahwah *Bergen*
Malaga *Gloucester*
Manahawkin *Ocean*
Manasquan *Monmouth*
Mantoloking *Ocean*
Mantua *Gloucester*
Manville *Somerset*
Maple Shade *Burlington*
Maplewood *Essex*
Margate City *Atlantic*
Marlboro *Monmouth*
Marlton *Burlington*
Marmora *Cape May*
Martinsville *Somerset*
Matawan *Monmouth*
Mauricetown *Cumberland*
Mays Landing *Atlantic*
Maywood *Bergen*
Medford *Burlington*
Medford Lakes *Burlington*
Mendham *Morris*
Mercerville *Mercer*
Merchantville *Camden*
Metuchen *Middlesex*
Mickleton *Gloucester*
Middlesex *Middlesex*
Middletown *Monmouth*
Middleville *Sussex*
Midland Park *Bergen*
Milford *Hunterdon*
Millburn *Essex*
Millington *Morris*
Milltown *Middlesex*
Millville *Cumberland*
Milmay *Atlantic*
Mine Hill *Morris*
Minotola *Atlantic*
Mizpah *Atlantic*
Monmouth Beach
    Monmouth
Monmouth Junction
    Middlesex
Monroeville *Salem*
Montclair *Essex*
Montvale *Bergen*
Montville *Morris*
Moonachie *Bergen*
Moorestown *Burlington*
Morganville *Monmouth*
Morris Plains *Morris*
Morristown *Morris*
Mountain Lakes *Morris*
Mountainside *Union*
Mount Arlington *Morris*
Mount Ephraim *Camden*
Mount Freedom *Morris*
Mount Holly *Burlington*
Mount Laurel *Burlington*
Mount Royal *Gloucester*
Mullica Hill *Gloucester*
National Park *Gloucester*
Navesink *Monmouth*
Neptune *Monmouth*
Neptune City *Monmouth*
Neshanic Station *Somerset*
Netcong *Morris*
Newark *Essex*
New Brunswick *Middlesex*

New Egypt *Ocean*
Newfield *Gloucester*
Newfoundland *Passaic*
New Gretna *Burlington*
New Lisbon *Burlington*
New Milford *Bergen*
Newport *Cumberland*
New Providence *Union*
Newton *Sussex*
Newtonville *Atlantic*
New Vernon *Morris*
Norma *Salem*
Normandy Beach *Ocean*
North Arlington *Bergen*
North Bergen *Hudson*
North Branch *Somerset*
North Brunswick *Somerset*
North Caldwell *Essex*
North Cape May *Cape May*
Northfield *Atlantic*
North Haledon *Passaic*
North Plainfield *Somerset*
Northvale *Bergen*
North Wildwood *Cape May*
Norwood *Bergen*
Nutley *Essex*
Oakhurst *Monmouth*
Oakland *Bergen*
Oaklyn *Camden*
Oak Ridge *Passaic*
Oak Valley *Gloucester*
Ocean City *Cape May*
Ocean Gate *Ocean*
Ocean Grove *Monmouth*
Oceanport *Monmouth*
Ocean View *Cape May*
Oceanville *Atlantic*
Ogdensburg *Sussex*
Old Bridge *Middlesex*
Old Tappan *Bergen*
Oldwick *Hunterdon*
Oradell *Bergen*
Orange *Essex*
Oxford *Warren*
Palisades Park *Bergen*
Palmyra *Burlington*
Paramus *Bergen*
Park Ridge *Bergen*
Parkway Pines *Monmouth*
Parlin *Middlesex*
Parsippany *Morris*
Passaic *Passaic*
Paterson *Passaic*
Paulsboro *Gloucester*
Peapack *Somerset*
Pedricktown *Salem*
Pemberton *Burlington*
Pennington *Mercer*
Penns Grove *Salem*
Pennsville *Salem*
Pequannock *Morris*
Perrineville *Monmouth*
Perth Amboy *Middlesex*
Phillipsburg *Warren*
Pine Beach *Ocean*
Pine Brook *Morris*
Pine Hill *Camden*
Piscataway *Middlesex*
Pitman *Gloucester*
Pittstown *Hunterdon*
Plainfield *Union*
Plainsboro *Middlesex*
Pleasantville *Atlantic*

Pluckemin *Somerset*
Point Pleasant *Monmouth*
Point Pleasant Beach
  Ocean
Pomona *Atlantic*
Pompton Lakes *Passaic*
Pompton Plains *Morris*
Port Elizabeth *Cumberland*
Port Monmouth *Monmouth*
Port Murray *Warren*
Port Norris *Cumberland*
Port Reading *Middlesex*
Port Republic *Atlantic*
Pottersville *Somerset*
Princeton *Mercer*
Princeton Junction *Mercer*
Prospect Park *Passaic*
Quakertown *Hunterdon*
Quinton *Salem*
Rahway *Union*
Ramsey *Bergen*
Rancocas *Burlington*
Rancocas Woods
  Burlington
Raritan *Somerset*
Readington *Hunterdon*
Red Bank *Monmouth*
Richland *Atlantic*
Richwood *Gloucester*
Ridgefield *Bergen*
Ridgefield Park *Bergen*
Ridgewood *Bergen*
Ringoes *Hunterdon*
Ringwood *Passaic*
Rio Grande *Cape May*
Riverdale *Morris*
River Edge *Bergen*
River Plaza *Monmouth*
Riverside *Burlington*
Riverton *Burlington*
River Vale *Bergen*
Robertsville *Monmouth*
Rochelle Park *Bergen*
Rockaway *Morris*
Rocky Hill *Somerset*
Roebling *Burlington*
Roosevelt *Monmouth*
Roseland *Essex*
Roselle *Union*
Roselle Park *Union*
Rosemont *Hunterdon*
Rosenhayn *Cumberland*
Rumson *Monmouth*
Runnemede *Camden*
Rutherford *Bergen*
Saddle Brook *Bergen*
Saddle River *Bergen*
Salem *Salem*
Sayreville *Middlesex*
Sayre Woods South
  Middlesex
Schooleys Mountain
  Morris
Scotch Plains *Union*
Sea Bright *Monmouth*
Seabrook *Cumberland*
Sea Girt *Monmouth*
Sea Isle City *Cape May*
Seaside Heights *Ocean*
Seaside Park *Ocean*
Secaucus *Hudson*
Sergeantsville *Hunterdon*
Sewaren *Middlesex*
Sewell *Gloucester*
Shiloh *Cumberland*

Ship Bottom *Ocean*
Short Hills *Essex*
Shrewsbury *Monmouth*
Sicklerville *Camden*
Silverton *Ocean*
Skillman *Somerset*
Slackwood *Mercer*
Somerdale *Camden*
Somerset *Somerset*
Somers Point *Atlantic*
Somerville *Somerset*
South Amboy *Middlesex*
South Belmar *Monmouth*
South Bound Brook
  Somerset
South Dennis *Cape May*
South Hackensack *Bergen*
South Orange *Essex*
South Plainfield *Middlesex*
South River *Middlesex*
South Seaville *Cape May*
South Toms River *Ocean*
Sparta *Sussex*
Spotswood *Middlesex*
Springfield *Union*
Spring Lake *Monmouth*
Spring Lake Heights
  Monmouth
Stanhope *Sussex*
Stanton *Hunterdon*
Stewartsville *Warren*
Stillwater *Sussex*
Stirling *Morris*
Stockholm *Sussex*
Stockton *Hunterdon*
Stone Harbor *Cape May*
Stratford *Camden*
Strathmere *Cape May*
Succasunna *Morris*
Summit *Union*
Surf City *Ocean*
Sussex *Sussex*
Swartswood *Sussex*
Swedesboro *Gloucester*
Mount Tabor *Morris*
Teaneck *Bergen*
Tenafly *Bergen*
Tennent *Monmouth*
Thorofare *Gloucester*
Three Bridges *Hunterdon*
Tinton Falls *Monmouth*
Titusville *Mercer*
Toms River *Ocean*
Towaco *Morris*
Tranquility *Sussex*
Trenton *Mercer*
Tuckahoe *Cape May*
Tuckerton *Ocean*
Twin Rivers *Mercer*
Union *Union*
Union Beach *Monmouth*
Union City *Hudson*
Upper Saddle River *Bergen*
Vauxhall *Union*
Ventnor City *Atlantic*
Vernon *Sussex*
Verona *Essex*
Vienna *Warren*
Victory Gardens *Morris*
Villas *Cape May*
Vincentown *Burlington*
Vineland *Cumberland*
Waldwick *Bergen*
Wallington *Bergen*
Wallpack Center *Sussex*

Wanaque *Passaic*
Waretown *Ocean*
Warren *Somerset*
Washington *Warren*
Watchung *Somerset*
Waterford Works *Camden*
Wayne *Passaic*
Weehawken *Hudson*
Wenonah *Gloucester*
West Berlin *Camden*
West Caldwell *Essex*
West Cape May *Cape May*
West Creek *Ocean*
Westfield *Union*
West Long Branch
  Monmouth
West Milford *Passaic*
Westmont *Camden*
West New York *Hudson*
West Orange *Essex*
West Patterson *Passaic*
Westville *Gloucester*
Westville Grove
  Gloucester
Westwood *Bergen*
Wharton *Morris*
Whippany *Morris*
Whitehouse *Hunterdon*
White House Station
  Hunterdon
Whitesboro *Cape May*
Whitman Square
  Gloucester
Wickatunk *Monmouth*
Wildwood *Cape May*
Wildwood Crest *Cape May*
Williamstown *Gloucester*
Willingboro *Burlington*
Windsor *Mercer*
Winslow *Camden*
Woodbine *Cape May*
Woodbridge *Middlesex*
Woodbury *Gloucester*
Woodbury Heights
  Gloucester
Woodlynne *Camden*
Woodstown *Salem*
Wood-Ridge *Bergen*
Wrightstown *Burlington*
Wyckoff *Bergen*
Yardville *Mercer*

New Mexico

All thirty three (33) New Mexico counties reported that criminal records are available for employment screening purposes. Thirty two (32) counties make their records available by phone or mail, and a few by fax. Civil records for $5,000 and greater are filed in District court.

For more information or for offices not listed, contact the state's information hot line at (505) 827-4011.

Driving Records

Motor Vehicle Division
Driver Services
PO Box 1028
Santa Fe, NM 87504
(505) 827-2234
Fax (505) 827-2267
Driving records are available by mail. $4 fee per request. Turnaround time is 48 hours. Written request must include job applicant's full name, date of birth and social security number; include license number, if available. Make check payable to Motor Vehicle Division.

Worker's Compensation Records

Worker's Compensation Division
Claims Assistance Bureau
1820 Randolph S.E.
PO Box 27125-7198
Albuquerque, NM 87125-7198
(505) 841-6000
Worker's compensation records are available by mail. No search fee. Written request must include subject's full name, SSN and date of injury. $.25 fee per copy. A signed release is not required.

Vital Statistics

Vital Statistics Bureau
1190 Saint Francis Drive
Santa Fe, NM 87504-0968
(505) 827-0121
Fax (505) 827-2338)
Birth records are available for $10.00 each and death records for $5.00 each. State office has records since 1920. Make certified check or money order payable to Vital Statistics Bureau.
Marriage records are available at county level, County Clerk's Office, where married. Divorce records are available at county level, Magistrate Court, where divorce granted.

Department of Education

State Department of Education
Education Bldg.
Licensing Unit
Sante Fe, NM 87561-2786
(505) 827-6587
Fax (505) 827-6696
Field of certification, effective date, expiration date is available by mail or phone. Include name and SSN.

Medical Licensing

Board of Medical Examiners
PO Box 20001
Sante Fe, NM 87504
(505) 827-9933
Licensing information for listing of all MDs in New Mexico is available by mail for $15.00. For other licenses not mentioned, contact the above office. Include name, date of birth, license number and SSN.

New Mexico Board of Nursing
4253 Montgomery NE, Suite 130
Albuquerque, NM 87109
(505) 841-8340
Will confirm license by phone. No fee. Include name, SSN or license number.

Bar Association

State Bar Association of New Mexico
PO Box 25883
Albuquuerque, NM 87125
(505) 824-6132
Will confirm licenses by mail or phone. No fee. Include name.

Accountancy Board

New Mexico State Board of Accountancy
1650 University Blvd. NE
Suite 400A
Albuquuerque, NM 87102
(505) 841-9108
Will confirm licenses by mail or phone. No fee. Include name.

Securities Commission

Regulation and Licensing Department
Securities Division
PO Box 25101
Santa Fe, NM 87504
(505) 827-7140
Will confirm licenses by mail or phone. No fee. Include name and SSN.

Secretary of State

State Corporation Commission
Corporation Department
PO Drawer 1269
Santa Fe, NM 87504-1269
(505) 827-4504
Service agent and address, date incorporated are available by mail or phone. No fee. Contact the above office for additional information.

Criminal Records

State Repository

New Mexico Department of Public Safety
Records Bureau
PO Box 1628
Santa Fe, NM 87504-1628
(505) 827-9181
Felony and misdemeanor records available. Written requests must include subject's name, date of birth, SSN and a signed, notarized release. There is a $5.00 fee.

Bernalillo County

Felony records
District Court Clerk, Criminal Records
PO Box 488
Albuquerque, NM 87103
(505) 841-7425
Felony records are available by mail. No release necessary. No search fee. Search information required: name, SSN, date of birth, years to search, SASE.

Civil records
District Court Clerk
PO Box 488
Albuquerque, NM 87103
(505) 841-7425
Civil records are available by mail. No release necessary. $1.50 search fee. $.35 fee per copy. $1.50 for certification. Make company check or money order payable to Clerk of District Court. Search information required: name, date of birth, years to search. Specify plaintiff or defendant.

Misdemeanor records
Bernalillo County Metropolitan Court
PO Box 133
Albuquerque, NM 87103-0133
(505) 841-8100
Misdemeanor records are available by mail. A release is required. $1.00 fee per copy, $1.50 fee per certification. Search information required: name, date of birth, SSN, reason for request.

Civil records
Bernalillo County Metropolitan Court
PO Box 133
Albuquerque, NM 87103-0133
(505) 841-8100
Civil records are available by mail. No release necessary. No search fee. $.50 fee per copy. $1.50 for certification. Search information required: name, date of birth, years to search. Specify plaintiff or defendant.

Catron County

District Court Clerk, Criminal Records
PO Drawer 1129
Socorro, NM 87801
(505) 835-0050
Felony and misdemeanor records are available by mail or phone. No release necessary. No search fee. Search information required: name, years to search.

Civil records are available by mail or phone. No release necessary. $.35 search fee. $1.50 fee per copy. Search information required: name, date of birth, years to search. Specify plaintiff or defendant.

Chaves County

District Court Clerk, Criminal Records
PO Box 1776
Roswell, NM 88201
(505) 622-2212
Felony and misdemeanor records are available for physical inspection at the District Court Clerk's Office. No phone or mail searches.

Civil records are available by mail. A release is required. No search fee. $.35 fee per copy. $1.50 for certification. Search information required: name, date of birth, years to search. Specify plaintiff or defendant.

Cibola County

District Court Clerk, Criminal Records
PO Box 758
Grants, NM 87020
(505) 287-8831
Felony records are available by mail or phone (since 1981). A release is required. No search fee. $.35 fee per copy $1.50 for certification. Search information required: name, years to search.

Civil records are available by mail. A release is required. No search fee. $.35 fee per copy. $1.50 for certification. Search information required: name, date of birth, years to search. Specify plaintiff or defendant.

Colfax County

Felony records
District Court Clerk, Criminal Records
PO Box 160
Raton, NM 87740
(505) 445-5585
Felony records are available by mail. No release necessary. No search fee. Search information required: name, years to search.

Civil records
District Court Clerk
PO Box 160
Raton, NM 87740
(505) 445-5585
Civil records are available by mail or phone. No release necessary. No search fee. $1.50 fee per copy. $.35 for certification. Search information required: name, date of birth, years to search. Specify plaintiff or defendant.

Misdemeanor records
Colfax County Magistrate Court
PO Box 68
Raton, NM 87740
(505) 445-2220
Misdemeanor records are available by mail. No release necessary. No search fee. $.35 fee per copy. $1.50 for certificaiton. Search information required: name, date of birth, SSN, years to search, SASE.

Civil records
Colfax County Magistrate Court
PO Box 68
Raton, NM 87740
(505) 445-2220
Civil records are available by mail. No release necessary. No search fee. $.50 fee per copy. $.50 for certification. Search information required: name, date of birth, years to search, SASE. Specify plaintiff or defendant.

Curry County

Felony records
District Court Clerk, Criminal Records
2nd Floor
Curry County Courthouse
Clovis, NM 88101
(505) 762-9148
Felony records are available by mail or phone. No release necessary. No search fee. Search information required: name, SSN, date of birth, years to search.

Civil records
District Court Clerk
2nd Floor
Curry County Courthouse
Clovis, NM 88101
(505) 762-9148
Civil records are available by mail. No release necessary. No search fee. $.35 fee per copy. $1.50 for certification. Search information required: name, date of birth, years to search. Specify plaintiff or defendant.

Misdemeanor records
Curry County Magistrate's Court
820 Main St.
Clovis, NM 88101
(505) 762-3766
Misdemeanor records are available by mail or phone. No release necessary. No fee. Search information required: name, date of birth, SSN, years to search.

Civil records
Curry County Magistrate's Court
820 Main St.
Clovis, NM 88101
(505) 762-3766
Civil records are available by mail. No release necessary. No search fee. $.50 fee per copy. $1.50 for certification. Search information required: name, date of birth, years to search. Specify plaintiff or defendant.

De Baca County

District Court Clerk, Criminal Records
Box 910
Ft. Sumner, NM 88119
(505) 355-2896
Felony and misdemeanor records are available by mail or phone. No release necessary. No search fee. Search information required: name.

Civil records are available by mail. No release necessary. No search fee. $.35 fee per copy. $1.50 for certification. Search information required: name, date of birth, years to search. Specify plaintiff or defendant.

Dona Ana County

3rd Judicial District Court, Criminal Records
151 N. Church St.
Las Cruces, NM 88001
(505) 524-6335
Felony records are available by mail or phone. No release necessary. No search fee. Search information required: name, years to search.

Civil records are available by mail or phone. No release necessary. No search fee. $.35 fee per copy. $1.50 for certification. Search information required: name, date of birth, years to search. Specify plaintiff or defendant.

Eddy County

Felony records
District Court Clerk, Criminal Records
PO Box 98
Carlsbad, NM 88220
(505) 885-4740
Fax (505) 887-7095
Felony records are available by mail, fax or phone. No release necessary. No search fee. Search information required: name, date of birth.

Civil records
District Court Clerk
PO Box 98
Carlsbad, NM 88220
(505) 885-4740
Fax (505) 887-7095
Civil records are available by mail, fax or phone. No release necessary. No search fee. $.35 fee per copy. $1.50 for certification. Search information required: name, date of birth, years to search. Specify plaintiff or defendant.

Misdemeanor records
Eddy County Magistrate's Court
302 North Main St.
Carlsbad, NM 88220
(505) 887-7119
Misdemeanor records are available by mail or phone. No release necessary. No search fee. Search information required: name, date of birth, SSN, date of offense.

Civil records
Eddy County Magistrate's Court
302 North Main St.
Carlsbad, NM 88220
(505) 887-7119
Civil records are available by mail or phone. No release necessary. No search fee. $.50 fee per copy. $1.50 for certification. Search information required: name, date of birth, years to search. Specify plaintiff or defendant.

Grant County

Felony records
District Court Clerk, Criminal Records
PO Box 2339
Silver City, NM 88062
(505) 538-3250
Felony records are available by mail or phone. No release necessary. No search fee. Search information required: name, years to search.

Civil records
District Court Clerk
PO Box 2339
Silver City, NM 88062
(505) 538-3250
Civil records are available by mail or phone. No release necessary. No search fee. $.35 fee per copy. $1.50 for certification. Search information required: name, date of birth, years to search. Specify plaintiff or defendant.

Misdemeanor records
Grant County Magistrate's Court
PO Box 1089
Silver City, NM 88062
(505) 538-3811
Misdemeanor records are available by mail. No release necessary. No search fee. Search information required: name, date of birth, SSN.

Civil records
Grant County Magistrate's Court
PO Box 1089
Silver City, NM 88062
(505) 538-3811
Civil records are available by mail. No release necessary. No search fee. $.50 fee per copy. $1.50 for certification. Search information required: name, date of birth, years to search. Specify plaintiff or defendant.

Guadalupe County

Deputy District Court Clerk, Criminal Records
Guadalupe County Courthouse
Santa Rosa, NM 88435
(505) 472-3888
Felony and misdemeanor records are available by mail or phone. No release necessary. No search fee. Search information required: name, SSN, date of birth, sex, race, years to search.

Civil records are available by mail or phone. A release is required No search fee. $.35 fee per copy. $1.50 for certification. Search information required: name, date of birth, years to search. Specify plaintiff or defendant.

Harding County

District Court, Criminal Records
Harding County
Mosquero, NM 87733
(505) 673-2252
Felony and misdemeanor records are available by mail. No release necessary. No search fee. $.35 fee per copy. $1.50 for certification. Search information required: name, years to search.

Civil records are available by mail. No release necessary. No search fee. $.35 fee per copy. $1.50 for certification. Search information required: name, date of birth, years to search. Specify plaintiff or defendant.

Hidalgo County

Felony records
District Court Clerk, Criminal Records
PO Drawer E
Lordsburg, NM 88045
(505) 542-3411
Felony records are available by mail or phone. No release necessary. No search fee. $.35 fee per copy. $1.50 for certification. Search information required: name, date of birth, years to search.

Civil records
District Court Clerk
PO Drawer E
Lordsburg, NM 88045
(505) 542-3411
Civil records are available by mail. No release necessary. No search fee. $.35 fee per copy. $1.50 for certification. Search information required: name, date of birth, years to search. Specify plaintiff or defendant.

Misdemeanor records
Hildago County Magistrate's Court
205 E. Second St.
Lordsburg, NM 88045
(505) 542-3582
Misdemeanor records are available by mail or phone. No release necessary. No search fee. $.50 fee per copy. $1.50 for certification. Search information required: name, date of birth, years to search.

Civil records
Hildago County Magistrate's Court
205 E. Second St.
Lordsburg, NM 88045
(505) 542-3582
Civil records are available by mail. No release necessary. No search fee. $.50 fee per copy. $1.50 for certification. Search information required: name, date of birth, years to search. Specify plaintiff or defendant.

Lea County

District Court Clerk, Criminal Records
Lea County
100 N. Main, Box 6C
Lovington, NM 88260
(505) 396-8571
Felony and misdemeanor records are available by mail or phone. No release necessary. No search fee. Search information required: name, years to search.

Civil records are available by mail or phone. No release necessary. No search fee. $.35 fee per copy. $1.50 for certification. Search information required: name, date of birth, years to search, SASE. Specify plaintiff or defendant.

Lincoln County

Felony records
District Court Clerk, Criminal Records
PO Box 725
Carrizozo, NM 88301
(505) 648-2432
Fax (505) 648-2454
Felony records are available by mail or fax. No release necessary. No search fee. $.50 fee per copy, $1.50 fee per certification. Search information required: name, years to search.

Civil records
District Court Clerk
PO Box 725
Carrizozo, NM 88301
(505) 648-2432
Fax (505) 648-2454
Civil records are available by mail or fax. No release necessary. No search fee. $.35 fee per copy. $1.50 for certification. Search information required: name, date of birth, years to search, SASE. Specify plaintiff or defendant.

Misdemeanor records
Lincoln County Magistrate Court
PO Box 488
Carrizozo, NM 88301
(505) 648-2389
Misdemeanor records are available by mail. No release necessary. No search fee. $.50 fee per copy, $1.50 fee per certification. Search information required: name, date of birth, SSN, offense.

Civil records
Lincoln County Magistrate Court
PO Box 488
Carrizozo, NM 88301
(505) 648-2389
Civil records are available by mail. A release is required. No search fee. $.50 fee per copy. $1.50 for certification. Search information required: name, date of birth, years to search, SASE. Specify plaintiff or defendant.

Los Alamos County

Felony records
District Court Clerk, Criminal Records
PO Box 2268
Santa Fe, NM 87504
(505) 827-5035
Felony records are available by mail or phone. No release necessary. No search fee. $.35 fee per copy. $1.50 for certification. Search information required: name, years to search.

Civil records
District Court Clerk
PO Box 2268
Santa Fe, NM 87504
(505) 827-5035
Civil records are available by mail or phone. No release necessary. No search fee. $.35 fee per copy. $1.50 for certification. Search information required: name, date of birth, years to search. Specify plaintiff or defendant.

Misdemeanor records
Los Alamos County Magistrate's Court
600 Sixth St. #104
Los Alamos, NM 87544
(505) 662-2727
Misdemeanor records are available by mail or phone. No release necessary. No search fee. Search information required: name, date of birth, SSN, offense, date of offense, years to search.

Civil records
Los Alamos County Magistrate's Court
600 Sixth St. #104
Los Alamos, NM 87544
(505) 662-2727
Civil records are available by mail. No release necessary. No search fee. $.505 fee per copy. $1.50 for certification. Search information required: name, date of birth, years to search. Specify plaintiff or defendant.

Luna County

Felony records
District Court Clerk, Criminal Records
Room 40
Luna County
Deming, NM 88030
(505) 546-9611
Felony records are available by mail or phone. No release necessary. No search fee. Search information required: name, date of birth, years to search.

Civil records
District Court Clerk
Room 40
Luna County
Deming, NM 88030
(505) 546-9611
Civil records are available by mail. No release necessary. No search fee. $.35 fee per copy. $1.50 for certification. Search information required: name, date of birth, years to search. Specify plaintiff or defendant.

Misdemeanor records
Luna county Magistrate Court
121 W. Spruce
Deming, NM 88030
(505) 546-9321
Misdemeanor records are available by mail. A release is required. No search fee. Search information required: name, date of birth, SSN, date of offense.

Civil records
Luna County Magistrate Court
121 W. Spruce
Deming, NM 88030
(505) 546-9321
Civil records are available by mail. No release necessary. No search fee. $.50 fee per copy. $1.50 for certification. Search information required: name, date of birth, years to search. Specify plaintiff or defendant.

McKinley County

District Court Clerk, Criminal Records
201 W. Hill, Rm 21
Gallup, NM 87301
(505) 863-6816
Felony records are available by mail. No release necessary. No search fee. Search information required: name.

Civil records are available by mail. No release necessary. No search fee. $.35 fee per copy. $1.50 for certification. Search information required: name, date of birth, years to search. Specify plaintiff or defendant.

Mora County

Criminal Records
PO Box 131
Mora, NM 87732
(505) 387-2448
Felony and misdemeanor records are available by mail or phone. A release is required. No search fee. Search information required: name.

Civil records are available by mail. No release necessary. No search fee. $.50 fee per copy. $1.50 for certification. Search information required: name, date of birth, years to search. Specify plaintiff or defendant.

Otero County

Felony records
District Court Clerk, Criminal Records
Otero County Courthouse
Room 209
Alamogordo, NM 88310
(505) 437-7310
Felony records are available by mail. No release necessary. No search fee. Search information required: name, years to search, SASE.

Civil records
District Court Clerk
Otero County Courthouse
Room 209
Alamogordo, NM 88310
(505) 437-7310
Civil records are available by mail. No release necessary. No search fee. $.35 fee per copy. $1.50 for certification. Search information required: name, date of birth, years to search. Specify plaintiff or defendant.

Misdemeanor records
Magistrate's Court
1106 New York
Alamogordo, NM 88310
(505) 437-9000
Misdemeanor records are available by mail. No release necessary. No search fee. Search information required: name, date of birth, years to search.

Civil records
Magistrate's Court
1106 New York
Alamogordo, NM 88310
(505) 437-9000
Civil records are available by mail. No release necessary. No search fee. $.50 fee per copy. $1.50 for certification. Search information required: name, date of birth, years to search. Specify plaintiff or defendant.

Quay County

District Court Clerk, Criminal Records
PO Box 1067
Tucumcari, NM 88401
(505) 461-2764
Fax (505) 461-4498
Felony and misdemeanor records are available by mail, phone or fax. No release necessary. No search fee. Search information required: name.

Civil records are available by mail or phone. No release necessary. No search fee. $.35 fee per copy. $1.50 for certification. Search information required: name, date of birth, years to search. Specify plaintiff or defendant.

Rio Arriba County

District Court Clerk, Criminal Records
PO Box 2268
Santa Fe, NM 87504-2268
(505) 827-5035
Felony records are available by mail or phone. No release necessary. No search fee. $.35 fee per copy. $1.50 for certification. Search information required: name, date of birth, SSN, years to search.

Civil records are available by mail. No release necessary. No search fee. $.35 fee per copy. $1.50 for certification. Search information required: name, date of birth, years to search. Specify plaintiff or defendant.

Roosevelt County

Felony records
District Court Clerk, Criminal Records
Roosevelt County Courthouse
Portales, NM 88130
(505) 356-4463
Fax (505) 356-5168
Felony records are available by mail, phone or fax. No release necessary. No search fee. Search information required: name.

Civil records
District Court Clerk
Roosevelt County Courthouse
Portales, NM 88130
(505) 356-4463
Fax (505) 356-5168
Civil records are available by mail. No release necessary. No search fee. $.35 fee per copy. $1.50 for certification. Search information required: name, date of birth, years to search. Specify plaintiff or defendant.

Misdemeanor records
Roosevelt County Magistrate Court
1700 North Boston St.
Portales, NM 88130
(505) 356-8569
Misdemeanor records are available by mail. A release is required. No search fee. Search information required: name, date of birth, SSN.

Civil records
Roosevelt County Magistrate Court
1700 North Boston St.
Portales, NM 88130
(505) 356-8569
Civil records are available by mail. No release necessary. No search fee. $.50 fee per copy. $1.50 for certification. Search information required: name, date of birth, years to search. Specify plaintiff or defendant.

San Juan County

District Court Clerk, Criminal Records
103 S. Oliver
Aztec, NM 87410
(505) 334-6151
Felony records are available by mail. No release necessary. No search fee. Search information required: name, SSN, date of birth, sex, years to search.

Civil records are available by mail. No release necessary. No search fee. $.35 fee per copy. $1.50 for certification. Search information required: name, date of birth, years to search. Specify plaintiff or defendant.

San Miguel County

Felony records
San Miguel County, Criminal Records
4th Judicial District Court
PO Bin-N
Las Vegas, NM 87701
(505) 425-7281
Fax (505) 425-6307
Felony records are available by mail or phone. No release necessary. No search fee. Search information required: name, years to search.

Civil records
San Miguel County
4th Judicial District Court
PO Bin-N
Las Vegas, NM 87701
(505) 425-7281
Fax (505) 425-6307
Civil records are available by mail. No release necessary. No search fee. $.35 fee per copy. $1.50 for certification. Search information required: name, date of birth, years to search. Specify plaintiff or defendant.

Misdemeanor records
San Miguel Magistrate Court
1900 Hot Springs Blvd.
Las Vegas, NM 87701
(505) 425-5204
Misdemeanor records are available by mail. No release required. No search fee. $.50 fee per copy. Search information required: name, date of birth, SSN.

Civil records
San Miguel Magistrate Court
1900 Hot Springs Blvd.
Las Vegas, NM 87701
(505) 425-5204
Civil records are available by mail or phone. No release necessary. No search fee. $.50 fee per copy. $1.50 for certification. Search information required: name, date of birth, years to search. Specify plaintiff or defendant.

Sandoval County

Felony records
District Court Clerk, Criminal Records
PO Box 130
Bernalillo, NM 87004
(505) 867-2376
Felony records are available by mail or phone. A release necessary. No search fee. $.35 fee per copy. $1.50 for certification. Search information required: name, years to search, SSN. SASE.

Civil records
District Court Clerk
PO Box 130
Bernalillo, NM 87004
(505) 867-2376
Civil records are available by mail. No release necessary. No search fee. $.35 fee per copy. $1.50 for certification. Search information required: name, date of birth, years to search. Specify plaintiff or defendant.

Misdemeanor records
Sandoval County Magistrate Court
PO Box 431
Bernalillo, NM 87004
(505) 867-5202
Misdemeanor records are available by mail. No release necessary. No search fee. $.50 fee per copy. $1.50 for certification. Search information required: name, years to search.

Civil records
Sandoval County Magistrate Court
PO Box 431
Bernalillo, NM 87004
(505) 867-5202
Civil records are available by mail. No release necessary. No search fee. $.50 fee per copy. $1.50 for certification. Search information required: name, date of birth, years to search. Specify plaintiff or defendant.

Santa Fe County

District Court Clerk, Criminal Records
PO Box 2268
Santa Fe, NM 87504-2268
(505) 827-5035
Felony records are available by mail or phone. No release necessary. No search fee. $.35 fee per copy. $1.50 for certification. Search information required: name, SSN, date of birth.

Civil records are available by mail. No release necessary. No search fee. $.35 fee per copy. $1.50 for certification. Search information required: name, date of birth, years to search. Specify plaintiff or defendant.

Sierra County

District Court Clerk, Criminal Records
PO Box 32
Truth or Consequences, NM 87901
(505) 894-7167
Felony and misdemeanor records are available by mail or phone. No release necessary. No search fee. Search information required: name, years to search, SASE.

Civil records are available by mail. No release necessary. No search fee. $.50 fee per copy. $1.50 for certification. Search information required: name, date of birth, years to search. Specify plaintiff or defendant.

Socorro County

Felony records
7th Judicial District Court, Criminal Records
PO Drawer 1129
Socorro, NM 87801
(505) 835-0050
Felony records are available by mail or phone. No release necessary. No search fee. Search information required: name, years to search.

Civil records
7th Judicial District Court
PO Drawer 1129
Socorro, NM 87801
(505) 835-0050
Civil records are available by mail. No release necessary. No search fee. $.35 fee per copy. $1.50 for certification. Search information required: name, date of birth, years to search. Specify plaintiff or defendant.

Misdemeanor records
Socorro County Magistrate Court
PO Box 1022
Socorro, NM 87801
(505) 835-2500
Misdemeanor records are available by mail. No release necessary. No search fee. Search information required: name, date of birth, SSN, years to search.

Civil records
Socorro County Magistrate Court
PO Box 1022
Socorro, NM 87801
(505) 835-2500
Civil records are available by mail. No release necessary. No search fee. $.35 fee per copy. $1.50 for certification. Search information required: name, date of birth, years to search. Specify plaintiff or defendant.

Taos County

District Court Clerk, Criminal Records
PO Box 1715
Taos, NM 87571
(505) 758-3173
Fax (505) 758-0597
Felony records are available by mail, phone or fax. No release necessary. No search fee. $.50 fee per copy. $1.50 for certification. Search information required: name, years to search.

Civil records are available by mail or phone. No release necessary. No search fee. $.35 fee per copy. $1.50 for certification. Search information required: name, date of birth, years to search. Specify plaintiff or defendant.

Torrance County

District Court Clerk
County Courthouse
PO Box 78
Estancia, NM 87016
(505) 384-2974
Felony and misdemeanor records are available by mail or phone. No search fee. $.35 fee per copy. Search information required: name, years to search.

Civil records are available by mail or phone. No release necessary. No search fee. $.35 fee per copy. $1.50 for certification. Search information required: name, date of birth, years to search. Specify plaintiff or defendant.

Union County

District Court Clerk, Criminal Records
PO Box 310
Clayton, NM 88415
(505) 374-9577
Felony records are available by mail. No release necessary. No search fee. $.35 fee per copy. $1.50 for certification. Search information required: name, years to search.

Civil records are available by mail. No release necessary. No search fee. $.35 fee per copy. $1.50 for certification. Search information required: name, date of birth, years to search. Specify plaintiff or defendant.

Valencia County

District Court Clerk, Criminal Records
PO Box 1089
Los Lunas, NM 87031
(505) 865-4630
Felony records are available by mail or
phone. No release necessary. No search fee.
Search information required: name, years to
search.

Civil records are available by mail or
phone. No release necessary. No search fee.
$.35 fee per copy. $1.50 for certification.
Search information required: name, date of
birth, years to search. Specify plaintiff or
defendant.

City-County Cross Reference

Abiquiu *Rio Arriba*
Acomita *Cibola*
Adobe Acres *Bernalillo*
Agua Fria *Santa Fe*
Alameda *Bernalillo*
Alamogordo *Otero*
Albuquerque *Bernalillo*
Alcalde *Rio Arriba*
Alto *Lincoln*
Amalia *Taos*
Amistad *Union*
Angel Fire *Colfax*
Animas *Hidalgo*
Anthony *Dona Ana*
Anton Chico *Guadalupe*
Aragon *Catron*
Arenas Valley *Grant*
Armijo *Bernalillo*
Arrey *Sierra*
Arroyo Hondo *Taos*
Arroyo Seco *Taos*
Artesia *Eddy*
Aztec *San Juan*
Bard *Quay*
Bayard *Grant*
Belen *Valencia*
Bellview *Curry*
Bent *Otero*
Bernalillo *Sandoval*
Bingham *Socorro*
Black Rock *McKinley*
Blanco *San Juan*
Bloomfield *San Juan*
Bluewater *Cibola*
Bosque *Valencia*
Bosque Farms *Valencia*
Broadview *Curry*
Buckhorn *Grant*
Buena Vista *Mora*
Bueyeros *Harding*
Caballo *Sierra*
Canjilon *Rio Arriba*
Canones *Rio Arriba*
Capitan *Lincoln*
Caprock *Lea*
Capulin *Union*
Carlsbad *Eddy*
Carrizozo *Lincoln*
Carson *Taos*
Casa Blanca *Cibola*
Causey *Roosevelt*
Cebolla *Rio Arriba*
Cedar Crest *Bernalillo*
Cedarvale *Torrance*
Central *Grant*
Cerrillos *Santa Fe*

Cerro *Taos*
Chacon *Mora*
Chama *Rio Arriba*
Chamberino *Dona Ana*
Chamisal *Taos*
Chimayo *Rio Arriba*
Church Rock *McKinley*
Cimarron *Colfax*
Claunch *Socorro*
Clayton *Union*
Cleveland *Mora*
Cliff *Grant*
Cloudcroft *Otero*
Clovis *Curry*
Columbus *Luna*
Cochiti *Los Alamos*
Continental Divide
   McKinley
Cordova *Rio Arriba*
Corona *Lincoln*
Corrales *Sandoval*
Costilla *Taos*
Coyote *Rio Arriba*
Crossroads *Lea*
Crownpoint *McKinley*
Cuba *Sandoval*
Cubero *Cibola*
Cuchillo *Sierra*
Cuervo *Guadalupe*
Datil *Catron*
Deming *Luna*
Derry *Sierra*
Des Moines *Union*
Dexter *Chaves*
Dixon *Rio Arriba*
Dona Ana *Dona Ana*
Dora *Roosevelt*
Dulce *Rio Arriba*
Duran *Torrance*
Eagle Nest *Colfax*
Edgewood *Santa Fe*
Elephant Butte *Sierra*
Elida *Roosevelt*
El Prado *Taos*
El Rito *Rio Arriba*
Embudo *Rio Arriba*
Encino *Torrance*
Espanola *Rio Arriba*
Estancia *Torrance*
Eunice *Lea*
Fairacres *Dona Ana*
Farmington *San Juan*
Faywood *Grant*
Fence Lake *Cibola*
Five Points *Bernalillo*
Flora Vista *San Juan*

Floyd *Roosevelt*
Flying H *Chaves*
Folsom *Union*
Fort Stanton *Lincoln*
Fort Sumner *DeBaca*
Fort Wingate *McKinley*
Fruitland *San Juan*
Gallina *Rio Arriba*
Gallup *McKinley*
Gamerco *McKinley*
Garfield *Dona Ana*
Garita *San Miguel*
Gila *Grant*
Gladstone *Union*
Glencoe *Lincoln*
Glenrio *Quay*
Glenwood *Catron*
Glorieta *Santa Fe*
Gonzales Ranch *San
   Miguel*
Grady *Curry*
Grants *Cibola*
Grenville *Union*
Guadalupita *Mora*
Hachita *Grant*
Hacienda Acres *Dona Ana*
Hagerman *Chaves*
Hanover *Grant*
Hatch *Dona Ana*
High Rolls *Otero*
High Rolls Mountain Park
   Otero
Hillsboro *Sierra*
Hobbs *Lea*
Holloman Air Force Base
   Otero
Holman *Mora*
Hondo *Lincoln*
Hope *Eddy*
House *Quay*
Hurley *Grant*
Isleta *Bernalillo*
Jal *Lea*
Jarales *Valencia*
Jemez Pueblo *Sandoval*
Jemez Springs *Sandoval*
Kenna *Roosevelt*
Kirtland *San Juan*
Laguna *Cibola*
LaJara *Sandoval*
Lajoya *Socorro*
Lake Arthur *Chaves*
Lake Valley *San Juan*
Lakewood *Eddy*
LaLoma *Guadalupe*
LaLuz *Otero*

LaMadera *Rio Arriba*
LaMesa *Dona Ana*
LaPlata *San Juan*
La Union *Dona Ana*
Las Chavez *Valencia*
Las Cruces *Dona Ana*
Las Tablas *Rio Arriba*
Las Vegas *San Miguel*
Ledoux *Mora*
Lemitar *Socorro*
Lincoln *Lincoln*
Lindrith *Rio Arriba*
Loco Hills *Eddy*
Logan *Quay*
Lordsburg *Hidalgo*
Los Alamos *Los Alamos*
Los Lunas *Valencia*
Los Ojos *Rio Arriba*
Los Padillas *Bernalillo*
Loving *Eddy*
Lovington *Lea*
Lumberton *Rio Arriba*
Luna *Catron*
McAlister *Quay*
McCartys *Cibola*
McDonald *Lea*
McIntosh *Torrance*
Magdalena *Socorro*
Malaga *Eddy*
Maljamar *Lea*
Maxwell *Colfax*
Mayhill *Otero*
Medanales *Rio Arriba*
Melrose *Curry*
Mescalero *Otero*
Mesilla *Dona Ana*
Mesilla Park *Dona Ana*
Mesquite *Dona Ana*
Mexican Springs *McKinley*
Mills *Harding*
Milnesand *Roosevelt*
Mimbres *Grant*
Montezuma *San Miguel*
Monticello *Sierra*
Monument *Lea*
Mora *Mora*
Moriarty *Torrance*
Mosquero *Harding*
Mount Dora *Union*
Mountainair *Torrance*
Mountain Park *Otero*
Mountain View *Bernalillo*
Mule Creek *Grant*
Nageezi *San Juan*
Nambe *Santa Fe*
Nara Visa *Quay*

Navajo Dam *San Juan*
Newkirk *Guadalupe*
New Laguna *Cibola*
Nogal *Lincoln*
Ocate *Mora*
Oil Center *Lea*
Ojo Caliente *Taos*
Ojo Sarco *Rio Arriba*
Organ *Dona Ana*
Orogrande *Otero*
Paguate *Cibola*
Pajarito *Bernalillo*
Pecos *San Miguel*
Pena Blanca *Sandoval*
Penasco *Taos*
Pep *Roosevelt*
Peralta *Valencia*
Petaca *Rio Arriba*
Picacho *Lincoln*
Pie Town *Catron*
Pinon *Otero*
Placitas *Sandoval*
Playas *Hidalgo*
Pojoaque *Santa Fe*
Polvadera *Socorro*
Ponderosa *Sandoval*
Portales *Roosevelt*
Prewitt *McKinley*
Pueblo Pintado *McKinley*
Quay *Quay*
Quemado *Catron*
Questa *Taos*
Radium Springs *Dona Ana*
Rainsville *Mora*
Ramah *McKinley*
Ranchos DeTaos *Taos*
Raton *Colfax*
Red River *Taos*
Rehoboth *McKinley*
Reserve *Catron*
Ribera *San Miguel*
Rincon *Dona Ana*
Rio Rancho *Sandoval*
Rociada *San Miguel*
Rodeo *Hidalgo*
Rogers *Roosevelt*
Roswell *Chaves*
Rowe *San Miguel*
Roy *Harding*
Ruidoso *Lincoln*
Ruidoso Downs *Lincoln*
Rutheron *Rio Arriba*
Sacramento *Otero*
Saint Vrain *Curry*
Salem *Dona Ana*
San Acacia *Socorro*
San Antonio *Socorro*
San Cristobal *Taos*
Sandia Park *Bernalillo*
San Felipe Pueblo
 Sandoval
San Fidel *Cibola*
San Jon *Quay*
San Jose *San Miguel*
San Juan Pueblo *Rio
 Arriba*
San Mateo *Cibola*
San Miguel *Dona Ana*
San Patricio *Lincoln*
San Rafael *Cibola*
Santa Cruz *Santa Fe*
Santa Fe *Santa Fe*
Santa Rosa *Guadalupe*
Santo Domingo Pueblo
 Sandoval

San Ysidro *Sandoval*
Seboyeta *Cibola*
Sedan *Union*
Sena *San Miguel*
Seneca *Union*
Serafina *San Miguel*
Shiprock *San Juan*
Silver City *Grant*
Socorro *Socorro*
Solano *Harding*
Springer *Colfax*
Stead *Union*
Sunland Park *Dona Ana*
Sunspot *Otero*
Taiban *DeBaca*
Talpa *Taos*
Taos *Taos*
Taos Pueblo *Taos*
Tatum *Lea*
Tererro *San Miguel*
Tesuque *Santa Fe*
Texico *Curry*
Thoreau *McKinley*
Tierra Amarilla *Rio Arriba*
Tijeras *Bernalillo*
Tinnie *Lincoln*
Toadlena *San Juan*
Tohatchi *McKinley*
Tome *Valencia*
Torreon *Torrance*
Trampas *Taos*
Trementina *San Miguel*
Tres Piedras *Taos*
Truchas *Rio Arriba*
Truth Or Consequences
 Sierra
Tucumcari *Quay*
Tularosa *Otero*
Tyrone *Grant*
University Park *Dona Ana*
Ute Park *Colfax*
Vadito *Taos*
Valdez *Taos*
Vallecitos *Rio Arriba*
Vanadium *Grant*
Vanderwagen *McKinley*
Vaughn *Guadalupe*
Veguita *Socorro*
Velarde *Rio Arriba*
Villanueva *San Miguel*
Wagon Mound *Mora*
Waterflow *San Juan*
Watrous *Mora*
Weed *Otero*
Whites City *Eddy*
Willard *Torrance*
Williamsburg *Sierra*
Winston *Sierra*
Yeso *DeBaca*
Youngsville *Rio Arriba*
Zuni *McKinley*

New York

Sixty one (61) of New York's sixty two (62) counties report that criminal records are available for employment screening purposes by phone and/or mail. Eight (8) counties indicate that requests may be made by facsimile. The superior court holds civil court records for $25,000 and more.

For more information or for offices not listed, contact the state's information hot line at (518) 474-2121.

Driving Records

Department of Motor Vehicles
Data Prep Unit
Empire State Plaza
Albany, NY 12228
(518) 474-0841
Driving records are available by mail. $5.00 fee per request, $2.50 if certified. Turnaround time is 4-5 weeks. Written request must include job applicant's full name, date of birth and license number. Make check payable to the Commission of Motor Vehicles.

Worker's Compensation Records

Director's Office
Claims Department
180 Livingston Street
Room 416
Brooklyn, NY 11248
(718) 802-6621
Worker's compensation records are available by mail only. Written request must include job applicant's full name, case number, name of employer involved in claim and date of accident. Notarized release required. $.10 fee per copy (letter size), $.15 fee per copy (legal size) plus tax. $10.00 fee for mailing and handling.

Vital Statistics

New York City
Bureau of Vital Statistics
Department of Health
125 Worth Street, Rm 133
New York, NY 10013
(212) 619-4530
Birth, death and divorce records are available for $15.00 each. State office has records since 1880. For records before 1914 in Albany, Buffalo, and Yonkers or before 1880 in any other city, write to Registrar of Vital Statistics in city where event occurred. For remainder of State, except New York City, write to State office.

Marriage records are available for $10.00 at the local registrar in city or town where license was issued. Also available through the State Health Dept. Divorce records prior to July 1, 1963 are available for $5.00 at the County Clerk's office where divorce was granted.

Birth and death records are available for $5.00. Office has birth records since 1898 to 1920. For Old City of New York (Manhattan and part of the Bronx) birth records from 1865 to 1919, write to Municipal Archives and Records Retention, 31 Chambers Street, New York, NY 10006. Records are public and are also accessible by computer. An employer can obtain records with a notarized, written release. Make certified check or money order payable to Department of Health. Search information required: full name, date of birth, mother's full maiden name, fathers full name, place and name of hospital where born, reason for request, SASE. Use US Postal Service only.

Department of Education

New York State Department
Division of Teacher Certification
CEC-5A11 Madison Avenue
Albany, NY 12230
(518) 474-3901
Field of certification, effective date, expiration date are available by mail or phone. No fee. Include name and SSN.

Medical Licensing

State Education Department
Division of Professional Licensing
Cultural Education Center
Albany, NY 12230
(518) 474-3817 or (800) 342-3729
Will confirm license by mail or by phone limited to one name. No fee for phone confirmations. $10.00 fee for written confirmation.

State Education Department
Division of Professional Licensing
Cultural Education Center
Albany, NY 12230
(518) 474-3817 or (800) 342-3729
Will confirm license by phone. No fee. Include name, license number, if available. Limit one name per call.

Bar Association

New York State Court Administration
80 Center Street, Room 549
New York, NY 10013
(212) 417-5872
Will confirm licenses by mail or by phone. By mail, the first name is free, $2.50 fee for additional name. One confirmation per phone request. Include name.

Accountancy Board

Division of Professional Licensing
Cultural Education Center
Albany, NY 12230
(518) 474-3817
Will confirm licenses by mail or phone. No fee. Include name.

Securities Commission

Bureau of Investor Protection and Securities
120 Broadway, 23rd Floor
New York, NY 10271
(212) 416-8000 or 416-8233
Will confirm licenses by phone. No fee. Include name and SSN.

Secretary of State

Division of State
Division of Corporation
162 Washington Avenue
Albany, NY 12231
(518) 474-6200 (Record searches)
(518) 473-2492 (General information)
Service agent and address, date incorporated, corporate names are available by mail. $10.00 fee for certified copies. $5.00 fee for plain copies.

Criminal Records

State Repository

New York State Division of Criminal Justice
Services
Executive Park Tower
Stuyvesant Plaza
Albany, NY 12203
Attention: Director, Bureau of Identification
(518) 457-6050
Access to criminal records maintained by central repository is limited to criminal justice and other governmental agencies and those private entities specifically authorized access by New York State or local laws. For authorized searches, there is a $44.00 fee for fingerprint card checks. Contact the above office or counties listed below for additional information and instructions. Turnaround time is normally 3-6 weeks.

Albany County

Albany County Court, Criminal Records
Room 128, Albany County Courthouse
Columbia and Eagle Street
Albany, NY 12207
(518) 487-5100
Fax (518) 487-5099

Felony and misdemeanor records are available by mail. No release necessary. Search fee is $5.00 per year, minimum of two years. Each additional year is $2.50. $.50 fee per copy. $4.00 for certification. Certified check only, payable to Albany County Clerk. Search information required: name, date of birth, years to search.

Civil records are available by mail. No release necessary. $5.00 search fee. $.50 fee per copy. $4.00 for certification. Search information required: name, date of birth, years to search. Specify plaintiff or defendant.

Allegany County

Chief Clerk's Office, Criminal Records
Courthouse
Belmont, NY 14813
(716) 268-5813
Fax (716) 268-9446 requests only.

Felony records are available by mail or phone. No release necessary. No search fee. $4.00 fee per copy. $4.00 for certification. Search information required: name, date of birth.

Civil records are available by mail or phone. No release necessary. No search fee. $4.00 fee per copy. $4.00 for certification. Search information required: name, date of birth, years to search. Specify plaintiff or defendant.

Bronx County

Office of Court Administration
Criminal History Search Dept.
80 Centre St.
Room 544
New York City, NY 10013
(212) 417-5854

Felony and misdemeanor records are available by mail. No release necessary. $4.00 search fee per name per borough prepaid. Search information required: name, date of birth, address, boroughs to be checked, two SASE.

Civil records are available by mail. No release necessary. $4.00 search fee. Search information required: name, date of birth, years to search, SASE. Specify plaintiff or defendant.

Broome County

Broome County Clerk
County Office Bldg.
Governmental Plaza
Binghamton, NY 13902
(607) 778-2451

Felony records are available by mail. $5.00 search fee for each two years searched with a maximum of ten years searched. No release necessary. Search information required: name, years to search.

Civil records are available by mail. No release necessary. $5.00 search fee. $.50 fee per copy. $.50 fee for each page certified, $4.00 minute fee. Search information required: name, date of birth, years to search. Specify plaintiff or defendant.

Cattaraugus County

Court Clerk's Office, Criminal Records
303 Court Street
Little Valley, NY 14755
(716) 938-9111 Ext. 387 or 388

Felony records are available by mail or by phone from 1982 forward. No release necessary. No search fee. $5.00 for certificate of conviction. Search information required: name.

Civil records are available by mail or phone. No release necessary. No search fee. $5.00 for certification. Search information required: name, date of birth, years to search. Specify plaintiff or defendant.

Cayuga County

Cayuga County Courthouse, Criminal Records
Genesee St.
Auburn, NY 13021
(315) 253-1400
Fax (315) 253-1176

Felony records are available by mail, phone or fax. A release is required. No search fee. $1.00 fee per copy. Search information required: name, date of birth, SASE.

Civil records are available by mail, phone or fax. No release necessary. No search fee. $1.00 fee per copy. Search information required: name, date of birth, years to search, SASE. Specify plaintiff or defendant.

Chautauqua County

Court Clerk, Criminal Records
District Attorney
PO Box 292
Mayville, NY 14757
(716) 753-4266

Felony and misdemeanor records are available by mail or phone. A signed release within the last 6 months is required. No search fee. $5.00 for certification. Search information required: name, date of birth.

Civil records are available by mail or phone. A signed release is required. No search fee. $5.00 for certification. Search information required: name, date of birth, years to search. Specify plaintiff or defendant.

Chemung County

Chemung County Clerk, Criminal Records
PO Box 588
Elmira, NY 14902
(607) 737-2084

Felony records are available by mail or phone. No release necessary. No search fee. $.50 fee per copy. $1.00 for certification. Search information required: name, date of birth.

Civil records are available by mail. No release necessary. No search fee. $.50 fee per copy. $1.00 for certification. Search information required: name, date of birth, years to search. Specify plaintiff or defendant.

Chenango County

Chenango County Supreme and County Court, Criminal Records
County Office Bldg.
5 Court Street
Norwich, NY 13815
(607) 335-4572

Felony records are available by mail or phone. No release necessary. $5.00 search fee. $.50 fee per copy. $1.00 for certification. Search information required: name, date of birth, if available.

Civil records are available by mail or phone. No release necessary. $5.00 search fee. $.50 fee per copy. $1.00 for certification. Search information required: name, date of birth, years to search. Specify plaintiff or defendant.

Clinton County

Clerk of Supreme and County Courts, Criminal Records Office
Clinton County Government Center
137 Margaret Street
Plattsburgh, NY 12901
(518) 565-4715

Felony records are available by mail. No release necessary. No search fee. $5.00 for certification of conviction. Search information required: name, years to search.

Civil records are available in person only. See New York state repository for additional information

Columbia County

Clerk of Criminal Court, Criminal Records
Columbia County Courthouse
Allen Street
Hudson, NY 12534
(518) 828-7858

Felony records are available by mail. A release is required. $5.00 search fee. Make check payable to Columbia County Clerk. Search information required: name, date of birth, years to search, SASE.

Civil records are available in person only. See New York state repository for additional information

Cortland County

Court Clerk, Criminal Records
Cortland County Courthouse
46 Greenbush Street
Suite 301
Cortland, NY 13045
(607) 753-5013

Felony and misdemeanor records are available by mail or phone. No release necessary. $5.00 search fee. $.50 fee per copy. $5.00 for certification. Make check payable to Cortland County Clerk. Search information required: name, date of birth, years to search.

Civil records are available in person only. See New York state repository for additional information

Delaware County

Court Clerk, Criminal Records
PO Box 426
3 Court Street
Delhi, NY 13753
(607) 746-2131
Felony records are available by mail. A signed release is required. No search fee. $.50 fee per copy. $1.00 for certification. Search information required: name, date of birth.

Civil records are available by mail. A signed release is required. No search fee. $.50 fee per copy. $1.00 for certification. Search information required: name, date of birth, years to search. Specify plaintiff or defendant.

Dutchess County

Dutchess County Clerk's Office, Criminal Records
22 Market Street
Poughkeepsie, NY 12601
(914) 431-2125
Felony and misdemeanor records are available by mail. No release necessary. Search fee is $5.00 for every 2 years searched. $4.00 for certification. Make check payable to Dutchess County Clerk. Search information required: name.

Civil records are available by mail. No release necessary. Search fee is$5.00 for every 2 years searched. $4.00 for certification. Search information required: name, date of birth, years to search. Specify plaintiff or defendant.

Erie County

Erie County Clerk, Criminal Records
25 Delaware Ave.
Buffalo, NY 14202
(716) 858-7877
Fax (716) 858-6550
Felony records are available by mail or fax. No release necessary. Search fee is $5.00 for every 2 years searched. $1.00 fee per copy. $5.00 for certification. $2.50 fee for first page of fax requests or response. $2.00 for 2nd page of fax, $1.00 each additional page. Make check payable to Erie County Clerk. Search information required: name, date of birth, years to search.

Civil records are available by mail. No release necessary. Search fee is $5.00 for every 2 years searched. $1.00 fee per copy. $5.00 for certification. $2.50 fee for first page of fax requests or response. $2.00 for 2nd page of fax, $1.00 each additional page. Search information required: name, date of birth, years to search. Specify plaintiff or defendant.

Essex County

Court Clerk's Office, Criminal Records
Essex County Government Center
Elizabethtown, NY 12932
(518) 873-6301 Extension 283
Felony and misdemeanor records are available by mail. No release necessary. No search fee. $.50 fee per copy. $5.00 for certification. Search information required: name, date of birth.

Civil records are available by mail. No release necessary. No search fee. $.50 fee per copy. $5.00 for certification. Search information required: name, date of birth, years to search. Specify plaintiff or defendant.

Franklin County

Chief Clerk of Court, Criminal Records
Courthouse
63 W. Main Street
Malone, NY 12953
(518) 483-6767 Ext. 749
Felony records are available by mail or phone. No release necessary.No search fee. $.50 fee per copy. $5.00 for certification. Search information required: name, date of birth.

Civil records are available by mail. No release necessary. No search fee. $.50 fee per copy. $5.00 for certification. Search information required: name, date of birth, years to search. Specify plaintiff or defendant.

Fulton County

Chief Clerk, Criminal Records
West Main Street
Johnstown, NY 12095
(518) 762-0539
Felony and some misdemeanor records are available by mail or phone. No release necessary. No search fee. $1.00 fee per copy. $4.00 for certification. Search information required: name, date of birth.

Civil records are available by mail. No release necessary. No search fee. $1.00 fee per copy. $4.00 for certification. Search information required: name, date of birth, years to search. Specify plaintiff or defendant.

Genesee County

County Clerk, Criminal Records
PO Box 379
Batavia, NY 14021-0379
(716) 344-2550 Ext. 242
Fax (716) 344-2442
Felony and misdemeanor records are available by mail or fax. No release necessary. Fee is $5.00 for every 5 years searched. $5.00 fee for fax returns. Make check payable to Genesee County Clerk. Search information required: name, SSN, date of birth, years to search.

Civil records are available by mail. No release necessary. $Fee is $5.00 for every 5 years searched. $5.00 fee for fax returns. $.50 fee per copy. $4.00 for certification. Search information required: name, date of birth, years to search. Specify plaintiff or defendant.

Greene County

Greene County Clerk, Legal Dept.
Courthouse
PO Box 446
Main St.
Catskill, NY 12414
(518) 943-2050
Felony and misdemeanor records are available by mail or phone. No release necessary. No search fee. $1.00 fee per copy. $4.00 for certification. Search information required: name.

Civil records are available by mail. No release necessary. No search fee. $1.00 fee per copy. $4.00 for certification. Search information required: name, date of birth, years to search. Specify plaintiff or defendant.

Hamilton County

County Court Clerk, Criminal Records
PO Box 204, Route 8
Lake Pleasant, NY 12108
(518) 548-7111
Felony and misdemeanor records are available by mail or phone. No release necessary. No search fee. $4.00 fee per copy. $4.00 for certification. Search information required: name, years to search.

Civil records are available by mail or phone. No release necessary. $0.00 search fee. $4.00 fee per copy. $4.00 for certification. Search information required: name, date of birth, years to search. Specify plaintiff or defendant.

Herkimer County

County Clerk, Criminal Records
PO Box 111
Herkimer, NY 13350-0111
(315) 867-1138
Felony records are available by mail. No release necessary. $5.00 search fee. $.50 fee per copy. $4.00 for certification. Company checks only, payable to Herkimer County Clerk. Search information required: name, date of birth, years to search.

Civil records are available by mail. No release necessary. $5.00 search fee. $.50 fee per copy. $4.00 for certification. Search information required: name, date of birth, years to search. Specify plaintiff or defendant.

Jefferson County

County Clerk, Criminal Records
175 Arsenal Street
Watertown, NY 13601
(315) 785-3081
Felony and misdemeanor records are available by mail only. No release necessary. $5.00 search fee. $1.00 fee per copy. $4.00 for certification. Make check payable to Jefferson County Clerk. Search information required: name, years to search.

Civil records are available by mail. No release necessary. $5.00 search fee. $1.00 fee per copy. $4.00 for certification. Search information required: name, date of birth, years to search. Specify plaintiff or defendant.

Kings County

Supreme Court Bldg., Criminal Records
Brooklyn, NY 11201
(718) 643-3993
Records are not currently available by mail or phone. See New York state repository.

Civil records are available in person only. See New York state repository for additional information.

Lewis County

County Clerk, Criminal Records
7660 State Street
Lowville, NY 13367
(315) 376-5333
Felony and misdemeanor records are available by mail. No release necessary. $5.00 search fee. $1.00 fee per copy. $4.00 for certification. Make check payable to Lewis County. Search information required: name.

Civil records are available by mail. No release necessary. $5.00 search fee. $1.00 fee per copy. $4.00 for certification. Search information required: name, date of birth, years to search. Specify plaintiff or defendant.

Livingston County

Livingston County Clerk's Office
Courthouse, Criminal Records
Geneseo, NY 14454
(716) 243-7000

Felony records are available by mail. No release necessary. $1.00 fee for each year searched. Make check payable to Livingston County Clerk. Search information required: name, years to search.

Civil records are available by mail. No release necessary. $1.00 fee for each year searched. $5.00 for certification. Search information required: name, date of birth, years to search. Specify plaintiff or defendant.

Madison County

Chief Clerk, Criminal Records
PO Box 668
Wampsville, NY 13163
(315) 366-2267

Felony records are available by mail. No release necessary. $5.00 search fee. Search information required: name, date of birth.

Civil records are available by mail. No release necessary. $5.00 search fee. Search information required: name, date of birth, years to search. Specify plaintiff or defendant.

Monroe County

County Office Bldg., Criminal Records
Room B18
39 W. Main Street
Rochester, NY 14614
(716) 428-5159
Fax (716) 428-5447

Felony records are available by mail. or fax. No release necessary. Fee is $5.00 for every 2 years searched. $5.00 for certification. Company checks only, payable to Monroe County Court Clerk. Search information required: name, years to search.

Civil records are available by mail. No release necessary. Fee is $5.00 for every 2 years searched. $5.00 for certification. Search information required: name, date of birth, years to search. Specify plaintiff or defendant.

Montgomery County

Montgomery County Chief Clerk
Montgomery County Courthouse
Criminal Records
Fonda, NY 12068
(518) 853-4516

Felony and misdemeanor records are available by mail. A release is required. No search fee. $.25 fee per copy. Search information required: name, SSN, date of birth, sex.

Civil records are available by mail. A release is required. No search fee. $.25 fee per copy. Search information required: name, date of birth, years to search. Specify plaintiff or defendant.

Nassau County

County Court Clerk's Office, Criminal Records
Room 215 N
262 Old Country Road
Mineola, NY 11501
(516) 535-2800

Felony records are available by mail. No release necessary. $5.00 fee for every two years searched. $.25 fee per copy. $4.00 for certification. Make check payable to Clerk of Court. Search information required: name, date of birth, SASE.

Civil records are available by mail. No release necessary. $5.00 fee for every two years searched. $.25 fee per copy. $4.00 for certification. Search information required: name, date of birth, years to search. Specify plaintiff or defendant.

New York County

Supreme Court Bldg., Criminal Records
Room 1000
100 Centre Street
New York, NY 10013
(212) 374-4976

Felony and misdemeanor records are available by mail. $4.00 search fee. $4.00 fee per copy includes certification.Search information required: name, date of birth, years to search.

Civil records are available by mail. No release necessary. $4.00 search fee. $4.00 fee per copy includes certification. Search information required: name, date of birth, years to search. Specify plaintiff or defendant.

Niagara County

County Clerk, Filing Room
175 Hawley Street
PO Box 461
Lockport, NY 14095-0461
(716) 439-7022

Felony records are available by mail. No release necessary. $5.00 fee for every 2 years searched. $1.00 fee per copy. $4.00 for certification.Company check payable to Niagara County Clerk. Search information required: name, date of birth, years to search.

Civil records are available by mail. No release necessary. $5.00 fee for every 2 years searched. $1.00 fee per copy. $4.00 for certification. Search information required: name, date of birth, years to search. Specify plaintiff or defendant.

Oneida County

County Clerk, Criminal Records
800 Park Ave.
Utica, NY 13501
(315) 798-5797

Felony records are available by mail. No release necessary. $5.00 search fee. $1.00 fee per copy. $4.00 for certification. Make check payable to Oneida County Clerk. Search information required: name, years to search.

Civil records are available by mail. No release necessary. $5.00 search fee. $1.00 fee per copy. $4.00 for certification. Search information required: name, date of birth, years to search. Specify plaintiff or defendant.

Onondaga County

Felony amd misdemeanor records
Onondaga County Clerk, Criminal Records
Room 200, Courthouse
Syracuse, NY 13202
(315) 435-2236

Felony records are available by mail. No release necessary. $2.50 fee for each year searched. Certified check only, payable to Onondaga County Clerk. Search information required: name, date of birth, years to search.

Civil records
Onondaga County Clerk
Room 200, Courthouse
Syracuse, NY 13202
(315) 435-2236 Ext. 2234

Civil records are available by mail. No release necessary. $2.50 fee for each year searched. Search information required: name, date of birth, years to search. Specify plaintiff or defendant.

Ontario County

County Clerk's Office, Criminal Records
25 Pleasant Street
Canandaigua, NY 14424
(716) 396-4202

Felony records are available by mail or phone. No release necessary. No search fee. $.50 fee per copy. $5.00 for certification. Search information required: name, years to search, SASE.

Civil records are available by mail or phone. No release necessary. No search fee. $.50 fee per copy. $5.00 for certification. Search information required: name, date of birth, years to search, SASE. Specify plaintiff or defendant.

Orange County

Orange County Clerk, Criminal Records
Orange County Government Center
255-275 Main Street
Goshen, NY 10924
(914) 294-5151

Felony and misdemeanor records are available by mail. No release necessary. Fee is $5.00 for every 2 years searched. $2.50 fee per copy. $4.00 for certification. Make check or money order payable to Orange County Clerk. Search information required: name, SSN, date of birth, sex, race, years to search, SASE.

Civil records are available by mail. No release necessary. Fee is $5.00 for every 2 years searched. $2.50 fee per copy. $4.00 for certification. Search information required: name, date of birth, years to search, SASE. Specify plaintiff or defendant.

Orleans County

Felony and misdemeanor records
County Court Clerk, Criminal Records
Courthouse Square
Main Street
Albion, NY 14411
(716) 589-5458

Felony records are available by mail or phone. No release necessary. No fee. Search information required: name, date of birth.

Civil records
County Court Clerk
Courthouse Square
Main Street
Albion, NY 14411
(716) 589-5334
Civil records are available by mail. No release necessary. No search fee. $1.00 fee per copy. $4.00 for certification. Search information required: name, date of birth, years to search. Specify plaintiff or defendant.

Oswego County

Oswego County Clerk, Criminal Records
46 E. Bridge Street
Oswego, NY 13126
(315) 349-8391
Felony records are available by mail. No release necessary. $5.00 search fee. Fee is $10.00 for search of records over 13 years old. $1.00 fee per copy. $5.00 for certification. Company checks only, payable to Oswego County Clerk. Search information required: name, date of birth, years to search.

Civil records are available by mail. No release necessary. $5.00 search fee. Fee is $10.00 for search of records over 13 years old. $1.00 fee per copy. $5.00 for certification. Search information required: name, date of birth, years to search. Specify plaintiff or defendant.

Otsego County

Otsego County Clerk, Criminal Records
PO Box 710
197 Main Street
Cooperstown, NY 13326
(607) 547-4388
Felony records are available by mail. No release necessary. $5.00 search fee. $1.00 fee per copy includes certification. Search information required: name, date of birth.

Civil records are available by mail. No release necessary. $5.00 search fee. $1.00 fee per copy includes certification. Search information required: name, date of birth, years to search. Specify plaintiff or defendant.

Putnam County

Putnam Combined Courts, Criminal Records
2 County Center, 3rd Floor, Rm 310
Carmel, NY 10512
(914) 225-3641 Extension 336 or 337
Felony records are available by mail. No release necessary. No search fee. Search information required: name, SASE.

Civil records are available by mail. No release necessary. No search fee. Search information required: name, date of birth, years to search, SASE. Specify plaintiff or defendant.

Queens County

Felony records
Clerk's Office of Supreme Court, Criminal Records
125-01 Queens Blvd, Rm G64
Kew Gardens, NY 11415
(718) 520-3137 or 520-3542
Records are available by mail or phone. A release is required. No search fee. $5.00 fee for certification. Search information required: name, years to search.

Civil records
Clerk's Office of Supreme Court
125-01 Queens Blvd, Rm G64
Kew Gardens, NY 11415
(718) 520-3137 or 520-3542
Civil records are available by mail. No release necessary. No search fee. $5.00 fee for certification. Search information required: name, date of birth, years to search. Specify plaintiff or defendant.

Misdemeanor records
Office of Court Administration
Court Operational Services
80 Centre St., Rm. 544A
New York, NY 10013
(718) 520-3595
Misdemeanor records are available by mail. No release necessary. $5.00 fee per name per borough, money order or certified check. Search information required: name, address, date of birth, number of boroughs to be checked, docket number (if available).

Civil records
Office of Court Administration
Court Operational Services
80 Centre St., Rm. 544A
New York, NY 10013
(718) 520-3595
Civil records are available by mail. No release necessary. $5.00 fee per name per borough. Search information required: name, date of birth, years to search. Specify plaintiff or defendant.

Rensselaer County

Rensselaer County Courthouse, Criminal Records
Congress and 2nd Street
Troy, NY 12180
(518) 270-3711
Felony and misdemeanor records are available by mail. No release necessary. $5.00 fee for every 2 years searched includes certification. Make check payable to Rensselaer County Clerk. Search information required: name, date of birth, previous address, years to search.

Civil records are available by mail. No release necessary. $5.00 fee for every 2 years searched includes certification. Search information required: name, date of birth, years to search. Specify plaintiff or defendant.

Richmond County

Office of Court Administration
Court Operational Services
80 Centre St., Rm. 544
New York, NY 10013
(212) 417-5854
Felony and misdemeanor records are available by mail. No release necessary. $4.00 search fee per name per borough, prepaid. Search information required: name, address, date of birth, two SASE, number of boroughs to be checked.

Civil records are available by mail. No release necessary. $4.00 search fee per name per borough, prepaid. Search information required: name, date of birth, years to search, SASE. Specify plaintiff or defendant.

Rockland County

County Clerk, Criminal Records
27 New Hempstead Road
New City, NY 10956
(914) 638-5077
Felony records are available by mail. No release necessary. Fee is $5.00 for every 2 years searched. Company checks only, payable to Rockland County Clerk. Search information required: name, date of birth, years to search.

Civil records are available by mail. No release necessary. Fee is $5.00 for every 2 years searched. Search information required: name, date of birth, years to search. Specify plaintiff or defendant.

Saratoga County

Supreme Court, Criminal Records
30 McMaster Street
Ballston Spa, NY 12020
(518) 885-2224
Felony records are available by mail. No release necessary. No search fee. $5.00 for certification. Search information required: name, SSN, date of birth, years to search, SASE.

Civil records are available by mail. No release necessary. No search fee. $5.00 for certification. Search information required: name, date of birth, years to search, SASE. Specify plaintiff or defendant.

Schenectady County

Calendar Clerk's Office, Criminal Records
620 State Street
Schenectady, NY 12305
(518) 388-4220
Felony records are available by mail. A release is required. $5.00 fee for every 2 years searched. $.50 fee per copy. $4.00 for certification. Search information required: name, date of birth.

Civil records are available by mail. No release necessary. $5.00 fee for every 2 years searched. $.50 fee per copy. $4.00 for certification. Search information required: name, date of birth, years to search. Specify plaintiff or defendant.

Schoharie County

Courthouse, Criminal Records
30 Main Street
Schoharie, NY 12157
(518) 295-8316
Felony and misdemeanor records are available by mail or phone. A release is required. $5.00 search fee. $.50 fee per copy. $4.00 for certification. $5.00 search fee. $.50 fee per copy. $4.00 for certification. Search information required: name.

Civil records are available by mail. No release necessary. $5.00 search fee. $.50 fee per copy. $4.00 for certification. Search information required: name, date of birth, years to search. Specify plaintiff or defendant.

Schuyler County

County Clerk's Office, Criminal
Records
PO Box 8
105 Ninth Street
Watkins Glen, NY 14891
(607) 535-2132
Felony records are available by mail. No release necessary. No search fee. $.50 fee per copy. $4.00 for certification. Search information required: name, date of birth.

Civil records are available by mail. No release necessary. No search fee. $.50 fee per copy. $4.00 for certification. Search information required: name, date of birth, years to search. Specify plaintiff or defendant.

Seneca County

County Clerk, Criminal Records
PO Box 638
Waterloo, NY 13165
(315) 539-5655 Ext. 2041
Felony records are available by mail or phone. No release necessary. No search fee. $.50 fee per copy. $4.00 for certification. Search information required: name, SASE.

Civil records are available by mail. No release necessary. No search fee. $.50 fee per copy. $4.00 for certification. Search information required: name, date of birth, years to search. Specify plaintiff or defendant.

Steuben County

Felony records
Chief Clerk of Court, Criminal
Records
3 Pulteney Square
Bath, NY 14810
(607) 776-7879
Felony records are available by mail or phone. No release necessary. No search fee. $.50 fee per copy. $4.00 for certification. Search information required: name.

Civil records
Chief Clerk of Court
3 Pulteney Square
Bath, NY 14810
(607) 776-9631 Ext. 3210
Civil records are available by mail or phone. No release necessary. No search fee. $.50 fee per copy. $4.00 for certification. Search information required: name, date of birth, years to search. Specify plaintiff or defendant.

St. Lawrence County

Courthouse, Criminal Records
Canton, NY 13617
(315) 379-2200
Fax (315) 379-2333
Felony and records are available by mail or fax. No release necessary. No search fee. $2.00 fee per copy. $5.00 for certification. Search information required: name, date of birth, SASE, years to search.

Civil records are available by mail or fax. No release necessary. No search fee. $2.00 fee per copy. $5.00 for certification. Search information required: name, date of birth, years to search. Specify plaintiff or defendant.

Suffolk County

Suffolk County Clerk, Room E18A
County Center
Riverhead, NY 11901
(516) 852-2016
Felony records are available by mail. No release necessary. Fee is $5.00 for every 2 consecutive years searched. $4.00 for certification. Make check payable to Suffolk County Clerk. Search information required: name, date of birth, years to search.

Civil records are available by mail from 1984 forward. No release necessary. Fee is $5.00 for every 2 consecutive years searched. $4.00 for certification. Search information required: name, date of birth, years to search. Specify plaintiff or defendant.

Sullivan County

Felony records
County Clerk's Office
Government Center
100 N. Street.
Monticello, NY 12701
(914) 794-3000 Ext. 3160
Felony records from 1985 forward are available by mail. No release necessary. $5.00 search fee includes certification. $1.00 fee per copy. Search information required: name, date of birth, address, SASE.

Civil records
County Clerk's Office
Government Center
100 N. Street.
Monticello, NY 12701
(914) 794-3000 Ext. 5012
Civil records are available by mail. No release necessary. $5.00 search fee includes certification. $1.00 fee per copy. Search information required: name, date of birth, years to search, SASE. Specify plaintiff or defendant.

Misdemeanor records
County Clerk's Office
18 Pleasant Street
Monticello, NY 12701
(914) 794-3000 Ext. 3160
Misdemeanor records prior to 1985 are available by mail. No release necessary. $5.00 search fee. $1.00 fee per copy. $4.00 for certification. Search information required: name, date of birth, SASE.

Civil records
County Clerk's Office
18 Pleasant Stree
Monticello, NY 12701
(914) 794-3000 Ext. 3160
Civil records are available by mail. No release necessary. $5.00 search fee. $1.00 fee per copy. $4.00 for certification. Search information required: name, date of birth, years to search. Specify plaintiff or defendant.

Tioga County

Clerk's Office, Criminal Records
16 Court Street
PO Box 307
Owego, NY 13827
(607) 687-3133
Felony records are available by mail or phone. No release necessary. No search fee. $.50 fee per copy. $4.00 for certification. Search information required: name, date of birth.

Civil records are available by mail or phone. No release necessary. No search fee. $.50 fee per copy. $4.00 for certification. Search information required: name, date of birth, years to search. Specify plaintiff or defendant.

Tompkins County

Felony and misdemeanor records
County Clerk's Office, Criminal
Records
320 N. Tioga St.
PO Box 720
Ithaca, NY 14850
(607) 272-0466 Ext. 252
Felony records are available by mail. A release is required. $5.00 fee for 5 years searched. $.50 fee per copy. $5.00 for certification. Make check payable to Tompkins County Clerk. Search information required: name, date of birth, years to search.

Civil records
County Clerk's Office
320 N. Tioga St.
PO Box 720
Ithaca, NY 14850
(607) 272-0466
Civil records are available by mail. A release is required. $5.00 fee for 5 years searched. $.50 fee per copy. $5.00 for certification. Search information required: name, date of birth, years to search. Specify plaintiff or defendant.

Ulster County

Ulster County Clerk, Criminal Records
Box 1800
Kingston, NY 12401
(914) 331-9300 Ext. 252
Felony records are available by mail. No release necessary. $5.00 fee for every 2 years searched. $.50 fee per copy. $4.00 for certification. Make check payable to Ulster County Clerk. Search information required: name, SSN, date of birth, years to search.

Civil records are available by mail. No release necessary. $5.00 fee for every 2 years searched. $.50 fee per copy. $4.00 for certification. Search information required: name, date of birth, years to search. Specify plaintiff or defendant.

Warren County

Warren County Clerk, Criminal
Records
Warren County Municipal Center
Lake George, NY 12845
(518) 761-6429 (Felony)
(518) 761-6430 (Misdemeanor)
Fax (518) 761-6551
Felony and misdemeanor records are available by mail or phone. No release necessary. No search fee. $.50 fee per copy. $4.00 for certification. $1.00 fee per fax requests. $3.00 fee per outgoing fax response. Search information required: name, years to search, SASE.

Civil records are available by mail. No release necessary. No search fee. $.50 fee per copy. $4.00 for certification. $1.00 fee per fax requests. $3.00 fee per outgoing fax response. Search information required: name, date of birth, years to search, SASE. Specify plaintiff or defendant.

Washington County

Washington County Clerk, Criminal Records
Upper Broadway
Fort Edward, NY 12828
(518) 747-4115

Felony records are available by mail or phone. No release necessary. No search fee. $5.00 for certification. Search information required: name, date of birth, years to search.

Civil records are available in person only. See New York state repository for additional information.

Wayne County

County Clerk, Criminal Records
9 Pearl Street
PO Box 608
Lyons, NY 14489
(315) 946-5870
Fax (315) 946-5978

Felony records are available by mail, phone or fax. No release necessary. $5.00 search fee for written requests. No fee for phone requests. $.50 fee per copy. $4.00 for certification. Company checks only, payable to Wayne County Clerk. Search information required: name, date of birth, years to search.

Civil records are available by mail. No release necessary. $5.00 search fee written requests. No fee for phone requests. $.50 per copy. $4.00 for certification. Search information required: name, date of birth, years to search. Specify plaintiff or defendant.

Westchester County

Westchester County Clerk, Criminal Records
Room 330
110 Grove St.
White Plains, NY 10601
(914) 285-2000

Felony records are available by mail. No release necessary. Fee is $5.00 for every 2 years searched. $4.00 for certification. Company checks only, payable to Westchester County Clerk. Search information required: name, date of birth, years to search.

Civil records are available by mail. No release necessary. Fee is $5.00 for every 2 years searched. $4.00 for certification. Search information required: name, date of birth, years to search. Specify plaintiff or defendant.

Wyoming County

Wyoming County Clerk, Criminal Records
PO Box 70
143 N. Main
Warsaw, NY 14569
(716) 786-8810
Fax (716) 786-3703

Felony and misdemeanor records are available by mail, fax or phone. No release necessary. No search fee. $.50 fee per copy. $4.00 for certification. Search information required: name, date of birth.

Civil records are available by mail, fax or phone. No release necessary. No search fee. $.50 fee per copy. $4.00 for certification. Search information required: name, date of birth, years to search. Specify plaintiff or defendant.

Yates County

County Clerk, Criminal Records
110 Court Street
Penn Yan, NY 14527
(315) 536-4011
Fax (315) 536-5120

Felony and misdemeanor records are available by mail, phone or fax. No release necessary. $10.00 search fee. $.50 fee per copy. $1.00 for certification. $3.00 fee for fax response plus $1.00 for each page. Company checks only, payable to Yates County Clerk. Search information required: name, years to search.

Civil records are available by mail. No release necessary. $10.00 search fee. $.50 fee per copy. $1.00 for certification. $3.00 fee for fax response plus $1.00 for each page. Search information required: name, date of birth, years to search. Specify plaintiff or defendant.

City-County Cross Reference

Accord *Ulster*
Acra *Greene*
Adams *Jefferson*
Adams Basin *Monroe*
Adams Center *Jefferson*
Addison *Steuben*
Adirondack *Warren*
Afton *Chenango*
Akron *Erie*
Airmont *Rockland*
Alabama *Genesee*
Albany *Albany*
Albertson *Nassau*
Albion *Orleans*
Alcove *Albany*
Alden *Erie*
Alder Creek *Oneida*
Alexander *Genesee*
Alexandria Bay *Jefferson*
Alfred *Allegany*
Alfred Station *Allegany*
Allegany *Cattaraugus*
Allentown *Allegany*
Alma *Allegany*
Almond *Allegany*
Alpine *Schuyler*
Altamont *Albany*
Altmar *Oswego*
Alton *Wayne*
Altona *Clinton*
Amagansett *Suffolk*

Amawalk *Westchester*
Amenia *Dutchess*
Amherst *Erie*
Amityville *Suffolk*
Amsterdam *Montgomery*
Ancram *Columbia*
Ancramdale *Columbia*
Andes *Delaware*
Andover *Allegany*
Angelica *Allegany*
Angola *Erie*
Angola On The Lake *Erie*
Antwerp *Jefferson*
Apalachin *Tioga*
Appleton *Niagara*
Apulia Station *Onondaga*
Aquebogue *Suffolk*
Arcade *Wyoming*
Arden *Orange*
Ardsley *Westchester*
Ardsley-*on-Hudson
   Westchester
Argyle *Washington*
Arkport *Steuben*
Arkville *Delaware*
Arlington *Dutchess*
Armonk *Westchester*
Armor *Erie*
Ashland *Greene*
Ashville *Chautauqua*
Athens *Greene*

Athol *Warren*
Athol Springs *Erie*
Atlanta *Steuben*
Atlantic Beach *Nassau*
Attica *Wyoming*
Auburn *Cayuga*
Aurora *Cayuga*
Au Sable Chasm *Clinton*
Au Sable Forks *Essex*
Austerlitz *Columbia*
Ava *Oneida*
Averill Park *Rensselaer*
Avoca *Steuben*
Avon *Livingston*
Babylon *Suffolk*
Bainbridge *Chenango*
Bakers Mills *Warren*
Baldwin *Nassau*
Baldwin Place *Putnam*
Baldwinsville *Onondaga*
Ballston Lake *Saratoga*
Ballston Spa *Saratoga*
Balmat *Saint Lawrence*
Balmville *Orange*
Bangall *Dutchess*
Barker *Niagara*
Barnes Corners *Lewis*
Barneveld *Oneida*
Barryville *Sullivan*
Barton *Tioga*
Basom *Genesee*

Batavia *Genesee*
Bath *Steuben*
Baxter Estates *Nassau*
Baybery *Onodaga*
Bayport *Suffolk*
Bay Shore *Suffolk*
Bayville *Nassau*
Beacon *Dutchess*
Bear Mountain *Rockland*
Bearsville *Ulster*
Beaver Dams *Schuyler*
Beaver Falls *Lewis*
Bedford *Westchester*
Bedford Hills *Westchester*
Belfast *Allegany*
Bellerose *Nassau*
Bellerose Terrace *Nassau*
Belleville *Jefferson*
Belle Terre *Suffolk*
Bellmore *Nassau*
Bellona *Yates*
Bellport *Suffolk*
Bellvale *Orange*
Belmont *Allegany*
Bemus Point *Chautauqua*
Bergen *Genesee*
Berkshire *Tioga*
Berlin *Rensselaer*
Berne *Albany*
Bernhards Bay *Oswego*
Bethel *Sullivan*

Bethpage *Nassau*
Bible School Park *Broome*
Big Flats *Chemung*
Big Indian *Ulster*
Big Tree *Erie*
Billings *Dutchess*
Binghamton *Broome*
Black Creek *Allegany*
Black River *Jefferson*
Blasdell *Erie*
Blauvelt *Rockland*
Bliss *Wyoming*
Blodgett Mills *Cortland*
Bloomfield *Ontario*
Bloomingburg *Sullivan*
Bloomingdale *Essex*
Blooming Grove *Orange*
Bloomington *Ulster*
Bloomville *Delaware*
Blossvale *Oneida*
Blue Mountain Lake
  Hamilton
Blue Point *Suffolk*
Bohemia *Suffolk*
Boiceville *Ulster*
Bolivar *Allegany*
Bolton Landing *Warren*
Bombay *Franklin*
Boonville *Oneida*
Boston *Erie*
Bouckville *Madison*
Bovina Center *Delaware*
Bowmansville *Erie*
Bradford *Steuben*
Brainard *Rensselaer*
Brainardsville *Franklin*
Branchport *Yates*
Brant *Erie*
Brantingham *Lewis*
Brant Lake *Warren*
Brasher Falls *Saint*
  Lawrence
Breesport *Chemung*
Brentwood *Suffolk*
Brewerton *Onondaga*
Brewster *Putnam*
Briarcliff Manor
  Westchester
Bridgehampton *Suffolk*
Bridgeport *Madison*
Bridgewater *Oneida*
Brier Hill *Saint Lawrence*
Brightwaters *Suffolk*
Broadalbin *Fulton*
Brockport *Monroe*
Brocton *Chautauqua*
Bronx *Bronx*
Bronxville *Westchester*
Brookfield *Madison*
Brookhaven *Suffolk*
Brooklyn *Kings*
Brooktondale *Tompkins*
Brookview *Rensselaer*
Brownville *Jefferson*
Brushton *Franklin*
Buchanan *Westchester*
Buffalo *Erie*
Bullville *Orange*
Burdett *Schuyler*
Burke *Franklin*
Burlingham *Sullivan*
Burlington Flats *Otsego*
Burnt Hills *Saratoga*
Burt *Niagara*
Buskirk *Rensselaer*
Byron *Genesee*

Cadyville *Clinton*
Cairo *Greene*
Calcium *Jefferson*
Caledonia *Livingston*
Callicoon *Sullivan*
Callicoon Center *Sullivan*
Calverton *Suffolk*
Cambridge *Washington*
Camden *Oneida*
Cameron *Steuben*
Cameron Mills *Steuben*
Camillus *Onondaga*
Campbell *Steuben*
Campbell Hall *Orange*
Canaan *Columbia*
Canajoharie *Montgomery*
Canandaigua *Ontario*
Canaseraga *Allegany*
Canastota *Madison*
Candor *Tioga*
Caneadea *Allegany*
Canisteo *Steuben*
Canton *Saint Lawrence*
Cape Vincent *Jefferson*
Carle Place *Nassau*
Carlisle *Schoharie*
Carmel *Putnam*
Caroga Lake *Fulton*
Carthage *Jefferson*
Cassadaga *Chautauqua*
Cassville *Oneida*
Castile *Wyoming*
Castle Creek *Broome*
Castle Point *Dutchess*
Castleton *on Hudson
  Rensselaer
Castorland *Lewis*
Cato *Cayuga*
Catskill *Greene*
Cattaraugus *Cattaraugus*
Cayuga *Cayuga*
Cayuga Heights *Tompkns*
Cayuta *Schuyler*
Cazenovia *Madison*
Cedarhurst *Nassau*
Celoron *Chautauqua*
Cementon *Greene*
Centereach *Suffolk*
Center Moriches *Suffolk*
Centerport *Suffolk*
Centerville *Allegany*
Central Bridge *Schoharie*
Central Islip *Suffolk*
Central Nyack *Rockland*
Central Square *Oswego*
Central Valley *Orange*
Ceres *Allegany*
Chadwicks *Oneida*
Chaffee *Erie*
Champlain *Clinton*
Champlain Park *Clinton*
Chappaqua *Westchester*
Charlotteville *Schoharie*
Chase Mills *Saint*
  Lawrence
Chateaugay *Franklin*
Chatham *Columbia*
Chaumont *Jefferson*
Chautauqua *Chautauqua*
Chazy *Clinton*
Cheektowaga *Erie*
Chelsea *Dutchess*
Chemung *Chemung*
Chenango Bridge *Broome*
Chenango Forks *Broome*
Cherry Creek *Chautauqua*

Cherry Plain *Rensselaer*
Cherry Valley *Otsego*
Chester *Orange*
Chestertown *Warren*
Chestnut Ridge *Rockland*
Chichester *Ulster*
Childwold *Saint Lawrence*
Chili Center *Monroe*
Chippewa Bay *Saint*
  Lawrence
Chittenango *Madison*
Churchville *Monroe*
Churubusco *Clinton*
Cicero *Onondaga*
Cincinnatus *Cortland*
Circleville *Orange*
Clarence *Erie*
Clarence Center *Erie*
Clarendon *Orleans*
Clark Mills *Oneida*
Clarkson *Monroe*
Clarksville *Albany*
Claryville *Sullivan*
Claverack *Columbia*
Clay *Onondaga*
Clayton *Jefferson*
Clayville *Oneida*
Clemons *Washington*
Cleveland *Oswego*
Cleverdale *Warren*
Clifton *Monroe*
Clifton Park *Saratoga*
Clifton Springs *Ontario*
Climax *Greene*
Clinton *Oneida*
Clinton Corners *Dutchess*
Clinton Park *Rensselaer*
Clintondale *Ulster*
Clockville *Madison*
Clyde *Wayne*
Clymer *Chautauqua*
Cobleskill *Schoharie*
Cochecton *Sullivan*
Cochecton Center *Sullivan*
Coeymans *Albany*
Coeymans Hollow *Albany*
Cohocton *Steuben*
Cohoes *Albany*
Colchester *Delaware*
Cold Brook *Herkimer*
Colden *Erie*
Cold Spring *Putnam*
Cold Spring Harbor *Suffolk*
Colliersville *Otsego*
Collins *Erie*
Collins Center *Erie*
Colonie *Albany*
Colton *Saint Lawrence*
Columbia *Herkimer*
Columbiaville *Columbia*
Commack *Suffolk*
Comstock *Washington*
Conesus *Livingston*
Conewango Valley
  Cattaraugus
Congers *Rockland*
Conklin *Broome*
Connelly *Ulster*
Constable *Franklin*
Constableville *Lewis*
Constantia *Oswego*
Cooks Falls *Delaware*
Coopers Plains *Steuben*
Cooperstown *Otsego*
Copake *Columbia*
Copake Falls *Columbia*

Copenhagen *Lewis*
Copiague *Suffolk*
Coram *Suffolk*
Corbettsville *Broome*
Corfu *Genesee*
Corinth *Saratoga*
Corning *Steuben*
Cornwall *Orange*
Cornwall On Hudson
  Orange
Cornwallville *Greene*
Cortland *Cortland*
Cossayuna *Washington*
Cottekill *Ulster*
Cowlesville *Wyoming*
Coxsackie *Greene*
Cragsmoor *Ulster*
Cranberry Lake *Saint*
  Lawrence
Craryville *Columbia*
Crittenden *Erie*
Croghan *Lewis*
Crompond *Westchester*
Cropseyville *Rensselaer*
Cross River *Westchester*
Croton Falls *Westchester*
Croton-*on-Hudson
  Westchester
Crown Point *Essex*
Crugers *Westchester*
Cuba *Allegany*
Cuddebackville *Orange*
Cutchogue *Suffolk*
Cuyler *Cortland*
Dale *Wyoming*
Dalton *Livingston*
Dannemora *Clinton*
Dansville *Livingston*
Dandee *Herkimer*
Darien Center *Genesee*
Davenport *Delaware*
Davenport Center
  Delaware
Dayton *Cattaraugus*
Deansboro *Oneida*
Deer Park *Suffolk*
Deer River *Lewis*
Deferiet *Jefferson*
Defreetsville *Rensselaer*
DeKalb Junction *Saint*
  Lawrence
DeLancey *Delaware*
Delanson *Schenectady*
Delevan *Cattaraugus*
Delhi *Delaware*
Delmar *Albany*
Delphi Falls *Onondaga*
Denmark *Lewis*
Denver *Delaware*
Depauville *Jefferson*
Depew *Erie*
DePeyster *Saint Lawrence*
Deposit *Broome*
Derby *Erie*
DeRuyter *Madison*
De Witt *Onondaga*
Dewittville *Chautauqua*
Dexter *Jefferson*
Diamond Point *Warren*
Dickinson Center *Franklin*
Dix Hills *Suffolk*
Dobbs Ferry *Westchester*
Dolgeville *Herkimer*
Dorloo *Schoharie*
Dover Plains *Dutchess*
Downsville *Delaware*

Dresden *Yates*
Dryden *Tompkins*
Duanesburg *Schenectady*
Dundee *Yates*
Dunkirk *Chautauqua*
Durham *Greene*
Durhamville *Oneida*
Eagle Bay *Herkimer*
Eagle Bridge *Rensselaer*
Eagle Harbor *Orleans*
Earlton *Greene*
Earlville *Madison*
East Amherst *Erie*
East Atlantic Beach
    Nassau
East Aurora *Erie*
East Berne *Albany*
East Bethany *Genesee*
East Bloomfield *Ontario*
East Branch *Delaware*
East Cayuga Heights
    Tompkins
East Chatham *Columbia*
East Chester *Westchester*
East Concord *Erie*
East Durham *Greene*
East Freetown *Cortland*
East Glenville *Schenectady*
East Greenbush *Rensselaer*
East Greenwich
    Washington
East Hills *Nassau*
East Hampton *Suffolk*
East Homer *Cortland*
East Irvington *Westchester*
East Islip *Suffolk*
East Jewett *Greene*
East Marion *Suffolk*
East Meadow *Nassau*
East Meredith *Delaware*
East Middletown *Orange*
East Moriches *Suffolk*
East Nassau *Rensselaer*
East Northport *Suffolk*
East Norwich *Nassau*
East Otto *Cattaraugus*
East Palmyra *Wayne*
East Patchogue *Suffolk*
East Pembroke *Genesee*
East Pharsalia *Chenango*
Eastport *Suffolk*
East Quogue *Suffolk*
East Randolph *Cattaraugus*
East Rochester *Monroe*
East Rockaway *Nassau*
East Schodack *Rensselaer*
East Setauket *Suffolk*
East Springfield *Otsego*
East Syracuse *Onondaga*
East Williamson *Wayne*
East Worcester *Otsego*
Eaton *Madison*
Eddyville *Ulster*
Eden *Erie*
Edmeston *Otsego*
Edwards *Saint Lawrence*
Elba *Genesee*
Elbridge *Onondaga*
Eldred *Sullivan*
Elizabethtown *Essex*
Elizaville *Columbia*
Elka Park *Greene*
Ellenburg *Clinton*
Ellenburg Center *Clinton*
Ellenburg Depot *Clinton*
Ellenville *Ulster*

Ellicottville *Cattaraugus*
Ellington *Chautauqua*
Ellisburg *Jefferson*
Elma *Erie*
Elmira *Chemung*
Elmira Heights *Chemung*
Elmont *Nassau*
Elmsford *Westchester*
Elsmere *Albany*
Elwood *Suffolk*
Endicott *Broome*
Endwell *Broome*
Erieville *Madison*
Erin *Chemung*
Esopus *Ulster*
Esperance *Schoharie*
Essex *Essex*
Etna *Tompkins*
Evans Mills *Jefferson*
Fabius *Onondaga*
Fairfield *Herkimer*
Fair Haven *Cayuga*
Fairmount *Onondaga*
Fairport *Monroe*
Fairview *Westchester*
Falconer *Chautauqua*
Fallsburg *Sullivan*
Fancher *Orleans*
Farmersville Station
    Cattaraugus
Farmingdale *Nassau*
Farmingville *Suffolk*
Farnham *Erie*
Far Rockaway *Queens*
Fayette *Seneca*
Fayetteville *Onondaga*
Felts Mills *Jefferson*
Ferndale *Sullivan*
Fernwood *Saratoga*
Feura Bush *Albany*
Fillmore *Allegany*
Findley Lake *Chautauqua*
Fine *Saint Lawrence*
Fineview *Jefferson*
Fishers *Ontario*
Fishers Island *Suffolk*
Fishers Landing *Jefferson*
Fishkill *Dutchess*
Fishs Eddy *Delaware*
Flanders *Suffolk*
Fleischmanns *Delaware*
Floral Park *Nassau*
Florida *Orange*
Flower Hill *Nassau*
Flushing *Queens*
Fluvanna *Chautauqua*
Fly Creek *Otsego*
Fonda *Montgomery*
Forestport *Oneida*
Forestville *Chautauqua*
Fort Ann *Washington*
Fort Covington *Franklin*
Fort Edward *Washington*
Fort Hunter *Montgomery*
Fort Johnson *Montgomery*
Fort Montgomery *Orange*
Fort Plain *Montgomery*
Fort Solonga *Suffolk*
Frankfort *Herkimer*
Franklin *Delaware*
Franklin Springs *Oneida*
Franklin Square *Nassau*
Franklinville *Cattaraugus*
Fredonia *Chautauqua*
Freedom *Cattaraugus*
Freehold *Greene*

Freeport *Nassau*
Freeville *Tompkins*
Fremont Center *Sullivan*
Frewsburg *Chautauqua*
Friendship *Allegany*
Fulton *Oswego*
Fultonham *Schoharie*
Fultonville *Montgomery*
Gabriels *Franklin*
Gainesville *Wyoming*
Gallupville *Schoharie*
Galway *Saratoga*
Gang Mills *Steuben*
Gansevoort *Saratoga*
Garden City *Nassau*
Gardiner *Ulster*
Gardnertown *Orange*
Garnerville *Rockland*
Garrattsville *Otsego*
Garrison *Putnam*
Gasport *Niagara*
Gates *Monroe*
Geneseo *Livingston*
Geneva *Ontario*
Genoa *Cayuga*
Georgetown *Madison*
German Flatts *Herkimer*
Germantown *Columbia*
Gerry *Chautauqua*
Getzville *Erie*
Ghent *Columbia*
Gilbertsville *Otsego*
Gilboa *Schoharie*
Glasco *Ulster*
Glen Aubrey *Broome*
Glen Cove *Nassau*
Glenfield *Lewis*
Glenford *Ulster*
Glenham *Dutchess*
Glen Head *Nassau*
Glenmont *Albany*
Glens Falls *Warren*
Glen Spey *Sullivan*
Glen Wild *Sullivan*
Glenwood *Erie*
Glenwood Landing *Nassau*
Gloversville *Fulton*
Godeffroy *Orange*
Goldens Bridge
    Westchester
Gorham *Ontario*
Goshen *Orange*
Gouverneur *Saint
    Lawrence*
Gowanda *Cattaraugus*
Grafton *Rensselaer*
Grahamsville *Sullivan*
Grand Gorge *Delaware*
Grand Island *Erie*
Grandyle Village *Erie*
Granite Springs
    Westchester
Granville *Washington*
Great Bend *Jefferson*
Great Neck *Nassau*
Great Neck Estates *Nassau*
Great River *Suffolk*
Great Valley *Cattaraugus*
Greece *Monroe*
Greene *Chenango*
Greenfield Center *Saratoga*
Greenfield Park *Ulster*
Greenhurst *Chautauqua*
Greenlawn *Suffolk*
Greenport *Suffolk*
Greenvale *Nassau*

Greenville *Greene*
Greenwich *Washington*
Greenwood *Steuben*
Greenwood Lake *Orange*
Green Island *Albany*
Greig *Lewis*
Groton *Tompkins*
Groveland *Livingston*
Guilderland *Albany*
Guilderland Center *Albany*
Guilford *Chenango*
Hadley *Saratoga*
Hagaman *Montgomery*
Hague *Warren*
Hailesboro *Saint Lawrence*
Haines Falls *Greene*
Halcottsville *Delaware*
Halesite *Suffolk*
Half Hollow Hills *Suffolk*
Hall *Ontario*
Hamburg *Erie*
Hamden *Delaware*
Hamilton *Madison*
Hamlin *Monroe*
Hammond *Saint Lawrence*
Hammondsport *Steuben*
Hampton *Washington*
Hampton Bays *Suffolk*
Hancock *Delaware*
Hankins *Sullivan*
Hannacroix *Greene*
Hannawa Falls *Saint
    Lawrence*
Hannibal *Oswego*
Harbour Hills *Nassau*
Harford *Cortland*
Harford Mills *Cortland*
Harpersfield *Delaware*
Harpursville *Broome*
Harriman *Orange*
Harris *Sullivan*
Harris Hills *Erie*
Harrison *Westchester*
Harrisville *Lewis*
Hartford *Washington*
Hartsdale *Westchester*
Harts Hill *Oneida*
Hartwick *Otsego*
Hartwick Seminary *Otsego*
Hastings *Oswego*
Hastings On Hudson
    Westchester
Hauppauge *Suffolk*
Haverstraw *Rockland*
Hawthorne *Westchester*
Head Of The Harbour
    Suffolk
Hector *Schuyler*
Helena *Saint Lawrence*
Helmuth *Erie*
Hemlock *Livingston*
Hempstead *Nassau*
Henderson *Jefferson*
Henderson Harbor
    Jefferson
Henrietta *Monroe*
Hensonville *Greene*
Herkimer *Herkimer*
Hermon *Saint Lawrence*
Herrings *Jefferson*
Heuvelton *Saint Lawrence*
Hewlett *Nassau*
Hicksville *Nassau*
High Falls *Ulster*
Highland *Ulster*
Highland Falls *Orange*

Highland Lake *Sullivan*
Highland Mills *Orange*
Highland On The Lake *Erie*
Highmount *Ulster*
Hillburn *Rockland*
Hillcrest *Rockland*
Hillsdale *Columbia*
Hilton *Monroe*
Himrod *Yates*
Hinckley *Oneida*
Hinsdale *Cattaraugus*
Hobart *Delaware*
Hoffmeister *Hamilton*
Hogansburg *Franklin*
Holbrook *Suffolk*
Holcomb *Ontario*
Holland *Erie*
Holland Patent *Oneida*
Holley *Orleans*
Hollowville *Columbia*
Holmes *Dutchess*
Holmesville *Chenango*
Holtsville *Suffolk*
Homer *Cortland*
Honeoye *Ontario*
Honeoye Falls *Monroe*
Hoosick *Rensselaer*
Hoosick Falls *Rensselaer*
Hopewell Junction *Dutchess*
Hornell *Steuben*
Horseheads *Chemung*
Hortonville *Sullivan*
Houghton *Allegany*
Howells *Orange*
Howes Cave *Schoharie*
Hubbardsville *Madison*
Hudson *Columbia*
Hudson Falls *Washington*
Hughsonville *Dutchess*
Huguenot *Orange*
Huletts Landing *Washington*
Hume *Allegany*
Hunt *Livingston*
Hunter *Greene*
Huntington *Suffolk*
Huntington Bay *Suffolk*
Huntington Station *Suffolk*
Hurley *Ulster*
Hurleyville *Sullivan*
Hyde Park *Dutchess*
Ilion *Herkimer*
Indian Lake *Hamilton*
Indian Village *Onondaga*
Industry *Monroe*
Inlet *Hamilton*
Interlaken *Seneca*
Inwood *Nassau*
Ionia *Ontario*
Irondequoit *Monroe*
Irving *Chautauqua*
Irvington *Westchester*
Island Park *Nassau*
Islip *Suffolk*
Islip Terrace *Suffolk*
Ithaca *Tompkins*
Jacksonville *Tompkins*
Jamaica *Queens*
Jamesport *Suffolk*
Jamestown *Chautauqua*
Jamesville *Onondaga*
Jasper *Steuben*
Java Center *Wyoming*

Java Village *Wyoming*
Jay *Essex*
Jefferson *Schoharie*
Jefferson Valley *Westchester*
Jeffersonville *Sullivan*
Jericho *Nassau*
Jewett *Greene*
Johnsburg *Warren*
Johnson *Orange*
Johnson City *Broome*
Johnsonville *Rensselaer*
Johnstown *Fulton*
Jordan *Onondaga*
Jordanville *Herkimer*
Kanona *Steuben*
Katonah *Westchester*
Kattelville *Broome*
Kattskill Bay *Warren*
Kauneonga Lake *Sullivan*
Keene *Essex*
Keene Valley *Essex*
Keeseville *Essex*
Kelly Corners *Delaware*
Kendall *Orleans*
Kenmore *Erie*
Kennedy *Chautauqua*
Kenoza Lake *Sullivan*
Kensington *Nassau*
Kent *Orleans*
Kerhonkson *Ulster*
Keuka Park *Yates*
Kiamesha Lake *Sullivan*
Killawog *Broome*
Kill Buck *Cattaraugus*
Kinderhook *Columbia*
King Ferry *Cayuga*
Kings Park *Suffolk*
Kings Point *Nassau*
Kingston *Ulster*
Kirkville *Onondaga*
Kirkwood *Broome*
Knapp Creek *Cattaraugus*
Knowlesville *Orleans*
Knox *Albany*
Knoxboro *Oneida*
Kortright *Delaware*
Lacona *Oswego*
LaFargeville *Jefferson*
LaFayette *Onondaga*
Lackawanna *Erie*
Lagrangeville *Dutchess*
Lake Clear *Franklin*
Lake Erie Beach *Erie*
Lake George *Warren*
Lake Grove *Suffolk*
Lake Hill *Ulster*
Lake Huntington *Sullivan*
Lake Katrine *Ulster*
Lake Luzerne *Warren*
Lakeland *Onondaga*
Lakemont *Yates*
Lake Peekskill *Putnam*
Lake Placid *Essex*
Lake Pleasant *Hamilton*
Lake Ronkonkoma *Suffolk*
Lake View *Erie*
Lakeville *Livingston*
Lakewood *Chautauqua*
Lancaster *Erie*
Lansing *Tompkins*
Lanesville *Greene*
Larchmont *Westchester*
Latham *Albany*
Lattingtown *Nassau*

Laurel *Suffolk*
Laurens *Otsego*
Lawrence *Nassau*
Lawrenceville *Saint Lawrence*
Lawtons *Erie*
Lawyersville *Schoharie*
Lebanon *Madison*
Lebanon Springs *Columbia*
Lee Center *Oneida*
Leeds *Greene*
Leicester *Livingston*
Leon *Cattaraugus*
Leonardsville *Madison*
Le Roy *Genesee*
Levittown *Nassau*
Lewbeach *Sullivan*
Lewis *Essex*
Lewiston *Niagara*
Lexington *Greene*
Liberty *Sullivan*
Lido Beach *Nassau*
Lily Dale *Chautauqua*
Lima *Livingston*
Limerick *Jefferson*
Limestone *Cattaraugus*
Lincolndale *Westchester*
Lindenhurst *Suffolk*
Lindley *Steuben*
Linwood *Livingston*
Lisbon *Saint Lawrence*
Lisle *Broome*
Litchfield *Herkimer*
Little Falls *Herkimer*
Little Genesee *Allegany*
Little Valley *Cattaraugus*
Little York *Cortland*
Liverpool *Onondaga*
Livingston *Columbia*
Livingston Manor *Sullivan*
Livonia *Livingston*
Livonia Center *Livingston*
Lloyd Harbour *Suffolk*
Loch Sheldrake *Sullivan*
Locke *Cayuga*
Lockport *Niagara*
Lockwood *Tioga*
Locust Grove *Nassau*
Locust Valley *Nassau*
Lodi *Seneca*
Long Beach *Nassau*
Long Eddy *Sullivan*
Long Island City *Queens*
Long Lake *Hamilton*
Lorraine *Jefferson*
Lowman *Chemung*
Lowville *Lewis*
Lycoming *Oswego*
Lynbrook *Nassau*
Lyndon *Onondaga*
Lyndonville *Orleans*
Lyon Mountain *Clinton*
Lyons *Wayne*
Lyons Falls *Lewis*
Lysander *Onondaga*
McConnellsville *Oneida*
McDonough *Chenango*
McGraw *Cortland*
McKnownville *Albany*
McLean *Tompkins*
Macedon *Wayne*
Machias *Cattaraugus*
Madison *Madison*
Madrid *Saint Lawrence*
Mahopac *Putnam*

Mahopac Falls *Putnam*
Maine *Broome*
Malden Bridge *Columbia*
Malden on Hudson *Ulster*
Mallory *Oswego*
Malone *Franklin*
Malverne *Nassau*
Mamaroneck *Westchester*
Manchester *Ontario*
Manhasset *Nassau*
Manhein *Herkimer*
Manlius *Onondaga*
Mannsville *Jefferson*
Manorhaven *Nassau*
Manorville *Suffolk*
Maplecrest *Greene*
Maple Springs *Chautauqua*
Maple View *Oswego*
Maplewood *Albany*
Marathon *Cortland*
Marcellus *Onondaga*
Marcy *Oneida*
Margaretville *Delaware*
Marietta *Onondaga*
Marilla *Erie*
Marion *Wayne*
Marlboro *Ulster*
Martinsburg *Lewis*
Martville *Cayuga*
Maryknoll *Westchester*
Maryland *Otsego*
Masonville *Delaware*
Massapequa *Nassau*
Massapequa Park *Nassau*
Massena *Saint Lawrence*
Mastic *Suffolk*
Mastic Beach *Suffolk*
Mattituck *Suffolk*
Mattydale *Onondaga*
Maybrook *Orange*
Mayfield *Fulton*
Mayville *Chautauqua*
Mechanicville *Saratoga*
Mecklenburg *Schuyler*
Medford *Suffolk*
Medina *Orleans*
Medusa *Albany*
Mellenville *Columbia*
Melrose *Rensselaer*
Melville *Suffolk*
Memphis *Onondaga*
Menands *Albany*
Mendon *Monroe*
Meredith *Delarare*
Meridale *Delaware*
Meridian *Cayuga*
Merrick *Nassau*
Mexico *Oswego*
Middleburgh *Schoharie*
Middle Falls *Washington*
Middle Granville *Washington*
Middle Grove *Saratoga*
Middle Hope *Orange*
Middle Island *Suffolk*
Middleport *Niagara*
Middlesex *Yates*
Middletown *Orange*
Middleville *Herkimer*
Milford *Otsego*
Millbrook *Dutchess*
Miller Place *Suffolk*
Millerton *Dutchess*
Mill Neck *Nassau*
Millport *Chemung*

Millwood *Westchester*
Milton *Ulster*
Mineola *Nassau*
Minerva *Essex*
Minetto *Oswego*
Mineville *Essex*
Minoa *Onondaga*
Model City *Niagara*
Modena *Ulster*
Mohawk *Herkimer*
Mohegan Lake *Westchester*
Moira *Franklin*
Mongaup Valley *Sullivan*
Monroe *Orange*
Monsey *Rockland*
Montauk *Suffolk*
Montebello *Rockland*
Montezuma *Cayuga*
Montgomery *Orange*
Monticello *Sullivan*
Montour Falls *Schuyler*
Montrose *Westchester*
Mooers *Clinton*
Mooers Forks *Clinton*
Moravia *Cayuga*
Moriah *Essex*
Moriah Center *Essex*
Moriches *Suffolk*
Morris *Otsego*
Morrisonville *Clinton*
Morristown *Saint
  Lawrence*
Morrisville *Madison*
Morton *Orleans*
Mottville *Onondaga*
Mountain Dale *Sullivan*
Mountainville *Orange*
Mount Kisco *Westchester*
Mount Marion *Ulster*
Mount Morris *Livingston*
Mount Sinai *Suffolk*
Mount Tremper *Ulster*
Mount Upton *Chenango*
Mount Vernon *Westchester*
Mount Vision *Otsego*
Mumford *Monroe*
Munsey Park *Nassau*
Munnsville *Madison*
Muttontown *Nassau*
Nanuet *Rockland*
Napanoch *Ulster*
Naples *Ontario*
Narrowsburg *Sullivan*
Nassau *Rensselaer*
Natural Bridge *Jefferson*
Nedrow *Onondaga*
Nelliston *Montgomery*
Nesconset *Suffolk*
Neversink *Sullivan*
Newark *Wayne*
Newark Valley *Tioga*
New Baltimore *Greene*
New Berlin *Chenango*
New Bremen *Lewis*
Newburgh *Orange*
New City *Rockland*
Newcomb *Essex*
Newfane *Niagara*
Newfield *Tompkins*
New Hamburg *Dutchess*
New Hampton *Orange*
New Hartford *Oneida*
New Haven *Oswego*
New Hempstead *Rockland*
New Hyde Park *Nassau*
New Kingston *Delaware*

New Lebanon *Columbia*
New Lebanon Center
  Columbia
New Lisbon *Otsego*
New Milford *Orange*
New Paltz *Ulster*
Newport *Herkimer*
New Rochelle *Westchester*
New Russia *Essex*
New Scotland *Albany*
New Square *Rockland*
New Suffolk *Suffolk*
Newton Falls *Saint
  Lawrence*
Newtonville *Albany*
New Woodstock *Madison*
New York *New York*
New York Mills *Oneida*
Niagara Falls *Niagara*
Niagara University
  Niagara
Nichols *Tioga*
Nicholville *Saint Lawrence*
Nimmonsburg *Broome*
Nineveh *Broome*
Niobe *Chautauqua*
Niskayuna *Schenectady*
Nissequogue *Suffolk*
Niverville *Columbia*
Norfolk *Saint Lawrence*
North Bangor *Franklin*
North Bay *Oneida*
North Bellmore *Nassau*
North Bellport *Suffolk*
North Blenheim *Schoharie*
North Bloomfield *Ontario*
North Boston *Erie*
North Branch *Sullivan*
North Brookfield *Madison*
North Chatham *Columbia*
North Chili *Monroe*
North Clymer *Chautauqua*
North Cohocton *Steuben*
North Collins *Erie*
North Creek *Warren*
North Evans *Erie*
North Granville
  Washington
North Greece *Monroe*
North Hoosick *Rensselaer*
North Hudson *Essex*
North Java *Wyoming*
North Lawrence *Saint
  Lawrence*
North New Hyde Park
  Nassau
North Norwich *Chenango*
North Pitcher *Chenango*
Northport *Suffolk*
North River *Warren*
North Rose *Wayne*
North Salem *Westchester*
North Syracuse *Onondaga*
North Tarrytown
  Westchester
North Tonawanda *Niagara*
North Valley Stream
  Nassau
Northville *Fulton*
North Western *Oneida*
Norton Hill *Greene*
Norway *Herkimer*
Norwich *Chenango*
Norwood *Saint Lawrence*
Nunda *Livingston*
Nyack *Rockland*

Oakdale *Suffolk*
Oakfield *Genesee*
Oak Hill *Greene*
Oaks Corners *Ontario*
Obernburg *Sullivan*
Ocean Beach *Suffolk*
Oceanside *Nassau*
Odessa *Schuyler*
Ogdensburg *Saint
  Lawrence*
Ohio *Herkimer*
Olcott *Niagara*
Old Chatham *Columbia*
Old Forge *Herkimer*
Olean *Cattaraugus*
Olivebridge *Ulster*
Oliverea *Ulster*
Olmstedville *Essex*
Onchiota *Franklin*
Oneida *Madison*
Oneonta *Otsego*
Ontario *Wayne*
Ontario Center *Wayne*
Oran *Onondaga*
Orangeburg *Rockland*
Orchard Park *Erie*
Orient *Suffolk*
Oriskany *Oneida*
Oriskany Falls *Oneida*
Orwell *Oswego*
Ossining *Westchester*
Oswegatchie *Saint
  Lawrence*
Oswego *Oswego*
Otego *Otsego*
Otisville *Orange*
Otselic *Chenango*
Otto *Cattaraugus*
Ouaquaga *Broome*
Ovid *Seneca*
Owasco *Cayuga*
Owego *Tioga*
Owls Head *Franklin*
Oxford *Chenango*
Oyster Bay *Nassau*
Oyster Bay Cove *Nassau*
Painted Post *Steuben*
Palatine Bridge
  Montgomery
Palenville *Greene*
Palisades *Rockland*
Palmyra *Wayne*
Panama *Chautauqua*
Paris *Oneida*
Parish *Oswego*
Parishville *Saint Lawrence*
Parksville *Sullivan*
Patchogue *Suffolk*
Patterson *Putnam*
Pattersonville *Schenectady*
Paul Smiths *Franklin*
Pavilion *Genesee*
Pawling *Dutchess*
Pearl River *Rockland*
Peconic *Suffolk*
Peekskill *Westchester*
Pelham *Westchester*
Pelham Manor *Westchester*
Penfield *Monroe*
Pennellville *Oswego*
Penn Yan *Yates*
Perkinsville *Steuben*
Perry *Wyoming*
Perrysburg *Cattaraugus*
Perryville *Madison*
Peru *Clinton*

Peterboro *Madison*
Petersburg *Rensselaer*
Phelps *Ontario*
Philadelphia *Jefferson*
Phillipsport *Sullivan*
Philmont *Columbia*
Phoenicia *Ulster*
Phoenix *Oswego*
Piercefield *Saint Lawrence*
Piermont *Rockland*
Pierrepont Manor *Jefferson*
Piffard *Livingston*
Pike *Wyoming*
Pine Bush *Orange*
Pine City *Chemung*
Pine Hill *Ulster*
Pine Island *Orange*
Pine Plains *Dutchess*
Pine Valley *Chemung*
Piseco *Hamilton*
Pitcher *Chenango*
Pittsford *Monroe*
Plainview *Nassau*
Plainville *Onondaga*
Plandome Heights *Nassau*
Plandome Manor *Nassau*
Plattekill *Ulster*
Plattsburgh *Clinton*
Pleasant Valley *Dutchess*
Pleasantville *Westchester*
Plessis *Jefferson*
Plymouth *Chenango*
Poestenkill *Rensselaer*
Point Lookout *Nassau*
Poland *Herkimer*
Pomona *Rockland*
Pompey *Onondaga*
Pond Eddy *Sullivan*
Poolville *Madison*
Poplar Ridge *Cayuga*
Portageville *Wyoming*
Port Byron *Cayuga*
Port Chester *Westchester*
Port Crane *Broome*
Porter Corners *Saratoga*
Port Dickinson *Broome*
Port Ewen *Ulster*
Port Gibson *Ontario*
Port Henry *Essex*
Port Jefferson *Suffolk*
Port Jefferson Station
  Suffolk
Port Jervis *Orange*
Port Kent *Essex*
Portland *Chautauqua*
Portlandville *Otsego*
Port Leyden *Lewis*
Portville *Cattaraugus*
Port Washington *Nassau*
Potsdam *Saint Lawrence*
Pottersville *Warren*
Poughkeepsie *Dutchess*
Poughquag *Dutchess*
Pound Ridge *Westchester*
Prattsburg *Steuben*
Pratts Hollow *Madison*
Prattsville *Greene*
Preble *Cortland*
Preston Hollow *Albany*
Prospect *Oneida*
Pulaski *Oswego*
Pulteney *Steuben*
Pultneyville *Wayne*
Purchase *Westchester*
Purdys *Westchester*
Purling *Greene*

Putnam Lake *Putnam*
Putnam Station *Washington*
Putnam Valley *Putnam*
Pyrites *Saint Lawrence*
Quaker Street *Schenectady*
Queens Burg *Warren*
Quogue *Suffolk*
Rainbow Lake *Franklin*
Randolph *Cattaraugus*
Ransomville *Niagara*
Raquette Lake *Hamilton*
Ravena *Albany*
Ray Brook *Essex*
Raymondville *Saint Lawrence*
Reading Center *Schuyler*
Red Creek *Wayne*
Redfield *Oswego*
Redford *Clinton*
Red Hook *Dutchess*
Redwood *Jefferson*
Remsen *Oneida*
Remsenburg *Suffolk*
Rensselaer *Rensselaer*
Rensselaer Falls *Saint Lawrence*
Rensselaerville *Albany*
Retsof *Livingston*
Rexford *Saratoga*
Rexville *Steuben*
Rhinebeck *Dutchess*
Rhinecliff *Dutchess*
Richburg *Allegany*
Richfield Springs *Otsego*
Richford *Tioga*
Richland *Oswego*
Richmondville *Schoharie*
Richville *Saint Lawrence*
Ridge *Suffolk*
Ridgewood *Oneida*
Rifton *Ulster*
Riparius *Warren*
Ripley *Chautauqua*
Riverhead *Suffolk*
Rochester *Monroe*
Rock City Falls *Saratoga*
Rock Hill *Sullivan*
Rock Stream *Yates*
Rock Tavern *Orange*
Rockville Centre *Nassau*
Rocky Point *Suffolk*
Rodman *Jefferson*
Rome *Oneida*
Romulus *Seneca*
Ronkonkoma *Suffolk*
Roosevelt *Nassau*
Rooseveltown *Saint Lawrence*
Roscoe *Sullivan*
Rose *Wayne*
Roseboom *Otsego*
Rosendale *Ulster*
Roslyn *Nassau*
Roslyn Heights *Nassau*
Rossburg *Allegany*
Ross Corners *Broome*
Rotterdam *Schenectady*
Rotterdam Junction *Schenectady*
Round Lake *Saratoga*
Round Top *Greene*
Rouses Point *Clinton*
Roxbury *Delaware*
Ruby *Ulster*
Rush *Monroe*

Rushford *Allegany*
Rushville *Yates*
Russell *Saint Lawrence*
Russell Gardens *Nassau*
Russia *Herkimer*
Rye *Westchester*
Rye Brook *Westchester*
Sabael *Hamilton*
Sackets Harbor *Jefferson*
Saddle Rock *Nassau*
Sagaponack *Suffolk*
Sag Harbor *Suffolk*
Saint Bonaventure *Cattaraugus*
Saint James *Suffolk*
Saint Johnsville *Montgomery*
Saint Regis Falls *Franklin*
Salamanca *Cattaraugus*
Salem *Washington*
Salisbury Center *Herkimer*
Salisbury Mills *Orange*
Salt Point *Dutchess*
Sanborn *Niagara*
Sand Lake *Rensselaer*
Sands Point *Nassau*
Sandusky *Cattaraugus*
Sandy Beach *Niagra*
Sandy Creek *Oswego*
Sangerfield *Oneida*
Sanitaria Springs *Broome*
San Remo *Suffolk*
Saranac *Clinton*
Saranac Lake *Franklin*
Saratoga Springs *Saratoga*
Sardinia *Erie*
Saugerties *Ulster*
Sauquoit *Oneida*
Savannah *Wayne*
Savona *Steuben*
Sayville *Suffolk*
Scarsdale *Westchester*
Schaghticoke *Rensselaer*
Schenectady *Schenectady*
Schenevus *Otsego*
Schodack Landing *Rensselaer*
Schoharie *Schoharie*
Schroon Lake *Essex*
Schuyler *Herkimer*
Schuyler Falls *Clinton*
Schuyler Lake *Otsego*
Schuylerville *Saratoga*
Scio *Allegany*
Scipio Center *Cayuga*
Scottsville *Monroe*
Sea Cliff *Nassau*
Seaford *Nassau*
Selden *Suffolk*
Selkirk *Albany*
Seneca Castle *Ontario*
Seneca Falls *Seneca*
Sennett *Cayuga*
Setauket *Suffolk*
Severance *Essex*
Shady *Ulster*
Shandaken *Ulster*
Sharon Springs *Schoharie*
Sheds *Madison*
Shelter Island *Suffolk*
Shelter Island Heights *Suffolk*
Shenorock *Westchester*
Sherburne *Chenango*
Sheridan *Chautauqua*

Sherman *Chautauqua*
Sherrill *Oneida*
Shinhopple *Delaware*
Shirley *Suffolk*
Shokan *Ulster*
Shoreham *Suffolk*
Shortsville *Ontario*
Shrub Oak *Westchester*
Shushan *Washington*
Sidney *Delaware*
Sidney Center *Delaware*
Silver Bay *Warren*
Silver Creek *Chautauqua*
Silver Lake *Wyoming*
Silver Springs *Wyoming*
Sinclairville *Chautauqua*
Skaneateles *Onondaga*
Skaneateles Falls *Onondaga*
Slate Hill *Orange*
Slaterville Springs *Tompkins*
Slingerlands *Albany*
Sloan *Erie*
Sloansville *Schoharie*
Sloatsburg *Rockland*
Smallwood *Sullivan*
Smithboro *Tioga*
Smithtown *Suffolk*
Smithville *Jefferson*
Smithville Flats *Chenango*
Smyrna *Chenango*
Sodus *Wayne*
Sodus Center *Wayne*
Sodus Point *Wayne*
Solvay *Onondaga*
Solsville *Madison*
Somers *Westchester*
Sonyea *Livingston*
Sound Beach *Suffolk*
Southampton *Suffolk*
South Bethlehem *Albany*
South Butler *Wayne*
South Byron *Genesee*
South Cairo *Greene*
South Colton *Saint Lawrence*
South Corning *Steuben*
South Dayton *Cattaraugus*
South Edmeston *Otsego*
South Fallsburg *Sullivan*
Southfields *Orange*
South Glen Falls *Saratoga*
South Jamesport *Suffolk*
South Kortright *Delaware*
South Lima *Livingston*
South New Berlin *Chenango*
South Nyack *Rockland*
Southold *Suffolk*
South Otselic *Chenango*
South Plymouth *Chenango*
South Rutland *Jefferson*
South Salem *Westchester*
South Schodack *Rensselaer*
South Schroon *Essex*
South Valley Stream *Nassau*
South Wales *Erie*
South Westerlo *Albany*
Sparkill *Rockland*
Sparrow Bush *Orange*
Speculator *Hamilton*
Speigletown *Rensselaer*

Spencer *Tioga*
Spencerport *Monroe*
Spencertown *Columbia*
Speonk *Suffolk*
Sprakers *Montgomery*
Spring Brook *Erie*
Springfield Center *Otsego*
Spring Glen *Ulster*
Spring Valley *Rockland*
Springville *Erie*
Springwater *Livingston*
Staatsburg *Dutchess*
Stafford *Genesee*
Stamford *Delaware*
Stanford Heights *Albany*
Stanfordville *Dutchess*
Stanley *Ontario*
Star Lake *Saint Lawrence*
Stark *Herkimer*
Staten Island *Richmond*
Steamburg *Cattaraugus*
Stella Niagara *Niagara*
Stephentown *Rensselaer*
Sterling *Cayuga*
Sterling Forest *Orange*
Stillwater *Saratoga*
Stittville *Oneida*
Stockport *Columbia*
Stockton *Chautauqua*
Stone Ridge *Ulster*
Stony Brook *Suffolk*
Stony Creek *Warren*
Stony Point *Rockland*
Stormville *Dutchess*
Stottville *Columbia*
Stow *Chautauqua*
Stratford *Fulton*
Strykersville *Wyoming*
Stuyvesant *Columbia*
Stuyvesant Falls *Columbia*
Suffern *Rockland*
Sugar Loaf *Orange*
Summit *Schoharie*
Summitville *Sullivan*
Surprise *Greene*
Swain *Allegany*
Swan Lake *Sullivan*
Swormville *Erie*
Sylvan Beach *Oneida*
Sycaway *Rensselaer*
Syosset *Nassau*
Syracuse *Onondaga*
Taberg *Oneida*
Tallman *Rockland*
Tannersville *Greene*
Tappan *Rockland*
Tarrytown *Westchester*
Taunton *Onondaga*
Terryville *Suffolk*
Thendara *Herkimer*
Theresa *Jefferson*
Thiells *Rockland*
Thomaston *Nassau*
Thompson Ridge *Orange*
Thompsonville *Sullivan*
Thornwood *Westchester*
Thousand Island Park *Jefferson*
Three Mile Bay *Jefferson*
Ticonderoga *Essex*
Tillson *Ulster*
Tioga Center *Tioga*
Tivoli *Dutchess*
Tomkins Cove *Rockland*
Tompkins *Delaware*

Tonawanda *Erie*
Treadwell *Delaware*
Tribes Hill *Montgomery*
Troupsburg *Steuben*
Trout Creek *Delaware*
Troy *Rensselaer*
Trumansburg *Tompkins*
Truxton *Cortland*
Tuckahoe *Westchester*
Tully *Onondaga*
Tunnel *Broome*
Tupper Lake *Franklin*
Turin *Lewis*
Tuscarora *Livingston*
Tuxedo Park *Orange*
Twin Orchards *Broome*
Tyrone *Schuyler*
Ulster Park *Ulster*
Unadilla *Otsego*
Union Center *Broome*
Uniondale *Nassau*
Union Hill *Monroe*
Union Springs *Cayuga*
Unionville *Orange*
University Gardens *Nassau*
Upper Jay *Essex*
Upper Nyack *Rockland*
Upton *Suffolk*
Utica *Oneida*
Vails Gate *Orange*
Valatie *Columbia*
Valhalla *Westchester*
Valley Cottage *Rockland*
Valley Falls *Rensselaer*
Valley Stream *Nassau*
Valois *Schuyler*
Van Etten *Chemung*
Van Hornesville *Herkimer*
Van Keurens *Dutchess*
Varysburg *Wyoming*
Venice Center *Cayuga*
Verbank *Dutchess*
Verdoy *Albany*
Vermontville *Franklin*
Vernon *Oneida*
Vernon Center *Oneida*
Verona *Oneida*
Verona Beach *Oneida*
Verplanck *Westchester*
Versailles *Cattaraugus*
Vestal *Broome*
Vestal Center *Broome*
Victor *Ontario*
Victory Mills *Saratoga*
Village Of The Branch
  Suffolk
Voorheesville *Albany*
Waccabuc *Westchester*
Waddington *Saint*
  Lawrence
Wadhams *Essex*
Wading River *Suffolk*
Wainscott *Suffolk*
Walden *Orange*
Wales Center *Erie*
Walker Valley *Ulster*
Wallkill *Ulster*
Walton *Delaware*
Walworth *Wayne*
Wampsville *Madison*
Wanakah *Erie*
Wanakena *Saint Lawrence*
Wantagh *Nassau*
Wappingers Falls *Dutchess*
Warners *Onondaga*

Warnerville *Schoharie*
Warren *Herkimer*
Warrensburg *Warren*
Warsaw *Wyoming*
Warwick *Orange*
Washington Mills *Oneida*
Washingtonville *Orange*
Wassaic *Dutchess*
Waterford *Saratoga*
Waterloo *Seneca*
Water Mill *Suffolk*
Waterport *Orleans*
Watertown *Jefferson*
Waterville *Oneida*
Watervliet *Albany*
Watkins Glen *Schuyler*
Waverly *Tioga*
Wawarsing *Ulster*
Wayland *Steuben*
Wayne *Schuyler*
Webb *Herkimer*
Webster *Monroe*
Webster Crossing
  Livingston
Weedsport *Cayuga*
Wells *Hamilton*
Wells Bridge *Otsego*
Wellsburg *Chemung*
Wellsville *Allegany*
West Babylon *Suffolk*
West Bloomfield *Ontario*
West Burlington *Otsego*
Westbury *Nassau*
West Camp *Ulster*
West Carthage *Jefferson*
West Chazy *Clinton*
West Clarksville *Allegany*
West Copake *Columbia*
West Corners *Broome*
Westdale *Oneida*
West Danby *Tompkins*
West Davenport *Delaware*
West Eaton *Madison*
West Edmeston *Otsego*
West Elmira *Chemung*
Westerlo *Albany*
Westernville *Oneida*
West Exeter *Otsego*
West Falls *Erie*
Westfield *Chautauqua*
Westford *Otsego*
West Fulton *Schoharie*
West Glen Falls
  Washington
Westhampton *Suffolk*
Westhampton Beach
  Suffolk
West Haverstraw *Rockland*
West Henrietta *Monroe*
West Hurley *Ulster*
West Islip *Suffolk*
West Kill *Greene*
West Lebanon *Columbia*
West Leyden *Lewis*
West Monroe *Oswego*
Westmoreland *Oneida*
West Nyack *Rockland*
West Oneonta *Otsego*
Westons Mills *Cattaraugus*
West Park *Ulster*
West Point *Orange*
Westport *Essex*
West Rush *Monroe*
West Sand Lake *Rensselaer*
West Sayville *Suffolk*

West Seneca *Erie*
West Shokan *Ulster*
West Stockholm *Saint*
  Lawrence
Westtown *Orange*
West Valley *Cattaraugus*
West Webster *Monroe*
West Winfield *Herkimer*
West Winsor *Broome*
Wevertown *Warren*
Whallonsburg *Essex*
Whippleville *Franklin*
Whitehall *Washington*
White Lake *Sullivan*
White Plains *Westchester*
Whitesboro *Oneida*
White Sulphur Springs
  Sullivan
Whitesville *Allegany*
Whitney Point *Broome*
Willard *Seneca*
Willet *Cortland*
Williamson *Wayne*
Williamstown *Oswego*
Williamsville *Erie*
Williston Park *Nassau*
Willow *Ulster*
Willow Point *Broome*
Willsboro *Essex*
Willseyville *Tioga*
Wilmington *Essex*
Wilson *Niagara*
Windham *Greene*
Windsor *Broome*
Winfield *Herkimer*
Wingdale *Dutchess*
Winthrop *Saint Lawrence*
Witherbee *Essex*
Wolcott *Wayne*
Woodbourne *Sullivan*
Woodbury *Nassau*
Woodgate *Oneida*
Woodhull *Steuben*
Woodmere *Nassau*
Woodridge *Sullivan*
Woodstock *Ulster*
Woodville *Jefferson*
Worcester *Otsego*
Wurtsboro *Sullivan*
Wyandanch *Suffolk*
Wynantskill *Rensselaer*
Wyoming *Wyoming*
Yaphank *Suffolk*
Yonkers *Westchester*
York *Livingston*
Yorkshire *Cattaraugus*
Yorktown Heights
  Westchester
Yorkville *Oneida*
Youngstown *Niagara*
Youngsville *Sullivan*
Yulan *Sullivan*

North Carolina

North Carolina worker's compensation claim histories are available free of charge for employment screening purposes.

The central repository for criminal records in the state, the North Carolina Bureau of Investigation, operates with tight restrictions on the dissemination of criminal history information. However, all 100 of the state's counties reported that they do release conviction records for employment screening purposes by phone and/or mail. All civil court records are held at Superior court.

For more information or for offices not listed, contact the state's information hot line at (919) 733-1110.

Driving Records

Department of Motor Vehicles
Driver License Section
1100 New Bern Avenue
Raleigh, NC 27697-0001
(919) 733-4241
Driving records are available by mail. $4.00 fee per request. Turnaround time is 7 to 10 days. Written request must include job applicant's full name and license number or full name and date of birth. Make check payable to Department of Motor Vehicles.

Worker's Compensation Records

North Carolina Industrial Commission
430 N. Salisbury Street
Raleigh, NC 27611
(919) 733-5020
Worker's compensation records are available by mail only. Written authorization from job applicant is required. Request must include applicant's complete name and SSN. If known, also include name of previous employer involved in claim. There is no fee.

Vital Statistics

Department of Human Resources
Vital Records Section
PO Box 27687
Raleigh, NC 27611
(919) 733-3526
Birth and death records are available for $10.00 each . State office has birth records since October 1913 and death records since January 1, 1930. For birth records include name, date of birth, place of birth, father's name, mother's maiden name, requestor's relationship and why certification is needed. For death records include name, date of birth, place of death, age or date of birth, spouse, race, requetor's relationship and why certification is needed. Death records from 1913 through 1929 are available from Archives and Records Section, State Records Center, 215 North Blount Street, Raleigh, NC 27602. Records are also available through county. Some records (1944-present) are accessible by computer. Make check or money order payable to Vital Records.

Marriage records since 1962 are available. Fee of $10.00. Checks acceptable. Include name, marriage date, spouse's name, and place of marriage, requestor's relationship and why certification is needed. Divorce records available from 1958 forward at county level, County Clerk's Office. Include plaintiff's name, defendant's name, date of divorce, place of divorce, requestor's relationship and why certification is needed. Urgent requests taken over the phone will be processed the same day received when payment is made by credit card. In such cases, a $20.00 fee is charged in addition to all commercial and shipping charges. Make all checks payable to the Vital Records Section.

Department of Education

Department of Education
Division of Teacher Certification
116 W. Edeton
Raleigh, NC 27603-1712
(919) 733-0377
Field of certification, effective date, expiration date are available by phone or mail. Include name and SSN.

Medical Licensing

Board of Medical Examiners
PO Box 26808
Raleigh, NC 27611-6808
(919) 828-1212
Will confirm licenses for MDs and DOs by phone or mail. $15.00 search fee. Make check payable to North Carolina Board of Medical Examiners. For licenses not mentioned, contact the above office.

North Carolina Board of Nursing
PO Box 2129
Raleigh, NC 27602
(919) 782-3211
Will confirm license by phone. No fee. Include name, license number.

Bar Association

North Carolina State Bar Association
PO Box 25908
Raleigh, NC 27611
(919) 828-4620
Will confirm licenses by phone. No fee. Include name.

Accountancy Board

North Carolina State Board of Accountancy
PO Box 12827
Raleigh, NC 27605-2827
(919) 733-4222
Will confirm licenses by phone. No fee. Include name.

Securities Commission

Department of State
Securities Division
300 North Salisbury Street, Suite 404
Raleigh, NC 27603
(919) 733-3924
Will confirm licenses by phone. No fee. Include name and SSN.

Secretary of State

Secretary of State Office
Corporation Division
300 N. Salisbury St.
Raleigh, NC 27603-5909
(919) 733-4201
Fax (919) 832-4909
Service agent and address, date incorporated, standing with tax commission, trade names are available by phone or mail. Contact the above office for additional information.

Criminal Records

State Repository

North Carolina Bureau of Investigation
Division of Criminal Information
Identification Section
407 North Blount Street
Raleigh, NC 27601-1009
(919) 662-4500

Access to criminal records maintained by State's central repository is primarily limited to criminal justice agencies. Government agencies may gain access if they have a state statute requiring a background investigation for employment or licensing purposes. The state statute must be reviewed and approved by the North Carolina Attorney General's Office, under the Fee For Service Program. A users agreement must be executed. Contact the above office for additional information and instructions.

Alamance County

Clerk of Superior Court, Records Division
Alamance County
Graham, NC 27253
(919) 570-6867

Felony and misdemeanor records are available by mail. No release necessary. $5.00 search fee. Certified check only, payable to Clerk of Superior Court. Search information required: name, date of birth, previous address.

Civil records are available in person only. See North Carolina state repository for additional information.

Alexander County

Clerk of Superior Court, Criminal Records
Alexander County Courthouse
Taylorsville, NC 28681
(704) 632-2215

Felony and misdemeanor records are available by mail or phone. No release necessary. $5.00 search fee. Company checks only, payable to Clerk of Superior Court. Search information required: name, date of birth, previous address.

Civil records are available by mail or phone. No release necessary. No search fee. $.25 fee per copy. Search information required: name, date of birth, years to search. Specify plaintiff or defendant.

Alleghany County

Alleghany Clerk of Superior Court, Criminal Records
PO Box 61
Sparta, NC 28675
(919) 372-8949

Felony and misdemeanor records are available by mail. A release is required. $5.00 search fee. Money order or certified checks, payable to Clerk of Superior Court. Search information required: name, date of birth.

Civil records are available by mail. A release is required. $5.00 search fee. Search information required: name, date of birth, SSN, years to search. Specify plaintiff or defendant.

Anson County

Clerk of Superior Court, Criminal Records
Anson County Courthouse
Wadesboro, NC 28170
(704) 694-2314

Felony and misdemeanor records are available by mail. No release necessary. $5.00 search fee. Search information required: name, date of birth, years to search.

Civil records are available by mail. No release necessary. $5.00 search fee. Search information required: name, date of birth, years to search. Specify plaintiff or defendant.

Ashe County

Clerk of Superior Court, Criminal Records
PO Box 95
Jefferson, NC 28640
(919) 246-5641

Felony and misdemeanor records are available by mail. No release necessary. $5.00 fee. Certified check only, payable to Clerk of Superior Court. Search information required: name, date of birth, address.

Civil records are available by mail. A release is required. $5.00 search fee. $1.00 fee for first copy, $.25 each additional copy. $2.00 for certification. Search information required: name, date of birth, years to search. Specify plaintiff or defendant.

Avery County

Clerk of Superior Court, Criminal Records
PO Box 115
Avery County
Newland, NC 28657
(704) 733-2900

Felony and misdemeanor records are available by mail. A release is required. $5.00 search fee. Certified check only, payable to Clerk of Superior Court. Search information required: name, date of birth, previous address, years to search.

Civil records are available by mail. No release necessary. $5.00 search fee. $.25 fee per copy. $2.00 for certification. Search information required: name, date of birth, years to search. Specify plaintiff or defendant.

Beaufort County

Clerk of Superior Court, Criminal Records
Box 1403
Washington, NC 27889
(919) 946-5184

Felony and misdemeanor records are available by mail. No release necessary. $5.00 search fee. $1.00 fee for first copy, $.25 each additional copy. $2.00 for certification. Certified check only, payable to Clerk of Superior Court. Search information required: name, date of birth, years to search.

Civil records are available in person only. See North Carolina state repository for additional information.

Bertie County

Clerk of Superior Court, Criminal Records
PO Box 370
Windsor, NC 27983
(919) 794-3039

Felony and misdemeanor records are available by mail. No release necessary. $5.00 search fee, $2.00 fee for certification (if requested). Company checks only, payable to Clerk of Superior Court. Search information required: name, date of birth, previous address.

Civil records are available by mail or phone. No release necessary. $1.00 fee for first copy, $.25 each additional copy. $2.00 for certification. Search information required: name, date of birth, years to search. Specify plaintiff or defendant.

Bladen County

Clerk of Superior Court, Criminal Records
PO Box 547
Elizabethtown, NC 28337
(919) 862-2143
Fax (919) 862-2818

Felony and misdemeanor records are available by mail. No release necessary. $5.00 fee. Certified check only, payable to Clerk of Superior Court. Search information required: name, date of birth, previous address, years to search.

Civil records are available by mail. No release necessary. $5.00 search fee. $1.00 fee for first copy, $.25 each additional copy. $2.00 for certification. Search information required: name, date of birth, years to search. Specify plaintiff or defendant.

Brunswick County

Clerk of Superior Court, Criminal Records
PO Box 127
Bolivia, NC 28422
(919) 253-4445
Fax (919) 253-4320

Felony and misdemeanor records are available by mail or fax. No release necessary. $5.00 search fee. Make company check payable to Clerk of Superior Court. Search information required: name, date of birth.

Civil records are available by mail or fax. No release necessary. No release necessary. $5.00 search fee. $1.00 fee for first copy, $.25 each additional copy. $2.00 for certification. Search information required: name, date of birth, years to search. Specify plaintiff or defendant.

Buncombe County

Clerk of Superior Court, Criminal Records
Buncombe County Courthouse
Asheville, NC 28801-3519
(704) 255-4703

Felony and misdemeanor records are available by mail. No release necessary. $5.00 search fee. Certified check or money order, payable to Clerk of Superior Court. Search information required: name, date of birth, sex, race.

Civil records are available in person only. See North Carolina state repository for additional information.

Burke County

Clerk of Superior Court, Criminal Records
PO Box 796
Morganton, NC 28655
(704) 438-5540
Felony and misdemeanor records are available by mail. No release necessary. $5.00 search fee. Company checks only, payable to Clerk of Superior Court. Search information required: name, date of birth, previous address, years to search.

Civil records are available by mail. No release necessary. No search fee. $1.00 fee for first copy, $.25 each additional copy. $2.00 for certification. Search information required: name, date of birth, years to search. Specify plaintiff or defendant.

Cabarrus County

Clerk of Superior Court, Criminal Records
PO Box 70
Concord, NC 28026-0070
(704) 786-4137
Felony and misdemeanor records are available by mail. No release necessary. $5.00 search fee. Certified check only, payable to Clerk of Superior Court. Search information required: name, date of birth.

Civil records are available in person only. See North Carolina state repository for additional information.

Caldwell County

Clerk of Superior Court, Criminal Records
PO Box 1376
Caldwell County
Lenoir, NC 28645-1376
(704) 757-1375
Felony and misdemeanor records are available by mail. No release necessary. $5.00 search fee. $1.00 fee per copy. $.25 fee per copy. $2.00 for certification. Certified check only, payable to Clerk of Court. Search information required: name, date of birth, years to search.

Civil records are available in person only. See North Carolina state repository for additional information.

Camden County

Camden County Clerk of Superior Court, Criminal Records
PO Box 219
Camden, NC 27921
(919) 335-7942
Felony and misdemeanor records are available by mail. No release necessary. $5.00 search fee. Certified check or money order, payable to Clerk of Superior Court. Search information required: name, address, date of birth, sex, race, years to search.

Civil records are available in person only. See North Carolina state repository for additional information.

Carteret County

Clerk of Superior Court, Criminal Records
Carteret County
Beaufort, NC 28516
(919) 728-8510
Felony and misdemeanor records are available by mail. No release necessary. $5.00 search fee. Certified check only, payable to Clerk of Superior Court. Search information required: name, date of birth, sex, race, previous address, years to search. Phone inquiries must prepay before information will be released.

Civil records are available in person only. See North Carolina state repository for additional information.

Caswell County

Clerk of Superior Court, Criminal Records
PO Drawer 790
Yanceyville, NC 27379
(919) 694-4171
Felony and misdemeanor records are available by mail. No release necessary. $5.00 search fee. Certified check only, payable to Clerk of Superior Court. Search information required: name, date of birth, race, previous address.

Civil records are available by mail. No release necessary. $5.00 search fee. $1.00 fee for first copy, $.25 each additional copy. $5.00 for certification. Search information required: name, date of birth, years to search. Specify plaintiff or defendant.

Catawba County

Clerk of Superior Court, Criminal Records
PO Box 728
Newton, NC 28658
(704) 464-5216
Felony and misdemeanor records are available by mail. No release necessary. $5.00 search fee. Certified check or money order, payable to Clerk of Superior Court. Search information required: name, date of birth, sex, race, current address.

Civil records are available in person only. See North Carolina state repository for additional information.

Chatham County

Clerk of Superior Court, Criminal Records
Chatham County
PO Box 368
Pittsboro, NC 27312
(704) 633-4126
Felony and misdemeanor records are available by mail. No release necessary. $5.00 search fee. Company checks only, payable to Clerk of Superior Court. Search information required: name, date of birth, current address, years to search.

Civil records are available in person only. See North Carolina state repository for additional information.

Cherokee County

Clerk of Superior Court, Criminal Records
Cherokee County
Murphy, NC 28906
(704) 837-2522
Felony and misdemeanor records are available by mail or phone. No release necessary. No search fee. Search information required: name, date of birth, previous address, years to search.

Civil records are available in person only. See North Carolina state repository for additional information.

Chowan County

Clerk of Superior Court, Criminal Records
Chowan County Courthouse
PO Box 588
Edenton, NC 27932
(919) 482-2323
Felony and misdemeanor records are available by mail. No release necessary. $5.00 search fee. Certified check only, payable to Clerk of Superior Court. Search information required: name, SSN, previous address, years to search, date of birth.

Civil records are available by mail. No release necessary. $5.00 search fee. $1.00 fee for first copy, $.25 each additional copy. $2.00 for certification. Search information required: name, date of birth, years to search. Specify plaintiff or defendant.

Clay County

Clerk of Superior Court, Criminal Records
PO Box 506
Hayesville, NC 28904
(704) 389-8334
Felony and misdemeanor records are available by mail. A release is required. $5.00 search fee. Certified check only, payable to Clerk of Superior Court. Search information required: name, SSN, date of birth, sex, race.

Civil records are available by mail. No release necessary. $5.00 search fee. Search information required: name, date of birth, years to search. Specify plaintiff or defendant.

Cleveland County

Clerk of Superior Court, Criminal Records
100 Justice Pl.
Shelby, NC 28150
(704) 484-4893
Felony and misdemeanor records are available by mail. A release is required. $5.00 search fee. Certified check only, payable to Clerk of Superior Court. Search information required: name, date of birth, sex, race, previous address.

Civil records are available in person only. See North Carolina state repository for additional information.

Columbus County

Clerk of Superior Court, Criminal
Records
Columbus County
Whiteville, NC 28472
(919) 642-3119

Felony and misdemeanor records are available by mail. No release necessary. $5.00 search fee. Certified check only, payable to Clerk of Superior Court. Search information required: name, SSN, date of birth, previous address.

Civil records are available in person only. See North Carolina state repository for additional information.

Craven County

Clerk of Superior Court, Criminal
Records
PO Box 1187
New Bern, NC 28560
(919) 633-3126

Felony and misdemeanor records are available by mail. No release necessary. $5.00 search fee. Company checks only, payable to Clerk of Superior Court. Search information required: full name, date of birth, sex. and race

Civil records are available in person only. See North Carolina state repository for additional information.

Cumberland County

Clerk of the Superior Court, Criminal
Records
PO Box 363
Fayetteville, NC 28302
(919) 678-2902

Felony and misdemeanor records are available by mail. No release necessary. $5.00 search fee. Certified check only, payable to Clerk of Superior Court. Search information required: name, date of birth, years to search, SASE.

Civil records are available by mail. No release necessary. $5.00 search fee. $2.00 for certification. Search information required: name, date of birth, years to search. Specify plaintiff or defendant.

Currituck County

Clerk of Superior Court, Criminal
Records
PO Box 175
Currituck, NC 27929
(919) 232-2010

Felony and misdemeanor records are available by mail. A release is required. $5.00 fee. Certified check only, payable to Clerk of Superior Court. Search information required: name, previous and current address, date of birth, SSN.

Civil records are available in person only. See North Carolina state repository for additional information.

Dare County

Clerk of Superior Court
PO Box 1849
Manteo, NC 27954
(919) 473-2143
Fax (919) 473-2950

Felony and misdemeanor records are available by mail, fax or phone. A release is required. $5.00 search fee. Certified check or money order payable to Clerk of Superior Court. Search information required: name, SSN, date of birth.

Civil records are available by mail. No release necessary. $5.00 search fee. $1.00 fee for first copy, $.25 each additional copy. $2.00 for certification. Search information required: name, date of birth, years to search. Specify plaintiff or defendant.

Davidson County

Clerk of Court, Criminal Records
PO Box 1064
Lexington, NC 27293-1064
(704) 249-0351

Felony and misdemeanor records are available by mail. No release necessary. $5.00 search fee. Certified check only, payable to Clerk of Court. Search information required: name, date of birth, sex and race.

Civil records are available by mail. No release necessary. $5.00 search fee. Search information required: name, date of birth, years to search. Specify plaintiff or defendant.

Davie County

Clerk of Court, Criminal Records
140 S. Main Street
Mocksville, NC 27028
(704) 634-3508

Felony and misdemeanor records are available by mail. No release necessary. $5.00 search fee. Make check payable to Clerk of Court. Search information required: name, date of birth, address, driver's license, if available.

Civil records are available by mail. No release necessary. $5.00 search fee. $1.00 fee for first copy, $.25 each additional copy. $2.00 for certification. Search information required: name, date of birth, years to search. Specify plaintiff or defendant.

Duplin County

Clerk of Superior Court, Criminal
Records
PO Box 188
Kenansville, NC 28349
(919) 296-0110

Felony and misdemeanor records are available by mail. No release necessary. $5.00 search fee. Company checks only, payable to Clerk of Superior Court. Search information required: name, date of birth, sex, race, years to search.

Civil records are available by mail. A release is required. $5.00 search fee. $1.00 fee for first copy, $.25 each additional copy. $2.00 for certification. Search information required: name, date of birth, years to search. Specify plaintiff or defendant.

Durham County

Clerk of Superior Court, Criminal
Records
PO Box 1772
Durham, NC 27702
(919) 560-6833

Felony and misdemeanor records are available by mail or phone. No release necessary. $5.00 fee. Certified check only, payable to Clerk of Court. Search information required: name, date of birth, sex, race, previous addresses and current address.

Civil records are available in person only. See North Carolina state repository for additional information.

Edgecombe County

Clerk of Superior Court, Criminal
Records
Edgecombe County
PO Drawer 9
Tarboro, NC 27886
(919) 823-2056

Felony and misdemeanor records are available by mail. No release necessary. $5.00 fee. Certified check or money order payable to Clerk of Superior Court. Search information required: name, date of birth, sex, race, previous address, years to search, SASE.

Civil records are available in person only. See North Carolina state repository for additional information.

Forsyth County

Clerk of Superior Court, Criminal
Records
Courthouse, Room 205
PO Box 20099
Winston-Salem, NC 27120-0099
(919) 761-2366

Felony and misdemeanor records are available by mail. No release necessary. $5.00 search fee. Certified check only, payable to Clerk of Superior Court. Search information required: name, date of birth, race.

Civil records are available in person only. See North Carolina state repository for additional information.

Franklin County

Clerk of Superior Court, Criminal
Records
Franklin County
102 South Main St.
Louisburg, NC 27549
(919) 496-5104

Felony and misdemeanor records are available by mail. No release necessary. $5.00 search fee. Company checks only, payable to Clerk of Superior Court. Search information required: name, date of birth, previous address.

Civil records are available by mail. No release necessary. $5.00 search fee. Search information required: name, date of birth, years to search. Specify plaintiff or defendant.

Gaston County

Clerk of Superior Court, District
Criminal Records
Gaston County
PO Box 340
Gastonia, NC 28053
(704) 868-5800

Felony records are available by mail. No release necessary. $5.00 search fee. Money order, payable to Clerk of Superior Court. Search information required: name, date of birth, sex, race.

Civil records are available by mail. No release necessary. $5.00 search fee. $1.00 fee for first copy, $.25 each additional copy. $2.00 for certification. Search information required: name, date of birth, years to search. Specify plaintiff or defendant.

Gates County

Clerk of Superior Court, Criminal
Records
PO Box 31
Gatesville, NC 27938
(919) 357-1365

Felony and misdemeanor records are available by mail. No release necessary. $5.00 search fee. $1.00 fee for first copy, $.25 each additional copy. $2.00 for certification. Company checks only, payable to Clerk of Superior Court. Search information required: name, date of birth, years to search.

Civil records are available by mail. No release necessary. $5.00 search fee. $1.00 fee for first copy, $.25 each additional copy. $2.00 for certification. Search information required: name, date of birth, years to search. Specify plaintiff or defendant.

Graham County

Clerk of Superior Court, Criminal
Records
PO Box 1179
Robbinsville, NC 28771
(704) 479-3361

Felony and misdemeanor records are available by mail. No release necessary. $5.00 search fee. Company checks only, payable to Clerk of Superior Court. Search information required: name, date of birth.

Civil records are available by mail. No release necessary. $5.00 search fee. $1.00 fee for first copy, $.25 each additional copy. $2.00 for certification. Search information required: name, date of birth, years to search. Specify plaintiff or defendant.

Granville County

Clerk of Superior Court, Criminal
Records
Granville County
Oxford, NC 27565
(919) 693-2649

Felony and misdemeanor records are available by mail. A release is required. $5.00 search fee. $1.00 fee for first copy, $.25 each additional copy. $2.00 for certification. Company checks only, payable to Clerk of Superior Court. Search information required: name, date of birth, current address, years to search.

Civil records are available in person only. See North Carolina state repository for additional information.

Greene County

Clerk of Superior Court
PO Box 675
Snow Hill, NC 28580
(919) 747-3505

Felony and misdemeanor records are available by mail. No release necessary. $5.00 search fee. $1.00 fee for first copy, $.25 each additional copy. $2.00 for certification. Certified check only, payable to Clerk of Superior Court. Search information required: name, date of birth, previous address, years to search.

Civil records are available by mail. No release necessary. $5.00 search fee. $1.00 fee for first copy, $.25 each additional copy. $2.00 for certification. Search information required: name, date of birth, years to search. Specify plaintiff or defendant.

Guilford County

Clerk of Superior Court, Criminal
Records
201 South Eugene Street
Drawer T-5
Greensboro, NC 27402
(919) 574-4300

Felony and misdemeanor records are available by mail. No release necessary. $5.00 search fee. Certified check only, payable to Clerk of Superior Court. Search information required: name, date of birth, sex, race, SASE.

Civil records are available in person only. See North Carolina state repository for additional information.

Halifax County

Clerk of the Superior Court, Criminal
Records
PO Box 66
Halifax, NC 27839
(919) 583-5061

Felony and misdemeanor records are available by mail. No release necessary. $5.00 search fee. Certified check or money order, payable to Clerk of Superior Court. Search information required: name, date of birth, previous address, years to search.

Civil records are available in person only. See North Carolina state repository for additional information.

Harnett County

Clerk of Superior Court, Criminal
Records
PO Box 849
Lillington, NC 27546
(919) 893-5164

Felony and misdemeanor records are available by mail. No release necessary. $5.00 search fee. Certified check only, payable to Clerk of Superior Court. Search information required: name, date of birth, previous address, years to search.

Civil records are available in person only. See North Carolina state repository for additional information.

Haywood County

Clerk of Superior Court, Criminal
Records
Haywood County
Waynesville, NC 28786
(704) 456-3540

Felony and misdemeanor records are available by mail. No release necessary. $5.00 search fee. Make company check payable to Clerk of Superior Court. Search information required: name, date of birth, sex, race, years to search.

Civil records are available by mail. A release is required. $5.00 search fee. $1.00 fee for first copy, $.25 each additional copy. $2.00 for certification. Search information required: name, date of birth, years to search. Specify plaintiff or defendant.

Henderson County

Felony and misdemeanor records
Clerk of Superior Court, Criminal
Records
Henderson County Courthouse
PO Box 965
Hendersonville, NC 28793-0965
(704) 697-4859

Felony and misdemeanor records are available by mail or phone. $5.00 search fee. Make check payable to Clerk of Superior Court. Search information required: name, SSN, date of birth, years to search.

Civil records
Clerk of Superior Court, Criminal
Records
Henderson County Courthouse
PO Box 965
Hendersonville, NC 28793-0965
(704) 697-4851

Civil records are available by mail. No release necessary. $5.00 search fee. $1.00 fee for first copy, $.25 each additional copy. $2.00 for certification. Search information required: name, date of birth, years to search. Specify plaintiff or defendant.

Hertford County

Clerk of Superior Court, Criminal
Records
PO Box 86
Winton, NC 27986
(919) 358-7845

Felony and misdemeanor records are available by mail. No release necessary. $5.00 search fee. Certified check only, payable to Clerk of Superior Court. Search information required: name, date of birth, years to search.

Civil records are available by mail. No release necessary. $5.00 search fee. $1.00 fee for first copy, $.25 each additional copy. $2.00 for certification. Search information required: name, date of birth, years to search. Specify plaintiff or defendant.

Hoke County

Clerk of Superior Court, Criminal
Records
Hoke County
PO Drawer 410
Raeford, NC 28376
(919) 875-3728

Felony and misdemeanor records are available by mail. A release is required. $5.00 searchfee. Certified check only, payable to Clerk of Superior Court. Search information required: name, date of birth, previous address.

Civil records are available in person only. See North Carolina state repository for additional information.

Hyde County

Clerk of Superior Court, Criminal Records
PO Box 337
Swanquarter, NC 27885
(919) 926-4101

Felony and misdemeanor records are available by mail. No release necessary. $5.00 search fee. Company checks only, payable to Clerk of Superior Court. Search information required: name, date of birth, previous address, years to search.

Civil records are available by mail. A release is required. $5.00 search fee. $1.00 fee for first copy, $.25 each additional copy. $2.00 for certification. Search information required: name, date of birth, years to search. Specify plaintiff or defendant.

Iredell County

Clerk of Superior Court, Criminal Records
PO Box 186
Statesville, NC 28677
(704) 878-4204

Felony and misdemeanor records are available by mail. No release necessary. $5.00 search fee. Certified check only, payable to Clerk of Superior Court. Search information required: name, date of birth, previous address, years to search.

Civil records are available by mail. No release necessary. $5.00 search fee. $1.00 fee for first copy, $.25 each additional copy. $2.00 for certification. Search information required: name, date of birth, years to search. Specify plaintiff or defendant.

Jackson County

Clerk of Superior Court, Criminal Records
Jackson County
Sylva, NC 28779
(704) 586-4312

Felony and misdemeanor records are available by mail. No release necessary. $5.00 search fee. Company checks only, payable to Clerk of Superior Court. Search information required: name, date of birth.

Civil records are available by mail. No release necessary. $5.00 search fee. $.25 fee per copy. $2.00 for certification. Search information required: name, date of birth, years to search. Specify plaintiff or defendant.

Johnston County

Clerk of Superior Court, Criminal Records
PO Box 297
Smithfield, NC 27577
(919) 934-3191

Felony and misdemeanor records are available by mail. No release necessary. $5.00 search fee. Certified check only, payable to Clerk of Superior Court. Search information required: name, SSN, date of birth, race, years to search.

Civil records are available by mail. No release necessary. No search fee. $1.00 fee for first copy, $.25 each additional copy. $2.00 for certification. Search information required: name, date of birth, race, years to search. Specify plaintiff or defendant.

Jones County

Clerk of Superior Court, Criminal Records
PO Box 280
Trenton, NC 28585
(919) 448-7351

Felony and misdemeanor records are available by mail. No release necessary. $5.00 search fee. Company checks only, payable to Clerk of Superior Court. Search information required: name, date of birth, previous address, years to search.

Civil records are available by mail. No release necessary. $5.00 search fee. $1.00 fee for first copy, $.25 each additional copy. $2.00 for certification. Search information required: name, date of birth, years to search. Specify plaintiff or defendant.

Lee County

Clerk of Superior Court, Criminal Records
PO Box 4209
Sanford, NC 27331
(919) 775-5606

Felony and misdemeanor records are available by mail. No release necessary. $5.00 search fee. Company checks only, payable to Clerk of Superior Court. Search information required: name, SSN, date of birth, previous address, years to search.

Civil records are available in person only. See North Carolina state repository for additional information.

Lenoir County

Clerk of Superior Court, Criminal Records
PO Box 68
Kinston, NC 28502-0068
(919) 527-6231

Felony and misdemeanor records are available by mail. No release necessary. $5.00 search fee. Certified check or money order only, payable to Clerk of Superior Court. Search information required: name, date of birth, previous address, years to search.

Civil records are available in person only. See North Carolina state repository for additional information.

Lincoln County

Clerk of Superior Court, Criminal Records
PO Box 8
Lincolnton, NC 28093
(704) 732-3361

Felony and misdemeanor records are available by mail. No release necessary. $5.00 fee. Company checks only, payable to Clerk of Superior Court. Search information required: name, date of birth, previous address, years to search.

Civil records are available by mail. No release necessary. No search fee. $1.00 fee for first copy, $.25 each additional copy. $2.00 for certification. Search information required: name, date of birth, race, years to search. Specify plaintiff or defendant.

Macon County

Clerk of Superior Court, Criminal Records
PO Box 288
Franklin, NC 28734
(704) 524-6421

Felony and misdemeanor records are available by mail. No release necessary. No search fee. Search information required: name, date of birth.

Civil records are available in person only. See North Carolina state repository for additional information.

Madison County

Clerk of Court, Criminal Records
PO Box 684
Marshall, NC 28753
(704) 649-2531

Felony and misdemeanor records are available by mail or phone. No release necessary. $5.00 search fee. Company checks only, payable to Clerk of Court. Search information required: name, date of birth.

Civil records are available by mail. No release necessary. $5.00 search fee. $1.00 fee for first copy, $.25 each additional copy. $2.00 for certification. Search information required: name, date of birth, years to search. Specify plaintiff or defendant.

Martin County

Clerk of Superior Court, Criminal Records
PO Box 807
Williamston, NC 27892
(919) 792-2515

Felony and misdemeanor records are available by mail. No release necessary. $5.00 search fee. Certified check only, payable to Clerk of Superior Court. Search information required: name, date of birth, SASE.

Civil records are available by mail. No release necessary. $5.00 search fee. Search information required: name, date of birth, years to search. Specify plaintiff or defendant.

McDowell County

Clerk of Superior Court, Criminal Records
McDowell County
Marion, NC 28752
(704) 652-7717

Felony and misdemeanor records are available by mail. A release is required. $5.00 search fee. Certified check only, payable to Clerk of Superior Court. Search information required: name, date of birth, previous address, years to search.

Civil records are available by mail. No release necessary. $5.00 search fee. $1.00 fee for first copy, $.25 each additional copy. $2.00 for certification. Search information required: name, date of birth, years to search. Specify plaintiff or defendant.

Mecklenburg County

Clerk of Court, Criminal Records
800 E. 4th Street
Charlotte, NC 28202
(704) 347-7809
Felony and misdemeanor records are available by mail. Turnaround time is 1 day. No release necessary. $5.00 search fee. Certified check only, payable to Clerk of Court. Search information required: name, date of birth, previous address, race, sex.

Civil records are available by mail. No release necessary. No search fee. $1.00 fee for first copy, $.25 each additional copy. $2.00 for certification. Search information required: name, date of birth, years to search. Specify plaintiff or defendant.

Mitchell County

Clerk Of Superior Court, Criminal Records
PO Box 402
Bakersville, NC 28705
(704) 688-2161
Felony and misdemeanor records are available by mail or phone. No release necessary. $5.00 search fee. $1.00 fee for first copy, $.25 each additional copy. $4.00 for certification. Company checks only, payable to Clerk of Superior Court. Search information required: name, date of birth, address, if available.

Civil records are available by mail. No release necessary. $5.00 search fee. $1.00 fee for first copy, $.25 each additional copy. $4.00 for certification. Search information required: name, date of birth, years to search. Specify plaintiff or defendant.

Montgomery County

Clerk of Court, Criminal Records
PO Box 182
Troy, NC 27371
(919) 576-4211
Felony and misdemeanor records are available by mail. A release is required. $5.00 search fee. Certified check only, payable to Clerk of Court. Search information required: name, date of birth, address.

Civil records are available in person only. See North Carolina state repository for additional information.

Moore County

Clerk of Superior Court, Criminal Records
PO Box 936
Carthage, NC 28327
(919) 947-2396
Felony and misdemeanor records are available by mail. $5.00 search fee. No release necessary. Certified check only, payable to Clerk of Superior Court. Search information required: name, date of birth, previous address, years to search.

Civil records are available in person only. See North Carolina state repository for additional information.

Nash County

Felony and misdemeanor records
Clerk of Superior Court, Criminal Records
Nash County
PO Box 759
Nashville, NC 27856
(919) 459-4085
Felony and misdemeanor records are available by mail. No release necessary. $5.00 search fee. $1.00 fee for first copy, $.25 each additional copy. $2.00 for certification. Certified check only, payable to Clerk of Superior Court. Search information required: name, SSN, date of birth, previous address if available, years to search.

Civil records
Clerk of Superior Court
Nash County
PO Box 759
Nashville, NC 27856
(919) 459-4081
Civil records are available in person only. See North Carolina state repository for additional information.

New Hanover County

Clerk of Superior Court, Criminal Records
PO Box 2023
New Hanover County
Wilmington, NC 28402
(919) 341-4430
Felony and misdemeanor records are available by mail. No release necessary. $5.00 search fee. Certified check only, payable to Clerk of Superior Court. Search information required: name, date of birth, previous address, years to search.

Civil records are available in person only. See North Carolina state repository for additional information.

Northampton County

Clerk of Superior Court, Criminal Records
PO Box 217
Jackson, NC 27845
(919) 534-1631
Felony and misdemeanor records are available by mail. No release necessary. $5.00 search fee. Certified check only, payable to Clerk of Superior Court. Search information required: name, SSN, date of birth, sex, race, previous address.

Civil records are available by mail. No release necessary. $5.00 search fee. $1.00 fee for first copy, $.25 each additional copy. $2.00 for certification. Search information required: name, date of birth, years to search. Specify plaintiff or defendant.

Onslow County

Clerk of Court, Criminal Records
625 Court Street
Jacksonville, NC 28540
(919) 455-4458
Felony and misdemeanor records are available by mail. No release necessary. $5.00 search fee. Company checks only, payable to Clerk of Superior Court. Search information required: name, date of birth, years to search. Records accessible from 1975.

Civil records are available by mail. No release necessary. $5.00 search fee. Search information required: name, date of birth, previous address, years to search, SASE. Specify plaintiff or defendant.

Orange County

Clerk of Superior Court, Criminal Records
106 Margaret Lane
Orange County
Hillsborough, NC 27278
(919) 732-8181
Felony and misdemeanor records are available by mail. No release necessary. $5.00 search fee. $1.00 fee for first copy, $.25 each additional copy. $2.00 for certification. Certified check only, payable to Clerk of Superior Court. Search information required: name, date of birth. Records accessible from 1982, years to search, SASE.

Civil records are available in person only. See North Carolina state repository for additional information.

Pamlico County

Clerk of Superior Court, Criminal Records
PO Box 38
Bayboro, NC 28515
(919) 745-3881
Felony and misdemeanor records are available by mail. No release necessary. $5.00 search fee. Certified check only, payable to Clerk of Superior Court. Search information required: name, date of birth, sex, race, previous address.

Civil records are available by mail. No release necessary.$5.00 search fee. $1.00 fee for first copy, $.25 each additional copy. $2.00 for certification. Search information required: name, date of birth, years to search. Specify plaintiff or defendant.

Pasquotank County

Clerk of Superior Court, Criminal Records
Pasquotank County
PO Box 449
Elizabeth City, NC 27907-0449
(919) 338-0175
Felony and misdemeanor records are available by mail. A release is required. $5.00 search fee. Certified check only, payable to Clerk of Superior Court. Search information required: name, date of birth, sex, race, previous address.

Civil records are available in person only. See North Carolina state repository for additional information.

Pender County

Clerk of Superior Court, Criminal Records
PO Box 308
Burgaw, NC 28425
(919) 259-1229
Felony and misdemeanor records are available by mail. No release necessary. $5.00 search fee. $1.00 fee for first copy, $.25 each additional copy. $2.00 for certification. Certified check or money order only, payable to Clerk of Superior Court. Search information required: name, date of birth, previous address if available, years to search.

Civil records are available in person only. See North Carolina state repository for additional information.

Perquimans County

Clerk of Superior Court, Criminal Records
Perquimans County
PO Box 33
Hertford, NC 27944
(919) 426-5676

Felony and misdemeanor records are available by mail. No release necessary. $5.00 search fee. $1.00 fee for first copy, $.25 each additional copy. $2.00 for certification. Certified check only, payable to Clerk of Superior Court. Search information required: name, date of birth, previous address, years to search.

Civil records are available in person only. See North Carolina state repository for additional information.

Person County

Clerk of Superior Court, Criminal Records
Person County
Roxboro, NC 27573
(919) 597-7230, 597-7231, 597-7232

Felony and misdemeanor records are available by mail. No release necessary. $5.00 search fee. $2.00 fee for certification. Certified check only, payable to Clerk of Superior Court. Search information required: name, date of birth, previous address, years to search.

Civil records are available by mail. No release necessary. $5.00 search fee. $1.00 fee for first copy, $.25 each additional copy. $2.00 for certification. Search information required: name, date of birth, years to search. Specify plaintiff or defendant.

Pitt County

Clerk of Court, Criminal Records
PO Box 6067
Greenville, NC 27834
(919) 830-6400

Felony and misdemeanor records are available by mail. No release necessary. $5.00 fee. Company checks only, payable to Clerk of Court. Search information required: name, date of birth, previous address.

Civil records are available in person only. See North Carolina state repository for additional information.

Polk County

Clerk of Court, Criminal Records
Polk County
PO Box 38
Columbus, NC 28722
(704) 894-8231

Felony and misdemeanor records are available by mail. No release necessary. $5.00 fee. Company checks only, payable to Clerk of Court. Search information required: name, date of birth, sex, race.

Civil records are available by mail. No release necessary. $5.00 search fee. $1.00 fee for first copy, $.25 each additional copy. $2.00 for certification. Search information required: name, date of birth, years to search. Specify plaintiff or defendant.

Randolph County

Clerk of Superior Court, Criminal Division
Randolph County
PO Box 1925
Asheboro, NC 27204-1925
(919) 629-2131 Extension 2108

Felony and misdemeanor records are available by mail. No release necessary. $5.00 fee. Certified check only, payable to Clerk of Court. Search information required: name, date of birth, years to search.

Civil records are available in person only. See North Carolina state repository for additional information.

Richmond County

Clerk of Superior Court, Criminal Records
PO Box 724
Rockingham, NC 28379
(919) 997-9101 or 997-9102

Felony and misdemeanor records are available by mail. No release necessary. $5.00 search fee. Certified check only, payable to Clerk of Superior Court. Search information required: name, date of birth, years to search.

Civil records are available in person only. See North Carolina state repository for additional information.

Robeson County

Clerk of Superior Court, Criminal Records
PO Box 1084
Lumberton, NC 28358
(919) 671-3390

Felony and misdemeanor records are available by mail. No release necessary. $5.00 search fee. Company checks only, payable to Clerk of Superior Court. Search information required: name, date of birth, previous address, race.

Civil records are available in person only. See North Carolina state repository for additional information.

Rockingham County

Clerk of Superior Court, Criminal Records
Rockingham County
PO Box 26
Wentworth, NC 27375
(919) 342-8700

Felony and misdemeanor records are available by mail. No release necessary. $5.00 search fee. Certified check only, payable to Clerk of Superior Court. Search information required: name, date of birth, sex, race, previous address.

Civil records are available in person only. See North Carolina state repository for additional information.

Rowan County

Clerk of Superior Court, Criminal Records
Rowan County
Salisbury, NC 28144
(704) 639-7505

Felony and misdemeanor records are available by mail. No release necessary. $5.00 search fee. Company checks only, payable to Clerk of Superior Court. Search information required: name, date of birth, race.

Civil records are available in person only. See North Carolina state repository for additional information.

Rutherford County

Clerk of Superior Court, Criminal Records
PO Box 630
Rutherfordton, NC 28139
(704) 286-9136

Felony and misdemeanor records are available by mail. No release necessary. $5.00 search fee. Certified check only, payable to Clerk of Superior Court. Search information required: name, SSN, date of birth, sex, race, years to search.

Civil records are available in person only. See North Carolina state repository for additional information.

Sampson County

Clerk of Superior Court, Criminal Records
Sampson County
Clinton, NC 28328
(919) 592-5191

Felony and misdemeanor records are available by mail. No release necessary. $5.00 search fee. Certified check or money order, payable to Clerk of Superior Court. Search information required: name, date of birth, previous address, years to search.

Civil records are available in person only. See North Carolina state repository for additional information.

Scotland County

Clerk of Superior Court, Criminal Records
PO Box 769
Laurinburg, NC 28352
(919) 276-1951

Felony and misdemeanor records are available by mail. No release necessary. $5.00 search fee. $1.00 fee for first copy, $.25 each additional copy. $2.00 for certification. Certified check only, payable to Clerk of Superior Court. Search information required: name, date of birth, previous address if available, years to search.

Civil records are available in person only. See North Carolina state repository for additional information.

Stanley County

Clerk of Superior Court, Criminal Records
PO Box 668
Albemarle, NC 28002-0668
(704) 982-2161

Felony and misdemeanor records are available by mail. A release is required. $5.00 search fee. Certified check only, payable to Clerk of Superior Court. Search information required: name, date of birth, sex, race, previous address, years to search.

Civil records are available by mail. A release is required. $5.00 search fee. $1.00 fee for first copy, $.25 each additional copy. $2.00 for certification. Search information required: name, date of birth, years to search. Specify plaintiff or defendant.

Stokes County

Clerk of Superior Court, Criminal
Records
Stokes County
PO Box 56
Danbury, NC 27016
(919) 593- 2416

Felony and misdemeanor records are available by mail. No release necessary. $5.00 search fee. Company checks only, payable to Clerk of Superior Court. Search information required: name, SSN, date of birth, sex, race, previous address.

Civil records are available by mail. No release necessary. $5.00 search fee. $1.00 fee for first copy, $.25 each additional copy. Search information required: name, date of birth, years to search. Specify plaintiff or defendant.

Surry County

Clerk of Superior Court, Criminal
Records
PO Box 345
Dobson, NC 27017
(919) 386-8131

Felony and misdemeanor records are available by mail. No release necessary. $5.00 search fee. Certified check only, payable to Clerk of Superior Court. Search information required: name, date of birth, previous address.

Civil records are available in person only. See North Carolina state repository for additional information.

Swain County

Clerk of Superior Court, Criminal
Records
PO Box 1397
Bryson City, NC 28713
(704) 488-9273 Ext. 243
Fax (704) 488-2754

Felony and misdemeanor records are available by mail, fax or phone. No release necessary. $5.00 search fee. Certified check only, payable to Clerk of Superior Court. Search information required: name, date of birth.

Civil records are available by mail. No release necessary. No search fee. $1.00 fee for first copy, $.25 each additional copy. $1.00 for certification. Search information required: name, date of birth, years to search. Specify plaintiff or defendant.

Transylvania County

Clerk of Superior Court, Criminal
Records
Transylvania County
Brevard, NC 28712
(704) 884-3120

Felony and misdemeanor records are available by mail. No release necessary. $5.00 search fee. $1.00 fee for first copy, $.25 each additional copy. $2.00 for certification. Certified check only, payable to Clerk of Superior Court. Search information required: name, date of birth, previous address, years to search .

Civil records are available in person only. See North Carolina state repository for additional information.

Tyrrell County

Clerk of Superior Court, Criminal
Records
PO Box 406
Columbia, NC 27925
(919) 796-6281

Felony and misdemeanor records are available by mail or phone. No release necessary. $5.00 search fee. Certified check only, payable to Clerk of Court. Search information required: name, date of birth.

Civil records are available by mail. No release necessary. $5.00 search fee. $1.00 fee for first copy, $.25 each additional copy. $2.00 for certification. Search information required: name, date of birth, years to search. Specify plaintiff or defendant.

Union County

Clerk of Superior Court, Criminal
Records
PO Box 985
Monroe, NC 28110
(704) 283-4313

Felony and misdemeanor records are available by mail. No release necessary. $5.00 search fee. $1.00 fee for first copy, $.25 each additional copy. $2.00 for certification. Certified check only, payable to Clerk of Superior Court. Search information required: name, date of birth, sex, race, previous address. Records accessible from 1976.

Civil records are available in person only. See North Carolina state repository for additional information.

Vance County

Clerk of Superior Court, Criminal
Records
Vance County
Henderson, NC 27536
(919) 492-0031

Felony and misdemeanor records are available by mail. No release necessary. $5.00 search fee. $1.00 fee for first copy, $.25 each additional copy. $2.00 for certification. Certified check only, payable to Clerk of Superior Court. Search information required: name, date of birth, previous address if available, years to search.

Civil records are available in person only. See North Carolina state repository for additional infromation.

Wake County

Clerk of Superior Court
Wake County
PO Box 351
Raleigh, NC 27602
(919) 755-4110

Felony and misdemeanor records are available by mail. No release necessary. $5.00 search fee. Certified check only, payable to Clerk of Superior Court. Search information required: name, date of birth, years to search.

Civil records are available in person only. See North Carolina state repository for additional information.

Warren County

Clerk of Superior Court, Criminal
Records
PO Box 709
Warrenton, NC 27589
(919) 257-3261

Felony and misdemeanor records are available by mail or phone. No release necessary. $5.00 search fee on mail requests. Certified check only, payable to Clerk of Superior Court. Search information required: name, date of birth, sex, race, previous address, years to search.

Civil records are available by mail. No release necessary. $5.00 search fee. $1.00 fee for first copy, $.25 each additional copy. $2.00 for certification. Search information required: name, date of birth, years to search. Specify plaintiff or defendant.

Washington County

Clerk of Court, Criminal Records
PO Box 901
Plymouth, NC 27962
(919) 793-3013

Felony and misdemeanor records are available by mail. No release necessary. $5.00 fee. Company checks only, payable to Clerk of Superior Court. Search information required: name, date of birth, sex, race, years to search.

Civil records are available in person only. See North Carolina state repository for additional information.

Watauga County

Clerk of Superior Court, Criminal
Records
Watauga County Courthouse
Courthouse Box 13
403 W. King Street
Boone, NC 28607-3525
(704) 265-5364

Felony and misdemeanor records are available by mail. No release necessary. $5.00 search fee. Company checks only, payable to Clerk of Superior Court. Search information required: full name, date of birth.

Civil records are available in person only. See North Carolina state repository for additional information.

Wayne County

Clerk of Superior Court, Criminal
Records
PO Box 267
Goldsboro, NC 27530
(919) 731-7919

Felony and misdemeanor records are available by mail. No release necessary. $5.00 search fee. Company checks only, payable to Clerk of Superior Court. Search information required: name, date of birth, sex, race, previous address.

Civil records are available by mail. No release necessary. No search fee. $1.00 fee for first copy, $.25 each additional copy. $2.00 for certification. Search information required: name, date of birth, years to search. Specify plaintiff or defendant.

Wilkes County

Wilkes County Courthouse, Criminal
Records
Wilkesboro, NC 28697
(919) 667-5266
Felony and misdemeanor records are available by mail. No release necessary. $5.00 search fee. Company checks only, payable to Clerk of Superior Court. Search information required: name, date of birth, sex, race.

Civil records are available in person only. See North Carolina state repository for additional information.

Wilson County

Clerk of Court, Criminal Records
PO Box 1608
Wilson, NC 27893
(919) 291-7500
Felony and misdemeanor records are available by mail or phone. No release necessary. $5.00 fee. Certified check only, payable to Clerk of Superior Court. Search information required: name, SSN, date of birth, sex, race. Records accessible from September 1976.

Civil records are available in person only. See North Carolina state repository for additional information.

Yadkin County

Clerk of Superior Court, Criminal
Records
PO Box 95
Yadkinville, NC 27055
(919) 679-8838
Felony and misdemeanor records since 1983 are available by mail. No release necessary. $5.00 search fee. Certified check or money order, payable to Clerk of Superior Court. Search information required: name, date of birth, previous address, years to search.

Civil records are available in person only. See North Carolina state repository for additional information.

Yancey County

Clerk of Superior Court, Criminal
Records
Room 5, Yancey Courthouse
Burnsville, NC 28714
(704) 682-2122 Extension 416
Felony and misdemeanor records are available by mail or phone. No release necessary. $5.00 search fee. $.25 fee per copy. $2.00 for certification. Certified check only, payable to Clerk of Superior Court. Search information required: name, date of birth, sex, race, years to search.

Civil records are available in person only. See North Carolina state repository for additional information.

City-County Cross Reference

Aberdeen *Moore*
Advance *Davie*
Ahoskie *Hertford*
Alamance *Alamance*
Albemarle *Stanley*
Albertson *Duplin*
Alexander *Buncombe*
Alexander Mills *Rutherford*
Alexis *Gaston*
Alliance *Pamlico*
Almond *Swain*
Altamahaw *Alamance*
Andrews *Cherokee*
Angier *Harnett*
Ansonville *Anson*
Apex *Wake*
Aquone *Macon*
Arapahoe *Pamlico*
Ararat *Surry*
Archdale *Randolph*
Arden *Buncombe*
Arlington *Yadkin*
Ash *Brunswick*
Asheboro *Randolph*
Asheville *Buncombe*
Atkinson *Pender*
Atlantic *Carteret*
Atlantic Beach *Carteret*
Aulander *Bertie*
Aurora *Beaufort*
Autryville *Sampson*
Avon *Dare*
Ayden *Pitt*
Aydlett *Currituck*
Badin *Stanly*
Bahama *Durham*
Bailey *Nash*
Bakersville *Mitchell*
Balfour *Henderson*
Balsam *Jackson*
Balsam Grove
  Transylvania
Banner Elk *Avery*
Bannertown *Surry*

Barber *Rowan*
Barco *Currituck*
Barium Springs *Iredell*
Barnardsville *Buncombe*
Barnesville *Robeson*
Bat Cave *Henderson*
Bath *Beaufort*
Battleboro *Nash*
Bayboro *Pamlico*
Bear Creek *Chatham*
Beaufort *Carteret*
Belews Creek *Forsyth*
Belhaven *Beaufort*
Bellarthur *Pitt*
Belmont *Gaston*
Belvidere *Perquimans*
Belwood *Cleveland*
Bennett *Chatham*
Benson *Johnston*
Bessemer City *Gaston*
Bethania *Forsyth*
Bethel *Pitt*
Bethesda *Durham*
Beulaville *Duplin*
Biltmore Forest *Buncombe*
Biscoe *Montgomery*
Black Creek *Wilson*
Black Mountain *Buncombe*
Bladenboro *Bladen*
Blanch *Caswell*
Blounts Creek *Beaufort*
Blowing Rock *Watauga*
Boger City *Lincoln*
Boiling Springs *Cleveland*
Boiling Spring Lakes
  Brunswick
Bolivia *Brunswick*
Bolton *Columbus*
Bonlee *Chatham*
Bonnie Doone *Cumberland*
Boomer *Wilkes*
Boone *Watauga*
Boonville *Yadkin*
Bostic *Rutherford*

Brasstown *Clay*
Brevard *Transylvania*
Bridgeton *Craven*
Broadway *Lee*
Browns Summit *Guilford*
Brunswick *Columbus*
Bryson City *Swain*
Buies Creek *Harnett*
Bullock *Granville*
Bunn *Franklin*
Bunnlevel *Harnett*
Burgaw *Pender*
Burlington *Alamance*
Burnsville *Yancey*
Butner *Granville*
Butters *Bladen*
Buxton *Dare*
Calypso *Duplin*
Camden *Camden*
Cameron *Moore*
Candler *Buncombe*
Candor *Montgomery*
Canton *Haywood*
Cape Carteret *Carteret*
Caroleen *Rutherford*
Carolina Beach *New
  Hanover*
Carrboro *Orange*
Carthage *Moore*
Cary *Wake*
Casar *Cleveland*
Cashiers *Jackson*
Castalia *Nash*
Castle Hayne *New Hanover*
Catawba *Catawba*
Cedar Falls *Randolph*
Cedar Grove *Orange*
Cedar Island *Carteret*
Cedar Mountain
  Transylvania
Cerro Gordo *Columbus*
Chadbourn *Columbus*
Chapel Hill *Orange*
Charlotte *Mecklenburg*

Cherokee *Swain*
Cherryville *Gaston*
Chimney Rock *Rutherford*
China Grove *Rowan*
Chinquapin *Duplin*
Chocowinity *Beaufort*
Claremont *Catawba*
Clarendon *Columbus*
Clarkton *Bladen*
Clayton *Johnston*
Clemmons *Forsyth*
Cleveland *Rowan*
Cliffside *Rutherford*
Climax *Guilford*
Clinton *Sampson*
Clyde *Haywood*
Coats *Harnett*
Cofield *Hertford*
Coinjock *Currituck*
Colerain *Bertie*
Coleridge *Randolph*
Colfax *Guilford*
Collettsville *Caldwell*
Columbia *Tyrrell*
Columbus *Polk*
Comfort *Jones*
Como *Hertford*
Concord *Cabarrus*
Conetoe *Edgecombe*
Connellys Springs *Burke*
Conover *Catawba*
Conway *Northampton*
Cooleemee *Davie*
Corapeake *Gates*
Cordova *Richmond*
Cornelius *Mecklenburg*
Corolla *Currituck*
Council *Bladen*
Cove City *Craven*
Cramerton *Gaston*
Cranberry *Avery*
Creedmoor *Granville*
Creston *Ashe*
Creswell *Washington*

Crossnore *Avery*
Crouse *Lincoln*
Crumpler *Ashe*
Culberson *Cherokee*
Cullowhee *Jackson*
Cumberland *Cumberland*
Currie *Pender*
Currituck *Currituck*
Dallas *Gaston*
Dana *Henderson*
Danbury *Stokes*
Davidson *Mecklenburg*
Davis *Carteret*
Deep Gap *Watauga*
Deep Run *Lenoir*
Delco *Columbus*
Denton *Davidson*
Denver *Lincoln*
Dillsboro *Jackson*
Dobson *Surry*
Dover *Craven*
Drexel *Burke*
Dublin *Bladen*
Dudley *Wayne*
Dunn *Harnett*
Durham *Durham*
Eagle Rock *Wake*
Eagle Springs *Moore*
Earl *Cleveland*
East Bend *Yadkin*
East Flat Rock *Henderson*
East Lake *Dare*
Eastover *Cumberland*
East Spencer *Rowan*
Eden *Rockingham*
Edenton *Chowan*
Edneyville *Henderson*
Edward *Beaufort*
Efland *Orange*
Elizabeth City *Pasquotank*
Elizabethtown *Bladen*
Elkin *Surry*
Elk Park *Avery*
Ellenboro *Rutherford*
Ellerbe *Richmond*
Elm City *Wilson*
Elon College *Alamance*
Enfield *Halifax*
Engelhard *Hyde*
Enka *Buncombe*
Ennice *Alleghany*
Ernul *Craven*
Erwin *Harnett*
Ether *Montgomery*
Etowah *Henderson*
Eure *Gates*
Everetts *Martin*
Evergreen *Columbus*
Fair Bluff *Columbus*
Fairfield *Hyde*
Fairmont *Robeson*
Fairplains *Wilkis*
Fairview *Buncombe*
Faison *Duplin*
Faith *Rowan*
Falcon *Cumberland*
Falkland *Pitt*
Fallston *Cleveland*
Farmville *Pitt*
Fayetteville *Cumberland*
Ferguson *Wilkes*
Flat Rock *Henderson*
Fleetwood *Ashe*
Fletcher *Henderson*
Fontana Dam *Graham*

Forest City *Rutherford*
Fountain *Pitt*
Four Oaks *Johnston*
Franklin *Macon*
Franklinton *Franklin*
Franklinville *Randolph*
Fremont *Wayne*
Frisco *Dare*
Fuquay-Varina *Wake*
Garland *Sampson*
Gamewell *Caldwell*
Garner *Wake*
Garysburg *Northampton*
Gaston *Northampton*
Gastonia *Gaston*
Gates *Gates*
Gatesville *Gates*
George *Northampton*
Germanton *Stokes*
Gerton *Henderson*
Gibson *Scotland*
Gibsonville *Guilford*
Glade Valley *Alleghany*
Glen Alpine *Burke*
Glendale Springs *Ashe*
Glendon *Moore*
Glenville *Jackson*
Glenwood *McDowell*
Gloucester *Carteret*
Godwin *Cumberland*
Gold Hill *Rowan*
Goldsboro *Wayne*
Goldston *Chatham*
Gorman *Durham*
Graham *Alamance*
Grandy *Currituck*
Granite Falls *Caldwell*
Granite Quarry *Rowan*
Grantsboro *Pamlico*
Grassy Creek *Ashe*
Grayson *Ashe*
Greenmountain *Yancey*
Greensboro *Guilford*
Greenville *Pitt*
Grifton *Pitt*
Grimesland *Pitt*
Grover *Cleveland*
Gulf *Chatham*
Gumberry *Northampton*
Halifax *Halifax*
Hallsboro *Columbus*
Hamilton *Martin*
Hamlet *Richmond*
Hampstead *Pender*
Hamptonville *Yadkin*
Harbinger *Currituck*
Harkers Island *Carteret*
Harmony *Iredell*
Harrells *Sampson*
Harrellsville *Hertford*
Harris *Rutherford*
Harrisburg *Cabarrus*
Hassell *Martin*
Hatteras *Dare*
Havelock *Craven*
Haw River *Alamance*
Hayesville *Clay*
Hays *Wilkes*
Hazelwood *Haywood*
Henderson *Vance*
Hendersonville *Henderson*
Henrico *Northampton*
Henrietta *Rutherford*
Hertford *Perquimans*
Hickory *Catawba*

Hiddenite *Alexander*
Highfalls *Moore*
Highlands *Macon*
High Point *Guilford*
High Shoals *Gaston*
Hildebran *Burke*
Hillsborough *Orange*
Hillsdale *Guilford*
Hobbsville *Gates*
Hobgood *Halifax*
Hobucken *Pamlico*
Hoffman *Richmond*
Hollister *Halifax*
Holly Ridge *Onslow*
Holly Springs *Wake*
Hookerton *Greene*
Hope Mills *Cumberland*
Horse Shoe *Henderson*
Hot Springs *Madison*
Hubert *Onslow*
Hudson *Caldwell*
Huntersville *Mecklenburg*
Hurdle Mills *Person*
Husk *Ashe*
Icard *Burke*
Indian Trail *Union*
Ingold *Sampson*
Iron Station *Lincoln*
Ivanhoe *Sampson*
Jackson *Northampton*
Jackson Springs *Moore*
Jacksonville *Onslow*
Jamestown *Guilford*
Jamesville *Martin*
Jarvisburg *Currituck*
Jefferson *Ashe*
Jonas Ridge *Burke*
Jonesville *Yadkin*
Julian *Guilford*
Kannapolis *Cabarrus*
Kelford *Bertie*
Kelly *Bladen*
Kenansville *Duplin*
Kenly *Johnston*
Kernersville *Forsyth*
Kill Devil Hills *Dare*
King *Stokes*
Kings Mountain *Cleveland*
Kinston *Lenoir*
Kipling *Harnett*
Kittrell *Vance*
Kitty Hawk *Dare*
Knightdale *Wake*
Knotts Island *Currituck*
Kure Beach *New Hanover*
LaGrange *Lenoir*
Lake Junaluska *Haywood*
Lake Lure *Rutherford*
Lake Toxaway
   Transylvania
Lakeview *Moore*
Lake Waccamaw
   Columbus
Landis *Rowan*
Lansing *Ashe*
Lasker *Northampton*
Lattimore *Cleveland*
Laurel Hill *Scotland*
Laurel Springs *Alleghany*
Laurinburg *Scotland*
Lawndale *Cleveland*
Lawsonville *Stokes*
Leasburg *Caswell*
Leicester *Buncombe*
Leland *Brunswick*

Lemon Springs *Lee*
Lenoir *Caldwell*
Lewiston Woodville *Bertie*
Lewisville *Forsyth*
Lexington *Davidson*
Liberty *Randolph*
Lilesville *Anson*
Lillington *Harnett*
Lincolnton *Lincoln*
Linden *Cumberland*
Linville *Avery*
Linville Falls *Burke*
Linwood *Davidson*
Little Switzerland
   McDowell
Littleton *Halifax*
Locust *Stanly*
Longisland *Catawba*
Long Beach *Brunswick*
Longwood *Brunswick*
Louisburg *Franklin*
Lowell *Gaston*
Lowgap *Surry*
Lowland *Pamlico*
Lucama *Wilson*
Lumber Bridge *Robeson*
Lumberton *Robeson*
Lynn *Polk*
McAdenville *Gaston*
McFarlan *Anson*
McGrady *Wilkes*
McLeansville *Guilford*
Macclesfield *Edgecombe*
Macon *Warren*
Madison *Rockingham*
Maggie Valley *Haywood*
Magnolia *Duplin*
Maiden *Catawba*
Mamers *Harnett*
Manns Harbor *Dare*
Manson *Warren*
Manteo *Dare*
Maple *Currituck*
Maple Hill *Pender*
Marble *Cherokee*
Margarettsville
   Northampton
Marietta *Robeson*
Marion *McDowell*
Marshall *Madison*
Marshallberg *Carteret*
Mars Hill *Madison*
Marshville *Union*
Marston *Richmond*
Matthews *Mecklenburg*
Maury *Greene*
Maxton *Robeson*
Mayodan *Rockingham*
Maysville *Jones*
Mebane *Alamance*
Merritt *Pamlico*
Merry Hill *Bertie*
Micaville *Yancey*
Micro *Johnston*
Middleburg *Vance*
Middlesex *Nash*
Midland *Cabarrus*
Millers Creek *Wilkes*
Mill Spring *Polk*
Milton *Caswell*
Milwaukee *Northampton*
Mineral Springs *Union*
Minneapolis *Avery*
Mint Hill *Mecklenburg*
Misenheimer *Stanly*

Mocksville *Davie*
Moncure *Chatham*
Monroe *Union*
Montezuma *Avery*
Montreat *Buncombe*
Mooresboro *Cleveland*
Mooresville *Iredell*
Moravian Falls *Wilkes*
Morehead City *Carteret*
Morganton *Burke*
Morrisville *Wake*
Morven *Anson*
Mountain Home
    Henderson
Mount Airy *Surry*
Mount Gilead *Montgomery*
Mount Holly *Gaston*
Mount Mourne *Iredell*
Mount Olive *Wayne*
Mount Pleasant *Cabarrus*
Mount Ulla *Rowan*
Moyock *Currituck*
Murfreesboro *Hertford*
Murphy *Cherokee*
Nags Head *Dare*
Nakina *Columbus*
Naples *Henderson*
Nashville *Nash*
Nebo *McDowell*
New Bern *Craven*
Newell *Mecklenburg*
New Hill *Wake*
New Hope *Wake*
Newland *Avery*
New London *Stanly*
Newport *Carteret*
Newton *Catawba*
Newton Grove *Sampson*
Norlina *Warren*
Norman *Richmond*
North Wilkesboro *Wilkes*
Norwood *Stanly*
Oakboro *Stanly*
Oak City *Martin*
Oak Ridge *Guilford*
Ocracoke *Hyde*
Old Fort *McDowell*
Olin *Iredell*
Olivia *Harnett*
Oriental *Pamlico*
Orrum *Robeson*
Oteen *Buncombe*
Otto *Macon*
Oxford *Granville*
Palmyra *Halifax*
Pantego *Beaufort*
Parkton *Robeson*
Parmele *Martin*
Patterson *Caldwell*
Paw Creek *Mecklenburg*
Peachland *Anson*
Pelham *Caswell*
Pembroke *Robeson*
Pendleton *Northampton*
Penland *Mitchell*
Penrose *Transylvania*
Pfafftown *Forsyth*
Pikeville *Wayne*
Pilot Mountain *Surry*
Pinebluff *Moore*
Pine Hall *Stokes*
Pinehurst *Moore*
Pine Level *Johnston*
Pineola *Avery*
Pinetops *Edgecombe*

Pinetown *Beaufort*
Pineville *Mecklenburg*
Piney Creek *Alleghany*
Pink Hill *Lenoir*
Pinnacle *Stokes*
Pisgah Forest *Transylvania*
Pittsboro *Chatham*
Pleasant Garden *Guilford*
Pleasant Hill *Northampton*
Plumtree *Avery*
Plymouth *Washington*
Point Harbor *Currituck*
Polkton *Anson*
Polkville *Cleveland*
Pollocksville *Jones*
Poplar Branch *Currituck*
Potecasi *Northampton*
Powells Point *Currituck*
Powellsville *Bertie*
Princeton *Johnston*
Proctorville *Robeson*
Prospect Hill *Caswell*
Providence *Caswell*
Purlear *Wilkes*
Raeford *Hoke*
Raleigh *Wake*
Ramseur *Randolph*
Randleman *Randolph*
Ranlo *Gaston*
Red Oak *Nash*
Red Springs *Robeson*
Reidsville *Rockingham*
Rex *Robeson*
Rhodhiss *Caldwell*
Richfield *Stanly*
Richlands *Onslow*
Rich Square *Northampton*
Ridgecrest *Buncombe*
Ridgeway *Warren*
Riegelwood *Columbus*
Roanoke Rapids *Halifax*
Roaring Gap *Alleghany*
Roaring River *Wilkes*
Robbins *Moore*
Robbinsville *Graham*
Robersonville *Martin*
Rockingham *Richmond*
Rockwell *Rowan*
Rocky Mount *Edgecombe*
Rocky Point *Pender*
Rodanthe *Dare*
Roduco *Gates*
Rolesville *Wake*
Ronda *Wilkes*
Roper *Washington*
Roseboro *Sampson*
Rose Hill *Duplin*
Rosman *Transylvania*
Rougemont *Durham*
Rowland *Robeson*
Roxboro *Person*
Roxobel *Bertie*
Ruffin *Rockingham*
Rural Hall *Forsyth*
Rutherford College *Burke*
Rutherfordton *Rutherford*
Saint Pauls *Robeson*
Salemburg *Sampson*
Salisbury *Rowan*
Salter Path *Carteret*
Saluda *Polk*
Salvo *Dare*
Sandy Ridge *Stokes*
Sanford *Lee*
Sapphire *Transylvania*

Saratoga *Wilson*
Saxapahaw *Alamance*
Scaly Mountain *Macon*
Scotland Neck *Halifax*
Scotts *Iredell*
Scottville *Ashe*
Scranton *Hyde*
Seaboard *Northampton*
Seagrove *Randolph*
Sealevel *Carteret*
Sedalia *Guilford*
Selma *Johnston*
Semora *Caswell*
Seven Springs *Wayne*
Severn *Northampton*
Shallotte *Brunswick*
Shannon *Robeson*
Sharpsburg *Nash*
Shawboro *Currituck*
Shelby *Cleveland*
Sherrills Ford *Catawba*
Shiloh *Camden*
Siler City *Chatham*
Siloam *Surry*
Silver City *Hoke*
Simpson *Pitt*
Sims *Wilson*
Skyland *Buncombe*
Smithfield *Johnston*
Smyrna *Carteret*
Sneads Ferry *Onslow*
Snow Camp *Alamance*
Snow Hill *Greene*
Sophia *Randolph*
Southern Pines *Moore*
South Mills *Camden*
Southmont *Davidson*
Southport *Brunswick*
Sparta *Alleghany*
Speed *Edgecombe*
Spencer *Rowan*
Spindale *Rutherford*
Spring Hope *Nash*
Spring Lake *Cumberland*
Spruce Pine *Mitchell*
Staley *Randolph*
Stallings *Union*
Stanfield *Stanly*
Stanley *Gaston*
Stanlyville *Forsythe*
Stantonsburg *Wilson*
Star *Montgomery*
State Road *Surry*
Statesville *Iredell*
Stedman *Cumberland*
Stella *Carteret*
Stem *Granville*
Stokes *Pitt*
Stokesdale *Guilford*
Stoneville *Rockingham*
Stonewall *Pamlico*
Stony Point *Alexander*
Stovall *Granville*
Stumpy Point *Dare*
Sugar Grove *Watauga*
Summerfield *Guilford*
Sunbury *Gates*
Supply *Brunswick*
Swannanoa *Buncombe*
Swanquarter *Hyde*
Swansboro *Onslow*
Swepsonville *Alamance*
Sylva *Jackson*
Tabor City *Columbus*
Tapoco *Graham*

Tarboro *Edgecombe*
Tar Heel *Bladen*
Taylorsville *Alexander*
Teachey *Duplin*
Terrell *Catawba*
Thomasville *Davidson*
Thurmond *Wilkes*
Tillery *Halifax*
Timberlake *Person*
Toast *Surry*
Tobaccoville *Forsyth*
Todd *Ashe*
Topton *Cherokee*
Townsville *Vance*
Traphill *Wilkes*
Trenton *Jones*
Trinity *Randolph*
Triplett *Watauga*
Troutman *Iredell*
Troy *Montgomery*
Tryon *Polk*
Tuckasegee *Jackson*
Turkey *Sampson*
Turnersburg *Iredell*
Tuxedo *Henderson*
Tyner *Chowan*
Union Grove *Iredell*
Union Mills *Rutherford*
Valdese *Burke*
Vale *Lincoln*
Vanceboro *Craven*
Vandemere *Pamlico*
Vander *Cumberland*
Vass *Moore*
Vaughan *Warren*
Vilas *Watauga*
Waco *Cleveland*
Wade *Cumberland*
Wadesboro *Anson*
Wagram *Scotland*
Wake Forest *Wake*
Wakulla *Robeson*
Walkertown *Forsyth*
Wallace *Duplin*
Wallburg *Davidson*
Walnut Cove *Stokes*
Walstonburg *Greene*
Wanchese *Dare*
Warne *Clay*
Warrensville *Ashe*
Warrenton *Warren*
Warsaw *Duplin*
Washington *Beaufort*
Watha *Pender*
Waves *Dare*
Waxhaw *Union*
Waynesville *Haywood*
Weaverville *Buncombe*
Webster *Jackson*
Weddington *Union*
Welcome *Davidson*
Weldon *Halifax*
Wendell *Wake*
Wentworth *Rockingham*
West End *Moore*
Westfield *Surry*
West Jefferson *Ashe*
Whispering Pines *Moore*
Whitakers *Nash*
Whitehead *Alleghany*
White Lake *Bladen*
White Oak *Bladen*
Whiteville *Columbus*
Whitsett *Guilford*
Whittier *Jackson*

Wilbar *Wilkes*
Wilkesboro *Wilkes*
Willard *Pender*
Williamston *Martin*
Williston *Carteret*
Willow Spring *Wake*
Wilmington *New Hanover*
Wilson *Wilson*
Wilsons Mills *Johnston*
Windsor *Bertie*
Winfall *Perquimans*
Wingate *Union*
Winnabow *Brunswick*
Winter Park *New Hanover*
Winston-Salem *Forsyth*
Winterville *Pitt*
Winton *Hertford*
Wise *Warren*
Woodfin *Buncombe*
Woodland *Northampton*
Woodleaf *Rowan*
Wrightsville Beach *New Hanover*
Yadkinville *Yadkin*
Yanceyville *Caswell*
Youngsville *Franklin*
Zebulon *Wake*
Zionville *Watauga*
Zirconia *Henderson*

North Dakota

While the State Bureau of Investigation, the central repository for criminal records, charges an unusually high fee for criminal record searches, fifty (50) of North Dakota's fifty three (53) counties make criminal records available for employment screening purposes by phone and/or mail. Twenty four (24) counties will accept a request via facsimile.

Claims for civil court records are divided between district and county court by $2,000.

For more information or for offices not listed, contact the state's information hot line at (701) 224-2000.

Driving Records

Driver's License Division
Records
608 East Boulevard
Bismarck, ND 58505
(701) 224-2600
Driving records are available by mail. $3.00 fee per request. Turnaround time is 1 week. Written request must include job applicant's full name, date of birth and, if available, license number. Make check payable to Driver's License Division.

Worker's Compensation Records

Claims Department
Russel Building, Highway 83 North
4007 N. State Street
Bismarck, ND 58501
(701) 224-3800
Worker's compensation records are available by phone or mail. Phone inquiries should be limited to one or two requests. Requests must contain full name, date of birth and SSN. There is no fee. A signed release is not required for verification of claim or basic information. A signed release is required for all medical records.

Vital Statistics

Division of Vital Records
State Department of Health
Office of Statistical Services
Bismarck, ND 58505
(701) 224-2360
Birth records are available for $7.00 and death records are available for $5.00. Additional copies of birth certificates are $4.00 each. Additional copies of death certificates are $2.00 each. State office has some records since July 1893. Years from 1894 to 1920 are incomplete. Records are accessible by computer. An employer can obtain records with a written release. Make certified check or money order payable to Vital Records.

Marriage records since July 1925 are available. $5.00 fee. Include name, marriage date, spouse's name, city where married, where resided, and county where license issued. Turnaround time is 2 days. Permission in writing to release copy of marriage license is required. Divorce records are available at county level, County Court House where divorce occurred.

Department of Education

Department of Public Instruction
Teacher Certification Division
600 East Blvd. Avenue
Bismark, ND 58505-0440
(701) 224-2264
Field of certification, effective date, expiration date are available by mail or phone. Include name.

Medical Licensing

State Board of Medical Examiners
418 East Broadway Avenue
Suite 12
Bismarck, ND 58501
(701) 223-9485
Fax (701) 223-4756
Will confirm licenses for MDs and DOs by mail or phone. No fee.

North Dakota Board of Nursing
919 South 7th St., Suite 504
Bismarck, ND 58504
(701) 224-2974
Will confirm license by phone. No fee. Include name, regional certificate, if available.

Bar Association

North Dakota State Bar Association
PO Box 2136
Bismarck, ND 58502
(701) 255-1404
Will confirm licenses by phone. No fee. Include name.

Accountancy Board

North Dakota State Board of Accountancy
PO Box 88104
University Station
Grand Forks, ND 58202
(701) 777-3869
Will confirm licenses by phone. No fee. Include name.

Securities Commission

Office of Securities
600 East Blvd.
Fifth Floor, State Capitol
Bismarck, ND 58502
(701) 224-4712
Will confirm licenses by phone. No fee. Include name and SSN.

Secretary of State

Secretary of State
State Capitol
Bismarck, ND 58505
(701) 224-4284
Fax (701) 224-2992
Service agent and address, date incorporated, trade names are available by mail or phone. $5.00 fee. Contact the above office for additional information.

Criminal Records

State Repository

State Bureau of Criminal Investigation
PO Box 1054
Bismarck, ND 58502
(701) 221-6180
Fax (701) 221-6158
Criminal records are available by mail only. All requests must include the subject's full name, date of birth and SSN. All requests must also include either the current address of the subject for notification by the state or a signed release authorizing the record check. There is a $20.00 fee. Make check

payable to Attorney General. Conviction data only is released. Turnaround time is 24 to 48 hours plus mail time.

Civil records are available by mail. No release necessary. $0.00 search fee. $0.00 fee per copy. $0.00 for certification. Search information required: name, date of birth, years to search. Specify plaintiff or defendant.

Adams County

Clerk of District Court, Criminal Records
PO Box 469
Hettinger, ND 58639
(701) 567-2460
Fax (701) 567-2910

Felony and misdemeanor records are available by mail or phone. No release necessary. No search fee. Search information required: name.

Civil records are available by mail or phone. No release necessary. No search fee. $.25 fee per copy. $5.00 for first certification, $2.00 each additional page. Search information required: name, date of birth, years to search. Specify plaintiff or defendant.

Barnes County

Felony records
Clerk of District Court, Criminal Records
Barnes County Courthouse
230-4th Street Northwest
Valley City, ND 58072
(701) 845-8512

Felony records are available by mail or phone. No release necessary. No fee for phone responses. $5.00 search fee if employer requests written confirmation of search results. Search information required: name, SSN, date of birth, sex, race.

Civil records
Clerk of District Court
Barnes County Courthouse
230-4th Street Northwest
Valley City, ND 58072
(701) 845-8512

Civil records are available by mail. A release is required. $5.00 search fee. $.25 fee per copy. $5.00 for first certification, $2.00 each additional page. Search information required: name, date of birth, years to search. Specify plaintiff or defendant.

Misdemeanor records
Barnes County Court
County Courthouse
Valley City, ND 58072
(701) 845-8503

Misdemeanor records are available by mail or phone. No release necessary. $5.00 search fee per name. $.20 fee per copy. $5.00 for certification. Search information required: name, date of birth, social security number.

Civil records
Barnes County Court
County Courthouse
Valley City, ND 58072
(701) 845-8503

Civil records are available by mail. No release necessary. $5.00 search fee. $.20 fee per copy. $5.00 for first certification. Search information required: name, date of birth, years to search. Specify plaintiff or defendant.

Benson County

Clerk of District Court, Criminal Records
Box 213
Minnewaukan, ND 58351
(701) 473-5345

Felony and misdemeanor records are available by mail. No release necessary. $5.00 search fee. Search information required: name, SSN, date of birth, sex, race.

Civil records are available by mail. No release necessary. $5.00 search fee. $1.00 fee per copy. $5.00 for certification. Search information required: name, date of birth, years to search. Specify plaintiff or defendant.

Billings County

Clerk of District Court, Criminal Records
PO Box 138
Medora, ND 58645
(701) 623-4492

Felony and misdemeanor records are available by mail. No release necessary. $5.00 search fee. $5.00 for certification. Search information required: name, SSN, date of birth, years to search.

Civil records are available by mail. No release necessary. $5.00 search fee. $5.00 for certification. Search information required: name, date of birth, years to search. Specify plaintiff or defendant.

Bottineau County

Clerk of Courts, Criminal Records
Courthouse
Bottineau, ND 58318
(701) 228-3983

Felony and misdemeanor records are available by mail or phone. No release necessary. $5.00 search fee. Search information required: name, SSN, date of birth, sex, race.

Civil records are available by mail. No release necessary. $5.00 search fee. $5.00 for first certification. Search information required: name, date of birth, years to search. Specify plaintiff or defendant.

Bowman County

Clerk of District Court
PO Box 379
Bowman, ND 58623
(701) 523-3450
Fax (701) 523-5443

Felony records are not currently available by mail or phone. See North Dakota State Repository.

Civil records are available by mail. No release necessary. No search fee. $1.00 fee per copy. $5.00 for certification. Search information required: name, years to search. Specify plaintiff or defendant.

Burke County

Clerk of Court, Criminal Records
PO Box 219
Bowbells, ND 58721
(701) 377-2718
Fax (701) 377-2020

Felony and misdemeanor records are available by mail or phone. No release necessary. No search fee. Search information required: name, SSN, date of birth, sex, race.

Civil records are available by mail. A release is required. No search fee. $.50 fee per copy. $5.00 for certification. Search information required: name, years to search. Specify plaintiff or defendant.

Burleigh County

Felony records
Clerk of District Court, Criminal Records
PO Box 1055
Bismarck, ND 58502
(701) 222-6690

Felony records are available by mail. No release necessary. $5.00 search fee. Company checks only, payable to Clerk of District Court. Search information required: name, date of birth.

Civil records
Clerk of District Court
PO Box 1055
Bismarck, ND 58502
(701) 222-6690

Civil records are available by mail. No release necessary. $5.00 search fee. $.20 fee per copy. $5.00 for certification. Search information required: name, date of birth, years to search. Specify plaintiff or defendant.

Misdemeanor records
Burleigh County Court
PO Box 5518
Bismarck, ND 58502
(701) 222-6702

Misdemeanor records are available by mail. No release necessary. $5.00 search fee. Company check payable to Burleigh County Court. Search information required: name, date of birth.

Civil records
Burleigh County Court
PO Box 5518
Bismarck, ND 58502
(701) 222-6702

Civil records are available by mail. No release necessary. $5.00 search fee. $.20 fee per copy. $5.00 for certification. Search information required: name, date of birth, years to search. Specify plaintiff or defendant.

Cass County

Felony records
Clerk of District Court, Criminal Records
PO Box 2806
Fargo, ND 58108
(701) 241-5645

Felony records are available by mail. No release necessary. $5.00 search fee. $.25 fee per copy. $5.00 for certification. Certified check only, payable to Clerk of District Court. Search information required: name, date of birth, years to search .

Civil records
Clerk of District Court
PO Box 2806
Fargo, ND 58108
(701) 241-5645

Civil records are available by mail. No release necessary. $5.00 search fee. $.25 fee per copy. $5.00 for certification. Search information required: name, date of birth, years to search. Specify plaintiff or defendant.

Misdemeanor records
Cass County Court
PO Box 2806
Fargo, ND 58108
(701) 241-5660
Fax (701) 241-5728
Misdemeanor records are available by mail or phone. No release necessary. $5.00 search fee. Search information required: name.

Civil records
Cass County Court
PO Box 2806
Fargo, ND 58108
(701) 241-5660
Fax (701) 241-5728
Civil records are available by mail. No release necessary. $5.00 search fee. $.25 fee per copy. $5.00 for certification. Search information required: name, date of birth, years to search. Specify plaintiff or defendant.

Cavalier County

Clerk of Court, Criminal Records
Courthouse
901 Third St.
Langdon, ND 58249
(701) 256-2124
Felony and misdemeanor records are available by mail or phone. No release necessary. $5.00 search fee. Search information required: name, date of birth, address.

Civil records are available by mail. No release necessary. $5.00 search fee. Search information required: name, date of birth, years to search. Specify plaintiff or defendant.

Dickey County

Clerk of Court, Criminal Records
PO Box 336
Ellendale, ND 58436
(701) 349-3560
Felony and misdemeanor records are available by mail or phone. A release is required. $5.00 search fee. Certified check only, payable to Clerk of Court. Search information required: name.

Civil records are available by mail. No release necessary. $5.00 search fee. $5.00 for certification. Search information required: name, date of birth, years to search. Specify plaintiff or defendant.

Divide County

Clerk of District Court, Criminal Records
PO Box 68
Crosby, ND 58730
(701) 965-6831
Fax (701) 965-6943
Felony and misdemeanor records are available by mail or phone. No release necessary. No search fee. Search information required: name.

Civil records are available by mail. No release necessary. $5.00 search fee. $.25 fee per copy. $5.00 for certification. Search information required: name, date of birth, years to search. Specify plaintiff or defendant.

Dunn County

Dunn County Clerk of Court, Criminal Records
PO Box 136
Manning, ND 58642-0136
(701) 573-4447
Felony and misdemeanor records are available by mail. No release necessary. $5.00 search fee. $5.00 for certification. Make company check payable to Dunn County Clerk of Court. Search information required: name, SSN, date of birth, previous address, years to search.

Civil records are available by mail. No release necessary. $5.00 search fee. $5.00 for certification. Search information required: name, date of birth, years to search. Specify plaintiff or defendant.

Eddy County

Clerk of County and District Courts, Criminal Records
524 Central Ave.
New Rockford, ND 58356
(701) 947-2816
Fax (701) 947-2067
Felony and misdemeanor records are available by mail. No release necessary. $5.00 search fee. Certified check only, payable to Clerk of Court. Search information required: name.

Civil records are available by mail. No release necessary. No search fee. $1.00 fee per copy. $5.00 for certification. Search information required: name, date of birth, years to search. Specify plaintiff or defendant.

Emmons County

District Clerk, Criminal Records
PO Box 905
Linton, ND 58552
(701) 254-4812
Fax (701) 254-4012
Felony and misdemeanor records are available by mail or fax. No release necessary. $5.00 search fee. $.20 fee per copy. $5.00 for certification. $3.00 fee for first page of fax response, $2.00 for each additional page. Search information required: name, date of birth, years to search.

Civil records are available by mail. No release necessary. $5.00 search fee. $.20 fee per copy. $5.00 for certification. $3.00 fee for first page of fax response, $2.00 for each additional page. Search information required: name, date of birth, years to search. Specify plaintiff or defendant.

Foster County

Clerk of Court, Criminal Records
PO 257
Carrington, ND 58421
(701) 652-2491
Fax (701) 652-2173
Felony and misdemeanor records are available by mail. No release necessary. No search fee. Make check payable to Clerk of Court. Search information required: name.

Civil records are available by mail. No release necessary. No search fee. $.50 fee per copy. $5.00 for certification. Search information required: name, date of birth, years to search. Specify plaintiff or defendant.

Golden Valley County

Clerk of Court, Criminal Records
Box 596
Beach, ND 58621
(701) 872-4352
Felony and misdemeanor records are available by mail. No release necessary. No fee. Search information required: name, SSN, date of birth.

Civil records are available by mail or phone. No release necessary. No search fee. $.50 fee per copy. $5.00 for certification. Search information required: name, date of birth, years to search. Specify plaintiff or defendant.

Grand Forks County

Felony records
Clerk of District Court
PO Box 1035
Grand Forks, ND 58206-1035
(701) 780-8214
Fax (701) 780-8400
Felony records are available by mail or fax. No release necessary. $5.00 search fee. $.25 fee per copy. $5.00 for certification. Make check payable to District Court Clerk. Search information required: name.

Civil records
Clerk of District Court
PO Box 1035
Grand Forks, ND 58206-1035
(701) 780-8214
Fax (701) 780-8400
Civil records are available by mail. No release necessary. $5.00 search fee. $.25 fee per copy. $5.00 for certification. Search information required: name, date of birth, years to search. Specify plaintiff or defendant.

Misdemeanor records
Grand Forks County Court
PO Box 1477
Grand Forks, ND 58206
(701) 780-8238
Misdemeanor records are available in person only. See North Dakota state repository for additional information.

Civil records
Grand Forks County Court
PO Box 1477
Grand Forks, ND 58206
(701) 780-8238
Civil records are available by mail. No release necessary. $5.00 search fee. $.25 fee per copy. $5.00 for certification. Search information required: name, date of birth, years to search. Specify plaintiff or defendant.

Grant County

Clerk of Court, Criminal Records
Box 258
Carson, ND 58529
(701) 622-3615
Felony and misdemeanor records are available by mail or phone. No release necessary. No search fee. $5.00 for written certification. Search information required: name, SSN, date of birth.

Civil records are available by mail. No release necessary. $5.00 search fee. $.25 fee per copy. $5.00 for certification. Search information required: name, date of birth, years to search. Specify plaintiff or defendant.

Griggs County

Clerk of Court
PO Box 326
Cooperstown, ND 58425
(701) 797-2772
Fax (701) 797-3170
Felony and misdemeanor records are available by mail. No release necessary. $5.00 fee. Make check payable to Clerk of Court. Search information required: name, date of birth, years to search.

Civil records are available by mail. No release necessary. $5.00 search fee. $.50 fee per copy. $5.00 for certification. Search information required: name, date of birth, years to search. Specify plaintiff or defendant.

Hettinger County

Clerk of District Court, Criminal Records
Courthouse
Box 668
Mott, ND 58646
(701) 824-2645
Fax (701) 824-2717
Felony records are available by mail. No release necessary. $5.00 search fee. Search information required: name, years to search. Turnaround time is one day.

Civil records are available by mail or phone. No release necessary. $5.00 search fee. $.25 fee per copy. $5.00 for certification. Search information required: name, date of birth, years to search. Specify plaintiff or defendant.

Kidder County

Clerk of Court, Criminal Records
PO Box 66
Steele, ND 58482
(701) 475-2663
Fax (701) 475-2022
Felony and misdemeanor records are available by mail or fax. No release necessary. $5.00 search fee. $1.00 fee per copy. $5.00 for certification. Search information required: name, years to search.

Civil records are available by mail. No release necessary. $5.00 search fee. $1.00 fee per copy. $5.00 for certification. Search information required: name, date of birth, years to search. Specify plaintiff or defendant.

La Moure County

Clerk of Court, Criminal Records
Box 5
La Moure, ND 58458
(701) 883-5179
Felony and misdemeanor records are available by mail or phone. No release necessary. $5.00 search fee. Certified check only, payable to Clerk of Court. Search information required: name.

Civil records are available by mail. No release necessary. $5.00 search fee. $.50 fee per copy. $5.00 for certification. Search information required: name, date of birth, years to search. Specify plaintiff or defendant.

Logan County

Felony records
Clerk of Court
Logan County Courthouse
Napoleon, ND 58561
(701) 254-4812
Fax (701) 254-4012
Felony records are not available by mail. No release necessary. $5.00 search fee. $.20 fee per copy. $5.00 for certification. Search information required: name, date of birth, years to search.

Civil records
Clerk of Court
Logan County Courthouse
Napoleon, ND 58561
(701) 254-4812
Fax (701) 254-4012
Civil records are available by mail. No release necessary. $5.00 search fee. $.20 fee per copy. $5.00 for certification. Search information required: name, date of birth, years to search. Specify plaintiff or defendant.

Misdemeanor records
Logan County Court
PO Box 6
Napoleon, ND 58561
(701) 754-2751
Fax (701) 754-2270
Misdemeanor records are available by mail or fax. No release necessary. $5.00 search fee. Search information required: name, date of birth, years to search, date of offense.

Civil records
Logan County Court
PO Box 6
Napoleon, ND 58561
(701) 754-2751
Fax (701) 254-4012
Civil records are available by mail. No release necessary. $5.00 search fee. $.20 fee per copy. $5.00 for certification. Search information required: name, date of birth, years to search. Specify plaintiff or defendant.

McHenry County

Clerk of Court, Criminal Records
PO Box 117
Towner, ND 58788
(701) 537-5729
Felony and misdemeanor records are available by mail. No release necessary. No search fee. $.50 fee per copy. $5.00 for certification. Search information required: name, date of birth.

Civil records are available by mail or phone. No release necessary. No search fee. $.50 fee per copy. $5.00 for certification. Search information required: name, date of birth, years to search. Specify plaintiff or defendant.

McIntosh County

Clerk of County & District Court, Criminal Records
PO Box 179
Ashley, ND 58413
(701) 288-3450
Felony and misdemeanor records are available by mail. No release necessary. No search fee. Search information required: name, years to search.

Civil records are available by mail. No release necessary. $5.00 search fee. $.15 fee per copy. $5.00 for certification. Search information required: name, date of birth, years to search. Specify plaintiff or defendant.

McKenzie County

Felony records
Clerk of Court, Criminal Records
Box 524
Watford City, ND 58854
(701) 842-3452
Felony records are available by mail. No release necessary. No search fee. Search information required: name, date of birth, SASE.

Civil records
Clerk of Court
Box 524
Watford City, ND 58854
(701) 842-3452
Civil records are available by mail. No release necessary. $5.00 search fee. $.25 fee per copy. $5.00 for certification. Search information required: name, date of birth, years to search, SASE. Specify plaintiff or defendant.

Misdemeanor records
Mackenzie County Court
Box 546
Watford City, ND 58854
(701) 842-3616 Extension 24
Fax (701) 842-3916
Misdemeanor records are available by mail, phone or fax. No release necessary. $5.00 search fee. $.25 fee per copy. $5.00 for certification. Search information required: name, date of birth.

Civil records
Mackenzie County Court
Box 546
Watford City, ND 58854
(701) 842-3616 Extension 24
Fax (701) 842-3916
Civil records are available by mail. No release necessary. $5.00 search fee. $.25 fee per copy. $5.00 for certification. Search information required: name, date of birth, years to search. Specify plaintiff or defendant.

McLean County

Clerk of Court, Criminal Records
PO Box H
Washburn, ND 58577
(701) 462-8541 Ext. 227
Felony and misdemeanor records are available by mail. No release necessary. $5.00 search fee. Make check payable to Clerk of Court. Search information required: name.

Civil records are available by mail. No release necessary. $5.00 search fee. $.25 fee per copy. $5.00 for certification. Search information required: name, date of birth, years to search. Specify plaintiff or defendant.

Mercer County

Mercer County Court Clerk, Criminal Records
PO Box 39
Stanton, ND 58571
(701) 745-3262
Fax (701) 745-3347

Felony and misdemeanor records are available by mail. A release is required. $5.00 search fee. Certified check only, payable to Clerk of Court. Search information required: name.

Civil records are available by mail. A release is required. $5.00 search fee. $1.00 fee per copy. $5.00 for certification. Search information required: name, date of birth, years to search. Specify plaintiff or defendant.

Morton County

Clerk of Court, Criminal Records
Morton County Courthouse
210 2nd Ave. N.W.
Mandan, ND 58554
(701) 667-3358

Felony records are available by mail. No release necessary. $5.00 search fee. Search information required: name, date of birth.

Civil records are available by mail. No release necessary. $5.00 search fee. $.25 fee per copy. $5.00 for certification. Search information required: name, date of birth, years to search. Specify plaintiff or defendant.

Mountrail County

Mountrail County Court, Criminal Records
Clerk of Court
PO Box 69
Stanley, ND 58784
(701) 628-2915
Fax (701) 628-3975

Felony and misdemeanor records are available by mail or phone. No release necessary. $5.00 search fee. Make check payable to Clerk of Court. Search information required: name, date of birth, years to search.

Civil records are available by mail. No release necessary. $5.00 search fee. $.25 fee per copy. $5.00 for certification. Search information required: name, date of birth, years to search. Specify plaintiff or defendant.

Nelson County

Clerk of Court, Criminal Records
PO Box 565
Lakota, ND 58344
(701) 247-2462
Fax (701) 247-2412

Felony and misdemeanor records are available by mail. No release necessary. $5.00 search fee. Make check payable to Clerk of Court. Search information required: name, date of birth.

Civil records are available by mail. A release is required. $5.00 search fee. $.25 fee per copy. $5.00 for certification. Search information required: name, date of birth, years to search. Specify plaintiff or defendant.

Oliver County

Clerk of Court, Criminal Records
Box 125
Center, ND 58530
(701) 794-8777
Fax (701) 794-3476

Misdemeanor records are available by mail. No release necessary. No search fee. Search information required: name. Felony request subject to district court approval.

Civil records are available by mail or phone. No release necessary. No search fee. $1.00 fee per copy. $5.00 for certification. Search information required: name, date of birth, years to search. Specify plaintiff or defendant.

Pembina County

Pembina District Court, Criminal Records
PO Box 357
Cavalier, ND 58220
(701) 265-4275

Felony and misdemeanor records are available by mail or phone. No release necessary. $5.00 search fee. Make company check payable to Clerk of Court. Search information required: name, years to search.

Civil records are available by mail. No release necessary. $5.00 search fe. $5.00 for certification. Search information required: name, date of birth, years to search. Specify plaintiff or defendant.

Pierce County

Pierce County Courthouse, Criminal Records
240 SE 2nd Street
Rugby, ND 58368
(701) 776-6161

Felony and misdemeanor records are available by mail or phone. No release necessary. No search fee. $.25 fee per copy. $5.00 for certification. Make company check payable to Clerk of Court. Search information required: name, years to search.

Civil records are available by mail. A release is required. No search fee. $.25 fee per copy. $5.00 for certification. Search information required: name, date of birth, years to search. Specify plaintiff or defendant.

Ramsey County

Ramsey County Courthouse, Criminal Records
524 4th Ave. #4
Devils Lake, ND 58301
(701) 662-7066
Fax (701) 662-7049

Felony and misdemeanor records are available by mail or phone. No release necessary. $5.00 search fee. Search information required: name, SSN, date of birth.

Civil records are available by mail. No release necessary. $5.00 search fee. $.50 fee per copy. $5.00 for certification. Search information required: name, date of birth, years to search. Specify plaintiff or defendant.

Ransom County

District Court Clerk, Criminal Records
PO Box 626
Lisbon, ND 58054
(701) 683-5823
Fax (701) 683-5827

Felony and misdemeanor records are available by mail or phone. No release necessary. No search fee. Search information required: name, date of birth.

Civil records are available by mail. No release necessary. $5.00 search fee. $.20 fee per copy. $5.00 for certification. Search information required: name, date of birth, years to search. Specify plaintiff or defendant.

Renville County

Renville County Courthouse, Criminal Records
PO Box 68
Mohall, ND 58761
(701) 756-6398
Fax (701) 756-7158

Records are not available by mail or phone. See North Dakota State Repository for additional information.

Civil records are available by mail. No release necessary. No search fee. $1.00 fee per copy. $5.00 for certification. Search information required: name, date of birth, years to search. Specify plaintiff or defendant.

Richland County

Felony records
Clerk of District Court, Criminal Records
PO Box 966
Wahpeton, ND 58074
(701) 642-7818
Fax (701) 642-3023

Felony records are available by mail or phone. No release necessary. $5.00 search fee. Search information required: name.

Civil records
Clerk of District Court
PO Box 966
Wahpeton, ND 58074
(701) 642-7818
Fax (701) 642-3023

Civil records are available by mail. No release necessary. No search fee. $.50 per copy. $5.00 for first certification, $2.00 each additional page. Search information required: name, date of birth, years to search. Specify plaintiff or defendant.

Misdemeanor records
Richland County Court
PO Box 665
Wahpeton, ND 58074
(701) 642-7781

Misdemeanor records are available by mail only. No release necessary. $3.00 search fee. $.25 fee per copy. $5.00 for certification. Search information required: name, date of birth, years to search.

Civil records
Richland County Court
PO Box 665
Wahpeton, ND 58074
(701) 642-7781

Civil records are available by mail. No release necessary. $3.00 search fee. $.25 fee per copy. $5.00 for certification. Search information required: name, date of birth, years to search. Specify plaintiff or defendant.

Rolette County

Rolette County Courthouse, Criminal
Records
Box 460
Rolla, ND 58367
(701) 477-3816

Felony records are available by mail. No release necessary. $5.00 search fee. $.25 fee per copy. $5.00 for certification. Search information required: name, date of birth, years to search.

Civil records are available by mail. No release necessary. $5.00 search fee. $.25 fee per copy. $5.00 for certification. Search information required: name, date of birth, years to search. Specify plaintiff or defendant.

Sargent County

Sargent County
Sheriff's Dept.
Box 157
Forman, ND 58032
(701) 724-3302
Fax (701) 724-6244

Records are not available by mail or phone. See North Dakota State Repository.

Civil records are available by mail. No release necessary. No search fee. $2.00 fee per copy. Search information required: name, date of birth, years to search. Specify plaintiff or defendant.

Sheridan County

Clerk of Court, Criminal Records
PO Box 668
McClusky, ND 58463
(701) 363-2207

Felony and misdemeanor records are available by mail. A release is required. No search fee. Search information required: name, years to search.

Civil records are available by mail. No release necessary. No search fee. $1.00 fee per copy. $5.00 for certification. Search information required: name, date of birth, years to search. Specify plaintiff or defendant.

Sioux County

Sioux County Courthouse
Box L
Fort Yates, ND 58538
(701) 854-3853

Felony records are not available by mail or phone. See North Dakota State Repository.

Civil records are available by mail. No release necessary. $5.00 search fee. $.25 fee per copy. $5.00 for certification. Search information required: name, date of birth, years to search. Specify plaintiff or defendant.

Slope County

Clerk of Court, Criminal Records
PO Box JJ
Amidon, ND 58620
(701) 879-6275
Fax (701) 879-6278

Felony and misdemeanor records are available by mail or phone. No release necessary. $10.00 search fee. Certified check only, payable to Clerk of Court. Search information required: name, date of birth, previous address, years to search.

Civil records are available by mail. No release necessary. $5.00 search fee. $.15 fee per copy. $5.00 for certification. Search information required: name, date of birth, years to search. Specify plaintiff or defendant.

Stark County

Felony records
Clerk of District Court, Criminal
Records
PO Box 130
Dickinson, ND 58602
(701) 264-7634

Felony records are available by mail. No release necessary. $5.00 search fee. Make check payable to Clerk of District Court. Search information required: name, date of birth, previous address.

Civil records
Clerk of District Court
PO Box 130
Dickinson, ND 58602
(701) 264-7634

Civil records are available by mail. No release necessary. $5.00 search fee. $.50 fee per copy. $5.00 for certification. Search information required: name, date of birth, years to search. Specify plaintiff or defendant.

Misdemeanor records
Stark County Court
PO Box 130
Dickinson, ND 58602
(701) 264-7636

Misdemeanor records are available by mail or phone. No release necessary. $5.00 search fee. Make company check payable to Stark County Court. Search information required: name, date of birth.

Civil records
Stark County Court
PO Box 130
Dickinson, ND 58602
(701) 264-7636

Civil records are available by mail. No release necessary. $5.00 search fee. $.25 fee per copy. $5.00 for certification. Search information required: name, date of birth, years to search. Specify plaintiff or defendant.

Steele County

Clerk of Court, Criminal Records
PO Box 296
Finley, ND 58230
(701) 524-2790

Felony and misdemeanor records are available by mail . A release is required. No search fee. Search information required: name, SSN, date of birth, previous address, years to search.

Civil records are available by mail. No release necessary. No search fee. $.25 fee per copy. $5.00 for certification. Search information required: name, date of birth, years to search. Specify plaintiff or defendant.

Stutsman County

Felony records
Stutsman District Courthouse,
Criminal Records
511 2nd Ave. S.E.
Jamestown, ND 58401
(701) 252-9042

Felony records are available by mail. No release necessary. $5.00 search fee. $5.00 for certification. Company checks only, payable to District Court Clerk. Search information required: name, date of birth, years to search.

Civil records
Stutsman District Courthouse
511 2nd Ave. S.E.
Jamestown, ND 58401
(701) 252-9042

Civil records are available by mail. No release necessary. $5.00 search fee. $5.00 for certification. Search information required: name, date of birth, years to search. Specify plaintiff or defendant.

Misdemeanor records
Stutsman County Courthouse,
Criminal Records
511 2nd Ave. S.E.
Jamestown, ND 58401
(701) 252-9037

Misdemeanor records are available by mail. No release necessary. $5.00 search fee. $5.00 for certification. Company checks only, payable to District Court Clerk. Search information required: name, date of birth, years to search.

Towner County

Clerk of Court, Criminal Records
Box 517
Cando, ND 58324
(701) 968-3424
Fax (701) 968-4511

Felony and misdemeanor records are available by mail or phone. No release necessary. No search fee. Search information required: name, SSN, date of birth, years to search.

Civil records are available by mail or phone. A release is required. No search fee. $1.00 fee per copy. $5.00 for certification. Search information required: name, date of birth, years to search. Specify plaintiff or defendant.

Traill County

Clerk of Court, Criminal Records
Box 805
Hillsboro, ND 58045
(701) 436-4454

Felony and misdemeanor records are available by mail. A signed release is required. $5.00 search fee. $.25 fee per copy. $5.00 for certification. Company checks only, payable to Clerk of Court. Search information required: name, date of birth, years to search.

Civil records are available by mail. No release necessary. $5.00 search fee. $.25 fee per copy. $5.00 for certification. Search information required: name, date of birth, years to search. Specify plaintiff or defendant.

Walsh County

Felony records
Clerk of District Court, Criminal
Records
Grafton, ND 58237
(701) 352-0350
Fax (701) 352-1104
Felony records are available by mail, phone
or fax. No release necessary. No search fee.
Search information required: name, date of
birth, years to search.

Civil records
Clerk of District Court
Grafton, ND 58237
(701) 352-0350
Fax (701) 352-1104
Civil records are available by mail. No release necessary. $5.00 search fee. $.50 fee
per copy. $5.00 for certification. Search in-
formation required: name, date of birth,
years to search. Specify plaintiff or defendant.

Misdemeanor records
Walsh County Court
County Courthouse
Grafton, ND 58237
(701) 352-2490
Fax (701) 352-1104
Misdemeanor records are available by mail
or fax. No release necessary. $5.00 search
fee. Search information required: name,
date of birth, social security number.

Civil records
Walsh County Court
County Courthouse
Grafton, ND 58237
(701) 352-2490
Fax (701) 352-1104
Civil records are available by mail. No release necessary. No search fee. $.25 fee per
copy. $5.00 for certification. Search infor-
mation required: name, date of birth, years
to search. Specify plaintiff or defendant.

Ward County

Felony records
Clerk of District Court, Criminal
Records, 2nd Floor
Ward County
Minot, ND 58701
(701) 857-6460
Felony records are available by mail. A re-
lease is required. $5.00 search fee. $.50 fee
per copy. $5.00 for certification. Make
check payable to Clerk of District Court.
Search information required: name, date of
birth, years to search.

Civil records
Clerk of District Court
Ward County
Minot, ND 58701
(701) 857-6460
Civil records are available by mail. No release necessary. $5.00 search fee. $.50 fee
per copy. $5.00 for certification. Search in-
formation required: name, date of birth,
years to search. Specify plaintiff or defendant.

Misdemeanor records
Clerk of County Court Office,
3nd Floor
Ward County
Minot, ND 58701
(701) 857-6470
Misdemeanor records are available by mail.
A release is required. $5.00 search fee. $.50
fee per copy. $5.50 for certification. Make
check payable to Clerk of District Court.
Search information required: name, years to
search.

Wells County

Clerk of Court, Criminal Records
Box 596
Fessenden, ND 58438
(701) 547-3122
Felony and misdemeanor records are available by mail. A signed release is required.
$5.00 search fee. Company checks only,
payable to Clerk of County Court. Search
information required: name, alias, date of
birth.

Civil records are available by mail. A release is required. No search fee. $.25 fee
per copy. $5.00 for certification. Search in-
formation required: name, date of birth,
years to search. Specify plaintiff or defendant.

Williams County

Felony records
District Court, Criminal Records
PO Box 2047
Williston, ND 58801
(701) 572-1720
Felony records are available by mail. A re-
lease is required. $5.00 fee. Search informa-
tion required: name, years to search.

Civil records
District Court
PO Box 2047
Williston, ND 58801
(701) 572-1720
Civil records are available by mail. A release is required. $5.00 search fee. $2.00
fee for first copy, $.50 each additional copy.
$5.00 for certification. Search information
required: name, date of birth, years to
search. Specify plaintiff or defendant.

Misdemeanor records
Williams County Courthouse, Criminal
Records
PO Box 2047
Williston, ND 58801
(701) 572-1729
Misdemeanor records are available by mail.
No release necessary. $5.00 search fee.
Make check payable to County Court.
Search information required: name, date of
birth, years to search.

Civil records
Williams County Courthouse
PO Box 2047
Williston, ND 58801
(701) 572-1729
Civil records are available by mail. No release necessary. $5.00 search fee. $2.00 fee
for first copy, $.50 each additional copy.
$5.00 for certification. Search information
required: name, date of birth, years to
search. Specify plaintiff or defendant.

City-County Cross Reference

Dickey *LaMoure*
Dickinson *Stark*
Dodge *Dunn*
Donnybrook *Ward*
Douglas *Ward*
Doyon *Ramsey*
Drake *McHenry*
Drayton *Pembina*
Driscoll *Burleigh*
Dunn Center *Dunn*
Dunseith *Rolette*
Edgeley *LaMoure*
Edinburg *Walsh*
Edmore *Ramsey*
Egeland *Towner*
Elgin *Grant*
Ellendale *Dickey*
Emerado *Grand Forks*
Enderlin *Ransom*
Epping *Williams*
Erie *Cass*
Esmond *Benson*
Fairdale *Walsh*
Fairfield *Billings*
Fairmount *Richland*
Fargo *Cass*
Fessenden *Wells*
Fillmore *Benson*
Fingal *Barnes*
Finley *Steele*
Flasher *Morton*
Flaxton *Burke*
Forbes *Dickey*
Fordville *Walsh*
Forest River *Walsh*
Forman *Sargent*
Fort Ransom *Ransom*
Fort Rice *Morton*
Fort Totten *Benson*
Fortuna *Divide*
Fort Yates *Sioux*
Fredonia *Logan*
Fullerton *Dickey*
Gackle *Logan*
Galesburg *Traill*
Gardner *Cass*
Garrison *McLean*
Geneseo *Sargent*
Gilby *Grand Forks*
Gladstone *Stark*
Glasston *Pembina*
Glenburn *Renville*
Glenfield *Foster*
Glen Ullin *Morton*
Golden Valley *Mercer*
Golva *Golden Valley*
Goodrich *Sheridan*
Grace City *Foster*
Grafton *Walsh*
Grand Forks *Grand Forks*
Grandin *Cass*
Granville *McHenry*
Grassy Butte *McKenzie*
Grenora *Williams*
Guelph *Dickey*
Gwinner *Sargent*
Hague *Emmons*
Halliday *Dunn*
Hamberg *Wells*
Hamilton *Pembina*
Hampden *Ramsey*
Hankinson *Richland*
Hannaford *Griggs*
Hannah *Cavalier*
Harvey *Wells*

Harwood *Cass*
Hatton *Traill*
Havana *Sargent*
Haynes *Adams*
Hazelton *Emmons*
Hazen *Mercer*
Heaton *Wells*
Hebron *Morton*
Heimdal *Wells*
Hensel *Pembina*
Hensler *Oliver*
Hettinger *Adams*
Hillsboro *Traill*
Hoople *Walsh*
Hope *Steele*
Horace *Cass*
Hunter *Cass*
Hurdsfield *Wells*
Inkster *Grand Forks*
Jamestown *Stutsman*
Jessie *Griggs*
Joliette *Pembina*
Jud *LaMoure*
Karlsruhe *McHenry*
Kathryn *Barnes*
Keene *McKenzie*
Kenmare *Ward*
Kensal *Stutsman*
Kief *McHenry*
Killdeer *Dunn*
Kindred *Cass*
Kintyre *Emmons*
Kloten *Nelson*
Knox *Benson*
Kramer *Bottineau*
Kulm *LaMoure*
Lakota *Nelson*
LaMoure *LaMoure*
Landa *Bottineau*
Langdon *Cavalier*
Lankin *Walsh*
Lansford *Bottineau*
Larimore *Grand Forks*
Lawton *Ramsey*
Leeds *Benson*
Lefor *Stark*
Lehr *McIntosh*
Leith *Grant*
Leonard *Cass*
Lidgerwood *Richland*
Lignite *Burke*
Lincoln *Burleigh*
Linton *Emmons*
Lisbon *Ransom*
Litchville *Barnes*
Luverne *Steele*
Mccanna *Grand Forks*
McClusky *Sheridan*
McGregor *Williams*
McHenry *Foster*
Mcleod *Ransom*
Mcville *Nelson*
Maddock *Benson*
Makoti *Ward*
Mandan *Morton*
Mandaree *McKenzie*
Manfred *Wells*
Manning *Dunn*
Mantador *Richland*
Manvel *Grand Forks*
Mapleton *Cass*
Marion *LaMoure*
Marshall *Dunn*
Martin *Sheridan*
Max *McLean*

Maxbass *Bottineau*
Mayville *Traill*
Medina *Stutsman*
Medora *Billings*
Mekinock *Grand Forks*
Menoken *Burleigh*
Mercer *McLean*
Merricourt *Dickey*
Michigan *Nelson*
Milnor *Sargent*
Milton *Cavalier*
Minnewaukan *Benson*
Minot *Ward*
Minto *Walsh*
Moffit *Burleigh*
Mohall *Renville*
Monango *Dickey*
Montpelier *Stutsman*
Mooreton *Richland*
Mott *Hettinger*
Mountain *Pembina*
Munich *Cavalier*
Mylo *Rolette*
Napoleon *Logan*
Nash *Walsh*
Neche *Pembina*
Nekoma *Cavalier*
Newburg *Bottineau*
New England *Hettinger*
New Hradec *Dunn*
New Leipzig *Grant*
New Rockford *Eddy*
New Salem *Morton*
New Town *Mountrail*
Niagara *Grand Forks*
Nome *Barnes*
Noonan *Divide*
Northwood *Grand Forks*
Norwich *McHenry*
Oakes *Dickey*
Oberon *Benson*
Oriska *Barnes*
Orrin *Pierce*
Osnabrock *Cavalier*
Overly *Bottineau*
Page *Cass*
Palermo *Mountrail*
Park River *Walsh*
Parshall *Mountrail*
Pekin *Nelson*
Pembina *Pembina*
Penn *Ramsey*
Petersburg *Nelson*
Pettibone *Kidder*
Pillsbury *Barnes*
Pingree *Stutsman*
Pisek *Walsh*
Plaza *Mountrail*
Portal *Burke*
Portland *Traill*
Powers Lake *Burke*
Ray *Williams*
Reeder *Adams*
Regan *Burleigh*
Regent *Hettinger*
Reynolds *Grand Forks*
Rhame *Bowman*
Richardton *Stark*
Riverdale *McLean*
Robinson *Kidder*
Rocklake *Towner*
Rogers *Barnes*
Rolette *Rolette*
Rolla *Rolette*
Roseglen *McLean*

Ross *Mountrail*
Rugby *Pierce*
Ruso *McLean*
Rutland *Sargent*
Ryder *Ward*
Saint Anthony *Morton*
Saint John *Rolette*
Saint Michael *Benson*
Saint Thomas *Pembina*
Sanborn *Barnes*
San Haven *Rolette*
Sarles *Cavalier*
Sawyer *Ward*
Scranton *Bowman*
Selfridge *Sioux*
Selz *Pierce*
Sentinel Butte *Golden Valley*
Sharon *Steele*
Sheldon *Ransom*
Sherwood *Renville*
Sheyenne *Eddy*
Solen *Sioux*
Souris *Bottineau*
South Heart *Stark*
Spiritwood *Stutsman*
Spring Brook *Williams*
Stanley *Mountrail*
Stanton *Mercer*
Starkweather *Ramsey*
Steele *Kidder*
Sterling *Burleigh*
Strasburg *Emmons*
Streeter *Stutsman*
Surrey *Ward*
Sutton *Griggs*
Sykeston *Wells*
Tappen *Kidder*
Taylor *Stark*
Thompson *Grand Forks*
Tioga *Williams*
Tokio *Benson*
Tolley *Renville*
Tolna *Nelson*
Tower City *Cass*
Towner *McHenry*
Trenton *Williams*
Trotters *Golden Valley*
Turtle Lake *McLean*
Tuttle *Kidder*
Underwood *McLean*
Union *Cavalier*
Upham *McHenry*
Valley City *Barnes*
Velva *McHenry*
Venturia *McIntosh*
Verona *LaMoure*
Voltaire *McHenry*
Wahpeton *Richland*
Walcott *Richland*
Wales *Cavalier*
Walhalla *Pembina*
Warwick *Benson*
Washburn *McLean*
Watford City *McKenzie*
Webster *Ramsey*
West Fargo *Cass*
Westhope *Bottineau*
Wheatland *Cass*
White Earth *Mountrail*
Wildrose *Williams*
Williston *Williams*
Willow City *Bottineau*
Wilton *McLean*
Wimbledon *Barnes*

Wing *Burleigh*
Wishek *McIntosh*
Wolford *Pierce*
Woodworth *Stutsman*
Wyndmere *Richland*
York *Benson*
Ypsilanti *Stutsman*
Zahl *Williams*
Zap *Mercer*
Zeeland *McIntosh*

Ohio

Fifty eight (58) of Ohio's eighty eight (88) counties make their criminal records available for employment screening purposes by phone and/or mail. A handful will allow requests to be made by fax.

Civil court records for $10,000 and more are filed in Common Pleas Court.

For more information or for offices not listed, contact the state's information hot line at (614) 466-2000.

Driving Records

Bureau of Motor Vehicles
Attn: ABST
PO Box 16520
Columbus, OH 43266-0020
(614) 752-7600
Driving records available by mail. $2.00 fee per request. Turnaround time is 3 weeks. Written request must include job applicant's full name and one of the following: date of birth, SSN or license number. Make check payable to Treasury, State of Ohio.

Worker's Compensation Records

Ohio Bureau of Worker's
Compensation
Correspondence Section
246 N. High Street
Columbus, OH 43266-0581
(614) 466-1000 or 466-2000
Limited access to records. For employment screening purposes State will inform the prospective employer if the job applicant has filed a "lost time injury." Request by telephone or mail must include the applicant's SSN. There is no fee. A signed release is not required for a claim number.

Vital Statistics

Ohio Department of Health
Bureau of Vital Statistics
246 N. High Street
PO Box 15098
Columbus, OH 43215-0098
(614) 466-2531
Birth and death records are available for $7.00 each. State office has records since December 20, 1908. For earlier records write to Probate Court in county where event occurred. Make check or money order payable to State Treasury.
Marriage records available through Probate Court in county where marriage took place. Divorce records are available through Probate Court in county where divorce granted.

Department of Education

Department of Education
Teacher Certification Division
65 South Front Street
Room 1012
Columbus, OH 43266-0308
(614) 466-3593
Field of certification, effective date, expiration date are available by mail or phone. Include name and SSN.

Medical Licensing

State Medical Board
Records Department
77 South High Street, 17th Floor
Columbus, OH 43266-0315
(614) 466-3934
Will confirm licenses for MDs, DOs, and PODs by mail. No fee. For licenses not mentioned, contact the above office.

Ohio Board of Nursing Education and Nurse Registration
77 S. High St., 17 Floor
Columbus, OH 43266-0316
(614) 466-3947
Will confirm license by phone. No fee. Include name, license number or SSN.

Bar Association

Ohio State Bar Association
1700 Lake Shore Drive
PO Box 16562
Columbus, OH 43216-6562
(614) 487-2050
Will confirm licenses by phone. No fee. Include name.

Accountancy Board

CPA Registration Association
Accounting Board of Ohio
77 SSouth High Street, 18th Floor
Columbus, OH 43266-0301
(614) 466-4135
Will confirm licenses by mail. $10.00 fee for written response. Include name and SSN.

Securities Commission

Division of Securities
77 South High Streeet, 22nd Floor
Columbus, OH 43266-0548
(614) 644-7381
Will confirm licenses by phone. No fee. Include name and SSN.

Secretary of State

Secretary of State
14th Floor
State Office Tower
Columbus, OH 43266-0418
(614) 466-3910
Service agent and address, date incorporated, standing with tax commission, trade names are available by mail or phone. Contact the above office for additional information.

Criminal Records

State Repository

Ohio Bureau of Criminal Identification and Investigation
PO Box 365
1580 State Route 56
London, OH 43140
(614) 466-8204
Criminal records are available by mail only. All requests must include a full set of fingerprints and a signed release by the subject witnessed by a third party. There is a $15.00 fee. Money order or certified check only. Make check payable to: Bureau of Criminal Identification and Investigation (BCI). Request forms (ID Cards) are available at the above address for $3.00 per hundred. Information released includes both conviction and arrest data. Turnaround time is 7-10 working days. Billing procedures are available. Contact the BCI to obtain a number for billing purposes.

Adams County

Felony records
Clerk of Courts, Criminal Records
Adams County Courthouse
110 W Main St.
West Union, OH 45693
(513) 544-2344
Felony records are available by mail. No release necessary. No search fee. $.50 fee per copy. $1.00 for each certified page. Search information required: name, SSN, date of birth, SASE.

Civil records
Clerk of Courts
Adams County Courthouse
110 W Main St.
West Union, OH 45693
(513) 544-2344
Civil records are available by mail. No release necessary. No search fee. $.50 fee per copy. $1.00 for each certified page. Search information required: name, date of birth, years to search, SASE. Specify plaintiff or defendant.

Misdemeanor records
Adams County Court
Rm. 202, Courthouse
West Union, OH 45693
(513) 544-2011
Misdemeanor records are available by mail or phone. No release necessary. No search fee. $.50 fee per copy. $1.00 for each certified page. Search information required: name, SSN, years to search.

Civil records
Adams County Court
Rm. 202, Courthouse
West Union, OH 45693
(513) 544-2011
Civil records are available by mail. No release necessary. No search fee. $.50 fee per copy. $1.00 for each certified page. Search information required: name, date of birth, years to search. Specify plaintiff or defendant.

Allen County

Felony records
Clerk of Court, Criminal Records
PO Box 1243
Lima, OH 45802
(419) 228-3700
Records are available in person only. See Ohio state repository for additional information.

Civil records
Clerk of Court
PO Box 1243
Lima, OH 45802
(419) 228-3700
Civil records are available in person only. See Ohio state repository for additional information.

Misdemeanor records
Allen County Municipal Court
109 North Union St.
Lima, OH 45801
(419) 221-5275
Misdemeanor records are available in person only. See Ohio state repository for additional information.

Civil records
Allen County Municipal Court
109 North Union St.
Lima, OH 45801
(419) 221-5275
Civil records are available in person only. See Ohio state repository for additional information.

Ashland County

Felony records
Clerk of Court, Criminal Records
PO Box 365
Ashland, OH 44805
(419) 289-0000 Extension 203
Felony records are available by mail. No release necessary. $5.00 search fee. Search information required: name, date of birth, SSN

Civil records
Clerk of Court
PO Box 365
Ashland, OH 44805
(419) 289-0000 Extension 203
Civil records are available by mail. No release necessary. No search fee. $1.00 fee per copy. $1.00 for certification. Search information required: name, date of birth, years to search. Specify plaintiff or defendant.

Misdemeanor records
Municipal Court
PO Box 354
Ashland, OH 44805
(419) 289-8137
Misdemeanor records are available by mail or phone. No release necessary. $1.00 fee for certified copy. No search fee. Search information required: name, years to search.

Civil records
Municipal Court
PO Box 354
Ashland, OH 44805
(419) 289-8137
Civil records are available by mail. No release necessary. No search fee. $1.00 fee per copy. $1.00 for certification. Search information required: name, date of birth, years to search. Specify plaintiff or defendant.

Ashtabula County

Clerk of Court
25 W. Jefferson Street
Jefferson, OH 44047
(216) 576-3637
Records are not available by mail or phone. See Ohio state repository.

Civil records are available in person only. See Ohio state repository for additional information.

Athens County

Felony records
Clerk of Court, Criminal Records
Courthouse
Athens, OH 45701
(614) 592-3242
Felony records are available in person only. See Ohio state repository for additional information.

Civil records
Clerk of Court
Courthouse
Athens, OH 45701
(614) 592-3242
Civil records are available in person only. See Ohio state repository for additional information.

Misdemeanor records
Athens County Municipal Court
City Hall
Washington St.
Athens, OH 45701
(614) 592-3328
Misdemeanor records are in person only. See Ohio state repository for additional information.

Civil records
Athens County Municipal Court
City Hall
Washington St.
Athens, OH 45701
(614) 592-3328
Civil records are available in person only. See Ohio state repository for additional information.

Auglaize County

Clerk of Court, Criminal Records
PO Box 1958
Wapakoneta, OH 45895-0958
(419) 738-4219
Felony records are available by mail. A release is required. No search fee. Search information required: name.

Civil records are available by mail. No release necessary. No search fee. $.50 fee per copy. $1.00 for certification. Search information required: name, date of birth, years to search. Specify plaintiff or defendant.

Belmont County

Clerk of Court, Criminal Records
Main Street
St. Clairsville, OH 43950
(614) 695-2121 Extension 241
Felony records are available by mail. No release necessary. $3.00 search fee. Search information required: name, years to search.

Civil records are available by mail. No release necessary. $3.00 search fee. $1.00 for certification. Search information required: name, date of birth, years to search. Specify plaintiff or defendant.

Brown County

Clerk of Court, Criminal Records
Courthouse
Georgetown, OH 45121
(513) 378-3100
Felony records are available by mail or phone. No release necessary. No search fee. Search information required: name, years to search.

Civil records are available by mail. No release necessary. No search fee. $.25 fee per copy. $1.00 for certification. Search information required: name, date of birth, years to search. Specify plaintiff or defendant.

Butler County

Clerk of Court, Criminal Records
Butler County Courthouse
Hamilton, OH 45011
(513) 887-3276
Felony records are available in person only. See Ohio state repository for additional information.

Civil records are available in person only. See Ohio state repository for additional information.

Carroll County

Felony records
Clerk of Court, Criminal Records
PO Box 367
Carrollton, OH 44615
(216) 627-4886
Felony records are available by mail or phone. No release necessary. No fee. Search information required: name, SSN, date of birth.

Civil records
Clerk of Court
PO Box 367
Carrollton, OH 44615
(216) 627-4886Civil records are available in person only. See Ohio state repository for additional information.

Misdemeanor records
Carroll County Court
Public Square, 3rd Floor
Carrollton, OH 44615
(216) 627-5049
Misdemeanor records are available by mail or phone. No release necessary. No search fee. $1.00 fee per copy. Search information required: name, date of birth, SSN, SASE.

Civil records
Carroll County Court
Public Square, 3rd Floor
Carrollton, OH 44615
(216) 627-5049
Civil records are available by mail. No release necessary. No search fee. $1.00 fee per copy. $1.00 for certification. Search information required: name, date of birth, years to search, SASE. Specify plaintiff or defendant.

Champaign County

Felony records
Clerk of Court, Criminal Records
214 N. Main Street
Urbana, OH 43078
(513) 653-4152
Records are not available by mail or phone. See Ohio state repository.

Civil records
Clerk of Court
214 N. Main Street
Urbana, OH 43078
(513) 653-4152
Civil records are available in person only. See Ohio state repository for additional information.

Misdemeanor records
Champaign County Municipal Court
PO Box 85
Urbana, OH 43078
(513) 653-7376
Fax (513) 653-8109
Misdemeanor records are available by mail. No release necessary. No search fee. $.25 fee per copy. $2.50 for certification. Search information required: name, SSN, years to search, SASE.

Civil records
Champaign County Municipal Court
PO Box 85
Urbana, OH 43078
(513) 653-7376
Fax (513) 653-8109
Civil records are available by mail. No release necessary. No search fee. $.25 fee per copy. $2.50 for certification. Search information required: name, SSN, years to search, SASE. Specify plaintiff or defendant.

Clark County

Felony records
Clerk of Court
PO Box 1008
101 N. Limestone Street
Springfield, OH 45502
(513) 328-3700
Records are available by mail. No release necessary. No search fee. $1.00 fee per copy. $1.00 for certification. Search information required: name, date of birth, SSN, years to search, SASE.

Civil records
Clerk of Court
PO Box 1008
101 N. Limestone Street
Springfield, OH 45502
(513) 328-3700
Civil records are available by mail. No release necessary. No search fee. $1.00 fee per copy. $1.00 for certification. Search information required: name, date of birth, SSN, years to search, SASE. Specify plaintiff or defendant.

Misdemeanor records
Clark County Municipal Court
50 East Columbia St.
Springfield, OH 45502
(513) 328-3700
Misdemeanor records are available by mail or phone. No release necessary. No search fee. Search information required: name, date of birth, SSN.

Civil records
Clark County Municipal Court
50 East Columbia St.
Springfield, OH 45502
(513) 328-3700
Civil records are available by mail. No release necessary. No search fee. $1.00 fee per copy. $1.00 for certification. Search information required: name, date of birth, years to search. Specify plaintiff or defendant.

Clermont County

Felony records
Clerk of Court, Criminal Records
270 Main Street
Batavia, OH 45103
(513) 732-7130
Felony records are available by mail. No release necessary. No search fee. $.25 fee per copy. $1.00 for certification. Search information required: name, date of birth, SSN, SASE.

Civil records
Clerk of Court
270 Main Street
Batavia, OH 45103
(513) 732-7130
Civil records are available by mail. No release necessary. No search fee. $.25 fee per copy. $1.00 for certification. Search information required: name, date of birth, SSN, years to search, SASE. Specify plaintiff or defendant.

Misdemeanor records
Clermont County Court
289 Main Street
Batavia, OH 45103
(513) 732-7290
Fax (513) 732-7831
Misdemeanor records are available by mail. No release necessary. No search fee. Search information required: name, date of birth, SSN, years to search.

Civil records
Clermont County Court
289 Main Street
Batavia, OH 45103
(513) 732-7290
Fax (513) 732-7831
Civil records are available by mail. No release necessary. No search fee. $.25 fee per copy. $1.00 for certification. Search information required: name, date of birth, SSN, years to search, SASE. Specify plaintiff or defendant.

Clinton County

Felony records
Clerk of Court, Criminal Records
46 So. South St.
3rd Floor, Courthouse
Wilmington, OH 45177
(513) 382-2316
Felony records are available by mail. No release necessary. $5.00 search fee. $.25 fee per copy. $1.00 for certification. Search information required: name, date of birth, SSN, years to search, SASE.

Civil records
Clerk of Court
46 So. South St.
3rd Floor, Courthouse
Wilmington, OH 45177
(513) 382-2316
Civil records are available by mail. No release necessary. $5.00 search fee. $.25 fee per copy. $1.00 for certification. Search information required: name, date of birth, SSN, years to search. Specify plaintiff or defendant.

Misdemeanor records
Wilmington Municipal Court
56 West Locust St.
Wilmington, OH 45177
(513) 382-8985
Misdemeanor records are available by mail or phone. No release necessary. No search fee. $.25 fee per copy. $0.00 for certification. Search information required: name, date of birth, SSN, years to search.

Civil records
Wilmington Municipal Court
56 West Locust St.
Wilmington, OH 45177
(513) 382-8985
Civil records are available by mail or phone. No release necessary. No search fee. $.25 fee per copy. Search information required: name, date of birth, SSN, years to search. Specify plaintiff or defendant.

Columbiana County

Clerk of Court, Criminal Records
105 S. Market Street
Lisbon, OH 44432
(216) 424-9511 Extension 239
Felony and misdemeanor records are available in person only. See Ohio state repository for additional information.

Civil records are available in person only. See Ohio state repository for additional information.

Coshocton County

Felony records
Clerk of Court, Criminal Records
Courthouse
Coshocton, OH 43812
(614) 622-1456
Felony records are available in person only. See Ohio state repository for additional information.

Civil records
Clerk of Court
Courthouse
Coshocton, OH 43812
(614) 622-1456
Civil records are available in person only. See Ohio state repository for additional information.

Misdemeanor records
Coshocton County Municipal Court
760 Chestnut St.
Coshocton, OH 43812
(614) 622-2871
Misdemeanor records are available by mail or phone. No release necessary. No search fee. $1.00 fee per copy. $1.00 for certification. Search information required: full name, date of birth, SSN.

Civil records
Coshocton County Municipal Court
760 Chestnut St.
Coshocton, OH 43812
(614) 622-2871
Civil records are available by mail or phone. No release necessary. No search fee. $1.00 fee per copy. $1.00 for certification. Search information required: name, date of birth, years to search. Specify plaintiff or defendant.

Crawford County

Clerk of Court, Criminal Records
PO Box 470
Bucyrus, OH 44820
(419) 562-2766
Felony records are available by mail. No release necessary. No search fee. Search information required: name, SASE.

Civil records are available by mail or phone. No release necessary. No search fee. $.50 fee per copy. $1.00 for certification. Search information required: name, date of birth, years to search, SASE. Specify plaintiff or defendant.

Cuyahoga County

Clerk of Court, Criminal Records
Common Pleas Court, 1200 Ontario Street
3rd Floor Justice Center
Cleveland, OH 44113
(216) 443-7950
Felony records are available by mail or phone. No release necessary. No search fee. $1.00 for certification. Search information required: name, years to search,

Civil records are available by mail or phone. No release necessary. No search fee. $1.00 for certification. Search information required: name, date of birth, years to search. Specify plaintiff or defendant.

Darke County

Felony records
Darke County Clerk of Court, Criminal Records
Courthouse, 2nd Floor
Greenville, OH 45331
(513) 547-7335
Felony records are available by mail or phone. No release necessary. No fee. Search information required: name, years to search.

Civil records
Darke County Clerk of Court
Courthouse, 2nd Floor
Greenville, OH 45331
(513) 547-7335
Civil records are available by mail. No release necessary. No search fee. $.25 fee per copy. $1.00 for first certified page, $.25 each additional page. Search information required: name, date of birth, years to search. Specify plaintiff or defendant.

Misdemeanor records
Darke County Court
Courthouse, 3rd Floor
Greenville, OH 45331
(513) 547-7340
Fax (513) 547-7323
Misdemeanor records are available by mail. No release necessary. No search fee. $.25 fee per copy. $1.00 for certification. Search information required: name, years to search, SSN, date of birth. Turnaround time is 5-7 working days.

Civil records
Darke County Court
Courthouse, 3rd Floor
Greenville, OH 45331
(513) 547-7340
Fax (513) 547-7323
Civil records are available by mail. No release necessary. No search fee. $.25 fee per copy. $1.00 for certification. Search information required: name, date of birth, years to search. Specify plaintiff or defendant.

Defiance County

Clerk of Court, Criminal Records
PO Box 716
Defiance, OH 43512
(419) 782-1936
Fax (419) 784-2761
Felony and misdemeanor records are available by mail or phone. No release necessary. No search fee. $1.00 fee per copy. $1.00 for certification. Search information required: name, years to search.

Civil records are available by mail or phone. No release necessary. No search fee. $1.00 fee per copy. $1.00 for certification. Search information required: name, date of birth, years to search. Specify plaintiff or defendant.

Delaware County

Felony records
Courthouse, Criminal Records
921 N. Sandusky
Delaware, OH 43015
(614) 369-8761 Extension 261
Felony records are available by mail. No release necessary. Possible search fee. $.25 fee per copy, $1.25 fee for certification. Search information required: name, years to search, SASE.

Civil records
Courthouse, Civil Records
921 N. Sandusky
Delaware, OH 43015
(614) 369-1551
Civil records are available by mail or phone. No release necessary. No search fee. first four copies free, $.25 each additional copy. Search information required: name, date of birth, years to search, SASE. Specify plaintiff or defendant.

Misdemeanor records
Delaware County Municipal Court
Attn: Criminal & Traffic Department
1 South Sandusky St.
Delaware, OH 43015
(614) 368-1555
Misdemeanor records are available by mail. No release necessary. No search fee. Search information required: name, date of birth, SSN, years to search.

Civil records
Delaware County Municipal Court
1 South Sandusky St.
Delaware, OH 43015
(614) 368-1555
Civil records are available by mail. No release necessary. No search fee. Search information required: name, date of birth, SSN, years to search, SASE. Specify plaintiff or defendant.

Erie County

Clerk of Court, Criminal Records
323 Colubus Avenue
Sandusky, OH 44870
(419) 627-7705
Felony records are available by mail or phone. No release necessary. No search fee. Search information required: name, years to search.

Civil records are available by mail or phone. No release necessary. No search fee. $.50 fee per copy. $.50 for certification. Search information required: name, date of birth, years to search, case number if known. Specify plaintiff or defendant.

Fairfield County

Clerk of Court, Criminal Records
PO Box 370
Lancaster, OH 43130
(614) 687-7030
Felony records are available in person only. See Ohio state repository for additional information.

Civil records are available n person only. See Ohio state repository for additional information.

Fayette County

Felony records
Fayette County Clerk of Court,
Criminal Records
110 E. Court Street
Washington Court House, OH 43160
(614) 335-6371
Felony records are available by mail. No release necessary. No search fee. $1.00 fee per copy. $1.00 for certification. Search information required: name, date of birth, years to search, SASE.

Civil records
Fayette County Clerk of Court
110 E. Court Street
Washington Court House, OH 43160
(614) 335-6371
Civil records are available by mail. No release necessary. No search fee. $1.00 fee per copy. $1.00 for certification. Search information required: name, date of birth, years to search, SASE. Specify plaintiff or defendant.

Misdemeanor records
Washington Court House Municipal Court
130 N. Fayette St.
Washington Court House, OH 43160
(614) 335-2901
Misdemeanor records are available by mail. A release is required. No search fee. $1.00 fee per copy. $2.00 for certification. Search information required: name, date of birth, SSN.

Civil records
Washington Court House Municipal Court
130 N. Fayette St.
Washington Court House, OH 43160
(614) 335-2901
Civil records are available by mail. A release is required. No search fee. $1.00 fee per copy. $2.00 for certification. Search information required: name, date of birth, SSN, years to search. Specify plaintiff or defendant.

Franklin County

Clerk of Court
Criminal Division
369 S. High Street
Columbus, OH 43215
(614) 462-3650
Felony records are available by mail. A release is required. $4.00 search fee. $1.00 fee per copy. $1.00 for certification. Certified check only, payable to Clerk of Court. Search information required: name, SSN, date of birth.

Civil records are available by mail. A release is required. $4.00 search fee. $1.00 fee per copy. $1.00 for certification. Search information required: name, date of birth, years to search. Specify plaintiff or defendant.

Fulton County

Clerk of Court
Room 203, Courthouse
210 S Fulton
Wauseon, OH 43567
(419) 337-9230
Felony records are not available by mail or phone. See Ohio state repository for additional information.

Civil records are available in person only. See Ohio state repository for additional information.

Gallia County

Felony records
Clerk of Court, Criminal Records
Gallia County Courthouse
Gallipolis, OH 45631
(614) 446-1221 Extension 268
Felony records are available by mail or phone. No release necessary. No search fee. Search information required: name, date of birth, years to search.

Civil records
Clerk of Court
Gallia County Courthouse
Gallipolis, OH 45631
(614) 446-1221 Extension 268
Civil records are available by mail. A release is required. No search fee. Search information required: name, date of birth, years to search, SSN. Specify plaintiff or defendant.

Misdemeanor records
Gallipolis Municipal Court
518 Second Ave.
Gallipolis, OH 45631
(614) 446-9400
Misdemeanor records are available by mail or phone. No release necessary. No search fee. Search information required: full name, date of birth, SSN, address.

Civil records
Gallipolis Municipal Court
518 Second Ave.
Gallipolis, OH 45631
(614) 446-9400
Civil records are available in person only. See Ohio state repository for additional information.

Geauga County

Felony records
Geauga County Clerk of Court,
Criminal Records
Geauga County Courthouse
Chardon, OH 44024
(216) 285-2222 Extension 231
Fax (216) 285-2063
Felony records are available in person only. See Ohio state repository for additional information.

Civil records
Geauga County Clerk of Court
Geauga County Courthouse
Chardon, OH 44024
(216) 285-2222 Extension 231
Fax (216) 285-2063
Civil records are available in person only. See Ohio state repository for additional information.

Misdemeanor records
Chardon Municipal Court
108 S. Hambden St.
Chardon, OH 44024
(216) 285-2222 Ext. 538
Fax (216) 285-2063
Misdemeanor records are available by mail or fax. No release necessary. No search fee. $.50 fee per copy, $1.50 fee for certification. Search information required: name, date of birth, SSN.

Civil records
Chardon Municipal Court
108 S. Hambden St.
Chardon, OH 44024
(216) 285-2222 Ext. 538
Fax (216) 285-2063
Civil records are available in person only. See Ohio state repository for additional information.

Greene County

Clerk of Court, Criminal Records
PO Box 156
45 N. Detroit Street
Xenia, OH 45385
(513) 376-5292
Felony records are available by mail. No release necessary. $5.00 search fee. Company checks only, payable to Clerk of Court. Search information required: name, date of birth, SSN, years to search.

Civil records are available in person only. See Ohio state repository for additional information.

Guernsey County

Felony records
Clerk of Court, Criminal Records
PO Box 766
Cambridge, OH 43725
(614) 432-2139
Felony records are available in person only. See Ohio state repository for additional information.

Civil records
Clerk of Court
PO Box 766
Cambridge, OH 43725
(614) 432-2139
Civil records are available in person only. See Ohio state repository for additional information.

Misdemeanor records
Cambridge Municipal Court
PO Box 1468
Cambridge, OH 43725
(614) 439-1430
Fax (6140 439-5666
Misdemeanor records are available by mail or phone. No release necessary. No search fee. $1.00 fee per copy. Search information required: full name, date of birth, years to search, SSN. .

Civil records
Cambridge Municipal Court
PO Box 1468
Cambridge, OH 43725
(614) 439-1430
Civil records are available by mail. No release necessary. No search fee. $1.00 fee per copy. Search information required: name, date of birth, years to search, SSN. Specify plaintiff or defendant.

Hamilton County

Clerk of Court
County Sheriff Office
1000 Main Street
Room 100
Cincinnati, OH 45202
(513) 632-8284
Felony record are available by mail. A release is required. $4.00 search fee. Search information required: name, years to search, date of birth, race, sex, SSN, SASE.

Civil records are available by mail. No release necessary. $4.00 search fee. Search information required: name, date of birth, years to search, case number, SASE. Specify plaintiff or defendant.

Hancock County

Felony records
Clerk of Court
Legal Department
300 S. Main Street
Findlay, OH 45840
(419) 424-7037

Felony records are available by mail. A release is required. $5.00 search fee. $1.00 fee per copy includes certification. Make check payable to Clerk of Court. Search information required: name, SSN, date of birth.

Civil records
Clerk of Court
Legal Department
300 S. Main Street
Findlay, OH 45840
(419) 424-7037

Civil records are available by mail. A release is required. $5.00 search fee. $1.00 fee per copy includes certification. Search information required: name, date of birth, years to search. Specify plaintiff or defendant.

Misdemeanor records
Findlay Municipal Court
PO Box 826
Findlay, OH 45839
(419) 424-7141
Fax (419) 424-7803

Misdemeanor records are available by mail or phone. No release necessary. $5.00 search fee. Search information required: name, date of birth, SSN, years to search.

Civil records
Findlay Municipal Court
PO Box 826
Findlay, OH 45839
(419) 424-7141
Fax (419) 424-7803

Civil records are available by mail or phone. No release necessary. $5.00 search fee. Search information required: name, date of birth, SSN, years to search. Specify plaintiff or defendant.

Hardin County

Felony records
Clerk of Court, Criminal Records
3rd Floor, Courthouse
Kenton, OH 43326
(419) 674-2278

Felony records are available by mail. A release is required. No search fee. Search information required: name, date of birth, sex, race, SASE.

Civil records
Clerk of Court
3rd Floor, Courthouse
Kenton, OH 43326
(419) 674-2278

Civil records are available in person only. See Ohio state repository for additional information.

Misdemeanor records
Clerk of Municipal Court
Kenton Municipal Court
PO Box 220
Kenton, OH 43326
(419) 674-4850
Fax (419) 673-1721

Misdemeanor records are available by mail or phone. No release necessary. No search fee. Search information required: name, date of birth, SSN, years to search.

Civil records
Clerk of Municipal Court
Kenton Municipal Court
PO Box 220
Kenton, OH 43326
(419) 674-4850
Fax (419) 673-1721

Civil records are available in person only. See Ohio state repository for additional information.

Harrison County

Felony records
Clerk of Court, Criminal Records
PO Box 242
Cadiz, OH 43907
(614) 942-8861 Extension 28

Felony records are available in person only. See Ohio state repository for additional information.

Civil records
Clerk of Court
PO Box 242
Cadiz, OH 43907
(614) 942-8861 Extension 28

Civil records are available in person only. See Ohio state repository for additional information.

Misdemeanor records
Harrison County Court
Courthouse
100 W. Market
Cadiz, OH 43907
(614) 942-8861 Ext. 29, 30
Fax (614) 942-4693

Misdemeanor records are available by mail or phone. No release necessary. No search fee. Search information required: name, date of birth, SSN, address.

Civil records
Harrison County Court
Courthouse
100 W. Market
Cadiz, OH 43907
(614) 942-8861 Ext. 29, 30
Fax (614) 942-4693

Civil records are available in person only. See Ohio state repository for additional information.

Henry County

Felony records
Clerk of Common Pleas Court, Criminal Records
PO Box 71
Napoleon, OH 43545
(419) 592-5886

Felony records are available in person only. See Ohio state repository for additional information.

Civil records
Clerk of Common Pleas Court
PO Box 71
Napoleon, OH 43545
(419) 592-5886

Civil records are available in person only. See Ohio state repository for additional information.

Misdemeanor records
Napoleon Municipal Court
PO Box 502
Napoleon, OH 43545
(419) 592-2851
Fax (419) 599-8393

Misdemeanor records are available by mail or phone. No release necessary. No search fee. Search information required: name, date of birth, SSN, years to search.

Civil records
Napoleon Municipal Court
PO Box 502
Napoleon, OH 43545
(419) 592-2851
Fax (419) 599-8393

Civil records are available by mail. No release necessary. No search fee. $1.00 for certification. Search information required: name, date of birth, years to search. Specify plaintiff or defendant.

Highland County

Felony records
Clerk of Court, Criminal Records
PO Box 821
Hillsboro, OH 45133
(513) 393-9957

Felony records are available by mail or phone. No release necessary. No search fee. $.25 fee per copy. $1.00 for certification. Search information required: name, SASE.

Civil records
Clerk of Court
PO Box 821
Hillsboro, OH 45133
(513) 393-9957

Civil records are available by mail. No release necessary. No search fee. $.25 fee per copy. $1.00 for certification. Search information required: name, date of birth, years to search, SASE. Specify plaintiff or defendant.

Misdemeanor records
Highland County Municipal Court
108 Governor Trimble Place
Hillsboro, OH 45133
(513) 393-3022

Misdemeanor records are available by mail. No release necessary. No search fee. Search information required: name, date of birth, SSN.

Civil records
Highland County Municipal Court
108 Governor Trimble Place
Hillsboro, OH 45133
(513) 393-3022

Civil records are available by mail. No release necessary. No search fee. Search information required: name, date of birth, SSN, years to search. Specify plaintiff or defendant.

Hocking County

Felony records
Clerk of Court, Criminal Records
PO Box 108
Logan, OH 43138
(614) 385-2616
Felony records are available by mail. No release necessary. No search fee. $1.00 fee per copy. $1.00 for certification. Search information required: name, years to search, SASE.

Civil records
Clerk of Court
PO Box 108
Logan, OH 43138
(614) 385-2616
Civil records are available by mail. No release necessary. No search fee. $1.00 fee per copy. $1.00 for certification. Search information required: name, date of birth, years to search, SASE. Specify plaintiff or defendant.

Misdemeanor records
Hocking County Municipal Court
Courthouse, 1st Floor
Logan, OH 43138
(614) 385-2250
Misdemeanor records are available in person only. See Ohio state repository for additional information.

Civil records
Hocking County Municipal Court
Courthouse, 1st Floor
Logan, OH 43138
(614) 385-2250
Civil records are available by mail. No release necessary. No search fee. $.50 fee per copy. $1.00 for certification. Search information required: name, date of birth, years to search. Specify plaintiff or defendant.

Holmes County

Felony records
Clerk of Common Pleas Court,
Criminal Records
1 E. Jackson Street, Suite 306
Holmes County Courthouse, 3rd Floor
Millersburg, OH 44654
(216) 674-1876
Felony records are available by mail or phone. No release necessary. $5.00 fee. Make check payable to Clerk of Court. Search information required: name.

Civil records
Clerk of Common Pleas Court
1 E. Jackson Street, Suite 306
Holmes County Courthouse, 3rd Floor
Millersburg, OH 44654
(216) 674-1876
Civil records are available in person only. See Ohio state repository for additional information.

Misdemeanor records
Holmes County Court
1 E. Jackson Street, Suite 304
Millersburg, OH 44654
(216) 674-4901
Misdemeanor records are available in person only. See Ohio state repository for additional information.

Civil records
Holmes County Court
1 E. Jackson Street, Suite 304
Millersburg, OH 44654
(216) 674-4901
Civil records are available in person only. See Ohio state repository for additional information.

Huron County

Huron County Courthouse, Criminal Records
Clerk of Courts
2 E. Main Street
Norwalk, OH 44857
(419) 668-5113
Felony records are available by mail. No release necessary. $1.00 search fee, payable to Clerk of Court. Search information required: name, years to search, SASE.

Civil records are available by mail. No release necessary. $1.00 search fee. Search information required: name, date of birth, SSN, years to search, SASE. Specify plaintiff or defendant.

Jackson County

Felony records
Clerk of Court, Criminal Records
Courthouse, 226 Main Street
Jackson, OH 45640
(614) 286-2006
Felony records are available by mail or phone. No release necessary. No search fee. $.50 fee per copy. Search information required: name, SASE.

Civil records
Clerk of Court
Courthouse, 226 Main Street
Jackson, OH 45640
(614) 286-2006
Civil records are available in person only. See Ohio state repository for additional information.

Misdemeanor records
Jackson County Municipal Court
226 Main St.
Jackson, OH 45640
(614) 286-2718
Misdemeanor records are available by mail. No release necessary. $$5.00 search fee. $.50 fee per copy. $1.00 for certification. Search information required: name, date of birth, SSN, years to search.

Civil records
Jackson County Municipal Court
226 Main St.
Jackson, OH 45640
(614) 286-2718
Civil records are available by mail. No release necessary. $5.00 search fee. $.50 fee per copy. $1.00 for certification. Search information required: name, date of birth, years to search, SASE. Specify plaintiff or defendant.

Jefferson County

Clerk of Court, Criminal Records
PO Box 1326
Steubenville, OH 43952
(614) 283-8583
Felony records are available by mail. No release necessary. $5.00 search fee. Company checks only, payable to Clerk of Court. Search information required: name, SSN, date of birth, sex, race, years to search, SASE.

Civil records are available by mail. No release necessary. $5.00 search fee. Company check or money order payable to Clerk of Court. Search information required: name, date of birth, years to search. Specify plaintiff or defendant.

Knox County

Felony records
Clerk of Court, Criminal Records
114 E. Chestnut Street
Mount Vernon, OH 43050
(614) 393-6788
Felony records are available by mail or phone. A release is required. No search fee. $1.00 fee per copy. Search information required: name, SASE, years to search.

Civil records
Clerk of Court
114 E. Chestnut Street
Mount Vernon, OH 43050
(614) 393-6788
Civil records are available in person only. See Ohio state repository for additional information.

Misdemeanor records
Mount Vernon Municipal Court
5 North Gay St.
Mount Vernon, OH 43050
(614) 393-9510
Fax (614) 393-1406
Misdemeanor records are available by mail, fax or phone. No release necessary. No fee. Search information required: name, date of birth.

Civil records
Mount Vernon Municipal Court
5 North Gay St.
Mount Vernon, OH 43050
(614) 393-9510
Fax (614) 393-1406
Civil records are available in person only. See Ohio state repository for additional information.

Lake County

Lake County Clerk of Court
PO Box 490
Painesville, OH 44077
(216) 357-2657
Records are not available by mail or phone. See Ohio state repository.

Civil records are available in person only. See Ohio state repository for additional information.

Lawrence County

Clerk of Court, Criminal Records
Lawrence County Courthouse
PO Box 208
Ironton, OH 45638
(614) 533-4355
Felony records are available in person only. See Ohio State Repository for additional information..

Civil records are available in person only. See Ohio state repository for additional information.

Licking County

Felony records
Clerk of Common Pleas Court, Legal
Dept.
PO Box 878
Newark, OH 43055-0878
(614) 349-6171
Felony records are available in person only.
See Ohio state repository for additional information.

Civil records
Clerk of Common Pleas Court, Legal
Dept.
PO Box 878
Newark, OH 43055-0878
(614) 349-6171
Civil records are available in person only.
See Ohio state repository for additional information.

Misdemeanor records
Licking County Municipal Court
Criminal and Traffic Dept.
40 West Main St.
Newark, OH 43055
(614) 349-6627
Misdemeanor records are available in person only. See Ohio state repository for additional information.

Civil records
Licking County Municipal Court
Criminal and Traffic Dept.
40 West Main St.
Newark, OH 43055
(614) 349-6627
Civil records are available in person only.
See Ohio state repository for additional information.

Logan County

Felony records
Clerk of Court, Criminal Records
PO Box 429
Bellefontaine, OH 43311
(513) 599-7275
Felony records are available in person only.
See Ohio state repository for additional information.

Civil records
Clerk of Court
PO Box 429
Bellefontaine, OH 43311
(513) 599-7275
Civil records are available in person only.
See Ohio state repository for additional information.

Misdemeanor records
Logan County Municipal Court
135 N. Detroit Street
Bellefontaine, OH 43311
(513) 599-6127
Fax (513) 592-4218
Misdemeanor records are available by mail
or by phone from 1986. No release necessary. No search fee. $.25 fee per copy.
$1.00 for certification. Search information
required: name, date of birth, SSN, address.

Civil records
Logan County Municipal Court
135 N. Detroit Street
Bellefontaine, OH 43311
(513) 599-6127
Fax (513) 592-4218
Civil records are available in person only.
See Ohio state repository for additional information.

Lorain County

Clerk of Court, Criminal Records
PO Box 749
Elyria, OH 44036
(216) 329-5536
Felony records are available in person only.
See Ohio state repository for additional information.

Civil records are available in person only.
See Ohio state repository for additional information.

Lucas County

Clerk of Court, Criminal Records
Lucas County Courthouse
Adams & Erie Streets
Toledo, OH 43624
(419) 245-4483
Felony records are available by mail only.
No release necessary. $5.00 fee per name
searched. Check payable to Clerk of Court.
Search information required: name, date of
birth.

Civil records are available by mail. No release necessary. $2.00 search fee. $1.00 fee
per copy. $1.00 for certification. Search information required: name, date of birth,
years to search. Specify plaintiff or defendant.

Madison County

Felony records
Clerk of Court, Criminal Records
Madison County Courthouse
PO Box 227
London, OH 43140
(614) 852-9776
Felony records are available by mail. A release is required. No search fee. $.50 fee
per copy. $1.00 for certification. Search information required: name, SASE.

Civil records
Clerk of Court
Madison County Courthouse
PO Box 227
London, OH 43140
(614) 852-9776
Civil records are available n person only.
See Ohio state repository for additional information.

Misdemeanor records
Madison County Municipal Court
Main and High St.
London, OH 43140
(614) 852-1669
Misdemeanor records are available by mail.
A release is required. No search fee. Search
information required: name, date of birth,
SSN, SASE.

Civil records
Madison County Municipal Court
Main and High St.
London, OH 43140
(614) 852-1669
Civil records are available by mail. No release necessary. No search fee. $.50 fee per
copy. $1.00 for certification. Search information required: name, date of birth, years
to search, SASE. Specify plaintiff or defendant.

Mahoning County

Clerk of Court, Criminal Records
120 Market Street
Youngstown, OH 44503
(216) 740-2104
Felony records are available by mail. No release necessary. $1.00 search fee. Search
information required: name, years to
search, SASE.

Civil records are availablein person only.
See Ohio state repository for additional information.

Marion County

Felony records
Courthouse, Criminal Records
114 N. Main Street
Marion, OH 43302
(614) 387-5871 Extension 221
Felony records are available in person only.
See Ohio state repository for additional information.

Civil records
Courthouse
114 N. Main Street
Marion, OH 43302
(614) 387-5871 Extension 221
Civil records are available in person only.
See Ohio state repository for additional information.

Misdemeanor records
Marion County Municipal Court
233 West Center St.
Marion, OH 43302-0326
(614) 387-2020
Misdemeanor records are available by mail.
A release is required. $3.00 search fee.
Search information required: name, date of
birth, SSN, years to search.

Civil records
Marion County Municipal Court
233 West Center St.
Marion, OH 43302-0326
(614) 387-2020
Civil records are available in person only.
See Ohio state repository for additional information.

Medina County

Felony records
Clerk of Court, Criminal Records
93 Public Square
Medina, OH 44256
(216) 723-3641
Felony records are available by mail or
phone. No release necessary. No search fee.
Search information required: name.

Civil records
Clerk of Court
93 Public Square
Medina, OH 44256
(216) 723-3641
Civil records are available by mail. No release necessary. No search fee. $.25 fee per copy. $1.00 for certification. Search information required: name, date of birth, years to search. Specify plaintiff or defendant.

Misdemeanor records
Medina Municipal Court
135 N. Elmwood
Medina, OH 44256
(216) 723-3287
Fax (216) 225-1108
Misdemeanor records are available by mail or fax. A release is required. No search fee. Search information required: name, date of birth, SSN, years to search.

Civil records
Medina Municipal Court
135 N. Elmwood
Medina, OH 44256
(216) 723-3287
Fax (216) 225-1108
Civil records are available by mail. No release necessary. No search fee. $1.00 fee per copy. $2.00 for certification. Search information required: name, date of birth, SSN, years to search, SASE. Specify plaintiff or defendant.

Meigs County

Felony records
Clerk of Court, Criminal Records
PO Box 151
Pomeroy, OH 45769
(614) 992-5290
Felony records are available by mail or phone. No release necessary. No search fee. Search information required: name.

Civil records
Clerk of Court
PO Box 151
Pomeroy, OH 45769
(614) 992-5290
Civil records are available in person only. See Ohio state repository for additional information.

Misdemeanor records
Meigs County Court
Courthouse
Pomeroy, OH 45769
(614) 992-2279
Fax (614) 992-2270
Misdemeanor records are available by mail. No release necessary. No search fee. Search information required: name, address, years to search.

Civil records
Meigs County Court
Courthouse
Pomeroy, OH 45769
(614) 992-2279
Fax (614) 992-2270
Civil records are available by mail. No release necessary. No search fee. Search information required: name, date of birth, years to search. Specify plaintiff or defendant.

Mercer County

Felony records
Clerk of Court, Criminal Records
PO Box 28
Celina, OH 45822
(419) 586-6461
Fax (419) 586-1714
Felony records are available in person only. See Ohio state repository for additional information.

Civil records
Clerk of Court
101 N. Main Street, Room 306
Celina, OH 45822
(419) 586-6461
Fax (419) 586-1714
Civil records are available in person only. See Ohio state repository for additional information.

Misdemeanor records
Celina Municipal Court
City Hall
PO Box 362
Celina, OH 45822
(419) 586-6491
Misdemeanor records are available by mail. A release is required. No search fee. Search information required: name, date of birth, SSN, years to search.

Civil records
Celina Municipal Court
City Hall
PO Box 362
Celina, OH 45822
(419) 586-6491
Civil records are available by mail. A release is required. No search fee. Search information required: name, date of birth, years to search. Specify plaintiff or defendant.

Miami County

Felony records
Clerk of Court, Criminal Records
Safety Bldg.
201 West Main Street
Troy, OH 45373
(513) 332-6855
Felony records are available by mail. A release is required. $5.00 search fee. Company checks only, payable to Clerk of Court. Search information required: name, SSN, date of birth, years to search.

Civil records
Clerk of Court
Safety Bldg.
201 West Main Street
Troy, OH 45373
(513) 332-6855
Civil records are available by mail. No release necessary. $5.00 search fee. Search information required: name, date of birth, years to search. Specify plaintiff or defendant.

Misdemeanor records
Miami County Municipal Court
201 West Main Street
Troy, OH 45373
(513) 332-6877
Fax (513) 332-7019
Misdemeanor records are available by mail or phone. A release is required. $5.00 search fee. Search information required: name, date of birth, SSN, years to search.

Civil records
Miami County Municipal Court
201 West Main Street
Troy, OH 45373
(513) 332-6909
Fax (513) 332-7019
Civil records are available by mail. A release is required. No search fee. $1.00 fee per copy. $2.00 for certification. Search information required: name, date of birth, years to search. Specify plaintiff or defendant.

Monroe County

Felony records
Clerk of Court, Criminal Records
PO Box 556
Woodsfield, OH 43793
(614) 472-0761
Felony records are available by mail. A release is required. $2.00 search fee. Company checks only, payable to Clerk of Court. Search information required: name, SSN, sex, race.

Civil records
Clerk of Court
PO Box 556
Woodsfield, OH 43793
(614) 472-0761
Civil records are available in person only. See Ohio state repository for additional information.

Misdemeanor records
Monroe County Court
PO Box 574
Woodsfield, OH 43793
(614) 472-5181
Misdemeanor records are available by mail or phone. No release necessary. No search fee. Search information required: name, date of birth, SSN.

Civil records
Monroe County Court
PO Box 574
Woodsfield, OH 43793
(614) 472-5181
Civil records are available in person only. See Ohio state repository for additional information.

Montgomery County

Clerk of Court
Criminal Division
41 N. Perry Street
Dayton, OH 45422
(513) 225-4536
Felony records are available by mail. No release necessary. No search fee. Search information required: name, date of birth, SSN.

Civil records are available in person only. See Ohio state repository for additional information.

Morgan County

Clerk of Court, Criminal Records
Courthouse
19 East Main Street
McConnelsville, OH 43756
(614) 962-4752
Fax (614) 962-4589
Felony and misdemeanor records are available by mail or phone. No release necessary. No fee. Search information required: name, SASE, years to search.

Civil records are available by mail. No release necessary. No search fee. $.25 fee per copy. $1.00 for certification. Search information required: name, date of birth, years to search, SASE. Specify plaintiff or defendant.

Morrow County

Felony records
Clerk of Court, Criminal Records
48 East High St.
Morrow County Courthouse
Mount Gilead, OH 43338
(419) 947-2085
Fax (419) 947-1860
Felony records are available by mail or phone. No release necessary. No search fee. Search information required: name, SASE.

Civil records
Clerk of Court
48 East High St.
Morrow County Courthouse
Mount Gilead, OH 43338
(419) 947-2085
Fax (419) 947-1860
Civil records are available by mail or phone. No release necessary. No search fee. $1.00 fee per copy. $1.00 for certification. Search information required: name, date of birth, years to search. Specify plaintiff or defendant.

Misdemeanor records
Morrow County Court
48 East High St.
Mount Gilead, OH 43338
(419) 947-5045
Fax (419) 947-1860
Misdemeanor records are available by mail. No release necessary. No search fee. Search information required: name, date of birth, SSN, years to search.

Civil records
Morrow County Court
48 East High St.
Mount Gilead, OH 43338
(419) 947-5045
Fax (419) 947-1860
Civil records are available by mail. No release necessary. No search fee. $1.00 fee per copy. $1.00 for certification. Search information required: name, date of birth, years to search. Specify plaintiff or defendant.

Muskingum County

Clerk of Common Pleas Court, Criminal Records
PO Box 268
Zanesville, OH 43702-0268
(614) 455-7104
Felony records are available by mail or phone. No release necessary. No search fee. $1.00 fee per copy. $5.00 for certification. Search information required: name, SASE, years to search.

Civil records are available by mail. No release necessary. No search fee. $1.00 fee per copy. $5.00 for certification. Search information required: name, date of birth, years to search, SASE. Specify plaintiff or defendant.

Noble County

Felony records
Clerk of Court, Criminal Records
350 Courthouse, 3rd Floor
Caldwell, OH 43724
(614) 732-4408
Felony records are available by mail or phone. No release necessary. No search fee. $.50 fee per copy. Search information required: name.

Civil records
Clerk of Court
350 Courthouse, 3rd Floor
Caldwell, OH 43724
(614) 732-4408
Civil records are available by mail. No release necessary. No search fee. $.50 fee per copy. $.50 for certification. Search information required: name, date of birth, years to search. Specify plaintiff or defendant.

Misdemeanor records
Noble County Court
1st Floor, Court House
Caldwell, OH 43724
(614) 732-5795
Misdemeanor records are available by mail or phone. No release necessary. No search fee. Search information required: full name, date of birth, SSN, address at time of offense.

Civil records
Noble County Court
1st Floor, Court House
Caldwell, OH 43724
(614) 732-5795
Civil records are available in person only. See Ohio state repository for additional information.

Ottawa County

Felony records
Clerk of Court, Criminal Records
315 Madison Street
Room 304, Courthouse
Port Clinton, OH 43452
(419) 734-6755
Felony records are available in person only. See Ohio state repository for additional information.

Civil records
Clerk of Court
315 Madison Street
Room 304, Courthouse
Port Clinton, OH 43452
(419) 734-6755
Civil records are available in person only. See Ohio state repository for additional information.

Misdemeanor records
Port Clinton Municipal Court
PO Box Q
Port Clinton, OH 43452
(419) 734-4143
Misdemeanor records are available iin person only. See Ohio state repository for additional information.

Civil records
Port Clinton Municipal Court
PO Box Q
Port Clinton, OH 43452
(419) 734-4143
Civil records are available in person only. See Ohio state repository for additional information.

Paulding County

Felony records
Clerk of Courts, Criminal Records
1st Floor
Paulding, OH 45879
(419) 399-8210
Felony records are available by mail. A release is required. $5.00 search fee. Search information required: name, date of birth, SSN, years to search.

Civil records
Clerk of Courts
1st Floor
Paulding, OH 45879
(419) 399-8210
Civil records are available by mail. A release is required. $5.00 search fee. Search information required: name, date of birth, SSN, years to search. Specify plaintiff or defendant.

Misdemeanor records
Paulding County Court
1st Floor, Courthouse
103 B E. Perry Street
Paulding, OH 45879
(419) 399-8235
Misdemeanor records are available by mail. No release necessary. No fee. Search information required: name.

Civil records
Paulding County Court
1st Floor, Courthouse
103 B E. Perry Street
Paulding, OH 45879
(419) 399-8235
Civil records are available by mail. No release necessary. No search fee. $.25 fee per copy. $2.00 for certification. Search information required: name, date of birth, years to search, SASE. Specify plaintiff or defendant.

Perry County

Felony records
Clerk of Court, Criminal Records
PO Box 67
New Lexington, OH 43764
(614) 342-1022
Felony records are available in person only. See Ohio state repository for additional information.

Civil records
Clerk of Court
PO Box 67
New Lexington, OH 43764
(614) 342-1022
Civil records are available by mail. No release necessary. No search fee. $.50 fee per copy. Search information required: name, date of birth, years to search. Specify plaintiff or defendant.

Misdemeanor records
Perry County Court
PO Box 207
New Lexington, OH 43764
(614) 342-3156
Fax (614) 342-2189
Misdemeanor records are available by mail or phone. No release necessary. No search fee. Search information required: name, SSN, years to search.

Civil records
Perry County Court
PO Box 207
New Lexington, OH 43764
(614) 342-3156
Fax (614) 342-2189
Civil records are available in person only. See Ohio state repository for additional information.

Pickaway County

Felony records
Clerk of Court, Criminal Records
Pickaway County Courthouse
Circleville, OH 43113
(614) 474-5231
Felony records are available by mail. A release is required. No search fee. $1.00 fee per copy. $1.00 for certification. Search information required: name, years to search.

Civil records
Clerk of Court
Pickaway County Courthouse
Circleville, OH 43113
(614) 474-5231
Civil records are available by mail. A release is required. No search fee. $1.00 fee per copy. $1.00 for certification. Search information required: name, date of birth, years to search. Specify plaintiff or defendant.

Misdemeanor records
Circleville Municipal Court
PO Box 128
Circleville, OH 43113
(614) 474-3171
Misdemeanor records are available by mail. A release is required. No search fee. Search information required: name, SSN, years to search.

Civil records
Circleville Municipal Court
PO Box 128
Circleville, OH 43113
(614) 474-3171
Civil records are available in person only. See Ohio state repository for additional information.

Pike County

Felony records
Clerk of Court, Criminal Records
Pike County Courthouse
100 East Second St.
Waverly, OH 45690
(614) 947-2715
Felony records are available by mail. No release necessary. No search fee. $.25 fee per copy. $1.00 for certification. Search information required: full name, date of birth, years to search, SASE.

Civil records
Clerk of Court
Pike County Courthouse
100 East Second St.
Waverly, OH 45690
(614) 947-2715
Civil records are available by mail. No release necessary. No search fee. $.25 fee per copy. $1.00 for certification. Search information required: full name, date of birth, years to search, SASE. Specify plaintiff or defendant.

Misdemeanor records
Pike County Court
106 N. Market St.
Waverly, OH 45690
(614) 947-4003
Misdemeanor records are available in person only. See Ohio state repository for additional information.

Civil records
Pike County Court
106 N. Market St.
Waverly, OH 45690
(614) 947-4003
Civil records are available in person only. See Ohio state repository for additional information.

Portage County

Clerk of Court, Criminal Records
203 W. Main
Ravenna, OH 44266
(216) 297-3644
Felony records are available in person only. See Ohio State Repository for additional information.

Civil records are available in person only. See Ohio state repository for additional information.

Preble County

Felony records
Clerk of Court, Criminal Records
Preble County Courthouse
100 Main Street
Eaton, OH 45320
(513) 456-8160
Felony records are available by mail or phone. No release necessary. No search fee. $1.00 fee per copy. $1.00 for certification. Search information required: name, SASE.

Civil records
Clerk of Court
Preble County Courthouse
100 Main Street
Eaton, OH 45320
(513) 456-8160
Civil records are available by mail. A release is required. No search fee. $1.00 fee per copy. $1.00 for certification. Search information required: name, date of birth, years to search, SASE. Specify plaintiff or defendant.

Misdemeanor records
Eaton Municipal Court
PO Box 65
Eaton, OH 45320
(513) 456-4941
Misdemeanor records are available by mail. A release is required. No search fee. Search information required: full name, date of birth, SSN, years to search.

Civil records
Eaton Municipal Court
PO Box 65
Eaton, OH 45320
(513) 456-4941
Civil records are available by mail. No release necessary. No search fee. $.50 fee per copy. $1.00 for certification. Search information required: name, date of birth, years to search. Specify plaintiff or defendant.

Putnam County

Clerk of Courts, Criminal Records
Putnam County Courthouse
245 E. Main Street
Ottawa, OH 45875
(419) 523-3110
Fax (419) 523-5284
Felony and misdemeanor records are available by mail or phone. No release necessary. No search fee. Search information required: name.

Civil records are available by mail. No release necessary. No search fee. $.25 fee per copy. $1.50 for certification. Search information required: name, date of birth, years to search. Specify plaintiff or defendant.

Richland County

Clerk of Court, Criminal Records
PO Box 127
Mansfield, OH 44901
(419) 755-5690
Felony records are available in person only. See Ohio state repository for additional information.

Civil records are available in person only. See Ohio state repository for additional information.

Ross County

Felony records
Clerk of Court, Criminal Records
Ross County Courthouse
Chillicothe, OH 45601
(614) 773-2330
Felony records are available in person only. See Ohio state repository for additional information.

Civil records
Clerk of Court
Ross County Courthouse
Chillicothe, OH 45601
(614) 773-2330
Civil records are available in person only. See Ohio state repository for additional information.

Misdemeanor records
Chillicothe Municipal Court
City Building
26 South Paint St
Chillicothe, OH 45601
(614) 773-3515
Misdemeanor records are available in person only. See Ohio state repository for additional information.

Civil records
Chillicothe Municipal Court
City Building
26 South Paint St
Chillicothe, OH 45601
(614) 773-3515
Civil records are available in person only. See Ohio state repository for additional information.

Sandusky County

Felony records
Clerk of Court, Criminal Records
PO Box 1150
Fremont, OH 43420
(419) 334-6161
Felony records are available by mail. No release necessary. No search fee. $.50 fee per copy. $1.00 for certification. Search information required: name.

Civil records
Clerk of Court
PO Box 1150
Fremont, OH 43420
(419) 334-6161
Civil records are available by mail. No release necessary. No search fee. $.50 fee per copy. $1.00 for certification. Search information required: name, date of birth, years to search. Specify plaintiff or defendant.

Misdemeanor records
Municiple Court
323 S. Front Street
Fremont, OH 43420
(419) 332-1579
Misdemeanor records are available by mail. A release is required. No search fee. $.50 fee per copy. $1.00 for certification. Search information required: name.

Civil records
Municiple Court
323 S. Front Street
Fremont, OH 43420
(419) 332-1579
Civil records are available by mail. No release necessary. No search fee. $.50 fee per copy. $1.00 for certification. Search information required: name, date of birth, years to search. Specify plaintiff or defendant.

Scioto County

Felony records
Scioto County Courthouse, Criminal Records
602 7th Street
Room 205
Portsmouth, OH 45662
(614) 355-8210
Fax (614) 354-2057
Felony records are available by mail or phone. No release necessary. No search fee. Search information required: name, years to search.

Civil records
Scioto County Courthouse
602 7th Street
Room 205
Portsmouth, OH 45662
(614) 355-8210
Fax (614) 354-2057
Civil records are available by mail. No release necessary. $10.00 search fee. $1.00 fee per copy. $1.00 for certification. Search information required: name, date of birth, years to search. Specify plaintiff or defendant.

Misdemeanor records
Portsmouth Municipal Court
728 Second St.
Portsmouth, OH 45662
(614) 354-3283
Misdemeanor records are available by mail. A release is required. No search fee. Search information required: name, date of birth, SSN, years to search.

Civil records
Portsmouth Municipal Court
728 Second St.
Portsmouth, OH 45662
(614) 354-3283
Civil records are available by mail or phone from November 1989 forward. No release necessary. No search fee. $.25 fee per copy. $1.00 for certification. Search information required: name, date of birth, years to search, SASE. Specify plaintiff or defendant.

Seneca County

Clerk of Court
Courthouse
103 S. Washington
Tiffin, OH 44883
(419) 447-0671
Felony records are available in person only. See Ohio state repository for additional information.

Civil records are available in person only. See Ohio state repository for additional information.

Shelby County

Felony records
Shelby County Clerk of Court, Criminal Records
PO Box 809
Sidney, OH 45365
(513) 498-7221
Felony records are available by mail. No release necessary. $1.00 search fee. Search information required: name, SSN, date of birth, sex, race, SASE.

Civil records
Shelby County Clerk of Court, Criminal Records
PO Box 809
Sidney, OH 45365
(513) 498-7221
Civil records are available by mail. A release is required. $1.00 search fee. $1.00 fee per copy. $1.00 for certification. Search information required: name, date of birth, years to search, SASE. Specify plaintiff or defendant.

Misdemeanor records
Municipal Court
201 West Poplar
Sidney, OH 45365
(513) 498-2335
Fax (513) 498-8119
Misdemeanor records are available by mail. Fax requests may be made, however court will not reply by fax. No release necessary. No search fee. $1.00 fee per copy. Search information required: name, date of birth, SSN, years to search.

Civil records
Municipal Court
201 West Poplar
Sidney, OH 45365
(513) 498-2335
Fax (513) 498-8119
Civil records are available by mail. A release is required. $0.00 search fee. $.50 fee per copy. $1.00 for certification. Search information required: name, address, SSN, date of birth, years to search. Specify plaintiff or defendant.

Stark County

Prosecuting Attorney, Stark County
Criminal Division
PO Box 20049
Canton, OH 44701-0049
(216) 438-0897
Felony Records are available by mail. No search fee. Search information required: name, date of birth, SSN, SASE.

Civil records are available by mail. No release necessary. No search fee. Search information required: name, date of birth, SSN, years to search, SASE. Specify plaintiff or defendant.

Summit County

Clerk of Court
Criminal Division
209 S. High Street
Akron, OH 44308
(216) 379-2282
Felony records are available by mail. No release necessary. No search fee. Search information required: name, SSN, date of birth, sex, race.

Civil records are available by mail. No release necessary. No search fee. $.50 fee per copy. $1.00 for certification. Search information required: full name, date of birth, years to search. Specify plaintiff or defendant.

Trumbull County

Trumbull County Clerk of Court, Criminal Records
160 High Street
Warren, OH 44481
(216) 841-0560
Felony records are available by mail. No release necessary. $5.00 search fee. Certified check only, payable to Clerk of Court. Search information required: name, previous address, years to search, SASE.

Civil records are available in person only. See Ohio state repository for additional information.

Tuscarawas County

Clerk of Court
PO Box 628
New Philadelphia, OH 44663
(216) 364-8811 Extension 243
Records are available in person only. See Ohio state repository.

Civil records are available in person only. See Ohio state repository for additional information.

Union County

Felony records
Clerk of Court, Criminal Records
Courthouse
PO Box 605
215 W. 5th Street
Marysville, OH 43040
(513) 642-5906
Felony records are available in person only. See Ohio State Repository for additional information.

Civil records
Clerk of Court
Courthouse
PO Box 605
215 W. 5th Street
Marysville, OH 43040
(513) 642-5906
Fax (513) 642-5906
Civil records are available in person only. See Ohio state repository for additional information.

Misdemeanor records
Marysville Municipal Court
PO Box 322
Marysville, OH 43040
(513) 644-9102
Fax (513) 642-1228
Misdemeanor records are available by mail. No release necessary. No search fee. Search information required: name, date of birth, SSN, address, SASE.

Civil records
Marysville Municipal Court
PO Box 322
Marysville, OH 43040
(513) 644-9102
Fax (513) 642-1228
Civil records are available by mail. A release is required. No search fee. Search information required: name, date of birth, years to search. Specify plaintiff or defendant.

Van Wert County

Clerk of Court, Criminal Records
PO Box 366
Van Wert, OH 45891
(419) 238-1022
Felony and misdemeanor records are available by mail. No release necessary. No search fee. $1.00 for certification. Search information required: name, years to search, SASE.

Civil records are available by mail. No release necessary. No search fee. $1.00 for certification. Search information required: name, date of birth, years to search, SASE. Specify plaintiff or defendant.

Vinton County

Felony records
Clerk of Court, Criminal Records
100 E. Main Street, Courthouse
Main and Market St.
McArthur, OH 45651
(614) 596-5401
Felony records are available by mail or phone. No release necessary. No search fee. Search information required: name, years to search.

Civil records
Clerk of Court
100 E. Main Street, Courthouse
Main and Market St.
McArthur, OH 45651
(614) 596-5401Civil records are available by mail. No release necessary. No search fee. $.25 fee per copy. $1.00 for certification. Search information required: name, date of birth, years to search, SASE. Specify plaintiff or defendant.

Misdemeanor records
Vinton County Court
Courthouse
McArthur, OH 45651
(614) 596-5000
Misdemeanor records are available by mail or phone. No release necessary. No search fee. Search information required: name, date of birth.

Civil records
Vinton County Court
Courthouse
McArthur, OH 45651
(614) 596-5000
Civil records are available by mail. No release necessary. No search fee. $.25 fee per copy. $1.00 for certification. Search information required: name, date of birth, years to search, SASE. Specify plaintiff or defendant.

Warren County

Felony records
Clerk of Court, Criminal Records
500 Justice Drive
Lebanon, OH 45036
(513) 933-1120
Felony records are available by mail or phone. No release necessary. No search fee. Search information required: name.

Civil records
Clerk of Court
500 Justice Drive
Lebanon, OH 45036
(513) 933-1120
Civil records are available by mail or phone. No release necessary. No search fee. $.20 fee per copy. $1.00 for certification. Search information required: name, date of birth, years to search, SASE. Specify plaintiff or defendant.

Misdemeanor records
Clerk of Court
550 Justice Drive
Lebanon, OH 45036
(513) 933-1371
Fax (513) 933-2990
Misdemeanor records are available by mail or by phone from 1990 forward. No release necessary. No search fee. Search information required: name, date of birth, years to search, SASE.

Civil records
Clerk of Court
550 Justice Drive
Lebanon, OH 45036
(513) 933-1371
Fax (513) 933-2990
Civil records are available by mail or phone. No release necessary. No search fee. $.20 fee per copy. $1.00 for certification. Search information required: name, date of birth, years to search. Specify plaintiff or defendant.

Washington County

Felony records
Clerk of Court, Criminal Records
205 Putnam St.
Washington County Courthouse
Marietta, OH 45750
(614) 373-6623
Records are not available by mail or phone but are available for physical inspection at the above office. See Ohio state repository.

Civil records
Clerk of Court
205 Putnam St.
Washington County Courthouse
Marietta, OH 45750
(614) 373-6623
Civil records are available in person only. See Ohio state repository for additional information.

Misdemeanor records
Marietta Municipal Court
301 Putnam St.
PO Box 615
Marietta, OH 45750
(614) 373-4474
Fax (614) 373-0483
Misdemeanor records are available by mail or phone. No release necessary. No seasrch fee. Search information required: name, date of birth, SSN.

Civil records
Marietta Municipal Court
301 Putnam St.
PO Box 615
Marietta, OH 45750
(614) 373-4474
Civil records are available by mail. No release necessary. No search fee. $.25 fee per copy. $1.50 for certification. Search information required: name, date of birth, years to search. Specify plaintiff or defendant.

Wayne County

Wayne County Clerk of Court,
Criminal Records
PO Box 113
Wooster, OH 44691
(216) 287-5590
Felony records are available by mail or phone. No release necessary. No search fee. Search information required: name.

Civil records are available by mail. No release necessary. No search fee. $1.00 per copy. $1.00 for certification. Search information required: name, date of birth, years to search, SASE. Specify plaintiff or defendant.

Williams County

Williams County Courthouse,
Criminal Records
3rd Floor Court
Bryan, OH 43506
(419) 636-1551
Felony records are available in person only. See Ohio state repository for additional information.

Civil records are available by mail. No release necessary. No search fee. $1.00 fee per copy. $1.00 for certification. Search information required: name, date of birth, years to search. Specify plaintiff or defendant.

Wood County

Clerk of Court, Criminal Records
Courthouse
PO Box 829
Bowling Green, OH 43402
(419) 354-9280
Fax (419) 354-9241
Felony records are available by mail. No release necessary. $3.00 search fee. $1.00 fee per copy. $1.00 for certification. Make check payable to Clerk of Court. Search information required: name, years to search.

Civil records are available by mail. No release necessary. $3.00 search fee. $1.00 fee per copy. $1.00 for certification. Search information required: name, date of birth, years to search. Specify plaintiff or defendant.

Wyandot County

Felony records
Clerk of Court, Criminal Records
Wyandot County Courthouse
Upper Sandusky, OH 43351
(419) 294-1432
Felony records are available by mail or phone. No release necessary. No search fee. Search information required: name, years to search, date of birth, years to search, SSN, SASE..

Civil records
Clerk of Court
Wyandot County Courthouse
Upper Sandusky, OH 43351
(419) 294-1432
Civil records are available by mail. No release necessary. No search fee. $.50 fee per copy. $1.00 for certification. Search information required: name, date of birth, years to search, SSN, SASE. Specify plaintiff or defendant.

Misdemeanor records
Upper Sandusky Municipal Court
119 N. 7th St.
Upper Sandusky, OH 43351
(419) 294-3809
Fax (419) 294-6765
Misdemeanor records are available by mail or phone. No release necessary. No search fee. Search information required: name, date of birth, SSN.

Civil records
Upper Sandusky Municipal Court
119 N. 7th St.
Upper Sandusky, OH 43351
(419) 294-3809
Fax (419) 294-6765
Civil records are available by mail. No release necessary. No search fee. Search information required: name, date of birth, years to search. Specify plaintiff or defendant.

City-County Cross Reference

Aberdeen *Brown*
Academia *Knox*
Ada *Hardin*
Adams Mills *Muskingum*
Adamsville *Muskingum*
Addyston *Hamilton*
Adelphi *Ross*
Adena *Jefferson*
Adrian *Seneca*
Akron *Summit*
Albany *Athens*
Alexandria *Licking*
Alger *Hardin*
Alledonia *Belmont*
Allensville *Vinton*
Alliance *Stark*
Alpha *Greene*
Alvada *Seneca*
Alvordton *Williams*
Amanda *Fairfield*
Amberley *Hamilton*
Amberly *Franklin*
Amelia *Clermont*
Amesville *Athens*
Amherst *Lorain*
Amlin *Franklin*
Amsden *Seneca*
Amsterdam *Jefferson*
Andover *Ashtabula*
Anna *Shelby*
Ansonia *Darke*
Antioch *Monroe*
Antwerp *Paulding*
Apple Creek *Wayne*
Arcadia *Hancock*
Arcanum *Darke*
Archbold *Fulton*
Arlington *Hancock*
Arlington Heights
   Hamilton
Ashland *Ashland*
Ashley *Delaware*
Ashtabula *Ashtabula*
Ashville *Pickaway*
Athens *Athens*
Attica *Seneca*
Atwater *Portage*
Augusta *Carroll*
Aurora *Portage*

Austinburg *Ashtabula*
Austintown *Mahoning*
Ava *Noble*
Avon *Lorain*
Avondale *Stark*
Avon Lake *Lorain*
Bainbridge *Ross*
Bakersville *Coshocton*
Ballville *Sandusky*
Baltic *Tuscarawas*
Baltimore *Fairfield*
Bannock *Belmont*
Barberton *Summit*
Barlow *Washington*
Barnesville *Belmont*
Bartlett *Washington*
Barton *Belmont*
Bascom *Seneca*
Batavia *Clermont*
Bath *Summit*
Bay View *Erie*
Bay Village *Cuyahoga*
Beach City *Stark*
Beachwood *Cuyahoga*
Beallsville *Monroe*
Beaver *Pike*
Bedford Heights *Cuyahoga*
Bellaire *Belmont*
Bellbrook *Greene*
Belle Center *Logan*
Bellefontaine *Logan*
Belle Valley *Noble*
Bellevue *Huron*
Bellville *Richland*
Belmont *Belmont*
Beloit *Mahoning*
Belpre *Washington*
Benton Ridge *Hancock*
Bentonville *Adams*
Berea *Cuyahoga*
Bergholz *Jefferson*
Berkey *Lucas*
Berlin *Holmes*
Berlin Center *Mahoning*
Berlin Heights *Erie*
Bethel *Clermont*
Bethesda *Belmont*
Bettsville *Seneca*
Beverly *Washington*

Bevis *Hamilton*
Bexely *Franklin*
Bidwell *Gallia*
Big Prairie *Holmes*
Birmingham *Erie*
Black Horse *Portage*
Blacklick *Franklin*
Bladensburg *Knox*
Blaine *Belmont*
Blakeslee *Williams*
Blanchester *Clinton*
Blissfield *Coshocton*
Bloomdale *Wood*
Bloomingburg *Fayette*
Bloomingdale *Jefferson*
Bloomville *Seneca*
Blue Ash *Hamilton*
Blue Creek *Adams*
Blue Rock *Muskingum*
Bluffton *Allen*
Boardman *Mahoning*
Bolivar *Tuscarawas*
Boston Heights *Summit*
Botkins *Shelby*
Bourneville *Ross*
Bowerston *Harrison*
Bowersville *Greene*
Bowling Green *Wood*
Bradford *Miami*
Bradner *Wood*
Bratenahl *Cuyahoga*
Brecksville *Cuyahoga*
Bremen *Fairfield*
Brentwood *Hamilton*
Brentwood Lake *Lorain*
Brewster *Stark*
Briarwood Beach *Medina*
Brice *Franklin*
Bridgeport *Belmont*
Bridgetown *Hamilton*
Brilliant *Jefferson*
Brimfield *Portage*
Brinkhaven *Knox*
Bristolville *Trumbull*
Broadview Heights
   Cuyahoga
Broadway *Union*
Brookfield *Trumbull*
Brooklyn *Cuyahoga*

Brook Park *Cuyahoga*
Brookside *Cuyahoga*
Brookville *Montgomery*
Brookside Estates *Franklin*
Brown Heights *Guernsey*
Brownsville *Licking*
Brunswick *Medina*
Bryan *Williams*
Buchtel *Athens*
Buckeye Lake *Licking*
Bucyrus *Crawford*
Buffalo *Guernsey*
Buford *Highland*
Burbank *Wayne*
Burghill *Trumbull*
Burgoon *Sandusky*
Burkettsville *Mercer*
Burlington *Lawrence*
Burton *Geauga*
Butler *Richland*
Byesville *Guernsey*
Cable *Champaign*
Cadiz *Harrison*
Cairo *Allen*
Calcutta *Columbiana*
Caldwell *Noble*
Caledonia *Marion*
Cambridge *Guernsey*
Camden *Preble*
Cameron *Monroe*
Campbell *Mahoning*
Camp Dennison *Hamilton*
Canal Fulton *Stark*
Canal Winchester *Franklin*
Canfield *Mahoning*
Canton *Stark*
Carbon Hill *Hocking*
Cardington *Morrow*
Carey *Wyandot*
Carroll *Fairfield*
Carrollton *Carroll*
Carrothers *Seneca*
Casstown *Miami*
Castalia *Erie*
Catawba *Clark*
Cecil *Paulding*
Cedarville *Greene*
Celina *Mercer*
Centerburg *Knox*

Centerville *Montgomery*
Chagrin Falls *Cuyahoga*
Champion *Trumbull*
Chandlersville *Muskingum*
Chardon *Geauga*
Charm *Holmes*
Chatfield *Crawford*
Chauncey *Athens*
Cherry Fork *Adams*
Cherry Grove *Hamilton*
Chesapeake *Lawrence*
Cheshire *Gallia*
Chester *Meigs*
Chesterhill *Morgan*
Chesterland *Geauga*
Chesterville *Morrow*
Chevoit *Hamilton*
Chillicothe *Ross*
Chilo *Clermont*
Chippewa Lake *Medina*
Christiansburg *Champaign*
Churchhill *Trumbull*
Cincinnati *Hamilton*
Circleville *Pickaway*
Clarington *Monroe*
Clarksburg *Ross*
Clarksville *Clinton*
Clay Center *Ottawa*
Claysville *Guernsey*
Clayton *Montgomery*
Clearview *Lorain*
Cleveland *Cuyahoga*
Cleveland Heights
   Cuyahoga
Cleves *Hamilton*
Clifton *Greene*
Clinton *Summit*
Cloverdale *Putnam*
Clyde *Sandusky*
Coal Grove *Lawrence*
Coal Run *Washington*
Coalton *Jackson*
Coldwater *Mercer*
Colerain *Belmont*
Colerian Heights *Hamilton*
College Corner *Butler*
Collins *Huron*
Collinsville *Butler*
Colton *Henry*
Columbiana *Columbiana*
Columbia Station *Lorain*
Columbus *Franklin*
Columbus Grove *Putnam*
Columbus Park *Erie*
Commercial Point
   Pickaway
Conesville *Coshocton*
Conneaut *Ashtabula*
Conover *Miami*
Continental *Putnam*
Convoy *Van Wert*
Coolville *Athens*
Copley *Summit*
Corning *Perry*
Cortland *Trumbull*
Coshocton *Coshocton*
Covedale *Hamilton*
Covington *Miami*
Craig Beach *Mahoning*
Creola *Vinton*
Crestline *Crawford*
Creston *Wayne*
Cridersville *Auglaize*
Crooksville *Perry*
Croton *Licking*

Crown City *Gallia*
Crystal Lakes *Clark*
Cuyahoga Heights
   Cuyahoga
Cuba *Clinton*
Cumberland *Guernsey*
Curtice *Ottawa*
Custar *Wood*
Cutler *Washington*
Cuyahoga Falls *Summit*
Cygnet *Wood*
Cynthiana *Pike*
Dalton *Wayne*
Damascus *Mahoning*
Danville *Knox*
Darbydale *Franklin*
Dayton *Montgomery*
Decatur *Brown*
Deerfield *Portage*
Deersville *Harrison*
Defiance *Defiance*
De Forest *Trumbull*
DeGraff *Logan*
Delaware *Delaware*
Dellroy *Carroll*
Delphos *Allen*
Delta *Fulton*
Dennison *Tuscarawas*
Dent *Hamilton*
Derby *Pickaway*
Derwent *Guernsey*
Deshler *Henry*
Devola *Washington*
Dexter City *Noble*
Diamond *Portage*
Dillonvale *Jefferson*
Dola *Hardin*
Donnelsville *Clark*
Dorset *Ashtabula*
Dover *Tuscarawas*
Doylestown *Wayne*
Dresden *Muskingum*
Drexel *Montgomery*
Dublin *Franklin*
Dunbridge *Wood*
Duncan Falls *Muskingum*
Dundee *Tuscarawas*
Dunkirk *Hardin*
East Alliance *Columbiana*
East Canton *Stark*
East Claridon *Geauga*
East Cleveland *Cuyahoga*
East Fultonham
   Muskingum
Eastlake *Lake*
East Liberty *Logan*
East Liverpool
   Columbiana
East Palestine *Columbiana*
East Rochester
   Columbiana
East Sparta *Stark*
East Springfield *Jefferson*
Eastview *Montgomery*
Eaton *Preble*
Eaton Estatus *Lorain*
Eden Park *Scioto*
Edgerton *Williams*
Edison *Morrow*
Edon *Williams*
Eldorado *Preble*
Elgin *Van Wert*
Elida *Allen*
Elkton *Columbiana*
Ellsworth *Mahoning*

Elmore *Ottawa*
Elmwood Place *Hamilton*
Elyria *Lorain*
Empire *Jefferson*
Englewood *Montgomery*
Enon *Clark*
Epworth Heights *Warren*
Etna *Licking*
Euclid *Cuyahoga*
Evansport *Defiance*
Evendale *Hamilton*
Excello *Butler*
Fairborn *Greene*
Fairpoint *Belmont*
Fairview *Guernsey*
Fairfax *Hamilton*
Fairfield *Butler*
Fairhope *Stark*
Fairlawn *Summit*
Fairport Harbour *Lake*
Farmdale *Trumbull*
Farmer *Defiance*
Farmersville *Montgomery*
Fayette *Fulton*
Fayetteville *Brown*
Feesburg *Brown*
Felicity *Clermont*
Findlay *Hancock*
Flat Rock *Seneca*
Fleming *Washington*
Fletcher *Miami*
Flushing *Belmont*
Fly *Monroe*
Forest *Hardin*
Forest Hills *Clark*
Forest Park *Hamilton*
Forestville *Hamilton*
Fort Jennings *Putnam*
Fort Loramie *Shelby*
Fort Shawnee *Allen*
Fort Recovery *Mercer*
Fort Seneca *Seneca*
Fostoria *Seneca*
Fowler *Trumbull*
Fox Chase *Franklin*
Frankfort *Ross*
Franklin *Warren*
Franklin Furnace *Scioto*
Frazeysburg *Muskingum*
Fredericksburg *Wayne*
Fredericktown *Knox*
Freeport *Harrison*
Fremont *Sandusky*
Fresno *Coshocton*
Friendship *Scioto*
Fruit Hill *Hamilton*
Fulton *Morrow*
Fultonham *Muskingum*
Gahanna *Franklin*
Galena *Delaware*
Galion *Crawford*
Gallipolis *Gallia*
Galloway *Franklin*
Gambier *Knox*
Garfield Heights *Cuyahoga*
Garrettsville *Portage*
Gates Mills *Cuyahoga*
Geneva *Ashtabula*
Geneva On The Lake
   Ashtabula
Genoa *Ottawa*
Georgetown *Brown*
Germantown *Montgomery*
Gettysburg *Darke*
Ghent *Summit*

Gibsonburg *Sandusky*
Girard *Trumbull*
Glandorf *Putnam*
Glencoe *Belmont*
Glendale *Hamilton*
Glenford *Perry*
Glenmont *Holmes*
Glenmoor *Columbiana*
Glouster *Athens*
Gnadenhutten *Tuscarawas*
Golf Manor *Hamilton*
Gordon *Darke*
Goshen *Clermont*
Grafton *Lorain*
Grand Rapids *Wood*
Grand River *Lake*
Grandview Heights
   Franklin
Granville *Licking*
Gratiot *Licking*
Gratis *Preble*
Graysville *Monroe*
Graytown *Ottawa*
Green Camp *Marion*
Greenfield *Highland*
Greenford *Mahoning*
Greenhills *Hamilton*
Greensburg *Summit*
Green Springs *Seneca*
Greentown *Stark*
Greenview *Montgomery*
Greenville *Darke*
Greenwich *Huron*
Groesbeck *Hamilton*
Grove City *Franklin*
Groveport *Franklin*
Grover Hill *Paulding*
Guysville *Athens*
Gypsum *Ottawa*
Hallsville *Ross*
Hamden *Vinton*
Hamersville *Brown*
Hamilton *Butler*
Hamilton Meadows
   Franklin
Hamler *Henry*
Hamlet *Clermont*
Hammondsville *Jefferson*
Hannibal *Monroe*
Hanover *Licking*
Hanoverton *Columbiana*
Harbor View *Lucas*
Harlem Springs *Carroll*
Harpster *Wyandot*
Harrisburg *Franklin*
Harrison *Hamilton*
Harrisville *Harrison*
Harrod *Allen*
Hartford *Trumbull*
Hartville *Stark*
Harveysburg *Warren*
Haskins *Wood*
Haverhill *Scioto*
Haviland *Paulding*
Haydenville *Hocking*
Hayesville *Ashland*
Heath *Licking*
Hebron *Licking*
Helena *Sandusky*
Hemlock *Perry*
Hicksville *Defiance*
Higginsport *Brown*
Highland *Highland*
Highland Heights
   Cuyahoga

Highland Park *Stark*
High Point *Hamilton*
Hilliard *Franklin*
Hillsboro *Highland*
Hinckley *Medina*
Hiram *Portage*
Hockingport *Athens*
Holgate *Henry*
Holland *Lucas*
Hollansburg *Darke*
Holloway *Belmont*
Holmesville *Holmes*
Homer *Licking*
Homerville *Medina*
Homewood *Butler*
Homeworth *Columbiana*
Hooven *Hamilton*
Hopedale *Harrison*
Hopewell *Muskingum*
Houston *Shelby*
Howard *Knox*
Hoytville *Wood*
Hubbard *Trumbull*
Huber Heights
   Montgomery
Huber Ridge *Franklin*
Hudson *Summit*
Huntsburg *Geauga*
Huntsville *Logan*
Huron *Erie*
Iberia *Morrow*
Independence *Cuyahoga*
Irondale *Jefferson*
Ironton *Lawrence*
Irwin *Union*
Isle Saint George *Ottawa*
Jackson *Jackson*
Jackson Center *Shelby*
Jacksontown *Licking*
Jacksonville *Athens*
Jacobsburg *Belmont*
Jamestown *Greene*
Jasper *Pike*
Jefferson *Ashtabula*
Jeffersonville *Fayette*
Jeromesville *Ashland*
Jerry City *Wood*
Jerusalem *Monroe*
Jewell *Defiance*
Jewett *Harrison*
Johnstown *Licking*
Junction City *Perry*
Kalida *Putnam*
Kansas *Seneca*
Keene *Coshocton*
Kelleys Island *Erie*
Kendall Heights *Stark*
Kensington *Columbiana*
Kent *Portage*
Kenton *Hardin*
Kenwood *Hamilton*
Kerr *Gallia*
Kettering *Montgomery*
Kettlersville *Shelby*
Kidron *Wayne*
Kilbourne *Delaware*
Killbuck *Holmes*
Kimbolton *Guernsey*
Kings Mills *Warren*
Kingston *Ross*
Kingsville *Ashtabula*
Kinsman *Trumbull*
Kipling *Guernsey*
Kipton *Lorain*
Kirby *Wyandot*

Kirkersville *Licking*
Kirtland *Lake*
Kitts Hill *Lawrence*
Kunkle *Williams*
Lacarne *Ottawa*
Lafferty *Belmont*
Lagrange *Lorain*
Laings *Monroe*
Lake Cable *Stark*
Lake Milton *Mahoning*
Lakemore *Summit*
Lakeside *Ottowa*
Lakeside-Marblehead
   Ottawa
Lakeview *Logan*
Lakeville *Holmes*
Lakewood *Cuyahoga*
Lancaster *Fairfield*
Langsville *Meigs*
Lansing *Belmont*
LaRue *Marion*
Latham *Pike*
Latty *Paulding*
Laura *Miami*
Laurel Ridge *Stark*
Laurelville *Hocking*
Leavittsburg *Trumbull*
Lebanon *Warren*
Leesburg *Highland*
Lees Creek *Clinton*
Leesville *Carroll*
Leetonia *Columbiana*
Leipsic *Putnam*
Lemoyne *Wood*
Lewisburg *Preble*
Lewis Center *Delaware*
Lewistown *Logan*
Lewisville *Monroe*
Lexington *Richland*
Liberty Center *Henry*
Lima *Allen*
Limaville *Stark*
Limecrest *Clark*
Lincoln Heights *Hamilton*
Lincoln Village *Franklin*
Lindsey *Sandusky*
Lisbon *Columbiana*
Litchfield *Medina*
Lithopolis *Fairfield*
Little Farms *Franklin*
Little Hocking *Washington*
Lockbourne *Franklin*
Lockland *Hamilton*
Lodi *Medina*
Logan *Hocking*
London *Madison*
Londonderry *Ross*
Long Bottom *Meigs*
Lorain *Lorain*
Lordstown *Trumbull*
Lore City *Guernsey*
Loudonville *Ashland*
Louisville *Stark*
Loveland *Hamilton*
Loveland Park *Warren*
Lowell *Washington*
Lowellville *Mahoning*
Lower Salem *Washington*
Lucas *Richland*
Lucasville *Scioto*
Luckey *Wood*
Ludlow Falls *Miami*
Lynchburg *Highland*
Lyndhurst *Cuyahoga*
Lynx *Adams*

Lyons *Fulton*
McArthur *Vinton*
McClure *Henry*
McComb *Hancock*
McConnelsville *Morgan*
McCutchenville *Wyandot*
McDermott *Scioto*
McDonald *Trumbull*
McGuffey *Hardin*
McKinley Heights
   Trumbull
Macedonia *Summit*
Mack *Hamilton*
Macksburg *Washington*
Madeira *Hamilton*
Madison *Lake*
Madison On The Lake
   Lake
Magnetic Springs *Union*
Magnolia *Stark*
Maineville *Warren*
Malaga *Monroe*
Malinta *Henry*
Malta *Morgan*
Malvern *Carroll*
Manchester *Adams*
Mansfield *Richland*
Mantua *Portage*
Maple Heights *Cuyahoga*
Maplewood *Shelby*
Marathon *Clermont*
Marble Cliff *Franklin*
Marengo *Morrow*
Maria Stein *Mercer*
Mariemont *Hamilton*
Marietta *Washington*
Marion *Marion*
Mark Center *Defiance*
Marshallville *Wayne*
Martel *Marion*
Martin *Ottawa*
Martinsburg *Knox*
Martins Ferry *Belmont*
Martinsville *Clinton*
Marysville *Union*
Mason *Warren*
Massillon *Stark*
Masury *Trumbull*
Mauds *Butler*
Maumee *Lucas*
Maximo *Stark*
Mayfield *Cuyahoga*
Mayfield Heights
   Cuyahoga
Maynard *Belmont*
Mechanicsburg *Champaign*
Mechanicstown *Carroll*
Medina *Medina*
Medway *Clark*
Melmore *Seneca*
Melrose *Paulding*
Mendon *Mercer*
Mentor *Lake*
Mentor On The Lake *Lake*
Mesopotamia *Trumbull*
Metamora *Fulton*
Miamisburg *Montgomery*
Miamitown *Hamilton*
Miamiville *Clermont*
Middle Bass *Ottawa*
Middlebranch *Stark*
Middleburg *Logan*
Middleburg Heights
   Cuyahoga
Middlefield *Geauga*

Middle Point *Van Wert*
Middleport *Meigs*
Middletown *Butler*
Midland *Clinton*
Midvale *Tuscarawas*
Milan *Erie*
Milford *Clermont*
Milford Center *Union*
Millbury *Wood*
Milledgeville *Fayette*
Miller City *Putnam*
Millersburg *Holmes*
Millersport *Fairfield*
Millfield *Athens*
Millville *Butler*
Milton Center *Wood*
Mineral City *Tuscarawas*
Mineral Ridge *Trumbull*
Minerva *Stark*
Minerva Park *Franklin*
Minford *Scioto*
Mingo *Champaign*
Mingo Junction *Jefferson*
Minster *Auglaize*
Mogadore *Summit*
Monclova *Lucas*
Monfort Heights *Hamilton*
Monroe *Butler*
Monroeville *Huron*
Montezuma *Mercer*
Montgomery *Hamilton*
Montpelier *Williams*
Montville *Geauga*
Moorefield *Harrison*
Moraine *Montgomery*
Moreland Hills *Cuyahoga*
Morral *Marion*
Morristown *Belmont*
Morrow *Warren*
Moscow *Clermont*
Mount Blanchard *Hancock*
Mount Carmel *Clermont*
Mount Cory *Hancock*
Mount Eaton *Wayne*
Mount Gilead *Morrow*
Mount Healthy *Hamilton*
Mount Hope *Holmes*
Mount Liberty *Knox*
Mount Orab *Brown*
Mount Perry *Perry*
Mount Pleasant *Jefferson*
Mount Repose *Clermont*
Mount Saint Joseph
   Hamilton
Mount Sterling *Madison*
Mount Vernon *Knox*
Mount Victory *Hardin*
Mowrystown *Highland*
Moxahala *Perry*
Mulberry *Clermont*
Munroe Falls *Summit*
Murlin Heights
   Montgomery
Murray City *Hocking*
Nankin *Ashland*
Napoleon *Henry*
Nashport *Muskingum*
Nashville *Holmes*
Navarre *Stark*
Neapolis *Lucas*
Neffs *Belmont*
Negley *Columbiana*
Nelsonville *Athens*
Nevada *Wyandot*
Neville *Clermont*

New Albany *Franklin*
Newark *Licking*
New Athens *Harrison*
New Bavaria *Henry*
New Bloomington *Marion*
New Boston *Scioto*
New Bremen *Auglaize*
Newburgh Heights
  Cuyahoga
Newbury *Geauga*
New Carlisle *Clark*
Newcomerstown
  Tuscarawas
New Concord *Muskingum*
New Hampshire *Auglaize*
New Haven *Huron*
New Holland *Pickaway*
New Knoxville *Auglaize*
New Lebanon *Montgomery*
New Lexington *Perry*
New London *Huron*
New Lyme *Ashtabula*
New Madison *Darke*
New Marshfield *Athens*
New Matamoras
  Washington
New Miami *Butler*
New Middletown
  Mahoning
New Paris *Preble*
New Philadelphia
  Tuscarawas
New Plymouth *Vinton*
Newport *Washington*
New Richmond *Clermont*
New Riegel *Seneca*
New Rumley *Harrison*
New Springfield *Mahoning*
New Straitsville *Perry*
Newton Falls *Trumbull*
Newtonsville *Clermont*
Newtown *Hamilton*
New Vienna *Clinton*
New Washington *Crawford*
New Waterford
  Columbiana
Ney *Defiance*
Niles *Trumbull*
North Baltimore *Wood*
North Bend *Hamilton*
North Benton *Mahoning*
North Bloomfield *Trumbull*
Northbrook *Hamilton*
North Canton *Stark*
North Fairfield *Huron*
Northfield *Summit*
Northfield Center *Stark*
North Georgetown
  Columbiana
North Hampton *Clark*
North Industry *Stark*
North Jackson *Mahoning*
North Kingsville *Ashtabula*
North Lawrence *Stark*
North Lewisburg
  Champaign
North Lima *Mahoning*
North Olmsted *Cuyahoga*
North Perry *Lake*
North Robinson *Crawford*
North Star *Darke*
Northridge *Clark*
Northup *Gallia*
Norton *Summit*
Norwalk *Huron*

Norwich *Muskingum*
Norwood *Hamilton*
Nova *Ashland*
Novelty *Geauga*
Oak Harbor *Ottawa*
Oak Hill *Jackson*
Oakwood *Paulding*
Oberlin *Lorain*
Obetz *Butler*
Oceola *Crawford*
Ohio City *Van Wert*
Okeana *Butler*
Okolona *Henry*
Old Fort *Seneca*
Old Washington *Guernsey*
Olmsted Falls *Cuyahoga*
Oneida *Butler*
Ontario *Richland*
Orange *Cuyahoga*
Orangeville *Trumbull*
Oregon *Lucas*
Oregonia *Warren*
Orient *Pickaway*
Orrville *Wayne*
Orwell *Ashtabula*
Osgood *Darke*
Ostrander *Delaware*
Ottawa *Putnam*
Ottawa Hills *Lucas*
Ottoville *Putnam*
Otway *Scioto*
Overpeck *Butler*
Owensville *Clermont*
Oxford *Butler*
Page Manor *Montgomery*
Painesville *Lake*
Painesville On-The-Lake
  Lake
Palestine *Darke*
Pandora *Putnam*
Parma *Cuyahoga*
Parma Heights *Cuyahoga*
Paris *Stark*
Parkman *Geauga*
Pataskala *Licking*
Patriot *Gallia*
Paulding *Paulding*
Payne *Paulding*
Pedro *Lawrence*
Peebles *Adams*
Pemberton *Shelby*
Pemberville *Wood*
Peninsula *Summit*
Pennsville *Morgan*
Pepper Pike *Cuyahoga*
Perry *Lake*
Perry Heights *Stark*
Perrysburg *Wood*
Perrysville *Ashland*
Petersburg *Mahoning*
Pettisville *Fulton*
Phillipsburg *Montgomery*
Philo *Muskingum*
Pickerington *Fairfield*
Piedmont *Harrison*
Pierpont *Ashtabula*
Piketon *Pike*
Piney Fork *Jefferson*
Pioneer *Williams*
Piqua *Miami*
Pisgah *Butler*
Pitsburg *Darke*
Plain City *Madison*
Plainfield *Coshocton*
Pleasant City *Guernsey*

Pleasant Hill *Miami*
Pleasant Plain *Warren*
Pleasant Run Farms
  Hamilton
Pleasant Valley *Ross*
Pleasantville *Fairfield*
Plymouth *Richland*
Poland *Mahoning*
Polk *Ashland*
Pomeroy *Meigs*
Portage *Wood*
Portage Lakes *Summit*
Port Clinton *Ottawa*
Port Jefferson *Shelby*
Portland *Meigs*
Portsmouth *Scioto*
Port Washington
  Tuscarawas
Port William *Clinton*
Potsdam *Miami*
Powell *Delaware*
Powhatan Point *Belmont*
Proctorville *Lawrence*
Prospect *Marion*
Put-In- Bay *Ottawa*
Quaker City *Guernsey*
Queen Acres *Butler*
Quincy *Logan*
Racine *Meigs*
Radcliff *Vinton*
Radnor *Delaware*
Randolph *Portage*
Rarden *Scioto*
Ravenna *Portage*
Rawson *Hancock*
Ray *Vinton*
Rayland *Jefferson*
Raymond *Union*
Reading *Hamilton*
Redbird *Lake*
Reedsville *Meigs*
Reedurban *Stark*
Reesville *Clinton*
Remonderville *Summit*
Reno *Washington*
Reno Beach *Lucas*
Rensselaer *Hamilton*
Republic *Seneca*
Reynoldsburg *Franklin*
Richfield *Summit*
Richmond *Jefferson*
Richmond Dale *Ross*
Richmond Heights
  Cuyahoga
Richwood *Union*
Ridgeville Corners *Henry*
Ridgeway *Hardin*
Ridgewood Heights
  Montgomery
Rinard Mills *Monroe*
Rio Grande *Gallia*
Ripley *Brown*
Risingsun *Wood*
Rittman *Wayne*
Riverside *Montgomery*
Robertsville *Stark*
Rockbridge *Hocking*
Rock Camp *Lawrence*
Rock Creek *Ashtabula*
Rockford *Mercer*
Rocky Ridge *Ottawa*
Rocky River *Cuyahoga*
Rogers *Columbiana*
Rome *Ashtabula*
Rootstown *Portage*

Roseville *Muskingum*
Rosewood *Champaign*
Ross *Butler*
Rossburg *Darke*
Rossford *Wood*
Roundhead *Hardin*
Rudolph *Wood*
Rushsylvania *Logan*
Rushville *Fairfield*
Russells Point *Logan*
Russellville *Brown*
Russia *Shelby*
Rutland *Meigs*
Sabina *Clinton*
Sagamore Hills *Summit*
Sahara Sands *Stark*
Saint Bernard *Hamilton*
Saint Clairsville *Belmont*
Saint Henry *Mercer*
Saint Johns *Auglaize*
Saint Louisville *Licking*
Saint Marys *Auglaize*
Saint Paris *Champaign*
Salem *Columbiana*
Salesville *Guernsey*
Salineville *Columbiana*
Sandusky *Erie*
Sandyville *Tuscarawas*
Sarahsville *Noble*
Sardinia *Brown*
Sardis *Monroe*
Savannah *Ashland*
Sawyerwood *Summit*
Scio *Harrison*
Scioto Furnace *Scioto*
Sciotodale *Scioto*
Scott *Van Wert*
Scottown *Lawrence*
Seaman *Adams*
Sebring *Mahoning*
Sedalia *Madison*
Senecaville *Guernsey*
Seven Hills *Cuyahoga*
Seven Mile *Butler*
Seville *Medina*
Shade *Athens*
Shadyside *Belmont*
Shaker Heights *Cuyahoga*
Shandon *Butler*
Sharon Center *Medina*
Sharonville *Hamilton*
Shauck *Morrow*
Shawnee *Perry*
Sheffield *Lorain*
Sheffield Lake *Lorain*
Shelby *Richland*
Sherrodsville *Carroll*
Sherwood *Defiance*
Shiloh *Richland*
Short Creek *Harrison*
Shreve *Wayne*
Sidney *Shelby*
Silver Lake *Summit*
Singing Hills *Montgomery*
Sinking Spring *Highland*
Skyline Acres *Hamilton*
Smithfield *Jefferson*
Smithville *Wayne*
Solon *Cuyahoga*
Somerdale *Tuscarawas*
Somerset *Perry*
Somerton *Belmont*
Somerville *Butler*
Sonora *Muskingum*
South Amherst *Lorain*

South Bloomfield *Pickaway*
South Charleston *Clark*
South Euclid *Cuyahoga*
Southington *Trumbull*
South Lebanon *Warren*
South Mount Vernon *Knox*
South Point *Lawrence*
South Russell *Geauga*
South Salem *Ross*
South Solon *Madison*
South Vienna *Clark*
South Webster *Scioto*
South West Hubbard *Trumbull*
South Zainesville *Muskingum*
Sparta *Morrow*
Spencer *Medina*
Spencerville *Allen*
Springboro *Warren*
Springdale *Hamilton*
Springfield *Clark*
Spring Valley *Greene*
Stafford *Monroe*
Sterling *Wayne*
Steubenville *Jefferson*
Stewart *Athens*
Stewartsville *Belmont*
Stillwater *Tuscarawas*
Stockdale *Pike*
Stockport *Morgan*
Stone Creek *Tuscarawas*
Stony Ridge *Wood*
Stout *Adams*
Stoutsville *Fairfield*
Strasburg *Tuscarawas*
Stratton *Jefferson*
Streetsboro *Portage*
Struthers *Mahoning*
Stryker *Williams*
Sugarcreek *Tuscarawas*
Sugar Grove *Fairfield*
Sullivan *Ashland*
Sulphur Springs *Crawford*
Summerfield *Noble*
Summerside Estates *Clermont*
Summit Station *Licking*
Summitville *Columbiana*
Sunbury *Delaware*
Sunnyland *Clark*
Sun Valley *Franklin*
Surrey Hill *Trumbull*
Swanton *Fulton*
Sycamore *Wyandot*
Sycamore Valley *Monroe*
Sylvania *Lucas*
Syracuse *Meigs*
Tallmadge *Summit*
Tarlton *Pickaway*
Terrace Park *Hamilton*
The Plains *Athens*
The Village Of Indian Hill *Hamilton*
Thompson *Geauga*
Thornville *Perry*
Thurman *Gallia*
Thurston *Fairfield*
Tiffin *Seneca*
Tiltonsville *Jefferson*
Timberlake *Lake*
Tipp City *Miami*
Tippecanoe *Harrison*
Tiro *Crawford*

Toledo *Lucas*
Tontogany *Wood*
Torch *Athens*
Toronto *Jefferson*
Tremont City *Clark*
Trenton *Butler*
Trimble *Athens*
Trinway *Muskingum*
Trotwood *Montgomery*
Troy *Miami*
Tuppers Plains *Meigs*
Turpin Hills *Hamilton*
Tuscarawas *Tuscarawas*
Twinsburg *Summit*
Uhrichsville *Tuscarawas*
Union *Montgomery*
Union City *Darke*
Union Furnace *Hocking*
Unionport *Jefferson*
Uniontown *Stark*
Unionville *Ashtabula*
Unionville Center *Union*
Uniopolis *Auglaize*
University Heights *Cuyahoga*
University View *Franklin*
Upper Arlington *Franklin*
Upper Sandusky *Wyandot*
Urbana *Champaign*
Urbancrest *Franklin*
Utica *Licking*
Valley City *Medina*
Valley View *Cuyahoga*
Valleyview *Franklin*
Van Buren *Hancock*
Vandalia *Montgomery*
Vanlue *Hancock*
Van Wert *Van Wert*
Vaughnsville *Putnam*
Venedocia *Van Wert*
Venice Heights *Trumbull*
Vermilion *Erie*
Verona *Preble*
Versailles *Darke*
Vickery *Sandusky*
Vienna *Trumbull*
Viking Village *Clermont*
Villa Nova *Auglaize*
Vincent *Washington*
Vinton *Gallia*
Wadsworth *Medina*
Wakefield *Pike*
Wakeman *Huron*
Walbridge *Wood*
Waldo *Marion*
Walhonding *Coshocton*
Walnut Creek *Holmes*
Walton Hills *Cuyahoga*
Wapakoneta *Auglaize*
Warner *Washington*
Warnock *Belmont*
Warren *Trumbull*
Warrensville Heights *Cuyahoga*
Warsaw *Coshocton*
Washington Court House *Fayette*
Washingtonville *Columbiana*
Waterford *Washington*
Waterloo *Lawrence*
Watertown *Washington*
Waterville *Lucas*
Wauseon *Fulton*
Waverly *Pike*

Wayland *Portage*
Wayne *Wood*
Wayne Lakes *Darke*
Waynesburg *Stark*
Waynesfield *Auglaize*
Waynesville *Warren*
Wellington *Lorain*
Wellston *Jackson*
Wellsville *Columbiana*
West Alexandria *Preble*
West Carrollton City *Montgomery*
West Chester *Butler*
West Elkton *Preble*
Westerville *Franklin*
West Farmington *Trumbull*
Westfield Center *Medina*
West Jefferson *Madison*
West Lafayette *Coshocton*
Westlake *Cuyahoga*
West Liberty *Logan*
West Manchester *Preble*
West Mansfield *Logan*
West Millgrove *Wood*
West Milton *Miami*
Weston *Wood*
West Point *Columbiana*
West Portsmouth *Scioto*
West Rushville *Fairfield*
West Salem *Wayne*
West Union *Adams*
West Unity *Williams*
Westview *Lorain*
Westville *Champaign*
Wharton *Wyandot*
Wheelersburg *Scioto*
Whipple *Washington*
White Cottage *Muskingum*
Whitehall *Franklin*
Whitehouse *Lucas*
Wickliffe *Lake*
Wilberforce *Greene*
Wilkesville *Vinton*
Willard *Huron*
Williamsburg *Clermont*
Williamsdale *Butler*
Williamsfield *Ashtabula*
Williamsport *Pickaway*
Williamstown *Hancock*
Williston *Ottawa*
Willoughby *Lake*
Willoughby Hills *Lake*
Willow Wood *Lawrence*
Willshire *Van Wert*
Wilmington *Clinton*
Wilmot *Stark*
Winchester *Adams*
Windham *Portage*
Windsor *Ashtabula*
Winesburg *Holmes*
Wingett Run *Washington*
Winona *Columbiana*
Wintersville *Jefferson*
Withamsville *Clermont*
Wolf Run *Jefferson*
Woodlawn *Hamilton*
Woodmere *Cuyahoga*
Woodsfield *Monroe*
Woodstock *Champaign*
Woodville *Sandusky*
Woodworth *Mahoning*
Wooster *Wayne*
Wooster Heights *Richland*
Worthington *Franklin*
Wren *Van Wert*

Wyoming *Hamilton*
Xenia *Greene*
Yellow Springs *Greene*
Yorkshire *Darke*
Yorkville *Jefferson*
Youngstown *Mahoning*
Zaleski *Vinton*
Zanesfield *Logan*
Zanesville *Muskingum*
Zoar *Tuscarawas*

Oklahoma

Both the Oklahoma State Bureau of Investigation and all seventy seven (77) of the state's counties make criminal records available for employment screening purposes. Seventy four (74) counties reported that requests may be made by phone and/or mail. Claims for $2,500 and more are filed in civil court while claims for less than $2,500 are filed in small claims court.

For more information or for offices not listed, contact the state's information hot line at (405) 521-1601 or (800) 522-8555 (in state).

Driving Records

Department of Public Safety
Driving Records
PO Box 11415
Oklahoma City, OK 73136
(405) 425-2262
Driving records are available by mail. $5 fee per request. Written request must include job applicant's full name, date of birth and license number. Make check payable to Department of Public Safety.

Worker's Compensation Records

Worker's Compensation Court
Records Search
1915 N. Stiles
Oklahoma City, OK 73105
(405) 557-7640
Worker's compensation information available by phone or mail. Request must include subject's full name and SSN. There is no fee. A signed release is not required.

Vital Statistics

Vital Records Section
State Department of Health
PO Box 53551
Oklahoma City, OK 73152
(405) 271-4040 or 271-5108
Birth and death records are available for $5.00 each. State office has records since October 1908. An employer can obtain records with a written release. Make certified check or money order payable to Oklahoma State Health Department.

Department of Education

State Department of Education
Professional Standards
2500 North Lincoln Blvd.
Room 211
Oklahoma City, OK 73105-4599
(405) 521-3337
Field of certification, effective date, expiration date are available by mail or phone. Include name and SSN.

Medical Licensing

Board of Medical Licensing
PO Box 18256
Oklahoma City, OK 73154
(405) 848-2189
Will confirm licenses for MDs by mail or phone. $20.00 fee. For licenses not mentioned, contact the above office.

Oklahoma State Board of Osteopathic Examiners
4848 N. Linclon, #100
Oklahoma City, OK 73105
(405) 528-8625
Will confirm license for DOs by mail or phone. $10.00 fee. No fee for phone inquiries.

Oklahoma Board of Nurse Registration & Nursing Education
2915 N. Classen Blvd., Suite 524
Oklahoma City, OK 73106
(405) 525-2076
Will confirm license by phone. No fee. Include name, license number, if available.

Bar Association

Oklahoma State Bar Association
PO Box 53036
Oklahoma City, OK 73105
(405) 524-2365
Will confirm license by phone. No fee. Include name.

Accountancy Board

Oklahoma State Board of Accountancy
4545 N. Lincoln Blvd., Suite 165
Oklahoma City, OK 73105-4313
(405) 521-2387
Will confirm license by phone. No fee. Include name.

Securities Commission

Department of Securities
PO Box 53595
2401 N. Lincoln Blvd., Room 408
Oklahoma City, OK 73152
(405) 521-2451
Will confirm license by phone. No fee. Include name and SSN.

Secretary of State

Office of Secretary of State
Corporation Division
101 State Capitol
Oklahoma City, OK 73105
(405) 521-3911
(900) 820-2424
Service agent and address, date incorporated, standing with tax commission, trade names are available by mail or phone. $5.00 search fee by mail. Money order or cashier's check will expedite process. $3.00 search fee by phone when dialing 900-820-2424. Contact the above office for additional information.

Criminal Records

State Repository

Oklahoma State Bureau of Investigation
Criminal History Information
PO Box 11497
Oklahoma City, OK 73136
(405) 427-5421
Criminal records are available by mail only. All requests must include subject's full name, date of birth, SSN, race, sex and SASE. There is a $10.00 fee. Make money order or company check payable to O.S.B.I. Information released includes both conviction and arrest data. Turnaround time is normally 24 to 48 hours plus mail time.

Adair County

Adair County Courthouse, Criminal Records
Court Clerk
Stillwell, OK 74960
(918) 696-7633

Felony and misdemeanor records are available by mail. No release necessary. $5.00 search fee. $1.00 fee for first copy, $.50 each additional copy. $.50 for certification. Search information required: name, date of birth, years to search, SASE.

Civil records are available by mail. No release necessary. $5.00 search fee. $1.00 fee for first copy, $.50 each additional copy. $.50 for certification. Search information required: name, date of birth, years to search, SASE. Specify plaintiff or defendant.

Alfalfa County

Court Clerk, Criminal Records
Alfalfa County Courthouse
300 S. Grand
Cherokee, OK 73728
(405) 596-3523

Felony and misdemeanor records are available by mail. No release necessary. $5.00 search fee. $1.00 fee for first copy, $.50 per copy thereafter. $.50 for certification. Search information required: name, date of birth, years to search, SASE.

Civil records are available by mail. No release necessary. $5.00 search fee. $1.00 fee for first copy, $.50 each additional copy. $.50 for certification. Search information required: name, date of birth, years to search, SASE. Specify plaintiff or defendant.

Atoka County

Court Clerk, Criminal Records
Courthouse
200 E. Court Street
Atoka, OK 74525
(405) 889-3565

Felony and misdemeanor records are available by mail or phone. No release necessary. $5.00 search fee. $1.00 fee for first copy, $.50 each additional copy. $.50 for certification. Search information required: name, years to search.

Civil records are available by mail or phone. No release necessary. $5.00 search fee. $1.00 fee for first copy, $.50 each additional copy. $.50 for certification. Search information required: name, date of birth, years to search. Specify plaintiff or defendant.

Beaver County

Court Clerk, Criminal Records
PO Box 237
Beaver, OK 73932
(405) 625-3191

Felony and misdemeanor records are available by mail. No release necessary. No search fee. $1.00 fee for first copy, $.50 each additional copy. $.50 for certification. Search information required: name, SSN, date of birth.

Civil records are available by mail. No release necessary. No search fee. $1.00 fee for first copy, $.50 each additional copy. $.50 for certification. Search information required: name, date of birth, SSN, years to search. Specify plaintiff or defendant.

Beckham County

Court Clerk, Criminal Records
Beckham County
PO Box 520
Sayre, OK 73662
(405) 928-3330

Felony and misdemeanor records are available by mail or phone. No release necessary. No search fee. $1.00 fee for first copy, $.50 each additional copy. $.50 for certification. Search information required: name, years to search.

Civil records are available by mail or phone. No release necessary. No search fee. $1.00 fee for first copy, $.50 each additional copy. $.50 for certification. Search information required: name, date of birth, years to search. Specify plaintiff or defendant.

Blaine County

Court Clerk, Criminal Records
PO Box 399
Watonga, OK 73772
(405) 623-5970

Felony and misdemeanor records are available by mail. No release necessary. $5.00 search fee. $1.00 fee for first copy, $.50 each additional copy. $.50 for certification. Search information required: name, years to search.

Civil records are available by mail. No release necessary. $5.00 search fee. $1.00 fee for first copy, $.50 each additional copy. $.50 for certification. Search information required: name, date of birth, years to search. Specify plaintiff or defendant.

Bryan County

Court Clerk, Criminal Records
Courthouse,
4th and Evergreen, 3rd Floor
Durant, OK 74701
(405) 924-1446

Felony and misdemeanor records are available by mail. No release necessary. No search fee. $1.00 fee for first copy, $.50 each additional copy. $.50 for certification. Search information required: name, date of birth, years to search.

Civil records are available by mail. No release necessary. No search fee. $1.00 fee for first copy, $.50 each additional copy. $.50 for certification. Search information required: name, date of birth, years to search. Specify plaintiff or defendant.

Caddo County

Court Clerk, Criminal Records
PO Box 10
Anadarko, OK 73005
(405) 247-3393

Felony and misdemeanor records are available by mail. No release necessary. No search fee. $1.00 fee for first copy, $.50 each additional copy. $1.50 for first certification, $.50 each additional page. Search information required: name, date of birth, years to search, SASE.

Civil records are available by mail. No release necessary. No search fee. $1.00 fee for first copy, $.50 each additional copy. $1.50 for first certification, $.50 each additional page. Search information required: name, date of birth, years to search, SASE. Specify plaintiff or defendant.

Canadian County

Court Clerk, Criminal Records
PO Box 730
El Reno, OK 73036
(405) 262-1070 Extension 271

Felony and misdemeanor records are available by mail. No release necessary. $5.00 search fee. $1.00 fee for first copy, $.50 per copy thereafter, $.50 fee for certification. Search information required: name, years to search, case number, SASE.

Civil records are available by mail. No release necessary. $5.00 search fee. $1.00 fee for first copy, $.50 per copy thereafter, $.50 fee for certification. Search information required: name, date of birth, years to search, SASE. Specify plaintiff or defendant.

Carter County

Court Clerk, Criminal Records
PO Box 37
Ardmore, OK 73402
(405) 223-5253

Felony and misdemeanor records are available by mail. No release necessary. $5.00 search fee. $1.00 fee for first copy, $.50 per copy thereafter. Search information required: name, years to search, SASE.

Civil records are available by mail. No release necessary. $5.00 search fee. $1.00 fee for first copy, $.50 per copy thereafter. Search information required: name, date of birth, years to search. Specify plaintiff or defendant.

Cherokee County

Court Clerk, Criminal Records
Cherokee County Courthouse
213 W. Delaware, Room 300
Tahlequah, OK 74464
(918) 456-0691

Felony and misdemeanor records are available by mail or phone. No release necessary. No search fee. $.25 fee per copy. $1.00 for certification. Search information required: name, date of birth, years to search.

Civil records are available by mail. No release necessary. No search fee. $.25 fee per copy. $1.00 for certification. Search information required: name, date of birth, years to search. Specify plaintiff or defendant.

Choctaw County

Court Clerk, Criminal Records
Choctaw County Courthouse
300 East Duke
Hugo, OK 74743
(405) 326-3241

Felony and misdemeanor records are available by mail. A release is required. $5.00 search fee. $1.00 fee for first copy, $.50 each additional copy. $1.50 for first certification, $.50 each additional page. Search information required: name, date of birth, years to search, SASE.

Civil records are available by mail. A release is required. $5.00 search fee. $1.00 fee for first copy, $.50 each additional copy. $1.50 for first certification, $.50 each additional page. Search information required: name, date of birth, years to search, SASE. Specify plaintiff or defendant.

Cimarron County

Court Clerk, Criminal Records
PO Box 788
Boise City, OK 73933
(405) 544-2221

Felony and misdemeanor records are available by mail. No release necessary. No search fee. $1.00 fee for first copy, $.50 per copy thereafter. $.50 for certification. Search information required: name, years to search, and offense, if available.

Civil records are available by mail. No release necessary. No search fee. $1.00 fee for first copy, $.50 per copy thereafter. $.50 for certification. Search information required: name, date of birth, years to search. Specify plaintiff or defendant.

Cleveland County

Clerk's Office
200 S. Peters
Norman, OK 73069
(405) 321-6402 or 366-7174

Felony records are available by mail or by phone for requests from 1989 forward. Misdemeanor records are available in person only. No release necessary. No search fee. $1.00 fee for first copy, $.50 per copy thereafter. $.50 for certification. Search information required: full name, years to search.

Civil records are available by mail or phone. No release necessary. No search fee. $1.00 fee for first copy, $.50 per copy thereafter. $.50 for certification. Search information required: name, date of birth, years to search. Specify plaintiff or defendant.

Coal County

Court Clerk's Office, Criminal Records
3 N. Main
Coalgate, OK 74538
(405) 927-2281

Felony and misdemeanor records are available by mail. No release necessary. No search fee. $1.00 fee for first copy, $.50 per copy thereafter. $.50 for certification. Search information required: name, date of birth, years to search.

Civil records are available by mail. No release necessary. No search fee. $1.00 fee for first copy, $.50 per copy thereafter. $.50 for certification. Search information required: name, date of birth, years to search. Specify plaintiff or defendant.

Comanche County

District Court Clerk, Criminal Records
Comanche County
Room 504
Lawton, OK 73501
(405) 355-4017

Felony and misdemeanor records are available by mail. No release necessary. No search fee. $1.00 fee for first copy, $.50 per copy thereafter. $.50 for certification. Search information required: name, file number, or date of charge.

Civil records are available by mail. No release necessary. No search fee. $1.00 fee for first copy, $.50 per copy thereafter. $.50 for certification. Search information required: name, date of birth, years to search. Specify plaintiff or defendant.

Cotton County

Court Clerk's Office, Criminal Records
301 N. Broadway
Walters, OK 73572
(405) 875-3029

Felony and misdemeanor records are available by mail or phone. No release necessary. No search fee. $1.00 fee for first copy, $.50 per copy thereafter. $.50 for certification. Search information required: name, years to search.

Civil records are available by mail. No release necessary. No search fee. $1.00 fee for first copy, $.50 per copy thereafter. $.50 for certification. Search information required: name, date of birth, years to search. Specify plaintiff or defendant.

Craig County

Craig County Courthouse, Criminal Records
Court Clerk's Office
301 W. Canadian
Vinita, OK 74301
(918) 256-6451

Felony and misdemeanor records are available by mail. No release necessary. $5.00 search fee. $1.00 fee for first copy, $.50 per copy thereafter. $.50 for certification. Search information required: name, date of birth, years to search.

Civil records are available by mail. No release necessary. $5.00 search fee. $1.00 fee for first copy, $.50 per copy thereafter. $.50 for certification. Search information required: name, date of birth, years to search. Specify plaintiff or defendant.

Creek County

Court Clerk's Office, Criminal Records
PO Box 1410
Sapulpa, OK 74067
(918) 227-2525

Felony and misdemeanor records are available in person only. See Oklahoma state repository for additional information.

Civil records are available in person only. See Oklahoma state repository for additional information.

Custer County

Court Clerk's Office, Criminal Records
PO Box D
Arapaho, OK 73620
(405) 323-3233

Felony and misdemeanor records are available by mail. No release necessary. $5.00 search fee. $1.00 fee for first copy, $.50 per copy thereafter. $.50 for certification. Search information required: name, date of birth, SSN, years to search.

Civil records are available by mail. No release necessary. $5.00 search fee. $1.00 fee for first copy, $.50 per copy thereafter. $.50 for certification. Search information required: name, date of birth, years to search. Specify plaintiff or defendant.

Delaware County

Court Clerk, Criminal Records
Delaware County
Box 407
Jay, OK 74346
(918) 253-4420

Felony and misdemeanor records are available by mail. No release necessary. $5.00 search fee. $.50 for certification. Make check payable to Court Clerk Office. Search information required: name, years to search.

Civil records are available by mail. No release necessary. No search fee. $.50 for certification. Search information required: name, date of birth, years to search. Specify plaintiff or defendant.

Dewey County

Court Clerk, Criminal Records
PO Box 278
Taloga, OK 73667
(405) 328-5521

Felony and misdemeanor records are available by mail or phone. No release necessary. No search fee. $1.00 fee for first copy, $.50 per copy thereafter. $.50 for certification. Search information required: name, years to search.

Civil records are available by mail or phone. No release necessary. No search fee. $1.00 fee for first copy, $.50 per copy thereafter. $.50 for certification. Search information required: name, date of birth, years to search. Specify plaintiff or defendant.

Ellis County

Court Clerk, Criminal Records
PO Box 217
Arnette, OK 73832
(405) 885-7255

Felony and misdemeanor records are available by mail or phone. No release necessary. No search fee. $1.00 fee for first copy, $.50 per copy thereafter. $.50 for certification. Search information required: name.

Civil records are available by mail or phone. No release necessary. No search fee. $1.00 fee for first copy, $.50 per copy thereafter. $.50 for certification. Search information required: name, date of birth, years to search. Specify plaintiff or defendant.

Garfield County

Court Clerk, Criminal Records
Garfield County
PO Box 3340
Enid, OK 73702
(405) 237-0232

Felony and misdemeanor records are available by mail. No release necessary. $5.00 search fee. $1.00 fee for first copy, $.50 per copy thereafter. $.50 for certification. Make check payable to Court Clerk. Search information required: name, years to search, type of case.

Civil records are available by mail. No release necessary. $5.00 search fee. $1.00 fee for first copy, $.50 per copy thereafter. $.50 for certification. Search information required: name, date of birth, years to search. Specify plaintiff or defendant.

Garvin County

Court Clerk, Criminal Records
PO Box 239
Pauls Valley, OK 73075
(405) 238-5596

Felony and misdemeanor records are available by mail or phone. A release is required. $5.00 search fee. $1.00 fee for first copy, $.50 per copy thereafter. $.50 for certification. Search information required: name, date of birth, years to search, SASE.

Civil records are available by mail. A release is required. $5.00 search fee. $1.00 fee for first copy, $.50 per copy thereafter. $.50 for certification. Search information required: name, date of birth, years to search, SASE. Specify plaintiff or defendant.

Grady County

Court Clerk, Criminal Records
PO Box 605
Chickasha, OK 73023
(405) 224-7388 Extension 349

Felony and misdemeanor records are available by mail. No release necessary. $20.00 fee per record search. $1.00 fee for first copy, $.50 per copy thereafter. $.50 for certification. Certified check only, payable to Court Clerk. Search information required: name, date of birth, years to search, SSN.

Civil records are available by mail. No release necessary. $20.00 search fee. $1.00 fee for first copy, $.50 per copy thereafter. $.50 for certification. Search information required: name, date of birth, SSN, years to search. Specify plaintiff or defendant.

Grant County

Court Clerk, Criminal Records
Grant County Courthouse
Medford, OK 73759
(405) 395-2828

Felony and misdemeanor records are available by mail or phone. No release necessary. No search fee. $1.00 fee for first copy, $.50 per copy thereafter. $.50 for certification. Search information required: name, date of birth, years to search.

Civil records are available by mail or phone. No release necessary. No search fee. $1.00 fee for first copy, $.50 per copy thereafter. $.50 for certification. Search information required: name, date of birth, years to search. Specify plaintiff or defendant.

Greer County

Court Clerk, Criminal Records
PO Box 216
Mangum, OK 73554
(405) 782-3665

Felony and misdemeanor records are available by mail or phone. No release necessary. $5.00 search fee for first 15 minutes. $1.00 fee for first copy, $.50 per copy thereafter. $.50 for certification. Search information required: name.

Civil records are available by mail or phone. No release necessary. $5.00 search fee for first 15 minutes. $1.00 fee for first copy, $.50 per copy thereafter. $.50 for certification. Search information required: name, date of birth, years to search. Specify plaintiff or defendant.

Harmon County

Court Clerk, Criminal Records
Courthouse
114 W. Hollis
Hollis, OK 73550
(405) 688-3617

Felony and misdemeanor records are available by mail or phone. No release necessary. No search fee. $1.00 fee for first copy, $.50 per copy thereafter. $.50 for certification. Search information required: name, years to search.

Civil records are available by mail or phone. No release necessary. No search fee. $1.00 fee for first copy, $.50 per copy thereafter. $.50 for certification. Search information required: name, date of birth, years to search. Specify plaintiff or defendant.

Harper County

Harper County Court Clerk, Criminal Records
PO Box 347
Buffalo, OK 73834
(405) 735-2010

Felony and misdemeanor records are available by mail or phone. No release necessary. No search fee. $1.00 fee for first copy, $.50 per copy thereafter. $.50 for certification. Search information required: name, years to search, SASE.

Civil records are available by mail or phone. No release necessary. No search fee. $1.00 fee for first copy, $.50 per copy thereafter. $.50 for certification. Search information required: name, date of birth, years to search, SASE. Specify plaintiff or defendant.

Haskell County

Court Clerk, Criminal Records
Haskell County Courthouse
202 E. Main
Stigler, OK 74462
(918) 967-3323

Felony and misdemeanor records are available by mail. No release necessary. No search fee. $1.00 fee for first copy, $.50 per copy thereafter. $1.00 for certification. Search information required: name, years to search.

Civil records are available by mail. No release necessary. No search fee. $1.00 fee for first copy, $.50 per copy thereafter. $1.00 for certification. Search information required: name, date of birth, years to search. Specify plaintiff or defendant.

Hughes County

Court Clerk, Criminal Records
PO Box 32
Holdenville, OK 74848
(405) 379-3384

Felony and misdemeanor records are available by mail or phone. No release necessary. No search fee. $1.00 fee for first copy, $.50 per copy thereafter. $.50 for certification. Search information required: name, years to search.

Civil records are available by mail or phone. No release necessary. No search fee. $1.00 fee for first copy, $.50 per copy thereafter. $.50 for certification. Search information required: name, date of birth, years to search. Specify plaintiff or defendant.

Jackson County

County Court Clerk, Criminal Records
Jackson County Court House, Room 303
Altus, OK 73521
(405) 482-0448

Felony and misdemeanor records are available by mail. No release necessary. $5.00 search fee. $1.00 fee for first copy, $.50 per copy thereafter. $.50 for certification. Search information required: name, years to search.

Civil records are available by mail. No release necessary. $5.00 search fee. $1.00 fee for first copy, $.50 per copy thereafter. $.50 for certification. Search information required: name, date of birth, years to search. Specify plaintiff or defendant.

Jefferson County

Court Clerk, Criminal Records
220 N. Main, Room 302
Waurika, OK 73573
(405) 228-2961

Felony and misdemeanor records are available by mail. No release necessary. No search fee. $1.00 fee for first copy, $.50 per copy thereafter. $.50 for certification. Search information required: name.

Civil records are available by mail. No release necessary. No search fee. $1.00 fee for first copy, $.50 per copy thereafter. $.50 for certification. Search information required: name, date of birth, years to search. Specify plaintiff or defendant.

Johnston County

Court Clerk's Office, Criminal Records
Johnston County Courthouse
PO Box 218
Tishomingo, OK 73460
(405) 371-3281

Felony records are available by mail. No release necessary. No search fee. $1.00 fee for first copy, $.50 per copy thereafter. $.50 for certification. Search information required: name, years to search.

Civil records are available by mail. No release necessary. No search fee. $1.00 fee for first copy, $.50 per copy thereafter. $.50 for certification. Search information required: name, date of birth, years to search. Specify plaintiff or defendant.

Kay County

Kay County Court Clerk, Criminal Records
PO Box 428
Newkirk, OK 74647
(405) 362-3350

Felony and misdemeanor records are available by mail. No release necessary. $5.00 search fee. $1.00 fee for first copy, $.50 per copy thereafter. $.50 for certification. Make check payable to Court Clerk. Search information required: name, years to search.

Civil records are available by mail. No release necessary. $5.00 search fee. $1.00 fee for first copy, $.50 per copy thereafter. $.50 for certification. Search information required: name, date of birth, years to search. Specify plaintiff or defendant.

Kingfisher County

Court Clerk, Criminal Records
PO Box 328
Kingfisher, OK 73750
(405) 375-3813

Felony and misdemeanor records are available by mail or phone. No release necessary. No search fee. $1.00 fee for first copy, $.50 per copy thereafter. $.50 for certification. Search information required: name, years to search.

Civil records are available by mail or phone. No release necessary. No search fee. $1.00 fee for first copy, $.50 per copy thereafter. $.50 for certification. Search information required: name, date of birth, years to search. Specify plaintiff or defendant.

Kiowa County

Court Clerk, Criminal Records
PO Box 854
Hobart, OK 73651
(405) 726-5125

Felony and misdemeanor records are available by mail or phone. No release necessary. No search fee. $1.00 fee for first copy, $.50 per copy thereafter. $.50 for certification. Search information required: name, years to search.

Civil records are available by mail or phone. No release necessary. No search fee. $1.00 fee for first copy, $.50 per copy thereafter. $.50 for certification. Search information required: name, date of birth, years to search. Specify plaintiff or defendant.

Latimer County

Court Clerk, Criminal Records
109 N. Central, Room 202
Wilburton, OK 74578
(918) 465-2011

Felony and misdemeanor records are available by mail. No release necessary. $5.00 search fee. $1.00 fee for first copy, $.50 per copy thereafter. $.50 for certification. Search information required: name, years to search.

Civil records are available by mail. No release necessary. $5.00 search fee. $1.00 fee for first copy, $.50 per copy thereafter. $.50 for certification. Search information required: name, date of birth, years to search. Specify plaintiff or defendant.

Le Flore County

Court Clerk, Criminal Records
Le Flore County Courthouse, Rm. 14
100 South Broadway
Poteau, OK 74953
(918) 647-3181

Felony and misdemeanor records are available by mail. No release necessary. $5.00 search fee. $1.00 fee for first copy, $.50 per copy thereafter. $.50 for certification. Search information required: name, years to search.

Civil records are available by mail. No release necessary. $5.00 search fee. $1.00 fee for first copy, $.50 per copy thereafter. $.50 for certification. Search information required: name, date of birth, years to search. Specify plaintiff or defendant.

Lincoln County

Court Clerk, Criminal Records
PO Box 307
Chandler, OK 74834
(405) 258-1309

Felony and misdemeanor records are available by mail or phone. No release necessary. No search fee. $1.00 fee for first copy, $.50 per copy thereafter. $.50 for certification. Search information required: name, years to search.

Civil records are available by mail or phone. No release necessary. No search fee. $1.00 fee for first copy, $.50 per copy thereafter. $.50 for certification. Search information required: name, date of birth, years to search. Specify plaintiff or defendant.

Logan County

Court Clerk, Criminal Records
Logan County Courthouse
301 E. Harrison
Guthrie, OK 73044
(405) 282-0123

Felony and misdemeanor records are available by mail. No release necessary. $5.00 search fee. $1.00 fee for first copy, $.50 per copy thereafter. $.50 for certification. Make check payable to Court Clerk. Search information required: name, years to search.

Civil records are available by mail. No release necessary. $5.00 search fee. $1.00 fee for first copy, $.50 per copy thereafter. $.50 for certification. Search information required: name, date of birth, years to search. Specify plaintiff or defendant.

Love County

Court Clerk, Criminal Records
405 W. Main, Suite 201
Marietta, OK 73448
(405) 276-2235

Felony and misdemeanor records are available by mail or phone. No release necessary. No search fee. $1.00 fee for first copy, $.50 per copy thereafter. Search information required: name, years to search.

Civil records are available by mail or phone. No release necessary. No search fee. $1.00 fee for first copy, $.50 per copy thereafter. Search information required: name, date of birth, years to search. Specify plaintiff or defendant.

Major County

Office of Court Clerk, Criminal Records
Major County Courthouse
Fairview, OK 73737
(405) 227-4690 Extension 204

Felony and misdemeanor records are available by mail or phone. No release necessary. No search fee. $1.00 fee for first copy, $.50 per copy thereafter. $.50 for certification. Search information required: name, SSN, date of birth, sex, race, years to search, SASE.

Civil records are available by mail. No release necessary. No search fee. $1.00 fee for first copy, $.50 per copy thereafter. $.50 for certification. Search information required: name, date of birth, SSN, years to search, SASE. Specify plaintiff or defendant.

Marshall County

Marshall County Court Clerk, Criminal Records
PO Box 58
Madill, OK 73446
(405) 795-3278

Felony and misdemeanor records are available by mail or phone. No release necessary. No search fee. $1.00 fee for first copy, $.50 per copy thereafter. $.50 for certification. Search information required: name, years to search.

Civil records are available by mail or phone. No release necessary. No search fee. $1.00 fee for first copy, $.50 per copy thereafter. $.50 for certification. Search information required: name, date of birth, years to search. Specify plaintiff or defendant.

Mayes County

Mayes County Court Clerk, Criminal Records
PO Box 867
Pryor, OK 74362
(918) 825-2185

Felony and misdemeanor records are available by mail or phone. No release necessary. No search fee. $1.00 fee for first copy, $.50 per copy thereafter. $.50 for certification. Search information required: name, years to search. Court will provide disclaimer for requestor to sign.

Civil records are available by mail or phone. No release necessary. No search fee. $1.00 fee for first copy, $.50 per copy thereafter. $.50 for certification. Search information required: name, date of birth, years to search. Specify plaintiff or defendant. Court will provide disclaimer for requestor to sign.

McClain County

McClain County Court Clerk, Criminal Records
PO Box 631
Purcell, OK 73080
(405) 527-3221

Felony and misdemeanor records are available by mail or phone. No release necessary. $10.00 search fee for 5 years searched. $1.00 fee for first copy, $.50 per copy thereafter. $.50 for certification. Search information required: name, years to search.

Civil records are available by mail. No release necessary. $10.00 search fee for 5 years searched. $1.00 fee for first copy, $.50 per copy thereafter. $.50 for certification. Search information required: name, date of birth, years to search. Specify plaintiff or defendant.

McCurtain County

Court Clerk, Criminal Records
PO Box 1378
Idabel, OK 74745
(405) 286-3693

Felony and misdemeanor records are available by mail. A release if available. No search fee. $1.00 fee for first copy, $.50 per copy thereafter. $1.00 for first certification, $.50 each additional page. Search information required: name, date of birth, years to search.

Civil records are available by mail. A release if available. No search fee. $1.00 fee for first copy, $.50 per copy thereafter. $1.00 for first certification, $.50 each additional page. Search information required: name, date of birth, years to search. Specify plaintiff or defendant.

McIntosh County

McIntosh County Court Clerk,
Criminal Records
PO Box 426
Eufaula, OK 74432
(918) 689-2282

Felony and misdemeanor records are available by mail. No release necessary. $5.00 search fee. $1.00 fee for first copy, $.50 per copy thereafter. $.50 for certification. Search information required: name, years to search, specify type of search.

Civil records are available by mail. No release necessary. $5.00 search fee. $1.00 fee for first copy, $.50 per copy thereafter. $.50 for certification. Search information required: name, date of birth, years to search. Specify plaintiff or defendant.

Murray County

Murray County Court Clerk, Criminal
Records
PO Box 578
Sulphur, OK 73086
(405) 622-3223
Fax (405) 622-3804

Felony and misdemeanor records are available by mail. No release necessary. $5.00 search fee. $1.00 fee for first copy, $.50 per copy thereafter. $.50 for certification. Search information required: name, years to search.

Civil records are available by mail. No release necessary. $5.00 search fee. $1.00 fee for first copy, $.50 per copy thereafter. $.50 for certification. Search information required: name, date of birth, years to search. Specify plaintiff or defendant.

Muskogee County

Muskogee County Courthouse,
Criminal Records
PO Box 1350
Muskogee, OK 74402
(918) 682-7873

Felony and misdemeanor records are available by mail. No release necessary. No search fee. $1.00 fee for first copy, $.50 per copy thereafter. $.50 for certification. Search information required: name, years to search.

Civil records are available by mail. No release necessary. No search fee. $1.00 fee for first copy, $.50 per copy thereafter. $.50 for certification. Search information required: name, date of birth, years to search. Specify plaintiff or defendant.

Noble County

Court Clerk, Criminal Records
PO Box 793
Perry, OK 73077
(405) 336-5187

Felony and misdemeanor records are available by mail. No release necessary. $5.00 search fee. $1.00 fee for first copy, $.50 per copy thereafter. $.50 for certification. Search information required: name, years to search.

Civil records are available by mail. No release necessary. $5.00 search fee. $1.00 fee for first copy, $.50 per copy thereafter. $.50 for certification. Search information required: name, date of birth, years to search. Specify plaintiff or defendant.

Nowata County

Court Clerk, Criminal Records
229 N. Maple
Nowata, OK 74048
(918) 273-0127

Felony and misdemeanor records are available by mail or phone. No release necessary. No search fee. $1.00 fee for first copy, $.50 per copy thereafter. $.50 for certification. Search information required: name, years to search.

Civil records are available by mail or phone. No release necessary. No search fee. $1.00 fee for first copy, $.50 per copy thereafter. $.50 for certification. Search information required: name, date of birth, years to search. Specify plaintiff or defendant.

Okfuskee County

Okfuskee County Court Clerk,
Criminal Records
PO Box 30
Okemah, OK 74859
(918) 623-0525

Felony and misdemeanor records are available by mail. No release necessary. $5.00 search fee. $1.00 fee for first copy, $.50 per copy thereafter. $.50 for certification. Company checks only, payable to Clerk of Court. Search information required: name, years to search.

Civil records are available by mail. No release necessary. $5.00 search fee. $1.00 fee for first copy, $.50 per copy thereafter. $.50 for certification. Search information required: name, date of birth, years to search. Specify plaintiff or defendant.

Oklahoma County

Court Clerk, Criminal Records
Oklahoma County Office Building
320 Robert S. Kerr Street, Room 405
Oklahoma City, OK 73102
(405) 236-2727 Extension 1702

Felony and misdemeanor records are available by mail or phone. No release necessary. No search fee. $1.00 fee for first copy, $.50 per copy thereafter. $.50 for certification. Search information required: name, SSN, date of birth, years to search, SASE.

Civil records are available by mail. No release necessary. No search fee. $1.00 fee for first copy, $.50 per copy thereafter. $.50 for certification. Search information required: name, date of birth, years to search, SASE. Specify plaintiff or defendant.

Okmulgee County

Courthouse, Criminal Records
7th and Seminole
Okmulgee, OK 74447
(918) 7581219

Felony and misdemeanor records are available by mail. No release necessary. $5.00 search fee. $1.00 fee for first copy, $.50 per copy thereafter. $.50 for certification. Certified check only, payable to Court Clerk. Search information required: name, years to search.

Civil records are available by mail. No release necessary. $5.00 search fee. $1.00 fee for first copy, $.50 per copy thereafter. $.50 for certification. Search information required: name, date of birth, years to search. Specify plaintiff or defendant.

Osage County

Court Clerk, Criminal Records
Osage County Courthouse
600 Grandview, Room 301
Pawhuska, OK 74056-4253
(918) 287-4104

Felony and misdemeanor records are available by mail. No release necessary. $5.00 search fee. $1.00 fee for first copy, $.50 per copy thereafter. $.50 for certification. Certified check only, payable to Court Clerk Criminal Records. Search information required: name, date of birth, years to search.

Civil records are available by mail. No release necessary. $5.00 search fee. $1.00 fee for first copy, $.50 per copy thereafter. $.50 for certification. Search information required: name, date of birth, years to search. Specify plaintiff or defendant.

Ottawa County

Court Clerk, Criminal Records
102 E. Central Ave., Suite 300
Miami, OK 74354-7043
(918) 542-2801

Felony and misdemeanor records are available in person only. See Oklahoma state repository for additional information.

Civil records are available in person only. See Oklahoma state repository for additional information.

Pawnee County

Pawnee County Court Clerk, Criminal
Records
Courthouse
500 Harrison, Room 300
Pawnee, OK 74058
(918) 762-2547

Felony and misdemeanor records are available by mail or phone. No release necessary. $5.00 search fee. $1.00 fee for first copy, $.50 per copy thereafter. $.50 for certification. Search information required: name, years to search.

Civil records are available by mail or phone. No release necessary. $5.00 search fee. $1.00 fee for first copy, $.50 per copy thereafter. $.50 for certification. Search information required: name, date of birth, years to search. Specify plaintiff or defendant.

Payne County

Payne County Court Clerk, Criminal
Records
6th and Husband, Room 308
Payne County Courthouse
Stillwater, OK 74074
(405) 372-4774

Felony and misdemeanor records are available by mail. No release necessary. Search fee is $5.00 for any five years searched, $10.00 for any ten years searched, $15.00 for any eleven years or more searched. $1.00 fee for first copy, $.50 per copy thereafter. $.50 for certification. Search information required: name, date of birth, previous address, years to search.

Civil records are available by mail. No release necessary. Search fee is $5.00 for any five years searched, $10.00 for any ten years searched, $15.00 for any eleven years or more searched. $1.00 fee for first copy, $.50 per copy thereafter. $.50 for certification. Search information required: name, date of birth, years to search. Specify plaintiff or defendant.

Pittsburg County

Court Clerk, Criminal Records
PO Box 460
McAlester, OK 74502
(918) 423-4859

Felony and misdemeanor records are available by mail. No release necessary. No search fee. $1.00 fee for first copy, $.50 per copy thereafter. $.50 for certification. Search information required: name, years to search.

Civil records are available by mail. No release necessary. No search fee. $1.00 fee for first copy, $.50 per copy thereafter. $.50 for certification. Search information required: name, date of birth, years to search. Specify plaintiff or defendant.

Pontotoc County

Court Clerk, Criminal Records
PO Box 427
Ada, OK 74820
(405) 332-5763

Felony and misdemeanor records are available by mail or phone. No release necessary. No search fee. $1.00 fee for first copy, $.50 per copy thereafter. $.50 for certification. Search information required: name, date of birth.

Civil records are available by mail. No release necessary. No search fee. $1.00 fee for first copy, $.50 per copy thereafter. $.50 for certification. Search information required: name, date of birth, years to search. Specify plaintiff or defendant.

Pottawatomie County

Court Clerk, Criminal Records
325 N. Broadway
Shawnee, OK 74801
(405) 273-3624

Felony and misdemeanor records are available by mail. No release necessary. $5.00 search fee. $1.00 fee for first copy, $.50 per copy thereafter. $.50 for certification. Search information required: name.

Civil records are available by mail. No release necessary. $5.00 search fee. $1.00 fee for first copy, $.50 per copy thereafter. $.50 for certification. Search information required: name, date of birth, years to search. Specify plaintiff or defendant.

Pushmataha County

Court Clerk
Courthouse, Criminal Records
Antlers, OK 74523
(405) 298-2274

Felony and misdemeanor records are available by mail or phone. No release necessary. No search fee. $1.00 fee for first copy, $.50 per copy thereafter. $.50 for certification. Search information required: name, years to search.

Civil records are available by mail or phone. No release necessary. No search fee. $1.00 fee for first copy, $.50 per copy thereafter. $11.50 for certification. Search information required: name, date of birth, years to search. Specify plaintiff or defendant.

Roger Mills County

Court Clerk, Criminal Records
PO Box 409
Cheyenne, OK 73628
(405) 497-3361

Felony and misdemeanor records are available by mail. No release necessary. No search fee. $1.00 fee for first copy, $.50 per copy thereafter. $.50 for certification. Search information required: name, years to search.

Civil records are available by mail. No release necessary. No search fee. $1.00 fee for first copy, $.50 per copy thereafter. $.50 for certification. Search information required: name, date of birth, years to search. Specify plaintiff or defendant.

Rogers County

Court Clerk, Criminal Records
PO Box 839
Claremore, OK 74018
(918) 341-5711

Felony and misdemeanor records are available from 1987 forward by mail. Prior to 1987, may search in person. No release necessary. $5.00 search fee. $1.00 fee for first copy, $.50 per copy thereafter. $.50 for certification. Certified check only, payable to Court Clerk. Search information required: name, years to search.

Civil records are available from 1987 forward by mail. Prior to 1987, may search in person. No release necessary. $5.00 search fee. $1.00 fee for first copy, $.50 per copy thereafter. $.50 for certification. Search information required: name, date of birth, years to search. Specify plaintiff or defendant.

Seminole County

Court Clerk, Criminal Records
PO Box 130
Wewoka, OK 74884
(405) 257-6236

Felony and misdemeanor records are available by mail or phone. No release necessary. $5.00 search fee. $1.00 fee for first copy, $.50 per copy thereafter. $.50 for certification. Search information required: name, years to search.

Civil records are available by mail or phone. No release necessary. $5.00 search fee. $1.00 fee for first copy, $.50 per copy thereafter. $.50 for certification. Search information required: name, date of birth, years to search. Specify plaintiff or defendant.

Sequoyah County

Sequoyah County Court Clerk,
Criminal Records
Room 10
Courthouse
Sallisaw, OK 74955
(918) 775-4411

Felony and misdemeanor records are available by mail or phone. No release necessary. $5.00 search fee. $1.00 fee for first copy, $.50 per copy thereafter. Search information required: name, years to search.

Civil records are available by mail or phone. No release necessary. $5.00 search fee. $1.00 fee for first copy, $.50 per copy thereafter. Search information required: name, date of birth, years to search. Specify plaintiff or defendant.

Stephens County

Court Clerk, Criminal Records
Stephens County Courthouse
101 S. 11th Street
Duncan, OK 73533
(405) 255-8460

Felony and misdemeanor records are available by mail. No release necessary. $5.00 fee for first copy, $.50 per copy thereafter. $.50 for certification. Make check payable to Clerk of Court. Search information required: name, years to search.

Civil records are available by mail. No release necessary. $5.00 search fee. $1.00 fee for first copy, $.50 per copy thereafter. $.50 for certification. Search information required: name, date of birth, years to search. Specify plaintiff or defendant.

Texas County

Court Clerk, Criminal Records
PO Box 1081
Guymon, OK 73942
(405) 338-3003

Felony and misdemeanor records are available by mail or phone. No release necessary. $5.00 search fee. $.50 fee per copy. $.50 for certification. Search information required: name, years to search.

Civil records are available by mail. No release necessary. $5.00 search fee. $.50 fee per copy. $.50 for certification. Search information required: name, date of birth, years to search. Specify plaintiff or defendant.

Tillman County

Court Clerk, Criminal Records
PO Box 116
Frederick, OK 73542
(405) 335-3023

Felony and misdemeanor records are available by mail or phone. No release necessary. No search fee. $1.00 fee for first copy, $.50 per copy thereafter. Search information required: name, years to search.

Civil records are available by mail. No release necessary. No search fee. $1.00 fee for first copy, $.50 per copy thereafter. Search information required: name, date of birth, years to search. Specify plaintiff or defendant.

Tulsa County

District Court Clerk, Criminal Records
Tulsa County Courthouse
500 S. Denver
Tulsa, OK 74103
(918) 586-5000

Felony and misdemeanor records are available in person only. See Oklahoma state repository for additional information.

Civil records are available in person only. See Oklahoma state repository for additional information.

Wagoner County

Court Clerk, Criminal Records
PO Box 249
Wagoner, OK 74477
(918) 485-4508

Felony and misdemeanor records are available by mail. No release necessary. $5.00 search fee. $1.00 fee for first copy, $.50 per copy thereafter. Search information required: name, years to search, SASE.

Civil records are available by mail. No release necessary. $5.00 search fee. $1.00 fee for first copy, $.50 per copy thereafter. Search information required: name, date of birth, years to search, SASE. Specify plaintiff or defendant.

Washington County

Court Clerk, Criminal Records
Washington County Courthouse
5th and Johnstone, Room 212
Bartlesville, OK 74003
(918) 336-2674

Felony and misdemeanor records are available by mail. No release necessary. $5.00 search fee. $1.00 fee for first copy, $.50 per copy thereafter. Search information required: name, years to search, case number, if available.

Civil records are available by mail. No release necessary. $5.00 search fee. $1.00 fee for first copy, $.50 per copy thereafter. Search information required: name, date of birth, years to search. Specify plaintiff or defendant.

Washita County

Court Clerk, Criminal Records
PO Box 397
Cordell, OK 73632
(405) 832-3836

Felony and misdemeanor records are available by mail. No release necessary. $5.00 search fee. $1.00 fee for first copy, $.50 per copy thereafter. Search information required: name, years to search.

Civil records are available by mail. No release necessary. $5.00 search fee. $1.00 fee for first copy, $.50 per copy thereafter. Search information required: name, date of birth, years to search. Specify plaintiff or defendant.

Woods County

Woods County Court Clerk, Criminal Records
PO Box 924
Alva, OK 73717
(405) 327-3119

Felony and misdemeanor records are available by mail. A release is required. No search fee. $1.00 fee for first copy, $.50 per copy thereafter. Search information required: name, years to search.

Civil records are available by mail. A release is required. No search fee. $1.00 fee for first copy, $.50 per copy thereafter. Search information required: name, date of birth, years to search. Specify plaintiff or defendant.

Woodward County

Woodward County Court Clerk, Criminal Records
1600 Main
Woodward, OK 73801
(405) 256-3413

Felony and misdemeanor records are available by mail or phone. No release necessary. No search fee. $1.00 fee for first copy, $.50 per copy thereafter. Search information required: name, years to search.

Civil records are available by mail or phone. No release necessary. No search fee. $1.00 fee for first copy, $.50 per copy thereafter. Search information required: name, date of birth, years to search. Specify plaintiff or defendant.

City-County Cross Reference

Achille *Bryan*
Ada *Pontotoc*
Adair *Mayes*
Adams *Texas*
Addington *Jefferson*
Afton *Ottawa*
Agra *Lincoln*
Albany *Bryan*
Albert *Caddo*
Albion *Pushmataha*
Alderson *Pittsburg*
Alex *Grady*
Aline *Alfalfa*
Allen *Pontotoc*
Altus *Jackson*
Alva *Woods*
Amber *Grady*
Ames *Major*
Amorita *Alfalfa*
Anadarko *Caddo*
Antlers *Pushmataha*
Apache *Caddo*
Arapaho *Custer*
Arcadia *Oklahoma*
Ardmore *Carter*
Arkoma *Le Flore*
Arnett *Ellis*
Asher *Pottawatomie*
Atoka *Atoka*
Atwood *Hughes*
Avant *Osage*
Bache *Pittsburg*
Balko *Beaver*
Barnsdall *Osage*

Bartlesville *Washington*
Battiest *McCurtain*
Beaver *Beaver*
Beggs *Okmulgee*
Bennington *Bryan*
Bessie *Washita*
Bethany *Oklahoma*
Bethel *McCurtain*
Bethel Acres *Pottawatomie*
Big Cabin *Craig*
Billings *Noble*
Binger *Caddo*
Bison *Garfield*
Bixby *Tulsa*
Blackwell *Kay*
Blair *Jackson*
Blanchard *McClain*
Blanco *Pittsburg*
Blocker *Pittsburg*
Bluejacket *Craig*
Boise City *Cimarron*
Bokchito *Bryan*
Bokoshe *Le Flore*
Boley *Okfuskee*
Boswell *Choctaw*
Bowlegs *Seminole*
Boynton *Muskogee*
Bradley *Grady*
Braggs *Muskogee*
Braman *Kay*
Bristow *Creek*
Broken Arrow *Tulsa*
Broken Bow *McCurtain*
Bromide *Johnston*

Buffalo *Harper*
Bunch *Adair*
Burbank *Osage*
Burlington *Alfalfa*
Burneyville *Love*
Burns Flat *Washita*
Butler *Custer*
Byars *McClain*
Byron *Alfalfa*
Cache *Comanche*
Caddo *Bryan*
Calera *Bryan*
Calumet *Canadian*
Calvin *Hughes*
Camargo *Dewey*
Cameron *Le Flore*
Canadian *Pittsburg*
Caney *Atoka*
Canton *Blaine*
Canute *Washita*
Capron *Woods*
Cardin *Ottawa*
Carmen *Alfalfa*
Carnegie *Caddo*
Carney *Lincoln*
Carrier *Garfield*
Carter *Beckham*
Cartwright *Bryan*
Cashion *Kingfisher*
Castle *Okfuskee*
Catoosa *Rogers*
Cement *Caddo*
Centrahoma *Coal*
Centralia *Craig*

Chandler *Lincoln*
Chattanooga *Comanche*
Checotah *McIntosh*
Chelsea *Rogers*
Cherokee *Alfalfa*
Chester *Major*
Cheyenne *Roger Mills*
Chickasha *Grady*
Choctaw *Oklahoma*
Chouteau *Mayes*
Claremore *Rogers*
Clarita *Coal*
Clayton *Pushmataha*
Clearview *Okfuskee*
Cleo Springs *Major*
Cleveland *Pawnee*
Clinton *Custer*
Coalgate *Coal*
Colbert *Bryan*
Colcord *Delaware*
Coleman *Johnston*
Collinsville *Tulsa*
Colony *Washita*
Comanche *Stephens*
Commerce *Ottawa*
Concho *Canadian*
Connerville *Johnston*
Cookson *Cherokee*
Copan *Washington*
Cordell *Washita*
Corn *Washita*
Council Hill *Muskogee*
Countyline *Stephens*
Covington *Garfield*

Coweta *Wagoner*
Cowlington *Le Flore*
Coyle *Logan*
Crawford *Roger Mills*
Crescent *Logan*
Cromwell *Seminole*
Crowder *Pittsburg*
Cushing *Payne*
Custer City *Custer*
Cyril *Caddo*
Dacoma *Woods*
Daisy *Atoka*
Davenport *Lincoln*
Davidson *Tillman*
Davis *Murray*
Deer Creek *Grant*
Delaware *Nowata*
Del City *Oklahoma*
Depew *Creek*
Devol *Cotton*
Dewar *Okmulgee*
Dewey *Washington*
Dibble *McClain*
Dickson *Carter*
Dill City *Washita*
Disney *Mayes*
Dougherty *Murray*
Douglas *Garfield*
Dover *Kingfisher*
Drummond *Garfield*
Drumright *Creek*
Duke *Jackson*
Duncan *Stephens*
Durant *Bryan*
Durham *Roger Mills*
Dustin *Hughes*
Eagletown *McCurtain*
Eakly *Caddo*
Earlsboro *Pottawatomie*
Edmond *Oklahoma*
Eldorado *Jackson*
Elgin *Comanche*
Elk City *Beckham*
Elmer *Jackson*
Elmore City *Garvin*
Elmwood *Beaver*
El Reno *Canadian*
Enid *Garfield*
Erick *Beckham*
Eucha *Delaware*
Eufaula *McIntosh*
Fairfax *Osage*
Fairland *Ottawa*
Fairmont *Garfield*
Fairview *Major*
Fanshawe *Le Flore*
Fargo *Ellis*
Faxon *Comanche*
Fay *Dewey*
Felt *Cimarron*
Finley *Pushmataha*
Fittstown *Pontotoc*
Fitzhugh *Pontotoc*
Fletcher *Comanche*
Forest Park *Oklahoma*
Forgan *Beaver*
Fort Cobb *Caddo*
Fort Gibson *Muskogee*
Fort Supply *Woodward*
Fort Towson *Choctaw*
Foss *Washita*
Foster *Garvin*
Fox *Carter*
Foyil *Rogers*
Francis *Pontotoc*
Frederick *Tillman*

Freedom *Woods*
Gage *Ellis*
Gans *Sequoyah*
Garber *Garfield*
Garvin *McCurtain*
Gate *Beaver*
Geary *Blaine*
Gene Autry *Carter*
Geronimo *Comanche*
Glencoe *Payne*
Glenpool *Tulsa*
Golden *McCurtain*
Goltry *Alfalfa*
Goodwell *Texas*
Gore *Sequoyah*
Gotebo *Kiowa*
Gould *Harmon*
Gowen *Latimer*
Gracemont *Caddo*
Graham *Carter*
Grandfield *Tillman*
Granite *Greer*
Grant *Choctaw*
Greenfield *Blaine*
Grove *Delaware*
Guthrie *Logan*
Guymon *Texas*
Haileyville *Pittsburg*
Hallett *Pawnee*
Hammon *Roger Mills*
Hanna *McIntosh*
Hardesty *Texas*
Harrah *Oklahoma*
Hartshorne *Pittsburg*
Haskell *Muskogee*
Hastings *Jefferson*
Haworth *McCurtain*
Haywood *Pittsburg*
Headrick *Jackson*
Healdton *Carter*
Heavener *Le Flore*
Helena *Alfalfa*
Hendrix *Bryan*
Hennepin *Garvin*
Hennessey *Kingfisher*
Henryetta *Okmulgee*
Hillsdale *Garfield*
Hinton *Caddo*
Hitchcock *Blaine*
Hitchita *McIntosh*
Hobart *Kiowa*
Hodgen *Le Flore*
Holdenville *Hughes*
Hollis *Harmon*
Hollister *Tillman*
Hominy *Osage*
Honobia *Pushmataha*
Hooker *Texas*
Hopeton *Woods*
Howe *Le Flore*
Hoyt *Haskell*
Hugo *Choctaw*
Hulbert *Cherokee*
Hunter *Garfield*
Hydro *Caddo*
Idabel *McCurtain*
Indiahoma *Comanche*
Indianola *Pittsburg*
Inola *Rogers*
Isabella *Major*
Jay *Delaware*
Jenks *Tulsa*
Jennings *Pawnee*
Jet *Alfalfa*
Jones *Oklahoma*
Kansas *Delaware*

Kaw City *Kay*
Kellyville *Creek*
Kemp *Bryan*
Kenefic *Bryan*
Kenton *Cimarron*
Keota *Haskell*
Ketchum *Craig*
Keyes *Cimarron*
Kiefer *Creek*
Kingfisher *Kingfisher*
Kingston *Marshall*
Kinta *Haskell*
Kiowa *Pittsburg*
Knowles *Beaver*
Konawa *Seminole*
Krebs *Pittsburg*
Kremlin *Garfield*
Lahoma *Garfield*
Lamar *Hughes*
Lamont *Grant*
Lane *Atoka*
Langley *Mayes*
Langston *Logan*
Laverne *Harper*
Lawton *Comanche*
Lebanon *Marshall*
Leedey *Dewey*
Leflore *Le Flore*
Lehigh *Coal*
Lenapah *Nowata*
Leon *Love*
Leonard *Tulsa*
Lequire *Haskell*
Lexington *Cleveland*
Lindsay *Garvin*
Loco *Stephens*
Locust Grove *Mayes*
Logan *Beaver*
Lone Grove *Carter*
Lone Wolf *Kiowa*
Longdale *Blaine*
Lookeba *Caddo*
Loveland *Tillman*
Loyal *Kingfisher*
Lucien *Noble*
Luther *Oklahoma*
McAlester *Pittsburg*
McCurtain *Haskell*
McLoud *Pottawatomie*
Macomb *Pottawatomie*
Madill *Marshall*
Manchester *Grant*
Mangum *Greer*
Manitou *Tillman*
Mannford *Creek*
Mannsville *Johnston*
Maramec *Pawnee*
Marble City *Sequoyah*
Marietta *Love*
Marland *Noble*
Marlow *Stephens*
Marshall *Logan*
Martha *Jackson*
Maud *Pottawatomie*
May *Harper*
Maysville *Garvin*
Mead *Bryan*
Medford *Grant*
Medicine Park *Comanche*
Meeker *Lincoln*
Meno *Major*
Meridian *Logan*
Miami *Ottawa*
Milburn *Johnston*
Midwest City *Oklahoma*
Milfay *Creek*

Mill Creek *Johnston*
Millerton *McCurtain*
Minco *Grady*
Moffett *Sequoyah*
Monroe *Le Flore*
Moodys *Cherokee*
Moore *Cleveland*
Mooreland *Woodward*
Morris *Okmulgee*
Morrison *Noble*
Mounds *Creek*
Mountain Park *Kiowa*
Mountain View *Kiowa*
Moyers *Pushmataha*
Muldrow *Sequoyah*
Mulhall *Logan*
Muse *Le Flore*
Muskogee *Muskogee*
Mustang *Canadian*
Mutual *Woodward*
Nardin *Kay*
Nash *Grant*
Nashoba *Pushmataha*
Newalla *Oklahoma*
Newcastle *McClain*
Newkirk *Kay*
Nicoma Park *Oklahoma*
Nichols Hills *Oklahoma*
Ninnekah *Grady*
Noble *Cleveland*
Norman *Cleveland*
North Miami *Ottawa*
Nowata *Nowata*
Oakhurst *Tulsa*
Oakland *Marshall*
Oaks *Delaware*
Oakwood *Dewey*
Ochelata *Washington*
Oilton *Creek*
Okarche *Kingfisher*
Okay *Wagoner*
Okeene *Blaine*
Okemah *Okfuskee*
Oklahoma City *Oklahoma*
Okmulgee *Okmulgee*
Oktaha *Muskogee*
Olustee *Jackson*
Omega *Kingfisher*
Oologah *Rogers*
Optima *Texas*
Orlando *Logan*
Osage *Osage*
Overbrook *Love*
Owasso *Tulsa*
Paden *Okfuskee*
Panama *Le Flore*
Panola *Latimer*
Paoli *Garvin*
Park Hill *Cherokee*
Pauls Valley *Garvin*
Pawhuska *Osage*
Pawnee *Pawnee*
Peggs *Cherokee*
Perkins *Payne*
Pernell *Garvin*
Perry *Noble*
Pharoah *Okfuskee*
Picher *Ottawa*
Pickens *McCurtain*
Piedmont *Canadian*
Pittsburg *Pittsburg*
Platter *Bryan*
Pocasset *Grady*
Pocola *Le Flore*
Ponca City *Kay*
Pond Creek *Grant*

Porter *Wagoner*
Porum *Muskogee*
Poteau *Le Flore*
Prague *Lincoln*
Preston *Okmulgee*
Proctor *Adair*
Prue *Osage*
Pryor *Mayes*
Purcell *McClain*
Putnam *Dewey*
Quapaw *Ottawa*
Quinton *Pittsburg*
Ralston *Pawnee*
Ramona *Washington*
Randlett *Cotton*
Ratliff City *Carter*
Rattan *Pushmataha*
Ravia *Johnston*
Redbird *Wagoner*
Red Oak *Latimer*
Red Rock *Noble*
Reed *Greer*
Rentiesville *McIntosh*
Reydon *Roger Mills*
Ringling *Jefferson*
Ringold *McCurtain*
Ringwood *Major*
Ripley *Payne*
Rocky *Washita*
Roff *Pontotoc*
Roland *Sequoyah*
Roosevelt *Kiowa*
Rose *Mayes*
Rosston *Harper*
Rufe *McCurtain*
Rush Springs *Grady*
Ryan *Jefferson*
Saint Louis *Pottawatomie*
Salina *Mayes*
Sallisaw *Sequoyah*
Sand Springs *Tulsa*
Sapulpa *Creek*
Sasakwa *Seminole*
Savanna *Pittsburg*
Sawyer *Choctaw*
Sayre *Beckham*
Schulter *Okmulgee*
Seiling *Dewey*
Seminole *Seminole*
Sentinel *Washita*
Shady Point *Le Flore*
Shamrock *Creek*
Sharon *Woodward*
Shattuck *Ellis*
Shawnee *Pottawatomie*
Shidler *Osage*
Skiatook *Tulsa*
Slaughterville *Cleveland*
Slick *Creek*
Smithville *McCurtain*
Snow *Pushmataha*
Snyder *Kiowa*
Soper *Choctaw*
Southard *Blaine*
South Coffeyville *Nowata*
Sparks *Lincoln*
Spavinaw *Mayes*
Spencer *Oklahoma*
Spencerville *Choctaw*
Sperry *Tulsa*
Spiro *Le Flore*
Springer *Carter*
Sterling *Comanche*
Stidham *McIntosh*
Stigler *Haskell*
Stillwater *Payne*

Stilwell *Adair*
Stonewall *Pontotoc*
Strang *Mayes*
Stratford *Garvin*
Stringtown *Atoka*
Stroud *Lincoln*
Stuart *Hughes*
Sulphur *Murray*
Sweetwater *Roger Mills*
Swink *Choctaw*
Taft *Muskogee*
Tahlequah *Cherokee*
Talala *Rogers*
Talihina *Le Flore*
Taloga *Dewey*
Tatums *Carter*
Tecumseh *Pottawatomie*
Temple *Cotton*
Terlton *Pawnee*
Terral *Jefferson*
Texhoma *Texas*
Texola *Beckham*
Thackerville *Love*
Thomas *Custer*
Tipton *Tillman*
Tishomingo *Johnston*
Tonkawa *Kay*
Tryon *Lincoln*
Tullahassee *Wagoner*
Tulsa *Tulsa*
Tupelo *Coal*
Turley *Tulsa*
Turpin *Beaver*
Tuskahoma *Pushmataha*
Tussy *Carter*
Tuttle *Grady*
Twin Oaks *Delaware*
Tyrone *Texas*
Union City *Canadian*
Valley Brook *Oklahoma*
Valliant *McCurtain*
Velma *Stephens*
Vera *Washington*
Verden *Grady*
Vernon *McIntosh*
Vian *Sequoyah*
Vici *Dewey*
Village *Oklahoma*
Vinita *Craig*
Vinson *Harmon*
Wagoner *Wagoner*
Wainwright *Muskogee*
Wakita *Grant*
Walters *Cotton*
Wanette *Pottawatomie*
Wann *Nowata*
Wapanucka *Johnston*
Wardville *Atoka*
Warner *Muskogee*
Warr Acres *Oklahoma*
Washington *McClain*
Watonga *Blaine*
Watson *McCurtain*
Watts *Adair*
Waukomis *Garfield*
Waurika *Jefferson*
Wayne *McClain*
Waynoka *Woods*
Weatherford *Custer*
Webbers Falls *Muskogee*
Welch *Craig*
Weleetka *Okfuskee*
Welling *Cherokee*
Wellston *Lincoln*
Welty *Okfuskee*
Westville *Adair*

Wetumka *Hughes*
Wewoka *Seminole*
Wheatland *Oklahoma*
Whitefield *Haskell*
Whitesboro *Le Flore*
Wilburton *Latimer*
Willow *Greer*
Wilson *Carter*
Wister *Le Flore*
Woodward *Woodward*
Wright City *McCurtain*
Wyandotte *Ottawa*
Wynnewood *Garvin*
Wynona *Osage*
Yale *Payne*
Yukon *Canadian*

Oregon

All thirty six (36) Oregon counties reported that they make criminal records available for employment screening purposes with only one county requesting the search in person only. Five (5) will honor fax requests. Circuit court holds civil court records for $10,000 and more.

For more information or for offices not listed, contact the state's information hot line at (503) 378-3131.

Driving Records

Motor Vehicle Division
1905 Lana Avenue NE
Salem, OR 97314
(503) 378-4085
Driving records are available by mail. $1.50-$2.000 fee. Turnaround time is 2 to 3 days. Written request must include driver's full name, date of birth, license number and reason for request. Request must be on Oregon Form 735-48 (9-85). Contact above office to obtain copies of this form. Larger volume accounts may establish a billing program by contacting the Finance Section at (503) 378-6912. There is a $25 fee for this service.

Worker's Compensation Records

Department of Insurance & Finance
Worker's Compensation Division
Compliance Section
21 Labor and Industry Building
Salem, OR 97310
(503) 378-4956
Fax (503) 378-2009
Requests are available by mail or fax. All inquiries must include the subject's name, date of birth if possible, SSN. Inquiries should be submitted on company letterhead. $1.50 search fee. A signed release is not required. Contact the above office to obtain a requestor ID number.

Vital Statistics

Oregon State Health Division
Vital Statistics Section
PO Box 14050
Portland, OR 97214-0050
(503) 731-4108
Birth and death records are available for $13.00 each. State office has records since January 1864. Some earlier records for the City of Portland since approximately 1880 are available from the Oregon State Archives, 1005 Broadway Northeast, Salem, OR 97310. Inquiries must include name at birth, date of birth, place of birth, mother's maiden name, and father's name. For death records, include name, date and place of death, relationship or reason for needing record. An employer can obtain records with a notorized release. Make certified check or money order payable to Oregon Health Division.

Marriage records from 1906 are available. $13.00 fee. Include name, marriage date, spouse's name, maiden name, city or county where married. Divorce records available at County Courthouse where divorce granted.

Department of Education

Teacher Standards and Practices Commission
630 Center Street NE
Suite 200
Salem, OR 97310-0320
(503) 378-3586
Fax (503) 378-4448
Field of certification is available by mail, fax or phone. Include full name and SSN.

Medical Licensing

Board of Medical Examiners
620 Crown Plaza
1500 Southwest First Avenue
Portland, OR 97201-5826
(503) 229-5027
Will confirm licenses for MDs by mail or phone. $10.00 fee. For licenses not mentioned, contact the above office.

Oregon State Board of Nursing
10445 S.W. Banyon Rd., Suite 200
Beaverton, OR 97005
(503) 644-2767
Will confirm license by phone. No fee. Include name, SSN or license number, first license date.

Bar Association

Oregon State Bar Association
PO Box 1689
Lake Oswego, OR 97035
(503) 224-4280
Will confirm licenses by phone. No fee. Include name.

Accountancy Board

Oregon Board of Accountancy
158 12th Street NE
Salem ,OR 97310
(503) 378-3131
Will confirm license by phone. No fee. Include name.

Securities Commission

Division of Finance and Corporate Securities
21 Labor & Industries Building
Salem, OR 97310
(503) 378-4387
Will confirm license by phone. No fee. Include name and SSN.

Secretary of State

Secretary of State
Corporation Division
158 12 Street NE
Salem, OR 97310
(503) 378-4166

Service agent and address, date incorporated, standing with tax commission, trade names are available by mail or phone. Contact the above office for additional information.

Criminal Records

State Repository

Oregon State Police
Bureau of Criminal Identification
3772 Portland Road, NE
Salem, OR 97310
(503) 378-3070
Written request must include subject's full name, date of birth, and, if available, SSN. Requests must also include the subject's present address. If a record exists, notification of the search is sent to the subject. After 14 days the record will be forwarded to the requesting party. There is a $10.00 fee for each request. Make check payable to Oregon State Police. Information released contains conviction data only and arrests that are less than a year old. Turnaround time is normally 24 hours for "no hits" and 24 hours plus the 14 holding period for "hits".

Baker County

Baker Circuit Court, Criminal Records
1995 Third Street
Baker, OR 97814
(503) 523-6303
Felony and misdemeanor records are available by mail or phone. No release necessary. No search fee. $.25 fee per copy. $3.75 for certification. Search information required: name, years to search.

Civil records are available by mail or phone. No release necessary. No search fee. Search information required: name, date of birth, years to search. Specify plaintiff or defendant.

Benton County

Felony and misdemeanor records
Criminal Clerk of the Circuit Court, Felony check
PO Box 1870
Coravallis, OR 97339
(503) 757-6875
Felony and misdemeanor records are available by mail. No release necessary. No search fee. $.25 fee per copy. $3.75 for certification. Search information required: name, years to search.

Civil records
Clerk of the Circuit Court
PO Box 1870
Coravallis, OR 97339
(503) 757-6829
Civil records are available by mail. No release necessary. No search fee. $.25 fee per copy. $3.75 for certification. Search information required: name, date of birth, years to search. Specify plaintiff or defendant.

Clackamas County

Clackamas County Courthouse
File Room-Felony check
807 Main Street
Oregon City, OR 97045
(503) 655-8447
Felony and misdemeanor records are available by mail from June, 1986 forward. Records prior to 1986 are available in person. No release necessary. No search fee. $.25 fee per copy. $4.00 for certification. Search information required: name, date of birth, years to search. Request for misdemeanor records ask for District Court–for felony records ask for Circuit Court.

Civil records are available by mail. No release necessary. No search fee. $.25 fee per copy. $4.00 for certification. Search information required: name, date of birth, years to search. Specify plaintiff or defendant.

Clatsop County

Trial Court Clerk, Felony Records
PO Box 835
Astoria, OR 97103
(503) 325-8583
Felony and misdemeanor records are available by maile. A release is required. No search fee. $.25 fee per copy. $3.75 for certification. Search information required: name, years to search.

Civil records are available by mail. A release is required. No search fee. $.25 fee per copy. $3.75 for certification. Search information required: name, date of birth, years to search. Specify plaintiff or defendant.

Columbia County

Trial Court Administrator, Felony Check
Columbia County Courthouse
St. Helens, OR 97051
(503) 397-2327
Felony and misdemeanor records are available by mail. No release necessary. $3.75 search fee. $.25 fee per copy. $4.00 for certification. Certified check only, payable to Trial Court Clerk. Search information required: name, date of birth.

Civil records are available by mail. No release necessary. $3.75 search fee. $.25 fee per copy. $4.00 for certification. Search information required: name, date of birth, years to search. Specify plaintiff or defendant.

Coos County

Circuit Court, Felony Check
Coos County Courthouse
Coquille, OR 97423
(503) 396-3121
Felony and misdemeanor records are available by mail. No release necessary. No search fee. $.25 fee per copy. $3.50 for certification. Search information required: name, date of birth, SASE, years to search.

Civil records are available by mail. No release necessary. No search fee. $.25 fee per copy. $3.75 for certification. Search information required: name, date of birth, years to search. Specify plaintiff or defendant.

Crook County

Courthouse, Felony Check
Circuit Court Clerk
Prineville, OR 97754
(503) 447-6541
Felony and misdemeanor records are available by mail or phone. No release necessary. No search fee. Copies are $.25 per page, $3.75 for certified copy. Search information required: name, years to search.

Civil records are available in person only. See Oregon state repository for additional information.

Curry County

Court Clerk, Felony Check
PO Box -H
Gold Beach, OR 97444
(503) 247-4511
Felony and misdemeanor records are available by mail. No release necessary. No search fee. $.25 per copy. Search information required: name, years to search.

Civil records are available by mail. No release necessary. No search fee. $.25 fee per copy. $4.00 for certification. Search information required: name, date of birth, years to search. Specify plaintiff or defendant.

Deschutes County

Clerk of the Circuit Court, Felony Check
1100 N.W. Bond
Bend, OR 97701
(503) 388-5300
Felony and misdemeanor records are available by mail or phone for records from July 1986 forward. No release necessary. No search fee. Search information required: name, SSN, date of birth, sex, race, years to search.

Civil records are available by mail or phone. No release necessary. No search fee. $.25 fee per copy. $4.00 for certification. Search information required: name, date of birth, years to search. Specify plaintiff or defendant.

Douglas County

Douglas County Circuit Court, Felony Records
Room 202, Justice Bldg.
Roseburg, OR 97470
(503) 440-4363
Felony and misdemeanor records are available by mail. No release necessary. No search fee. $.25 fee per copy. $3.75 for certification. Search information required: name, date of birth, years to search.

Civil records are available by mail. No release necessary. No search fee. $.25 fee per copy. $3.75 for certification. Search information required: name, date of birth, years to search. Specify plaintiff or defendant.

Gilliam County

Gilliam Circuit Court, Felony Check
PO Box 622
Condon, OR 97823
(503) 384-3572
Felony and misdemeanor records are available by mail or phone. No release necessary. No search fee. $.25 fee per copy. $4.00 for certification. Search information required: name.

Civil records are available by mail. No release necessary. No search fee. $.25 fee per copy. $4.00 for certification. Search information required: name, date of birth, years to search. Specify plaintiff or defendant.

Grant County

Trial Court Clerk, Felony Check
PO Box 159
Canyon City, OR 97820
(503) 575-1438
Fax (503) 575-2165
Felony and misdemeanor records are available by mail, phone or fax. A release is required. No search fee. $.25 fee per copy. $3.75 for certification. Search information required: name, years to search.

Civil records are available by mail. No release necessary. No search fee. $.25 fee per copy. $3.75 for certification. Search information required: name, date of birth, years to search. Specify plaintiff or defendant.

Harney County

Clerk of the Circuit Court, Criminal Records
450 N. Buena Vista
Burns, OR 97720
(503) 573-5207
Fax (503) 573-5715
Felony and misdemeanor records are available by mail, phone or fax. No release necessary. No search fee. $.25 fee per copy. $3.75 for certification. Search information required: name, years to search, SASE.

Civil records are available by mail or fax. No release necessary. No search fee. $.25 fee per copy. $3.75 for certification. Search information required: name, date of birth, years to search, SASE. Specify plaintiff or defendant.

Hood River County

Trial Court Operations
Circuit Court of District Court and
Felony Check
Courthouse
309 State St.
Hood River, OR 97031
(503) 386-1862

Felony and misdemeanor records are available by mail. No release necessary. No search fee. $.25 fee per copy. $3.75 for certification. Search information required: name, date of birth, years to search.

Civil records are available by mail. No release necessary. No search fee. $.25 fee per copy. $3.75 for certification. Search information required: name, date of birth, years to search. Specify plaintiff or defendant.

Jackson County

Circuit Court, Felony Check
Jackson County Circuit Court
100 S. Oakdale
Medford, OR 97501
(503) 776-7171 Ext. 297

Felony records are available by mail or phone. No release necessary. No search fee. $.25 fee per copy. $3.75 for certification. Search information required: name, date of birth.

Civil records are available by mail or phone. No release necessary. No search fee. $.25 fee per copy. $3.75 for certification. Search information required: name, date of birth, years to search. Specify plaintiff or defendant.

Jefferson County

Circuit Court, Felony Check
Jefferson County Courthouse
Madras, OR 97741
(503) 475-3317

Felony and misdemeanor records are available by mail or phone. No release necessary. No search fee. $.25 fee per copy. $3.75 for certification. Search information required: name, date of birth, years to search.

Civil records are available by mail or phone. No release necessary. No search fee. $.25 fee per copy. $3.75 for certification. Search information required: name, date of birth, years to search. Specify plaintiff or defendant.

Josephine County

Felony records
Josephine County Courts, Criminal
Clerk
Courthouse, Room 254
Grants Pass, OR 97526
(503) 474-5181

Felony records are available by mail or phone. No release necessary. No search fee. $.25 fee per copy. $3.75 for certification. Search information required: name, years to search.

Civil records
Josephine County Courts, Civil
Department
Courthouse, Room 252
Grants Pass, OR 97526
(503) 474-5181

Civil records are available by mail. No release necessary. No search fee. $.25 fee per copy. $3.75 for certification. Search information required: name, date of birth, years to search. Specify plaintiff or defendant.

Misdemeanor records
Josephine County Courts, Criminal
Clerk
Courthouse, Rm. 254
Grants Pass, OR 97526
(503) 474-5181 Ext. 45

Misdemeanor records are available by mail. No release necessary. No search fee. $.25 fee per copy. $3.75 for certification. Search information required: name, date of birth, years to search, date of offense, if known, SASE.

Klamath County

Felony records
Circuit Court, Criminal Records
316 Main
Klamath Falls, OR 97601
(503) 883-5504

Felony records are available by mail. No release necessary. No search fee. $.25 fee per copy. $3.75 for certification. Search information required: name, date of birth, years to search.

Civil records
Circuit Court
316 Main
Klamath Falls, OR 97601
(503) 883-5504

Civil records are available by mail. No release necessary. $7.50 search fee. $.25 fee per copy. $3.75 for certification. Search information required: name, date of birth, years to search. Specify plaintiff or defendant.

Misdemeanor records
Klamath County District Court
Courthouse, Records Dept.
316 Main
Klamath Falls, OR 97601
(503) 883-5504 Ext. 26

Misdemeanor records are available by mail. No release necessary. No search fee. $.25 fee per copy. $3.75 for certification. Search information required: name, date of birth, years to search.

Civil records
Klamath County District Court
Courthouse, Records Dept.
316 Main
Klamath Falls, OR 97601
(503) 883-5504 Ext. 26

Civil records are available by mail. No release necessary. $7.50 search fee. $.25 fee per copy. $3.75 for certification. Search information required: name, date of birth, years to search. Specify plaintiff or defendant.

Lake County

Circuit Court Clerk, Felony Check
513 Center Street
Lakeview, OR 97630
(503) 947-6051
Fax (503) 947-3724

Felony and misdemeanor records are available by mail or fax. No release necessary. $7.50 search fee. $.25 fee per copy. $3.75 for certification. Make check payable to Lake County Circuit Court. Search information required: name, years to search.

Civil records are available by mail or fax. No release necessary. $7.50 search fee. $.25 fee per copy. $3.75 for certification. Search information required: name, date of birth, years to search. Specify plaintiff or defendant.

Lane County

Circuit Court, Criminal Records
125 E. 8th Ave.
Eugene, OR 97401
(503) 687-4335

Felony and misdemeanor records are available by mail. No release necessary. No search fee. $.25 fee per copy. $4.00 for certification. Search information required: name, years to search, SASE.

Civil records are available by mail. No release necessary. No search fee. $.25 fee per copy. $4.00 for certification. Search information required: name, date of birth, years to search, SASE. Specify plaintiff or defendant.

Lincoln County

Circuit Court, Felony Check
PO Box 100
Newport, OR 97365
(503) 265-4236

Felony and misdemeanor records are available by mail. No release necessary. No search fee. Search information required: name, date of birth, SSN if available, years to search.

Civil records are available by mail from 1988 forward. Records prior to 1988 are available in person. No release necessary. No search fee. Search information required: name, date of birth, years to search. Specify plaintiff or defendant.

Linn County

Circuit Court, Felony Check
PO Box 1749
Albany, OR 97321
(503) 967-3841

Felony and misdemeanor records are available by mail or by phone for requests from May 1987 forward. No release necessary. No search fee. $.25 fee per copy, $3.75 fee for certification. Search information required: name, date of birth, SSN, offense, if known, years to search, SASE.

Civil records are available by mail. No release necessary. No search fee. $.25 fee per copy. $3.75 for certification. Search information required: name, date of birth, years to search. Specify plaintiff or defendant.

Malheur County

Circuit Court, Felony Check
251 B Street West
Box 3
Vale, OR 97918
(503) 473-5171
Fax (503) 473-5174

Felony and misdemeanor records are available by mail or phone. No release necessary. No search fee. $.25 fee per copy. $3.75 for certification. Search information required: name, date of birth, years to search.

Civil records are available by mail or phone. No release necessary. No search fee. $.25 fee per copy. $3.75 for certification. Search information required: name, date of birth, years to search. Specify plaintiff or defendant.

Marion County

Felony and misdemeanor records

Marion County Courthouse
100 High Street N.E.
Salem, OR 97301
(503) 588-5101

Felony and misdemeanor records are available by mail or phone (post November 1986). No release necessary. No search fee. $.25 fee per copy. $3.75 for certification. Search information required: name, years to search.

Civil records

Marion County Courthouse
100 High Street N.E.
Salem, OR 97301
(503) 588-5228

Civil records are available by mail or phone. No release necessary. No search fee. $.25 fee per copy. $3.75 for certification. Search information required: name, date of birth, years to search. Specify plaintiff or defendant.

Morrow County

Morrow County Circuit Court, Felony Check
PO Box 609
Heppner, OR 97836
(503) 676-5264

Felony and misdemeanor records are available by mail or phone. No release necessary. No search fee. $.25 fee per copy. $4.00 for certification. Search information required: name.

Civil records are available by mail. No release necessary. No search fee. $.25 fee per copy. $4.00 for certification. Search information required: name, date of birth, years to search. Specify plaintiff or defendant.

Multnomah County

Felony records

Multnomah County Courthouse, Felony Check
1021 S.W. 4th Ave.
Room 131
Portland, OR 97204
(503) 248-3003

Felony records are available by mail. No release necessary. No search fee. $.25 fee per copy. $3.75 for certification. Search information required: name, date of birth, years to search.

Civil records

Multnomah County Courthouse
1021 S.W. 4th Ave.
Room 131
Portland, OR 97204
(503) 248-3003

Civil records are available by mail. No release necessary. No search fee. $.25 fee per copy. $3.75 for certification. Search information required: name, date of birth, years to search. Specify plaintiff or defendant.

Misdemeanor records

District Court
1021 SW 4th Ave.
Courthouse, Room 106
Portland, OR 97204
(503) 248-3235

Misdemeanor records are available by mail. No release necessary. No search fee. $.25 fee per copy. $3.75 for certification. Search information required: name, date of birth, SSN, years to search.

Civil records

District Court
1021 SW 4th Ave.
Courthouse, Room 106
Portland, OR 97204
(503) 248-3235

Civil records are available in person only. See Oregon state repository for additional information.

Polk County

Felony records

Court Records Office, Felony Check
Room 301
Polk County Courthouse
Dallas, OR 97338
(503) 623-3154

Felony records are available by mail or phone. No release necessary. No search fee. $.25 fee per copy. $3.75 for certification. Make check payable to Trial Court Clerk. Search information required: name, years to search.

Civil records

Court Records Office
Room 301
Polk County Courthouse
Dallas, OR 97338
(503) 623-3154

Civil records are available by mail or phone. No release necessary. No search fee. $.25 fee per copy. $3.75 for certification. Search information required: name, date of birth, years to search. Specify plaintiff or defendant.

Misdemeanor records

District Court
Room 301
Polk County Courthouse
Dallas, OR 97338
(503) 623-9266

Misdemeanor records are available by mail or phone. No release necessary. No search fee. $.25 fee per copy. $3.75 for certification. Search information required: name, date of birth, years to search.

Civil records

District Court
Room 301
Polk County Courthouse
Dallas, OR 97338
(503) 623-9266

Civil records are available by mail or phone. No release necessary. No search fee. $.25 fee per copy. $3.75 for certification. Search information required: name, date of birth, years to search. Specify plaintiff or defendant.

Sherman County

Circuit Court, Felony Check
PO Box 402
Moro, OR 97039
(503) 565-3650

Felony and misdemeanor records are available by mail or phone. No release necessary. No search fee. $.25 fee per copy, $3.75 fee for certification. Search information required: name, date of birth, years to search.

Civil records are available by mail or phone. No release necessary. No search fee. $.25 fee per copy. $3.75 for certification. Search information required: name, date of birth, years to search. Specify plaintiff or defendant.

Tillamook County

Tillamook County Circuit Clerk, Felony Check
201 Laurel Ave.
Tillamook, OR 97141
(503) 842-8014
Fax (503) 842-2597

Felony and misdemeanor records are available in person only. See Oregon state repository for additional information.

Civil records are available by mail or phone. No release necessary. No search fee. $.25 fee per copy. $3.75 for certification. Search information required: name, date of birth, years to search. Specify plaintiff or defendant.

Umatilla County

Trial Court Administrator, Felony Check
PO Box 1307
Pendleton, OR 97801
(503) 278-0341

Felony and misdemeanor records are available by mail. No release necessary. No search fee. $.25 fee per copy. $3.75 for certification. Search information required: name, years to search.

Civil records are available by mail or phone. No release necessary. No search fee. $.25 fee per copy. $3.75 for certification. Search information required: name, date of birth, years to search. Specify plaintiff or defendant.

Union County

Felony records

Circuit Court Records, Felony Check
PO Box 2950
La Grande, OR 97850
(503) 963-2167

Felony records are available by mail or phone. No release necessary. No search fee. Search information required: name, date of birth, years to search.

Civil records
Circuit Court Records
PO Box 2950
La Grande, OR 97850
(503) 963-1029
Civil records are available by mail. No release necessary. $10.00 search fee. $.25 fee per copy. $3.75 for certification. Search information required: name, date of birth, years to search. Specify plaintiff or defendant.

Misdemeanor records
District Court
1007 Fourth St.
La Grande, OR 97850
(503) 963-1008
Misdemeanor records are available by mail. A release is required. No search fee. $5.00 fee for first 4 copies, $.50 each additional copy. $3.75 for certification. Search information required: name, date of birth, SASE.

Civil records
District Court
1007 Fourth St.
La Grande, OR 97850
(503) 963-1008
Civil records are available by mail or phone. No release necessary. $10.00 search fee. $.25 fee per copy. $3.75 for certification. Search information required: name, date of birth, years to search, SASE. Specify plaintiff or defendant.

Wallowa County

Circuit Court, Felony Check
101 S. River Street, Room 204
Enterprise, OR 97828
(503) 426-4991
Felony and misdemeanor records are available by mail or phone. No release necessary. No search fee. Search information required: name, years to search.

Civil records are available by mail or phone. No release necessary. No search fee. $.25 fee per copy. $4.00 for first certification, $.25 for each additional certified copy. Search information required: name, date of birth, years to search. Specify plaintiff or defendant.

Wasco County

Felony records
Wasco County Circuit Clerk, Felony Check
Courthouse
PO Box 821
The Dalles, OR 97058
(503) 296-3196
Felony records are available by mail or phone. No release necessary. No search fee. Search information required: name, SASE, years to search.

Civil records
Wasco County Circuit Clerk
Courthouse
PO Box 821
The Dalles, OR 97058
(503) 296-3196
Civil records are available by mail or phone. No release necessary. No search fee. $.25 fee per copy. $3.75 for certification. Search information required: name, date of birth, years to search, SASE. Specify plaintiff or defendant.

Misdemeanor records
Wasco County District Court
Courthouse
PO Box 415
The Dalles, OR 97058
(503) 296-2209
Misdemeanor records are available by mail or phone. No release necessary. No search fee. Search information required: name, date of birth.

Civil records
Wasco County District Court
Courthouse
PO Box 415
The Dalles, OR 97058
(503) 296-2209
Civil records are available by mail or phone. No release necessary. No search fee. $.25 fee per copy. $3.75 for certification. Search information required: name, date of birth, years to search. Specify plaintiff or defendant.

Washington County

Felony records
Court Clerk, Felony Check
145 N. E. 2nd
Hillsboro, OR 97124
(503) 648-8841
Felony records are available by mail or phone. No release necessary. No search fee. $.25 fee per copy. $3.75 for certification. Search information required: name, date of birth, years to search.

Civil records
Court Clerk
145 N. E. 2nd
Hillsboro, OR 97124
(503) 648-8841
Civil records are available by mail or phone. No release necessary. No search fee. $.25 fee per copy. $3.75 for certification. Search information required: name, date of birth, years to search. Specify plaintiff or defendant.

Misdemeanor records
District Court
145 NE. 2nd St.
Hillsboro, OR 97124
(503) 640-3505
Misdemeanor records are available by mail or phone. No release necessary. No search fee. $.25 fee per copy. $3.75 for certification. Search information required: name, date of birth, years to search, category of search.

Civil records
District Court
145 NE. 2nd St.
Hillsboro, OR 97124
(503) 640-3505
Civil records are available by mail or phone. No release necessary. No search fee. $.25 fee per copy. $3.75 for certification. Search information required: name, date of birth, years to search. Specify plaintiff or defendant.

Wheeler County

Wheeler County Circuit Court, Felony Check
Courthouse
Fossil, OR 97830
(503) 763-2541
Felony and misdemeanor records are available by mail or phone. No release necessary. No search fee. $.25 fee per copy. $3.75 for certification. Search information required: name, years to search.

Civil records are available by mail or phone. No release necessary. No search fee. $.25 fee per copy. $3.75 for certification. Search information required: name, date of birth, years to search. Specify plaintiff or defendant.

Yamhill County

Yamhill County Trial Court, Felony Check
Yamhill County Courthouse, Room 206
5th and Evans
McMinnville, OR 97128
(503) 434-7530
Felony and misdemeanor records are available by mail. No release necessary. $12.50 search fee. $.25 fee per copy. $3.75 for certification. Make company check payable to Trial Court. Search information required: name, date of birth, SASE, years to search.

Civil records are available by mail or phone. No release necessary. $5.00 search fee. $.25 fee per copy. $3.75 for certification. Search information required: name, date of birth, years to search, SASE. Specify plaintiff or defendant.

City-County Cross Reference

Adams *Umatilla*
Adel *Lake*
Adrian *Malheur*
Agness *Curry*
Albany *Linn*
Allegany *Coos*
Aloha *Washington*
Alsea *Benton*
Altamont *Klamath*
Alvadore *Lane*
Amity *Yamhill*
Antelope *Wasco*
Applegate *Jackson*
Arlington *Gilliam*
Arock *Malheur*
Ashland *Jackson*
Ashwood *Jefferson*
Astoria *Clatsop*
Athena *Umatilla*
Aumsville *Marion*
Aurora *Marion*
Azalea *Douglas*
Baker *Baker*
Baker City *Baker*
Bandon *Coos*
Banks *Washington*
Barview *Coos*
Bay City *Tillamook*
Beatty *Klamath*
Beavercreek *Clackamas*
Beaverton *Washington*
Bend *Deschutes*
Blodgett *Benton*
Blue River *Lane*
Bly *Klamath*
Boardman *Morrow*
Bonanza *Klamath*
Boring *Clackamas*
Bridal Veil *Multnomah*
Brightwood *Clackamas*
Broadbent *Coos*
Brookings *Curry*
Brothers *Deschutes*
Brownsville *Linn*
Bunker Hill *Coos*
Burns *Harney*
Butte Falls *Jackson*
Camas Valley *Douglas*
Camp Sherman *Jefferson*
Canby *Clackamas*
Cannon Beach *Clatsop*
Canyon City *Grant*
Canyonville *Douglas*
Carlton *Yamhill*
Cascade Locks *Hood River*
Cascadia *Linn*
Cave Junction *Josephine*
Cayuse *Umatilla*
Central Point *Jackson*
Charleston *Coos*
Chemult *Klamath*
Chenoweth *Wasco*
Cheshire *Lane*
Chiloquin *Klamath*
Clackamas *Clackamas*
Clatskanie *Columbia*
Cloverdale *Tillamook*
Coberg *Lane*
Colton *Clackamas*
Columbia City *Columbia*
Condon *Gilliam*
Coos Bay *Coos*
Coquille *Coos*

Corbett *Multnomah*
Cornelius *Washington*
Corvallis *Benton*
Cottage Grove *Lane*
Cove *Union*
Crabtree *Linn*
Crane *Harney*
Crawfordsville *Linn*
Crescent *Klamath*
Crescent Lake *Klamath*
Creswell *Lane*
Culp Creek *Lane*
Culver *Jefferson*
Curtin *Douglas*
Dallas *Polk*
Days Creek *Douglas*
Dayton *Yamhill*
Dayville *Grant*
Deadwood *Lane*
Depoe Bay *Lincoln*
Detroit *Marion*
Dexter *Lane*
Dillard *Douglas*
Donald *Marion*
Dorena *Lane*
Drain *Douglas*
Drewsey *Harney*
Dufur *Wasco*
Dundee *Yamhill*
Durham *Washington*
Durkee *Baker*
Eagle Creek *Clackamas*
Eagle Point *Jackson*
Echo *Umatilla*
Eddyville *Lincoln*
Elgin *Union*
Elkton *Douglas*
Elmira *Lane*
Enterprise *Wallowa*
Errol Heights *Multnomah*
Estacada *Clackamas*
Eugene *Lane*
Fairview *Multnomah*
Falcon Heights *Klamath*
Falls City *Polk*
Florence *Lane*
Forest Grove *Washington*
Fort Klamath *Klamath*
Fort Rock *Lake*
Fossil *Wheeler*
Foster *Linn*
Fox *Grant*
Frenchglen *Harney*
Garden Home *Washington*
Gardiner *Douglas*
Garibaldi *Tillamook*
Gaston *Washington*
Gearhart *Glatsop*
Gervais *Marion*
Gilbert *Multnomah*
Gilchrist *Klamath*
Gladstone *Clackamas*
Glendale *Douglas*
Gleneden Beach *Lincoln*
Glenwood *Washington*
Glide *Douglas*
Gold Beach *Curry*
Gold Hill *Jackson*
Government Camp
  Clackamas
Grand Ronde *Polk*
Grants Pass *Josephine*
Grass Valley *Sherman*

Green *Douglas*
Greenleaf *Lane*
Gresham *Multnomah*
Haines *Baker*
Halfway *Baker*
Halsey *Linn*
Hammond *Clatsop*
Happy Valley *Clackamas*
Harbour *Curry*
Harper *Malheur*
Harrisburg *Linn*
Hayesville *Marion*
Hebo *Tillamook*
Helix *Umatilla*
Heppner *Morrow*
Hereford *Baker*
Hermiston *Umatilla*
Hillsboro *Washington*
Hines *Harney*
Hood River *Hood River*
Hubbard *Marion*
Huntington *Baker*
Idanha *Marion*
Idleyld Park *Douglas*
Imbler *Union*
Imnaha *Wallowa*
Independence *Polk*
Ione *Morrow*
Irrigon *Morrow*
Jacksonville *Jackson*
Jamieson *Malheur*
Jefferson *Marion*
John Day *Grant*
Jordan Valley *Malheur*
Joseph *Wallowa*
Junction City *Lane*
Juntura *Malheur*
Keizer *Marion*
Keno *Klamath*
Kent *Sherman*
Kimberly *Grant*
Klamath Falls *Klamath*
Lafayette *Yamhill*
LaGrande *Union*
Lake Oswego *Clackamas*
Lakeside *Coos*
Lakeview *Lake*
Langlois *Curry*
LaPine *Deschutes*
Lawen *Harney*
Lebanon *Linn*
Lincoln City *Lincoln*
Long Creek *Grant*
Lorane *Lane*
Lostine *Wallowa*
Lowell *Lane*
Lyons *Linn*
McMinnville *Yamhill*
Madras *Jefferson*
Malin *Klamath*
Manzanita *Tillamook*
Mapleton *Lane*
Marcola *Lane*
Marylhurst *Clackamas*
Maupin *Wasco*
Maywood Park *Multnomah*
Medford *Jackson*
Merlin *Josephine*
Merrill *Klamath*
Metzger *Washington*
Midland *Klamath*
Mill City *Linn*
Milton-Freewater *Umatilla*

Milwaukie *Clackamas*
Mitchell *Wheeler*
Molalla *Clackamas*
Monmouth *Polk*
Monroe *Benton*
Monument *Grant*
Moro *Sherman*
Mosier *Wasco*
Mount Angel *Marion*
Mount Hood-Parkdale
  Hood River
Mount Vernon *Grant*
Mulino *Clackamas*
Murphy *Josephine*
Myrtle Creek *Douglas*
Myrtle Point *Coos*
Nehalem *Tillamook*
Neotsu *Lincoln*
Newberg *Yamhill*
New Pine Creek *Lake*
Newport *Lincoln*
North Bend *Coos*
North Plains *Washington*
North Powder *Union*
Norway *Coos*
Noti *Lane*
Nyssa *Malheur*
Oak Grove *Clackamas*
Oakland *Douglas*
Oakridge *Lane*
O'Brien *Josephine*
Oceanside *Tillamook*
Odell *Hood River*
Ontario *Malheur*
Ophir *Curry*
Oregon City *Clackamas*
Otis *Lincoln*
Oxbow *Baker*
Pacific City *Tillamook*
Paisley *Lake*
Parkrose *Multnomah*
Paulina *Crook*
Pendleton *Umatilla*
Philomath *Benton*
Phoenix *Jackson*
Pilot Rock *Umatilla*
Plush *Lake*
Portland *Multnomah*
Port Orford *Curry*
Post *Crook*
Powell Butte *Crook*
Powers *Coos*
Prairie City *Grant*
Prineville *Crook*
Prospect *Jackson*
Rainier *Columbia*
Raleigh Hills *Washington*
Redmond *Deschutes*
Reedsport *Douglas*
Remote *Coos*
Rhododendron *Clackamas*
Richland *Baker*
Rickreall *Polk*
Riddle *Douglas*
Riley *Harney*
Ritter *Grant*
Riverside *Malheur*
Rockaway *Tillamook*
Rogue River *Jackson*
Roseburg *Douglas*
Rufus *Sherman*
Russellville *Multnomah*
Saint Benedict *Marion*

Saint Helens *Columbia*
Saint Paul *Marion*
Salem *Marion*
Sandy *Clackamas*
Santa Clara *Lane*
Scappoose *Columbia*
Scio *Linn*
Scottsburg *Douglas*
Scotts Mills *Marion*
Seaside *Clatsop*
Selma *Josephine*
Seneca *Grant*
Shady Cove *Jackson*
Shaniko *Wasco*
Shedd *Linn*
Sheridan *Yamhill*
Sherwood *Washington*
Siletz *Lincoln*
Silver Lake *Lake*
Silverton *Marion*
Sisters *Deschutes*
Sixes *Curry*
Spray *Wheeler*
Springfield *Lane*
Stanfield *Umatilla*
Stayton *Marion*
Sublimity *Marion*
Summer Lake *Lake*
Sumpter *Baker*
Sutherlin *Douglas*
Svensen *Clatsop*
Sweet Home *Linn*
Swisshome *Lane*
Talent *Jackson*
Tangent *Linn*
Tenmile *Douglas*
Terrebonne *Deschutes*
The Dalles *Wasco*
Tidewater *Lincoln*
Tigard *Washington*
Tillamook *Tillamook*
Tiller *Douglas*
Timber *Washington*
Toledo *Lincoln*
Trail *Jackson*
Tri-City *Douglas*
Troutdale *Multnomah*
Tualatin *Washington*
Turner *Marion*
Tygh Valley *Wasco*
Ukiah *Umatilla*
Umatilla *Umatilla*
Umpqua *Douglas*
Union *Union*
Unity *Baker*
Vale *Malheur*
Veneta *Lane*
Vernonia *Columbia*
Vida *Lane*
Waldport *Lincoln*
Wallowa *Wallowa*
Walterville *Lane*
Walton *Lane*
Warm Springs *Jefferson*
Warren *Columbia*
Warrenton *Clatsop*
Wasco *Sherman*
Wedderburn *Curry*
Welches *Clackamas*
Westfall *Malheur*
Westfir *Lane*
Westlake *Lane*
West Linn *Clackamas*
Weston *Umatilla*
Westport *Clatsop*

West Slope *Washington*
Wheeler *Tillamook*
White City *Jackson*
Wilbur *Douglas*
Willamina *Yamhill*
Williams *Josephine*
Wilsonville *Clackamas*
Winchester *Douglas*
Winchester Bay *Douglas*
Winston *Douglas*
Wolf Creek *Josephine*
Woodburn *Marion*
Yachats *Lincoln*
Yamhill *Yamhill*
Yoncalla *Douglas*

Pennsylvania

Sixty three (63) of Pennsylvania's sixty seven (67) counties reported that their criminal records are available by phone or mail for employment screening purposes and a handful available by fax. Civil suits for $4,000 and more are filed in the court of Common Pleas while suits less than $4,000 are in the District Magistrate court.

For more information or for offices not listed, contact the state's information hot line at (717) 787-2121.

Driving Records

Bureau of Driver Licensing
Certified Driver Records
PO Box 8695
Harrisburg, PA 17105
(717) 787-3130
Driving records are available by mail. $10.00 fee per request. Turnaround time is 7 to 10 days. Written request must include job applicant's full name, date of birth and license number. Request must be on Form DL-2(7-90). Contact the above office to obtain copies of this form. Make check payable to Penndot.

Worker's Compensation Records

Bureau of Worker's Compensation
Petitions Department
1171 S. Cameron St., Rm 103
Harrisburg, PA 17104-2501
(717) 783-5421
In accordance with the Pennsylvania Human Relation Act, Worker's Compensation records are not available for pre-employment purposes. Employers may request a record check if the applicant has been offered a job. The request must be in writing, and both the employer and employee's signature need to be on the request stating that a job offer has been made.

Vital Statistics

Division of Vital Statistics
State Department of Health
Central Building
101 South Mercer Street
PO Box 1528
New Castle, PA 16103
Death (412) 656-3279
Birth (412) 656-3100
Administration Office (412) 656-3117
Birth records are available for $4.00. Death records are available for $3.00. State office has records since January 1906. For earlier records, write to Register of Wills, Orphans Court, in county seat where event occurred. Persons born in Pittsburgh from 1870 to 1905 or in Allegheny City, now part of Pittsburgh, from 1882 to 1905 should write to Office of Statistics, Pittsburgh Health Department, City-County Building,

Pittsburgh, PA 15219. For event occurring in City of Philadelphia, Department of Public Health, 401 N. Broad St., Rm. 920, Philadelphia, PA 19108. An employer can obtain records with a written release, and must state reason for requesting certificate. Make check or money order payable to Vital Records

Marriage records are available at County level, county court house in area where married. Divorce records available at county level, court where divorce granted.

Department of Education

Department of Education
Bureau of Teacher Preparation and Certification
333 Market Street
Harrisburg, PA 17126-0333
(717) 787-2967
Field of certification, effective date, expiration date are available by mail or phone. Include name and SSN.

Medical Licensing

State Board of Medicine
PO Box 2649
Harrisburg, PA 17105
(717) 783-1400
Will confirm licenses for MDs by mail or phone. For licenses not mentioned, contact the above office.

State Board of Osteopathic Medicine
PO Box 2649
Harrisburg, PA 17105
(717) 783-1400
Will confirm licenses for DOs by mail or phone. No fee. Include name and license number.

Pennsylvania Bureau of Professional & Occupational Affairs
PO Box 1753
Harrisburg, PA 17105-1753
(717) 787-8503
Will confirm license by phone. No fee. Include name, license number.

Bar Association

Pennsylvania State Bar Association
PO Box 186
Harrisburg, PA 17108
(717) 238-6715
Will confirm licenses by phone. No fee. Include name.

Accountancy Board

Pennsylvania State Board of Accountancy
PO Box 2649
Harrisburg, PA 17105
(717) 783-14-4
Will confirm license by phone. No fee. Include name.

Securities Commission

Securities Commission
Eastgate Office Building
1010 N. Seventh Street, 2nd Floor
Harrisburg, PA 17102-1410
(717) 787-5675
Will confirm license by phone. No fee. Include name and SSN.

Secretary of State

Department of State
Corporation Bureau
308 North Office Bldg.
Harrisburg, PA 17120
(717) 787-1057
Service agent and address, date incorporated, standing with tax commission, trade names are available by mail or phone. Contact the above office for additional information.

Criminal Records

State Repository

Director, Records & Identification
Attention: Central Repository
1800 Elmerton Avenue
Harrisburg, PA 17110
(717) 783-5592

All written requests must be submitted on the state form "Request For Criminal History Record Information." The form requires the subject's full name, date of birth, SSN, race, sex, aliases and the reason for the request. There is a $10.00 fee for each search. Make check payable to Commonwealth of Pennsylvania. Contact the above office for the special 2-part form. Information released contains conviction data only. Turnaround time for "no hits" is seven to ten days. "Hits" may take up to 30 days to process.

Adams County

Clerk of Court, Criminal Records
Adams County Courthouse
1111 to 1117 Baltimore Street
Room 103
Gettysburg, PA 17325
(717) 334-6781

Felony and misdemeanor records are available by mail. A release is required. $5.00 search fee. $.25 fee per copy, $5.00 fee for certifcation. Check payable to Clerk of Court. Search information required: name, date of birth.

Civil records are available by mail. No release necessary. $12.00 search fee. $1.00 fee per copy. $3.00 for certification. Search information required: name, date of birth, years to search. Specify plaintiff or defendant.

Allegheny County

Clerk of Court, Criminal Records
Grant Street, Room 114, Courthouse
Pittsburgh, PA 15219
(412) 355-5322

Felony and misdemeanor records are available by mail. A release is required. $10.00 fee. $.25 fee per copy, $5.00 fee for certifcation. Make check payable to Clerk of Court. Search information required: name, SSN, date of birth, years to search.

Civil records are available by mail. No release necessary. No search fee. $.50 fee per copy. $8.00 for certification. Search information required: name, date of birth, years to search. Specify plaintiff or defendant.

Armstrong County

Clerk of Court, Criminal Records
Armstrong County Courthouse
Kittanning, PA 16201
(412) 548-3252

Felony and misdemeanor records are available by mail. A release is required. $10.00 fee. $.50 fee per copy, $3.00 fee for certification. Search information required: name, SSN, date of birth, address, SASE.

Civil records are available in person only. See Pennsylvania state repository for additional information.

Beaver County

Clerk of Court, Criminal Records
Beaver County Courthouse
3rd Street
Beaver, PA 15009
(412) 728-5700

Felony and misdemeanor records are available by mail. No release necessary. $10.00 fee. Copies are available in person only. Make check payable to Clerk of Court. Search information required: name, SSN, date of birth, years to search.

Civil records are available in person only. See Pennsylvania state repository for additional information.

Bedford County

Clerk of Court, Criminal Records
Bedford County Courthouse
Bedford, PA 15522
(814) 623-4807
Fax (814) 623-4833

Felony and misdemeanor records are available by mail or fax. No release necessary. $10.00 search fee. Search information required: name, date of birth, years to search.

Civil records are available by mail. No release necessary. $12.00 search fee. $.50 fee per copy. $3.00 for certification. Search information required: name, date of birth, years to search. Specify plaintiff or defendant.

Berks County

Clerk of Common Pleas
Criminal Division, Berks County Courthouse
33 N. 6th St, 4th Floor
Reading, PA 19601
(215) 378-8119

Felony and misdemeanor records are available in person only. See Pennsylvania state repository for additional information.

Civil records are available in person only. See Pennsylvania state repository for additional information.

Blair County

Clerk of Court, Criminal Records
PO Box 719
Hollidaysburg, PA 16648
(814) 695-5541 Extension 311

Felony and misdemeanor records are available by mail. No release necessary. $10.00 search fee. Make check payable to Clerk of Court. Search information required: name, date of birth.

Civil records are available by mail. No release necessary. No search fee. $.50 fee per copy. $3.00 for certification. Search information required: name, date of birth, years to search. Specify plaintiff or defendant.

Bradford County

Clerk of Court, Criminal Records
Courthouse
Main Street
Towanda, PA 18848
(717) 265-5700 Extension 132

Felony and misdemeanor records are available by mail. No release necessary. $5.00 search fee. $.25 fee per copy. $5.00 for certification. Search information required: name, SSN, date of birth, SASE, years to search.

Civil records are available by mail. No release necessary. $5.00 search fee. $.25 fee per copy. $3.00 for certification. Search information required: name, date of birth, years to search, SASE. Specify plaintiff or defendant.

Bucks County

Clerk of Court
Criminal Division
Bucks County Courthouse
Doylestown, PA 18901
(215) 348-6389

Felony and misdemeanor records are available by mail. No release necessary. No search fee. $1.00 fee per copy, $5.00 for certification. Search information required: name, date of birth, years to search.

Civil records are available in person only. See Pennsylvania state repository for additional information.

Butler County

Clerk of Court, Criminal Records
Butler County Courthouse
PO Box 1208
Butler, PA 16001-1208
(412) 285-4731
Fax (412) 284-5238

Felony and misdemeanor records are available by mail or fax. A release is required. $5.00 search fee, prepaid. Payable to Clerk of Court. Search information required: name, SSN, date of birth, SASE.

Civil records are available in person only. See Pennsylvania state repository for additional information.

Cambria County

Office of Clerk of Court, Criminal Records
Cambria County Courthouse
Ebensburg, PA 15931
(814) 472-5440

Felony and misdemeanor records are available by mail. No release necessary. $1.00 search fee. Make check payable to Clerk of Court. Search information required: name, SSN, date of birth, sex, race.

Civil records are available in person only. See Pennsylvania state repository for additional information.

Cameron County

Clerk of Court, Criminal Records
Cameron County Courthouse
Emporium, PA 15834
(814) 486-3355
Fax (814) 486-0464

Felony and misdemeanor records are available by mail, fax or phone. No release necessary. $10.00 search fee. Search information required: name, years to search.

Civil records are available in person only. See Pennsylvania state repository for additional information.

Carbon County

Clerk of Court, Criminal Records
Carbon County Courthouse
Jim Thorpe, PA 18229
(717) 325-3637 or 3638

Felony and misdemeanor records are available by mail or phone. No release necessary. No search fee. Search information required: name, date of birth.

Civil records are available by mail. No release necessary. $1.00 search fee. $1.00 fee per copy. Search information required: name, date of birth, years to search, SASE. Specify plaintiff or defendant.

Centre County

Clerk of Court, Criminal Records
Centre County Courthouse
Bellefonte, PA 16823
(814) 355-6796

Felony and misdemeanor records are available by mail. Release, if available. $5.00 search fee. Search information required: name, date of birth, previous address, years to search.

Civil records are available in person only. See Pennsylvania state repository for additional information.

Chester County

Clerk of Court, Criminal Records
2 N. High Street, Suite 2
West Chester, PA 19380
(215) 344-6135

Felony and misdemeanor records are available by mail. A release is required. $10.00 fee. Make check payable to Clerk of Court. Search information required: name, SSN, date of birth, present address of individual, previous address, years to search, SASE.

Civil records are available by mail. A release is required. $10.00 search fee. Search information required: name, date of birth, years to search. Specify plaintiff or defendant.

Clarion County

Prothonotary–Clerk of Court, Criminal Records
Clarion County Courthouse
Main Street
Clarion, PA 16214
(814) 226-4000

Felony and misdemeanor records are available by mail or phone. No release necessary. $10.00 fee. Make check payable to Clerk of Court. Search information required: name.

Civil records are available by mail or phone. No release necessary. $12.00 search fee. $.25 fee per copy. $5.00 for certification. Search information required: name, date of birth, years to search. Specify plaintiff or defendant.

Clearfield County

Prothonotary's Office
231 1/2 E. Market St.
Clearfield, PA 16830
(814) 765-2641 Extension 22

Felony and misdemeanor records are available by mail. No release necessary. No search fee. $.50 fee per copy. Search information required: name, date of birth , address.

Civil records are available in person only. See Pennsylvania state repository for additional information.

Clinton County

Clerk of Court, Criminal Records
PO Box 630
Lock Haven, PA 17745
(717) 893-4007

Felony and misdemeanor records are available by mail or phone. No release necessary. No search fee. Copies are released only with written consent of defendant. Search information required: name, date of birth.

Civil records are available in person only. See Pennsylvania state repository for additional information.

Columbia County

Clerk of Court, Criminal Records
PO Box 380
Bloomsburg, PA 17815
(717) 389-5614

Felony and misdemeanor records are available by mail. A release is required. $10.00 fee. Make check payable to Clerk of Court. Search information required: name, SSN, date of birth, previous address, years to search.

Civil records are available by mail. No release necessary. $12.00 search fee. $.25 fee per copy. $3.00 for certification. Search information required: name, date of birth, years to search. Specify plaintiff or defendant.

Crawford County

Clerk of Court, Criminal Records
Courthouse
Meadville, PA 16335
(814) 336-1151

Felony and misdemeanor records are available by mail. A release is required. $10.00 fee. Make check payable to Clerk of Court. Search information required: name, SSN, date of birth, years to search.

Civil records are available in person only. See Pennsylvania state repository for additional information.

Cumberland County

Clerk of Court, Criminal Records
Cumberland County Courthouse
Carlisle, PA 17013
(717) 240-6250

Felony and misdemeanor records are available by mail. A release is required. $10.00 search fee. Make check payable to Clerk of Court. Search information required: name, SSN, date of birth, sex, race, years to search.

Civil records are available in person only. See Pennsylvania state repository for additional information.

Dauphin County

Clerk of Court, Criminal Records
Dauphin County Courthouse
Front & Market Street
Harrisburg, PA 17101
(717) 255-2692

Felony and misdemeanor records are available by mail. No release necessary. $10.00 search fee. Search information required: name, date of birth, SSN, SASE, years to search.

Civil records are available by mail or phone. No release necessary. $10.00 fee per 5 years searched. $1.00 fee per copy. $3.00 for first certification, $1.00 each additional certification. Search information required: name, date of birth, years to search. Specify plaintiff or defendant.

Delaware County

Clerk of Court, Criminal Records
Judicial Support, Veteran's Square Courthouse
PO Box 1056
Media, PA 19063
(215) 891-4363
Fax (215) 891-7294

Felony and misdemeanor records are available by mail. A release is required. $10.00 search fee. Search information required: name, SSN, date of birth.

Civil records are available in person only. See Pennsylvania state repository for additional information.

Elk County

Clerk of Court, Criminal Records
PO Box 237
Ridgway, PA 15853
(814) 776-1161 Ext. 344

Felony and misdemeanor records are available by mail or phone. No release necessary. $10.00 fee. Make check payable to Clerk of Court. Search information required: name, date of birth, years to search. Will only search last 15 years.

Civil records are available by mail. No release necessary. $5.00 search fee. $1.00 fee per each case found. $.50 fee per copy. $3.00 for certification. Search information required: name, date of birth, years to search. Specify plaintiff or defendant.

Erie County

Clerk of the District Court, Criminal Records
Erie County Courthouse
140 West 6th St.
Erie, PA 16501
(814) 451-6250

Felony and misdemeanor records are available by mail or phone. No release necessary. $10.00 fee. Make check payable to Clerk of Court. Search information required: name, date of birth.

Civil records are available in person only. See Pennsylvania state repository for additional information.

Fayette County

Felony and misdemeanor records
Clerk of Court, Criminal Records
61 E. Main Street
Uniontown, PA 15401
(412) 430-1253

Felony and misdemeanor records are available by mail. A release is required. Court will bill $10 fee if record is found. Search information required: name, date of birth.

Civil records
Clerk of Court
61 E. Main Street
Uniontown, PA 15401
(412) 430-1272

Civil records are available by mail or phone. No release necessary. No search fee. $.50 fee per copy. $3.00 for certification. Search information required: name, date of birth, years to search. Specify plaintiff or defendant.

Forest County

Clerk of Court, Criminal Records
PO Box 423
Forest County Courthouse
Tionesta, PA 16353
(814) 755-3526
Fax (814) 755-8837
Felony and misdemeanor records are available by mail or fax. No release necessary. No search fee. Search information required: name.

Civil records are available by mail, fax or phone. No release necessary. No search fee. $.25 fee per copy. $1.50 for certification. Search information required: name, date of birth, years to search, SASE. Specify plaintiff or defendant.

Franklin County

Felony and misdemeanor records
Clerk of Court, Criminal Records
157 Lincoln Way East
Chambersburg, PA 17201
(717) 261-3805
Felony and misdemeanor records are available by mail. A release is required. $10.00 fee. Make check payable to Clerk of Court. Search information required: name, SSN, date of birth, sex, race.

Civil records
Clerk of Court
157 Lincoln Way East
Chambersburg, PA 17201
(717) 261-3848
Civil records are available by mail. No release necessary. $10.00 search fee. Search information required: name, date of birth, years to search. Specify plaintiff or defendant.

Fulton County

Clerk of Court, Criminal Records
Fulton County Courthouse
McConnellsburg, PA 17233
(717) 485-4212
Felony and misdemeanor records are available by mail. No release necessary. $5.00 search fee. $.50 fee per copy. $5.00 for certificaiton. Search information required: name, date of birth, years to search.

Civil records are available in person only. See Pennsylvania state repository for additional information.

Greene County

Clerk of Court, Criminal Records
Greene County Courthouse
Waynesburg, PA 15370
(412) 852-1171
Felony and misdemeanor records are available by mail. No release necessary. $10.00 search fee. $.50 fee per copy. $5.00 for certificaiton. Search information required: name, date of birth, SSN, years to search.

Civil records are available by mail. No release necessary. $12.00 search fee. $.40 fee per copy. Search information required: name, date of birth, years to search. Specify plaintiff or defendant.

Huntingdon County

Clerk of Court, Criminal Records
PO Box 39
Courthouse
Huntingdon, PA 16652
(814) 643-1610
Felony and misdemeanor records are available by mail or phone. No release necessary. $5.00 search fee. $.25 fee per copy. $5.00 for certification. Search information required: name, date of birth, years to search.

Civil records are available by mail. No release necessary. $5.00 search fee. $.20 fee per copy. $3.00 for certification.Search information required: name, date of birth, years to search. Specify plaintiff or defendant.

Indiana County

Clerk of Court, Criminal Records
Prothonotary's Office
Indiana County Courthouse
825 Philadelphia St.
Indiana, PA 15701
(412) 465-3855
Felony and misdemeanor records are available by mail. No release necessary. $10.00 search fee. Make check payable to Clerk of Court. Search information required: name, date of birth.

Civil records are available in person only. See Pennsylvania state repository for additional information.

Jefferson County

Clerk of Court, Criminal Records
Jefferson County Courthouse
200 Main Street
Brookville, PA 15825
(814) 849-1606
Felony and misdemeanor records are available by mail. No release necessary. $5.00 search fee. Search information required: name, date of birth.

Civil records are available in person only. See Pennsylvania state repository for additional information.

Juniata County

Clerk of Court, Criminal Records
Juniata County Courthouse
Mifflintown, PA 17059
(717) 436-8991
Felony and misdemeanor records are available by mail. No release necessary. No search fee. Search information required: name, date of birth, years to search.

Civil records are available by mail. A release is required. $5.00 search fee. $.30 fee per copy. $1.00 for certification. Search information required: name, date of birth, years to search. Specify plaintiff or defendant.

Lackawanna County

Clerk of Judicial Records, Criminal Division
3rd Floor
Lackawanna County Courthouse
Scranton, PA 18503
(717) 963-6759
Felony and misdemeanor records are available by mail. No release necessary. $10.00 fee. Make check payable to Clerk of Judicial Records. Search information required: name, date of birth, years to search.

Civil records are available in person only. See Pennsylvania state repository for additional information.

Lancaster County

Clerk of Court, Criminal Records
50 N. Duke Street
Lancaster, PA 17602
(717) 299-8275 Extension 1
Felony and misdemeanor records are available by mail. A release is required. $10.00 search fee. Make check payable to Clerk of Court. Search information required: name, date of birth, years to search.

Civil records are available in person only. See Pennsylvania state repository for additional information.

Lawrence County

Clerk of Court, Criminal Records
Lawrence County Government Center
Court Street
New Castle, PA 16101
(412) 658-2541, Ext. 189
Felony and misdemeanor records are available by mail. A release is required. $10.00 search fee. Certified check only, payable to Clerk of Court. Search information required: name, date of birth, years to search.

Civil records are available by mail or phone. A release required. No search fee. $.30 fee per copy. $1.00 for certification. Search information required: name, years to search. Specify plaintiff or defendant.

Lebanon County

Clerk of Court, Criminal Records
Room 106, Municipal Bldg.
400 S. 8th Street
Lebanon, PA 17042
(717) 274-2801
Felony and misdemeanor records are available by mail. No release necessary. $10.00 search fee. $.25 fee per copy. $5.00 for certification. Certified check or money order, payable to Clerk of Court. Search information required: name, SSN, date of birth, years to search.

Civil records are available in person only. See Pennsylvania state repository for additional information.

Lehigh County

Clerk of Court, Criminal Records
PO Box 1548
Allentown, PA 18105
(215) 820-3077
Felony and misdemeanor records are available by mail. No release necessary. $10.00 search fee. $10.00 additional fee for alias search or maiden name search. Company checks only, payable to Clerk of Court. Search information required: name, date of birth, SSN, address.

Civil records are available in person only. See Pennsylvania state repository for additional information.

Luzerne County

Clerk of Court, Criminal Records
200 North River Street
Wilkes–Barre, PA 18711
(717) 825-1585
Fax (717) 825-1843

Felony and misdemeanor records are available by fax or mail. No release necessary. $10.00 search fee. $.25 fee per copy. $5.00 for certification. Company checks only, payable to Clerk of Court. Search information required: name, date of birth, years to search.

Civil records are available by mail or fax. No release necessary. $10.00 search fee. $1.00 fee per copy. $3.00 for certification. Search information required: name, date of birth, years to search. Specify plaintiff or defendant.

Lycoming County

Lycoming County Prothonotary's Office, Criminal Records
48 W. 3rd
Williamsport, PA 17701
(717) 327-2200

Felony and misdemeanor records are available by mail. No release necessary. $10.00 search fee. Company checks only, payable to Lycoming County Prothonotary. Search information required: name, date of birth.

Civil records are available in person only. See Pennsylvania state repository for additional information.

McKean County

Clerk of Court, Criminal Records
PO Box 273
Smethport, PA 16749
(814) 887-5571 Extension 270
Fax (814) 2242

Felony and misdemeanor records are available by mail, fax or phone. No release necessary. $10.00 search fee. $2.00 fee per page faxed. Company checks only, payable to Clerk of Court. Search information required: name, date of birth, years to search.

Civil records are available by mail. No release necessary. $12.00 search fee. $.50 fee per copy. $3.50 for certification. Search information required: name, date of birth, years to search. Specify plaintiff or defendant.

Mercer County

Clerk of Court, Criminal Records
112 Mercer County Courthouse
Mercer, PA 16137
(412) 662-3800

Felony and misdemeanor records are available by mail. A release is required. $10.00 search fee. Company checks only, payable to Clerk of Court. Search information required: name, SSN, date of birth, sex, race, years to search.

Civil records are available in person only. See Pennsylvania state repository for additional information.

Mifflin County

Prothonotary's Office, Criminal Records
20 N. Wayne Street
Lewistown, PA 17044
(717) 248-8146

Felony and misdemeanor records are available by mail or phone. No release necessary. No search fee. Search information required: name, date of birth, years to search.

Civil records are available by mail or phone. No release necessary. No search fee. $.25 fee per copy. $3.00 for certification. Search information required: name, date of birth, years to search. Specify plaintiff or defendant.

Monroe County

Prothonotary, Criminal Records
Monroe County Courthouse
Stroudsburg, PA 18360
(717) 424-5100

Felony and misdemeanor records are available by mail. No release necessary. $5.00 search fee. $1.00 fee per copy. Make check payable to Clerk of Court. Search information required: name, date of birth, years to search.

Civil records are available by mail. No release necessary. $5.00 search fee. $1.00 fee per copy. $3.00 for certification. Search information required: name, date of birth, years to search. Specify plaintiff or defendant.

Montgomery County

Clerk of Court, Criminal Records
Montgomery County Courthouse
Airy & Swede Street
Norristown, PA 19404
(215) 278-3000

Felony and misdemeanor records are available by mail. A release is required. $5.00 search fee. Search information required: name, date of birth, years to search, SASE.

Civil records are available in person only. See Pennsylvania state repository for additional information.

Montour County

Prothonotary's Office, Criminal Records
Montour County Courthouse
29 Mill Street
Danville, PA 17821
(717) 271-3010

Felony and misdemeanor records are available by mail or phone. No release necessary. No search fee. Make check payable to Clerk of Court. Search information required: name, date of birth.

Civil records are available in person only. See Pennsylvania state repository for additional information.

Northampton County

Criminal Division
Northampton County Government Center
7th and Washington St.
Easton, PA 18042
(215) 559-3000 Ext. 2114

Felony and misdemeanor records are available by mail. No release necessary. $5.00 search fee, prepaid. Make check payable to Northampton County Criminal Division. Search information required: name, SSN, date of birth, years to search.

Civil records are available by mail. No release necessary. No search fee. $1.00 fee for copy, $.25 each additional copy. $3.00 for certification. Search information required: name, date of birth, years to search. Specify plaintiff or defendant.

Northumberland County

Clerk of Court, Criminal Records
Northumberland County Courthouse
2nd and Market Street
Sunbury, PA 17801
(717) 988-4148

Felony and misdemeanor records are available by mail. No release necessary. $5.00 search fee. Make check payable to Clerk of Court. Search information required: name, date of birth.

Civil records are available by mail. No release necessary. $12.00 search fee. $1.00 fee per case found. $.50 fee per copy. $10.00 for certification. Search information required: name, date of birth, years to search. Specify plaintiff or defendant.

Perry County

Prothonotary's Office, Criminal Records
PO Box 325
New Bloomfield, PA 17068
(717) 582-2131

Felony and misdemeanor records are available by mail or phone. No release necessary. No search fee. Search information required: name, date of birth.

Civil records are available in person only. See Pennsylvania state repository for additional information.

Philadelphia County

Clerk of Quarter Sessions, 2nd Deputy
Room 663 City Hall
Philadelphia, PA 19107
(215) 686-4280

Felony and misdemeanor records are available by mail. Each name searched must be on separate request letter. No release necessary. $10.00 search fee. Make check payable to Clerk of Quarter Sessions. Search information required: name, date of birth, years to search, race, sex, address, SASE.

Civil records are available by mail. No release necessary. $30.00 search fee. Search information required: name, date of birth, years to search, SASE. Specify plaintiff or defendant.

Pike County

Prothonotary's Office, Criminal
Records
412 Broad Street
Milford, PA 18337
(717) 296-7231

Felony and misdemeanor records are available by mail. No release necessary. No search fee. Search information required: name, years to search, SASE.

Civil records are available in person only. See Pennsylvania state repository for additional information.

Potter County

Prothonotary, Criminal Records
1 East 2nd Street
Coudersport, PA 16915
(814) 274-9740
Fax (814) 274-0584

Felony and misdemeanor records are available by mail or phone. No release necessary. No search fee. Search information required: name, date of birth.

Civil records are available by mail or phone. No release necessary. No search fee. $.25 fee per copy. $3.00 for certification. Search information required: name, date of birth, years to search. Specify plaintiff or defendant.

Schuylkill County

Clerk of Court
Schuylkill County Courthouse
401 N. 2nd Street.
Pottsville, PA 17901-2520
(717) 628-1140
Fax (717) 628-1108

Felony and misdemeanor records are available by mail. No release necessary. $10.00 search fee. Check or money order payable to Clerk of Court. Search information required: name, date of birth, previous address.

Civil records are available by mail . No release necessary. No search fee. $.25 fee per copy. Search information required: name, date of birth, years to search. Specify plaintiff or defendant.

Snyder County

Prothonotary, Criminal Records
Snyder County Courthouse
PO Box 217
Middleburg, PA 17842
(717) 837-4202

Felony and misdemeanor records are available by mail or phone. No release necessary. $5.00 search fee. Company checks only, payable to Snyder County Prothonotary. Search information required: name, date of birth, years to search.

Civil records are available by mail. A releaseis required. No search fee. $.25 fee per copy. $3.00 for certification. Search information required: name, date of birth, years to search. Specify plaintiff or defendant.

Somerset County

Clerk of Court, Criminal Records
PO Box 494
Somerset, PA 15501
(814) 443-3049
Fax (814) 445-5154

Felony and misdemeanor records are available by mail or fax. No release necessary. $5.00 search fee. Company checks only, payable to Clerk of Court. Search information required: name, SSN, date of birth, years to search.

Civil records are available in person only. See Pennsylvania state repository for additional information.

Sullivan County

Sullivan County Courthouse, Criminal
Records
Clerk of Court
Main Street
LaPorte, PA 18626
(717) 946-7351

Felony and misdemeanor records are available by mail. No release necessary. $25.00 search fee. $.25 fee per copy. $3.00 for certification. Search information required: name, date of birth, years to search, SASE.

Civil records are available by mail. No release necessary. $25.00 search fee. $.25 fee per copy. $3.00 for certification. Search information required: name, date of birth, years to search, SASE. Specify plaintiff or defendant.

Susquehanna County

Prothonotary's Office, Criminal
Records
Susquehanna County Courthouse
Montrose, PA 18801
(717) 278-4600 Ext. 320

Felony and misdemeanor records are available by mail or phone. No release necessary. No search fee. Search information required: name, date of birth, years to search.

Civil records are available by mail or phone. No release necessary. $5.00 search fee. $1.00 fee per each item found. $1.00 fee per copy. $3.00 for certification. Search information required: name, date of birth, years to search. Specify plaintiff or defendant.

Tioga County

Clerk of Court, Criminal Records
Main Street
Wellsboro, PA 16901
(717) 724-1906

Felony and misdemeanor records are available by mail. A release is required. $5.00 fee. Make check payable to Tioga County Prothonotary. Search information required: name, SSN, date of birth, previous address, years to search.

Civil records are available in person only. See Pennsylvania state repository for additional information.

Union County

Clerk of Court, Criminal Records
Union County Courthouse
Lewisburg, PA 17837
(717) 524-8751

Felony and misdemeanor records are available by mail or phone. A release is required. No search fee. Search information required: name, date of birth, previous address.

Civil records are available in person only. See Pennsylvania state repository for additional information.

Venango County

Clerk of Court, Criminal Records
Venango County Courthouse
Franklin, PA 16323
(814) 437-6871 Extension 254

Felony and misdemeanor records are available by mail or phone. No release necessary. $5.00 search fee. Certified check only, payable to Clerk of Court. Search information required: name, date of birth. Prepayment required on phone searches.

Civil records are available by mail. No release necessary. $5.00 search fee. $.25 fee per copy. $5.00 for certification. Search information required: name, date of birth, years to search. Specify plaintiff or defendant.

Warren County

Clerk of Court, Criminal Records
4th and Market Street
Warren, PA 16365
(814) 723-7550

Felony and misdemeanor records are available by mail. A release is required. $5.00 search fee. $1.00 fee per copy. $3.00 for certification. Search information required: name, date of birth, previous address, years to search.

Civil records are available by mail. No release necessary. $12.00 search fee. $1.00 fee per copy. $3.00 for certification. Search information required: name, date of birth, years to search. Specify plaintiff or defendant.

Washington County

Clerk of Court, Criminal Records
Courthouse
Washington, PA 15301
(412) 228-6787

Felony and misdemeanor records are available by mail. No release necessary. $5.00 search fee. Company checks only, payable to Clerk of Court. Search information required: name, date of birth.

Civil records are available in person only. See Pennsylvania state repository for additional information.

Wayne County

Wayne County Courthouse
925 Court Street
Honesdale, PA 18431-1996
(717) 253-5970

Records are available in person only. See Pennsylvania state repository for additional information.

Civil records are available in person only. See Pennsylvania state repository for additional information.

Westmoreland County

Court of Common Pleas
Criminal Division
203 Courthouse Square
Greensburg, PA 15601-1168
(412) 830-3734
Fax (412) 830-3042
Felony and misdemeanor records are available by mail or fax. No release necessary. $10.00 search fee. Company checks only, payable to Clerk of Court. Search information required: name, alias, SSN, date of birth, previous address, years to search.

Civil records are available in person only. See Pennsylvania state repository for additional information.

Wyoming County

Prothonotary's Office, Criminal Records
Wyoming County Courthouse
Tunkhannock, PA 18657
(717) 836-3200
Records are not available by mail or phone. See Pennsylvania state repository.

Civil records are available in person only. See Pennsylvania state repository for additional information.

York County

Clerk of Court
York County Courthouse
York, PA 17401
(717) 771-9612
Records are not available by mail or phone. See Pennsylvania state repository for additional information.

Civil records are available in person only. See Pennsylvania state repository for additional information.

City-County Cross Reference

Aaronsburg *Centre*
Abbottstown *Adams*
Abington *Montgomery*
Acme *Westmoreland*
Acmetonia *Allegheny*
Acosta *Somerset*
Adah *Fayette*
Adamsburg *Westmoreland*
Adamstown *Lancaster*
Adamsville *Crawford*
Addison *Somerset*
Adrian *Armstrong*
Airville *York*
Akron *Lancaster*
Alba *Bradford*
Albion *Erie*
Albrightsville *Carbon*
Alburtis *Lehigh*
Aldan *Delaware*
Alden *Luzerne*
Aleppo *Greene*
Alexandria *Huntingdon*
Aliquippa *Beaver*
Allenport *Washington*
Allensville *Mifflin*
Allentown *Lehigh*
Allenwood *Union*
Allison *Fayette*
Allison Park *Allegheny*
Allport *Clearfield*
Almedia *Columbia*
Altoona *Blair*
Alum Bank *Bedford*
Alverda *Indiana*
Alverton *Westmoreland*
Amberson *Franklin*
Ambler *Montgomery*
Ambridge *Beaver*
Amity *Washington*
Analomink *Monroe*
Ancient Oaks *Lehigh*
Andreas *Schuylkill*
Anita *Jefferson*
Annville *Lebanon*
Antes Fort *Lycoming*
Apollo *Armstrong*
Aquashicola *Carbon*
Arcadia *Indiana*
Archbald *Lackawanna*
Arcola *Montgomery*
Ardara *Westmoreland*
Ardmore *Montgomery*
Arendtsville *Adams*

Aristes *Columbia*
Armagh *Indiana*
Armbrust *Westmoreland*
Arnold *Allegheny*
Arnot *Tioga*
Arona *Westmoreland*
Artemas *Bedford*
Ashfield *Carbon*
Ashland *Schuylkill*
Ashley *Luzerne*
Ashville *Cambria*
Aspers *Adams*
Aspinwall *Allegheny*
Atglen *Chester*
Athens *Bradford*
Atlantic *Crawford*
Atlas *Northumberland*
Atlasburg *Washington*
Auburn *Schuylkill*
Audubon *Montgomery*
Aultman *Indiana*
Austin *Potter*
Avalon *Allegheny*
Avella *Washington*
Avis *Clinton*
Avoca *Luzerne*
Avon *Lebanon*
Avondale *Chester*
Avonmore *Westmoreland*
Baden *Beaver*
Bainbridge *Lancaster*
Bairdford *Allegheny*
Bakers Summit *Bedford*
Bakerstown *Allegheny*
Bala-Cynwyd *Montgomery*
Baldwin *Allegheny*
Bally *Berks*
Bangor *Northampton*
Baresville *York*
Bareville *Lancaster*
Barnesboro *Cambria*
Barnesville *Schuylkill*
Barree *Huntingdon*
Bart *Lancaster*
Barto *Berks*
Bartonsville *Monroe*
Bath *Northampton*
Bausman *Lancaster*
Beach Haven *Luzerne*
Beach Lake *Wayne*
Beallsville *Washington*
Bear Lake *Warren*
Beaver *Beaver*

Beaverdale *Cambria*
Beaver Falls *Beaver*
Beaver Meadows *Carbon*
Beaver Springs *Snyder*
Beavertown *Snyder*
Beccaria *Clearfield*
Bechtelsville *Berks*
Bedford *Bedford*
Bedminster *Bucks*
Beech Creek *Clinton*
Belfast *Northampton*
Bell Acres *Allegheny*
Bellefonte *Centre*
Belle Vernon *Fayette*
Belleville *Mifflin*
Bellevue *Allegheny*
Bellwood *Blair*
Belmont *Cambria*
Belsano *Cambria*
Bendersville *Adams*
Benezett *Elk*
Bensalem *Bucks*
Bentleyville *Washington*
Benton *Columbia*
Berlin *Somerset*
Bernville *Berks*
Berrysburg *Dauphin*
Berwick *Columbia*
Berwyn *Chester*
Bessemer *Lawrence*
Bethel *Berks*
Bethel Park *Allegheny*
Bethlehem *Northampton*
Beyer *Indiana*
Big Beaver *Beaver*
Bigler *Clearfield*
Biglerville *Adams*
Big Run *Jefferson*
Birchrunville *Chester*
Bird In Hand *Lancaster*
Birdsboro *Berks*
Black Lick *Indiana*
Blain *Perry*
Blairs Mills *Huntingdon*
Blairsville *Indiana*
Blakely *Lackawanna*
Blakeslee *Monroe*
Blanchard *Centre*
Blandburg *Cambria*
Blawnox *Allegheny*
Blandon *Berks*
Blooming Glen *Bucks*
Bloomsburg *Columbia*

Blossburg *Tioga*
Blue Ball *Lancaster*
Blue Bell *Montgomery*
Blue Ridge Summit
 Franklin
Boalsburg *Centre*
Bobtown *Greene*
Boiling Springs
 Cumberland
Bolivar *Westmoreland*
Bonneauville *Adams*
Boston *Allegheny*
Boswell *Somerset*
Bovard *Westmoreland*
Bowers *Berks*
Bowmansdale *Cumberland*
Bowmanstown *Carbon*
Bowmansville *Lancaster*
Boyers *Butler*
Boyertown *Berks*
Boynton *Somerset*
Brackenridge *Allegheny*
Brackney *Susquehanna*
Braddock *Allegheny*
Braddock Hills *Allegheny*
Bradenville *Westmoreland*
Bradford *McKean*
Bradfordwoods *Allegheny*
Branch Dale *Schuylkill*
Branchton *Butler*
Brandamore *Chester*
Brandy Camp *Elk*
Brave *Greene*
Breezewood *Bedford*
Breinigsville *Lehigh*
Brentwood *Allegheny*
Breslau *Luzerne*
Bridgeport *Montgomery*
Bridgeville *Allegheny*
Brier Hill *Fayette*
Brisbin *Clearfield*
Bristol *Bucks*
Broad Top *Huntingdon*
Brockport *Elk*
Brockton *Schuylkill*
Brockway *Jefferson*
Brodheadsville *Monroe*
Brogue *York*
Brookhaven *Delaware*
Brooklyn *Susquehanna*
Brookside *Erie*
Brookville *Jefferson*
Broomall *Delaware*

Browndale *Wayne*
Brownfield *Fayette*
Brownstown *Lancaster*
Brownsville *Fayette*
Bruin *Butler*
Brush Valley *Indiana*
Bryn Athyn *Montgomery*
Bryn Mawr *Montgomery*
Buck Hill Falls *Monroe*
Buckingham *Bucks*
Buena Vista *Allegheny*
Buffalo Mills *Bedford*
Bulger *Washington*
Bunola *Allegheny*
Burgettstown *Washington*
Burlington *Bradford*
Burnham *Mifflin*
Burnside *Clearfield*
Burnt Cabins *Fulton*
Bushkill *Pike*
Butler *Butler*
Byrnedale *Elk*
Cabot *Butler*
Cadogan *Armstrong*
Cairnbrook *Somerset*
California *Washington*
Callensburg *Clarion*
Callery *Butler*
Calumet *Westmoreland*
Calvin *Huntingdon*
Cambra *Luzerne*
Cambridge Springs *Crawford*
Cammal *Lycoming*
Campbelltown *Lebanon*
Camp Hill *Cumberland*
Camptown *Bradford*
Canadensis *Monroe*
Canadohta Lake *Crawford*
Canonsburg *Washington*
Canton *Bradford*
Carbondale *Lackawanna*
Cardale *Fayette*
Carlisle *Cumberland*
Carlton *Mercer*
Carmichaels *Greene*
Carnegie *Allegheny*
Carnot *Allegheny*
Carrolltown *Cambria*
Carversville *Bucks*
Cashtown *Adams*
Cassandra *Cambria*
Cassville *Huntingdon*
Castanea *Clinton*
Castle Shannon *Allegheny*
Catasauqua *Lehigh*
Catawissa *Columbia*
Cecil *Washington*
Cedars *Montgomery*
Cementon *Northampton*
Centerport *Berks*
Center Square *Montgomery*
Center Valley *Lehigh*
Centerville *Crawford*
Central City *Somerset*
Centralia *Columbia*
Centre Hall *Centre*
Cetronia *Lehigh*
Chadds Ford *Delaware*
Chalfont *Bucks*
Chalkhill *Fayette*
Chambersburg *Franklin*
Chambersville *Indiana*
Champion *Westmoreland*
Chandlers Valley *Warren*

Charleroi *Washington*
Chatham *Chester*
Chatewood *Chester*
Cheltenham *Montgomery*
Cherry Tree *Indiana*
Cherryville *Northampton*
Cherokee Ranch *Berks*
Chester *Delaware*
Chester Heights *Delaware*
Chester Hill *Clearfield*
Chester Springs *Chester*
Chestnut Ridge *Fayette*
Chest Springs *Cambria*
Cheswick *Allegheny*
Chevy Chase Heights *Indiana*
Cheyney *Delaware*
Chicora *Butler*
Chinchilla *Lackawanna*
Christiana *Lancaster*
Churchill *Allegheny*
Churchville *Bucks*
Clairton *Allegheny*
Clarence *Centre*
Clarendon *Warren*
Claridge *Westmoreland*
Clarington *Forest*
Clarion *Clarion*
Clark *Mercer*
Clarksburg *Indiana*
Clarks Mills *Mercer*
Clarks Summit *Lackawanna*
Clarksville *Greene*
Claysburg *Blair*
Claysville *Washington*
Clearfield *Clearfield*
Clearville *Bedford*
Cleona *Lebanon*
Clifford *Susquehanna*
Clifton Heights *Delaware*
Climax *Armstrong*
Clinton *Allegheny*
Clintonville *Venango*
Clune *Indiana*
Clymer *Indiana*
Coal Center *Washington*
Coaldale *Schuylkill*
Coaltown *Lawrence*
Coalport *Clearfield*
Coatesville *Chester*
Coburn *Centre*
Cochranton *Crawford*
Cochranville *Chester*
Cocolamus *Juniata*
Codorus *York*
Cogan Station *Lycoming*
Cokeburg *Washington*
Colebrook *Lebanon*
Collegeville *Montgomery*
Collingdale *Delaware*
Colmar *Montgomery*
Colonial Park *Dauphin*
Columbia *Lancaster*
Columbia Cross Roads *Bradford*
Columbus *Warren*
Colver *Cambria*
Commodore *Indiana*
Concord *Franklin*
Concordville *Delaware*
Conestoga *Lancaster*
Confluence *Somerset*
Conneaut Lake *Crawford*
Conneautville *Crawford*

Connellsville *Fayette*
Connoquenessing *Butler*
Conshohocken *Montgomery*
Conway *Beaver*
Conyngham *Luzerne*
Cooksburg *Forest*
Coopersburg *Lehigh*
Cooperstown *Venango*
Coplay *Lehigh*
Coral *Indiana*
Coraopolis *Allegheny*
Cornwall *Lebanon*
Corry *Erie*
Corsica *Jefferson*
Coudersport *Potter*
Coulters *Allegheny*
Courtdale *Luzerne*
Courtney *Washington*
Covington *Tioga*
Cowanesque *Tioga*
Cowansville *Armstrong*
Crabtree *Westmoreland*
Crafton *Allegheny*
Craigsville *Armstrong*
Craley *York*
Cranberry *Venango*
Cranesville *Erie*
Creamery *Montgomery*
Creekside *Indiana*
Creighton *Allegheny*
Cresco *Monroe*
Cresson *Cambria*
Cressona *Schuylkill*
Crosby *McKean*
Cross Fork *Potter*
Crown *Clarion*
Crucible *Greene*
Crystal Spring *Fulton*
Cuddy *Allegheny*
Cumbola *Schuylkill*
Curllsville *Clarion*
Curryville *Blair*
Curtisville *Allegheny*
Curwensville *Clearfield*
Custer City *McKean*
Cyclone *McKean*
Dagus Mines *Elk*
Daisytown *Washington*
Dale *Cambria*
Dallas *Luzerne*
Dallastown *York*
Dalmatia *Northumberland*
Dalton *Lackawanna*
Damascus *Wayne*
Danboro *Bucks*
Danielsville *Northampton*
Danville *Montour*
Darby *Delaware*
Darlington *Beaver*
Darragh *Westmoreland*
Dauphin *Dauphin*
Davidsville *Somerset*
Dawson *Fayette*
Dawson Ridge *Beaver*
Dayton *Armstrong*
Deemston *Washington*
Defiance *Bedford*
DeLancey *Jefferson*
Delano *Schuylkill*
Delaware Water Gap *Monroe*
Delmont *Westmoreland*
Delta *York*
Denbo *Washington*

Denver *Lancaster*
Derrick City *McKean*
Derry *Westmoreland*
Devault *Chester*
Devon *Chester*
Dewart *Northumberland*
DeYoung *Elk*
Dickerson Run *Fayette*
Dickinson *Cumberland*
Dickson City *Lackawanna*
Dilliner *Greene*
Dillsburg *York*
Dilltown *Indiana*
Dimock *Susquehanna*
Dingmans Ferry *Pike*
Distant *Armstrong*
Dixonville *Indiana*
Donegal *Westmoreland*
Donora *Washington*
Dormont *Allegheny*
Dorneyville *Lehigh*
Dornsife *Northumberland*
Douglassville *Berks*
Downingtown *Chester*
Dover *York*
Doylestown *Bucks*
Dravosburg *Allegheny*
Drexel Hill *Delaware*
Drifting *Clearfield*
Drifton *Luzerne*
Driftwood *Cameron*
Drumore *Lancaster*
Drums *Luzerne*
Dry Run *Franklin*
Dublin *Bucks*
Du Bois *Clearfield*
Duboistown *Lycoming*
Dudley *Huntingdon*
Duke Center *McKean*
Dunbar *Fayette*
Duncannon *Perry*
Duncansville *Blair*
Dunlevy *Washington*
Dunlo *Cambria*
Dunnstown *Clinton*
Duquesne *Allegheny*
Durham *Bucks*
Duryea *Luzerne*
Dushore *Sullivan*
Dysart *Cambria*
Eagles Mere *Sullivan*
Eagleville *Montgomery*
Earlington *Montgomery*
Earlville *Berks*
East Bangor *Northampton*
East Berlin *Adams*
East Berwick *Luzerne*
East Brady *Clarion*
East Butler *Butler*
East Conemaugh *Cambria*
East Earl *Lancaster*
East Freedom *Blair*
East Greenville *Montgomery*
East Hickory *Forest*
East Lansdowne *Delaware*
East McKeesport *Allegheny*
East Millsboro *Fayette*
Easton *Northampton*
East Petersburg *Lancaster*
East Pittsburgh *Allegheny*
East Prospect *York*
Easr Rochester *Beaver*
East Smethport *McKean*

East Smithfield *Bradford*
East Springfield *Erie*
East Stroudsburg *Monroe*
East Texas *Lehigh*
East Uniontown *Fayette*
East Vandergrift
    Westmoreland
East Washington
    Washington
East Waterford *Juniata*
Eau Claire *Butler*
Ebensburg *Cambria*
Ebervale *Luzerne*
Economy *Beaver*
Eddystone *Delaware*
Eden *Lancaster*
Edgemont *Delaware*
Edgewood *Allegheny*
Edgeworth *Allegheny*
Edinboro *Erie*
Edinburg *Lawrence*
Edmon *Armstrong*
Edwardsville *Luzerne*
Effort *Monroe*
Egypt *Lehigh*
Eighty Four *Washington*
Elco *Washington*
Eldersville *Washington*
Elderton *Armstrong*
Eldred *McKean*
Elgin *Erie*
Elizabeth *Allegheny*
Elizabethtown *Lancaster*
Elizabethville *Dauphin*
Elkland *Tioga*
Elliottsburg *Perry*
Ellport *Beaver*
Ellsworth *Washington*
Ellwood City *Lawrence*
Elm *Lancaster*
Elmhurst *Lackawanna*
Elmora *Cambria*
Elrama *Washington*
Elton *Cambria*
Elverson *Chester*
Elysburg *Northumberland*
Emeigh *Cambria*
Emigsville *York*
Emlenton *Venango*
Emmaus *Lehigh*
Emporium *Cameron*
Endeavor *Forest*
Enola *Cumberland*
Enon Valley *Lawrence*
Entriken *Huntingdon*
Ephrata *Lancaster*
Equinunk *Wayne*
Erie *Erie*
Erwinna *Bucks*
Essington *Delaware*
Estherton *Cumberland*
Etna *Allegheny*
Etters *York*
Evans City *Butler*
Evansburg *Montgomery*
Evansville *Berks*
Everett *Bedford*
Everson *Fayette*
Excelsior *Northumberland*
Export *Westmoreland*
Exton *Chester*
Factoryville *Wyoming*
Fairbank *Fayette*
Fairchance *Fayette*
Fairfield *Adams*

Fairhope *Somerset*
Fairless Hills *Bucks*
Fairmount City *Clarion*
Fairview *Erie*
Fallentimber *Cambria*
Falls *Wyoming*
Falls Creek *Jefferson*
Fannettsburg *Franklin*
Farmington *Fayette*
Farrandsville *Clinton*
Farrell *Mercer*
Fawn Grove *York*
Fayette City *Fayette*
Fayetteville *Franklin*
Faxon *Lycoming*
Felton *York*
Fellsburg *Westmoreland*
Fenelton *Butler*
Ferndale *Bucks*
Fernway *Butler*
Filbert *Fayette*
Finleyville *Washington*
Fisher *Clarion*
Fishertown *Bedford*
Five Points *Beaver*
Fleetville *Lackawanna*
Fleetwood *Berks*
Fleming *Centre*
Flemington *Clinton*
Flinton *Cambria*
Flourtown *Montgomery*
Fogelsville *Lehigh*
Folcroft *Delaware*
Folsom *Delaware*
Fombell *Beaver*
Forbes Road *Westmoreland*
Force *Elk*
Ford City *Armstrong*
Ford Cliff *Armstrong*
Forest City *Susquehanna*
Forest Grove *Bucks*
Forest Hills *Allegheny*
Forestville *Butler*
Forksville *Sullivan*
Fort Hill *Somerset*
Fort Loudon *Franklin*
Fort Washington
    Montgomery
Forty Fort *Luzerne*
Foster Brook *McKean*
Fountain Hill *Lehigh*
Fountainville *Bucks*
Foxburg *Clarion*
Fox Chapel *Allegheny*
Frackville *Schuylkill*
Franklin *Venango*
Franklin Park *Allegheny*
Franklintown *York*
Frazer *Chester*
Frederick *Montgomery*
Fredericksburg *Lebanon*
Fredericktown *Washington*
Fredonia *Mercer*
Freeburg *Snyder*
Freedom *Beaver*
Freeland *Luzerne*
Freemansburg
    Northampton
Freeport *Armstrong*
Frenchville *Clearfield*
Friedens *Somerset*
Friedensburg *Schuylkill*
Friendsville *Susquehanna*
Frisco *Beaver*
Fryburg *Clarion*

Furlong *Bucks*
Gabby Heights *Washington*
Gaines *Tioga*
Galeton *Potter*
Gallitzin *Cambria*
Gap *Lancaster*
Garards Fort *Greene*
Garden View *Lycoming*
Gardenville *Bucks*
Gardners *Adams*
Garland *Warren*
Garrett *Somerset*
Gastonville *Washington*
Geigertown *Berks*
Geistown *Cambria*
Genesee *Potter*
Georgetown *Beaver*
Germansville *Lehigh*
Gettysburg *Adams*
Ghennes Heights
    Washington
Gibbon Glade *Fayette*
Gibson *Susquehanna*
Gibsonia *Allegheny*
Gifford *McKean*
Gilbert *Monroe*
Gilberton *Schuylkill*
Gilbertsville *Montgomery*
Gillett *Bradford*
Gipsy *Indiana*
Girard *Erie*
Girardville *Schuylkill*
Gladwyne *Montgomery*
Glasgow *Cambria*
Glassport *Allegheny*
Glen Campbell *Indiana*
Glencoe *Somerset*
Glen Lyon *Luzerne*
Glen Mills *Delaware*
Glenmoore *Chester*
Glenolden *Delaware*
Glen Rock *York*
Glenshaw *Allegheny*
Glenside *Montgomery*
Glenville *York*
Glenwillard *Allegheny*
Glenwood *Cumberland*
Goodville *Lancaster*
Gordon *Schuylkill*
Gordonville *Lancaster*
Gouldsboro *Wayne*
Gowen City
    Northumberland
Gradyville *Delaware*
Grampian *Clearfield*
Grand Valley *Warren*
Grangeville *York*
Grantham *Cumberland*
Grantville *Dauphin*
Granville *Mifflin*
Granville Summit *Bradford*
Grapeville *Westmoreland*
Grassflat *Clearfield*
Graterford *Montgomery*
Gratz *Dauphin*
Gray *Somerset*
Graysville *Greene*
Great Bend *Susquehanna*
Greeley *Pike*
Greenawalds *Lehigh*
Greencastle *Franklin*
Green Lane *Montgomery*
Greenock *Allegheny*
Green Park *Perry*
Greensboro *Greene*

Greensburg *Westmoreland*
Greentown *Pike*
Green Tree *Chester*
Greenville *Mercer*
Greenwood *Blair*
Grindstone *Fayette*
Grove City *Mercer*
Grover *Bradford*
Guys Mills *Crawford*
Gwynedd Valley
    Montgomery
Hadley *Mercer*
Halifax *Dauphin*
Hallam *York*
Hallstead *Susquehanna*
Hamburg *Berks*
Hamilton *Jefferson*
Hamlin *Wayne*
Hannastown *Westmoreland*
Hanover *York*
Harborcreek *Erie*
Harford *Susquehanna*
Harleigh *Luzerne*
Harleysville *Montgomery*
Harmonsburg *Crawford*
Harmony *Butler*
Harrisburg *Dauphin*
Harrison City
    Westmoreland
Harrisville *Butler*
Hartleton *Union*
Hartstown *Crawford*
Harveys Lake *Luzerne*
Harwick *Allegheny*
Hastings *Cambria*
Hatboro *Montgomery*
Hatfield *Montgomery*
Haverford *Montgomery*
Hawk Run *Clearfield*
Hawley *Wayne*
Hawthorn *Clarion*
Hayti *Chester*
Hazel Hurst *McKean*
Hazleton *Luzerne*
Hecktown *Northampton*
Hegins *Schuylkill*
Heidelberg *Allegheny*
Heilwood *Indiana*
Helfenstein *Schuylkill*
Hellertown *Northampton*
Hendersonville *Washington*
Henryville *Monroe*
Hereford *Berks*
Herman *Butler*
Herminie *Westmoreland*
Hermitage *Mercer*
Herndon *Northumberland*
Herrick Center
    Susquehanna
Hershey *Dauphin*
Hesston *Huntingdon*
Hibbs *Fayette*
Hickory *Washington*
Highland Park *Cumberland*
Highspire *Dauphin*
Hiller *Fayette*
Hilliards *Butler*
Hillsdale *Indiana*
Hillsgrove *Sullivan*
Hillsville *Lawrence*
Hilltown *Bucks*
Holbrook *Greene*
Holicong *Bucks*
Holland *Bucks*
Hollidaysburg *Blair*

Hollsopple *Somerset*
Holmes *Delaware*
Hometown *Schuylkill*
Holtwood *Lancaster*
Home *Indiana*
Homer City *Indiana*
Homestead *Allegheny*
Honesdale *Wayne*
Honey Brook *Chester*
Honey Grove *Juniata*
Hookstown *Beaver*
Hooversville *Somerset*
Hop Bottom *Susquehanna*
Hopeland *Lancaster*
Hopewell *Bedford*
Hopwood *Fayette*
Horsham *Montgomery*
Hostetter *Westmoreland*
Houserville *Centre*
Houston *Washington*
Houtzdale *Clearfield*
Howard *Centre*
Hudson *Luzerne*
Huey *Clarion*
Hughestown *Luzerne*
Hughesville *Lycoming*
Hulmeville *Bucks*
Hummelstown *Dauphin*
Hummels Wharf *Snyder*
Hunker *Westmoreland*
Hunlock Creek *Luzerne*
Huntingdon *Huntingdon*
Huntingdon Valley
    Montgomery
Huntington Mills *Luzerne*
Hustontown *Fulton*
Hutchinson *Westmoreland*
Hyde *Clearfield*
Hyde Park *Westmoreland*
Hydetown *Crawford*
Hyndman *Bedford*
Ickesburg *Perry*
Idaville *Adams*
Imler *Bedford*
Immaculata *Chester*
Imperial *Allegheny*
Indiana *Indiana*
Indian Head *Fayette*
Indianola *Allegheny*
Industry *Beaver*
Ingomar *Allegheny*
Ingram *Allegheny*
Intercourse *Lancaster*
Iona *Lebanon*
Irvine *Warren*
Irvona *Clearfield*
Irwin *Westmoreland*
Isabella *Fayette*
Jackson *Susquehanna*
Jackson Center *Mercer*
Jacksonwald *Berks*
Jacobs Creek
    Westmoreland
Jacobus *York*
James City *Elk*
James Creek *Huntingdon*
Jamestown *Mercer*
Jamison *Bucks*
Jeannette *Westmoreland*
Jefferson *Greene*
Jenkintown *Montgomery*
Jenners *Somerset*
Jennerstown *Somerset*
Jermyn *Lackawanna*
Jerome *Somerset*

Jersey Mills *Lycoming*
Jersey Shore *Lycoming*
Jessup *Lackawanna*
Jim Thorpe *Carbon*
Joffre *Washington*
Johnsonburg *Elk*
Johnstown *Cambria*
Jones Mills *Westmoreland*
Jonestown *Lebanon*
Josephine *Indiana*
Julian *Centre*
Juneau *Indiana*
Junedale *Carbon*
Juniata Gap *Blair*
Juniata Terrace *Mifflin*
Kane *McKean*
Kantner *Somerset*
Karns City *Butler*
Karthaus *Clearfield*
Kaska *Schuylkill*
Keisterville *Fayette*
Kelayres *Schuylkill*
Kelton *Chester*
Kemblesville *Chester*
Kempton *Berks*
Kenhorst *Berks*
Kennerdell *Venango*
Kennett Square *Chester*
Kent *Indiana*
Kersey *Elk*
Kimberton *Chester*
Kingsley *Susquehanna*
Kingston *Luzerne*
Kintnersville *Bucks*
Kinzers *Lancaster*
Kirkwood *Lancaster*
Kittanning *Armstrong*
Kleinfeltersville *Lebanon*
Klingerstown *Schuylkill*
Knox *Clarion*
Knox Dale *Jefferson*
Knoxville *Tioga*
Koppel *Beaver*
Korn Krest *Luzerne*
Kossuth *Clarion*
Kreamer *Snyder*
Kresgeville *Monroe*
Kulpmont *Northumberland*
Kulpsville *Montgomery*
Kunkletown *Monroe*
Kutztown *Berks*
Kylertown *Clearfield*
LaBelle *Fayette*
Laceyville *Wyoming*
Lackawaxen *Pike*
Lafayette Hill *Montgomery*
Laflin *Luzerne*
Lahaska *Bucks*
Lairdsville *Lycoming*
LaJose *Clearfield*
Lake Ariel *Wayne*
Lake City *Erie*
Lake Como *Wayne*
Lake Harmony *Carbon*
Lake Lynn *Fayette*
Lake Winola *Wyoming*
Lakewood *Wayne*
Lamar *Clinton*
Lamartine *Clarion*
Lampeter *Lancaster*
Lancaster *Lancaster*
Landenberg *Chester*
Landingville *Schuylkill*
Landisburg *Perry*
Landisville *Lancaster*

Lanesboro *Susquehanna*
Langeloth *Washington*
Langhorne *Bucks*
Lansdale *Montgomery*
Lansdowne *Delaware*
Lanse *Clearfield*
Lansford *Carbon*
LaPlume *Lackawanna*
Laporte *Sullivan*
Larimer *Westmoreland*
Latrobe *Westmoreland*
Lattimer Mines *Luzerne*
Laughlintown
    Westmoreland
Laureldale *Berks*
Laurel Run *Luzerne*
Laurelton *Union*
Laurys Station *Lehigh*
Lavelle *Schuylkill*
Lawn *Lebanon*
Lawrence *Washington*
Lawrence Park *Erie*
Lawrenceville *Tioga*
Lawton *Susquehanna*
Leaders Heights *York*
Lebanon *Lebanon*
Leck Kill *Northumberland*
Leckrone *Fayette*
Lederach *Montgomery*
Leechburg *Armstrong*
Lee Park *Luzerne*
Leeper *Clarion*
Leesport *Berks*
Leetsdale *Allegheny*
Lehighton *Carbon*
Lehman *Luzerne*
Leisenring *Fayette*
Leith *Fayette*
Lemasters *Franklin*
Lemont *Centre*
Lemont Furnace *Fayette*
Lemoyne *Cumberland*
Lenhartsville *Berks*
Lenni *Delaware*
Leola *Lancaster*
Le Raysville *Bradford*
Le Roy *Bradford*
Level Green *Westmoreland*
Levittown *Bucks*
Lewisberry *York*
Lewisburg *Union*
Lewis Run *McKean*
Lewistown *Mifflin*
Lewisville *Chester*
Liberty *Tioga*
Library *Allegheny*
Lickingville *Clarion*
Light Street *Columbia*
Ligonier *Westmoreland*
Lilly *Cambria*
Limekiln *Berks*
Limeport *Lehigh*
Limerick *Montgomery*
Limestone *Clarion*
Lincoln University *Chester*
Lincoln Heights
    Westmoreland
Lincoln Park *Berks*
Linden *Lycoming*
Line Lexington *Bucks*
Linesville *Crawford*
Linglestown *Dauphin*
Linntown *Union*
Linwood *Delaware*
Listie *Somerset*

Lititz *Lancaster*
Little Marsh *Tioga*
Little Meadows
    Susquehanna
Littlestown *Adams*
Liverpool *Perry*
Llewellyn *Schuylkill*
Lock Haven *Clinton*
Locustdale *Schuylkill*
Locust Gap
    Northumberland
Loganton *Clinton*
Loganville *York*
Long Pond *Monroe*
Lopez *Sullivan*
Lorain *Cambria*
Lorane *Berks*
Loretto *Cambria*
Lost Creek *Schuylkill*
Lowber *Westmoreland*
Lower Burrell
    Westmoreland
Loyalhanna *Westmoreland*
Loysburg *Bedford*
Loysville *Perry*
Lucernemines *Indiana*
Lucinda *Clarion*
Ludlow *McKean*
Lurgan *Franklin*
Luthersburg *Clearfield*
Luxor *Westmoreland*
Lykens *Dauphin*
Lyndell *Chester*
Lyndon *Lancaster*
Lyndora *Butler*
Lyon Station *Berks*
McAdoo *Schuylkill*
McAlisterville *Juniata*
McCandless *Allegheny*
McClellandtown *Fayette*
McClure *Snyder*
McConnellsburg *Fulton*
McConnellstown
    Huntingdon
McDonald *Washington*
McElhattan *Clinton*
McEwensville
    Northumberland
McGovern *Washington*
McGrann *Armstrong*
McIntyre *Indiana*
McKean *Erie*
McKeesport *Allegheny*
McKees Rocks *Allegheny*
McKnightstown *Adams*
McMurray *Washington*
McSherrystown *Adams*
McVeytown *Mifflin*
Mackeyville *Clinton*
Macungie *Lehigh*
Madera *Clearfield*
Madison *Westmoreland*
Madisonburg *Centre*
Mahaffey *Clearfield*
Mahanoy City *Schuylkill*
Mahanoy Plane *Schuylkill*
Mainesburg *Tioga*
Mainland *Montgomery*
Malvern *Chester*
Mammoth *Westmoreland*
Manchester *York*
Manheim *Lancaster*
Manns Choice *Bedford*
Manor *Westmoreland*
Manor Ridge *Lancaster*

Manorville *Armstrong*
Mansfield *Tioga*
Mapleton Depot
   Huntingdon
Marble *Clarion*
Marchand *Indiana*
Marcus Hook *Delaware*
Marianna *Washington*
Marienville *Forest*
Marietta *Lancaster*
Marion *Franklin*
Marion Center *Indiana*
Marion Heights
   Northumberland
Markleton *Somerset*
Markleysburg *Fayette*
Mar Lin *Schuylkill*
Mars *Butler*
Marshalls Creek *Monroe*
Marshallton
   Northumberland
Marsteller *Cambria*
Martin *Fayette*
Martinsburg *Blair*
Martins Creek
   Northampton
Mary D *Schuylkill*
Marysville *Perry*
Masontown *Fayette*
Matamoras *Pike*
Mather *Greene*
Mattawana *Mifflin*
Maxatawny *Berks*
Mayfield *Lackawanna*
Mayport *Clarion*
Maytown *Lancaster*
Meadow Lands
   Washington
Meadville *Crawford*
Mechanicsburg
   Cumberland
Mechanicsville *Bucks*
Media *Delaware*
Mehoopany *Wyoming*
Melcroft *Fayette*
Mendenhall *Chester*
Mentcle *Indiana*
Mercer *Mercer*
Mercersburg *Franklin*
Meridian *Butler*
Merion Station
   Montgomery
Merrittstown *Fayette*
Mertztown *Berks*
Meshoppen *Wyoming*
Mexico *Juniata*
Meyersdale *Somerset*
Middleburg *Snyder*
Middlebury Center *Tioga*
Middleport *Schuylkill*
Middletown *Dauphin*
Midland *Beaver*
Midway *Washington*
Mifflin *Juniata*
Mifflinburg *Union*
Mifflintown *Juniata*
Mifflinville *Columbia*
Milan *Bradford*
Milanville *Wayne*
Mildred *Sullivan*
Milesburg *Centre*
Milford *Pike*
Milford Square *Bucks*
Mill Creek *Huntingdon*
Millersburg *Dauphin*

Millerstown *Perry*
Millersville *Lancaster*
Millerton *Tioga*
Mill Hall *Clinton*
Millheim *Centre*
Millmont *Union*
Millrift *Pike*
Mill Run *Fayette*
Mills *Potter*
Millsboro *Washington*
Millvale *Allegheny*
Mill Village *Erie*
Millville *Columbia*
Milnesville *Luzerne*
Milroy *Mifflin*
Milton *Northumberland*
Mineral Point *Cambria*
Mineral Springs *Clearfield*
Minersville *Schuylkill*
Mingoville *Centre*
Minisink Hills *Monroe*
Miquon *Montgomery*
Mocanaqua *Luzerne*
Modena *Chester*
Mohnton *Berks*
Mohrsville *Berks*
Monaca *Beaver*
Monessen *Westmoreland*
Monocacy Station *Berks*
Monongahela *Washington*
Monroeton *Bradford*
Monroeville *Allegheny*
Mont Alto *Franklin*
Montandon
   Northumberland
Mont Clare *Montgomery*
Montgomery *Lycoming*
Montgomeryville
   Montgomery
Montoursville *Lycoming*
Montrose *Susquehanna*
Moon *Allegheny*
Moon Run *Allegheny*
Moosic *Lackawanna*
Morann *Clearfield*
Morgan *Allegheny*
Morgantown *Berks*
Morris *Tioga*
Morrisdale *Clearfield*
Morris Run *Tioga*
Morrisville *Bucks*
Morton *Delaware*
Moscow *Lackawanna*
Moshannon *Centre*
Mount Aetna *Berks*
Mountainhome *Monroe*
Mountain Top *Luzerne*
Mount Allen *Cumberland*
Mount Bethel
   Northampton
Mount Braddock *Fayette*
Mount Carmel
   Northumberland
Mount Cobb *Lackawanna*
Mount Gretna *Lebanon*
Mount Holly Springs
   Cumberland
Mount Jewett *McKean*
Mount Joy *Lancaster*
Mount Lebanon *Allegheny*
Mount Morris *Greene*
Mount Oliver *Allegheny*
Mount Penn *Berks*
Mount Pleasant
   Westmoreland

Mount Pleasant Mills
   Snyder
Mount Pocono *Monroe*
Mount Union *Huntingdon*
Mountville *Lancaster*
Mount Wolf *York*
Muir *Schuylkill*
Muncy *Lycoming*
Muncy Valley *Sullivan*
Munhall *Allegheny*
Munson *Clearfield*
Murrysville *Westmoreland*
Muse *Washington*
Myerstown *Lebanon*
Nanticoke *Luzerne*
Nanty Glo *Cambria*
Narberth *Montgomery*
Narvon *Lancaster*
Natrona Heights *Allegheny*
Nazareth *Northampton*
Needmore *Fulton*
Neelyton *Huntingdon*
Neffs *Lehigh*
Nelson *Tioga*
Nemacolin *Greene*
Nescopeck *Luzerne*
Nesquehoning *Carbon*
New Albany *Bradford*
New Alexandria
   Westmoreland
New Baltimore *Somerset*
New Beaver *Lawrence*
New Bedford *Lawrence*
New Berlin *Union*
New Berlinville *Berks*
New Bethlehem *Clarion*
New Bloomfield *Perry*
New Brighton *Beaver*
New Buffalo *Perry*
Newburg *Cumberland*
New Castle *Lawrence*
New Cumberland
   Cumberland
New Derry *Westmoreland*
New Eagle *Washington*
Newell *Fayette*
New Enterprise *Bedford*
New Florence
   Westmoreland
Newfoundland *Wayne*
New Freedom *York*
New Freeport *Greene*
New Galilee *Beaver*
New Geneva *Fayette*
New Germantown *Perry*
New Holland *Lancaster*
New Hope *Bucks*
New Kensington
   Westmoreland
New Kingstown
   Cumberland
New London *Chester*
Newmanstown *Lebanon*
New Milford *Susquehanna*
New Millport *Clearfield*
New Oxford *Adams*
New Paris *Bedford*
New Park *York*
New Philadelphia
   Schuylkill
Newport *Perry*
New Providence *Lancaster*
New Ringgold *Schuylkill*
Newry *Blair*
New Salem *Fayette*

New Stanton *Westmoreland*
Newton Hamilton *Mifflin*
Newtown *Bucks*
Newtown Square *Delaware*
New Tripoli *Lehigh*
Newville *Cumberland*
New Wilmington *Lawrence*
Nicholson *Wyoming*
Nicktown *Cambria*
Nineveh *Greene*
Nisbet *Lycoming*
Normalville *Fayette*
Norristown *Montgomery*
Northampton *Northampton*
North Apollo *Armstrong*
North Belle Vernon
   Westmoreland
North Bend *Clinton*
North Braddock *Allegheny*
North Catasauqua
   Northampton
North Charleroi
   Washington
North East *Erie*
North Springfield *Erie*
Northumberland
   Northumberland
North Versailles *Allegheny*
North Wales *Montgomery*
North Warren *Warren*
North Washington *Butler*
North York *York*
Norvelt *Westmoreland*
Norwood *Delaware*
Nottingham *Chester*
Noxen *Wyoming*
Nuangola *Luzerne*
Numidia *Columbia*
Nu Mine *Armstrong*
Nuremberg *Schuylkill*
Oakdale *Allegheny*
Oakland Mills *Juniata*
Oakmont *Allegheny*
Oak Park *Montgomery*
Oak Ridge *Armstrong*
Oaks *Montgomery*
Ohiopyle *Fayette*
Ohioville *Beaver*
Oil City *Venango*
Oklahoma *Westmoreland*
Olanta *Clearfield*
Old Forge *Lackawanna*
Old Zionsville *Lehigh*
Oley *Berks*
Oliveburg *Jefferson*
Oliver *Fayette*
Olyphant *Lackawanna*
Oneida *Schuylkill*
Ono *Lebanon*
Orangeville *Columbia*
Orbisonia *Huntingdon*
Orchard Hills *Armstrong*
Orefield *Lehigh*
Oreland *Montgomery*
Orrstown *Franklin*
Orrtanna *Adams*
Orson *Wayne*
Orwigsburg *Schuylkill*
Osceola *Tioga*
Osceola Mills *Clearfield*
Osterburg *Bedford*
Ottsville *Bucks*
Oxford *Chester*
Paint *Somerset*
Palm *Montgomery*

Palmer Heights *Northampton*
Palmerton *Carbon*
Palmyra *Lebanon*
Palo Alto *Schuykill*
Paoli *Chester*
Paradise *Lancaster*
Pardeesville *Luzerne*
Paris *Washington*
Parker *Armstrong*
Parker Ford *Chester*
Parkesburg *Chester*
Parkhill *Cambria*
Parkville *York*
Parryville *Carbon*
Patterson Heights *Beaver*
Patton *Cambria*
Paupack *Pike*
Paxinos *Northumberland*
Paxtonia *Cumberland*
Paxtonville *Snyder*
Peach Bottom *Lancaster*
Peckville *Lackawanna*
Pen Argyl *Northampton*
Penfield *Clearfield*
Penn *Westmoreland*
Penndel *Bucks*
Penn Hills *Allegheny*
Penn Run *Indiana*
Penns Creek *Snyder*
Penns Park *Bucks*
Pennsylvania Furnace *Huntingdon*
Penryn *Lancaster*
Pequea *Lancaster*
Perkasie *Bucks*
Perkiomenville *Montgomery*
Perryopolis *Fayette*
Petersburg *Huntingdon*
Petrolia *Butler*
Philadelphia *Philadelphia*
Philipsburg *Centre*
Phoenixville *Chester*
Picture Rocks *Lycoming*
Pillow *Dauphin*
Pine Bank *Greene*
Pine Forge *Berks*
Pine Grove *Schuylkill*
Pine Grove Mills *Centre*
Pineville *Bucks*
Pipersville *Bucks*
Pitcairn *Allegheny*
Pitman *Schuylkill*
Pittsburgh *Allegheny*
Pittsfield *Warren*
Pittston *Luzerne*
Plainfield *Cumberland*
Plains *Luzerne*
Pleasant Gap *Centre*
Pleasant Hall *Franklin*
Pleasant Hills *Allegheny*
Pleasant Mount *Wayne*
Pleasant Unity *Westmoreland*
Pleasantville *Venango*
Pleasurville *York*
Plum *Allegheny*
Plumsteadville *Bucks*
Plumville *Indiana*
Plymouth *Luzerne*
Plymouth Meeting *Montgomery*
Plymptonville *Clearfield*
Pocono Lake *Monroe*

Pocono Manor *Monroe*
Pocono Pines *Monroe*
Pocono Summit *Monroe*
Pocopson *Chester*
Point Marion *Fayette*
Point Pleasant *Bucks*
Polk *Venango*
Pomeroy *Chester*
Portage *Cambria*
Port Allegany *McKean*
Port Carbon *Schuylkill*
Port Clinton *Schuylkill*
Portersville *Butler*
Portland *Northampton*
Port Matilda *Centre*
Port Royal *Juniata*
Port Trevorton *Snyder*
Port Vue *Allegheny*
Potts Grove *Northumberland*
Pottstown *Montgomery*
Pottsville *Schuylkill*
Poyntelle *Wayne*
Presto *Allegheny*
Preston Park *Wayne*
Pricedale *Westmoreland*
Primrose *Schuylkill*
Progress *Cumberland*
Prompton *Wayne*
Prospect *Butler*
Prospect Park *Delaware*
Prosperity *Washington*
Pulaski *Lawrence*
Punxsutawney *Jefferson*
Quakake *Schuylkill*
Quakertown *Bucks*
Quarryville *Lancaster*
Quecreek *Somerset*
Queen *Bedford*
Quentin *Lebanon*
Quincy *Franklin*
Railroad *York*
Rahns *Montgomery*
Ralston *Lycoming*
Ramey *Clearfield*
Rankin *Allegheny*
Ransom *Lackawanna*
Ravine *Schuylkill*
Rea *Washington*
Reading *Berks*
Reamstown *Lancaster*
Rebersburg *Centre*
Rebuck *Northumberland*
Rector *Westmoreland*
Red Hill *Montgomery*
Red Lion *York*
Reeders *Monroe*
Reedsville *Mifflin*
Refton *Lancaster*
Rehrersburg *Berks*
Reiffton *Berks*
Reinholds *Lancaster*
Renfrew *Butler*
Reno *Venango*
Renovo *Clinton*
Republic *Fayette*
Revere *Bucks*
Revloc *Cambria*
Rew *McKean*
Rexmont *Lebanon*
Reynoldsville *Jefferson*
Rheems *Lancaster*
Rices Landing *Greene*
Riceville *Crawford*
Richeyville *Washington*

Richfield *Juniata*
Richland *Lebanon*
Richlandtown *Bucks*
Riddlesburg *Bedford*
Ridgway *Elk*
Ridley Park *Delaware*
Riegelsville *Bucks*
Rillton *Westmoreland*
Rimersburg *Clarion*
Ringgold *Jefferson*
Ringtown *Schuylkill*
Riverside *Northumberland*
Rixford *McKean*
Roaring Branch *Tioga*
Roaring Spring *Blair*
Robertsdale *Huntingdon*
Robesonia *Berks*
Robinson *Indiana*
Rochester *Beaver*
Rochester Mills *Indiana*
Rock Glen *Luzerne*
Rockhill Furnace *Huntingdon*
Rockledge *Montgomery*
Rockton *Clearfield*
Rockwood *Somerset*
Rogersville *Greene*
Rohrerstown *Lancaster*
Rome *Bradford*
Ronco *Fayette*
Ronks *Lancaster*
Roscoe *Washington*
Roseto *Northampton*
Rose Valley *Delaware*
Rossiter *Indiana*
Rossmoyne *Cumberland*
Rossville *York*
Roulette *Potter*
Rouseville *Venango*
Rouzerville *Franklin*
Rowes Run *Fayette*
Rowland *Pike*
Roxbury *Franklin*
Royersford *Montgomery*
Ruffs Dale *Westmoreland*
Rural Ridge *Allegheny*
Rural Valley *Armstrong*
Rushland *Bucks*
Rushville *Susquehanna*
Russell *Warren*
Russellton *Allegheny*
Rutledge *Delaware*
Sabinsville *Tioga*
Sacramento *Schuylkill*
Sadsburyville *Chester*
Saegertown *Crawford*
Sagamore *Armstrong*
Saint Benedict *Cambria*
Saint Boniface *Cambria*
Saint Clair *Schuylkill*
Saint Johns *Luzerne*
Saint Lawrence *Berks*
Saint Marys *Elk*
Saint Michael *Cambria*
Saint Peters *Chester*
Saint Petersburg *Clarion*
Saint Thomas *Franklin*
Salford *Montgomery*
Salfordville *Montgomery*
Salina *Westmoreland*
Salisbury *Somerset*
Salix *Cambria*
Saltillo *Huntingdon*
Saltsburg *Indiana*
Salunga *Lancaster*

Sand Hill *Lebanon*
Sandy *Clearfield*
Sandy Lake *Mercer*
Sankertown *Cambria*
Sarver *Butler*
Sassamansville *Montgomery*
Saxonburg *Butler*
Saxton *Bedford*
Saylorsburg *Monroe*
Sayre *Bradford*
Scalp Level *Cambria*
Scenery Hill *Washington*
Schaefferstown *Lebanon*
Schellsburg *Bedford*
Schenley *Armstrong*
Schnecksville *Lehigh*
Schuylkill Haven *Schuylkill*
Schwenksville *Montgomery*
Sciota *Monroe*
Scotland *Franklin*
Scotrun *Monroe*
Scottdale *Westmoreland*
Scranton *Lackawanna*
Seanor *Somerset*
Selinsgrove *Snyder*
Sellersville *Bucks*
Seltzer *Schuylkill*
Seminole *Armstrong*
Seneca *Venango*
Seven Valleys *York*
Seward *Westmoreland*
Sewickley *Allegheny*
Shade Gap *Huntingdon*
Shady Grove *Franklin*
Shamokin *Northumberland*
Shamokin Dam *Snyder*
Shanksville *Somerset*
Sharon *Mercer*
Sharon Hill *Delaware*
Sharpsburg *Allegheny*
Sharpsville *Mercer*
Shartlesville *Berks*
Shavertown *Luzerne*
Shawanese *Luzerne*
Shawnee On Delaware *Monroe*
Shawville *Clearfield*
Sheakleyville *Mercer*
Sheffield *Warren*
Shelocta *Indiana*
Shenandoah *Schuylkill*
Shenandoah Heights *Schuylkill*
Sheppton *Schuylkill*
Shermans Dale *Perry*
Shickshinny *Luzerne*
Shillington *Berks*
Shiloh *York*
Shinglehouse *Potter*
Shippensburg *Cumberland*
Shippenville *Clarion*
Shippingport *Beaver*
Shiremanstown *Cumberland*
Shirleysburg *Huntingdon*
Shoemakersville *Berks*
Shohola *Pike*
Shrewsbury *York*
Shunk *Sullivan*
Sidman *Cambria*
Sigel *Jefferson*
Silverdale *Bucks*

Silver Spring *Lancaster*
Simpson *Lackawanna*
Sinking Spring *Berks*
Sinnamahoning *Cameron*
Sipesville *Somerset*
Six Mile Run *Bedford*
Skippack *Montgomery*
Skytop *Monroe*
Slatedale *Lehigh*
Slateford *Northampton*
Slate Run *Lycoming*
Slatington *Lehigh*
Slickville *Westmoreland*
Sligo *Clarion*
Slippery Rock *Butler*
Slovan *Washington*
Smethport *McKean*
Smicksburg *Indiana*
Smithfield *Fayette*
Smithmill *Clearfield*
Smithton *Westmoreland*
Smock *Fayette*
Smokerun *Clearfield*
Smoketown *Lancaster*
Snow Shoe *Centre*
Snydersburg *Clarion*
Solebury *Bucks*
Somerset *Somerset*
Soudersburg *Lancaster*
Souderton *Montgomery*
Southampton *Bucks*
South Canaan *Wayne*
South Coatsville *Chester*
South Fork *Cambria*
South Gibson *Susquehanna*
South Greensburg
    Westmoreland
South Heights *Beaver*
Southmont *Cambria*
South Montrose
    Susquehanna
South Mountain *Franklin*
South Pottstown *Chester*
South Sterling *Wayne*
South Temple *Berks*
South Uniontown *Fayette*
Southview *Washington*
South Waverly *Bradford*
Southwest *Westmoreland*
South Williamsport
    Lycoming
Spangler *Cambria*
Spartansburg *Crawford*
Spinnerstown *Bucks*
Spraggs *Greene*
Springboro *Crawford*
Spring Church *Armstrong*
Spring City *Chester*
Spring Creek *Warren*
Springdale *Allegheny*
Springfield *Delaware*
Spring Gardens York
Spring Glen *Schuylkill*
Spring Grove *York*
Spring House *Montgomery*
Spring Mills *Centre*
Spring Mount *Montgomery*
Spring Run *Franklin*
Springs *Somerset*
Springtown *Bucks*
Springville *Susquehanna*
Sproul *Blair*
Spruce Creek *Huntingdon*
Stahlstown *Westmoreland*

Stafore Estates
    Northampton
Starford *Indiana*
Star Brick *Warren*
Star Junction *Fayette*
Starlight *Wayne*
Starrucca *Wayne*
State College *Centre*
State Line *Franklin*
Steelton *Dauphin*
Steelville *Chester*
Sterling *Wayne*
Stevens *Lancaster*
Stevensville *Bradford*
Stewartstown *York*
Stiles *Lehigh*
Stillwater *Columbia*
Stockdale *Washington*
Stockertown *Northampton*
Stoneboro *Mercer*
Stoneybrook *York*
Stoney Creek Mills *Berks*
Stony Run *Berks*
Stowe *Montgomery*
Stoystown *Somerset*
Strabane *Washington*
Strasburg *Lancaster*
Strattanville *Clarion*
Strausstown *Berks*
Stroudsburg *Monroe*
Stump Creek *Jefferson*
Sturgeon *Allegheny*
Sugargrove *Warren*
Sugarloaf *Luzerne*
Sugar Notch *Luzerne*
Sugar Run *Bradford*
Summerdale *Cumberland*
Summerhill *Cambria*
Summerville *Jefferson*
Summit Hill *Carbon*
Summit Station *Schuylkill*
Sumneytown *Montgomery*
Sunbury *Northumberland*
Sunset Valley
    Westmoreland
Suplee *Chester*
Susquehanna *Susquehanna*
Sutersville *Westmoreland*
Swarthmore *Delaware*
Sweet Valley *Luzerne*
Swengel *Union*
Swiftwater *Monroe*
Swissvale *Allegheny*
Swoyerville *Luzerne*
Sybertsville *Luzerne*
Sycamore *Greene*
Sykesville *Jefferson*
Sylvan Hills *Blair*
Sylvania *Bradford*
Tafton *Pike*
Talmage *Lancaster*
Tamaqua *Schuylkill*
Tannersville *Monroe*
Tarentum *Allegheny*
Tarrs *Westmoreland*
Tatamy *Northampton*
Taylor *Lackawanna*
Taylorstown *Washington*
Telford *Montgomery*
Temple *Berks*
Templeton *Armstrong*
Terre Hill *Lancaster*
Thomasville *York*
Thompson *Susquehanna*
Thompsontown *Juniata*

Thorndale *Chester*
Thornton *Delaware*
Three Springs *Huntingdon*
Tidioute *Warren*
Timblin *Jefferson*
Tioga *Tioga*
Tiona *Warren*
Tionesta *Forest*
Tipton *Blair*
Tire Hill *Somerset*
Titusville *Crawford*
Tobyhanna *Monroe*
Todd *Huntingdon*
Topton *Berks*
Torrance *Westmoreland*
Toughkenamon *Chester*
Towanda *Bradford*
Tower City *Schuylkill*
Townville *Crawford*
Trafford *Westmoreland*
Trainer *Delaware*
Transfer *Mercer*
Trappe *Montgomery*
Treichlers *Northampton*
Tremont *Schuylkill*
Tresckow *Carbon*
Trevorton *Northumberland*
Trexlertown *Lehigh*
Trooper *Montgomery*
Trout Run *Lycoming*
Troutville *Clearfield*
Troxelville *Snyder*
Troy *Bradford*
Trucksville *Luzerne*
Tullytown *Bucks*
Trumbauersville *Bucks*
Tunkhannock *Wyoming*
Turbotville
    Northumberland
Turkey City *Clarion*
Turtle Creek *Allegheny*
Turtlepoint *McKean*
Tuscarora *Schuylkill*
Twin Rocks *Cambria*
Tyler Hill *Wayne*
Tylersburg *Clarion*
Tylersport *Montgomery*
Tylersville *Clinton*
Tyrone *Blair*
Uledi *Fayette*
Ulster *Bradford*
Ulysses *Potter*
Union City *Erie*
Union Dale *Susquehanna*
Union Deposit *Dauphin*
Uniontown *Fayette*
Unionville *Chester*
United *Westmoreland*
Unityville *Lycoming*
Upland *Delaware*
Upper Black Eddy *Bucks*
Upper Darby *Delaware*
Upperstrasburg *Franklin*
Ursina *Somerset*
Utica *Venango*
Uwchland *Chester*
Valencia *Butler*
Valier *Jefferson*
Valley Forge *Chester*
Valley View *Schuylkill*
Vanderbilt *Fayette*
Vandergrift *Westmoreland*
Vanport *Beaver*
Van Voorhis *Washington*
Venango *Crawford*

Venetia *Washington*
Venus *Venango*
Verona *Allegheny*
Versailles *Allegheny*
Vestaburg *Washington*
Vicksburg *Union*
Villa Maria *Lawrence*
Villanova *Delaware*
Vintondale *Cambria*
Virginville *Berks*
Volant *Lawrence*
Vowinckel *Clarion*
Wagontown *Chester*
Wall *Allegheny*
Wallaceton *Clearfield*
Walnut Bottom
    Cumberland
Walnutport *Northampton*
Walston *Jefferson*
Waltersburg *Fayette*
Wampum *Lawrence*
Wapwallopen *Luzerne*
Warfordsburg *Fulton*
Warminster *Bucks*
Warren *Warren*
Warren Center *Bradford*
Warrendale *Allegheny*
Warrington *Bucks*
Warriors Mark *Huntingdon*
Warrior Run *Luzerne*
Washington *Washington*
Washington Boro
    Lancaster
Washington Crossing
    Bucks
Washingtonville *Montour*
Waterfall *Fulton*
Waterford *Erie*
Waterville *Lycoming*
Watsontown
    Northumberland
Wattsburg *Erie*
Waverly *Lackawanna*
Waymart *Wayne*
Wayne *Delaware*
Wayne Heights *Franklin*
Waynesboro *Franklin*
Waynesburg *Greene*
Weatherly *Carbon*
Webster *Westmoreland*
Weedville *Elk*
Weigelstown *York*
Weikert *Union*
Wellsboro *Tioga*
Wells Tannery *Fulton*
Wellsville *York*
Wendel *Westmoreland*
Wernersville *Berks*
Wescosville *Lehigh*
Wesleyville *Erie*
West Alexander
    Washington
West Bridgewater *Beaver*
West Brownsville
    Washington
West Catasauqua *Lehigh*
West Chester *Chester*
West Conshohocken
    Montgomery
West Decatur *Clearfield*
West Elizabeth *Allegheny*
West Fairview *Cumberland*
Westfield *Tioga*
West Finley *Washington*

Westgate Hills *Northampton*
West Grove *Chester*
West Hazelton *Luzerne*
West Hickory *Forest*
West Kittanning *Armstrong*
West Lancaster *Lancaster*
Westland *Washington*
West Lawn *Berks*
West Lebanon *Indiana*
West Leechburg *Westmoreland*
West Leisenring *Fayette*
West Middlesex *Mercer*
West Middletown *Washington*
West Milton *Union*
West Mayfield *Beaver*
West Mifflin *Allegheny*
Westmoreland City *Westmoreland*
West Nanticoke *Luzerne*
West Newton *Westmoreland*
Weston *Luzerne*
Westover *Clearfield*
West Pittsburg *Lawrence*
West Pittston *Luzerne*
West Point *Montgomery*
Westport *Clinton*
West Reading *Berks*
West Salisbury *Somerset*
West Springfield *Erie*
West Sunbury *Butler*
Westtown *Chester*
West View *Allegheny*
West Willow *Lancaster*
West Wyomissing *Berks*
West York *York*
Wexford *Allegheny*
Wheatland *Mercer*
Whitaker *Allegheny*
White *Fayette*
White Deer *Union*
Whitehall *Lehigh*
White Haven *Luzerne*
White Mills *Wayne*
White Oak *Allegheny*
Whitney *Westmoreland*
Whitsett *Fayette*
Wickhaven *Fayette*
Wiconisco *Dauphin*
Widnoon *Armstrong*
Wilburton *Columbia*
Wilcox *Elk*
Wildwood *Allegheny*
Wilkes-Barre *Luzerne*
Wilkinsburg *Allegheny*
Williamsburg *Blair*
Williamson *Franklin*
Williamsport *Lycoming*
Williamstown *Dauphin*
Willow Grove *Montgomery*
Willow Hill *Franklin*
Willow Street *Lancaster*
Wilmerding *Allegheny*
Wilmore *Cambria*
Wilson *Northampton*
Winburne *Clearfield*
Windber *Somerset*
Windgap *Northampton*
Wind Ridge *Greene*
Windsor *York*
Windsor Park *Cumberland*
Winfield *Union*

Witmer *Lancaster*
Wolfdale *Washington*
Womelsdorf *Berks*
Wood *Huntingdon*
Woodbury *Bedford*
Woodland *Clearfield*
Woodland Park *Lycoming*
Woodlawn *Lehigh*
Woodlyn *Delaware*
Woodside *Luzerne*
Woodward *Centre*
Woolrich *Clinton*
Worcester *Montgomery*
Worthington *Armstrong*
Worthville *Jefferson*
Woxall *Montgomery*
Wrightsville *York*
Wyalusing *Bradford*
Wyano *Westmoreland*
Wycombe *Bucks*
Wyncote *Montgomery*
Wynnewood *Montgomery*
Wyoming *Luzerne*
Wyomissing *Berks*
Wyomissing Hills *Berks*
Wysox *Bradford*
Yardley *Bucks*
Yatesboro *Armstrong*
Yeadon *Delaware*
Yeagertown *Mifflin*
Yoe *York*
York *York*
York Haven *York*
York New Salem *York*
Yorkshire *York*
York Springs *Adams*
Youngstown *Westmoreland*
Youngsville *Warren*
Youngwood *Westmoreland*
Yukon *Westmoreland*
Zelienople *Butler*
Zieglerville *Montgomery*
Zion Grove *Schuylkill*
Zionhill *Bucks*
Zionsville *Lehigh*
Zullinger *Franklin*

Rhode Island

All five (5) Rhode Island counties reported that their criminal records are available for employment screening purposes, although two require that records requests be made in person. Civil records $5,000 and above are filed in Superior Court.

For more information or for offices not listed, contact the state's information hot line at (401) 277-2000.

Driving Records

Division of Motor Vehicles
Room 212
345 Harris Avenue
Providence, RI 02909
(401) 277-2994
Driving records are available by mail. $10.00 fee per request. Turnaround time is 2-3 weeks. Written request must include job applicant's full name, date of birth and license number. Make certified check or money order payable to Division of Motor Vehicles.

Worker's Compensation Records

Department of Labor/Worker's Compensation
Records Department
610 Manton Avenue
PO Box 3500
Providence, RI 02909
(401) 272-0700
Fax (401) 277-2127
Worker's compensation records are available by mail or fax. Information may be obtained from the Department by persons not directly involved in the worker's compensation claim when the request is accompanied by a release signed by the individual identified in the requested information. The request must be specific as to the information requested. No fee for first 30 minutes searched. $15.00 fee per hour over 30 minutes. $.40 for fax copies. $.15 fee per copy. $3.00 for certification.

Vital Statistics

Division of Vital Statistics
State Department of Health
Room 101
Cannon Building, 3 Capital Hill
Providence, RI 02908-5097
(401) 277-2811 or (401) 277-2812
Birth and death records are available for $10.00 each. State office has records since 1853. For earlier records contact town clerk in town where event occurred. If exact date is not known fee is $10.00 for the first two years searched and $.25 for each year thereafter. An employer can obtain records with a written release. Make certified check or money order payable to General Treasury, State of Rhode Island.

Marriage records available. Fee of $10.00 includes two years searched. $.25 for each additional year searched. Include name, marriage date if known, spouse's name and city or town. Divorce records available at county level, court where divorce granted.

Department of Education

Department of Education
Teacher Certification Division
22 Hayes Street
Providence, RI 02908
(401)277-2675
Fax (401) 277-6178
Field of certification, effective date, expiration date are available by mail or phone. Include name and SSN.

Medical Licensing

Board of Medical Licensure
Cannon Building, Room 205
3 Capitol Hill
Providence, RI 02908-5097
(401) 277-3855
Will confirm licenses for MDs and DOs by mail or phone. For licenses not mentioned, contact the above office.

Rhode Island Board of Nurse Registration & Nursing Education
3 Capitol Hill
Providence, RI 02904-5097
(401) 277-2827
Will confirm license by phone. No fee. Include name, license number.

Bar Association

Rhode Island State Bar Association
115 Cedar Street
Providence, RI 02903
(401) 421-5740
Will confirm licenses by phone. No fee. Include name.

Accountancy Board

Rhode Island State Board of Accountancy
233 Richmond S.
Providence, RI 02903
(401) 277-3185
Will confirm license by phone. No fee. Include name.

Securities Commission

Department of Business Regulation
Securities
233 Richmond Street, Suite 232
Providence, RI 02903-4232
(401) 277-3048
Will confirm license by phone. No fee. Include name and SSN.

Secretary of State

Department of State
Corporations Division
100 N. Main Street
Providence, RI 02903
(401) 277-2357
Service agent and address, date incorporated, standing with tax commission, trade names are available by mail or phone. Contact the above office for additional information.

Criminal Records

State Repository

Department of Attorney General
Bureau of Criminal Identification
72 Pine Street
Providence, RI 02903
(401) 274-4400
Access by non-criminal justice agencies to criminal records maintained by State's central repository is primarily limited to criminal justice and other governmental agencies. Contact the above office or counties listed below for additional information and instructions.

Bristol County

District Court–First Division, Criminal Records
516 Main Street
Warren, RI 02885
(401) 245-7977

Felony and misdemeanor records are being held at Providence County and are available by mail. No release necessary. No search fee. $.50 fee per copy. $1.00 for certification. Search information required: name, date of birth, years to search.

Civil records are available held at Providence County and are available by mail. No release necessary. No search fee. Search information required: name, date of birth, years to search. Specify plaintiff or defendant.

Kent County

Clerk of Superior Court, Criminal Records
222 Quaker Lane
Warwick, RI 02886-0107
(401) 822-1311

Records are not available by mail or phone but are available for physical inspection at the above office. See Rhode Island state repository.

Civil records are available by mail. No release necessary. No search fee. $.50 fee per copy. $1.00 for certification. Search information required: name, date of birth, years to search. Specify plaintiff or defendant.

Newport County

Felony records
Clerk of District Court, Criminal Records
2nd Division
Washington Square
Newport, RI 02840
(401) 841-8350

Felony records are available by mail or by phone from 1983 forward. A release is required. No search fee. Search information required: name, date of birth, years to search.

Civil records
Clerk of District Court
2nd Division
Washington Square
Newport, RI 02840
(401) 841-8350

Civil records are available by mail or phone. No release necessary. No search fee. Search information required: name, date of birth, years to search. Specify plaintiff or defendant.

Misdemeanor records
Clerk of District Court
Isenhower Square
Newport, RI 02840
(401) 841-8350

Misdemeanor records are availabe by mail. A release is required. No search fee. Search information required: name, date of birth.

Civilr records
Clerk of District Court
Isenhower Square
Newport, RI 02840
(401) 841-8350

Civil records are available by mail. No release necessary. No search fee. $.50 fee per copy. $1.00 for certification. Search information required: name, date of birth, years to search. Specify plaintiff or defendant.

Providence County

Felony and misdemeanor records
Bureau of Criminal Identification
6th District Court
1 Dorrance Plaza
2nd Floor
Providence, RI 02903
(401) 277-6710

Felony and misdemeanor records are available by mail. No release necessary. No search fee. $.50 fee per copy. $1.00 for certification. Search information required: name, years to search.

Civil records
250 Benefit Street
Providence, RI 02903
(401) 277-3235

Civil records are available by mail or phone. No release necessary. No search fee. Search information required: name, date of birth, years to search. Specify plaintiff or defendant.

Washington County

Clerk of 4th Division–District Court, Criminal Records
PO Box 248
1693 Kingstown Road
West Kingston, RI 02892
(401) 782-4131

Felony and misdemeanor records are available in person only.

Civil records are available in person only. See Rhode Island state repository for additional information.

City-County Cross Reference

Adamsville *Newport*
Albion *Providence*
Allentown *Washington*
Annex *Providence*
Anthony *Kent*
Arnold Mills *Providence*
Ashaway *Washington*
Ashton *Pawtucket*
Barrington *Bristol*
Berkeley *Providence*
Block Island *Newport*
Bradford *Washington*
Bristol *Bristol*
Broadway *Newport*
Brown *Providence*
Carolina *Washington*
Centerdale *Providence*
Central Falls *Pawtucket*
Charlestown *Washington*
Chepachet *Providence*
Clayville *Providence*
Coddington Point *Newport*
Common Fence Point *Newport*
Conimicut *Warwick*
Coventry *Kent*
Cranston *Providence*
Cumberland *Pawtucket*
Cumberland Hill *Pawtucket*
Darlington *Pawtucket*

Davisville *North Kingstown*
Diamond Hill *Providence*
East Greenwich *Kent*
East Providence *Providence*
East Side *Providence*
Edgewood *Providence*
Elmwood *Providence*
Escoheag *Washington*
Esmond *Providence*
Exeter *Washington*
Fiskeville *Providence*
Forestdale *Providence*
Foster *Providence*
Friar *Providence*
Garden City *Providence*
Glendale *Providence*
Greene *Kent*
Greenville *Providence*
Harmony *Providence*
Harris *Kent*
Harrisville *Providence*
Hope *Providence*
Hope Valley *Washington*
Hopkinton *Washington*
Island Park *Newport*
Jamestown *Newport*
Johnston *Providence*
Kenyon *Washington*
Kingston *Wakefield*

Lincoln *Pawtucket*
Little Compton *Newport*
Lonsdale *Providence*
Manville *Providence*
Mapleville *Providence*
Matunuck *Washington*
Middletown *Newport*
Misquamicut *Westerly*
Mount View *Washington*
Narragansett *Wakefield*
Newport *Newport*
North *Providence*
North Providence *Providence*
North Kingstown *Washington*
North Scituate *Providence*
Oakland *Providence*
Olneyville *Providence*
Pascoag *Providence*
Pawtucket *Providence*
Peace Dale *Wakefield*
Pilgrim *Warwick*
Portsmouth *Newport*
Providence *Providence*
Prudence Island *Newport*
Quidnessett *Washington*
Quidnick *Kent*
Quonochontaug *Washington*
Riverside *Providence*

Rockville *Washington*
Rumford *Providence*
Saunderstown *Washington*
Saylesville *Providence*
Shannock *Washington*
Slatersville *Providence*
Slocum *Washington*
South Hopkinton *Washington*
Tiverton *Newport*
Union Village *Providence*
Vally Falls *Providence*
Wakefield *Washington*
Walnut Hill *Woonsocket*
Warren *Bristol*
Warwick *Kent*
Warwick Neck *Warwick*
Watch Hill *Westerly*
Weekapaug *Westerly*
Westerly *Washington*
West Kingston *Washington*
West Warwick *Kent*
Weybosset Hill *Providence*
Wickford *Washington*
Wildes Corner *Warwick*
Wood River Junction *Washington*
Woonsocket *Providence*
Wyoming *Washington*

South Carolina

Both South Carolina's central repository and all forty six (46) of its counties report that criminal records are available for employment screening purposes. Only four of those counties require records requests to be made in person, with the remaining forty two (42) accepting mail and/or phone requests. A handful will honor fax requests. Civil suits for $2,500 and more are filed in County Court while suits less than $2,500 are filed in Magistrate Court.

For more information or for offices not listed, contact the state's information hot line at (803) 734-1000.

Driving Records

South Carolina State Highway Department
Motor Vehicle Division
PO Box 1498
Columbia, SC 29216-0030
(803) 251-2940
Driving records are available by mail. $2.00 fee per request. Turnaround time is 24 hours. Written request must include job applicant's full name, date of birth and license number. Make check payable to South Carolina State Highway Department

Worker's Compensation Records

Worker's Compensation Commission
Research Department
PO Box 1715
Columbia, SC 29202-1715
(803) 737-5713
Worker's compensation records are available by mail only. Written request must include subject's full name, date of birth and SSN, SASE. No fee. A signed release is required.

Vital Statistics

Vital Records and Public Health Statistics
SC Dept of Health and Env. Control
2600 Bull Street
Columbia, SC 29201
(803) 734-4830
Fax (803) 734-5131
Birth and death records are available for $8.00 each. State office has records since January 1915. City of Charleston births from 1877 and deaths from 1821 are on file at Charleston County Health Department. Ledger entries of Florence City births and deaths from late 1800's are on file at Newberry County Health Department. An employer can obtain records with a written release. Make certified check or money order payable to SCDHEC.

Marriage records from July, 1950 forward are available. $8.00 fee. Turnaround time is 3-4 weeks. Include name, marriage date, spouse's name, county where marriage took place.

Marriage records before July, 1950 are available in county where license was obtained. Release is required. Divorce records from July 1962 forward are available for $8.00, divorce records prior to July 1962 are located at county level, Clerk of Court, where divorce occurred.

Department of Education

Office of Teacher Certification
1015 Rutledge Bldg.
Columbia, SC 29201
(803) 734-8466
Field of certification, effective date, expiration date are available by mail or phone. Include name and SSN.

Medical Licensing

State Board of Medicical Examiners
PO Box 12245
Columbia, SC 29211
(803) 734-8901
Will confirm licenses for MDs or DO's by mail or phone. For licenses not mentioned, contact the above office.

State Board of Nursing for South Carolina
220 Executive Center Drive
Columbia, SC 29210
(803) 253-6281
Will confirm license by phone. No fee. Include name, license number.

Bar Association

South Carolina State Bar Association
PO Box 608
Columbia, SC 29202
(803) 799-6653
Will confirm licenses by phone. No fee. Include name.

Accountancy Board

South Carolina State Board of Accountancy
800 Dutch Square Blvd., Suite 260
Columbia, SC 29210
(803) 731-1677
Will confirm license by phone. No fee. Include name.

Securities Commission

Department of State
Securities Division
1205 Pendleton Street
Edgar Brown Building
Suite 501
Columbia, SC 29201
(803) 734-1095
Will confirm license by phone. No fee. Include name and SSN.

Secretary of State

Department of State
Corporation Division
PO Box 11350.
Columbia, SC 29211
(803) 734-2158
Fax (803) 734-2164
Service agent and address, date incorporated, standing with tax commission, trade names are available by mail, fax or phone. Contact the above office for additional information.

Criminal Records

State Repository

South Carolina Law Enforcement Division
Attention: Criminal Records Section
PO Box 21398
Columbia, SC 29221
(803) 737-9000 or 737-9078
Written requests must include subject's full name, maiden name, alias, date of birth, race, sex and SSN. There is a $10.00 fee for each search. Make check payable to S.C. Law Enforcement Division. Information released includes all records with dispositions and records that are less than a year old.

Abbeville County

Clerk of Court, Criminal Records
PO Box 99
Abbeville, SC 29620
(803) 459-5074
Felony and misdemeanor records are available by mail. No release necessary. No search fee. $.25 fee per copy. $1.00 for certification. Search information required: name, years to search.

Civil records are available by mail. No release necessary. No search fee. $.25 fee per copy. $1.00 for certification. Search information required: name, date of birth, years to search. Specify plaintiff or defendant.

Aiken County

Clerk of Court
PO Box 583
Aiken, SC 29802
(803) 642-2099
Felony and misdemeanor records are available in person only. See South Carolina state repository for additional information.

Civil records are available in person only. See South Carolina state repository for additional information.

Allendale County

Clerk of Court, Criminal Records
PO Box 126
Allendale, SC 29810
(803) 584-2737
Felony and misdemeanor records are available by mail or phone. Turnaround time is 2 days. No release necessary. No search fee. Search information required: name, SSN, date of birth, years to search.

Civil records are available by mail. A release is required. $5.00 search fee. $1.00 for certification. Search information required: name, date of birth, years to search. Specify plaintiff or defendant.

Anderson County

Clerk of Court, Criminal Records
PO Box 1656
Anderson, SC 29622
(803) 260-4053
Felony records are available by mail. A release is required. $3.00 search fee. Make check payable to Clerk of Court. Search information required: name, SSN, date of birth, years to search.

Civil records are available by mail or phone. A release is required. $3.00 search fee. Search information required: name, date of birth, years to search. Specify plaintiff or defendant.

Bamberg County

Felony records
Clerk of Court, Criminal Records
PO Box 150
Bamberg, SC 29003
(803) 245-3025
Felony records are available by mail. No release necessary. $5.00 search fee. Make company check payable to Clerk of Court. Search information required: name, SSN, years to search, SASE.

Civil records
Clerk of Court
PO Box 150
Bamberg, SC 29003
(803) 245-3025
Civil records are available by mail or phone. No release necessary. $5.00 search fee. Search information required: name, date of birth, years to search, SASE. Specify plaintiff or defendant.

Misdemeanor records
Bamberg County Magistrates Office
PO Box 187
Bamberg, SC 29003
(803) 245-3016
Misdemeanor records are available in person only. See South Carolina state repository for additional information.

Civil records
Bamberg County Magistrates Office
PO Box 187
Bamberg, SC 29003
(803) 245-3016
Civil records are available in person only. See South Carolina state repository for additional information.

Barnwell County

Clerk of Court Office, Criminal Records
PO Box 723
Barnwell, SC 29812
(803) 259-3485
Fax (803) 259-1466
Felony and misdemeanor records are available by mail or fax. Turnaround time is 2 days. No release necessary. No search fee. Search information required: name, date of birth.

Civil records are available by mail or fax. No release necessary. No search fee. $.50 fee per copy. $1.00 for certification. Search information required: name, date of birth, years to search. Specify plaintiff or defendant.

Beaufort County

Clerk of Court Office, Criminal Records
PO Drawer 1128
Beaufort, SC 29901
(803) 525-7306
Felony and misdemeanor records are available by mail. Turnaround time is 1 week. No release necessary. No search fee. Search information required: name, date of birth, SSN, years to search.

Civil records are available by mail. No release necessary. No search fee. $.25 fee per copy. $2.00 for certification. Search information required: name, date of birth, SSN, years to search. Specify plaintiff or defendant.

Berkeley County

Clerk of Court, Criminal Records
223 N. Live Oak Drive
Moncks Corner, SC 29461
(803) 761-8179
Felony records are available in person only. See South Carolina state repository for additional information.

Civil records are available in person only. See South Carolina state repository for additional information.

Calhoun County

Clerk of Court, Criminal Records
302 S. Railroad Ave.
St. Matthews, SC 29135
(803) 874-3524
Felony records are available by mail. Turnaround time is 2 days. No release necessary. $5.00 search fee. Search information required: name, SSN, date of birth.

Civil records are available by mail or phone. No release necessary. No search fee. $.25 for certification. Search information required: name, date of birth, years to search. Specify plaintiff or defendant.

Charleston County

Clerk of Court, Criminal Records
PO Box 293
Charleston, SC 29402
(803) 740-5700
Felony records are available by mail. Turnaround time is 3 days. No release necessary. $10.00 fee. Certified check or money order, payable to Clerk of Court. Search information required: name, SSN, date of birth, years to search.

Civil records are available in person only. See South Carolina state repository for additional information.

Cherokee County

Clerk of Court, Criminal Records
PO Drawer 2289
Gaffney, SC 29342
(803) 487-2571
Fax (803) 487-2754
Felony records are available by mail. Turnaround time is 2 days. No release necessary. $5.00 search fee. Make check payable to Clerk of Court. Search information required: name, SSN, date of birth, years to search.

Civil records are available by mail. No release necessary. $5.00 search fee. $.50 fee per copy. $1.50 for certification. Search information required: name, date of birth, years to search. Specify plaintiff or defendant.

Chester County

Clerk of Court, Criminal Records
PO Drawer 580
Chester, SC 29706
(803) 385-2605
Fax (803) 385-2022
Felony records are available by mail or fax. Turnaround time is 3 days. A release is required. $2.00 search fee. Search information required: name, SSN, date of birth, previous address.

Civil records are available by mail or fax. No release necessary. No search fee. $.25 fee per copy. $1.00 for certification. Search information required: name, date of birth, years to search. Specify plaintiff or defendant.

Chesterfield County

Clerk of Court, Criminal Records
PO Box 529
Chesterfield, SC 29709
(803) 623-2574

Felony and misdemeanor records are available by mail. Turnaround time is 2 days. No release necessary. $5.00 search fee. Make check payable to Clerk of Court. Search information required: name, SSN, date of birth, sex, race.

Civil records are available by mail. No release necessary. $5.00 search fee. Search information required: name, date of birth, SSN, years to search. Specify plaintiff or defendant.

Clarendon County

Clerk of Court, Criminal Records
Drawer E
Manning, SC 29102
(803) 435-4444

Felony records are available by mail. Turnaround time is 2 days. No release necessary. $4.00 search fee. Company checks only, payable to Clerk of Court. Search information required: name, SSN, date of birth.

Civil records are available by mail. No release necessary. $4.00 search fee. $.25 fee per copy. Search information required: name, date of birth, years to search. Specify plaintiff or defendant.

Colleton County

Clerk of Court, Criminal Records
PO Box 620
Walterboro, SC 29488
(803) 549-5791

Felony and misdemeanor records are available by mail. No release necessary. No search fee. $1.00 certification fee per copy. Search information required: name, SSN, date of birth, sex, race, years to search .

Civil records are available in person only. See South Carolina state repository for additional information.

Darlington County

Clerk of Court, Criminal Records
Darlington Courthouse
Darlington, SC 29532
(803) 393-3836
Fax (803) 398-4330

Felony and misdemeanor records are available by mail or fax . Turnaround time is 3 days. No release necessary. $6.00 search fee. Company checks only, payable to Clerk of Court. Search information required: name, SSN, date of birth, sex, race, years to search.

Civil records are available by mail or fax. No release necessary. $6.00 search fee. $1.00 fee per copy. Search information required: name, date of birth, years to search. Specify plaintiff or defendant.

Dillon County

Clerk of Court, Criminal Records
PO Box 1220
Dillon, SC 29536
(803) 774-1425
Fax (803) 774-1443

Felony and misdemeanor records are available by mail or fax. No release necessary. $5.00 search fee. Make check payable to Clerk of Court. Search information required: name, date of birth, SSN.

Civil records are available by mail or fax. No release necessary. $5.00 search fee. Search information required: name, date of birth, years to search. Specify plaintiff or defendant.

Dorchester County

Clerk of Court, Criminal Records
PO Box 158
St. George, SC 29477
(803) 563-2331

Felony records are available by mail or phone. No release necessary. No search fee. $.25 fee per copy. Search information required: name, years to search.

Civil records are available by mail or phone. No release necessary. No search fee. $.25 fee per copy. Search information required: name, date of birth, years to search. Specify plaintiff or defendant.

Edgefield County

Felony records
Clerk of Court, Criminal Records
PO Box 34
Edgefield, SC 29824
(803) 637-4080

Felony records are available by mail. Turnaround time is 2 days. No release necessary. No search fee. Search information required: name, SSN, date of birth, sex, race, years to search.

Civil records
Clerk of Court
PO Box 34
Edgefield, SC 29824
(803) 637-4080

Civil records are available in person only. See South Carolina state repository for additional information.

Misdemeanor records
Magistrate Court
PO Box 664
Edgefield, SC 29824
(803) 637-4090

Misdemeanor records are available in person only. See South Carolina state repository for additional information.

Civil records
Magistrate Court
PO Box 664
Edgefield, SC 29824
(803) 637-4090

Civil records are available by mail. No release necessary. No search fee. Search information required: name, date of birth, years to search. Specify plaintiff or defendant.

Fairfield County

Clerk of Court
PO Drawer 299
Winnsboro, SC 29180
(803) 635-1411

Felony records are available in person only. See South Carolina state repository for additional information.

Civil records are available in person only. See South Carolina state repository for additional information.

Florence County

Clerk of Court, Criminal Records
Drawer E, City County Complex
Florence, SC 29501
(803) 665-3031

Felony records are available by mail. Turnaround time is 1 day. A release is required. $5.00 search fee. Certified check only, payable to Clerk of Court. Search information required: name, SSN, date of birth, years to search.

Civil records are available by mail. No release necessary. $2.00 search fee. $1.00 for certification. Search information required: name, date of birth, years to search. Specify plaintiff or defendant.

Georgetown County

Clerk of Court, Criminal Records
PO Box 1270
Georgetown, SC 29442
(803) 527-6314
Fax (803) 546-2144

Felony and misdemeanor records are available by mail or fax. Turnaround time is 1 week. No release necessary. $2.00 search fee. Certified check only, payable to Clerk of Court. Search information required: name, SSN, date of birth.

Civil records are available in person only. See South Carolina state repository for additional information.

Greenville County

Criminal Justice Support Records Division
4 McGee Street/Box 600
Greenville, SC 29601
(803) 271-5257

Felony and misdemeanor records are available by mail. No release necessary. $5.00 search fee. Check payable to Greenville County. Search information required: full name, date of birth,

Civil records are available in person only. See South Carolina state repository for additional information.

Greenwood County

Clerk of Court, Criminal Records
Room 114, Courthouse
Greenwood, SC 29646
(803) 942-8546

Felony records are available by mail. Turnaround time is 3 days. A release is required. $2.00 search fee. Search information required: name, SSN, date of birth.

Civil records are available in person only. See South Carolina state repository for additional information.

Hampton County

Clerk of Court, Criminal Records
PO Box 7
Hampton, SC 29924
(803) 943-3668

Felony records are available by mai. No release necessary. No search fee. $.50 fee per copy. $1.00 for certification. Search information required: name, SSN, years to search.

Civil records are available by mail or phone. No release necessary. No search fee. $.50 fee per copy. $1.00 for certification. Search information required: name, SSN, years to search. Specify plaintiff or defendant.

Horry County

Clerk of Court, Criminal Records
PO Box 677
Conway, SC 29526
(803) 248-1270

Felony and misdemeanor records are available by mail. No release necessary. $3.00 search fee. $.25 fee per copy. $1.00 for certification. Search information required: name, date of birth.

Civil records are available by mail. No release necessary. $3.00 search fee. $.25 fee per copy. $1.00 for certification. Search information required: name, date of birth, years to search. Specify plaintiff or defendant.

Jasper County

Clerk of Court, Criminal Records
PO Box 248
Ridgeland, SC 29936
(803) 726-7710

Felony and misdemeanor records are available by mail. Turnaround time is 3 days. A release is required. $5.00 search fee. Search information required: name, SSN, date of birth.

Civil records are available in person only. See South Carolina state repository for additional information.

Kershaw County

Clerk of Court, Criminal Records
Room 313
Kershaw County Courthouse
Camden, SC 29020
(803) 425-1527

Felony and misdemeanor records are available by mail. Turnaround time is 2 days. A release is required. $5.00 search fee. Search information required: name, date of birth.

Civil records are available in person only. See South Carolina state repository for additional information.

Lancaster County

Clerk of Court, Criminal Records
PO Box 1809
Lancaster, SC 29720
(803) 285-1581

Felony and misdemeanor records are available by mail. Turnaround time is 3 days. No release necessary. $5.00 search fee. Certified check only, payable to Clerk of Court. Search information required: name, SSN, date of birth, SASE, years to search.

Civil records are available by mail. A release is required. $5.00 search fee. $.25 fee per copy. $2.00 for certification. Search information required: name, date of birth, years to search. Specify plaintiff or defendant.

Laurens County

Clerk of Court Office, Criminal Records
PO Box 287
Laurens, SC 29360
(803) 984-3538

Felony and misdemeanor records are available by mail. No release necessary. $5.00 search fee. $.50 fee per copy. $1.00 for certification. Search information required: name, SSN, date of birth, years to search.

Civil records are available by mail. No release necessary. $5.00 search fee. $.50 fee per copy. $1.00 for certification. Search information required: name, date of birth, years to search. Specify plaintiff or defendant.

Lee County

Felony records
Clerk of Court, Criminal Records
PO Box 281
Bishopville, SC 29010
(803) 484-5341
Fax (803) 484-5043

Felony records are available by mail or fax. A release is required. No search fee. Search information required: name, SSN, date of birth, years to search.

Civil records
Clerk of Court
PO Box 281
Bishopville, SC 29010
(803) 484-5341
Fax (803) 484-5043

Civil records are available by mail or fax. A release is required. No search fee. $1.00 fee per copy. $2.00 for certification. Search information required: name, date of birth, years to search. Specify plaintiff or defendant.

Misdemeanor records
Magistrate Court
PO Box 2
Bishopville, SC 29010
(803) 484-5341 Ext. 47

Misdemeanor records are available by mail or phone. No release necessary. No search fee. Search information required: name, years to search.

Civil records
Magistrate Court
PO Box 2
Bishopville, SC 29010
(803) 484-5341 Ext. 47

Civil records are available by mail or phone. No release necessary. No search fee. Search information required: name, years to search. Specify plaintiff or defendant.

Lexington County

Clerk of Court, Criminal Records
Room 107
County Courthouse
Lexington, SC 29072
(803) 359-8212

Felony records are available by mail. Turnaround time is 3 days. A release is required. $3.00 search fee. Certified check only, payable to Clerk of Court. Search information required: name, SSN, date of birth, sex, race.

Civil records are available by mail. No release necessary. $3.00 search fee. Search information required: name, date of birth, years to search. Specify plaintiff or defendant.

Marion County

Clerk of Court, Criminal Records
PO Box 295
Marion, SC 29571
(803) 423-8240

Felony and misdemeanor records are available by mail. Turnaround time is 1 week. A release is required. $2.00 search fee. Search information required: name, date of birth, years to search, SASE.

Civil records are available by mail or phone. No release necessary. $2.00 search fee. $.20 fee per copy. $1.00 for certification. Search information required: name, date of birth, years to search. Specify plaintiff or defendant.

Marlboro County

Clerk of Court, Criminal Records
PO Drawer 996
Bennettsville, SC 29512
(803) 479-5613
Fax (803) 479-5640

Felony and some misdemeanor records are available by mail, phone or fax. Turnaround time is 5 days. A release is required. $5.00 search fee. Certified check only, payable to Clerk of Court. Search information required: name, SSN, date of birth, sex, race.

Civil records are available by mail or fax. No release necessary. $5.00 search fee. $.25 fee per copy. $2.00 for certification. Search information required: name, date of birth, SSN, years to search. Specify plaintiff or defendant.

McCormick County

Clerk of Court
PO Box 86
McCormick, SC 29835
(803) 465-2195

Felony and misdemeanor records are available by mail. Turnaround time is 5 days. No search fee. Search information required: name, SSN, date of birth, SASE, previous address.

Civil records are available by mail. No release necessary. $5.00 search fee. $.50 fee per copy. $1.00 for certification. Search information required: name, date of birth, years to search. Specify plaintiff or defendant.

Newberry County

Clerk of Court, Criminal Records
PO Box 278
Newberry, SC 29108
(803) 321-2110

Felony and misdemeanor records are available in person only. See South Carolina state repository for additional information.

Civil records are available in person only. See South Carolina state repository for additional information.

Oconee County

Clerk of Court, Criminal Records
PO Box 158
Walhalla, SC 29691
(803) 638-4280

Felony and misdemeanor records are available by mail. No release necessary. $5.00 search fee. Make check payable to Clerk of Court. Search information required: name, SSN, date of birth, years to search, SASE.

Civil records are available by mail. No release necessary. $5.00 search fee. $2.00 for certification. Search information required: name, date of birth, years to search. Specify plaintiff or defendant.

Orangeburg County

Clerk of Court, Criminal Records
PO Box 1000
Orangeburg, SC 29116
(803) 533-1000

Felony records are available by mail. Turnaround time is 2 days. No release necessary. No search fee. Search information required: name, date of birth and or SSN, years to search, SASE.

Civil records are available by mail or phone. No release necessary. No search fee. $.50 fee per copy. $2.00 for certification. Search information required: name, date of birth, years to search, SASE. Specify plaintiff or defendant.

Pickens County

Clerk of Court, Criminal Records
PO Box 215
Pickens, SC 29671
(803) 878-5866

Felony and misdemeanor records are available by mail. Turnaround time is 2 days. No release necessary. $2.00 search fee. $.25 fee per copy. Certified check only, payable to Clerk of Court. Search information required: name, date of birth, SASE.

Civil records are available by mail. A release is required. $2.00 search fee. $.25 fee per copy. $1.00 for certification. Search information required: name, date of birth, years to search. Specify plaintiff or defendant.

Richland County

Clerk of Court, Criminal Records
PO Box 1781
Columbia, SC 29202
(803) 748-4684

Felony and misdemeanor records are available by mail. Turnaround time is 1 week. A release is required. $5.00 search fee. Make check payable to Richland County Clerk of Court. Search information required: name, SSN, date of birth, sex, race.

Civil records are available by mail. No release necessary. $2.00 search fee. Search information required: name, date of birth, years to search. Specify plaintiff or defendant.

Saluda County

Clerk of Court, Criminal Records
Saluda County Courthouse
Saluda, SC 29138
(803) 445-3303

Felony and misdemeanor records are available by mail. No release necessary. No search fee. $.50 fee per copy. $2.00 for certification. Search information required: name, SSN, years to search.

Civil records are available by mail. No release necessary. No search fee. $.50 fee per copy. $2.00 for certification. Search information required: name, date of birth, years to search. Specify plaintiff or defendant.

Spartanburg County

Clerk of Court, Criminal Records
Spartanburg County Courthouse
Magnolia Street
Spartanburg, SC 29301
(803) 596-2591

Felony and misdemeanor records are available by mail. No release necessary. $2.00 search fee. Certified check only, payable to Clerk of Court. Search information required: name, SSN, date of birth, sex, race.

Civil records are available by mail. No release necessary. $2.00 search fee. $.25 fee per copy. $1.00 for certification. Search information required: name, date of birth, years to search. Specify plaintiff or defendant.

Sumter County

Clerk of Court, Criminal Records
Sumter County Courthouse
Sumter, SC 29150
(803) 773-1581

Felony and misdemeanor records are available by mail. Turnaround time is 2 days. No release necessary. $2.00 search fee. Make check payable to Clerk of Court. Search information required: name, SSN, date of birth, years to search.

Civil records are available by mail. No release necessary. $5.00 search fee. $.50 fee per copy. $1.00 for certification. Search information required: name, date of birth, years to search. Specify plaintiff or defendant.

Union County

Clerk of Court, Criminal Records
PO Drawer G
Union, SC 29379
(803) 429-1630
Fax (803) 429-1628

Felony and misdemeanor records are available by mail or fax. Turnaround time is 2 days. No release necessary. $1.00 search fee. Certified check only, payable to Clerk of Court. Search information required: name, SSN, date of birth, sex, race.

Civil records are available by mail or fax. No release necessary. $1.00 search fee. $.25 fee per copy. $2.00 for certification. Search information required: name, date of birth, years to search. Specify plaintiff or defendant.

Williamsburg County

Clerk of Court, Criminal Records
PO Box 86
Kingstree, SC 29556
(803) 354-6855

Felony and misdemeanor records are available by mail or phone. No release necessary. $5.00 search fee. Search information required: name, SSN, date of birth, years to search, SASE.

Civil records are available by mail or phone. No release necessary. $5.00 search fee. Search information required: name, date of birth, years to search, SASE. Specify plaintiff or defendant.

York County

Clerk of Court, Criminal Records
PO Box 649
York, SC 29745
(803) 684-8505

Felony and misdemeanor records are available by mail. Turnaround time is 1 day. No release necessary. $1.00 search fee. Certified check only, payable to Clerk of Court. Search information required: name, SSN, date of birth.

Civil records are available in person only. See South Carolina state repository for additional infomation.

City-County Cross Reference

Abbeville *Abbeville*
Adams Run *Charleston*
Aiken *Aiken*
Alcolu *Clarendon*
Allendale *Allendale*
Alvin *Berkeley*
Anderson *Anderson*
Andrews *Georgetown*

Arcadia *Spartanburg*
Arkwright *Spartanburg*
Awendaw *Charleston*
Aynor *Horry*
Ballentine *Richland*
Bamberg *Bamberg*
Barnwell *Barnwell*
Batesburg *Lexington*

Bath *Aiken*
Beaufort *Beaufort*
Beech Island *Aiken*
Belton *Anderson*
Bennettsville *Marlboro*
Berea *Greenville*
Bethera *Berkeley*
Bethune *Kershaw*

Bishopville *Lee*
Blacksburg *Cherokee*
Blackstock *Chester*
Blackville *Barnwell*
Blair *Fairfield*
Blenheim *Marlboro*
Bluffton *Beaufort*
Blythewood *Richland*

Bonneau *Berkeley*
Bowling Green *York*
Bowman *Orangeburg*
Bradley *Greenwood*
Branchville *Orangeburg*
Brunson *Hampton*
Bucksport *Horry*
Buffalo *Union*
Cades *Williamsburg*
Calhoun Falls *Abbeville*
Camden *Kershaw*
Cameron *Calhoun*
Campobello *Spartanburg*
Canadys *Colleton*
Capitol View *Richland*
Carlisle *Union*
Cassatt *Kershaw*
Catawba *York*
Cayce-West Columbia
   Lexington
Centenary *Marion*
Central *Pickens*
Chapin *Lexington*
Chappells *Newberry*
Charleston *Charleston*
Cheraw *Chesterfield*
Cherokee Falls *Cherokee*
Chesnee *Spartanburg*
Chester *Chester*
Chesterfield *Chesterfield*
City View *Greenville*
Clarks Hill *McCormick*
Clearwater *Aiken*
Clemson *Pickens*
Cleveland *Greenville*
Clifton *Spartanburg*
Clinton *Laurens*
Clio *Marlboro*
Clover *York*
Columbia *Richland*
Conestee *Greenville*
Converse *Spartanburg*
Conway *Horry*
Cope *Orangeburg*
Cordesville *Berkeley*
Cordova *Orangeburg*
Cottageville *Colleton*
Coward *Florence*
Cowpens *Spartanburg*
Cross *Berkeley*
Cross Anchor *Spartanburg*
Cross Hill *Laurens*
Dalzell *Sumter*
Darlington *Darlington*
Daufuskie Island *Beaufort*
Davis Station *Clarendon*
Denmark *Bamberg*
Denny Terrace *Richland*
Dillon *Dillon*
Donalds *Abbeville*
Dorchester *Dorchester*
Drayton *Spartanburg*
Due West *Abbeville*
Duncan *Spartanburg*
Dunean *Greenville*
Early Branch *Hampton*
Easley *Pickens*
Eastover *Richland*
Edgefield *Edgefield*
Edgemoor *Chester*
Edisto Island *Charleston*
Effingham *Florence*
Ehrhardt *Bamberg*
Elgin *Kershaw*
Elko *Barnwell*

Elliott *Lee*
Elloree *Orangeburg*
Enoree *Spartanburg*
Estill *Hampton*
Eutawville *Orangeburg*
Fairfax *Allendale*
Fairforest *Spartanburg*
Fair Play *Oconee*
Fingerville *Spartanburg*
Florence *Florence*
Floyd Dale *Dillon*
Folly Beach *Charleston*
Forest Acres *Richland*
Fork *Dillon*
Fort Lawn *Chester*
Fort Mill *York*
Fort Motte *Calhoun*
Fountain Inn *Greenville*
Frogmore *Beaufort*
Furman *Hampton*
Gable *Clarendon*
Gadsden *Richland*
Gaffney *Cherokee*
Galivants Ferry *Horry*
Gantt *Anderson*
Garnett *Hampton*
Gaston *Lexington*
Georgetown *Georgetown*
Gifford *Hampton*
Gilbert *Lexington*
Glendale *Spartanburg*
Gloverville *Aiken*
Gluck *Anderson*
Goose Creek *Berkeley*
Gramling *Spartanburg*
Graniteville *Aiken*
Gray Court *Laurens*
Great Falls *Chester*
Greeleyville *Williamsburg*
Green Pond *Colleton*
Green Sea *Horry*
Greenville *Greenville*
Greenwood *Greenwood*
Greer *Greenville*
Gresham *Marion*
Grover *Dorchester*
Hamer *Dillon*
Hampton *Hampton*
Hanahan *Berkeley*
Hardeeville *Jasper*
Harleyville *Dorchester*
Hartsville *Darlington*
Heath Springs *Lancaster*
Hemingway *Williamsburg*
Hickory Grove *York*
Hilton Head Island
   Beaufort
Hodges *Greenwood*
Holly Hill *Orangeburg*
Hollywood *Charleston*
Honea Path *Anderson*
Hopkins *Richland*
Horatio *Sumter*
Huger *Berkeley*
Inman *Spartanburg*
Inman Mills *Spartanburg*
Irmo *Lexington*
Islandton *Colleton*
Isle Of Palms *Charleston*
Iva *Anderson*
Jackson *Aiken*
Jacksonboro *Colleton*
James Island *Charleston*
Jamestown *Berkeley*
Jefferson *Chesterfield*

Jenkinsville *Fairfield*
Joanna *Laurens*
Johns Island *Charleston*
Johnsonville *Florence*
Johnston *Edgefield*
Jonesville *Union*
Judson *Greenville*
Kensington *Georgetown*
Kershaw *Lancaster*
Kinards *Newberry*
Kings Creek *Cherokee*
Kingstree *Williamsburg*
Ladson *Charleston*
LaFrance *Anderson*
Lake City *Florence*
Lake View *Dillon*
Lamar *Darlington*
Lancaster *Lancaster*
Lando *Chester*
Landrum *Spartanburg*
Lane *Williamsburg*
Langley *Aiken*
Latta *Dillon*
Laurel Bay *Jasper*
Laurens *Laurens*
Leesville *Lexington*
Lesslie *York*
Lexington *Lexington*
Liberty *Pickens*
Liberty Hill *Kershaw*
Little Mountain *Newberry*
Little River *Horry*
Little Rock *Dillon*
Lobeco *Beaufort*
Lockhart *Union*
Lodge *Colleton*
Longcreek *Oconee*
Longs *Horry*
Loris *Horry*
Lowndesville *Abbeville*
Lugoff *Kershaw*
Luray *Hampton*
Lydia *Darlington*
Lyman *Spartanburg*
Lynchburg *Lee*
McBee *Chesterfield*
McClellanville *Charleston*
McColl *Marlboro*
McConnells *York*
McCormick *McCormick*
Manning *Clarendon*
Marietta *Greenville*
Marion *Marion*
Martin *Allendale*
Mauldin *Greenville*
Mayesville *Sumter*
Mayo *Spartanburg*
Miley *Hampton*
Minturn *Dillon*
Modoc *McCormick*
Monarch Mills *Union*
Moncks Corner *Berkeley*
Monetta *Saluda*
Montmorenci *Aiken*
Moore *Spartanburg*
Mountain Rest *Oconee*
Mount Carmel *McCormick*
Mount Croghan
   Chesterfield
Mount Holly *Berkeley*
Mount Pleasant *Charleston*
Mountville *Laurens*
Mullins *Marion*
Murrells Inlet *Georgetown*
Myrtle Beach *Horry*

Neeses *Orangeburg*
Nesmith *Williamsburg*
Newberry *Newberry*
New Ellenton *Aiken*
Newry *Oconee*
New Zion *Clarendon*
Nichols *Marion*
Ninety Six *Greenwood*
Norris *Pickens*
North Charleston *Berkeley*
North *Orangeburg*
North Augusta *Aiken*
North Myrtle Beach *Horry*
Norway *Orangeburg*
Olanta *Florence*
Olar *Bamberg*
Orangeburg *Orangeburg*
Pacolet *Spartanburg*
Pacolet Mills *Spartanburg*
Pageland *Chesterfield*
Pamplico *Florence*
Park Place *Greenville*
Parksville *McCormick*
Patrick *Chesterfield*
Pauline *Spartanburg*
Pawleys Island
   Georgetown
Peak *Newberry*
Peedee *Marion*
Pelion *Lexington*
Pelzer *Anderson*
Pendleton *Anderson*
Perry *Aiken*
Pickens *Pickens*
Piedmont *Greenville*
Pineland *Jasper*
Pineville *Berkeley*
Pinewood *Sumter*
Pinopolis *Berkeley*
Plum Branch *McCormick*
Pomaria *Newberry*
Port Royal *Beaufort*
Poston *Florence*
Prosperity *Newberry*
Quinby *Florence*
Rains *Marion*
Ravenel *Charleston*
Reevesville *Dorchester*
Reidville *Spartanburg*
Rembert *Sumter*
Richburg *Chester*
Richland *Oconee*
Ridgeland *Jasper*
Ridge Spring *Saluda*
Ridgeville *Dorchester*
Ridgeway *Fairfield*
Rimini *Clarendon*
Rion *Fairfield*
Riverside *Greenville*
Rock Hill *York*
Roebuck *Spartanburg*
Round O *Colleton*
Rowesville *Orangeburg*
Ruby *Chesterfield*
Ruffin *Colleton*
Russellville *Berkeley*
Saint Andrews *Charleston*
Saint Andrews *Richland*
Saint George *Dorchester*
Saint Matthews *Calhoun*
St. Stephen *Berkeley*
Salem *Oconee*
Salley *Aiken*
Salters *Williamsburg*
Saluda *Saluda*

Sandy Springs *Anderson*
Sans Souci *Greenville*
Santee *Orangeburg*
Scranton *Florence*
Seabrook *Beaufort*
Sellers *Marion*
Seneca *Oconee*
Shannontown *Sumter*
Sharon *York*
Sheldon *Beaufort*
Shulerville *Berkeley*
Silverstreet *Newberry*
Simpsonville *Greenville*
Six Mile *Pickens*
Slater *Greenville*
Smoaks *Colleton*
Smyrna *York*
Socastee *Horry*
Society Hill *Darlington*
South Congaree *Lexington*
Spartanburg *Spartanburg*
Springdale *Lexington*
Springfield *Orangeburg*
Starr *Anderson*
Startex *Spartanburg*
State Park *Richland*
Sullivans Island
   Charleston
Summerton *Clarendon*
Summerville *Dorchester*
Sumter *Sumter*
Sunset *Pickens*
Surfside Beach *Horry*
Swansea *Lexington*
Sycamore *Allendale*
Tamassee *Oconee*
Tatum *Marlboro*
Taylors *Greenville*
Tega Cay *York*
Tigerville *Greenville*
Tillman *Jasper*
Timmonsville *Florence*
Townville *Anderson*
Travelers Rest *Greenville*
Trenton *Edgefield*
Trio *Williamsburg*
Troy *Greenwood*
Turbeville *Clarendon*
Ulmer *Allendale*
Una *Spartanburg*
Union *Union*
Utica *Ocohee*
Vance *Orangeburg*
Van Wyck *Lancaster*
Varnville *Hampton*
Vaucluse *Aiken*
Wadmalaw Island
   Charleston
Wagener *Aiken*
Walhalla *Oconee*
Wallace *Marlboro*
Walterboro *Colleton*
Wando *Berkeley*
Ward *Saluda*
Ware Shoals *Greenwood*
Warrenville *Aiken*
Waterloo *Laurens*
Watts Mills *Laurens*
Wedgefield *Sumter*
Wellford *Spartanburg*
West Columbia *Lexington*
West Pelzer *Anderson*
Westminster *Oconee*
West Union *Oconee*
West View *Spartanburg*

Westville *Kershaw*
White Oak *Fairfield*
White Rock *Richland*
White Stone *Spartanburg*
Whitmire *Newberry*
Whitney *Spartanburg*
Williams *Colleton*
Williamston *Anderson*
Williston *Barnwell*
Windsor *Aiken*
Winnsboro *Fairfield*
Winnsboro Mills *Fairfield*
Wisacky *Lee*
Woodruff *Spartanburg*
Yemassee *Hampton*
Yonges Island *Charleston*
York *York*

South Dakota

Forty nine (49) of South Dakota's sixty six (66) counties reported that their criminal records are available by phone or mail for employment screening purposes. As of July 1, 1992, civil suits for more than $4,000 are filed in circuit court. Prior to July1, 1992, civil court held records for $2,000 and greater.

For more information or for offices not listed, contact the state's information hot line at (605) 773-3011.

Driving Records

Department of Commerce
Driver's License Issuance
118 West Capitol
Pierre, SD 57501
(605) 773-4127
Driving records are available by mail. $4.00 fee per request. Turnaround time is 4 days. Written request must include job applicant's full name, date of birth and license number. Make check payable to Department of Commerce.

Worker's Compensation Records

Labor and Management
Department of Labor
700 Governor's Drive
Pierre, SD 57501
(605) 773-3681
Worker's compensation records are available by mail from July, 1989 forward. A release is required with original copy of claimant's signature. $10.00 fee for a South Dakota employer, $20.00 fee for out of state employer. No copies will be made. Must submit form for office to fill out. Injury date, type of injury and employer information will be released. Fax requests are not accepted. Written request must include full name.

Vital Statistics

South Dakota Department of Health
Vital Records Program
523 East Capital
Pierre, SD 57501
(605) 773-4961
Birth and death records are available for $5.00 each. State office has records since July 1905. Most records are public and those entered from 1959 are issued by computer. An employer can obtain records with a written release. Make certified check or money order payable to Department of Health. Mastercard and Visa are also accepted for an additional $5.00.

Marriage records are available. $5.00 fee. Include name, marriage date, spouse's name, and place marriage occurred. Turnaround time is 2 weeks. Divorce records are available at county level, Clerk of Court, where divorce granted. Certified copies of divorce transcripts are also available in the state office for $5.00 each Mastercard and Visa are also accepted for an additional $5.00 per name searched.

Department of Education

Division of Education Records
Teacher Education and Certification
700 Governor Drive
Pierre, SD 57501
(605) 773-3553
Field of certification, effective date, expiration date are available by mail or phone. Include name and SSN.

Medical Licensing

State Medical Examiners
1323 South Minnesota Avenue
Souix Falls, SD 57105
(605) 336-1965
Fax (605) 336-0270
Will confirm licenses for MDs and DOs by mail or by phone for up to 2 requests. For licenses not mentioned, contact the above office.

South Dakota Board of Nursing
304 South Phillips Ave., Suite 205
Sioux Falls, SD 57102
(605) 335-4973
Will confirm license by phone. No fee. Include name, license number.

Bar Association

State Bar South Dakota
222 E. Capitol
Pierre, SD 57501
(605) 224-7554
Will confirm licenses by phone. No fee. Include name.

Accountancy Board

State Board of Accountancy
301 E. 14th Street. Suite 200
Sioux Falls, SD 57104
(605) 339-6746
Will confirm license by phone. No fee. Include name.

Securities Commission

Registrar Assistant
910 E. Sioux
Pierre, SD 57501-3940
(605) 773-3187
Will confirm license by phone. No fee. Include name and SSN.

Secretary of State

Secretary of State
Corporation Commission
500 East Capitol
Pierre, SD 57510
(605) 773-4845
Service agent and address and date incorporated are available by mail or phone. Contact the above office for additional information.

Criminal Records

State Repository

Division of Criminal Investigation
Office of Attorney General
East Highway 34
c/o 500 East Capitol
Pierre, SD 57501
(605) 773-3331
Fax (605) 773-4629
All written requests must include subject's signed release and a set of fully rolled fingerprints. Card releases are available by contacting the state at the above address. There is a $15.00 fee for each request. Make check payable to Division of Criminal Investigation. Information released contains both conviction and arrest information. Turnaround time is normally 48 to 72 hours.

Aurora County

Clerk of Court, Criminal Records
PO Box 333
Plankinton, SD 57368
(605) 942-7736
Felony and misdemeanor records are available in person only. See South Dakota state repository for additional information.

Civil records are available by mail. A release is required. No search fee. Search information required: name, date of birth, years to search. Specify plaintiff or defendant.

Beadle County

Clerk of Court, Criminal Records
PO Box 1358
Huron, SD 57350
(605) 353-7165

Felony and misdemeanor records are available in person only. See South Dakota State Repository for additional information.

Civil records are available by mail. No release necessary. $2.00 search fee. $.10 fee per copy. $2.00 for certification. Search information required: name, date of birth, years to search. Specify plaintiff or defendant.

Bennett County

Bennett County Clerk of Court, Criminal Records
PO Box 281
Martin, SD 57551
(605) 685-6969

Felony and misdemeanor records are available in person only. See South Dakota state repository for additional information.

Civil records are available by mail. No release necessary. $2.00 search fee. $.25 fee for first copy. $.10 each additional copy. $3.00 for certification. Search information required: name, date of birth, years to search. Specify plaintiff or defendant.

Bon Homme County

Clerk of Court, Criminal Records
PO Box 6
Tyndall, SD 57066
(605) 589-3382

Felony and misdemeanor records are available by mail. Turnaround time is 1-2 days. No release necessary. $2.00 search fee. Certified check only, payable to Clerk of Court. Search information required: name.

Civil records are available by mail. No release necessary. $2.00 search fee. $.10 fee per copy. $2.00 for certification. Search information required: name, date of birth, years to search. Specify plaintiff or defendant.

Brookings County

Clerk of Court, Criminal Records
Brookings County Courthouse
314 6th Avenue
Brookings, SD 57006
(605) 688-4200

Felony and misdemeanor records are available by mail. $2.00 search fee. $.10 fee per copy. $2.00 for certification. Certified check only, payable to Clerk of Court. Search information required: name, date of birth, years to search.

Civil records are available by mail. No release necessary. $2.00 search fee. $.10 fee per copy. $2.00 for certification. Search information required: name, date of birth, years to search. Specify plaintiff or defendant.

Brown County

Clerk of Circuit Court, Criminal Records
101 1st Ave. S.E.
Aberdeen, SD 57401
(605) 622-2451

Felony and misdemeanor records are available by mail or phone. Turnaround time is 3 days. No release necessary. $2.00 search fee. Make company check payable to Clerk of Circuit Court. Search information required: name.

Civil records are available by mail. No release necessary. $2.00 search fee. $.50 fee per copy. $2.50 for certification. Search information required: name, date of birth, years to search. Specify plaintiff or defendant.

Brule County

Brule County Courthouse, Criminal Records
300 S. Courtland
Chamberlain, SD 57325
(605) 734-5443

Felony and misdemeanor records are available by mail. No release necessary. No search fee. $.15 fee per copy. $2.50 for certification. Search information required: name, SSN, date of birth, SASE.

Civil records are available by mail. No release necessary. No search fee. $.15 fee per copy. $2.50 for certification. Search information required: name, date of birth, years to search, SASE. Specify plaintiff or defendant.

Buffalo County

Clerk of Court, Criminal Records
PO Box 148
Gann Valley, SD 57341
(605) 293-3234

Felony and misdemeanor records are available by mail. No release necessary. $2.00 search fee. Make check payable to Buffalo County Clerk. Search information required: name, date of birth.

Civil records are available by mail. No release necessary. $2.00 search fee. $.15 fee per copy. $2.00 for certification. Search information required: name, date of birth, years to search. Specify plaintiff or defendant.

Butte County

Clerk of Court, Criminal Records
PO Box 237
Belle Fourche, SD 57717
(605) 892-2516

Felony and misdemeanor records are available in person only. See South Dakota state repository for additional information.

Civil records are available by mail. No release necessary. $2.00 search fee. $.25 fee per copy. $2.00 for certification. Search information required: name, date of birth, years to search. Specify plaintiff or defendant.

Campbell County

Clerk of Court, Criminal Records
PO Box 146
Mound City, SD 57646
(605) 955-3536

Felony and misdemeanor records are available in person only. Contact the South Dakota state repository for additional information.

Civil records are available by mail. No release necessary. $2.00 search fee. $.25 fee per copy. $2.00 for certification. Search information required: name, date of birth, years to search. Specify plaintiff or defendant.

Charles Mix County

Clerk of Court, Criminal Records
PO Box 640
Lake Andes, SD 57356
(605) 487-7511

Felony and misdemeanor records are available by mail or phone. Turnaround time is 1 week. No release necessary. $2.00 search fee. Make check payable to Clerk of Court. Search information required: name, date of birth, sex, race.

Civil records are available by mail. No release necessary. $2.00 search fee. $.15 fee per copy. $2.00 for certification. Search information required: name, date of birth, years to search. Specify plaintiff or defendant.

Clark County

Clerk of Court, Criminal Records
PO Box 294
Clark, SD 57225
(605) 532-5851

Felony and misdemeanor records are available by mail. Turnaround time is 1 week. A release is required. $2.00 search fee. Make check payable to Clerk of Court. Search information required: name, date of birth, SASE, years to search.

Civil records are available by mail. No release necessary. $2.00 search fee. $.20 fee per copy. $2.00 for certification. Search information required: name, date of birth, years to search. Specify plaintiff or defendant.

Clay County

Clay County Clerk of Court, Criminal Records
PO Box 377
Vermillion, SD 57069
(605) 624-3371

Felony and misdemeanor records are available by mail. No release necessary. $2.00 search fee. $.10 fee per copy. $2.00 for certification. Search information required: name, years to search.

Civil records are available by mail. No release necessary. $2.00 search fee. $.25 fee per copy. $2.00 for certification. Search information required: name, date of birth, years to search. Specify plaintiff or defendant.

Codington County

Clerk of Court, Criminal Records
PO Box 1054
Watertown, SD 57201
(605) 886-4850

Felony and misdemeanor records are available by mail. Turnaround time is 3 days. A release is required. $2.00 search fee. Search information required: name, date of birth, years to search. SASE.

Civil records are available by mail or phone. No release necessary. 2.00 search fee. $.20 fee per copy. $2.00 for certification. Search information required: name, date of birth, years to search, SASE. Specify plaintiff or defendant.

Corson County

Clerk of Court, Criminal Records
PO Box 175
McIntosh, SD 57641
(605) 273-4201

Felony and misdemeanor records are available in person only. Contact the South Dakota state repository for additional information.

Civil records are available in person only. Contact the South Dakota state repository for additional information.

Custer County

Clerk of Court, Criminal Records
420 Mt. Rushmore Road
Custer, SD 57730
(605) 673-4816

Felony and misdemeanor records are available in person only. See the South Dakota state repository for additional information.

Civil records are available by mail. No release necessary. $2.00 search fee. $.10 fee per copy. $2.00 for certification. Search information required: name, date of birth, years to search. Specify plaintiff or defendant.

Davison County

Clerk of Court, Criminal Records
PO Box 927
Mitchell, SD 57301
(605) 996-2450

Felony and misdemeanor records are available in person only. See the South Dakota state repository for additional information.

Civil records are available by mail. No release necessary. $2.00 search fee. $.25 fee per copy. $2.00 for certification. Search information required: name, date of birth, years to search. Specify plaintiff or defendant.

Day County

Clerk of Court, Criminal Records
710 W. 1st Street
Webster, SD 57274
(605) 345-3771

Felony and misdemeanor records are available in person only. See the South Dakota state repository for additional information.

Civil records are available by mail. No release necessary. $2.00 search fee. $.20 fee per copy. $2.00 for certification. Search information required: name, date of birth, years to search. Specify plaintiff or defendant.

Deuel County

Clerk of Court, Criminal Records
PO Box 125
Clear Lake, SD 57226
(605) 874-2120

Felony and misdemeanor records are available by mail or phone. No release necessary. No search fee. $.15 fee per copy. $2.00 for certification. Search information required: name, date of birth, years to search.

Civil records are available by mail. No release necessary. $2.00 search fee. $.15 fee per copy. $2.00 for certification. Search information required: name, date of birth, years to search. Specify plaintiff or defendant.

Dewey County

Clerk of Court, Criminal Records
PO Box 96
Timber Lake, SD 57656
(605) 865-3566

Felony and misdemeanor records are available by mail. A release is required. $2.00 search fee. Make check payable to Clerk of Court. Search information required: name, date of birth, years to search.

Civil records are available by mail. No release necessary. $2.00 search fee. $.25 fee per copy. $2.00 for certification. Search information required: name, date of birth, years to search. Specify plaintiff or defendant.

Douglas County

Clerk of Court, Criminal Records
PO Box 36
Armour, SD 57313
(605) 724-2585

Felony and misdemeanor records are available by mail. $2.00 search fee. $.25 fee per copy. $2.00 for certification. Make company check payable to Clerk of Court. Search information required: name, SSN, years to search, SASE.

Civil records are available by mail. No release necessary. $2.00 search fee. $.25 fee per copy. $2.00 for certification. Search information required: name, date of birth, years to search. Specify plaintiff or defendant.

Edmunds County

Clerk of Court, Criminal Records
PO Box 384
Ipswich, SD 57451
(605) 426-6671

Felony and misdemeanor records are available by mail. Turnaround time is 1 day. No release necessary. $2.00 search fee. Make company check payable to Clerk of Court. Search information required: name, date of birth, years to search.

Civil records are available by mail. No release necessary. $2.00 search fee. $.25 fee per copy. $2.00 for certification. Search information required: name, date of birth, years to search. Specify plaintiff or defendant.

Fall River County

Clerk of Court, Criminal Records
Fall River County Courthouse
Hot Springs, SD 57747
(605) 745-5131

Felony and misdemeanor records are available by mail. Turnaround time is 1 day. A release is required. $2.00 search fee. Company checks only, payable to Clerk of Court. Search information required: name.

Civil records are available by mail. No release necessary. $2.00 search fee. $1.00 fee per copy. $2.00 for certification. Search information required: name, date of birth, years to search. Specify plaintiff or defendant.

Faulk County

Clerk of Court, Criminal Records
PO Box 357
Faulkton, SD 57438
(605) 598-6223

Felony and misdemeanor records are available by mail. No release necessary. $2.00 search fee. $.25 fee per copy. $1.00 for certification. Make check payable to Clerk of Court. Search information required: name, SSN, date of birth.

Civil records are available by mail. No release necessary. $2.00 search fee. $.25 fee per copy. $1.00 for certification. Search information required: name, date of birth, years to search. Specify plaintiff or defendant.

Grant County

Clerk of Court, Criminal Records
PO Box 509
Milbank, SD 57252
(605) 432-5482

Felony and misdemeanor records are available by mail or phone. Turnaround time is 3 days. No release necessary. No search fee. Search information required: name, date of birth.

Civil records are available by mail or phone. No release necessary. $2.00 search fee. $.25 fee per copy. $2.00 for certification. Search information required: name, date of birth, years to search. Specify plaintiff or defendant.

Gregory County

Clerk of Court, Criminal Records
Gregory County
PO Box 430
Burke, SD 57523
(605) 775-2665

Felony and misdemeanor records are available by mail. No release necessary. $2.00 search fee. $.15 fee per copy. $2.00 for certification. Certified check only, payable to Clerk of Court. Search information required: name, years to search.

Civil records are available by mail. No release necessary. $2.00 search fee. $.15 fee per copy. $2.00 for certification. Search information required: name, date of birth, years to search. Specify plaintiff or defendant.

Haakon County

Clerk of Court, Criminal Records
PO Box 70
Philip, SD 57567
(605) 859-2627

Felony and misdemeanor records are available by mail or phone. Office hours are Monday-Friday, 1-5 pm mountain time. No release necessary. $2.00 search fee. $.25 fee per copy. $2.00 for certification. Search information required: name, date of birth, years to search.

Civil records are available by mail or phone. No release necessary. $2.00 search fee. $.25 fee per copy. $2.00 for certification. Search information required: name, date of birth, years to search. Specify plaintiff or defendant.

Hamlin County

Clerk of Court, Criminal Records
PO Box 256
Hayti, SD 57241
(605) 783-3751

Felony and misdemeanor records are available by mail. Turnaround time is 2 days. No release necessary. $2.00 search fee. Search information required: name, date of birth.

Civil records are available by mail. No release necessary. $2.00 search fee. $.50 fee per copy. $2.00 for certification. Search information required: name, date of birth, years to search. Specify plaintiff or defendant.

Hand County

Clerk of Court, Criminal Records
PO Box 122
Miller, SD 57362
(605) 853-3337

Felony and misdemeanor records are available in person only. See South Dakota State Repository for additional information.

Civil records are available by mail. No release necessary. $2.00 search fee. $.20 fee per copy. $2.00 for certification. Search information required: name, date of birth, years to search. Specify plaintiff or defendant.

Hanson County

Clerk of Court, Criminal Records
PO Box 127
Alexandria, SD 57311
(605) 239-4446

Felony and misdemeanor records are available by mail or phone. No release necessary. No search fee. $.25 fee per copy. $2.00 for certification. Search information required: name.

Civil records are available by mail or phone. No release necessary. No search fee. $.25 fee per copy. $2.00 for certification. Search information required: name, date of birth, years to search. Specify plaintiff or defendant.

Harding County

Clerk of Court, Criminal Records
PO Box 534
Buffalo, SD 57720
(605) 375-3351

Felony and misdemeanor records are available in person or by mail. A release, if available. $2.00 search fee. Search information required: name, date of birth, years to search

Civil records are available by mail. No release necessary. $2.00 search fee. $.25 fee per copy. $2.00 for certification. Search information required: name, date of birth, years to search. Specify plaintiff or defendant.

Hughes County

Clerk of Court
104 E. Capitol
Pierre, SD 57501
(605) 773-3713

Felony and misdemeanor records are available by mail. No release necessary. $2.00 search fee. $2.00 for certification. Search information required: name, date of birth, years to search.

Civil records are available by mail. No release necessary. $2.00 search fee. $2.00 for certification. Search information required: name, date of birth, years to search. Specify plaintiff or defendant.

Hutchinson County

Clerk of Court, Criminal Records
PO Box 7
Olivet, SD 57052
(605) 387-5335

Felony and misdemeanor records are available by mail. No release necessary. No search fee. $.25 fee per copy. $2.00 for certification. Make company check payable to Hutchinson County Clerk. Search information required: name, years to search.

Civil records are available by mail. No release necessary. No search fee. $.25 fee per copy. $2.00 for certification. Search information required: name, date of birth, years to search. Specify plaintiff or defendant.

Hyde County

Clerk of Court, Criminal Records
PO Box 306
Highmore, SD 57345
(605) 852-2512

Felony and misdemeanor records are available by mail. No release necessary. $2.00 search fee. $.25 fee per copy. $2.00 for certification. Make check payable to Clerk of Court. Search information required: name.

Civil records are available by mail. No release necessary. $2.00 search fee. $.25 fee per copy. $2.00 for certification. Search information required: name, date of birth, years to search. Specify plaintiff or defendant.

Jackson County

Clerk of Court, Criminal Records
PO Box 128
Kadoka, SD 57543
(605) 837-2121

Felony and misdemeanor records are available by mail. Turnaround time is 1 day. No release necessary. $2.00 search fee. Company checks only, payable to Clerk of Court. Search information required: name, years to search.

Civil records are available by mail. No release necessary. $2.00 search fee. $.15 fee per copy. $2.00 for certification. Search information required: name, date of birth, years to search. Specify plaintiff or defendant.

Jerauld County

Clerk of Court, Criminal Records
Box 435
Wessington Springs, SD 57382
(605) 539-1202

Felony and misdemeanor records are available in person only. See South Dakota state repository for additional information.

Civil records are available by mail. No release necessary. $2.00 search fee. $.50 fee per copy. $2.00 for certification. Search information required: name, date of birth, years to search. Specify plaintiff or defendant.

Jones County

Clerk of Court, Criminal Records
PO Box 448
Murdo, SD 57559
(605) 669-2361

Felony and misdemeanor records are available by mail. A release is required. No search fee. $.25 fee per copy. Search information required: name, SSN, date of birth, sex, race.

Civil records are available by mail. A release is required. $2.00 search fee. $.25 fee per copy. $2.00 for certification. Search information required: name, date of birth, years to search. Specify plaintiff or defendant.

Kingsbury County

Clerk of Court, Criminal Records
PO Box 176
DeSmet, SD 57231
(605) 854-3811

Felony and misdemeanor records are available in person only. See South Dakota state repository for additional information.

Civil records are available by mail. No release necessary. $2.00 search fee. $.50 fee per copy. $2.00 for certification. Search information required: name, date of birth, years to search. Specify plaintiff or defendant.

Lake County

Lake County Courthouse, Criminal Records
PO Box 447
Madison, SD 57042
(605) 256-4876

Felony and misdemeanor records are available by mail. A release is required. $2.00 search fee. $.25 fee per copy. $2.00 for certification. Certified check only, payable to Clerk of Court. Search information required: name, years to search.

Civil records are available by mail. No release necessary. $2.00 search fee. $.25 fee per copy. $2.00 for certification. Search information required: name, date of birth, years to search. Specify plaintiff or defendant.

Lawrence County

Clerk of Court, Criminal Records
PO Box 626
Deadwood, SD 57732
(605) 578-2040

Felony and misdemeanor records are available by mail. No release necessary. $5.00 search fee. $.25 fee per copy. $2.00 for certification. Search information required: name, date of birth, years to search.

Civil records are available by mail. No release necessary. $5.00 search fee. $.25 fee per copy. $2.00 for certification. Search information required: name, date of birth, years to search. Specify plaintiff or defendant.

Lincoln County

Clerk of Court, Criminal Records
100 E. 5th Street
Canton, SD 57013
(605) 987-5891

Felony and misdemeanor records are available by mail. No release necessary. $2.00 search fee. $.50 fee per copy. $2.00 for certification. Search information required: name, date of birth, years to search.

Civil records are available by mail. No release necessary. $2.00 search fee. $.50 fee per copy. $2.00 for certification. Search information required: name, date of birth, years to search. Specify plaintiff or defendant.

Lyman County

Lyman County Courthouse, Criminal Records
PO Box 235
Kennebec, SD 57544
(605) 869-2277

Felony and misdemeanor records are available by mail. Turnaround time is 2 days. A release is required. $2.00 search fee. Make check payable to Lyman County Clerk. Search information required: name, years to search.

Civil records are available by mail or phone. No release necessary. $2.00 search fee. $.50 fee per copy. $2.00 for certification. Search information required: name, date of birth, years to search. Specify plaintiff or defendant.

Marshall County

Clerk of Court, Criminal Records
PO Box 130
Britton, SD 57430
(605) 448-5213

Felony and misdemeanor records are available by mail or phone. Turnaround time is 2 days. No release necessary. No search fee. $.10 fee per copy. $2.00 for certification. Search information required: name.

Civil records are available by mail or phone. No release necessary. No search fee. $.10 fee per copy. $2.00 for certification. Search information required: name, date of birth, years to search. Specify plaintiff or defendant.

McCook County

Clerk of Court, Criminal Records
PO Box 504
Salem, SD 57058
(605) 425-2781

Felony and misdemeanor records are available in person only. See South Dakota State Repository for additional information.

Civil records are available by mail. No release necessary. $2.00 search fee. $.15 fee per copy. $2.00 for certification. Search information required: name, date of birth, years to search. Specify plaintiff or defendant.

McPherson County

Clerk of Court, Criminal Records
PO Box 248
Leola, SD 57456
(605) 439-3361

Felony records are available in person only and misdemeanor records are available by mail. No release necessary. $2.00 search fee. $.30 fee per copy. Make check payable to Clerk of Court. Search information required: name, SSN, date of birth, sex, race, SASE.

Civil records are available by mail. No release necessary. $2.00 search fee. $.25 fee per copy. $2.00 for certification. Search information required: name, date of birth, years to search, SASE Specify plaintiff or defendant.

Meade County

Clerk of Court, Criminal Records
PO Box 939
Sturgis, SD 57785
(605) 347-4411

Felony and misdemeanor records for this county are open to the public only through the South Dakota state repository. Contact the state repository for more information.

Civil records are available by mail. No release necessary. $2.00 search fee. $.25 fee per copy. $2.00 for certification. Search information required: name, date of birth, years to search. Specify plaintiff or defendant.

Mellette County

Mellette County Courthouse, Criminal Records
PO Box 257
White River, SD 57579
(605) 259-9404 or 259-3230

Felony and misdemeanor records are available by mail. No release necessary. $2.00 search fee. $.25 fee per copy. $2.00 for certification. Make check payable to Clerk of Court. Search information required: name, years to search.

Civil records are available by mail or phone. No release necessary. $2.00 search fee. $.25 fee per copy. $2.00 for certification. Search information required: name, date of birth, years to search. Specify plaintiff or defendant.

Miner County

Miner County Courthouse, Criminal Records
PO Box 265
Howard, SD 57349
(605) 772-4612

Felony and misdemeanor records are available by mail. No release necessary. $2.00 search fee. $.25 fee per copy. $2.00 for certification. Search information required: name.

Civil records are available by mail No release necessary. $2.00 search fee. $.25 fee per copy. $2.00 for certification. Search information required: name, date of birth, years to search. Specify plaintiff or defendant.

Minnehaha County

Minnehaha County Courthouse, Criminal Records
415 N. Dakota Ave.
Sioux Falls, SD 57102
(605) 339-6418

Felony and misdemeanor records are available by mail. No release necessary. $2.00 search fee. $.25 fee per copy. $2.00 for certification. Company checks only, payable to Clerk of Court. Search information required: name, date of birth, years to search.

Civil records are available by mail No release necessary. $2.00 search fee. $.25 fee per copy. $2.00 for certification. Search information required: name, date of birth, years to search. Specify plaintiff or defendant.

Moody County

Clerk of Court, Criminal Records
PO Box 226
Flandreau, SD 57028
(605) 997-3181

Felony and misdemeanor records are available in person only. See South Dakota state repository for additional information.

Civil records are available by mail. No release necessary. $2.00 search fee. $.10 fee per copy. $2.00 for certification. Search information required: name, date of birth, years to search. Specify plaintiff or defendant.

Pennington County

Felony records
Clerk of Court, Criminal Records
PO Box 230
Rapid City, SD 57709
(605) 394-2575

Felony records are available by mail or phone. No release necessary. $2.00 search fee. Search information required: name, date of birth, years to search.

Civil records
Clerk of Court
PO Box 230
Rapid City, SD 57709
(605) 394-2575

Civil records are available by mail or phone. No release necessary. $2.00 search fee. $.25 fee per copy. $2.00 for certification. Search information required: name, date of birth, years to search. Specify plaintiff or defendant.

Misdemeanor records
Magistrate's Court
PO Box 230
Rapid City, SD 57709
(605) 394-2570

Misdemeanor records are available in person only. See South Dakota state repository for additional information.

Civil records
Magistrate's Court
PO Box 230
Rapid City, SD 57709
(605) 394-2570

Civil records are available in person only. See South Dakota state repository for additional information.

Perkins County

Clerk of Court, Criminal Records
PO Box 27
Bison, SD 57620
(605) 244-5626

Felony and misdemeanor records are available by mail. A release is required. $2.00 search fee. Make check payable to Clerk of Court. Search information required: name, date of birth, years to search.

Civil records are available by mail No release necessary. $2.00 search fee. $.25 fee per copy. $2.00 for certification. Search information required: name, date of birth, years to search. Specify plaintiff or defendant.

Potter County

Clerk of Court, Criminal Records
201 S. Exene
Gettysburg, SD 57442
(605) 765-9472

Felony and misdemeanor records are available by mail. No release necessary. $2.00 search fee. $.25 fee per copy. $2.00 for certification. Make check payable to Clerk of Court. Search information required: name, years to search.

Civil records are available by mail. No release necessary. $2.00 search fee. $.25 fee per copy. $2.00 for certification. Search information required: name, date of birth, years to search. Specify plaintiff or defendant.

Roberts County

Clerk of Court, Criminal Records
411 2nd Ave. E.
Sisseton, SD 57262
(605) 698-3395

Felony and misdemeanor records are available in person only. See South Dakota state repository for additional information.

Civil records are available by mail. No release necessary. $2.00 search fee. $.15 fee per copy. $2.00 for certification. Search information required: name, date of birth, years to search. Specify plaintiff or defendant.

Sanborn County

Clerk of Court, Criminal Records
PO Box 56
Woonsocket, SD 57385
(605) 796-4515

Felony and misdemeanor records are available in person only. See South Dakota state repository for additional information.

Civil records are available in person only. See South Dakota state repository for additional information.

Shannon County

Clerk of Court, Criminal Records
Fall River County Courthouse
Hot Springs, SD 57747
(605) 745-5131

Felony and misdemeanor records are available by mail. A release is required. $2.00 search fee. $1.00 fee per copy. $2.00 for certification. Make check payable to Clerk of Court. Search information required: name, years to search.

Civil records are available by mail. A release is required. $2.00 search fee. $1.00 fee per copy. $2.00 for certification. Search information required: name, date of birth, years to search. Specify plaintiff or defendant.

Spink County

Clerk of Court & Magistrate's Office, Criminal Records
210 E. 7th Ave.
Redfield, SD 57469-1299
(605) 472-1922

Felony and misdemeanor records are available by mail. No release necessary. $2.00 search fee. $.15 fee per copy. $2.00 for certification. Make check payable to Clerk of Court. Search information required: name, years to search.

Civil records are available by mail. No release necessary. $2.00 search fee. $.15 fee per copy. $2.00 for certification. Search information required: name, date of birth, years to search. Specify plaintiff or defendant.

Stanley County

Clerk of Court, Criminal Records
PO Box 758
104 East Capital
Fort Pierre, SD 57532
(605) 773-3992

Felony and misdemeanor records are available by mail or phone. No release necessary. $2.00 search fee. $.15 fee per copy. $2.00 for certification. Certified check only, payable to Clerk of Court. Search information required: name, date of birth, years to search.

Civil records are available by mail or phone. No release necessary. $2.00 search fee. $.15 fee per copy. $2.00 for certification. Search information required: name, date of birth, years to search. Specify plaintiff or defendant.

Sully County

Clerk of Court, Criminal Records
PO Box 188
Onida, SD 57564
(605) 258-2535

Felony and misdemeanor records are available by mail or phone. No release necessary. $2.00 search fee. Make check payable to Clerk of Court. Search information required: name, SSN, date of birth, sex, race, years to search.

Civil records are available by mail. No release necessary. $2.00 search fee. $.15 fee per copy. $2.00 for certification. Search information required: name, date of birth, years to search. Specify plaintiff or defendant.

Todd County

Clerk of Court, Criminal Records
200 E. 3rd Street
Winner, SD 57580
(605) 842-2266

Felony and misdemeanor records are available by mail. Turnaround time is 1 day. No release necessary. $2.00 search fee. Certified check only, payable to Todd County Clerk of Court. Search information required: name, years to search.

Civil records are available by mail. No release necessary. $2.00 search fee. $.10 fee per copy. $2.00 for certification. Search information required: name, date of birth, years to search. Specify plaintiff or defendant.

Tripp County

Clerk of Court, Criminal Records
200 E. 3rd
Winner, SD 57580
(605) 842-2266

Felony and misdemeanor records are available by mail or phone. Turnaround time is 1 day. No release necessary. $2.00 search fee. Company checks only, payable to Trip County Clerk of Court. Search information required: name, years to search.

Civil records are available by mail No release necessary. $2.00 search fee. $.10 fee per copy. $2.00 for certification. Search information required: name, date of birth, years to search. Specify plaintiff or defendant.

Turner County

Clerk of Court, Criminal Records
PO Box 446
Parker, SD 57053
(605) 297-3115

Felony and misdemeanor records are available in person only. See South Dakota State Repository for additional information.

Civil records are available by mail No release necessary. $2.00 search fee. $.25 fee per copy. $2.00 for certification. Search information required: name, date of birth, years to search. Specify plaintiff or defendant.

Union County

Clerk of Court
PO Box 757
Elk Point, SD 57025
(605) 356-2132

Felony records are available by mail. $2.00 search fee. $.20 fee per copy. $2.00 for certification. Make certified check payable to Clerk of Court. Search information required: name, years to search.

Civil records are available by mail No release necessary. $2.00 search fee. $.10 fee per copy. $2.00 for certification. Search information required: name, date of birth, years to search. Specify plaintiff or defendant.

Walworth County

Clerk of Court, Criminal Records
PO Box 328
Selby, SD 57472
(605) 649-7311

Felony and misdemeanor records are available by mail. No release necessary. $2.00 search fee. $.25 fee per copy. $2.00 for certification. Search information required: name, date of birth, years to search.

Civil records are available by mail. No release necessary. $2.00 search fee. $.25 fee per copy. $2.00 for certification. Search information required: name, date of birth, years to search. Specify plaintiff or defendant.

Yankton County

Clerk of Court, Criminal Records
PO Box 155
Yankton, SD 57078
(605) 668-3438

Felony and misdemeanor records in person only. See South Dakota state repository for additional information.

Civil records are available by mail or phone. No release necessary. $2.00 search fee. $.20 fee per copy. $2.00 for certification. Search information required: name, date of birth, years to search. Specify plaintiff or defendant.

Ziebach County

Clerk of Court, Criminal Records
PO Box 306
Dupree, SD 57623
(605) 365-5159

Felony and misdemeanor records are available in person only. See South Dakota state repository for additional information.

Civil records are available by mail. No release necessary. $2.00 search fee. $.25 fee per copy. $2.00 for certification. Search information required: name, date of birth, years to search. Specify plaintiff or defendant.

City-County Cross Reference

Aberdeen *Brown*
Academy *Charles Mix*
Agar *Sully*
Akaska *Walworth*
Albee *Grant*
Alcester *Union*
Alexandria *Hanson*
Allen *Bennett*
Alpena *Jerauld*
Amherst *Marshall*
Andover *Day*
Arlington *Kingsbury*
Armour *Douglas*
Artas *Campbell*
Artesian *Sanborn*
Ashton *Spink*
Astoria *Deuel*
Athol *Spink*
Aurora *Brookings*
Avon *Bon Homme*
Badger *Kingsbury*
Baltic *Minnehaha*
Bancroft *Kingsbury*
Barnard *Brown*
Batesland *Shannon*
Bath *Brown*
Belle Fourche *Butte*
Belvidere *Jackson*
Beresford *Union*
Big Stone City *Grant*
Bison *Perkins*
Black Hawk *Meade*
Blunt *Hughes*
Bonesteel *Gregory*
Bowdle *Edmunds*
Box Elder *Pennington*
Bradley *Clark*
Brandon *Minnehaha*
Brandt *Deuel*
Brentford *Spink*
Bridgewater *McCook*
Bristol *Day*
Britton *Marshall*
Brookings *Brookings*
Bruce *Brookings*
Bryant *Hamlin*
Buffalo *Harding*
Buffalo Gap *Custer*
Bullhead *Corson*
Burbank *Clay*
Burke *Gregory*
Butler *Day*
Camp Crook *Harding*
Canistota *McCook*
Canova *Miner*
Canton *Lincoln*
Caputa *Pennington*
Carpenter *Clark*
Carter *Tripp*
Carthage *Miner*
Castlewood *Hamlin*
Cavour *Beadle*
Cedarbutte *Mellette*
Centerville *Turner*
Chamberlain *Brule*
Chancellor *Turner*
Cherry Creek *Ziebach*
Chester *Lake*
Claire City *Roberts*
Claremont *Brown*
Clark *Clark*
Clear Lake *Deuel*

Colman *Moody*
Colome *Tripp*
Colton *Minnehaha*
Columbia *Brown*
Conde *Spink*
Corona *Roberts*
Corsica *Douglas*
Corson *Minnehaha*
Cresbard *Faulk*
Crooks *Minnehaha*
Custer *Custer*
Dante *Charles Mix*
Davis *Turner*
Deadwood *Lawrence*
Dell Rapids *Minnehaha*
Delmont *Douglas*
Dempster *Hamlin*
DeSmet *Kingsbury*
Dimock *Hutchinson*
Doland *Spink*
Dolton *Turner*
Draper *Jones*
Dupree *Ziebach*
Eagle Butte *Ziebach*
Eden *Marshall*
Edgemont *Fall River*
Egan *Moody*
Elk Point *Union*
Elkton *Brookings*
Elm Springs *Meade*
Emery *Hanson*
Enning *Meade*
Erwin *Kingsbury*
Estelline *Hamlin*
Ethan *Davison*
Eureka *McPherson*
Fairburn *Custer*
Fairfax *Gregory*
Fairview *Lincoln*
Faith *Meade*
Farmer *Hanson*
Faulkton *Faulk*
Fedora *Miner*
Firesteel *Dewey*
Flandreau *Moody*
Florence *Codington*
Forestburg *Sanborn*
Fort Meade *Meade*
Fort Pierre *Stanley*
Fort Thompson *Buffalo*
Frankfort *Spink*
Frederick *Brown*
Freeman *Hutchinson*
Fulton *Hanson*
Gannvalley *Buffalo*
Garden City *Clark*
Garretson *Minnehaha*
Gary *Deuel*
Gayville *Yankton*
Geddes *Charles Mix*
Gettysburg *Potter*
Glad Valley *Ziebach*
Glencross *Dewey*
Glenham *Walworth*
Goodwin *Deuel*
Gregory *Gregory*
Grenville *Day*
Groton *Brown*
Hamill *Tripp*
Harrisburg *Lincoln*
Harrold *Hughes*
Hartford *Minnehaha*

Hayti *Hamlin*
Hazel *Hamlin*
Hecla *Brown*
Henry *Codington*
Hermosa *Custer*
Herreid *Campbell*
Herrick *Gregory*
Hetland *Kingsbury*
Highmore *Hyde*
Hill City *Pennington*
Hitchcock *Beadle*
Holabird *Hyde*
Hosmer *Edmunds*
Hot Springs *Fall River*
Hoven *Potter*
Howard *Miner*
Howes *Meade*
Hudson *Lincoln*
Humboldt *Minnehaha*
Hurley *Turner*
Huron *Beadle*
Ideal *Tripp*
Interior *Jackson*
Iona *Lyman*
Ipswich *Edmunds*
Irene *Clay*
Iroquois *Kingsbury*
Isabel *Dewey*
Java *Walworth*
Jefferson *Union*
Kadoka *Jackson*
Kaylor *Hutchinson*
Keldron *Corson*
Kennebec *Lyman*
Keyapaha *Tripp*
Keystone *Pennington*
Kimball *Brule*
Kranzburg *Codington*
Kyle *Shannon*
Lake Andes *Charles Mix*
Lake City *Marshall*
Lake Norden *Hamlin*
Lake Preston *Kingsbury*
Langford *Marshall*
Lantry *Dewey*
Lead *Lawrence*
Lebanon *Potter*
Lemmon *Perkins*
Lennox *Lincoln*
Leola *McPherson*
Lesterville *Yankton*
Letcher *Sanborn*
Lily *Day*
Little Eagle *Corson*
Lodgepole *Perkins*
Longlake *McPherson*
Longvalley *Jackson*
Lower Brule *Lyman*
Ludlow *Harding*
Lyons *Minnehaha*
McIntosh *Corson*
McLaughlin *Corson*
Madison *Lake*
Manderson *Shannon*
Mansfield *Spink*
Marcus *Meade*
Marion *Turner*
Martin *Bennett*
Marty *Charles Mix*
Marvin *Grant*
Meadow *Perkins*
Meckling *Clay*

Mellette *Spink*
Menno *Hutchinson*
Midland *Haakon*
Milbank *Grant*
Milesville *Haakon*
Miller *Hand*
Mission *Todd*
Mission Hill *Yankton*
Mission Ridge *Stanley*
Mitchell *Davison*
Mobridge *Walworth*
Montrose *McCook*
Morristown *Corson*
Mound City *Campbell*
Mount Vernon *Davison*
Mud Butte *Meade*
Murdo *Jones*
Nemo *Lawrence*
New Effington *Roberts*
Newell *Butte*
New Holland *Douglas*
New Underwood
    Pennington
Nisland *Butte*
Norris *Mellette*
North Eagle Butte *Ziebach*
North Sioux City *Union*
Northville *Spink*
Nunda *Lake*
Oacoma *Lyman*
Oelrichs *Fall River*
Oglala *Shannon*
Okaton *Jones*
Okreek *Todd*
Oldham *Kingsbury*
Olivet *Hutchinson*
Onaka *Faulk*
Onida *Sully*
Opal *Meade*
Oral *Fall River*
Orient *Faulk*
Owanka *Pennington*
Parade *Dewey*
Parker *Turner*
Parkston *Hutchinson*
Parmelee *Todd*
Peever *Roberts*
Philip *Haakon*
Pickstown *Charles Mix*
Piedmont *Meade*
Pierpont *Day*
Pierre *Hughes*
Pine Ridge *Shannon*
Plankinton *Aurora*
Platte *Charles Mix*
Pollock *Campbell*
Porcupine *Shannon*
Prairie City *Perkins*
Presho *Lyman*
Pringle *Custer*
Provo *Fall River*
Pukwana *Brule*
Quinn *Pennington*
Ramona *Lake*
Rapid City *Pennington*
Raymond *Clark*
Redfield *Spink*
Redig *Harding*
Redowl *Meade*
Ree Heights *Hand*
Reliance *Lyman*
Reva *Harding*

Revillo *Grant*
Ridgeview *Dewey*
Rockham *Faulk*
Roscoe *Edmunds*
Rosebud *Todd*
Rosholt *Roberts*
Roslyn *Day*
Saint Francis *Todd*
Saint Lawrence *Hand*
Saint Onge *Lawrence*
Salem *McCook*
Scenic *Pennington*
Scotland *Bon Homme*
Selby *Walworth*
Seneca *Faulk*
Sherman *Minnehaha*
Sinai *Brookings*
Sioux Falls *Minnehaha*
Sisseton *Roberts*
Smithwick *Fall River*
South Shore *Codington*
Spearfish *Lawrence*
Spencer *McCook*
Springfield *Bon Homme*
Stickney *Aurora*
Stockholm *Grant*
Strandburg *Grant*
Sturgis *Meade*
Summit *Roberts*
Tabor *Bon Homme*
Tea *Lincoln*
Timber Lake *Dewey*
Tolstoy *Potter*
Toronto *Deuel*
Trail City *Dewey*
Trent *Moody*
Tripp *Hutchinson*
Tulare *Spink*
Turton *Spink*
Tuthill *Bennett*
Twin Brooks *Grant*
Tyndall *Bon Homme*
Union Center *Meade*
Utica *Yankton*
Vale *Butte*
Valley Springs *Minnehaha*
Veblen *Marshall*
Vermillion *Clay*
Viborg *Turner*
Vivian *Lyman*
Volga *Brookings*
Volin *Yankton*
Wagner *Charles Mix*
Wakonda *Clay*
Wakpala *Corson*
Wall *Pennington*
Wallace *Codington*
Wanblee *Jackson*
Warner *Brown*
Wasta *Pennington*
Watauga *Corson*
Watertown *Codington*
Waubay *Day*
Webster *Day*
Wentworth *Lake*
Wessington *Beadle*
Wessington Springs
    Jerauld
Westport *Brown*
Wewela *Tripp*
White *Brookings*
Whitehorse *Dewey*
White Lake *Aurora*
White Owl *Meade*
White River *Mellette*

Whitewood *Lawrence*
Willow Lake *Clark*
Wilmot *Roberts*
Winfred *Lake*
Winner *Tripp*
Witten *Tripp*
Wolsey *Beadle*
Wood *Mellette*
Woonsocket *Sanborn*
Worthing *Lincoln*
Wounded Knee *Shannon*
Yale *Beadle*
Yankton *Yankton*
Zell *Faulk*
Zeona *Perkins*

Tennessee

The Tennessee Bureau of Investigation, the central repository in the state for criminal records, reported that access to its files is limited to criminal justice agencies. In contrast, the state's ninety five (95) counties indicated that they do release conviction data for employment screening purposes. Seventy eight (78) accept mail and/or phone requests, and a handful will allow requests to be made by fax. Civil records for $10,000 and greater are filed in circuit court.

For more information or for offices not listed, contact the state's information hot line at (615) 741-3011.

Driving Records

Tennessee Department of Safety
1150 Foster Avenue
Nashville, TN 37249-4000
(615) 741-3954
Driving records are available by mail. $5.00 fee per request. Turnaround time is 2 to 3 weeks. Written request must include job applicant's full name, date of birth and license number. Make check payable to Tennessee Department of Safety.

Worker's Compensation Records

Department of Labor
Division of Worker's Compensation
501 Union Building, 2nd Floor
Nashville, TN 37219
(615) 741-2395
Currently worker's compensation records are stored under the name of the previous employer involved in the claim. For this reason written requests must include the name of that employer along with the applicant's full name, date of birth and SSN, date of the injury. The state has automated records beginning September, 1991, which allows access by name and SSN. There is no fee. A signed release is not required.

Vital Statistics

Tennessee Vital Records
Department of Health and Environment
C3-324 Cordell Hull Building
Nashville, TN 37247-0350
(615) 741-1763
Birth records are available in both long and short form. Fee of $10.00 for the long form, and a fee of $5.00 for the short form. Additional copies of birth records at the same time are $2.00 per copy. Death records are available for $5.00. State office has birth records for entire State since January, 1914 and death records for entire State since January, 1942.

Marriage and divorce records are available. $10.00 fee. State office has records since July 1, 1945. Check or money order.

Include name, marriage or divorce date, spouse's name, and county where marriage or divorce took place. Turnaround time is 10-14 days. Written release required.

Department of Education

Teacher Licensing
6th Floor, North Wing
Cordell Hull Bldg.
Nashville, TN 37243-0377
(615) 741-1644
Fax (615) 741-6236
Field of certification, effective date, expiration date are available by mai. Include name, teacher number and SSN.

Medical Licensing

Board of Medical Examiners
Health and Environment
283 Plus Park Blvd.l
Nashville, TN 37247-1010H
(615) 367-6231
Will confirm licenses for MDs by mail or phone. No fee. For licenses not mentioned, contact the above office.

Tennessee State Board of Nursing
419 Cordell Hull
Nashville, TN 37247-1010
(615) 741-1954
Will supply a printout of current licenses for RNs and LPNs. $100.00 fee for each printout.

Bar Association

Tennessee State Board of Law Examiners
Nashville City Center
511 Union Street, Suite 1420
Nasville, TN 37243-0740
(615) 741-3234
Will confirm licenses by phone. No fee. Include name.

Accountancy Board

Tennessee State Board of Accountancy
500 James Robertson Parkway
2nd Floor
Nashville, TN 37243-1141
(615) 741-2550
Will confirm license by phone. No fee. Include name.

Securities Commission

Department of Commerce and Insurance
500 James Robertson Parkway
Suite 680
Nashville, TN 37243-0583
(615) 741-3187
Will confirm license by phone. No fee. Include name and SSN.

Secretary of State

Department of State
Division of Services
Attn: Certification
Suite 1800
James K. Polk Bldg.
Nashville, TN 37243-0306
(615) 741-2816
Service agent and address, date incorporated, trade names are available by mail. $20.00 fee. Corporation name may be verified by phone. Contact the above office for additional information.

Criminal Records

State Repository

Tennessee Bureau of Investigation
c/o Criminal Records Unit
PO Box 100940
Nashville, TN 37224
(615) 741-0430
Non-criminal justice agencies are not currently allowed access to criminal record information at the state repository level. See the appropriate Tennessee county listing.

Anderson County

Anderson County Courthouse, Criminal Records
100 Main Street, Rm. 301
Clinton, TN 37716
(615) 457-5400

Felony and misdemeanor records are available in person only.

Civil records are available in person only. See Tennessee state repository for additional information.

Bedford County

Circuit Court Clerk, Criminal Records
1 Public Square, Suite 200
Bedford County Courthouse
Shelbyville, TN 37160
(615) 684-3223

Felony and misdemeanor records are available by mail. No release necessary. No search fee. $1.00 for certification. Search information required: name, SASE, years to search.

Civil records are available by mail. No release necessary. No search fee. $1.00 for certification. Search information required: name, date of birth, years to search, SASE. Specify plaintiff or defendant.

Benton County

Circuit Court Clerk, Criminal Records
PO Box 466
Camden, TN 38320
(901) 584-6711

Felony and misdemeanor records are available by mail. No release necessary. No search fee. Search information required: name, years to search.

Civil records are available by mail. No release necessary. No search fee. Search information required: name, date of birth, years to search. Specify plaintiff or defendant.

Bledsoe County

Circuit Court Clerk, Criminal Records
PO Box 455
Pikeville, TN 37367
(615) 447-6488

Felony and misdemeanor records are available in person only. See Tennessee state repository for additional information.

Civil records are available in person only. See Tennessee state repository for additional information.

Blount County

Circuit Court Clerk, Criminal Records
301 Court St.
Maryville, TN 37801
(615) 982-5263

Felony records are available by mail. A release is required. $15.00 fee. Search information required: name, SSN, date of birth, sex, race, years to search.

Civil records are available in person only. See Tennessee state repository for additional information.

Bradley County

Bradley County Courthouse, Criminal Records
Cleveland, TN 37311
(615) 476-0590

Felony and misdemeanor records are available by mail. No release necessary. $10.00 search fee. $6.50 fee for first certified copy, $1.00 each additional page. Search information required: name, previous address, years to search, date of birth.

Civil records are available by mail. No release necessary. $10.00 search fee. $.30 fee per copy. $10.00 for certification. Search information required: name, date of birth, years to search. Specify plaintiff or defendant.

Campbell County

Circuit Court Clerk, Criminal Records
PO Box 26
Jacksboro, TN 37757
(615) 562-2624

Felony and misdemeanor records are available in person only. See Tennessee State Repository for additional information.

Civil records are available by mail or phone. No release necessary. $5.00 search fee. $1.00 fee per copy. $5.00 for certification. Search information required: name, date of birth, years to search. Specify plaintiff or defendant.

Cannon County

Circuit Court Clerk, Criminal Records
Cannon County Courthouse
Woodbury, TN 37190
(615) 563-4461

Felony and misdemeanor records are available by mail. No release necessary. $3.00 search fee. Search information required: name.

Civil records are available by mail. No release necessary. $6.00 search fee. $.25 fee per copy. $3.00 for certification. Search information required: name, date of birth, years to search. Specify plaintiff or defendant.

Carroll County

Circuit Court Clerk, Criminal Records
PO 487
Huntingdon, TN 38344
(901) 986-3031

Felony and misdemeanor records are available by mail .No release necessary. $4.00 search fee. $6.00 fee for certification. Checks payable to Circuit and General Sessions Court. Search information required: name, date of birth, race, sex, address, years to search.

Civil records are available by mail. No release necessary. $6.00 search fee. $.25 fee per copy. $6.00 for certification. Search information required: name, date of birth, years to search. Specify plaintiff or defendant.

Carter County

Circuit Court Clerk, Criminal Records
Courthouse Annex
900 E. Elk Ave.
Elizabethton, TN 37643
(615) 542-1835

Felony and misdemeanor records are available in person only.

Civil records are available in person only. See Tennessee state repository for additional information.

Cheatham County

Circuit Court Clerk, Criminal Records
Ashland City, TN 37015
(615) 792-3272

Felony and misdemeanor records are available by mail or phone. No release necessary. $2.00 search fee. Search information required: name, years to search.

Civil records are available by mail. No release necessary. No search fee. $2.50 fee per copy. $5.00 for certification. Search information required: name, date of birth, years to search. Specify plaintiff or defendant.

Chester County

Circuit Court Clerk, Criminal Records
PO Box 133
Henderson, TN 38340
(901) 989-2454
Fax (901) 989-4755

Felony and misdemeanor records are available by mail, fax or phone. No release necessary. No search fee. $1.00 fee per copy, $5.00 fee for certified copy. Search information required: name, date of birth, SASE. Include individual's driver's license number.

Civil records are available by mail or phone. No release necessary. No search fee. $1.00 fee per copy. Search information required: name, date of birth, years to search, SASE. Specify plaintiff or defendant.

Claiborne County

Circuit Court Clerk, Criminal Records
PO Box 34
Tazewell, TN 37879
(615) 626-3334

Felony and misdemeanor records are available by mail or phone. A release is required. No search fee. Search information required: name, date of birth, SSN.

Civil records are available by mail. No release necessary. No search fee. $.50 fee per copy. $3.50 for certification. Search information required: name, date of birth, years to search. Specify plaintiff or defendant.

Clay County

Circuit Court Clerk, Criminal Records
PO Box 156
Celina, TN 38551
(615) 243-2557

Felony and misdemeanor records are available in person only.

Civil records are available in person only. See Tennessee state repository for additional information.

Cocke County

Felony records
Circuit Court Clerk, Criminal Records
Cocke County Courthouse
Newport, TN 37821
(615) 623-6124

Felony records are available by mail or phone. No release necessary. No search fee. $2.00 fee per copy, $5.00 fee for certified copy. Search information required: name.

Civil records
Circuit Court Clerk
Cocke County Courthouse
Newport, TN 37821
(615) 623-6124
Civil records are available by mail or phone. No release necessary. No search fee. $.25 fee per copy. Search information required: name, date of birth, years to search. Specify plaintiff or defendant.

Misdemeanor records
General Sessions Court
Cocke County Courthouse
Newport, TN 37821
(615) 623-8619
Misdemeanor records are available by mail or phone. No release necessary. $3.00 search fee. Search information required: name, date of birth, address, years to search.

Civil records
General Sessions Court
Cocke County Courthouse
Newport, TN 37821
(615) 623-8619
Civil records are available by mail. No release necessary. No search fee. $3.00 fee per copy. $3.00 for certification. Search information required: name, date of birth, years to search. Specify plaintiff or defendant.

Coffee County

Circuit Court Clerk, Criminal Records
PO Box 629
Manchester, TN 37355
(615) 723-5110
Felony and misdemeanor records are available by mail. No release necessary. $5.00 search fee. $3.50 fee for certification. Company checks only, payable to Clerk of Circuit Court. Search information required: name, years to search.

Civil records are available by mail. No release necessary. $5.00 search fee. $3.50 fee for first copy, $.50 each additional copy. $3.50 for certification. Search information required: name, date of birth, years to search. Specify plaintiff or defendant.

Crockett County

Circuit Court Clerk, Criminal Records
Crockett County Courthouse
Alamo, TN 38001
(901) 696-5462
Felony and misdemeanor records are available by mail or phone. No release necessary. No search fee. $1.00 fee per copy, $2.00 fee for certification. Search information required: name, date of birth, years to search.

Civil records are available by mail or phone. No release necessary. No search fee. $1.00 fee per copy, $2.00 fee for certification. Search information required: name, date of birth, years to search. Specify plaintiff or defendant.

Cumberland County

Criminal Records
Courthouse Box 7
Crossville, TN 38555
(615) 484-6647
Felony and misdemeanor records are available by mail or phone. No release necessary. No search fee. Search information required: name, SSN, date of birth, sex, race.

Civil records are available by mail or phone. No release necessary. No search fee. Search information required: name, date of birth, years to search. Specify plaintiff or defendant.

Davidson County

Felony and misdemeanor records
Criminal Court, Criminal Records
303 Metro Courthouse
Nashville, TN 37201
(615) 862-5656
Felony and misdemeanor records are available by mail. No release necessary. $5.00 search fee. Make check payable to Criminal Court Clerk. Search information required: name, date of birth, SASE.

Civil records
100 James Robertson Parkway
Benwest Bldg., Room 2
Nashville, TN 37201
(615) 862-5195
Civil records are available in person only. See Tennessee state repository for additional information.

DeKalb County

DeKalb County Courthouse, Criminal Records
Smithville, TN 37166
(615) 597-5711
Felony and misdemeanor records are available by mail. No release necessary. $5.00 search fee. $.25 fee per copy, $5.00 fee for certified copy. Certified check only, payable to Clerk of Circuit Court. Search information required: name, years to search.

Civil records are available by mail. No release necessary. $5.00 search fee. $.25 fee per copy. $5.00 for certification. Search information required: name, date of birth, years to search. Specify plaintiff or defendant.

Decatur County

Circuit Court Clerk, Criminal Records
Decaturville, TN 38329
(901) 852-3125
Felony and misdemeanor records are available by mail. No release necessary. No search fee. $.25 fee per copy. $5.00 for certification. Search information required: name, SSN, date of birth, years to search.

Civil records are available by mail. No release necessary. No search fee. $.25 fee per copy. $5.00 for certification. Search information required: name, date of birth, years to search. Specify plaintiff or defendant.

Dickson County

Circuit Court Clerk, Criminal Records
Court Square
PO Box 220
Charlotte, TN 37036
(615) 789-4171 Extension 40
Fax (615) 789-7010
Felony and misdemeanor records are available by mail, fax or phone. No release necessary. No search fee. $.25 fee per copy, $2.00 fee for certified copy. Search information required: name, date of birth, SASE, years to search.

Civil records are available by mail, fax or phone. No release necessary. No search fee. $.25 fee per copy. $2.00 for certification. Search information required: name, date of birth, years to search, SASE. Specify plaintiff or defendant.

Dyer County

Dyer County Courthouse, Criminal Records
Circuit Court Clerk
PO Box 1360
Dyersburg, TN 38024
(901) 286-7809
Felony and misdemeanor records are available by mail. No release necessary. $25.00 search fee. Search information required: name, date of birth, years to search.

Civil records are available by mail. No release necessary. $25.00 search fee. Search information required: name, date of birth, years to search, SASE. Specify plaintiff or defendant.

Fayette County

Circuit Court Clerk, Criminal Records
PO Box 177
Somerville, TN 38068
(901) 465-5205
Felony records are available by mail. No release necessary. $10.00 search fee. Search information required: name, years to search.

Civil records are available by mail. No release necessary. $10.00 search fee. $3.00 for certification. Search information required: name, date of birth, years to search. Specify plaintiff or defendant.

Fentress County

Circuit Court Clerk, Criminal Records
PO Box 699
Jamestown, TN 38556
(615) 879-7919
Fax (615) 879-7919
Felony and misdemeanor records are available by mail, phone or fax. No release necessary. No search fee. Search information required: name, date of birth.

Civil records are available by mail, phone or fax. No release necessary. No search fee. $.50 fee per copy. $6.00 for certification. Search information required: name, date of birth, years to search. Specify plaintiff or defendant.

Franklin County

Circuit Court Clerk, Criminal Records
Franklin County Courthouse
Winchester, TN 37398
(615) 967-2923
Felony and misdemeanor records are available by mail or phone. No release necessary. No search fee. $4.00 fee per certified copy. Search information required: name, date of offense, date of birth, SSN.

Civil records are available by mail. No release necessary. $10.00 search fee. $4.00 for certification. Search information required: name, date of birth, years to search. Specify plaintiff or defendant.

Gibson County

Courthouse, Criminal Records
Trenton, TN 38382
(901) 855-7615
Fax (901) 855-7650
Felony and misdemeanor records are available by mail, fax or phone. No release necessary. No search fee. $3.00 fee for certified copy. Search information required: name, date of birth, sex, race.

Civil records are available by mail, fax or phone. No release necessary. No search fee. $.50 fee per copy. $3.00 for certification. Search information required: name, date of birth, years to search. Specify plaintiff or defendant.

Giles County

Circuit Court Clerk, Criminal Records
PO Box 678
Pulaski, TN 38478
(615) 363-5495 or 363-7528

Felony records are available by mail. A release is required. $5.00 search fee. $.50 fee per copy. $3.00 for certification. Search information required: name, date of birth, years to search.

Civil records are available in person only. See Tennessee state repository for additional information.

Grainger County

Circuit Court Clerk, Criminal Records
PO Box 157
Rutledge, TN 37861
(615) 828-3605

Felony and misdemeanor records are available by mail or phone. No release necessary. No search fee. $4.00 fee for certified copy. Make check payable to Clerk of Circuit Court. Search information required: name, date of birth, years to search.

Civil records are available by mail. No release necessary. No search fee. $4.00 for certification. Search information required: name, date of birth, years to search. Specify plaintiff or defendant.

Greene County

Greene County Courthouse, Criminal Records
Greenville, TN 37743
(615) 639-9732

Felony and misdemeanor records are available by mail. No release necessary. No search fee. $1.00 fee per copy. $3.00 for certification. Search information required: name, date of birth, years to search.

Civil records are available by mail. No release necessary. No search fee. $1.00 fee per copy. $3.00 for certification. Search information required: name, date of birth, years to search. Specify plaintiff or defendant.

Grundy County

Circuit Court Clerk, Criminal Records
PO Box 161
Altamont, TN 37301
(615) 692-3368

Felony and misdemeanor records are available by mail. A release is required. No search fee. $.25 fee per copy. $1.50 for certification. Search information required: name, date of birth, years to search.

Civil records are available by mail. A release is required. No search fee. $.25 fee per copy. $1.50 for certification. Search information required: name, date of birth, years to search. Specify plaintiff or defendant.

Hamblen County

Circuit Court Clerk, Criminal Records
510 Allison Street
Morristown, TN 37814
(615) 586-5640

Felony and misdemeanor records are available by mail. A release is required. $5.00 search fee. Company checks only, payable to Circuit Court Clerk. Search information required: name, SSN, date of birth, years to search.

Civil records are available by mail. No release necessary. $5.00 search fee. $.25 fee per copy. $3.00 for certification. Search information required: name, date of birth, years to search. Specify plaintiff or defendant.

Hamilton County

Criminal Court Clerk
Justice Bldg.
6th & Walnut St., Room 313
Chattanooga, TN 37402
(615) 757-2366

Felony and misdemeanor records are available by mail. No release necessary. $10.00 search fee. $2.00 fee for first copy, $1.00 each additional copy. $2.00 for certification. All checks and money payable to Criminal Court Clerk. Search information required: name, date of birth, SSN, race, years to search.

Civil records are available by mail. No release necessary. $10.00 search fee. $2.00 fee for first copy, $1.00 each additional copy. $2.00 for certification. Search information required: name, date of birth, years to search. Specify plaintiff or defendant.

Hancock County

Hancock County Courthouse, Criminal Records
Sneedville, TN 37869
(615) 733-2954

Felony records are available by mail or phone. No release necessary. $5.00 search fee. $.25 fee per copy. $2.00 for certification. Check or money order payable to Clerk of Circuit Court. Search information required: name, address, SSN, years to search, SASE.

Civil records are available by mail or phone. No release necessary. $5.00 search fee. $.25 fee per copy. $2.00 for certification. Search information required: name, date of birth, years to search, SASE. Specify plaintiff or defendant.

Hardeman County

General Session and Circuit Court, Criminal Records
Hardeman County
Bolivar, TN 38008
(901) 658-6524

Felony and misdemeanor records are available by mail or phone. No release necessary. No search fee. $.25 fee per copy. $2.50 for certification. Search information required: name, SSN, date of birth, years to search.

Civil records are available by mail or phone. No release necessary. No search fee. $.25 fee per copy. $2.50 for certification. Search information required: name, date of birth, years to search. Specify plaintiff or defendant.

Hardin County

Felony records
Circuit Court Clerk, Criminal Records
Savannah, TN 38372
(901) 925-3583

Felony records are available by mail or phone. No release necessary. No search fee from 1980 forward. $.50 fee per copy. $5.00 for certification. Search information required: name, years to search.

Civil records
Circuit Court Clerk
Savannah, TN 38372
(901) 925-3583

Civil records are available in person only. See Tennessee state repository for additional information.

Misdemeanor records
Circuit Court Clerk, Criminal Records
Savannah, TN 38372
(901) 925-3583

Misdemeanor records are available in person only.

Civil records
Circuit Court Clerk
Savannah, TN 38372
(901) 925-3583

Civil records are available in person only. See Tennessee state repository for additional information.

Hawkins County

Courthouse, Criminal Records
PO Box 9
Rogersville, TN 37857
(615) 272-3397

Felony and misdemeanor records are available in person only.

Civil records are available in person only. See Tennessee state repository for additional information.

Haywood County

General Sessions and Court Clerk, Criminal Records
Courthouse
Brownsville, TN 38012
(901) 772-1112

Felony and misdemeanor records are available by mail or phone. A release is required. No search fee. $2.50 for certification. Search information required: name, date of birth, years to search.

Civil records are available in person only. See Tennessee state repository for additional information.

Henderson County

Circuit Court Clerk, Criminal Records
Henderson County Courthouse
Lexington, TN 38351
(901) 968-2031

Felony and misdemeanor records are available by mail. No release necessary. $5.00 search fee. $1.00 fee per copy. $2.00 for certification. Search information required: name, years to search.

Civil records are available by mail. No release necessary. $5.00 search fee. $1.00 fee per copy. $2.00 for certification. Search information required: name, date of birth, years to search. Specify plaintiff or defendant.

Henry County

Circuit Court Clerk, Criminal Records
PO Box 429
Paris, TN 38242
(901) 642-0461
Felony and misdemeanor records are available by phone. No release necessary. No fee. Search information required: name, date of birth, address, year offense took place.

Civil records are available in person only. See Tennessee state repository for additional information.

Hickman County

Hickman County Courthouse
Circuit Court Clerk
Criminal Records
Centerville, TN 37033
(615) 729-2211
Felony and misdemeanor records are available in person only. See Tennessee state repository for additional information.

Civil records are available in person only. See Tennessee state repository for additional information.

Houston County

Circuit Court Clerk, Criminal Records
PO Box 403
Erin, TN 37061
(615) 289-4673
Felony and misdemeanor records are available by mail or phone. No release necessary. $5.00 search fee. Search information required: name, years to search.

Civil records are available by mail or phone. No release necessary. $5.00 search fee. $.25 fee per copy. Search information required: name, date of birth, years to search. Specify plaintiff or defendant.

Humphreys County

Circuit Court Clerk, Criminal Records
Humphreys County Courthouse
Room 106
Waverly, TN 37185
(615) 296-2461
Felony and misdemeanor records are available by mail. No release necessary. Fee is $5.00 for up to five years searched, $1.00 fee per year thereafter. Company checks only, payable to Deputy Clerk. Search information required: name, SSN, date of birth, sex, race.

Civil records are available by mail. A release is required. $1.00 search fee per year. $3.00 for certification. Search information required: name, date of birth, years to search. Specify plaintiff or defendant.

Jackson County

Circuit Court Clerk, Criminal Records
PO Box 205
Gainesboro, TN 38562
(615) 268-9314
Felony and misdemeanor records are available by mail. No release necessary. $3.00 search fee. $.50 fee per copy. $3.00 for certification. Certified check only, payable to Circuit Court Clerk. Search information required: name, years to search.

Civil records are available by mail. No release necessary. $3.00 search fee. $.50 fee per copy. $3.00 for certification. Search information required: name, date of birth, years to search. Specify plaintiff or defendant.

Jefferson County

Felony records
Circuit Court Clerk, Criminal Records
PO Box 671
Dandridge, TN 37725
(615) 397-2786
Felony records are available by mail or phone from 1985 forward. No release necessary. $5.00 search fee. $.25 fee per copy. $2.50 for certification. Search information required: name, years to search, SASE.

Civil records
Circuit Court Clerk
PO Box 671
Dandridge, TN 37725
(615) 397-2786
Civil records are available by mail or phone. No release necessary. $5.00 search fee. $.25 fee per copy. $2.50 for certification. Search information required: name, date of birth, years to search, SASE. Specify plaintiff or defendant.

Misdemeanor records
General Sessions Clerk, Criminal Records
PO Box 33
Dandridge, TN 37725
(615) 397-2786
Misdemeanor records are available in person only. See Tennessee state repository for additional information.

Civil records
General Sessions Clerk
PO Box 33
Dandridge, TN 37725
(615) 397-2786
Civil records are available by mail. No release necessary. $5.00 search fee. $.25 fee per copy. $2.00 for certification. Search information required: name, date of birth, years to search. Specify plaintiff or defendant.

Johnson County

Circuit Court Clerk, Criminal Records
PO Box 73
Mountain City, TN 37683
(615) 586-5640
Fax (615) 727-9012
Felony and misdemeanor records are available by mail. A release is required. $5.00 fee. $4.00 for certification. Search information required: name, date of birth, previous address, years to search.

Civil records are available by mail or phone. No release necessary. $5.00 search fee. $.25 fee per copy. $4.00 for certification. Search information required: name, date of birth, years to search. Specify plaintiff or defendant.

Knox County

Criminal Court, Criminal Records
Room 149
400 Main Street, City-County Bldg.
Knoxville, TN 37902
(615) 521-2492
Felony and misdemeanor records are available by mail or phone. No release necessary. $1.00 search fee. Search information required: name, date of birth, SASE.

Civil records are available by mail. No release necessary. $3.00 search fee. $.50 fee per copy. $3.00 for certification. Search information required: name, date of birth, years to search. Specify plaintiff or defendant.

Lake County

Lake County Courthouse, Criminal Records
227 Church Street, Box 11
Tiptonville, TN 38079
(901) 253-7137
Felony and misdemeanor records are available by mail or phone. No release necessary. No search fee. Search information required: name, date of birth, SSN, years to search, style of case.

Civil records are available by mail. No release necessary. No search fee. $1.00 fee per copy. $3.00 for certification. Search information required: name, date of birth, years to search. Specify plaintiff or defendant.

Lauderdale County

Lauderdale County Courthouse, Circuit Court Clerk
Criminal Records
Ripley, TN 38063
(901) 635-0101
Fax (901) 635-9682
Felony records are available by mail or phone. No release necessary. No search fee. Search information required: name, SSN, date of birth, sex, race, years to search.

Civil records are available by mail. No release necessary. No search fee. $.50 fee per copy. Search information required: name, date of birth, years to search. Specify plaintiff or defendant.

Lawrence County

Lawrence County Circuit NBU #12
Court, Criminal Records
Lawrenceburg, TN 38464
(615) 762-4398
Fax(615) 766-2219
Felony and misdemeanor records are available by mail and fax. No release necessary. $5.00 search fee. $3.00 for certification. Company, cashier's check or money order, payable to Circuit Court Clerk. Search information required: name, SSN, date of birth, years to search, SASE.

Civil records are available by mail or fax. No release necessary. $5.00 search fee. $3.00 for certification. Search information required: name, date of birth, years to search, SASE. Specify plaintiff or defendant.

Lewis County

Lewis County Courthouse, Criminal Records
Hohenwald, TN 38462
(615) 796-3724
Felony and misdemeanor records are available by mail or phone. No release necessary. No search fee. $4.50 fee for certified copy. Search information required: name.

Civil records are available by mail or phone. No release necessary. No search fee. $.25 fee per copy. $2.50 for certification. Search information required: name, date of birth, years to search. Specify plaintiff or defendant.

Lincoln County

Circuit Court Clerk, Criminal Records
PO Box 78
Fayetteville, TN 37334
(615) 433-2334

Felony and misdemeanor records are available by mail. No release necessary. $7.00 search fee. Certified, cashier's check or money order, payable to Circuit Court Clerk. Search information required: name, years to search.

Civil records are available by mail. No release necessary. $5.00 search fee. $.25 per copy. $5.00 for certification. Search information required: name, date of birth, years to search. Specify plaintiff or defendant.

Loudon County

Loudon County Sherriff's Dept.
Criminal Records
PO Box 349
Loudon, TN 37774
(615) 986-9081
Fax (615) 986-3621

Felony and misdemeanor records are available by mail or fax. $4.00 search fee. $5.00 fee for fax response. A release is required. Search information required: name, date of birth, SSN, years to search.

Civil records are available by mail or fax. A release is required. $4.00 search fee. $5.00 fee for fax response. Search information required: name, date of birth, years to search. Specify plaintiff or defendant.

Macon County

Macon County Courthouse, Clerk
Circuit & General Sessions Court
Room 202
Lafayette, TN 37083
(615) 666-2354

Felony and misdemeanor records are available in person only. See Tennessee State Repository for additional information.

Civil records are available in person only. See Tennessee State Repository for additional information.

Madison County

Circuit Court Clerk
2nd Floor, Room 203
Jackson, TN 38301
(901) 423-6035

Felony and misdemeanor records are available in person only. See Tennessee state repository for additional information.

Civil records are available in person only. See Tennessee State Repository for additional information.

Marion County

Marion County Courthouse, Criminal Records
PO Box 789
Jasper, TN 37347
(615) 942-2134
Fax (615) 942-4160

Felony and misdemeanor records are available by mail, phone or fax. A release is required. No search fee. Search information required: name, date of birth.

Civil records are available by mail. No release necessary. $5.00 search fee. $1.00 fee per copy. Search information required: name, date of birth, years to search. Specify plaintiff or defendant.

Marshall County

Courthouse, Criminal Records
Lewisburg, TN 37091
(615) 359-1312

Felony and misdemeanor records are available by mail or phone. No release necessary. No search fee. $.35 fee per copy. Search information required: name, years to search.

Civil records are available by mail or phone. No release necessary. No search fee. $.35 fee per copy. Search information required: name, date of birth, years to search. Specify plaintiff or defendant.

Maury County

Maury County Courthouse, Criminal Records
General Session Court
Room 203
Columbia, TN 38401
(615) 381-3690

Felony and misdemeanor records are available by mail. A release is required. No search fee. $4.00 fee for certification. Search information required: name, SSN, date of birth.

Civil records are available by mail. A release is required. No search fee. $.50 fee per copy. $4.00 for certification. Search information required: name, date of birth, years to search. Specify plaintiff or defendant.

McMinn County

Circuit Court Clerk, Criminal Records
PO Box 506
Athens, TN 37303
(615) 745-1923

Felony and misdemeanor records are available by mail or phone. No release necessary. No search fee. $1.00 fee per copy. $3.00 for certification. Search information required: name, SSN, date of birth, years to search.

Civil records are available by mail or phone. No release necessary. No search fee. $1.00 fee per copy. $3.00 for certification. Search information required: name, date of birth, years to search. Specify plaintiff or defendant.

McNairy County

Courthouse, Criminal Records
Selmer, TN 38375
(901) 645-5561

Felony and misdemeanor records are available by mail. No release necessary. $5.00 search fee. No fee for phone searches. $1.00 fee per copy. $3.00 for certification. Make check payable to Circuit Court Clerk. Search information required: name, years to search.

Civil records are available by mail or phone. No release necessary. $5.00 search fee. No fee for phone searches. $1.00 fee per copy. $3.00 for certification. Search information required: name, date of birth, years to search. Specify plaintiff or defendant.

Meigs County

Circuit Court Clerk, Criminal Records
PO Box 205
Decatur, TN 37322
(615) 334-5821

Felony and misdemeanor records are available by mail or phone. No release necessary. No search fee. $.25 fee per copy. $2.50 for certification. Search information required: name, years to search, SASE.

Civil records are available by mail or phone. No release necessary. No search fee. $.25 fee per copy. $2.50 for certification. Search information required: name, date of birth, years to search, SASE. Specify plaintiff or defendant.

Monroe County

Felony records

Clerk of Criminal & Circuit Court, Criminal Records
Madisonville, TN 37354
(615) 442-2396

Felony records are available by mail. No release necessary. $10.00 fee. Make check payable to Circuit Court Clerk. Search information required: name, SSN, years to search.

Civil records

Clerk of Circuit Court
Madisonville, TN 37354
(615) 442-2396

Civil records are available by mail. No release necessary. $10.00 search fee. Search information required: name, date of birth, years to search. Specify plaintiff or defendant.

Misdemeanor records

Clerk of General Sessions, Criminal Records
Madisonville, TN 37354
(615) 442-9537

Misdemeanor records are available by mail or phone. No release necessary. $10.00 fee. Make check payable to Circuit Court Clerk. Search information required: name, SSN, years to search..

Civil records

Clerk of General Sessions
Madisonville, TN 37354
(615) 442-9537

Civil records are available by mail. No release necessary. $10.00 search fee. Search information required: name, date of birth, years to search. Specify plaintiff or defendant.

Montgomery County

Circuit Court Clerk, Criminal Records
PO Box 384
Clarksville, TN 37041-0384
(615) 648-5700

Felony and misdemeanor records are available by mail. No release necessary. $5.00 search fee. $.25 fee per copy. $3.00 for certification. Search information required: name, SSN, date of birth, sex, race, years to search.

Civil records are available by mail. No release necessary. $5.00 search fee. $.25 fee per copy. $3.00 for certification. Search information required: name, date of birth, years to search. Specify plaintiff or defendant.

Moore County

Courthouse, Criminal Records
Lynchburg, TN 37352
(615) 759-7208
Felony and misdemeanor records are available by mail or phone. A release necessary. $5.00 search fee. $1.00 fee per copy. $2.00 for certification. Search information required: name, SASE.

Civil records are available by mail. No release necessary. $5.00 search fee. $1.00 fee per copy. $2.00 for certification. Search information required: name, date of birth, years to search, SASE. Specify plaintiff or defendant.

Morgan County

Circuit Court Clerk, Criminal Records
PO Box 163
Wartburg, TN 37887
(615) 346-3503
Felony and misdemeanor records are available by mail or phone. A release required. $10.00 search fee. Make check payable to Circuit Court Clerk. Search information required: name, date of birth, years to search, SASE.

Civil records are available by mail. No release necessary. $10.00 search fee. $1.00 fee per copy. $6.00 for certification. Search information required: name, date of birth, years to search, SASE. Specify plaintiff or defendant.

Obion County

Circuit Court Clerk, Criminal Records
Obion County Courthouse
Union City, TN 38261
(901) 885-1372
Felony and misdemeanor records are available in person only.

Civil records are available in person only. See Tennessee state repository for additional information.

Overton County

Circuit Court Clerk, Criminal Records
Courthouse
Livingston, TN 38570
(615) 823-2312
Felony and misdemeanor records are available by mail. No release necessary. No search fee. $5.00 for certification. Search information required: name, date of birth, SSN, SASE, years to search.

Civil records are available by mail. No release necessary. No search fee. $5.00 for certification. Search information required: name, date of birth, years to search, SASE. Specify plaintiff or defendant.

Perry County

Circuit Court Clerk, Criminal Records
PO Box 91
Linden, TN 37096
(615) 589-2218
Felony and misdemeanor records are available by mail or phone. No release necessary. No search fee. $4.00 fee for certification. Certified check only, payable to Circuit Court Clerk. Search information required: name, years to search.

Civil records are available by mail or phone. No release necessary. No search fee. $4.00 for certification. Search information required: name, date of birth, years to search. Specify plaintiff or defendant.

Pickett County

Circuit Court Clerk, Criminal Records
PO Box 5
Byrdstown, TN 38549
(615) 864-3958
Felony and misdemeanor records are available by mail or phone. No release necessary. $5.00 search fee. $3.00 for certification. Search information required: name, date of birth, SSN, years to search.

Civil records are available by mail or phone. No release necessary. $5.00 search fee. $3.00 for certification. Search information required: name, date of birth, years to search. Specify plaintiff or defendant.

Polk County

Circuit Court Clerk, Criminal Records
PO Box 256
Benton, TN 37307
(615) 338-4524
Felony and misdemeanor records are available by mail or phone. No release necessary. $5.00 search fee. $.25 fee per copy. $5.50 fee for certified copies. Search information required: name, date of birth or driver's license, if available, years to search, SASE.

Civil records are available by mail or phone. No release necessary. $5.00 search fee. $.25 fee per copy. $5.50 for certification. Search information required: name, date of birth, years to search, SASE. Specify plaintiff or defendant.

Putnam County

Circuit Court
Putnam County Courthouse
Room 9
Cookeville, TN 38501
(615) 528-1508
Felony and misdemeanor records are available in person only. See Tennessee state repository for additional information.

Civil records are available in person only. See Tennessee state repository for additional information.

Rhea County

Circuit Court Clerk
Rhea County Courthouse, Criminal Records
Room 200
Dayton, TN 37321
(615) 775-7805
Felony records are available by mail. No release necessary. $10.00 fee for 5 years searched, $15.00 fee for 6-10 years, $20.00 fee for over 10 years. Search information required: full name, date of birth, SSN, years to search.

Civil records are available by mail. No release necessary. $5.00 search fee. $.50 fee per copy. $3.50 for certification. Search information required: name, date of birth, years to search. Specify plaintiff or defendant.

Roane County

Felony records
Circuit Court Clerk, Criminal Records
PO Box 73
Kingston, TN 37763
(615) 376-2390
Felony records are available by mail or phone. A release is required. $5.00 search fee. No fee for phone searches. Make check payable to Circuit Court Clerk. Search information required: name, SSN, date of birth, sex, race.

Civil records
Circuit Court Clerk
PO Box 73
Kingston, TN 37763
(615) 376-2390
Civil records are available by mail. A release is required. $5.00 search fee. $.25 fee per copy. $5.00 for certification. Search information required: name, date of birth, years to search. Specify plaintiff or defendant.

Misdemeanor records
General Sessions
PO Box 73
Kingston, TN 37763
(615) 376-5584
Misdemeanor records are available by mail. No release necessary. $5.00 search fee. Search information required: name, sex, race, years to search.

Civil records
General Sessions
PO Box 73
Kingston, TN 37763
(615) 376-5584
Civil records are available by mail. No release necessary. $5.00 search fee. $.25 fee per copy. $5.00 for certification. Search information required: name, date of birth, years to search. Specify plaintiff or defendant.

Robertson County

Courthouse, Criminal Records
Room 200
Springfield, TN 37172
(615) 384-7864
Felony and misdemeanor records are available by mail or phone. No release necessary. No search fee. $.25 fee per copy. $5.00 for certification. Search information required: name, date of birth, years to search.

Civil records are available by mail. No release necessary. No search fee. $.25 fee per copy. $5.00 for certification. Search information required: name, date of birth, years to search. Specify plaintiff or defendant.

Rutherford County

Circuit Court Clerk, Criminal Records
Judicial Bldg.
2nd Floor
Murfreesboro, TN 37130
(615) 898-7813
Felony and misdemeanor records are available in person only.

Civil records are available in person only. See Tennessee state repository for additional information.

Scott County

Circuit Court Clerk, Criminal Records
PO Box 73
Huntsville, TN 37756
(615) 663-2440
Felony and misdemeanor records are available by mail or phone. No release necessary. $1.00 search fee. make check payable to Circuit Court Clerk. Search information required: name, years to search.

Civil records are available by mail. A release is required. $1.00 search fee per year. $.50 fee per copy. $2.00 for certification. Search information required: name, date of birth, years to search. Specify plaintiff or defendant.

Sequatchie County

Circuit Court Clerk, Criminal Records
PO Box 551
Dunlap, TN 37327
(615) 949-2618
Felony and misdemeanor records are available by mail or phone. No release necessary. No search fee. $.25 fee per copy. $3.00 for certification. Search information required: name, years to search.

Civil records are available by mail or phone. No release necessary. No search fee. $.25 fee per copy. $3.00 for certification. Search information required: name, date of birth, years to search. Specify plaintiff or defendant.

Sevier County

Felony records
Circuit Court Clerk, Criminal Records
Room 207
Sevierville, TN 37862
(615) 453-5536
Felony records are available by mail or phone. No release necessary. No search fee. $.25 fee per copy. $3.00 for certification. Search information required: name, date of birth, years to search.

Civil records
Circuit Court Clerk
Room 207
Sevierville, TN 37862
(615) 453-5536
Civil records are available by mail or phone. No release necessary. No search fee. $.25 fee per copy. $3.00 for certification. Search information required: name, date of birth, years to search. Specify plaintiff or defendant.

Misdemeanor records
Trial Justice Court
Sevier County Courthouse
Sevierville, TN 37862
(615) 453-6116
Misdemeanor records are available in person only. See Tennessee state repository for additional information.

Civil records
Trial Justice Court
Sevier County Courthouse
Sevierville, TN 37862
(615) 453-6116
Civil records are available in person only. See Tennessee state repository for additional information.

Shelby County

Criminal Court Clerk, Criminal Records
Suite 401
201 Poplar Ave.
Memphis, TN 38103
(901) 576-5001
Felony and misdemeanor records are available by mail or phone. No release necessary. $5.00 search fee. No fee for phone searches. Make check payable to Criminal Court Clerk. Search information required: name, date of birth, sex, race.

Civil records are available in person only. See Tennessee state repository for additional information.

Smith County

Smith County Courthouse, Criminal Records
Carthage, TN 37030
(615) 735-0500
Felony and misdemeanor records are by mail. No release necessary. No search fee. $1.00 fee per copy. $6.00 for certification. Search information required: name, date of birth, years to search.

Civil records are available by mail. No release necessary. No search fee. $1.00 fee per copy. $6.00 for certification. Search information required: name, date of birth, years to search. Specify plaintiff or defendant.

Stewart County

Circuit Court Clerk, Criminal Records
PO Box 193
Dover, TN 37058
(615) 232-7042
Felony and misdemeanor records are available in person only.

Civil records are available in person only. See Tennessee state repository for additional information.

Sullivan County

Circuit Court Clerk
140 Blockville Bypass
PO Box 585
Blountville, TN 37617
(615) 323-5158
Records are not available by mail or phone. See Tennessee state repository.

Civil records are available in person only. See Tennessee state repository for additional information.

Sumner County

Sumner County Courthouse
4th Floor
Public Square
PO Box 549
Gallatin, TN 37066
(615) 452-4367
Records are not available by mail or phone. See Tennessee state repository.

Civil records are available in person only. See Tennessee state repository for additional information.

Tipton County

Circuit Court Clerk, Criminal Records
Box 308
Covington, TN 38019
(901) 476-0216
Felony and misdemeanor records are available by mail or phone. No release necessary. $10.00 search fee, prepaid for phone searches. Make check payable to Circuit Court Clerk. Search information required: name, date of birth, years to search.

Civil records are available by mail. No release necessary. $50.00 search fee. $.25 fee per copy. $5.00 for certification. Search information required: name, date of birth, years to search. Specify plaintiff or defendant.

Trousdale County

Trousdale County Courthouse, Criminal Records
PO Box 119
Room 5
Hartsville, TN 37074
(615) 374-3411
Felony and misdemeanor records are available in person only.

Civil records are available in person only. See Tennessee state repository for additional information.

Unicoi County

Circuit Court Clerk, Criminal Records
PO Box 376
Erwin, TN 37650
(615) 743-3541
Felony and misdemeanor records are available by mail. A release is required. No search fee. Search information required: name, date of birth, previous address, years to search, SASE.

Civil records are available in person only. See Tennessee state repository for additional information.

Union County

Circuit Court Clerk, Criminal Records
PO Box 306
Maynardsville, TN 37807
(615) 992-5493
Felony and misdemeanor records are available by mail or phone. No release necessary. No search fee. Search information required: name, date of birth, address.

Civil records are available by mail. A release is required. No search fee. $.25 fee per copy. $1.50 for certification. Search information required: name, date of birth, years to search. Specify plaintiff or defendant.

Van Buren County

Circuit Court Clerk, Criminal Records
PO Box 126
Spencer, TN 38585
(615) 946-2153
Felony and misdemeanor records are available by mail or phone. No release necessary. No search fee. Search information required: name, SSN, date of birth, sex, race, SASE.

Civil records are available by mail. No release necessary. No search fee. $.50 fee per copy. $.75 for certification. Search information required: name, date of birth, years to search. Specify plaintiff or defendant.

Warren County

Warren County Courthouse, Criminal
Records
McMinnville, TN 37110
(615) 473-2373
Felony and misdemeanor records are available by mail. A release is required. $5.00 search fee. Search information required: name, years to search.

Civil records are available by mail. A release is required. $5.00 search fee. $.25 fee per copy. $3.00 for certification. Search information required: name, date of birth, years to search. Specify plaintiff or defendant.

Washington County

Felony records
Circuit Court Clerk, Criminal Records
PO Box 356
Jonesboro, TN 37659
(615) 753-1611
Felony records are available by mail. No release necessary. $5.00 search fee. Make check payable to Circuit Court Clerk. Search information required: name, SSN, date of birth, SASE, years to search.

Civil records
Circuit Court Clerk
PO Box 356
Jonesboro, TN 37659
(615) 753-1611
Civil records are available by mail. No release necessary. $5.00 search fee. $.25 fee per copy. $4.00 for certification. Search information required: name, date of birth, years to search. Specify plaintiff or defendant.

Misdemeanor records
Circuit Court Clerk
PO Box 356
Jonesboro, TN 37659
(615) 753-1611
Misdemeanor records are available by mail. A signed release is required. $ 5.00 search fee. Search information required: name, date of birth, years to search.

Civil records
Circuit Court Clerk
PO Box 356
Jonesboro, TN 37659
(615) 753-1611
Civil records are available by mail or phone. No release necessary. $5.00 search fee. $.25 fee per copy. $4.00 for certification. Search information required: name, date of birth, years to search. Specify plaintiff or defendant.

Wayne County

Clerk of Circuit Court, Criminal
Records
PO Box 869
Waynesboro, TN 38485
(615) 722-5519
Felony and misdemeanor records are available by mail. No release necessary. No search fee. $.25 fee per copy. Search information required: name, date of birth, years to search, SASE.

Civil records are available by mail. No release necessary. No search fee. $.25 fee per copy. Search information required: name, date of birth, years to search. Specify plaintiff or defendant.

Weakley County

Circuit Court Clerk, Criminal Records
PO Box 11
Dresden, TN 38225
(901) 364-3455
Felony and misdemeanor records are available by mail. No release necessary. Search fee: 1-3 year check, $5.00; 3-5 year check, $10.00; 5-7 year check, $15.00. Certified or cashier check, payable to Circuit Court Clerk. Search information required: name, offense, and year of offense,years to search.

Civil records are available by mail. No release necessary. Search fee: 1-3 year check, $5.00; 3-5 year check, $10.00; 5-7 year check, $15.00. Search information required: name, date of birth, years to search. Specify plaintiff or defendant.

White County

Circuit Court Clerk, Criminal Records
Room 304
Sparta, TN 38583
(615) 836-3205
Felony and misdemeanor records are available by mail or phone. A release is required. $10.00 search fee. Certified or personal check, payable to Circuit Court Clerk. Search information required: name, date of birth, sex, race, years to search, SASE.

Civil records are available by mail. No release necessary. $10.00 search fee. $.50 fee per copy. $3.50 for certification. Search information required: name, date of birth, years to search, SASE. Specify plaintiff or defendant.

Williamson County

Williamson County Courthouse
Circuit Court Clerk
Room 107, Criminal Records
Franklin, TN 37064
(615) 790-5454
Felony records are available by mail. A release is required. No search fee. $1.00 fee per copy. $4.00 for certification. Search information required: name, date of birth, SSN, years to search, SASE.

Civil records are available by mail or phone. No release necessary. No search fee. $1.00 fee per copy. $4.00 for certification. Search information required: name, date of birth, years to search, SASE. Specify plaintiff or defendant.

Wilson County

Circuit Court Clerk, Criminal Records
PO Box 1366
Lebanon, TN 37087
(615) 444-2042
Felony and misdemeanor records are available in person only.

Civil records are available in person only. See Tennessee state repository for additional information.

City-County Cross Reference

Adams *Robertson*
Adamsville *McNairy*
Afton *Greene*
Alamo *Crockett*
Alcoa *Blount*
Alexandria *DeKalb*
Allardt *Fentress*
Allgood *Putnam*
Allons *Overton*
Allred *Overton*
Alpine *Overton*
Altamont *Grundy*
Andersonville *Anderson*
Antioch *Davidson*
Apison *Hamilton*
Ardmore *Giles*
Arlington *Shelby*
Arrington *Williamson*
Arthur *Claiborne*
Ashland City *Cheatham*
Ashwood *Maury*
Athens *McMinn*
Atoka *Tipton*

Atwood *Carroll*
Auburntown *Cannon*
Bartlett *Shelby*
Bath Springs *Decatur*
Baxter *Putnam*
Bean Station *Grainger*
Beech Bluff *Madison*
Beechgrove *Coffee*
Beersheba Springs *Grundy*
Belfast *Marshall*
Bell Buckle *Bedford*
Belle Meade *Davidison*
Bells *Crockett*
Belvidere *Franklin*
Benton *Polk*
Berry Hill *Davidison*
Berry's Chapel *Williamson*
Bethel Springs *McNairy*
Bethpage *Sumner*
Big Rock *Stewart*
Big Sandy *Benton*
Birchwood *Hamilton*
Blaine *Grainger*

Bloomingdale *Sullivan*
Bloomington Springs *Putnam*
Blountville *Sullivan*
Bluff City *Sullivan*
Bogota *Dyer*
Bolivar *Hardeman*
Bon Aqua *Hickman*
Braden *Fayette*
Bradford *Gibson*
Bradyville *Cannon*
Brentwood *Williamson*
Briarwood *Montgomery*
Briceville *Anderson*
Brighton *Tipton*
Bristol *Sullivan*
Brownsville *Haywood*
Bruceton *Carroll*
Brunswick *Shelby*
Brush Creek *Smith*
Buchanan *Henry*
Buena Vista *Carroll*
Buffalo Valley *Putnam*

Bulls Gap *Hawkins*
Bumpus Mills *Stewart*
Burlison *Tipton*
Burns *Dickson*
Butler *Johnson*
Bybee *Cocke*
Byrdstown *Pickett*
Calhoun *McMinn*
Camden *Benton*
Campaign *Warren*
Capleville *Shelby*
Carson Springs *Cocke*
Carter *Carter*
Carthage *Smith*
Caryville *Campbell*
Castalian Springs *Sumner*
Cedar Grove *Carroll*
Cedar Hill *Robertson*
Celina *Clay*
Centerville *Hickman*
Chapel Hill *Marshall*
Chapmansboro *Cheatham*
Charleston *Bradley*

Charlotte *Dickson*
Chattanooga *Hamilton*
Chestnut Mound *Smith*
Chewalla *McNairy*
Christiana *Rutherford*
Chuckey *Greene*
Church Hill *Hawkins*
Clairfield *Claiborne*
Clarkrange *Fentress*
Clarksburg *Carroll*
Clarksville *Montgomery*
Cleveland *Bradley*
Clifton *Wayne*
Clinton *Anderson*
Coalfield *Morgan*
Coalmont *Grundy*
Cokercreek *Monroe*
Collegedale *Hamilton*
College Grove *Williamson*
Collierville *Shelby*
Collinwood *Wayne*
Columbia *Maury*
Como *Henry*
Conasauga *Polk*
Cookeville *Putnam*
Copperhill *Polk*
Cordova *Shelby*
Cornersville *Marshall*
Corryton *Knox*
Cosby *Cocke*
Cottage Grove *Henry*
Cottontown *Sumner*
Counce *Hardin*
Covington *Tipton*
Cowan *Franklin*
Crab Orchard *Cumberland*
Crawford *Overton*
Crockett Mills *Crockett*
Cross Plains *Robertson*
Crossville *Cumberland*
Crump *Hardin*
Culleoka *Maury*
Cumberland City *Stewart*
Cumberland Furnace
    Dickson
Cumberland Gap
    Claiborne
Cunningham *Montgomery*
Cypress Inn *Wayne*
Dandridge *Jefferson*
Darden *Henderson*
Dayton *Rhea*
Decatur *Meigs*
Decaturville *Decatur*
Decherd *Franklin*
Deer Lodge *Morgan*
Delano *Polk*
Del Rio *Cocke*
Denmark *Madison*
Denver *Humphreys*
Dickson *Dickson*
Dixon Springs *Smith*
Dover *Stewart*
Dowelltown *DeKalb*
Doyle *White*
Dresden *Weakley*
Drummonds *Tipton*
Duck River *Hickman*
Ducktown *Polk*
Duff *Campbell*
Dukedom *Weakley*
Dunlap *Sequatchie*
Dyer *Gibson*
Dyersburg *Dyer*
Eads *Shelby*

Eagan *Claiborne*
Eagleville *Rutherford*
East Ridge *Hamilton*
Eaton *Gibson*
Edgemont *Cocke*
Eidson *Hawkins*
Elbridge *Obion*
Elgin *Scott*
Elizabethton *Carter*
Elkton *Giles*
Ellendale *Shelby*
Elmwood *Smith*
Elora *Lincoln*
Englewood *McMinn*
Enville *Chester*
Erin *Houston*
Erwin *Unicoi*
Estill Springs *Franklin*
Ethridge *Lawrence*
Etowah *McMinn*
Eva *Benton*
Evensville *Rhea*
Fairview *Williamson*
Fall Branch *Washington*
Farner *Polk*
Farragut *Knox*
Fayetteville *Lincoln*
Finger *McNairy*
Finley *Dyer*
Five Points *Lawrence*
Flag Pond *Unicoi*
Flatwoods *Perry*
Flintville *Lincoln*
Forest Hills *Davidson*
Fosterville *Rutherford*
Fowlkes *Dyer*
Frankewing *Giles*
Franklin *Williamson*
Friendship *Crockett*
Friendsville *Blount*
Fruitvale *Crockett*
Gadsden *Crockett*
Gainesboro *Jackson*
Gallatin *Sumner*
Gallaway *Fayette*
Gates *Lauderdale*
Gatlinburg *Sevier*
Georgetown *Meigs*
Germantown *Shelby*
Gibson *Gibson*
Gilt Edge *Tipton*
Gladeville *Wilson*
Gleason *Weakley*
Goodlettsville *Davidson*
Goodspring *Giles*
Gordonsville *Smith*
Grand Junction *Hardeman*
Grandview *Rhea*
Granville *Jackson*
Gray *Washington*
Graysville *Rhea*
Greenback *Loudon*
Greenbrier *Robertson*
Greeneville *Greene*
Greenfield *Weakley*
Green Hill *Wilson*
Grimsley *Fentress*
Gruetli-Laager *Grundy*
Guild *Marion*
Guys *McNairy*
Haletown (Guild) *Marion*
Halls *Lauderdale*
Halls Crossroads *Knox*
Hampshire *Maury*
Hampton *Carter*

Harriman *Roane*
Harrison *Hamilton*
Harrogate *Claiborne*
Hartford *Cocke*
Hartsville *Trousdale*
Heiskell *Knox*
Helenwood *Scott*
Henderson *Chester*
Hendersonville *Sumner*
Henning *Lauderdale*
Henry *Henry*
Hermitage *Davidson*
Hickman *Smith*
Hickory Valley *Hardeman*
Hickory Withe *Fayette*
Hilham *Overton*
Hillsboro *Coffee*
Hixson *Hamilton*
Hohenwald *Lewis*
Holladay *Benton*
Hollow Rock *Carroll*
Hornbeak *Obion*
Hornsby *Hardeman*
Humboldt *Gibson*
Huntingdon *Carroll*
Huntland *Franklin*
Huntsville *Scott*
Huron *Henderson*
Hurricane Mills
    Humphreys
Idlewild *Gibson*
Indian Mound *Stewart*
Iron City *Lawrence*
Isabella *Polk*
Jacksboro *Campbell*
Jacks Creek *Chester*
Jackson *Madison*
Jakestown *Rutherford*
Jamestown *Fentress*
Jasper *Marion*
Jefferson City *Jefferson*
Jellico *Campbell*
Joelton *Davidson*
Johnson City *Washington*
Jonesborough *Washington*
Karns *Knox*
Kelso *Lincoln*
Kenton *Obion*
Kimball *Marion*
Kingsport *Sullivan*
Kingston *Roane*
Kingston Springs
    Cheatham
Knoxville *Knox*
Kodak *Sevier*
Kyles Ford *Hancock*
Laconia *Fayette*
Lafayette *Macon*
LaFollette *Campbell*
LaGrange *Fayette*
Lake City *Anderson*
Lakeland *Shelby*
Lake Tansi Village
    Cumberland
Lakewood *Davidson*
Lancaster *Smith*
Lancing *Morgan*
Lascassas *Rutherford*
Laurel Bloomery *Johnson*
LaVergne *Rutherford*
Lavinia *Carroll*
Lawrenceburg *Lawrence*
Leach *Carroll*
Lebanon *Wilson*
Lenoir City *Loudon*

Lenox *Dyer*
Leoma *Lawrence*
Lewisburg *Marshall*
Lexington *Henderson*
Liberty *DeKalb*
Limestone *Washington*
Linden *Perry*
Livingston *Overton*
Lobelville *Perry*
Lone Mountain *Claiborne*
Lookout Mountain
    Hamilton
Loretto *Lawrence*
Loudon *Loudon*
Louisville *Blount*
Lowland *Hamblen*
Lupton City *Hamilton*
Luray *Henderson*
Luttrell *Union*
Lutts *Wayne*
Lyles *Hickman*
Lynchburg *Moore*
Lynnville *Giles*
McDonald *Bradley*
McEwen *Humphreys*
McKenzie *Carroll*
McLemoresville *Carroll*
McMinnville *Warren*
Macon *Fayette*
Madison *Davidson*
Madisonville *Monroe*
Manchester *Coffee*
Mansfield *Henry*
Martin *Weakley*
Maryville *Blount*
Mascot *Knox*
Mason *Tipton*
Maury City *Crockett*
Maynardville *Union*
Medina *Gibson*
Medon *Madison*
Memphis *Shelby*
Mercer *Madison*
Michie *McNairy*
Middle Valley *Hamilton*
Middleton *Hardeman*
Midtown *Roane*
Midway *Greene*
Milan *Gibson*
Milledgeville *McNairy*
Millersville *Sumner*
Milligan College *Carter*
Millington *Shelby*
Milton *Rutherford*
Minor Hill *Giles*
Miston *Dyer*
Mitchellville *Sumner*
Mohawk *Greene*
Monoville *Smith*
Monroe *Overton*
Monteagle *Grundy*
Monterey *Putnam*
Mooresburg *Hawkins*
Morgantown *Rhea*
Morley *Campbell*
Morris Chapel *Hardin*
Morrison *Warren*
Morristown *Hamblen*
Moscow *Fayette*
Mosheim *Greene*
Moss *Clay*
Mountain City *Johnson*
Mountain Home
    Washington
Mount Carmel *Hawkins*

Mount Juliet *Wilson*
Mount Pleasant *Maury*
Mount Vernon *Monroe*
Mulberry *Lincoln*
Munford *Tipton*
Murfreesboro *Rutherford*
Nashville *Davidson*
Newbern *Dyer*
Newcomb *Campbell*
New Johnsonville
    Humphreys
New Market *Jefferson*
Newport *Cocke*
New Tazewell *Claiborne*
Niota *McMinn*
Nolensville *Williamson*
Norene *Wilson*
Normandy *Bedford*
Norris *Anderson*
Nunnelly *Hickman*
Oakdale *Morgan*
Oakfield *Madison*
Oak Hill *Davidison*
Oakland *Fayette*
Oak Ridge *Anderson*
Obion *Obion*
Ocoee *Polk*
Oldfort *Polk*
Old Hickory *Davidson*
Olivehill *Hardin*
Oliver Springs *Roane*
Oneida *Scott*
Only *Hickman*
Ooltewah *Hamilton*
Orlinda *Robertson*
Ozone *Cumberland*
Pall Mall *Fentress*
Palmer *Grundy*
Palmersville *Weakley*
Palmyra *Montgomery*
Paris *Henry*
Parrottsville *Cocke*
Parsons *Decatur*
Pegram *Cheatham*
Pelham *Grundy*
Petersburg *Lincoln*
Petros *Morgan*
Philadelphia *Loudon*
Pickwick Dam *Hardin*
Pigeon Forge *Sevier*
Pikeville *Bledsoe*
Piney Flats *Sullivan*
Pinson *Madison*
Pioneer *Campbell*
Piperton *Fayette*
Pleasant Hill *Cumberland*
Pleasant Shade *Smith*
Pleasant View *Cheatham*
Pleasantville *Hickman*
Pocahontas *Hardeman*
Portland *Sumner*
Postelle *Polk*
Powder Springs *Grainger*
Powell *Knox*
Powells Crossroads
    Sequatchie
Primm Springs *Hickman*
Prospect *Giles*
Pruden *Claiborne*
Pulaski *Giles*
Puryear *Henry*
Quebeck *White*
Ramer *McNairy*
Ramsey *Knox*
Readyville *Cannon*

Reagan *Henderson*
Red Bank *Hamilton*
Red Boiling Springs
    Macon
Reliance *Polk*
Riceville *McMinn*
Rickman *Overton*
Riddleton *Smith*
Ridgely *Lake*
Ridgeside *Hamilton*
Ridgetop *Robertson*
Ripley *Lauderdale*
Rives *Obion*
Roan Mountain *Carter*
Robbins *Scott*
Rockford *Blount*
Rock Island *Warren*
Rockvale *Rutherford*
Rockwood *Roane*
Rogersville *Hawkins*
Rossville *Fayette*
Russellville *Hamblen*
Rutherford *Gibson*
Rutledge *Grainger*
Saint Andrews *Franklin*
Saint Bethlehem
    Montgomery
Saint Joseph *Lawrence*
Sale Creek *Hamilton*
Saltillo *Hardin*
Samburg *Obion*
Santa Fe *Maury*
Sardis *Henderson*
Saulsbury *Hardeman*
Savannah *Hardin*
Scotts Hill *Henderson*
Selmer *McNairy*
Sequatchie *Marion*
Sevierville *Sevier*
Sewanee *Franklin*
Seymour *Sevier*
Shady Valley *Johnson*
Sharon *Weakley*
Sharps Chapel *Union*
Shawanee *Claiborne*
Shelbyville *Bedford*
Sherwood *Franklin*
Shiloh *Hardin*
Signal Mountain *Hamilton*
Silerton *Hardeman*
Silver Point *Putnam*
Slayden *Dickson*
Smartt *Warren*
Smithville *DeKalb*
Smyrna *Rutherford*
Sneedville *Hancock*
Soddy-Daisy *Hamilton*
Somerville *Fayette*
South Carthage *Smith*
South Fulton *Obion*
South Pittsburg *Marion*
Southside *Montgomery*
Sparta *White*
Speedwell *Claiborne*
Spencer *Van Buren*
Spring City *Rhea*
Spring Creek *Madison*
Springfield *Robertson*
Spring Hill *Maury*
Springville *Henry*
Stanton *Haywood*
Stantonville *McNairy*
Stewart *Houston*
Strawberry Plains *Jefferson*
Sugar Tree *Decatur*

Sullivan Gardens *Sullivan*
Summertown *Lawrence*
Summitville *Coffee*
Sunbright *Morgan*
Surgoinsville *Hawkins*
Sweetwater *Monroe*
Taft *Lincoln*
Talbott *Hamblen*
Tallassee *Blount*
Tazewell *Claiborne*
Telford *Washington*
Tellico Plains *Monroe*
Ten Mile *Meigs*
Tennessee Ridge *Houston*
Thompsons Station
    Williamson
Thorn Hill *Grainger*
Tigrett *Dyer*
Tipton *Tipton*
Tiptonville *Lake*
Toone *Hardeman*
Townsend *Blount*
Tracy City *Grundy*
Trade *Johnson*
Treadway *Hancock*
Trenton *Gibson*
Trentville *Knox*
Trezevant *Carroll*
Trimble *Dyer*
Troy *Obion*
Tullahoma *Coffee*
Turtletown *Polk*
Tuscullum *Greene*
Unicoi *Unicoi*
Union City *Obion*
Unionville *Bedford*
Vanleer *Dickson*
Viola *Warren*
Vonore *Monroe*
Walden *Hamilton*
Walland *Blount*
Walling *White*
Wartburg *Morgan*
Wartrace *Bedford*
Washburn *Grainger*
Watauga *Carter*
Watertown *Wilson*
Watts Bar Dam *Rhea*
Waverly *Humphreys*
Waynesboro *Wayne*
Westmoreland *Sumner*
Westover *Madison*
Westpoint *Lawrence*
Westport *Carroll*
Westwood *Maury*
White Bluff *Dickson*
White House *Robertson*
White Pine *Jefferson*
Whitesburg *Hamblen*
Whites Creek *Davidson*
Whiteside *Marion*
Whiteville *Hardeman*
Whitleyville *Jackson*
Whitwell *Marion*
Wilder *Fentress*
Wildersville *Henderson*
Williamsport *Maury*
Williston *Fayette*
Winchester *Franklin*
Winfield *Scott*
Winona *Scott*
Woodbury *Cannon*
Woodland Mills *Obion*
Woodlawn *Montgomery*
Wrigley *Hickman*

Wynnburg *Lake*
Yorkville *Gibson*
Yuma *Carroll*

Texas

Of the state's 254 counties, 253 indicated that they release conviction data for employment screening purposes by phone or mail. A handful will honor facsimile requests. A few counties will allow fees to be paid with credit cards.

Civil court records are divided between District and County courts by a monetary value of $50,000.

For more information or for offices not listed, contact the state's information hot line at (512) 463-4630.

Driving Records

Texas Department of Public Safety
PO Box 15999
Austin, TX 78761-5999
(512) 465-2000
Driving records are available by mail. $6.00 fee for three 3 years. Turnaround time is 2 to 4 weeks. Written request must include job applicant's full name, date of birth and license number. Make check payable to Texas Department of Public Safety.

Worker's Compensation Records

Industrial Accident Board
200 East Riverside Drive, 1st Floor
Austin, TX 78704
(512) 448-7930
Service limited to Texas employers only. For detailed instructions and the forms necessary to process requests, contact the Industrial Accident Board at the above listed address or phone number. $5.00 fee for any 5 years searched. $20.00 fee for any 10 years searched. A signed release is required. Search information required: SSN, date of inquiry.

Vital Statistics

Bureau of Vital Statistics
Texas Department of Health
1100 West 49th Street
Austin, TX 78756-3191
(512) 458-7364 or 458-7111
Fax (512) 458-7297
Birth records are available for $11.00 each and death records for $9.00 each. State office has records since 1903. Some records are accessible by computer. Search information required: relationship to the person, name of person, father's full name, mother's maiden name, county where birth or death occurred, date of birth or death. Make check or money order payable to Texas Department of Health.

Marriage records are available for $9.00 each from 1966 forward at county level where license purchased. Divorce records are available from 1968 forward at county level, District Clerk's Office where divorce was granted.

Department of Education

Teacher Education Agency
William B. Travis Bldg.
1701 North Congress Avenue
Austin, TX 78701
(512) 463-9734
Field of certification is available by mail or phone. Include name and SSN.

Medical Licensing

State Board of Medical Examiners
Registration Division
PO Box 149134
Austin, TX 78714
(512) 834-7860
Will confirm licenses for MDs and DOs by mail or phone. For licenses not mentioned, contact the above office.

Board of Nurse Examiners for the State of Texas
Box 140466
Austin, TX 78714
(512) 835-4880
Will confirm license by phone. No fee. Include name, license number or SSN.

Bar Association

Texas State Bar Association
PO Box 12487
Capitol Station
Austin, TX 78711
(512) 463-1463
Will confirm licenses by phone. No fee. Include name.

Accountancy Board

Texas State Board of Accountancy
1033 La Posada, Suite 340
Austin, TX 78752-3892
(512) 451-0241
Will confirm license by phone. No fee. Include name.

Securities Commission

State securities Board
PO Box 13167
Austin, TX 78711-3167
(512) 474-2233
Will confirm license by phone. No fee. Include name and SSN.

Secretary of State

Secretary of State
Corporation Division
PO Box 13697
Austin, TX 78711
(512) 463-5555
Fax (512) 463-5709
Registered agent and address, date incorporated, officers and directors, trade names are available by mail or phone. Contact the above office for additional information.

Criminal Records

State Repository

Crime Records Division
PO Box 4143
Austin, TX 78765
(512) 465-2079
Access by non-criminal justice agencies to criminal records held by State's central repository is primarily limited to criminal justice agencies. No reciprocity. Contact the above office for additional information and instructions.

Anderson County

District Clerk's Office, Criminal Records
PO Box 1159
Palestine, TX 75802-1159
(903) 723-7412
Felony and misdemeanor records are available by mail. No release necessary. $5.00 search fee. Search information required: name, date of birth, years to search, and SASE.

Civil records are available by mail. No release necessary. $5.00 search fee. $.10 fee per copy. $1.00 for certification. Search information required: name, date of birth, years to search. Specify plaintiff or defendant.

Andrews County

Felony records
District Clerk, Criminal Records
PO Box 328
Andrews, TX 79714
(915) 524-1417
Felony records are available by mail (for past 5 years). No release necessary. $5.00 search fee. Search information required: name, years to search, and SASE.

Civil records
District Clerk
PO Box 328
Andrews, TX 79714
(915) 524-1417
Civil records are available by mail. No release necessary. $5.00 search fee. $.15 fee per copy. $1.00 for certification. Search information required: name, date of birth, years to search. Specify plaintiff or defendant.

Misdemeanor records
County Clerk
PO Box 727
Andrews, TX 79714
(915) 524-1426
Misdemeanor records are available by mail or phone. No release necessary. No search fee. Search information required: name, years to search, date of offense.

Civil records
County Clerk
PO Box 727
Andrews, TX 79714
(915) 524-1426
Civil records are available by mail or phone. No release necessary. No search fee. $1.00 fee per copy. $1.00 for certification. Search information required: name, date of birth, years to search. Specify plaintiff or defendant.

Angelina County

Felony records
District Clerk's Office, Criminal Records
PO Box 908
Lufkin, TX 75902-0908
(409) 634-4312
Fax (409) 634-5915
Felony records are available by mail. No release necessary. $5.00 search fee, prepaid. Search information required: name, years to search, SASE.

Civil records
District Clerk's Office
PO Box 908
Lufkin, TX 75902-0908
(409) 634-4312
Fax (409) 634-5915
Civil records are available by mail. No release necessary. $5.00 search fee. $1.00 fee per copy. $1.00 for certification. Search information required: name, date of birth, years to search. Specify plaintiff or defendant.

Misdemeanor records
County Clerk's Office, Criminal Records
PO Box 908
Lufkin, TX 75902-0908
(409) 634-8339
Misdemeanor records are available by mail or phone. No release necessary. $5.00 search fee. Search information required: name, years to search, offense (if available), address.

Civil records
County Clerk's Office
PO Box 908
Lufkin, TX 75902-0908
(409) 634-8339
Civil records are available by mail. No release necessary. $10.00 search fee. $.50 fee per copy. $1.00 for each certification. Search information required: name, date of birth, years to search. Specify plaintiff or defendant.

Aransas County

Felony records
District Clerk's Office, Criminal Records
301 N. Live Oak
Rockport, TX 78382
(512) 729-2519
Fax (512) 790-0128
Felony records are available by mail or phone. No release necessary. $5.00 search fee. Certified or personal check, payable to District Clerk. Prepayment required for phone requests. Search information required: name, years to search, SASE.

Civil records
District Clerk's Office, Criminal Records
301 N. Live Oak
Rockport, TX 78382
(512) 729-2519
Civil records are available by mail. No release necessary. $5.00 search fee. Search information required: name, date of birth, years to search, SASE. Specify plaintiff or defendant.

Misdemeanor records
County Clerk's Office
301 N. Live Oak
Rockport, TX 78382
(512) 790-0123
Misdemeanor records are available by mail. No release necessary. $5.00 search fee. Certified or personal check, payable to County Clerk. Search information required: name, years to search.

Civil records
County Clerk's Office
301 N. Live Oak
Rockport, TX 78382
(512) 729-7430
Civil records are available by mail. No release necessary. $5.00 search fee. Search information required: name, date of birth, years to search. Specify plaintiff or defendant.

Archer County

District Clerk's Office, Criminal Records
PO Box 815
Archer City, TX 76351
(817) 574-4615
Felony and misdemeanor records are available by mail or phone. No release necessary. No search fee. $1.00 fee per copy. Search information required: name, years to search, SASE.

Civil records are available by mail. No release necessary. No search fee. $1.00 fee per copy. Search information required: name, date of birth, years to search, SASE. Specify plaintiff or defendant.

Armstrong County

District Clerk's Office, Criminal Records
PO Box 309
Claude, TX 79019
(806) 226-2081
Felony and misdemeanor records are available by mail. No release necessary. $5.00 search fee. Search information required: name, SASE.

Civil records are available by mail. No release necessary. $5.00 search fee. Search information required: name, date of birth, years to search, SASE. Specify plaintiff or defendant.

Atascosa County

Felony records
District Clerk's Office, Criminal Records
#52 Courthouse Circle
Jourdanton, TX 78026
(512) 769-3011
Felony records are available by mail or phone for past 5 years. No release necessary. $5.00 search fee. Search information required: name, years to search, SASE.

Civil records
District Clerk's Office
#52 Courthouse Circle
Jourdanton, TX 78026
(512) 769-3011
Civil records are available by mail. No release necessary. $5.00 search fee. Search information required: name, date of birth, years to search, SASE. Specify plaintiff or defendant.

Misdemeanor records
County Clerk
Circle Drive, Room 6-1
Jourdanton, TX 78026
(512) 769-2511
Misdemeanor records are available by mail or phone. No release necessary. No search fee. Search information required: name, years to search.

Civil records
County Clerk
Circle Drive, Room 6-1
Jourdanton, TX 78026
(512) 769-2511
Civil records are available by mail. No release necessary. $5.00 search fee. $.50 fee per copy. $1.00 for each certification. Search information required: name, date of birth, years to search. Specify plaintiff or defendant.

Austin County

Felony records
District Clerk's Office, Criminal Records
1 East Main
Bellville, TX 77418
(409) 865-5911 Extension 121
Felony records are available by mail. No release necessary. $5.00 search fee. Search information required: name, years to search.

Civil records
District Clerk's Office
1 East Main
Bellville, TX 77418
(409) 865-5911 Extension 201
Civil records are available by mail. No release necessary. $5.00 search fee. Search information required: name, date of birth, years to search. Specify plaintiff or defendant.

Misdemeanor records
County Clerk's Office, Criminal Records
1 East Main
Bellville, TX 77418
(409) 865-5911
Misdemeanor records are available by mail. A release is required. $5.00 search fee. Search information required: name, years to search.

Civil records
County Clerk's Office
1 East Main
Bellville, TX 77418
(409) 865-5911
Civil records are available by mail. A release is required. $5.00 search fee.$1.00 fee per copy. $1.00 for each certification. Search information required: name, date of birth, years to search. Specify plaintiff or defendant.

Bailey County

Felony records
District Clerk's Office, Criminal Records
300 S. 1st
Muleshoe, TX 79347
(806) 272-3165
Felony records are available by mail or phone. No release necessary. $1.00 search fee. Company or personal checks, payable to District Clerk. Search information required: name.

Civil records
District Clerk's Office
300 S. 1st
Muleshoe, TX 79347
(806) 272-3165
Civil records are available by mail or phone. No release necessary. No search fee. $.25 fee per copy. $1.00 for each certification. Search information required: name, date of birth, years to search. Specify plaintiff or defendant.

Misdemeanor records
County Clerk's Office
300 S. 1st
Muleshoe, TX 79347
(806) 272-3044
Misdemeanor records are available by mail or phone. No release necessary. $1.00 search fee. Company or personal checks, payable to County Clerk. Search information required: name.

Civil records
County Clerk's Office
300 S. 1st
Muleshoe, TX 79347
(806) 272-3044
Civil records are available by mail or phone. No release necessary. No search fee. $.50 fee per copy. $1.00 for certification. Search information required: name, date of birth, years to search. Specify plaintiff or defendant.

Bandera County

District Clerk's Office, Criminal Records
PO Box 823
Bandera, TX 78003
(512) 796-3332
Fax (512) 796-8323
Felony and misdemeanor records are available by mail or phone. A release is required. $5.00 search fee. Search information required: name.

Civil records are available by mail. A release is required. $5.00 search fee. Search information required: name, date of birth, years to search. Specify plaintiff or defendant.

Bastrop County

Felony records
District Clerk's Office, Criminal Records
PO Box 770
Bastrop, TX 78602
(512) 321-2114
Felony records are available by mail. No release necessary. $5.00 search fee. Make check payable to District Clerk's Office. Search information required: name, case number.

Civil records
District Clerk's Office
PO Box 770
Bastrop, TX 78602
(512) 321-2114
Civil records are available by mail. No release necessary. $5.00 search fee. $1.00 fee per copy. $1.00 for certification. Search information required: name, date of birth, years to search. Specify plaintiff or defendant.

Misdemeanor records
County Clerk's Office, Criminal Records
PO Box 577
Bastrop, TX 78602
(512 321-4443
Misdemeanor records are available by mail or phone. $5.00 search fee. Search information required: name, date of offense, date of birth.

Civil records
County Clerk's Office
PO Box 577
Bastrop, TX 78602
(512 321-4443
Civil records are available by mail or phone. No release necessary. $5.00 search fee. Search information required: name, date of birth, years to search. Specify plaintiff or defendant.

Baylor County

District Clerk's Office, Criminal Records
PO Box 689
Seymour, TX 76380
(817) 888-3322
Felony and misdemeanor records are available by mail or phone. No release necessary. No search fee. Search information required: name, years to search.

Civil records are available by mail or phone. No release necessary. No search fee.Search information required: name, date of birth, years to search. Specify plaintiff or defendant.

Bee County

Felony records
District Clerk's Office, Criminal Records
Box 666
Beeville, TX 78104
(512) 358-3081
Felony records are available by mail. No release necessary. $5.00 search fee. Search information required: name, years to search.

Civil records
District Clerk's Office
Box 666
Beeville, TX 78104
(512) 358-3081
Civil records are available by mail. No release necessary. $5.00 search fee.Search information required: name, date of birth, years to search. Specify plaintiff or defendant.

Misdemeanor records
County Clerk's Office
105 W. Corpus Christi St. Room 103
Beeville, TX 78102
(512) 358-3664
Misdemeanor records are available by mail. No release necessary. $5.00 fee for 5 to 10 years searched. $1.00 fee per copy. $2.00 for certification. Search information required: name, date of offense.

Civil records
County Clerk's Office
105 W. Corpus Christi St. Room 103
Beeville, TX 78102
(512) 358-3664
Civil records are available by mail. No release necessary. $5.00 fee for 5 to 10 years searched. $1.00 fee per copy. $2.00 for certification. Search information required: name, date of birth, years to search. Specify plaintiff or defendant.

Bell County

Felony records
District Clerk's Office, Criminal Records
PO Box 909
Belton, TX 76513
(817) 939-3521 Extension 365
Felony records are available by mail. A release is required. $10.00 search fee. $1.00 fee per copy. $2.00 for certification. Written request required. Company checks, payable to District Court. Search information required: name, date of birth, years to search.

Civil records
District Clerk's Office
PO Box 909
Belton, TX 76513
(817) 939-3521 Extension 365
Civil records are available by mail. A release is required. $10.00 search fee. $1.00 fee per copy. $2.00 for certification. Search information required: name, date of birth, years to search. Specify plaintiff or defendant.

Misdemeanor records
County Clerk's Office
PO Box 480
Belton TX 76513
(817) 939-3521 Ext. 261
Misdemeanor records are available by mail. No release necessary. $5.00 fee for 5 years searched, $10.00 fee for 10 years searched. Make checks payable to Bell County Clerk. Search information required: name, date of birth, date of offense.

Civil records
County Clerk's Office
PO Box 480
Belton TX 76513
(817) 939-3521 Ext. 261
Civil records are available by mail. No release necessary. $5.00 fee for 5 years searched, $10.00 fee for 10 years searched. Search information required: name, date of birth, years to search. Specify plaintiff or defendant.

Bexar County

District Clerk's Office, Criminal Division
Bexar County Courthouse
San Antonio, TX 78205
(512) 220-2217
Felony and misdemeanor records are available in person only.

Civil records are available in person only. See Texas state repository for additional information.

Blanco County

District Clerk's Office, Criminal Records
PO Box 65
Johnson City, TX 78636
(512) 868-7357
Felony and misdemeanor records are available by mail. No release necessary. $5.00 search fee. $1.00 fee per copy. $2.00 for certification. Search information required: name, SSN, date of birth, SASE.

Civil records are available by mail. No release necessary. $5.00 search fee. $1.00 fee per copy. $2.00 for certification. Search information required: name, date of birth, years to search, SASE. Specify plaintiff or defendant.

Borden County

Borden County Clerk's Office, Criminal Records
Box 124
Gail, TX 79738
(806) 756-4312
Felony and misdemeanor records are available by mail. No release necessary. $5.00 search fee. Written request required. Make check payable to District Clerk's Office. Search information required: name, SASE.

Civil records are available by mail. No release necessary. $5.00 search fee. $1.00 fee per copy. $2.00 for certification. Search information required: name, date of birth, years to search, SASE. Specify plaintiff or defendant.

Bosque County

Felony records
District Clerk's Office, Criminal Records
PO Box 647
Meridian, TX 76665
(817) 435-2334
Felony records are available by mail. No release necessary. $5.00 search fee. $1.00 fee per copy. $2.00 for certification. Company checks only, payable to District Clerk's Office. Search information required: name, years to search.

Civil records
District Clerk's Office
PO Box 647
Meridian, TX 76665
(817) 435-2334
Civil records are available by mail. No release necessary. $5.00 search fee. $1.00 fee per copy. $2.00 for certification. Search information required: name, date of birth, years to search. Specify plaintiff or defendant.

Misdemeanor records
County Clerk's Office, County Court
PO Box 617
Meridian, TX 76665
(817) 435-2382
Misdemeanor records are available by mail or phone. $5.00 search fee. $1.00 fee per copy. $2.00 for certification. No release necessary. Search information required: name, date of birth, years to search.

Civil records
County Clerk's Office, County Court
PO Box 617
Meridian, TX 76665
(817) 435-2382
Civil records are available by mail. No release necessary. $5.00 search fee. $1.00 fee per copy. $2.00 for certification. Search information required: name, date of birth, years to search. Specify plaintiff or defendant.

Bowie County

District Clerk's Office, Criminal Records
PO Box 248
New Boston, TX 75570
(903) 628-2571 Extension 309
Felony and misdemeanor records are available by mail. No release necessary. $5.00 search fee. Company checks only, payable to District Clerk. Search information required: name, date of birth, years to search.

Civil records are available by mail. No release necessary. $5.00 search fee. $2.00 for certification. Search information required: name, date of birth, years to search. Specify plaintiff or defendant.

Brazoria County

Felony records
District Clerk's Office, Criminal Records
PO Box 1869
Room 400
Angelton, TX 77516-1869
(409) 849-5711 Extension 1317
Felony records are available by mail. A release is required. $5.00 search fee. Company checks only, payable to District Clerk. Search information required: name, SSN, date of birth.

Civil records
District Clerk's Office
PO Box 1869
Room 400
Angelton, TX 77516-1869
(409) 849-5711 Extension 1317
Civil records are available by mail. A release is required. $5.00 search fee. Search information required: name, date of birth, years to search. Specify plaintiff or defendant.

Misdemeanor records
County Clerk's Office
PO Box 1989
Angelton, TX 77516
(409) 849-5711
Misdemeanor records are available by mail. $5.00 search fee. Certified checks, cashiers checks, or money order, payable to County Clerk. Search information required: name, date of birth.

Civil records
County Clerk's Office
PO Box 1989
Angelton, TX 77516
(409) 849-5711
Civil records are available by mail. No release necessary. $5.00 search fee. Search information required: name, date of birth, years to search. Specify plaintiff or defendant.

Brazos County

Felony records
District Clerk's Office, Criminal Records
300 E. 26th Street, Suite 216
Bryan, TX 77803
(409) 361-4233
Felony records are available by mail. No release necessary. $5.00 search fee. $.50 fee per copy. $2.00 for certification. Search information required: name, years to search.

Civil records
District Clerk's Office
300 E. 26th Street, Suite 216
Bryan, TX 77803
(409) 361-4233
Civil records are available by mail. No release necessary. $5.00 search fee. $.50 fee per copy. $2.00 for certification. Search information required: name, date of birth, years to search. Specify plaintiff or defendant.

Misdemeanor records
County Clerk's Office
Brazos County Courthouse
300 E. 26th Street, Suite 120
Bryan, TX 77803
(409) 361-4128
Misdemeanor records are available by mail. $5.00 search fee. No release necessary. Search information required: name, address, years to search.

Civil records
County Clerk's Office
Brazos County Courthouse
300 E. 26th Street, Suite 120
Bryan, TX 77803
(409) 361-4128 Civil records are available by mail. No release necessary. $5.00 search fee. Search information required: name, date of birth, years to search. Specify plaintiff or defendant.

Brewster County

District Clerk's Office, Criminal Records
PO Drawer 119
Alpine, TX 79831
(915) 837-3366
Fax (915) 837-3488

Felony and misdemeanor records are available by mail, phone or fax. No release necessary. $5.00 search fee for mail searches only. Make check payable to District Clerk's Office. Search information required: name, SSN, sex, date of birth, years to search.

Civil records are available by mail. No release necessary. $5.00 search fee. $.10 fee per copy. $1.00 for certification. Search information required: name, date of birth, years to search. Specify plaintiff or defendant.

Briscoe County

District Clerk's Office, Criminal Records
PO Box 70
Silverton, TX 79257
(806) 823-2131

Felony and misdemeanor records are available by mail or phone. No release necessary. No search fee. Company checks only, payable to District Court. Search information required: name, date of birth, years to search.

Civil records are available by mail or phone. No release necessary. No search fee. Search information required: name, date of birth, years to search. Specify plaintiff or defendant.

Brooks County

District Clerk's Office, Criminal Records
PO Box 534
Falfurrias, TX 78355
(512) 325-5604 Ext. 236

Felony and misdemeanor records are available by mail or phone. No release necessary. $5.00 search fee. Certified check only, payable to District Clerk's Office. Search information required: name, date of birth, years to search.

Civil records are available by mail or phone. No release necessary. $1.00 search fee. Search information required: name, date of birth, years to search. Specify plaintiff or defendant.

Brown County

Felony records
District Clerk's Office, Criminal Records
Brownwood Courthouse
200 S. Broadway
Brownwood, TX 76801
(915) 646-5514

Felony records are available by mail. No release necessary. No search fee. Search information required: name, SASE, years to search.

Civil records
District Clerk's Office
Brownwood Courthouse
200 S. Broadway
Brownwood, TX 76801
(915) 646-5514

Civil records are available by mail. No release necessary. No search fee. Search information required: name, date of birth, years to search, SASE. Specify plaintiff or defendant.

Misdemeanor records
County Clerk
200 S. Broadway
Brownwood, TX 76801
(915) 643-2594

Misdemeanor records are available by mail. No release necessary. $5.00 search fee. $1.00 fee per copy. $1.00 for each certification. Search information required: name, date of birth, years to search. Specify plaintiff or defendant.

Civil records
County Clerk
200 S. Broadway
Brownwood, TX 76801
(915) 643-2594

Civil records are available by mail. No release necessary. $5.00 search fee. $1.00 fee per copy. $1.00 for each certification. Search information required: name, date of birth, years to search. Specify plaintiff or defendant.

Burleson County

District Clerk's Office, Criminal Records
PO Box 179
Caldwell, TX 77836
(409) 567-4237

Felony records are available by mail or phone. No release necessary. $5.00 search fee. $1.00 fee per copy. $2.00 for each certification. Search information required: name, SASE, years to search.

Civil records are available by mail. No release necessary. $5.00 search fee. $1.00 fee per copy. $1.00 for each certification. Search information required: name, date of birth, years to search, SASE. Specify plaintiff or defendant.

Burnet County

Felony records
District Clerk's Office, Criminal Records
220 S. Pierce
Burnet, TX 78611
(512) 756-5450

Felony records are available by mail. No release necessary. $5.00 search fee. Make check payable to District Clerk's Office. Search information required: name, date of offense, years to search.

Civil records
District Clerk's Office
220 S. Pierce
Burnet, TX 78611
(512) 756-5450

Civil records are available by mail. No release necessary. $5.00 search fee. Search information required: name, date of birth, years to search. Specify plaintiff or defendant.

Misdemeanor records
County Courts Office, Criminal Records
220 S. Pierce
Burnet, TX 78611
(512) 756-5403
Fax (512) 756-4091

Misdemeanor records are available by mail or phone. $5.00 search fee. Checks payable to County Court Clerk of Burnet. Search information required: name, date of birth, date of offense, if available, years to search.

Civil records
County Courts Office
220 S. Pierce
Burnet, TX 78611
(512) 756-5403

Civil records are available by mail or phone. $5.00 search fee. Search information required: name, date of birth, years to search. Specify plaintiff or defendant.

Caldwell County

Felony records
District Clerk's Office, Criminal Records
PO Box 749
Lockhart, TX 78644
(512) 398-2428

Felony records are available by mail or by phone for one request. No release necessary. $5.00 search fee. Search information required: name, date of birth, previous address, years to search.

Civil records
District Clerk's Office
PO Box 749
Lockhart, TX 78644
(512) 398-2428

Civil records are available by mail or by phone for one request. No release necessary. $5.00 search fee. Search information required: name, date of birth, years to search. Specify plaintiff or defendant.

Misdemeanor records
County Clerk's Office
PO Box 906
Lockhart, TX 78644
(512) 398-2424

Misdemeanor records are available by mail. $5.00 search fee. $1.00 fee per copy, $1.00 per certification. No release necessary. Search information required: name, date of birth, date of offense.

Civil records
County Clerk's Office
PO Box 906
Lockhart, TX 78644
(512) 398-2424

Civil records are available by mail. $5.00 search fee. $1.00 fee per copy, $1.00 per certification. Search information required: name, date of birth, years to search. Specify plaintiff or defendant.

Calhoun County

Felony records
District Clerk's Office, Criminal Records
211 S. Ann
Port Lavaca, TX 77979
(512) 553-4630

Felony records are available by mail. No release necessary. $5.00 search fee. Certified check only. Search information required: name, SASE.

Civil records
District Clerk's Office
211 S. Ann
Port Lavaca, TX 77979
(512) 553-4630
Civil records are available by mail. No release necessary. $5.00 search fee. Search information required: name, date of birth, years to search, SASE. Specify plaintiff or defendant.

Misdemeanor records
County Clerk's Office
211 S. Ann St.
Port Lavaca, TX 77979
(512) 553-4411
Misdemeanor records are available by mail. $5.00 search fee. Checks payable to Calhoun County Clerk. Search information required: name, years to search.

Civil records
County Clerk's Office
211 S. Ann St.
Port Lavaca, TX 77979
(512) 553-4411
Civil records are available by mail. No release necessary. $5.00 search fee. Search information required: name, date of birth, years to search. Specify plaintiff or defendant.

Callahan County

Felony records
District Clerk's Office, Criminal Records
Callahan County Courthouse
Baird, TX 79504
(915) 854-1800
Felony records are available by mail or phone. No release necessary. $5.00 search fee. Search information required: name.

Civil records
District Clerk's Office
Callahan County Courthouse
Baird, TX 79504
(915) 854-1800
Civil records are available by mail. No release necessary. $5.00 search fee. $1.00 fee per copy. $2.00 for certification. Search information required: name, date of birth, years to search. Specify plaintiff or defendant.

Misdemeanor records
County Clerk's Office
PO Box 1088
Baird, TX 79504
(915) 854-1217
Misdemeanor records are available by mail or phone. $5.00 search fee. $1.00 fee per copy. $2.00 for certification. No release necessary. Search information required: name, years to search.

Civil records
County Clerk's Office
PO Box 1088
Baird, TX 79504
(915) 854-1217
Civil records are available by mail or phone. No release necessary. $5.00 search fee. $1.00 fee per copy. $2.00 for certification. Search information required: name, date of birth, years to search. Specify plaintiff or defendant.

Cameron County

Felony records
District Clerk's Office, Criminal Records Bureau
PO Box 3570
Brownsville, TX 78523-3570
(512) 544-0838
Felony records are available by mail. A release is required. $5.00 search fee. Cashier's check or money order, payable to District Clerk's Office. Search information required: name, SSN, date of birth, sex, race, years to search.

Civil records
District Clerk's Office
PO Box 3570
Brownsville, TX 78523-3570
(512) 544-0838
Civil records are available by mail. No release necessary. $5.00 search fee. $1.00 fee per copy. $1.00 for certification. Search information required: name, date of birth, years to search. Specify plaintiff or defendant.

Misdemeanor records
County Clerk's Office, Criminal Records
PO Box 2178
Brownsville, TX 78520
(512) 544-0848
Misdemeanor records are available by mail. $5.00 search fee. $1.00 fee per copy, $1.00 fee for certification. Checks payable to County Clerk's Office. Search information required: name, date of birth, years to search.

Civil records
County Clerk's Office
PO Box 2178
Brownsville, TX 78520
(512) 544-0848
Civil records are available by mail. No release necessary. $5.00 search fee. $1.00 fee per copy, $1.00 fee for certification. Search information required: name, date of birth, years to search. Specify plaintiff or defendant.

Camp County

Felony records
District Clerk's Office, Criminal Records
Room 203
126 Church Street
Pittsburg, TX 75686
(903) 856-3221
Felony records are available by mail. No release necessary. $5.00 search fee. Search information required: name, SASE.

Civil records
District Clerk's Office
Room 203
126 Church Street
Pittsburg, TX 75686
(903) 856-3221
Civil records are available by mail. No release necessary. $5.00 search fee. Search information required: name, date of birth, years to search, SASE. Specify plaintiff or defendant.

Misdemeanor records
County Court's Office, County Clerk
126 Church St., Room 102
Pittsburg, TX 75686
(903) 856-2731
Misdemeanor records are available by mail. Written request required. No release necessary. No search fee. Search information required: name, year of offense, SASE.

Civil records
County Court's Office, County Clerk
126 Church St., Room 102
Pittsburg, TX 75686
(903) 856-2731
Civil records are available by mail. Written release required. No search fee. Search information required: name, date of birth, years to search, SASE. Specify plaintiff or defendant.

Carson County

District Clerk's Office, Criminal Records
PO Box 487
Panhandle, TX 79068
(806) 537-3873
Felony and misdemeanor records are available by mail or phone. No release necessary. $5.00 search fee. Make check payable to District Clerk's Office. Search information required: name.

Civil records are available by mail or phone. No release necessary. $5.00 search fee. Search information required: name, date of birth, years to search. Specify plaintiff or defendant.

Cass County

Felony records
District Clerk's Office, Criminal Records
PO Box 510
Linden, TX 75563
(903) 756-7514
Felony records are available by mail. No release necessary. $5.00 search fee. $1.00 fee per copy, $5.00 fee per certification. Certified check only, payable to District Clerk. Search information required: name, years to search.

Civil records
District Clerk's Office
PO Box 510
Linden, TX 75563
(903) 756-7514
Civil records are available by mail. No release necessary. $5.00 search fee. $1.00 fee for first copy, $.25 each additional copy. $2.00 for first certification, $1.00 each additional page. Search information required: name, date of birth, years to search. Specify plaintiff or defendant.

Misdemeanor records
County Courthouse
PO Box 468
Linden, TX 75563
(903) 756-5071
Misdemeanor records since 1983 are available by mail or phone. $5.00 search fee. Checks payable to Associate Cass County Clerk. No release necessary. Search information required: name.

Civil records
County Courthouse
PO Box 468
Linden, TX 75563
(903) 756-5071
Civil records are available by mail or phone. No release necessary. $5.00 search fee. Search information required: name, date of birth, years to search. Specify plaintiff or defendant.

Castro County

District Clerk's Office, Criminal Records
100 E. Bedford
Dimmitt, TX 79027
(806) 647-3338
Felony and misdemeanor records are available by mail. No release necessary. $5.00 search fee. $1.00 fee per copy, $5.00 for certification. Search information required: name, years to search.

Civil records are available by mail. No release necessary. $5.00 search fee. $1.00 per copy, $5.00 for certification. Search information required: name, date of birth, years to search. Specify plaintiff or defendant.

Chambers County

Felony records
District Clerk's Office, Criminal Records
Drawer NN
Anahuac, TX 77514
(409) 267-3175
Felony records are available by mail. No release necessary. $5.00 search fee. Make check payable to District Clerk. Search information required: name, years to search.

Civil records
District Clerk's Office
Drawer NN
Anahuac, TX 77514
(409) 267-3175
Civil records are available by mail. No release necessary. $5.00 search fee. Search information required: name, date of birth, years to search. Specify plaintiff or defendant.

Misdemeanor records
County Clerk's Office
PO Box 728
Anahuac, TX 77514
(409) 267-3471
Misdemeanor records are available by mail. $5.00 search fee. $1.00 fee per copy. $2.00 for certification. No release necessary. Search information required: name, date of offense if available, years to search.

Civil records
County Clerk's Office
PO Box 728
Anahuac, TX 77514
(409) 267-3471
Civil records are available by mail. No release necessary. $5.00 search fee. $1.00 fee per copy. $2.00 for certification. Search information required: name, date of birth, years to search. Specify plaintiff or defendant.

Cherokee County

Felony records
District Clerk's Office, Criminal Records
Drawer C
Rusk, TX 75785
(903) 683-4533
Felony records are available by mail. No release necessary. $5.00 search fee. $2.00 for certification. Search information required: name, years to search.

Civil records
District Clerk's Office
Drawer C
Rusk, TX 75785
(903) 683-4533
Civil records are available by mail. No release necessary. $5.00 search fee. $2.00 for certification. Search information required: name, date of birth, years to search. Specify plaintiff or defendant.

Misdemeanor records
County Clerk's Office
Courthouse, Cherokee County
Rusk, TX 75785
(903) 683-2350
Misdemeanor records are available by mail or phone. No search fee. $1.00 fee per copy. $1.00 for certification. No release necessary. Search information required: name, years to search.

Civil records
County Clerk's Office
Courthouse, Cherokee County
Rusk, TX 75785
(903) 683-2350
Civil records are available by mail. No release necessary. No search fee. $1.00 fee per copy. $1.00 for certification. Search information required: name, date of birth, years to search. Specify plaintiff or defendant.

Childress County

Felony records
District Clerk's Office, Criminal Records
Courthouse Box 4
Childress, TX 79201
(817) 937-6143
Felony records are available by mail or phone. No release necessary. No search fee. $1.00 fee per copy. Certified check only, payable to District Clerk. Search information required: name, date of birth, sex, years to search, SASE.

Civil records
District Clerk's Office
Courthouse Box 4
Childress, TX 79201
(817) 937-6143
Civil records are available by mail or phone. No release necessary. No search fee. $1.00 fee per copy. Search information required: name, date of birth, years to search, SASE. Specify plaintiff or defendant.

Misdemeanor records
County Clerk's Office
Courthouse Box 4
Childress, TX 79201
(817)) 937-6143
Misdemeanor records are available by mail. $10.00 search fee. $1.00 fee per copy. No release necessary. Search information required: name, years to search.

Civil records
County Clerk's Office
Courthouse Box 4
Childress, TX 79201
(817)) 937-6143
Civil records are available by mail. No release necessary. $10.00 search fee. $1.00 fee per copy. Search information required: name, years to search. Specify plaintiff or defendant.

Clay County

Felony records
District Clerk's Office, Criminal Records
PO Box 554
Henrietta, TX 76365
(817) 538-4561
Fax (817) 538-4431
Felony records are available by mail. No release necessary. No search fee. Search information required: name, date of birth, SSN.

Civil records
District Clerk's Office
PO Box 554
Henrietta, TX 76365
(817) 538-4561
Civil records are available by mail or phone. No release necessary. No search fee. $.50 fee per copy. $1.00 for certification. Search information required: name, date of birth, years to search. Specify plaintiff or defendant.

Misdemeanor records
County Clerk's Office
PO Box 548
Henrietta, TX 76365
(817) 538-4631
Misdemeanor records are available by mail or phone. No search fee. $.50 fee per copy. $1.00 for certification. No release necessary. Search information required: name, years to search.

Civil records
County Clerk's Office
PO Box 548
Henrietta, TX 76365
(817) 538-4631
Civil records are available by mail or phone. No release necessary. No search fee. $.50 fee per copy. $1.00 for certification. Search information required: name, date of birth, years to search. Specify plaintiff or defendant.

Cochran County

District Clerk's Office, Criminal Records
Cochran County Courthouse
Room 102
Morton, TX 79346
(806) 266-5450
Felony and misdemeanor records are available by mail. No release necessary. $5.00 search fee. Certified check only, payable to Rita Tyson. Search information required: name, SSN, date of birth, sex, race, SASE, years to search.

Civil records are available by mail. No release necessary. $5.00 search fee. Search information required: name, date of birth, years to search, SASE. Specify plaintiff or defendant.

Coke County

County and District Clerk, Criminal Records
PO Box 150
Robert Lee, TX 76945
(915) 453-2631

Felony and misdemeanor records are available by mail or phone. No release necessary. No search fee. $1.00 fee per copy. $2.00 for certification. Search information required: name, SSN, date of birth, years to search.

Civil records are available by mail or phone. No release necessary. No search fee. $1.00 fee per copy. $2.00 for certification. Search information required: name, date of birth, years to search. Specify plaintiff or defendant.

Coleman County

Felony records
District Clerk's Office, Criminal Records
PO Box 957
Coleman, TX 76834
(915) 625-2568

Felony records are available by mail. No release necessary. $5.00 search fee. Search information required: name, years to search. Secify plaintiff or defendant.

Civil records
District Clerk's Office
PO Box 957
Coleman, TX 76834
(915) 625-2568

Civil records are available by mail. No release necessary. $5.00 search fee. Search information required: name, date of birth, years to search. Specify plaintiff or defendant.

Misdemeanor records
County Clerk's Office
PO Box 591
Coleman, TX 76834
(915) 625-2889

Misdemeanor records are available by mail or phone. No release necessary. No search fee. $1.00 fee per copy. $2.00 for certification. Search information required: name, years to search.

Civil records
County Clerk's Office
PO Box 591
Coleman, TX 76834
(915) 625-2889

Civil records are available by mail or phone. No release necessary. No search fee. $1.00 fee per copy. $2.00 for certification. Search information required: name, date of birth, years to search. Specify plaintiff or defendant.

Collin County

Felony records
District Clerk's Office, Criminal Records
PO Box 578
McKinney, TX 75069
(214) 548-4318

Felony records are available by mail. No release necessary. $5.00 search fee. Make check payable to District Clerk. Search information required: name, SASE.

Civil records
District Clerk's Office
PO Box 578
McKinney, TX 75069
(214) 548-4318

Civil records are available by mail or phone. No release necessary. $5.00 search fee. $1.00 fee per copy. Search information required: name, years to search, SASE. Specify plaintiff or defendant.

Misdemeanor records
County Court at Law
210 S. McDonald
McKinney, TX 75069
(214) 548-4134 Ext. 4549
Fax (214) 542-1014

Misdemeanor records are available by mail. No release necessary. $5.00 search fee. Checks payable to County Clerk. Search information required: name, date of birth, drivers license or SSN if available.

Civil records
County Court at Law
210 S. McDonald
McKinney, TX 75069
(214) 548-4134 Ext. 4549
Fax (214) 542-1014

Civil records are available by mail. No release necessary. $5.00 search fee. $1.00 fee per copy. $2.00 for certification. Search information required: name, date of birth, years to search. Specify plaintiff or defendant.

Collingsworth County

Felony records
District Clerk's Office, Criminal Records
First Floor, Room 3
County Courthouse
Wellington, TX 79095
(806) 447-2408

Felony records are available by mail. No release necessary. $5.00 search fee. Search information required: name, date of birth.

CIvil records
District Clerk's Office
First Floor, Room 3
County Courthouse
Wellington, TX 79095
(806) 447-2408

Civil records are available by mail. No release necessary. $5.00 search fee. Search information required: name, date of birth, years to search. Specify plaintiff or defendant.

Misdemeanor records
County Clerk's Office
Courthouse, Room 3
Wellington, TX 79095
(806) 447-2408

Misdemeanor records are available by mail. $5.00 search fee. No release necessary. Checks made payable to County Clerk. Search information required: name, date of offense.

Civil records
County Clerk's Office
Courthouse, Room 3
Wellington, TX 79095
(806) 447-2408

Civil records are available by mail. No release necessary. $5.00 search fee. Search information required: name, date of birth, years to search. Specify plaintiff or defendant.

Colorado County

District Clerk's Office, Criminal Records
Colorado County Courthouse
Columbus, TX 78934
(409) 732-2536

Felony records are available by mail. No release necessary. $5.00 search fee. Search information required: name.

Civil records are available by mail. No release necessary. $5.00 search fee. Search information required: name, date of birth, years to search. Specify plaintiff or defendant.

Comal County

Felony records
District Clerk's Office, Criminal Records
150 N. Seguin, Suite 304
New Braunfels, TX 78130
(512) 620-5574

Felony records are available by mail. A release is required. $5.00 search fee. Company checks only, payable to District Clerk's Office. Search information required: name, date of birth, years to search.

Civil records
District Clerk's Office
150 N. Seguin, Suite 304
New Braunfels, TX 78130
(512) 620-5574

Civil records are available by mail. A release is required. $5.00 search fee. Search information required: name, date of birth, years to search. Specify plaintiff or defendant.

Misdemeanor records
County Court at Law
100 Main Plaza, Suite 203
New Braunfels, TX 78130
(512) 620-5582
Fax (512) 620-5592

Misdemeanor records are available by mail or phone. $5.00 search fee. Search information required: name, alias, date of birth.

Civil records
County Court at Law
100 Main Plaza, Suite 203
New Braunfels, TX 78130
(512) 620-5582
Fax (512) 620-5592

Civil records are available by mail. No release necessary. $5.00 search fee. Search information required: name, date of birth, years to search. Specify plaintiff or defendant.

Comanche County

Felony records
District Clerk's Office, Criminal Records
County Courthouse
Comanche, TX 76442
(915) 356-2342

Felony records are available by mail or phone. No release necessary. No search fee. $1.00 fee per copy. Search information required: name.

Civil records
District Clerk's Office
County Courthouse
Comanche, TX 76442
(915) 356-2342
Civil records are available by mail or phone. No release necessary. No search fee. $1.00 fee per copy. Search information required: name, date of birth, years to search. Specify plaintiff or defendant.

Misdemeanor records
County Clerk's Office
Comanche Courthouse
Comanche, TX 76442
(915) 356-2655
Misdemeanor records are available by mail. No release necessary. $5.00 search fee. Search information required: name.

Civil records
County Clerk's Office
Comanche Courthouse
Comanche, TX 76442
(915) 356-2655
Civil records are available by mail. No release necessary. $5.00 search fee. Search information required: name, date of birth, years to search. Specify plaintiff or defendant.

Concho County

Felony and misdemeanor records
District Clerk's Office, Criminal Records
PO Box 98
Paint Rock, TX 76866
(915) 732-4322
Felony and misdemeanor records are available by mail or phone. No release necessary. No search fee. Search information required: name, SSN, date of birth.

Civil records
County & District Clerk's Office, Civil Records
PO Box 98
Paint Rock, TX 76866
(915) 732-4322
Civil records are available by mail. No release necessary. No search fee. Search information required: name, date of birth, years to search. Specify plaintiff or defendant.

Cooke County

Felony records
District Clerk's Office, Criminal Records
Cooke County Courthouse
Gainesville, TX 76240
(817) 668-5422
Felony records are available by mail. No release necessary. $5.00 search fee. Certified check only, payable to District Clerk. Search information required: name, years to search.

Civil records
District Clerk's Office
Cooke County Courthouse
Gainesville, TX 76240
(817) 668-5450
Civil records are available by mail. No release necessary. $5.00 search fee. Search information required: name, date of birth, years to search. Specify plaintiff or defendant.

Misdemeanor records
County Clerk's Office
Cooke County Courthouse
Gainesvelle, TX 76240
(817) 668-5420
Misdemeanor records are available by mail or phone. No search fee. No release necessary. Search information required: name, years to search.

Civil records
County Clerk's Office
Cooke County Courthouse
Gainesvelle, TX 76240
(817) 668-5420
Civil records are available by mail. No release necessary. No search fee. $1.00 fee per copy. $2.00 for certification. Search information required: name, date of birth, years to search. Specify plaintiff or defendant.

Coryell County

Felony records
District Clerk's Office, Criminal Records
PO Box 4
Gatesville, TX 76528
(817) 865-6115
Felony records are available by mail or phone. No release necessary. $5.00 search fee. Search information required: name, SASE, years to search.

Civil records
District Clerk's Office
PO Box 4
Gatesville, TX 76528
(817) 865-6115
Civil records are available by mail or phone. No release necessary. No search fee. Search information required: name, date of birth, years to search. Specify plaintiff or defendant.

Misdemeanor records
County Clerk's Office
PO Box 237
Gatesville, TX 76528
(817) 865-5016
Misdemeanor records are available by mail. $5.00 search fee. Make cashier's check payable to County Clerk. Search information required: name, years to search.

Civil records
County Clerk's Office
PO Box 237
Gatesville, TX 76528
(817) 865-5016
Civil records are available by mail. No release necessary. No search fee. Search information required: name, date of birth, years to search. Specify plaintiff or defendant.

Cottle County

District Clerk's Office, Criminal Records
PO Box 717
Paducah, TX 79248
(806) 492-3823
Felony and misdemeanor records are available by mail or phone. No release necessary. $5.00 search fee. Make check payable to District Clerk. Search information required: name.

Civil records are available by mail. No release necessary. $5.00 search fee. $1.00 fee per copy. $2.00 for certification. Search information required: name, date of birth, years to search. Specify plaintiff or defendant.

Crane County

Felony records
District Clerk's Office, Criminal Records
PO Box 578
6th and Alford
Crane, TX 79731
(915) 558-3581
Felony records are available by mail. No release necessary. $5.00 fee for 10 years searched. $1.00 fee per copy. $1.00 fee for certification. Search information required: name, SSN, date of birth, sex.

Civil records
District Clerk's Office
PO Box 578
6th and Alford
Crane, TX 79731
(915) 558-3581
Civil records are available by mail. No release necessary. $5.00 fee for 10 years searched. $1.00 fee per copy. $1.00 fee for certification. Search information required: name, date of birth, years to search. Specify plaintiff or defendant.

Misdemeanor records
County Clerk
PO Box 578
Crane, TX 79731
(915) 558-3581
Misdemeanor records are available by mail. $5.00 search fee. $1.00 fee per copy. $1.00 for certification. Checks payable to County Clerk. Search information required: name, years to search.

Civil records
County Clerk
PO Box 578
Crane, TX 79731
(915) 558-3581
Civil records are available by mail. No release necessary. $5.00 search fee. $1.00 fee per copy. $1.00 for certification. Search information required: name, date of birth, years to search. Specify plaintiff or defendant.

Crockett County

Felony records
District Clerk's Office
Courthouse
PO Drawer C
Ozona, TX 76943
(915) 392-2022
Felony records are available by mail. No search fee. Checks payable to District Clerk. Search information required: name, date of offense.

Civil records
District Clerk's Office
Courthouse
PO Drawer C
Ozona, TX 76943
(915) 392-2022
Civil records are available by mail. No release necessary. $10.00 search fee. $1.00 fee per copy. $2.00 for certification. Search information required: name, date of birth, years to search. Specify plaintiff or defendant.

Misdemeanor records
County Clerk's Office
Courthouse
PO Box Drawer C
Ozona, TX 76943
(915) 392-2022
Misdemeanor records are available by mail or phone. $10.00 fee. $1.00 fee per copy. $2.00 for certification. Search information required: name, years to search.

Civil records
County Clerk's Office
Courthouse
PO Box Drawer C
Ozona, TX 76943
(915) 392-2022
Civil records are available by mail or phone. No release necessary. $10.00 search fee. $1.00 fee per copy. $2.00 for certification. Search information required: name, date of birth, years to search. Specify plaintiff or defendant.

Crosby County

Felony records
District Clerk's Office, Criminal Records
PO Box 495
Crosbyton, TX 79322
(806) 675-2071
Fax (806) 675-2804
Felony records are available by mail or phone. No release necessary. No search fee. $1.00 fee per copy. Certified checks only, payable to District Clerk. Search information required: name.

Civil records
District Clerk's Office
PO Box 495
Crosbyton, TX 79322
(806) 675-2071
Civil records are available by mail or phone. No release necessary. No search fee. $1.00 fee per copy. Search information required: name, date of birth, years to search. Specify plaintiff or defendant.

Misdemeanor records
County Clerk's Office
PO Box 218
Crosbyton, TX 79322
(806) 675-2334
Misdemeanor records are available by mail or phone. No search fee. No release necessary. Search information required: name, years to search.

Civil records
County Clerk's Office
PO Box 218
Crosbyton, TX 79322
(806) 675-2334
Civil records are available by mail or phone. No release necessary. No search fee. Search information required: name, date of birth, years to search. Specify plaintiff or defendant.

Culberson County

District Clerk's Office, Criminal Records
PO Box 158
Van Horn, TX 79855
(915) 283-2058
Felony and misdemeanor records are available by mail or phone. A release is required. No search fee. $1.00 fee per copy. Search information required: name, years to search.

Civil records are available by mail or phone. A release is required. No search fee. $1.00 fee per copy. Search information required: name, date of birth, years to search. Specify plaintiff or defendant.

Dallam County

District Clerk's Office
PO Box 1352
Dalhart, TX 79022
(806) 249-4751
Felony and misdemeanor records are available by mail. No release necessary. $5.00 search fee. Make check payable to District Clerk. Search information required: name, date of offense.

Civil records are available by mail. No release necessary. $5.00 search fee. Search information required: name, date of birth, years to search. Specify plaintiff or defendant.

Dallas County

Felony records
District Clerk's Office, Criminal Section
Frank Crowley Courts Building
133 N. Industrial Blvd.
Dallas, TX 75207-4313
(214) 653-7421
Felony records are available by mail. No release necessary. $5.00 search fee. $1.00 fee per copy. $2.00 for certification. Check payable to District Clerk. Search information required: name, years to search, SASE.

Civil records
District Clerk's Office
600 Commerce Street
Dallas County Courthouse
Dallas, TX 75202
(214) 653-7421
Civil records are available by mail. No release necessary. $5.00 search fee. $1.00 fee per copy. $2.00 for certification. Search information required: name, date of birth, years to search. Specify plaintiff or defendant.

Misdemeanor records
County Clerk's Office
Dallas County Courthouse
600 Commerce Street
Dallas, TX 75202
(214) 653-7541
Misdemeanor records are available by mail. $5.00 search fee. Checks payable to County Clerk. Search information required: name, date of birth.

Civil records
County Clerk's Office
Dallas County Courthouse
600 Commerce Street
Dallas, TX 75202
(214) 653-7541
Civil records are available by mail. No release necessary. $5.00 search fee. Search information required: name, date of birth, years to search. Specify plaintiff or defendant.

Dawson County

Felony records
District Clerk's Office, Criminal Records
Drawer 1268
Lamesa, TX 79331
(806) 872-7373
Felony records are available by mail or phone. No release necessary. No search fee. $.25 fee per copy. $1.00 for certification. Search information required: name, years to search.

Civil records
District Clerk's Office
Drawer 1268
Lamesa, TX 79331
(806) 872-7373
Civil records are available by mail or phone. No release necessary. No search fee. $.25 fee per copy. $1.00 for certification. Search information required: name, date of birth, years to search. Specify plaintiff or defendant.

Misdemeanor records
County Clerk's Office
PO Box 1268
La Mesa, TX 79331
(806) 872-3778
Misdemeanor records are available by mail. No search fee. $1.00 fee per copy. $2.00 for certification. A release is required. Search information required: name, date of offense if available, years to search.

Civil records
County Clerk's Office
PO Box 1268
La Mesa, TX 79331
(806) 872-3778
Civil records are available by mail. A release is required. No search fee. $1.00 fee per copy. $2.00 for certification. Search information required: name, date of birth, years to search. Specify plaintiff or defendant.

De Witt County

Felony records
District Clerk's Office, Criminal Records
PO Box 224
Cuero, TX 77954
(512) 275-2221
Felony records are available by mail or phone. No release necessary. $5.00 search fee. $1.00 fee per copy. Search information required: name, date of birth, years to search.

Civil records
District Clerk's Office
PO Box 224
Cuero, TX 77954
(512) 275-2221
Civil records are available by mail or phone. No release necessary. $5.00 search fee. $1.00 fee per copy. Search information required: name, date of birth, years to search. Specify plaintiff or defendant.

Misdemeanor records
County Clerk, De Witt County
307 N. Gonzales
Cuero, TX 77954
(512) 275-3724
Misdemeanor records are available by mail or phone. No search fee. $1.00 fee per copy. $2.00 for certification. No release necessary. Search information required: name, date of birth, years to search.

Civil records
County Clerk, De Witt County
307 N. Gonzales
Cuero, TX 77954
(512) 275-3724
Civil records are available by mail. No release necessary. No search fee. $1.00 fee per copy. $2.00 for certification. Search information required: name, date of birth, years to search. Specify plaintiff or defendant.

Deaf Smith County

Felony records
District Clerk's Office, Criminal Records
Deaf Smith Courthouse
235 E. 3rd, Room 304
Hereford, TX 79045
(806) 364-3901
Fax (806) 364-8830
Felony records are available by mail or phone. No release necessary. No search fee. Search information required: name.

Civil records
District Clerk's Office
Deaf Smith Courthouse
Hereford, TX 79045
(806) 364-3901
Fax (806) 364-8830
Civil records are available by mail or phone. No release necessary. No search fee.$ Search information required: name, date of birth, years to search. Specify plaintiff or defendant.

Misdemeanor records
Deaf Smith County Clerk's Office
Courthouse
235 E. 3rd, Room 203
Hereford, TX 79045-5593
(806) 364-1746
Misdemeanor records are available by mail. $5.00 search fee. Checks payable to County Clerk. No release necessary. Search information required: name, year of offense, years to search.

Civil records
Deaf Smith County Clerk's Office
Courthouse
Hereford, TX 79045
(806) 364-1746
Civil records are available by mail. No release necessary. $5.00 search fee. Search information required: name, date of birth, years to search. Specify plaintiff or defendant.

Delta County

District Clerk's Office, Criminal Records
PO Box 455
Cooper, TX 75432
(214) 395-4110
Fax (903) 395-4110
Felony and misdemeanor records are available by mail or phone. No release necessary. $5.00 search fee. Search information required: name.

Civil records are available by mail. No release necessary. $5.00 search fee. Search information required: name, date of birth, years to search. Specify plaintiff or defendant.

Denton County

Felony records
District Clerk's Office, Criminal Records
PO Box 2146
Denton, TX 76202
(817) 565-8532
Felony records are available by mail. No release necessary. $5.00 search fee. Make check payable to District Clerk. Search information required: name, date of birth, SASE.

Civil records
District Clerk's Office
PO Box 2146
Denton, TX 76202
(817) 565-8532
Civil records are available by mail. No release necessary. $5.00 search fee. $1.00 fee per copy. $2.00 for certification. Search information required: name, date of birth, years to search, SASE. Specify plaintiff or defendant.

Misdemeanor records
County Clerk, Criminal Records
Carroll Court Bldg.
PO Box 2187
Denton, TX 76202
(817) 565-8501 or (800) 356-5639
Misdemeanor records are available by mail. $5.00 fee for 5 years searched. Make cashier's check or money order payable to County Clerk. No release necessary. Search information required: name, alias, date of birth, SSN, if available, years to search.

Civil records
County Clerk
Carroll Court Bldg.
PO Box 2187
Denton, TX 76202
(817) 565-8501 or (800) 356-5639
Civil records are available by mail or phone. No release necessary. $5.00 search fee if done by mail, $1.00 fee per year searched. $2.00 for certification. Search information required: name, date of birth, years to search. Specify plaintiff or defendant.

Dickens County

District Clerk's Office, Criminal Records
PO Box 120
Dickens, TX 79229
(806) 623-5531
Felony and misdemeanor records are available by mail. No release necessary. $5.00 search fee. $1.00 fee per copy. $2.00 for certification. Make check payable to District Clerk. Search information required: name, date of birth, years to search.

Civil records are available by mail or phone. No release necessary. $5.00 search fee. $1.00 fee per copy. $2.00 for certification. Search information required: name, date of birth, years to search. Specify plaintiff or defendant.

Dimmit County

Felony records
District Clerk's Office, Criminal Records
103 N. 5th
Carrizo Springs, TX 78834
(512) 876-2321
Felony records are available by mail. No release necessary. $5.00 search fee. $1.00 fee per copy. $2.00 for certification. Search information required: name, SSN, years to search.

Civil records
District Clerk's Office
103 N. 5th
Carrizo Springs, TX 78834
(512) 876-2321
Civil records are available by mail. No release necessary. $5.00 search fee. $1.00 fee per copy. $2.00 for certification. Search information required: name, date of birth, years to search. Specify plaintiff or defendant.

Misdemeanor records
County Clerk
103 N. 5th
Carrizo Springs, TX 78834
(512) 876-3569
Misdemeanor records are available by mail. $5.00 search fee. $1.00 fee per copy. $2.00 for certification. No release necessary. Make cashier's check or money order payable to County Clerk. Search information required: name, date of birth, date of-fense if available, years to search .

Civil records
County Clerk
103 N. 5th
Carrizo Springs, TX 78834
(512) 876-3569
Civil records are available by mail. No release necessary. $5.00 search fee. $1.00 fee per copy. $2.00 for certification. Search information required: name, date of birth, years to search. Specify plaintiff or defendant.

Donley County

District Clerk's Office, Criminal Records
PO Drawer U
Clarendon, TX 79226
(806) 874-3436
Felony and misdemeanor records are available by mail. Written release is required. $5.00 search fee. $1.00 fee per copy. $2.00 for certification. Make check payable to District Clerk. Search information required: name, alias, SSN, date of birth, years to search.

Civil records are available by mail. Written release is required. $5.00 search fee. $1.00 fee per copy. $2.00 for certification. Search information required: name, date of birth, years to search. Specify plaintiff or defendant.

Duval County

Felony records
District Clerk's Office, Criminal Records
PO Box 487
San Diego, TX 78384
(512) 279-3322 Extension 239
Felony records are available by mail. No release necessary. $15.00 search fee. $1.00 fee per copy, $2.00 for certifcation. Checks payable to District Clerk. Search information required: name, SASE.

Civil records
District Clerk's Office
PO Box 487
San Diego, TX 78384
(512) 279-3322 Extension 239
Civil records are available by mail. No release necessary. $15.00 search fee. $1.00 fee per copy, $2.00 for certifcation. Search information required: name, date of birth, years to search, SASE. Specify plaintiff or defendant.

Misdemeanor records
County Clerk's Office
PO Box 248
San Diego, TX 78384
(512) 279-3322
Misdemeanor records are available by mail. $10.00 search fee. $1.00 fee per copy, $2.00 for certifcation. Make checks payable to County Clerk. No release necessary. Search information required: name, date of offense, years to search, driver's license.

Civil records
County Clerk's Office
PO Box 248
San Diego, TX 78384
(512) 279-3322
Civil records are available by mail. No release necessary. $10.00 search fee. $1.00 fee per copy, $2.00 for certifcation. Search information required: name, date of birth, years to search. Specify plaintiff or defendant.

Eastland County

Felony records
District Clerk's Office, Criminal Records
PO Box 670
Eastland, TX 76448
(817) 629-2664
Fax (817) 629-2080
Felony and misdemeanor prior to May 1987 records are available by mail or phone. No release necessary. No search fee. $2.00 fee per page for fax response. Search information required: name, years to search, offense, case number (if available).

Civil records
District Clerk's Office
PO Box 670
Eastland, TX 76448
(817) 629-2664
Civil records are available by mail or phone. No release necessary. No search fee. Search information required: name, date of birth, years to search. Specify plaintiff or defendant.

Misdemeanor records
County Clerk
PO Box 110
Eastland, TX 76448
(817) 629-1583
Misdemeanor records from April, 1987 are available by mail. $5.00 search fee. No release necessary. Search information required: name, date of birth, date of offense.

Ector County

Felony records
District Clerk's Office, Criminal Records
Ector County Courthouse, Room 301
Odessa, TX 79761
(915) 335-3144
Felony records are available by mail or phone. No release necessary. $10.00 search fee. Make check payable to District Clerk's Office. Search information required: name, date of birth, SSN, years to search.

Civil records
District Clerk's Office
Ector County Courthouse, Room 301
Odessa, TX 79761
(915) 335-3144
Civil records are available by mail or phone. No release necessary. $10.00 search fee. Search information required: name, date of birth, years to search. Specify plaintiff or defendant.

Misdemeanor records
County Clerk's Office
PO Box 707
Odessa, TX 79760
(915) 335-3045
Misdemeanor records are available by mail. No search fee. $1.00 fee per copy. $2.00 for certification. No release necessary. Search information required: name, years to search.

Civil records
County Clerk's Office
PO Box 707
Odessa, TX 79760
(915) 335-3045
Civil records are available by mail. No release necessary. No search fee. $1.00 fee per copy. $2.00 for certification. Search information required: name, date of birth, years to search. Specify plaintiff or defendant.

Edwards County

District Clerk's Office, Criminal Records
PO Box 184
Rocksprings, TX 78880
(512) 683-2235
Fax (512) 683-5376
Felony and misdemeanor records are available by mail. No release necessary. $10.00 search fee. Make check payable to District Clerk's Office. Search information required: name.

Civil records are available by mail. No release necessary. $10.00 search fee. Search information required: name, date of birth, years to search. Specify plaintiff or defendant.

El Paso County

Felony records
District Clerk's Office, Criminal Records
1403 City County Bldg.
El Paso, TX 79901
(915) 546-2021
Felony records are available by mail. No release necessary. $5.00 search fee. $1.00 fee per copy. Make check payable to District Clerk. Search information required: name, date of birth, years to search.

Civil records
District Clerk's Office
1403 City County Bldg.
El Paso, TX 79901
(915) 546-2021
Civil records are available by mail. No release necessary. $5.00 search fee. $1.00 fee per copy. Search information required: name, date of birth, years to search. Specify plaintiff or defendant.

Misdemeanor records
County Clerk's Office
City County Bldg.
500 E. San Antonio St., Room 104
El Paso, TX 79901
(915) 546-2071
Misdemeanor records are available by mail. Records available by phone if case number is available. $5.00 search fee. No release necessary. Search information required: name, date of birth, years to search.

Civil records
County Clerk's Office
City County Bldg.
500 E. San Antonio St., Room 104
El Paso, TX 79901
(915) 546-2071
Civil records are available by mail. No release necessary. $5.00 search fee. $1.00 fee per copy. $1.00 for certification. Search information required: name, date of birth, years to search. Specify plaintiff or defendant.

Ellis County

Felony records
District Clerk's Office, Criminal Records
Ellis County Courthouse
101 W. Main Street
Waxahachie, TX 75165
(214) 937-8620
Felony records are available by mail. No release necessary. $5.00 search fee. Search information required: name, date of birth.

Civil records
District Clerk's Office
Ellis County Courthouse
Waxahachie, TX 75165
(214) 937-8620
Civil records are available by mail. No release necessary. $5.00 search fee. $1.00 fee per copy. $2.00 for certification. Search information required: name, date of birth, years to search. Specify plaintiff or defendant.

Misdemeanor records
County Clerk's Office
Ellis County Courthouse
PO Box 250
Waxahachie, TX 75165
(214) 937-6370
Misdemeanor records are available by mail. $10.00 fee per 5 years searched. No release necessary. Checks payable to County Clerk. Search information required: name, years to search.

Civil records
County Clerk's Office
Ellis County Courthouse
PO Box 250
Waxahachie, TX 75165
(214) 937-6370
Civil records are available by mail. No release necessary. $5.00 fee for each 5 years searched. Search information required: name, date of birth, years to search. Specify plaintiff or defendant.

Erath County

Felony records
District Clerk's Office, Criminal
Records
Erath Courthouse
Stephenville, TX 76401
(817) 965-1431
Felony records are available by mail. No release necessary. $5.00 search fee. Make check payable to District Clerk. Search information required: name.

Civil records
District Clerk's Office
Erath Courthouse
Stephenville, TX 76401
(817) 965-1431
Civil records are available by mail. No release necessary. $5.00 search fee. Search information required: name, date of birth, years to search. Specify plaintiff or defendant.

Misdemeanor records
County Clerk's Office
Erath Courthouse
Stephenville, TX 76401
(817) 965-3219
Misdemeanor records are available by mail. $5.00 search fee. $1.00 fee per copied page. No release necessary. Search information required: name, year of offense.

Civil records
County Clerk's Office
Erath Courthouse
Stephenville, TX 76401
(817) 965-3219
Civil records are available by mail. No release necessary. $5.00 search fee. $1.00 fee per copy. Search information required: name, date of birth, years to search. Specify plaintiff or defendant.

Falls County

Felony records
District Clerk's Office, Criminal
Records
PO Box 229
Marlin, TX 76661
(817) 883-3181
Felony and misdemeanor records are available by mail or phone. No release necessary. No search fee. $1.00 fee per copy. $2.00 for certification. Search information required: name, years to search.

Civil records
District Clerk's Office
PO Box 229
Marlin, TX 76661
(817) 883-3181
Civil records are available by mail or phone. No release necessary. No search fee. $1.00 fee per copy. $2.00 for certification. Search information required: name, date of birth, years to search. Must have plaintiff's name.

Misdemeanor records
County Clerk's Office
PO Box 458
Marlin, TX 76661
(817) 883-2061
Misdemeanor records since 1985 available by mail or phone. No search fee. Release is required. Search information required: name.

Civil records
County Clerk's Office
PO Box 458
Marlin, TX 76661
(817) 883-2061
Civil records are available by mail or phone. A release is required. No search fee. Search information required: name, date of birth, years to search. Specify plaintiff or defendant.

Fannin County

Felony records
District Clerk's Office, Criminal
Records
Fannin County Courthouse
Bonham, TX 75418
(903) 583-7459 Extension 33
Felony and misdemeanor records are available by mail or phone. $5.00 search fee. Checks payable to District Clerk. No release necessary. Search information required: full name, years to search.

Civil records
District Clerk's Office
Fannin County Courthouse
Bonham, TX 75418
(903) 583-7459 Extension 33
Civil records are available by mail. No release necessary. $5.00 search fee. $1.00 fee per copy. $2.00 for certification. Search information required: name, date of birth, years to search. Specify plaintiff or defendant.

Misdemeanor records
Fannin County Curthouse
Bonham, TX 75418
(214) 583-7486
Midemeanor records are available by mail. $5.00 search fee. No release necessary. Search information required: name, years to search.

Civil records
Fannin County Curthouse
Bonham, TX 75418
(214) 583-7486
Civil records are available by mail. No release necessary. $5.00 search fee. Search information required: name, date of birth, years to search. Specify plaintiff or defendant.

Fayette County

Felony records
District Clerk's Office, Criminal
Records
Fayette County Courthouse
LaGrange, TX 78945
(409) 968-3548
Felony records are available by mail. No release necessary. $5.00 search fee. Search information required: name, years to search.

Civil records
District Clerk's Office
Fayette County Courthouse
LaGrange, TX 78945
(409) 968-3548
Civil records are available by mail. No release necessary. $5.00 search fee. Search information required: name, date of birth, years to search. Specify plaintiff or defendant.

Misdemeanor records
County Clerk
Fayette County Courthouse
PO Box 296
La Grange, TX 78945
(409) 968-3251
Misdemeanor records are available by mail or phone. No search fee. No release necessary. Search information required: name, years to search, year of offense.

Civil records
County Clerk
Fayette County Courthouse
PO Box 296
La Grange, TX 78945
(409) 968-3251
Civil records are available by mail or phone. No release necessary. No search fee. Search information required: name, date of birth, years to search. Specify plaintiff or defendant.

Fisher County

Felony records
Fisher County Courthouse, Criminal
Records
District Clerk's Office
PO Box 88
Roby, TX 79543
(915) 776-2279
Felony records are available by mail. Written request required. A release is required if the case is pending or has been closed. $5.00 search fee. Checks payable to District Clerk. Search information required: name, years to search, SASE.

Civil records
Fisher County Courthouse
District Clerk's Office
PO Box 88
Roby, TX 79543
(915) 776-2279
Civil records are available by mail. No release necessary. $5.00 search fee. $1.00 fee per copy. $1.00 for certification. Search information required: name, date of birth, years to search, SASE. Specify plaintiff or defendant.

Misdemeanor records
County Clerk
Fisher County Courthouse
PO Box 368
Roby, TX 79543
(915) 776-2401
Misdemeanor records are available by mail. No search fee. A release is required. Search information required: name, year of offense.

Civil records
County Clerk
Fisher County Courthouse
PO Box 368
Roby, TX 79543
(915) 776-2401
Civil records are available by mail. A release is required. No search fee. Search information required: name, date of birth, years to search. Specify plaintiff or defendant.

Floyd County

Felony records
District Clerk's Office, Criminal
Records
PO Box 67
Floydada, TX 79235
(806) 983-2232
Felony records are available by mail. No release necessary. $5.00 search fee. Checks payable to District Clerk. Search information required: name, years to search.

Civil records
District Clerk's Office
PO Box 67
Floydada, TX 79235
(806) 983-2232
Civil records are available by mail. No release necessary. $5.00 search fee. Search information required: name, date of birth, years to search. Specify plaintiff or defendant.

Misdemeanor records
County Clerk's Office
PO Box 476
Floydada, TX 79235
(806) 983-3236
Misdemeanor records are available by mail. $5.00 search fee. Checks payable to County Clerk. No release necessary. Search information required: name, date of birth, years to search.

Civil records
County Clerk's Office
PO Box 476
Floydada, TX 79235
(806) 983-3236
Civil records are available by mail. No release necessary. No search fee. Search information required: name, date of birth, years to search. Specify plaintiff or defendant.

Foard County

District Clerk's Office, Criminal
Records
PO Box 539
Crowell, TX 79227
(817) 684-1365
Felony and misdemeanor records are available by mail. No release necessary. No search fee. $1.00 fee per copy. $1.00 for certification. Search information required: name, date of birth, years to search.

Civil records are available by mail. No release necessary. No search fee. $1.00 fee per copy. $1.00 for certification. Search information required: name, date of birth, years to search. Specify plaintiff or defendant.

Fort Bend County

Felony records
District Clerk's Office, Criminal
Records
PO Drawer E
Richmond, TX 77469
(713) 342-4506
Fax (713) 341-4519 or 341-4520
Felony records are available by mail. No release necessary. $7.00 search fee. Certified check only, payable to District Clerk. Search information required: name, date of birth. Contact the above office for required form.

Civil records
District Clerk's Office
PO Drawer E
Richmond, TX 77469
(713) 342-4506
Fax (713) 341-4519 or 341-4520
Civil records are available by mail. No release necessary. $7.00 search fee. $1.00 fee per copy. Search information required: name, date of birth, years to search. Specify plaintiff or defendant.

Misdemeanor records
County Clerk's Office
PO Box 520
Richmond, TX 77469
(713) 342-3411
Fax (713) 341-8696
Misdemeanor records are available by mail. $5.00 search fee. Checks payable to County Clerk. No release necessary. Search information required: name, date of birth, years to search.

Civil records
County Clerk's Office
PO Box 520
Richmond, TX 77469
(713) 342-3411
Fax (713) 341-8696
Civil records are available by mail. No release necessary. $5.00 search fee. Search information required: name, date of birth, years to search. Specify plaintiff or defendant.

Franklin County

Felony records
District Clerk's Office, Criminal
Records
PO Box 68
Mount Vernon, TX 75457
(214) 537-4786
Felony records are available by mail or phone. No release necessary. $5.00 search fee. Certified check only, payable to District Clerk's Office. Search information required: name.

Civil records
District Clerk's Office
PO Box 68
Mount Vernon, TX 75457
(214) 537-4786
Civil records are available by mail or phone. No release necessary. $5.00 search fee. Search information required: name, date of birth, years to search. Specify plaintiff or defendant.

Misdemeanor records
County Clerk's Office
PO Box 68
Mount Vernon, TX 75457
(214) 537-4252
Misdemeanor records are available by mail. $5.00 search fee. No release necessary. Search information required: name, years to search.

Civil records are available by mail. No release necessary. $5.00 search fee. Search information required: name, date of birth, years to search. Specify plaintiff or defendant.

Freestone County

Felony records
District Clerk's Office, Criminal
Records
PO Box 722
Fairfield, TX 75840
(903) 389-2534
Felony records are available by mail or phone. No release necessary. No search fee. $1.00 fee per copy. $1.50 for certification. Search information required: name, SASE, years to search.

Civil records
District Clerk's Office
PO Box 722
Fairfield, TX 75840
(903) 389-2534
Civil records are available by mail or phone. No release necessary. No search fee. $1.00 fee per copy. $1.50 for certification. Search information required: name, date of birth, years to search. Specify plaintiff or defendant.

Misdemeanor records
County Clerk's Office
PO Box 1017
Fairfield, TX 75840
(903) 389-2635
Misdemeanor records are available by mail. No search fee. $1.00 fee per copy. No release necessary. Search information required: name, years to search.

Civil records
County Clerk's Office
PO Box 1017
Fairfield, TX 75840
(903) 389-2635
Civil records are available by mail. No release necessary. No search fee. $1.00 fee per copy. Search information required: name, date of birth, years to search. Specify plaintiff or defendant.

Frio County

District Clerk's Office, Criminal
Records
PO Box 242
Pearsall, TX 78061
(512) 334-8073
Felony and misdemeanor records are available by mail or phone. No release necessary. $5.00 search fee. Certified or personal checks, payable to District Clerk. Search information required: name, SSN, date of birth, previous address, years to search.

Civil records are available by mail or phone. No release necessary. $5.00 search fee. Search information required: name, date of birth, years to search. Specify plaintiff or defendant.

Gaines County

Felony records
District Clerk's Office, Criminal
Records
Gaines County Courthouse
Seminole, TX 79360
(915) 758-5491
Fax (915) 758-9258
Felony records are available by mail or phone. Case number required for phone seaches. No release necessary. $5.00 search fee. Make check payable to District Clerk. Search information required: name, years to search.

Civil records
District Clerk's Office
Gaines County Courthouse
Seminole, TX 79360
(915) 758-5491
Fax (915) 758-9258
Civil records are available by mail or phone. Case number required for phone seaches. No release necessary. $5.00 search fee. Search information required: name, date of birth, years to search. Specify plaintiff or defendant.

Misdemeanor records
County Clerk's Office
Gaines County Courthouse
Seminole, TX 79360
(915) 758-3521
Misdemeanor records are available by mail. No search fee. Make cashier's check payable to County Clerk. No release necessary. Search information required: name, years to search.

Civilr records
County Clerk's Office
Gaines County Courthouse
Seminole, TX 79360
(915) 758-3521
Civil records are available by mail. No release necessary. No search fee. Search information required: name, date of birth, years to search. Specify plaintiff or defendant.

Galveston County

Felony records
District Clerk's Office, Criminal Records
722 Moody Room 404
Galveston, TX 77550
(409) 766-2424
Felony records are available by mail. No release necessary. $5.00 search fee. No fee for records after 1983. Make check payable to District Clerk. Search information required: name, date of birth, years to search.

Civil records
District Clerk's Office
722 Moody Room 404
Galveston, TX 77550
(409) 766-2424
Civil records are available by mail. No release necessary. $5.00 search fee. $1.00 fee per copy. $1.00 for certification. Search information required: name, date of birth, years to search. Specify plaintiff or defendant.

Misdemeanor records
County Clerk's Office
PO Box 2450
Galveston, TX 77550
(409) 766-2200
Misdemeanor records are available by mail. No release necessary. $5.00 search fee. Search information required: name, years to search.

Civil records
County Clerk's Office
PO Box 2450
Galveston, TX 77550
(409) 766-2200
Civil records are available by mail. No release necessary. $5.00 search fee. Search information required: name of each individual, years to search. Specify plaintiff or defendant.

Garza County

District Clerk's Office, Criminal Records
Garza County Courthouse
Post, TX 79356
(806) 495-3535
Felony and misdemeanor records are available by mail. No release necessary. $5.00 search fee. $1.00 fee per copy. Make check payable to District Clerk. Search information required: name, years to search.

Civil records are available by mail. No release necessary. $5.00 search fee. $1.00 fee per copy. Search information required: name, date of birth, years to search. Specify plaintiff or defendant.

Gillespie County

Felony records
District Clerk's Office, Criminal Records
101 W. Main Street, #204
Fredericksburg, TX 78624-3700
(512) 997-6517
Felony records are available by mail. No release necessary. $5.00 search fee. Make check payable to District Clerk. Search information required: name.

Civil records
District Clerk's Office
101 W. Main Street, #204
Fredericksburg, TX 78624-3700
(512) 997-6517
Civil records are available by mail. No release necessary. $5.00 search fee. Search information required: name, date of birth, years to search. Specify plaintiff or defendant.

Misdemeanor records
County Clerk's Office
101 W. Main Street, #13
Fredericksburg, TX 78624
(512) 997-6515
Misdemeanor records are available by mail. $5.00 search fee. $1.00 fee per copy. $3.00 for certification. No release necessary. Search information required: name, alias , if known, years to search.

Civil records
County Clerk's Office
101 W. Main Street, #13
Fredericksburg, TX 78624
(512) 997-6515
Civil records are available by mail. No release necessary. $5.00 search fee. $1.00 fee per copy. $3.00 for certification. Search information required: name, date of birth, years to search. Specify plaintiff or defendant.

Glasscock County

Clerk of District Court
Courthouse
Garden City, TX 79739
(915) 354-2371
Felony and misdemeanor records are available by mail. No release necessary. $10.00 search fee. $1.00 fee per copy. $1.00 for each certification. Search information required: name, date of birth, years to search. Specify plaintiff or defendant.

Civil records are available by mail. No release necessary. $10.00 search fee. $1.00 fee per copy. $1.00 for each certification. Search information required: name, date of birth, years to search. Specify plaintiff or defendant.

Goliad County

District Clerk's Office, Criminal Records
PO Box 5
Goliad, TX 77963
(512) 645-2443
Felony and misdemeanor records are available by mail or phone. No release necessary. No search fee. $1.00 fee per copy. Search information required: full name, date of birth.

Civil records are available by mail or phone. No release necessary. No search fee. $1.00 fee per copy. Search information required: name, date of birth, years to search. Specify plaintiff or defendant.

Gonzales County

Felony records
District Clerk's Office, Criminal Records
PO Box 34
Gonzales, TX 78629
(512) 672-2326
Felony records are available by mail or phone. No release necessary. No search fee. Search information required: name, years to search.

Civil records
District Clerk's Office
PO Box 34
Gonzales, TX 78629
(512) 672-2326
Civil records are available by mail. No release necessary. $5.00 search fee. $1.00 fee per copy. $2.00 for certification. Search information required: name, date of birth, years to search. Specify plaintiff or defendant.

Misdemeanor records
County Clerk's Office
PO Box 77
Gonzales, TX 78629
(512) 672-2801
Misdemeanor records are available by mail. No search fee. $1.00 fee per copy. No release necessary. Search information required: name, date of offense, years to search.

Civil records
County Clerk's Office
PO Box 77
Gonzales, TX 78629
(512) 672-2801
Civil records are available by mail. No release necessary. No search fee. $1.00 fee per copy. Search information required: name, date of birth, years to search. Specify plaintiff or defendant.

Gray County

Felony records
District Clerk's Office, Criminal Records
PO Box 1139
Pampa, TX 79066-1902
(806) 669-6856
Felony records are available by mail from 1980. A release is required. $5.00 search fee. Company checks only, payable to Gray County District Clerk. Search information required: name, years to search.

Civil records
District Clerk's Office
PO Box 1139
Pampa, TX 79066-1902
(806) 669-6856
Civil records are available by mail. A release is required. $5.00 search fee. Search information required: name, date of birth, years to search. Specify plaintiff or defendant.

Misdemeanor records
County Clerk's Office
PO Box 1902
Pampa, TX 79066-1902
(806) 669-8004
Misdemeanor records are available by mail. $5.00 search fee. No release necessary. Search information required: name, years to search.

Civil records
County Clerk's Office
PO Box 1902
Pampa, TX 79066-1902
(806) 669-8004
Civil records are available by mail. No release necessary. $5.00 search fee. Search information required: name, date of birth, years to search. Specify plaintiff or defendant.

Grayson County

District Clerk's Office, Criminal Records
200 S. Crockett
Sherman, TX 75090
(903) 868-9515 Extension 306
Felony and misdemeanor records are available by mail. No release necessary. $5.00 search fee. $1.00 fee per copy. $1.00 for certification. Company or personal checks, payable to District Court. Search information required: name, date of birth, years to search.

Civil records are available by mail. No release necessary. $5.00 search fee. $1.00 fee per copy. $1.00 for certification. Search information required: name, date of birth, years to search. Specify plaintiff or defendant.

Gregg County

Felony records
District Clerk's Office, Criminal Records
PO Box 711
Longview, TX 75606
(903) 237-2656
Fax (903) 236-8456
Felony records are available by mail or phone. No release necessary. $5.00 search fee, prepaid. Search information required: name, years to search.

Civil records
District Clerk's Office
PO Box 711
Longview, TX 75606
(903) 237-2656
Civil records are available by mail or phone. No release necessary. $5.00 search fee, prepaid. Search information required: name, date of birth, years to search. Specify plaintiff or defendant.

Misdemeanor records
County Clerk's Office
PO Box 3049
Longview, TX 75606
(903) 236-8430
Fax (903) 236-8456
Misdemeanor records are available by mail or phone. No fee by phone from 1983 forward. $5.00 search fee. No release necessary. Search information required: name, date of birth.

Civil records
County Clerk's Office
PO Box 3049
Longview, TX 75606
(903) 236-8430
Fax (903) 236-8456
Civil records are available by mail or phone. No release necessary. No search fee. $1.00 fee per copy. $1.00 for certification. Search information required: name, date of birth, years to search. Specify plaintiff or defendant.

Grimes County

Felony records
District Clerk's Office, Criminal Records
PO Box 234
Anderson, TX 77830
(409) 873-2111
Fax (409) 873-2514
Felony records are available by mail or phone. Written request preferred. No release necessary. $5.00 search fee. $2.00 fee for first 3 pages of fax response, $1.00 each page therafter. Make check payable to District Clerk. Search information required: name, alias.

Civil records
District Clerk's Office
PO Box 234
Anderson, TX 77830
(409) 873-2982
Fax (409) 873-2514
Civil records are available by mail or phone. Written request preferred. No release necessary. $5.00 search fee. $2.00 fee for first 3 pages of fax response, $1.00 each page therafter. Search information required: name, date of birth, years to search. Specify plaintiff or defendant.

Misdemeanor records
County Clerk's Office
PO Box 209
Anderson, TX 77830
(903) 873-2111
Misdemeanor records are available by mail. No search fee. No release necessary. Search information required: name, date of offense.

Civil records
County Clerk's Office
PO Box 209
Anderson, TX 77830
(903) 873-2662
Civil records are available by mail. No release necessary. No search fee. Search information required: name, years to search. Specify plaintiff or defendant.

Guadalupe County

Felony records
District Clerk's Office, Criminal Records
Guadalupe County Courthouse
101 E. Court St.
Seguin, TX 78155
(512) 379-4188
Felony records are available by mail or phone. No release necessary. $5.00 search fee. Checks payable to District Clerk's Office. Search information required: name.

Civil records
District Clerk's Office
Guadalupe County Courthouse
101 E. Court St.
Seguin, TX 78155
(512) 379-4188
Civil records are available by mail or phone. No release necessary. No search fee. $1.00 fee per copy. Search information required: name, date of birth, years to search. Specify plaintiff or defendant.

Misdemeanor records
County Clerk
Guadalupe County Courthouse
101 E. Court St.
Seguin, TX 78155
(512) 379-4188
Fax (512) 379-9491
Misdemeanor records are available by mail or phone. No search fee. No release necessary. Search information required: name, date of birth, years to search, SASE.

Civil records
County Clerk
Guadalupe County Courthouse
101 E. Court St.
Seguin, TX 78155
(512) 379-4188
Civil records are available by mail. No release necessary. No search fee. Search information required: plaintiff's name, defendant's name, date of birth, years to search, SASE.

Hale County

Felony records
District Clerk
Hale County Courthouse
Plainview, TX 79072
(806) 293-0327 Ext. 228
Felony records are available by mail or phone. $5.00 search fee. Checks payable to Hale County District Clerk. Search information required: name, SSN, date of birth.

Civil records
District Clerk
Hale County Courthouse
Plainview, TX 79072
(806) 293-0327 Ext. 227 or 229
Civil records are available by mail or phone. No release necessary. No search fee. $1.00 fee per copy. Search information required: name, date of birth, years to search. Specify plaintiff or defendant.

Misdemeanor records
County Clerk, Hale County
PO Box 710
Plainview, TX 79072
(806) 293-8481
Misdemeanor records are available by mail or by phone Monday – Thursday. No search fee. No release necessary. Search information required: name, years to search.

Civil records
County Clerk, Hale County
PO Box 710
Plainview, TX 79072
(806) 293-8481
Civil records are available by mail or phone. No release necessary. No search fee. Search information required: name, date of birth, years to search. Specify plaintiff or defendant.

Hall County

District Clerk's Office, Criminal Records
Hall County Courthouse
Memphis, TX 79245
(806) 259-2627
Felony and misdemeanor records are available by mail or phone. No release necessary. $5.00 search fee. $1.00 fee per copy. No fee for phone searches. Make check payable to District Clerk's Office. Search information required: full name, years to search.

Civil records are available by mail or phone. No release necessary. $5.00 search fee. $1.00 fee per copy. No fee for phone searches. Search information required: name, date of birth, years to search. Specify plaintiff or defendant.

Hamilton County

Felony records
District Clerk's Office, Criminal Records
Hamilton County Courthouse
Hamilton, TX 76531
(817) 386-3417
Felony records are available by mail or phone. No release necessary. $5.00 search fee. $1.00 fee per copy. $2.00 for certification. Checks payable to Hamilton District Clerk. Search information required: name, years to search.

Civil records
District Clerk's Office
Hamilton County Courthouse
Hamilton, TX 76531
(817) 386-3417
Civil records are available by mail. No release necessary. $5.00 search fee. $1.00 fee per copy. $2.00 for certification. Search information required: name, date of birth, years to search. Specify plaintiff or defendant.

Misdemeanor records
County Clerk's Office
Hamilton County Courthouse
Hamilton, TX 76531
(817) 386-3518
Fax (817) 386-8727
Misdemeanor records are available by mail or phone. $10.00 search fee. Checks payable to County Clerk. No release necessary. Search information required: name, date of birth.

Civil records
County Clerk's Office
Hamilton County Courthouse
Hamilton, TX 76531
(817) 386-3518
Civil records are available by mail. No release necessary. $5.00 search fee. $1.00 fee per copy. $1.00 for certification. Search information required: name, date of birth, years to search. Specify plaintiff or defendant.

Hansford County

District Clerk's Office, Criminal Records
PO Box 397
Spearman, TX 79081
(806) 659-2666
FAx (806) 659-2025
Felony and misdemeanor records are available by mail or phone. No release necessary. $5.00 search fee. Search information required: name, years to search.

Civil records are available by mail or phone. No release necessary. No search fee. $1.00 fee per copy. $1.00 for certification. Search information required: name, date of birth, years to search. Specify plaintiff or defendant.

Hardeman County

District Clerk's Office, Criminal Records
PO Box 30
Quanah, TX 79252
(817) 663-2901
Felony and misdemeanor records are available by mail. No release necessary. $10.00 search fee. Certified or personal checks, payable to District Clerk. Search information required: name, SSN.

Civil records are available by mail. No release necessary. $10.00 search fee. $.25 fee per copy. $1.00 for certification. Search information required: name, date of birth, years to search. Specify plaintiff or defendant.

Hardin County

Felony records
District Clerk's Office, Criminal Records
PO Box 2997
Kountze, TX 77625
(409) 246-5150
Felony records are available by mail or phone. No release necessary. $1.00 fee for mail searches. No fee for phone searches. Certified check only, payable to District Clerk. Search information required: name, years to search.

Civil records
District Clerk's Office
PO Box 2997
Kountze, TX 77625
(409) 246-5150
Civil records are available by mail. No release necessary. $5.00 search fee. $1.00 fee per copy. $1.00 for certification. Search information required: name, date of birth, years to search. Specify plaintiff or defendant.

Misdemeanor records
County Clerk's Office
PO Box 38
Kountze, TX 77625
(409) 246-5185
Misdemeanor records are available by mail. $5.00 search fee. No release necessary. Search information required: name, offense, years to search.

Civil records
County Clerk's Office
PO Box 38
Kountze, TX 77625
(409) 246-5185
Civil records are available by mail or phone. No release necessary. No search fee. $1.00 fee per copy. $1.00 for certification. Search information required: name, date of birth, years to search. Specify plaintiff or defendant.

Harris County

District Clerk's Office, Correspondence
301 San Jacinto
Houston, TX 77002
(713) 221-5734
Felony and misdemeanor records are available by mail or phone. No release necessary. No search fee. Search information required: name, date of birth.

Civil records are available by mail or phone. No release necessary. No search fee. Search information required: name, date of birth, years to search. Specify plaintiff or defendant.

Harrison County

Felony records
District Clerk's Office, Criminal Records
Harrison County Courthouse
Marshall, TX 75670
(903) 935-4845 or 935-4846
Felony records are available by mail. No release necessary. $5.00 fee for 5 years searched, $10.00 fee over 5 years. Make check payable to District Clerk. Search information required: name, date of birth, SASE.

Civil records
District Clerk's Office
Harrison County Courthouse
Marshall, TX 75670
(903) 935-4845 or 935-4846
Civil records are available by mail. No release necessary. $5.00 fee for 5 years searched, $10.00 fee over 5 years. Search information required: name, date of birth, years to search, SASE. Specify plaintiff or defendant.

Misdemeanor records
County Clerk's Office
PO Box 1365
Marshall, TX 75671
(903) 938-4858
Misdemeanor records are available by mail. $2.00 search fee. Cashier's check or money order payable to County Clerk. Search information required: name, years to search, offense (if available).

Civil records
County Clerk's Office
PO Box 1365
Marshall, TX 75671
(903) 938-4858
Civil records are available by mail. No release necessary. $2.00 search fee. Search information required: name, date of birth, years to search. Specify plaintiff or defendant.

Hartley County

District Clerk's Office, Criminal
Records
PO Box T
Channing, TX 79018
(806) 235-3582
Felony and misdemeanor records are available by mail or phone. No release necessary. $5.00 search fee. Search information required: name, SSN.

Civil records are available by mail. No release necessary. $5.00 search fee. $1.00 fee per copy. $1.00 for certification. Search information required: name, date of birth, years to search. Specify plaintiff or defendant.

Haskell County

Felony records
District Clerk's Office, Criminal
Records
PO Box 27
Haskell, TX 79521
(817) 864-2030
Felony records are available by mail. A notarized release required. $5.00 search fee. Certified checks only, payable to District Clerk. Search information required: name, SASE.

Civil records
District Clerk's Office
PO Box 27
Haskell, TX 79521
(817) 864-2030
Civil records are available by mail. No release necessary. $5.00 search fee. $.50 fee per copy. $1.00 for certification. Search information required: name, date of birth, years to search, SASE. Specify plaintiff or defendant.

Misdemeanor records
County Clerk's Office
PO Box 725
Haskell, TX 79521
(817) 864-2451
Misdemeanor records are available by mail. No release necessary. $5.00 search fee. $1.00 fee per copy. $1.00 for certification. Search information required: name, years to search.

Civil records
County Clerk's Office
PO Box 725
Haskell, TX 79521
(817) 864-2451
Civil records are available by mail. No release necessary. $5.00 search fee. $1.00 fee per copy. $1.00 for certification. Search information required: name, date of birth, years to search. Specify plaintiff or defendant.

Hays County

Felony records
District Clerk's Office, Criminal
Records
Room 304, Hays County Courthouse
San Marcos, TX 78666
(512) 353-4346
Felony records are available by mail or phone. $5.00 search fee. $1.00 fee per copy. $1.00 for certification. Checks payable to District Clerk's Office. Search information required: name, date of birth, years to search.

Civil records
District Clerk's Office
Room 304, Hays County Courthouse
San Marcos, TX 78666
(512) 353-4346
Civil records are available by mail or phone. No release necessary. $5.00 search fee. $1.00 fee per copy. $1.00 for certification. Search information required: name, date of birth, years to search. Specify plaintiff or defendant.

Misdemeanor records
County Clerk's Office
Hays County Courthouse
San Marcos, TX 78666
(512) 396-2601
Fax (512) 396-2280
Misdemeanor records are available by mail. $5.00 search fee, prepaid. Checks payable to County Clerk. No release necessary. Search information required: name, years to search.

Civil records
County Clerk's Office
Hays County Courthouse
San Marcos, TX 78666
(512) 396-2601
Fax (512) 396-2280
Civil records are available by mail. No release necessary. $5.00 search fee, prepaid. Search information required: name, date of birth, years to search. Specify plaintiff or defendant.

Hemphill County

District Clerk's Office, Criminal
Records
PO Box 867
Canadian, TX 79014
(806) 323-6212
Felony and misdemeanor records are available by mail or phone. No release necessary. No search fee. Search information required: name, years to search.

Civil records are available by mail or phone. No release necessary. No search fee. $.40 fee per copy. $2.00 for first certification, $.40 each page thereafter. Search information required: name, date of birth, years to search. Specify plaintiff or defendant.

Henderson County

Felony records
District Clerk's Office, Kathryn
Bullock
Henderson County Courthouse
Athens, TX 75751
(903) 675-6115
Felony records are available by mail. No release necessary. $5.00 search fee. Certified check only, payable to District Clerk. Search information required: name, date of birth, SASE, years to search.

Civil records
District Clerk's Office,
Henderson County Courthouse
Athens, TX 75751
(903) 675-6115
Civil records are available by mail. No release necessary. $5.00 search fee. $1.00 fee per copy. $2.00 for certification. Search information required: name, date of birth, years to search, SASE. Specify plaintiff or defendant.

Misdemeanor records
County Clerk's Office
PO Box 632
Athens, TX 75751
(214) 675-6140
Misdemeanor records are available by mail or phone. No search fee. No release necessary. Search information required: name, date of birth, years to search.

Civil records
County Clerk's Office
PO Box 632
Athens, TX 75751
(214) 675-6140
Civil records are available by mail or phone. No release necessary. No search fee. Search information required: name, date of birth, years to search. Specify plaintiff or defendant.

Hidalgo County

Felony records
District Clerk's Office, Index Clerk
PO Box 87
100 S. Closner
Edinburg, TX 78540
(512) 318-2250
Fax (512) 380-6780
Felony records are available by mail or phone. No release necessary. $5.00 search fee. Company checks only, payable to District Clerk. Search information required: name.

Civil records
District Clerk's Office, Index Clerk
PO Box 87
100 S. Closner
Edinburg, TX 78540
(512) 318-2250
Fax (512) 380-6780
Civil records are available by mail. No release necessary. $5.00 search fee. $1.00 fee per copy. $2.00 for certification. Search information required: name, date of birth, years to search. Specify plaintiff or defendant.

Misdemeanor records
County Clerk's Office
PO Box 58
Edinburg, TX 78540
(512) 318-2100
Fax (512) 383-2751 or 318-2105
Misdemeanor records are available by mail, phone or fax. No search fee. No release necessary. Search information required: name, date of birth, date of offense.

Civil records
County Clerk's Office
PO Box 58
Edinburg, TX 78540
(512) 318-2100
Fax (512) 383-2751
Civil records are available by mail. No release necessary. No search fee. Search information required: name, date of birth, years to search. Specify plaintiff or defendant.

Hill County

District Clerk's Office, Criminal Records
PO Box 634
Hillsboro, TX 76645
(817) 582-3512

Felony and misdemeanor records are available by mail. No release necessary. $5.00 search fee. Certified check only, payable to District Clerk. Search information required: name, years to search.

Civil records are available by mail. No release necessary. No search fee. Search information required: name, date of birth, years to search. Specify plaintiff or defendant.

Hockley County

Felony records
District Clerk's Office, Criminal Records
Hockley County Courthouse #16
Levelland, TX 79336
(806) 894-8527

Felony records are available by mail or phone. No release necessary. No search fee. $1.00 fee per copy. $2.00 for certification. Search information required: name, case number if available, SASE.

Civil records
District Clerk's Office
Hockley County Courthouse #16
Levelland, TX 79336
(806) 894-8527

Civil records are available by mail or phone. No release necessary. No search fee. $1.00 fee per copy. $2.00 for certification. Search information required: name, date of birth, years to search. Specify plaintiff or defendant.

Misdemeanor records
County Clerk
Courthouse Box 13
Levelland, TX 79336
(806) 894-3185

Misdemeanor records are available by mail or phone. No search fee. No release necessary. Search information required: name, years to search.

Civil records
County Clerk
Courthouse Box 13
Levelland, TX 79336
(806) 894-3185

Civil records are available by mail or phone. No release necessary. No search fee. Search information required: name, date of birth, years to search. Specify plaintiff or defendant.

Hood County

Felony records
District Clerk's Office, Criminal Records
Hood County Courthouse, Room 21
Granbury, TX 76048
(817) 579-3236

Felony records are available by mail. No release necessary. $5.00 search fee. Make check payable to District Clerk. Search information required: name.

Civil records
District Clerk's Office
Hood County Courthouse, Room 21
Granbury, TX 76048
(817) 579-3236

Civil records are available by mail. A release is required. $5.00 search fee. $1.00 fee for first copy, $.75 each additional copy. $1.00 for certification. Search information required: name, date of birth, years to search. Specify plaintiff or defendant.

Misdemeanor records
County Clerk's Office
PO Box 339
Granbury, TX 76048
(817) 579-3222

Misdemeanor records are available by mail. $5.00 search fee. Checks payable to County Clerk. A release is required. Search information required: name, date of birth, driver's license number, case number (if available).

Civil records
County Clerk's Office
PO Box 339
Granbury, TX 76048
(817) 579-3222

Civil records are available by mail. No release necessary. $5.00 search fee. Search information required: name, date of birth, years to search. Specify plaintiff or defendant.

Hopkins County

Felony records
District Clerk's Office, Criminal Records
PO Box 391
Sulphur Springs, TX 75482
(903) 885-2656

Felony records are available by mail. No release necessary. $5.00 search fee. $1.00 fee per copy. $2.00 for certification. Checks payable to District Clerk. Search information required: name, years to search..

Civil records
District Clerk's Office
PO Box 391
Sulphur Springs, TX 75482
(903) 885-2656

Civil records are available by mail. No release necessary. $5.00 search fee. $1.00 fee per copy. $2.00 for certification. Search information required: name, date of birth, years to search. Specify plaintiff or defendant.

Misdemeanor records
County Clerk's Office
PO Box 288
Sulphur Springs, TX 75482
(903) 885-3929

Misdemeanor records are available by mail or phone. $5.00 search fee. No release necessary. Search information required: name, years to search.

Civil records
County Clerk's Office
PO Box 288
Sulphur Springs, TX 75482
(903) 885-3929

Civil records are available by mail. No release necessary. No search fee. $1.00 fee per copy. $2.00 for certification. Search information required: name, date of birth, years to search. Specify plaintiff or defendant.

Houston County

Felony records
District Clerk's Office, Criminal Records
Houston County Courthouse
Crockett, TX 75835
(409) 544-3256

Felony records are available by mail. No release necessary. $5.00 search fee. Checks payable to District Clerk. Search information required: name, date of birth, SASE.

Civil records
District Clerk's Office
Houston County Courthouse
Crockett, TX 75835
(409) 544-3256

Civil records are available by mail. A release is required. $5.00 search fee. $1.00 fee per copy. $1.00 for certification. Search information required: name, date of birth, years to search. Specify plaintiff or defendant.

Misdemeanor records
County Clerk's Office
PO Box 370
Crockett, TX 75835
(409) 544-3255 Ext. 31

Misdemeanor records are available by mail or phone. No search fee. A release is required. Search information required: full name, years to search.

Civil records
County Clerk's Office
PO Box 370
Crockett, TX 75835
(409) 544-3255 Ext. 31

Civil records are available by mail or phone. No release necessary. No search fee. $1.00 fee per copy. $1.00 for certification. Search information required: name, date of birth, years to search. Specify plaintiff or defendant.

Howard County

Felony records
District Clerk's Office, Criminal Records
PO Box 2138
Big Spring, TX 79721
(915) 267-6211

Felony records are available by mail or phone. No release necessary. $5.00 search fee. Search information required: name.

Civil records
District Clerk's Office
PO Box 2138
Big Spring, TX 79721
(915) 267-6211

Civil records are available by mail. No release necessary. $5.00 search fee. Search information required: name, date of birth, years to search. Specify plaintiff or defendant.

Misdemeanor records
County Clerk's Office
PO Box 1468
Big Spring, TX 79721
(915) 267-2881

Misdemeanor records available by mail or phone. No search fee. $1.00 fee per copy. $1.00 for certification. No release necessary. Search information required: name, offense (if available), years to search.

Civil records
County Clerk's Office
PO Box 1468
Big Spring, TX 79721
(915) 267-2881
Civil records are available by mail. No release necessary. $5.00 search fee. Search information required: name, date of birth, years to search. Specify plaintiff or defendant.

Hudspeth County

District Clerk's Office, Criminal Records
PO Drawer A
Sierra Blanca, TX 79851
(915) 369-2301
Fax (915) 369-2361
Felony and misdemeanor records are available by mail or phone. No release necessary. No search fee. $.50 fee per copy. $1.00 for certification. Search information required: name, years to search.

Civil records are available by mail or phone. No release necessary. No search fee. $.50 fee per copy. $1.00 for certification. Search information required: name, date of birth, years to search. Specify plaintiff or defendant.

Hunt County

Felony records
District Clerk's Office, Criminal Records
PO Box 1627
Greenville, TX 75401
(903) 455-4525
Felony records are available by mail. No release necessary. $5.00 search fee. Search information required: name, date of birth, SSN, case number (if available), years to search.

Civil records
District Clerk's Office
PO Box 1627
Greenville, TX 75401
(903) 455-4525
Civil records are available by mail. No release necessary. $5.00 search fee. $1.00 fee per copy. Search information required: name, date of birth, SSN, years to search, SASE. Specify plaintiff or defendant.

Misdemeanor records
County Clerk's Office
PO Box 1316
Greenville, TX 75401
(903) 455-6460
Misdemeanor records are available by mail or phone. $5.00 search fee. $1.00 fee per copied page. No release necessary. Search information required: name, offense, years to search.

Civil records
County Clerk's Office
PO Box 1316
Greenville, TX 75401
(903) 455-6460
Civil records are available by mail. No release necessary. $5.00 search fee. $1.00 fee per copy. Search information required: name, date of birth, years to search. Specify plaintiff or defendant.

Hutchinson County

Felony records
District Clerk's Office, Criminal Records
PO Box 580
Stinnett, TX 79083
(806) 878-2881
Felony records are available by mail or phone. A release is required. $5.00 search fee. Search information required: name.

Civil records
District Clerk's Office
PO Box 580
Stinnett, TX 79083
(806) 878-2881
Civil records are available by mail. A release is required. No search fee. $.25 fee per copy. $1.00 for certification. Search information required: name, date of birth, years to search. Specify plaintiff or defendant.

Misdemeanor records
County Clerk's Office
Drawer F
Stinnett, TX 79083
(806) 878-2829
Misdemeanor records are available by mail. A release is required. $5.00 search fee. $.50 fee per copied page. Search information required: name, years to search, SASE.

Civil records
County Clerk's Office
Drawer F
Stinnett, TX 79083
(806) 878-2829
Civil records are available by mail. A release is required. $5.00 search fee. $.50 fee per copy. Search information required: name, date of birth, years to search. Specify plaintiff or defendant.

Irion County

District County Clerk, Criminal Records
PO Box 736
Mertzon, TX 76941
(915) 835-2421
Felony and misdemeanor records are available by mail. No release necessary. $5.00 search fee. $1.00 fee per copy. $1.00 for certification. Search information required: name, years to search.

Civil records are available by mail. No release necessary. $5.00 search fee. $1.00 fee per copy. $1.00 for certification. Search information required: name, date of birth, years to search. Specify plaintiff or defendant.

Jack County

Felony records
District Clerk's Office, Criminal Records
Jack County Courthouse
Jacksboro, TX 76458
(817) 567-2141
Felony records are available by mail or phone. No release necessary. $10.00 search fee. Certified or personal checks, payable to District Clerk. Search information required: name, years to search.

Civil records
District Clerk's Office
Jack County Courthouse
Jacksboro, TX 76056
(817) 567-2141
Civil records are available by mail. No release necessary. $5.00 search fee. Search information required: name, date of birth, years to search. Specify plaintiff or defendant.

Misdemeanor records
County Clerk's Office
100 Main
Jacksboro, TX 76458
(817) 567-2111
Misdemeanor records are available by mail. No search fee. $.50 fee per page copy. $1.00 for certification, plus $1.00 per page. No release necessary. Search information required: name, case number, year of offense.

Civil records
County Clerk's Office
100 Main
Jacksboro, TX 76458
(817) 567-2111
Civil records are available by mail or phone. No release necessary. No search fee. $.50 fee per page copy. $1.00 for certification, plus $1.00 per page. Search information required: name, date of birth, years to search. Specify plaintiff or defendant.

Jackson County

Felony records
District Clerk's Office, Criminal Records
115 W. Main, Room 203
Edna, TX 77957
(512) 782-3812
Felony records are available by mail or phone. No release necessary. $5.00 search fee. $1.00 fee per copy. $1.00 for certification. Check or money order payable to District Clerk. Search information required: name, years to search.

Civil records
District Clerk's Office
115 W. Main, Room 203
Edna, TX 77957
(512) 782-3812
Civil records are available by mail or phone. No release necessary. $5.00 search fee. $1.00 fee per copy. $1.00 for certification. Search information required: name, date of birth, years to search. Specify reason for requesting records. Specify plaintiff or defendant.

Misdemeanor records
County Clerk's Office
115 W. Main
Edna, TX 77957
(512) 782-3563
Misdemeanor records are available by mail or phone. $5.00 search fee. $1.00 fee per copied page, $1.00 fee for certification. No release necessary. Search information required: name, years to search.

Civil records
County Clerk's Office
115 W. Main
Edna, TX 77957
(512) 782-3563
Civil records are available by mail. No release necessary. $5.00 search fee. $1.00 fee per copied page, $1.00 fee for certification. Search information required: name, date of birth, years to search. Specify plaintiff or defendant.

Jasper County

Felony records
District Clerk's Office, Criminal Records
202 County Courthouse
Jasper, TX 75951
(409) 384-2721
Felony records are available by mail or phone. No release necessary. $5.00 search fee. Search information required: name, SASE.

Civil records
District Clerk's Office
202 County Courthouse
Jasper, TX 75951
(409) 384-2721
Civil records are available by mail. No release necessary. $5.00 search fee. $1.00 fee per copied page, $1.00 fee for certification. Search information required: name, date of birth, years to search, SASE. Specify plaintiff or defendant.

Misdemeanor records
County Clerk's Office
Jasper County Courthouse, Room 104
Jasper, TX 75951
(409) 384-2632
Misdemeanor records are available by mail. $10.00 search fee. $1.00 fee per copied page. Checks payable to County Clerk. A release is required. Search information required: full name, date of birth, driver's license (if available).

Civil records
County Clerk's Office
Jasper County Courthouse, Room 104
Jasper, TX 75951
(409) 384-2632
Civil records are available by mail or phone. No release necessary. $10.00 search fee. $1.00 fee per copy. $1.00 for certification. Search information required: name, date of birth, years to search. Specify plaintiff or defendant.

Jeff Davis County

District Clerk's Office, Criminal Records
PO Box 398
Ft. Davis, TX 79734
(915) 426-3251
Felony and misdemeanor records are available by mail or phone. No release necessary. $5.00 search fee. $1.00 fee per copy. $1.00 for certification. Certified or personal checks, payable to Jeff Davis County District Clerk. Search information required: name, years to search.

Civil records are available by mail. No release necessary. $5.00 search fee. $1.00 fee per copy. $1.00 for certification. Search information required: name, date of birth, years to search. Specify plaintiff or defendant.

Jefferson County

Felony records
District Clerk's Office, Criminal Records
PO Box 3707
Beaumont, TX 77704
(409) 835-8580
Felony records are available by mail. No release necessary. $7.00 search fee. $.25 fee per copy. $1.00 for certification. Search information required: name, date of birth, SASE.

Civil records
District Clerk's Office
PO Box 3707
Beaumont, TX 77704
(409) 835-8580
Civil records are available by mail. No release necessary. $5.00 search fee. $.25 fee per copy. $1.00 for certification. Search information required: name, date of birth, years to search, SASE. Specify plaintiff or defendant.

Misdemeanor records
County Clerk's Office
PO Box 1151
Beaumont, TX 77704
(409) 835-8475
Misdemeanor records are available by mail. $1.00 fee per page copied if employer sends a case number. Search information required: name, date of birth, date of offense, case number, SASE. Specify plaintiff or defendant.

Civil records
County Clerk's Office
PO Box 1151
Beaumont, TX 77704
(409) 835-8475
Civil records are available in person only. See Texas state repository for additional information.

Jim Hogg County

District Clerk's Office, Criminal Records
PO Box 729
Hebbronville, TX 78361
(512) 527-4031
Fax (512) 527-4611
Felony and misdemeanor records are available by mail or phone. No release necessary. No search fee. $1.00 fee per copy. $1.00 for certification. Search information required: name, years to search.

Civil records are available by mail. No release necessary. No search fee. $1.00 fee per copy. $1.00 for certification. Search information required: name, date of birth, years to search. Specify plaintiff or defendant.

Jim Wells County

District Clerk's Office, Criminal Records
PO Box Drawer 2219
Alice, TX 78333
(512) 668-5717
Fax (512) 664-6855
Felony records are available by mail or fax. No release necessary. $5.00 search fee. $1.00 fee per copy. $1.00 for certification. Certified and personal checks, payable to District Clerk. Search information required: name, date of birth, years to search.

Civil records are available by mail. No release necessary. $5.00 search fee. $1.00 fee per copy. $1.00 for certification. Search information required: name, date of birth, years to search. Specify plaintiff or defendant.

Johnson County

District Clerk's Office, Criminal Records
PO Box 495
Cleburne, TX 76033
(817) 556-6835 or 556-6836
Felony and misdemeanor records are available by mail. No release necessary. $5.00 search fee. Certified checks only, payable to District Clerk. Search information required: name, years to search. For Misdemeanor inquiries mail to: Court at Law, PO Box 662, Cleburen, TX 76033.

Civil records are available by mail. No release necessary. $5.00 search fee. $1.00 fee for first copy, $.25 each additional copy. $2.00 for certification. Search information required: name, date of birth, years to search. Specify plaintiff or defendant.

Jones County

District Clerk's Office, Criminal Records
PO Box 308
Anson, TX 79501
(915) 823-3731
Felony and misdemeanor records are available by mail. A release is required. $5.00 search fee. $1.00 fee per copy. $2.00 for certification. Make check payable to District Clerk. Search information required: name, years to search.

Civil records are available by mail. A release is required. $5.00 search fee. $1.00 fee per copy. $2.00 for certification. Search information required: name, date of birth, years to search. Specify plaintiff or defendant.

Karnes County

Felony records
District Clerk's Office, Criminal Records
Karnes County Courthouse
Karnes City, TX 78118
(512) 780-2562
Felony records are available by mail or phone. No release necessary. No search fee. $1.00 fee per copy. $1.00 for certification. Certified or personal checks, payable to District Clerk. Search information required: name, previous address if available, years to search.

Civil records
District Clerk's Office
Karnes County Courthouse
Karnes City, TX 78118
(512) 780-2562
Civil records are available by mail. No release necessary. No search fee. $1.00 fee per copy. $1.00 for certification. Search information required: name, date of birth, years to search. Specify plaintiff or defendant.

Misdemeanor records
County Clerk's Office
Karnes County Courthouse
Karnes City, TX 78118
(512) 780-3939
Misdemeanor records are available by mail.
No search fee. No release necessary. Search
information required: name, date of birth.

Civilr records
County Clerk's Office
Karnes County Courthouse
Karnes City, TX 78118
(512) 780-3939
Civil records are available by mail. A release is required. No search fee. $1.00 fee
per copy. $2.00 for certification. Search in-
formation required: name, date of birth,
years to search. Specify plaintiff or defendant.

Kaufman County

Felony records
District Clerk's Office, Criminal
Records
Kaufman County Courthouse
Kaufman, TX 75142
(214) 932-4331 Ext. 133
Felony records are available by mail or
phone. No release necessary. $5.00 search
fee. Search information required: name,
SASE.

Civil records
District Clerk's Office
Kaufman County Courthouse
Kaufman, TX 75142
(214) 932-4331 Ext. 133
Civil records are available by mail. No release necessary. $5.00 search fee for each 5
years searched. $1.00 fee per copy. $2.00
for certification. Search information required: name, date of birth, years to search,
SASE. Specify plaintiff or defendant.

Misdemeanor records
County Clerk's Office
Kaufman County Courthouse
Kaufman, TX 75142
(214) 932-4331
Misdemeanor records are available by mail.
No search fee. No release necessary. Search
information required: name, years to
search.

Civil records
County Clerk's Office
Kaufman County Courthouse
Kaufman, TX 75142
(214) 932-4331
Civil records are available by mail. No release necessary. No search fee. $1.00 fee
per copy. $5.00 for certification. Search in-
formation required: name, date of birth,
years to search. Specify plaintiff or defendant.

Kendall County

Felony records
District Clerk's Office, Criminal
Records
204 E. San Antonio
Suite 3
Boerne, TX 78006
(512) 249-9343 Ext. 13
Felony records are available by mail. No re-
lease necessary. $5.00 search fee. Certified
or personal checks, payable to District
Clerk. Search information required: name.

Civil records
District Clerk's Office
204 E. San Antonio
Suite 3
Boerne, TX 78006
(512) 249-9343
Civil records are available by mail. No release necessary. $10.00 search fee. $1.00
fee per copy. $1.00 for certification. Search
information required: name, date of birth,
years to search. Specify plaintiff or defendant.

Misdemeanor records
County Clerk
204 E. San Antonio St.
Suite 2
Boerne, TX 78006
(512) 249-9343
Misdemeanor records are available by mail.
No search fee. No release necessary. Search
information required: name, years to
search.

Civil records
County Clerk
204 E. San Antonio St.
Suite 2
Boerne, TX 78006
(512) 249-9343
Civil records are available by mail. No release necessary. $10.00 search fee. $1.00
fee per copy. $1.00 for certification. Search
information required: name, date of birth,
years to search. Specify plaintiff or defendant.

Kenedy County

District Clerk's Office, Criminal
Records
PO Box 1519
Sarita, TX 78385
(512) 294-5220
Felony and misdemeanor records are available by mail or phone. No release necessary. $5.00 search fee. Certified checks
only, payable to District Clerk. Search information required: name.

Civil records are available by mail or
phone. No release necessary. $5.00 search
fee. $1.00 fee per copy. $1.00 for certification. Search information required: name,
date of birth, years to search. Specify plaintiff or defendant.

Kent County

District Clerk's Office, Criminal
Records
PO Box 9
Jayton, TX 79528
(806) 237-3881
Felony and misdemeanor records are avail-
able by mail. No release necessary. $5.00
search fee. $1.00 fee per copy. Certified
check only, payable to District Clerk.
Search information required: name.

Civil records are available by mail. No release necessary. No search fee. $1.00 fee
per copy. Search information required:
name, date of birth, years to search. Specify
plaintiff or defendant.

Kerr County

Felony records
District Clerk's Office, Criminal
Records
Kerr County Courthouse
Kerrville, TX 78028
(512) 257-4396
Felony records are available by mail or
phone. No release necessary. $5.00 search
fee. Certified or personal checks, payable to
District Clerk. Search information required:
name, years to search.

Civil records
District Clerk's Office
Kerr County Courthouse
Kerrville, TX 78028
(512) 257-4396
Civil records are available by mail or
phone. No release necessary. $5.00 search
fee. Search information required: name,
date of birth, years to search. Specify plaintiff or defendant.

Misdemeanor records
County Clerk's Office
Kerr County Courthouse
Kerrville, TX 78028
(512) 257-6181
Misdemeanor records are available by mail
or phone. $10.00 search fee for extensive
searches of 10 minutes or more. No fee otherwise. $.50 fee per copy. $1.00 for certification. No release necessary. Search information required: name, date of birth,
drivers license if available, years to search.

Civil records
County Clerk's Office
Kerr County Courthouse
Kerrville, TX 78028
(512) 257-6181
Civil records are available by mail or
phone. No release necessary. No search fee.
$.50 fee per copy. $1.00 for certification,
plus $1.00 per page. Search information re-
quired: name, date of birth, years to search.
Specify plaintiff or defendant.

Kimble County

Courthouse, Louise Oliver County
Clerk
501 Main Street
Junction, TX 76849
(915) 446-3353
Felony and misdemeanor records are available by mail. No search fee. No release necessary. Certified or personal checks payable
to Kimble County Clerk. Search information required: name, years to search.

Civil records are available by mail. No release necessary. No search fee. $1.00 fee
per copy. $2.00 for certification. Search in-
formation required: name, date of birth,
years to search. Specify plaintiff or defendant.

King County

District Clerk's Office, Criminal
Records
PO Box 71
Guthrie, TX 79236
(806) 596-4412
Felony and misdemeanor records are available by mail or phone. No release necessary. No search fee. Search information required: name.

Civil records are available by mail or phone. No release necessary. No search fee. $1.00 fee per copy. $1.00 for certification. Search information required: name, date of birth, years to search. Specify plaintiff or defendant.

Kinney County

District Clerk's Office, Criminal Records
PO Drawer 9
Bracketville, TX 78832
(512) 563-2521

Felony and misdemeanor records are available by mail or phone. Written request required. A release is required. $5.00 search fee. Certified check only, payable to District Clerk. Search information required: name, SSN, date of birth.

Civil records are available by mail. A release is required. $10.00 search fee. $1.00 fee per copy. $1.00 for certification. Search information required: name, date of birth, years to search. Specify plaintiff or defendant.

Kleberg County

Felony records
District Clerk's Office, Criminal Records
PO Box 312
Kingsville, TX 78364-0312
(512) 595-8561
Fax (512) 595-8525

Felony records are available by mail or phone. No release necessary. $10.00 search fee. Search information required: name.

Civil records
District Clerk's Office
PO Box 312
Kingsville, TX 78364-0312
(512) 595-8561
Fax (512) 595-8525

Civil records are available by mail. No release necessary. $5.00 search fee. $1.00 fee per copy. $1.00 for certification. Search information required: name, date of birth, years to search. Specify plaintiff or defendant.

Misdemeanor records
County Clerk's Office
PO Box 1327
Kingsville, TX 78364-1327
(512) 595-8548

Misdemeanor records are available by mail. $5.00 search fee. No release necessary. Search information required: name, years to search.

Civil records
County Clerk's Office
PO Box 1327
Kingsville, TX 78364-1327
(512) 595-8548

Civil records are available by mail. No release necessary. $10.00 search fee. Search information required: name, date of birth, years to search. Specify plaintiff or defendant.

Knox County

District Clerk's Office, Criminal Records
PO Box 196
Benjamin, TX 79505
(817) 454-2441

Felony and misdemeanor records are available by mail or phone. No release necessary. No search fee. Search information required: name.

Civil records are available by mail or phone. No release necessary. No search fee. $1.00 fee per copy. $1.00 for certification. Search information required: name, date of birth, years to search. Specify plaintiff or defendant.

La Salle County

Felony records
District Clerk's Office, Criminal Records
PO Box 340
Cotulla, TX 78014
(512) 879-2421

Felony records are available by mail or phone. No release necessary. No search fee. $1.00 fee per copy. $1.00 for certification. Search information required: name, years to search.

Civil records
District Clerk's Office
PO Box 340
Cotulla, TX 78014
(512) 879-2421

Civil records are available by mail. No release necessary. No search fee. $1.00 fee per copy. $1.00 for certification. Search information required: name, date of birth, years to search. Specify plaintiff or defendant.

Misdemeanor records
County Clerk's Office
PO Box 340
Cotulla, TX 78014
(512) 879-2117
Fax (512) 879-2713

Misdemeanor records are available by mail or phone. No search fee. $1.00 fee per copy. $1.00 for certification. Checks payable to County Clerk. No release necessary. Search information required: name, date of birth, years to search.

Civil records
County Clerk's Office
PO Box 340
Cotulla, TX 78014
(512) 879-2117
Fax (512) 879-2713

Civil records are available by mail. No release necessary. No search fee. $1.00 fee per copy. $1.00 for certification. Search information required: name, date of birth, years to search. Specify plaintiff or defendant.

Lamar County

Felony records
District Clerk's Office, Criminal Records
Lamar County Courthouse
Paris, TX 75460
(903) 737-2427

Felony records are available by mail. No release necessary. $5.00 search fee, $1.00 per page. Certified or personal checks, payable to District Clerk. Search information required: name, date of birth, sex and race.

Civil records
District Clerk's Office
Lamar County Courthouse
Paris, TX 75460
(903) 737-2427

Civil records are available by mail. No release necessary. $5.00 search fee, $1.00 per page. Search information required: name, date of birth, years to search. Specify plaintiff or defendant.

Misdemeanor records
County Clerk's Office
119 N. Main
Paris, TX 75460
(903) 737-2420

Misdemeanor records are available by mail. $10.00 search fee. $1.00 fee per copy. $1.00 for certification. Checks payable to County Clerk. No release necessary. Search information required: name, years to search.

Civil records
County Clerk's Office
119 N. Main
Paris, TX 75460
(903) 737-2420

Civil records are available by mail. No release necessary. $10.00 search fee. $1.00 fee per copy. $1.00 for certification. Search information required: name, date of birth, years to search. Specify plaintiff or defendant.

Lamb County

Felony records
District Clerk's Office, Criminal Records
PO Box 689
Littlefield, TX 79339-3366
(806) 385-3840

Felony records are available by mail or phone. No release necessary. $5.00 search fee. Search information required: name, years to search.

Civil records
District Clerk's Office
PO Box 689
Littlefield, TX 79339-3366
(806) 385-3840

Civil records are available by mail or phone. No release necessary. No search fee. Search information required: name, date of birth, years to search. Specify plaintiff or defendant.

Misdemeanor records
County Clerk's Office
Lamb County Courthouse, Room 103
Box 3
Littlefield, TX 79339-3366
(806) 385-5173

Misdemeanor records are available by mail. $5.00 search fee. $1.00 fee per copy. Checks payable to County Clerk. No release necessary. Search information required: name, years to search, address.

Civil records
County Clerk's Office
Lamb County Courthouse, Room 103
Box 3
Littlefield, TX 79339-3366
(806) 385-5173

Civil records are available by mail or phone. No release necessary. $5.00 search fee by phone. $1.00 fee per copy. $1.00 for certification. Search information required: name, date of birth, years to search. Specify plaintiff or defendant.

Lampasas County

Felony records
District Clerk's Office, Criminal Records
PO Box 327
Lampasas, TX 76550
(512) 556-8271 Ext. 22

Felony records are available by mail or phone. No release necessary. $5.00 search fee for extensive searches. Search information required: name, years to search.

Civil records
District Clerk's Office
PO Box 327
Lampasas, TX 76550
(512) 556-8271 Ext. 22
Civil records are available by mail or phone. No release necessary. $5.00 search fee for extensive searches. Search information required: name, date of birth, years to search. Specify plaintiff or defendant.

Misdemeanor records
County Clerk's Office
PO Box 347
Lampasas, TX 76550
(512) 556-8271 Ext. 37
Misdemeanor records are available by mail or phone. No search fee. $1.00 fee per copy. No release necessary. Search information required: name, years to search.

Civil records
County Clerk's Office
PO Box 347
Lampasas, TX 76550
(512) 556-8271 Ext. 37
Civil records are available by mail or phone. No release necessary. No search fee. $1.00 fee per copy.Search information required: name, date of birth, years to search. Specify plaintiff or defendant.

Lavaca County

Felony records
District Clerk's Office, Criminal Records
PO Box 306
Hallettsville, TX 77964
(512) 798-2351
Felony records are available by mail. No release necessary. $5.00 search fee. Certified or personal checks, payable to District Clerk. Search information required: name, case number (if available).

Civil records
District Clerk's Office
PO Box 306
Hallettsville, TX 77964
(512) 798-2351
Civil records are available by mail. No release necessary. $5.00 search fee. Search information required: name, date of birth, years to search. Specify plaintiff or defendant.

Misdemeanor records
County Clerk's Office
PO Box 326
Hallettsville, TX 77964
(512) 798-3612
Misdemeanor records are available by mail or phone. $5.00 search fee. No release necessary. Search information required: name, offense, years to search.

Civil records
County Clerk's Office
PO Box 326
Hallettsville, TX 77964
(512) 798-3612
Civil records are available by mail or phone. No release necessary. No search fee. Search information required: name, date of birth, years to search. Specify plaintiff or defendant.

Lee County

Felony records
District Clerk's Office, Criminal Records
PO Box 176
Giddings, TX 78942
(409) 542-2947
Fax (409) 542-2623
Felony records are available by mail or phone. No release necessary. $5.00 search fee. Search information required: name, years to search.

Civil records
District Clerk's Office
PO Box 176
Giddings, TX 78942
(409) 542-2947
Civil records are available by mail or phone. No release necessary. No search fee. Search information required: name, date of birth, years to search. Specify plaintiff or defendant.

Misdemeanor records
County Clerk's Office
PO Box 419
Giddings, TX 78942
(409) 542-3684
Misdemeanor records are available by mail or phone. $5.00 search fee. $1.00 fee per copy. No release necessary. Search information required: name, years to search.

Civil records
County Clerk's Office
PO Box 419
Giddings, TX 78942
(409) 542-3684
Civil records are available by mail. No release necessary. $5.00 search fee. $1.00 fee per copy. Search information required: name, date of birth, years to search. Specify plaintiff or defendant.

Leon County

Felony records
District Clerk's Office, Criminal Records
PO Box 39
Leon County
Centerville, TX 75833
(903) 536-2227
Felony records are available by mail. No release necessary. $5.00 search fee. Certified or personal checks, payable to District Clerk. Search information required: name, SASE, years to search.

Civil records
District Clerk's Office
PO Box 39
Leon County
Centerville, TX 75833
(903) 536-2227
Civil records are available by mail. No release necessary. $5.00 search fee. Search information required: name, date of birth, years to search. Specify plaintiff or defendant.

Misdemeanor records
County Clerk's Office
PO Box 98
Centerville, TX 75833
(903) 536-2352
Misdemeanor records are available by mail. $5.00 search fee. A release is required. Search information required: name, date of offense, years to search.

Civil records
County Clerk's Office
PO Box 98
Centerville, TX 75833
(903) 536-2352
Civil records are available by mail. No release necessary. $5.00 search fee. Search information required: name, date of birth, years to search. Specify plaintiff or defendant.

Liberty County

Felony records
District Clerk's Office, Criminal Records
1923 Sam Houston, Room 303
Liberty, TX 77575
(409) 336-8071 Extension 236
Felony records are available by mail. No release necessary. $5.00 search fee. Make check payable to District Clerk's Office. Search information required: name, years to search.

Civil records
District Clerk's Office
1923 Sam Houston, Room 303
Liberty, TX 77575
(409) 336-8071 Extension 236
Civil records are available by mail. No release necessary. $5.00 search fee. Search information required: name, date of birth, years to search. Specify plaintiff or defendant.

Misdemeanor records
County Clerk's Office
PO Box 369
Liberty, TX 77575
(409) 336-8071
Misdemeanor records are available in person only. See Texas state repository for additional information.

Civil records
County Clerk's Office
PO Box 369
Liberty, TX 77575
(409) 336-8071
Civil records are available in person only. See Texas state repository for additional information.

Limestone County

Felony records
District Clerk's Office, Criminal Records
PO Box 230
Groesbeck, TX 76642
(817) 729-3206
Felony records are available by mail or phone. No release necessary. No search fee. Search information required: name, years to search.

Civil records
District Clerk's Office
PO Box 230
Groesbeck, TX 76642
(817) 729-3206
Civil records are available by mail. No release necessary. No search fee. $1 .00 fee per copy. $2.00 for certification. Search information required: parties names, date of birth, case number, style of case, years to search.

Misdemeanor records
County Clerk's Office
PO Box 350
Groesbeck, TX 76642
(817) 729-5504
Misdemeanor records are available by mail or phone. No search fee. No release necessary. Search information required: name, date of birth, years to search.

Civil records
County Clerk's Office
PO Box 350
Groesbeck, TX 76642
(817) 729-5504
Civil records are available by mail. No release necessary. No search fee. $1.00 fee per copy. $2.00 for certification. Search information required: name, date of birth, years to search. Specify plaintiff or defendant.

Lipscomb County

District Clerk's Office, Criminal Records
PO Box 70
Lipscomb, TX 79056
(806) 862-3091
Fax (806) 862-2603
Felony and misdemeanor records are available by mail or phone. No release necessary. No search fee. Search information required: name, years to search.

Civil records are available by mail or phone. No release necessary. $5.00 search fee if case number is not furnished. $1.00 fee per copy. $1.00 for certification. Search information required: name, date of birth, years to search. Specify plaintiff or defendant.

Live Oak County

Felony records
District Clerk's Office, Criminal Records
PO Drawer O
George West, TX 78022
(512) 449-2733 Ext. 105
Felony records are available by mail or phone. No release necessary. No search fee. Search information required: name, date of birth.

Civil records
District Clerk's Office
PO Drawer O
George West, TX 78022
(512) 449-2733
Civil records are available by mail. No release necessary. $5.00 search fee if cause number is not furnished. Search information required: name, date of birth, years to search. Specify plaintiff or defendant.

Misdemeanor records
County Clerk
PO Box 280
George West, TX 78022
(512) 449-2733 Ext. 103
Misdemeanor records are available by mail. A release is required. $10.00 search fee. Checks payable to County Clerk. Search information required: name, date of birth.

Civil records
County Clerk
PO Box 280
George West, TX 78022
(512) 449-2733
Civil records are available by mail. A release is required. $10.00 search fee. $1.00 fee per copy. $1.00 for certification. Search information required: name, date of birth, years to search. Specify plaintiff or defendant.

Llano County

Felony records
District Clerk's Office, Criminal Records
Llano County Courthouse
801 Ford, Room 209
Llano, TX 78643
(915) 247-5036
Felony records are available by mail. No release necessary. $1.00 fee per year searched. Certified check only, payable to District Clerk. Search information required: name, SASE.

Civil records
District Clerk's Office
Llano County Courthouse
801 Ford, Room 209
Llano, TX 78643
(915) 247-5036
Civil records are available by mail. No release necessary. $5.00 search fee. $1.00 fee per copy. $2.00 for certification. Search information required: name, date of birth, years to search, SASE. Specify plaintiff or defendant.

Misdemeanor records
County Clerk's Office
107 W. Sandstone
Llano, TX 78643
(915) 247-4455
Misdemeanor records are available by mail. $5.00 search fee. A release is required. Search information required: name, date of birth, sex, race, years to search.

Civil records
County Clerk's Office
107 W. Sandstone
Llano, TX 78643
(915) 247-4455
Civil records are available by mail or phone. No release necessary. No search fee. $1.00 fee per copy. $1.00 for certification. Search information required: name, date of birth, years to search. Specify plaintiff or defendant.

Loving County

District Clerk's Office, Criminal Records
Loving County Courthouse
Box 194
Mentone, TX 79754
(915) 377-2441
Felony and misdemeanor records are available by mail or phone. No release necessary. $5.00 search fee. $.25 fee per copy. $1.00 for certification plus $1.00 per page. Search information required: name, date of birth, years to search.

Civil records are available by mail. No release necessary. $5.00 search fee. $.25 fee per copy. $1.00 for certification plus $1.00 per page. Search information required: name, date of birth, years to search. Specify plaintiff or defendant.

Lubbock County

Felony records
District Clerk's Office, Criminal Records
Room 305 Courthouse
PO Box 10536
Lubbock, TX 79408
(806) 767-1311
Felony records are available by mail or phone. No release necessary. No search fee. $5.00 fee for searching records prior to 1978. $1.00 fee for first copy, $.25 each additional copy. $1.00 for certification. Certified or personal checks, payable to District Clerk. Search information required: name, years to search.

Civil records
District Clerk's Office
Room 305 Courthouse
PO Box 10536
Lubbock, TX 79408
(806) 767-1311
Civil records are available by mail. No release necessary. No search fee. $1.00 fee for first copy, $.25 each additional copy. $1.00 for certification. Search information required: name, date of birth, years to search. Specify plaintiff or defendant.

Misdemeanor records
County Clerk's Office
Lubbock County Courthouse
PO Box 10536, Room 207
Lubbock, TX 79408
(806) 741-1004
Misdemeanor records are available by mail. $5.00 fee for searches up to ten years. Over ten years fee is $7.00. Checks payable to County Clerk. No release necessary. Search information required: name, years to search, date of birth.

Civil records
County Clerk's Office
Lubbock County Courthouse
PO Box 10536, Room 207
Lubbock, TX 79408
(806) 741-1051
Civil records are available by mail. No release necessary. $5.00 search fee. $1.00 fee per copy. $1.00 for certification. Checks payable to County Clerk. Search information required: name, date of birth if available, years to search. Specify plaintiff or defendant.

Lynn County

Felony records
District Clerk's Office, Criminal Records
PO Box 1142
Tahoka, TX 79373
(806) 998-4274
Felony records are available by mail or phone. No release necessary. No search fee. $1.00 fee per copy. $1.00 for certification. Search information required: name, years to search.

Civil records
District Clerk's Office
PO Box 1142
Tahoka, TX 79373
(806) 998-4274
Civil records are available by mail. No release necessary. No search fee. $1.00 fee per copy. $1.00 for certification. Search information required: name, date of birth, years to search. Specify plaintiff or defendant.

Misdemeanor records
County Clerk's Office
PO Box 937
Tahoka, TX 79373
(806) 998-4750
Misdemeanor records are available by mail or phone. No search fee. $1.00 fee per copied page. Search information required: name, SASE.

Civil records
County Clerk's Office
PO Box 937
Tahoka, TX 79373
(806) 998-4750
Civil records are available by mail. No release necessary. No search fee. $1.00 fee per copy. $1.00 for certification plus $1.00 per page. Search information required: name, date of birth, years to search, SASE. Specify plaintiff or defendant.

Madison County

District Clerk's Office, Criminal Records
Madison Courthouse, Room 226
Madisonville, TX 77864
(409) 348-9203
Felony records are available by mail. A release is required. $5.00 search fee. Checks payable to District Clerk. Search information required: name, SSN, date of birth.

Civil records are available by mail. No release necessary. No search fee. $1.00 fee per copy. $1.00 for certification. Search information required: name, date of birth, years to search. Specify plaintiff or defendant.

Marion County

Felony records
District Clerk's Office, Criminal Records
PO Box 628
Jefferson, TX 75657
(214) 665-2441 or 2013
Felony records are available by mail. A release is required. $5.00 search fee. Certified check only, payable to District Clerk. Search information required: name, SSN, date of birth, address.

Civil records
District Clerk's Office
PO Box 628
Jefferson, TX 75657
(214) 665-2441 or 2013
Civil records are available by mail. A release is required. $5.00 search fee. Search information required: name, date of birth, years to search, address, SSN. Specify plaintiff or defendant.

Misdemeanor records
County Clerk's Office
PO Drawer F
Jefferson, TX 75657
(903) 665-3971
Misdemeanor records are available by mail. No search fee. No release necessary. Search information required: name, offense, year of offense.

Martin County

Felony records
District Clerk's Office, Criminal Records
PO Box 906
Stanton, TX 79782
(915) 756-3412
Felony records are available by mail or phone. No release necessary. $5.00 search fee. Certified check only, payable to District Court Clerk. Search information required: name, SSN, date of birth, sex, years to search.

Civil records
District Clerk's Office
PO Box 906
Stanton, TX 79782
(915) 756-3412
Civil records are available by mail or phone. No release necessary. $5.00 search fee. $1.00 fee per copy. $1.00 for certification. Search information required: name, date of birth, years to search. Specify plaintiff or defendant.

Misdemeanor records
County Clerk's Office
PO Box 906
Stanton, TX 79782
(915) 756-3412
Misdemeanor records are available by mail. $5.00 search fee. No release necessary. Search information required: name, years to search.

Civil records
County Clerk's Office
PO Box 906
Stanton, TX 79782
(915) 756-3412
Civil records are available by mail. No release necessary. $5.00 search fee. $1.00 fee per copy. $1.00 for certification. Search information required: name, date of birth, years to search. Specify plaintiff or defendant.

Mason County

District Clerk's Office, Criminal Records
PO Box 702
Mason, TX 76856
(915) 347-5253
Felony and misdemeanor records are available by mail. No release necessary. $10.00 search fee. Make check payable to District Clerk. Search information required: name, SSN, date of birth, sex.

Civil records are available by mail. No release necessary. $10.00 search fee. $1.00 fee per copy. $1.00 for certification. Search information required: name, date of birth, years to search. Specify plaintiff or defendant.

Matagorda County

Felony records
District Clerk's Office, Criminal Records
PO Drawer 188
Bay City, TX 77414
(409) 244-7621
Felony records are available by mail. No release necessary. $5.00 search fee. Certified or personal checks, payable to District Clerk. Search information required: name, years to search, SASE.

Civil records
District Clerk's Office
PO Drawer 188
Bay City, TX 77414
(409) 244-7621
Civil records are available by mail. No release necessary. $5.00 search fee. $1.00 fee per copy. $1.00 for certification. Search information required: name, date of birth, years to search. Specify plaintiff or defendant.

Misdemeanor records
County Clerk's Office
PO Box 69
Bay City, TX 77414
(409) 244-7680
Misdemeanor records are available by mail. $5.00 search fee. Make checks payable to County Clerk. No release necessary. Search information required: name, date of offense, years to search.

Civil records
County Clerk's Office
PO Box 69
Bay City, TX 77414
(409) 244-7680
Civil records are available by mail. No release necessary. $5.00 search fee. $1.00 fee per copy. $1.00 for certification. Search information required: name, date of birth, years to search. Specify plaintiff or defendant.

Maverick County

Felony records
District Clerk's Office, Criminal Records
PO Box 3659
Eagle Pass, TX 78853
(512) 773-2629
Felony records are available by mail. No release necessary. $5.00 search fee. Make check payable to District Clerk. Search information required: name, date of birth.

Civil records
District Clerk's Office
PO Box 3659
Eagle Pass, TX 78853
(512) 773-2629
Civil records are available by mail. No release necessary. $5.00 search fee. $1.00 fee per copy. $1.00 for certification. Search information required: name, date of birth, years to search. Specify plaintiff or defendant.

Misdemeanor records
County Clerk's Office
PO Box 4050
Eagle Pass, TX 78853
(512) 773-2829
Misdemeanor records are available by mail. $5.00 search fee. $1.00 fee per copy. $1.00 for certification. No release necessary. Search information required: name, years to search.

Civil records
County Clerk's Office
PO Box 4050
Eagle Pass, TX 78853
(512) 773-2829
Civil records are available by mail. No release necessary. $5.00 search fee. $1.00 fee per copy. $1.00 for certification. Search information required: name, date of birth, years to search. Specify plaintiff or defendant.

McCulloch County

Felony records
District Clerk's Office, Criminal
Records
McCulloch County Courthouse
Room 205
Brady, TX 76825
(915) 597-0733
Felony records are available by mail or
phone. No release necessary. $10.00 search
fee. $1.00 fee per copy. $1.00 for certification. Search information required: name,
date of birth, years to search, year of offense (if available).

Civil records
District Clerk's Office
McCulloch County Courthouse
Room 205
Brady, TX 76825
(915) 597-0733
Civil records are available by mail. No release necessary. $10.00 search fee. $1.00
fee per copy. $1.00 for certification. Search
information required: name, date of birth,
years to search. Specify plaintiff or defendant.

Misdemeanor records
County Clerk's Office
McCulloch County Courthouse
Brady, TX 76825
(915) 597-0733
Misdemeanor records are available by mail.
No search fee. No release necessary. Search
information required: name, date of of-
fense.

Civil records
County Clerk's Office
McCulloch County Courthouse
Brady, TX 76825
(915) 597-0733
Civil records are available by mail. No release necessary. $10.00 search fee. $1.00
fee per copy. $1.00 for certification. Search
information required: name, date of birth,
years to search. Specify plaintiff or defendant.

McLennan County

District Clerk's Office, Criminal
Records
PO Box 2451
Waco, TX 76703
(817) 757-5054
Fax (817) 757-5060
Felony records are available by mail. No re-
lease necessary. $5.00 search fee. Make
check payable to District Clerk. Search in-
formation required: name, date of birth,
SSN, SASE.

Civil records are available by mail. No release necessary. $5.00 search fee. $.15 fee
per copy. $1.00 for certification. Search in-
formation required: name, date of birth,
years to search, SASE. Specify plaintiff or
defendant.

McMullen County

District Clerk's Office, Criminal
Records
PO Box 235
Tilden, TX 78072
(512) 274-3215
Fax (512) 274-3618
Felony and misdemeanor records are available by mail or phone. No release necessary. $5.00 search fee. Company checks
only, payable to District Clerk. Search information required: name, years to search.

Civil records are available by mail. No release necessary. $5.00 search fee. $1.00 fee
per copy. $2.00 for certification. Search in-
formation required: name, date of birth,
years to search. Specify plaintiff or defendant.

Medina County

Criminal Records
District Court
Medina County Courthouse
Hondo, TX 78861
(512) 426-5381
Felony and misdemeanor records are available by mail. No release necessary. $5.00
search fee. Company checks only, payable
to Medina County District Clerk. Search information required: name, years to search.

Civil records are available by mail or
phone. No release necessary. No search fee.
$.50 fee per copy. $1.00 for certification
plus $1.00 per page. Search information re-
quired: name, date of birth, years to search.
Specify plaintiff or defendant.

Menard County

District Clerk's Office, Criminal
Records
PO Box 1028
Menard, TX 76859
(915) 396-4682
Felony and misdemeanor records are avail-
able by mail or phone. No release neces-
sary. No search fee. $1.00 fee per copy.
Search information required: name, SSN,
driver's license.

Civil records are available by mail or
phone. No release necessary. No search fee.
$1.00 fee per copy. $1.00 for certification.
Search information required: name, date of
birth, years to search. Specify plaintiff or
defendant.

Midland County

Felony records
District Clerk's Office, Criminal
Records
PO Box 1922
Midland, TX 79702
(915) 688-1107
Fax (915) 688-1218
Felony records are available by mail. $5.00
search fee. No release necessary. Search in-
formation required: name, years to search.

Civil records
District Clerk's Office
PO Box 1922
Midland, TX 79702
(915) 688-1107
Fax (915) 688-1218
Civil records are available by mail. No re-
lease necessary. $5.00 search fee. $1.00 fee
per copy. $1.00 for certification. Search in

formation required: name, date of birth,
years to search. Specify plaintiff or defendant.

Misdemeanor records
County Clerk's Office
PO Box 211
Midland, TX 79702
(915) 688-1070
Fax (915) 688-8973
Misdemeanor records are available by mail
or phone. $5.00 search fee. No release nec-
essary. Search information required: name,
date of birth, SASE, date of offense, years
to search.

Civil records
County Clerk's Office
PO Box 211
Midland, TX 79702
(915) 688-1070
Fax (915) 688-8973
Civil records are available by mail. No release necessary. $5.00 search fee. $1.00 fee
per copy. $1.00 for certification. Search in-
formation required: name, date of birth,
years to search, SASE. Specify plaintiff or
defendant.

Milam County

Felony records
District Clerk's Office, Criminal
Records
PO Box 999
Cameron, TX 76520
(817) 697-3952
Fax (817) 697-4433
Felony records are available by mail or
phone. A release is required. $5.00 search
fee. Certified or personal checks, payable to
District Clerk. Search information required:
name.

Civil records
District Clerk's Office
PO Box 999
Cameron, TX 76520
(817) 697-3952
Civil records are available by mail. No release necessary. $5.00 search fee. $1.00 fee
per copy. $1.00 for certification. Search in-
formation required: name, date of birth,
years to search. Specify plaintiff or defendant.

Misdemeanor records
County Clerk's Office
PO Box 191
Cameron, TX 76520
(817) 697-6596
Fax (817) 697-4433
Misdemeanor records are available by mail
or phone. No search fee. $1.00 fee per copy.
A release is required. Search information
required: name, address, date of offense.

Civil records
County Clerk's Office
PO Box 191
Cameron, TX 76520
(817) 697-6596
Fax (817) 697-4433
Civil records are available by mail. A release is required. No search fee. $1.00 fee
per copy. $1.00 for certification. Search in-
formation required: name, date of birth,
years to search. Specify plaintiff or defendant.

Mills County

District Clerk's Office, Criminal Records
PO Box 646
Goldthwaite, TX 76844
(915) 648-2711
Felony and misdemeanor records are available by mail. No release necessary. $5.00 search fee. Checks payable to District Clerk. Search information required: name, years to search.

Civil records are available by mail. No release necessary.$5.00 search fee. $1.00 fee per copy. $2.00 for certification. Search information required: name, date of birth, years to search. Specify plaintiff or defendant.

Mitchell County

Felony records
District Clerk's Office
Mitchell County Courthouse
Colorado City, TX 79512
(915) 728-5918
Felony records are available by mail. No release necessary. $5.00 search fee. $1.00 fee per copy. $1.00 for certification. Search information required: name, years to search.

Civil records
District Clerk's Office
Mitchell County Courthouse
Colorado City, TX 79512
(915) 728-5918
Civil records are available by mail. No release necessary. $5.00 search fee. $1.00 fee per copy. $1.00 for certification. Search information required: name, date of birth, years to search. Specify plaintiff or defendant.

Misdemeanor records
County Clerk's Office
PO Box 1166
Colorado City, TX 79512
(915) 728-3481
Fax (915) 728-8697
Misdemeanor records are available by mail. A release is required. No search fee. $3.00 for certification. Search information required: name, years to search.

Civil records
County Clerk's Office
PO Box 1166
Colorado City, TX 79512
(915) 728-3481
Civil records are available by mail. A release is required. No search fee. $3.00 for certification. Search information required: name, date of birth, years to search. Specify plaintiff or defendant.

Montague County

Felony records
District Clerk's Office, Criminal Records
PO Box 155
Montague, TX 76251
(817) 894-2571
Felony records are available by mail or phone. No release necessary. No search fee. $1.00 fee per copy. $1.00 for certification. Search information required: name, years to search.

Civil records
District Clerk's Office
PO Box 155
Montague, TX 76251
(817) 894-2571
Civil records are available by mail or phone. No release necessary. No search fee. $1.00 fee per copy. $1.00 for certification. Search information required: name, date of birth, years to search. Specify plaintiff or defendant.

Misdemeanor records
County Clerk's Office
PO Box 77
Montague, TX 76251
(817) 894-2461
Misdemeanor records are available by mail. $5.00 search fee. $1.00 fee per copy. $1.00 for certification. No release necessary. Search information required: name, date of offense if available, years to search.

Civil records
County Clerk's Office
PO Box 77
Montague, TX 76251
(817) 894-2461
Civil records are available by mail. No release necessary. $5.00 search fee. $1.00 fee per copy. $1.00 for certification. Search information required: name, date of birth, years to search. Specify plaintiff or defendant.

Montgomery County

Felony records
District Clerk's Office, Criminal Records
PO Box 2985
Conroe, TX 77305
(409) 539-7855 or 760-6931
Felony records are available by mail. No release necessary. No search fee. Search information required: name, SASE.

Civil records
District Clerk's Office
PO Box 2985
Conroe, TX 77305
(409) 539-7855
Civil records are available by mail. No release necessary. $5.00 search fee. $1.00 fee per copy. Search information required: name, date of birth, years to search, SASE. Specify plaintiff or defendant.

Misdemeanor records
County Clerk's Office
PO Box 959
Conroe, TX 77305-0959
(409) 539-7885
Misdemeanor records are available by mail or phone. No search fee. $1.00 fee per copy. $2.00 for certification. No release necessary. Search information required: name, date of birth, years to search.

Civil records
County Clerk's Office
PO Box 959
Conroe, TX 77305-0959
(409) 539-7889
Civil records are available by mail or phone. No release necessary. No search fee. $1.00 fee per copy. $2.00 for certification. Search information required: name, date of birth, years to search. Specify plaintiff or defendant.

Moore County

Felony records
District Clerk's Office, Criminal Records
715 Dumas Ave. #105
Dumas, TX 79029
(806) 935-4218
Fax (806) 935-2699
Felony records are available by mail, phone or fax. No release necessary. $5.00 search fee. $1.00 fee per copy. $1.00 for certification. Search information required: name, years to search.

Civil records
District Clerk's Office
715 Dumas Ave. #109
Dumas, TX 79029
(806) 935-4218
Fax (806) 935-2699
Civil records are available by mail, phone or fax. No release necessary. $5.00 search fee. $1.00 fee per copy. $1.00 for certification. Search information required: name, date of birth, years to search. Specify plaintiff or defendant.

Misdemeanor records
County Clerk's Office
PO Box 396
Dumas, TX 79029
(806) 935-6164
Fax (806) 935-2699
Misdemeanor records are available by mail or fax. A release is required. 5.00 search fee. $1.00 fee per copy. $5.00 fee plus $1.00 per page for fax response. Search information required: full name, years to search.

Civil records
County Clerk's Office
PO Box 396
Dumas, TX 79029
(806) 935-6164
Fax (806) 935-2699
Civil records are available by mail. No release necessary. $5.00 search fee. $1.00 fee per copy. $1.00 for certification. Search information required: name, date of birth, years to search. Specify plaintiff or defendant.

Morris County

Felony records
District Clerk's Office, Criminal Records
500 Brodnax
Daingerfield, TX 75638
(903) 645-2321
Felony records are available by mail or phone. No release necessary. $5.00 search fee. $1.00 fee per copy. $1.00 for certification. Search information required: name, years to search.

Civil records
District Clerk's Office
500 Brodnax
Daingerfield, TX 75638
(903) 645-2321
Civil records are available by mail or phone. No release necessary. $5.00 search fee. $1.00 fee per copy. $1.00 for certification. Search information required: name, date of birth, years to search. Specify plaintiff or defendant.

Misdemeanor records
County Clerk's Office
500 Brodnax
Daingerfield, TX 75638
(214) 645-3911
Misdemeanor records are available by mail. $5.00 search fee. A release is required. Search information required: full name, years to search.

Motley County

District Clerk's Office, Criminal Records
PO Box 66
Matador, TX 79244
(806) 347-2621
Felony and misdemeanor records are available by mail or phone. $10.00 search fee. Copies are $1.00 per page ($1.00 if certified). Search information required: name.

Civil records are available by mail. No release necessary. $10.00 search fee. $.50 fee per copy. $1.00 for certification. Search information required: name, date of birth, years to search. Specify plaintiff or defendant.

Nacogdoches County

Felony records
District Clerk's Office, Criminal Records
101 West Main Street
Nacogdoches, TX 75961
(409) 560-7730
Felony records are available by mail or by phone from 1986 forward. No release necessary. $5.00 search fee. Certified or personal checks, payable to District Clerk. Search information required: name.

Civil records
District Clerk's Office
101 West Main Street
Nacogdoches, TX 75961
(409) 560-7730
Civil records are available by mail. No release necessary. $5.00 search fee. $1.00 fee per copy. $1.00 for certification. Search information required: name, date of birth, years to search. Specify plaintiff or defendant.

Misdemeanor records
County Clerk's Office
101 West Main
Nacogdoches, TX 75961
(409) 560-7733
Misdemeanor records are available by mail or by phone from 1986 forward. $5.00 search fee. $1.00 fee per copy. $2.00 for certification. Make checks payable to County Clerk. No release necessary. Search information required: name, years to search, year of offense.

Civil records
County Clerk's Office
101 West Main
Nacogdoches, TX 75961
(409) 560-7733
Civil records are available by mail or phone. No release necessary. $5.00 search fee. $1.00 fee per copy. $2.00 for certification. Search information required: name, date of birth, years to search. Specify plaintiff or defendant.

Navarro County

Felony records
District Clerk's Office, Criminal Records
PO Box 1439
Corsicana, TX 75151-1439
(903) 654-3040
Felony records are available by mail or phone. No release necessary. $5.00 search fee. All checks accepted, payable to District Clerk. Search information required: name, years to search.

Civil records
District Clerk's Office
PO Box 1439
Corsicana, TX 75151-1439
(903) 654-3040
Civil records are available by mail or phone. No release necessary. $5.00 search fee. Search information required: name, date of birth, years to search. Specify plaintiff or defendant.

Misdemeanor records
County Clerk's Office
PO Box 423
Corsicana, TX 75110
(903) 654-3035
Misdemeanor records are available by mail. $5.00 search fee. No release necessary. Search information required: name, years to search.

Civil records
County Clerk's Office
PO Box 423
Corsicana, TX 75110
(903) 654-3035
Civil records are available by mail. No release necessary. $5.00 fee per 10 years searched. $1.00 fee per copy. $2.00 for certification. Search information required: name, date of birth, years to search. Specify plaintiff or defendant.

Newton County

Felony records
District Clerk's Office, Criminal Records
PO Box 535
Newton, TX 75966
(409) 379-3951
Felony records are available by mail. No release necessary. $5.00 search fee. Certified check only, payable to Newton District Clerk. Search information required: name, years to search, SASE.

Civil records
District Clerk's Office
PO Box 535
Newton, TX 75966
(409) 379-3951
Civil records are available by mail. No release necessary. $5.00 search fee. $1.00 fee per copy. $1.00 for certification. Search information required: name, date of birth, years to search, SASE. Specify plaintiff or defendant.

Misdemeanor records
County Clerk's Office
PO Box 484
Newton, TX 75966
(409) 379-5341
Misdemeanor records are available by mail. $5.00 fee for extensive searches. $1.00 fee per copy. $2.00 for certification. No release necessary. Search information required: name, years to search.

Civil records
County Clerk's Office
PO Box 484
Newton, TX 75966
(409) 379-5341
Civil records are available by mail. No release necessary. $5.00 fee for extensive searches. $1.00 fee per copy. $2.00 for certification. Search information required: name, date of birth, years to search. Specify plaintiff or defendant.

Nolan County

Felony records
District Clerk's Office, Criminal Records
PO Box 1236
Sweetwater, TX 79556
(915) 235-2111
Felony records are available by mail or phone. No release necessary. $5.00 search fee. Search information required: name, SASE.

Civil records
District Clerk's Office
PO Box 1236
Sweetwater, TX 79556
(915) 235-2111
Civil records are available by mail. No release necessary. $5.00 search fee. $1.00 fee for first copy, $.50 each additional copy. $1.00 for certification. Search information required: name, date of birth, years to search, SASE. Specify plaintiff or defendant.

Misdemeanor records
County Clerk's Office
PO Drawer 98
Sweetwater, TX 79556
(915) 235-2462
Misdemeanor records are available by mail. $5.00 search fee. $1.00 fee per copy. $3.00 for certification. No release necessary. Search information required: name, years to search.

Civil records
County Clerk's Office
PO Drawer 98
Sweetwater, TX 79556
(915) 235-2462
Civil records are available by mail. No release necessary. $5.00 search fee. $1.00 fee per copy. $3.00 for certification. Search information required: name, date of birth, years to search. Specify plaintiff or defendant.

Nueces County

Felony records
District Clerk's Office, Criminal Records
PO Box 2987
Corpus Christi, TX 78403
(512) 888-0450
Felony records are available by mail. No release necessary. $5.00 search fee. Certified or personal checks, payable to District Clerk. Search information required: name, date of birth.

Civil records
District Clerk's Office
PO Box 2987
Corpus Christi, TX 78403
(512) 888-0450
Civil records are available by mail. No release necessary. $5.00 search fee. $.25 fee per copy. $1.00 for certification. Search information required: name, date of birth, years to search. Specify plaintiff or defendant.

Misdemeanor records
County Clerk's Office
PO Box 2627
Corpus Christi, TX 78403
(512) 888-0757
Misdemeanor records are available by mail. $5.00 search fee. Checks payable to County Clerk. No release necessary. Search information required: name, date of birth, date of offense, years to search.

Civil records
County Clerk's Office
PO Box 2627
Corpus Christi, TX 78403
(512) 888-0757
Civil records are available by mail. No release necessary. 5.00 search fee. $1.00 fee per copy. $1.00 for certification. Search information required: name, date of birth, years to search. Specify plaintiff or defendant.

Ochiltree County

Felony records
District Clerk's Office, Criminal Records
511 S. Main
Perryton, TX 79070
(806) 435-8160
Felony records are available by mail. No release necessary. $5.00 search fee. $1.00 fee per copy. $1.00 for certification. Search information required: name, date of birth, years to search.

Civil records
District Clerk's Office
511 S. Main
Perryton, TX 79070
(806) 435-8160
Civil records are available by mail. No release necessary. $5.00 search fee. $1.00 fee per copy. $1.00 for certification. Search information required: name, date of birth, years to search. Specify plaintiff or defendant.

Misdemeanor records
County Clerk's Office
511 South Main
Perryton, TX 79070
(806) 435-8105
Misdemeanor records are available by mail. No search fee. No release necessary. Search information required: name, years to search.

Civil records
County Clerk's Office
511 South Main
Perryton, TX 79070
(806) 435-8105
Civil records are available by mail. No release necessary. No search fee. $1.00 fee per copy. $1.00 for certification. Search information required: name, date of birth, years to search. Specify plaintiff or defendant.

Oldham County

District Clerk's Office, Criminal Records
PO Box 469
Vega, TX 79092
(806) 267-2667
Felony and misdemeanor records are available by mail or phone. No release necessary. No search fee. $1.00 fee per copy. $1.00 for certification. Make check payable to District Clerk. Search information required: name, date of birth, SSN, years to search.

Civil records are available by mail or phone. No release necessary. No search fee. $1.00 fee per copy. $1.00 for certification. Search information required: name, SSN, date of birth, years to search. Specify plaintiff or defendant.

Orange County

Felony records
District Clerk's Office, Criminal Records
PO Box 427
Orange, TX 77630
(409) 883-7740 Ext. 298
Fax (409) 883-4449
Felony records are available by mail. No release necessary. $5.00 search fee. Company or personal checks, payable to District Clerk. Search information required: name, years to search.

Civil records
District Clerk's Office
PO Box 427
Orange, TX 77630
(409) 883-7740 Ext. 298
Fax (409) 883-4449
Civil records are available in person only. See Texas state repository for additional information.

Misdemeanor records
County Clerk's Office
PO Box 1536
Orange, TX 77631-1536
(409) 883-7740 Ext. 231
Misdemeanor records are available by phone from 1982 forward. No release necessary. No search fee. $1.00 fee per copy. $1.00 for certification. Search information required: name, years to search.

Civil records
County Clerk's Office
PO Box 1536
Orange, TX 77631-1536
(409) 883-7740 Ext. 231
Civil records are available by phone from 1982 forward. No release necessary. No search fee. $1.00 fee per copy. $1.00 for certification. Search information required: name, years to search. Specify plaintiff or defendant.

Palo Pinto County

Felony records
District Clerk's Office, Criminal Records
PO Box 189
Palo Pinto, TX 76484-0189
(817) 659-3651 or 659-1279
Felony records are available by mail or phone. No release necessary. No search fee. Certified check only, payable to District Clerk. Search information required: name, SSN, date of birth, years to search.

Civil records
District Clerk's Office
PO Box 189
Palo Pinto, TX 76484-0189
(817) 659-3651 or 659-1279
Civil records are available by mail. No release necessary. $5.00 search fee. $1.00 fee per copy. $1.00 for certification. Search information required: name, date of birth, years to search. Specify plaintiff or defendant.

Misdemeanor records
County Clerk's Office
PO Box 8
Palo Pinto, TX 76072
(817) 659-3651
Misdemeanor records are available by mail. No release necessary. $5.00 search fee. $1.00 fee per copy. $1.00 for certification. Search information required: name, date of birth, offense, years to search.

Civil records
County Clerk's Office
PO Box 8
Palo Pinto, TX 76072
(817) 659-3651
Civil records are available by mail. No release necessary. No search fee. $1.00 fee per copy. $1.00 for certification. Search information required: name, date of birth, years to search. Specify plaintiff or defendant.

Panola County

Felony records
District Clerk's Office, Criminal Records
Panola County Courthouse
Carthage, TX 75633
(903) 693-0306
Felony records are available by mail or phone. No release necessary. $5.00 search fee. Search information required: name, years to search.

Civil records
District Clerk's Office
Panola County Courthouse
Carthage, TX 75633
(903) 693-0306
Civil records are available by mail. No release necessary. $5.00 search fee. $.50 fee per copy. $2.00 for certification. Search information required: name, date of birth, years to search. Specify plaintiff or defendant.

Misdemeanor records
County Clerk's Office
201 Panola County Courthouse Bldg.
Carthage, TX 75633
(903) 693-0302
Misdemeanor records are available by mail. $5.00 search fee. Make checks payable to County Clerk. No release necessary. Search information required: name, date of birth, years to search.

Civil records
County Clerk's Office
201 Panola County Courthouse Bldg.
Carthage, TX 75633
(903) 693-0302
Civil records are available by mail. No release necessary. $5.00 search fee. Search information required: name, date of birth, years to search. Specify plaintiff or defendant.

Parker County

Felony records
District Clerk's Office, Criminal
Records
PO Box 340
Weatherford, TX 76086-0340
(817) 599-6591 Extension 111
Felony records are available by mail. No release necessary. $5.00 search fee. Make check payable to District Clerk. Search information required: name, SSN, date of birth, years to search.

Civil records
District Clerk's Office
PO Box 340
Weatherford, TX 76086-0340
(817) 599-6591 Extension 111
Civil records are available by mail. No release necessary. $5.00 search fee. Search information required: name, date of birth, years to search. Specify plaintiff or defendant.

Misdemeanor records
Parker County Court Clerk
PO Box 819
Weatherford, TX 76086-0819
(817) 599-6591 Extension 177
Fax (817) 599-6591 Extension 177
Misdemeanor records are available by mail. $5.00 search fee. No release necessary. Search information required: name, offense, years to search, date of birth.

Civil records
Parker County Court Clerk
PO Box 819
Weatherford, TX 76086-0819
(817) 599-6591 Extension 177
Fax (817) 599-6591 Extension 177
Civil records are available by mail. No release necessary. $5.00 search fee. $1.00 fee per copy. $1.00 for certification. Search information required: name, date of birth, years to search. Specify plaintiff or defendant.

Parmer County

Felony records
District Clerk's Office, Criminal
Records
PO Box 888
Farwell, TX 79325
(806) 481-3419
Felony records are available by mail. A release is required. $5.00 search fee. Checks payable to District Clerk. Search information required: name, date of indictment.

Civil records
District Clerk's Office
PO Box 888
Farwell, TX 79325
(806) 481-3419
Civil records are available by mail. No release necessary. $5.00 search fee. $1.00 fee per copy. $1.00 for certification. Search information required: name, date of birth, years to search. Specify plaintiff or defendant.

Misdemeanor records
County Clerk's Office
PO Box 356
Farwell, TX 79325
(806) 481-3691
Misdemeanor records are available by mail or phone. $5.00 search fee. Make checks payable to County Clerk. No release necessary. Search information required: name, years to search.

Civil records
County Clerk's Office
PO Box 356
Farwell, TX 79325
(806) 481-3691
Civil records are available by mail. No release necessary. $5.00 search fee. $1.00 fee per copy. $1.00 for certification. Search information required: name, date of birth, years to search. Specify plaintiff or defendant.

Pecos County

Felony records
District Clerk's Office, Criminal
Records
400 S. Nelson
Fort Stockton, TX 79735
(915) 336-3503
Felony records are available by mail or phone. No release necessary. 5.00 search fee. $1.00 fee per copy. Make check payable to District Clerk. Search information required: name.

Civil records
District Clerk's Office
400 S. Nelson
Fort Stockton, TX 79735
(915) 336-3503
Civil records are available by mail. No release necessary. $5.00 search fee. $1.00 fee per copy. $1.00 for certification. Search information required: name, date of birth, years to search. Specify plaintiff or defendant.

Misdemeanor records
County Clerk's Office
103 W. Callaghan
Fort Stockton, TX 79735
(915) 336-7555
Misdemeanor records are available by mail. $5.00 search fee. $1.00 fee per copy. $1.00 for certification. No release necessary. Search information required: name, years to search.

Civil records
County Clerk's Office
103 W. Callaghan
Fort Stockton, TX 79735
(915) 336-7555
Civil records are available by mail. No release necessary. $5.00 search fee. $1.00 fee per copy. $1.00 for certification. Search information required: name, date of birth, years to search. Specify plaintiff or defendant.

Polk County

Felony records
District Clerk's Office, Criminal
Records
101 West Church Street
Polk County Courthouse
Livingston, TX 77351
(409) 327-8314
Felony records are available by mail. No release necessary. $5.00 search fee. $1.00 fee per copy. $2.00 for certification. Certified check only, payable to District Clerk. Search information required: name, years to search.

Civil records
District Clerk's Office
101 West Church Street
Polk County Courthouse
Livingston, TX 77351
(409) 327-8314
Civil records are available by mail. No release necessary. $5.00 search fee. $1.00 fee per copy. $1.00 for certification. Search information required: name, date of birth, years to search. Specify plaintiff or defendant.

Misdemeanor records
County Clerk's Office
PO Drawer 2119
Livingston, TX 77351
(409) 327-8210
Misdemeanor records are available by mail. No search fee. No release necessary. Search information required: name, years to search.

Civil records
County Clerk's Office
PO Drawer 2119
Livingston, TX 77351
(409) 327-8398
Civil records are available by mail. No release necessary. $10.00 search fee. $1.00 fee per copy. $2.00 for certification. Search information required: name, date of birth, years to search. Specify plaintiff or defendant.

Potter County

Felony records
District Clerk's Office, Criminal
Records
PO Box 9570
Amarillo, TX 79105
(806) 379-2313
Felony records are available by mail. No release necessary. $5.00 search fee. Company checks only, payable to District Clerk. Search information required: name, years to search.

Civil records
District Clerk's Office
PO Box 9570
Amarillo, TX 79105
(806) 379-2313
Civil records are available by mail. No release necessary. $5.00 search fee. $.10 fee per copy. $1.00 for certification. Search information required: name, date of birth, years to search. Specify plaintiff or defendant.

Misdemeanor records
County Clerk's Office
PO Box 9638
Amarillo, TX 79105
(806) 379-2280
Misdemeanor records are available by mail. $6.00 search fee. Money orders only, payable to County Clerk. No release necessary. Search information required: name, years to search.

Civil records
County Clerk's Office
PO Box 9638
Amarillo, TX 79105
(806) 379-2275
Civil records are available by mail. No release necessary. $6.00 search fee. $.50 fee per copy. $1.00 for certification. Search information required: name, date of birth, years to search. Specify plaintiff or defendant.

Presidio County

District Clerk's Office, Criminal Records
PO Box 789
Marfa, TX 79843
(915) 729-4812

Felony and misdemeanor records are available by mail or phone. No release necessary. $5.00 search fee. Check payable to District Clerk. Search information required: name, years to search.

Civil records are available by mail. No release necessary. $5.00 search fee. $1.00 fee per copy. $1.00 for certification. Search information required: name, date of birth, years to search. Specify plaintiff or defendant.

Rains County

District Clerk's Office, Criminal Records
PO Box 187
Emory, TX 75440
(903) 473-2461

Felony and misdemeanor records are available by mail. No release necessary. $5.00 search fee. Checks payable to County Clerk. Search information required: name, years to search.

Civil records are available by mail. No release necessary. $5.00 search fee. $1.00 fee per copy. $2.00 for certification. Search information required: name, date of birth, years to search. Specify plaintiff or defendant.

Randall County

Felony records
District Clerk's Office, Criminal Records
PO Box 1096
Canyon, TX 79015
(806) 655-6205
Fax (806) 655-7469

Felony records are available by mail. No release necessary. $5.00 search fee. Make certified check payable to District Clerk. Fees may be charged to Master Card or Visa. Include card number, card holder's name and expiration date. Search information required: name, years to search.

Civil records
District Clerk's Office
PO Box 1096
Canyon, TX 79015
(806) 655-6200
Fax (806) 655-7469

Civil records are available by mail. No release necessary. $5.00 search fee. $.25 fee per copy. $1.00 for certification. Search information required: name, date of birth, years to search. Specify plaintiff or defendant.

Misdemeanor records
County Clerk's Office
PO Box 660
Canyon, TX 79015
(806) 655-6333
Fax (806) 655-6331

Misdemeanor records are available by mail. No search fee. No release necessary. Search information required: name, date of offense.

Civil records
County Clerk's Office
PO Box 660
Canyon, TX 79015
(806) 655-6333
Fax (806) 655-6331

Civil records are available by mail. No release necessary. $5.00 search fee. $1.00 fee per copy. $1.00 for certification. Search information required: name, date of birth, years to search. Specify plaintiff or defendant.

Reagan County

District Clerk's Office, Criminal Records
PO Box 100
Big Lake, TX 76932
(915) 884-2442

Felony and misdemeanor records are available by mail or phone. No release necessary. No search fee. Search information required: name, SASE, specify misdemeanor of felony, years to search.

Civil records are available by mail. No release necessary. $10.00 search fee. $1.00 for certification. Search information required: name, date of birth, years to search, SASE. Specify plaintiff or defendant.

Real County

District Clerk's Office, Criminal Records
PO Box 656
Leakey, TX 78873
(512) 232-5202
Fax (512) 232-6040

Felony and misdemeanor records are available by mail or phone. No release necessary. $5.00 search fee. $1.00 fee per copy, $1.00 fee for certification. Make check payable to District Court Clerk. Search information required: name.

Civil records are available by mail. No release necessary. $5.00 search fee. $1.00 fee per copy, $1.00 fee for certification. Search information required: name, date of birth, years to search. Specify plaintiff or defendant.

Red River County

Felony records
District Clerk's Office, Criminal Records
Red River County Courthouse
Clarksville, TX 75426
(903) 427-3761

Felony records are available by mail or phone. No release necessary. $5.00 fee. Checks payable to District Clerk. Search information required: name, years to search.

Civil records
District Clerk's Office
Red River County Courthouse
Clarksville, TX 75426
(903) 427-3761

Civil records are available by mail. No release necessary. $5.00 search fee. $1.00 fee per copy, $2.00 fee for certification. Search information required: name, date of birth, years to search. Specify plaintiff or defendant.

Misdemeanor records
County Clerk's Office
200 N. Walnut - Courthouse Annex
Clarksville, TX 75426
(903) 427-2401

Misdemeanor records are available by mail. $5.00 fee for 10 years searched. Make checks payable to County Clerk. No release necessary. Search information required: name, years to search.

Reeves County

Felony records
District Clerk's Office, Criminal Records
PO Box 848
Pecos, TX 79772
(915) 445-2714

Felony records are available by mail or phone. No release necessary. No search fee. Search information required: name, date of birth, years to search.

Civil records
District Clerk's Office
PO Box 848
Pecos, TX 79772
(915) 445-2714

Civil records are available by mail. No release necessary. No search fee. $1.00 fee per copy. $1.00 for certification. Search information required: name, date of birth, years to search. Specify plaintiff or defendant.

Misdemeanor records
County Clerk's Office
PO Box 867
Pecos, TX 79772
(915) 445-5467

Misdemeanor records are available by mail. $10.00 search fee. $1.00 fee per copy. Search information required: name, date of birth, SSN.

Civil records
County Clerk's Office
PO Box 867
Pecos, TX 79772
(915) 445-5467

Civil records are available by mail. No release necessary. $10.00 search fee. $1.00 fee per copy. $1.00 for certification. Search information required: name, date of birth, years to search. Specify plaintiff or defendant.

Refugio County

Felony records
District Clerk's Office, Criminal Records
PO Box 736
Refugio, TX 78377
(512) 526-2721

Felony records are available by mail. A release is required. $5.00 search fee. $1.00 fee per copied page. Certified check only, payable to District Clerk. Search information required: name.

Civil records
District Clerk's Office
PO Box 736
Refugio, TX 78377
(512) 526-2721

Civil records are available by mail. No release necessary. $5.00 search fee. $1.00 fee per copy. $1.00 for certification. Search information required: name, date of birth, years to search. Specify plaintiff or defendant.

Misdemeanor records
County Clerk's Office
PO Box 704
Refugio, TX 78377
(512) 526-2233
Misdemeanor records are available by mail or phone. $10.00 search fee. $1.00 fee per copy, $1.00 fee for certification. Checks payable to County Clerk. No release necessary. Search information required: name, years to search.

Civil records
County Clerk's Office
PO Box 704
Refugio, TX 78377
(512) 526-2233
Civil records are available by mail. No release necessary. $10.00 search fee. $1.00 fee per copy. $1.00 for certification. Search information required: name, date of birth, years to search. Specify plaintiff or defendant.

Roberts County

District Clerk's Office, Criminal Records
PO Box 477
Miami, TX 79059
(806) 868-2341
Felony and misdemeanor records are available by mail or phone. No release necessary. $5.00 search fee. Checks payable to Roberts County Texas. Search information required: name, SASE.

Civil records are available by mail or phone. No release necessary. No search fee. $.50 fee per copy. $1.00 for certification. Search information required: name, date of birth, years to search. Specify plaintiff or defendant.

Robertson County

Felony records
District Clerk's Office, Criminal Records
PO Box 250
Franklin, TX 77856
(409) 828-3636
Fax (409) 828-3300
Felony records are available by mail or phone. A release is required. $5.00 search fee. $10.00 fee for fax response. Search information required: name.

Civil records
District Clerk's Office
PO Box 250
Franklin, TX 77856
(409) 828-3636
Civil records are available by mail. No release necessary. $5.00 search fee. $1.00 fee per copy. $1.00 for certification. Search information required: name, date of birth, years to search. Specify plaintiff or defendant.

Misdemeanor records
County Clerk's Office
PO Drawer L
Franklin, TX 77856
(409) 828-4130
Fax (214) 722-0242
Misdemeanor records are available by mail. No search fee. No release necessary. Search information required: name, type of offense, date of deposition, if available. years to search.

Civil records
County Clerk's Office
PO Drawer L
Franklin, TX 77856
(409) 828-4130
Civil records are available by mail. No release necessary. $5.00 search fee. $.25 fee per copy. $1.00 for certification. Search information required: name, date of birth, years to search. Specify plaintiff or defendant.

Rockwall County

Felony records
District Clerk's Office, Criminal Records
Rockwall County Courthouse
Rockwall, TX 75087
(214) 722-3382
Fax (214) 771-3382
Felony records are available by mail, phone or fax. No release necessary. $5.00 search fee. Make check payable to District Clerk. Search information required: name.

Civil records
District Clerk's Office
Rockwall County Courthouse
Rockwall, TX 75087
(214) 722-3382
Fax (214) 771-3382
Civil records are available by mail. No release necessary. $5.00 search fee. $1.00 fee per copy. $1.00 for certification. Search information required: name, date of birth, years to search. Specify plaintiff or defendant.

Misdemeanor records
County Clerk's Office
Rockwall County Courthouse
Rockwall, TX 75087
(214) 771-5141
Misdemeanor records are available by mail. $5.00 search fee. $1.00 fee per copied page. Checks payable to County Clerk. Search information required: name, years to search.

Civil records
County Clerk's Office
Rockwall County Courthouse
Rockwall, TX 75087
(214) 771-5141
Civil records are available by mail. No release necessary.$5.00 search fee. $1.00 fee per copy. $1.00 for certification. Search information required: name, date of birth, years to search. Specify plaintiff or defendant.

Runnels County

Felony records
District Clerk's Office, Criminal Records
PO Box 166
Ballinger, TX 76821
(915) 365-2638
Felony records are available by mail or phone. No release necessary. No search fee. Search information required: name.

Civil records
District Clerk's Office
PO Box 166
Ballinger, TX 76821
(915) 365-2638
Civil records are available by mail or phone. No release necessary. No search fee. $.50 fee per copy. $1.00 for certification. Search information required: name, date of birth, years to search. Specify plaintiff or defendant.

Misdemeanor records
County Clerk's Office
PO Box 189
Ballinger, TX 76821
(915) 365-2720
Misdemeanor records are available by mail, or phone. No search fee. $1.00 fee per copy, $1.00 for certification, prepaid. No release necessary. Search information required: full name, date of birth, years to search.

Civil records
County Clerk's Office
PO Box 189
Ballinger, TX 76821
(915) 365-2720
Civil records are available by mail. No release necessary. No search fee. $1.00 fee per copy. $1.00 for certification. Search information required: name, date of birth, years to search. Specify plaintiff or defendant.

Rusk County

Felony records
District Clerk's Office, Criminal Records
Rusk County Courthouse
115 N. Main
Henderson, TX 75652
(903) 657-0353
Felony records are available by mail. No release necessary. $5.00 search fee. Certified check only, payable to District Clerk. Search information required: name, SASE, years to search.

Civil records
District Clerk's Office
Rusk County Courthouse
115 N. Main
Henderson, TX 75652
(903) 657-0353
Civil records are available by mail. A release ia required. $5.00 search fee. $.10 fee per copy. $1.00 for certification. Search information required: name, date of birth, years to search, SASE. Specify plaintiff or defendant.

Misdemeanor records
County Clerk's Office
PO Box 758
Henderson, TX 75653
(903) 657-0330
Misdemeanor records are available by mail or phone. No search fee. No release required for verification only. Search information required: name, years to search.

Civil records
County Clerk's Office
PO Box 758
Henderson, TX 75653
(903) 657-0330
Civil records are available by mail. No release necessary. $10.00 search fee. $1.00 fee per copy. $1.00 for certification. Search information required: name, date of birth, years to search. Specify plaintiff or defendant.

Sabine County

Felony records
District Clerk's Office, Criminal
Records
PO Box 850
Hemphill, TX 75948
(409) 787-2912
Felony records are available by mail or
phone. No release necessary. No search fee.
$1.00 fee per copy, $5.00 fee for certification. Search information required: name,
years to search.

Civil records
District Clerk's Office
PO Box 850
Hemphill, TX 75948
(409) 787-2912
Civil records are available by mail or
phone. No release necessary. No search fee.
$1.00 fee per copy, $5.00 fee for certification. Search information required: name,
date of birth, years to search. Specify plaintiff or defendant.

Misdemeanor records
County Clerk's Office
PO Drawer 580
Hemphill, TX 75948-0580
(409) 787-3786
Fax (409) 787-2044
Misdemeanor records are available by mail
or phone. No search fee. No release neces-
sary. Search information required: name,
years to search.

Civil records
County Clerk's Office
PO Drawer 580
Hemphill, TX 75948-0580
(409) 787-3786
Civil records are available in person only.
See Texas state repository for additional in-
formation.

San Augustine County

Felony records
District Clerk's Office, Criminal
Records
Room 202, Courthouse
San Augustine, TX 75972
(409) 275-2231
Felony records are available by mail. No re-
lease necessary. No search fee. $.50 fee per
copy. Search information required: name,
years to search.

Civil records
District Clerk's Office
Room 202, Courthouse
San Augustine, TX 75972
(409) 275-2231
Civil records are available by mail or
phone. No release necessary. No search fee.
$.50 fee per copy. $1.50 for certification.
Search information required: name, date of
birth, years to search. Specify plaintiff or
defendant.

Misdemeanor records
County Clerk's Office
Room 106 Courthouse
San Augustine, TX 75972
(409) 275-2452
Misdemeanor records are available by mail.
No search fee. $1.00 fee per copied page.
No release necessary. Search information
required: name, date of conviction or filing,
address, years to search.

San Jacinto County

Felony records
District Clerk's Office, Criminal
Records
PO Box 369
Cold Springs, TX 77331
(409) 653-2909
Felony records are available by mail or
phone. No release necessary. $5.00 search
fee. Company or certified checks only,
payable to District Clerk. Search information required: name.

Civil records
District Clerk's Office
PO Box 369
Cold Springs, TX 77331
(409) 653-2909
Civil records are available by mail. No release necessary. $5.00 search fee. $1.00 fee
per copy. $1.00 for certification. Search in-
formation required: name, date of birth,
years to search. Only check by plaintiff.

Misdemeanor records
County Clerk's Office
PO Box 669
Cold Springs, TX 77331
(409) 653-2324
Misdemeanor records are available by
phone. $10.00 search fee. $1.00 fee per
copied page. No release necessary. Search
information required: name, years to
search.

Civil records
County Clerk's Office
PO Box 669
Cold Springs, TX 77331
(409) 653-2324
Civil records are available by mail. A release is required. $10.00 search fee. $1.00
fee per copy. $1.00 for certification. Search
information required: name, date of birth,
years to search. Specify plaintiff or defendant.

San Patricio County

Felony records
District Clerk's Office, Criminal
Records
PO Box 1084
Sinton, TX 78387
(512) 364-1725
Felony records are available by mail. No re-
lease necessary. $5.00 search fee. Search
information required: name, years to
search.

Civil records
District Clerk's Office
PO Box 1084
Sinton, TX 78387
(512) 364-1725
Civil records are available by mail. No release necessary. $5.00 search fee. $1.00 fee
per copy. $1.00 for certification. Search in-
formation required: name, date of birth,
years to search. Specify plaintiff or defendant.

Misdemeanor records
County Clerk's Office
PO Box 578
Sinton, TX 78387
(512) 364-2490
Misdemeanor records are available by mail
or phone. No search fee. No release necessary. Search information required: name,
date of birth.

Civil records
County Clerk's Office
PO Box 578
Sinton, TX 78387
(512) 364-2490
Civil records are available by mail. No release necessary. No search fee. $1.00 fee
per copy. $1.00 for certification. Search in-
formation required: name, date of birth,
years to search. Specify plaintiff or defendant.

San Saba County

District Clerk's Office, Criminal
Records
San Saba County Courthouse
San Saba, TX 76877
(915) 372-3375
Felony and misdemeanor records are available by mail or phone. No release necessary. No search fee. Search information required: name, SASE, years to search.

Civil records are available by mail or
phone. No release necessary. No search fee.
$1.00 fee per copy. $1.00 for certification.
Search information required: name, date of
birth, years to search, SASE. Specify plaintiff or defendant.

Schleicher County

District Clerk's Office, Criminal
Records
PO Drawer 580
El Dorado, TX 76936
(915) 853-2833
Felony and misdemeanor records are available by mail or phone. No release necessary. $10.00 search fee. Certified checks
only, payable to County Clerk. Search information required: name.

Civil records are available by mail. No release necessary. $8.00 search fee. $1.00 fee
per copy. $1.00 for certification. Search in-
formation required: name, date of birth,
years to search. Specify plaintiff or defendant.

Scurry County

Felony records
District Clerk's Office, Criminal
Records
Scurry County Courthouse
Snyder, TX 79549
(915) 573-5641
Felony records are available by mail or
phone. No release necessary. $5.00 search
fee. Make check payable to District Clerk.
Search information required: name.

Civil records
District Clerk's Office
Scurry County Courthouse
Snyder, TX 79549
(915) 573-5641
Civil records are available by mail. No release necessary. $5.00 search fee. $1.00 fee
per copy. $1.00 for certification. Search in-
formation required: name, date of birth,
years to search. Specify plaintiff or defendant.

Misdemeanor records
County Clerk's Office
Scurry County Courthouse
Snyder, TX 79549
(915) 573-5332
Misdemeanor records are available by mail.
$5.00 search fee. $1.00 fee per copy. $1.00
for certification. A release is required.
Search information required: name, years to
search.

Civil records
County Clerk's Office
Scurry County Courthouse
Snyder, TX 79549
(915) 573-5332
Civil records are available by mail. No release necessary. $5.00 search fee. $1.00 fee per copy, $1.00 for certification. Search information required: name, date of birth, years to search. Specify plaintiff or defendant.

Shackelford County

District Clerk's Office, Criminal Records
PO Box 247
Albany, TX 76430
(915) 762-2232
Felony and misdemeanor records are available by mail. No release necessary. No search fee. Search information required: name, years to search.

Civil records are available by mail. No release necessary. $5.00 search fee. $1.00 fee per copy, $1.00 for certification. Search information required: name, date of birth, years to search. Specify plaintiff or defendant.

Shelby County

Felony records
District Clerk's Office, Criminal Records
PO Box 1546
Center, TX 75935
(409) 598-4164
Felony records are available by mail from 1967 to present. No release necessary. $5.00 search fee. Checks payable to District Clerk. Search information required: name years to search.

Civil records
District Clerk's Office
PO Box 1546
Center, TX 75935
(409) 598-4164
Civil records are available by mail. No release necessary. $5.00 search fee. $1.00 fee per copy, $1.00 for certification. Search information required: name, date of birth, years to search. Specify plaintiff or defendant.

Misdemeanor records
County Clerk's Office
PO Box 592
Center, TX 75935
(409) 598-6361
Misdemeanor records are available by mail. $10.00 search fee. Money order only, payable to County Clerk. A release is required. Search information required: name, date of birth, address.

Civilr records
County Clerk's Office
PO Box 592
Center, TX 75935
(409) 598-6361
Civil records are available by mail. No release necessary. $5.00 search fee. $1.00 fee per copy, $1.00 for certification. Search information required: name, date of birth, years to search. Specify plaintiff or defendant.

Sherman County

District Clerk's Office, Criminal Records
PO Box 270
Stratford, TX 79084
(806) 396-2371
Felony and misdemeanor records are available by mail or phone. No release necessary. $5.00 search fee. $1.00 fee per copy, $1.00 for certification. Search information required: name, years to search.

Civil records are available by mail or phone. No release necessary. $5.00 search fee. $1.00 fee per copy, $1.00 for certification. Search information required: name, date of birth, years to search. Specify plaintiff or defendant.

Smith County

Felony records
District Clerk's Office, Criminal Records
PO Box 1077
Tyler, TX 75710
(903) 535-0666
Felony records are available by mail. A release is required. $5.00 search fee. Certified or personal checks, payable to District Clerk. Search information required: name, years to search, sex, date of birth.

Civil records
District Clerk's Office
PO Box 1077
Tyler, TX 75710
(903) 535-0666
Civil records are available by mail. No release necessary. $5.00 search fee. $1.00 fee per copy, $1.00 for certification. Search information required: name, date of birth, years to search. Specify plaintiff or defendant.

Misdemeanor records
County Clerk's Office
PO Box 1018
Tyler, TX 75710
(903) 535-0642
Misdemeanor records are available by mail or phone. $5.00 search fee. Make checks payable to County Clerk. No release necessary. Search information required: name, date of birth, date of offense, years to search.

Civil records
County Clerk's Office
PO Box 1018
Tyler, TX 75710
(903) 535-0642
Civil records are available by mail or phone. No release necessary. $5.00 search fee. $1.00 fee per copy, $1.00 for certification. Search information required: name, date of birth, years to search. Specify plaintiff or defendant.

Somervell County

District Clerk's Office, Criminal Records
PO Box 1098
Glen Rose, TX 76043
(817) 897-4427
Felony and misdemeanor records are available by mail. A release is required. $5.00 search fee. Certified or personal checks, payable to County Clerk's Office. Search information required: name, date of birth.

Civil records are available by mail. No release necessary. $5.00 search fee. $1.00 fee per copy, $1.00 for certification. Search information required: name, date of birth, years to search. Specify plaintiff or defendant.

Starr County

District Clerk's Office, Criminal Records
Starr County
Courthouse Bldg.
4th & Britton Ave.
Rio Grande City, TX 78582
(512) 487-2610
Felony and misdemeanor records are available by mail or phone. No release necessary. $5.00 search fee, prepaid. Search information required: name, years to search.

Civil records are available by mail. No release necessary. $5.00 search fee. $1.00 fee per copy, $1.00 for certification. Search information required: name, date of birth, years to search. Specify plaintiff or defendant.

Stephens County

District Clerk's Office, Criminal Records
200 W. Walker
Breckenridge, TX 76424
(817) 559-3151
Felony and misdemeanor records are available by mail. No release necessary. $5.00 search fee. Search information required: name, years to search.

Civil records are available by mail. No release necessary. $5.00 search fee. $1.00 fee per copy, $1.00 for certification. Search information required: name, date of birth, years to search. Specify plaintiff or defendant.

Sterling County

District Clerk's Office, Criminal Records
PO Box 55
Sterling City, TX 76951
(915) 378-5191
Felony and misdemeanor records are available by mail. No release necessary. No search fee. Search information required: name, years to search.

Civil records are available by mail. No release necessary. $5.00 search fee. $1.00 for certification. Search information required: name, date of birth, years to search. Specify plaintiff or defendant.

Stonewall County

District Clerk's Office, Criminal Records
Drawer P
Aspermont, TX 79502
(817) 989-2272
Felony and misdemeanor records are available by mail or phone. No release necessary. No search fee. $1.00 fee per copy, $1.00 for certification. Search information required: name, years to search.

Civil records are available by mail. No release necessary. No search fee. $1.00 fee per copy, $1.00 for certification. Search information required: name, date of birth, years to search. Specify plaintiff or defendant.

Sutton County

District Clerk's Office, Criminal Records
300 East Oak, Suite 3
Sonora, TX 76950
(915) 387-3815
Felony and misdemeanor records are available by mail. No release necessary. $5.00 search fee. Check payable to District Clerk. Search information required: name, years to search.

Civil records are available by mail. No release necessary. No search fee. $1.00 fee per copy. $2.00 for certification. Search information required: name, date of birth, years to search. Specify plaintiff or defendant.

Swisher County

Felony records
District Clerk's Office, Criminal Records
Swisher County Courthouse
Tulia, TX 79088
(806) 995-3294
Fax (806) 995-2214
Felony records are available by mail or phone. No release necessary. $5.00 fee. Company checks only, payable to District Clerk. Search information required: name.

Civil records
District Clerk's Office
Swisher County Courthouse
Tulia, TX 79088
(806) 995-3294
Civil records are available by mail. No release necessary. $5.00 search fee. $.50 fee per copy, $1.00 for certification. Search information required: name, date of birth, years to search. Specify plaintiff or defendant.

Misdemeanor records
County Clerk's Office
Swisher County Courthouse
Tulia, TX 79088
(806) 995-3294
Misdemeanor records are available by mail. $5.00 search fee. $1.00 fee per copy, $1.00 for certification. No release necessary. Search information required: name, offense if available, years to search.

Civil records
County Clerk's Office
Swisher County Courthouse
Tulia, TX 79088
(806) 995-3294
Civil records are available by mail. No release necessary. $5.00 search fee. $1.00 fee per copy, $1.00 for certification. Search information required: name, date of birth, years to search. Specify plaintiff or defendant.

Tarrant County

Felony records
District Clerk's Office
Criminal Courts Bldg.
300 West Belknap
Fort Worth, TX 76196-0402
(817) 884-1342 or 884-1343
Felony records are available by mail. No release necessary. $5.00 search fee. Company checks only, payable to District Clerk. Search information required: full name, maiden name, if available, date of birth.

Civil records
District Clerk's Office
Criminal Courts Bldg.
300 West Belknap
Fort Worth, TX 76196-0402
(817) 884-1342
Civil records are available by mail. No release necessary. $5.00 search fee. $1.00 for certification. Search information required: name, date of birth, years to search. Specify plaintiff or defendant.

Misdemeanor records
County Clerk's Office
100 W. Weatherford
Fort Worth, TX 76196-0401
(817) 884-1066
Misdemeanor records are available by mail. $1.00 fee per year searched. $1.00 fee per copy, $1.00 for certification. No release necessary. Search information required: name, date of birth, SASE.

Civil records
County Clerk's Office
100 W. Weatherford
Fort Worth, TX 76196-0401
(817) 884-1066
Civil records are available by mail. No release necessary. $5.00 search fee. $1.00 fee per copy. $1.00 for certification. Search information required: name, date of birth, years to search, SASE. Specify plaintiff or defendant.

Taylor County

Felony records
District Clerk's Office, Criminal Records
300 Oak Street
Abilene, TX 79602
(915) 674-1316
Felony records are available by mail. No release necessary. $5.00 search fee. Check payable to District Clerk. Search information required: name.

Civil records
District Clerk's Office
300 Oak Street
Abilene, TX 79602
(915) 674-1316
Civil records are available by mail. No release necessary. $5.00 search fee. $1.00 fee per copy. $1.00 for certification. Search information required: name, date of birth, years to search. Specify plaintiff or defendant.

Misdemeanor records
County Clerk's Office
PO Box 5497
Abilene, TX 79608
(915) 674-1202
Misdemeanor records are available by mail. $5.00 search fee. $1.00 fee per copy. No release necessary. Search information required: name, date of birth, years to search.

Civil records
County Clerk's Office
PO Box 5497
Abilene, TX 79608
(915) 674-1202
Civil records are available by mail. No release necessary. $5.00 fee per 10 years seasrched. $1.00 fee per copy. $1.00 for certification. Search information required: name, date of birth, years to search. Specify plaintiff or defendant.

Terrell County

District Clerk's Office, Criminal Records
PO Drawer 410
Sanderson, TX 79848
(915) 345-2391
Felony and misdemeanor records are available by mail or phone. No release necessary. No search fee. $1.00 fee per copy. $1.00 for certification. Make check payable to District Clerk. Search information required: name, years to search.

Civil records are available by mail. No release necessary. No search fee. $1.00 fee per copy. $1.00 for certification. Search information required: name, date of birth, years to search. Specify plaintiff or defendant.

Terry County

Felony records
District Clerk's Office, Criminal Records
Terry County Courthouse
Brownfield, TX 79316
(806) 637-4202
Felony records are available by mail. No release necessary. $5.00 search fee. Make check payable to District Clerk. Search information required: name, years to search.

Civil records
District Clerk's Office
Terry County Courthouse
Brownfield, TX 79316
(806) 637-4202
Civil records are available by mail. No release necessary. $5.00 search fee. $1.00 fee per copy. $2.00 for certification. Search information required: name, date of birth, years to search. Specify plaintiff or defendant.

Misdemeanor records
County Clerk's Office
5th Main
Brownfield, TX 79316
(806) 637-8551
Misdemeanor records are available by mail or phone. $5.00 search fee. No release necessary. Search information required: name.

Civil records
County Clerk's Office
5th Main
Brownfield, TX 79316
(806) 637-8551
Civil records are available by mail. No release necessary. $5.00 search fee. $1.00 fee per copy. $2.00 for certification. Search information required: name, date of birth, years to search. Specify plaintiff or defendant.

Throckmorton County

District Clerk's Office, Criminal Records
PO Box 309
Throckmorton, TX 76083
(817) 849-2501
Felony and misdemeanor records are available by mail or by phone for one name search. No release necessary. No search fee. Search information required: name, years to search.

Civil records are available by mail. No release necessary. $10.00 search fee. $1.00 fee per copy. Search information required: name, date of birth, years to search. Specify plaintiff or defendant.

Titus County

Felony records
District Clerk's Office, Criminal
Records
Titus County Courthouse
Mt. Pleasant, TX 75455
(903) 577-6721
Felony records are available by mail or
phone. No release necessary. No search fee.
Search information required: full name,
years to search.

Civil records
District Clerk's Office
Titus County Courthouse
Mt. Pleasant, TX 75455
(903) 577-6721
Civil records are available by mail. No release necessary. $5.00 search fee. $1.00 fee
per copy. Search information required:
name, date of birth, years to search. Specify
plaintiff or defendant.

Misdemeanor records
County Clerk's Office
Titus County Courthouse
100 W. 1st, Suite 204
Mt. Pleasant, TX 75455
(903) 577-6796
Misdemeanor records are available by mail
or phone. No search fee. No release necessary. Search information required: name,
date of offense.

Civil records
County Clerk's Office
Titus County Courthouse
100 W. 1st, Suite 204
Mt. Pleasant, TX 75455
(903) 577-6796
Civil records are available by mail. No release necessary. $10.00 search fee. $1.00
fee per copy. $1.00 for certification. Search
information required: name, date of birth,
years to search. Specify plaintiff or defendant.

Tom Green County

Felony records
District Clerk's Office, Criminal
Records
Tom Green County Courthouse
San Angelo, TX 76903
(915) 659-6582
Felony records are available by mail or
phone. No release necessary. No search fee.
$1.00 fee per copy. Checks payable to
District Clerk. Search information required:
name, years to search.

Civil records
District Clerk's Office
Tom Green County Courthouse
San Angelo, TX 76903
(915) 659-6579
Civil records are available by mail. No release necessary. $5.00 search fee. $1.00 fee
per copy. $1.00 for certification. Search
information required: name, date of birth,
years to search. Specify plaintiff or defendant.

Misdemeanor records
County Clerk's Office, Criminal
Division
112 W. Beaureguard
San Angelo, TX 76903
(915) 659-6551
Misdemeanor records are available by mail
or phone. $5.00 search fee No release nec-
essary. Search information required: name,
years to search. Contact the above office to
set up a deposit account.

Civil records
County Clerk's Office
112 W. Beaureguard
San Angelo, TX 76903
(915) 659-6551
Civil records are available by mail. No release necessary. $5.00 search fee. $1.00 fee
per copy. $1.00 for certification. Search in-
formation required: name, date of birth,
years to search. Specify plaintiff or defendant.

Travis County

Felony records
District Clerk's Office, Criminal
Records
PO Box 1748
Austin, TX 78767
(512) 473-9420
Felony records are available by mail. No re-
lease necessary. $5.00 search fee. $1.00 fee
per copy. $1.00 for certification. Search in-
formation required: name, years to search. .

Civil records
District Clerk's Office
PO Box 1748
Austin, TX 78767
(512) 473-9420
Civil records are available by mail. No release necessary. $5.00 search fee. $1.00 fee
per copy. $1.00 for certification. Search in-
formation required: name, date of birth,
years to search. Specify plaintiff or defendant.

Misdemeanor records
County Clerk's Office, Criminal
Division
PO Box 1748
Austin, TX 78767
(512) 473-9440
Misdemeanor records are available by mail.
$5.00 search fee. $1.00 fee per copied page.
Checks payable to County Clerk. No re-
lease necessary. Search information re-
quired: name, date of birth.

Civil records
County Clerk's Office
PO Box 1748
Austin, TX 78767
(512) 473-5244
Civil records are available by mail form
1981. No release necessary. $5.00 search
fee. $10.00 search fee prior to 1981. $1.00
fee per copy. $1.00 for certification. Search
information required: name, date of birth,
years to search. Specify plaintiff or defendant.

Trinity County

District Clerk's Office, Criminal
Records
PO Box 548
Groveton, TX 75845
(409) 642-1118
Felony and misdemeanor records are avail-
able by mail. No release necessary. $5.00
search fee. Checks payable to District
Clerk. Search information required: name,
years to search.

Civil records are available by mail. No release necessary. $5.00 search fee. $1.00 fee
per copy. $1.00 for certification. Search in-
formation required: name, date of birth,
years to search. Specify plaintiff or defendant.

Tyler County

Felony records
District Clerk's Office, Criminal
Records
Room 203, County Courthouse
Woodville, TX 75979
(409) 283-2162
Felony records are available by mail. No re-
lease necessary. $5.00 search fee. Certified
check only, payable to District Clerk.
Search information required: name, SSN,
date of birth, sex, race, years to search,
SASE.

Civil records
District Clerk's Office
Room 203, County Courthouse
Woodville, TX 75979
(409) 283-2162
Civil records are available by mail. No release necessary. $5.00 search fee. $1.00 fee
per copy. $1.00 for certification. Search in-
formation required: name, date of birth,
years to search, SASE. Specify plaintiff or
defendant.

Misdemeanor records
County Clerk's Office
100 Courthouse
Woodville, TX 75979
(409) 283-2281
Misdemeanor records are available by mail.
$5.00 search fee. No release necessary.
Search information required: name, offense
if available, years to search.

Civil records
County Clerk's Office
100 Courthouse
Woodville, TX 75979
(409) 283-2281
Civil records are available by mail. No release necessary. $5.00 search fee. $.50 fee
per copy. $1.00 for certification. Search in-
formation required: name, date of birth,
years to search. Specify plaintiff or defendant.

Upshur County

Felony records
District Clerk's Office, Criminal
Records
PO Box 960
Gilmer, TX 75644
(903) 843-5031
Felony records are available by mail. No re-
lease necessary. $5.00 search fee. $1.00 fee
per copy. Search information required:
name.

Civil records
District Clerk's Office
PO Box 960
Gilmer, TX 75644
(903) 843-5031
Civil records are available by mail. No release necessary. $5.00 search fee. $1.00 fee per copy. $1.00 for certification. Search information required: name, date of birth, years to search. Specify plaintiff or defendant.

Misdemeanor records
County Clerk's Office
PO Box 730
Gilmer, TX 75644-0730
(903) 843-3083
Misdemeanor records are available by mail. $5.00 search fee. Search information required: name, year of conviction, years to search.

Civil records
County Clerk's Office
PO Box 730
Gilmer, TX 75644-0730
(903) 843-3083
Civil records are available by mail. No release necessary. $5.00 search fee. $1.00 fee per copy. $1.00 for certification. Search information required: name, date of birth, years to search. Specify plaintiff or defendant.

Upton County

District Clerk's Office, Criminal Records
PO Box 465
Rankin, TX 79778
(915) 693-2861
Felony and misdemeanor records are available by mail. A release is required. No search fee. Search information required: name, years to search.

Civil records are available by mail. No release necessary. $5.00 search fee. $1.00 fee per copy. Search information required: name, date of birth, years to search. Specify plaintiff or defendant.

Uvalde County

District Clerk's Office, Criminal Records
#15 County Courthouse
Uvalde, TX 78801
(512) 278-3918
Felony and misdemeanor records are available by mail or phone. No release necessary. $5.00 search fee. Checks payable to District Clerk. Search information required: name.

Civil records are available by mail. No release necessary. $5.00 search fee. $1.00 fee per copy. Search information required: name, date of birth, years to search. Specify plaintiff or defendant.

Val Verde County

Felony records
District Clerk's Office, Criminal Records
PO Box 1544
Del Rio, TX 78841
(512) 774-7538
Felony records are available by mail or phone. No release necessary. $5.00 search fee. $1.00 for certification. Certified checks only, payable to District Clerk. Search information required: name, years to search.

Civil records
District Clerk's Office
PO Box 1544
Del Rio, TX 78841
(512) 774-7538
Civil records are available by mail. No release necessary. $5.00 search fee. $1.00 for certification. Search information required: name, date of birth, years to search. Specify plaintiff or defendant.

Misdemeanor records
County Clerk's Office
PO Box 1201
Del Rio, TX 78841-1201
(512) 774-7520
Misdemeanor records are available by mail. $5.00 search fee. $1.00 fee per copy. $1.00 for certification. No release necessary. Search information required: name, SSN, years to search.

Civil records
County Clerk's Office
PO Box 1201
Del Rio, TX 78841-1201
(512) 774-7520
Civil records are available by mail. No release necessary. $5.00 search fee. $1.00 fee per copy. $1.00 for certification. Search information required: name, date of birth, years to search. Specify plaintiff or defendant.

Van Zandt County

Felony records
District Clerk's Office, Criminal Records
Van Zandt County Courthouse
Canton, TX 75103
(903) 567-6576
Felony records are available by mail. No release necessary. $5.00 search fee. $1.00 fee per copy. $2.00 for certification. Certified or personal checks, payable to District Clerk. Search information required: name.

Civil records
District Clerk's Office
Van Zandt County Courthouse
Canton, TX 75103
(903) 567-6576
Civil records are available by mail. No release necessary. $5.00 search fee. $1.00 fee per copy. $2.00 for certification. Search information required: name, date of birth, years to search. Specify plaintiff or defendant.

Misdemeanor records
County Clerk's Office
PO Box 515
Canton, TX 75103
(903) 567-6503
Misdemeanor records are available by mail. No search fee. No release necessary. Search information required: name, offense if available, years to search.

Civil records
County Clerk's Office
PO Box 515
Canton, TX 75103
(903) 567-6503
Civil records are available by mail. No release necessary. $5.00 search fee. $1.00 fee per copy. $1.00 for certification. Search information required: name, date of birth, years to search. Specify plaintiff or defendant.

Victoria County

Felony records
District Clerk's Office, Criminal Records
PO Box 1357
Victoria, TX 77902
(512) 575-0581
Felony records are available by mail or phone. No release necessary. $5.00 search fee. Search information required: name, years to search.

Civil records
District Clerk's Office
PO Box 1357
Victoria, TX 77902
(512) 575-0581
Civil records are available by mail. No release necessary. $5.00 search fee. $1.00 fee per copy. Search information required: name, date of birth, years to search. Specify plaintiff or defendant.

Misdemeanor records
County Clerk's Office
PO Box 2410
Victoria, TX 77902-2410
(512) 575-1478
Misdemeanor records are available by mail or phone. $5.00 search fee. $1.00 fee per copy. $1.00 for certification. No release necessary. Search information required: name, date of birth, years to search.

Civil records
County Clerk's Office
PO Box 2410
Victoria, TX 77902-2410
(512) 575-1478
Civil records are available by mail. No release necessary. $5.00 search fee. $1.00 fee per copy. $1.00 for certification. Search information required: name, date of birth, years to search. Specify plaintiff or defendant.

Walker County

Felony records
District Clerk's Office, Criminal Records
1100 University Ave.
Room 301, Walker County Courthouse
Huntsville, TX 77340
(409) 291-9500
Felony records are available by mail. No release necessary. $5.00 search fee. Company checks only, payable to District Clerk. Search information required: name, years to search, date of birth, SSN.

Civil records
District Clerk's Office
1100 University Ave.
Room 301, Walker County Courthouse
Huntsville, TX 77340
(409) 291-9500
Civil records are available by mail. No release necessary. $5.00 search fee. $1.00 fee per copy. $1.00 for certification. Search information required: name, date of birth, years to search. Specify plaintiff or defendant.

Misdemeanor records
County Clerk's Office
PO Box 210
Huntsville, TX 77340
(409) 291-9500
Misdemeanor records are available by mail. $5.00 search fee. Search information required: name, years to search.

Civil records
County Clerk's Office
PO Box 210
Huntsville, TX 77340
(409) 291-9500
Civil records are available by mail. No release necessary. $5.00 search fee. $1.00 fee per copy. $1.00 for certification. Search information required: name, date of birth, years to search. Specify plaintiff or defendant.

Waller County

Felony records
District Clerk's Office, Criminal Records
836 Austin Street
Room 318
Hempstead, TX 77445
(409) 826-3357 Ext. 135
Felony records are available by mail. A release is required. $5.00 search fee. Certified or personal checks, payable to District Clerk. Search information required: name, years to search.

Civil records
District Clerk's Office
836 Austin Street
Room 318
Hempstead, TX 77445
(409) 826-3357 Ext. 135
Civil records are available by mail. No release necessary. $5.00 search fee. $1.00 fee per copy. $1.00 for certification. Search information required: name, date of birth, years to search. Specify plaintiff or defendant.

Misdemeanor records
County Clerk's Office
836 Austin Street
Room 217
Hempstead, TX 77445
(409) 826-3357 Ext. 110
Misdemeanor records are available by mail. $1.00 fee per year searched. No release necessary. Search information required: name, years to search.

Civil records
County Clerk's Office
836 Austin Street
Room 217
Hempstead, TX 77445
(409) 826-3357 Ext. 112
Civil records are available by mail. No release necessary. $1.00 fee per year searched. $.50 fee per copy. $1.00 for certification plus $1.00 per page. Search information required: name, date of birth, years to search. Specify plaintiff or defendant.

Ward County

Felony records
District Clerk's Office, Criminal Records
Ward County Courthouse
Monahans, TX 79756
(915) 943-2751
Felony records are available by mail or phone. No release necessary. $5.00 search fee. Search information required: name.

Civil records
District Clerk's Office
Ward County Courthouse
Monahans, TX 79756
(915) 943-2751
Civil records are available by mail or phone. No release necessary. No search fee.$.50 fee per copy. $1.00 for certification. Search information required: name, date of birth, years to search. Specify plaintiff or defendant.

Misdemeanor records
County Clerk's Office
Ward County Courthouse
Monahans, TX 79756
(915) 943-3294
Misdemeanor records are available by mail. $5.00 search fee. Checks payable to County Clerk. No release necessary. Search information required: name, years to search.

Civil records
County Clerk's Office
Ward County Courthouse
Monahans, TX 79756
(915) 943-3294
Civil records are available by mail. No release necessary. $5.00 search fee. $1.00 fee per copy. $1.00 for certification. Search information required: name, date of birth, years to search. Specify plaintiff or defendant.

Washington County

Felony records
District Clerk's Office, Criminal Records
PO Box 1041
Brenham, TX 77834-1041
(409) 836-3763
Felony records are available by mail or phone. No release necessary. $5.00 search fee. Search information required: name.

Civil records
District Clerk's Office
PO Box 1041
Brenham, TX 77834-1041
(409) 836-3763
Civil records are available by mail or phone. No release necessary. No search fee.$1.00 fee per copy. $1.00 for certification. Search information required: name, date of birth, years to search. Specify plaintiff or defendant.

Misdemeanor records
County Clerk's Office
PO Box 609
Brenham, TX 77833
(409) 836-4300
Misdemeanor records are available by mail. $5.00 search fee. A release is required. Search information required: name, years to search.

Civil records
County Clerk's Office
PO Box 609
Brenham, TX 77833
(409) 836-4300
Civil records are available by mail. No release necessary. $5.00 search fee. $1.00 fee per copy. Search information required: name, date of birth, years to search. Specify plaintiff or defendant.

Webb County

Felony records
District Clerk's Office, Criminal Records
PO Box 667
Laredo, TX 78042-0667
(512) 721-2455
Felony records are available by mail. No release necessary. $5.00 search fee. $1.00 fee per copy. Search information required: name, SSN, date of birth, sex, race.

Civil records
District Clerk's Office
PO Box 667
Laredo, TX 78042-0667
(512) 721-2455
Civil records are available by mail. No release necessary. $5.00 search fee. $1.00 fee per copy. $1.00 for certification. Search information required: name, date of birth, years to search. Specify plaintiff or defendant.

Misdemeanor records
County Clerk's Office, Criminal Division
PO Box 599
Laredo, TX 78040-0667
(512) 727-7272 Extension 654
Fax (512) 721-2651 or 721-2653
Misdemeanor records are available by mail, phone or fax. $5.00 search fee. $1.00 fee per copy. $1.00 for certification. No release necessary. Search information required: name, date of birth, years to search.

Civil records
County Clerk's Office
PO Box 599
Laredo, TX 78040-0667
(512) 727-7272 Extension 654
Fax (512) 721-2651 or 721-2653
Civil records are available by mail. No release necessary. $5.00 search fee. $1.00 fee per copy. $1.00 for certification. Search information required: name, date of birth, years to search. Specify plaintiff or defendant.

Wharton County

Felony records
District Clerk's Office, Criminal Records
PO Drawer 391
Wharton, TX 77488
(409) 532-5542
Fax (409) 532-1299
Felony records are available by mail or phone. No release necessary. $5.00 search fee. Make check payable to District Clerk. Search information required: name.

Civil records
District Clerk's Office
PO Drawer 391
Wharton, TX 77488
(409) 532-5542
Fax (409) 532-1299
Civil records are available by mail. No release necessary. $5.00 search fee. $1.00 fee per copy. $1.00 for certification. Search information required: name, date of birth, years to search. Specify plaintiff or defendant.

Misdemeanor records
County Clerk's Office
PO Box 69
Wharton, TX 77488
(409) 532-2381
Misdemeanor records are available by mail. No search fee. A release is required. Search information required: name, date of birth, years to search.

Civil records
County Clerk's Office
PO Box 69
Wharton, TX 77488
(409) 532-2381
Civil records are available by mail. No release necessary. No search fee. $1.00 fee per copy. $1.00 for certification. Search information required: name, date of birth, years to search. Specify plaintiff or defendant.

Wheeler County

Felony records
District Clerk's Office, Criminal Records
PO Box 528
Wheeler, TX 79096
(806) 826-5931
Felony records are available by mail. No release necessary. $5.00 search fee. Make check payable to District Clerk. Search information required: name, years to search, SASE.

Civil records
District Clerk's Office
PO Box 528
Wheeler, TX 79096
(806) 826-5931
Civil records are available by mail. No release necessary. $5.00 search fee. $1.00 fee per copy. $2.00 for certification. Search information required: name, date of birth, years to search. Specify plaintiff or defendant.

Misdemeanor records
County Clerk's Office
PO Box 465
Wheeler, TX 79096
(806) 826-5544
Misdemeanor records are available by mail or phone. No search fee. $1.00 fee per copy. $1.00 for certification. No release necessary. Search information required: name, years to search.

Civil records
County Clerk's Office
PO Box 465
Wheeler, TX 79096
(806) 826-5544
Civil records are available by mail. No release necessary. No search fee. $1.00 fee per copy. $1.00 for certification. Search information required: name, date of birth, years to search. Specify plaintiff or defendant.

Wichita County

Felony records
District Clerk's Office, Criminal Records
PO Box 718
Wichita Falls, TX 76307
(817) 766-8100 Ext. 187
Felony records are available by mail or phone. No release necessary. No search fee for years searched from 1984 forward. $5.00 search fee prior to 1984. Checks payable to District Clerk. Search information required: name, SASE.

Civil records
District Clerk's Office
PO Box 718
Wichita Falls, TX 76307
(817) 766-8100 Ext. 187
Civil records are available by mail. No release necessary. $5.00 search fee. $1.00 fee per copy. $1.00 for certification. Search information required: name, date of birth, years to search, SASE. Specify plaintiff or defendant.

Misdemeanor records
County Clerk's Office, Criminal Section
PO Box 1679
Wichita Falls, TX 76307
(817) 766-8100
Misdemeanor records are available by mail or phone. No search fee. No release necessary. Search information required: name, date of birth, date of offense, years to search.

Civil records
County Clerk's Office
PO Box 1679
Wichita Falls, TX 76307
(817) 766-8100
Civil records are available by mail. No release necessary. $5.00 search fee. $1.00 fee per copy. $1.00 for certification. Search information required: name, date of birth, years to search. Specify plaintiff or defendant.

Wilbarger County

Felony records
District Clerk's Office, Criminal Records
Wilbarger County Courthouse
Vernon, TX 76384
(817) 553-3411
Felony records are available by mail or phone. No release necessary. $5.00 search fee. Make check payable to District Clerk. Search information required: name, years to search.

Civil records
District Clerk's Office
Wilbarger County Courthouse
Vernon, TX 76384
(817) 553-3411
Civil records are available by mail. No release necessary. $5.00 search fee. $1.00 fee per copy. $1.00 for certification. Search information required: name, date of birth, years to search. Specify plaintiff or defendant.

Misdemeanor records
County Clerk's Office
Wilbarger County Courthouse
Vernon, TX 76384
(817) 552-5486
Misdemeanor records are available by mail or phone. No search fee. Checks payable to County Clerk. No release necessary. Search information required: name, years to search.

Civil records
County Clerk's Office
Wilbarger County Courthouse
Vernon, TX 76384
(817) 552-5486
Civil records are available by mail. No release necessary. $10.00 search fee. $1.00 fee per copy. $1.00 for certification. Search information required: name, date of birth, years to search. Specify plaintiff or defendant.

Willacy County

Felony records
District Clerk's Office
2nd Floor
Willacy County Courthouse
Raymondville, TX 78580
(512) 689-2532
Felony records are available by mail or phone. No release necessary. $8.00 search fee. Make check payable to District Clerk. Search information required: name, years to search.

Civil records
District Clerk's Office
2nd Floor
Willacy County Courthouse
Raymondville, TX 78580
(512) 689-2532
Civil records are available by mail. No release necessary. $8.00 search fee. $1.00 fee per copy. $2.00 for certification. Search information required: name, date of birth, years to search. Specify plaintiff or defendant.

Misdemeanor records
County Clerk's Office
Willacy County Courthouse
Raymondville, TX 78580
(512) 689-2710
Misdemeanor records are available by mail or phone. No fee. No release necessary. Search information required: name, date of birth, years to search.

Civil records
County Clerk's Office
Willacy County Courthouse
Raymondville, TX 78580
(512) 689-2710
Civil records are available by mail or phone. No release necessary. No search fee. $.50 fee per copy. $5.00 for certification plus $1.00 per page. Search information required: name, date of birth, years to search. Specify plaintiff or defendant.

Williamson County

Felony records
District Clerk's Office, Lisa David
PO Box 24
Georgetown, TX 78627
(512) 869-4426 Extension 345
Felony records are available by mail. No release necessary. $5.00 search fee. Make check payable to District Clerk. Search information required: name, date of birth, years to search.

Civil records
District Clerk's Office, Lisa David
PO Box 24
Georgetown, TX 78627
(512) 869-4426 Extension 345
Civil records are available by mail. No release necessary. $5.00 search fee. $1.00 fee per copy. $1.00 for certification. Search information required: name, date of birth, years to search. Specify plaintiff or defendant.

Misdemeanor records
County Clerk's Office
PO Box 18
Georgetown, TX 78626
(512) 869-4373
Misdemeanor records are available by mail or by phone for two names. No search fee. No release necessary. Search information required: name, years to search.

Civil records
County Clerk's Office
PO Box 18
Georgetown, TX 78626
(512) 869-4373
Civil records are available by mail. No release necessary. $5.00 search fee. $1.00 fee per copy. Search information required: name, date of birth, years to search. Specify plaintiff or defendant.

Wilson County

Felony records
District Clerk's Office, Criminal Records
PO Box 812
Floresville, TX 78114
(512) 393-7322
Fax (512) 393-7319
Felony records are available by mail or phone. No release necessary. $5.00 search fee. Make check payable to District Clerk. Search information required: name, years to search.

Felony records
District Clerk's Office, Criminal Records
PO Box 812
Floresville, TX 78114
(512) 393-7322
Fax (512) 393-7319
Civil records are available by mail. No release necessary. $8.00 search fee. $.50 fee per copy. $1.00 for certification. Search information required: name, date of birth, years to search. Specify plaintiff or defendant.

Misdemeanor records
County Clerk's Office
PO Box 27
Floresville, TX 78114
(512) 393-7308
Misdemeanor records are available by mail. No search fee. $1.00 fee per copied page. Release, if available. Search information required: name, years to search, date of offense.

Civil records
County Clerk's Office
PO Box 27
Floresville, TX 78114
(512) 393-7308
Civil records are available by mail. No release necessary. No search fee. $.50 fee per copy. $1.00 for certification plus $1.00 per page. Search information required: name, date of birth, years to search. Specify plaintiff or defendant.

Winkler County

Felony records
District Clerk's Office, Criminal Records
PO Box 1065
Kermit, TX 79745
(915) 586-3359
Felony records are available by mail or phone. No release necessary. $5.00 search fee. $1.00 fee per copy. Checks payable to District Clerk. Search information required: name, years to search.

Civil records
District Clerk's Office
PO Box 1065
Kermit, TX 79745
(915) 586-3359
Civil records are available by mail. No release necessary. $5.00 search fee. $1.00 fee per copy. Search information required: name, date of birth, years to search. Specify plaintiff or defendant.

Misdemeanor records
County Clerk's Office
Box 1007
Kermit, TX 79745
(915) 586-3401
Misdemeanor records are available by mail or phone. No search fee. $1.00 fee per copy, $1.00 for certification. A release is required. Search information required: name, years to search.

Civil records
County Clerk's Office
Box 1007
Kermit, TX 79745
(915) 586-3401
Civil records are available by mail or phone. No release necessary. $5.00 search fee. $1.00 fee per copy. $1.00 for certification. Search information required: name, date of birth, years to search. Specify plaintiff or defendant.

Wise County

Felony records
District Clerk's Office, Criminal Records
PO Box 308
Decatur, TX 76234
(817) 627-5535
Fax (817) 627-6404
Felony records are available by mail or phone. No release necessary. $5.00 search fee. Certified or personal checks, payable to District Clerk. Search information required: name.

Civil records
District Clerk's Office
PO Box 308
Decatur, TX 76234
(817) 627-5535
Civil records are available by mail or phone. No release necessary. No search fee. $1.00 fee per copy. $5.00 for certification. Search information required: name, date of birth, years to search. Specify plaintiff or defendant.

Misdemeanor records
County Clerk's Office
PO Box 359
Decatur, TX 76234
(817) 627-3351
Misdemeanor records are available by mail. $10.00 search fee. Checks payable to County Clerk. No release necessary. Search information required: name, years to search.

Civil records
County Clerk's Office
PO Box 359
Decatur, TX 76234
(817) 627-3351
Civil records are available by mail or phone. No release necessary. No search fee. $1.00 fee per copy. $5.00 for certification. Search information required: name, date of birth, years to search. Specify plaintiff or defendant.

Wood County

Felony records
District Clerk's Office, Criminal Records
PO Box 447
Quitman, TX 75783
(903) 763-2361
Felony records are available by mail or phone. A release is required. $5.00 search fee. Search information required: name, SSN, years to search.

Civil records
District Clerk's Office
PO Box 447
Quitman, TX 75783
(903) 763-2361
Civil records are available by mail or phone. No release necessary. $5.00 search fee. $1.00 fee per copy. $1.00 for certification. Search information required: name, date of birth, years to search. Specify plaintiff or defendant.

Misdemeanor records
County Clerk's Office
PO Box 338
Quitman, TX 75783
(903) 763-2711
Fax (903) 763-5549
Misdemeanor records are available by mail or phone. No search fee. No release necessary. Search information required: name, years to search.

Civil records
County Clerk's Office
PO Box 338
Quitman, TX 75783
(903) 763-2711
Civil records are available by mail or phone. No release necessary. No search fee. $1.00 fee per copy. $1.00 for certification. Search information required: name, date of birth, years to search. Specify plaintiff or defendant.

Yoakum County

Felony records
District Clerk's Office, Mae Barnett
PO Box 899
Plains, TX 79355
(806) 456-7453
Fax (806) 456-6175
Felony records are available by mail or phone. No release necessary. $5.00 search fee. Make check payable to District Clerk. Search information required: name, SSN.

Civil records
District Clerk's Office, Mae Barnett
PO Box 899
Plains, TX 79355
(806) 456-7453
Fax (806) 456-6175
Civil records are available by mail. No release necessary. $5.00 search fee. $1.00 fee per copy. $1.00 for certification. Search information required: name, date of birth, years to search. Specify plaintiff or defendant.

Misdemeanor records
County Clerk's Office
PO Box 309
Plains, TX 79355
(806) 456-2721
Fax (806) 456-6175
Misdemeanor records are available by mail. $5.00 search fee. $1.00 fee per copy. $1.00 for certification. No release necessary. Search information required: name, offense, years to search.

Civil records
County Clerk's Office
PO Box 309
Plains, TX 79355
(806) 456-2721
Civil records are available by mail. No release necessary. $5.00 search fee. $1.00 fee per copy. $1.00 for certification. Search information required: name, date of birth, years to search. Specify plaintiff or defendant.

Young County

District Clerk's Office, Criminal Records
PO Box 1138
Graham, TX 76046
(817) 549-0029
Felony and misdemeanor records are available by mail or phone. No release necessary. $5.00 search fee. Make check payable to District Clerk. Search information required: name.

Civil records are available by mail. No release necessary. $5.00 search fee. $1.00 fee per copy. $2.00 for certification. Search information required: name, date of birth, years to search. Specify plaintiff or defendant.

Zapata County

Felony records
District Clerk's Office, Criminal Records
PO Box 789
Zapata, TX 78076
(512) 765-9930
Fax (512) 765-9784
Felony records are available by mail, phone or fax. No release necessary. No search fee. Search information required: name.

Civil records
District Clerk's Office
PO Box 789
Zapata, TX 78076
(512) 765-9930
Fax (512) 765-9784
Civil records are available by mail. No release necessary. $5.00 search fee. $1.00 fee per copy. $1.00 for certification plus $1.00 per page. Search information required: name, date of birth, years to search. Specify plaintiff or defendant.

Misdemeanor records
County Clerk's Office
PO Box 789
Zapata, TX 78076
(512) 765-9915
Fax (512) 765-9036
Misdemeanor records are available by mail or phone. $5.00 search fee. Checks payable to County Clerk. No release necessary. Search information required: name, years to search.

Civil records
County Clerk's Office
PO Box 789
Zapata, TX 78076
(512) 765-9915
Civil records are available by mail. No release necessary. $5.00 search fee. $1.00 fee per copy. Search information required: name, date of birth, years to search. Specify plaintiff or defendant.

Zavala County

District Clerk's Office, Criminal Records
PO Box 704
Crystal City, TX 78839
(512) 374-3456
Felony records are available by mail or phone. No release necessary. $5.00 search fee. $1.00 fee per copy. Company checks only, payable to District Clerk. Search information required: name, SSN, date of birth, sex, race.

Civil records are available by mail. No release necessary. $5.00 search fee. $1.00 fee per copy. $1.00 for certification. Search information required: name, date of birth, years to search. Specify plaintiff or defendant.

City-County Cross Reference

Abbott *Hill*
Abernathy *Hale*
Abilene *Taylor*
Ace *Polk*
Ackerly *Dawson*
Addison *Dallas*
Adkins *Bexar*
Adrian *Oldham*
Afton *Dickens*
Agua Dulce *Nueces*
Aiken *Floyd*
Alamo *Hidalgo*
Alamo Heights *Bexar*
Alanreed *Gray*
Alba *Wood*
Albany *Shackelford*
Albert *Gillespie*
Aldine *Harris*
Aledo *Parker*
Algoa *Galveston*
Alice *Jim Wells*
Alief *Harris*
Allen *Collin*
Allison *Wheeler*
Alpine *Brewster*
Altair *Colorado*
Alto *Cherokee*
Alvarado *Johnson*
Alvin *Brazoria*
Alvord *Wise*
Amarillo *Potter*

Ames *Liberty*
Amherst *Lamb*
Anahuac *Chambers*
Anderson *Grimes*
Andrews *Andrews*
Angleton *Brazoria*
Anna *Collin*
Annona *Red River*
Anson *Jones*
Antelope *Jack*
Anthony *El Paso*
Anton *Hockley*
Apple Springs *Trinity*
Aquilla *Hill*
Aransas Pass *San Patricio*
Archer City *Archer*
Argyle *Denton*
Arlington *Tarrant*
Armstrong *Kenedy*
Arp *Smith*
Art *Mason*
Arthur City *Lamar*
Asherton *Dimmit*
Aspermont *Stonewall*
Atascosa *Bexar*
Athens *Henderson*
Atlanta *Cass*
Aubrey *Denton*
Austin *Travis*
Austwell *Refugio*
Avalon *Ellis*

Avery *Red River*
Avinger *Cass*
Axtell *McLennan*
Azle *Tarrant*
Bacliff *Galveston*
Bagwell *Red River*
Bailey *Fannin*
Baird *Callahan*
Balch Springs *Dallas*
Ballinger *Runnels*
Balmorhea *Reeves*
Bandera *Bandera*
Bangs *Brown*
Banquete *Nueces*
Bardwell *Ellis*
Barker *Harris*
Barksdale *Edwards*
Barnhart *Irion*
Barry *Navarro*
Barstow *Ward*
Bartlett *Bell*
Bastrop *Bastrop*
Batesville *Zavala*
Batson *Hardin*
Bay City *Matagorda*
Bayside *Refugio*
Baytown *Harris*
Beasley *Fort Bend*
Beaumont *Jefferson*
Beaumont Place *Harris*
Bebe *Gonzales*

Beckville *Panola*
Bedford *Tarrant*
Bedias *Grimes*
Bee House *Coryell*
Beeville *Bee*
Bellaire *Harris*
Bellevue *Clay*
Bellmead *McLennan*
Bells *Grayson*
Bellville *Austin*
Belmont *Gonzales*
Belton *Bell*
Ben Arnold *Milam*
Benavides *Duval*
Benbrook *Tarrant*
Bend *San Saba*
Ben Franklin *Delta*
Benjamin *Knox*
Ben Wheeler *Van Zandt*
Berclair *Goliad*
Bertram *Burnet*
Best *Reagan*
Big Bend National Park *Brewster*
Bigfoot *Frio*
Big Lake *Reagan*
Big Sandy *Upshur*
Big Spring *Howard*
Big Wells *Dimmit*
Birome *Hill*
Bishop *Nueces*

Bivins *Cass*
Blackwell *Nolan*
Blanco *Blanco*
Blanket *Brown*
Bledsoe *Cochran*
Bleiblerville *Austin*
Blessing *Matagorda*
Bloomburg *Cass*
Blooming Grove *Navarro*
Bloomington *Victoria*
Blossom *Lamar*
Bluegrove *Clay*
Blue Mound *Tarrant*
Blue Ridge *Collin*
Bluff Dale *Erath*
Bluffton *Llano*
Blum *Hill*
Boerne *Kendall*
Bogata *Red River*
Boling *Wharton*
Bonham *Fannin*
Bon Wier *Newton*
Booker *Lipscomb*
Borger *Hutchinson*
Bosqueville *McLennan*
Boston *Bowie*
Bovina *Parmer*
Bowie *Montague*
Boyd *Wise*
Boys Ranch *Oldham*
Brackettville *Kinney*
Brady *McCulloch*
Brandon *Hill*
Brashear *Hopkins*
Brazoria *Brazoria*
Breckenridge *Stephens*
Bremond *Robertson*
Brenham *Washington*
Bridge City *Orange*
Bridgeport *Wise*
Briggs *Burnet*
Briscoe *Wheeler*
Broaddus *San Augustine*
Bronson *Sabine*
Bronte *Coke*
Brookeland *Sabine*
Brookesmith *Brown*
Brookshire *Waller*
Brookston *Lamar*
Brownfield *Terry*
Brownsboro *Henderson*
Brownsville *Cameron*
Brownwood *Brown*
Bruceville *McLennan*
Bruni *Webb*
Bryan *Brazos*
Bryson *Jack*
Buchanan Dam *Llano*
Buckholts *Milam*
Buda *Hays*
Buffalo *Leon*
Buffalo Gap *Taylor*
Bula *Bailey*
Bullard *Smith*
Buna *Jasper*
Bunker Hill Village *Harris*
Burkburnett *Wichita*
Burkett *Coleman*
Burkeville *Newton*
Burleson *Johnson*
Burlington *Milam*
Burnet *Burnet*
Burton *Washington*
Bushland *Potter*
Byers *Clay*

Bynum *Hill*
Cactus *Moore*
Caddo *Stephens*
Caddo Mills *Hunt*
Caldwell *Burleson*
Call *Newton*
Calliham *McMullen*
Calvert *Robertson*
Camden *Polk*
Cameron *Milam*
Campbell *Hunt*
Campbellton *Atascosa*
Camp Wood *Real*
Canadian *Hemphill*
Canton *Van Zandt*
Canutillo *El Paso*
Canyon *Randall*
Carbon *Eastland*
Carey *Childress*
Carlsbad *Tom Green*
Carlton *Hamilton*
Carmine *Fayette*
Carrizo Springs *Dimmit*
Carrollton *Dallas*
Carthage *Panola*
Cason *Morris*
Castell *Llano*
Castle Hills *Bexar*
Castroville *Medina*
Catarina *Dimmit*
Cat Spring *Austin*
Cayuga *Anderson*
Cedar Creek *Bastrop*
Cedar Hill *Dallas*
Cedar Lane *Matagorda*
Cedar Park *Williamson*
Cee Vee *Cottle*
Celeste *Hunt*
Celina *Collin*
Center *Shelby*
Center Point *Kerr*
Centerville *Leon*
Centralia *Trinity*
Chalk *Cottle*
Chandler *Henderson*
Channelview *Harris*
Channing *Hartley*
Chapman Ranch *Nueces*
Chappell Hill *Washington*
Charlotte *Atascosa*
Chatfield *Navarro*
Cheapside *Gonzales*
Cherokee *San Saba*
Chester *Tyler*
Chico *Wise*
Chicota *Lamar*
Childress *Childress*
Chillicothe *Hardeman*
Chilton *Falls*
China *Jefferson*
China Spring *McLennan*
Chireno *Nacogdoches*
Chriesman *Burleson*
Christine *Atascosa*
Christoval *Tom Green*
Cibolo *Guadalupe*
Cisco *Eastland*
Clarendon *Donley*
Clarksville *Red River*
Claude *Armstrong*
Clayton *Panola*
Cleburne *Johnson*
Cleveland *Liberty*
Clifton *Bosque*
Clint *El Paso*

Cloverleaf *Harris*
Clute *Brazoria*
Clyde *Callahan*
Coahoma *Howard*
Cockrell Hill *Dallas*
Coldspring *San Jacinto*
Coleman *Coleman*
Collegeport *Matagorda*
College Station *Brazos*
Colleyville *Tarrant*
Collinsville *Grayson*
Colmesneil *Tyler*
Colorado City *Mitchell*
Columbus *Colorado*
Comanche *Comanche*
Combes *Cameron*
Comfort *Kendall*
Commerce *Hunt*
Como *Hopkins*
Comstock *Val Verde*
Concan *Uvalde*
Concepcion *Duval*
Concord *Leon*
Cone *Crosby*
Conroe *Montgomery*
Converse *Bexar*
Cookville *Titus*
Coolidge *Limestone*
Cooper *Delta*
Copeville *Collin*
Coppell *Dallas*
Copperas Cove *Coryell*
Corinth *Denton*
Corpus Christi *Nueces*
Corrigan *Polk*
Corsicana *Navarro*
Cost *Gonzales*
Cotton Center *Hale*
Cotulla *LaSalle*
Coupland *Williamson*
Covington *Hill*
Coyanosa *Pecos*
Crandall *Kaufman*
Crane *Crane*
Cranfills Gap *Bosque*
Crawford *McLennan*
Cresson *Hood*
Crockett *Houston*
Crosby *Harris*
Crosbyton *Crosby*
Cross Plains *Callahan*
Crowell *Foard*
Crowley *Tarrant*
Crystal City *Zavala*
Cuero *DeWitt*
Cumby *Hopkins*
Cuney *Cherokee*
Cunningham *Lamar*
Cushing *Nacogdoches*
Cut And Shoot
   Montgomery
Cypress *Harris*
Daingerfield *Morris*
Daisetta *Liberty*
Dale *Caldwell*
Dalhart *Dallam*
Dallardsville *Polk*
Dallas *Dallas*
Dalworthington Gardens
   Tarrant
Damon *Brazoria*
Danbury *Brazoria*
Danciger *Brazoria*
Danevang *Wharton*
Darrouzett *Lipscomb*

Davilla *Milam*
Dawn *Deaf Smith*
Dawson *Navarro*
Dayton *Liberty*
Deanville *Burleson*
DeBerry *Panola*
Decatur *Wise*
Deer Park *Harris*
DeKalb *Bowie*
DeLeon *Comanche*
Dell City *Hudspeth*
Delmita *Starr*
Del Rio *Val Verde*
Del Valle *Travis*
Denison *Grayson*
Dennis *Parker*
Denton *Denton*
Denver City *Yoakum*
Deport *Lamar*
Dermott *Scurry*
Desdemona *Eastland*
DeSoto *Dallas*
Detroit *Red River*
Devers *Liberty*
Devine *Medina*
Deweyville *Newton*
D' Hanis *Medina*
Diana *Upshur*
Diboll *Angelina*
Dickens *Dickens*
Dickinson *Galveston*
Dike *Hopkins*
Dilley *Frio*
Dime Box *Lee*
Dimmitt *Castro*
Dobbin *Montgomery*
Dodd City *Fannin*
Dodge *Walker*
Dodson *Collingsworth*
Donie *Freestone*
Donna *Hidalgo*
Doole *McCulloch*
Doss *Gillespie*
Doucette *Tyler*
Dougherty *Floyd*
Douglass *Nacogdoches*
Douglassville *Cass*
Driftwood *Hays*
Dripping Springs *Hays*
Driscoll *Nueces*
Dryden *Terrell*
Dublin *Erath*
Duffau *Erath*
Dumas *Moore*
Dumont *King*
Duncanville *Dallas*
Dunn *Scurry*
Eagle Lake *Colorado*
Eagle Pass *Maverick*
Early *Brown*
Earth *Lamb*
East Bernard *Wharton*
Eastland *Eastland*
Easton *Gregg*
Ector *Fannin*
Edcouch *Hidalgo*
Eddy *McLennan*
Eden *Concho*
Edgecliff *Tarrant*
Edgewood *Van Zandt*
Edinburg *Hidalgo*
Edmonson *Hale*
Edna *Jackson*
Edroy *San Patricio*
Egypt *Wharton*

Elbert *Throckmorton*
El Campo *Wharton*
El Dorado *Schleicher*
Electra *Wichita*
Elgin *Bastrop*
Eliasville *Young*
El Indio *Maverick*
Elkhart *Anderson*
Ellinger *Fayette*
Elmaton *Matagorda*
Elmendorf *Bexar*
Elm Mott *McLennan*
Elmo *Kaufman*
El Paso *El Paso*
Elsa *Hidalgo*
Elysian Fields *Harrison*
Emory *Rains*
Encinal *LaSalle*
Encino *Brooks*
Energy *Comanche*
Enloe *Delta*
Ennis *Ellis*
Enochs *Bailey*
Eola *Concho*
Era *Cooke*
Estelline *Hall*
Etoile *Nacogdoches*
Euless *Tarrant*
Eustace *Henderson*
Evadale *Jasper*
Evant *Coryell*
Everman *Tarrant*
Fabens *El Paso*
Fairfield *Freestone*
Fairview *Collin*
Falcon Heights *Starr*
Falfurrias *Brooks*
Falls City *Karnes*
Fannin *Goliad*
Farmers Branch *Dallas*
Farmersville *Collin*
Farnsworth *Ochiltree*
Farwell *Parmer*
Fashing *Atascosa*
Fate *Rockwall*
Fayetteville *Fayette*
Fentress *Caldwell*
Ferris *Ellis*
Fieldton *Lamb*
Fife *McCulloch*
Fischer *Comal*
Flat *Coryell*
Flatonia *Fayette*
Flint *Smith*
Flomot *Motley*
Florence *Williamson*
Floresville *Wilson*
Floydada *Floyd*
Fluvanna *Scurry*
Flynn *Leon*
Follett *Lipscomb*
Forestburg *Montague*
Forest Hill *Tarrant*
Forney *Kaufman*
Forreston *Ellis*
Forsan *Howard*
Fort Davis *Jeff Davis*
Fort Hancock *Hudspeth*
Fort McKavett *Menard*
Fort Stockton *Pecos*
Fort Worth *Tarrant*
Fowlerton *LaSalle*
Francitas *Jackson*
Franklin *Robertson*
Frankston *Anderson*

Fred *Tyler*
Fredericksburg *Gillespie*
Fredonia *Mason*
Freeport *Brazoria*
Freer *Duval*
Fresno *Fort Bend*
Friendswood *Galveston*
Friona *Parmer*
Frisco *Collin*
Fritch *Hutchinson*
Frost *Navarro*
Fruitvale *Van Zandt*
Fulshear *Fort Bend*
Fulton *Aransas*
Gail *Borden*
Gainesville *Cooke*
Galena Park *Harris*
Gallatin *Cherokee*
Galveston *Galveston*
Ganado *Jackson*
Garciasville *Starr*
Garden City *Glasscock*
Gardendale *Ector*
Garland *Dallas*
Garrison *Nacogdoches*
Garwood *Colorado*
Gary *Panola*
Gatesville *Coryell*
Gause *Milam*
Geneva *Sabine*
Georgetown *Williamson*
George West *Live Oak*
Geronimo *Guadalupe*
Giddings *Lee*
Gilchrist *Galveston*
Gillett *Karnes*
Gilmer *Upshur*
Girard *Kent*
Girvin *Pecos*
Gladewater *Gregg*
Glen Flora *Wharton*
Glen Rose *Somervell*
Gober *Fannin*
Godley *Johnson*
Golden *Wood*
Goldsboro *Coleman*
Goldsmith *Ector*
Goldthwaite *Mills*
Goliad *Goliad*
Gonzales *Gonzales*
Goodland *Bailey*
Goodrich *Polk*
Gordon *Palo Pinto*
Gordonville *Grayson*
Goree *Knox*
Gorman *Eastland*
Gouldbusk *Coleman*
Graford *Palo Pinto*
Graham *Young*
Granbury *Hood*
Grandfalls *Ward*
Grand Prairie *Dallas*
Grand Saline *Van Zandt*
Grandview *Johnson*
Granger *Williamson*
Grapeland *Houston*
Grapevine *Tarrant*
Greenville *Hunt*
Greenwood *Wise*
Gregory *San Patricio*
Groesbeck *Limestone*
Groom *Carson*
Groves *Jefferson*
Groveton *Trinity*
Grulla *Starr*

Gruver *Hansford*
Guerra *Jim Hogg*
Gun Barrel City *Henderson*
Gunter *Grayson*
Gustine *Comanche*
Guthrie *King*
Guy *Fort Bend*
Hale Center *Hale*
Hallettsville *Lavaca*
Hallsville *Harrison*
Haltom City *Tarrant*
Hamilton *Hamilton*
Hamlin *Jones*
Hamshire *Jefferson*
Hankamer *Chambers*
Happy *Swisher*
Hardin *Liberty*
Hargill *Hidalgo*
Harker Heights *Bell*
Harleton *Harrison*
Harlingen *Cameron*
Harper *Gillespie*
Harrold *Wilbarger*
Hart *Castro*
Hartley *Hartley*
Harwood *Gonzales*
Haskell *Haskell*
Haslet *Tarrant*
Hasse *Comanche*
Hawkins *Wood*
Hawley *Jones*
Hearne *Robertson*
Hebbronville *Jim Hogg*
Hedley *Donley*
Hedwig Village *Harris*
Heidenheimer *Bell*
Helotes *Bexar*
Hemphill *Sabine*
Hempstead *Waller*
Henderson *Rusk*
Henrietta *Clay*
Hereford *Deaf Smith*
Hermleigh *Scurry*
Hewitt *McLennan*
Hext *Menard*
Hico *Hamilton*
Hidalgo *Hidalgo*
Higgins *Lipscomb*
High Island *Galveston*
Highland Park *Dallas*
Highlands *Harris*
Hillister *Tyler*
Hillsboro *Hill*
Hilshire Village *Harris*
Hitchcock *Galveston*
Hobson *Karnes*
Hochheim *DeWitt*
Hockley *Harris*
Holland *Bell*
Holliday *Archer*
Hondo *Medina*
Honey Grove *Fannin*
Hooks *Bowie*
Horizon City *El Paso*
Houston *Harris*
Howe *Grayson*
Hubbard *Hill*
Huffman *Harris*
Hughes Springs *Cass*
Hull *Liberty*
Humble *Harris*
Hungerford *Wharton*
Hunt *Kerr*
Hunters Creek Village
   Harris

Huntington *Angelina*
Huntsville *Walker*
Hurst *Tarrant*
Hutchins *Dallas*
Hutto *Williamson*
Hye *Blanco*
Idalou *Lubbock*
Imperial *Pecos*
Industry *Austin*
Inez *Victoria*
Ingleside *San Patricio*
Ingram *Kerr*
Iola *Grimes*
Iowa Park *Wichita*
Ira *Scurry*
Iraan *Pecos*
Iredell *Bosque*
Irene *Hill*
Irving *Dallas*
Italy *Ellis*
Itasca *Hill*
Ivanhoe *Fannin*
Jacinto City *Harris*
Jacksboro *Jack*
Jacksonville *Cherokee*
Jarrell *Williamson*
Jasper *Jasper*
Jayton *Kent*
Jefferson *Marion*
Jermyn *Jack*
Jewett *Leon*
Joaquin *Shelby*
Johnson City *Blanco*
Joinerville *Rusk*
Jonesboro *Coryell*
Jones Creek *Brazoria*
Jonesville *Harrison*
Josephine *Collin*
Joshua *Johnson*
Jourdanton *Atascosa*
Judson *Gregg*
Junction *Kimble*
Justiceburg *Garza*
Justin *Denton*
Kamay *Wichita*
Karnack *Harrison*
Karnes City *Karnes*
Katemcy *Mason*
Katy *Harris*
Kaufman *Kaufman*
Keene *Johnson*
Keller *Tarrant*
Kemah *Galveston*
Kemp *Kaufman*
Kempner *Lampasas*
Kendalia *Kendall*
Kendleton *Fort Bend*
Kenedy *Karnes*
Kennard *Houston*
Kennedale *Tarrant*
Kenney *Austin*
Kerens *Navarro*
Kermit *Winkler*
Kerrville *Kerr*
Kildare *Cass*
Kilgore *Gregg*
Killeen *Bell*
Kingsbury *Guadalupe*
Kingsland *Llano*
Kingsville *Kleberg*
Kingwood *Harris*
Kirby *Bexar*
Kirbyville *Jasper*
Kirkland *Childress*
Kirvin *Freestone*

Klondike *Delta*
Knickerbocker *Tom Green*
Knippa *Uvalde*
Knott *Howard*
Knox City *Knox*
Kopperl *Bosque*
Kosse *Limestone*
Kountze *Hardin*
Kress *Swisher*
Krum *Denton*
Kurten *Brazos*
Kyle *Hays*
LaBlanca *Hidalgo*
Lacy-Lakeview *McLennan*
LaCoste *Medina*
Ladonia *Fannin*
LaFeria *Cameron*
LaGrange *Fayette*
Laird Hill *Rusk*
LaJoya *Hidalgo*
Lake Creek *Delta*
Lake Dallas *Denton*
Lake Jackson *Brazoria*
Lakeport *Gregg*
Lakeview *Hall*
Lakeway *Travis*
Lake Worth *Tarrant*
LaMarque *Galveston*
Lamesa *Dawson*
Lampasas *Lampasas*
Lancaster *Dallas*
Lane City *Wharton*
Laneville *Rusk*
Langtry *Val Verde*
LaPorte *Harris*
LaPryor *Zavala*
Laredo *Webb*
Larue *Henderson*
LaSalle *Jackson*
Lasara *Willacy*
Latexo *Houston*
LaVernia *Wilson*
LaVilla *Hidalgo*
Lavon *Collin*
LaWard *Jackson*
Lawn *Taylor*
Lazbuddie *Parmer*
Leaday *Coleman*
League City *Galveston*
Leakey *Real*
Leander *Williamson*
Ledbetter *Fayette*
Leesburg *Camp*
Leesville *Gonzales*
Lefors *Gray*
Leggett *Polk*
Lelia Lake *Donley*
Leming *Atascosa*
Lenorah *Martin*
Leon Valley *Bexar*
Leona *Leon*
Leonard *Fannin*
Leon Junction *Coryell*
Leroy *McLennan*
Levelland *Hockley*
Lewisville *Denton*
Lexington *Lee*
Liberty *Liberty*
Liberty Hill *Williamson*
Lillian *Johnson*
Lincoln *Lee*
Lindale *Smith*
Linden *Cass*
Lindsay *Cooke*
Lingleville *Erath*

Linn *Hidalgo*
Lipan *Hood*
Lipscomb *Lipscomb*
Lissie *Wharton*
Little Elm *Denton*
Littlefield *Lamb*
Little River *Bell*
Live Oak *Bexar*
Liverpool *Brazoria*
Livingston *Polk*
Llano *Llano*
Lockhart *Caldwell*
Lockney *Floyd*
Lodi *Marion*
Lohn *McCulloch*
Lolita *Jackson*
Lometa *Lampasas*
London *Kimble*
Lone Oak *Hunt*
Lone Star *Morris*
Long Branch *Panola*
Long Mott *Calhoun*
Longview *Gregg*
Loop *Gaines*
Lopeno *Zapata*
Loraine *Mitchell*
Lorena *McLennan*
Lorenzo *Crosby*
Los Ebanos *Hidalgo*
Los Fresnos *Cameron*
Los Indios *Cameron*
Lott *Falls*
Louise *Wharton*
Lovelady *Houston*
Loving *Young*
Lowake *Concho*
Lozano *Cameron*
Lubbock *Lubbock*
Lucas *Collin*
Lueders *Jones*
Lufkin *Angelina*
Luling *Caldwell*
Lumberton *Hardin*
Lyford *Willacy*
Lyons *Burleson*
Lytle *Atascosa*
McAdoo *Dickens*
McAllen *Hidalgo*
McCamey *Upton*
McCaulley *Fisher*
McCoy *Atascosa*
McDade *Bastrop*
McFaddin *Victoria*
McGregor *McLennan*
McKinney *Collin*
McLean *Gray*
McLeod *Cass*
McNeil *Travis*
McQueeney *Guadalupe*
Mabank *Kaufman*
Macdona *Bexar*
Madisonville *Madison*
Magnolia *Montgomery*
Magnolia Springs *Jasper*
Malakoff *Henderson*
Malone *Hill*
Manchaca *Travis*
Manor *Travis*
Mansfield *Tarrant*
Manvel *Brazoria*
Maple *Bailey*
Marathon *Brewster*
Marble Falls *Burnet*
Marfa *Presidio*
Marietta *Cass*

Marion *Guadalupe*
Markham *Matagorda*
Marlin *Falls*
Marquez *Leon*
Marshall *Harrison*
Mart *McLennan*
Martindale *Caldwell*
Martinsville *Nacogdoches*
Maryneal *Nolan*
Mason *Mason*
Masterson *Moore*
Matador *Motley*
Matagorda *Matagorda*
Mathis *San Patricio*
Maud *Bowie*
Mauriceville *Orange*
Maxwell *Caldwell*
May *Brown*
Maydelle *Cherokee*
Maypearl *Ellis*
Maysfield *Milam*
Meadow *Terry*
Medina *Bandera*
Megargel *Archer*
Melissa *Collin*
Melvin *McCulloch*
Memphis *Hall*
Menard *Menard*
Mentone *Loving*
Mercedes *Hidalgo*
Mereta *Tom Green*
Meridian *Bosque*
Merit *Hunt*
Merkel *Taylor*
Mertens *Hill*
Mertzon *Irion*
Mesquite *Dallas*
Mexia *Limestone*
Meyersville *DeWitt*
Miami *Roberts*
Midfield *Matagorda*
Midkiff *Upton*
Midland *Midland*
Midlothian *Ellis*
Midway *Madison*
Milam *Sabine*
Milano *Milam*
Miles *Runnels*
Milford *Ellis*
Millersview *Concho*
Millican *Brazos*
Millsap *Parker*
Minden *Rusk*
Mineola *Wood*
Mineral Wells *Palo Pinto*
Mingus *Palo Pinto*
Mirando City *Webb*
Mission *Hidalgo*
Missouri City *Fort Bend*
Mobeetie *Wheeler*
Monahans *Ward*
Monroe City *Chambers*
Montague *Montague*
Montalba *Anderson*
Mont Belvieu *Chambers*
Monte Alto *Hidalgo*
Montgomery *Montgomery*
Moody *McLennan*
Moore *Frio*
Moran *Shackelford*
Morgan *Bosque*
Morgan Mill *Erath*
Morse *Hansford*
Morton *Cochran*
Moscow *Polk*

Moulton *Lavaca*
Mound *Coryell*
Mountain Home *Kerr*
Mount Calm *Hill*
Mount Enterprise *Rusk*
Mount Pleasant *Titus*
Mount Vernon *Franklin*
Muenster *Cooke*
Muldoon *Fayette*
Muleshoe *Bailey*
Mullin *Mills*
Mumford *Robertson*
Munday *Knox*
Murchison *Henderson*
Myra *Cooke*
Nacogdoches *Nacogdoches*
Nada *Colorado*
Naples *Morris*
Nash *Bowie*
Nassau Bay *Harris*
Natalia *Medina*
Navasota *Grimes*
Nazareth *Castro*
Neches *Anderson*
Nederland *Jefferson*
Needville *Fort Bend*
Nemo *Somervell*
Nevada *Collin*
Newark *Wise*
New Baden *Robertson*
New Boston *Bowie*
New Braunfels *Comal*
New Caney *Montgomery*
Newcastle *Young*
New Deal *Lubbock*
Newgulf *Wharton*
New London *Rusk*
Newport *Clay*
New Summerfield
    Cherokee
Newton *Newton*
New Ulm *Austin*
New Waverly *Walker*
Nixon *Gonzales*
Nocona *Montague*
Nolan *Nolan*
Nolanville *Bell*
Nome *Jefferson*
Nordheim *DeWitt*
Normangee *Leon*
Normanna *Bee*
Northcrest *McLennan*
Northfield *Motley*
North Houston *Harris*
North Richland Hills
    Tarrant
North Zulch *Madison*
Norton *Runnels*
Notrees *Ector*
Novice *Coleman*
Nursery *Victoria*
Oakhurst *San Jacinto*
Oakland *Colorado*
Oakwood *Leon*
O'Brien *Haskell*
Odell *Wilbarger*
Odem *San Patricio*
Odessa *Ector*
O'Donnell *Lynn*
Oglesby *Coryell*
Oilton *Webb*
Oklaunion *Wilbarger*
Olden *Eastland*
Old Glory *Stonewall*
Old Ocean *Brazoria*

Olmito *Cameron*
Olmos Park *Bexar*
Olney *Young*
Olton *Lamb*
Omaha *Morris*
Onalaska *Polk*
Orange *Orange*
Orangefield *Orange*
Orange Grove *Jim Wells*
Orchard *Fort Bend*
Ore City *Upshur*
Orla *Reeves*
Ottine *Gonzales*
Otto *Falls*
Ovalo *Taylor*
Overton *Rusk*
Oyster Creek *Brazoria*
Ozona *Crockett*
Paducah *Cottle*
Paige *Bastrop*
Paint Rock *Concho*
Palacios *Matagorda*
Palestine *Anderson*
Palmer *Ellis*
Palo Pinto *Palo Pinto*
Paluxy *Hood*
Pampa *Gray*
Pandora *Wilson*
Panhandle *Carson*
Panna Maria *Karnes*
Panola *Panola*
Pantego *Tarrant*
Paradise *Wise*
Paris *Lamar*
Pasadena *Harris*
Pattison *Waller*
Pattonville *Lamar*
Pawnee *Bee*
Peacock *Stonewall*
Pearland *Brazoria*
Pearsall *Frio*
Pear Valley *McCulloch*
Peaster *Parker*
Pecan Gap *Delta*
Pecos *Reeves*
Peggy *Atascosa*
Pendleton *Bell*
Penelope *Hill*
Penitas *Hidalgo*
Pennington *Trinity*
Penwell *Ector*
Pep *Hockley*
Perrin *Jack*
Perry *Falls*
Perryton *Ochiltree*
Petersburg *Hale*
Petrolia *Clay*
Pettit *Hockley*
Pettus *Bee*
Petty *Lamar*
Pflugerville *Travis*
Pharr *Hidalgo*
Phillips *Hutchinson*
Pickton *Hopkins*
Pierce *Wharton*
Pilot Point *Denton*
Pinehurst *Montgomery*
Pineland *Sabine*
Piney Point Village *Harris*
Pipe Creek *Bandera*
Pittsburg *Camp*
Placedo *Victoria*
Plains *Yoakum*
Plainview *Hale*
Plano *Collin*

Plantersville *Grimes*
Pleasanton *Atascosa*
Pledger *Matagorda*
Plum *Fayette*
Point *Rains*
Pointblank *San Jacinto*
Point Comfort *Calhoun*
Pollok *Angelina*
Ponder *Denton*
Pontotoc *Mason*
Poolville *Parker*
Port Aransas *Nueces*
Port Arthur *Jefferson*
Port Bolivar *Galveston*
Porter *Montgomery*
Port Isabel *Cameron*
Portland *San Patricio*
Port Lavaca *Calhoun*
Port Neches *Jefferson*
Port O'Connor *Calhoun*
Post *Garza*
Poteet *Atascosa*
Poth *Wilson*
Pottsboro *Grayson*
Pottsville *Hamilton*
Powderly *Lamar*
Powell *Navarro*
Poynor *Henderson*
Prairie Hill *Limestone*
Prairie Lea *Caldwell*
Prairie View *Waller*
Premont *Jim Wells*
Presidio *Presidio*
Preston Shores *Grayson*
Price *Rusk*
Priddy *Mills*
Princeton *Collin*
Proctor *Comanche*
Progreso *Hidalgo*
Prosper *Collin*
Purdon *Navarro*
Purmela *Coryell*
Putnam *Callahan*
Pyote *Ward*
Quail *Collingsworth*
Quanah *Hardeman*
Queen City *Cass*
Quemado *Maverick*
Quinlan *Hunt*
Quitaque *Briscoe*
Quitman *Wood*
Rainbow *Somervell*
Ralls *Crosby*
Randolph *Fannin*
Ranger *Eastland*
Rankin *Upton*
Ratcliff *Houston*
Ravenna *Fannin*
Raymondville *Willacy*
Raywood *Liberty*
Reagan *Falls*
Realitos *Duval*
Redford *Presidio*
Red Oak *Ellis*
Red Rock *Bastrop*
Red Springs *Baylor*
Redwater *Bowie*
Refugio *Refugio*
Reklaw *Cherokee*
Reno *Parker*
Rhome *Wise*
Rice *Navarro*
Richards *Grimes*
Richardson *Dallas*
Richland *Navarro*

Richland Hills *Tarrant*
Richland Springs *San Saba*
Richmond *Fort Bend*
Riesel *McLennan*
Ringgold *Montague*
Rio Frio *Real*
Rio Grande City *Starr*
Rio Hondo *Cameron*
Riomedina *Medina*
Rio Vista *Johnson*
Rising Star *Eastland*
River Oaks *Tarrant*
Riverside *Walker*
Riviera *Kleberg*
Roanoke *Denton*
Roaring Springs *Motley*
Robert Lee *Coke*
Robinson *McLennan*
Robstown *Nueces*
Roby *Fisher*
Rochelle *McCulloch*
Rochester *Haskell*
Rockdale *Milam*
Rock Island *Colorado*
Rockland *Tyler*
Rockport *Aransas*
Rocksprings *Edwards*
Rockwall *Rockwall*
Rockwood *Coleman*
Rogers *Bell*
Rollingwood *Travis*
Roma *Starr*
Romayor *Liberty*
Roosevelt *Kimble*
Ropesville *Hockley*
Rosanky *Bastrop*
Roscoe *Nolan*
Rosebud *Falls*
Rose City *Jefferson*
Rosenberg *Fort Bend*
Rosharon *Brazoria*
Ross *McLennan*
Rosser *Kaufman*
Rosston *Cooke*
Rotan *Fisher*
Round Mountain *Blanco*
Round Rock *Williamson*
Round Top *Fayette*
Rowena *Runnels*
Rowlett *Dallas*
Roxton *Lamar*
Royalty *Ward*
Royse City *Rockwall*
Rule *Haskell*
Runge *Karnes*
Rusk *Cherokee*
Rye *Liberty*
Sabinal *Uvalde*
Sabine Pass *Jefferson*
Sachse *Dallas*
Sacul *Nacogdoches*
Sadler *Grayson*
Saginaw *Tarrant*
Saint Francis Village *Tarrant*
Saint Hedwig *Bexar*
Saint Jo *Montague*
Salado *Bell*
Salineno *Starr*
Salt Flat *Hudspeth*
Saltillo *Hopkins*
Samnorwood *Collingsworth*
San Angelo *Tom Green*
San Antonio *Bexar*

San Augustine *San Augustine*
San Benito *Cameron*
Sanderson *Terrell*
Sandia *Jim Wells*
San Diego *Duval*
Sand Springs *Howard*
Sandy *Blanco*
San Elizario *El Paso*
San Felipe *Austin*
Sanford *Hutchinson*
Sanger *Denton*
San Isidro *Starr*
San Juan *Hidalgo*
San Marcos *Hays*
San Perlita *Willacy*
San Saba *San Saba*
Sansom Park *Tarrant*
Santa Anna *Coleman*
Santa Elena *Starr*
Santa Fe *Galveston*
Santa Maria *Cameron*
Santa Rosa *Cameron*
Santo *Palo Pinto*
San Ygnacio *Zapata*
Saragosa *Reeves*
Saratoga *Hardin*
Sarita *Kenedy*
Saspamco *Wilson*
Satin *Falls*
Savoy *Fannin*
Schertz *Guadalupe*
Schulenburg *Fayette*
Schwertner *Williamson*
Scotland *Archer*
Scottsville *Harrison*
Scroggins *Franklin*
Scurry *Kaufman*
Seabrook *Harris*
Seadrift *Calhoun*
Seagoville *Dallas*
Seagraves *Gaines*
Sealy *Austin*
Sebastian *Willacy*
Seguin *Guadalupe*
Selman City *Rusk*
Seminole *Gaines*
Seth Ward *Hale*
Seymour *Baylor*
Shafter *Presidio*
Shallowater *Lubbock*
Shamrock *Wheeler*
Sheffield *Pecos*
Shelbyville *Shelby*
Sheldon *Harris*
Shenandoah *Montgomery*
Shepherd *San Jacinto*
Sheridan *Colorado*
Sherman *Grayson*
Shiner *Lavaca*
Shiro *Grimes*
Shoreacres *Harris*
Sidney *Comanche*
Sierra Blanca *Hudspeth*
Silsbee *Hardin*
Silver *Coke*
Silverton *Briscoe*
Simms *Bowie*
Simonton *Fort Bend*
Sinton *San Patricio*
Skellytown *Carson*
Skidmore *Bee*
Slaton *Lubbock*
Slidell *Wise*
Smiley *Gonzales*

Smithville *Bastrop*
Smyer *Hockley*
Snook *Burleson*
Snyder *Scurry*
Socorro *El Paso*
Somerset *Bexar*
Somerville *Burleson*
Sonora *Sutton*
Sour Lake *Hardin*
South Bend *Young*
South Houston *Harris*
South Lake *Tarrant*
Southmayd *Grayson*
South Padre Island
   Cameron
South Plains *Floyd*
Southside Place *Harris*
Spade *Lamb*
Speaks *Lavaca*
Spearman *Hansford*
Spicewood *Burnet*
Splendora *Montgomery*
Spring *Harris*
Spring Branch *Comal*
Springlake *Lamb*
Springtown *Parker*
Spring Valley *Harris*
Spur *Dickens*
Spurger *Tyler*
Stafford *Fort Bend*
Stamford *Jones*
Stanton *Martin*
Staples *Guadalupe*
Star *Mills*
Stephenville *Erath*
Sterling City *Sterling*
Stinnett *Hutchinson*
Stockdale *Wilson*
Stonewall *Gillespie*
Stowell *Chambers*
Stratford *Sherman*
Strawn *Palo Pinto*
Streetman *Freestone*
Sublime *Lavaca*
Sudan *Lamb*
Sugar Land *Fort Bend*
Sullivan City *Hidalgo*
Sulphur Bluff *Hopkins*
Sulphur Springs *Hopkins*
Sumner *Lamar*
Sundown *Hockley*
Sunnyvale *Dallas*
Sunray *Moore*
Sunset *Montague*
Sutherland Springs *Wilson*
Sweeny *Brazoria*
Sweet Home *Lavaca*
Sweetwater *Nolan*
Sylvester *Fisher*
Taft *San Patricio*
Tahoka *Lynn*
Talco *Titus*
Talpa *Coleman*
Tarpley *Bandera*
Tarzan *Martin*
Tatum *Rusk*
Taylor *Williamson*
Teague *Freestone*
Tehuacana *Limestone*
Telegraph *Kimble*
Telephone *Fannin*
Telferner *Victoria*
Tell *Childress*
Temple *Bell*
Tenaha *Shelby*

Tennessee Colony
   Anderson
Tennyson *Coke*
Terlingua *Brewster*
Terrell *Kaufman*
Terrell Hills *Bexar*
Texarkana *Bowie*
Texas City *Galveston*
Texhoma *Texas, Ok*
Texline *Dallam*
Texon *Reagan*
The Colony *Collin*
Thicket *Hardin*
Thomaston *DeWitt*
Thompsons *Fort Bend*
Thorndale *Milam*
Thornton *Limestone*
Thrall *Williamson*
Three Rivers *Live Oak*
Throckmorton
   Throckmorton
Tilden *McMullen*
Timpson *Shelby*
Tioga *Grayson*
Tivoli *Refugio*
Tokio *Terry*
Tolar *Hood*
Tomball *Harris*
Tom Bean *Grayson*
Tornillo *El Paso*
Tow *Llano*
Toyah *Reeves*
Toyahvale *Reeves*
Trent *Taylor*
Trenton *Fannin*
Trinidad *Henderson*
Trinity *Trinity*
Troup *Smith*
Troy *Bell*
Truscott *Knox*
Tuleta *Bee*
Tulia *Swisher*
Turkey *Hall*
Turnersville *Coryell*
Tuscola *Taylor*
Tye *Taylor*
Tyler *Smith*
Tynan *Bee*
Umbarger *Randall*
Universal City *Bexar*
University Park *Dallas*
Utopia *Uvalde*
Uvalde *Uvalde*
Valentine *Jeff Davis*
Valera *Coleman*
Valley Mills *Bosque*
Valley Spring *Llano*
Valley View *Cooke*
Van *Van Zandt*
Van Alstyne *Grayson*
Vancourt *Tom Green*
Vanderbilt *Jackson*
Vanderpool *Bandera*
Van Horn *Culberson*
Van Vleck *Matagorda*
Vega *Oldham*
Venus *Johnson*
Vera *Knox*
Veribest *Tom Green*
Vernon *Wilbarger*
Victoria *Victoria*
Vidor *Orange*
Village Mills *Hardin*
Voca *McCulloch*
Von Ormy *Bexar*

Voss *Coleman*
Votaw *Hardin*
Waco *McLennan*
Wadsworth *Matagorda*
Waelder *Gonzales*
Waka *Ochiltree*
Wake Village *Bowie*
Walburg *Williamson*
Wall *Tom Green*
Waller *Waller*
Wallis *Austin*
Wallisville *Chambers*
Walnut Springs *Bosque*
Warda *Fayette*
Waring *Kendall*
Warren *Tyler*
Washington *Washington*
Waskom *Harrison*
Watauga *Tarrant*
Water Valley *Tom Green*
Waxahachie *Ellis*
Weatherford *Parker*
Webster *Harris*
Weesatche *Goliad*
Weimar *Colorado*
Weinert *Haskell*
Weir *Williamson*
Welch *Dawson*
Wellborn *Brazos*
Wellington *Collingsworth*
Wellman *Terry*
Wells *Cherokee*
Weslaco *Hidalgo*
West *McLennan*
Westbrook *Mitchell*
West Columbia *Brazoria*
Westfield *Harris*
Westhoff *DeWitt*
West Lake Hills *Travis*
Westminster *Collin*
Weston *Collin*
West Orange *Orange*
West Point *Fayette*
West Tawakoni *Hunt*
West University Place
   Harris
Westworth Village *Tarrant*
Wharton *Wharton*
Wheeler *Wheeler*
Wheelock *Robertson*
White Deer *Carson*
Whiteface *Cochran*
Whitehouse *Smith*
White Oak *Gregg*
Whitesboro *Grayson*
White Settlement *Tarrant*
Whitewright *Grayson*
Whitharral *Hockley*
Whitney *Hill*
Whitsett *Live Oak*
Whitt *Parker*
Whon *Coleman*
Wichita Falls *Wichita*
Wickett *Ward*
Wiergate *Newton*
Wildorado *Oldham*
Willis *Montgomery*
Willow City *Gillespie*
Wills Point *Van Zandt*
Wilmer *Dallas*
Wilson *Lynn*
Wimberley *Hays*
Winchester *Fayette*
Windcrest *Bexar*
Windom *Fannin*

Windthorst *Archer*
Winfield *Titus*
Wingate *Runnels*
Wink *Winkler*
Winnie *Chambers*
Winnsboro *Wood*
Winona *Smith*
Winters *Runnels*
Woden *Nacogdoches*
Wolfe City *Hunt*
Wolfforth *Lubbock*
Woodlake *Trinity*
Woodlawn *Harrison*
Woodsboro *Refugio*
Woodson *Throckmorton*
Woodville *Tyler*
Woodway *McLennan*
Wortham *Freestone*
Wrightsboro *Gonzales*
Wylie *Collin*
Yancey *Medina*
Yantis *Wood*
Yoakum *Lavaca*
Yorktown *DeWitt*
Zapata *Zapata*
Zavalla *Angelina*
Zephyr *Brown*

Utah

While the state criminal record repository reported fairly tight restriction on the release of its records, twenty seven (27) of Utah's twenty nine (29) counties do disseminate conviction records for employment screening by phone or mail. Eighteen counties allow requests to be made by fax. Civil records for $20,000 and more are filed with the District Court Clerk.

For more information or for offices not listed, contact the state's information hot line at (801) 538-3000.

Driving Records

Driver License Services
Motor Vehicle Records Section
PO Box 30560
4501 South 2700 West
West Valley City, UT 84130-0560
(801) 965-4437
Fax (801) 965-4496
Driving records are available by mail. $3.00 fee per request. Turnaround time is 24 hours. Written request must include job applicant's full name, date of birth and license number. Make check payable to Driver's License Division.

Worker's Compensation Records

Industrial Commission of Utah
Industrial Accidents Division
160 East 3rd South, 3rd Floor
PO Box 146610
Salt Lake City, UT 84114-6610
(801) 530-6800
All requests must include job applicant's full name, SSN, date of injury and name of employer involved in claim, if available, years to search. $15.00 fee per hour. $.50 fee per copy, plus postage. A signed, notarized release is required.

Vital Statistics

Bureau of Vital Records
PO Box 16700
Salt Lake City, UT 84116-0700
(801) 538-6380
Birth and death records are available for $9.00. State office has records since 1905. If event occurred from 1890 to 1904 in Salt Lake City or Ogden, write to City Board of Health. For records elsewhere in the State from 1898 to 1904, write to County Clerk in county where event occurred. An employer can obtain records with a written release. Birth certificates are available for $12.00 to immediate family or designated representative only. Make certified check or money order payable to Vital Records.

Marriage records prior to 1978 are available for a $9.00 fee at county level, county clerk, where license was purchased . Divorce records prior to 1978 are available at county level, county clerk's office for $9.00.

Department of Education

State Office of Education
Teacher Certification
250 E 500 South
Salt Lake City, UT 84111
(801) 538-7740
Certificate information is currently not considered public information. Information will be released to school districts.

Medical Licensing

D.O.P.L.
Medical Board
160 E. 300 South
PO Box 45805
Salt Lake City, UT 84145-0805
(801) 530-6634
Will confirm licenses for 42 professions by phone or mail. No fee.

Utah State Board of Nursing
Division of Occupational and
Professional Licensing
Heber M. Wells Bldg., 4th Floor
160 East 300 South
PO Box 45805
Salt Lake City, UT 84145-0805
(801) 530-6628
Will confirm license by mail or phone. No fee. Include name, license number, if available.

Bar Association

Utah State Bar Association
645 S. 200 East
Salt Lake City, UT 84111
(801) 531-9077
Will confirm licenses by phone. No fee. Include name.

Accountancy Board

Department of Professional Licensing
PO Box 45805
Salt Lake City, UT 84145-0805
(801) 530-6633
Will confirm license by phone. No fee. Include name.

Securities Commission

Division of Commerce
Division of Securities
PO Box 45808
Salt Lake City, UT 84145-0808
Will confirm license by phone. No fee. Include name and SSN.

Secretary of State

Department of Commerce
Utah Division of Corporation
PO Box 45801
Salt Lake City, UT 84145-0801
(801) 530-4849
Service agent and address, date incorporated, standing with tax commission, trade names are available by phone or mail. Contact the above office for additional information.

Criminal Records

State Repository

Bureau Chief
Utah Bureau of Criminal Identification
4501 South 2700 West
Salt Lake City, UT 84119
(801) 965-4561
Access by non-criminal justice agencies to criminal records maintained by State's central repository is limited to those entities specifically authorized access by law. Contact the above office for additional information and instructions.

Beaver County

County Clerk, Criminal Records
PO Box 523
Beaver, UT 84713
(801) 438-2352
Felony and misdemeanor records are available by mail. No release necessary. $5.00 search fee. Make check payable to Beaver County Clerk. Search information required: name, SASE. Fee must be paid in advance on phone inquiries.

Civil records are available by mail. No release necessary. $5.00 search fee. $.25 fee per copy. $2.50 for certification. Search information required: name, date of birth, years to search, SASE. Specify plaintiff or defendant.

Box Elder County

Felony records
District Court, Criminal Records
Box Elder County Courthouse
1 South Main
Brigham City, UT 84302
(801) 734-2433
Felony records are available by mail. No release necessary. No search fee. $.25 fee per copy. $2.00 for certification. Search information required: name, date of birth, SASE, years to search.

Civil records
District Court
Box Elder County Courthouse
1 South Main
Brigham City, UT 84302
(801) 734-2433
Civil records are available by mail. No release necessary. No search fee. $.25 fee per copy. $2.00 for certification. Search information required: name, date of birth, years to search, SASE. Specify plaintiff or defendant.

Misdemeanor records
1st Circuit Court
PO Box 1005
Brigham City, UT 84302
(801) 723-2862
Misdemeanor records are available by mail or phone. No release necessary. No search fee. Search information required: name, date of birth if available, years to search.

Civil records
1st Circuit Court
PO Box 1005
Brigham City, UT 84302
(801) 723-2862
Civil records are available in person only. See Utah state repository for additional information.

Cache County

First District Court
140 N. 100 West
Logan, UT 84321
(801) 752-3230
Fax (801) 753-0372
Felony records are available by mail or phone. No release necessary. No search fee. $.25 fee per copy. $2.00 for certification. Search information required: name, SASE, years to search.

Civil records are available by mail or phone. No release necessary. No search fee. $.25 fee per copy. $2.00 for certification. Search information required: name, date of birth, years to search. Specify plaintiff or defendant.

Carbon County

Felony records
7th District Court
County Clerk, Criminal Records
149 E. 100 South
Price, UT 84501
(801) 637-0180
Fax (801) 637-2102
Felony records are available by mail, fax or phone. A release is required. $8.20 fee per hour, no fee for first 20 minutes. $.25 fee per copy. $2.00 for certification. Search information required: name, years to search.

Civil records
7th District Court
County Clerk
149 E. 100 South
Price, UT 84501
(801) 637-0180
Fax (801) 637-2102
Civil records are available by mail, fax or phone. A release is required. No search fee. $.25 fee per copy. $2.00 for certification. Search information required: name, date of birth, years to search. Specify plaintiff or defendant.

Misdemeanor records
7th Circuit Court
149 E. 100 S. #2
Price, UT 84501
(801) 637-2150
Fax (801) 637-2102
Misdemeanor records are available by mail or fax. $8.20 fee per hour, no fee for first 20 minutes. $.25 fee per copy. $1.00 for certification. Search information required: name, date of birth.

Civil records
7th Circuit Court
149 E. 100 S. #2
Price, UT 84501
(801) 637-2150
Fax (801) 637-2102
Civil records are available by mail or fax. No release necessary. No search fee. $.25 fee per copy. $1.00 for certification. Search information required: name, date of birth, years to search. Specify plaintiff or defendant.

Daggett County

County Clerk
PO Box 218
Manila, UT 84046
(801) 784-3154
Fax (801) 784-3335
Felony and misdemeanor records are available by mail or fax. No search fee. $.25 fee per copy. $2.00 for certification. No release necessary. Search information required: name, date of birth, years to search, SASE.

Civil records are available by mail or fax. No release necessary. No search fee. $.25 fee per copy. $2.00 for certification. earch information required: name, date of birth, years to search, SASE. Specify plaintiff or defendant.

Davis County

Second District Court
Criminal Records
PO Box 769
Farmington, UT 84025
(801) 451-4406
Fax (801) 451-4470
Felony records are available by mail, fax or phone. No release necessary. No search fee. $.25 fee per copy. $2.00 for certification. Search information required: name, SSN, date of birth, SASE, years to search.

Civil records are available by mail, fax or phone. No release necessary. No search fee. $.25 fee per copy. $2.00 for certification. Search information required: name, date of birth, years to search. Specify plaintiff or defendant.

Duchesne County

County Clerk
Drawer 270
Duchesne, UT 84021
(801) 738-2435
Felony records are available by mail. A release is required. $10.00 search fee. $.30 fee per copy. $2.00 for certification. Search information required: name, date of birth, SSN, years to search.

Civil records are available by mail. A release is required. $10.00 search fee. $.30 fee per copy. $2.00 for certification. Search information required: name, date of birth, SSN, years to search. Specify plaintiff or defendant.

Emery County

County Clerk, Criminal Records
PO Box 907
Castle Dale, UT 84513
(801) 381-2465
Fax (801) 381-5183
Felony and misdemeanor records are available by mail, phone or fax. No release necessary. No fee for first 20 minutes searched. $8.00 search fee per hour. $1.00 fee for first page of fax request, $.50 thereafter. $2.00 fee for fax response, $1.00 thereafter. $.25 fee per copy. $5.00 for certification. Make check payable to County Clerk. Search information required: name, date of birth.

Civil records are available by mail, fax or phone. No release necessary. No fee for first 20 minutes searched. $8.00 search fee per hour. $1.00 fee for first page of fax request, $.50 thereafter. $2.00 fee for fax response, $1.00 thereafter. $.25 fee per copy. $5.00 for certification. Search information required: name, date of birth, years to search. Specify plaintiff or defendant.

Garfield County

County Clerk, Criminal Records
PO Box 77
Panguitch, UT 84759
(801) 676-8826 Extension 15
Fax (801) 676-8239
Felony and misdemeanor records are available by mail. A release is required. No search fee. $.25 fee per copy. $2.00 for certification. $3.00 fee for first page of fax response, $1.00 fee for each additional page. Search information required: name, date of birth, years to search.

Civil records are available by mail. No release necessary. No search fee. $.25 fee per copy. $2.00 for certification. $3.00 fee for first page of fax response, $1.00 fee for each additional page. Search information required: name, date of birth, years to search. Specify plaintiff or defendant.

Grand County

Felony records
Clerk of District Court, Criminal Records
125 E. Center
Moab, UT 84532
(801) 259-5986
Felony records are available by mail or phone. No release necessary. No search fee. Search information required: name, SSN, date of birth, sex, race, SASE.

Civil records
Clerk of District Court
125 E. Center
Moab, UT 84532
(801) 259-5986
Civil records are available by mail. No release necessary. $8.00 fee for each 20 minutes searched. $.25 fee per copy. $2.00 for certification. Search information required: name, date of birth, years to search, SASE. Specify plaintiff or defendant.

Misdemeanor records
District Court
125 E. Center
Moab, UT 84532
(801) 259-5986
Misdemeanor records are available by mail or phone. No release necessary. No search fee. Search information required: name, date of birth.

Civil records
District Court
125 E. Center
Moab, UT 84532
(801) 259-5986
Civil records are available by mail. No release necessary. $7.65 search fee after 20 minutes. $.25 fee per copy. $1.00 for certification. Search information required: name, date of birth, years to search. Specify plaintiff or defendant.

Iron County

County Clerk, Criminal Records
5th District Court
40 North & 100 East
Cedar City, UT 84720
(801) 586-7440
Fax (801) 586-4801
Felony and misdemeanor records are available by mail or phone. No release necessary. No search fee. $.25 fee per copy. $2.00 for certification. Search information required: name, date of birth, years to search.

Civil records are available by mail or phone. No release necessary. No search fee. $.25 fee per copy. $2.00 for certification. Search information required: name, date of birth, years to search. Specify plaintiff or defendant.

Juab County

County Clerk, Criminal Records
160 N. Main
Nephi, UT 84648
(801) 623-0271
Fax (801) 623-4609
Felony and misdemeanor records are available by phone or fax. No release necessary. $5.00 search fee. $.20 fee per copy. $2.00 for certification. $2.00 fee for fax response. Search information required: name, date of birth, years to search.

Civil records are available by mail, fax or phone. No release necessary. $5.00 search fee. $.20 fee per copy. $2.00 for certification. $2.00 fee for fax response. Search information required: name, date of birth, years to search. Specify plaintiff or defendant.

Kane County

Kane County Clerk, Criminal Records
PO Box 728
Kanab, UT 84741
(801) 644-2458
Fax (801) 644-2096
Felony and misdemeanor records are available by mail. No release necessary. No search fee. $.25 fee per copy. $2.00 fee for certification. Search information required: name, date of birth, SASE.

Civil records are available by mail or phone. No release necessary. No search fee. $.25 fee per copy. Search information required: name, date of birth, years to search, case number if available, SASE. Specify plaintiff or defendant.

Millard County

County Clerk, Criminal Records
PO Box 226
Fillmore, UT 84631
(801) 743-6223
Fax (801) 743-6923
Felony and misdemeanor records are available by mail, fax or phone. No release necessary. No fee. Search information required: name, SSN, SASE.

Civil records are available by mail or fax. No release necessary. $10.00 search fee. $.25 fee per copy. $2.00 for certification. Search information required: name, date of birth, years to search. Specify plaintiff or defendant.

Morgan County

Clerk of District Court, Criminal Records
48 W. Young St.
Morgan, UT 84050
(801) 829-6811
Felony and misdemeanor records in person only. See Utah state repository for additional information.

Civil records are available in person only. See Utah state repository for additional information.

Piute County

County Clerk, Criminal Records
PO Box 99
Junction, UT 84740
(801) 577-2840
Felony and misdemeanor records are available by mail or phone. A release is required. No search fee. $.25 fee per copy. $2.00 for certification. Search information required: name, date of birth, address, years to search.

Civil records are available by mail or phone. A release is required. No search fee. $.25 fee per copy. $2.00 for certification. Search information required: name, date of birth, years to search. Specify plaintiff or defendant.

Rich County

Clerk of District Court, Criminal Records
PO Box 218
Randolph, UT 84064
(801) 793-2415
Fax (801) 793-3122
Felony and misdemeanor records are available by mail, fax or phone. No release necessary. No search fee. $.50 fee per copy. Search information required: name, date of birth.

Civil records are available by mail or fax. A release is required. No search fee. $.25 fee per copy. $2.00 for certification. Search information required: name, date of birth, years to search. Specify plaintiff or defendant.

Salt Lake County

Felony records
3rd District Court, Rm 205
Salt Lake County, Criminal Division
240 E. 4th South.
Salt Lake City, UT 84111
(801) 535-5401
Felony records are available by mail, fax or phone. No release necessary. No search fee. $.25 fee per copy. $2.00 fee for certifation. Search information required: name, date of birth.

Civil records
3rd District Court, Rm 205
Salt Lake County
240 E. 4th South.
Salt Lake City, UT 84111
(801) 535-5111
Civil records are available by mail, fax or phone. No release necessary. No search fee. $.25 fee per copy. $2.00 fee for certifation. Search information required: name, date of birth, years to search. Specify plaintiff or defendant.

Misdemeanor records
3rd Circuit Court
451 S. 200 East
Salt Lake City, UT 84111
(801) 533-3921
Misdemeanor records are available by mail or phone. No release necessary. No fee. Search information required: name, date of birth.

Civil records
3rd Circuit Court
451 S. 200 East
Salt Lake City, UT 84111
(801) 533-3911
Civil records are available by mail or phone. No release necessary. No search fee. $.25 fee per copy. $1.00 fee for certifation. Search information required: name, date of birth, years to search. Specify plaintiff or defendant.

San Juan County

7th Circuit Court, Criminal Records
PO Box 68
Monticello, UT 84535
(801) 587-2122
Fax (801) 587-2013
Felony and misdemeanor records are available by mail or fax. No release necessary. $8.00 per hour search fee. $.25 fee per copy. $2.00 for certification. Search information required: name, years to search.

Civil records are available by mail or fax. A release is required. $8.00 per hour search fee. $.25 fee per copy. $2.00 for certification. Search information required: name, date of birth, years to search, names of both parties. Specify plaintiff or defendant.

Sanpete County

Sanpete County Clerk, Criminal
Records
160 N. Main
Manti, UT 84642
(801) 835-2131
Fax (801) 835-2143
Felony and misdemeanor records are available in person only. See Utah state repository for additional information.

Civil records are available in person only. See Utah state repository for additional information.

Sevier County

Felony records
6th District Court
Criminal Records
250 N. Main
Richfield, UT 84701
(801) 896-9256
Fax (801) 896-8047
Felony records are available by mail or fax. No release necessary. No search fee. Search information required: name, years to search.

Civil records
6th District Court
250 N. Main
Richfield, UT 84701
(801) 896-9256
Fax (801) 896-8047
Civil records are available by mail or phone. No release necessary. No search fee. Search information required: name, date of birth, years to search. Specify plaintiff or defendant.

Misdemeanor records
District Court
Criminal Records
250 N. Main
Richfield, UT 84701
(801) 896-9262
Fax (801) 896-8888
Felony records are available by mail, phone or fax. No release necessary. No search fee. $3.00 fee for fax response. Search information required: name, years to search.

Civil records
District Court
250 N. Main, Room6
Richfield, UT 84701
(801) 896-9262
Fax (801) 896-8888
Civil records are available by mail, fax or phone. No release necessary. No search fee. $3.00 fee for fax response. Search information required: name, date of birth, years to search. Specify plaintiff or defendant.

Summit County

Summit County Clerk, Criminal
Records
PO Box 128
Coalville, UT 84017
(801) 336-4451 Extension 202 or 205
Fax (801) 336-4450
Felony and misdemeanor records are available by mail or phone. No release necessary. $8.00 search fee per hour. No search fee for first twenty minutes. Search information required: name, date of birth, SASE.

Civil records are available by mail or fax. No release necessary. $8.00 per hour search fee. $.25 fee per copy. $2.00 for certification. $3.00 fee for first page of fax request, $1.00 for each page thereafter. $4.00 fee for first page of fax response, $1.00 for each page thereafter. Search information required: name, date of birth, years to search. Specify plaintiff or defendant.

Tooele County

Felony and misdemeanor records
3rd District Court, Criminal Records
47 S. Main
Tooele, UT 84074
(801) 882-9215 or 882-9212
Felony and misdemeanor records are available by mail or phone. No release necessary. No search fee. Search information required: name, SASE.

Civil records
3rd District Court
47 S. Main
Tooele, UT 84074
(801) 882-9212
Civil records are available by mail. No release necessary. No search fee. $2.00 for certification. Search information required: name, date of birth, years to search, SASE. Specify plaintiff or defendant.

Uintah County

7th Judicial District, Criminal Records
Uintah County
147 E. Main.
Vernal, UT 84078
(801) 789-7534
Fax (801) 789-0564
Felony and misdemeanor records are available by mail, phone or fax. No release necessary. No search fee. $.25 fee per copy. $2.00 for certification. Search information required: name, years to search

Civil records are available by mail or fax. No release necessary. No search fee. $.25 fee per copy. $2.00 for certification. Search information required: name, date of birth, years to search, case number.. Specify plaintiff or defendant.

Utah County

4th District Court, Criminal Records
PO Box 1847
Provo, UT 84603
(801) 429-1039
Felony and misdemeanor records are available by mail. No release necessary. $8.00 fee per hour. Make check payable to 4th District Court. Search information required: name, years to search, SASE.

Civil records are available by mail. No release necessary. $8.00 search fee per hour after first 20 minutes. $.25 fee per copy. $2.00 for certification. Search information required: name, date of birth, years to search, SASE. Specify plaintiff or defendant.

Wasatch County

Wasatch County Clerk, Criminal
Records
25 N. Main
Heber City, UT 84032
(801) 654-3211
Felony and misdemeanor records are available by mail. No release necessary. No search fee. $.25 fee per copy. $2.00 for certification. Search information required: name, years to search.

Civil records are available by mail. A release is required. No search fee. $.25 fee per copy. $2.00 for certification.Search information required: name, date of birth, years to search. Specify plaintiff or defendant.

Washington County

Felony records
5th District Court, District Court Clerk
220 N. 200 E.
St. George, UT 84770
(801) 673-7225
Fax (801) 628-7870
Felony records are available by mail or fax. No release necessary. No search fee. $.25 fee per copy. $2.00 for certification. Search information required: name, date of birth, years to search.

Civil records
5th District Court, District Court Clerk
220 N. 200 E.
St. George, UT 84770
(801) 673-7225
Fax (801) 628-7870
Civil records are available by mail or fax. No release necessary. No search fee. $.25 fee per copy. $2.00 for certification. Search information required: name, date of birth, years to search. Specify plaintiff or defendant.

Misdemeanor records
Circuit Court
220 N. 200 E.
St. George, UT 84771
(801) 673-6001
Misdemeanor records are available by mail. No release necessary. Search fee varies. $.25 fee per copy. $1.00 for certification. Search information required: name, date of birth.

Civil records
Circuit Court
220 N. 200 E.
St. George, UT 84771
(801) 673-6001
Civil records are available by mail. No release necessary. No search fee. $.25 fee per copy. $1.00 for certification. Search information required: name, date of birth, years to search. Specify plaintiff or defendant.

Wayne County

County Clerk
18 South Main
Loa, UT 84747
(801)836-2731
Fax (801) 836-2479
Records are available by mail, phone or fax. No search fee. $3.00 fee for first page of fax, $1.00 per page thereafter. No release necessary. Search information required: name, date of birth, SSN, SASE.

Civil records are available by mail. No release necessary. No search fee for first 15 minutes, $8.00 fee per hour thereafter. $.50 fee per copy. $2.00 for certification. Search information required: name, date of birth, years to search, SASE. Specify plaintiff or defendant.

Weber County

Weber County Clerk, Criminal
Records
2549 Washington Blvd.
Ogden, UT 84401
(801) 399-8481
Felony records are available by mail or
phone. No release necessary. No search fee
for first 20 minutes, $2.00 fee thereafter.
Search information required: name, years to
search.

Civil records are available by mail. No release necessary. $2.00 search fee after first
20 minutes. $.25 fee per copy. $2.00 for
certification. Search information required:
name, date of birth, years to search. Specify
plaintiff or defendant.

City-County Cross Reference

Alta *Salt Lake*
Altamont *Duchesne*
American Fork *Utah*
Annabella *Sevier*
Aurora *Sevier*
Axtell *Sanpete*
Ballard *Uintah*
Bear River City *Box Elder*
Beaver *Beaver*
Belmont Heights *Salt Lake*
Bennion *Salt Lake*
Beryl *Iron*
Bicknell *Wayne*
Bingham Canyon *Salt Lake*
Blanding *San Juan*
Bluebell *Duchesne*
Bluff *San Juan*
Bluffdale *Salt Lake*
Bountiful *Davis*
Bridgeland *Duchesne*
Brigham City *Box Elder*
Castle Dale *Emery*
Cedar City *Iron*
Cedar Valley *Utah*
Centerfield *Sanpete*
Centerville *Davis*
Circleville *Piute*
Clarkston *Cache*
Clawson *Emery*
Clearfield *Davis*
Cleveland *Emery*
Coalville *Summit*
Copperton *Salt Lake*
Corinne *Box Elder*
Cottonwood *Salt Lake*
Cottonwood Heights *Salt Lake*
Croydon *Morgan*
Delta *Millard*
Draper *Salt Lake*
Duchesne *Duchesne*
Dugway *Tooele*
Dutch John *Daggett*
East Carbon *Carbon*
Eastwood Hills *Salt Lake*
Echo *Summit*
Eden *Weber*
Elberta *Utah*
Elmo *Emery*
Elsinore *Sevier*
Emery *Emery*
Enterprise *Washington*
Ephraim *Sanpete*
Escalante *Garfield*
Eureka *Juab*
Fairview *Sanpete*
Farmington *Davis*
Ferron *Emery*
Fielding *Box Elder*

Fillmore *Millard*
Fort Duchesne *Uintah*
Fountain Green *Sanpete*
Garden City *Rich*
Garland *Box Elder*
Garrison *Millard*
Glendale *Kane*
Goshen *Utah*
Granite *Salt Lake*
Granite Park *Salt Lake*
Grantsville *Tooele*
Green River *Emery*
Greenville *Beaver*
Greenwich *Piute*
Grouse Creek *Box Elder*
Gunlock *Washington*
Gunnison *Sanpete*
Hanksville *Wayne*
Hanna *Duchesne*
Harrisville *Weber*
Hatch *Garfield*
Heber City *Wasatch*
Helper *Carbon*
Henefer *Summit*
Henrieville *Garfield*
Hiawatha *Carbon*
Hildale *Washington*
Hinckley *Millard*
Holden *Millard*
Holladay *Salt Lake*
Honeyville *Box Elder*
Hooper *Weber*
Howell *Box Elder*
Huntington *Emery*
Huntsville *Weber*
Hurricane *Washington*
Hyde Park *Cache*
Hyrum *Cache*
Jensen *Uintah*
Junction *Piute*
Kamas *Summit*
Kanab *Kane*
Kanosh *Millard*
Kaysville *Davis*
Kearns *Salt Lake*
Laketown *Rich*
Lapoint *Uintah*
LaSal *San Juan*
LaVerkin *Washington*
Layton *Davis*
Lehi *Utah*
Levan *Juab*
Lewiston *Cache*
Loa *Wayne*
Logan *Cache*
Lyman *Wayne*
Lynndyl *Millard*
Maeser *Uintah*
Magna *Salt Lake*

Manila *Daggett*
Manti *Sanpete*
Mapleton *Utah*
Marysvale *Piute*
Mayfield *Sanpete*
Meadow *Millard*
Mendon *Cache*
Midvale *Salt Lake*
Midway *Wasatch*
Milford *Beaver*
Millcreek *Salt Lake*
Millville *Cache*
Minersville *Beaver*
Moab *Grand*
Mona *Juab*
Monroe *Sevier*
Montezuma Creek *San Juan*
Monticello *San Juan*
Morgan *Morgan*
Moroni *Sanpete*
Mount Carmel *Kane*
Mount Olympus *Salt Lake*
Mount Pleasant *Sanpete*
Murray *Salt Lake*
Myton *Duchesne*
Naples *Uintah*
Neola *Duchesne*
Nephi *Juab*
Newcastle *Iron*
New Harmony *Washington*
Newton *Cache*
North Ogden *Weber*
North Salt Lake *Davis*
Oak City *Millard*
Oakley *Summit*
Oasis *Millard*
Ogden *Weber*
Orangeville *Emery*
Orderville *Kane*
Orem *Utah*
Panguitch *Garfield*
Paradise *Cache*
Park City *Summit*
Park Terrace *Salt Lake*
Park Valley *Box Elder*
Parowan *Iron*
Payson *Utah*
Peoa *Summit*
Perry *Box Elder*
Peruvian Park *Salt Lake*
Pleasant Grove *Utah*
Plymouth *Box Elder*
Portage *Box Elder*
Price *Carbon*
Providence *Cache*
Provo *Utah*
Randolph *Rich*
Redmond *Sevier*

Redwood *Salt Lake*
Richfield *Sevier*
Richmond *Cache*
Riverdale *Weber*
Riverside *Box Elder*
Riverton *Salt Lake*
Roosevelt *Duchesne*
Roy *Weber*
Rush Valley *Tooele*
Saint George *Washington*
Salem *Utah*
Salina *Sevier*
Salt Lake City *Salt Lake*
Sandy *Salt Lake*
Santa Clara *Washington*
Santaquin *Utah*
Smithfield *Cache*
Snowville *Box Elder*
South Salt Lake *Salt Lake*
South Weber *Davis*
Spanish Fork *Utah*
Spring City *Sanpete*
Springdale *Washington*
Springville *Utah*
St George *Washington*
Stockton *Tooele*
Sunnyside *Carbon*
Sunset *Davis*
Tabiona *Duchesne*
Taylorsville *Salt Lake*
Teasdale *Wayne*
Tooele *Tooele*
Toquerville *Washington*
Tremonton *Box Elder*
Trenton *Cache*
Tropic *Garfield*
Uintah *Morgan*
Union *Salt Lake*
Vernal *Uintah*
Vernon *Tooele*
Wallsburg *Wasatch*
Washington *Washington*
Washington Terrace *Weber*
Wellington *Carbon*
Wellsville *Cache*
Wendover *Tooele*
West Jordan *Salt Lake*
West Point *Davis*
West Valley City *Salt Lake*
Whiterocks *Uintah*
Willard *Box Elder*
Woodruff *Rich*
Woods Cross *Davis*

Vermont

Vermont worker's compensation histories are available at no charge for employment screening purposes. Two (2) of the state's fourteen (14) counties make criminal records available to employers by either phone or mail.

Civil court records for $2,000 and higher are located in Superior Court.

For more information or for offices not listed, contact the state's information hot line at (802) 828-1110.

Driving Records

Department of Motor Vehicles
Driver Improvement
120 State Street
Montpelier, VT 05603
(802) 828-2050

Driving records available by mail. $4.00 fee for 3-year record, $8.00 fee for complete record. Turnaround time is 2 to 3 days. Written request must include subject's full name, date of birth and, if available, license number. Make check payable to Department of Motor Vehicles.

Worker's Compensation Records

Department of Labor and Industry
Worker's Compensation Division
120 State Street
Montpelier, VT 05602
(802) 828-2286
Fax (802) 828-2195

Worker's compensation records are available by mail only. Inquiries on claims filed prior to July 1985 must include job applicant's full name, SSN and the name of the employer involved in the claim. Inquiries on claims after July 1985 are available using applicant's full name and SSN. All requests must include a signed release authorizing access. There is no fee.

Vital Statistics

Vermont Department of Public Health
Vital Records Section
Box 70
60 Main Street
Burlington, VT 05402
(802) 863-7275

Birth and death records are available for $5.00 each. Records are public and an employer can obtain records with a written release. Make certified check or money order payable to Vermont Department of Public Health.

Marriage records are available. $5.00 per copy. Check or money order. Include name, marriage date, spouse's name, town or city where married. Turnaround time is 48 hours. Divorce records are available. Include: name, court where divorce was granted and date of decree.

Department of Education

Department of Education
Licensing Office
120 State Street
Montpelier, VT 05620
(802) 828-2445

Field of certification, effective date, expiration date are available by phone or mail. Include name and SSN.

Medical Licensing

Board of Medical Practice
Secretary of State Office
109 State Street
Montpelier, VT 05609-1106
(802) 828-2363
Fax (802) 828-2496

Will confirm licenses for MDs and PODs by phone or mail. No search fee. $20.00 fee for written physician verification. For licenses not mentioned, contact the above office.

Vermont State Board of Nursing
Secretary of State
109 State Street
Montpelier, VT 05609-1106
(802) 828-2396
Fax (802) 828-2496

Will confirm license by phone. No search fee. Include name, license number, if available.

Bar Association

Vermont State Bar Association
PO Box 100
Montpelier, VT 05601
(802) 223-2020

Will confirm licenses by phone. No fee. Include name.

Accountancy Board

Vermont State Board of Accountancy
109 State Street
Montpelier, VT 05609
(802) 828-2363

Will confirm license by phone. No fee. Include name.

Securities Commission

Department of Banking, Insurance and Securities
120 State Street
Montpelier, VT 05620-3101
(802) 828-3420

Will confirm license by phone. No fee. Include name and SSN.

Secretary of State

Secretary of State
Corporation Division
Pavilion Office Building
Montpelier, VT 05602
(802) 828-2386

Service agent and address, date incorporated, standing with tax commission, trade names are available by phone or mail. Contact the above office for additional information.

Criminal Records

State Repository

Vermont Criminal Information Center
PO Box 189
Waterbury, VT 05676-0850
(802) 244-8727

Non-criminal justice agencies wishing access to criminal records through Vermont's central repository must submit a request to the above office along with any supporting statute, executive order or charter demand. If access is granted, there is no fee. Information released contains conviction data with dispositions. Turnaround time is normally 24 to 48 hours.

Addison County

Felony and misdemeanor records
Vermont District Court, Criminal Records
5 Court Street
Middlebury, VT 05753
(802) 388-4237

Felony and misdemeanor records are available in person only. See Vermont state repository for additional information.

Civil records
Vermont District Court, Criminal Records
5 Court Street
Middlebury, VT 05753
(802) 388-7741
Civil records are available by mail. No release necessary. No search fee. $.25 fee per copy. $2.00 for certification. Search information required: name, date of birth, years to search. Specify plaintiff or defendant.

Bennington County

Felony and misdemeanor records
Bennington District Court
1 Veterans Memorial Dr.
Bennington, VT 05201
(802) 447-2727
Records are not available by mail or phone but are available to the public for physical inspection at the above office. See Vermont state repository for additional information.

Civil records
Bennington District Court
PO Box 157
Bennington, VT 05201
(802) 447-2700
Civil records are available by mail. No release necessary. No search fee. $.50 fee per copy. $3.00 for certification. Search information required: name, years to search. Specify plaintiff or defendant.

Caledonia County

Felony and misdemeanor records
District Court of Vermont, Criminal Records
27 Main Street
St. Johnsbury, VT 05819
(802) 748-3811 or 748-6610
Felony and misdemeanor records are available in person only. See Vermont state repository for additional information.

Civil records
District Court of Vermont
PO Box 4129
St. Johnsbury, VT 05819
(802) 748-6600
Civil records are available by mail. No release necessary. No search fee. $.25 fee per copy. $2.00 for first page certified, $.25 each additional page. Search information required: name, date of birth, years to search, SASE. Specify plaintiff or defendant.

Chittenden County

Vermont District Court, Criminal Records
Chittenden Unit 2
PO Box 268
Burlington, VT 05402
(802) 863-7575
Felony and misdemeanor records are available in person only. See Vermont state repository for additional information.

Civil records are available in person only. See Vermont state repository for additional information.

Essex County

District Court of Vermont, Criminal Records
PO Box 75
Guildhall, VT 05905
(802) 676-3910
Felony and misdemeanor records are available by mail. No release necessary. No search fee. $.25 fee per copy. $2.00 for first certification, $.25 each page thereafter. Search information required: name, date of birth, years to search, SASE.

Civil records are available by mail. No release necessary. No search fee. $.25 fee per copy. $2.00 for first certification, $.25 each page thereafter. Search information required: name, date of birth, years to search, SASE. Specify plaintiff or defendant.

Franklin County

Felony and misdemeanor records
Vermont District Court, Criminal Records
PO Box 314
St. Albans, VT 05478
(802) 524-7998
Felony and misdemeanor records are available in person only. See Vermont state repository for additional information.

Civil records
Vermont District Court
PO Box 808
St. Albans, VT 05478
(802) 524-3863
Civil records are available by mail or phone. No release necessary. No search fee. $.25 fee per copy. $2.00 for first certification. Search information required: name, date of birth, years to search. Specify plaintiff or defendant.

Grand Isle County

Felony and misdemeanor records
Grand Isle Courts Clerk, Criminal Records
PO Box 7
North Hero, VT 05474
(802) 372-8350
Felony and misdemeanor records are available in person only. See Vermont state repository for additional information.

Civil records
Grand Isle Courts Clerk
PO Box 303
North Hero, VT 05655
(802) 888-2207
Civil records are available by mail. No release necessary. No search fee. $.10 fee per copy. $2.25 for certification. Search information required: name, date of birth, years to search. Specify plaintiff or defendant.

Lamoille County

Vermont District Court, Criminal Records
Unit 3, Lamoille Circuit
Hyde Park, VT 05655
(802) 888-3887
Felony and misdemeanor records are available by mail. No release necessary. No search fee. Search information required: name, date of birth.

Civil records are available by mail. No release necessary. No search fee. $.25 fee per copy. $2.25 for certification. Search information required: name, date of birth, years to search. Specify plaintiff or defendant.

Orange County

Vermont District Court
PO Box 267
Chelsea, VT 05038
(802) 685-4870
Records are not available by mail or phone. See Vermont state repository for additional information.

Civil records are available by mail. No release necessary. No search fee. $.25 fee per copy. $2.00 for certification. Search information required: name, date of birth, years to search. Specify plaintiff or defendant.

Orleans County

Felony and misdemeanor records
Clerk of District Court, Criminal Records
81 Main Street
Newport, VT 05855
(802) 334-3325
Felony and misdemeanor records are available in person only. See Vermont state repository for additional information.

Civil records
Clerk of District Court
PO Box 787
Newport, VT 05855
(802) 334-3355
Civil records are available by mail. No release necessary. No search fee. $.25 fee per copy. $2.25 for certification. Search information required: name, date of birth, years to search. Specify plaintiff or defendant.

Rutland County

Felony and misdemeanor records
Clerk of District Court
PO Box 147
92 State St.
Rutland, VT 05701
(802) 773-5880
Records are not available by mail or phone. Records available for physical inspection at above office. See Vermont state repository. for additional information

Civil records
Clerk of Superior Court
PO Box 339
83 Center St.
Rutland, VT 05702
(802) 775-4394
Civil records are available by mail. No release necessary. No search fee. $.25 fee per copy. $2.00 for certification. Search information required: name, date of birth, years to search. Specify plaintiff or defendant.

Washington County

Felony and misdemeanor records
Clerk of District Court, Criminal Records
255 N. Main
Barrie, VT 05641
(802) 479-4252
Records are not available by mail or phone. See Vermont state repository for additional information.

Civil records
Clerk of Superior Court
PO Box 426
Montpelier, VT 05602
(802) 223-2091
Civil records are available by mail or phone. No release necessary. No search fee. $.50 fee per copy. $4.00 for certification. Search information required: name, date of birth, years to search. Specify plaintiff or defendant.

Windham County

Felony and misdemeanor records
Vermont District Court
6 Putney Road
Brattleboro, VT
(802) 257-2800
Records are not available by mail or phone. See Vermont state repository for additional information.

Civil records
Vermont Superior Court
6 Putney Road
Newfane, VT 05345
(802) 365-7979
Civil records are available in person only. See Vermont state repository for additional information.

Windsor County

Felony and misdemeanor records
Vermont District Court
Unit #1
Windsor Circuit
White River Junction, VT 05001
(802) 295-8865
Records are not available by mail or phone. See Vermont state repository for additional information.

Civil records
Vermont Superior Court
PO Box 458
Woodstock, VT 05091
(802) 457-2121
Civil records are available by mail or phone. No release necessary. No search fee. $.25 fee pre copy. $2.00 for first page certified, $.25 each additional page. Search information required: name, years to search. Specify plaintiff or defendant.

City-County Cross Reference

Adamant *Washington*
Albany *Orleans*
Alburg *Grand Isle*
Arlington *Bennington*
Ascutney *Windsor*
Bakersfield *Franklin*
Barnard *Windsor*
Barnet *Caledonia*
Barre *Washington*
Barton *Orleans*
Beebe Plain *Orleans*
Beecher Falls *Essex*
Bellows Falls *Windham*
Belmont *Rutland*
Belvidere Center *Lamoille*
Bennington *Bennington*
Berlin Corners *Washington*
Bethel *Windsor*
Bomoseen *Rutland*
Bondville *Bennington*
Bradford *Orange*
Brandon *Rutland*
Brattleboro *Windham*
Bridgewater *Windsor*
Bridgewater Corners
 Windsor
Bridport *Addison*
Bristol *Addison*
Brookfield *Orange*
Brownsville *Windsor*
Burlington *Chittenden*
Cabot *Washington*
Calais *Washington*
Cambridge *Lamoille*
Cambridgeport *Windham*
Canaan *Essex*
Castleton *Rutland*
Cavendish *Windsor*
Center Rutland *Rutland*
Charlotte *Chittenden*
Chelsea *Orange*
Chester *Windsor*
Chester Depot *Windsor*
Chittenden *Rutland*
Clarendon *Rutland*
Colchester *Chittenden*
Concord *Essex*
Corinth *Orange*
Coventry *Orleans*

Craftsbury *Orleans*
Craftsbury Common
 Orleans
Cuttingsville *Rutland*
Danby *Rutland*
Danville *Caledonia*
Derby *Orleans*
Derby Line *Orleans*
Dorset *Bennington*
East Arlington *Bennington*
East Barre *Washington*
East Berkshire *Franklin*
East Burke *Caledonia*
East Calais *Washington*
East Charleston *Orleans*
East Corinth *Orange*
East Dorset *Bennington*
East Dover *Windham*
East Fairfield *Franklin*
East Hardwick *Caledonia*
East Haven *Essex*
East Middlebury *Addison*
East Montpelier
 Washington
East Poultney *Rutland*
East Randolph *Orange*
East Ryegate *Caledonia*
East Saint Johnsbury
 Caledonia
East Thetford *Orange*
East Wallingford *Rutland*
Eden *Lamoille*
Ely *Orange*
Enosburg Falls *Franklin*
Essex *Chittenden*
Essex Junction *Chittenden*
Fairfax *Franklin*
Fairfield *Franklin*
Fair Haven *Rutland*
Fairlee *Orange*
Ferrisburg *Addison*
Florence *Rutland*
Forest Dale *Rutland*
Foxville *Orange*
Franklin *Franklin*
Gaysville *Windsor*
Gilman *Essex*
Glover *Orleans*
Grafton *Windham*

Granby *Essex*
Grand Isle *Grand Isle*
Graniteville *Washington*
Granville *Addison*
Greensboro *Orleans*
Greensboro Bend *Orleans*
Groton *Caledonia*
Guildhall *Essex*
Hancock *Addison*
Hardwick *Caledonia*
Hartford *Windsor*
Hartland *Windsor*
Hartland Four Corners
 Windsor
Highgate Center *Franklin*
Highgate Springs *Franklin*
Hinesburg *Chittenden*
Huntington *Chittenden*
Hyde Park *Lamoille*
Hydeville *Rutland*
Irasburg *Orleans*
Island Pond *Essex*
Isle LaMotte *Grand Isle*
Jacksonville *Windham*
Jamaica *Windham*
Jeffersonville *Lamoille*
Jericho *Chittenden*
Johnson *Lamoille*
Jonesville *Chittenden*
Killington *Rutland*
Leicester Junction *Addison*
Londonderry *Windham*
Lowell *Orleans*
Lower Village *Lamoille*
Lower Waterford
 Caledonia
Ludlow *Windsor*
Lunenburg *Essex*
Lyndon *Caledonia*
Lyndon Center *Caledonia*
Lyndonville *Caledonia*
McIndoe Falls *Caledonia*
Manchester *Bennington*
Manchester Center
 Bennington
Marlboro *Windham*
Marshfield *Washington*
Middlebury *Addison*
Middletown Springs

 Rutland
Milton *Chittenden*
Monkton *Addison*
Montgomery *Franklin*
Montgomery Center
 Franklin
Montpelier *Washington*
Moretown *Washington*
Morgan *Orleans*
Morgan Center *Orleans*
Morrisville *Lamoille*
Moscow *Lamoille*
Mount Holly *Rutland*
Newbury *Orange*
Newfane *Windham*
New Haven *Addison*
Newport *Orleans*
Newport Center *Orleans*
North Bennington
 Bennington
North Clarendon *Rutland*
North Concord *Essex*
North Ferrisburg *Addison*
Northfield *Washington*
Northfield Falls
 Washington
North Hartland *Windsor*
North Hero *Grand Isle*
North Hyde Park *Lamoille*
North Pomfret *Windsor*
North Pownal *Bennington*
North Springfield *Windsor*
North Thetford *Orange*
North Troy *Orleans*
Norton *Essex*
Norwich *Windsor*
Orleans *Orleans*
Orwell *Addison*
Passumpsic *Caledonia*
Pawlet *Rutland*
Peacham *Caledonia*
Perkinsville *Windsor*
Peru *Bennington*
Pittsfield *Rutland*
Pittsford *Rutland*
Plainfield *Washington*
Plymouth *Windsor*
Post Mills *Orange*
Poultney *Rutland*

Pownal *Bennington*
Pownal Center *Bennington*
Proctor *Rutland*
Proctorsville *Windsor*
Putney *Windham*
Quechee *Windsor*
Randolph *Orange*
Randolph Center *Orange*
Reading *Windsor*
Readsboro *Bennington*
Richford *Franklin*
Richmond *Chittenden*
Riverton *Washington*
Rochester *Windsor*
Roxbury *Washington*
Rupert *Bennington*
Rutland *Rutland*
Saint Albans *Franklin*
Saint Albans Bay *Franklin*
Saint Johnsbury *Caledonia*
Saint Johnsbury Center
    Caledonia
Salisbury *Addison*
Saxtons River *Windham*
Shaftsbury *Bennington*
Sharon *Windsor*
Sheffield *Caledonia*
Shelburne *Chittenden*
Sheldon *Franklin*
Sheldon Springs *Franklin*
Shoreham *Addison*
South Barre *Washington*
South Burlington
    Chittenden
South Dorset *Bennington*
South Hero *Grand Isle*
South Londonderry
    Windham
South Pomfret *Windsor*
South Royalton *Windsor*
South Ryegate *Caledonia*
South Strafford *Orange*
South Woodstock *Windsor*
Springfield *Windsor*
Starksboro *Addison*
Stockbridge *Windsor*
Stowe *Lamoille*
Strafford *Orange*
Sutton *Caledonia*
Swanton *Franklin*
Taftsville *Windsor*
Thetford *Orange*
Thetford Center *Orange*
Topsham *Orange*
Townshend *Windham*
Trow Hill *Washington*
Troy *Orleans*
Tunbridge *Orange*
Underhill *Chittenden*
Underhill Center
    Chittenden
Vergennes *Addison*
Vernon *Windham*
Vershire *Orange*
Waitsfield *Washington*
Wallingford *Rutland*
Wardsboro *Windham*
Warren *Washington*
Washington *Orange*
Waterbury *Washington*
Waterbury Center
    Washington
Waterville *Lamoille*
Websterville *Washington*
Wells *Rutland*

Wells River *Orange*
West Branch *Lamoille*
West Burke *Caledonia*
West Charleston *Orleans*
West Danville *Caledonia*
West Dover *Windham*
West Dummerston
    Windham
West Fairlee *Orange*
Westfield *Orleans*
Westford *Chittenden*
West Halifax *Windham*
West Hartford *Windsor*
Westminster *Windham*
Westminster Station
    Windham
West Newbury *Orange*
Weston *Windsor*
West Pawlet *Rutland*
West Rupert *Bennington*
West Rutland *Rutland*
West Topsham *Orange*
West Wardsboro *Windham*
White River Junction
    Windsor
Whiting *Addison*
Whitingham *Windham*
Wilder *Windsor*
Williamstown *Orange*
Williamsville *Windham*
Williston *Chittenden*
Wilmington *Windham*
Windsor *Windsor*
Winooski *Chittenden*
Winooski Park *Chittenden*
Wolcott *Lamoille*
Woodbury *Washington*
Woodstock *Windsor*
Worcester *Washington*

Virginia

While forty seven (47) of Virginia's ninety five (95) counties report that their criminal records are available in person only for employment screening purposes, the Virginia State Police offer statewide searches at a reasonable fee.

Civil court records filed in circuit court are for $7,000 and more.

For more information or for offices not listed, contact the state's information hot line at (804) 786-0000.

Driving Records

Department of Motor Vehicles
Information Department
PO Box 27412
Richmond, VA 23269
(804) 367-0538
Driving records are available by mail. $5.00 fee per request. $10.00 fee for certification. Turnaround time is 7 to 10 days. Written request must include job applicant's full name, date of birth, license number and signed release. Make check payable to Department of Motor Vehicles.

Worker's Compensation Records

Virginia Worker's Compensation
Commission
1000 DMV Drive
Richmond, VA 23220
(804) 367-8615
Worker's compensation records are available by mail. Request must include subject's full name and SSN. There is a $10.00 search fee. $.50 fee per copy. A notarized release is required.

Vital Statistics

Bureau of Vital Records
State Department of Health
PO Box 1000
Richmond, VA 23208-1000
(804) 786-6228
Birth and death records are available for $5.00 each. State office has records from January 1853 to December 1896 and since June 14, 1912. For records between those dates, write to the Health Department in the city where event occurred. An employer can obtain records with a written release. Make certified check or money order payable to State Health Department. Marriage records are available for $5.00. Include name, spouse's name, maiden name, date, city or county where license issued and reason for request. Turnaround time is 8 weeks. Divorce records are available for $5.00. Include name, spouse's name, maiden name, divorce date and place, reason for request. Turnaround time is 8 weeks.

Department of Education

Department of Education
Certification Office
PO Box 6Q
Richmond, VA 23216-2060
(804) 225-2022
Field of certification, effective date, expiration date are available by phone or mail. Include name and SSN.

Medical Licensing

Department of Health Professions
Board of Medicine
1601 Rollinghills Drive
Richmond, VA 23229-5005
(804) 662-9908
Will confirm licenses for MDs, PODs and DOs by phone or mail. No fee. Include name, license number. For licenses not mentioned, contact the above office.

Virginia State Board of Nursing
1601 Rolling Hills Drive
Richmond, VA 23229-5005
(804) 662-9909
Will confirm license by phone. No fee. Include name, license number.

Bar Association

Virginia State Bar Association
707 East Main STreet
Suite1500
Richmond, VA 23219-2803
(804) 775-0500
Will confirm licenses by phone. No fee. Include name.

Accountancy Board

Virginia State Board of Accountancy
3600 W. Broad Street, 5th Floor
Richmond, VA 23230
(804) 367-8505
Will confirm license by phone. No fee. Include name.

Securities Commission

State Corporation Commission
Division of Securities
220 Bank Street, 4th Floor
Richmond, VA 23230
(804) 786-7751

Will confirm license by phone. No fee. Include name and SSN.

Secretary of State

State Corporation Commission
Jefferson Building, 1st floor
1220 Bank St.
Richmond, VA 23219
(804) 786-9733
Service agent and address, date incorporated, standing with tax commission, trade names are available by phone or mail. Contact the above office for additional information.

Criminal Records

State Repository

Virginia State Police
Records Management Division
Central Criminal Records Exchange
PO Box C-85076
Richmond, VA 23261-7472
(804) 674-2021
(804) 674-2024 – Dissemination Clerk
All written requests must be submitted on the state's "Criminal History Record Request" form. Request must include subject's full name, sex, race, date of birth, place of birth, SSN and a signed, notarized release. There is a $5.00 fee for each request. Make check payable to Virginia State Police. Information released is conviction data only. Turnaround time is normally 72 hours plus mail time.

Accomack County

Clerk of Circuit Court, Criminal
Records
PO Box 126
Accomac, VA 23301
(804) 787-5776
Records are not available by mail or phone. See Virginia state repository.

Civil records are available in person only. See Virginia state repository for additional information.

Albemarle County

Albemarle County, Court Services
Circuit Court Clerk's Office
Room 225, Court Square
501 E. Jefferson Street
Charlottesville, VA 22902-5176
(804) 296-6621

Felony and misdemeanor records are available by mail. No release necessary. $5.00 fee. Make check payable to Clerk of Circuit Court. Search information required: name, SSN, date of birth, sex, race.

Civil records are available by mail or phone. No release necessary. No search fee. $2.00 fee for first copy, $.50 each additional copy. $2.50 for certification. Search information required: name, date of birth, years to search. Specify plaintiff or defendant.

The City of Alexandria

Clerk of Circuit Court, Felony Check
520 King Street
Room 307
Alexandria, VA 22314
(703) 838-4044

Felony and misdemeanor records are available in person only. See Virginia state repository for additional information.

Civil records are available in person only. See Virginia state repository for additional information.

Alleghany County

Felony records
Clerk of Circuit Court, Felony Check
PO Box 670
Covington, VA 24426
(703) 965-1730

Felony records are available by mail. No release necessary. No search fee. Search information required: name, SSN, date of birth.

Civil records
Clerk of Circuit Court
PO Box 670
Covington, VA 24426
(703) 962-3906

Civil records are available in person only. See Virginia state repository for additional information.

Misdemeanor records
Alleghany District Court
PO Box 139
Covington, VA 24426
(703) 965-1720

Misdemeanor records are available by mail. No search fee. No release necessary. Search information required: name, date of birth, years to search, SASE.

Civil records
Alleghany District Court
PO Box 139
Covington, VA 24426
(703) 965-1720

Civil records are available by mail. No release necessary. No search fee. Search information required: name, date of birth, years to search, SASE. Specify plaintiff or defendant.

Amelia County

Clerk of the Circuit Court, Felony Check
PO Box 237
Amelia, VA 23002
(804) 561-2128

Felony and misdemeanor records are available by mail or phone. No release necessary. No search fee. $1.00 fee per copy. Search information required: name, SSN, date of birth, years to search, SASE.

Civil records are available by mail or phone. No release necessary. No search fee. $1.00 fee per copy. Search information required: name, date of birth, years to search, SASE. Specify plaintiff or defendant.

Amherst County

Amherst Circuit Court, Felony Check
PO Box 462
Amherst, VA 24521
(804) 929-9321

Felony and misdemeanor records are available by mail. No release necessary. No search fee. Search information required: name, SSN, date of birth, years to search, SASE.

Civil records are available by mail or phone. No release necessary. No search fee. $.50 fee per copy. $1.00 for certification. Search information required: name, date of birth, years to search. Specify plaintiff or defendant.

Appomattox County

Clerk of Circuit Court, Felony Check
PO Box 672
Appomattox, VA 24522
(804) 352-5275

Felony and misdemeanor records are available by mail. A signed release is required. No search fee. Search information required: name, SSN, date of birth, sex, race, years to search.

Civil records are available by mail. A signed release is required. No search fee. $1.00 fee for first copy, $.50 each additional copy. Search information required: name, date of birth, years to search. Specify plaintiff or defendant.

Arlington County

Felony records
Clerk of the Circuit Court
Room 400
Arlington County Courthouse
1400 N. Courthouse Rd.
Arlington, VA 22201
(703) 358-7010

Felony records are available in person only. See Virginia state repository for more information.

Civil records
Clerk of the Circuit Court
Room 400
Arlington County Courthouse
1400 N. Courthouse Rd.
Arlington, VA 22201
(703) 358-7010

Civil records are available in person only. See Virginia state repository for more information.

Misdemeanor records
General District Court
1400 N. Courthouse Road
Alrington, VA 22201
(703) 358-4590

Misdemeanor records are available by mail. No release necessary. $1.00 fee per copy. No search fee. Search information required: name, years to search, SASE.

Civil records
General District Court
1400 N. Courthouse Road
Alrington, VA 22201
(703) 358-4590

Civil records for defendants only are available by mail or phone. No release necessary. No search fee. Search information required: name, date of birth, years to search.

Augusta County

Clerk of Circuit Court, Felony Check
PO Box 689
Staunton, VA 24401
(703) 245-5321

Felony and misdemeanor records are available by mail or phone. No search fee. $1.00 fee per copy. $2.00 for certification. No release necessary. Search information required: name, years to search.

Civil records are available by mail. No release necessary. No search fee. $1.00 fee per copy. $2.00 for certification. Search information required: name, date of birth, years to search. Specify plaintiff or defendant.

Bath County

Bath County Circuit Court, Felony Check
PO Box 180
Warm Springs, VA 24484
(703) 839-7226

Felony and misdemeanor records are available in person only. For additional information see Virginia state repository.

Civil records are available in person only. See Virginia state repository for additional information .

Bedford County

Clerk of the Circuit Court, Felony Check
PO Box 235
Bedford, VA 24523
(703) 586-7632

Felony and misdemeanor records are available by mail. No release necessary. $5.00 search fee. Company checks only, payable to Clerk of Circuit Court. Search information required: name, SSN, date of birth, sex, race.

Civil records are available by mail. No release necessary. $5.00 search fee. $.50 fee per copy. Search information required: name, date of birth, years to search. Specify plaintiff or defendant.

The City of Bedford

Clerk of Circuit Court, Felony Check
PO Box 235
Bedford, VA 24523
(703) 586-7632

Felony and misdemeanor records are available by mail. A release is required. $5.00 fee. Company checks only, payable to Clerk of Circuit Court. Search information required: name, SSN, date of birth, sex.

Civil records are available by mail. No release necessary. $5.00 search fee. $.50 fee per copy. Search information required: name, date of birth, years to search. Specify plaintiff or defendant.

Bland County

Circuit Court, Felony Check
PO Box 295
Bland, VA 24315
(703) 688-4562

Felony and misdemeanor records are available by mail. A release is required. $10.00 search fee. Company checks only, payable to Clerk of Circuit Court. Search information required: name, date of birth, SSN.

Civil records are available by mail. A release is required. $10.00 search fee. $.50 fee per copy. $1.00 for first certification, $.50 each additional page. Search information required: name, date of birth, years to search. Specify plaintiff or defendant.

Botetourt County

Clerk of Circuit Court, Criminal Records
PO Box 219
Fincastle, VA 24090
(703) 473-8274

Felony and misdemeanor records are available by mail. No release necessary. No search fee. $1.00 fee per copy. Search information required: name, date of birth.

Civil records are available by mail. A release is required. No search fee. $1.00 fee per copy. Search information required: name, date of birth, years to search. Specify plaintiff or defendant.

The City of Bristol

Police Department
415 Cumberland St.
Bristol, VA 24201
(703) 466-2121

Felony and misdemeanore records are available by mail only. Notarized release is required. $3.00 search fee. Check payable to City of Bristol. Search information required: name, date of birth, address, SSN, SASE.

Civil records are available by mail. A notorized release is required. $3.00 search fee. Search information required: name, date of birth, SSN, years to search. Specify plaintiff or defendant.

Brunswick County

Clerk of the Circuit Court, Felony Check
PO Box 929
Lawrenceville, VA 23868
(804) 848-2215

Felony and misdemeanor records are available in person only. See Virginia state repository for more information.

Civil records are available in person only. See Virginia state repository for more information.

Buchanan County

Clerk of Circuit Court, Criminal Records
PO Box 929
Grundy, VA 24614
(703) 935-6575

Felony and misdemeanor records are available by mail or phone. No release necessary. No search fee. Search information required: name, date of birth, SSN, years to search.

Civil records are available by mail or phone. A release is required. No search fee. $.25 fee per copy. $.50 for certification. Search information required: name, date of birth, years to search. Specify plaintiff or defendant.

Buckingham County

Felony records

Clerk of Circuit Court, Felony Check
PO Box 107
Buckingham, VA 23921
(804) 969-4734

Felony records are available by mail. A release is requird. No search fee. $1.00 fee per copy. Search information required: name, date of birth, SSN, sex, race, previous address, years to search.

Civil records

Clerk of Circuit Court
PO Box 107
Buckingham, VA 23921
(804) 969-4734

Civil records are available in person only. See Virginia state repository for more information.

Misdemeanor records

District Court
PO Box 127
Buckingham, VA 23921
(804) 969-47555

Misdemeanor records are available by mail. No release necessary. No search fee. Search information required: name, date of birth, years to search.

Civil records

District Court
PO Box 127
Buckingham, VA 23921
(804) 969-47555

Civil records are available by mail. No release necessary. No search fee. Search information required: name, date of birth, years to search.

The City of Buena Vista

Clerk of Circuit Court, Felony Check
2039 Sycamore Avenue
Buena Vista, VA 24416
(703) 261-6121 Extension 127, 128

Felony and misdemeanor records are available by mail. A release is required. $5.00 search fee. $1.00 fee for first two copies, $.50 fee per copy thereafter. Search information required: name, SSN, date of birth, sex, race, SASE.

Civil records are available by mail. A release is required. No search fee. $.50 fee per copy. $3.00 for certification. Search information required: name, date of birth, years to search. Specify plaintiff or defendant.

Campbell County

Clerk of Circuit Court
PO Box 7
Rustburg, VA 24588
(804) 847-0961

Records are available in person only. See Virginia state repository.

Civil records are available in person only. See Virginia state repository for additional information.

Caroline County

Clerk of Circuit Court, Criminal Records
PO Box 309
Bowling Green, VA 22427
(804) 633-5800

Felony records are available in person only. See Virginia state repository for additional information.

Civil records are available in person only. See Virginia state repository for additional information.

Carroll County

Clerk of Circuit Court, Criminal Records
PO Box 218
Hillsville, VA 24343
(703) 728-3117

Felony and misdemeanor records are available by mail. No release necessary. $5.00 search fee, $1.00 fee per copy. Search information required: name, SSN, date of birth, years to search.

Civil records are available by mail. No release necessary. $5.00 search fee. $.50 fee per copy. $2.00 for certification. Search information required: name, date of birth, years to search. Specify plaintiff or defendant.

Charles City County

Clerk of Circuit Court, Criminal Records
PO Box 86
Charles City, VA 23030-0086
(804) 829-9212

Felony and misdemeanor records are available by mail. A release is required. No search fee. Search information required: name, SSN, date of birth, sex, race, previous address, years to search.

Civil records are available by mail. No release necessary. No search fee. $1.00 fee per copy. $2.00 for certification. Search information required: name, date of birth, years to search. Specify plaintiff or defendant.

Charlotte County

Clerk of Circuit Court, Criminal Records
PO Box 38
Charlotte Courthouse, VA 23923
(804) 748-1241

Felony and misdemeanor records are available by mail. No release necessary. $3.00 search fee. $.50 fee per copy. Search information required: name, date of birth, years to search. Specify plaintiff or defendant.

Civil records are available by mail. No release necessary. $3.00 search fee. $.50 fee per copy. Search information required: name, date of birth, years to search. Specify plaintiff or defendant.

The City of Charlottesville

Clerk of the Circuit Court, Criminal Records
315 E. High Street
Charlottesville, VA 22901
(804) 295-3182

Felony records are available in person only. See Virginia state repository for additional information.

Civil records are available by mail. No release necessary. No search fee. $1.00 fee for first copy, $.50 each additional copy. $2.00 for certification. Search information required: name, date of birth, years to search. Specify plaintiff or defendant.

The City of Chesapeake

Clerk of the Circuit Court, Criminal Dept.
PO Box 15205
Chesapeake, VA 23320
(804) 547-6111

Felony records are available by mail. A release is required. 5.00 search fee. $1.00 fee for first copy, $.50 each additional copy. . $1.50 for certification. Company checks only, payable to Clerk of Circuit Court. Search information required: name, SSN, date of birth, years to search.

Civil records are available by mail. A release is required. $5.00 search fee. $1.00 fee for first copy, $.50 each additional copy. $1.50 for certification. Search information required: name, date of birth, years to search. Specify plaintiff or defendant.

Chesterfield County

Clerk of Circuit Court, Criminal Division
PO Box 125
Chesterfield, VA 23832
(804) 748-1406

Felony and misdemeanor records are available by mail. A release is required. $3.00 search fee. Search information required: name, SSN, date of birth.

Civil records are available by mail. No release necessary. $3.00 search fee. $.50 fee per copy. Search information required: name, date of birth, years to search. Specify plaintiff or defendant.

Clarke County

Clerk of Circuit Court, Criminal Records
PO Box 189
Berryville, VA 22611
(703) 955-1309

Records are not available by mail or phone. See Virginia state repository.

Civil records are available by mail. No release necessary. No search fee. $.50 fee per copy. Search information required: name, date of birth, years to search. Specify plaintiff or defendant.

The City of Clifton Forge

Felony records
Clerk of Circuit Court, Criminal Records
PO Box 27
Clifton Forge, VA 24422
(703) 863-8536

Felony and misdemeanor records are available by mail. No release necessary. No search fee. Search information required: name, SASE.

Civil records
Clerk of Circuit Court
PO Box 27
Clifton Forge, VA 24422
(703) 863-8536

Civil records are available by mail. No release necessary. No search fee. $.50 fee per copy. Search information required: name, date of birth, years to search, SASE. Specify plaintiff or defendant.

Misdemenor records
General District Court
Clifton Forge, VA 24422
(703)-863-5676

Misdemeanor records are available by mail or phone. 5.00 search fee. $.50 fee per copy. $2.00 for certification. No release necessary. Search information required: name, years to search.

Civil records
General District Court
Clifton Forge, VA 24422
(703)-863-5676

Civil records are available by mail. No release necessary. $5.00 search fee. $.50 fee per copy. $2.00 for certification. Search information required: name, date of birth, years to search. Specify plaintiff or defendant.

The City of Colonial Heights

Colonial Heights Circuit Court, Criminal Records
401 Temple Ave.
Colonial Heights, VA 23834
(804) 520-9364

Felony and misdemeanor records are available by mail. No release necessary. $10.00 search fee. Search information required: name, years to search, SASE.

Civil records are available in person only. See Virginia state repository.

The City of Covington

Clerk of Circuit Court, Criminal Records
PO Box 670
Covington, VA 24426
(703) 962-3906

Felony and misdemeanor records are available by mail. No release necessary. No search fee. Search information required: name, years to search.

Civil records are available by mail. No release necessary. No search fee. $1.00 fee per copy. Search information required: name, date of birth, years to search. Specify plaintiff or defendant.

Craig County

Clerk of Circuit Court, Criminal Records
PO Box 185
New Castle, VA 24127
(703) 864-5989

Felony and misdemeanor records are available in person only. For additional information see Virginia state repository.

Civil records are available in person only. See Virginia state repository.

Culpeper County

Clerk of Circuit Court, Criminal Records
135 West Cameron Street
Culpeper, VA 22701
(703) 825-8086

Felony and misdemeanor records are available by mail. A release is required. $5.00 search fee. Company checks only, payable to Clerk of Court. Search information required: name, SSN, date of birth, SASE, previous address, years to search.

Civil records are available by mail. No release necessary. $5.00 search fee. $1.00 fee for first copy, $.50 each additional copy. $2.00 for certification. Search information required: name, date of birth, years to search. Specify plaintiff or defendant.

Cumberland County

Felony records
Circuit Court, Criminal Records
PO Box 8
Cumberland, VA 23040
(804) 492-9224
Fax (804) 492-4441

Felony records are available by mail, fax or phone. A release is required. No search fee. $1.00 fee per copy. Search information required: name, date of birth, SASE, years to search.

Civil records
Circuit Court
PO Box 8
Cumberland, VA 23040
(804) 492-9224
Fax (804) 492-4441

Civil records are available by mail, fax or phone. A release is required. No search fee. $1.00 fee per copy. Search information required: name, date of birth, years to search, SASE. Specify plaintiff or defendant.

Misdemeanor records
General District Court
PO Box 24
Cumberland, VA 23040
(804) 492-4848

Records are available by phone. Release required. No search fee. Search information required: name, date of birth, and years to search.

Civil records
General District Court
PO Box 24
Cumberland, VA 23040
(804) 492-4848

Civil records are available by mail or phone. No release necessary. No search fee. Search information required: name, date of birth, years to search. Specify plaintiff or defendant.

The City of Danville

Clerk of Circuit Court
PO Box 3300
Danville, VA 24543
(804) 799-5168
Records are not available by mail or phone. See Virginia state repository.

Civil records are available in person only. See Virginia state repository for additional information.

Dickenson County

Clerk of Circuit Court, Criminal Records
PO Box 190
Clintwood, VA 24228
(703) 926-1616
Felony and misdemeanor records are available by mail or phone. No release necessary. No search fee. $.50 fee per copy. Search information required: name, SSN, date of birth, sex, race.

Civil records are available by mail. No release necessary. No search fee. $1.00 fee per copy. Search information required: name, date of birth, years to search. Specify plaintiff or defendant.

Dinwiddie County

Clerk of Circuit Court
PO Box 63
Dinwiddie, VA 23841
(804) 469-4540
Felony and misdemeanor records are available by mail. No release necessary. No search fee. $.25 fee per copy. $2.00 for certification. Search information required: name, date of birth, years to search, SASE, previous address.

Civil records are available by mail. No release necessary. No search fee. $.25 fee per copy. $2.00 for certification. Search information required: name, date of birth, years to search, SASE. Specify plaintiff or defendant.

The City of Emporia

Clerk of Circuit Court, Criminal Records
PO Box 631
Emporia, VA 23847
(804) 348-4215
Felony and misdemeanor records are available by mail. No release necessary. No fee. Search information required: name, year to search.

Civil records are available in person only. See Virginia state repository for additional information.

Essex County

Courthouse
PO Box 445
Tappahannock, VA 22560
(804) 443-3541
Records are available in person only. See Virginia state repository.

Civil records are available in person only. See Virginia state repository for additional information.

Fairfax County

Clerk of Circuit Court, Criminal Records
4110 Chain Bridge Road
Fairfax, VA 22030
(703) 246-2228
Felony records are available in person only. See Virginia state repository for additional information.

Civil records are available in person only. See Virginia state repository for additional information.

The City of Fairfax

Clerk of Circuit Court, Criminal Records
4110 Chain Bridge Road
Fairfax, VA 22030
(703) 246-2228
Felony and misdemeanor records are available in person only. See Virginia state repository for additional information.

Civil records are available in person only. See Virginia state repository for additional information.

The City of Falls Church

Clerk of Circuit Court, Criminal Records
1400 N. Courthouse Road, Room 201
Arlington, VA 22201
(703) 358-4399
Felony and misdemeanor records are available in person only. See Virginia state repository for additional information.

Civil records are available in person only. See Virginia state repository for additional information.

Fauquier County

Clerk of Circuit Court
PO Box 985
Warrenton, VA 22186
(703) 347-8600
Records are not available by mail or phone. See Virginia state repository.

Civil records are available in person only. See Virginia state repository for additional information.

Floyd County

Clerk of Circuit Court, Criminal Records
100 East Main Street - Room 200
Floyd, VA 24091
(703) 745-9330
Felony and misdemeanor records are available by mail. A release is required. $5.00 search fee. Check payable to Clerk of Circuit Court. Search information required: name, SSN, date of birth, years to search.

Civil records are available by mail. No release necessary. $5.00 search fee. $1.00 fee per copy. $3.00 for certification. Search information required: name, date of birth, years to search. Specify plaintiff or defendant.

Fluvanna County

Clerk of Circuit Court
PO box 299
Palmyra, VA 22963
(804) 589-8011
Felony and misdemeanor records by mail. No release necessary. $5.00 search fee. $.50 fee per copy. $3.00 for certification. Search information required: name, years to search.

Civil records are available in person only. See Virginia state repository for more information.

Franklin County

Clerk of Circuit Court, Criminal Records
PO Box 126
Courtland, VA 23837
(804) 653-2200
Felony and misdemeanor records are available by mail. A release is required. $5.00 search fee. Certified check only, payable to Clerk of Circuit Court. Search information required: name, SSN, years to search.

Civil records are available by mail. No release necessary. $5.00 search fee. $1.00 fee for first copy, $.50 each additional copy. Search information required: name, date of birth, years to search. Will only search for plaintiff.

Frederick County

Clerk of Circuit Court, Criminal Records
5 North Kent Street
Winchester, VA 22601
(703) 667-5770
Records are not available by mail. No release necessary. No search fee. $.50 fee per copy. $1.00 for certification. Search information required: name, years to search.

Civil records are available by mail. No release necessary. No search fee. $.50 fee per copy. $1.00 for certification. Search information required: name, years to search. Specify plaintiff or defendant.

The City of Fredericksburg

Felony records
Clerk of Circuit Court, Criminal Records
PO Box 359
Fredericksburg, VA 22404-0359
(703) 376-1066
Felony and misdemeanor records up to Dec. 1984 are available by mail. A release is required. No search fee. $.50 fee per copy. $2.00 for certification. Search information required: name, years to search, SASE.

Civil records
Clerk of Circuit Court
PO Box 359
Fredericksburg, VA 22404-0359
(703) 376-1066
Civil records are available by mail. A release is required. No search fee. $.50 fee per copy. $2.00 for certification. Search information required: name, date of birth, years to search, SASE. Specify plaintiff or defendant.

Misdemeanor records
General District Court
615 Princess Ann St.
Fredericksburg, VA 22401
(703) 372-1042

Misdemeanor records from 1985 forward are available by mail. No search fee. $.50 fee per copy. $2.00 for certification. No release necessary. Search information required: name, years to search.

Civil records are available by mail. No release necessary. No search fee. $.50 fee per copy. $2.00 for certification. Search information required: name, date of birth, years to search. Specify plaintiff or defendant.

The City of Galax

Clerk of Circuit Court
PO Box 130
Independence, VA 24348
(703) 773-2231

Records are not available by mail or phone. See Virginia state repository.

Civil records are available in person only. See Virginia state repository for more information.

Giles County

Clerk of Circuit Court
PO Box 502
Pearisburg, VA 24134
(703) 921-1722

Felony and misdemeanor records are available in person only. See Virginia state repository for more information.

Civil records are available in person only. See Virginia state repository for more information.

Gloucester County

Clerk of Circuit Court, Criminal Records
Box N
Gloucester, VA 23061
(804) 693-2502
Fax (804) 693-9425

Felony and misdemeanor records are available by mail or fax. No release necessary. No search fee. Search information required: name, SSN, date of birth, sex, race.

Civil records are available by mail. No release necessary. No search fee. $1.00 fee per copy. $2.00 for certification. Search information required: name, date of birth, years to search. Specify plaintiff or defendant.

Goochland County

Clerk of Circuit Court, Criminal Records
PO Box 196
Goochland, VA 23063
(804) 556-5353

Felony records are available in person only. See Virginia state repository for more information.

Civil records are available in person only. See Virginia state repository for more information.

Grayson County

Clerk of Circuit Court
PO Box 130
Independence, VA 24348
(703) 773-2231

Records are not available by mail or phone. See Virginia state repository.

Civil records are available in person only. See Virginia state repository for more information.

Greene County

Clerk of Circuit Court, Criminal Records
PO Box 386
Stanardsville, VA 22973
(804) 985-5208

Felony and misdemeanor records are available by mail. A release is required. No fee. Search information required: name, date of birth, years to search.

Civil records are available by mail. No release necessary. No search fee. $1.00 fee for first copy, $.50 each additional copy. Search information required: name, date of birth, years to search. Specify plaintiff or defendant.

Greensville County

Clerk of Circuit Court, Criminal Records
PO Box 631
Emporia, VA 23847
(804) 348-4215

Felony and misdemeanor records are available by mail. A release is required. No search fee. $1.00 fee per copy. $1.00 for certification. Search information required: name, years to search.

Civil records are available by mail. A release is required. No search fee. $1.00 fee per copy. $1.00 for certification. Search information required: name, date of birth, years to search. Specify plaintiff or defendant.

Halifax County

Clerk of Circuit Court
PO Box 729
Halifax, VA 24558
(804) 476-6211

Records are not available by mail. No release necessary. $5.00 search fee. $1.00 fee per copy. $1.00 for certification. Search information required: name, years to search. .

Civil records are available by mail. No release necessary. $5.00 search fee. $1.00 fee per copy. $1.00 for certification. Search information required: name, date of birth, years to search. Specify plaintiff or defendant.

The City of Hampton

Clerk of Circuit Court
PO Box 40
Hampton, VA 23669
(804) 727-6105

Records are not available by mail or phone. See Virginia state repository.

Civil records are available by mail or phone. No release necessary. No search fee. $1.00 fee for first copy, $.50 each additional copy. . $2.00 for certification. Search information required: name, date of birth, years to search. Specify plaintiff or defendant.

Hanover County

Clerk of Circuit Court
PO Box 39
Hanover, VA 23069
(804) 537-6000 Extension 6151

Records are not available in person only. See Virginia state repository for more information.

Civil records are availablein person only. See Virginia state repository for more information.

The City of Harrisonburg

Rockingham County
Harrisonburg, VA 22801
(703) 564-3000

Records are available in person only. See Virginia state repository.

Civil records are available in person only. See Virginia state repository for more information.

Henrico County

Henrico Circuit Court, Criminal Records
PO Box 27032
Richmond, VA 23273
(804) 672-4764

Felony and misdemeanor records are available by mail. No search fee. A release is required. Search informatin required: name, date of birth, SSN, years to search.

Civil records are available in person only. See Virginia state repository for more information.

Henry County

Clerk of Circuit Court, Criminal Records
PO Box 1049
Martinsville, VA 24114
(703) 638-3961

Felony and misdemeanor records are available by mail. No release necessary. $5.00 search fee. Search information required: name, SSN, date of birth, sex, race, years to search.

Civil records are available in person only. See Virginia state repository for more information.

Highland County

Highland County Circuit Court, Criminal Records
PO Box 190
Monterey, VA 24465
(703) 468-2447

Felony and misdemeanor records are available by mail. No release necessary. No search fee. $1.00 fee per copy. $3.00 for certification. Search information required: name, SSN, date of birth, years to search.

Civil records are available by mail. No release necessary. No search fee. $1.00 fee per copy. $3.00 for certification. Search information required: name, SSN, date of birth, years to search. Specify plaintiff or defendant.

The City of Hopewell

Clerk of Circuit Court
PO Box 354
Hopewell, VA 23860
(804) 541-2239

Records are not available in person only. See Virginia state repository for more information.

Civil records are available in person only. See Virginia state repository for more information.

Isle of Wight County

Clerk of Circuit Court
Isle of Wight, VA 23397
(804) 562-3275

Records are not available in person only. See Virginia state repository for more information.

Civil records are available in person only. See Virginia state repository for more information.

James City County

Clerk of Circuit Court, Criminal Records
PO Box 3045
Williamsburg, VA 23187
(804) 229-2552

Felony and misdemeanor records are available by mail. A release is required. $2.00 search fee. Search information required: name, SSN, date of birth, sex, race, SASE, years to search.

Civil records are available by mail. No release necessary. $2.00 search fee. $1.00 fee for first copy, $.50 each additional. $.50 for certification. Search information required: name, date of birth, years to search. Specify plaintiff or defendant.

King and Queen County

Clerk of Circuit Court, Criminal Records
PO Box 67
King and Queen, VA 23085
(804) 785-2460

Felony and misdemeanor records are available by mail. No release necessary. No search fee. $.50 fee per copy. $1.00 for certification. Search information required: name, date of birth, years to search, SASE.

Civil records are available by mail. No release necessary. No search fee. $.50 fee per copy. $1.00 for certification. Search information required: name, date of birth, years to search, SASE. Specify plaintiff or defendant.

King George County

Clerk of Circuit Court, Criminal Records
PO Box 105
King George, VA 22485
(703) 775-3322

Felony and misdemeanor records are available by mail. No release necessary. $10.00 search fee. Search information required: name, SSN, date of birth, sex, race.

Civil records are available by mail. No release necessary. $10.00 search fee. Search information required: name, date of birth, years to search. Specify plaintiff or defendant.

King William County

Clerk of Circuit Court, Criminal Records
PO Box 216
King William, VA 23086
(804) 769-2311

Felony and misdemeanor records are available by mail or phone. A release is required. No search fee. Search information required: name, SSN, date of birth, sex, race.

Civil records are available in person only. See Virginia state repository for additional information.

Lancaster County

Clerk of Circuit Court
Lancaster, VA 22503
(804) 462-5611

Records are available in person only. See Virginia state repository.

Civil records are available in person only. See Virginia state repository for additional information.

Lee County

Clerk of Circuit Court, Criminal Records
PO Box 326
Jonesville, VA 24263
(703) 376-7763

Felony and misdemeanor records are available by mail. No release necessary. No fee. Search information required: name, SSN.

Civil records are available in person only. See Virginia state repository for additional information.

The City of Lexington

Rockbridge County Circuit Court, Criminal Records
Courthouse
Lexington, VA 24450
(703) 463-2232

Felony and misdemeanor records are available in person only.

Civil records are available in person only. See Virginia state repository for additional information.

Loudoun County

Clerk of Circuit Court
18 E. Market Street
PO Box 550
Leesburg, VA 22075
(703) 777-0270

Records are not available by mail or phone. See Virginia state repository.

Civil records are available by mail from 1987 forward. No release necessary. No search fee. $.50 fee per copy. $2.00 for certification. Search information required: name, date of birth, years to search. Specify plaintiff or defendant.

Louisa County

Clerk of Circuit Court
PO Box 37
Louisa, VA 23093
(703) 967-0401

Records are not available by mail or phone. See Virginia state repository.

Civil records are available in person only. See Virginia state repository for additional information.

Lunenburg County

Clerk of Circuit Court, Criminal Records
Lunenberg, VA 23952
(804) 696-2230

Felony and misdemeanor records are available by mail. A release is required. $3.00 search fee. $1.00 fee per copy. Search information required: name, years to search.

Civil records are available in person only. See Virginia state repository for additional information.

The City of Lynchburg

Clerk of Circuit Court
PO Box 4
Lynchburg, VA 24505-0004
(804) 847-1590

Records are not available by mail or phone. See Virginia state repository.

Civil records are available in person only. See Virginia state repository for additional information.

Madison County

General District, Criminal Records
PO Box 470
Madison, VA 22727
(703) 948-4657

Felony and misdemeanor records are available by mail. No release necessary. No search fee. Search information required: name. Has most misdemeanor records through 1985.

Civil records are available by mail or phone. No release necessary. No search fee. Search information required: name, date of birth, years to search. Specify plaintiff or defendant.

The City of Manassas Park

Clerk of Circuit Court, Criminal Records
9311 Lee Avenue
Manassas, VA 22110
(703) 335-8800

Felony and misdemeanor records are available by mail. No release necessary. $10.00 fee. Certified check only, payable to Clerk of Circuit Court. Search information required: name, SSN, date of birth, sex, race. Misdemeanor records are available through 1985.

Civil records are available by mail. No release necessary. No search fee. $2.00 for certification. Search information required: name, date of birth, years to search, SASE. Specify plaintiff or defendant.

The City of Manassas

Clerk of Circuit Court, Criminal
Records
PO Box 191
Manassas, VA 22110
(703) 792-6149

Felony and misdemeanor records are available by mail. No release necessary. $10.00 search fee. Certified check only, payable to Clerk of Circuit Court. Search information required: name, SSN, date of birth, sex. Misdemeanor records are available through 1985.

Civil records are available by mail. No release necessary. No search fee. $2.00 for certification. Search information required: name, date of birth, years to search, SASE. Specify plaintiff or defendant.

The City of Martinsville

Martinsville Circuit Court, Criminal
Records
Clerk of Circuit Court
PO Box 1206
Martinsville, VA 24114-1206
(703) 638-3971

Felony and misdemeanor records are available by mail or phone. No release necessary. No search fee. Search information required: name, SSN, date of birth, sex, race, years to search.

Civil records are available by mail or phone. No release necessary. No search fee. $1.00 fee for first copy, $.50 each additional copy. $3.00 for certification. Search information required: name, date of birth, years to search. Specify plaintiff or defendant.

Mathews County

Felony records
Clerk of Circuit Court, Criminal
Records
PO Box 463
Mathews, VA 23109
(804) 725-2550

Felony and misdemeanor records are available by mail. No release necessary. No search fee. $1.00 fee per copy. Search information required: name, SSN, date of birth, sex, race.

Civil records
Clerk of Circuit Court
PO Box 463
Mathews, VA 23109
(804) 725-2550

Civil records are available by mail or phone. No release necessary. No search fee. $1.00 fee per copy. $2.00 for certification. Search information required: name, date of birth, years to search. Specify plaintiff or defendant.

Misdemeanor records
General District Court
PO Box 169
Saluda, VA 23149
(804) 758-4312
Misdemeanor records from 1985 forward are available in person only.

Civil records
General District Court
PO Box 169
Saluda, VA 23149
(804) 758-4312
Civil records are available in person only. See Virginia state repository for additional information.

Mecklenburg County

Clerk of Circuit Court
PO Box 530
Boydton, VA 23917
(804) 738-6191 Extension 209

Felony and misdemeanor records are available by mail form 1987 forward. A release is required. No search fee. Search information required: name, years to search.

Civil records are available by mail. A release is required. No search fee. Search information required: name, date of birth, years to search. Specify plaintiff or defendant.

Middlesex County

Clerk of Circuit Court
PO Box 158
Saluda, VA 23149
(804) 758-5317

Felony and misdemeanor records are available by mail. A release is required. No search fee. Search information required: name, years to search.

Civil records are available by mail. No release necessary. No search fee. $1.00 fee per copy. $2.00 for certification. Search information required: name, date of birth, years to search. Specify plaintiff or defendant.

Montgomery County

Clerk of Circuit Court
PO Box 209
Christiansburg, VA 24073
(703) 382-5760

Records are available in person only. See Virginia state repository for additional information.

Civil records are available in person only. See Virginia state repository for additional information.

Nelson County

Clerk of Circuit Court
PO Box 10
Lovingston, VA 22949
(804) 263-4069

Records are not available by mail or phone. See Virginia state repository.

Civil records are available in person only. See Virginia state repository for additional information.

New Kent County

Clerk of Circuit Court
PO Box 98
New Kent, VA 23124
(804) 966-9601

Records are available in person only. See Virginia state repository for additional information.

Civil records are available by mail. No release necessary. No search fee. Search information required: name, date of birth, years to search. Specify plaintiff or defendant.

The City of Newport News

Newport News Police Department,
Record Division
224 26th St.
PO Box 336
Newport News, VA 23607
(804) 247-8794

Felony and misdemeanor records are available by mail. A notarized release required. $5.00 search fee. Make check payable to City of Newport News. Search information required: full name, SSN or drivers license, date of birth

Civil records are available by mail. A notarized release required. $5.00 search fee. Search information required: name, date of birth, years to search. Specify plaintiff or defendant.

The City of Norfolk

Clerk of Circuit Court, Criminal
Records
Virginia State Police
Records Management Division
100 St. Paul Blvd.
Norfolk, VA 23510
(804) 441-2193

Felony and misdemeanor records are available by mail. No release necessary. $10.00 search fee, prepaid. Check or money order payable to Virginia State Police. Search information required: name, years to search.

Civil records are available by mail. No release necessary. $10.00 search fee, prepaid. Search information required: name, years to search. Specify plaintiff or defendant.

Northampton County

Clerk of Circuit Court, Criminal
Records
PO Box 36
Eastville, VA 23347
(804) 678-0465

Felony and misdemeanor records are available by mail. No release necessary. No search fee. Search information required: name, SSN, date of birth, sex, race.

Civil records are available in person only. See Virginia state repository for additional information.

Northumberland County

Clerk of Circuit Court, Criminal
Records
PO Box 217
Heathsville, VA 22473
(804) 580-3700

Felony and misdemeanor records are available by mail. No release necessary. No search fee. $1.00 for certification. Search information required: name, SSN, date of birth, years to search.

Civil records are available by mail. No release necessary. No search fee. $1.00 for certification. Search information required: name, date of birth, years to search. Specify plaintiff or defendant.

The City of Norton

Clerk of Circuit Court, Criminal
Records
PO Box 1248
Wise, VA 24293
(703) 328-6111

Records are available by mail. A signed release is required. $10.00 search fee. Search information required: name, SSN, date of birth, years to search.

Civil records are available by mail. A release is required. $10.00 search fee. $.25 fee per copy. $3.00 for certification. Search information required: name, date of birth, years to search. Specify plaintiff or defendant.

Nottoway County

Nottoway Circuit Court, Criminal
Records
Nottoway, VA 23955
(804) 645-9043

Felony and misdemeanor records are available by mail. A release is required. No search fee. $1.00 fee per copy. $1.00 for certification. Search information required: name, SSN, date of birth, years to search. Misdemeanor records are available through 1984.

Civil records are available by mail. No release necessary. No search fee. $1.00 fee per copy. $1.00 for certification. Search information required: name, date of birth, years to search. Specify plaintiff or defendant.

Orange County

Clerk of Circuit Court
PO Box 230
Orange, VA 22960
(703) 672-4030

Records are not available by mail or phone. See Virginia state repository.

Civil records are available in person only. See Virginia state repository for additional information.

Page County

Clerk of Court
116 South Court Street
Luray, VA 22835
(703) 743-4064

Records are not available in person only. See Virginia state repository for additional information.

Civil records are available in person only. See Virginia state repository for additional information.

Patrick County

Clerk of Circuit Court, Criminal
Records
PO Box 148
Stuart, VA 24171
(703) 694-7213

Felony and misdemeanor records are available by mail. A release is required. $3.00 search fee. $.50 fee per copy. Make check payable to Clerk of Circuit Court. Search information required: name, SSN, date of birth, sex, race.

Civil records are available by mail. A release is required. $3.00 search fee. $.50 fee per copy. Search information required: name, date of birth, years to search. Specify plaintiff or defendant.

The City of Petersburg

Clerk of Circuit Court
Courthouse Hill
Petersburg, VA 23803
(804) 733-2367

Felony and misdemeanor records are available in person only. See Virginia state repository for more information.

Civil records are available in person only. See Virginia state repository for more information.

Pittsylvania County

Clerk of Circuit Court
PO Box 31
Chatham, VA 24531
(804) 432-2041

Felony and misdemeanor records are available by mail. A release form is required. $5.00 search fee. Search information required: name, SSN, date of birth, previous address, years to search.

Civil records are available in person only. See Virginia state repository for more information.

The City of Poquoson

Clerk of Circuit Court, Criminal
Records
PO Box 371
Yorktown, VA 23690
(804) 890-3350

Felony and misdemeanor records are available by mail. No release necessary. No search fee. $1.00 fee for first copy, $.50 each additional copy. Search information required: name, years to search.

Civil records are available by mail. No release necessary. No search fee. $1.00 fee for first copy, $.50 each additional copy. Search information required: name, date of birth, years to search. Specify plaintiff or defendant.

The City of Portsmouth

Clerk of Circuit Court, Criminal
Records
PO Drawer 1217
Portsmouth, VA 23705
(804) 393-8671

Felony and misdemeanor records are available in person only. See Virginia state repository for more information.

Civil records are available in person only. See Virginia state repository for more information.

Powhatan County

Clerk of Circuit Court, Criminal
Records
PO Box 37
Powhatan, VA 23139
(804) 598-5660

Felony and misdemeanor records are available by mail. A release is required. No search fee. $.50 fee per copy. $1.00 for certification. Search information required: name, SSN, date of birth, years to search.

Civil records are available by mail. A release is required. No search fee. $.50 fee per copy. $1.00 for certification. Search information required: name, SSN, date of birth, years to search. Specify plaintiff or defendant.

Prince Edward County

Clerk of Circuit Court
PO Box 304
Farmville, VA 23901
(804) 392-5145

Felony and misdemeanor records are available in person only. Contact Central Criminal Records Exchange for additional information.

Civil records are available by mail. No release necessary. $10.00 search fee. $1.00 fee per copy. $2.00 for certification. Search information required: name, date of birth, SSN, years to search. Specify plaintiff or defendant.

Prince George County

Clerk of Circuit Court, Criminal
Records
PO Box 98
Prince George, VA 23875
(804) 733-2640

Felony records are available by mail. No release necessary. $5.00 search fee. Make check payable to Circuit Court. Search information required: name, SSN, date of birth, sex, race, years to search. Misdemeanors available through 1984.

Civil records are available by mail. No release necessary. $5.00 search fee. $1.00 fee for first copy, $50 each additional copy. Search information required: name, date of birth, years to search. Specify plaintiff or defendant.

Prince William County

Clerk of Circuit Court, Criminal
Records
PO Box 191
Manassas, VA 22110
(703) 792-6015

Felony and misdemeanor records are available from 1968 by mail. No release necessary. $10.00 search fee. $.50 fee per copy. $2.00 for certification. Make check or money order payable to Clerk of Circuit Court. Search information required: name, SSN, date of birth, SASE. Misdemeanors available through 1984.

Civil records are available in person only. See Virginia state repository for more information.

Pulaski County

Clerk of Circuit Court
PO Box 270
Pulaski, VA 24301
(703) 980-7825

Records are not available by mail or phone. See Virginia state repository.

Civil records are available in person only. See Virginia state repository for more information.

The City of Radford

Clerk of Circuit Court, Criminal
Records
619 Second Street
Radford, VA 24141
(703) 731-3610

Felony and misdemeanor records are available by mail. A release is required. No fsearch ee. Search information required: name, SSN, date of birth, sex, race.

Civil records are available by mail. A release is required. No search fee. $.50 fee per copy. $2.00 for certification. Search information required: name, date of birth, years to search. Specify plaintiff or defendant.

Rappahannock County

Clerk of Circuit Court
PO Box 116
Washington, VA 22747
(703) 675-3621
Records are available for physical inspection at above office. See Virginia state repository for additional information.

Civil records are available by mail. No release necessary. No search fee. $1.50 for first copy, $1.00 each additional copy. Search information required: name, date of birth, years to search. Specify plaintiff or defendant.

Richmond County

Circuit Court of Richmond County, Criminal Records
PO Box 956
Warsaw, VA 22572
(804) 333-3781
Felony records are available by mail. No release necessary. No search fee. Search information required: name, SSN, date of birth, sex, race.

Civil records are available by mail. No release necessary. No search fee. $.50 fee per copy. $2.00 for certification. Search information required: name, date of birth, years to search, SASE. Specify plaintiff or defendant.

The City of Richmond

Circuit Court, Criminal Records
Manchester Courthouse
10th & Hull Street
Richmond, VA 23224-0129
(804) 780-5370
Felony and misdemeanor records are available by mail. No release necessary. No search fee. $.50 fee per copy. $1.00 for certification. Search information required: name. years to search. Additional records are available from Circuit Court, John Marshall Courts Bldg. 800 E. Marshall St. Richmond, VA. 23219 (804) 780-6553.

Civil records are available by mail. No release necessary. No search fee. $.50 fee per copy. $1.00 for certification. Search information required: name, date of birth, years to search. Specify plaintiff or defendant.

Roanoke County

Clerk of Circuit Court, Criminal Records
PO Box 1126
Salem, VA 24153
(703) 387-6261
Felony and misdemeanor records are available by mail. A release is required. $5.00 search fee. $.50 fee per copy. $2.00 for certification. Certified check only, payable to Clerk of Court. Search information required: name, SSN, date of birth, years to search.

Civil records are available by mail. A release is required. $5.00 search fee. $.50 fee per copy. $2.00 for certification. Search information required: name, date of birth, years to search. Specify plaintiff or defendant.

The City of Roanoke

Clerk of Circuit Court, Criminal Records
PO Box 2610
Roanoke, VA 24010
(703) 981-2324
Felony and misdemeanor records are available by mail. A release is required. $5.00 search fee. Search information required: name, date of birth, SSN, years to search.

Civil records are available in person only. See Virginia state repository for additional information.

Rockbridge County

Clerk of Rockbridge County, Criminal Records
Courthouse Square
Lexington, VA 24450
(703) 463-2232
Felony and misdemeanor records are available in person only.

Civil records are available in person only. See Virginia state repository for additional information.

Rockingham County

Circuit Court Clerk, Criminal Records
Harrisonburg, VA 22801
(703) 564-3000
Records are not available by mail or phone. See Virginia state repository.

Civil records are available in person only. See Virginia state repository for additional information.

Russell County

Clerk of Circuit Court, Criminal Records
PO Box 435
Lebanon, VA 24266
(703) 889-8023
Felony and misdemeanor records are available by mail. A release is required. $5.00 search fee. Make check payable to Circuit Court. Search information required: name, SSN, date of birth, sex, race.

Civil records are available in person only. See Virginia state repository for additional information.

The City of Salem

Clerk of Circuit Court, Criminal Records
PO Box 891
Salem, VA 24153
(703) 387-6205
Records are not available by mail or phone. Records are available for physical inspection at above office. See Virginia state repository.

Civil records are available in person only. See Virginia state repository for additional information.

Scott County

Clerk of Circuit Court
Suite 2
104 E. Jackson St.
Gate City, VA 24251
(703) 386-3801
Felony and misdemeanor records are available by mail. No release necessary. $5.00 search fee. $1.00 fee per copy. $2.00 for certification. Make check payable to Circuit Clerk. Search information required: name, date of birth, SSN, years to search. Circuit Court has misdemeanor records through 1985. For pre-1985 records contact: General District Court, 104 E. Jackson, Suite 9, Gate City, VA 24251. (703) 386-7341.

Civil records are available by mail. No release necessary. $5.00 search fee. $1.00 fee per copy. $2.00 for certification. Search information required: name, date of birth, years to search. Specify plaintiff or defendant.

Shenandoah County

Clerk of Circuit Court, Criminal Records
PO Box 406
Woodstock, VA 22664
(703) 459-3791
Felony and misdemeanor records are available in person only. See Virginia state repository for additional information.

Civil records are available in person only. See Virginia state repository for additional information.

Smyth County

Clerk of Circuit Court, Criminal Records
PO Box 1025
Marion, VA 24354
(703) 783-7186
Felony and misdemeanor records are available by mail. No release necessary. $5.00 search fee. Certified check only, payable to Circuit Clerk. Search information required: name, SSN, date of birth, years to search.

Civil records are available by mail. No release necessary. $5.00 search fee. $1.00 fee per copy. $1.00 for certification. Search information required: name, date of birth, years to search. Specify plaintiff or defendant.

The City of South Boston

Clerk of Circuit Court
PO Box 729
Halifax, VA 24558
(804) 476-6211
Felony records are available in person only.

Civil records are available by mail. A release is required. $5.00 search fee. $1.00 fee per copy. Search information required: name, date of birth, years to search. Specify plaintiff or defendant.

Southampton County

Clerk of Circuit Court
22350 Main Street
PO Box 190
Courtland, VA 23837
(804) 653-2200 or 653-9245

Felony records are available by mail. $5.00 search fee. A release is required. 1.00 fee for first copy, $.50 each additional copy. Search information required: name, SSN, years to search.

Civil records are available by mail. A release is required. $5.00 search fee. $1.00 fee for first copy, $.50 each additional copy. Search information required: name, date of birth, years to search. Specify plaintiff or defendant.

Spotsylvania County

Clerk of Circuit Court
PO Box 96
Spotsylvania, VA 22553
(703) 582-7090

Records are available in person only. See Virginia state repository for additional information.

Civil records are available in person only. See Virginia state repository for additional information.

Stafford County

Clerk of Circuit Court
PO Box 69
Stafford, VA 22554
(703) 659-8750

Records are not available by mail or phone. See Virginia state repository.

Civil records are available in person only. See Virginia state repository for additional information.

The City of Staunton

Clerk of Circuit Court, Criminal Records
PO Box 58
Staunton, VA 24401
(703) 885-5121

Records are not available by mail or phone. See Virginia state repository.

Civil records are available in person only. See Virginia state repository for additional information.

The City of Suffolk

Clerk of Circuit Court
PO Box 1604
Suffolk, VA 23434
(804) 925-6450

Records are not available by mail or phone. See Virginia state repository.

Civil records are available in person only. See Virginia state repository for additional information.

Surry County

Clerk of Circuit Court
PO Box 203
Surry, VA 23883
(804) 294-3161

Records are not available by mail or phone. See Virginia state repository.

Civil records are available in person only. See Virginia state repository for additional information.

Sussex County

Clerk of Circuit Court, Criminal Records
PO Box 1337
Sussex, VA 23884
(804) 246-5511 Extension 276

Felony records are available by mail. A release is required. No search fee. $1.00 fee per copy. Make check payable to Clerk of Circuit Court. Search information required: name, SSN, date of birth, years to search. Misdemeanor records are available through 1984.

Civil records are available by mail. A release is required. No search fee. $1.00 fee per copy. Search information required: name, date of birth, years to search. Specify plaintiff or defendant.

Tazewell County

Clerk of Circuit Court, Criminal Records
PO Box 968
Tazewell, VA 24651
(703) 988-7541 Extension 311

Felony and misdemeanor records are available by mail. A release is required. No seasrch fee. Search information required: name, SSN, date of birth, years to search.

Civil records are available in person only. See Virginia state repository for addtional information.

The City of Virginia Beach

Clerk of Circuit Court
Princess Ann Station
Virginia Beach, VA 23456-9002
(804) 427-4181

Records are not available by mail or phone. See Virginia state repository.

Civil records are available in person only. See Virginia state repository for addtional information.

Warren County

Warren County Circuit Court
1 East Main Street
Front Royal, VA 22630
(703) 635-2435

Records are available in person only. See Virginia state repository for addtional information.

Civil records are available by mail. A release is required. No search fee. $.50 fee per copy. $2.50 for certification. Search information required: name, date of birth, years to search. Specify plaintiff or defendant.

Washington County

Clerk of Circuit Court
Court Street
Abingdon, VA 24210
(703) 628-3761

Records are available in person only. See Virginia State Repository for additional information.

Civil records are available in person only. See Virginia state repository for addtional information.

The City of Waynesboro

Clerk of Circuit Court, Criminal Records
PO Box 910
Waynesboro, VA 22980
(703) 942-6616

Felony and misdemeanor records are available in person only. See Virginia state repository for addtional information.

Civil records are available in person only. See Virginia state repository for addtional information.

Westmoreland County

Clerk of the Circuit Court, Criminal Records
PO Box 307
Montross, VA 22520
(804) 493-8911 Extension 343

Felony and misdemeanor records are available in person only. See Virginia state repository for addtional information.

Civil records are available in person only. See Virginia state repository for addtional information.

The City of Williamsburg

Clerk of Circuit Court, Criminal Records
PO Box 3045
Williamsburg, VA 23187
(804) 229-2552

Felony and misdemeanor records are available by mail. A release is required. $2.00 search fee. Search information required: name, SSN, date of birth, sex, race, SASE, years to search.

Civil records are available by mail. No release necessary. $2.00 search fee. $1.00 fee for first copy, $.50 each additional. $.50 for certification. Search information required: name, date of birth, years to search. Specify plaintiff or defendant.

The City of Winchester

Clerk of Circuit Court
Judicial Center
Winchester, VA 22601
(703) 667-5770

Records are not available by mail or phone. See Virginia state repository.

Civil records are available in person only. See Virginia state repository for addtional information.

Wise County

Clerk of Circuit Court
PO Box 1248
Wise, VA 24293
(703) 328-6111 Extension 21

Felony and misdemeanor records are available by mail. A release is required. $10.00 search fee. Search information required: name, SSN, date of birth.

Civil records are available in person only. See Virginia state repository for addtional information.

Wythe County

Clerk of Circuit Court, Criminal
Records
225 S. 4th Street, Room 105
Wytheville, VA 24382
(703) 223-6050
Felony and misdemeanor records are available by mail or phone. No release necessary. No search fee. Search information required: name, SSN, date of birth.

Civil records are available by mail. A release is required. No search fee. $.50 fee per copy. Search information required: name, date of birth, years to search. Specify plaintiff or defendant.

York County

Clerk of Circuit Court, Criminal
Records
PO Box 371
Yorktown, VA 23690
(804) 890-3350
Felony and misdemeanor records are available by mail. A release is required. No search fee. $1.00 fee for first copy, $.50 each additional copy. Check or money order payable to Virginia State Police. Search information required: name, SSN, date of birth, years to search. Contact Criminal Records Exchange of the Virginia State Police, PO Box 27472, Richmond VA, 23261-7472.

Civil records are available by mail. No release inecessary. No search fee. $1.00 fee for first copy, $.50 each additional copy. Search information required: name, date of birth, years to search. Specify plaintiff or defendant.

City-County Cross Reference

Abingdon *Washington*
Accomac *Accomack*
Achilles *Gloucester*
Adwolf *Smyth*
Afton *Nelson*
Alberta *Brunswick*
Aldie *Loudoun*
Alexandria *Independent City*
Alfonso *Lancaster*
Allison Gap *Smyth*
Altavista *Campbell*
Alton *Halifax*
Amelia Court House *Amelia*
Amherst *Amherst*
Amissville *Rappahannock*
Amonate *Tazewell*
Andover *Wise*
Annalee Heights *Fairfax*
Annandale *Fairfax*
Appalachia *Wise*
Appomattox *Appomattox*
Ararat *Patrick*
Arcola *Loudoun*
Ark *Gloucester*
Arlington *Arlington*
Aroda *Madison*
Arrington *Nelson*
Arvonia *Buckingham*
Ashburn *Loudoun*
Ashland *Hanover*
Assawoman *Accomack*
Atkins *Smyth*
Atlantic *Accomack*
Augusta Springs *Augusta*
Austinville *Wythe*
Axton *Henry*
Aylett *King William*
Bacova *Bath*
Baileys Crossroads *Fairfax*
Banco *Madison*
Bandy *Tazewell*
Banner *Russell*
Barboursville *Orange*
Barhamsville *New Kent*
Barren Springs *Wythe*
Baskerville *Mecklenburg*
Bassett *Henry*
Bastian *Bland*
Basye *Shenandoah*
Batesville *Albemarle*
Battery Park *Isle Of Wight*
Bavon *Mathews*

Bealeton *Fauquier*
Beaverdam *Hanover*
Beaverlett *Mathews*
Bedford *Independent City*
Bee *Dickenson*
Bel Aire *Fairfax*
Bellamy *Gloucester*
Belle Haven *Accomack*
Belle View *Fairfax*
Belspring *Pulaski*
Belvedere *Fairfax*
Bena *Gloucester*
Ben Hur *Lee*
Bensley *Chesterfield*
Bent Mountain *Roanoke*
Bentonville *Warren*
Bergton *Rockingham*
Berryville *Clarke*
Big Island *Bedford*
Big Rock *Buchanan*
Big Stone Gap *Wise*
Birchleaf *Dickenson*
Birdsnest *Northampton*
Bishop *Tazewell*
Blackridge *Mecklenburg*
Blacksburg *Montgomery*
Blackstone *Nottoway*
Blackwater *Lee*
Blairs *Pittsylvania*
Blakes *Mathews*
Bland *Bland*
Bloxom *Accomack*
Bluefield *Tazewell*
Blue Grass *Highland*
Bluemont *Loudoun*
Blue Ridge *Botetourt*
Bohannon *Mathews*
Boissevain *Tazewell*
Bon Aire *Chesterfield*
Boones Mill *Franklin*
Boston *Culpeper*
Bowling Green *Caroline*
Boyce *Clarke*
Boydton *Mecklenburg*
Boykins *Southampton*
Bracey *Mecklenburg*
Branchville *Southampton*
Brandy Station *Culpeper*
Breaks *Dickenson*
Bremo Bluff *Fluvanna*
Bridgewater *Rockingham*
Brightwood *Madison*
Bristol *Independent City*
Bristow *Prince William*

Broadford *Smyth*
Broad Run *Prince William*
Broad Run Farms *Loudon*
Broadway *Rockingham*
Brodnax *Brunswick*
Brooke *Stafford*
Brookneal *Campbell*
Brownsburg *Rockbridge*
Broyhill Park *Fairfax*
Brucetown *Frederick*
Bruington *King And Queen*
Buchanan *Botetourt*
Buckingham *Buckingham*
Bucknell Manor *Fairfax*
Buena Vista *Independent City*
Buffalo Junction *Mecklenburg*
Bumpass *Louisa*
Burgess *Northumberland*
Burke *Fairfax*
Burkeville *Nottoway*
Burnsville *Bath*
Burr Hill *Orange*
Butylo *Middlesex*
Callands *Pittsylvania*
Callao *Northumberland*
Callaway *Franklin*
Calverton *Fauquier*
Cana *Carroll*
Cape Charles *Northampton*
Capeville *Northampton*
Capron *Southampton*
Cardinal *Mathews*
Caret *Essex*
Carrollton *Isle Of Wight*
Carrsbrook *Albemarle*
Carrsville *Isle Of Wight*
Carson *Dinwiddie*
Cartersville *Cumberland*
Carver Gardens *York*
Casanova *Fauquier*
Cascade *Pittsylvania*
Castleton *Rappahannock*
Castlewood *Russell*
Catawba *Roanoke*
Catharpin *Prince William*
Catlett *Fauquier*
Cave Springs *Roanoke*
Cauthornville *King And Queen*
Cedar Bluff *Tazewell*
Center Cross *Essex*
Centreville *Fairfax*

Ceres *Bland*
Champlain *Essex*
Chance *Essex*
Charles City *Charles City*
Charlotte Court House *Charlotte*
Charlottesville *Independent City*
Chase City *Mecklenburg*
Chatham *Pittsylvania*
Check *Floyd*
Cheriton *Northampton*
Chesapeake *Independent City*
Chester *Chesterfield*
Chesterbrook *Fairfax*
Chesterfield *Chesterfield*
Chester Gap *Rappahannock*
Chilhowie *Smyth*
Chincoteague *Accomack*
Christiansburg *Montgomery*
Church Road *Dinwiddie*
Church View *Middlesex*
Churchville *Augusta*
Claremont *Surry*
Clarksville *Mecklenburg*
Claudville *Patrick*
Claypod Hill *Tazewell*
Clear Brook *Frederick*
Cleveland *Russell*
Clifford *Amherst*
Clifton *Fairfax*
Clifton Forge *Independent City*
Clinchco *Dickenson*
Clintwood *Dickenson*
Clover *Halifax*
Cloverdale *Botetourt*
Cluster Springs *Halifax*
Cobbs Creek *Mathews*
Coeburn *Wise*
Coleman Falls *Bedford*
Coles Point *Westmoreland*
Collinsville *Henry*
Colonial Beach *Westmoreland*
Colonial Heights *Independent City*
Columbia *Fluvanna*
Conaway *Buchanan*
Concord *Campbell*
Copper Hill *Floyd*

Corbin *Caroline*
Courtland *Southampton*
Covesville *Albemarle*
Covington *Independent City*
Craddockville *Accomack*
Craigsville *Augusta*
Crewe *Nottoway*
Criders *Rockingham*
Crimora *Augusta*
Cripple Creek *Wythe*
Critz *Patrick*
Crockett *Wythe*
Cross Junction *Frederick*
Crozet *Albemarle*
Crozier *Goochland*
Crystal Hill *Halifax*
Cullen *Charlotte*
Culmore *Fairfax*
Culpeper *Culpeper*
Cumberland *Cumberland*
Dabneys *Louisa*
Dahlgren *King George*
Dale City *Prince William*
Daleville *Botetourt*
Damascus *Washington*
Dante *Russell*
Danville *Independent City*
Darlington Heights *Prince Edward*
Davenport *Buchanan*
Davis Wharf *Accomack*
Dayton *Rockingham*
Deerfield *Augusta*
Delaplane *Fauquier*
Deltaville *Middlesex*
Dendron *Surry*
Dewitt *Dinwiddie*
Diggs *Mathews*
Dillwyn *Buckingham*
Dinwiddie *Dinwiddie*
Disputanta *Prince George*
Doe Hill *Highland*
Dogue *King George*
Dolphin *Brunswick*
Dooms *Albemarle*
Doran *Tazewell*
Doswell *Hanover*
Drakes Branch *Charlotte*
Draper *Pulaski*
Drewryville *Southampton*
Dryden *Lee*
Dry Fork *Pittsylvania*
Dublin *Pulaski*
Duffield *Scott*
Dugspur *Carroll*
Dumfries *Prince William*
Dundas *Lunenburg*
Dungannon *Scott*
Dunn Loring *Fairfax*
Dunnsville *Essex*
Dutton *Gloucester*
Dyke *Greene*
Eagle Rock *Botetourt*
Earlysville *Albemarle*
East Stone Gap *Wise*
Eastville *Northampton*
Ebony *Brunswick*
Edinburg *Shenandoah*
Edwardsville *Northumberland*
Eggleston *Giles*
Elberon *Surry*
Elk Creek *Grayson*
Elkton *Rockingham*

Elkwood *Culpeper*
Elliston *Montgomery*
Emory *Washington*
Emporia *Independent City*
Engleside *Fairfax*
Esmont *Albemarle*
Evergreen *Appomattox*
Evington *Campbell*
Ewing *Lee*
Exeter *Wise*
Exmore *Northampton*
Faber *Nelson*
Fairfax *Independent City*
Fairfield *Rockbridge*
Fairlawn *Pulaski*
Falls Church *Independent City*
Falls Mills *Tazewell*
Falmouth *Stafford*
Fancy Gap *Carroll*
Farmville *Prince Edward*
Farnham *Richmond*
Ferrum *Franklin*
Ferry Farms *Stafford*
Fieldale *Henry*
Fife *Goochland*
Fincastle *Botetourt*
Fishers Hill *Shenandoah*
Fishersville *Augusta*
Five Mile Fork *Spotsylvania*
Flint Hill *Rappahannock*
Floyd *Floyd*
Foneswood *Richmond*
Ford *Dinwiddie*
Forest *Bedford*
Forksville *Mecklenburg*
Fork Union *Fluvanna*
Fort Belvoir *Fairfax*
Fort Blackmore *Scott*
Fort Defiance *Augusta*
Fort Mitchell *Lunenburg*
Foster *Mathews*
Fosters Falls *Wythe*
Franklin *Independent City*
Franktown *Northampton*
Fredericksburg *Independent City*
Freeman *Brunswick*
Free Union *Albemarle*
Fries *Grayson*
Front Royal *Warren*
Fulks Run *Rockingham*
Gainesville *Prince William*
Galax *Independent City*
Garrisonville *Stafford*
Gasburg *Brunswick*
Gate City *Scott*
Gladehill *Franklin*
Glade Spring *Washington*
Gladstone *Nelson*
Gladys *Campbell*
Glasgow *Rockbridge*
Glen Allen *Henrico*
Glen Lyn *Giles*
Glen Wilton *Botetourt*
Gloucester *Gloucester*
Gloucester Point *Gloucester*
Goldbond *Giles*
Goldvein *Fauquier*
Goochland *Goochland*
Goode *Bedford*
Goodview *Bedford*
Gordonsville *Orange*

Gore *Frederick*
Goshen *Rockbridge*
Graves Mill *Madison*
Great Falls *Fairfax*
Greenbackville *Accomack*
Green Bay *Prince Edward*
Greenbush *Accomack*
Greenville *Augusta*
Greenwood *Albemarle*
Gretna *Pittsylvania*
Grimstead *Mathews*
Grindall Creek *Chesterfield*
Grottoes *Rockingham*
Grove *James City*
Groveton *Fairfax*
Groveton Gardens *Fairfax*
Grundy *Buchanan*
Gum Spring *Louisa*
Gwynn *Mathews*
Hacksneck *Accomack*
Hadensville *Goochland*
Hague *Westmoreland*
Halifax *Halifax*
Hallieford *Mathews*
Hallwood *Accomack*
Hamilton *Loudoun*
Hampden Sydney *Prince Edward*
Hampton *Independent City*
Handsom *Southampton*
Hanover *Hanover*
Harborton *Accomack*
Hardy *Bedford*
Hardyville *Middlesex*
Harman *Buchanan*
Harrisonburg *Independent City*
Hartfield *Middlesex*
Hartwood *Stafford*
Hayes *Gloucester*
Hayfield *Fairfax*
Haymarket *Prince William*
Haynesville *Richmond*
Haysi *Dickenson*
Head Waters *Highland*
Heathsville *Northumberland*
Henry *Franklin*
Herndon *Fairfax*
Hightown *Highland*
Hillsville *Carroll*
Hillwood *Fairfax*
Hiltons *Scott*
Hinton *Rockingham*
Hiwassee *Pulaski*
Hollin Hall Village *Fairfax*
Hollins *Roanoke*
Holmes Run Acres *Fairfax*
Honaker *Russell*
Hood *Madison*
Hopewell *Independent City*
Horntown *Accomack*
Horse Pasture *Henry*
Horsepen *Tazewell*
Hot Springs *Bath*
Howertons *Essex*
Huddleston *Bedford*
Hudgins *Mathews*
Hume *Fauquier*
Hunterdale *Southampton*
Huntington *Fairfax*
Huntly *Rappahannock*
Hurley *Buchanan*

Hurt *Pittsylvania*
Hustle *Essex*
Hyacinth *Northumberland*
Hybla Valley *Fairfax*
Independence *Grayson*
Indian Springs *Fairfax*
Indian Valley *Floyd*
Ingram *Halifax*
Iron Gate *Alleghany*
Irvington *Lancaster*
Isle of Wight *Isle Of Wight*
Ivanhoe *Wythe*
Ivor *Southampton*
Ivy *Albemarle*
Jamaica *Middlesex*
James Store *Gloucester*
Jamesville *Northampton*
Jarratt *Sussex*
Java *Pittsylvania*
Jeffersonton *Culpeper*
Jefferson Village *Fairfax*
Jenkins Bridge *Accomack*
Jersey *King George*
Jetersville *Amelia*
Jewell Ridge *Tazewell*
Jewell Valley *Buchanan*
Jonesville *Lee*
Jordan Mines *Alleghany*
Keeling *Pittsylvania*
Keene *Albemarle*
Keen Mountain *Buchanan*
Keezletown *Rockingham*
Keller *Accomack*
Kenbridge *Lunenburg*
Kents Store *Fluvanna*
Keokee *Lee*
Keswick *Albemarle*
Keysville *Charlotte*
Kilmarnock *Lancaster*
King And Queen Court House *King And Queen*
King George *King George*
King William *King William*
Kings Park *Fairfax*
Kinsale *Westmoreland*
Lacey Spring *Rockingham*
Lackey *York*
LaCrosse *Mecklenburg*
Ladd *Augusta*
Ladysmith *Caroline*
Lafayette *Montgomery*
Lahore *Orange*
Lambsburg *Carroll*
Lancaster *Lancaster*
Laneview *Essex*
Lanexa *New Kent*
Langley *Fairfax*
Laurel *Henrico*
Laurel Fork *Carroll*
Lawrenceville *Brunswick*
Lebanon *Russell*
Lebanon Church *Shenandoah*
Lee Mont *Accomack*
Leesburg *Loudoun*
Leon *Madison*
Lewisetta *Northumberland*
Lexington *Independent City*
Lightfoot *James City*
Lignum *Culpeper*
Lincolnia Heights *Fairfax*
Linden *Warren*
Linville *Rockingham*
Lively *Lancaster*

Locust Dale *Madison*
Locust Grove *Orange*
Locust Hill *Middlesex*
Locustville *Accomack*
Long Island *Campbell*
Loretto *Essex*
Lorton *Fairfax*
Lottsburg *Northumberland*
Louisa *Louisa*
Lovettsville *Loudoun*
Lovingston *Nelson*
Lowesville *Amherst*
Lowmoor *Alleghany*
Lowry *Bedford*
Lunenburg *Lunenburg*
Luray *Page*
Lynchburg *Independent City*
Lynch Station *Campbell*
Lyndhurst *Augusta*
McClure *Dickenson*
McCoy *Montgomery*
McDowell *Highland*
McGaheysville *Rockingham*
McKenney *Dinwiddie*
McLean *Fairfax*
Machipongo *Northampton*
Macon *Powhatan*
Madison *Madison*
Madison Heights *Amherst*
Madison Mills *Madison*
Maidens *Goochland*
Manakin Sabot *Goochland*
Manassas *Independent City*
Mangohick *King William*
Mannboro *Amelia*
Manquin *King William*
Mappsville *Accomack*
Marion *Smyth*
Marionville *Northampton*
Markham *Fauquier*
Marshall *Fauquier*
Martinsville *Independent City*
Maryus *Gloucester*
Mascot *King And Queen*
Massies Mill *Nelson*
Mathews *Mathews*
Mattaponi *King And Queen*
Maurertown *Shenandoah*
Mavisdale *Buchanan*
Maxie *Buchanan*
Max Meadows *Wythe*
Meadows of Dan *Patrick*
Meadowview *Washington*
Mears *Accomack*
Mechanicsville *Hanover*
Meherrin *Prince Edward*
Melfa *Accomack*
Mendota *Washington*
Meredithville *Brunswick*
Merrifield *Fairfax*
Merry Point *Lancaster*
Middlebrook *Augusta*
Middleburg *Loudoun*
Middletown *Frederick*
Midland *Fauquier*
Midlothian *Chesterfield*
Miles *Mathews*
Milford *Caroline*
Millboro *Bath*
Millers Tavern *Essex*
Millwood *Clarke*
Mineral *Louisa*

Mint Spring *Augusta*
Mitchells *Culpeper*
Mobjack *Mathews*
Modest Town *Accomack*
Mollusk *Lancaster*
Moneta *Bedford*
Monroe *Amherst*
Montebello *Nelson*
Monterey *Highland*
Montpelier *Hanover*
Montpelier Station *Orange*
Montross *Westmoreland*
Montvale *Bedford*
Moon *Mathews*
Morattico *Lancaster*
Moseley *Powhatan*
Mount Crawford *Rockingham*
Mount Holly *Westmoreland*
Mount Jackson *Shenandoah*
Mount Sidney *Augusta*
Mount Solon *Augusta*
Mount Vernon *Fairfax*
Mouth *of Wilson *Grayson*
Mustoe *Highland*
Narrows *Giles*
Naruna *Campbell*
Nassawadox *Northampton*
Nathalie *Halifax*
Natural Bridge *Rockbridge*
Natural Bridge Station *Rockbridge*
Naxera *Gloucester*
Nellysford *Nelson*
Nelson *Mecklenburg*
Nelsonia *Accomack*
Newbern *Pulaski*
New Alexandria *Fairfax*
New Canton *Buckingham*
New Castle *Craig*
New Church *Accomack*
New Hope *Augusta*
Newington *Fairfax*
New Kent *New Kent*
New Market *Shenandoah*
New Point *Mathews*
Newport *Giles*
Newport News *Independent City*
New River *Pulaski*
Newsoms *Southampton*
Newtown *King And Queen*
Nickelsville *Scott*
Ninde *King George*
Nokesville *Prince William*
Nomini Grove *Westmoreland*
Nora *Dickenson*
Norfolk *Independent City*
Norge *James City*
North *Mathews*
North Garden *Albemarle*
North Springfield *Fairfax*
North Tazewell *Tazewell*
Norton *Independent City*
Norwood *Nelson*
Nottoway *Nottoway*
Nuttsville *Lancaster*
Oak Hall *Accomack*
Oakpark *Madison*
Oakwood *Buchanan*
Occoquan *Prince William*
Oilville *Goochland*
Oldhams *Westmoreland*

Onancock *Accomack*
Onemo *Mathews*
Onley *Accomack*
Ophelia *Northumberland*
Orange *Orange*
Ordinary *Gloucester*
Oriskany *Botetourt*
Orkney Springs *Shenandoah*
Orlean *Fauquier*
Oyster *Northampton*
Paeonian Springs *Loudoun*
Paint Bank *Craig*
Painter *Accomack*
Palmyra *Fluvanna*
Pamplin *Appomattox*
Paris *Fauquier*
Parklawn *Fairfax*
Parksley *Accomack*
Parrott *Pulaski*
Partlow *Spotsylvania*
Patrick Springs *Patrick*
Patterson *Buchanan*
Pearisburg *Giles*
Pembroke *Giles*
Penhook *Franklin*
Pennington Gap *Lee*
Penn Laird *Rockingham*
Petersburg *Independent City*
Phenix *Charlotte*
Philomont *Loudoun*
Pilgrims Knob *Buchanan*
Pilot *Montgomery*
Pimmit Hills *Fairfax*
Pinero *Gloucester*
Piney River *Nelson*
Pittsville *Pittsylvania*
Plain View *King And Queen*
Plasterco *Washington*
Pleasant Valley *Rockingham*
Pocahontas *Tazewell*
Port Haywood *Mathews*
Port Republic *Rockingham*
Port Royal *Caroline*
Portsmouth *Independent City*
Pound *Wise*
Pounding Mill *Tazewell*
Powhatan *Powhatan*
Pratts *Madison*
Prince George *Prince George*
Prospect *Prince Edward*
Providence Forge *New Kent*
Pulaski *Pulaski*
Pungoteague *Accomack*
Purcellville *Loudoun*
Quantico *Prince William*
Queens Lake *York*
Quicksburg *Shenandoah*
Quinby *Accomack*
Quinque *Greene*
Quinton *New Kent*
Radford *Independent City*
Radiant *Madison*
Randolph *Charlotte*
Raphine *Rockbridge*
Rapidan *Culpeper*
Rappahannock Academy *Caroline*
Raven *Tazewell*

Ravensworth *Fairfax*
Ravenwood *Fairfax*
Rawlings *Brunswick*
Rectortown *Fauquier*
Redart *Mathews*
Red Ash *Tazewell*
Red House *Charlotte*
Red Oak *Charlotte*
Redwood *Franklin*
Reedville *Northumberland*
Regina *Lancaster*
Remington *Fauquier*
Republican Grove *Halifax*
Rescue *Isle Of Wight*
Reston *Fairfax*
Reva *Culpeper*
Rhoadesville *Orange*
Rice *Prince Edward*
Richardsville *Culpeper*
Rich Creek *Giles*
Richlands *Tazewell*
Richmond *Independent City*
Ridgeway *Henry*
Rileyville *Page*
Riner *Montgomery*
Ringgold *Pittsylvania*
Ripplemead *Giles*
Riverdale *Halifax*
Riverton *Warren*
Rixeyville *Culpeper*
Roanoke *Independent City*
Rochelle *Madison*
Rockbridge Baths *Rockbridge*
Rockville *Hanover*
Rocky Gap *Bland*
Rocky Mount *Franklin*
Rollins Fork *King George*
Rosedale *Russell*
Rose Hill *Lee*
Roseland *Nelson*
Round Hill *Loudoun*
Rowe *Buchanan*
Ruby *Stafford*
Ruckersville *Greene*
Rural Retreat *Wythe*
Rustburg *Campbell*
Ruther Glen *Caroline*
Ruthville *Charles City*
Saint Charles *Lee*
Saint Davids Church *Shenandoah*
Saint Paul *Wise*
Saint Stephens Church *King And Queen*
Salem *Independent City*
Saltville *Smyth*
Saluda *Middlesex*
Sandston *Henrico*
Sandy Hook *Goochland*
Sandy Level *Pittsylvania*
Sanford *Accomack*
Saxe *Charlotte*
Saxis *Accomack*
Schley *Gloucester*
Schuyler *Nelson*
Scottsburg *Halifax*
Scottsville *Albemarle*
Seaford *York*
Sealston *King George*
Seaview *Northampton*
Sedley *Southampton*
Selma *Alleghany*

Seven Fountains *Shenandoah*
Seven Mile Ford *Smyth*
Severn *Gloucester*
Shacklefords *King And Queen*
Shadow *Mathews*
Sharps *Richmond*
Shawsville *Montgomery*
Shenandoah *Page*
Shiloh *King George*
Shipman *Nelson*
Singers Glen *Rockingham*
Skippers *Greensville*
Skipwith *Mecklenburg*
Sleepy Hollow *Fairfax*
Smithfield *Isle Of Wight*
Somerset *Orange*
Somerville *Fauquier*
South Boston *Independent City*
South Hill *Mecklenburg*
Sparta *Caroline*
Speedwell *Wythe*
Spencer *Henry*
Sperryville *Rappahannock*
Spotsylvania *Spotsylvania*
Spottswood *Augusta*
Spout Spring *Appomattox*
Springfield *Fairfax*
Spring Grove *Surry*
Stafford *Stafford*
Staffordsville *Giles*
Stanardsville *Greene*
Stanley *Page*
Stanleytown *Henry*
Star Tannery *Frederick*
State Farm *Goochland*
Staunton *Independent City*
Steeles Tavern *Augusta*
Stephens *Wise*
Stephens City *Frederick*
Stephenson *Frederick*
Sterling *Loudoun*
Stevensburg *Culpeper*
Stevensville *King And Queen*
Stonega *Wise*
Stony Creek *Sussex*
Strasburg *Shenandoah*
Stuart *Patrick*
Stuarts Draft *Augusta*
Studley *Hanover*
Suffolk *Independent City*
Sugar Grove *Smyth*
Sugar Loaf *Roanoke*
Sumerduck *Fauquier*
Supply *Essex*
Surry *Surry*
Susan *Mathews*
Sussex *Sussex*
Sutherland *Dinwiddie*
Sutherlin *Pittsylvania*
Sweet Briar *Amherst*
Swoope *Augusta*
Swords Creek *Russell*
Syria *Madison*
Syringa *Middlesex*
Tabb *York*
Tangier *Accomack*
Tannersville *Tazewell*
Tappahannock *Essex*
Tasley *Accomack*
Tazewell *Tazewell*
Temperanceville *Accomack*

Thaxton *Bedford*
The Plains *Fauquier*
Thornburg *Spotsylvania*
Timberlake *Campbell*
Timberville *Rockingham*
Tiptop *Tazewell*
Toano *James City*
Toms Brook *Shenandoah*
Tookland *Buchanan*
Topping *Middlesex*
Townsend *Northampton*
Trammel *Dickenson*
Triangle *Prince William*
Trout Dale *Grayson*
Troutville *Botetourt*
Troy *Fluvanna*
Turbeville *Halifax*
Tyler Park *Fairfax*
Union Hall *Franklin*
Union Level *Mecklenburg*
Unionville *Orange*
Upperville *Fauquier*
Urbanna *Middlesex*
Valentines *Brunswick*
Vansant *Buchanan*
Varina *Chesterfield*
Vernon Hill *Halifax*
Verona *Augusta*
Vesta *Patrick*
Vesuvius *Rockbridge*
Victoria *Lunenburg*
Vienna *Fairfax*
Viewtown *Rappahannock*
Village *Richmond*
Villamont *Bedford*
Vinton *Roanoke*
Virgilina *Halifax*
Virginia Beach *Independent City*
Virginia Hills *Fairfax*
Volney *Grayson*
Wachapreague *Accomack*
Wake *Middlesex*
Wakefield *Sussex*
Walkerton *King And Queen*
Wardtown *Northampton*
Ware Neck *Gloucester*
Warfield *Brunswick*
Warm Springs *Bath*
Warner *Middlesex*
Warrenton *Fauquier*
Warsaw *Richmond*
Washington *Rappahannock*
Waterford *Loudoun*
Water View *Middlesex*
Wattsville *Accomack*
Waverly *Sussex*
Waynesboro *Independent City*
Waynewood *Fairfax*
Weber City *Scott*
Weems *Lancaster*
Weirwood *Northampton*
Wellington *Fairfax*
West Augusta *Augusta*
Westmoreland *Westmoreland*
West Point *King William*
West Springfield *Fairfax*
Weyanoke *Fairfax*
Weyers Cave *Augusta*
Whitacre *Frederick*
White Hall *Albemarle*
White Marsh *Gloucester*
White Plains *Brunswick*

White Post *Clarke*
White Stone *Lancaster*
Whitetop *Grayson*
Whitewood *Buchanan*
Wicomico *Gloucester*
Wicomico Church *Northumberland*
Williamsburg *Independent City*
Williamsville *Bath*
Willis *Floyd*
Willis Wharf *Northampton*
Wilsons *Dinwiddie*
Wilton Woods *Fairfax*
Winchester *Independent City*
Windsor *Isle Of Wight*
Wingina *Nelson*
Wirtz *Franklin*
Wise *Wise*
Withams *Accomack*
Wolford *Buchanan*
Wolftown *Madison*
Woodbridge *Prince William*
Woodford *Caroline*
Woodlawn *Carroll*
Woods Cross Roads *Gloucester*
Woodstock *Shenandoah*
Woolwine *Patrick*
Wylliesburg *Charlotte*
Wytheville *Wythe*
Yale *Sussex*
Yards *Tazewell*
York Terrace *York*
Yorktown *York*
Zacata *Westmoreland*
Zanoni *Gloucester*
Zuni *Isle Of Wight*

Washington

All thirty nine (39) of Washington's counties reported that they release conviction data for employment screening purposes by phone and/or mail. Sixteen (16) counties reported that requests may be made by fax. Superior Court holds civil records for $25,000 and more.

For more information or for offices not listed, contact the state's information hot line at (206) 753-5000.

Driving Records

Department of Licensing
Driving Records
Olympia, WA 98504
(206) 753-6960
Driving records are available by mail. $4.50 fee per request. Turnaround time is 7 to 10 days. Written request must include job applicant's full name, date of birth, license number and reason for request (i.e. employment, insurance, etc.). Make check payable to Department of Licensing.

Worker's Compensation Records

Department of Labor and Industry
General Administration Building
PO Box 44001
Olympia, WA 98504
(206) 753-6341
Signed authorization of job applicant required to process a request. Authorization must include applicant's SSN, date of birth, complete name and, if available, the claim number. There is no fee.

Vital Statistics

Department of Health
Center for Health Statistics
PO Box 9709
Olympia, WA 98507-9709
(206) 753-5936
Birth and death records are available for $11.00 each. State Office has records since July 1907. For King, Pierce, and Spokane counties copies may also be obtained from county health departments. County Auditor in county of birth has registered births prior to July 1907. An employer can obtain records with a written release. Search information required: name of child, date of birth, place of birth, father's name, mother's full maiden name. Make certified check or money order payable to Department of Health.

Marriage records are available from 1968. Records prior to 1968 available at county level. $11.00 fee. Check or money order. Include name, marriage date, spouse's name, city or county where married. Turnaround time is 3 weeks. Divorce records are available at county level, County Clerk's office where divorce filed.

Department of Education

S.P.I.
Old Capitol Building
Teacher Certification
Olympia, WA 98504-3211
(206) 753-6773
Field of certification is available by phone or mail. Include name.

Medical Licensing

Board of Medical Examiners
PO Box 1099
Olympia, WA 98507
(206) 753-2205
Will confirm licenses for MDs by phone or mail. No fee. For licenses not mentioned, contact the above office.

Washington State Board of Nursing
PO Box 47864
Olympia, WA 98504-7864
(206) 753-2206
Will confirm NA and RN license by phone. No fee. Include full name, license number, DOB or reference number.

Bar Association

Washington State Bar Association
500 Westin Building
2001 6th Avenue
Seattle, WA 98121-2599
Will confirm licenses by phone. No fee. Include name.

Accountancy Board

CPA Registration Association
PO Box 9131
Olympia, WA 98507-9131
(206) 753-2585
Will confirm license by phone. No fee. Include name.

Securities Commission

Department of Licensing
Securities Division
405 Blacklake Blvd. SW, 2nd Floor
Plympia, WA 98502
(206) 753-6928
Will confirm license by phone. No fee. Include name and SSN.

Secretary of State

Secretary of State
Corporation Division
2nd Fl. Republic Building
PO Box 40234
Olympia, WA 98504-0234
(206) 753-7115
Service agent and address and date incorporated are available by phone or mail. Contact the above office for additional information.

Criminal Records

State Repository

Washington State Patrol
PO Box 42633
Olympia, WA 98504-2633
(206) 753-7272
Fax (206) 753-0444
Criminal conviction information through the State's central repository is available on employees or prospective employees who hold a position of trust. All requests must include the subject's full name, date of birth, physical description and fingerprints. The fingerprints should be taken on a standard "Applicant" fingerprint card supplied by the state. To obtain the cards and special instructions regarding the release that must be included on each card, contact the state at the above address. There is a $10.00 fee for each request. Make cashier's check, company check, or money order payable to Washington State Patrol.

Adams County

Adams County Clerk, Felony check
PO Box 187
Ritzville, WA 99169
(509) 659-0090 Extension 230
Fax (509) 659-0118
Felony records are available by mail, phone or fax. No release necessary. $8.00 search fee per hour. $.50 fee per copy. $2.00 for first certification, $1.00 each additional page. $1.50 fee per page for fax response. Company or personal checks made payable to Adams County Clerk. Search information required: name.

Civil records are available by mail. No release necessary. $8.00 search fee per hour. $.50 fee per copy. $2.00 for first certification, $1.00 each additional page. $1.50 fee per page for fax response. Search information required: name, date of birth, years to search. Specify plaintiff or defendant.

Asotin County

Felony records
Clerk of Superior Court, Felony check
PO Box 159
Asotin, WA 99402
(509) 243-2081
Fax (509) 243-4978
Felony records are available by mail, phone or fax. No release necessary. No search fee. $2.00 fee for first copy, $1.00 each additional page includes certification. Search information required: name, years to search, SASE.

Civil records
Clerk of Superior Court
PO Box 159
Asotin, WA 99402
(509) 243-2081
Fax (509) 243-4978
Civil records are available by mail, phone or fax. No release necessary. No search fee. $2.00 fee for first copy, $1.00 each additional page includes certification. Search information required: name, date of birth, years to search, SASE. Specify plaintiff or defendant.

Misdemeanor records
District Court
PO Box 429
Asotin, WA 99402
(509) 243-4127
Misdemeanor records are available by mail. No release necessary. $5.00 search fee. $6.00 for certification. Make check payable to Asotin District Court. Search information required: name, date of birth, date of conviction, SASE.

Civil records
District Court
PO Box 429
Asotin, WA 99402
(509) 243-4127
Civil records are available by mail. No release necessary. $5.00 search fee. $6.00 for certification. Search information required: name, date of birth, years to search, SASE. Specify plaintiff or defendant.

Benton County

Felony records
Benton County Clerk, Criminal Department
7320 W. Quinault
Kennewick, WA 99336
(509) 735-8388
Felony records are available by mail. No release necessary. 2.00 search fee. $.25 fee per copy. $2.00 for first certification, $1.00 each additional page. Make check payable to Benton County Clerk. Search information required: name, date of birth, years to search, SASE.

Civil records
Benton County Clerk
7320 W. Quinault
Kennewick, WA 99336
(509) 735-8388
Civil records are available by mail. No release necessary. $2.00 search fee. $.25 fee per copy. $2.00 for first certification, $1.00 each additional page. Search information required: name, date of birth, years to search, SASE. Specify plaintiff or defendant.

Misdemeanor records
Benton District Court
7320 W. Quinualt
Kennewick, WA 99336
(509) 735-8476
Misdemeanor records are available by mail. No release necessary. $5.00 search fee. $.25 fee per copy. $5.00 for certification. Make check payable to District Court. Search information required: name, date of birth.

Civil records
Benton District Court
7320 W. Quinualt
Kennewick, WA 99336
(509) 735-8476
Civil records are available by mail. No release necessary. $5.00 search fee. $.25 fee per copy. $5.00 for certification. Search information required: name, date of birth, years to search. Specify plaintiff or defendant.

Chelan County

Felony records
County Clerk of the Superior Court, Felony Check
Box 3025
Wenatchee, WA 98807
(509) 664-5380
Felony records are available by mail or phone. No release necessary. No search fee. $2.00 fee for first copy, $1.00 each additional page includes certification. Search information required: name, years to search, SASE.

Civil records
County Clerk of the Superior Court
Box 3025
Wenatchee, WA 98807
(509) 664-5380
Civil records are available by mail. No release necessary. No search fee. $2.00 fee for first copy, $1.00 each additional page includes certification. Search information required: name, date of birth, years to search. Specify plaintiff or defendant.

Misdemeanor records
District Court
PO Box 2182
Wenatchee, WA 98807
(509) 664-5393
Misdemeanor records are available by mail. No release necessary. $15.00 search fee. $2.00 fee for first copy, $1.00 each additional copy. $5.00 for certification. Search information required: name, date of birth, alias, SASE.

Civil records
District Court
PO Box 2182
Wenatchee, WA 98807
(509) 664-5393
Civil records are available by mail. No release necessary. $15.00 search fee. $2.00 fee for first copy, $1.00 each additional copy. $5.00 for certification. Search information required: name, date of birth, years to search. Specify plaintiff or defendant.

Clallam County

County Clerk, Felony Check
223 E. 4th Street
Port Angeles, WA 98362
(206) 452-7831 Ext. 333
Felony and misdemeanor records are available by mail. No release necessary. $8.00 search fee plus $8.00 fee per hour searched. Search information required: name, date of birth.

Civil records are available in person only. See Washington state repository for more information.

Clark County

Felony records
County Clerk, Felony Check
PO Box 5000
Vancouver, WA 98668
(206) 699-2295
Felony records are available by mail. No release necessary. 8.00 search fee per hour. $2.00 fee for first copy, $1.00 each additional copy includes certification. Search information required: name, date of birth, SASE.

Civil records
County Clerk
PO Box 5000
Vancouver, WA 98668
(206) 699-2295
Civil records are available by mail. No release necessary. 8.00 search fee per hour. $2.00 fee for first copy, $1.00 each additional copy includes certification. Search information required: name, date of birth, years to search SASE. Specify plaintiff or defendant.

Misdemeanor records
District Court
PO Box 5000
Vancouver, WA 98668
(206) 699-2424
Misdemeanor records are available by mail, or phone. A release is required. $10.00 search fee. $2.00 fee per copy includes certification. Search information required: name, date of birth, last known address, drivers license number, if known, SASE.

Civil records
District Court
PO Box 5000
Vancouver, WA 98668
(206) 699-2424
Civil records are available by mail. A release is required. $10.00 search fee. $2.00 fee per copy includes certification. Search information required: name, date of birth, years to search, SASE. Specify plaintiff or defendant.

Columbia County

County Clerk of Superior Court
341 E. Main Street
Dayton, WA 99328
(509) 382-4321
Fax (509) 382-4830
Felony and misdemeanor records are available by mail or fax. $8.00 search fee per hour. $1.00 fee per copy. $2.00 for certification. Company checks only, payable to Columbia County Clerk. Search information required: name, SASE, years to search.

Civil records are available by mail or fax. No release necessary. $8.00 search fee per hour. $1.00 fee per copy. $2.00 for certification. Search information required: name, date of birth, years to search. Specify plaintiff or defendant.

Cowlitz County

Felony records
Cowlitz County Clerk, Felony Check
Hall of Justice
312 S.W. First
Kelso, WA 98626
(206) 577-3016
Felony records are available by mail. No release necessary. $4.00 search fee. $1.00 fee per copy. $1.00 for certification. Certified check only, payable to Cowlitz County Clerk. Search information required: name, date of birth, years to search.

Civil records
Cowlitz County Clerk
Hall of Justice
312 S.W. First
Kelso, WA 98626
(206) 577-3016
Civil records are available by mail. No release necessary. $4.00 search fee. $1.00 fee per copy. $1.00 for certification. Search information required: name, date of birth, years to search. Specify plaintiff or defendant.

Misdemeanor records
District Court
312 S.W. First Ave.
Kelso, WA 98626
(206) 577-3073
Misdemeanor records are available by mail. No search fee. Search information required: name, date of birth, years to search, SASE.

Civil records
District Court
312 S.W. First Ave.
Kelso, WA 98626
(206) 577-3073
Civil records are available by mail. No release necessary. No search fee. $5.00 for certification. Search information required: name, date of birth, years to search, SASE. Specify plaintiff or defendant.

Douglas County

County Clerk, Felony Check
PO Box 516
Waterville, WA 98858
(509) 745-8529
Fax (509) 745-8027
Felony and misdemeanor records are available by mail or fax No release necessary. No search fee. $2.00 fee for first copy, $1.00 fee per copy thereafter. $2.00 for certification. $2.00 fee for first page of fax response, $1.00 each additional page. Search information required: name, years to search.

Civil records are available by mail or fax No release necessary. No search fee. $2.00 fee for first copy, $1.00 fee per copy thereafter. $2.00 for certification. $2.00 fee for first page of fax response, $1.00 each additional page. Search information required: name, date of birth, years to search. Specify plaintiff or defendant.

Ferry County

Ferry County Clerk, Felony Check
PO Box 302
Republic, WA 99166
(509) 775-5245 or 775-5232
Felony records are available by mail. No release necessary. $8.00 fee per hour. $.50 fee per copy. $2.00 for first certification. $1.00 each additional page. Certified check only, payable to Ferry County Clerk. Search information required: name, SSN, date of birth, sex, race.

Civil records are available by mail. No release necessary. $8.00 fee per hour. $.50 fee per copy. $2.00 for first certification. $1.00 each additional page. Search information required: name, date of birth, years to search. Specify plaintiff or defendant.

Franklin County

Franklin County Clerk, Felony Check
1016 N. 4th Street
Pasco, WA 99301
(509) 545-3525
Felony records are available by mail. No release necessary. $8.00 fee per hour. $2.00 fee for first copy, $1.00 each additional page, includes certification. Make check payable to County Clerk. Search information required: name, date of birth, SASE, years to search.

Civil records are available by mail. No release necessary. $8.00 fee per hour. $2.00 fee for first copy, $1.00 each additional page, includes certification. Search information required: name, date of birth, years to search. Specify plaintiff or defendant.

Garfield County

County Clerk of Superior Court, Felony Check
Box 915
Pomeroy, WA 99347
(509) 843-3731
Fax (509) 843-1224
Felony and misdemeanor records are available by mail, phone or fax. No release necessary. No search fee. $.25 fee per copy. $2.00 for first certification. $1.00 each additional page. Search information required: name.

Civil records are available by mail. No release necessary. No search fee. $.25 fee per copy. $2.00 for first certification. $1.00 each additional page. Search information required: name, date of birth, years to search. Specify plaintiff or defendant.

Grant County

Felony records
Grant County Superior Court Clerk
Felony Check
PO Box 37
Ephrata, WA 98823
(509) 754-2011
Fax (509) 754-5638
Felony records are available by mail or fax. No release necessary. $8.00 search fee. $2.00 fee per copy. $2.00 for first copy. $1.00 each additional copy includes certification. $2.00 fee for first page of fax request, $1.00 each additional page. Search information required: name.

Civil records
Grant County Superior Court Clerk
PO Box 37
Ephrata, WA 98823
(509) 754-2011
Fax (509) 754-5638
Civil records are available by mail or fax. No release necessary. $8.00 search fee. $2.00 fee per copy. $2.00 for first copy. $1.00 each additional copy includes certification. $2.00 fee for first page of fax request, $1.00 each additional page. Search information required: name, date of birth, years to search. Specify plaintiff or defendant.

Misdemeanor records
Grant County Clerk
District Court, Misdemeanor Records
PO Box 37
Ephrata, WA 98823
(509) 754-2011 Ext. 389
Misdemeanor records are available by mail or fax. No release necessary. $8.00 search fee. $2.00 fee per copy. $2.00 for first copy. $1.00 each additional copy includes certification. $2.00 fee for first page of fax request, $1.00 each additional page. Search information required: name, date of birth, years to search. Specify plaintiff or defendant.

Civil records
Grant County Clerk
District Court
PO Box 37
Ephrata, WA 98823
(509) 754-2011 Ext. 389
Civil records are available by mail or fax. No release necessary. $8.00 search fee. $2.00 for first copy. $1.00 each additional copy includes certification. $2.00 fee for first page of fax request, $1.00 each additional page. Search information required: name, date of birth, years to search. Specify plaintiff or defendant.

Grays Harbor County

Grays Harbor County Clerk, Felony Check
PO Box 711
Montesano, WA 98563
(206) 249-3842
Fax (206) 249-6381

Felony and misdemeanor records are available by mail or phone. No release necessary. No search fee. $2.00 for first copy. $1.00 each additional copy includes certification. $.15 fee for fax request. $2.00 fee for first page of fax response, $.35 each additional page. Company checks only, payable to Grays Harbor County Clerk. Search information required: name, date of birth.

Civil records are available by mail or phone. No release necessary. No search fee. $2.00 for first copy, $1.00 each additional copy includes certification. $.15 fee for fax request. $2.00 fee for first page of fax response, $.35 each additional page. Search information required: name, date of birth, years to search. Specify plaintiff or defendant.

Island County

District and Municipal Court
4114 400 Avenue West
Oak Harbor, WA 98277
(206) 675-5988

Felony and misdemeanor records are available by mail. No release necessary. No search fee. $2.00 for first copy, $.25 each additional copy. $2.00 for certification. Search information required: name, years to search, SASE.

Civil records are available by mail. No release necessary. No search fee. $2.00 for first copy, $.25 each additional copy. $2.00 for certification. Search information required: name, date of birth, years to search. Specify plaintiff or defendant.

Jefferson County

Jefferson County Clerk, Felony Check
PO Box 1220
Port Townsend, WA 98368
(206) 385-9125
Fax (206) 385-5672

Felony records are available by mail. No release necessary. $8.00 search per hour fee. $4.00 minimum. $1.00 for first copy, $.50 each additional copy. $2.00 for first certification, $1.00 each additional page. Company checks only, payable to Jefferson County Clerk. Search information required: name.

Civil records are available by mail. No release necessary. $8.00 search per hour fee. $4.00 minimum. $1.00 for first copy, $.50 each additional copy. $2.00 for first certification, $1.00 each additional page. Search information required: name, date of birth, years to search. Specify plaintiff or defendant.

King County

King County Courthouse, Customer Service
Room E-609
Seattle, WA 98104
(206) 296-9300

Pre-1979 felony records are available by mail or phone. $8.00 search fee per hour. $2.00 fee for first copy, $1.00 each additional copy. $2.00 fee for certification. Certified check only, payable to King Court Superior Court Clerk. Search information required: name, previous address, years to search, SASE.

Civil records are available by mail or phone. $8.00 search fee per hour. $2.00 fee for first copy, $1.00 each additional copy. $2.00 fee for certification. Search information required: name, date of birth, years to search. Specify plaintiff or defendant.

Kitsap County

County Clerk of Superior Court, Felony Check
614 Division Street - MS-34
Port Orchard, WA 98366
(206) 876-7164
Fax (206) 895-4927

Felony records are available by mail, phone or fax. No release necessary. No search fee for records from 1978 and forward. $8.00 search fee per hour for records prior to 1978. $2.00 fee for first copy, $1.00 each additional copy, includes certification. Make check payable to County Clerk. Search information required: name, years to search.

Civil records are available by mail. No release necessary. $8.00 search fee per hour. $2.00 fee for first copy, $1.00 each additional copy, includes certification. Search information required: name, date of birth, years to search. Specify plaintiff or defendant.

Kittitas County

Kittitas County Clerk, Felony Check
205 W. 5th
Ellensburg, WA 98926
(509) 962-7531
Fax (509) 962-7667

Felony records are available by mail, phone or fax. No release necessary. No search fee. $1.00 fee per copy. $1.00 for certification. Certified check only, payable to Kittitas County Clerk. Search information required: name, years to search, SASE.

Civil records are available by mail. No release necessary. No search fee. $1.00 fee per copy. $1.00 for certification. Search information required: name, date of birth, years to search. Specify plaintiff or defendant.

Klickitat County

Felony records
County Clerk, Felony Check
205 S. Columbus Ave.
Room 204
Goldendale, WA 98620
(509) 773-5744
Fax (509) 773-4559

Felony records are available by mail, phone or fax. No release necessary. $8.00 search fee per hour. $2.00 fee for first copy, $1.00 each additional copy, includes certification. Search information required: name, SASE

Civil records
County Clerk, Felony Check
205 S. Columbus Ave.
Room 204
Goldendale, WA 98620
(509) 773-5744
Fax (509) 773-4559

Civil records are available by mail, phone or fax. No release necessary. $8.00 search fee per hour. $2.00 fee for first copy, $1.00 each additional copy, includes certification. Search information required: name, date of birth, years to search, SASE. Specify plaintiff or defendant.

Misdemeanor records
East District Court, Room 107
205 S. Columbus
Goldendale, WA 98620
(509) 773-4670
Fax (509) 773-6575

Misdemeanor records are available by mail or fax. No release necessary. No search fee. $5.00 for certification. Search information required: name.

Civil records
East District Court, Room 107
205 S. Columbus
Goldendale, WA 98620
(509) 773-4670
Fax (509) 773-6575

Civil records are available by mail or fax. No release necessary. No search fee. $5.00 for certification. Search information required: name, date of birth, years to search. Specify plaintiff or defendant.

Lewis County

Felony records
County Clerk, Felony Check
PO Box 1124
Chehalis, WA 98532
(206) 748-9121 Ext. 177

Felony records are available by mail. No release necessary. $8.00 search fee per hour. $2.00 fee per copy, $1.00 for additional pages. Make check payable to County Clerk. Search information required: name, date of birth, previous address.

Civil records
County Clerk
PO Box 1124
Chehalis, WA 98532
(206) 748-9121 Ext. 177

Civil records are available by mail. No release necessary. $8.00 search fee per hour. $2.00 fee per copy, $1.00 for additional pages. Search information required: name, date of birth, years to search. Specify plaintiff or defendant.

Misdemeanor records
District Court
PO Box 1124
Chehalis, WA 98532
(206) 748-9121 Ext. 200

Misdemeanor records are available by mail. No release necessary. No search fee. Search information required: name, date of birth, driver's license number, if available.

Civil records
District Court
PO Box 1124
Chehalis, WA 98532
(206) 748-9121 Ext. 200
Civil records are available by mail. No release necessary. No search fee. Search information required: name, date of birth, years to search. Specify plaintiff or defendant.

Lincoln County

Felony records
County Clerk, Felony Check
Box 369
Davenport, WA 99122
(509) 725-1401
Felony records are available by mail or phone. No release necessary. $8.00 search fee per hour. $.25 fee per copy. $5.00 for certification. Certified check only, payable to County Clerk. Search information required: name, years to search.

Civil records
County Clerk, Felony Check
Box 369
Davenport, WA 99122
(509) 725-1401
Civil records are available by mail. No release necessary. $8.00 search fee per hour. $.25 fee per copy. $5.00 for certification. Search information required: name, date of birth, years to search. Specify plaintiff or defendant.

Misdemeanor records
District Court
PO Box 118
Davenport, WA 99122
(509) 725-2281
Misdemeanor records are available by mail or phone. No release necessary. $8.00 search fee per hour. $.25 fee per copy. $5.00 for certification. Certified check only, payable to County Clerk. Search information required: name, years to search.

Civil records
District Court
PO Box 118
Davenport, WA 99122
(509) 725-2281
Civil records are available by mail. No release necessary. No search fee. $8.00 search fee per hour. $.25 fee per copy. $5.00 for certification. Search information required: name, date of birth, years to search. Specify plaintiff or defendant.

Mason County

Felony records
County Clerk, Felony Check
PO Box 340
Shelton, WA 98584
(206) 427-9670
Felony records are available by mail. No release necessary. $8.00 search fee per hour. $2.00 fee for first copy, $1.00 each additional copy, includes certification. Certified check only, payable to County Clerk. Search information required: name, years to search.

Civil records
County Clerk
PO Box 340
Shelton, WA 98584
(206) 427-9670
Civil records are available by mail. No release necessary. $8.00 search fee per hour. $2.00 fee for first copy, $1.00 each additional copy, includes certification. Search information required: name, date of birth, years to search. Specify plaintiff or defendant.

Misdemeanor records
Mason County District Court
Misdemeanor Records
4th Alder
PO Box 0
Shelton, WA 98584
(206) 427-9670
Misdemeanor records are available in person only. See Virginia state repository for additional information.

Civil records
Mason County District Court
4th Alder
PO Box 0
Shelton, WA 98584
(206) 427-9670
Civil records are available n person only. See Virginia state repository for additional information.

Okanogan County

County Clerk, Felony Check
PO Box 72
Okanogan, WA 98840
(509) 422-3650 7275
Felony and misdemeanor records are available by mail or phone. No release necessary. No search fee. $1.00 fee per copy. $2.00 for first certification, $1.00 each additional page. Search information required: name.

Civil records are available by mail. No release necessary. No search fee. $1.00 fee per copy. $2.00 for first certification, $1.00 each additional page. Search information required: name, date of birth, years to search. Specify plaintiff or defendant.

Pacific County

County Clerk, Felony Check
PO Box 67
South Bend, WA 98586
(206) 875-9320
Fax (206) 875-9321
Felony records are available by mail, fax or phone. No release necessary. No search fee. $2.00 fee for first copy, $1.00 each additional copy, includes certification. Certified or personal check made payable to County Clerk. Search information required: name.

Civil records are available by mail, fax or phone. No release necessary. No search fee. $2.00 fee for first copy, $1.00 each additional copy, includes certification. Search information required: name, date of birth, years to search. Specify plaintiff or defendant.

Pend Oreille County

Pend Oreille County Clerk, Felony Check
PO Box 5000
Hall of Justice
Newport, WA 99156-5020
(509) 447-2435
Fax (509) 447-2734
Felony records are available by mail, fax or phone. No release necessary. No search fee. $2.00 fee for first copy, $1.00 each additional copy, includes certification. Company checks only, payable to County Clerk. Search information required: name, years to search.

Civil records are available by mail, fax or phone. No release necessary. No search fee. $2.00 fee for first copy, $1.00 each additional copy, includes certification. Search information required: name, date of birth, years to search. Specify plaintiff or defendant.

Pierce County

County Clerk, Felony Check
County - City Bldg., Room 110
Tacoma, WA 98402
(206) 593-2521
Felony records are available by mail. No release necessary. $8.00 search fee per hour. $2.00 fee for first copy, $1.00 each additional copy, includes certification. Certified check only, payable to County Clerk. Search information required: name, SSN, date of birth.

Civil records are available by mail. No release necessary. No search fee. $2.00 fee for first copy, $1.00 each additional copy, includes certification. Search information required: name, date of birth, years to search. Specify plaintiff or defendant.

San Juan County

County Clerk, Felony Check
PO Box 1249
Friday Harbor, WA 98250
(206) 378-2163
Fax (206) 378-3967
Felony records are available by mail, fax or phone. No release necessary. No search fee. $2.00 fee for first copy, $1.00 each additional copy, includes certification. $5.00 fee for first page of fax response, $1.00 each additional page. Search information required: name, date of offense.

Civil records are available by mail, fax or phone. No release necessary. No search fee. $2.00 fee for first copy, $1.00 each additional copy, includes certification. $5.00 fee for first page of fax response, $1.00 each additional page. Search information required: name, date of birth, years to search. Specify plaintiff or defendant.

Skagit County

County Clerk, Felony Check
PO Box 837
Mount Vernon, WA 98273
(206) 336-9440
Felony records are available by mail. No release necessary. $8.00 search fee per hour. $2.00 fee for first copy, $1.00 each additional copy. $2.00 fee for certification. Make check payable to Skagit County Clerk. Search information required: name, date of birth, SASE

Civil records are available by mail. No release necessary. $8.00 search fee per hour. $2.00 fee for first copy, $1.00 each additional copy. $2.00 fee for certification. Search information required: name, date of birth, years to search, SASE. Specify plaintiff or defendant.

Skamania County

County Clerk, Felony Check
PO Box 790
Stevenson, WA 98648
(509) 427-5141
Felony records are available by mail. No release necessary. $8.00 search fee per hour. $2.00 fee for first copy, $1.00 each additional copy, includes certification. Certified check only, payable to County Clerk. Search information required: name, SASE.

Civil records are available by mail. No release necessary. $8.00 search fee per hour. $2.00 fee for first copy, $1.00 each additional copy, includes certification. Search information required: name, date of birth, years to search, SASE. Specify plaintiff or defendant.

Snohomish County

Snohomish County Clerk, Felony Check
Snohomish County Courthouse, Room 246
3000 Rockefeller
Everett, WA 98201
(206) 388-3466 Ext. 2714
Felony records are available by mail or phone. No release necessary. $8.00 fee for 1 search. $12.00 fee for 2-10 requests. Certified check only, payable to County Clerk. Search information required: name, years to search, SASE.

Civil records are available bymail or phone. No release necessary. $8.00 fee for 1 search. $12.00 fee for 2-10 requests. Search information required: name, date of birth, years to search. Specify plaintiff or defendant.

Spokane County

Clerk of Superior Court, Felony Check
W. 1116 Broadway, Room300
Spokane, WA 99260-0090
(509) 456-2211
Felony records are available by mail. No release necessary. $8.00 search fee per hour. $2.00 fee for first copy, $1.00 each additional copy, includes certification. Certified check or money order payable to Spokane County Clerk. Search information required: full name, date of birth, years to search, SASE.

Civil records are available by mail. No release necessary. $8.00 search fee per hour. $2.00 fee for first copy, $1.00 each additional copy, includes certification. Search information required: name, date of birth, years to search. Specify plaintiff or defendant.

Stevens County

Stevens County Clerk, Felony Check
PO Box 350
Colville, WA 99114-0350
(509) 684-6111
Felony and misdemeanor records are available by mail. No release necessary. $8.00 search fee per hour. $2.00 fee for first copy, $1.00 each additional copy, includes certifi

cation. Certified check only, payable to County Clerk. Search information required: name, years to search.

Civil records are available by mail. No release necessary. $8.00 search fee per hour. $2.00 fee for first copy, $1.00 each additional copy, includes certification. Search information required: name, date of birth, years to search. Specify plaintiff or defendant.

Thurston County

County Clerk
2000 Lakeridge Dr.
SW Building #2
Olympia, WA 98502
(206) 786-5430
Felony and misdemeanor records are available by mail or phone. No search fee. $2.00 fee for first copy, $1.00 each additional copy, includes certification. Certified check only, payable to Thurston County Clerk. Search information required: name, SSN.

Civil records are available by mail. No release necessary. No search fee. $2.00 fee for first copy, $1.00 each additional copy, includes certification. Search information required: name, date of birth, years to search. Specify plaintiff or defendant.

Wahkiakum County

Wahkiakum County Clerk, Felony Check
PO Box 116
Cathlamet, WA 98612
(206) 795-3558
Fax (206) 795-8813
Felony and misdemeanor records are available by mail or fax. No release necessary. $8.00 search fee per hour. $2.00 fee for first copy, $1.00 each additional copy, includes certification. Make check payable to County Clerk. Search information required: name.

Civil records are available by mail or fax. No release necessary. $8.00 search fee per hour. $2.00 fee for first copy, $1.00 each additional copy, includes certification. Search information required: name, date of birth, years to search. Specify plaintiff or defendant.

Walla Walla County

Felony records
County Clerk, Felony Check
PO Box 836
Walla Walla, WA 99362
(509) 527-3221
Felony records are available by mail. No release necessary. No search fee. $2.00 fee for first copy, $1.00 each additional copy, includes certification. Certified check only, payable to County Clerk. Search information required: name, years to search.

Civil records
County Clerk
PO Box 836
Walla Walla, WA 99362
(509) 527-3221
Civil records are available by mail. No release necessary. No search fee.$2.00 fee for first copy, $1.00 each additional copy, includes certification. Search information required: name, date of birth, years to search. Specify plaintiff or defendant.

Misdemeanor records
District Court
PO Box 641
Walla Walla, WA 99362
(509) 527-3236
Misdemeanor records are available by mail or phone. No release necessary. $5.00 search fee. $.50 fee per copy. $5.00 for certification. Make check payable to District Court. Search information required: name, date of birth.

Civil records
District Court
PO Box 641
Walla Walla, WA 99362
(509) 527-3236
Civil records are available by mail. No release necessary. $5.00 search fee. $.50 fee per copy. $5.00 for certification. Search information required: name, date of birth, years to search. Specify plaintiff or defendant.

Whatcom County

Whatcom County Clerk, Felony Check
PO Box 1144
Bellingham, WA 98227
(206) 676-6777
Felony records are available by mail or phone. No release necessary. $8.00 search fee per hour. $2.00 fee for first copy, $1.00 each additional copy, includes certification. Make check payable to County Clerk. Search information required: name.

Civil records are available by mail. No release necessary. $8.00 search fee per hour. $2.00 fee for first copy, $1.00 each additional copy, includes certification. Search information required: name, date of birth, years to search. Specify plaintiff or defendant.

Whitman County

County Clerk, Felony Check
N. 404 Main Street
Colfax, WA 99111
(509) 397-6240
Fax (509) 397-3546
Felony records are available by mail, phone or fax. No release necessary. No search fee. $1.00 fee per copy. $2.00 for first certification, $1.00 each additional page. Search information required: name.

Civil records are available by mail, phone or fax. No release necessary. No search fee. $1.00 fee per copy. $2.00 for first certification, $1.00 each additional page. Search information required: name, date of birth, years to search. Specify plaintiff or defendant.

Yakima County

Yakima County Clerk, Felony Check
128 N 2nd St.
Room 323
Yakima, WA 98901
(509) 575-4120
Felony records are available by mail or phone. No release necessary. $8.00 search fee per hour, $4.00 minimum fee. $2.00 fee for first copy, $1.00 each additional copy, includes certification. Search information required: name, years to search.

Civil records are available by mail. No release necessary. $8.00 search fee per hour, $4.00 minimum fee. $2.00 fee for first copy, $1.00 each additional copy, includes certification. Search information required: name, date of birth, years to search. Specify plaintiff or defendant.

City-County Cross Reference

Aberdeen *Grays Harbor*
Acme *Whatcom*
Addy *Stevens*
Adna *Lewis*
Airway Heights *Spokane*
Albion *Whitman*
Alderwood Manor
   Snohomish
Algona *King*
Allyn *Mason*
Almira *Lincoln*
Amanda Park *Grays*
   Harbor
Amboy *Clark*
Anacortes *Skagit*
Anatone *Asotin*
Appleton *Klickitat*
Ardenvoir *Chelan*
Ariel *Cowlitz*
Arlington *Snohomish*
Ashford *Pierce*
Asotin *Asotin*
Auburn *King*
Baring *King*
Battle Ground *Clark*
Bay Center *Pacific*
Beaver *Clallam*
Belfair *Mason*
Bellevue *King*
Bellingham *Whatcom*
Benge *Adams*
Benton City *Benton*
Beverly *Grant*
Bickleton *Klickitat*
Bingen *Klickitat*
Black Diamond *King*
Blaine *Whatcom*
Bonny Lake *Pierce*
Bothell *King*
Bow *Skagit*
Bremerton *Kitsap*
Brewster *Okanogan*
Bridgeport *Douglas*
Brinnon *Jefferson*
Browns Point *Pierce*
Brownstown *Yakima*
Brush Prairie *Clark*
Buckley *Pierce*
Bucoda *Thurston*
Buena *Yakima*
Burbank *Walla Walla*
Burien *Kittitas*
Burley *Kitsap*
Burlington *Skagit*
Camas *Clark*
Carbonado *Pierce*
Carlsborg *Clallam*
Carlton *Okanogan*
Carnation *King*
Carrolls *Cowlitz*
Carson *Skamania*
Cashmere *Chelan*
Castle Rock *Cowlitz*
Cathlamet *Wahkiakum*
Centerville *Klickitat*
Centralia *Lewis*
Central Park *Grays Harbor*
Chattaroy *Spokane*
Chehalis *Lewis*
Chelan *Chelan*
Chelan Falls *Chelan*
Cheney *Spokane*

Chewelah *Stevens*
Chico *Kitsap*
Chimacum *Jefferson*
Chinook *Pacific*
Cinebar *Lewis*
Clallam Bay *Clallam*
Clarkston *Asotin*
Clayton *Stevens*
Clearlake *Skagit*
Clearview *Snohomish*
Cle Elum *Kittitas*
Clinton *Island*
Clyde Hill *King*
Colbert *Spokane*
Colfax *Whitman*
College Place *Walla Walla*
Colton *Whitman*
Colville *Stevens*
Conconully *Okanogan*
Concrete *Skagit*
Connell *Franklin*
Conway *Skagit*
Copalis Beach *Grays*
   Harbor
Copalis Crossing *Grays*
   Harbor
Cosmopolis *Grays Harbor*
Cougar *Cowlitz*
Coulee City *Grant*
Coulee Dam *Okanogan*
Country Homes *Spokane*
Coupeville *Island*
Cowiche *Yakima*
Creston *Lincoln*
Cunningham *Adams*
Curlew *Ferry*
Curtis *Lewis*
Cusick *Pend Oreille*
Custer *Whatcom*
Dallesport *Klickitat*
Danville *Ferry*
Darrington *Snohomish*
Davenport *Lincoln*
Dayton *Columbia*
Deer Harbor *San Juan*
Deer Park *Spokane*
Deming *Whatcom*
Des Moines *King*
Dishman *Spokane*
Dixie *Walla Walla*
Doty *Lewis*
Dryden *Chelan*
Du Pont *Pierce*
Duvall *King*
East Olympia *Thurston*
Easton *Kittitas*
Eastsound *San Juan*
East Wenatchee *Douglas*
Eatonville *Pierce*
Edgewood *King*
Edmonds *Snohomish*
Edwall *Lincoln*
Elbe *Pierce*
Electric City *Grant*
Elk *Spokane*
Ellensburg *Kittitas*
Elma *Grays Harbor*
Elmer City *Okanogan*
Eltopia *Franklin*
Endicott *Whitman*
Entiat *Chelan*
Enumclaw *King*

Ephrata *Grant*
Ethel *Lewis*
Everett *Snohomish*
Everson *Whatcom*
Fairchild Air Force Base
   Spokane
Fairfield *Spokane*
Fairwood *King*
Fall City *King*
Farmington *Whitman*
Federal Way *King*
Ferndale *Whatcom*
Fife *Pierce*
Fircrest *Pierce*
Ford *Stevens*
Fords Prairie *Lewis*
Forks *Clallam*
Four Lakes *Spokane*
Fox Island *Pierce*
Freeland *Island*
Friday Harbor *San Juan*
Galvin *Lewis*
Garfield *Whitman*
Gifford *Stevens*
Gig Harbor *Pierce*
Glenoma *Lewis*
Glenwood *Klickitat*
Gold Bar *Snohomish*
Goldendale *Klickitat*
Graham *Pierce*
Grand Coulee *Grant*
Grandview *Yakima*
Granger *Yakima*
Granite Falls *Snohomish*
Grapeview *Mason*
Grayland *Grays Harbor*
Grays River *Wahkiakum*
Greenacres *Spokane*
Greenbank *Island*
Hadlock *Jefferson*
Hamilton *Skagit*
Hansville *Kitsap*
Harrah *Yakima*
Harrington *Lincoln*
Hartline *Grant*
Heisson *Clark*
Hobart *King*
Hoodsport *Mason*
Hooper *Whitman*
Hoquiam *Grays Harbor*
Humptulips *Grays Harbor*
Hunters *Stevens*
Husum *Klickitat*
Ilwaco *Pacific*
Inchelium *Ferry*
Index *Snohomish*
Indianola *Kitsap*
Inglewood *King*
Ione *Pend Oreille*
Issaquah *King*
Joyce *Clallam*
Kahlotus *Franklin*
Kalama *Cowlitz*
Kapowsin *Pierce*
Keller *Ferry*
Kelso *Cowlitz*
Kenmore *King*
Kennewick *Benton*
Kent *King*
Kettle Falls *Stevens*
Keyport *Kitsap*
Kingston *Kitsap*

Kirkland *King*
Kittitas *Kittitas*
Klickitat *Klickitat*
LaCenter *Clark*
LaConner *Skagit*
Lacrosse *Whitman*
Lacey *Thurston*
LaGrande *Pierce*
Lakebay *Pierce*
Lake Forest Park *King*
Lakes District *Pierce*
Lake Stevens *Snohomish*
Lakewood *Snohomish*
Langley *Island*
LaPush *Clallam*
Latah *Spokane*
Laurier *Ferry*
Leavenworth *Chelan*
Lebam *Pacific*
Lexington *Cowlitz*
Liberty Lake *Spokane*
Lilliwaup *Mason*
Lind *Adams*
Littlerock *Thurston*
Long Beach *Pacific*
Longview *Cowlitz*
Loomis *Okanogan*
Loon Lake *Stevens*
Lopez *San Juan*
Lummi Island *Whatcom*
Lyle *Klickitat*
Lyman *Skagit*
Lynden *Whatcom*
Lynnwood *Snohomish*
Lynwood Center *Kitsap*
McCleary *Grays Harbor*
McKenna *Pierce*
McMillin *Pierce*
Mabton *Yakima*
Malaga *Chelan*
Malden *Whitman*
Malo *Ferry*
Malone *Grays Harbor*
Malott *Okanogan*
Manchester *Kitsap*
Mansfield *Douglas*
Manson *Chelan*
Maple Falls *Whatcom*
Maple Valley *King*
Marblemount *Skagit*
Marcus *Stevens*
Marlin *Grant*
Marshall *Spokane*
Marysville *Snohomish*
Matlock *Mason*
Mead *Spokane*
Medical Lake *Spokane*
Medina *King*
Menlo *Pacific*
Mercer Island *King*
Mesa *Franklin*
Metaline *Pend Oreille*
Metaline Falls *Pend Oreille*
Methow *Okanogan*
Midland *Pierce*
Mill Creek *Snohomish*
Millwood *Spokane*
Milton *Pierce*
Mineral *Lewis*
Moclips *Grays Harbor*
Monitor *Chelan*
Monroe *Snohomish*

Montesano *Grays Harbor*
Morgan Acres *Spokane*
Morton *Lewis*
Moses Lake *Grant*
Mossyrock *Lewis*
Mountlake Terrace *Snohomish*
Mount Vernon *Skagit*
Moxee City *Yakima*
Mukilteo *Snohomish*
Naches *Yakima*
Napavine *Lewis*
Naselle *Pacific*
Neah Bay *Clallam*
Neilton *Grays Harbor*
Nespelem *Okanogan*
Newman Lake *Spokane*
Newport *Pend Oreille*
Newport Hills *King*
Nine Mile Falls *Spokane*
Nooksack *Whatcom*
Nordland *Jefferson*
Normandy Park *King*
North Bend *King*
North Bonneville *Skamania*
Northport *Stevens*
North Puyallup *Pierce*
Oakesdale *Whitman*
Oak Harbor *Island*
Oakville *Grays Harbor*
Ocean City/shores *Grays Harbor*
Ocean Park *Pacific*
Odessa *Lincoln*
Okanogan *Okanogan*
Olalla *Kitsap*
Olga *San Juan*
Olympia *Thurston*
Omak *Okanogan*
Onalaska *Lewis*
Opportunity *Spokane*
Orcas *San Juan*
Orondo *Douglas*
Oroville *Okanogan*
Orting *Pierce*
Othello *Adams*
Otis Orchards *Spokane*
Outlook *Yakima*
Oysterville *Pacific*
Pacific *King*
Pacific Beach *Grays Harbor*
Packwood *Lewis*
Palisades *Douglas*
Palouse *Whitman*
Parker *Yakima*
Parkland *Pierce*
Parkwater *Spokane*
Pasadena Park *Spokane*
Pasco *Franklin*
Pateros *Okanogan*
Paterson *Benton*
Pe Ell *Lewis*
Peshastin *Chelan*
Plymouth *Benton*
Point Roberts *Whatcom*
Pomeroy *Garfield*
Port Angeles *Clallam*
Port Gamble *Kitsap*
Port Orchard *Kitsap*
Port Townsend *Jefferson*
Poulsbo *Kitsap*
Prescott *Walla Walla*
Preston *King*

Prosser *Benton*
Pullman *Whitman*
Puyallup *Pierce*
Quilcene *Jefferson*
Quincy *Grant*
Quinault *Grays Harbor*
Rainier *Thurston*
Randle *Lewis*
Ravensdale *King*
Raymond *Pacific*
Reardan *Lincoln*
Redmond *King*
Redondo *Kittilas*
Renton *King*
Republic *Ferry*
Rice *Stevens*
Richland *Benton*
Richmond Beach *King*
Ridgefield *Clark*
Ritzville *Adams*
Riverside *Okanogan*
Riverton Heights *King*
Rochester *Thurston*
Rockford *Spokane*
Rock Island *Douglas*
Rockport *Skagit*
Rollingbay *Kitsap*
Ronald *Kittitas*
Roosevelt *Klickitat*
Rosalia *Whitman*
Rosburg *Wahkiakum*
Roslyn *Kittitas*
Roy *Pierce*
Royal City *Grant*
Ruston *Pierce*
Ryderwood *Cowlitz*
Saint John *Whitman*
Salkum *Lewis*
Salmon Creek *Clark*
Satsop *Grays Harbor*
Seabeck *Kitsap*
Seahurst *King*
Seattle *King*
Seaview *Pacific*
Sedro Woolley *Skagit*
Sekiu *Clallam*
Selah *Yakima*
Sequim *Clallam*
Shaw Island *San Juan*
Shelton *Mason*
Sheridan Beach *King*
Silvana *Snohomish*
Silver Creek *Lewis*
Silverdale *Kitsap*
Silverlake *Cowlitz*
Skamokawa *Wahkiakum*
Skykomish *King*
Skyway *King*
Snohomish *Snohomish*
Snoqualmie *King*
Soap Lake *Grant*
South Bend *Pacific*
South Cle Elum *Kittitas*
South Colby *Kitsap*
South Prairie *Pierce*
South Wenatchee *Chelan*
Southworth *Kitsap*
Spanaway *Pierce*
Spangle *Spokane*
Spokane *Spokane*
Sprague *Lincoln*
Springdale *Stevens*
Stanwood *Snohomish*
Starbuck *Columbia*
Startup *Snohomish*

Stehekin *Chelan*
Steilacoom *Pierce*
Steptoe *Whitman*
Stevenson *Skamania*
Stratford *Grant*
Sultan *Snohomish*
Sumas *Whatcom*
Sumner *Pierce*
Sunnyside *Yakima*
Suquamish *Kitsap*
Tacoma *Pierce*
Taholah *Grays Harbor*
Tahuya *Mason*
Tekoa *Whitman*
Tenino *Thurston*
Thornton *Whitman*
Thorp *Kittitas*
Tieton *Yakima*
Tokeland *Pacific*
Toledo *Lewis*
Tonasket *Okanogan*
Toppenish *Yakima*
Touchet *Walla Walla*
Toutle *Cowlitz*
Tracyton *Kitsap*
Trentwood *Spokane*
Trout Lake *Klickitat*
Tukwila *King*
Tumwater *Thurston*
Twisp *Okanogan*
Underwood *Skamania*
Union *Mason*
Union Gap *Yakima*
Uniontown *Whitman*
Usk *Pend Oreille*
Vader *Lewis*
Valley *Stevens*
Valleyford *Spokane*
Vancouver *Clark*
Vashon *King*
Vaughn *Pierce*
Veradale *Spokane*
Wahkiacus *Klickitat*
Waitsburg *Walla Walla*
Waldron *San Juan*
Walla Walla *Walla Walla*
Wallula *Walla Walla*
Wapato *Yakima*
Warden *Grant*
Washougal *Clark*
Washtucna *Adams*
Waterville *Douglas*
Wauconda *Okanogan*
Wauna *Pierce*
Waverly *Spokane*
Wellpinit *Stevens*
Wenatchee *Chelan*
Westport *Grays Harbor*
White Center *King*
White Salmon *Klickitat*
White Swan *Yakima*
Wilbur *Lincoln*
Wilkeson *Pierce*
Wilson Creek *Grant*
Winlock *Lewis*
Winslow *Kitsap*
Winthrop *Okanogan*
Wishram *Klickitat*
Wollochet *Pierce*
Woodinville *King*
Woodland *Cowlitz*
Woodway *Snohomish*
Yacolt *Clark*
Yakima *Yakima*
Yarrow Point *King*

Yelm *Thurston*
Zenith *King*
Zillah *Yakima*

West Virginia

Fifty two (52) of West Virginia's fifty five (55) counties indicated that they release conviction records to employers for employment screening purposes by mail or phone. The vast majority do not require a release. None of the counties charge a fee for their services at this time. A few counties allow fax requests.

Civil suits are divided between Circuit and Magistrate Courts by a monetary value of $3,000.

For more information or for offices not listed, contact the state's information hot line at (304) 348-3456.

Driving Records

Department of Motor Vehicles
Driving Records
1800 Washington Street, East
Charleston, WV 25317
(304) 348-0238
Driving records are available by mail. $5.00 fee per request. Turnaround time is 24 hours. Written request must include job applicant's full name and license number. Make check payable to Department of Motor Vehicles.

Worker's Compensation Records

Worker's Compensation Fund
PO Box 3151
Charleston, WV 25332
(304) 348-0653
Worker's compensation records are available by phone or mail on current employees only. Information may not be used for pre-employment screening purposes. Written request should include the employee's full name, SSN and a photocopy of the applicant's signed W-4 form. A signed release is required.

Vital Statistics

Birth and death records
Vital Registration Office
Bureau of Public Health
State Capitol Complex
Building 3, Room 516
Charleston, WV 25305
(304) 558-2931
Birth and death records are available for $5.00 each. State office has birth records since January 1917, and death records since 1853. For earlier records, write to Clerk of Court, Commission of Kanawha County. An employer can obtain records with a written release. Make check or money order payable to Vital Registration.

Marriage and divorce records
Kanawha Clerk's Office
PO Box 3226
Charleston, WV 25332
(304) 357-0130 Extension 0241
Marriage records are available for a $5.00 fee. Certified copies from 1964 are available. Prior to 1964 contact county clerk in county where license was issued.. Include name, marriage date, and spouse's name. Turnaround time is 3-4 days. Divorce records from 1968 are available for $5.00. Cerified copies are not available from state office. Records prior to 1968 are available at county level, circuit clerk. Include name, spouse's name, and if known, civil action number.

Department of Education

Department of Education
Certification Unit
Capitol Complex
Bldg. 6 Room B-337
Charleston, WV 25305
(304) 348-7010 or (800) 982-2378
Field of certification is available by mail. Include name and SSN.

Medical Licensing

West Virginia Board of Medicine Verification
101 Dee Drive
Charleston, WV 25311
(304) 348-2921
Will confirm licenses for MD by mail. No fee. For licenses not mentioned, contact the above office.

West Virginia Board of Examiners for Registered Nurses
922 Quarrier St.
Suite 309, Embleton Bldg.
Charleston, WV 25301
(304) 348-3596
Will confirm license by mail. $1.00 fee. Include name, SSN, license number, if available.

Bar Association

West Virginia State Bar Association
2006 Kanawha Blvd. East
Charleston, WV 25311
(304) 548-2456
Will confirm licenses by phone. No fee. Include name.

Accountancy Board

West Virginia State Board of Accountancy
201 L and S Building
812 Quarrier Street
Charleston, WV 25305
(304) 348-2257
Will confirm license by phone. No fee. Include name.

Securities Commission

State Auditor's Office
Securities Division
Room W-118, State Capitol
Charleston, WV 25305
(304) 348-2257
Will confirm license by phone. No fee. Include name and SSN.

Secretary of State

Secretary of State
Corporation Division
State Capitol
Charleston, WV 25305
(304) 342-8000
Fax (304) 348-0900
Service agent and address, date incorporated, standing with tax commission, trade names are available by phone or mail. Contact the above office for additional information.

Criminal Records

State Repository

West Virginia State Police
Criminal Identification Bureau
Records Section
725 Jefferson Road
South Charleston, WV 25309
(304) 746-2177

All written requests must be submitted on a special "Record Request Check" card available from the state at the above address. Each request must include the applicant's full name, address, sex, race, date of birth, SSN, signed release and thumbprint. Each request must be accompanied by an alphabetical list of the individuals to be checked, including name, date of birth, and SSN on each party. There is a $5.00 fee for each request. Make check payable to the Superintendent, Department of Public Safety. Information released contains conviction data and arrest records that are less than a year old. Turnaround time is normally 24 to 48 hours.

Barbour County

Clerk of Circuit Court, Criminal
Records
PO Box 249
Philippi, WV 26416
(304) 457-3454

Felony and misdemeanor records are available by mail or phone. A release is required. No search fee. Search information required: name, date of birth, SASE, years to search.

Civil records are available by mail or phone. A release is required. No search fee. $.25 fee per copy. $1.00 for certification. Search information required: name, date of birth, years to search. Specify plaintiff or defendant.

Berkeley County

Circuit Court Clerk, Criminal Records
100 W. King Street
Martinsburg, WV 25401
(304) 267-3000
Fax (304) 267-9723

Felony and misdemeanor records are available by mail or fax. A release is required. No search fee. Search information required: name, date of birth, sex, race, years to search, SASE.

Civil records are available by mail. No release necessary. No search fee. $.25 fee per copy. Search information required: name, date of birth, years to search. Specify plaintiff or defendant.

Boone County

Circuit Clerk, Criminal Records
State Street
Madison, WV 25130
(304) 369-3925

Felony and misdemeanor records are available by mail or phone. No release necessary. No fee. Search information required: name, date of birth, sex, race, previous address, SSN, years to search.

Civil records are available by mail. No release necessary. No search fee. Search information required: name, date of birth, years to search. Specify plaintiff or defendant.

Braxton County

Clerk of Circuit Court, Criminal
Records
Braxton County Courthouse
Sutton, WV 26601
(304) 765-2837

Felony and misdemeanor records are available by mail or phone. No release necessary. No search fee. $.25 fee per copy. Search information required: name, years to search.

Civil records are available by mail or phone. No release necessary. No search fee. $.25 fee per copy. Search information required: name, date of birth, years to search. Specify plaintiff or defendant.

Brooke County

Clerk of Circuit Court, Criminal
Records
PO Box 474
Wellsburg, WV 26070
(304) 737-3662

Felony and misdemeanor records are available by mail or phone. No release necessary. No search fee. Search information required: name, SSN, date of birth, sex, race, years to search.

Civil records are available by mail or phone. No release necessary. No search fee. $.25 fee per copy. $.50 for certification. Search information required: name, date of birth, years to search. Specify plaintiff or defendant.

Cabell County

Clerk of Circuit Court, Criminal
Records
PO Box 698
Huntington, WV 25711
(304) 526-8622

Felony and misdemeanor records are available by mail. No release necessary. No search fee. Search information required: name, years to search.

Civil records are available by mail. No release necessary. No search fee. $.25 fee per copy. Search information required: name, SSN, date of birth, years to search, SASE. Specify plaintiff or defendant.

Calhoun County

Clerk of Circuit Court, Criminal
Records
PO Box 266
Grantsville, WV 26147
(304) 354-6910

Felony and misdemeanor records are available by mail or phone. No release necessary. No search fee. Search information required: name, SSN, date of birth, sex, race, years to search.

Civil records are available by mail. No release necessary. No search fee. $.25 fee per copy. $.50 for certification. Search information required: name, date of birth, years to search. Specify plaintiff or defendant.

Clay County

Clerk of Circuit Court, Criminal
Records
PO Box 129
Clay, WV 25043
(304) 587-4256

Felony and misdemeanor records are available by mail or phone. No release neces

sary. No search fee. Search information required: name.

Civil records are available by mail or phone. No release necessary. No search fee. $.25 fee per copy. Search information required: name, date of birth, years to search. Specify plaintiff or defendant.

Doddridge County

Circuit Court Clerk, Criminal Records
118 E. Court Street
West Union, WV 26456
(304) 873-2331
Fax (304) 873-1840

Felony and misdemeanor records are available by mail, phone or fax. A release is required. No search fee. $.25 fee per copy. Search information required: name, years to search, SASE.

Civil records are available by mail or phone. No release necessary. No search fee. $.25 fee per copy. Search information required: name, date of birth, years to search, SASE. Specify plaintiff or defendant.

Fayette County

Clerk of Court, Criminal Records
Fayette County Courthouse
Fayetteville, WV 25840
(304) 574-1200 Extension 50

Felony and misdemeanor records are available by mail or phone. No release necessary. No search fee. $.25 fee per copy. Search information required: name, date of birth, SASE, previous address, years to search, SSN.

Civil records are available by mail. No release necessary. No search fee. $.25 fee per copy. Search information required: name, SSN, date of birth, years to search, SASE. Specify plaintiff or defendant.

Gilmer County

Clerk of Circuit Court, Criminal
Records
Gilmer County Courthouse
Glenville, WV 26351
(304) 462-7241

Felony and misdemeanor records are available by mail or phone. No release necessary. No search fee. Search information required: name.

Civil records are available by mail or phone. No release necessary. No search fee. $.25 fee per copy. Search information required: name, date of birth, years to search. Specify plaintiff or defendant.

Grant County

Grant County Circuit Clerk, Criminal
Records
5 Highland Ave.
Petersburg, WV 26847
(304) 257-4545

Felony and misdemeanor records are available in person only. See West Virginia state repository for additional information.

Civil records are available by mail or phone. No release necessary. No search fee. $.25 fee per copy. Search information required: name, date of birth, years to search. Specify plaintiff or defendant.

Greenbrier County

Greenbrier County Circuit Court, Criminal Records
PO Drawer 751
Lewisburg, WV 24901
(304) 647-6626
Fax (304) 647-6666

Felony and misdemeanor records are available by mail or fax. No release necessary. No search fee. Search information required: name, SSN, date of birth, sex, race, years to search.

Civil records are available by mail or phone. No release necessary. No search fee. $.25 fee per copy. $1.00 for certification. Search information required: name, date of birth, years to search. Specify plaintiff or defendant.

Hampshire County

Clerk of Circuit Court, Criminal Records
PO Box 343
Romney, WV 26757
(304) 822-5022

Felony and misdemeanor records are available by mail. No release necessary. No search fee. $.25 fee per copy. Search information required: name, SSN, date of birth, years to search.

Civil records are available by mail. No release necessary. No search fee. $0.00 fee per copy. Search information required: name, date of birth, years to search. Specify plaintiff or defendant.

Hancock County

Circuit Clerk, Criminal Records
PO Box 428
New Cumberland, WV 26047
(304) 564-3311 Extension 260
Fax (304) 564-4059

Felony and misdemeanor records are available by mail. No release necessary. No search fee. Search information required: name.

Civil records are available by mail or fax. No release necessary. No search fee. Search information required: name, date of birth, years to search. Specify plaintiff or defendant.

Hardy County

Circuit Clerk, Criminal Records
Hardy County
Moorefield, WV 26836
(304) 538-2590

Felony and misdemeanor records are available in person only. See West Virginia state repository for additional information.

Civil records are available in person only. See West Virginia state repository for additional information.

Harrison County

Circuit Clerk, Criminal Records
301 W. Main Street
Courthouse Bldg.
Clarksburg, WV 26301
(304) 624-8636

Felony and misdemeanor records are available by mail. A release is required. No search fee. Search information required: name, year of offense, years to search, SASE.

Civil records are available by mail or phone. No release necessary. No search fee. $.25 fee per copy. $.50 for certification. Search information required: name, date of birth, years to search, SASE (triple amount of postage). Specify plaintiff or defendant.

Jackson County

Clerk of Circuit Court, Criminal Records
PO Box 427
Ripley, WV 25271
(304) 372-2011 Extension 326

Felony and misdemeanor records are available by mail or phone. No release necessary. No search fee. Search information required: name.

Civil records are available by mail or phone. No release necessary. No search fee. $.25 fee per copy. Search information required: name, date of birth, years to search. Specify plaintiff or defendant.

Jefferson County

Jefferson County Circuit Clerk, Criminal Records
PO Box 584
Charles Town, WV 25414
(304) 725-9761 Extension 232

Felony and misdemeanor records are available by mail. No release necessary. No search fee. $.25 fee per copy. $.50 for certification. Search information required: name, date of birth, years to search.

Civil records are available by mail. No release necessary. No search fee. $.25 fee per copy. $.50 for certification. Search information required: name, date of birth, years to search. Specify plaintiff or defendant.

Kanawha County

Clerk of Circuit Court, Criminal Records
PO Drawer 2351
Charleston, WV 25328
(304) 357-0440

Felony and misdemeanor records are available by mail. No release necessary. No search fee. Search information required: name, SSN, date of birth, years to search, SASE.

Civil records are available by mail. No release necessary. No search fee. $.25 fee per copy. Search information required: name, date of birth, years to search. Specify plaintiff or defendant.

Lewis County

Circuit Court Clerk, Criminal Records
PO Box 69
Weston, WV 26452
(304) 269-8210

Felony and misdemeanor records are available by mail. A release is required. No search fee. Search information required: name, SSN, date of birth, sex, race, years to search.

Civil records are available by mail. No release necessary. No search fee. $.25 fee per copy. $.50 for certification. Search information required: name, date of birth, years to search. Specify plaintiff or defendant.

Lincoln County

Clerk of Circuit Court, Criminal Records
PO Box 338
Hamlin, WV 25523
(304) 824-7887

Felony and misdemeanor records are available by mail or phone. No release necessary. No search fee. $.25 fee per copy. Search information required: name, date of birth, years to search.

Civil records are available by mail. No release necessary. No search fee. $.25 fee per copy. Search information required: name, date of birth, years to search. Specify plaintiff or defendant.

Logan County

Logan County Courthouse, Criminal Records
Room 311
Logan, WV 25601
(304) 752-2000 Extension 234

Felony and misdemeanor records are available by mail. No release necessary. No search fee. $.25 fee per copy. Search information required: name, date of birth, years to search.

Civil records are available by mail. No release necessary. No search fee. $.25 fee per copy. Search information required: name, date of birth, years to search. Specify plaintiff or defendant.

Marion County

Circuit Court Clerk, Criminal Records
PO Box 1269
Fairmont, WV 26554
(304) 367-5360
Fax (304) 367-5374

Felony and misdemeanor records are available in person only. See West Virginia state repository for additional information.

Civil records are available by mail or phone. No release necessary. No search fee. $.25 fee per copy. Search information required: name, date of birth, years to search. Specify plaintiff or defendant.

Marshall County

Clerk of Circuit Court, Criminal Records
7th St. Courthouse
Moundsville, WV 26041
(304) 845-2130

Felony and misdemeanor records are available by mail or phone. No release necessary. No search fee. Search information required: name, years to search.

Civil records are available by mail. No release necessary. No search fee. $.25 fee per copy. $.50 for certification. Search information required: name, date of birth, years to search. Specify plaintiff or defendant.

Mason County

Circuit Court Clerk, Criminal Records
PO Box 402
Point Pleasant, WV 25550
(304) 675-4400

Felony and misdemeanor records are available by mail or phone. No release necessary. No search fee. Search information required: name, years to search.

Civil records are available by mail. No release necessary. No search fee. $.25 fee per copy. Search information required: name, date of birth, years to search. Specify plaintiff or defendant.

McDowell County

Circuit Court Clerk, Criminal Records
PO Box 400
Welch, WV 24801
(304) 436-8332

Felony and misdemeanor records are available by mail or phone. No release necessary. No fee. Search information required: name, date of birth, years to search.

Civil records are available by mail. A release is required. No search fee. $.25 fee per copy. Search information required: name, date of birth, years to search. Specify plaintiff or defendant.

Mercer County

Mercer County Courthouse, Criminal Records
Circuit Court Clerk
1501 W. Main Street
Princeton, WV 24740-2626
(304) 487-8372
Fax (304) 487-8351

Felony and misdemeanor records are available by mail or fax. Call before faxing request. A release is required. No search fee. Search information required: name, SSN, date of birth, SASE.

Civil records are available by mail. No release necessary. No search fee. $.25 fee per copy. $.50 for certification. Search information required: name, date of birth, years to search. Specify plaintiff or defendant.

Mineral County

Clerk of Circuit Court, Criminal Records
Mineral County Courthouse
Keyser, WV 26726
(304) 788-1562

Felony and misdemeanor records are available by mail. No release necessary. No search fee. Search information required: name.

Civil records are available by mail. A release is required. No search fee. $.25 fee per copy. Search information required: name, date of birth, years to search. Specify plaintiff or defendant.

Mingo County

Circuit Court Clerk, Criminal Records
PO Box 435
Williamson, WV 25661
(304) 235-4994

Felony and misdemeanor records are available by mail or phone. No release necessary. No search fee. Search information required: name.

Civil records are available by mail. No release necessary. No search fee. Search information required: name, date of birth, years to search. Specify plaintiff or defendant.

Monongalia County

Monongalia County Courthouse, Criminal Records
Clerk of Circuit Court
Morgantown, WV 26505
(304) 291-7240
Fax (304) 291-7273

Felony and misdemeanor records are available by mail. No release necessary. No search fee. Search information required: name, date of birth, years to search.

Civil records are available in person only. See West Virginia state repository for additional information.

Monroe County

Circuit Court Clerk, Criminal Records
Monroe County Courthouse
Union, WV 24983
(304) 772-3017

Felony and misdemeanor records are available by mail or phone. No release necessary. No search fee. Search information required: name, date of birth, years to search.

Civil records are available by mail or phone. No release necessary. No search fee. $.25 fee per copy. $1.00 for certification. Search information required: name, date of birth, years to search. Specify plaintiff or defendant.

Morgan County

Clerk of Circuit Court, Criminal Records
Morgan County Courthouse
Berkeley Springs, WV 25411
(304) 258-2367

Felony and misdemeanor records are available by mail or phone. No release necessary. No search fee. Postage fee varies. $.25 fee per copy. Search information required: name, date of birth, years to search.

Civil records are available by mail or phone. No release necessary. No search fee. Postage fees varies. $.25 fee per copy. Search information required: name, date of birth, years to search. Specify plaintiff or defendant.

Nicholas County

Circuit Clerk's Office, Criminal Records
Courthouse
700 Main St.
Summersville, WV 26651
(304) 872-3630

Felony and misdemeanor records are available by mail or phone. No release necessary. No search fee. $.25 fee per copy. Search information required: name, sex, years to search.

Civil records are available by mail. A release is required. No search fee. $.25 fee per copy. Search information required: name, date of birth, years to search, SASE. Specify plaintiff or defendant.

Ohio County

Circuit Court Clerk, Criminal Records
1500 Chapline Street
Wheeling, WV 26003
(304) 234-3611

Felony and misdemeanor records are available by mail or phone. No release necessary. No search fee. $.25 fee per copy.

$1.50 for certification. Search information required: name, SSN, date of birth, years to search, SASE.

Civil records are available by mail or phone. No release necessary. No search fee. $.25 fee per copy. $1.50 for certification. Search information required: name, date of birth, years to search, SASE. Specify plaintiff or defendant.

Pendleton County

Circuit Court Clerk, Criminal Records
PO Box 846
Franklin, WV 26807
(304) 358-7067

Felony and misdemeanor records are available by mail or phone. No release necessary. No search fee. Search information required: name, years to search.

Civil records are available by mail. No release necessary. No search fee. $.25 fee per copy. $1.50 for certification. Search information required: name, date of birth, years to search. Specify plaintiff or defendant.

Pleasants County

Circuit Clerk's Office, Criminal Records
Pleasant County Courthouse
301 Courl Lane, Room 201
St. Marys, WV 26170
(304) 684-3513

Felony and misdemeanor records are available by mail or phone. A release is required. No search fee. Search information required: name, years to search.

Civil records are available by mail or phone. No release necessary. No search fee. $.25 fee per copy. Search information required: name, date of birth, years to search. Specify plaintiff or defendant.

Pocahontas County

Circuit Court of Pocahontas County, Criminal Records
900 D, 10th Ave.
Marlinton, WV 24954
(304) 799-4604

Felony and misdemeanor records are available by mail or phone. No release necessary. No search fee. Search information required: name, years to search.

Civil records are available by mail or phone. No release necessary. No search fee. $.25 fee per copy. Search information required: name, date of birth, years to search. Specify plaintiff or defendant.

Preston County

Circuit Clerk, Criminal Records
101 W. Main Street
Kingwood, WV 26537
(304) 329-0047

Felony and misdemeanor records are available by mail or phone. No release necessary. No search fee. $.25 fee per copy. Search information required: name, years to search.

Civil records are available by mali or phone. No release necessary. No search fee. $.25 fee per copy. Search information required: name, date of birth, years to search. Specify plaintiff or defendant.

Putnam County

Circuit Court Clerk, Criminal Records
PO Box 358
Winfield, WV 25213
(304) 586-0203
Fax (304) 586-0200

Felony and misdemeanor records are available by mail, fax or phone. No release necessary. No search fee. Search information required: name, SSN, date of birth, sex, race, years to search.

Civil records are available by mail, fax or phone. No release necessary. No search fee. $.25 fee per copy. Search information required: name, date of birth, years to search. Specify plaintiff or defendant.

Raleigh County

Circuit Clerk's Office, Criminal Records
Raleigh County Courthouse
215 Main St.
Beckley, WV 25801
(304) 255-9135

Felony and misdemeanor records are available by mail or phone. No release necessary. No search fee. $.25 fee per copy. Search information required: name, SSN, date of birth, years to search.

Civil records are available by mail or phone. No release necessary. No search fee. $.25 fee per copy. Search information required: name, date of birth, years to search. Specify plaintiff or defendant.

Randolph County

Circuit Clerk's Office, Criminal Records
Randolph County Courthouse
Elkins, WV 26241
(304) 636-2765

Felony and misdemeanor records are available by mail or phone. No release necessary. No search fee. $.25 fee per copy. Search information required: name, years to search.

Civil records are available by mail or phone. No release necessary. No search fee. $.25 fee per copy. Search information required: name, date of birth, years to search. Specify plaintiff or defendant.

Ritchie County

Clerk of Circuit Court, Criminal Records
Ritchie County Courthouse
Harrisville, WV 26362
(304) 643-2163

Felony and misdemeanor records are available by mail or phone. No release necessary. No search fee. Search information required: name, years to search.

Civil records are available by mail or phone. No release necessary. No search fee. $.25 fee per copy. $.50 for certification. Search information required: name, date of birth, years to search. Specify plaintiff or defendant.

Roane County

Circuit Court Clerk, Criminal Records
PO Box 122
Spencer, WV 25276
(304) 927-2750

Felony and misdemeanor records are available by mail or phone. No release necessary. No search fee. $.25 fee per copy. Search information required: name, date of birth, years to search.

Civil records are available by mail. No release necessary. No search fee. $.25 fee per copy. Search information required: name, date of birth, years to search. Specify plaintiff or defendant.

Summers County

Circuit Clerk's Office, Criminal Records
PO Box 1058
Hinton, WV 25951
(304) 466-7103

Felony and misdemeanor records are available by mail or phone. A release is required. No search fee. Search information required: name.

Civil records are available by mail or phone. No release necessary. No search fee. $.25 fee per copy. Search information required: name, date of birth, SSN, years to search. Specify plaintiff or defendant.

Taylor County

Circuit Court Clerk, Criminal Records
Taylor County Courthouse
Grafton, WV 26354
(304) 265-2480
Fax (304) 265-3016

Felony records are available by mail, fax or phone. No release necessary. No search fee. Search information required: name, date of birth.

Civil records are available by mail or fax. No release necessary. No search fee. $.25 fee per copy. $.50 for certification. Search information required: name, date of birth, years to search. Specify plaintiff or defendant.

Tucker County

Circuit Clerk's Office, Criminal Records
215 First St.
Parsons, WV 26287
(304) 478-2606

Felony and misdemeanor records are available by mail or phone. No release necessary. No search fee. Search information required: name, years to search.

Civil records are available by mail or phone. No release necessary. No search fee. $.25 fee per copy. Search information required: name, date of birth, years to search. Specify plaintiff or defendant.

Tyler County

Circuit Court Clerk, Criminal Records
PO Box 8
Middlebourne, WV 26149
(304) 758-4811

Felony and misdemeanor records are available by mail or phone. No release necessary. No search fee. Search information required: name, years to search.

Civil records are available by mail. No release necessary. No search fee. $.25 fee per copy. Search information required: name, date of birth, years to search. Specify plaintiff or defendant.

Upshur County

Upshur County Courthouse, Criminal Records
Circuit Clerk's Office
Main Street
Buckhannon, WV 26201
(304) 472-2370

Felony and misdemeanor records are available by mail or phone. No release necessary. No search fee. Search information required: name.

Civil records are available by mail. or phone No release necessary. No search fee. $.25 fee per copy. $.50 for certification. Search information required: name, date of birth, years to search. Specify plaintiff or defendant.

Wayne County

Circuit Court Clerk, Criminal Records
PO Box 38
Wayne, WV 25570
(304) 272-5101

Felony and misdemeanor records are available by mail or phone. No release necessary. No search fee. $.50 fee per copy. Search information required: name, years to search.

Civil records are available by mail or phone. No release necessary. No search fee. $.25 fee per copy. Search information required: name, date of birth, years to search. Specify plaintiff or defendant.

Webster County

Webster County Courthouse, Criminal Records
Circuit Clerk's Office
Webster Springs, WV 26288
(304) 847-2421

Felony and misdemeanor records are available by mail or phone. No release necessary. No search fee. $.25 fee per copy. Search information required: name, date of birth, years to search.

Civil records are available by mail. No release necessary. No search fee. $.25 fee per copy. Search information required: name, date of birth, years to search. Specify plaintiff or defendant.

Wetzel County

Circuit Court Clerk, Criminal Records
PO Box 263
New Martinsville, WV 26155
(304) 455-1420

Felony and misdemeanor records are available by mail or phone. No release necessary. No search fee. Search information required: name, SSN, date of birth, sex, race, previous address.

Civil records are available by mail. No release necessary. No search fee. $.25 fee per copy. Search information required: name, date of birth, years to search. Specify plaintiff or defendant.

Wirt County

Wirt County Circuit Clerk
PO Box 465
Elizabeth, WV 26143
(304) 275-6597

Felony and misdemeanor records are available by mail or phone. No release necessary. No search fee. $.25 fee per copy. Search information required: name, date of birth, years to search.

Civil records are available by mail. No release necessary. No search fee. $.25 fee per copy. $.50 for certification. Search information required: name, date of birth, years to search, SASE. Specify plaintiff or defendant.

Wood County

Wood County Clerk of Circuit Court, Criminal Records
PO Box 1701
Parkersburg, WV 26101
(304) 424-1700
Felony and misdemeanor records are available by mail or phone. No release necessary. No search fee. Search information required: name, years to search.

Civil records are available by mail. No release necessary. No search fee. $.25 fee per copy. $.50 for certification. Search information required: name, date of birth, years to search. Specify plaintiff or defendant.

Wyoming County

Circuit Court Clerk, Criminal Records
PO Box 529
Pineville, WV 24874
(304) 732-8000 Extension 238
Felony and misdemeanor records are available in person only. See West Virginia state repository for additional information.

Civil records are available in person only. See West Virginia state repository for additional information.

City-County Cross Reference

Accoville *Logan*
Adrian *Upshur*
Advent *Jackson*
Albright *Preston*
Alderson *Monroe*
Algoma *McDowell*
Alkol *Lincoln*
Allen Junction *Wyoming*
Alloy *Fayette*
Alma *Tyler*
Alpoca *Wyoming*
Alum Bridge *Lewis*
Alum Creek *Kanawha*
Alvy *Tyler*
Ameagle *Raleigh*
Amherstdale *Logan*
Amigo *Wyoming*
Amma *Roane*
Anawalt *McDowell*
Anmoore *Harrison*
Annamoriah *Calhoun*
Ansted *Fayette*
Anthony *Greenbrier*
Apple Grove *Mason*
Arbovale *Pocahontas*
Arnett *Raleigh*
Arnoldsburg *Calhoun*
Arthur *Grant*
Arthurdale *Preston*
Artie *Raleigh*
Asbury *Greenbrier*
Asco *McDowell*
Ashford *Boone*
Ashland *McDowell*
Ashton *Mason*
Athens *Mercer*
Auburn *Ritchie*
Augusta *Hampshire*
Aurora *Preston*
Auto *Greenbrier*
Avondale *McDowell*
Baisden *Mingo*
Baker *Hardy*
Bald Knob *Boone*
Ballard *Monroe*
Ballengee *Summers*
Bancroft *Putnam*
Bandytown *Boone*
Barboursville *Cabell*
Barnabus *Logan*
Barrackville *Marion*
Barrett *Boone*
Bartley *McDowell*
Bartow *Pocahontas*

Bayard *Grant*
Beards Fork *Fayette*
Beaver *Raleigh*
Beckley *Raleigh*
Beckwith *Fayette*
Beech Bottom *Brooke*
Beeson *Mercer*
Belington *Barbour*
Belle *Kanawha*
Belleville *Wood*
Belmont *Pleasants*
Belva *Nicholas*
Bens Run *Tyler*
Bentree *Clay*
Benwood *Marshall*
Berea *Ritchie*
Bergoo *Webster*
Berkeley Springs *Morgan*
Berwind *McDowell*
Bethany *Brooke*
Bethlehem *Marshall*
Beverly *Randolph*
Bickmore *Clay*
Bigbend *Calhoun*
Big Chimney *Kanawha*
Big Creek *Logan*
Big Run *Wetzel*
Big Sandy *McDowell*
Big Springs *Calhoun*
Bim *Boone*
Birch River *Nicholas*
Blacksville *Monongalia*
Blair *Logan*
Blandville *Doddridge*
Blennerhassett *Wood*
Bloomery *Hampshire*
Bloomingrose *Boone*
Blount *Kanawha*
Blue Creek *Kanawha*
Bluefield *Mercer*
Blue Jay *Raleigh*
Bob White *Boone*
Boggs *Webster*
Bolivar *Jefferson*
Bolt *Raleigh*
Bomont *Clay*
Boomer *Fayette*
Booth *Monongalia*
Borderland *Mingo*
Bowden *Randolph*
Bozoo *Monroe*
Bradley *Raleigh*
Bradshaw *McDowell*
Bramwell *Mercer*

Branchland *Lincoln*
Brandonville *Preston*
Brandywine *Pendleton*
Breeden *Mingo*
Brenton *Wyoming*
Bretz *Preston*
Bridgeport *Harrison*
Bristol *Harrison*
Brohard *Wirt*
Brooks *Summers*
Brownton *Barbour*
Bruceton Mills *Preston*
Bruno *Logan*
Buckeye *Pocahontas*
Buckhannon *Upshur*
Bud *Wyoming*
Buffalo *Putnam*
Bunker Hill *Berkeley*
Burlington *Mineral*
Burnsville *Braxton*
Burnwell *Kanawha*
Burton *Wetzel*
Cabin Creek *Kanawha*
Cabins *Grant*
Cairo *Ritchie*
Caldwell *Greenbrier*
Calvin *Nicholas*
Camden *Lewis*
Camden On Gauley *Webster*
Cameron *Marshall*
Camp Creek *Mercer*
Canebrake *McDowell*
Cannelton *Fayette*
Canvas *Nicholas*
Capels *McDowell*
Capon Bridge *Hampshire*
Capon Springs *Hampshire*
Carbon *Kanawha*
Caretta *McDowell*
Carolina *Marion*
Cass *Pocahontas*
Cassville *Monongalia*
Cedar Grove *Kanawha*
Cedarville *Gilmer*
Center Point *Doddridge*
Centralia *Braxton*
Century *Barbour*
Ceredo *Wayne*
Chapmanville *Logan*
Charleston *Kanawha*
Charles Town *Jefferson*
Charlton Heights *Fayette*
Charmco *Greenbrier*

Chattaroy *Mingo*
Chauncey *Logan*
Cherry Grove *Pendleton*
Chesapeake *Kanawha*
Chester *Hancock*
Chloe *Calhoun*
Circleville *Pendleton*
Clarksburg *Harrison*
Clay *Clay*
Clear Creek *Raleigh*
Clear Fork *Wyoming*
Clearview *Ohio*
Clendenin *Kanawha*
Clifton *Mason*
Clintonville *Greenbrier*
Clio *Roane*
Clothier *Logan*
Coal City *Raleigh*
Coaldale *Mercer*
Coal Mountain *Wyoming*
Coalton *Randolph*
Coalwood *McDowell*
Colcord *Raleigh*
Colfax *Marion*
Colliers *Brooke*
Comfort *Boone*
Cool Ridge *Raleigh*
Cora *Logan*
Core *Monongalia*
Corinne *Wyoming*
Corinth *Preston*
Corley *Braxton*
Corton *Kanawha*
Costa *Boone*
Cottageville *Jackson*
Cottle *Nicholas*
Cove Gap *Wayne*
Covel *Wyoming*
Cowen *Webster*
Coxs Mills *Gilmer*
Crab Orchard *Raleigh*
Craigsville *Nicholas*
Cranberry *Raleigh*
Crawford *Lewis*
Crawley *Greenbrier*
Creston *Wirt*
Crichton *Greenbrier*
Cross Lanes *Kanawha*
Crown Hill *Kanawha*
Crum *Wayne*
Crumpler *McDowell*
Cucumber *McDowell*
Culloden *Cabell*
Curtin *Webster*

Cuzzart *Preston*
Cyclone *Wyoming*
Dailey *Randolph*
Dallas *Marshall*
Danese *Fayette*
Daniels *Raleigh*
Danville *Boone*
Davin *Logan*
Davis *Tucker*
Davisville *Wood*
Davy *McDowell*
Dawes *Kanawha*
Dawmont *Harrison*
Dawson *Greenbrier*
Deep Water *Fayette*
Dehue *Logan*
Delbarton *Mingo*
Dellslow *Monongalia*
Delray *Hampshire*
Despard *Harrison*
Diana *Webster*
Dille *Clay*
Dingess *Mingo*
Dixie *Nicholas*
Dorcas *Grant*
Dorothy *Raleigh*
Dothan *Fayette*
Dott *Mercer*
Drennen *Nicholas*
Droop *Pocahontas*
Drybranch *Kanawha*
Dry Creek *Raleigh*
Dryfork *Randolph*
Duck *Clay*
Duhring *Mercer*
Dunbar *Kanawha*
Duncan *Jackson*
Dunlow *Wayne*
Dunmore *Pocahontas*
Durbin *Pocahontas*
Earling *Logan*
East Bank *Kanawha*
East Lynn *Wayne*
Eccles *Raleigh*
Eckman *McDowell*
Edgarton *Mingo*
Edmond *Fayette*
Eglon *Preston*
Elbert *McDowell*
Eleanor *Putnam*
Elgood *Mercer*
Elizabeth *Wirt*
Elk Garden *Mineral*
Elkhorn *McDowell*
Elkins *Randolph*
Elkview *Kanawha*
Ellamore *Randolph*
Ellenboro *Ritchie*
Elm Grove *Ohio*
Elmira *Braxton*
Elton *Summers*
Emmett *Logan*
English *McDowell*
Enterprise *Harrison*
Erbacon *Webster*
Eskdale *Kanawha*
Ethel *Logan*
Eureka *Pleasants*
Evans *Jackson*
Everettville *Monongalia*
Exchange *Braxton*
Fairdale *Raleigh*
Fairmont *Marion*
Fairview *Marion*
Falling Rock *Kanawha*

Falling Waters *Berkeley*
Falls Mill *Braxton*
Fanrock *Wyoming*
Farmington *Marion*
Fayetteville *Fayette*
Fenwick *Nicholas*
Ferrellsburg *Lincoln*
Filbert *McDowell*
Fisher *Hardy*
Five Forks *Calhoun*
Flat Top *Mercer*
Flatwoods *Braxton*
Flemington *Taylor*
Floe *Clay*
Fola *Clay*
Follansbee *Brooke*
Folsom *Wetzel*
Forest Hill *Summers*
Fort Ashby *Mineral*
Fort Gay *Wayne*
Fort Seybert *Pendleton*
Fort Spring *Greenbrier*
Foster *Boone*
Four States *Marion*
Frametown *Braxton*
Frankford *Greenbrier*
Franklin *Pendleton*
Fraziers Bottom *Putnam*
Freeman *Mercer*
French Creek *Upshur*
Friars Hill *Greenbrier*
Friendly *Tyler*
Gallagher *Kanawha*
Gallipolis Ferry *Mason*
Galloway *Barbour*
Gandeeville *Roane*
Gap Mills *Monroe*
Garrison *Boone*
Gary *McDowell*
Gassaway *Braxton*
Gauley Bridge *Fayette*
Gay *Jackson*
Gem *Braxton*
Genoa *Wayne*
Gerrardstown *Berkeley*
Ghent *Raleigh*
Gilbert *Mingo*
Gilboa *Nicholas*
Gilliam *McDowell*
Gilmer *Gilmer*
Given *Jackson*
Glace *Monroe*
Glady *Randolph*
Glasgow *Kanawha*
Glen *Clay*
Glen Dale *Marshall*
Glen Daniel *Raleigh*
Glendon *Braxton*
Glen Easton *Marshall*
Glen Ferris *Fayette*
Glen Fork *Wyoming*
Glengary *Berkeley*
Glenhayes *Wayne*
Glen Jean *Fayette*
Glen Morgan *Raleigh*
Glen Rogers *Wyoming*
Glenville *Gilmer*
Glen White *Raleigh*
Glenwood *Mason*
Gordon *Boone*
Gormania *Grant*
Grafton *Taylor*
Grantsville *Calhoun*
Grant Town *Marion*
Granville *Monongalia*

Grassy Meadows
   Greenbrier
Great Cacapon *Morgan*
Green Bank *Pocahontas*
Green Spring *Hampshire*
Green Sulphur Springs
   Summers
Greenville *Monroe*
Greenwood *Doddridge*
Griffithsville *Lincoln*
Grimms Landing *Mason*
Guardian *Webster*
Guthrie *Kanawha*
Gypsy *Harrison*
Hacker Valley *Webster*
Halltown *Jefferson*
Hambleton *Tucker*
Hamlin *Lincoln*
Hampden *Mingo*
Hancock *Morgan*
Handley *Kanawha*
Hanover *Wyoming*
Hansford *Kanawha*
Harman *Randolph*
Harmony *Roane*
Harper *Raleigh*
Harpers Ferry *Jefferson*
Harrison *Clay*
Harrisville *Ritchie*
Hartford *Mason*
Harts *Lincoln*
Harvey *Fayette*
Havaco *McDowell*
Haywood *Harrison*
Hazelgreen *Ritchie*
Hazelton *Preston*
Heaters *Braxton*
Hebron *Pleasants*
Hedgesville *Berkeley*
Helen *Raleigh*
Helvetia *Randolph*
Hemphill *McDowell*
Henderson *Mason*
Hendricks *Tucker*
Henlawson *Logan*
Hensley *McDowell*
Hepzibah *Harrison*
Herndon *Wyoming*
Hernshaw *Kanawha*
Hewett *Boone*
Hiawatha *Mercer*
Hico *Fayette*
High View *Hampshire*
Hillsboro *Pocahontas*
Hilltop *Fayette*
Hines *Greenbrier*
Hinton *Summers*
Holden *Logan*
Hometown *Putnam*
Horner *Lewis*
Hugheston *Kanawha*
Hundred *Wetzel*
Huntington *Cabell*
Hurricane *Putnam*
Huttonsville *Randolph*
Iaeger *McDowell*
Idamay *Marion*
Ikes Fork *Wyoming*
Independence *Preston*
Indian Mills *Summers*
Indore *Clay*
Industrial *Harrison*
Institute *Kanawha*
Inwood *Berkeley*
Ireland *Lewis*

Isaban *McDowell*
Itmann *Wyoming*
Ivydale *Clay*
Jacksonburg *Wetzel*
Jane Lew *Lewis*
Jeffrey *Boone*
Jenkinjones *McDowell*
Jesse *Wyoming*
Jodie *Fayette*
Jolo *McDowell*
Jonben *Raleigh*
Josephine *Raleigh*
Julian *Boone*
Jumping Branch *Summers*
Junction *Hampshire*
Junior *Barbour*
Justice *Mingo*
Kanawha Falls *Fayette*
Kanawha Head *Upshur*
Kearneysville *Jefferson*
Kegley *Mercer*
Kellysville *Mercer*
Kenna *Jackson*
Kenova *Wayne*
Kentuck *Jackson*
Kerens *Randolph*
Kermit *Mingo*
Keslers Cross Lanes
   Nicholas
Keyser *Mineral*
Keystone *McDowell*
Kiahsville *Wayne*
Kieffer *Greenbrier*
Kilsyth *Fayette*
Kimball *McDowell*
Kimberly *Fayette*
Kincaid *Fayette*
Kingmont *Marion*
Kingston *Fayette*
Kingwood *Preston*
Kirby *Hampshire*
Kistler *Logan*
Kopperston *Wyoming*
Kyle *McDowell*
Lahmansville *Grant*
Lake *Logan*
Lakin *Mason*
Lanark *Raleigh*
Landville *Logan*
Lansing *Fayette*
Lashmeet *Mercer*
Lavalette *Wayne*
Layland *Fayette*
Leckie *McDowell*
Leet *Lincoln*
Leewood *Kanawha*
Left Hand *Roane*
Leivasy *Nicholas*
Lenore *Mingo*
Leon *Mason*
Lerona *Mercer*
Le Roy *Jackson*
Lesage *Cabell*
Leslie *Greenbrier*
Lester *Raleigh*
Letart *Mason*
Letter Gap *Gilmer*
Levels *Hampshire*
Lewisburg *Greenbrier*
Liberty *Putnam*
Lima *Tyler*
Linden *Roane*
Lindside *Monroe*
Linn *Gilmer*
Little Birch *Braxton*

Littleton *Wetzel*
Liverpool *Jackson*
Lizemores *Clay*
Lobata *Mingo*
Lochgelly *Fayette*
Lockbridge *Summers*
Lockney *Gilmer*
Logan *Logan*
London *Kanawha*
Long Branch *Fayette*
Lookout *Fayette*
Looneyville *Roane*
Lorado *Logan*
Lorentz *Upshur*
Lost City *Hardy*
Lost Creek *Harrison*
Lost River *Hardy*
Lubeck *Wood*
Lumberport *Harrison*
Lundale *Logan*
Lyburn *Logan*
Lynco *Wyoming*
McComas *Mercer*
McConnell *Logan*
McDowell *McDowell*
McGraws *Wyoming*
McMechen *Marshall*
McWhorter *Harrison*
Maben *Wyoming*
Mabie *Randolph*
Mabscott *Raleigh*
Mac Arthur *Raleigh*
Macfarlan *Ritchie*
Madison *Boone*
Mahan *Fayette*
Maidsville *Monongalia*
Malden *Kanawha*
Mallory *Logan*
Mammoth *Kanawha*
Man *Logan*
Mannington *Marion*
Maplewood *Fayette*
Marfrance *Greenbrier*
Marlinton *Pocahontas*
Marlowe *Berkley*
Marmet *Kanawha*
Martinsburg *Berkeley*
Mason *Mason*
Masontown *Preston*
Matewan *Mingo*
Matheny *Wyoming*
Mathias *Hardy*
Matoaka *Mercer*
Maxwelton *Greenbrier*
Maybeury *McDowell*
Maysel *Clay*
Maysville *Grant*
Mead *Raleigh*
Meador *Mingo*
Meadow Bluff *Greenbrier*
Meadow Bridge *Fayette*
Meadowbrook *Harrison*
Meadow Creek *Summers*
Medley *Grant*
Metz *Marion*
Miami *Kanawha*
Middlebourne *Tyler*
Midkiff *Lincoln*
Midway *Raleigh*
Milam *Hardy*
Mill Creek *Randolph*
Mill Point *Pocahontas*
Millstone *Calhoun*
Millville *Jefferson*
Millwood *Jackson*

Milton *Cabell*
Minden *Fayette*
Mineralwells *Wood*
Mingo *Randolph*
Minnehaha Springs
   Pocahontas
Moatsville *Barbour*
Mohawk *McDowell*
Monaville *Logan*
Monongah *Marion*
Montana Mines *Marion*
Montcalm *Mercer*
Montcoal *Raleigh*
Monterville *Randolph*
Montgomery *Fayette*
Montrose *Randolph*
Moorefield *Hardy*
Morgantown *Monongalia*
Morrisvale *Boone*
Moundsville *Marshall*
Mountain *Ritchie*
Mount Alto *Jackson*
Mount Carbon *Fayette*
Mount Clare *Harrison*
Mount Gay *Logan*
Mount Hope *Fayette*
Mount Lookout *Nicholas*
Mount Nebo *Nicholas*
Mount Storm *Grant*
Mount Zion *Calhoun*
Moyers *Pendleton*
Mullens *Wyoming*
Munday *Wirt*
Murraysville *Jackson*
Myra *Lincoln*
Myrtle *Mingo*
Nallen *Fayette*
Naoma *Raleigh*
Napier *Braxton*
Naugatuck *Mingo*
Nebo *Clay*
Nellis *Boone*
Nemours *Mercer*
Nettie *Nicholas*
Newberne *Gilmer*
Newburg *Preston*
New Creek *Mineral*
New Cumberland *Hancock*
Newell *Hancock*
Newhall *McDowell*
New Haven *Mason*
New Manchester *Hancock*
New Martinsville *Wetzel*
New Milton *Doddridge*
New Richmond *Wyoming*
Newton *Roane*
Newtown *Mingo*
Nicut *Calhoun*
Nimitz *Summers*
Nitro *Kanawha*
Nolan *Mingo*
Normantown *Gilmer*
Northfork *McDowell*
North Matewan *Mingo*
North Spring *Wyoming*
Norton *Randolph*
Nutter Fort *Harrison*
Oak Hill *Fayette*
Oceana *Wyoming*
Odd *Raleigh*
Ohley *Kanawha*
Old Fields *Hardy*
Omar *Logan*
Ona *Cabell*
Onego *Pendleton*

Orgas *Boone*
Orlando *Lewis*
Orma *Calhoun*
Osage *Monongalia*
Ottawa *Boone*
Ovapa *Clay*
Paden City *Wetzel*
Page *Fayette*
Pageton *McDowell*
Palermo *Lincoln*
Palestine *Wirt*
Panther *McDowell*
Parcoal *Webster*
Parkersburg *Wood*
Parsons *Tucker*
Paw Paw *Morgan*
Pax *Fayette*
Paynesville *McDowell*
Peach Creek *Logan*
Pecks Mill *Logan*
Pemberton *Raleigh*
Pence Springs *Summers*
Pennsboro *Ritchie*
Pentress *Monongalia*
Perkins *Gilmer*
Petersburg *Grant*
Peterstown *Monroe*
Petroleum *Ritchie*
Peytona *Boone*
Philippi *Barbour*
Pickaway *Monroe*
Pickens *Randolph*
Piedmont *Mineral*
Pinch *Kanawha*
Pine Grove *Wetzel*
Pineville *Wyoming*
Piney View *Raleigh*
Pipestem *Summers*
Pleasant Valley *Marion*
Pliny *Putnam*
Poca *Putnam*
Pocatalico *Putnam*
Poe *Nicholas*
Point Pleasant *Mason*
Points *Hampshire*
Pond Gap *Kanawha*
Pool *Nicholas*
Porters Falls *Wetzel*
Powellton *Fayette*
Powhatan *McDowell*
Pratt *Kanawha*
Premier *McDowell*
Prenter *Boone*
Prichard *Wayne*
Prince *Fayette*
Princeton *Mercer*
Princewick *Raleigh*
Procious *Clay*
Proctor *Wetzel*
Prosperity *Raleigh*
Pullman *Ritchie*
Purgitsville *Hampshire*
Pursglove *Monongalia*
Quinnimont *Fayette*
Quinwood *Greenbrier*
Rachel *Marion*
Racine *Boone*
Radnor *Wayne*
Ragland *Mingo*
Rainelle *Greenbrier*
Raleigh *Raleigh*
Ramage *Boone*
Ramsey *Fayette*
Rand *Kanawha*
Ranger *Lincoln*

Ranson *Jefferson*
Ravencliff *Wyoming*
Ravenswood *Jackson*
Rawl *Mingo*
Raysal *McDowell*
Reader *Wetzel*
Red Creek *Tucker*
Red House *Putnam*
Red Jacket *Mingo*
Redstar *Fayette*
Reedsville *Preston*
Reedy *Roane*
Renick *Greenbrier*
Replete *Webster*
Reynoldsville *Harrison*
Rhodell *Raleigh*
Richwood *Nicholas*
Ridgeley *Mineral*
Ridgeview *Boone*
Ridgeway *Berkeley*
Rio *Hampshire*
Ripley *Jackson*
Rippon *Jefferson*
Riverton *Pendleton*
Rivesville *Marion*
Roanoke *Lewis*
Robertsburg *Putnam*
Robinette *Logan*
Robson *Fayette*
Rock *Mercer*
Rock Castle *Jackson*
Rock Cave *Upshur*
Rock Creek *Raleigh*
Rockport *Wood*
Rock View *Wyoming*
Roderfield *McDowell*
Romney *Hampshire*
Ronceverte *Greenbrier*
Rosedale *Gilmer*
Rosemont *Taylor*
Rossmore *Logan*
Rowlesburg *Preston*
Runa *Nicholas*
Rupert *Greenbrier*
Russellville *Greenbrier*
Sabine *Wyoming*
Saint Albans *Kanawha*
Saint George *Tucker*
Saint Marys *Pleasants*
Salem *Harrison*
Salt Rock *Cabell*
Sand Fork *Gilmer*
Sand Ridge *Calhoun*
Sandstone *Summers*
Sandyville *Jackson*
Sarah Ann *Logan*
Sarton *Monroe*
Saxon *Raleigh*
Scarbro *Fayette*
Scott Depot *Putnam*
Secondcreek *Monroe*
Seebert *Pocahontas*
Selbyville *Upshur*
Seneca Rocks *Pendleton*
Seth *Boone*
Shady Spring *Raleigh*
Shanks *Hampshire*
Sharon *Kanawha*
Sharples *Logan*
Shenandoah Junction
   Jefferson
Shepherdstown *Jefferson*
Sherman *Jackson*
Shinnston *Harrison*
Shirley *Tyler*

Shoals *Wayne*
Shock *Gilmer*
Short Creek *Brooke*
Sias *Lincoln*
Simon *Wyoming*
Simpson *Taylor*
Sinks Grove *Monroe*
Sissonville *Kanawha*
Sistersville *Tyler*
Skelton *Raleigh*
Skygusty *McDowell*
Slab Fork *Raleigh*
Slanesville *Hampshire*
Slatyfork *Pocahontas*
Smithburg *Doddridge*
Smithers *Fayette*
Smithfield *Wetzel*
Smithville *Ritchie*
Smoot *Greenbrier*
Sod *Lincoln*
Sophia *Raleigh*
South Charleston *Kanawha*
Southside *Mason*
Spanishburg *Mercer*
Spelter *Harrison*
Spencer *Roane*
Sprigg *Mingo*
Spring Dale *Fayette*
Springfield *Hampshire*
Spring Valley *Wayne*
Spurlockville *Lincoln*
Squire *McDowell*
Stanaford *Raleigh*
Statts Mills *Jackson*
Stephenson *Wyoming*
Stickney *Raleigh*
Stirrat *Logan*
Stollings *Logan*
Stonewood *Harrison*
Stony Bottom *Pocahontas*
Stouts Mills *Gilmer*
Strange Creek *Braxton*
Streeter *Summers*
Stumptown *Gilmer*
Sugar Grove *Pendleton*
Sumerco *Lincoln*
Summerlee *Fayette*
Summersville *Nicholas*
Summit Point *Jefferson*
Sundial *Raleigh*
Superior *McDowell*
Surveyor *Raleigh*
Sutton *Braxton*
Sweetland *Lincoln*
Sweet Springs *Monroe*
Swiss *Nicholas*
Switchback *McDowell*
Switzer *Logan*
Sylvester *Boone*
Tad *Kanawha*
Talcott *Summers*
Tallmansville *Upshur*
Tams *Raleigh*
Tanner *Gilmer*
Taplin *Logan*
Tariff *Roane*
Teays *Putnam*
Terra Alta *Preston*
Terry *Raleigh*
Tesla *Braxton*
Thacker *Mingo*
Thomas *Tucker*
Thornton *Taylor*
Thorpe *McDowell*
Three Churches *Hampshire*

Thurmond *Fayette*
Tioga *Nicholas*
Tornado *Kanawha*
Triadelphia *Ohio*
Trout *Greenbrier*
Troy *Gilmer*
True *Summers*
Tunnelton *Preston*
Turtle Creek *Boone*
Twilight *Boone*
Twin Branch *McDowell*
Uler *Roane*
Uneeda *Boone*
Unger *Morgan*
Union *Monroe*
Upperglade *Webster*
Upper Tract *Pendleton*
Vadis *Lewis*
Valley Bend *Randolph*
Valley Chapel *Lewis*
Valley Fork *Clay*
Valley Grove *Ohio*
Valley Head *Randolph*
Vallscreek *McDowell*
Van *Boone*
Varney *Mingo*
Verdunville *Logan*
Verner *Mingo*
Victor *Fayette*
Vienna *Wood*
Vivian *McDowell*
Volga *Barbour*
Vulcan *Mingo*
Wadestown *Monongalia*
Waiteville *Monroe*
Walker *Wood*
Walkersville *Lewis*
Wallace *Harrison*
Wallback *Clay*
Walton *Roane*
Wana *Monongalia*
War *McDowell*
Wardensville *Hardy*
Warriormine *McDowell*
Washington *Wood*
Waverly *Wood*
Wayne *Wayne*
Wayside *Monroe*
Webster Springs *Webster*
Weirton *Hancock*
Welch *McDowell*
Wellsburg *Brooke*
West Columbia *Mason*
West Hamlin *Lincoln*
West Liberty *Ohio*
West Logan *Logan*
West Milford *Harrison*
Weston *Lewis*
Westover *Monongalia*
West Pea Ridge *Cabell*
West Union *Doddridge*
Wharncliffe *Mingo*
Wharton *Boone*
Wheeling *Ohio*
Whitby *Raleigh*
White Oak *Raleigh*
White Sulphur Springs
    Greenbrier
Whitesville *Boone*
Whitman *Logan*
Whitmer *Randolph*
Whittaker *Kanawha*
Wick *Tyler*
Widen *Clay*
Wilbur *Tyler*

Wilcoe *McDowell*
Wiley Ford *Mineral*
Wileyville *Wetzel*
Wilkinson *Logan*
Williamsburg *Greenbrier*
Williamson *Mingo*
Williamstown *Wood*
Willow Island *Pleasants*
Wilsie *Braxton*
Wilson *Grant*
Wilsondale *Wayne*
Windsor Heights *Brooke*
Winfield *Putnam*
Winifrede *Kanawha*
Winona *Fayette*
Wolfcreek *Monroe*
Wolfe *Mercer*
Wolf Pen *Wyoming*
Wolf Summit *Harrison*
Woodville *Lincoln*
Worth *McDowell*
Worthington *Marion*
Wyatt *Harrison*
Wyco *Wyoming*
Wymer *Randolph*
Wyoming *Wyoming*
Yawkey *Lincoln*
Yellow Spring *Hampshire*
Yolyn *Logan*
Yukon *McDowell*

Wisconsin

Both the Wisconsin Crime Information Bureau and seventy one (71) of the state's seventy two (72) counties report that criminal records are available for employment screening purposes by phone or mail. Twenty seven (27) counties reported that requests may be submitted by fax. Claims for civil suits are split between Circuit and Small Claims with a monetary value of $2,000.

For more information or for offices not listed, contact the state's information hot line at (608) 266-2211.

Driving Records

Wisconsin Department of Transportation
Driver Record Files
PO Box 7918
Madison, WI 53707-7918
(608) 266-2353
Driving records are available by mail. $2.00 fee per request. Turnaround time is 24 hours. Written request must include job applicant's full name, date of birth and license number. Make check payable to Registration Fee Trust.

Worker's Compensation Records

Worker's Compensation Department
PO Box 7901
Madison, WI 53707
(608) 266-1340
Worker's compensation records are not available for pre-employment screening purposes. Records are only available to employees involved in the claim.

Vital Statistics

Bureau of Health Statistics
Wisconsin Division of Health
PO Box 309
Madison, WI 53701
(608) 266-1371
Birth records are available for $10.00 and death records are available for $7.00. State Office has scattered records earlier than 1857. Records before October 1, 1907, are very incomplete. Duplicate copies at the time of the initial request are $2.00 each. An employer can obtain records with a written release. Make check or money order payable to Center for Health Statistics.

Marriage records are available. Fee of $7.00, plus $2.00 for each additional copy. Send self addressed, stamped envelope. Include name, marriage date, maiden name, city and county where married. Specify relationship to either party or other reason for request. Divorce records are available. Fee of $7.00, $2.00 each additional copy. Include name, maiden name, divorce date, city and county. Specify relationship to either party or other reason for request.

Department of Education

Department of Public Instruction
Bureau for Teacher Education, Licensing and Placement
PO Box 7841
Madison, WI 53707
Fax (608) 267-1052
Field of certification is available by phone or mail. Include name and SSN.

Medical Licensing

Medical Board
PO Box 8935
Madison, WI 53708
(608) 266-1626
Will confirm licenses for MDs, DOs, PODs, and VET by phone or mail. No fee. For licenses not mentioned, contact the above office.

Wisconsin Bureau of Health Professions
PO Box 8935
Madison, WI 53708-8935
(608) 266-3735
Will confirm license by phone. No fee. Include name, license number, if available.

Bar Association

Wisconsin State Bar Association
PO Box 7158
Madison, WI 53707
(608) 257-3838
Will confirm licenses by phone. No fee. Include name.

Accountancy Board

Wisconsin State Board of Accountancy
Department of Registration & Licensing
PO Box 8935
Madison, WI 53708
(608) 266-2112
Will confirm license by phone. No fee. Include name.

Securities Commission

Office of Commissioner of Securities
111 West Wilson Street
Madison, WI 53703
(608) 266-3693
Will confirm license by phone. No fee. Include name and SSN.

Secretary of State

Secretary of State Wisconsin Corporation Division
PO Box 7846
Madison, WI 53707
(608) 266-3590
Service agent and address and date incorporated are available by phone or mail. Contact the above office for additional information.

Criminal Records

State Repository

Crime Information Bureau
Attention: Records
PO Box 2718
Madison, WI 53701-2718
(608) 266-7314
All written requests must include full name, date of birth, race, sex, SASE and, if available, SSN. $10.00 search fee. Check payable to Wisconsin Department of Justice. Turnaround time is 3-5 working days.

Adams County

Clerk of Circuit Court, Criminal Records
PO Box 220
Friendship, WI 53934
(608) 339-4208
Fax (608) 339-6414
Felony and misdemeanor records are available by mail or fax. No release necessary. $5.00 base fee. Additional $5.00 fee is charged if record is found. $1.25 fee per copy. $5.00 for certification. Make check payable to Clerk of Circuit Court. Search information required: name.

Civil records are available by mail or fax. No release necessary. $5.00 fee for each record found. Additional $5.00 fee is charged if record is found. $1.25 fee per copy. $5.00 for certification. Search information required: name, date of birth, years to search. Specify plaintiff or defendant.

Ashland County

Clerk of Circuit Court, Criminal Records
Ashland County Courthouse
201 W. Main, Room 307
Ashland, WI 54806
(715) 682-7016
Felony and misdemeanor records are available by mail. No release necessary. $5.00 fee. $1.25 fee per copy. $5.00 for certification. Certified check only, payable to Clerk of Circuit Court. Search information required: name, date of birth.

Civil records are available by mail. No release necessary. No search fee. $1.25 fee per copy. $5.00 for certification. Search information required: name, date of birth, years to search. Specify plaintiff or defendant.

Barron County

Barron County Courthouse, Criminal Records
Clerk of Circuit Court
330 E. LaSalle
Barron, WI 54812
(715) 537-6265
Records are not available by mail or phone. See Wisconsin state repository.

Civil records are available in person. See Wisconsin state repository for additional information.

Bayfield County

Clerk of Circuit Court, Criminal Records
117 E. 5th
PO Box 536
Washburn, WI 54891
(715) 373-6108
Felony and misdemeanor records are available by mail. No release necessary. $5.00 search fee. $1.25 fee per copy. $5.00 for certification. Make check payable to Clerk of Circuit Court. Search information required: name, date of birth, present address, previous address.

Civil records are available by mail. No release necessary. $5.00 search fee. $1.25 fee per copy. $5.00 for certification. Search information required: name, date of birth, years to search. Specify plaintiff or defendant.

Brown County

Brown County Clerk of Courts, Criminal Records
PO Box 23600
Green Bay, WI 54305-3600
(414) 448-4161
Fax (414) 448-4156
Felony and misdemeanor records are available by mail. No release necessary. $5.00 search fee. $1.25 fee per copy. Make check payable to Clerk of Courts. Search information required: name, date of birth. SASE.

Civil records are available by mail. No release necessary. No search fee. $1.25 fee per copy. $5.00 for certification. Search information required: name, date of birth, years to search. Specify plaintiff or defendant.

Buffalo County

Clerk of Court, Criminal Records
Courthouse
Alma, WI 54610
(608) 685-6212
Fax (608) 685-6240
Felony and misdemeanor records are available by mail or fax. A release is required. No release necessary. $5.00 search fee. $1.25 fee per copy. $5.00 for certification. $2.00 fee for fax response. Company checks only, payable to Clerk of Circuit Court. Search information required: name, date of birth, years to search.

Civil records are available by mail or fax. A release is required. $5.00 search fee. $1.25 fee per copy. $5.00 for certification. $2.00 fee for fax response. Search information required: name, date of birth, years to search. Specify plaintiff or defendant.

Burnett County

Burnett County Clerk of Court, Criminal Records
7410 County Road K, #115
Siren, WI 54872
(715) 349-2147
Fax (715) 349-2102
Felony and misdemeanor records are available by mail. No release necessary. $5.00 search fee. $1.25 fee per copy. $5.00 for certification. $2.00 fee for fax response. Make check payable to Clerk of Circuit Court. Search information required: name, date of birth.

Civil records are available by mail. No release necessary. $5.00 search fee. $1.25 fee per copy. $5.00 for certification. $2.00 fee for fax response. Search information required: name, date of birth, years to search. Specify plaintiff or defendant.

Calumet County

Courthouse
206 Court Street
Chilton, WI 53014
(414) 849-2361 Extension 218
Fax (414) 849-1431
Records are available by mail or fax. No release necessary. $5.00 search fee. $1.25 fee per copy. $5.00 for certification. $2.00 fee for fax response. Search information required: name, date of birth.

Civil records are available by mail or fax. No release necessary. $5.00 search fee. $1.25 fee per copy. $5.00 for certification. $2.00 fee for fax response. Search information required: name, date of birth, years to search. Specify plaintiff or defendant.

Chippewa County

Courthouse, Criminal Records
PO Box 550
Chippewa Falls, WI 54729
(715) 723-1831 Extension 255
Felony and misdemeanor records are available by mail. No release necessary. $5.00 search fee, paid in advance. Make check payable to Clerk of Circuit Court. Search information required: name, date of birth, years to search.

Civil records are available by mail. No release necessary. $5.00 search fee. $.25 fee per copy. $5.00 for certification. Search information required: name, date of birth, years to search. Specify plaintiff or defendant.

Clark County

Courthouse, Criminal Records
517 Court Street
Neillsville, WI 54456
(715) 743-5183
Felony and misdemeanor records are available by mail. No release necessary. $5.00 search fee. Check payable to Clerk of Circuit Court. Search information required: name, date of birth, years to search.

Civil records are available by mail. No release necessary. $5.00 search fee. $.15 fee per copy. $5.00 for certification. Search information required: name, date of birth, years to search. Specify plaintiff or defendant.

Columbia County

Clerk of Circuit Court, Criminal Records
PO Box 405
Portage, WI 53901
(608) 742-2191 Extension 273
Fax (608) 742-1605
Felony and misdemeanor records are available by mail or fax. No release necessary. No search fee. $1.25 fee per copy. $5.00 for certification. Search information required: name, SASE.

Civil records are available by mail or fax. No release necessary. $5.00 search fee. $1.25 fee per copy. $5.00 for certification. Search information required: name, date of birth, years to search, SASE. Specify plaintiff or defendant.

Crawford County

Crawford County Courthouse, Criminal Records
220 N. Beaumont Road
Prairie Du Chien, WI 53821
(608) 326-0209
Felony and misdemeanor records are available by mail. No release necessary. No search fee. $1.25 fee per copy. $5.00 for certification. Search information required: name, date of birth, years to search.

Civil records are available by mail. No release necessary. No search fee. $1.25 fee per copy. $5.00 for certification. Search information required: name, date of birth, years to search. Specify plaintiff or defendant.

Dane County

Criminal and Traffic Court, Criminal Records
City-County Bldg. - Room 202
210 Martin Luther King Jr. Boulevard
Madison, WI 53709
(608) 266-4311
Felony and misdemeanor records are available by mail form 1976 forward. No release necessary. $5.00 search fee. $.50 fee per copy. $5.00 for certification. Make check payable to Clerk of Criminal Court. Search information required: name, date of birth, years to search.

Civil records are available by mail. No release necessary. $5.00 search fee. $.50 fee per copy. $5.00 for certification. Search information required: name, date of birth, years to search. Specify plaintiff or defendant.

Dodge County

Clerk of Court, Criminal Records
105 N. Main
Juneau, WI 53039
(414) 386-4411
Fax (414) 386-3587

Felony and misdemeanor records are available by mail, fax or phone. No release necessary. $5.00 search fee. $1.25 fee per copy. $5.00 for certification. $1.50 fee for fax response. Certified check only, payable to Clerk of Court. Search information required: name, date of birth, SASE.

Civil records are available by mail, fax or phone. No release necessary. $5.00 search fee. $1.25 fee per copy. $5.00 for certification. $1.50 fee for fax response. Search information required: name, date of birth, years to search. Specify plaintiff or defendant.

Door County

Clerk of Circuit Court, Criminal Records
PO Box 670
Sturgeon Bay, WI 54235
(414) 746-2205
Fax (414) 723-1333

Felony and misdemeanor records are available by mail or fax. No release necessary. $5.00 search fee. $1.25 fee per copy. $5.00 for certification. $4.00 fee for first page of fax response, $1.25 each additional page. Make check payable to Clerk of Court. Search information required: name, date of birth, years to search.

Civil records are available by mail or fax. No release necessary. $5.00 search fee. $1.25 fee per copy. $5.00 for certification. $4.00 fee for first page of fax response, $1.25 each additional page. Search information required: name, date of birth, years to search. Specify plaintiff or defendant.

Douglas County

Clerk of Court, Criminal Records
1313 Belknap Street
Superior, WI 54880
(715) 394-0240

Felony and misdemeanor records are available by mail. No release necessary. $5.00 search fee. $1.25 fee per copy. $5.00 for certification. Certified check only, payable to Clerk of Court. Search information required: name, date of birth, SASE.

Civil records are available by mail. No release necessary. $5.00 search fee. $1.25 fee per copy. $5.00 for certification. Search information required: name, date of birth, years to search, SASE. Specify plaintiff or defendant.

Dunn County

Clerk of Circuit Court, Criminal Records
800 Wilson Ave.
Menomonie, WI 54751
(715) 232-2611

Felony and misdemeanor records are available by mail. No release necessary. No search fee. $1.25 fee per copy. $5.00 for certification. Certified check or money order, payable to Clerk of Circuit Court. Search information required: name, date of birth, sex.

Civil records are available by mail. No release necessary. $5.00 search fee. $.25 fee per copy. $5.00 for certification. Search information required: name, date of birth, years to search. Specify plaintiff or defendant.

Eau Claire County

Clerk of Courts, Criminal Records
721 Oxford Ave.
Courthouse
Eau Claire, WI 54703
(715) 839-1866
Fax (715) 839-4854

Felony and misdemeanor records are available by mail, fax or phone. No release necessary. $5.00 search fee. $1.25 fee per copy. $5.00 for certification. $5.00 fee for first page of fax response, $1.25 each additional page. Check payable to Clerk of Courts. Search information required: name, date of birth, years to search.

Civil records are available by mail, fax or phone. No release necessary. $5.00 search fee. $1.25 fee per copy. $5.00 for certification. $5.00 fee for first page of fax response, $1.25 each additional page. Search information required: name, date of birth, years to search. Specify plaintiff or defendant.

Florence County

Clerk of Circuit Court, Criminal Records
PO Box 410
Courthouse
Florence, WI 54121
(715) 528-3205
Fax (715) 528-5470

Felony and misdemeanor records are available by mail. No release necessary. $4.00 search fee. $1.25 fee per copy. $5.00 for certification. Certified check only, payable to Clerk of Circuit Court. Search information required: name, years to search.

Civil records are available by mail. No release necessary. $4.00 search fee. $1.25 fee per copy. $5.00 for certification. Search information required: name, date of birth, years to search. Specify plaintiff or defendant.

Fond du Lac County

Clerk of Circuit Court, Criminal Records
City-County Government Center
PO Box 1355
Fond du Lac, WI 54936-1355
(414) 929-3041

Felony and misdemeanor records are available by mail. No release necessary. $5.00 search fee. $1.25 fee per copy. $5.00 for certification. Company checks only, payable to Clerk of Circuit Court. Search information required: name, date of birth.

Civil records are available by mail. No release necessary. $5.00 search fee. $1.25 fee per copy. $5.00 for certification. Search information required: name, date of birth, years to search. Specify plaintiff or defendant.

Forest County

Courthouse, Clerk of Court
Criminal Records
200 E. Madison
Crandon, WI 54520
(715) 478-3323
Fax (715) 478-2430

Felony and misdemeanor records are available by mail. No release necessary. $5.00 search fee. $1.25 fee per copy. $5.00 for certification. Make check payable to Clerk of Circuit Court. Search information required: name, date of birth, if available.

Civil records are available by mail. No release necessary. $5.00 search fee. $1.25 fee per copy. $5.00 for certification. Search information required: name, date of birth, years to search. Specify plaintiff or defendant.

Grant County

Clerk of Court, Criminal Records
PO Box 46
Lancaster, WI 53813
(608) 723-2752
Fax (608-723-7370

Felony and misdemeanor records are available by mail, phone or fax. No release necessary. No search fee. $.50 fee per copy. $1.25 for certification. Search information required: name, date of birth, years to search, SASE.

Civil records are available by mail. No release necessary. No search fee. $.50 fee per copy. $1.25 for certification. Search information required: name, date of birth, years to search. Specify plaintiff or defendant.

Green County

Courthouse, Criminal Records
Monroe, WI 53566
(608) 328-9433
Fax (608) 328-9433

Felony and misdemeanor records are available by mail. No release necessary. $5.00 search fee. $1.25 fee per copy. $5.00 for certification. Certified check only, payable to Clerk of Circuit Court. Search information required: name, years to search.

Civil records are available by mail. No release necessary. $5.00 search fee. $1.25 fee per copy. $5.00 for certification. Search information required: name, date of birth, years to search. Specify plaintiff or defendant.

Green Lake County

Clerk of Circuit Court, Criminal Records
492 Hill Street
Green Lake, WI 54941
(414) 294-4142
Fax (414) 294-6216

Felony and misdemeanor records are available by mail or fax. A release is required. $5.00 search fee. $1.25 fee per copy. $5.00 for certification. Certified check only, payable to Clerk of Circuit Court. Search information required: name, date of birth, sex.

Civil records are available by mail or fax. A release is required. $5.00 search fee. $1.25 fee per copy. $5.00 for certification. Search information required: name, date of birth, years to search. Specify plaintiff or defendant.

Iowa County

Clerk of Circuit Court, Criminal Records
222 N. Iowa Street
Dodgeville, WI 53533
(608) 935-5052
Fax (608) 935-3024

Felony and misdemeanor records are available by mail. No release necessary. $5.00 search fee. $1.25 fee per copy. $5.00 for certification. Make check payable to Clerk of Circuit Court. Search information required: name, date of birth.

Civil records are available by mail. No release necessary. $5.00 search fee. $1.25 fee per copy. $5.00 for certification. Search information required: name, date of birth, years to search. Specify plaintiff or defendant.

Iron County

Clerk of Circuit Court, Criminal Records
300 Taconite Street
Hurley, WI 54534
(715) 561-4084
Fax (715) 561-2822

Felony and misdemeanor records are available by mail or phone. No release necessary. $5.00 search fee. $1.25 fee per copy. $5.00 for certification. Certified check only, payable to Clerk of Circuit Court. Search information required: name, date of birth, years to search.

Civil records are available by mail or phone. No release necessary. $5.00 search fee. $1.25 fee per copy. $5.00 for certification. Search information required: name, date of birth, years to search. Specify plaintiff or defendant.

Jackson County

Clerk of Circuit Court, Criminal Records
307 Main Street
Black River Falls, WI 54615
(715) 284-0208 Extension 243

Felony and misdemeanor records are available by mail or phone. No release necessary. $5.00 search fee. $.30 fee per copy. $5.00 for certification. Certified check only, payable to Clerk of Circuit Court. Search information required: name, date of birth.

Civil records are available by mail. No release necessary. $5.00 search fee. $.30 fee per copy. $5.00 for certification. Search information required: name, date of birth, years to search. Specify plaintiff or defendant.

Jefferson County

Criminal Clerk, Criminal Records
320 S. Main Street
Jefferson, WI 53549
(414) 674-7153 or 674-7154

Felony and misdemeanor records are available by mail or phone. No release necessary. $5.00 search fee. $1.25 fee per copy. $5.00 for certification. Company checks only, payable to Clerk of Circuit Court. Search information required: name, date of birth.

Civil records are available by mail or phone. No release necessary. $5.00 search fee. $1.25 fee per copy. $5.00 for certification. Search information required: name, date of birth, years to search. Specify plaintiff or defendant.

Juneau County

Clerk of Circuit Court, Criminal Records
220 E. State Street
Mouston, WI 53948
(608) 847-9356
Fax (608) 847-9369

Felony and misdemeanor records are available by mail, fax or phone. No release necessary. $5.00 search fee. $1.25 fee per copy. $5.00 for certification. $2.00 fee for fax response. Make check payable to Clerk of Circuit Court. Search information required: name.

Civil records are available by mail, fax or phone. No release necessary. No search fee. $5.00 search fee. $1.25 fee per copy. $5.00 for certification. $2.00 fee for fax response. Search information required: name, date of birth, years to search. Specify plaintiff or defendant.

Kenosha County

Clerk of Circuit Court, Criminal Records
912 56th Street
Kenosha, WI 53140
(414) 653-6664
Fax (414) 653-7088

Felony and misdemeanor records are available by mail or fax. No release necessary. $5.00 search fee. $1.25 fee per copy. $5.00 for certification. Company checks or money orders payable to Clerk of Circuit Court. Search information required: name, date of birth.

Civil records are available by mail. No release necessary. $5.00 search fee. $1.25 fee per copy. $5.00 for certification. Search information required: name, date of birth, years to search. Specify plaintiff or defendant.

Kewaunee County

Clerk of Circuit Court, Criminal Records
613 Dodge Street
Kewaunee, WI 54216
(414) 388-4410 Extension 144
Fax (414) 388-4410

Felony and misdemeanor records are available by mail. No release necessary. $5.00 search fee. Make check payable to Clerk of Circuit Court. Search information required: name, date of birth.

Civil records are available by mail. No release necessary. $5.00 search fee. $1.25 fee per copy. $5.00 for certification. Search information required: name, date of birth, years to search. Specify plaintiff or defendant.

La Crosse County

Clerk of Circuit Court, Criminal Records
400 N. 4th St.
La Crosse, WI 54601
(608) 785-9691

Felony and misdemeanor records are available by mail. No release necessary. $5.00 search fee. $1.25 fee per copy. $5.00 for certification. Make check payable to Clerk of Circuit Court. Search information required: name, date of birth.

Civil records are available by mail. No release necessary. $5.00 search fee. $1.25 fee per copy. $5.00 for certification. Search information required: name, date of birth, years to search. Specify plaintiff or defendant.

Lafayette County

Clerk of Court, Criminal Records
626 Main Street
Darlington, WI 53530
(608) 776-4832

Felony and misdemeanor records are available by mail. No release necessary. $5.00 search fee, prepaid. $1.25 fee per copy. $5.00 for certification. Make check payable to Clerk of Court. Search information required: name, years to search.

Civil records are available by mail. No release necessary. $5.00 search fee. $1.25 fee per copy. $5.00 for certification. Search information required: name, date of birth, years to search. Specify plaintiff or defendant.

Langlade County

Langlade County Courthouse, Clerk of Court
800 Clermont Street
Antigo, WI 54409
(715) 627-6215

Felony and misdemeanor records are available by mail. No release necessary. $5.00 search fee, prepaid. Make check payable to Clerk of Circuit Court. Search information required: name, date of birth, sex, race, years to search.

Civil records are available by mail. No release necessary. $5.00 search fee. $1.25 fee per copy. $5.00 for certification. Search information required: name, date of birth, years to search. Specify plaintiff or defendant.

Lincoln County

Courthouse, Criminal Records
Merrill, WI 54452
(715) 536-0320

Felony and misdemeanor records are available by mail. No release necessary. $5.00 search fee. $1.25 fee per copy. $5.00 for certification. Certified check only, payable to Clerk of Court. Search information required: name, date of birth.

Civil records are available by mail. No release necessary. $5.00 search fee. $1.25 fee per copy. $5.00 for certification. Search information required: name, date of birth, years to search. Specify plaintiff or defendant.

Manitowoc County

Clerk of Court, Criminal Records
PO Box 2000
Manitowoc, WI 54220-0900
(414) 683-4030

Felony and misdemeanor records are available by mail. For phone requests contact Manitowoc County for Search Fee Agreement Form. No release necessary. $5.00 search fee plus $5.00 for each record found. $1.25 fee per copy. Make check payable to Clerk of Court. Search information required: name, date of birth.

Civil records are available by mail. No release necessary. $5.00 search fee. $1.25 fee per copy. Search information required: name, date of birth, years to search. Specify plaintiff or defendant.

Marathon County

Clerk of Court, Criminal Records
Marathon County
PO Box 726
Wausau, WI 54401
(715) 847-5495

Felony and misdemeanor records are available by mail. No release necessary. $5.00 search fee. Certified check only, payable to Clerk of Court. Search information required: name, date of birth.

Civil records are available by mail. No release necessary. $5.00 search fee. $1.25 fee per copy. $5.00 for certification. Search information required: name, date of birth, years to search. Specify plaintiff or defendant.

Marinette County

Clerk of Circuit Court, Criminal Records
Marinette County Courthouse
PO Box 320
Marinette, WI 54143
(715) 732-7450

Felony and misdemeanor records are available by mail or phone. No release necessary. $5.00 search fee. Check payable to Clerk of Court. Search information required: name, date of birth.

Civil records are available in person only. See Wisconsin state respository for additional information.

Marquette County

Clerk of Circuit Court, Criminal Records
PO Box 187
Montello, WI 53949
(608) 297-9102
Fax (608) 247-2019

Felony and misdemeanor records are available by mail. No release necessary. $5.00 search fee. Make check payable to Clerk of Circuit Court. Search information required: name, date of birth.

Civil records are available by mail. No release necessary. $5.00 search fee. $1.25 fee per copy. $5.00 for certification. Search information required: name, date of birth, years to search. Specify plaintiff or defendant.

Menominee County

Clerk of Circuit Court, Criminal Records
PO Box 428
Keshena, WI 54135
(715) 799-3313

Felony and misdemeanor records are available by mail. No release necessary. $5.00 search fee. $1.25 fee per copy. $5.00 for certification. Certified check or money order payable to Clerk of Circuit Court. Search information required: name.

Civil records are available by mail. No release necessary. No search fee. $5.00 search fee. $1.25 fee per copy. $5.00 for certification. Search information required: name, date of birth, years to search. Specify plaintiff or defendant.

Milwaukee County

Clerk of Court, Criminal Records
Milwaukee Safety Bldg.
Room 136, 821 W. State Street
Milwaukee, WI 53233
(414) 278-4588

Felony and misdemeanor records are available by mail or phone. No release necessary. No search fee. Search information required: name, date of birth.

Civil records are available by mail. No release necessary. No search fee. $1.25 fee per copy. $5.00 for certification. Search information required: name, date of birth, years to search. Specify plaintiff or defendant.

Monroe County

Clerk of Circuit Court, Criminal Records
PO Box 186
Sparta, WI 54656
(608) 269-8745 Extension 8741

Felony and misdemeanor records are available by mail. No release necessary. $5.00 search fee. Certified check only, payable to Clerk of Circuit Court. Search information required: name, date of birth, years to search.

Civil records are available by mail. No release necessary. $5.00 search fee. $1.25 fee per copy. $5.00 for certification. Search information required: name, date of birth, years to search. Specify plaintiff or defendant.

Oconto County

Clerk of Circuit Court, Criminal Records
300 Washington St.
Oconto, WI 54153
(414) 834-5322 Extension 254
Fax (414) 834-3423

Felony and misdemeanor records are available by mail or fax. No release necessary. $5.00 search fee. Make check payable to Clerk of Circuit Court. Search information required: name, date of birth, years to search.

Civil records are available by mail. No release necessary. $5.00 search fee. $1.25 fee per copy. $5.00 for certification. Search information required: name, date of birth, years to search. Specify plaintiff or defendant.

Oneida County

Clerk of Circuit Court, Criminal Records
PO Box 400
Rhinelander, WI 54501
(715) 369-6120

Felony and misdemeanor records are available by mail. No release necessary. $5.00 fee for each ten years searched. Make check payable to Clerk of Circuit Court. Search information required: full name, date of birth, years to search.

Civil records are available by mail. No release necessary. $5.00 search fee. $1.25 fee per copy. $5.00 for certification. Search information required: name, date of birth, years to search. Specify plaintiff or defendant.

Outagamie County

Clerk of Circuit Court, Criminal Records
410 S. Walnut Street
Appleton, WI 54911
(414) 832-5131

Felony and misdemeanor records are available by mail. No release necessary. $5.00 search fee. Company checks only, payable to Clerk of Circuit Court. Search information required: name, date of birth, previous address, years to search.

Civil records are available in person only. See Winconsin state repository for additional information.

Ozaukee County

Ozaukee Clerk of Courts
Ozaukee County Justice Center
1201 S. Spring Street
Port Washington, WI 53074
(414) 238-8421

Felony and misdemeanor records are available by mail. No release necessary. $5.00 search fee. Make check payable to Clerk of Circuit Court. Search information required: name, date of birth.

Civil records are available by mail. No release necessary. $5.00 search fee. $1.25 fee per copy. $5.00 for certification. Search information required: name, date of birth, years to search. Specify plaintiff or defendant.

Pepin County

Clerk of Circuit Court, Criminal Records
550 7 Ave West
PO Box 39
Durand, WI 54736
(715) 672-8861

Felony and misdemeanor records are available by mail. No release necessary. $5.00 search fee. Make check payable to Clerk of Circuit Court. Search information required: name, date of birth.

Civil records are available by mail. No release necessary. $5.00 search fee. $1.00 fee per copy. $5.00 for certification. Search information required: name, date of birth, years to search. Specify plaintiff or defendant.

Pierce County

Clerk of Court, Criminal Records
PO Box 129
Ellsworth, WI 54011
(715) 273-3531 Extension 228

Felony and misdemeanor records are available by mail. No release necessary. $5.00 search fee. Make check payable to Clerk of Court. Search information required: name, date of birth.

Civil records are available by mail. No release necessary. $5.00 search fee. $1.25 fee per copy. $5.00 for certification. Search information required: name, date of birth, years to search. Specify plaintiff or defendant.

Polk County

Clerk of Court, Criminal Records
Courthouse Traffic & Criminal Office
Balsam Lake, WI 54810
(715) 485-3161 Extension 215
Felony and misdemeanor records are
available by mail. No release necessary.
$5.00 search fee. $1.25 fee per copy. $7.00
for certification. Make check payable to
Traffic and Criminal Office. Search information required: name, date of birth, years
to search.

Civil records are available by mail. No release necessary. $5.00 search fee. $1.25 fee
per copy. $7.00 for certification. Search in-
formation required: name, date of birth,
years to search. Specify plaintiff or defendant.

Portage County

Clerk of Court, Criminal Records
1516 Church Street
Stevens Point, WI 54481
(715) 346-1364
Felony and misdemeanor records are available by mail. No release necessary. $5.00
search fee. $1.25 fee per copy. Certified
check only, payable to Clerk of Court.
Search information required: name, date of
birth, years to search.

Civil records are available by mail. No release necessary. $5.00 search fee. $1.25 fee
per copy. $5.00 for certification. Search in-
formation required: name, date of birth,
years to search. Specify plaintiff or defendant.

Price County

Price County Courthouse, Criminal
Records
Phillips, WI 54555
(715) 339-2353
Felony and misdemeanor records are available by mail or phone. No release necessary. $5.00 search fee. Make check payable
to Clerk of Circuit Court. Search information required: name, date of birth.

Civil records are available by mail. No release necessary. $5.00 search fee. $1.25 fee
per copy. $5.00 for certification. Search in-
formation required: name, date of birth,
years to search. Specify plaintiff or defendant.

Racine County

Clerk of Circuit Court, Criminal
Records
717 Wisconsin Ave.
Racine, WI 53403
(414) 636-3242
Fax (414) 636-3341
Felony and misdemeanor records are avail-
able by mail or fax. No release necessary.
$5.00 search fee. Make check payable to
Clerk of Circuit Court. Search information
required: name, date of birth.

Civil records are available by mail or fax.
No release necessary. $5.00 search fee.
$1.25 fee per copy. $5.00 for certification.
Search information required: name, date of
birth, years to search. Specify plaintiff or
defendant.

Richland County

Clerk of Circuit Court, Criminal
Records
PO Box 655
Richland Center, WI 53581
(608) 647-3956
Felony and misdemeanor records are avail-
able by mail. No release necessary. $5.00
search fee. Certified check only, payable to
Clerk of Circuit Court. Search information
required: name, date of birth.

Civil records are available by mail. No release necessary. $5.00 search fee. $1.25 fee
per copy. $5.00 for certification. Search in-
formation required: name, date of birth,
years to search. Specify plaintiff or defendant.

Rock County

Northern Half of County,
Clerk of Circuit Court, Criminal
Records
51 S. Main
Janesville, WI 53545
(608) 757-5624
Felony and misdemeanor records for
Northern half of county are available by
mail or phone. No release necessary. $5.00
search fee. Make check payable to Clerk of
Circuit Court. Search information required:
name.

Southern Half of County,
Clerk of Circuit Court, Criminal
Records
250 Garden Lane
Beloit, WI 53511
(608) 364-2000
Felony and misdemeanor records for
Southern half of county are available by
mail or phone. No release necessary. $5.00
search fee. Make check payable to Clerk of
Circuit Court. Search information required:
name.

Civil records are available by mail. No release necessary. $5.00 search fee. $1.25 fee
per copy. $5.00 for certification. Search in-
formation required: name, date of birth,
years to search. Specify plaintiff or defendant.

Rusk County

Clerk of Circuit Court, Criminal
Records
311 Miner Ave. E.
Ladysmith, WI 54848
(715) 532-2108
Felony and misdemeanor records are available by mail. No release necessary. $5.00
search fee. Make check payable to Clerk of
Circuit Court. Search information required:
name, date of birth.

Civil records are available by mail. No release necessary. $5.00 search fee. $1.25 fee
per copy. $5.00 for certification. Search in-
formation required: name, date of birth,
years to search. Specify plaintiff or defendant.

Sauk County

Clerk of Court, Criminal Records
PO Box 449
Baraboo, WI 53913
(608) 356-5581 Extension 3406
Felony and misdemeanor records are available by mail. No release necessary. $5.00
search fee. Make check payable to Clerk of
Court. Search information required: name,
date of birth.

Civil records are available by mail. No release necessary. $5.00 search fee. $1.25 fee
per copy. $5.00 for certification. Search in-
formation required: name, date of birth,
years to search. Specify plaintiff or defendant.

Sawyer County

Clerk of Circuit Court, Criminal
Records
PO Box 508
Hayward, WI 54843
(715) 634-4887
Felony and misdemeanor records are avail-
able by mail. No release necessary. $5.00
search fee. Make check payable to Clerk of
Circuit Court. Search information required:
name, date of birth, SASE.

Civil records are available by mail. No release necessary. $5.00 search fee. $1.25 fee
per copy. $5.00 for certification. Search in-
formation required: name, date of birth,
years to search, SASE. Specify plaintiff or
defendant.

Shawano County

Clerk of Circuit Court, Criminal
Records
311 N. Main
Room 206
Shawano, WI 54166
(715) 526-9347
Felony and misdemeanor records are available by mail. No release necessary. $5.00
search fee. Make check payable to Clerk of
Circuit Court. Search information required:
name, date of birth, years to search.

Civil records are available by mail. No release necessary. $5.00 search fee. $1.25 fee
per copy. $5.00 for certification. Search in-
formation required: name, date of birth,
years to search. Specify plaintiff or defendant.

Sheboygan County

Clerk of Court, Criminal Records
615 N. 6th Street
Sheboygan, WI 53081
(414) 459-3068
Fax (414) 459-4383
Felony and misdemeanor records are available by mail or phone. No release necessary. $5.00 search fee. $.25 fee per copy.
$1.25 for certification. Make check payable
to Sheboygan County Clerk of Courts.
Search information required: name, date of
birth, SASE, previous address.

Civil records are available by mail. No release necessary. $5.00 search fee. $1.25 fee
per copy. $5.00 for certification. Search in-
formation required: name, date of birth,
years to search. Specify plaintiff or defendant.

St. Croix County

St. Croix County Courthouse,
Criminal Records
911 4th Street
Hudson, WI 54016
(715) 386-4630 Extension 272
Felony and misdemeanor records are available by mail or phone. No release necessary. $5.00 search fee. Make check payable
to Clerk of Circuit Court. Search information required: name, date of birth.

Civil records are available by mail. No release necessary. $5.00 search fee. $1.25 fee per copy. $5.00 for certification. Search information required: name, date of birth, years to search. Specify plaintiff or defendant.

Taylor County

Clerk of Circuit Court, Criminal Records
PO Box 97
Medford, WI 54451
(715) 748-3131 Extension 127
Felony and misdemeanor records are available by mail. No release necessary. $5.00 search fee. Make check payable to Clerk of Circuit Court. Search information required: name, date of birth.

Civil records are available by mail. No release necessary. $5.00 search fee. $1.25 fee per copy. $5.00 for certification. Search information required: name, date of birth, years to search. Specify plaintiff or defendant.

Trempealeau County

Courthouse, Criminal Records
Whitehall, WI 54773
(715) 538-2311 Extension 241
Felony and misdemeanor records are available by mail. No release necessary. $5.00 search fee. $1.25 fee per copy. $5.00 for certification. Make check payable to Clerk of Circuit Court. Search information required: name, date of birth, years to search.

Civil records are available by mail. No release necessary. $5.00 search fee. $1.25 fee per copy. $5.00 for certification. Search information required: name, date of birth, years to search. Specify plaintiff or defendant.

Vernon County

Clerk of Court, Criminal Records
PO Box 426
Viroqua, WI 54665
(608) 637-3220
Felony and misdemeanor records are available by mail or phone. No release necessary. No search fee. Make check payable to Clerk of Court. Search information required: name.

Civil records are available by mail. No release necessary. $5.00 search fee. $.25 fee per copy. $5.00 for certification. Search information required: name, date of birth, years to search. Specify plaintiff or defendant.

Vilas County

Clerk of Circuit Court, Criminal Records
PO Box 369
Eagle River, WI 54521
(715) 479-3632
Fax (715) 479-3605
Felony and misdemeanor records are available by mail or fax. No release necessary. $5.00 search fee. Make check payable to Clerk of Circuit Court. Search information required: name, date of birth.

Civil records are available by mail or fax. No release necessary. $5.00 search fee. $1.25 fee per copy. $5.00 for certification. Search information required: name, date of birth, years to search. Specify plaintiff or defendant.

Walworth County

Clerk of Court, Criminal Records
PO Box 1001
Elkhorn, WI 53121
(414) 741-4224
Fax (414) 741-4379
Felony and misdemeanor records are available by mail, phone or fax. No release necessary. $5.00 search fee. Make check payable to Clerk of Court. Search information required: name, date of birth.

Civil records are available by mail or fax. No release necessary. $5.00 search fee. $1.25 fee per copy. $5.00 for certification. Search information required: name, date of birth, years to search. Specify plaintiff or defendant.

Washburn County

Clerk of Circuit Court, Criminal Records
PO Box 339
Shell Lake, WI 54871
(715) 468-7468
Fax (715) 468-7836
Felony and misdemeanor records are available by mail or fax. No release necessary. $5.00 search fee. Company checks only, payable to Clerk of Court. Search information required: name, date of birth.

Civil records are available by mail or fax. No release necessary. $5.00 search fee. $1.25 fee per copy. $5.00 for certification. Search information required: name, date of birth, years to search. Specify plaintiff or defendant.

Washington County

Clerk of Court, Criminal Records
PO Box 1986
West Bend, WI 53095
(414) 335-4350
Felony and misdemeanor records are available by mail. No release necessary. $5.00 search fee. Make check payable to Clerk of Court. Search information required: name, date of birth.

Civil records are available by mail. No release necessary. $5.00 search fee. $1.00 fee per copy. $5.00 for certification. Search information required: name, date of birth, years to search. Specify plaintiff or defendant.

Waukesha County

Criminal and Traffic Court Clerk
515 Westmoreland
Waukesha, WI 53188
(414) 548-7484
Fax (414) 548-7043
Felony and misdemeanor records are available by mail, fax or phone. No release necessary. $5.00 search fee. $1.25 fee per copy. $5.00 for certification. Make check payable to Clerk of Court. Search information required: name, date of birth.

Civil records are available by mail, fax or phone. No release necessary. $5.00 search fee. $1.25 fee per copy. $5.00 for certification. Search information required: name, date of birth, years to search. Specify plaintiff or defendant.

Waupaca County

Clerk of Circuit Court, Criminal Records
PO Box 354
Waupaca, WI 54981
(715) 258-6460
Felony and misdemeanor records are available by mail. No release necessary. $5.00 search fee. Make check payable to Clerk of Court. Search information required: name, date of birth, years to search.

Civil records are available by mail. No release necessary. $5.00 search fee. $1.25 fee per copy. $5.00 for certification. Search information required: name, date of birth, years to search. Specify plaintiff or defendant.

Waushara County

Clerk of Circuit Court, Criminal Records
PO Box 507
Wautoma, WI 54982
(414) 787-4631
Felony and misdemeanor records are available by mail. No release necessary. $5.00 search fee. Certified check only, payable to Clerk of Circuit Court. Search information required: name, date of birth.

Civil records are available by mail. No release necessary. $5.00 search fee. $1.25 fee per copy. $5.00 for certification. Search information required: name, date of birth, years to search. Specify plaintiff or defendant.

Winnebago County

Criminal and Traffic Court
415 Jackson Drive
Oshkosh, WI 54903
(414) 235-2500 Extension 495
Fax (414) 236-4855
Felony and misdemeanor records are available by mail or fax. No release necessary. $5.00 search fee. Company checks only, payable to Clerk of Court. Search information required: name, date of birth.

Civil records are available by mail or fax. No release necessary. $5.00 search fee. $1.25 fee per copy. $5.00 for certification. Search information required: name, date of birth, years to search. Specify plaintiff or defendant.

Wood County

Courthouse, Criminal Records
400 Market Street
Wisconsin Rapids, WI 54494
(715) 236-4855
Felony and misdemeanor records are available by mail or phone. No release necessary. $5.00 search fee. Make check payable to Circuit Court Clerk. Search information required: name, date of birth.

Civil records are available by mail. No release necessary. $5.00 search fee. $1.25 fee per copy. $5.00 for certification. Search information required: name, date of birth, years to search. Specify plaintiff or defendant.

City-County Cross Reference

Abbotsford *Clark*
Abrams *Oconto*
Adams *Adams*
Adell *Sheboygan*
Afton *Rock*
Albany *Green*
Algoma *Kewaunee*
Allenton *Washington*
Allouz *Brown*
Alma *Buffalo*
Alma Center *Jackson*
Almena *Barron*
Almond *Portage*
Altoona *Eau Claire*
Amberg *Marinette*
Amery *Polk*
Amherst *Portage*
Amherst Junction *Portage*
Aniwa *Shawano*
Antigo *Langlade*
Appleton *Outagamie*
Arcadia *Trempealeau*
Arena *Iowa*
Argonne *Forest*
Argyle *Lafayette*
Arkansaw *Pepin*
Arkdale *Adams*
Arlington *Columbia*
Armstrong Creek *Forest*
Arpin *Wood*
Ashippun *Dodge*
Ashland *Ashland*
Ashwaubenon *Brown*
Athelstane *Marinette*
Athens *Marathon*
Auburndale *Wood*
Augusta *Eau Claire*
Avalon *Rock*
Avoca *Iowa*
Babcock *Wood*
Bagley *Grant*
Baileys Harbor *Door*
Baldwin *Saint Croix*
Balsam Lake *Polk*
Bancroft *Portage*
Bangor *LaCrosse*
Baraboo *Sauk*
Barneveld *Iowa*
Barron *Barron*
Barronett *Barron*
Bassett *Kenosha*
Bay City *Pierce*
Bayfield *Bayfield*
Bayside *Milwaukee*
Bear Creek *Outagamie*
Beaver Dam *Dodge*
Beetown *Grant*
Beldenville *Pierce*
Belgium *Ozaukee*
Belleville *Dane*
Belmont *Lafayette*
Beloit *Rock*
Benton *Lafayette*
Berlin *Green Lake*
Big Bend *Waukesha*
Big Falls *Waupaca*
Birchwood *Washburn*
Birnamwood *Shawano*
Biron *Wood*
Black Creek *Outagamie*
Black Earth *Dane*
Black River Falls *Jackson*
Blair *Trempealeau*

Blanchardville *Lafayette*
Blenker *Wood*
Bloomer *Chippewa*
Bloomington *Grant*
Blue Mounds *Dane*
Blue River *Grant*
Bonduel *Shawano*
Boscobel *Grant*
Boulder Junction *Vilas*
Bowler *Shawano*
Boyceville *Dunn*
Boyd *Chippewa*
Branch *Manitowoc*
Brandon *Fond Du Lac*
Brantwood *Price*
Briggsville *Marquette*
Brill *Barron*
Brillion *Calumet*
Bristol *Kenosha*
Brodhead *Green*
Brokaw *Marathon*
Brookfield *Waukesha*
Brooklyn *Green*
Brooks *Adams*
Brown Deer *Milwaukee*
Brownsville *Dodge*
Browntown *Green*
Bruce *Rusk*
Brule *Douglas*
Brussels *Door*
Bryant *Langlade*
Buffalo *Buffalo*
Burlington *Racine*
Burnett *Dodge*
Butler *Waukesha*
Butte Des Morts
    Winnebago
Butternut *Ashland*
Cable *Bayfield*
Cadott *Chippewa*
Caledonia *Racine*
Cambria *Columbia*
Cambridge *Dane*
Cameron *Barron*
Campbellsport *Fond Du Lac*
Camp Douglas *Juneau*
Camp Lake *Kenosha*
Caroline *Shawano*
Cascade *Sheboygan*
Casco *Kewaunee*
Cashton *Monroe*
Cassville *Grant*
Cataract *Monroe*
Catawba *Price*
Cato *Manitowoc*
Cazenovia *Richland*
Cecil *Shawano*
Cedarburg *Ozaukee*
Cedar Grove *Sheboygan*
Centuria *Polk*
Chaseburg *Vernon*
Chelsea *Taylor*
Chetek *Barron*
Chili *Clark*
Chilton *Calumet*
Chippewa Falls *Chippewa*
Clam Lake *Ashland*
Clayton *Polk*
Clear Lake *Polk*
Cleveland *Manitowoc*
Clinton *Rock*
Clintonville *Waupaca*

Clyman *Dodge*
Cobb *Iowa*
Cochrane *Buffalo*
Colby *Clark*
Coleman *Marinette*
Colfax *Dunn*
Colgate *Washington*
Collins *Manitowoc*
Coloma *Waushara*
Columbus *Columbia*
Combined Locks
    Outagamie
Comstock *Barron*
Conover *Vilas*
Conrath *Rusk*
Coon Valley *Vernon*
Cornell *Chippewa*
Cornucopia *Bayfield*
Cottage Grove *Dane*
Couderay *Sawyer*
Crandon *Forest*
Crivitz *Marinette*
Cross Plains *Dane*
Cuba City *Grant*
Cudahy *Milwaukee*
Cumberland *Barron*
Curtiss *Clark*
Cushing *Polk*
Custer *Portage*
Dale *Outagamie*
Dallas *Barron*
Dalton *Green Lake*
Danbury *Burnett*
Dane *Dane*
Darien *Walworth*
Darlington *Lafayette*
Deerbrook *Langlade*
Deerfield *Dane*
Deer Park *Saint Croix*
DeForest *Dane*
Delafield *Waukesha*
Delavan *Walworth*
Denmark *Brown*
DePere *Brown*
DeSoto *Vernon*
Dickeyville *Grant*
Dodge *Trempealeau*
Dodgeville *Iowa*
Dorchester *Clark*
Dousman *Waukesha*
Downing *Dunn*
Downsville *Dunn*
Doylestown *Columbia*
Dresser *Polk*
Drummond *Bayfield*
Durand *Pepin*
Eagle *Waukesha*
Eagle River *Vilas*
Eastman *Crawford*
East Troy *Walworth*
Eau Claire *Eau Claire*
Eau Galle *Dunn*
Eden *Fond Du Lac*
Edgar *Marathon*
Edgerton *Rock*
Edgewater *Sawyer*
Edmund *Iowa*
Egg Harbor *Door*
Eland *Shawano*
Elcho *Langlade*
Elderon *Marathon*
Eldorado *Fond Du Lac*
Eleva *Trempealeau*

Elkhart Lake *Sheboygan*
Elkhorn *Walworth*
Elk Mound *Dunn*
Ellison Bay *Door*
Ellsworth *Pierce*
Elm Grove *Waukesha*
Elmwood *Pierce*
Elroy *Juneau*
Elton *Langlade*
Embarrass *Waupaca*
Endeavor *Marquette*
Ephraim *Door*
Ettrick *Trempealeau*
Eureka *Winnebago*
Evansville *Rock*
Exeland *Sawyer*
Fairchild *Eau Claire*
Fair Water *Fond Du Lac*
Fall Creek *Eau Claire*
Fall River *Columbia*
Fence *Florence*
Fennimore *Grant*
Ferryville *Crawford*
Fifield *Price*
Fish Creek *Door*
Fitchburg *Dane*
Florence *Florence*
Fond du Lac *Fond du Lac*
Fontana *Walworth*
Footville *Rock*
Forest Junction *Calumet*
Forestville *Door*
Fort Atkinson *Jefferson*
Fountain City *Buffalo*
Fox Lake *Dodge*
Fox Point *Waukesha*
Francis Creek *Manitowoc*
Franklin *Waukesha*
Franksville *Racine*
Frederic *Polk*
Fredonia *Ozaukee*
Fremont *Waupaca*
French Island *La Crosse*
Friendship *Adams*
Friesland *Columbia*
Galesville *Trempealeau*
Gays Mills *Crawford*
Genesee Depot *Waukesha*
Genoa *Vernon*
Genoa City *Walworth*
Germantown *Washington*
Gile *Iron*
Gillett *Oconto*
Gilman *Taylor*
Gilmanton *Buffalo*
Gleason *Lincoln*
Glenbeulah *Sheboygan*
Glendale *Milwaukee*
Glen Flora *Rusk*
Glen Haven *Grant*
Glenwood City *Saint Croix*
Glidden *Ashland*
Goodman *Marinette*
Gordon *Douglas*
Gotham *Richland*
Grafton *Ozaukee*
Grand Marsh *Adams*
Grand View *Bayfield*
Granton *Clark*
Grantsburg *Burnett*
Gratiot *Lafayette*
Green Bay *Brown*
Greenbush *Sheboygan*

Greendale *Milwaukee*
Greenfield *Milwaukee*
Green Lake *Green Lake*
Greenleaf *Brown*
Green Valley *Shawano*
Greenville *Outagamie*
Greenwood *Clark*
Gresham *Shawano*
Gurney *Iron*
Hager City *Pierce*
Hales Corners *Milwaukee*
Hammond *Saint Croix*
Hancock *Waushara*
Hannibal *Taylor*
Harshaw *Oneida*
Hartford *Washington*
Hartland *Waukesha*
Hatley *Marathon*
Haugen *Barron*
Hawkins *Rusk*
Hawthorne *Douglas*
Hayward *Sawyer*
Hazel Green *Grant*
Hazelhurst *Oneida*
Helenville *Jefferson*
Herbster *Bayfield*
Hertel *Burnett*
Hewitt *Wood*
High Bridge *Ashland*
Highland *Iowa*
Hilbert *Calumet*
Hillpoint *Sauk*
Hillsboro *Vernon*
Hingham *Sheboygan*
Hixton *Jackson*
Holcombe *Chippewa*
Hollandale *Iowa*
Holmen *LaCrosse*
Honey Creek *Walworth*
Horicon *Dodge*
Hortonville *Outagamie*
Howard *Brown*
Howards Grove-Millersville
    Sheboygan
Hubertus *Washington*
Hudson *Saint Croix*
Humbird *Clark*
Hurley *Iron*
Hustisford *Dodge*
Independence *Trempealeau*
Iola *Waupaca*
Irma *Lincoln*
Iron Belt *Iron*
Iron Ridge *Dodge*
Iron River *Bayfield*
Ixonia *Jefferson*
Jackson *Washington*
Janesville *Rock*
Jefferson *Jefferson*
Jim Falls *Chippewa*
Johnson Creek *Jefferson*
Juda *Green*
Junction City *Portage*
Juneau *Dodge*
Kansasville *Racine*
Kaukauna *Outagamie*
Kellnersville *Manitowoc*
Kempster *Langlade*
Kendall *Monroe*
Kennan *Price*
Kenosha *Kenosha*
Keshena *Menominee*
Kewaskum *Washington*
Kewaunee *Kewaunee*
Kiel *Manitowoc*
Kieler *Grant*

Kimberly *Outagamie*
King *Waupaca*
Kingston *Green Lake*
Knapp *Dunn*
Kohler *Sheboygan*
Krakow *Shawano*
Lac Du Flambeau *Vilas*
LaCrosse *LaCrosse*
Ladysmith *Rusk*
LaFarge *Vernon*
Lake Delton *Sauk*
Lake Geneva *Walworth*
Lake Mills *Jefferson*
Lake Nebagamon *Douglas*
Lake Tomahawk *Oneida*
Lakewood *Oconto*
Lancaster *Grant*
Land O'Lakes *Vilas*
Lannon *Waukesha*
Laona *Forest*
LaPointe *Ashland*
Larsen *Winnebago*
LaValle *Sauk*
Lebanon *Dodge*
Lena *Oconto*
Leopolis *Shawano*
Lewis *Polk*
Limeridge *Sauk*
Linden *Iowa*
Little Chute *Outagamie*
Little Suamico *Oconto*
Livingston *Grant*
Lodi *Columbia*
Loganville *Sauk*
Lomira *Dodge*
Lone Rock *Richland*
Long Lake *Florence*
Lowell *Dodge*
Loyal *Clark*
Lublin *Taylor*
Luck *Polk*
Luxemburg *Kewaunee*
Lyndon Station *Juneau*
Lyons *Walworth*
McFarland *Dane*
McNaughton *Oneida*
Madison *Dane*
Maiden Rock *Pierce*
Malone *Fond Du Lac*
Manawa *Waupaca*
Manchester *Green Lake*
Manitowish Waters *Vilas*
Manitowoc *Manitowoc*
Maple *Douglas*
Maple Bluff *Dane*
Maplewood *Door*
Marathon *Marathon*
Marengo *Ashland*
Maribel *Manitowoc*
Marinette *Marinette*
Marion *Waupaca*
Markesan *Green Lake*
Marquette *Green Lake*
Mequon *Ozaukee*
Marshall *Dane*
Marshfield *Wood*
Mason *Bayfield*
Mather *Juneau*
Mattoon *Shawano*
Mauston *Juneau*
Mayville *Dodge*
Mazomanie *Dane*
Medford *Taylor*
Mellen *Ashland*
Melrose *Jackson*
Menasha *Winnebago*

Menomonee Falls
    Waukesha
Menomonie *Dunn*
Mequon *Ozaukee*
Mercer *Iron*
Merrill *Lincoln*
Merrillan *Jackson*
Merrimac *Sauk*
Merton *Waukesha*
Middleton *Dane*
Mikana *Barron*
Milan *Marathon*
Milladore *Wood*
Millston *Jackson*
Milltown *Polk*
Milton *Rock*
Milwaukee *Milwaukee*
Mindoro *LaCrosse*
Mineral Point *Iowa*
Minocqua *Oneida*
Minong *Washburn*
Mishicot *Manitowoc*
Mondovi *Buffalo*
Monico *Oneida*
Monona *Dane*
Monroe *Green*
Montello *Marquette*
Montfort *Grant*
Monticello *Green*
Montreal *Iron*
Morrisonville *Dane*
Mosinee *Marathon*
Mountain *Oconto*
Mount Calvary *Fond Du Lac*
Mount Hope *Grant*
Mount Horeb *Dane*
Mount Sterling *Crawford*
Mukwonago *Waukesha*
Muscoda *Grant*
Muskego *Waukesha*
Nashotah *Waukesha*
Necedah *Juneau*
Neenah *Winnebago*
Neillsville *Clark*
Nekoosa *Wood*
Nelson *Buffalo*
Nelsonville *Portage*
Neopit *Menominee*
Neosho *Dodge*
Neshkoro *Marquette*
New Auburn *Chippewa*
New Berlin *Waukesha*
Newburg *Washington*
New Franken *Brown*
New Glarus *Green*
New Holstein *Calumet*
New Lisbon *Juneau*
New London *Waupaca*
New Munster *Kenosha*
New Richmond *Saint Croix*
Newton *Manitowoc*
Niagara *Marinette*
Nichols *Outagamie*
North Fond Du Lac *Fon
    Du Lac*
North Freedom *Sauk*
North Hudson *Saint Croix*
North Lake *Waukesha*
North Prairie *Waukesha*
Norwalk *Monroe*
Oak Creek *Milwaukee*
Oakdale *Monroe*
Oakfield *Fond Du Lac*
Oconomowoc *Waukesha*
Oconto *Oconto*

Oconto Falls *Oconto*
Odanah *Ashland*
Ogdensburg *Waupaca*
Ogema *Price*
Ojibwa *Sawyer*
Okauchee *Waukesha*
Omro *Winnebago*
Onalaska *LaCrosse*
Oneida *Outagamie*
Ontario *Vernon*
Oostburg *Sheboygan*
Oregon *Dane*
Orfordville *Rock*
Osceola *Polk*
Oshkosh *Winnebago*
Osseo *Trempealeau*
Owen *Clark*
Oxford *Marquette*
Packwaukee *Marquette*
Paddock Lake *Kenosha*
Palmyra *Jefferson*
Pardeeville *Columbia*
Park Falls *Price*
Patch Grove *Grant*
Pearson *Langlade*
Pelican Lake *Oneida*
Pell Lake *Walworth*
Pembine *Marinette*
Pepin *Pepin*
Peshtigo *Marinette*
Pewaukee *Waukesha*
Phelps *Vilas*
Phillips *Price*
Pickerel *Forest*
Pickett *Winnebago*
Pigeon Falls *Trempealeau*
Pine River *Waushara*
Pittsville *Wood*
Plain *Sauk*
Plainfield *Waushara*
Platteville *Grant*
Pleasant Prairie *Kenosha*
Plover *Portage*
Plum City *Pierce*
Plymouth *Sheboygan*
Poplar *Douglas*
Portage *Columbia*
Port Edwards *Wood*
Porterfield *Marinette*
Port Washington *Ozaukee*
Port Wing *Bayfield*
Poskin *Barron*
Potosi *Grant*
Potter *Calumet*
Pound *Marinette*
Powers Lake *Kenosha*
Poynette *Columbia*
Poy Sippi *Waushara*
Prairie Du Chien *Crawford*
Prairie Du Sac *Sauk*
Prairie Farm *Barron*
Prentice *Price*
Prescott *Pierce*
Presque Isle *Vilas*
Princeton *Green Lake*
Pulaski *Brown*
Racine *Racine*
Radisson *Sawyer*
Randolph *Columbia*
Random Lake *Sheboygan*
Readfield *Waupaca*
Readstown *Vernon*
Redgranite *Waushara*
Reedsburg *Sauk*
Reedsville *Manitowoc*
Reeseville *Dodge*

Rewey *Iowa*
Rhinelander *Oneida*
Rib Lake *Taylor*
Rice Lake *Barron*
Richfield *Washington*
Richland Center *Richland*
Ridgeland *Dunn*
Ridgeway *Iowa*
Ringle *Marathon*
Rio *Columbia*
Ripon *Fond Du Lac*
River Falls *Pierce*
River Hills *Milwaukee*
Roberts *Saint Croix*
Rochester *Racine*
Rockfield *Washington*
Rockland *LaCrosse*
Rock Springs *Sauk*
Rosendale *Fond Du Lac*
Rosholt *Portage*
Rothschild *Marathon*
Royalton *Waupaca*
Rubicon *Dodge*
Rudolph *Wood*
Saint Cloud *Fond Du Lac*
Saint Croix Falls *Polk*
Saint Francis *Milwaukee*
Saint Germain *Vilas*
Saint Nazianz *Manitowoc*
Salem *Kenosha*
Sand Creek *Dunn*
Sarona *Washburn*
Sauk City *Sauk*
Saukville *Ozaukee*
Saxeville *Waushara*
Saxon *Iron*
Sayner *Vilas*
Scandinavia *Waupaca*
Schofield *Marathon*
Seneca *Crawford*
Sextonville *Richland*
Seymour *Outagamie*
Sharon *Walworth*
Shawano *Shawano*
Sheboygan *Sheboygan*
Sheboygan Falls
   Sheboygan
Sheldon *Rusk*
Shell Lake *Washburn*
Sherwood *Calumet*
Shiocton *Outagamie*
Shorewood *Milwaukee*
Shorewood Hills *Dane*
Shullsburg *Lafayette*
Silver Lake *Kenosha*
Sinsinawa *Grant*
Siren *Burnett*
Sister Bay *Door*
Slinger *Washington*
Soldiers Grove *Crawford*
Solon Springs *Douglas*
Somers *Kenosha*
Somerset *Saint Croix*
South Kenosha *Kenosha*
South Milwaukee
   Milwaukee
South Range *Douglas*
South Wayne *Lafayette*
Sparta *Monroe*
Spencer *Marathon*
Spooner *Washburn*
Springbrook *Washburn*
Springfield *Walworth*
Spring Green *Sauk*
Spring Valley *Pierce*

Stanley *Chippewa*
Starlake *Vilas*
Star Prairie *Saint Croix*
Stetsonville *Taylor*
Steuben *Crawford*
Stevens Point *Portage*
Stitzer *Grant*
Stockbridge *Calumet*
Stockholm *Pepin*
Stoddard *Vernon*
Stone Lake *Sawyer*
Stoughton *Dane*
Stratford *Marathon*
Strum *Trempealeau*
Sturgeon Bay *Door*
Sturtevant *Racine*
Suamico *Brown*
Sullivan *Jefferson*
Summit Lake *Langlade*
Sun Prairie *Dane*
Superior *Douglas*
Suring *Oconto*
Sussex *Waukesha*
Taylor *Jackson*
Theresa *Dodge*
Thiensville *Ozaukee*
Thorp *Clark*
Three Lakes *Oneida*
Tigerton *Shawano*
Tilleda *Shawano*
Tisch Mills *Manitowoc*
Tomah *Monroe*
Tomahawk *Lincoln*
Tony *Rusk*
Townsend *Oconto*
Trego *Washburn*
Trempealeau *Trempealeau*
Trevor *Kenosha*
Tripoli *Oneida*
Tunnel City *Monroe*
Turtle Lake *Barron*
Twin Lakes *Kenosha*
Two Rivers *Manitowoc*
Union Center *Juneau*
Union Grove *Racine*
Unity *Marathon*
Valders *Manitowoc*
Vandyne *Fond Du Lac*
Vesper *Wood*
Verona *Dane*
Viola *Richland*
Viroqua *Vernon*
Wabeno *Forest*
Waldo *Sheboygan*
Wales *Waukesha*
Walworth *Walworth*
Warrens *Monroe*
Wascott *Douglas*
Washburn *Bayfield*
Washington Island *Door*
Waterford *Racine*
Waterloo *Jefferson*
Watertown *Jefferson*
Waukau *Winnebago*
Waukesha *Waukesha*
Waunakee *Dane*
Waupaca *Waupaca*
Waupun *Fond Du Lac*
Wausau *Marathon*
Wausaukee *Marinette*
Wautoma *Waushara*
Wauwatosa *Milwaukee*
Wauzeka *Crawford*
Webster *Burnett*
West Allis *Waukesha*

West Baraboo *Sauk*
Westboro *Taylor*
Westby *Vernon*
Westfield *Marquette*
West Milwaukee
   Milwaukee
West Salem *LaCrosse*
Weyauwega *Waupaca*
Weyerhaeuser *Rusk*
Wheeler *Dunn*
Whitefish Bay *Milwaukee*
Whitehall *Trempealeau*
White Lake *Langlade*
Whitelaw *Manitowoc*
Whitewater *Walworth*
Whiting *Portage*
Wild Rose *Waushara*
Willard *Clark*
Williams Bay *Walworth*
Wilmot *Kenosha*
Wilson *Saint Croix*
Wilton *Monroe*
Wind Lake *Racine*
Windsor *Dane*
Winnebago *Winnebago*
Winneconne *Winnebago*
Winter *Sawyer*
Wisconsin Dells *Columbia*
Wisconsin Rapids *Wood*
Withee *Clark*
Wittenberg *Shawano*
Wonewoc *Juneau*
Wood *Milwaukee*
Woodford *Lafayette*
Woodland *Dodge*
Woodman *Grant*
Woodruff *Oneida*
Woodville *Saint Croix*
Woodworth *Kenosha*
Wrightstown *Brown*
Wyeville *Monroe*
Wyocena *Columbia*
Zachow *Shawano*
Zenda *Walworth*

Wyoming

The Wyoming Division of Criminal Investigation, the state's central repository for criminal records, now allows dissemination of data in its files. However procedures for release of their information is quite strict. All twenty three (23) of Wyoming's counties reported that conviction records are accessible for employment screening services. Seven (7) counties will accept fax requests.

Civil court claims for $7,000 and more are filed in District court.

For more information or for offices not listed, contact the state's information hot line at (307) 777-7011.

Driving Records

Department of Revenue and Taxation
Driving Records
Herschler Building
122 W. 25th Street
Cheyenne, WY 82002-0110
(307) 777-7971
Driving records are available by mail. $5.00 fee per request. Turnaround time is 24 hours. Written request must include job applicant's full name, date of birth, license number, and self-addressed, stamped envelope. Make check or money order payable to Department of Transportation.

Worker's Compensation Records

Worker's Compensation Division
Herschler Building
122 West 25th Street
Cheyenne, WY 82002-0700
(307) 777-7441
Fax (307) 777-5946
Worker's compensation records are available by mail or fax. Written request must include subject's full name, SSN and a signed release authorizing access. There is no search fee. $.25 fee per copy.

Vital Statistics

Vital Records Services
Division of Health And Medical Services
Hathaway Building
Cheyenne, WY 82002
(307) 777-7591
Birth records are available for $8.00, and death records for $6.00. State office has records since July 1909. An employer can obtain records with a written release. Make certified check or money order payable to Vital Records.

Marriage and divorce records are available from 1941 by mail. $8.00 fee. A release is required. Search information required: full names of husband and wife, date of event, county where event occured. Turnaround time is one week.

Department of Education

Certification and Licensing
Department of Education
Hathaway Building
Cheyenne, WY 82002
(307) 777-6261
Field of certification is available by phone or mail. Include name and SSN.

Medical Licensing Board

Board of Medicine
Barrett Building
2nd Floor
Cheyenne, WY 82002
(307) 777-6463
Will confirm licenses for MDs and DOs by phone or mail. For licenses not mentioned, contact the above office.

Wyoming State Board of Nursing
Barrett Bldg., 3rd Floor
2301 Central Ave.
Cheyenne, WY 82002
(307) 777-7601
Will confirm license by phone. No fee. Include name, license number, if available.

Bar Association

Wyoming State Bar Association
PO Box 109
Cheyenne, WY 82003
(307) 632-9061
Will confirm licenses by phone. No fee. Include name.

Accountancy Board

Wyoming State Board of Accountancy
Barrett Building, 2nd Floor
Cheyenne, WY 82002
(307) 777-7551
Will confirm license by phone. No fee. Include name.

Securities Commission

Office of Secretary of State
Securities Division
State Capitol Building
Cheyenne, WY 82002
(307) 777-7370
Will confirm license by phone. No fee. Include name and SSN.

Secretary of State

Secretary of State
The Capitol
Cheyenne, WY 82002-0020
(307) 777-7311
Fax (307) 777-5339
Service agent and address, date incorporated, standing with tax commission, trade names are available by phone or mail. Contact the above office for additional information.

Criminal Records

State Repository

Division of Criminal Investigation
Criminal Justice Information Section
Identification Unit
316 W. 22nd St.
Cheyenne, WY 85002
(307) 777-7545
Fax (307) 777-7252
Criminal History Record Information will be provided by the Division indicating arrest and convictions on record within the State of Wyoming. Each individual/agency requesting a fingerprint clearance will submit to the Division of Criminal Investigation, one (1) set of properly rolled fingerprint impressions. Fingerprints MUST be submitted on the standard 8x8 BLUE Applicant Fingerprint Card. Applicant must sign the fingerprint card. Be sure to include a return address and telephone number if request is made by mail. Every application must be accompanied by a signed notarized Waiver, printed on the reverse side of each fingerprint card, of the record subject, on forms provided by the Division, listing to whom dissemination should be made and the address of the person or organization to whom dissemniation should be made. The completed fingerprint

card, waiver and $20.00 fee must then be forwarded to the Division. Make money order or certified check payable to the Office of the Attorney General.

Albany County

Clerk of District Court, Criminal Records
Albany County Courthouse
Room 305
Laramie, WY 82070
(307) 721-2508
Felony records are available by mail or phone. No release necessary. No search fee. Search information required: name.

Civil records are available by mail or phone. No release necessary. No search fee. $.25 fee per copy. $.25 for certification. Search information required: name, date of birth, years to search. Specify plaintiff or defendant.

Big Horn County

Felony records
Clerk of District Court, Criminal Records
PO Box 670
Basin, WY 82410
(307) 568-2381
Felony records are available by mail or phone. No release necessary. No search fee. Search information required: name, years to search, SASE.

Civil records
Clerk of District Court
PO Box 670
Basin, WY 82410
(307) 568-2381
Civil records are available by mail. No release necessary. $5.00 search fee. $1.00 fee per copy. $.50 for certification. Search information required: name, date of birth, years to search. Specify plaintiff or defendant.

Misdemeanor records
Justice Court
PO Box 749
Basin, WY 82410
(307) 568-2361
Misdemeanor records are available by mail. No release necessary. No search fee. $.50 fee per copy. $1.50 for certification. Search information required: name, years to search, SASE.

Civil records
Justice Court
PO Box 749
Basin, WY 82410
(307) 568-2361
Civil records are available by mail. No release necessary. No search fee. $.50 fee per copy. $1.50 for certification. Search information required: name, date of birth, years to search, SASE. Specify plaintiff or defendant.

Campbell County

Felony records
Clerk of District Court, Criminal Records
500 S. Gillette
Gillette, WY 82716
(307) 686-8177
Fax (307) 687-6209

Felony records are available by mail or fax. No release necessary. $2.00 search fee. $1.00 fee per copy for first page, $.50 fee per copy thereafter. $1.00 fee per copy faxed. Search information required: name.

Civil records
Clerk of District Court
500 S. Gillette
Gillette, WY 82716
(307) 686-8177
Fax (307) 687-6209
Civil records are available by mail. No release necessary. $5.00 search fee. $1.00 fee per copy. $.50 for certification. Search information required: name, date of birth, years to search. Specify plaintiff or defendant.

Misdemeanor records
County Court
500 S. Gillette Ave.
Gillette, WY 82716
(307) 682-2190
Misdemeanor records since 1983 are available by mail. No release necessary. $5.00 search fee. $.25 fee per copy. Make check payable to County Court of Campbell County. Search information required: full name, SASE.

Civil records
County Court
500 S. Gillette Ave.
Gillette, WY 82716
(307) 682-2190
Civil records are available by mail. No release necessary. $5.00 search fee. $.25 fee per copy. Search information required: name, date of birth, years to search, SASE. Specify plaintiff or defendant.

Carbon County

Felony records
Clerk of District Court, Criminal Records
PO Box 67
Rawlins, WY 82301
(307) 328-2628
Felony records are available by mail. No release necessary. No search fee. Search information required: name, SSN.

Civil records
Clerk of District Court
PO Box 67
Rawlins, WY 82301
(307) 328-2628
Civil records are available by mail or phone. No release necessary. No search fee. $.25 fee per copy. $1.00 for certification. Search information required: name, date of birth, years to search. Specify plaintiff or defendant.

Misdemeanor records
County Court of Carbon County
Courthouse, Attn: Chief Clerk
Rawlins, WY 82301
(307) 324-6655
Misdemeanor records since 1984 are available by mail or phone. No release necessary. $5.00 search fee. Search information required: name, date of birth, if available.

Civil records
County Court of Carbon County
Courthouse, Attn: Chief Clerk
Rawlins, WY 82301
(307) 324-6655
Civil records are available by mail. No release necessary. No search fee. Search information required: name, date of birth, years to search. Specify plaintiff or defendant.

Converse County

Clerk of District Court, Criminal Records
Box 189
Douglas, WY 82633
(307) 358-3165
Felony records are available by mail or phone. No release necessary. No search fee. Search information required: name.

Civil records are available by mail or phone. No release necessary. No search fee. $.25 fee per copy. $1.50 for first certification, $.50 each additional page. Search information required: name, date of birth, years to search. Specify plaintiff or defendant.

Crook County

Clerk of District Court, Criminal Records
PO Box 904
Sundance, WY 82729
(307) 283-2523
Fax (307) 283-2996
Felony and misdemeanor records are available by mail or phone. No release necessary. No search fee. Search information required: name.

Civil records are available by mail. A release is required. No search fee. $2.50 for certification. Search information required: name, date of birth, years to search. Specify plaintiff or defendant.

Fremont County

Clerk of District Court, Criminal Records
PO Box 373
Lander, WY 82520
(307) 332-2368
Felony records are available by mail or phone. No release necessary. No search fee. Search information required: name, SASE, years to search.

Civil records are available by mail or phone. No release necessary. No search fee. $1.00 fee for first copy, $.25 each additional copy. Search information required: name, date of birth, years to search, SASE. Specify plaintiff or defendant.

Goshen County

Felony records
Clerk of District Court, Criminal Records
PO Box 818
Torrington, WY 82240
(307) 532-2155
Felony records are available by mail. No release necessary. $5.00 search fee. $1.00 fee for first copy, $.50 per copy thereafter. Search information required: name, SASE.

Civil records
Clerk of District Court
PO Box 818
Torrington, WY 82240
(307) 532-2155
Civil records are available by mail. A release is required. $5.00 search fee. $1.00 fee for first copy, $.50 per copy thereafter. $.50 for certification. Search information required: name, date of birth, years to search, SASE. Specify plaintiff or defendant.

Misdemeanor records
County Court
PO Drawer BB
Torrington, WY 82240
(307) 532-2938
Misdemeanor records since 1984 are available by mail. No release necessary. $5.00 search fee. Search information required: name, address, date of birth.

Civil records
County Court
PO Drawer BB
Torrington, WY 82240
(307) 532-2938
Civil records are available by mail. No release necessary. $5.00 search fee. $.50 fee per copy. $.50 for certification. Search information required: name, date of birth, years to search. Specify plaintiff or defendant.

Hot Springs County

Clerk of District Court, Criminal Records
Courthouse
Thermopolis, WY 82443
(307) 864-3323
Felony and misdemeanor records are available by mail. No release necessary. No search fee. Search information required: name, date of birth.

Civil records are available by mail. No release necessary. No search fee. $.25 fee per copy. $1.00 for first certification, $.50 each additional page. Search information required: name, date of birth, years to search. Specify plaintiff or defendant.

Johnson County

Clerk of District Court, Criminal Records
76 N. Main
Buffalo, WY 82834
(307) 684-7271
Felony and misdemeanor records are available by mail or phone. No release necessary. No search fee. Search information required: full name, years to search.

Civil records are available by mail. No release necessary. No search fee. $1.00 fee for first copy, $.50 each additional copy. $.50 for certification. Search information required: name, date of birth, years to search. Specify plaintiff or defendant.

Laramie County

Felony records
Clerk of District Court, Criminal Records
PO Box 743
Cheyenne, WY 82003
(307) 638-4270
Felony records are available by mail. No release necessary. $5.00 search fee. $1.00 fee

for first copy, $.50 each additional copy. $.50 for certification. Search information required: name, years to search.

Civil records
Clerk of District Court
PO Box 743
Cheyenne, WY 82003
(307) 638-4270
Civil records are available by mail. No release necessary. $5.00 search fee. $1.00 fee for first copy, $.50 each additional copy. $.50 for certification. Search information required: name, date of birth, years to search. Specify plaintiff or defendant.

Misdemeanor records
County Court
19th Carey Avenue, Room 108
Cheyenne, WY 82001
(307) 638-4296
Misdemeanor records since 1979 are available by mail. No release necessary. $5.00 search fee. $.50 fee per copy. $.50 for certification. Search information required: name, date of offense, date of birth, years to search.

Civil records
County Court
19th Carey Avenue, Room 108
Cheyenne, WY 82001
(307) 638-4296
Civil records are available by mail. No release necessary. $5.00 search fee. $.50 fee per copy. $.50 for certification. Search information required: name, date of birth, years to search. Specify plaintiff or defendant.

Lincoln County

Clerk of District Court, Criminal Records
PO Drawer 510
Kemmerer, WY 83101
(307) 877-9056
Fax (307) 877-6263
Felony and misdemeanor records are available by mail, phone or fax. No release necessary. No search fee. $5.00 for court to send fax. Search information required: name.

Civil records are available by mail or phone. No release necessary. No search fee. $1.00 fee for first copy, $.50 each additional copy. $2.50 for certification. Search information required: name, date of birth, years to search. Specify plaintiff or defendant.

Natrona County

Felony records
Clerk of District Court, Criminal Records
PO Box 3120
Casper, WY 82602
(307) 235-9243
Fax (307) 235-9493
Felony records are available by mail or phone. No release necessary. No search fee. $1.00 fee for first copy, $.50 each additional copy. Search information required: name, years to search.

Civil records
Clerk of District Court
PO Box 3120
Casper, WY 82602
(307) 235-9243
Fax (307) 235-9493
Civil records are available by mail or phone. No release necessary. No search fee. $1.00 fee for first copy, $.50 each additional copy. $.50 for certification. Search information required: name, date of birth, years to search. Specify plaintiff or defendant.

Misdemeanor records
County Court
PO Box 1339
Casper, WY 82062
(307) 235-9266
Misdemeanor records are available by mail. No release necessary. $5.00 search fee. Search information required: name, date of birth, years to search.

Civil records
County Court
PO Box 1339
Casper, WY 82062
(307) 235-9266
Civil records are available by mail. No release necessary. $5.00 search fee. $.25 fee per copy. $.25 for certification. Search information required: name, date of birth, years to search. Specify plaintiff or defendant.

Niobrara County

Clerk of District Court, Criminal Records
PO Box 1318
Lusk, WY 82225
(307) 334-2736
Felony and misdemeanor records are available by mail. A release is required. No search fee. Search information required: name, date of birth, years to search.

Civil records are available by mail. No release necessary. No search fee. $1.00 fee for first copy, $.50 each additional copy. $.50 for certification. Search information required: name, date of birth, years to search. Specify plaintiff or defendant.

Park County

Clerk of District Court
PO Box 1960
Cody, WY 82414
(307) 587-2204 Extension 218
Felony and misdemeanor records are available by mail. No release necessary. No search fee. Search information required: name, SSN, years to search.

Civil records are available by mail. No release necessary. No search fee. $1.00 fee for first copy, $.50 each additional copy. $1.00 for certification. Search information required: name, date of birth, years to search. Specify plaintiff or defendant.

Platte County

Clerk of District Court, Criminal Records
PO Box 158
Wheatland, WY 82201
(307) 322-3857
Felony and misdemeanor records are available by mail or phone. No release necessary. $5.00 search fee. Search information required: name, years to search, SASE.

Civil records are available by mail. No release necessary. $5.00 search fee. Search information required: name, date of birth, years to search, SASE. Specify plaintiff or defendant.

Sheridan County

Felony records
Clerk of District Court, Criminal Records
224 South Main
Suite B-11
Sheridan, WY 82801
(307) 674-4821
Felony records are available by mail. No release necessary. $5.00 search fee. $.50 fee for first copy, $.25 each additional copy. Search information required: name.

Civil records
Clerk of District Court
224 South Main
Suite B-11
Sheridan, WY 82801
(307) 674-4821
Civil records are available by mail. No release necessary. $5.00 search fee. $.25 fee per copy. $.50 for first certification, $.25 each additional page. Search information required: name, date of birth, years to search. Specify plaintiff or defendant.

Misdemeanor records
County Court
224 South Main St.
Suite B-7
Sheridan, WY 82801
(307) 672-9718
Misdemeanor records since 1983 are available by mail. No release necessary. $5.00 search fee. $.25 per copy. Search information: name, date of birth, SSN, offense, date charged.

Civil records
County Court
224 South Main St.
Suite B-7
Sheridan, WY 82801
(307) 672-9718
Civil records are available by mail. No release necessary. $5.00 search fee. $.25 fee per copy. $.50 for certification. Search information required: name, date of birth, years to search, SASE. Specify plaintiff or defendant.

Sublette County

Clerk of District Court, Criminal Records
PO Box 292
Pinedale, WY 82941
(307) 367-4376
Fax (307) 367-6396
Felony records are available by mail, phone or fax. No release necessary. No search fee. $1.00 fee for first copy, $.50 each additional copy. Search information required: name, years to search .

Civil records are available by mail. No release necessary. No search fee. $1.00 fee for first copy, $.50 each additional copy. Search information required: name, date of birth, years to search. Specify plaintiff or defendant.

Sweetwater County

Clerk of District Court, Criminal Records
PO Box 430
Green River, WY 82935
(307) 875-5343
Fax (307) 875-8439
Felony records are available by mail, phone or fax. No release necessary. No search fee. $1.00 fee for first copy or fax. $.50 for each additional copy. Search information required: name, SASE.

Civil records are available by mail. No release necessary. $5.00 search fee. $.25 fee per copy. $.50 for certification. Search information required: name, date of birth, years to search. Specify plaintiff or defendant.

Teton County

Clerk of District Court, Criminal Records
Box 1727
Jackson, WY 83001
(307) 733-2533
Fax (307) 733-5343
Felony and misdemeanor records are available by mail or phone. No release necessary. No search fee. $1.00 fee for first copy, $.50 each additional copy. $.50 for certification. Search information required: name, years to search .

Civil records are available by mail. No release necessary. No search fee. $1.00 fee for first copy, $.50 each additional copy. $.50 for certification. Search information required: name, date of birth, years to search. Specify plaintiff or defendant.

Uinta County

Felony records
Clerk of District Court, Criminal Records
PO Box 1906
Evanston, WY 82931
(307) 789-1780
Felony records are available by mail. No release necessary. No fee. Search information required: name, SSN, date of birth, previous address, years to search, docket number, if available.

Civil records
Clerk of District Court
PO Box 1906
Evanston, WY 82931
(307) 789-1780
Civil records are available by mail. No release necessary. No search fee. Search information required: name, date of birth, years to search. Specify plaintiff or defendant.

Misdemeanor records
County Court
225 9th Street
Evanston, WY 82930
(307) 789-2471
Misdemeanor records since 1982 are available by mail. No release necessary. $5.00 search fee. Search information required: name, date of birth if available, SSN, years to search, SASE.

Civilr records
County Court
225 9th Street
Evanston, WY 82930
(307) 789-2471
Civil records are available by mail. A release is required. $5.00 search fee. Search information required: name, date of birth, years to search. Specify plaintiff or defendant.

Washakie County

Clerk of District Court, Criminal Records
PO Box 862
Worland, WY 82401
(307) 347-4821
Felony and misdemeanor records are available by mail. No release necessary. No search fee. Search information required: name.

Civil records are available by mail. No release necessary. No search fee. $1.00 fee for first copy, $.50 each additional copy. $.50 for certification. Search information required: name, date of birth, years to search. Specify plaintiff or defendant.

Weston County

Felony records
Clerk of District Court, Criminal Records
1 W. Main
Newcastle, WY 82701
(307) 746-4778
Felony records are available by mail or phone. No release necessary. No search fee. $.50 fee per copy. $.50 for certification. Search information required: name, years to search.

Civil records
Clerk of District Court
1 W. Main
Newcastle, WY 82701
(307) 746-4778
Civil records are available by mail. No release necessary. No search fee. $.50 fee per copy. $.50 for certification. Search information required: name, date of birth, years to search. Specify plaintiff or defendant.

Misdemeanor records
Justice Court
PO Box 173
Newcastle, WY 82701
(307) 746-3547
Misdemeanor records since 1983 are available by mail or phone. No release necessary. No fee. Search information required: name, date of offense, years to search.

Civil records
Justice Court
PO Box 173
Newcastle, WY 82701
(307) 746-3547
Civil records are available by mail. No release necessary. No search fee. $.25 fee per copy. $.50 for certification. Search information required: name, date of birth, years to search. Specify plaintiff or defendant.

City-County Cross Reference

Afton *Lincoln*
Albin *Laramie*
Alcova *Natrona*
Alva *Crook*
Arvada *Sheridan*
Auburn *Lincoln*
Baggs *Carbon*
Bairoil *Sweetwater*
Banner *Sheridan*
Bar Nunn *Natrona*
Basin *Big Horn*
Beulah *Crook*
Big Horn *Sheridan*
Big Piney *Sublette*
Bill *Converse*
Bondurant *Sublette*
Bosler *Albany*
Boulder *Sublette*
Buffalo *Johnson*
Buford *Albany*
Burlington *Big Horn*
Burns *Laramie*
Byron *Big Horn*
Carpenter *Laramie*
Casper *Natrona*
Centennial *Albany*
Cheyenne *Laramie*
Chugwater *Platte*
Clearmont *Sheridan*
Cody *Park*
Cokeville *Lincoln*
Cora *Sublette*
Cowley *Big Horn*
Crowheart *Fremont*
Daniel *Sublette*
Dayton *Sheridan*
Deaver *Big Horn*
Devils Tower *Crook*
Diamondville *Lincoln*
Dixon *Carbon*
Douglas *Converse*
Dubois *Fremont*
East Thermopolis *Hot Springs*
Eden *Sweetwater*
Edgerton *Natrona*
Elk Mountain *Carbon*
Emblem *Big Horn*
Encampment *Carbon*
Etna *Lincoln*
Evanston *Uinta*
Evansville *Natrona*
Fairview *Lincoln*
Farson *Sweetwater*
Fort Bridger *Uinta*
Fort Laramie *Goshen*
Fort Washakie *Fremont*
Frannie *Park*
Freedom *Lincoln*
Frontier *Lincoln*
Gillette *Campbell*
Glendo *Platte*
Glenrock *Converse*
Granger *Sweetwater*
Granite Canon *Laramie*
Grass Creek *Hot Springs*
Green River *Sweetwater*
Greybull *Big Horn*
Grover *Lincoln*
Guernsey *Platte*
Hamilton Dome *Hot Springs*
Hanna *Carbon*

Hartville *Platte*
Hawk Springs *Goshen*
Hillsdale *Laramie*
Horse Creek *Laramie*
Hudson *Fremont*
Hulett *Crook*
Huntley *Goshen*
Hyattville *Big Horn*
Iron Mountain *Laramie*
Jackson *Teton*
Jay Em *Goshen*
Jeffery City *Fremont*
Kaycee *Johnson*
Keeline *Niobrara*
Kelly *Teton*
Kemmerer *Lincoln*
Kinnear *Fremont*
LaBarge *Lincoln*
Lagrange *Goshen*
Lance Creek *Niobrara*
Lander *Fremont*
Laramie *Albany*
Leiter *Sheridan*
Linch *Johnson*
Lingle *Goshen*
Little America *Sweetwater*
Lonetree *Uinta*
Lost Springs *Converse*
Lovell *Big Horn*
Lusk *Niobrara*
Lyman *Uinta*
Lysite *Fremont*
McFadden *Carbon*
Manderson *Big Horn*
Manville *Niobrara*
Marbleton *Sublette*
Medicine Bow *Carbon*
Meeteetse *Park*
Meriden *Laramie*
Midwest *Natrona*
Mills *Natrona*
Moorcroft *Crook*
Moose *Teton*
Moran *Teton*
Mountain View *Uinta*
Newcastle *Weston*
Node *Niobrara*
Opal *Lincoln*
Orchard Valley *Laramie*
Osage *Weston*
Oshoto *Crook*
Otto *Big Horn*
Parkman *Sheridan*
Pavillion *Fremont*
Pine Bluffs *Laramie*
Pinedale *Sublette*
Powder River *Natrona*
Powell *Park*
Ralston *Park*
Ranchester *Sheridan*
Rawlins *Carbon*
Recluse *Campbell*
Reliance *Sweetwater*
Riverton *Fremont*
Robertson *Uinta*
Rock River *Albany*
Rock Springs *Sweetwater*
Rolling Hills *Converse*
Rozet *Campbell*
Saint Stephens *Fremont*
Saratoga *Carbon*
Savery *Carbon*
Shawnee *Converse*

Shell *Big Horn*
Sheridan *Sheridan*
Shirley Basin *Carbon*
Shoshoni *Fremont*
Sinclair *Carbon*
Smoot *Lincoln*
Story *Sheridan*
Sundance *Crook*
Superior *Sweetwater*
Ten Sleep *Washakie*
Thayne *Lincoln*
Thermopolis *Hot Springs*
Tie Siding *Albany*
Torrington *Goshen*
Upton *Weston*
Van Tassell *Niobrara*
Veteran *Goshen*
Walcott *Carbon*
Wamsutter *Sweetwater*
Wapiti *Park*
Weston *Campbell*
Wheatland *Platte*
Wilson *Teton*
Wolf *Sheridan*
Worland *Washakie*
Wyarno *Sheridan*
Yellowstone National Park *Park*
Yoder *Goshen*

THE STATE MAPS DIRECTORY

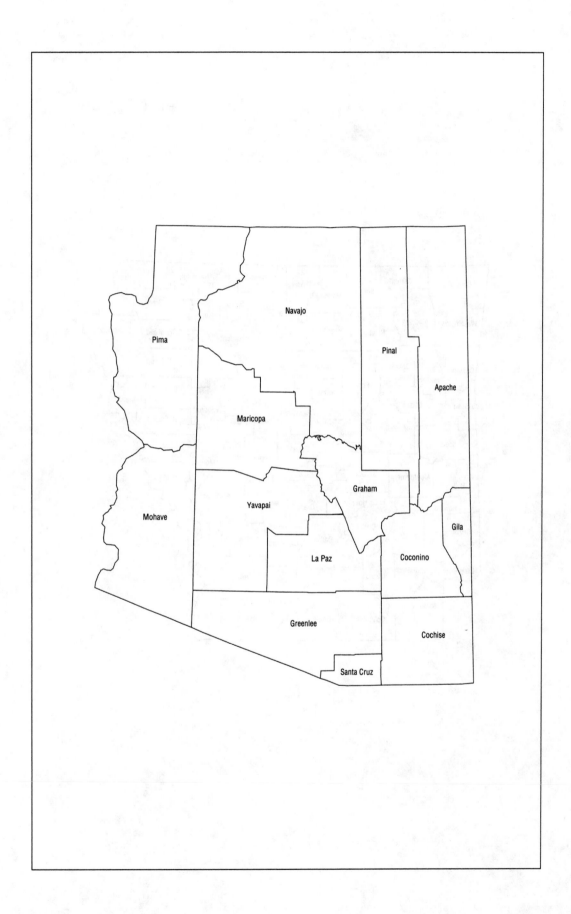

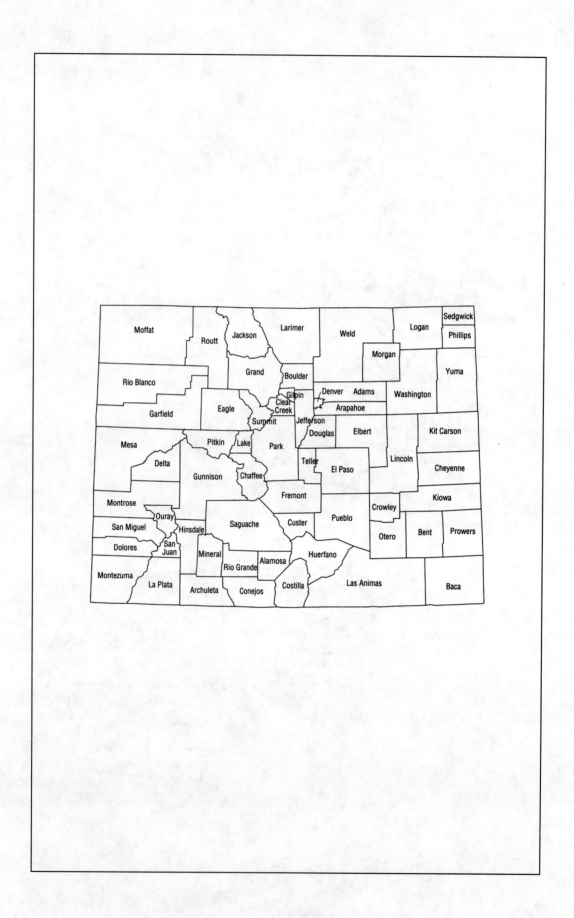

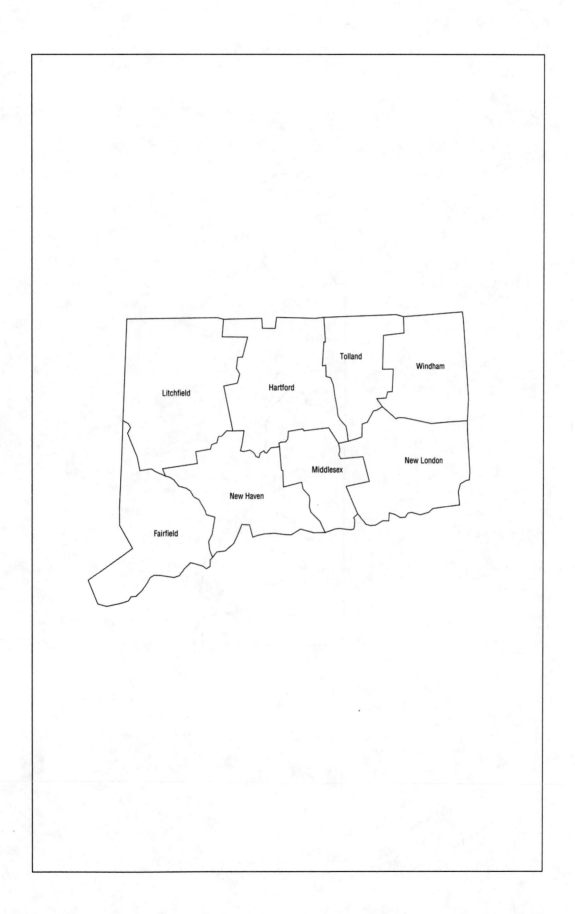

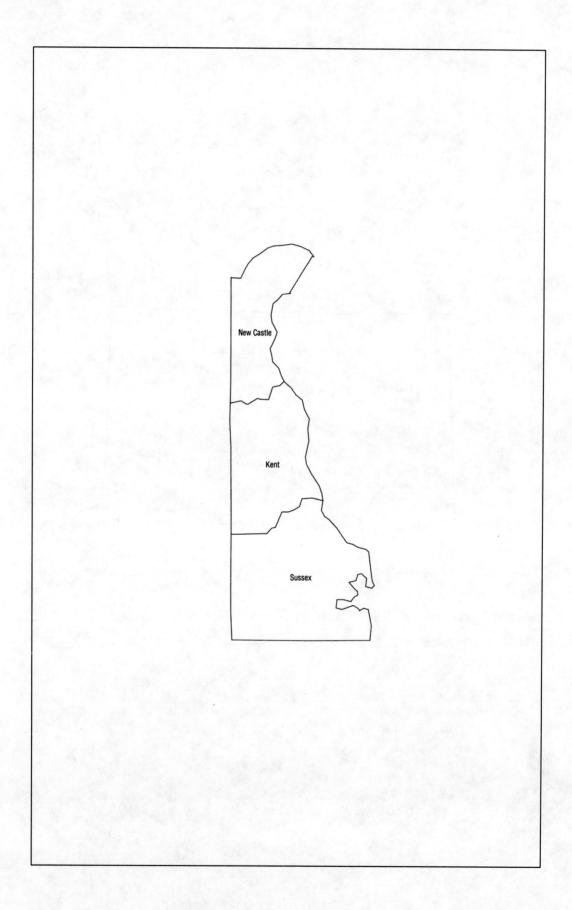

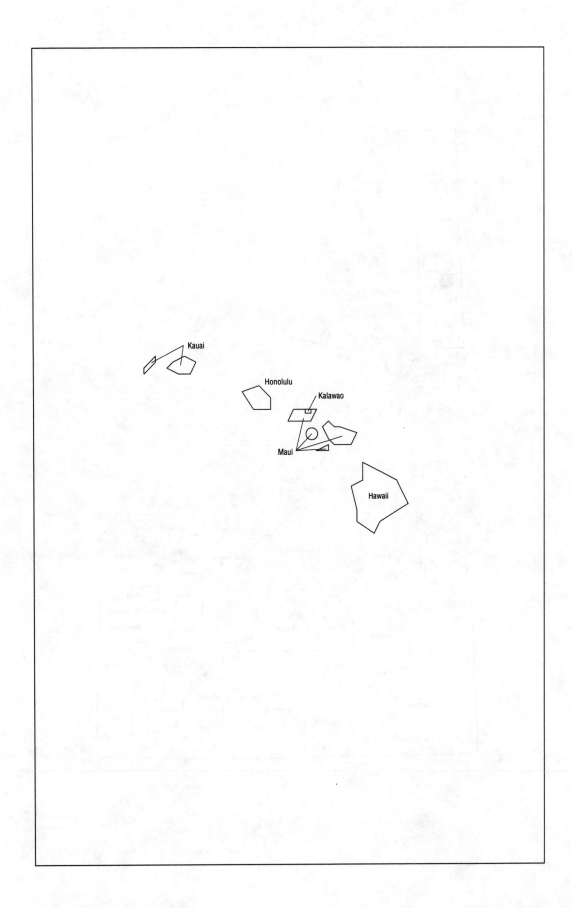

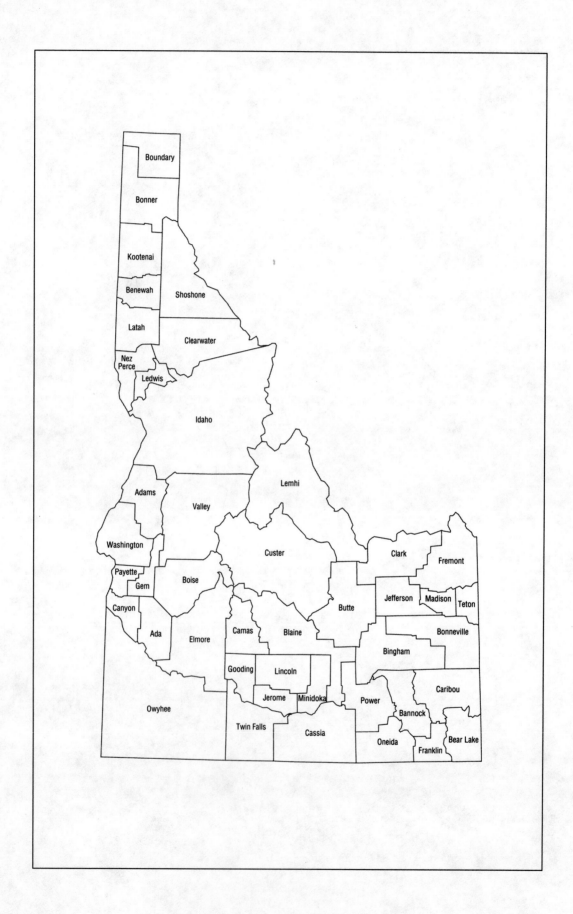

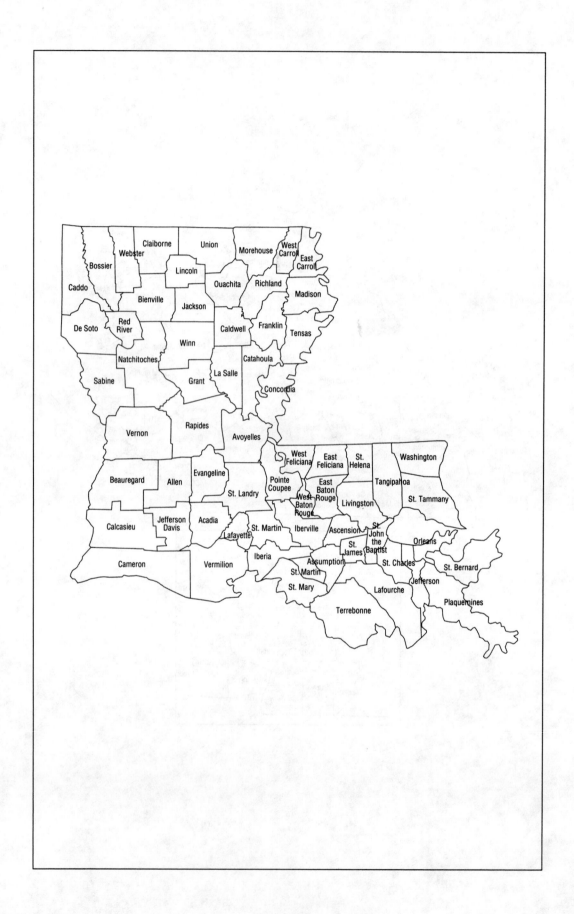

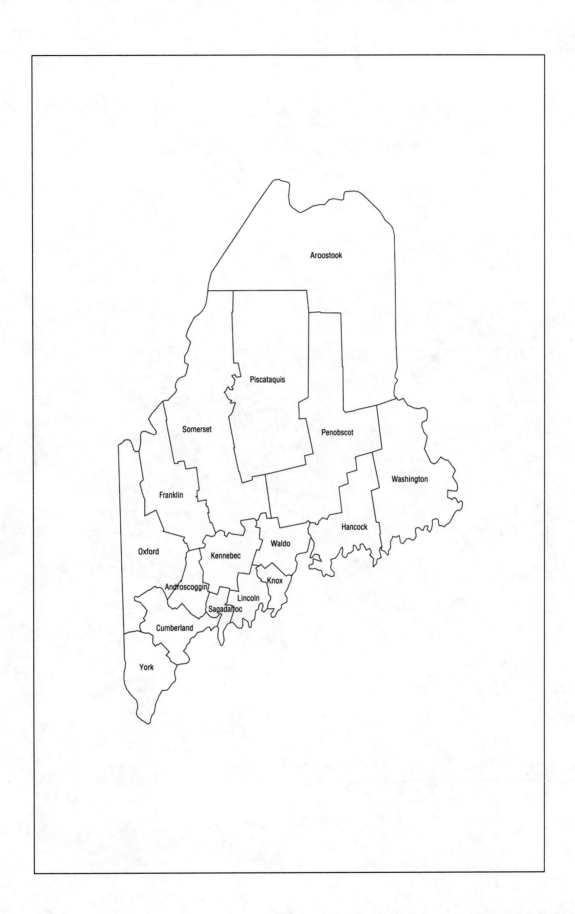

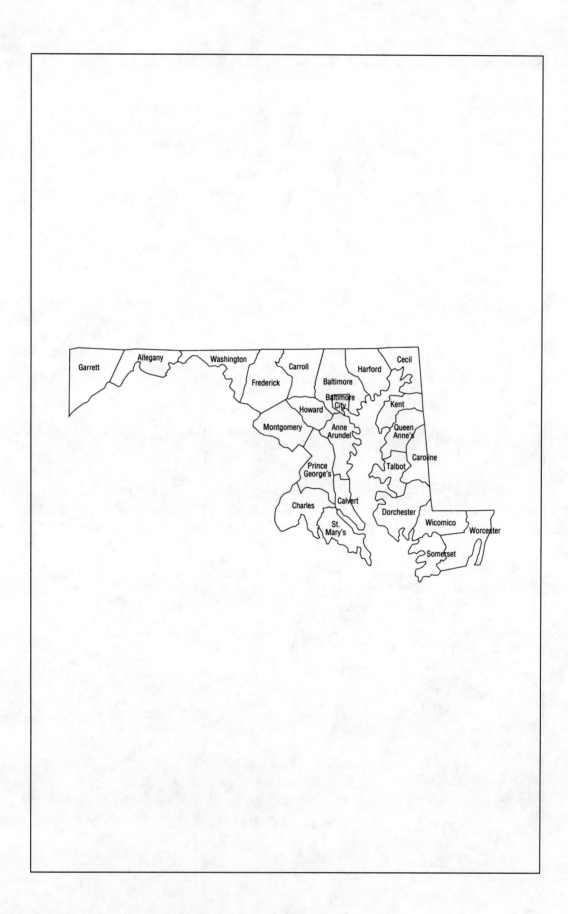

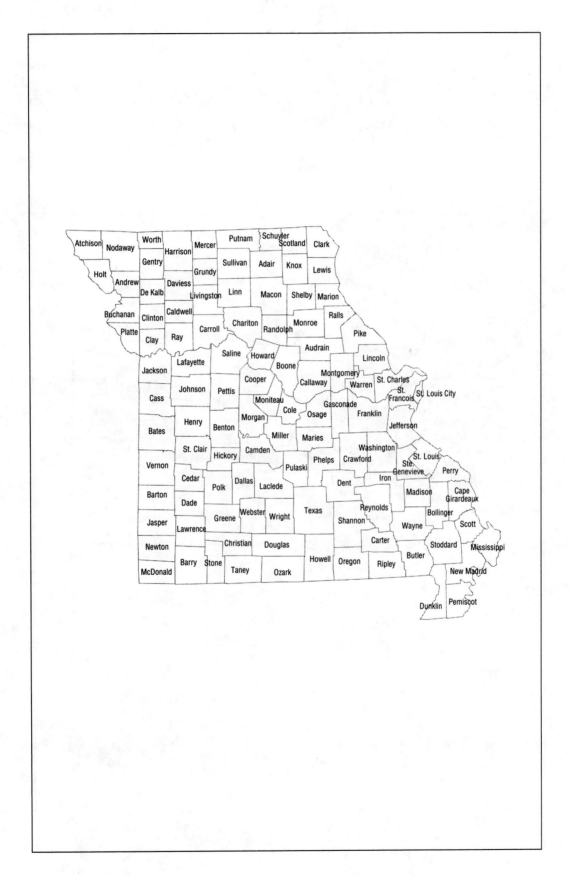

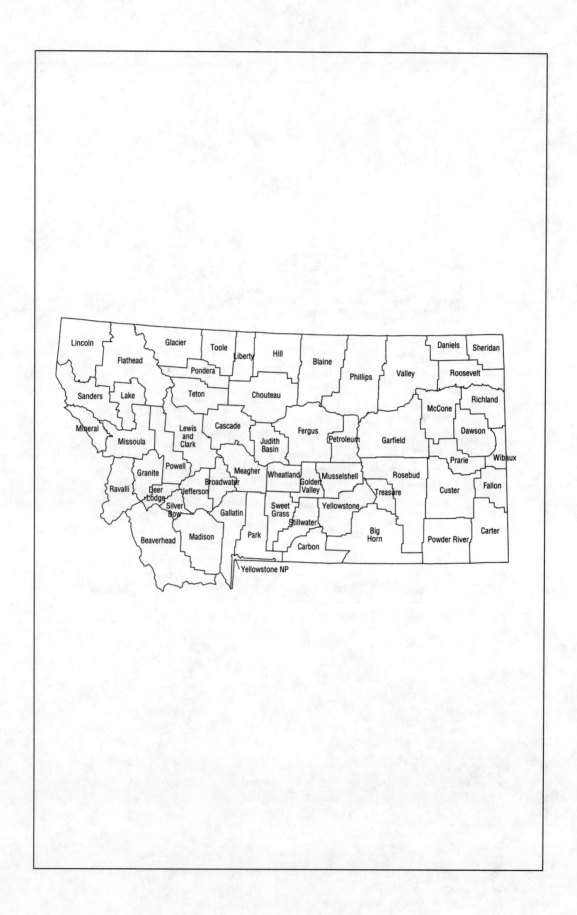

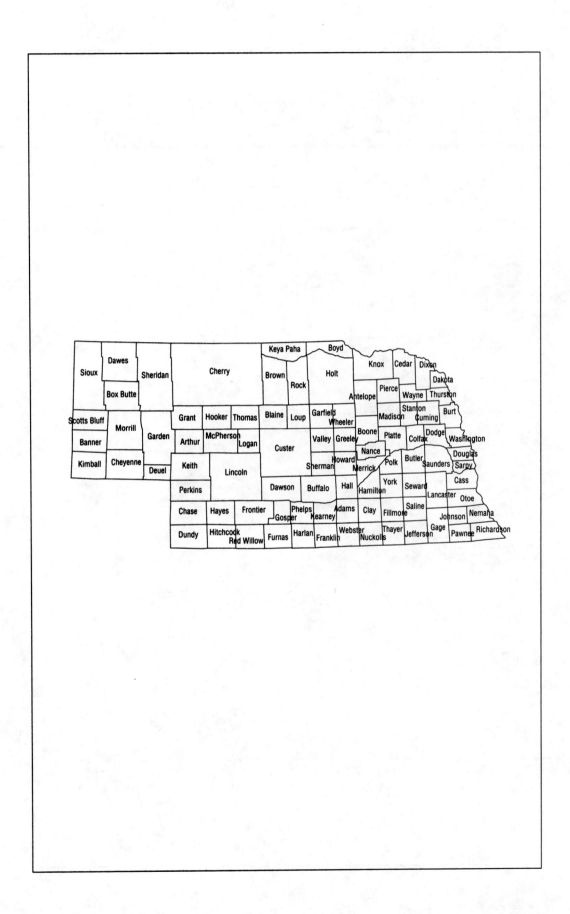

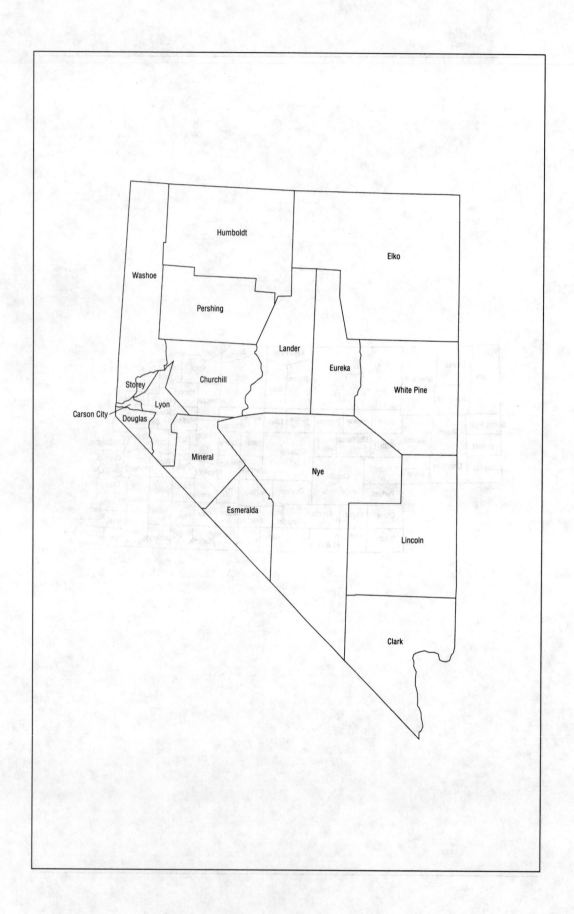

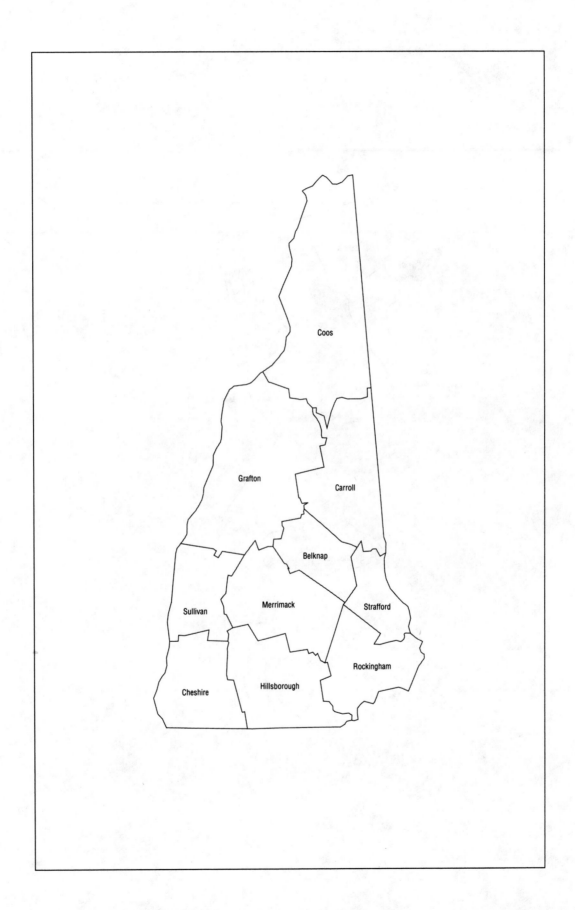

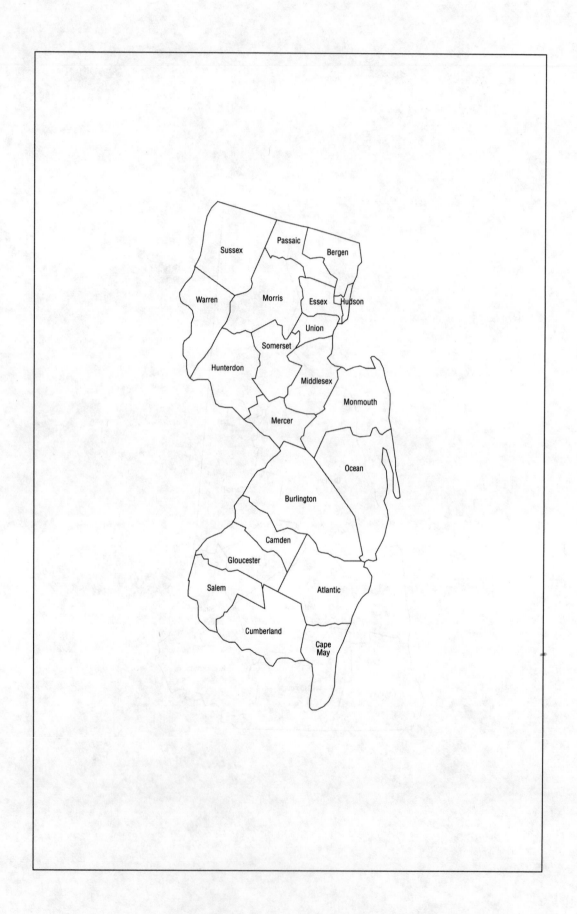

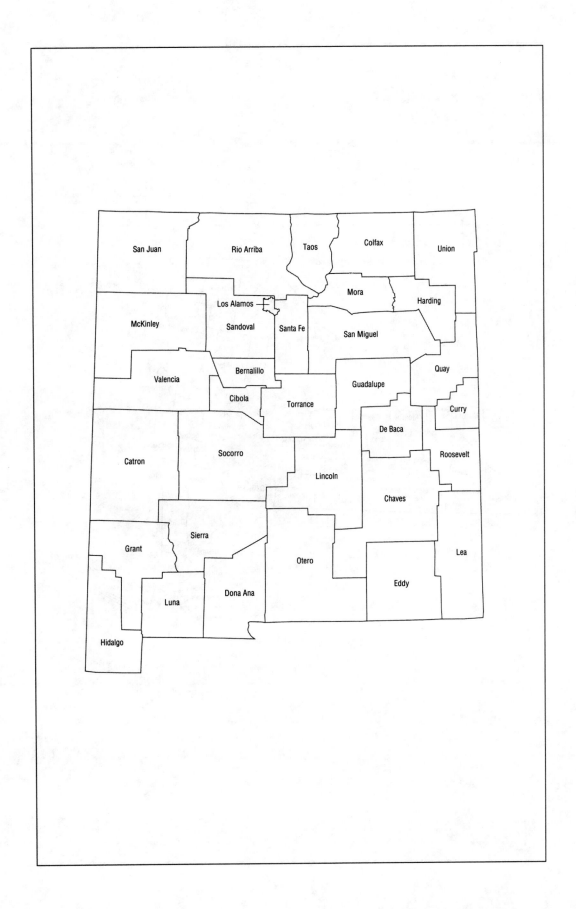

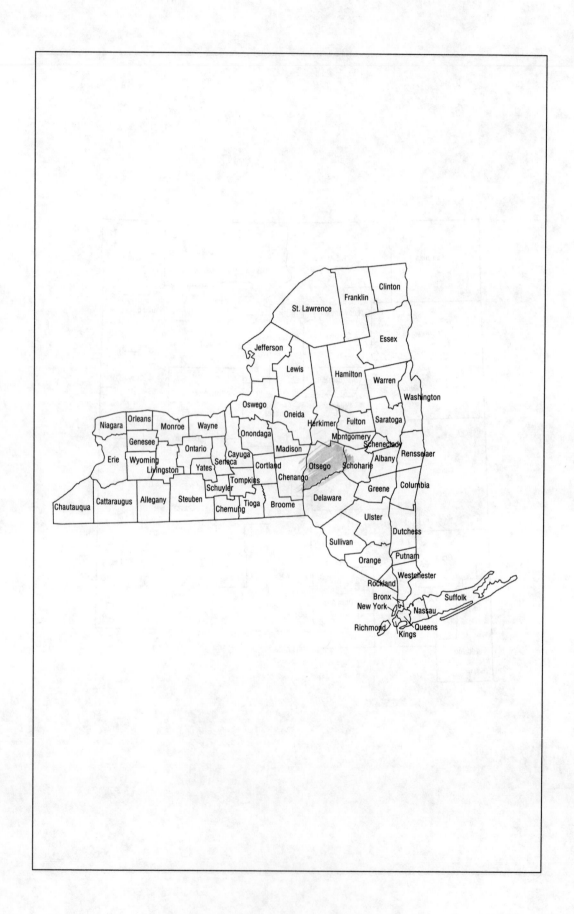

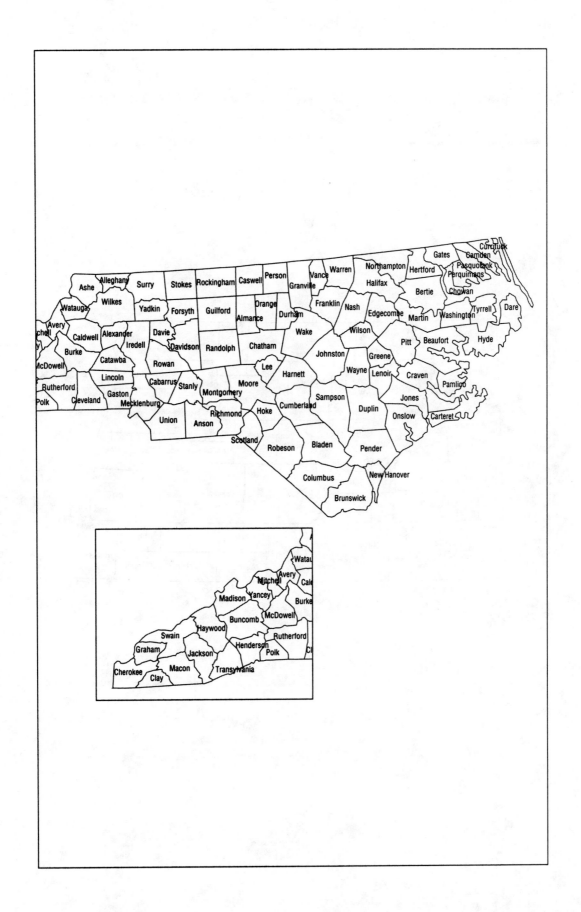

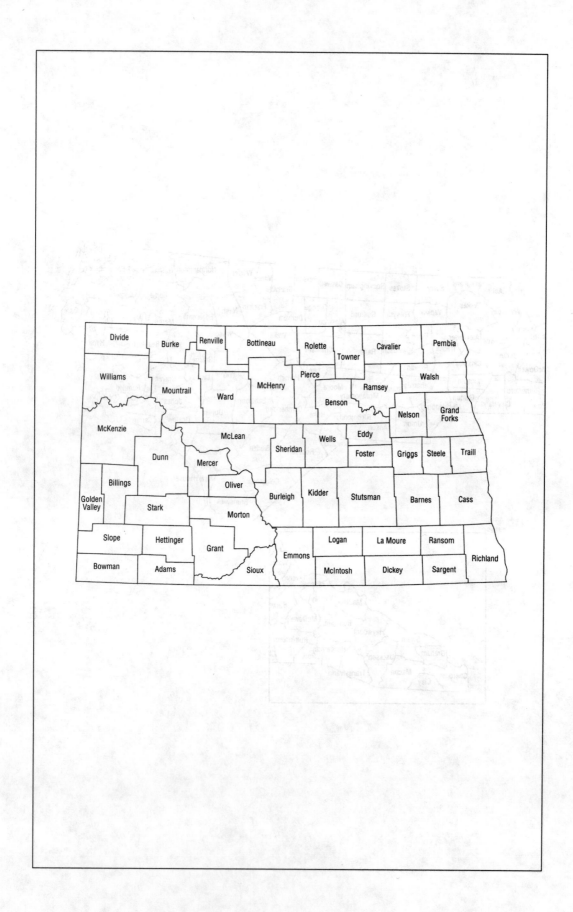

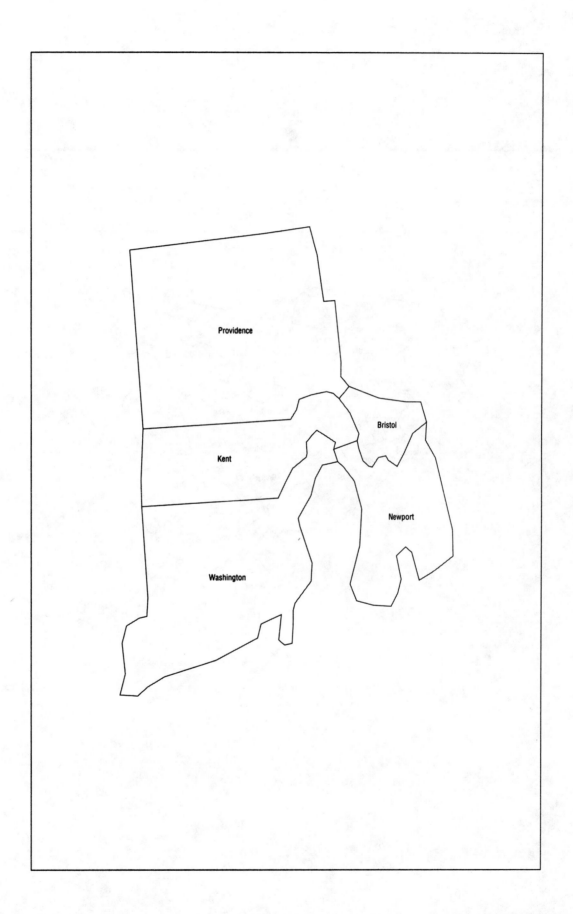

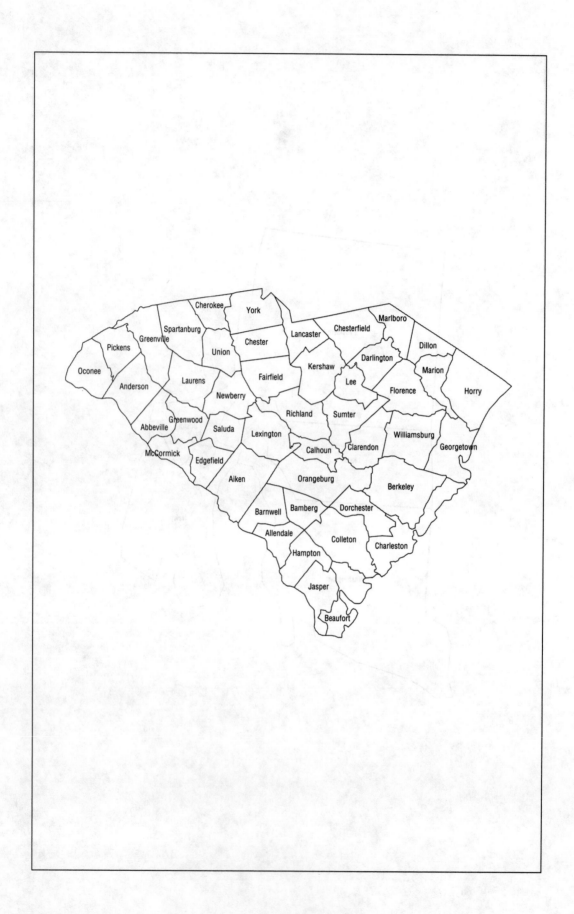

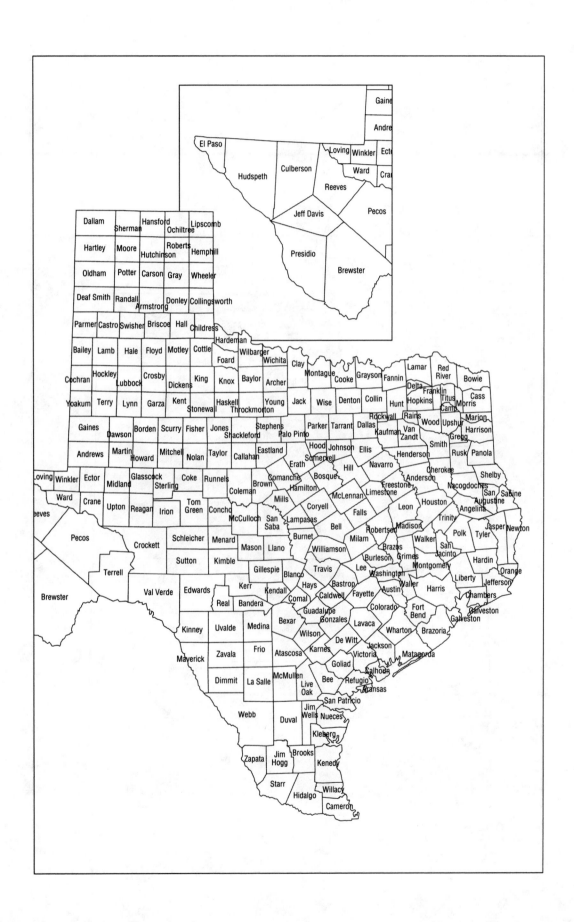

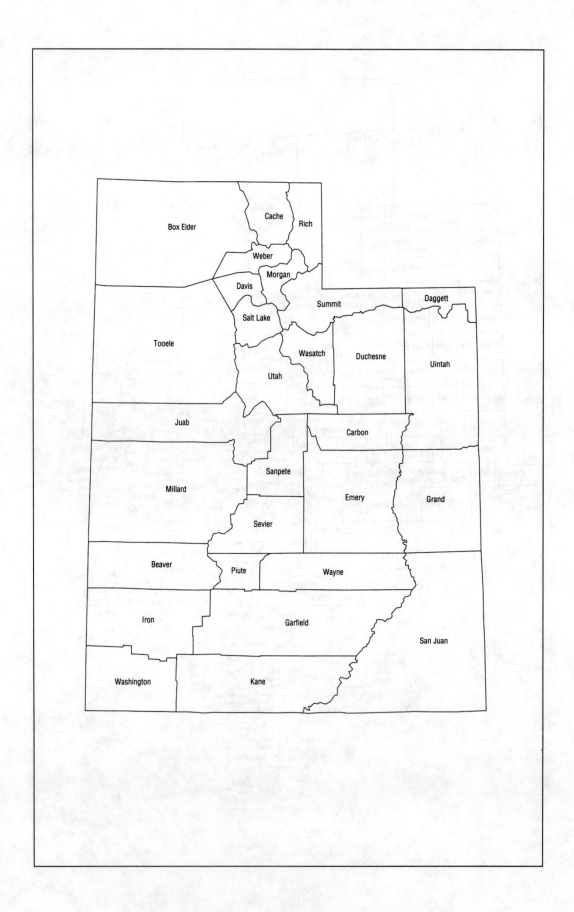

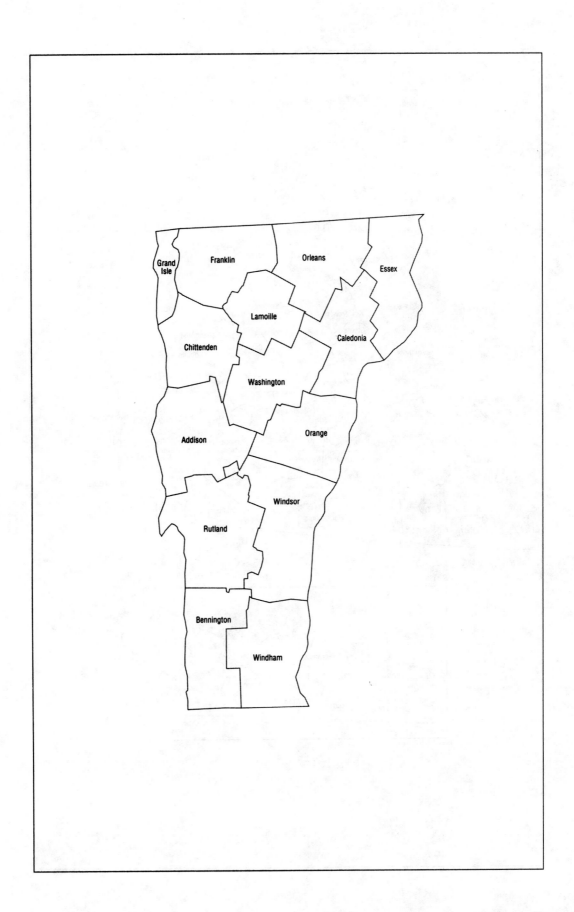

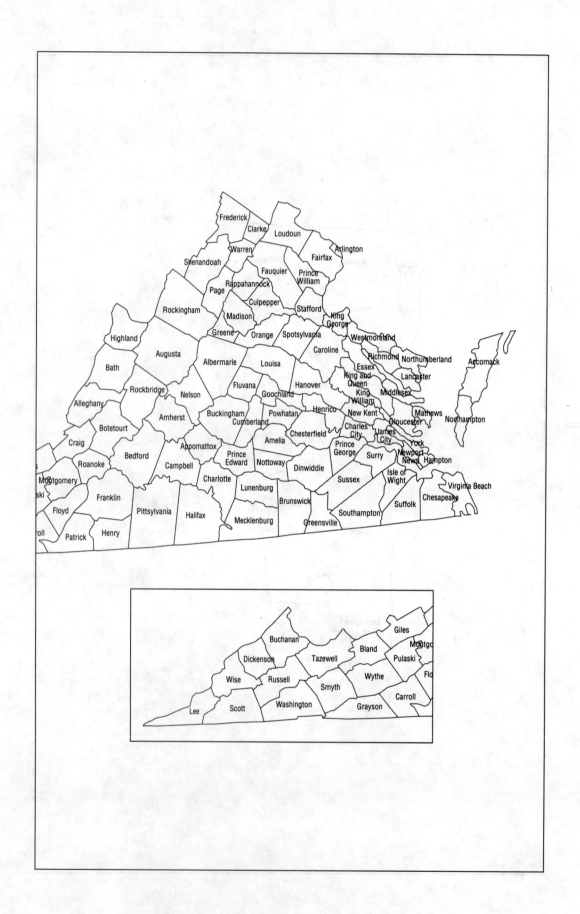

THE FEDERAL RECORDS DIRECTORY

INTRODUCTION

As important as state-held records are, they represent only half of the public records pool which may be used in pre-employment screening. Every citizen falls under the dominion of both a state, commonwealth or district and the federal government itself. Each of these dual authorities imposes its own legal obligations on those under its jurisdiction.

Though sometimes overlapping, the two legal systems are distinct. Any employer ignoring the federal courts risks a failure to uncover potentially relevant information about a job candidate.

First introduced in the *Second Edition* of the GUIDE, the *Federal Records Directory* facilitates access to a vast field of helpful data available at the federal level.

THE FEDERAL COURT SYSTEM.

A basic familiarity with the federal court system is essential for any professional aiming to tap into these resources.

The United States is divided into ninety-three (93) federal judicial districts. The boundary lines have been drawn in an attempt to achieve some parity in the various districts' caseload as well as to maintain geographic sensibility. Thus, while some of the smaller or less populous states (New Jersey, Montana) may constitute a single federal judicial district, bigger states may have as many as three or four (California, Illinois).

Each district's boundaries are contained wholly within the borders of a single state. This geographic division is inherently logical and, additionally, allows for easy identification of the various districts. The New Jersey court, for example, is known as the United States District Court for New Jersey. The northernmost court in Texas is identified as the United States District Court for the Northern District of Texas.

The federal court system handles three distinct types of controversies:

1. Civil Cases. While most legal disputes between private parties are settled in state court, the federal courts provide a forum when the case involves alleged violations of federal statutory or constitutional rights. These civil cases, brought by individuals, businesses or governmental entities, may seek money damages, request injunctions to stop an allegedly illegal behavior or pursue some other remedy provided by law.

2. Criminal Cases. These are different from civil cases. A criminal complaint is always brought by the federal government itself.

In the name of the United States of America, federal prosecutors try to convince the court that a named defendant has violated federal criminal law. Whether involving mail fraud, interstate drug trafficking, civil rights violations or some other matter, the essence of these cases is always the same – the defendant is alleged to have committed a crime and prosecutors seek a conviction and punishment.

3. Bankruptcy Cases. Bankruptcy, the third category, in recent years has claimed an increasing share of the federal judiciary's time and efforts.

The bankruptcy courts differ from the civil and criminal district courts in the way they are organized and operated. They have their own rules of evidence and procedures. In fact, the origin of the bankruptcy courts is even traceable to a different part of the Constitution than the other federal courts.

Bankruptcy actions may be brought by individuals and businesses whose indebtedness burden becomes too heavy to manage. The bankruptcy court seeks to provide the debtor with both protection and a "fresh start," while also considering the rights and interests of the creditors. Under certain circumstances, creditors may force a debtor into bankruptcy. These "involuntary" proceedings are allowed when it is shown that intervention is necessary to prevent the debtor from squandering assets which should be preserved for the creditors.

The *Federal Records Directory* shows how to access records relating to all three types of cases.

USING THE FEDERAL RECORDS DIRECTORY.

To use the *Federal Records Directory* on a given job applicant, first isolate the geographic areas with which you will be most concerned.

The employment application will be the first source to which you should look. It will reveal locations in which the individual has lived, worked or had other significant contacts. (For tips on other pointers to relevant locales, see *Using The Guide to Background Investigations* and the introduction to the *State Records Directory*.)

Determining which federal district court controls records for the locations you have identified can be easily done. The federal courts are listed alphabetically by state and then by district within the state. Thus, in California, you will find first the Central District and then the Eastern, Northern and Southern Districts, respectively.

Each of the federal courts included here begins with a listing of the counties under its jurisdiction. If you are unsure in which county a given city lies, the city-county cross references in the *State Records Directory* can eliminate any doubts.

What You Will Find.

Essentially every district will have at least two separate record repositories listed. This is because civil and criminal files are usually maintained separately from those of the district's bankruptcy court. Bigger districts with a heavier caseload may have several more record repositories, each maintaining records for a geographic subdivision within the district.

For every repository within a district, the *Federal Records Directory* will include the address and phone number of the court office as well as a summary of the procedures that office follows in releasing records for employment screening purposes. You can see what information must be supplied to conduct a records search on a given applicant as well as what fees are involved.

FEDERAL RECORDS CENTERS.

The court itself will retain records of cases in process. The court clerks will also usually retain closed files for several years (often in the one to five year range). Older records are stored in one of eleven regional "Federal Record Centers" (FRCs), also sometimes called the "federal archives."

Obtaining records through a FRC is a fairly simple matter with the *Federal Records Directory*, though two steps are involved.

In any search, however, you should always start with the district court, even if you suspect that any records on a given individual are probably more than a few years old. The district court will be able to tell you whether any records on the individual have actually been sent to the FRC. When a record has been forwarded to the FRC, the court will also supply the identification numbers required for the FRC to pull the file. Without the identification number, access to FRC files is difficult or impossible.

Note that the district court can contact the appropriate FRC to obtain the records for you. However, most districts charge an additional $25 (on top of their regular search fee) for this service. If you simply contact the FRC yourself with the required access information the FRC search can often be conducted at no charge.

To facilitate these inquiries, the *Federal Records Directory* shows the controlling FRC for each district court. All the FRCs are listed at the end of the *Directory*, with summaries of their individual search procedures.

United States District Courts

Middle District of Alabama

AUTAUGA, BARBOUR, BULLOCK, BUTLER, CHAMBERS, CHILTON, COFFEE, COOSA, COVINGTON, CRENSHAW, DALE, ELMORE, GENEVA, HENRY, HOUSTON, LEE, LOWNDES, MACON, MONTGOMERY, PIKE, RANDOLPH, RUSSELL, TALLAPOOSA.

Civil and Criminal Records

Clerk, US District Court Records Search
PO Box 711
Montgomery, AL 36101
(205) 223-7308

Records are available by mail. $15.00 search fee. $.50 fee per copy, $5.00 for certified copy. Search information required: name, SSN, previous address. Turnaround time: 48 hours. For pre 1987 closed files, see Atlanta Federal Records Center.

Bankruptcy Records

US Bankruptcy Court Clerk
PO Box 1248
Montgomery, AL 36102
(205) 223-7348 or 223-7250

Records are available by mail. No release necessary. $15.00 search fee. $.50 fee per copy, $5.00 for certified copy. Company check payable to Clerk, US Bankruptcy Court. Search information required: name, SSN, previous address. Turnaround time: 2-3 days. For closed files prior to 1988, as directed by court clerk, see Atlanta Federal Records Center.

Northern District of Alabama

BIBB, BLOUNT, CALHOUN, CHEROKEE, CLAY, CLEBURNE, COLBERT, CULMAN, DEKALB, ETOWAH, FAYETTE, FRANKLIN, GREENE, JACKSON, JEFFERSON, LAMAR, LAUDERDALE, LAWRENCE, LIMESTONE, MADISON, MARION, MARSHALL, MORGAN, PICKENS, SAINT CLAIR, SHELBY, SUMTER, TALLADEGA, TUSCALOOSA, WALKER, WINSTON.

Civil and Criminal Records

US District Court
Room 140
US Courthouse
1729 5th Ave. North
Birmingham, AL 35203
(205) 731-1701

Records are available by mail. $15.00 search fee. $.50 fee per copy, $5.00 for certified copy. Search information required: name. Turnaround time: 48 hours. For closed files prior to 1987, as directed by court clerk, see Atlanta Federal Records Center.

Bankruptcy Records

Clerk of Bankruptcy Court Northern District
1800 5th Avenue N.
Room 120
Birmingham, AL 35203
(205) 731-1614

Records are available by mail. $15.00 search fee. $.50 fee per copy, $5.00 for certified copy. Make check payable to Clerk, US Bankruptcy Court. Search information required: name, SSN, years to search. Turnaround time: 24 hours. Include your phone number with request. For closed files prior to 1991, as directed by court clerk, see Atlanta Federal Records Center.

Southern District of Alabama

BALDWIN, CHOCTAW, CLARKE, CONECUH, DALLAS, ESCAMBIA, HALE, MARENGO, MOBILE, MONROE, PERRY, WASHINGTON, WILCOX.

Civil and Criminal Records

District Clerk of Court
113 St. Joseph St.
Mobile, AL 36602
(205) 690-2371

Records are available by mail or phone. $15.00 search fee. $.50 fee per copy, $5.00 for certified copy. Make check payable to Clerk, US District Court. Search information required: name. Turnaround time: 7 days. For closed files prior to 1985, as directed by court clerk, see Atlanta Federal Records Center.

Bankruptcy Records

US Bankruptcy Court Clerk
PO Box 2865
Mobile, AL 36652
(205) 690-2391

Records are available by mail. $15.00 search fee. $.50 fee per copy, $5.00 for certified copy. Company check payable to US Bankruptcy Court. Search information required: name, SSN. Turnaround time: 2-3 days. For closed files prior to 1987, as directed by court clerk, see Atlanta Federal Records Center.

District of Alaska

FAIRBANKS, JUNEAU, KETCHIKAN, NOME.

Civil and Criminal Records

US Federal Building
222 W. 7th Ave.
Box 4
Anchorage, AK 99513
(907) 271-5568

Records are available by mail or phone. $15.00 search fee. Make check payable to Clerk, US District Court. Search information required: name. Turnaround time: 7 days. For closed files prior to 1959, as directed by court clerk, see Seattle Federal Records Center.

US District Court
101 12th Avenue
Box 1
Fairbanks, AK 99701
(907) 452-3163

Records are available by mail or phone. $15.00 search fee. $.50 fee per copy, $5.00 for certified copy. Make check payable to Clerk, US District Court. Search information required: name, years to search. Turnaround time: 7-10 days. For closed files, as directed by court clerk, see Seattle Federal Records Center.

Ketchikan Criminal Courts
415 Main Street
Room 400
Ketchikan, AK 99901
(907) 225-3195

Records are available by mail. $15.00 search fee. $.25 fee per copy, $5.00 fee for certified copy. Search information required: name, years to search, SASE. Turnaround time: 1-2 weeks. For closed files prior to 1987, as directed by court clerk, see Seattle Federal Records Center.

Nome Trial Courts
Box 100
Nome, AK 99762
(907) 443-5216

Records are available by mail or phone. $15.00 search fee. $.20 fee per copy, $5.00 fee for certification. Make check payable to Alaska Court System. Search information required: name, date of birth, SASE. Turnaround time: 5 days. For closed files prior to 1960, as directed by court clerk, see Seattle Federal Records Center.

Bankruptcy Records

US Bankruptcy Court
605 W. 4th Ave., Suite 138
Anchorage, AK 99501-2296
(907) 271-2655

Records are available by mail. $15.00 search fee. $.50 fee per copy, $5.00 for certified copy. Make check payable to US Bankruptcy Court. Search information required: name, years to search, SASE. Turnaround time: 24 hours. For closed files prior to 1992, as directed by court clerk, see Seattle Federal Records Center.

District of Arizona

THIS DISTRICT COMPRISES THE ENTIRE STATE.

Civil and Criminal Records

Clerk, US Courthouse
230 N. 1st Ave.
Room 1400
Phoenix, AZ 85025
(602) 379-6407

Records are available by mail. $15.00 search fee. $.50 fee per copy, $5.00 for certified copy. Company check payable to Clerk, US District Court. Search information required: name, years to search, SASE. Turnaround time: 2 weeks. For closed files prior to 1987, as directed by court clerk, see Los Angeles Federal Records Center.

US District Court
55 East Broadway
Tucson, AZ 85701
(602) 670-6559

Records are available by mail. $15.00 search fee. $.50 fee per copy, $5.00 for certified copy. Make check payable to US District Court Clerk. Search information required: name, years to search. Turnaround time: 1 week. For closed files prior to 1985, as directed by court clerk, see Los Angeles Federal Records Center.

Bankruptcy Records

US Bankruptcy Court
110 S. Church, Suite #81112
Tucson, AZ 85701
(602) 670-6304

Records are available by mail. $15.00 search fee. $.50 fee per copy, $5.00 for certified copy. Make check payable to US Bankruptcy Court. Search information required: name, address, approximate year case filed, SASE. Turnaround time: 4-5 days. For pre 1983 closed files, see Los Angeles Federal Records Center.

US Bankruptcy Court
Room 5000
230 North 1st Avenue
Phoenix, AZ 85025
(602) 379-6935 or 379-6965

Records are available by mail. $15.00 search fee. $.50 fee per copy, $5.00 fee for certification. Certified check only, payable to Clerk, US Bankruptcy Court. Search information required: name, years to search or case number, SASE. Turnaround time: 2 weeks. For closed files, as directed by court clerk, see Los Angeles Federal Records Center.

Eastern District of Arkansas

ARKANSAS, CHICOT, CLAY, CLEBURNE, CLEVELAND, CONWAY, CRAIGHEAD, CRITTENDEN, CROSS, DALLAS, DESHA, DREW, FAULKNER, FULTON, GRANT, GREENE, INDEPENDENCE, IZARD, JACKSON, JEFFERSON, LAWRENCE, LEE, LINCOLN, LONOKE, MISSISSIPPI, MONROE, PERRY, PHILLIPS, POINSETT, POPE, PRAIRIE, PULASKI, RANDOLPH, SAINT FRANCIS, SALINE, SHARP, STONE, VAN BUREN, WHITE, WOODRUFF, YELL.

Civil and Criminal Records

US District Court Clerk
PO Box 869
Little Rock, AR 72203
(501) 324-5351

Records are available by mail. $15.00 search fee. $.50 fee per copy, $5.00 for certified copy. Make check payable to US District Court. Search information required: name. Turnaround time: 7 days. For pre 1988 closed files, see Fort Worth Federal Records Center.

Bankruptcy Records

US Bankruptcy Court
PO Box 2381
Little Rock, AR 72203
(501) 324-6357

Records are available by phone or mail. $15.00 search fee. $.50 fee per copy, $5.00 for certified copy. Make check payable to Clerk, US Bankruptcy Court. Search information required: name, SSN, address, SASE. Turnaround time: 1-2 weeks. For pre 1983 closed files, see Fort Worth Federal Records Center.

Western District of Arkansas

ASHLEY, BAXTER, BENTON, BOONE, BRADLEY, CALHOUN, CARROLL, CLARK, COLUMBIA, CRAWFORD, FRANKLIN, GARLAND, HEMPSTEAD, HOT SPRING, HOWARD, JOHNSON, LA FAYETTE, LITTLE RIVER, LOGAN, MADISON, MARION, MILLER, MONTGOMERY, NEVADA, NEWTON, OUACHITA, PIKE, POLK, SCOTT, SEARCY, SEBASTIAN, SEVIER, UNION, WASHINGTON.

Civil and Criminal Records

US District Court
35 East Mountain
Room 523
Fayetteville, AR 72701
(501) 521-6980
Fax (501) 575-0774

Records are available by mail or phone. $15.00 search fee. $.50 fee per copy, $5.00 for certified copy. Make check payable to US District Clerk. Search information required: name. Turnaround time: 24 hours. For pre 1985 closed files, see Atlanta Federal Records Center.

US District Court Clerk
PO Box 1566
101 S. Jackson, Rm 205
El Dorado, AR 71731-1566
(501) 862-1202

Records are available by mail. $15.00 search fee. $.50 fee per copy, $5.00 for certified copy. No fee to check index by phone. Make check payable to Clerk, US District Court. Search information required: name. Turnaround time: 24 hours. For pre 1985 closed files, see Fort Worth Federal Records Center.

US District Court
PO Box 1523
Fort Smith, AR 72902
(501) 783-6833

Records are available by mail or phone. $15.00 search fee. $.50 fee per copy, $5.00 for certified copy. Make check payable to Clerk, US District Court. Search information required: name. Turnaround time: 1 week. For closed files, as directed by court clerk, see Fort Worth Federal Records Center.

Clerk, US District Court
PO Box 2746
Texarkana, AR 75504
(501) 773-3381

Records are available by mail or phone. No release necessary. $15.00 search fee. $.50 fee per copy, $5.00 for certified copy. Make check payable to Clerk, US District Court. Search information required: name. Turnaround time: 2-3 days. For closed files prior to 1987, as directed by court clerk, see Fort Worth Federal Records Center.

US District Court
PO Drawer I
Hot Springs, AR 71902
(501) 623-6411

Records are available by mail or phone. $15.00 search fee. $.50 fee per copy, $5.00 for certified copy. Company check payable to US District Court. Search information required: name. Turnaround time: 2 days. For closed files prior to 1986, as directed by court clerk, see Fort Worth Federal Records Center. Files go back to 1940.

Bankruptcy Records

US Bankruptcy Court
PO Box 2381
Little Rock, AR 72203
(501) 324-6357

Records are available by mail or phone. $15.00 search fee. $.50 fee per copy, $5.00 for certified copy. Make check payable to Clerk, US Bankruptcy Court. Search information required: name, previous address, years to search. Turnaround time: 1-2 weeks. For pre August 1988 closed files, see Fort Worth Federal Records Center.

Central District of California

LOS ANGELES, ORANGE, RIVERSIDE, SAN BERNARDINO, SAN LUIS OBISPO, SANTA BARBARA, VENTURA.

Civil and Criminal Records

US Courthouse Records Department
312 North Spring Street
Los Angeles, CA 90012
(213) 894-3649 or 894-5261

Records are available by mail. No release necessary. $15.00 search fee. $.50 fee per copy, $5.00 for certified copy. Certified check only, payable to Clerk, US District Court. Search information required: name. Turnaround time: 7 days. For pre 1989 closed files, see Los Angeles Federal Records Center.

Bankruptcy Records

US Bankruptcy Court Clerk
Room 906
312 North Spring Street
Los Angeles, CA 90012
(213) 894-5978
Records are available by mail. $15.00 search fee. $.50 fee per copy, $5.00 for certified copy. Make check payable to US Bankruptcy Court. Search information required: name. Turnaround time: 2 weeks. For pre 1989 closed files, see Los Angeles Federal Records Center.

Eastern District of California

ALPINE, AMADOR, BUTTE, CALAVERAS, COLUSA, EL DORADO, FRESNO, GLENN, INYO, KERN, KINGS, LASSEN, MADERA, MARIPOSA, MERCED, MODOC, MONO, NEVADA, PLACER, PLUMAS, SACRAMENTO, SAN JOAQUIN, SHASTA, SIERRA, SISKIYOU, SOLANO, STANISLAUS, SUTTER, TEHAMA, TRINITY, TULARE, TUOLUMNE, YOLO, YUBA.

Civil and Criminal Records

US Courthouse
Room 5408
1130 O Street
Fresno, CA 93721
(209) 487-5083
Records are available by mail. $15.00 search fee. $.50 fee per copy, $5.00 for certified copy. Make check payable to US District Court. Search information required: name. Turnaround time: 2 days. For pre 1985 closed files, see San Francisco Federal Records Center.

US District Court
650 Capital Mall
Sacramento, CA 95814-4797
(916) 551-2615
Records are available by mail. $15.00 search fee. $.50 fee per copy, $5.00 for certified copy. Make check payable to Clerk, US District Court. Search information required: name, years to search. Turnaround time: 48 hours. For pre 1987 closed files, see San Francisco Federal Records Center.

Bankruptcy Records

US Bankruptcy Court Clerk
PO Box 5276
Modesto, CA 95352
(209) 521-5160
Records are available by mail. $15.00 search fee. $.50 fee per copy, $5.00 for certified copy. Make check payable to US Bankruptcy Court. Search information required: name. Turnaround time: 2 weeks. For closed files, as directed by court clerk, see San Francisco Federal Records Center.

US Bankruptcy Court Clerk
5301 Federal Courthouse
1130 O Street
Fresno, CA 93721
(209) 487-5219
Records are available by mail. $15.00 search fee. $.50 fee per copy, $5.00 for certified copy. Make check payable to US Bankruptcy Court Clerk. Search information required: name. Turnaround time: 2 weeks. For closed files, as directed by court clerk, see San Francisco Federal Records Center.

US Bankruptcy Court Clerk
650 Capital Mall
Sacramento, CA 95814
(916) 551-2674
Records are available by mail. $15.00 search fee. $.50 fee per copy, $5.00 for certified copy. Make check payable to US Bankruptcy Court. Search information required: name, years to search. Turnaround time: 1 week. For closed files, as directed by court clerk, see San Francisco Federal Records Center.

Northern District of California

ALAMEDA, CONTRA COSTA, DEL NORTE, HUMBOLDT, LAKE, MARIN, MENDOCINO, MONTEREY, NAPA, SAN BENITO, SANTA CLARA, SANTA CRUZ, SAN FRANCISCO, SAN MATEO, SONOMA.

Civil and Criminal Records

US Courthouse
280 South First Street - Room 2112
San Jose, CA 95113
(408) 291-7783
Records are available by mail. $15.00 search fee. $.50 fee per copy, $5.00 for certified copy. Make check payable to Clerk, US District Court. Search information required: name. Turnaround time: 7 days. For pre 1988 closed files, see San Bruno Federal Records Center.

US District Court Clerk
PO Box 36060
450 Golden Gate Ave., R-18425
San Francisco, CA 94102
(415) 556-3031
Fax (415) 705-3141
Records are available by mail or phone. No search fee. $.50 fee per copy, $5.00 for certified copy. Search information required: name. Turnaround time: 5 days. For closed files prior to 1990, as directed by court clerk, see San Francisco Federal Records Center.

Bankruptcy Records

US Bankruptcy Court Clerk
PO Box 36053
450 Golden Gate Ave.
San Francisco, CA 94102
(415) 556-2250
Records are available by mail or phone. $15.00 search fee. $.50 fee per copy, $5.00 for certified copy. Company check payable to US Bankruptcy Court Clerk. Search information required: name, SSN, approximately date case filed, address, SASE. Turnaround time: 1-2 weeks. For closed files, as directed by court clerk, see San Francisco Federal Records Center.

Southern District of California

IMPERIAL, SAN DIEGO.

Civil and Criminal Records

US District Courthouse
940 Front Street, Room #1 North 20
San Diego, CA 92189
(619) 557-5602
Records are available by mail. $15.00 search fee. $.50 fee per copy, $5.00 for certified copy. Make check payable to US District Court. Search information required: name. Turnaround time: 7-10 days. For closed files, as directed by court clerk, see Los Angeles Federal Records Center.

Bankruptcy Records

US Bankruptcy Court
Room 5 N 26
940 Front Street
San Diego, CA 92189-0020
(619) 557-5620
Records are available by mail. $15.00 search fee. $.50 fee per copy, $5.00 for certified copy. Make check payable to US Bankruptcy Court. Search information required: name, case number if available. For all closed files, see Los Angeles Federal Records Center.

District of Colorado

THIS DISTRICT COMPRISES THE ENTIRE STATE.

Civil and Criminal Records

US Courthouse
1929 Stout Street
Room C-161
Denver, CO 80294
(303) 844-2115
Records are available by mail or phone. No search fee. $.50 fee per copy, $5.00 for certified copy. Search information required: name. Turnaround time: 1-2 days. For closed files prior to 1980, as directed by court clerk, see Denver Federal Records Center.

Bankruptcy Records

US Bankruptcy Court Clerk
US Custom House
721 19th Street
Denver, CO 80203-2508
(303) 844-4045
Records are available by mail. $15.00 search fee. $.50 fee per copy, $5.00 for certified copy. Make check payable to US Bankruptcy Court. Search information required: name. Turnaround time: 2-3 weeks. For pre 1989 closed files, see Denver Federal Records Center.

District of Connecticut

THIS DISTRICT COMPRISES THE ENTIRE STATE.

Civil and Criminal Records

US District Court
450 Main Street
Hartford, CT 06103
(203) 240-3200
Records are available by mail. $15.00 search fee. $.50 fee per copy, $5.00 for certified copy. Make check payable to US District Court. Search information required: name, years to search. Turnaround time: 3-4 days. For pre 1986 closed files, see Boston Federal Records Center.

Office of the Clerk
US District Court
915 Lafayette Boulevard, Room 400
Bridgeport, CT 06604
(203) 579-5864
Records are available by mail. $15.00 search fee. $.50 fee per copy, $5.00 for certified copy. Search information required: name, years to search. A one name search is free. Multiple name searches, $15.00 per name. For pre 1987 closed files, see Boston Federal Records Center.

US District Court Clerk
141 Church Street
New Haven, CT 06510
(203) 773-2140
Records are available by mail or phone. No search fee for first request. $15.00 each additional request. $.50 fee per copy, $5.00 for certified copy. Make check payable to District Court Clerk. Search information required: name. Turnaround time: 24 hours. A one name search is free. Multiple name searches, $15.00 per name. For pre 1986 closed files, see Boston Federal Records Center.

Bankruptcy Records

US Bankruptcy Court
450 Main Street
Hartford, CT 06103
(203) 240-3677
Records are available by mail. $15.00 search fee. $.50 fee per copy, $5.00 for certified copy. Make check payable to Clerk of Bankruptcy Court. Search information required: name, previous address, approximate date case filed. Turnaround time: 7-10 days. For pre 1989 closed files, see Boston Federal Records Center.

District of Delaware

THIS DISTRICT COMPRISES THE ENTIRE STATE.

Civil and Criminal Records

US Courthouse
844 N. King Street
Lock Box 18
Wilmington, DE 19801
(302) 573-6170
Records are available by mail. $15.00 search fee. $.50 fee per copy, $5.00 for certified copy. Make company check payable to Clerk of US District Court. Search information required: name, years to search. Turnaround time: 2 days. For closed files, as directed by court clerk, see Philadelphia Federal Records Center.

Bankruptcy Records

US Bankruptcy Court
844 N. King Street - Federal Building
Lock Box 38
Wilmington, DE 19801
(302) 573-6174
Records are available by mail. $15.00 search fee. $.50 fee per copy, $5.00 for certified copy. Make check payable to US Bankruptcy Court. Search information required: name. Turnaround time: 2-3 weeks. For closed files, as directed by court clerk, see Philadelphia Federal Records Center.

District of Columbia

THIS DISTRICT COMPRISES ALL THE DISTRICT OF COLUMBIA.

Civil and Criminal Records

US Courthouse
US District Court - Clerk's Office
3rd & Constitution Avenue Northwest
Washington, DC 20001
(202) 535-3520
Records are available by mail or phone. $15.00 minimum search fee. $.50 fee per copy, $5.00 for certified copy. Search information required: name. Turnaround time: 7 days.

Bankruptcy Records

US Bankruptcy Court Clerk
Room 4400
3rd & Constitution Avenue Northwest
Washington, DC 20001
(202) 535-3042
Records are available by mail. No release necessary. $15.00 search fee. $.50 fee per copy, $5.00 for certified copy. Make company check payable to US Bankruptcy Court. Search information required: name. Turnaround time: 2 days.

Middle District of Florida

BAKER, BRADFORD, BREVARD, CHARLOTTE, CITRUS, CLAY, COLLIER, COLUMBIA, DESOTO, DUVAL, FLAGLER, GLADES, HAMILTON, HARDEE, HENDRY HERNANDO, HILLSBOROUGH, LAKE, LEE, MANATEE, MARION, NASSAU, ORANGE, OSCEOLA, PASCO, PINELLAS, POLK, PUTNAM, SARASOTA, SEMINOLE, ST. JOHNS, SUMTER, SUWANNEE UNION, VOLUSIA.

Civil and Criminal Records

US Courthouse
611 North Florida Avenue
Tampa, FL 33602
(813) 228-2105
Records are available by mail. $15.00 search fee. $.50 fee per copy, $5.00 for certified copy. Make check payable to Clerk, US District Court. Search information required: name. For closed files prior to 1989, as directed by court clerk, see Atlanta Federal Records Center.

US District Court
80 North Hughey Avenue
Room 218
Orlando, FL 32801
(407) 648-6366
Records are available by mail. $15.00 search fee. $.50 fee per copy, $5.00 for certified copy. Make check payable to Clerk, US District Court. Search information required: name. Turnaround time: 3 days. For pre 1990 closed files, see Atlanta Federal Records Center.

US District Court
311 West Monroe Street
Suite 110
Jacksonville, FL 32202
(904) 791-3357
Records are available by mail. $15.00 search fee. $.50 fee per copy, $5.00 for certified copy. Company check payable to Clerk, US District Court. Search information required: name. Turnaround time: 24 hours. For pre 1987 closed files, see Atlanta Federal Records Center.

Bankruptcy Records

US Bankruptcy Court
PO Box 559
Jacksonville, FL 32201
(904) 791-3357
Records are available by mail. $15.00 search fee. $5.00 fee for copying, plus $.25 fee per copy. $14.00 for certified copy. Make check payable to US Bankruptcy Court. Search information required: name. Turnaround time: 3 days. For pre 1987 closed files, see Atlanta Federal Records Center.

US Bankruptcy Court Clerk
4921 Memorial Highway
Suite 200
Tampa, FL 33634
(813) 225-7064
Records are available by mail. $15.00 search fee. $5.00 fee for copying, plus $.25 fee per copy. $14.00 for certified copy. Make check payable to US Bankruptcy Clerk. Search information required: name, SSN. Turnaround time: 24 hours. For closed files prior to 1987, as directed by court clerk, see Atlanta Federal Records Center.

Northern District of Florida

ALACHUA, BAY, CALHOUN, DIXIE, ESCAMBIA, FRANKLIN, GADSDEN, GILCHRIST, GULF, HOLMES, JACKSON, JEFFERSON, LAFAYETTE, LEON, LEVY, LIBERTY, MADISON, OKALOOSA, SANTA ROSA, TAYLOR, WAKULLA, WALTON, WASHINGTON.

Civil and Criminal Records

US District Court
110 East Park Avenue
Suite 122
Tallahassee, FL 32301
(904) 942-8826
Records are available by mail. $15.00 search fee. $.50 fee per copy, $5.00 for certified copy. Make check payable to US District Court Clerk. Search information required: name. Turnaround time: 3 days. For closed files, as directed by court clerk, see Atlanta Federal Records Center. For closed files prior to 1987, as directed by court clerk, see Atlanta Federal Records Center.

US Courthouse
100 North Palafox Street
Room 129
Pensacola, FL 32501
(904) 435-8441
Records are available by mail. $15.00 search fee. $.50 fee per copy, $5.00 for certified copy. Make check payable to Clerk, US District Court. Search information required: name. Turnaround time: 7 days. For pre 1985 closed files, see Atlanta Federal Records Center.

Bankruptcy Records

US Bankruptcy Court Clerk
Room 3120
227 North Bronough Street
Tallahassee, FL 32301
(904) 681-7500
Records are available by mail or limited information available by phone. $15.00 search fee. $.50 fee per copy, $5.00 for certified copy. Make check payable to US Bankruptcy Court. Search information required: name. Turnaround time: 7 days. For pre 1989 closed files, see Atlanta Federal Records Center. Contact the above office for Accession Numbers.

Southern District of Florida

BROWARD, DADE, HIGHLANDS, INDIAN RIVER, MARTIN, MONROE, OKEECHOBEE, PALM BEACH, ST. LUCIE.

Civil and Criminal Records

US District Court
701 Clematis Street
Room 402
West Palm Beach, FL 33401
(407) 655-8710
Records are available by mail. $15.00 search fee. $.50 fee per copy, $5.00 for certified copy. Company check payable to Clerk, US District Court. Search information required: name. Turnaround time: 7 days. For pre 1983 closed files, see Atlanta Federal Records Center.

US District Court
301 North Miami Avenue, Room 150
Miami, FL 33128-7788
(305) 536-4131 or 536-5504
Records are available by mail. No release necessary. $15.00 search fee. $.50 fee per copy, $5.00 for certified copy. Make check payable to Clerk, US District Court. Search information required: name, years to search. Turnaround time: 1 week. For pre 1981 closed files, see Atlanta Federal Records Center.

US District Courthouse
299 East Broward Boulevard
Room 201
Ft. Lauderdale, FL 33301
(305) 356-7075
Records are available by mail. $15.00 search fee. $.50 fee per copy, $5.00 for certified copy. Company check payable to US District Court Clerk. Search information required: name, years to search. Turnaround time: 3-5 days. For pre 1988 closed files, see Atlanta Federal Records Center.

Bankruptcy Records

US Bankruptcy Court Clerk
51 Southwest First Avenue, Rm. 1401
Miami, FL 33101
(305) 536-5216
Records are available by mail. $15.00 search fee. $.50 fee per copy, $5.00 for certified copy. Certified check or money order, payable to US Bankruptcy Court. Search information required: name. Turnaround time: 1 week. For pre 1990 closed files, see Atlanta Federal Records Center.

Middle District of Georgia

BAKER, BALDWIN, BEN HILL, BERRIEN, BIBB, BLECKLEY, BROOKS, BUTTS, CALHOUN, CHATTAHOOCHEE, CLARKE, CLAY, CLINCH, COLQUITT, COOK, CRAWFORD, CRISP, DECATUR, DOOLEY, DOUGHERTY, EARLY, ECHOLS, ELBERT, FRANKLIN, GRADY, GREENE, HANCOCK, HARRIS, HART, HOUSTON, IRWIN, JASPER, JONES, LAMAR, LANIER, LEE, LOWNDES, MACON, MADISON, MARION, MILLER, MITCHELL, MONROE, MORGAN, MUSCOGEE, OCONEE, OGLETHORPE, PEACH, PULASKI, PUTNAM, QUITMAN, RANDOLPH, SCHLEY, SEMINOLE, STEWART, SUMPTER, TALBOT, TAYLOR, TERRILL, THOMAS, TIFT, TURNER, TWIGGS, UPSON, WALTON, WASHINGTON, WEBSTER, WILCOX, WILKINSON, WORTH.

Civil and Criminal Records

Clerk, US District Court
PO Box 1906
Albany, GA 31702
(912) 430-8432
Records are available by mail or phone. $15.00 search fee. $.50 fee per copy, $5.00 for certified copy. Certified check only, payable to Clerk, US District Court. Search information required: name. Turnaround time: 24 hours. For pre 1983 closed files, as directed by court clerk, see Atlanta Federal Records Center.

Clerk, US District Court
PO Box 124
Columbus, GA 31902
(404) 649-7816
Records are available by mail or phone. No release necessary. $15.00 search fee. $.50 fee per copy, $5.00 for certified copy. Make check payable to Clerk, US District Court. Search information required: name. Turnaround time: 2 days. For closed files prior to 1986, as directed by court clerk, see Atlanta Federal Records Center.

Clerk of Superior Court
PO Box 1015
Macon, GA 31202
(912) 749-6527
Records open to public.

Bankruptcy Records

US Bankruptcy Court Clerk
PO Box 1957
Macon, GA 31202-1957
(912) 752-3506
Records are available by mail. $15.00 search fee, prepaid. $.50 fee per copy, $5.00 for certified copy. Make check payable to Clerk, US Bankruptcy Court. Search information required: name. Turnaround time: 5 days. For closed files, as directed by court clerk, see Atlanta Federal Records Center.

Northern District of Georgia

BANKS, BARROW, BARTOW, CARROLL, CATOOSA, CHATTOOGA, CHEROKEE, CLAYTON, COBB, COWETA, DADE, DAWSON, DEKALB, DOUGLAS, FANNIN, FAYETTE, FLOYD, FORSYTH, FULTON, GILMER, GORDON, GWINNETT, HABERSHAM, HALL, HARALSON, HEARD, HENRY, JACKSON, LUMPKIN, MERIWETHER, MURRAY, NEWTON, PAULDING, PICKENS, PIKE, POLK, RABUN, ROCKDALE, SPAULDING, STEPHENS, TOWNS, TROUP, UNION, WALKER, WHITE, WHITFIELD.

Civil and Criminal Records

Clerk, US District Court
126 Washington Southeast
Room 201 Federal Bldg.
Gainesville, GA 30501
(404) 534-5954
Records are available by mail. $15.00 search fee. $.50 fee per copy, $5.00 for certified copy. Certified check or money order, payable to Clerk, US District Court. Search information required: name. Turnaround time: 24 hours. For pre 1928 closed files, see Atlanta Federal Records Center.

Clerk, US District Court
PO Box 939
Newnan, GA 30264
(404) 253-8847
Records are available by mail. $15.00 search fee. $.50 fee per copy, $5.00 for certified copy. Make cashier's check or money order payable to Clerk, US District Court. Search information required: name, SSN. Turnaround time: 2 days. For 1939-1983 closed files, see Atlanta Federal Records Center.

Clerk, US District Court
PO Box 1186
Rome, GA 30162-1186
(404) 291-5629

Records are available by mail. $15.00 search fee. $.50 fee per copy, $5.00 for certified copy. Cashiers check or US Postal money order only, payable to Clerk, US District Court. Search information required: name. Turnaround time: 2 days. For pre 1982 closed files, see Atlanta Federal Records Center.

2211 US District Court
75 Spring Street Southwest
Atlanta, GA 30335
(404) 331-6197

Records are available by mail. $15.00 search fee. $.50 fee per copy, $5.00 for certified copy. Cashiers check or US Postal money order only, payable to Clerk, US District Court. Search information required: name, years to search. Turnaround time: 24 hours. For pre 1985 closed files, see Atlanta Federal Records Center.

Bankruptcy Records

US Bankruptcy Court Clerk
1340 US Courthouse
75 Spring Street Southwest
Atlanta, GA 30303
(404) 331-5411

Records are available by mail. $15.00 search fee. $.50 fee per copy, $5.00 for certified copy. Make check payable to Clerk, US Bankruptcy Court. Search information required: name. Turnaround time: 1-2 days. For closed files, as directed by court clerk, see Atlanta Federal Records Center. For copies of closed files contact the Atlanta copying service at (404) 688-6476

Southern District of Georgia

APPLING, ATKINSON, BACON, BRANTLEY, BRYAN, BULLOCH, BURKE, CAMDEN, CANDLER, CHARLTON, CHATHAM, COFFEE, COLUMBIA, DODGE, EFFINGHAM, EMANUEL, EVANS, GLASCOCK, GLYNN, JEFF DAVIS, JEFFERSON, JENKINS, JOHNSON, LAURENS, LIBERTY, LINCOLN, LONG, MCDUFFIE, MCINTOSH, MONTGOMERY, PIERCE, RICHMOND, SCREVEN, TALIAFERRO, TATTNALL, TELFAIR, TOOMBS, TREUTLEN, WARE, WARREN, WAYNE, WHEELER, WILKES.

Civil and Criminal Records

Clerk, US District Court
PO Box 1130
Augusta, GA 30903
(404) 722-2074

Records are available by mail. $15.00 search fee. $.50 fee per copy, $5.00 for certified copy. Make check payable to Clerk, US District Court. Search information required: name. Turnaround time: 1-2 weeks. For pre 1985 closed files, see Atlanta Federal Records Center.

Clerk, US District Court
PO Box 1636
Brunswick, GA 31521
(912) 265-1758

Records are available by mail. $15.00 search fee. $.50 fee per copy, $5.00 for certified copy. Make check payable to Clerk, US District Court. Search information required: name. Turnaround time: 2 days. For closed files, as directed by court clerk, see Atlanta Federal Records Center.

Clerk, US District Court
PO Box 8286
Savannah, GA 31412
(912) 652-4013

Records are available by mail. No release necessary. $15.00 search fee. $.50 fee per copy, $5.00 for certified copy. Make check payable to Clerk, US District Court. Search information required: name. Turnaround time: 1 to 2 days. For pre 1989 closed files, see Atlanta Federal Records Center.

Bankruptcy Records

US Bankruptcy Court Clerk
PO Box 8347
Savannah, GA 31412
(912) 652-4100

Records are available by mail. $15.00 search fee. $.50 fee per copy, $5.00 for certified copy. Make check payable to Clerk, US Bankruptcy Court. Search information required: name, SSN. Turnaround time: 7 days. For closed files, as directed by court clerk, see Atlanta Federal Records Center.

District of Hawaii

HAWAII CONSTITUTES ONE JUDICIAL DISTRICT WHICH INCLUDES THE HAWAIIAN ISLANDS, THE MIDWAY ISLANDS, WAKE ISLAND, JOHNSTON ISLAND, SAND ISLAND, KINGMAN REEF, PALMYRA ISLAND, BAKER ISLAND, HOWLAND ISLAND, CANTON ISLAND, JARVIS ISLAND, AND ENDERBURY ISLAND.

Civil and Criminal Records

Clerk, US District Court
PO Box 50129
Honolulu, HI 96850
(808) 541-1300

Records are available by mail or phone. No search fee. $.50 fee per copy, $5.00 for certified copy. Search information required: name. Turnaround time: 2 weeks. For closed files prior to 1988, as directed by court clerk, see San Francisco Federal Records Center.

Bankruptcy Records

US Bankruptcy Court Clerk
PO Box 50121
Honolulu, HI 96850
(808) 541-1791

Records are available by mail. $15.00 search fee. $.50 fee per copy, $5.00 for certified copy. Make check payable to Clerk, US Bankruptcy Court. Search information required: name. Turnaround time: 2 weeks. For closed files, as directed by court clerk, see San Francisco Federal Records Center.

District of Idaho

THIS DISTRICT COMPRISES THE ENTIRE STATE.

Civil and Criminal Records

US District Court
Box 039
Federal Building
550 West Fort Street
Boise, ID 83724
(208) 334-1361

Records are available by mail or phone. No release necessary. $15.00 search fee. $.50 fee per copy, $5.00 for certified copy. Make check payable to US District Court Clerk. Search information required: name. Turnaround time: 1 week. For pre 1983 closed files, see Seattle Federal Records Center.

Bankruptcy Records

US Bankruptcy Court
US Courthouse & Federal Bldg
550 West Fort Street, Box 42
Boise, ID 83724
(208) 334-1074

Records are available by mail. $15.00 search fee. $.50 fee per copy, $5.00 for certified copy. Make check payable to US Bankruptcy Court. Search information required: name, case number (if available), SASE. Turnaround time: 24 hours. For closed files, as directed by court clerk, see Seattle Federal Records Center.

Central District of Illinois

ADAMS, BROWN, BUREAU, CASS, CHAMPAIGN, CHRISTIAN, COLES, DEWITT, DOUGLAS, EDGAR, FORD, FULTON, GREENE, HANCOCK, HENDERSON, HENRY, IROQUOIS, KANKAKEE, KNOX, LIVINGSTON, LOGAN, MACON, MACOUPIN, MARSHALL, MASON, MCDONOUGH, MCLEAN, MENARD, MERCER, MONTGOMERY, MORGAN, MOULTRIE, PEORIA, PIATT, PIKE, PUTNAM, ROCK ISLAND, SANGAMON, SCHUYLER, SCOTT, SHELBY, STARK, TAZEWELL, VERMILION, WARREN, WOODFORD.

Civil and Criminal Records

US District Court Clerk
PO Box 315
Springfield, IL 62705
(217) 492-4020

Records are available by mail. $15.00 search fee. $.50 fee per copy, $5.00 for certified copy. Make check payable to US District Court Clerk. Search information required: name. Turnaround time: 1 week. For closed files, as directed by court clerk, see Chicago Federal Records Center.

US District Court Clerk
Room 174
100 Northeast Monroe Street
Peoria, IL 61602
(309) 671-7117

Records are available by mail or phone. $15.00 search fee. $.50 fee per copy. $5.00 for certification. Certified check only, payable to Clerk, US District Court. Search information required: name. Turnaround time: 2-3 days. For closed files prior to 1986, as directed by court clerk, see Chicago Federal Records Center.

US District Court
211 19th Street
Room 40
Rock Island, IL 61201
(309) 793-5778
Records are available by mail. $15.00
search fee. $.50 fee per copy, $5.00 for
certified copy. Make check payable to
Clerk, US District Court. Search
information required: name. Turnaround
time: 1-2 days. For closed files prior to
1985 for civil and prior to 1983 for
criminal, as directed by court clerk, see
Chicago Federal Records Center.

US District Court
PO Box 786
201 North Vermilion Street
Danville, IL 61832
(217) 431-4805
Records are available by mail or phone.
$15.00 search fee. $.50 fee per copy, $5.00
for certified copy. Check payable to U.S.
District Court. Search information required:
name, case number (if available), specific
information to search. Turnaround time: 24
hours. For closed files prior to 1989, as
directed by court clerk, see Chicago
Federal Records Center.

Bankruptcy Records

US Bankruptcy Court Clerk
PO Box 2438
Springfield, IL 62705
(217) 492-4550
Records are available by mail. $15.00
search fee. $.50 fee per copy, $5.00 for
certified copy. Company check payable to
Clerk, US Bankruptcy Court. Search
information required: name, specific
information to search. Turnaround time: 10
days. For closed files, as directed by court
clerk, see Chicago Federal Records Center.

Northern District of Illinois

BOONE, CARROLL, COOK, DEKALB,
DUPAGE, GRUNDY, JO DAVIESS, KANE,
KENDALL, LAKE, LASALLE, LEE,
MCHENRY, OGLE, STEPHENSON,
WHITESIDE, WILL, WINNEBAGO.

Civil and Criminal Records

US District Court Clerk Copy Desk
219 South Dearborn Street
Chicago, IL 60604
(312) 435-5670
Records are available by mail. $15.00
search fee. $.50 fee per copy, $5.00 for
certified copy. Make check payable to
Clerk, US District Court. Search
information required: name, specific
information to search. Turnaround time: 2
days. For closed files prior to 1989, as
directed by court clerk, see Chicago
Federal Records Center.

US District Court Clerk
211 Court Street
Room 252
Rockford, IL 61101
(815) 987-4354
Records are available by mail. $15.00
search fee. $.50 fee per copy, $5.00 for
certified copy. Make check payable to US
District Court Clerk. Search information
required: name, case number. Turnaround
time: 1-2 days. For closed files, as directed
by court clerk, see Chicago Federal
Records Center.

Bankruptcy Records

US Bankruptcy Court Clerk
219 South Dearborn
Chicago, IL 60604
(312) 435-5593
Records are available by mail. $15.00
search fee. $.50 fee per copy, $5.00 for
certified copy. Make check payable to
Clerk, US Bankruptcy Court. Search
information required: name (business),
specific information to search. Turnaround
time: 10 days. For closed files, as directed
by court clerk, see Chicago Federal
Records Center.

Southern District of Illinois

ALEXANDER, BOND, CALHOUN, CLARK,
CLAY, CLINTON, CRAWFORD,
CUMBERLAND, EDWARDS, EFFINGHAM,
FAYETTE, FRANKLIN, GALLATIN,
HAMILTON, HARDIN, JACKSON, JASPER,
JEFFERSON, JERSEY, JOHNSON,
LAWRENCE, MADISON, MARION, MASSAC,
MONROE, PERRY, POPE, PULASKI,
RANDOLPH, RICHLAND, ST. CLAIR,
SALINE, UNION, WABASH, WASHINGTON,
WAYNE, WHITE, WILLIAMSON.

Civil and Criminal Records

US District Court
750 Missouri Ave.
East St. Louis, IL 62002
(618) 482-9371
Records are available by mail. $15.00
search fee. $.50 fee per copy, $5.00 for
certified copy. Make check payable to
Clerk, US District Court. Search
information required: name, specific
information to search. Turnaround time: 2
days. For closed files, as directed by court
clerk, see Chicago Federal Records Center.

US District Court Clerk
750 Missouri Avenue
PO Box 249
East St. Louis, IL 62202
(618) 482-9371
Records are available by mail. $15.00
search fee. $.50 fee per copy, $5.00 for
certified copy. Make check payable to
Clerk, US District Court. Search
information required: name, specific
information to search. Turnaround time: 24
hours. For closed files, as directed by court
clerk, see Chicago Federal Records Center.

US District Court
301 West Main
Benton, IL 62812
(618) 438-0671
Records are available by mail. $15.00
search fee. $.50 fee per copy, $5.00 for
certified copy. Make check payable to
Clerk, US District Court. Search
information required: name. Turnaround
time: 1-2 weeks. For closed files, as
directed by court clerk, see Chicago Federal
Records Center.

Bankruptcy Records

US Bankruptcy Court Clerk
PO Box 309
East St. Louis, IL 62201
(618) 482-9400
Records are available by mail. $15.00
search fee. $.50 fee per copy, $5.00 for
certified copy. Make check payable to
Clerk, US Bankruptcy Court. Search
information required: name, specific

information to search. Turnaround time: 1-2
days. For closed files, as directed by court
clerk, see Chicago Federal Records Center.

Northern District of Indiana

ADAMS, ALLEN, BENTON, BLACKFORD,
CARROLL, CASS, DEKALB, ELKHART,
FULTON, GRANT, HUNTINGTON, JASPER,
JAY, KOSCIUSKO, LAGRANGE, LAKE,
LAPORTE, MARSHALL, MIAMI, NEWTON,
NOBEL, PORTER, PULASKI, STARKE,
STEUBEN, ST. JOSEPH, TIPPECANOE,
WABASH, WARREN, WELLS, WHITE,
WHITLEY.

Civil and Criminal Records

US District Court Clerk
Room 1108, Federal Bldg.
1300 South Harrison Street
Fort Wayne, IN 46802
(219) 424-7360
Records are available by mail or phone.
$15.00 search fee. $.50 fee per copy, $5.00
for certified copy. Make check payable to
Clerk, US District Court. Search
information required: name. Turnaround
time: 48 hours. For closed files, as directed
by court clerk, see Chicago Federal
Records Center.

US District Court Clerk
204 South Main
Room 102
South Bend, IN 46601
(219) 236-8260
Records are available by mail. $15.00
search fee. $.50 fee per copy, $5.00 for
certified copy. Make check payable to
Clerk, US District Court. Search
information required: name, specific
information to search. Turnaround time: 2-3
days. For closed files, as directed by court
clerk, see Chicago Federal Records Center.

US District Court Clerk
232 North 4th Street
PO Box 1498
Lafayette, IN 47902
(317) 742-0512
Records are available by mail or phone. No
release necessary. $15.00 search fee. $.50
fee per copy, $5.00 for certified copy. Make
check payable to Clerk, US District Court.
Search information required: name, specific
information to search. Turnaround time: 3-4
days. For closed files, as directed by court
clerk, see Chicago Federal Records Center.

US District Court, Clerk
Room 101
507 State Street
Hammond, IN 46320
(219) 937-5235
Records are available by mail or phone.
$15.00 search fee. $.50 fee per copy, $5.00
for certified copy. Make check payable to
Clerk, US District Court. Search
information required: name, specific
information to search. Turnaround time: 2-7
days. For closed files prior to 1988, as
directed by court clerk, see Chicago Federal
Records Center.

Bankruptcy Records

US Bankruptcy Court Clerk
Room 224
204 South Main
South Bend, IN 46601
(219) 236-8247
Fax (219) 236-8886
Records are available by mail or phone. $15.00 search fee. $.50 fee per copy, $5.00 for certified copy. Make check payable to US Bankruptcy Court Clerk. Search information required: name, specific information to search. Turnaround time: 2 weeks. For closed files, as directed by court clerk, see Chicago Federal Records Center.

US Bankruptcy Court Clerk
221 Federal Building
610 Connecticut Street
Gary, IN 46402
(219) 881-3335
Records are available by phone or mail. $15.00 search fee. $.50 fee per copy, $5.00 for certified copy. Make check payable to US Bankruptcy Court. Search information required: name, specific information to search. Turnaround time: 24 hours. For closed files, as directed by court clerk, see Chicago Federal Records Center.

Southern District of Indiana

BARTHOLOMEW, BOONE, BROWN, CLARK, CLAY, CLINTON, CRAWFORD, DAVIES, DEARBORN, DECATUR, DELAWARE, DUBOIS, FAYETTE, FLOYD, FOUNTAIN, FRANKLIN, GIBSON, GREEN, HAMILTON, HANCOCK, HARRISON, HENDRICKS, HENRY, HOWARD, JACKSON, JEFFERSON, JENNINGS, JOHNSON, KNOX, LAWRENCE, MADISON, MARION, MARTIN, MONROE, MONTGOMERY, MORGAN, OHIO, ORANGE, OWEN, PARKE, PERRY, PIKE, POSEY, PUTNAM, RANDOLPH, RIPLEY, RUSH, SCOTT, SHELBY, SPENCER, SULLIVAN, SWITZERLAND, TIPTON, UNION, VANDERBURGH, VERMILION, VIGO, WARRICK, WASHINGTON, WAYNE.

Civil and Criminal Records

US District Court Clerk
304 Federal Building
101 Northwest 7th Street
Evansville, IN 47708
(812) 465-6427
Records are available by mail. $15.00 search fee. $.50 fee per copy, $5.00 for certified copy. Make check payable to Clerk, US District Court. Search information required: name, specific information to search. Turnaround time: 24 hours. For closed files, as directed by court clerk, see Chicago Federal Records Center.

US District Court Clerk
46 East Ohio Street
Room 105
Indianapolis, IN 46204
(317) 226-6670
Records are available by mail. $15.00 search fee. $.50 fee per copy. Make check payable to Clerk, US District Court. Search information required: name, case number, specific information to search. Turnaround time: 2-3 days. For closed files, as directed by court clerk, see Chicago Federal Records Center.

US District Court Clerk
121 W. Spring St.
New Albany, IN 47150
(812) 948-5239
Records are available by mail or phone. $15.00 search fee. $.50 fee per copy, $5.00 for certified copy. Make check payable to Clerk, US District Court. Search information required: name, date of birth, case number or date when filed, specific information to search. Turnaround time: 2 days. For closed files, as directed by court clerk, see Chicago Federal Records Center.

US District Court Clerk
207 Federal Building
Terre Haute, IN 47808
(812) 234-9484
Records are available by mail. $15.00 search fee. $.50 fee per copy, $5.00 for certified copy. Make check payable to Clerk, US District Court. Search information required: name, specific information to search. For closed files, as directed by court clerk, see Chicago Federal Records Center.

Bankruptcy Records

US Bankruptcy Court Clerk
123 US Courthouse
46 East Ohio
Indianapolis, IN 46204
(317) 226-6710
Records are available by mail. $15.00 search fee. $.50 fee per copy, $5.00 for certified copy. Make check payable to US Bankruptcy. Search information required: name, SASE, specific information to search. Turnaround time: 1 day. For closed files, as directed by court clerk, see Chicago Federal Records Center.

Northern District of Iowa

ALLAMAKEE, BENTON, BLACK HAWK, BREMER, BUCHANAN, BUENA VISTA, BUTLER, CALHOUN, CARROLL, CEDAR, CERRO GORDO, CHEROKEE, CHICKASAW, CLAY, CLAYTON, CRAWFORD, DELAWARE, DICKINSON, DUBUQUE, EMMET, FAYETTE, FLOYD, FRANKLIN, GRUNDY, HAMILTON, HANCOCK, HARDIN, HAWK, HOWARD, HUMBOLDT, IDA, IOWA, JACKSON, JONES, KOSSUTH, LINN, LYON, MITCHELL, MONONA, OSCEOLA, O'BRIEN, PALO ALTO, PLYMOUTH, POCAHONTAS, SAC, SIOUX, TAMA, WEBSTER, WINNEBAGO, WINNESHIEK, WOODBURY, WORTH, WRIGHT.

Civil and Criminal Records

US District Court
320 6th Street
Room 301, Federal Bldg.
Sioux City, IA 51101
(712) 252-3336
Records are available by phone. $15.00 search fee. $.50 fee per copy, $5.00 for certified copy. Make check payable to Clerk, US District Court. Search information required: name, specific information to search. For closed files, as directed by court clerk, see Kansas City Federal Records Center.

US District Court Clerk
Federal Bldg. US Court House
101 1st St. SE, Room 313
Cedar Rapids, IA 52407
(319) 364-2447
Records are available by mail. $15.00 search fee. $.50 fee per copy, $5.00 for certified copy. Make check payable to Clerk, US District Court. Search information required: name, specific information to search. Turnaround time: 2 weeks. For closed files, as directed by court clerk, see Kansas City Federal Records Center.

Bankruptcy Records

US Bankruptcy Court Clerk
PO Box 74890
Cedar Rapids, IA 52407
(319) 362-9696
Records are available by mail or phone. $15.00 search fee. $.50 fee per copy, $5.00 for certified copy. Make check payable to Clerk, US Bankruptcy Court or supply Mastercard/Visa number for faster service. Search information required: name, specific information to search. Turnaround time: 7 days. For closed files, as directed by court clerk, see Kansas City Federal Records Center.

Southern District of Iowa

ADAIR, ADAMS, APPANOOSE, AUDUBON, BOONE, CASS, CLARKE, CLINTON, DALLAS, DAVIS, DECATUR, DES MOINES, FREMONT, GREENE, GUTHRIE, HARRISON, HENRY, JASPER, JEFFERSON, JOHNSON, KEOKUK, LEE, LOUISA, LUCAS, MADISON, MAHASKA, MARION, MARSHALL, MILLS, MONROE, MONTGOMERY, MUSCATINE, PAGE, POLK, POTTAWATTAMIE, POWESHIEK, RINGGOLD, SCOTT, SHELBY, STORY, TAYLOR, UNION, VAN BUREN, WAPELLO, WARREN, WASHINGTON, WAYNE.

Civil and Criminal Records

US District Court Clerk
East 1st & Walnut Street
Room 200
Des Moines, IA 50309
(515) 284-6248
Fax (515) 284-6210
Records are available by mail or phone. $15.00 search fee. Search information required: name, specific information to search. Turnaround time: 1-2 days. For closed files, as directed by court clerk, see Kansas City Federal Records Center.

Bankruptcy Records

US Bankruptcy Court Clerk
PO Box 9264
Des Moines, IA 50306-9264
(515) 284-6230
Records are available by mail or phone. $15.00 search fee. $.50 fee per copy, $5.00 for certified copy. Make check payable to Clerk, US Bankruptcy Court. Search information required: name, case number, specific information to search. Turnaround time: 3-4 days. For closed files prior to 1982, as directed by court clerk, see Kansas City Federal Records Center.

District of Kansas

THIS DISTRICT COMPRISES THE ENTIRE STATE.

Civil and Criminal Records

US District Court, Clerk
444 S. E. Quincy, Rm. 490
Topeka, KS 66683
(913) 295-2610
Records are available by mail. No search fee. $.50 fee per copy, $5.00 for certified copy. Make check payable to Clerk, US District Court. Search information required: name, specific information to search. Turnaround time: 2 days. For closed files prior to 1987, as directed by court clerk, see Kansas City Federal Records Center.

US District Court Clerk
Room 204
401 North Market Street
Wichita, KS 67202-2096
(316) 269-6491
Records are available by mail. $15.00 search fee. Search information required: name, specific information to search. Turnaround time: 2 days. For closed files prior to 1986, as directed by court clerk, see Kansas City Federal Records Center.

US District Court, Clerk
812 North 7th Street
Kansas City, KS 66101
(913) 236-3719
Records are available by mail or phone. No search fee. $.50 fee per copy, $5.00 for certified copy. Search information required: name, specific information to search. For closed files prior to 1989, as directed by court clerk, see Kansas City Federal Records Center.

Bankruptcy Records

US Bankruptcy Court Clerk
167 US Courthouse
401 North Market
Wichita, KS 67202
(316) 269-6486
Records are available by mail. $15.00 search fee. $.50 fee per copy. Make check payable to Clerk, US Bankruptcy Court. Search information required: name. Turnaround time: 1-2 weeks. For closed files, as directed by court clerk, see Kansas City Federal Records Center.

Eastern District of Kentucky

ANDERSON, BATH, BELL, BOONE, BOURBON, BOYD, BOYLE, BRACKEN, BREATHITT, CAMPBELL, CARROLL, CARTER, CLARK, CLAY, ELLIOTT, ESTILL, FAYETTE, FLEMING, FLOYD, FRANKLIN, GALLATIN, GARRARD, GRANT, GREENUP, HARLAN, HARRISON, HENRY, JACKSON, JESSAMINE, JOHNSON, KENTON, KNOTT, KNOX, LAUREL, LAWRENCE, LEE, LESLIE, LETCHER, LEWIS, LINCOLN, MCCREARY, MADISON, MAGOFFIN, MARTIN, MASON, MENIFEE, MERCER, MONTGOMERY, MORGAN, NICHOLAS, OWEN, OWSLEY, PENDLETON, PERRY, PIKE, POWELL, PULASKI, ROBERTSON, ROCKCASTLE, ROWAN, SCOTT, SHELBY, TRIMBLE, WAYNE, WHITLEY, WOLFE, WOODFORD.

Civil and Criminal Records

US District Court Clerk
PO Box 1073
Covington, KY 41012
(606) 292-3167
Fax (606) 292-8280
Records are available by mail, fax or phone. $15.00 search fee. $.50 fee per copy, $5.00 for certified copy. Make check payable to Clerk, US District Court. Search information required: name, specific information to search. Turnaround time: 24 hours. For closed files, as directed by court clerk, see Atlanta Federal Records Center.

US District Court Clerk
1405 Greenup, Suite 336
Ashland, KY 41101
(606) 329-2465
Records are available by mail or phone. No release necessary. $15.00 search fee. $.50 fee per copy, $5.00 for certified copy. Make check payable to Clerk, US District Court. Search information required: name, specific information to search. Turnaround time: 1-3 days. For closed files, as directed by court clerk, see Atlanta Federal Records Center.

US District Court Clerk
203 Federal Building
102 Main Street
Pikeville, KY 41501-1144
(606) 437-6160
Records are available by mail or phone (case number needed). $15.00 search fee. $.50 fee per copy, $5.00 for certified copy. Make check payable to Clerk, US District Court. Search information required: name, specific information to search. Turnaround time: 3 days. For closed files, as directed by court clerk, see Atlanta Federal Records Center.

US District Court Clerk
124 US Courthouse
3rd Main St.
PO Box 5121
London, KY 40745
(606) 864-5137
Records are available by mail or phone (with case number). $15.00 search fee. $.50 fee per copy, $5.00 for certified copy. Make check payable to Clerk, US District Court. Search information required: name, specific information to search. Turnaround time: 48 hours. For closed files prior to 1987, as directed by court clerk, see Atlanta Federal Records Center.

US District Court Clerk
313 John C. Watts Federal Bldg.
330 West Broadway
Frankfort, KY 40601
(502) 223-5225
Records are available by mail or phone. $15.00 search fee. $.50 fee per copy, $5.00 for certified copy. Make check payable to Clerk, US District Court. Search information required: name, specific information to search. Turnaround time: 1-2 days. For closed files, as directed by court clerk, see Atlanta Federal Records Center.

US District Court Clerk
PO Box 3074
Lexington, KY 40596
(606) 233-2503
Records are available by mail or phone. $15.00 search fee. $.50 fee per copy, $5.00 for certified copy. Make check payable to Clerk, US District Court. Search information required: name, specific information to search. Turnaround time: 2-3 days. For closed files, as directed by court clerk, see Atlanta Federal Records Center.

Bankruptcy Records

US Bankruptcy Court Clerk
PO Box 1050
Lexington, KY 40588
(606) 233-2608
Records are available by mail or phone. $15.00 search fee. $.50 fee per copy, $5.00 for certified copy. Make check payable to Clerk, US Bankruptcy Court. Search information required: name, specific information to search. Turnaround time: 2 weeks. For closed files, as directed by court clerk, see Atlanta Federal Records Center.

Western District of Kentucky

ADAIR, ALLEN, BALLARD, BRECKENRIDGE, BULLITT, BUTLER, CALDWELL, CALLOWAY, CARLISLE, CASEY, CHRISTIAN, CLINTON, CRITTENDEN, CUMBERLAND, DAVIESS, EDMONDSON, FULTON, GRAVES, GRAYSON, GREEN, HANCOCK, HARDIN, HART, HENDERSON, HICKMAN, HOPKINS, JEFFERSON, LARUE, LIVINGSTON, LOGAN, LYON, MCCRACKEN, MCCLEAN, MARION, MARSHALL, MEADE, METCALFE, MONROE, MUHLENBERG, NELSON, OHIO, OLDHAM, RUSSELL, SIMPSON, SPENCER, TAYLOR, TODD, TRIGG, UNION, WARREN, WASHINGTON, WEBSTER.

Civil and Criminal Records

US District Court Clerk
601 W. Broadway, Room 231
Louisville, KY 40202
(502) 582-5156
Records are available by mail. $15.00 search fee. $.50 fee per copy, $5.00 for certified copy. Make check payable to Clerk, US District Court. Search information required: name, date of birth, specific information to search. Turnaround time: 5 days. For closed files, as directed by court clerk, see Atlanta Federal Records Center.

US District Court Clerk
Room 322
Federal Building
Paducah, KY 42001
(502) 443-1337
Records are available by mail or phone. $15.00 search fee. $.50 fee per copy. $5.00 for certification. Make check payable to Clerk, US District Court. Search information required: name, date of birth. Turnaround time: 5 days. For closed files, prior to 1987 as directed by court clerk, see Atlanta Federal Records Center.

US District Court Clerk
PO Box 538
423 Frederica Street - 210 Federal Bldg.
Owensboro, KY 42302-0538
(502) 683-0221
Records are available by mail or phone. $15.00 search fee. Make check payable to US District Court Clerk. Search information required: name, date of birth. Turnaround time: 1 week. For closed files, as directed by court clerk, see Atlanta Federal Records Center.

US District Court Clerk
214 E. Main
Federal Building, Room 213
Bowling Green, KY 42101
(502) 781-1110
Records are available by mail or phone.
$15.00 search fee. Make check payable to
Clerk, US District Court. Search
information required: name, date of birth.
Turnaround time: 24 hours. For closed files
prior to 1987, as directed by court clerk, see
Atlanta Federal Records Center.

Bankruptcy Records

US Bankruptcy Court
601 West Broadway, Suite 546
Louisville, KY 40202
(502) 582-5140
Records are available by mail or phone. No
release necessary. $15.00 search fee. $.50
fee per copy, $5.00 for certified copy.
Company check payable to Clerk, US
Bankruptcy Court. Search information
required: name, specific information to
search. Turnaround time: 2 days. For closed
files, as directed by court clerk, see Atlanta
Federal Records Center. To receive a closed
file from Atlanta, the fee is $25.00

Eastern District of Louisiana

ASSUMPTION, JEFFERSON, LAFOURCHE,
ORLEANS, PLAQUEMINES, SAINT
BERNARD, SAINT CHARLES, SAINT JAMES,
SAINT JOHN THE BAPTIST, SAINT
TAMMANY, TANGIPAHOA, TERREBONNE,
WASHINGTON.

Civil and Criminal Records

US District Court Clerk
Room C 151
500 Camp Street
New Orleans, LA 70130
(504) 589-4474
Fax (504) 589-3199
Records are available by mail or phone.
$15.00 search fee. $.50 fee per copy, $5.00
for certified copy. Make check payable to
Clerk, US District Court. Search
information required: name, specific
information to search. Turnaround time: 1-2
days. For closed files, as directed by court
clerk, see Fort Worth Federal Records
Center.

Bankruptcy Records

US Bankruptcy Court Clerk
500 Camp Street
New Orleans, LA 70130
(504) 589-6506
Fax (504) 589-2076
Records are available by mail or fax.
Records are available by phone from 9:00-
10:30 a.m. & 1:00-2:30 p.m. central time.
$15.00 search fee. $.50 fee per copy, $5.00
for certified copy. Make check payable to
Clerk, US Bankruptcy Court. Search
information required: name, specific
information to search. Turnaround time: 2-3
days. For closed files, as directed by court
clerk, see Fort Worth Federal Records
Center.

Middle District of Louisiana

ASCENSION, EAST BATON ROUGE, EAST
FELICIANA, IBERVILLE, LIVINGSTON,
POINTE COUPEE, SAINT HELENA, WEST
BATON ROUGE, WEST FELICIANA.

Civil and Criminal Records

US District Court Clerk
PO Box 2630
Baton Rouge, LA 70821
(504) 389-0321
Records are available by mail or phone.
$15.00 search fee. $.50 fee per copy, $5.00
for certified copy. Make check payable to
Clerk, US District Court. Search
information required: name, specific
information to search. Turnaround time: 2-3
days. For closed files, as directed by court
clerk, see Fort Worth Federal Records
Center.

Bankruptcy Records

US Bankruptcy Court Clerk
412 North 4th Street
Baton Rouge, LA 70802
(504) 389-0211
Records are available by mail. $15.00
search fee. $.50 fee per copy, $5.00 for
certified copy. Make check payable to
Clerk, US Bankruptcy Court. Search
information required: name, specific
information to search. Turnaround time: 1
week. For closed files prior to 1987, as
directed by court clerk, see Fort Worth
Federal Records Center.

Western District of Louisiana

ACADIA, ALLEN, AVOYELLES,
BEAUREGARD, BIENVILLE, BOSSIER,
CADDO, CALCASIEU, CALDWELL,
CAMERON, CATAHOULA, CLAIBORNE,
CONCORDIA, DESOTO, EAST CARROLL,
EVANGELINE, FRANKLIN, GRANT, IBERIA,
JACKSON, JEFFERSON DAVIS, LAFAYETTE,
LASALLE, LINCOLN, MADISON,
MOREHOUSE, NATCHITOCHES, OUACHITA,
RAPIDES, RED RIVER, RICHLAND, SABINE,
SAINT LANDRY, SAINT MARTIN, SAINT
MARY, TENSAS, UNION, VERMILION,
VERNON, WEBSTER, WEST CARROLL,
WINN.

Civil and Criminal Records

US District Court Clerk
Room 106
500 Fannin Street
Shreveport, LA 71101
(318) 226-5273
Records are available by mail or phone.
$15.00 search fee. $.50 fee per copy, $5.00
for certified copy. Make check payable to
Clerk, US District Court. Search
information required: name, specific
information to search. Turnaround time: 1-2
days. For closed files, as directed by court
clerk, see Fort Worth Federal Records
Center.

US District Court Clerk
Box Drawer J
306 Federal Building
Opelousas, LA 70571-1909
(318) 948-8594
Records are held at Shreveport, LA.

US District Court Clerk
PO Box 1269
Alexandria, LA 71309
(318) 473-7415
Records are available by mail. $15.00
search fee. $.50 fee per copy, $5.00 for
certified copy. Company check payable to
Clerk, US District Court. Search
information required: name, years to
search, specific information to search.
Turnaround time: 2-3 days. For closed files,
as directed by court clerk, see Fort Worth
Federal Records Center.

Bankruptcy Records

US Bankruptcy Court Clerk
Room 4 A 18
500 Fannin
Shreveport, LA 71109
(318) 226-5267
Voice Case Information System –
(800) 326-4026

District of Maine

THIS DISTRICT COMPRISES THE ENTIRE
STATE.

Civil and Criminal Records

US District Court Clerk
PO Box 1007
Bangor, ME 04402-1007
(207) 945-0575
Records are available by mail. $15.00 fee
for computer name searches from 1980
forward. $15.00 fee if written certificate is
requested. $.50 fee per copy. Search
information required: name, specific
information to search. Turnaround time: 1-2
days. Make check payable to Clerk, US
District Court. For closed files prior to
1987, as directed by court clerk, see Boston
Federal Records Center.

US District Court Clerk
156 Federal Street
Portland, ME 04101
(207) 780-3356
Records are available by mail. No search
fee for computer name searches from 1980
forward. $15.00 fee if written certificate is
requested. $.50 fee per copy, $5.00 for
certified copy. Make check payable to
Clerk, US District Court. Search
information required: name, specific
information to search. Turnaround time: 1-2
days. For pre 1989 closed files, see Boston
Federal Records Center.

Bankruptcy Records

US Bankruptcy Court Clerk
PO Box 48 DTS
156 Federal
Portland, ME 04112
(207) 780-3482
Records are available by mail or phone.
$15.00 search fee. $.50 fee per copy, $5.00
for certified copy. Company check payable
to Clerk, US Bankruptcy Court. Search
information required: name, specific
information to search. Turnaround time: 1-2
days. For closed files prior to 1983, as
directed by court clerk, see Boston Federal
Records Center.

District of Maryland

THIS DISTRICT COMPRISES THE ENTIRE STATE.

Civil and Criminal Records

US District Court Clerk
101 West Lombard
Room 404
Baltimore, MD 21201
(301) 962-2600

Records are available by mail. $15.00 search fee. $.50 fee per copy. Make check payable to Clerk, US District Court. Search information required: name, specific information to search. Turnaround time: 3-4 days. For closed files prior to 1987, as directed by court clerk, see Philadelphia Federal Records Center.

Bankruptcy Records

US Bankruptcy Court-District of Maryland
US Courthouse
101 West Lombard
Baltimore, MD 21201
(410) 962-2688

Records are available by mail. $15.00 search fee. $.50 fee per copy, $5.00 for certified copy. Company check payable to Clerk, US Bankruptcy Court. Search information required: name, specific information to search. Turnaround time: 2-3 weeks. For closed files prior to 1989, as directed by court clerk, see Philadelphia Federal Records Center.

District of Massachusetts

THIS DISTRICT COMPRISES THE ENTIRE STATE.

Civil and Criminal Records

US District Court Clerk
PO Square
Room 607
Boston, MA 02109
(617) 223-9083

Records are available by mail. $15.00 search fee. $.50 fee per copy, $5.00 for certified copy. Company check payable to Clerk, US District Court. Search information required: name, specific information to search. Turnaround time: 7 days. For closed files, as directed by court clerk, see Boston Federal Records Center.

Bankruptcy Records

US Bankruptcy Court Clerk
Room 1101
10 Causeway
Boston, MA 02222
(617) 565-6051

Records are available by mail. $15.00 search fee. $.50 fee per copy, $5.00 for certified copy. Company check payable to Clerk, US Bankruptcy Court. Search information required: name, specific information to search. Turnaround time: 1 week. For pre 1977 closed files, see Boston Federal Records Center.

Eastern District of Michigan

ALCONA, ALPENA, ARENAC, BAY, CHEBOYGAN, CLARE, CRAWFORD, GENESEE, GLADWIN, GRATIOT, HURON, JACKSON, IOSCO, ISABELLA, LAPEER, LENAWEE, LIVINGSTON, MACOMB, MIDLAND, MONROE, MONTMORENCY, OAKLAND, OGEMAW, OSCODA, OTSEGO, PRESQUE ISLE, ROSCOMMON, SAINT CLAIR, SAGINAW, SANILAC, SHIAWASSEE, TUSCOLA, WASHTENAW, WAYNE.

Civil and Criminal Records

US District Court Clerk
PO Box X913
Bay City, MI 48707
(517) 892-6571

Records are available by mail or phone. $15.00 search fee. $.50 fee per copy, $5.00 for certified copy. Company check payable to Clerk, US District Court. Search information required: name, specific information to search. Turnaround time: 1-2 days. For closed files prior to 1987, as directed by court clerk, see Chicago Federal Records Center.

US District Court Clerk
PO Box 8199
Ann Arbor, MI 48107
(313) 668-2380
Fax (313) 668-2065

Records are available by mail or phone. $15.00 search fee. $.50 fee per copy, $5.00 for certified copy. Company check payable to Clerk, US District Court. Search information required: name, specific information to search. Turnaround time: 3 days. For closed files prior to 1986, as directed by court clerk, see Chicago Federal Records Center.

US District Court Clerk
Federal Bldg, Room 140
600 Church Street
Flint, MI 48502
(313) 766-5020

Records are available by mail or phone. $15.00 search fee. $.50 fee per copy, $5.00 for certified copy. Company check payable to Clerk, US District Court. Search information required: name, specific information to search. Turnaround time: 1 day. For closed files prior to 1988, as directed by court clerk, see Chicago Federal Records Center.

US District Court Clerk
133 Federal Building
Detroit, MI 48226
(313) 226-7455

Records are available by mail. $15.00 search fee. $.50 fee per copy, $5.00 for certified copy. Company check payable to Clerk, US District Court. Search information required: name, specific information to search. Turnaround time: 3 days. For closed files prior to 1986, as directed by court clerk, see Chicago Federal Records Center.

Bankruptcy Records

US Bankruptcy Court Clerk
231 West Lafayette Room 1002
Detroit, MI 48226
(313) 226-7064

Records are available by mail. $15.00 search fee. $.50 fee per copy, $5.00 for certified copy. Search information required: name, specific information to search. Turnaround time: 2 days. For pre 1988 closed files, see Chicago Federal Records Center.

Western District of Michigan

ACONA, ALGER, ALLEGAN, ANTRIM, APENA, ARENAC, BARAGA, BARRY, BAY, BENZIE, BERRIEN, BRANCH, CALHOUN, CASS, CHARLEVOIX, CHEBOYGAN, CHIPPEWA, CLINTON, COLDWATER, DELTA, DICKINSON, EATON, EMMET, GOGEBIC, GRAND TRAVERSE, HILLSDALE, HOUGHTON, INGHAM, IONIA, IRON, KALAMAZOO, KALKASKA, KENT, KEWEENAW, LAKE, LEELANAU, LUCE, MACKINAC, MANISTEE, MARQUETTE, MASON, MECOSTA, MENOMINEE, MISSAUKEE, MONTCALM, MUSKEGON, NEWAYGO, OCEANA, ONTONAGON, OSCEOLA, OTTAWA, SAINT JOSEPH, SCHOOLCRAFT, VAN BUREN, WEXFORD.

Civil and Criminal Records

US District Court Clerk
452 Federal Building
110 Michigan Street Northwest
Grand Rapids, MI 49503
(616) 456-2381

Records are available by mail or phone. $15.00 search fee. $.50 fee per copy, $5.00 for certified copy. Company check payable to Clerk, US District Court. Search information required: name, specific information to search. Turnaround time: 1 week. For closed files prior to 1986, as directed by court clerk, see Chicago Federal Records Center.

Bankruptcy Records

US Bankruptcy Court Clerk
PO Box 3310
Grand Rapids, MI 49501
(616) 456-2540

Records are available by mail. $15.00 search fee. $.50 fee per copy, $5.00 for certified copy. Company check payable to Clerk, US Bankruptcy Court. Search information required: name, specific information to search, SASE. Turnaround time: 1 week. For closed files prior to 1988, as directed by court clerk, see Chicago Federal Records Center.

District of Minnesota

AITKIN, ANOKA, BECKER, BELTRAMI, BENTON, BIG STONE, BLUE EARTH, BROWN, CARLTON, CARVER, CASS, CHIPPEWA, CHISAGO, CLAY, CLEARWATER, COOK, COTTONWOOD, CROW WING, DAKOTA, DODGE, DOUGLAS, FAIRBAULT, FILLMORE, FREEBORN, GOODHUE, GRANT, HENNEPIN, HOUSTON, HUBBARD, ISANTI, ITASCA, JACKSON, KANABEC, KANDIYOHI, KITTSON, KOOCHICHING, LACQUI PARLE, LAKE, LAKE OF THE WOODS, LE SUEUR, LINCOLN, LYON, MAHNOMEN, MARSHALL, MARTIN, MCLEOD, MEEKER, MILLE LACS, MORRISON, MOWER, MURRAY, NICOLLET, NOBLES, NORMAN, OLMSTED, OTTER TAIL, PENNINGTON, PINE, PIPESTONE, POLK, POPE, RAMSEY, RED LAKE, REDWOOD, RENVILLE, RICE, ROCK, ROUSEAU, SAINT LOUIS, SCOTT, SHERBURNE, SIBLEY, STEARNS, STEELE, STEVENS, SWIFT, TODD, TRAVERSE, WABASHA, WADENA, WASHINGTON, WATONWAN, WESECA, WILKIN, WINONA, WRIGHT, YELLOW MEDICINE.

Civil and Criminal Records

US District Court Clerk
110 South 4th, Room 514
Minneapolis, MN 55401
(612) 348-1821
Records are available by mail or phone. $15.00 search fee. $.50 fee per copy, $5.00 for certified copy. Specify civil or criminal. Company check payable to Clerk, US District Court. Search information required: full name. Turnaround time: 1 day. For closed files prior to 1980, as directed by court clerk, see Chicago Federal Records Center.

US District Court
417 Federal Bldg.
Duluth, MN 55802
(218) 720-5250
Records are available by mail or by phone for one name search. $15.00 search fee. $.50 fee per copy, $5.00 for certified copy. Make check payable to Clerk, US District Court. Search information required: name. Turnaround time: 24 hours. For closed files prior to 1987, as directed by court clerk, see Chicago Federal Records Center.

US District Court Clerk
708 Federal Building
316 North Robert
St. Paul, MN 55101
(612) 290-3212
Records are available by mail or phone. $15.00 search fee. $.50 fee per copy, $5.00 for certified copy. Make check payable to US District Court. Search information required: name. Turnaround time: 24 hours. For closed files prior to 1989, as directed by court clerk, see Chicago Federal Records Center.

Bankruptcy Records

US Bankruptcy Court
600 Towle Building
330 2nd Avenue South
Minneapolis, MN 55401
(612) 348-1855
Records are available by mail or phone. No search fee. Search information required: name. Turnaround time: 1 week. For closed files, as directed by court clerk, see Chicago Federal Records Center.

US Bankruptcy Court Clerk
416 US Courthouse
Duluth, MN 55802
(218) 720-5249
Records are available by mail or phone. $15.00 search fee. $.50 fee per copy, $5.00 for certified copy. Company check payable to Clerk, US Bankruptcy Court. Search information required: name. Turnaround time: 3 days. For closed files prior to 1990, as directed by court clerk, see Chicago Federal Records Center.

US Bankruptcy Court Clerk
200 Federal Building
316 North Robert
St. Paul, MN 55101
(612) 290-3184
Records are available by mail or phone. $15.00 search fee for certificate. $.50 fee per copy, $5.00 for certified copy. Make check payable to Clerk, US Bankruptcy Court. Search information required: name. Turnaround time: 2-3 days. For closed files prior to 1989, as directed by court clerk, see Chicago Federal Records Center.

Northern District of Mississippi

ALCORN, ATTALA, BENTON, BLIVAR, CALHOUN, CARROLL, CHICKASAW, CHOCTAW, CLAY, COAHOMA, DESOTO, GRENADA, HUMPHREYS, ITAWAMBA, LAFAYETTE, LEE, LEFLORE, LOWANDES, MARSHALL, MONROE, MONTGOMERY, OKTIBBEHA, PANOLA, PONTOTOC, PRENTISS, QUITMAN, SUNFLOWER, TALLAHATCHIE, TATE, TIPPAH, TISHOMINGO, TUNICA, UNION, WASHINGTON, WEBSTER, WINSTON, YALOBUSHA.

Civil and Criminal Records

US District Court Clerk
PO Box 727
Oxford, MS 38655
(601) 234-1971
Records are available by mail or phone. $15.00 search fee. $.50 fee per copy, $5.00 for certified copy. Make check payable to Clerk, US District Court. Search information required: name. Turnaround time: 24 hours. For closed civil files prior to 1987 and closed criminal files prior to 1982, as directed by court clerk, see Chicago Federal Records Center.

Bankruptcy Records

US Bankruptcy Court Clerk
PO Box 867
Aberdeen, MS 39730
(601) 369-2596
Records are available by mail. $15.00 search fee. $.50 fee per page, $5.00 for certified copy. All fees prepaid. Make check payable to Clerk US Bankruptcy Court. Search information required: name. Turnaround time: 2 weeks. For closed files prior to 1987, as directed by court clerk, see Atlanta, Georgia Archives.

Southern District of Mississippi

ADAMS, AMITE, CLAIBORNE, CLARKE, COPIAH, COVINGTON, FORREST, FRANKLIN, GEORGE, GREENE, HANCOCK, HARRISON, HINDS, HOLMES, ISSAQUENA, JACKSON, JASPER, JEFFERSON, JEFFERSON DAVIS, JONES, KEMPER, LAMAR, LAUDERDALE, LAWRENCE, LEAKE, LINCOLN, MADISON, MARION, NESHOBA, NEWTON, NOXUBEE, PEARL RIVER, PERRY, PIKE, RANKIN, SCOTT, SHARKEY, SIMPSON, SMITH, STONE, WALTHALL, WARREN, WAYNE, WILKINSON, YAZOO.

Civil and Criminal Records

US District Court
245 E. Capitol, Suite 416
Jackson, MS 39201
(601) 965-4439
Records are available by mail or phone. $15.00 search fee. $.50 fee per copy, $5.00 for certification. Make check payable to Clerk, US District Court. Search information required: name. Turnaround time: 2-3 days. For pre 1987 closed files, see Atlanta Federal Records Center.

US District Court Clerk
PO Box 369
Biloxi, MS 39533
(601) 432-8623
Records are available by mail or phone. $15.00 search fee. $.50 fee per copy, $5.00 for certified copy. Make check payable to Clerk, US District Court. Search information required: name. Turnaround time: 2-3 days. For closed files prior to 1989, as directed by court clerk, see Atlanta Federal Records Center.

US District Court Clerk
245 E. Capitol St., Suite 416
Jackson, MS 39201
(601) 965-4439
Records are available by mail only. $15.00 search fee. Make check payable to US District Court. Search information required: name, SASE. Turnaround time: 2 days. For pre 1982 closed files, see Atlanta Federal Records Center.

US District Court Clerk
701 Main Street, Suite 200
Hattiesburg, MS 39403
(601) 583-2433
Records are available by mail. $15.00 search fee. $.50 fee per copy. $5.00 for certification. Make check payable to Clerk, US District Court. Search information required: name, SASE. Turnaround time: 3-5 days. For closed files, prior to 1989 as directed by court clerk, see Atlanta Federal Records Center.

Bankruptcy Records

US Bankruptcy Court
PO Drawer 2448
Jackson, MS 39225-2448
(601) 965-5301
Records are available by mail or phone. $15.00 search fee. $.50 fee per copy, $5.00 for certified copy. Make check payable to Clerk, US Bankruptcy Court. Search information required: name, SSN, address if available. Turnaround time: 5-7 days. For closed files prior to 1979, as directed by court clerk, see Atlanta Federal Records Center.

Eastern District of Missouri

ADAIR, AUDRAIN, BOLLINGER, BUTLER, CAPE GIRARDEAU, CARTER, CHARITON, CITY OF ST. LOUIS, CLARK, CRAWFORD, DENT, DUNKLIN, FRANKLIN, GASCONADE, IRON, JEFFERSON, KNOX, LEWIS, LINCOLN, LINN, MACON, MADISON, MARIES, MARION, MISSISSIPPI, MONROE, MONTGOMERY, NEW MADRID, PEMISCOT, PERRY, PHELPS, PIKE, RALLS, RANDOLPH, REYNOLDS, RIPLEY, SAINT CHARLES, SAINT FRANCOIS, SAINT GENEVIEVE, SCHUYLER, SCOTLAND, SCOTT, SHANNON, SHELBY, STODDARD, ST. LOUIS, WARREN, WASHINGTON, WAYNE.

Civil and Criminal Records

US District Court Clerk
Room 302
1114 Market Street
St. Louis, MO 63101
(314) 539-6056
Records are available by mail. $15.00 search fee. $.50 fee per copy, $5.00 for certified copy. Make check payable to Clerk, US District Court. Search information required: name. Turnaround time: 5-7 days. For closed files, as directed by court clerk, see Kansas City Federal Records Center.

US District Court Clerk
SE Division
339 Broadway
Cape Girardeau, MO 63701
(314) 335-8538
Records are available by mail. $15.00 search fee. $.50 fee per copy, $5.00 for certified copy. Make check payable to Clerk, US District Court. Search information required: name. Turnaround time: 1-2 days. For closed files prior to 1987, as directed by court clerk, see Kansas City Federal Records Center.

Bankruptcy Records

US Bankruptcy Court Clerk
Room 702
1114 Market St.
St. Louis, MO 63101
(314) 539-2222
Records are available by mail or phone. $15.00 search fee. Make check payable to Clerk, US Bankruptcy Court. Search information required: name, SSN, SASE. Turnaround time: 3-5 days. For closed files, as directed by court clerk, see Kansas City Federal Records Center.

Western District of Missouri

ANDREW, ATCHISON, BARRY, BARTON, BATES, BENTON, BOONE, BUCHANAN, CALDWELL, CALLAWAY, CAMDEN, CARROLL, CASS, CEDAR, CHRISTIAN, CLAY, CLINTON, COLE, COOPER, DADE, DALLAS, DAVIESS, DEKALB, DOUGLAS, GENTRY, GREEN, GRUNDY, HARRISON, HENRY, HICKORY, HOLT, HOWARD, HOWELL, JACKSON, JASPER, JOHNSON, LACIEDE, LAFAYETTE, LAWRENCE, LIVINGSTON, MCDONALD, MERCER, MILLER, MONITEAU, MORGAN, NEWTON, NODAWAY, OREGON, OSAGE, OZARK, PETTIS, PLATTE, POLK, PULASKI, PUTNAM, RAY, SAINT CLAIR, SALINE, STONE, SULLIVAN, TANEY, TEXAS, VERNON, WEBSTER, WORTH, WRIGHT.

Civil and Criminal Records

US District Court
222 N. John Q. Hammons Pkwy.
Suite 1400
Springfield, MO 65806
(417) 865-3869
Records are available by mail only. $15.00 search fee. Make check payable to Clerk, US District Court. Search information required: name. Turnaround time: 1 week. For closed files prior to 1985, as directed by court clerk, see Kansas City Federal Records Center.

US District Court Clerk
PO Box 387
201 South 8th Street
St. Joseph, MO 64502
(816) 279-2428
Records are available by mail only. $15.00 search fee. $.50 fee per copy. $5.00 for certification. Make check payable to Clerk, US District Courts. Search information required: name. Turnaround time: 1-2 days. For closed files prior to 1987, as directed by court clerk, see Kansas City Federal Records Center.

US District Court Clerk
201 US Courthouse
811 Grand Avenue
Kansas City, MO 64106
(816) 426-2811
Fax (816) 426-2819
Records are available by mail only. $15.00 search fee. Make check payable to US District Court Clerk. Search information required: name, years to search. Turnaround time: 24 hours. For closed files prior to 1987, as directed by court clerk, see Kansas City Federal Records Center.

Bankruptcy Records

US Bankruptcy Court Clerk
811 Grand Avenue
Kansas City, MO 64106
(816) 426-3321
Records are available by mail or phone. $15.00 search fee. Company check payable to US Bankruptcy Court. Search information required: name. Turnaround time: 10 days. For closed files prior to 1987, as directed by court clerk, see Kansas City Federal Records Center.

District of Montana

THIS DISTRICT COMPRISES THE ENTIRE STATE.

Civil and Criminal Records

US District Court Clerk
PO Box 8537
Missoula, MT 59807
(406) 329-3598
Records are available by mail or phone. $15.00 search fee. $.50 fee per copy, $5.00 for certified copy. Make check payable to US District Court. Search information required: name, SSN. Turnaround time: 24 hours. For closed files, prior to 1987 as directed by court clerk, see Denver Federal Records Center.

US District Court Clerk
Room 5405, Federal Bldg.
316 North 26th Street
Billings, MT 59101
(406) 657-6366
Records are available by mail or phone. $15.00 search fee. $.50 fee per copy, $5.00 for certified copy. Make check payable to Clerk, US District Court. Search information required: name. Turnaround time: 24 hours. For closed files prior to 1989, see Denver Federal Records Center.

US District Court Clerk
301 South Park Ave, Room 542
Federal Bldg.
Drawer 10015
Helena, MT 59626
(406) 449-5356
Records are available by mail or phone. $15.00 search fee. $.50 fee per copy, $5.00 for certified copy. Make check payable to Clerk, US District Court. Search information required: name. Turnaround time: 24 hours. For closed files prior to 1987, as directed by court clerk, see Denver Federal Records Center.

Cascade County
US District Court Clerk
PO Box 2186
Great Falls, MT 59403
(406) 727-1922
Records are available by mail or phone. No search fee. $.50 fee per copy, $5.00 for certified copy. Search information required: name, years to search. Turnaround time: 24 hours. For closed files prior to 1988, as directed by court clerk, see Denver Federal Records Center.

US District Court Clerk
Room 273
Federal Building
Butte, MT 59701
(406) 782-0432
Records are available by mail or phone. $15.00 search fee. $.50 fee per copy, $5.00 for certified copy. Company check payable to Clerk, US District Court. Search information required: name. Turnaround time: 2-3 days. For closed files prior to 1986, as directed by court clerk, see Denver Federal Records Center.

Bankruptcy Records

US Bankruptcy Court Clerk
273 Federal Building
Butte, MT 59701
(406) 782-3354
Records are available by mail or phone. $15.00 search fee. $.50 fee per copy. Make check payable to US Bankruptcy Court. Search information required: name. Turnaround time: 3-5 days. For closed files, prior to 1986 as directed by court clerk, see Denver Federal Records Center.

District of Nebraska

THIS DISTRICT COMPRISES THE ENTIRE STATE.

Civil and Criminal Records

US District Court
593 Federal Building
100 Centennial Mall North
Lincoln, NE 68508
(402) 437-5225

Records are available by mail. $15.00 search fee. $.50 fee per copy, $5.00 for certified copy; prepaid. Make check payable to Clerk US District Court. Search information required: name. Turnaround time: 1-2 days. For closed files prior to 1987, as directed by court clerk, see Kansas City Federal Records Center.

US District Court Clerk
PO Box 129, DTS
Omaha, NE 68101
(402) 221-4761

Records are available by mail. $15.00 search fee. $.50 fee per copy, $5.00 for certified copy; prepaid. Make check payable to Clerk, US District Court. Search information required: name, years to search. Turnaround time: 24 hours. For closed files prior to 1989, as directed by court clerk, see Kansas City Federal Records Center.

Bankruptcy Records

US Bankruptcy Court Clerk
PO Box 428 DTS
Omaha, NE 68101-0428
(402) 221-4687
Fax (402) 221-3209

Records are available by mail or phone. $15.00 search fee, prepaid. $.50 fee per copy, $5.00 for certified copy; prepaid. Make check payable to US Bankruptcy Court. Search information required: name. Turnaround time: 5 days. For closed files, as directed by court clerk, see Kansas City Federal Records Center.

District of Nevada

THIS DISTRICT COMPRISES THE ENTIRE STATE.

Civil and Criminal Records

US District Court Clerk
300 Booth Street, Room 5003
Reno, NV 89509
(702) 784-5515

Records are available by mail. $15.00 search fee. $.50 fee per copy, $5.00 for certification. Make check payable to Clerk, US District Court. Search information required: name, years to search. Turnaround time: 2 days. For closed files prior to 1987, as directed by court clerk, see San Francisco Federal Records Center.

US District Court Clerk
300 Las Vegas Boulevard South
Las Vegas, NV 89101
(702) 388-6351

Records are available by mail. $15.00 search fee. $.50 fee per copy. $5.00 for certification. Make check payable to Clerk, US District Court. Search information required: name. Turnaround time: 2 days. For closed files prior to 1989, as directed by court clerk, see San Francisco Federal Records Center.

Bankruptcy Records

US Bankruptcy Court Clerk
300 Las Vegas Boulevard South
Las Vegas, NV 89101
(702) 388-6633

Records are available by mail or phone. $15.00 search fee, prepaid. $.50 fee per copy, $5.00 for certified copy; prepaid. Make check payable to US Bankruptcy Court Clerk. Search information required: name. Turnaround time: 2 weeks. For closed files prior to 1991, as directed by court clerk, see San Francisco Federal Records Center.

District of New Hampshire

THIS DISTRICT COMPRISES THE ENTIRE STATE.

Civil and Criminal Records

Clerk, US District Court
55 Pleasant St.
PO Box 1498
Concord, NH 03302-1498
(603) 225-1423

Records are available by mail or phone. No release necessary. $15.00 search fee. $.50 fee per copy, $5.00 for certified copy. Company check payable to Clerk, US District Court. Search information required: name. Turnaround time: 7-10 days. For closed files, as directed by court clerk, see Boston Federal Records Center.

Bankruptcy Records

US Bankruptcy Court Clerk
275 Chestnut Street, Room 715
Manchester, NH 03101
(603) 666-7624

Records are available by mail. $15.00 search fee. $.50 fee per copy, $5.00 for certified copy; prepaid. Make check payable to Clerk, US Bankruptcy Court. Search information required: case name, SASE. Turnaround time: 3-4 weeks. For closed files, as directed by court clerk, see Boston Federal Records Center.

District of New Jersey

THIS DISTRICT COMPRISES THE ENTIRE STATE.

Civil and Criminal Records

US District Court Clerk
PO Box 515
Trenton, NJ 08608
(609) 989-2065

Records are available by mail. $15.00 search fee. Make check payable to Clerk, US District Court. Search information required: name, years to search. Turnaround time: 2-3 days. For closed civil records prior to 1986 and closed criminal prior to 1981, as directed by court clerk, see New York Federal Records Center.

US County Courthouse
500 Federal Square
PO Box 419
Newark, NJ 07102-1681
(201) 645-3730

Records are available by mail. No release necessary. $15.00 search fee. $.50 fee per copy, $5.00 for certified copy; prepaid. Company check payable to Clerk, US District Court. Search information required: name, date of birth, SSN, years to search, SASE. Turnaround time: 1-2 days. For closed files, as directed by court clerk, see New York Federal Records Center.

Bankruptcy Records

US Bankruptcy Court
15 N. 7th St.
Camden, NJ 08102
(609) 757-5485

Records are available by mail. $15.00 search fee. $.50 fee per copy. $5.00 for certification. Make check payable to Clerk, US Bankruptcy Court. Search information required: name, SSN, previous address. Turnaround time: 2 weeks. For closed files prior to 1991, as directed by court clerk, see New York Federal Records Center.

US Bankruptcy Court
970 Broadstreet
Newark, NJ 07102
(201) 645-4764

Records are available by mail or phone. $15.00 search fee. $.50 fee per copy. $5.00 for certification. Make check payable to US Bankruptcy Court. Search information required: name. Turnaround time: 3-5 days. For closed files prior to 1989, as directed by court clerk, see New York Federal Records Center.

Clerk, US Bankruptcy Court
PO Box 1568
Trenton, NJ 08607
(609) 989-2129

Records are available by mail. $15.00 search fee. $.50 fee per copy. $5.00 for certification. Make check payable to US Bankruptcy Court. Search information required: name. Turnaround time: 1 week. For closed files prior to 1983, as directed by court clerk, see New York Federal Records Center.

District of New Mexico

THIS DISTRICT COMPRISES THE ENTIRE STATE.

Civil and Criminal Records

US District Court
PO Box 689
Albuquerque, NM 87103
(505) 766-2851
Fax (505) 766-8448
Records are available by mail. $15.00 search fee. $.50 fee per copy, $5.00 for certified copy. Make check payable to Clerk, US District Court. Search information required: name, SASE. Turnaround time: 1 week. For closed files prior to 1988, as directed by court clerk, see Fort Worth Federal Records Center.

Clerk, US District Court
200 East Griggs
Room E-202
Las Cruces, NM 88001
(505) 525-2304
Records are available by mail. $15.00 search fee. $.50 fee per copy, $5.00 for certification. Make check payable to Clerk, US District Court. Search information required: name, SASE. Turnaround time: 1 week. Contact Albuquerque for additional records. For closed files prior to 1991, as directed by court clerk, see Fort Worth Federal Records Center.

Bankruptcy Records

US Bankruptcy Court
PO Box 546
Albuquerque, NM 87103
(505) 766-2051
Records are available by mail or phone. $15.00 search fee. $.50 fee per copy, $5.00 for certified copy; prepaid. Make check payable to US Bankruptcy Court. Search information required: name, SASE. Turnaround time: 5 days. For closed files prior to 1983, as directed by court clerk, see Fort Worth Federal Records Center.

Eastern District of New York

KINGS, NASSAU, QUEENS, RICHMOND, SUFFOLK (INCLUDED IN THIS DISTRICT, CONCURRENTLY WITH THE SOUTHERN DISTRICT, ARE THE WATERS WITHIN THE COUNTIES OF BRONX AND NEW YORK).

Civil and Criminal Records

Clerk, US District Court
225 Cadman Plaza East
Brooklyn, NY 11201
(718) 330-2105
Records are available by mail only. $15.00 search fee. $.50 fee per copy, $5.00 for certified copy; prepaid. Make check payable to Clerk, US District Court. Search information required: name, years to search. Turnaround time: 1 week. For closed files prior to 1987, as directed by court clerk, see New York Federal Records Center.

Bankruptcy Records

US Bankruptcy Court
75 Clinton Street
Brooklyn, NY 11201
(718) 330-2188
Records are available by mail. $15.00 search fee. $.50 fee per copy, $5.00 for certified copy; prepaid. Make check payable to Clerk, US Bankruptcy Court. Search information required: name, SSN, previous address. Turnaround time: 1 week. For closed files prior to 1985, as directed by court clerk, see New York Federal Records Center.

Northern District of New York

ALBANY, BROOME, CAYUGA, CHENANGO, CLINTON, COLUMBIA, CORTLAND, DELAWARE, ESSEX, FRANKLIN, FULTON, GREENE, HAMILTON, HERKIMER, JEFFERSON, LEWIS, MADISON, MONTGOMERY, ONEIDA, ONONDAGA, OSWEGO, OTSEGO, RENSSELAER, SAINT LAWRENCE, SARATOGA, SCHENECTADY, SCHOHARIE, TIOGA, TOMPKINS, ULSTER, WARREN, WASHINGTON.

Civil and Criminal Records

Clerk, US District Court
Alexander Pirnie Building
10 Broad Street
Utica, NY 13501
(315) 793-8151
Records are available by mail. $15.00 search fee. $.50 fee per copy, $5.00 for certified copy; prepaid. Make check payable to Clerk, US District Court. Search information required: name. Turnaround time: 1 week. This is the main office for Northern District of New York. For closed files, as directed by court clerk, see New York Federal Records Center.

Bankruptcy Records

US Bankruptcy Court
J.T. Foley Courthouse
PO Box 398
Albany, NY 12201-0398
(518) 472-4226
Records are available by mail. $15.00 search fee. Make check payable to Clerk, US Bankruptcy Court. Search information required: name. Turnaround time: 1-2 weeks. For closed files, as directed by court clerk, see New York Federal Records Center.

Southern District of New York

BRONX, DUTCHESS, NEW YORK, ORANGE, PUTNAM, ROCKLAND, SULLIVAN, WESTCHESTER. THIS DISTRICT INCLUDES, CONCURRENTLY WITH THE EASTERN DISTRICT, THE WATERS WITHIN THE EASTERN DISTRICT.

Civil and Criminal Records

US District Courthouse
Southern District of New York
40 Foley Square
New York, NY 10007
(212) 791-0108
Records are available by mail. $15.00 search fee. $.50 fee per copy, $5.00 for certification. Make check payable to Clerk, US District Court. Search information required: name. For closed files prior to 1989, as directed by court clerk, see New York Federal Records Center.

Bankruptcy Records

US Bankruptcy Court
1 Bowling Green
6th Floor
New York, NY 10004-1408
(212) 791-2249
Records are available by mail. $15.00 search fee. $.50 fee per copy. $5.00 for certification. Make check payable to Clerk, US Bankruptcy Court. Search information required: name. Turnaround time: 1 month. For closed files prior to 1987, as directed by court clerk, see New York Federal Records Center.

Western District of New York

ALLEGANY, CATTARAUGUS, CHAUTAUQUA, CHEMUNG, ERIE, GENESEE, LIVINGSTON, MONROE, NIAGARA, ONTARIO, ORLEANS, SCHUYLER, SENECA, STEUBEN, WAYNE, WYOMING, YATES.

Civil and Criminal Records

Clerk, US District Court
282 US Courthouse
100 State Street
Rochester, NY 14614
(716) 263-6263
Records are available by mail or phone. $15.00 search fee. $.50 fee per copy. $5.00 for certification. Company check payable to Clerk, US District Court. Search information required: name. Turnaround time: 2-7 days. For closed files, prior to 1987 as directed by court clerk, see New York Federal Records Center.

US District Court
304 US Courthouse
68 Court Street
Buffalo, NY 14202
(716) 846-4211
Records are available by mail or phone. $15.00 search fee. $.50 fee per copy, $5.00 for certified copy; prepaid. Make check payable to Clerk, US District Court. Search information required: name, SASE. Turnaround time: 1 day. For closed files prior to 1981, as directed by court clerk, see New York Federal Records Center.

Bankruptcy Records

US Bankruptcy Court
310 US Courthouse
68 Court Street
Buffalo, NY 14202
(716) 846-4130
Touchtone automated system
(716) 846-5311
Records are available by mail or phone.
$15.00 search fee. $.50 fee per copy, $5.00
fee for certification. Make check payable to
Clerk, US Bankruptcy Court. Search
information required: name. Turnaround
time: 1 week. For closed files, as directed
by court clerk, see New York Federal
Records Center.

US Bankruptcy Court
100 State Street
Room 212
Rochester, NY 14614
(716) 263-3148
Touchtone automated system
(716) 846-5311
Records are available by mail. $15.00
search fee. $.50 fee per copy, $5.00 for
certified copy; prepaid. Company check
payable to Clerk, US Bankruptcy Court.
Search information required: name,
information to search, SASE. Turnaround
time: 2-3 days.

Eastern District of North Carolina

BEAUFORT, BERTIE, BLADEN,
BRUNSWICK, CAMDEN, CARTERET,
CHOWAN, COLUMBUS, CRAVEN,
CUMBERLAND, CURRITUCK, DARE,
DUPLIN, EDGECOMBE, FRANKLIN, GATES,
GRANVILLE, GREENE, HALIFAX,
HARNETT, HERTFORD, HYDE, JOHNSTON,
JONES, LENOIR, MARTIN, NASH, NEW
HANOVER, NORTHHAMPTON, ONSLOW,
PAMLICO, PASQUOTANK, PENDER,
PERQUIMANS, PITT, ROBESON, SAMPSON,
TYRRELL, VANCE, WAKE, WARREN,
WASHINGTON, WAYNE, WILSON.

Civil and Criminal Records

Clerk, US District Court Criminal
Division
PO Box 25670
Raleigh, NC 27611
(919) 856-4418
Records are available by mail. $15.00
search fee. $.50 fee per copy, $5.00 for
certified copy, prepaid. Make check
payable to Clerk, US District Court. Search
information required: name. Turnaround
time: 10 days. For closed files prior to
1985, as directed by court clerk, see Atlanta
Federal Records Center.

Clerk, US District Court
PO Box 43
Fayetteville, NC 28302
(919) 483-9509
Records are available by mail. $15.00
search fee. $.50 fee per copy. $5.00 for
certification. Certified check or money
order, payable to Clerk, US District Court.
Search information required: name, years to
search. Turnaround time: 10 days. For
closed files prior to 1987, as directed by
court clerk, see Atlanta Federal Records
Center.

Clerk, US District Court
PO Box 1336
New Bern, NC 28563
(919) 638-8534
Fax (919) 638-1529
Records are available by mail. $15.00
search fee. $.50 fee per copy. $5.00 for
certification. Certified check or money
order, payable to Clerk, US District Court.
Search information required: name, SASE.
Turnaround time: 7-10 days. For closed
files prior to 1987, as directed by court
clerk, see Atlanta Federal Records Center.

Bankruptcy Records

US Bankruptcy Court
PO Drawer 2807
Wilson, NC 27894-2807
(919) 237-0248
Records are available by mail or phone.
$15.00 search fee. $.50 fee per copy, $5.00
for certified copy, prepaid. Make check
payable to Clerk, US Bankruptcy Court.
Search information required: name.
Turnaround time: 2-3 days. For closed files
prior to 1992, as directed by court clerk, see
Atlanta Federal Records Center.

Middle District of North Carolina

ALAMANCE, CABARRUS, CASWELL,
CHATHAM, DAVIDSON, DAVIE, DURHAM,
FORSYTH, GUILFORD, HOKE, LEE,
MONTGOMERY, MOORE, ORANGE,
PERSON, RANDOLPH, RICHMOND,
ROCKINGHAM, ROWAN, SCOTLAND,
STANLEY, STOKES, SURRY, YADKIN.

Civil and Criminal Records

US District Court
Clerk's Office
PO Box V-1
Greensboro, NC 27402
(919) 333-5347
Records are available by mail. $15.00
search fee. $.50 fee per copy. $5.00 for
certification. Make check payable to Clerk,
US District Court. Search information
required: name. Turnaround time: 7 days.
For closed files prior to 1987, as directed
by court clerk, see Atlanta Federal Records
Center.

Bankruptcy Records

US Bankruptcy Court
PO Box 26100
Greensboro, NC 27420-6100
(919) 333-5647
Records are available by mail or phone.
$15.00 search fee. $.50 fee per copy, $5.00
fee for certification. Make check payable to
Clerk, US Bankruptcy Court. Search
information required: name, specific
information to search. Turnaround time: 1-2
days. For closed files prior to 1991, as
directed by court clerk, see Atlanta Federal
Records Center.

Western District of North Carolina

ALEXANDER, ALLEGHANY, ANSON, ASHE,
AVERY, BUNCOMBE, BURKE, CALDWELL,
CATAWBA, CHEROKEE, CLAY,
CLEVELAND, GASTON, GRAHAM,
HAYWOOD, HENDERSON, IREDELL,
JACKSON, LINCOLN, MACON, MADISON,
MCDOWELL, MECKLENBURG, MITCHELL,
POLK, RUTHERFORD, SWAIN,
TRANSYLVANIA, UNION, WATAUGA,
WILKES, YANCEY.

Civil and Criminal Records

Clerk, US District Court
PO Box 466
Statesville, NC 28677
(704) 873-7112
Fax (704) 873-9544
Records are available by mail or phone.
$15.00 search fee. $.50 fee per copy, $5.00
for certified copy; prepaid. Search
information required: name. Turnaround
time: 2 days. For closed files prior to 1987,
as directed by court clerk, see Atlanta
Federal Records Center.

Clerk, US District Court
401 West Trade Street
Room 204
Charlotte, NC 28202
(704) 344-6101
Records are available by mail. $15.00
search fee. $.50 fee per copy, $5.00 for
certified copy; prepaid. Make check
payable to Clerk, US District Court. Search
information required: name. Turnaround
time: 7-10 days. For closed files, prior to
1986 as directed by court clerk, see Atlanta
Federal Records Center.

Clerk, US District Court
100 Otis Street
Asheville, NC 28801-2611
(704) 259-0648
Records are available by mail. $15.00
search fee. $.50 fee per copy, $5.00 for
certified copy; prepaid. Make check
payable to Clerk, US District Court. Search
information required: name. Turnaround
time: 7 days. For closed files, prior to 1987
as directed by court clerk, see Atlanta
Federal Records Center.

Bankruptcy Records

US Bankruptcy Court
401 West Trade Street
Charlotte, NC 28202
(704) 344-6103
Records are available by mail. $15.00
search fee. $.50 fee per copy, $5.00 for
certified copy; prepaid. Company check
payable to Clerk, US Bankruptcy Court.
Search information required: name, SASE.
Turnaround time: 7-10 days. For closed
files prior to 1986, as directed by court
clerk, see Atlanta Federal Records Center.

District of North Dakota

THIS DISTRICT COMPRISES THE ENTIRE STATE.

Civil and Criminal Records

US District Court
PO Box 1193
Bismarck, ND 58502
(701) 250-4295

Records are available by mail. $15.00 search fee. $.50 fee per copy, $5.00 for certified copy. Make check payable to Clerk, US District Court. Search information required: name, years to search. Turnaround time: Within 24 hours after receipt of check. For closed files, as directed by court clerk, see Denver Federal Records Center.

Bankruptcy Records

US Bankruptcy Court
PO Box 1110
Fargo, ND 58107
(701) 239-5129

Records are available by mail or phone. No search fee. $.50 fee per copy, $5.00 for certified copy. Make check payable to Clerk, US Bankruptcy Court. Search information required: name. Turnaround time: 2-3 days. For closed files, as directed by court clerk, see Denver Federal Records Center.

Northern District of Ohio

ALLEN, ASHLAND, ASHTABULA, AUGLAIZE, CARROLL, COLUMBIANA, CRAWFORD, CUYAHOGA, DEFIANCE, ERIE, FULTON, GEAUGA, HANCOCK, HARDIN, HENRY, HOLMES, HURON, LAKE, LORAIN, LUCAS, MAHONING, MARION, MEDINA, MERCER, OTTAWA, PAULDING, PORTAGE, PUTNAM, RICHLAND, SANDUSKY, SENECA, STARK, SUMMIT, TRUMBULL, TUSCARAWAS, VAN WERT, WAYNE, WILLIAMS, WOODS, WYANDOT.

Civil and Criminal Records

Clerk, US District Court
201 Superior Avenue
Cleveland, OH 44114
(216) 522-4355

Records are available by mail or phone. No search fee. $.50 fee per copy, $5.00 for certified copy; prepaid. Make check payable to Clerk, US District Court. Search information required: name. Turnaround time: 2-3 days. For closed files prior to 1987, as directed by court clerk, see Chicago Federal Records Center.

Clerk, US District Court
568 Federal Building
2 South Main Street
Akron, OH 44308
(216) 375-5544

Records are available by mail or phone. $15.00 search fee. $.50 fee per copy. $5.00 for certification. Search information required: name. Turnaround time: 1-2 days. For closed files prior to 1987, as directed by court clerk, see Chicago Federal Records Center.

Clerk, US District Court
114 US Courthouse
1716 Spielbusch, Room 114
Toledo, OH 43624
(419) 259-6412

Records are available by mail or phone. $15.00 search fee. $.50 fee per copy, $5.00 for certified copy; prepaid. Make check payable to Clerk, US District Court. Search information required: name, SASE. Turnaround time: 7 days. For closed files, as directed by court clerk, see Chicago Federal Records Center.

Bankruptcy Records

US Bankruptcy Court
9 West Front Street
PO Box 147
City Hall Annex
Youngstown, OH 44501
(216) 746-7027

Records are available by mail. $15.00 search fee. $.50 fee per copy, $5.00 for certified copy; prepaid. Make check payable to Clerk, US Bankruptcy Court. Search information required: name. Turnaround time: 10 days. For closed files, as directed by court clerk, see Chicago Federal Records Center.

US Bankruptcy Court
2 South Main
455 Federal Building
Akron, OH 44308
(216) 375-5840

Records are available by mail. $15.00 search fee. $.50 fee per copy, $5.00 for certified copy, prepaid. Make check payable to Clerk, US Bankruptcy Court. Search information required: name, SASE. Turnaround time: 2-3 days. For closed files prior to 1992, as directed by court clerk, see Chicago Federal Records Center.

US Bankruptcy Court
1716 Spielbusch Ave.
Room 411
Toledo, OH 43624
(419) 259-6440

Records are available by mail. $15.00 search fee. $.50 fee per copy, $5.00 for certified copy; prepaid, include company telephone number to verify copying fees for prepayment. Make check payable to US Bankruptcy Court. Search information required: name. Turnaround time: 10 days. For closed files, as directed by court clerk, see Chicago Federal Records Center.

US Bankruptcy Court
Frank T. Bow Federal Building
201 Cleveland Avenue Southwest
Canton, OH 44702
(216) 489-4426
Fax (216) 489-4434

Records are available by mail. $15.00 search fee. $.50 fee per copy, $5.00 for certified copy; prepaid. Make check payable to Clerk, US Bankruptcy Court. Search information required: name, SASE. Turnaround time: 1 week. For closed files, as directed by court clerk, see Chicago Federal Records Center.

US Bankruptcy Court
201 Superior
Cleveland, OH 44114
(216) 522-4373

Records are available by mail. $15.00 search fee. $.50 fee per copy, $5.00 for certified copy; prepaid. Make check payable to Clerk, US Bankruptcy Court. Search information required: name, phone number of person requesting information,

SASE. Turnaround time: 1-2 days. For closed files, as directed by court clerk, see Chicago Federal Records Center.

Southern District of Ohio

ADAMS, ATHENS, BELMONT, BROWN, BUTLER, CHAMPAIGN, CLARK, CLERMONT, CLINTON, COSCHOCTON, DARKE, DELAWARE, FAIRFIELD, FAYETTE, FRANKLIN, GALLIA, GREENE, GUERNSEY, HAMILTON, HARRISON, HIGHLAND, HOCKING, JACKSON, JEFFERSON, KNOX, LAWRENCE, LICKING, LOGAN, MADISON, MEIGS, MIAMI, MONROE, MONTGOMERY, MORGAN, MORROW, MUSKINGUM, NOBLE, PERRY, PICKAWAY, PIKE, PREBLE, ROSS, SCIOTO, SHELBY, UNION, VINTON, WARREN, WASHINGTON.

Civil and Criminal Records

US Clerk's Office
PO Box 970
200 W. 2nd St.
Dayton, OH 45402
(513) 225-2896

Records are available by mail or phone. $15.00 search fee. $.50 fee per copy, $5.00 for certified copy; prepaid. Make check payable to Clerk, US District Court. Search information required: name, SASE. Turnaround time: 1-2 days. For closed files prior to 1992, as directed by court clerk, see Chicago Federal Records Center.

Office of the Clerk
Room 260
85 Marconi Boulevard
Columbus, OH 43215
(614) 469-6638

Records are available by mail or phone. $15.00 search fee. $.50 fee per copy, $5.00 for certified copy; prepaid. Make check payable to Clerk, US District Court. Search information required: name, SSN, address if available. Turnaround time: 5 working days. For closed files prior to 1989, as directed by court clerk, see Chicago Federal Records Center.

Clerk, US District Court
324 Post Office & Courthouse
5th & Main St.
Cincinnati, OH 45202
(513) 684-2777

Records are available by mail. $15.00 search fee. $.50 fee per copy, $5.00 for certified copy; prepaid. Make check payable to Clerk, US District Court. Search information required: name. Turnaround time: 1-2 days. For closed files prior to 1989 for civil and prior to 1987 for criminal, as directed by court clerk, see Chicago Federal Records Center.

Bankruptcy Records

US Bankruptcy Court
735 US PO & Courthouse Building
Cincinnati, OH 45202
(513) 684-2573

Records are available by mail. $15.00 search fee. $.50 fee per copy, $5.00 for certified copy; prepaid. Make check payable to Clerk, US Bankruptcy Court. Search information required: name. Turnaround time: 1-2 days. For closed files, as directed by court clerk, see Chicago Federal Records Center.

Clerk, US Bankruptcy Court
200 West Second Street
Room 705
Dayton, OH 45402
(513) 225-7274

Records are available by mail. $15.00 search fee. $.50 fee per copy, $5.00 for certified copy, prepaid. Company check payable to Clerk, US Bankruptcy Court. Search information required: name. Turnaround time: 2 days. For closed files, as directed by court clerk, see Chicago Federal Records Center.

US Bankruptcy Court
124 US Courthouse
85 Marconi Boulevard
Columbus, OH 43215
(614) 469-2087

Records are available by mail. No release necessary. $15.00 search fee. $.50 fee per copy, $5.00 fee for certification. Make check payable to Clerk, US Bankruptcy Court. Search information required: name, SASE. Turnaround time: 3-4 days. For closed files, as directed by court clerk, see Chicago Federal Records Center.

Eastern District of Oklahoma

ADAIR, ATOKA, BRYAN, CARTER, CHEROKEE, CHOCTAW, COAL, HESKELL, HUGHES, JOHNSTON, LATIMER, LEFLORE, LOVE, MARSHALL, MCCURTIN, MCINTOSH, MURRAY, MUSKOGEE, OKFUSKEE, OKMULGEE, PITTSBURG, PONTOTOC, PUSHMATAHA, SEMINOLE, SEQUOYAH, WAGONER.

Civil and Criminal Records

Clerk, US District Court
PO Box 607
Muskogee, OK 74401
(918) 687-2471

Records are available by mail. $15.00 search fee. $.50 fee per copy, $5.00 for certified copy; prepaid. Certified check only, payable to Clerk, US District Court. Search information required: name, SASE. Turnaround time: 1-2 days. For closed files, as directed by court clerk, see Fort. Worth Federal Records Center.

Bankruptcy Records

US Bankruptcy Court
PO Box 1347
Okmulgee, OK 74447
(918) 758-0126
(918) 756-8617 Voice Case Information System

Records are available by mail. $15.00 search fee. $.50 fee per copy, $5.00 for certified copy; prepaid. Make check payable to US Bankruptcy Court. Search information required: name. Turnaround time: 3-4 days. For closed files, as directed by court clerk, see Fort Worth Federal Records Center.

Northern District of Oklahoma

CRAIG, CREEK, DELAWARE, MAYES, NOWATA, OSAGE, OTTAWA, PAWNEE, ROGERS, TULSA, WASHINGTON.

Civil and Criminal Records

Clerk, US District Court
411 US Courthouse
333 W. 4th Street
Tulsa, OK 74103
(918) 581-7796

Records are available by mail or phone. $15.00 search fee. $.50 fee per copy, $5.00 for certified copy. Make check payable to Clerk, US District Court. Search information required: name, specific information to search, SASE. Turnaround time: 1-2 days. For closed files, as directed by court clerk, see Fort Worth Federal Records Center.

Bankruptcy Records

US Bankruptcy Court
111 W. 5th St.
Suite 320
Tulsa, OK 74103
(918) 581-7181

Records are available by mail. $15.00 search fee. $.50 fee per copy, $5.00 for certified copy. Make check payable to Clerk, US Bankruptcy. Search information required: name. Turnaround time: 2 weeks. For closed files prior to 1990, see Fort Worth Federal Records Center.

Western District of Oklahoma

ALFALFA, BEAVER, BECKHAM, BLAINE, CADDO, CANADIAN, CIMARRON, CLEVELAND, COMANCHE, COTTON, CUSTER, DEWEY, ELLIS, GARFIELD, GARVIN, GRADY, GRANT, GREER, HARMON, HARPER, JACKSON, JEFFERSON, KAY, KINGFISHER, KIOWA, LINCOLN, LOGAN, MAJOR, MCCLAIN, NOBLE, OKLAHOMA, PAYNE, POTTAWATOMIE, ROGER MILLS, STEPHENS, TEXAS, TILLMAN, WASHITA, WOODS, WOODWARD.

Civil and Criminal Records

Clerk, US District Court
Room 3210
200 Northwest 4th Street
Oklahoma City, OK 73102
(405) 231-4792

Records are available by mail. $15.00 search fee. $.50 fee per copy, $5.00 for certified copy. Make check payable to Clerk, US District Court. Search information required: name, SASE. Turnaround time: 2-3 days. For closed files, as directed by court clerk, see Fort Worth Federal Records Center.

Bankruptcy Records

US Bankruptcy Court
215 Dean McGee Avenue
Attn: Research Dept.
Oklahoma City, OK 73102
(405) 231-5141

Records are available by mail only. $15.00 search fee. $.50 fee per copy, $5.00 for certification. Make check payable to US Bankruptcy Court Clerk. Search information required: name, SASE. Turnaround time: 1 week. For closed files, prior to 1991 as directed by court clerk, see Fort Worth Federal Records Center.

District of Oregon

THIS DISTRICT COMPRISES THE ENTIRE STATE.

Civil and Criminal Records

Clerk, US District Court
531 Gus J. Solomon Courthouse
620 SW Main
Portland, OR 97205
(503) 326-5412

Records are available by mail. $15.00 search fee. $.50 fee per copy, $5.00 for certified copy. Make check payable to Clerk, US District Court. Search information required: full name, date of birth, dates to search. Turnaround time: 1 week. For closed files, as directed by court clerk, see Seattle Federal Records Center.

US District Court Clerk
102 US Courthouse
211 East Seventh Avenue
Eugene, OR 97401
(503) 465-6423

Records are available by mail or phone. No search fee. $.50 fee per copy, $5.00 for certified copy. Search information required: name. Turnaround time: 1-2 days. For closed files prior to 1988, as directed by court clerk, see Seattle Federal Records Center.

Bankruptcy Records

US Bankruptcy Court
PO Box 1335
Eugene, OR 97440
Touchtone automated system
(503) 326-2249
(800) 326-2227

Records are available by mail or phone. $15.00 search fee. $.50 fee per copy, $5.00 for certified copy. Make check payable to Clerk, US Bankruptcy Court. Search information required: name. Turnaround time: 1-2 days. For closed files, as directed by court clerk, see Seattle Federal Records Center.

US Bankruptcy Court
1001 Southwest 5th Avenue
#900
Portland, OR 97204
(503) 326-2231

Records are available by mail or phone. $15.00 search fee. $.50 fee per copy, $5.00 for certified copy. Make check payable to Clerk, US Bankruptcy Court. Search information required: name, specific information to search. Turnaround time: 1-3 days. For closed files prior to 1987, as directed by court clerk, see Seattle Federal Records Center.

Eastern District of Pennsylvania

BERKS, BUCKS, CHESTER, DELAWARE, LANCASTER, LEHIGH, MONTGOMERY, NORTHAMPTON, PHILADELPHIA, SCHUYKILL.

Civil and Criminal Records

US District Court
Room 2609 US Courthouse
601 Market Street
Philadelphia, PA 19106-1797
(215) 597-7704
Records are available by mail. $15.00 search fee. $.50 fee per copy, $5.00 for certified copy. Make check payable to Clerk, US District Court. Search information required: name, SASE. Turnaround time: 14 days. For closed files prior to 1988, see Philadelphia Federal Records Center.

Bankruptcy Records

US Bankruptcy Court
601 Market Street, Rm. 3726
Philadelphia, PA 19106
(215) 597-1644
Records are available by mail or phone. $15.00 search fee. $.50 fee per copy, $5.00 for certified copy. Make check payable to Clerk, US Bankruptcy Court. Search information required: name, SASE. Turnaround time: 1 week. For closed files prior to 1992, as directed by court clerk, see Philadelphia Federal Records Center.

Middle District of Pennsylvania

ADAMS, BRADFORD, CAMERON, CARBON, CENTRE, CLINTON, COLUMBIA, CUMBERLAND, DAUPHIN, FRANKLIN, FULTON, HUNTINGTON, JUNIATA, LACKAWANNA, LEBANON, LUZERNE, LYCOMING, MIFFLIN, MONROE, MONTOUR, NORTHUMBERLAND, PERRY, PIKE, POTTER, SNYDER, SULLIVAN, SUSQUEHANNA, TIOGA, UNION, WAYNE, WYOMING, YORK.

Civil and Criminal Records

Clerks Office
US District Court
PO Box 1148
Washington Ave, Linden St.
Scranton, PA 18501
(717) 347-0205
Records are available by mail. $15.00 search fee. $.50 fee per copy, $5.00 for certified copy. Make check payable to Clerk of Courts. Search information required: name. Turnaround time: 7 days. Central office for Middle District of Pennsylvania. For closed files, as directed by court clerk, see Philadelphia Federal Records Center.

Bankruptcy Records

Clerk, US Bankruptcy Court
217 Federal Building
197 South Main Street
Wilkes Barre, PA 18701
(717) 826-6450
Records are available by mail. $15.00 search fee. $.50 fee per copy, $5.00 for certified copy. Make check payable to Louise Cannon Copy Service. Search information required: name, SASE, Pennsylvania address. Turnaround time: 7 days. For closed files, as directed by court clerk, see Philadelphia Federal Records Center.

Western District of Pennsylvania

ALLEGHENY, ARMSTRONG, BEAVER, BEDFORD, BLAIR, BUTLER, CAMBRIA, CLARION, CLEARFIELD, CRAWFORD, ELK, ERIE, FAYETTE, FOREST, GREENE, INDIANA, JEFFERSON, LAWRENCE, MCKEAN, MERCER, SOMERSET, VENANGO, WARREN, WASHINGTON, WESTMORELAND.

Civil and Criminal Records

Clerk's Office
US District Court & PO Rm 829
7th & Grant St.
Pittsburgh, PA 15219
(412) 644-3527
Records are available by phone. No release necessary. $15.00 search fee. $.50 fee per copy, $5.00 for certified copy. Search information required: name. Turnaround time: 1 day. For pre 1984 closed files, see Philadelphia Federal Records Center.

Bankruptcy Records

Clerk, US Bankruptcy Court
1602 Federal Building
1000 Liberty Ave.
Pittsburgh, PA 15222
(412) 644-2700
Records are available by mail or phone. $15.00 search fee. $.50 fee per copy, $5.00 for certification. Make check payable to Clerk, US Bankruptcy Court. Search information required: name. Turnaround time: 2 weeks. For closed files prior to 1987, as directed by court clerk, see Philadelphia Federal Records Center.

District of Rhode Island

THIS DISTRICT COMPRISES THE ENTIRE STATE.

Civil and Criminal Records

US District Court
Rm 119, Federal Bldg.
Clerk's Office
Providence, RI 02903
(401) 528-5100
Fax (401) 528-5112
Records are available by mail. $15.00 search fee. $.50 fee per copy, $5.00 for certified copy; prepaid. Make check payable to Clerk, US District Court. Search

information required: name. Turnaround time: 1-2 days. For closed files, as directed by court clerk, see Boston Federal Records Center.

Bankruptcy Records

US Bankruptcy Court
380 Westminster Mall
6th Floor
Providence, RI 02903
(401) 528-4477
(401) 528-4476 VCIS
Records are available by mail or phone. $15.00 search fee. $.50 fee per copy, $5.00 for certified copy. Make check payable to Clerk, US Bankruptcy Court. Search information required: name, SASE. Turnaround time: 1-2 days. For closed files, as directed by court clerk, see Boston Federal Records Center.

District of South Carolina

THIS DISTRICT COMPRISES THE ENTIRE STATE.

Civil and Criminal Records

Clerk, US District Court
PO Box 10768
Greenville, SC 29603
(803) 233-2781
Records are available by mail or phone. $15.00 search fee. $.50 fee per copy, $5.00 fee for certification. Make check payable to Clerk, US District Court. Search information required: name, SASE. Turnaround time: 1 day. For closed files, as directed by court clerk, see Atlanta Federal Records Center.

US District Court
PO Box 2317
Florence, SC 29503
(803) 662-1223
Records are available by mail. $15.00 search fee. $.50 fee per copy, $5.00 for certified copy. Make check payable to Clerk, US District Court. Search information required: full name. Turnaround time: 2-3 days. For closed files prior to 1987, as directed by court clerk, see Atlanta Federal Records Center.

Clerk of Court
1845 Assembly Street
Columbia, SC 29201
(803) 765-5353
Records are available by mail. $15.00 search fee. $.50 fee per copy, $5.00 for certified copy. Make check payable to Clerk, US District Court. Search information required: name, years to search. Turnaround time: 1 week. Central office for District of South Carolina. For closed files prior to 1989, as directed by court clerk, see Atlanta Federal Records Center.

Bankruptcy Records

US Bankruptcy Court
PO Box 1448
Columbia, SC 29202
(803) 765-5436
(803) 765-5211 VCIS

Records are available by mail or phone. $15.00 search fee. $.50 fee per copy, $5.00 for certified copy. Make check payable to Clerk, US Bankruptcy Court. Search information required: name, SASE. Turnaround time: 1 week. For closed files, as directed by court clerk, see Atlanta Federal Records Center. For copies of documents contact copy service at (803) 799-2679 or (800) 772-2679.

District of South Dakota

THIS DISTRICT COMPRISES THE ENTIRE STATE.

Civil and Criminal Records

US District Court
Clerk's Office
515 9th St., Rm 302
Rapid City, SD 57701
(605) 342-3066

Records are available by mail or phone. $15.00 search fee, prepaid. $.50 fee per copy. $5.00 for certification. Make check payable to Clerk, US District Court. Search information required: name. Turnaround time: 1-2 day. For closed files prior to 1987, as directed by court clerk, see Denver Federal Records Center.

Clerk, US District Court
400 South Phillips Avenue
Sioux Falls, SD 57102
(605) 338-5566

Records are available by mail. $15.00 search fee, prepaid. $.50 fee per copy, $5.00 for certified copy. Make check payable to Clerk, US District Court. Search information required: name. Turnaround time: 1-2 days. Central office for District of South Dakota. For closed files prior to 1985, as directed by court clerk, see Denver Federal Records Center.

US District Court Clerk
Federal Building & Courthouse
225 S. Pierre St., Rm. 405
Pierre, SD 57501
(605) 224-5849

Records are available by mail or phone. $15.00 search fee. $.50 fee per copy, $5.00 for certified copy. Search information required: name. Turnaround time: 1-2 days. For closed files, as directed by court clerk, see Denver Federal Records Center.

Bankruptcy Records

US Bankruptcy Court
PO Box 5060
Sioux Falls, SD 57117-5060
(605) 330-4541

Records are available by mail or phone. $15.00 search fee. $.50 fee per copy, $5.00 for certified copy. Company check payable to Clerk, US Bankruptcy Court. Search information required: name, SASE. Turnaround time: 1 day. For closed files, as directed by court clerk, see Denver Federal Records Center.

Eastern District of Tennessee

ANDERSON, BEDFORD, BLEDSOE, BLOUNT, BRADLEY, CAMPBELL, CARTER, CLAIRBORNE, COCKE, COFFEE, FRANKLIN, GRAINGER, GREENE, GRUNDY, HAMBLEN, HAMILTON, HANCOCK, HAWKINS, JEFFERSON, JOHNSON, KNOX, LINCOLN, LOUDON, MARION, MCMINN, MEIGS, MONROE, MOORE, MORGAN, POLK, RHEA, ROANE, SCOTT, SEQUATCHIE, SEVIER, SULLIVAN, UNICOI, UNION, VAN BUREN, WARREN, WASHINGTON.

Civil and Criminal Records

Clerk, US District Court
101 Summer Street West
Greenville, TN 37743
(615) 639-3105

Records are available by mail or phone. $15.00 search fee. $.50 fee per copy, $5.00 for certified copy. Make check payable to Clerk, US District Court. Search information required: name. Turnaround time: 3 days. For closed files, as directed by court clerk, see Atlanta Federal Records Center.

US District Court
Clerk's Office
PO Box 2348
Knoxville, TN 37901
(615) 673-4227

Records are available by mail. $15.00 search fee. $.50 fee per copy, $5.00 for certified copy, prepaid. Make check payable to US District Court. Search information required: name. Turnaround time: 1-2 days. For closed files prior to 1984, as directed by court clerk, see Atlanta Federal Records Center.

US District Court
Clerk's Office
PO Box 591
Chattanooga, TN 37401
(615) 752-5200

Records are available by mail or phone. $15.00 search fee. $.50 fee per copy, $5.00 for certified copy. Search information required: name. Turnaround time: 1 to 2 days. For closed files prior to 1985, as directed by court clerk, see Atlanta Federal Records Center.

Bankruptcy Records

US Bankruptcy Court
Suite 1501
Plaza Tower
Knoxville, TN 37929-1501
(615) 673-4525

Records are available by mail or phone. $15.00 search fee. $.50 fee per copy, $5.00 for certified copy. Make check payable to Clerk, US Bankruptcy Court. Search information required: name. Turnaround time: 1 week. For closed files prior to 1989, as directed by court clerk, see Atlanta Federal Records Center.

Middle District of Tennessee

CANNON, CHEATHAM, CLAY, CUMBERLAND, DAVIDSON, DEKALB, DICKSON, FENTRESS, GILES, HICKMAN, HOUSTON, HUMPHREYS, JACKSON, LAWRENCE, LEWIS, MACON, MARSHALL, MAURY, MONTGOMERY, OVERTON, PICKETT, PUTNAM, ROBERTSON, RUTHERFORD, SMITH, STEWART, SUMNER, TROUSDALE, WAYNE, WHITE, WILLIAMSON, WILSON.

Civil and Criminal Records

US District Court Clerk's Office
US Courthouse - Room 800
801 Broadway
Nashville, TN 37203
(615) 736-7763

Records are available by mail only. $15.00 search fee. Make check payable to Clerk, US District Court. Search information required: name. Turnaround time: 2-3 days. For closed files, as directed by court clerk, see Atlanta Federal Records Center.

Bankruptcy Records

US Bankruptcy Court
Room 207 Customs House
701 Broadway
Nashville, TN 37203
(615) 736-5590

Records are available by mail or phone. $15.00 search fee. $.50 fee per copy, $5.00 for certified copy, prepaid. Certified check only, payable to Clerk, US Bankruptcy. Search information required: name. Turnaround time: 1 week. For closed files, see Atlanta Federal Records Center.

Western District of Tennessee

BENTON, CARROLL, CHESTER, CROCKETT, DECATUR, DYER, FAYETTE, GIBSON, HARDEMAN, HARDIN, HAYWOOD, HENDERSON, HENRY, LAKE, LAUDERDALE, MCNAIRY, MADISON, OBION, PERRY, SHELBY, TIPTON, WEAKLEY THIS DISTRICT INCLUDES THE WATERS OF THE TENNESSEE RIVER TO LOW-WATER MARK ON THE EASTERN SHORE THEREOF WHEREVER SUCH RIVER FORMS THE BOUNDARY LINE BETWEEN THE WESTERN AND MIDDLE DISTRICTS OF TENNESSEE FROM THE NORTH LINE OF THE STATE OF ALABAMA NORTH TO THE POINT IN HENRY COUNTY, TENNESSEE WHERE THE SOUTH BOUNDARY LINE OF THE STATE OF KENTUCKY STRIKES THE EAST BANK OF THE RIVER.

Civil and Criminal Records

US District Court Clerk
206 Federal Building
109 South Highland Street
Jackson, TN 38301
(901) 427-6586

Records are available by mail or phone. $15.00 search fee. $.50 fee per copy, $5.00 for certified copy; prepaid. Make check payable to Clerk, US District Court. Search information required: name, years to search. Turnaround time: 1-2 days. For closed files, as directed by court clerk, see Atlanta Federal Records Center.

US District Court Clerk's Office
Federal Building Room 978
167 North Main
Memphis, TN 38103
(901) 544-3315

Records are available by mail. $15.00 search fee. $.50 fee per copy, $5.00 for certified copy; prepaid. Make check payable to Clerk, US District Court. Search information required: name. Turnaround time: 1 week. For closed files , as directed by court clerk, see Atlanta Federal Records Center.

Bankruptcy Records

US Bankruptcy Court
200 Jefferson, Suite 500
Memphis, TN 38103
(901) 544-3202
(901) 544-4325 VCIS

Records are available by mail or phone. $15.00 search fee. $.50 fee per copy, $5.00 for certified copy. Certified check or money order, payable to US Bankruptcy Court. Search information required: full name. Turnaround time: 3-4 weeks. For closed files prior to 1991, as directed by court clerk, see Atlanta Federal Records Center. The Voice Case Information System is available to the public 24 hours a day at (901) 544-4325, with basic information on any case filed after July 1, 1992.

Eastern District of Texas

ANDERSON, ANGELINA, BOWIE, CAMP, CASS, CHEROKEE, COLLIN, COOK, DELTA, DENTON, FANNIN, FRANKLIN, GRAYSON, GREGG, HARDIN, HARRISON, HENDERSON, HOPKINS, HOUSTON, JASPER, JEFFERSON, LAMAR, LIBERTY, MARION, MORRIS, NACOGDOCHES, NEWTON, ORANGE, PANOLA, POLK, RAINS, RED RIVER, RUSK, SABINE, SAN AUGUSTINE, SHELBY, SMITH, TITUS, TRINITY, TYLER, UPSHUR, VAN ZANDT.

Civil and Criminal Records

US District Court
Clerk's Office
PO Box 3507
Beaumont, TX 77704
(409) 839-2645

Records are available by mail. $15.00 fee. $.50 fee per copy, $5.00 for certified copy; prepaid. Make check payable to Clerk, US District Court. Search information required: name, case number. Turnaround time: 1 week. For closed files, as directed by court clerk, see Fort Worth Federal Records Center.

Clerk, US District Court
211 West Ferguson
Room 106
Tyler, TX 75702
(214) 592-8195

Records are available by mail. $15.00 search fee. $.50 fee per copy, $5.00 for certified copy. Make check payable to Clerk, US District Clerk. Search information required: name. Turnaround time: 1 week. For closed files, as directed by court clerk, see Fort Worth Federal Records Center.

US District Court
PO Box 1499
Marshall, TX 75671-1499
(214) 935-2912

Records are available by mail. $15.00 search fee. Make check payable to Clerk, US District Court. Search information required: name. Turnaround time: 2 weeks. For closed files, as directed by court clerk, see Fort Worth Federal Records Center.

US District Court
Clerk's Office
PO Box 2667
Texarkana, TX 75504
(214) 794-8561

Records are available by mail. $15.00 search fee. Search information required: name. Turnaround time: 1 week. For closed files, as directed by court clerk, see Fort Worth Federal Records Center.

Bankruptcy Records

US Bankruptcy Court
211 West Ferguson
4th Floor
Tyler, TX 75702
(214) 592-1212

Records are available by mail or phone. $15.00 search fee. Company check payable to Clerk, US Bankruptcy Court. Search information required: name. Turnaround time: 2-3 days. For closed files, as directed by court clerk, see Fort Worth Federal Records Center.

Northern District of Texas

ARCHER, ARMSTRONG, BAILEY, BAYLOR, BORDEN, BRISCO, BROWN, CALLAHAN, CARSON, CASTRO, CHILDRESS, CLAY, COCHRAN, COKE, COLEMAN, COLLINGSWORTH, COMANCHE, CONCHO, COTTLE, CROCKETT, CROSBY, DALLAM, DALLAS, DAWSON, DEAF SMITH, DICKENS, DONLEY, EASTLAND, ELLIS, ERATH, FISHER, FLOYD, FOARD, GAINES, GARZA, GLASCOCK, GRAY, HALE, HALL, HANSFORD, HARDEMAN, HARTLEY, HASKELL, HEMPHILL, HOCKLEY, HOOD, HOWARD, HUNT, HUTCHINSON, IRION, JACK, JOHNSON, JONES, KAUFMAN, KENT, KING, KNOX, LAMB, LIPS-COMB, LUBBOCK, LYNN, MENARD, MILLS, MITCHELL, MONTAGUE, MOORE, MOTLEY, NAVARRO, NOLAN, OCHILTREE, OLDHAM, PALO, PARKER, PARMER, PINTO, POTTER, RANDALL, REAGAN, ROBERTS, ROCKWALL, RUNNELS, SCHLEICHER, SCURRY, SHACKLEFORD, SHERMAN, STEPHENS, STERLING, STONEWALL, SUTTON, SWISHER, TARRANT, TAYLOR, TERRY, THROCKMORTON, TOM GREEN, WHEELER, WICHITA, WILBARGER, WISE, YOAKUM, YOUNG.

Civil and Criminal Records

Clerk, US District Court
205 East Fifth Street, F-13240
Amarillo, TX 79101
(806) 376-2352

Records are available by mail or phone. $15.00 search fee. $.50 fee per copy, $5.00 for certified copy. Make check payable to Clerk, US District Court. Search information required: name. Turnaround time: 2-3 days. For closed files, as directed by court clerk, see Fort Worth Federal Records Center.

US District Court
Clerk Offices
202 US Courthouse
10th & Lamar
Fort Worth, TX 76102
(817) 334-3132

Records are available by mail. $15.00 search fee. $.50 fee per copy, $5.00 for certified copy, $3.00 for microfilm; prepaid. Make check payable to Clerk, US District Court. Search information required: name. Turnaround time: 1 week. For closed files, as directed by court clerk, see Fort Worth Federal Records Center.

US District Court Clerk
PO Box 1234
Wichita Falls, TX 76307
(817) 767-1902

Records are available by mail. $15.00 search fee. $.50 fee per copy, $5.00 for certified copy; prepaid. Make check payable to Clerk, US District Court. Search information required: name. Turnaround time: 1-2 days. For closed files, as directed by court clerk, see Fort Worth Federal Records Center.

US District Court Clerk's Office
Room 14A20
1100 Commerce Street
Dallas, TX 75242
(214) 767-0787

Records are available by mail. $15.00 search fee. $.50 fee per copy, $5.00 for certified copy; prepaid. Make check payable to Clerk, US District Court. Search information required: name. Turnaround time: 2 days. For closed files, as directed by court clerk, see Fort Worth Federal Records Center.

Clerk, US District Court
1205 Texas Avenue
Room C-221
Lubbock, TX 79401
(806) 743-7624

Records are available by mail. $15.00 search fee. $.50 fee per copy, $5.00 for certified copy; prepaid. Make check payable to Clerk, US District Court. Search information required: name. Turnaround time: 1 day. For closed files, as directed by court clerk, see Fort Worth Federal Records Center.

US District Court Clerk
PO Box 1218
Abilene, TX 79604
(915) 677-6311

Records are available by mail. $15.00 search fee. $.50 fee per copy, $5.00 for certified copy. Make check payable to Clerk, US District Court. Search information required: name, years to search. Turnaround time: 1-2 days. For closed files, as directed by court clerk, see Fort Worth Federal Records Center.

US District Court Clerk's Office
33 East Twohig, Room 202
San Angelo, TX 76903
(915) 655-4506

Records are available by mail or phone. $15.00 search fee. $.50 fee per copy, $5.00 for certified copy; prepaid. Make check payable to Clerk, US District Court. Search information required: name. Turnaround time: 1-2 days. For closed files, as directed by court clerk, see Fort Worth Federal Records Center.

Bankruptcy Records

US Bankruptcy Court
1100 Commerce Street
Room 14 A 7
Dallas, TX 75242-1496
(214) 767-0814
Records are available by mail or phone. No search fee. $.50 fee per copy, $5.00 for certified copy; prepaid. To obtain uncertified copies overnight contact (214) 220-0430. Make check payable to US Bankruptcy Court. Search information required: name. Turnaround time: 2-3 days. For closed files, as directed by court clerk, see Fort Worth Federal Records Center.

US Bankruptcy Court
501 West 10th
Room 501
Ft. Worth, TX 76102
(817) 334-3802
Records are available by mail or phone. $15.00 search fee. $.50 fee per copy, $5.00 for certified copy; prepaid. Make check payable to US Bankruptcy Court. Search information required: name. Turnaround time: 1-2 days. For closed files, as directed by court clerk, see Fort Worth Federal Records Center.

US Bankruptcy Court
102 Federal Building
1205 Texas Avenue
Lubbock, TX 79401
(806) 743-7336
Records are available by mail or phone. $15.00 search fee. $.50 fee per copy, $5.00 for certified copy; prepaid. Make check payable to Clerk, US Bankruptcy Court. Search information required: name. Turnaround time: 2-3 days. For closed files, as directed by court clerk, see Fort Worth Federal Records Center.

Southern District of Texas

ARANSAS, AUSTIN, BEE, BRAZORIA, BRAZOS, BROOKS, CALHOUN, CAMERON, CHAMBERS, COLORADO, DEWITT, DUVAL, FAYETTE, FORT BEND, GALESTON, GOLAID, GRIMES, HARRIS, HIDALGO, JACKSON, JIM HOGG, JIM WELLS, KENEDY, KLEBERG, LASALLE, LAVACA, LIVE OAK, MADISON, MATAGORDA, MCMULLEN, MONTGOMERY, NUECES, REFUGIO, SAN JACINTO, SAN PATRICIO, STARR, VICTORIA, WALKER, WALLER, WEBB, WHARTON, WILLACY, ZAPATA.

Civil and Criminal Records

US District Court
Clerk's Office
PO Drawer 2300
Galveston, TX 77553
(409) 766-3530
Fax (409) 766-3562
Records are available by mail. $15.00 search fee. $.50 fee per copy, $5.00 for certified copy. Make check payable to Clerk, US District Court. Search information required: name. Turnaround time: 1-2 days.

US District Clerk Criminal Division
PO Box 2299
Brownsville, TX 78520
(512) 548-2500
Records are available by mail or phone. $15.00 search fee. Make check payable to Clerk, US District Court. Search information required: name, date of birth, years to search. Turnaround time: 2-3 days. For closed files, as directed by court clerk, see Fort Worth Federal Records Center.

US District Courts
PO Box 61010
Houston, TX 77208
(713) 221-9543
Records are available by mail. $15.00 search fee. $.50 fee per copy, $5.00 for certified copy; prepaid. Make check payable to Clerk, US District Court. Search information required: name, years to search. Direct inquiries to: Files Management. Turnaround time: 2-3 days. For closed files, as directed by court clerk, see Fort Worth Federal Records Center.

US District Court
PO Box 597
Laredo, TX 78042-0597
(512) 723-3542
Records are available by mail. $15.00 search fee. $.50 fee per copy, $5.00 for certified copy; prepaid. Make check payable to Clerk, US District Court. Search information required: name. Turnaround time: 1-2 days. For closed files, as directed by court clerk, see Fort Worth Federal Records Center.

US District Court
Clerk's Office
521 Starr Street
Corpus Christi, TX
(512) 888-3142
Records are available by mail. $15.00 search fee. $.50 fee per copy, $5.00 for certified copy; prepaid. Make check payable to Clerk, US District Court. Search information required: name, years to search. Turnaround time: 1 week. For closed files, as directed by court clerk, see Fort Worth Federal Records Center.

Clerk, US District Court
PO Box 1541
Victoria, TX 77902
(512) 575-3512
Records are available by mail. $15.00 search fee. $.50 fee per copy, $5.00 for certified copy; prepaid. Make check payable to Clerk, US District Court. Search information required: name, years to search. Turnaround time: 1-2 days. For closed files, as directed by court clerk, see Fort Worth Federal Records Center.

Bankruptcy Records

US Bankruptcy Court
515 Rusk Avenue, Room 4603
Houston, TX 77002
(713) 250-5114
Records are available by mail. For automated records from 1991 forward contact 800-745-4459. For copies of records contact (713) 223-8141. $15.00 search fee. Company check payable to Clerk, US Bankruptcy Court. Search information required: name. Turnaround time: 5-7 days. For closed files, as directed by court clerk, see Fort Worth Federal Records Center.

Western District of Texas

ANDREWS, ATASCOSA, BANDERA, BASTROP, BELL, BEXAR, BLANCO, BOSQUE, BREWSTER, BURLESON, BURNET, CALDWELL, COMAL, CORYELL, CRANE, CULBERSON, DIMMIT, ECTOR, EDWARDS, EL PASO, FALLS, FREESTONE, FRIO, GILLESPIE, GONZALES, GUADALUPE, HAMILTON, HAYS, HILL, HUDSPETH, JEFF DAVIS, KARNES, KENDALL, KERR, KIMBLE, KINNEY, LAMPASAS, LEE, LEON, LIMESTONE, LLANO, LOVING, MARTIN, MASON, MAVERICK, MCCULLOCH, MCLENNAN, MEDINA, MIDLAND, MILAM, PECOS, PRESIDIO, REAL, REEVES, ROBERTSON, SAN SABA, SOMERVELL, TERRELL, TRAVIS, UPTON, UVALDE, VAL VERDE, WARD, WASHINGTON, WILLIAMSON, WILSON, WINKLER, ZAVALLA.

Civil and Criminal Records

Clerk, US District Court
200 West 8th Street
Austin, TX 78701
(512) 482-5896
Records are available by mail. $15.00 search fee. $.50 fee per copy, $5.00 for certified copy; prepaid. Make check payable to Clerk, US District Court. Search information required: name. Turnaround time: 7-10 days. For closed files, as directed by court clerk, see Fort Worth Federal Records Center.

US Courthouse
US District Clerk's Office - Room 108
511 East San Antonio
El Paso, TX 79901
(915) 534-6725
Records are available by mail. $15.00 search fee. $.50 fee per copy, $5.00 for certified copy. Make check payable to Clerk, US District Court. Search information required: name, specific information to search. Turnaround time: 7-10 days. For closed files, as directed by court clerk, see Fort Worth Federal Records Center.

US Clerk's Office
US Courthouse
655 East Durango
San Antonio, TX 78206
(512) 229-6627
Records are available by mail. $15.00 search fee. $.50 fee per copy, $5.00 for certified copy; prepaid. Make check payable to Clerk, US District Court. Search information required: name. Turnaround time: 1 week. For closed files, as directed by court clerk, see Fort Worth Federal Records Center.

US District Court
Clerk's Office
PO Box 10708
Midland, TX 79702
(915) 683-2001
Records are available by mail. $15.00 search fee. $.50 fee per copy, $5.00 for certified copy; prepaid. Make money order payable to Clerk, US District Court. Search information required: name, SASE. Turnaround time: 1 week. For closed files, as directed by court clerk, see Fort Worth Federal Records Center.

US District Court, Clerk
PO Box 1349
Del Rio, TX 78841
(512) 775-2021
Records are available by mail or phone. $15.00 search fee. $.50 fee per copy, $5.00 for certified copy; prepaid. Make check payable to Clerk, US District Court. Search information required: name. Turnaround time: 1-2 days. For closed files, as directed by court clerk, see Fort Worth Federal Records Center.

Clerk, US District Court
PO Box 608
Waco, TX 76703
(817) 756-0307
Records are available by mail. $15.00 search fee. $.50 fee per copy, $5.00 for certified copy; prepaid. Make check payable to Clerk, US District Court. Search information required: name, case number, specific information to search. Turnaround time: 1-2 days. For closed files, as directed by court clerk, see Fort Worth Federal Records Center.

US District Court
PO Box 191
Pecos, TX 79772
(915) 445-4228
Records are available by mail. $15.00 search fee. Certified check only, payable to Clerk, US District Court. Search information required: name, SSN, date of birth. Turnaround time: 7-10 days. For closed files, as directed by court clerk, see Fort Worth Federal Records Center.

Bankruptcy Records

US Bankruptcy Court
PO Box 1439
San Antonio, TX 78295
(512) 229-6555
Records are available by mail. $15.00 search fee. $.50 fee per copy, $5.00 for certified copy; prepaid. Make check payable to Clerk, US District Court. Search information required: name. Turnaround time: 1 week. For closed files, as directed by court clerk, see Fort Worth Federal Records Center.

District of Utah

THIS DISTRICT COMPRISES THE ENTIRE STATE.

Civil and Criminal Records

US District Court
Clerk's Office, Rm 150
350 South Main Street
Salt Lake City, UT 84101
(801) 524-5161
Records are available by mail. $15.00 search fee. $.50 fee per copy, $5.00 for certified copy; prepaid. Check payable to Clerk, US District Court. Search information required: name. Turnaround time: 7-10 days. For closed files, as directed by court clerk, see Denver Federal Records Center.

Bankruptcy Records

US Bankruptcy Court
350 South Main Street, Room 361
Salt Lake City, UT 84101
(801) 524-5157
Records are available by mail or phone. $15.00 search fee. $.50 fee per copy, $5.00 for certified copy; prepaid. Make check payable to Clerk, US Bankruptcy Court. Search information required: name. Turnaround time: 1 week. For closed files, as directed by court clerk, see Denver Federal Records Center.

District of Vermont

THIS DISTRICT COMPRISES THE ENTIRE STATE.

Civil and Criminal Records

US District Court
Clerk's Office
PO Box 945
Burlington, VT 05402
(802) 951-6301
Records are available by mail. $15.00 search fee. $.50 fee per copy, $5.00 for certified copy; prepaid. Make check payable to Clerk, US District Court. Search information required: name, years to search. Turnaround time: 1 week. For closed files, as directed by court clerk, see Boston Federal Records Center.

Bankruptcy Records

US Bankruptcy Court
PO Box 6648
Rutland, VT 05702
(802) 773-0219
Records are available by mail or phone. $15.00 search fee. $.50 fee per copy, $5.00 for certified copy. Make check payable to Clerk, US Bankruptcy. Search information required: name. Turnaround time: 2-3 weeks. For closed files, as directed by court clerk, see Boston Federal Records Center.

Eastern District of Virginia

ACCOMACK, AMELIA, ARLINGTON, BRUNSWICK, CAROLINE, CHARLES CITY, CHESTERFIELD, CULPEPER, DINWIDDIE, ESSEX, FAIRFAX, FAUQUIER, GLOUCESTER, GOOCHLAND, GREENSVILLE, HANOVER, HENRICO, ISLE OF WIGHT, JAMES CITY, KING AND QUEEN, KING GEORGE, KING WILLIAM, LANCASTER, LOUDOUN, LOUISA, LUNENBERG, MATHEWS, MECKLENBERG, MIDDLESEX, NEW KENT, NORTHAMPTON, NORTHUMBERLAND, NOTTOWAY, ORANGE, POWHATAN, PRINCE EDWARD, PRINCE GEORGE, PRINCE WILLIAM, RICHMOND, SOUTHAMPTON, SPOTSYLVANIA, STAFFORD, SURRY, SUSSEX, WESTMORELAND, YORK (CITIES AND INCORPORATED TOWNS WITHIN THE EXTERIOR BOUNDARIES OF THE ABOVE COUNTIES, OR OUT OF THE TERRITORY OF WHICH THEY HAVE BEEN INCORPORATED, ARE INCLUDED WITHIN DISTRICT).

Civil and Criminal Records

US District Court Clerk
PO Box 21449
Alexandria, VA 22320
(703) 557-5132
Records are available by mail or phone. $15.00 search fee. $.50 fee per copy, $5.00 for certified copy. Make check payable to Clerk, US District Court. Search information required: name, date of birth. Turnaround time: 2-3 days. For closed files, as directed by court clerk, see Philadelphia Federal Records Center.

US District Court Clerk
PO Box 2-AD
Richmond, VA 23205
(804) 771-2612
Records are available by mail or phone. No release necessary. $15.00 search fee. Company check payable to Clerk, US District Court. Search information required: name. Turnaround time: 2-3 days. For closed files, as directed by court clerk, see Philadelphia Federal Records Center.

US District Court
Clerk's Office
PO Box 494
Newport News, VA 23607
(804) 244-0539
Records are available by mail. $15.00 search fee. $.50 fee per copy, $5.00 for certified copy. Make check payable to Clerk, US District Court. Search information required: name. Turnaround time: 2 days. For pre 1983 closed files, see Philadelphia Federal Records Center.

US Courthouse
Room 193
600 Granby Street
Norfolk, VA 23510
(804) 441-3250 or 441-3253
Records are available by mail. $15.00 search fee. $.50 fee per copy, $5.00 for certified copy. Make check payable to Clerk, US District Court. Search information required: name, case number, date filed, trustee, city. Turnaround time: 1 week. For pre 1981 closed files, see Philadelphia Federal Records Center.

Bankruptcy Records

US Bankruptcy Court
206 North Washington Street
Suite 408
Alexandria, VA 22314
(703) 557-1716
Records are available by mail or phone. $15.00 search fee. $.50 fee per copy, $5.00 for certified copy. Make check payable to Clerk, US Bankruptcy Court. Search information required: name. Turnaround time: 1-2 days. For pre 1991 closed files, see Philadelphia Federal Records Center.

US Bankruptcy Court
PO Box 1938
Norfolk, VA 23501-1938
(804) 441-6651
Records are available by mail. $15.00 search fee. $.50 fee per copy, $5.00 for certified copy. Make check payable to Clerk US Bankruptcy Court. Search information required: name. Turnaround time: 2-3 days. Contact the above office for copying procedures. For pre 1986 closed files, see Philadelphia Federal Records Center.

US Bankruptcy Court
PO Box 676
Richmond, VA 23206
(804) 771-2878
Records are available by mail or phone.
$15.00 search fee. $.50 fee per copy, $5.00
for certified copy. Make check payable to
Clerk, US Bankruptcy Court. Search
information required: name. Turnaround
time: 2 weeks. For pre July,1991 closed
files, see Philadelphia Federal Records
Center.

US Bankruptcy Court
PO Box 497
Newport News, VA 23607
(804) 247-0196
Records are available by mail or phone.
$15.00 search fee. $.50 fee per copy, $5.00
for certified copy. Make check payable to
Clerk, US Bankruptcy Court. Search
information required: name. Turnaround
time: 1-2 days. For pre 1986 closed files,
see Philadelphia Federal Records Center.

Western District of Virginia

ALBEMARLE, ALLEGHENY, AMHERST,
APPOMATTOX, AUGUSTA, BATH,
BEDFORD, BLAND, BOTECOURT,
BUCHANAN, BUCKINGHAM, CAMPBELL,
CARROLL, CHARLOTTE, CLARKE, CRAIG,
CUMBERLAND, DICKENSON, FLOYD,
FLUVANNA, FRANKLIN, FREDERICK,
GILES, GRAYSON, GREENE, HALIFAX,
HENRY, HIGHLAND, LEE, MADISON,
MONTGOMERY, NELSON, PAGE, PATRICK,
PITTSYLVANIA, PULASKI,
RAPPAHANNOCK, ROANOKE,
ROCKBRIDGE, ROCKINGHAM, RUSSELL,
SCOTT, SHENANDOAH, SMYTH,
TAZEWELL, WARREN, WASHINGTON,
WISE, WYTHE (CITIES AND
INCORPORATED TOWNS WITHIN THE
EXTERIOR BOUNDARIES OF THE ABOVE
NAMED COUNTIES, OR OUT OF THE
TERRITORY OF WHICH THEY HAVE BEEN
INCORPORATED, ARE INCLUDED WITHIN
THE DISTRICT).

Civil and Criminal Records

US District Court Clerk
PO Box 1207
Harrisonburg, VA 22801
(703) 434-3181
Records are available by mail. $15.00
search fee. $.50 fee per copy, $5.00 for
certified copy. Search information required:
name. Turnaround time: 1-2 days. For pre
1981 closed files, see Philadelphia Federal
Records Center.

US District Court
Clerk's Office
PO Box 398
Abingdon, VA 24210
(703) 628-5116
Fax (703) 628-1028
Records are available by mail or phone. No
search fee. $.50 fee per copy, $5.00 for
certified copy. Search information required:
name. Turnaround time: 2-3 days. For pre
1985 closed files, see Philadelphia Federal
Records Center.

Clerk, US District Court
Room 304
255 West Main Street
Charlottesville, VA 22901
(804) 296-9284
Records are available by mail. $15.00
search fee. $.50 fee per copy, $5.00 for
certification. Make check payable to Clerk,
US District Court. Search information
required: name. Turnaround time: 2-3 days.
For closed files prior to 1987, as directed
by court clerk, see Philadelphia Federal
Records Center.

US District Court Clerk
PO Box 1234
Roanoke, VA 24006
(703) 982-6224
Records are available by mail. $15.00
search fee. $.50 fee per copy, $5.00 for
certified copy. Make check payable to
Clerk, US District Court. Search
information required: name. Turnaround
time: 1 week. For pre 1983 closed files, see
Philadelphia Federal Records Center.

Bankruptcy Records

US Bankruptcy Court
PO Box 2390
Roanoke, VA 24010
(703) 982-6391
Records are available by mail. $15.00
search fee. $.50 fee per copy, $5.00 for
certified copy. Make check payable to US
Bankruptcy Court. Search information
required: name, SSN. Turnaround time: 1
week. For closed files, as directed by court
clerk, see Philadelphia Federal Records
Center.

Eastern District of Washington

ADAMS, ASOTIN, BENTON, CHELAN,
COLUMBIA, DOUGLAS, FERRY, FRANKLIN,
GARFIELD, GRANT, KITTITAS, KLICKITAT,
LINCOLN, OKANOGAN, PEND OREILLE,
SPOKANE, STEVENS, WALLA WALLA,
WHITMAN, YAKIMA.

Civil and Criminal Records

Clerk, US District Court
Eastern District of Washington
PO Box 1493
Spokane, WA 99210-1493
(509) 353-2150
Records are available by mail or phone.
$15.00 search fee. $.50 fee per copy, $5.00
for certified copy. Make check payable to
Clerk, US District Court. Search
information required: name. Turnaround
time: 1 week. For pre 1989 closed files, see
Seattle Federal Records Center.

Bankruptcy Records

US Bankruptcy Court
PO Box 2164
West 904 Riverside
Spokane, WA 99201
(509) 353-2404
Records are available by mail or phone.
$15.00 search fee. $.50 fee per copy, $5.00
for certified copy. Make check payable to
Clerk, US Bankruptcy Court. Search
information required: name, case number,
date filed. Turnaround time: 3 days. For pre
1987 closed files, see Seattle Federal
Records Center.

Western District of Washington

CLALLAM, CLARK, COWLITZ, GRAYS
HARBOR, ISLAND, JEFFERSON, KING,
KITSAP, LEWIS, MASON, PACIFIC, PIERCE,
SAN JUAN, SKAGIT, SKAMANIA,
SNOHOMISH, THURSTON, WHAKIAKUM,
WHATCOM.

Civil and Criminal Records

Clerk US District Court
1010 5th Avenue
215 US Courthouse
Seattle, WA 98104
(206) 442-5598
Records are available by mail. $15.00
search fee. $.50 fee per copy, $5.00 for
certified copy. Make check payable to
Clerk, US District Court. Search
information required: name, case number.
Turnaround time: 1 week after receipt of
payment. For pre 1989 closed files, see
Seattle Federal Records Center.

Bankruptcy Records

US Bankruptcy Court Clerk
315 Park Place Bldg.
1200 6th Avenue
Seattle, WA 98101
(206) 553-7545
Records are available by mail or phone.
$15.00 search fee. $.50 fee per copy, $5.00
for certified copy; prepaid. Make check
payable to Clerk, US Bankruptcy Court.
Search information required: name.
Turnaround time: 2-3 days. For closed files,
as directed by court clerk, see Seattle
Federal Records Center.

Northern District of West Virginia

BARBOUR, BERKELEY, BRAXTON,
BROOKE, CALHOUN, DODDRIDGE,
GILMER, GRANT, HAMPSHIRE, HANCOCK,
HARDY, HARRISON, JEFFERSON, LEWIS,
MARION, MARSHALL, MINERAL,
MONONGALIA, MORGAN, OHIO,
PENDLETON, PLEASANTS, POCAHONTAS,
PRESTON, RANDOLPH, RITCHIE, TAYLOR,
TUCKER, TYLER, UPSHUR, WEBSTER,
WETZEL.

Civil and Criminal Records

US District Court
PO Box 1518
Elkins, WV 26241
(304) 636-1445
Fax (304) 636-5746
Records are available by mail. $15.00
search fee. $.50 fee per copy, $5.00 for
certified copy. Make check payable to
Clerk, US District Court. Search
information required: name. Turnaround
time: 1-2 days. Central office for Northern
District of West Virginia. For pre 1968
closed files, see Philadelphia Federal
Records Center.

Bankruptcy Records

US Bankruptcy Court
PO Box 70
Wheeling, WV 26003
(304) 233-1655
Records are available by mail. $15.00 search fee. $.50 fee per copy, $5.00 for certified copy. Company checks accepted, payable to Clerk, US Bankruptcy Court. Search information required: name, specific information to search. Turnaround time: 1 week. For pre 1987 closed files, see Philadelphia Federal Records Center.

Southern District of West Virginia

BOONE, CABELL, CLAY, FAYETTE, GREENBRIER, JACKSON, KANAWHA, LINCOLN, LOGAN, MASON, MCDOWELL, MERCER, MINGO, MONROE, NICHOLAS, PUTNAM, RALEIGH, ROANE, SUMMERS, WAYNE, WEBSTER, WIRT, WOOD, WYOMING.

Civil and Criminal Records

US District Court
Clerk's Office
PO Box 4128
Bluefield, WV 24701
(304) 327-9798
Records are available by mail or phone. $15.00 search fee. $.50 fee per copy, $5.00 for certified copy. Search information required: name, years to search. Turnaround time: 1-2 days. For pre 1985 closed files, see Philadelphia Federal Records Center.

US District Court
PO Box 1526
Parkersburg, WV 26102
(304) 420-6490
Fax (304) 420-6363
Records are available by mail or phone. $15.00 search fee. $.50 fee per copy, $5.00 for certified copy. Search information required: name. Turnaround time: 1-2 days. For pre 1985 closed files, see Philadelphia Federal Records Center.

US District Court
Clerk's Office
PO Box 1570
Huntington, WV 25716
(304) 529-5588
Fax (304) 529-5131
Records are available by mail or phone. No search fee. $.50 fee per copy, $5.00 for certified copy. Search information required: name, years to search. Turnaround time: 2-3 days. For pre 1985 closed files, see Philadelphia Federal Records Center.

Clerk, US District Court
PO Box 2546
Charleston, WV 25329
(304) 342-5154
Records are available by mail or phone. $15.00 search fee. $.50 fee per copy, $5.00 for certified copy. Make check payable to Clerk, US District Court. Search information required: name, years to search. Turnaround time: 4 days. For pre 1988 closed files, see Philadelphia Federal Records Center.

US District Court
PO Drawer 5009
Beckley, WV 25801
(304) 253-7481
Records are available by mail. No release necessary. $15.00 search fee. $.50 fee per copy. $5.00 for certification. Make check payable to Clerk, US Bankruptcy Court. Search information required: name. Turnaround time: 1-2 days. For closed files prior to 1988, as directed by court clerk, see Philadelphia Federal Records Center.

Bankruptcy Records

US Bankruptcy Court
PO Box 3924
Charleston, WV 25301
(304) 347-5114
Records are available by mail or phone. $15.00 search fee. Make check payable to Clerk, US Bankruptcy Court. Search information required: name. Turnaround time: 7-10 days. For closed files, as directed by court clerk, see Philadelphia Federal Records Center.

Eastern District of Wisconsin

BROWN, CALUMET, DODGE, DOOR, FLORENCE, FOND DU LAC, FOREST, GREEN LAKE, KENOSHA, KEWAUNEE, LANGLADE, MANITOWOC, MARINETTE, MARQUETTE, MENOMINEE, MILWAUKEE, OCONTO, OUTAGAMIE, OZAUKEE, RACINE, SHAWANO, SHEBOYGAN, WALWORTH, WASHINGTON, WAUKESHA, WAUPACA, WAUSHARA, WINNEBAGO.

Civil and Criminal Records

US District Court
Clerk's Office
517 East Wisconsin Avenue
Room 362
Milwaukee, WI 53202
(414) 297-3372
Records are available by mail. $15.00 search fee for one name searched. $.50 fee per copy, $5.00 for certified copy. Make check payable to Clerk, US District Court. Search information required: name or case number. Turnaround time: 2-3 days. For pre 1986 closed files, see Chicago Federal Records Center.

Bankruptcy Records

US Bankruptcy Court
517 East Wisconsin Avenue
Room 216
Milwaukee, WI 53202
(414) 297-4070
Records are available by mail or phone. $15.00 search fee. $.50 fee per copy. $5.00 for certification. Company check payable to Clerk, US Bankruptcy Court. Search information required: name. Turnaround time: 2 weeks. For closed files, as directed by court clerk, see Chicago Federal Records Center.

Western District of Wisconsin

ADAMS, ASHLAND, BARRON, BAYFIELD, BUFFALO, BURNETT, CHIPPEWA, CLARK, COLUMBIA, CRAWFORD, DANE, DOUGLAS, DUNN, EAU CLAIRE, GRANT, GREEN, IOWA, IRON, JACKSON, JEFFERSON, JUNEAU, LACROSSE, LAFAYETTE, LINCOLN, MARATHON, MONROE, ONEIDA, PEPIN, PIERCE, POLK, PORTAGE, PRICE, RICHLAND, ROCK, RUSK, SAINT CROIX, SAUK, SAWYER, TAYLOR, TREMPEALEAU, VERNON, VILAS, WASHBURN, WOOD.

Civil and Criminal Records

US District Court
Clerk's Office
120 N. Henry, Rm 320
Madison, WI 53701
(608) 264-5156
Fax (608) 264-5925
Records are available by mail. $15.00 search fee. $.50 fee per copy, $5.00 for certified copy. Make check payable to Clerk, US District Court. Search information required: name. Turnaround time: 1-2 days. For pre 1986 closed files, see Chicago Federal Records Center.

Bankruptcy Records

US Bankruptcy Court
PO Box 548
Madison, WI 53701
(608) 264-5178
Records are available by mail or phone. $15.00 search fee. $.50 fee per copy, $5.00 for certified copy. Make check payable to Clerk, US Bankruptcy. Search information required: name. Turnaround time: 2-3 days. For pre 1968 closed files, see Chicago Federal Records Center. Files closed prior to 1990 are located in the archives. A $25.00 retrieval fee is required.

District of Wyoming

THIS DISTRICT COMPRISES THE STATE OF WYOMING AND THOSE PORTIONS OF YELLOWSTONE NATIONAL PARK SITUATED IN THE STATES OF MONTANA AND IDAHO.

Civil and Criminal Records

Clerk, US District Court
PO Box 727
Cheyenne, WY 82003
(307) 772-2145
Records are available by mail. $15.00 search fee. Make check payable to Clerk, US District Court. Search information required: name. Turnaround time: 48 hours after receipt of payment. For closed files, as directed by court clerk, see Denver Federal Records Center.

Bankruptcy Records

US Bankruptcy Court
PO Box 1107
Cheyenne, WY 82003
(307) 772-2191
Records are available by mail. $15.00 search fee. Make check payable to Clerk, US Bankruptcy Court. Search information required: name. Turnaround time: 1-2 days. For closed files, as directed by court clerk, see Denver Federal Records Center.

Federal Records Centers

Atlanta

SERVES ALABAMA, GEORGIA, FLORIDA, KENTUCKY, MISSISSIPPI, NORTH CAROLINA, SOUTH CAROLINA, AND TENNESSEE.

1557 St. Joseph Avenue
East Point, GA 30344
(404) 763-7477
Records are available by mail. No search fee. $.25 fee per copy with a $6.00 minimum fee. $5.00 for certification. For each inquiry, obtain from U.S. District Court the following items: name, date filed, case number, accession number, agency box number, FRC location number.

Boston

SERVES CONNECTICUT, MAINE, MASSACHUSETTS, NEW HAMPSHIRE, RHODE ISLAND, AND VERMONT.

380 Trapelo Road
Waltham, MA 02154
(617) 647-8104
Records are available by mail. No search fee. $.50 fee per copy. $5.00 for certification. For each inquiry, obtain from U.S. District Court the following items: name, date filed, case number, accession number, agency box number, FRC location number.

Chicago

SERVES ILLINOIS, INDIANA, MICHIGAN, MINNESOTA, OHIO, AND WISCONSIN.

7358 South Pulaski Road
Chicago, IL 60629
(312) 353-0162
Records are available in person by appointment.

Denver

SERVES COLORADO, MONTANA, NEW MEXICO, NORTH DAKOTA, SOUTH DAKOTA, UTAH, AND WYOMING.

Building 48, Denver Federal Center
Denver, CO 80225
(303) 236-0804
Records are available by mail. No search fee. $.50 fee per copy. $5.00 for certification. For each inquiry, obtain from U.S. District Court the following items: name, date filed, case number, accession number, agency box number, FRC location number.

Fort Worth

SERVES ARKANSAS, LOUISIANA, OKLAHOMA, AND TEXAS.

PO Box 6216
501 W. Felix Street
Fort Worth, TX 76115
(817) 334-5525
Records are available by mail. No search fee. $1.00 fee per copy. $2.00 for certification. For each inquiry, obtain from U.S. District Court the following items: name, date filed, case number, accession number, agency box number, FRC location number.

Kansas City

SERVES IOWA, KANSAS, MISSOURI, AND NEBRASKA.

2312 East Bannister Road
Kansas City, MO 64131
(816) 926-7272
Records are available by mail. No search fee. $.50 fee per copy with a $5.00 minimum fee. $5.00 for certification. For each inquiry, obtain from U.S. District Court the following items: name, date filed, case number, accession number, agency box number, FRC location number.

Los Angeles

SERVES ARIZONA, THE SOUTHERN CALIFORNIA COUNTIES OF IMPERIAL, INYO, KERN, LOS ANGELES, ORANGE, RIVERSIDE, SAN BERNARDINO, SAN DIEGO, SAN LUIS OBISPO, SANTA BARBARA, AND VENTURA; AND CLARK COUNTY, NEVADA.

24000 Avila Road
Laguna Niguel, CA 92607-6719
(714) 643-4220
Records are available by mail. No search fee. Copying fees vary. For each inquiry, obtain from U.S. District Court the following items: name, date filed, case number, accession number, agency box number, FRC location number.

New York

SERVES NEW JERSEY, NEW YORK, PUERTO RICO, AND THE VIRGIN ISLANDS.

Building 22-M O T Bayonne
Bayonne, NJ 07002
(201) 823-7545 or 823-7242
Records are available by mail. No search fee. $.50 fee per copy. $5.00 for certification. For each inquiry, obtain from U.S. District Court the following items: name, date filed, case number, accession number, agency box number, FRC location number. For records prior to 1967 contact New York Northeast Region, 201 Varick Street, New York, NY 10014.

Philadelphia

SERVES DELAWARE, PENNSYLVANIA, MARYLAND, VIRGINIA, AND WEST VIRGINIA.

5000 Wissahickon Avenue
Philadelphia, PA 19144
(215) 951-5588
Records are available by mail. No search fee. $.50 fee per copy. $5.00 for certification. For each inquiry, obtain from U.S. District Court the following items: name, date filed, case number, accession number, agency box number, FRC location number.

San Francisco

SERVES CALIFORNIA EXCEPT SOUTHERN CALIFORNIA, HAWAII, NEVADA EXCEPT CLARK COUNTY, AND THE PACIFIC OCEAN AREA.

1000 Commodore Drive
San Bruno, CA 94066
(415) 876-9001
Records are available by mail. No search fee. $.50 fee per copy. $5.00 for certification. For each inquiry, obtain from U.S. District Court the following items: name, date filed, case number, accession number, agency box number, FRC location number.

Seattle

SERVICES ALASKA, IDAHO, OREGON , AND WASHINGTON.

6125 Sand Point Way NE
Seattle, WA 98115
(206) 553-4501
Records are available by mail. No search fee. $.50 fee per copy. $5.00 for certification. For each inquiry, obtain from U.S. District Court the following items: name, date filed, case number, accession number, agency box number, FRC location number.

FEDERAL AVIATION ADMINISTRATION

Federal Aviation Administration Records

Airmen Certification

US Department of Transportation
Federal Aviation Administration
Mike Monroney Aeronautical Center
PO Box 25082
AAC – 260
Oklahoma City, OK 73125
(405) 680-3261 press 3
Will confirm license, rating, type and medical record by phone. No fee. Search information required: name, date of birth or SSN if available.

Aircraft Records

US Department of Transportation
Federal Aviation Administration
Mike Monroney Aeronautical Center
PO Box 25082
AAC – 250
Oklahoma City, OK 73125
(405) 680-3261 press 1
Will confirm ownership, address, date of registration and description by phone. Records are computerized by the N number (tail number). If N number is not known, a record search may be done by using the owner's name.

CANADA DRIVING RECORDS

Canada Driving Records

Alberta

Motor Vehicles Divsion
Driving Abstracts
15220 114th Avenue
Edmondton, Alberta T5M2Z2
(403) 427-7013
Driving records are available by mail.
$6.00 search fee per request. A written
release is required. Search information
required: full name, date of birth, and
license number.

British Columbia

Motor Vehicle Department
Driver License Division
2631 Douglas Street
Victoria, BC V8T5A3
(604) 387-6824
Driving records are available by mail.
$5.00 search fee per request. A written
release is necessary. Search information
required: name, date of birth, and license
number.

Manitoba

Division of Driver & Vehicle
Licensing
Suspension & Records
1075 Portage Avenue
Winnipeg, Manitoba R3G0S1
(204) 945-6943
Driving records are available by mail.
$4.00 search fee per request. A written
release is necessary. Search information
required: name, date of birth, license
number. Send inquiries to the attention of
Driver Records.

New Brunswick

Motor Vehicle Registration
Driver Records
PO Box 6000
Fredericton, New Brunswick E3B5H1
(506) 453-2410
Driving records are available by mail.
$7.00 search fee per request. Make check
payable to Minister of Finance. Search
information required: full name, date of
birth, license number.

Newfoundland

Motor Vehicle Registration
Driver Records
PO Box 8710
St. Johns, Newfoundland A1B4J5
(709) 729-2518 or (709) 729-2519
Driving records are available by mail.
$5.00 search fee. Search information
required: full name, date of birth, license
number, address, if available.

Nova Scotia

Department of Vehicle Registration
PO Box 1652
Halifax, Nova Scotia B3J2Z3
(902) 424-5851
Driving records are available by mail.
$10.00 search fee. A written release is
necessary. Search information required: full
name, date of birth.

Ontario

Department of Motor Vehicles
2680 Keele
Downsdiew, Ontario M3M1J8
(613) 731-3731
Contact the above office for a motor
vehicle records application form. $5.00
search fee. Search information required:
full name, date of birth.

Prince Edward Island

Department of Highway Safety
Records Division
PO Box 2000
Charlottetown, PEI C1A7N8
(902) 368-5210
Driving records are available by mail. $7.00
search fee. A release is necessary. Search
information required: full name, date of
birth or license number.

Northwest Territories

Motor Vehicles Division
Department of Transportation
Government of the Northwest
Territories
PO Box 1320
Yellowknife, NT
Canada X1A2L9
(403) 873-7406
Driving records are available by mail. $7.00
search fee. A written release is necessary.
Search information: full name, date of birth,
license number.

Quebec

Driving Records Division
Information & Refund Services
SAAQ
333 Jean Lesage
PO Box 19600, 6th Floor
Quebec, Quebec G1K8J6
(418) 643-7620
Driving records are available by mail. $8.00
search fee. A written release is necessary.
Make checks payable to Regie Insurance
Automobile. Search information required:
name, license number, issue date, reason for
requesting information.

Saskatchewan

Driver History
Saskatchewan Government Insurance
2260 11th Avenue
Regina, Saskatchewan S4P2N7
(306) 566-6198
Driving records are available by mail.
$10.00 search fee. A written release is
necessary. Search information required: full
name, date of birth.

Yukon Territory

Registrar of Motor Vehicles
Box 2703
Whitehorse, Yukon Y1A2C6
(403) 667-5315
Driving records are available by mail. $6.00
search fee. A written release is necessary.
Search information required: full name,
date of birth and license number.

THE EDUCATIONAL RECORDS DIRECTORY

INTRODUCTION

Educational credentials say much about an individual's motivation, initiative, qualifications, leadership abilities, or lack thereof. While certainly not the only measure of a person's capabilities, past academic achievements do indicate a great deal about what an individual could accomplish in the future.

As a result, education is among the first inquiries on most employment applications. However, the same companies which ask about job applicants' schooling seldom take the follow-up step of verifying the information they are given.

This is unfortunate because the sad fact is that inadvertent and intentional misstatements of academic background present a real and serious danger for American business. False, exaggerated and misleading educational claims saddle employers with workers of both the wrong qualifications and the wrong character.

Why don't employers as a matter of standard practice verify the educational background of their job applicants? Certainly inertia plays a big part. It's easier to stay with the status quo, unless and until some unscrupulous candidate slips through, causes a problem and forces the issue.

But another hurdle has loomed even larger. With our increasingly mobile society, companies are seeing more applicants from locations and institutions with which they are unfamiliar. Thorough educational verification practices would require the employer to be ready to check credentials from literally thousands of possible institutions. The enormous data management requirements this would entail are simply more than most companies have been willing to meet.

THE PROBLEMS SOLVED.

The *Educational Records Directory* removes most of the stumbling blocks that have prevented verification from being a standard part of companies' screening procedures.

Included are over 3000 post-secondary institutions and programs from across the United States. Each of these schools was contacted directly prior to publication of the *Fifth Edition* to determine the specific procedures it follows in verifying degrees and attendance for employment purposes. The results of those contacts are included here.

Are schools willing to cooperate with employers in confirming degrees and/or attendance? Overwhelmingly so. Schools have a vested interest in seeing that their current and former students are employed. Potential employers who contact a school's registrar are generally seen as friends, not enemies.

A few statistics confirm this general rule. Over 97% of the schools reported that they will verify for employers a job applicant's degree and/or attendance. And some 84% will even confirm this information over the phone when supplied with the appropriate identifiers. For those rare cases when an exact academic record is required, about 60% also reported that employers can directly obtain a student's actual transcript when they follow the school's guidelines.

INS AND OUTS.

The *Educational Records Directory* has evolved from a list first supplied to NESS by the Department of Education (DOE). To be chosen for inclusion in the Department's original list, a school had to meet three criteria.

First, it had to offer the equivalent of at least a one year college level program creditable toward a degree. Second, it had to be accredited by a nationally recognized agency or fit DOE's other special accreditation requirements. Third, the institution had to have submitted all required informational reports to DOE.

The DOE list included only basic information on the institution—its name, address and basic program descriptions. NESS has taken the data much further, developing verification procedures through numerous phone conversations and correspondence with the responsible parties at each institution.

While appropriate additions and deletions of schools and programs have occurred with each edition of the GUIDE, the current list is certainly not to be taken as 100% inclusive of all existing or accredited institutions in the country. An omission from the *Educational Records Directory* may be due to something as serious as an accreditation problem or as inconsequential as a failure to return to DOE a requested report in a timely manner.

UNDERSTANDING THE SCHOOL AND PROGRAM LISTINGS.

Entries in the *Educational Records Directory* are in alphabetical order. Each listing follows a consistent pattern for both format and content. To familiarize yourself with what you will encounter as you use the *Directory,* consider the following example:

Angelo State University

2601 West Avenue N
San Angelo, TX 76909
(915) 942-2043

Will confirm attendance and degree by phone or mail. Inquiry must include student's name, social security number. Employers may obtain transcripts upon written request accompanied by a $3.00 fee and a signed release from the student. Requests should be directed to: Registrar's Office.

A comprehensive institution with no medical school, with an enrollment of 6,128. Highest level of offering: master's.

ACCREDITATIONS: SC NLN/AD MUS

The components of this typical entry may be broken down as follows:

1. *Locating Information.*

Immediately beneath the school's name will be the address and phone number of the office that handles record requests. Wherever possible, the phone number listed is a direct line or an extension number to the actual office that handles employer informational requests. If the school operates on a switchboard system, the listing will give the main institutional number from which an operator will connect you to the appropriate office. Many schools have also supplied their FAX phone numbers by which users can quickly make a written verification request.

2. *Confirmation Policy.*

The next two to three lines contain the school's basic policy on confirming a student's degree and/or attendance. You can quickly see whether and how the institution allows employers to verify these facts on a job applicant.

For the vast majority that do release this information for employment purposes, the summary will include the manner in which inquiries must be made (mail, phone or FAX) and what identifiers the office requires to find a student's record. In the case of Angelo State, for example, the Registrar's Office will provide either mail or phone verifications when a student's name and social security number are furnished.

3. *Transcript Policy.*

Occasionally, an employer will want more detail on an applicant's academic performance than a simple verification of the basics of attendance or degree. The demands of the job may require a background in specific courses. Only a full transcript from the school would show the extent of the applicant's qualification for the position.

Many schools will furnish employers with a student's transcript under certain conditions. Where this is possible, the *Directory* gives a general summary of what procedures the employer should follow.

Users will quickly see that the requirements for transcript release are normally much stricter than those for degree and attendance verification. The entry may note, for example, that only students can request transcripts. Even when the school allows the employer to make the request directly, a written release from the student is almost always required. Contact the school directly for further details on requests for this type of more complete record.

4. Descriptive Information.

This last section contains essential information about the school and its program. Two basic components will be included:

a. General description. The National Center for Education Statistics (NCES) several years ago adopted a system for identifying and organizing institutions according to the number and type of degrees they award. There are five basic types of classifications:

i. Doctoral-level institutions. Schools with a significant number of doctoral offerings and degrees.

ii. Comprehensive institutions. Offer diverse undergraduate and postgraduate programs, but few degrees at the doctoral level.

iii. General baccalaureate institutions. Primary offerings and emphasis are on undergraduate programs and degrees.

iv. Specialized institutions. May offer either bachelor's or graduate level studies, but offerings are concentrated in one area of study (engineering, business, law, performing arts, etc.)

v. Institutions newly admitted. A temporary designation for institutions that are either newly created or at least new participants in the NCES educational survey.

The general description will also include an approximate count on the school's enrollment. This fact will help give a broad picture of the educational context from which an applicant has come.

b. Highest level of offering. While not necessarily describing the "typical" course of study at the institution, this category does show the highest degree, program or award offered by the school. This will allow you to determine whether a claimed degree from a given institution is even possible.

An applicant may claim a master's degree, for example, from an institution that only offers undergraduate degrees. A discrepancy between a claimed credential and what is reported in this category will at least suggest the need for a deeper inquiry.

There are ten possible categories into which a school may fall. In order of decreasing complexity, they are:

i. Postdoctoral research only

ii. Doctorate

iii. Beyond master's but less than doctorate

iv. Master's

v. First professional degree (offers the first, basic degree in at least one profession – J.D., M.D., D.D.S., etc.)

vi. Graduate non-degree granting

vii. Four or five year baccalaureate

viii. Undergraduate non-degree granting (offers at least four years of undergraduate studies but does not award bachelor's degrees)

ix. One but less than four years (includes junior colleges and others offering less than full bachelor's program)

x. Less than 1 year (offers less than one year of accredited, college level courses)

Note that an institution may be listed as awarding a "first professional degree" and yet be called a "general baccalaureate institution." This would simply indicate that its primary emphasis is on undergraduate studies while at least one professional degree is among its offerings.

5. Accreditations.

All of the institutions appearing in this listing have been accredited by some nationally recognized organization. The final item of general information included in each school's listing is a summary of those bodies that have passed on and approved some segment of the school's program.

For most institutions with liberal arts programs, one of the six regional associations of colleges and schools takes primary accrediting responsibility for the entire school. (On occasion, a 4 year college will be accredited by one of these regional associations as a junior college. An accreditation of this type will be indicated in the *Directory* by the initials of the association, preceded by the letter "J".)

Other specialized accrediting bodies may review specific programs within a larger institution. These specialized bodies also take primary responsibility for independent professional and vocational schools not affiliated with a larger university system.

Users are cautioned that some accreditations shown here may be limited.

Full accreditation is often not the first award given to an institution or program. A "preaccreditation" or "candidate for accreditation" status is often the first step. Some schools listed in the *Directory* as accredited may actually have a preaccreditation status.

This designation generally means that the school or program is progressing toward full accreditation. A preaccreditation award is not a guarantee that full accreditation will be achieved. Any number of problems could derail the process. Nevertheless, schools in this posture can be presumed to be on track for gaining full accreditation if no further complications arise.

The following list of abbreviations details the various accreditations awarded by both the regional and specialized accrediting agencies. Included in parenthesis after the accreditation abbreviations are abbreviations that have been adopted by the Department of Education. In subsequent editions of the GUIDE only the standard abbreviations will be used; however, during this transitional phase both are listed.

3IC *Three-Institutional Certification procedure*

ADNUR (NLN/AD) *National League for Nursing, Inc. (associate degree programs in nursing)*

ADVET (AVMA/CVTAT) *American Veterinary Medical Association (associate degree program in animal technology)*

AHE (ABHES/HE) *Accrediting Bureau of Health Education Schools (applied health education)*

ANEST (AANA) *American Association of Nurse Anesthetists (nurse anesthesia)*

APCP (AMA/APCP) *American Medical Association (assistant to the primary care physician)*

ARCH (NAAB) *National Architectural Accrediting Board, Inc. (architecture)*

ART (NASAD) *National Association of Schools of Art and Design (art)*

AUD (ASLH/A) *American Speech, Language, and Hearing Association (audiology)*

BBT (AABB) *American Medical Association (blood bank technology)*

BI (AABC) *American Association of Bible Colleges (Bible college education)*

BUS (AACSB) *American Assembly of Collegiate Schools of Business (business)*

CHE (CEPH/HE) *Council on Education for Public Health (community health education)*

CHIRO (CCE) *Council on Chiropractic Education (chiropractic)*

CHM (ACS) *American Chemical Society*

CHPM (CEPH/PM) *Council on Education for Public Health (community health, preventive medicine)*

CLA (AMA/LT) *American Medical Association (certified laboratory technician education)*

CLPSY (APA) *American Psychological Association (clinical psychology)*

COPSY (APA/C) *American Psychological Association (counseling psychology)*

CYTO (AMA/CY) *American Medical Association (cytotechnology)*

DANCE (NASD) *National Association of Schools of Dance (dance)*

DA (ADA/DA) *American Dental Association (dental assisting)*

DENT (ADA/D) *American Dental Association (dentistry)*

DH (ADA/DH) *American Dental Association (dental hygiene)*

DIETI (ADI) *American Dietetic Association (postbaccalaureate dietetics internship programs)*

DIET (AD) *American Dietetic Association (undergraduate dietetics programs)*

DMS (AMA/DMS) *American Medical Association (diagnostic medical sonographer)*

DNUR (NLN/N) *National League for Nursing, Inc. (nursing)*

DT (ADA/DT) *American Dental Association (dental technology)*

EEG (AMA/ET) *American Medical Association (electroencephalographic technologist)*

EH (NEASC) *New England Association of Schools and Colleges, Commission on Institutions of Higher Education*

EMT (AMA/EMT)*American Medical Association (emergency medical technician–paramedic)*

ENGT (ABET/T) *Accreditation Board for Engineering and Technology, Inc. (engineering technology)*

ENG (ABET) *Accreditation Board for Engineering and Technology, Inc. (engineering)*

EV (NEASC/V) *New England Association of Schools and Colleges, Commission on Vocational, Technical, Career Institutions*

E (NEASC) *New England Association of Schools and Colleges, Commission on Institutions of Higher Education*

FIDER *Foundation for Interior Design Education Research (interior design)*

FOR (SAF) *Society for American Foresters (forestry)*

FUSER (ABFSE) *American Board of Funeral Service Education (funeral service education)*

HA (ACESHA/HA) *Accrediting Commission on Education for Health Services Administration (hospital administration)*

HSA (ACESHA) *Accrediting Commission on Education for Health Services Administration (health services administration)*

HT (AMA/HT) *American Medical Association (histologic technician)*

ID (FIDER) *Foundation for Interior Design Education Research (interior design)*

IPSY (APA/IPSY) *American Psychological Association (predoctoral internships in professional psychology)*

JOUR (ACEJMC) *Accrediting Council on Education in Journalism and Mass Communication (journalism)*

JRCB (AICS/JR) *Association of Independent Colleges and Schools (junior colleges of business)*

LAW (ABA) *American Bar Association (law)*

LDAR (ASLA) *American Society of Landscape Architects (landscape architecture)*

LIB (ALA)*American Library Association (librarianship)*

LSAR (ASLA)*American Society of Landscape Architects (landscape architecture)*

MAAB (ABHES/MA) *Accrediting Bureau of Health Education Schools (Medical Assistant)*

MAC (AMA/MA)*American Medical Association (Medical Assistant)*

MAE (ABHES) *Accrediting Bureau of Health Education Schools (medical assistant education)*

MA (AMA/MAE) *American Medical Association (Medical Assistant Education)*

MEDB *Liaison Committee on Medical Education (basic medical science)*

MED *Liaison Committee on Medical Education (medicine)*

MFCC (AAMFI/CT) *American Association for Marriage and Family Therapy (clinical training programs in marriage and family therapy)*

MFCD (AAMFI/CT) *American Association for Marriage and Family Therapy (graduate degree programs in marriage and family therapy)*

MICB (AAM) *American Academy of microbiology (microbiology)*

MIDWF (ACNM) *American College of Nurse-Midwives (nursing midwifery)*

MLTAB (ABHES/TEC) *Accrediting Bureau of Health Education Schools (medical laboratory technician)*

MLTAD (AMA/MLTAD) *American Medical Association (associate degrees for medical laboratory technicians)*

MLTC (AMA/MLTC) *American Medical Association (certificate programs for medical laboratory technicians)*

MLTE (AMA/MLTE) *American Medical Association (medical laboratory technician education)*

MLT (ABHES/TECED) *Accrediting Bureau of Health Education Schools (medical laboratory technician education)*

MRA (AMA/MRA) *American Medical Association (medical record administrator)*

MRT (AMA/MRT) *American Medical Association (medical record technician)*

MT (AMA/MT) *American Medical Association (medical technology)*

MUS (NASM) *National Association of Schools of Music (music)*

M (MSA/CHE) *Middle States Association of Colleges and Schools, Commission on Higher Education*

NATTS *National Association of Trade and Technical Schools (associate and baccalaureate degree programs in occupational, trade and technical education)*

NHSC *National Home Study Council (associate degree programs in home study education)*

NH (NCA) *North Central Association of Colleges and Schools, Commission on Institutions of Higher Education*

NMT (AMA/NMT) *American Medical Association (nuclear medicine technology)*

NURS (NLN/TX) *National League for Nursing, Inc. (nursing–University of Texas System only)*

NUR (NLN) *National League for Nursing, Inc. (baccalaureate or higher degree programs in nursing)*

NW (NASC) *Northwest Association of Schools and Colleges, Commission on Colleges*

NY (NYSBR) *New York State Board of Regents (degree-granting programs offered by institutions of higher education within New York state)*

N (NCA/S) *North Central Association of Colleges and Secondary Schools, Commission on Institutions of Higher Education*

OMA (AMA/OMA) *American Medical Association (opthalmic medical assistant)*

OPTR (AOA/R) *American Optometric Association (optometry-residency program)*

OPTT (AOA/T) *American Optometric Association (optometry-technician program)*

OPT (AOA) *American Optometric Association (optometry)*

ORT (AMA/ORT) *American Medical Association (operating room technician)*

OSTEO *American Osteopathic Association (osteopathic medicine)*

OT (AOTA) *American Medical Association (occupational therapy)*

PERF (AMA/P) *American Medical Association (perfusionist)*

PHAR (ACPE) *American Council on Pharmaceutical Education (pharmacy)*

PH (CEPH) *Council on Education for Public Health (schools of public health)*

PNE (*National Association for Practical Nurse Education and Service, Inc. (practical nursing)*

PNUR (NLN/PN) *National League for Nursing, Inc. (practical nursing)*

PN (NLN/PN) *National League for Nursing, Inc. (practical nursing)*

PODA *American Podiatry Association (podiatry assistant)*

POD *American Podiatry Association (podiatry)*

PSPSY (APA/P) *American Psychological Association (professional/scientific psychology)*

PTAA (APTAA) *American Physical Therapy Association (physical therapist assistant)*

PTA (APTA) *American Physical Therapy Association (physical therapist)*

PTC (AMA/PTC) *American Medical Association (physical therapy)*

PT (AMA/PT) *American Medical Association (physical therapist)*

RABN (AARTS) *Association of Advanced Rabbinical and Talmudic Schools (rabbinical and Talmudic education)*

RAD (AMA/RD) *American Medical Association (radiography)*

RESTH (AMA/R) *American Medical Association (respiratory)*

RSTHT (AMA/RTT) *American Medical Association (respiratory therapy technician)*

RSTH (AMA/RT) *American Medical Association (respiratory therapy)*

RTT (AMA/RAD) *American Medical Association (radiation therapy technology)*

RT (AMA/RADT) *American Medical Association (radiologic technologist)*

SBBT (AMA/SBBT) *American Medical Association (specialist in blood bank technology)*

SCPSY (APA/SP) *American Psychological Association (school psychology)*

SC (SACS) *Southern Association of Colleges and Schools, Commission on Colleges*

SP (ASLA/P) *American Speech, Language, and Hearing Association (speech-language pathology)*

SRCB (AICS) *Association of Independent Colleges and Schools, Accrediting Commission (senior colleges of business)*

SURGA (AMA/SA) *American Medical Association (Surgeon's Assistant)*

SURGT (AMA/ST) *American Medical Association (Surgical Technology)*

SV (SACS/COEI) *Southern Association of Colleges and Schools, Commission on Occupational Educational Institutions*

SW (CSWE) *Council on Social Work Education (social work)*

S (SACS) *Southern Association of Colleges and Schools, Commission on Colleges*

TECH (ABET/T) *Accreditation Board for Engineering and Technology, Inc. (engineering technology)*

TED (NCATE) *National Council for Accreditation of Teacher Education (teacher education)*

THEA (NAST) *National Association of Schools of Theatre (theatre)*

THEOL (ATS) *Association of Theological Schools in the United States and Canada (theology)*

VET (AVMA) *American Veterinary Medical Association (veterinary medicine)*

WC (WASC/SR) *Western Association of Schools and Colleges, Accrediting Commission for Senior Colleges and Universities*

WJ (WASC/JR) *Western Association of Schools and Colleges, Accrediting Commission for Community and Junior Colleges*

W *Western Association of Schools and Colleges, Accrediting Commission for Senior Colleges and Universities and Junior Colleges*

USING THE EDUCATIONAL RECORDS DIRECTORY.

All schools and institutions in the *Educational Records Directory* are listed in alphabetical order. Once you have located the school you need, your next step(s) will be dictated principally by what the listing shows.

Assuming your school is among the 97% that will cooperate with employers, its listing will detail the data you need to confirm a student's attendance or degree. Hopefully, the required identifiers will be on the employment application. If not, contact the applicant to obtain the missing pieces of information – and modify your form so this kind of delay won't happen in the future. The school's entry will also indicate whether verification requests may be made by mail or by phone. If written requests can be submitted by FAX, the listing will include the appropriate number to dial.

If only one of the options is available, your next step is easy. Contact the school by mail or phone, as directed. When the school accepts both types of inquiries, you will have a decision to make.

A phone request can obviously be made much more quickly. However, there is also some advantage to having a written educational verification in your files. A request via FAX, if possible, will minimize some of the delays inherent in written verifications. You will have to make a choice based on your priorities. In some cases, a phone confirmation with a mail followup may be desirable.

A LESS AMBITIOUS TECHNIQUE.

The individual listings can also be used for other more limited purposes. For example, assume an applicant lists a master's degree in law from James College in Arlington, Texas. The *Educational Records Directory* itself can provide answers to the following important questions without any additional research or work:

1. Is there a James College?

2. Does it offer a program in law?

3. Does it offer degrees at the master's level?

4. Is the school accredited through any of the regional accrediting associations?

5. Does this particular program of study have any special accreditations?

A "no" answer to any questions would suggest a potential problem with this candidate's educational claims. At a minimum, the company should contact the individual to see if there is an explanation for the apparent inconsistency.

A

A T E S Technical Institute

2076 Youngstown–Warren Road
Niles, OH 44446
(216) 652-9919

Will confirm attendance and degree by mail. Inquiry must include student's name, date of birth, social security number, years attended, program of study (if available). Employers may obtain transcripts upon written request accompanied by a $2.00 fee and a signed release from the student.

A single program two-year institution, with an enrollment of 200. Highest level of offering: one year but less than four years.
ACCREDITATIONS: NATTS

Abilene Christian University

A C U Box 7940
Abilene, TX 79699
(915) 674-2236
Fax (915) 674-2238

Will confirm attendance and degree by phone or mail. Inquiry must include student's name, social security number, years attended. Employers may obtain transcripts upon written request accompanied by a signed release from the student. Requests should be directed to: Registrar's Office.

A comprehensive institution with no medical school, with an enrollment of 3,946. Highest level of offering: doctorate.
ACCREDITATIONS: SC AAMFI/GD NASM NLN CSWE TED

Abraham Baldwin Agricultural College

A B A C Station Box 3
Tifton, GA 31794-2693
(912) 386-3236

Will confirm attendance and degree by mail. Inquiry must include student's name, date of birth, social security number, years attended. Employers may obtain transcripts upon written request accompanied by a signed release from the student.

A multiprogram two-year institution, with an enrollment of 2,665. Highest level of offering: one year but less than four years.
ACCREDITATIONS: SC NLN/AD AVVMA/CVTTAT

Academy of Aeronautics

See College of Aeronautics

Academy of the New Church College

PO Box 717
2895 College Drive
Bryn Athyn, PA 19009
(215) 938-2543
Fax (215) 938-2637

Will confirm attendance and degree by mail, phone or fax. Inquiry must include student's name, years attended. Employers may obtain transcripts upon written request accompanied by a $3.00 fee and a signed release from the student.

A general baccalaureate institution, with an enrollment of 120. Highest level of offering: first professional degree.
ACCREDITATIONS: M NCATE ATS

Adams State College

Alamosa, CO 81102
(719) 589-7321
Fax (719) 589-7522

Will confirm attendance and degree by mail or phone. Inquiry must include student's name, date of birth, social security number, years attended. Employers may obtain transcripts upon written request accompanied by a $2.00 fee and a signed release from the student. Requests should be directed to: Records Department.

A comprehensive institution with no medical school, with an enrollment of 2,540. Highest level of offering: master's.
ACCREDITATIONS: NH TED

Adelphi University

South Avenue
Garden City, NY 11530
(516) 877-3300

Will confirm attendance and degree by phone or mail. Inquiry must include student's name, social security number, years attended. Employers may obtain transcripts upon written request accompanied by a $7.50 fee and a signed release from the student. Requests should be directed to: Office of the Registrar.

A doctoral-level institution with no medical school, with an enrollment of 10,717. Highest level of offering: doctorate.
ACCREDITATIONS: M CLPSY DANCE NLN NY SP CSWE

Adirondack Community College

Bay Road
Glens Falls, NY 12801
(518) 793-4491 Ext. 272
Fax (518) 793-4491

Will confirm attendance and degree by phone or mail. Inquiry must include student's name, date of birth, social security number, years attended. Employers may obtain transcripts upon written request accompanied by a $3.00 fee and a signed release from the student.

A multiprogram two-year institution, with an enrollment of 2,878. Highest level of offering: one year but less than four years.
ACCREDITATIONS: M NY

Adler School of Professional Phychology

(Formerly Alfred Adler Institute of Chicago)
65 Wacker Place
Chicago, IL 60601
(312) 201-5900
Fax (312) 201-5917

Will confirm attendance and degree by mail. Inquiry must include student's name, social security number, years attended. A release is required. Employers may obtain transcripts upon written request accompanied by a $5.00 fee and a signed release from the student.

A specialized school, with an enrollment of 350. Highest level of offering: doctorate.
ACCREDITATIONS: NH

Adrian College

110 South Madison
Adrian, MI 49221
(517) 265-5161 Ext. 4313
Fax (517) 264-3331

Will confirm attendance and degree by phone or mail. Inquiry must include student's name, date of birth, social security number, years attended. Requests should be directed to: Registrar's Office. Employers may obtain transcripts upon written request accompanied by a $2.00 fee and a signed release from the student.

A general baccalaureate institution, with an enrollment of 1,200. Highest level of offering: four or five year baccalaureate.
ACCREDITATIONS: NH TED

Agnes Scott College

Decatur, GA 30030
(404) 371-6306
Fax (404) 371-6177

Will confirm attendance and degree by phone, fax or mail. Inquiry must include student's name, date of birth, years attended. Requests should be directed to: Registrar's Office. Employers may obtain transcripts upon written request accompanied by a $1.00 fee with first free and a signed release from the student specifically requesting that a transcript be sent to the company.

A general baccalaureate institution, with an enrollment of 591. Highest level of offering: four year baccalaureate.
ACCREDITATIONS: SC

Aiken Technical College

PO Drawer 696
Aiken, SC 29802
(803) 593-9231 Ext. 244

Will confirm attendance and degree by mail. Inquiry must include student's name, social security number, years attended. Requests should be directed to: Records Department. Employers may obtain transcripts upon written request accompanied by a $5.00 fee and a signed release from the student.

A multiprogram two-year institution, with an enrollment of 1,500. Highest level of offering: two years.
ACCREDITATIONS: SC

Aims Community College

Box 69
Greeley, CO 80632
(303) 330-8008 Ext. 404
Fax (303) 339-9001

Will confirm attendance and degree by mail, phone or fax. Inquiry must include student's name, date of birth, social security number, years attended. Employers may obtain transcripts upon written request accompanied by a signed release from the student. Requests should be directed to: Records Office.

A multiprogram two-year institution, with an enrollment of 7,500. Highest level of offering: one year but less than four years.
ACCREDITATIONS: NH RAD RSTHT

Alabama Agricultural and Mechanical University

PO Box 908
Normal, AL 35762
(205) 851-5254

Will confirm attendance and degree by phone or mail. Inquiry must include student's name, date of birth, social security number, years attended. Written request from the student is required. Employers may obtain transcripts upon written request accompanied by a $3.00 fee and a signed release from the student. Requests should be directed to: Registrar's Office.

A comprehensive institution with no medical school, with an enrollment of 4,415. Highest level of offering: beyond master's but less than doctorate.

ACCREDITATIONS: SC ENGT CSWE TED

Alabama Aviation & Technical College

PO Box 1209
Ozark, AL 36361
(205) 774-5113

Will confirm attendance and degree by phone or mail. Inquiry must include student's name, social security number, years attended. Employers may obtain transcripts upon written request accompanied by a $2.00 fee and a signed release from the student.

A two-year institution newly admitted to NCES, with an enrollment of 374. Highest level of offering: one year but less than four years.

ACCREDITATIONS: SV

Alabama Christian College

(See Faulkner University)

Alabama Southern Community College

(Formerly Patrick Henry Community College)
PO Drawer 5311
Martinsville, VA 24115
(703) 638-8777

Will confirm attendance and degree by mail or phone. Inquiry must include student's name, social security number, years attended, release. Employers may obtain transcripts upon written request accompanied by a signed release from the student.

A multiprogram two-year institution, with an enrollment of 2,000. Highest level of offering: one year but less than four years.

ACCREDITATIONS: SC

Alabama State University

915 South Jackson Street
Montgomery, AL 36195
(205) 293-4243
Fax (205) 832-0336

Will confirm attendance and degree by phone, fax or mail. Inquiry must include student's name, date of birth, social security number, years attended. Employers may obtain transcripts upon written request accompanied by a $2.00 fee and a signed release from the student. Requests should be directed to: Registrar's Office.

A comprehensive institution with no medical school, with an enrollment of 4,456. Highest level of offering: beyond master's but less than doctorate.

ACCREDITATIONS: SC NASM TED

Alabama Technical College

(See Gadsden State Community College)

Alamance Community College

(Formerly Technical College of Alamance)
PO Box 8000
Graham, NC 27253
(919) 578-2002 Ext. 111

Will confirmattendance and degree by mail. Inquiry must include studen's name, date of birth, social security number, years attended. Employers may obtain transcript upon written request accompanied by a $2.00 fee and a written release from the student

A multiprogram two-year institution, with an enrollment of 3,500. Highest level of offering: one year but less than four years.

ACCREDITATIONS: SC DA ENGT

Alaska Bible College

Box 289
Glennallen, AK 99588
(907) 822-3201 Ext. 33

Will confirm attendance and degree by phone or mail. Inquiry must include student's name. Employers may obtain transcripts upon written request accompanied by a $4.00 fee and a signed release from the student.

A school of philosophy, religion and theology, with an enrollment of 62. Highest level of offering: four or five year baccalaureate.

ACCREDITATIONS: BI

Alaska Pacific University

4101 University Drive
Anchorage, AK 99508
(907) 564-8210
Fax (907) 562-4276

Will confirm attendance and degree by phone or mail. Inquiry must include student's name and years attended. Employers may obtain transcripts upon written request accompanied by a $3.00 fee and a signed release from the student. Requests should be directed to: Registrar's Office.

A specialized school, with an enrollment of 688. Highest level of offering: master's.

ACCREDITATIONS: NW

Albany Business College

(See Bryant and Stratton)

Albany College of Pharmacy

106 New Scotland Avenue
Albany, NY 12208
(518) 445-7221
Fax (518) 445-7202

Will confirm attendance and degree by phone or mail. Inquiry must include student's name, date of birth, social security number, maiden name (if any). Requests should be directed to: Registrar's Office. Employers may obtain transcripts upon written request accompanied by a $3.00 fee and a signed release from the student.

A health institution, with an enrollment of 650. Highest level of offering: five year baccalaureate, two-year post BS Pharm D.

ACCREDITATIONS: M NY PHAR

Albany Junior College

(See Darton College)

Albany Law School

80 New Scotland Avenue
Albany, NY 12208
(518) 445-2324
Fax (518) 445-2315

Will confirm attendance and degree by phone or mail. Inquiry must include student's name, years attended. Employers may obtain transcripts upon written request accompanied by a $2.00 fee and a signed release from the student.

A law school, with an enrollment of 820. Highest level of offering: first professional degree.

ACCREDITATIONS: NY LAW

Albany Medical College

47 New Scotland Avenue, A3
Albany, NY 12208
(518) 445-5523
Fax (518) 445-5887

Will confirm attendance and degree by mail or phone. Inquiry must include student's name, social security number, year graduated. Requests should be directed to: Office of Student Records. Employers may obtain transcripts upon written request accompanied by a $3.00 fee and a signed release from the student specifically requesting that a transcript be sent to the company.

A medical school, with an enrollment of 615. Highest level of offering: doctorate.

ACCREDITATIONS: M APCP IPSY MED NY

Albany State College

504 College Drive
Albany, GA 31705
(912) 430-4638

Will confirm attendance and degree by phone or mail. Inquiry must include student's name, social security number, years attended. Employers may obtain transcripts upon written request accompanied by a $1.00 fee and a signed release or written letter from the student. Requests should be directed to: Registrar's Office.

A general baccalaureate institution, with an enrollment of 2,746. Highest level of offering: master's.

ACCREDITATIONS: SC NLN TED

Albertson College of Idaho

(Formerly College of Idaho)
2112 Cleveland Boulevard
Caldwell, ID 83605
(208) 459-5201
Fax (208) 454-2077

Will confirm attendance and degree by phone or mail. Inquiry must include student's name, date of birth. Employers may obtain transcripts upon written request accompanied by a $3.00 fee and a signed release from the student.

A general baccalaureate institution, with an enrollment of 975. Highest level of offering: master's.

ACCREDITATIONS: NW

Albertus Magnus College

700 Prospect Street–Room 120
New Haven, CT 06511
(203) 773-8514

Will confirm attendance and degree by phone or mail. Inquiry must include student's name or maiden name (if any), years attended. Requests should be directed to: Registrar's Office. Employers may obtain transcripts upon written request accompanied by a $3.00 fee and a signed release from the student.

A general baccalaureate institution, with an enrollment of 700. Highest level of offering: four or five year baccalaureate.

ACCREDITATIONS: EH

Albion College

Albion, MI 49224
(517) 629-5511 Ext. 216
Fax (517) 629-0477

Will confirm attendance and degree by phone or mail. Inquiry must include student's name, date of birth, social security number, years attended. Employers may obtain transcripts upon written request accompanied by a $3.00 fee and a signed release from the student. Requests should be directed to: Registrar's Office.

A general baccalaureate institution, with an enrollment of 1,586. Highest level of offering: four or five year baccalaureate.

ACCREDITATIONS: NH NASM

Albright College

Box 15234
Reading, PA 19612-5234
(215) 921-2381 Ext. 7256
Fax (215) 921-7530

Will confirm attendance and degree by phone or mail. Inquiry must include student's name and social security number. Requests should be directed to: Registrar's Office. Employers may obtain transcripts upon written request accompanied by a signed release from the student.

A general baccalaureate institution, with an enrollment of 1,500. Highest level of offering: four or five year baccalaureate.

ACCREDITATIONS: M NLN CHE CSWE TED

Alcorn State University

Box 420
Lorman, MS 39096
(601) 877-6100

Will confirm attendance and degree by phone or mail. Inquiry must include student's name, date of birth, social security number, years attended. Employers may obtain transcripts upon written request accompanied by a $2.00 fee and a signed release from the student. Requests should be directed to: Registrar's Office.

A general baccalaureate institution, with an enrollment of 2,857. Highest level of offering: master's.

ACCREDITATIONS: SC NLN/AD NASM NLN TED

Alderson–Broaddus College

Philippi, WV 26416
(304) 457-1700 Ext. 278

Will confirm attendance and degree by phone or mail. Inquiry must include student's name, social security number, years attended. Requests should be directed to: Registrar's Office. Employers may obtain transcripts upon written request accompanied by signed release or written letter from the student.

A general baccalaureate institution, with an enrollment of 776. Highest level of offering: four or five year baccalaureate.

ACCREDITATIONS: NH APCP NLN CSWE

Alexander City State Junior College

(See Central Alabama Community College)

Alexandria Technical College

1601 Jefferson Street
Alexandria, MN 56308
(612) 762-0221 Ext. 4470
Fax (612) 762-4501

Will confirm attendance and degree by phone or mail. Inquiry must include student's name and years attended. Employers may obtain transcripts upon written request accompanied by a $.50 fee (per name) and a signed release.

A two-year institution with an enrollment of 1,800. Highest level of offering: one year but less than four years.

ACCREDITATIONS: NCA FIDER AMA/MLTC

Alfred Adler Institute of Chicago

(See Adler School of Professional Phychology)

Alfred State College

Alfred, NY 14802
(607) 587-4796
Fax (607) 587-3294

Will confirm attendance and degree by phone, fax or mail. Inquiry must include student's name, date of birth, social security number, years attended. Employers may obtain transcripts upon written request accompanied by a $5.00 fee and a signed release from the student.

A multiprogram two-year institution, with an enrollment of 3,600. Highest level of offering: one year but less than four years.

ACCREDITATIONS: M NLN/AD ENGT MLTAD MRT NY

Alfred University

PO Box 805
Alfred, NY 14802
(607) 871-2122

Will confirm attendance and degree by phone or mail. Inquiry must include student's name and years attended. Employers may obtain transcripts upon written request accompanied by a $5.00 fee and a signed release from the student.

A comprehensive institution with no medical school, with an enrollment of 2,035. Highest level of offering: doctorate.

ACCREDITATIONS: M NLN NY

Alice Lloyd College

Pippa Passes, KY 41844
(606) 368-2101 Ext. 4502

Will confirm attendance and degree by phone or mail. Inquiry must include student's name, date of birth, years attended. Employers may obtain transcripts upon written request accompanied by a $2.00 fee and a signed release from the student.

A multiprogram four-year institution, with an enrollment of 548. Highest level of offering: four or five year baccalaureate.

ACCREDITATIONS: SC

Allan Hancock College

800 South College Drive
Santa Maria, CA 93454
(805) 922-6966 Ext. 272

Will confirm attendance and degree by phone or mail. Inquiry must include student's name, date of birth, social security number, years attended. Employers may obtain transcripts upon written request accompanied by a $2.00 fee and a signed release from the student.

A multiprogram two-year institution, with an enrollment of 8,528. Highest level of offering: one year but less than four years.

ACCREDITATIONS: WJ MAC DA

Allegany Community College

Willow Brook Road
Cumberland, MD 21502
(301) 724-7700 Ext. 212
Fax (301) 724-6892

Will confirm attendance and degree by phone or mail. Inquiry must include student's name and social security number. Employers may obtain transcripts upon written request accompanied by a $2.00 fee and a signed release from the student. Requests should be directed to: Registrar's Office.

A multiprogram two-year institution, with an enrollment of 2,655. Highest level of offering: one year but less than four years.

ACCREDITATIONS: M DA DH MLTAD RSTH

Allegheny College

North Main
Meadville, PA 16335
(814) 724-2357
Fax (814) 337-0955

Will confirm attendance and degree by mail or phone. Inquiry must include student's name and years attended. Employers may obtain transcripts upon written request accompanied by a $2.00 fee and a signed release from the student. Requests should be directed to: Registrar's Office.

A general baccalaureate institution, with an enrollment of 1,955. Highest level of offering: master's.

ACCREDITATIONS: M NASM

Allen County Community College

1801 North Cottonwood
Iola, KS 66749
(316) 365-5116
Fax (316) 365-3284

Will confirm attendance and degree by phone, fax or mail. Inquiry must include student's name, social security number, years attended. Employers may obtain transcripts upon written request accompanied by a $2.00 fee and a signed release from the student. Requests should be directed to: Registrar's Office.

A multiprogram two-year institution, with an enrollment of 2,012. Highest level of offering: one year but less than four years.

ACCREDITATIONS: NH

Allen University

1530 Harden Street
Columbia, SC 29204
(803) 376-5712

Will confirm attendance and degree by mail or phone. Inquiry must include student's name and social security number.

Employers may obtain transcripts upon written request accompanied by a $3.00 fee and a signed release from the student.

A general baccalaureate institution, with an enrollment of 223. Highest level of offering: four or five year baccalaureate.

ACCREDITATIONS: 3IC

Allentown College of St. Francis De Sales

2755 Station Ave.
Center Valley, PA 18034
(215) 282-1100 Ext. 1223
Fax (215) 282-2342

Will confirm attendance and degree by phone, fax or mail. Inquiry must include student's name and years attended. Employers may obtain transcripts upon written request accompanied by a $2.00 fee and a signed release from the student.

A general baccalaureate institution, with an enrollment of 1,298. Highest level of offering: master's.

ACCREDITATIONS: M NLN

Alliance College

c/o Mercy Hurst College
501 E. 38th
Erie, PA 16546
(814) 398-5100

Records are maintained at the above address. Will confirm attendance and degree by phone or mail. Inquiry must include student's name, social security number, years attended. Employers may obtain transcripts upon written request accompanied by a $3.00 fee and a signed release from the student. Requests should be directed to: Registrar's Office.

Alma College

Alma, MI 48801
(517) 463-7348
Fax (517) 463-7277

Will confirm attendance and degree by phone or mail. Inquiry must include student's name, date of birth, years attended. Employers may obtain transcripts upon written request accompanied by a $2.00 fee and a signed release from the student. Requests should be directed to: Registrar's Office.

A general baccalaureate institution, with an enrollment of 1,165. Highest level of offering: four or five year baccalaureate.

ACCREDITATIONS: NH NASM TED

Alpena Community College

666 Johnson Street
Alpena, MI 49707
(517) 356-9021 Ext. 223

Will confirm attendance and degree by phone or mail. Inquiry must include student's name, date of birth, social security number, years attended. Employers may obtain transcripts upon written request accompanied by a $1.00 fee and a signed release from the student. Requests should be directed to: Registrar's Office.

A multiprogram two-year institution, with an enrollment of 2,542. Highest level of offering: one year but less than four years.

ACCREDITATIONS: NH

Alvernia College

Reading, PA 19607-1799
(215) 777-5411
Fax (215) 777-6632

Will confirm attendance and degree by phone or mail. Inquiry must include student's name, social security number, years attended, and year graduated (if applicable). Employers may obtain transcripts upon written request accompanied by a $3.00 fee and a signed release from the student. Requests should be directed to: Registrar's Office.

A general baccalaureate institution, with an enrollment of 1238. Highest level of offering: four year baccalaureate.

ACCREDITATIONS: NLN/AD APTAA

Alverno College

3401 South 39th Street
Milwaukee, WI 53215
(414) 382-6070

Will confirm attendance and degree by mail. Inquiry must include student's name, date of birth, social security number. Employers may obtain transcripts upon written request accompanied by a $3.00 fee

and a signed release from the student. Requests should be directed to: Registrar's Office.

A general baccalaureate institution, with an enrollment of 2,291. Highest level of offering: four or five year baccalaureate.

ACCREDITATIONS: NH NASM NLN TED

Alvin Community College

3110 Mustang Road
Alvin, TX 77511
(713) 388-4615

Will confirm attendance and degree by mail. Inquiry must include student's name, date of birth, social security number, years attended, release. Employers may obtain transcripts upon written request accompanied by a signed release from the student. Requests should be directed to: Records Office.

A multiprogram two-year institution, with an enrollment of 4,000. Highest level of offering: one year but less than four years.

ACCREDITATIONS: SC NLN/AD MLTAD RSTH RSTHT

Amarillo College

PO Box 447
Amarillo, TX 79178
(806) 371-5030
Fax (806) 371-5370

Will confirm attendance and degree by mail. Inquiry must include student's name, date of birth, social security number, years attended. Employers may obtain transcripts upon written request accompanied by a $2.00 fee and a signed release from the student. Requests should be directed to: Registrar's Office.

A multiprogram two-year institution, with an enrollment of 6,500. Highest level of offering: one year but less than four years.

ACCREDITATIONS: SC NLN/AD DA DH MLTAD NASM PTAA RAD RSTH RTT

Amber University

1700 Eastgate Drive
Garland, TX 75041
(214) 279-6511
Fax (214) 279-9773

Will confirm attendance and degree by mail. Inquiry must include student's name, social security number, years attended, release. Employers may obtain transcripts upon written request accompanied by a $5.00 fee and a signed release from the student.

A comprehensive institution with no medical school, with an enrollment of 1,600. Highest level of offering: master's.

ACCREDITATIONS: SC

American Academy McAllister Institute of Funeral Service

450 West 56th Street
New York, NY 10019
(212) 757-1190
Fax (212) 765-5923

Will confirm attendance and degree by phone or mail. Inquiry must include student's name, social security number, years attended. Employers may obtain transcripts upon written request accompanied by a $2.00 fee and a signed release from the student.

A two-year institution newly admitted to NCES, with an enrollment of 125. Highest level of offering: one year but less than four years.
ACCREDITATIONS: NY FUSER

American Academy of Art

122 South Michigan
Chicago, IL 60603
(312) 939-3883
Fax (312) 939-5429

Will confirm attendance and degree by mail. Inquiry must include student's name, social security number, years attended. Employers may obtain transcripts upon written request accompanied by a $3.00 fee and a signed release from the student.

A single program two-year institution, with an enrollment of 775. Highest level of offering: one year but less than four years.
ACCREDITATIONS: NATTS

American Academy of Dramatic Arts–West

2550 Paloma Street
Pasadena, CA 91107
(818) 798-0777
Fax (818) 798-5047

Will confirm attendance and degree by phone or mail. Inquiry must include student's name, social security number, years attended. Employers may obtain transcripts upon written request accompanied by a $3.00 fee and a signed release from the student. Requests should be directed to: Registrar's Office.

A single program two-year institution, with an enrollment of 200. Highest level of offering: one year but less than four years.
ACCREDITATIONS: WJ

American Academy of Dramatic Arts

120 Madison Avenue
New York, NY 10016
(212) 686-9244
Fax (212) 545-7934

Will confirm attendance and degree by mail. Inquiry must include student's name, social security number, years attended, days or evenings, release. Employers may obtain transcripts upon written request accompanied by a $6.00 money order and a signed release from the student. Requests should be directed to: Registrar's Office.

A single program two-year institution, with an enrollment of 249. Highest level of offering: one year but less than four years.
ACCREDITATIONS: M NY THEA

American Baptist Seminary of the West

2606 Dwight Way
Berkeley, CA 94704
(510) 841-1905

Will confirm attendance and degree by phone or mail. Inquiry must include student's name and social security number. Requests should be directed to: Registrar's Office. Employers may obtain transcripts upon written request accompanied by a $5.00 fee and a signed release from the student.

A school of philosophy, religion and theology, with an enrollment of 53. Highest level of offering: doctorate.
ACCREDITATIONS: THEOL

American Baptist College

1800 Baptist World Center Drive
Nashville, TN 37207
(615) 262-3433

Will confirm attendance and degree by phone or mail. Inquiry must include student's name and years attended. Requests should be directed to: Registrar's Office. Employers may obtain transcripts upon written request accompanied by a $2.00 fee and a signed release from the student.

A school of philosophy, religion and theology, with an enrollment of 200. Highest level of offering: four or five year baccalaureate.
ACCREDITATIONS: BI

American Conservatory of Music

16 N. Wabash Ave.
Suite 1850
Chicago, IL 60602
(312) 263-4161
Fax (312) 263-5832

Will confirm attendance and degree by phone or mail. Inquiry must include student's name, social security number, years attended. Employers may obtain transcripts upon written request accompanied by a $5.00 fee and a signed release from the student. Requests should be directed to: Dr. A. C. Sligting.

A visual and performing arts school, with an enrollment of 175. Highest level of offering: doctorate.
ACCREDITATIONS: NASM

American Conservatory Theatre

450 Geary Street
San Francisco, CA 94102
(415) 749-2350
Fax (415) 771-4859

Will confirm attendance and degree by phone or fax. Inquiry must include student's name and years attended. Employers may obtain transcripts upon written request accompanied by a $4.00 fee and a signed release from the student. Requests should be directed to: Registrar's Office.

A multiprogram two-year institution, with an enrollment of 150. Highest level of offering: master's.
ACCREDITATIONS: WC

American Film Institute–Center for Advanced Film Studies

2021 North Western Avenue
Los Angeles, CA 90027
(213) 856-7628
Fax (213) 467-4578

Will confirm attendance and degree by phone or mail. Inquiry must include student's name and years attended. Employers may obtain transcripts upon written request accompanied by a signed release from the student and a $5.00 fee.

A bachelor's or higher institution newly admitted to NCES, with an enrollment of 196. Highest level of offering: master's.
ACCREDITATIONS: NASAD

American Graduate School of International Management

Thunderbird Campus
Glendale, AZ 85306
(602) 978-7210
Fax (602) 439-5432

Will confirm attendance and degree by phone, fax or mail. Inquiry must include student's name, date of birth, years attended. Employers may obtain transcripts upon written request accompanied by a $5.00 fee and a signed release from the student. Requests should be directed to: Registrar's Office.

A business school, with an enrollment of 1,300. Highest level of offering: master's.
ACCREDITATIONS: NH

American Indian Bible College

10020 North 15th Avenue
Phoenix, AZ 85021
(602) 944-3335 Ext. 15

Will confirm attendance and degree by mail. Inquiry must include student's name, social security number, years attended. Employers may obtain transcripts upon written request accompanied by a signed release from the student.

A bachelor's or higher institution newly admitted to NCES, with an enrollment of 92. Highest level of offering: four or five year baccalaureate.
ACCREDITATIONS: NH

American Institute of Business

2500 Fleur Drive
Des Moines, IA 50321
(515) 244-4221
Fax (515) 244-6773

Will confirm attendance and degree by phone or mail. Inquiry must include student's name, social security number, years attended. Employers may obtain transcripts upon written request accompanied by a $2.00 fee and a signed release from the student. Requests should be directed to: Registrar's Office.

A multiprogram two-year institution, with an enrollment of 1,063. Highest level of offering: one year but less than four years.
ACCREDITATIONS: NH JRCB

American Institute of Design

1616 Orthodox Street
Philadelphia, PA 19124
(215) 288-8200 Ext. 23
Fax (215) 288-0466

Will confirm attendance by phone or mail. Inquiry must include student's name, date of birth, years attended. Employers may obtain transcripts upon written request accompanied by a $5.00 fee and a signed release from the student. Requests should be sent to: Attn: Registrar's Office.

A two-year institution newly admitted to NCES, with an enrollment of 450. Highest level of offering: one year but less than four years.
ACCREDITATIONS: NATTS

American International College

1000 State Street
Springfield, MA 01109
(413) 737-7000 Ext. 212

Will confirm attendance and degree by phone or mail. Inquiry must include student's name, date of birth, social security number, years attended. Employers may obtain transcripts upon written request accompanied by a $3.00 fee and a signed release from the student. Requests should be directed to: Registrar's Office.

A comprehensive institution with no medical school, with an enrollment of 1,859. Highest level of offering: doctorate.
ACCREDITATIONS: EH TED NLN

American Islamic College

640 West Irving Park Road
Chicago, IL 60613
(312) 281-4700 Ext. 26
Fax (312) 281-8552

Will confirm attendance and degree by phone or mail. Inquiry must include student's name, social security number. A release is required. Employers may obtain transcripts upon written request accompanied by a signed release from the student and a $3.00 fee.

A bachelor's or higher institution newly admitted to NCES, with an enrollment of 62. Highest level of offering: four or five year baccalaureate.
ACCREDITATIONS: NH

American River College

4700 College Oak Drive
Sacramento, CA 95841
(916) 484-8171

Will confirm attendance and degree by mail. Inquiry must include student's name, date of birth, social security number, years attended. A signed release is required. Employers may obtain transcripts upon written request accompanied by a $2.00 fee and a signed release from the student. Requests should be directed to: Records.

A multiprogram two-year institution, with an enrollment of 22,659. Highest level of offering: one year but less than four years.
ACCREDITATIONS: WJ RSTH

American Technological University

(See University of Central Texas)

American Trade Insitute

(Formerly Flagler Career Institute)
3225 University Boulevard South
Jacksonville, FL 32216
(904) 721-1622

Will confirm attendance and degree by phone or mail. Inquiry must include student's name, social security number, and years attended. Employers may obtain transcripts upon written request accompanied by a $2.00 fee and a signed release from the student.

A two-year institution newly admitted to NCES, with an enrollment of 150. Highest level of offering: one year but less than four years.
ACCREDITATIONS: NATTS

American Trade Institute Health Education Center

(Formerly Flagler Career Institute)
1395 SW 167th St., Suite 200
Miami, FL 33169
(305)561-8452
Fax (305) 628-1461

Will confirm attendance and degree by phone, fax or mail. Inquiry must include student's name, social security number, and years attended. Employers may obtain transcripts upon written request accompanied by a $3.00 fee and a signed release from the student.

A two-year institution newly admitted to NCES, with an enrollment of 220. Highest level of offering: one year but less than four years.
ACCREDITATIONS: NATTS

American University

4400 Mass Avenue North West
Washington, DC 20016
(202) 885-2232
Fax (202) 885-1052

Will confirm attendance and degree by phone or mail. Inquiry must include student's name, social security number, years attended. Employers may obtain transcripts upon written request accompanied by a $2.00 fee and a signed release from the student. Requests should be directed to: Registrar's Office Transcript Dept.

A doctoral-level institution with no medical school, with an enrollment of 11,764. Highest level of offering: doctorate.
ACCREDITATIONS: M CLPSY JOUR LAW NASM NLN TED

Amherst College

PO Box 2211
Amherst, MA 01002
(413) 542-2225
Fax (413) 542-2327

Will confirm attendance and degree by phone or mail. Inquiry must include student's name and years attended. Employers may obtain transcripts upon written request accompanied by a $2.00 fee and a signed release from the student. Requests should be directed to: Registrar's Office.

A general baccalaureate institution, with an enrollment of 1,588. Highest level of offering: four or five year baccalaureate.
ACCREDITATIONS: EH

Anchorage Community College

(See University of Alaska Anchorage)

Ancilla Domini College

Union Road, Box 1
Donaldson, IN 46513
(219) 936-8898 Ext. 321

Will confirm attendance and degree by phone or mail. Inquiry must include student's name and years attended. Employers may obtain transcripts upon written request accompanied by a $2.00 fee and a signed release from the student. Requests should

be directed to: Registrar's Office.

A multiprogram two-year institution, with an enrollment of 473. Highest level of offering: one year but less than four years.
ACCREDITATIONS: NH

Anderson College

1100 East 5th Street
Anderson, IN 40612
(317) 649-9071
Fax (317) 641-3851

Will confirm attendance and degree by mail. Inquiry must include student's name, date of birth, social security number, years attended. Employers may obtain transcripts upon written request accompanied by a $3.00 fee and a signed release from the student. Requests should be directed to: Registrar's Office.

A general baccalaureate institution, with an enrollment of 2,150. Highest level of offering: first professional degree.
ACCREDITATIONS: NH NLN/AD NASM CSWE TED THEOL

Anderson College

316 Boulevard
Anderson, SC 29621-4035
(803) 231-2120
Fax (803) 231-2004

Will confirm attendance and degree by phone, fax or mail. Inquiry must include student's name, social security number, years attended. Employers may obtain transcripts upon written request accompanied by a signed release from the student. Requests should be directed to: Registrar's Office.

A multiprogram four-year institution, with an enrollment of 1,100. Highest level of offering: one year but less than four years.
ACCREDITATIONS: SC NASM

Andover College

901 Washington Avenue
Portland, ME 04103
(207) 774-6126
Fax (207) 774-1715

Will confirm attendance by mail. Inquiry must include student's name and release. Employers may obtain transcripts upon written request accompanied by a $3.00 fee and a signed release from the student. Requests should be directed to: Registrar's Office.

A multiprogram two-year institution, with an enrollment of 500. Highest level of offering: one year but less than four years.
ACCREDITATIONS: JRCB

Andover Newton Theological School

210 Herrick Road
Newton Centre, MA 02159
(617) 964-1100 Ext. 212

Will confirm attendance and degree by mail or phone. Inquiry must include student's name, social security number, years attended. Employers may obtain transcripts upon written request accompanied by a $2.00 fee and a signed release from the student. Requests should be directed to: Registrar's Office.

A school of philosophy, religion and theology, with an enrollment of 467. Highest level of offering: doctorate.
ACCREDITATIONS: EH THEOL PAST

Andrew College

413 College Street
Cuthbert, GA 31740
(912) 732-2171 Ext. 130

Will confirm attendance and degree by phone or mail. Inquiry must include student's name and years attended. Employers may obtain transcripts upon written request accompanied by a $2.00 fee and a signed release from the student.

A multiprogram two-year institution, with an enrollment of 295. Highest level of offering: Associate Degree.
ACCREDITATIONS: SC

Andrews University

Records Office
Berrien Springs, MI 49104
(616) 471-3375

Will confirm attendance and degree by mail. Inquiry must include student's name, date of birth, social security number, years attended. Employers may obtain transcripts upon written request accompanied by a $5.00 fee and a signed release from the student. Requests should be directed to: Records Office.

A comprehensive institution with no medical school, with an enrollment of 2,890. Highest level of offering: doctorate.
ACCREDITATIONS: NH DIET NASM NLN TED THEOL

Angelina College

PO Box 1768
Lufkin, TX 75902
(409) 639-1301
Fax (409) 639-4299

Will confirm attendance and degree by phone, fax or mail. Inquiry must include student's name, date of birth, social security number, years attended. Employers may obtain transcripts upon written request accompanied by a $2.00 fee and a signed release from the student.

A multiprogram two-year institution, with an enrollment of 3,000. Highest level of offering: one year but less than four years.
ACCREDITATIONS: SC NLN/AD RAD

Angelo State University

2601 West Avenue N
San Angelo, TX 76909
(915) 942-2043

Will confirm attendance and degree by phone or mail. Inquiry must include student's name and social security number. Employers may obtain transcripts upon written request accompanied by a $3.00 fee and a signed release from the student. Requests should be directed to: Registrar's Office.

A comprehensive institution with no medical school, with an enrollment of 6,128. Highest level of offering: master's.
ACCREDITATIONS: SC NLN/AD NASM NLN

Anna Maria College

Paxton, MA 01612-1198
(508) 757-4586 Ext. 275
Fax (508) 756-2970

Will confirm attendance and degree by phone, fax or mail. Inquiry must include student's name, social security number, years attended. Employers may obtain transcripts upon written request accompanied by a $3.00 fee and a signed release from the student.

A comprehensive institution with no medical school, with an enrollment of 1,395. Highest level of offering: beyond master's but less than doctorate.
ACCREDITATIONS: AMA MLTAD CSWE NEASC NLN

Anne Arundel Community College

101 College Parkway
Arnold, MD 21012
(410) 541-2241
Fax (410) 541-2489

Will confirm attendance by phone or mail. Inquiry must include student's name and social security number, years attended and a release. Employers may obtain transcripts upon written request accompanied by a $2.00 fee and a signed release from the student.

A multiprogram two-year institution, with an enrollment of 12,000. Highest level of offering: one year but less than four years.
ACCREDITATIONS: M NLN/AD

Annenberg Research Institute

420 Walnut St.
Philadelphia, PA 19106
(215) 238-1290

Will confirm attendance and degree by phone or mail. Inquiry must include student's name, date of birth, social security number. Employers may obtain transcripts upon written request accompanied by a $4.00 fee and a signed release from the student. Degrees will no longer be awarded after May 1992

A specialized school, with an enrollment of 4. Highest level of offering: doctorate.
ACCREDITATIONS: M

Anoka–Ramsey Community College

11200 Mississippi Boulevard
Coon Rapids, MN 55433
(612) 422-3418

Will confirm attendance and degree by phone or mail. Inquiry must include student's name, date of birth, social security number. Employers may obtain transcripts upon written request accompanied by a signed release from the student. Requests should be directed to: Records Dept.

A multiprogram two-year institution, with an enrollment of 5,200. Highest level of offering: one year but less than four years.
ACCREDITATIONS: NH NLN/AD ENGT

Anson Community College

PO Box 126
Polkton, NC 28135
(704) 272-7635
Fax (704) 272-8904

Will confirm attendance and degree by mail or phone. Inquiry must include student's name, date of birth, social security number, years attended. Employers may obtain transcripts upon written request accompanied by a $1.00 fee and a signed release from the student. Requests should be directed to: Registrar's Office.

A multiprogram two-year institution, with an enrollment of 662. Highest level of offering: one year but less than four years.
ACCREDITATIONS: SC

Antelope Valley College

3041 West Avenue K
Lancaster, CA 93536
(805) 943-3241 Ext. 620

Will confirm attendance and degree by mail. Inquiry must include student's name, date of birth, social security number, years attended. A signed release is required. Employers may obtain transcripts upon written request accompanied by a $1.00 fee and a signed release from the student.

A multiprogram two-year institution, with an enrollment of 8,637. Highest level of offering: one year but less than four years.
ACCREDITATIONS: WJ RAD

Antioch University

795 Livermore
Yellow Springs, OH 45387
(513) 767-6401

Will confirm attendance and degree by phone or mail. Inquiry must include student's name, social security number, years attended. Employers may obtain transcripts upon written request accompanied by a $5.00 fee and a signed release from the student. Requests should be directed to: Registrar's Office.

A comprehensive institution with no medical school, with an enrollment of 3,426. Highest level of offering: doctorate.
ACCREDITATIONS: NH LAW

Antonelli Institute of Art and Photography

124 East Seventh Street
Cincinnati, OH 45202
(513) 241-4338
Fax (513) 241-9396

Will confirm attendance and degree by phone or mail. Inquiry must include student's name, social security number and years attended. Employers may obtain transcripts upon written request accompanied by a $5.00 fee and a signed release from the student. Requests should be directed to: Registrar's Office.

A two-year institution, with an enrollment of 175. Highest level of offering: one year but less than four years.
ACCREDITATIONS: NATTS

Antonelli Institute of Art and Photography

2910 Jolly Road–PO Box 570
Plymouth Meeting, PA 19462
(215) 275-3040
Fax (215) 275-5630

Will confirm attendance and degree by mail. Inquiry must include student's name, social security number, years attended. Employers may obtain transcripts upon written request accompanied by a signed release from the student. Requests should be directed to: Registrar's Office.

A single program two-year institution, with an enrollment of 346. Highest level of offering: one year but less than four years.
ACCREDITATIONS: NATTS

Appalachian Bible College

PO Box ABC
Bradley, WV 25818-1353
(304) 877-6428 Ext. 233
Fax (304) 877-6423

Will confirm attendance and degree by phone or mail. Inquiry must include student's name and years attended. Employers may obtain transcripts upon written request accompanied by a $2.00 fee and a signed release from the student. Requests should be directed to: Registrar's Office.

A school of Bible and theology, with an enrollment of 191. Highest level of offering: four or five year baccalaureate.

ACCREDITATIONS: AABC

Appalachian State University

Boone, NC 28608
(704) 262-2050 Ext. 23
Fax (704) 262-3136

Will confirm attendance and degree by phone or mail. Inquiry must include student's name, social security number, years attended. Employers may obtain transcripts upon written request accompanied by a $2.00 fee and a signed release from the student. Requests should be directed to: Registrar's Office.

A comprehensive institution with no medical school, with an enrollment of 11,501. Highest level of offering: beyond master's but less than doctorate.

ACCREDITATIONS: SC BUS NASM TED

Aquinas College

1607 Robinson Road South East
Grand Rapids, MI 49506
(616) 459-8281 Ext. 5,107

Will confirm attendance and degree by phone or mail. Inquiry must include student's name, social security number, years attended. Employers may obtain transcripts upon written request accompanied by a $3.00 fee and a signed release from the student.

A general baccalaureate institution, with an enrollment of 2,831. Highest level of offering: master's.

ACCREDITATIONS: NH

Aquinas Institute of Theology

3642 Lindell Boulevard
St Louis, MO 63108
(314) 658-3882
Fax (314) 652-0935

Will confirm attendance and degree by mail or phone. Inquiry must include student's name, date of birth, social security number, years attended. Employers may obtain transcripts upon written request accompanied by a $3.00 fee and a signed release from the student.

A school of philosophy, religion and theology, with an enrollment of 110. Highest level of offering: doctorate until 1985, masters since 1985.

ACCREDITATIONS: NH THEOL

Aquinas Junior College at Milton

303 Adams Street
Milton, MA 02186
(617) 696-3100

Will confirm attendance and degree by phone or mail. Inquiry must include student's name, social security number and years attended. Employers may obtain transcripts upon written request accompanied by a $2.00 fee and a signed release from the student. Requests should be directed to: Registrar's Office.

A multiprogram two-year institution, with an enrollment of 225 . Highest level of offering: one year but less than four years.

ACCREDITATIONS: EV MAC

Aquinas Junior College at Newton

15 Walnut Park
Newton, MA 02158
(617) 969-4400

Will confirm attendance and degree by mail or phone. Inquiry must include student's name, social security number, years attended. Employers may obtain transcripts upon written request accompanied by a $2.00 fee and a signed release from the student. Requests should be directed to: Registrar's Office.

A multiprogram two-year institution, with an enrollment of 367. Highest level of offering: one year but less than four years.

ACCREDITATIONS: EV

Aquinas Junior College

4210 Harding Road
Nashville, TN 37205
(615) 297-7545
Fax (615) 297-7557

Will confirm attendance and degree by phone or mail. Inquiry must include student's name, date of birth, social security number, years attended. Employers may obtain transcripts upon written request accompanied by a $3.00 fee and a signed release from the student.

A multiprogram two-year institution, with an enrollment of 425. Highest level of offering: one year but less than four years.

ACCREDITATIONS: SC RAD

Arapahoe Community College

2500 West College Drive
PO Box 9002
Littleton, CO 80160-9002
(303) 797-5621

Will confirm attendance and degree by phone or mail. Inquiry must include student's name, social security number, years attended. Employers may obtain transcripts upon written request accompanied by a $2.00 fee and a signed release from the student.

A multiprogram two-year institution, with an enrollment of 7,400. Highest level of offering: one year but less than four years.

ACCREDITATIONS: NH MAC MLTAD MRT

Arizona Automotive Institute

6829 North 46th Avenue
Glendale, AZ 85301
(602) 934-7273 Ext. 139

Will confirm attendance and degree by mail. Inquiry must include student's name, social security number, years attended. Employers may obtain transcripts upon written request accompanied by signed release from the student. Requests should be directed to: Director of Graduate Placement.

A two-year institution newly admitted to NCES, with an enrollment of 1,111. Highest level of offering: one year but less than four years.

ACCREDITATIONS: NATTS

Arizona College of the Bible

2045 West Northern Avenue
Phoenix, AZ 85021
(602) 995-2670

Will confirm attendance and degree by mail or phone. Inquiry must include student's name (and maiden name if available), social security number, years attended. Employers may obtain transcripts upon written request accompanied by a $2.00 fee and a signed release from the student. Requests should be directed to: Registrar's Office.

A school of philosophy, religion and theology, with an enrollment of 115. Highest level of offering: four or five year baccalaureate.

ACCREDITATIONS: BI

Arizona State University

Tempe, AZ 85287-0312
(602) 965-7276

Will confirm by mail or phone. Inquiry must include student's name (and maiden name if available), date of birth, social security number, years attended. Employers may obtain transcripts upon written request accompanied by a $5.00 fee and a signed release from the student, specifically stating to whom transcript should be sent. Requests should be directed to: Registrar's Office.

A doctoral-level institution with no medical school, with an enrollment of 42,626. Highest level of offering: doctorate.

ACCREDITATIONS: NH ARCH AUD BUS CLPSY COPSY ENG ENGT HSA JOUR LAW MT TED NASM NLN SCPSY SP CSWE DANCE

Arizona Western College

PO Box 929
Yuma, AZ 85366
(602) 726-1050

Will confirm attendance and degree by phone or mail. Inquiry must include student's name, date of birth, social security number, years attended, release. Employers may obtain transcripts upon written request accompanied by a $2.00 fee and a signed release from the student. Requests should be directed to: Registrar's Office.

A multiprogram two-year institution, with an enrollment of 7,000. Highest level of offering: one year but less than four years.

ACCREDITATIONS: NH NLN/AD

Arkansas Baptist College

1600 Bishop Street
Little Rock, AR 72202
(501) 374-7856

Will confirm attendance and degree by mail. Inquiry must include student's name, date of birth, social security number, years attended, release. Employers may obtain transcripts upon written request accompanied by a $1.50 fee and a signed release from the student.

A general baccalaureate institution, with an enrollment of 150. Highest level of offering: four or five year baccalaureate.

ACCREDITATIONS: NH

Arkansas College

PO Box 2317
Batesville, AR 72501
(501) 793-9813 Ext. 203
Fax (501) 698-4622

Will confirm attendance and degree by phone or mail. Inquiry must include student's name, date of birth, social security number. Employers may obtain transcripts upon written request accompanied by a $3.00 fee and a signed release from the student.

A general baccalaureate institution, with an enrollment of 800. Highest level of offering: four or five year baccalaureate.

ACCREDITATIONS: NH MT TED CSWE

Arkansas State University Beebe Branch

PO Drawer H
Beebe, AR 72012
(501) 882-6452 Ext. 61

Will confirm attendance and degree by mail. Inquiry must include student's name, social security number, years attended. Employers may obtain transcripts upon written request accompanied by a $1.00 fee and a signed release from the student.

A multiprogram two-year institution, with an enrollment of 1,600. Highest level of offering: one year but less than four years.

ACCREDITATIONS: NH

Arkansas State University Main Campus

PO Box 1630
State University, AR 72467
(501) 972-2031

Will confirm attendance and degree by phone or mail. Inquiry must include student's name, date of birth, social security number, years attended. Employers may obtain transcripts upon written request accompanied by a $2.00 fee and a signed release from the student. Requests should be directed to: Admission & Records Office.

A comprehensive institution with no medical school, with an enrollment of 9,700. Highest level of offering: doctorate.

ACCREDITATIONS: NH NLN/AD BUS ENG JOUR MT NASM NLN RAD CSWE TED

Arkansas Tech University

Russellville, AR 72801-2222
(501) 968-0272
Fax (501) 968-0683

Will confirm attendance and degree by phone, fax or mail. Inquiry must include student's name, date of birth, maiden name (if available), social security number, years attended. Employers may obtain transcripts upon written request accompanied by a $1.00 fee and a signed release from the student. Requests should be directed to: Registrar's Office.

A general baccalaureate institution, with an enrollment of 4,333. Highest level of offering: master's.

ACCREDITATIONS: NH MAC MRA NASM TED NLN ENG

Arlington Baptist College

3001 West Division
Arlington, TX 76012
(817) 461-8741 Ext. 108

Will confirm attendance and degree by phone or mail. Inquiry must include student's name. Employers may obtain transcripts upon written request accompanied by a $4.00 fee and a signed release from the student. Requests should be directed to: Registrar's Office.

A bachelor's or higher institution newly admitted to NCES, with an enrollment of 134. Highest level of offering: four or five year baccalaureate.

ACCREDITATIONS: BI

Armstrong College

2222 Harold Way
Berkeley, CA 94704
(510) 848-2500

Will confirm attendance and degree by mail. Inquiry must include student's name, social security number, years attended. Employers may obtain transcripts upon written request accompanied by a $5.00 fee and a signed release from the student. Requests should be directed to: Registrar's Office.

A business school, with an enrollment of 180. Highest level of offering: master's.

ACCREDITATIONS: WC JRCB

Armstrong State College

11935 Abercorn Street
Savannah, GA 31419-1997
(912) 927-5275
Fax (912) 927-5209

Will confirm attendance and degree by phone, fax or mail. Inquiry must include student's name, social security number, years attended. Employers may obtain transcripts upon written request accompanied by a $2.00 fee and a signed release from the student.

A comprehensive institution with no medical school, with an enrollment of 5,000. Highest level of offering: beyond master's but less than doctorate.

ACCREDITATIONS: SC NLN/AD DH MRT NASM NLN RSTH TED MT RAD

Arrowhead Community College–Hibbing Campus

(See Hibbing Community Campus)

Art Academy of Cincinnati

1125 St. Gregory Street
Cincinnati, OH 45202
(513) 721-5205

Will confirm degree by phone or mail. Inquiry must include student's name, date of birth, social security number, years attended. Employers may obtain transcripts upon written request accompanied by a $2.00 fee and a signed release from the student. Requests should be directed to: Registrar's Office.

A visual and performing arts school, with an enrollment of 235. Highest level of offering: four or five year baccalaureate.

ACCREDITATIONS: NH

Art Center College of Design

1700 Lida Street
Pasadena, CA 91103-1999
(818) 584-5040
Fax (818) 405-9104

Will confirm attendance and degree by mail, phone or fax. Inquiry must include student's name and date of birth. Employers may obtain transcripts upon written request accompanied by a $2.00 fee and a signed release from the student.

A visual and performing arts school, with an enrollment of 1,200. Highest level of offering: master's.

ACCREDITATIONS: WASC NASAD

Art Institute of Atlanta

3376 Peachtree Road North East
Atlanta, GA 30326
(404) 266-1341 Ext. 350
Fax (404) 266-2662 Ext. 408

Will confirm degree by mail or fax. Inquiry must include student's name, social security number, years attended and a signed release from student. Employers may obtain transcripts upon written request accompanied by a $2.00 fee and a signed release from the student. Requests should be directed to: Registrar's Office.

A multiple program two-year institution, with an enrollment of 1,300. Highest level of offering: one year but less than four years.

ACCREDITATIONS: SC

Art Institute of Dallas

2 No. Park, 8080 Park Lane
Dallas, TX 75231
(214) 692-8080

Will confirm attendance and degree by mail. Inquiry must include student's name, social security number, years attended. Employers may obtain transcripts upon written request accompanied by a $2.00 fee and a signed release from the student.

A two-year institution newly admitted to NCES, with an enrollment of 900. Highest level of offering: one year but less than four years.

ACCREDITATIONS: SC

Art Institute of Fort Lauderdale

1799 South East 17th Street
Fort Lauderdale, FL 33316
(305) 463-3000 Ext. 451

Will confirm attendance and degree by mail or phone. Inquiry must include student's name, social security number, years attended. Employers may obtain transcripts upon written request accompanied by a $3.00 fee and a signed release from the student. Requests should be directed to: Registrar's Office.

A single program two-year institution, with an enrollment of 2,500. Highest level of offering: one year but less than four years.
ACCREDITATIONS: NATTS

Art Institute of Houston

1900 Yorktown
Houston, TX 77056
(713) 623-2040 Ext. 750

Will confirm attendance and degree by mail or phone. Inquiry must include student's name and social security number. Employers may obtain transcripts upon written request accompanied by a $2.00 fee and a signed release from the student. Requests should be directed to: Registrar's Office.

A two-year institution newly admitted to NCES, with an enrollment of 1,000. Highest level of offering: one year but less than four years.
ACCREDITATIONS: NATTS

Art Institute of Philadelphia

1622 Chestnut Street
Philadelphia, PA 19103
(215) 567-7080
Fax (215) 246-3339

Will confirm attendance and degree by mail. Inquiry must include student's name, social security number, years attended. Employers may obtain transcripts upon written request accompanied by a $2.00 fee and a signed release from the student. Requests should be directed to: Registrar's Office.

A single program two-year institution, with an enrollment of 1,200. Highest level of offering: one year but less than four years.
ACCREDITATIONS: NATTS

Art Institute of Pittsburgh

526 Penn Avenue
Pittsburgh, PA 15222
(412) 263-6600 Ext. 252
Fax (412) 263-6600 Ext. 313

Will confirm attendance and degree by mail, phone or fax. Inquiry must include student's name, social security number, years attended. Employers may obtain transcripts upon written request accompanied by a $2.00 fee and a signed release from the student. Attn: Registrar's Office.

A single program two-year institution, with an enrollment of 1,961. Highest level of offering: one year but less than four years.
ACCREDITATIONS: NATTS

Art Institute of Seattle

2323 Elliot Avenue
Seattle, WA 98121
(206) 448-0900 Ext. 884

Will confirm attendance and degree by phone or mail. Inquiry must include student's name and social security number. Employers may obtain transcripts upon written request accompanied by a $2.00 fee and a signed release from the student.

A two-year institution newly admitted to NCES, with an enrollment of 602. Highest level of offering: one year but less than four years.
ACCREDITATIONS: NATTS

Arthur D. Little Management Education Institute

35 Acorn Park
Cambridge, MA 02140
(617) 864-5657 Ext. 3268
Fax (617) 864-5411

Will confirm attendance and degree by phone, fax or mail. Inquiry must include student's name and years attended. Employers may obtain transcripts upon written request accompanied by a signed release from the student.

A business school, with an enrollment of 67. Highest level of offering: master's.
ACCREDITATIONS: EH

Asbury College

1 Macklem Drive
Wilmore, KY 40390
(606) 858-3511 Ext. 325

Will confirm attendance and degree by mail or phone. Inquiry must include student's name, date of birth, social security number, years attended. Requests should be directed to: Registrar's Office. Employers may obtain transcripts upon written request accompanied by a $3.00 fee and a signed release from the student.

A general baccalaureate institution, with an enrollment of 1,882. Highest level of offering: four or five year baccalaureate.
ACCREDITATIONS: SC NASM

Asbury Theological Seminary

204 North Lexington Avenue
Wilmore, KY 40390
(606) 858-3581 Ext. 208

Will confirm attendance and degree by phone or mail. Inquiry must include student's name and social security number. Employers may obtain transcripts upon written request accompanied by a $2.00 fee and a signed release from the student.

A school of philosophy, religion and theology, with an enrollment of 742. Highest level of offering: doctorate.
ACCREDITATIONS: SC THEOL

Asheville Buncombe Technical College

340 Victoria Road
Asheville, NC 28801
(704) 254-1921 Ext. 147
Fax (704) 251-6355

Will confirm attendance and degree by phone or mail. Inquiry must include student's name, date of birth, social security number. Employers may obtain transcripts upon written request accompanied by a signed release from the student.

A multiprogram two-year institution, with an enrollment of 3,200. Highest level of offering: one year but less than four years.
ACCREDITATIONS: SC DA DH MLTAD RAD

Ashland University

401 College Avenue
Ashland, OH 44805
(419) 289-4142 Ext. 5031

Will confirm attendance and degree by phone or mail. Inquiry must include student's name, social security number, years attended. Requests should be directed to: Registrar's Office. Employers may obtain transcripts upon written request accompanied by a $2.00 fee and a signed release from the student.

A comprehensive institution with no medical school, with an enrollment of 5,100. Highest level of offering: doctorate.
ACCREDITATIONS: NH NASM TED THEOL

Asnuntuck Community College

170 Elm St.
Enfield, CT 06082
(203) 253-3017
Fax (203) 253-3029

Will confirm attendance and degree by phone or mail. Inquiry must include student's name and social security number. Employers may obtain transcripts upon written request accompanied by a signed release from the student.

A multiprogram two-year institution, with an enrollment of 1,970. Highest level of offering: one year but less than four years.
ACCREDITATIONS: EH

Assemblies of God Theological Seminary

1445 Boonville Avenue
Springfield, MO 65802
(417) 862-3344 Ext. 5611

Will confirm attendance and degree by phone or mail. Inquiry must include student's name and social security number. Employers may obtain transcripts upon written request by student accompanied by a $3.00 fee and a signed release from the student.

A school of philosophy, religion and theology, with an enrollment of 305. Highest level of offering: beyond master's but less than doctorate.
ACCREDITATIONS: NH

Associated Beth Rivkah Schools

310 Crown Street
Brooklyn, NY 11225
(718) 735-0414
Fax (718) 735-0422

Will confirm attendance and degree by mail. Inquiry must include student's name, date of birth, social security number, years attended, release. Employers may obtain transcripts upon written request accompanied by a $15.00 fee and a signed release from the student.

A specialized non-degree granting institution, with an enrollment of 343. Highest level of offering: undergraduate non-degree granting.

ACCREDITATIONS: 3IC

Assumption College for Sisters

Hilltop Road
Mendham, NJ 07945
(201) 543-6528

Will confirm attendance and degree by mail. Inquiry must include student's name, date of birth, social security number, years attended. Employers may obtain transcripts upon written request accompanied by a signed release from the student. Requests should be directed to: Registrar's Office.

A multiprogram two-year institution, with an enrollment of 40. Highest level of offering: one year but less than four years.

ACCREDITATIONS: M

Assumption College

500 Salisbury Street
Worcester, MA 01609
(508) 752-5615 Ext. 355

Will confirm attendance and degree by phone or mail. Inquiry must include student's name, social security number, years attended. Employers may obtain transcripts upon written request accompanied by a $2.00 fee and a signed release from the student.

A comprehensive institution with no medical school, with an enrollment of 2,474. Highest level of offering: beyond master's but less than doctorate.

ACCREDITATIONS: EH NLN

Athenaeum of Ohio

6616 Beechmont Avenue
Cincinnati, OH 45230
(513) 231-2223 Ext. 18
Fax (513) 231-3254

Will confirm attendance and degree by mail or phone. Inquiry must include student's name, social security number, years attended. Employers may obtain transcripts upon written request accompanied by a $2.00 fee and a signed release from the student.

A school of philosophy, religion and theology, with an enrollment of 272. Highest level of offering: master's.

ACCREDITATIONS: NH THEOL

Athens State College

Athens, AL 35611
(205) 233-8100 Ext. 167
Fax (205) 233-8164

Will confirm attendance and degree by phone, fax or mail. Inquiry must include student's name, date of birth, social security number, years attended. Employers may obtain transcripts upon written request accompanied by a $3.00 fee and a signed release from the student. Requests should be directed to: Registrar's Office.

A general baccalaureate institution, with an enrollment of 2,520. Highest level of offering: four or five year baccalaureate.

ACCREDITATIONS: SC

Atlanta Christian College

2605 Ben Hill Road
East Point, GA 30344
(404) 669-2095
Fax (404) 669-2024

Will confirm attendance and degree by phone or mail. Inquiry must include student's name, date of birth, years attended. Employers may obtain transcripts upon written request accompanied by a $2.00 fee and a signed release from the student.

A school of biblical studies, arts and sciences, with an enrollment of 225. Highest level of offering: four or five year baccalaureate.

ACCREDITATIONS: BI SACS

Atlanta College of Art

1280 Peachtree Street North East
Atlanta, GA 30309
(404) 898-1164 Ext. 555
Fax (404) 898-9577

Will confirm attendance and degree by phone or mail. Inquiry must include student's name and social security number. Employers may obtain transcripts upon written request accompanied by a $2.00 fee and a signed release from the student.

A visual and performing arts school, with an enrollment of 247. Highest level of offering: four or five year baccalaureate.

ACCREDITATIONS: SC ART

Atlanta Junior College

1630 Stewart Avenue South West
Atlanta, GA 30310
(404) 756-4001

Will confirm attendance and degree by phone or mail. Inquiry must include student's name, social security number, years attended. Employers may obtain transcripts upon written request accompanied by a $1.00 fee and a signed release from the student. Requests should be directed to: Student Service Office.

A multiprogram two-year institution, with an enrollment of 1,453. Highest level of offering: one year but less than four years.

ACCREDITATIONS: SC

Atlanta University

(See Clark Atlanta University)

Atlantic Christian College

(See Barton College)

Atlantic Community College

Black Horse Pike
Mays Landing, NJ 08330
(609) 343-4927
Fax (609) 343-4914

Will confirm attendance and degree by mail or fax. Inquiry must include student's name, social security number, years attended. Employers may obtain transcripts upon written request accompanied by a $1.00 fee and a signed release from the student.

A multiprogram two-year institution, with an enrollment of 5,562. Highest level of offering: two years but less than four years.

ACCREDITATIONS: M NLN/AD ENGT MLTAD PTAA RSTH RSTHT

Atlantic Union College

South Lancaster, MA 01561
(617) 368-2000 Ext. 2215

Will confirm attendance and degree by mail. Inquiry must include student's name, years attended, release. Employers may obtain transcripts upon written request accompanied by a $3.00 fee and a signed release from the student. Requests should be directed to: Office of Academic Records.

A general baccalaureate institution, with an enrollment of 600. Highest level of offering: four or five year baccalaureate.

ACCREDITATIONS: EH NLN/AD TED CSWE

Auburn University at Montgomery

7300 University Drive
Montgomery, AL 36117
(205) 244-3000 or (205) 244-3762

Will confirm attendance and degree by phone or mail. Inquiry must include student's name and social security number. Employers may obtain transcripts upon written request accompanied by a $3.00 fee and a signed release from the student.

A comprehensive institution with no medical school, with an enrollment of 6,690. Highest level of offering: beyond master's but less than doctorate.

ACCREDITATIONS: SC MT NLN TED

Auburn University Main Campus

100 Mary Martin Hall
Auburn, AL 36849-5146
(205) 844-4770

Will confirm attendance and degree by phone or mail. Inquiry must include student's name, date of birth, social security number, years attended. Employers may obtain transcripts upon written request accompanied by a $3.00 fee and a signed release from the student. Requests should be directed to: Registrar's Office.

A doctoral-level institution with a veterinary medical school, with an enrollment of 21,836. Highest level of offering: doctorate.

ACCREDITATIONS: SC ARCH ART AUD BUS CLPSY DIET ENG ENGT FIDER FOR MUS TED VET LSAR MFCD NUN PHAR SP SW

Augsburg College

731 21st Avenue South
Minneapolis, MN 55454
(612) 330-1036
Fax (612) 330-1649

Will confirm attendance and degree by phone or mail. Inquiry must include student's name and years attended. Employers may obtain transcripts upon written request accompanied by a $2.00 fee and a signed release from the student.

A general baccalaureate institution, with an enrollment of 2,800. Highest level of offering: master's.

ACCREDITATIONS: NH NLN CSWE TED

Augusta College

2500 Walton Way
Augusta, GA 30910
(404) 737-1408
Fax (404) 737-1777

Will confirm attendance and degree by phone or mail. Inquiry must include student's name and social security number. Employers may obtain transcripts upon written request accompanied by a $3.00 fee and a signed release from the student.

A comprehensive institution with no medical school, with an enrollment of 5,300. Highest level of offering: beyond master's but less than doctorate.

ACCREDITATIONS: SDE

Augustana College

639–38th Street
Rock Island, IL 61201
(309) 794-7211
Fax (309) 784-7422

Will confirm attendance and degree by phone or mail. Inquiry must include student's name, social security number, years attended. Employers may obtain transcripts upon written request accompanied by a $2.00 fee and a signed release from the student.

A general baccalaureate institution, with an enrollment of 2,158. Highest level of offering: bachelor's.

ACCREDITATIONS: NH

Augustana College

29th and Summit
Sioux Falls, SD 57197
(605) 336-4121

Will confirm attendance and degree by phone or mail. Inquiry must include student's name, social security number, years attended. Employers may obtain transcripts upon written request accompanied by a signed release from the student.

A general baccalaureate institution, with an enrollment of 1,914. Highest level of offering: master's.

ACCREDITATIONS: NH NASM NLN CSWE TED

Aurora University

347 South Gladstone Avenue
Aurora, IL 60506-4892
(708) 892-6431
Fax (708) 844-5463

Will confirm attendance and degree by phone or mail. Inquiry must include student's name, date of birth, social security number, years attended. Employers may obtain transcripts upon written request accompanied by a $3.00 fee and a signed release from the student.

A general baccalaureate institution, with an enrollment of 2,102. Highest level of offering: master's.

ACCREDITATIONS: CSWE

Austin College

Attn: Registrar's Office
Sherman, TX 75091-1177
(903) 813-2000

Will confirm attendance and degree by phone or mail. Inquiry must include student's name, date of birth, social security number, years attended. Employers may obtain transcripts upon written request accompanied by a $2.00 fee and a signed release from the student.

A general baccalaureate institution, with an enrollment of 1,200. Highest level of offering: master's.

ACCREDITATIONS: SC

Austin Community College

1600 8th Avenue North West
Austin, MN 55912
(507) 433-0517
Fax (507) 433-0515

Will confirm attendance and degree by phone, fax or mail. Inquiry must include student's name, date of birth, social security number. Employers may obtain transcripts upon written request accompanied by a signed release from the student.

A multiprogram two-year institution, with an enrollment of 1,200. Highest level of offering: two years.

ACCREDITATIONS: NH NLN/AD

Austin Community College

5930 Middle Fiskville Road
Austin, TX 78752
(512) 495-7503

Will confirm attendance and degree by phone or mail. Inquiry must include student's name, date of birth, social security number, years attended. Employers may obtain transcripts upon written request accompanied by a $3.00 fee and a signed release from the student.

A multiprogram two-year institution, with an enrollment of 17,807. Highest level of offering: one year but less than four years.

ACCREDITATIONS: SC NLN/AD MLTAD PTAA RAD SURGT

Austin Peay State University

Registrar's Office
PO Box 4448
Clarksville, TN 37044
(615) 648-7121
Fax (615) 648-7475

Will confirm attendance and degree by phone, fax or mail. Inquiry must include student's name, social security number, years attended. Employers may obtain transcripts upon written request accompanied by a signed release from the student.

A comprehensive institution with no medical school, with an enrollment of 5,282. Highest level of offering: beyond master's but less than doctorate.

ACCREDITATIONS: SC NASM NLN TED

Austin Presbyterian Theological Seminary

100 East 27th Street
Austin, TX 78705
(512) 472-6736 Ext. 28

Will confirm attendance and degree by mail. Inquiry must include student's name and years attended. Employers may obtain transcripts upon written request accompanied by a $3.00 fee and a signed release from the student.

A school of philosophy, religion and theology, with an enrollment of 177. Highest level of offering: doctorate.

ACCREDITATIONS: SC THEOL

Authority

(See Eastern Virginia Medical School.)

Averett College

420 West Main Street
Danville, VA 24541
(804) 791-5600
Fax (804) 799-0658

Will confirm attendance by phone or mail. Inquiry must include student's name, social security number, years attended. Employers may obtain transcripts upon written request accompanied by a $4.00 fee and a signed release from the student.

A general baccalaureate institution, with an enrollment of 1,209. Highest level of offering: master's.

ACCREDITATIONS: SC CSWE

Avila College

11901 Wornall Road
Kansas City, MO 64145
(816) 942-8400 Ext. 210
Fax (816) 942-3362

Will confirm attendance and degree by phone, fax or mail. Inquiry must include student's name, date of birth, social security number. Employers may obtain transcripts upon written request accompanied by a $2.00 fee and a signed release from the student.

A general baccalaureate institution, with an enrollment of 1,662. Highest level of offering: master's.

ACCREDITATIONS: NH NLN RAD CSWE

Azusa Pacific University

Citrus and Alosta
Azusa, CA 91702
(818) 969-3434 Ext. 3391

Will confirm attendance and degree by phone or mail. Inquiry must include student's name, date of birth, social security number. Employers may obtain transcripts upon written request accompanied by a $4.00 fee and a signed release from the student.

A comprehensive institution with no medical school, with an enrollment of 2,578. Highest level of offering: master's.

ACCREDITATIONS: WC NLN CSWE

B

Babson College

Babson Park, MA 02157
(617) 239-5438
Fax (617) 239-4194

Will confirm attendance and degree by phone, fax or mail. Inquiry must include student's name, years attended. Employers may obtain transcripts upon written request and a signed release from the student.

A business school, with an enrollment of 3,187. Highest level of offering: beyond master's but less than doctorate.

ACCREDITATIONS: EH BUS

Bacone College

9903 W. Bacone Rd.
Muskogee, OK 74403-1597
(918) 683-4581 Ext. 275

Will confirm attendance and degree by phone or mail. Inquiry must include student's name, maiden name, date of birth, social security number, years attended. Employers may obtain transcripts upon written request accompanied by a signed release from the student.

A multiprogram two-year institution, with an enrollment of 6129. Highest level of offering: one year but less than four years.

ACCREDITATIONS: NH NLN/AD RAD

Bailey Technical School-Kansas City

(See ITT Technical Institute in Kansas City, MO)

Bailey Technical School-St. Louis

(See ITT technical Institute in St. Louis, MO)

Bainbridge College

Highway 84 East
Bainbridge, GA 31717
(912) 248-2500
Fax (912) 248-2589

Will confirm attendance and degree by mail. Inquiry must include student's name, social security number, years attended, release. Employers may obtain transcripts upon written request accompanied by a $1.00 fee and a signed release from the student.

A multiprogram two-year institution, with an enrollment of 975. Highest level of offering: one year but less than four years.

ACCREDITATIONS: SC

Bainbridge Junior College

(See Bainbridge College)

Bais Binyomin Academy

132 Prospect Street
Stamford, CT 06901
(203) 325-4351

Will confirm attendance and degree by mail. Inquiry must include student's name and date of birth. Employers may obtain transcripts upon written request accompanied by a $5.00 fee and a signed release from the student.

A school of philosophy, religion and theology, with an enrollment of 33. Highest level of offering: first professional degree.

ACCREDITATIONS: RABN

Bais Fruma

4601 14th Ave.
Brooklyn, NY 11219
(718)633-2305

Will confirm attendance and degree by mail. Inquiry must include student's name, date of birth, social security number, years attended. Employers may obtain transcripts upon written request accompanied by a signed release from the student.

A bachelor's or higher institution newly admitted to NCES, with an enrollment of 1,000. Highest level of offering: undergraduate non-degree granting.

ACCREDITATIONS: 3IC

Baker College of Flint

G150 W. Bristol Road
Flint, MI 48507
(313) 766-4115 or 766-4117
Fax (313) 766-4049

Will confirm attendance and degree by phone, fax or mail. Inquiry must include student's name, date of birth, social security number, years attended. Employers may obtain transcripts upon written request accompanied by a $2.00 fee and a signed release from the student. Requests should be directed to: Registrar's Office.

A multiprogram four-year institution, with an enrollment of 6,500. Highest level of offering: one year but less than four years.

ACCREDITATIONS: NH JRCB MAC

Baker College of Mt. Clemens

34950 Little Mack
Mt. Clemens, MI 48043-7192
(313) 465-1700
Fax (313) 791-6611

Will confirm attendance and degree by phone or mail. Inquiry must include student's name, date of birth, social security number, years attended. Employers may obtain transcripts upon written request accompanied by a $2.00 fee and a signed release from the student. Requests should be directed to: Registrar's Office.

A multiprogram four-year institution, with an enrollment of 300. Highest level of offering: one year but less than four years

ACCREDITATIONS: NH

Baker College of Muskegon

(Formerly Muskegon Business College)
34950 Little Mack
Mt. Clemens, MI 48043-7192
(313) 465-1700
Fax (313) 791-6611

Will confirm attendance and degree by phone or mail. Inquiry must include student's name, date of birth, social security number, years attended. Employers may obtain transcripts upon written request accompanied by a $2.00 fee and a signed release from the student. Requests should be directed to: Registrar's Office.

A multiprogram four-year institution, with an enrollment of 300. Highest level of offering: one year but less than four years

ACCREDITATIONS: NH

Baker College of Owosso

1020 S. Washington Street
Owosso, MI 48867
(517) 723-5251
Fax (517) 723-3355

Will confirm attendance and degree by phone or mail. Inquiry must include student's name, date of birth, social security number, years attended. Employers may obtain transcripts upon written request accompanied by a $2.00 fee and a signed release from the student. Requests should be directed to: Registrar's Office.

A multiprogram four-year institution, with an enrollment of 1,000. Highest level of offering: one year but less than four years

ACCREDITATIONS: NH

Baker College of Pontiac

1500 University Drive
Auburn Hills, MI 48326
(313) 340-0600
Fax (313) 340-0608

Will confirm attendance and degree by mail. Inquiry must include student's name, date of birth, social security number, years attended. Employers may obtain transcripts upon written request accompanied by a $1.00 fee and a signed release from the student. Requests should be directed to: Registrar's Office.

A multiprogram four-year institution, with an enrollment of 175. Highest level of offering: one year but less than four years

ACCREDITATIONS: NH

Baker College of Port Huron

3403 Lapeer Rd.
Port Huron, MI 48060
(313) 985-7000
Fax (313) 985-7066

Will confirm attendance and degree by phone or mail. Inquiry must include student's name, date of birth, social security number, years attended. Employers may obtain transcripts upon written request accompanied by a signed release from the student. Requests should be directed to: Registrar's Office.

A multiprogram four-year institution, with an enrollment of 185. Highest level of offering: one year but less than four years

ACCREDITATIONS: NH JRCB MAC

Baker University

8th & Grove St.
Baldwin City, KS 66006
(913) 594-6451 Ext. 530
Fax (913) 594-2252

Will confirm attendance and degree by phone, fax or mail. Inquiry must include student's name, social security number, and dates attended. Employers may obtain transcripts upon written request accompanied by a $3.00 fee and a signed release from the student.

A general baccalaureate institution, with an enrollment of 16673. Highest level of offering: master's.

ACCREDITATIONS: NCA

Bakersfield College

1801 Panorama Drive
Bakersfield, CA 93305
(805) 395-4011

Will confirm attendance and degree by phone or mail. Inquiry must include student's name, date of birth, social security number, years attended. Requests should be directed to: Transcript Department. Employers may obtain transcripts upon written request accompanied by a $2.00 fee and a signed release from the student.

A multiprogram two-year institution, with an enrollment of 10,500. Highest level of offering: one year but less than four years.

ACCREDITATIONS: WJ DA RAD

Baldwin–Wallace College

275 Eastland Road
Berea, OH 44017
(216) 826-2126;2127;2128;2129
Fax (216) 826-2329

Will confirm attendance and degree by phone or mail. Inquiry must include student's name, social security number, years attended. Employers may obtain transcripts upon written request accompanied by a $3.00 fee and a signed release from the student.

A general baccalaureate institution, with an enrollment of 3,705. Highest level of offering: master's.

ACCREDITATIONS: NH NASM TED

Ball State University

Registrar's Office
Muncie, IN 47306
(317) 285-1722
Fax (317) 285-8765

Will confirm degree by phone or mail. Inquiry must include student's name, date of birth, social security number, years attended. Employers may obtain transcripts upon written request accompanied by a signed release from the student.

A doctoral-level institution with no medical school, with an enrollment of 20,000. Highest level of offering: doctorate.

ACCREDITATIONS: NH NLN/AD ARCH AUD BUS COPSY IPSY JOUR TED LSAR NASM NLN PTA SP CSWE SCPSY

Baltimore Hebrew University

5800 Park Heights Avenue
Baltimore, MD 21215
(410) 578-6900 or 578-6918

Will confirm attendance and degree by mail or phone. Inquiry must include student's name, social security number, years attended. Employers may obtain transcripts upon written request accompanied by a $5.00 fee and a signed release from the student.

A school of Jewish studies, with an enrollment of 231. Highest level of offering: doctorate.

ACCREDITATIONS: M

Bangor Theological Seminary

300 Union Street
Bangor, ME 04401
(207) 942-6781 Ext. 36
Fax (207) 942-4914

Will confirm attendance and degree by mail or fax. Inquiry must include student's name, date of birth, years attended. Employers may obtain transcripts upon written request accompanied by a $2.00 fee and a signed release from the student.

A school of philosophy, religion and theology, with an enrollment of 164. Highest level of offering: doctorate.

ACCREDITATIONS: NEAS&C ATS

Bank Street College of Education

Attn: Registrar
610 West 112th Street
New York, NY 10025
(212) 222-6700 Ext. 525

Will confirm attendance and degree by mail. Inquiry must include student's name, date of birth, social security number, years attended, release. Employers may obtain transcripts upon written request accompanied by a $7.00 fee and a signed release from the student.

A school of education, with an enrollment of 869. Highest level of offering: master's.

ACCREDITATIONS: M NY

Baptist Bible College of Pennsylvania

PO Box 800
538 Venard Road
Clarks Summit, PA 18411
(717) 587-1172
Fax (717) 586-1753

Will confirm attendance and degree by phone or mail. Inquiry must include student's name, social security number, years attended. Employers may obtain transcripts upon written request accompanied by a signed release from the student.

A school specializing in Christian ministry vocations, with an enrollment of 685. Highest level of offering: master's.

ACCREDITATIONS: M BI

Baptist Bible College

628 East Kearney
Springfield, MO 65803
(417) 869-6000 Ext. 2220 or 2219
Fax (417) 831-8029

Will confirm attendance and degree by phone or mail. Inquiry must include student's name, date of birth, social security number, years attended. Employers may obtain transcripts upon written request accompanied by a $3.00 fee and a signed release from the student.

A school of philosophy, religion and theology, with an enrollment of 715. Highest level of offering: four or five year baccalaureate.

ACCREDITATIONS: BI

Baptist Bible Institute

(See Florida Baptist Theological College)

Baptist College at Charleston

(See Charleston Southern University)

Barat College

700 East Westleigh Road
Lake Forest, IL 60045
(708) 234-3000
Fax (708) 615-5000

Will confirm attendance and degree by mail. Inquiry must include student's name, social security number, years attended. Employers may obtain transcripts upon written request accompanied by a $3.00 fee and a signed release from the student.

A general baccalaureate institution, with an enrollment of 688. Highest level of offering: four or five year baccalaureate.

ACCREDITATIONS: NH

Barber–Scotia College

145 Cabarrus Avenue West
Concord, NC 28025
(704) 786-5171 Ext. 221
Fax (704) 784-3817

Will confirm attendance and degree by mail. Inquiry must include student's name and years attended. Employers may obtain transcripts upon written request accompanied by a $2.00 fee and a signed release from the student.

A general baccalaureate institution, with an enrollment of 362. Highest level of offering: four or five year baccalaureate.

ACCREDITATIONS: SC

Barclay College

(Formerly Friends Bible College)
PO Box 288
Haviland, KS 67059
(316) 862-5252

Will confirm attendance and degree by
phone or mail. Inquiry must include student's name and social security number.
Employers may obtain transcripts upon
written request accompanied by a $3.00 fee
and a signed release from the student. A
school of philosophy, religion and theology,
with an enrollment of 116. Highest level of
offering: four or five year baccaleaureate.
ACCREDITATIONS: BI

Bard College

Annandale–On–Hudson, NY 12504
(914) 758-6822 Ext. 458
Fax (914) 758-4294

Will confirm attendance and degree by
phone or mail. Inquiry must include student's name and years attended. Employers
may obtain transcripts upon written request
accompanied by a $2.00 fee and a signed
release from the student.

A general baccalaureate institution, with an
enrollment of 1,080. Highest level of offering: master's.

ACCREDITATIONS: M NY

Barnard College

3009 Broadway
New York, NY 10027-6598
(212) 854-2011

Will confirm attendance and degree by
mail. Inquiry must include student's name,
date of birth, years attended. Employers
may obtain transcripts upon written request
accompanied by a $3.00 fee and a signed
release from the student.

A general baccalaureate institution, with an
enrollment of 2,187. Highest level of offering: four or five year baccalaureate.

ACCREDITATIONS: M DANCE NY

Barrington College

(See Gordon College)

Barry University

11300 North East 2nd Avenue
Miami Shore, FL 33161
(305) 899-3660

Will confirm attendance and degree by
phone or mail. Inquiry must include student's name, date of birth, social security
number, years attended. Employers may obtain transcripts upon written request accompanied by a $2.00 fee and a signed release
from the student.

A comprehensive institution with no medical school, with an enrollment of 6,701.
Highest level of offering: doctorate.

ACCREDITATIONS: SC NLN CSWE POD

Barstow College

2700 Barstow Road
Barstow, CA 92311
(619) 252-2411 Ext. 295

Will confirm attendance and degree by
mail. Inquiry must include student's name,
social security number, years attended, release. Requests should be directed to:
Student Records. Employers may obtain
transcripts upon written request accompanied by a $2.00 fee and a signed release
from the student.

A multiprogram two-year institution, with
an enrollment of 2,129. Highest level of offering: one year but less than four years.

ACCREDITATIONS: WJ

Bartlesville Wesleyan College

2201 Silver–Lake Road
Bartlesville, OK 74006
(918) 333-6151 Ext. 217
Fax (918) 333-6210

Will confirm attendance and degree by
phone or mail. Inquiry must include student's name, date of birth, years attended.
Employers may obtain transcripts upon
written request accompanied by a $2.00 fee
and a signed release from the student.

A general baccalaureate institution, with an
enrollment of 448. Highest level of offering: four or five year baccalaureate.

ACCREDITATIONS: NH

Barton College

(Formerly Atlantic Christian College)
College Station
Wilson, NC 27893
(919) 399-6300
Fax (919) 237-4957

Will confirm attendance and degree by mail
or phone. Inquiry must include student's
name, date of birth, social security number,
years attended. Employers may obtain transcripts upon written request accompanied
by a $2.00 fee and a signed release from the
student. Requests should be directed to:
Registrar's Office.

A general baccalaureate institution, with an
enrollment of 1,348. Highest level of offering: four or five year baccalaureate.

ACCREDITATIONS: SC NLN TED

Barton County Community College

Rural Route 3
Great Bend, KS 67530
(316) 792-2701 Ext. 212

Will confirm attendance and degree by
phone or mail. Inquiry must include student's name, social security number, years
attended. Employers may obtain transcripts
upon written request accompanied by a
$2.00 fee and a signed release from the stu-
dent.

A multiprogram two-year institution, with
an enrollment of 5,113. Highest level of offering: one year but less than four years.

ACCREDITATIONS: NH NLN/AD MLTAD

Basic Institute of Technology

4455 Chippewa
Saint Louis, MO 63116
(314) 771-1200

Will confirm attendance and degree by
mail. Inquiry must include student's name,
date of birth, social security number, years
attended. Employers may obtain transcripts
upon written request accompanied by a
$4.00 fee and a signed release from the stu-
dent.

A single program two-year institution, with
an enrollment of 80. Highest level of offering: one year but less than four years.

ACCREDITATIONS: NATTS

Bassist College

2000 South West Fifth Avenue
Portland, OR 97201-4972
(503) 228-6528
Fax (503) 228-4227

Will confirm attendance (and degree with a
written request from the student) by phone.
Inquiry must include student's name, date
of birth, social security number. Employers
may obtain transcripts upon written request
accompanied by a $5.00 fee and a signed
release from the student.

A multiprogram two and four year institution, with an enrollment of 250. Highest
level of offering: four or five year baccalaureate.

ACCREDITATIONS: NW

Bastyr College of Naturopathic Medicine

(Formerly John Bastyr College of
Naturopathic Medicine)
144 North East 54th Street
Seattle, WA 98105
(206) 523-9585 Ext. 29

Will confirm attendance and degree by
phone or mail. Inquiry must include student's name. Employers may obtain transcripts upon written request accompanied
by a $3.00 fee and a signed release from the
student.

A bachelor's or higher institution newly admitted to NCES, with an enrollment of 180.
Highest level of offering: first professional
degree.

ACCREDITATIONS: NW

Bates College

Lewiston, ME 04240
(207) 786-6096

Will confirm attendance and degree by
phone or mail. Inquiry must include student's name, date of birth, years attended.
Employers may obtain transcripts upon
written request accompanied by a $2.00 fee
and a signed release from the student.

A general baccalaureate institution, with an
enrollment of 1,519. Highest level of offering: four or five year baccalaureate.

ACCREDITATIONS: EH

Bauder Fashion College

508 South Center
Arlington, TX 76010
(817) 277-6666 Ext. 33
Fax (817) 274-9701

Will confirm attendance and degree by phone or mail. Inquiry must include student's name, social security number, years attended. Employers may obtain transcripts upon written request accompanied by a signed release from the student and a $10.00 fee.

A single program two-year institution, with an enrollment of 476. Highest level of offering: one year but less than four years.
ACCREDITATIONS: SC NATTS

Bauder Fashion College

3500 Peachtree Road North East
Atlanta, GA 30326
(404) 237-7573
Fax (404) 237-1641

Will confirm attendance and degree by phone or mail. Inquiry must include student's name, social security number, years attended, release. Employers may obtain transcripts upon written request accompanied by a $2.00 fee and a signed release from the student.

A single program two-year institution, with an enrollment of 675. Highest level of offering: one year but less than four years.
ACCREDITATIONS: SC NATTS

Bay–Valley Technical Institute

c/o Institute of Business and Technology
2550 Scott Boulevard
Santa Clara, CA 95050
(408) 727-1060

Will confirm attendance and degree by mail. Inquiry must include student's name, social security number, years attended, release. Employers may obtain transcripts upon written request accompanied by a signed release from the student.

A single program two-year institution, with an enrollment of 515. Highest level of offering: one year but less than four years.
ACCREDITATIONS: NATTS

Bay De Noc Community College

2001 North Lincoln Road
Escanaba, MI 49829--2511
(906) 786-5802 Ext. 148
Fax (906) 786-6555

Will confirm attendance and degree by phone or mail. Inquiry must include student's name, social security number, years attended. Employers may obtain transcripts upon written request accompanied by a $1.00 fee and a signed release from the student. Requests should be directed to: Student Records Department.

A multiprogram two-year institution, with an enrollment of 1,801. Highest level of offering: one year but less than four years.
ACCREDITATIONS: NH

Bay Path Junior College

588 Longmeadow Street
Longmeadow, MA 01106
(413) 567-0621 Ext. 222

Will confirm attendance and degree by phone or mail. Inquiry must include student's name, social security number, years attended. Employers may obtain transcripts upon written request accompanied by a $4.00 fee and a signed release from the student.

A multiprogram two-year institution, with an enrollment of 550. Highest level of offering: one year but less than four years.
ACCREDITATIONS: EH MAC

Bay State College of Business

122 Commonwealth Avenue
Boston, MA 02116
(617) 236-8035 Ext. 29

Will confirm attendance and degree by phone or mail. Inquiry must include student's name, date of birth, social security number, years attended. Employers may obtain transcripts upon written request accompanied by a $3.00 fee and a signed release from the student.

A multiprogram two-year institution, with an enrollment of 750. Highest level of offering: one year but less than four years.
ACCREDITATIONS: EH EV JRCB MAAB

Baylor College of Dentistry

3302 Gaston Avenue
Dallas, TX 75246
(214) 828-8230
Fax (214) 828-8346

Will confirm attendance and degree by phone or mail. Inquiry must include student's name, social security number, years attended. Employers may obtain transcripts upon written request accompanied by a $2.00 fee and a signed release from the student.

A dental school, with an enrollment of 450. Highest level of offering: doctorate.
ACCREDITATIONS: SC DENT DH

Baylor College of Medicine

Office of Student Affairs
One Baylor Plaza
Houston, TX 77030
(713) 798-4600
Fax (713) 798-7951

Will confirm attendance and degree by phone or mail. Inquiry must include student's name, social security number. Employers may obtain transcripts upon written request accompanied by a signed release from the student.

A medical school, with an enrollment of 1,042. Highest level of offering: doctorate.
ACCREDITATIONS: SC ANEST APCP IPSY MED MICB MIDWF NMT PERF RTT

Baylor University

Box 7068
Waco, TX 76798
(817) 755-1813
Fax (817) 755-2233

Will confirm attendance and degree by phone or mail. Inquiry must include student's name, social security number, type of degree, years attended. Employers may obtain transcripts upon written request accompanied by a $5.00 fee and a signed release from the student. Requests should be directed to: Registrar's Office.

A comprehensive institution with no medical school, with an enrollment of 10,943. Highest level of offering: doctorate.
ACCREDITATIONS: SC BUS CLPSY DIETI HSA LAW MT NASM NLN RAD RTT BUSA CSWE TED PAST

Beal College

629 Main Street
Bangor, ME 04401
(207) 947-4591

Will confirm attendance and degree by mail. Inquiry must include student's name, social security number, years attended, release. Employers may obtain transcripts upon written request accompanied by a $2.00 fee, a signed release from the student, and student's phone number.

A multiprogram two-year institution, with an enrollment of 456. Highest level of offering: one year but less than four years.
ACCREDITATIONS: EV JRCB

Beaufort County Community College

PO Box 1069
Washington, NC 27889
(919) 946-6194 Ext. 236
Fax (919) 946-0271

Will confirm attendance and degree by phone or mail. Inquiry must include student's name and social security number. Employers may obtain transcripts upon written request accompanied by a signed release from the student.

A multiprogram two-year institution, with an enrollment of 1,086. Highest level of offering: one year but less than four years.
ACCREDITATIONS: SC MLTAD

Beaufort Technical College

(See Technical College of the Low Country)

Beaver College

Attn: Registrar
Glenside, PA 19038
(215) 572-2968
Fax (215) 572-0240

Will confirm attendance and degree by phone, fax or mail. Inquiry must include student's name and years attended. Employers may obtain transcripts upon written request accompanied by a $2.00 fee and a signed release from the student.

A school of education, with an enrollment of 2,294. Highest level of offering: beyond master's but less than doctorate.
ACCREDITATIONS: M ART PTA

Becker College Leicester

3 Paxton Street
Leicester, MA 01524
(508) 791-9241 Ext. 434
Fax (508) 831-7505

Will confirm attendance and degree by phone or mail. Inquiry must include student's name, social security number, years attended. Employers may obtain transcripts upon written request accompanied by a $3.00 fee and a signed release from the student.

A multiprogram two-year institution, with an enrollment of 374. Highest level of offering: one year but less than four years.
ACCREDITATIONS: AVVMA/CVTTAT

Becker College Worcester

61 Sever Street
Worcester, MA 01609
(508) 791-9241

Will confirm attendance and degree by mail. Inquiry must include student's name, social security number, year graduated, and maiden name (if applicable). Employers may obtain transcripts upon written request by the student, accompanied by a $3.00 fee. Requests should be directed to: Registrar's Office

A multiprogram two-year institution, with an enrollment of 911. Highest level of offering: one year but less than four years.
ACCREDITATIONS: EV MAC PTAA

Beckley College

(See The College of West Virginia)

Bee County College

3800 Charco Road
Beeville, TX 78102
(512) 358-3130 Ext. 244,245,255,256
Fax (512) 358-3973

Will confirm attendance and degree by mail. Inquiry must include student's name, social security number, years attended. Employers may obtain transcripts upon written request accompanied by a $2.00 fee and a signed release from the student.

A multiprogram two-year institution, with an enrollment of 2,240. Highest level of offering: associate degree.
ACCREDITATIONS: SC DH

Bel–Rea Institute of Animal Technology

1681 South Dayton Street
Denver, CO 80231
(303) 751-8700
Fax (303) 751-9969

Will confirm attendance and degree by phone or mail. Inquiry must include student's name, social security number, and date graduated. Employers may obtain transcripts upon written request accompanied by a $2.00 fee and a signed release from the student.

A two-year institution, with an enrollment of 223. Highest level of offering: one year but less than four years.
ACCREDITATIONS: AVVMA/CVTTAT CCA

Belhaven College

1500 Peachtree
Jackson, MS 39202
(601) 968-5922

Will confirm attendance and degree by phone or mail. Inquiry must include student's name, date of birth, social security number. Employers may obtain transcripts upon written request accompanied by a $2.00 fee and a signed release from the student.

A general baccalaureate institution, with an enrollment of 965. Highest level of offering: four or five year baccalaureate.
ACCREDITATIONS: SC NASM

Bellarmine College

Newburg Road
Louisville, KY 40205
(502) 452-8211 Ext. 133
Fax (502) 456-1844

Will confirm attendance and degree by phone, fax or mail. Inquiry must include student's name, date of birth, social security number, years attended. Employers may obtain transcripts upon written request accompanied by a $3.00 fee and a signed release from the student.

A general baccalaureate institution, with an enrollment of 2,660. Highest level of offering: master's.
ACCREDITATIONS: ART SC

Belleville Area College

2500 Carlyle Road
Belleville, IL 62221
(618) 235-2700 Ext. 216
Fax (618) 235-1578

Will confirm attendance and degree by phone, fax or mail. Inquiry must include student's name, date of birth, social security number, years attended. Employers may obtain transcripts upon written request accompanied by a $2.00 fee and a signed release from the student.

A multiprogram two-year institution, with an enrollment of 16,500. Highest level of offering: one year but less than four years.
ACCREDITATIONS: NH NLN/AD ENGT MAC MLTAD MRT PTAA RAD RSTHT RTT

Bellevue College

Galvin Road at Harvell Drive
Bellevue, NE 68005
(402) 293-3778
Fax (402) 293-3819

Will confirm attendance and degree by mail. Inquiry must include student's name, date of birth, social security number. Employers may obtain transcripts upon written request accompanied by a $3.00 fee and a signed release from the student.

A business school, with an enrollment of 2,605. Highest level of offering: graduate level and master's.
ACCREDITATIONS: NH

Bellevue Community College

3000 Landerholm Circle S.E.
Room #A105
Bellevue, WA 98009-6484
(206) 641-2761

Will confirm attendance and degree by phone or mail. Inquiry must include student's name, date of birth, social security number, years attended. Employers may obtain transcripts upon written request accompanied by a signed release from the student.

A multiprogram two-year institution, with an enrollment of 7,779. Highest level of offering: one year but less than four years.
ACCREDITATIONS: NW NLN/AD RAD

Belmont Abbey College

Belmont-Mt. Holly Road
Belmont, NC 28012
(704) 825-6732

Will confirm attendance and degree by phone or mail. Inquiry must include student's name, date of birth, social security number, years attended. Employers may obtain transcripts upon written request accompanied by a $2.00 fee and a signed release from the student.

A general baccalaureate institution, with an enrollment of 1,052. Highest level of offering: four or five year baccalaureate.
ACCREDITATIONS: SC

Belmont College

1900 Belmont Boulevard
Nashville, TN 37212-3757
(615) 383-7001 Ext. 6619

Will confirm attendance and degree by phone or mail. Inquiry must include student's name, date of birth, social security number. Employers may obtain transcripts upon written request accompanied by a $1.00 fee and a signed release from the student.

A general baccalaureate institution, with an enrollment of 2,125. Highest level of offering master's degree.
ACCREDITATIONS: SC NLN/AD NASM

Belmont Technical College

120 Fox–Shannon Place
Saint Clairsville, OH 43950
(614) 695-9500 Ext. 57

Will confirm attendance and degree by phone or mail. Inquiry must include student's name, date of birth, social security number, years attended. Employers may obtain transcripts upon written request accompanied by a signed release from the student.

A multiprogram two-year institution, with an enrollment of 2,056. Highest level of offering: one year but less than four years.
ACCREDITATIONS: NH

Beloit College

700 College Street
Beloit, WI 53511
(608) 363-2640
Fax (608) 363-2718

Will confirm attendance and degree by phone, fax or mail. Inquiry must include student's name, date of birth, social security number. Employers may obtain transcripts upon written request accompanied by a $2.00 fee and a signed release from the student.

A general baccalaureate institution, with an enrollment of 1,097. Highest level of offering: master's.

ACCREDITATIONS: NH

Belzer Yeshiva–Machzikei Torah Seminary

4814 16th Avenue
Brooklyn, NY 11204
(718) 435-9633
Fax (718) 972-2782

Will confirm attendance and degree by mail, phone or fax. Inquiry must include student's name, social security number, years attended. Employers may obtain transcripts upon written request accompanied by a $3.00 fee and a signed release from the student.

A specialized non-degree granting institution, with an enrollment of 1,000. Highest level of offering: first professional degree.

ACCREDITATIONS: 3IC

Bemidji State University

1500 Birchmont Drive North East
Bemidji, MN 56601
(218) 755-2020
Fax (218) 755-4048

Will confirm attendance and degree by phone, fax or mail. Inquiry must include student's name, social security number, years attended. Employers may obtain transcripts upon written request accompanied by a $2.00 fee and a signed release from the student.

A comprehensive institution with no medical school, with an enrollment of 5,400. Highest level of offering: master's.

ACCREDITATIONS: NH CSWE TED ACS

Benedict College

Harden and Blanding Streets
Columbia, SC 29204
(803) 253-5143

Will confirm attendance and degree by phone or mail. Inquiry must include student's name, date of birth, social security number, years attended. Employers may obtain transcripts upon written request accompanied by a $2.00 fee and a signed release from the student. Requests should be directed to: Admissions & Records Office.

A general baccalaureate institution, with an enrollment of 1,495. Highest level of offering: four or five year baccalaureate.

ACCREDITATIONS: SC CSWE

Benedictine College

Atchison, KS 66002
(913) 367-5340 Ext. 2550
Fax (913) 367-6102

Will confirm attendance and degree by phone, fax or mail. Inquiry must include student's name, date of birth, social security number, years attended. Employers may obtain transcripts upon written request accompanied by a $3.00 fee and a signed release from the student.

A general baccalaureate institution, with an enrollment of 1,130. Highest level of offering: four or five year master's.

ACCREDITATIONS: NH NASM TED

Benjamin Franklin University

(See George Washington University)

Bennett College

900 Washington Street
Greensboro, NC 27401-3239
(919) 370-8620

Will confirm attendance and degree by phone or mail. Inquiry must include student's name, years attended, date graduated. Employers may obtain transcripts upon written request accompanied by a $2.00 fee and a signed release from the student. Requests should be directed to: Records Department.

A general baccalaureate institution, with an enrollment of 575. Highest level of offering: four or five year baccalaureate.

ACCREDITATIONS: SACS

Bennington College

Bennington, VT 05201
(802) 442-5401 Ext. 242
Fax (802) 442-5402

Will confirm attendance and degree by phone or mail. Inquiry must include student's name and years attended. Employers may obtain transcripts upon written request accompanied by a $3.00 fee and a signed release from the student.

A general baccalaureate institution, with an enrollment of 584. Highest level of offering: master's.

ACCREDITATIONS: EH

Bentley College

Beaver and Forest Street
Waltham, MA 02254
(617) 891-2000
Fax (617) 891-2192

Will confirm degree by phone or mail. Inquiry must include student's name, social security number, years attended. Employers may obtain transcripts upon written request accompanied by a $2.00 fee and a signed release from the student. Requests should be directed to: Transcript Coordinator.

A business school, with an enrollment of 8,085. Highest level of offering: master's.

ACCREDITATIONS: EH

Berea College

College PO Box 2305
Berea, KY 40404
(606) 986-9341 Ext. 5180

Will confirm degree by phone or mail. Inquiry must include student's name, social security number, years attended. Employers may obtain transcripts upon written request accompanied by a $2.00 fee and a signed release from the student.

A general baccalaureate institution, with an enrollment of 1,586. Highest level of offering: four or five year baccalaureate.

ACCREDITATIONS: SC NLN TED

Berean Institute

1901 West Girard Avenue
Philadelphia, PA 19130
(215) 763-4833

Will confirm attendance and degree by phone or mail. Inquiry must include student's name, social security number, years attended, release. Employers may obtain transcripts upon written request accompanied by a $2.00 fee and a signed release from the student.

A multiprogram two-year institution, with an enrollment of 287. Highest level of offering: one year but less than four years.

ACCREDITATIONS: NATTS

Bergen Community College

400 Paramus Road
Paramus, NJ 07652
(201) 447-7100 or 447-7997

Will confirm attendance and degree by mail or phone with written release from student. Inquiry must include student's name, maiden name (if applicable), date of birth, social security number, years attended. Employers may obtain transcripts upon written request accompanied by a $3.00 fee and a signed release from the student. Requests should be directed to: Registrar's Office.

A multiprogram two-year institution, with an enrollment of 11,247. Highest level of offering: one year but less than four years.

ACCREDITATIONS: M NLN/AD DH MAC MLTAD RAD RSTH SURGT

Berkeley School–Hicksville

Records are being held at Berkley School-New York. Will confirm attendance and degree by mail or phone. Inquiry must include student's name, social security number, years attended. Employers may obtain transcripts upon written request accompanied by a signed release from the student.

A single program two-year institution, with an enrollment of 352. Highest level of offering: one year but less than four years.

ACCREDITATIONS: NY

Berkeley School–New York

3 East 43 Street
New York, NY 10017
(212) 986-4343
Fax (212) 697-3371

Will confirm attendance and degree by phone, fax or mail. Inquiry must include student's name, social security number, years attended, program of study. Employers may obtain transcripts upon written request accompanied by a signed release from the student.

A single program two-year institution, with an enrollment of 491. Highest level of offering: one year but less than four years.
ACCREDITATIONS: NY JRCB

Berklee College of Music

1140 Boylston Street
Boston, MA 02215
(617) 266-1400
Fax (617) 247-6878

Will confirm attendance and degree by phone, fax or mail. Inquiry must include student's name and years attended. Requests should be directed to: Registrar's Office. Employers may obtain transcripts upon written request accompanied by a signed release from the student.

A visual and performing arts school, with an enrollment of 2,425. Highest level of offering: four or five year baccalaureate.
ACCREDITATIONS: EH

Berkshire Christian College

PO Box 826
Haverhill, MA 01831
(508) 372-8122

Will confirm attendance and degree by phone or mail. Inquiry must include student's name and social security number. Employers may obtain transcripts upon written request accompanied by a $5.00 fee and a signed release from the student.

A school of philosophy, religion and theology, with an enrollment of 126. Highest level of offering: four or five year baccalaureate.
ACCREDITATIONS: BI

Berkshire Community College

West Street
Pittsfield, MA 01201
(413) 499-4660

Will confirm attendance and degree by mail or phone. Inquiry must include student's name, social security number, release, dates attended. Employers may obtain transcripts upon written request accompanied by a signed release from the student.

A multiprogram two-year institution, with an enrollment of 3,017. Highest level of offering: one year but less than four years.
ACCREDITATIONS: EH NLN/AD RSTHT

Berry College

PO Box 400
Mount Berry Station
Rome, GA 30149
(404) 236-2282

Will confirm attendance and degree by phone or mail. Inquiry must include student's name, date of birth, social security number, years attended. Employers may obtain transcripts upon written request by student accompanied by a $2.00 fee and a signed release from the student. Requests should be directed to: Registrar's Office.

A general baccalaureate institution, with an enrollment of 1,715. Highest level of offering: master's.
ACCREDITATIONS: SACS NCATE

Bessemer State Technical College

PO Box 308
Bessemer, AL 35021
(205) 428-6391 Ext. 125

Will confirm attendance and degree by phone or mail. Inquiry must include student's name, date of birth, social security number. Employers may obtain transcripts upon written request accompanied by a signed release from the student.

A two-year institution with an enrollment of 1,800. Highest level of offering: one year but less than four years.
ACCREDITATIONS: SV

Beth Hamedrash Shaarei Yosher Institute

4102–10 16th Avenue
Brooklyn, NY 11204
(718) 854-2290

Will confirm attendance and degree by mail. Inquiry must include student's name, date of birth, social security number and address. Employers may obtain transcripts upon written request accompanied by a signed release from the student.

A specialized non-degree granting institution, with an enrollment of 140. Highest level of offering: graduate non-degree granting.
ACCREDITATIONS: RABN

Beth Hatalmud Rabbinical College

2127 82nd St.
PO Box 140085
Brooklyn, NY 11214
(718) 259-2525

Will confirm attendance and degree by mail. Inquiry must include student's name, years attended and social security number. Employers may obtain transcripts upon written request accompanied by a signed release from the student.

A specialized non-degree granting institution, with an enrollment of 171. Highest level of offering: graduate non-degree granting.
ACCREDITATIONS: RABN

Beth Israel School of Nursing

(See Phillips Beth Israel School of Nursing)

Beth Jacob Hebrew Teachers College

1213–23 Elm Avenue
Brooklyn, NY 11230
(718) 339-4747

Will confirm attendance and degree by phone or mail. Inquiry must include student's name, social security number, years attended. Employers may obtain transcripts upon written request accompanied by a $15.00 fee and a signed release from the student.

A specialized non-degree granting institution, with an enrollment of 595. Highest level of offering: undergraduate non-degree granting.
ACCREDITATIONS: 3IC

Beth Medrash Eeyun Hatalmud

14 Fred Eller Drive
Monsey, NY 10952
(914) 356-0477
Fax (914) 356-7867

Will confirm attendance and degree by mail, phone or fax. Inquiry must include student's name, years attended and social security number. Employers may obtain transcripts upon written request accompanied by a $5.00 fee and a signed release from the student.

A specialized non-degree granting institution, with an enrollment of 500. Highest level of offering: first professional degree.
ACCREDITATIONS: 3IC

Beth Medrash Emek Halacha Rabbinical College

1763 63rd Street
Brooklyn, NY 11204
(718) 232-1600

Will confirm attendance and degree by mail. Inquiry must include student's name, social security number, years attended. Employers may obtain transcripts upon written request accompanied by a signed release from the student.

A specialized non-degree granting institution, with an enrollment of 54. Highest level of offering: graduate non-degree granting.
ACCREDITATIONS: RABN

Beth Medrash Govoha

617 6th Street
Lakewood, NJ 08701
(908) 367-1060

Will confirm attendance and degree by mail. Inquiry must include student's name, social security number, release. Employers may obtain transcripts upon written request accompanied by a signed release from the student.

A school of philosophy, religion and theology, with an enrollment of 1,425. Highest level of offering: beyond master's but less than doctorate.
ACCREDITATIONS: RABN

Beth Rochel Seminary

PO Box 302
145 Saddle River Road
Monsey, NY 10952
(914) 352-5000

Will confirm attendance and degree by
mail. Inquiry must include student's name,
social security number, years attended.
Employers may obtain transcripts upon
written request accompanied by a signed release from the student.

A specialized non-degree granting institution. Highest level of offering: undergraduate non-degree granting.
ACCREDITATIONS: 3IC

Bethany Bible College

800 Bethany Drive
Scotts Valley, CA 95066
(408) 438-3800
Fax (408) 438-1621

Will confirm attendance and degree by
phone, fax or mail. Inquiry must include
student's name, date of birth, social security
number, years attended and current address.
Requests should be directed to: Records &
Registrar's Office. Employers may obtain
transcripts upon written request accompanied by a $5.00 fee and a signed release
from the student.

A general baccalaureate institution, with an
enrollment of 539. Highest level of offering: four or five year baccalaureate.
ACCREDITATIONS: WC BI

Bethany College

421 North First Street
Lindsborg, KS 67456
(913) 227-3311

Will confirm attendance and degree by
phone or mail. Inquiry must include student's name, social security number, dates
attended. Requests should be directed to:
Enrollment Services. Employers may obtain transcripts upon written request accompanied by a $3.00 fee and a signed release
from the student.

A general baccalaureate institution, with an
enrollment of 822. Highest level of offering: four or five year baccalaureate.
ACCREDITATIONS: NH NASM CSWE TED

Bethany College

Bethany, WV 26032
(304) 829-7831

Will confirm attendance and degree by
phone or mail. Inquiry must include student's name and years attended. Employers
may obtain transcripts upon written request
accompanied by a $1.00 fee and a signed
release from the student. Requests should
be directed to: Registrar's Office.

A general baccalaureate institution, with an
enrollment of 822. Highest level of offering: four or five year baccalaureate.
ACCREDITATIONS: NH CSWE TED

Bethany Lutheran College

734 Marsh Street
Mankato, MN 56001
(507) 625-2977

Will confirm attendance and degree by
phone or mail. Inquiry must include student's name, social security number, years
attended. Employers may obtain transcripts
upon written request accompanied by a
$2.00 fee and a signed release from the stu-
dent.

A multiprogram two-year institution, with
an enrollment of 296. Highest level of offering: two year.
ACCREDITATIONS: NH

Bethany Nazarene College

(See Southern Nazarene University)

Bethany Theological Seminary

Butterfield & Meyers Roads
Oak Brook, IL 60521
(708) 620-2206
Fax (708) 620-9014

Will confirm attendance and degree by
phone or mail. Inquiry must include student's name and years attended. Requests
should be directed to: Registrar's Office.
Employers may obtain transcripts upon
written request accompanied by a $4.00 fee
and a signed release from the student.

A school of philosophy, religion and theology, with an enrollment of 110. Highest
level of offering: doctorate.
ACCREDITATIONS: NH THEOL

Bethel College

1001 West McKinley Avenue
Mishawaka, IN 46545
(219) 259-8511 Ext. 308

Will confirm attendance and degree by
mail. Inquiry must include student's name
and years attended. Employers may obtain
transcripts upon written request accompanied by a $4.00 fee and a signed release
from the student. Requests should be directed to: Registrar's Office.

A general baccalaureate institution, with an
enrollment of 8000. Highest level of offering: master's.
ACCREDITATIONS: NH

Bethel College

300 East 27th Street
North Newton, KS 67117
(316) 283-2500 Ext. 315

Will confirm attendance and degree by
phone or mail. Inquiry must include student's name, social security number, years
attended. Employers may obtain transcripts
upon written request accompanied by a
$2.00 fee and a signed release from the stu-
dent.Requests should be directed to:
Registrar's Office.

A general baccalaureate institution, with an
enrollment of 667. Highest level of offering: four or five year baccalaureate.
ACCREDITATIONS: NH NLN CSWE

Bethel College

212 Cherry Street
McKenzie, TN 38201
(901) 352-1000
Fax (901) 352-1008

Will confirm attendance and degree by
phone or mail. Inquiry must include student's name, date of birth, social security
number, years attended. Employers may obtain transcripts upon written request accompanied by a $2.00 fee and a signed release
from the student. Inquiries should be directed to Registrar.

A general baccalaureate institution, with an
enrollment of 520. Highest level of offering: master's.
ACCREDITATIONS: SC

Bethel College

3900 Bethel Drive
Saint Paul, MN 55112
(612) 638-6250

Will confirm attendance and degree by
phone or mail. Inquiry must include student's name, social security number, years
attended. Employers may obtain transcripts
upon written request accompanied by a
$1.00 fee and a signed release from the stu-
dent.

A general baccalaureate institution, with an
enrollment of 1,861. Highest level of offering: four or five year baccalaureate.
ACCREDITATIONS: NH CSWE TED NLN

Bethel Theological Seminary

3949 Bethel Drive
Saint Paul, MN 55112
(612) 638-6181

Will confirm attendance and degree by
phone or mail. Inquiry must include student's name, social security number, years
attended. Employers may obtain transcripts
upon written request accompanied by a
$2.00 fee and a signed release from the stu-
dent. Requests should be directed to:
Registrar's Office.

A school of philosophy, religion and
theology, with an enrollment of 466.
Highest level of offering: doctorate.
ACCREDITATIONS: NH THEOL

Bethune Cookman College

640 Second Avenue
Daytona Beach, FL 32015
(904) 255-1401
Fax (904) 257-5338

Will confirm attendance and degree by
phone or mail. Inquiry must include
student's name, years attended and social
security number. Requests should be directed to: Registrar's Office. Employers may
obtain transcripts upon written request accompanied by a $2.00 fee and a signed re-
lease from the student.

A general baccalaureate institution, with an
enrollment of 1,827. Highest level of offering: four or five year baccalaureate.
ACCREDITATIONS: SC MT

Big Bend Community College

7662 Chanute St.
Moses Lake, WA 98837-3299
(509) 762-6226
Fax (509) 762-6329

Will confirm attendance and degree by mail or fax. Inquiry must include student's name, social security number, years attended. Employers may obtain transcripts upon written request accompanied by $2.00 transcript fee and a signed release from the student. Requests should be directed to: Registrar's Office.

A multiprogram two-year institution, with an enrollment of 2,100. Highest level of offering: one year but less than four years.
ACCREDITATIONS: NW

Biola University

13800 Biola Avenue
La Mirada, CA 90639
(310) 903-4720
Fax (310) 903-4748
(Fax to attn. of Registrar's Office)

Will confirm attendance and degree by phone, fax or mail. Inquiry must include student's name, social security number, date of birth and years attended. Employers may obtain transcripts upon written request accompanied by a $5.00 fee and a signed release from the student.

A comprehensive institution with no medical school, with an enrollment of 3,027. Highest level of offering: doctorate.
ACCREDITATIONS: WC BI CLPSY NASM NLN THEOL

Birmingham Southern College

900 Arkadelphia Road
Birmingham, AL 35254
(205) 226-4698

Will confirm attendance and degree by phone or mail. Inquiry must include student's name and social security number. Employers may obtain transcripts upon written request accompanied by a $2.00 fee and a signed release from the student.

A general baccalaureate institution, with an enrollment of 1,800. Highest level of offering: master's.
ACCREDITATIONS: SC NASM TED

Bishop Clarkson College

333 South 44th Street
Omaha, NE 68131-3799
(402) 552-3033
Fax (402) 552-2899

Will confirm attendance and degree by phone or mail. Inquiry must include student's name, social security number, years attended, and maiden name (if applicable). Employers may obtain transcripts upon written request accompanied by a $3.00 fee and a signed release from the student.

A bachelor's or higher institution newly admitted to NCES, with an enrollment of 664. Highest level of offering: four year baccalaureate, masters
ACCREDITATIONS: NCA DNUR NLN/N

Bishop College

(See Paul Quinn College)

Bismarck State College

1500 Edwards Avenue
Bismarck, ND 58501
(701) 224-5429
Fax (701) 224-5550

Will confirm attendance and degree by phone or mail. Inquiry must include student's name, date of birth, social security number, years attended. Employers may obtain transcripts upon written request and a signed release from the student.

A multiprogram two-year institution, with an enrollment of 2,600. Highest level of offering: one year but less than four years.
ACCREDITATIONS: NH MLTAD

Black Hawk College East Campus

Box 489
Kewanee, IL 61443
(309) 852-5671 Ext. 220

Will confirm attendance and degree by phone or mail. Inquiry must include student's name, social security number, years attended. Employers may obtain transcripts upon written request accompanied by a signed release from the student. Requests should be directed to: Records & Admission Office.

A multiprogram two-year institution, with an enrollment of 835. Highest level of offering: one year but less than four years.
ACCREDITATIONS: NH

Black Hawk College Quad–Cities Campus

6600 34th Avenue
Moline, IL 61265
(309) 796-1311 Ext. 1260
Fax (309) 792-5976

Will confirm attendance and degree by mail or fax. Inquiry must include student's name and social security number. Employers may obtain transcripts upon written request accompanied by a signed release from the student.

A multiprogram two-year institution, with an enrollment of 5,272. Highest level of offering: two years.
ACCREDITATIONS: NH NLN/AD DA RSTH RSTHT

Black Hills State University

1200 University
University Station Box 9502
Spearfish, SD 57799
(800) 255-2478
Fax (605) 642-6214

Will confirm attendance and degree by phone, fax or mail. Inquiry must include student's name, date of birth, social security number, years attended. Employers may obtain transcripts upon written request accompanied by a $2.00 fee and a signed release from the student. Requests should be directed to: Office of Admissions and Records.

A general baccalaureate institution, with an enrollment of 2,400. Highest level of offering: master's.
ACCREDITATIONS: NH NASM TED

Blackburn College

Carlinville, IL 62626
(217) 854-3231 Ext. 210

Will confirm attendance and degree by phone or mail. Inquiry must include student's name and years attended. Employers may obtain transcripts upon written request accompanied by a $1.00 fee and a signed release from the student. Requests should be directed to: Records Department.

A general baccalaureate institution, with an enrollment of 465. Highest level of offering: four or five year baccalaureate.
ACCREDITATIONS: NH

Blackfeet Community College

Box 819
Browning, MT 59417
(406) 338-5441 Ext. 221

Will confirm attendance and degree by phone or mail. Inquiry must include student's name and years attended. Employers may obtain transcripts upon written request accompanied by a $1.00 fee and a signed release from the student.

A multiprogram two-year institution, with an enrollment of 300. Highest level of offering: one year but less than four years.
ACCREDITATIONS: NW

Blackhawk Technical College

PO Box 5009
Janesville, WI 53547
(608) 757-7713

Will confirm attendance and degree by mail. Inquiry must include student's name, social security number, years attended. Employers may obtain transcripts upon written request accompanied by a signed release from the student. Requests should be directed to: Records Office.

A muliprogram two-year institution, with an enrollment of 2,300. Highest level of offering: one year but less than four years
ACCREDITATIONS: NH NLN/AD DA

Bladen Community College

PO Box 266
Dublin, NC 28332
(919) 862-2164 Ext. 208
Fax (919) 862-3484

Will confirm attendance and degree by mail or phone. Inquiry must include student's name, date of birth, social security number, release. Employers may obtain transcripts upon written request accompanied by a signed release from the student.

A multiprogram two-year institution, with an enrollment of 650. Highest level of offering: two years.
ACCREDITATIONS: SACS

Bladen Technical Institute

(See Bladen Community College)

Blair Junior College

828 Wooten Road
Colorado Springs, CO 80915
(719) 574-1082

Will confirm attendance and degree by mail
or phone. Inquiry must include student's
name, social security number, years attended. Employers may obtain transcripts upon
written request accompanied by a $2.00 fee
and a signed release from the student.
Requests should be directed to: Student's
Records.

A two-year institution newly admitted to
NCES, with an enrollment of 739. Highest
level of offering: one year but less than four
years.
ACCREDITATIONS: NH JRCB

Blanton's College

126 College Street
Asheville, NC 28801
(704) 252-7346

Will confirm attendance and degree by
mail. Inquiry must include student's name,
social security number, years attended.
Employers may obtain transcripts upon
written request accompanied by a $2.00 fee
and a signed release from the student.

A single program two-year institution, with
an enrollment of 191. Highest level of offering: one year but less than four years.
ACCREDITATIONS: JRCB

Blinn College

902 College Avenue
Brenham, TX 77833
(409) 830-4000
Fax (409) 830-4116

Will confirm attendance and degree by mail
or fax. Inquiry must include student's name,
social security number, years attended.
Employers may obtain transcripts upon
written request accompanied by a $3.00 fee
and a signed release from the student.
Requests should be directed to: Admissions
Office.

A multiprogram two-year institution, with
an enrollment of 2,000. Highest level of offering: one year but less than four years.
ACCREDITATIONS: SC

Bloomfield College

467 Franklin Street
Bloomfield, NJ 07003
(201) 748-9000 Ext. 218

Will confirm attendance and degree by mail
or phone. Inquiry must include student's
name, date of birth, years attended.
Employers may obtain transcripts upon
written request accompanied by a signed release from the student.

A business school, with an enrollment of
1,631. Highest level of offering: four or
five year baccalaureate.
ACCREDITATIONS: M NLN

Bloomsburg University of Pennsylvania

Bloomsburg, PA 17815
(717) 389-4263
Fax (717) 389-4001

Will confirm attendance and degree by
phone or mail. Inquiry must include student's name, social security number, years
attended. Employers may obtain transcripts
upon written request accompanied by a
$2.00 fee and a signed release from the stu-
dent. Requests should be directed to:
Registrar's Office. A comprehensive institution with no medical school, with an enrollment of 7,700. Highest level of offering:
master's.
ACCREDITATIONS: M NLN TED

Blue Hills Regional Technical Institute

(See Massasoit Community College)

Blue Mountain College

Blue Mountain, MS 38610
(601) 685-4771 Ext. 35

Will confirm attendance and degree by
phone or mail. Inquiry must include student's name and years attended. Employers
may obtain transcripts upon written request
accompanied by a $2.00 fee and a signed
release from the student.

A general baccalaureate institution, with an
enrollment of 318. Highest level of offering: four or five year baccalaureate.
ACCREDITATIONS: SC

Blue Mountain Community College

PO Box 100
Pendleton, OR 97801
(503) 276-1260 Ext. 291

Will confirm attendance and degree by mail
or phone. Inquiry must include student's
name, date of birth, social security number.
Employers may obtain transcripts upon
written request accompanied by a $2.00 fee
and a signed release from the student.

A multiprogram two-year institution, with
an enrollment of 2,511. Highest level of offering: one year but less than four years.
ACCREDITATIONS: NW DA ENGT

Blue Ridge Community College

PO Box 80
Weyers Cave, VA 24486
(703) 234-9261 Ext. 217
Fax (703) 234-9066

Will confirm attendance and degree by
phone, fax or mail. Inquiry must include
student's name and social security number.
Only students may obtain transcripts.

A multiprogram two-year institution, with
an enrollment of 2,579. Highest level of offering: one year but less than four years.
ACCREDITATIONS: SACS AVVMA/CVTTAT

Blue Ridge Technical College

(See Blue Ridge Community College)

Bluefield College

3000 College Drive
Bluefield, VA. 24605
(703) 326-3682 Ext. 220
Fax (703) 326-3682

Will confirm attendance and degree by
phone, fax or mail. Inquiry must include
student's name, date of birth, social security
number, years attended. Employers may obtain transcripts upon written request accompanied by a $3.00 fee and a signed release
from the student.

A general baccalaureate institution, with an
enrollment of 621. Highest level of offering: four or five year baccalaureate.
ACCREDITATIONS: SC

Bluefield State College

219 Rock Street
Bluefield, WV 24701
(304) 327-4063

Will confirm attendance and degree by
phone or mail. Inquiry must include student's name, date of birth, social security
number, years attended. Employers may obtain transcripts upon written request accompanied by a $3.00 fee and a signed release
from the student. Requests should be directed to: Registrar's Office.

A general baccalaureate institution, with an
enrollment of 2,597. Highest level of offering: four or five year baccalaureate.
ACCREDITATIONS: NH NLN/AD ENGT RAD

Bluffton College

Bluffton, OH 45817
(419) 358-3321

Will confirm attendance and degree by
phone or mail. Inquiry must include student's name, social security number, years
attended. Employers may obtain transcripts
upon written request accompanied by a
$3.00 fee and a signed release from the stu-
dent.

A general baccalaureate institution, with an
enrollment of 700. Highest level of offering: four or five year baccalaureate.
ACCREDITATIONS: NH NASM CSWE NLN

Bnos Jerusalem Seminary

1273 53rd Street
Brooklyn, NY 11218
(718) 435-6355

Will confirm attendance and degree by mail
or phone. Inquiry must include student's
name and social security number.
Employers may obtain transcripts upon
written request accompanied by a signed release from the student. Requests should be
directed to: Registrar's Office.

A bachelor's or higher institution newly admitted to NCES, with an enrollment of
1,050. Highest level of offering: undergraduate non-degree granting.
ACCREDITATIONS: 3IC

Bob Jones University

Greenville, SC 29614
(803) 242-5100 Ext. 2010
Fax (803) 242-5100 Ext. 3015

Will confirm attendance and degree by phone, fax or mail. Inquiry must include student's name, date of birth, years attended, release. Employers may obtain transcripts upon written request accompanied by a signed release from the student. Requests should be directed to: Records Office.

A comprehensive institution with no medical school, with an enrollment of 4,287. Highest level of offering: doctorate.
ACCREDITATIONS: 3IC

Boise Bible College

8695 Marigold
Boise, ID 83714
(208) 376-7731

Will confirm attendance and degree by mail or phone. Inquiry must include student's name, date of birth, years attended. Employers may obtain transcripts upon written request accompanied by a $5.00 fee and a signed release from the student. Requests should be directed to: Academic Dean.

A bachelor's or higher institution newly admitted to NCES, with an enrollment of 80. Highest level of offering: four or five year baccalaureate.
ACCREDITATIONS: BI

Boise State University

1910 University Drive
Boise, ID 83725
(208) 385-3486

Will confirm attendance and degree by phone or mail. Inquiry must include student's name, date of birth, social security number. Employers may obtain transcripts upon written request accompanied by a $2.00 fee and a signed release from the student. Requests should be directed to: Registrar's Office.

A comprehensive institution with no medical school, with an enrollment of 13,500. Highest level of offering: master's.
ACCREDITATIONS: NW NLN/AD BUS DA MRT NASM NLN RAD RSTH SURGT CSWE TED

Boricua College

3755 Broadway
New York, NY 10032
(212) 694-1000

Will confirm attendance and degree by phone or mail. Inquiry must include student's name, social security number, years attended. Requests should be directed to: Registrar's Office. Only students may obtain transcripts, $3.00 fee.

A multiprogram two-year institution, with an enrollment of 1,100. Highest level of offering: four or five year baccalaureate.
ACCREDITATIONS: M NY

Borromeo College of Ohio

(See Center for Pastoral Leadership)

Bossier Parish Community College

2719 Airline Drive North
Bossier City, LA 71111
(318) 746-9851
Fax (318) 742-8664

Will confirm attendance and degree by phone, fax or mail. Inquiry must include student's name, social security number, years attended. Employers may obtain transcripts upon written request accompanied by a signed release from the student.

A multiprogram two-year institution, with an enrollment of 2,950. Highest level of offering: one year but less than four years.
ACCREDITATIONS: SC RSTHT

Boston Architectural Center

320 Newbury Street
Boston, MA 02115
(617) 536-3170

Will confirm attendance and degree by phone or mail. Inquiry must include student's name and years attended. Employers may obtain transcripts upon written request accompanied by a $3.00 fee and a signed release from the student. Requests should be directed to: Registrar's Office.

A bachelor's or higher institution newly admitted to NCES, with an enrollment of 642. Highest level of offering: four or five year baccalaureate.
ACCREDITATIONS: ARCH

Boston College

Registrar's Office Lyons 101
Chestnut Hill, MA 02167
(617) 552-4977
Fax (617) 552-4975

Will confirm attendance and degree by phone, fax or mail. Inquiry must include student's name, date of birth, social security number, years attended. Employers may obtain transcripts upon written request accompanied by a $2.00 fee and a signed release from the student. Requests should be directed to: Registrar's Office.

A doctoral-level institution with no medical school, with an enrollment of 14,500. Highest level of offering: doctorate.
ACCREDITATIONS: EH BUS COPSY LAW NLN CSWE TED

Boston Conservatory

8 The Fenway
Boston, MA 02215
(617) 536-6340 Ext. 46

Will confirm attendance and degree by mail or phone. Inquiry must include student's name and years attended. Employers may obtain transcripts upon written request accompanied by a $3.00 fee and a signed release from the student.

A visual and performing arts school, with an enrollment of 420. Highest level of offering: master's.
ACCREDITATIONS: EH DANCE NASM

Boston University

881 Commonwealth Avenue–2nd Floor
Boston, MA 02215
(617) 353-3623
Fax (617) 353-9770

Will confirm attendance and degree by phone or mail. Inquiry must include student's name, social security number, years attended. Employers may obtain transcripts upon written request accompanied by a $3.00 fee and a signed release from the student. Requests should be directed to: Transcript Office.

A doctoral-level institution with a medical school, with an enrollment of 27,630. Highest level of offering: doctorate.
ACCREDITATIONS: EH BUS CLPSY COPSY DA DENT ENG HSA PAST LAW MED NASM NLN TED THEOL DT OT PH PTA SP CSWE OMA

Bowdoin College

Brunswick, ME 04011
(207) 725-3226
Fax (207) 725-3795

Will confirm attendance and degree by phone, fax or mail. Inquiry must include student's name and years attended. Employers may obtain transcripts upon written request accompanied by a $2.00 fee and a signed release from the student. Requests should be directed to: Registrar's Office.

A general baccalaureate institution, with an enrollment of 1,350. Highest level of offering: four or five year baccalaureate.
ACCREDITATIONS: EH

Bowie State University

Registrar's Office
Jericho Park Road
Bowie, MD 20715
(301) 464-3000

Will confirm attendance and degree by phone or mail. Inquiry must include student's name, social security number, years attended. Employers may obtain transcripts upon written request accompanied by a $2.00 fee and a signed release from the student. Requests should be directed to: Admissions & Records Office.

A comprehensive institution with no medical school, with an enrollment of 2,361. Highest level of offering: master's.
ACCREDITATIONS: M CSWE TED

Bowling Green Junior College of Business

(See Western Kentucky University)

Bowling Green State University Firelands Campus

Registration & Records Office
110 Administration and Records Bldg.
Bowling Green, OH 43403
(419) 372-8441

Will confirm attendance and degree by mail or phone. Inquiry must include student's name, social security number, years attended. Employers may obtain transcripts upon written request accompanied by a $3.00 fee and a signed release from the student. Requests should be directed to: Office of Registration and Records.

A multiprogram two-year institution, with an enrollment of 1,074. Highest level of offering: one year but less than four years.
ACCREDITATIONS: NH MRT

Bowling Green State University Main Campus

Office of Registration & Records
110 Administration Bldg.
Bowling Green, OH 43403
(419) 372-8441
Fax (419) 372-7977

Will confirm attendance and degree by phone or mail. Inquiry must include student's name, social security number, years attended. Requests should be directed to: Registrar's Office. Employers may obtain transcripts upon written request accompanied by a $3.00 fee and a signed release from the student. Requests should be directed to : Office of Registration & Records.

A doctoral-level institution with no medical school, with an enrollment of 17,428. Highest level of offering: doctorate.
ACCREDITATIONS: NH ART AUD BUS CLPSY JOUR MRA MT NASM NLN SP CSWE TED PTA THEA

Bradford College

320 South Main Street
Bradford, MA 01835
(508) 372-7161 Ext. 261, 262
Fax (508) 521-0480

Will confirm attendance and degree by phone or mail. Inquiry must include student's name, social security number, years attended. Employers may obtain transcripts upon written request accompanied by a $3.00 fee and a signed release from the student.

A general baccalaureate institution, with an enrollment of 404. Highest level of offering: four or five year baccalaureate.
ACCREDITATIONS: EH

Bradley University

Peoria, IL 61625
(309) 677-3101
Fax (309) 677-2715

Will confirm attendance and degree by phone or mail. Inquiry must include student's name, date of birth, social security number, years attended. Employers may obtain transcripts upon written request accompanied by a $2.00 fee and a signed release from the student.

A comprehensive institution with no medical school, with an enrollment of 5,658. Highest level of offering: beyond master's but less than doctorate.
ACCREDITATIONS: NH ART BUS ENG ENGT NASM NLN SP TED BUSA

Brainerd Community College

Col Drive at South West 4th Street
Brainerd, MN 56401
(218) 828-2508

Will confirm attendance and degree by phone or mail. Inquiry must include student's name, date of birth, social security number, years attended. Employers may obtain transcripts upon written request accompanied by a signed release from the student. Requests should be directed to: Student Records Department.

A multiprogram two-year institution, with an enrollment of 1,644. Highest level of offering: one year but less than four years.
ACCREDITATIONS: NH

Bramson Ort Technical Institute

69-30 Austin St.
Forest Hills, NY 11375
(718) 261-5800

Will confirm attendance and degree by mail. Inquiry must include student's name and release. Employers may obtain transcripts upon written request accompanied by a $2.00 fee and a signed release from the student.

A multiprogram two-year institution, with an enrollment of 1,510. Highest level of offering: one year but less than four years.
ACCREDITATIONS: M NY

Brandeis University

Registrar's Office
PO Box 9110
Waltham, MA 02254-9110
(617) 736-2010
Fax (617) 736-3485

Will confirm attendance and degree by phone or mail. Inquiry must include student's name, years attended, date graduated. Only students may obtain transcripts. $5.00 fee.

A doctoral-level institution with no medical school, with an enrollment of 3,536. Highest level of offering: doctorate.
ACCREDITATIONS: EH

Brandywine College of Widener University

(See Widener University of Law)

Brazosport College

500 College Drive
Lake Jackson, TX 77566
(409) 265-6131 Ext. 221

Will confirm attendance and degree by phone or mail. Inquiry must include student's name, social security number, years attended. Employers may obtain transcripts upon written request accompanied by a signed release from the student.

A multiprogram two-year institution, with an enrollment of 3,729. Highest level of offering: one year but less than four years.
ACCREDITATIONS: SC

Brenau College

Gainesville, GA 30501
(404) 534-6115

Will confirm attendance and degree by phone or mail. Inquiry must include student's name, date of birth, social security number, years attended. Employers may obtain transcripts upon written request accompanied by a $5.00 fee and a signed release from the student.

A general baccalaureate institution, with an enrollment of 2,000. Highest level of offering: master's.
ACCREDITATIONS: SC

Brescia College

717 Frederica Street
Owensboro, KY 42301
(502) 686-4248

Will confirm attendance and degree by mail. Inquiry must include student's name, maiden name, date of birth, social security number. Employers may obtain transcripts upon written request accompanied by a $2.00 fee and a signed release from the student.

A general baccalaureate institution, with an enrollment of 815. Highest level of offering: four or five year baccalaureate.
ACCREDITATIONS: SC

Brevard College

Brevard, NC 28712
(704) 883-8292 Ext. 255
Fax (704(884-3790

Will confirm attendance and degree by mail. Inquiry must include student's name, date of birth, social security number, years attended. A signed release is required. Employers may obtain transcripts upon written request accompanied by a signed release from the student.

A multiprogram two-year liberal arts institution, with an enrollment of 750. Highest level of offering: two years but less than four years.
ACCREDITATIONS: SC NASM

Brevard Community College

1519 Clearlake Road
Cocoa, FL 32922
(407) 632-1111 Ext. 2150

Will confirm attendance and degree by phone or mail. Inquiry must include student's name, date of birth, social security number, years attended. Requests should be directed to: College Records. Employers may obtain transcripts upon written request accompanied by a signed release from the student.

A multiprogram two-year institution, with an enrollment of 10,709. Highest level of offering: one year but less than four years.
ACCREDITATIONS: SC DA MLTAD RAD RSTHT

Brewer State Junior College

2631 Temple Avenue North
Fayettc, AL 35555
(205) 932-3221 Ext. 112
Fax (205) 932-6974

Will confirm attendance and degree by phone, fax or mail. Inquiry must include student's name date of birth, SSN, years to search. Requests should be directed to: Registrar's Office. Employers may obtain transcripts upon written request accompanied by a signed release from the student.

A multiprogram two-year institution, with an enrollment of 1,1000. Highest level of offering: one year but less than four years.
ACCREDITATIONS: SC

Brewton–Parker College

Mount Vernon, GA 30445
(912) 583-2241
Fax (912) 583-4498

Will confirm attendance and degree by phone or mail. Inquiry must include student's name, date of birth, social security number, years attended. Employers may obtain transcripts upon written request accompanied by a signed release from the student.

A multiprogram four-year institution, with an enrollment of 2,014. Highest level of offering: four or five year baccalaureate.
ACCREDITATIONS: SC

Briar Cliff College

Box 2100
3303 Rebecca Street
Sioux City, IA 51104-2100
(712) 279-5448

Will confirm attendance and degree by phone or mail. Inquiry must include student's name, date of birth, social security number, years attended. Requests should be directed to: Registrar's Office. Employers may obtain transcripts upon written request accompanied by a signed release from the student.

A general baccalaureate institution, with an enrollment of 1,293. Highest level of offering: four or five year baccalaureate.
ACCREDITATIONS: NH NLN CSWE

Briarcliffe Secretarial School

(See The College for Business)

Briarcliffe – The College of Business

(Formerly Briarcliffe Secretarial School)
55 North Broadway
Hicksville, NY 11801
(516) 681-1100

Will confirm attendance and degree by mail. Inquiry must include student's name, date of birth, social security number, years attended. Employers may obtain transcripts upon written request accompanied by a $2.00 fee and a signed release from the student.

A two-year institution newly admitted to NCES, with an enrollment of 622. Highest level of offering: one year but less than four years.
ACCREDITATIONS: NY

(Formerly Briarcliffe Secretarial School)
55 North Broadway
Hicksville, NY 11801
(516) 681-1100

Will confirm attendance and degree by mail. Inquiry must include student's name, date of birth, social security number, years attended. Employers may obtain transcripts upon written request accompanied by a $2.00 fee and a signed release from the student.

A two-year institution newly admitted to NCES, with an enrollment of 622. Highest level of offering: one year but less than four years.
ACCREDITATIONS: NY

Briarwood College

2279 Mount Vernon Road
Southington, CT 06489
(203) 628-4751
Fax (203) 628-6444

Will confirm attendance and degree by fax or mail. Inquiry must include student's name, date of birth, social security number, years attended. Employers may obtain transcripts upon written request accompanied by a $2.00 fee and a signed release from the student.

A multiprogram two-year institution, with an enrollment of 350. Highest level of offering: one year but less than four years.
ACCREDITATIONS: EV DA NEASC CADDAEADA AMAAHEA

Bridgeport Engineering Institute

785 Unquowa Road
Fairfield, CT 06430
(203) 259-5717
Fax (203) 259-9372

Will confirm attendance and degree by mail or phone. Inquiry must include student's name, date of birth, social security number. Employers may obtain transcripts upon written request accompanied by a $2.00 fee and a signed release from the student.

An engineering school, with an enrollment of 372. Highest level of offering: four or five year baccalaureate.
ACCREDITATIONS: EH

Bridgewater College

Bridgewater, VA 22812
(703) 828-2501 Ext. 313

Will confirm attendance and degree by phone or mail. Inquiry must include student's name, date of birth, social security number, years attended. Employers may obtain transcripts upon written request accompanied by a $2.00 fee and a signed release from the student.

A general baccalaureate institution, with an enrollment of 985. Highest level of offering: four or five year baccalaureate.
ACCREDITATIONS: SC

Bridgewater State College

Bridgewater, MA 02324
(617) 697-1200 Ext. 1231

Will confirm attendance and degree by phone or mail. Inquiry must include student's name, social security number, years attended. Employers may obtain transcripts upon written request accompanied by a signed release from the student.

A comprehensive institution with no medical school, with an enrollment of 8,313. Highest level of offering: beyond master's but less than doctorate.
ACCREDITATIONS: EH CSWE TED

Brigham Young University Hawaii Campus

BYUH Box 1974
Laie, HI 96762
(808) 293-3736

Will confirm attendance and degree by phone or mail. Inquiry must include student's name, date of birth, social security number, years attended. Employers may obtain transcripts upon written request accompanied by a signed release from the student.

A general baccalaureate institution, with an enrollment of 1,936. Highest level of offering: four or five year baccalaureate.
ACCREDITATIONS: WC

Brigham Young University Main Campus

Records Department B150 ASB
Provo, UT 84602
(801) 378-2631

Will confirm attendance and degree by phone or mail. Inquiry must include student's name, date of birth, social security number, years attended. Requests should be directed to: Records Department. Employers may obtain transcripts upon written request accompanied by a $2.00 fee and a signed release from the student.

A doctoral-level institution with no medical school, with an enrollment of 29,571. Highest level of offering: doctorate.
ACCREDITATIONS: NW AVVMA/CVTTAT AUD BUS CLPSY ENG ENGT JOUR LAW LIB AAMFI/GD DIET TED MT NASM NLN SP CSWE THEA

Brisk Rabbinical College

2965 West Peterson
Chicago, IL 60659
(312) 275-5166

Will confirm attendance and degree by phone or mail. Inquiry must include student's name and years attended. Employers may obtain transcripts upon written request accompanied by a signed release from the student.

A bachelor's or higher institution newly admitted to NCES, with an enrollment of 26. Highest level of offering: master's.
ACCREDITATIONS: RABN

Bristol University

(Formerly Bristol College)
1241 Volunteer Parkway
Bristol, TN 37625
(615) 968-1442
Fax (615) 989-5828

Will confirm attendance and degree by phone or mail. Inquiry must include student's name, social security number, years attended. Employers may obtain transcripts upon written request accompanied by a signed release from the student.

A single program two-year institution, with an enrollment of 200. Highest level of offering: four or five year baccalaureate.
ACCREDITATIONS: SRCB

Bristol Community College

777 Elsbree Street
Fall River, MA 02720
(508) 678-2811 Ext. 240

Will confirm attendance and degree by phone or mail. Inquiry must include student's name, social security number, years attended, release. Employers may obtain transcripts upon written request accompanied by a $1.00 fee and a signed release from the student.

A multiprogram two-year institution, with an enrollment of 4,718. Highest level of offering: one year but less than four years.
ACCREDITATIONS: EH NLN/AD DH MLTAD

Bronx Community College-City of New York

(Formerly City University of New York Bronx Community College)
West 181 Street & University Avenue
Colston Hall, Room 513
Bronx, NY 10453
(212) 220-6935

Will confirm attendance by phone or mail. Inquiry must include student's name, date of birth, social security number, years attended. Employers may obtain transcripts upon written request accompanied by a $4.00 fee and a signed release from the student.

A multiprogram two-year institution, with an enrollment of 7,095. Highest level of offering: one year but less than four years.
ACCREDITATIONS: M NLN/AD ENGT NMT NY

Brookdale Community College

Newman Springs Road
Lincroft, NJ 07738
(908) 842-1900

Will confirm attendance and degree by mail. Inquiry must include student's name, date of birth, social security number, years attended, release. Requests should be directed to: Records Department. Employers may obtain transcripts upon written request accompanied by a $2.00 fee and a signed release from the student.

A multiprogram two-year institution, with an enrollment of 11,089. Highest level of offering: one year but less than four years.
ACCREDITATIONS: M NLN/AD MLTAD RSTH

Brookhaven College

3939 Valley View Lane
Farmers Branch, TX 75244
(214) 620-4700
Fax (214) 620-4897

Will confirm attendance and degree by mail or fax. Inquiry must include student's name, social security number, years attended, release. Employers may obtain transcripts upon written request accompanied by a $1.00 fee and a signed release from the student. Requests should be directed to: Admissions Office.

A multiprogram two-year institution, with an enrollment of 8,200. Highest level of offering: one year but less than four years.
ACCREDITATIONS: SC

Brooklyn Law School

250 Joralemon Street
Brooklyn, NY 11201
(718) 625-2200

Will confirm attendance and degree by phone or mail. Inquiry must include student's name, date of birth, social security number, years attended. Employers may obtain transcripts upon written request accompanied by a $4.00 fee and a signed release from the student.

A law school, with an enrollment of 1,183. Highest level of offering: first professional degree.
ACCREDITATIONS: NY LAW

Brooks College

4825 East Pacific Coast Highway
Long Beach, CA 90804
(310) 597-6611
Fax (310) 597-7412

Will confirm attendance and degree by mail or fax. Inquiry must include student's name, social security number, years attended. Employers may obtain transcripts upon written request accompanied by a $2.00 fee and a signed release from the student.

A single program two-year institution, with an enrollment of 700. Highest level of offering: two years but less than four years.
ACCREDITATIONS: WJ NATTS

Brooks Institute of Photography

801 Alston Road
Santa Barbara, CA 93108
(805) 966-3888 Ext. 220
Fax (805) 564-1475

Will confirm attendance and degree by phone or mail. Inquiry must include student's name, date of birth, social security number, years attended. Only students may obtain transcripts. $4.00 fee.

A visual and preforming arts school, with an enrollment of 662. Highest level of offering: four or five year baccalaureate.
ACCREDITATIONS: JRCB

Brooks Institute of Technology

801 Alston Road
Santa Barbara, CA 93108
(805) 966-3888 Ext. 220

Will confirm attendance and degree by phone or mail. Inquiry must include student's name, date of birth, social security number, years attended. Only students may obtain transcripts. $4.00 fee.

A visual and performing arts school, with an enrollment of 662. Highest level of offering: four or five year baccalaureate.
ACCREDITATIONS: JRCB

Brookstone College of Business

7815 National Service Road
Greensboro, NC 27409
(919) 668-2627

Will confirm attendance and degree by mail. Inquiry must include student's name, social security number, years attended, release. Employers may obtain transcripts upon written request accompanied by a signed release from the student.

A multiprogram two-year institution, with an enrollment of 140. Highest level of offering: less than one year.

Broome Community College

PO Box 1017
Binghamton, NY 13902
(607) 778-5000 Ext. 5349

Will confirm attendance and degree by phone or mail. Inquiry must include student's name and social security number. Employers may obtain transcripts upon written request accompanied by a $2.00 fee and a signed release from the student.

A multiprogram two-year institution, with an enrollment of 6,700. Highest level of offering: one year but less than four years. Attn: Registrar's Office.
ACCREDITATIONS: M NLN/AD DH ENGT MAC MLTAD MRT NY RAD

Broward Community College

225 East Las Olas Boulevard
Fort Lauderdale, FL 33301
(305) 761-7472

Will confirm attendance and degree by phone or mail. Inquiry must include student's name, social security number, release. Requests should be directed to: Records Department. Employers may obtain transcripts upon written request accompanied by a signed release from the student.

A multiprogram two-year institution, with an enrollment of 19,500. Highest level of offering: one year but less than four years.
ACCREDITATIONS: SC NLN/AD DA MAC MLTAD PTAA RAD RSTH RSTHT RTT

Brown University

Box 1883
Providence, RI 02912
(401) 863-1851

Will confirm attendance and degree by phone. Inquiry must include student's name and years attended. Employers may obtain transcripts upon written request accompanied by a $4.00 fee and a signed release from the student.

A doctoral-level institution with a medical school, with an enrollment of 7,099. Highest level of offering: doctorate.
ACCREDITATIONS: EH ENG IPSY MED

Brunswick College

Altama at Fourth Street
Brunswick, Ga 31523
(912) 264-7235

Will confirm attendance and degree by phone or mail. Inquiry must include student's name, social security number, years attended. Employers may obtain transcripts upon written request accompanied by a $1.00 fee and a signed release from the student.

A multiprogram two-year institution, with an enrollment of 1,332. Highest level of offering: one year but less than four years.
ACCREDITATIONS: SC NLN/AD MLTAD RAD RSTHT

Brunswick Community College

PO Box 30
Supply, NC 28462
(919) 754-6950 Ext. 325
Fax (919) 754-7805

Will confirm attendance and degree by phone or mail. Inquiry must include student's name, social security number, years attended. Employers may obtain transcripts upon written request accompanied by a signed release from the student.

A two-year institution newly admitted to NCES, with an enrollment of 750. Highest level of offering: two year.
ACCREDITATIONS: SACS

Bryan College

Box 7000
Dayton, TN 37321-7000
(615) 775-2041 Ext. 237
Fax (615) 775-7330

Will confirm attendance and degree by phone, fax or mail. Inquiry must include student's name, social security number, date of birth, years attended. Employers may obtain transcripts upon written request accompanied by a signed release from the student.

A general baccalaureate institution, with an enrollment of 413. Highest level of offering: four or five year baccalaureate.
ACCREDITATIONS: SC

Bryant & Stratton

(Formerly Albany Business College)
1259 Central Avenue
Albany, NY 12205
(518) 437-1802

Will confirm attendance and degree by mail. Inquiry must include student's name, date of birth, social security number, years attended. Employers may obtain transcripts upon written request accompanied by a signed release from the student.

A multiprogram two-year institution, with an enrollment of 236. Highest level of offering: one year but less than four years.
ACCREDITATIONS: NY

Bryant & Stratton Business Institute

1028 Main Street
Buffalo, NY 14202
(716) 884-9120 Ext. 221
Fax (716) 884-0091

Will confirm attendance and degree by mail or fax. Inquiry must include student's name, years attended, SSN, date of birth, release. Employers may obtain transcripts upon written request accompanied by a $5.00 fee and a signed release from the student.

A multiprogram two-year institution, with an enrollment of 5,704. Highest level of offering: one year but less than four years.
ACCREDITATIONS: NY MAC

Bryant & Stratton Business Institute

400 Montgomery Street
Syracuse, NY 13202
(315) 472-6603 Ext. 312

Will confirm attendance and degree by phone or mail. Inquiry must include student's name, social security number, years attended,. Employers may obtain transcripts upon written request accompanied by a $5.00 fee and a signed release from the student.

A multiprogram two-year institution, with an enrollment of 1,561. Highest level of offering: one year but less than four years.
ACCREDITATIONS: NY

Bryant & Stratton Business Institute

82 St. Paul Street
Rochester, NY 14604
(716) 359-2130

Will confirm attendance and degree by phone or mail. Inquiry must include student's name, social security number, years attended. Employers may obtain transcripts upon written request accompanied by a $5.00 fee and a signed release from the student.

A multiprogram two-year institution, with an enrollment of 750. Highest level of offering: one year but less than four years.
ACCREDITATIONS: NY MAC

Bryant and Stratton Business Institute, Great Northern

26700 Brook Park Road Ext
North Olmsted, OH 44070
(216) 777-3151 Ext. 22
Fax (216) 777-4093

Will confirm attendance and degree by mail. Inquiry must include student's name, date of birth, social security number, years attended, release. Employers may obtain transcripts upon written request accompanied by a signed release from the student.

A two-year institution newly admitted to NCES. Highest level of offering: one year but less than four years.
ACCREDITATIONS: SRCB

Bryant College of Business Administration

450 Douglas Pike
Smithfield, RI 02917-1284
(401) 232-6080

Will confirm attendance and degree by phone or mail. Inquiry must include student's name, date of birth, social security number, years attended. Employers may obtain transcripts upon written request accompanied by a $2.00 fee and a signed release from the student.

A business school, with an enrollment of 6,505. Highest level of offering: master's.
ACCREDITATIONS: EH

Bryn Mawr College

Bryn Mawr, PA 19010
(215) 526-5141

Will confirm attendance and degree by mail or phone. Inquiry must include student's name and years attended. Requests should be directed to: Registrar's Office. Employers may obtain transcripts upon written request accompanied by a $3.00 fee and a signed release from the student.

A doctoral-level institution with no medical school, with an enrollment of 1,839. Highest level of offering: doctorate.
ACCREDITATIONS: M CSWE

Bucknell University

Office of the Registrar
Lewisburg, PA 17837
(717) 524-1201

Will confirm attendance and degree by phone or mail. Inquiry must include student's name, date of birth, social security number, years attended. Employers may obtain transcripts upon written request accompanied by a $3.00 fee and a signed release from the student.

A comprehensive institution with no medical school, with an enrollment of 3,439. Highest level of offering: master's.
ACCREDITATIONS: M ENG NASM ACS

Bucks County Community College

Swamp Road
Newtown, PA 18940
(215) 968-8101

Will confirm attendance and degree by mail or phone. Inquiry must include student's name, student ID. number, or social security number and years attended. Employers may obtain transcripts upon written request accompanied by a $1.00 fee and a signed release from the student. Requests should be directed to: Admissions Office.

A multiprogram two-year institution, with an enrollment of 10,300. Highest level of offering: one year but less than four years.
ACCREDITATIONS: M NLN/AD ART

Buena Vista College

4th and College
Storm Lake, IA 50588
(712) 749-2233
Fax (712) 749-2037

Will confirm attendance and degree by phone or mail. Inquiry must include student's name, date of birth, social security number, years attended. Employers may obtain transcripts upon written request accompanied by a $3.00 fee and a signed release from the student.

A general baccalaureate institution, with an enrollment of 2,240. Highest level of offering: four or five year baccalaureate.
ACCREDITATIONS: NH CSWE TED

Bunker Hill Community College

New Rutherford Avenue
Boston, MA 02129
(617) 241-8600 Ext. 312
Fax (617) 241-8600-404

Will confirm attendance and degree by phone, fax or mail. Inquiry must include student's name, date of birth, social security number, years attended. Employers may obtain transcripts upon written request accompanied by a $1.00 fee and a signed release from the student. Attn: Registrar's Office.

A multiprogram two-year institution, with an enrollment of 6,977. Highest level of offering: one year but less than four years.

ACCREDITATIONS: EH NLN/AD NMT RAD

Burlington College

95 North Avenue
Burlington, VT 05401
(802) 862-9616

Will confirm attendance and degree by phone or mail. Inquiry must include student's name, social security number, years attended. Employers may obtain transcripts upon written request accompanied by a signed release from the student.

A general baccalaureate institution, with an enrollment of 200. Highest level of offering: four or five year baccalaureate.

ACCREDITATIONS: EH

Burlington County College

Pemberton–Browns Mills Road
Pemberton, NJ 08068
(609) 894-9311 Ext. 277
Fax (609) 894-0183

Will confirm attendance and degree by fax or mail. Inquiry must include student's name, social security number, signed release and years attended. Employers may obtain transcripts upon written request accompanied by a $2.00 fee and a signed release from the student.

A multiprogram two-year institution, with an enrollment of 5,835. Highest level of offering: one year but less than four years.

ACCREDITATIONS: M

Butler County Community College

901 South Haverhill Road
El Dorado, KS 67042
(316) 321-5083 Ext. 123
Fax (316) 321-5122

Will confirm attendance and degree by phone or mail. Inquiry must include student's name, date of birth, social security number, years attended. Employers may obtain transcripts upon written request accompanied by a $3.00 fee and a signed release from the student.

A multiprogram two-year institution, with an enrollment of 6,000. Highest level of offering: one year but less than four years.

ACCREDITATIONS: NH NLN/AD

Butler County Community College

College Drive Oak Hills
Butler, PA 16001
(412) 287-8711 Ext. 256

Will confirm attendance and degree by phone or mail. Inquiry must include student's name, date of birth and release. Employers may obtain transcripts upon written request accompanied by a $1.00 fee and a signed release from the student.

A multiprogram two-year institution, with an enrollment of 2,109. Highest level of offering: one year but less than four years.

ACCREDITATIONS: M

Butler University

4600 & Sunset
Indianapolis, IN 46208
(317) 283-9203

Will confirm attendance and degree by phone or mail. Inquiry must include student's name, date of birth, social security number, years attended and a release. Employers may obtain transcripts upon written request accompanied by a $5.00 fee and a signed release from the student.

A comprehensive institution with no medical school, with an enrollment of 4,058. Highest level of offering: beyond master's but less than doctorate.

ACCREDITATIONS: NH NASM PHAR NCATE CHEM RSTHT TED NMT RAD

Butte College

3536 Butte Campus Drive
Oroville, CA 95965
(916) 895-2511

Will confirm attendance and degree by mail. Inquiry must include student's name, date of birth, social security number, years attended, release. Employers may obtain transcripts upon written request accompanied by a $3.00 fee and a signed release from the student. Requests should be directed to: Admissions & Records Department.

A multiprogram two-year institution, with an enrollment of 13,000. Highest level of offering: one year but less than four years.

ACCREDITATIONS: WJ RSTH

C

C B N University
(See Rengent University)

Cabrillo College

6500 Soquel Drive
Adminssions and Records Office
Aptos, CA 95003
(408) 479-6212 or 479-6201

Will confirm attendance and degree by mail. Inquiry must include student's name, social security number, years attended, release. Requests should be directed to: Admissions and Records Office, Attn: Records. Employers may obtain transcripts upon written request and a signed release from the student. $2.00 fee per copy.

A multiprogram two-year institution, with an enrollment of 14,500. Highest level of offering: one year but less than four years.

ACCREDITATIONS: WJ DA DH RAD THEA

Cabrini College

Radnor, PA 19087
(215) 971-8545
Fax (215) 971-8309

Will confirm attendance and degree by phone or mail. Inquiry must include student's name, years attended. Employers may obtain transcripts upon written request accompanied by a $2.00 fee and a signed release from the student. Requests should be directed to: Registrar's Office.

A general baccalaureate institution, with an enrollment of 935. Highest level of offering: master's.

ACCREDITATIONS: M

Caldwell College

Ryerson Avenue
Caldwell, NJ 07006
(201) 228-4424 Ext. 201

Will confirm attendance and degree by mail. Inquiry must include student's name, date of birth, years attended. Employers may obtain transcripts upon written request accompanied by a $3.00 fee and a signed release from the student. Requests should be directed to: Registrar's Office.

A general baccalaureate institution, with an enrollment of 704. Highest level of offering: four or five year baccalaureate.

ACCREDITATIONS: M

Caldwell Community College and Technical Institute

1000 Hickory Boulevard
Hudson, NC 28645
(704) 726-2200

Will confirm attendance and degree by phone or mail. Inquiry must include student's name, date of birth, social security number, years attended. Employers may obtain transcripts upon written request accompanied by a signed release from the student. Requests should be directed to: Student Development–Records Department.

A multiprogram two-year institution, with an enrollment of 2,600. Highest level of offering: one year but less than four years.

ACCREDITATIONS: SC NMT RAD

California Baptist College

8432 Magnolia Avenue
Riverside, CA 92504
(714) 689-5771 Ext. 223
Fax (714) 351-1808

Will confirm attendance and degree by phone or mail. Inquiry must include student's name, date of birth, social security number, years attended. Employers may obtain transcripts upon written request accompanied by a $3.00 fee and a signed release from the student.

A general baccalaureate institution, with an enrollment of 687. Highest level of offering: master's.

ACCREDITATIONS: WC NASM

California College of Arts and Crafts

5212 Broadway
Oakland, CA 94618
(415) 653-8118 Ext. 112

Will confirm attendance and degree by phone or mail. Inquiry must include student's name, date of birth, years attended. Employers may obtain transcripts upon written request accompanied by a $3.00 fee and a signed release from the student.

A visual and performing arts school, with an enrollment of 1,035. Highest level of offering: master's.

ACCREDITATIONS: WC ART FIDER

California College of Podiatric Medicine

1210 Scott Street
San Francisco, CA 94115
(415) 292-0414

Will confirm attendance and degree by mail or phone. Inquiry must include student's name, years attended, social security number. Requests should be directed to: Registrar's Office. Employers may obtain transcripts upon written request accompanied by a $4.00 fee and a signed release from the student.

A health institution, with an enrollment of 360. Highest level of offering: masters.

ACCREDITATIONS: WC POD

California Family Study Center

5433 Laurel Canyon Boulevard
North Hollywood, CA 91607
(818) 509-5959 Ext. 252

Will confirm degree and attendance by mail. Inquiry must include student's name, date of birth, social security number, years attended, release. Employers may obtain transcripts upon written request accompanied by a $4.00 fee and a signed release from the student.

A bachelor's or higher institution . Highest level of offering: master's.

ACCREDITATIONS: WC

California Institute of Integral Studies

765 Ashbury Street
San Francisco, CA 94117
(415) 753-6100 Ext. 13
Fax (415) 753-1167

Will confirm attendance and degree by phone or mail. Inquiry must include student's name. Employers may obtain transcripts upon written request accompanied by a $3.00 fee and a signed release from the student. Requests should be directed to: Registrar's Office.

A specialized school, with an enrollment of 650. Highest level of offering: doctorate.

ACCREDITATIONS: WC

California Institute of Technology

1201 East California Boulevard
M/C 110-31
Pasadena, CA 91125
818-356-6354

Will confirm attendance and degree by phone or mail. Inquiry must include student's name, date of birth, years attended. Employers may obtain transcripts upon written request accompanied by a $1.00 fee and a signed release from the student.

A doctoral-level institution with no medical school, with an enrollment of 1,816. Highest level of offering: doctorate.

ACCREDITATIONS: WC ENG

California Institute of the Arts

24700 Mcbean Parkway
Valencia, CA 91355
(805) 255-1050

Will confirm attendance and degree by mail. Inquiry must include student's name, social security number, years attended. Employers may obtain transcripts upon written request accompanied by a $2.00 fee and a signed release from the student.

A visual and performing arts school, with an enrollment of 842. Highest level of offering: master's.

ACCREDITATIONS: WC ART NASM

California Institute of Transpersonal Psychology

250 Oak Grove Avenue
Menlo Park, CA 94025
(415) 326-1960 Ext. 14

Will confirm attendance and degree by phone or mail. Inquiry must include student's name. Employers may obtain transcripts upon written request accompanied by a $10.00 fee and a signed release from the student.

A bachelor's or higher institution newly admitted to NCES, with an enrollment of 175. Highest level of offering: doctorate

ACCREDITATIONS: 3IC

California Lutheran College

60 West Olsen Road
Thousand Oaks, CA 91360
(805) 493-3105

Will confirm attendance and degree by phone or mail. Inquiry must include student's name, date of birth, years attended. Employers may obtain transcripts upon written request accompanied by a $2.00 fee and a signed release from the student. Requests should be directed to: Registrar Department.

A comprehensive institution with no medical school, with an enrollment of 2,282. Highest level of offering: master's.

ACCREDITATIONS: WC

California Maritime Academy

PO Box 1392
Vallejo, CA 94590
(707) 648-4262
Fax (707) 648-4204

Will confirm attendance and degree by mail or fax. Inquiry must include student's name, years attended. Employers may obtain transcripts upon written request accompanied by a $4.00 fee and a signed release from the student. Requests should be directed to: Records Office.

An engineering school, with an enrollment of 456. Highest level of offering: four or five year baccalaureate.

ACCREDITATIONS: WC ENGT

California Polytechnic State University–San Luis Obispo

San Luis Obispo, CA 93407
(805) 756-2531
Fax (805) 756-7237

Will confirm attendance and degree by phone or mail. Inquiry must include student's name, social security number, years attended. Requests should be directed to: Records Office–Transcript Department. Employers may obtain transcripts upon written request accompanied by a $4.00 fee and a signed release from the student.

A comprehensive institution with no medical school, with an enrollment of 15,968. Highest level of offering: master's.

ACCREDITATIONS: WC ARCH BUS ENG ENGT LSAR

California School of Professional Psychology at Berkeley

1005 Atlantic Avenue
Alamed, CA 94501
(510) 523-2300

Will confirm attendance and degree by mail. Inquiry must include student's name, date of birth, social security number, years attended, release, self addressed stamped envelope.

A specialized school, with an enrollment of 348. Highest level of offering: doctorate.

ACCREDITATIONS: WC CLPSY

California School of Professional Psychology at Fresno

1350 M Street
Fresno, CA 93721
(209) 486-8420 Ext. 22

Will confirm attendance and degree by mail. Inquiry must include student's name, social security number, years attended. Employers may obtain transcripts upon written request accompanied by a $4.00 fee and a signed release from the student.

A specialized school, with an enrollment of 341. Highest level of offering: doctorate.

ACCREDITATIONS: WC CLPSY

California School of Professional Psychology at Los Angeles

1000 S. Fremont
Alhambra, CA 91803-1360
(818) 284-2777

Will confirm attendance and degree by mail. Inquiry must include student's name, years attended. Only students may request transcripts. Employers may obtain transcripts upon written request accompanied by a $5.00 fee and a signed release from the student.

A specialized school, with an enrollment of 505. Highest level of offering: doctorate.
ACCREDITATIONS: WC CLPSY

California School of Professional Psychology at San Diego

6212 Ferris Square
San Diego, CA 92121
(619) 452-1664

Will confirm attendance and degree by phone or mail. Inquiry must include student's name. Employers may obtain transcripts upon written request accompanied by a $3.00 fee and a signed release from the student. Requests should be directed to: Registrar's Office.

A specialized school, with an enrollment of 420. Highest level of offering: doctorate.
ACCREDITATIONS: WC CLPSY

California School of Professional Psychology Central Office

2749 Hyde Street
San Francisco, CA 94109
(415) 346-4500

Will confirm attendance and degree by mail. Inquiry must include student's name, social security number, years attended. Employers may obtain transcripts upon written request accompanied by a $3.00 fee and a signed release from the student.

California State College–Bakersfield

9001 Stockdale Highway
Bakersfield, CA 93311-1099
(805) 664-2147

Will confirm attendance and degree by mail or phone. Inquiry must include student's name, social security number, date of birth. Employers may obtain transcripts upon written request accompanied by a $4.00 fee and a signed release from the student. Requests should be directed to: Records Office.

A comprehensive institution with no medical school, with an enrollment of 5,245. Highest level of offering: master's.
ACCREDITATIONS: WC BUS MT NLN

California State College–San Bernardino

5500 University Parkway
San Bernardino, CA 92407-2397
(714) 880-5000

Will confirm attendance and degree by phone or mail. Inquiry must include student's name, social security number. Employers may obtain transcripts upon written request accompanied by a $4.00 fee and a signed release from the student.

A comprehensive institution with no medical school, with an enrollment of 11,000. Highest level of offering: master's
ACCREDITATIONS: WC ART NLN

California State Polytechnic University–Pomona

3801 West Temple Avenue
Pomona, CA 91768
(714) 869-3000

Will confirm attendance and degree by phone or mail. Inquiry must include student's name, date of birth, social security number, years attended. Employers may obtain transcripts upon written request accompanied by a $4.00 fee and a signed release from the student. Requests should be directed to: Records Department.

A comprehensive institution with no medical school, with an enrollment of 17,024. Highest level of offering: master's.
ACCREDITATIONS: WC ARCH ENG ENGT LSAR CSWE

California State University & College System All Institutions

5151 State University Drive
Los Angeles, CA 90032
(213) 224-2177
Fax (213) 343-3840

Will confirm attendance and degree by phone or mail. Inquiry must include student's name, social security number, years attended. Employers may obtain transcripts upon written request accompanied by a $4.00 fee and a signed release from the student.

California State University–Chico

Chico, CA 95929-0720
(916) 895-5142

Will confirm attendance and degree by phone or mail. Inquiry must include student's name, social security number, years attended. Employers may obtain transcripts upon written request accompanied by a $4.00 fee and a signed release from the student. Requests should be directed to: Records & Admissions Office.

A comprehensive institution with no medical school, with an enrollment of 14,196. Highest level of offering: master's.
ACCREDITATIONS: WC ART BUS ENG NASM NLN CSWE TED

California State University–Fresno

Joyal Administrative Bldg.
Fresno, CA 93740-0057
(209) 294-2328

Will confirm attendance and degree by phone or mail. Inquiry must include student's name, social security number, years attended. Employers may obtain transcripts upon written request accompanied by a $4.00 fee and a signed release from the student. Requests should be directed to: Registrar's Office.

A comprehensive institution with no medical school, with an enrollment of 16,454. Highest level of offering: master's.
ACCREDITATIONS: WC BUS ENG JOUR NASM NLN PTA SP CSWE TED

California State University–Fullerton

PO Box 34080
Fullerton, CA 92634-9480
(714) 773-2300

Will confirm attendance and degree by phone or mail. Inquiry must include student's name, date of birth, social security number, years attended. Requests should be directed to: Record's Office. Employers may obtain transcripts upon written request accompanied by a $4.00 fee and a signed release from the student.

A comprehensive institution with no medical school, with an enrollment of 25,000. Highest level of offering: master's.
ACCREDITATIONS: WC ART BUS DANCE ENG JOUR NASM NLN SP TED THEA

California State University–Hayward

Hayward, CA 94542
(510) 881-3075

Will confirm attendance and degree by mail or phone. Inquiry must include student's name, date of birth, social security number. Employers may obtain transcripts upon written request accompanied by a $4.00 fee and a signed release from the student. Requests should be directed to: Records Office.

A comprehensive institution with no medical school, with an enrollment of 12,072. Highest level of offering: master's.
ACCREDITATIONS: WC ART BUS NASM NLN TED CHEM

California State University–Long Beach

1250 Bellflower Boulevard
Long Beach, CA 90840
(310) 985-4111 Ext. 6077
Fax (310) 985-8887

Will confirm attendance and degree by phone or mail. Inquiry must include student's name, date of birth, social security number, years attended. Requests should be directed to: Admission & Records Dept. Only students may obtain transcripts. There is a $4.00 fee.

A comprehensive institution with no medical school, with an enrollment of 35,000. Highest level of offering: master's.
ACCREDITATIONS: WC ART BUS DANCE ENG FIDER JOUR NASM NLN PTA CSWE THEA AUD

California State University–Los Angeles

5151 State University Drive
Los Angeles, CA 90032
(213) 224-2158
Fax (213) 343-3840

Will confirm attendance and degree by phone or mail. Inquiry must include student's name, date of birth, social security number, years attended. Employers may obtain transcripts upon written request accompanied by a $4.00 fee and a signed release from the student. Requests should be directed to: Verifications Office.

A comprehensive institution with no medical school, with an enrollment of 19,576. Highest level of offering: doctorate.
ACCREDITATIONS: WC ART BUS DIET ENG NASM NLN CSWE TED

California State University–Northridge

18111 Nordhoff Street
Northridge, CA 91330
(818) 885-3731
Fax (818) 885-3766

Will confirm attendance and degree by mail. Inquiry must include student's name, date of birth, social security number, years attended, and a release from the student. Employers may obtain transcripts upon written request accompanied by a $4.00 fee.

A comprehensive institution with no medical school, with an enrollment of 28,144. Highest level of offering: master's.
ACCREDITATIONS: WC BUS CHE ENG JOUR NASM PTA RAD SP

California State University–Sacramento

6000 J Street
Sacramento, CA 95819
(916) 278-7111
(10:00 a.m – 2:00 p.m. Pacific time)

Will confirm degree by phone or mail. Inquiry must include student's name, date of birth, social security number, field of study. Employers may obtain transcripts upon written request accompanied by a $4.00 fee and a signed release from the student. Requests should be directed to: Registrar's Office.

A comprehensive institution with no medical school, with an enrollment of 24,974. Highest level of offering: master's.
ACCREDITATIONS: WC ART BUS ENG ENGT NASM NLN CSWE TED THEA

California State University–San Bernardino

5500 University Parkway
San Bernardino, CA 92407-2397
(714) 880-5212

Will confirm attendance and degree by phone or mail. Inquiry must include student's name, social security number. Employers may obtain transcripts upon written request accompanied by a $4.00 fee and a signed release from the student. Requests should be directed to: Records Office.

A comprehensive institution with no medical school, with an enrollment of 10,450. Highest level of offering: master's.
ACCREDITATIONS: WC ART NLN

California State University–Stanislaus

801 West Monte Vista
Turlock, CA 95380
(209) 667-3264

Will confirm attendance and degree by phone or mail. Inquiry must include student's name, social security number. Employers may obtain transcripts upon written request accompanied by a $4.00 fee and a signed release from the student. Requests should be directed to: Records Office.

A comprehensive institution with no medical school, with an enrollment of 5,800. Highest level of offering: master's.
ACCREDITATIONS: WC ART NASM SP THEA

California State University–Statewide Nursing Program

Domingues Hills, 1000 East Victoria Street
Carson, CA 90747
(310) 516-4065

Will confirm attendance and degree by phone or mail. Inquiry must include student's name, social security number, years attended. Requests should be directed to: Records Clerk. Employers may obtain transcripts upon written request accompanied by a $4.00 fee and a signed release from the student.

A bachelor's or higher institution newly admitted to NCES, with an enrollment of 4,000. Highest level of offering: master's.
ACCREDITATIONS: WC NLN

California State University Dominguez Hills

1000 East Victoria Street
Carson, CA 90747
(213) 516-3601

Will confirm attendance and degree by mail or phone (Mon.-Thurs. 10a.m.-1p.m.; 3p.m.-6p.m. and Fri. 8a.m.-12 noon Pacific time). Inquiry must include student's name, date of birth, social security number, years attended. Employers may obtain transcripts upon written request accompanied by a $4.00 fee and a signed release from the student. Requests should be directed to: Transcripts.

A comprehensive institution with no medical school, with an enrollment of 8,000. Highest level of offering: master's.
ACCREDITATIONS: WC ART MT NASM TED

California University of Pennsylvania

250 University Ave.
California, PA 15419-1394
(412) 938-4434
Fax (412) 938-4434

Will confirm attendance and degree by phone, fax or mail. Inquiry must include student's name, social security number. Employers may obtain transcripts upon written request accompanied by a $2.00 fee and a signed release from the student. Requests should be directed to: Academic Records.

A comprehensive institution with no medical school, with an enrollment of 7,000. Highest level of offering: beyond master's but less than doctorate.
ACCREDITATIONS: M ANEST CSWE TED

California Western School of Law

350 Cedar Street
San Diego, CA 92101
(619) 239-0391 Ext. 408
Fax (619) 696-9999

Will confirm attendance and degree by phone or mail. Inquiry must include student's name, years attended. Employers may obtain transcripts upon written request accompanied by a $3.00 fee and a signed release from the student.

A law school, with an enrollment of 750. Highest level of offering: master's.
ACCREDITATIONS: LAW

Calumet College of St. Joseph

2400 New York Avenue
Whiting, IN 46394
(219) 473-4211
Fax (219) 473-4259

Will confirm attendance and degree by phone or mail. Inquiry must include student's name, date of birth. Employers may obtain transcripts upon written request accompanied by a $3.00 fee and a signed release from the student.

A general baccalaureate institution, with an enrollment of 1,130. Highest level of offering: four or five year baccalaureate.
ACCREDITATIONS: NH

Calvary Bible College

15800 Calvary Boulevard
Kansas City, MO 64147-1341
(816) 322-0110 Ext. 1306
Fax (816) 331-4474

Will confirm attendance and degree by phone or mail. Inquiry must include student's name, date of birth, years attended. Employers may obtain transcripts upon written request accompanied by a $2.00 fee and a signed release from the student. Requests should be directed to: Registrar's Office.

A school of philosophy, religion and theology, with an enrollment of 280. Highest level of offering: master's.
ACCREDITATIONS: BI

Calvin College

3201 Burton South East
Grand Rapids, MI 49546
(616) 957-6155
Fax (616) 957-8551

Will confirm attendance and degree by phone, fax or mail. Inquiry must include student's name, date of birth, years attended. Employers may obtain transcripts upon written request accompanied by a $2.00 fee and a signed release from the student. Requests should be directed to: Registrar's Office.

A general baccalaureate institution, with an enrollment of 4,025. Highest level of offering: master's.

ACCREDITATIONS: NCA

Calvin Theological Seminary

3233 Burton Street South East
Grand Rapids, MI 49546
(616) 957-6036

Will confirm attendance and degree by mail or phone. Inquiry must include student's name. Requests should be directed to: Academics Secretary. Employers may obtain transcripts upon written request accompanied by a $2.00 fee and a signed release from the student.

A school of philosophy, religion and theology, with an enrollment of 238. Highest level of offering: master's.

ACCREDITATIONS: THEOL

Cambridge College

15 Mifflin Place
Cambridge, MA 02138
(617) 492-5108
Fax (617) 349-3545

Will confirm attendance and degree by phone or mail. Inquiry must include student's name, social security number, years attended. Requests should be directed to: Registrar's Office. Only students may obtain transcripts, $3.00 fee.

A bachelor's or higher institution newly admitted to NCES, with an enrollment of 600. Highest level of offering: master's.

ACCREDITATIONS: EH

Camden County College

PO Box 200–College Drive
Blackwood, NJ 08012-0200
(609) 227-7200 Ext. 200

Will confirm attendance and degree by mail. Inquiry must include student's name, social security number, years attended, release. Employers may obtain transcripts upon written request accompanied by a signed release from the student.

A multiprogram two-year institution, with an enrollment of 10,411. Highest level of offering: one year but less than four years.

ACCREDITATIONS: M AVVMA/CVTTAT DH MLTAD

Cameron University

2800 West Gore Boulevard
Lawton, OK 73505
(405) 581-2238
Fax (405) 581-2235

Will confirm attendance and degree by phone, fax or mail. Inquiry must include student's name, date of birth, social security number, years attended. Employers may obtain transcripts upon written request accompanied by a $1.00 fee and a signed release from the student.

A general baccalaureate institution, with an enrollment of 5,496. Highest level of offering: four or five year baccalaureate.

ACCREDITATIONS: NH NLN/AD NASM

Campbell University

PO Box 367
Buies Creek, NC 27506
(919) 893-4111

Will confirm attendance and degree by phone or mail. Inquiry must include student's name, date of birth, social security number, years attended, release. Employers may obtain transcripts upon written request accompanied by a $3.00 fee and a signed release from the student.

A comprehensive institution with no medical school, with an enrollment of 3,338. Highest level of offering: doctorate.

ACCREDITATIONS: SC LAW TED

Campbellsville College

200 West College Street
Campbellsville, KY 42718-2799
(502) 465-8158 Ext. 6233
Fax (502) 789-5020

Will confirm attendance and degree by phone or mail. Inquiry must include student's name, date of birth, social security number, years attended. Employers may obtain transcripts upon written request accompanied by a $2.00 fee and a signed release from the student.

A general baccalaureate institution, with an enrollment of 1,010. Highest level of offering: four or five year baccalaureate.

ACCREDITATIONS: SACA NASM

Canada College

4200 Farm Hill Boulevard
Redwood City, CA 94061
(415) 364-1212 Ext. 228

Will confirm attendance and degree by mail or phone. Inquiry must include student's name, social security number, years attended. Employers may obtain transcripts upon written request accompanied by a $3.00 fee and a signed release from the student.

A multiprogram two-year institution, with an enrollment of 7,082. Highest level of offering: one year but less than four years.

ACCREDITATIONS: WJ RAD

Canisius College

2001 Main Street
Buffalo, NY 14208
(716) 888-2998
Fax (716) 888-2525

Will confirm attendance and degree by phone or mail. Inquiry must include student's name, date of birth, social security number, years attended. Employers may obtain transcripts upon written request accompanied by a $3.00 fee and a signed release from the student.

A comprehensive institution with no medical school, with an enrollment of 4,383. Highest level of offering: beyond master's but less than doctorate.

ACCREDITATIONS: M BUS NY TED

Canton

Canton, NY 13617
(315) 386-7042
Fax (315) 386-7930

Will confirm attendance and degree by phone or mail. Inquiry must include student's name, social security number, years attended. Employers may obtain transcripts upon written request accompanied by a $5.00 fee and a signed release from the student. Requests should be directed to: Registrar's Office.

A multiprogram two-year institution, with an enrollment of 2,326. Highest level of offering: one year but less than four.

ACCREDITATIONS: M NLN/AD AVVMA/CVTTAT ENGT FUSER MLTAD NY

Cape Cod Community College

Route 132
West Barnstable, MA 02668
(508) 362-2131 Ext. 313

Will confirm attendance and degree by phone or mail. Inquiry must include student's name, date of birth. Requests should be directed to: Records Department. Employers may obtain transcripts upon written request accompanied by a signed release from the student.

A multiprogram two-year institution, with an enrollment of 4,251. Highest level of offering: one year but less than four years.

ACCREDITATIONS: EH NLN/AD DH

Cape Fear Technical Institute

411 North Front Street
Wilmington, NC 28401
(919) 343-0481

Will confirm attendance and degree by phone or mail. Inquiry must include student's name, social security number, years attended. Employers may obtain transcripts upon written request accompanied by a signed release from the student.

A multiprogram two-year institution, with an enrollment of 2,600. Highest level of offering: one year but less than four years.

ACCREDITATIONS: SC

Capital City Junior College

PO Box 4818
7723 Asher Avenue
Little Rock, AR 72214
(501) 562-0700
Fax (501) 565-7591

Will confirm attendance and degree by phone or mail. Inquiry must include student's name, social security number, years attended. Employers may obtain transcripts upon written request accompanied by a $2.00 fee and a signed release from the student.

A multiprogram two-year institution, with an enrollment of 304. Highest level of offering: one year but less than four years.

ACCREDITATIONS: NH JRCB

Capital University

2199 East Main Street
Columbus, OH 43209
(614) 236-6150
Fax (614) 236-6490

Will confirm attenda nce and degree by phone, fax or mail. Inquiry must include student's name, date of birth, social security number, years attended. Employers may obtain transcripts upon written request accompanied by a $2.00 fee and a signed release from the student.

A general baccalaureate institution, with an enrollment of 3,008. Highest level of offering: master's.

ACCREDITATIONS: NH LAW NASM NLN CSWE TED

Capitol Institute of Technology

11301 Springfield Road
Laurel, MD 20708
(301) 953-0060
Fax (301) 953-3876

Will confirm attendance and degree by phone, fax or mail. Inquiry must include student's name, date of birth, social security number, years attended. Employers may obtain transcripts upon written request accompanied by a $3.00 fee and a signed release from the student. Requests should be directed to: Registrar's Office.

An engineering school, with an enrollment of 850. Highest level of offering: four or five year baccalaureate.

ACCREDITATIONS: M ENGT

Cardinal Glennon College and Seminary

5200 Glennon Drive
Saint Louis, MO 63119
(314) 644-0266

Cardinal Glennon College and Seminary closed in June 1987. Records are maintained at the above address. Will confirm attendance and degree by phone or mail. Inquiry must include student's name, social security number and address. Employers may obtain transcripts upon written request accompanied by a $2.00 fee and a signed release from the student.

Cardinal Newman College

c/o Fontbonne College
6800 Wydown
Saint Louis, MO 63105
(314) 889-1421
Fax (314) 889-1451

Records for this school are being handled by Fontbonne College. Will confirm attendance and degree by phone. Inquiry must include student's name, social security number. Employers may obtain transcripts upon written request accompanied by a $2.00 fee and a signed release from the student.

Cardinal Stritch College

6801 North Yates Road
Milwaukee, WI 53217
(414) 352-5400

Will confirm attendance and degree by mail. Inquiry must include student's name, date of birth, social security number, years attended. Requests should be directed to: Registrar's Office. Employers may obtain transcripts upon written request accompanied by a $3.00 fee and a signed release from the student.

A general baccalaureate institution, with an enrollment of 4,000. Highest level of offering: master's.

ACCREDITATIONS: NH NLN/AD TED

CareerCom Junior College

(See Franklin College)

Carl Albert Junior College

PO Box 606
Poteau, OK 74953
(918) 647-8660 Ext. 237
Fax (918) 647-2980

Will confirm attendance and degree by phone or mail. Inquiry must include student's name, date of birth, social security number, years attended. Employers may obtain transcripts upon written request accompanied by a $1.00 fee and a signed release from the student. Requests should be directed to: Registrar's Office.

A multiprogram two-year institution, with an enrollment of 1,972. Highest level of offering: two years but less than four years.

ACCREDITATIONS: NCA

Carl Sandburg College

2232 South Lake Storey Road
Galesburg, IL 61401
(309) 344-2518

Will confirm attendance and degree by phone or mail. Inquiry must include student's name, date of birth, social security number. Employers may obtain transcripts upon written request accompanied by a $2.00 fee and a signed release from the student.

A multiprogram two-year institution, with an enrollment of 2,144. Highest level of offering: one year but less than four years.

ACCREDITATIONS: NH RAD

Carleton College

1 North College Street
Northfield, MN 55057
(507) 663-4289

Will confirm attendance and degree by phone or mail. Inquiry must include student's name, social security number, years attended. Requests should be directed to: Registrar's Office. Employers may obtain transcripts upon written request accompanied by a $2.00 fee and a signed release from the student.

A general baccalaureate institution, with an enrollment of 1,855. Highest level of offering: four or five year baccalaureate.

ACCREDITATIONS: NH TED

Carlow College

3333 Fifth Avenue
Pittsburgh, PA 15213
(412) 578-6084

Will confirm attendance and degree by phone or mail. Inquiry must include student's name, date of birth, social security number. Employers may obtain transcripts upon written request accompanied by a $4.00 fee and a signed release from the student.

A general baccalaureate institution, with an enrollment of 1,246. Highest level of offering: master's.

ACCREDITATIONS: M NLN

Carnegie–Mellon University

5000 Forbes Avenue
Pittsburgh, PA 15213
(412) 268-2000 Ext. 2004 or 2006
Fax (412) 268-5249

Will confirm attendance and degree by phone, fax or mail. Inquiry must include student's name, social security number, years attended. Employers may obtain transcripts upon written request accompanied by a $2.00 fee and a signed release from the student.

A doctoral-level institution with no medical school, with an enrollment of 7,000. Highest level of offering: doctorate.

ACCREDITATIONS: M ARCH ART BUS ENG NASM

Carroll College

100 North East Avenue
Waukesha, WI 53186
(414) 524-7210

Will confirm attendance and degree by phone or mail. Inquiry must include student's name, date of birth, social security number. Employers may obtain transcripts upon written request accompanied by a $3.00 fee and a signed release from the student.

A liberal arts baccalaureate institution, with an enrollment of 1,365. Highest level of offering: master's.

ACCREDITATIONS: NH CSWE

Carroll College

North Benton Avenue
Helena, MT 59625
(406) 442-3450 Ext. 236
Fax (406) 442-9291

Will confirm attendance and degree by phone, fax or mail. Inquiry must include student's name, date of birth, social security number. Employers may obtain transcripts upon written request accompanied by a $3.00 fee and a signed release from the student.

A general baccalaureate institution, with an enrollment of 1,300. Highest level of offering: four or five year baccalaureate.

ACCREDITATIONS: NW MRA NLN CSWE

Carson–Newman College

Jefferson City, TN 37760
(615) 475-9061 Ext. 3240
Fax (615) 471-3502

Will confirm attendance and degree by phone or mail. Inquiry must include student's name, social security number, years attended. Employers may obtain transcripts upon written request accompanied by a $3.00 fee and a signed release from the student.

A general baccalaureate institution, with an enrollment of 2,016. Highest level of offering: master's degree.

ACCREDITATIONS: SC NASM TED

Carteret Technical College

3505 Arendell Street
Morehead City, NC 28557
(919) 247-6000
Fax (919) 247-4142

Will confirm attendance and degree by mail. Inquiry must include student's name, date of birth, social security number, years attended, release. Employers may obtain transcripts upon written request accompanied by a $1.00 fee and a signed release from the student.

A multiprogram two-year institution, with an enrollment of 1,600. Highest level of offering: one year but less than four years.

ACCREDITATIONS: SC MAC RAD RSTH RSTHT

Carthage College

2001 Alford Drive
Kenosha, WI 53141
(414) 551-8500 Ext. 285

Will confirm attendance and degree by phone or mail. Inquiry must include student's name, date of birth, years attended. Requests should be directed to: Registrar's Office. Employers may obtain transcripts upon written request accompanied by a $2.00 fee and a signed release from the student.

A general baccalaureate institution, with enrollment of 1,502. Highest level of offering: master's.

ACCREDITATIONS: NH NASM CSWE

Casco Bay College

477 Congress Street
Portland, ME 04101
(207) 772-0196

Will confirm attendance and degree by mail or phone. Inquiry must include student's name, years attended, social security number and release. Employers may obtain transcripts upon written request accompanied by a $5.00 fee and a signed release from the student.

A multiprogram two-year institution, with an enrollment of 245. Highest level of offering: two years but less than four years.

ACCREDITATIONS: JRCB

Case Western Reserve University

10900 Euclid Avenue
235 Pardee Hall
Cleveland, OH 44106
(216) 368-4323
Fax (216) 368-4633

Will confirm attendance and degree by mail or fax. Inquiry must include student's name, date of birth, social security number, years attended, self addressed stamped envelope. Requests should be directed to: Transcript Office–Pardee Hall. Employers may obtain transcripts upon written request accompanied by a $2.00 fee and a signed release from the student.

A doctoral-level institution with a medical school, with an enrollment of 8,352. Highest level of offering: doctorate.

ACCREDITATIONS: NH AUD BUS CLPSY DENT DIET DIETI ENG IPSY LAW LIB MED NASM NLN SP CSWE MIDWF

Casper College

125 College Drive
Casper, WY 82601
(307) 268-2211
Fax (307) 235-1461

Will confirm attendance and degree by phone or mail. Inquiry must include student's name, social security number. Employers may obtain transcripts upon written request accompanied by a signed release from the student.

A multiprogram two-year institution, with an enrollment of 4,053. Highest level of offering: one year but less than four years.

ACCREDITATIONS: NH NLN/AD PNUR RAD

Castle College

Searles Road
Windham, NH 03087
(603) 893-6111

Will confirm attendance and degree by mail. Inquiry must include student's name, date of birth, social security number, years attended. Employers may obtain transcripts upon written request and a signed release from the student.

A single program two-year institution, with an enrollment of 149. Highest level of offering: one year but less than four years.

ACCREDITATIONS: NEASC

Castleton State College

Castleton, VT 05735
(802) 468-5611 Ext. 274

Will confirm attendance and degree by phone or mail. Inquiry must include student's name, social security number, years attended, degree earned. Employers may obtain transcripts upon written request accompanied by a $3.00 fee and a signed release from the student.

A general baccalaureate institution, with an enrollment of 2,043. Highest level of offering: beyond master's but less than doctorate.

ACCREDITATIONS: EH NLN/AD CSWE

Catawba College

2300 West Innes Street
Salisbury, NC 28144
(704) 637-4111 Ext. 411

Will confirm attendance and degree by phone or mail. Inquiry must include student's name, date of birth, social security number, years attended. Employers may obtain transcripts upon written request accompanied by a $2.00 fee and a signed release from the student.

A general baccalaureate institution, with an enrollment of 910. Highest level of offering: four or five year baccalaureate.

ACCREDITATIONS: SC CSWE

Catawba Valley Technical College

Route 3 Box 283
Hickory, NC 28602
(704) 327-9124 Ext. 221

Will confirm attendance and degree by phone or mail. Inquiry must include student's name, date of birth, social security number, years attended. Employers may obtain transcripts upon written request accompanied by a signed release from the student. Requests should be directed to: Records Office.

A multiprogram two-year institution, with an enrollment of 3,200. Highest level of offering: one year but less than four years.

ACCREDITATIONS: SC ENGT

Cathedral Residence of the Immaculate Conception Center

(See Imaculate Conception Center)

Catherine College

(See Labore College)

Catholic Theological Union–At Chicago

5401 South Cornell Avenue
Chicago, IL 60615
(312) 324-8000 Ext. 30
Fax (312) 324-8490

Will confirm attendance and degree by phone or mail. Inquiry must include student's name, date of birth, social security number, years attended. Requests should be directed to: Student Services.

A school of religion and theology, with an enrollment of 351. Highest level of offering: doctorate. Employers may obtain transcripts upon written request accompanied by a $5.00 fee and a signed release from the student.

ACCREDITATIONS: NCA ATS

Catholic University of America

629 Michigan Avenue North East
Washington, DC 20064
(202) 635-5300

Will confirm attendance and degree by phone or mail. Inquiry must include student's name, date of birth, social security number. Employers may obtain transcripts upon written request accompanied by a $4.00 fee and a signed release from the student.

A doctoral-level institution with no medical school, with an enrollment of 6,780. Highest level of offering: doctorate.
ACCREDITATIONS: M ARCH CLPSY ENG LAW LIB MT NASM NLN CSWE TED THEOL PAST

Catonsville Community College

800 South Rolling Road
Catonsville, MD 21228
(301) 455-4555

Will confirm attendance and degree by phone or mail. Inquiry must include student's name, social security number, years attended. Employers may obtain transcripts upon written request accompanied by a signed release from the student. Requests should be directed to: Records Department.

A multiprogram two-year institution, with an enrollment of 13,462. Highest level of offering: two years.
ACCREDITATIONS: M FUSER

Cayuga County Community College

Franklin Street
Auburn, NY 13021
(315) 255-1743 Ext. 216

Will confirm attendance and degree by phone or mail. Inquiry must include student's name, date of birth, social security number. Employers may obtain transcripts upon written request accompanied by a $2.00 fee and a signed release from the student. Requests should be directed to: Records Office.

A multiprogram two-year institution, with an enrollment of 3,053. Highest level of offering: one year but less than four years.
ACCREDITATIONS: M NY NLN/AD

Cazenovia College

Cazenovia, NY 13035
(315) 655-9446
Fax (315) 655-2190

Will confirm attendance and degree by phone or mail. Inquiry must include student's name, social security number, years attended. Employers may obtain transcripts upon written request accompanied by a signed release from the student.

A multiprogram four-year institution, with an enrollment of 1055. Highest level of offering: a general baccalaureate institution..
ACCREDITATIONS: M NY

Cecil Community College

1000 North East Road
North East, MD 21901
(301) 287-6060

Will confirm attendance and degree by mail or phone. Inquiry must include student's name, social security number, years attended, release. Employers may obtain transcripts upon written request accompanied by a signed release from the student.

A multiprogram two-year institution, with an enrollment of 1,423. Highest level of offering: one year but less than four years.
ACCREDITATIONS: M NLN/AD

Cecils Junior College

PO Box 6407
Asheville, NC 28816
(704) 252-2486
Fax (704) 252-8558

Will confirm attendance and degree by phone or mail. Inquiry must include student's name, social security number. Employers may obtain transcripts upon written request accompanied by a $2.00 fee and a signed release from the student.

A multiprogram two-year institution, with an enrollment of 192. Highest level of offering: one year but less than four years.
ACCREDITATIONS: SC JRCB

Cedar Crest College

100 College Drive
Allentown, PA 18104
(215) 437-4471 Ext. 345
Fax (215) 740-3766

Will confirm attendance and degree by phone, fax or mail. Inquiry must include student's name, social security number, years attended. Employers may obtain transcripts upon written request accompanied by a $3.00 fee and a signed release from the student. Requests should be directed to: Registrar's Office.

A general baccalaureate institution, with an enrollment of 1,085. Highest level of offering: four or five year baccalaureate.
ACCREDITATIONS: M NMT NLN CSWE

Cedar Valley College

3030 North Dallas Avenue
Lancaster, TX 75134-3799
(214) 372-8200
Fax (214) 372-8207

Will confirm attendance and degree by phone or mail. Inquiry must include student's name, social security number. Employers may obtain transcripts upon written request and a signed release from the student. Requests should be directed to: Admission Office.

A multiprogram two-year institution, with an enrollment of 3,300. Highest level of offering: one year but less than four years.
ACCREDITATIONS: SC AVVMA/CVTTAT

Cedarville College

Box 601
Cedarville, OH 45314
(513) 766-2211
Fax (513) 766-2760

Will confirm attendance and degree by phone or mail. Inquiry must include student's name. Employers may obtain transcripts upon written request accompanied by a $2.00 fee and a signed release from the student.

A general baccalaureate institution, with an enrollment of 2,046. Highest level of offering: four or five year baccalaureate.
ACCREDITATIONS: NH

Centenary College of Louisiana

PO Box 41188
Shreveport, LA 71134-1188
(318) 869-5146
Fax (318) 869-5026

Will confirm attendance and degree by phone, fax or mail. Inquiry must include student's name, years attended, social security number, date of birth. Employers may obtain transcripts upon written request accompanied by a $2.00 fee and a signed release from the student.

A general baccalaureate institution, with an enrollment of 1,120. Highest level of offering: master's.
ACCREDITATIONS: SC NASM

Centenary College

400 Jefferson Street
Hackettstown, NJ 07840
(908) 852-1400

Will confirm attendance and degree by phone or mail. Inquiry must include student's name, years attended. Employers may obtain transcripts upon written request accompanied by a $3.00 fee and a signed release from the student. Requests should be directed to: Registrar's Office.

A general baccalaureate institution, with an enrollment of 1,160. Highest level of offering: four or five year baccalaureate.
ACCREDITATIONS: M

Center for Creative Studies–College of Art and Design

245 East Kirby
Detroit, MI 48202
(313) 872-3118 Ext. 288

Will confirm attendance and degree by phone or mail. Inquiry must include student's name, social security number. Requests should be directed to: Registrar's Office. Employers may obtain transcripts upon written request accompanied by a $2.00 fee and a signed release from the student.

A visual and performing arts school, with an enrollment of 1,141. Highest level of offering: four or five year baccalaureate.
ACCREDITATIONS: NH ART

Center for Degree Studies

Oak and Pawnee Streets
Scranton, PA 18515
(717) 342-7701

Will confirm attendance and degree by mail. Inquiry must include student's name, years attended, release. Requests should be directed to: Student Services. Employers may obtain transcripts upon written request accompanied by a $5.00 fee and a signed release from the student.

A multiprogram two-year institution, with an enrollment of 778. Highest level of offering: one year but less than four years.
ACCREDITATIONS: NHSC

Center for Early Education

563 North Alfred Street
Los Angeles, CA 90048
(213) 651-0707
Fax (213) 8651-0860

Records are held at the above address. Will confirm attendance and degree by mail or phone or fax. Inquiry must include student's name, social security number, years attended, release. Employers may obtain transcripts upon written request accompanied by a $5.00 fee and a signed release from the student.

A multiprogram two-year institution, with an enrollment of 48. Highest level of offering: master's.
ACCREDITATIONS: WC

Center for Humanistic Studies

40 East Ferry Avenue
Detroit, MI 48202
(313) 875-7440
Fax (313) 875-7442

Will confirm attendance and degree by phone or mail. Inquiry must include student's name, years attended. Employers may obtain transcripts upon written request by student accompanied by a $6.00 fee.

A bachelor's or higher institution newly admitted to NCES, with an enrollment of 75. Highest level of offering: beyond master's but less than doctorate.
ACCREDITATIONS: NH

Center for Pastoral Leadership Diocese of Cleveland

(Formerly Borromeo College of Ohio)
28700 Euclid Avenue
Wickliffe, OH 44092
(216) 943-7600 Ext. 7666
Fax (216) 943-7577

Will confirm attendance and degree by phone or mail. Inquiry must include student's name, social security number, years attended. Employers may obtain transcripts upon written request accompanied by a $3.00 fee and a signed release from the student. Requests should be directed to: Records Office.

A specialized school, with an enrollment of 122. Highest level of offering: four or five year baccalaureate.
ACCREDITATIONS: NH

Central Alabama Community College

(Formerly Alexander City State Junior College & N F Nunnelly State Technical College)
PO Box 699
Alexander City, AL 35010
(205) 234-6346

Will confirm attendance and degree by mail. Inquiry must include student's name, date of birth, years attended. Employers may obtain transcripts upon written request accompanied by a signed release from the student.

A multiprogram two-year institution, with an enrollment of 2,616. Highest level of offering: one year but less than four years.
ACCREDITATIONS: SACS

Central Arizona College

8470 N. Overfield Road
Coolidge, AZ 85228
(602) 723-4141 Ext. 263

Will confirm attendance and degree by mail. Inquiry must include student's name, date of birth, social security number, years attended. Employers may obtain transcripts upon written request accompanied by a $2.00 fee and a signed release from the student.

A multiprogram two-year institution, with an enrollment of 5,500. Highest level of offering: one year but less than four years.
ACCREDITATIONS: NH NLN/AD EMT

Central Baptist College

Conway, AR 72032
(501) 329-6872 Ext. 14

Will confirm attendance and degree by phone or mail. Inquiry must include student's name, date of birth, social security number, years attended. Employers may obtain transcripts upon written request accompanied by a $3.00 fee and a signed release from the student.

A specialized school, with an enrollment of 238. Highest level of offering: baccalaureate.
ACCREDITATIONS: NH BI

Central Baptist Theological Seminary

Seminary Heights
741 N. 31st Street
Kansas City, KS 66102
(913) 371-5313 Ext. 20

Will confirm attendance and degree by phone or mail. Inquiry must include student's name, date of birth, social security number, years attended. Requests should be directed to: Registrar's Office. Employers may obtain transcripts upon written request accompanied by a $3.00 fee and a signed release from the student.

A school of philosophy, religion and theology, with an enrollment of 120. Highest level of offering: first professional degree.
ACCREDITATIONS: NH THEOL

Central Bible College

3000 North Grant Avenue
Springfield, MO 65803
(417) 833-2551
Fax (417) 833-5141

Will confirm attendance and degree by phone or mail. Inquiry must include student's name, date of birth, social security number. Employers may obtain transcripts upon written request accompanied by a $5.00 fee and a signed release from the student.

A school of philosophy, religion and theology, with an enrollment of 1,038. Highest level of offering: four or five year baccalaureate.
ACCREDITATIONS: BI

Central Carolina Community College

1105 Kelly Drive
Sanford, NC 27330
(919) 775-5401 Ext. 239

Will confirm attendance and degree by phone or mail. Inquiry must include student's name, social security number, years attended. Employers may obtain transcripts upon written request accompanied by a signed release from the student.

A multiprogram two-year institution, with an enrollment of 2,688. Highest level of offering: one year but less than four years.
ACCREDITATIONS: SC AVVMA/CVTTAT

Central Christian College of the Bible

911 Urbandale Drive East
Moberly, MO 65270-1997
(816) 263-3900

Will confirm attendance and degree by mail. Inquiry must include student's name, years attended, release. Employers may obtain transcripts upon written request accompanied by a $3.00 fee and a signed release from the student.

A school of philosophy, religion and theology, with an enrollment of 100. Highest level of offering: four or five year baccalaureate.
ACCREDITATIONS: BI

Central City Business Institute

Attn: Academic Dean
953 James Street
Syracuse, NY 13203
(315) 472-6233 Ext. 120
Fax (315) 472-6201

Will confirm attendance and degree by phone, fax or mail. Inquiry must include student's name, date of birth, social security number, years attended. Employers may obtain transcripts upon written request accompanied by a signed release from the student.

A single program two-year institution, with an enrollment of 700. Highest level of offering: one year but less than four years.
ACCREDITATIONS: NY

Central College

1200 South Main
McPherson, KS 67460
(316) 241-0723 Ext. 319

Will confirm attendance and degree by phone or mail. Inquiry must include student's name, date of birth, social security number, years attended. Employers may obtain transcripts upon written request accompanied by a $3.00 fee and a signed release from the student. Requests should be directed to: Registrar's Office.

A multiprogram two-year institution, with an enrollment of 275. Highest level of offering: four years.
ACCREDITATIONS: NH NCA

Central Community College Area

PO Box 4903
Grand Island, NE 68802
(308) 384-5220

Will confirm by mail. Inquiry must include student's name, social security number, years attended, release. Only students may obtain transcripts.

A multiprogram two-year institution, with an enrollment of 8,209. Highest level of offering: one year but less than four years.
ACCREDITATIONS: NH DA DH DT MAC PNUR

Central Connecticut State University

1615 Stanley Street
New Britain, CT 06050
(203) 827-7561

Will confirm attendance and degree by phone or mail. Inquiry must include student's name, social security number, years attended. Employers may obtain transcripts upon written request accompanied by a signed release from the student.

A comprehensive institution with no medical school, with an enrollment of 14,400. Highest level of offering: beyond master's but less than doctorate.
ACCREDITATIONS: EH TED

Central Florida Community College

PO Box 1388
Ocala, FL 32678
(904) 237-2111
Fax (904) 237-3747

Will confirm attendance and degree by mail or fax. Inquiry must include student's name, social security number, years attended. Employers may obtain transcripts upon written request accompanied by a signed release from the student, $2.00 fee.

A multiprogram two-year institution, with an enrollment of 2,522. Highest level of offering: one year but less than four years.
ACCREDITATIONS: SC

Central Maine Medical Center School of Nursing

300 Main Street
Lewiston, ME 04240
(207) 795-2858
Fax (207) 795-2303

Will confirm attendance and degree by phone or mail. Inquiry must include student's name, social security number. Employers may obtain transcripts upon written request accompanied by a $2.00 fee and a signed release from the student.

A two-year institution with an enrollment of 99. Highest level of offering: two years but less than four years.
ACCREDITATIONS: EV PAST NLN

Central Maine Technical College

1250 Turner Street
Auburn, ME 04210
(207) 784-2385 Ext. 246

Will confirm attendance and degree by phone or mail. Inquiry must include student's name. Employers may obtain transcripts upon written request accompanied by a $3.00 fee and a signed release from the student.

A multiprogram two-year institution, with an enrollment of 780. Highest level of offering: two years but less than four years.
ACCREDITATIONS: EV ENGT

Central Methodist College

411 Central Methodist Square
Fayette, MO 65248
(816) 248-3391 Ext. 208

Will confirm attendance and degree by mail. Inquiry must include student's name, date of birth, social security number, years attended. Employers may obtain transcripts upon written request accompanied by a $2.00 fee and a signed release from the student.

A general baccalaureate institution, with an enrollment of 611. Highest level of offering: four or five year baccalaureate.
ACCREDITATIONS: NH NASM TED

Central Michigan University

Mount Pleasant, MI 48859
(517) 774-3261

Will confirm attendance and degree by phone or mail. Inquiry must include student's name, date of birth, social security number, years attended. Employers may obtain transcripts upon written request accompanied by a $2.00 fee and a signed release from the student. Requests should be sent to: Registrar's Office.

A comprehensive institution with no medical school, with an enrollment of 17,229. Highest level of offering: doctorate.
ACCREDITATIONS: NH AUD BUS NASM SP TED

Central Missouri State University

Warrensburg, MO 64093
(816) 429-4900
Fax (816) 747-1653

Will confirm attendance and degree by phone or mail. Inquiry must include student's name, date of birth, social security number, years attended. Employers may obtain transcripts upon written request accompanied by a signed release from the student.

A comprehensive institution with no medical school, with an enrollment of 11,300. Highest level of offering: beyond master's but less than doctorate.
ACCREDITATIONS: NH AUD NASM NLN SP TED

Central New England College

c/o Nichols College
Dudley, MA 01571-5000
(508) 943-1560

Will confirm attendance and degree by phone or mail. Inquiry must include student's name, social security number. Employers may obtain transcripts upon written request accompanied by a $10.00 fee and a signed release from the student. Requests should be addressed to: Registrar's Office.

Central Ohio Technical College

University Drive
Newark, OH 43055
(614) 366-9208 Ext. 208
Fax (614) 366-5047

Will confirm attendance and degree by mail or phone. Inquiry must include student's name, social security number, years attended. Employers may obtain transcripts upon written request accompanied by a $2.00 fee and a signed release from the student.

A multiprogram two-year institution, with an enrollment of 1,700. Highest level of offering: two years but less than four years.
ACCREDITATIONS: NH NLN/AD RAD

Central Oregon Community College

2600 North West College Way
Bend, OR 97701
(503) 385-5522
Fax (503) 385-5978

Will confirm attendance and degree by phone or fax. Inquiry must include student's name, social security number, years attended. Employers may obtain transcripts upon written request accompanied by a $3.00 fee and a signed release from the student.

A multiprogram two-year institution, with an enrollment of 3,000. Highest level of offering: one year but less than four years.
ACCREDITATIONS: NW MRT

Central Pennsylvania Business School

College Hill Road
Summerdale, PA 17093
(717) 732-0702 Ext. 205
Fax (717) 732-5254

Will confirm attendance and degree by phone or mail. Inquiry must include student's name, social security number, years attended. Employers may obtain transcripts upon written request accompanied by a signed release from the student. Requests should be directed to: Registrar's Office.

A multiprogram two-year institution, with an enrollment of 722. Highest level of offering: one year but less than four years.
ACCREDITATIONS: M MAC

Central Piedmont Community College

PO Box 35009
Charlotte, NC 28235
(704) 342-6959
fax (704) 342-5935

Will confirm attendance and degree by phone or mail. Inquiry must include student's name, social security number. Employers may obtain transcripts upon written request accompanied by a $1.00 fee and a signed release from the student. Requests should be directed to: Student Records.

A multiprogram two-year institution, with an enrollment of 26,235. Highest level of offering: one year but less than four years.
ACCREDITATIONS: SC DA DH ENGT MAC MRT PTAA RSTH

Central State University

100 North University Drive
Edmond, OK 73060-0151
(405) 341-2980 Ext. 2331
Fax (405) 341-4964

Will confirm attendance and degree by phone, fax or mail. Inquiry must include student's name, date of birth, social security number, years attended. Requests should be directed to: Office of the Registrar. Employers may obtain transcripts upon written request accompanied by a $3.00 fee and a signed release from the student.

A comprehensive institution with no medical school, with an enrollment of 15,250. Highest level of offering: master's.
ACCREDITATIONS: NH FUSER NLN TED NCATE

Central State University

Wilberforce, OH 45384
(513) 376-6150

Will confirm attendance and degree by phone or mail. Inquiry must include student's name, social security number, years attended. Employers may obtain transcripts upon written request accompanied by a $3.00 fee and a signed release from the student.

A general baccalaureate institution, with an enrollment of 2,600. Highest level of offering: four or five year baccalaureate.
ACCREDITATIONS: NH NASM TED

Central Texas College

PO Box 1800
Killeen, TX 76540-9990
(817) 526-1211
Fax (817) 526-0817

Will confirm attendance and degree by mail or fax. Inquiry must include student's name, social security number. Employers may obtain transcripts upon written request accompanied by a signed release from the student and dates attended.

A multiprogram two-year institution, with an enrollment of 6,410. Highest level of offering: one year but less than four years.
ACCREDITATIONS: SACS NLN/AD

Central University of Iowa

812 University
Pella, IA 50219
(515) 628-5267

Will confirm attendance and degree by phone or mail. Inquiry must include student's name, years attended. Employers may obtain transcripts upon written request accompanied by a $3.00 fee and a signed release from the student.

A general baccalaureate institution, with an enrollment of 1,751. Highest level of offering: four or five year baccalaureate.
ACCREDITATIONS: NH NASM TED

Central Virginia Community College

3506 Wards Road
Lynchburg, VA 24502-2498
(804) 386-4575
Fax (804) 386-4681

Will confirm attendance and degree by phone or mail. Inquiry must include student's name, social security number, years attended. Employers may obtain transcripts upon written request accompanied by a signed release from the student.

A multiprogram two-year institution, with an enrollment of 4,000. Highest level of offering: one year but less than four years.
ACCREDITATIONS: SC MLTAD MRT RAD RSTHT

Central Washington University

Ellensburg, WA 98926
(509) 963-3001
Fax (509) 963-3022

Will confirm attendance and degree by phone, fax or mail. Inquiry must include student's name, date of birth, social security number, years attended. Employers may obtain transcripts upon written request accompanied by a $3.00 fee and a signed release from the student. Requests should be directed to: Registrar's Office.

A comprehensive institution with no medical school, with an enrollment of 7,383. Highest level of offering: master's.
ACCREDITATIONS: NW MT NASM TED

Central Wesleyan College

1 Wesleyan Drive
Central, SC 29630
(803) 639-2453 Ext. 325
Fax (803) 639-0826

Will confirm attendance and degree by phone or mail. Inquiry must include student's name, social security number. Employers may obtain transcripts upon written request accompanied by a $3.00 fee and a signed release from the student.

A general baccalaureate institution, with an enrollment of 1,091. Highest level of offering: master's degree.
ACCREDITATIONS: SC

Central Wyoming College

2660 Peck Avenue
Riverton, WY 82501
(307) 856-9291
Fax (307) 856-9291 Ext. 191

Will confirm attendance and degree by phone, fax or mail. Inquiry must include student's name, date of birth, social security number, years attended, release. Employers may obtain transcripts upon written request accompanied by a $1.00 fee and a signed release from the student. Requests should be directed to: Admissions Office.

A multiprogram two-year institution, with an enrollment of 1,736. Highest level of offering: one year but less than four years.
ACCREDITATIONS: NH

Central Yeshiva Tomchei Tmimim Lubavitch

841-853 Ocean Parkway
Brooklyn, NY 11230
(718) 434-0784

Will confirm attendance and degree by mail. Inquiry must include student's name, date of birth, social security number, years attended, release. Employers may obtain transcripts upon written request accompanied by a $25.00 fee and a signed release from the student.

A specialized non-degree granting institution, with an enrollment of 400. Highest level of offering: graduate non-degree granting.
ACCREDITATIONS: RABN

Centralia College

600 West Locust Street
Centralia, WA 98531
(206) 736-9391 Ext. 221
Fax 206) 753-3404

Will confirm attendance and degree by phone or mail. Inquiry must include student's name, social security number, years attended. Employers may obtain transcripts upon written request accompanied by a $2.00 fee and a signed release from the student. Requests should be directed to: Admissions and Records Office.

A multiprogram two-year institution, with an enrollment of 3,000. Highest level of offering: one year but less than four years.
ACCREDITATIONS: NW

Centre College

West Walnut Street
Danville, KY 40422
(606) 238-5630

Will confirm attendance and degree by phone or mail. Inquiry must include student's name, date of birth, social security number. Employers may obtain transcripts upon written request accompanied by a signed release from the student. Requests should be directed to: Registrar's Office.

A general baccalaureate institution, with an enrollment of 850. Highest level of offering: four or five year baccalaureate.
ACCREDITATIONS: SC

Cerritos College

11110 East Alondra Boulevard
Norwalk, CA 90650
(213) 860-2451 Ext. 211

Will confirm attendance and degree by
phone. Inquiry must include student's
name, date of birth, social security number,
years attended. Employers may obtain transcripts upon written request accompanied
by a $2.00 fee and a signed release from the
student. Direct inquiries to Admissions.

A multiprogram two-year institution, with
an enrollment of 18,308. Highest level of
offering: one year but less than four years.
ACCREDITATIONS: WJ DA DH PTAA

Cerro Coso Community College

3000 College Heights Boulevard
Ridgecrest, CA 93555
(619) 375-5001 Ext. 357
Fax (619) 375-5001 Ext. 252

Will confirm attendance and degree by
phone, fax or mail. Inquiry must include
student's name, date of birth, social security
number, years attended. Employers may obtain transcripts upon written request accompanied by a $5.00 fee and a signed release
from the student.

A multiprogram two-year institution, with
an enrollment of 5,133. Highest level of offering: one year but less than four years.
ACCREDITATIONS: WJ

Chabot College

25555 Hesperian Blvd
Hayward, CA 94545
(510) 786-6710

Will confirm attendance and degree by
mail. Employers may obtain transcripts
upon written request accompanied by a
$2.00 fee and a signed release from the stu-
dent.

A multiprogram two-year institution, with
an enrollment of 20,000. Highest level of
offering: one year but less than four years.
ACCREDITATIONS: WJ DA DH MAC MRT

Chadron State College

Chadron, NE 69337
(308) 432-6221

Will confirm attendance and degree by
phone or mail. Inquiry must include student's name, date of birth, social security
number. Employers may obtain transcripts
upon written request accompanied by a
$2.00 fee and a signed release from the stu-
dent. Attn: Registrar's Office.

A general baccalaureate institution, with an
enrollment of 2,674. Highest level of offering: beyond master's but less than doctorate.
ACCREDITATIONS: NH TED

Chaffey Community College

5885 Haven Avenue
Rancho Cucamonga, CA 91701
(714) 987-1737 Ext. 261
Fax (714) 941-2783

Will confirm attendance and degree by
mail. Inquiry must include student's name,
social security number, release. Employers
may obtain transcripts upon written request
accompanied by a $3.00 fee and a signed
release from the student.

A multiprogram two-year institution, with
an enrollment of 13,000. Highest level of
offering: one year but less than four years.
ACCREDITATIONS: WJ NLN/AD DA RAD

Chamberlayne Junior College

(See Mount Ida College)

Chaminade University of Honolulu

3140 Waialae Avenue
Honolulu, HI 96816
(808) 735-4722 or 735-4724

Will confirm attendance and degree by mail
or phone. Inquiry must include student's
name, date of birth, social security number,
years attended. Employers may obtain transcripts upon written request accompanied
by a $5.00 fee and a signed release from the
student.

A general baccalaureate institution, with an
enrollment of 2,481. Highest level of offering: master's.
ACCREDITATIONS: WC

Champlain College

163 South Willard Street–PO Box 670
Burlington, VT 05401
(802) 658-0800 Ext. 2322
Fax (802) 860-2750

Will confirm attendance and degree by
phone, fax or mail. Inquiry must include
student's name, social security number.
Employers may obtain transcripts upon
written request accompanied by a $1.00 fee
and a signed release from the student.

A multiprogram two-year institution, with
an enrollment of 1,801. Highest level of offering: two years, bachelor'ds degree in
Accounting and Business Management.
ACCREDITATIONS: EV DA

Chapman College

Orange, CA 92666
(714) 997-6701

Will confirm attendance and degree by
phone or mail. Inquiry must include student's name, social security number.
Employers may obtain transcripts upon
written request accompanied by a $5.00 fee
and a signed release from the student. Attn:
Registrar's Office.

A comprehensive institution with no medi-
cal school, with an enrollment of 6,200.
Highest level of offering: master's.
ACCREDITATIONS: WC

Charles County Community College

Registrar's Office
PO Box 910–Mitchell Road
La Plata, MD 20646-0910
(301) 934-2251 Ext. 506-8

Will confirm attendance and degree by
phone or mail. Inquiry must include student's name, social security number, years
attended. Employers may obtain transcripts
upon written request accompanied by a
$2.00 fee and a signed release from the stu-
dent. Attn: transcripts.

A multiprogram two-year institution, with
an enrollment of 5,000. Highest level of offering: one year but less than four years.
ACCREDITATIONS: M PNUR

Charles S. Mott Community College

(See Mott Community College)

Charleston Southern University

(Formerly Baptist College at
Charleston)
PO Box 10087
Charleston, SC 29411
(803) 863-7000
Fax (800) 863-8074

Will confirm attendance and degree by
phone or mail. Inquiry must include student's name, date of birth, social security
number, years attended. Employers may obtain transcripts upon written request accompanied by a $3.00 fee and a signed release
from the student.

A liberal arts baccalaureate institution, with
an enrollment of 2,500. Highest level of offering: master's.
ACCREDITATIONS: SC NASM

Charter Oak College

The Exchange Suite 171–270
Farmington Avenue
Farmington, CT 06032-1934
(203) 677-0076
Fax (203) 677-5147

Will confirm attendance and degree by
phone or mail. Inquiry must include student's name, date of birth, social security
number, years attended. Employers may obtain transcripts upon written request accompanied by a $3.00 fee and a signed release
from the student.

A general baccalaureate institution, with an
enrollment of 940. Highest level of offering: four baccalaureate.
ACCREDITATIONS: EH

Chatfield College

20918 State Route 251
Saint Martin, OH 45118
(513) 875-3344

Will confirm attendance and degree by
phone or mail. Inquiry must include student's name, social security number.
Employers may obtain transcripts upon
written request accompanied by a $2.00 fee
and a signed release from the student.

A multiprogram two-year institution, with
an enrollment of 250. Highest level of offering: two years but less than four years.
ACCREDITATIONS: NCA

Chatham College

Woodland Road
Pittsburgh, PA 15232-9705
(412) 365-1121

Will confirm attendance and degree by
phone or mail. Inquiry must include student's name, social security number, years
attended. Employers may obtain transcripts
upon written request accompanied by a
$3.00 fee and a signed release from the stu-
dent.

A general baccalaureate institution, with an
enrollment of 650. Highest level of offering: four or five year baccalaureate.
ACCREDITATIONS: M

Chattahoochee Valley Community College

2602 College Drive
Phenix City, AL 36869
(205) 291-4900
Fax (205) 291-4980

Will confirm attendance and degree by mail or fax. Inquiry must include student's name, date of birth, social security number, years attended, release. Employers may obtain transcripts upon written request accompanied by a $2.00 fee and a signed release from the student.

A multiprogram two-year institution, with an enrollment of 1,730. Highest level of offering: two years but less than four years.
ACCREDITATIONS: SC NLN/AD

Chattanooga State Technical Community College

4501 Amnicola Highway
Chattanooga, TN 37406
(615) 697-4404
Fax (615) 697-4709

Will confirm attendance and degree by phone or mail. Inquiry must include student's name, social security number. Employers may obtain transcripts upon written request accompanied by a signed release from the student. Attn: Record's Office.

A multiprogram two-year institution, with an enrollment of 8,000. Highest level of offering: one year but less than four years.
ACCREDITATIONS: SC DA DH DT ENGT MRT PTAA RAD RSTH

Chauncey Sparks State Technical College

PO Drawer 580
Eufala, AL 36072-0580
(205) 687-3543
Fax (205) 687-0255

Will confirm attendance and degree by phone or mail. Inquiry must include student's name, date of birth, social security number, years attended. Employers may obtain transcripts upon written request accompanied by a signed release from the student. Requests should be directed to: Registrar's Office.

A two-year institution newly admitted to NCES. Highest level of offering: one year but less than four years.
ACCREDITATIONS: SV

Chemeketa Community College

PO Box 14007
Salem, OR 97309
(503) 399-5001
Fax (503) 399-3918

Will confirm attendance and degree by phone, fax or mail. Inquiry must include student's name, date of birth, social security number. Employers may obtain transcripts upon written request accompanied by a signed release from the student and a $2.00 fee. Requests should be directed to: Registrar's Office.

A multiprogram two-year institution, with an enrollment of 860. Highest level of offering: two years but less than four years.
ACCREDITATIONS: NW NLN/AD DA MAC

Chesapeake College

PO Box 8
Wye Mills, MD 21679
(301) 822-5400 Ext. 245

Will confirm attendance and degree by phone or mail. Inquiry must include student's name, date of birth, social security number years attended. Employers may obtain transcripts upon written request accompanied by a $2.00 fee and a signed release from the student. Requests should be directed to: Records Office.

A multiprogram two-year institution, with an enrollment of 2,100. Highest level of offering: one year but less than four years.
ACCREDITATIONS: M MLTAD

Chesterfield–Marlboro Technical College

Drawer 1007
Cheraw, SC 29520
(803) 537-5286 Ext. 18
Fax (803) 537-6148

Will confirm attendance and degree by mail or fax. Inquiry must include student's name, date of birth, social security number. Employers may obtain transcripts upon written request accompanied by a $2.00 fee and a signed release from the student.

A multiprogram two-year institution, with an enrollment of 602. Highest level of offering: one year but less than four years.
ACCREDITATIONS: SC

Chestnut Hill College

Philadelphia, PA 19118-2695
(215) 248-7005

Will confirm attendance and degree by phone or mail. Inquiry must include student's name, date of birth, social security number, years attended. Employers may obtain transcripts upon written request accompanied by a $2.00 fee and a signed release from the student. Requests should be directed to: Registrar's Office.

A general baccalaureate institution, with an enrollment of 1,184. Highest level of offering: master's.
ACCREDITATIONS: M

Cheyney University of Pennsylvania

Cheyney, PA 19319
(215) 399-2225
Fax (215) 399-2415

Will confirm attendance and degree by phone, fax or mail. Inquiry must include student's name, social security number, years attended. Employers may obtain transcripts upon written request accompanied by a $5.00 fee, student's SSN and a signed release from the student. Attn: Registrar's Office.

A comprehensive institution with no medical school, with an enrollment of 1,646. Highest level of offering: master's.
ACCREDITATIONS: M TED

Chicago City–Wide College

See City Colleges of Chicago-Chicago City-Wide College

Chicago College of Osteopathic Medicine

555 31st St.
Downers Grove, IL 60515
(708) 515-6074
Fax (708) 515-6384

Will confirm attendance and degree by mail. Inquiry must include student's name, release. Employers may obtain transcripts upon written request accompanied by a $5.00 fee and a signed release from the student.

A medical school, with an enrollment of 513. Highest level of offering: first professional degree.
ACCREDITATIONS: OSTEO

Chicago School of Professional Psychology

806 South Plymouth Court
Chicago, IL 60605
(312) 786-9443

Will confirm attendance and degree by phone or mail. Inquiry must include student's name, years attended. Employers may obtain transcripts upon written request accompanied by a $4.00 fee and a signed release from the student.

A bachelor's or higher institution newly admitted to NCES, with an enrollment of 131. Highest level of offering: first professional degree.
ACCREDITATIONS: NH

Chicago State University

95th Street at King Drive
Chicago, IL 60628
(312) 995-2522

Will confirm attendance and degree by mail. Inquiry must include student's name, social security number years attended. Employers may obtain transcripts upon written request accompanied by a $2.00 fee and a signed release from the student. Requests should be directed to: Registrar's Office.

A comprehensive institution with no medical school, with an enrollment of 6,500. Highest level of offering: master's.
ACCREDITATIONS: NH DIET MRA NLN OT RTT TED

Chicago Theological Seminary

5757 South University Avenue
Chicago, IL 60637
(312) 752-5757
Fax (312) 752-5925

Will confirm attendance and degree by mail, phone or fax. Inquiry must include student's name and years attended. Employers may obtain transcripts upon written request accompanied by a $2.00 fee and a signed release from the student.

A school of philosophy, religion and theology, with an enrollment of 185. Highest level of offering: doctorate.
ACCREDITATIONS: NH THEOL

Chipola Junior College

3094 Indian Circle
Marianna, FL 32446
(904) 526-2761 Ext. 211
Fax (904) 526-4153

Will confirm attendance and degree by
phone, fax or mail. Inquiry must include
student's name, date of birth, social security
number, years attended. Employers may obtain transcripts upon written request accompanied by a $1.00 fee and a signed release
from the student.

A multiprogram two-year institution, with
an enrollment of 2,000. Highest level of offering: one year but less than four years.
ACCREDITATIONS: SC

Chippewa Valley Technical College

(Formerly District One Technical
Institute)
620 West Clairmont Avenue
Eau Claire, WI 54701
(715) 833-6269
Fax (715) 833-6470

Will confirm attendance and degree by
phone, fax or mail. Inquiry must include
student's name, social security number,
years attended. Employers may obtain transcripts upon written request accompanied
by a signed release from the student.

A multiprogram two-year institution, with
an enrollment of 3,037. Highest level of offering: one year but less than four years.
ACCREDITATIONS: SC

Chowan College

Murfreesboro, NC 27855
(919) 398-4101 Ext. 235

Will confirm attendance and degree by
phone or mail. Inquiry must include student's name, social security number, years
attended. Employers may obtain transcripts
upon written request accompanied by a
$3.00 fee and a signed release from the student. Requests should be directed to:
Registrar's Office.

A multiprogram four-year institution, with
an enrollment of 911. Highest level of offering: one year but less than four years.
ACCREDITATIONS: SC

Christ College Irvine

1530 Concordia
Irvine, CA 92715
(714) 854-8002 Ext. 219
Fax (714) 854-6854

Will confirm attendance and degree by
phone, fax or mail. Inquiry must include
student's name, social security number.
Employers may obtain transcripts upon
written request accompanied by a $5.00 fee
and a signed release from the student.
Requests should be directed to: Registrar's
Office.

A general baccalaureate institution, with an
enrollment of 575. Highest level of offering: master's.
ACCREDITATIONS: WC

Christ Seminary–Seminex

1100 East 55 Street
Chicago, IL 60615
(312) 753-0700 Ext.717

Will confirm attendance and degree by
mail. Inquiry must include student's name,
years attended. Employers may obtain transcripts upon written request accompanied
by a $2.00 fee and a signed release from the
student.

A school of philosophy, religion and theology, with an enrollment of 401. Highest
level of offering: doctorate.
ACCREDITATIONS: THEOL

Christ The King Seminary

711 Knox Road Box 607
East Aurora, NY 14052
(716) 652-8900 Ext. 24

Will confirm attendance and degree by
phone or mail. Inquiry must include student's name, social security number, years
attended. Employers may obtain transcripts
upon written request accompanied by a
$3.00 fee and a signed release from the student.

A school of theology, with an enrollment of
114. Highest level of offering: master's.
ACCREDITATIONS: M NYSBR THEOL

Christendon College

Route 3 Box 87
Front Royal, VA 22630
(703) 636-2908
Fax (703) 636-1655

Will confirm attendance and degree by
phone or mail. Inquiry must include student's name, date of birth, social security
number, years attended. Employers may obtain transcripts upon written request accompanied by a $3.00 fee and a signed release
from the student.

A bachelor's or higher institution newly admitted to NCES. Highest level of offering:
four or five year baccalaureate.
ACCREDITATIONS: SC

Christian Brothers College

650 East Parkway South
Memphis, TN 38104
(901) 722-0239

Will confirm attendance and degree by
phone or mail. Inquiry must include student's name, date of birth, social security
number, years attended. Employers may obtain transcripts upon written request
accompanied by a $2.00 fee and a signed
release from the student.

A general baccalaureate institution, with an
enrollment of 1,774. Highest level of offering: master's.
ACCREDITATIONS: SC ENG

Christian Heritage College

2100 Greenfield Drive
El Cajon, CA 92019
(619) 441-2200 Ext. 1219
Fax (619) 440-0209

Will confirm attendance and degree by
phone, fax or mail. Inquiry must include
student's name, date of birth, social security
number, years attended. Employers may obtain transcripts upon written request accompanied by a $2.00 fee and a signed release
from the student.

A general baccalaureate institution, with an
enrollment of 350. Highest level of offering: four or five year baccalaureate.
ACCREDITATIONS: WC

Christian Theological Seminary

1000 West 42nd Street
Indianapolis, IN 46208
(317) 924-1331 Ext. 283
Fax (317) 923-1961＊2

Will confirm attendance and degree by
phone, fax or mail. Inquiry must include
student's name, date of birth, social security
number, years attended, self addressed
stamped envelope. Employers may obtain
transcripts upon written request accompanied by a $5.00 fee and a signed release
from the student. Attn: Registrar's Office.

A school of philosophy, religion and theology, with an enrollment of 328. Highest
level of offering: doctorate.
ACCREDITATIONS: NH THEOL

Christopher Newport College

50 Shoe Lane
Newport News, VA 23606
(804) 594-7155
Fax (804) 594-7713

Will confirm attendance and degree by
phone or mail. Inquiry must include student's name, social security number.
Employers may obtain transcripts upon
written request accompanied by a signed release from the student.

A general baccalaureate institution, with an
enrollment of 4,268. Highest level of offering: four or five year baccalaureate.
ACCREDITATIONS: SC CSWE

Church Divinity School of the Pacific

2451 Ridge Road
Berkeley, CA 94709
(510) 848-3282 Ext. 38

Will confirm attendance and degree by
phone or mail. Inquiry must include student's name, years attended, self addressed
stamped envelope, release. Employers may
obtain transcripts upon written request accompanied by a $4.00 fee and a signed release from the student.

A school of philosophy, religion and theology, with an enrollment of 95. Highest level
of offering: master's.
ACCREDITATIONS: WC THEOL

Church of God School of Theology

900 Walker St. NE
Cleveland, TN 37311
(615) 478-7725
Fax (615) 478-7711

Will confirm attendance and degree by phone or mail. Inquiry must include student's name, social security number, years attended. Employers may obtain transcripts upon written request accompanied by a signed release from the student.

A bachelor's or higher institution newly admitted to NCES, with an enrollment of 210. Highest level of offering: master's.

ACCREDITATIONS: SC

Cincinnati Bible College and Seminary

PO Box 43200
Cincinnati, OH 45204-3200
(513) 244-8162
Fax (513) 244-8140

Will confirm attendance and degree by phone or mail. Inquiry must include student's name, date of birth, social security number, years attended, self addressed stamped envelope. Employers may obtain transcripts upon written request accompanied by a $2.00 fee and a signed release from the student.

A school of philosophy, religion and theology, with an enrollment of 892. Highest level of offering: beyond master's but less than doctorate.

ACCREDITATIONS: BI NH

Cincinnati College of Mortuary Science

3860 Pacific Avenue
Cohen Center
Cincinnati, OH 45212
(513) 745-3631

Will confirm attendance and degree by mail. Inquiry must include student's name, date of birth, social security number, years attended, release, self addressed stamped envelope. Requests should be directed to: Records Department. Employers may obtain transcripts upon written request accompanied by a $2.00 fee and a signed release from the student.

A two-year institution newly admitted to NCES, with an enrollment of 110. Highest level of offering: one year but less than four years.

ACCREDITATIONS: NH FUSER

Cincinnati Technical College

Registrar's Office
3520 Central Parkway
Cincinnati, OH 45223-2690
(513) 569-1522

Will confirm attendance and degree by phone or mail. Inquiry must include student's name, social security number. Employers may obtain transcripts upon written request accompanied by a $3.00 fee and a signed release from the student.

A multiprogram two-year institution, with an enrollment of 5,500. Highest level of offering: one year but less than four years.

ACCREDITATIONS: NH ENGT MAC MLTAD MRT RSTH RSTHT SURGT

Circleville Bible College

Box 458
Circleville, OH 43113
(614) 474-8896 Ext. 223

Will confirm attendance and degree by phone or mail. Inquiry must include student's name, years attended. Employers may obtain transcripts upon written request accompanied by a $3.00 fee and a signed release from the student. Requests should be directed to: Records Department.

A school of philosophy, religion and theology, with an enrollment of 186. Highest level of offering: four or five year baccalaureate.

ACCREDITATIONS: BI

Cisco Junior College

Route 3 Box 3
Cisco, TX 76437
(817) 442-2567 Ext. 132

Will confirm attendance and degree by phone or mail. Inquiry must include student's name, social security number, years attended. Employers may obtain transcripts upon written request accompanied by a $2.00 fee and a signed release from the student.

A multiprogram two-year institution, with an enrollment of 1,774. Highest level of offering: one year but less than four years.

ACCREDITATIONS: SC PNUR

Citadel Military College of South Carolina

Charleston, SC 29409
(803) 792-5001
Fax (803) 792-7084

Will confirm attendance and degree by phone, fax or mail. Inquiry must include student's name, social security number, years attended. Employers may obtain transcripts upon written request accompanied by a $3.00 fee and a signed release from the student. Requests should be directed to: Citadel Record's Office.

A comprehensive institution with no medical school, with an enrollment of 3,670. Highest level of offering: beyond master's but less than doctorate.

ACCREDITATIONS: SC ENG TED

Citrus College

1000 West Foothill Boulevard
Glendora, CA 91740-1899
(818) 914-8511
Fax (818) 335-3159

Will confirm attendance and degree by mail. Inquiry must include student's name, date of birth, social security number. Employers may obtain transcripts upon written request accompanied by a $2.00 fee and a signed release from the student.

A multiprogram two-year institution, with an enrollment of 9,326. Highest level of offering: one year but less than four years.

ACCREDITATIONS: WJ DA

City Colleges of Chicago–Chicago City-Wide College

Formerly Chicago City-Wide College
Jackson Boulevard
Chicago, IL 60606
(312) 368-7159
Fax (312) 443-5202

Will confirm attendance and degree by phone, fax or mail. Inquiry must include student's name, social security number, release. Employers may obtain transcripts upon written request accompanied by a $2.00 fee and a signed release from the student.

A multiprogram two-year institution, with an enrollment of 9,835. Highest level of offering: one year but less than four years.

ACCREDITATIONS: NH

City Colleges of Chicago–Kennedy–King College

6800 South Wentworth Avenue
Chicago, IL 60621
(312) 962-3200 Ext. 708

Will confirm attendance and degree by mail. Inquiry must include student's name, date of birth, social security number, years attended, release. Employers may obtain transcripts upon written request accompanied by a $2.00 fee and a signed release from the student.

A multiprogram two-year institution, with an enrollment of 8,081. Highest level of offering: one year but less than four years.

ACCREDITATIONS: NH

City Colleges of Chicago–Malcolm X College

1900 West Ban Buren Street
Chicago, IL 60612
(312) 942-3000 Ext. 319

Will confirm attendance and degree by mail. Inquiry must include student's name, social security number, years attended, release. Employers may obtain transcripts upon written request accompanied by a $2.00 fee and a signed release from the student.

A multiprogram two-year institution, with an enrollment of 6,437. Highest level of offering: one year but less than four years.

ACCREDITATIONS: NH MLTAD RAD RSTH

City Colleges of Chicago–Olive–Harvey College

10001 South Woodlawn Avenue
Chicago, IL 60628
(312) 568-3700

Will confirm attendance and degree by phone or mail. Inquiry must include student's name, date of birth, social security number. Employers may obtain transcripts upon written request accompanied by a $2.00 fee and a signed release from the student.

A multiprogram two-year institution, with an enrollment of 8,314. Highest level of offering: one year but less than four years.
ACCREDITATIONS: NH

City Colleges of Chicago–Richard J. Daley College

7500 South Pulaski Road
Chicago, IL 60652
(312) 838-4863
Fax (312) 838-4876

Will confirm attendance and degree by phone or fax. Inquiry must include student's name, social security number, years attended. Employers may obtain transcripts upon written request accompanied by a $2.00 fee and a signed release from the student.

A multiprogram two-year institution, with an enrollment of 10,502. Highest level of offering: one year but less than four years.
ACCREDITATIONS: NH

City Colleges of Chicago–The Harold Washington College

30 East Lake Street
Chicago, IL 60601
(312) 984-2787

Will confirm attendance and degree by mail. Inquiry must include student's name, social security number, years attended, date of birth, release. Direct inquiries to Registrar's Office. Employers may obtain transcripts upon written request accompanied by a $2.00 fee and a signed release from the student.

A multiprogram two-year institution, with an enrollment of 6,268. Highest level of offering: one year but less than four.
ACCREDITATIONS: NH DA

City Colleges of Chicago–Truman College

1145 West Willson Avenue
Chicago, IL 60640
(312) 878-1700

Will confirm attendance and degree by mail. Inquiry must include student's name, date of birth, social security number, years attended, release. Employers may obtain transcripts upon written request accompanied by a $2.00 fee and a signed release from the student.

A multiprogram two-year institution, with an enrollment of 11,151. Highest level of offering: one year but less than four years.
ACCREDITATIONS: NH MRT

City Colleges of Chicago Chicago City–Wide College

226 West Jackson Boulevard
Chicago, IL 60606
(312) 641-2595

Will confirm attendance and degree by mail. Inquiry must include student's name, social security number, release. Employers may obtain transcripts upon written request accompanied by a $2.00 fee and a signed release from the student.

A multiprogram two-year institution, with an enrollment of 7,841. Highest level of offering: one year but less than four years.
ACCREDITATIONS: NH

City Colleges of Chicago-Wright College

3400 North Austin
Chicago, IL 60634
312-794-3100
Fax 9312) 794-4982

Will confirm attendance and degree by phone, fax or mail. Inquiry must include student's name, date of birth, social security number, years attended. Employers may obtain transcripts upon written request accompanied by a $2.00 fee and a signed release from the student.

A multiprogram two-year institution, with an enrollment of 11,000. Highest level of offering: one year but less than four years.
ACCREDITATIONS: NH RAD

City University of New York Bernard Baruch College

155 East 24th Street
New York, NY 10010
(212) 447-3800

Will confirm attendance and degree by mail. Inquiry must include student's name, date of birth, social security number, years attended, release. Employers may obtain transcripts upon written request accompanied by a $4.00 fee and a signed release from the student.

A business school, with an enrollment of 15,581. Highest level of offering: doctorate.
ACCREDITATIONS: M BUS HSA NY BUSA

City University of New York-Borough of Manhattan Community College

Registrar's Office
199 Chambers Street Rm. S-310
New York, NY 10007
(212) 618-1210

Will confirm attendance and degree by phone or mail. Inquiry must include student's name, date of birth, social security number, years attended. Employers may obtain transcripts upon written request accompanied by a $4.00 fee and a signed release from the student.

A multiprogram two-year institution, with an enrollment of 12,076. Highest level of offering: one year but less than four years.
ACCREDITATIONS: M NLN/AD MRT NY RSTH

City University of New York Bronx Community College

(See Bronx Community College -City of New York)

City University of New York Brooklyn College

Bedford Avenue & Avenue H
Brooklyn, NY 11210
(718) 780-5485

Will confirm by mail. Inquiry must include student's name, social security number, years attended, release. Requests should be directed to: Student Records. Employers may obtain transcripts upon written request accompanied by a $4.00 fee and a signed release from the student.

A comprehensive institution with no medical school, with an enrollment of 14,607. Highest level of offering: beyond master's but less than doctorate.
ACCREDITATIONS: M AUD NY SP TED

City University of New York City College

Convent Ave at 138th St
New York, NY 10031
(212) 650-7000

Will confirm attendance and degree by phone or mail. Inquiry must include student's name, date of birth, social security number, years attended. Employers may obtain transcripts upon written request accompanied by a $4.00 fee and a signed release from the student.

A comprehensive institution with no medical school, with an enrollment of 13,024. Highest level of offering: doctorate.
ACCREDITATIONS: M APCP ARCH CLPSY DANCE ENG ENGT LSAR NLN NY TED

City University of New York College of Staten Island

715 Ocean Terrace
Staten Island, NY 10301
(718) 390-7733

Will confirm attendance and degree by mail. Inquiry must include student's name, social security number, years attended, release. Employers may obtain transcripts upon written request accompanied by a $4.00 fee and a signed release from the student.

A comprehensive institution with no medical school, with an enrollment of 12,200. Highest level of offering: beyond master's but less than doctorate.
ACCREDITATIONS: M NLN/AD ENGT MLTAD NY ENG

City University of New York Graduate School and University Center

33 West 42nd Street
New York, NY 10036
(212) 642-1600

Will confirm attendance and degree by phone or mail. Inquiry must include student's name, social security number, years attended. Employers may obtain transcripts upon written request accompanied by a $4.00 fee and a signed release from the student.

A doctoral-level institution with no medical school, with an enrollment of 3,800. Highest level of offering: doctorate.

ACCREDITATIONS: M NY

City University of New York Herbert H. Lehman College

250 Bedford Park Boulevard
West–Schuster Hall, Room 114
Bronx, NY 10468
(212) 960-8611

Will confirm degree by mail. Inquiry must include student's name, date of birth, social security number, years attended. Employers may obtain transcripts upon written request accompanied by a $4.00 fee and a signed release from the student.

A comprehensive institution with no medical school, with an enrollment of 9,810. Highest level of offering: doctorate.

ACCREDITATIONS: M NLN NY SP CSWE TED

City University of New York Hostos Community College

500 Grand Concourse
Bronx, NY 10451
(212) 518-4444

Will confirm by mail. Inquiry must include student's name, social security number, release. Employers may obtain transcripts upon written request accompanied by a $4.00 fee and a signed release from the student. Direct inquiries to Registrar's Office.

A multiprogram two-year institution, with an enrollment of 4,000. Highest level of offering: one year but less than four years.

ACCREDITATIONS: M DH NY RAD

City University of New York Hunter College

695 Park Avenue
New York, NY 10021
(212) 772-4000

Will confirm attendance and degree by mail. Inquiry must include student's name, date of birth, social security number, years attended, release. Employers may obtain transcripts upon written request accompanied by a $4.00 fee and a signed release from the student. Direct inquiries to Registrar's Office.

A comprehensive institution with no medical school, with an enrollment of 20,000. Highest level of offering: beyond master's but less than doctorate.

ACCREDITATIONS: M AUD CHE NLN NY PTA SP CSWE TED

City University of New York John Jay College of Criminal Justice

445 West 59th Street
New York, NY 10019
(212) 237-8000

Will confirm attendance and degree by mail. Inquiry must include student's name, social security number, date of birth years attended, release. Employers may obtain transcripts upon written request accompanied by a $4.00 fee and a signed release from the student. Requests should be directed to: Registrar's Office.

A comprehensive institution with no medical school, with an enrollment of 6,518. Highest level of offering: doctorate.

ACCREDITATIONS: M NY

City University of New York Kingsborough Community College

2001 Oriental Boulevard
Brooklyn, NY 11235
(718) 368-5000

Will confirm attendance and degree by mail. Inquiry must include student's name, date of birth, social security number, years attended, release. Employers may obtain transcripts upon written request accompanied by a $4.00 fee and a signed release from the student.

A multiprogram two-year institution, with an enrollment of 10,206. Highest level of offering: one year but less than four years.

ACCREDITATIONS: M NLN/AD NY

City University of New York La Guardia Community College

Office of Registrar
31-10 Thomson Avenue
Long Island City, NY 11101
(718) 368-7232

Will confirm attendance and degree by mail. Inquiry must include student's name, social security number, years attended, release. Employers may obtain transcripts upon written request accompanied by a $4.00 fee and a signed release from the student.

A multiprogram two-year institution, with an enrollment of 9,000. Highest level of offering: one year but less than four years.

ACCREDITATIONS: M

City University of New York Medgar Evers College

1150 Carroll Street
Brooklyn, NY 11225
(718) 270-4900

Will confirm attendance and degree by mail. Inquiry must include student's name, social security number, years attended, release. Employers may obtain transcripts upon written request accompanied by a $4.00 fee and a signed release from the student.

A general baccalaureate institution, with an enrollment of 3,000. Highest level of offering: four or five year baccalaureate.

ACCREDITATIONS: M NLN NY

City University of New York New York City Technical College

300 Jay Street–Registrar Office
Brooklyn, NY 11201
(718) 260-5000

Will confirm attendance by phone or mail. Inquiry must include student's name, date of birth, social security number, years attended. Employers may obtain transcripts upon written request accompanied by a $4.00 fee and a signed release from the student.

A multiprogram two-year institution, with an enrollment of 10,500. Highest level of offering: four or five year baccalaureate.

ACCREDITATIONS: M NLN/AD DH DT ENGT NY RAD

City University of New York Queens College

65–30 Kissena Boulevard
Flushing, NY 11367
(718) 997-4400
Fax (718) 997-3134

Will confirm attendance and degree by phone or mail. Inquiry must include student's name, social security number. Requests should be directed to: Administrative Department. Employers may obtain transcripts upon written request accompanied by a $4.00 fee and a signed release from the student.

A comprehensive institution with no medical school, with an enrollment of 16,646. Highest level of offering: beyond master's but less than doctorate.

ACCREDITATIONS: M AUD LIB NY SP

City University of New York Queensborough Community College

56th Avenue–Springfield Boulevard
New York, NY 11364
(718) 631-6262

Will confirm attendance and degree by mail. Inquiry must include student's name, social security number, years attended, graduation date. Employers may obtain transcripts upon written request accompanied by a $4.00 fee and a signed release from the student.

A multiprogram two-year institution, with an enrollment of 13,176. Highest level of offering: one year but less than four years.

ACCREDITATIONS: M NLN/AD ENGT NY

City University of New York York College

94–20 Guy R Brewer Boulevard
Jamaica, NY 11451
(718) 262-2000 Ext. 2148
Fax (718) 262-2027

Will confirm attendance and degree by mail or fax. Inquiry must include student's name, social security number, release. Employers may obtain transcripts upon written request accompanied by a $4.00 fee and a signed release from the student. Requests should be directed to: Registrar's Office.

A general baccalaureate institution, with an enrollment of 4,843. Highest level of offering: four or five year baccalaureate.
ACCREDITATIONS: M NY OT

City University
16661 Northrup Way
Bellevue, WA 98008
(800) 426-5596 Ext. 270
Fax (206) 746-2567

Will confirm attendance and degree by phone, fax or mail. Inquiry must include student's name, social security number, years attended. Employers may obtain transcripts upon written request accompanied by a $3.00 fee and a signed release from the student.

A business school, with an enrollment of 6,500. Highest level of offering: master's.
ACCREDITATIONS: NW

Clackamas Community College
19600 Molalla Avenue
Oregon City, OR 97045
(503) 657-8400 Ext. 254
Fax (503) 650-6654

Will confirm enrollment and degree by phone or mail. Inquiry must include student's name, date of birth, social security number, years attended. Employers may obtain transcripts upon written request accompanied by a $3.00 fee and a signed release from the student. Requests should be directed to: Registrar's Office.

A multiprogram two-year institution, with an enrollment of 4,677. Highest level of offering: two years.
ACCREDITATIONS: NW

Claflin College
College Avenue North East
Orangeburg, SC 29115
(803) 534-2710 Ext. 340

Will confirm attendance and degree by phone or mail. Inquiry must include student's name, maiden name, social security number, years attended. Employers may obtain transcripts upon written request accompanied by a $4.00 fee and a signed release from the student. Requests should be directed to: Registrar's Office.

A general baccalaureate institution, with an enrollment of 850. Highest level of offering: four or five year baccalaureate.
ACCREDITATIONS: SC

Claremont Graduate School
McManus 131–170 East 10th Street
Claremont, CA 91711
(714) 621-8285

Will confirm attendance and degree by phone or mail. Inquiry must include student's name, date of birth, social security number, years attended. Employers may obtain transcripts upon written request accompanied by a $4.00 fee and a signed release from the student.

A doctoral-level institution with no medical school, with an enrollment of 1,742. Highest level of offering: doctorate.
ACCREDITATIONS: WC

Claremont McKenna College
500 East 9th Street
Claremont, CA 91711
(714) 621-8101

Will confirm attendance and degree by phone or mail. Inquiry must include student's name, social security number. Employers may obtain transcripts upon written request accompanied by a $1.00 fee and a signed release from the student.

A general baccalaureate institution, with an enrollment of 843. Highest level of offering: four or five year baccalaureate.
ACCREDITATIONS: WC

Clarendon College
PO Box 968
Clarendon, TX 79226
(806) 874-3571

Will confirm attendance and degree by mail. Inquiry must include student's name, date of birth, social security number, years attended. Employers may obtain transcripts upon written request accompanied by a $2.00 fee and a signed release from the student. Requests should be directed to: Registrar's Office.

A multiprogram two-year institution, with an enrollment of 723. Highest level of offering: one year but less than four years.
ACCREDITATIONS: SC

Clarion University of Pennsylvania Main Campus
122 Carrier
Clarion, PA 16214
(814) 226-2229
Fax (814) 226-2039

Will confirm attendance and degree by phone, fax or mail. Inquiry must include student's name, social security number. Employers may obtain transcripts upon written request accompanied by a $3.00 fee and a signed release from the student. Requests should be directed to: Registrar's Office.

A comprehensive institution with no medical school, with an enrollment of 6,500. Highest level of offering: master's.
ACCREDITATIONS: M NLN/AD LIB TED

Clarion University of Pennsylvania
122 Carrier Hall
Clarion, PA 16214
(814) 226-2229
Fax (814) 226-2039

Will confirm attendance and degree by phone, fax or mail. Inquiry must include student's name, social security number. Employers may obtain transcripts upon written request accompanied by a $3.00 fee and a signed release from the student. Requests should be directed to: Registrar's Office.

A multiprogram four-year institution, with an enrollment of 6,000. Highest level of offering: master's.
ACCREDITATIONS: M

Clark Atlanta University
(Formerly Clark College and Atlanta University)
James P Brawley Dr. at Fair St., S.W.
Atlanta, GA 30314
(404) 880-8759

Will confirm attendance and degree by mail. Inquiry must include student's name, date of birth, social security number, years attended. Employers may obtain transcripts upon written request accompanied by a $3.00 fee and a signed release from the student.

A comprehensive institution with no medical school, with an enrollment of 3,523. Highest level of offering: doctorate.
ACCREDITATIONS: SC BUS LIB CSWE TED

Clark College
c/o State Indianapolis Commission of Proprietory Education
32 East Washington, Suite 804
Indianpolis, ID 46204
(800) 227-5695

School closed. Records are being held at the above location. Will confirm attendance and degree by phone or mail. Inquiry must include student's name, social security number, years attended. Employers may obtain transcripts upon written request accompanied by a $2.00 fee and a signed release from the student.

A multiprogram two-year institution, with an enrollment of 400. Highest level of offering: one year but less than four years.
ACCREDITATIONS: JRCB MAC

Clark College
1800 East Mcloughlin Boulevard
Vancouver, WA 98663
(206) 699-0135
Fax (206) 690-7228

Will confirm attendance and degree by phone, fax or mail. Inquiry must include student's name, social security number, years attended. Employers may obtain transcripts upon written request accompanied by a signed release from the student.

A multiprogram two-year institution, with an enrollment of 6,217. Highest level of offering: one year but less than four years.
ACCREDITATIONS: NW NLN/AD DH

Clark County Community College
Office of Records, Sort Code C1K
3200 East Cheyenne Avenue
North Las Vegas, NV 89030
(702) 648-0830

Will confirm attendance and degree by phone or mail. Inquiry must include student's name, social security number, years attended. Employers may obtain transcripts upon written request accompanied by a $2.00 fee and a signed release from the student.

A multiprogram two-year institution, with an enrollment of 9,824. Highest level of offering: one year but less than four years.
ACCREDITATIONS: NW DH RSTHT

Clark Technical College

570 East Leffels Lane
Springfield, OH 45501
(513) 328-6015
Fax (513) 328-6133

Will confirm degree by phone, fax or mail. Inquiry must include student's name, social security number. Employers may obtain transcripts upon written request accompanied by a $2.00 fee and a signed release from the student.

A multiprogram two-year institution, with an enrollment of 2,399. Highest level of offering: two years but less than four years.
ACCREDITATIONS: NH NLN/AD MLTAD

Clark University

950 Main Street
Worcester, MA 01610
(508) 793-7426

Will confirm attendance and degree by phone or mail. Inquiry must include student's name, years attended. Employers may obtain transcripts upon written request accompanied by a $3.00 fee and a signed release from the student.

A doctoral-level institution with no medical school, with an enrollment of 3,185. Highest level of offering: doctorate.
ACCREDITATIONS: EH CLPSY

Clarke College

PO Box 440
Newton, MS 39345
(601) 683-2061

Will confirm attendance and degree by mail or phone. Inquiry must include student's name, date of birth, social security number, years attended. Employers may obtain transcripts upon written request accompanied by a $2.00 fee and a signed release from the student.

A multiprogram two-year institution, with an enrollment of 166. Highest level of offering: one year but less than four years.
ACCREDITATIONS: SC

Clarke College

1550 Clarke Drive
Dubuque, IA 52001
(319) 588-6300
Fax (319) 588-6789

Will confirm attendance and degree by phone. Inquiry must include student's name, SSN, years attended. Employers may obtain transcripts upon written request accompanied by a $2.00 fee and a signed release from the student.

A general baccalaureate institution, with an enrollment of 922. Highest level of offering: master's.
ACCREDITATIONS: NH NASM CSWE TED NCN

Clarkson University

Registrar's Office
Snell Hall
Clarkson University
Potsdam, NY 13699-5575
(315) 268-6451

Will confirm attendance and degree by phone. Inquiry must include student's name. Employers may obtain transcripts upon written request accompanied by a $4.00 fee and a signed release from the student.

An engineering school, with an enrollment of 3,006. Highest level of offering: doctorate.
ACCREDITATIONS: M NYSBR ABET AACSB

Clatsop Community College

16th & Jerome
Astoria, OR 97103
(503) 325-0910
Fax (503) 325-5738

Will confirm attendance and degree by phone. Inquiry must include student's name, social security number, years attended. Employers may obtain transcripts upon written request accompanied by a $2.00 fee and a signed release from the student.

A multiprogram two-year institution, with an enrollment of 2,500. Highest level of offering: two years but less than four years.
ACCREDITATIONS: NW

Clayton Junior College

(See Clayton State College)

Clayton State College

PO Box 285
5900 Lee Street
Morrow, GA 30260
(404) 961-3500
Fax (404) 961-3700

Will confirm attendance and degree by phone, fax or mail. Inquiry must include student's name, social security number, years attended. Employers may obtain transcripts upon written request accompanied by a signed release from the student. No fax requests. Requests should be directed to: Admissions Office.

A multiprogram four-year institution, with an enrollment of 3,600. Highest level of offering: four years.
ACCREDITATIONS: SC NLN/AD DH

Clayton University

PO Box 16941
St. Louis , MO 63105
(314) 727-6100

Will confirm attendance and degree by mail. Inquiry must include student's name, social security number, release. Employers may obtain transcripts upon written request accompanied by a $20.00 fee and a signed release from the student.

A bachelor's or higher institution newly admitted to NCES, with an enrollment of 300. Highest level of offering: doctorate.
ACCREDITATIONS: 3IC

Clearwater Christian College

3400 Gulf–To–Bay Boulevard
Clearwater, FL 34614
(813) 726-1153 Ext. 239

Will confirm attendance and degree by mail. Inquiry must include student's name, social security number, years attended, release. Employers may obtain transcripts upon written request by student accompanied by a $2.00 fee and a signed release from the student.

A general baccalaureate institution, with an enrollment of 430. Highest level of offering: four or five year baccalaureate.
ACCREDITATIONS: SC

Cleary College

2170 Washtenaw Avenue
Ypsilanti, MI 48197
(313) 483-4400
Fax (313) 483-0090

Will confirm attendance by phone, fax or mail. Inquiry must include student's name, date of birth, social security number, years attended. Employers may obtain transcripts upon written request accompanied by a $5.00 fee and a signed release from the student.

A business school, with an enrollment of 1,081. Highest level of offering: four or five year baccalaureate.
ACCREDITATIONS: NCA SRCB

Clemson University

104 Sikes Hall
Clemson, SC 29634-5125
(803) 656-2173

Will confirm attendance and degree by mail. Inquiry must include student's name, date of birth, social security number, years attended. Employers may obtain transcripts upon written request accompanied by a $3.00 fee and a signed release from the student.

A doctoral-level institution with no medical school, with an enrollment of 12,926. Highest level of offering: doctorate.
ACCREDITATIONS: SC ARCH BUS ENG ENGT FOR NLN TED

Cleveland Chiropractic College

590 North Vermont Avenue
Los Angeles, CA 90004
(213) 660-6166
Fax (213) 665-1931

Will confirm attendance and degree by mail or fax. Inquiry must include student's name, social security number, years attended, release. Employers may obtain transcripts upon written request accompanied by a $5.00 fee and a signed release from the student.

A health institution, with an enrollment of 419. Highest level of offering: first professional degree.
ACCREDITATIONS: CHIRO

Cleveland Chiropractic College

6401 Rockhill Road
Kansas City, MO 64131
(816) 333-8230
Fax (816) 361-0272

Will confirm attendance and degree by mail or fax. Inquiry must include student's name, social security number. Employers may obtain transcripts upon written request accompanied by a signed release from the student. Attn: Registrar.

A health institution, with an enrollment of 375. Highest level of offering: first professional degree.
ACCREDITATIONS: NH CHIRO

Cleveland College of Jewish Studies

26500 Shaker Boulevard
Beachwood, OH 44122
(216) 464-4050
Fax (216) 464-5827

Will confirm attendance and degree by phone, fax or mail. Inquiry must include student's name, social security number. Employers may obtain transcripts upon written request accompanied by a $3.00 fee and a signed release from the student.

A specialized school, with an enrollment of 183. Highest level of offering: master's.
ACCREDITATIONS: NH

Cleveland Community College

(Formerly Cleveland Technical College)
137 South Post Road
Shelby, NC 28150
(704) 484-4099

Will confirm attendance and degree by mail or phone. Inquiry must include student's name, social security number. Employers may obtain transcripts upon written request accompanied by a signed release from the student.

A multiprogram two-year institution, with an enrollment of 1,700. Highest level of offering: two year but less than four years.
ACCREDITATIONS: SACS

Cleveland Institute of Art

11141 East Boulevard
Cleveland, OH 44106
(216) 421-7321
Fax (216) 229-0904

Will confirm attendance and degree by phone, fax or mail. Inquiry must include student's name, social security number, years attended. Employers may obtain transcripts upon written request accompanied by a signed release from the student.

A visual arts school, with an enrollment of 442. Highest level of offering: four or five year baccalaureate.
ACCREDITATIONS: NH ART

Cleveland Institute of Electronics

1776 East 17th Street
Cleveland, OH 44114
(216) 781-9400
Fax (216) 781-0331

Will confirm attendance and degree by phone, fax or mail. Inquiry must include student's name, social security number. Employers may obtain transcripts upon written request accompanied by a $25.00 fee and a signed release from the student. Requests should be directed to: Students Service Department.

A two-year institution newly admitted to NCES, with an enrollment of 23,373. Highest level of offering: one year but less than four years.
ACCREDITATIONS: NHSC

Cleveland Institute of Music

11021 East Boulevard
Cleveland, OH 44106
(216) 791-5165
Fax (216) 791-3063

Will confirm attendance and degree by phone, fax or mail. Inquiry must include student's name, date of birth, social security number, years attended. Employers may obtain transcripts upon written request accompanied by $2.00 fee and a signed release from the student.

A visual and performing arts school, with an enrollment of 290. Highest level of offering: doctorate.
ACCREDITATIONS: NH NASM

Cleveland State Community College

PO Box 3570
Cleveland, TN 37320-3570
(615) 472-7141 Ext. 268
Fax (615) 478-6255

Will confirm attendance and degree by phone or mail. Inquiry must include student's name, social security number. Employers may obtain transcripts upon written request accompanied by a signed release from the student.

A multiprogram two-year institution, with an enrollment of 3,500. Highest level of offering: one year but less than four years.
ACCREDITATIONS: SC NLN/AD MLTAD DT

Cleveland State University

East 24th and Euclid Avenue
Cleveland, OH 44115
(216) 687-3700

Will confirm attendance and degree by mail. Inquiry must include student's name, social security number, years attended. Employers may obtain transcripts upon written request accompanied by a signed release from the student.

A comprehensive institution with no medical school, with an enrollment of 18,535. Highest level of offering: doctorate.
ACCREDITATIONS: NCA AUD BUS ENG LAW NASM NLN OT PTA SP CSWE TED BUSA ACS

Cleveland Technical College

(See Cleveland Community College)

Clinton Community College

Bluff Point
Plattsburgh, NY 12901
(518) 562-4122
Fax (518) 561-8621

Will confirm attendance and degree by phone or mail. Inquiry must include student's name, social security number. Employers may obtain transcripts upon written request accompanied by a $5.00 fee and a signed release from the student.

A multiprogram two-year institution, with an enrollment of 2,000. Highest level of offering: one year but less than four years.
ACCREDITATIONS: M NY

Clinton Junior College

PO Box 968
Rock Hill, SC 29731
(803) 327-7402

Will confirm attendance and degree by phone or mail. Inquiry must include student's name, social security number, years attended. Employers may obtain transcripts upon written request accompanied by a $2.00 fee and a signed release from the student.

A multiprogram two-year institution, with an enrollment of 95. Highest level of offering: one year but less than four years.
ACCREDITATIONS: 3IC

Cloud County Community College

2221 Campus Drive-Box 1002
Concordia, KS 66901
(913) 243-1435 Ext. 205
Fax (913) 243-1459

Will confirm attendance and degree by phone or mail. Inquiry must include student's name, social security number, years attended. Employers may obtain transcripts upon written request accompanied by a $2.00 fee and a signed release from the student.

A multiprogram two-year institution, with an enrollment of 3,184. Highest level of offering: one year but less than four years.
ACCREDITATIONS: NCA NLN/AD

Coahoma Junior College

Route 1 Box 616
Clarksdale, MS 38614
(601) 627-2571
Fax (601) 627-2571

Will confirm attendance and degree by phone, fax or mail. Inquiry must include student's name, date of birth, social security number, years attended, release. Employers may obtain transcripts upon written request accompanied by a $1.00 fee and a signed release from the student.

A multiprogram two-year institution, with an enrollment of 1,700. Highest level of offering: one year but less than four years.
ACCREDITATIONS: SC

Coastal Carolina Community College

444 Western Boulevard
Jacksonville, NC 28546
(919) 455-1221 Ext. 323
Fax (919) 455-7027

Will confirm attendance and degree by phone, fax or mail. Inquiry must include student's name, date of birth, social security number, years attended. Employers may obtain transcripts upon written request accompanied by a signed release from the student.

A multiprogram two-year institution, with an enrollment of 3,750. Highest level of offering: one year but less than four years.
ACCREDITATIONS: SC DA DH MLTAD SURGT

Coastline Community College

11460 Warner Avenue
Fountain Valley, CA 92708
(714) 546-7600
Fax (714) 241-6248

Will confirm attendance and degree by phone, fax or mail. Inquiry must include student's name, date of birth, social security number. Employers may obtain transcripts upon written request accompanied by a $2.00 fee and a signed release from the student.

A multiprogram two-year institution, with an enrollment of 12,286. Highest level of offering: one year but less than four years.
ACCREDITATIONS: WJ

Cobleskill

Knapp Hall
Cobleskill, NY 12043
(518) 234-5521
Fax (518) 234-5333

Will confirm attendance and degree by phone, fax or mail. Inquiry must include student's name, social security number. Employers may obtain transcripts upon written request accompanied by a $3.00 fee and a signed release from the student.

A multiprogram two-year institution, with an enrollment of 12,286. Highest level of offering: one year but less than four years.
ACCREDITATIONS: M HT NY

Cochise College

Rt. 1 Box 100
Douglas, AZ 85607
(602) 364-0241
Fax (602) 364-0326

Will confirm attendance and degree by phone, fax or mail. Inquiry must include student's name, social security number. Employers may obtain transcripts upon written request accompanied by a $2.50 fee and a signed release from the student.

A multiprogram two-year institution, with an enrollment of 4,800. Highest level of offering: one year but less than four years.
ACCREDITATIONS: NH NLN/AD

Cochran School of Nursing-St Johns

967 North Broadway
Yonkers, NY 10701
(914) 964-4283

Will confirm attendance and degree by phone or mail. Inquiry must include student's name, years attended. Employers may obtain transcripts upon written request accompanied by a $3.00 fee and a signed release from the student.

A two-year institution newly admitted to NCES, with an enrollment of 126. Highest level of offering: one year but less than four years.
ACCREDITATIONS: NY NYSBR

Coe College

1220 1st Avenue East
Cedar Rapids, IA 52402
(319) 399-8000 Ext. 8526

Will confirm attendance and degree by phone or mail. Inquiry must include student's name, years attended. Employers may obtain transcripts upon written request accompanied by a $3.00 fee and a signed release from the student. Attn: Registrar.

A general baccalaureate institution, with an enrollment of 1,302. Highest level of offering: four or five year baccalaureate.
ACCREDITATIONS: NH NASM

Coffeyville Community College

11th And Willow
Coffeyville, KS 67337
(316) 251-7700 Ext. 2021
Fax (316) 251-7798

Will confirm attendance and degree by phone or mail. Inquiry must include student's name, date of birth, social security number, years attended. Employers may obtain transcripts upon written request accompanied by a $1.00 fee and a signed release from the student.

A multiprogram two-year institution, with an enrollment of 1,420. Highest level of offering: one year but less than four years.
ACCREDITATIONS: NCA MLTAD

Cogswell College North

c/o Cogswell Polytechnical College
10420 Bubb Road
Cupertino, CA 95014
(408) 252-5550

Records for this school are being handled by Cogswell Polytechnical College. Will confirm attendance and degree by mail or phone. Inquiry must include student's name, social security number, years attended. Employers may obtain transcripts upon written request accompanied by a signed release from the student.

A bachelor's or higher institution newly admitted to NCES. Highest level of offering: four or five year baccalaureate.
ACCREDITATIONS: NW

Cogswell Polytechnical College

10420 Bubb Road
Cupertino, CA 95014
(408) 252-5550
Fax (408) 253-2413

Will confirm attendance and degree by mail. Inquiry must include student's name, date of birth, social security number, years attended, release. Employers may obtain transcripts upon written request accompanied by a signed release from the student.

An engineering school, with an enrollment of 285. Highest level of offering: four or five year baccalaureate.
ACCREDITATIONS: WC ENGT

Coker College

College Avenue
Hartsville, SC 29550
(803) 383-8022
Fax (803) 383-8095

Will confirm attendance and degree by phone or mail. Inquiry must include student's name, social security number, years attended. Employers may obtain transcripts upon written request accompanied by a $3.00 fee and a signed release from the student.

A general baccalaureate institution, with an enrollment of 740. Highest level of offering: four or five year baccalaureate.
ACCREDITATIONS: SC NASM

Colby–Sawyer College

Main Street
New London, NH 03257
(603) 526-2010 Ext. 770

Will confirm attendance and degree by phone or mail. Inquiry must include student's name, years attended. Employers may obtain transcripts upon written request accompanied by a $3.00 fee and a signed release from the student.

A general baccalaureate institution, with an enrollment of 449. Highest level of offering: four or five year baccalaureate.
ACCREDITATIONS: EH

Colby College

Waterville, ME 04901
(207) 872-3198
Fax (207) 872-3555

Will confirm attendance and degree by phone, fax or mail. Inquiry must include student's name, years attended. Employers may obtain transcripts upon written request accompanied by a $1.00 fee and a signed release from the student.

A general baccalaureate institution, with an enrollment of 1,695. Highest level of offering: four or five year baccalaureate.
ACCREDITATIONS: EH

Colby Community College

1255 South Range
Colby, KS 67701
(913) 462-3984 Ext. 297
Fax (913) 462-8315

Will confirm attendance and degree by phone or mail. Inquiry must include student's name, date of birth, social security number, years attended. Employers may obtain transcripts upon written request accompanied by a $1.00 fee and a signed release from the student.

A multiprogram two-year institution, with an enrollment of 1,663. Highest level of offering: two year degree.
ACCREDITATIONS: NH AVVMA/CVTTAT PNUR PTAA

Coleman College

7380 Parkway Drive
La Mesa, CA 91942
(619) 465-3990
Fax (619) 463-0162

Will confirm attendance and degree by phone, fax or mail. Inquiry must include student's name, date of birth, social security number, years attended. Employers may obtain transcripts upon written request accompanied by a $3.00 fee and a signed release from the student.

A specialized school, with an enrollment of 988. Highest level of offering: master's.
ACCREDITATIONS: SRCB

Colgate Divinity School

1100 South Goodman Street
Rochester, NY 14620
(716) 271-1320 Ext. 243
Fax (716) 271-2166

Will confirm attendance and degree by phone or mail. Inquiry must include student's name, social security number. Employers may obtain transcripts upon written request accompanied by a $5.00 fee and a signed release from the student.

A school of religion and theology, with an enrollment of 220. Highest level of offering:doctorate.
ACCREDITATIONS: NY THEOL

Colgate University

Hamilton, NY 13346
(315) 824-7406
Fax (315) 824-7831

Will confirm attendance and degree by phone, fax or mail. Inquiry must include student's name, date of birth, social security number, years attended. Employers may obtain transcripts upon written request accompanied by $3.00 fee and a signed release from the student. Requests should be directed to: Registrar's Office.

A comprehensive institution with no medical school, with an enrollment of 2,734. Highest level of offering: master's.
ACCREDITATIONS: M NY

College for Human Services

345 Hudson Street
New York, NY 10014
(212) 989-2002

Will confirm attendance and degree by mail. Inquiry must include student's name, social security number, release. Employers may obtain transcripts upon written request accompanied by a $2.00 fee and a signed release from the student. Requests should be directed to: Registrar's Office.

A specialized school, with an enrollment of 2,000. Highest level of offering: master's.
ACCREDITATIONS: M NY

College Misericordia

Lake Street
Dallas, PA 18612
(717) 675-2181 Ext. 297
Fax (717) 675-2441

Will confirm attendance and degree by phone, fax or mail. Inquiry must include student's name, social security number, years attended. Requests should be directed to: Registrar's Office. Employers may obtain transcripts upon written request accompanied by a $4.00 fee and a signed release from the student.

A general baccalaureate institution, with an enrollment of 1,292. Highest level of offering: master's.
ACCREDITATIONS: M NASM NLN RAD CSWE

College of Aeronautics

(Formerly Academy of Aeronautics)
La Guardia Airport
Flushing, NY 11371
(718) 429-6600 Ext. 53

Will confirm attendance and degree by mail. Inquiry must include student's name. Employers may obtain transcripts upon written request accompanied by a $3.00 fee and a signed release from the student. Requests should be directed to: Records Office.

A single program four-year institution, with an enrollment of 1,230. Highest level of offering: bachelor.
ACCREDITATIONS: M ENGT NY

College of Alameda

555 Atlantic Avenue
Alameda, CA 94501
(510) 748-2228

Will confirm attendance and degree by mail or fax. Inquiry must include student's name, social security number, date of birth. Employers may obtain transcripts upon written request accompanied by a $1.00 fee and a signed release from the student. Requests should be directed to: Admissions & Records.

A multiprogram two-year institution, with an enrollment of 5,001. Highest level of offering: one year but less than four years.
ACCREDITATIONS: WJ DA MAC

College of Boca Raton

3601 N Military Trail
Boca Raton, FL 33431
(407) 994-0770 Ext. 177

Will confirm attendance and degree by phone or mail. Inquiry must include student's name, social security number. Employers may obtain transcripts upon written request accompanied by a $2.00 fee and a signed release from the student. Requests should be directed to: Registrar's Office.

A multiprogram two-year institution, with an enrollment of 1,000. Highest level of offering: four or five year baccalaureate.
ACCREDITATIONS: SC FUSER

College of Charleston

66 George Street
Charleston, SC 29424
(803) 792-5507
Fax (803) 792-4831

Will confirm attendance and degree by phone, fax or mail. Inquiry must include student's name, social security number, years attended. Employers may obtain transcripts upon written request accompanied by a $3.00 fee and a signed release from the student. Requests should be directed to: Registrar's Office.

A comprehensive institution with no medical school, with an enrollment of 8,000. Highest level of offering: master's.
ACCREDITATIONS: SC

College of Du Page

Records Office
Lambert Road & 22nd Street
Glen Ellyn, IL 60137-6599
(312) 858-2800
Fax (312) 858-9390

Will confirm attendance and degree by phone, fax or mail. Inquiry must include student's name, social security number. Requests should be directed to: Records Office. Employers may obtain transcripts upon written request accompanied by a $2.00 fee and a signed release from the student.

A multiprogram two-year institution, with an enrollment of 32,500. Highest level of offering: one year but less than four years.
ACCREDITATIONS: NH NLN/AD MRT NMT RAD RSTHT

College of Eastern Utah

451 East 400 North
Price, UT 84501
(801) 637-2120 Ext. 200
Fax (801) 637-4102

Will confirm attendance and degree by phone, fax or mail. Inquiry must include student's name, social security number, date of birth, years attended. Employers may obtain transcripts upon written request accompanied by a $2.00 fee and a signed release from the student.

A multiprogram two-year institution, with an enrollment of 2,200. Highest level of offering: one year but less than four years.
ACCREDITATIONS: NW

College of Ganado

c/o Navajo Community College
Tsaile, AZ 86556
(602) 724-3311 Ext. 110

Will confirm attendance and degree by mail. Inquiry must include student's name, date of birth, social security number, years attended. Employers may obtain transcripts upon written request accompanied by a $2.00 fee and a signed release from the student.

A multiprogram two-year institution, with an enrollment of 268. Highest level of offering: one year but less than four years.
ACCREDITATIONS: NH

College of Great Falls

1301 Twentieth Street South
Great Falls, MT 59405
(406) 761-8210

Will confirm attendance and degree by mail. Inquiry must include student's name, date of birth, years attended, release. Requests should be directed to: Registrar's Office. Employers may obtain transcripts upon written request accompanied by a $2.00 fee and a signed release from the student.

A general baccalaureate institution, with an enrollment of 1,360. Highest level of offering: master's.
ACCREDITATIONS: NW

College of Idaho

(See Albertson College of Idaho)

College of Insurance

101 Murray Street
New York, NY 10007
(212) 962-4111 Ext. 326
Fax (212) 964-3381

Will confirm attendance and degree by mail or fax. Inquiry must include student's name, date of birth, social security number, years attended, release. Employers may obtain transcripts upon written request accompanied by a $4.00 fee and a signed release from the student.

A business school, with an enrollment of 1,093. Highest level of offering: master's.
ACCREDITATIONS: M NY

College of Lake County

19351 West Washington Street
Grayslake, IL 60030
(708) 223-6601
Fax (708) 223-1017

Will confirm attendance and degree by phone or mail. Inquiry must include student's name, social security number. Employers may obtain transcripts upon written request accompanied by a $1.00 fee and a signed release from the student.

A multiprogram two-year institution, with an enrollment of 13,689. Highest level of offering: one year but less than four years.
ACCREDITATIONS: NH NLN/AD DA MLTAD MRT RAD

College of Marin

835 College Avenue
Kentfield, CA 94904
(415) 457-8811

Records prior to 1990 are being held at: Indian Valley Campus, Novata, CA, 94940. Direct inquiries to Transcript Department, (415) 883-2211, Ext. 8822. Will confirm attendance and degree by mail. Inquiry must include student's name, social security number, years attended, release. Employers may obtain transcripts upon written request accompanied by a $5.00 fee and a signed release from the student.

A multiprogram two-year institution, with an enrollment of 12,000. Highest level of offering: one year but less than four years.
ACCREDITATIONS: WJ NLN/AD DA

Colleges of Miran Novato Campus

(Formerly Miran Community College and Kentfield College)
1800 Ignacio Boulevard
Novato, CA 94949
(415) 883-2211
Fax (415) 883-6878

Will confirm attendance and degree by mail. Inquiry must include student's name, social security number, years attended, release. Employers may obtain transcripts upon written request accompanied by a $5.00 fee and a signed release from the student. Requests should be directed to: Admissions & Records.

A multiprogram two-year institution, with an enrollment of 10,000. Highest level of offering: one year but less than four years.
ACCREDITATIONS: WJ NLN/AD DA

College of Mount Saint Joseph

5701 Delhi Road
Cincinnati, OH 45233-1670
(513) 244-4621
Fax (513) 244-4222

Will confirm attendance and degree by phone, fax or mail. Inquiry must include student's name, social security number. Employers may obtain transcripts upon written request accompanied by a $2.00 fee and a signed release from the student.

A general baccalaureate institution, with an enrollment of 2,600. Highest level of offering: master's.
ACCREDITATIONS: NH MLTAD NASM NLN RSTH

College of Mount Saint Vincent

Riverdale, NY 10471
(212) 405-3200

Will confirm attendance and degree by phone or mail. Inquiry must include student's name, years attended. Employers may obtain transcripts upon written request accompanied by a $5.00 fee and a signed release from the student.

A general baccalaureate institution, with an enrollment of 1,079. Highest level of offering: four or five year baccalaureate.
ACCREDITATIONS: M NLN NY

College of New Rochelle

29 Castle Place
New Rochelle, NY 10805-2308
(914) 654-5245

Will confirm attendance and degree by mail. Inquiry must include student's name, social security number. Employers may obtain transcripts upon written request accompanied by a $4.00 fee and a signed release from the student.

A comprehensive institution with no medical school, with an enrollment of 5,138. Highest level of offering: master's.
ACCREDITATIONS: M NLN NY CSWE

College of Notre Dame of Maryland

4701 North Charles Street
Baltimore, MD 21210
(301) 435-0100 or 532-5318

Will confirm attendance and degree by mail or phone. Inquiry must include student's name, social security number, years attended. Employers may obtain transcripts upon written request accompanied by a $2.00 fee and a signed release from the student.

A general baccalaureate institution, with an enrollment of 2,100. Highest level of offering: four or five year baccalaureate.
ACCREDITATIONS: M

College of Notre Dame

1500 Ralston Avenue
Belmont, CA 94002
(415) 595-3521 Ext. 221

Will confirm attendance and degree by phone or mail. Inquiry must include student's name, social security number date of birth. Employers may obtain transcripts upon written request accompanied by a $3.00 fee and a signed release from the student.

A comprehensive institution with no medical school, with an enrollment of 1,300. Highest level of offering: master's.
ACCREDITATIONS: WC NASM TED

College of Oceaneering

272 South Fries Avenue
Wilmington, CA 90744
(213) 834-2501
Fax (213) 834-7132

Will confirm attendance and degree by mail or fax. Inquiry must include student's name, social security number, years attended. Employers may obtain transcripts upon written request accompanied by a $5.00 fee and a signed release from the student.

A two-year institution newly admitted to NCES, with an enrollment of 92. Highest level of offering: less than one year.
ACCREDITATIONS: WJ

College of Osteopathic Medicine of the Pacific

College Plaza
Pomona, CA 91766
(714) 623-6116 Ext. 243
Fax (714) 623-9623

Will confirm attendance and degree by phone or mail. Inquiry must include student's name, years attended. Employers may obtain transcripts upon written request accompanied by a $2.00 fee and a signed release from the student. Attn: Student Affairs.

A medical school, with an enrollment of 476. Highest level of offering: first professional degree.
ACCREDITATIONS: OSTEO

College of Our Lady of the Elms

291 Springfield Street
Chicopee, MA 01013-2839
(413) 594-2761 Ext. 236
Fax (413) 592-4871

Will confirm attendance and degree by phone or mail. Inquiry must include student's name, maiden name, and marriage name, if available, years attended. Employers may obtain transcripts upon written request accompanied by a $3.00 fee and a signed release from the student.

A general baccalaureate institution, with an enrollment of 1,100. Highest level of offering: master's.

ACCREDITATIONS: EH NLN CSWE

College of Saint Benedict

37 South College Avenue
Saint Joseph, MN 56374
(612) 363-5304
Fax (612) 363-2115

Will confirm attendance and degree by phone, fax or mail. Inquiry must include student's name, social security number, years attended. Employers may obtain transcripts upon written request accompanied by a $2.00 fee and a signed release from the student.

A general baccalaureate institution, with an enrollment of 2,035. Highest level of offering: four or five year baccalaureate.

ACCREDITATIONS: NCA NLN CSWE TED

College of Saint Catherine

2004 Randolph Avenue
Saint Paul, MN 55105
(612) 690-6000

Will confirm attendance and degree by phone or mail. Inquiry must include student's name, maiden name (if any), social security number, years attended. Employers may obtain transcripts upon written request accompanied by a $3.00 fee and a signed release from the student.

A general baccalaureate institution, with an enrollment of 2,585. Highest level of offering: four or five year baccalaureate.

ACCREDITATIONS: NH NASM NLN OT CSWE TED

College of Saint Elizabeth

2 Convent Road
Morristown, NJ 07960-6989
(201) 292-6308

Will confirm attendance and degree by phone or mail. Inquiry must include student's name, maiden name (if any), date of birth, years attended, release. Employers may obtain transcripts upon written request accompanied by a $3.00 fee and a signed release from the student.

A general baccalaureate institution, with an enrollment of 919. Highest level of offering: four or five year baccalaureate.

ACCREDITATIONS: M

College of Saint Francis

500 North Wilcox Street
Joliet, IL 60435
(815) 740-3391
Fax (815) 740-4285

Will confirm attendance and degree by phone or mail. Inquiry must include student's name, social security number, address. Employers may obtain transcripts upon written request accompanied by a $2.00 fee and a signed release from the student.

A liberal arts institution, with an enrollment of 3,850. Highest level of offering: master's.

ACCREDITATIONS: NH CSWE

College of Saint Joseph in Vermont

Clement Road
Rutland, VT 05701
(802) 773-5900

Will confirm attendance and degree by phone or mail. Inquiry must include student's name, social security number, date of birth. Employers may obtain transcripts upon written request accompanied by a $4.00 fee and a signed release from the student.

A school of education, with an enrollment of 500. Highest level of offering: master's.

ACCREDITATIONS: EH

College of Saint Mary

1901 South 72nd Street
Omaha, NE 68124
(402) 399-2400
Fax (402) 399-2441

Will confirm attendance and degree by phone, fax or mail. Inquiry must include student's name, date of birth, social security number, years attended. Employers may obtain transcripts upon written request accompanied by a $2.00 fee and a signed release from the student.

A health institution, with an enrollment of 1,125. Highest level of offering: four or five year baccalaureate.

ACCREDITATIONS: NH NLN/AD MRA

College of Saint Rose

432 Western Avenue
Albany, NY 12203
(518) 454-5213

Will confirm attendance and degree by phone or mail. Inquiry must include student's name, maiden name (if any), social security number, date of birth. Employers may obtain transcripts upon written request accompanied by a $3.00 fee and a signed release from the student.

A comprehensive institution with no medical school, with an enrollment of 3,600. Highest level of offering: master's.

ACCREDITATIONS: NY M MT

College of Saint Scholastica

1200 Kenwood Avenue
Duluth, MN 55811
(218) 723-6563
Fax (218) 723-6290

Will confirm attendance and degree by mail. Inquiry must include student's name, maiden name (if any), date of birth, social security number, years attended. Employers may obtain transcripts upon written request accompanied by a $2.00 fee and a signed release from the student.

A general baccalaureate institution, with an enrollment of 1,900. Highest level of offering: master's.

ACCREDITATIONS: NH MRA MT NLN PTA CSWE

College of Saint Teresa

c/o Assisi Heights
PO Box 4900
Rochester, MN 55901
(507) 282-7441

Will confirm attendance and degree by mail. Inquiry must include student's maiden name, (if any), date of birth, social security number. Employers may obtain transcripts upon written request accompanied by a $3.00 fee and a signed release from the student.

College of Saint Thomas

2115 Summit Avenue
Saint Paul, MN 55105
(612) 647-5000 Ext. 5336
Fax (612) 647-4378

Will confirm attendance and degree by phone, fax or mail. Inquiry must include student's name, social security number, years attended. Employers may obtain transcripts upon written request accompanied by a signed release from the student.

A comprehensive institution with no medical school, with an enrollment of 10,000. Highest level of offering: beyond master's but less than doctorate.

ACCREDITATIONS: NH NASM CSWE TED

College of San Mateo

1700 West Hillsdale Blvd
San Mateo, CA 94402
(415) 574-6165

Will confirm attendance and degree by phone or mail. Inquiry must include student's name, date of birth, social security number. Employers may obtain transcripts upon written request accompanied by a $3.00 fee and a signed release from the student.

A multiprogram two-year institution, with an enrollment of 14,055. Highest level of offering: one year but less than four years.

ACCREDITATIONS: WJ NLN/AD DA

College of Santa Fe

Saint Michaels Drive
Santa Fe, NM 87501
(505) 473-6320
Fax (505) 473-6504

Will confirm attendance and degree by phone, fax or mail. Inquiry must include student's name, social security number, years attended. Employers may obtain transcripts upon written request accompanied by a $3.00 fee ($5.00 fee to expedite) and a signed release from the student. Requests should be directed to: Registrar's Office.

A general baccalaureate institution, with an enrollment of 1,205. Highest level of offering: four or five year baccalaureate.
ACCREDITATIONS: NH

College of Southern Idaho

PO Box 1238
Twin Falls, ID 83303
(208) 733-9554 Ext. 234
Fax (208) 736-3014

Will confirm attendance and degree by phone, fax or mail. Inquiry must include student's name, social security number. Employers may obtain transcripts upon written request accompanied by a $2.00 fee and a signed release from the student.

A multiprogram two-year institution, with an enrollment of 3,014. Highest level of offering: one year but less than four years.
ACCREDITATIONS: NW NLN/AD

College of the Albemarle

PO Box 2327
Elizabeth City, NC 27909
(919) 335-0821 Ext. 252

Will confirm attendance and degree by phone or mail. Inquiry must include student's name, social security number. Employers may obtain transcripts upon written request accompanied by a signed release from the student.

A multiprogram two-year institution, with an enrollment of 1,843. Highest level of offering: two years but less than four years.
ACCREDITATIONS: SC

College of the Associated Arts

(Formerly School of the Associated Arts)
344 Summit Avenue
St. Paul, MN 55102
(612) 224-3416
Fax (612)224-8854

Will confirm attendance and degree by fax or mail. Inquiry must include student's name, social security number. Employers may obtain transcripts upon written request accompanied by a $2.00 fee and a signed release from the student.

A specialized school, with an enrollment of 150. Highest level of offering: four or five year baccalaureate.
ACCREDITATIONS: NATTS

College of the Atlantic

105 Eden Street
Bar Harbor, ME 04609
(207) 288-5015
Fax (207) 288-2328

Will confirm attendance and degree by phone, fax or mail. Inquiry must include student's name, years attended. Employers may obtain transcripts upon written request accompanied by a $2.00 fee and a signed release from the student.

A general baccalaureate institution, with an enrollment of 207. Highest level of offering: four or five year baccalaureate.
ACCREDITATIONS: EH

College of the Canyons

26455 North Rockwell Canyon Road
Valencia, CA 91355
(805) 259-7800
Fax (805) 259-8302

Will confirm attendance and degree by phone, fax or mail. Inquiry must include student's name, maiden name (if any), date of birth, social security number. Employers may obtain transcripts upon written request accompanied by a $2.00 fee and a signed release from the student.

A multiprogram two-year institution, with an enrollment of 5,600. Highest level of offering: one year but less than four years.
ACCREDITATIONS: WJ

College of the Desert

43-500 Monterey Avenue
Palm Desert, CA 92260
(619) 346-8041 Ext. 330
Fax (619) 341-8678

Will confirm attendance and degree by mail or fax. Inquiry must include student's name, date of birth, social security number, years attended. Employers may obtain transcripts upon written request accompanied by a $3.00 fee and a signed release from the student.

A multiprogram two-year institution, with an enrollment of 5,110. Highest level of offering: one year but less than four years.
ACCREDITATIONS: WJ NLN/AD RSTH

College of the Holy Cross

Worcester, MA 01610
(617) 793-2511

Will confirm attendance and degree by phone or mail. Inquiry must include student's name, years attended. Employers may obtain transcripts upon written request accompanied by a signed release from the student.

A general baccalaureate institution, with an enrollment of 2,590. Highest level of offering: four or five year baccalaureate.
ACCREDITATIONS: EH

College of the Mainland

1200 Amburn Road
Texas City, TX 77591
(409) 938-1211
Fax (409) 938-1306

Will confirm attendance and degree by mail. Inquiry must include student's name, social security number, years attended. Employers may obtain transcripts upon written request accompanied by a $1.00 fee and a signed release from the student.

A multiprogram two-year institution, with an enrollment of 2,901. Highest level of offering: one year but less than four years.
ACCREDITATIONS: SC NLN/AD

College of the Ozarks

415 College Avenue
Clarksville, AR 72830
(501) 754-3839
Fax (501) 754-3431 (Evenings)
Fax (501) 754-3839 (Daytime)

Will confirm attendance and degree by phone or mail. Inquiry must include student's name, date of birth, social security number, years attended. Employers may obtain transcripts upon written request accompanied by a $2.00 fee and a signed release from the student.

A general baccalaureate institution, with an enrollment of 794. Highest level of offering: four or five year baccalaureate.
ACCREDITATIONS: NH TED

College of the Redwoods

7351 Thompkins Hill Road
Eureka, CA 95501-9302
(707) 445-6720
Fax (707) 445-6991

Will confirm attendance and degree by phone, fax or mail. Inquiry must include student's name, social security number, years attended. Employers may obtain transcripts upon written request accompanied by a $5.00 fee and a signed release from the student.

A multiprogram two-year institution, with an enrollment of 7,952. Highest level of offering: one year but less than four years.
ACCREDITATIONS: WJ DA

College of the Sequoias

915 South Mooney Boulevard
Visalia, CA 93277
(209) 730-3775

Will confirm attendance and degree by mail. Inquiry must include student's name, date of birth, social security number, years attended. Employers may obtain transcripts upon written request accompanied by a $4.00 fee and a signed release from the student. Requests should be directed to: Records Department.

A multiprogram two-year institution, with an enrollment of 9,500. Highest level of offering: two year AA and AS.
ACCREDITATIONS: WJ

College of the Siskiyous

800 College Avenue
Weed, CA 96094
(916) 938-4462
Fax (916) 938-5226

Will confirm attendance and degree by phone, fax or mail. Inquiry must include student's name, date of birth, social security number, years attended, release. Employers may obtain transcripts upon written request accompanied by a $2.00 fee and a signed release from the student.

A multiprogram two-year institution, with an enrollment of 4,000. Highest level of offering: one year but less than four years.
ACCREDITATIONS: WJ

College of the Southwest

6610 Lovington Highway
Hobbs, NM 88240-9987
(505) 392-6561
Fax (505) 392-6006

Will confirm attendance and degree by phone or mail. Inquiry must include student's name, date of birth, social security number, years attended. Employers may obtain transcripts upon written request accompanied by a $2.00 fee and a signed release from the student.

A general baccalaureate institution, with an enrollment of 250. Highest level of offering: four or five year baccalaureate.

ACCREDITATIONS: NH

College of William and Mary

PO Box 8795
Williamsburg, VA 23187-8795
(804) 253-4245
Fax (804) 221-1773

Will confirm attendance and degree by phone or mail. Inquiry must include student's name, date of birth, social security number, years attended. Employers may obtain transcripts upon written request accompanied by a signed release from the student.

A comprehensive institution with no medical school, with an enrollment of 7,200. Highest level of offering: doctorate.

ACCREDITATIONS: SC BUS LAW TED BUSA

College of Wooster

Wooster, OH 44691
(216) 263-2366
Fax (216) 263-2260

Will confirm attendance and degree by mail or fax. Inquiry must include student's name, date of birth, social security number, years attended. Employers may obtain transcripts upon written request accompanied by a $3.00 fee and a signed release from the student.

A general baccalaureate institution, with an enrollment of 1,800. Highest level of offering: four or five year baccalaureate.

ACCREDITATIONS: NH NASM

Colorado Christian University

(Formerly Western Bible College and Rockmont College)
180 South Garrison
Lakewood, CO 80226
(303) 238-5386 Ext. 140

Will confirm attendance and degree by mail. Inquiry must include student's name, social security number, years attended. Employers may obtain transcripts upon written request accompanied by a $3.00 fee and a signed release from the student.

A school of liberal arts, business, religion and theology, with an enrollment of 1,300. Highest level of offering: four or five year baccalaureate.

ACCREDITATIONS: BI NH

Colorado College

Attn: Office of Registrar
Colorado Springs, CO 80903
(719) 389-6610
Fax (719) 389-6932

Will confirm degree and attendance by phone, fax or mail. Inquiry must include student's name, date of birth, years attended. Employers may obtain transcripts upon written request accompanied by a signed release from the student.

A general baccalaureate institution, with an enrollment of 1,923. Highest level of offering: master's.

ACCREDITATIONS: NH NASM

Colorado Institute of Art

200 East Ninth Avenue
Denver, CO 80203
(303) 837-0825
Fax (303) 837-0825 Ext. 549

Will confirm attendance and degree by phone, fax or mail. Inquiry must include student's name, social security number, years attended. Employers may obtain transcripts upon written request accompanied by a $2.00 fee and a signed release from the student.

A two-year institution newly admitted to NCES, with an enrollment of 1,300. Highest level of offering: one year but less than four years.

ACCREDITATIONS: NATTS

Colorado Mountain College

PO Box 10001
Glenwood Springs, CO 81602
(303) 945-8691

Will confirm attendance and degree by mail. Inquiry must include student's name, date of birth, social security number, years attended and release from student. Employers may obtain transcripts upon written request accompanied by a $2.00 fee and a signed release from the student.

A multiprogram two-year institution, with an enrollment of 8,155. Highest level of offering: one year but less than four years.

ACCREDITATIONS: NH AVVMA/CVTTAT

Colorado Northwestern Community College

500 Kennedy Drive
Rangely, CO 81648
(303) 675-3218
Fax (303) 675-3330

Will confirm attendance and degree by phone, fax or mail. Inquiry must include student's name, date of birth, social security number, years attended. Employers may obtain transcripts upon written request accompanied by a $2.00 fee and a signed release from the student.

A multiprogram two-year institution, with an enrollment of 700. Highest level of offering: one year but less than four years.

ACCREDITATIONS: NH DH

Colorado School of Mines

Golden, CO 80401
(303) 273-3200
Fax (303) 273-3278

Will confirm attendance and degree by phone, fax or mail. Inquiry must include student's name, date of birth, and SSN. Employers may obtain transcripts upon written request accompanied by a $2.00 fee and a signed release from the student.

An engineering school, with an enrollment of 2,882. Highest level of offering: doctorate.

ACCREDITATIONS: NH ENG

Colorado State University

Admin. Annex Room 100
Fort Collins, CO 80523
(303) 491-7148

Will confirm attendance and degree by phone or mail. Inquiry must include student's name, date of birth, years attended. Employers may obtain transcripts upon written request accompanied by a $2.00 fee and a signed release from the student. Requests should be directed to: Office of Admissions & Records.

A doctoral-level institution including a veterinary medicine and biomedical sciences college. with an enrollment of 20,094. Highest level of offering: doctorate.

ACCREDITATIONS: NH AUD BUS COPSY ENG FOR IPSY JOUR LSAR NASM OT SP TED VET CSWE

Colorado Technical College

4435 North Chestnut
Colorado Springs, CO 80907
(719) 598-0200

Will confirm attendance and degree by mail. Inquiry must include student's name, date of birth, social security number, release. Employers may obtain transcripts upon written request accompanied by a $10.00 fee and a signed release from the student.

An engineering school, with an enrollment of 1,300. Highest level of offering: master's.

ACCREDITATIONS: NH ENGT

Columbia–Greene Community College

PO Box 1000
Hudson, NY 12534
(518) 828-4181 Ext. 371
Fax (518) 828-8543

Will confirm attendance and degree by phone, fax or mail. Inquiry must include student's name, date of birth, social security number. Requests should be directed to: Student Services. Employers may obtain transcripts upon written request accompanied by a $3.00 fee and a signed release from the student.

A multiprogram two-year institution, with an enrollment of 1,600. Highest level of offering: one year but less than four years.

ACCREDITATIONS: M NY

Columbia Basin College

2600 North 20th Avenue
Pasco, WA 99301
(509) 547-0511
Fax (509) 546-0401

Will confirm attendance and degree by mail, phone or fax. Inquiry must include student's name, date of birth, social security number, years attended. Employers may obtain transcripts upon written request accompanied by a $2.00 fee and a signed release from the student.

A multiprogram two-year institution, with an enrollment of 5,500. Highest level of offering: two years.
ACCREDITATIONS: NW

Columbia Bible College & Seminary

PO Box 3122
Columbia, SC 29230
(803) 754-4100

Will confirm attendance and degree by phone or mail. Inquiry must include student's name, years attended. Employers may obtain transcripts upon written request accompanied by a $3.00 fee and a signed release from the student.

A school of education, religion and theology, with an enrollment of 885. Highest level of offering: doctorate.
ACCREDITATIONS: SC BI THEOL

Columbia Christian College

9101 East Burnside
Portland, OR 97216-1515
(503) 255-7060

Will confirm attendance and degree by phone or mail. Inquiry must include student's name, social security number. Employers may obtain transcripts upon written request accompanied by a $3.00 fee and a signed release from the student.

A general baccalaureate institution, with an enrollment of 330. Highest level of offering: four or five year baccalaureate.
ACCREDITATIONS: NW

Columbia College–Columbia

PO Box 1849
Columbia, CA 95310
(209) 533-5100
Fax (209) 533-5104

Will confirm attendance and degree by mail. Inquiry must include student's name, date of birth, social security number, years attended, release. Requests should be directed to: Record & Admissions Office. Employers may obtain transcripts upon written request accompanied by a $3.00 fee and a signed release from the student.

A multiprogram two-year institution, with an enrollment of 3,800. Highest level of offering: one year but less than four years.
ACCREDITATIONS: WJ

Columbia College–Hollywood

925 North La Brea Avenue
Los Angeles, CA 90038
(213) 851-0550
Fax (213) 851-6401

Will confirm attendance and degree by phone, fax or mail. Inquiry must include student's name, social security number, years attended. Employers may obtain transcripts upon written request accompanied by a $6.00 fee and a signed release from the student.

A single program two-year institution, with an enrollment of 200. Highest level of offering: four or five year baccalaureate.
ACCREDITATIONS: NATTS

Columbia College

600 South Michigan
Chicago, IL 60605
(312) 663-1600 Ext. 438

Will confirm attendance and degree by phone or mail. Inquiry must include student's name, social security number, years attended. Employers may obtain transcripts upon written request accompanied by a $3.00 fee and a signed release from the student.

A general baccalaureate institution, with an enrollment of 6,500. Highest level of offering: master's.
ACCREDITATIONS: NH

Columbia College

Columbia College Drive
Columbia, SC 29203
(803) 786-3672
Fax (803) 786-3771

Will confirm attendance and degree by phone or mail. Inquiry must include student's name, social security number, years attended. Employers may obtain transcripts upon written request accompanied by a $2.00 fee and a signed release from the student.

A general baccalaureate institution, with an enrollment of 1,186. Highest level of offering: master's.
ACCREDITATIONS: SACS NASM CSWE TED

Columbia College

1001 Rogers
Columbia, MO 65216
(314) 875-8700

Will confirm attendance and degree by phone or mail. Inquiry must include student's name, date of birth, social security number, years attended. Employers may obtain transcripts upon written request accompanied by a $2.00 fee and a signed release from the student.

A general baccalaureate institution, with an enrollment of 2,745. Highest level of offering: four or five year baccalaureate.
ACCREDITATIONS: NH

Columbia Junior College of Business

3810 Main Street
Columbia, SC 29203
(803) 799-9082 Ext. 20

Will confirm attendance and degree by phone or mail. Inquiry must include student's name, social security number, years attended. Employers may obtain transcripts upon written request accompanied by a $2.00 fee and a signed release from the student.

A multiprogram two-year institution, with an enrollment of 475. Highest level of offering: one year but less than four years.
ACCREDITATIONS: JRCB

Columbia State Community College

PO Box 1315
Columbia, TN 38402-1315
(615) 388-0120 Ext. 324

Will confirm attendance and degree by phone or mail. Inquiry must include student's name, social security number. Employers may obtain transcripts upon written request accompanied by a signed release from the student.

A multiprogram two-year institution, with an enrollment of 2,556. Highest level of offering: one year but less than four years.
ACCREDITATIONS: SC NLN/AD AVVMA/CVTTAT MLTAD RAD RSTH

Columbia Theological Seminary

PO Box 520
Decatur, GA 30031
(404) 378-8821 Ext. 21
Fax (404) 377-9696

Will confirm attendance and degree by phone or mail. Inquiry must include student's name, date of birth, social security number, years attended. Employers may obtain transcripts upon written request accompanied by a $2.00 fee and a signed release from the student.

A school of philosophy, religion and theology, with an enrollment of 547. Highest level of offering: doctorate.
ACCREDITATIONS: SC THEOL

Columbia Union College

7600 Flower Avenue
Takoma Park, MD 20912
(301) 891-4118

Will confirm attendance and degree by phone or mail. Inquiry must include student's name, social security number, years attended. Employers may obtain transcripts upon written request accompanied by a $3.00 fee and a signed release from the student.

A general baccalaureate institution, with an enrollment of 886. Highest level of offering: four or five year baccalaureate.
ACCREDITATIONS: M MLTAD MT NASM NLN RSTH

Columbia University Main Division

Philosophy Hall Room 207
Office of Registrar, Transcript Dept.
New York, NY 10027
(212) 854-3056

Will confirm attendance and degree by mail. Inquiry must include student's name, social security number, years attended, degree awarded. Employers may obtain transcripts upon written request accompanied by a $5.00 fee and a signed release from the student.

A doctoral-level institution with a medical school, with an enrollment of 17,017. Highest level of offering: doctorate.

ACCREDITATIONS: NY ANEST ARCH BUS DENT DH ENG JOUR LAW LIB M MED NLN OT PH PTA CSWE MIDWF

Columbia University Teachers College

525 West 120 Street
Attn: Registrar's Office
New York, NY 10027
(212) 678-4065 or 678-4071

Will confirm attendance and degree by phone or mail. Inquiry must include student's name, social security number, years attended. Employers may obtain transcripts upon written request accompanied by a $5.00 fee and a signed release from the student.

A school of education, with an enrollment of 4,064. Highest level of offering: doctorate.

ACCREDITATIONS: M AUD CLPSY COPSY NLN NY SP TED

Columbus College of Art and Design

107 N. Ninth St.
Columbus, OH 43215-1758
(614) 222-3295
Fax (614) 222-4040

Will confirm attendance and degree by mail. Inquiry must include student's name, social security number, years attended. Employers may obtain transcripts upon written request accompanied by a $5.00 fee and a signed release from the student.

A visual and performing arts school, with an enrollment of 1,285. Highest level of offering: four or five year baccalaureate.

ACCREDITATIONS: NH ART

Columbus College

3600 Algonquin Drive
Columbus, GA 31993
(404) 568-2237

Will confirm attendance and degree by phone or mail. Inquiry must include student's name, social security number, years attended. Employers may obtain transcripts upon written request accompanied by a $2.00 fee and a signed release from the student. Attn: Mrs. Morris.

A comprehensive institution with no medical school, with an enrollment of 3,500. Highest level of offering: beyond master's but less than doctorate.

ACCREDITATIONS: SC NLN/AD DH MT NASM RSTH TED

Columbus IVY Tech

4475 Central Avenue
Attention: Records
Columbus, IN 47203
(812) 372-9925 Ext. 30

Will confirm attendance and degree by phone or mail. Inquiry must include student's name, social security number, years attended. Employers may obtain transcripts upon written request from the student.

A multiprogram two-year institution, with an enrollment of 1,840. Highest level of offering: one year but less than four years

ACCREDITATIONS: NCA RSTHT

Columbus State Community College

(Formerly Columbus Technical Institute)
Madison Hall-Records 550
East Spring Street–Box 1609
Columbus, OH 43215
(614) 227-2643
Fax (614) 227-5117

Will confirm attendance and degree by phone or mail. Inquiry must include student's name, social security number, years attended. Employers may obtain transcripts upon written request accompanied by a $1.00 fee and a signed release from the student.

A multiprogram two-year institution, with an enrollment of 15,209. Highest level of offering: one year but less than four years.

ACCREDITATIONS: NCA NLN/AD AVVMA/CVTTAT DT ENGT MLTAD OPTT RSTH RSTHT

Columbus Technical Institute

(See Columbus State Community College)

Combs College of Music

7500 Germantown Avenue
Philadelphia, PA 19119
No listing with directory assistance.

Community College of Allegheny County Allegheny Campus

808 Ridge Avenue
Pittsburgh, PA 15212
(412) 237-2525, Ext. 2700

Will confirm attendance and degree by mail. Inquiry must include student's name, social security number, years attended, release. Employers may obtain transcripts upon written request accompanied by a $1.00 fee and a signed release from the student. Requests should be directed to: Records Office, Byers Hall.

A multiprogram two-year institution, with an enrollment of 7,474. Highest level of offering: one year but less than four years.

ACCREDITATIONS: M NLN/AD APCP MAC MLTAD MRT NMT RSTH RSTHT RTT

Community College of Allegheny County Boyce Campus

595 Beatty Road
Monroeville, PA 15146
(412) 733-4298
Fax (412) 733-4397

Will confirm attendance and degree by phone or mail. Inquiry must include student's name, social security number, years attended. Employers may obtain transcripts upon written request accompanied by a $1.00 fee and a signed release from the student. Requests should be directed to: Students Records.

A multiprogram two-year institution, with an enrollment of 4,736. Highest level of offering: one year but less than four years.

ACCREDITATIONS: M RAD

Community College of Allegheny County North Campus

8701 Perry Highway
Pittsburgh, PA 15237
(412) 369-3700

Will confirm attendance and degree by mail. Inquiry must include student's name, social security number. Employers may obtain transcripts upon written request accompanied by a $1.00 fee and a signed release from the student.

A multiprogram two-year institution, with an enrollment of 3,968. Highest level of offering: one year but less than four years.

ACCREDITATIONS: M

Community College of Allegheny County College Office

800 Allegheny Ave.
Attn: Registrar's Office
Pittsburgh, PA 15233
(412) 237-3185
Fax (412) 237-3195

Will confirm attendance and degree by phone or mail. Inquiry must include student's name, social security number, years attended. Employers may obtain transcripts upon written request accompanied by a $1.00 fee and a signed release from the student.

Community College of Allegheny County South Campus

1750 Clairton Road
West Mifflin, PA 15122
(412) 469-6202

Will confirm attendance and degree by mail. Inquiry must include student's name, social security number. Employers may obtain transcripts upon written request accompanied by a $1.00 fee and a signed release from the student. Requests should be directed to: Student Records.

A multiprogram two-year institution, with an enrollment of 5,300. Highest level of offering: one year but less than four years.

ACCREDITATIONS: M NLN/AD MLTAD

Community College of Aurora

16000 E. Centretech Parkway
Aurora, CO 80011-9036
(303) 360-4761

Will confirm attendance and degree by phone or mail. Inquiry must include student's name, social security number. Employers may obtain transcripts upon written request accompanied by a $2.00 fee and a signed release from the student. Requests should be directed to: Registrar's Office.

A two-year institution newly admitted to NCES, with an enrollment of 4,600. Highest level of offering: one year but less than four years.

ACCREDITATIONS: NH

Community College of Baltimore

2901 Liberty Heights Avenue
Baltimore, MD 21215
(301) 333-5525

Will confirm attendance and degree by phone or mail. Inquiry must include student's name, social security number, years attended. Requests should be directed to: Student Records. Employers may obtain transcripts upon written request accompanied by a $2.00 fee and a signed release from the student.

A multiprogram two-year institution, with an enrollment of 5,297. Highest level of offering: one year but less than four years.

ACCREDITATIONS: M NLN/AD DA DH DT MRT PTAA RSTH

Community College of Beaver County

1 Campus Drive
Monaca, PA 15061
(412) 775-8561 Ext. 106

Will confirm attendance and degree by phone or mail. Inquiry must include student's name, social security number, release. Requests should be directed to: Student Records. Employers may obtain transcripts upon written request accompanied by a $1.00 fee and a signed release from the student.

A multiprogram two-year institution, with an enrollment of 2,579. Highest level of offering: one year but less than four years.

ACCREDITATIONS: M MLTAD

Community College of Denver

1111 West Colfax Avenue–Box 201
Denver, CO 80204
(303) 556-2430
Fax (303) 556-8555

Will confirm attendance and degree by phone or mail. Inquiry must include student's name, social security number, years attended. Employers may obtain transcripts upon written request accompanied by a $1.00 fee and a signed release from the student. Requests should be directed to: Registrar's Office.

A multiprogram two-year institution, with an enrollment of 2,995. Highest level of offering: one year but less than four years.

ACCREDITATIONS: NH NMT RAD RTT SURGT DA

Community College of Philadelphia

1700 Spring Garden Street
Philadelphia, PA 19130
(215) 751-8261

Will confirm attendance and degree by phone or mail. Inquiry must include student's name, social security number. Requests should be directed to: Student Records. Employers may obtain transcripts upon written request accompanied by a $1.00 fee and a signed release from the student.

A multiprogram two-year institution, with an enrollment of 14,965. Highest level of offering: one year but less than four years.

ACCREDITATIONS: M NLN/AD DA DH MAC MLTAD MRT RAD RSTH

Community College of Rhode Island

Attn: Admission & Records
400 East Avenue
Warwick, RI 02886
(401) 825-2125

Will confirm attendance and degree by phone or mail. Inquiry must include student's name, social security number. Employers may obtain transcripts upon written request accompanied by a $2.00 fee and a signed release from the student. Requests should be directed to: Records Office.

A multiprogram two-year institution, with an enrollment of 15,000. Highest level of offering: one year but less than four years.

ACCREDITATIONS: EH NLN/AD DA MLTAD PNUR RAD

Community College of the Finger Lakes

Lincoln Hill
Canandaigua, NY 14424
(716) 394-3500 Ext. 291

Will confirm attendance and degree by phone or mail. Inquiry must include student's name, social security number. Requests should be directed to: Registrar's Office. Employers may obtain transcripts upon written request accompanied by a $2.00 fee and a signed release from the student.

A multiprogram two-year institution, with an enrollment of 2,952. Highest level of offering: two years.

ACCREDITATIONS: M NLN/AD NY

Community College of Vermont

PO Box 120
Waterbury, VT 05676
(802) 241-3535
Fax (802) 241-3526

Will confirm attendance and degree by phone or mail. Inquiry must include student's name, date of birth, social security number, years attended. Employers may obtain transcripts upon written request accompanied by a $5.00 fee and a signed release from the student. Requests should be directed to: Registrar's Office.

A multiprogram two-year institution, with an enrollment of 4,500. Highest level of offering: two years.

ACCREDITATIONS: EH

Community Hospital of Roanoke Valley/College of Health Sciences

PO Box 13186
Roanoke, VA 24031-3186
(703) 985-8481

Will confirm attendance and degree by phone or mail. Inquiry must include student's name, social security number, years attended. Employers may obtain transcripts upon written request accompanied by a $2.00 fee and a signed release from the student.

A two-year education with an enrollment of 351. Highest level of offering: one year but less than four years.

ACCREDITATIONS: DNUR RSTH

Compton Community College

1111 East Artesia Boulevard
Compton, CA 90221-5393
(310) 637-2660 Ext. 2044
Fax (310) 639-8260

Will confirm attendance and degree by phone or mail. Inquiry must include student's name, date of birth, years attended. Employers may obtain transcripts upon written request accompanied by a $2.00 fee and a signed release from the student.

A multiprogram two-year institution, with an enrollment of 5,598. Highest level of offering: one year but less than four years.

ACCREDITATIONS: WJ

Conception Seminary College

Attn: Registrar's Office
Conception, MO 64433
(816) 944-2218

Will confirm attendance and degree by phone or mail. Inquiry must include student's name, years attended. Employers may obtain transcripts upon written request accompanied by a $2.00 fee and a signed release from the student.

A specialized school, with an enrollment of 96. Highest level of offering: four or five year baccalaureate.

ACCREDITATIONS: NH

Concord College

Attn: Registrar's Office
Athens, WV 24712
(304) 384-5237

Will confirm attendance and degree by mail or phone. Inquiry must include student's name, social security number, years attended, release. Employers may obtain transcripts upon written request accompanied by a $3.00 fee and a signed release from the student.

A general baccalaureate institution, with an enrollment of 2,900. Highest level of offering: four or five year baccalaureate.

ACCREDITATIONS: NH CSWE TED

Concordia College–Saint Paul

275 N. Syndicate
Saint Paul, MN 55104
612-641-8498

Will confirm attendance and degree by phone or mail. Inquiry must include student's name, social security number, years attended, release. Employers may obtain transcripts upon written request accompanied by a $2.00 fee and a signed release from the student.

A general baccalaureate institution, with an enrollment of 1,010. Highest level of offering: four or five year baccalaureate.
ACCREDITATIONS: NH TED

Concordia College at Moorhead

Attn: Registrar
Moorhead, MN 56562
(218) 299-3250

Will confirm attendance and degree by phone or mail. Inquiry must include student's name, date of birth, SSN, years attended. Employers may obtain transcripts upon written request accompanied by a $1.00 fee and a signed release from the student.

A general baccalaureate institution, with an enrollment of 2,933. Highest level of offering: four or five year baccalaureate.
ACCREDITATIONS: NH NASM TED CSWE

Concordia University Wisconsin

12800 North Lake Shore Drive
Mequon, WI 53092
(414) 243-5700 Ext. 345
Fax (414) 243-4351

Will confirm attendance and degree by phone or mail. Employers may obtain transcripts upon written request accompanied by a $3.00 fee and a signed release from the student.

A general baccalaureate institution, with an enrollment of 2,074. Highest level of offering: master's.
ACCREDITATIONS: NH NCA

Concordia College

2811 North East Holman
Portland, OR 97211
(503) 280-8510
Fax (503) 280-8518

Will confirm attendance and degree by phone or mail. Inquiry must include student's name, social security number, years attended. Employers may obtain transcripts upon written request accompanied by a $5.00 fee and a signed release from the student.

A general baccalaureate institution, with an enrollment of 889. Highest level of offering: four or five year baccalaureate.
ACCREDITATIONS: NW

Concordia College

1804 Green Street
Selma, AL 36701
(205) 874-5700 Ext. 703

Will confirm attendance and degree by phone or mail. Inquiry must include student's name, social security number. Employers may obtain transcripts upon written request accompanied by a $3.00 fee and a signed release from the student.

A multiprogram two-year institution, with an enrollment of 376. Highest level of offering: one year but less than four years.
ACCREDITATIONS: SC

Concordia College

171 White Plains Road
Bronxville, NY 10708
(914) 337-9300 Ext. 2103

Will confirm attendance and degree by phone or mail. Inquiry must include student's name, date of birth, social security number. Employers may obtain transcripts upon written request accompanied by a $3.00 fee and a signed release from the student.

A general baccalaureate institution, with an enrollment of 526. Highest level of offering: four or five year baccalaureate.
ACCREDITATIONS: M NY CSWE

Concordia College

4090 Geddes Road
Ann Arbor, MI 48105
(313) 995-7300, Ext. 325

Will confirm attendance and degree by phone or mail. Inquiry must include student's name. Employers may obtain transcripts upon written request accompanied by a $2.00 fee and a signed release from the student.

A general baccalaureate institution, with an enrollment of 560. Highest level of offering: four or five year baccalaureate.
ACCREDITATIONS: NH

Concordia College

7400 Augusta
River Forest, IL 60305
(708) 771-8300, Ext. 3163

Will confirm attendance and degree by mail. Inquiry must include student's name, social security number, years attended. Employers may obtain transcripts upon written request accompanied by a signed release from the student.

A school of education, with an enrollment of 1,721. Highest level of offering: beyond master's but less than doctorate.
ACCREDITATIONS: NH TED

Concordia Lutheran College

3400 Interstate 35 North
Austin, TX 78705
(512) 452-7661 Ext. 146 or 292

Will confirm attendance and degree by phone or mail. Inquiry must include student's name, social security number, years attended. Employers may obtain transcripts upon written request accompanied by a $3.00 fee and a signed release from the student.

A multiprogram four-year institution, with an enrollment of 700. Highest level of offering: four or five year baccalaureate.
ACCREDITATIONS: SACS

Concordia Seminary

Attn: Office of Registrar
801 Demun Avenue
Saint Louis, MO 63105
(314) 721-5934 Ext. 206

Will confirm attendance and degree by phone or mail. Inquiry must include student's name, social security number. Employers may obtain transcripts upon written request accompanied by a $3.00 fee and a signed release from the student.

A school of philosophy, religion and theology, with an enrollment of 485. Highest level of offering: doctorate.
ACCREDITATIONS: NH THEOL

Concordia Teachers College

800 N. Columbia Ave.
Seward, NE 68434
(402) 643-3651 Ext. 230
Fax (402) 643-4073

Will confirm attendance and degree by phone or mail. Inquiry must include student's name, social security number, years attended. Employers may obtain transcripts upon written request accompanied by a $5.00 fee and a signed release from the student.

A school of education, with an enrollment of 830. Highest level of offering: master's.
ACCREDITATIONS: NH TED

Concordia Theological Seminary

6600 North Clinton Street
Fort Wayne, IN 46825
(219) 481-2100
Fax (219) 481-2121

Will confirm attendance and degree by phone or mail. Inquiry must include student's name, social security number, years attended. Employers may obtain transcripts upon written request accompanied by a $4.00 fee and a signed release from the student.

A school of philosophy, religion and theology, with an enrollment of 389. Highest level of offering: doctorate.
ACCREDITATIONS: NH THEOL

Condie Junior College

(See Phillips Junior College-Condie Campus)

Connecticut College

270 Mohegan Ave.
New London, CT 06320-4196
(203) 447-7515
Fax (203) 439-2700

Will confirm attendance and degree by phone or mail. Inquiry must include student's name, social security number, years attended. Employers may obtain transcripts upon written request accompanied by a $2.00 fee and a signed release from the student. Requests should be directed to: Registrar's Office.

A general baccalaureate institution, with an enrollment of 1,677. Highest level of offering: master's.
ACCREDITATIONS: EH

Connors State College

Attn: Office of Registrar
Route 1 Box 1000
Warner, OK 74469
(918) 463--2931 Ext. 241

Will confirm attendance and degree by phone or mail. Inquiry must include student's name, social security number, years attended, release. Employers may obtain transcripts upon written request accompanied by a $2.00 fee and a signed release from the student.

A multiprogram two-year institution, with an enrollment of 2,100. Highest level of offering: one year but less than four years.
ACCREDITATIONS: NCA

Consortium of California State University

(See California State University-Statewide Nursing Program)

Contra Costa College

2600 Mission Bell Drive
San Pablo, CA 94806
(510) 235-7800 Ext. 210

Will confirm attendance and degree by phone or mail. Inquiry must include student's name, social security number, years attended. Employers may obtain transcripts upon written request accompanied by a $3.00 fee and a signed release from the student.

A multiprogram two-year institution, with an enrollment of 7,989. Highest level of offering: one year but less than four years.
ACCREDITATIONS: WJ DA

Converse College

580 East Main
Spartanburg, SC 29302-0006
(803) 596-9094

Will confirm attendance and degree by mail. Inquiry must include student's name, social security number, years attended. Employers may obtain transcripts upon written request accompanied by a $5.00 fee and a signed release from the student.

A general baccalaureate institution, with an enrollment of 1,329. Highest level of offering: beyond master's but less than doctorate.
ACCREDITATIONS: SC NASM NASTACT

Conway School of Landscape Design

Delabarre Avenue
Conway, MA 01341
(413) 369-4044

Will confirm attendance and degree by phone or mail. Inquiry must include student's name, years attended. Employers may obtain transcripts upon written request accompanied by a signed release from the student.

A bachelor's or higher institution newly admitted to NCES. Highest level of offering: master's.
ACCREDITATIONS: EH

Cooke County College

1525 West California
Gainesville, TX 76240
(817) 668-7731 Ext. 243

Will confirm attendance and degree by phone or mail. Inquiry must include student's name, date of birth, social security number, years attended. Employers may obtain transcripts upon written request accompanied by a $2.00 fee and a signed release from the student.

A multiprogram two-year institution, with an enrollment of 3,472. Highest level of offering: two years but less than four years.
ACCREDITATIONS: SC NLN/AD

Cooper Institute/Knoxville Business College

720 N. 5th Ave.
Knoxville, TN 37917
(615) 637-3573, Ext. 22

Will confirm attendance and degree by phone or mail. Employers may obtain transcripts upon written request accompanied by a signed release from the student.

A two-year institution newly admitted to NCES, with an enrollment of 410. Highest level of offering: one year but less than four years.
ACCREDITATIONS: JRCB

Cooper Union

Attn: Admissions and Records
41 Cooper Square
New York, NY 10003
(212) 253-4124
Fax (212) 353-4343

Will confirm attendance and degree by phone or mail. Inquiry must include student's name, years attended. Employers may obtain transcripts upon written request accompanied by a $2.00 fee and a signed release from the student.

An engineering school, with an enrollment of 1,085. Highest level of offering: master's in Engineering.
ACCREDITATIONS: M ARCH ART ENG NY

Copiah–Lincoln Junior College

Attn: Admissions Office
PO Box 371
Wesson, MS 39191
(601) 643-8307

Will confirm attendance and degree by phone or mail. Inquiry must include student's name, social security number, years attended. Employers may obtain transcripts upon written request accompanied by a $2.00 fee and a signed release from the student.

A multiprogram two-year institution, with an enrollment of 1,400. Highest level of offering: one year but less than four years.
ACCREDITATIONS: SC MLTAD RAD

Coppin State College

2500 West North Avenue
Attn: Registrar
Baltimore, MD 21216-3698
(410) 383-5550

Will confirm attendance and degree by phone or mail. Inquiry must include student's name, years attended, social security number. Employers may obtain transcripts upon written request accompanied by a signed release from the student.

A general baccalaureate institution, with an enrollment of 2,000. Highest level of offering: master's.
ACCREDITATIONS: M NLN CSWE TED

Corcoran School of Art

500 17th NW
Washington, DC 20006-4899
(202) 628-9484

Will confirm attendance and degree by phone or mail. Inquiry must include student's name, date of birth, social security number. Employers may obtain transcripts upon written request accompanied by a $5.00 fee and a signed release from the student.

A visual and performing arts school, with an enrollment of 1,100. Highest level of offering: four or five year baccalaureate.
ACCREDITATIONS: M ART

Cornell College

600 First Street West
Mount Vernon, IA 52314
(319) 895-4372
Fax (319) 895-4492

Will confirm attendance and degree by phone or mail. Inquiry must include student's name, years attended. Employers may obtain transcripts upon written request accompanied by a $2.00 fee and a signed release from the student. Attn: Registrar.

A general baccalaureate institution, with an enrollment of 1,111. Highest level of offering: four or five year baccalaureate.
ACCREDITATIONS: NH NASM

Cornell University

University Registrar
222 Day Hall
Ithaca, NY 14853
(607) 255-4232
Fax (607) 255-6262

Will confirm attendance and degree by phone or mail. Inquiry must include student's name, date of birth, social security number, years attended. Requests should be directed to: Registrar's Office. Employers may obtain transcripts upon written request accompanied by a $2.00 fee and a signed release from the student.

A doctoral-level institution with no medical school, with an enrollment of 18,243. Highest level of offering: doctorate.
ACCREDITATIONS: M ARCH BUS ENG HSA LAW NY

C

Cornell University Endowed Colleges

222 Day Hall
Ithaca, NY 14853
(607) 255-4232
Fax (607) 255-6262

Will confirm attendance and degree by phone or mail. Inquiry must include student's name, date of birth, social security number, years attended. Employers may obtain transcripts upon written request accompanied by a $2.00 fee and a signed release from the student.

A doctoral-level institution with no medical school, with an enrollment of 18,243. Highest level of offering: doctorate
ACCREDITATIONS: M ARCH BUS ENG HSA LAW NY

Cornell University Graduate School of Medical Sciences

1300 York Avenue Rm. A-139
New York, NY 10021
(212) 746-6565
Fax (212) 746-8906

Will confirm attendance and degree by phone or mail. Inquiry must include student's name, years attended. Requests should be directed to: Registrar's Office Room A-1398. Employers may obtain transcripts upon written request accompanied by a signed release from the student.

A medical school, with an enrollment of 200. Highest level of offering: doctorate.
ACCREDITATIONS: NYSBR

Cornell University Medical College

1300 York Avenue Room C-118
New York, NY 10021
(212) 746-1056

Will confirm attendance and degree by phone or mail. Inquiry must include student's name, years attended. Requests should be directed to: Registrar's Office Room C-118. Employers may obtain transcripts upon written request accompanied by a signed release from the student.

A medical school, with an enrollment of 405. Highest level of offering: doctorate.
ACCREDITATIONS: NYSBR IPSY MED

Cornell University Statutory Colleges

222 Day Hall
Ithaca, NY 14853
(607) 255-4232
Fax (607) 255-6262

Will confirm attendance and degree by phone or mail. Inquiry must include student's name, date of birth, social security number, years attended. Employers may obtain transcripts upon written request accompanied by a $2.00 fee and a signed release from the student.

A doctoral-level institution with a medical school. Highest level of offering: doctorate.
ACCREDITATIONS: M LSAR NY CSWE VET

Corning Community College

Spencer Hill
Corning, NY 14830
(607) 962-9230

Will confirm attendance and degree by phone or mail. Inquiry must include student's name, social security number. Employers may obtain transcripts upon written request accompanied by a $2.00 fee and a signed release from the student.

A multiprogram two-year institution, with an enrollment of 3,136. Highest level of offering: one year but less than four years.
ACCREDITATIONS: M NLN/AD NY

Cornish College of the Arts

710 East Roy
Seattle, WA 98102
(206) 323-1400 Ext. 212

Will confirm attendance and degree by phone or mail. Inquiry must include student's name, date of birth, years attended. Employers may obtain transcripts upon written request accompanied by a $2.00 fee and a signed release from the student.

A visual and performing arts school, with an enrollment of 555. Highest level of offering: four or five year baccalaureate.
ACCREDITATIONS: NW

Corpus Christi State University

6300 Ocean Drive
Corpus Christi, TX 78412
(512) 991-6810 Ext. 632

Will confirm attendance and degree by phone or mail. Inquiry must include student's name, date of birth, social security number, years attended. Employers may obtain transcripts upon written request accompanied by a $2.00 fee and a signed release from the student.

A comprehensive institution with no medical school, with an enrollment of 3,808. Highest level of offering: master's.
ACCREDITATIONS: SC MT NASM NLN

Cosumnes River College

8401 Center Parkway
Sacramento, CA 95823
(916) 688-7410

Will confirm attendance and degree by mail. Inquiry must include student's name, date of birth, social security number, years attended. Employers may obtain transcripts upon written request. No search fee and a signed release from the student.

A multiprogram two-year institution, with an enrollment of 10,000. Highest level of offering: one year but less than four years.
ACCREDITATIONS: WJ AVVMA/CVTTAT MAC

Cottey College

1000 West Austin
Nevada, MO 64772
(417) 667-8181 Ext. 125

Will confirm attendance and degree by phone or mail. Inquiry must include student's name, social security number, years attended. Employers may obtain transcripts upon written request accompanied by a $2.00 fee and a signed release from the student. Requests should be directed to: Registrar's Office.

A multiprogram two-year institution, with an enrollment of 348. Highest level of offering: one year but less than four years.
ACCREDITATIONS: NH NASM

County College of Morris

214 Center Grove Road
Randolph, NJ 07869
(201) 328-5200

Will confirm attendance and degree by phone or mail. Inquiry must include student's name, social security number. Employers may obtain transcripts upon written request accompanied by a $2.00 fee and a signed release from the student.

A multiprogram two-year institution, with an enrollment of 11,000. Highest level of offering: one year but less than four years.
ACCREDITATIONS: M NLN/AD DA MLTAD ENGT

Covenant College

Lookout Mountain, GA 30750
(404) 820-1560 Ext. 133

Will confirm attendance and degree by phone or mail. Inquiry must include student's name, date of birth, social security number. Employers may obtain transcripts upon written request accompanied by a $2.00 fee and a signed release from the student.

A general baccalaureate institution, with an enrollment of 511. Highest level of offering: four or five year baccalaureate.
ACCREDITATIONS: SC

Covenant Theological Seminary

12330 Conway Road
Saint Louis, MO 63141
(314) 434-4044

Will confirm attendance and degree by phone or mail. Inquiry must include student's name, social security number. Employers may obtain transcripts upon written request accompanied by a $3.00 fee and a signed release from the student.

A school of philosophy, religion and theology, with an enrollment of 254. Highest level of offering: doctorate.
ACCREDITATIONS: NH THEOL

Cowley County Community College

125 South Second Street
Arkansas City, KS 67005
(316) 442-0430

Will confirm attendance and degree by mail or phone. Inquiry must include student's name, date of birth, social security number, years attended, release. Employers may obtain transcripts upon written request accompanied by a $2.00 fee and a signed release from the student.

A multiprogram two-year institution, with an enrollment of 1,679. Highest level of offering: one year but less than four years.
ACCREDITATIONS: NH

Crafton Hills College

11711 Sand Canyon Road
Yucaipa, CA 92399
(714) 794-2161, Ext. 350

Will confirm attendance and degree by mail or phone. Inquiry must include student's name, social security number, years attended, date of birth, release. Employers may obtain transcripts upon written request accompanied by a $3.00 fee and a signed release from the student.

A multiprogram two-year institution, with an enrollment of 5,000. Highest level of offering: one year but less than four years.
ACCREDITATIONS: WJ RSTH RSTHT

Cranbrook Academy of Art

500 Lone Pine Road Box 801
Bloomfield Hills, MI 48303-0801
(313) 645-3303

Will confirm attendance and degree by phone or mail. Inquiry must include student's name. Employers may obtain transcripts upon written request accompanied by a $2.00 fee and a signed release from the student. Requests should be directed to: Registrar's Office.

A visual and performing arts school, with an enrollment of 147. Highest level of offering: master's.
ACCREDITATIONS: NH ART

Crandall Junior College

2490 Riverside Drive
Macon, GA 31204
(912) 745-6593

Will confirm attendance and degree by phone or mail. Inquiry must include student's name, social security number, years attended. Employers may obtain transcripts upon written request accompanied by a $2.00 fee and a signed release from the student.

A multiprogram two-year institution, with an enrollment of 547. Highest level of offering: one year but less than four years.
ACCREDITATIONS: JRCB

Craven Community College

PO Box 885
New Bern, NC 28560
(919) 638-4131, Ext. 226
Fax (919) 638-4232

Will confirm attendance and degree by mail. Inquiry must include student's name, social security number. Employers may obtain transcripts upon written request accompanied by a $1.00 fee and a signed release from the student.

A multiprogram two-year institution, with an enrollment of 2,200. Highest level of offering: one year but less than four years.
ACCREDITATIONS: SC

Creighton University

California Street at 24th
Omaha, NE 68178
(402) 280-2701

Will confirm attendance and degree by phone or mail. Inquiry must include student's name, social security number, years attended. Employers may obtain transcripts upon written request by student accompanied by a $2.00 fee.

A comprehensive institution with a medical school, with an enrollment of 5,913. Highest level of offering: doctorate.
ACCREDITATIONS: NH ANEST BUS DENT EMT LAW MED MT NLN PHAR RSTH BUSA TED

Crichton College

(Fomerly Mid-South Bible College)
PO Box 757830
Memphis, TN 38175-7830
(901) 367-9800

Will confirm attendance and degree by phone or mail. Inquiry must include student's name. Employers may obtain transcripts upon written request accompanied by a $2.00 fee and a signed release from the student.

A school of philosophy, religion and theology, with an enrollment of 357. Highest level of offering: four or five year baccalaureate.
ACCREDITATIONS: SC BI

Criswell College

Registrar's Office
4010 Gaston Ave.
Dallas, TX 75246
(214) 821-5433
Fax (214) 818-1310

Will confirm attendance and degree by phone or mail. Inquiry must include student's name. Employers may obtain transcripts upon written request accompanied by a $2.00 fee and a signed release from the student.

A bachelor's or higher institution newly admitted to NCES, with an enrollment of 335. Highest level of offering: master's.
ACCREDITATIONS: SACS

Crosier Seminary

PO Box 400
Onamia, MN 56359
(612) 532-3103, Ext. 232

Will confirm attendance and degree by phone or mail. Inquiry must include student's name, date of birth, social security number, years attended. Employers may obtain transcripts upon written request accompanied by a $3.00 fee and a signed release from the student.

A multiprogram two-year institution, with an enrollment of 26. Highest level of offering: one year but less than four years.
ACCREDITATIONS: NH

Crowder College

601 Laclede Street
Neosho, MO 64850
(417) 451-3223
Fax (417) 451-4280

Will confirm attendance and degree by mail or phone. Inquiry must include student's name, social security number. Employers may obtain transcripts upon written request accompanied by a $1.00 fee and a signed release from the student.

A multiprogram two-year institution, with an enrollment of 1,300. Highest level of offering: one year but less than four years.
ACCREDITATIONS: NH

Crowley's Ridge College

100 College Drive
Paragould, AR 72450
(501) 236-6901

Will confirm attendance and degree by mail. Inquiry must include student's name, social security number, years attended, release. Employers may obtain transcripts upon written request accompanied by a $2.00 fee and a signed release from the student.

A multiprogram two-year institution, with an enrollment of 145. Highest level of offering: one year but less than four years.
ACCREDITATIONS: 3IC

Crown College

(Formerly Saint Paul Bible College)
6425 County Road 30
St. Bonifacius, MN 55375-9001

Will confirm attendance and degree by mail. Inquiry must include student's name, social security number, years attended, release. Employers may obtain transcripts upon written request accompanied by a $2.00 fee and a signed release from the student.

A multiprogram two-year institution, with an enrollment of 145. Highest level of offering: one year but less than four years.
ACCREDITATIONS: 3IC

Cuesta College

PO Box 8106
San Luis Obispo, CA 93403-8106
(805) 546-3139
Fax (805) 546-3904

Will confirm attendance and degree by mail. Inquiry must include student's name, maiden name (if any), date of birth, social security number, years attended, release. Employers may obtain transcripts upon written request accompanied by a $2.00 fee and a signed release from the student. Requests should be directed to: Registrar's Office.

A multiprogram two-year institution, with an enrollment of 5,440. Highest level of offering: one year but less than four years.
ACCREDITATIONS: WJ

Culinary Institute of America

PO Box 53 North Road
Hyde Park, NY 12538
(914) 452-9600 Ext. 1267

Will confirm attendance and degree by phone or mail. Inquiry must include student's name, date of birth, years attended. Employers may obtain transcripts upon written request accompanied by a $2.00 fee and a signed release from the student.

A single program two-year institution, with an enrollment of 1,841. Highest level of offering: one year but less than four years.
ACCREDITATIONS: NY NATTS

Culver–Stockton College

Canton, MO 63435
(314) 288-5221 Ext. 330

Will confirm attendance and degree by phone or mail. Inquiry must include student's name, social security number, years attended. Employers may obtain transcripts upon written request accompanied by a $2.00 fee and a signed release from the student.

A general baccalaureate institution, with an enrollment of 999. Highest level of offering: four or five year baccalaureate.
ACCREDITATIONS: NH

Cumberland College of Tennessee

S. Greenwood St.
Lebanon, TN 37087
(615) 444-2562 Ext. 25

Will confirm attendance and degree by phone or mail. Inquiry must include student's name, social security number, years attended. Employers may obtain transcripts upon written request accompanied by a $3.00 fee and a signed release from the student.

A multiprogram two-year institution, with an enrollment of 726. Highest level of offering: four or five year baccalaureate.
ACCREDITATIONS: SC

Cumberland College

Registrar's Office
Williamsburg, KY 40769
(606) 549-2200 Ext. 3
Fax (606) 549-2200 Ext. 4490

Will confirm attendance and degree by phone or mail. Inquiry must include student's name, date of birth, social security number. Employers may obtain transcripts upon written request accompanied by a $2.00 fee and a signed release from the student.

A general baccalaureate institution, with an enrollment of 2,106. Highest level of offering: master's.
ACCREDITATIONS: SC NASM

Cumberland County College

PO Box 517
Vineland, NJ 08360
(609) 691-8600 Ext. 220

Will confirm attendance and degree by phone or mail. Inquiry must include student's name, social security number, years attended. Employers may obtain transcripts upon written request accompanied by a signed release from the student.

A multiprogram two-year institution, with an enrollment of 2,700. Highest level of offering: one year but less than four years.
ACCREDITATIONS: M NLN/AD

Cumberland University

South Greenwood St.
Lebanon, TN 37087
(615) 444-2562 Ext. 25
Fax (615) 444-2569

Will confirm attendance and degree by phone or mail. Inquiry must include student's name, social security number, years attended. Employers may obtain transcripts upon written request accompanied by a $3.00 fee and a signed release from the student.

A multiprogram two-year institution, with an enrollment of 565. Highest level of offering: four or five year baccalaureate.
ACCREDITATIONS: SACS

Curry College

Attn: Registrar
Milton, MA 02186
(617) 333-0500 Ext. 2255
Fax (617) 333-6860

Will confirm attendance and degree by phone or mail. Inquiry must include student's name, years attended. Employers may obtain transcripts upon written request accompanied by a $2.00 fee and a signed release from the student.

A general baccalaureate institution, with an enrollment of 1,244. Highest level of offering: master's.
ACCREDITATIONS: EH NLN

Curtis Institute of Music

1726 Locust Street
Philadelphia, PA 19103
(215) 893-5257
Fax (215) 893-9065

Will confirm attendance and degree by phone or mail. Inquiry must include student's name, years attended. Employers may obtain transcripts upon written request accompanied by a signed release from the student.

A visual and performing arts school, with an enrollment of 166. Highest level of offering: master's.
ACCREDITATIONS: NASM

Cuyahoga Community College District

2900 Community College Avenue
Cleveland, OH 44115
(216) 987-4200

Will confirm attendance and degree by phone or mail. Inquiry must include student's name, social security number, date of birth, release. Employers may obtain transcripts upon written request accompanied by a $1.00 fee and a signed release from the student.

A multiprogram two-year institution, with an enrollment of 20,662. Highest level of offering: one year but less than four years.
ACCREDITATIONS: NH NLN/AD APCP DH MAC MLTAD MRT PTAA RAD RSTH RSTHT SURGA

Cuyamaca College

2950 Jamacha Road
El Cajon, CA 92019-4304
(619) 670-1980, Ext. 276

Will confirm attendance and degree by mail. Inquiry must include student's name, social security number, release. Employers may obtain transcripts upon written request accompanied by a $2.00 fee and a signed release from the student.

A multiprogram two-year institution, with an enrollment of 5,000. Highest level of offering: one year but less than four years.
ACCREDITATIONS: WJ

Cypress College

9200 Valley View Street
Cypress, CA 90630
(714) 826-2220 Ext. 347

Will confirm attendance and degree by phone or mail. Inquiry must include student's name, date of birth. Requests should be directed to: Record & Admissions Office. Employers may obtain transcripts upon written request accompanied by a $2.00 fee and a signed release from the student.

A multiprogram two-year institution, with an enrollment of 20,000. Highest level of offering: one year but less than four years.
ACCREDITATIONS: WJ DA DH FUSER MAC MRT RAD

D

D-Q University

PO Box 409
Davifs, CA 95617
(916) 758-0470

Will confirm attendance and degree by mail. Inquiry must include student's name and social security number. Employers may obtain transcripts upon written request accompanied by a $3.00 fee and a signed release from the student.

A multiprogram two-year institution, with an enrollment of 206. Highest level of offering: four or five year baccalaureate.
ACCREDITATIONS: WJ

D'youville College

320 Porter Avenue
Buffalo, NY 14201
(716) 881-7626

Will confirm attendance and degree by phone or mail. Inquiry must include student's name, social security number, years attended. Employers may obtain transcripts upon written request by student accompanied by a $5.00 fee.

A health institution, with an enrollment of 1,286. Highest level of offering: master's.
ACCREDITATIONS: M NUR NY

Dabney S. Lancaster Community College

Attn: Registrar
PO Box 1000
Clifton Forge, VA 24422-1000
(703) 862-4246 Ext 242

Will confirm attendance and degree by phone or mail. Inquiry must include student's name and social security number. Employers may obtain transcripts upon written request by student.

A multiprogram two-year institution, with an enrollment of 1,213. Highest level of offering: one year but less than four years.
ACCREDITATIONS: SC

Daemen College

4380 Main Street
Amherst, NY 14226
(716) 839-8214

Will confirm attendance by phone or mail. Will confirm degree by mail. Inquiry must include student's name and social security number. Employers may obtain transcripts upon written request by student accompanied by a $3.00 fee.

A general baccalaureate institution, with an enrollment of 1,603. Highest level of offering: four year baccalaureate.
ACCREDITATIONS: M MRA MT NUR NY PTA SW

Dakota County Technical College

1300 East 145th Street
Rosemount, MN 55068
(612) 423-2281 Ext. 301
Fax (612) 423-7028

Will confirm attendance and degree by phone, fax or mail. Inquiry must include student's name, date of birth, years attended, major field of study. Requests should be directed to: Student Services. Employers may obtain transcripts upon written request accompanied by a signed release from the student.

A two-year institution newly admitted to NCES, with an enrollment of 2000+. Highest level of offering: two year or less .
ACCREDITATIONS: NCA

Dakota State University

Madison, SD 57042
(605) 256-5139
Fax (605) 256-5316

Will confirm attendance and degree by mail, phone or fax. Inquiry must include student's name, date of birth, social security number, years attended. Requests should be directed to: Records. Employers may obtain transcripts upon written request accompanied by a $2.00 fee and a signed release from the student.

A general baccalaureate institution, with an enrollment of 1465. Highest level of offering: four or five year baccalaureate.
ACCREDITATIONS: NH MRA MRT RSTH RSTHT TED

Dakota Wesleyan University

1200 West University Avenue
Mitchell, SD 57301
(605) 995-2642
Fax (605) 995-2699

Will confirm attendance and degree by phone or mail. Inquiry must include student's name, social security number, years attended. Employers may obtain transcripts upon written request accompanied by a signed release from the student.

A general baccalaureate institution, with an enrollment of 720. Highest level of offering: four or five year baccalaureate, masters.
ACCREDITATIONS: NCA ADNUR SW

Dallas Baptist University

7777 West Kiest Boulevard
Dallas, TX 75211
(214) 333-5334
Fax (214) 333-5115

Will confirm attendance and degree by phone or mail. Inquiry must include student's name and social security number. Employers may obtain transcripts upon written request accompanied by a signed release from the student. Attn: Registrar's Office.

A general baccalaureate institution, with a Fall, 1991, enrollment of 2,635. Highest level of offering: master's.
ACCREDITATIONS: SACS

Dallas Bible College

c/o Criswell College
4010 Gaston Ave.
Dallas, TX 75246
(214) 821-5433
Fax (214) 818-1310

Records for this school are being handled by Criswell College. Will confirm attendance and degree by phone, fax or mail. Inquiry must include student's name. Employers may obtain transcripts upon written request accompanied by a $5.00 fee and a signed release from the student.

Dallas Christian College

2700 Christian Parkway
Dallas, TX 75234
(214) 241-3371 Ext. 113

Will confirm attendance and degree by phone or mail. Inquiry must include student's name and social security number. Employers may obtain transcripts upon written request accompanied by a signed release from the student.

A school of philosophy, religion and theology, with an enrollment of 132. Highest level of offering: four or five year baccalaureate.
ACCREDITATIONS: BI

Dallas County Community–Brook Haven College

(See Brook Haven College)

Dallas County Community College District-All Institutions

701 Elm and Lamar
Dallas, TX 75202
214-746-2311

Will confirm attendance and degree by phone or mail. Inquiry must include student's name and social security number. Employers may obtain transcripts upon written request accompanied by a $1.00 fee and a signed release from the student.

Dallas County Community–Cedar Valley College

3030 North Dallas Avenue
Lancaster, TX 75134
(214) 372-8201

Will confirm attendance and degree by phone or mail. Inquiry must include student's name, social security number, years attended. Employers may obtain transcripts upon written request accompanied by a signed release from the student.

Dallas County Community–East Field College

3737 Motley
Mesquite, TX 75150
(214) 324-7100

Will confirm attendance and degree by mail. Inquiry must include student's name and social security number, and release. Employers may obtain transcripts upon written request accompanied by a signed release from the student. Requests should be directed to: Admissions Office.

Dallas County Community–El Centro College

Main Street & Lamar
Dallas, TX 75202
(214) 746-2311
Fax (214) 746-2011

Will confirm attendance and degree by mail, phone or fax. Inquiry must include student's name and social security number. Employers may obtain transcripts upon written request accompanied by a $1.00 fee and a signed release from the student.

Dallas County Community–Mt. View College

4849 West Illinois
Dallas, TX 75211
(214) 333-8600
Fax (214) 333-8570

Will confirm attendance and degree by mail. Requests and release should be directed to: Admissions Office. Employers may obtain transcripts upon written request accompanied by a signed release from the student.

Dallas County Community–North Lake College

5001 North MacAurthur Boulevard
Irving, TX 75038
(214) 659-5220

Will confirm attendance and degree by mail. Inquiry must include student's name, social security number, years attended. Employers may obtain transcripts upon written request accompanied by a signed release from the student.

Dallas County Community–Richland College

12800 Abarms Road
Dallas, TX 75243-2199
(214) 238-6100

Will confirm attendance and degree by mail. Requests should be directed to: Admissions Office. Inquiry must include student's name, social security number, release. Employers may obtain transcript upon written request by student.

Dallas Theological Seminary

3909 Swiss Avenue
Dallas, TX 75204
(214) 841-3608
FAX (214) 841-3664

Will confirm attendance and degree by phone or mail. Inquiry must include student's name and years attended. Employers may obtain transcripts upon written request accompanied by a signed release from the student.

A school of philosophy, religion and theology, with an enrollment of 1,300. Highest level of offering: doctorate.
ACCREDITATIONS: SC

Dalton Junior College

213 North College Drive
Dalton, GA 30720
(404) 272-4436
Fax 9404) 272-4588

Will confirm attendance and degree by phone, fax or mail. Inquiry must include student's name and social security number. Employers may obtain transcripts upon written request accompanied by a signed release from the student and a $1.00 fee.

A multiprogram two-year institution, with an enrollment of 2,621 Highest level of offering: one year but less than four years.
ACCREDITATIONS: SC ADNUR MLTAD

Dana College

2848 College Drive
Attn: Registrar
Blair, NE 68008
(402) 426-7208
Fax (402) 426-7386

Will confirm attendance and degree by phone or mail. Inquiry must include student's name, social security number, years attended. Employers may obtain transcripts upon written request accompanied by a $3.00 fee and a signed release from the student.

A general baccalaureate institution, with an enrollment of 461. Highest level of offering: four or five year baccalaureate.
ACCREDITATIONS: NH TED

Daniel Webster College

20 University Drive
Nashua, NH 03063
(603) 883-3556 Ext. 230

Will confirm attendance and degree by phone or mail. Inquiry must include student's name and social security number. Employers may obtain transcripts upon written request accompanied by a $2.00 fee and a signed release from the student.

A business school, with an enrollment of 1,000. Highest level of offering: four or five year baccalaureate.
ACCREDITATIONS: EH

Danville Area Community College

2000 East Main Street
Danville, IL 61832
(217) 443-8803

Will confirm attendance and degree by phone or mail. Inquiry must include student's name, social security number, major field of study, years attended. Employers may obtain transcripts upon written request accompanied by a signed release from the student.

A multiprogram two-year institution, with an enrollment of 3,072. Highest level of offering: one year but less than four years.
ACCREDITATIONS: NH

Danville Community College

1008 South Main Street
Danville, VA 24541
(804) 797-3553

Will confirm attendance and degree by phone or mail. Inquiry must include student's name, social security number, years attended. Employers may obtain transcripts upon written request and a signed release from the student.

A multiprogram two-year institution, with an enrollment of 3,443. Highest level of offering: one year but less than four years.
ACCREDITATIONS: SC

Darkei No'am Rabbinical College

1535 49th Street
Brooklyn, NY 11219
(718) 377-3767

Will confirm attendance and degree by phone or mail. Inquiry must include student's name and social security number. Employers may obtain transcripts upon written request accompanied by a $2.00 fee and a signed release from the student.

A bachelor's or higher institution newly admitted to NCES, with an enrollment of 55. Highest level of offering: four or five year baccalaureate.
ACCREDITATIONS: RABN

Dartmouth College

4 McMutt Hall
Hanover, NH 03755
(603) 646-2246

Will confirm attendance and degree by phone or mail. Inquiry must include student's name, social security number, years attended. A $1.00 fee is charged for written confirmation. Requests should be directed to: Registrar's Office. Employers may obtain transcripts upon written request accompanied by a $2.00 fee and a signed release from the student.

A doctoral-level institution with a medical school, with an enrollment of 4,908. Highest level of offering: doctorate.
ACCREDITATIONS: EH BUS ENG IPSY MED THEA

Darton College

(Formerly Albany Junior College)
2400 Gillionville Road
Albany, GA 31707
(912) 888-8742

Will confirm attendance and degree by phone or mail. Inquiry must include student's name, date of birth, social security number. Employers may obtain transcripts upon written request accompanied by a $1.00 fee and a signed release from the student.

A multiprogram two-year institution, with an enrollment of 1,770. Highest level of offering: one year but less than four years.
ACCREDITATIONS: SC ADNUR DH MLTAD

Davenport College

415 East Fulton
Grand Rapids, MI 49503
(616) 451-3734
Fax (616) 732-1142

Will confirm attendance and degree by phone, fax or mail. Inquiry must include student's name, date of birth, social security number, years attended. Only students may obtain transcripts.

A multiprogram two-year institution, with an enrollment of 4,219. Highest level of offering: four or five year baccalaureate.
ACCREDITATIONS: NH JRCB MAAB MAC

David Lipscomb University

Nashville, TN 37204-3951
(615) 269-1788
Fax (615) 269-1808

Will confirm attendance and degree by phone, fax or mail. Inquiry must include student's name and social security number. Employers may obtain transcripts upon written request accompanied by a signed release from the student.

A general baccalaureate institution, with an enrollment of 2,518. Highest level of offering: master's.
ACCREDITATIONS: SC TED

Davidson College

Attn: Registrar
Davidson, NC 28036
(704) 892-2000 Ext. 227

Will confirm attendance and degree by phone or mail. Inquiry must include student's name and years attended. Employers may obtain transcripts upon written request accompanied by a $1.00 fee and a signed release from the student.

A general baccalaureate institution, with an enrollment of 1,373. Highest level of offering: four or five year baccalaureate.
ACCREDITATIONS: SC

Davidson County Community College

Attn: Records Office
PO Box 1287
Lexington, NC 27293
(704) 249-8186 Ext. 234

Will confirm attendance and degree by phone or mail. Inquiry must include student's name, date of birth, social security number, years attended. Employers may obtain transcripts upon written request accompanied by a $1.00 fee and a signed release from the student.

A multiprogram two-year institution, with an enrollment of 2,169. Highest level of offering: one year but less than four years.
ACCREDITATIONS: SC

Davis and Elkins College

Attn: Office of Registrar
100 Sycamore Street
Elkins, WV 26241
(304) 636-1900 Ext. 223
Fax (304) 636-8624

Will confirm attendance and degree by mail. Inquiry must include student's name, social security number, years attended, release. Employers may obtain transcripts upon written request accompanied by a $3.00 fee and a signed release from the student.

A general baccalaureate institution, with an enrollment of 860. Highest level of offering: four or five year baccalaureate.
ACCREDITATIONS: NH

Davis Junior College

4747 Monroe Street
Toledo, OH 43623
(419) 473-2700

Will confirm attendance and degree by phone or mail. Inquiry must include student's name and years attended. Employers may obtain transcripts upon written request accompanied by a $2.00 fee and a signed release from the student.

A multiprogram two-year institution, with an enrollment of 450. Highest level of offering: one year but less than four years.
ACCREDITATIONS: JRCB

Dawson Community College

Box 421
Glendive, MT 59330
(406) 365-3396
Fax (406) 365-8132

Will confirm attendance and degree by phone or mail. Inquiry must include student's name and social security number. Employers may obtain transcripts upon written request accompanied by a signed release from the student.

A multiprogram two-year institution, with an enrollment of 753. Highest level of offering: one year but less than four years.
ACCREDITATIONS: NW

Daytona Beach Community College

PO Box 2811
1200 Volusia Avenue
Daytona Beach, FL 32120
(904) 255-8131

Will confirm attendance and degree by mail. Inquiry must include student's name and social security number. Employers may obtain transcripts upon written request accompanied by a $2.00 fee and a signed release from the student.

A multiprogram two-year institution, with an enrollment of 11,718. Highest level of offering: one year but less than four years.
ACCREDITATIONS: SC ADNUR DA MRT RSTH RSTHT SURGT

De Anza College

21250 Stevens Creek Boulevard
Cupertino, CA 95014
(408) 996-4419
Fax (408) 864-8329

Will confirm attendance and degree by mail or fax. Fax inquiries will be responded by mail. Inquiry must include student's name, social security number, written release. Requests should be directed to: Admissions & Records Office. Employers may obtain transcripts upon written request accompanied by a signed release from the student.

A multiprogram two-year institution, with an enrollment of 26,256. Highest level of offering: one year but less than four years.
ACCREDITATIONS: WJ MAC PTAA

De Lourdes College

c/o Holy Family College
Grant & Frankford Avenues
Philadelphia, PA 19114
(215) 637-7700 637-7700 Ext. 210
Fax (215) 632-8067

Records for this school are being handled by Holy Family College. Will confirm attendance and degree by phone or mail. Inquiry must include student's name, social security number. Employers may obtain transcripts upon written request accompanied by a $2.00 fee and a signed release from the student.

De Paul University

243 South Wabash
Chicago, IL 60604
(312) 362-8610

Will confirm attendance and degree by phone or mail. Inquiry must include student's name, social security number, years attended. Employers may obtain transcripts upon written request accompanied by a $3.00 fee and a signed release from the student.

A comprehensive institution with no medical school, with an enrollment of 16,414 Highest level of offering: doctorate.
ACCREDITATIONS: NH BUS CLPSY LAW MUS NUR RAD TED BUSA

De Pauw University

Attn: Office of Registrar
Greencastle, IN 46135
(317) 658-4000
Fax (317) 658-4177

Will confirm attendance and degree by phone, fax or mail. Inquiry must include student's name, date of birth, social security number, years attended. Employers may obtain transcripts upon written request accompanied by a $2.00 fee and a signed release from the student.

A comprehensive institution with no medical school, with an enrollment of 2,220. Highest level of offering: four or five year baccalaureate.

ACCREDITATIONS: NCA MUS NUR TED

De Sales School of Theology

721 Lawrence Street North East
Washington, DC 20017
(202) 269-9412

Will confirm attendance and degree by phone or mail. Inquiry must include student's name and social security number. Employers may obtain transcripts upon written request accompanied by a $3.00 fee and a signed release from the student.

A school of philosophy, religion and theology, with an enrollment of 54. Highest level of offering: master's.

ACCREDITATIONS: M THEOL

Dean Institute of Technology

1501 West Liberty Avenue
Pittsburgh, PA 15226
(412) 531-4433

Will confirm attendance and degree by phone or mail. Inquiry must include student's name. Employers may obtain transcripts upon written request accompanied by a signed release from the student.

A single program two-year institution, with an enrollment of 202-9803. Highest level of offering: one year but less than four years.

ACCREDITATIONS: NATTS

Dean Junior College

99 Main Street
Franklin, MA 02038
(508) 528-9100 Ext. 235
Fax (508) 528-7846

Will confirm attendance and degree by phone, fax or mail. Inquiry must include student's name, social security number, years attended. Employers may obtain transcripts upon written request accompanied by a $2.00 fee and a signed release from the student.

A multiprogram two-year institution, with an enrollment of 2,550. Highest level of offering: one year but less than four years.

ACCREDITATIONS: EH

Deep Springs College

Deep Springs, California via Dyer,
NV 89010-9803
(619) 872-2000

Will confirm attendance and degree by phone or mail. Inquiry must include student's name and years attended. Employers may obtain transcripts upon written request accompanied by a signed release from the student.

A multiprogram two-year institution, with an enrollment of 24. Highest level of offering: one year but less than four years.

ACCREDITATIONS: WJ

Defense Intelligence College

Washington, DC 20340-5485
(202) 373-4545

Will confirm attendance and degree by mail. Inquiry must include student's name, social security number, years attended, release. Employers may obtain transcripts upon written request accompanied by a signed release from the student.

A bachelor's or higher institution newly admitted to NCES, with an enrollment of 618. Highest level of offering: master's.

ACCREDITATIONS: M

DeKalb Community College

District Admission & Records
555 N. Indian Creek Drive
Clarkston, GA 30021
(404) 299-4564
Fax (404) 299-4574

Will confirm attendance and degree by mail phone or fax. Inquiry must include student's name, release and social security number. Requests should be directed to: Admissions Office. Employers may obtain transcripts upon written request accompanied by a signed release from the student.

A multiprogram two-year institution, with an enrollment of 14,877. Highest level of offering: one year but less than four years.

ACCREDITATIONS: SC ADNUR DH MLTAD SURGT

Del Mar College

101 Baldwin Street
Corpus Christi, TX 78404-3897
(512) 886-1200

Will confirm attendance and degree by phone or mail. Inquiry must include student's name, social security number, years attended. Employers may obtain transcripts upon written request accompanied by a $2.00 fee and a signed release from the student.

A multiprogram two-year institution, with an enrollment of 9,639. Highest level of offering: one year but less than four years.

ACCREDITATIONS: SC ADNUR DA DH ENGT MLTAD MUS RAD RSTH RSTHT SURGT

Delaware County Community College

Media, PA 19063
(215) 359-5335

Will confirm attendance and degree by phone or mail. Inquiry must include student's name and social security number. Employers may obtain transcripts upon written request accompanied by a $1.00 fee and a signed release from the student.

A multiprogram two-year institution, with an enrollment of 10,000. Highest level of offering: one year but less than four years.

ACCREDITATIONS: M ADNUR RSTH

Delaware State College

1200 North Dupont Highway
Dover, DE 19901
(302) 739-4915

Will confirm attendance and degree by phone or mail. Inquiry must include student's name, social security number, years attended, release. Requests should be directed to: Records Department. Employers may obtain transcripts upon written request accompanied by a $2.00 fee and a signed release from the student.

A general baccalaureate institution, with an enrollment of 2,209. Highest level of offering: master's.

ACCREDITATIONS: M SW

Delaware Technical and Community College Southern Campus

Box 610
Georgetown, DE 19947
(302) 856-5400

Will confirm attendance and degree by phone or mail. Inquiry must include student's name, social security number, release. Employers may obtain transcripts upon written request by student accompanied by a $1.00 fee.

A multiprogram two-year institution, with an enrollment of 1,808. Highest level of offering: one year but less than four years.

ACCREDITATIONS: M MLTAD

Delaware Technical and Community College Terry Campus

1832 North Dupont Highway
Dover, DE 19901
(302) 736-5412
Fax (302) 739-5451

Will confirm attendance and degree by phone or mail. Inquiry must include student's name and social security number. Employers may obtain transcripts upon written request accompanied by a $1.00 fee and a signed release from the student.

A multiprogram two-year institution, with an enrollment of 1,400. Highest level of offering: one year but less than four years.

ACCREDITATIONS: M RSTH

Delaware Technical Community College–Wilmington Campus

333 Shipley Street
Wilmington, DE 19801
(302) 571-5317

Will confirm attendance and degree by phone or mail. Inquiry must include student's name and social security number. Employers may obtain transcripts upon written request accompanied by a $1.00 fee and a signed release from the student.

Delaware Technical Community College Stanton

400 Stanton–Christiana Road
Newark, DE 19702
(302) 454-3900

Will confirm attendance and degree by mail or phone. Inquiry must include student's name and social security number. Employers may obtain transcripts upon written request accompanied by a $1.00 fee and a signed release from the student.

A multiprogram two-year institution, with an enrollment of 4,025. Highest level of offering: Associate in Applied Science Degree.
ACCREDITATIONS: MSA/CHE

Delaware Valley College of Science and Agriculture

Doylestown, PA 18901
700 E. Butler Ave.
(215) 345-1500 Ext. 2378

Will confirm attendance and degree by phone or mail. Inquiry must include student's name and years attended. Employers may obtain transcripts upon written request accompanied by a signed release from the student.

A general baccalaureate institution, with an enrollment of 1,534. Highest level of offering: four or five year baccalaureate.
ACCREDITATIONS: M

Delgado Community College

615 City Park Avenue
New Orleans, LA 70119
(504) 483-4153

Will confirm attendance and degree by phone or mail. Inquiry must include student's name, social security number, years attended. Employers may obtain transcripts upon written request and a signed release from the student.

A multiprogram two-year institution, with an enrollment of 9,600. Highest level of offering: one year but less than four years.
ACCREDITATIONS: SC RAD RSTH RSTHT FUSER

Delta College

Registrar's Office
University Center, MI 48710
(517) 686-9305

Will confirm attendance and degree by phone or mail. Inquiry must include student's name, date of birth, social security number, years attended. Employers may obtain transcripts upon written request accompanied by a $2.00 fee and a signed release from the student.

A multiprogram two-year institution, with an enrollment of 12,664. Highest level of offering: one year but less than four years.
ACCREDITATIONS: NH ADNUR DA DH ENGT PTAA RAD RSTH RSTHT

Delta State University

Registrar's Office
109 Kethley
Cleveland, MS 38733
(601) 846-4040

Will confirm attendance and degree by phone or mail. Inquiry must include student's name, years attended and social security number. Employers may obtain transcripts upon written request accompanied by a $2.00 fee and a signed release from the student.

A comprehensive institution with no medical school, with an enrollment of 3,475. Highest level of offering: doctorate.
ACCREDITATIONS: SC MUS NUR SW TED

Denison University

PO Box B
Granville, OH 43023
(614) 587-6296

Will confirm attendance and degree by phone or mail. Inquiry must include student's name, date of birth, social security number, years attended. Employers may obtain transcripts upon written request accompanied by a $2.00 fee and a signed release from the student.

A general baccalaureate institution, with an enrollment of 2,121. Highest level of offering: four or five year baccalaureate.
ACCREDITATIONS: NH MUS

Denmark Technical College

PO Box 327
Denmark, SC 29042
(803) 793-3301 Ext. 206 or 208
Fax (803) 793-5942

Will confirm attendance and degree by mail or fax. Inquiry must include student's name and social security number. Employers may obtain transcripts upon written request accompanied by a $2.00 fee and a signed release from the student.

A multiprogram two-year institution, with an enrollment of 657. Highest level of offering: one year but less than four years.
ACCREDITATIONS: SC

Denver Conservative Baptist Seminary

PO Box 10000
Denver, CO 80210
(303) 761-2482 Ext. 221
Fax (303) 761-8060

Will confirm attendance and degree by phone or mail. Inquiry must include student's name and years attended. Employers may obtain transcripts upon written request accompanied by a $2.00 fee and a signed release from the student.

A school of philosophy, religion and theology, with an enrollment of 544. Highest level of offering: doctorate.
ACCREDITATIONS: NCA ATS

Denver Technical College

925 S. Niagara St.
Registrar's Office
Denver, CO 80224
(303) 329-3000 Ext. 50
Fax (303) 321-3412

Will confirm attendance and degree by phone, fax or mail. Inquiry must include student's name, social security number, years attended. Employers may obtain transcripts upon written request accompanied by a $2.00 fee and a signed release from the student.

A two-year institution newly admitted to NCES, with an enrollment of 700. Highest level of offering: one year to four years.
ACCREDITATIONS: NATTS

Derech Ayson Rabbinical Seminary

802 Hicksville Road
Far Rockaway, NY 11691
(718) 327-7600

Will confirm attendance and degree by mail. Inquiry must include student's name, social security number, years attended, release. Employers may obtain transcripts upon written request accompanied by a signed release from the student.

A bachelor's or higher institution newly admitted to NCES, with an enrollment of 130. Highest level of offering: four or five year baccalaureate.
ACCREDITATIONS: 3IC

Des Moines Area Community College

2006 South Ankeny Boulevard
Ankeny, IA 50021
(515) 964-6224
Fax (515) 964-6655

Will confirm attendance and degree by phone, fax or mail. Inquiry must include student's name and social security number. Employers may obtain transcripts upon written request accompanied by a $1.00 fee and a signed release from the student.

A multiprogram two-year institution, with an enrollment of 10,000. Highest level of offering: one year but less than four years.
ACCREDITATIONS: NH DA DH MAC MLTAD PNUR RSTH

Detroit College of Business

4801 Oakman Boulevard
Dearborn, MI 48126
(313) 581-4400
Fax (313) 581-6822

Will confirm attendance and degree by phone, fax or mail. Inquiry must include student's name, date of birth, social security, years attended. Employers may obtain transcripts upon written request accompanied by a $2.00 fee and a signed release from the student.

A business school, with an enrollment of 4,787. Highest level of offering: four or five year baccalaureate.

ACCREDITATIONS: NH

Detroit College of Law

130 East Elizabeth Street
Detroit, MI 48201
(313) 965-0150 Ext. 62 or 63

Will confirm attendance and degree by phone or mail. Inquiry must include student's name, date of birth, years attended. Employers may obtain transcripts upon written request accompanied by a $3.00 fee and a signed release from the student.

A law school, with an enrollment of 809. Highest level of offering: first professional degree.

ACCREDITATIONS: LAW

Devry Institute of Technology

2000 South Finley Road
Lombard, IL 60148
(708) 953-1300 Ext. 356

Will confirm attendance and degree by phone or mail. Inquiry must include student's name, social security number, release. Employers may obtain transcripts upon written request accompanied by a $2.00 fee and a signed release from the student.

An associate and bachelor's institution, with an enrollment of 2,600.

ACCREDITATIONS: NCA ABET

Devry Institute of Technology

250 North Arcadia Avenue
Decatur, GA 30030
(404) 292-7900 Ext. 491

Will confirm attendance and degree by phone or mail. Inquiry must include student's name and social security number. Employers may obtain transcripts upon written request accompanied by a $2.00 fee and a signed release from the student.

An engineering school, with an enrollment of 3,100. Highest level of offering: four or five year baccalaureate.

ACCREDITATIONS: NCA ENGT

Devry Institute of Technology

11224 Holmes Road, Rm. 214
Kansas City, MO 64131
(816) 941-0430 Ext. 460

Will confirm attendance and degree by phone or mail. Inquiry must include student's name, social security number, years attended. Employers may obtain transcripts upon written request by student accompanied by a $2.00 fee.

An engineering school, with an enrollment of 2,081. Highest level of offering: four or five year baccalaureate.

ACCREDITATIONS: NCA ABET

Devry Institute of Technology

1350 Alum Creek Drive
Columbus, OH 43209
(614) 253-7291
Fax (614) 252-4108

Will confirm attendance and degree by phone, fax or mail. Inquiry must include student's name and social security number. Employers may obtain transcripts upon written request accompanied by a $2.00 fee and a signed release from the student.

A multiprogram two-year institution, with an enrollment of 3,630. Highest level of offering: four or five year baccalaureate.

ACCREDITATIONS: ENGT NH NATTS

Devry Institute of Technology

4250 North Beltline Road
Irving, TX 75038-4299
(214) 258-6767 Ext. 116

Will confirm attendance and degree by phone or mail. Inquiry must include student's name, social security number, years attended. Employers may obtain transcripts upon written request accompanied by a $2.00 fee and a signed release from the student.

A multiprogram two-year institution, with an enrollment of 2,300. Highest level of offering: four or five year baccalaureate.

ACCREDITATIONS: NH ENGT NATTS

Devry Institute of Technology

3300 North Campbell Avenue
Chicago, IL 60618
(312) 929-8500 Ext. 2060
Fax (312) 348-1780

Will confirm attendance and degree by phone, fax or mail. Inquiry must include student's name, social security number, years attended. Employers may obtain transcripts upon written request accompanied by a $2.00 fee and a signed release from the student.

An engineering school, with an enrollment of 7,049. Highest level of offering: four or five year baccalaureate.

ACCREDITATIONS: ENGT NATTS

Diablo Valley College

321 Golf Club Road
Pleasant Hill, CA 94523
(510) 685-1310

Will confirm attendance by phone or mail. Inquiry must include student's name, date of birth, social security number. Employers may obtain transcripts upon written request accompanied by a signed release from the student and a $3.00 transcript fee.

A multiprogram two-year institution, with an enrollment of 22,483. Highest level of offering: two years but less than four years.

ACCREDITATIONS: WJ DA DH DT

Dickinson College

PO Box 1773
Carlisle, PA 17013
(717) 245-1315

Will confirm attendance and degree by phone or mail. Inquiry must include student's name, years attended. Only students may obtain transcripts.

A general baccalaureate institution, with an enrollment of 1,888. Highest level of offering: four or five year baccalaureate.

ACCREDITATIONS: M

Dickinson School of Law

150 South College Street
Carlisle, PA 17013
(717) 243-4611 Ext. 304
Fax (717) 243-4443

Will confirm attendance and degree by phone, fax or mail. Inquiry must include student's name, social security number, years attended. Employers may obtain transcripts upon written request accompanied by a $2.00 fee and a signed release from the student.

A law school, with an enrollment of 520. Highest level of offering: master's.

ACCREDITATIONS: LAW

Dickinson State University

(Formerly Dickinson State College)
Campus Box 288
Dickinson, ND 58601
(701) 227-2332

Will confirm attendance and degree by phone or mail. Inquiry must include student's name, date of birth, social security number, years attended. Employers may obtain transcripts upon written request accompanied by a $2.00 fee and a signed release from the student.

A general baccalaureate institution, with an enrollment of 1,248. Highest level of offering: four or five year baccalaureate

ACCREDITATIONS: NH ADNUR TED

Dillard University

Office of Registrar
2601 Gentilly Boulevard
New Orleans, LA 70122
(504) 283-8822

Will confirm attendance and degree by phone or mail. Inquiry must include student's name, social security number, years attended. Employers may obtain transcripts upon written request accompanied by a $2.00 fee and a signed release from the student.

A general baccalaureate institution, with an enrollment of 1,214. Highest level of offering: four or five year baccalaureate.
ACCREDITATIONS: SC MUS NUR

District One Technical Institute

620 West Clairemont Avenue
Eau Claire, WI 54701
(715) 833-6269
Fax (715) 833-6470

Will confirm attendance and degree by phone, fax or mail. Inquiry must include student's name, social security number, years attended. Employers may obtain transcripts upon written request accompanied by a signed release from the student.

A multiprogram two-year institution, with an enrollment of 3,037. Highest level of offering: one year but less than four years.
ACCREDITATIONS: NH ADNUR HT MLTAD MRT RAD

Divine Word College

Registrar's Office
South Center Avenue
Epworth, IA 52045
(319) 876-3353 Ext. 205

Will confirm attendance and degree by phone or mail. Inquiry must include student's name and social security number. Employers may obtain transcripts upon written request accompanied by a $5.00 fee and a signed release from the student.

A general baccalaureate institution, with an enrollment of 72. Highest level of offering: four or five year baccalaureate.
ACCREDITATIONS: NH

Dixie College

225 South 700 East
Saint George, UT 84770
(801) 673-4811 Ext. 348

Will confirm attendance and degree by phone or mail. Inquiry must include student's name, social security number, years attended. Employers may obtain transcripts upon written request accompanied by a $2.00 fee and a signed release from the student.

A multiprogram two-year institution, with an enrollment of 2,383. Highest level of offering: one year but less than four years.
ACCREDITATIONS: NW ADNUR

Doane College

Crete, NE 68333
(402) 826-8251 Ext. 8251

Will confirm attendance and degree by phone or mail. Inquiry must include student's name, social security number, years attended. Employers may obtain transcripts upon written request accompanied by a $2.00 fee and a signed release from the student.

A general baccalaureate institution, with an enrollment of 736. Highest level of offering: four or five year baccalaureate.
ACCREDITATIONS: NH TED

Dodge City Community College

2501 North 14th Avenue
Dodge City, KS 67801
(316) 225-1321 Ext. 208

Will confirm attendance and degree by phone or mail. Inquiry must include student's name, social security number, years attended. Employers may obtain transcripts upon written request accompanied by a signed release from the student.

A multiprogram two-year institution, with an enrollment of 1,379. Highest level of offering: one year but less than four years.
ACCREDITATIONS: NH ADNUR PNUR

Dominican College of Blauvelt

10 Western Highway
Orangeburg, NY 10962
(914) 359-7800 Ext. 231

Will confirm attendance and degree by phone or mail. Inquiry must include student's name, social security number, years attended. Employers may obtain transcripts upon written request accompanied by a $3.00 fee and a signed release from the student.

A general baccalaureate institution, with an enrollment of 1,565. Highest level of offering: four or five year baccalaureate.
ACCREDITATIONS: M NUR NY SW

Dominican College of San Rafael

52 Acacia
San Rafael, CA 94901
(415) 457-4440 Ext. 260

Will confirm attendance and degree by phone or mail. Inquiry must include student's name, years attended. Employers may obtain transcripts upon written request accompanied by a $5.00 fee and a signed release from the student.

A comprehensive institution with no medical school, with an enrollment of 725. Highest level of offering: master's.
ACCREDITATIONS: WC

Dominican House of Studies

487 Michigan Avenue North East
Washington, DC 20017
(202) 529-5300 Ext. 167
Fax (202) 636-4460

Will confirm attendance and degree by phone, fax or mail. Inquiry must include student's name and social security number. Employers may obtain transcripts upon written request by student accompanied by a $2.00 fee. Requests should be directed to: Registrar's Office.

A school of philosophy, religion and theology, with an enrollment of 38. Highest level of offering: doctorate.
ACCREDITATIONS: M THEOL

Dominican School of Philosophy and Theology

2401 Ridge Road
Berkeley, CA 94709
(510) 849-2030

Will confirm attendance and degree by phone or mail. Inquiry must include student's name, social security number, date of birth, signed release. Employers may obtain transcripts upon written request accompanied by a $3.00 fee and a signed release from the student.

A school of philosophy, religion and theology, with an enrollment of 82. Highest level of offering: master's.
ACCREDITATIONS: WC THEOL

Don Bosco College

Registrar's Office
College Hill
Newton, NJ 07860
(201) 579-5400
Fax (914) 636-0159

Records are maintained at the above address. Will confirm attendance and degree by mail. Inquiry must include student's namr, social security number, release. Employers may obtain transcripts upon written request by student accompanied by a $2.00 fee.

Don Bosco Technical Institute

1151 San Gabriel Blvd
Rosemead, CA 91770-4299
(818) 307-6522

Will confirm attendance and degree by phone or mail. Inquiry must include student's name, date of birth, social security number, years attended. Employers may obtain transcripts upon written request accompanied by a $2.00 fee and a signed release from the student.

A multiprogram two-year institution, with an enrollment of 282. Highest level of offering: two years but less than four years.
ACCREDITATIONS: WJ

Donnelly College

608 North 18th Street
Kansas City, KS 66102
(913) 621-6070 Ext. 33
Fax (913) 621-0354

Will confirm attendance and degree by phone or mail. Inquiry must include student's name, date of birth, social security number. Employers may obtain transcripts upon written request accompanied by a $1.00 fee and a signed release from the student.

A multiprogram two-year institution, with an enrollment of 712. Highest level of offering: one year but less than four years.
ACCREDITATIONS: NH

Dordt College

498 4th Avenue North East
Sioux Center, IA 51250
(712) 722-6030
Fax (712) 722-1198 or 722-1967

Will confirm attendance and degree by
phone, fax or mail. Inquiry must include
student's name, date of birth, social security
number. Employers may obtain transcripts
upon written request accompanied by a
signed release from the student.

A general baccalaureate institution, with an
enrollment of 1,039. Highest level of offering: four or five year baccalaureate.
ACCREDITATIONS: NH

Douglas MacArthur State Technical College

PO Box 649
Opp, AL 36467
(205) 493-3573 Ext. 233

Will confirm attendance and degree by
phone or mail. Inquiry must include student's name and social security number.
Employers may obtain transcripts upon
written request accompanied by a signed release from the student.

A two-year institution newly admitted to
NCES, with an enrollment of 600. Highest
level of offering: one year but less than four
years.
ACCREDITATIONS: SV

Dowling College

Idle Hour Boulevard
Oakdale, Long Island, NY 11769
(516) 244-3250

Will confirm attendance and degree by
phone or mail. Inquiry must include student's name, social security number, years
attended. Employers may obtain transcripts
upon written request accompanied by a
$3.00 fee and a signed release from the stu-
dent.

A general baccalaureate institution, with an
enrollment of 3,100. Highest level of offering: master's.
ACCREDITATIONS: M NY

Dr. William M. Scholl College of Podiatric Medicine

1001 North Dearborn
Chicago, IL 60610
(312) 280-2943

Will confirm attendance and degree by
phone or mail. Inquiry must include student's name, years attended. Employers
may obtain transcripts upon written request
accompanied by a $2.00 fee and a signed
release from the student.

A health institution, with an enrollment of
500. Highest level of offering: first professional degree.
ACCREDITATIONS: NCA POD

Dr. Martin Luther College

1884 College Heights
New Ulm, MN 56073
(507) 354-8221

Will confirm attendance and degree by mail
or phone. Inquiry must include student's
name and social security number.
Employers may obtain transcripts upon
written request accompanied by a $2.00 fee
and a signed release from the student.

A school of education, with an enrollment
of 559. Highest level of offering: four or
five year baccalaureate.
ACCREDITATIONS: NH

Drake University

26th Street & Old Main Bldg.
Des Moines, IA 50311
(515) 271-3901 Ext. 3091
Fax (515) 271-3977

Will confirm attendance and degree by
phone or fax. Inquiry must include student's name, date of birth, social security
number. Employers may obtain transcripts
upon written request accompanied by a
$4.00 fee and a signed release from the stu-
dent. Attn: Registrar's Office.

A comprehensive institution with no medi-
cal school, with an enrollment of 7,000.
Highest level of offering: doctorate.
ACCREDITATIONS: NH ART BUS JOUR LAW
MUS PHAR TED

Draughon's College of Business

(See Franklin College)

Draughons Junior College–Knoxville

315 Erin Street
Attn: Academic Dean
Knoxville, TN 37919
(615) 588-72171 Ext. 207

Records for Draughon's at Johnson City
and Draughons at Chattanooga are being
held here. Will confirm attendance and degree by mail. Inquiry must include student's
name, date of birth, social security number,
years attended. Employers may obtain transcripts upon written request accompanied
by a signed release from the student.

A single program two-year institution, with
an enrollment of 1,741. Highest level of offering: one year but less than four years.
ACCREDITATIONS: JRCB

Draughons Junior College of Business–Nashville

PO Box 17386
Nashville, TN 37217
(615) 361-7555
Fax (615) 367-2736

Will confirm attendance and degree by
phone, fax or mail. Inquiry must include
student's name, social security number,
years attended. Employers may obtain transcripts upon written request accompanied
by a $1.00 fee and a signed release from the
student.

A multiprogram two-year institution, with
an enrollment of 545. Highest level of offering: one year but less than four years.
ACCREDITATIONS: JRCB

Draughons Junior College

3200 Elvis Presley Boulevard
Memphis, TN 38116
(901) 332-7800

Will confirm attendance and degree by
phone or mail. Inquiry must include student's name, date of birth, social security
number, years graduated, release. Requests
should be directed to: Dean's Office.
Employers may obtain transcripts upon
written request accompanied by a $1.00 fee
and a signed release from the student.

A multiprogram two-year institution, with
an enrollment of 783. Highest level of offering: one year but less than four years.
ACCREDITATIONS: JRCB

Draughons Junior College

(See South College)

Drew University

Madison, NJ 07940
(201) 408-3000 Ext. 3245

Will confirm attendance and degree by
phone or mail. Inquiry must include student's name, date of birth, social security
number, years attended. Employers may obtain transcripts upon written request accompanied by a $5.00 fee and a signed release
from the student.

A doctoral-level institution with no medical
school, with an enrollment of 2,100.
Highest level of offering: doctorate.
ACCREDITATIONS: M THEOL

Drexel University

32 and Chestnut Street
Philadelphia, PA 19104
(215) 895-2305
Fax (215) 895-2307

Will confirm attendance and degree by
phone or mail. Inquiry must include student's name, date of birth, social security
number, years attended. Requests should be
directed to: Student Information & Records.
Employers may obtain transcripts upon
written request accompanied by a $2.00 fee
and a signed release from the student.

A comprehensive institution with no medi-
cal school, with an enrollment of 12,566.
Highest level of offering: doctorate.
ACCREDITATIONS: M ARCH BUS DIET ENG
FIDER LIB

Dropsie College

(See Annenberg Research Institute)

Drury College

900 North Benton Avenue
Springfield, MO 65802
(417) 865-8731 Ext. 211
Fax (417) 865-6502 (Attn: Registrar's
Office)

Will confirm attendance and degree by
mail. Inquiry must include student's name,
date of birth, social security number, years
attended. Employers may obtain transcripts

upon written request by student accompanied by a $5.00 fee and a signed release from the student.

A general baccalaureate institution, with an enrollment of 1,140. Highest level of offering: master's.

ACCREDITATIONS: NH TED

Duke University

103 Allen Bldg.
Durham, NC 27706
(919) 684-2813
Fax (919) 684-4500

Will confirm attendance and degree by phone, fax or mail. Inquiry must include student's name, social security number, years attended. Employers may obtain transcripts upon written request accompanied by a $3.00 fee and a signed release from the student.

A doctoral-level institution with a medical school, with an enrollment of 10,025. Highest level of offering: doctorate.

ACCREDITATIONS: SC APCP BBT BUS CLPSY CYTO ENG FOR HSA PAST IPSY LAW MED TED THEOL MT PTA RAD EEG

Dull Knife Memorial College

PO Box 98
Lame Deer, MT 59043
(406) 477-6215 Ext. 305
Fax (406) 477-6219

Will confirm attendance and degree by phone, fax or mail. Inquiry must include student's name, date of birth, years attended. Employers may obtain transcripts upon written request accompanied by a signed release from the student.

A multiprogram two-year institution, with an enrollment of 237. Highest level of offering: one year but less than four years.

ACCREDITATIONS: NW

Dundalk Community College

7200 Sollers Point Road
Dundalk, MD 21222
(301) 285-9823
Fax (301) 285-9903

Will confirm attendance and degree by phone, fax or mail. Inquiry must include student's name, social security number, years attended. Employers may obtain transcripts upon written request accompanied by a signed release from the student.

A multiprogram two-year institution, with an enrollment of 3,300. Highest level of offering: one year but less than four years.

ACCREDITATIONS: M

Duquesne University

600 Forbes Avenue
Pittsburgh, PA 15282
(412) 434-6212

Will confirm attendance and degree by phone or mail. Inquiry must include student's name, date of birth, social security number, years attended. Employers may obtain transcripts upon written request accompanied by a $3.00 fee and a signed release from the student.

A comprehensive institution with no medical school, with an enrollment of 6,598. Highest level of offering: doctorate.

ACCREDITATIONS: M BUS LAW MUS NUR PHAR

Durham Technical Community College

1637 Lawson Street
Durham, NC 27703
(919) 598-9384

Will confirm attendance and degree by phone or mail. Inquiry must include student's name, social security number, years attended. Employers may obtain transcripts upon written request accompanied by a $1.00 fee and a signed release from the student.

A multiprogram two-year institution, with an enrollment of 4,875. Highest level of offering: one year but less than four years.

ACCREDITATIONS: SC DT RSTH

Dutchess Community College

Pendell Road
Poughkeepsie, NY 12601
(914) 471-4500 Ext. 1800
Fax (914) 471-8467

Will confirm attendance and degree by mail or fax. Inquiry must include student's name, social security number, release. Requests should be directed to: Counseling and Career Services Center. Employers may obtain transcripts upon written request by student accompanied by a $3.00 fee.

A multiprogram two-year institution, with an enrollment of 7,000. Highest level of offering: one year certificate or two year associate.

ACCREDITATIONS: M ADNUR DA DT MAC MLTAD NY

Dyersburg State Community College

PO Box 648
Dyersburg, TN 38024-0648
(901) 286-3330
Fax (901) 286-3333

Will confirm attendance and degree by phone or mail. Inquiry must include student's name, date of birth, social security number, years attended. Requests should be directed to: Admissions and Records Office. Employers may obtain transcripts upon written request accompanied by a signed release from the student.

A multiprogram two-year institution, with an enrollment of 2,112. Highest level of offering: two years but less than four years.

ACCREDITATIONS: SACS ADNUR

Dyke College

112 Prospect Avenue
Cleveland, OH 44115
(216) 696-9000 Ext. 833

Will confirm attendance and degree by phone or mail. Inquiry must include student's name, maiden name (if any), date of birth, social security number, years attended. Requests should be directed to: Student Records Office-Room 212. Employers may obtain transcripts upon written request accompanied by a $2.00 fee and a signed release from the student.

A business school, with an enrollment of 1,313. Highest level of offering: four or five year baccalaureate.

ACCREDITATIONS: NH

E

Earlham College

Registrar's Office
Richmond, IN 47374
(317) 983-1515

Will confirm attendance and degree by phone or mail. Inquiry must include student's name, social security number, and years attended. Employers may obtain transcripts upon written request accompanied by a $2.00 fee and a signed release from the student.

A general baccalaureate institution, with an enrollment of 1,106. Highest level of offering: master's.

ACCREDITATIONS: NH THEOL

East-West University

816 South Michigan Avenue
Chicago, IL 60605
(312) 939-0111
Fax (312) 939-0083

Will confirm attendance and degree by phone or mail. Inquiry must include student's name, date of birth, social security number, and years attended. Requests should be directed to: Records Department. Employers may obtain transcripts upon written request accompanied by a $2.00 fee and a signed release from the student ($5.00 for expedited services).

A four-year institution , with an enrollment of 242. Highest level of offering: bachelor's

ACCREDITATIONS: NH

East Arkansas Community College

Forest City, AR 72335-9598
(501) 633-4480

Will confirm attendance and degree by phone or mail. Inquiry must include student's name, date of birth, social security number, and years attended. Employers may obtain transcripts upon written request accompanied by a $1.00 fee and a signed release from the student.

A multiprogram two-year institution, with an enrollment of 1,311. Highest level of offering: one year but less than four years.

ACCREDITATIONS: NH

East Carolina University

East Fifth Street
Greenville, NC 27858-4353
(919) 757-6524
Fax (919) 757-4232

Will confirm attendance and degree by phone or mail. Inquiry must include student's name, date of birth, social security number, and years attended. Employers may obtain transcripts upon written request accompanied by a $3.00 fee and a signed release from the student. Attention: Registrar's Office.

A comprehensive institution with a medical school, with an enrollment of 15,140. Highest level of offering: doctorate.

ACCREDITATIONS: SC ART BUS DIET MED MRA MT MUS NUR OT PTA SW

East Central College

PO Box 529
Union, MO 63084
(314) 583-5193 Ext. 220
Fax (314) 583-5195 Ext. 2432

Will confirm attendance and degree by phone, fax or mail. Inquiry must include student's name and social security number. Employers may obtain transcripts upon written request accompanied by a $2.00 fee and a signed release from the student.

A multiprogram two-year institution, with an enrollment of 2,800. Highest level of offering: one year but less than four years.

ACCREDITATIONS: NH DA

East Central Community College

Decatur, MS 39327
(601) 635-2111 Ext. 206

Will confirm attendance and degree by phone or mail. Inquiry must include student's name and social security number. Requests should be directed to: Admission's Office. Employers may obtain transcripts upon written request accompanied by a $2.00 fee and a signed release from the student.

A multiprogram two-year institution, with an enrollment of 1,395 Highest level of offering: two year.

ACCREDITATIONS: SC

East Central University

Ada, OK 74820
(405) 332-8000 Ext. 234
Fax (405) 521-6516

Will confirm attendance and degree by phone, fax or mail. Inquiry must include student's name, date of birth, social security number, and years attended. Employers may obtain transcripts upon written request accompanied by a $1.00 fee and a signed release from the student.

A comprehensive institution with no medical school, with an enrollment of 4,046. Highest level of offering: master's.

ACCREDITATIONS: NH MRA NUR RAD SW TED

East Coast Bible College

6900 Wilkinson Boulevard
Charlotte, NC 28214
(704) 394-2307
Fax (704) 394-2308

Will confirm attendance and degree by phone or mail. Inquiry must include student's name social security number, and years attended. Requests should be directed to: Admissions Office. Employers may obtain transcripts upon written request accompanied by a signed release from the student.

A bachelor's or higher institution newly admitted to NCES, with an enrollment of 303. Highest level of offering: four or five year baccalaureate.

ACCREDITATIONS: BI,SACS

East Los Angeles College

1301 Brooklyn Avenue
Monterey Park, CA 91754
(213) 265-8650

Will confirm attendance and degree by mail. Inquiry must include student's name, date of birth, social security number, years attended, release. Requests should be directed to: Record & Admissions Office. Employers may obtain transcripts upon written request accompanied by a $1.00 fee and a signed release from the student.

A multiprogram two-year institution, with an enrollment of 17,300. Highest level of offering: one year but less than four years.

ACCREDITATIONS: WJ MRT RSTH

East Mississippi Community College

PO Box 158
Scooba, MS 39358
(601) 476-8442 Ext. 219

Will confirm degree and attendance by phone or mail. Inquiry must include student's name, social security number, and years attended. Requests should be directed to: Dean's Office. Employers may obtain transcripts upon written request accompanied by a $2.00 fee and a signed release from the student.

A multiprogram two-year institution, with an enrollment of 1,200. Highest level of offering: one year but less than four years.

ACCREDITATIONS: SC FUSER

East Stroudsburg University of Pennsylvania

East Stroudsburg, PA 18301
(717) 424-3148

Will confirm attendance and degree by phone or mail. Inquiry must include student's name, social security number, and years attended. Employers may obtain transcripts upon written request accompanied by a signed release from the student.

A comprehensive institution with no medical school, with an enrollment of 4,235. Highest level of offering: master's.

ACCREDITATIONS: M NUR TED

East Tennessee State University

Box 19330A
Johnson City, TN 37614
(615) 929-4230
Fax (615) 929-6604

Will confirm attendance and degree by phone, fax or mail. Inquiry must include student's name, social security number, and years attended. Employers may obtain transcripts upon written request accompanied by a signed release from the student. Direct inquiries to: Office of the Registrar, Box 70561, Johnson City, TN 37614.

A comprehensive institution with a medical school, with an enrollment of 11,500. Highest level of offering: doctorate.

ACCREDITATIONS: SC ADNUR ART DA DH DT ENGT MAC MED MLTAD MUS NUR TED RAD RSTHT SURGT SW

East Texas Baptist University

1209 North Grove
Marshall, TX 75670
(214) 935-7963 Ext. 202
Fax (903) 935-3447

Will confirm attendance and degree by phone or mail. Inquiry must include student's name, date of birth, social security number, years attended, self addressed stamped envelope. Employers may obtain transcripts upon written request accompanied by a $2.00 fee and a signed release from the student.

A general baccalaureate institution, with an enrollment of 1,015. Highest level of offering: four or five year baccalaureate.

ACCREDITATIONS: SC MUS

East Texas State University at Texarkana

PO Box 5518
Texarkana, TX 75505
(903) 838-6514

Will confirm attendance and degree by phone or mail. Inquiry must include student's name and social security number. Requests should be directed to: Admission's Office. Employers may obtain transcripts upon written request accompanied by a $2.00 fee and a signed release from the student.

A bachelor's or higher institution newly admitted to NCES, with an enrollment of 1,410. Highest level of offering: master's.

ACCREDITATIONS: SC

East Texas State University

East Texas Station
Commerce, TX 75429
(214) 886-5068
Fax (903) 886-5888

Will confirm attendance and degree by phone, fax or mail. Inquiry must include student's name, social security number, and years attended. Requests should be directed to: Registrar's Office. Employers may obtain transcripts upon written request accompanied by a $2.00 fee and a signed release from the student.

A comprehensive institution with no medical school, with an enrollment of 7,100. Highest level of offering: doctorate.

ACCREDITATIONS: SC BUS MFCD MUS SW TED

Eastern Arizona College

Church Street
Thatcher, AZ 85552-0769
(602) 428-8250
Fax (602) 428-8462

Will confirm attendance and degree by phone, fax or mail. Inquiry must include student's name, date of birth, social security number, years attended, self addressed stamped envelope. Requests should be directed to: Admissions & Registrar's Office. Employers may obtain transcripts upon written request accompanied by a $3.00 fee and a signed release from the student.

A multiprogram two-year institution, with an enrollment of 4,521. Highest level of offering: one year but less than four years.

ACCREDITATIONS: NH

Eastern Baptist Theological Seminary

City Line & Lancaster Avenue
Philadelphia, PA 19151
(215) 645-9330

Will confirm attendance and degree by mail. Inquiry must include student's name, date of birth, social security number, and years attended. Employers may obtain transcripts upon written request by student accompanied by a $5.00 fee and a signed release from the student. Requests should be addressed to: Registrar's Office.

A school of philosophy, religion and theology, with an enrollment of 391. Highest level of offering: doctorate.

ACCREDITATIONS: M THEOL

Eastern Christian College

PO Box 629
Bel Air, MD 21014
(301) 734-7727 Ext. 209

Will confirm attendance and degree by phone or mail. Inquiry must include student's name, social security number, years attended, self addressed stamped envelope. Employers may obtain transcripts upon written request accompanied by a $3.00 fee and a signed release from the student.

A bachelor's or higher institution newly admitted to NCES, with an enrollment of 30. Highest level of offering: four or five year baccalaureate.

ACCREDITATIONS: 3IC

Eastern College

Fair View Drive
Saint Davids, PA 19087
(215) 341-5853
Fax (215) 341-1375

Will confirm attendance and degree by phone, fax or mail. Inquiry must include student's name social security number, and years attended. Employers may obtain transcripts upon written request accompanied by a $2.00 fee and a signed release from the student. Attn: Registrar's Office.

A general baccalaureate institution, with an enrollment of 1,300. Highest level of offering: master's.

ACCREDITATIONS: M SW NUR

Eastern Connecticut State University

83 Windham Street
Willimantic, CT 06226
(203) 456-5223
FAX (203) 456-5520

Will confirm attendance and degree by phone or mail. Inquiry must include student's name, date of birth, social security number, years attended, release. Employers may obtain transcripts upon written request accompanied by a $2.00 fee and a signed release from the student.

A comprehensive institution with no medical school, with an enrollment of 3,873. Highest level of offering: master's.

ACCREDITATIONS: EH

Eastern Illinois University

Records Office
Charleston, IL 61920-3099
(217) 581-3511

Will confirm attendance and degree by phone or mail. Inquiry must include student's name, date of birth, and social security number. Employers may obtain transcripts upon written request accompanied by a $2.00 fee and a signed release from the student.

A comprehensive institution with no medical school, with an enrollment of 9,837. Highest level of offering: beyond master's but less than doctorate.

ACCREDITATIONS: NH JOUR MUS SP TED

Eastern Iowa Community College District

500 Belmont Road
Battendarf, IA 52722
(319) 359-7531 Ext. 316

Will confirm attendance and degree by mail. Inquiry must include student's name, date of birth, social security number, years attended, self addressed stamped envelope. Employers may obtain transcripts upon written request accompanied by a signed release from the student.

A multiprogram two-year institution, with an enrollment of 3,026. Highest level of offering: one year but less than four years.

ACCREDITATIONS: NH MLTAD RAD SURGT

Eastern Kentucky University

Richmond, KY 40475-3101
(606) 622-3876

Will confirm attendance and degree by phone or mail. Inquiry must include student's name, date of birth, social security number, and years attended. Requests should be directed to: Registrar's Office. Employers may obtain transcripts upon written request accompanied by a $3.00 fee and a signed release from the student.

A comprehensive institution with no medical school, with an enrollment of 16,525. Highest level of offering: beyond master's but less than doctorate.

ACCREDITATIONS: SC ADNUR FIDER MAC MLTAD MRA MRT MUS NUR OT SP SW TED EMT

Eastern Maine Vocational and Technical Institute

354 Hogan Road
Bangor, ME 04401
(207) 941-4625
Fax (207) 941-4608

Will confirm attendance and degree by phone, fax or mail. Inquiry must include student's name, date of birth, social security number, and years attended. Employers may obtain transcripts upon written request accompanied by a $2.00 fee and a signed release from the student.

A multiprogram two-year institution, with an enrollment of 858. Highest level of offering: one year but less than four years.

ACCREDITATIONS: EV ENGT MLTAD RAD

Eastern Mennonite College

1200 Park Road
Harrisonburg, VA 22801
(703) 432-4110

Will confirm attendance and degree by phone or mail. Inquiry must include student's name, social security number, date of birth, and years attended. Employers may obtain transcripts upon written request accompanied by a $2.00 fee and a signed release from the student.

A general baccalaureate institution, with an enrollment of 919. Highest level of offering: first professional degree.

ACCREDITATIONS: SC NUR SW TED THEOL

Eastern Michigan University

Pierce Hall–Room 302
Ypsilanti, MI 48197
(313) 487-4111

Will confirm attendance and degree by phone or mail. Inquiry must include student's name, social security number, and years attended. Employers may obtain transcripts upon written request accompanied by a $5.00 fee and a signed release from the student. Requests should be directed to: Registrar's Office.

A comprehensive institution with no medical school, with an enrollment of 24,000. Highest level of offering: doctorate.

ACCREDITATIONS: NH BUS DIET MT MUS NUR OT SP SW TED

Eastern Montana College

1500 North 30th Street
Billings, MT 59101
(406) 657-2303

Will confirm attendance and degree by phone or mail. Inquiry must include student's name, date of birth, social security number, self addressed stamped envelope. Employers may obtain transcripts upon written request accompanied by a $2.00 fee and a signed release from the student.

A general baccalaureate institution, with an enrollment of 3,576. Highest level of offering: master's.

ACCREDITATIONS: NW ART MUS TED

Eastern Nazarene College

23 East Elm Avenue
Quincy, MA 02170
(617) 773-6350 Ext. 227

Will confirm attendance and degree by phone or mail. Inquiry must include student's name, date of birth, and years attended. Employers may obtain transcripts upon written request accompanied by a $2.00 fee and a signed release from the student.

A general baccalaureate institution, with an enrollment of 889. Highest level of offering: master's.

ACCREDITATIONS: EH SW

Eastern New Mexico University–Roswell

PO Box 6000
Roswell, NM 88202-6000
(505) 624-7144
Fax (505) 624-7119

Will confirm attendance and degree by phone or mail. Inquiry must include student's name, date of birth, social security number, years attended, date graduated. Employers may obtain transcripts upon written request accompanied by a signed release from the student.

A multiprogram two-year institution, with an enrollment of 1,285. Highest level of offering: one year but less than four years.

ACCREDITATIONS: NH ADNUR

Eastern New Mexico University Main Campus

Station No. 5
Portales, NM 88130
(505) 562-2175
Fax (505) 562-2566

Will confirm attendance and degree by phone or mail. Inquiry must include student's name, social security number, years attended, date graduated. Requests should be directed to: Registrar's Office. Employers may obtain transcripts upon written request accompanied by a $2.00 fee and a signed release from the student.

A comprehensive institution with no medical school, with an enrollment of 3,571. Highest level of offering: beyond master's but less than doctorate.

ACCREDITATIONS: NH MUS TED

Eastern Oklahoma State College

1301 West Main
Wilburton, OK 74578
(918) 465-2361 Ext. 346
Fax (918) 465-2431

Will confirm attendance and degree by phone or mail. Inquiry must include student's name, date of birth, social security number, and years attended. Employers may obtain transcripts upon written request accompanied by a $2.00 fee and a signed release from the student.

A multiprogram two-year institution, with an enrollment of 1,675. Highest level of offering: one year but less than four years.

ACCREDITATIONS: NH ADNUR

Eastern Oregon State College

La Grande, OR 97850
(503) 962-3519

Registrar's Office will confirm attendance and degree by phone or mail. Inquiry must include student's name, date of birth, social security number, and years attended. Requests should be directed to: Registrar's Office. Employers may obtain transcripts upon written request accompanied by a $1.00 fee per copy, $5.00 per certified copy and a signed release from the student.

A general baccalaureate institution, with an enrollment of 1,602. Highest level of offering: beyond master's but less than doctorate.

ACCREDITATIONS: NW TED

Eastern Shore Community College

Route 1 Box 6
Melfa, VA 23410
(804) 787-5900 Ext. 15
Fax (804) 787-5919

Will confirm attendance and degree by phone, fax or mail. Inquiry must include student's name, social security number, and years attended. Employers may obtain transcripts upon written request accompanied by a signed release from the student.

A multiprogram two-year institution, with an enrollment of 516. Highest level of offering: one year but less than four years.

ACCREDITATIONS: SC

Eastern Virginia Medical School

(Formerly Authority)
PO Box 1980
Norfolk, VA 23501
(804) 446-5244

Will confirm attendance and degree by mail. Inquiry must include student's name, social security number, years attended. Employers may obtain transcripts upon written request accompanied by a $1.00 fee and signed release from the student. Contact the above office for required form.

A medical School, with an enrollment of 430. Highest level of offering: doctorate.

Eastern Washington University

MS 150
Cheney, WA 99004
(509) 359-2321
Fax (509) 359-6594

Will confirm attendance and degree by phone or mail. Inquiry must include student's name, date of birth, social security number, and years attended. Requests should be directed to: Records Department. Employers may obtain transcripts upon written request accompanied by a $3.00 fee and a signed release from the student.

A comprehensive institution with no medical school, with an enrollment of 7,712. Highest level of offering: beyond master's but less than doctorate.

ACCREDITATIONS: NW BUS DH DIET MUS NUR SW TED

Eastern Wyoming College

3200 West C Street
Torrington, WY 82240
(307) 532-7111 Ext. 271
Fax (307) 532-2316

Will confirm attendance and degree by phone, fax or mail. Inquiry must include student's name, social security number, and years attended. Employers may obtain transcripts upon written request accompanied by a signed release from the student.

A multiprogram two-year institution, with an enrollment of 2,000 Highest level of offering: two year but less than four years.

ACCREDITATIONS: NH ADVET NCA

Eastfield College

3737 Motley Drive
Mesquite, TX 75150
(214) 324-7100

Will confirm attendance and degree by mail. Inquiry must include student's name and social security number. Requests should be directed to: Admissions Office. Employers may obtain transcripts upon written request accompanied by a signed release from the student.

A multiprogram two-year institution, with an enrollment of 9,000. Highest level of offering: one year but less than four years.

ACCREDITATIONS: SC

Eckerd College

PO Box 12560
Saint Petersburg, FL 33733
(813) 864-8217
Fax (813) 866-2304

Will confirm attendance and degree by phone or mail. Inquiry must include student's name, date of birth, social security number, and years attended. Employers may obtain transcripts upon written request accompanied by a $2.00 fee and a signed release from the student.

A general baccalaureate institution, with an enrollment of 1,350. Highest level of offering: four or five year baccalaureate.

ACCREDITATIONS: SC

Eden Theological Seminary

475 East Lockwood Avenue
St. Louis, MO 63119
(314) 961-3627

Will confirm attendance and degree by phone or mail. Inquiry must include student's name and years attended. Employers may obtain transcripts upon written request by student accompanied by a $5.00 fee and a signed release from the student.

A school of philosophy, religion and theology, with an enrollment of 231. Highest level of offering: doctorate.

ACCREDITATIONS: NH THEOL

Edgecombe Community College

(Formerly Edgecombe Technical College)
2009 West Wilson
Tarboro, NC 27886
(919) 823-5166

Will confirm attendance and degree by mail or phone. Inquiry must include student's name, date of birth, social security number, years attended, and release. Employers may obtain transcripts upon written request accompanied by a $1.00 fee and a signed release from the student.

A multiprogram two-year institution, with an enrollment of 1,700. Highest level of offering: one year but less than four years.

ACCREDITATIONS: SC RAD

Edgewood College

855 Woodrow
Madison, WI 53711
(608) 257-4861 Ext. 2202

Will confirm attendance and degree by phone or mail. Inquiry must include student's name, date of birth, and years attended. Employers may obtain transcripts upon written request accompanied by a $2.00 fee and a signed release from the student.

A general baccalaureate institution, with an enrollment of 1,609 Highest level of offering: master's.

ACCREDITATIONS: NH NUR TED

Edinboro University of Pennsylvania

Edinboro, PA 16444
(814) 732-2726

Will confirm attendance and degree by phone or mail. Inquiry must include student's name, social security number, and years attended. Employers may obtain transcripts upon written request accompanied by a $3.00 fee and a signed release from the student. Requests should be directed to: Office.of Records & Registration.

A comprehensive institution with no medical school, with an enrollment of 7,000. Highest level of offering: beyond master's but less than doctorate.

ACCREDITATIONS: M ANEST DIET DT TED

Edison Community College

PO Box 06210
8099 College Parkway South West
Fort Myers, FL 33906-6210
(813) 489-9221

Will confirm attendance and degree by mail. Inquiry must include student's name, social security number and release. Employers may obtain transcripts upon written request accompanied by a signed release from the student. Requests should be directed to: Records Department.

A multiprogram two-year institution, with an enrollment of 9,190 Highest level of offering: one year but less than four years.

ACCREDITATIONS: SC

Edison State Community College

1973 Edison Drive
Piqua, OH 45356
(513) 778-8600 Ext. 213

Will confirm attendance and degree by phone or mail. Inquiry must include student's name, social security number, and years attended. Employers may obtain transcripts upon written request accompanied by a $2.00 fee and a signed release from the student. Requests should be directed to: Enrollment Services.

A multiprogram two-year institution, with an enrollment of 3,000. Highest level of offering: two year but less than four years.

ACCREDITATIONS: NH REGIONAL

Edmonds Community College

20000 68th Avenue West
Lynnwood, WA 98036
(206) 771-7456
Fax (206) 771-3366

Will confirm attendance and degree by mail. Inquiry must include student's name, date of birth, social security number, and years attended. Employers may obtain transcripts upon written request accompanied by a signed release from the student.

A multiprogram two-year institution, with an enrollment of 8,000. Highest level of offering: one year but less than four years.

ACCREDITATIONS: NW DA MAC

Edmondson Junior College

3635 Brainerd Road
Chattanooga, TN 37411
(615) 698-3885
Fax (615) 493-1129

Will confirm attendance and degree by phone or mail. Inquiry must include student's name, social security number, and years attended. Employers may obtain transcripts upon written request accompanied by a $2.00 fee and a signed release from the student.

A multiprogram two-year institution, with an enrollment of 559. Highest level of offering: two years but less than four years.

ACCREDITATIONS: JRCB MAC AICS AAMA NSRA AATS NHA THEC TBCA SBCA

Edward Waters College

1658 Kings Road
Jacksonville, FL 32209
(904) 366-2717

Will confirm attendance and degree by mail. Inquiry must include student's name, date of birth, social security number, and years attended. Requests should be directed to: Admission & Record Office. Employers may obtain transcripts upon written request accompanied by a $5.00 fee and a signed release from the student.

A general baccalaureate institution, with an enrollment of 748. Highest level of offering: four or five year baccalaureate.

ACCREDITATIONS: SC

El Camino College

16007 Crenshaw Boulevard
Torrance, CA 90506
(213) 715-3418
Fax (310) 715-7818

Will confirm attendance and degree by mail or fax. Inquiry must include student's name, date of birth, social security number, and years attended. Requests should be directed to: Admissions Office. Employers may obtain transcripts upon written request accompanied by a $1.00 fee and a signed release from the student.

A multiprogram two-year institution, with an enrollment of 24,476. Highest level of offering: one year but less than four years.

ACCREDITATIONS: WJ MAC RAD RSTH

El Centro College

Main and Lamar
Dallas, TX 75202-3604
(214) 746-2311
Fax (214) 746-2011

Will confirm attendance and degree by mail or fax. Inquiry must include student's name, social security number, release. Requests should be directed to: Admissions Office. Employers may obtain transcripts upon written request accompanied by a signed release from the student.

A multiprogram two-year institution, with an enrollment of 5,506. Highest level of offering: one year but less than four years.

ACCREDITATIONS: SC ADNUR DA FIDER MAC MLTAD RAD RSTHT SURGT

El Paso Community College

PO Box 20500
El Paso, TX 79998
(915) 594-2264

Will confirm attendance and degree by mail. Inquiry must include student's name, date of birth, social security number, and years attended. Employers may obtain transcripts upon written request accompanied by a $2.00 fee and a signed release from the student. Requests should be directed to: Records Department.

A multiprogram two-year institution, with an enrollment of 17,098. Highest level of offering: one year but less than four years.

ACCREDITATIONS: SC ADNUR DA DH MAC MLTAD RAD RSTH RTT SURGT

El Reno Junior College

(See Redlands Community College)

Electronic Institute–Middletown

19 Jamesway Plaza
Middletown, PA 17057-4851
(717) 944-2731

Will confirm attendance and degree by phone or mail. Inquiry must include student's name, social security number, and years attended. Employers may obtain transcripts upon written request accompanied by a signed release from the student.

A multiprogram two-year institution, with an enrollment of 197 Highest level of offering: one year but less than four years.

ACCREDITATIONS: NATTS

Electronic Institute–Pittsburgh

4634 Browns Hill Road
Pittsburgh, PA 15217
(412) 521-8686
FAX (412) 521-9277

Will confirm attendance and degree by phone or mail. Inquiry must include student's name, date of birth, and social security number. Employers may obtain transcripts upon written request accompanied by a signed release from the student.

A multiprogram two-year institution, with an enrollment of 356. Highest level of offering: one year but less than four years.

ACCREDITATIONS: NATTS

Electronic Institutes

19 Jamesway Plaza
Middletown, PA 17057
(717) 944-2731

Will confirm attendance and degree by phone or mail. Inquiry must include student's name, social security number, and years attended. Employers may obtain transcripts upon written request accompanied by a signed release from the student.

A multiprogram two-year institution, with an enrollment of 279. Highest level of offering: one year but less than four years.
ACCREDITATIONS: NATTS

Electronic Technical Institute

11059 E. Bethany Drive
Aurora, CO 80011
Will confirm attendance and degree by phone or mail. Inquiry must include student's name, social security number, and years attended. Employers may obtain transcripts upon written request accompanied by a $5.00 fee and a signed release from the student.

A two-year institution newly admitted to NCES, with an enrollment of 161. Highest level of offering: one year but less than four years.
ACCREDITATIONS: NATTS

Electronic Technology Institute

4300 Euclid Avenue
Cleveland, OH 44103
(216) 391-9696

Will confirm attendance and degree by mail. Inquiry must include student's name, social security number, and years attended. Employers may obtain transcripts upon written request accompanied by a $5.00 fee and a signed release from the student. Attn: Transcript Dept.

A single program two-year institution, with an enrollment of 450 Highest level of offering: one year but less than four years.
ACCREDITATIONS: NATTS

Elgin Community College

1700 Spartan Drive
Elgin, IL 60123
(312) 888-7386

Will confirm attendance and degree by phone or mail. Inquiry must include student's name, social security number, and years attended. Employers may obtain transcripts upon written request accompanied by a $1.00 fee and a signed release from the student. Requests should be directed to: Registrar's Office.

A multiprogram two-year institution, with an enrollment of 5,533. Highest level of offering: one year but less than four years.
ACCREDITATIONS: NH ADNUR DA

Elizabeth City State University

1704 Weeksville Road
Elizabeth City, NC 27909
(919) 335-3300

Will confirm attendance and degree by phone or mail. Inquiry must include student's name, social security number, and years attended. Employers may obtain transcripts upon written request accompanied by a $2.00 fee and a signed release from the student. Attn: Registrar's Office.

A general baccalaureate institution, with an enrollment of 1,762. Highest level of offering: four or five year baccalaureate.
ACCREDITATIONS: SC

Elizabeth Seton Iona College

1061 North Broadway
Yonkers, NY 10701
(914) 969-4000
Fax (914) 969-4106

Will confirm attendance and degree by mail or fax. Inquiry must include student's name, social security number, years attended, release. Employers may obtain transcripts upon written request accompanied by a $3.00 fee and a signed release from the student.

A multiprogram two-year institution, with an enrollment of 1,291. Highest level of offering: one year but less than four years.
ACCREDITATIONS: M NY PNUR

Elizabethtown College

1 Alpha Drive
Elizabethtown, PA 17022-2298
(717) 367-1151

Will confirm attendance and degree by phone or mail. Inquiry must include student's name and years attended. Employers may obtain transcripts upon written request accompanied by a $2.00 fee and a signed release from the student.

A general baccalaureate institution, with an enrollment of 1,788. Highest level of offering: four or five year baccalaureate.
ACCREDITATIONS: M MUS OT SW

Ellsworth Community College

1100 College Avenue
Iowa Falls, IA 50126
(515) 648-4611
Fax (515) 648-3128

Will confirm attendance and degree by phone or mail. Inquiry must include student's name social security number, and years attended. Employers may obtain transcripts upon written request accompanied by a $3.00 fee and a signed release from the student.

A multiprogram two-year institution, with an enrollment of 850. Highest level of offering: one year but less than four years.
ACCREDITATIONS: NCA

Elmhurst College

190 Prospect Avenue
Elmhurst, IL 60126-3296
(708) 617-3200
Fax (708) 617-3245

Will confirm attendance and degree by phone, fax or mail. Inquiry must include student's name, social security number, and years attended. Employers may obtain transcripts upon written request accompanied by a $3.00 fee and a signed release from the student.

A general baccalaureate institution, with an enrollment of 3,100. Highest level of offering: four or five year baccalaureate.
ACCREDITATIONS: NH NUR TED

Elmira College

Park Place
Elmira, NY 14901
(607) 734-3911
Fax (607) 734-9401

Will confirm attendance and degree by phone or mail. Inquiry must include student's name and social security number. Employers may obtain transcripts upon written request accompanied by a $3.00 fee and a signed release from the student.

A comprehensive institution with no medical school, with an enrollment of 2,090. Highest level of offering: master's.
ACCREDITATIONS: M NUR NY

Elon College

Campus Box 2106
Elon College, NC 27244
(919) 584-2376

Will confirm attendance and degree by phone or mail. Inquiry must include student's name and social security number. Employers may obtain transcripts upon written request accompanied by a $3.00 fee and a signed release from the student.

A general baccalaureate institution, with an enrollment of 3,368. Highest level of offering: master's.
ACCREDITATIONS: SC

Emanuel County Junior College

237 Thigpen Drive
Swainsboro, GA 30401
(912) 237-7831

Will confirm attendance and degree by phone or mail. Inquiry must include student's name and social security number. Employers may obtain transcripts upon written request accompanied by a signed release from the student.

A multiprogram two-year institution, with an enrollment of 777. Highest level of offering: one year but less than four years.
ACCREDITATIONS: SC

Embry–Riddle Aeronautical University

Spruance Hall 600 S. Clyde Morris
Daytona, FL 32114-3900
(904) 226-6030

Will confirm attendance and degree by phone or mail. Inquiry must include student's name, social security number, campus attended, and years attended. Employers may obtain transcripts upon written request accompanied by a $4.00 fee and a signed release from the student.

A general baccalaureate institution, with an enrollment of 12,189. Highest level of offering: master's.

ACCREDITATIONS: SC ENG ENGT

Emerson College

100 Beacon Street
Boston, MA 02116
(617) 578-8660

Will confirm attendance and degree by phone or mail. Inquiry must include student's name, social security number, and years attended. Employers may obtain transcripts upon written request accompanied by a $2.00 fee and a signed release from the student.

A comprehensive institution with no medical school, with an enrollment of 2,600. Highest level of offering: master's.

ACCREDITATIONS: EH SP

Emmanuel College

400 The Fenway
Boston, MA 02115
(617) 735-9960

Will confirm attendance and degree by phone or mail. Inquiry must include student's name and social security number. Employers may obtain transcripts upon written request accompanied by a $2.00 fee and a signed release from the student.

A general baccalaureate institution, with an enrollment of 1,103. Highest level of offering: master's.

ACCREDITATIONS: EH

Emmanuel College

Box 129,
Franklin Springs, GA 30639
(404) 245-7226
(404) 245-4424

Will confirm attendance and degree by phone or mail. Inquiry must include student's name, social security number, and years attended. Employers may obtain transcripts upon written request accompanied by a $2.00 fee and a signed release from the student. Attn: Record's Office.

A multiprogram four-year institution, with an enrollment of 425. Highest level of offering: bachelor's

ACCREDITATIONS: SC

Emmanuel School of Religion

1 Walker Drive
Johnson City, TN 37601
(615) 461-1520

Will confirm attendance and degree by phone or mail. Inquiry must include student's name and social security number. Requests should be directed to: Academic Dean. Employers may obtain transcripts upon written request accompanied by a $2.00 fee and a signed release from the student.

A school of philosophy, religion and theology, with an enrollment of 139. Highest level of offering: master's.

ACCREDITATIONS: THEOL S

Emory and Henry College

Emory, VA 24327
(703) 944-4121
Fax (703) 944-4438

Will confirm attendance and degree by phone or mail. Inquiry must include student's name, social security number, and years attended. Employers may obtain transcripts upon written request accompanied by a $3.00 fee and a signed release from the student. Attn: Registrar's Office.

A general baccalaureate institution, with an enrollment of 768. Highest level of offering: four or five year baccalaureate.

ACCREDITATIONS: SC

Emory University

Atlanta, GA 30322
(404) 727-6042

Will confirm attendance and degree by phone or mail. Inquiry must include student's name and years attended. Employers may obtain transcripts upon written request accompanied by a $1.00 fee and a signed release from the student.

A doctoral-level institution with a medical school, with an enrollment of 9,793. Highest level of offering: doctorate.

ACCREDITATIONS: SC APCP BUS CHPM CLPSY DENT DIETI IPSY LAW LIB MED MT MUS NMT NUR PTA RAD RSTH THEOL MIDWF OMA PAST

Emporia State University

1200 Commercial Street
Emporia, KS 66801-5087
(316) 343-1200 Ext. 5155
Fax (316) 341-5073

Will confirm attendance and degree by phone or mail. Inquiry must include student's name, social security number, and years attended. Requests should be directed to: Records Department. Employers may obtain transcripts upon written request accompanied by a $3.00 fee and a signed release from the student.

A comprehensive institution with no medical school, with an enrollment of 6,021. Highest level of offering: beyond master's but less than doctorate.

ACCREDITATIONS: NH MUS TED LIB

Endicott College

376 Hale Street
Beverly, MA 01915
(508) 927-0585 Ext. 2065

Will confirm attendance and degree by phone or mail. Inquiry must include student's name and years attended. Employers may obtain transcripts upon written request accompanied by a $2.00 fee and a signed release from the student.

A multiprogram two-year institution, with an enrollment of 805. Highest level of offering: one year but less than four years.

ACCREDITATIONS: EH

Enterprise State Junior College

PO Box 1300
Enterprise, AL 36331
(205) 393-3752 Ext. 233

Will confirm attendance and degree by phone or mail. Inquiry must include student's name, social security number, and years attended. Employers may obtain transcripts upon written request accompanied by a signed release from the student.

A multiprogram two-year institution, with an enrollment of 2,073. Highest level of offering: one year but less than four years.

ACCREDITATIONS: SC

Episcopal Divinity School

99 Brattle Street
Cambridge, MA 02138
(617) 868-3450

Will confirm attendance and degree by phone or mail. Inquiry must include student's name, date of birth, and years attended. Employers may obtain transcripts upon written request accompanied by a $2.00 fee and a signed release from the student.

A school of philosophy, religion and theology, with an enrollment of 128. Highest level of offering: beyond master's but less than doctorate.

ACCREDITATIONS: THEOL

Episcopal Theological Seminary of the Southwest

Box 2247
Austin, TX 78768
(512) 472-4133
Fax (512) 472-3098

Will confirm attendance and degree by phone or mail. Inquiry must include student's name and social security number. Employers may obtain transcripts upon written request accompanied by a $2.00 fee and a signed release from the student.

A school of philosophy, religion and theology, with an enrollment of 74. Highest level of offering: master's.

ACCREDITATIONS: SC THEOL PAST

Erie Business Center

246 West Ninth Street
Erie, PA 16501
(814) 456-7504
Fax (814) 456-4882

Will confirm attendance and degree by phone or mail. Inquiry must include student's name, social security number, and years attended. Employers may obtain transcripts upon written request by student accompanied by a $3.00 fee and a signed release from the student.

A 20 month associate degree (ASB) institution newly admitted to NCES, with an enrollment of 300. Highest level of offering: one year but less than four years.

ACCREDITATIONS: CCA ACICS

Erie Community College City Campus

121 Ellicott Street
Buffalo, NY 14203
(716) 842-2770 Ext. 319

Will confirm attendance and degree by phone or mail. Inquiry must include student's name, social security number, years attended, and release. Employers may obtain transcripts upon written request accompanied by a $3.00 fee and a signed release from the student.

A multiprogram two-year institution, with an enrollment of 3,400. Highest level of offering: one year but less than four years.

ACCREDITATIONS: M NY RTT

Erie Community College North Campus

Main Street and Youngs Road
Williamsville, NY 14221
(716)851-1466, 851-1467, 851-1468
Fax (716) 851-1469

Will confirm attendance and degree by mail. Inquiry must include student's name, social security number, and years attended. Employers may obtain transcripts upon written request accompanied by a $3.00 fee and a signed release from the student.

A multiprogram two-year institution, with an enrollment of 5,549. Highest level of offering: one year but less than four years.

ACCREDITATIONS: M ADNUR DH ENGT MLTAD NY RSTH

Erie Community College South Campus

4140 Southwestern Boulevard
Orchard Park, NY 14127
(716)851-1666

Will confirm attendance and degree by phone or mail. Inquiry must include student's name, social security number, and years attended. Employers may obtain transcripts upon written request accompanied by a $3.00 fee and a signed release from the student.

A multiprogram two-year institution, with an enrollment of 3,500. Highest level of offering: one year but less than four years.

ACCREDITATIONS: M NY

Erskine College and Seminary

Due West, SC 29639
(803) 379-2131

Will confirm attendance and degree by phone or mail. Inquiry must include student's name and social security number. Employers may obtain transcripts upon written request accompanied by a $5.00 fee and a signed release from the student.

A general baccalaureate institution, with an enrollment of 525. Highest level of offering: doctorate.

ACCREDITATIONS: SC THEOL

Essex Community College

7201 Rossville Boulevard
Baltimore County, MD 21237
(301) 522-1263

Will confirm attendance and degree by phone or mail. Inquiry must include student's name and social security number. Employers may obtain transcripts upon written request accompanied by a signed release from the student.

A multiprogram two-year institution, with an enrollment of 9,861. Highest level of offering: one year but less than four years.

ACCREDITATIONS: M ADNUR ADVET APCP DA MLTAD MUS NMT RAD RSTHT RTT THEA

Essex County College

303 University Avenue
Newark, NJ 07102
(201) 877-3111

Will confirm attendance and degree by mail. Inquiry must include student's name, social security number, years attended, release. Employers may obtain transcripts upon written request accompanied by a $2.00 fee and a signed release from the student.

A multiprogram two-year institution, with an enrollment of 6,087. Highest level of offering: one year but less than four years.

ACCREDITATIONS: M PTAA RAD

Eugene Bible College

2155 Bailey Hill Road
Eugene, OR 97405
(503) 485-1780
Fax (503) 343-5801

Will confirm attendance and degree by mail. Inquiry must include student's name, release. Employers may obtain transcripts upon written request accompanied by a $2.00 fee and a signed release from the student.

A bachelor's or higher institution newly admitted to NCES, with an enrollment of 171. Highest level of offering: four or five year baccalaureate.

ACCREDITATIONS: BI

Eureka College

300 College Avenue
Eureka, IL 61530
(309) 467-3721
Fax (309) 467-6325

Will confirm attendance and degree by phone, fax or mail. Inquiry must include student's name, social security number, and years attended. Employers may obtain tran-

scripts upon written request accompanied by a $2.00 fee and a signed release from the student.

A general baccalaureate institution, with an enrollment of 460. Highest level of offering: four or five year baccalaureate.

ACCREDITATIONS: NH

Evangel College

1111 North Glenstone
Springfield, MO 65802
(417) 865-2811 Ext. 7205
Fax (417) 865-9599

Will confirm attendance and degree by phone or mail. Inquiry must include student's name, social security number, and years attended. Employers may obtain transcripts upon written request accompanied by a $3.00 fee and a signed release from the student.

A general baccalaureate institution, with an enrollment of 1,777. Highest level of offering: four or five year baccalaureate.

ACCREDITATIONS: NH MUS TED

Evangelical School of Theology

121 South College Street
Myerstown, PA 17067
(717) 866-5775

Will confirm attendance and degree by phone or mail. Inquiry must include student's name and social security number. Employers may obtain transcripts upon written request accompanied by a $2.00 fee and a signed release from the student. Requests should be directed to: Registrar's Office.

A school of philosophy, religion and theology, with an enrollment of 145. Highest level of offering: master's.

ACCREDITATIONS: M THEOL

Everett Community College

801 Wetmore
Everett, WA 98201
(206) 259-7151
Fax (206) 339-9129

Will confirm attendance and degree by phone, fax or mail. Inquiry must include student's name and social security number. Employers may obtain transcripts upon written request and a signed release from the student.

A multiprogram two-year institution, with an enrollment of 6,473. Highest level of offering: one year but less than four years.

ACCREDITATIONS: NW

Evergreen State College

Olympia, WA 98505
(206) 866-6000 Ext. 6180

Will confirm attendance and degree by phone or mail. Inquiry must include student's name and social security number. Employers may obtain transcripts upon written request accompanied by a $10.00 fee and a signed release from the student. Requests should be directed to: Registration and Records Office.

A general baccalaureate institution, with an enrollment of 3,000. Highest level of offering: master's.

ACCREDITATIONS: NW

Evergreen Valley College

3095 Yerba Buena Road
San Jose, CA 95135
(408) 270-6423

Will confirm attendance and degree by phone or mail. Inquiry must include student's name, social security number, a confirmation fee of $2.00. Employers may obtain transcripts upon written request accompanied by a $2.00 fee and a signed release from the student.

A multiprogram two-year institution, with an enrollment of 12,0700. Highest level of offering: one year but less than four years.
ACCREDITATIONS: WJ ADNUR

F

Fairfield University

North Benson Road
Fairfield, CT 06430-7524
(203) 254-4000 Ext. 2224

Will confirm attendance and degree by phone or mail. Inquiry must include student's name, social security number, years attended. Employers may obtain transcripts upon written request accompanied by a $4.00 fee and a signed release from the student.

A comprehensive institution with no medical school, with an enrollment of 5,104. Highest level of offering: beyond master's but less than doctorate.
ACCREDITATIONS: EH NUR

Fairleigh Dickinson University Edward Williams College

150 Kotte Place
Hackensack, NJ 07601
(201) 692-2000
Fax (201) 692-2503

Will confirm attendance and degree by phone or mail. Inquiry must include student's name, social security number, years attended. Requests should be directed to: Records Department. Employers may obtain transcripts upon written request accompanied by a $3.00 fee and a signed release from the student.

A multiprogram two-year institution, with an enrollment of 1,061. Highest level of offering: one year but less than four years.
ACCREDITATIONS: NUR IPSY ENGT CHM RTT RSTHT RAD PTA

Fairleigh Dickinson University Florhan–Madison Campus

285 Madison Avenue
Madison, NJ 07940
(201) 593-8500

Will confirm attendance and degree by phone or mail. Inquiry must include student's name, social security number, years attended. Employers may obtain transcripts upon written request accompanied by a $5.00 fee and a signed release from the student.

A business school, with an enrollment of 4,275. Highest level of offering: doctorate.
ACCREDITATIONS: M PTAA RAD RSTH

Fairleigh Dickinson University Rutherford Campus

W Passaic & Montross Ave
Rutherford, NJ 07070
(201) 460-5470

Will confirm degree by phone or mail. Inquiry must include student's name, social security number, and last date of attendance. Employers may obtain transcripts upon written request accompanied by a $5.00 fee and a signed release from the student. Requests should be directed to: Records Office.

A comprehensive institution with no medical school, with an enrollment of 3,090. Highest level of offering: doctorate.
ACCREDITATIONS: M NUR

Fairleigh Dickinson University Teaneck Campus

1000 River Road
Teaneck, NJ 07666
(201) 692-2380
Fax (201) 692-2560

Will confirm attendance and degree by phone or mail. Inquiry must include student's name and social security number. Employers may obtain transcripts upon written request accompanied by a $4.00 fee and a signed release from the student. Requests should be directed to: Registrar's Office.

A comprehensive institution with a medical school, with an enrollment of 7,011. Highest level of offering: doctorate.
ACCREDITATIONS: M ENG SW

Fairmont State College

Fairmont, WV 26554
(304) 367-4141

Will confirm attendance and degree by phone or mail. Inquiry must include student's name and social security number. Employers may obtain transcripts upon written request accompanied by a $3.00 fee and a signed release from the student.

A general baccalaureate institution, with an enrollment of 6,368. Highest level of offering: four or five year baccalaureate.
ACCREDITATIONS: NH ADNUR ADVET MLTAD MRT NCATE

Faith Baptist Bible College and Theological Seminary

1900 North West 4th Street
Ankeny, IA 50021
(515) 964-0601
Fax (515) 964-1638

Will confirm attendance and degree by phone or mail. Inquiry must include student's name and social security number. Employers may obtain transcripts upon written request accompanied by a $2.25 fee and a signed release from the student.

A school of philosophy, religion and theology, with an enrollment of 275. Highest level of offering: master's.
ACCREDITATIONS: BI NCA

Faith Theological Seminary

920 Spring Avenue
Elkins Park, PA 19117
(215) 635-3300

Will confirm attendance and degree by phone or mail. Inquiry must include student's name and date of birth. Employers may obtain transcripts upon written request accompanied by a $5.00 fee and a signed release from the student.

A school of philosophy, religion and theology, with an enrollment of 21. Highest level of offering: doctorate.
ACCREDITATIONS: 3IC

Farmingdale

Melville Road
Farmingdale, NY 11735
(516) 420-2124

Will confirm attendance and degree by phone. Inquiry must include student's name, social security number, years attended. Employers may obtain transcripts upon written request accompanied by a $5.00 fee and a signed release from the student.

A multiprogram two-year institution, with an enrollment of 12,987. Highest level of offering: one year but less than four years.
ACCREDITATIONS: M ADNUR DH ENGT FUSER NY

Fashion and Art Institute of Dallas

2 North Park East
8080 Park Lane
Dallas, TX 75231
(214) 692-8080

Will confirm attendance and degree by mail. Inquiry must include student's name, social security number, years attended. Employers may obtain transcripts upon written request accompanied by a $2.00 fee and a signed release from the student.

A two-year institution with an enrollment of 1,023. Highest level of offering: one year but less than four years.
ACCREDITATIONS: SACS

Fashion Institute of Design and Merchandising

919 South Grant
Los Angeles, CA 90015
(213) 624-1200 Ext. 3420

Will confirm attendance and degree by phone or mail. Inquiry must include student's name and social security number. Employers may obtain transcripts upon written request accompanied by a $2.00 fee and a signed release from the student. Requests should be directed to: Attn: Student Records.

A single program two-year institution, with an enrollment of 2,700. Highest level of offering: one year but less than four years.

ACCREDITATIONS: WJ FIDER JRCB

Fashion Institute of Technology

227 West 27th Street
New York, NY 10001
(212) 760-7676

Will confirm attendance and degree by phone or mail. Inquiry must include student's name, address, social security number, years attended. Employers may obtain transcripts upon written request accompanied by a $5.00 fee and a signed release from the student.

A multiprogram two-year institution, with an enrollment of 5,000. Highest level of offering: four or five year baccalaureate.

ACCREDITATIONS: M ART FIDER NY

Faulkner University

(Formerly Alabama Christian College)
5345 Atlanta Highway
Montgomery, AL 36109-3398
(205) 272-5820 Ext. 377

Will confirm attendance and degree by phone or mail. Inquiry must include student's name, social security number, years attended. Employers may obtain transcripts upon written request accompanied by a $3.00 fee and a signed release from the student.

A multiprogram four-year institution, with an enrollment of 1,589. Highest level of offering: four or five year baccalaureate.

ACCREDITATIONS: SC

Fayetteville State University

Murchison Road
Fayetteville, NC 28301
(919) 486-1185

Will confirm attendance and degree by phone or mail. Inquiry must include student's name and social security number. Employers may obtain transcripts upon written request accompanied by a $3.00 fee and a signed release from the student.

A general baccalaureate institution, with an enrollment of 2,679. Highest level of offering: master's.

ACCREDITATIONS: SC TED

Fayetteville Technical Community College

PO Box 35236
Fayetteville, NC 28303-0236
(919) 678-8416
Fax (919) 484-6600

Will confirm attendance and degree by phone, fax or mail. Inquiry must include student's name, social security number, years attended. Employers may obtain transcripts upon written request accompanied by a signed release from the student.

A multiprogram two-year institution, with an enrollment of 6,824. Highest level of offering: one year but less than four years.

ACCREDITATIONS: SC ADNUR DA DH ENGT FUSER PTAA RAD RSTH SURGT

Feather River College

PO Box 11110
Quincy, CA 95971
(916) 283-0202 Ext. 246

Will confirm attendance and degree by mail. Inquiry must include student's name, social security number and release. Requests should be directed to: Records Office. Employers may obtain transcripts upon written request accompanied by a $1.00 fee and a signed release from the student.

A multiprogram two-year institution, with an enrollment of 1,400. Highest level of offering: one year but less than four years.

ACCREDITATIONS: WJ

Felician College

260 South Main Street
Lodi, NJ 07644
(201) 778-1190

Will confirm attendance and degree by mail. Inquiry must include student's name and social security number. Employers may obtain transcripts upon written request accompanied by a $3.00 fee and a signed release from the student.

A multiprogram four-year institution, with an enrollment of 900. Highest level of offering: four or five year baccalaureate.

ACCREDITATIONS: M ADNUR MLTAD NUR

Felician College

(See Montay College)

Fergus Falls Community College

1414 College Way
Fergus Falls, MN 56537
(218) 739-7500
Fax (218) 739-7475

Will confirm attendance and degree by phone, fax or mail. Inquiry must include student's name, date of birth, social security number, years attended. Employers may obtain transcripts upon written request accompanied by a signed release from the student.

A multiprogram two-year institution, with an enrollment of 1,200. Highest level of offering: two years but less than four years.

ACCREDITATIONS: NH HT MLTAD

Ferris State University

Prakken-Room 202
Big Rapids, MI 49307
(616) 592-2790

Will confirm attendance and degree by phone or mail. Inquiry must include student's name, date of birth, social security number, years attended. Employers may obtain transcripts upon written request accompanied by a signed release from the student. Direct inquiries to Registrar's Office.

A general baccalaureate institution, with an enrollment of 11,775. Highest level of offering: doctorate.

ACCREDITATIONS: NH DA DH DT MLTAD MRA MRT MT NMT OPT OPTT PHAR RAD RSTH

Ferrum College

Ferrum, VA 24088
(703) 365-4275

Will confirm attendance and degree by phone or mail. Inquiry must include student's name, social security number, years attended. Employers may obtain transcripts upon written request accompanied by a $3.00 fee and a signed release from the student.

A multiprogram two-year institution, with an enrollment of 1,211. Highest level of offering: four or five year baccalaureate.

ACCREDITATIONS: SC SW

Fielding Institute

2112 Santa Barbara Street
Santa Barbara, CA 93105
(805) 687-1099
Fax (805) 687-4590

Will confirm attendance and degree by phone, fax or mail. Inquiry must include student's name and social security number. Employers may obtain transcripts upon written request accompanied by a $5.00 fee and a signed release from the student.

A specialized school, with an enrollment of 830. Highest level of offering: doctorate.

ACCREDITATIONS: WC

Findlay College

1000 North Main Street
Findlay, OH 45840
(419) 424-4556

Will confirm attendance and degree by phone or mail. Inquiry must include student's name, social security number, years attended. Employers may obtain transcripts upon written request accompanied by a signed release from the student.

A general baccalaureate institution, with an enrollment of 1,796. Highest level of offering: master's.

ACCREDITATIONS: NH NCATE

Fisher College

118 Beacon Street
Boston, MA 02116
(617) 236-8800 Ext. 825

Will confirm attendance and degree by phone or mail. Inquiry must include student's name, maiden name (if any), social security number, years attended and campus attended. Employers may obtain transcripts upon written request accompanied by a $3.00 fee and a signed release from the student.

A multiprogram two-year institution, with an enrollment of 2,500. Highest level of offering: two years but less than four years.
ACCREDITATIONS: EH MAC

Fisk University
1000 17th Avenue North
Nashville, TN 37208-3051
(615) 329-8587

Will confirm attendance and degree by phone or mail. Inquiry must include student's name, social security number, years attended. Employers may obtain transcripts upon written request accompanied by a $2.00 fee and a signed release from the student.

A general baccalaureate institution, with an enrollment of 694. Highest level of offering: master's.
ACCREDITATIONS: SC MUS

Fitchburg State College
160 Pearl Street
Fitchburg, MA 01420
(508) 345-2151 Ext. 3138

Will confirm attendance and degree by phone or mail. Inquiry must include student's name and social security number. Employers may obtain transcripts upon written request accompanied by a $1.00 fee and a signed release from the student.

A comprehensive institution with no medical school, with an enrollment of 6,693. Highest level of offering: master's.
ACCREDITATIONS: EH NUR

Five Towns College
2165 Seaford Avenue
Seaford, NY 11783
(516) 783-8800

Will confirm attendance and degree by mail. Inquiry must include student's name, date of birth, social security number, release. Employers may obtain transcripts upon written request accompanied by a $2.00 fee and a signed release from the student.

A single program two-year institution, with an enrollment of 450. Highest level of offering: one year but less than four years.
ACCREDITATIONS: M NY

Flagler Career Institute
(See American Trade Institute)

Flagler Career Institute
(See American Trade Institute Health Education Center)

Flagler College
PO Box 1027
Saint Augustine, FL 32085
(904) 829-6481 Ext. 204

Will confirm attendance and degree by phone or mail. Inquiry must include student's name, date of attendance and social security number. Employers may obtain transcripts upon written request accompanied by a $2.00 fee and a signed release from the student.

A general baccalaureate institution, with an enrollment of 1,100. Highest level of offering: four or five year baccalaureate.
ACCREDITATIONS: SC

Flaming Rainbow University
419 North 2nd Street
Stilwell, OK 74960
(918) 696-3644

Will confirm attendance and degree by phone or mail. Inquiry must include student's name and social security number. Employers may obtain transcripts upon written request accompanied by a $3.00 fee and a signed release from the student. Requests should be sent to: Attn: Registrar's Office.

A general baccalaureate institution, with an enrollment of 221. Highest level of offering: four or five year baccalaureate.
ACCREDITATIONS: NH

Flathead Valley Community College
777 Grandview Drivet
Kalispell, MT 59901
(406) 756-3851

Will confirm attendance by phone or mail. Inquiry must include student's name, date of birth, social security number. Employers may obtain transcripts upon written request accompanied by a signed release from the student.

A multiprogram two-year institution, with an enrollment of 1,874. Highest level of offering: one year but less than four years.
ACCREDITATIONS: NW

Florence Darlington Technical College
PO Drawer 100548
Florence, SC 29501
(803) 661-8155

Will confirm attendance and degree by phone or mail. Inquiry must include student's name, social security number, years attended. Employers may obtain transcripts upon written request accompanied by a $2.00 fee and a signed release from the student.

A multiprogram two-year institution, with an enrollment of 2,275. Highest level of offering: one year but less than four years.
ACCREDITATIONS: SC ADNUR DA DH ENGT MLTAD RAD RSTHT SURGT

Florida Agricultural and Mechanical University
Tallahassee, FL 32307
(904) 599-3115
Fax (904) 599-3067

Will confirm attendance and degree by phone, fax or mail. Inquiry must include student's name, social security number, years attended. Employers may obtain transcripts upon written request accompanied by a signed release from the student.

A comprehensive institution with no medical school, with an enrollment of 9,243. Highest level of offering: doctorate.
ACCREDITATIONS: SC ARCH ENGT JOUR NUR PHAR PTA SW TED

Florida Atlantic University
PO Box 3091
Boca Raton, FL 33431
(305) 367-2711

Will confirm attendance and degree by phone or mail. Inquiry must include student's name, social security number, years attended. Employers may obtain transcripts upon written request accompanied by a signed release from the student.

A comprehensive institution with no medical school, with an enrollment of 10,956. Highest level of offering: doctorate.
ACCREDITATIONS: SC BUS ENG MT MUS NUR SW TED

Florida Baptist Theological College
(Formerly Baptist Bible Institute)
1306 College Drive
Graceville, FL 32440
(800) 328-2660

Will confirm attendance and degree by phone or mail. Inquiry must include student's name and social security number and years attended. Employers may obtain transcripts upon written request accompanied by a $2.00 fee and a signed release from the student.

A bachelor's or higher institution newly admitted to NCES, with an enrollment of 378. Highest level of offering: four or five year baccalaureate.
ACCREDITATIONS: SC

Florida College
Temple Terrace, FL 33617
(813) 988-5131 Ext. 222
Fax (813) 985-9654

Will confirm attendance and degree by phone, fax or mail. Inquiry must include student's name, social security number, years attended. Employers may obtain transcripts upon written request accompanied by a $2.00 fee and a signed release from the student.

A multiprogram two-year institution, with an enrollment of 395. Highest level of offering: one year but less than four years.
ACCREDITATIONS: SC

Florida Community College at Jacksonville
501 West State Street
Jacksonville, FL 32202
(904) 632-3100
Fax (904) 632-3109

Will confirm attendance and degree by phone, fax or mail. Inquiry must include student's name and social security number. Employers may obtain transcripts upon written request accompanied by a signed release from the student.

A multiprogram two-year institution, with an enrollment of 16,722. Highest level of offering: one year but less than four years.
ACCREDITATIONS: SC ADNUR DA DH MLTAD RSTH

Florida Institute of Technology

150 West University Boulevard
Melbourne, FL 32901
(407) 768-8000 Ext. 8115
Fax (407) 727-2419

Will confirm attendance and degree by mail. Inquiry must include student's name, date of birth, social security number. Employers may obtain transcripts upon written request accompanied by a $4.00 fee and a signed release from the student.

A comprehensive institution with no medical school, with an enrollment of 5,754. Highest level of offering: doctorate.
ACCREDITATIONS: SC CLPSY ENG MLTAD

Florida International University–Tamiami Campus

Miami, FL 33199
(305) 348-2392

Will confirm attendance and degree by mail. Inquiry must include student's name, social security number, release. Employers may obtain transcripts upon written request accompanied by a signed release from the student. Requests should be directed to: Registration & Records Office.

A comprehensive institution with no medical school, with an enrollment of 22,000. Highest level of offering: doctorate.
ACCREDITATIONS: SC BUS DIET ENGT MRA MT OT PTA SW BUSA NUR

Florida Keys Community College

5901 West Jr. College Road
Key West, FL 33040
(305) 296-9081 Ext. 201

Will confirm attendance and degree by phone or mail. Inquiry must include student's name, date of birth, social security number. Employers may obtain transcripts upon written requestaccompanied with a $2.00 fee and a signed release from the student.

A multiprogram two-year institution, with an enrollment of 4,400. Highest level of offering: two years.
ACCREDITATIONS: SC

Florida Memorial College

15800 North West 42nd Avenue
Miami, FL 33054
(305) 625-4141 Ext. 104

Will confirm attendance and degree by mail. Inquiry must include student's name, date of birth, social security number. Employers may obtain transcripts upon written request accompanied by a $3.00 fee and a signed release from the student.

A general baccalaureate institution, with an enrollment of 3,100. Highest level of offering: four or five year baccalaureate.
ACCREDITATIONS: SC

Florida Southern College

111 Lake Hollingsworth Drive
Lakeland, FL 33801-5698
(813) 680-4127
Fax (813) 680-4126

Will confirm attendance and degree by phone, fax or mail. Inquiry must include student's name, date of birth, social security number, years attended. Employers may obtain transcripts upon written request accompanied by a $2.00 fee and a signed release from the student.

A general baccalaureate institution, with an enrollment of 2,700. Highest level of offering: master's.
ACCREDITATIONS: SC

Florida State University

214 William Johnston Bldg.
Tallahassee, FL 32306
(904) 644-1251 or 644-1050

Will confirm attendance and degree by phone or mail. Inquiry must include student's name, social security number, years attended. Employers may obtain transcripts upon written request accompanied by a signed release from the student.

A doctoral-level institution with no medical school, with an enrollment of 20,984. Highest level of offering: doctorate.
ACCREDITATIONS: SC AUD BUS CLPSY FIDER LAW LIB MUS NUR SCPSY DANCE THEA SP TED SW BUSA MFCD

Floyd Junior College

PO Box 1864
Rome, GA 30163
(404) 295-6339
Fax (404) 295-6610

Will confirm attendance and degree by phone, fax or mail. Inquiry must include student's name, social security number, years attended. Requests should be directed to: Records & Admissions Office. Employers may obtain transcripts upon written request accompanied by a signed release from the student.

A multiprogram two-year institution, with an enrollment of 1,278. Highest level of offering: one year but less than four years.
ACCREDITATIONS: SC ADNUR MLTAD

Fontbonne College

6800 Wydown Boulevard
Saint Louis, MO 63105
(314) 889-1421 or 862-3456

Will confirm attendance and degree by mail or phone. Inquiry must include student's name and social security number. Employers may obtain transcripts upon written request accompanied by a $2.00 fee and a signed release from the student.

A general baccalaureate institution, with an enrollment of 1108. Highest level of offering: master's.
ACCREDITATIONS: NH MUS TED

Foothill College

12345 El Monte Road
Los Altos Hills, CA 94022-4599
(415) 949-7777

Will confirm attendance and degree by phone or mail. Inquiry must include student's name, date of birth, social security number, years attended. Employers may obtain transcripts upon written request accom-

panied by a $3.00 fee and a signed release from the student. Requests should be directed to: Admissions & Records Office.

A multiprogram two-year institution, with an enrollment of 19,144. Highest level of offering: one year but less than four years.
ACCREDITATIONS: WJ DA DH RAD RSTH RTT

Fordham University

East Fordham Road
Bronx, NY 10458
(212) 579-2130

Will confirm attendance and degree by phone or mail. Inquiry must include student's name, date of birth, social security number, years attended. Employers may obtain transcripts upon written request accompanied by a $5.00 fee and a signed release from the student. Requests should be directed to: Registrar's Office.

A doctoral-level institution with no medical school, with an enrollment of 12,340. Highest level of offering: doctorate.
ACCREDITATIONS: M BUS CLPSY LAW NY SCPSY SW TED

Forest Institute of Professional Psychology

200 North Glendale
Wheeling, IL 60090
(708) 215-7870

Will confirm attendance and degree by mail. Inquiry must include student's name, social security number, years attended, release. Employers may obtain transcripts upon written request by student.

A specialized school, with an enrollment of 250. Highest level of offering: doctorate.
ACCREDITATIONS: NCA

Forest Institute

(Formerly Professional Psychology)
2611 Leeman Ferry Rd.
Huntsville, AL 35801
(205) 536-9088
Fax (205) 533-7405

Will confirm attendance and degree by mail or fax. Inquiry must include student's name, date of birth, social security number. Employers may obtain transcripts upon written request by student accompanied by a signed release from the student.

A specialized school, with an enrollment of 250. Highest level of offering: doctorate.
ACCREDITATIONS: NH

Forsyth School of Dental Hygienists

140 Fenway
Boston, MA 02115
(617) 262-5200 Ext. 211
Fax (617) 262-4021

Will confirm attendance and degree by phone or mail. Inquiry must include student's name, social security number, mother's maiden name, years attended. Employers may obtain transcripts upon written request accompanied by a $2.00 fee and a signed release from the student.

A single program two year - four year institution, with an enrollment of 100. Highest level of offering: baccalaureate.
ACCREDITATIONS: DH

Forsyth Technical College

2100 Silas Creek Parkway
Winston–Salem, NC 27103
(919) 723-0371

Will confirm attendance and degree by mail. Inquiry must include student's name, social security number, years attended, release. Employers may obtain transcripts upon written request accompanied by a signed release from the student.

A multiprogram two-year institution, with an enrollment of 4,00. Highest level of offering: one year but less than four years.
ACCREDITATIONS: SC ENGT NMT RAD RSTH RSTHT

Fort Berthold Community College

PO Box 490
New Town, ND 58763
(701) 627-3665

Will confirm attendance and degree by phone or mail. Inquiry must include student's name, date of birth, social security number, years attended. Employers may obtain transcripts upon written request accompanied by a $2.00 fee and a signed release from the student.

A two-year institution newly admitted to NCES, with an enrollment of 200. Highest level of offering: one year but less than four years.
ACCREDITATIONS: NH

Fort Hays State University

600 Park Street
Hays, KS 67601-4099
(913) 628-4222
Fax (913) 628-4046

Will confirm attendance and degree by phone, fax or mail. Inquiry must include student's name, date of birth, social security number, years attended. Employers may obtain transcripts upon written request accompanied by a signed release from the student.

A comprehensive institution with no medical school, with an enrollment of 5,599. Highest level of offering: beyond master's but less than doctorate.
ACCREDITATIONS: NH MUS NUR RAD TED

Fort Lauderdale College

1040 Bayview Drive
Fort Lauderdale, FL 33304
(305) 568-1600
Fax (617) 262-4021

Will confirm attendance and degree by mail. Inquiry must include student's name social security number and release. Employers may obtain transcripts upon written request accompanied by a $2.00 fee and a signed release from the student.

A business school, with an enrollment of 1250. Highest level of offering: four or five year baccalaureate.
ACCREDITATIONS: SRCB

Fort Lewis College

Durango, CO 81301-3999
(303) 247-7350

Will confirm attendance and degree by phone or mail. Inquiry must include student's name, social security number, years attended. Employers may obtain transcripts upon written request accompanied by a $2.00 fee and a signed release from the student. Requests should be directed to: College Records Office.

A general baccalaureate institution, with an enrollment of 3,984. Highest level of offering: four or five year baccalaureate.
ACCREDITATIONS: NH BUS MUS TED

Fort Scott Community College

2108 South Horton
Fort Scott, KS 66701
(316) 223-2700

Will confirm attendance and degree by mail. Inquiry must include student's name, social security number, dates attended, release. Employers may obtain transcripts upon written request accompanied by a $1.00 fee and a signed release from the student.

A multiprogram two-year institution, with an enrollment of 2,100. Highest level of offering: one year but less than four years.
ACCREDITATIONS: NH

Fort Steilacoom Community College

9401 Farwest Drive South West
Tacoma, WA 98498
(206) 964-6622

Will confirm attendance and degree by phone or mail. Inquiry must include student's name, date of birth, social security number. Only students may obtain transcripts.

A multiprogram two-year institution, with an enrollment of 6,865. Highest level of offering: one year but less than four years.
ACCREDITATIONS: NW ADVET DH

Fort Valley State College

1005 State College Drive
Fort Valley, GA 31030
(912) 825-6282

Will confirm attendance and degree by phone or mail. Inquiry must include student's name or maiden name (if applicable), social security number, years attended. Employers may obtain transcripts upon written request accompanied by a $1.00 fee and a signed release from the student.

A general baccalaureate institution, with an enrollment of 2,360. Highest level of offering: master's.
ACCREDITATIONS: SC ADVET ENGT TED

Fort Wayne Bible College

(See Taylor University-Fort Wayne)

Fox Valley Technical College

PO Box 2277
Appleton, WI 54913-2277
(414) 735-5712

Will confirm attendance and degree by phone or mail. Inquiry must include student's name, date of birth, social security number. Employers may obtain transcripts upon written request accompanied by a $1.00 fee and a signed release from the student.

A multiprogram two-year institution, with an enrollment of 3,601. Highest level of offering: one year but less than four years.
ACCREDITATIONS: NH ADNUR DA RSTHT

Framingham State College

100 State Street
Framingham, MA 01701
(508) 626-4545
Fax (508) 626-4592

Will confirm attendance and degree by phone, fax or mail. Inquiry must include student's name, social security number, years attended. Employers may obtain transcripts upon written request accompanied by a $1.00 fee and a signed release from the student.

A comprehensive institution with no medical school, with an enrollment of 5,653. Highest level of offering: master's.
ACCREDITATIONS: EH DIET

Francis Marion College

Box F-7500
Florence, SC 29501
(803) 661-1362

Will confirm attendance and degree by mail. Inquiry must include student's name and social security number. Employers may obtain transcripts upon written request accompanied by a $2.00 fee and a signed release from the student. Requests should be directed to: Registrar's Office.

A general baccalaureate institution, with an enrollment of 3,232. Highest level of offering: master's.
ACCREDITATIONS: SC

Franciscan School of Theology

1712 Euclid Avenue
Berkeley, CA 94709
(510) 848-5232

Will confirm attendance and degree by phone or mail. Inquiry must include student's name and dates attended. Employers may obtain transcripts upon written request accompanied by a $3.00 fee and a signed release from the student.

A school of philosophy, religion and theology, with an enrollment of 100. Highest level of offering: master's.
ACCREDITATIONS: WC THEOL

Frank Phillips College

PO Box 5118
Borger, TX 79008
(806) 274-5311 Ext. 40

Will confirm attendance and degree by phone or mail. Inquiry must include student's name, social security number, years attended. Employers may obtain transcripts upon written request accompanied by a $3.00 fee and a signed release from the student.

A multiprogram two-year institution, with an enrollment of 959. Highest level of offering: one year but less than four years.
ACCREDITATIONS: SC

Franklin and Marshall College

PO Box 3003
Lancaster, PA 17604-3003
(717) 291-3931

Will confirm attendance and degree by phone or mail. Inquiry must include student's name, social security number, years attended. Employers may obtain transcripts upon written request accompanied by a signed release from the student.

A general baccalaureate institution, with an enrollment of 1,800. Highest level of offering: four or five year baccalaureate.

ACCREDITATIONS: M

Franklin College

(Formerly CareerCom Junior College and formerly Draughon's College of Business)
218 North Fifth Street
Paducah, KY 42001
(502) 443-8478
Fax (502) 442-5329

Will confirm attendance and degree by phone or mail. Inquiry must include student's name, date of birth, social security number, years attended. Employers may obtain transcripts upon written request accompanied by a signed release from the student.

A multiprogram two-year institution, with an enrollment of 150. Highest level of offering: one year but less than four years.

ACCREDITATIONS: JRCB

Franklin College of Indiana

501 East Monroe
Franklin, IN 46131
(317) 738-8018

Will confirm attendance and degree by phone or mail. Inquiry must include student's name, date of birth, social security number. Employers may obtain transcripts upon written request accompanied by a $2.00 fee and a signed release from the student.

A general baccalaureate institution, with an enrollment of 850. Highest level of offering: four or five year baccalaureate.

ACCREDITATIONS: NH

Franklin Institute of Boston

41 Berkeley Street
Boston, MA 02116
(617) 423-4630 Ext. 23
Fax (617) 482-3706

Will confirm attendance and degree by phone or mail. Inquiry must include student's name, field of study, years attended. Employers may obtain transcripts upon written request accompanied by a $2.00 fee and a signed release from the student.

A multiprogram two-year institution, with an enrollment of 449. Highest level of offering: one year but less than four years.

ACCREDITATIONS: ABET NEASC

Franklin Pierce College

College Road
PO Box 60
Rindge, NH 03461
(603) 899-5111 Ext. 230
Fax (603) 899-6448

Will confirm attendance and degree by phone, fax or mail. Inquiry must include student's name, social security number, years attended. Employers may obtain transcripts upon written request accompanied by a $3.00 fee and a signed release from the student.

A general baccalaureate institution, with an enrollment of 1,795. Highest level of offering: four or five year baccalaureate.

ACCREDITATIONS: EH

Franklin Pierce Law Center

2 White Street
Concord, NH 03301
(603) 228-1541
Fax (603) 225-4016 or 224-3342

Will confirm attendance and degree by phone, fax or mail. Inquiry must include student's name and social security number. Employers may obtain transcripts upon written request accompanied by a $1.00 fee per copy, $3.00 for certified copy and a signed release from the student.

A law school, with an enrollment of 350. Highest level of offering: first professional degree.

ACCREDITATIONS: LAW

Franklin University

201 South Grant Avenue
Columbus, OH 43215
(614) 224-6237
Fax (614) 221-7723

Will confirm attendance and degree by mail or fax. Inquiry must include student's name, date of birth, social security number. Employers may obtain transcripts upon written request accompanied by a signed release from the student. Requests should be directed to: Records Office.

A business school, with an enrollment of 3,700. Highest level of offering: four or five year baccalaureate.

ACCREDITATIONS: NH ENGT

Fransciscan University of Steubenville

Fransciscan Way
Steubenville, OH 43952
(614) 283-6207
Fax (614) 283-6472

Will confirm attendance and degree by phone, fax or mail. Inquiry must include student's name and social security number. Employers may obtain transcripts upon written request accompanied by a $2.00 fee and a signed release from the student.

A general baccalaureate institution, with an enrollment of 1676 Highest level of offering: master's

Frederick Community College

7932 Opossumtown Pike
Frederick, MD 21701
(301) 846-2433
Fax (301) 846-2498

Will confirm attendance and degree by phone, fax or mail. Inquiry must include student's name and social security number. Employers may obtain transcripts upon written request accompanied by a $2.00 fee and a signed release from the student. Direct inquiries to Registrar's Office.

A multiprogram two-year institution, with an enrollment of 4,255. Highest level of offering: one year but less than four years.

ACCREDITATIONS: M DA

Free Will Baptist Bible College

3606 West End Avenue
Nashville, TN 37205
(615) 383-1340 Ext. 2232

Will confirm attendance and degree by phone or mail. Inquiry must include student's name, SSN, years attended. Employers may obtain transcripts upon written request accompanied by a $2.00 fee and a signed release from the student.

A school of philosophy, religion and theology, with an enrollment of 281. Highest level of offering: master's.

ACCREDITATIONS: BI

Freed–Hardeman University

158 East Main
Henderson, TN 38340
(901) 989-6000
Fax (901) 989-6065

Will confirm attendance and degree by phone or mail. Inquiry must include student's name, social security number, release. Employers may obtain transcripts upon written request accompanied by a $5.00 fee and a signed release from the student.

A general baccalaureate institution, with an enrollment of 1,247. Highest level of offering: master's.

ACCREDITATIONS: SC SW TED

Freeman Academy

748 South Main Box 1000
Freeman, SD 57029
(605) 925-4237

Will confirm attendance and degree by phone or mail. Inquiry must include student's name and social security number. Employers may obtain transcripts upon written request accompanied by a $2.00 fee and a signed release from the student.

A multiprogram two-year institution, with an enrollment of 54. Highest level of offering: one year but less than four years.

ACCREDITATIONS: NH

Fresno City College

1101 East University Avenue
Fresno, CA 93741
(209) 442-4600

Will confirm attendance and degree by mail. Inquiry must include student's name, social security number, release. Requests should be directed to: Records. Employers may obtain transcripts upon written request accompanied by a $2.00 fee and a signed release from the student.

A multiprogram two-year institution, with an enrollment of 18,000. Highest level of offering: one year but less than four years.
ACCREDITATIONS: WJ DH RAD RSTH

Fresno Pacific College

1717 South Chestnut Avenue
Fresno, CA 93702
(209) 453-2037

Will confirm attendance and degree by phone or mail. Inquiry must include student's name, date of birth, social security number. Employers may obtain transcripts upon written request accompanied by a $4.00 fee and a signed release from the student.

A Christian liberal arts/graduate education, with an enrollment of 1,450. Highest level of offering: master's.
ACCREDITATIONS: WC

Friends University

Registrar's Office
2100 University
Wichita, KS 67213
(316) 261-5860
Fax (316) 263-1092

Will confirm attendance and degree by phone, fax or mail. Inquiry must include student's name, social security number, years attended. Employers may obtain transcripts upon written request accompanied by a $3.00 fee and a signed release from the student.

A general baccalaureate institution, with an enrollment of 1,510. Highest level of offering: four or five year baccalaureate.
ACCREDITATIONS: NH MUS TED

Friends World College

239 Montauk Highway
South Hampton, NY 11968
(516) 283-4000

Will confirm attendance and degree by phone or mail. Inquiry must include student's name. Employers may obtain transcripts upon written request accompanied by a $5.00 fee and a signed release from the student.

A general baccalaureate institution, with an enrollment of 238. Highest level of offering: four or five year baccalaureate.
ACCREDITATIONS: M NY

Front Range Community College

Records Center
3645 West 112th Avenue
Westminster, CO 80030
(303) 466-8811 Ext. 313

Will confirm enrollment and degree by phone or mail. Inquiry must include student's name and social security number. Employers may obtain transcripts upon written request accompanied by a $2.00 fee and a signed release from the student. Requests should be directed to: Records Department.

A multiprogram two-year institution, with an enrollment of 7,500. Highest level of offering: one year but less than four years.
ACCREDITATIONS: NH RSTH

Frostburg State University

Frostburg, MD 21532-1099
(301) 689-4346

Will confirm attendance and degree by phone or mail. Inquiry must include student's name and social security number. Employers may obtain transcripts upon written request accompanied by a signed release from the student. Attn: Registrar's Office.

A comprehensive institution with no medical school, with an enrollment of 4,937. Highest level of offering: master's.
ACCREDITATIONS: M TED

Fuller Theological Seminary

135 N. Oakland
Pasadena, CA 91101
(818) 584-5408
Fax (818) 584-5449

Will confirm attendance and degree by phone or mail. Inquiry must include student's name, date of birth, social security number. Employers may obtain transcripts upon written request accompanied by a $3.00 fee and a signed release from the student. Attn: Registrar's Office.

A school of philosophy, religion and theology, with an enrollment of 2,800. Highest level of offering: doctorate.
ACCREDITATIONS: WC CLPSY THEOL MFCD

Fullerton Community College

321 East Chapman Avenue
Fullerton, CA 92634
(714) 992-7577 Ext. 7568

Will confirm attendance and degree by mail. Inquiry must include student's name, date of birth, social security number, years attended. Employers may obtain transcripts upon written request accompanied by a $2.00 fee and a signed release from the student. Requests should be directed to: Admissions & Records Department.

A multiprogram two-year institution, with an enrollment of 21,000. Highest level of offering: one year but less than four years.
ACCREDITATIONS: WJ

Fulton–Montgomery Community College

Johnstown, NY 12095
(518) 762-4651 Ext. 222

Will confirm attendance and degree by phone or mail. Inquiry must include student's name and social security number. Employers may obtain transcripts upon written request accompanied by a $3.00 fee and a signed release from the student.

A multiprogram two-year institution, with an enrollment of 2,300. Highest level of offering: two years but less than four years.
ACCREDITATIONS: M NY

Furman University

Greenville, SC 29613
(803) 294-2031
Fax (803) 294-3001

Will confirm attendance and degree by fax or mail. Inquiry must include student's name, maiden name (if any), social security number, years attended. Employers may obtain transcripts upon written request accompanied by a $2.00 fee and a signed release from the student. Requests should be directed to: Registrar's Office.

A comprehensive institution with no medical school, with an enrollment of 2,969. Highest level of offering: master's.
ACCREDITATIONS: SC MUS

G

Gadsden State Community College

PO Box 227
Gadsden, AL 35902-0227
(205) 549-8261

Will confirm attendance and degree by phone or mail. Inquiry must include student's name, social security number, years attended. Employers may obtain transcripts upon written request by student accompanied by a $3.00 fee.

A multiprogram two-year institution, with an enrollment of 586. Highest level of offering: one year but less than four years.
ACCREDITATIONS: SV

Gadsden State Community College

PO Box 227
Gadsden, AL 35902-0227
(205) 549-8261

Will confirm attendance and degree by phone or mail. Inquiry must include student's name, social security number, years attended. Employers may obtain transcripts upon written request by student accompanied by a $3.00 fee.

A multiprogram two-year institution, with an enrollment of 5,088. Highest level of offering: one year but less than four years.
ACCREDITATIONS: SC ADNUR MLTAD RAD

Gainesville College

Box 1358
Gainesville, GA 30503
(404) 535-6244

Will confirm attendance and degree by phone or mail. Inquiry must include student's name and social security number. Employers may obtain transcripts upon written request accompanied by a signed release from the student.

A multiprogram two-year institution, with an enrollment of 2,350. Highest level of offering: one year but less than four years.
ACCREDITATIONS: SC

Gallaudet University

800 Florida Avenue North East
Washington, DC 20002
(202) 651-5393

Will confirm attendance and degree by
phone or mail. Inquiry must include student's name. Employers may obtain transcripts upon written request accompanied
by a $5.00 fee and a signed release from the
student.

A comprehensive institution with no medi-
cal school, with an enrollment of 2,300.
Highest level of offering: doctorate.
ACCREDITATIONS: M AUD SW TED

Galveston College

4015 Avenue Q
Galveston, TX 77550
(409) 763-6551

Will confirm attendance and degree by mail
or phone. Inquiry must include student's
name, social security number, and release.
Employers may obtain transcripts upon
written request accompanied by a $2.00 fee
and a signed release from the student.

A multiprogram two-year institution, with
an enrollment of 2,001. Highest level of offering: one year but less than four years.
ACCREDITATIONS: SC ADNUR NMT RAD
SURGT

Gannon University

(Villa Maria College merged with the
above)
University Square
Erie, PA 16541
(814) 871-7612

Will confirm attendance and degree by
phone or mail. Inquiry must include student's name, date of birth, social security
number, and years attended. Employers
may obtain transcripts upon written request
accompanied by a signed release from the
student.

A comprehensive institution with no medi-
cal school, with an enrollment of 4,185.
Highest level of offering: master's.
ACCREDITATIONS: M APCP ENG MAC RAD
RSTH SW TED

Gannon University

(Formerly Villa Maria College)
University Square
Erie, PA 16541
(814) 838-1966 Ext. 304

Will confirm attendance and degree by
phone or mail. Inquiry must include student's name, date of birth, social security
number, years attended. Employers may obtain transcripts upon written request accompanied by a signed release from the student.

A health institution, with an enrollment of
4,491. Highest level of offering: four or
five year baccalaureate.
ACCREDITATIONS: M DIET NUR

Garden City Community College

801 Campus Drive
Garden City, KS 67846
(316) 276-9605
Fax (316) 276-9630

Will confirm attendance and degree by
phone, fax or mail. Inquiry must include
student's name and social security number.
Employers may obtain transcripts upon

written request accompanied by a signed release from the student.

A multiprogram two-year institution, with
an enrollment of 1,800. Highest level of offering: one year but less than four years.
ACCREDITATIONS: NH ADNUR

Gardner–Webb College

PO Box 997
Boiling Springs, NC 28017
(704) 434-2361 Ext. 222

Will confirm attendance and degree by
phone or mail. Inquiry must include student's name, social security number, and
years attended. Employers may obtain transcripts upon written request accompanied
by a $3.00 fee and a signed release from the
student.

A general baccalaureate institution, with an
enrollment of 1,885. Highest level of offering: master's.
ACCREDITATIONS: SC ADNUR MUS

Garland County Community College

Mid-America Blvd.
100 College Drive
Hot Springs, AR 71913
(501) 767-9371 Ext. 202
Fax (501) 767-6896

Will confirm attendance and degree by
phone or mail. Inquiry must include student's name and social security number.
Employers may obtain transcripts upon
written request accompanied by a signed release from the student.

A multiprogram two-year institution, with
an enrollment of 2,209. Highest level of offering: two years but less than four years.
ACCREDITATIONS: NH ADNUR MLTAD

Garrett Community College

PO Box 151
McHenry, MD 21541
(301) 387-6666 Ext. 140
Fax (301) 387-7469

Will confirm attendance and degree by
phone or mail. Inquiry must include student's name, SSN, release. Employers may
obtain transcripts upon written request accompanied by a $2.00 fee and a signed re-
lease from the student.

A multiprogram two-year institution, with
an enrollment of 649. Highest level of
offering: one year but less than four years.
ACCREDITATIONS: M ADVET

Garrett Evangelical Theological Seminary

2121 Sheridan Road
Evanston, IL 60201
(708) 866-3907

Will confirm attendance and degree by
phone or mail. Inquiry must include student's name, social security number, and
years attended. Employers may obtain transcripts upon written request accompanied
by a $2.00 fee and a signed release from the
student.

A school of philosophy, religion and theology, with an enrollment of 512. Highest
level of offering: doctorate.
ACCREDITATIONS: NCA THEOL

Gaston College

201 Highway 321 South
Dallas, NC 28034
(704) 922-6233
Fax (704) 922-6440

Will confirm attendance and degree by mail
or fax. Inquiry must include student's name,
date of birth, social security number, years
attended, and release. Employers may obtain transcripts upon written request accompanied by a signed release from the student.
Attn: Records & Transcripts.

A multiprogram two-year institution, with
an enrollment of 3,800. Highest level of offering: one year but less than four years.
ACCREDITATIONS: SC ENGT

Gateway Community College

108 North 40th Street
Phoenix, AZ 85034
(602) 275-8500
Fax (602) 392-5329

Will confirm attendance by phone or mail
and degree by mail only. Inquiry must include student's name and social security
number. Employers may obtain transcripts
upon written request accompanied by a
$2.00 fee and a signed release from the stu-
dent. Requests should be directed to:
Registrar's Office.

A multiprogram two-year institution, with
an enrollment of 8,547. Highest level of offering: two years but less than four years.
ACCREDITATIONS: NCA ADNUR RAD RSTH
RSTHT

Gateway Technical College

3520–30th Avenue
Kenosha, WI 53142-1690
(414) 656-6900

Will confirm attendance and degree by
phone or mail. Inquiry must include student's name, social security number, and
years attended. Employers may obtain transcripts upon written request accompanied
by a $3.00 fee and a signed release from the
student.

A multiprogram two-year institution, with
an enrollment of 6,175. Highest level of offering: one year but less than four years.
ACCREDITATIONS: NH ADNUR DA MAC

Gavilan College

5055 Santa Teresa Boulevard
Gilroy, CA 95020
(408) 848-4735

Will confirm attendance by mail. Inquiry
must include student's name and social security number. Employers may obtain transcripts upon written request accompanied
by a $2.00 fee and a signed release from the
student.

A multiprogram two-year institution, with
an enrollment of 4,300. Highest level of offering: one year but less than four years.
ACCREDITATIONS: WJ

Gem City College

PO Box 179
Quincy, IL 62306
(217) 222-0391

Will confirm attendance and degree by
phone or mail. Inquiry must include stu-

dent's name. Employers may obtain transcripts upon written request accompanied by a $5.00 fee and a signed release from the student.

A multiprogram two-year institution, with an enrollment of 190. Highest level of offering: one year but less than four years.

ACCREDITATIONS: MAAB NATTS

Genesee Community College

One College Road
Batavia, NY 14020
(716) 343-0055 Ext. 218
Fax (716) 343-0055 Ext. 203

Will confirm attendance and degree by phone, fax or mail. Inquiry must include student's name and social security number. Employers may obtain transcripts upon written request accompanied by a $1.00 fee , student's social security number, and a signed release from the student.

A multiprogram two-year institution, with an enrollment of 2,700. Highest level of offering: one year but less than four years.

ACCREDITATIONS: M ADNUR NY

Geneva College

College Avenue
Beaver Falls, PA 15010
(412) 847-6600

Will confirm attendance and degree by phone or mail. Inquiry must include student's name and social security number. Employers may obtain transcripts upon written request accompanied by a $2.00 fee and a signed release from the student.

A general baccalaureate institution, with an enrollment of 1,225. Highest level of offering: master's degree.

ACCREDITATIONS: M

George Corley Wallace State Community College at Dothan

Route 6, Box 62
Dothan, AL 36303
(205) 983-3521 Ext. 302

Will confirm attendance and degree by phone or mail. Inquiry must include student's name, social security number, and years attended. Employers may obtain transcripts upon written request accompanied by a signed release from the student.

A multiprogram two-year institution, with an enrollment of 3,600. Highest level of offering: one year but less than four years.

ACCREDITATIONS: SC ADNUR MLTAD RSTH

George C. Wallace State Community College–Hanceville

Hanceville, AL 35077
(205) 352-6403 Ext. 129

Will confirm attendance and degree by phone. Inquiry must include student's name and years attended. Employers may obtain transcripts upon written request accompanied by a $2.00 fee and a signed release from the student.

A multiprogram two-year institution, with an enrollment of 3,735. Highest level of offering: one year but less than four years.

ACCREDITATIONS: SC ADNUR DA MLTAD MRT RAD

George Fox College

Newberg, OR 97132
(503) 538-8383
Fax (503) 538-7234

Will confirm attendance and degree by phone or mail. Inquiry must include student's name and social security number. Employers may obtain transcripts upon written request accompanied by a $2.00 fee and a signed release from the student.

A general baccalaureate institution, with an enrollment of 1,223. Highest level of offering: doctorate.

ACCREDITATIONS: NW MUS

George Mason University

4400 University Drive
Fairfax, VA 22030
(703) 993-2440

Will confirm attendance and degree by phone or mail. Inquiry must include student's name, social security number, and years attended. Employers may obtain transcripts upon written request accompanied by a $2.00 fee and a signed release from the student.

A comprehensive institution with no medical school, with an enrollment of 15,534. Highest level of offering: doctorate.

ACCREDITATIONS: SC LAW NUR SW TED

George Wallace State Community College at Selma

PO Drawer 1049
Selma, AL 36702
(205) 875-2634 Ext. 36
Fax (205) 874-7116

Will confirm attendance and degree by phone or mail. Inquiry must include student's name, date of birth, and social security number. Employers may obtain transcripts upon written request accompanied by a $2.00 fee and a signed release from the student.

A multiprogram two-year institution, with an enrollment of 1,801. Highest level of offering: one year but less than four years.

ACCREDITATIONS: SC ADNUR PNUR RSTH

George Washington University

2121 I Street
Washington, DC 20052
(202) 994-4909

Will confirm attendance and degree by phone or mail. Inquiry must include student's name and social security number. Employers may obtain transcripts upon written request accompanied by a $3.00 fee and a signed release from the student.

A doctoral-level institution with a medical school, with an enrollment of 19,322. Highest level of offering: doctorate.

ACCREDITATIONS: M ANEST APCP AUD BUS CLPSY ENG HSA IPSY LAW MED MT TED MUS NMT RTT SP

George Williams College

Box 1476
Downers Grove, IL 60515
(708) 964-3100

Records are maintained at the above address. Will confirm attendance and degree by phone or mail. Inquiry must include student's name and social security number. Employers may obtain transcripts upon written request accompanied by a $10.00 fee and a signed release from the student. Money order or certified checks accepted.

Georgetown College

400 East College Street
Georgetown, KY 40324
(502) 863-8024

Will confirm attendance and degree by phone or mail. Inquiry must include student's name, date of birth, social security number, and years attended. Employers may obtain transcripts upon written request accompanied by a $2.00 fee and a signed release from the student.

A general baccalaureate institution, with an enrollment of 1,290. Highest level of offering: master's.

ACCREDITATIONS: SACS

Georgetown University

37th & O Street North West
Washington, DC 20057
(202) 687-4020

Will confirm attendance and degree by mail or phone. Inquiry must include student's name, date of birth, social security number, and years attended. Employers may obtain transcripts upon written request accompanied by a $2.00 fee and a signed release from the student. Requests should be directed to: Registrar's Office.

A doctoral-level institution with a medical school, with an enrollment of 11,861. Highest level of offering: doctorate.

ACCREDITATIONS: M BUS DENT LAW MED MIDWF NMT NUR OMA

Georgia College

Campus Box 23
Milledgeville, GA 31061
(912) 453-5234

Will confirm attendance and degree by mail. Inquiry must include student's name, date of birth, and social security number. Employers may obtain transcripts upon written request accompanied by a $1.00 fee and a signed release from the student.

A comprehensive institution with no medical school, with an enrollment of 4,830. Highest level of offering: beyond master's but less than doctorate.

ACCREDITATIONS: SC MUS NUR TED

Georgia Institute of Technology Main Campus

225 North Avenue
Atlanta, GA 30332-0312
(404) 894-4151
Fax (404) 853-0167

Will confirm attendance and degree by phone or mail. Inquiry must include student's name and social security number. Employers may obtain transcripts upon written request accompanied by a $3.00 fee and a signed release from the student. Requests should be directed to: Records Office.

An engineering school, with an enrollment of 11,258. Highest level of offering: doctorate.

ACCREDITATIONS: SC ARCH BUS ENG

Georgia Military College

201 East Greene Street
Milledgeville, GA 31061
(912) 453-3481 Ext. 228

Will confirm attendance and degree by mail. Inquiry must include student's name, social security number, years attended, and release. Employers may obtain transcripts upon written request accompanied by a $2.00 fee and a signed release from the student.

A multiprogram two-year institution, with an enrollment of 1,403. Highest level of offering: one year but less than four years.
ACCREDITATIONS: SC

Georgia Southern College

Office of Registrar
Landrum-Box 8092
Statesboro, GA 30460
(912) 681-5152

Will confirm attendance and degree by phone or mail. Inquiry must include student's name, social security number and years attended. Employers may obtain transcripts upon written request accompanied by a signed release from the student.

A comprehensive institution with no medical school, with an enrollment of 12,500. Highest level of offering: beyond master's but less than doctorate.
ACCREDITATIONS: SC BUS ENGT MUS TED NUR

Georgia Southwestern College

Wheatley Street
Americus, GA 31709
(912) 928-1331
Fax (912) 928-1630

Will confirm attendance and degree by phone, fax or mail. Inquiry must include student's name, date of birth, and social security number. Employers may obtain transcripts upon written request accompanied by a $1.00 fee and a signed release from the student.

A comprehensive institution with no medical school, with an enrollment of 2,302. Highest level of offering: beyond master's but less than doctorate.
ACCREDITATIONS: SC ADNUR NUR TED

Georgia State University

University Plaza
Atlanta, GA 30303-3084
(404) 651-3207

Will confirm attendance and degree by phone or mail. Inquiry must include student's name, date of birth, social security number, and years attended. Employers may obtain transcripts upon written request accompanied by a $2.00 fee and a signed release from the student. Requests should be directed to: Records.

A doctoral-level institution with no medical school, with an enrollment of 21,366. Highest level of offering: doctorate.
ACCREDITATIONS: SC ART BUS CLPSY COPSY DIET HSA IPSY LAW MFCD MT MUS TED NUR PTA RSTH RSTHT SCPSY SW

Georgian Court College

Lakewood Avenue
Lakewood, NJ 08701
(908) 364-2200 Ext. 228
Fax (908) 367-3920

Will confirm attendance and degree by phone or mail. Inquiry must include student's name and social security number. Employers may obtain transcripts upon written request accompanied by a $2.00 fee and a signed release from the student.

A general baccalaureate institution, with an enrollment of 2,000. Highest level of offering: master's.
ACCREDITATIONS: M

Germanna Community College

PO Box 339
Locust Grove, VA 22508
(703) 423-1333
Fax (703) 423-1009

Will confirm attendance and degree by phone, fax or mail. Inquiry must include student's name, social security number and release. Employers may obtain transcripts upon written request accompanied by a signed release from the student.

A multiprogram two-year institution, with an enrollment of 2,500. Highest level of offering: one year but less than four years.
ACCREDITATIONS: SC ADNUR

Gettysburg College

North Washington Street
Gettysburg, PA 17325
(717) 337-6240

Will confirm attendance and degree by phone or mail. Inquiry must include student's name and years attended. Employers may obtain transcripts upon written request accompanied by a signed release from the student.

A general baccalaureate institution, with an enrollment of 1,951. Highest level of offering: four or five year baccalaureate.
ACCREDITATIONS: M

Glassboro State College

Glassboro, NJ 08028
(609) 863-6032

Will confirm attendance and degree by phone or mail. Inquiry must include student's name and social security number. Employers may obtain transcripts upon written request accompanied by a $5.00 fee and a signed release from the student. Requests should be directed to: Registrar's Office.

A general baccalaureate institution, with an enrollment of 7,000. Highest level of offering: beyond master's but less than doctorate.
ACCREDITATIONS: M MUS TED

Glen Oaks Community College

62249 Shimmel Road
Centreville, MI 49032
(616) 467-9945 Ext. 243
Fax (616) 467-4114

Will confirm attendance and degree by phone, fax or mail. Inquiry must include student's name, social security number release. Employers may obtain transcripts upon written request accompanied by a $2.00 fee and a signed release from the student.

A multiprogram two-year institution, with an enrollment of 1,300. Highest level of offering: one year but less than four years.
ACCREDITATIONS: NH

Glendale Community College

1500 North Verdugo Road
Glendale, CA 91208
(818) 240-1000 Ext. 284
Fax (818) 549-9436

Will confirm attendance and degree by mail. Inquiry must include student's name and date of birth, release. Employers may obtain transcripts upon written request accompanied by a $2.00 fee and a signed release from the student.

A multiprogram two-year institution, with an enrollment of 15,553. Highest level of offering: two years but less than four years.
ACCREDITATIONS: WJ

Glendale Community College

6000 West Olive Avenue
Glendale, AZ 85302
(602) 435-3319

Will confirm attendance and degree by phone or mail. Inquiry must include student's name, social security number, years attended, release. Employers may obtain transcripts upon written request accompanied by a $5.00 fee and a signed release from the student.

A multiprogram two-year institution, with an enrollment of 18,240. Highest level of offering: one year but less than four years.
ACCREDITATIONS: NH ADNUR ENGT

Glenville State College

200 High Street
Glenville, WV 26351
(304) 462-7361 Ext. 117
Fax (304) 462-4407

Will confirm attendance and degree by phone or mail. Inquiry must include student's name. Employers may obtain transcripts upon written request accompanied by a $3.00 fee and a signed release from the student.

A general baccalaureate institution, with an enrollment of 2,186. Highest level of offering: four or five year baccalaureate.
ACCREDITATIONS: NH TED

Gloucester County College

Tanyard Road–Deptford PO
Sewell, NJ 08080
(609) 468-5000 Ext. 282

Will confirm attendance and degree by phone or mail. Inquiry must include student's name and social security number. Employers may obtain transcripts upon written request accompanied by a $2.00 fee and a signed release from the student.

A multiprogram two-year institution, with an enrollment of 4,110. Highest level of offering: one year but less than four years.

ACCREDITATIONS: M ADNUR NMT RSTHT

GMI Engineering and Management Institute

1700 West Third Avenue
Flint, MI 48504
(313) 762-7862

Will confirm attendance and degree by phone or mail. Inquiry must include student's name and social security number. Employers may obtain transcripts upon written request accompanied by a $3.00 fee and a signed release from the student.

An engineering school, with an enrollment of 2,998. Highest level of offering: master's.

ACCREDITATIONS: NH ENG

Goddard College

Plainfield, VT 05667
(802) 454-8311 Ext. 13
Fax (802) 454-8017

Will confirm attendance and degree by phone or mail. Inquiry must include student's name. Employers may obtain transcripts upon written request accompanied by a $5.00 fee and a signed release from the student.

A comprehensive institution with no medical school, with an enrollment of 308. Highest level of offering: master's.

ACCREDITATIONS: EH

God's Bible School and College

1810 Young Street
Cincinnati, OH 45210
(513) 721-7944 Ext. 251

Will confirm attendance and degree by phone or mail. Inquiry must include student's name and years attended. Employers may obtain transcripts upon written request accompanied by a $2.00 fee and a signed release from the student.

A bachelor's or higher institution newly admitted to NCES, with an enrollment of 210. Highest level of offering: four or five year baccalaureate.ACCREDITATIONS: BI

Gogebic Community College

East 4946 Jackson Road
Ironwood, MI 49938
(906) 932-4231 Ext. 212

Will confirm attendance and degree by phone. Inquiry must include student's name and social security number. Employers may obtain transcripts upon written request accompanied by a $3.00 fee and a signed release from the student.

A multiprogram two-year institution, with an enrollment of 1,600. Highest level of offering: one year but less than four years.

ACCREDITATIONS: NH

Golden Gate Baptist Theological Seminary

Strawberry Point
Mill Valley, CA 94941
(415) 388-8080 Ext. 209

Will confirm attendance and degree by phone or mail. Inquiry must include student's name. Employers may obtain transcripts upon written request accompanied by a $5.00 fee and a signed release from the student.

A school of philosophy, religion and theology, with an enrollment of 571. Highest level of offering: doctorate.

ACCREDITATIONS: WC MUS THEOL

Golden Gate University

536 Mission Street
San Francisco, CA 94105
(415) 442-7273

Will confirm attendance and degree by phone or mail. Inquiry must include student's name, date of birth, and social security number. Employers may obtain transcripts upon written request accompanied by a $5.00 fee and a signed release from the student. Requests should be directed to: Records Office.

A comprehensive institution with no medical school, with an enrollment of 10,441. Highest level of offering: doctorate.

ACCREDITATIONS: WC LAW

Golden Valley Lutheran College

3718 Macalaster Drive NE
Minneapolis, MN 55421
(612) 788-7616

Records are maintained at the above address. Will confirm attendance and degree by phone or mail. Inquiry must include student's name and social security number. Employers may obtain transcripts upon written request accompanied by a $5.00 fee and a signed release from the student. Requests should be directed to: Registrar's Office.

Golden West College

15744 Golden West
Huntington Beach, CA 92647
(714) 895-8121

Will confirm attendance and degree by phone or mail. Inquiry must include student's name and date of birth. Employers may obtain transcripts upon written request accompanied by a $2.00 fee and a signed release from the student.

A multiprogram two-year institution, with an enrollment of 15,079. Highest level of offering: one year but less than four years.

ACCREDITATIONS: WJ ADNUR

Goldey Beacom College

4701 Limestone Road
Wilmington, DE 19808
(302) 998-8814
Fax (302) 998-3467

Will confirm attendance and degree by mail or fax. Inquiry must include student's name, social security number, and years attended. Employers may obtain transcripts upon written request accompanied by a signed release from the student.

A business school, with an enrollment of 1,918. Highest level of offering: four or five year baccalaureate.

ACCREDITATIONS: M

Gonzaga University

Spokane, WA 99258-0001
(509) 328-4220 Ext. 3192
Fax (509) 484-2818

Will confirm attendance and degree by phone, fax or mail. Inquiry must include student's name, date of birth, social security number, and years attended. Employers may obtain transcripts upon written request accompanied by a $5.00 fee and a signed release from the student. Requests should be directed to: Registrar's Office.

A comprehensive institution with no medical school, with an enrollment of 3,930. Highest level of offering: doctorate.

ACCREDITATIONS: NW ANEST LAW NUR TED ENG BUS

Gordon College

103 College Drive
Barnesville, CA 30204
(404) 358-5022
Fax (404) 358-3031

Will confirm attendance and degree by phone or mail. Inquiry must include student's name, social security number, and years attended. Employers may obtain transcripts upon written request accompanied by a signed release from the student.

A multiprogram two-year institution, with an enrollment of 1,365. Highest level of offering: one year but less than four years.

ACCREDITATIONS: SC ADNUR

Gordon College

255 Grapevine Road
Wenham, MA 01984
(508) 927-2300 Ext. 4242
Fax (508) 921-1398

Will confirm attendance and degree by phone or mail. Inquiry must include student's name, date of birth, and years attended. Employers may obtain transcripts upon written request accompanied by a $3.00 fee and a signed release from the student.

A general baccalaureate institution, with an enrollment of 1,200. Highest level of offering: four or five year baccalaureate.

ACCREDITATIONS: EH MUS CSWE

Gordon Junior College

419 College Drive
Barnesville, GA 30204
(404) 358-5022 Ext. 4250

Will confirm attendance and degree by phone or mail. Inquiry must include student's name, maiden name (if any), social security number, and years attended. Employers may obtain transcripts upon written request accompanied by a signed release from the student.

A multiprogram two-year institution, with an enrollment of 1,500. Highest level of offering: one year but less than four years.

ACCREDITATIONS: SC ADNUR

Gordon–Conwell Theological Seminary

130 Essex Street
South Hamilton, MA 01982
(508) 468-7111 Ext. 380

Will confirm attendance and degree by phone or mail. Inquiry must include student's name. Employers may obtain transcripts upon written request accompanied by a $3.00 fee and a signed release from the student.

A school of religion and theology, with an enrollment of 470. Highest level of offering: doctorate.
ACCREDITATIONS: THEOL

Goshen Biblical Seminary

3003 Benham Avenue
Elkhart, IN 46517
(219) 295-3726 Ext. 200

Will confirm attendance and degree by mail or phone. Inquiry must include student's name. Employers may obtain transcripts upon written request accompanied by a $3.00 fee and a signed release from the student.

A school of philosophy, religion and theology, with an enrollment of 108. Highest level of offering: master's.
ACCREDITATIONS: NCA THEOL

Goshen College

1700 South Main
Goshen, IN 46526
(219) 535-7517
Fax (219) 535-7660

Will confirm attendance and degree by phone, fax or mail. Inquiry must include student's name and years attended. Employers may obtain transcripts upon written request accompanied by a $2.00 fee and a signed release from the student.

A general baccalaureate institution, with an enrollment of 1,152. Highest level of offering: four or five year baccalaureate.
ACCREDITATIONS: NH NUR SW TED

Goucher College

Dulaney Dalley Road
Towson, MD 21204
(301) 337-6090
Fax (301) 337-6123

Will confirm attendance and degree by phone, fax or mail. Inquiry must include student's name and years attended. Employers may obtain transcripts upon written request accompanied by a $2.00 fee and a signed release from the student.

A general baccalaureate institution, with an enrollment of 964. Highest level of offering: master's.
ACCREDITATIONS: M

Governors State University

Governors Highway and Stuenkel Road
University Park, IL 60466
(708) 534-5000 Ext. 2148

Will confirm attendance and degree by phone or mail. Inquiry must include student's name, social security number, and years attended. Employers may obtain tran-

scripts upon written request accompanied by a $2.00 fee and a signed release from the student. Requests should be directed to: Registrar's Office.

A comprehensive institution with no medical school, with an enrollment of 5,000. Highest level of offering: master's.
ACCREDITATIONS: NH HSA MT NUR

Grace Bible College

1011 Aldon Street South West Box 910
Grand Rapids, MI 49509
(616) 538-2330
Fax (616) 538-0599

Will confirm attendance and degree by phone or mail. Inquiry must include student's name. Employers may obtain transcripts upon written request accompanied by a $2.00 fee and a signed release from the student.

A specialized school, with an enrollment of 100. Highest level of offering: four or five year baccalaureate.
ACCREDITATIONS: NCA BI

Grace College

200 Seminary Drive
Winona Lake, IN 46590
(219) 372-5100

Will confirm attendance and degree by phone or mail. Inquiry must include student's name. Employers may obtain transcripts upon written request accompanied by a $2.00 fee and a signed release from the student.

A general baccalaureate institution, with an enrollment of 845. Highest level of offering: four or five year baccalaureate.
ACCREDITATIONS: NH

Grace College of the Bible

1515 South 10th Street
Omaha, NE 68108
(402) 449-2811

Will confirm attendance and degree by phone or mail. Inquiry must include student's name and date of birth. Employers may obtain transcripts upon written request accompanied by a signed release from the student.

A school of Biblical studies, with an enrollment of 272. Highest level of offering: four or five year baccalaureate.
ACCREDITATIONS: AABC

Graceland College

Lamoni, IA 50140
(515) 784-5000 Ext. 5222
Fax (515) 784-5474

Will confirm attendance and degree by phone, fax or mail. Inquiry must include student's name, maiden name (if any), date of birth, and social security number. Employers may obtain transcripts upon written request accompanied by a $3.00 fee and a signed release from the student.

A general baccalaureate institution, with an enrollment of 1,600. Highest level of offering: four or five year baccalaureate.
ACCREDITATIONS: NH NUR TED

Graduate Theological Union

2400 Ridge Road
Berkeley, CA 94709
(510) 649-2400

Will confirm attendance and degree by mail. Inquiry must include student's name. Employers may obtain transcripts upon written request accompanied by a $3.00 fee and a signed release from the student.

A school of philosophy, religion and theology, with an enrollment of 372. Highest level of offering: doctorate.
ACCREDITATIONS: WC THEOL

Graham Bible College

PO Box 1630
Bristol, VA 24203
(615) 968-4201

Will confirm attendance and degree by phone or mail. Inquiry must include student's name and social security number. Employers may obtain transcripts upon written request accompanied by a $2.00 fee and a signed release from the student.

A bachelor's or higher institution newly admitted to NCES, with an enrollment of 31. Highest level of offering: four or five year baccalaureate.

Grambling State University

PO Box 589
Grambling, LA 71245
(318) 274-2385

Will confirm attendance and degree by phone or mail. Inquiry must include student's name, date of birth, and social security number. Employers may obtain transcripts upon written request accompanied by a $2.00 fee and a signed release from the student. Attn: Enrollment Center.

A general baccalaureate institution, with an enrollment of 6,200. Highest level of offering: master's.
ACCREDITATIONS: SC MUS TED SW

Grand Canyon University

PO Box 11097
Phoenix, AZ 85061
(602) 589-2850
Fax (602) 589-2895

Will confirm attendance and degree by phone, fax or mail. Inquiry must include student's name, date of birth, and social security number. Employers may obtain transcripts upon written request accompanied by a $3.00 fee and a signed release from the student.

A general baccalaureate institution, with an enrollment of 1,800. Highest level of offering: four or five year baccalaureate.
ACCREDITATIONS: NH NUR

Grand Rapids Baptist College and Seminary

1001 E Beltline Ave N E
Grand Rapids, MI 49505
(616) 949-5300 Ext. 264

Will confirm attendance and degree by phone or mail. Inquiry must include student's name and social security number. Employers may obtain transcripts upon written request accompanied by a $3.00 fee and a signed release from the student.

A general baccalaureate institution, with an enrollment of 925. Highest level of offering: doctorate.

ACCREDITATIONS: NH

Grand Rapids Junior College

143 Bostwick Avenue North East
Grand Rapids, MI 49503
(616) 771-4000
Fax (616) 456-4886

Will confirm attendance and degree by mail or fax. Inquiry must include student's name, date of birth, social security number, and release. Employers may obtain transcripts upon written request accompanied by a $2.00 fee and a signed release from the student.

A multiprogram two-year institution, with an enrollment of 8,913. Highest level of offering: one year but less than four years.

ACCREDITATIONS: NH ADNUR DA DH MUS PNUR RAD

Grand Valley State University

Allendale, MI 49401
(616) 895-3327
Fax (616) 895-3180

Will confirm attendance and degree by phone, fax or mail. Inquiry must include student's name and social security number. Employers may obtain transcripts upon written request accompanied by a $3.00 fee and a signed release from the student. Requests should be directed to: Records Office.

A comprehensive institution with no medical school, with an enrollment of 12,565. Highest level of offering: master's.

ACCREDITATIONS: NH ART CHM MUS NUR SW PTA NCATE ABET

Grand View College

1200 Grand View Avenue
Des Moines, IA 50316
(515) 263-2818

Will confirm attendance and degree by phone or mail. Inquiry must include student's name. Employers may obtain transcripts upon written request accompanied by a $3.00 fee and a signed release from the student.

A general baccalaureate institution, with an enrollment of 1,323. Highest level of offering: four or five year baccalaureate.

ACCREDITATIONS: NH NUR

Grantham College of Engineering

10570 Humbolt
Los Alamitos, CA 90720
(213) 493-4421

Will confirm attendance and degree by phone or mail. Inquiry must include student's name, release. Employers may obtain transcripts upon written request accompanied by a $5.00 fee and a signed release from the student.

A bachelor's or higher institution newly admitted to NCES, with an enrollment of 975. Highest level of offering: four or five year baccalaureate.

ACCREDITATIONS: NHSC

Gratz College

Old York Road & Melrose Ave.
Melrose, PA 19126
(215) 635-7300

Will confirm attendance and degree by mail. Inquiry must include student's name, years attended, release. Employers may obtain transcripts upon written request accompanied by a $4.00 fee and a signed release from the student.

A specialized school, with an enrollment of 309. Highest level of offering: master's.

ACCREDITATIONS: M

Grays Harbor College

1620 Edward P. Smith Drive
Aberdeen, WA 98520
(206) 532-9020 Ext. 262
Fax (206) 532-6716

Will confirm attendance and degree by phone, fax or mail. Inquiry must include student's name, social security number, release. Employers may obtain transcripts upon written request accompanied by a signed release from the student.

A multiprogram two-year institution, with an enrollment of 3,200. Highest level of offering: one year but less than four years.

ACCREDITATIONS: NW

Grayson County College

6101 Grayson Drive
Denison, TX 75020
(903) 465-6030 Ext. 733
Fax (903) 463-5284

Will confirm attendance and degree by phone, fax or mail. Inquiry must include student's name and social security number. Employers may obtain transcripts upon written request accompanied by a $2.00 fee and a signed release from the student. An additional $5.00 fee will be charged for faxed copies.

A multiprogram two-year institution, with an enrollment of 3,500. Highest level of offering: one year but less than four years.

ACCREDITATIONS: SC ADNUR DA

Great Lakes Bible College

6211 W. Willow Highway
Lansing, MI 48917
(517) 321-0242 Ext. 24

Will confirm attendance and degree by phone or mail. Inquiry must include student's name and social security number. Employers may obtain transcripts upon written request accompanied by a $5.00 fee and a signed release from the student.

A school of philosophy, religion and theology, with an enrollment of 141. Highest level of offering: four or five year baccalaureate.

ACCREDITATIONS: BI

Great Lakes Junior College

(Formerly Saginaw Business School)
310 South Washington Ave
Saginaw, MI 48607
(517) 755-3444
Fax (517) 752-3453

Will confirm attendance and degree by phone, fax or mail. Inquiry must include student's name and social security number. Employers may obtain transcripts upon written request accompanied by a signed release from the student.

A two-year institution. with an enrollment of 2,227. Highest level of offering: associates degree.

ACCREDITATIONS: JRCB CCA

Greater Hartford Community College

61 Woodland Street
Hartford, CT 06105
(203) 520-7828

Will confirm attendance and degree by phone or mail. Inquiry must include student's name and social security number. Employers may obtain transcripts upon written request accompanied by a signed release from the student.

A multiprogram two-year institution, with an enrollment of 3,430. Highest level of offering: one year but less than four years.

ACCREDITATIONS: EH ADNUR

Greater New Haven State Technical College

88 Bassett Road
North Haven, CT 06473
(203) 234-3325
Fax (203) 234-0693

Will confirm attendance and degree by mail or fax. Inquiry must include student's name, social security number, and release. Employers may obtain transcripts upon written request accompanied by a signed release from the student.

A multiprogram two-year institution, with an enrollment of 1,125. Highest level of offering: one year but less than four years.

ACCREDITATIONS: EV ENGT ABET

Green Mountain College

16 College Street
Poultney, VT 05764
(802) 287-9313 Ext. 215

Will confirm attendance and degree by phone or mail. Inquiry must include student's name and years attended. Employers may obtain transcripts upon written request accompanied by a $2.00 fee and a signed release from the student.

A multiprogram four-year institution, with an enrollment of 600. Highest level of offering: four or five year baccalaureate.

ACCREDITATIONS: EH MAC

Green River Community College

12401 South East 320th Street
Auburn, WA 98002
(206) 833-9111 Ext. 248
Fax (206) 939-5135

Will confirm attendance by phone, fax or mail. Inquiry must include student's name and social security number. Employers may obtain transcripts upon written request accompanied by a signed release from the student.

A multiprogram two-year institution, with an enrollment of 7,000. Highest level of offering: one year but less than four years.
ACCREDITATIONS: NW PTAA

Greenfield Community College

1 College Drive
Greenfield, MA 01301
(413) 774-3131 Ext. 234
Fax (413) 773-5129

Will confirm attendance and degree by phone or mail. Inquiry must include student's name, date of birth, and years attended. Employers may obtain transcripts upon written request accompanied by a $2.00 fee and a signed release from the student.

A multiprogram two-year institution, with an enrollment of 2,364. Highest level of offering: one year but less than four years.
ACCREDITATIONS: EH ADNUR

Greensboro College

815 West Market Street
Greensboro, NC 27401-1875
(919) 271-2207
Fax (919) 271-2237

Will confirm attendance and degree by phone or mail. Inquiry must include student's name and years attended. Employers may obtain transcripts upon written request accompanied by a $2.00 fee and a signed release from the student.

A general baccalaureate institution, with an enrollment of 1,078. Highest level of offering: four or five year baccalaureate.
ACCREDITATIONS: SC

Greenville College

315 E. College Avenue
Greenville, IL 62246
(618) 664-1840 Ext. 216
Fax (618) 664-4084

Will confirm attendance and degree by phone, fax or mail. Inquiry must include student's name, social security number, and years attended. Employers may obtain transcripts upon written request accompanied by a $3.00 fee and a signed release from the student.

A general baccalaureate institution, with an enrollment of 750. Highest level of offering: four or five year baccalaureate.
ACCREDITATIONS: NH TED

Greenville Technical College

PO Box 5616 Station B
Greenville, SC 29606
(803) 239-3014

Will confirm attendance and degree by mail or phone. Inquiry must include student's name, social security number, years attended, self addressed stamped envelope. Employers may obtain transcripts upon written request accompanied by a $3.00 fee and a signed release from the student.

A multiprogram two-year institution, with an enrollment of 7,000. Highest level of offering: two years but less than four years.
ACCREDITATIONS: SC ADNUR DA DH ENGT MLTAD OPTT PTAA RAD RSTH SURGT

Griffin College

2505 2nd Avenue
Seattle, WA 98121
(206) 728-0987 Ext. 103

Will confirm attendance and degree by phone or mail. Inquiry must include student's name, social security number, and years attended. Employers may obtain transcripts upon written request accompanied by a $5.00 fee and a signed release from the student.

A general baccalaureate institution, with an enrollment of 1,472. Highest level of offering: four or five year baccalaureate.
ACCREDITATIONS: NW

Grinnell College

PO Box 805
Grinnell, IA 50112
(515) 269-3450

Will confirm attendance and degree by phone or mail. Inquiry must include student's name, social security number, and years attended. Employers may obtain transcripts upon written request accompanied by a $1.00 fee and a signed release from the student.

A general baccalaureate institution, with an enrollment of 1,270. Highest level of offering: four or five year baccalaureate.
ACCREDITATIONS: NH

Grossmont College

8800 Grossmont College Drive
El Cajon, CA 92020
(619) 589-0800

Will confirm attendance and degree by mail. Inquiry must include student's name, date of birth, social security number, years attended, and release. Employers may obtain transcripts upon written request accompanied by a $2.00 fee and a signed release from the student.

A multiprogram two-year institution, with an enrollment of 15,000. Highest level of offering: one year but less than four years.
ACCREDITATIONS: WJ RSTH

Grove City College

Grove City, PA 16127
(412) 458-2172

Will confirm attendance and degree by phone or mail. Inquiry must include student's name, date of birth, social security number, and years attended. Employers may obtain transcripts upon written request accompanied by a $2.00 fee and a signed release from the student.

A general baccalaureate institution, with an enrollment of 2,184. Highest level of offering: four or five year baccalaureate.
ACCREDITATIONS: M

Gruss Girls School

15 Isabel Avenue
Spring Valley, NY 10977
(914) 354-0874

Will confirm attendance by phone or mail. Inquiry must include student's name, date of birth, and social security number. Employers may obtain transcripts upon

written request accompanied by a signed release from the student.

A specialized non-degree granting institution, with an enrollment of 228. Highest level of offering: undergraduate non-degree granting.
ACCREDITATIONS: NY

Guilford College

5800 West Friendly Avenue
Greensboro, NC 27410
(919) 292-5511 Ext. 132
Fax (919) 316-2951

Will confirm attendance and degree by phone or mail. Inquiry must include student's name. Employers may obtain transcripts upon written request accompanied by a $2.00 fee and a signed release from the student.

A general baccalaureate institution, with an enrollment of 1,636. Highest level of offering: four or five year baccalaureate.
ACCREDITATIONS: SC

Guilford Technical Community College

PO Box 309
Jamestown, NC 27282
(919) 292-1101 Ext. 2234
Fax (919) 454-2510

Will confirm attendance and degree by phone or mail. Inquiry must include student's name, social security number, and years attended. Requests should be directed to: Records Office. Employers may obtain transcripts upon written request accompanied by a $1.00 fee and a signed release from the student.

A multiprogram two-year institution, with an enrollment of 7,350. Highest level of offering: one year but less than four years.
ACCREDITATIONS: SC DA DH ENGT

Gulf Coast Community College

5230 West Highway 98
Panama City, FL 32401
(904) 769-1551 Ext. 4893

Will confirm attendance and degree by mail. Inquiry must include student's name, social security number, years attended, and release. Employers may obtain transcripts upon written request accompanied by a signed release from the student. Requests should be directed to: Admission's Office.

A multiprogram two-year institution, with an enrollment of 7,000. Highest level of offering: one year but less than four years.
ACCREDITATIONS: SC DA RSTHT

Gupton Jones College of Funeral Service

5141 Snapfinger Woods Drive
Decatur GA 30035
(404) 761-3118

Will confirm attendance and degree by phone or mail. Inquiry must include student's name. Employers may obtain transcripts upon written request accompanied by a $2.00 fee and a signed release from the student.

A two-year institution with an enrollment of 225. Highest level of offering: one year but less than four years.
ACCREDITATIONS: FUSER

Gustavus Adolphus College

Saint Peter, MN 56082
(507) 933-7495
Fax (507) 933-7041

Will confirm attendance and degree by phone or mail. Inquiry must include student's name and years attended. Employers may obtain transcripts upon written request accompanied by a $2.00 fee and a signed release from the student. Requests should be directed to: Registrar's Office.

A general baccalaureate institution, with an enrollment of 2,214. Highest level of offering: four or five year baccalaureate.
ACCREDITATIONS: NH MUS NUR TED

Gwynedd–Mercy College

Sumneytown Pike
Gwynedd Valley, PA 19437
(215) 646-7300 Ext. 437

Will confirm attendance and degree by phone or mail. Inquiry must include student's name, social security number, and years attended. Employers may obtain transcripts upon written request by student and a $3.00 fee. Requests should be directed to: Registrar's Office.

A health institution, with an enrollment of 2,107. Highest level of offering: master's.
ACCREDITATIONS: M ADNUR MLTAD MRT NMT NUR RAD RSTH RSTHT RTT

H

Hadar Hatorah Rabbinical Seminary

824 Eastern Parkway
Brooklyn, NY 11213
(718) 735-0250

Will confirm attendance and degree by mail. Inquiry must include student's name, social security number. Employers may obtain transcripts upon written request accompanied by a signed release from the student. Requests should be directed to: Registrar's Office.

A bachelor's or higher institution newly admitted to NCES, with an enrollment of 50. Highest level of offering: four or five year baccalaureate.
ACCREDITATIONS: 3IC

Hagerstown Business College

1050 Crestwood Drive
Hagerstown, MD 21740
(301) 739-2670 Ext. 28

Will confirm attendance and degree by phone or mail. Inquiry must include student's name, date of birth, social security number, years attended. Employers may obtain transcripts upon written request accompanied by a $2.00 fee and a signed release from the student. Requests should be directed to: Registrar's Office.

A single program two-year institution, with an enrollment of 259. Highest level of offering: one year but less than four years.
ACCREDITATIONS: JRCB

Hagerstown Junior College

11400 Robinwood Drive
Hagerstown, MD 21742
(301) 790-2800 Ext. 239
Fax (301) 790-2800 Ext 386

Will confirm attendance and degree by phone, fax or mail. Inquiry must include student's name, social security number. Employers may obtain transcripts upon written request accompanied by a $2.00 fee and a signed release from the student. Requests should be directed to: Records Office.

A multiprogram two-year institution, with an enrollment of 3,200. Highest level of offering: one year but less than four years.
ACCREDITATIONS: M RAD

Hahnemann University

Broad and Vine
Philadelphia, PA 19102-1192
(215) 448-7601

Will confirm attendance and degree by phone or mail. Inquiry must include student's name and social security number. Employers may obtain transcripts upon written request accompanied by a $3.00 fee and a signed release from the student. Requests should be directed to: Registrar's Office.

A medical school, with an enrollment of 2,069. Highest level of offering: doctorate.
ACCREDITATIONS: M ADNUR APCP CLPSY MED MLTAD MT NUR PTA RAD RSTH MFCD

Halifax Community College

PO Drawer 809
Weldon, NC 27890
(919) 536-2551 Ext. 221

Will confirm attendance and degree by phone or mail. Inquiry must include student's name, date of birth, social security number, years attended. Employers may obtain transcripts upon written request accompanied by a signed release from the student. Requests should be directed to: Registrar's Office.

A multiprogram two-year institution, with an enrollment of 1,050. Highest level of offering: one year but less than four years.
ACCREDITATIONS: SC MLTAD

Hamilton College

Clinton, NY 13323
(315) 859-4637
Fax (315) 859-4632

Will confirm attendance and degree by phone, fax or mail. Inquiry must include student's name, date of birth, social security number, years attended. Employers may obtain transcripts upon written request accompanied by a $2.00 fee and a signed release from the student. Requests should be directed to: Registrar's Office.

A general baccalaureate institution, with an enrollment of 1,626. Highest level of offering: four or five year baccalaureate.
ACCREDITATIONS: M NY

Hamilton Technical College

1011 East 53rd Street
Davenport, IA 52807
(319) 386-3570 Ext. 51

Will confirm attendance and degree by phone or mail. Inquiry must include student's name and years attended. Employers may obtain transcripts upon written request accompanied by a $2.00 fee and a signed release from the student.

A multiprogram two-year institution, with an enrollment of 447. Highest level of offering: one year but less than four years.
ACCREDITATIONS: NATTS

Hamline University

1536 Hewitt Avenue
Saint Paul, MN 55104
(612) 641-2209
Fax (612) 641-2956

Will confirm attendance and degree by phone, fax or mail. Inquiry must include student's name, social security number, years attended. Requests should be directed to: Registrar's Office. Employers may obtain transcripts upon written request accompanied by a $3.00 fee and a signed release from the student.

A general baccalaureate institution, with an enrollment of 1,854. Highest level of offering: master's.
ACCREDITATIONS: NH LAW MUS TED

Hampden–Sydney College

Hampden–Sydney, VA 23943
(804) 223-6274 or 223-6203

Will confirm attendance and degree by phone or mail. Inquiry must include student's name and social security number. Requests should be directed to: Student Aid & Records Office. Employers may obtain transcripts upon written request accompanied by a $1.00 fee and a signed release from the student.

A private Presbyterian general baccalaureate institution, with an enrollment of 944. Highest level of offering: four or five year baccalaureate, four year liberal arts.
ACCREDITATIONS: SACS

Hampshire College

Amherst, MA 01002
(413) 549-4600 Ext. 421

Will confirm attendance and degree by phone or mail. Inquiry must include student's name, date of entry. Employers may obtain transcripts upon written request by student. Requests should be directed to: Central Records Office.

A general baccalaureate institution, with an enrollment of 1,049. Highest level of offering: four or five year baccalaureate.
ACCREDITATIONS: EH

Hampton University

Hampton, VA 23668
(804) 727-5323

Will confirm attendance and degree by mail. Inquiry must include student's name, social security number, years attended. Employers may obtain transcripts upon written request accompanied by a $3.00 fee and a signed release from the student.

Requests should be directed to: Registrar's Office.

A comprehensive institution with no medical school, with an enrollment of 5,342. Highest level of offering: master's.
ACCREDITATIONS: SC ARCH MUS NUR TED SW

Hannibal–La Grange College

2800 Palmyra Road
Hannibal, MO 63401
(314) 221-3675 Ext. 255

Will confirm attendance and degree by phone or mail. Inquiry must include student's name, date of birth, social security number, years attended. Employers may obtain transcripts upon written request accompanied by a $4.00 fee and a signed release from the student. Requests should be directed to: Registrar's Office.

A general baccalaureate institution, with an enrollment of 950. Highest level of offering: four or five year baccalaureate.
ACCREDITATIONS: NH

Hanover College

Hanover, IN 47243
(812) 866-7051
Fax (812) 866-2164

Will confirm attendance and degree by phone, fax or mail. Inquiry must include student's name, date of birth, social security number. Employers may obtain transcripts upon written request accompanied by a $5.00 fee and a signed release from the student. Requests should be directed to: Registrar's Office.

A general baccalaureate institution, with an enrollment of 1,070. Highest level of offering: four or five year baccalaureate.
ACCREDITATIONS: NH

Harcum Junior College

Bryn Mawr, PA 19010
(215) 526-6007
Fax (215) 526-6086

Will confirm attendance and degree by phone, fax or mail. Inquiry must include student's name, social security number, years attended. Employers may obtain transcripts upon written request accompanied by a $2.00 fee and a signed release from the student. Requests should be directed to: Registrar's Office.

A multiprogram two-year institution, with an enrollment of 784. Highest level of offering:two years but less than four years.
ACCREDITATIONS: M ADVET DA MLTAD PTAA

Hardbarger Junior College of Business

c/o Department
109 E. Jones Street
Raleigh, NC 27611
(919) 733-3952

Records are now held at Archives in Raleigh, NC, 27604. Will confirm attendance and degree by mail. Inquiry must include student's name, social security number, dates attended, release. Employers may obtain transcripts upon written request accompanied by a $3.00 fee and a signed release from the student. Requests should be directed to: Registrar's Office.

A multiprogram two-year institution, with

an enrollment of 710. Highest level of offering: one year but less than four years.
ACCREDITATIONS: JRCB

Hardin–Simmons University

H. S. U. Station Drawer G
Abilene, TX 79698
(915) 670-1200

Will confirm attendance and degree by phone or mail. Inquiry must include student's name, social security number, years attended. Requests should be directed to: Registrar's Office. Employers may obtain transcripts upon written request accompanied by a $5.00 fee and a signed release from the student.

A comprehensive institution with no medical school, with an enrollment of 1,709. Highest level of offering: master's.
ACCREDITATIONS: SC MUS NUR TED SW

Harding Graduate School of Religion

1000 Cherry Road
Memphis, TN 38117
(901) 761-1353
Fax (901) 761-1358

Will confirm attendance and degree by phone or mail. Inquiry must include student's name, social security number. Requests should be directed to: Registrar's Office. Employers may obtain transcripts upon written request accompanied by a $2.00 fee and a signed release from the student.

A school of philosophy, religion and theology, with an enrollment of 159. Highest level of offering: doctorate.
ACCREDITATIONS: SC

Harding University Main Campus

Box 766 Station A
Searcy, AR 72143
(501) 279-4403

Will confirm attendance and degree by phone or mail. Inquiry must include student's name, date of birth, social security number. Requests should be directed to: Registrar's Office. Employers may obtain transcripts upon written request accompanied by a $3.00 fee and a signed release from the student.

A general baccalaureate institution, with an enrollment of 3,341. Highest level of offering: master's.
ACCREDITATIONS: NH MUS NUR SW TED

Harford Community College

401 Thomas Run Road
Bel Air, MD 21014
(410) 836-4221 Ext. 222
Fax (410) 836-4169

Will confirm attendance and degree by mail. Inquiry must include student's name and social security number. Employers may obtain transcripts upon written request accompanied by a signed release from the student.

A multiprogram two-year institution, with an enrollment of 4,285. Highest level of offering: one year but less than four years.
ACCREDITATIONS: M ADNUR HT

Harrington Institute of Interior Design

410 S Michigan Avenue
Chicago, IL 60605
(312) 939-4975
Fax (312) 939-8005

Will confirm attendance and degree by phone, fax or mail. Inquiry must include student's name, social security number, years attended. Employers may obtain transcripts upon written request accompanied by a $3.00 fee and a signed release from the student.

A single program three and four year institution, with an enrollment of 395. Highest level of offering: four or five year baccalaureate.
ACCREDITATIONS: FIDER

Harris–Stowe State College

3026 Laclede Avenue
Saint Louis, MO 63103
(314) 533-3366

Will confirm attendance and degree by mail. Inquiry must include student's name, social security number, date of birth, dates attended. Employers may obtain transcripts upon written request accompanied by a $3.00 fee and a signed release from the student. Requests should be directed to: Registrar's Office.

A school of education, with an enrollment of 1,360. Highest level of offering: four or five year baccalaureate.
ACCREDITATIONS: NCA NCATE

Harrisburg Area Community College

3300 North Cameron Street Road
Harrisburg, PA 17110
(717) 780-2376
Fax (717) 780-2428

Will confirm attendance and degree by phone, fax or mail. Inquiry must include student's name, social security number, dates attended. Requests should be directed to: Records Office. Employers may obtain transcripts upon written request accompanied by a $3.00 fee and a signed release from the student.

A multiprogram two-year institution, with an enrollment of 8,123. Highest level of offering: one year but less than four years.
ACCREDITATIONS: M MLTAD RSTH RSTHT

Harry M. Ayers State Technical College

PO Box 1647
Anniston, AL 36202
(205) 831-4540 Ext. 6

Will confirm attendance and degree by mail. Inquiry must include student's name and social security number. Employers may obtain transcripts upon written request accompanied by a signed release from the student. Requests should be directed to: Registrar's Office.

A two-year institution newly admitted to NCES. Highest level of offering: one year but less than four years.
ACCREDITATIONS: SV

Hartford College for Women

1265 Asylum Avenue
Hartford, CT 06105
(203) 236-1215 Ext. 9

Will confirm attendance and degree by phone or mail. Inquiry must include student's name, social security number, years attended. Requests should be directed to: Registrar's Office. Employers may obtain transcripts upon written request accompanied by a $3.00 fee and a signed release from the student.

A multiprogram two-year institution, with an enrollment of 197. Highest level of offering: one year but less than four years.
ACCREDITATIONS: EH

Hartford Seminary

77 Sherman Street
Hartford, CT 06105
(203) 232-4451 Ext. 316

Will confirm attendance and degree by mail. Inquiry must include student's name and years attended. Employers may obtain transcripts upon written request accompanied by a $3.00 fee and a signed release from the student. Requests should be directed to: Registrar's Office.

A school of religion and theology, with an enrollment of 200. Highest level of offering: doctorate.
ACCREDITATIONS: EH THEOL

Hartford State Technical College

401 Flatbush Avenue
Hartford, CT 06106
(203) 527-4111 Ext. 165

Will confirm attendance and degree by mail. Inquiry must include student's name, social security number, years attended. Employers may obtain transcripts upon written request accompanied by a signed release from the student. Requests should be directed to: Registrar's Office.

A multiprogram two-year institution, with an enrollment of 1,858. Highest level of offering: one year but less than four years.
ACCREDITATIONS: EV ENGT

Hartnell College

Admissions Office
156 Homestead Avenue
Salinas, CA 93901
(408) 755-6711
Fax (408) 755-6751

Will confirm degree by mail or fax. Inquiry must include student's name, social security number, date of birth, years attended. Requests should be directed to: Registrar's Office. Employers may obtain transcripts upon written request accompanied by a $2.00 fee and a signed release from the student. Direct inquiries to Admissions Office.

A multiprogram two-year institution, with an enrollment of 7,455. Highest level of offering: one year but less than four years.
ACCREDITATIONS: WJ ADVET

Hartwick College

Oneonta, NY 13820
(607) 431-4460
Fax (607) 431-4318

Will confirm attendance and degree by phone, fax or mail. Inquiry must include student's name and years attended. Employers may obtain transcripts upon written request accompanied by a $3.00 fee and a signed release from the student. Requests should be directed to: Registrar's Office.

A general baccalaureate institution, with an enrollment of 1,441. Highest level of offering: four or five year baccalaureate.
ACCREDITATIONS: M NUR NY

Harvard University

1350 Massachuttes Avenue
Cambridge, MA 02138
(617) 495-1543

Will confirm attendance and degree by phone or mail. Inquiry must include student's name, type of degree, years attended. Employers may obtain transcripts upon written request accompanied by a $3.00 fee for first copy, $2.00 fee for addtional and a signed release from the student. Requests should be directed to: Registrar's Office.

A doctoral-level institution with a medical school, with an enrollment of 17,762. Highest level of offering: doctorate.
ACCREDITATIONS: EH ARCH BUS DENT ENG IPSY LAW LSAR MED PH TED THEOL

Harvey Mudd College

301 East 12th Street
Claremont, CA 91711
(714) 621-8090

Will confirm attendance and degree by phone or mail. Inquiry must include student's name, date of birth, social security number. Employers may obtain transcripts upon written request accompanied by a $2.00 fee and a signed release from the student. Requests should be directed to: Registrar's Office.

An engineering school, with an enrollment of 556. Highest level of offering: master's.
ACCREDITATIONS: WC ENG

Haskell Indian Junior College

Box 461282
Lawrence, KS 66046
(913) 749-8454
Fax (913) 749-8429

Will confirm attendance and degree by phone or mail. Inquiry must include student's name and social security number. Requests should be directed to: Admissions & Records Office. Employers may obtain transcripts upon written request accompanied by a signed release from the student.

A multiprogram two-year institution, with an enrollment of 774. Highest level of offering: one year but less than four years.
ACCREDITATIONS: NCA DA

Hastings College

Box 269
Hastings, NE 68902
(402) 463-2402 Ext. 306
Fax (402) 463-3002

Will confirm attendance and degree by phone, fax or mail. Inquiry must include student's name, date of birth, social security number. Requests should be directed to: Registrar's Office. Employers may obtain transcripts upon written request accompanied by a $2.00 fee and a signed release from the student.

A general baccalaureate institution, with an enrollment of 930. Highest level of offering: master of art in teaching.
ACCREDITATIONS: NH MUS TED

Haverford College

Haverford, PA 19041
(215) 896-1022

Will confirm attendance and degree by phone or mail. Inquiry must include student's name, social security number, years attended. Requests should be directed to: Registrar's Office. Employers may obtain transcripts upon written request accompanied by a $4.00 fee and a signed release from the student.

A general baccalaureate institution, with an enrollment of 1,100. Highest level of offering: four or five year baccalaureate.
ACCREDITATIONS: M

Hawaii Loa College

45-045 Kamehameha Highway
Kaneohe, HI 96744
(808) 233-3137
Fax (808) 233-3190

Will confirm attendance and degree by phone or mail. Inquiry must include student's name, social security number, years attended. Employers may obtain transcripts upon written request accompanied by a $3.00 fee and a signed release from the student. Requests should be directed to: Registrar's Office.

A general baccalaureate institution, with an enrollment of 510. Highest level of offering: four or five year baccalaureate.
ACCREDITATIONS: WASC

Hawaii Pacific College

1164 Bishop Street–Suite 200
Honolulu, HI 96813
(808) 544-0239
Fax (808) 544-1168

Will confirm attendance and degree by phone, fax or mail. Inquiry must include student's name, social security number, years attended, last date attended. Employers may obtain transcripts upon written request accompanied by a $4.00 fee and a signed release from the student.

A business school, with an enrollment of 5,000. Highest level of offering: four or five year baccalaureate.
ACCREDITATIONS: WC

Hawkeye Institute of Technology

Box 8015
Waterloo, IA 50704
(319) 296-2320 Ext. 208
Fax (319) 296-2874

Will confirm attendance and degree by phone, fax or mail. Inquiry must include student's name, date of birth, social security number, years attended. Employers may obtain transcripts upon written request accompanied by a $1.00 fee and a signed release from the student. Requests should be directed to: Enrollment Services Office.

A multiprogram two-year institution, with an enrollment of 1,844. Highest level of offering: two years but less than four years.
ACCREDITATIONS: NH DA DH ENGT MLTAD RSTHT

Haywood Community College

Freedlander Drive
Clyde, NC 28721
(704) 627-4504
Fax (704) 627-3606

Will confirm attendance and degree by phone, fax or mail. Inquiry must include student's name, social security number, years attended. Employers may obtain transcripts upon written request accompanied by a signed release from the student. Requests should be directed to: Registrar's Office.

A multiprogram two-year institution, with an enrollment of 1,350. Highest level of offering: two years but less than four years.
ACCREDITATIONS: SC

Heald Business College–San Francisco

1453 Mission Street
San Francisco, CA 94103
(415) 673-5500
Fax (415)626-1404

Will confirm attendance and degree by mail or fax. Inquiry must include student's name, date of birth, social security number, release. Employers may obtain transcripts upon written request accompanied by a $2.00 fee and a signed release from the student. Requests should be directed to: Dean's Office.

A two-year institution newly admitted to NCES. Highest level of offering: one year but less than four years.
ACCREDITATIONS: WJ

Heald Business College

684 El Paseo De Saratoga
San Jose, CA 95130
(408) 370-2400
Fax (408) 374-3224

Will confirm attendance and degree by mail or fax. Inquiry must include student's name, date of birth, social security number, release, years attended, degree. Employers may obtain transcripts upon written request accompanied by a signed release from the student.

A two-year institution newly admitted to NCES, with an enrollment of 450. Highest level of offering: one year but less than four years.
ACCREDITATIONS: WJ

Heald Business College–Fresno

255 West Bullard
Fresno, CA 93704
(209) 438-4222
Fax (209) 438-6368

Will confirm attendance and degree by mail or fax. Inquiry must include student's name, social security number, release. Employers may obtain transcripts upon written request accompanied by a signed release from the student.

A two-year institution newly admitted to NCES. Highest level of offering: one year but less than four years.
ACCREDITATIONS: WJ

Heald Business College–Sacramento

2910 Prospect Park Drive
Rancho Cordova, CA 95670-6005
(916) 638-1616
Fax (916) 638-1580

Will confirm attendance and degree by mail or fax. Inquiry must include student's name, social security number, years attended, release. Employers may obtain transcripts upon written request accompanied by a signed release from the student.

A two-year institution. Highest level of offering: one year but less than four years.
ACCREDITATIONS: WJ

Heald Business College–San Jose

684 El Paseo de Saratoga
San Jose, CA 95130
(408) 370-2400
Fax (408) 374-3224

Will confirm attendance and degree by mail or fax. Inquiry must include student's name, social security number, release. Employers may obtain transcripts upon written request accompanied by a signed release from the student. Requests should be directed to: Dean's Office.

A two-year institution newly admitted to NCES, with an enrollment of 960. Highest level of offering: one year but less than four years.
ACCREDITATIONS: WJ

Heald Business College–Santa Rosa

100 Professional Center Drive
Rohnert Park, CA 94928
(707) 584-5900
Fax (707) 584-3735

Will confirm attendance and degree by phone, fax or mail. Inquiry must include student's name and social security number. Employers may obtain transcripts upon written request accompanied by a signed release from the student. Requests should be directed to: Dean's Office.

A two-year institution newly admitted to NCES. Highest level of offering: one year but less than four years.
ACCREDITATIONS: WJ

Heald Business College–Walnut Creek

2085 North Broadway
Walnut Creek, CA 94596
(510) 933-2436
Fax (510) 933-1839

Will confirm attendance and degree by phone, fax or mail. Inquiry must include student's name and social security number. Employers may obtain transcripts upon written request accompanied by a signed release from the student. Requests should be directed to: Dean of Instruction.

A two-year institution newly admitted to NCES, with an enrollment of 200. Highest level of offering: one year but less than four years.
ACCREDITATIONS: WJ

Heald College-Martinez

2860 Howe Road
Martinez, CA 94553
(510) 228-9000 Ext. 10
Fax (510) 229-3792

Will confirm attendance and degree by phone, fax or mail. Inquiry must include student's name, social security number, and graduation date. Employers may obtain transcripts upon written request accompanied by a signed release from the student.

A two-year institution newly admitted to NCES, with an enrollment of 300. Highest level of offering: one year but less than four years.
ACCREDITATIONS: MJ

Heald College–Santa Clara

684 El Paso de Saratoga
San Jose, CA 95130
(408) 370-2400
Fax (408) 374-3224

Will confirm attendance and degree by mail or fax. Inquiry must include student's name, date of birth, social security number, release. Employers may obtain transcripts upon written request accompanied by a signed release from the student.

A two-year institution newly admitted to NCES, with an enrollment of 450. Highest level of offering: one year but less than four years.
ACCREDITATIONS: WJ

Heald Institute of Technology-San Francisco

150 4th Street
San Francisco, CA 94103
(415) 441-5555 Ext. 320
Fax (415) 543-9530

Will confirm attendance and degree by phone, fax or mail. Inquiry must include student's name, social security number, years attended. Employers may obtain transcripts upon written request accompanied by a $3.00 fee and a signed release from the student. Requests should be directed to: Transcript.

A single program two-year institution, with an enrollment of 895. Highest level of offering: four or five year baccalaureate.
ACCREDITATIONS: WJ

Health Science Center at Brooklyn

(See State University of New York)

Hebrew College

43 Hawes Street
Brookline, MA 02146
(617) 232-8710
Fax (617) 734-9769

Will confirm attendance and degree by phone or mail. Inquiry must include student's name and years attended. Employers may obtain transcripts upon written request accompanied by a $3.00 fee and a signed release from the student. Requests should be directed to: Registrar's Office.

A general baccalaureate institution, with an enrollment of 160. Highest level of offering: master's.

ACCREDITATIONS: EH

Hebrew Theological College

7135 North Carpenter Road
Skokie, IL 60077
(708) 674-7750
Fax (708) 674-6381

Will confirm attendance and degree by mail or fax. Inquiry must include student's name, date of birth, social security number and release. Requests should be directed to: Education Office. Employers may obtain transcripts upon written request accompanied by a signed release from the student.

A school of philosophy, religion and theology, with an enrollment of 235. Highest level of offering: doctorate.

ACCREDITATIONS: 3IC

Hebrew Union College California Branch

3077 University Avenue–32nd & Hoover Streets
Los Angeles, CA 90007-3796
(213) 749-3424

Will confirm attendance and degree by phone or mail. Inquiry must include student's name and social security number. Requests should be directed to: Registrar's Office. Employers may obtain transcripts upon written request accompanied by a $2.00 fee and a signed release from the student.

A school of philosophy, religion and theology, with an enrollment of 78. Highest level of offering: doctorate.

ACCREDITATIONS: WC

Hebrew Union College New York Branch

1 West Fourth Street
New York, NY 10012
(212) 674-5300 Ext. 220

Will confirm attendance and degree by phone or mail. Inquiry must include student's name and years attended. Requests should be directed to: Registrar's Office. Employers may obtain transcripts upon written request accompanied by a $2.00 fee and a signed release from the student.

A school of philosophy, religion and theology, with an enrollment of 100. Highest level of offering: doctorate.

ACCREDITATIONS: NY M

Hebrew Union College–Jewish Institute of Religion

3101 Clifton Avenue
Cincinnati, OH 45220
(513) 221-1875 Ext. 235
Fax (513) 221-0321

Will confirm attendance and degree by phone, fax or mail. Inquiry must include student's name and years attended. Employers may obtain transcripts upon written request accompanied by a $2.00 fee and a signed release from the student. Requests should be directed to: Registrar's Office.

A school of philosophy, religion and theology, with an enrollment of 140. Highest level of offering: doctorate.

ACCREDITATIONS: NH

Heidelberg College

310 East Market Street
Tiffin, OH 44883
(419) 448-2000 Ext. 2090
Fax (419) 448-2124

Will confirm attendance and degree by phone, fax or mail. Inquiry must include student's name and years attended. Employers may obtain transcripts upon written request accompanied by a $3.00 fee and a signed release from the student. Requests should be directed to: Registrar's Office.

A general baccalaureate institution, with an enrollment of 968. Highest level of offering: master's degree.

ACCREDITATIONS: NCA MUS

Hellenic College–Holy Cross Greek Orthodox School of Theology

50 Goddard Avenue
Brookline, MA 02146
(617) 731-3500 Ext. 261

Will confirm attendance and degree by phone or mail. Inquiry must include student's name, date of birth, social security number. Employers may obtain transcripts upon written request accompanied by a $2.00 fee and a signed release from the student. Requests should be directed to: Registrar's Office.

A school of philosophy, religion and theology, with an enrollment of 138. Highest level of offering: master's.

ACCREDITATIONS: EH THEOL

Henderson County Junior College

(See Trinity Community College)

Henderson State University

Box 7534
Arkadelphia, AR 71923-0001
(501) 246-5511 Ext. 3293

Will confirm attendance and degree by phone or mail. Inquiry must include student's name, date of birth, years attended. Employers may obtain transcripts upon written request accompanied by a $3.00 fee and a signed release from the student.

A comprehensive institution with no medical school, with an enrollment of 3,369. Highest level of offering: master's.

ACCREDITATIONS: NH MUS NUR TED

Hendrix College

Conway, AR 72032
(501) 450-1226
Fax (501) 450-1200

Will confirm attendance and degree by phone or mail. Inquiry must include student's name and years attended. Employers may obtain transcripts upon written request accompanied by a $1.00 fee and a signed release from the student.

A general baccalaureate institution, with an enrollment of 1,000. Highest level of offering: four or five year baccalaureate.

ACCREDITATIONS: NH MUS TED

Henry Ford Community College

5101 Evergreen Road
Dearborn, MI 48128-1495
(313) 845-9614

Will confirm attendance and degree by phone or mail. Inquiry must include student's name, date of birth, social security number. Employers may obtain transcripts upon written request accompanied by a $3.00 fee and a signed release from the student. Direct inquiries to Registrar's Office.

A multiprogram two-year institution, with an enrollment of 16,555. Highest level of offering: one year but less than four years.

ACCREDITATIONS: NH ADNUR MAC MRT RSTH

Heritage College

3240 Fort Road
Toppenish, WA 98948
(509) 865-2244 Ext. 1605
Fax (509) 865-4469 or 865-4144

Will confirm attendance and degree by phone, fax or mail. Inquiry must include student's name, date of birth, social security number. Employers may obtain transcripts upon written request accompanied by a $5.00 fee and a signed release from the student.

A comprehensive institution with no medical school, with an enrollment of 1,000. Highest level of offering: master's.

ACCREDITATIONS: NW

Herkimer County Community College

100 Reservoir Road
Herkimer, NY 13350
(315) 866-0300

Will confirm attendance and degree by phone or mail. Inquiry must include student's name and social security number. Employers may obtain transcripts upon written request accompanied by a $4.00 fee and a signed release from the student. Requests should be directed to: Registrar's Office.

A multiprogram two-year institution, with an enrollment of 2,011. Highest level of offering: one year but less than four years.

ACCREDITATIONS: M NY

Hesser College

3 Sundial Avenue
Manchester, NH 03103
(603) 668-6660 Ext. 230

Will confirm attendance and degree by
phone or mail. Inquiry must include student's name, date of birth, social security
number, years attended. Employers may
obtain transcripts upon written request accompanied by a $4.00 feesigned release
from the student.

A multiprogram two-year institution, with
an enrollment of 1,983. Highest level of offering: one year but less than four years.
ACCREDITATIONS: EV JRCB

Hesston College

Box 3000
Hesston, KS 67062
(316) 327-8231

Will confirm attendance and degree by
phone or mail. Inquiry must include student's name and social security number.
Employers may obtain transcripts upon
written request accompanied by a $2.00 fee
and a signed release from the student.

A multiprogram two-year institution, with
an enrollment of 501. Highest level of offering: two years but less than four years.
ACCREDITATIONS: NCA ADNUR

Hibbing Community Campus

(Formerly Arrowhead Community
College-Hibbing Campus)
1515 East 25th Street
Hibbing, MN 55746
(218) 262-6735

Will confirm attendance and degree by
phone or mail. Inquiry must include student's name, date of birth, social security
number, years attended. Employers may obtain transcripts upon written request accompanied by a signed release from the student.

A multiprogram two-year institution, with
an enrollment of 3,160. Highest level of offering: one year but less than four years.
ACCREDITATIONS: NH

High Point University

University Station, Montieu Avenue
High Point, NC 27262-3598
(919) 841-9205
Fax (919) 841-5123

Will confirm attendance and degree by
phone or mail. Inquiry must include student's name and years attended. Employers
may obtain transcripts upon written request
accompanied by a $2.00 fee and a signed
release from the student.

A general baccalaureate institution, with an
enrollment of 2,300. Highest level of offering: four or five year baccalaureate.
ACCREDITATIONS: SC TED

Highland Community College

Pearl City Road
Freeport, IL 61032
(815) 235-6121 Ext. 285
Fax (815) 235-6130

Will confirm attendance and degree by
phone, fax or mail. Inquiry must include
student's name and social security number.
Employers may obtain transcripts upon
written request accompanied by a $1.00 fee
and a signed release from the student.

A multiprogram two-year institution, with
an enrollment of 2,665. Highest level of offering: one year but less than four years.
ACCREDITATIONS: NH

Highland Community College

PO Box 68
Highland, KS 66035
(913) 442-3236 Ext. 222

Will confirm attendance and degree by
phone or mail. Inquiry must include student's name, social security number, years
attended. Employers may obtain transcripts
upon written request accompanied by a
$2.00 fee and a signed release from the stu-
dent.

A multiprogram two-year institution, with
an enrollment of 550. Highest level of offering: one year but less than four years.
ACCREDITATIONS: NH

Highland Park Community College

Glendale at Third
Highland Park, MI 48203
(313) 252-0475 Ext. 238

Will confirm attendance and degree by
phone or mail. Inquiry must include student's name, date of birth, social security
number, years attended. Employers may
obtain transcripts upon written request accompanied by a $2.00 fee and a signed re-
lease from the student.

A multiprogram two-year institution, with
an enrollment of 2,353. Highest level of offering: one year but less than four years.
ACCREDITATIONS: NH RSTH RSTHT

Highline Community College

PO Box 98000
Des Moines, WA 98198-9800
(206) 878-3710 Ext. 559

Will confirm attendance and degree by
phone or mail. Inquiry must include student's name and social security number.
Employers may obtain transcripts upon
written request accompanied by a signed release from the student.

A multiprogram two-year institution, with
an enrollment of 10,000. Highest level of
offering: one year but less than four years.
ACCREDITATIONS: NW ADNUR DA MAC
RSTH

Hilbert College

5200 South Park Avenue
Hamburg, NY 14075
(716) 649-7900 Ext. 241
Fax (716) 649-0702

Will confirm attendance and degree by
phone or mail. Inquiry must include student's name. Employers may obtain transcripts upon written request accompanied
by a $3.00 fee and a signed release from the
student.

A multiprogram two-year institution, with
an enrollment of 709. Highest level of offering: baccalaureate.
ACCREDITATIONS: M NY

Hill College

112 Lamar Drive
Hillsboro, TX 76645
(817) 582-2555 Ext. 214

Will confirm attendance and degree by
phone or mail. Inquiry must include student's name, date of birth, social security
number, years attended. Employers may
obtain transcripts upon written request accompanied by a $2.00 fee and a signed re-
lease from the student.

A multiprogram two-year institution, with
an enrollment of 1,159. Highest level of offering: one year but less than four years.
ACCREDITATIONS: SC

Hillsborough Community College

PO Box 31127
Tampa, FL 33631-3127
(813) 253-7004
Fax (813) 253-7136

Will confirm attendance and degree by
phone or mail. Inquiry must include student's name and social security number.
Employers may obtain transcripts upon
written request accompanied by a $2.00 fee
and a signed release from the student.
Requests should be directed to: Admissions
& Records Office.

A multiprogram two-year institution, with
an enrollment of 19,926. Highest level of
offering: one year but less than four years.
ACCREDITATIONS: SC NMT RAD RTT

Hillsdale College

33 East College
Hillsdale, MI 49242
(517) 437-7341 Ext. 360

Will confirm attendance and degree by
phone or mail. Inquiry must include student's name and date of birth. Employers
may obtain transcripts upon written request
accompanied by a $1.00 fee and a signed
release from the student.

A general baccalaureate institution, with an
enrollment of 1,033. Highest level of offering: four or five year baccalaureate.
ACCREDITATIONS: NH

Hillsdale Free Will Baptist College

PO Box 7208
Moore, OK 73153
(405) 794-6661 Ext. 201

Will confirm attendance and degree by phone or mail. Inquiry must include student's name and social security number. Employers may obtain transcripts upon written request accompanied by a $2.00 fee and a signed release from the student.

A specialized school, with an enrollment of 138. Highest level of offering: four or five year baccalaureate.

ACCREDITATIONS: 3IC

Hinds Community College

(Formerly Hinds Junior College and Utica Junior College)
Utica Campus
Utica, MS 39175
(601) 885-6062 Ext. 225

Will confirm attendance and degree by phone or mail. Inquiry must include student's name, social security number, release. Employers may obtain transcripts upon written request accompanied by a $2.00 fee and a signed release from the student.

A multiprogram two-year institution, with an enrollment of 640. Highest level of offering: one year but less than four years.

ACCREDITATIONS: SC

Hinds Community College District

(Formerly Hinds Junior College)
Raymond, MS 39154
(601) 857-3212

Will confirm attendance and degree by phone or mail. Inquiry must include student's name, social security number, years attended. Employers may obtain transcripts upon written request accompanied by a $2.00 fee and a signed release from the student. Requests should be directed to: Admissions & Records Office.

A multiprogram two-year institution, with an enrollment of 7,358. Highest level of offering: one year but less than four years.

ACCREDITATIONS: SC ADNUR DA MLTAD MRT RSTH RSTHT SURGT

Hiram College

Hiram, OH 44234
(216) 569-5210
Fax (216) 569-5211

Will confirm attendance and degree by phone, fax or mail. Inquiry must include student's name and social security number. Employers may obtain transcripts upon written request accompanied by a $3.00 fee ($5.00 if faxed) and a signed release from the student.

A general baccalaureate institution, with an enrollment of 924. Highest level of offering: four or five year baccalaureate.

ACCREDITATIONS: NH MUS TED

Hiwassee College

Madisonville, TN 37354
(615) 442-2001 Ext. 215

Will confirm attendance and degree by phone or mail. Inquiry must include student's name and social security number. Employers may obtain transcripts upon written request accompanied by a $2.00 fee and a signed release from the student.

A multiprogram two-year institution, with an enrollment of 543. Highest level of offering: one year but less than four years.

ACCREDITATIONS: SC

Hobart William Smith Colleges

Geneva, NY 14456
(315) 781-3650

Will confirm attendance and degree by phone or mail. Inquiry must include student's name, social security number, years attended. Employers may obtain transcripts upon written request accompanied by a $5.00 fee and a signed release from the student.

A general baccalaureate institution, with an enrollment of 1,933. Highest level of offering: four or five year baccalaureate.

ACCREDITATIONS: M NY

Hobe Sound Bible College

PO Box 1065
Hobe Sound, FL 33475
(407) 546-5534 Ext. 213

Will confirm attendance and degree by phone or mail. Inquiry must include student's name and social security number. Employers may obtain transcripts upon written request accompanied by a $2.00 fee and a signed release from the student.

A bachelor's or higher institution with an enrollment of 265. Highest level of offering: four or five year baccalaureate.

ACCREDITATIONS: BI

Hobson State Technical College

Highway 43 South, PO Box 489
Thomasville, AL 36784
(205) 636-9642 Ext. 39
Fax (205) 636-8123

Will confirm attendance and degree by phone or mail. Inquiry must include student's name and years attended. Employers may obtain transcripts upon written request accompanied by a signed release from the student.

A two-year institution newly admitted to NCES, with an enrollment of 500. Highest level of offering: one year but less than four years.

ACCREDITATIONS: SV

Hocking Technical College

3301 Hocking Parkway
Nelsonville, OH 45764-9704
(614) 753-3591 Ext. 2118

Will confirm attendance and degree by phone or mail. Inquiry must include student's name and social security number. Employers may obtain transcripts upon written request accompanied by a $2.00 fee and a signed release from the student. Requests should be directed to: Cashier's Office.

A multiprogram two-year institution, with an enrollment of 3,665. Highest level of offering: one year but less than four years.

ACCREDITATIONS: NH MAC MRT

Hofstra University

Registrar's Office
Hempstead, NY 11550
(516) 560-6738

Will confirm attendance and degree by phone or mail. Inquiry must include student's name and social security number. Employers may obtain transcripts upon written request accompanied by a $3.00 fee and a signed release from the student. Requests should be directed to: Registrar's Office.

A comprehensive institution with no medical school, with an enrollment of 11,414. Highest level of offering: doctorate.

ACCREDITATIONS: M AUD BUS ENG LAW NY PSPSY SP TED

Hollins College

Roanoke, VA 24020
(703) 362-6312

Will confirm attendance and degree by phone or mail. Inquiry must include student's name and years attended. Employers may obtain transcripts upon written request accompanied by a $4.00 fee and a signed release from the student.

A comprehensive institution with no medical school, with an enrollment of 982. Highest level of offering: master's.

ACCREDITATIONS: SC

Holmes Community College

PO Box 398
Hill Street
Goodman, MS 39079
(601) 472-2312 Ext. 23
Fax (601) 472-2566

Will confirm attendance and degree by phone, fax or mail. Inquiry must include student's name, date of birth, social security number. Employers may obtain transcripts upon written request accompanied by a $2.00 fee and a signed release from the student. Requests should be directed to: Admissions & Records Office.

A multiprogram two-year institution, with an enrollment of 1,986. Highest level of offering: one year but less than four years.

ACCREDITATIONS: SC

Holy Apostles College

33 Prospect Hill Road
Cromwell, CT 06416
(203) 632-3000
Fax (203) 632-3007

Will confirm attendance and degree by mail. Inquiry must include student's name, social security number, release. Employers may obtain transcripts upon written request accompanied by a $5.00 fee and a signed release from the student.

A school of philosophy, religion and theology, with an enrollment of 125. Highest level of offering: master's.
ACCREDITATIONS: EH

Holy Cross College

Box 308
Notre Dame, IN 46556
(219) 233-6813 Ext. 372
Fax (219) 233-7427

Will confirm attendance and degree by phone or mail. Inquiry must include student's name. Employers may obtain transcripts upon written request accompanied by a $2.00 fee and a signed release from the student.

A multiprogram two-year institution, with an enrollment of 414. Highest level of offering: two years.
ACCREDITATIONS: NCA

Holy Family College

c/o Sisters of the Holy Family
PO Box 3248
Fremont, CA 94539
(510) 490-8657

Records for this school are being handled by Sisters of the Holy Family. Will confirm attendance and degree by mail only. Inquiry must include student's name, years attended. Only students may obtain transcripts.

Holy Names College

3500 Mountain Boulevard
Oakland, CA 94619
(510) 436-1133

Will confirm attendance and degree by phone or mail. Inquiry must include student's name, date of birth, social security number. Employers may obtain transcripts upon written request accompanied by a $5.00 fee and a signed release from the student.

A comprehensive institution with no medical school, with an enrollment of 645. Highest level of offering: master's.
ACCREDITATIONS: WC MUS NUR

Holy Trinity Orthodox Seminary

PO Box 36
Jordanville, NY 13361
(315) 858-0940

Will confirm attendance and degree by phone or mail. Inquiry must include student's name. Employers may obtain transcripts upon written request accompanied by a $3.00 fee and a signed release from the student.

A school of religion and theology, with an enrollment of 37. Highest level of offering: four or five year baccalaureate.
ACCREDITATIONS: NY

Holyoke Community College

303 Homestead Avenue
Holyoke, MA 01040
(413) 538-7000 Ext. 247
Fax (413) 534-8975

Will confirm attendance and degree by phone or mail. Inquiry must include student's name, any former name, social security number. Employers may obtain transcripts upon written request accompanied by a $3.00 fee and a signed release from the student.

A multiprogram two-year institution, with an enrollment of 5,200. Highest level of offering: two years but less than four years.
ACCREDITATIONS: EH ADNUR MRT RAD

Honolulu Community College

874 Dillingham Boulevard
Honolulu, HI 96817
(808) 845-9211 Ext. 120
Fax (808) 845-9173

Will confirm attendance and degree by phone or mail. Inquiry must include student's name, social security number, years attended. Employers may obtain transcripts upon written request accompanied by a $1.00 fee and a signed release from the student.

A multiprogram two-year institution, with an enrollment of 4,000. Highest level of offering: two years but less than four years.
ACCREDITATIONS: WJ

Hood College

Rosemont Avenue
Frederick, MD 21701
(301) 663-3131 Ext. 367
Fax (301) 694-7653

Will confirm attendance and degree by phone or mail. Inquiry must include student's name, social security number, years attended. Employers may obtain transcripts upon written request accompanied by a $3.00 fee and a signed release from the student.

A comprehensive institution with no medical school, with an enrollment of 1,736. Highest level of offering: master's.
ACCREDITATIONS: M DIET SW

Hope College

Holland, MI 49423
(616) 394-7760
Fax (616) 394-7950

Will confirm attendance and degree by phone or mail. Inquiry must include student's name and social security number. Employers may obtain transcripts upon written request accompanied by a $3.00 fee and a signed release from the student.

A general baccalaureate institution, with an enrollment of 2,770. Highest level of offering: four or five year baccalaureate.
ACCREDITATIONS: NH ART DANCE MUS TED

Horry–Georgetown Technical College

Highway 501 East PO Box 1966
Conway, SC 29526
(803) 347-3186 Ext. 244

Will confirm attendance and degree by phone or mail. Inquiry must include student's name, social security number, years attended. Employers may obtain transcripts upon written request accompanied by a $2.00 fee and a signed release from the student.

A multiprogram two-year institution, with an enrollment of 2,294. Highest level of offering: two years but less than four years.
ACCREDITATIONS: SACS

Houghton College

1 Willard Avenue
Houghton, NY 14744
(716) 567-2211 Ext. 350
Fax (716) 567-9572

Will confirm attendance and degree by phone or mail. Inquiry must include student's name and years attended. Employers may obtain transcripts upon written request accompanied by a $2.00 fee and a signed release from the student.

A general baccalaureate institution, with an enrollment of 1,169. Highest level of offering: four or five year baccalaureate.
ACCREDITATIONS: M MUS NY

Housatonic Community College

510 Barnum Avenue
Bridgeport, CT 06608
(203) 579-6400

Will confirm attendance and degree by phone or mail. Inquiry must include student's name and social security number. Employers may obtain transcripts upon written request accompanied by a signed release from the student.

A multiprogram two-year institution, with an enrollment of 2,386. Highest level of offering: one year but less than four years.
ACCREDITATIONS: EH MLTAD

Houston Baptist University

7502 Fondren Road
Houston, TX 77074
(713) 774-7661

Will confirm attendance and degree by mail. Inquiry must include student's name, social security number, years attended, release. $3.00 fee for verification. Employers may obtain transcripts upon written request accompanied by a $3.00 fee and a signed release from the student.

A comprehensive institution with no medical school, with an enrollment of 2,624. Highest level of offering: master's.
ACCREDITATIONS: SC NUR

Houston Community College

PO Box 7849
Houston, TX 77270-7849
(713) 868-0763

Will confirm attendance and degree by mail. Inquiry must include student's name, social security number, years attended, release. Employers may obtain transcripts upon written request accompanied by a $3.00 fee and a signed release from the student. Requests should be directed to: Admissions & Records Office.

A multiprogram two-year institution, with an enrollment of 25,547. Highest level of offering: one year but less than four years.
ACCREDITATIONS: SC DA ENGT MLTAD NMT PTAA RAD RSTH RSTHT SURGT

Howard Community College

Little Patuxent Parkway
Columbia, MD 21044
(301) 992-4800

Will confirm by mail. Inquiry must include student's name, social security number, years attended, release. Requests should be directed to: Student Services Office. Employers may obtain transcripts upon written request accompanied by a $2.00 fee and a signed release from the student.

A multiprogram two-year institution, with an enrollment of 3,420. Highest level of offering: one year but less than four years.
ACCREDITATIONS: M ADNUR

Howard County Junior College District

1001 Birdwell Lane
Big Spring, TX 79720
(915) 264-5109

Will confirm attendance and degree by phone or mail. Inquiry must include student's name, social security number, years attended. Employers may obtain transcripts upon written request accompanied by a $2.00 fee and a signed release from the student.

A multiprogram two-year institution, with an enrollment of 1,784. Highest level of offering: one year but less than four years.
ACCREDITATIONS: SC ADNUR DH

Howard Payne University

1000 Fisk Avenue
Brownwood, TX 76801
(915) 643-7805
Fax (915) 643-7835

Will confirm attendance and degree by phone or mail. Inquiry must include student's name, date of birth, social security number. Employers may obtain transcripts upon written request accompanied by a $3.00 fee and a signed release from the student.

A general baccalaureate institution, with an enrollment of 1,017. Highest level of offering: four or five year baccalaureate.
ACCREDITATIONS: SC

Howard University

2400 Sixth Street North West
Washington, DC 20059
(202) 806-2700

Will confirm attendance and degree by phone or mail. Inquiry must include student's name, social security number, release. Employers may obtain transcripts upon written request accompanied by a $5.00 fee and a signed release from the student.

A doctoral-level institution with a medical school, with an enrollment of 11,454. Highest level of offering: doctorate.
ACCREDITATIONS: M APCP ARCH ART BUS DENT DH DIET ENG HSA IPSY LAW THEOL MED MT MUS NUR OT PHAR PTA RAD RTT SP SW

Hudson County Community College

168 Sip Avenue–Room 109
Jersey City, NJ 07306
(201) 656-2020
Fax (201) 656-8961

Will confirm attendance and degree by mail. Inquiry must include student's name and social security number. Employers may obtain transcripts upon written request accompanied by a $2.00 fee and a signed release from the student.

A multiprogram two-year institution, with an enrollment of 3,000. Highest level of offering: one year but less than four years.
ACCREDITATIONS: M MAC MRT ENGT

Hudson Valley Community College

80 Vandenburgh Avenue
Troy, NY 12180
(518) 270-1574

Will confirm attendance and degree by phone or mail. Inquiry must include student's name, date of birth, social security number, years attended. Employers may obtain transcripts upon written request accompanied by a $3.00 fee and a signed release from the student.

A multiprogram two-year institution, with an enrollment of 8,040. Highest level of offering: one year but less than four years.
ACCREDITATIONS: M ADNUR APCP DA DH ENGT FUSER NY RAD RSTH

Humboldt State University

Arcata, CA 95521
(707) 826-4101 or 826- 4314
Fax (707) 826-5555

Will confirm attendance and degree by phone, fax or mail. Inquiry must include student's name, release, social security number. Requests should be directed to: Records Office. Employers may obtain transcripts upon written request accompanied by a $4.00 fee and a signed release from the student.

A comprehensive institution with no medical school, with an enrollment of 7,400. Highest level of offering: master's.
ACCREDITATIONS: WC ART ENG FOR JOUR MUS NUR THEA

Humphreys College

6650 Inglewood Avenue
Stockton, CA 95207
(209) 478-0800

Will confirm attendance and degree by mail. Inquiry must include student's name, date of birth, social security number, years attended, release. Employers may obtain transcripts upon written request accompanied by a $2.00 fee and a signed release from the student.

A multiprogram two-year institution, with an enrollment of 450. Highest level of offering: one year but less than four years.
ACCREDITATIONS: WC

Huntingdon College

1500 East Fairview Avenue
Montgomery, AL 36106-2148
(205) 265-0511 Ext. 430

Will confirm attendance and degree by phone or mail. Inquiry must include student's name, date of birth, years attended. Employers may obtain transcripts upon written request accompanied by a $3.00 fee and a signed release from the student.

A general baccalaureate institution, with an enrollment of 800. Highest level of offering: four or five year baccalaureate.
ACCREDITATIONS: SC MUS

Huntington College

College Avenue
Huntington, IN 46750
(219) 356-6000 Ext. 1011

Will confirm attendance and degree by phone or mail. Inquiry must include student's name and years attended. Employers may obtain transcripts upon written request accompanied by a $2.00 fee and a signed release from the student.

A general baccalaureate institution, with an enrollment of 600. Highest level of offering: master's.
ACCREDITATIONS: NCA

Huntington Junior College

900 5th Avenue
Huntington, WV 25701
(304) 697-7550
Fax (304) 697-7554

Will confirm attendance and degree by phone or mail. Inquiry must include student's name, social security number, years attended, release. Employers may obtain transcripts upon written request accompanied by a signed release from the student.

A two-year institution newly admitted to NCES, with an enrollment of 470. Highest level of offering: one year but less than four years.
ACCREDITATIONS: JRCB

Huron College

333 9th Street SW
Huron, SD 57350
(605) 352-8721 Ext. 23

Will confirm attendance and degree by mail. Inquiry must include student's name and social security number. Employers may obtain transcripts upon written request accompanied by a $4.00 fee and a signed release from the student.

A general baccalaureate institution, with an enrollment of 476. Highest level of offering: four or five year baccalaureate.
ACCREDITATIONS: NH

Hussian School of Art

1010 Arch Street
Philadelphia, PA 19107
(215) 238-9000
Fax (215) 238-0848

Will confirm attendance and degree by phone or mail. Inquiry must include student's name and years attended. Employers may obtain transcripts upon written request accompanied by a signed release from the student.

A two-year institution newly admitted to NCES, with an enrollment of 155. Highest level of offering: one year but less than four years.
ACCREDITATIONS: NATTS

Husson College

1 College Circle
Bangor, ME 04401
(207) 947-1121 Ext. 231

Will confirm attendance and degree by phone or mail. Faxed inquiries will be confirmed by phone or mail. Inquiry must include student's name, date of birth, social security number, years attended.
Employers may obtain transcripts upon written request accompanied by a $3.00 fee and a signed release from the student.

A business school, with an enrollment of 1,800. Highest level of offering: master's.
ACCREDITATIONS: EH

Huston–Tillotson College

1820 East 8th Street
Austin, TX 78702
(512) 476-7421 Ext. 247

Will confirm attendance and degree by phone or mail. Inquiry must include student's name, date of birth, social security number. Employers may obtain transcripts upon written request accompanied by a $3.00 fee and a signed release from the student.

A general baccalaureate institution, with an enrollment of 587. Highest level of offering: four or five year baccalaureate.
ACCREDITATIONS: SC

Hutchinson Community College

1300 North Plum Street
Hutchinson, KS 67501
(316) 665-3520

Will confirm attendance and degree by phone or mail. Inquiry must include student's name, social security number, years attended. Employers may obtain transcripts upon written request accompanied by a $2.00 fee and a signed release from the student.

A multiprogram two-year institution, with an enrollment of 5,003. Highest level of offering: one year but less than four years.
ACCREDITATIONS: NH ADNUR MRT RAD

I

Idaho State University

Museum 319–Box 8196
Pocatello, ID 83209
(208) 236-2661

Will confirm attendance and degree by phone or mail. Inquiry must include student's name, date of birth, social security number, years attended. Employers may obtain transcripts upon written request accompanied by a $2.00 fee and a signed release from the student. Requests should be directed to: Registrar's Office.

A comprehensive institution with no medical school, with an enrollment of 8,025. Highest level of offering: doctorate.
ACCREDITATIONS: NW AUD BUS DH MUS NUR PHAR RAD SP SW TED ENG

Iliff School of Theology

2201 South University Boulevard
Denver, CO 80210
(303) 744-1287 Ext. 227

Will confirm attendance and degree by mail. Inquiry must include student's name, social security number, last year attended. Employers may obtain transcripts upon written request accompanied by a $2.00 fee and a signed release from the student.

A school of philosophy, religion and theology, with an enrollment of 350. Highest level of offering: doctorate.
ACCREDITATIONS: NH THEOL

Illinois Benedictine College

5700 College Road
Lisle, IL 60532
(708) 960-1500

Will confirm attendance and degree by phone or mail. Inquiry must include student's name, social security number, years attended. Employers may obtain transcripts upon written request accompanied by a signed release from the student.

A general baccalaureate institution, with an enrollment of 2,500. Highest level of offering: master's.
ACCREDITATIONS: NH NUR

Illinois Central College

East Peoria, IL 61635
(309) 694-5235

Will confirm attendance and degree by phone or mail. Inquiry must include student's name and social security number. Employers may obtain transcripts upon written request accompanied by a $2.00 fee and a signed release from the student. Requests should be directed to: Admissions & Records Office.

A multiprogram two-year institution, with an enrollment of 12,350. Highest level of offering: one year but less than four years.
ACCREDITATIONS: NH ADNUR DA DH MLTAD MUS PNUR PTAA RAD SURGT

Illinois College of Optometry

3241 South Michigan Avenue
Chicago, IL 60616
(312) 225-1700 Ext. 606

Will confirm attendance and degree by phone or mail. Inquiry must include student's name, date of birth, social security number. Employers may obtain transcripts upon written request accompanied by a $10.00 fee and a signed release from the student.

A health institution, with an enrollment of 531. Highest level of offering: first professional degree.
ACCREDITATIONS: NH OPT

Illinois College

1101 West College Avenue
Jacksonville, IL 62650
(217) 245-3013

Will confirm attendance and degree by phone or mail. Inquiry must include student's name, social security number, years attended. Employers may obtain transcripts upon written request accompanied by a signed release from the student.

A general baccalaureate institution, with an enrollment of 800. Highest level of offering: four or five year baccalaureate.
ACCREDITATIONS: NH

Illinois Eastern Community College Frontier Community College

Lot 2 Frontier Drive
Fairfield, IL 62837
(618) 842-3711
Fax (618) 842-3711 Ext. 4496

Will confirm attendance and degree by mail. Inquiry must include student's name, social security number, release. Requests should be directed to: Admissions & Records Office. Employers may obtain transcripts upon written request accompanied by a $1.00 fee and a signed release from the student.

A multiprogram two-year institution, with an enrollment of 3,844. Highest level of offering: one year but less than four years.
ACCREDITATIONS: NH

Illinois Eastern Community College Lincoln Trail College

Route 3 Box 82-A
Robinson, IL 62454
(618) 544-8657 Ext. 1137
Fax (618) 544-1161

Will confirm attendance and degree by mail or fax. Inquiry must include student's name, social security number, release. Employers may obtain transcripts upon written request accompanied by a $1.00 fee and a signed release from the student. Requests should be directed to: Records Office.

A multiprogram two-year institution, with an enrollment of 1,446. Highest level of offering: one year but less than four years.

Illinois Eastern Community College Olney Central College

305 North West Street
Olney, IL 62450
(618) 395-4351
Fax (618) 392-3293

Will confirm attendance and degree by mail or fax. Inquiry must include student's name, social security number, years attended, release. Employers may obtain transcripts upon written request accompanied by a $1.00 fee and a signed release from the student.

A multiprogram two-year institution, with an enrollment of 2,554. Highest level of offering: one year but less than four years.

Illinois Eastern Community College Wabash Valley College

2200 College Drive
Mount Carmel, IL 62863
(618) 262-8641 Ext. 3248
Fax (618) 262-8641 Ext. 3247

Will confirm attendance and degree by phone, fax or mail. Inquiry must include student's name and social security number. Employers may obtain transcripts upon written request accompanied by a $1.00 fee and a signed release from the student. Requests should be directed to: Admissions and Records Office.

A multiprogram two-year institution, with an enrollment of 2,313. Highest level of offering: two years but less than four years.

Illinois Institute of Technology

Registrar's Office, Room 104
3300 South Federal Street
Chicago, IL 60616
(312) 567-3310
Fax (312) 567-3313

Will confirm attendance and degree by phone, fax or mail. Inquiry must include student's name, social security number, years attended. Employers may obtain transcripts upon written request accompanied by a $3.00 fee and a signed release from the student.

A doctoral-level institution with no medical school, with an enrollment of 6,432. Highest level of offering: doctorate.
ACCREDITATIONS: NH ARCH ART CLPSY ENG LAW

Illinois Institute of Technology

(Formerly Midwest College of Engineering)
201 E. Loop Road
Wheaton, IL 60187
(312) 567-3900
Fax (708) 790-1826

Will confirm attendance and degree by phone, fax or mail. Inquiry must include student's name, social security number, years attended. Employers may obtain transcripts upon written request accompanied by a $3.00 fee and a signed release from the student. Requests should be sent to: Illinois Institute of Technology.

Illinois School of Professional Psychology

220 South State Street
Chicago, IL 60604
(312) 341-6500 Ext. 533
Fax (312) 922-1730

Will confirm attendance and degree by phone or mail. Inquiry must include student's name and social security number. Employers may obtain transcripts upon written request accompanied by a signed release from the student.

A bachelor's or higher institution newly admitted to NCES, with an enrollment of 581. Highest level of offering: doctorate.
ACCREDITATIONS: NH

Illinois State University

201 Hovey Hall
Normal, IL 61761-6901
(309) 438-2188 or 438-2181

Will confirm attendance and degree by phone or mail. Inquiry must include student's name, social security number, years attended. Employers may obtain transcripts upon written request accompanied by a $3.00 fee and a signed release from the student. Requests should be directed to: Records Office.

A doctoral-level institution with no medical school, with an enrollment of 20,903. Highest level of offering: doctorate.
ACCREDITATIONS: NH ART AUD BUS IPSY MRA MUS SP SW TED THEA

Illinois Technical College

33 East Congress Parkway
Chicago, IL 60605
(312) 922-9000
Fax (312) 922-9007

Will confirm attendance and degree by mail or fax. Inquiry must include student's name, social security number, years attended. Employers may obtain transcripts upon written request accompanied by a $5.00 fee and a signed release from the student. Requests should be directed to: Records Office.

A single program two-year institution, with an enrollment of 342. Highest level of offering: one year but less than four years.
ACCREDITATIONS: NH NATTS

Illinois Valley Community College

2578 East 350th Road
Oglesby, IL 61099
(815) 224-2720 Ext. 448
Fax (815) 224-3033

Will confirm attendance and degree by phone, fax or mail. Inquiry must include student's name and social security number. Employers may obtain transcripts upon written request accompanied by a $2.00 fee and a signed release from the student. Requests should be directed to: Records Office.

A multiprogram two-year institution, with an enrollment of 3,983. Highest level of offering: one year but less than four years.
ACCREDITATIONS: NH ADNUR DA

Illinois Wesleyan University

Holmes Hall Room 106
Bloomington, IL 61702
(309) 556-3161
Fax (309) 556-3411

Will confirm attendance and degree by phone, fax or mail. Inquiry must include student's name. Employers may obtain transcripts upon written request accompanied by a $1.00 fee and a signed release from the student.

A general baccalaureate institution, with an enrollment of 1,641. Highest level of offering: four or five year baccalaureate.
ACCREDITATIONS: NCA MUS NUR ACS

Immaculata College

Immaculata, PA 19345
(215) 647-4400 Ext. 302
Fax (215) 251-1668

Will confirm attendance and degree by phone or mail. Inquiry must include student's name, date of birth, social security number, years attended. Employers may obtain transcripts upon written request accompanied by a $2.00 fee and a signed release from the student.

A general baccalaureate institution, with an enrollment of 2,345. Highest level of offering: doctorate.
ACCREDITATIONS: M DIET MUS

Immaculate Conception Center

(Formerly Cathedral Residence of the Immaculate Conception)
7200 Douglaston Parkway
Douglaston, NY 11326-1997
(718)229-8001 Ext. 203

Will confirm attendance and degree by phone or mail. Inquiry must include student's name date of birth, social security number years attended. Employers may obtain transcripts upon written request accompanied by a $3.00 fee and a signed release from the student.

Immaculate Conception Seminary

400 South Orange Avenue
South Orange, NJ 07079
(201) 761-9575 Ext. 9016

Will confirm attendance and degree by phone or mail. Inquiry must include student's name and years attended. Employers may obtain transcripts upon written request accompanied by a $2.00 fee and a signed release from the student.

A school of theology, with an enrollment of 200. Highest level of offering: master's.
ACCREDITATIONS: M THEOL

Imperial Valley College

PO Box 158
Imperial, CA 92251-0158
(619) 352-8320 Ext. 201
Fax (619) 355-2663

Will confirm attendance and degree by phone, fax or mail. Inquiry must include student's name, date of birth, social security number, years attended. Employers may obtain transcripts upon written request accompanied by a $2.00 fee and a signed release from the student.

A multiprogram two-year institution, with an enrollment of 4,200. Highest level of offering: one year but less than four years.
ACCREDITATIONS: WJ

Incarnate Word College

4301 Broadway
San Antonio, TX 78209
(512) 829-6006

Will confirm attendance and degree by phone or mail. Inquiry must include student's name and social security number. Employers may obtain transcripts upon written request accompanied by a $3.00 fee and a signed release from the student.

A comprehensive institution with no medical school, with an enrollment of 2,500. Highest level of offering: master's.
ACCREDITATIONS: SC MRA NMT NUR TED

Independence Community College

PO Box 708–Brookside Drive & College Avenue
Independence, KS 67301
(316) 331-4100 Ext. 277

Will confirm attendance and degree by phone or mail. Inquiry must include student's name and social security number. Employers may obtain transcripts upon written request accompanied by a $3.00 fee and a signed release from the student.

A multiprogram two-year institution, with an enrollment of 2,000. Highest level of offering: one year but less than four years.
ACCREDITATIONS: NH

Indian Hills Community College

525 Grandview
Ottumwa, IA 52501
(515) 683-5151
Fax (515) 683-5184

Will confirm attendance and degree by phone, fax or mail. Inquiry must include student's name and social security number. Employers may obtain transcripts upon written request accompanied by a signed release from the student.

A multiprogram two-year institution, with an enrollment of 2,800. Highest level of offering: one year but less than four years.
ACCREDITATIONS: NH MRT RAD

Indian River Community College

3209 Virginia Avenue
Fort Pierce, FL 34981
(407) 468-4700
Fax (407) 468-4796

Will confirm attendance and degree by mail or fax. Inquiry must include student's name, date of birth, social security number, release. Employers may obtain transcripts upon written request accompanied by a signed release from the student.

A multiprogram two-year institution, with an enrollment of 6,104. Highest level of offering: one year but less than four years.
ACCREDITATIONS: SC ADNUR DA DT MLTAD RAD

Indian Valley Colleges

(See College of Miran.)

Indian Vocational Technical College

One West 26th Street, Box 1763
Indianapolis, IN 46206
(317) 921-4745
Fax (317) 921-4753

Will confirm attendance and degree by phone, fax or mail. Inquiry must include student's name, date of birth, social security number, years attended. Employers may obtain transcripts upon written request accompanied by a signed release from the student.

A multiprogram two-year institution, with an enrollment of 4,427. Highest level of offering: one year but less than four years.
ACCREDITATIONS: NH MAC MLTAD PNUR RAD RSTHT SURGT

Indiana Central University

1400 East Hanna Avenue
Indianapolis, IN 46227
(317) 788-3368 Ext. 3220
Fax (317) 788-3300

Will confirm attendance and degree by phone, fax or mail. Inquiry must include student's name, date of birth, social security number, years attended. Employers may obtain transcripts upon written request accompanied by a $2.00 fee and a signed release from the student.

A comprehensive institution with no medical school, with an enrollment of 2,999. Highest level of offering: master's.
ACCREDITATIONS: NH ADNUR MUS PTA TED

Indiana Institute of Technology

1600 East Washington Boulevard
Fort Wayne, IN 46803
(219) 422-5561 Ext. 231
Fax (219) 422-7696

Will confirm attendance and degree by phone, fax or mail. Inquiry must include student's name and years attended. Employers may obtain transcripts upon written request accompanied by a $2.00 fee and a signed release from the student.

A general baccalaureate institution, with an enrollment of 557. Highest level of offering: four or five year baccalaureate.
ACCREDITATIONS: NH

Indiana State University

217 North 6th Street
Terre Haute, IN 47809
(812) 237-2020

Will confirm attendance by mail and degree by phone. Inquiry must include student's name, social security number, years attended. Employers may obtain transcripts upon written request accompanied by a $2.00 fee and a signed release from the student.

A comprehensive institution with no medical school, with an enrollment of 11,618. Highest level of offering: doctorate.
ACCREDITATIONS: NH ADNUR ART BUS COPSY DIET FIDER MLTAD MT MUS NUR SCPSY TED SP

Indiana University–Purdue University at Fort Wayne

Registrar's Office
2101 Coliseum Boulevard East
Fort Wayne, IN 46805-1499
(219) 481-6815
Fax (219) 481-6880

Will confirm attendance and degree by phone or mail. Inquiry must include student's name and social security number. Employers may obtain transcripts upon written request accompanied by a $5.00 fee and a signed release from the student.

A comprehensive institution with no medical school, with an enrollment of 11,422. Highest level of offering: beyond master's but less than doctorate.
ACCREDITATIONS: NCA ADNUR ACS DA DH DT ENGT MUS NUR

Indiana University–Purdue University at Indianapolis

425 University Blvd.
Indianapolis, IN 46202-5144
(317) 274-1501

Will confirm attendance and degree by phone or mail. Inquiry must include student's name and social security number. Employers may obtain transcripts upon written request accompanied by a $5.25 fee and a signed release from the student.

A comprehensive institution with a medical school, with an enrollment of 23,366. Highest level of offering: doctorate.
ACCREDITATIONS: NH ADNUR ART CYTO DA DENT DH DIETI ENG ENGT HSA PAST LAW MED MRA MT NMT NUR OT PTA RAD RSTH RTT SW IPSY

Indiana University at Kokomo

PO Box 9003
Kokomo, IN 46904-9003
(317) 455-9391
Fax (317) 455-9276

Will confirm attendance and degree by phone, fax or mail. Inquiry must include student's name and social security number. Employers may obtain transcripts upon written request accompanied by a $5.25 search fee and a signed release from the student.

A general baccalaureate institution, with an enrollment of 3,300. Highest level of offering: master's.
ACCREDITATIONS: NH ADNUR ENGT TED

Indiana University at South Bend

1700 Mishawaka Ave.
PO Box 7111
South Bend, IN 46634
(219) 237-4451
Fax (219) 237-4599

Will confirm attendance and degree by phone, fax or mail. Inquiry must include student's name, social security number, years attended. Employers may obtain transcripts upon written request accompanied by a $5.25 fee and a signed release from the student.

A comprehensive institution with no medical school, with an enrollment of 7,000. Highest level of offering: master's.
ACCREDITATIONS: NH DA DH TED

Indiana University Bloomington

Student Services Bldg.–Room 100
Bloomington, IN 47405
(812) 335-0121

Will confirm attendance and degree by phone or mail. Inquiry must include student's name, social security number, years attended. Employers may obtain transcripts upon written request accompanied by a $5.25 fee and a signed release from the student. Requests should be directed to: Office of the Registrar, Transcripts.

A doctoral-level institution with no medical school, with an enrollment of 35,489. Highest level of offering: doctorate.
ACCREDITATIONS: NH AUD BUS CLPSY JOUR LAW LIB MUS OPT OPTT SCPSY SP TED

Indiana University East

2325 Chester Boulevard
Richmond, IN 47374
(317) 966-8261 Ext. 251
Fax (317) 973-8315

Will confirm attendance and degree by phone, fax or mail. Inquiry must include student's name and social security number, years attended. Employers may obtain transcripts upon written request accompanied by a $5.25 fee and a signed release from the student.

A multiprogram four-year institution, with an enrollment of 2,080. Highest level of offering: one year but less than four years.
ACCREDITATIONS: NCA

Indiana University Northwest

3400 Broadway
Gary, IN 46408
(219) 980-6815

Will confirm attendance and degree by phone or mail. Inquiry must include student's name, social security number, years attended. Employers may obtain transcripts upon written request accompanied by a $5.25 fee and a signed release from the student.

A comprehensive institution with no medical school, with an enrollment of 5,591. Highest level of offering: master's.
ACCREDITATIONS: NH ADNUR DA DH MRT RAD RSTH TED

Indiana University of Pennsylvania

G-5 Sutton Hall
Indiana, PA 15705
(412) 357-2217

Will confirm attendance and degree by phone or mail. Inquiry must include student's name, social security number, years attended. Employers may obtain transcripts upon written request accompanied by a $3.00 fee and a signed release from the student.

A comprehensive institution with no medical school, with an enrollment of 13,000. Highest level of offering: doctorate.
ACCREDITATIONS: M MUS NUR RSTH TED

Indiana University Southeast

4201 Grant Line Road
New Albany, IN 47150
(812) 941-2240
Fax (812) 941-2493

Will confirm attendance and degree by phone, fax or mail. Inquiry must include student's name and social security number. Employers may obtain transcripts upon written request accompanied by a $5.00 fee and a signed release from the student.

A general baccalaureate institution, with an enrollment of 5,500. Highest level of offering: master's.
ACCREDITATIONS: NH

Indiana Vocational Technical College–Kokomo Technical Institute

PO Box 1373
Kokomo, IN 46903-1373
(317) 459-0561

Will confirm attendance and degree by phone or mail. Inquiry must include student's name, social security number, years attended. Employers may obtain transcripts upon written request accompanied by a signed release from the student.

A multiprogram two-year institution, with an enrollment of 2,085. Highest level of offering: one year but less than four years.
ACCREDITATIONS: NH MAC

Indiana Vocational Technical College–Lafayette Technical Institute

3208 Ross Road Box 6299
Lafayette, IN 47903
(317) 477-9119
Fax (317) 477-9214

Will confirm attendance and degree by phone or mail. Inquiry must include student's name, social security number, years attended. Employers may obtain transcripts upon written request accompanied by a signed release from the student. Requests should be directed to: Office of the Registrar.

A multiprogram two-year institution, with an enrollment of 1,891. Highest level of offering: one year but less than four years.
ACCREDITATIONS: NCA DA MAC MLTAD RSTHT SURGT

Indiana Vocational Technical College–Northeast Technical Institute

3800 North Anthony Boulevard
Fort Wayne, IN 46805
(219) 482-9171 Ext. 255
Fax (219) 480-4177

Will confirm attendance and degree by phone, fax or mail. Inquiry must include student's name and social security number. Employers may obtain transcripts upon written request accompanied by a signed release from the student.

A multiprogram two-year institution, with an enrollment of 3,318. Highest level of offering: one year but less than four years.
ACCREDITATIONS: NH MAC RSTHT

Indiana Vocational Technical College–Northwest

1440 East 35th Avenue
Gary, IN 46409
(219) 981-1111 Ext. 272
Fax (219) 981-1111 Ext. 212

Will confirm degree by phone, fax or mail. Inquiry must include student's name, date of birth, social security number. Employers may obtain transcripts upon written request.

A multiprogram two-year institution, with an enrollment of 2,800. Highest level of offering: one year but less than four years.
ACCREDITATIONS: NH RSTHT

Indiana Vocational Technical College–Southeast Technical Institute

PO Box 209
Hwy. 62, Ivy Tech Drive
Madison, IN 47250
(812) 265-2580 Ext. 32

Will confirm attendance and degree by phone or mail. Inquiry must include student's name, date of birth, social security number. Employers may obtain transcripts upon written request accompanied by a signed release from the student.

A multiprogram two-year institution, with an enrollment of 939. Highest level of offering: one year but less than four years.
ACCREDITATIONS: NH MAC

Indiana Vocational Technical College–Wabash Valley Technical

7999 US Highway 41 South
Terre Haute, IN 47802-9990
(812) 299-1121 Ext. 207

Will confirm attendance and degree by phone or mail. Inquiry must include student's name, date of birth, social security number. Requests should be directed to: Student Services. Employers may obtain transcripts upon written request and a signed release from the student.

A multiprogram two-year institution, with an enrollment of 1,667. Highest level of offering: one year but less than four years.
ACCREDITATIONS: NH MAC MLTAD RAD

Indiana Vocational Technical College Central Office

PO Box 1763–1 West 26th Street
Indianapolis, IN 46206
(317) 921-4823
Fax (317) 921-4753

Will confirm attendance and degree by phone, fax or mail. Inquiry must include student's name and social security number. Employers may obtain transcripts upon written request accompanied by a signed release from the student. Enrollment is 4,800
ACCREDITATIONS: NH MAC

Indiana Vocational Technical College

4475 Central Avenue
Columbus, IN 47203
(812) 372-9925 Ext. 30

Will confirm attendance and degree by phone or mail. Inquiry must include student's name, date of birth, social security number. Employers may obtain transcripts upon written request accompanied by a signed release from the student.

A multiprogram two-year institution, with an enrollment of 2,000. Highest level of offering: one year but less than four years.
ACCREDITATIONS: NH RSTHT

Indiana Vocational Technical College

3501 First Avenue
Evansville, IN 47710
(812) 426-2865 Ext. 434
Fax (812) 429-1483

Will confirm attendance and degree by phone, fax or mail. Inquiry must include student's name and social security number. Employers may obtain transcripts upon written request accompanied by a signed release from the student.

A multiprogram two-year institution, with an enrollment of 2,500. Highest level of offering: one year but less than four years.
ACCREDITATIONS: NH MAC

Indiana Vocational Technical College

PO Box 3100
Muncie, IN 47307
(317) 289-2291 Ext. 374

Will confirm attendance and degree by phone or mail. Inquiry must include student's name, social security number, years attended. Employers may obtain transcripts upon written request accompanied by a signed release from the student.

A multiprogram two-year institution, with an enrollment of 2,200. Highest level of offering: one year but less than four years.
ACCREDITATIONS: NH MAC

Indiana Vocational Technical College

2325 Chester Boulevard
Richmond, IN 47374
(317) 966-2656 Ext. 37
Fax (317) 966-2656

Will confirm attendance and degree by phone, fax or mail. Inquiry must include student's name, date of birth, social security number, years attended, release. Employers may obtain transcripts upon written request accompanied by a signed release from the student.

A multiprogram two-year institution, with an enrollment of 1,005. Highest level of offering: one year but less than four years.
ACCREDITATIONS: NH MLTC

Indiana Vocational Technical College

8204 Highway 311
Sellersburg, IN 47172
(812) 246-3301 Ext. 139

Will confirm attendance and degree by phone or mail. Inquiry must include student's name and social security number. Employers may obtain transcripts upon written request accompanied by a signed release from the student.

A multiprogram two-year institution, with an enrollment of 1,370. Highest level of offering: one year but less than four years.
ACCREDITATIONS: NH MAC

Indiana Vocational Technical College

1534 West Sample Street
South Bend, IN 46619
(219) 289-7001 Ext. 229

Will confirm attendance and degree by phone or mail. Inquiry must include student's name, social security number, years attended, release. Employers may obtain transcripts upon written request and a signed release from the student.

A multiprogram two-year institution, with an enrollment of 2,352. Highest level of offering: one year but less than four years.
ACCREDITATIONS: NH MAC MLTAD

Institute of American Indian Arts

PO Box 20007
Santa Fe, NM 87504
(505) 988-6493
Fax (505) 988-6446

Will confirm attendance and degree by phone, fax or mail. Inquiry must include student's name, years attended, release. Employers may obtain transcripts upon written request accompanied by a signed release from the student.

A multiprogram two-year institution, with an enrollment of 214. Highest level of offering: one year but less than four years.
ACCREDITATIONS: NH ART

Institute of Design and Construction

141 Willoughby Street
Brooklyn, NY 11201
(718) 855-3661
Fax (718) 852-5889

Will confirm attendance and degree by mail or fax. Inquiry must include student's name, social security number, years attended, release. Employers may obtain transcripts upon written request accompanied by a $5.00 fee and a signed release from the student.

A single program two-year institution, with an enrollment of 250. Highest level of offering: one year but less than four years.
ACCREDITATIONS: NY

Institute of Electronic Technology

509 South 30th Street
Paducah, KY 42001
(502) 444-9676

Will confirm attendance and degree by phone or mail. Inquiry must include student's name, social security number, years attended. Employers may obtain transcripts upon written request accompanied by a signed release from the student.

A single program two-year institution, with an enrollment of 185. Highest level of offering: one year but less than four years.
ACCREDITATIONS: NATTS

Institute of Paper Science & Technology

575 14th Street, N.W.
Atlanta, GA 30318
(404) 853-9500
Fax (404) 853-9510

Will confirm attendance and degree by phone or mail. Inquiry must include student's name and years attended. Employers may obtain transcripts upon written request accompanied by a signed release from the student.

A specialized school, with an enrollment of 104. Highest level of offering: doctorate.
ACCREDITATIONS: NH

Institute of Transpersonal Psychology

250 Oak Grove Avenue
Menlo Park, CA 94025
(415) 326-1960

Will confirm attendance and degree by phone or mail. Inquiry must include student's name. Employers may obtain transcripts upon written request accompanied by a $10.00 fee and a signed release from the student.

A bachelor's or higher institution newly admitted to NCES, with an enrollment of 175. Highest level of offering: doctorate.
ACCREDITATIONS: 3IC

Interboro Institute

450 West 56th Street
New York, NY 10019
(212) 399-0091

Will confirm attendance and degree by mail. Inquiry must include student's name, social security number, years attended, release. Employers may obtain transcripts upon written request accompanied by a $4.00 fee and a signed release from the student.

A multiprogram two-year institution, with an enrollment of 854. Highest level of offering: one year but less than four years.

ACCREDITATIONS: NY JRCB

Interdenominational Theological Center

671 Beckwith Street South West
Atlanta, GA 30314
(404) 527-7700
Fax (404) 527-0901

Will confirm attendance and degree by phone, fax or mail. Inquiry must include student's name, social security number, years attended, release. Employers may obtain transcripts upon written request accompanied by a $2.00 fee and a signed release from the student.

A school of philosophy, religion and theology, with an enrollment of 311. Highest level of offering: doctorate.

ACCREDITATIONS: SC THEOL

Intermountain Bible College

2101 Patterson Road
Grand Junction, CO 81501
(303) 243-3870

Will confirm attendance and degree by mail. Inquiry must include student's name and years attended. Employers may obtain transcripts upon written request accompanied by a signed release from the student.

A school of philosophy, religion and theology. Highest level of offering: four or five year baccalaureate.

International Bible College

PO Box Ibc
Florence, AL 35630
(205) 766-6610 Ext. 46

Will confirm attendance and degree by phone or mail. Inquiry must include student's name and social security number. Employers may obtain transcripts upon written request accompanied by a $2.00 fee and a signed release from the student.

A bachelor's or higher institution newly admitted to NCES, with an enrollment of 107. Highest level of offering: four or five year baccalaureate.

ACCREDITATIONS: BI

International Bible College

(See International Christian University & Seminary)

International Broadcasting School

6 South Smithville Road
Dayton, OH 45431
(513) 258-8251

Will confirm attendance and degree by mail. Inquiry must include student's name and social security number. Employers may obtain transcripts upon written request accompanied by a $2.00 fee and a signed release from the student.

A two-year institution newly admitted to NCES, with an enrollment of 65. Highest level of offering: one year but less than four years.

ACCREDITATIONS: NATTS

International Business College

3811 Old Illinois Road
Fort Wayne, IN 46804
(219) 432-8702 Ext. 50

Will confirm attendance and degree by phone or mail. Inquiry must include student's name, maiden name, social security number, years attended, day or evening student. Employers may obtain transcripts upon written request accompanied by a $4.00 fee and a signed release from the student.

A single program two-year institution, with an enrollment of 482. Highest level of offering: one year but less than four years.

ACCREDITATIONS: JRCB

International Christian University & Seminary

(Formerly International Bible College)
1218 S. Fairfax Ave.
Los Angeles, CA 90019
(213) 939-7179
Fax (213) 939-2422

Will confirm attendance and degree by phone or mail. Inquiry must include student's name, social security number, years attended. Employers may obtain transcripts upon written request accompanied by a $10.00 fee and a signed release from the student.

A doctoral-level institution with no medical school, with an enrollment of 120. Highest level of offering: doctorate.

ACCREDITATIONS: 3IC

International Fine Arts College

1737 North Bayshore Drive
Miami, FL 33132
(305) 373-4684
Fax (305) 374-5933

Will confirm attendance and degree by mail or fax. Inquiry must include student's name, social security number, years attended.Employers may obtain transcripts upon written request accompanied by a fee (ranging from $5.00 to $10.00) and a signed release from the student.

A single program two-year institution, with an enrollment of 400. Highest level of offering: one year but less than four years.

ACCREDITATIONS: SC

International School of Theology

PO Box 50015
San Bernadino, CA 92412
(714) 886-7876 Ext. 7066

Will confirm attendance and degree by phone or mail. Inquiry must include student's name and years attended. Employers may obtain transcripts upon written request accompanied by a $2.00 fee and a signed release from the student.

A bachelor's or higher institution, with an enrollment of 131. Highest level of offering: master's.

ACCREDITATIONS: THEOL

Interstate Technical Institute

2402 Medford Drive
Fort Wayne, IN 46803
(219) 749-8583

Will confirm attendance and degree by phone or mail. Inquiry must include student's name and years attended. Employers may obtain transcripts upon written request accompanied by a $3.00 fee and a signed release from the student.

A two-year institution newly admitted to NCES, with an enrollment of 150. Highest level of offering: one year but less than four years.

ACCREDITATIONS: NATTS

Inver Hills Community College

8445 College Trail
Inver Grove Heights, MN 55075
(612) 450-8502
Fax (612) 450-8506

Will confirm attendance and degree by phone or mail. Inquiry must include student's name and social security number. Employers may obtain transcripts upon written request accompanied by a signed release from the student.

A multiprogram two-year institution, with an enrollment of 5,500. Highest level of offering: one year but less than four years.

ACCREDITATIONS: NCA ADNUR

Iona College

715 North Avenue
New Rochelle, NY 10801
(914) 633-2509

Will confirm attendance and degree by phone or mail. Inquiry must include student's name, social security number, years attended. Employers may obtain transcripts upon written request accompanied by a $3.00 fee and a signed release from the student.

A comprehensive institution with no medical school, with an enrollment of 6,140.

Highest level of offering: beyond master's but less than doctorate.

ACCREDITATIONS: M NY SW

Iowa Central Community College

330 Avenue M
Fort Dodge, IA 50501
(515) 576-7201 Ext. 2409

Will confirm attendance and degree by phone or mail. Inquiry must include student's name, social security number, years attended. Employers may obtain transcripts upon written request accompanied by a $1.00 fee and a signed release from the student.

A multiprogram two-year institution, with an enrollment of 2,867. Highest level of offering: one year but less than four years.
ACCREDITATIONS: NH DA MAC

Iowa Lakes Community College

300 South 18th Street
Estherville, IA 51334
(712) 362-2604 Ext. 122
Fax (712) 362-7649

Will confirm attendance and degree by phone, fax or mail. Inquiry must include student's name and social security number. Employers may obtain transcripts upon written request accompanied by a $2.00 fee and a signed release from the student.

A multiprogram two-year institution, with an enrollment of 1,755. Highest level of offering: one year but less than four years.
ACCREDITATIONS: NH

Iowa Lakes Community College

3200 College Drive
Emmetsburg, IA 50536
(712) 852-3554 Ext. 265
Fax (712) 852-2152

Will confirm attendance and degree by phone, fax or mail. Inquiry must include student's name and social security number. Employers may obtain transcripts upon written request accompanied by a $2.00 fee and a signed release from the student.

A multiprogram two-year institution, with an enrollment of 1,755. Highest level of offering: one year but less than four years.
ACCREDITATIONS: NH

Iowa State University of Science and Technology

214 Alumni Hall
Ames, IA 50011
(515) 294-1840

Will confirm attendance and degree by phone or mail. Inquiry must include student's name, social security number, release. Employers may obtain transcripts upon written request accompanied by a $3.00 fee and a signed release from the student. Attn: Registrar's Office.

A doctoral-level institution with a veterinary medicine school, with an enrollment of 25,489. Highest level of offering: doctorate.

ACCREDITATIONS: NH ARCH COPSY DIET ENG FIDER FOR IPSY JOUR LSAR MUS SW TED VET

Iowa Wesleyan College

601 North Main
Mount Pleasant, IA 52641
(319) 385-8021 Ext. 225 or 227

Will confirm attendance and degree by phone or mail. Inquiry must include student's name, date of birth, years attended. Employers may obtain transcripts upon written request accompanied by a $2.00 fee and a signed release from the student.

A general baccalaureate institution, with an enrollment of 900. Highest level of offering: four or five year baccalaureate.
ACCREDITATIONS: NH NUR

Iowa Western Community College

Box 4C 2700 College Road
Council Bluffs, IA 51502
(712) 325-3285

Will confirm attendance and degree by phone or mail. Inquiry must include student's name, social security number, years attended. Employers may obtain transcripts upon written request accompanied by a $1.00 fee and a signed release from the student.

A multiprogram two-year institution, with an enrollment of 3,527. Highest level of offering: one year but less than four years.
ACCREDITATIONS: NCA DA MAC SURGT ABET

Islands Community College

(See University of Alaska Southeast Sitka Campus)

Isothermal Community College

PO Box 804
Spindale, NC 28160
(704) 286-3636 Ext. 267

Will confirm attendance and degree by phone or mail. Inquiry must include student's name and social security number. Requests should be directed to: Student Services. Employers may obtain transcripts upon written request accompanied by a signed release from the student.

A multiprogram two-year institution, with an enrollment of 1,700. Highest level of offering: one year but less than four years.
ACCREDITATIONS: SC

Itawamba Community College

(Formerly Itawamba Junior College)
Fulton, MS 38843
(601) 862-3101 Ext. 243
Fax (601) 862-9540

Will confirm attendance and degree by phone, fax or mail. Inquiry must include student's name, date of birth, social security number. Employers may obtain transcripts upon written request accompanied by a $2.00 fee and a signed release from the student.

A multiprogram two-year institution, with an enrollment of 2,560. Highest level of offering: one year but less than four years.
ACCREDITATIONS: SC RAD RSTH RSTHT

Ithaca College

Attn: Registrar
953 Danby Road
Ithaca, NY 14850
(607) 274-3127
Fax (607) 274-1366

Will confirm attendance and degree by phone, fax or mail. Inquiry must include student's name, social security number, years attended. Employers may obtain transcripts upon written request accompanied by a $2.00 fee and a signed release from the student.

A comprehensive institution with no medical school, with an enrollment of 6,488. Highest level of offering: master's.
ACCREDITATIONS: M AUD MRA MUS NY PTA SP THEA

ITT Career Institute-Jacksonville

(See Flagler Career Institute in Jacksonville, FL)

ITT Career Institute-Miami

(See Flagler Career Institute in Miami, FL)

ITT Peterson School of Business

(See ITT Technical Institute in Seattle, WA)

ITT Technical Institute–Evansville

5115 Oak Grove Road
Evansville, IN 47715
(812) 479-1441 Ext. 205

Will confirm attendance and degree by mail. Inquiry must include student's name, social security number, years attended, field of study. Employers may obtain transcripts upon written request accompanied by a signed release from the student.

A single program two-year institution, with an enrollment of 452. Highest level of offering: one year but less than four years.
ACCREDITATIONS: NATTS

ITT Technical Institute–Fort Wayne

4919 Coldwater Road
Fort Wayne, IN 46825
(219) 484-4107 Ext. 209

Will confirm attendance and degree by phone or mail. Inquiry must include student's name and social security number. Employers may obtain transcripts upon written request accompanied by a $1.00 fee and a signed release from the student.

A single program two-year institution, with an enrollment of 1,252. Highest level of offering: one year but less than four years.
ACCREDITATIONS: NATTS

ITT Technical Institute–Indianapolis

9511 Angola Court
Indianapolis, IN 46268
(317) 875-8640 Ext. 249
Fax (317) 875-8641

Will confirm attendance and degree by phone or mail. Inquiry must include student's name and years attended. Employers may obtain transcripts upon written request accompanied by a signed release from the student.

A multiprogram two-year institution, with an enrollment of 1,430. Highest level of offering: one year but less than four years.
ACCREDITATIONS: NATTS

ITT Technical Institute–La Mesa

9680 Granite Ridge Drive
San Diego, CA 92123
(619) 571-8500 Ext. 25

Will confirm attendance and degree by phone or mail. Inquiry must include student's name and years attended. Employers may obtain transcripts upon written request accompanied by a signed release from the student.

A two-year institution newly admitted to NCES with an enrollment of 400. Highest level of offering: one year but less than four years.
ACCREDITATIONS: NATTS

ITT Technical Institute

3325 Stop Eight Road
Dayton, OH 45414
(513) 454-2267
Fax (513) 454-2278

Will confirm attendance and degree by phone or mail. Inquiry must include student's name and years attended. Employers may obtain transcripts upon written request accompanied by a signed release from the student.

A multiprogram two-year institution, with an enrollment of 556. Highest level of offering: one year but less than four years.
ACCREDITATIONS: NATTS

ITT Technical Institute

(See Tad Technical Institute)

ITT Technical Institute

4837 East McDowell Road
Phoenix, AZ 85008
(602) 252-2331 Ext. 123

Will confirm attendance and degree by mail. Inquiry must include student's name, social security number, years attended, release. Employers may obtain transcripts upon written request accompanied by a signed release from the student.

A two-year institution newly admitted to NCES, with an enrollment of 900. Highest level of offering: one year but less than four years.
ACCREDITATIONS: NATTS

ITT Technical Institute

6035 N.E. 78th Court
Portland, OR 97218
(503) 760-5690

Will confirm attendance and degree by phone or mail. Inquiry must include student's name, social security number years attended, release. Employers may obtain transcripts upon written request accompanied by a $2.00 fee and a signed release from the student.

A two-year institution newly admitted to NCES, with an enrollment of 500. Highest level of offering: four or five year baccalaureate.
ACCREDITATIONS: NATTS

ITT Technical Institute

13505 Lake Front
Earth City, MO 63045
(314) 298-7800 Ext. 22
Fax (314) 298-0559

Will confirm attendance and degree by phone or mail. Inquiry must include student's name and years attended. Requests should be directed to: Department of Education. Employers may obtain transcripts upon written request accompanied by a signed release from the student.

A two-year institution newly admitted to NCES, with an enrollment of 600. Highest level of offering: one year but less than four years.
ACCREDITATIONS: NATTS

ITT Technical Institute

(Formerly ITT Peterson School of Business)
12720 Gateway Drive
Suite 100
Seattle, WA 98168
(206) 244-3300
Fax (206) 246-7635

Will confirm attendance and degree by phone, fax or mail. Inquiry must include student's name, date of birth, years attended. Employers may obtain transcripts upon written request accompanied by a signed release from the student.

A two-year institution newly admitted to NCES, with an enrollment of 407. Highest level of offering: one year but less than four years.
ACCREDITATIONS: NATTS

ITT Technical Institute

5225 Memorial Highway
Tampa, FL 33634
(813) 885-2244

Will confirm attendance and degree by phone or mail. Inquiry must include student's name and social security number. Employers may obtain transcripts upon written request accompanied by a signed release from the student.

A two-year institution newly admitted to NCES. Highest level of offering: one year but less than four years.
ACCREDITATIONS: NATTS

ITT Technical Institute

655 Wick Avenue–PO Box 779
Youngstown, OH 44501
(216) 747-5555 Ext. 21

Will confirm attendance and degree by phone or mail. Inquiry must include student's name, social security number, years attended. Employers may obtain transcripts upon written request accompanied by a $2.00 fee and a signed release from the student.

A multiprogram two-year institution, with an enrollment of 500. Highest level of offering: one year but less than four years.

ITT Technical Institute–West Covina

1530 West Cameron
West Covina, CA 91790
(818) 960-8681

Will confirm attendance and degree by phone or mail. Inquiry must include student's name and social security number. Employers may obtain transcripts upon written request accompanied by a signed release from the student.

A bachelor's or higher institution newly admitted to NCES, with an enrollment of 800. Highest level of offering: one year but less than four years.
ACCREDITATIONS: NATTS

J

J F Drake State Technical College

3421 Meridan Street, North
Huntsville, AL 35811
(205) 539-8161 Ext. 110

Will confirm attendance and degree by phone or mail. Inquiry must include student's name, social security number, years attended. Employers may obtain transcripts upon written request accompanied by a $2.00 fee and a signed release from the student.

A two-year institution newly admitted to NCES. Highest level of offering: one year but less than four years.
ACCREDITATIONS: SV

J. Sargeant Reynolds Community College

Central Admissions
PO Box 85622
Richmond, VA 23285-5622
(804) 371-3029
Fax (804) 371-3386

Will confirm attendance and degree by phone or mail. Inquiry must include student's name, social security number. Only students may obtain transcripts. Employers may obtain transcripts upon written request accompanied by a signed release from the student.

A multiprogram two-year institution, with an enrollment of 12,954. Highest level of offering: two years but less than four years.
ACCREDITATIONS: SC ADNUR DA DT MAC MLTAD RSTH RSTHT

Jackson Community College

2111 Emmons Road
Jackson, MI 49201
(517) 787-0800 Ext. 122
Fax (517) 789-1631

Will confirm attendance and degree by phone, fax or mail. Inquiry must include student's name, maiden name (if any), date of birth, social security number, years attended. Employers may obtain transcripts upon written request accompanied by a signed release from the student.

A multiprogram two-year institution, with an enrollment of 7,500. Highest level of offering: two year but less than four years.
ACCREDITATIONS: NH RAD

Jackson State Community College

2046 N. Parkway Street
Jackson, TN 38301-3797
(901) 424-2654

Will confirm attendance and degree by phone or mail. Inquiry must include student's name, social security number, release. Employers may obtain transcripts upon written request accompanied by a signed release from the student.

A multiprogram two-year institution, with an enrollment of 2,776. Highest level of offering: one year but less than four years.
ACCREDITATIONS: SC MLTAD RAD RSTH

Jackson State University

PO Box 17125
1400 J R Lynch Street-0125
Jackson, MS 39217-0125
(601) 968-2300

Will confirm attendance and degree by phone or mail. Inquiry must include student's name, social security number, years attended. Requests should be directed to: Registrar's Office. Employers may obtain transcripts upon written request accompanied by a $2.00 fee and a signed release from the student.

A comprehensive institution with no medical school, with an enrollment of 7,152. Highest level of offering: doctorate.
ACCREDITATIONS: SC ART MUS SW TED JOUR

Jacksonville College

500 West Pine Street
Jacksonville, TX 75766
(903) 586-2518 Ext. 24
Fax (903) 586-0743

Will confirm attendance and degree by phone or mail. Inquiry must include student's name. Employers may obtain transcripts upon written request accompanied by a $2.00 fee and a signed release from the student.

A multiprogram two-year institution, with an enrollment of 275. Highest level of offering: one year but less than four years.
ACCREDITATIONS: SC

Jacksonville State University

Admissions and Records
700 Pelham Road North
Jacksonville, AL 36265-9982
(205) 782-5400
Fax (205) 782-5291

Will confirm attendance and degree by phone or mail. Inquiry must include student's name, date of birth, social security number, years attended. Employers may obtain transcripts upon written request accompanied by a $3.00 fee and a signed release from the student.

A comprehensive institution with no medical school, with an enrollment of 8,240. Highest level of offering: beyond master's but less than doctorate.
ACCREDITATIONS: SC NUR TED

Jacksonville University

2800 University Boulevard North
Jacksonville, FL 32211
(904) 744-3950 Ext. 2260
Fax (904) 744-0101

Will confirm attendance and degree by phone or mail. Inquiry must include student's name. Employers may obtain transcripts upon written request accompanied by a $2.00 fee and a signed release from the student.

A comprehensive institution with no medical school, with an enrollment of 2,500. Highest level of offering: master's.
ACCREDITATIONS: SC DANCE MUS

James H. Faulkner State Junior College

1900 Hwy 31 South
Bay Minette, AL 36507
(205) 937-9581 Ext. 311

Will confirm attendance and degree by phone or mail. Inquiry must include student's name. Requests should be directed to: Admissions Office. Employers may obtain transcripts upon written request accompanied by a signed release from the student.

A multiprogram two-year institution, with an enrollment of 2,921. Highest level of offering: one year but less than four years.
ACCREDITATIONS: SC DA

James Madison University

Records Department
Harrisonburg, VA 22807
(703) 568-6281

Will confirm attendance and degree by phone or mail. Inquiry must include student's name, social security number. Requests should be directed to: Registration and Records Office. Employers may obtain transcripts upon written request accompanied by a signed release from the student.

A comprehensive institution with no medical school, with an enrollment of 11,000. Highest level of offering: beyond master's but less than doctorate.
ACCREDITATIONS: SC ART AUD BUS MUS NUR SP SW TED THEA BUSA

James Sprunt Community College

PO Box 398
Kenansville, NC 28349
(919) 296-2400
Fax (919) 296-1636

Will confirm attendance and degree by phone or mail. Inquiry must include student's name, social security number. Requests should be directed to: Student Services. Employers may obtain transcripts upon written request accompanied by a signed release from the student.

A multiprogram two-year institution, with an enrollment of 809. Highest level of offering: two years but less than four years.
ACCREDITATIONS: SC

Jamestown Business College

7 Fairmount Avenue
Jamestown, NY 14701
(716) 664-5100
Fax (716) 664-3144

Will confirm attendance and degree by phone, fax or mail. Inquiry must include student's name. Employers may obtain transcripts upon written request accompanied by a signed release from the student.

A single program two-year institution, with an enrollment of 312. Highest level of offering: one year but less than four years.
ACCREDITATIONS: NY JRCB

Jamestown College

Registrar's Office
Jamestown, ND 58401
(701) 252-3467 Ext. 2554
Fax (701) 253-2318

Will confirm attendance and degree by phone or mail. Inquiry must include student's name. Employers may obtain transcripts upon written request accompanied by a $3.00 fee and a signed release from the student.

A general baccalaureate institution, with an enrollment of 1,029. Highest level of offering: four or five year baccalaureate.
ACCREDITATIONS: NH NUR

Jamestown Community College

525 Falconer Street
Jamestown, NY 14701
(716) 665-5220 Ext. 332

Will confirm attendance and degree by phone or mail. Inquiry must include student's name, social security number, years attended. Employers may obtain transcripts upon written request accompanied by a signed release from the student.

A multiprogram two-year institution, with an enrollment of 3,947. Highest level of offering: one year but less than four years.
ACCREDITATIONS: M ADNUR NY

Jarvis Christian College

Registrar's Office
Drawer G
Hawkins, TX 75765
(214) 769-2174 Ext. 239

Will confirm attendance and degree by phone or mail. Inquiry must include student's name and social security number. Employers may obtain transcripts upon written request accompanied by a $3.00 fee and a signed release from the student.

A general baccalaureate institution, with an enrollment of 481. Highest level of offering: four or five year baccalaureate.
ACCREDITATIONS: SC

Jefferson College

PO Box 1000
Hillsboro, MO 63050
(314) 789-3951 Ext. 205
Fax (314) 789-4012

Will confirm attendance and degree by phone or mail. Inquiry must include student's name, social security number, years attended. Requests should be directed to: Student Services. Employers may obtain transcripts upon written request accompanied by a signed release from the student.

A multiprogram two-year institution, with an enrollment of 3,700. Highest level of offering: one year but less than four years.
ACCREDITATIONS: NH ADVET

Jefferson Community College

Outer Coffeen Street
Watertown, NY 13601
(315) 786-2200 Ext. 2417

Will confirm attendance and degree by phone or mail. Inquiry must include student's name, social security number, years attended. Employers may obtain transcripts upon written request accompanied by a $5.00 fee and a signed release from the student.

A multiprogram two-year institution, with an enrollment of 1,300. Highest level of offering: one year but less than four years.
ACCREDITATIONS: M ADNUR NY

Jefferson Davis State Junior College

220 Alco Drive
Brewton, AL 36426
(205) 867-4832 Ext. 45

Will confirm attendance and degree by mail. Inquiry must include student's name, date of birth, years attended. Employers may obtain transcripts upon written request accompanied by a signed release from the student.

A multiprogram two-year institution, with an enrollment of 1,019. Highest level of offering: one year but less than four years.
ACCREDITATIONS: SC ADNUR

Jefferson State Junior College

2601 Carson Road
Birmingham, AL 35215
(205) 853-1200 Ext. 1272

Will confirm attendance and degree by phone or mail. Inquiry must include student's name, social security number. Employers may obtain transcripts upon written request accompanied by a signed release from the student.

A multiprogram two-year institution, with an enrollment of 6,030. Highest level of offering: one year but less than four years.
ACCREDITATIONS: SC ADNUR FUSER MLTAD RAD ENGT

Jefferson Technical College

4000 Sunset Boulevard
Steubenville, OH 43952
(614) 264-5591 Ext. 289
Fax (614) 1338

Will confirm attendance and degree by phone, fax or mail. Inquiry must include student's name, social security number. Employers may obtain transcripts upon written request accompanied by a $2.00 fee and a signed release from the student.

A multiprogram two-year institution, with an enrollment of 1,449. Highest level of offering: one year but less than four years.
ACCREDITATIONS: NH DA MAC MLTAD RAD

Jersey City State College

2039 Kennedy Boulevard
Jersey City, NJ 07305
(201) 200-3333

Will confirm attendance by phone or mail. Inquiry must include student's name, social security number. Employers may obtain transcripts upon written request accompanied by a $2.00 fee and a signed release from the student.

A comprehensive institution with no medical school, with an enrollment of 8,449. Highest level of offering: beyond master's but less than doctorate.
ACCREDITATIONS: M ART MUS NUR TED

Jesuit School of Theology at Berkley

1735 LeRoy Avenue
Berkeley, CA 94709-1193
(510) 841-8804
Fax (501) 841-8536

Will confirm attendance and degree by phone or mail. Inquiry must include student's name, date of birth. Employers may obtain transcripts upon written request accompanied by a $3.00 fee and a signed release from the student.

A school of theology, with an enrollment of 211. Highest level of offering: beyond master's but less than doctorate.
ACCREDITATIONS: WC THEOL

Jewish Theological Seminary of America

3080 Broadway
New York, NY 10027
(212) 678-8000

Will confirm attendance and degree by mail. Inquiry must include student's name, years attended. Requests should be directed to: Records Office. Employers may obtain transcripts upon written request accompanied by a $5.00 fee and a signed release from the student.

A comprehensive institution with no medical school, with an enrollment of 475. Highest level of offering: doctorate.
ACCREDITATIONS: M NY

John A. Gupton College

2507 West End Avenue
Nashville, TN 37203
(615) 327-3927

Will confirm attendance and degree by mail. Inquiry must include student's name, social security number, years attended. Requests should be directed to: Dean's Office. Employers may obtain transcripts upon written request accompanied by a $5.00 fee and a signed release from the student.

A single program two-year institution, with an enrollment of 50. Highest level of offering: one year but less than four years.
ACCREDITATIONS: SC FUSER

John A. Logan College

Carterville, IL 62918
(618) 985-3741 Ext. 291

Will confirm attendance and degree by phone or mail. Inquiry must include student's name, social security number, years attended. Requests should be directed to: Admissions Office. Employers may obtain transcripts upon written request accompanied by a signed release from the student.

A multiprogram two-year institution, with an enrollment of 4,800. Highest level of offering: associates degree.
ACCREDITATIONS: NH ADNUR

John Bastyr College of Naturopathic Medicine

(See Bastyr College of Naturopathathic Medicine)

John Brown University

Siloam Springs, AR 72761
(501) 524-3131
Fax (501) 524-9548

Will confirm attendance and degree by phone, fax or mail. Inquiry must include student's name, years attended. Employers may obtain transcripts upon written request accompanied by a $2.00 fee and a signed release from the student.

A general baccalaureate institution, with an enrollment of 929. Highest level of offering: four or five year baccalaureate.
ACCREDITATIONS: NH TED

John C. Calhoun State Community College

PO 2216
Decatur, AL 35602
(205) 353-3102

Will confirm attendance and degree by mail. Inquiry must include student's name, date of birth, social security number, release. Requests should be directed to: Admissions Office. Employers may obtain transcripts upon written request accompanied by a signed release from the student.

A multiprogram two-year institution, with an enrollment of 8,000. Highest level of offering: one year but less than four years.
ACCREDITATIONS: SC ADNUR DA PNUR

John Carroll University

20700 North Park Blvd.
University Heights, OH 44118
(216) 397-4291
Fax (216) 397-4256

Will confirm attendance and degree by phone or mail. Inquiry must include student's name, social security number, years attended. Employers may obtain transcripts upon written request accompanied by a $3.00 fee and a signed release from the student.

A comprehensive institution with no medical school, with an enrollment of 4,423. Highest level of offering: master's.
ACCREDITATIONS: AACSB NCA TED

John F. Kennedy University

12 Altarinda Road
Orinda, CA 94563
(415) 254-0200

Will confirm attendance and degree by mail or phone. Inquiry must include student's name, years attended. Employers may obtain transcripts upon written request accompanied by a $3.00 fee and a signed release from the student.

A comprehensive institution with no medical school, with an enrollment of 1,791. Highest level of offering: master's.
ACCREDITATIONS: WC

John M. Patterson State Technical College

3920 Troy Highway
Montgomery, AL 36116-2699
(205) 284-9356
Fax (205) 284-9357

Will confirm attendance and degree by phone, fax or mail. Inquiry must include student's name, social security number, years attended. Employers may obtain transcripts upon written request accompanied by a signed release from the student.

A two-year institution newly admitted to NCES with an enrollment of 700. Highest level of offering: one year but less than four years.
ACCREDITATIONS: SV

John Marshall Law School

315 South Plymouth Court
Chicago, IL 60604
(312) 427-2737 Ext. 466

Will confirm attendance and degree by phone or mail. Inquiry must include student's name, social security number, years attended. Employers may obtain transcripts upon written request accompanied by a $2.00 fee and a signed release from the student.

A law school, with an enrollment of 1,218. Highest level of offering: master's.
ACCREDITATIONS: LAW

John Tyler Community College

13101 Jefferson Davis Highway
Chester, VA 23831
(804) 796-4154
Fax (804) 796-4163

Will confirm attendance and degree by phone, fax or mail. Inquiry must include student's name, social security number, and release. Employers may obtain transcripts upon written request accompanied by a $1.00 fee and a signed release from the student.

A multiprogram two-year institution, with an enrollment of 5,421. Highest level of offering: one year but less than four years.
ACCREDITATIONS: SC ADNUR ENGT FUSER

John Wesley College

2314 North Centennial Street
High Point, NC 27265
(919) 889-2262

Will confirm attendance and degree by phone or mail. Inquiry must include student's name, social security number. Employers may obtain transcripts upon written request accompanied by a $2.00 fee and a signed release from the student.

A school of philosophy, religion and theology, with an enrollment of 94. Highest level of offering: four or five year baccalaureate.
ACCREDITATIONS: BI

John Wood Community College

150 South 48th Street
Quincy, IL 62301
(217) 224-6500 Ext. 140
Fax (217) 224-4208

Will confirm attendance and degree by phone, fax or mail. Inquiry must include student's name, social security number, years attended. Employers may obtain transcripts upon written request accompanied by a $2.00 fee and a signed release from the student.

A multiprogram two-year institution, with an enrollment of 3,664. Highest level of offering: one year but less than four years.
ACCREDITATIONS: NH

Johns Hopkins University

3400 N. Charles Street
Baltimore, MD 21218
(301) 516-8499

Will confirm attendance and degree by phone or mail. Inquiry must include student's name, social security number. Requests should be directed to: Registrar's Office. Employers may obtain transcripts upon written request accompanied by a $3.00 fee and a signed release from the student.

A doctoral-level institution with a medical school, with an enrollment of 10,586. Highest level of offering: doctorate.
ACCREDITATIONS: M ENG MED PH

Johnson and Wales College

Abbott Park Place
Providence, RI 02903
(401) 456-1088
Fax (401) 455-2837

Will confirm attendance and degree by phone, fax or mail. Inquiry must include student's name, social security number, years attended. Employers may obtain transcripts upon written request accompanied by a $2.00 fee and a signed release from the student.

A multiprogram two-year institution, with an enrollment of 3,591. Highest level of offering: four or five year baccalaureate.
ACCREDITATIONS: SRCB

Johnson Bible College

7900 Johnson Drive
Knoxville, TN 37998
(615) 579-2302

Will confirm attendance and degree by phone or mail. Inquiry must include student's name, years attended. Employers may obtain transcripts upon written request accompanied by a $2.00 fee and a signed release from the student.

A general baccalaureate institution, with an enrollment of 400. Highest level of offering: master's.
ACCREDITATIONS: SC BI

Johnson C. Smith University

100 Beatties Ford Road
Charlotte, NC 28216
(704) 378-1013
Fax (704) 372-5746

Will confirm attendance and degree by phone or mail. Inquiry must include student's name, social security number, years attended. Employers may obtain transcripts upon written request accompanied by a $3.00 fee and a signed release from the student.

A general baccalaureate institution, with an enrollment of 1,442. Highest level of offering: four or five year baccalaureate.
ACCREDITATIONS: SACS

Johnson County Community College

12345 College Boulevard at Quivira Road
Overland Park, KS 66210-1299
(913) 469-8500 Ext. 3803

Will confirm attendance and degree by phone or mail. Inquiry must include student's name, social security number. Employers may obtain transcripts upon written request accompanied by a $2.00 fee and a signed release from the student.

A multiprogram two-year institution, with an enrollment of 16,000. Highest level of offering: one year but less than four years.
ACCREDITATIONS: NH ADNUR DH

Johnson State College

Johnson, VT 05656
(802) 635-2356 Ext. 229
Fax (802) 635-2069

Will confirm attendance and degree by phone, fax or mail. Inquiry must include student's name, social security number, years attended. Employers may obtain transcripts upon written request accompanied by a $3.00 fee and a signed release from the student.

A general baccalaureate institution, with an enrollment of 1,600. Highest level of offering: master's.
ACCREDITATIONS: EH

Johnston Community College

PO Box 2350
Smithfield, NC 27577
(919) 934-3051 Ext. 218
Fax (919) 934-2823

Will confirm attendance and degree by phone or mail. Inquiry must include student's name, social security number. Employers may obtain transcripts upon written request accompanied by a signed release from the student.

A multiprogram two-year institution, with an enrollment of 2,222. Highest level of offering: one year but less than four years.
ACCREDITATIONS: SC RAD

Joliet Junior College

1216 Houbolt Avenue
Joliet, IL 60436
(815) 744-2200 Ext 2242 or 2290
Fax (815) 744-5507

Will confirm attendance and degree by phone, fax or mail. Inquiry must include student's name, social security number, years attended. Employers may obtain transcripts upon written request accompanied by a $3.00 fee and a signed release from the student.

A multiprogram two-year institution, with an enrollment of 9,845. Highest level of offering: one year but less than four years.
ACCREDITATIONS: NH ADNUR

Jones College Jacksonville

5353 Arlington Expressway
Jacksonville, FL 32211
(904) 743-1122
Fax (904) 743-1122

Will confirm attendance and degree by mail or fax. Inquiry must include student's name, social security number, years attended, release. Employers may obtain transcripts upon written request accompanied by a $2.00 fee and a signed release from the student.

A business school, with an enrollment of 800. Highest level of offering: four or five year baccalaureate.
ACCREDITATIONS: SRCB

Jones County Junior College

Ellisville, MS 39437
(601) 477-4047 or 477-4036

Will confirm attendance and degree by phone or mail. Inquiry must include student's name, social security number, years attended. Employers may obtain transcripts upon written request accompanied by a $1.00 fee and a signed release from the student.

A multiprogram two-year institution, with an enrollment of 3,693. Highest level of offering: one year but less than four years.
ACCREDITATIONS: SC

Jordan College

360 West Pine Street
Cedar Springs, MI 49319
(616) 696-1180 Ext. 20
Fax (616) 696-3790

Will confirm attendance and degree by phone or mail. Inquiry must include student's name, social security number, years attended. Employers may obtain transcripts upon written request accompanied by a $2.00 fee and a signed release from the student.

A multiprogram two-year institution, with an enrollment of 1,711. Highest level of offering: four or five year baccalaureate.
ACCREDITATIONS: 3IC

Judson Baptist College

c/o Southwestern College
2625 E. Cactus Road
Phoenix, AR 85032
(602) 992-6101

Will confirm attendance and degree by mail. Inquiry must include student's name, social security number, years attended. Employers may obtain transcripts upon written request accompanied by a $2.00 fee and a signed release from the student.

Judson College

1151 North State
Elgin, IL 60123
(708) 695-2500 Ext. 143
Fax (708) 695-0407

Will confirm attendance and degree by phone, fax or mail. Inquiry must include student's name, date of birth, social security number, SASE. Employers may obtain transcripts upon written request accompanied by a signed release from the student.

A general baccalaureate institution, with an enrollment of 509. Highest level of offering: four or five year baccalaureate.
ACCREDITATIONS: NH

Judson College

Bibb Street PO Box 120
Marion, AL 36756
(205) 683-6161 Ext. 809

Will confirm attendance and degree by mail. Inquiry must include student's full name, date of birth, social security number, years attended, release. Employers may obtain transcripts upon written request accompanied by a $5.00 fee and a signed release from the student.

A general baccalaureate institution, with an enrollment of 401. Highest level of offering: four or five year baccalaureate.
ACCREDITATIONS: SC MUS

Juniata College

1700 Moore Street
Huntingdon, PA 16652
(814) 643-4310 Ext. 270

Will confirm attendance and degree by phone or mail. Inquiry must include student's name, years attended. Employers may obtain transcripts upon written request accompanied by a signed release from the student.

A general baccalaureate institution, with an enrollment of 1,185. Highest level of offering: four or five year baccalaureate.
ACCREDITATIONS: M SW

K

Kalamazoo College

1200 Academy Street
Kalamazoo, MI 49007
(616) 383-8448
Fax (616) 383-5688

Will confirm attendance and degree by phone, fax or mail. Inquiry must include student's name, date of birth, years attended. Employers may obtain transcripts upon written request accompanied by a $2.00 fee and a signed release from the student. Requests should be directed to: Records Office.

A general baccalaureate institution, with an enrollment of 1,270. Highest level of offering: four or five year baccalaureate.
ACCREDITATIONS: NH

Kalamazoo Valley Community College

6767 West O Avenue
Kalamazoo, MI 49009
(616) 372-5000 Ext. 281

Will confirm attendance and degree by phone or mail. Inquiry must include student's name, date of birth, social security number, years attended. Employers may obtain transcripts upon written request accompanied by a $1.00 fee and a signed release from the student.

A multiprogram two-year institution, with an enrollment of 10,500. Highest level of offering: one year but less than four years.

ACCREDITATIONS: NH DH MAC RSTH RSTHT

Kankakee Community College

PO Box 888
Kankakee, IL 60901
(815) 933-0242

Will confirm attendance and degree by phone or mail. Inquiry must include student's name, social security number, years attended. Employers may obtain transcripts upon written request accompanied by a $1.00 fee and a signed release from the student.

A multiprogram two-year institution, with an enrollment of 3,881. Highest level of offering: one year but less than four years.

ACCREDITATIONS: NH MLTAD RAD RSTHT

Kansas City Art Institute

4415 Warwick Boulevard
Kansas City, MO 64111
(816) 561-4852 Ext. 244

Will confirm attendance and degree by phone or mail. Inquiry must include student's name, date of birth, social security number, years attended. Requests should be directed to: Records Office. Employers may obtain transcripts upon written request by student accompanied by a $2.00 fee and a signed release from the student.

A visual and performing arts school, with an enrollment of 600. Highest level of offering: four or five year baccalaureate.

ACCREDITATIONS: NH ART

Kansas City College and Bible School

7401 Metcalf
Overland Park, KS 66204
(913) 722-0272 Ext. 25

Will confirm attendance and degree by phone or mail. Inquiry must include student's name, date of birth, social security number, years attended. Employers may obtain transcripts upon written request accompanied by a $2.00 fee and a signed release from the student.

A bachelor's or higher institution newly admitted to NCES. Highest level of offering: four or five year baccalaureate.

Kansas City Kansas Community College

7250 State Avenue
Kansas City, KS 66112
(913) 334-1100 Ext. 601

Will confirm attendance and degree by phone or mail. Inquiry must include student's name, social security number, years attended, self addressed stamped envelope. Employers may obtain transcripts upon written request accompanied by a $1.00 fee and a signed release from the student.

A multiprogram two-year institution, with an enrollment of 6,000. Highest level of offering: one year but less than four years.

ACCREDITATIONS: NH ADNUR FUSER

Kansas College of Technology

(See Kansas State University - Salina, The College of Technology)

Kansas Newman College

3100 McCormick Avenue
Wichita, KS 67213
(316) 942-4291 Ext. 121

Will confirm attendance and degree by phone or mail. Inquiry must include student's name, date of birth, social security number, years attended. Requests should be directed to: Registrar's Office. Employers may obtain transcripts upon written request accompanied by a $2.00 fee and a signed release from the student.

A general baccalaureate institution, with an enrollment of 1,444. Highest level of offering: four or five year baccalaureate.

ACCREDITATIONS: NH ADNUR ANEST NUR

Kansas State University of Agriculture and Applied Science

118 Anderson Hall
Manhattan, KS 66506
(913) 532-6254

Will confirm attendance and degree by phone or mail. Inquiry must include student's name, date of birth, social security number, years attended, self addressed stamped envelope. Employers may obtain transcripts upon written request accompanied by a $3.00 fee and a signed release from the student. Requests should be directed to: Records Department.

A doctoral-level institution with a medical school, with an enrollment of 18,089. Highest level of offering: doctorate.

ACCREDITATIONS: NH ARCH BUS ENG ENGT FIDER JOUR LSAR MFCD MUS SP TED VET SW THEA

Kansas State University

118 Anderson Hall
Manhattan, KS 66506
(913) 532-6254

Will confirm attendance and degree by phone or mail. Inquiry must include student's name, date of birth, social security number, years attended, self addressed stamped envelope. Employers may obtain transcripts upon written request accompanied by a $3.00 fee and a signed release from the student.

A doctoral-level institution with a medical school, with an enrollment of 18,089. Highest level of offering: doctorate.

ACCREDITATIONS: NH ARCH BUS DIET ENG ENGT FIDER JOUR LSAR MFCD MUS SP TED VET SW THEA

Kansas State University-Salina, The College of Technology

(Formerly Kansas College of Technology)
2409 Scanlan Avenue
Salina, KS 67401-8186
(913) 825-0275 Ext. 463
Fax (913) 825-8475

Will confirm attendance and degree by phone or mail. Inquiry must include student's name, date of birth, social security number, years attended. Employers may obtain transcripts upon written request accompanied by a $1.00 fee and a signed release from the student.

A multiprogram two-year institution, with an enrollment of 629. Highest level of offering: one year but less than four years.

ACCREDITATIONS: NH ENGT

Kansas Technical Institute

(See Kansas College of Technology)

Kansas Wesleyan University

Attn: Registrar
100 East Claflin
Salina, KS 67401
(913) 827-5541
Fax (913) 827-0927

Will confirm attendance and degree by phone or mail. Inquiry must include student's name, social security number, years attended. Employers may obtain transcripts upon written request accompanied by a $3.00 fee and a signed release from the student.

A general baccalaureate institution, with an enrollment of 750. Highest level of offering: four or five year baccalaureate.

ACCREDITATIONS: NCA

Kapiolani Community College

4303 Diamond Head Road
Honolulu, HI 96816
(808) 734-9532 or 734-9533

Will confirm attendance and degree by phone or mail. Inquiry must include student's name, social security number. Employers may obtain transcripts upon written request accompanied by a $1.00 fee and a signed release from the student. Requests should be directed to: Registration & Records.

A multiprogram two-year institution, with an enrollment of 6,500. Highest level of offering: one year but less than four years.

ACCREDITATIONS: WJ DA MAC MLTAD RAD RSTH RSTHT

Kaskaskia College

Shattuc Road
Centralia, IL 62801
(618) 532-1981 Ext. 241

Will confirm attendance and degree by phone or mail. Inquiry must include student's name, date of birth, social security number, years attended. Employers may obtain transcripts upon written request accompanied by a $1.00 fee and a signed release from the student. Requests should be directed to: Admissions Office.

A multiprogram two-year institution, with an enrollment of 2,644. Highest level of offering: one year but less than four years.
ACCREDITATIONS: NH ADNUR DA RAD

Katharine Gibbs School

5 Arlingtion Street
Boston, MA 02116
(617) 262-2250 Ext. 110
Fax (617) 262-6210

Will confirm attendance and degree by phone, fax or mail. Inquiry must include student's name, maiden name, social security number, day or evening classes. Employers may obtain transcripts upon written request accompanied by a $3.00 fee and a signed release from the student. Requests should be directed to: Registrar's Office.

A single program two-year institution, with an enrollment of 810. Highest level of offering: one year but less than four years.
ACCREDITATIONS: JRCB

Katharine Gibbs School

535 Broad Hollow Road
Melville, NY 11747
(516) 293-2460

Will confirm attendance and degree by mail. Inquiry must include student's name, years attended. Requests should be directed to: Transcript Coordinator. Employers may obtain transcripts upon written request accompanied by a $3.00 fee and a signed release from the student.

A two-year institution newly admitted to NCES, with an enrollment of 273. Highest level of offering: one year but less than four years.
ACCREDITATIONS: NY

Kauai Community College

3–1901 Kaumualii Hwy
Lihue, HI 96766
(808) 245-8311

Will confirm attendance and degree by phone or mail. Inquiry must include student's name, date of birth, social security number, years attended. Requests should be directed to: Admissions & Records. Employers may obtain transcripts upon written request accompanied by a $1.00 fee and a signed release from the student. Make check payable to Univ. of Hawaii.

A multiprogram two-year institution, with an enrollment of 1,159. Highest level of offering: one year but less than four years.
ACCREDITATIONS: WJ ADNUR

Kean College of New Jersey

Morris Avenue
Union, NJ 07083
(908) 527-2023

Will confirm attendance and degree by mail. Inquiry must include student's name, social security number, years attended. Requests should be directed to: Registrar's Office. Employers may obtain transcripts upon written request accompanied by a $3.00 fee and a signed release from the student.

A comprehensive institution with no medical school, with an enrollment of 12,758. Highest level of offering: beyond master's but less than doctorate.
ACCREDITATIONS: M MRA MUS NUR OT PTA SW TED

Kearney State College

25th Street & 9th Avenue
Kearney, NE 68849
(308) 234-8527

Will confirm attendance and degree by phone or mail. Inquiry must include student's name, social security number, years attended. Employers may obtain transcripts upon written request accompanied by a $2.00 fee and a signed release from the student.

A comprehensive institution with no medical school, with an enrollment of 10,000. Highest level of offering: beyond master's but less than doctorate.
ACCREDITATIONS: CHM NH MUS NUR SP SW TED

Keene State College

229 Main Street
Keene, NH 03431
(603) 352-1909 Ext. 283

Will confirm attendance and degree by phone or mail. Inquiry must include student's name, social security number, years attended. Employers may obtain transcripts upon written request accompanied by a $2.00 fee and a signed release from the student. Requests should be directed to: Registrar's Office.

A general baccalaureate institute, with an enrollment of 3,512. Highest level of offering: master's
ACCREDITATIONS: EH TED

Kehilath Yakov Rabbinical Seminary

206 Wilson Street
Brooklyn, NY 11211
(718) 963-1212

Will confirm attendance and degree by mail. Inquiry must include student's name, date of birth, social security number, years attended. Employers may obtain transcripts upon written request accompanied by a signed release from the student.

A specialized non-degree granting institution, with an enrollment of 1500. Highest level of offering: four or five year baccalaureate.
ACCREDITATIONS: RABN

Keller Graduate School of Management

10 South Riverside Plaza
Chicago, IL 60606
(312) 454-0880

Will confirm attendance and degree by phone or mail. Inquiry must include student's name, social security number, years attended. Employers may obtain transcripts upon written request accompanied by a $2.00 fee and a signed release from the student.

A business school, with an enrollment of 2,000. Highest level of offering: master's.
ACCREDITATIONS: NCA

Kellogg Community College

450 North Avenue
Battle Creek, MI 49016
(616) 965-3931 Ext. 2614
Fax (616) 965-4133

Will confirm attendance by phone or mail. Include student's name and social security number. Will confirm degree by phone or mail. Inquiry must include student's name, date of birth, social security number, release. Requests should be directed to: Records Office. Employers may obtain transcripts upon written request accompanied by a $2.00 fee and a signed release from the student.

A multiprogram two-year institution, with an enrollment of 7,553. Highest level of offering: one year but less than four years.
ACCREDITATIONS: NH DH MLTAD PTAA RAD

Kemper Military School and College

701 Third Street
Boonville, MO 65233
(816) 882-5623 Ext. 55

Will confirm attendance and degree by phone or mail. Inquiry must include student's name, date of birth, years attended. Requests should be directed to: Academics/Registrar's Office. Employers may obtain transcripts upon written request accompanied by a $2.00 fee and a signed release from the student.

A multiprogram two-year institution, with an enrollment of 230. Highest level of offering: one year but less than four years.
ACCREDITATIONS: NH

Kenai Peninsula Community College

34820 College Drive
Soldotna, AK 99669
(907) 262-5801 Ext. 27

Will confirm attendance and degree by mail. Inquiry must include student's name, social security number, years attended. Employers may obtain transcripts upon written request accompanied by a $4.00 fee and a signed release from the student.

A multiprogram two-year institution, with an enrollment of 1,155. Highest level of offering: one year but less than four years.
ACCREDITATIONS: NW

Kendall College of Art and Design

111 North Division
Grand Rapids, MI 49503
(616) 451-2787 Ext. 40
Fax (616) 451-9867

Will confirm attendance and degree by phone or mail. Inquiry must include student's name, date of birth, social security number, years attended. Employers may obtain transcripts upon written request accompanied by a $3.00 fee and a signed release from the student.

A general baccalaureate institution, with an enrollment of 687. Highest level of offering: four or five year baccalaureate.
ACCREDITATIONS: NH ART FIDER

Kendall College

2408 Orrington Avenue
Evanston, IL 60201
(708) 866-1324

Will confirm attendance and degree by
phone or mail. Inquiry must include student's name, date of birth, years attended.
Employers may obtain transcripts upon
written request by student accompanied by
a $3.00 fee and a signed release from the
student.

A general baccalaureate institution, with an
enrollment of 4008. Highest level of offering: four or five year baccalaureate.

ACCREDITATIONS: NH

Kennebec Valley Vocational Technical Institute

PO Box 29
Fairfield, ME 04937
(207) 453-9762 Ext. 127

Will confirm attendance and degree by mail
or phone. Inquiry must include student's
name, date of birth, social security number,
years attended, release. Employers may obtain transcripts upon written request accompanied by a $2.00 fee and a signed release
from the student.

A two-year institution newly admitted to
NCES, with an enrollment of 681. Highest
level of offering: one year but less than four
years.

ACCREDITATIONS: EV ADNUR RSTHT

Kennedy–King College

Attn: Registrar
6800 South Wentworth Avenue
Chicago, IL 60621
(312) 962-3200
Fax (312) 962-0391

Will confirm attendance and degree by
mail. Inquiry must include student's name,
date of birth, years attended, release.
Employers may obtain transcripts upon
written request accompanied by a $2.00 fee
and a signed release from the student.

A multiprogram two-year institution, with
an enrollment of 8,081. Highest level of offering: one year but less than four years.

ACCREDITATIONS: NH

Kennesaw State College

PO Box 444
Marietta, GA 30061
(404) 423-6200
Fax (404) 423-6541

Will confirm attendance and degree by
phone or mail. Inquiry must include student's name, social security number, years
attended. Employers may obtain transcripts
upon written request accompanied by a
signed release from the student.

A general baccalaureate institution, with an
enrollment of 10,800. Highest level of offering: master's.

ACCREDITATIONS: SC ADNUR

Kenrick Seminary

5200 Glennon Drive
St. Louis, MO 63119
(314) 644-0266 Ext. 108

Will confirm attendance and degree by
phone or mail. Inquiry must include student's name, years attended. Employers
may obtain transcripts upon written request
accompanied by a $3.00 fee and a signed
release from the student.

A school of philosophy, religion and theology, with an enrollment of 70. Highest level
of offering: master's.

ACCREDITATIONS: NH THEOL

Kent State University Ashtabula Regional Campus

3325 West 13th Street
Ashtabula, OH 44004
(216) 964-3322 Ext. 216

Will confirm attendance and degree by
phone or mail. Inquiry must include student's name, date of birth, social security
number, years attended. Requests should be
directed to: Records Department.
Employers may obtain transcripts upon
written request accompanied by a signed release from the student.

A multiprogram two-year institution, with
an enrollment of 950. Highest level of offering: two years but less than four years.

ACCREDITATIONS: NH ADNUR

Kent State University East Liverpool Regional Campus

400 E. Fourth Street
East Liverpool, OH 43920
(216) 385-3805

Will confirm attendance and degree by
phone or mail. Inquiry must include student's name, date of birth, social security
number, years attended, self addressed
stamped envelope. Employers may obtain
transcripts upon written request accompanied by a $3.00 fee and a signed release
from the student.

A multiprogram two-year institution, with
an enrollment of 800. Highest level of offering: associate.

ACCREDITATIONS: NH ADNUR

Kent State University Main Campus

Kent, OH 44242
(216) 672-3131

Will confirm attendance and degree by
phone or mail. Inquiry must include student's name, date of birth, social security
number, years attended. Employers may obtain transcripts upon written request accompanied by a signed release from the student.

A doctoral-level institution with no medical
school, with an enrollment of 22,000 to
24,000. Highest level of offering: doctorate.

ACCREDITATIONS: NH ARCH ART AUD
BUS CLPSY FIDER JOUR LIB MUS NUR
SCPSY TED SP

Kent State University Salem Campus

2491 State Rt. 45 South
Salem, OH 44460
(216) 332-0361 Ext. 19

Will confirm attendance and degree by
phone or mail. Inquiry must include student's name, social security number, years
attended. Employers may obtain transcripts
upon written request accompanied by a
signed release from the student.

A multiprogram two-year institution, with
an enrollment of 900. Highest level of offering: one year but less than four years.

ACCREDITATIONS: NH

Kent State University Stark County Regional Campus

6000 Frank Avenue North West
Canton, OH 44720
(216) 499-9600 Ext. 241
Fax (216) 494-6121

Will confirm attendance and degree by
phone, fax or mail. Inquiry must include
student's name, social security number,
years attended. Employers may obtain transcripts upon written request accompanied
by a signed release from the student.

A multiprogram two-year institution, with
an enrollment of 2,000. Highest level of offering: one year but less than four years.

ACCREDITATIONS: NH

Kent State University Trumbull Regional Campus

4314 Mahoning Ave. North West
Warren, OH 44483
(216) 847-0571 Ext. 335
Fax (216) 847-6172

Will confirm attendance and degree by
phone or mail. Inquiry must include student's name, date of birth, social security
number, years attended. Requests should be
directed to: Student Services. Employers
may obtain transcripts upon written request
accompanied by a signed release from the
student.

A multiprogram two-year institution, with
an enrollment of 1,800. Highest level of offering: one year but less than four years.

ACCREDITATIONS: NH

Kent State University Tuscarawas Regional Campus

University Drive North East
New Philadelphia, OH 44663
(216) 339-3391 Ext. 221
Fax (216) 339-3321

Will confirm attendance and degree by
phone, fax or mail. Inquiry must include
student's name, date of birth, social security
number, years attended. Request should be
directed to: Registrar's Office. Employers
may obtain transcripts upon written request
accompanied by a signed release from the
student.

A multiprogram two-year institution, with
an enrollment of 1,020. Highest level of offering: one year but less than four years.

ACCREDITATIONS: NH ADNUR ENGT

Kentucky Christian College

617 North Carol Malone Boulevard
Grayson, KY 41143
(606) 474-6613 Ext. 2212
Fax (606) 474-3502

Will confirm attendance and degree by phone, fax or mail. Inquiry must include student's name. Employers may obtain transcripts upon written request accompanied by a $2.00 fee and a signed release from the student.

A school of philosophy, religion and theology, with an enrollment of 505. Highest level of offering: four or five year baccalaureate.

ACCREDITATIONS: SACS BI

Kentucky College of Business

628 East Main Street
Lexington, KY 40508
(606) 253-0621
Fax (606) 233-3054

Will confirm attendance and degree by phone or mail. Inquiry must include student's name, date of birth, social security number, years attended. Employers may obtain transcripts upon written request accompanied by a $2.00 fee and a signed release from the student. Attn: Registrar's Office.

A multiprogram two-year institution, with an enrollment of 418. Highest level of offering: one year but less than four years.

ACCREDITATIONS: JRCB

Kentucky State University

Frankfort, KY 40601
(502) 227-6000
Fax (502) 227-6890

Will confirm attendance and degree by mail. Inquiry must include student's name, date of birth, social security number, years attended, release. Employers may obtain transcripts upon written request accompanied by a $2.00 fee and a signed release from the student. Requests should be directed to: Registrar's / Records Office.

A general baccalaureate institution, with an enrollment of 2,066. Highest level of offering: master's.

ACCREDITATIONS: SC ADNUR MUS SW TED

Kentucky Wesleyan College

3000 Frederica St.
Owensboro, KY 42302
(502) 926-3111 Ext. 118
Fax (502) 926-3196

Will confirm attendance and degree by phone or mail. Inquiry must include student's name, social security number, years attended. Employers may obtain transcripts upon written request accompanied by a $2.00 fee and a signed release from the student.

A general baccalaureate institution, with an enrollment of 821. Highest level of offering: four or five year baccalaureate.

ACCREDITATIONS: SC

Kenyon College

Gambier, OH 43022
(614) 427-5121

Will confirm attendance and degree by phone or mail. Inquiry must include student's name, date of birth, years attended. Employers may obtain transcripts upon written request accompanied by a $2.00 fee and a signed release from the student.

A general baccalaureate institution, with an enrollment of 1,500. Highest level of offering: four or five year baccalaureate.

ACCREDITATIONS: NCA

Ketchikan College

7th And Madison
Ketchikan, AK 99901
(907) 225-6177

Will confirm attendance and degree by phone or mail. Inquiry must include student's name, years attended, release. Requests should be directed to: Student Services. Employers may obtain transcripts upon written request accompanied by a $2.00 fee and a signed release from the student. Request should be mailed to: University of Alaska Southeast; 11120 Glacier Highway, Juneau, AK 99801.

A multiprogram two-year institution, with an enrollment of 800. Highest level of offering: one year but less than four years.

ACCREDITATIONS: NW

Kettering College of Medical Arts

3737 Southern Boulevard
Kettering, OH 45429
(513) 296-7228

Will confirm attendance and degree by phone or mail. Inquiry must include student's name, date of birth, social security number, years attended. Employers may obtain transcripts upon written request accompanied by a $2.00 fee and a signed release from the student.

A single program two-year institution, with an enrollment of 463. Highest level of offering: one year but less than four years.

ACCREDITATIONS: NCA APCP MLTAD RAD RSTH PAST

Keuka College

Keuka Park, NY 14478
(315) 536-4411 Ext. 204

Will confirm attendance and degree by phone or mail. Inquiry must include student's name, years attended, social security number. Requests should be directed to: Registrar's Office. Employers may obtain transcripts upon written request accompanied by a $4.00 fee and a signed release from the student.

A general baccalaureate institution, with an enrollment of 750. Highest level of offering: four or five year baccalaureate.

ACCREDITATIONS: M NUR NY SW OT

Keystone Junior College

PO Box 50
La Plume, PA 18440
(717) 945-5141 Ext. 2301

Will confirm attendance and degree by phone or mail. Inquiry must include student's name, years attended. Employers may obtain transcripts upon written request accompanied by a $3.00 fee and a signed release from the student.

A multiprogram two-year institution, with an enrollment of 1,092. Highest level of offering: one year but less than four years.

ACCREDITATIONS: M

Kilgore College

1100 Broadway
Kilgore, TX 75662
(903) 984-8531

Will confirm attendance and degree by phone or mail. Inquiry must include student's name, date of birth, social security number, years attended. Employers may obtain transcripts upon written request accompanied by a $2.00 fee and a signed release from the student.

A multiprogram two-year institution, with an enrollment of 4,469. Highest level of offering: one year but less than four years.

ACCREDITATIONS: SC ADNUR

Kilian Community College

1600 South Menlo Avenue
Sioux Falls, SD 57105
(605) 336-1711

Will confirm attendance and degree by phone or mail. Inquiry must include student's name, date of birth, social security number, years attended, release. Employers may obtain transcripts upon written request accompanied by a $2.00 fee and a signed release from the student.

A multiprogram two-year institution, with an enrollment of 230. Highest level of offering: one year but less than four years.

ACCREDITATIONS: NCA

King College

1350 King College Road
Bristol, TN 37620-2699
(615) 968-1187 Ext. 232

Will confirm attendance and degree by phone or mail. Inquiry must include student's name, date of birth, social security number, years attended. Employers may obtain transcripts upon written request accompanied by a $3.00 fee and a signed release from the student.

A general baccalaureate institution, with an enrollment of 589. Highest level of offering: four or five year baccalaureate.

ACCREDITATIONS: SC

King's College

133 North River Street
Wilkes–Barre, PA 18711
(717) 826-5870 Ext. 870

Will confirm attendance and degree by phone or mail. Inquiry must include student's name, date of birth, social security number, years attended, release. Employers may obtain transcripts upon written request accompanied by a $4.00 fee and a signed release from the student.

A general baccalaureate institution, with an enrollment of 1,639. Highest level of offering: four or five year baccalaureate.

ACCREDITATIONS: M APCP TED

King's College

Briarcliff Manor, NY 10510
(914) 944-5519

Will confirm attendance and degree by phone or mail. Inquiry must include student's name, years attended. Employers may obtain transcripts upon written request accompanied by a $3.00 fee and a signed release from the student.

A general baccalaureate institution, with an enrollment of 513. Highest level of offering: four or five year baccalaureate.
ACCREDITATIONS: M NY

Kings River Community College

995 North Reed
Reedley, CA 93654
(209) 638-3641 Ext. 221

Will confirm attendance and degree by phone or mail. Inquiry must include student's name, date of birth, social security number, years attended, release. Employers may obtain transcripts upon written request accompanied by a $2.00 fee and a signed release from the student. Requests should be directed to: Admissions & Records Office.

A multiprogram two-year institution, with an enrollment of 5,500. Highest level of offering: one year but less than four years.
ACCREDITATIONS: WJ DA

Kirksville College of Osteopathic Medicine

800 West Jefferson
Kirksville, MO 63501
(816) 626-2356
Fax (816) 626-2483

Will confirm attendance and degree by phone or mail. Inquiry must include student's name, years attended.

A medical school, with an enrollment of 536. Highest level of offering: first professional degree.
ACCREDITATIONS: OSTEO

Kirkwood Community College

PO Box 2068
Cedar Rapids, IA 52406
(319) 398-5603

Will confirm attendance and degree by phone or mail. Inquiry must include student's name, date of birth, social security number, years attended. Employers may obtain transcripts upon written request accompanied by a signed release from the student.

A multiprogram two-year institution, with an enrollment of 7,800. Highest level of offering: one year but less than four years.
ACCREDITATIONS: NCA DA DT EEG MAC MRT RSTH

Kirtland Community College

10775 North St. Helen Road
Roscommon, MI 48653
(517) 275-5121 Ext. 248

Will confirm attendance and degree by phone or mail. Inquiry must include student's name, date of birth, social security number, years attended. Employers may obtain transcripts upon written request accompanied by a $3.00 fee and a signed release from the student. Requests should be directed to: Student Services.

A multiprogram two-year institution, with an enrollment of 1,400. Highest level of offering: one year but less than four years.
ACCREDITATIONS: NCA

Kishwaukee College

Highway 38 and Malta Road
Malta, IL 60150
(815) 825-2086 Ext. 274
Fax (815) 825-2072

Will confirm attendance and degree by phone or mail. Inquiry must include student's name, date of birth, social security number. Requests should be directed to: Student Services. Employers may obtain transcripts upon written request accompanied by a $2.00 fee and a signed release from the student.

A multiprogram two-year institution, with an enrollment of 1,500. Highest level of offering: one year but less than four years.
ACCREDITATIONS: NCA RAD

Knox College

Galesburg, IL 61401
(309) 343-0112 Ext. 205

Will confirm attendance and degree by phone or mail. Inquiry must include student's name, years attended, release. Requests should be directed to: Registrar's Office. Employers may obtain transcripts upon written request accompanied by a $3.00 fee and a signed release from the student.

A general baccalaureate institution, with an enrollment of 975. Highest level of offering: four or five year baccalaureate.
ACCREDITATIONS: NCA

Knoxville Business College

720 North Fifth Avenue
Knoxville, TN 37917
(615) 524-3043 Ext. 22

Will confirm attendance and degree by phone or mail. Inquiry must include student's name, date of birth, social security number, years attended. Employers may obtain transcripts upon written request accompanied by a signed release from the student.

A multiprogram two-year institution, with an enrollment of 350. Highest level of offering: one year but less than four years.
ACCREDITATIONS: JRCB

Knoxville College - Morristown Campus

901 College Street
Knoxville, TN 37921
(615) 524-6513 Ext. 510

Will confirm attendance and degree by mail. Inquiry must include student's name, date of birth, social security number, years attended. Employers may obtain transcripts upon written request accompanied by a $3.00 fee and a signed release from the student.

A two year institution, with an enrollment of 1,200. Highest level of offering: associate's.
ACCREDITATIONS: SACS

Knoxville College

(Formerly Morristown College)
417 N. James Street
Morristown, TN 37814
(615) 586-5262

Will confirm attendance and degree by phone or mail. Inquiry must include student's name, date of birth, social security number, years attended. Employers may obtain transacsripts upon written request accompanied by a $3.00 fee and a signed release from the student.

A general baccalaureate institution, with an enrollment of 178. Highest level of offering: four or five year baccalaureate.
ACCREDITATIONS: SACS

Kodiak Community College

117 Benny Benson Drive
Kodiak, AK 99615
(907) 486-4161 Ext. 44
Fax (907) 486-4166

Will confirm attendance and degree by phone, fax or mail. Inquiry must include student's name, social security number, release. Employers may obtain transacsripts upon written request accompanied by a $4.00 fee and a signed release from the student.

A multiprogram two-year institution, with an enrollment of 830. Highest level of offering: one year but less than four years.
ACCREDITATIONS: NW

Kol Yaakov Torah Center

PO Box 402
Monsey, NY 10952
(914) 425-3863

Will confirm attendance and degree by phone or mail. Inquiry must include student's name, date of birth, social security number, years attended. Employers may obtain transacsripts upon written request accompanied by a signed release from the student.

A bachelor's or higher institution newly admitted to NCES. Highest level of offering: beyond master's but less than doctorate.
ACCREDITATIONS: RABN

Kuskokwim College

(See University of Alaska Fairbanks.)

Kutztown University of Pennsylvania

PO Box 730
Kutztown, PA 19530
(215) 683-4485

Will confirm attendance and degree by phone or mail. Inquiry must include student's name, social security number, years attended. Employers may obtain transcripts upon written request accompanied by a $2.00 fee and a signed release from the student. Requests should be directed to: Registrar's Office.

A comprehensive institution with no medical sacschool, with an enrollment of 6,001. Highest level of offering: master's.
ACCREDITATIONS: M TED NUR

L

La Grange College

601 Broad Street
La Grange, GA 30240
(404) 882-2911 Ext. 237

Will confirm attendance and degree by phone or mail. Inquiry must include student's name, date of birth, social security number, years attended. Requests should be directed to: Registrar's Office. Employers may obtain transcripts upon written request accompanied by a signed release from the student.

A general baccalaureate institution, with an enrollment of 947. Highest level of offering: master's.
ACCREDITATIONS: SACS ADNUR

La Roche College

9000 Babcock Boulevard
Pittsburgh, PA 15237
(412) 367-9300 Ext. 118
Fax (412) 367-9368

Will confirm attendance and degree by phone or mail. Inquiry must include student's name, years attended. Employers may obtain transcripts upon written request accompanied by a $3.00 fee and a signed release from the student.

A general baccalaureate institution, with an enrollment of 1,868. Highest level of offering: master's.
ACCREDITATIONS: M ANEST NUR FIDER

La Salle University

20th Street and Olney Avenue
Philadelphia, PA 19141
(215) 951-1021

Will confirm attendance and degree by phone or mail. Inquiry must include student's name, date of birth, social security number, years attended. Employers may obtain transcripts upon written request accompanied by a $2.00 fee and a signed release from the student.

A general baccalaureate institution, with an enrollment of 6,333. Highest level of offering: master's.
ACCREDITATIONS: M NUR SW

Labette Community College

200 South 14th Street
Parsons, KS 67357
(316) 421-6700 Ext. 26

Will confirm attendance and degree by phone or mail. Inquiry must include student's name, date of birth, social security number, years attended. Employers may obtain transcripts upon written request accompanied by a $1.00 fee and a signed release from the student.

A multiprogram two-year institution, with an enrollment of 2,413. Highest level of offering: one year but less than four years.
ACCREDITATIONS: NCA ADNUR RAD RSTH RSTHT

Laboratory Institute of Merchandising

12 East 53rd Street, 2nd Floor
New York, NY 10022
(212) 752-1530
Fax (212) 832-6708

Will confirm attendance and degree by mail. Inquiry must include student's name, years attended. Requests should be directed to: Academic Dean. Employers may obtain transcripts upon written request accompanied by a $3.00 fee and a signed release from the student.

A single program four-year institution, with an enrollment of 259. Highest level of offering: four or five year baccalaureate.
ACCREDITATIONS: M NY

Labore College

(Formerly Catherine College)
2120 Dorchester Avenue
Boston MA 02124
(617) 296-8300

Will confirm attendance and degree by phone or mail. Inquiry must include student's name, date of birth, social security number, years attended. Employers may obtain transcripts upon written request accompanied by a $3.00 fee and a signed release from the student.

A single program two-year institution, with an enrollment of 681. Highest level of offering: one year but less than four years.
ACCREDITATIONS: EV ADNUR EEG MRT RSTH RTT

Lackawanna Junior College

901 Prospect Avenue
Sacsranton, PA 18505
(717) 961-7810
Fax (717) 961-7858

Will confirm attendance and degree by mail. Inquiry must include student's name, social security number, years attended, release, self addressed stamped envelope. Employers may obtain transcripts upon written request accompanied by a $3.00 fee and a signed release from the student.

A multiprogram two-year institution, with an enrollment of 1,060. Highest level of offering: one year but less than four years.
ACCREDITATIONS: M

Lafayette College

Easton, PA 18042
(215) 250-5090

Will confirm attendance and degree by phone or mail. Inquiry must include student's name, years attended. Employers may obtain transcripts upon written request accompanied by a $1.00 fee and a signed release from the student.

A general baccalaureate institution, with an enrollment of 2,332. Highest level of offering: four or five year baccalaureate.
ACCREDITATIONS: M ENG

Lake–Sumter Community College

9501 US Highway 441
Leesburg, FL 34788
(904) 365-3572
Fax (904) 365-3501

Will confirm attendance and degree by mail or fax. Inquiry must include student's name, date of birth, social security number, years attended, release. Employers may obtain transcripts upon written request accompanied by a signed release from the student. Requests should be directed to Attn: Records Department.

A multiprogram two-year institution, with an enrollment of 1,722. Highest level of offering: one year but less than four years.
ACCREDITATIONS: SACS

Lake City Community College

Rt 3 Box 7
Lake City, FL 32055
(904) 752-1822 Ext. 203

Will confirm attendance and degree by phone or mail. Inquiry must include student's name, date of birth, social security number, years attended. Employers may obtain transcripts upon written request accompanied by a signed release from the student.

A multiprogram two-year institution, with an enrollment of 2,500. Highest level of offering: one year but less than four years.
ACCREDITATIONS: SACS

Lake Erie College

391 West Washington Street
Painesville, OH 44077
(216) 352-3361 Ext. 246

Will confirm attendance and degree by phone or mail. Inquiry must include student's name, social security number, years attended. Employers may obtain transcripts upon written request accompanied by a $2.00 fee and a signed release from the student.

A general baccalaureate institution, with an enrollment of 949. Highest level of offering: master's.
ACCREDITATIONS: NCA APCP

Lake Forest College

Lake Forest, IL 60045
(708) 234-3100 Ext. 211
Fax (708) 234-6487

Will confirm attendance and degree by phone, fax or mail. Inquiry must include student's name, years attended. Requests should be directed to Registrar's Office. Employers may obtain transcripts upon written request accompanied by a $1.00 fee and a signed release from the student.

A general baccalaureate institution, with an enrollment of 1,050. Highest level of offering: master's.
ACCREDITATIONS: NCA

Lake Forest Graduate Sacshool of Management

Lake Forest, IL 60045
(708) 295-3657 or 234-5005
Fax (708) 295-3656

Will confirm attendance and degree by phone, fax or mail. Inquiry must include student's name, years attended. Requests should be directed to: Registrar's Office. Employers may obtain transcripts upon written request accompanied by a $2.00 fee and a signed release from the student.

A business sacshool, with an enrollment of 697. Highest level of offering: master's.
ACCREDITATIONS: NCA

Lake Land College

5001 Lake Land Blvd.
Mattoon, IL 61938
(217) 235-3131 Ext. 252

Will confirm attendance and degree by phone or mail. Inquiry must include student's name, date of birth, social security number, years attended. Requests should be directed to: Records Office. Employers may obtain transcripts upon written request accompanied by a $2.00 fee and a signed release from the student.

A multiprogram two-year institution, with an enrollment of 4,835. Highest level of offering: one year but less than four years.
ACCREDITATIONS: NCA DA DH PNUR

Lake Michigan College

2755 East Napier
Benton Harbor, MI 49022
(616) 927-3571 Ext. 253

Will confirm attendance by phone or mail. Inquiry must include student's name, date of birth, social security number. Employers may obtain transcripts upon written request accompanied by a $3.00 fee and a signed release from the student.

A multiprogram two-year institution, with an enrollment of 3,340. Highest level of offering: one year but less than four years.
ACCREDITATIONS: NCA ADNUR DA MLTAD RAD

Lake Region Community College

(See University of North Dakota Lake Region)

Lake Superior State College

Sault Sainte Marie, MI 49783
(906) 635-2681

Will confirm attendance and degree by phone or mail. Inquiry must include student's name, date of birth, social security number, years attended. Employers may obtain transcripts upon written request accompanied by a $5.00 fee and a signed release from the student.

A general baccalaureate institution, with an enrollment of 3,500. Highest level of offering: master's.
ACCREDITATIONS: NCA ADNUR ENGT NUR

Lake Tahoe Community College

Admissions & Records
PO Box 14445
S. Lake Tahoe, CA 96151
(916) 541-1651
Fax (916) 541-7852

Will confirm attendance by phone, fax or mail and degree by mail with a signed release. Inquiry must include student's name, date of birth, social security number, years attended. Employers may obtain transcripts upon written request accompanied by a signed release from the student.

A multiprogram two-year institution, with an enrollment of 2,800. Highest level of offering: one year but less than four years.
ACCREDITATIONS: WJ

Lakeland College of Business

(See Tampa College of Lakeland)

Lakeland College

PO Box 359
Sheboygan, WI 53082-0359
(414) 565-1216

Will confirm attendance and degree by phone or mail. Inquiry must include student's name, date of birth, social security number, years attended. Employers may obtain transcripts upon written request accompanied by a $2.50 fee and a signed release from the student.

A general baccalaureate institution, with an enrollment of 2,300. Highest level of offering: four or five year baccalaureate.
ACCREDITATIONS: NCA

Lakeland Community College

7700 Clocktower Drive
Mentor, OH 44060
(216) 953-7246

Will confirm attendance by phone or mail. Inquiry must include student's name, social security number, years attended. Employers may obtain transcripts upon written request accompanied by a $1.00 fee and a signed release from the student.

A multiprogram two-year institution, with an enrollment of 9,209. Highest level of offering: one year but less than four years.
ACCREDITATIONS: NCA DH ADNUR MLTAD RSTH

Lakeshore Technical College

1290 North Avenue
Cleveland, WI 53015-9761
(414) 458-4183

Will confirm attendance and degree by phone or mail. Inquiry must include student's name, date of birth, social security number. Employers may obtain transcripts upon written request accompanied by a signed release from the student.

A multiprogram two-year institution, with an enrollment of 3,249. Highest level of offering: one year but less than four years.
ACCREDITATIONS: NCA ADNUR DA MAC PNUR

Lakeshore Technical Institute

1290 North Avenue
Cleveland, OH 53015-9761
(510) 684-4408

Will confirm attendance and degree by phone or mail. Inquiry must include student's name, date of birth, social security number. Employers may obtain transcripts upon written request accompanied by a signed release from the student.

A multiprogram two-year institution, with an enrollment of 3,249 Highest level of offering: one year but less than four years.
ACCREDITATIONS: NCA ADNUR DA MAC PNUR

Lakewood Community College

3401 Century Avenue North
White Bear Lake, MN 55110-5697
(612) 779-3298

Will confirm attendance and degree by phone or mail. Inquiry must include student's name, social security number. Employers may obtain transcripts upon written request accompanied by a signed release from the student.

A multiprogram two-year institution, with an enrollment of 5,721. Highest level of offering: one year but less than four years.
ACCREDITATIONS: NCA

Lamar Community College

2401 South Main
Lamar, CO 81052
(719) 336-2248

Will confirm attendance and degree by mail. Inquiry must include student's name, social security number, years attended. Employers may obtain transcripts upon written request accompanied by a $2.00 fee and a signed release from the student.

A multiprogram two-year institution, with an enrollment of 1,005. Highest level of offering: one year but less than four years.
ACCREDITATIONS: NCA

Lamar University

PO Box 10010
Beaumont, TX 77710
(409) 880-8365
Fax (409) 880-8463

Will confirm attendance and degree by phone or mail. Inquiry must include student's name, date of birth, social security number. Employers may obtain transcripts upon written request accompanied by a $2.00 fee and a signed release from the student. Requests should be directed to: Records Office.

A comprehensive institution with no medical school, with enrollment of 15,835. Highest level of offering: doctorate.
ACCREDITATIONS: SACS ADNUR BUS DH ENG MUS NUR PNE RAD RSTHT SP SW TED

Lambuth College

Jackson, TN 38301-5296
(901) 425-3207
Fax (901) 423-1990

Will confirm attendance and degree by phone, fax or mail. Inquiry must include student's name. Employers may obtain transcripts upon written request accompanied by a $2.00 fee and a signed release from the student. Requests should be directed to: Registrar's Office.

A general baccalaureate institution, with an enrollment of 804. Highest level of offering: four or five year baccalaureate.

ACCREDITATIONS: SACS

Lancaster Bible College

901 Eden Road
Lancaster, PA 17601
(717) 560-8258
Fax (717) 560-8213

Will confirm attendance and degree by phone or mail. Inquiry must include student's name, social security number, date of birth. Employers may obtain transcripts upon written request accompanied by a $2.00 fee and a signed release from the student.

A school of philosophy, religion and theology, with an enrollment of 425. Highest level of offering: four or five year baccalaureate.

ACCREDITATIONS: M BI

Lancaster Theological Seminary

555 West James Street
Lancaster, PA 17603
(717) 393-0654

Will confirm attendance and degree by mail. Inquiry must include student's name, social security number. Employers may obtain transcripts upon written request accompanied by a $2.00 fee and a signed release from the student.

A school of philosophy, religion and theology, with an enrollment of 244. Highest level of offering: doctorate.

ACCREDITATIONS: M THEOL

Lander College

Stanley Avenue
Greenwood, SACS 29649
(803) 229-8398
Fax (803) 229-8890

Will confirm attendance and degree by phone, fax or mail. Inquiry must include student's name, social security number. Employers may obtain transcripts upon written request accompanied by a $5.00 fee and a signed release from the student.

A general baccalaureate institution, with an enrollment of 2,323. Highest level of offering: master's.

ACCREDITATIONS: SACS ADNUR

Lane College

545 Lane Avenue
Jackson, TN 38301-4598
(901) 426-7600 or 426-7601

Will confirm attendance and degree by phone or mail. Inquiry must include student's name, social security number, years attended. Employers may obtain transcripts upon written request accompanied by a $2.00 fee and a signed release from the student.

A general baccalaureate institution, with an enrollment of 496. Highest level of offering: four or five year baccalaureate.

ACCREDITATIONS: SACS

Lane Community College

4000 East 30th Avenue
Eugene, OR 97405
(503) 726-2213

Will confirm attendance and degree by phone or mail. Inquiry must include student's name, social security number. Employers may obtain transcripts upon written request accompanied by a $2.00 fee and a signed release from the student.

A multiprogram two-year institution, with an enrollment of 12,600. Highest level of offering: one year but less than four years.

ACCREDITATIONS: NW ADNUR DA DH RSTH

Laney College

900 Fallon Street
Oakland, CA 94607
(510) 834-5740

Will confirm attendance and degree by mail. Inquiry must include student's name, social security number, release. Employers may obtain transcripts upon written request accompanied by a $1.00 fee and a signed release from the student.

A multiprogram two-year institution, with an enrollment of 9,651. Highest level of offering: one year but less than four years.

ACCREDITATIONS: WJ

Langston University

PO Box 728
Langston, OK 73050
(405) 466-2231 Ext. 227
Fax (405) 466-3381

Will confirm attendance and degree by phone or mail. Inquiry must include student's name, social security number, years attended. Employers may obtain transcripts upon written request accompanied by a $2.00 fee and a signed release from the student.

A general baccalaureate institution, with an enrollment of 1,802. Highest level of offering: four or five year baccalaureate.

ACCREDITATIONS: NCA TED

Lansing Community College

Mail Code 26–PO Box 40010
Lansing, MI 48901-7210
(517) 483-1266
Fax (517) 483-9795

Will confirm attendance and degree by mail. Inquiry must include student's name, social security number. Employers may obtain transcripts upon written request accom-

panied by a $2.00 fee and a signed release from the student.

A multiprogram two-year institution, with an enrollment of 21,781. Highest level of offering: one year but less than four years.

ACCREDITATIONS: NCA ADNUR DA DH RAD RSTH RSTHT RTT

Laramie County Community College

1400 East College Drive
Cheyenne, WY 82007
(307) 778-5222

Will confirm attendance and degree by mail. Inquiry must include student's name, social security number, years attended, release. Employers may obtain transcripts upon written request accompanied by a signed release from the student.

A multiprogram two-year institution, with an enrollment of 4,125. Highest level of offering: one year but less than four years.

ACCREDITATIONS: NCA PNUR RAD

Laredo Junior College

West End Washington Street
Laredo, TX 78040
(512) 722-0521 Ext. 109
Fax (512) 721-5109

Will confirm attendance and degree by phone or mail. Inquiry must include student's name, date of birth, social security number. Employers may obtain transcripts upon written request accompanied by a $2.00 fee and a signed release from the student. Requests should be directed to: Admissions Office.

A multiprogram two-year institution, with an enrollment of 4,038. Highest level of offering: one year but less than four years.

ACCREDITATIONS: SACS ADNUR MLTAD RAD

Laredo State University

West End Washington Street
Laredo, TX 78040
(512) 722-8001

Will confirm attendance and degree by phone or mail. Inquiry must include student's name, date of birth, social security number, years attended. Requests should be directed to: Admissions Office. Employers may obtain transcripts upon written request accompanied by a $3.00 fee and a signed release from the student.

A general baccalaureate institution, with an enrollment of 1,382. Highest level of offering: master's.

ACCREDITATIONS: SACS

Lasell College

Newton, MA 02166
(617) 243-2133
Fax (617) 243-2389

Will confirm attendance and degree by phone or mail. Inquiry must include student's name, date of birth, years attended. Employers may obtain transcripts upon written request accompanied by a $2.00 fee and a signed release from the student.

A general baccalaureate institution, with an enrollment of 492. Highest level of offering: four year baccalaureate.

ACCREDITATIONS: EH MAC MLTAD PTAA

Lassen College

PO Box 3000
Susanville, CA 96130
(916) 257-6181

Will confirm attendance and degree by mail. Inquiry must include student's name, date of birth, years attended, social security number, release. Employers may obtain transcripts upon written request accompanied by a $3.00 fee and a signed release from the student.

A multiprogram two-year institution, with an enrollment of 3,400. Highest level of offering: one year but less than four years.
ACCREDITATIONS: WJ

Latter–Day Saints Business College

411 East South Temple
Salt Lake City, UT 84111
(801) 363-2765

Will confirm attendance and degree by phone or mail. Inquiry must include student's name, social security number, years attended, release. Employers may obtain transcripts upon written request accompanied by a $2.00 fee and a signed release from the student.

A multiprogram two-year institution, with an enrollment of 1,148. Highest level of offering: one year but less than four years.
ACCREDITATIONS: NW

Lawrence Institute of Technology

21000 West Ten Mile Road
Southfield, MI 48075
(313) 356-0200

Will confirm attendance and degree by phone or mail. Inquiry must include student's name, date of birth. Employers may obtain transcripts upon written request accompanied by a $3.00 fee and a signed release from the student.

A general baccalaureate institution, with an enrollment of 5,509. Highest level of offering: master's.
ACCREDITATIONS: NCA ARCH ENG ENGT

Lawrence University

PO Box 599
Appleton, WI 54912
(414) 832-6578

Will confirm attendance and degree by phone or mail. Inquiry must include student's name, maiden name, years attended. Employers may obtain transcripts upon written request accompanied by a $2.00 fee and a signed release from the student.

A general baccalaureate institution, with an enrollment of 1,201. Highest level of offering: four or five year baccalaureate.
ACCREDITATIONS: NCA MUS

Lawson State Community College

3060 Wilson Road South West
Birmingham, AL 35221
(205) 925-2515 Ext. 232
Fax (205) 929-6316

Will confirm attendance and degree by phone or mail. Inquiry must include student's name, social security number, years attended. Employers may obtain transcripts upon written request accompanied by a $2.00 fee and a signed release from the student.

A multiprogram two-year institution, with an enrollment of 1,958. Highest level of offering: one year but less than four years.
ACCREDITATIONS: SACS

Le Moyne–Owen College

807 Walker Avenue
Memphis, TN 38126
(901) 942-7322
Fax (901) 942-7810

Will confirm attendance and degree by phone, fax or mail. Inquiry must include student's name, social security number. Employers may obtain transcripts upon written request accompanied by a $2.00 fee and a signed release from the student.

A general baccalaureate institution, with an enrollment of 1,041. Highest level of offering: four or five year baccalaureate.
ACCREDITATIONS: SACS

Le Moyne College

Syracuse, NY 13214
(315) 445-4100
Fax (315) 445-4540

Will confirm attendance and degree by mail or fax. Inquiry must include student's name, years attended. Employers may obtain transcripts upon written request accompanied by a $1.00 fee and a signed release from the student. Requests should be directed to: Registrar's Office.

A general baccalaureate institution, with an enrollment of 2,213. Highest level of offering: four or five year baccalaureate.
ACCREDITATIONS: M NY

Le Tourneau University

PO Box 7001
Longview, TX 75607
(214) 753-0231 Ext. 380
Fax (903) 237-2732

Will confirm attendance and degree by phone, fax or mail. Inquiry must include student's name, social security number. Employers may obtain transcripts upon written request accompanied by a $3.00 fee and a signed release from the student.

An engineering school, with an enrollment of 800. Highest level of offering: four or five year baccalaureate.
ACCREDITATIONS: SACS ENG

Lebanon Valley College

101 College Avenue
Annville, PA 17003-0501
(717) 867-6215

Will confirm attendance and degree by phone or mail. Inquiry must include student's name, date of birth, social security number. Employers may obtain transcripts upon written request accompanied by a $2.00 fee and a signed release from the student.

A general baccalaureate institution, with an enrollment of 1,287. Highest level of offering: four or five year baccalaureate.
ACCREDITATIONS: M MUS ACS

Lee College

Cleveland, TN 37311
(615) 478-7319
Fax (615) 478-7075

Will confirm attendance and degree by phone, fax or mail. Inquiry must include student's name, social security number. Employers may obtain transcripts upon written request accompanied by a $2.00 fee and a signed release from the student.

A general baccalaureate institution, with an enrollment of 1,642. Highest level of offering: four or five year baccalaureate.
ACCREDITATIONS: SACS

Lee College

511 South Whiting
Baytown, TX 77520-4703
(713) 425-6393

Will confirm attendance and degree by phone or mail. Inquiry must include student's name, social security number. Employers may obtain transcripts upon written request accompanied by a $2.00 fee and a signed release from the student.

A multiprogram two-year institution, with an enrollment of 4,879. Highest level of offering: one year but less than four years.
ACCREDITATIONS: SACS

Lees–McRae College

Registrar's Office
PO Box 128
Banner Elk, NC 28604
(704) 898-5241

Will confirm attendance and degree by phone or mail. Inquiry must include student's name, social security number, years attended. Employers may obtain transcripts upon written request accompanied by a $1.00 fee and a signed release from the student. Requests should be directed to: Academic Fairs.

A general baccalaureate institution, with an enrollment of 833. Highest level of offering: four or five year baccalaureate.
ACCREDITATIONS: SACS

Lees College

Jackson, KY 41339
(606) 666-7521
Fax (606) 666-8910

Will confirm attendance and degree by phone, fax or mail. Inquiry must include student's name, social security number, years attended. Employers may obtain transcripts upon written request accompanied by a $2.00 fee and a signed release from the student. Requests should be directed to: Office of Registrar.

A multiprogram two-year institution, with an enrollment of 329. Highest level of offering: one year but less than four years.
ACCREDITATIONS: SACS

Leeward Community College

96–045 Ala Ike
Pearl City, HI 96782
(808) 455-0219

Will confirm attendance and degree by phone or mail. Inquiry must include student's name, social security number, reason for request. Employers may obtain transcripts upon written request accompanied by a $1.00 fee and a signed release from the student.

A multiprogram two-year institution, with an enrollment of 5,751. Highest level of offering: one year but less than four years.
ACCREDITATIONS: WJ

Lehigh County Community College

2370 Main Street
Sacshnecksville, PA 18078
(215) 799-1172

Will confirm attendance and degree by phone or mail. Inquiry must include student's name, date of birth, social security number. Employers may obtain transcripts upon written request accompanied by a $2.00 fee and a signed release from the student.

A multiprogram two-year institution, with an enrollment of 4,649. Highest level of offering: one year but less than four years.
ACCREDITATIONS: M MAC PTAA RSTHT OTAA

Lehigh University

Alumni Bldg. #27
Bethlehem, PA 18015
(215) 758-3200
Fax (215) 758-4361

Will confirm attendance and degree by phone, fax or mail. Inquiry must include student's name, social security number. Employers may obtain transcripts upon written request accompanied by a signed release from the student.

A doctoral-level institution with no medical school, with an enrollment of 6,280. Highest level of offering: doctorate.
ACCREDITATIONS: M BUS ENG TED BUSA

Lenoir–Rhyne College

Hickory, NC 28603
(704) 328-7278

Will confirm attendance and degree by phone or mail. Inquiry must include student's name, social security number, years attended. Requests should be directed to Registrar's Office. Employers may obtain transcripts upon written request accompanied by a $3.00 fee and a signed release from the student.

A general baccalaureate institution, with an enrollment of 1,532. Highest level of offering: master's.
ACCREDITATIONS: SACS NUR TED

Lenoir Community College

PO Box 188
Kinston, NC 28501
(919) 527-6223 Ext. 323

Will confirm attendance and degree by phone or mail. Inquiry must include student's name, social security number, years attended. Employers may obtain transcripts upon written request accompanied by a signed release from the student.

A multiprogram two-year institution, with an enrollment of 1,980. Highest level of offering: one year but less than four years.
ACCREDITATIONS: SACS SURGT

Lesley College

29 Everett Street
Cambridge, MA 02138
(617) 868-9600 Ext. 8734

Will confirm attendance and degree by mail. Inquiry must include student's name, social security number, years attended, release. Employers may obtain transcripts upon written request accompanied by a $5.00 fee and a signed release from the student.

A school of education, with an enrollment of 2,980. Highest level of offering: beyond master's but less than doctorate.
ACCREDITATIONS: EH

Lewis–Clark State College

8th Avenue & 6th Street
Lewiston, ID 83501
(208) 799-2223
Fax (208) 746-7354

Will confirm attendance by mail and degree by phone or fax. Inquiry must include student's name, social security number. Employers may obtain transcripts upon written request accompanied by a $2.00 fee and a signed release from the student.

A general baccalaureate institution, with an enrollment of 2,033. Highest level of offering: four or five year baccalaureate.
ACCREDITATIONS: NW ADNUR TED

Lewis and Clark College

0165 South West Palatine Hill Road
Portland, OR 97219
(503) 768-7000

Will confirm attendance and degree by phone or mail. Inquiry must include student's name, years attended. Employers may obtain transcripts upon written request accompanied by a $5.00 fee and a signed release from the student.

A comprehensive institution with no medical school, with an enrollment of 3,322. Highest level of offering: beyond master's but less than doctorate.
ACCREDITATIONS: NW LAW MUS TED

Lewis and Clark Community College

5800 Godfrey Road
Godfrey, IL 62035
(618) 466-3411
Fax (618) 466-2798

Will confirm attendance and degree by phone, fax or mail. Inquiry must include student's name, social security number. Employers may obtain transcripts upon

written request accompanied by a signed release from the student.

A multiprogram two-year institution, with an enrollment of 6,000. Highest level of offering: one year but less than four years.
ACCREDITATIONS: NCA ADNUR DA DT MLTAD

Lewis College of Business

17370 Meyers Road
Detroit, MI 48235
(313) 862-6300 Ext. 33

Will confirm attendance and degree by phone or mail. Inquiry must include student's name, social security number. Employers may obtain transcripts upon written request accompanied by a $3.00 fee and a signed release from the student.

A single program two-year institution, with an enrollment of 377. Highest level of offering: one year but less than four years.
ACCREDITATIONS: NCA

Lewis University

Route 53
Romeoville, IL 60441
(815) 838-0500 Ext. 217

Will confirm attendance and degree by phone or mail. Inquiry must include student's name, social security number, years attended. Employers may obtain transcripts upon written request accompanied by a $3.00 fee and a signed release from the student.

A comprehensive institution with no medical school, with an enrollment of 2,826. Highest level of offering: master's.
ACCREDITATIONS: NCA NUR

Lexington Community College

203 Oswald Bldg.
Lexington, KY 40506-0235
(606) 257-6064

Will confirm attendance and degree by phone or mail. Inquiry must include student's name, date of birth, social security number. Employers may obtain transcripts upon written request accompanied by a $1.00 fee and a signed release from the student.

A multiprogram two-year institution, with an enrollment of 3,000.
ACCREDITATIONS: SACS ADNUR COPSY DH DT MLTAD PTAA RSTH

Lexington Theological Seminary

631 South Limestone
Lexington, KY 40508
(606) 252-0361

Will confirm attendance and degree by phone or mail. Inquiry must include student's name, date of birth, social security number. Employers may obtain transcripts upon written request accompanied by a $3.00 fee and a signed release from the student.

A school of religion and theology, with an enrollment of 134. Highest level of offering: doctorate.
ACCREDITATIONS: SACS THEOL

Liberty University

Box 20,000
Lynchburg, VA 24506-8001
(804) 582-2000

Will confirm attendance and degree by phone or mail. Inquiry must include student's name, social security number. Employers may obtain transcripts upon written request accompanied by a $2.00 fee and a signed release from the student. Requests should be directed to: Registrar's Office.

A general baccalaureate institution, with an enrollment of 4,207. Highest level of offering: master's.

ACCREDITATIONS: SACS

Life Bible College

1100 Glendale Boulevard
Los Angeles, CA 90026
(213) 413-1234 Ext. 246

Will confirm attendance and degree by mail. Inquiry must include student's name, date of birth, social security number, years attended. Employers may obtain transcripts upon written request accompanied by a $3.00 fee and a signed release from the student.

A school, religion and theology, with an enrollment of 453. Highest level of offering: four or five year baccalaureate.

ACCREDITATIONS: BI

Life Chiropractic College–West

2005 Via Barrett
San Lorenzo, CA 94580
(510) 276-9013 Ext. 35

Will confirm attendance and degree by phone or mail. Inquiry must include student's name, years attended. Employers may obtain transcripts upon written request accompanied by a $5.00 fee and a signed release from the student.

A bachelor's or higher institution newly admitted to NCES, with an enrollment of 417. Highest level of offering: first professional degree.

ACCREDITATIONS: CHIRO

Life Chiropractic College

1269 Barclay Cir
Marietta, GA 30060
(404) 424-0554
Fax (404) 429-8359

Will confirm attendance and degree by mail or fax. Inquiry must include student's name, social security number. Employers may obtain transcripts upon written request accompanied by a $5.00 fee and a signed release from the student.

A health institution, with an enrollment of 1,596. Highest level of offering: first professional degree.

ACCREDITATIONS: SACS CHIRO

Lima Technical College

4240 Campus Drive
Lima, OH 45804
(419) 221-1112
Fax (419) 221-0450

Will confirm attendance and degree by phone or mail. Inquiry must include student's name, social security number, years attended. Employers may obtain transcripts upon written request accompanied by a $1.00 fee and a signed release from the student.

A multiprogram two-year institution, with an enrollment of 2,300. Highest level of offering: one year but less than four years.

ACCREDITATIONS: NCA ADNUR DH RAD RSTHT

Limestone College

1115 College Drive
Gaffney, SACS 29340
(803) 489-7151 Ext. 307

Will confirm attendance and degree by phone or mail. Inquiry must include student's name, social security number, years attended. Employers may obtain transcripts upon written request accompanied by a $3.00 fee and a signed release from the student.

A general baccalaureate, with an enrollment of 1,151. Highest level of offering: four or five year baccalaureate.

ACCREDITATIONS: SACS MUS

Lincoln Christian College and Seminary

100 Campus View Drive
Lincoln, IL 62656
(217) 732-3168 Ext. 212
Fax (217) 732-5914

Will confirm attendance by phone or mail. Inquiry must include student's name, years attended. Employers may obtain transcripts upon written request accompanied by a $3.00 fee and a signed release from the student.

A school of religion and theology, with an enrollment of 731. Highest level of offering: beyond master's but less than doctorate.

ACCREDITATIONS: NCA AABC ATS

Lincoln College

300 Keokuk Street
Lincoln, IL 62656
(217) 732-3155

Will confirm attendance by mail. Inquiry must include student's name, social security number, years attended, release. Requests should be directed to: Registrar's Office. Employers may obtain transcripts upon written request accompanied by a $2.00 fee and a signed release from the student.

A multiprogram two-year institution, with an enrollment of 520. Highest level of offering: one year but less than four years.

ACCREDITATIONS: NCA

Lincoln Land Community College

Shepherd Road
Springfield, IL 62794-9256
(217) 786-2290

Will confirm attendance and degree by phone or mail. Inquiry must include student's name, social security number. Employers may obtain transcripts upon written request accompanied by a $1.00 fee and a signed release from the student.

A multiprogram two-year institution, with an enrollment of 6,610. Highest level of offering: one year but less than four years.

ACCREDITATIONS: NCA ADNUR DA RAD RSTH

Lincoln Memorial University

Highway 25 East
Harrogate, TN 37752
(615) 869-3611 Ext. 302
Fax (615) 869-4825

Will confirm attendance and degree by phone, fax or mail. Inquiry must include student's name, social security number. Employers may obtain transcripts upon written request accompanied by a $3.00 fee and a signed release from the student. Requests should be directed to: Registrar's Office.

A general baccalaureate institution, with an enrollment of 1,859. Highest level of offering: master's.

ACCREDITATIONS: SACS ADNUR

Lincoln Technical Institute

5151 Tilghman Street
Allentown, PA 18104
(215) 398-5300

Will confirm attendance and degree by phone or mail. Inquiry must include student's name, years attended. Employers may obtain transcripts upon written request accompanied by a $1.00 fee and a signed release from the student.

A multiprogram two-year institution, with an enrollment of 932. Highest level of offering: one year but less than four years.

ACCREDITATIONS: NATTS

Lincoln Technical Institute

2501 Vine Street
West Des Moines, IA 50265
(515) 225-8433

Will confirm attendance and degree by mail. Inquiry must include student's name, social security number, years attended, release. Employers may obtain transcripts upon written request accompanied by a signed release from the student.

A two-year institution newly admitted to NCES. Highest level of offering: one year but less than four years.

ACCREDITATIONS: NATTS

Lincoln University

Lincoln University, PA 19352
(215) 932-8300 Ext. 282

Will confirm attendance and degree by mail. Inquiry must include student's name, social security number, years attended. Employers may obtain transcripts upon written request accompanied by a $5.00 fee and a signed release from the student. Requests should be directed to: Registrar's Office.

A general baccalaureate institution, with an enrollment of 1,450. Highest level of offering: master's.

ACCREDITATIONS: M

Lincoln University

281 Masonic Avenue
San Francisacso, CA 94118
(415) 221-1212

Will confirm attendance and degree by mail. Inquiry must include student's name, date of birth, years attended. Employers may obtain transcripts upon written request accompanied by a $2.00 fee and a signed release from the student.

Highest level of offering: master's.

Lincoln University

820 Chestnut
Jefferson City, MO 65101
(314) 681-5011

Will confirm attendance and degree by phone or mail. Inquiry must include student's name, date of birth, social security number. Employers may obtain transcripts upon written request accompanied by a $2.00 fee and a signed release from the student.

A comprehensive institution with no medical school, with an enrollment of 3,051. Highest level of offering: master's.

ACCREDITATIONS: NCA MUS TED

Lindenwood College

209 S. King's Highway
Saint Charles, MO 63301
(314) 949-2000 Ext. 304

Will confirm attendance and degree by phone or mail. Inquiry must include student's name, date of birth, social security number, years attended. Employers may obtain transcripts upon written request accompanied by a $3.00 fee and a signed release from the student.

A comprehensive institution with no medical school, with an enrollment of 2,500. Highest level of offering: master's.

ACCREDITATIONS: NCA TED

Lindsey Wilson College

210 Lindsey Wilson Street
Columbia, KY 42728
(502) 384-2126 Ext. 2024
Fax (502) 384-8200

Will confirm attendance and degree by mail. Inquiry must include student's name, social security number, years attended. Employers may obtain transcripts upon written request accompanied by a $2.00 fee and a signed release from the student.

A multiprogram four-year institution, with an enrollment of 1,507. Highest level of offering: baccalaureate.

ACCREDITATIONS: SACS

Linfield College

500 South Baker
McMinnville, OR 97128
(503) 472-4121 Ext. 211

Will confirm attendance and degree by phone or mail. Inquiry must include student's name, social security number, years attended. Employers may obtain transcripts upon written request accompanied by a signed release from the student.

A general baccalaureate institution, with an enrollment of 1,966. Highest level of offering: master's.

ACCREDITATIONS: NW MUS

Linn–Benton Community College

6500 South West Pacific Boulevard
Albany, OR 97321
(503) 967-8801
Fax (503) 928-6352

Will confirm attendance and degree by mail or fax. Inquiry must include student's name, date of birth, social security number. Employers may obtain transcripts upon written request accompanied by a $2.00 fee and a signed release from the student.

A multiprogram two-year institution, with an enrollment of 6,385. Highest level of offering: one year but less than four years.

ACCREDITATIONS: NW ADNUR DA

Little Big Horn College

PO Box 370
Crow Agency, MT 59022
(406) 638-2228

Will confirm attendance and degree by phone or mail. Inquiry must include student's name, date of birth, social security number. Employers may obtain transcripts upon written request accompanied by a signed release from the student.

A two-year institution newly admitted to NCES. Highest level of offering: one year but less than four years.

ACCREDITATIONS: NW

Little Hoop Community College

Box 269
Fort Totten, ND 58335
(701) 766-4415

Will confirm attendance and degree by phone or mail. Inquiry must include student's name, date of birth. Employers may obtain transcripts upon written request accompanied by a $1.00 fee and a signed release from the student.

A two-year institution newly admitted to NCES, with an enrollment of 109. Highest level of offering: one year but less than four years.

ACCREDITATIONS: NCA

Livingston University

Station Four
Livingston, AL 35470
(205) 652-9661 Ext. 361

Will confirm attendance and degree by phone or mail. Inquiry must include student's name, social security number. Employers may obtain transcripts upon written request accompanied by a $2.00 fee and a signed release from the student.

A comprehensive institution with no medical school, with an enrollment of 1,500. Highest level of offering: beyond master's but less than doctorate.

ACCREDITATIONS: SACS ADNUR TED

Livingstone College

701 West Monroe Street
Salisbury, NC 28144
(704) 638-5524

Will confirm attendance and degree by phone or mail. Inquiry must include student's name, date of birth, social security number. Employers may obtain transcripts upon written request accompanied by a $2.00 fee and a signed release from the student.

A general baccalaureate institution, with an enrollment of 570. Highest level of offering: four or five year baccalaureate.

ACCREDITATIONS: SACS SW

Lock Haven University of Pennsylvania

Lock Haven, PA 17745
(717) 893-2006
Fax (717) 893-2432

Will confirm attendance and degree by phone or mail. Inquiry must include student's name, social security number. Employers may obtain transcripts upon written request accompanied by a $2.00 fee and a signed release from the student.

A general baccalaureate institution, with an enrollment of 3,500. Highest level of offering: four or five year baccalaureate.

ACCREDITATIONS: M SW TED

Lockyear College

209–221 North West 5th Street
Evansville, IN 47706
(812) 425-8157

Will confirm attendance and degree by phone or mail. Inquiry must include student's name, date of birth, social security number. Employers may obtain transcripts upon written request accompanied by a $2.00 fee and a signed release from the student.

A general baccalaureate institution, with an enrollment of 650. Highest level of offering: one year but less than four years.

ACCREDITATIONS: JRCB

Logan College of Chiropractic

1851 Sacshoettler Road–PO Box 1065
Chesterfield, MO 63006-1065
(314) 227-2100 Ext. 139
Fax (314) 227-9338

Will confirm attendance and degree by phone or mail. Inquiry must include student's name, social security number. Employers may obtain transcripts upon written request accompanied by a $5.00 fee and a signed release from the student.

A health institution, with an enrollment of 630. Highest level of offering: first professional degree.

ACCREDITATIONS: NCA CHIRO

Loma Linda University

1113 Anderson Street
Loma Linda, CA 92350
(714) 824-4508

Will confirm attendance and degree by mail. Inquiry must include student's name, social security number, years attended. Employers may obtain transcripts upon written request accompanied by a $2.00 fee and a signed release from the student.

A medical school, with an enrollment of 4,610. Highest level of offering: doctorate.

ACCREDITATIONS: WC ADNUR ANEST CYTO DA DENT DH DIET MED MFCD MRA MT NMT NUR OT PH PTA RAD RSTH RTT SW DMS PAST

Lomax–Hannon Junior College

c/o Rev. James E. Cook
151 School Highland Road
Greenville, AL 36037
(205) 382-8594

Will confirm attendance and degree by mail or phone. Inquiry must include student's name, social security number, years attended. Employers may obtain transcripts upon written request accompanied by a $5.00 fee and a signed release from the student.

Lon Morris College

Jacksonville, TX 75766
(903) 586-2471 Ext. 26

Will confirm attendance and degree by phone or mail. Inquiry must include student's name, social security number, years attended. Employers may obtain transcripts upon written request accompanied by a $2.00 fee and a signed release from the student.

A multiprogram two-year institution, with an enrollment of 300. Highest level of offering: one year but less than four years.

ACCREDITATIONS: SACS

Long Beach City College

4901 East Carson Street
Long Beach, CA 90808
(213) 420-4145

Will confirm attendance and degree by mail. Inquiry must include student's name, date of birth, social security number, years attended, release. Employers may obtain transcripts upon written request accompanied by a $2.00 fee and a signed release from the student.

A multiprogram two-year institution, with an enrollment of 22,245. Highest level of offering: one year but less than four years.

ACCREDITATIONS: WJ ADNUR RAD RSTH

Long Island College Hospital School of Nursing

397 Hicks Street
Brooklyn, NY 11201
(718) 780-1952

Will confirm attendance and degree by mail. Inquiry must include student's name, years attended. Employers may obtain transcripts upon written request accompanied by a $4.00 fee and a signed release from the student. Requests should be directed to: Student Services.

A single program two-year institution, with an enrollment of 151. Highest level of offering: one year but less than four years.

ACCREDITATIONS: NY ADNUR

Long Island Seminary of Jewish Studies for Women

(See Torah Academy for Girls)

Long Island University Brooklyn Campus

University Plaza
Brooklyn, NY 11201
(718) 488-1000

Will confirm attendance and degree by phone or mail. Inquiry must include student's name, date of birth, years attended. Employers may obtain transcripts upon written request accompanied by a $3.00 fee and a signed release from the student. Attn: Office of Bursar.

A comprehensive institution with no medical school, with an enrollment of 6,888. Highest level of offering: doctorate.

ACCREDITATIONS: M APCP CLPSY NUR NY PHAR PTA RSTH

Long Island University C W Post Center

Northern Boulevard
Brookville, NY 11548
(516) 299-2588

Will confirm attendance and degree by phone or mail. Inquiry must include student's name, social security number, years attended. Employers may obtain transcripts upon written request accompanied by a $3.00 fee and a signed release from the student. Direct inquiries to Record's Office.

A comprehensive institution with no medical school, with an enrollment of 8,209. Highest level of offering: beyond master's but less than doctorate.

ACCREDITATIONS: M LIB MT NY RAD

Long Island University Southampton Center

Southampton, NY 11968
(516) 283-4000 Ext. 325

Will confirm attendance and degree by phone or mail. Inquiry must include student's name, social security number. Employers may obtain transcripts upon written request accompanied by a $3.00 fee and a signed release from the student.

A general baccalaureate institution, with an enrollment of 1,288. Highest level of offering: master's.

ACCREDITATIONS: M NY

Longview Community College

500 Longview Road
Lee's Summit, MO 64081
(816) 763-7777 Ext. 247
Fax (816) 761-4457

Will confirm attendance and degree by phone or mail. Inquiry must include student's name, social security number. Employers may obtain transcripts upon written request accompanied by a $2.00 fee and a signed release from the student.

A multiprogram two-year institution, with an enrollment of 5,703. Highest level of offering: one year but less than four years.

ACCREDITATIONS: NCA ENGT

Longwood College

201 High Street
Farmville, VA 23909-1899
(804) 395-2063
Fax (804) 395-2635

Will confirm attendance and degree by phone, fax or mail. Inquiry must include student's name, social security number. Employers may obtain transcripts upon written request accompanied by a $3.00 fee and a signed release from the student.

A general baccalaureate institution, with an enrollment of 3,100. Highest level of offering: master's.

ACCREDITATIONS: SACS MUS SW TED

Lorain County Community College

1005 North Abbe Road
Elyria, OH 44035
(216) 365-4191 Ext. 228
Fax (216) 365-6519

Will confirm attendance and degree by phone, fax or mail. Inquiry must include student's name, , date of birth, social security number. Employers may obtain transcripts upon written request accompanied by a $2.00 fee and a signed release from the student.

A multiprogram two-year institution, with an enrollment of 7,746. Highest level of offering: one year but less than four years.

ACCREDITATIONS: NCA ADNUR MLTAD PNUR RAD

Loras College

Dubuque, IA 52004-0178
(319) 588-7106

Will confirm attendance and degree by phone or mail. Inquiry must include student's name, social security number, years attended. Employers may obtain transcripts upon written request accompanied by a $2.00 fee and a signed release from the student.

A general baccalaureate institution, with an enrollment of 1,800. Highest level of offering: master's.

ACCREDITATIONS: NCA SW TED

Lord Fairfax Community College

PO Box 47
Middletown, VA 22645
(703) 869-1120 Ext. 126
Fax (703) 869-7881

Will confirm attendance and degree by phone, fax or mail. Inquiry must include student's name, social security number, release. Employers may obtain transcripts upon written request accompanied by a signed release from the student. Release must be dated and no more than 12 months old.

A multiprogram two-year institution, with an enrollment of 2,948. Highest level of offering: two years.

ACCREDITATIONS: SACS

Loretto Heights College

West 50th Avenue & Lowell Boulevard
Denver, CO 80221
(303) 458-4114

Will confirm attendance and degree by phone or mail. Inquiry must include student's name, date of birth, social security number. Employers may obtain transcripts upon written request accompanied by a $2.00 fee and a signed release from the student. Requests should be directed to: Registrar.

A general baccalaureate institution, with an enrollment of 717. Highest level of offering: four or five year baccalaureate.

ACCREDITATIONS: NCA NUR

Los Angeles City College

855 North Vermont Avenue
Los Angeles, CA 90029
(213) 669-4000

Will confirm attendance and degree by mail. Inquiry must include student's name, social security number. Employers may obtain transcripts upon written request accompanied by a $1.00 fee and a signed release from the student. Requests should be directed to: Admissions Office.

A multiprogram two-year institution, with an enrollment of 15,184. Highest level of offering: one year but less than four years.

ACCREDITATIONS: WJ ADNUR DA DT NMT RAD

Los Angeles College of Chiropractic

16200 East Amber Valley Drive
Whittier, CA 90604
(213) 947-8755 Ext. 220

Will confirm attendance and degree by mail. Inquiry must include student's name, social security number, years attended, release. Employers may obtain transcripts upon written request accompanied by a $10.00 fee and a signed release from the student.

A health institution, with an enrollment of 775. Highest level of offering: first professional degree.

ACCREDITATIONS: CHIRO

Los Angeles Harbor College

1111 Figueroa Place
Wilmington, CA 90744
(310) 522-8255

Will confirm attendance and degree by mail. Inquiry must include student's name, date of birth, social security number, years attended. Employers may obtain transcripts upon written request accompanied by a $1.00 fee and a signed release from the student. Requests should be directed to: Records Office.

A multiprogram two-year institution, with an enrollment of 9,000. Highest level of offering: one year but less than four years.

ACCREDITATIONS: WJ

Los Angeles Master's College

(See Master's College)

Los Angeles Mission College

13356 Eldridge Ave.
Sylmar, CA 91342-3244
(818) 364-7600 Ext. 7660

Will confirm attendance and degree by mail. Inquiry must include student's name, social security number, release. Employers may obtain transcripts upon written request accompanied by a $1.00 fee and a signed release from the student.

A multiprogram two-year institution, with an enrollment of 3,082. Highest level of offering: one year but less than four years.

ACCREDITATIONS: WJ

Los Angeles Pierce College

6201 Winnetka Avenue
Woodland Hills, CA 91371
(818) 719-6404

Will confirm attendance and degree by mail. Inquiry must include student's name, date of birth, social security number, release. Employers may obtain transcripts upon written request accompanied by a $1.00 fee and a signed release from the student. Requests should be directed to: Admissions/Records Office.

A multiprogram two-year institution, with an enrollment of 18,906. Highest level of offering: one year but less than four years.

ACCREDITATIONS: WJ ADNUR ADVET PTAA

Los Angeles Southwest College

1600 West Imperial Highway
Los Angeles, CA 90047
(213) 777-3515

Will confirm attendance and degree by mail. Inquiry must include student's name, social security number, release. Employers may obtain transcripts upon written request accompanied by a $1.00 fee and a signed release from the student.

A multiprogram two-year institution, with an enrollment of 4,153. Highest level of offering: one year but less than four years.

ACCREDITATIONS: WJ

Los Angeles Trade–Technical College

400 West Washington Boulevard
Los Angeles, CA 90015
(213) 744-9420
Fax (213) 748-1946

Will confirm attendance and degree by mail. Inquiry must include student's name, social security number, years attended, release. Employers may obtain transcripts upon written request accompanied by a $1.00 fee and a signed release from the student. Requests should be directed to: Admissions Records Office (for verification)–Transcript Office (for transcripts).

A multiprogram two-year institution, with an enrollment of 11,888. Highest level of offering: one year but less than four years.

ACCREDITATIONS: WJ SURGT

Los Angeles Valley College

5800 Fulton Avenue
Van Nuys, CA 91401-4096
(818) 781-1200 Ext. 253

Will confirm attendance and degree by mail. Inquiry must include student's name, date of birth, social security number, years attended, release. Employers may obtain transcripts upon written request accompanied by a $1.00 fee and a signed release from the student. Requests should be directed to: Transacsript Office.

A multiprogram two-year institution, with an enrollment of 20,000. Highest level of offering: one year but less than four years.

ACCREDITATIONS: WJ ADNUR RSTH

Los Medanos College

2700 East Leland Road
Pittsburg, CA 94565
(510) 439-2181 Ext. 251

Will confirm attendance and degree by phone or mail. Inquiry must include student's name, date of birth, social security number. Employers may obtain transcripts upon written request accompanied by a $3.00 fee and a signed release from the student. Requests should be directed to: Records Office.

A multiprogram two-year institution, with an enrollment of 8,500. Highest level of offering: one year but less than four years.

ACCREDITATIONS: WJ

Louisburg College

501 N. Main
Louisburg, NC 27549
Fax (919) 496-2521

Will confirm attendance and degree by mail or fax. Inquiry must include student's name, years attended, release. Employers may obtain transcripts upon written request accompanied by a signed release from the student.

A multiprogram two-year institution, with an enrollment of 841. Highest level of offering: one year but less than four years.

ACCREDITATIONS: SACS

Louisiana College

PO Box 568–1140 College Drive
Pineville, LA 71359
(318) 487-7222
Fax (318) 487-7191

Will confirm attendance and degree by phone, fax or mail. Inquiry must include student's name, social security number. Employers may obtain transcripts upon written request accompanied by a signed release from the student.

A general baccalaureate institution, with an enrollment of 1,062. Highest level of offering: four or five year baccalaureate.
ACCREDITATIONS: SACS MUS

Louisiana State University at Alexandria

Admissions and Records
8100 Hwy. 71 South
Alexandria, LA 71302-9633
(318) 473-6413
Fax (318) 473-6418

Will confirm attendance and degree by phone, fax or mail. Inquiry must include student's name, social security number. Employers may obtain transcripts upon written request accompanied by a $5.00 fee and a signed release from the student.

A multiprogram two-year institution, with an enrollment of 1,985. Highest level of offering: one year but less than four years.
ACCREDITATIONS: SACS ADNUR

Louisiana State University at Eunice

PO Box 1129
Eunice, LA 70535
(318) 457-7311 Ext. 302
Fax (318) 546-6620

Will confirm attendance and degree by phone, fax or mail. Inquiry must include student's name, social security number. Employers may obtain transcripts upon written request accompanied by a signed release from the student.

A multiprogram two-year institution, with an enrollment of 1,886. Highest level of offering: one year but less than four years.
ACCREDITATIONS: SACS RSTHT

Louisiana State University in Shreveport

One University Place
Shreveport, LA 71115
(318) 797-5061
Fax (318) 797-5180

Will confirm attendance and degree by phone or mail. Inquiry must include student's name, social security number. Employers may obtain transcripts upon written request accompanied by a $3.00 fee and a signed release from the student.

A general baccalaureate institution, with an enrollment of 4,690. Highest level of offering: beyond master's but less than doctorate.
ACCREDITATIONS: SACS AUD MED SP TED ACS

Louisiana State University Medical Center

Registrar's Office
433 Bolivar Street
New Orleans, LA 70112
(504) 568-4829
Fax (504) 568-7399

Will confirm attendance and degree by phone or mail. Inquiry must include student's name, social security number, years attended, date degree granted. Employers may obtain transcripts upon written request accompanied by a $2.00 fee and a signed release from the student.

A medical center, with an enrollment of 2,639. Highest level of offering: doctorate.
ACCREDITATIONS: ADNUR AUD CYTO DENT DH DT IPSY MED MT DA NUR OT PTA RAD RSTH SACS SP

Louisiana State University System Office

112 Thomas Boyd Hall
Baton Rouge, LA 70803
(504) 388-1686
Fax (504) 388-5991

Will confirm attendance and degree by phone, fax or mail. Inquiry must include student's name, social security number, years attended. Employers may obtain transcripts upon written request accompanied by a signed release from the student.

Louisiana Tech University

PO Box 3155 Tech Station
Ruston, LA 71272
(318) 257-2176
Fax (318) 257-4041

Will confirm attendance and degree by mail, phone or fax. Inquiry must include student's name, social security number. Employers may obtain transcripts upon written request accompanied by a signed release from the student.

A comprehensive institution with no medical school, with an enrollment of 10,825. Highest level of offering: doctorate.
ACCREDITATIONS: SACS ADNUR ARCH ART BUS DIET ENG ENGT FIDER MRA MRT FOR MUS TED SP BUSA

Louisville Presbyterian Theological Seminary

1044 Alta Vista Road
Louisville, KY 40205
(502) 895-3411 Ext. 269

Will confirm attendance and degree by phone or mail. Inquiry must include student's name, years attended. Employers may obtain transcripts upon written request accompanied by a $5.00 fee and a signed release from the student.

A school of philosophy, religion and theology, with an enrollment of 190. Highest level of offering: doctorate.
ACCREDITATIONS: SACS THEOL

Louisville Technical Institute

3901 Atkinson Drive
Louisville, KY 40218
(502) 459-6011
Fax (502) 454-4880

Will confirm attendance and degree by phone or mail. Inquiry must include student's name, social security number. Employers may obtain transcripts upon written request accompanied by a $5.00 fee and a signed release from the student.

A single program two-year institution, with an enrollment of 450. Highest level of offering: one year but less than four years.
ACCREDITATIONS: CCA CA TTSS

Lourdes College

6832 Convent Boulevard
Sylvania, OH 43560
(419) 885-3211 Ext. 207

Will confirm attendance and degree by mail. Inquiry must include student's name, social security number. Employers may obtain transcripts upon written request accompanied by a $3.00 fee and a signed release from the student.

A multiprogram four-year institution, with an enrollment of 1,400. Highest level of offering: four or five year baccalaureate.
ACCREDITATIONS: NCA

Lower Columbia College

PO Box 3010
1600 Maple Street
Longview, WA 98632
(206) 577-2304
Fax (206) 577-3400

Will confirm attendance and degree by phone or mail. Inquiry must include student's name, social security number, release. Employers may obtain transcripts upon written request accompanied by a signed release from the student.

A multiprogram two-year institution, with an enrollment of 4,000. Highest level of offering: two-year associate.
ACCREDITATIONS: NWASC

Loyola College

4501 North Charles Street
Baltimore, MD 21210
(301) 323-1010 Ext. 2659

Will confirm attendance and degree by phone or mail. Inquiry must include student's name, social security number. Employers may obtain transcripts upon written request accompanied by a $3.00 fee and a signed release from the student. Requests should be directed to: Records Office.

A comprehensive institution with no medical school, with an enrollment of 5,171. Highest level of offering: beyond master's but less than doctorate.
ACCREDITATIONS: M

Loyola Marymount University

Loyola Boulevard at West 80th Street
Los Angeles, CA 90045
(213) 642-2740

Will confirm attendance and degree by phone or mail. Inquiry must include student's name, social security number, years attended. Employers may obtain transcripts upon written request accompanied by a $2.00 fee and a signed release from the student.

A comprehensive institution with no medical school, with an enrollment of 6,410. Highest level of offering: master's.
ACCREDITATIONS: WC BUS ENG LAW

Loyola University in New Orleans

Office of the Registrar
Box 2
6363 Saint Charles Avenue
New Orleans, LA 70118
(504) 865-3237
Fax (504) 865-2110

Will confirm attendance and degree by phone, fax or mail. Inquiry must include student's name, social security number, years attended. Employers may obtain transcripts upon written request accompanied by a $2.00 fee and a signed release from the student.

A comprehensive institution with no medical school, with an enrollment of 4,859. Highest level of offering: master's.
ACCREDITATIONS: SACS BUS DH LAW MUS NUR

Loyola University of Chicago

(Formerly Mundelein College)
6525 North Sheridan Road
Chicago, IL 60626
(312) 262-8100 Ext. 435

Will confirm attendance and degree by phone or mail. Inquiry must include student's name, social security number, years attended. Employers may obtain transcripts upon written request accompanied by a $3.00 fee and a signed release from the student.

A general baccalaureate institution, with an enrollment of 1,171. Highest level of offering: master's.
ACCREDITATIONS: NH TED

Loyola University of Chicago

820 North Michigan Avenue
Chicago, IL 60611
(312) 915-7221
Fax (312) 915-6448

Will confirm attendance and degree by phone or mail. Inquiry must include student's name, social security number, years attended. Employers may obtain transcripts upon written request accompanied by a $3.00 fee and a signed release from the student.

A doctoral-level institution with a medical school, with an enrollment of 14,174. Highest level of offering: doctorate.
ACCREDITATIONS: NCA BUS CLPSY DENT DH LAW MED MT NUR SW TED COPSY

Loyola University at Mallinckrodt Campus

(Formerly Mallinckrodt Colege)
1041 Ridge Road
Wilmette, IL 60091
(708) 256-1094

Will confirm attendance and degree by mail. Inquiry must include student's name, social security number, release. Employers may obtain transcripts upon written request accompanied by a $4.00 fee and a signed release from the student.

A multiprogram two-year institution, with an enrollment of 287. Highest level of offering: four or five year baccalaureate.
ACCREDITATIONS: NH

Lubbock Christian University

5601 19th Street
Lubbock, TX 79407-2099
(806) 796-8800 Ext. 226
Fax (806) 796-8917

Will confirm attendance and degree by phone, fax or mail. Inquiry must include student's name, social security number, years attended. Employers may obtain transcripts upon written request accompanied by a $3.00 fee and a signed release from the student.

A general baccalaureate institution, with an enrollment of 1,055. Highest level of offering: four or five year baccalaureate.
ACCREDITATIONS: SACS TED SW

Lurleen B. Wallace State Junior College

PO Drawer 1418
Andalusia, AL 36420
(205) 222-6591 Ext. 273

Will confirm attendance and degree by phone or mail. Inquiry must include student's name, social security number. Employers may obtain transcripts upon written request accompanied by a $1.00 fee and a signed release from the student.

A multiprogram two-year institution, with an enrollment of 774. Highest level of offering: one year but less than four years.
ACCREDITATIONS: SACS

Luther College

700 College Drive
Decorah, IA 52101-1045
(319) 387-1167

Will confirm attendance and degree by phone or mail. Inquiry must include student's name, social security number, years attended. Employers may obtain transcripts upon written request accompanied by a $4.00 fee and a signed release from the student.

A general baccalaureate institution, with an enrollment of 2,350. Highest level of offering: four or five year baccalaureate.
ACCREDITATIONS: NCA MUS NUR SW TED

Luther Northwestern Theological Seminary

2481 Como Street
Saint Paul, MN 55108
(612) 641-3473

Will confirm attendance and degree by phone or mail. Inquiry must include student's name. Employers may obtain transcripts upon written request accompanied by a $2.00 fee and a signed release from the student.

A school of philosophy, religion and theology, with an enrollment of 755. Highest level of offering: doctorate.
ACCREDITATIONS: NCA THEOL

Lutheran Bible Institute of Seattle

4221 228th Avenue SE
Issaquah, WA 98027
(206) 392-0400 Ext. 218

Will confirm attendance and degree by phone or mail. Inquiry must include student's name, years attended. Employers may obtain transcripts upon written request accompanied by a $3.00 fee and a signed release from the student.

A school of philosophy, religion and theology, with an enrollment of 174. Highest level of offering: four or five year baccalaureate.
ACCREDITATIONS: NW BI

Lutheran School of Theology at Chicago

1100 East 55th Street
Chicago, IL 60615
(312) 753-0700
Fax (312) 753-0700

Will confirm attendance and degree by phone, fax or mail. Inquiry must include student's name, years attended. Employers may obtain transcripts upon written request accompanied by a $2.00 fee and a signed release from the student.

A school of philosophy, religion and theology, with an enrollment of 401. Highest level of offering: doctorate.
ACCREDITATIONS: NCA THEOL

Lutheran Theological Seminary at Gettysburg

61 Northwest Confederate Avenue
Gettysburg, PA 17325
(717) 334-6286 Ext. 201

Will confirm attendance and degree by phone or mail. Inquiry must include student's name. Employers may obtain transcripts upon written request accompanied by a $2.00 fee and a signed release from the student.

A school of philosophy, religion and theology, with an enrollment of 270. Highest level of offering: master's.
ACCREDITATIONS: M THEOL

Lutheran Theological Seminary at Philadelphia

7301 Germantown Avenue
Philadelphia, PA 19119
(215) 248-4616 Ext. 16

Will confirm attendance and degree by phone or mail. Inquiry must include student's name. Employers may obtain transcripts upon written request accompanied by a $2.00 fee and a signed release from student.

A school of philosophy, religion and theology, with an enrollment of 288. Highest level of offering: doctorate.
ACCREDITATIONS: M THEOL

Lutheran Theological Southern Seminary

4201 North Main Street
Columbia, SACS 29203
(803) 786-5150 Ext. 210

Will confirm attendance and degree by phone or mail. Inquiry must include student's name, social security number, years attended. Employers may obtain transcripts upon written request accompanied by a $2.00 fee and a signed release from the student.

A school of philosophy, religion and theology, with an enrollment of 168. Highest level of offering: doctorate.
ACCREDITATIONS: SACS THEOL

Luzerne County Community College

Prospect Street
Nanticoke, PA 18634
(717) 829-7340

Will confirm attendance and degree by phone or mail. Inquiry must include student's name, social security number. Employers may obtain transcripts upon written request accompanied by a $2.00 fee and a signed release from the student.

A multiprogram two-year institution, with an enrollment of 6,950. Highest level of offering: one year but less than four years.
ACCREDITATIONS: M ADNUR DA DH RSTHT

Lycoming College

Williamsport, PA 17701
(717) 321-4045
Fax (717) 321-4337

Will confirm attendance and degree by mail or phone. Inquiry must include student's name, social security number. Employers may obtain transcripts upon written request accompanied by a $3.00 fee and a signed release from the student.

A general baccalaureate institution, with an enrollment of 1,258. Highest level of offering: four or five year baccalaureate.
ACCREDITATIONS: M

Lynchburg College

1501 Lakeside Drive
Lynchburg, VA 24501
(804) 522-8100 Ext. 218
Fax (804) 522-0658

Will confirm attendance and degree by phone or mail. Inquiry must include student's name, social security number. Employers may obtain transcripts upon written request accompanied by a $3.00 fee and a signed release from the student.

A comprehensive institution with no medical school, with an enrollment of 2,400.
ACCREDITATIONS: SACS

Lyndon State College

Lyndonville, VT 05851
(802) 626-9371 Ext. 194

Will confirm attendance and degree by phone or mail. Inquiry must include student's name, social security number, years attended. Employers may obtain transcripts upon written request accompanied by a $5.00 fee and a signed release from the student.

A general baccalaureate institution, with an enrollment of 1,300. Highest level of offering: master's.
ACCREDITATIONS: EH

M

Macalester College

1600 Grand Avenue
Saint Paul, MN 55105
(612) 696-6200

Will confirm attendance and degree by phone or mail. Inquiry must include student's name, date of birth, years attended. Employers may obtain transcripts upon written request accompanied by a $3.00 fee and a signed release from the student. Requests should be directed to: Registrar's Office.

A general baccalaureate institution, with an enrollment of 1,896. Highest level of offering: four or five year baccalaureate.
ACCREDITATIONS: NH MUS

MacCormac College

327 South Lasalle Street
Chicago, IL 60604
(312) 922-1885

Will confirm attendance and degree by mail. Inquiry must include student's name, social security number, years attended. Employers may obtain transcripts upon written request accompanied by a $3.00 fee and a signed release from the student.

A single program two-year institution, with an enrollment of 600. Highest level of offering: one year but less than four years.
ACCREDITATIONS: NH

MacMurray College

East College Avenue
Jacksonville, IL 62650
(217) 479-7012
Fax (217) 245-5214

Will confirm attendance and degree by phone, fax or mail. Inquiry must include student's name, social security number. Employers may obtain transcripts upon written request accompanied by a $3.00 fee and a signed release from the student.

A general baccalaureate institution, with an enrollment of 626. Highest level of offering: four or five year baccalaureate.
ACCREDITATIONS: NH NUR

Macomb Community College

14500 Twelve Mile Road
Warren, MI 48093-3896
(313) 445-7999
Fax (313) 445-7157

Will confirm attendance by phone, fax or mail. Inquiry must include student's name, social security number. Employers may obtain transcripts upon written request accompanied by a $3.00 fee and a signed release from the student. Requests should be directed to: Records Office.

A multiprogram two-year institution, with an enrollment of 32,000. Highest level of offering: one year but less than four years.
ACCREDITATIONS: NH ADNUR ADVET DA PTAA RSTH OPTT

Macon College

100 College Station Drive
Macon, GA 31297
(912) 471-2855 or 471-2856

Will confirm attendance and degree by phone or mail. Inquiry must include student's name, social security number. Employers may obtain transcripts upon written request accompanied by a signed release from the student. Requests should be directed to: Registrar's Office.

A multiprogram two-year institution, with an enrollment of 4,600. Highest level of offering: two year associate degree.
ACCREDITATIONS: SC ADNUR DH

Madison Area Technical College

3550 Anderson Street
Madison, WI 53704
(608) 246-6210
Fax (608) 246-6880

Will confirm attendance by mail and degree by phone or mail. Inquiry must include student's name, social security number, years attended. Employers may obtain transcripts upon written request accompanied by a signed release from the student.

A multiprogram two-year institution, with an enrollment of 5,930. Highest level of offering: two years but less than four years.
ACCREDITATIONS: NH ADNUR ADVET DA DIET DH MAC MLTAD PNUR RSTH

Madison Business College

1110 Spring Harbor Drive
Madison, WI 53705
(608) 238-4266
Fax (608) 238-9905

Will confirm attendance and degree by phone or mail. Inquiry must include student's name. Employers may obtain transcripts upon written request accompanied by a $2.00 fee and a signed release from the student.

A single program two-year institution, with an enrollment of 350. Highest level of offering: one year but less than four years.
ACCREDITATIONS: JRCB OPTT

Madonna College

36600 Schoolcraft Road
Livonia, MI 48150
(313) 591-5038
Fax (313) 591-0156

Will confirm attendance and degree by phone, fax or mail. Inquiry must include student's name, social security number, years attended. Employers may obtain transcripts upon written request accompanied by a $4.00 fee and a signed release from the student.

A general baccalaureate institution, with an enrollment of 3,878. Highest level of offering: master's.
ACCREDITATIONS: NH NUR SW TED

Magdalen College

Tory Hill Road
RFD #2, Box 375
Warner, NH 03102
(603) 456-2656
Fax (603) 456-2660

Will confirm attendance and degree by phone, fax or mail. Inquiry must include student's name. Employers may obtain transcripts upon written request accompanied by a $5.00 fee and a signed release from the student.

A bachelor's or higher institution newly admitted to NCES, with an enrollment of 70. Highest level of offering: four or five year baccalaureate.
ACCREDITATIONS: EH

Maharishi International University

Office of Registrar, Box 1104
Fairfield, IA 52556
(515) 472-1144

Will confirm attendance and degree by phone or mail. Inquiry must include student's name, social security number, years attended. Employers may obtain transcripts upon written request accompanied by a $3.00 fee and a signed release from the student.

A general baccalaureate institution, with an enrollment of 3,231. Highest level of offering: doctorate.
ACCREDITATIONS: NH

Maine Maritime Academy

Registrar
Castine, ME 04420
(207) 326-4311 Ext. 426

Will confirm attendance and degree by phone or mail. Inquiry must include student's name, SSN, years attended. Employers may obtain transcripts upon written request by student accompanied by a $2.50 fee. Requests should be directed to: Registrar.

An engineering school, with an enrollment of 621. Highest level of offering: master's.
ACCREDITATIONS: EH

Malcolm X College

1900 West Van Buren Street
Chicago, IL 60612
(312) 942-3000

Will confirm attendance and degree by mail. Inquiry must include student's name, social security number, years attended, release. Employers may obtain transcripts upon written request accompanied by a $2.00 fee and a signed release from the student.

A multiprogram two-year institution, with an enrollment of 3,000. Highest level of offering: one year but less than four years.
ACCREDITATIONS: NH MLTAD RAD RSTH

Mallinckrodt College

(See Loyola University Mallinckrodt Campus)

Malone College

515 25th Street North West
Canton, OH 44709
(216) 471-8128
Fax (216) 454-6977

Will confirm attendance and degree by phone or mail. Inquiry must include student's name, social security number. Employers may obtain transcripts upon written request accompanied by a $3.00 fee and a signed release from the student.

A general baccalaureate institution, with an enrollment of 1,701. Highest level of offering: master's.
ACCREDITATIONS: NH SW

Manatee Community College

PO Box 1849
Bradenton, FL 34206
(813) 755-1511 Ext. 4212

Will confirm attendance and degree by phone or mail. Inquiry must include student's name, social security number. Employers may obtain transcripts upon written request accompanied by a signed release from the student.

A multiprogram two-year institution, with an enrollment of 8,500. Highest level of offering: two years but less than four years.
ACCREDITATIONS: SC ADNUR MLTAD RAD RSTH

Manchester College

Office of Registrar
North Manchester, IN 46962
(219) 982-2141 Ext. 234
Fax (219) 982-6868

Will confirm attendance and degree by phone, fax or mail. Inquiry must include student's name. Employers may obtain transcripts upon written request accompanied by a $2.00 fee and a signed release from the student.

A general baccalaureate institution, with an enrollment of 1,028. Highest level of offering: master's.
ACCREDITATIONS: NCA SW TED

Manchester Community College

PO Box 1046
Manchester, CT 06040
(203) 647-6147

Will confirm attendance and degree by phone or mail. Inquiry must include student's name, social security number. Employers may obtain transcripts upon written request accompanied by a signed release from the student.

A multiprogram two-year institution, with an enrollment of 6,633. Highest level of offering: one year but less than four years.
ACCREDITATIONS: EH MLTAD RSTH SURGT

Manhattan Christian College

1415 Anderson Avenue
Manhattan, KS 66502
(913) 539-3571 Ext. 16
Fax (913) 539-0832

Will confirm attendance and degree by phone or mail. Inquiry must include student's name, social security number, years attended. Employers may obtain transcripts upon written request accompanied by a $2.00 fee and a signed release from the student.

A school of religion and theology, with an enrollment of 229. Highest level of offering: four or five year baccalaureate.
ACCREDITATIONS: BI

Manhattan College

Registrar's Office
Riverdale, NY 10471
(212) 920-0310

Will confirm attendance and degree by phone or mail. Inquiry must include student's name, years attended, date graduated. Employers may obtain transcripts upon written request accompanied by a $5.00 fee and a signed release from the student. Requests should be directed to: Registrar's Office.

A comprehensive institution with no medical school, with an enrollment of 4,500. Highest level of offering: master's.
ACCREDITATIONS: M CHM ENG NMT NY

Manhattan School of Music

120 Claremont Avenue
New York, NY 10027
(212) 749-2802 Ext. 479
Fax (212) 749-5471

Will confirm attendance and degree by phone or mail. Inquiry must include student's name, social security number, years attended. Employers may obtain transcripts upon written request accompanied by a $3.00 fee and a signed release from the student. Requests should be directed to: Registrar's Office.

A visual and performing arts school, with an enrollment of 801. Highest level of offering: doctorate.
ACCREDITATIONS: M NY

Manhattanville College

125 Purchase Street
Purchase, NY 10577
(914) 694-2200 Ext. 264

Will confirm attendance and degree by phone or mail. Inquiry must include student's name, social security number, years attended. Employers may obtain transcripts upon written request accompanied by a $5.00 fee and a signed release from the student. Requests should be directed to: Registrar's Office.

A comprehensive institution with no medical school, with an enrollment of 1,275. Highest level of offering: master's.
ACCREDITATIONS: M MUS NY

Mankato State University

South Road & Ellis Avenue
Mankato, MN 56002-8400
(507) 389-6268

Will confirm attendance and degree by phone or mail. Inquiry must include student's name, social security number. Employers may obtain transcripts upon written request accompanied by a $2.00 fee and a signed release from the student. Requests should be directed to: Registrar's Office.

A comprehensive institution with no medical school, with an enrollment of 14,000. Highest level of offering: beyond master's but less than doctorate.
ACCREDITATIONS: NH ART DA DH ENGT MUS NUR SW TED

Mannes College of Music

150 West 85th
New York, NY 10024
(212) 580-0210
Fax (212) 580-1738

Will confirm attendance and degree by phone, fax or mail. Inquiry must include student's name, social security number, years attended. Employers may obtain transcripts upon written request accompanied by a $5.00 fee and a signed release from the student.

A performing arts school, with an enrollment of 205. Highest level of offering: master's.
ACCREDITATIONS: M NY

Manor Junior College

Fox Chase Road and Forest Avenue
Jenkintown, PA 19046
(215) 885-2360 Ext. 13

Will confirm attendance by phone or mail. Inquiry must include student's name, years attended. Employers may obtain transcripts upon written request accompanied by a $2.00 fee and a signed release from the student. Requests should be directed to: Registrar's Office.

A multiprogram two-year institution, with an enrollment of 450. Highest level of offering: one year but less than four years.
ACCREDITATIONS: M DA MLTAD

Mansfield University of Pennsylvania

112 South Hall
Mansfield, PA 16933
(717) 662-4112
Fax (717) 662-4995

Will confirm attendance and degree by phone, fax or mail. Inquiry must include student's name, social security number. Employers may obtain transcripts upon written request accompanied by a $2.00 fee and a signed release from the student. Requests should be directed to: Registrar's Office.

A comprehensive institution with no medical school, with an enrollment of 3,009. Highest level of offering: master's.
ACCREDITATIONS: M MUS RSTH SW TED RAD

Maple Woods Community College

2601 North East Barry Road
Kansas City, MO 64156
(816) 436-6500 Ext. 188
Fax (816) 734-2963

Will confirm attendance and degree by phone, fax or mail. Inquiry must include student's name, social security number. Employers may obtain transcripts upon written request accompanied by a $2.00 fee and a signed release from the student. Requests should be directed to: Admissions Office.

A multiprogram two-year institution, with an enrollment of 4,200. Highest level of offering: one year but less than four years.
ACCREDITATIONS: NH ADVET

Maranatha Baptist Bible College

745 West Main Street
Watertown, WI 53094
(414) 261-9300
Fax (414) 261-9109

Will confirm attendance and degree by phone, fax or mail. Inquiry must include student's name. Employers may obtain transcripts upon written request accompanied by a $3.00 fee and a signed release from the student. Requests should be directed to: Registrar's Office.

A bachelor's or higher institution newly admitted to NCES, with an enrollment of 475. Highest level of offering: master's.
ACCREDITATIONS: 3IC

Maria College of Albany

700 New Scotland Avenue
Albany, NY 12208
(518) 438-3111 Ext. 24

Will confirm attendance and degree by phone or mail. Inquiry must include student's name, social security number. Employers may obtain transcripts upon written request accompanied by a $2.00 fee and a signed release from the student. Requests should be directed to: Registrar's Office.

A multiprogram two-year institution, with an enrollment of 957. Highest level of offering: one year but less than four years.
ACCREDITATIONS: M ADNUR NY PTAA

Maria Regina Center

1118 Court Street
Syracuse, NY 13208
(315) 478-1217

Records are maintained at above addres. Will confirm attendance and degree by phone or mail. Inquiry must include student's name. Employers may obtain transcripts upon written request accompanied by a $3.00 fee and a signed release from the student. Requests should be directed to: Registrar's Office.

Marian College of Fond Du Lac

45 South National Avenue
Fond Du Lac, WI 54935
(414) 923-7618

Will confirm attendance and degree by phone or mail. Inquiry must include student's name. Employers may obtain transcripts upon written request accompanied by a $2.00 fee and a signed release from the student. Requests should be directed to: Registrar's Office.

A general baccalaureate institution, with an enrollment of 456. Highest level of offering: master's.
ACCREDITATIONS: NH NUR SW TED

Marian College

3200 Cold Spring Road
Indianapolis, IN 46222-1997
(317) 929-0213
Fax (317) 929-0263

Will confirm attendance and degree by phone, fax or mail. Inquiry must include student's name. Requests should be directed to: Registrar's Office. Employers may obtain transcripts upon written request accompanied by a $2.00 fee and a signed release from the student.

A general baccalaureate institution, with an enrollment of 1,228. Highest level of offering: four or five year baccalaureate.
ACCREDITATIONS: ADNUR NH RAD RSTH RSTHT TED

Marian Court Junior College

35 Littles Point Road
Swampscott, MA 01907
(617) 595-6768

Will confirm attendance and degree by mail. Inquiry must include student's name, social security number, years attended, release. Employers may obtain transcripts upon written request accompanied by a $2.00 fee and a signed release from the student. Requests should be directed to: Registrar's Office.

A two-year institution newly admitted to NCES, with an enrollment of 250. Highest level of offering: one year but less than four years.
ACCREDITATIONS: JRCB

Maricopa Technical Community College

c/o Gateway Community College
108 North 40th Street
Phoenix, AZ 85034
(602) 275-8500

Records for this school are being handled by Gateway Community College. Will confirm attendance and degree by phone or mail. Inquiry must include student's name, social security number.

Marietta College

Records Office
215 Fifth Street
Marietta, OH 45750
(614) 374-4728
Fax (614) 374-4896

Will confirm attendance and degree by phone, fax or mail. Inquiry must include student's name, maiden name, date of birth. Employers may obtain transcripts upon written request accompanied by a signed release from the student. Requests should be directed to: Records Office.

A general baccalaureate institution, with an enrollment of 1,365. Highest level of offering: master's.
ACCREDITATIONS: NH

Marin Community College

1800 Ignacia Boulevard
Navato, CA 94949
(415) 883-2211

Will confirm attendance and degree by mail. Inquiry must include student's name, date of birth, social security number, release. Requests should be directed to: Admissions & Records Office. Only students may obtain transcripts.

A multiprogram two-year institution, with an enrollment of 2,954. Highest level of offering: one year but less than four years.
ACCREDITATIONS: WJ

Marion College

4201 South Washington Street
Marion, IN 46953
(317) 674-6901 Ext. 131
Fax (317) 677-2131

Will confirm attendance and degree by phone or mail. Inquiry must include student's name, years attended. Employers may obtain transcripts upon written request accompanied by a $2.00 fee and a signed release from the student. Requests should be directed to: Records Office.

A general baccalaureate institution, with an enrollment of 2,700. Highest level of offering: master's.
ACCREDITATIONS: NH MLTAD NUR SW

Marion Military Institute

Marion, AL 36756
(205) 683-2300

Will confirm attendance and degree by phone or mail. Employers may obtain transcripts upon written request accompanied by a $5.00 fee and a signed release from the student. Requests should be directed to: Registrar's Office.

A multiprogram two-year institution, with an enrollment of 350. Highest level of offering: one year but less than four years.
ACCREDITATIONS: SC

Marion Technical College

1465 Mount Vernon Avenue
Marion, OH 43302
(614) 389-4636

Will confirm attendance and degree by mail. Inquiry must include student's name, social security number, years attended, release. Employers may obtain transcripts upon written request accompanied by a $2.00 fee and a signed release from the student. Requests should be directed to: Records Office.

A multiprogram two-year institution, with an enrollment of 1,366. Highest level of offering: one year but less than four years.
ACCREDITATIONS: NH ADNUR MLTAD

Marist College

290 North Road
Poughkeepsie, NY 12601
(914) 575-3000

Will confirm attendance and degree by mail. Inquiry must include student's name, date of birth, social security number, release. Employers may obtain transcripts upon written request accompanied by a $3.00 fee and a signed release from the student. Requests should be directed to: Registrar's Office.

A general baccalaureate institution, with an enrollment of 4,219. Highest level of offering: master's.
ACCREDITATIONS: M NY SW

Marlboro College

Marlboro, VT 05344
(802) 257-4333 Ext. 233

Will confirm attendance and degree by phone or mail. Inquiry must include student's name. Employers may obtain transcripts upon written request accompanied by a signed release from the student. Requests should be directed to: Registrar's Office.

A general baccalaureate institution, with an enrollment of 240. Highest level of offering: four or five year baccalaureate.
ACCREDITATIONS: EH

Marquette University

1217 West Wisconsin Avenue
Milwaukee, WI 53233
(414) 288-6326

Will confirm attendance and degree by phone or mail. Inquiry must include student's name, social security number, years attended. Employers may obtain transcripts upon written request accompanied by a $3.00 fee and a signed release from the student. Requests should be directed to: Registrar's Office.

A doctoral-level institution with a medical school, with an enrollment of 11,630. Highest level of offering: doctorate.
ACCREDITATIONS: NH BUS DENT DH ENG LAW NUR PTA SP SW TED

Mars Hill College

Mars Hill, NC 28754
(704) 689-1151

Will confirm attendance and degree by phone or mail. Inquiry must include student's name, social security number. Employers may obtain transcripts upon written request accompanied by a $2.00 fee and a signed release from the student. Requests should be directed to: Registrar's Office.

A general baccalaureate institution, with an enrollment of 1,357. Highest level of offering: four or five year baccalaureate.
ACCREDITATIONS: SC MUS SW

Marshall University

Huntington, WV 25701
(304) 696-6410
Fax (304) 696-2252

Will confirm attendance and degree by mail or fax. Inquiry must include student's name, social security number, years attended. Employers may obtain transcripts upon written request accompanied by a $3.00 fee and a signed release from the student. Requests should be directed to: Registrar's Office.

A comprehensive institution with a medical school, with an enrollment of 12,500. Highest level of offering: first professional degree.
ACCREDITATIONS: NH ADNUR JOUR MED MLTAD MUS NUR TED

Marshalltown Community College

3700 South Center Street
Marshalltown, IA 50158
(515) 752-7106 Ext. 217
Fax (515) 752-8149

Will confirm attendance and degree by phone, fax or mail. Inquiry must include student's name, social security number, years attended. Employers may obtain transcripts upon written request accompanied by a signed release from the student. Requests should be directed to: Registrar's Office.

A multiprogram two-year institution, with an enrollment of 1,383. Highest level of offering: one year but less than four years.
ACCREDITATIONS: NH DA MAC SURGT

Martin Center College

PO Box 18567
2171 Avendale Place
Indianapolis, IN 46218
(317) 543-3240

Will confirm attendance and degree by mail. Inquiry must include student's name, social security number, release. Employers may obtain transcripts upon written request accompanied by a $5.00 fee and a signed release from the student. Requests should be directed to: Registrar's Office.

A specialized school, with an enrollment of 765. Highest level of offering: four or five year baccalaureate.

ACCREDITATIONS: NH

Martin Community College

Kehukee Park Road
Williamston, NC 27892
(919) 792-1521 Ext. 243
Fax (919) 792-4425

Will confirm attendance and degree by phone or mail. Inquiry must include student's name, social security number, dates of enrollment. Employers may obtain transcripts upon written request accompanied by a signed release from the student. Requests should be directed to: Registrar's Office.

A multiprogram two-year institution, with an enrollment of 750. Highest level of offering: one year but less than four years.

ACCREDITATIONS: SACS

Martin Methodist College

433 West Madison Street
Pulaski, TN 38478
(615) 363-9809
Fax (615) 363-9818

Will confirm attendance and degree by phone or mail. Inquiry must include student's name, social security number, years attended. Employers may obtain transcripts upon written request accompanied by a signed release from the student. Requests should be directed to: Records Office.

A multiprogram two-year institution, with an enrollment of 327. Highest level of offering: one year but less than four years.

ACCREDITATIONS: SC

Mary Baldwin College

Staunton, VA 24401
(703) 887-7071
Fax (703) 886-5561

Will confirm attendance and degree by phone or mail. Inquiry must include student's name. Employers may obtain transcripts upon written request accompanied by a $2.00 fee and a signed release from the student. Requests should be directed to: Registrar's Office.

A general baccalaureate institution, with an enrollment of 1,177. Highest level of offering: four or five year baccalaureate.

ACCREDITATIONS: SC

Mary Holmes College

PO Drawer 2157
West Point, MS 39773
(601) 494-6820 Ext. 136

Will confirm attendance and degree by phone. Inquiry must include student's name, social security number. Employers may obtain transcripts upon written request accompanied by a $2.00 fee and a signed release from the student. Requests should be directed to: Registrar's Office.

A multiprogram two-year institution, with an enrollment of 704. Highest level of offering: one year but less than four years.

ACCREDITATIONS: SC

Mary Immaculate Seminary

300 Cherryville Road
Northampton, PA 18067
(215) 262-7866
Fax (215) 262-6766

Records are maintained at the above address. Will confirm attendance and degree by phone or mail. Inquiry must include student's name, years attended. Employers may obtain transcripts upon written request accompanied by a $3.00 fee and a signed release from the student.

Mary Washington College

Fredericksburg, VA 22401-5358
(703) 899-4691

Will confirm attendance and degree by phone or mail. Inquiry must include student's name, years attended. Employers may obtain transcripts upon written request accompanied by a $2.00 fee and a signed release from the student. Requests should be directed to: Student Records Office.

A general baccalaureate institution, with an enrollment of 3,700. Highest level of offering: master's.

ACCREDITATIONS: SC MUS

Marycrest College

1607 West 12th Street
Davenport, IA 52804
(319) 326-9216

Will confirm attendance and degree by phone or mail. Inquiry must include student's name, social security number. Requests should be directed to: Registrar's Office. Employers may obtain transcripts upon written request accompanied by a $5.00 fee and a signed release from the student.

A general baccalaureate institution, with an enrollment of 1,453. Highest level of offering: master's.

ACCREDITATIONS: NH NUR SW

Marygrove College

8425 West Mcnichols Road
Detroit, MI 48221
(313) 862-8000 Ext. 262
Fax (313) 864-6670

Will confirm attendance and degree by phone, fax or mail. Inquiry must include student's name, social security number. Employers may obtain transcripts upon written request accompanied by a $3.00 fee and a signed release from the student. Requests should be directed to: Registrar's Office.

A comprehensive institution with no medical school, with an enrollment of 1,182. Highest level of offering: master's.

ACCREDITATIONS: NH RAD SW TED

Maryknoll School of Theology

Maryknoll, NY 10545
(914) 941-7590 Ext. 409

Will confirm attendance and degree by mail. Inquiry must include student's name, years attended. Employers may obtain transcripts upon written request accompanied by a $3.00 fee and a signed release from the student. Requests should be directed to: Registrar's Office.

A school of philosophy, religion and theology, with an enrollment of 123. Highest level of offering: beyond master's but less than doctorate.

ACCREDITATIONS: M NY THEOL

Maryland College of Art and Design

10500 Georgia Avenue
Silver Spring, MD 20902
(301) 649-4454

Will confirm attendance and degree by phone or mail. Inquiry must include student's name. Employers may obtain transcripts upon written request accompanied by a $3.50 fee and a signed release from the student.

A single program two-year institution, with an enrollment of 83. Highest level of offering: one year but less than four years.

ACCREDITATIONS: ART

Maryland Institute College of Art

1300 Mount Royal Avenue
Baltimore, MD 21217
(301) 225-2234

Will confirm attendance and degree by phone or mail. Inquiry must include student's name, social security number. Employers may obtain transcripts upon written request accompanied by a $2.00 fee and a signed release from the student.

A visual and performing arts school, with an enrollment of 1,280. Highest level of offering: master's.

ACCREDITATIONS: M ART

Marylhurst College for Lifelong Learning

Marylhurst, OR 97036
(503) 636-8141 Ext. 324

Will confirm attendance and degree by phone or mail. Inquiry must include student's name, social security number, years attended. Employers may obtain transcripts upon written request accompanied by a $6.00 fee and a signed release from the student. Requests should be directed to: Registrar's Office.

A general baccalaureate institution, with an enrollment of 1,500. Highest level of offering: master's.

ACCREDITATIONS: NW MUS

Marymount College of Kansas

St. Mary of the Plains College
PO Box 980
Salina, KS 67402-0980
(913) 827-8746

Will confirm attendance and degree by
mail. Inquiry must include student's name,
years attended. Employers may obtain transcripts upon written request accompanied
by a $2.00 fee and a signed release from the
student. Requests should be directed to: St.
Mary of the Plains College, 240 San Jose
Drive, Dodge City, KS 67801.

Marymount College of Virginia

Office of Registrar
2807 North Glebe Road
Arlington, VA 22207
(703) 284-1520

Will confirm attendance and degree by
phone or mail. Inquiry must include student's name, social security number.
Employers may obtain transcripts upon
written request accompanied by a $3.00 fee
and a signed release from the student.

An independent coeducational institution,
with an enrollment of 3,400. Highest level
of offering: master's
ACCREDITATIONS: SACS ADNUR NUR
FIDER NCATE

Marymount College

Tarrytown, NY 10591-3796
(914) 631-3200 Ext. 211

Will confirm attendance and degree by
phone or mail. Inquiry must include student's name. Employers may obtain transcripts upon written request accompanied
by a $2.00 fee and a signed release from the
student.

A general baccalaureate institution, with an
enrollment of 1,202. Highest level of offering: four or five year baccalaureate.
ACCREDITATIONS: M NY SW

Marymount Manhattan College

221 East 71st Street
New York, NY 10021
(212) 517-0400
Fax (212) 517-0413

Will confirm attendance and degree by mail
or fax. Inquiry must include student's name,
social security number, release. Requests
should be directed to: Registrar's Office.
Employers may obtain transcripts upon
written request accompanied by a $4.00 fee
and a signed release from the student.

A general baccalaureate institution, with an
enrollment of 1,250. Highest level of offering: four or five year baccalaureate.
ACCREDITATIONS: M NY

Marymount Palos Verdes College

30800 Palos Verdes Dr. East
Rancho Palos Verdes, CA 90274
(310) 377-5501 Ext. 214
Fax (310) 377-6223

Will confirm attendance and degree by
phone or mail. Inquiry must include student's name, social security number.
Employers may obtain transcripts upon
written request accompanied by a $3.00 fee
and a signed release from the student.
Requests should be directed to: Registrar's
Office.

A multiprogram two-year institution, with
an enrollment of 755. Highest level of offering: two years but less than four years.
ACCREDITATIONS: WJ

Marymount University

2807 North Glebe Road
Arlington, VA 22207
(703) 284-1520

Will confirm attendance and degree by
phone or mail. Inquiry must include student's name, social security number.
Employers may obtain transcripts upon
written request accompanied by a $3.00 fee
and a signed release from the student.
Requests should be directed to: Registrar's
Office.

A general baccalaureate institution, with an
enrollment of 2,088. Highest level of offering: master's.
ACCREDITATIONS: SC ADNUR NUR FIDER

Maryville College

Maryville, TN 37801
(615) 981-8212
Fax (615) 983-0581

Will confirm attendance and degree by
phone or mail. Inquiry must include student's name, social security number, years
attended. Employers may obtain transcripts
upon written request accompanied by a
$2.00 fee and a signed release from the stu-
dent. Requests should be directed to:
Registrar's Office.

A general baccalaureate institution, with an
enrollment of 900. Highest level of offering: four or five year baccalaureate.
ACCREDITATIONS: SC MUS

Maryville University

13550 Conway Road
Saint Louis, MO 63141
(314) 576-9300 Ext. 370
Fax (314) 542-9085

Will confirm attendance and degree by mail
or fax. Inquiry must include student's name,
social security number. Employers may obtain transcripts upon written request accompanied by a $2.00 fee and a signed release
from the student. Requests should be directed to: Registrar's Office.

A general baccalaureate institution, with an
enrollment of 3,143. Highest level of offering: master's.
ACCREDITATIONS: NH ADNUR FIDER NUR
PTA TED

Marywood College

Registrar's Office
2300 Adams Avenue
Scranton, PA 18509
(717) 348-6211

Will confirm attendance and degree by
mail. Inquiry must include student's name,
social security number, release. Employers
may obtain transcripts upon written request
by student accompanied by a $4.00 fee.

A comprehensive institution with no medi-
cal school, with an enrollment of 2,927.
Highest level of offering: master's.
ACCREDITATIONS: M ART DIET MUS SW
TED NLN/AD

Massachusetts Bay Community College

50 Oakland Street
Wellesley Hills, MA 02181
(617) 237-1100

Will confirm attendance and degree by
mail. Inquiry must include student's name,
social security number, release. Requests
should be directed to: Registrar's Office.
Employers may obtain transcripts upon
written request accompanied by a signed release from the student.

A multiprogram two-year institution, with
an enrollment of 4,236. Highest level of offering: one year but less than four years.
ACCREDITATIONS: EH MLTAD MRT RAD

Massachusetts College of Art

621 Huntington Avenue
Boston, MA 02115
(617) 232-1555 Ext. 243
Fax (617) 566-4034

Will confirm attendance and degree by
mail. Inquiry must include student's name,
date of birth, social security number, release. Employers may obtain transcripts
upon written request accompanied by a
$2.00 fee and a signed release from the stu-
dent. Requests should be directed to:
Registrar's Office.

A visual and performing arts school, with
an enrollment of 1,730. Highest level of offering: master's.
ACCREDITATIONS: EH ART

Massachusetts College of Pharmacy and Allied Health Sciences

179 Longwood Avenue
Boston, MA 02115
(617) 732-2800 Ext. 2855

Will confirm attendance and degree by
phone. Inquiry must include student's
name, years attended. Employers may obtain transcripts upon written request accompanied by a $3.00 fee and a signed release
from the student. Requests should be directed to: Registrar's Office.

A health institution, with an enrollment of
1,194. Highest level of offering: doctorate.
ACCREDITATIONS: EH NMT PHAR

Massachusetts Institute of Technology

77 Massachusetts Avenue–Building E
19 Room 335
Cambridge, MA 02139
(617) 253-4784

Will confirm attendance and degree by mail. Inquiry must include student's name, date of birth, social security number. Employers may obtain transcripts upon written request accompanied by a $2.00 fee and a signed release from the student. Requests should be directed to: Registrar's Office.

A doctoral-level institution with no medical school, with an enrollment of 9,608. Highest level of offering: doctorate.

ACCREDITATIONS: EH ARCH BUS ENG

Massachusetts Maritime Academy

PO Box D
Buzzards Bay, MA 02532
(617) 759-5761
Fax (508) 759-4116

Will confirm attendance and degree by phone, fax or mail. Inquiry must include student's name, social security number. Requests should be directed to: Registrar's Office. Employers may obtain transcripts upon written request accompanied by a $1.00 fee and a signed release from the student.

An engineering school, with an enrollment of 803. Highest level of offering: four or five year baccalaureate.

ACCREDITATIONS: EH

Massachusetts School of Professional Psychology

322 Sprague St.
Dedham, MA 02026
(617) 329-6777
Fax (617) 329-5339

Will confirm attendance and degree by phone, fax or mail. Inquiry must include student's name, social security number, date of birth. Employers may obtain transcripts upon written request accompanied by a $2.00 fee and a signed release from the student.

A bachelor's or higher institution newly admitted to NCES, with an enrollment of 179. Highest level of offering: doctorate.

ACCREDITATIONS: EH

Massasoit Community College

(Formerly Blue Hills Regional Technical Institute)
One Massasoit Boulevard
Brockton, MA 02402
(508) 588-9100 Ext. 2

Will confirm attendance and degree by phone or mail. Inquiry must include student's name, social security number, years attended. Employers may obtain transcripts upon written request accompanied by a $1.00 fee and a signed release from the student. Requests should be directed to: Registrar's Office.

A multiprogram two-year institution, with an enrollment of 6,113. Highest level of offering: one year but less than four years.

ACCREDITATIONS: EH ADNUR RSTH

Master's College

(Formerly Los Angeles Master's College)
PO Box 878
Newhall, CA 91321-0878
(805) 259-3540 Ext. 317

Will confirm attendance and degree by phone or mail. Inquiry must include student's name, social security number. Employers may obtain transcripts upon written request accompanied by a $3.00 fee and a signed release from the student.

A general baccalaureate institution, with an enrollment of 815. Highest level of offering: four or five year baccalaureate.

ACCREDITATIONS: WC

Matanuska–Susitna Community College

PO Box 2889
Palmer, AK 99645
(907) 745-9774
Fax (907) 745-9711

Will confirm attendance and degree by phone or fax. Inquiry must include student's name, social security number. Employers may obtain transcripts upon written request accompanied by a $4.00 fee and a signed release from the student. Contact the above address to obtain the proper form for requesting transcript information.

A multiprogram two-year institution, with an enrollment of 3,200. Highest level of offering: one year but less than four years.

ACCREDITATIONS: NW

Mater Dei College

Rural Route #2, Box 45
Ogdensburg, NY 13669-9699
(315) 393-5930

Will confirm attendance and degree by mail. Inquiry must include student's name, date of birth, social security number, release. Requests should be directed to: Registrar's Office. Employers may obtain transcripts upon written request accompanied by a signed release from the student.

A multiprogram two-year institution, with an enrollment of 550. Highest level of offering: one year but less than four years.

ACCREDITATIONS: M NY

Mattatuck Community College

750 Chase Parkway
Waterbury, CT 06708
(203) 575-8011
Fax (203) 575-8228

Will confirm attendance and degree by phone, fax or mail. Inquiry must include student's name, social security number. Employers may obtain transcripts upon written request accompanied by a signed release from the student. Requests should be directed to: Registrar's Office.

A multiprogram two-year institution, with an enrollment of 4,100. Highest level of offering: one year but less than four years.

ACCREDITATIONS: EH ADNUR RAD

Maui Community College

310 Kaahumanu Avenue
Kahului, HI 96732
(808) 244-9181
Fax (808) 242-9618

Will confirm attendance and degree by mail or fax. Inquiry must include student's name, social security number. Employers may obtain transcripts upon written request accompanied by a $1.00 fee and a signed release from the student. Requests should be directed to: Registrar's Office.

A multiprogram two-year institution, with an enrollment of 2,440. Highest level of offering: one year but less than four years.

ACCREDITATIONS: WJ

Mayland Technical College

PO Box 547
Spruce Pine, NC 28777
(704) 765-7351

Will confirm attendance and degree by mail. Inquiry must include student's name, social security number, years attended, release. Employers may obtain transcripts upon written request accompanied by a signed release from the student.

A multiprogram two-year institution, with an enrollment of 940. Highest level of offering: one year but less than four years.

ACCREDITATIONS: SC

Mayo Graduate School

200 First Street Southwest
Rochester, MN 55905
(507) 284-4339
Fax (507) 284-0532

Will confirm attendance and degree by phone or mail. Inquiry must include student's name, years attended. Employers may obtain transcripts upon written request accompanied by a signed release from the student. Requests should be directed to: Registrar's Office.

A graduate school of medicine affiliated with a health institution, with an enrollment of 1,114. Highest level of offering: graduate non-degree granting.

ACCREDITATIONS: NCA MICB ACDME ADA/A

Mayville State College

330 Third Street North East
Mayville, ND 58257
(701) 786-2301 Ext. 774
Fax (701) 786-4748

Will confirm attendance and degree by phone, fax or mail. Inquiry must include student's name, social security number, date of birth. Employers may obtain transcripts upon written request accompanied by a $2.00 fee and a signed release from the student.

A general baccalaureate institution, with an enrollment of 775. Highest level of offering: four or five year baccalaureate.

ACCREDITATIONS: NH TED

McCarrie School of Health Sciences and Technology

512 S. Broad Street
Philadelphia, PA 19146
(215) 545-7772

Will confirm attendance and degree by mail. Inquiry must include student's name, social security number, years attended, release. Employers may obtain transcripts upon written request accompanied by a $2.00 fee and a signed release from the student. Requests should be directed to: Records Department.

A multiprogram two-year institution, with an enrollment of 251. Highest level of offering: one year but less than four years.

ACCREDITATIONS: AHE NATTS

McCormick Theological Seminary

5555 South Woodlawn Avenue
Chicago, IL 60637
(312) 241-7800
Fax (312) 947-6273

Will confirm attendance and degree by phone, fax or mail. Inquiry must include student's name, years attended. Employers may obtain transcripts upon written request accompanied by a $2.00 fee and a signed release from the student. Requests should be directed to: Registrar's Office.

A school of philosophy, religion and theology, with an enrollment of 548. Highest level of offering: doctorate.

ACCREDITATIONS: NH THEOL

McDowell Technical Community College

Route 1 Box 170
Marion, NC 28752
(704) 652-6021 Ext. 401

Will confirm attendance and degree by phone or mail. Inquiry must include student's name. Employers may obtain transcripts upon written request accompanied by a signed release from the student.

A multiprogram two-year institution, with an enrollment of 688. Highest level of offering: one year but less than four years.

ACCREDITATIONS: SC

McHenry County College

8900 US Highway 14
Crystal Lake, IL 60012-2761
(815) 455-3700 Ext. 231
Fax (815) 455-3999

Will confirm attendance and degree by phone, fax or mail. Inquiry must include student's name, social security number. Employers may obtain transcripts upon written request accompanied by a $2.00 fee and a signed release from the student. Requests should be directed to: Records Office.

A multiprogram two-year institution, with an enrollment of 3,497. Highest level of offering: one year but less than four years.

ACCREDITATIONS: NH

McIntosh College

23 Cataract Avenue
Dover, NH 03820
(603) 742-1234
Fax (603) 742-7292

Will confirm attendance and degree by mail. Inquiry must include student's name, social security number, date of birth. Employers may obtain transcripts upon written request accompanied by a $2.00 fee and a signed release from the student. Requests should be directed to: Registrar's Office.

A two-year institution, with an enrollment of 900. Highest level of offering: two years.

ACCREDITATIONS: EV JRCB

McKendree College

701 College Road
Lebanon, IL 62254
(618) 537-4481 Ext. 131
Fax (618) 537-6259

Will confirm attendance and degree by phone or fax. Inquiry must include student's name, social security number, years attended. Employers may obtain transcripts upon written request accompanied by a $3.00 fee and a signed release from the student. Requests should be directed to: Academic Records.

A general baccalaureate institution, with an enrollment of 973. Highest level of offering: four or five year baccalaureate.

ACCREDITATIONS: NH NUR

McKenzie College

1000 Riverfront Parkway
Chattanooga, TN 37402
(615) 756-7042

Will confirm attendance and degree by mail. Inquiry must include student's name, release. Employers may obtain transcripts upon written request accompanied by a $2.00 fee and a signed release from the student. Requests should be directed to: Registrar's Office.

A single program two-year institution, with an enrollment of 376. Highest level of offering: one year but less than four years.

ACCREDITATIONS: JRCB

McLennan Community College

1400 College Drive
Waco, TX 76708
(817) 756-6551 Ext. 522
Fax (817) 750-3529

Will confirm attendance and degree by phone or mail. Inquiry must include student's name, social security number. Employers may obtain transcripts upon written request accompanied by a $3.00 fee and a signed release from the student.

A multiprogram two-year institution, with an enrollment of 5,800. Highest level of offering: one year but less than four years.

ACCREDITATIONS: SC ADNUR NMT RAD RSTHT MLTAD

McMurry University

Box 338 McMurry Station
Abilene, TX 79697
(915) 691-6401
Fax (915) 691-6599

Will confirm attendance and degree by phone or mail. Inquiry must include student's name, social security number, years attended. Employers may obtain transcripts upon written request accompanied by a $5.00 fee and a signed release from the student. Requests should be directed to: Registrar's Office.

A general baccalaureate institution, with an enrollment of 1,482. Highest level of offering: four or five year baccalaureate.

ACCREDITATIONS: SC TED

McNeese State University

PO Box 92495
Lake Charles, LA 70609
(318) 475-5145

Will confirm attendance and degree by phone or mail. Inquiry must include student's name, date of birth, social security number. Employers may obtain transcripts upon written request accompanied by a $2.00 fee and a signed release from the student. Requests should be directed to: Registrar's Office.

A comprehensive institution with no medical school, with an enrollment of 7,600. Highest level of offering: beyond master's but less than doctorate.

ACCREDITATIONS: SC ENG MUS NUR RAD TED

McPherson College

PO Box 1402
McPherson, KS 67460
(316) 241-0731 Ext. 122

Will confirm attendance and degree by phone or mail. Inquiry must include student's name. Employers may obtain transcripts upon written request accompanied by a $3.00 fee and a signed release from the student. Requests should be directed to: Registrar's Office.

A general baccalaureate institution, with an enrollment of 484. Highest level of offering: four or five year baccalaureate.

ACCREDITATIONS: NH

Meadows Junior College

1170 Brown Avenue
Columbus, GA 31906
(404) 327-7668
Fax (404) 324-4696

Will confirm attendance and degree by phone, fax or mail. Inquiry must include student's name, social security number. Employers may obtain transcripts upon written request accompanied by a signed release from the student.

A two-year institution newly admitted to NCES, with an enrollment of 327. Highest level of offering: one year but less than four years.

ACCREDITATIONS: JRCB

Meadville–Lombard Theological School

5701 S. Woodlawn Avenue
Chicago, IL 60637
(312) 753-3198

Will confirm attendance and degree by mail. Inquiry must include student's name, social security number, release. Employers may obtain transcripts upon written request accompanied by a $4.00 fee and a signed release from the student. Requests should be directed to: Registrar's Office.

A school of philosophy, religion and theology, with an enrollment of 35. Highest level of offering: doctorate.

ACCREDITATIONS: THEOL

Medaille College

18 Agassiz Circle
Buffalo, NY 14214
(716) 884-3281 Ext. 261
Fax (716) 884-0291

Will confirm attendance and degree by phone, fax or mail. Inquiry must include student's name, social security number. Employers may obtain transcripts upon written request accompanied by a $2.00 fee and a signed release from the student. Requests should be directed to: Registrar's Office.

A general baccalaureate institution, with an enrollment of 787. Highest level of offering: four or five year baccalaureate.

ACCREDITATIONS: M NY

Median School of Allied Health Careers

125 7th Street
Pittsburgh, PA 15222
(412) 391-0422

Will confirm attendance and degree by phone or mail. Inquiry must include student's name, years attended. Employers may obtain transcripts upon written request accompanied by a $2.00 fee and a signed release from the student. Requests should be directed to: Education Secretary.

A two-year institution newly admitted to NCES, with an enrollment of 250. Highest level of offering: one year but less than four years.

ACCREDITATIONS: ADVET DA

Medical College of Georgia

1120 Fifteenth Street–Administration Building Room 171
Augusta, GA 30912-7310
(404) 721-2201
Fax (404) 721-3461

Will confirm attendance and degree by phone, fax or mail. Inquiry must include student's name, social security number. Employers may obtain transcripts upon written request accompanied by a signed release from the student. Requests should be directed to: Registrar's Office.

A health sciences university, with an enrollment of 2,320. Highest level of offering: doctorate.

ACCREDITATIONS: SC APCP DENT DH IPSY MED MRA MT NMT NUR OT PTA PTAA RAD RSTH RTT DMS

Medical College of Ohio at Toledo

PO Box 10008
Toledo, OH 43699
(419) 381-4198

Will confirm attendance and degree by phone or mail. Inquiry must include student's name. Requests should be directed to: Registrar's Office. Employers may obtain transcripts upon written request by student accompanied by a $3.00 fee and a signed release from the student. Contact college for appropriate form.

A medical school, with an enrollment of 838. Highest level of offering: first professional degree.

ACCREDITATIONS: NH MED PTA NUR

Medical College of Wisconsin

8701 Watertown Plank Road
Milwaukee, WI 53226
(414) 257-8248

Will confirm attendance and degree by phone or mail. Inquiry must include student's name, years attended. Requests should be directed to: Admissions Office. Employers may obtain transcripts upon written request accompanied by a $1.00 fee and a signed release from the student.

A medical school, with an enrollment of 1,150. Highest level of offering: doctorate.

ACCREDITATIONS: NH MED RTT

Medical Institute of Minnesota

5503 Greenvalley Drive
W. Bloomington, MN 55437
(612) 871-8481

Will confirm attendance and degree by phone or mail. Inquiry must include student's name, years attended. Employers may obtain transcripts upon written request accompanied by a $4.00 fee and a signed release from the student. Requests should be directed to: Student Resources.

A single program two-year institution, with an enrollment of 550. Highest level of offering: one year but less than four years.

ACCREDITATIONS: ADVET AHE MAC NATTS

Medical University of South Carolina

171 Ashley Avenue
Charleston, SC 29425-3281
(803) 792-3281

Will confirm attendance and degree by phone or mail. Inquiry must include student's name, social security number. Employers may obtain transcripts upon written request accompanied by a $3.00 fee and a signed release from the student. Requests should be directed to: Registrar's Office.

A medical school, with an enrollment of 2,194. Highest level of offering: doctorate.

ACCREDITATIONS: SC ANEST BBT CYTO DENT HT IPSY MED MIDWF MT NMT NUR OT PHAR PTA RTT OMA PERF

Meharry Medical College

1005 D B Todd Boulevard
Nashville, TN 37208
(615) 327-6223

Will confirm attendance and degree by phone or mail. Inquiry must include student's name, social security number. Requests should be directed to: Admissions Office. Employers may obtain transcripts upon written request accompanied by a $2.00 fee and a signed release from the student.

A medical school, with an enrollment of 715. Highest level of offering: doctorate.

ACCREDITATIONS: SC DENT DH MED MIDWF MT

Memphis College of Art

Overton Park
Memphis, TN 38112
(901) 726-4085 Ext. 29
Fax (901) 726-9371

Will confirm attendance and degree by phone or mail. Inquiry must include student's name, years attended. Employers may obtain transcripts upon written request accompanied by a signed release from the student.

A visual and performing arts school, with an enrollment of 244. Highest level of offering: four or five year baccalaureate.

ACCREDITATIONS: SC ART

Memphis State University

Memphis, TN 38152
(901) 678-2671

Will confirm attendance and degree by phone or mail. Inquiry must include student's name, social security number. Employers may obtain transcripts upon written request accompanied by a signed release from the student. Requests should be directed to: Records Office–Transcripts, room 143.

A doctoral-level institution with no medical school, with an enrollment of 20,728. Highest level of offering: doctorate.

ACCREDITATIONS: SC ART AUD BUS CLPSY ENG ENGT JOUR LAW MUS NUR BUSA SP TED SW

Memphis Theological Seminary

168 East Parkway South
Memphis, TN 38104
(901) 458-8232
Fax (901) 452-4051

Will confirm attendance and degree by phone or mail. Inquiry must include student's name. Employers may obtain transcripts upon written request accompanied by a $3.00 fee and a signed release from the student. Requests should be directed to: Registrar's Office.

A school of religion and theology, with an enrollment of 189. Highest level of offering: master's.

ACCREDITATIONS: SACS THEOL

Mendocino College

PO Box 3000
Ukiah, CA 95482
(707) 468-3100

Will confirm attendance and degree by mail. Inquiry must include student's name, social security number, release. Employers may obtain transcripts upon written request accompanied by a $2.00 fee and asigned release from the student.

A multiprogram two-year institution, with an enrollment of 4,750. Highest level of offering: one year but less than four years.
ACCREDITATIONS: WJ

Menlo College

1000 El Camino Real
Atherton, CA 94027
(415) 688-3764
Fax (415) 324-2347

Will confirm attendance and degree by phone, fax or mail. Inquiry must include student's name, date of birth, social security number, years attended. Employers may obtain transcripts upon written request accompanied by a $4.00 fee and a signed release from the student.

A specialized school, with an enrollment of 550. Highest level of offering: four or five year baccalaureate.
ACCREDITATIONS: WC

Mennonite Biblical Seminary

3003 Benham Avenue
Elkhart, IN 46517
(219) 295-3726 Ext. 213

Will confirm attendance and degree by phone or mail. Inquiry must include student's name. Employers may obtain transcripts upon written request accompanied by a $3.00 fee and a signed release from the student. Requests should be directed to: Registrar's Office.

A school of religion and theology, with an enrollment of 89. Highest level of offering: master's.
ACCREDITATIONS: NCA THEOL

Mennonite Brethren Biblical Seminary

4824 East Butler
Fresno, CA 93727-5097
(209) 251-8628
Fax (209) 251-1432

Will confirm attendance and degree by mail or fax. Inquiry must include student's name, social security number. Requests should be directed to: Registrar's Office. Employers may obtain transcripts upon written request accompanied by a signed release from the student.

A school of religion and theology, with an enrollment of 120. Highest level of offering: master's.
ACCREDITATIONS: WC THEOL MFCC

Mennonite College of Nursing

804 North East Street
Bloomington, IL 61701
(309) 829-0715

Will confirm attendance and degree by phone or mail. Inquiry must include student's name, social security number. Employers may obtain transcripts upon written request accompanied by a $2.00 fee and a signed release from the student.

A bachelor's or higher institution with an enrollment of 146. Highest level of offering: first professional degree.
ACCREDITATIONS: NH NUR

Merced College

3600 M Street
Merced, CA 95348-2898
(209) 384-6000

Will confirm attendance and degree by mail. Inquiry must include student's name, social security number, release. Employers may obtain transcripts upon written request accompanied by a $3.00 fee and a signed release from the student. Requests should be directed to: Admission & Records Office.

A multiprogram two-year institution, with an enrollment of 5,736. Highest level of offering: one year but less than four years.
ACCREDITATIONS: WJ DA DT RAD

Mercer County Community College

PO Box B
Trenton, NJ 08690
(609) 586-4800
Fax (609) 586-6944

Will confirm attendance and degree by mail or fax. Inquiry must include student's name, social security number, release. Employers may obtain transcripts upon written request accompanied by a $2.00 fee and a signed release from the student. Requests should be directed to: Student's Records Office.

A multiprogram two-year institution, with an enrollment of 9,171. Highest level of offering: one year but less than four years.
ACCREDITATIONS: M ADNUR DA ENGT FUSER MLTAD RAD

Mercer University Registrar's Office

1400 Coleman Avenue
Macon, GA 31207
(912) 752-2680

Will confirm attendance and degree by phone from 1987 forward or by mail. Inquiry must include student's name, social security number, date of birth. Employers may obtain transcripts upon written request accompanied by a $2.00 fee and a signed release from the student

Mercer University in Atlanta

3001 Mercer University Dr
Atlanta, GA 30341
(404) 986-3129
Fax (404) 986-3135

Will confirm attendance and degree by phone or mail. Inquiry must include student's name, social security number. Employers may obtain transcripts upon written request accompanied by a signed release from the student. Requests should be directed to: Registrar's Office.

A general baccalaureate institution, with an enrollment of 1,975. Highest level of offering: master's.
ACCREDITATIONS: SACS MUS

Mercer University Main Campus

1400 Coleman Avenue
Macon, GA 31207
(912) 752-2680

Will confirm attendance and degree by phone or mail. Inquiry must include student's name, social security number. Employers may obtain transcripts upon written request accompanied by a $2.00 fee and a signed release from the student. Requests should be directed to: Registrar's Office.

A comprehensive institution with no medical school, with an enrollment of 2,771. Highest level of offering: master's.
ACCREDITATIONS: SC LAW MED MUS TED

Mercer University Southern School of Pharmacy

3001 Mercer University Drive
Atlanta, GA 30341
(404) 653-3129
Fax (404) 986-3135

Will confirm attendance and degree by phone or mail. Inquiry must include student's full name and social security number. Employers may obtain transcripts upon written request accompanied by a signed release from the student.

A health institution, with an enrollment of 500. Highest level of offering: ph.d.
ACCREDITATIONS: SACS ACPE

Mercy College of Detroit

(See University of Detroit Mercy-Outer Drive)

Mercy College

555 Broadway
Dobbs Ferry, NY 10522
(914) 693-4500 Ext. 266
Fax (914) 693-9455 Ext 410

Will confirm attendance and degree by mail or fax. Inquiry must include student's name, social security number, years attended, release. Employers may obtain transcripts upon written request accompanied by a $4.00 fee and a signed release from the student.

A general baccalaureate institution, with an enrollment of 5,000. Highest level of offering: master's.
ACCREDITATIONS: M NUR NY SW

Mercyhurst College

501 East 38th Street
Erie, PA 16546
(814) 824-2250
Fax (814) 824-2438

Will confirm attendance and degree by phone. Inquiry must include student's name, social security number. Employers may obtain transcripts upon written request accompanied by a $2.00 fee and a signed release from the student.

A general baccalaureate institution, with an enrollment of 2,194. Highest level of offering: master's.

ACCREDITATIONS: M DIET SW

Meredith College

3800 Hillsborough Street
Raleigh, NC 27607-5298
(919) 829-8593

Will confirm attendance and degree by mail. Inquiry must include student's name, maiden name, social security number, years to search. Employers may obtain transcripts upon written request accompanied by a $2.00 fee and a signed release from the student, SASE.

A general baccalaureate institution, with an enrollment of 2,211. Highest level of offering: master's.

ACCREDITATIONS: SC MUS SW

Meridian Community College

5500 Highway 19 North
Meridian, MS 39301-39305
(601) 483-8241 Ext. 136
Fax (601) 484-8636

Will confirm attendance and degree by phone or mail. Inquiry must include student's name, social security number. Employers may obtain transcripts upon written request accompanied by a $2.00 fee and a signed release from the student.

A multiprogram two-year institution, with an enrollment of 2,541. Highest level of offering: one year but less than four years.

ACCREDITATIONS: SC ADNUR DH MLTAD MRT PNUR RAD RSTHT SURGT

Meridian Junior College

5500 Highway 19 North
Meridian, MS 39301-39305
(601) 484-8636

Will confirm attendance and degree by phone or mail. Inquiry must include student's name, social security number. Employers may obtain transcripts upon written request accompanied by a $2.00 fee and a signed release from the student.

A multiprogram two-year institution, with an enrollment of 2,541. Highest level of offering: one year but less than four years.

ACCREDITATIONS: SC ADNUR DH MLTAD MRT PNUR RAD RSTHT SURGT

Merrimack College

North Andover, MA 01845
(617) 683-7111

Will confirm attendance and degree by phone or mail. Inquiry must include student's name, years attended. Employers may obtain transcripts upon written request accompanied by a $2.00 fee and a signed release from the student.

A general baccalaureate institution, with an enrollment of 3,643. Highest level of offering: four or five year baccalaureate.

ACCREDITATIONS: EH ENG

Merrimack Valley College

(See University of New Hampshire at Manchester)

Merritt College

12500 Campus Drive
Oakland, CA 94619
(510) 436-2487

Will confirm attendance and degree by mail. Inquiry must include student's name, social security number, years attended, release. Employers may obtain transcripts upon written request accompanied by a $1.00 fee and a signed release from the student.

A multiprogram two-year institution, with an enrollment of 6,156. Highest level of offering: two years but less than four years.

ACCREDITATIONS: WJ RAD

Mesa College

PO Box 2647
Grand Junction, CO 81502
(303) 248-1613

Will confirm attendance and degree by phone or mail. Inquiry must include student's name, social security number, years attended. Employers may obtain transcripts upon written request accompanied by a $2.00 fee and a signed release from the student.

A general baccalaureate institution, with an enrollment of 4,188. Highest level of offering: four or five year baccalaureate.

ACCREDITATIONS: NH ADNUR DA NUR RAD

Mesa Community College

1833 West Southern Avenue
Mesa, AZ 85202
(602) 461-7000
Fax (602) 461-7805

Will confirm attendance and degree by phone, fax or mail. Inquiry must include student's name, date of birth, social security number, years attended. Employers may obtain transcripts upon written request accompanied by a $2.00 fee and a signed release from the student.

A multiprogram two-year institution, with an enrollment of 20,000. Highest level of offering: one year but less than four years.

ACCREDITATIONS: NCA ADNUR

Mesivta Eastern Parkway Rabbinical Seminary

510 Dayhill Road
Brooklyn, NY 11218
(718) 438-1002
Fax (718) 438-2591

Will confirm attendance and degree by mail or fax. Inquiry must include student's name, date of birth. Employers may obtain transcripts upon written request accompanied by a $10.00 fee and a signed release from the student.

A specialized non-degree granting institution, with an enrollment of 45. Highest level of offering: graduate non-degree granting.

ACCREDITATIONS: RABN

Mesivta Torah Vodaath Rabbinical Seminary

425 East 9th Street
Brooklyn, NY 11218
(718) 941-8000

Will confirm attendance and degree by mail. Inquiry must include student's name, date of birth, years attended. Employers may obtain transcripts upon written request accompanied by a signed release from the student.

A specialized non-degree granting institution, with an enrollment of 506. Highest level of offering: first professional degree.

ACCREDITATIONS: RABN

Mesivtha Tifereth Jerusalem of America

145 East Broadway
New York, NY 10002
(212) 964-2830

Will confirm attendance and degree by mail. Inquiry must include student's name, years attended. Employers may obtain transcripts upon written request accompanied by a $5.00 fee and a signed release from the student.

A specialized non-degree granting institution, with an enrollment of 105. Highest level of offering: graduate non-degree granting.

ACCREDITATIONS: RABN

Messiah College

Grantham, PA 17027
(717) 691-6034
Fax (717) 691-6025

Will confirm attendance and degree by phone, fax or mail. Inquiry must include student's name, years attended. Employers may obtain transcripts upon written request accompanied by a $2.00 fee and a signed release from the student.

A general baccalaureate institution, with an enrollment of 2,246. Highest level of offering: four or five year baccalaureate.

ACCREDITATIONS: M

Methodist College

5400 Ramsey Street
Fayetteville, NC 28311-1499
(919) 630-7036
Fax (919) 630-7119

Will confirm attendance and degree by phone or mail. Inquiry must include student's name, social security number, years attended, date of birth. Employers may obtain transcripts upon written request accompanied by a $5.00 fee and a signed release from the student.

A general baccalaureate institution, with an enrollment of 1,581. Highest level of offering: four or five year baccalaureate.

ACCREDITATIONS: SC

Methodist Theological School of Ohio

PO Box 1204
Registrar's Office
Delaware, OH 43015
(614) 363-1146

Will confirm attendance and degree by phone or mail. Inquiry must include student's name. Employers may obtain transcripts upon written request accompanied by a $5.00 fee and a signed release from the student.

A school of philosophy, religion and theology, with an enrollment of 240. Highest level of offering: doctorate.

ACCREDITATIONS: NH THEOL

Metropolitan Business College

2658 West 95th Street
Evergreen Park, IL 60642
(708) 424-3000

Will confirm attendance and degree by mail. Inquiry must include student's name, years attended, release, field of study. Employers may obtain transcripts upon written request accompanied by a $2.00 fee and a signed release from the student.

A two-year institution newly admitted to NCES, with an enrollment of 270. Highest level of offering: one year but less than four years.

ACCREDITATIONS: SRCB

Metropolitan Community College Area

PO Box 3777
Omaha, NE 68103
(402) 449-8400

Will confirm attendance and degree by mail. Inquiry must include student's name, social security number, years attended. Requests should be directed to: Records Department. Employers may obtain transcripts upon written request accompanied by a signed release from the student.

A multiprogram two-year institution, with an enrollment of 7,383. Highest level of offering: one year but less than four years.

ACCREDITATIONS: NH DA RSTHT SURGT

Metropolitan State College

PO Box 173362
Denver, CO 80217-3362
(303) 556-3067
Fax (303) 556-3999

Will confirm attendance and degree by mail or fax. Inquiry must include student's name, date of birth, social security number. Employers may obtain transcripts upon written request accompanied by a $1.00 fee and a signed release from the student.

A general baccalaureate institution, with an enrollment of 16,800. Highest level of offering: four or five year baccalaureate.

ACCREDITATIONS: NH ENGT MUS NUR TED

Metropolitan State University

121 Metro Square
Saint Paul, MN 55101
(612) 296-4453

Will confirm attendance and degree by phone or mail. Inquiry must include student's name, social security number. Employers may obtain transcripts upon written request accompanied by a $2.00 fee and a signed release from the student.

A general baccalaureate institution, with an enrollment of 6,602. Highest level of offering: master's.

ACCREDITATIONS: NH

Mgh Institute of Health Professions

Ruth Speeper Hall–Massachusetts General Hospital
40 Parkman Street
Boston, MA 02114-2696
(617) 726-3140

Will confirm attendance and degree by mail. Inquiry must include student's name, years attended, release, name of school attended. Employers may obtain transcripts upon written request accompanied by a $4.00 fee and a signed release from the student.

A bachelor's or higher institution newly admitted to NCES, with an enrollment of 300. Highest level of offering: master's.

ACCREDITATIONS: EH DMS ADNUR

Miami–Dade Community College–South Campus

11011 South West 104 Street
Miami, FL 33176
(305) 237-2222

Will confirm attendance and degree by phone or mail. Inquiry must include student's name, social security number. Employers may obtain transcripts upon written request accompanied by a signed release from the student.

A multiprogram two-year institution, with an enrollment of 49,145. Highest level of offering: one year but less than four years.

ACCREDITATIONS: SC ADNUR DH EEG FUSER MLTAD MRT OPTT PTAA RAD RSTH RSTHT

Miami–Jacobs Junior College of Business

400 East 2nd Street
Dayton, OH 45401
(513) 461-5174 Ext. 20

Will confirm attendance and degree by mail. Inquiry must include student's name, social security number, years attended. Employers may obtain transcripts upon written request accompanied by a $3.00 fee and a signed release from the student.

A multiprogram two-year institution, with an enrollment of 569. Highest level of offering: one year but less than four years.

ACCREDITATIONS: JRCB

Miami Christian College

PO Box 019674
Miami, FL 33101-9674
(305) 577-4600

Will confirm attendance and degree by phone or mail. Inquiry must include student's name, years attended. Employers may obtain transcripts upon written request accompanied by a $2.00 fee and a signed release from the student.

A school of philosophy, religion and theology, with an enrollment of 353. Highest level of offering: four or five year baccalaureate.

ACCREDITATIONS: BI

Miami University All Campuses

Oxford, OH 45056
(513) 529-1809 or 529-3314

Will confirm attendance and degree by phone or mail. Inquiry must include student's name, date of birth, social security number, years attended. Requests should be directed to: Records Department. Employers may obtain transcripts upon written request accompanied by a signed release from the student.

Highest level of offering: doctorate.

Miami University Hamilton Campus

1601 Peck Boulevard
Hamilton, OH 45011
(513) 863-8833 Ext. 202

Will confirm attendance and degree by phone or mail. Inquiry must include student's name, social security number, years attended. Employers may obtain transcripts upon written request accompanied by a signed release from the student.

A multiprogram two-year institution, with an enrollment of 2,000. Highest level of offering: one year but less than four years.

ACCREDITATIONS: NH ADNUR

Miami University Middletown Campus

4200 East University Boulevard
Middletown, OH 45052
(513) 424-4444 Ext. 217
Fax (513) 424-4632

Will confirm attendance and degree by phone, fax or mail. Inquiry must include student's name, social security number, years attended. Employers may obtain transcripts upon written request accompanied by a signed release from the student.

A multiprogram two-year institution, with an enrollment of 2,050. Highest level of offering: one year but less than four years.

ACCREDITATIONS: NH ADNUR

Miami University Oxford Campus

500 E. High Street
Oxford, OH 45056
(513) 529-3314
Fax (513) 529-7255

Will confirm attendance and degree by phone, fax or mail. Inquiry must include student's name, social security number, years attended. Employers may obtain transcripts upon written request accompanied by a signed release from the student. Requests should be directed to: Records Department.

A doctoral-level institution with no medical school, with an enrollment of 15,430. Highest level of offering: doctorate.

ACCREDITATIONS: NH ARCH BUS CLPSY MUS NUR SP TED BUSA

Michigan Christian College

800 West Avon Road
Rochester Hills, MI 48063
(313) 651-5800

Will confirm attendance and degree by mail. Inquiry must include student's name, social security number, release. Employers may obtain transcripts upon written request from the student accompanied by a $3.00 fee.

A multiprogram two-year institution, with an enrollment of 257. Highest level of offering: four or five year baccalaureate.

ACCREDITATIONS: NH

Michigan State University

Room 50
East Lansing, MI 48824
(517) 353-5206
Fax (517) 336-1649

Will confirm attendance and degree by phone, fax or mail. Inquiry must include student's name. Employers may obtain transcripts upon written request accompanied by a $5.00 fee and a signed release from the student.

A doctoral-level institution with a medical school, with an enrollment of 42,866. Highest level of offering: doctorate.

ACCREDITATIONS: NH ADVET AUD BUS CLPSY COPSY ENG FIDER FOR IPSY JOUR TED LSAR VET BUSA MED MUS NUR OSTEO SP SW

Michigan Technological University

Houghton, MI 49931
(906) 487-2319

Will confirm attendance and degree by phone or mail. Inquiry must include student's name, social security number. Employers may obtain transcripts upon written request accompanied by a $3.00 fee and a signed release from the student.

An engineering school, with an enrollment of 6,565. Highest level of offering: doctorate.

ACCREDITATIONS: NH ENG ENGT FOR

Mid–America Baptist Theological Seminary

1255 Poplar Avenue
Memphis, TN 38104
(901) 726-9171 Ext. 18
Fax (901) 726-6791

Will confirm attendance and degree by phone, fax or mail. Inquiry must include student's name. Employers may obtain transcripts upon written request accompanied by a $3.00 fee and a signed release from the student.

A school of philosophy, religion and theology, with an enrollment of 466. Highest level of offering: doctorate.

ACCREDITATIONS: SC

Mid–America Bible College

3500 South West 119 Street
Oklahoma City, OK 73170
(405) 691-3800 Ext. 102
Fax (405) 692-3165

Will confirm attendance and degree by phone or mail. Inquiry must include student's name and social security number. Employers may obtain transcripts upon written request accompanied by a $2.00 fee and a signed release from the student.

A school of philosophy, religion and theology, with an enrollment of 225. Highest level of offering: four or five year baccalaureate.

ACCREDITATIONS: NH BI

Mid–America College of Funeral Service

3111 Hamburg Pike
Jeffersonville, IN 47130
(812) 288-8878
Fax (812) 288-5942

Will confirm attendance and degree by phone or mail. Inquiry must include student's name, social security number. Employers may obtain transcripts upon written request accompanied by a $2.00 fee and a signed release from the student.

A single program two-year institution, with an enrollment of 93. Highest level of offering: one year but less than four years.

ACCREDITATIONS: FUSER

Mid–America Nazarene College

2030 College Way
Olathe, KS 66061
(913) 782-3750 Ext. 222

Will confirm attendance and degree by phone or mail. Inquiry must include student's name, years attended. Employers may obtain transcripts upon written request accompanied by a $2.00 fee and a signed release from the student.

A general baccalaureate institution, with an enrollment of 1,189. Highest level of offering: master's.

ACCREDITATIONS: NH NUR

Mid–Continent Baptist Bible College

Route 2 PO Box 7010
Mayfield, KY 42066
(502) 247-8521 Ext. 15

Will confirm attendance and degree by mail. Inquiry must include student's name, date of birth, social security number, release. Employers may obtain transcripts upon written request accompanied by a $3.00 fee and a signed release from the student.

A bachelor's or higher institution newly admitted to NCES. Highest level of offering: four or five year baccalaureate.

ACCREDITATIONS: SC

Mid–South Bible College

(See Crichton College)

Mid State Technical College

Registrar
500 32nd Street North
Wisconsin Rapids, WI 54494
(715) 423-5502
Fax (715) 422-5345

Will confirm attendance and degree by phone or mail. Inquiry must include student's name, social security number. Employers may obtain transcripts upon written request accompanied by a signed release from the student.

A multiprogram two-year institution, with an enrollment of 2,000. Highest level of offering: one year but less than four years.

ACCREDITATIONS: NH PNUR RSTH SURGT

Mid Michigan Community College

1375 South Clare Avenue
Harrison, MI 48625
(517) 386-7792 Ext. 273

Will confirm attendance and degree by phone or mail. Inquiry must include student's name, social security number, years attended. Employers may obtain transcripts upon written request accompanied by a $2.00 fee and a signed release from the student.

A multiprogram two-year institution, with an enrollment of 2,237. Highest level of offering: one year but less than four years.

ACCREDITATIONS: NH MLTAD RAD

Mid Plains Community College Area

Rt. 4 Box 1
North Platte, NE 69101
(308) 532-8740
Fax (308) 532-8494

Will confirm attendance and degree by phone or mail. Employers may obtain transcripts upon written request accompanied by a $2.00 fee and a signed release from the student.

A multiprogram two-year institution, with an enrollment of 2,497. Highest level of offering: one year but less than four years.

ACCREDITATIONS: NH DA MLTAD

Middle Georgia College

Cochran, GA 31014
(912) 934-3165
Fax (912) 934-3199

Will confirm attendance and degree by phone or mail. Inquiry must include student's name, social security number. Employers may obtain transcripts upon written request accompanied by a $3.00 fee and a signed release from the student. Requests should be directed to: Registrar's Office.

A multiprogram two-year institution, with an enrollment of 1,293. Highest level of offering: one year but less than four years.
ACCREDITATIONS: SC ADNUR

Middle Tennessee State University

Murfreesboro, TN 37132
(615) 898-2600

Will confirm attendance and degree by phone or mail. Inquiry must include student's name, date of birth, social security number. Employers may obtain transcripts upon written request accompanied by a signed release from the student. Requests should be directed to: Records Office.

A comprehensive institution with no medical school, with an enrollment of 14,000. Highest level of offering: doctorate.
ACCREDITATIONS: SC ADNUR BUS MUS SW TED

Middlebury College

Old Chapel Building
Middlebury, VT 05753
(802) 388-3711 Ext. 5389
Fax (802) 388-9646

Will confirm attendance and degree by phone, fax or mail. Inquiry must include student's name, social security number. Requests should be directed to: Records Office. Employers may obtain transcripts upon written request accompanied by a $2.00 fee and a signed release from the student.

A comprehensive institution with no medical school, with an enrollment of 2,012. Highest level of offering: doctorate.
ACCREDITATIONS: EH

Middlesex Community College

Springs Road
Bedford, MA 01730
(617) 275-8910 Ext. 220
Fax (617) 275-2590

Will confirm attendance and degree by mail or fax. Inquiry must include student's name, social security number, maiden name, years attended. Employers may obtain transcripts upon written request accompanied by a $2.00 fee and a signed release from the student.

A multiprogram two-year institution, with an enrollment of 6,772. Highest level of offering: one year but less than four years.
ACCREDITATIONS: EH ADNUR DA DH DT MAC MLTAD RAD

Middlesex Community College

100 Training Hill Road
Middletown, CT 06457
(203) 344-3027
Fax (203) 344-7488

Will confirm attendance and degree by phone or mail. Inquiry must include student's name, social security number. Employers may obtain transcripts upon written request accompanied by a signed release from the student. Requests should be directed to: Records Office.

A multiprogram two-year institution, with an enrollment of 2,690. Highest level of offering: one year but less than four years.
ACCREDITATIONS: EH RAD

Middlesex County College

155 Mill Road–PO Box 3050
Edison, NJ 08818-3050
(201) 906-2523

Will confirm attendance and degree by phone or mail. Inquiry must include student's name, social security number. Employers may obtain transcripts upon written request accompanied by a $3.00 fee and a signed release from the student.

A multiprogram two-year institution, with an enrollment of 11,197. Highest level of offering: one year but less than four years.
ACCREDITATIONS: M ADNUR DH ENGT MLTAD RAD

Midland College

Attn: Registrar
3600 North Garfield
Midland, TX 79705
(915) 685-4508
Fax (915) 685-4714

Will confirm attendance and degree by phone or mail. Inquiry must include student's name, social security number, years attended. Employers may obtain transcripts upon written request accompanied by a $1.00 fee and a signed release from the student.

A multiprogram two-year institution, with an enrollment of 3,817. Highest level of offering: one year but less than four years.
ACCREDITATIONS: SC ADNUR RSTH RSTHT

Midland Lutheran College

900 North Clarkson
Fremont, NE 68025
(402) 721-5480 Ext. 5057
Fax (402) 727-2348

Will confirm attendance and degree by phone or mail. Inquiry must include student's name, social security number. Employers may obtain transcripts upon written request accompanied by a $5.00 fee and a signed release from the student.

A general baccalaureate institution, with an enrollment of 1,003. Highest level of offering: four or five year baccalaureate.
ACCREDITATIONS: NH NUR RSTH

Midlands Technical College

PO Box 2408
Columbia, SC 29202
(803) 738-7798

Will confirm attendance and degree by phone or mail. Inquiry must include student's name, social security number. Employers may obtain transcripts upon written request accompanied by a $2.00 fee and a signed release from the student. Requests should be directed to: Student Records.

A multiprogram two-year institution, with an enrollment of 6,954. Highest level of offering: one year but less than four years.
ACCREDITATIONS: SC DA DH ENGT MLTAD NMT PNUR RAD RSTH RSTHT SURGT

Midstate College

244 South West Jefferson
Peoria, IL 61602
(309) 673-6365 Ext. 20
Fax (309) 673-5814

Will confirm attendance and degree by phone, fax or mail. Inquiry must include student's name, social security number. Employers may obtain transcripts upon written request accompanied by a $3.00 fee and a signed release from the student.

A multiprogram two-year institution, with an enrollment of 446. Highest level of offering: two years but less than four years.
ACCREDITATIONS: NH APCP

Midway College

512 E. Stephens Street
Midway, KY 40347-1120
(606) 846-5728
Fax (606) 846-5349

Will confirm attendance and degree by phone, fax. Inquiry must include student's name, social security number. Employers may obtain transcripts upon written request accompanied by a $2.00 fee and a signed release from the student.

A multiprogram four-year institution, with an enrollment of 725. Highest level of offering: four year baccaeloreate.
ACCREDITATIONS: SC ADNUR

Midwest College of Engineering

(See Illinois Institute of Technology)

Midwestern Baptist Theological Seminary

5001 North Oak Street Trafficway
Kansas City, MO 64118
(816) 453-4600 Ext. 220
Fax (816) 455-3528

Will confirm attendance and degree by phone or mail. Inquiry must include student's name. Employers may obtain transcripts upon written request accompanied by a signed release from the student.

A school of philosophy, religion and theology, with an enrollment of 450. Highest level of offering: doctorate.
ACCREDITATIONS: NH THEOL

Midwestern State University

3400 Taft Boulevard
Wichita Falls, TX 76308
(817) 692-6611 Ext. 4321

Will confirm attendance and degree by phone or mail. Inquiry must include student's name, social security number, years attended. Employers may obtain transcripts upon written request accompanied by a $3.00 fee and a signed release from the student.

A comprehensive institution with no medical school, with an enrollment of 5,512. Highest level of offering: master's.
ACCREDITATIONS: SC ADNUR DH MUS RAD TED

Miles College

PO Box 3800
Birmingham, AL 35208
(205) 923-2771 Ext. 290

Will confirm attendance and degree by phone or mail. Inquiry must include student's name, social security number, years attended. Employers may obtain transcripts upon written request accompanied by a $3.00 fee and a signed release from the student.

A general baccalaureate institution, with an enrollment of 677. Highest level of offering: four or five year baccalaureate.
ACCREDITATIONS: SACS

Miles Community College

2715 Dickinson
Miles City, MT 59301
(406) 232-3031 Ext. 22
Fax (406) 232-5705

Will confirm attendance and degree by phone, fax or mail. Inquiry must include student's name. Employers may obtain transcripts upon written request accompanied by a $2.00 fee and a signed release from the student.

A multiprogram two-year institution, with an enrollment of 813. Highest level of offering: one year but less than four years.
ACCREDITATIONS: NW

Miller Institute

(See ITT Technology Institute)

Millersville University of Pennsylvania

Millersville, PA 17551
(717) 872-3035

Will confirm attendance and degree by phone or mail. Inquiry must include student's name, social security number, years attended. Employers may obtain transcripts upon written request accompanied by a $3.00 fee and a signed release from the student.

A comprehensive institution with no medical school, with an enrollment of 7,708. Highest level of offering: beyond master's but less than doctorate.
ACCREDITATIONS: M MUS RSTH SW TED

Milligan College

Milligan College, TN 37682
(615) 929-0116

Will confirm attendance and degree by mail. Inquiry must include student's name, social security number, years attended, release. Employers may obtain transcripts upon written request accompanied by a $2.00 fee and a signed release from the student.

A general baccalaureate institution, with an enrollment of 760. Highest level of offering: master's.
ACCREDITATIONS: SC TED

Millikin University

1184 West Main Street
Decatur, IL 62522
(217) 424-6217
Fax (217) 424-3993

Will confirm attendance and degree by phone, fax or mail. Inquiry must include student's name, date of birth, social security number, years attended. Employers may obtain transcripts upon written request accompanied by a signed release from the student.

A general baccalaureate institution, with an enrollment of 1,857. Highest level of offering: four or five year baccalaureate.
ACCREDITATIONS: NH MUS NUR

Mills College

500 MacArthur Boulevard
Oakland, CA 94613
(510) 430-2083

Will confirm attendance and degree by phone or mail. Inquiry must include student's name, years attended. Employers may obtain transcripts upon written request accompanied by a $3.00 fee and a signed release from the student. Requests should be directed to: Registrar's Office.

A comprehensive institution with no medical school, with an enrollment of 1,041. Highest level of offering: master's.
ACCREDITATIONS: WC

Millsaps College

1701 N. State Street
Jackson, MS 39210
(601) 974-1000

Will confirm attendance and degree by phone or mail. Inquiry must include student's name, date of birth, social security number, years attended. Employers may obtain transcripts upon written request accompanied by a $2.00 fee and a signed release from the student. Requests should be directed to: Records Office.

A general baccalaureate institution, with an enrollment of 1,450. Highest level of offering: master's.
ACCREDITATIONS: SC

Milwaukee Area Technical College

700 W. State Street
Milwaukee, WI 53233
(414) 278-6256

Will confirm attendance and degree by phone or mail. Inquiry must include student's name, social security number, years attended. Employers may obtain transcripts upon written request accompanied by a $2.00 fee and a signed release from the student.

A multiprogram two-year institution, with an enrollment of 22,782. Highest level of offering: one year but less than four years.
ACCREDITATIONS: NH ADNUR DA DH DT FUSER MAC MLTAD PNUR PTAA RAD RSTH RSTHT SURGT

Milwaukee Institute of Art and Design

342 North Water Street
Milwaukee, WI 53202
(414) 276-7889

Will confirm attendance and degree by phone or mail. Inquiry must include student's name. Requests should be directed to: Registrar's Office. Employers may obtain transcripts upon written request accompanied by a $3.00 fee and a signed release from the student.

A visual and performing arts school, with an enrollment of 450. Highest level of offering: four or five year baccalaureate.
ACCREDITATIONS: ART

Milwaukee School of Engineering

PO Box 644
Milwaukee, WI 53201-0644
(414) 277-7220

Will confirm attendance and degree by phone or mail. Inquiry must include student's name, date of birth, social security number, years attended. Employers may obtain transcripts upon written request accompanied by a $5.00 fee and a signed release from the student.

An engineering school, with an enrollment of 3,000. Highest level of offering: master's.
ACCREDITATIONS: NH ENG ENGT PERF

Mineral Area College

Flat River, MO 63601
(314) 431-4593 Ext. 22

Will confirm attendance and degree by phone or mail. Inquiry must include student's name, date of birth, social security number. Employers may obtain transcripts upon written request accompanied by a $2.00 fee and a signed release from the student.

A multiprogram two-year institution, with an enrollment of 2,700. Highest level of offering: one year but less than four years.
ACCREDITATIONS: NH DA

Minneapolis College of Art and Design

2501 Stevens Avenue South
Minneapolis, MN 55404
(612) 874-3700
Fax (612) 874-3704

Will confirm attendance and degree by phone, fax or mail. Inquiry must include student's name, social security number. Employers may obtain transcripts upon written request accompanied by a $5.00 fee and a signed release from the student.

A visual and performing arts school, with an enrollment of 660. Highest level of offering: four year baccalaureate.
ACCREDITATIONS: NH ART

Minneapolis Community College

1501 Hennepin Avenue
Minneapolis, MN 55403
(612) 341-701095

Will confirm attendance and degree by phone or mail. Inquiry must include student's name, date of birth, social security number. Employers may obtain transcripts upon written request accompanied by a signed release from the student.

A multiprogram two-year institution, with an enrollment of 3,729. Highest level of offering: one year but less than four years.
ACCREDITATIONS: NH ADNUR

Minnesota Bible College

920 Mayowood Road South West
Rochester, MN 55902
(507) 288-4563 Ext. 15
Fax (507) 288-9046

Will confirm attendance and degree by phone or mail. Inquiry must include student's name, social security number, years attended. Employers may obtain transcripts upon written request accompanied by a $2.00 fee and a signed release from the student.

A multiprogram two-year institution, with an enrollment of 100. Highest level of offering: four or five year baccalaureate.
ACCREDITATIONS: BI

Minot State University

Minot, ND 58701
(701) 857-3340
Fax (701) 839-6933

Will confirm attendance and degree by phone, fax or mail. Inquiry must include student's name, social security number, years attended. Employers may obtain transcripts upon written request accompanied by a $2.00 fee and a signed release from the student.

A general baccalaureate institution, with an enrollment of 3,600. Highest level of offering: master's
ACCREDITATIONS: NH MUS NUR SP SW TED

Mira Costa College

One Barnard Drive
Oceanside, CA 92056
(619) 757-2121 Ext. 287

Will confirm attendance and degree by mail. Inquiry must include student's name, date of birth, social security number, years attended. Requests should be directed to: Admissions & Records Office. Employers may obtain transcripts upon written request accompanied by a $2.00 fee and a signed release from the student.

A multiprogram two-year institution, with an enrollment of 10,000. Highest level of offering: one year but less than four years.
ACCREDITATIONS: WJ

Mirrer Yeshiva Central Institute

1791–5 Ocean Parkway
Brooklyn, NY 11223
(718) 645-0536
Fax (718) 645-9251

Will confirm attendance and degree by mail or fax. Inquiry must include student's name, social security number, years attended, release. Employers may obtain transcripts upon written request accompanied by a $25.00 fee and a signed release from the student.

A specialized non-degree granting institution, with an enrollment of 340. Highest level of offering: graduate non-degree granting.
ACCREDITATIONS: RABN

Miss Wade's Fashion Merchandising College

PO Box 586343
The Dallas Apparel Mart, Ste. M5120
Dallas, TX 75258
(214) 637-3530
Fax (214) 637-0827

Will confirm attendance and degree by phone, fax or mail. Inquiry must include student's name, social security number, years attended. Employers may obtain transcripts upon written request accompanied by a $5.00 fee and a signed release from the student.

A single program two-year institution, with an enrollment of 400. Highest level of offering: one year but less than four years.
ACCREDITATIONS: SC NATTS

Mission College

Registrar's Office
3000 Mission College Blvd
Santa Clara, CA 95054
(408) 988-2200 Ext. 1502
Fax (408) 980-8980

Will confirm attendance and degree by phone, fax or mail. Inquiry must include student's name, date of birth, social security number, years attended, self addressed stamped envelope. Requests should be directed to: Records Office. Employers may obtain transcripts upon written request accompanied by a $3.00 fee and a signed release from the student.

A multiprogram two-year institution, with an enrollment of 12,000. Highest level of offering: one year but less than four years.
ACCREDITATIONS: WJ

Mississippi College

Box 4087
Clinton, MS 39058
(601) 925-3210

Will confirm attendance and degree by phone or mail. Inquiry must include student's name, date of birth, social security number, years attended, self addressed stamped envelope. Employers may obtain transcripts upon written request accompanied by a $2.00 fee and a signed release from the student.

A comprehensive institution with no medical school, with an enrollment of 3,609. Highest level of offering: beyond master's but less than doctorate.
ACCREDITATIONS: SC LAW MUS NUR TED

Mississippi County Community College

PO Drawer 1109
Blytheville, AR 72316
(501) 762-1020 Ext. 105

Will confirm attendance and degree by phone or mail. Inquiry must include student's name, social security number. Employers may obtain transcripts upon written request accompanied by a signed release from the student.

A multiprogram two-year institution, with an enrollment of 1,214. Highest level of offering: one year but less than four years.
ACCREDITATIONS: NH

Mississippi Delta Junior College

PO Box 668
Moorhead, MS 38761
(601) 246-5631 Ext. 107

Will confirm attendance and degree by phone or mail. Inquiry must include student's name, date of birth, social security number, years attended. Employers may obtain transcripts upon written request accompanied by a $2.00 fee and a signed release from the student.

A multiprogram two-year institution, with an enrollment of 1,627. Highest level of offering: one year but less than four years.
ACCREDITATIONS: SC ADNUR MLTAD RAD

Mississippi Gulf Coast Community College

PO Box 47
Perkinston, MS 39573
(601) 928-5211 Ext. 206
Fax (601) 928-6386

Will confirm attendance and degree by phone, fax or mail. Inquiry must include student's name, social security number, years attended. Employers may obtain transcripts upon written request accompanied by a signed release from the student.

A multiprogram two-year institution, with an enrollment of 6,967. Highest level of offering: one year but less than four years.
ACCREDITATIONS: SC ADNUR MLTAD RAD RSTHT

Mississippi Industrial College

c/o Lane College
545 Lane Avenue
Jackson, TN 38301
(901) 426-7600 or 426-7601
Will confirm attendance and degree by mail. Inquiry must include student's name, maiden name, social security number. Employers may obtain transcripts upon written request accompanied by a $3.00 fee and a signed release from the student.

Mississippi State University

PO Box 5268
Mississippi State, MS 39762
(601) 325-1843

Will confirm attendance and degree by phone or mail. Inquiry must include student's name, date of birth, social security number, years attended. Employers may obtain transcripts upon written request accompanied by a $2.00 fee and a signed release from the student.

A doctoral-level institution with a medical school, with an enrollment of 12,775. Highest level of offering: doctorate.
ACCREDITATIONS: SC ARCH BUS ENG FOR LSAR TED VET

Mississippi University for Women

PO Box W-1605
Columbus, MS 39701
(601) 329-7131
Fax (601) 329-7297

Will confirm attendance and degree by phone, fax or mail. Inquiry must include student's name, date of birth, social security number, years attended. Employers may obtain transcripts upon written request accompanied by a $2.00 fee and a signed release from the student. Requests should be directed to Attn: Registrar's Office.

A comprehensive institution with no medical school, with an enrollment of 2,197. Highest level of offering: beyond master's but less than doctorate.
ACCREDITATIONS: SC ADNUR MUS NUR TED

Mississippi Valley State University

PO Box 1116 MVSU
Itta Bena, MS 38941
(601) 254-9041 Ext. 6436

Will confirm attendance and degree by phone or mail. Inquiry must include student's name, social security number, years attended. Employers may obtain transcripts upon written request accompanied by a $2.00 fee and a signed release from the student.

A general baccalaureate institution, with an enrollment of 2,000. Highest level of offering: master's.
ACCREDITATIONS: SC ART SW TED

Missouri Baptist College

12542 Conway Road
Saint Louis, MO 63141
(314) 434-1115 Ext. 275
Fax (314) 434-7596

Will confirm attendance and degree by phone or mail. Inquiry must include student's name, social security number, years attended. Requests should be directed to: Records Office. Employers may obtain transcripts upon written request accompanied by a $5.00 fee and a signed release from the student.

A general baccalaureate institution, with an enrollment of 1,200. Highest level of offering: four or five year baccalaureate.
ACCREDITATIONS: NCA

Missouri Southern State College

Joplin, MO 64801
(417) 625-9300
Fax (417) 625-3121

Will confirm attendance and degree by phone, fax or mail. Inquiry must include student's name, social security number, years attended. Employers may obtain transcripts upon written request accompanied by a $1.00 fee and a signed release from the student.

A general baccalaureate institution, with an enrollment of 4,323. Highest level of offering: four or five year baccalaureate.
ACCREDITATIONS: NH ADNUR DA DH RAD

Missouri Valley College

500 East College
Marshall, MO 65340
(816) 886-6924 Ext. 122
Fax (816) 886-9818

Will confirm attendance and degree by phone or mail. Inquiry must include student's name, years attended. Employers may obtain transcripts upon written request accompanied by a $4.00 fee and a signed release from the student.

A general baccalaureate institution, with an enrollment of 1,000. Highest level of offering: four or five year baccalaureate.
ACCREDITATIONS: NH

Missouri Western State College

4525 Downs Drive
Saint Joseph, MO 64507
(816) 271-4215

Will confirm attendance and degree by phone or mail. Inquiry must include student's name, social security number, years attended. Employers may obtain transcripts upon written request accompanied by a $2.00 fee and a signed release from the student.

A general baccalaureate institution, with an enrollment of 4,500. Highest level of offering: four or five year baccalaureate.
ACCREDITATIONS: NH ADNUR MUS SW TED

Mitchell College

437 Pequot Avenue
New London, CT 06320
(203) 443-2811 Ext. 204
Fax (203) 437-0632

Will confirm attendance and degree by phone, fax or mail. Inquiry must include student's name, years attended. Employers may obtain transcripts upon written request accompanied by a $3.00 fee and a signed release from the student.

A multiprogram two-year institution, with an enrollment of 1,500. Highest level of offering: one year but less than four years.
ACCREDITATIONS: EH

Mitchell Community College

West Broad Street
Statesville, NC 28677
(704) 878-3246
Fax (704) 878-0872

Will confirm attendance and degree by phone or mail. Inquiry must include student's name, social security number, years attended. Employers may obtain transcripts upon written request accompanied by a signed release from the student.

A multiprogram two-year institution, with an enrollment of 1,332. Highest level of offering: one year but less than four years.
ACCREDITATIONS: SC

Moberly Area Junior College

College & Rollins Streets
Moberly, MO 65270
(816) 263-4110
Fax (816) 263-6252

Will confirm attendance and degree by mail. Inquiry must include student's name, social security number, years attended, release. Employers may obtain transcripts upon written request accompanied by a $1.00 fee and a signed release from the student.

A multiprogram two-year institution, with an enrollment of 1,600. Highest level of offering: one year but less than four years.
ACCREDITATIONS: NH

Mobile College

PO Box 13220
Mobile, AL 36663-0220
(205) 675-5990 Ext. 236
Fax (205) 675-3404

Will confirm attendance and degree by phone, fax or mail. Inquiry must include student's name, social security number, years attended. Employers may obtain transcripts upon written request accompanied by a $.75 fee per copy, $5.00 for certified copy and a signed release from the student.

A general baccalaureate institution, with an enrollment of 1,190. Highest level of offering: master's.
ACCREDITATIONS: SC ADNUR NUR

Modesto Junior College

435 College Avenue
Modesto, CA 95350
(209) 575-6014
Fax (209) 575-6666

Will confirm attendance and degree by phone, fax or mail. Inquiry must include student's name, social security number, years attended. Requests should be directed to: Records Office. Employers may obtain transcripts upon written request accompanied by a $3.00 fee and a signed release from the student.

A multiprogram two-year institution, with an enrollment of 14,900. Highest level of offering: one year but less than four years.
ACCREDITATIONS: WJ DA EMT MAC RSTHT

Mohave Community College

1971 Jagerson Avenue
Kingman, AZ 86401
(602) 757-4331
Fax (602) 757-0836

Will confirm attendance and degree by mail. Inquiry must include student's name, social security number, release. Employers may obtain transcripts upon written request accompanied by a $2.00 fee and a signed release from the student.

A multiprogram two-year institution, with an enrollment of 5,600. Highest level of offering: two years.
ACCREDITATIONS: NH

Mohawk Valley Community College

1101 Sherman Drive
Utica, NY 13501
(315) 792-5336

Will confirm attendance and degree by phone or mail. Inquiry must include student's name, social security number, years attended. Employers may obtain transcripts upon written request accompanied by a $2.00 fee and a signed release from the student.

A multiprogram two-year institution, with an enrollment of 7,653. Highest level of offering: one year but less than four years.

ACCREDITATIONS: M ADNUR ENGT NY RSTHT

Mohegan Community College

Mahan Drive
Norwich, CT 06360
(203) 886-1931

Will confirm attendance and degree by mail. Inquiry must include student's name, social security number, years attended. Employers may obtain transcripts upon written request accompanied by a signed release from the student.

A multiprogram two-year institution, with an enrollment of 3,000. Highest level of offering: one year but less than four years.

ACCREDITATIONS: EH ADNUR

Molloy College

1000 Hempstead Avenue
Rockville Center, NY 11570
(516) 678-5000

Will confirm attendance and degree by phone or mail. Inquiry must include student's name, social security number, years attended. Employers may obtain transcripts upon written request accompanied by a $5.00 fee and a signed release from the student.

A general baccalaureate institution, with an enrollment of 1,600. Highest level of offering: master's.

ACCREDITATIONS: M NUR NY SW

Monmouth College

Attn: Registrar
West Long Branch, NJ 07764
(201) 222-6600 Ext. 3477

Will confirm attendance and degree by phone or mail. Inquiry must include student's name, social security number, years attended. Employers may obtain transcripts upon written request accompanied by a $5.00 fee and a signed release from the student.

A comprehensive institution with no medical school, with an enrollment of 4,000. Highest level of offering: master's.

ACCREDITATIONS: M ENG SW

Monmouth College

700 East Broadway
Monmouth, IL 61462
(309) 457-2326

Will confirm attendance and degree by phone or mail. Inquiry must include student's name, years attended. Employers may obtain transcripts upon written request accompanied by a $2.00 fee and a signed release from the student.

A general baccalaureate institution, with an enrollment of 608. Highest level of offering: four or five year baccalaureate.

ACCREDITATIONS: NH

Monroe College

Attn: Registrar
29 East Fordham Road
Bronx, NY 10454
(212) 933-6700
Fax (212) 220-3032

Will confirm attendance and degree by mail or fax if accompained by student release. Inquiry must include student's name, date of birth, social security number, years attended, release. Employers may obtain transcripts upon written request accompanied by a $3.00 fee and a signed release from the student.

A multiprogram two-year institution, with an enrollment of 2,251. Highest level of offering: one year but less than four years.

ACCREDITATIONS: NY

Monroe Community College

1000 East Henrietta Road
Rochester, NY 14623
(716) 292-2300

Will confirm attendance and degree by phone or mail. Inquiry must include student's name, social security number, years attended. Employers may obtain transcripts upon written request accompanied by a $3.00 fee and a signed release from the student. Direct inquiries to Office of Registration and Records.

A multiprogram two-year institution, with an enrollment of 13,500. Highest level of offering: two years but less than four years.

ACCREDITATIONS: M ADNUR DH ENGT MLTAD MRT NY RAD

Monroe County Community College

1555 South Raisinville Road
Monroe, MI 48161
(313) 242-7300 Ext. 250
Fax (313) 242-9711

Will confirm attendance and degree by phone, fax or mail. Inquiry must include student's name, social security number. Employers may obtain transcripts upon written request accompanied by a $2.00 fee and a signed release from the student.

A multiprogram two-year institution, with an enrollment of 3,668. Highest level of offering: one year but less than four years.

ACCREDITATIONS: NH RSTH RSTHT

Montana College of Mineral Science and Technology

West Park Street
Butte, MT 59701
(406) 496-4256

Will confirm attendance and degree by phone or mail. Inquiry must include student's name, social security number. Employers may obtain transcripts upon written request accompanied by a $2.00 fee and a signed release from the student.

An engineering school, with an enrollment of 1,881. Highest level of offering: master's.

ACCREDITATIONS: NW ENG

Montana State University

101 Montana Hall
Bozeman, MT 59717-0012
(406) 994-2601

Will confirm attendance and degree by phone or mail. Inquiry must include student's name, date of birth, social security number, years attended. Employers may obtain transcripts upon written request accompanied by a $2.00 fee and a signed release from the student.

A comprehensive institution with no medical school, with an enrollment of 10,251. Highest level of offering: doctorate.

ACCREDITATIONS: NW ARCH ART BUS ENG ENGT MUS NUR TED

Montay College

3750 West Peterson Avenue
Chicago, IL 60659
(312) 539-1919

Will confirm attendance and degree by phone or mail. Inquiry must include student's name and social security number. Employers may obtain transcripts upon written request accompanied by a $3.00 fee and a signed release from the student.

A multiprogram two-year institution, with an enrollment of 510. Highest level of offering: two years but less than four years.

ACCREDITATIONS: NH

Montcalm Community College

2800 College Drive
Sidney, MI 48885
(517) 328-2111 Ext. 230
Fax (517) 328-2950

Will confirm attendance and degree by phone, fax or mail. Inquiry must include student's name, social security number, years attended. Employers may obtain transcripts upon written request accompanied by a $1.00 fee and a signed release from the student.

A multiprogram two-year institution, with an enrollment of 2,700. Highest level of offering: one year but less than four years.

ACCREDITATIONS: NH

Montclair State College

Registrar's Office
Upper Montclair, NJ 07043
(201) 893-4376
Fax (201) 893-5455

Will confirm attendance and degree by phone, fax or mail. Inquiry must include student's name, social security number, years attended. Employers may obtain transcripts upon written request accompanied by a $2.00 fee and a signed release from the student.

A comprehensive institution with no medical school, with an enrollment of 14,241. Highest level of offering: master's.

ACCREDITATIONS: M MUS TED

Monterey Institute of International Studies

425 Van Buren
Monterey, CA 93940
(408) 647-4121

Will confirm degree by phone or mail. Inquiry must include student's name, years attended. Employers may obtain transcripts upon written request accompanied by a $3.00 fee and a signed release from the student.

A comprehensive institution with no medical school, with an enrollment of 638. Highest level of offering: master's.
ACCREDITATIONS: WC

Monterey Peninsula College

980 Fremont
Monterey, CA 93940
(408) 646-4002

Will confirm attendance and degree by phone or mail. Inquiry must include student's name, date of birth, social security number, years attended. Employers may obtain transcripts upon written request accompanied by a $2.00 fee and a signed release from the student.

A multiprogram two-year institution, with an enrollment of 5,656. Highest level of offering: one year but less than four years.
ACCREDITATIONS: WJ DA

Montgomery College Central Office

51 Mannakee Street
Rockville, MD 20850
(301) 279-5046

Will confirm attendance and degree by mail. For Rockville, Germantown and Takoma Compuses, Inquiry must include student's name, social security number, release. Request should be directed to Admissions & Records Office. Employers may obtain transcripts upon written request accompanied by a $5.00 fee and a signed release from the student.

Montgomery College Germantown Campus

20200 Observation Drive
Germantown, MD 20876
(301) 353-7818

Will confirm attendance and degree by mail. Inquiry must include student's name, social security number, release. Requests should be directed to: Admissions Office. Employers may obtain transcripts upon written request accompanied by a $5.00 fee and a signed release from the student.

A multiprogram two-year institution, with an enrollment of 3,800. Highest level of offering: one year but less than four years.
ACCREDITATIONS: M

Montgomery College Rockville Campus

51 Mannakee Street
Rockville, MD 20850
(301) 279-5046

Will confirm attendance and degree by mail. Inquiry must include student's name, social security number, release. Requests should be directed to: Admissions & Records Office. Employers may obtain transcripts upon written request accompanied by a $5.00 fee and a signed release from the student.

A multiprogram two-year institution, with an enrollment of 13,834. Highest level of offering: one year but less than four years.
ACCREDITATIONS: M ENGT MUS

Montgomery College Takoma Park Campus

Takoma Avenue and Fenton Street
Takoma Park, MD 20912
(301) 650-1500

Will confirm attendance and degree by mail. Inquiry must include student's name, social security number, release. Requests should be directed to: Admissions & Records Office. Employers may obtain transcripts upon written request accompanied by a $5.00 fee and a signed release from the student.

A multiprogram two-year institution, with an enrollment of 4,350. Highest level of offering: one year but less than four years.
ACCREDITATIONS: M ADNUR DA DT MAC MLTAD RAD

Montgomery Community College

PO Box 787
Troy, NC 27371
(919) 572-3691

Will confirm attendance and degree by phone or mail. Inquiry must include student's name, social security number, years attended. Employers may obtain transcripts upon written request accompanied by a $1.00 fee and a signed release from the student.

A multiprogram two-year institution, with an enrollment of 506. Highest level of offering: one year but less than four years.
ACCREDITATIONS: SC

Montgomery County Community College

340 Dekalb Pike
Blue Bell, PA 19422
(215) 641-6551

Will confirm attendance and degree by phone or mail. Inquiry must include student's name, social security number. Requests should be directed to: Admissions & Records Office. Employers may obtain transcripts upon written request accompanied by a $3.00 fee and a signed release from the student.

A multiprogram two-year institution, with an enrollment of 7,239. Highest level of offering: one year but less than four years.
ACCREDITATIONS: M DH MLTAD

Montgomery Technical College

PO Box 787
Troy, NC 27371
(919) 572-3691

Will confirm attendance and degree by phone or mail. Inquiry must include student's name, social security number, years attended. Employers may obtain transcripts upon written request accompanied by a $1.00 fee and a signed release from the student.

A multiprogram two-year institution, with an enrollment of 593. Highest level of offering: one year but less than four years.
ACCREDITATIONS: SC

Montreat–Anderson College

Montreat, NC 28757
(704) 669-8011 Ext. 224
Fax (704) 669-9554

Will confirm attendance and degree by phone or mail. Inquiry must include student's name. Employers may obtain transcripts upon written request accompanied by a $1.00 fee and a signed release from the student.

A multiprogram four-year institution, with an enrollment of 440. Highest level of offering: one year but less than four years.
ACCREDITATIONS: SC

Moody Bible Institute

Registrar's Office
820 North Lasalle Drive
Chicago, IL 60610
(312) 329-4261
Fax (312) 329-4328

Will confirm attendance and degree by phone, fax or mail. Inquiry must include student's name, social security number, years attended. Employers may obtain transcripts upon written request accompanied by a $2.00 fee and a signed release from the student.

A school of philosophy, religion and theology, with an enrollment of 1,415. Highest level of offering: four or five year baccalaureate.
ACCREDITATIONS: NCA AABC NASM

Moore College of Art

20th And The Parkway
Philadelphia, PA 19103
(215) 568-4515 Ext. 1124
Fax (215) 568-8017

Will confirm attendance and degree by phone, fax or mail. Inquiry must include student's name, social security number, years attended. Employers may obtain transcripts upon written request accompanied by a $5.00 fee and a signed release from the student.

A visual and performing arts school, with an enrollment of 541. Highest level of offering: four or five year baccalaureate.
ACCREDITATIONS: M ART

Moorhead State University

1104 7th Avenue South
Moorhead, MN 56563
(218) 236-2557
Fax (218) 236-2168

Will confirm attendance and degree by phone, fax or mail. Inquiry must include student's name, social security number. Employers may obtain transcripts upon written request accompanied by a signed release from the student.

A comprehensive institution with no medical school, with an enrollment of 9,000. Highest level of offering: master's.

ACCREDITATIONS: NH ART MUS NUR SW TED ASLA/P

Moorpark College

7075 Campus Road
Moorpark, CA 93021
(805) 378-1429
Fax (805) 378-1429

Will confirm attendance and degree by mail or fax. Inquiry must include student's name, social security number, years attended. Employers may obtain transcripts upon written request accompanied by a $3.00 fee and a signed release from the student. Requests should be directed to: Records Office.

A multiprogram two-year institution, with an enrollment of 12,955. Highest level of offering: one year but less than four years.

ACCREDITATIONS: WJ

Moraine Park Technical Institute

PO Box 1940–235 North National Avenue
Fond Du Lac, WI 54936-1940
(414) 922-8611
Fax (414) 929-2478

Will confirm attendance and degree by mail. Inquiry must include student's name, social security number. Employers may obtain transcripts upon written request accompanied by a signed release from the student.

A multiprogram two-year institution, with an enrollment of 5,513. Highest level of offering: one year but less than four years.

ACCREDITATIONS: NCA ADNUR MRT PNUR SURGT

Moraine Valley Community College

10900 South 88th Avenue
Palos Hills, IL 60465
(708) 974-2110

Will confirm attendance and degree by mail. Requests should be directed to: College Service Center. Inquiry must include student's name, social security number. Employers may obtain transcripts upon written request accompanied by a $3.00 fee and a signed release from the student.

A multiprogram two-year institution, with an enrollment of 13,990. Highest level of offering: one year but less than four years.

ACCREDITATIONS: NH ADNUR MLTAD MRT RAD RSTH RSTHT

Moravian College

1210 Main Street
Bethlehem, PA 18018
(215) 861-1350
Fax (215) 861-3919

Will confirm attendance and degree by phone or mail. Inquiry must include student's name, years attended, release. Employers may obtain transcripts upon written request by student accompanied by a $3.00 fee and a signed release from the student.

A general baccalaureate institution, with an enrollment of 1,750. Highest level of offering: four or five year baccalaureate and master's in business.

ACCREDITATIONS: M THEOL

Morehead State University

Registrar's Office
Morehead, KY 40351
(606) 783-2221

Will confirm attendance and degree by mail. Inquiry must include student's name, date of birth, social security number, years attended. Employers may obtain transcripts upon written request accompanied by a $2.00 fee and a signed release from the student. Requests should be directed to Registrar's Office.

A comprehensive institution with no medical school, with an enrollment of 6,570. Highest level of offering: beyond master's but less than doctorate.

ACCREDITATIONS: SC ADNUR ADVET MUS RAD SW TED

Morehouse College

830 Westview Drive South West
Atlanta, GA 30314
(404) 215-2641
Fax (404) 681-2650

Will confirm attendance and degree by phone or mail. Inquiry must include student's name, social security number, years attended. Employers may obtain transcripts upon written request accompanied by a $2.00 fee and a signed release from the student.

A general baccalaureate institution, with an enrollment of 2,056. Highest level of offering: four or five year baccalaureate.

ACCREDITATIONS: SC

Morehouse School of Medicine

720 Westview Drive South West
Atlanta, GA 30310
(404) 752-1650

Will confirm attendance and degree by mail. Inquiry must include student's name, social security number, years attended. Requests should be directed to: Admissions & Student Affairs Office. Employers may obtain transcripts upon written request accompanied by a $2.00 fee and a signed release from the student.

A medical school, with an enrollment of 127. Highest level of offering: first professional degree.

ACCREDITATIONS: SC MED

Morgan Community College

17800 Road 20
Fort Morgan, CO 80701
(303) 867-3081 Ext. 113

Will confirm attendance and degree by mail. Inquiry must include student's name, date of birth, social security number, release. Requests should be directed to: Admissions & Records. Employers may obtain transcripts upon written request accompanied by a signed release from the student.

A multiprogram two-year institution, with an enrollment of 1,000. Highest level of offering: one year but less than four years.

ACCREDITATIONS: NH

Morgan State University

Cold Spring Hillen Road
Bldg. CGW–Room 303
Baltimore, MD 21239
(301) 444-3333

Will confirm attendance and degree by phone or mail. Inquiry must include student's name, social security number, years attended. Employers may obtain transcripts upon written request accompanied by a $2.00 fee and a signed release from the student.

A comprehensive institution with no medical school, with an enrollment of 4,208. Highest level of offering: doctorate.

ACCREDITATIONS: M ART MUS SW TED

Morningside College

1501 Morningside Avenue
Sioux City, IA 51106
(712) 274-5110
Fax (712) 274-5101

Will confirm attendance and degree by phone, fax or mail. Inquiry must include student's name, social security number, years attended. Employers may obtain transcripts upon written request accompanied by a $3.00 fee and a signed release from the student.

A general baccalaureate institution, with an enrollment of 1,205. Highest level of offering: master's.

ACCREDITATIONS: NH MUS TED NUR

Morris Brown College

643 Martin L. King Jr. Drive North West
Atlanta, GA 30314
(404) 220-0270 or 220-0145

Will confirm attendance and degree by phone or mail. Inquiry must include student's name, social security number, years attended. Employers may obtain transcripts upon written request accompanied by a $2.00 fee and a signed release from the student.

A general baccalaureate institution, with an enrollment of 1,800. Highest level of offering: four or five year baccalaureate.

ACCREDITATIONS: SC

Morris College

100 W. College Street
Sumter, SC 29150
(803) 775-9371 Ext. 225

Will confirm attendance and degree by phone or mail. Inquiry must include student's name, years attended. Employers may obtain transcripts upon written request accompanied by a $3.00 fee and a signed release from the student. Requests should be addressed to Admissions Office.

A general baccalaureate institution, with an enrollment of 700. Highest level of offering: four or five year baccalaureate.

ACCREDITATIONS: SC

Morris Junior College of Business

2401 North Harbor City Boulevard
Melbourne, FL 32935
(407) 254-6459

Will confirm attendance and degree by mail. Inquiry must include student's name, date of birth, social security number, years attended, release. Employers may obtain transcripts upon written request accompanied by a $2.00 fee and a signed release from the student.

A single program two-year institution, with an enrollment of 600. Highest level of offering: one year but less than four years.

ACCREDITATIONS: JRCB

Morrison Institute of Technology

PO Box 410
Morrison, IL 61270
(815) 772-7218

Will confirm attendance and degree by phone or mail. Inquiry must include student's name, social security number. Employers may obtain transcripts upon written request accompanied by a $2.00 fee and a signed release from the student. Requests should be directed to: Registrar's Office.

A single program two-year institution, with an enrollment of 202. Highest level of offering: one year but less than four years.

ACCREDITATIONS: ENGT

Morristown College

(See Knoxville College)

Morrisville College

Morrisville, NY 13408
(315) 684-6000 Ext. 6066

Will confirm attendance and degree by phone or mail. Inquiry must include student's name, date of birth, social security number, years attended. Employers may obtain transcripts upon written request accompanied by a $5.00 fee and a signed release from the student.

A multiprogram two-year institution, with an enrollment of 3,054. Highest level of offering: one year but less than four years.

ACCREDITATIONS: M ADNUR ENGT NY

Morton College

Attn: Admissions and Records
3801 South Central Avenue
Cicero, IL 60650
(708) 656-8000
Fax (708) 656-9592

Will confirm degree by phone or mail. Inquiry must include student's name, date of birth, social security number, years attended. Employers may obtain transcripts upon written request accompanied by a $2.00 fee and a signed release from the student.

A multiprogram two-year institution, with an enrollment of 3,489. Highest level of offering: one year but less than four years.

ACCREDITATIONS: NH DA PTAA

Motlow State Community College

PO Box 88100
Tullahoma, TN 37388-8100
(615) 455-8511 Ext. 207

Will confirm attendance and degree by phone or mail. Inquiry must include student's name, social security number, years attended. Employers may obtain transcripts upon written request by student. Requests should be directed to: Admissions Office.

A multiprogram two-year institution, with an enrollment of 3,032. Highest level of offering: one year but less than four years.

ACCREDITATIONS: SC ADNUR

Mott Community College

(Formerly Charles S. Mott Community College)
1401 East Court Street
Flint, MI 48503
(313) 762-0090
Fax (313) 762-0257

Will confirm attendance and degree by phone, fax or mail. Inquiry must include student's name, social security number, last year attended. Employers may obtain transcripts upon written request accompanied by a signed release from the student. Attn: Registrar's Office.

A multiprogram two-year institution, with an enrollment of 11,158. Highest level of offering: one year but less than four years.

ACCREDITATIONS: NH ADNUR DA DH RSTH RSTHT

Mount Aloysius College

Cresson, PA 16630
(814) 886-4131 Ext. 225

Will confirm attendance and degree by phone or mail. Inquiry must include student's name, social security number. Employers may obtain transcripts upon written request accompanied by a $2.00 fee and a signed release from the student. Requests should be directed to: Registrar's Office.

A multiprogram four-year institution, with an enrollment of 2,000. Highest level of offering: baccalaureate.

ACCREDITATIONS: M ADNUR MLTAD

Mount Angel Seminary

Saint Benedict, OR 97373
(503) 845-3951

Will confirm attendance and degree by phone or mail. Inquiry must include student's name, years attended. Employers may obtain transcripts upon written request accompanied by a $5.00 fee and a signed release from the student.

A school of philosophy, religion and theology, with an enrollment of 116. Highest level of offering: master's.

ACCREDITATIONS: NW THEOL

Mount Holyoke College

College Street
South Hadley, MA 01075
(413) 538-2000 Ext. 2025

Will confirm attendance and degree by phone or mail. Inquiry must include student's name, social security number, years attended. Employers may obtain transcripts upon written request accompanied by a $3.00 fee and a signed release from the student.

A general baccalaureate institution, with an enrollment of 1,966. Highest level of offering: master's.

ACCREDITATIONS: EH

Mount Ida College

(Formerly Chamberlayne Junior College)
777 Dedham Street
Newton Centre, MA 02159
(617) 536-4500 Ext. 117
Fax (617) 969-6993

Will confirm attendance and degree by phone, fax or mail. Inquiry must include student's name, social security number, years attended. Employers may obtain transcripts upon written request accompanied by a $2.00 fee and a signed release from the student.

A multiprogram two-year institution, with an enrollment of 1,800. Highest level of offering: four or five year baccalaureate.

ACCREDITATIONS: EH DA MAC

Mount Marty College

1105 West 8th
Yankton, SD 57078
(605) 668-1515

Will confirm attendance and degree by phone or mail. Inquiry must include student's name. Employers may obtain transcripts upon written request accompanied by a $2.00 fee and a signed release from the student.

A general baccalaureate institution, with an enrollment of 722. Highest level of offering: master's.

ACCREDITATIONS: NH ANEST MT NUR RSTH RSTHT SW

Mount Mary College

2900 Menomonee River Parkway
Milwaukee, WI 53222
(414) 258-4810 Ext. 206

Will confirm attendance and degree by mail. Inquiry must include student's name, social security number, years attended. Employers may obtain transcripts upon written request accompanied by a $2.00 fee and a signed release from the student.

A general baccalaureate institution, with an enrollment of 1,468. Highest level of offering: master's.
ACCREDITATIONS: NH DIET OT SW TED

Mount Mercy College

1330 Elmhurst Drive North East
Cedar Rapids, IA 52402
(319) 363-8213 Ext. 553

Will confirm attendance and degree by mail. Inquiry must include student's name, date of birth, social security number. Employers may obtain transcripts upon written request accompanied by a $3.00 fee and a signed release from the student.

A general baccalaureate institution, with an enrollment of 1,287. Highest level of offering: four or five year baccalaureate.
ACCREDITATIONS: NH NUR SW

Mount Olive College

514 Henderson Street
Mount Olive, NC 28365
(919) 658-2502 Ext. 151
Fax (919) 658-8934

Will confirm attendance and degree by phone, fax or mail. Inquiry must include student's name, years attended. Employers may obtain transcripts upon written request accompanied by a $2.00 fee and a signed release from the student.

A multiprogram two-year institution, with an enrollment of 665. Highest level of offering: four or five year baccalaureate.
ACCREDITATIONS: SC

Mount Sacred Heart College

265 Benham Street
Hamden, CT 06514
(203) 248-4225

Will confirm attendance and degree by mail. Inquiry must include student's name, release. Employers may obtain transcripts upon written request accompanied by a $2.00 fee and a signed release from the student.

A single program two-year institution. Highest level of offering: one year but less than four years.

Mount Saint Alphonsus Seminary

Route 9 West North
Esopus, NY 12429
(914) 384-6550

Will confirm degree by phone or mail. Inquiry must include student's name, years attended. Employers may obtain transcripts upon written request accompanied by a $5.00 fee and a signed release from the student.

A school of philosophy, religion and theology, with an enrollment of 30. Highest level of offering: master's.

Mount Saint Clare College

400 North Bluff Boulevard
Clinton, IA 52732
(319) 242-4023 Ext. 56
Fax (319) 242-2003

Will confirm attendance and degree by phone, fax or mail. Inquiry must include student's name, years attended. Employers may obtain transcripts upon written request accompanied by a $2.00 fee and a signed release from the student.

A multiprogram two-year institution, with an enrollment of 348. Highest level of offering: four or five year baccalaureate.
ACCREDITATIONS: NH

Mount Saint Mary College

330 Powell Avenue
Newburgh, NY 12550
(914) 561-0800 Ext. 237

Will confirm attendance and degree by phone or mail. Inquiry must include student's name, social security number. Employers may obtain transcripts upon written request accompanied by a $3.00 fee and a signed release from the student. Requests should be directed to: Registrar's Office.

A general baccalaureate institution, with an enrollment of 1,180. Highest level of offering: master's.
ACCREDITATIONS: M MT NUR NY

Mount Saint Mary's College

Emmitsburg, MD 21727
(301) 447-5215
Fax (301) 447-5755

Will confirm attendance and degree by phone or mail. Inquiry must include student's name, social security number, years attended. Requests should be directed to: Registrar's Office. Employers may obtain transcripts upon written request accompanied by a $2.00 fee and a signed release from the student.

A general baccalaureate institution, with an enrollment of 1,400. Highest level of offering: master's.
ACCREDITATIONS: M THEOL

Mount Saint Mary's College

12001 Chalon Road
Los Angeles, CA 90049
(310) 476-2237 Ext. 9560
Fax (310) 476-9296

Will confirm attendance and degree by mail. Inquiry must include student's name, social security number. Employers may obtain transcripts upon written request accompanied by a $4.00 fee and a signed release from the student.

A comprehensive institution with no medical school, with an enrollment of 1,200. Highest level of offering: master's.
ACCREDITATIONS: WC ADNUR MUS NUR PTA PTAA AOTA

Mount San Antonio College

1100 North Grand
Walnut, CA 91789
(714) 594-5611 Ext. 4415
Fax (714) 594-8060

Will confirm attendance and degree by phone, fax or mail. Inquiry must include student's name, date of birth, social security number. Employers may obtain transcripts upon written request accompanied by a $2.00 fee and a signed release from the student.

A multiprogram two-year institution, with an enrollment of 20,693. Highest level of offering: one year but less than four years.
ACCREDITATIONS: WJ ADVET RAD RSTH RSTHT

Mount San Jacinto College

1499 North State Street
San Jacinto, CA 92383
(714) 654-8011 Ext. 1410
Fax (714) 487-9240

Will confirm attendance and degree by mail. Inquiry must include student's name, social security number, years attended, release. Employers may obtain transcripts upon written request accompanied by a $2.00 fee and a signed release from the student. Requests should be directed to: Admissions & Records Office.

A multiprogram two-year institution, with an enrollment of 6,900. Highest level of offering: one year but less than four years.
ACCREDITATIONS: WASC

Mount Senario College

1500 College Avenue
Ladysmith, WI 54848
(715) 532-5511 Ext. 305
Fax (715) 532-7690

Will confirm attendance and degree by phone or mail. Inquiry must include student's name, social security number. Employers may obtain transcripts upon written request accompanied by a $5.00 fee and a signed release from the student.

A general baccalaureate institution, with an enrollment of 661. Highest level of offering: four or five year baccalaureate.
ACCREDITATIONS: NH

Mount Sinai School of Medicine

One Gustave L. Levy Place
New York, NY 10029
(212) 241-6500 Ext. 6691

Will confirm attendance and degree by phone or mail. Inquiry must include student's name, date of birth, years attended. Employers may obtain transcripts upon written request accompanied by a $2.00 fee and a signed release from the student.

A medical school, with an enrollment of 469. Highest level of offering: first professional degree.
ACCREDITATIONS: NY MED MICB

Mount Union College

1972 Clark Avenue
Alliance, OH 44601
(216) 821-5320 Ext. 6018

Will confirm attendance and degree by
phone or mail. Inquiry must include student's name, social security number, years
attended. Employers may obtain transcripts
upon written request accompanied by a
$3.00 fee and a signed release from the stu-
dent.

A general baccalaureate institution, with an
enrollment of 1,434. Highest level of offering: four or five year baccalaureate.
ACCREDITATIONS: NH MUS

Mount Vernon College

2100 Foxhall Road North West
Washington, DC 20007
(202) 625-4526

Will confirm attendance and degree by
phone or mail. Inquiry must include student's name, years attended. Employers
may obtain transcripts upon written request
accompanied by a signed release from the
student. Requests should be addressed to:
Registrar's Office.

A general baccalaureate institution, with an
enrollment of 500. Highest level of offering: four or five year baccalaureate.
ACCREDITATIONS: M FIDER

Mount Vernon Nazarene College

800 Martinsburg Road
Mount Vernon, OH 43050
(614) 397-1244 Ext. 232

Will confirm attendance and degree by
phone or mail. Inquiry must include student's name and SSN. Employers may obtain transcripts upon written request accompanied by a $3.00 fee or a $5.00 fee for ur-
gent request and a signed release from the
student.

A general baccalaureate institution, with an
enrollment of 1,065. Highest level of offering: four or five year baccalaureate.
ACCREDITATIONS: NH

Mount Wachusett Community College

444 Green Street
Gardner, MA 01440
(617) 632-6600 Ext. 106

Will confirm attendance and degree by
phone or mail. Inquiry must include student's name, social security number.
Employers may obtain transcripts upon
written request accompanied by a $1.00 fee
and a signed release from the student.

A multiprogram two-year institution, with
an enrollment of 2,900. Highest level of offering: one year but less than four years.
ACCREDITATIONS: EH ADNUR MLTAD

Mountain Empire Community College

Drawer 700
Big Stone Gap, VA 24219
(703) 523-2400 Ext. 209
Fax (703) 523-2400 Ext. 323

Will confirm attendance and degree by
phone, fax or mail. Inquiry must include
student's name, social security number.
Requests should be directed to: Admissions
Office. Employers may obtain transcripts
upon written request accompanied by a
signed release from the student.

A multiprogram two-year institution, with
an enrollment of 2,700. Highest level of offering: one year but less than four years.
ACCREDITATIONS: SC ADNUR RSTHT

Mountain View College

4849 West Illinois
Dallas, TX 75211
(214) 333-8680
Fax (214) 333-8708

Will confirm attendance and degree by
mail. Inquiry must include student's name,
social security number. Employers may obtain transcripts upon written request accompanied by a signed release from the student.
Requests should be addressed to:
Admissions Office.

A multiprogram two-year institution, with
an enrollment of 5,288. Highest level of offering: one year but less than four years.
ACCREDITATIONS: SC

Mt. Hood Community College

26000 South East Stark Street
Gresham, OR 97030
(503) 667-7391
Fax (503) 667-7275

Will confirm attendance and degree by
phone, fax or mail. Inquiry must include
student's name, social security number.
Employers may obtain transcripts upon
written request accompanied by a $3.00 fee
and a signed release from the student.
Requests should be directed to: Admissions
Office.

A multiprogram two-year institution, with
an enrollment of 6,524. Highest level of offering: one year but less than four years.
ACCREDITATIONS: NW ADNUR DH FUSER
PTAA RSTH SURGT

Muhlenberg College

2400 Chew Street
Allentown, PA 18104
(215) 821-3190
Fax (215) 821-3234

Will confirm attendance and degree by
phone, fax or mail. Inquiry must include
student's name, social security number,
years attended. Employers may obtain transcripts upon written request accompanied
by a $2.00 fee and a signed release from the
student.

A general baccalaureate institution, with an
enrollment of 1,617. Highest level of offering: four or five year baccalaureate.
ACCREDITATIONS: M TED CHM

Multnomah School of the Bible

8435 North East Glisan Street
Portland, OR 97220
(503) 255-0332 Ext. 372

Will confirm attendance and degree by
phone or mail. Inquiry must include student's name, years attended. Employers
may obtain transcripts upon written request
accompanied by a $3.00 fee and a signed
release from the student.

A school of philosophy, religion and theology, with an enrollment of 765. Highest
level of offering: master's.
ACCREDITATIONS: BI

Mundelein College

(See Loyola University)

Murray State College

Tishomingo, OK 73460
(405) 371-2371 Ext. 108
Fax (405) 371-9844

Will confirm attendance and degree by
phone or mail. Inquiry must include student's name, date of birth, social security
number, years attended. Employers may obtain transcripts upon written request accompanied by a $2.00 fee and a signed release
from the student.

A multiprogram two-year institution, with
an enrollment of 1,600. Highest level of offering: one year but less than four years.
ACCREDITATIONS: NH ADNUR ADVET

Murray State University

University Station–Sparks Hall
Murray, KY 42071
(502) 762-3753

Will confirm attendance and degree by
phone or mail. Inquiry must include student's name, date of birth, social security
number. Employers may obtain transcripts
upon written request accompanied by a
$3.00 fee and a signed release from the stu-
dent. Requests should be directed to:
Registrar's Office.

A comprehensive institution with no medi-
cal school, with an enrollment of 7,335.
Highest level of offering: beyond master's
but less than doctorate.
ACCREDITATIONS: SC BUS ENGT MLTAD
MUS NUR SP SW TED

Muscle Shoals State Technical College

PO Box 2545
Muscle Shoals, AL 35662
(205) 381-2813

Will confirm by mail. Inquiry must include
student's name, date of birth, release.
Employers may obtain transcripts upon
written request accompanied by a signed release from the student.

A two-year institution newly admitted to
NCES. Highest level of offering: one year
but less than four years.
ACCREDITATIONS: SV

Muskegon Business College

(See Baker College of Muskegon)

Muskegon Community College

221 South Quarterline Road
Muskegon, MI 49442
(616) 777-0230
Fax (616) 777-0255

Will confirm attendance and degree by phone, fax or mail. Inquiry must include student's name, date of birth, social security number, years attended. Employers may obtain transcripts upon written request accompanied by a $2.00 fee and a signed release from the student.

A multiprogram two-year institution, with an enrollment of 5,400. Highest level of offering: one year but less than four years.
ACCREDITATIONS: NH RSTHT DA

Muskingum Area Technical College

1555 Newark Road
Zanesville, OH 43701
(614) 454-2501 Ext. 212
Fax (614) 454-0035

Will confirm attendance and degree by phone, fax or mail. Inquiry must include student's name, social security number. Employers may obtain transcripts upon written request accompanied by a $2.00 fee and a signed release from the student.

A multiprogram two-year institution, with an enrollment of 2,403. Highest level of offering: one year but less than four years.
ACCREDITATIONS: NH MAC MLTAD RAD

Muskingum College

New Concord, OH 43762
(614) 826-8211 Ext. 165

Will confirm attendance and degree by phone or mail. Inquiry must include student's name, years attended. Employers may obtain transcripts upon written request accompanied by a $3.00 fee and a signed release from the student. Requests should be directed to: Registrar's Office.

A general baccalaureate institution, with an enrollment of 1,036. Highest level of offering: four or five year baccalaureate.
ACCREDITATIONS: NH MUS

N

N F Nunnelly State Technical College

(See Central Alabama Community College)

Naes College

2838 West Peterson Ave
Chicago, IL 60659
(312) 761-5000
Fax (312) 761-3808

Will confirm attendance and degree by phone, fax or mail. Inquiry must include student's name. Employers may obtain transcripts upon written request accompanied by a $5.00 fee and a signed release from the student.

A specialized school, with an enrollment of 143. Highest level of offering: four or five year baccalaureate.
ACCREDITATIONS: NH

Napa Valley College

Napa, CA 94558
(707) 253-3000

Will confirm attendance and degree by mail. Inquiry must include student's name, date of birth, social security number, years attended. Requests should be directed to: Admissions Office. Employers may obtain transcripts upon written request accompanied by a $2.00 fee and a signed release from the student.

A multiprogram two-year institution, with an enrollment of 7,000. Highest level of offering: one year but less than four years.
ACCREDITATIONS: WJ RSTH

Naropa Institute

2130 Arapahoe Avenue
Boulder, CO 80302
(303) 444-0202

Will confirm attendance and degree by phone or mail. Inquiry must include student's name. Employers may obtain transcripts upon written request accompanied by a signed release from the student.

A general baccalaureate institution, with an enrollment of 498. Highest level of offering: master's.
ACCREDITATIONS: NH

Nash Community College

PO Box 7488
Rocky Mount, NC 27804-7488
(919) 443-4011 Ext. 274
Fax (919) 443-0828

Will confirm attendance and degree by phone or mail. Inquiry must include student's name, social security number. Requests should be directed to: Registrar's Office–Room 104. Employers may obtain transcripts upon written request accompanied by a $1.00 fee and a signed release from the student.

A multiprogram two-year institution, with an enrollment of 1,500. Highest level of offering: one year but less than four years.
ACCREDITATIONS: SACS APTA

Nashotah House

2777 Mission Road
Nashotah, WI 53058
(414) 646-3371

Will confirm attendance and degree by phone or mail. Inquiry must include student's name, social security number, release. Employers may obtain transcripts upon written request accompanied by a $5.00 fee and a signed release from the student.

A school of philosophy, religion and theology, with an enrollment of 74. Highest level of offering: master's.
ACCREDITATIONS: THEOL

Nashville State Technical Institute

120 White Bridge Road
Nashville, TN 37209
(615) 353-3218
Fax (615) 353-3243

Will confirm attendance and degree by phone, fax or mail. Inquiry must include student's name, social security number. Employers may obtain transcripts upon written request accompanied by a signed release from the student.

A multiprogram two-year institution, with an enrollment of 4,946. Highest level of offering: one year but less than four years.
ACCREDITATIONS: SC ENGT MLTAD

Nassau Community College

One Education Drive
Garden City, NY 11530-6793
(516) 222-7500

Will confirm attendance and degree by phone or mail. Inquiry must include student's name, social security number, years attended. Employers may obtain transcripts upon written request accompanied by a $3.00 fee and a signed release from the student.

A multiprogram two-year institution, with an enrollment of 22,500. Highest level of offering: one year but less than four years.
ACCREDITATIONS: M ADNUR ENGT MUS NY PTAA RAD RSTH RTT SURGT

National Business College

PO Box 6400
Roanoke, VA 24017
(703) 986-1800

Will confirm attendance and degree by phone or mail. Inquiry must include student's name, date of birth, social security number, years attended. Requests should be directed to: Placement Center. -Employers may obtain transcripts upon written request accompanied by a signed release from the student.

A multiprogram two-year institution, with an enrollment of 1,196. Highest level of offering: one year but less than four years.
ACCREDITATIONS: JRCB

National College of Chiropractic

200 East Roosevelt Road
Lombard, IL 60148
(708) 629-2000
Fax (708) 268-6554

Will confirm attendance and degree by mail or fax. Inquiry must include student's name, years attended, release. Employers may obtain transcripts upon written request accompanied by a $5.00 fee and a signed release from the student. Requests should be directed to: Registrar's Office.

A health institution, with an enrollment of 908. Highest level of offering: first professional degree.
ACCREDITATIONS: NH CHIRO

National College of Education

(See Louis University)

National College

PO Box 1780
Rapid City, SD 57709
(605) 394-4800
Fax (605) 394-4871

Will confirm attendance and degree by phone, fax or mail. Inquiry must include student's name, years attended. Employers may obtain transcripts upon written request accompanied by a $2.00 fee and a signed release from the student. Requests should be directed to: Registrar's Office.

A business school, with an enrollment of 2,712. Highest level of offering: four or five year baccalaureate.

ACCREDITATIONS: NH ADVET MAAB MAC SRCB

National Education Center–Arkansas College of Technology Campus

9720 Rodney Parham Road
Little Rock, AR 72207
(501) 224-8200 Ext. 35
Fax (501) 227-9217

Will confirm attendance and degree by phone or mail. Inquiry must include student's name, social security number. Employers may obtain transcripts upon written request accompanied by a signed release from the student and a $5.00 fee.

A single program two-year institution, with an enrollment of 594. Highest level of offering: one year but less than four years.
ACCREDITATIONS: NATTS

National Education Center–Bauder College Campus

4801 North Dixie Highway
Fort Lauderdale, FL 33334
(305) 491-7171

Will confirm attendance and degree by mail. Inquiry must include student's name, years attended, field of study. Requests should be directed to: Education Department. Employers may obtain transcripts upon written request accompanied by a $5.00 fee (Money order) and a signed release from the student.

A single program two-year institution, with an enrollment of 6--5. Highest level of offering: one year but less than four years.
ACCREDITATIONS: NATTS

National Education Center–Brown Institute Campus

2225 East Lake Street
Minneapolis, MN 55407
(612) 721-2481 Ext. 222
Fax (612) 721-2179

Will confirm attendance and degree by phone or mail. Inquiry must include student's name, social security number, years attended. Employers may obtain transcripts upon written request accompanied by a $3.00 fee and a signed release from the student.

A multiprogram two-year institution, with an enrollment of 1,329. Highest level of offering: two years but less than four years.
ACCREDITATIONS: NATTS

National Education Center–Kentucky College of Technology Campus

300 Highrise Drive
Louisville, KY 40213
(502) 966-5555

Will confirm attendance and degree by phone or mail. Inquiry must include student's name, social security number, years attended. Employers may obtain transcripts upon written request accompanied by a $5.00 fee and a signed release from the student.

A single program two-year institution, with an enrollment of 330. Highest level of offering: one year but less than four years.
ACCREDITATIONS: NATTS

National Education Center–National Institute of Technology Campus

1119 5th Street
West Des Moines, IA 50265
(515) 223-1486

Will confirm attendance and degree by phone or mail. Inquiry must include student's name, social security number. Employers may obtain transcripts upon written request accompanied by a $5.00 fee and a signed release from the student.

A single program two-year institution, with an enrollment of 330. Highest level of offering: one year but less than four years.
ACCREDITATIONS: NATTS

National Institute of Technology Campus

Homewood, AL 35209
(714) 261-7206

Records are being held at National Education Center,1732 Reynolds, Irvine, CA 92714. Will confirm attendance and degree by phone or mail. Inquiry must include student's name, social security number. Employers may obtain transcripts upon written request accompanied by a $5.00 fee and a signed release from the student.

A two-year institution newly admitted to NCES, with an enrollment of 350. Highest level of offering: one year but less than four years.
ACCREDITATIONS: NATTS

National Education Center–National Institute of Technology Campus

5514 Big Tyler Road
Cross Lanes, WV 25313
(304) 776-6290 Ext. 18

Will confirm attendance and degree by phone or mail. Inquiry must include student's name, social security number, years attended. Employers may obtain transcripts upon written request by student accompanied by a $5.00 fee (contact the Registrar's Office to obtain a release form).

A single program two-year institution, with an enrollment of 350. Highest level of offering: one year but less than four years.
ACCREDITATIONS: NATTS

National Education Center–Spartan School of Aeronautics Campus

PO Box 582833
Tulsa, OK 74158-2833
(918) 836-6886 Ext. 118
Fax (918) 831-5387

Will confirm attendance and degree by phone, fax or mail. Inquiry must include student's name, years attended. Employers may obtain transcripts upon written request accompanied by a $5.00 fee and a signed release from the student

A single program two-year institution, with an enrollment of 1,675. Highest level of offering: one year but less than four years.
ACCREDITATIONS: NATTS

National Education Center–Tampa Technical Institute Campus

2410 E. Bush Blvd.
Tampa, FL 33612
(813) 935-5700
Fax (813) 239-2163

Will confirm attendance and degree by mail or fax. Inquiry must include student's name, social security number, years attended, release. Employers may obtain transcripts upon written request accompanied by a $5.00 fee and a signed release from the student.

A multiprogram two-year institution, with an enrollment of 1,198. Highest level of offering: one year but less than four years.
ACCREDITATIONS: NATTS

National Education Center–Vale Technical Institute Campus

135 West Market Street
Blairsville, PA 15717
(412) 459-9500 Ext. 318

Will confirm attendance and degree by mail. Inquiry must include student's name, years attended. Employers may obtain transcripts upon written request accompanied by a signed release from the student.

A single program two-year institution, with an enrollment of 350. Highest level of offering: one year but less than four years.
ACCREDITATIONS: NATTS

National Louis University
(Formerly National College of Education)
2840 Sheridan Road
Evanston, IL 60201
(708) 256-5150

Will confirm attendance and degree by phone or mail. Inquiry must include student's name, social security number. Employers may obtain transcripts upon written request accompanied by a $3.00 fee and a signed release from the student.

A multi-program institution, with an enrollment of 3,313. Highest level of offering: one year but less than four years.
ACCREDITATIONS: NH TED

National Technical Schools
(See United Education & Software)

National University
4025 Camino Del Rio South
San Diego, CA 92108
(619) 563-7100

Will confirm attendance and degree by phone or mail. Inquiry must include student's name, social security number. Employers may obtain transcripts upon written request accompanied by a $4.00 fee and a signed release from the student.

A specialized institution, with an enrollment of 9,000. Highest level of offering: doctorate.
ACCREDITATIONS: WC

Navajo Community College
Box 67
Tsaile, AZ 86556
(602) 724-3311 Ext. 110

Will confirm attendance and degree by phone or mail. Inquiry must include student's name, date of birth, social security number, years attended. Employers may obtain transcripts upon written request by student, accompanied by a $2.00 fee and a signed release from the student. Requests should be directed to: Records & Admission.

A multiprogram two-year institution, with an enrollment of 1,427. Highest level of offering: one year but less than four years.
ACCREDITATIONS: NH

Navarro College
3200 West 7th Avenue
Corsicana, TX 75110
(903) 874-6501 Ext. 221

Will confirm attendance and degree by phone or mail. Inquiry must include student's name, social security number. Employers may obtain transcripts upon written request accompanied by a $2.00 fee

and a signed release from the student.

A multiprogram two-year institution, with an enrollment of 2,930. Highest level of offering: one year but less than four years.
ACCREDITATIONS: SC MLTAB

Nazarene Bible College
1111 Chapman Drive
Colorado Springs, CO 80935
(719) 596-5110 Ext. 120

Will confirm attendance and degree by phone or mail. Inquiry must include student's name. Employers may obtain transcripts upon written request accompanied by a $2.00 fee and a signed release from the student.

A single program two-year institution, with an enrollment of 433. Highest level of offering: one year but less than four years.
ACCREDITATIONS: BI

Nazarene Theological Seminary
1700 East Meyer Boulevard
Kansas City, MO 64131
(816) 333-6254 Ext. 43
Fax (816) 822-9025

Will confirm attendance and degree by phone, fax or mail. Inquiry must include student's name. Employers may obtain transcripts upon written request accompanied by a $2.00 fee and a signed release from the student.

A school of philosophy, religion and theology, with an enrollment of 383. Highest level of offering: doctorate.
ACCREDITATIONS: THEOL

Nazareth College of Rochester
4245 East Avenue
Rochester, NY 14610
(716) 586-2525 Ext. 408

Will confirm attendance and degree by phone or mail. Inquiry must include student's name, social security number, years attended. Employers may obtain transcripts upon written request accompanied by a $5.00 fee and a signed release from the student.

A general baccalaureate institution, with an enrollment of 2,880. Highest level of offering: master's.
ACCREDITATIONS: M MUS NY SW NUR

Nazareth College
c/o Davenport College
4123 W. Main
Kalamazoo, MI 49001
(616) 382-2835
(800) 632-8928

Records are being held at the above location. Will confirm attendance and degree by phone or mail. Inquiry must include student's name, social security number. Employers may obtain transcripts upon written request by student accompanied by a $3.00 fee and a signed release from the student.

A health institution, with an enrollment of 820. Highest level of offering: master's.
ACCREDITATIONS: NH NUR SW TED

Nebraska Christian College
1800 Syracuse
Norfolk, NE 68701
(402) 371-5960 Ext. 16

Will confirm attendance and degree by phone or mail. Inquiry must include student's name. Employers may obtain transcripts upon written request accompanied by a $2.00 fee and a signed release from the student.

A school of philosophy, religion and theology, with an enrollment of 121. Highest level of offering: four or five year baccalaureate.
ACCREDITATIONS: BI

Nebraska Indian Community College
PO Box 752
Winnebago, NE 68071
(402) 878-2414
Fax (402) 878-2522

Will confirm attendance and degree by mail. Inquiry must include student's name, social security number, years attended, release. Employers may obtain transcripts upon written request accompanied by a $4.00 fee and a signed release from the student.

A two-year institution newly admitted to NCES, with an enrollment of 289. Highest level of offering: one year but less than four years.
ACCREDITATIONS: NH

Nebraska Wesleyan University
50th And Saint Paul Streets
Lincoln, NE 68504
(402) 465-2242
Fax (402) 465-2179

Will confirm attendance and degree by phone, fax or mail. Inquiry must include student's name, years attended. Employers may obtain transcripts upon written request accompanied by a $2.00 fee and a signed release from the student.

A general baccalaureate institution, with an enrollment of 1,600. Highest level of offering: four or five year baccalaureate.
ACCREDITATIONS: NH ANEST MT MUS SW TED

Neosho County Community College
1000 South Allen
Chanute, KS 66720
(316) 431-2820

Will confirm attendance and degree by phone or mail. Inquiry must include student's name, social security number. Employers may obtain transcripts upon written request accompanied by a signed release from the student. Attn: Registrar.

A multiprogram two-year institution, with an enrollment of 1,001. Highest level of offering: one year but less than four years.
ACCREDITATIONS: NH

Ner Israel Rabbinical College

400 Mount Wilson Lane
Baltimore, MD 21208
(301) 484-7200 Ext. 234
Fax (310) 484-3060

Will confirm attendance and degree by mail or fax. Inquiry must include student's name, social security number. Employers may obtain transcripts upon written request accompanied by a signed release from the student.

A school of philosophy, religion and theology, with an enrollment of 325. Highest level of offering: doctorate.

ACCREDITATIONS: RABN

Neumann College

Concord Road
Aston, PA 19014
(215) 459-0905 Ext. 221

Will confirm attendance and degree by phone or mail. Inquiry must include student's name, social security number, years attended. Employers may obtain transcripts upon written request accompanied by a $3.00 fee and a signed release from the student.

A general baccalaureate institution, with an enrollment of 982. Highest level of offering: master's.

ACCREDITATIONS: M MT NUR

New Brunswick Theological Seminary

17 Seminary Place
New Brunswick, NJ 08091
(201) 247-5241
Fax (908) 249-5412

Will confirm attendance and degree by phone or mail. Inquiry must include student's name. Employers may obtain transcripts upon written request accompanied by a $3.50 fee and a signed release from the student. Requests should be sent to: Attn: Registrar's Office.

A school of philosophy, religion and theology, with an enrollment of 178. Highest level of offering: master's.

ACCREDITATIONS: THEOL

New College of California

50 Fell Street
San Francisco, CA 94102
(415) 626-1694

Will confirm attendance and degree by phone or mail. Inquiry must include student's name, social security number, release. Employers may obtain transcripts upon written request accompanied by a $2.00 fee and a signed release from the student.

A comprehensive institution, with an enrollment of 800. Highest level of offering: master's.

ACCREDITATIONS: WC

New England College of Optometry

Registrar's Office
424 Beacon Street
Boston, MA 02115
(617) 236-6272

Will confirm attendance and degree by phone or mail. Inquiry must include student's name, social security number, date graduated. Employers may obtain transcripts upon written request directly by the student and accompanied by a $3.00 fee. Direct requests to the Registrar's Office.

A health institution, with an enrollment of 396. Highest level of offering: first professional degree.

ACCREDITATIONS: EH OPT OPTT

New England College

7 Main Street
Henniker, NH 03242
(603) 428-2203
Fax (603) 428-7230

Will confirm attendance and degree by phone, fax or mail. Inquiry must include student's name, years attended. Employers may obtain transcripts upon written request accompanied by a $5.00 fee and a signed release from the student.

A general baccalaureate institution, with an enrollment of 1,321. Highest level of offering: master's.

ACCREDITATIONS: EH ENG

New England Conservatory of Music

290 Huntington Avenue
Boston, MA 02115
(617) 262-1120 Ext. 270
Fax (617) 262-0500

Will confirm attendance and degree by phone, fax or mail. Inquiry must include student's name, date of birth, social security number. Employers may obtain transcripts upon written request accompanied by a $5.00 fee and a signed release from the student. Requests should be directed to: Registrar's Office.

A visual and performing arts school, with an enrollment of 745. Highest level of offering: doctorate.

ACCREDITATIONS: EH MUS

New England Institute of Applied Arts and Sciences

c/o Mount Ida College
Registrar's Office
777 Dedham St.
Newton Center, MA 02159
(617) 969-7000
Fax (617) 969-6993

Will confirm attendance and degree by phone or mail. Inquiry must include student's name, date of birth, social security number, years attended. Employers may obtain transcripts upon written request accompanied by a $2.00 fee and a signed release from the student.

New England Institute of Technology at Palm Beach

1126 53rd Court
West Palm Beach, FL 33407
(407) 848-2677

Will confirm attendance and degree by phone or mail. Inquiry must include student's name, social security number. Employers may obtain transcripts upon written request accompanied by a $2.00 fee and a signed release from the student.

A two-year institution with an enrollment of 600. Highest level of offering: one year but less than four years.

ACCREDITATIONS: NATTS

New England Institute of Technology

2500 Post Road
Warwick, RI 02886
(401) 467-7744

Will confirm attendance and degree by phone or mail. Inquiry must include student's name, social security number, years attended. Employers may obtain transcripts upon written request accompanied by a $2.00 fee and a signed release from the student.

A single program two-year institution, with an enrollment of 1,505. Highest level of offering: four or five year baccalaureate.

ACCREDITATIONS: EV NATTS

New England School of Law

154 Stuart Street
Boston, MA 02116
(617) 422-7215

Will confirm attendance and degree by phone or mail. Inquiry must include student's name, social security number. Employers may obtain transcripts upon written request accompanied by a $3.00 fee and a signed release from the student. Requests should be sent to: Attn: Registrar's Office.

A law school, with an enrollment of 1,150. Highest level of offering: first professional degree.

ACCREDITATIONS: LAW

New Hampshire College

2500 North River Road
Manchester, NH 03104
(603) 668-2211 Ext. 9619

Will confirm attendance and degree by phone or mail. Inquiry must include student's name, social security number, years attended. Employers may obtain transcripts upon written request accompanied by a $3.00 fee and a signed release from the student.

A business school, with an enrollment of 7,262. Highest level of offering: master's.

ACCREDITATIONS: EH SRCB

New Hampshire Technical College

One College Drive
Claremont, NH 03743
(603) 542-7744 Ext. 33

Will confirm attendance and degree by phone or mail. Inquiry must include student's name, years attended. Employers may obtain transcripts upon written request accompanied by a $3.00 fee and a signed release from the student.

A multiprogram two-year institution, with an enrollment of 375. Highest level of offering: one year but less than four years.

New Hampshire Technical Institute

Institute Drive
Concord, NH 03302
(603) 225-1804

Will confirm attendance and degree by phone or mail. Inquiry must include student's name, years attended. Employers may obtain transcripts upon written request by student accompanied by a $3.00 fee. Attn: Registrar's Office.

A multiprogram two-year institution, with an enrollment of 2,700. Highest level of offering: one year but less than four years.
ACCREDITATIONS: EV ADNUR DA DH ENGT RAD

New Hampshire Technical College at Stratham

277R Portsmouth Avenue
Stratham, NH 03885
(603) 772-1194 Ext. 18

Will confirm attendance and degree by phone or mail. Inquiry must include student's name, social security number. Employers may obtain transcripts upon written request accompanied by a $3.00 fee and a signed release from the student.

A multiprogram two-year institution, with an enrollment of 995. Highest level of offering: one year but less than four years.
ACCREDITATIONS: EV

New Hampshire Vocational–Technical College at Berlin

2020 Riverside Drive
Berlin, NH 03570
(603) 752-1113 Ext. 1003

Will confirm attendance and degree by phone or mail. Inquiry must include student's name, social security number. Employers may obtain transcripts upon written request accompanied by a $3.00 fee and a signed release from the student. Requests should be sent to: Attn: Registrar's Office.

A multiprogram two-year institution, with an enrollment of 650. Highest level of offering: one year but less than four years.
ACCREDITATIONS: EV

ACCREDITATIONS: EV MAC MLTAD MRT PTAA RSTH

New Hampshire Technical College at Laconia

Route 106 Prescott Hill
Laconia, NH 03246
(603) 524-3207 Ext. 18
Fax (603) 524-8084

Will confirm attendance and degree by phone or mail. Inquiry must include student's name, social security number. Employers may obtain transcripts upon written request accompanied by a $2.00 fee and a signed release from the student.

A multiprogram two-year institution, with an enrollment of 214. Highest level of offering: one year but less than four years.
ACCREDITATIONS: EV

New Hampshire Technical College at Manchester

1066 Front Street
Manchester, NH 03102
(603) 668-6706
Fax (603) 6668-5354

Will confirm attendance and degree by phone, fax or mail. Inquiry must include student's name, social security number. Employers may obtain transcripts upon written request accompanied by a $3.00 fee and a signed release from the student.

A single program two-year institution, with an enrollment of 1,534. Highest level of offering: one year but less than four years.
ACCREDITATIONS: EV

New Hampshire Vocational–Technical College at Nashua

505 Amherst Street–Room 98
Nashua, NH 03061
(603) 882-6923 Ext. 63

Will confirm attendance and degree by phone or mail. Inquiry must include student's name, social security number, years attended. Employers may obtain transcripts upon written request accompanied by a signed release from the student. A $3.00 fee will be charged for the the third copy of transcript.

A multiprogram two-year institution, with an enrollment of 1,079. Highest level of offering: one year but less than four years.
ACCREDITATIONS: EV

New Jersey Institute of Technology

323 Martin Luther King, Jr. Boulevard
Newark, NJ 07102
(201) 596-3236
Fax (201) 802-1802

Will confirm attendance and degree by phone, fax or mail. Inquiry must include student's name, date of birth, social security number. Employers may obtain transcripts upon written request accompanied by a $3.00 fee and a signed release from the student.

An engineering school, with an enrollment of 7,540. Highest level of offering: doctorate.
ACCREDITATIONS: M ARCH

New Mexico Highlands University

Las Vegas, NM 87701
(505) 424-3455
Fax (505) 454-3552

Will confirm attendance and degree by phone, fax or mail. Inquiry must include student's name, social security number. Employers may obtain transcripts upon written request accompanied by a $2.00 fee and a signed release from the student. Attn: Registrar.

A comprehensive institution with no medical school, with an enrollment of 2,602. Highest level of offering: bachelor's and master's.
ACCREDITATIONS: NH SW CHM

New Mexico Institute of Mining and Technology

PO Box E, Campus Station
Socorro, NM 87801
(505) 835-5133

Will confirm attendance and degree by mail. Inquiry must include student's name, social security number, release. Employers may obtain transcripts upon written request by student accompanied by a $2.00 fee.

A comprehensive institution with no medical school, with an enrollment of 1,244. Highest level of offering: doctorate.
ACCREDITATIONS: NH ENG

New Mexico Junior College

5317 Lovington Highway
Hobbs, NM 88240
(505) 392-5113
Fax (505) 392-2527

Will confirm attendance and degree by fax or mail. Inquiry must include student's name, social security number, release. Employers may obtain transcripts upon written request accompanied by a $2.00 fee and a signed release from the student.

A multiprogram two-year institution, with an enrollment of 2,612. Highest level of offering: one year but less than four years.
ACCREDITATIONS: NH ADNUR MLTAD

New Mexico Military Institute

101 W. College
Roswell, NM 88201-5173
(505) 622-6250 Ext. 217

Will confirm attendance and degree by phone or mail. Inquiry must include student's name, date of birth, social security number. Employers may obtain transcripts upon written request accompanied by a $1.00 fee and a signed release from the student.

A multiprogram two-year institution, with an enrollment of 475. Highest level of offering: one year but less than four years.
ACCREDITATIONS: NH

New Mexico State University Alamogordo Branch

Box 477
Alamogordo, NM 88310
(505) 434-3723
Fax (505) 437-8858

Will confirm attendance by phone, fax or mail. Inquiry must include student's name, social security number, years attended. Employers may obtain transcripts upon written request accompanied by a $3.00 fee and a signed release from the student.

A multiprogram two-year institution, with an enrollment of 1,900. Highest level of offering: one year but less than four years.
ACCREDITATIONS: NH MLTAD

New Mexico State University Carlsbad Branch

1500 University Drive–Room 111
Carlsbad, NM 88220
(505) 885-8831
Fax (505) 885-4951

Will confirm attendance and degree by phone or mail. Inquiry must include student's name, social security number, years attended. Requests should be directed to: Student Services, Office of Registrar, Box 3AR, University Park, NM 88003. Employers may obtain transcripts upon written request accompanied by a $3.00 fee and a signed release from the student.

A multiprogram two-year institution, with an enrollment of 1,100. Highest level of offering: one year but less than four years.
ACCREDITATIONS: NCA NLN

New Mexico State University Grants Branch

1500 3rd Street
Grants, NM 87020
(505) 287-7981 Ext. 108
Fax (505) 287-7992

Will confirm attendance and degree by phone, fax or mail. Inquiry must include student's name, social security number. Employers may obtain transcripts upon written request accompanied by a $3.00 fee and a signed release from the student.

A multiprogram two-year institution, with an enrollment of 507. Highest level of offering: one year but less than four years.
ACCREDITATIONS: NH

New Mexico State University Main Campus

Box 30001, Department 3AR
Las Cruces, NM 88003
(505) 646-3411

Will confirm attendance and degree by mail. Inquiry must include student's name, social security number. Employers may obtain transcripts upon written request accompanied by a $3.00 fee and a signed release from the student.

A doctoral-level institution with no medical school, with an enrollment of 13,540. Highest level of offering: doctorate.
ACCREDITATIONS: NH BUS ENG ENGT MUS RAD SW TED

New Orleans Baptist Theological Seminary

3939 Gentilly Boulevard
New Orleans, LA 70126
(504) 282-4455 Ext. 3304

Will confirm attendance and degree by phone or mail. Inquiry must include student's name, social security number. Employers may obtain transcripts upon written request by student accompanied by a $5.00 fee.

A school of philosophy, religion and theology, with an enrollment of 1,850. Highest level of offering: doctorate.
ACCREDITATIONS: SC MUS THEOL

New River Community College

Drawer 1127
Dublin, VA 24084
(703) 674-3603

Will confirm attendance and degree by phone or mail. Inquiry must include student's name, social security number. Employers may obtain transcripts upon written request accompanied by a signed release from the student. Requests should be directed to: Admissions Office.

A multiprogram two-year institution, with an enrollment of 3,845. Highest level of offering: one year but less than four years.
ACCREDITATIONS: SC

New School for Social Research

66 West 12th
New York, NY 10011
(212) 741-5720
Fax (212) 229-5359

Will confirm attendance and degree by phone or mail. Inquiry must include student's name, social security number. Employers may obtain transcripts upon written request accompanied by a $4.00 fee and a signed release from the student. Requests should be sent to: Attn: Records.

A doctoral-level institution with no medical school, with an enrollment of 6,371. Highest level of offering: doctorate.
ACCREDITATIONS: M ART CLPSY NY

New School of Music

c/o Temple University
Esther Boyer College of Music
13th & Norris St.
Philadelphia, PA 19122
(215) 787-8301

Will confirm attendance and degree by phone. Inquiry must include student's name, social security number. Employers may obtain transcripts upon written request accompanied by a $3.00 fee and a signed release from the student. Requests should be sent to: Attn: Graduate Coordinator.

A visual and performing arts school, with an enrollment of 600. Highest level of offering: four or five year baccalaureate.
ACCREDITATIONS: M

New York Chiropractic College

PO Box 800
Seneca Falls, NY 13148
(315) 568-3000 Ext. 60

Will confirm attendance and degree by phone or mail. Inquiry must include student's name, social security number. Employers may obtain transcripts upon written request accompanied by a $5.00 fee and a signed release from the student.

A health institution, with an enrollment of 600. Highest level of offering: first professional degree.
ACCREDITATIONS: M CHIRO NY

New York College of Podiatric Medicine

53 East 124th Street
New York, NY 10035
(212) 410-8000

Will confirm attendance and degree by mail or phone. Inquiry must include student's name, social security number, years attended. Requests should be directed to: Registrar's Office. Employers may obtain transcripts upon written request by student accompanied by a $5.00 fee. Requests should be sent to: Attn: Registrar

A health institution, with an enrollment of 414. Highest level of offering: first professional degree.
ACCREDITATIONS: NY POD

New York Institute of Technology Main Campus

Old Westbury, NY 11568
(516) 686-7580

Will confirm attendance and degree by phone or mail. Inquiry must include student's name, social security number, years attended. Employers may obtain transcripts upon written request accompanied by a $5.00 fee and a signed release from the student. Requests should be sent to: Attn: Student Records.

A comprehensive institution with a medical school, with an enrollment of 9,473. Highest level of offering: master's.
ACCREDITATIONS: NY M ARCH ENGT FIDER OSTEO

New York Institute of Technology New York City Campus

1855 Broadway
New York, NY 10023
(212) 399-8332
Fax (212) 977-3460

Will confirm attendance and degree by phone or mail. Inquiry must include student's name, social security number. Employers may obtain transcripts upon written request accompanied by a $5.00 fee and a signed release from the student.

A comprehensive institution with no medical school, with an enrollment of 3,605. Highest level of offering: master's.
ACCREDITATIONS: ENGT NY

New York Law School

57 Worth Street
New York, NY 10013
(212) 431-2300

Will confirm attendance and degree by mail. Inquiry must include student's name, social security number, years attended and written release from student. Employers may obtain transcripts upon written request accompanied by a $2.00 fee and a signed release from the student. Requests should be sent to: Attn: Registrar's Office.

A law school, with an enrollment of 1,216. Highest level of offering: first professional degree.

ACCREDITATIONS: NYSBR

New York Medical College

Sunshine Cottage
Valhalla, NY 10595
(914) 993-4495

Will confirm attendance and degree by phone or mail. Inquiry must include student's name, social security number, years attended. Employers may obtain transcripts upon written request accompanied by a $2.00 fee and a signed release from the student.

A medical school, with an enrollment of 1,268. Highest level of offering: doctorate.

ACCREDITATIONS: NY ANEST MED

New York School of Interior Design

155 East 56th Street
New York, NY 10022
(212) 753-5365
Fax (212) 826-9706

Will confirm attendance and degree by mail. Inquiry must include student's name, years attended. Employers may obtain transcripts upon written request accompanied by a $5.00 fee and a signed release from the student.

A multiprogram two-year institution, with an enrollment of 6287. Highest level of offering: four or five year baccalaureate.

ACCREDITATIONS: NY FIDER

New York State College of Ceramics at Alfred University

PO Box 805
Alfred, NY 14802
(607) 871-2122

Will confirm attendance and degree by phone or mail. Inquiry must include student's name, years attended. Employers may obtain transcripts upon written request accompanied by a $5.00 fee and a signed release from the student. Requests should be sent to: Attn: Registrar's Office.

A multi-program school, with an enrollment of 702. Highest level of offering: doctorate.

ACCREDITATIONS: ART ENG NY

New York Theological Seminary

5 West 29th Street-9th Floor
New York, NY 10001
(212) 532-4012
Fax (212) 684-0757

Will confirm attendance and degree by mail. Inquiry must include student's name, social security number. Employers may obtain transcripts upon written request accompanied by a $5.00 fee and a signed release from the student.

A school of philosophy, religion and theology, with an enrollment of 388. Highest level of offering: doctorate.

ACCREDITATIONS: NY THEOL ATS

New York University

100 Washington Square East
Room 201
New York, NY 10003
(212) 998-4800

Will confirm attendance and degree by mail. Inquiry must include student's name, social security number, years attended, release. Employers may obtain transcripts upon written request accompanied by a $3.00 fee and a signed release from the student.

A doctoral-level institution with a medical school, with an enrollment of 40,000. Highest level of offering: doctorate.

ACCREDITATIONS: M BUS CHE CLPSY COPSY DA DENT IPSY JOUR LAW BUSA HSA MED NY TED PTAA MUS NMT NUR OT PTA RSTH RTT SCPSY SP SW DANCE DMS

Newberry College

2100 College Street
Newberry, SC 29108
(803) 276-5010 Ext. 220
Fx (803) 321-5124

Will confirm attendance and degree by phone or mail. Inquiry must include student's name. Employers may obtain transcripts upon written request accompanied by a $5.00 fee and a signed release from the student.

A general baccalaureate institution, with an enrollment of 700. Highest level of offering: four or five year baccalaureate.

ACCREDITATIONS: SC MUS TED

Newbury College

129 Fisher Ave.
Brookline, MA 02146
(617) 262-9350 Ext. 225

Will confirm attendance and degree by phone or mail. Inquiry must include student's name, social security number. Employers may obtain transcripts upon written request accompanied by a $2.00 fee and a signed release from the student.

A multiprogram two-year institution, with an enrollment of 6,000. Highest level of offering: one year but less than four years.

ACCREDITATIONS: EV ADVET PTAA RSTH RSTHT

Niagara County Community College

3111 Saunders Settlement Road
Sanborn, NY 14132
(716) 731-3271 Ext. 111

Will confirm attendance and degree by phone or mail. Inquiry must include student's name, social security number. Employers may obtain transcripts upon written request accompanied by a $3.00 fee and a signed release from the student.

A multiprogram two-year institution, with an enrollment of 5,000. Highest level of offering: one year but less than four years.

ACCREDITATIONS: M ADNUR DA ENGT NY SURGT EEG

Niagara University

Niagara University, NY 14109
(716) 285-1212 Ext. 221

Will confirm attendance and degree by phone or mail. Inquiry must include student's name. Employers may obtain transcripts upon written request by student accompanied by a $3.00 fee. Requests should be directed to: Office of Admissions and Records.

A comprehensive institution with an enrollment of 3,347. Highest level of offering: beyond master's but less than doctorate.

ACCREDITATIONS: M NUR ACS SW NCATE NYSBR

Nicholls State University

PO Box 2004
University Station
Thibodaux, LA 70310
(504) 448-4151
Fax (504) 448-4929

Will confirm attendance and degree by phone, fax or mail. Inquiry must include student's name, date of birth, social security number. Employers may obtain transcripts upon written request accompanied by a $2.00 fee and a signed release from the student. Requests should be directed to: Records and Registration Department.

A comprehensive institution with no medical school, with an enrollment of 7,387. Highest level of offering: beyond master's but less than doctorate.

ACCREDITATIONS: SC ADNUR BUS MUS RSTHT TED

Nichols College

Dudley, MA 01571-5000
(508) 943-1560 Ext. 290

Will confirm attendance and degree by phone or mail. Inquiry must include student's name, social security number. Employers may obtain transcripts upon written request accompanied by a $2.00 fee and a signed release from the student.

A business school, with an enrollment of 1,092. Highest level of offering: master's.

ACCREDITATIONS: EH

Nicolet Technical College

Box 518
Rhinelander, WI 54501
(715) 369-4422
Fax (715) 369-4445

Will confirm attendance and degree by phone, fax or mail. Inquiry must include student's name, date of birth, social security number. Employers may obtain transcripts upon written request accompanied by a signed release from the student. Requests should be directed to: Student's Records Office.

A multiprogram two-year institution, with an enrollment of 1,168. Highest level of offering: one year but less than four years.

ACCREDITATIONS: NH

Nielsen Electronics Institute

1600 Meeting Street
Charleston, SC 29405
(803) 577-3350
Fax (803) 853-7171

Will confirm attendance and degree by phone or mail. Inquiry must include student's name, social security number. Employers may obtain transcripts upon written request accompanied by a signed release from the student.

A single program two-year institution, with an enrollment of 291. Highest level of offering: one year but less than four years.

ACCREDITATIONS: NATTS

Norfolk State University

2401 Corprew Avenue
Norfolk, VA 23504
(804) 683-8910

Will confirm attendance and degree by mail. Inquiry must include student's name, social security number, years attended. Employers may obtain transcripts upon written request accompanied by a $2.00 fee and a signed release from the student. Requests should be directed to: Registrar's Office.

A comprehensive institution with no medical school, with an enrollment of 7,233. Highest level of offering: master's.

ACCREDITATIONS: SC ADNUR MT MUS SW TED NUR

Normandale Community College

9700 France Avenue South
Bloomington, MN 55431
(612) 832-6314
Fax (612) 832-6571

Will confirm attendance and degree by phone or mail. Inquiry must include student's name, date of birth, social security number, years attended. Employers may obtain transcripts upon written request accompanied by a signed release from the student. Attn: Transcript Office.

A multiprogram two-year institution, with an enrollment of 7349. Highest level of offering: one year but less than four years.

ACCREDITATIONS: NH ADNUR DA DH MAC

North Adams State College

Church Street
North Adams, MA 01247
(413) 664-4511 Ext. 216

Will confirm attendance and degree by phone or mail. Inquiry must include student's name, social security number. Employers may obtain transcripts upon written request accompanied by a $1.00 fee and a signed release from the student.

A general baccalaureate institution, with an enrollment of 2,000. Highest level of offering: master's.

ACCREDITATIONS: EH TED

North American Baptist Seminary

1321 West 22nd Street
Sioux Falls, SD 57105
(605) 336-6588 Ext. 381

Will confirm attendance and degree by phone or mail. Inquiry must include student's name. Employers may obtain transcripts upon written request accompanied by a $2.00 fee and a signed release from the student.

A school of philosophy, religion and theology, with an enrollment of 170. Highest level of offering: doctorate.

ACCREDITATIONS: NH THEOL

North Arkansas Community College

Pioneer Ridge
Harrison, AR 72601
(501) 743-3000 Ext. 241

Will confirm attendance and degree by phone or mail. Inquiry must include student's name, social security number. Employers may obtain transcripts upon written request accompanied by a $2.00 fee and a signed release from the student. Requests should be directed to: Registrar's Office.

A multiprogram two-year institution, with an enrollment of 1,072. Highest level of offering: one year but less than four years.

ACCREDITATIONS: NH

North Carolina Agricultural and Technical State University

1601 East Market Street
Greensboro, NC 27411
(919) 334-7595

Will confirm attendance and degree by phone or mail. Inquiry must include student's name, date of birth, social security number, years attended. Employers may obtain transcripts upon written request accompanied by a $2.00 fee and a signed release from the student.

A comprehensive institution with no medical school, with an enrollment of 5,426. Highest level of offering: beyond master's but less than doctorate.

ACCREDITATIONS: SC BUS ENG NUR SW TED

North Carolina Central University

Office of the Registrar
Durham, NC 27707
(919) 560-5051

Will confirm attendance and degree by mail. Inquiry must include student's name, date of birth, social security number, years attended. Employers may obtain transcripts upon written request accompanied by a $2.00 fee and a signed release from the student. Requests should be directed to: Registrar's Office.

A comprehensive institution with no medical school, with an enrollment of 5,200. Highest level of offering: master's.

ACCREDITATIONS: SC LAW LIB NUR TED

North Carolina School of the Arts

200 Waughtown Street
Winston–Salem, NC 27117-2189
(919) 770-3294

Will confirm attendance and degree by phone or mail. Inquiry must include student's name. Employers may obtain transcripts upon written request accompanied by a $3.00 fee and a signed release from the student.

A visual and performing arts school, with an enrollment of 721. Highest level of offering: master's.

ACCREDITATIONS: SC

North Carolina State University at Raleigh

Box 7313
Raleigh, NC 27695-7313
(919) 515-2572
Fax (919) 515-2376

Will confirm attendance and degree by phone, fax or mail. Inquiry must include student's name, social security number, years attended. Employers may obtain transcripts upon written request accompanied by a $2.00 fee and a signed release from the student.

A doctoral-level institution with no medical school, with an enrollment of 28,000. Highest level of offering: doctorate.

ACCREDITATIONS: SC ARCH ENG FOR LSAR SW TED VET

North Carolina Wesleyan College

3400 N. Wesleyan Blvd.
Rocky Mount, NC 27804
(919) 977-7171 Ext. 228
Fax (919) 977-3701

Will confirm attendance and degree by phone, fax or mail. Inquiry must include student's name, social security number. Employers may obtain transcripts upon written request accompanied by a $2.00 fee and a signed release from the student.

A general baccalaureate institution, with an enrollment of 1,143. Highest level of offering: four or five year baccalaureate.

ACCREDITATIONS: SC

North Central Bible College

910 Elliot Avenue South
Minneapolis, MN 55404
(612) 332-3491 Ext. 4480
Fax (612) 343-4778

Will confirm attendance and degree by phone, fax or mail. Inquiry must include student's name, years attended. Employers may obtain transcripts upon written request accompanied by a $2.00 fee and a signed release from the student. Requests should be directed to: Admissions & Records.

A school of philosophy, religion and theology, with an enrollment of 1,130. Highest level of offering: four or five year baccalaureate.

ACCREDITATIONS: NH BI

North Central College

PO Box 3063
30 North Brainard Street
Naperville, IL 60566-7063
(708) 420-3430
Fax (708) 357-8393

Will confirm attendance and degree by phone, fax or mail. Inquiry must include student's name, years attended. Employers may obtain transcripts upon written request accompanied by a $2.00 fee and a signed release from the student.

A general baccalaureate institution, with an enrollment of 2,555. Highest level of offering: four or five year baccalaureate.

ACCREDITATIONS: NH

North Central Michigan College

1515 Howard Street
Petoskey, MI 49770
(616) 347-3973 Ext. 2110
Fax (616) 348-6625

Will confirm attendance and degree by phone or mail. Inquiry must include student's name, social security number, years attended. Employers may obtain transcripts upon written request accompanied by a $2.00 fee and a signed release from the student. Requests should be directed to: Student Services.

A multiprogram two-year institution, with an enrollment of 2,032. Highest level of offering: one year but less than four years.

ACCREDITATIONS: NCA RSTH

North Central Missouri College

(Formerly Trenton Junior College)
1301 Main Street, Box 107
Trenton, MO 64683
(816) 359-3948
Fax (816) 359-2211

Will confirm attendance and degree by phone or mail. Inquiry must include student's name, date of birth, social security number, years attended. Employers may obtain transcripts upon written request accompanied by a $1.00 fee and a signed release from the student.

A multiprogram two-year institution, with an enrollment of 865. Highest level of offering: one year but less than four years.

ACCREDITATIONS: NH

North Central Technical College

2441 Kenwood Circle–PO Box 698
Mansfield, OH 44901
(419) 755-4800 Ext. 837

Will confirm attendance and degree by phone or mail. Inquiry must include student's name, social security number. Employers may obtain transcripts upon written request accompanied by a $2.00 fee and a signed release from the student.

A multiprogram two-year institution, with an enrollment of 1,930. Highest level of offering: one year but less than four years.

ACCREDITATIONS: NH ADNUR RAD RSTHT

North Country Community College

PO Box 89
20 Winona Avenue
Saranac Lake, Ny 12983
(518) 891-2915
Fax 9518) 891-2915 Ext. 214

Will confirm attendance and degree by phone, fax or mail. Inquiry must include student's name, social security number. Employers may obtain transcripts upon written request accompanied by a $2.00 fee and a signed release from the student.

A multiprogram two-year institution, with an enrollment of 1,509. Highest level of offering: one year but less than four years.

ACCREDITATIONS: M MLTAD NY RAD

North Dakota State College of Science

800 North 6th Street
Wahpeton, ND 58075
(701) 671-1130
Fax (701) 671-2145

Will confirm attendance and degree by phone or mail. Inquiry must include student's name, social security number. Employers may obtain transcripts upon written request accompanied by a signed release from the student.

A multiprogram two-year institution, with an enrollment of 2,932. Highest level of offering: one year but less than four years.

ACCREDITATIONS: NH DA DH MRT

North Dakota State University Bottineau

1st & Sim Rall Boulevard
Bottineau, ND 58318
(701) 228-2277

Will confirm attendance and degree by phone or mail. Inquiry must include student's name, student ID number. Employers may obtain transcripts upon written request accompanied by a $2.00 fee and a signed release from the student.

A multiprogram two-year institution, with an enrollment of 475. Highest level of offering: one year but less than four years.

ACCREDITATIONS: NH

North Dakota State University Main Campus

PO Box 5196
Fargo, ND 58105
(701) 237-7981

Will confirm attendance and degree by phone or mail. Inquiry must include student's name, student ID number. Employers may obtain transcripts upon written request accompanied by a $2.00 fee and a signed release from the student.

A comprehensive institution with no medical school, with an enrollment of 9,998. Highest level of offering: doctorate.

ACCREDITATIONS: NH ADNUR ADVET ARCH DIET ENG MUS PHAR TED

North Florida Junior College

1000 Turner Davis Drive
Madison, FL 32340
(904) 973-2288 Ext. 169

Will confirm attendance and degree by phone or mail. Inquiry must include student's name, social security number, last date attended. Employers may obtain transcripts upon written request accompanied by a $1.00 fee and a signed release from the student.

A multiprogram two-year institution, with an enrollment of 1,200. Highest level of offering: one year but less than four years.

ACCREDITATIONS: SC

North Georgia College

Dahlonega, GA 30597
(404) 864-1400

Will confirm attendance and degree by phone or mail. Inquiry must include student's name, social security number. Employers may obtain transcripts upon written request accompanied by a $2.00 fee and a signed release from the student.

A comprehensive institution with no medical school, with an enrollment of 1,979. Highest level of offering: master's.

ACCREDITATIONS: SC ADNUR TED

North Greenville College

Records Office
Tigerville, SC 29688
(803) 895-1410 Ext. 317

Will confirm attendance and degree by phone or mail. Inquiry must include student's name. Employers may obtain transcripts upon written request accompanied by a $3.00 fee and a signed release from the student.

A multiprogram two-year institution, with an enrollment of 501. Highest level of offering: two years but less than four years.

ACCREDITATIONS: SACS

North Harris College

2700 W.W. Thorne
Houston, TX 77073
(713) 443-5420

Will confirm attendance and degree by phone or mail. Inquiry must include student's name, social security number and signature. Employers may obtain transcripts upon written request accompanied by a signed release from the student.

A multiprogram two-year institution, with an enrollment of 17,800. Highest level of offering: one year but less than four years.
ACCREDITATIONS: SC ADNUR

North Hennepin Community College

7411 85th Avenue North
Brooklyn Park, MN 55445
(612) 424-0719

Will confirm attendance and degree by mail. Inquiry must include student's name, SSN, date of birth and release. Employers may obtain transcripts upon written request accompanied by a signed release from the student.

A multiprogram two-year institution, with an enrollment of 6,000. Highest level of offering: one year but less than four years.
ACCREDITATIONS: NH ADNUR PERF

North Idaho College

1000 W. Garden Avenue
Coeur D'alene, ID 83814
(208) 769-3320

Will confirm attendance and degree by phone or mail. Inquiry must include student's name, date of birth, social security number. Employers may obtain transcripts upon written request accompanied by a $2.00 fee and a signed release from the student.

A multiprogram two-year institution, with an enrollment of 3,000. Highest level of offering: one year but less than four years.
ACCREDITATIONS: NW ADNUR

North Lake College

5001 N. Macarthur Blvd.
Irving, TX 75038-3899
(214) 659-5230

Will confirm attendance and degree by mail. Inquiry must include student's name, social security number. Employers may obtain transcripts upon written request accompanied by a $1.00 fee and a signed release from the student.

A multiprogram two-year institution, with an enrollment of 6,064. Highest level of offering: one year but less than four years.
ACCREDITATIONS: SC

North Park College and Theological Seminary

3225 W. Foster Ave.
Chicago, IL 60625
(312) 583-2700 Ext. 4031

Will confirm attendance and degree by phone or mail. Inquiry must include student's name, social security number, years attended. Employers may obtain transcripts upon written request accompanied by a $2.00 fee and a signed release from the student.

A general baccalaureate institution, with an enrollment of 1,491. Highest level of offering: first professional degree.
ACCREDITATIONS: NH MUS NUR THEOL

North Seattle Community College

9600 College Way North
Seattle, WA 98103
(206) 527-3669

Will confirm attendance and degree by phone or mail. Inquiry must include student's name, social security number. Employers may obtain transcripts upon written request accompanied by a $1.00 fee and a signed release from the student.

A multiprogram two-year institution, with an enrollment of 9,484. Highest level of offering: one year but less than four years.
ACCREDITATIONS: NW MAC

North Shore Community College

1 Ferncroft Road
Danvers, MA 01923
(508) 762-4000

Will confirm attendance and degree by phone or mail. Inquiry must include student's name, social security number. Employers may obtain transcripts upon written request accompanied by a $1.00 fee and a signed release from the student.

A multiprogram two-year institution, with an enrollment of 2,068. Highest level of offering: one year but less than four years.
ACCREDITATIONS: EH ADNUR PTAA RAD RSTH

North Texas State University

PO Box 13766
Denton, TX 76203
(817) 565-2111

Will confirm attendance and degree by phone or mail. Inquiry must include student's name, maiden name, date of birth, social security number, years attended. Employers may obtain transcripts upon written request accompanied by a $3.00 fee and a signed release from the student.

A doctoral-level institution with no medical school, with an enrollment of 26,519. Highest level of offering: doctorate.
ACCREDITATIONS: SC AUD BUS CLPSY COPSY FIDER JOUR LIB MUS SP SW TED

Northampton County Area Community College

3835 Green Pond Road
Bethlehem, PA 18017
(215) 861-5494
Fax (215) 861-5089

Will confirm attendance and degree by phone or mail. Inquiry must include student's name, release. Employers may obtain transcripts upon written request accompanied by a $2.00 fee and a signed release from the student.

A multiprogram two-year institution, with an enrollment of 6,000. Highest level of offering: one year but less than four years.
ACCREDITATIONS: M ADNUR DA DH FUSER MLTAD PNUR RAD

Northcentral Technical College

1000 Campus Drive
Wausau, WI 54401-1899
(715) 675-3331 Ext. 228

Will confirm attendance and degree by phone or mail. Inquiry must include student's name, maiden name, social security number, years attended. Employers may obtain transcripts upon written request accompanied by a signed release from the student.

A multiprogram two-year institution, with an enrollment of 4,850. Highest level of offering: one year but less than four years.
ACCREDITATIONS: NH DH RAD

Northeast Alabama State Junior College

Highway 35
PO Box 159
Rainsville, AL 35986
(205) 228-6001
Fax (205) 228-6558

Will confirm attendance and degree by phone or mail. Inquiry must include student's name, release. Employers may obtain transcripts upon written request accompanied by a $1.00 fee and a signed release from the student.

A multiprogram two-year institution, with an enrollment of 1,500. Highest level of offering: one year but less than four years.
ACCREDITATIONS: SACS NLN/AD

Northeast Community College

PO Box 469
801 East Benjamin
Norfolk, NE 68702-0469
(402) 371-2020

Will confirm attendance and degree by phone or mail. Inquiry must include student's name, years attended. Employers may obtain transcripts upon written request accompanied by a $1.00 fee and a signed release from the student.

A multiprogram two-year institution, with an enrollment of 2,298. Highest level of offering: two years but less than four years.
ACCREDITATIONS: NCA

Northeast Iowa Community College

(Formerly Northeast Iowa Technical Institute)
Box 400
Calmar, IA 52132
(319) 562-3263 Ext. 233
Fax (319) 562-3719

Will confirm attendance and degree by phone, fax or mail. Inquiry must include student's name, years attended. Employers may obtain transcripts upon written request accompanied by a $1.00 fee and a signed release from the student.

A multiprogram two-year institution, with an enrollment of 1,003. Highest level of offering: one year but less than four years.
ACCREDITATIONS: NCA

Northeast Louisiana University

700 University Avenue
Monroe, LA 71209
(318) 342-5262

Will confirm attendance and degree by phone or mail. Inquiry must include student's name, social security number. Employers may obtain transcripts upon written request accompanied by a signed release from the student.

A comprehensive institution with no medical school, with an enrollment of 10,250. Highest level of offering: doctorate.
ACCREDITATIONS: SC BUS DH MUS NUR OT PHAR RAD SW TED

Northeast Mississippi Community College

Cunningham Boulevard
Booneville, MS 38829
(601) 728-7751 Ext. 290

Will confirm attendance and degree by phone or mail. Inquiry must include student's name. Employers may obtain transcripts upon written request accompanied by a $2.00 fee and a signed release from the student.

A multiprogram two-year institution, with an enrollment of 2,277. Highest level of offering: one year but less than four years.
ACCREDITATIONS: SC ADNUR DH MAC MLTAD RSTHT

Northeast Missouri State University

AH104
Kirksville, MO 63501
(816) 785-4000 Ext. 4143
Fax (816) 785-4181

Will confirm attendance and degree by phone, fax or mail. Inquiry must include student's name, social security number, years attended. Employers may obtain transcripts upon written request accompanied by a $2.00 fee and a signed release from the student.

A comprehensive institution with no medical school, with an enrollment of 6,150. Highest level of offering: beyond master's but less than doctorate.
ACCREDITATIONS: NH ADVET MUS NUR SP TED

Northeast State Technical Community College

(Formerly Tri-Cities State Technical Institue)
PO Box 246
Blountville, TN 37617
(615) 323-3191 Ext. 329
Fax (615) 323-3083

Will confirm attendance and degree by phone or mail. Inquiry must include student's name, social security number. Employers may obtain transcripts upon written request accompanied by a signed release from the student.

A two-year institution newly admitted to NCES, with an enrollment of 1,733. Highest level of offering: one year but less than four years.
ACCREDITATIONS: SC ENGT

Northeast Wisconsin Technical College

PO Box 19042
2740 W. Mason Street
Green Bay, WI 54307-9042
(414) 498-5579
Fax (414) 498-6242

Will confirm attendance and degree by phone or mail. Inquiry must include student's name. Employers may obtain transcripts upon written request accompanied by a signed release from the student. Requests should be sent to: Attn: Transcripts.

A multiprogram two-year institution, with an enrollment of 7,682. Highest level of offering: one year but less than four years.
ACCREDITATIONS: NH ADNUR DA DH MAC RSTHT

Northeastern Bible College

Oak Lane
Essex Fells, NJ 07021
(201) 226-1074

Records are maintained at the above address. Will confirm attendance and degree by phone or mail. Inquiry must include student's name, social security number. Employers may obtain transcripts upon written request accompanied by a $3.00 fee and a signed release from the student.

Northeastern Christian Junior College

1860 Montgomery Avenue
Villanova, PA 19085
(215) 525-6780 Ext. 28
Fax (215) 520-9210

Will confirm attendance and degree by phone, fax or mail. Inquiry must include student's name, social security number. Employers may obtain transcripts upon written request accompanied by a $3.00 fee and a signed release from the student.

A liberal arts two-year institution, with an enrollment of 207. Highest level of offering: one year but less than four years.
ACCREDITATIONS: M

Northeastern Illinois University

5500 N. Saint Louis Avenue
Chicago, IL 60625-4699
(312) 583-4050

Will confirm attendance and degree by phone or mail. Inquiry must include student's name, social security number, years attended. Employers may obtain transcripts upon written request accompanied by a signed release from the student.

A comprehensive institution with no medical school, with an enrollment of 10,075. Highest level of offering: master's.
ACCREDITATIONS: NH TED

Northeastern Junior College

Sterling, CO 80751
(303) 522-6600 Ext. 658
Fax (303) 522-4945

Will confirm attendance and degree by mail, phone or fax. Inquiry must include student's name, social security number. Employers may obtain transcripts upon written request accompanied by a $3.00 fee and a signed release from the student.

A multiprogram two-year institution, with an enrollment of 1,635. Highest level of offering: one year but less than four years.
ACCREDITATIONS: NCA

Northeastern Ohio Universities College of Medicine

4209 State Route 44
Rootstown, OH 44272
(216) 325-2511 Ext. 504

Will confirm attendance and degree by phone or mail. Inquiry must include student's name. Employers may obtain transcripts upon written request by student and accompanied by a $2.00 fee and a signed release from the student.

A medical school, with an enrollment of 400. Highest level of offering: first professional degree.
ACCREDITATIONS: MED

Northeastern Oklahoma Agricultural and Mechanical College

200 I Streets N E
Miami, OK 743544-6497
(918) 542-8441 Ext. 212
Fax (918) 542-9759

Will confirm attendance and degree by phone, fax or mail. Inquiry must include student's name, social security number. Employers may obtain transcripts upon written request accompanied by a $2.00 fee and a signed release from the student.

A multiprogram two-year institution, with an enrollment of 2,536. Highest level of offering: one year but less than four years.
ACCREDITATIONS: NH ADNUR MLTAD

Northeastern Oklahoma State University

Tahlequah, OK 74464
(918) 456-5511 Ext. 2200

Will confirm attendance and degree by mail. Inquiry must include student's name. Employers may obtain transcripts upon written request accompanied by a $1.00 fee and a signed release from the student.

A school of education, with an enrollment of 9,100. Highest level of offering: doctorate.
ACCREDITATIONS: NH NUR OPT TED

Northeastern University

360 Huntington, Avenue
Boston, MA 02115
(617) 437-2300

Will confirm attendance and degree by
phone or mail. Inquiry must include student's name, social security number, date of
birth. Employers may obtain transcripts
upon written request accompanied by a
$2.00 fee and a signed release from the stu-
dent.

A comprehensive institution with no medical school, with an enrollment of 35,904.
Highest level of offering: doctorate.

ACCREDITATIONS: EH APCP AUD BUS DA
ENG ENGT LAW MLTAD MRA MT NUR TED
PHAR PTA RAD RSTH SP PERF

Northern Arizona University

PO Box 4103
Flagstaff, AZ 86011
(602) 523-2108

Will confirm attendance and degree by
phone or mail. Inquiry must include student's name, social security number.
Employers may obtain transcripts upon
written request accompanied by a $3.00 fee
and a signed release from the student.

A comprehensive institution with no medical school, with an enrollment of 17,047.
Highest level of offering: doctorate.

ACCREDITATIONS: NH BUS DH ENG ENGT
FOR MUS PTA RAD TED NUR

Northern Baptist Theological Seminary

660 East Butterfield Road
Lombard, IL 60148
(708) 620-2105
Fax (708) 620-2194

Will confirm attendance and degree by
phone, fax or mail. Inquiry must include
student's name, years attended. Employers
may obtain transcripts upon written request
accompanied by a $2.00 fee and a signed
release from the student.

A school of philosophy, religion and theology, with an enrollment of 215. Highest
level of offering: doctorate.

ACCREDITATIONS: NH THEOL

Northern Essex Community College

Elliott Way
Haverhill, MA 01830
(508) 374-3900

Will confirm attendance and degree by
phone or mail. Inquiry must include student's name, social security number, release. Employers may obtain transcripts
upon written request accompanied by a
$1.00 fee and a signed release from the stu-
dent.

A multiprogram two-year institution, with
an enrollment of 6,110. Highest level of offering: one year but less than four years.

ACCREDITATIONS: EH ADNUR MRT RAD
RSTH RSTHT

Northern Illinois University

De Kalb, IL 60115
(815) 753-0681
Fax (815) 753-0149

Will confirm attendance and degree by
phone, fax or mail. Inquiry must include
student's name, date of birth, social security
number, years attended. Employers may obtain transcripts upon written request accompanied by a $3.50 fee and a signed release
from the student.

A doctoral-level institution with no medical
institution, with an enrollment of 23,689.
Highest level of offering: doctorate.

ACCREDITATIONS: NH ART AUD BUS
CLPSY DIET JOUR LAW LIB MFCD MUS
NUR TED BUSA PTA SP DANCE THEA

Northern Kentucky University

Office of Registrar
301 Adminstration Center
University Drive
Highland Heights, KY 41099-7011
(606) 572-5226

Will confirm attendance and degree by
phone or mail. Inquiry must include
student's name, social security number.
Employers may obtain transcripts upon
written request accompanied by a signed release from the student. Direct inquiries to
Office of Registrar, 301 Administration
Center.

A multiprogram two-year institution, with
an enrollment of 5,625. Highest level of offering: beyond master's but less than doctorate.

ACCREDITATIONS: SC ADNUR LAW NUR
RAD SW

Northern Maine Vocational Technical Institute

33 Edgemont Drive
Presque Isle, ME 04769
(207) 769-2461 Ext. 238

Will confirm attendance and degree by
mail. Inquiry must include student's name,
maiden name, years attended. Employers
may obtain transcripts upon written request
accompanied by a $2.00 fee and a signed
release from the student.

A multiprogram two-year institution, with
an enrollment of 1,229. Highest level of offering: one year but less than four years.

ACCREDITATIONS: EV ADNUR

Northern Michigan University

Marquette, MI 49855
(906) 227-2322

Will confirm attendance and degree by
phone or mail. Inquiry must include student's name, social security number.
Employers may obtain transcripts upon
written request accompanied by a $2.00 fee
and an original signed release from the student.

A multiprogram tfour-year institution, with
an enrollment of 8,560. Highest level of offering: master's.

ACCREDITATIONS: NCA CSWE NCATE ACS
NLN NASM

Northern Montana College

PO Box 7751
Havre, MT 59501
(406) 265-3700

Will confirm attendance and degree by
phone or mail. Inquiry must include student's name, social security number, date of
birth. Employers may obtain transcripts
upon written request accompanied by a
signed release from the student.

A general baccalaureate institution, with an
enrollment of 1,811. Highest level of offering: master's.

ACCREDITATIONS: NW

Northern Nevada Community College

901 Elm Street
Elko, NV 89801
(702) 738-8493
Fax (702) 738-8771

Will confirm attendance and degree by
phone or mail. Inquiry must include student's name. Employers may obtain transcripts upon written request accompanied
by a signed release from the student.

A multiprogram two-year institution, with
an enrollment of 2,600. Highest level of offering: one year but less than four years.

ACCREDITATIONS: NW

Northern New Mexico Community College

1002 North Onate St.
Espanola, NM 87532
(505) 753-7141
Fax (505) 753-5237

Will confirm attendance and degree by
phone, fax or mail. Inquiry must include
student's name, social security number, date
of birth. Employers may obtain transcripts
upon written request accompanied by a
$2.00 fee and a signed release from the stu-
dent.

A multiprogram two-year institution, with
an enrollment of 1,500. Highest level of offering: one year but less than four years.

ACCREDITATIONS: NH PNE RAD RSTHT

Northern New Mexico Community College

PO Box 3650
Taos, NM 87571
(505) 758-9369

Will confirm attendance and degree by
phone or mail. Inquiry must include student's name, social security number, date of
birth. Employers may obtain transcripts
upon written request accompanied by a
$2.00 fee and a signed release from the stu-
dent.

A multiprogram two-year institution, with
an enrollment of 1,047. Highest level of offering: one year but less than four years.

ACCREDITATIONS: NH PNE RAD RSTHT

Northern Oklahoma College

1220 E. Grand Avenue
Tonkawa, OK 74653
(405) 628-2581
Fax (405) 628-5260

Will confirm attendance and degree by mail. Inquiry must include student's name, social security number, date of birth. Employers may obtain transcripts upon written request accompanied by a $1.00 fee and a signed release from the student.

A multiprogram two-year institution, with an enrollment of 2,100. Highest level of offering: one year but less than four years.
ACCREDITATIONS: NCA

Northern State University

Aberdeen, SD 57401
(605) 622-2012

Will confirm attendance and degree by phone or mail. Inquiry must include student's name, social security number, years attended. Employers may obtain transcripts upon written request accompanied by a $2.00 fee and a signed release from the student.

A general baccalaureate institution, with an enrollment of 3,108. Highest level of offering: master's.
ACCREDITATIONS: NH MUS TED

Northern Virginia Community College

8333 Lithel River Turnpike
Annandale, VA 22003
(703) 323-2925 3400
Fax (703) 323-3367

Will confirm attendance and degree by phone or mail. Inquiry must include student's name, social security number. Employers may obtain transcripts upon written request accompanied by a signed release from the student. Requests should be sent to: Attn: Admissions & Records.

A multiprogram two-year institution, with an enrollment of 32,053. Highest level of offering: one year but less than four years.
ACCREDITATIONS: SC ADNUR ADVET DA DH DT EMT MLTAD MRT PTAA RAD RSTH

Northland College

1411 Ellis Avenue
Ashland, WI 54806
(715) 682-4531 Ext. 227

Will confirm attendance and degree by phone or mail. Inquiry must include student's name, social security number. Employers may obtain transcripts upon written request accompanied by a $2.00 fee and a signed release from the student.

A general baccalaureate institution, with an enrollment of 650. Highest level of offering: four or five year baccalaureate.
ACCREDITATIONS: NH

Northland Community College

Highway 1 East
Thief River Falls, MN 56701
(218) 681-2181 Ext. 48
Fax (218) 681-6405

Will confirm attendance and degree by phone or mail. Inquiry must include student's name, social security number. Employers may obtain transcripts upon written request accompanied by a signed release from the student.

A multiprogram two-year institution, with an enrollment of 850. Highest level of offering: one year but less than four years.
ACCREDITATIONS: NCA

Northland Pioneer College

PO Box 610
Holbrook, AZ 86025
(602) 524-1993
Fax (602) 524-1997

Will confirm attendance and degree by phone, fax or mail. Inquiry must include student's name, social security number, year graduated. Employers may obtain transcripts upon written request accompanied by a signed release from the student.

A multiprogram two-year institution, with an enrollment of 6,500. Highest level of offering: one year but less than four years.
ACCREDITATIONS: NCA

Northrop University

5800 Arbor Vita
Los Angeles, CA 90045
(310) 337-4449
Fax (310) 645-4120

Records are being held at the above address. Will confirm attendance and degree by phone, fax or mail. Inquiry must include student's name, years attended. Employers may obtain transcripts upon written request accompanied by a $5.00 fee and a signed release from the student.

A engineering school, with an enrollment of 2,076. Highest level of offering: master's
ACCREDITATIONS: WC ENG ENGT

Northwest Alabama State Junior College

Route 3 Box 77
Phil Campbell, AL 35581
(205) 993-5331 Ext. 218

Will confirm attendance and degree by mail. Inquiry must include student's name, social security number. Employers may obtain transcripts upon written request accompanied by a $3.00 fee and a signed release from the student.

A multiprogram two-year institution, with an enrollment of 1,086. Highest level of offering: one year but less than four years.
ACCREDITATIONS: SACS NLN/AD

Northwest Alabama Community College

PO Box 9
Hamilton, AL 35570
(205) 921-3177
Fax (205) 921-3177 Ext. 300

Will confirm attendance and degree by phone, fax or mail. Inquiry must include student's name, social security number. Employers may obtain transcripts upon written request accompanied by a $2.00 fee and a signed release from the student.

A two-year institution with an enrollment of 1,500. Highest level of offering: one year but less than four years.
ACCREDITATIONS: SV

Northwest Christian College

828 East 11th Avenue
Eugene, OR 97401
(503) 343-1641 Ext. 15
Fax (503) 345-9159

Will confirm attendance and degree by phone, fax or mail. Inquiry must include student's name, social security number, years attended. Employers may obtain transcripts upon written request accompanied by a $6.00 fee and a signed release from the student.

A school of religion and theology, with an enrollment of 282. Highest level of offering: master's
ACCREDITATIONS: NW

Northwest College of the Assemblies of God

PO Box 579
Kirkland, WA 98083-0579
(206) 822-8266 Ext. 245
Fax (206) 827-0148

Will confirm attendance and degree by phone, fax or mail. Inquiry must include student's name. Employers may obtain transcripts upon written request accompanied by a $3.00 fee and a signed release from the student.

Highest level of offering: four or five year baccalaureate.
ACCREDITATIONS: NW BI NASC AABC

Northwest Community College

231 West 6th St.
Powell, WY 82435
(307) 754-6111
Fax (307) 754-6700

Will confirm attendance and degree by phone, fax or mail. Inquiry must include student's name, social security number, date of birth. Employers may obtain transcripts upon written request accompanied by a $1.00 fee and a signed release from the student.

A multiprogram two-year institution, with an enrollment of 2,200. Highest level of offering: two years but less than four years.
ACCREDITATIONS: NH MLTAB MLTAD PNUR

Northwest College/University of Alaska Fairbanks

Pouch 400
Nome, AK 99762
(907) 443-2201
Fax (907) 443-5602

Will not confirm attendance and degree by phone or mail. Employers may obtain transcripts by contacting the college and requesting an official transcript form accompanied by a $3.00 fee and a signed release from the student.

A single program two-year institution, with an enrollment of 141. Highest level of offering: one year but less than four years.
ACCREDITATIONS: NW

Northwest Iowa Technical College

Highway 18 West
Sheldon, IA 51201
(712) 324-5061

Will confirm attendance and degree by phone or mail. Inquiry must include student's name, social security number. Employers may obtain transcripts upon written request accompanied by a $1.00 fee and a signed release from the student.

A multiprogram two-year institution, with an enrollment of 587. Highest level of offering: one year but less than four years.
ACCREDITATIONS: NH

Northwest Mississippi Community College

Highway 51 North
Senatobia, MS 38668
(601) 562-3219

Will confirm attendance and degree by phone or mail. Inquiry must include student's name, social security number, years attended. Employers may obtain transcripts upon written request accompanied by a $2.00 fee and a signed release from the student.

A multiprogram two-year institution, with an enrollment of 4,136. Highest level of offering: one year but less than four years.
ACCREDITATIONS: SC ADNUR ENGT FUSER RSTH

Northwest Missouri State University

Maryville, MO 64468
(816) 562-1151

Will confirm attendance and degree by phone or mail. Inquiry must include student's name, social security number, year graduated. Employers may obtain transcripts upon written request accompanied by a $3.00 fee and a signed dated release from the student.

A comprehensive institution with no medical school, with an enrollment of 6,000. Highest level of offering: beyond master's but less than doctorate.
ACCREDITATIONS: NH MUS TED

Northwest Nazarene College

Nampa UD 83686
(208) 467-8541
Fax (208) 467-1098

Will confirm attendance and degree by phone or mail. Inquiry must include student's name, social security number, date of birth. Employers may obtain transcripts upon written request accompanied by a $2.50 fee and a signed release from the student.

A general baccalaureate institution, with an enrollment of 1,100. Highest level of offering: master's.
ACCREDITATIONS: NW MUS SW TED

Northwest Technical College

Route 1, Box 246A
Archbold, OH 43502
(419) 267-5511 Ext. 316
Fax (419) 267-3688

Will confirm attendance and degree by phone, fax or mail. Inquiry must include student's name, social security number. Employers may obtain transcripts upon written request accompanied by a $2.00 fee and a signed release from the student.

A multiprogram two-year institution, with an enrollment of 1,800. Highest level of offering: one year but less than four years.
ACCREDITATIONS: NH

Northwest Technical Institute

11995 Singletree Lane
Eden Prairie, MN 55344
(612) 944-0080

Will confirm attendance and degree by phone or mail. Inquiry must include student's name, social security number, years attended, release. Employers may obtain transcripts upon written request accompanied by a signed release from the student.

A single program two-year institution, with an enrollment of 126. Highest level of offering: one year but less than four years.
ACCREDITATIONS: NATTS

Northwestern Business College-Technical Center

1441 North Cable Road
Lima, OH 45805
(419) 227-3141 Ext. 232
Fax (419) 229-6926

Will confirm attendance and degree by phone or mail. Inquiry must include student's name, years attended. Employers may obtain transcripts upon written request accompanied by a $3.00 fee and a signed release from the student.

A multiprogram two-year institution, with an enrollment of 1,300. Highest level of offering: one year but less than four years.
ACCREDITATIONS: NCA

Northwestern College

3003 Snelling Ave. N
Saint Paul, MN 55113
(612) 631-5239
Fax (612) 631-5010

Will confirm attendance and degree by phone or mail. Inquiry must include student's name, social security number. Employers may obtain transcripts upon written request accompanied by a $1.00 fee and a signed release from the student.

A general baccalaureate institution, with an enrollment of 1,176. Highest level of offering: four or five year baccalaureate.
ACCREDITATIONS: NCA

Northwestern College

101 7th Street SW
Orange City, IA 51041
(712) 737-4821 Ext. 132

Will confirm attendance and degree by phone or mail. Inquiry must include student's name, years attended. Employers may obtain transcripts upon written request signed by the student accompanied by a $2.00 fee.

A general baccalaureate institution, with an enrollment of 1,021. Highest level of offering: master's.
ACCREDITATIONS: NH SW TED

Northwestern College of Chiropractic

2501 West 84th Street
Bloomington, MN 55431
(612) 888-4777
Fax (612) 888-6713

Will confirm attendance and degree by phone, fax or mail. Inquiry must include student's name, social security number. Employers may obtain transcripts upon written request accompanied by a signed release from the student.

A health institution, with an enrollment of 533. Highest level of offering: first professional degree.
ACCREDITATIONS: CHIRO

Northwestern Connecticut Community College

Park Place
Winsted, CT 06098
(203) 379-8543

Will confirm attendance and degree by phone or mail. Inquiry must include student's name, social security number. Employers may obtain transcripts upon written request accompanied by a signed release from the student.

A multiprogram two-year institution, with an enrollment of 2,343. Highest level of offering: one year but less than four years.
ACCREDITATIONS: EH

Northwestern Electronics Institute

825 41st Avenue N. E.
Columbia Heights, MN 55421
(612) 781-4881

Will confirm attendance and degree by phone or mail. Inquiry must include student's name, social security number, years attended. Only student may obtain transcripts.

A single program two-year institution, with an enrollment of 1,090. Highest level of offering: one year but less than four years.
ACCREDITATIONS: NATTS

Northwestern Michigan College

1701 E. Front Street
Traverse City, MI 49684
(616) 922-0650
Fax (616) 922-1570

Will confirm attendance and degree by phone, fax or mail. Inquiry must include student's name, social security number. Employers may obtain transcripts upon written request accompanied by a $2.00 fee and a signed release from the student.

A multiprogram two-year institution, with an enrollment of 4,698. Highest level of offering: one year but less than four years.
ACCREDITATIONS: NH DA

Northwestern Oklahoma State University

Alva, OK 73717
(405) 327-1700

Will confirm attendance and degree by phone or mail. Inquiry must include student's name, social security number. Employers may obtain transcripts upon written request and a signed release from the student.

A general baccalaureate institution, with an enrollment of 1,663. Highest level of offering: master's.
ACCREDITATIONS: NH TED

Northwestern State University of Louisiana

Natchitoches, LA 71497
(318) 357-6171

Will confirm attendance and degree by phone or mail. Inquiry must include student's name, social security number. Employers may obtain transcripts upon written request accompanied by a signed release from the student.

A comprehensive institution with no medical school, with an enrollment of 6,206. Highest level of offering: doctorate.
ACCREDITATIONS: SC ADNUR ADVET MUS NUR RAD SW TED

Northwestern University

633 Clark Street
Evanston, IL 60208
(708) 491-3741
Fax (708) 491-8458

Will confirm attendance and degree by phone, fax or mail. Inquiry must include student's name, social security number, last year attended. Employers may obtain transcripts upon written request accompanied by a $1.00 fee and a signed release from the student.

A doctoral-level institution with a medical school, with an enrollment of 15,829. Highest level of offering: doctorate.
ACCREDITATIONS: NH AUD BUS CLPSY DENT DH ENG HSA LAW MED MUS NUR PTA RSTH SP IPSY

Northwood Institute

3225 Cook Road
Midland, MI 48640
(517) 837-4213
Fax (517) 832-9590

Will confirm attendance and degree by phone, fax or mail. Inquiry must include student's name, social security number, years attended. Employers may obtain transcripts upon written request accompanied by a $2.00 fee and a signed release from the student.

A single program two-year institution, with an enrollment of 1,850. Highest level of offering: four or five year baccalaureate.
ACCREDITATIONS: NH

Norwalk Community College

333 Wilson Avenue
Norwalk, CT 06854
(203) 853-2040
Fax (203) 857-7007

Will confirm attendance and degree by mail. Inquiry must include student's name, social security number, years attended. Employers may obtain transcripts upon written request accompanied by a signed release from the student.

A multiprogram two-year institution, with an enrollment of 3,547. Highest level of offering: one year but less than four years.
ACCREDITATIONS: EH ADNUR

Norwalk State Technical College

181 Richards Avenue
Norwalk, CT 06854
(203) 855-6600 855-6627
Fax (203) 853-4125

Will confirm attendance and degree by phone or mail. Inquiry must include student's name, social security number, date of birth, release. Employers may obtain transcripts upon written request accompanied by a signed release from the student.

A multiprogram two-year institution, with an enrollment of 980. Highest level of offering: one year but less than four years.
ACCREDITATIONS: EV ENGT

Norwich University

Northfield, VT 05663
(802) 485-2035

Will confirm attendance and degree by mail. Inquiry must include student's name, social security number, date of birth. Employers may obtain transcripts upon written request accompanied by a $4.00 fee and a signed release from the student.

A general baccalaureate institution, with an enrollment of 2,500. Highest level of offering: master's.
ACCREDITATIONS: EH ENG ENGT

Notre Dame College

4545 College Road
Cleveland, OH 44121
(216) 381-1680 Ext. 243

Will confirm attendance and degree by mail. Inquiry must include student's name, social security number, years attended, date graduated. Employers may obtain transcripts upon written request accompanied by a $4.00 fee and a signed release from the student.

A general baccalaureate institution, with an enrollment of 827. Highest level of offering: four or five year baccalaureate.
ACCREDITATIONS: NH

Notre Dame College

Attn: Registrar's Office
2321 Elm Street
Manchester, NH 03104
(603) 669-4298

Will confirm attendance and degree by phone or mail. Inquiry must include student's name, social security number, years attended. Employers may obtain transcripts upon written request accompanied by a $3.00 fee and a signed release from the student.

A general baccalaureate institution, with an enrollment of 1,094. Highest level of offering: master's.
ACCREDITATIONS: EH MT

Notre Dame Seminary School of Theology

2901 S. Carrollton Avenue
New Orleans, LA 70118
(504) 866-7426 Ext. 24

Will confirm attendance by phone or mail. Inquiry must include student's name, social security number, years attended. Employers may obtain transcripts upon written request accompanied by a $2.00 fee and a signed release from the student.

A school of religion and theology, with an enrollment of 117. Highest level of offering: master's.
ACCREDITATIONS: SC THEOL

Nova University

3301 College Avenue
Fort Lauderdale, FL 33314
(305) 475-7300
Fax (305) 475-7621

Will confirm attendance and degree by mail or fax. Inquiry must include student's name, social security number. Employers may obtain transcripts upon written request accompanied by a $3.00 fee and a signed release from the student.

A school of education, with an enrollment of 1,200. Highest level of offering: first professional degree.
ACCREDITATIONS: SC CLPSY LAW

Nyack College

South Highland Ave.
Nyack, NY 10960
(914) 358-1710 Ext. 265

Will confirm attendance and degree by phone or mail. Inquiry must include student's name, date of birth, social security number, years attended. Employers may obtain transcripts upon written request accompanied by a $3.00 fee and a signed release from the student.

A general baccalaureate institution, with an enrollment of 540. Highest level of offering: master's.
ACCREDITATIONS: M MUS NY

O

Oakland City College

143 Lucretia Street
Oakland City, IN 47660
(812) 749-1237

Will confirm attendance and degree by phone or mail. Inquiry must include student's name, years attended. Employers may obtain transcripts upon written request accompanied by a $2.00 fee and a signed release from the student.

A multiprogram two-year institution, with an enrollment of 736. Highest level of offering: master's.
ACCREDITATIONS: NH

Oakland Community College

PO Box 812
Bloomfield Hills, MI 48013-0812
(313) 540-1548
Fax (313) 540-1841

Will confirm by mail. Inquiry must include student's name, social security number, years attended, release. Employers may obtain transcripts upon written request accompanied by a $2.00 fee and a signed release from the student.

A multiprogram two-year institution, with an enrollment of 28,000. Highest level of offering: two years but less than four years.
ACCREDITATIONS: NCA DH MAC MLTAD RSTH DMS

Oakland University

102 O'Dowd Hall
Rochester, MI 48309-4401
(313) 370-3452
Fax (313) 370-4475

Will confirm attendance and degree by phone, fax or mail. Inquiry must include student's name, maiden name, date of birth, social security number, years attended. Employers may obtain transcripts upon written request accompanied by a $5.00 fee and a signed release from the student. Requests should be directed to: Academics Records Office.

A comprehensive institution with no medical school, with an enrollment of 12,530. Highest level of offering: doctorate.
ACCREDITATIONS: NH ENG NUR PTA TED

Oakton Community College

1600 East Golf Road
Des Plaines, IL 60016
(708) 635-1700
Fax (708) 635-1706

Will confirm by mail. Inquiry must include student's name, date of birth, social security number, years attended, release. Requests should be directed to: Registration & Records. Employers may obtain transcripts upon written request accompanied by a $3.00 fee and a signed release from the student.

A multiprogram two-year institution, with an enrollment of 11,0272. Highest level of offering: one year but less than four years.
ACCREDITATIONS: NH MLTAD MRT PTAA RAD

Oakwood College

Oakwood Road North West
Huntsville, AL 35896
(205) 726-7000 Ext. 7348
Fax (205) 726-7409

Will confirm attendance and degree by phone, fax or mail. Inquiry must include student's name, date of birth, social security number, years attended. Employers may obtain transcripts upon written request accompanied by a $2.00 fee and a signed release from the student. Requests should be directed to: Records Office.

A general baccalaureate institution, with an enrollment of 1,330. Highest level of offering: four or five year baccalaureate.
ACCREDITATIONS: SC TED

Oberlin College

Registrar's Office, Peters Hall
Oberlin, OH 44074
(216) 775-8450

Will confirm attendance and degree by phone or mail. Inquiry must include student's name, date of birth, social security number, years attended. Employers may obtain transcripts upon written request accompanied by a $4.00 fee and a signed release from the student.

A general baccalaureate institution, with an enrollment of 2,700. Highest level of offering: master's.
ACCREDITATIONS: NH ART MUS

Oblate College

391 Michigan Avenue North East
Washington, DC 20017
(202) 529-6544

Will confirm attendance and degree by phone or mail. Inquiry must include student's name, date of birth, years attended. Employers may obtain transcripts upon written request accompanied by a $5.00 fee and a signed release from the student.

A specialized school, with an enrollment of 42. Highest level of offering: master's.
ACCREDITATIONS: M THEOL

Oblate School of Theology

285 Oblate Drive
San Antonio, TX 78216
(512) 341-1366

Will confirm attendance and degree by mail. Inquiry must include student's name, date of birth, social security number, years attended, self addressed stamped envelope. Employers may obtain transcripts upon written request accompanied by a $3.00 fee and a signed release from the student.

A school of philosophy, religion and theology, with an enrollment of 145. Highest level of offering: first professional degree.
ACCREDITATIONS: SC THEOL

Occidental College

1600 Campus Road
Los Angeles, CA 90041
(213) 259-2500

Will confirm attendance and degree by phone or mail. Inquiry must include student's name, social security number, years attended. Employers may obtain transcripts upon written request accompanied by a $2.00 fee and a signed release from the student.

A general baccalaureate institution, with an enrollment of 1,675. Highest level of offering: master's.
ACCREDITATIONS: WC

Ocean County College

College Drive–2001
PO Box 20
Toms River, NJ 08754-2001
(908) 255-0304

Will confirm attendance and degree by phone or mail. Inquiry must include student's name, social security number, years attended. Requests should be directed to: Admissions Office. Employers may obtain transcripts upon written request accompanied by a $2.00 fee and a signed release from the student.

A multiprogram two-year institution, with an enrollment of 6,774. Highest level of offering: one year but less than four years.
ACCREDITATIONS: M ADNUR ENGT

Odessa College

201 West University
Odessa, TX 79764
(915) 335-6404

Will confirm attendance and degree by mail. Inquiry must include student's name, date of birth, social security number, years attended. Employers may obtain transcripts upon written request accompanied by a $1.00 fee and a signed release from the student.

A multiprogram two-year institution, with an enrollment of 4,916. Highest level of offering: one year but less than four years.
ACCREDITATIONS: SC ADNUR MLTAD MUS RAD RSTH RSTHT SURGT

Oglala Lakota College

Box 490
Kyle, SD 57752
(605) 455-2321 Ext. 236

Will confirm attendance and degree by phone or mail or phone. Inquiry must include student's name, date of birth, social security number, years attended, release. Employers may obtain transcripts upon written request accompanied by a $2.00 fee and a signed release from the student.

A multiprogram two-year institution, with an enrollment of 1,053. Highest level of offering: four or five year baccalaureate.
ACCREDITATIONS: NH

Oglethorpe University

4484 Peachtree Road North East
Atlanta, GA 30319
(404) 261-1441 Ext. 316

Will confirm attendance and degree by phone or mail. Inquiry must include student's name, social security number, years attended. Employers may obtain transcripts upon written request accompanied by a $2.00 fee and a signed release from the student.

A general baccalaureate institution, with an enrollment of 1,075. Highest level of offering: master's.
ACCREDITATIONS: SACS

Ohio College of Podiatric Medicine

10515 Carnegie Avenue
Cleveland, OH 44106
(216) 231-3300
Fax (216) 231-0453

Will confirm attendance and degree by mail, phone or fax. Inquiry must include student's name, date of birth, social security number, years attended. Employers may obtain transcripts upon written request accompanied by a $2.00 fee and a signed release from the student.

A health institution, with an enrollment of 367. Highest level of offering: first professional degree.

ACCREDITATIONS: NH POD

Ohio Dominican College

1216 Sunbury Road
Columbus, OH 43219
(614) 251-4650
Fax (614) 252-0776

Will confirm attendance and degree by phone, fax or mail. Inquiry must include student's name, date of birth, social security number, years attended. Employers may obtain transcripts upon written request accompanied by a $3.00 fee and a signed release from the student.

A general baccalaureate institution, with an enrollment of 1,300. Highest level of offering: four or five year baccalaureate.

ACCREDITATIONS: NH

Ohio Northern University

Ada, OH 45810
(419) 772-2024
Fax (419) 772-1932

Will confirm attendance and degree by phone, fax or mail. Inquiry must include student's name, years attended. Employers may obtain transcripts upon written request accompanied by a $4.00 fee and a signed release from the student.

A general baccalaureate institution, with an enrollment of 2,791. Highest level of offering: first professional degree.

ACCREDITATIONS: ACS NH ENG LAW MUS PHAR

Ohio State University Agricultural Technical Institute

1328 Dover Road
Wooster, OH 44691
(216) 264-3911
Fax (216) 262-7634

Will confirm attendance and degree by mail or fax. Inquiry must include student's name, social security number. Employers may obtain transcripts upon written request accompanied by a $2.00 fee and a signed release from the student.

A single program two-year institution, with an enrollment of 790. Highest level of offering: one year but less than four years.

ACCREDITATIONS: NH

Ohio State University Main Campus

1800 Cannon Drive
Lincoln Tower–Room 320
Columbus, OH 43210
(614) 292-8500
Fax (614) 292-7199

Will confirm attendance and degree by fax or mail. $10.00 fee for fax response. Fax responses will also be mailed. Inquiry must include student's name, social security number, release. Requests should be directed to: Verification Department. Employers may obtain transcripts upon written request accompanied by a $2.00 fee and a signed release from the student. Check, money order, Visa or Mastercard accepted. Include expiration date on credit cards.

A doctoral-level institution with a medical school, with an enrollment of 53,446.

ACCREDITATIONS: NH ANEST ARCH AUD BBT BUS CLPSY COPSY DENT DH PAST THEA HSA IPSY JOUR LAW LSAR MED MRA MT MUS NMT NUR OPT DIET ENG TED VET OT PHAR PTA RAD RSTH SP SW DANCE PERF

Ohio State University–Lima Campus

4240 Campus Drive
Lima, OH 45804
(419) 221-1641
Fax (419) 221-1658

Will confirm attendance and degree by mail. Inquiry must include student's name, social security number, release. Employers may obtain transcripts upon written request accompanied by a $2.00 fee and a signed release from the student. Transcript requests should be directed to: OSU-Main Campus, 1800 Cannon Drive, Lincoln Tower-Room 320, Columbus, OH 43210.

A multiprogram two-year institution, with an enrollment of 939. Highest level of offering: four or five year baccalaureate.

ACCREDITATIONS: NH

Ohio State University–Mansfield Campus

1680 University Drive
Mansfield, OH 44906
(419) 755-4230

Will confirm attendance by phone or mail. Inquiry must include student's name, social security number. Employers may obtain transcripts upon written request accompanied by a $2.00 fee and a signed release from the student. Transcript requests should be directed to: OSU-Main Campus, 1800 Cannon Drive, Lincoln Tower-Room 320, Columbus, OH 43210.

A multiprogram two-year institution, with an enrollment of 1,336. Highest level of offering: four or five year baccalaureate.

ACCREDITATIONS: NH

Ohio State University–Marion Campus

1465 Mount Vernon Avenue
Marion, OH 43302
(614) 389-2361
Fax (614) 389-6786

Will confirm attendance by phone, fax or mail. Inquiry must include student's name, social security number. Employers may obtain transcripts upon written request accompanied by a $2.00 fee and a signed release from the student. Transcript requests should be directed to: OSU-Main Campus, 1800 Cannon Drive, Lincoln Tower-Room 320, Columbus, OH 43210.

A multiprogram two-year institution, with an enrollment of 1,331. Highest level of offering: four or five year baccalaureate.

ACCREDITATIONS: NH

Ohio State University–Newark Campus

University Drive
Newark, OH 43055
(614) 366-3321

Will confirm attendance by mail. Inquiry must include student's name, social security number. Employers may obtain transcripts upon written request accompanied by a $2.00 fee and a signed release from the student. Transcript requests should be directed to: OSU-Main Campus, 1800 Cannon Drive, Lincoln Tower-Room 320, Columbus, OH 43210.

A multiprogram two-year institution, with an enrollment of 1,600. Highest level of offering: four or five year baccalaureate.

ACCREDITATIONS: NH

Ohio University Belmont

45425 National Road
Saint Clairsville, OH 43950
(614) 695-1720

Will confirm attendance and degree by phone or mail. Inquiry must include student's name, social security number. Employers may obtain transcripts upon written request accompanied by a $2.00 fee and a signed release from the student. Transcript requests should be directed to: OU-Main Campus, 110 Chubbs Hall, Athens, OH 45701.

A multiprogram two-year institution, with an enrollment of 1,170. Highest level of offering: four or five year baccalaureate.

ACCREDITATIONS: NH

Ohio University Chillicothe Campus

PO Box 629
Chillicothe, OH 45601
(614) 774-7200 Ext. 241

Will confirm attendance and degree by mail. Inquiry must include student's name, social security number, release. Employers may obtain transcripts upon written request accompanied by a $2.00 fee and a signed release from the student. Transcript requests should be directed to: OU-Main Campus, Office of Student Records, 110 Chubb Hall, Ohio University, Athens, OH 45701.

A multiprogram two-year institution, with an enrollment of 1,600. Highest level of offering: four or five year baccalaureate.
ACCREDITATIONS: NH

Ohio University Lancaster Branch

1570 Granville Pike
Lancaster, OH 43130
(614) 654-6711

Will confirm attendance and degree by phone or mail. Inquiry must include student's name, social security number. Employers may obtain transcripts upon written request accompanied by a $2.00 fee and a signed release from the student. Transcript requests should be directed to: OU-Main Campus, 110 Chubbs Hall, Athens, OH 45701.

A multiprogram two-year institution, with an enrollment of 1,529. Highest level of offering: four or five year baccalaureate.
ACCREDITATIONS: NH

Ohio University Main Campus

110 Chubbs Hall
Athens, OH 45701
(614) 593-4191
Fax (614) 593-4184

Will confirm attendance and degree by phone or mail. Inquiry must include student's name, social security number. Only students may obtain transcripts.

A doctoral-level institution with a medical school, with an enrollment of 14,684. Highest level of offering: doctorate.
ACCREDITATIONS: NH AUD BUS CLPSY DANCE ENG JOUR MUS NUR OSTEO SP SW TED PTA

Ohio University Zanesville Branch

1425 Newark Road
Zanesville, OH 43701
(614) 453-0762

Will confirm attendance and degree by phone or mail. Inquiry must include student's name, social security number. Employers may obtain transcripts upon written request accompanied by a $2.00 fee and a signed release from the student. Transcript requests should be directed to: OU-Main Campus, 110 Chubb Hall, Athens, OH 45701.

A multiprogram two-year institution, with an enrollment of 1,700. Highest level of offering: four or five year baccalaureate.
ACCREDITATIONS: NH ADNUR

Ohio Valley College

College Parkway
Parkersburg, WV 26101
(304) 485-7384 Ext. 26

Will confirm attendance and degree by phone or mail. Inquiry must include student's name, social security number, years attended. Employers may obtain transcripts upon written request accompanied by a $5.00 fee and a signed release from the student.

A multiprogram two-year institution, with an enrollment of 220. Highest level of offering: four or five year baccalaureate.
ACCREDITATIONS: NH

Ohio Wesleyan University

Delaware, OH 43015
(614) 368-3200 Ext. 960
Fax (614) 368-3299

Will confirm attendance and degree by phone or mail. Inquiry must include student's name, date of birth, social security number, years attended. Employers may obtain transcripts upon written request accompanied by a $3.00 fee and a signed release from the student.

A general baccalaureate institution, with an enrollment of 1,900. Highest level of offering: four or five year baccalaureate.
ACCREDITATIONS: NH MUS NUR

Ohlone College

43600 Mission Blvd.
Fremont, CA 94539-5884
(510) 659-6100
Fax (510) 659-8817

Will confirm attendance and degree by phone or mail. Inquiry must include student's name, social security number, years attended. Requests should be directed to: Admissions & Records. Employers may obtain transcripts upon written request accompanied by a $2.00 fee and a signed release from the student.

A multiprogram two-year institution, with an enrollment of 9,000. Highest level of offering: one year but less than four years.
ACCREDITATIONS: WJ ADNUR MAC RSTH RSTHT

Ohr Hameir Theological Seminary

PO Box 2130
Peekskill, NY 10566
(914) 736-1500

Will confirm attendance and degree by phone or mail. Inquiry must include student's name, social security number, years attended. Employers may obtain transcripts upon written request accompanied by a signed release from the student.

A specialized non-degree granting institution, with an enrollment of 45. Highest level of offering: four or five year baccalaureate.
ACCREDITATIONS: RABN

Ohr Somayach Institutions

PO Box 334
Monsey, NY 10952
(914) 425-1370
Fax (914) 425-8865

Will confirm attendance and degree by phone, fax or mail. Inquiry must include student's name, social security number, years attended. Employers may obtain transcripts upon written request accompanied by a signed release from the student.

A bachelor's or higher institution newly admitted to NCES. Highest level of offering: graduate non-degree granting.
ACCREDITATIONS: RABN

Okaloosa–Walton Junior College

100 College Boulevard
Niceville, FL 32578
(904) 678-5111 Ext. 374

Will confirm attendance and degree by phone or mail. Inquiry must include student's name, date of birth, social security number, years attended. Employers may obtain transcripts upon written request accompanied by a signed release from the student.

A multiprogram two-year institution, with an enrollment of 3,592. Highest level of offering: one year but less than four years.
ACCREDITATIONS: SACS

Oklahoma Baptist University

500 West University
Shawnee, OK 74801
(405) 878-2023
Fax (405) 878-2069

Will confirm attendance and degree by phone or mail. Inquiry must include student's name, SSN, date of birth, years attended. Requests should be directed to: Academic Center. Employers may obtain transcripts upon written request accompanied by a signed release from the student.

A general baccalaureate institution, with an enrollment of 2,200. Highest level of offering: four or five year baccalaureate.
ACCREDITATIONS: NH MUS NUR TED

Oklahoma Christian University

Box 11000
Oklahoma City, OK 73136-1100
(405) 425-5203 or 425-5204
Fax (405) 425-5316

Will confirm attendance and degree by phone or mail. Inquiry must include student's name, social security number, years attended. Requests should be directed to: Records Department. Employers may obtain transcripts upon written request accompanied by a $2.00 fee and a signed release from the student.

A general baccalaureate institution, with an enrollment of 1,700. Highest level of offering: four or five year master's.
ACCREDITATIONS: NH TED

Oklahoma City Community College

7777 South May
Oklahoma City, OK 73159
(405) 682-1611
Fax (405) 682-7585

Will confirm attendance and degree by mail. Inquiry must include student's name, social security number, years attended, release. Requests should be directed to: Admissions Office. Employers may obtain transcripts upon written request accompanied by a signed release from the student.

A multiprogram two-year institution, with an enrollment of 10,222. Highest level of offering: one year but less than four years.
ACCREDITATIONS: NCA ADNUR PTAA

Oklahoma City University

2501 North Blackwelder
Oklahoma City, OK 73106
(405) 521-5296
Fax (405) 521-5264

Will confirm attendance and degree by phone, fax or mail. Inquiry must include student's name, date of birth, social security number. Employers may obtain transcripts upon written request accompanied by a $6.00 fee and a signed release from the student.

A comprehensive institution with no medical school, with an enrollment of 3,778. Highest level of offering: master's.
ACCREDITATIONS: NH LAW MUS

Oklahoma Junior College of Business and Technology

7370 E. 71st Street
Tulsa, OK 74133
(918) 459-0200
Fax (918) 250-4526

Will confirm attendance and degree by mail, phone or fax. Inquiry must include student's name, years attended, release. Employers may obtain transcripts upon written request accompanied by a $2.00 fee and a signed release from the student.

A multiprogram two-year institution, with an enrollment of 774. Highest level of offering: one year but less than four years.

Oklahoma Missionary Baptist College

PO Box 71
Marlow, OK 73055
(405) 658-5446

Will confirm attendance and degree by phone or mail. Inquiry must include student's name, years attended. Employers may obtain transcripts upon written request accompanied by a $1.00 fee and a signed release from the student.

A bachelor's or higher institution newly admitted to NCES, with an enrollment of 184. Highest level of offering: four or five year baccalaureate.
ACCREDITATIONS: 3IC

Oklahoma Panhandle State University

Box 430
Goodwell, OK 73939
(405) 349-2611 Ext. 223
Fax (405) 349-2302

Will confirm attendance and degree by phone, fax or mail. Inquiry must include student's name, social security number, years attended. Employers may obtain transcripts upon written request accompanied by a $1.00 fee and a signed release from the student.

A general baccalaureate institution, with an enrollment of 1,065. Highest level of offering: four or five year baccalaureate.
ACCREDITATIONS: NH TED

Oklahoma State University Main Campus

103 Whitehurst
Stillwater, OK 74078-0102
(405) 744-3078

Will confirm attendance and degree by phone or mail. Inquiry must include student's name, social security number. Employers may obtain transcripts upon written request accompanied by a $1.00 fee and a signed release from the student.

A doctoral-level institution with a medical school, with an enrollment of 22,237. Highest level of offering: doctorate.
ACCREDITATIONS: NH ARCH BUS CLPSY DIETI ENG ENGT FIDER FOR JOUR LSAR TED VET BUSA MUS SP

Oklahoma State University Oklahoma City

900 North Portland
Oklahoma City, OK 73107
(405) 945-3207

Will confirm degree by phone or mail. Inquiry must include student's name, social security number, years attended. Employers may obtain transcripts upon written request accompanied by a $2.00 fee and a signed release from the student.

A multiprogram two-year institution, with an enrollment of 4,3500. Highest level of offering: one year but less than four years.
ACCREDITATIONS: NH ADNUR

Oklahoma State University–Technical Branch

Okmulgee, OK 74447
(918) 756-6211 Ext. 304
Fax (918) 756-1315

Will confirm attendance and degree by phone or mail. Inquiry must include student's name, social security number, years attended. Employers may obtain transcripts upon written request accompanied by a $1.00 fee and a signed release from the student.

Old College

(See Turkey Meadows Community College)

Old Dominion University

Norfolk, VA 23529-0053
(804) 683-4425
Fax (804) 683-5357

Will confirm attendance and degree by phone or mail. Inquiry must include student's name, social security number, years attended. Employers may obtain transcripts upon written request accompanied by a $5.00 fee and a signed release from the student. Attn: Registrar's Office.

A comprehensive institution with no medical school, with an enrollment of 15,626. Highest level of offering: doctorate.
ACCREDITATIONS: SC BUS DA DH ENG ENGT MT MUS NUR PTA TED BUSA

Olean Business Institute

301 North Union Street
Olean, NY 14760
(716) 372-7978

Will confirm attendance and degree by phone or mail. Inquiry must include student's name, years attended. Employers may obtain transcripts upon written request accompanied by a $1.00 fee and a signed release from the student.

A single program two-year institution, with an enrollment of 156. Highest level of offering: one year but less than four years.
ACCREDITATIONS: NY JRCB

Olive–Harvey College

10001 South Woodlawn Avenue
Chicago, IL 60628
(312) 568-3700
Fax (312) 660-4847

Will confirm attendance and degree by mail, phone or fax. Inquiry must include student's name, date of birth, social security number. Employers may obtain transcripts upon written request accompanied by a $2.00 fee and a signed release from the student.

A multiprogram two-year institution, with an enrollment of 6,612. Highest level of offering: one year but less than four years.
ACCREDITATIONS: NH

Olivet College

Olivet, MI 49076
(616) 749-7637
Fax (616) 749-7121

Will confirm attendance and degree by phone or mail. Inquiry must include student's name, date of birth, social security number, years attended. Employers may obtain transcripts upon written request accompanied by a $2.00 fee and a signed release from the student.

A general baccalaureate institution, with an enrollment of 679. Highest level of offering: four or five year baccalaureate.
ACCREDITATIONS: NH

Olivet Nazarene University

Box 6
Kankakee, IL 60901
(815) 939-5201
Fax (815) 939-0416

Will confirm attendance and degree by phone or mail. Inquiry must include student's name, social security number. Employers may obtain transcripts upon written request accompanied by a signed release from the student.

A general baccalaureate institution, with an enrollment of 1,875. Highest level of offering: master's.
ACCREDITATIONS: NCA MUS NUR TED

Olympic College

1600 Chester Ave.
Bremerton, WA 98310-1699
(206) 478-4544
Fax (206) 478-7161

Will confirm attendance and degree by mail or fax. Inquiry must include student's name, social security number, date of birth, release from student. Requests should be directed to: Admissions & Records. Employers may obtain transcripts upon written request accompanied by a $2.00 fee and a signed release from the student.

A multiprogram two-year institution, with an enrollment of 5,692. Highest level of offering: one year but less than four years.
ACCREDITATIONS: NW

O'More College of Design

PO Box 908
Franklin, TN 37065
(615) 794-4254

Will confirm attendance and degree by phone or mail. Inquiry must include student's name, years attended. Employers may obtain transcripts upon written request accompanied by a $1.00 fee and a signed release from the student.

A visual arts school, with an enrollment of 130. Highest level of offering: four or five year baccalaureate.
ACCREDITATIONS: FIDER

Onondaga Community College

Onondaga Hill Road
Syracuse, NY 13215
(315) 469-7741

Will confirm attendance and degree by mail. Inquiry must include student's name, social security number, years attended. Employers may obtain transcripts upon written request accompanied by a $5.00 fee and a signed release from the student.

A multiprogram two-year institution, with an enrollment of 7,262. Highest level of offering: one year but less than four years.
ACCREDITATIONS: M ADNUR DH NY RSTH RSTHT SURGT

Oral Roberts University

7777 South Lewis Avenue
Tulsa, OK 74171
(918) 495-6549

Will confirm attendance and degree by phone or mail. Inquiry must include student's name, social security number. Employers may obtain transcripts upon written request accompanied by a signed release from the student.

A comprehensive institution with no medical school, with an enrollment of 4,351. Highest level of offering: doctorate.
ACCREDITATIONS: NH DENT MED MUS NUR SW THEOL

Orange Coast College

2701 Fairview Road
Costa Mesa, CA 92628-5005
(714) 432-5771

Will confirm attendance and degree by mail. Inquiry must include student's name, date of birth, release. Employers may obtain transcripts upon written request accompanied by a $2.00 fee and a signed release from the student. Requests should be directed to: Records Office.

A multiprogram two-year institution, with an enrollment of 25,000. Highest level of offering: one year but less than four years.
ACCREDITATIONS: WJ DA DT EEG MAC RAD RSTH RTT

Orange County Community College

115 South Street
Middletown, NY 10940
(914) 343-1121 Ext. 4140
Fax (914) 343-1228

Will confirm attendance and degree by phone, fax or mail. Inquiry must include student's name, social security number, years attended. Employers may obtain transcripts upon written request accompanied by a $3.00 fee and a signed release from the student.

A multiprogram two-year institution, with an enrollment of 6,000. Highest level of offering: one year but less than four years.
ACCREDITATIONS: M ADNUR DH ENGT MLTAD NY PTAA

Orangeburg Calhoun Technical College

3250 Saint Matthews Road
Orangeburg, SC 29115
(803) 536-0311 Ext. 324
Fax (803)531-4364

Will confirm attendance and degree by mail or fax. Inquiry must include student's name, social security number. Employers may obtain transcripts upon written request accompanied by a $3.00 fee and a signed release from the student.

A multiprogram two-year institution, with an enrollment of 1,307. Highest level of offering: one year but less than four years.
ACCREDITATIONS: SC MLTAD NUR RAD RSTHT

Oregon Graduate Institute

19600 NW Von Neumann Drive
Beaverton, OR 97006-1999
(503) 690-1028
Fax (503) 690-1387

Will confirm attendance and degree by phone, fax or mail. Inquiry must include student's name. Employers may obtain transcripts upon written request accompanied by a $4.00 fee and a signed release from the student.

A specialized school, with an enrollment of 224. Highest level of offering: doctorate.
ACCREDITATIONS: NW

Oregon Graduate School of Professional Psychology

(See Pacific University, School of Professional Psychology)

Oregon Health Sciences University

3181 South West Sam Jackson Park Road
Portland, OR 97201
(503) 494-7800
Fax (503) 494-4629

Will confirm attendance and degree by phone, fax or mail. Inquiry must include student's name, social security number. Employers may obtain transcripts upon written request accompanied by a $5.00 fee and a signed release from the student.

A medical school, with an enrollment of 1,317. Highest level of offering: doctorate.
ACCREDITATIONS: NW DENT DH DIETI IPSY MED MIDWF MT NUR RTT

Oregon Institute of Technology

3201 Campus Drive
Klamath Falls, OR 97601-8801
(503) 885-1300
Fax (503) 885-1115

Will confirm attendance and degree by phone, fax or mail. Inquiry must include student's name, social security number, years attended. Employers may obtain transcripts upon written request accompanied by a $1.00 fee and a signed release from the student.

An engineering school, with an enrollment of 2,700. Highest level of offering: four or five year baccalaureate.
ACCREDITATIONS: NW DH ENGT RAD AMA/MT

Oregon Polytechnic Institute

900 South East Sandy Boulevard
Portland, OR 97214
(503) 234-9333
Fax (503) 233-0195

Will confirm attendance and degree by phone, fax or mail. Inquiry must include student's name, date of birth, social security number. Employers may obtain transcripts upon written request accompanied by a $3.00 fee and a signed release from the student.

A single program two-year institution, with an enrollment of 300. Highest level of offering: one year but less than four years.
ACCREDITATIONS: NATTS

Oregon State University

Corvallis, OR 97331-2130
(503) 737-4331

Will confirm attendance and degree by phone or mail. Inquiry must include student's name, date of birth, social security number. Employers may obtain transcripts upon written request accompanied by a $5.00 fee and a signed release from the student. Requests should be directed to: Registrar's Office.

A doctoral-level institution with no medical school, with an enrollment of 14,915. Highest level of offering: doctorate.
ACCREDITATIONS: NW BUS ENG FOR JOUR MUS PHAR TED VET ACS

Orlando College

5500 Diplomat Circle
Orlando, FL 32810
(407) 628-5870 Ext. 43

Will confirm attendance and degree by phone or mail. Inquiry must include student's name, social security number. Employers may obtain transcripts upon written request accompanied by a $2.00 fee and a signed release from the student. Requests should be directed to: Registrar's Office.

A four-year business school, with an enrollment of 980. Highest level of offering: four or five year baccalaureate.
ACCREDITATIONS: SRCB

OS Johnson Technical Institute

3427 North Main Avenue
Scranton, PA 18508
(717) 342-6404
Fax (717) 348-2181

Will confirm attendance and degree by phone or mail. Inquiry must include student's name, years attended. Employers may obtain transcripts upon written request accompanied by a $2.00 fee and a signed release from the student.

A single program two-year institution, with an enrollment of 349. Highest level of offering: one year but less than four years.
ACCREDITATIONS: NATTS

Otero Junior College

18th & Colorado Ave.
La Junta, CO 81050
(719) 384-6842
Fax (719) 384-6880

Will confirm attendance and degree by phone, fax or mail. Inquiry must include student's name, social security number and dates of attendance. Employers may obtain transcripts upon written request accompanied by a $1.00 fee and a signed release from the student.

A multiprogram two-year institution, with an enrollment of 850. Highest level of offering: one year but less than four years.
ACCREDITATIONS: NH ADNUR

Otis/Parsons School of Art and Design

2401 Wilshire Boulevard
Los Angeles, CA 90057
(213) 251-0510

Will confirm attendance and degree by mail. Inquiry must include student's name, social security number, years attended. Employers may obtain transcripts upon written request accompanied by a $5.00 fee and a signed release from the student.

A visual and performing arts school, with an enrollment of 740. Highest level of offering: master's.
ACCREDITATIONS: WC ART

Ottawa University

Box 5
Ottawa, KS 66067-3399
(913) 242-5200 Ext. 240
Fax (913) 242-7429

Will confirm attendance and degree by phone, fax or mail. Inquiry must include student's name, date of birth, social security number, years attended. Employers may obtain transcripts upon written request accompanied by a $3.00 fee and a signed release from the student.

A general baccalaureate institution, with an enrollment of 1,704. Highest level of offering: four or five year baccalaureate.
ACCREDITATIONS: NH

Otterbein College

Westerville, OH 43081
(614) 898-1350
Fax (614) 898-1200

Will confirm attendance and degree by phone, fax or mail. Inquiry must include student's name, social security number. Employers may obtain transcripts upon written request accompanied by a $3.00 fee and a signed release from the student.

A general baccalaureate institution, with an enrollment of 2,490. Highest level of offering: master's.
ACCREDITATIONS: NCA/CIHE ADNUR MUS NUR TED

Ouachita Baptist University

Box 3757
Arkadelphia, AR 71998-0001
(501) 246-4531 Ext. 588

Will confirm attendance and degree by phone or mail. Inquiry must include student's name, date of birth. Employers may obtain transcripts upon written request accompanied by a $2.00 fee and a signed release from the student.

A comprehensive institution with no medical school, with an enrollment of 1,400. Highest level of offering: master's.
ACCREDITATIONS: NH MUS TED

Our Lady of Holy Cross College

4123 Woodland Drive
New Orleans, LA 70131
(504) 394-7744 Ext. 114

Will confirm attendance and degree by phone or mail. Inquiry must include student's name, social security number. Employers may obtain transcripts upon written request accompanied by a $5.00 fee and a signed release from the student.

A general baccalaureate institution, with an enrollment of 1,120. Highest level of offering: master's.
ACCREDITATIONS: SACS

Our Lady of the Lake University of San Antonio

411 South West 24th Street
San Antonio, TX 78285
(512) 434-6711 Ext. 316
Fax (512) 436-2314

Will confirm attendance and degree by phone, fax or mail. Inquiry must include student's name, date of birth, social security number, years attended. Employers may obtain transcripts upon written request accompanied by a $3.00 fee and a signed release from the student.

A comprehensive institution with no medical school, with an enrollment of 2,381. Highest level of offering: doctorate.
ACCREDITATIONS: SC SP SW

Owens Technical College

PO Box 10000
Toledo, OH 43699-1947
(419) 666-0580

Will confirm attendance and degree by mail. Inquiry must include student's name, social security number, release. Employers may obtain transcripts upon written request accompanied by a $2.00 fee and a signed release from the student. Requests should be directed to: Records Department.

A multiprogram two-year institution, with an enrollment of 7,000. Highest level of offering: one year but less than four years.
ACCREDITATIONS: NH ADNUR ENGT DH RAD RTT SURGT OPTT

Owensboro Junior College of Business

1515 East 18th Street–Box 1350
Owensboro, KY 42303
(502) 926-4040 Ext. 25

Will confirm attendance and degree by phone or mail. Inquiry must include student's name, maiden name, social security number, years attended. Employers may obtain transcripts upon written request accompanied by a $2.00 fee and a signed release from the student.

A multiprogram two-year institution, with an enrollment of 265. Highest level of offering: one year but less than four years.
ACCREDITATIONS: JRCB

Oxnard College

4000 South Rose Avenue
Oxnard, CA 93033
(805) 986-5844
Fax (805) 986-5843

Will confirm attendance and degree by mail, phone or fax. Inquiry must include student's name, social security number. Employers may obtain transcripts upon written request accompanied by a $3.00 fee and a signed release from the student.

A multiprogram two-year institution, with an enrollment of 6,800. Highest level of offering: one year but less than four years.
ACCREDITATIONS: WJ

Ozark Christian College

1111 North Main Street
Joplin, MO 64801
(417) 624-2518 Ext. 233
Fax (417) 624-0090

Will confirm attendance and degree by phone or mail. Inquiry must include student's name, date of birth. Employers may obtain transcripts upon written request accompanied by a $2.00 fee and a signed release from the student.

A bachelor's or higher institution newly admitted to NCES, with an enrollment of 578. Highest level of offering: four or five year baccalaureate.

ACCREDITATIONS: BI

P

Pace University White Plains Campus

1 Martine Avenue
White Plains, NY 10606
(914) 422-4040 (Undergraduate)
(914) 422-4044 (Graduate)
(914) 422-4213 (Law)

Will confirm attendance and degree by phone or by mail prior to 1985. Inquiry must include student's name, social security number, years attended. Employers may obtain transcripts upon written request accompanied by a $5.00 fee and a signed release from the student. Inquiries should be directed to: Registrar's Office.

A comprehensive institution with no medical school, with an enrollment of 3,432. Highest level of offering: master's.
ACCREDITATIONS: M LAW NY

Pace University New York Campus

One Pace Plaza
New York, NY 10038
(212) 346-1315

Will confirm attendance and degree by mail. Inquiry must include student's name, social security number, release. Employers may obtain transcripts upon written request accompanied by a signed release from the student. Requests should be directed to: Registrar's Office.

A business school, with an enrollment of 6,903. Highest level of offering: doctorate.
ACCREDITATIONS: M NY

Pace University Pleasantville–Briarcliff Campus

861 Bedford Road
Pleasantville, NY 10570
(914) 741-3431

Will confirm attendance and degree by phone or mail. Inquiry must include student's name, social security number, years attended. Employers may obtain transcripts upon written request accompanied by a $5.00 fee and a signed release from the student.

A general baccalaureate institution, with an enrollment of 4,894. Highest level of offering: master's.
ACCREDITATIONS: M ADNUR NUR NY

Pacific Christian College

2500 East Nutwood Avenue
Fullerton, CA 92631
(714) 879-3901 Ext. 256
Fax (714) 526-0231

Will confirm attendance and degree by phone, fax or mail. Inquiry must include student's name, date of birth, social security number. Employers may obtain transcripts upon written request accompanied by a signed release from the student.

A business school, with an enrollment of 600. Highest level of offering: master's.
ACCREDITATIONS: WC BI

Pacific Coast Baptist Bible College

1100 S. Valley Center
San Dimas, CA 917731
(714) 599-6843 Ext. 237

Will confirm attendance and degree by phone or mail. Inquiry must include student's name, social security number. Employers may obtain transcripts upon written request accompanied by a $3.00 fee and a signed release from the student.

A bachelor's or higher institution newly admitted to NCES, with an enrollment of 150. Highest level of offering: four or five year baccalaureate.
ACCREDITATIONS: 3IC

Pacific Coast College

1261 3rd Ave.
Chula Vista, CA 91911
(619) 691-0882
Fax (619) 691-0670

Will confirm attendance and degree by mail. Inquiry must include student's name, social security number. Employers may obtain transcripts upon written request accompanied by a signed release from the student. Inquiries should be directed to: Registrar's Office.

A two-year institution with an enrollment of 290. Highest level of offering: one year but less than four years.
ACCREDITATIONS: JRCB

Pacific Graduate School of Psychology

935 E. Meadow Dr.
Palo Alto, CA 94303
(415) 494-7477

Will confirm attendance and degree by phone or mail. Inquiry must include student's name, date of birth, social security number. Employers may obtain transcripts upon written request accompanied by a signed release from the student.

A specialized school, with an enrollment of 332. Highest level of offering: doctorate.
ACCREDITATIONS: WC

Pacific Lutheran Theological Seminary

2770 Marin Avenue
Berkeley, CA 94708
(510) 524-5264

Will confirm attendance and degree by phone or mail. Inquiry must include student's name, date of birth. Employers may obtain transcripts upon written request accompanied by a signed release from the student.

A school of philosophy, religion and theology, with an enrollment of 125. Highest level of offering: doctorate.
ACCREDITATIONS: THEOL

Pacific Lutheran University

Tacoma, WA 98447
(206) 535-7131
Fax (206) 535-8320

Will confirm attendance and degree by phone, fax or mail. Inquiry must include student's name, social security number. Employers may obtain transcripts upon written request accompanied by a signed release from the student.

A comprehensive institution with no medical school, with an enrollment of 3,694. Highest level of offering: master's.
ACCREDITATIONS: NW BUS MUS NUR SW TED BUSA

Pacific Northwest College of Art

1219 South West Park
Portland, OR 97205
(503) 226-4391

Will confirm attendance and degree by mail. Inquiry must include student's name. Employers may obtain transcripts upon written request accompanied by a $5.00 fee and a signed release from the student.

A visual and performing arts school, with an enrollment of 199. Highest level of offering: four or five year baccalaureate.
ACCREDITATIONS: NW ART

Pacific Oaks College

5 Westmoreland Place
Pasadena, CA 91103
(818) 397-1300
Fax (818) 397-1356

Will confirm attendance and degree by mail. Inquiry must include student's name, date of birth, social security number, years attended, release. Employers may obtain transcripts upon written request accompanied by a $5.00 fee and a signed release from the student.

A comprehensive institution with no medical school, with an enrollment of 500. Highest level of offering: master's.
ACCREDITATIONS: WC

Pacific School of Religion

1798 Scenic Avenue
Berkeley, CA 94709
(415) 848-0528
Fax (510) 845-8948

Will confirm attendance and degree by mail. Inquiry must include student's name, release. Requests should be directed to: Registrar. Only students may obtain transcripts.

A school of philosophy, religion and theology, with an enrollment of 200. Highest level of offering: doctorate.
ACCREDITATIONS: WC THEOL

Pacific Union College

Angwin, CA 94508
(707) 965-6673

Will confirm attendance and degree by phone or mail. Inquiry must include student's name, social security number, years attended. Employers may obtain transcripts upon written request accompanied by a $3.00 fee and a signed release from the student.

A general baccalaureate institution, with an enrollment of 1,403. Highest level of offering: master's.

ACCREDITATIONS: WC ADNUR MUS NUR SW

Pacific University

2043 College Way
Forest Grove, OR 97116
(503) 359-2234
Fax (503) 359-2242

Will confirm attendance and degree by phone, fax or mail. Inquiry must include student's name, date of birth, social security number. Requests should be directed to: Registrar's Office. Employers may obtain transcripts upon written request accompanied by a $2.00 fee and a signed release from the student.

A general baccalaureate institution, with an enrollment of 1,061. Highest level of offering: master's.

ACCREDITATIONS: NW MUS OPT PTA

Paier College of Art Incorporated

6 Prospect Court
Hamden, CT 06517
(203) 777-3851

Will confirm attendance and degree by phone or mail. Inquiry must include student's name, years attended. Employers may obtain transcripts upon written request accompanied by a $2.00 fee and a signed release from the student. Requests should be directed to: Registrar's Office.

A bachelor's or higher institution newly admitted to NCES, with an enrollment of 385. Highest level of offering: four or five year baccalaureate.

ACCREDITATIONS: NATTS

Paine College

1235 15th Street
Augusta, GA 30910-2799
(404) 722-4471 Ext. 323

Will confirm attendance and degree by phone or mail. Inquiry must include student's name, social security number. Employers may obtain transcripts upon written request by student accompanied by a $2.00 fee.

A general baccalaureate institution, with an enrollment of 752. Highest level of offering: four or five year baccalaureate.

ACCREDITATIONS: SC

Palm Beach Atlantic College

PO Box 24708
901 South Flagler Drive
West Palm Beach, FL 33416-4708
(407) 835-4347
Fax (407) 835-4342

Will confirm attendance and degree by mail. Inquiry must include student's name, social security number, release. Employers may obtain transcripts upon written request accompanied by a $2.00 fee and a signed release from the student.

A general baccalaureate institution, with an enrollment of 1,500. Highest level of offering: master's.

ACCREDITATIONS: SACS

Palm Beach Community College

4200 Congress Avenue
Lake Worth, FL 33461
(407) 439-8284
Fax (407) 439-8255

Will confirm attendance and degree by phone or mail. Inquiry must include student's name, social security number. Employers may obtain transcripts upon written request accompanied by a $3.00 fee and a signed release from the student.

A multiprogram two-year institution, with an enrollment of 16,500. Highest level of offering: one year but less than four years.

ACCREDITATIONS: SC DA DH DT

Palmer College of Chiropractic–West

1095 Dunford Way
Sunnyvale, CA 94087
(408) 983-4000
Fax (408) 983-4017

Will confirm attendance and degree by phone or mail. Inquiry must include student's name, date of birth, social security number. Employers may obtain transcripts upon written request accompanied by a $5.00 fee and a signed release from the student.

A bachelor's or higher institution newly admitted to NCES, with an enrollment of 656. Highest level of offering: first professional degree.

ACCREDITATIONS: CHIRO

Palmer College of Chiropractic

1000 Brady Street
Davenport, IA 52803
(319) 326-9862
Fax (319) 326-9897

Will confirm attendance and degree by phone or mail. Inquiry must include student's name, social security number. Employers may obtain transcripts upon written request accompanied by a $3.00 fee and a signed release from the student.

A health institution, with an enrollment of 1,816. Highest level of offering: first professional degree.

ACCREDITATIONS: NCA CHIRO

Palo Verde College

811 West Chanslorway
Blythe, CA 92225
(619) 922-6168

Will confirm attendance and degree by mail. Inquiry must include student's name, date of birth, years attended, release. Employers may obtain transcripts upon written request accompanied by a $2.00 fee and a signed release from the student.

A multiprogram two-year institution, with an enrollment of 1,250. Highest level of offering: one year but less than four years.

ACCREDITATIONS: WJ

Palomar College

1140 West Mission
San Marcos, CA 92069
(619) 744-1150 Ext. 2169
Fax (619) 744-8123

Will confirm attendance and degree by phone, fax or mail. Inquiry must include student's name, social security number. Employers may obtain transcripts upon written request accompanied by a $3.00 fee and a signed release from the student.

A multiprogram two-year institution, with an enrollment of 24,027. Highest level of offering: one year but less than four years.

ACCREDITATIONS: WJ ADNUR DA

Pamlico Community College

PO Box 185
Grantsboro, NC 28529
(919) 249-1851

Will confirm attendance and degree by phone or mail. Inquiry must include student's name, social security number. Employers may obtain transcripts upon written request accompanied by a signed release from the student. Requests should be directed to: Student Development Services.

A multiprogram two-year institution, with an enrollment of 134. Highest level of offering: one year but less than four years.

ACCREDITATIONS: SC

Pan American University

1201 West University Dr
Edinburg, TX 78539
(512) 381-2206
Fax (512) 381-2212

Will confirm attendance and degree by phone, fax or mail. Inquiry must include student's name, social security number. Employers may obtain transcripts upon written request accompanied by a $2.00 fee and a signed release from the student. Requests should be directed to: Admission Office.

A comprehensive institution with no medical school, with an enrollment of 11,843. Highest level of offering: master's.

ACCREDITATIONS: SC ADNUR BUS MT SW TED NUR

Panola Junior College

West Panola Street
Carthage, TX 75633
(214) 693-2038
Fax (214) 693-2018

Will confirm attendance and degree by phone, fax or mail. Inquiry must include student's name, social security number. Employers may obtain transcripts upon written request accompanied by a $2.00 fee and a signed release from the student.

A multiprogram two-year institution, with an enrollment of 1,600. Highest level of offering: one year but less than four years.

ACCREDITATIONS: SC

Paris Junior College

2400 Clarksville Street
Paris, TX 75460
(903) 784-9212

Will confirm attendance and degree by phone or mail. Inquiry must include student's name, social security number, years attended. Employers may obtain transcripts upon written request accompanied by a $2.00 fee and a signed release from the student.

A multiprogram two-year institution, with an enrollment of 2,400. Highest level of offering: one year but less than four years.
ACCREDITATIONS: SC ADNUR

Park College

Mackay Hall
Parkville, MO 64152
(816) 741-2000 Ext. 271

Will confirm attendance and degree by phone or mail. Inquiry must include student's name, social security number, years attended. Employers may obtain transcripts upon written request accompanied by a $4.00 fee and a signed release from the student.

A general baccalaureate institution, with an enrollment of 3,272. Highest level of offering: master's.
ACCREDITATIONS: NH

Parker College of Chiropractic

2500 Walnut Hill Lane
Dallas, TX 75229
(214) 438-6932
Fax (214) 357-3107

Will confirm attendance and degree by phone, fax or mail. Inquiry must include student's name, social security number. Employers may obtain transcripts upon written request accompanied by a $5.00 fee and signed release from the student. Requests should be directed to: Registrar's Office.

A bachelor's or higher institution newly admitted to NCES, with an enrollment of 600. Highest level of offering: first professional degree.
ACCREDITATIONS: CHIRO

Parkersburg Community College

(See West Virginia University at Parkersburg)

Parkland College

PO Box 3278
Champaign, IL 61826
(217) 351-2208

Will confirm attendance and degree by phone or mail. Inquiry must include student's name, social security number, release. Requests should be directed to: Admissions Office. Employers may obtain transcripts upon written request accompanied by a $2.00 fee and a signed release from the student.

A multiprogram two-year institution, with an enrollment of 8,483. Highest level of offering: one year but less than four years.
ACCREDITATIONS: NH ADNUR ADVET DA DH ENGT PNUR RAD RSTH SURGT

Parks College of Saint Louis University

500 Falling Springs Road
Cahokia, IL 62206
(618) 337-7500 Ext. 225
Fax (618) 332-6802

Will confirm attendance and degree by phone, fax or mail. Inquiry must include student's name, social security number. Employers may obtain transcripts upon written request accompanied by a signed release from the student.

A business school, with an enrollment of 1,112. Highest level of offering: four or five year baccalaureate.
ACCREDITATIONS: NH ENG

Parks Junior College

9065 Grant Street
Denver, CO 80229
(303) 457-2757
Fax (303) 457-4030

Will confirm attendance and degree by mail or fax. Inquiry must include student's name, social security number, years attended, release. Employers may obtain transcripts upon written request accompanied by a $2.00 fee and a signed release from the student. Direct inquiries to Financial Aid Office.

A single program two-year institution, with an enrollment of 425. Highest level of offering: one year but less than four years.
ACCREDITATIONS: NH MAC SRCB

Parsons School of Design

66 West 12th Street
New York, NY 10011
(212) 229-5720

Will confirm attendance and degree by phone or mail. Inquiry must include student's name, social security number, years attended. Employers may obtain transcripts upon written request accompanied by a $4.00 fee and a signed release from the student. Direct inquiries to University Records Office, 65 Fifth Ave., New York, NY 10003.

A visual and performing arts school, with and enrollment of 6,100. Highest level of offering: master's.

Pasadena City College

1570 East Colorado Boulevard
Pasadena, CA 91106
(818) 585-7175

Will confirm attendance and degree by phone or by mail prior to 1976. Inquiry must include student's name, date of birth, social security number, years attended, release. Employers may obtain transcripts upon written request accompanied by a $2.00 fee and a signed release from the student. Requests should be directed to: Admissions & Records Office.

A multiprogram two-year institution, with an enrollment of 20,000. Highest level of offering: two years.
ACCREDITATIONS: WJ

Pasadena College of Chiropractic

8420 Beverly Road
Pico Rivera, CA 90660
(213) 692-0331 Ext. 23

Will confirm attendance and degree by phone or mail. Inquiry must include student's name, date of birth, social security number. Employers may obtain transcripts upon written request accompanied by a $10.00 fee and a signed release from the student.

A health institution, with an enrollment of 150. Highest level of offering: first professional degree.
ACCREDITATIONS: CHIRO

Pasco–Hernando Community College East Campus

2401 County Road 41
Dade City, FL 33525-7599
(904) 567-6701 Ext. 1011
Fax (904) 567-6701 Ext. 1252

Will confirm attendance and degree by phone, fax or mail. Inquiry must include student's name, social security number. Employers may obtain transcripts upon written request accompanied by a signed release from the student. Requests should be directed to: Records Office.

A multiprogram two-year institution, with an enrollment of 5,663. Highest level of offering: one year but less than four years.
ACCREDITATIONS: SC

Passaic County Community College

College Boulevard
Paterson, NJ 07509
(201) 684-6400
Fax (201) 684-6778

Will confirm attendance and degree by fax or mail. Inquiry must include student's name, social security number. Requests should be directed to: Registrar's Office. Employers may obtain transcripts upon written request accompanied by a $2.00 fee and a signed release from the student.

A multiprogram two-year institution, with an enrollment of 3,550. Highest level of offering: one year but less than four years.
ACCREDITATIONS: M ADNUR RAD RSTHT

Patrick Henry Community College

(See Albama Southern Community College)

Patrick Henry State Junior College

PO Box 2000
Monroeville, AL 36460
(205) 575-3156 Ext. 252

Will confirm attendance and degree by phone or mail. Inquiry must include student's name, social security number. Employers may obtain transcripts upon written request accompanied by a signed release from the student.

A multiprogram two-year institution, with an enrollment of 1,153. Highest level of offering: one year but less than four years.
ACCREDITATIONS: SC

Patten College

2433 Coolidge Avenue
Oakland, CA 94601
(510) 533-8300
Fax (510) 534-8564

Will confirm attendance and degree by phone or mail. Inquiry must include student's name, years attended. Employers may obtain transcripts upon written request accompanied by a $5.00 fee and a signed release from the student.

A school of philosophy, religion and theology, with an enrollment of 360. Highest level of offering: four or five year baccalaureate.
ACCREDITATIONS: WC

Paul D. Camp Community College

PO Box 737–College Drive
Franklin, VA 23851
(804) 562-2171 Ext. 225
Fax (804) 562-7430

Will confirm attendance and degree by phone, fax or mail. Inquiry must include student's name, social security number. Employers may obtain transcripts upon written request accompanied by a signed release from the student. Requests should be directed to: Admissions Office.

A multiprogram two-year institution, with an enrollment of 1,154. Highest level of offering: one year but less than four years.
ACCREDITATIONS: SC

Paul Quinn College

(Formerly Bishop College)
3837 Simpson-Stuart Road
PO Box 411238
Dallas, TX 75241
(214) 371-1311

Will confirm attendance and degree by phone or mail. Inquiry must include student's name, social security number, years attended. Employers may obtain transcripts upon written request accompanied by a $5.00 fee and a signed release from the student.

A general baccalaureate institution, with an enrollment of 935. Highest level of offering: four or five year baccalaureate.
ACCREDITATIONS: SC

Paul Smith's College of Arts and Sciences

Paul Smiths, NY 12970
(518) 327-6231

Will confirm attendance and degree by phone or mail. Inquiry must include student's name, social security number, years attended. Employers may obtain transcripts upon written request accompanied by a $2.00 fee and a signed release from the student. Requests should be directed to: Registrar's Office.

A multiprogram two-year institution, with an enrollment of 891. Highest level of offering: one year but less than four years.
ACCREDITATIONS: M NY

Peabody Institute of Johns Hopkins University

1 East Mount Vernon Place
Baltimore, MD 21202-2397
(301) 659-8266
Fax (301) 659-8168

Will confirm attendance and degree by phone, fax or mail. Inquiry must include student's name, social security number, years attended. Employers may obtain transcripts upon written request accompanied by a $3.00 fee and a signed release from the student.

A visual and performing arts school, with an enrollment of 429. Highest level of offering: doctorate.
ACCREDITATIONS: M MUS

Peace College

15 East Peace Street
Raleigh, NC 27604
(919) 832-2881 Ext. 250
Fax (919) 834-6755

Will confirm attendance and degree by phone, fax or mail. Inquiry must include student's name, social security number, years attended. Employers may obtain transcripts upon written request accompanied by a $2.00 fee and a signed release from the student. Requests should be directed to: Registrar's Office.

A multiprogram two-year institution, with an enrollment of 464. Highest level of offering: one year but less than four years.
ACCREDITATIONS: SC

Pearl River Community College

Station–A
Poplarville, MS 39470
(601) 795-6801 Ext. 215

Will confirm attendance and degree by mail. Inquiry must include student's name, social security number, years attended. Requests should be directed to: Admissions & Records. Employers may obtain transcripts upon written request accompanied by a $1.00 fee and a signed release from the student.

A multiprogram two-year institution, with an enrollment of 2,100. Highest level of offering: one year but less than four years.
ACCREDITATIONS: SC RSTHT

Peirce Junior College

1420 Pine Street
Philadelphia, PA 19102
(215) 545-6400 Ext. 257

Will confirm attendance and degree by phone or mail. Inquiry must include student's name, date of birth, social security number. Employers may obtain transcripts upon written request accompanied by a $2.00 fee and a signed release from the student.

A multiprogram two-year institution, with an enrollment of 1,642. Highest level of offering: one year but less than four years.
ACCREDITATIONS: M

Pembroke State University

College Street
Pembroke, NC 28372
(919) 521-4214

Will confirm attendance and degree by phone or mail. Inquiry must include student's name, years attended. Employers may obtain transcripts upon written request accompanied by a $2.00 fee and a signed release from the student. Requests should be directed to: Registrar's Office.

A general baccalaureate institution, with an enrollment of 2,942. Highest level of offering: master's.
ACCREDITATIONS: SACS CSWE

Peninsula College

1502 E. Lauridsen Blvd.
Port Angeles, WA 98362
(206) 452-9277
Fax (206) 457-8100

Will confirm attendance and degree by phone, fax or mail. Inquiry must include student's name, social security number. Employers may obtain transcripts upon written request accompanied by a $1.00 fee and a signed release from the student.

A multiprogram two-year institution, with an enrollment of 2,800. Highest level of offering: one year but less than four years.
ACCREDITATIONS: NW

Penn Technical Institute

110 Ninth Street
Pittsburgh, PA 15222
(412) 355-0455

Will confirm attendance and degree by phone or mail. Inquiry must include student's name, social security number, and release. Employers may obtain transcripts upon written request accompanied by a signed release from the student.

A single program two-year institution, with an enrollment of 200. Highest level of offering: 21 mpnths.
ACCREDITATIONS: NATTS

Penn Valley Community College

3201 Southwest Trafficway
Kansas City, MO 64111
(816) 932-7610
Fax (816) 531-3374

Will confirm attendance and degree by phone, fax or mail. Inquiry must include student's name, social security number. Employers may obtain transcripts upon written request accompanied by a $2.00 fee and a signed release from the student. Requests should be directed to: Admissions Office.

A multiprogram two-year institution, with an enrollment of 5,500. Highest level of offering: one year but less than four years.
ACCREDITATIONS: NH ADNUR DA MLTAD PTAA RAD

Pennco Tech

3815 Otter Street
Bristol, PA 19007
(215) 824-3200

Will confirm attendance and degree by mail. Inquiry must include student's name, social security number, years attended, release. Employers may obtain transcripts upon written request accompanied by a $5.00 fee and a signed release from the student.

A single program two-year institution, with an enrollment of 700. Highest level of offering: one year but less than four years.
ACCREDITATIONS: NATTS

Pennsylvania College of Optometry

1200 West Godfrey Avenue
Philadelphia, PA 19141
(215) 276-6260
Fax (215) 276-6081

Will confirm attendance and degree by mail or fax. Inquiry must include student's name, years attended. Employers may obtain transcripts upon written request accompanied by a $2.00 fee and a signed release from the student.

A general baccalaureate institution, with an enrollment of 623. Highest level of offering: first professional degree.
ACCREDITATIONS: M OPT OPTR

Pennsylvania College of Podiatric Medicine

8th And Race Streets
Philadelphia, PA 19107
(215) 629-0300 Ext. 283
Fax (215) 629-1622

Will confirm attendance and degree by phone, fax or mail. Inquiry must include student's name, years attended, year graduated, release. Employers may obtain transcripts upon written release accompanied by a $5.00 fee and a signed release from the student.

A health institution, with an enrollment of 400. Highest level of offering: first professional degree.
ACCREDITATIONS: POD

Pennsylvania College of Straight Chiropractic

200 Tournament Drive, Suite 100
Hershman, PA 19044
(215) 957-6080

Will confirm attendance and degree by mail. Inquiry must include student's name, social security number, release. Requests should be directed to: Registrar's Office. Employers may obtain transcripts upon written request accompanied by a $10.00 fee and a signed release from the student.

A bachelor's or higher institution newly admitted to NCES, with an enrollment of 125. Highest level of offering: first professional degree.
ACCREDITATIONS: 3IC

Pennsylvania College of Technology

(Formerly Williamsport Area Community College)
1 College Ave.
Williamsport, PA 17701
(717) 326-3761
Fax (717) 327-4503

Will confirm attendance and degree by mail. Inquiry must include student's name, social security number. Requests should be directed to: Records Dept. Employers may obtain transcripts upon written request accompanied by a $1.00 fee and a signed release from the student.

A multi-program institution, with an enrollment of 4,156. Highest level of offering: first professional degree.
ACCREDITATIONS: M DH RAD ENGT

Pennsylvania Institute of Technology

800 Manchester Avenue
Media, PA 19063-4098
(215) 565-7900 Ext. 113

Will confirm attendance and degree by phone or mail. Inquiry must include student's name, social security number. Employers may obtain transcripts upon written request accompanied by a signed release from the student.

A single program two-year institution, with an enrollment of 399. Highest level of offering: one year but less than four years.
ACCREDITATIONS: M NATTS

Pennsylvania State University Allentown Campus

Registrar, Room 158
Academic Building
8400 Mohr Lane
Fogelsville, PA 18051-9999
(215) 285-5057
Fax (215) 285-5220

Will confirm attendance and degree by mail or fax. Inquiry must include student's name, social security number. Employers may obtain transcripts upon written request accompanied by a $4.00 fee and a signed release from the student. Transcript requests should be directed to: Pennsylvania State University-Main Campus, 112 Shields Bldg., University Park, PA 16802. Attn: Transcript Department.

A multiprogram two-year institution, with an enrollment of 783. Highest level of offering: one year but less than four years.
ACCREDITATIONS: M

Pennsylvania State University Altoona Campus

Smith Building
Altoona, PA 16603
(814) 949-5035

Will confirm attendance and degree by phone or mail. Inquiry must include student's name, social security number. Employers may obtain transcripts upon written request accompanied by a $4.00 fee and a signed release from the student. Transcript requests should be directed to: Pennsylvania State University-Main Campus, 112 Shields Bldg., University Park, PA 16802. Attn: Transcript Department.

A multiprogram two-year institution, with an enrollment of 2,500. Highest level of offering: two years.
ACCREDITATIONS: M ENGT

Pennsylvania State University Beaver Campus

Brodhead Road
Monaca, PA 15061
(412) 773-3785

Will confirm attendance and degree by phone or mail. Inquiry must include student's name, social security number. Employers may obtain transcripts upon written request accompanied by a $4.00 fee and a signed release from the student. Transcript requests should be directed to: Pennsylvania State University, 112 Shields Bldg., University Park, PA 16802. Attn: Transcript Department.

A multiprogram two-year institution, with an enrollment of 1,060. Highest level of offering: one year but less than four years.
ACCREDITATIONS: M ENGT

Pennsylvania State University at Erie Behrend College

Station Road
Erie, PA 16563
(814) 898-6000

Will confirm attendance by mail. For confirming degree contact University Registrar; 114 Shields Bldg.; University Park, PA 16802. Inquiry must include student's name, social security number. Employers may obtain transcripts upon written request accompanied by a $4.00 fee and a signed release from the student. Transcript requests should be directed to: Pennsylvania State University-Main Campus, 112 Shields Bldg., University Park, PA 16802. Attn: Transcript Department.

A general baccalaureate institution, with an enrollment of 2,893. Highest level of offering: master's.
ACCREDITATIONS: M ENGT

Pennsylvania State University Berks Campus

PO Box 7009
Tulpehocken Road
Reading, PA 19610-6009
(215) 320-4897

Will confirm attendance and degree by mail or phone. Inquiry must include student's name, social security number. Employers may obtain transcripts upon written request accompanied by a $4.00 fee and a signed release from the student. Transcript requests should be directed to: Pennsylvania State University-Main Campus, 112 Shields Bldg., University Park, PA 16802. Attn: Transcript Department.

A multiprogram two-year institution, with an enrollment of 1,600. Highest level of offering: one year but less than four years.

ACCREDITATIONS: M ENGT

Pennsylvania State University Harrisburg

777 West Harrisburg Pike
Middletown, PA 17057-4898
(717) 948-6020
Fax (717) 948-6008

Will confirm attendance and degree by phone, fax or mail. Inquiry must include student's name, social security number. Employers may obtain transcripts upon written request accompanied by a $4.00 fee and a signed release from the student. Transcript requests should be directed to: Pennsylvania State University-Main Campus, 112 Shields Bldg., University Park, PA 16802. Attn: Transcript Department.

A comprehensive institution with no medical school, with an enrollment of 3,276. Highest level of offering: doctorate.

ACCREDITATIONS: M ENGT

Pennsylvania State University Delaware Campus

25 Yearsley Mill Road
Media, PA 19063
(215) 892-1400

Will confirm attendance and degree by mail. Inquiry must include student's name, social security number. Employers may obtain transcripts upon written request accompanied by a $4.00 fee and a signed release from the student. Transcript requests should be directed to: Pennsylvania State University-Main Campus, 112 Shields Bldg., University Park, PA 16802. Attn: Transcript Department.

A multiprogram institution, with an enrollment of 1,975. Highest level of offering: baccalaureate.

ACCREDITATIONS: M ENGT

Pennsylvania State University Du Bois Campus

College Place
Du Bois, PA 15801
(814) 375-4700

Will confirm by mail or phone. Inquiry must include student's name, social security number, years attended. Employers may obtain transcripts upon written request accompanied by a $4.00 fee and a signed release from the student. Transcript requests should be directed to: Pennsylvania State University-Main Campus, 112 Shields Bldg., University Park, PA 16802. Attn: Transcript Department.

A multiprogram two-year institution, with an enrollment of 936. Highest level of offering: one year but less than four years.

ACCREDITATIONS: M ENGT

Pennsylvania State University Fayette Campus

PO Box 519 Route 119 North
Uniontown, PA 15401
(412) 430-4100

Will confirm by mail. Inquiry must include student's name, social security number, date of last attendance. Employers may obtain transcripts upon written request accompanied by a $4.00 fee and a signed release from the student. Transcript requests should be directed to: Pennsylvania State University-Main Campus, 112 Shields Bldg., University Park, PA 16802. Attn: Transcript Department.

A multiprogram two-year institution, with an enrollment of 939. Highest level of offering: one year but less than four years.

ACCREDITATIONS: M ENGT

Pennsylvania State University Hazleton Campus

Highacres
Hazleton, PA 18201
(717) 450-3185

Will confirm attendance and degree by mail. Inquiry must include student's name, date of birth, social security number, release. Employers may obtain transcripts upon written request accompanied by a $4.00 fee and a signed release from the student. Transcript requests should be directed to: Pennsylvania State University-Main Campus, 112 Shields Bldg., University Park, PA 16802. Attn: Transcript Department.

A multiprogram two-year institution, with an enrollment of 1,262. Highest level of offering: one year but less than four years.

ACCREDITATIONS: M ENGT MLTAD PTAA

Pennsylvania State University Main Campus

112 Shields Bldg.
University Park, PA 16802-1271
(814) 863-1923

Will confirm attendance and degree by mail. Inquiry must include student's name, social security number. Employers may obtain transcripts upon written request accompanied by a $4.00 fee and a signed release from the student. Requests should be directed to: Transcript Department.

A doctoral-level institution with no medical school, with an enrollment of 37,623. Highest level of offering: doctorate.

ACCREDITATIONS: M APCP ARCH ART AUD BUS CLPSY COPSY ENG FOR BUSA HSA IPSY TED JOUR LSAR MUS NUR SCPSY SP SW

Pennsylvania State University McKeesport Campus

University Drive
McKeesport, PA 15132
(412) 675-9170
Fax (814) 863-1923

Will confirm attendance and degree by phone or mail. Inquiry must include student's name, social security number. Employers may obtain transcripts upon written request accompanied by a $4.00 fee and a signed release from the student. Transcript requests should be directed to: Pennsylvania State University-Main Campus, 112 Shields Bldg., University Park, PA 16802. Attn: Transcript Department.

A multiprogram two-year institution, with an enrollment of 1,380. Highest level of offering: one year but less than four years.

ACCREDITATIONS: M ENGT

Pennsylvania State University Milton S. Hershey Medical Center

PO Box 850
Hershey, PA 17033
(717) 531-8755

Will confirm attendance and degree by phone or mail. Inquiry must include student's name, social security number. Employers may obtain transcripts upon written request by student accompanied by a $4.00 fee and a signed release from the student. Requests should be directed to: Sudent Affairs.

A medical school, with an enrollment of 451. Highest level of offering: doctorate.

ACCREDITATIONS: M MED RAD PAST PERF

Pennsylvania State University Mont Alto Campus

Campus Drive
Mont Alto, PA 17237
(717) 749-3111

Will confirm attendance and degree by mail. Inquiry must include student's name, social security number. Employers may obtain transcripts upon written request accompanied by a $4.00 fee and a signed release from the student. Transcript requests should be directed to: Pennsylvania State University-Main Campus, 112 Shields Bldg., University Park, PA 16802. Attn: Transcript Department.

A multiprogram two-year institution, with an enrollment of 942. Highest level of offering: one year but less than four years.
ACCREDITATIONS: M ENGT

Pennsylvania State University New Kensington Campus

3550 7th Street Road
New Kensington, PA 15068
(412) 339-5466
Fax (412) 339-5434

Will confirm attendance and degree by mail or fax. Inquiry must include student's name, social security number. Employers may obtain transcripts upon written request accompanied by a $4.00 fee and a signed release from the student. Transcript requests should be directed to: Pennsylvania State University, 112 Shields Bldg., University Park, PA 16802. Attn: Transcript Department.

A multiprogram two-year institution, with an enrollment of 1,492. Highest level of offering: one year but less than four years.
ACCREDITATIONS: M ENGT MLTAD RAD

Pennsylvania State University Ogontz Campus

1600 Woodland Road
Abington, PA 19001
(215) 886-9400

Will confirm attendance and degree by mail. Inquiry must include student's name, social security number. Employers may obtain transcripts upon written request accompanied by a $4.00 fee and a signed release from the student. Transcript requests should be directed to: Pennsylvania State University, 112 Shields Bldg., University Park, PA 16802-1271. Attn: Transcript Department.

A multiprogram two-year institution, with an enrollment of 3,330. Highest level of offering: one year but less than four years.
ACCREDITATIONS: M ENGT

Pennsylvania State University Schuylkill Campus

PO Box 308 State Highway
Schuylkill Haven, PA 17972
(717) 385-6125
Fax (717) 385-3672

Will confirm attendance and degree by phone, fax or mail. Inquiry must include student's name, social security number. Employers may obtain transcripts upon written request accompanied by a $4.00 fee and a signed release from the student. Transcript requests should be directed to: Pennsylvania State University-Main Campus, 112 Shields Bldg., University Park, PA 16802. Attn: Transcript Department.

A multiprogram two-year institution, with an enrollment of 1,230. Highest level of offering: one year but less than four years.
ACCREDITATIONS: M ENGT

Pennsylvania State University Shenango Valley Campus

147 Shenango Road
Sharon, PA 16146
(412) 983-5860

Will confirm attendance and degree by phone or mail. Inquiry must include student's name, social security number. Employers may obtain transcripts upon written request accompanied by a $4.00 fee and a signed release from the student. Transcript requests should be directed to: Pennsylvania State University-Main Campus, 112 Shields Bldg., University Park, PA 16802. Attn: Transcript Department.

A multiprogram two-year institution, with an enrollment of 1,196. Highest level of offering: one year but less than four years.
ACCREDITATIONS: M ENGT

Pennsylvania State University Wilkes–Barre Campus

PO Box PSU
Lehman, PA 18627
(717) 675-2171

Will confirm attendance and degree by mail. Inquiry must include student's name, social security number, release. Employers may obtain transcripts upon written request accompanied by a $3.00 fee and a signed release from the student. Transcript requests should be directed to: Pennsylvania State University-Main Campus, 112 Shields Bldg., University Park, PA 16802. Attn: Transcript Department.

A multiprogram two-year institution, with an enrollment of 948. Highest level of offering: one year but less than four years.
ACCREDITATIONS: M ENGT

Pennsylvania State University Worthington Scranton Campus

120 Ridge View Drive
Dunmore, PA 18512
(717) 963-4757

Will confirm by mail. Inquiry must include student's name, social security number. Employers may obtain transcripts upon written request accompanied by a $4.00 fee and a signed release from the student. Transcript requests should be directed to: Pennsylvania State University-Main Campus, 112 Shields Bldg., University Park, PA 16802. Attn: Transcript Department.

A multiprogram two-year institution, with an enrollment of 1,295. Highest level of offering: one year but less than four years.
ACCREDITATIONS: M ENGT

Pennsylvania State University York Campus

1031 Edgecomb Avenue
York, PA 17403
(717) 771-4057
Fax (717) 771-4062

Will confirm attendance and degree by phone, fax or mail. Inquiry must include student's name, social security number, years attended. Employers may obtain transcripts upon written request accompanied by a $4.00 fee and a signed release from the student. Transcript requests should be directed to: Pennsylvania State University-Main Campus, 112 Shields Bldg., University Park, PA 16802. Attn: Transcript Department.

A multiprogram two-year institution, with an enrollment of 1,946. Highest level of offering: one year but less than four years.
ACCREDITATIONS: M ENGT

Pennsylvania University College of Medicine

PO Box 850
Hershey, PA 17033
(717) 531-8755

Will confirm attendance and degree by phone or mail. Inquiry must include student's name, social security number. Employers may obtain transcripts upon written request accompanied by a $4.00 fee and a signed release from the student. Requests should be directed to: Student Services.

A medical school, with an enrollment of 346. Highest level of offering: doctorate
ACCREDITATIONS: M MED RAD PAST PERF

Pensacola Junior College

1000 College Boulevard
Pensacola, FL 32504
(904) 484-1611

Will confirm attendance and degree by phone or mail. Inquiry must include student's name, maiden name, social security number, years attended. Employers may obtain transcripts upon written request accompanied by a signed release from the student. Requests should be directed to: Registrar's Office.

A multiprogram two-year institution, with an enrollment of 7,653. Highest level of offering: one year but less than four years.
ACCREDITATIONS: SC DA DH DT RSTHT

Pepperdine University
24255 Pacific Coast Highway
Malibu, CA 90265
(310) 456-4542
Fax (310) 456-4358

Will confirm attendance and degree by phone or mail. Inquiry must include student's name, date of birth, social security number, years attended. Employers may obtain transcripts upon written request accompanied by a $4.00 fee and a signed release from the student.

A comprehensive institution with no medical school, with an enrollment of 6,836. Highest level of offering: doctorate.
ACCREDITATIONS: WC LAW MUS

Peralta Community Colleges System Office
333 East Eighth Street
Oakland, CA 94606
(510) 466-7200

Will confirm attendance and degree by mail. Inquiry must include student's name, date of birth, social security number, years attended, release. Employers may obtain transcripts upon written request accompanied by a $1.00 fee and a signed release from the student. Requests should be directed to: Admissions & Records Office.

Peru State College
Route Rte, Box 10
Peru, NE 68421
(402) 872-3815 Ext. 226

Will confirm attendance and degree by phone or mail. Inquiry must include student's name, social security number. Requests should be directed to: Registrar's Office. Employers may obtain transcripts upon written request accompanied by a $3.00 fee and a signed release from the student.

A general baccalaureate institution, with an enrollment of 1,650. Highest level of offering: master's.
ACCREDITATIONS: NH TED

Pfeiffer College
Highway 52 North
Misenheimer, NC 28109
(704) 463-7343 Ext. 2057

Will confirm attendance and degree by phone or mail. Inquiry must include student's name, date of birth, social security number, years attended. Employers may obtain transcripts upon written request accompanied by a $2.00 fee and a signed release from the student.

A general baccalaureate institution, with an enrollment of 954. Highest level of offering: master's.
ACCREDITATIONS: SC MUS

Philadelphia College of Art
(See The University of the Arts)

Philadelphia College of Osteopathic Medicine
4150 City Line Avenue
Philadelphia, PA 19131
(215) 871-1000

Will confirm attendance and degree by phone or mail. Inquiry must include student's name, social security number, year graduated. Requests should be directed to: Admissions Office and Registrar. Employers may obtain transcripts upon written request by student.

A medical school, with an enrollment of 833. Highest level of offering: first professional degree.
ACCREDITATIONS: M AHE EEG OSTEO

Philadelphia College of Pharmacy and Science
600 South Forty-Third Street
Philadelphia, PA 19104-4495
(215) 596-8813
Fax (215) 895-1100

Will confirm attendance and degree by phone or mail. Inquiry must include student's name, social security number. Employers may obtain transcripts upon written request accompanied by a $2.00 fee and a signed release from the student. Requests should be directed to: Registrar's Office.

A health institution, with an enrollment of 1,545. Highest level of offering: doctorate.
ACCREDITATIONS: M PHAR PTA ACS

Philadelphia College of Textiles and Science
4201 Henry Avenue
Philadelphia, PA 19144
(215) 951-2700

Will confirm attendance and degree by mail. Inquiry must include student's name, social security number, years attended, release. Employers may obtain transcripts upon written request accompanied by a signed release from the student. Requests should be directed to: Registrar's Office.

A business school, with an enrollment of 2,776. Highest level of offering: master's.
ACCREDITATIONS: M

Philadelphia College of the Bible
Langhorne Manor
Langhorne, PA 19047
(215) 752-5800 Ext. 245
Fax (215) 752-5812

Will confirm attendance and degree by phone or mail. Inquiry must include student's name, years attended. Employers may obtain transcripts upon written request accompanied by a $2.00 fee and a signed release from the student. Requests should be directed to: Records Office.

A school of philosophy, religion and theology, with an enrollment of 622. Highest level of offering: four or five year baccalaureate.
ACCREDITATIONS: M BI MUS SW

Philadelphia College of the Performing Arts
320 S. Broad Street
Philadelphia, PA 19102
(215) 875-4800

Will confirm attendance and degree by phone or mail. Inquiry must include student's name, social security number, date of birth. Employers may obtain transcripts upon written request accompanied by a $5.00 fee and a signed release from the student. Requests should be directed to: Registrar's Office.

A visual and performing arts school, with an enrollment of 414. Highest level of offering: master's.
ACCREDITATIONS: M MUS

Philander Smith College
812 West 13th
Little Rock, AR 72202
(501) 375-9845

Will confirm attendance and degree by phone or mail. Inquiry must include student's name, date of birth, social security number, years attended, release. Requests should be directed to: Registrar's Office. Employers may obtain transcripts upon written request accompanied by a $2.00 fee and a signed release from the student.

A general baccalaureate institution, with an enrollment of 761. Highest level of offering: four or five year baccalaureate.
ACCREDITATIONS: NH

Phillips Beth Israel School of Nursing
310 East 22nd Street
New York, NY 10010
(212) 614-6108
Fax (212) 614-6109

Will confirm attendance and degree by phone or mail. Inquiry must include student's name, social security number, years attended. Employers may obtain transcripts upon written request accompanied by a $5.00 fee and a signed release from the student.

A two-year institution with an enrollment of 184. Highest level of offering: two years but less than four years.
ACCREDITATIONS: NY

Phillips College of Jackson
2680 Insurance Center Drive
Jackson, MS 39216
(601) 362-6341

Will confirm attendance and degree by mail. Inquiry must include student's name, social security number, years attended, release. Employers may obtain transcripts upon written request accompanied by a $2.00 fee and a signed release from the student. Requests should be directed to: Academic Affairs.

A multiprogram two-year institution, with an enrollment of 633. Highest level of offering: one year but less than four years

Phillips County Community College

Box 785
Helena, AR 72342
(501) 338-6474 Ext. 236
Fax (501) 338-7542

Will confirm attendance and degree by phone, fax or mail. Inquiry must include student's name, maiden name, date of birth, years attended. Employers may obtain transcripts upon written request accompanied by a $1.00 fee and a signed release from the student. Requests should be directed to: Registrar's Office.

A multiprogram two-year institution, with an enrollment of 1,712. Highest level of offering: two years but less than four years.
ACCREDITATIONS: NH MLTAD

Phillips Junior College–Charleston

(Formerly Rutledge College Charleston)
c/o Phillips Colleges, Inc.
One Hancock Plaza, Suite 1408
Gulfport, MS 39501
(601) 864-6096

Records are held at the above location. Will confirm attendance and degree by phone or mail. Inquiry must include student's name, social security number. Employers may obtain transcripts upon written request by student accompanied by a $2.00 fee and a signed release from the student.

Phillips Junior College–Condie Campus

(Formerly Condie Junior College)
One West Campbell Avenue
Campbell, CA 95008
(408) 866-6666, Ext. 20

Will confirm attendance and degree by phone or mail. Inquiry must include student's name, social security number. Requests should be directed to: Academic Office. Employers may obtain transcripts upon written request accompanied by a $3.00 fee and a signed release from the student.

A two-year institution with an enrollment of 784. Highest level of offering: one year but less than four years.
ACCREDITATIONS: JRCB

Phillips Junior College–Greenville

(Formerly Rutledge College Greenville)
c/o Phillips Colleges, Inc.
One Hancock Plaza, Suite 1408
Gulfport, MS 39501
(601) 864-6096

Records are held at the above location. Will confirm attendance and degree by mail. Inquiry must include student's name, social security number, years attended, release. Employers may obtain transcripts upon written request accompanied by a $2.00 fee and a signed release from the student.

Phillips Junior College–Raleigh

(Formerly Rutledge College Raleigh)
c/o Phillips Colleges, Inc.
One Hancock Plaza, Suite 1408
Gulfport, MS 39501
(601) 864-6096

Records are held at the above location. Will confirm attendance and degree by phone or mail. Inquiry must include student's name, date of birth, social security number, years attended. Employers may obtain transcripts upon written request accompanied by a $2.00 fee and a signed release from the student.

Phillips Junior College–Spartanburg

(Formerly Rutledge College Spartanburg)
325 South Church Street
Spartanburg, SC 29301
(803) 585-3446

Will confirm attendance and degree by mail. Inquiry must include student's name, social security number, release. Employers may obtain transcripts upon written request accompanied by a $2.00 fee and a signed release from the student.

Phillips Junior College of Augusta

c/o Phillips Colleges, Inc.
One Hancock Plaza, Suite 1408
Gulfport, MS 39501
(601) 864-6096

Records are held at the above location. Will confirm attendance and degree by phone, fax or mail. Inquiry must include student's name, social security number, years attended. Employers may obtain transcripts upon written request accompanied by a $2.00 fee and a signed release from the student.

Phillips Junior College of Business

2401 North Harbor City Boulevard
Melbourne, FL 32935
(407) 254-6459 Ext. 20

Will confirm attendance and degree by mail. Inquiry must include student's name, date of birth, social security number, years attended, release. Employers may obtain transcripts upon written request accompanied by a $2.00 fee and a signed release from the student.

A single program two-year institution, with an enrollment of 278. Highest level of offering: one year but less than four years
ACCREDITATIONS: JRCB

Phillips Junior College of Charlotte

(Formerly Rutledge College of Charlotte)
c/o Phillips Colleges, Inc.
One Hancock Plaza, Suite 1408
Gulfport, MS 39501
(601) 864-6096

Records are held at the above location. Will confirm attendance and degree by mail or phone. Inquiry must include student's name, social security number, years attended, release. Employers may obtain transcripts upon written request accompanied by a $2.00 fee and a signed release from the student.

Phillips Junior College at Columbus

1622 13th Avenue
Columus, GA 31901
(404) 327-4381
Fax (404) 327-7772

Will confirm attendance and degree by mail or fax. Inquiry must include student's name, social security number, years attended. Employers may obtain transcripts upon written request accompanied by a $2.00 fee and a signed release from the student. Requests should be directed to: Registrar's Office.

A single program two-year institution, with an enrollment of 551. Highest level of offering: one year but less than four years.
ACCREDITATIONS: JRCB

Phillips Junior College of Fayettville

(Formerly Rutledge College-Fayetteville)
c/o Phillips Colleges, Inc.
One Hancock Plaza, Suite 1408
Gulfport, MS 39501
(601) 864-6096

Records are held at the above location. Will confirm attendance and degree by phone or mail. Inquiry must include student's name, social security number. Employers may obtain transcripts upon written request accompanied by a $2.00 fee and a signed release from the student.

Phillips Junior College of Greensboro

(Formerly Rutledge College of Greensboro)
c/o Phillips Colleges, Inc.
One Hancock Plaza, Suite 1408
Gulfport, MS 39501
(601) 864-6096

Records are held at the above location. Will confirm attendance and degree by phone or mail. Inquiry must include student's name. Employers may obtain transcripts upon written request accompanied by a $2.00 fee and a signed release from the student.

Phillips Junior College of Jackson

2680 Insurance Center Drive
Jackson, MS 39216
(601) 362-6341

Will confirm attendance and degree by phone or mail. Inquiry must include student's name, social security number, years attended, release. Employers may obtain transcripts upon written request accompanied by a $2.00 fee and a signed release from the student. Requests should be directed to: Academic Affairs.

A multiprogram two-year institution, with an enrollment of 633. Highest level of offering: one year but less than four years.
ACCREDITATIONS: JRCB

Phillips Junior College of the Mississippi Gulf Coast

942 Beach Drive
Gulfport, MS 39507
(601) 896-6465
Fax (601) 896-6501

Will confirm attendance and degree by phone or mail. Inquiry must include student's name, social security number, years attended. Employers may obtain transcripts upon written request accompanied by a $3.00 fee and a signed release from the student. Requests should be directed to: Registrar's Office.

A multiprogram two-year institution, with an enrollment of 753. Highest level of offering: four or five year baccalaureate.
ACCREDITATIONS: JRCB SRCB

Phillips Junior College of Springfield

(Formerly Rutledge College of Springfield)
1010 West Sunshine
Springfield, MO 65807
(417) 864-7220

Will confirm attendance and degree by phone or mail. Inquiry must include student's name, date of birth, social security number. Employers may obtain transcripts upon written request accompanied by a $3.00 fee and a signed release from the student.

A two-year institution newly admitted to NCES, with an enrollment of 750. Highest level of offering: one year but less than four years.
ACCREDITATIONS: JRCB MAC

Phillips Junior College of Winston–Salem

(Formerly Rutledge College of Winston-Salem)
c/o Phillips Colleges, Inc.
One Hancock Plaza, Suite 1408
Gulfport, MS 39501
(601) 864-6096

Records are held at the above location. Will confirm attendance and degree by phone or mail. Inquiry must include student's name, social security number, release. Employers may obtain transcripts upon written request accompanied by a $2.00 fee and a signed release from the student.

Phillips Junior College

(Formerly Rutledge Junior College)
1640 Sycamore View
Memphis, TN 38134
(901) 377-1200
Fax (901) 388-8105

Will confirm attendance and degree by phone, fax or mail. Inquiry must include student's name, social security number. Employers may obtain transcripts upon written request accompanied by a signed release from the student. Attn: Registrar's Office.

A two-year institution newly admitted to NCES, with an enrollment of 200. Highest level of offering: one year but less than four years.
ACCREDITATIONS: JRCB

Phillips Junior College

822 South Clearview Parkway
New Orleans, LA 70123
(504) 734-0123 Ext. 352

Will confirm attendance and degree by phone or mail. Inquiry must include student's name, social security number. Employers may obtain transcripts upon written request accompanied by a $2.00 fee and a signed release from the student. Requests should be directed to: Registrar's Office.

A multiprogram two-year institution, with an enrollment of 1,706. Highest level of offering: one year but less than four years.
ACCREDITATIONS: JRCB

Phillips Junior College

5001 Westbank Expressway
Marrero, LA 70072
(504) 348-1182
Fax (504) 340-5212

Will confirm attendance and degree by phone, fax or mail. Inquiry must include student's name, social security number. Employers may obtain transcripts upon written request accompanied by a $2.00 fee and a signed release from the student. Requests should be directed to: Registrar's Office.

Phillips University

Box 2000 University Station
Enid, OK 73702
(405) 237-4433 Ext. 416
Fax (405) 237-1607

Will confirm attendance and degree by phone, fax or mail. Inquiry must include student's name, social security number, years attended. Employers may obtain transcripts upon written request accompanied by a $2.00 fee and a signed release from the student. Requests should be directed to: Registrar's Office.

A comprehensive institution with no medical school, with an enrollment of 1,136. Highest level of offering: master's.
ACCREDITATIONS: NH MUS THEOL PAST

Phoenix College

1202 West Thomas Road
Phoenix, AZ 85013
(602) 264-2492
Fax (602) 285-7700

Will confirm attendance and degree by mail. Inquiry must include student's name, social security number, release. Employers may obtain transcripts upon written request accompanied by a $2.00 fee and a signed release from the student. Requests should be directed to: Admissions Office.

A multiprogram two-year institution, with an enrollment of 15,000. Highest level of offering: one year but less than four years.
ACCREDITATIONS: NH ADNUR DA DH ENGT MLTAD MLTC MRT

Piedmont Bible College

716 Franklin Street
Winston-Salem, NC 27101
(919) 725-8344 Ext. 282

Will confirm attendance and degree by phone or mail. Inquiry must include student's name. Employers may obtain transcripts upon written request accompanied by a $2.00 fee and a signed release from the student. Requests should be directed to: Registrar's Office.

A school of philosophy, religion and theology, with an enrollment of 290. Highest level of offering: four or five year baccalaureate.
ACCREDITATIONS: BI

Piedmont College

PO Box 10
Demorest, GA 30535
(404) 778-3000

Will confirm attendance and degree by phone or mail. Inquiry must include student's name, years attended. Employers may obtain transcripts upon written request accompanied by a $2.00 fee and a signed release from the student. Requests should be directed to: Registrar's Office.

A general baccalaureate institution, with an enrollment of 387. Highest level of offering: four or five year baccalaureate.
ACCREDITATIONS: SC

Piedmont Community College

PO Box 1197
Roxboro, NC 27573
(919) 599-1181 Ext. 242

Will confirm attendance and degree by phone or mail. Inquiry must include student's name, maiden name, social security number, years attended. Employers may obtain transcripts upon written request accompanied by a $3.00 fee and a signed release from the student. Requests should be directed to: Records Office.

A multiprogram two-year institution, with an enrollment of 947. Highest level of offering: one year but less than four years.
ACCREDITATIONS: SC

Piedmont Technical College

PO Box 1467 Emerald Road
Greenwood, SC 29646
(803) 941-8363
Fax (803) 941-8555

Will confirm attendance and degree by phone, fax or mail. Inquiry must include student's name, social security number. Employers may obtain transcripts upon written request accompanied by a $1.00 fee and a signed release from the student. Requests should be directed to: Students Records.

A multiprogram two-year institution, with an enrollment of 2,190. Highest level of offering: two years.
ACCREDITATIONS: SACS ENGT RAD RSTHT

Piedmont Virginia Community College

Route 6 Box 1
Charlottesville, VA 22902-8714
(804) 977-3900

Will confirm attendance and degree by phone or mail. Inquiry must include student's name, social security number. Employers may obtain transcripts upon written request accompanied by a $1.00 fee and a signed release from the student. Requests should be directed to: Admissions & Records Office.

A multiprogram two-year institution, with an enrollment of 4,240. Highest level of offering: one year but less than four years.
ACCREDITATIONS: SC ADNUR RSTH

Pierce College

9401 Farwest Drive South West
Tacoma, WA 98498
(206) 964-6622

Will confirm attendance and degree by phone or mail. Inquiry must include student's name, date of birth, social security number. Employers may obtain transcripts upon written request accompanied by a signed release from the student.

A multiprogram two-year institution, with an enrollment of 12,000. Highest level of offering: One year but less than four years.
ACCREDITATIONS: NW ADVET DH

Pikes Peak Community College

5675 South Academy Boulevard
Colorado Springs, CO 80906
(719) 540-7155 or 576-7711 Ext. 7158

Will confirm attendance and degree by phone or mail. Inquiry must include student's name, social security number. Employers may obtain transcripts upon written request accompanied by a $1.00 fee and a signed release from the student. Requests should be directed to: Records Office.

A multiprogram two-year institution, with an enrollment of 6,773. Highest level of offering: one year but less than four years.
ACCREDITATIONS: NH ADNUR DA

Pikeville College

Sycamore Street
Pikeville, KY 41501
(606) 432-9369

Will confirm attendance and degree by phone or mail. Inquiry must include student's name, social security number. Employers may obtain transcripts upon written request accompanied by a $2.00 fee and a signed release from the student.

A general baccalaureate institution, with an enrollment of 980. Highest level of offering: four or five year baccalaureate.
ACCREDITATIONS: SC

Pillsbury Baptist Bible College

315 South Grove
Owatonna, MN 55060
(507) 451-2710 Ext. 275
Fax (507) 451-6459

Will confirm attendance and degree by phone, fax or mail. Inquiry must include student's name, date of birth, social securtiy number, years attended. Employers may obtain transcripts upon written request accompanied by a $3.00 fee and a signed release from the student. Requests should be directed to: Registrar's Office.

A bachelor's or higher institution newly admitted to NCES, with an enrollment of 383. Highest level of offering: four or five year baccalaureate.
ACCREDITATIONS: 3IC

Pima Community College

2202 West Anklam Road
Tucson, AZ 85709
(602) 884-6640
Fax (602) 884-6209

Will confirm attendance and degree by phone, fax or mail. Inquiry must include student's name, date of birth, years attended. Employers may obtain transcripts upon written request accompanied by a $2.00 fee and a signed release from the student. Requests should be directed to: Admissions Office.

A multiprogram two-year institution, with an enrollment of 20,882. Highest level of offering: one year but less than four years.
ACCREDITATIONS: NH ADNUR DA DT RAD RSTH

Pine Manor College

400 Heath Street
Boston, MA 02167
(617) 731-7135
Fax (617) 731-7199

Will confirm attendance and degree by phone or mail. Inquiry must include student's name, social security number, years attended. Requests should be directed to: Registrar's Office. Employers may obtain transcripts upon written request accompanied by a $3.00 fee and a signed release from the student.

A multiprogram four-year institution, with an enrollment of 500. Highest level of offering: four or five year baccalaureate.
ACCREDITATIONS: EH

Pinebrook Junior College

c/o NYACK College
New York, NY 10960-9987
(914) 358-1710

Records are held at the above location. Will confirm attendance and degree by phone or mail. Inquiry must include student's name, years attended. Employers may obtain transcripts upon written request accompanied by a $2.00 fee and a signed release from the student. Requests should be directed to: Registrar's Office.

A multiprogram two-year institution. Highest level of offering: one year but less than four years.

Pioneer Community College

(See Penn Valley Community College)

Pitt Community College

PO Box 7007
Greenville, NC 27835
(919) 355-4232

Will confirm attendance and degree by mail. Inquiry must include student's name, social security number, years attended, release. Employers may obtain transcripts upon written request accompanied by a $1.00 fee and a signed release from the student. Requests should be directed to: Registrar's Office.

A multiprogram two-year institution, with an enrollment of 4,397. Highest level of offering: two years but less than four years.
ACCREDITATIONS: SACS RAD

Pittsburg State University

Pittsburg, KS 66762
(316) 235-4200
Fax (316) 232-7515

Will confirm attendance and degree by phone or mail. Inquiry must include student's name, social security number. Employers may obtain transcripts upon written request accompanied by a $3.00 fee and a signed release from the student. Requests should be directed to: Registrar's Office.

A comprehensive institution with no medical school, with an enrollment of 4,927. Highest level of offering: beyond master's but less than doctorate.
ACCREDITATIONS: NH ENGT MUS NUR SW TED

Pittsburgh Institute of Aeronautics

PO Box 10897
Pittsburgh, PA 15236-0897
(412) 462-9011
Fax (412) 466-0513

Will confirm attendance and degree by phone, fax or mail. Inquiry must include student's name, social security number, years attended. Employers may obtain transcripts upon written request accompanied by a signed release from the student. Requests should be directed to: Student Records.

A single program two-year institution, with an enrollment of 1,050. Highest level of offering: one year but less than four years.
ACCREDITATIONS: NATTS

Pittsburgh Technical Institute

635 Smithfield Street
Pittsburgh, PA 15222
(412) 471-1011
Fax (412) 471-9014

Will confirm attendance and degree by mail. Inquiry must include student's name, years attended. Employers may obtain transcripts upon written request accompanied by a signed release from the student. Requests should be directed to: Registrar.

A multiprogram two-year institution, with an enrollment of 254. Highest level of offering: one year but less than four years.
ACCREDITATIONS: NATTS

Pittsburgh Theological Seminary

616 North Highland Avenue
Pittsburgh, PA 15206
(412) 362-5610 Ext. 210

Will confirm attendance and degree by phone or mail. Inquiry must include student's name, social security number, years attended. Requests should be directed to: Registrar's Office. Employers may obtain transcripts upon written request by student accompanied by a $2.00 fee and a signed release from the student.

A school of religion and theology, with an enrollment of 311. Highest level of offering: doctorate.
ACCREDITATIONS: M THEOL

Pitzer College

1050 North Mills Avenue
Claremont, CA 91711
(714) 621-8363
Fax (714) 621-8521

Will confirm attendance and degree by phone, fax or mail. Inquiry must include student's name, social security number, years attended. Employers may obtain transcripts upon written request accompanied by a $2.00 fee and a signed release from the student. Requests should be directed to: Registrar's Office.

A general baccalaureate institution, with an enrollment of 761. Highest level of offering: four or five year baccalaureate.
ACCREDITATIONS: WC

Platt Junior College

4315 Pickett Road
Saint Joseph, MO 64503
(816) 233-9563

Will confirm attendance and degree by phone or mail. Inquiry must include student's name, years attended. Employers may obtain transcripts upon written request by student accompanied by a $2.00 fee and a signed release from the student. Requests should be directed to: Registrar's Office.

A two-year institution newly admitted to NCES, with an enrollment of 475. Highest level of offering: one year but less than four years.
ACCREDITATIONS: NH JRCB

Platte Valley Bible College

Box 1227
Scottsbluff, NE 69363-1227
(308) 632-6933

Will confirm attendance and degree by phone or mail. Inquiry must include student's name. Employers may obtain transcripts upon written request accompanied by a $2.00 fee and a signed release from the student. Requests should be directed to: Registrar's Office.

A school of philosophy, religion and theology, with an enrollment of 40. Highest level of offering: four or five year baccalaureate.

Plaza Business Institute

74-09 37th Avenue
Jackson Heights, NY 11372
(718) 779-1430
Fax (718) 779-1456

Will confirm attendance and degree by mail or fax. Inquiry must include student's name, social security number, years attended, release. Employers may obtain transcripts upon written request accompanied by a $5.00 fee and a signed release from the student. Requests should be directed to: Registrar's Office.

A two-year institution newly admitted to NCES, with an enrollment of 387. Highest level of offering: one year but less than four years.
ACCREDITATIONS: NY

Plymouth State College

Plymouth, NH 03264
(603) 535-5000 Ext. 2345

Will confirm attendance and degree by phone or mail. Inquiry must include student's name, social security number. Requests should be directed to: Registrar's Office. Employers may obtain transcripts upon written request accompanied by a $3.00 fee and a signed release from the student.

A general baccalaureate institution, with an enrollment of 4,400. Highest level of offering: master's
ACCREDITATIONS: EH TED

Point Loma Nazarene College

3900 Lomaland Drive
San Diego, CA 92106
(619) 221-2508

Will confirm attendance and degree by mail. Inquiry must include student's name, date of birth, social security number, years attended, release. Employers may obtain transcripts upon written request accompanied by a $4.00 fee and a signed release from the student.

A general baccalaureate institution, with an enrollment of 2,221. Highest level of offering: beyond master's but less than doctorate.
ACCREDITATIONS: WC NUR

Point Park College

201 Wood Street
Pittsburgh, PA 15222
(412) 392-3865

Will confirm attendance and degree by phone or mail. Inquiry must include student's name, date of birth, social security number. Employers may obtain transcripts upon written request accompanied by a $3.00 fee and a signed release from the student. Requests should be directed to: Student Records Office.

A general baccalaureate institution, with an enrollment of 2,700. Highest level of offering: master's.
ACCREDITATIONS: M

Polk Community College

999 Avenue H North East
Winter Haven, FL 33881-4299
(813) 297-1000
Fax (813) 297-1060

Will confirm attendance and degree by mail, fax. Inquiry must include student's name, date of birth, social security number, release. Employers may obtain transcripts upon written request accompanied by a signed release from the student. Requests should be directed to: Student Records.

A multiprogram two-year institution, with an enrollment of 4,488. Highest level of offering: one year but less than four years.
ACCREDITATIONS: SC RAD ADNUR

Polytechnic University

(Formerly Polytechnic Institute of New York)
333 Jay Street
Brooklyn, NY 11201
(718) 260-3900
Fax (718) 260-3136

Will confirm attendance and degree by mail, phone or fax. Inquiry must include student's name, social security number, years attended, release. Employers may obtain transcripts upon written request accompanied by a $4.00 fee and a signed release from the student. Requests should be directed to: Registrar's Office.

An engineering school, with an enrollment of 4,000. Highest level of offering: doctorate.
ACCREDITATIONS: M ENG NY

Pomona College

333 North College Way
Claremont, CA 91711
(714) 621-8131
Fax (714) 621-8403

Will confirm attendance and degree by phone or mail. Inquiry must include student's name, years attended, release. Employers may obtain transcripts upon written request accompanied by a $2.00 fee and a signed release from the student. Requests should be directed to: Registrar's Office.

A general baccalaureate institution, with an enrollment of 1,391. Highest level of offering: four or five year baccalaureate.
ACCREDITATIONS: WC

Pontifical College Josephinum

7625 North High
Columbus, OH 43235-1498
(614) 885-5585

Will confirm attendance and degree by phone or mail. Inquiry must include student's name. Employers may obtain transcripts upon written request accompanied by a $2.00 fee and a signed release from the student. Requests should be directed to: Registrar's Office.

A school of philosophy, religion and theology, with an enrollment of 220. Highest level of offering: master's.

ACCREDITATIONS: NH THEOL

Pope John XXIII National Seminary

558 South Avenue
Weston, MA 02193
(617) 899-5500

Will confirm attendance and degree by phone or mail. Inquiry must include student's name. Requests should be directed to: Dean of Admissions. Employers may obtain transcripts upon written request accompanied by a $3.00 fee and a signed release from the student.

A school of philosophy, religion and theology, with an enrollment of 70. Highest level of offering: master's.

ACCREDITATIONS: THEOL

Porterville College

900 South Main
Porterville, CA 93257
(209) 781-3130 Ext. 220
Fax (209) 781-3130 Ext. 375

Will confirm attendance and degree by phone, fax or mail. Inquiry must include student's name, social security number, years attended. Employers may obtain transcripts upon written request accompanied by a $2.00 fee and a signed release from the student. Requests should be directed to: Admissions Office.

A multiprogram two-year institution, with an enrollment of 1,887. Highest level of offering: one year but less than four years.

ACCREDITATIONS: WJ

Portland Community College

12000 South West 49th
Portland, OR 97280
(503) 244-6111

Will confirm attendance and degree by mail. Inquiry must include student's name, social security number, release. Employers may obtain transcripts upon written request accompanied by a $3.00 fee and a signed release from the student. Requests should be directed to: Student Records.

A multiprogram two-year institution, with an enrollment of 30,000. Highest level of offering: one year but less than four years.

ACCREDITATIONS: NW ADNUR DA DH DT MAC MLTAD MRT RAD ENGT

Portland School of Art

97 Spring Street
Portland, ME 04101
(207) 775-3052
Fax (207) 772-5069

Will confirm attendance and degree by mail. Inquiry must include student's name, years attended. Requests should be directed to: Registrar's Office. Employers may obtain transcripts upon written request by student accompanied by a $3.00 fee.

A visual and performing arts school, with an enrollment of 300. Highest level of offering: four or five year baccalaureate.

ACCREDITATIONS: EH ART

Portland State University

PO Box 751
Portland, OR 97207
(503) 725-4900
Fax (503) 725-3444

Will confirm attendance by mail and degree by phone or mail. Inquiry must include student's name, date of birth, social security number, years attended. Requests should be directed to: Registrar's Office. Employers may obtain transcripts upon written request accompanied by a $1.50 fee per copy, $5.00 for certified copy and a signed release from the student.

A comprehensive institution with no medical school, with an enrollment of 18,000. Highest level of offering: doctorate.

ACCREDITATIONS: NW AUD BUS CHM ENG MUS SP SW TED

Post College

800 Country Club Road
Waterbury, CT 06708
(203) 755-0121

Will confirm attendance and degree by phone or mail. Inquiry must include student's name, social security number, years attended, release. Employers may obtain transcripts upon written request accompanied by a $3.00 fee and a signed release from the student. Requests should be directed to: Records Office.

A multiprogram two-year institution, with an enrollment of 1,507. Highest level of offering: four or five year baccalaureate.

ACCREDITATIONS: EH

Potomac State College of West Virginia University

Keyser, WV 26726
(304) 788-3011 Ext. 226

Will confirm attendance and degree by phone or mail. Inquiry must include student's name, years attended. Employers may obtain transcripts upon written request accompanied by a $3.00 fee and a signed release from the student. Requests should be directed to: Admissions & Records Office.

A multiprogram two-year institution, with an enrollment of 1,133. Highest level of offering: two years but less than four years.

ACCREDITATIONS: NH

Prairie State College

202 South Halsted Street
Chicago Heights, IL 60411
(708) 756-3110 Ext. 121
Fax (708) 755-2587

Will confirm attendance and degree by phone, fax or mail. Inquiry must include student's name, social security number. Employers may obtain transcripts upon written request accompanied by a $2.00 fee and a signed release from the student. Requests should be directed to: Admissions Office.

A multiprogram two-year institution, with an enrollment of 5,234. Highest level of offering: one year but less than four years.

ACCREDITATIONS: NH ADNUR DH

Prairie View A&M University

PO Box 2610
Prairie View, TX 77446
(409) 857-2618

Will confirm attendance and degree by phone or mail. Inquiry must include student's name, social security number. Employers may obtain transcripts upon written request accompanied by a $3.00 fee and a signed release from the student. Requests should be directed to: Registrar's Office.

A comprehensive institution with no medical school, with an enrollment of 5,200. Highest level of offering: master's.

ACCREDITATIONS: SC ENG NUR SW TED

Pratt Community College

Highway 61
Pratt, KS 67124
(316) 672-5641 Ext. 153
Fax (316) 672-5288

Will confirm attendance and degree by phone or mail. Inquiry must include student's name, social security number, years attended. Employers may obtain transcripts upon written request accompanied by a $1.00 fee and a signed release from the student. Requests should be directed to: Registrar's Office.

A multiprogram two-year institution, with an enrollment of 3,000. Highest level of offering: two years but less than four years.

ACCREDITATIONS: NH

Pratt Institute

255 Ryerson Street
Brooklyn, NY 11205
(718) 636-3533

Will confirm attendance and degree by phone or mail. Inquiry must include student's name, years attended. Employers may obtain transcripts upon written request accompanied by a $5.00 fee and a signed release from the student.

A comprehensive institution with no medical school, with an enrollment of 3,527. Highest level of offering: beyond master's but less than doctorate.

ACCREDITATIONS: M ARCH ART ENG LIB NY

Presbyterian College

PO Box 975
Clinton, SC 29325
(803) 833-2820
Fax (803) 833-8481

Will confirm attendance and degree by phone, fax or mail. Inquiry must include student's name, social security number, years attended. Employers may obtain transcripts upon written request accompanied by a $2.00 fee and a signed release from the student. Requests should be directed to: Registrar's Office.

A general baccalaureate institution, with an enrollment of 1,087. Highest level of offering: four or five year baccalaureate.
ACCREDITATIONS: SC

Presbyterian School of Christian Education

1205 Palmyra Avenue
Richmond, VA 23227
(804) 359-5031
Fax (804) 254-8060

Will confirm attendance by phone or mail and degree by mail accompanied by release. Inquiry must include student's name, date of birth, social security number. Employers may obtain transcripts upon written request accompanied by a $2.00 fee and a signed release from the student.

A school of philosophy, religion and theology, with an enrollment of 136. Highest level of offering: doctorate.
ACCREDITATIONS: SC THEOL

Prescott College

220 Grove Avenue
Prescott, AZ 86301
(602) 778-2090

Will confirm attendance and degree by phone or mail. Inquiry must include student's name, date of birth, years attended. Employers may obtain transcripts upon written request accompanied by a $4.00 fee and a signed release from the student. Requests should be directed to: Registrar's Office.

A general baccalaureate institution, with an enrollment of 450. Highest level of offering: four or five year baccalaureate.
ACCREDITATIONS: NH

Presentation College

1500 North Main
Aberdeen, SD 57401
(605) 225-0420

Will confirm attendance and degree by mail. Inquiry must include student's name, social security number, years attended, release. Employers may obtain transcripts upon written request accompanied by a $2.00 fee and a signed release from the student. Requests should be directed to: Registrar's Office.

A multiprogram two-year institution, with an enrollment of 512. Highest level of offering: baccalaureate.
ACCREDITATIONS: NH ADNUR MLTAD

Prince Georges Community College

301 Largo Road
Largo, MD 20772
(301) 322-0801
Fax (301) 808-0960

Will confirm attendance and degree by phone or mail. Inquiry must include student's name, social security number. Employers may obtain transcripts upon written request accompanied by a $2.00 fee and a signed release from the student. Requests should be directed to: Registration & Records Office.

A multiprogram two-year institution, with an enrollment of 13,500. Highest level of offering: one year but less than four years.
ACCREDITATIONS: M ADNUR DA ENGT MLTAD MRT NMT RAD RSTH

Princeton Theological Seminary

Cn 8 21
Princeton, NJ 08542
(609) 921-8300

Will confirm attendance and degree by phone or mail. Inquiry must include student's name, date of birth, social security number. Employers may obtain transcripts upon written request accompanied by a $2.00 fee and a signed release from the student.

A school of philosophy, religion and theology, with an enrollment of 745. Highest level of offering: doctorate.
ACCREDITATIONS: M THEOL

Princeton University

PO Box 70
Princeton, NJ 08544-0070
(609) 258-3365

Will confirm attendance and degree by phone or mail. Inquiry must include student's name, social security number, years attended. Requests should be directed to: Registrar's Office. Employers may obtain transcripts upon written request accompanied by a $3.00 fee and a signed release from the student.

A doctoral-level institution with no medical school, with an enrollment of 6,277. Highest level of offering: doctorate.
ACCREDITATIONS: M ARCH ENG

Principia College

Elsah, IL 62028
(618) 374-5100 Ext. 200
Fax (618) 374-5122

Will confirm attendance and degree by phone or mail. Inquiry must include student's name, years attended. Employers may obtain transcripts upon written request accompanied by a signed release from the student. Requests should be directed to: Registrar's Office.

A general baccalaureate institution, with an enrollment of 765. Highest level of offering: four or five year baccalaureate.
ACCREDITATIONS: NCA

Professional Psychology

(See Forest Institute)

Protestant Episcopal Theological Seminary in Virginia

3737 Seminary Road
Alexandria, VA 22304
(703) 370-6600 Ext. 1723

Will confirm attendance and degree by phone or mail. Inquiry must include student's name, date of birth, social security number. Employers may obtain transcripts upon written request accompanied by a $2.00 fee and a signed release from the student. Requests should be directed to: Registrar's Office.

A school of philosophy, religion and theology, with an enrollment of 212. Highest level of offering: doctorate.
ACCREDITATIONS: THEOL

Providence College

Providence, RI 02918
(401) 865-2366

Will confirm attendance and degree by phone or mail. Inquiry must include student's name, social security number, years attended. Employers may obtain transcripts upon written request accompanied by a $2.00 fee and a signed release from the student. Requests should be directed to: Records Office.

A comprehensive institution with no medical school, with an enrollment of 5,679. Highest level of offering: doctorate.
ACCREDITATIONS: EH SW

Provincial Archives Redemptorist Fathers and Brothers

PO Box 6
Glenview, IL 60025
(708) 724-0425

Records are maintained at the above address. Will confirm attendance and degree by mail. Inquiry must include student's name, years attended, and release. Employers may obtain transcripts upon written request accompanied by a $3.00 fee and a signed release from the student.

Pueblo Community College

900 West Orman Avenue
Pueblo, CO 81004
(719) 549-3200

Will confirm attendance and degree by mail. Inquiry must include student's name, social security number. Employers may obtain transcripts upon written request accompanied by a $2.00 fee and a signed release from the student. Requests should be directed to: Records Office.

A multiprogram two-year institution, with an enrollment of 1,331. Highest level of offering: one year but less than four years.
ACCREDITATIONS: NH DH RAD RSTH

Puget Sound Christian College

410 4th Avenue North
Edmonds, WA 98020
(206) 775-8686

Will confirm attendance and degree by phone or mail. Inquiry must include student's name, social security number. Employers may obtain transcripts upon written request accompanied by a $5.00 fee and a signed release from the student. Requests should be directed to: Registrar's Office.

A school of philosophy, religion and theology, with an enrollment of 100. Highest level of offering: four or five year baccalaureate.

ACCREDITATIONS: BI

Purdue University All Campuses

Hovde Hall
West Lafayette, IN 47907
(317) 494-8581
Fax (317) 494-0570

Will confirm attendance and degree by phone, fax or mail. Inquiry must include student's name, social security number. Employers may obtain transcripts upon written request accompanied by a signed release from the student.

A doctoral-level institution with a medical school, with an enrollment of 31,852. Highest level of offering: doctorate.

ACCREDITATIONS: NH ADVET AUD BUS CLPSY DIET ENG MFCD ENGT FIDER FOR LSAR TED VET NUR PHAR SP

Purdue University Calumet

2233 171st Street
Hammond, IN 46323-2094
(219) 989-2210

Will confirm attendance and degree by phone or mail. Inquiry must include student's name, social security number, years attended. Employers may obtain transcripts upon written request accompanied by a signed release from the student. Transcript requests should be directed to: Purdue University, Hovde Hall, West Lafayette, IN 47907.

A comprehensive institution with no medical school, with an enrollment of 7,837. Highest level of offering: beyond master's but less than doctorate.

ACCREDITATIONS: NH ADNUR ENG ENGT NUR TED

Purdue University North Central Campus

1401 South U.S. Highway 421
Westville, IN 46391
(219) 785-5341

Will confirm attendance and degree by phone or mail. Inquiry must include student's name, social security number, years attended. Employers may obtain transcripts upon written request accompanied by a signed release from the student. Transcript requests should be directed to: Purdue University, Hovde Hall, West Lafayette, IN 47907.

A multiprogram two-year institution, with an enrollment of 3,552. Highest level of offering: four or five year baccalaureate.

ACCREDITATIONS: NH ADNUR RAD

Q

Queen of the Holy Rosary College

PO Box 3908
Mission San Jose, CA 94539
(510) 657-2468

Will confirm attendance and degree by mail. Inquiry must include student's name. Employers may obtain transcripts upon written request accompanied by a $3.00 fee and a signed release from the student. Requests should be directed to: Registrar's Office.

A two-year institution newly admitted to NCES, with an enrollment of 263. Highest level of offering: one year but less than four years.

ACCREDITATIONS: WJ

Queens College

1900 Selwyn Avenue
Charlotte, NC 28274-0001
(704) 337-2211
Fax (704) 337-2503

Will confirm attendance and degree by phone or mail. Inquiry must include student's name, date of birth, social security number. Employers may obtain transcripts upon written request accompanied by a $3.00 fee and a signed release from the student. Requests should be directed to: Registrar's Office.

A general baccalaureate institution, with an enrollment of 1,6000. Highest level of offering: master's.

ACCREDITATIONS: SC MUS NMT NUR

Quincy College

Attn: Registrar's Office
1800 College Avenue
Quincy, IL 62301
(217) 222-5285
Fax (217) 222-5354

Will confirm attendance and degree by phone, fax or mail. Inquiry must include student's name, date of birth, social security number, years of attendance. Employers may obtain transcripts upon written request accompanied by a $3.00 fee and a signed release from the student. Requests should be directed to: Registrar's Office.

A general baccalaureate institution, with an enrollment of 1,000. Highest level of offering: master's.

ACCREDITATIONS: NH MUS

Quincy Junior College

34 Coddington Street
Quincy, MA 02169
(617) 984-1600 (Voice mail-press 4 for Registrar's Office)

Will confirm attendance and degree by mail. Inquiry must include student's name, social security number, years attended, release. Employers may obtain transcripts upon written request accompanied by a $2.00 fee and a signed release from the student.

A multiprogram two-year institution, with an enrollment of 2,945. Highest level of offering: one year but less than four years.

ACCREDITATIONS: EH ADNUR DA DT PNUR

Quinebaug Valley Community College

742 Upper Maple Street
Danielson, CT 06239
(203) 774-1130

Will confirm attendance and degree by mail or phone. Inquiry must include student's name, maiden name, present address, social security number. Employers may obtain transcripts upon written request accompanied by a signed release from the student.

A multiprogram two-year institution, with an enrollment of 1,131. Highest level of offering: two years but less than four years.

ACCREDITATIONS: EH

Quinnipiac College

Mount Carmel Avenue
Hamden, CT 06518
(203) 281-8695

Will confirm attendance and degree by phone or mail. Inquiry must include student's name, date of birth, social security number, years attended. Employers may obtain transcripts upon written request accompanied by a signed release from the student. Attn: Registrar's Office.

A general baccalaureate institution, with an enrollment of 3,139. Highest level of offering: master's.

ACCREDITATIONS: EH ADNUR ADVET DMS MT NMT OT PTA RSTH

Quinsigamond Community College

670 West Boylston Street
Worcester, MA 01606
(508) 853-2300 Ext. 257

Will confirm attendance and degree by phone or mail. Inquiry must include student's name, social security number, years attended. Employers may obtain transcripts upon written request accompanied by a $1.00 fee and a signed release from the student

A multiprogram two-year institution, with an enrollment of 4,782. Highest level of offering: one year but less than four years.

ACCREDITATIONS: EH ADNUR DH RAD RSTH

R

Rabbi Isaac Elchanan Theological Seminary

Registrar's Office
500 West 185 Street
New York, NY 10033
(212) 960-5291

Will confirm attendance and degree by mail. Inquiry must include student's name, social security number, years attended, specific program. Employers may obtain transcripts upon written request accompanied by a $4.00 fee and a signed release from the student.

A specialized non-degree granting institution, with an enrollment of 236. Highest level of offering: graduate non-degree granting.
ACCREDITATIONS: NY

Rabbinical Academy Mesivta Rabbi Chaim Berlin

1593 Coney Island Avenue
Brooklyn, NY 11230
(718) 377-0777
Fax (718) 338-5578

Will confirm attendance and degree by mail. Inquiry must include student's name, years attended. Employers may obtain transcripts upon written request accompanied by a $15.00 fee and a signed release from the student.

A school of philosophy, religion and theology, with an enrollment of 270. Highest level of offering: first professional degree.
ACCREDITATIONS: RABN

Rabbinical College Beth Shraga

PO Box 412
28 Saddle River Road
Monsey, NY 10952
(914) 356-1980

Will confirm attendance and student's records by phone or mail. Inquiry must include student's name, date of birth, years attended. Employers may obtain transcripts upon written request accompanied by a signed release from the student.

A specialized non-degree granting institution, with an enrollment of 46. Highest level of offering: four or five year baccalaureate.
ACCREDITATIONS: RABN

Rabbinical College Bobover Yeshiva B'nei Zion

1577 48th Street
Brooklyn, NY 11219
(718) 438-2018

Will confirm attendance and degree by mail. Inquiry must include student's name, social security number. Employers may obtain transcripts upon written request accompanied by a signed release from the student.

A specialized non-degree granting institution, with an enrollment of 114. Highest level of offering: graduate non-degree granting.
ACCREDITATIONS: RABN

Rabbinical College Ch'san Sofer of New York

1876 50th Street
Brooklyn, NY 11204
(718) 236-1171

Will confirm attendance and degree by mail. Inquiry must include student's name, social security number, years attended. Inquiry must include student's name, social security number, years attended. Employers may obtain transcripts upon written request accompanied by a signed release from the student.

A specialized non-degree granting institution, with an enrollment of 118. Highest level of offering: graduate non-degree granting.
ACCREDITATIONS: RABN

Rabbinical College of America

226 Sussex Avenue
Morristown, NJ 07960
(201) 267-9404

Will confirm attendance and degree by phone or mail. Inquiry must include student's name, years attended. Employers may obtain transcripts upon written request accompanied by a $5.00 fee and a signed release from the student.

A school of philosophy, religion and theology, with an enrollment of 230. Highest level of offering: four or five year baccalaureate.
ACCREDITATIONS: RABN

Rabbinical College of Kamenitz Yeshiva

1650 56th Street
Brooklyn, NY 11204
(718) 851-4735

Will confirm attendance and degree by phone or mail. Inquiry must include student's name.

A specialized non-degree granting institution. Highest level of offering: undergraduate non-degree granting.

Rabbinical College of Long Island

Torah H.S. of Long Beach
205 West Beech Street
Long Beach, NY 11561
(516) 431-7414

Will confirm attendance and degree by phone or mail. Inquiry must include student's name, years attended. Employers may obtain transcripts upon written request accompanied by a signed release from the student.

A specialized non-degree granting institution, with an enrollment of 79. Highest level of offering: graduate non-degree granting.
ACCREDITATIONS: RABN

Rabbinical College of Telshe

28400 Euclid Avenue
Wickliffe, OH 44092
(216) 943-5300

Will confirm attendance and degree by phone or mail. Inquiry must include student's name, date of birth. Employers may obtain transcripts upon written request accompanied by a signed release from the student.

A school of philosophy, religion and theology, with an enrollment of 158. Highest level of offering: doctorate.
ACCREDITATIONS: RABN

Rabbinical Seminary Adas Yereim

185 Wilson Street
Brooklyn, NY 11211
(718) 388-1751

Will confirm attendance and degree by phone or mail. Inquiry must include student's name, date of birth, social security number, years attended. Employers may obtain transcripts upon written request accompanied by a signed release from the student.

A specialized non-degree granting institution, with an enrollment of 114. Highest level of offering: undergraduate non-degree granting.
ACCREDITATIONS: RABN

Rabbinical Seminary Beth Yitzchok D'spinka

192 Keap Street
Brooklyn, NY 11211
(718) 387-4597

Will confirm attendance by mail. A specialized non-degree granting institution, with an enrollment of 56. Highest level of offering: graduate non-degree granting.

Rabbinical Seminary M'kor Chaim

1571 55th Street
Brooklyn, NY 11219
(718) 851-0183

Will confirm attendance and degree by phone or mail. Inquiry must include student's name, date of birth, social security number. Employers may obtain transcripts upon written request accompanied by a signed release from the student.

A specialized non-degree granting institution, with an enrollment of 85. Highest level of offering: graduate non-degree granting.
ACCREDITATIONS: RABN

Rabbinical Seminary of America

92-15 69th Avenue
Forest Hills, NY 11375
(718) 268-4700

Will confirm attendance and degree by mail. Inquiry must include student's full name. Requests should be directed to: Registrar's Office. Employers may obtain transcripts upon written request by student.

A specialized institution, with an enrollment of 200. Highest level of offering: graduate non-degree granting.
ACCREDITATIONS: RABN

Rabbinical Seminary of Munkacs

4706 14th Avenue
Brooklyn, NY 11219
(718) 438-5246

Will confirm attendance and degree by mail. Inquiry must include student's name, social security number, date of birth. Employers may obtain transcripts upon written request accompanied by a signed release from the student.

A specialized non-degree granting institution, with an enrollment of 540. Highest level of offering: undergraduate non-degree granting.
ACCREDITATIONS: 3IC

Radcliffe College

Registrar's Office
1350 Mass Avenue, Room 831
Cambridge, MA 02138
(617) 495-1543

Will confirm attendance and degree by phone or mail. Inquiry must include student's name, date of birth. Employers may obtain transcripts upon written request accompanied by a $3.00 fee and a signed release from the student.

A general baccalaureate institution, with an enrollment of 6,493. Highest level of offering: four or five year baccalaureate.
ACCREDITATIONS: EH

Radford University

Box 6904
Radford, VA 24142
(703) 831-5271
Fax (703) 831-5138

Will confirm attendance and degree by phone or mail. Inquiry must include student's name, social security number. Employers may obtain transcripts upon written request accompanied by a $2.00 fee and a signed release from the student.

A comprehensive institution with no medical school, with an enrollment of 9,175. Highest level of offering: beyond master's but less than doctorate.
ACCREDITATIONS: SC MUS NUR SW TED

Ramapo College of New Jersey

505 Ramapo Valley Road
Mahwah, NJ 07430
(201) 529-7500
Fax (201) 529-7508

Will confirm attendance and degree by phone or mail. Inquiry must include student's name, social security number. Only students may request transcripts. Fee is $3.00.

A general baccalaureate institution, with an enrollment of 4,000. Highest level of offering: four or five year baccalaureate.
ACCREDITATIONS: M SW

Rancho Santiago

1530 W. 17th Street
Santa Ana, CA 92706
(714) 564-6000

Will confirm attendance and degree by phone or mail. Inquiry must include student's name, date of birth. Employers may obtain transcripts upon written request accompanied by a $2.00 fee and a signed release from the student.

A multiprogram two-year institution, with an enrollment of 27,441. Highest level of offering: one year but less than four years
ACCREDITATIONS: WJ

Rand Graduate Institute of Policy Studies

1700 Main Street
PO Box 2138
Santa Monica, CA 90407-2138
(310) 393-0411 Ext. 7690
Fax (310) 393-4818

Will confirm attendance and degree by phone, fax or mail. Inquiry must include student's name, years attended. Employers may obtain transcripts upon written request accompanied by a signed release from the student.

A doctoral-level institution with no medical school, with an enrollment of 60. Highest level of offering: doctorate.
ACCREDITATIONS: WC

Randolph–Macon College

PO Box 5005
Ashland, VA 23005-5505
(804) 798-8372 Ext. 227

Will confirm attendance and degree by phone. Inquiry must include student's name, social security number. Employers may obtain transcripts upon written request accompanied by a $1.00 fee and a signed release from the student.

A general baccalaureate institution, with an enrollment of 1,120. Highest level of offering: four or five year baccalaureate.
ACCREDITATIONS: SC

Randolph–Macon Woman's College

2500 Rivermont Avenue
Lynchburg, VA 24503
(804) 845-9599

Will confirm attendance and degree by phone or mail. Inquiry must include student's name, social security number, years attended. Employers may obtain transcripts upon written request accompanied by a $3.00 fee and a signed release from the student ($5.00 for same-day service). Direct inquiries to: Office of the Registrar.

A general baccalaureate institution, with an enrollment of 769. Highest level of offering: four year baccalaureate.
ACCREDITATIONS: SC

Randolph Community College

PO Box 1009
Asheboro, NC 27203
(919) 629-1471 Ext. 213
Fax (919) 629-4695

Will confirm attendance and degree by phone or mail. Inquiry must include student's name, date of birth, social security number, years attended. Employers may obtain transcripts upon written request accompanied by a signed release from the student.

A multiprogram two-year institution, with an enrollment of 1,500. Highest level of offering: one year but less than four years.
ACCREDITATIONS: SC

Ranger Junior College

College Circle
Ranger, TX 76470
(817) 647-3234 Ext. 113
Fax (817) 647-1656

Will confirm attendance and degree by phone or mail. Inquiry must include student's name, social security number. Employers may obtain transcripts upon written request accompanied by a $1.00 fee and a signed release from the student.

A multiprogram two-year institution, with an enrollment of 698. Highest level of offering: but less than four years.
ACCREDITATIONS: SC

Rappahannock Community College

PO Box 287
Glenns, VA 23149
(804) 758-5324 Ext. 214
Fax (804) 758-3852

Will confirm attendance and degree by phone, fax or mail. Inquiry must include student's name, social security number, years attended. Employers may obtain transcripts upon written request accompanied by a $1.00 fee and a signed release from the student.

A multiprogram two-year institution, with an enrollment of 1,318. Highest level of offering: one year but less than four years.
ACCREDITATIONS: SC

Raritan Valley Community College

(Formerly Somerset County College)
Attn: Registrar's Office
PO Box 3300
Somerville, NJ 08876
(201) 526-1200

Will confirm attendance and degree by mail or phone. Inquiry must include student's name, social security number, release. Employers may obtain transcripts upon written request accompanied by a $2.00 fee and a signed release from the student. Requests should be directed to: Registrar's Office.

A multiprogram two-year institution, with an enrollment of 5,050. Highest level of offering: one year but less than four years.
ACCREDITATIONS: M ADNUR

Reading Area Community College

PO Box 1706
Reading, PA 19603
(215) 372-4721 Ext. 224

Will confirm attendance and degree by phone or mail. Inquiry must include student's name, social security number. Employers may obtain transcripts upon written request accompanied by a $2.00 fee and a signed release from the student.

A multiprogram two-year institution, with an enrollment of 2,900. Highest level of offering: one year but less than four years.
ACCREDITATIONS: M MLTAD

Red Rocks Community College

13300 West Sixth Avenue
Lakewood, CO 80401-5398
(303) 988-6160 Ext. 357

Will confirm attendance and degree by phone or mail. Inquiry must include student's name, social security number, years attended. Employers may obtain transcripts upon written request accompanied by a signed release from the student.

A multiprogram two-year institution, with an enrollment of 6,500. Highest level of offering: one year but less than four years.

ACCREDITATIONS: NH

Redlands Community College

(Formerly Reno Junior College)
Box 370
El Reno, OK 73036
(405) 262-2552

Will confirm attendance and degree by phone or mail. Inquiry must include student's name, social security number, and years attended. Employers may obtain transcripts upon written request accompanied by a $1.00 fee and a signed release from the student.

A multiprogram two-year institution, with an enrollment of 186. Highest level of offering: one year but less than four years.

ACCREDITATIONS: NH ADNUR

Reed College

3203 South East Woodstock Boulevard
Portland, OR 97202
(503) 771-1112 Ext. 793
Fax (503) 777-7769

Will confirm attendance and degree by phone, fax or mail. Inquiry must include student's name, date of birth, social security number, years attended. Employers may obtain transcripts upon written request accompanied by a $3.00 fee and a signed release from the student.

A general baccalaureate institution, with an enrollment of 1,087. Highest level of offering: master's.

ACCREDITATIONS: NW

Reformed Bible College

3333 East Beltline NE
Grand Rapids, MI 49505
(616) 363-2050

Will confirm attendance and degree by phone or mail. Inquiry must include student's name, social security number, years attended. Employers may obtain transcripts upon written request accompanied by a $2.00 fee and a signed release from the student.

A school of philosophy, religion and theology, with an enrollment of 219. Highest level of offering: four or five year baccalaureate.

ACCREDITATIONS: BI

Reformed Theological Seminary

5422 Clinton Boulevard
Jackson, MS 39209
(601) 922-4988 Ext. 236
Fax (601) 922-1153

Will confirm attendance and degree by phone, fax or mail. Inquiry must include student's name, date of birth, social security number, years attended. Employers may obtain transcripts upon written request accompanied by a $3.00 fee and a signed release from the student.

A school of philosophy, religion and theology, with an enrollment of 399. Highest level of offering: doctorate.

ACCREDITATIONS: SC THEOL

Regent University

(Formerly CNB University)
Virginia Beach, VA 23464-9800
(804) 523-7406
Fax (804) 424-7051

Will confirm attendance and degree by phone, fax or mail. Inquiry must include student's name, social security number. Employers may obtain transcripts upon written request accompanied by a signed release from the student.

A bachelor's or higher insttution newly admitted to NCES, with an enrollment of 2121. Highest evel of offering: doctorate.

ACCREDITATIONS: SC

Regional Seminary of Saint Vincent De Paul in Florida, Inc.

10701 South Military Trail
Boynton Beach, FL 33436
(407) 732-4424

Will confirm attendance and degree by phone or mail. Inquiry must include student's name, date of birth, social security number, years attended. Employers may obtain transcripts upon written request accompanied by a $2.00 fee and a signed release from the student.

A school of philosophy, religion and theology, with an enrollment of 73. Highest level of offering: master's.

ACCREDITATIONS: SC THEOL

Regis College

235 Welesley
Weston, MA 02193
(617) 893-1820 Ext. 2060
Fax (617) 899-4725

Will confirm attendance and degree by phone, fax or mail. Inquiry must include student's name, date of birth, social security number, years attended. Employers may obtain transcripts upon written request accompanied by a $3.00 fee and a signed release from the student.

A general baccalaureate institution, with an enrollment of 1,180. Highest level of offering: master's.

ACCREDITATIONS: EH SW

Regis College

Registrar's Office
3333 Regis Boulevard
Denver, CO 80221
(303) 458-4114

Will confirm attendance and degree by phone or mail. Inquiry must include student's name, date of birth, social security number, years attended. Employers may obtain transcripts upon written request accompanied by a $5.00 fee and a signed release from the student.

A general baccalaureate institution, with an enrollment of 3,196. Highest level of offering: master's.

ACCREDITATIONS: NH MRA

Reid State Technical College

PO Box 588
Evergreen, AL 36401
(205) 578-1313 Ext. 107
Fax (205) 578-5355

Will confirm attendance and degree by phone, fax or mail. Inquiry must include student's name, social security number, years attended. Employers may obtain transcripts upon written request accompanied by a $2.00 fee and a signed release from the student.

A two-year institution newly admitted to NCES. Highest level of offering: one year but less than four years.

ACCREDITATIONS: SV

Reinhardt College

PO Box 128
Waleska, GA 30183
(404) 479-1454 Ext. 243
Fax (404) 479-9007

Will confirm attendance and degree by phone, fax or mail. Inquiry must include student's name, date of birth, social security number, years attended. Employers may obtain transcripts upon written request accompanied by a $2.00 fee and a signed release from the student.

A multiprogram two-year institution, with an enrollment of 679. Highest level of offering: two years but less than four years.

ACCREDITATIONS: SC

Rend Lake College

Rural Route 1
Ina, IL 62846
(618) 437-5321 Ext. 230

Will confirm attendance and degree by phone or mail. Inquiry must include student's name, date of birth, social security number, years attended. Requests should be directed to: Admissions Office. Employers may obtain transcripts upon written request accompanied by a signed release from the student.

A multiprogram two-year institution, with an enrollment of 4,000. Highest level of offering: one year but less than four years.

ACCREDITATIONS: NH ADNUR

Rensselaer Polytechnic Institute

110 8th Street
Troy, NY 12181-3590
(518) 276-6231

Will confirm attendance and degree by phone or mail. Inquiry must include student's name, social security number, years attended. Employers may obtain transcripts upon written request accompanied by a signed release from the student.

A doctoral-level institution with no medical school, with an enrollment of 6,811. Highest level of offering: doctorate.

ACCREDITATIONS: M ARCH BUS ENG NY

Research College of Nursing

(See Rockhurst College of Nursing)

RETS Electronic Institute

2812 12th Avenue North
Birmingham, AL 35234
(205) 251-7962

Will confirm attendance and degree by phone or mail. Inquiry must include student's name, date of birth, social security number, years attended. Employers may obtain transcripts upon written request accompanied by a $3.00 fee and a signed release from the student.

A two-year institution newly admitted to NCES, with an enrollment of 600. Highest level of offering: one year but less than four years.

ACCREDITATIONS: NATTS

RETS Electronic Institute

4146 Outer Loop
Louisville, KY 40219
(502) 968-7191 Ext. 271

Will confirm attendance and degree by phone or mail. Inquiry must include student's name, social security number, years attended. Employers may obtain transcripts upon written request accompanied by a $3.00 fee and a signed release from the student.

A two-year institution newly admitted to NCES, with an enrollment of 600. Highest level of offering: undergraduate non-degree granting.

ACCREDITATIONS: NATTS

RETS Technical Center

116 Westpark Road
Centerville, OH 45459
(513) 433-3410

Will confirm attendance and degree by phone or mail. Inquiry must include student's name, social security number, years attended. Employers may obtain transcripts upon written request accompanied by a $2.00 fee and a signed release from the student.

A two-year institution newly admitted to NCES, with an enrollment of 400. Highest level of offering: one year but less than four years.

ACCREDITATIONS: NATTS

Rhode Island College

600 Mount Pleasant Ave
Providence, RI 02908
(401) 456-8000
Fax (401) 456-8379

Will confirm attendance and degree by mail or fax. Inquiry must include student's name, social security number, years attended. Employers may obtain transcripts upon written request accompanied by a $2.00 fee and a signed release from the student.

A comprehensive institution with no medical school, with an enrollment of 8,750. Highest level of offering: beyond master's but less than doctorate.

ACCREDITATIONS: EH ART MUS NUR SW TED

Rhode Island School of Design

2 College Street
Providence, RI 02903
(401) 454-6100 Ext. 6151

Will confirm attendance and degree by phone or mail. Inquiry must include student's name, years attended. Employers may obtain transcripts upon written request accompanied by a $2.00 fee and a signed release from the student.

A visual and performing arts school, with an enrollment of 1,900. Highest level of offering: master's.

ACCREDITATIONS: EH ARCH ART FIDER LSAR

Rhodes College

2000 North Parkway
Memphis, TN 38112
(901) 726-3885

Will confirm attendance and degree by phone or mail. Inquiry must include student's name, years attended. Employers may obtain transcripts upon written request accompanied by a $2.00 fee and a signed release from the student.

A general baccalaureate institution, with an enrollment of 1,407 Highest level of offering: four or five year baccalaureate.

ACCREDITATIONS: SC MUS ACS

Rice University

PO Box 1892
Houston, TX 77251
(713) 527-8101

Will confirm attendance and degree by mail. Inquiry must include student's name, date of birth, social security number, years attended, release. Employers may obtain transcripts upon written request accompanied by a $1.00 fee and a signed release from the student.

A doctoral-level institution with no medical school, with an enrollment of 4,040. Highest level of offering: doctorate.

ACCREDITATIONS: SC ARCH ENG

Rich Mountain Community College

601 Bush Street
Mena, AR 71953
Fax (501) 394-2828
(501) 394-5012 Ext. 45

Will confirm attendance and degree by mail. Inquiry must include student's name, social security number. Employers may obtain transcripts upon written request accompanied by a $1.00 fee and a signed release from the student.

A two-year institution newly admitted to NCES, with an enrollment of 750. Highest level of offering: one year but less than four years.

ACCREDITATIONS: NH

Richard Bland College of the College of William and Mary

Route 1 Box 77-A
Petersburg, VA 23805
(804) 862-6225 Ext. 206
Fax (804) 862-6189

Will confirm attendance and degree by phone, fax or mail. Inquiry must include student's name, social security number, years attended. Employers may obtain transcripts upon written request accompanied by a signed release from the student.

A multiprogram two-year institution, with an enrollment of 1,100. Highest level of offering: one year but less than four years.

ACCREDITATIONS: SC SACS

Richard J. Daley College

Attn: Admissions
7500 South Pulaski Road
Chicago, IL 60652
(312) 735-3000

Will confirm attendance and degree by phone or mail. Inquiry must include student's name, social security number, years attended. Employers may obtain transcripts upon written request accompanied by a $2.00 fee and a signed release from the student.

A multiprogram two-year institution, with an enrollment of 9,638. Highest level of offering: one year but less than four years.

ACCREDITATIONS: NH

Richland College

12800 Abrams Road
Dallas, TX 75243-2199
(214) 238-6100

Will confirm attendance and degree by mail. Inquiry must include student's name, social security number, release. Employers may obtain transcripts upon written request accompanied by a signed release from the student. Requests should be directed to: Admissions Office.

A multiprogram two-year institution, with an enrollment of 12,577. Highest level of offering: one year but less than four years.

ACCREDITATIONS: SACS

Richland Community College

Attn: Student Records
1 College Park
Decatur, IL 62521
(217) 875-7200 Ext. 257

Will confirm attendance and degree by phone or mail. Inquiry must include student's name, social security number. Employers may obtain transcripts upon written request accompanied by a $1.00 fee and a signed release from the student.

A multiprogram two-year institution, with an enrollment of 4,000. Highest level of offering: one year but less than four years.

ACCREDITATIONS: NH

Richmond Community College

Box 1189
Hamlet, NC 28345
(919) 582-7113
Fax (919) 582-7028

Will confirm attendance and degree by mail or fax. Inquiry must include student's name, social security number, years attended, release. Employers may obtain transcripts upon written request accompanied by a signed release from the student.

A multiprogram two-year institution, with an enrollment of 786. Highest level of offering: one year but less than four years.
ACCREDITATIONS: SC

Ricks College

Registrar's Office
Rexburg, ID 83460-4125
(208) 356-1084
Fax (208) 356-1035

Will confirm attendance and degree by phone or mail. Inquiry must include student's name, date of birth, social security number, years attended. Employers may obtain transcripts upon written request accompanied by a $2.00 fee and a signed release from the student.

A multiprogram two-year institution, with an enrollment of 7,591. Highest level of offering: two years but less than four years.
ACCREDITATIONS: NW ADNUR ENGT MUS

Rider College

2083 Lawrenceville Road
Lawrenceville, NJ 08648-3099
(609) 896-5065

Will confirm attendance and degree by phone or mail. Inquiry must include student's name, social security number, years attended. Employers may obtain transcripts upon written request accompanied by a signed release from the student.

A comprehensive college, with an enrollment of 5,600. Highest level of offering: master's.
ACCREDITATIONS: M TED

Rika Breuer Teachers Seminary

85-93 Bennett Avenue
New York, NY 10033
(212) 568-6200

Will confirm attendance and degree by phone or mail. Inquiry must include student's name, years attended. Employers may obtain transcripts upon written request accompanied by a $4.00 fee and a signed release from the student.

A specialized non-degree granting institution, with an enrollment of 73. Highest level of offering: one year but less than four years.
ACCREDITATIONS: 3IC

Ringling School of Art and Design

2700 N. Tamiami Trail
Sarasota, FL 34234
(813) 351-4614

Will confirm attendance and degree by phone or mail. Inquiry must include student's name, social security number. Employers may obtain transcripts upon written request accompanied by a $2.00 fee and a signed release from the student.

A visual and performing arts school, with an enrollment of 500. Highest level of offering: four or five year baccalaureate.
ACCREDITATIONS: SC ART FIDER

Rio Grande College

(See University of Rio Grande)

Rio Hondo College

3600 Workman Mill Road
Whittier, CA 90608
(310) 692-0921 Ext. 301
Fax (310) 699-7386

Will confirm attendance and degree by phone, fax or mail. Inquiry must include student's name, date of birth, social security number, release. Employers may obtain transcripts upon written request accompanied by a $3.00 fee and a signed release from the student. Requests should be directed to: Registrar's Office.

A multiprogram two-year institution, with an enrollment of 13,512. Highest level of offering: one year but less than four years.
ACCREDITATIONS: WJ DA RSTH

Rio Salado Community College

640 North First Avenue
Phoenix, AZ 85003
(602) 223-4000
Fax (602) 223-4329

Will confirm attendance and degree by mail, phone or fax. Inquiry must include student's name, social security number, years attended. Employers may obtain transcripts upon written request accompanied by a $5.00 fee and a signed release from the student.

A multiprogram two-year institution, with an enrollment of 13,712. Highest level of offering: one year but less than four years.
ACCREDITATIONS: NH

Ripon College

300 Seward Street PO Box 248
Ripon, WI 54971
(414) 748-8119
Fax (414) 748-9262

Will confirm attendance and degree by phone or mail. Inquiry must include student's name, years attended. Employers may obtain transcripts upon written request accompanied by a $2.00 fee and a signed release from the student.

A general baccalaureate institution, with an enrollment of 801. Highest level of offering: four or five year baccalaureate.
ACCREDITATIONS: NCA

Riverside Community College

Attn: Enrollment Services
4800 Magnolia Avenue
Riverside, CA 92506
(714) 684-3240
Fax (714) 781-8574

Will confirm attendance and degree by mail or fax. Inquiry must include student's name, date of birth, social security number, release. Employers may obtain transcripts upon written request accompanied by a $2.00 fee and a signed release from the student. Requests should be directed to: Admissions Office.

A multiprogram two-year institution, with an enrollment of 22,073. Highest level of offering: two year but less than four years.
ACCREDITATIONS: WJ ADNUR DT

Rivier College

420 S. Main Street
Nashua, NH 03060
(603) 888-1311 Ext. 231

Will confirm attendance and degree by phone or mail. Inquiry must include student's name, social security number, years attended. Employers may obtain transcripts upon written request accompanied by a $3.00 fee and a signed release from the student.

A comprehensive institution with no medical school, with an enrollment of 2,500. Highest level of offering: master's.
ACCREDITATIONS: EH MLTAD

Roane State Community College

Patton Lane
Harriman, TN 37748
(615) 882-4523 Ext. 4523
Fax (615) 354-3000 Ext. 4462

Will confirm attendance and degree by phone, fax or mail. Inquiry must include student's name, social security number. Employers may obtain transcripts upon written request accompanied by a signed release from the student.

A multiprogram two-year institution, with an enrollment of 3,521. Highest level of offering: one year but less than four years.
ACCREDITATIONS: SC ADNUR ENGT MLTAD MRT RAD RSTH

Roanoke–Chowan Technical College

Route 2 Box 46a
Ahoskie, NC 27910
(919) 332-5921 Ext. 220

Will confirm attendance and degree by mail. Inquiry must include student's name. Employers may obtain transcripts upon written request accompanied by a $1.00 fee and a signed release from the student.

A multiprogram two-year institution, with an enrollment of 710. Highest level of offering: one year but less than four years.
ACCREDITATIONS: SC

Roanoke Bible College

714 First Street
Elizabeth City, NC 27909
(919) 338-5191 Ext. 9

Will confirm attendance and degree by phone or mail. Inquiry must include student's name, date of birth, social security number. Employers may obtain transcripts upon written request accompanied by a $3.00 fee and a signed release from the student.

A school of philosophy, religion and theology, with an enrollment of 142. Highest level of offering: four or five year baccalaureate.

ACCREDITATIONS: AABC

Roanoke College

Salem, VA 24153
(703) 375-2210
Fax (703) 375-2211

Will confirm attendance and degree by phone, fax or mail. Inquiry must include student's name, social security number. Employers may obtain transcripts upon written request accompanied by a $2.00 fee and a signed release from the student.

A general baccalaureate institution, with an enrollment of 1,600. Highest level of offering: four or five year baccalaureate.

ACCREDITATIONS: SACS

Robert Morris College

180 N. La Salle Drive
Chicago, IL 60601
(312) 836-4849

Will confirm attendance and degree by phone or mail. Inquiry must include student's name, social security number. Employers may obtain transcripts upon written request accompanied by a signed release from the student.

A two-year institution newly admitted to NCES, with an enrollment of 2,102. Highest level of offering: one year but less than four years.

ACCREDITATIONS: NH MAC

Robert Morris College

Narrows Run Road
Coraopolis, PA 15108
(412) 262-8213
(412) 262-8215 (Transcript requests)
Fax (412) 262-5958

Will confirm attendance and degree by phone. Inquiry must include student's name, social security number. Employers may obtain transcripts upon written request accompanied by a $2.00 fee and a signed release from the student. Requests should be directed to: Student Record Office.

A business school, with an enrollment of 4,848. Highest level of offering: master's.

ACCREDITATIONS: M RAD

Roberts Wesleyan College

2301 Westside Drive
Rochester, NY 14624
(716) 594-9471 Ext. 421
Fax (716) 594-9757

Will confirm attendance and degree by phone or mail. Inquiry must include student's name, years attended. Employers may obtain transcripts upon written request accompanied by a $5.00 fee and a signed release from the student.

A general baccalaureate institution, with an enrollment of 630. Highest level of offering: four or five year baccalaureate; master's in education

ACCREDITATIONS: M MUS NUR NY SW NASAD

Robeson Community College

PO Box 1420
Lumberton, NC 28359
(919) 738-7101 Ext. 241
Fax (919) 671-4143

Will confirm attendance and degree by phone or mail. Inquiry must include student's name, social security number. Employers may obtain transcripts upon written request accompanied by a $1.00 fee and a signed release from the student.

A multiprogram two-year institution, with an enrollment of 1,101. Highest level of offering: one year but less than four years.

ACCREDITATIONS: SACS

Rochester Business Institute

1850 East Ridge Road
Rochester, NY 14622
(716) 266-0430

Will confirm attendance and degree by phone or mail. Inquiry must include student's name, years attended. Employers may obtain transcripts upon written request accompanied by a $5.00 fee and a signed release from the student.

A multiprogram two-year institution, with an enrollment of 587. Highest level of offering: one year but less than four years.

ACCREDITATIONS: NY

Rochester Community College

851 30th Avenue South East
Rochester, MN 55904-4999
(507) 285-7265
Fax (507) 285-7496

Will confirm attendance and degree by phone, fax or mail. Inquiry must include student's name, date of birth, social security number. Employers may obtain transcripts upon written request accompanied by a signed release from the student.

A multiprogram two-year institution, with an enrollment of 3,999. Highest level of offering: one year but less than four years.

ACCREDITATIONS: NH ADNUR ENGT MAC RSTH

Rochester Institute of Technology

1 Lomb Memorial Drive
Rochester, NY 14623
(716) 475-2821
Fax (716) 475-7005

Will confirm attendance and degree by phone or fax. Inquiry must include student's name, social security number. Employers may obtain transcripts upon written request accompanied by a $4.00 fee and a signed release from the student.

A comprehensive institution with no medical school, with an enrollment of 13,298. Highest level of offering: master's.

ACCREDITATIONS: M ART DIET ENG ENGT MRT NMT NY SW

Rock Valley College

3301 North Mulford Road
Rockford, IL 61111
(815) 654-4306
Fax (815) 654-5568

Will confirm attendance and degree by phone or mail. Inquiry must include student's name, social security number. Employers may obtain transcripts upon written request accompanied by a signed release from the student.

A multiprogram two-year institution, with an enrollment of 8,363. Highest level of offering: two years but less than four years.

ACCREDITATIONS: NCA DA RSTH RSTHT

Rockefeller University

1230th York Avenue–Box 270
New York, NY 10021
(212) 570-8086
Fax (212) 570-8505

Will confirm attendance and degree by phone or mail. Inquiry must include student's name, date of birth. Employers may obtain transcripts upon written request accompanied by a signed release from the student. Requests should be directed to: Graduate Studies Office.

A doctoral-level institution with no medical school, with an enrollment of 117. Highest level of offering: doctorate.

ACCREDITATIONS: NY

Rockford College

5050 East State Street
Rockford, IL 61108
(815) 226-4070

Will confirm attendance and degree by phone or mail. Inquiry must include student's name, social security number, years attended. Employers may obtain transcripts upon written request by student accompanied by a $3.00 fee and a signed release from the student. Requests should be directed to: Registrar's Office.

A general baccalaureate institution, with an enrollment of 1,421. Highest level of offering: master's.

ACCREDITATIONS: NH

Rockhurst College

5225 Troost Avenue
Kansas City, MO 64110
(816) 926-4057
Fax (816) 926-4588

Will confirm attendance and degree by phone, fax or mail. Inquiry must include student's name, date of birth, social security number. Employers may obtain transcripts upon written request accompanied by a signed release from the student.

A business school, with an enrollment of 2,426. Highest level of offering: master's.

ACCREDITATIONS: NH

Rockhurst College of Nursing

(Formerly Research College of Nursing)
1100 Rockhurst Road
Kansas City, MO 64110
(816) 926-4057
Fax (816) 926-4588

Will confirm attendance and degree by phone, fax or mail. Inquiry must include student's name, social security number, years attended. Employers may obtain transcripts upon written request by student accompanied by a signed release from the student.

A bachelor's or higher institution newly admitted to NCES, with an enrollment of 110. Highest level of offering: four or five year baccalaureate.

ACCREDITATIONS: NH

Rockingham Community College

PO Box 38
Wentworth, NC 27375-0038
(919) 342-4261 Ext. 117
Fax (919) 349-9986

Will confirm attendance and degree by mail or fax. Inquiry must include student's name, social security number, release. Employers may obtain transcripts upon written request accompanied by a signed release from the student. Requests should be directed to: Records Office.

A multiprogram two-year institution, with an enrollment of 1,529. Highest level of offering: one year but less than four years.

ACCREDITATIONS: SC

Rockland Community College

145 College Road
Suffern, NY 10901
(914) 574-4225

Will confirm attendance and degree by mail. Inquiry must include student's name, social security number, release. Employers may obtain transcripts upon written request accompanied by a $3.00 fee and a signed release from the student.

A multiprogram two-year institution, with an enrollment of 8,500. Highest level of offering: one year but less than four years.

ACCREDITATIONS: M ADNUR DA MLTAD NY

Rockmont College

(See Colorado Christian University)

Rocky Mountain College

1511 Poly Drive
Billings, MT 59102
(406) 657-1030
Fax (406) 259-9751

Will confirm attendance and degree by phone or mail. Inquiry must include student's name, social security number, years attended. Employers may obtain transcripts upon written request accompanied by a $2.00 fee and a signed release from the student.

A general baccalaureate institution, with an enrollment of 800. Highest level of offering: four or five year baccalaureate.

ACCREDITATIONS: NW

Roger Williams College Main Campus

Old Ferry Road
Bristol, RI 02809
(401) 254-3510

Will confirm attendance and degree by phone or mail. Inquiry must include student's name, years attended. Employers

may obtain transcripts upon written request accompanied by a $2.00 fee and a signed release from the student.

A general baccalaureate institution, with an enrollment of 2,978. Highest level of offering: four or five year baccalaureate.

ACCREDITATIONS: EH ENGT

Roger Williams College Providence Branch

612 Academy Avenue
Providence, RI 02908
(401) 274-2200

Will confirm attendance and degree by phone. Inquiry must include student's name, years attended. Employers may obtain transcripts upon written request accompanied by a $2.00 fee and a signed release from the student.

A general baccalaureate institution, with an enrollment of 1,322. Highest level of offering: four or five year baccalaureate.

ACCREDITATIONS: RSTH

Rogers State College

College Hill
Claremore, OK 74017-2099
(918) 341-7510

Will confirm attendance and degree by mail. Inquiry must include student's name, date of birth, social security number, years attended. Employers may obtain transcripts upon written request accompanied by a $1.00 fee and a signed release from the student.

A multiprogram two-year institution, with an enrollment of 3,200. Highest level of offering: one year but less than four years.

ACCREDITATIONS: NH ADNUR

Rogue Community College

3345 Redwood Highway
Grants Pass, OR 97527
(503) 479-5541 Ext. 254

Will confirm attendance and degree by mail. Inquiry must include student's name, social security number. Employers may obtain transcripts upon written request accompanied by a $2.00 fee and a signed release from the student.

A multiprogram two-year institution, with an enrollment of 5,500. Highest level of offering: one year but less than four years.

ACCREDITATIONS: NW RSTH RSTHT

Rollins College

Campus Mail 2713
Winter Park, FL 32789
(305) 646-2144
Fax (407) 646-1576

Will confirm attendance and degree by phone, fax or mail. Inquiry must include student's name, social security number, years attended. Employers may obtain transcripts upon written request accompanied by a $3.00 fee and a signed release from the student.

A comprehensive institution with no medical school, with an enrollment of 3,648. Highest level of offering: beyond master's but less than doctorate.

ACCREDITATIONS: SC BUS MUS

Roosevelt University

430 South Michigan Avenue
Chicago, IL 60605
(312) 341-3526

Will confirm attendance and degree by phone or mail. Inquiry must include student's name, social security number, years attended. Employers may obtain transcripts upon written request by student accompanied by a $3.00 fee and a signed release from the student. Requests should be directed to: Registrar's Office.

A comprehensive institution with no medical school, with an enrollment of 6,400. Highest level of offering: doctorate.

ACCREDITATIONS: NH MUS SW TED

Rosary College

7900 West Division Street
River Forest, IL 60305
(708) 524-6802

Will confirm attendance and degree by phone or mail. Inquiry must include student's name, social security number. Employers may obtain transcripts upon written request by student accompanied by a $2.00 fee. Requests should be directed to: Registrar's Office.

A comprehensive institution with no medical school, with an enrollment of 1,898. Highest level of offering: master's.

ACCREDITATIONS: NCA LIB

Rose–Hulman Institute of Technology

5500 Wabash Avenue
Terre Haute, IN 47803
(812) 877-1511 Ext. 298
Fax (812) 877-8298

Will confirm attendance and degree by phone or mail. Inquiry must include student's name, years attended. Employers may obtain transcripts upon written request accompanied by a $2.00 fee and a signed release from the student.

An engineering school, with an enrollment of 1,346. Highest level of offering: master's.

ACCREDITATIONS: NCA ENG ACS CPTACS

Rose State College

6420 South East 15th
Midwest City, OK 73110
(405) 733-7308

Will confirm attendance and degree by phone or mail. Inquiry must include student's name, date of birth, social security number, years attended. Employers may obtain transcripts upon written request accompanied by a $2.00 fee and a signed release from the student. Requests should be directed to: Admissions Office.

A multiprogram two-year institution, with an enrollment of 9,876. Highest level of offering: one year but less than four years.

ACCREDITATIONS: NH DA DH DT MLTAD RAD RSTH RSTHT

Rosemont College

Montgomery Avenue at Wendover
Rosemont, PA 19010
(215) 527-0200 Ext. 306

Will confirm attendance and degree by
phone or mail. Inquiry must include student's name, social security number.
Employers may obtain transcripts upon
written request accompanied by a $4.00 fee
and a signed release from the student.

A general baccalaureate institution, with an
enrollment of 688. Highest level of offering: four or five year baccalaureate.
ACCREDITATIONS: M

Rowan–Cabarrus Community College

Box 1595
Salisbury, NC 28145-1595
(704) 637-0760 Ext. 272
Fax (704) 637-6642

Will confirm attendance and degree by
phone or mail. Inquiry must include student's name, social security number.
Employers may obtain transcripts upon
written request accompanied by a signed release from the student.

A multiprogram two-year institution, with
an enrollment of 3,000. Highest level of offering: two years but less than four years.
ACCREDITATIONS: SC DA RAD

Roxbury Community College

1234 Columbus Avenue
Boston, MA 02120
(617) 427-0060

Will confirm attendance and degree by mail
or phone. Inquiry must include student's
name, date of birth, social security number,
years attended. Employers may obtain transcripts upon written request accompanied
by a $1.00 fee and a signed release from the
student.

A multiprogram two-year institution, with
an enrollment of 1,444. Highest level of offering: one year but less than four years.
ACCREDITATIONS: EH

Rush University

1743 West Harrison
Chicago, IL 60612
(312) 942-5681
Fax (312) 942-2219

Will confirm attendance and degree by mail
or fax. Inquiry must include student's name,
date of birth, years attended. Employers
may obtain transcripts upon written request
accompanied by a signed release from the
student. Requests should be directed to:
Registrar's Office.

A health professions school, with an enrollment of 1,112. Highest level of offering:
doctorate.
ACCREDITATIONS: NH ANEST HSA MED
MIDWF MT NUR

Russell Sage College Main Campus

Troy, NY 12180
(518) 270-2205

Will confirm attendance and degree by
phone or mail. Inquiry must include student's name, date of birth, social security
number. Employers may obtain transcripts
upon written request accompanied by a
$2.00 fee and a signed release from the stu-
dent.

A comprehensive institution with no medi-
cal school, with an enrollment of 3,426.
Highest level of offering: master's.
ACCREDITATIONS: M NUR NY PTA

Rust College

1 Rust Avenue
Holly Springs, MS 38635
(601) 252-8000 Ext. 4057

Will confirm attendance and degree by
phone or mail. Inquiry must include student's name. Employers may obtain transcripts upon written request accompanied
by a $1.50 fee and a signed release from the
student. Requests should be directed to:
Registrar's Office.

A general baccalaureate institution, with an
enrollment of 1,075. Highest level of offering: four or five year baccalaureate.
ACCREDITATIONS: SACS

Rutgers The State University of New Jersey Camden Campus

311 North 5th Street
Camden, NJ 08102
(609) 757-6053
Fax (609) 757-6453

Will confirm attendance and degree by
phone, fax or mail. Inquiry must include
student's name, maiden name, social security number, years and campus attended.
Employers may obtain transcripts upon
written request accompanied by a $3.00 fee
and a signed release from the student.

A general baccalaureate institution, with an
enrollment of 5,000. Highest level of offering: master's.
ACCREDITATIONS: M LAW NUR SW TED

Rutgers The State University of New Jersey New Brunswick Campus

CN 1360
Picscataway, NJ 08854
(201) 932-3220
Fax (908) 932-3221

Will confirm attendance and degree by
phone or mail. Inquiry must include student's name, date of birth, social security
number, years attended. Employers may obtain transcripts upon written request accompanied by a $3.00 fee and a signed release
from the student.

A doctoral-level institution with no medical
school, with an enrollment of 33,728.
Highest level of offering: doctorate.
ACCREDITATIONS: M APCP CLPSY ENG
LSAR MUS PHAR SCPSY SW TED THEA LIB

Rutgers The State University of New Jersey Newark Campus

249 University Avenue
Newark, NJ 07102
(201) 648-1766

Will confirm attendance and degree by
phone or mail. Inquiry must include student's name, years attended. Employers
may obtain transcripts upon written request
accompanied by a $3.00 fee and a signed
release from the student. Requests should
be directed to: Registrar's Office.

A comprehensive institution with no medi-
cal school, with an enrollment of 9,381.
Highest level of offering: doctorate.
ACCREDITATIONS: M BUS LAW MUS NUR
SW TED

Rutledge College–Charleston

(See Phillips Junior College Charleston)

Rutledge College–Columbia

1700 Laurel Street
Columbia, SC 29201

Will confirm attendance and degree by
mail. Inquiry must include student's name,
social security number, years attended, release. Employers may obtain transcripts
upon written request accompanied by a
$2.00 fee and a signed release from the stu-
dent.

A two-year institution newly admitted to
NCES, with an enrollment of 504. Highest
level of offering: one year but less than four
years.
ACCREDITATIONS: JRCB

Rutledge College–Fayetteville

(See Phillips Junior College.)

Rutledge College–Greenville

(See Phillips Junior College Greenville)

Rutledge College–Raleigh

(See Phillips Junior College Raleigh)

Rutledge College–Spartanburg

(See Phillips Junior College Spartanburg)

Rutledge College of Charlotte

(See Phillips Junior College of Charlotte)

Rutledge College of Durham

410 West Chapel Hill Street
Durham, NC 27701

Will confirm attendance and degree by
phone or mail. Inquiry must include student's name, social security number, release. Employers may obtain transcripts
upon written request accompanied by a
$2.00 fee and a signed release from the stu-
dent.

A single program two-year institution, with
an enrollment of 123. Highest level of offering: one year but less than four years.
ACCREDITATIONS: JRCB

Rutledge College of Greensboro

(See Phillips Junior College of Greensboro)

Rutledge College of Springfield

(See Phillips Junior College of Springfield)

Rutledge College of Winston–Salem

(See Phillips Junior College of Winston-
Salem)

Rutledge College

(See Phillips Junior College)

S

Sacramento City College

3835 Freeport Boulevard
Sacramento, CA 95822
(916) 558-2351

Will confirm attendance and degree by
phone or mail. Inquiry must include student's name, social security number, release. Employers may obtain transcripts
upon written request accompanied by a
$2.00 fee and a signed release from the stu-
dent. Requests should be directed to:
Admissions Office.

A multiprogram two-year institution, with
an enrollment of 16,500. Highest level of
offering: one year but less than four years.
ACCREDITATIONS: WJ ADNUR DA DH

Sacred Heart College

c/o Division of Archives and History
State of North Carolina
109 East Jones STreet
Raleigh, NC 27611
(704) 829-5100

Will confirm attendance and degree by
mail. Inquiry must include student's name,
social security number, release. Employers
may obtain transcripts upon written request
accompanied by a $2.00 fee and a signed
release from the student.

Sacred Heart School of Theology

7335 South Highway 100–PO Box 429
Hales Corners, WI 53130
(414) 425-8300 Ext. 7228

Will confirm attendance and degree by
mail. Inquiry must include student's name.
Employers may obtain transcripts upon
written request accompanied by a $5.00 fee
and a signed release from the student.
Requests should be directed to: Registrar's
Office.

A school of philosophy, religion and theology, with an enrollment of 150. Highest
level of offering: first professional degree.
ACCREDITATIONS: THEOL

Sacred Heart Major Seminary College

2701 Chicago Boulevard
Detroit, MI 48206
(313) 883-8500

Will confirm attendance and degree by
phone. Inquiry must include student's
name, years attended. Employers may obtain transcripts upon written request accompanied by a $5.00 fee and a signed release
from the student. Requests should be directed to: Registrar's Office.

A school of philosophy, religion and theology, with an enrollment of 203. Highest
level of offering: four or five year baccalaureate.
ACCREDITATIONS: NCA ATS

Sacred Heart University

5151 Park Avenue
Fairfield, CT 06432
(203) 371-7894
Fax (203) 365-7500

Will confirm attendance and degree by
phone or mail. Inquiry must include student's name, social security number, years
attended. Employers may obtain transcripts
upon written request accompanied by a
$3.00 fee and a signed release from the stu-
dent. Requests should be directed to:
Registrar's Office.

A general baccalaureate institution, with an
enrollment of 4,581. Highest level of offering: master's.
ACCREDITATIONS: EH NUR RSTH SW

Saddleback College

28000 Marguerite Parkway
Mission Viejo, CA 92692
(714) 582-4555

Will confirm attendance and degree by
phone or mail. Inquiry must include student's name, date of birth, social security
number. Employers may obtain transcripts
upon written request accompanied by a
$3.00 fee and a signed release from the stu-
dent.

A multiprogram two-year institution, with
an enrollment of 24,000. Highest level of
offering: one year but less than four years.
ACCREDITATIONS: WJ

Sage Junior College of Albany

140 New Scotland Avenue
Albany, NY 12208
(518) 445-1715
Fax (518) 436-0539

Will confirm attendance and degree by
phone or mail. Inquiry must include student's name, social security number.
Employers may obtain transcripts upon
written request accompanied by a $2.00 fee
and a signed release from the student.

A multiprogram two-year institution, with
an enrollment of 1,126. Highest level of offering: two years but less than four years.
ACCREDITATIONS: M ADNUR ART NY

Saginaw Business School

(See Great Lakes Junior College)

Saginaw Valley State College

2250 Pierce Road
University Center, MI 48710
(517) 790-4088

Will confirm attendance and degree by
phone or mail. Inquiry must include student's name, social security number.
Employers may obtain transcripts upon
written request accompanied by a $4.00 fee
and a signed release from the student.

A comprehensive institution with no medi-
cal school, with an enrollment of 6,474.
Highest level of offering: master's.
ACCREDITATIONS: ENGR NUR SW

Saint Alphonsus College

c/o St. Johns University
Grand Central Utopia Parkway
Jamaka, NY 11439
(718) 990-6161

Records are held at the above address. Will
confirm attendance and degree by phone or
mail. Inquiry must include student's name.
Employers may obtain transcripts upon
written request accompanied by a $3.00 fee
and a signed release from the student.

A specialized school, with an enrollment of
43. Highest level of offering: four or five
year baccalaureate.
ACCREDITATIONS: EH

Saint Ambrose College

518 West Locust Street
Davenport, IA 52804
(319) 383-8747
Fax (319) 383-8791

Will confirm attendance and degree by
phone, fax or mail. Inquiry must include
student's name, date of birth, social security
number, years attended. Employers may obtain transcripts upon written request accompanied by a $.25 fee per copy, $2.00 for
certified copy and a signed release from the
student.

A general baccalaureate institution, with an
enrollment of 2,278. Highest level of offering: master's
ACCREDITATIONS: NH

Saint Andrew's Presbyterian College

1700 Dogwood
Laurinburg, NC 28352
(919) 277-5221
Fax (919) 277-5020

Will confirm attendance and degree by phone, fax or mail. Inquiry must include student's name, years attended. Employers may obtain transcripts upon written request accompanied by a $5.00 fee and a signed release from the student.

A general baccalaureate institution, with an enrollment of 751. Highest level of offering: four or five year baccalaureate.
ACCREDITATIONS: SC

Saint Anselm College

Manchester, NH 03102
(603) 641-7000

Will confirm attendance and degree by phone or mail. Inquiry must include student's name. Employers may obtain transcripts upon written request accompanied by a $2.00 fee and a signed release from the student.

A general baccalaureate institution, with an enrollment of 1,917. Highest level of offering: four or five year baccalaureate.
ACCREDITATIONS: EH NUR

Saint Augustine College

1333 West Argyle
Chicago, IL 60640
(312) 878-8756 Ext. 143

Will confirm attendance and degree by mail. Inquiry must include student's name, social security number. Employers may obtain transcripts upon written request accompanied by a $2.00 fee and a signed release from the student.

A two-year institution newly admitted to NCES, with an enrollment of 774. Highest level of offering: one year but less than four years.
ACCREDITATIONS: NH

Saint Augustine's College

1315 Oakwood Avenue
Raleigh, NC 27610-2298
(919) 828-4451

Will confirm attendance and degree by phone or mail. Inquiry must include student's name, social security number, years attended, release. Employers may obtain transcripts upon written request accompanied by a $5.00 fee and a signed release from the student.

A general baccalaureate institution, with an enrollment of 1,716. Highest level of offering: four or five year baccalaureate.
ACCREDITATIONS: SC

Saint Basil's College

195 Glenbrook Road
Stamford, CT 06902
(203) 324-4578

This college is closed. However, records are held at the above address. Will confirm attendance and degree by phone or mail. Inquiry must include student's name, social security number. Employers may obtain transcripts upon written request accompanied by a $5.00 fee and a signed release from the student. Attn: Dr. Edward Bordeau.

A bachelor's or higher institution newly admitted to NCES, with an enrollment of 3. Highest level of offering: four or five year baccalaureate.
ACCREDITATIONS: 3IC

Saint Bernard Parish Community College

2500 Palmisano Blvd.
Chalmette, LA 70043
(504) 277-1142

Will confirm attendance and degree by phone or mail. Inquiry must include student's name, date of birth, social security number, years attended. Employers may obtain transcripts upon written request accompanied by a $2.00 fee and a signed release from the student.

A single program two-year institution, with an enrollment of 950. Highest level of offering: one year but less than four years.
ACCREDITATIONS: SC

Saint Bernard's Institute

1100 South Goodman Street
Rochester, NY 14620
(716) 271-1320 Ext. 290
Fax (716) 271-2166

Will confirm attendance and degree by phone or mail. Inquiry must include student's name, social security number. Employers may obtain transcripts upon written request accompanied by a $5.00 fee and a signed release from the student.

A specialized institution, with an enrollment of 200. Highest level of offering: master's.
ACCREDITATIONS: NY THEOL

Saint Bonaventure University

Registrar's Office
Saint Bonaventure, NY 14778
(716) 375-2022
Fax (716) 375-2135

Will confirm attendance and degree by phone or mail. Inquiry must include student's name, date of birth, social security number. Employers may obtain transcripts upon written request accompanied by a $3.00 fee and a signed release from the student.

A comprehensive institution with no medical school, with an enrollment of 2,675. Highest level of offering: doctorate.
ACCREDITATIONS: M NY

Saint Catharine College

Saint Catharine, KY 40061
(606) 336-5082 Ext. 242
Fax (606) 336-5134

Will confirm attendance and degree by phone, fax or mail. Inquiry must include student's name, social security number, years attended. Employers may obtain transcripts upon written request accompanied by a $2.00 fee and a signed release from the student.

A multiprogram two-year institution, with an enrollment of 300. Highest level of offering: one year but less than four years.
ACCREDITATIONS: SC

Saint Charles Borromeo Seminary

1000 East Wynnewood Rd.
Overbrook , PA 19096
(215) 667-3394

Will confirm attendance and degree by phone or mail. Inquiry must include student's name, years attended, release. Employers may obtain transcripts upon written request accompanied by a $3.00 fee and a signed release from the student.

A school of philosophy, religion and theology, with an enrollment of 173. Highest level of offering: beyond master's but less than doctorate.
ACCREDITATIONS: M THEOL

Saint Clair County Community College

PO Box 5015
323 Erie Street
Port Huron, MI 48061-5015
(313) 984-3881 Ext. 220

Will confirm attendance and degree by mail. Inquiry must include student's name, date of birth, social security number. Employers may obtain transcripts upon written request accompanied by a $3.00 fee and a signed release from the student. Requests should be directed to: Records Office.

A multiprogram two-year institution, with an enrollment of 4,600. Highest level of offering: one year but less than four years.
ACCREDITATIONS: NH

Saint Cloud State University

Saint Cloud, MN 56301
(612) 255-2111

Will confirm attendance and degree by phone or mail. Inquiry must include student's name, social security number. Employers may obtain transcripts upon written request accompanied by a $2.00 fee and a signed release from the student. Requests should be directed to: Records & Registration Office.

A comprehensive institution with no medical school, with an enrollment of 16,500. Highest level of offering: beyond master's but less than doctorate.
ACCREDITATIONS: NH ART BUS JOUR MUS SW TED

Saint Edward's University

3001 South Congress Ave
Austin, TX 78704
(512) 448-8750
Fax (512) 448-8492

Will confirm attendance and degree by phone, fax or mail. Inquiry must include student's name, years attended. Employers may obtain transcripts upon written request accompanied by a $2.00 fee and a signed release from the student.

A general baccalaureate institution, with an enrollment of 2,980. Highest level of offering: master's.
ACCREDITATIONS: SC SW

Saint Francis College

2701 Spring Street
Fort Wayne, IN 46808-3994
(219) 434-3252

Will confirm attendance and degree by phone or mail. Inquiry must include student's name, social security number, years attended. Employers may obtain transcripts upon written request accompanied by a $2.00 fee and a signed release from the student.

A comprehensive institution with no medical school, with an enrollment of 1,012. Highest level of offering: beyond master's but less than doctorate.
ACCREDITATIONS: NH SW TED

Saint Francis College

180 Remsen Street
Brooklyn, NY 11201
(718) 522-2300

Will confirm attendance and degree by mail. Inquiry must include student's name, date of birth, social security number, years attended, release. Employers may obtain transcripts upon written request accompanied by a $5.00 fee and a signed release from the student.

A general baccalaureate institution, with an enrollment of 1,800. Highest level of offering: four or five year baccalaureate.
ACCREDITATIONS: M NY

Saint Francis College

Loretto, PA 15940
(814) 472-3009

Will confirm attendance and degree by phone or mail. Inquiry must include student's name, date of birth, social security number, years attended, release. Employers may obtain transcripts upon written request accompanied by a $3.00 fee and a signed release from the student.

A general baccalaureate institution, with an enrollment of 1,750. Highest level of offering: master's.
ACCREDITATIONS: M APCP SW

Saint Francis Seminary

3257 South Lake Drive
St. Francis, WI 53235
(414) 747-6450
Fax (414) 747-6442

Will confirm attendance and degree by phone or mail. Inquiry must include student's name, maiden name. Employers may obtain transcripts upon written request accompanied by a $4.00 fee and a signed release from the student.

A school of philosophy, religion and theology, with an enrollment of 98. Highest level of offering: master's.

Saint Gregory's College

1900 West Macarthur
Shawnee, OK 74801
(405) 878-5433

Will confirm attendance and degree by phone or mail. Inquiry must include student's name, social security number, release. Employers may obtain transcripts upon written request accompanied by a $2.00 fee and a signed release from the student.

A multiprogram two-year institution, with an enrollment of 261. Highest level of offering: one year but less than four years.
ACCREDITATIONS: NH

Saint Hyacinth College–Seminary

66 School Street
Granby, MA 01033
(413) 467-7191

Will confirm attendance and degree by phone or mail. Inquiry must include student's name, years attended, release. Requests should be directed to: Registrar's Office. Employers may obtain transcripts upon written request accompanied by a $3.00 fee and a signed release from the student.

A specialized school, with an enrollment of 39. Highest level of offering: four or five year baccalaureate.
ACCREDITATIONS: EH

Saint John Vianney College Seminary

2900 South West 87th Avenue
Miami, FL 33165
(305) 223-4561

Will confirm attendance and degree by mail. Inquiry must include student's name, release. Employers may obtain transcripts upon written request accompanied by a $2.00 fee and a signed release from the student.

A specialized school, with an enrollment of 54. Highest level of offering: four or five year baccalaureate.
ACCREDITATIONS: SACS

Saint John's College

c/o Concordia Teacher's College
Seward, NE 68434
(402) 643-7230
Fax (402) 643-4073

Will confirm attendance and degree by phone or mail. Inquiry must include student's name, maiden name, social security number, years attended. Employers may obtain transcrits upon written request accompanied by a $5.00 fee and a signed release from the student.

St. John's College

PO Box 2800
Annapolis, MD 21404
(301) 263-2371

Will confirm attendance and degree by mail. Inquiry must include student's name, social security number, years attended, release. Employers may obtain transcripts upon written request accompanied by a $2.00 fee and a signed release from the student.

Highest level of offering: master's.

Saint John's Provincial Seminary

c/o Sacred Heart Seminary
2701 W. Chicago Blvd.
Detroit, MI 48206
(313) 883-8500

Records are being maintained by Sacred Heart Major Seminary. Will confirm attendance and degree by mail. Inquiry must include student's name, social security number, years attended. Employers may obtain transcripts upon written request accompanied by a $5.00 fee and a signed release from the student.

Saint John's Seminary College

5012 East Seminary Road
Camarillo, CA 93012
(805) 482-4697
Fax (805) 484-4074

Will confirm attendance and degree by phone, fax or mail. Inquiry must include student's name, years attended. Employers may obtain transcripts upon written request accompanied by a $2.00 fee and a signed release from the student.

A school of philosophy, religion and theology, with an enrollment of 135. Highest level of offering: master's.
ACCREDITATIONS: WC THEOL

Saint John's Seminary

127 Lake Street
Brighton, MA 02135
(617) 254-2610

Will confirm attendance and degree by phone or mail. Inquiry must include student's name, years attended. Employers may obtain transcripts upon written request accompanied by a $2.00 fee and a signed release from the student.

A general baccalaureate institution, with an enrollment of 110. Highest level of offering: master's.
ACCREDITATIONS: EH THEOL

Saint John's University

Collegeville, MN 56321
(612) 363-3394

Will confirm attendance and degree by phone or mail. Inquiry must include student's name, date of birth, social security number. Employers may obtain transcripts upon written request accompanied by a $2.00 fee and a signed release from the student.

A general baccalaureate institution, with an enrollment of 1,956. Highest level of offering: master's.
ACCREDITATIONS: NCA SW TED THEOL

Saint John's University, New York

Grand Cen & Utopia Pkwys
Jamaica, NY 11439
(718) 990-6322

Will confirm attendance and degree by phone or mail. Inquiry must include student's name, social security number. Employers may obtain transcripts upon written request accompanied by a $3.00 fee and a signed release from the student. Requests should be directed to: Records Department.

A doctoral-level institution with no medical school, with an enrollment of 19,037. Highest level of offering: doctorate.
ACCREDITATIONS: M BUS LAW LIB NY PHAR CLPSY ACS ASLQ/P

Saint Johns River Community College

5001 Saint Johns Avenue
Palatka, FL 32077
(904) 328-1571

Will confirm attendance and degree by mail. Inquiry must include student's name, date of birth, social security number, release. Requests should be directed to: Records Office. Employers may obtain transcripts upon written request accompanied by a signed release from the student.

A multiprogram two-year institution, with an enrollment of 3,200. Highest level of offering: one year but less than four years.

ACCREDITATIONS: SC

Saint Joseph College

1678 Asylum Avenue
West Hartford, CT 06117
(203) 232-4571

Will confirm attendance and degree by phone or mail. Inquiry must include student's name, social security number. Employers may obtain transcripts upon written request accompanied by a $4.00 fee and a signed release from the student.

A comprehensive institution with no medical school, with an enrollment of 2,000. Highest level of offering: beyond master's but less than doctorate.

ACCREDITATIONS: EH DIET NUR SW

Saint Joseph Seminary College

Saint Benedict, LA 70457-9990
(504) 892-1800

Will confirm attendance and degree by phone or mail. Inquiry must include student's name, social security number, years attended. Employers may obtain transcripts upon written request accompanied by a $2.00 fee and a signed release from the student.

A general baccalaureate institution, with an enrollment of 89. Highest level of offering: four or five year baccalaureate.

ACCREDITATIONS: SC

Saint Joseph's College Main Campus

245 Clinton Avenue
Brooklyn, NY 11205
(718) 636-6800
Fax (718) 398-4936

Will confirm attendance and degree by mail or fax. Inquiry must include student's name, social security number, years attended. Employers may obtain transcripts upon written request accompanied by a $3.00 fee and a signed release from the student.

A health institution, with an enrollment of 928. Highest level of offering: four or five year baccalaureate.

ACCREDITATIONS: M NY

Saint Joseph's College Suffolk Campus

155 Roe Boulevard
Patchogue, NY 11772
(516) 447-3200

Will confirm attendance and degree or mail. Inquiry must include student's name, social security number. Employers may obtain transcripts upon written request accompanied by a $3.00 fee and a signed release from the student.

A general baccalaureate institution, with an enrollment of 1,400. Highest level of offering: four or five year baccalaureate.

ACCREDITATIONS: M NY

Saint Joseph's College

c/o St. Patrick Seminary
320 Middlefield Road
Menlo Park, CA 94025
(415) 325-5621

Records are held at the above address. Will confirm attendance and degree by mail. Inquiry must include student's name, years attended. Employers may obtain transcripts upon written request accompanied by a $4.00 fee and a signed release from the student.

A general baccalaureate institution, with an enrollment of 112. Highest level of offering: four or five year baccalaureate.

ACCREDITATIONS: WC

Saint Joseph's College

Whites Bridge Road
Windham, ME 04062-1198
(207) 892-6766 Ext. 1752
Fax (207) 892-7746

Will confirm attendance and degree by phone, fax or mail. Inquiry must include student's name, social security number. Employers may obtain transcripts upon written request accompanied by a $3.00 fee and a signed release from the student.

A health institution, with an enrollment of 600. Highest level of offering: four or five year baccalaureate.

ACCREDITATIONS: EH NUR

Saint Joseph's College

PO Box 929
Rensselaer, IN 47978
(219) 866-6161

Will confirm attendance and degree by phone or mail. Inquiry must include student's name, date of birth, social security number. Employers may obtain transcripts upon written request accompanied by a $3.00 fee and a signed release from the student. Requests should be directed to: Registrar's Office.

A general baccalaureate institution, with an enrollment of 1,021. Highest level of offering: master's.

ACCREDITATIONS: NCA TED

Saint Joseph's Seminary and College

201 Seminary Ave.
Yonkers, NY 10704
(914) 968-6200 Ext. 8208
Fax (914) 968-7912

Will confirm attendance and degree by phone, fax or mail. Inquiry must include student's name, social security number, years attended, release. Employers may obtain transcripts upon written request accompanied by a $2.00 fee and a signed release from the student.

A school of philosophy, religion and theology, with an enrollment of 77. Highest level of offering: master's.

ACCREDITATIONS: M NY THEOL

Saint Joseph's University

5600 City Avenue
Philadelphia, PA 19131
(215) 660-1015
Fax (215) 473-0001

Will confirm attendance and degree by phone or mail. Inquiry must include student's name, social security number, years attended. Employers may obtain transcripts upon written request accompanied by a $2.00 fee and a signed release from the student.

A comprehensive institution with no medical school, with an enrollment of 6,985. Highest level of offering: master's.

ACCREDITATIONS: M

Saint Lawrence University

University Avenue
Canton, NY 13617
(315) 379-5267

Will confirm attendance and degree by phone or mail. Inquiry must include student's name, date of birth, social security number, years attended. Employers may obtain transcripts upon written request accompanied by a $3.00 fee and a signed release from the student.

A general baccalaureate institution, with an enrollment of 2,129. Highest level of offering: master's.

ACCREDITATIONS: M NY

Saint Leo College

PO Box 2278
Saint Leo, FL 33574
(904) 588-8200
Fax (904) 588-8350

Will confirm attendance and degree by phone, fax or mail. Inquiry must include student's name, social security number, release. Employers may obtain transcripts upon written request accompanied by a $2.00 fee and a signed release from the student. Requests should be directed to: Records Office.

A general baccalaureate institution, with an enrollment of 7,012. Highest level of offering: four or five year baccalaureate.

ACCREDITATIONS: SACS SW

Saint Louis Christian College

1360 Grandview Drive
Florissant, MO 63033
(314) 837-6777

Will confirm attendance and degree by phone or mail. Inquiry must include student's name, years attended. Employers may obtain transcripts upon written request accompanied by a $2.00 fee and a signed release from the student. Requests should be directed to: Registrar's Office.

A school of philosophy, religion and theology, with an enrollment of 153. Highest level of offering: four or five year baccalaureate.

ACCREDITATIONS: BI

Saint Louis College of Pharmacy

4588 Parkview Place
Saint Louis, MO 63110
(314) 367-8700 Ext. 228
Fax (314) 367-2784 Ext. 284

Will confirm attendance and degree by phone, fax or mail. Inquiry must include student's name. Employers may obtain transcripts upon written request accompanied by a $2.00 fee and a signed release from the student.

A health institution, with an enrollment of 750. Highest level of offering: five year baccalaureate and master's.

ACCREDITATIONS: NCA PHAR

Saint Louis Community College at Florissant Valley

3400 Pershall Road
Saint Louis, MO 63135
(314) 595-4244

Will confirm attendance and degree by phone or mail. Inquiry must include student's name, social security number. Requests should be directed to: Admissions & Records Office. Employers may obtain transcripts upon written request accompanied by a $2.00 fee and a signed release from the student.

A multiprogram two-year institution, with an enrollment of 11,628. Highest level of offering: one year but less than four years.

ACCREDITATIONS: NH ADNUR ART ENGT

Saint Louis Community College at Forest Park

5600 Oakland Avenue
Saint Louis, MO 63110
(314) 602-9102

Will confirm attendance and degree by mail or phone, Monday-Thursday 1p.m. to 6:30 p.m. Central Time. Inquiry must include student's name, social security number. Requests should be directed to: Records U-200. Employers may obtain transcripts upon written request accompanied by a $2.00 fee and a signed release from the student.

A multiprogram two-year institution, with an enrollment of 6,564. Highest level of offering: one year but less than four years.

ACCREDITATIONS: NH ADNUR DA DH FUSER MAC MLTAD RAD RSTH RSTHT SURGT

Saint Louis Community College at Meramec

11333 Big Bend Boulevard
Kirkwood, MO 63122
(314) 966-7502

Will confirm attendance and degree by mail or phone. Inquiry must include student's name, date of birth, social security number, release. Requests should be directed to: Admissions Office. Employers may obtain transcripts upon written request accompanied by a $2.00 fee and a signed release from the student. Direct requests to Central Student Records, 5600 Oakland Ave., Room B013, St. Louis, MO 66310.

A multiprogram two-year institution, with an enrollment of 15,000. Highest level of offering: one year but less than four years.

ACCREDITATIONS: NH ADNUR DA DT PTAA

Saint Louis Conservatory of Music

560 Trinity at Delmar
Saint Louis, MO 63130
(314) 863-3033

Will confirm attendance and degree by phone or mail. Inquiry must include student's name, years attended, release. Employers may obtain transcripts upon written request accompanied by a $3.00 fee and a signed release from the student.

A visual and performing arts school, with an enrollment of 17,000.

ACCREDITATIONS: MUS

Saint Louis Rabbinical College

7400 Olive Road
Saint Louis, MO 63130
(314) 727-1379

Will confirm attendance and degree by phone or mail. Inquiry must include student's name, social security number. Employers may obtain transcripts upon written request accompanied by a $5.00 fee and a signed release from the student.

A school of philosophy, religion and theology, with an enrollment of 60. Highest level of offering: first professional degree.

ACCREDITATIONS: RABN

Saint Louis University All Campuses

221 North Grand Boulevard
St Louis, MO 63103
(314) 658-2269
Fax (314) 658-3874

Will confirm attendance and degree by phone, fax or mail. Inquiry must include student's name, social security number. Employers may obtain transcripts upon written request accompanied by a $3.00 fee and a signed release from the student.

Highest level of offering: doctorate.

Saint Martin's College

5300 Pacific Ave. SE
Lacey, WA 98503
(206) 438-4356
Fax (206) 459-4124

Will confirm attendance and degree by phone or mail. Inquiry must include student's name, date of birth, social security number. Employers may obtain transcripts upon written request by student, accompanied by a $2.00 fee. Requests should be directed to: Records Department.

A general baccalaureate institution, with an enrollment of 508. Highest level of offering: master's.

ACCREDITATIONS: NW ENG

Saint Mary–Of–The–Woods College

Saint Mary-Of-The-Woods, IN 47876
(812) 535-5269

Will confirm attendance and degree by phone or mail. Inquiry must include student's name, social security number. Requests should be directed to: Registrar's Office. Employers may obtain transcripts upon written request accompanied by a $2.00 fee and a signed release from the student.

A general baccalaureate institution, with an enrollment of 900. Highest level of offering: master's.

ACCREDITATIONS: NH MUS

Saint Mary College

4100 South 4th Street
Leavenworth, KS 66048-5082
(913) 682-5151 Ext. 235

Will confirm attendance and degree by phone or mail. Inquiry must include student's name, date of birth, social security number. Employers may obtain transcripts upon written request accompanied by a $3.00 fee and a signed release from the student.

A general baccalaureate institution, with an enrollment of 950. Highest level of offering: four or five year baccalaureate.

ACCREDITATIONS: NH NUR TED

Saint Mary of the Lake Seminary

(See University of Saint Mary of the Lake)

Saint Mary of the Plains College

240 San Jose Drive
Dodge City, KS 67801
(316) 225-4171 Ext. 166
Fax (316) 225-6212

Will confirm attendance and degree by phone or mail. Inquiry must include student's name, social security number. Employers may obtain transcripts upon written request accompanied by a $2.00 fee and a signed release from the student.

A general baccalaureate institution, with an enrollment of 906. Highest level of offering: four or five year baccalaureate.

ACCREDITATIONS: NCAADNUR MUS NUR SW TED

Saint Mary Seminary

28700 Euclid Ave.
Wickliffe, OH 44092
(216) 943-7600 Ext. 7666
Fax (216) 943-7577

Will confirm attendance and degree by phone, fax or mail. Inquiry must include student's name, social security number, years attended. Requests should be directed to: Kathy Simmons. Employers may obtain transcripts upon written request accompanied by a $3.00 fee and a signed release from the student.

A school of religion and theology, with an enrollment of 50. Highest level of offering: master's.

ACCREDITATIONS: NCA THEOL

Saint Mary's Campus

2500 South 6th Street
Minneapolis, MN 55454
(612) 332-5521 Ext. 229

Will confirm attendance and degree by phone or mail. Inquiry must include student's name, date of birth. Employers may obtain transcripts upon written request accompanied by a $3.00 fee and a signed release from the student. Requests should be directed to: Records Office.

A multiprogram two-year institution, with an enrollment of 825. Highest level of offering: one year but less than four years.

ACCREDITATIONS: NH ADNUR MLTAD MRT PTAA RSTH

Saint Mary's College of California

PO Box 4748
Moraga, CA 94575
(510) 631-4214

Will confirm attendance and degree by phone or mail. Inquiry must include student's name, date of birth, social security number, years attended. Employers may obtain transcripts upon written request accompanied by a $3.00 fee and a signed release from the student. Requests should be directed to: Registrar's Office.

A comprehensive institution with no medical school, with an enrollment of 3,590. Highest level of offering: master's.

ACCREDITATIONS: WC

Saint Mary's College of Maryland

Saint Mary's City, MD 20686
(301) 862-0336

Will confirm attendance and degree by phone or mail. Inquiry must include student's name, maiden name, social security number. Requests should be directed to: Record's Office. Employers may obtain transcripts upon written request accompanied by a $2.00 fee and a signed release from the student.

A general baccalaureate institution, with an enrollment of 1,500. Highest level of offering: four or five year baccalaureate.

ACCREDITATIONS: M MUS

Saint Mary's College of O'fallon

4601 Mid Rivers Mall Drive
Saint Peters, MO 63376
(314) 922-8000

Will confirm attendance and degree by mail. Inquiry must include student's name, social security number, years attended, release. Requests should be directed to: Registrar's Office. Employers may obtain transcripts upon written request by student, accompanied by a $3.00 fee.

A multiprogram two-year institution, with an enrollment of 3,500. Highest level of offering: one year but less than four years.

ACCREDITATIONS: NH ADNUR MRT

Saint Mary's College

900 Hillsborough Street
Raleigh, NC 27603
(919) 828-2521
Fax (919) 832-4831

Will confirm attendance and degree by phone, fax or mail. Inquiry must include student's name, years attended. Employers may obtain transcripts upon written request accompanied by a $2.00 fee and a signed release from the student.

A multiprogram two-year institution, with an enrollment of 400. Highest level of offering: one year but less than four years.

ACCREDITATIONS: SC

Saint Mary's College

Orchard Lake, MI 48324
(313) 682-1885
Fax (313) 683-0402

Will confirm attendance and degree by phone, fax or mail. Inquiry must include student's name, years attended. Requests should be directed to: Registrar's Office. Employers may obtain transcripts upon written request accompanied by a $3.00 fee and a signed release from the student.

A general baccalaureate institution, with an enrollment of 400. Highest level of offering: four or five year baccalaureate.

ACCREDITATIONS: NH

Saint Mary's College

Box 37
Winona, MN 55987
(507) 457-1428

Will confirm attendance and degree by phone or mail. Inquiry must include student's name. Employers may obtain transcripts upon written request accompanied by a $2.00 fee and a signed release from the student.

A comprehensive institution with no medical school, with an enrollment of 1,480. Highest level of offering: master's.

ACCREDITATIONS: NH ANEST NMT

Saint Mary's College

Notre Dame, IN 46556
(219) 284-4560
Fax (219) 284-4716

Will confirm attendance and degree by phone or mail. Inquiry must include student's name, social security number. Employers may obtain transcripts upon written request accompanied by a $2.00 fee and a signed release from the student.

A general baccalaureate institution, with an enrollment of 1,675. Highest level of offering: four or five year baccalaureate.

ACCREDITATIONS: NCA ART MUS NUR TED

Saint Mary's Dominican College

7300 Saint Charles Avenue
New Orleans, LA 70118
(504) 865-7761

Records are maintained at the above address. Will confirm attendance and degree by phone or mail. Inquiry must include student's name, date of birth, release. Employers may obtain transcripts upon written request accompanied by a $3.00 fee and a signed release from the student.

Saint Mary's Seminary and University

5400 Roland Avenue
Baltimore, MD 21210
(410) 323-3200
Fax (410) 323-3554

Will confirm attendance and degree by mail. Inquiry must include student's name, social security number, date of birth, release. Employers may obtain transcripts upon written request accompanied by a $3.00 fee and a signed release from the student.

A school of philosophy, religion and theology, with an enrollment of 348. Highest level of offering: master's.

ACCREDITATIONS: M THEOL

Saint Mary's Seminary

1701 West Street Joseph
Perryville, MO 63775-1599
(314) 547-6533
Fax (314) 547-6534

Records are maintained at the above address. Will confirm attendance. Inquiry must include student's name, social security number. Employer may obtain transcripts upon written request accompanied by a $5.00 fee and a signed release.

Saint Mary's University of San Antonio

One Camino Santa Maria
San Antonio, TX 78228-8576
(512) 436-3701
Fax (512) 436-3500

Will confirm attendance and degree by phone, fax or mail. Inquiry must include student's name, date of birth, social security number, years attended. Employers may obtain transcripts upon written request accompanied by a $3.00 fee and a signed release from the student.

A comprehensive institution with no medical school, with an enrollment of 4,000. Highest level of offering: master's.

ACCREDITATIONS: SC ENG LAW MUS MFCD

Saint Meinrad College

Saint Meinrad, IN 47577
(812) 357-6525

Will confirm attendance and degree by phone or mail. Inquiry must include student's name, social security number, years attended. Employers may obtain transcripts upon written request accompanied by a $2.00 fee and a signed release from the student. Requests should be directed to: Registrar's Office.

A general baccalaureate institution, with an enrollment of 168. Highest level of offering: four or five year baccalaureate.
ACCREDITATIONS: NH

Saint Meinrad School of Theology

Saint Meinrad, IN 47577
(812) 357-6522

Will confirm attendance and degree by phone or mail. Inquiry must include student's name, date of birth, years attended. Employers may obtain transcripts upon written request accompanied by a $2.00 fee and a signed release from the student. Will not give transcript if student owes money.

A school of philosophy, religion and theology, with an enrollment of 147. Highest level of offering: master's.
ACCREDITATIONS: NH THEOL

Saint Michael's College

Park Colchester, VT 05439
(802) 654-2571

Will confirm attendance and degree by phone or mail. Inquiry must include student's name, social security number. Employers may obtain transcripts upon written request accompanied by a $2.00 fee and a signed release from the student. Requests should be directed to: Registrar's Office.

A comprehensive institution with no medical school, with an enrollment of 2,009. Highest level of offering: master's.
ACCREDITATIONS: EH

Saint Norbert College

De Pere, WI 54115
(414) 337-3216

Will confirm attendance and degree by phone or mail. Inquiry must include student's name, social security number. Employers may obtain transcripts upon written request accompanied by a $2.00 fee and a signed release from the student. Requests should be directed to: Registrar's Office.

A general baccalaureate institution, with an enrollment of 1,741. Highest level of offering: four or five year baccalaureate.
ACCREDITATIONS: NH

Saint Olaf College

Northfield, MN 55057
(507) 646-3015

Will confirm attendance and degree by phone or mail. Inquiry must include student's name, social security number, years attended. Employers may obtain transcripts upon written request accompanied by a $2.00 fee and a signed release from the student. Requests should be directed to: Registrar's Office.

A general baccalaureate institution, with an enrollment of 3,010. Highest level of offering: four or five year baccalaureate.
ACCREDITATIONS: NCA ACS NAST

Saint Patrick's Seminary

320 Middlefield Road
Menlo Park, CA 94025
(415) 325-5621
Fax (415) 322-0997

Will confirm attendance and degree by phone, fax or mail. Inquiry must include student's name, social security number, date of birth, years attended. Employers may obtain transcripts upon written request accompanied by a $3.00 fee and a signed release from the student.

A school of philosophy, religion and theology, with an enrollment of 85. Highest level of offering: master's.
ACCREDITATIONS: WC THEOL

Saint Paul Bible College

(See Crown College)

Saint Paul School of Theology

5123 Truman Road
Kansas City, MO 64127
(816) 483-9600

Will confirm attendance and degree by mail. Inquiry must include student's name, social security number, years attended, release. Employers may obtain transcripts upon written request accompanied by a $5.00 fee and a signed release from the student. Requests should be directed to: Registrar's Office.

A school of philosophy, religion and theology, with an enrollment of 133. Highest level of offering: doctorate.
ACCREDITATIONS: NH THEOL

Saint Paul Seminary

School of Divinity
2260 Summit Ave.
Saint Paul, MN 55105-1096
(612) 647-5715

Will confirm attendance and degree by mail. Inquiry must include student's name, social security number, release. Employers may obtain transcripts upon written request accompanied by a signed release from the student.

A school of philosophy, religion and theology, with an enrollment of 114. Highest level of offering: master's.
ACCREDITATIONS: NH THEOL

Saint Paul's College

200 Main
Concordia, MO 64020
(816) 463-2238
Fax (816) 463-7621

Records are maintained at the above address. Will confirm attendance and degree by phone or mail. Inquiry must include student's name. Requests should be directed to: Principal. Employers may obtain transcripts upon written request accompanied by a $3.00 fee and a signed release from the student.

Saint Paul's College

406 Windsor Avenue
Lawrenceville, VA 23868
(804) 848-3111

Will confirm attendance and degree by phone or mail. Inquiry must include student's name, social security number. Employers may obtain transcripts upon written request accompanied by a $3.00 fee and a signed release from the student.

A general baccalaureate institution, with an enrollment of 697. Highest level of offering: four or five year baccalaureate.
ACCREDITATIONS: SC

Saint Peter's College

2641 Kennedy Boulevard
Jersey City, NJ 07306
(201) 915-9035

Will confirm attendance and degree by phone or mail. Inquiry must include student's name, social security number. Employers may obtain transcripts upon written request accompanied by a $2.00 fee and a signed release from the student.

A general baccalaureate institution, with an enrollment of 3,000. Highest level of offering: master's.
ACCREDITATIONS: M NUR

Saint Petersburg Junior College

PO Box 13489
Saint Petersburg, FL 33733
(813) 341-3600
Fax (813) 341-4792

Will confirm attendance and degree by phone, fax or mail. Inquiry must include student's name, date of birth, years attended. Employers may obtain transcripts upon written request accompanied by a signed release from the student.

A multiprogram two-year institution, with an enrollment of 15,865. Highest level of offering: one year but less than four years.
ACCREDITATIONS: SC ADNUR ADVET DH ENGT MLTAD OPTT PTAA RAD RSTH SURGT

Saint Philip's College

2111 Nevada Street
San Antonio, TX 78203
(512) 531-3296

Will confirm attendance and degree by mail. Inquiry must include student's name, social security number, release. Employers may obtain transcripts upon written request accompanied by a signed release from the student.

A multiprogram two-year institution, with an enrollment of 6,313. Highest level of offering: one year but less than four years.
ACCREDITATIONS: SC MLTAD MRT PNE PTAA RAD RSTHT SURGT PNUR

Saint Thomas Aquinas College

Route 340
Sparkill, NY 10976
(914) 359-9500 Ext. 250

Will confirm attendance and degree by phone or mail. Inquiry must include student's name, social security number. Employers may obtain transcripts upon written request by student, accompanied by a $3.00 fee and a signed release from the student.

A general baccalaureate institution, with an enrollment of 2,100. Highest level of offering: four or five year master's.
ACCREDITATIONS: M NY

Saint Thomas Theological Seminary

1300 South Steele Street
Denver, CO 80210
(303) 722-4687 Ext. 264
Fax (303) 722-7422

Will confirm attendance and degree by phone or mail. Inquiry must include student's name, years attended. Employers may obtain transcripts upon written request accompanied by a $5.00 fee and a signed release from the student. Requests should be directed to: Registrar's Office.
A school of religion and theology, with an enrollment of 170. Highest level of offering: master's.
ACCREDITATIONS: NH THEOL

Saint Vincent College and Seminary

Latrobe, PA 15650
(412) 537-4559

Will confirm attendance and degree by phone or mail. Inquiry must include student's name, date of birth, social security number. Employers may obtain transcripts upon written request accompanied by a $2.00 fee and a signed release from the student.
A school of philosophy, religion and theology, with an enrollment of 1,150. Highest level of offering: master's.
ACCREDITATIONS: M THEOL

Saint Vladimir Orthodox Theological Seminary

575 Scarsdale Road
Crestwood, NY 10707
(914) 961-8313

Will confirm attendance and degree by phone or mail. Inquiry must include student's name, date of birth, social security number. Employers may obtain transcripts upon written request accompanied by a $3.00 fee and a signed release from the student.
A school of philosophy, religion and theology, with an enrollment of 91. Highest level of offering: doctorate
ACCREDITATIONS: NY THEOL

Saint Xavier College

3700 West 103rd Street
Chicago, IL 60655
(312) 779-3300
Fax (312) 779-9061

Will confirm attendance and degree by phone, fax or mail. Inquiry must include student's name, social security number, release. Employers may obtain transcripts upon written request accompanied by a $3.00 fee and a signed release from the student.
A general baccalaureate institution, with an enrollment of 2,700. Highest level of offering: master's.
ACCREDITATIONS: NH NUR

Salem College at Clarksburg

Salem, WV 26426
(304) 782-5297

Will confirm attendance and degree by phone or mail. Inquiry must include student's name, date of birth, social security number, years attended. Employers may obtain transcripts upon written request accompanied by a $5.00 fee and a signed release from the student.
A multiprogram two-year institution, with an enrollment of 396. Highest level of offering: one year but less than four years.
ACCREDITATIONS: NH

Salem–Teikyo University

223 West Main Street
Salem, WV 26426
(304) 782-5297

Will confirm attendance and degree by phone or mail. Inquiry must include student's name, date of birth, social security number, years attended. Employers may obtain transcripts upon written request accompanied by a $5.00 fee and a signed release from the student. Requests should be directed to: Registrar's Office.
A general baccalaureate institution, with an enrollment of 600. Highest level of offering: master's.
ACCREDITATIONS: NCA

Salem College

Winston–Salem, NC 27108
(919) 721-2670

Will confirm attendance and degree by phone or mail. Inquiry must include student's name, social security number. Employers may obtain transcripts upon written request accompanied by a $2.00 fee and a signed release from the student. Requests should be directed to: Registrar's Office.
A general baccalaureate institution, with an enrollment of 672. Highest level of offering: four or five year baccalaureate.
ACCREDITATIONS: SC MUS

Salem Community College

460 Hollywood Avenue
Carneys Point, NJ 08069
(609) 299-2100 Ext. 232

Will confirm attendance and degree by mail. Inquiry must include student's name, social security number. Employers may obtain transcripts upon written request accompanied by a $3.00 fee and a signed release from the student.
A multiprogram two-year institution, with an enrollment of 1,490. Highest level of offering: one year but less than four years.
ACCREDITATIONS: M

Salem State College

352 Lafayette Street
Salem, MA 01970
(508) 741-6210

Will confirm attendance and degree by mail. Inquiry must include student's name, social security number, year graduated. Employers may obtain transcripts upon

written request accompanied by a $1.00 fee and a signed release from the student.
A comprehensive institution with no medical school, with an enrollment of 8,654. Highest level of offering: master's.
ACCREDITATIONS: EH NMT NUR SW TED

Salisbury State College

Salisbury, MD 21801
(301) 543-6150

Will confirm attendance and degree by phone or mail. Inquiry must include student's name, date of birth, social security number. Employers may obtain transcripts upon written request accompanied by a signed release from the student.
A comprehensive institution with no medical school, with an enrollment of 5,800. Highest level of offering: master's.
ACCREDITATIONS: M MT NUR SW TED

Salish Kootenai Community College

PO Box 117
Pablo, MT 59855
(406) 675-4800 Ext. 152 or 153

Will confirm attendance and degree by phone or mail. Inquiry must include student's name, date of birth, social security number, release. Employers may obtain transcripts upon written request accompanied by a $2.00 fee and a signed release from the student. Requests should be directed to: Registrar's Office.
A multiprogram two-year institution, with an enrollment of 850. Highest level of offering: one year but less than four years.
ACCREDITATIONS: NW

Salt Lake City Community College

(Formerly Utah Technical College at Salt Lake)
PO Box 30808
Salt Lake City, UT 84130-0808
(801) 967-4298
Fax (801) 967-4522

Will confirm attendance and degree by phone or mail. Inquiry must include student's name, social security number. Employers may obtain transcripts upon written request accompanied by a $2.00 fee and a signed release from the student.
A multiprogram two-year institution, with an enrollment of 15,900 Highest level of offering: two years.
ACCREDITATIONS: NW ADNUR PNUR

Salve Regina University

Ochre Point Avenue
Newport, RI 02840
(401) 847-6650

Will confirm attendance and degree by mail. Inquiry must include student's name, social security number, years attended. Employers may obtain transcripts upon written request accompanied by a $3.00 fee and a signed release from the student.
A comprehensive institution with no medical school, with an enrollment of 2,300. Highest level of offering: doctorate.
ACCREDITATIONS: EH NUR SW NASAD

Sam Houston State University

PO Box 2029
Huntsville, TX 77341
(409) 294-1040

Will confirm attendance and degree by phone or mail. Inquiry must include student's name, social security number. Employers may obtain transcripts upon written request accompanied by a $3.00 fee and a signed release from the student. Requests should be directed to: Registrar's Office.

A comprehensive institution with no medical school, with an enrollment of 12,359. Highest level of offering: doctorate.
ACCREDITATIONS: SC MUS TED

Samford University

800 Lakeshore Drive
Birmingham, AL 35229
(205) 870-2911

Will confirm attendance and degree by phone or mail. Inquiry must include student's name, social security number, years attended. Requests should be directed to: Student Records Office. Employers may obtain transcripts upon written request accompanied by a $5.00 fee and a signed release from the student.

A comprehensive institution with no medical school, with an enrollment of 4,248. Highest level of offering: beyond master's but less than doctorate.
ACCREDITATIONS: SC ADNUR ANEST LAW MUS NUR PHAR TED

Sampson Community College

PO Drawer 318
Clinton, NC 28328
(919) 592-8081
Fax (919) 592-8048

Will confirm attendance and degree by phone, fax or mail. Inquiry must include student's name, social security number, years attended. Employers may obtain transcripts upon written request accompanied by a signed release from the student.

A multiprogram two-year institution, with an enrollment of 836. Highest level of offering: one year but less than four years.
ACCREDITATIONS: SC

Sampson Technical Institute

(See Sampson Community College)

San Antonio College

1300 San Pedro Avenue
San Antonio, TX 78212
(512) 733-2583 or 733-2584

Will confirm attendance and degree by phone or mail. Inquiry must include student's name, social security number, years attended. Employers may obtain transcripts upon written request accompanied by a signed release from the student. Requests should be directed to: Admissions & Records Office.

A multiprogram two-year institution, with an enrollment of 22,274. Highest level of offering: one year but less than four years.
ACCREDITATIONS: SC ADNUR DA FUSER MAC

San Bernardino Valley College

701 South Mount Vernon Avenue
San Bernardino, CA 92410
(714) 888-6511
Fax (714) 381-4604

Will confirm attendance and degree by mail or fax. Inquiry must include student's name, date of birth, social security number, years attended, release. Requests should be directed to: Records Office. Employers may obtain transcripts upon written request accompanied by a $3.00 fee and a signed release from the student

A multiprogram two-year institution, with an enrollment of 11,350. Highest level of offering: one year but less than four years.
ACCREDITATIONS: WJ

San Diego City College

c/o San Diego Community College District
Student Records
3375 Camino Del Rio South
San Diego, CA 92108
(619) 230-2472 or 230-2473

Records for this school are being handled by San Diego Community College District. Will confirm attendance and degree by mail. Inquiry must include student's name, date of birth, social security number, years attended. Requests should be directed to: Admissions & Records Office. Employers may obtain transcripts upon written request accompanied by a $3.00 fee and a signed release from the student.

A multiprogram two-year institution, with an enrollment of 11,034. Highest level of offering: one year but less than four years.
ACCREDITATIONS: WJ

San Diego Mesa College

7250 Mesa College Drive
San Diego, CA 92111
(619) 627-2805

Will confirm attendance and degree by mail. Inquiry must include student's name, date of birth, social security number, release. Requests should be directed to: Records Department. Employers may obtain transcripts upon written request accompanied by a $3.00 fee and a signed release from the student.

A multiprogram two-year institution, with an enrollment of 29,000. Highest level of offering: one year but less than four years.
ACCREDITATIONS: WJ ADVET DA MAC MRT PTAA RAD

San Diego Miramar College

10440 Black Mountain Road
San Diego, CA 92126
(619) 536-7800

Will confirm attendance and degree by mail. Inquiry must include student's name, maiden name, date of birth, social security number, years attended, release. Employers may obtain transcripts upon written request accompanied by a $3.00 fee and a signed release from the student. Requests should be directed to: SDCCD, Transcript Office, 3375 Camino del Rio S., San Diego, CA 92108.

A multiprogram two-year institution, with an enrollment of 8,500. Highest level of offering: one year but less than four years.
ACCREDITATIONS: WJ

San Diego State University

San Diego, CA 92182-0771
(619) 594-5200

Will confirm attendance and degree by phone or mail. Inquiry must include student's name, date of birth, social security number, years attended. Employers may obtain transcripts upon written request accompanied by a $4.00 fee and a signed release from the student. Requests should be directed to: Admissions & Records Office.

A comprehensive institution with no medical school, with an enrollment of 33,898. Highest level of offering: doctorate.
ACCREDITATIONS: WC ART AUD BUS ENG FIDER HSA JOUR MUS NUR PH SP TED BUSA SW THEA

San Francisco Art Institute

800 Chestnut Street
San Francisco, CA 94133
(415) 771-7020 Ext. 74
Fax (415) 749-4590

Will confirm attendance and degree by phone or mail. Inquiry must include student's name, social security number. Employers may obtain transcripts upon written request accompanied by a $4.00 fee and a signed release from the student. Requests should be directed to: Registrar's Office.

A visual and performing arts school, with an enrollment of 716. Highest level of offering: master's.
ACCREDITATIONS: WC ART

San Francisco College of Mortuary Science

1363 Divisadero Street
San Francisco, CA 94115
(415) 567-0674

Will confirm attendance and degree by phone or mail. Inquiry must include student's name, social security number, years attended. Employers may obtain transcripts upon written request accompanied by a signed release from the student.

A single program two-year institution, with an enrollment of 70. Highest level of offering: one year but less than four years.
ACCREDITATIONS: WJ FUSER

San Francisco Community College District

50 Phelan Avenue
San Francisco, CA 94112
(415) 239-3285
Fax (415) 239-3936

Will confirm attendance and degree by phone or mail. Inquiry must include student's name, date of birth, social security number. Employers may obtain transcripts upon written request accompanied by a $3.00 fee and a signed release from the student. Requests should be directed to: Admissions & Records Department.

A multiprogram two-year institution, with an enrollment of 85,000. Highest level of offering: one year but less than four years.
ACCREDITATIONS: WJ DA DT ENGT MAC MRT RAD RTT

San Francisco Conservatory of Music

1201 Ortega Street
San Francisco, CA 94122
(415) 759-3428

Will confirm attendance and degree by phone or mail. Inquiry must include student's name, date of birth, social security number, years attended. Employers may obtain transcripts upon written request accompanied by a $3.00 fee and a signed release from the student.

A visual and performing arts school, with an enrollment of 250. Highest level of offering: master's.

ACCREDITATIONS: WC MUS

San Francisco State University

1600 Holloway Avenue
San Francisco, CA 94132
(415) 338-2787

Will confirm attendance and degree by phone or mail. Inquiry must include student's name, date of birth, years attended, release. Requests should be directed to: Records & Verification. Employers may obtain transcripts upon written request accompanied by a $4.00 fee and a signed release from the student.

A comprehensive institution with no medical school, with an enrollment of 24,170. Highest level of offering: doctorate.

ACCREDITATIONS: WC ART AUD BUS ENG JOUR MT MUS NUR SP SW TED THEA

San Francisco Theological Seminary

2 Kensington Road
San Anselmo, CA 94960
(415) 258-6553
Fax (415) 454-2493

Will confirm attendance and degree by phone or mail. Inquiry must include student's name. Employers may obtain transcripts upon written request accompanied by a $3.00 fee and a signed release from the student.

A school of philosophy, religion and theology, with an enrollment of 650. Highest level of offering: doctorate.

ACCREDITATIONS: WC THEOL

San Jacinto College Central Campus

8060 Spencer Highway
Pasadena, TX 77505
(713) 476-1844

Will confirm attendance and degree by phone or mail. Inquiry must include student's name, social security number. Employers may obtain transcripts upon written request accompanied by a $2.00 fee and a signed release from the student.

A multiprogram two-year institution, with an enrollment of 9,000. Highest level of offering: one year but less than four years.

ACCREDITATIONS: SC RAD RSTH RSTHT SURGT

San Jacinto College North Campus

5800 Uvalde Road
Houston, TX 77049
(713) 459-7102

Will confirm attendance and degree by phone or mail. Inquiry must include student's name, social security number. Employers may obtain transcripts upon written request accompanied by a $2.00 fee and a signed release from the student. Requests should be directed to: Registrar's Office.

A multiprogram two-year institution, with an enrollment of 4,000. Highest level of offering: one year but less than four years.

ACCREDITATIONS: SC

San Joaquin Delta College

5151 Pacific Avenue
Stockton, CA 95207
(209) 474-5636

Will confirm attendance and degree by phone or mail. Inquiry must include student's name, social security number, years attended. Employers may obtain transcripts upon written request accompanied by a $2.00 fee and a signed release from the student.

A multiprogram two-year institution, with an enrollment of 14,520. Highest level of offering: one year but less than four years.

ACCREDITATIONS: WJ ADNUR PNUR

San Jose Bible College

PO Box 1090
San Jose, CA 95108
(408) 293-9058

Will confirm attendance and degree by phone or mail. Inquiry must include student's name, social security number. Employers may obtain transcripts upon written request accompanied by a $3.00 fee and a signed release from the student.

A school of philosophy, religion and theology, with an enrollment of 190. Highest level of offering: four or five year baccalaureate.

ACCREDITATIONS: BI

San Jose City College

2100 Moorpark Avenue
San Jose, CA 95128
(408) 288-3700

Will confirm attendance and degree by phone or mail. Inquiry must include student's name, date of birth. Employers may obtain transcripts upon written request accompanied by a $2.00 fee and a signed release from the student. Requests should be directed to: Admissions & Records.

A multiprogram two-year institution, with an enrollment of 11,061. Highest level of offering: one year but less than four years.

ACCREDITATIONS: WJ DA

San Jose State University

1 Washington Square
San Jose, CA 95192-0009
(408) 924-1000

Will confirm attendance and degree by phone or mail. Inquiry must include student's name, date of birth, social security number, years attended. Employers may obtain transcripts upon written request accompanied by a $4.00 fee and a signed release from the student. Requests should be directed to: Admissions & Records.

A comprehensive institution with no medical school, with an enrollment of 28,559. Highest level of offering: master's.

ACCREDITATIONS: WC ART BUS CHE ENG JOUR LIB MUS NUR OT SP SW TED THEA

San Juan College

4601 College Boulevard
Farmington, NM 87401
(505) 326-3311 Ext. 335
Fax (505) 599-0385

Will confirm attendance and degree by phone or mail. Inquiry must include student's name, social security number. Employers may obtain transcripts upon written request accompanied by a $2.00 fee and a signed release from the student.

A multiprogram two-year institution, with an enrollment of 3,254. Highest level of offering: one year but less than four years.

ACCREDITATIONS: NH

San Mateo County Community College District Office

1700 West Hillsdale Boulevard
San Mateo, CA 94402
(415) 574-6165

Will confirm attendance and degree by phone or mail. Inquiry must include student's name, social security number, release. Requests should be directed to: Admissions Office. Employers may obtain transcripts upon written request accompanied by a $3.00 fee and a signed release from the student.

Sandhills Community College

2200 Airport Road
Pinehurst, NC 28374
(919) 692-6185 Ext. 226
Fax (919) 692-2756

Will confirm attendance and degree by phone or mail. Inquiry must include student's name, social security number, years attended. Employers may obtain transcripts upon written request accompanied by a $1.00 fee and a signed release from the student.

A multiprogram two-year institution, with an enrollment of 2,100. Highest level of offering: one year but less than four years.

ACCREDITATIONS: SC ADNUR MLTAD RAD RSTH

Sangamon State University

Shepherd Road Bldg. F–Room 20
Springfield, IL 62794-9243
(217) 786-6600

Will confirm attendance and degree by mail. Inquiry must include student's name, social security number, years attended. Employers may obtain transcripts upon written request accompanied by a $2.00 fee and a signed release from the student. Requests should be directed to: Admissions & Records Office.

A comprehensive institution with no medical school, with an enrollment of 4,500. Highest level of offering: master's.
ACCREDITATIONS: NCA MT NUR

Santa Ana College

(See Rancho Santiago College)

Santa Barbara City College

721 Cliff Drive
Santa Barbara, CA 93109-2394
(805) 965-0581
Fax (805) 963-7222

Will confirm attendance and degree by mail or fax. Inquiry must include student's name, date of birth, social security number, years attended, release. Requests should be directed to: Admissions Office. Employers may obtain transcripts upon written request accompanied by a $3.00 fee and a signed release from the student.

A multiprogram two-year institution, with an enrollment of 12,000. Highest level of offering: one year but less than four years.
ACCREDITATIONS: WJ ADNUR RAD

Santa Fe Community College

Po Box 4187
Santa Fe, NM 87502-4187
(505) 471-8200

Will confirm attendance and degree by phone or mail. Inquiry must include student's name, social security number. Employers may obtain transcripts upon written request accompanied by a $1.00 fee and a signed release from the student.

A two-year institution newly admitted to NCES, with an enrollment of 2,700. Highest level of offering: one year but less than four years.
ACCREDITATIONS: NCA

Santa Fe Community College

3000 North West 83rd Street
Gainesville, FL 32602
(904) 395-5443

Will confirm attendance and degree by phone or mail. Inquiry must include student's name, social security number, years attended. Employers may obtain transcripts upon written request accompanied by a signed release from the student.

A multiprogram two-year institution, with an enrollment of 10,500. Highest level of offering: one year but less than four years.
ACCREDITATIONS: SC DA DH NMT RAD RSTH PERF

Santa Monica College

1900 Pico Boulevard
Santa Monica, CA 90405
(213) 450-5150

Will confirm attendance and degree by mail. Inquiry must include student's name, date of birth, social security number, years attended, release. Requests should be directed to: Records and Admissions. Employers may obtain transcripts upon written request accompanied by a $3.00 fee and a signed release from the student.

A multiprogram two-year institution, with an enrollment of 26,000. Highest level of offering: one year but less than four years.
ACCREDITATIONS: WJ

Santa Rosa Junior College

1501 Mendocino Avenue
Santa Rosa, CA 95401
(707) 527-4685
Fax (707) 527-4816

Will confirm attendance and degree by phone, fax or mail. Inquiry must include student's name, social security number, release. Employers may obtain transcripts upon written request accompanied by a $1.00 fee and a signed release from the student.

A multiprogram two-year institution, with an enrollment of 33,300. Highest level of offering: one year but less than four years.
ACCREDITATIONS: WJ DA RAD

Sara Schenirer Teachers Seminary

4622 14th Avenue
Brooklyn, NY 11219
(718) 633-8557

Will confirm attendance and degree by phone or mail. Inquiry must include student's name, years attended. Employers may obtain transcripts upon written request accompanied by a $5.00 fee and a signed release from the student.

A specialized non-degree granting institution, with an enrollment of 154. Highest level of offering: four or five year baccalaureate.

Sarah Lawrence College

Bronxville, NY 10708
(914) 395-2301

Will confirm attendance and degree by phone or mail. Inquiry must include student's name, social security number. Employers may obtain transcripts upon written request accompanied by a $6.00 fee and a signed release from the student. Requests should be directed to: Registrar's Office.

A comprehensive institution with no medical school, with an enrollment of 1,063. Highest level of offering: master's.
ACCREDITATIONS: M NY

Sauk Valley Community College

173 Illinois Rt. 2
Dixon, IL 61021
(815) 288-5511 Ext. 297

Will confirm attendance and degree by phone or mail. Inquiry must include student's name, social security number, years attended. Employers may obtain transcripts upon written request accompanied by a $1.00 fee and a signed release from the student. Requests should be directed to: Attn: Admissions.

A multiprogram two-year institution, with an enrollment of 3,100. Highest level of offering: one year but less than four years.
ACCREDITATIONS: NH MLTAD RAD

Savannah College of Art and Design

PO Box 3146
Savannah, GA 31401-3146
(912) 238-2483

Will confirm attendance and degree by phone or mail. Inquiry must include student's name, social security number, years attended. Employers may obtain transcripts upon written request by student accompanied by a $10.00 fee.

A bachelor's or higher institution newly admitted to NCES, with an enrollment of 1,700. Highest level of offering: master's.
ACCREDITATIONS: SC

Savannah State College

State College Branch
PO Box 20479
Savannah, GA 31404
(912) 356-2212

Will confirm attendance and degree by phone or mail. Inquiry must include student's name, social security number, years attended. Employers may obtain transcripts upon written request accompanied by a $2.00 fee and a signed release from the student.

A general baccalaureate institution, with an enrollment of 2,011. Highest level of offering: master's.
ACCREDITATIONS: SC ENGT SW

Saybrook Institute

1550 Sutter Street
San Francisco, CA 94109
(415) 441-5034

Will confirm attendance and degree by phone or mail. Inquiry must include student's name, years attended. Employers may obtain transcripts upon written request accompanied by a $5.00 fee and a signed release from the student.

A specialized school, with an enrollment of 200. Highest level of offering: doctorate.
ACCREDITATIONS: WC

Sayre Junior College

(See Southwestern Oklahoma State University at Sayre)

Scarritt Foundation

1008 19 Ave. South
Nashville, TN 37212-2166
(615) 340-7460

Records are held at the above address. Will confirm attendance and degree by mail. Inquiry must include student's name, years attended. Employers may obtain transcripts upon written request accompanied by a $2.00 fee and a signed release from the student. Requests should be directed to: Registrar's Office.

A school of philosophy, religion and theology, with an enrollment of 96. Highest level of offering: master's.
ACCREDITATIONS: SC THEOL

Schenectady County Community College

78 Washington Avenue
Schenectady, NY 12305
(518) 346-6211 Ext. 148

Will confirm attendance and degree by phone or mail. Inquiry must include student's name, social security number. Employers may obtain transcripts upon written request accompanied by a $2.00 fee and a signed release from the student.

A multiprogram two-year institution, with an enrollment of 4,151. Highest level of offering: one year but less than four years.
ACCREDITATIONS: M NY

School for International Training

Kipling Road
Brattleboro, VT 05301
(802) 257-7751 Ext. 2014

Will confirm attendance and degree by phone or mail. Inquiry must include student's name. Requests should be directed to: Registrar's Office. Employers may obtain transcripts upon written request accompanied by a $3.00 fee and a signed release from the student.

A comprehensive institution with no medical school, with an enrollment of 438. Highest level of offering: master's.
ACCREDITATIONS: EH

School for Lifelong Learning

Dunlap Center
Durham, NH 03824
(603) 862-1692

Will confirm attendance and degree by phone or mail. Inquiry must include student's name, social security number, years attended. Employers may obtain transcripts upon written request accompanied by a $3.00 fee and a signed release from the student.

A bachelor's or higher institution newly admitted to NCES, with an enrollment of 1,600. Highest level of offering: four or five year baccalaureate.
ACCREDITATIONS: EH

School of the Art Institute of Chicago

37 South Wabash Avenue, Room 705
Chicago, IL 60603
(312) 899-5117
Fax (312) 263-0141

Will confirm attendance and degree by phone, fax or mail. Inquiry must include student's name, social security number, years attended. Employers may obtain transcripts upon written request accompanied by a $3.00 fee and a signed release from the student.

A visual and performing arts school, with an enrollment of 1,691. Highest level of offering: beyond master's but less than doctorate.
ACCREDITATIONS: NH ART NASAD

School of the Associated Arts

(See College of Associated Arts.)

School of the Museum of Fine Arts–Boston

230 The Fenway
Boston, MA 02115
(617) 267-6100

Will confirm attendance and degree by mail. Inquiry must include student's name, social security number, years attended, release. Requests should be directed to: Registrar's Office. Employers may obtain transcripts upon written request accompanied by a $2.00 fee and a signed release from the student.

A visual and performing arts school, with an enrollment of 750. Highest level of offering: master's.
ACCREDITATIONS: ART

School of the Ozarks

Point Lookout, MO 65726
(417) 334-6411 Ext. 4223

Will confirm attendance and degree by phone or mail. Inquiry must include student's name, social security number. Requests should be directed to: Registrar's Office. Employers may obtain transcripts upon written request accompanied by a $2.00 fee and a signed release from the student.

A general baccalaureate institution, with an enrollment of 1,222. Highest level of offering: four or five year baccalaureate.
ACCREDITATIONS: NH MUS TED

School of Theology at Claremont

1325 North College Avenue
Claremont, CA 91711-3199
(714) 626-3521

Will confirm attendance and degree by mail. Inquiry must include student's name, social security number, release. Employers may obtain transcripts upon written request accompanied by a $3.00 fee and a signed release from the student. Requests should be sent to: Attn: Registrar's Office.

A school of philosophy, religion and theology, with an enrollment of 233. Highest level of offering: doctorate.
ACCREDITATIONS: WC THEOL

School of Visual Arts

209 East 23rd Street
New York, NY 10010
(212) 679-7350
Fax (212) 725-3587

Will confirm attendance and degree by phone, fax or mail. Inquiry must include student's name, social security number, release. Employers may obtain transcripts upon written request accompanied by a $7.00 fee and a signed release from the student.

A general baccalaureate institution, with an enrollment of 4,765. Highest level of offering: master's.
ACCREDITATIONS: M ART NY

Schoolcraft College

18600 Haggerty Road
Livonia, MI 48152-2696
(313) 462-4430
Fax (313) 462-4506

Will confirm attendance and degree by phone, fax or mail. Inquiry must include student's name, date of birth, social security number. Employers may obtain transcripts upon written request accompanied by a $2.00 fee and a signed release from the student.

A multiprogram two-year institution, with an enrollment of 9,224. Highest level of offering: one year but less than four years.
ACCREDITATIONS: NH MLTAD MRT

Schreiner College

Box 4487
Kerrville, TX 78028
(512) 896-5411 Ext. 224
Fax (512) 896-3232

Will confirm attendance and degree by phone, fax or mail. Inquiry must include student's name, social security number, years attended. Employers may obtain transcripts upon written request accompanied by a $4.00 fee and a signed release from the student. Requests should be directed to: Registrar's Office.

A multiprogram four-year institution, with an enrollment of 625. Highest level of offering: four or five year baccalaureate.
ACCREDITATIONS: SC

Scottsdale Community College

9000 East Chaparral
Scottsdale, AZ 85250-2699
(602) 423-6125
Fax (602) 423-6200

Will confirm attendance and degree by mail or fax. Inquiry must include student's name, social security number, release. Employers may obtain transcripts upon written request accompanied by a $5.00 fee and a signed release from the student.

A multiprogram two-year institution, with an enrollment of 7,313. Highest level of offering: one year but less than four years.
ACCREDITATIONS: NH ADNUR

Scripps College

1030 Columbia Avenue
Claremont, CA 91711-3948
(714) 621-8273

Will confirm attendance and degree by
phone or mail. Inquiry must include student's name, years attended, release.
Employers may obtain transcripts upon
written request accompanied by a $3.00 fee
and a signed release from the student.

A general baccalaureate institution, with an
enrollment of 604. Highest level of offering: four or five year baccalaureate.
ACCREDITATIONS: WC

Sanford Dixon Bishop State Junior College

351 North Broad St.
Mobile, AL 36603-5898
(205) 690-6421

Will confirm attendance and degree by
phone or mail. Inquiry must include student's name, social security number, years
attended. Employers may obtain transcripts
upon written request accompanied by a
$3.00 fee and a signed release from the stu-
dent.

A multiprogram two-year institution, with
an enrollment of 2,500. Highest level of offering: one year but less than four years.
ACCREDITATIONS: SC ADNUR

Seabury-Western Theological Seminary

2122 North Sheridan Road
Evanston, IL 60201
(708) 328-9300

Will confirm attendance and degree by
phone or mail. Inquiry must include student's name. Employers may obtain transcripts upon written request accompanied
by a $2.00 fee and a signed release from the
student.

A school of philosophy, religion and theology, with an enrollment of 80. Highest level
of offering: master's.
ACCREDITATIONS: NH THEOL

Seattle Central Community College

1701 Broadway
Seattle, WA 98122
(206) 587-6918
Fax (206) 587-3805

Will confirm attendance and degree by
mail. Inquiry must include student's name,
social security number, date of birth, years
attended. Employers may obtain transcripts
upon written request accompanied by a
$3.00 fee for an official copy (no fee for
unofficial copy) and a signed release from
the student. Requests should be sent to:
Attn: Transcripts.

A multiprogram two-year institution, with
an enrollment of 9,000. Highest level of offering: one year but less than four years.
ACCREDITATIONS: NW DT RSTHT DA

Seattle Community College South Campus

6000 16th Avenue South West
Seattle, WA 98106
(206) 764-5300

Will confirm attendance and degree by
phone or mail. Inquiry must include student's name, social security number.
Employers may obtain transcripts upon
written request accompanied by a $3.00 fee
and a signed release from the student.

A multiprogram two-year institution, with
an enrollment of 7,500. Highest level of offering: two years.
ACCREDITATIONS: NW

Seattle Pacific University

Seattle, WA 98119
(206) 281-2031
Fax (206) 281-2669

Will confirm attendance and degree by
phone, fax or mail. Inquiry must include
student's name, social security number,
years attended. Employers may obtain transcripts upon written request accompanied
by a $3.00 fee and a signed release from the
student. Requests should be directed to:
Records Office.

A comprehensive institution with no medical school, with an enrollment of 2,935.
Highest level of offering: beyond master's
but less than doctorate.
ACCREDITATIONS: NW MUS NUR TED

Seattle University

12th and East Columbia
Seattle, WA 98122
(206) 296-5850
Fax (206) 296-2163

Will confirm attendance and degree by
phone or mail. Inquiry must include student's name, date of birth, social security
number, year graduated. Employers may
obtain transcripts upon written request accompanied by a signed release from the student.

A comprehensive institution with no medi-
cal school, with an enrollment of 4,626.
Highest level of offering: doctorate.
ACCREDITATIONS: NW BUS DMS ENG MRA
NMT NUR TED

Selma University

1501 Lapsley Street
Selma, AL 36701
(205) 872-2533 Ext. 24

Will confirm attendance and degree by
phone or mail. Inquiry must include student's name, date of birth, social security
number, years attended. Employers may obtain transcripts upon written request accompanied by a $2.00 fee and a signed release
from the student.

A multiprogram two-year institution, with
an enrollment of 300. Highest level of offering: four or five year baccalaureate.
ACCREDITATIONS: 3IC

Seminary of the Immaculate Conception

440 West Neck Road
Huntington, NY 11743
(516) 423-0483

Will confirm attendance and degree by
phone or mail. Inquiry must include student's name, years attended. Employers
may obtain transcripts upon written request
accompanied by a signed release from the
student.

A school of philosophy, religion and theology, with an enrollment of 180. Highest
level of offering: master's.
ACCREDITATIONS: M NY THEOL

Seminole Community College

100 Weldon Blvd.
Sanford, FL 32773-6199
(407) 323-1450 Ext. 368

Will confirm attendance and degree by
phone or mail. Inquiry must include student's name, social security number, years
attended. Employers may obtain transcripts
upon written request accompanied by a
signed release from the student. Requests
should be directed to: Student Records.

A multiprogram two-year institution, with
an enrollment of 7,000. Highest level of offering: one year but less than four years.
ACCREDITATIONS: SC RSTHT ADNUR

Seminole Junior College

PO Box 351
Seminole, OK 74868
(405) 382-9950 Ext. 248
Fax (405) 382-2998

Will confirm attendance and degree by
phone or mail. Inquiry must include student's name, social security number.
Employers may obtain transcripts upon
written request accompanied by a $2.00 fee
and a signed release from the student.

A multiprogram two-year institution, with
an enrollment of 1,481. Highest level of offering: one year but less than four years.
ACCREDITATIONS: NH ADNUR MLTAD

Seton Hall University

400 South Orange Avenue
South Orange, NJ 07079
(201) 761-9000 Ext. 9677

Will confirm attendance and degree by
phone or mail. Inquiry must include student's name, date of birth, social security
number, years attended. Employers may obtain transcripts upon written request accompanied by a $3.00 fee and a signed release
from the student.

A comprehensive institution with no medi-
cal school, with an enrollment of 8,965.
Highest level of offering: doctorate.
ACCREDITATIONS: M BUS LAW NUR SW
TED

Seton Hill College

Attn: Registrar's Office
Seton Hill Drive
Greensburg, PA 15601
(412) 834-2200 Ext. 219

Will confirm attendance and degree by
phone or mail. Inquiry must include student's name, social security number, years
attended. Employers may obtain transcripts
upon written request accompanied by a
$2.00 fee and a signed release from the stu-
dent.

A general baccalaureate institution, with an
enrollment of 919. Highest level of offering: four or five year baccalaureate.
ACCREDITATIONS: M DIET MUS

Seward County Community College

Box 1137
Liberal, KS 67905-1137
(316) 624-1951 Ext. 116

Will confirm attendance and degree by
phone or mail. Inquiry must include student's name, date of birth, social security
number. Employers may obtain transcripts
upon written request accompanied by a
signed release from the student.

A multiprogram two-year institution, with
an enrollment of 1,203. Highest level of offering: one year but less than four years.
ACCREDITATIONS: NH ADNUR MLTAD
PNUR

Sh'or Yoshuv Rabbinical College

1526 Central Avenue
Far Rockaway, NY 11691
(718) 327-2048

Will confirm attendance and degree by
mail. Inquiry must include student's name,
social security number, years attended.
Only students may obtain transcripts.

A specialized institution, with an enrollment of 120. Highest level of offering:
graduate non-degree granting.
ACCREDITATIONS: RABN

Shaarei Zion Academy

4206 15th Avenue
Brooklyn, NY 11219
(718) 851-0404

Will confirm attendance and degree by mail
or phone. Inquiry must include student's
name, date of birth, social security number,
years attended. Employers may obtain transcripts upon written request accompanied
by a signed release from the student.
Requests should be sent to: Attn:
Registrar's Office.

A bachelor's or higher institution newly admitted to NCES, with an enrollment of
1,400. Highest level of offering: four or
five year baccalaureate.
ACCREDITATIONS: 3IC

Shasta College

PO Box 496006
Redding, CA 96049-6006
(916) 225-4841

Will confirm attendance and degree by
mail. Inquiry must include student's name,
date of birth, social security number, release, years attended. Employers may obtain transcripts upon written request accompanied by a $3.00 fee and a signed release
from the student. Requests should be sent
to: Attn: Admissions and Records.

A multiprogram two-year institution, with
an enrollment of 13,000. Highest level of
offering: one year but less than four years.
ACCREDITATIONS: WJ

Shaw University

Records & Registration
118 East South Street
Raleigh, NC 27611
(919) 546-8415
Fax (919) 546-8301

Will confirm attendance and degree by
phone, fax or mail. Inquiry must include
student's name, social security number,
years attended. Employers may obtain transcripts upon written request accompanied
by a $4.00 fee and a signed release from the
student.

A general baccalaureate institution, with an
enrollment of 2,134. Highest level of offering: four or five year baccalaureate.
ACCREDITATIONS: SC

Shawnee College

Rural Rte. #1, Box 53
Ullin, IL 62992-9725
(618) 634-2242

Will confirm attendance and degree by
mail. Inquiry must include student's name,
social security number, release. Employers
may obtain transcripts upon written request
accompanied by a $2.00 fee and a signed
release from the student. Requests should
be directed to: Records Office.

A multiprogram two-year institution, with
an enrollment of 2,000. Highest level of offering: one year but less than four years.
ACCREDITATIONS: NH ADNUR

Shawnee State Community College

940 Second Street
Portsmouth, OH 45662
(614) 354-3205 Ext. 262
Fax (614) 355-2416

Will confirm attendance and degree by mail
or fax. Inquiry must include student's name,
social security number, release. Employers
may obtain transcripts upon written request
accompanied by a $2.00 fee and a signed
release from the student.

A multiprogram two-year institution, with
an enrollment of 3,000. Highest level of offering: one year but less than four years.
ACCREDITATIONS: NH DH MLTAD RAD
RSTH RSTHT

Shawnee State University

(See Shawnee State Community
College)

Shelby State Community College

PO Box 40568
Memphis, TN 38174-0568
(901) 528-6707

Will confirm attendance and degree by
phone or mail. Inquiry must include student's name, social security number.
Employers may obtain transcripts upon
written request by student.

A multiprogram two-year institution, with
an enrollment of 8,000. Highest level of offering: two years but less than four years.
ACCREDITATIONS: SACS EMT MLTAD MUS
PTAA ADNUR AD

Sheldon Jackson College

801 Lincoln Street
Sitka, AK 99835
(907) 747-5216
Fax (907) 747-5212

Will confirm attendance and degree by
phone, fax or mail. Inquiry must include
student's name, social security number.
Employers may obtain transcripts upon
written request accompanied by a $3.00 fee
and a signed release from the student.

A multiprogram two-year institution, with
an enrollment of 236. Highest level of offering: four or five year baccalaureate.
ACCREDITATIONS: NW

Shelton State Community College Technical Division

Attn: Transcripts
202 Skyland Blvd.
Tuscaloosa, AL 35405
(205) 759-1541
Fax (205) 759-2495

Will confirm attendance and degree by
phone or mail. Inquiry must include student's name, social security number.
Employers may obtain transcripts upon
written request accompanied by a $1.00 fee
and a signed release from the student.

A multiprogram two-year institution, with
an enrollment of 4,287. Highest level of offering: one year but less than four years.
ACCREDITATIONS: SC

Shenandoah University

1460 University Drive
Winchester, VA 22601
(703) 665-4536

Will confirm attendance and degree by
phone or mail. Inquiry must include student's name, social security number, years
attended. Employers may obtain transcripts
upon written request accompanied by a
$3.00 fee and a signed release from the stu-
dent.

A general baccalaureate institution, with an
enrollment of 932. Highest level of offering: master's.
ACCREDITATIONS: SC ADNUR MUS RSTH
RSTHT

Shepherd College

Shepherdstown, WV 25443
(304) 876-2511 Ext. 320
Fax (304) 876-3101

Will confirm attendance and degree by phone or mail. Inquiry must include student's name, social security number. Employers may obtain transcripts upon written request accompanied by a $3.00 fee with a 3 day turnaround, $10.00 fee for same day service, and a signed release from the student. Requests should be directed to: Registrar's Office.

A general baccalaureate institution, with an enrollment of 3,507. Highest level of offering: four or five year baccalaureate.

ACCREDITATIONS: NH ADNUR SW TED

Sheridan College

PO Box 1500
Sheridan, WY 82801
(307) 674-6446 Ext. 140
Fax (307) 674-4293

Will confirm attendance and degree by phone or mail. Inquiry must include student's name, social security number. Employers may obtain transcripts upon written request accompanied by a signed release from the student. Requests should be sent to: Attn: Records.

A multiprogram two-year institution, with an enrollment of 1,601. Highest level of offering: one year but less than four years.

ACCREDITATIONS: NH DA DH PNUR

Sherman College of Straight Chiropractic

PO Box 1452
Spartanburg, SC 29304
(803) 578-8770 Ext. 16
Fax (803) 578-8774

Will confirm attendance and degree by phone or mail. Inquiry must include student's name, date of birth, social security number, years attended. Employers may obtain transcripts upon written request by student accompanied by a $5.00 fee.

A health institution, with an enrollment of 150. Highest level of offering: first professional degree.

ACCREDITATIONS: SACSC

Sherwood Conservatory of Music

1014 South Michigan Avenue
Chicago, IL 60605
(312) 427-6267
Fax (312) 427-6677

Records are maintained at the above address. Will confirm attendance and degree by phone or mail. Inquiry must include student's name, years attended. Employers may obtain transcripts upon written request accompanied by a $2.00 fee and a signed release from the student. Direct inquiries to Registrar.

Shimer College

Box A500
Waukegan, IL 60079
(708) 623-8400 Ext. 24

Will confirm attendance and degree by phone or mail. Inquiry must include student's name, years attended. Employers may obtain transcripts upon written request accompanied by a $5.00 fee and a signed release from the student.

A general baccalaureate institution, with an enrollment of 90. Highest level of offering: four or five year baccalaureate.

ACCREDITATIONS: NH

Shippensburg University of Pennsylvania

Shippensburg, PA 17257
(717) 532-1381
Fax (717) 532-1388

Will confirm attendance and degree by phone or mail. Inquiry must include student's name, social security number, years attended. Employers may obtain transcripts upon written request accompanied by a $2.00 fee and a signed release from the student. Requests should be directed to: Registrar's Office.

A comprehensive institution with no medical school, with an enrollment of 6,121. Highest level of offering: beyond master's but less than doctorate.

ACCREDITATIONS: M BUS SW TED

Shoals Community College

(Formerly Muscle Shoals State Technical College)
PO Box 2545
Muscle Shoals, AL 35662
(205) 381-2813

Will confirm by mail. Inquiry must include student's name, date of birth, release. Employers may obtain transcripts upon written request accompanied by a $1.00 fee and a signed release from the student.

A two-year institution newly admitted to NCES. Highest level of offering: one year but less than four years.

ACCREDITATIONS: SACS

Shoreline Community College

16101 Greenwood Avenue North
Seattle, WA 98133
(206) 546-4610
Fax (206) 546-4599

Will confirm attendance and degree by mail. Inquiry must include student's name, social security number, date of birth, years attended, release. Employers may obtain transcripts upon written request accompanied by a $2.00 fee and a signed release from the student.

A multiprogram two-year institution, with an enrollment of 8,000. Highest level of offering: two years but less than four years.

ACCREDITATIONS: NW ADNUR DH HT MLTAD MRT

Shorter College

315 Shorter Ave.
Rome, GA 30165-4298
(404) 291-2121 Ext. 206

Will confirm attendance and degree by phone or mail. Inquiry must include student's name, social security number. Employers may obtain transcripts upon written request accompanied by a $1.00 fee and a signed release from the student. Requests should be directed to: Registrar's Office.

A general baccalaureate institution, with an enrollment of 800. Highest level of offering: four or five year baccalaureate.

ACCREDITATIONS: SC MUS

Shorter College

604 Locust Street
North Little Rock, AR 72114
(501) 374-6305

Will confirm attendance and degree by phone, fax or mail. Inquiry must include student's name, social security number, years attended. Employers may obtain transcripts upon written request accompanied by a $2.00 fee and a signed release from the student.

A multiprogram two-year institution, with an enrollment of 78. Highest level of offering: one year but less than four years.

ACCREDITATIONS: NH

Siena College

515 Louden Road
Loudonville, NY 12211
(518) 783-2369

Will confirm attendance and degree by phone or mail. Inquiry must include student's name, date of birth. Employers may obtain transcripts upon written request by student accompanied by a $2.00 fee and a signed release from the student. Requests should be directed to: Registrar's Office.

A business school, with an enrollment of 3,318. Highest level of offering: four or five year baccalaureate.

ACCREDITATIONS: M NY

Siena Heights College

1247 East Siena Heights Drive
Adrian, MI 49221
(517) 263-0731 Ext. 213

Will confirm attendance and degree by phone or mail. Inquiry must include student's name, social security number. Employers may obtain transcripts upon written request accompanied by a $2.00 fee and a signed release from the student. Requests should be directed to: Registrar's Office.

A general baccalaureate institution, with an enrollment of 1,480. Highest level of offering: master's.

ACCREDITATIONS: NH

Sierra College

Records Office
5000 Rocklin Road
Rocklin, CA 95677
(916) 624-3333 Ext. 2318

Will confirm attendance and degree by mail. Inquiry must include student's name, social security number, years attended, release. Employers may obtain transcripts upon written request accompanied by a

$2.00 fee and a signed release from the student.

A multiprogram two-year institution, with an enrollment of 13,146. Highest level of offering: two years but less than four years.
ACCREDITATIONS: WJ

Sierra Nevada College

PO Box 4269
Incline Village, NV 89450
(702) 831-1314 Ext. 24

Will confirm attendance and degree by phone or mail. Inquiry must include student's name, date of birth, social security number, years attended. Employers may obtain transcripts upon written request accompanied by a $3.00 fee and a signed release from the student.

A general baccalaureate institution, with an enrollment of 300. Highest level of offering: master's.
ACCREDITATIONS: NW

Sierra University

2900 Bristol Street
Suite D 207
Costa Mesa, CA 92626
(714) 545-1133

Will confirm attendance and degree by mail. Inquiry must include student's name. Employers may obtain transcripts upon written request accompanied by a $20.00 fee and a signed release from the student.

A bachelor's or higher institution newly admitted to NCES. Highest level of offering: four or five year baccalaureate.
ACCREDITATIONS: 3IC

Silver Lake College

2406 South Alverno Road
Manitowoc, WI 54220
(414) 684-6691 Ext. 131

Will confirm attendance and degree by phone or mail. Inquiry must include student's name, date of birth, social security number. Employers may obtain transcripts upon written request accompanied by a $2.00 fee and a signed release from the student.

A general baccalaureate institution, with an enrollment of 520. Highest level of offering: master's.
ACCREDITATIONS: NH TED

Simmons College

Office of the Registrar
300 The Fenway
Boston, MA 02115
(617) 738-2112

Will confirm attendance and degree by phone or mail. Inquiry must include student's name, maiden name, social security number, date of birth, years attended. Employers may obtain transcripts upon written request accompanied by a $3.00 fee and a signed release from the student.

A comprehensive institution with no medical school, with an enrollment of 3,138. Highest level of offering: doctorate.
ACCREDITATIONS: EH LIB NUR PTA SW

Simon's Rock College of Bard

84 Alford Road
Great Barrington, MA 01230
(413) 528-0771 Ext. 201
Fax (413) 528-7365

Will confirm attendance and degree by phone or mail. Inquiry must include student's name. Employers may obtain transcripts upon written request accompanied by a $2.00 fee and a signed release from the student.

A multiprogram four-year institution, with an enrollment of 300. Highest level of offering: four or five year baccalaureate.
ACCREDITATIONS: EH

Simpson College

2211 College View Drive
Redding, CA 96003
(916) 222-6360

Will confirm attendance and degree by phone, fax or mail. Inquiry must include student's name, social security number, years attended, release. Employers may obtain transcripts upon written request by student accompanied by a $3.00 fee.

A general baccalaureate institution, with an enrollment of 321. Highest level of offering: master's.
ACCREDITATIONS: WC BI

Simpson College

Registrar's Office
701 North C Street
Indianola, IA 50125
(515) 961-1642
Fax (515) 961-1498

Will confirm attendance and degree by phone, fax or mail. Inquiry must include student's name, date of birth, social security number. Employers may obtain transcripts upon written request by student accompanied by a $2.00 fee.

A general baccalaureate institution, with an enrollment of 1,737. Highest level of offering: four or five year baccalaureate.
ACCREDITATIONS: NH MUS TED

Sinclair Community College

444 West Third Street
Dayton, OH 45402
(513) 226-2736
Fax (513) 449-5192

Will confirm attendance and degree by phone or mail. Inquiry must include student's name, social security number. Requests should be directed to: Registrar's Office. Employers may obtain transcripts upon written request accompanied by a $2.00 fee and a signed release from the student.

A multiprogram two-year institution, with an enrollment of 17,000. Highest level of offering: associate.
ACCREDITATIONS: NCA ADNUR DH ENGT MRT PTAA RAD RSTH SURGT

Sinte Gleska College

Box 490
Rosebud, SD 57570
(605) 747-2263 Ext. 24

Will confirm attendance and degree by phone or mail. Inquiry must include student's name, social security number. Employers may obtain transcripts upon written request accompanied by a $3.00 fee and a signed release from the student.

A specialized school, with an enrollment of 540. Highest level of offering: four or five year baccalaureate.
ACCREDITATIONS: NH

Sioux Empire College

c/o University of Iowa
Registrar's Office
1 Jessup Hall
Iowa City, IA 52242
(319) 335-0229

Records of this school are being handled by University of Iowa. Will confirm attendance and degree by mail or phone. Inquiry must include student's name, date of birth. Employers may obtain transcripts upon written request accompanied by a $3.00 fee and a signed release from the student.

A multiprogram two-year institution, with an enrollment of 151. Highest level of offering: one year but less than four years.
ACCREDITATIONS: NH

Sioux Falls College

1501 South Prairie
Sioux Falls, SD 57105-1699
(605) 331-5000

Will confirm attendance and degree by phone or mail. Inquiry must include student's name, date of birth, social security number. Employers may obtain transcripts upon written request accompanied by a $2.00 fee and a signed release from the student.

A general baccalaureate institution, with an enrollment of 950. Highest level of offering: master's.
ACCREDITATIONS: NH SW TED

Skagit Valley College

2405 East College Way
Mount Vernon, WA 98273
(206) 428-1261 or 428-1155
Fax (206) 428-1612

Will confirm attendance and degree by mail or fax. Inquiry must include student's name, social security number, release. Employers may obtain transcripts upon written request accompanied by a $1.00 fee and a signed release from the student.

A multiprogram two-year institution, with an enrollment of 3,894. Highest level of offering: one year but less than four years.
ACCREDITATIONS: NW PNUR RSTHT

Skidmore College

Saratoga Springs, NY 12866
(518) 584-5000 Ext. 2211
Fax (518) 584-3023

Will confirm attendance and degree by phone, fax or mail. Inquiry must include student's name, years attended. Employers may obtain transcripts upon written request accompanied by a $2.00 fee and a signed release from the student. Requests should be directed to: Registrar's Office.

A general baccalaureate institution, with an enrollment of 2,537. Highest level of offering: four or five year baccalaureate.
ACCREDITATIONS: M ART NY SW AACSB

Skyline College

3300 College Drive
San Bruno, CA 94066
(415) 355-7000

Will confirm attendance and degree by mail. Inquiry must include student's name, social security number, years attended, release. Employers may obtain transcripts upon written request accompanied by a $3.00 fee and a signed release from the student.

A multiprogram two-year institution, with an enrollment of 10,000. Highest level of offering: one year but less than four years.
ACCREDITATIONS: WJ RSTH

Slippery Rock University of Pennsylvania

Slippery Rock, PA 16057-1326
(412) 738-2010
Fax (412) 738-2098

Will confirm attendance and degree by phone, fax or mail. Inquiry must include student's name, social security number, dates attended. Employers may obtain transcripts upon written request accompanied by a $2.00 fee and a signed release from the student. Requests should be directed to: Academic Records Office.

A comprehensive institution with no medical school, with an enrollment of 7,500. Highest level of offering: master's.
ACCREDITATIONS: M MUS NUR SW TED APTA

Smith College

Office of the Registrar
Northampton, MA 01063
(413) 584-2700 Ext. 2556

Will confirm attendance and degree by phone or mail. Inquiry must include student's name, date of birth, social security number. Employers may obtain transcripts upon written request by student accompanied by a $5.00 fee. Requests should be directed to: Registrar's Office.

A comprehensive institution with no medical school, with an enrollment of 2,752. Highest level of offering: doctorate.
ACCREDITATIONS: EH SW

Snead State Junior College

PO Drawer D
Boaz, AL 35957
(205) 593-5120 Ext. 207

Will confirm attendance and degree by phone or mail. Inquiry must include student's name, social security number, years attended. Employers may obtain transcripts upon written request accompanied by a $2.00 fee and a signed release from the student.

A multiprogram two-year institution, with an enrollment of 1,109. Highest level of offering: one year but less than four years.
ACCREDITATIONS: SC ADVET

Snow College

150 East College Avenue
Ephraim, UT 84627
(801) 283-4021
Fax (801) 283-6879

Will confirm attendance and degree by phone or mail. Inquiry must include student's name, social security number, years attended. Employers may obtain transcripts upon written request accompanied by a $2.00 fee and a signed release from the student.

A multiprogram two-year institution, with an enrollment of 2,025. Highest level of offering: one year but less than four years.
ACCREDITATIONS: NW

Sojourner–Douglas College

500 North Caroline Street
Baltimore, MD 21205
(410) 276-0306 Ext. 39
Fax (410) 675-1810

Will confirm attendance and degree by phone or mail. Inquiry must include student's name, social security number, years attended. Employers may obtain transcripts upon written request by student accompanied by a $3.00 fee. Requests should be directed to: Registrar's Office.

A specialized school, with an enrollment of 387. Highest level of offering: four or five year baccalaureate.
ACCREDITATIONS: M

Solano Community College

4000 Suisun Valley Road
Suisun, CA 94585
(707) 864-7000
Fax (707) 864-0361

Will confirm attendance and degree by mail. Inquiry must include student's name, social security number, release. Employers may obtain transcripts upon written request accompanied by a $2.00 fee and a signed release from the student. Requests should be directed to: Admissions & Records Office.

A multiprogram two-year institution, with an enrollment of 11,700. Highest level of offering: one year but less than four years.
ACCREDITATIONS: WJ

Somerset County College

(See Raritan Valley Community College)

Sonoma State University

1801 East Cotati Avenue
Rohnert Park, CA 94928
(707) 664-2778

Will confirm attendance and degree by phone or mail. Inquiry must include student's name, social security number, date of birth, years attended. Requests should be directed to: Admissions & Records Office. Employers may obtain transcripts upon written request accompanied by a $4.00 fee for first copy, $2.00 for additional copy and a signed release from the student.

A comprehensive institution with no medical school, with an enrollment of 5,364. Highest level of offering: master's.
ACCREDITATIONS: WC ART MUS NUR

South Carolina State College

PO Box 1627
Orangeburg, SC 29117
(803) 536-7185

Will confirm attendance and degree by phone or mail. Inquiry must include student's name, social security number, years attended. Employers may obtain transcripts upon written request accompanied by a $3.00 fee and a signed release from the student.

A general baccalaureate institution, with an enrollment of 5,000. Highest level of offering: doctorate.
ACCREDITATIONS: SC TED ENGT

South Central Community College

60 Sargent Drive
New Haven, CT 06511
(203) 789-7041

Will confirm attendance and degree by mail. Inquiry must include student's name, social security number, release. Employers may obtain transcripts upon written request accompanied by a signed release from the student. Requests should be directed to: Records Office.

A multiprogram two-year institution, with an enrollment of 3,301. Highest level of offering: one year but less than four years.
ACCREDITATIONS: EH NMT RAD RTT

South College

(Formerly Draughons Junior College)
Registrar's Office
709 Mall Blvd.
Savannah, GA 31406
(912) 651-8100

Will confirm attendance and degree by mail. Inquiry must include student's name, date of birth, social security number, attended. Employers may obtain transcripts upon written request accompanied by a $2.00 fee and a signed release from the student.

A multiprogram two-year institution, with an enrollment of 701. Highest level of offering: two years.
ACCREDITATIONS: SACS AICS/JR

South Dakota School of Mines and Technology

501 East Saint Joseph
Rapid City, SD 57701
(605) 394-2414
Fax (605) 394-6131

Will confirm attendance and degree by phone or mail. Inquiry must include student's name, date of birth, social security number. Employers may obtain transcripts upon written request accompanied by a $2.00 fee and a signed release from the student. Requests should be directed to: Registrar's Office.

An engineering school, with an enrollment of 2,583. Highest level of offering: doctorate.
ACCREDITATIONS: NH ENG

South Dakota State University

PO Box 2201
Brookings, SD 57007
(605) 688-4121

Will confirm attendance and degree by phone or mail. Inquiry must include student's name, date of birth, social security number, years attended. Employers may obtain transcripts upon written request accompanied by a $2.00 fee and a signed release from the student. Turnaround time is 3 days. Requests should be directed to: Registrar's Office.

A comprehensive institution with no medical school, with an enrollment of 8,090. Highest level of offering: doctorate.

ACCREDITATIONS: DIET ENG JOUR MUS NUR PHAR TED

South Florida Community College

600 West College Drive
Avon Park, FL 33825
(813) 453-6661
Fax (813) 452-6042

Will confirm attendance and degree by mail or fax. Inquiry must include student's name, social security number, release. Employers may obtain transcripts upon written request by student. Requests should be directed to: Registrar's Office.

A multiprogram two-year institution, with an enrollment of 847. Highest level of offering: one year but less than four years.

ACCREDITATIONS: SC

South Georgia College

Douglas, GA 31533
(912) 383-4200
Fax (912) 383-4322

Will confirm attendance and degree by phone or mail. Inquiry must include student's name, social security number. Employers may obtain transcripts upon written request accompanied by a $1.00 fee and a signed release from the student. Requests should be directed to: Registrar's Office.

A multiprogram two-year institution, with an enrollment of 1,059. Highest level of offering: one year but less than four years.

ACCREDITATIONS: SACS ADNUR

South Mountain Community College

7050 South 24th Street
Phoenix, AZ 85040
(602) 243-8123
Fax (602) 243-8329

Will confirm attendance and degree by phone or mail. Inquiry must include student's name, social security number, years attended. Employers may obtain transcripts upon written request by student accompanied by a $2.00 fee. Requests should be directed to: Admissions Office.

A multiprogram two-year institution, with an enrollment of 3,200. Highest level of offering: one year but less than four years.

ACCREDITATIONS: NH

South Plains College

1401 College Avenue
Levelland, TX 79336
(806) 894-9611 Ext. 372
Fax (806) 894-5274

Will confirm attendance and degree by phone, fax or mail. Inquiry must include student's name, social security number, years attended. Employers may obtain transcripts upon written request accompanied by a $1.00 fee and a signed release from the student.

A multiprogram two-year institution, with an enrollment of 5,000. Highest level of offering: one year but less than four years.

ACCREDITATIONS: SC MRT RAD RSTH RSTHT

South Puget Sound Community College

2011 Mottman Road South West
Olympia, WA 98502
(206) 754-7711 Ext. 244 .

Will confirm attendance and degree by phone or mail. Inquiry must include student's name, social security number, years attended. Employers may obtain transcripts upon written request accompanied by a $3.00 fee for official transcripts, $1.00 for unofficial transcripts; and a signed release from the student. Requests should be directed to: Registrar's Office.

A multiprogram two-year institution, with an enrollment of 4,500. Highest level of offering: one year but less than four years.

ACCREDITATIONS: NW

South Suburban College

(Formerly Thornton Community College)
15800 South State Street
South Holland, IL 60473
(708) 596-2000
Fax (708) 596-9957

Will confirm attendance and degree by phone or mail. Inquiry must include student's name, social security number, years attended. Employers may obtain transcripts upon written request accompanied by a $3.00 fee and a signed release from the student. Requests should be directed to: Registrar's Office.

A multiprogram two-year institution, with an enrollment of 7,378. Highest level of offering: one year but less than four years.

ACCREDITATIONS: NH ADNUR MUS PNUR RAD

South Texas College of Law

1303 San Jacinto Street
Houston, TX 77002
(713) 659-8040 Ext. 63

Will confirm degree by mail. Inquiry must include student's name, social security number, years attended, release. Employers may obtain transcripts upon written request accompanied by a $5.00 fee and a signed release from the student. Requests should be directed to: Registrar's Office.

A law school, with an enrollment of 1,186. Highest level of offering: first professional degree.

ACCREDITATIONS: LAW

Southeast Community College

(Formerly Southeastern Nebraska Technical Community College)
8800 "O" Street
Lincoln, NE 68520
(402) 437-2609
Fax (402) 437-2520

Will confirm attendance and degree by phone, fax or mail. Inquiry must include student's name, social security number. Employers may obtain transcripts upon written request accompanied by a signed release from the student. Requests should be directed to: Registrar's Office.

A multiprogram two-year institution, with an enrollment of 5,228. Highest level of offering: one year but less than four years.

ACCREDITATIONS: NH DA MAC MLTAD PNUR RAD RSTH RSTHT SURGT

Southeast Missouri State University

1 University Plaza
Cape Girardeau, MO 63701
(314) 651-2865
Fax (314) 651-2200

Will confirm attendance and degree by phone, fax or mail. Inquiry must include student's name, social security number. Employers may obtain transcripts upon written request accompanied by a $3.00 fee and a signed release from the student. Requests should be directed to: Registrar's Office.

A comprehensive institution with no medical school, with an enrollment of 8,061. Highest level of offering: specialist.

ACCREDITATIONS: NH MUS SP TED

Southeastern Baptist College

4229 Highway 15 North
Laurel, MS 39440
(601) 426-6346

Will confirm attendance and degree by phone or mail. Inquiry must include student's name, social security number, years attended. Employers may obtain transcripts upon written request accompanied by a $2.00 fee and a signed release from the student. Requests should be directed to: Registrar's Office.

A school of philosophy, religion and theology, with an enrollment of 72. Highest level of offering: four or five year baccalaureate.

ACCREDITATIONS: BI

Southeastern Baptist Theological Seminary

PO Box 1889
Wake Forest, NC 27588-1889
(919) 556-3101
Fax (919) 556-3101

Will confirm attendance and degree by phone, fax or mail. Inquiry must include student's name, social security number. Employers may obtain transcripts upon written request accompanied by a $2.00 fee and a signed release from the student. Requests should be directed to: Registrar's Office.

A school of philosophy, religion and theology, with an enrollment of 692. Highest level of offering: doctorate.

ACCREDITATIONS: SC THEOL

Southeastern Bible College

3001 Highway 280 East
Birmingham, AL 35243-4181
(205) 969-0880

Will confirm attendance and degree by phone. Inquiry must include student's name. Employers may obtain transcripts upon written request accompanied by a $2.00 fee and a signed release from the student. Requests should be directed to: Registrar's Office.

A school of philosophy, religion and theology, with an enrollment of 157. Highest level of offering: master's.
ACCREDITATIONS: BI

Southeastern College of Osteopathic Medicine

1750 North East 168th Street
North Miami Beach, FL 33162
(305) 949-4000 Ext. 1170 or 1171

Will confirm attendance and degree by phone or mail. Inquiry must include student's name. Employers may obtain transcripts upon written request accompanied by a $1.00 fee and a signed release from the student. Requests should be directed to: Mary Smith.

A bachelor's or higher institution newly admitted to NCES, with an enrollment of 273. Highest level of offering: first professional degree.
ACCREDITATIONS: OSTEO

Southeastern College of the Assemblies of God

1000 Longfellow Boulevard
Lakeland, FL 33801
(813) 665-4404 Ext. 212

Will confirm attendance and degree by phone. Inquiry must include student's name, social security number. Employers may obtain transcripts upon written request accompanied by a $3.00 fee and a signed release from the student. Requests should be directed to: Records Office.

A school of philosophy, religion and theology, with an enrollment of 1,130. Highest level of offering: four or five year baccalaureate.
ACCREDITATIONS: SC BI

Southeastern Community College

Drawer F Highway 406
W. Burlington, IA 52655
(319) 752-2731 Ext. 132
Fax (319) 752-4957

Will confirm attendance and degree by phone or mail. Inquiry must include student's name, years attended. Employers may obtain transcripts upon written request accompanied by a signed release from the student. Requests should be directed to: Registrar's Office.

A multiprogram two-year institution, with an enrollment of 2,800. Highest level of offering: one year but less than four years.
ACCREDITATIONS: NCA MAC

Southeastern Community College

PO Box 151
Whiteville, NC 28472
(919) 642-7141 Ext. 250
Fax (919) 642-5658

Will confirm attendance and degree by phone or mail. Inquiry must include student's name, date of birth, social security number. Employers may obtain transcripts upon written request accompanied by a signed release from the student. Requests should be directed to: Registrar's Office.

A multiprogram two-year institution, with an enrollment of 1,500. Highest level of offering: two years but less than four years.
ACCREDITATIONS: SACS

Southeastern Illinois College

3575 College Road
Harrisburg, IL 62946
(618) 252-6376

Will confirm attendance and degree by phone or mail. Inquiry must include student's name, social security number, years attended. Employers may obtain transcripts upon written request accompanied by a $1.00 fee and a signed release from the student. Requests should be directed to: Records Office.

A multiprogram two-year institution, with an enrollment of 2,252. Highest level of offering: one year but less than four years.
ACCREDITATIONS: NH ADNUR

Southeastern Louisiana University

PO Box 752SLU
Hammond, LA 70402
(504) 549-2062

Will confirm attendance and degree by phone or mail. Inquiry must include student's name, social security number, years attended. Employers may obtain transcripts upon written request accompanied by a signed release from the student. Requests should be directed to: Records Office.

A comprehensive institution with no medical school, with an enrollment of 11,392. Highest level of offering: beyond master's but less than doctorate.
ACCREDITATIONS: SC MUS NUR SW TED AACSB

Southeastern Massachusetts University

(See University of Massachusetts Dartmouth)

Southeastern Nebraska Technical Community College

(See Southeast Community College)

Southeastern Oklahoma State University

Station A Box 4139
Durant, OK 74701
(405) 924-0121 Ext. 240
Fax (405) 920-0758

Will confirm attendance and degree by phone or mail. Inquiry must include student's name, social security number. Employers may obtain transcripts upon written request accompanied by a $3.00 fee and a signed release from the student. Requests should be directed to: Registrar's Office.

A comprehensive institution with no medical school, with an enrollment of 4,000. Highest level of offering: master's.
ACCREDITATIONS: NCA MUS TEDACE

Southeastern University

501 I Street South West
Washington, DC 20024
(202) 488-8162

Will confirm attendance and degree by phone or mail. Inquiry must include student's name, social security number, release. Employers may obtain transcripts upon written request accompanied by a $5.00 fee and a signed release from the student. Requests should be directed to: Registrar's Office.

A business school, with an enrollment of 960. Highest level of offering: master's.
ACCREDITATIONS: M

Southern Arkansas University El Dorado Branch

300 South West Avenue
El Dorado, AR 71730
(501) 862-8131
Fax (501) 862-6412

Will confirm attendance and degree by phone or mail. Inquiry must include student's name, social security number, years attended. Employers may obtain transcripts upon written request accompanied by a signed release from the student. Requests should be directed to: Registrar.

A multiprogram two-year institution, with an enrollment of 950. Highest level of offering: one year but less than four years.
ACCREDITATIONS: NCA MLTAD RAD

Southern Arkansas University Main Campus

PO Box 1404
Magnolia, AR 71753
(501) 235-4031
Fax (501) 235-5005

Will confirm attendance and degree by phone or mail. Inquiry must include student's name, years attended. Employers may obtain transcripts upon written request accompanied by a $1.00 fee and a signed release from the student. Requests should be directed to: Registrar's Office.

A general baccalaureate institution, with an enrollment of 2,127. Highest level of offering: master's.
ACCREDITATIONS: NH ADNUR MUS TED

Southern Arkansas University Technical Branch

SAU Tech Station
Camden, AR 71701
(501) 574-4504

Will confirm attendance and degree by phone or mail. Inquiry must include student's name, social security number, years attended. Employers may obtain transcripts upon written request accompanied by a $2.00 fee and a signed release from the student. Requests should be directed to: Admissions Department.

A multiprogram two-year institution, with an enrollment of 988. Highest level of offering: one year but less than four years.
ACCREDITATIONS: NH

Southern Baptist College

PO Box 453
Walnut Ridge, AR 72476
(501) 886-6741 Ext. 104
Fax (501) 886-3924

Will confirm attendance and degree by phone, fax or mail. Inquiry must include student's name, social security number. Employers may obtain transcripts upon written request accompanied by a $2.00 fee and a signed release from the student. Requests should be directed to: Registrar's Office.

A multiprogram four-year institution, with an enrollment of 571. Highest level of offering: four or five year baccalaureate.
ACCREDITATIONS: NH

Southern Baptist Theological Seminary

2825 Lexington Road
Louisville, KY 40280
(502) 897-4011

Will confirm attendance and degree by phone or mail. Inquiry must include student's name, SSN, years attended. Requests should be directed to: Registrar's Office. Employers may obtain transcripts upon written request accompanied by a $3.00 fee and a signed release from the student.

A school of philosophy, religion and theology, with an enrollment of 2,335. Highest level of offering: doctorate.
ACCREDITATIONS: SC MUS THEOL SW

Southern California College of Optometry

2575 Yorba Linda Boulevard
Fullerton, CA 92631
(714) 449-7445

Will confirm attendance and degree by phone or mail. Inquiry must include student's name, social security number, years attended. Employers may obtain transcripts upon written request accompanied by a $2.00 fee and a signed release from the student.

A health institution, with an enrollment of 398. Highest level of offering: first professional degree.
ACCREDITATIONS: WC OPT OPTR OPTT

Southern California College

55 Fair Drive
Costa Mesa, CA 92626
(714) 556-3610 Ext. 209

Will confirm attendance and degree by phone or mail. Inquiry must include student's name, social security number. Employers may obtain transcripts upon written request accompanied by a $4.00 fee and a signed release from the student. Requests should be directed to: Records Office.

A general baccalaureate institution, with an enrollment of 917. Highest level of offering: master's.
ACCREDITATIONS: WC

Southern California College of Chiropractic

(Formerly Pasadena College of Chiropractic)
8420 Beverly Road
Pico Rivera, CA 90660
(213) 692-0331 Ext. 23

Will confirm attendance and degree by phone or mail. Inquiry must include student's name, date of birth, social security number. Employers may obtain transcripts upon written request accompanied by a $10.00 fee and a signed release from the student. .

A health institution, with an enrollment of 150. Highest level of offering: first professional degree.
ACCREDITATIONS: CHIRO

Southern California Institute of Architecture

5454 Beethoven Street
Los Angeles, CA 90066
(310) 574-1123
Fax (310) 574-3801

Will confirm attendance and degree by mail or fax. Inquiry must include student's name, date of birth, social security number, years attended, release. Employers may obtain transcripts upon written request accompanied by a $2.00 fee and a signed release from the student. Requests should be directed to: Registrar's Office.

A specialized school, with an enrollment of 425. Highest level of offering: master's.
ACCREDITATIONS: ARCH

Southern College of Optometry

1245 Madison Avenue
Memphis, TN 38104
(901) 722-3224
Fax (901) 722-3279

Will confirm attendance and degree by phone, fax or mail. Inquiry must include student's name, years attended. Employers may obtain transcripts upon written request accompanied by a signed release from the student. Requests should be directed to: Registrar's Office.

A health institution, with an enrollment of 422. Highest level of offering: first professional degree.
ACCREDITATIONS: SC OPT OPTR

Southern College of Seventh-Day Adventists

Box 370
Collegedale, TN 37315
(615) 238-2897
Fax (615) 238-3003

Will confirm attendance and degree by phone, fax or mail. Inquiry must include student's name, social security number, years attended. Employers may obtain transcripts upon written request accompanied by a $3.00 fee and a signed release from the student. Requests should be directed to: Records Office.

A general baccalaureate institution, with an enrollment of 1,532. Highest level of offering: four or five year baccalaureate.
ACCREDITATIONS: SC ADNUR MUS NUR

Southern Connecticut State University

501 Crescent Street
New Haven, CT 06515
(203) 397-4221

Will confirm attendance and degree by mail. Inquiry must include student's name, date of birth, social security number, last semester attended. Employers may obtain transcripts upon written request accompanied by a $3.00 fee and a signed release from the student. Requests should be directed to: Records Office.

A comprehensive institution with no medical school, with an enrollment of 10,733. Highest level of offering: beyond master's but less than doctorate.
ACCREDITATIONS: EH LIB MFCD NUR SP SW

Southern Illinois University at Carbondale

Woody Hall
Carbondale, IL 62901
(618) 453-4381

Will confirm attendance and degree by phone or mail. Inquiry must include student's name, years attended. Employers may obtain transcripts upon written request accompanied by a signed release from the student. Requests should be directed to: Transcript Department.

A doctoral-level institution with a medical school, with an enrollment of 22,776. Highest level of offering: doctorate.
ACCREDITATIONS: NH ADNUR ART BUS CLPSY COPSY DH DT ENG ENGT FIDER FOR FUSER IPSY JOUR LAW MED MUS PTAA RAD RSTH SP SW BUSA TED PAST

Southern Illinois University at Edwardsville

PO Box 1047
Edwardsville, IL 62026
(618) 692-2000

Will confirm attendance and degree by phone or mail. Inquiry must include student's name, social security number, years attended. Employers may obtain transcripts upon written request accompanied by a $2.00 fee and a signed release from the student. Requests should be directed to: Records Office.

A comprehensive institution with a medical school, with an enrollment of 10,820. Highest level of offering: doctorate.
ACCREDITATIONS: NH BUS DENT ENG JOUR MUS NUR SP SW TED

Southern Junior College of Business

115 Office Park Drive
Birmingham, AL 35223
(205) 879-5100

Will confirm attendance and degree by phone or mail. Inquiry must include student's name, social security number. Employers may obtain transcripts upon written request accompanied by a $2.00 fee and a signed release from the student. Requests should be directed to: Registrar's Office.

A multiprogram two-year institution, with an enrollment of 1,783. Highest level of offering: one year but less than four years.
ACCREDITATIONS: SC JRCB

Southern Maine Technical College

Fort Road
South Portland, ME 04106
(207) 767-9538
Fax (207) 767-2731

Will confirm attendance and degree by phone or mail. Inquiry must include student's name, social security number, years attended. Employers may obtain transcripts upon written request accompanied by a $3.00 fee and a signed release from the student. Requests should be directed to: Registrar's Office.

A multiprogram two-year institution, with an enrollment of 2,100. Highest level of offering: one year but less than four years.
ACCREDITATIONS: EV RAD RSTH RTT

Southern Methodist University

Box 276
Dallas, TX 75275
(214) 692-2045

Will confirm attendance and degree by phone or mail. Inquiry must include student's name, social security number, years attended. Employers may obtain transcripts upon written request accompanied by a $5.00 fee and a signed release from the student.

A doctoral-level institution with no medical school, with an enrollment of 8,746 Highest level of offering: doctorate.
ACCREDITATIONS: SC BUS DANCE ENG LAW MUS TED THEOL

Southern Nazarene University

6729 North West 39 Expressway
Bethany, OK 73008
(405) 491-6386

Will confirm attendance and degree by phone or mail. Inquiry must include student's name, social security number, years attended. Employers may obtain transcripts upon written request accompanied by a $3.00 fee and a signed release from the student.

A general baccalaureate institution, with an enrollment of 1,600. Highest level of offering: master's.
ACCREDITATIONS: NH TED

Southern Ohio College Technical Center

Registrar's Office
4641 Bach Lane
Fairfield, OH 45014
(513) 829-7100 Ext. 25

Will confirm attendance and degree by mail. Inquiry must include student's name, social security number, years attended. Employers may obtain transcripts upon written request accompanied by a $4.00 fee and a signed release from the student. Requests should be directed to: Student Services.

A multiprogram two-year institution, with an enrollment of 550. Highest level of offering: one year but less than four years.
ACCREDITATIONS: NCA JRCB

Southern Ohio College Technical Center

309 Buttermilk Pike
Ft. Mitchell, OH 41017
(606) 341-5627

Will confirm attendance and degree by mail. Inquiry must include student's name, social security number, years attended. Employers may obtain transcripts upon written request accompanied by a $4.00 fee and a signed release from the student. Requests should be directed to: Student Services.

A multiprogram two-year institution, with an enrollment of 289. Highest level of offering: one year but less than four years.
ACCREDITATIONS: NCA JRCB NATTS

Southern Oregon State College

1250 Siskiyou Boulevard–Britt
Room 242
Ashland, OR 97520
(503) 552-7672

Will confirm attendance and degree by phone or mail. Inquiry must include student's name, social security number, years attended. Employers may obtain transcripts upon written request accompanied by a $5.00 fee and a signed release from the student. Requests should be directed to: Registrar's Office.

A comprehensive institution with no medical school, with an enrollment of 4,432. Highest level of offering: master's.
ACCREDITATIONS: NW ADNUR MUS NUR TED

Southern Seminary College

Buena Vista, VA 24416
(703) 261-8430

Will confirm attendance and degree by phone or mail. Inquiry must include student's name, maiden name, social security number. Employers may obtain transcripts upon written request accompanied by a $2.00 fee and a signed release from the student. Requests should be directed to: Registrar's Office.

A multiprogram two-year institution, with an enrollment of 270. Highest level of offering: one year but less than four years.
ACCREDITATIONS: SC

Southern State Community College

200 Hobart Drive
Hillsboro, OH 45133
(513) 393-3431
Fax (513) 393-9370

Will confirm attendance and degree by phone, fax or mail. Inquiry must include student's name, social security number, years attended. Employers may obtain transcripts upon written request accompanied by a signed release from the student. Requests should be directed to: Records Office.

A multiprogram two-year institution, with an enrollment of 1,500. Highest level of offering: one year but less than four years.
ACCREDITATIONS: NH

Southern Technical College

401 Beacon Parkway West
Birmingham, AL 35209
(205) 956-8801

Will confirm attendance and degree by mail. Inquiry must include student's name, social security number, years attended, release. Employers may obtain transcripts upon written request accompanied by a signed release from the student. Requests should be directed to: Registrar's Office.

A two-year institution newly admitted to NCES, with an enrollment of 150. Highest level of offering: one year but less than four years.
ACCREDITATIONS: JRCB

Southern Technical Institute

1100 South Marietta
Marietta, GA 30060
(404) 528-7267
Fax (404) 528-7292

Will confirm attendance and degree by phone, fax or mail. Inquiry must include student's name, social security number. Employers may obtain transcripts upon written request by student accompanied by a $3.00 fee and a signed release from the student. Requests should be directed to: Registrar's office.

An engineering school, with an enrollment of 3,610. Highest level of offering: four or five year baccalaureate.
ACCREDITATIONS: SC ENGT

Southern Union State Junior College

Robert's Street
Wadley, AL 36276
(205) 395-2211
Fax (205) 395-2215

Will confirm attendance and degree by mail. Inquiry must include student's name, social security number, release. Employers may obtain transcripts upon written request accompanied by a $2.00 fee and a signed release from the student. Requests should be directed to: Records Office.

A multiprogram two-year institution, with an enrollment of 2,984. Highest level of offering: one year but less than four years.
ACCREDITATIONS: SC ADNUR

Southern University Agriculture and Mechanical College at Baton Rouge

PO Box 9454
Baton Rouge, LA 70813
(504) 771-5050

Will confirm attendance and degree by phone or mail. Inquiry must include student's name, social security number. Employers may obtain transcripts upon written request accompanied by a $2.00 fee and a signed release from the student. Requests should be directed to: Registrar's Office.

A comprehensive institution with no medical school, with an enrollment of 9,802. Highest level of offering: master's.
ACCREDITATIONS: SC ARCH ENG LAW MUS SW TED

Southern University at New Orleans

6400 Press Drive
New Orleans, LA 70126
(504) 286-5000
Fax (504) 286-5131

Will confirm attendance and degree by mail. Inquiry must include student's name, social security number, years attended. Employers may obtain transcripts upon written request accompanied by a $2.00 fee and a signed release from the student. Requests should be directed to: Records Office.

A general baccalaureate institution, with an enrollment of 2,870. Highest level of offering: master's.
ACCREDITATIONS: SC SW

Southern University Shreveport–Bossier City Campus

3050 Martin L. King Drive
Shreveport, LA 71107
(318) 674-3343

Will confirm attendance and degree by phone or mail. Inquiry must include student's name, social security number. Employers may obtain transcripts upon written request accompanied by a $1.00 fee and a signed release from the student. Requests should be directed to: Registrar's Office.

A multiprogram two-year institution, with an enrollment of 1,150. Highest level of offering: one year but less than four years.
ACCREDITATIONS: SC

Southern Utah State College

351 West Center
Cedar City, UT 84720
(801) 586-7715

Will confirm attendance and degree by phone or mail. Inquiry must include student's name, date of birth, social security number. Employers may obtain transcripts upon written request accompanied by a $2.00 fee and a signed release from the student. Requests should be directed to: SUSC Registrar's Office.

A general baccalaureate institution, with an enrollment of 3,800. Highest level of offering: master's.
ACCREDITATIONS: NW ADNUR SW TED

Southern Vermont College

Monument View Road
Bennington, VT 05201
(802) 442-5427 Ext. 228
Fax (802) 442-5529

Will confirm attendance and degree by phone or mail. Inquiry must include student's name, social security number, years attended. Employers may obtain transcripts upon written request accompanied by a $5.00 fee and a signed release from the student. Requests should be directed to: Registrar's Office.

A general baccalaureate institution, with an enrollment of 650. Highest level of offering: four or five year baccalaureate.
ACCREDITATIONS: EH

Southern West Virginia Community College

PO Box 2900
Logan, WV 25601
(304) 792-4300
Fax (304) 792-4399

Will confirm attendance and degree by phone, fax or mail. Inquiry must include student's full name, social security number, years attended. Employers may obtain transcripts upon written request accompanied by a $3.00 fee and a signed release from the student. Requests should be directed to: Records Office.

A multiprogram two-year institution, with an enrollment of 2,359. Highest level of offering: one year but less than four years.
ACCREDITATIONS: NH

Southside Virginia Community College

Rt. 1 Box 60
Alberta, VA 23821
(804) 949-7111
Fax (804) 949-7863

Will confirm attendance and degree by phone or mail. Inquiry must include student's name, social security number. Employers may obtain transcripts upon written request accompanied by a signed release from the student. Requests should be directed to: Records Office.

A multiprogram two-year institution, with an enrollment of 3,398. Highest level of offering: two years but less than four years.
ACCREDITATIONS: SACS

Southwest Baptist University

Bolivar, MO 65613
(417) 326-1605
Fax (417) 326-1514

Will confirm attendance and degree by phone or mail. Inquiry must include student's name, social security number, years attended. Employers may obtain transcripts upon written request accompanied by a $3.00 fee and a signed release from the student. Requests should be directed to: Registrar's Office.

A general baccalaureate institution, with an enrollment of 1,824. Highest level of offering: four or five year baccalaureate.
ACCREDITATIONS: NH MUS

Southwest Mississippi Community College

Summit, MS 39666
(601) 276-2000 Ext. 2001

Will confirm attendance and degree by phone or mail. Inquiry must include student's name, years attended. Employers may obtain transcripts upon written request accompanied by a $2.00 fee and a signed release from the student. Requests should be directed to: Admissions Office.

A multiprogram two-year institution, with an enrollment of 1,475. Highest level of offering: one year but less than four years.
ACCREDITATIONS: SC

Southwest Missouri State University

901 South National
Springfield, MO 65804
(417) 836-5517
Fax (417) 836-6334

Will confirm attendance and degree by phone, fax or mail. Inquiry must include student's name, social security number, years attended. Employers may obtain transcripts upon written request accompanied by a $3.00 fee and a signed release from the student. Requests should be directed to: Admissions & Records Office/Transcript Department.

A comprehensive institution with no medical school, with an enrollment of 20,672. Highest level of offering: beyond master's but less than doctorate.
ACCREDITATIONS: CHM DIET NH MUS NUR SW TED

Southwest State Technical College

925 Dauphin Island Pkwy
Mobile, AL 36605-3299
(205) 479-0003

Will confirm attendance and degree by phone or mail. Inquiry must include student's name, years attended. Employers may obtain transcripts upon written request accompanied by a $2.00 fee and a signed release from the student. Requests should be directed to: Student Service.

A two-year institution newly admitted to NCES, with an enrollment of 1,143. Highest level of offering: one year but less than four years.
ACCREDITATIONS: SV

Southwest State University

Marshall, MN 56258
(507) 537-6206
Fax (507) 537-7154

Will confirm attendance and degree by phone, fax or mail. Inquiry must include student's name, social security number. Employers may obtain transcripts upon written request accompanied by a signed release from the student. Requests should be directed to: Transcript Office.

A general baccalaureate institution, with an enrollment of 3,000. Highest level of offering: four or five year baccalaureate.
ACCREDITATIONS: NH

Southwest Texas Junior College

2401Garnerfield Road
Uvalde, TX 78801-6297
(512) 278-4401

Will confirm attendance and degree by phone or mail. Inquiry must include student's name, social security number. Employers may obtain transcripts upon written request accompanied by a $2.00 fee and a signed release from the student. Requests should be directed to: Admissions Office.

A multiprogram two-year institution, with an enrollment of 2,717. Highest level of offering: one year but less than four years.
ACCREDITATIONS: SC

Southwest Texas State University

San Marcos, TX 78666-4606
(512) 245-2367
Fax (512) 245-3040

Will confirm attendance and degree by phone or mail. Inquiry must include student's name, social security number. Employers may obtain transcripts upon written request accompanied by a $5.00 fee and a signed release from the student. Requests should be directed to: Registrar's Office.

A comprehensive institution with no medical school, with an enrollment of 21,587. Highest level of offering: beyond master's but less than doctorate.
ACCREDITATIONS: SC MRA MT MUS RSTH RSTHT SP SW TED

Southwest Virginia Community College

Box S V C C
Richlands, VA 24641
(703) 964-2555 Ext. 294
Fax (703) 964-9307

Will confirm attendance and degree by phone or mail. Inquiry must include student's name, social security number. Requests should be directed to: Registrar's Office. Employers may obtain transcripts upon written request accompanied by a signed release from the student.

A multiprogram two-year institution, with an enrollment of 7,021. Highest level of offering: one year but less than four years.
ACCREDITATIONS: SC ADNUR RAD RSTHT

Southwest Wisconsin Technical College

Rt.1 Box 500
Fennimore, WI 53809
(608) 822-3262 Ext. 135
Fax (608) 822-6019

Will confirm attendance and degree by phone or mail. Inquiry must include student's name, social security number. Employers may obtain transcripts upon written request accompanied by a $2.00 fee and a signed release from the student. Requests should be directed to: Student Services.

A multiprogram two-year institution, with an enrollment of 1,080. Highest level of offering: one year but less than four years.
ACCREDITATIONS: NH PNUR

Southwest Wisconsin Vocational Technical Institute

Rt. 1 Box 500
Fennimore, WI 53809
(608) 822-3262 Ext. 135
Fax (608) 822-6019

Will confirm attendance and degree by phone or mail. Inquiry must include student's name, social security number. Employers may obtain transcripts upon written request accompanied by a $2.00 fee and a signed release from the student.

A multiprogram two-year institution, with an enrollment of 1,080. Highest level of offering: one year but less than four years.
ACCREDITATIONS: NH PNUR

Southwestern Adventist College

PO Box 567
Keene, TX 76059
(817) 645-3921
Fax (817) 556-4744

Will confirm attendance and degree by phone or mail. Inquiry must include student's name, date of birth, social security number. Employers may obtain transcripts upon written request accompanied by a $2.00 fee and a signed release from the student. Requests should be directed to: Record's Office.

A general baccalaureate institution, with an enrollment of 871. Highest level of offering: master's.
ACCREDITATIONS: SC ADNUR

Southwestern Assemblies of God College

1200 Sycamore
Waxahachie, TX 75165
(214) 937-4010 Ext. 113

Will confirm attendance and degree by phone or mail. Inquiry must include student's name, social security number, years attended. Employers may obtain transcripts upon written request accompanied by a $5.00 fee and a signed release from the student. Requests should be directed to: Registrar's Office.

A school of philosophy, religion and theology, with an enrollment of 647. Highest level of offering: four or five year baccalaureate.
ACCREDITATIONS: SC BI

Southwestern Baptist Theological Seminary

PO Box 22000
Fort Worth, TX 76122
(817) 923-1921 Ext. 2000

Will confirm attendance and degree by phone or mail. Inquiry must include student's name, social security number. Employers may obtain transcripts upon written request accompanied by a $5.00 fee and a signed release from the student.

A school of religion and theology, with an enrollment of 3,232. Highest level of offering: doctorate.
ACCREDITATIONS: SC MUS THEOL

Southwestern Christian College

Box 10
Terrell, TX 75160
(214) 524-3341 Ext. 142
Fax (214) 563-7133

Will confirm attendance and degree by phone, fax or mail. Inquiry must include student's name, social security number. Employers may obtain transcripts upon written request accompanied by a $2.00 fee and a signed release from the student. Requests should be directed to: Registrar's Office.

A multiprogram two-year institution, with an enrollment of 272. Highest level of offering: one year but less than four years.
ACCREDITATIONS: SC

Southwestern College of Christian Ministries

PO Box 340
Bethany, OK 73008
(405) 789-7661

Will confirm attendance and degree by phone or mail. Inquiry must include student's name, date of birth, social security number. Employers may obtain transcripts upon written request accompanied by a $5.00 fee and a signed release from the student. Requests should be directed to: Registrar's Office.

A school of philosophy, religion and theology, with an enrollment of 151. Highest level of offering: four or five year baccalaureate.
ACCREDITATIONS: NH

Southwestern College

100 College Street
Winfield, KS 67156
(316) 221-4150 Ext. 208
Fax (316) 221-3725

Will confirm attendance and degree by phone, fax or mail. Inquiry must include student's name, social security number. Employers may obtain transcripts upon written request accompanied by a $2.00 fee and a signed release from the student.

A general baccalaureate institution, with an enrollment of 628. Highest level of offering: master's.
ACCREDITATIONS: NH MUS SW

Southwestern College

900 Otay Lakes Road
Chula Vista, CA 92010
(619) 421-6700
Fax (619) 482-6323

Will confirm attendance and degree by mail. Inquiry must include student's name, maiden name, date of birth, social security number, years of attendance, release. Employers may obtain transcripts upon written request accompanied by a $2.00 fee and a signed release from the student. Requests should be directed to: Admissions Office.

A multiprogram two-year institution, with an enrollment of 17,000. Highest level of offering: one year but less than four years.
ACCREDITATIONS: WJ

Southwestern Community College

1501 West Townline
Creston, IA 50801
(515) 782-7081
Fax (515) 782-3312

Will confirm attendance and degree by phone, fax or mail. Inquiry must include student's name, social security number, release. Employers may obtain transcripts upon written request accompanied by a $3.00 fee and a signed release from the student.

A multiprogram two-year institution, with an enrollment of 1,154. Highest level of offering: two years but less than four years.
ACCREDITATIONS: NH

Southwestern Community College

275 Webster Road
Sylva, NC 28779
(704) 586-4091 Ext. 219
Fax (704) 586-4091 Ext. 293

Will confirm attendance and degree by phone, fax or mail. Inquiry must include student's name, social security number, years attended. Employers may obtain transcripts upon written request accompanied by a signed release from the student. Requests should be directed to: Registrar's Office.

A multiprogram two-year institution, with an enrollment of 1,215. Highest level of offering: two years but less than four years.
ACCREDITATIONS: SC MLTAD

Southwestern Conservative Baptist Bible College

2625 East Cactus Road
Phoenix, AZ 85032
(602) 992-6101

Will confirm attendance and degree by phone or mail. Inquiry must include student's name, social security number, years attended. Employers may obtain transcripts upon written request accompanied by a $2.00 fee and a signed release from the student.

A school of philosophy, religion and theology, with an enrollment of 147. Highest level of offering: four or five year baccalaureate.
ACCREDITATIONS: BI

Southwestern Michigan College

Cherry Grove Road
Dowagiac, MI 49047
(616) 782-5113 Ext. 305
Fax (616) 782-8414

Will confirm attendance and degree by phone or mail. Inquiry must include student's name, social security number. Employers may obtain transcripts upon written request accompanied by a $2.00 fee and a signed release from the student. Requests should be directed to: Registrar's Office.

A multiprogram two-year institution, with an enrollment of 2,365. Highest level of offering: one year but less than four years.
ACCREDITATIONS: NH

Southwestern Oklahoma State University

100 Campus Drive
Weatherford, OK 73096
(405) 774-3777
Fax (405) 722-5447

Will confirm attendance and degree by phone, fax or mail. Inquiry must include student's name, date of birth, social security number. Requests should be directed to: Registrar's Office. Employers may obtain transcripts upon written request accompanied by a $1.00 fee and a signed release from the student.

A comprehensive institution with no medical school, with an enrollment of 4,657. Highest level of offering: master's.
ACCREDITATIONS: NH MRA MUS NUR PHAR TED

Southwestern Oklahoma State University at Sayre

(Formerly Sayre Junior College)
409 East Mississippi
Sayre, OK 73662
(405) 928-5533

Will confirm attendance and degree by phone or mail. Inquiry must include student's name, date of birth, social security number. Employers may obtain transcripts upon written request accompanied by a $1.00 fee and a signed release from the student.

A multiprogram two-year institution, with an enrollment of 510. Highest level of offering: one year but less than four years.
ACCREDITATIONS: MLTAB

Southwestern Oregon Community College

Coos Bay, OR 97420
(503) 888-2525

Will confirm attendance and degree by phone or mail. Inquiry must include student's name, social security number, years attended. Requests should be directed to: Records Office. Employers may obtain transcripts upon written request accompanied by a $4.00 fee and a signed release from the student.

A multiprogram two-year institution, with an enrollment of 5,000. Highest level of offering: one year but less than four years.
ACCREDITATIONS: NW

Southwestern University School of Law

675 South Westmoreland Avenue
Los Angeles, CA 90005
(213) 738-6734

Will confirm attendance and degree by mail. Inquiry must include student's name, social security number, years attended. Employers may obtain transcripts upon written request accompanied by a $4.00 fee and a signed release from the student. Attn: Registrar's Office.

A law school, with an enrollment of 1,015. Highest level of offering: first professional degree.
ACCREDITATIONS: LAW

Southwestern University

University Avenue
Georgetown, TX 78626
(512) 863-1952
Fax (512) 863-5788

Will confirm attendance and degree by phone or mail. Inquiry must include student's name, social security number, years attended. Requests should be directed to: Registrar's Office. Employers may obtain transcripts upon written request accompanied by a $2.00 fee and a signed release from the student.

A general baccalaureate institution, with an enrollment of 1,230. Highest level of offering: four or five year baccalaureate.
ACCREDITATIONS: SACS MUS

Spalding University

851 South Fourth Avenue
Louisville, KY 40203
(502) 585-9911 Ext. 210
Fax (502) 581-0108

Will confirm attendance and degree by phone, fax or mail. Inquiry must include student's name, social security number. Employers may obtain transcripts upon written request accompanied by a $4.00 fee and a signed release from the student.

A comprehensive institution with no medical school, with an enrollment of 1,126. Highest level of offering: doctorate.
ACCREDITATIONS: SC DIET NUR SW

Spartanburg Methodist College

1200 Textile Road
Spartanburg, SC 29301
(803) 587-4232
Fax (803) 574-6919

Will confirm attendance and degree by phone or mail. Inquiry must include student's name, date of birth, social security number, years attended. Employers may obtain transcripts upon written request accompanied by a $3.00 fee and a signed release from the student. Requests should be directed to: Registrar's Office.

A multiprogram two-year institution, with an enrollment of 1,005. Highest level of offering: one year but less than four years.
ACCREDITATIONS: SC

Spartanburg Technical College

PO Drawer 4386
Spartanburg, SC 29305-4386
(803) 591-3684

Will confirm attendance and degree by phone or mail. Inquiry must include student's name, social security number. Employers may obtain transcripts upon written request accompanied by a $1.00 fee and a signed release from the student. Requests should be directed to: Records Office.

A multiprogram two-year institution, with an enrollment of 1,653. Highest level of offering: one year but less than four years.
ACCREDITATIONS: SC DA ENGT MLTAD RAD RSTHT SURGT

Spelman College

350 Spelman Lane South West
Atlanta, GA 30314
(404) 681-3643 Ext. 2127
Fax (404) 223-1449

Will confirm attendance and degree by
phone or mail. Inquiry must include student's name, social security number.
Employers may obtain transcripts upon
written request accompanied by a $2.00 fee
and a signed release from the student.

A general baccalaureate institution, with an
enrollment of 1,788. Highest level of offering: four or five year baccalaureate.

ACCREDITATIONS: SC MUS TED

Spertus College of Judaica

618 South Michigan Avenue
Chicago, IL 60605
(312) 922-9012 Ext. 222

Will confirm attendance and degree by
mail. Inquiry must include student's name,
social security number, years attended.
Requests should be directed to: Registrar's
Office. Employers may obtain transcripts
upon written request accompanied by a
$2.00 fee and a signed release from the stu-
dent.

A general baccalaureate institution, with an
enrollment of 450. Highest level of offering: master's.

ACCREDITATIONS: NH

Spokane Community College

North 1810 Greene
Spokane, WA 99207
(509) 533-7012
Fax (509) 533-8839

Will confirm attendance and degree by
phone or mail. Inquiry must include student's name, social security number.
Employers may obtain transcripts upon
written request accompanied by a signed release from the student.

A multiprogram two-year institution, with
an enrollment of 6,065. Highest level of offering: one year but less than four years.

ACCREDITATIONS: NW DA MRT OPTT
RSTH SURGT

Spokane Falls Community College

West 3410 Ft George Wright Drive
Spokane, WA 99204-5288
(509) 459-3518
Fax (509) 533-3237

Will confirm enrollment and degree by
phone or mail. Inquiry must include student's name, social security number, release. Employers may obtain transcripts
upon written request accompanied by a
signed release from the student. Requests
should be directed to: Registrar's Office.

A multiprogram two-year institution, with
an enrollment of 5,547. Highest level of offering: one year but less than four years.

ACCREDITATIONS: NW FIDER

Spoon River College

Rural Route One
Canton, IL 61520
(309) 647-4645 Ext. 205
Fax (309) 647-6498

Will confirm attendance and degree by
phone or mail. Inquiry must include student's name, social security number.
Employers may obtain transcripts upon
written request accompanied by a $2.00 fee
and a signed release from the student.
Requests should be directed to: Records
Office.

A multiprogram two-year institution, with
an enrollment of 1,612. Highest level of offering: one year but less than four years.

ACCREDITATIONS: NCA

Spring Arbor College

106 Main Street
Spring Arbor, MI 49283
(517) 750-1200 Ext. 510

Will confirm attendance and degree by
phone or mail. Inquiry must include student's name, social security number.
Employers may obtain transcripts upon
written request accompanied by a $4.00 fee
and a signed release from the student.

A general baccalaureate institution, with an
enrollment of 1,867. Highest level of offering: four or five year baccalaureate.

ACCREDITATIONS: NCA

Spring Garden College

7500 German Town Avenue
Philadelphia, PA 19119
(215) 248-7908
Fax (215) 248-7938

Will confirm attendance and degree by
phone or mail. Inquiry must include student's name, social security number, years
attended. Employers may obtain transcripts
upon written request accompanied by a
$4.00 fee and a signed release from the stu-
dent. Requests should be directed to:
Registrar's Office.

An engineering school, with an enrollment
of 1,255. Highest level of offering: four or
five year baccalaureate.

ACCREDITATIONS: M ENGT MLTAD

Spring Hill College

4000 Dolphin Street
Mobile, AL 36608
(205) 460-2164

Will confirm attendance and degree by
phone or mail. Inquiry must include student's name, date of birth, social security
number. Requests should be directed to:
Student Records Office. Employers may
obtain transcripts upon written request accompanied by a $2.00 fee and a signed re-
lease from the student. Requests should be
directed to: Registrar's Office.

A general baccalaureate institution, with an
enrollment of 1,125. Highest level of offering: master's.

ACCREDITATIONS: SC

Springfield College in Illinois

1500 North Fifth Street
Springfield, IL 62702
(217) 525-1420 Ext. 13

Will confirm attendance and degree by
phone or mail. Inquiry must include student's name, date of birth, dates of attendance. Employers may obtain transcripts
upon written request accompanied by a
$2.00 fee and a signed release from the stu-
dent. Requests should be directed to:
Registrar's Office.

A multiprogram two-year institution, with
an enrollment of 507. Highest level of offering: one year but less than four years.

ACCREDITATIONS: NH MUS

Springfield College

263 Alden Street
Springfield, MA 01109
(413) 788-3149
Fax (413) 731-1681

Will confirm attendance and degree by
phone or mail. Inquiry must include student's name, social security number, years
attended. Employers may obtain transcripts
upon written request accompanied by a
$2.00 fee and a signed release from the stu-
dent. Requests should be directed to:
Registrar's Office.

A comprehensive institution with no medical school, with an enrollment of 2,353.
Highest level of offering: doctorate.

ACCREDITATIONS: EH

Springfield Technical Community College

1 Armory Square
Springfield, MA 01105
(413) 781-7822

Will confirm attendance and degree by
phone or mail. Inquiry must include student's name, social security number, years
attended. Employers may obtain transcripts
upon written request accompanied by a
$1.00 fee and a signed release from the stu-
dent.

A multiprogram two-year institution, with
an enrollment of 3,400. Highest level of offering: one year but less than four years.

ACCREDITATIONS: EH ADNUR DA DH MAC
MLTAD NMT PTAA RAD RSTH RTT SURGT

Spurgeon Baptist Bible College

4440 Spurgeon Drive
Mulberry, FL 33860
(813) 425-3429

Will confirm attendance and degree by
phone or mail. Inquiry must include student's name, years attended. Requests
should be directed to: Registrar's Office.
Employers may obtain transcripts upon
written request accompanied by a $2.00 fee
and a signed release from the student.

A bachelor's or higher institution newly admitted to NCES, with an enrollment of 65.
Highest level of offering: four or five year
baccalaureate.

ACCREDITATIONS: BI

St. Anthony On–Hudson Seminary

517 Washington Avenue
Rensselaer, NY 12144
(518) 463-2261

Records are maintained at the above address. Will confirm attendance and degree by mail. Inquiry must include student's name, years attended. Employers may obtain transcripts upon written request accompanied by a $3.00 fee and a signed release from the student. Requests should be directed to: Registrar.

A bachelor's or higher institution newly admitted to NCES, with an enrollment of 39. Highest level of offering: master's.
ACCREDITATIONS: NY

St. Paul Technical Vocational Institute

235 Marshall Avenue
St Paul, MN 55102
(612) 221-1434

Will confirm attendance and degree by phone or mail. Inquiry must include student's name, social security number, years attended. Employers may obtain transcripts upon written request accompanied by a $2.00 fee and a signed release from the student.

A two-year institution newly admitted to NCES, with an enrollment of 1,952. Highest level of offering: one year but less than four years.
ACCREDITATIONS: NH PNUR

St. John Fisher College

3690 East Avenue
Rochester, NY 14618
(716) 385-8015

Will confirm attendance and degree by phone or mail. Inquiry must include student's name, social security number, years attended. Employers may obtain transcripts upon written request accompanied by a $3.00 fee for official copy, $2.00 for unofficial copy and a signed release from the student.

A general baccalaureate institution, with an enrollment of 2,259. Highest level of offering: master's.
ACCREDITATIONS: M NY

St. John's College at Santa Fe New Mexico

1160 Camino Cruz Blanca
Santa Fe, NM 87501
(505) 982-3691 Ext. 266
Fax (505) 989-9269

Will confirm attendance and degree by phone or mail. Inquiry must include student's name, social security number. Employers may obtain transcripts upon written request accompanied by a $2.00 fee and a signed release from the student.

A general baccalaureate institution, with an enrollment of 385. Highest level of offering: master's.
ACCREDITATIONS: NCA

St. John's College Main Campus

PO Box 2800
Annapolis, MD 21404
(410) 626-2513
Fax (410) 263-4828

Will confirm attendance and degree by mail. Inquiry must include student's name, social security number, years attended, release. Employers may obtain transcripts upon written request accompanied by a $2.00 fee and a signed release from the student. Requests should be sent to: Registrar's Office.

A general baccalaureate institution, with an enrollment of 450. Highest level of offering: master's.
ACCREDITATIONS: M

St. Thomas University

16400 North West 32nd Avenue
Miami, FL 33054
(305) 628-6537
Fax (305) 628-6510

Will confirm attendance and degree by phone, fax or mail. Inquiry must include student's name, social security number, years attended. Employers may obtain transcripts upon written request accompanied by a $3.00 fee and a signed release from the student.

A comprehensive institution with no medical school, with an enrollment of 3,595. Highest level of offering: master's.
ACCREDITATIONS: SC

St. Vincent De Paul Regional Seminary

10701 South Military Trail
Boynton Beach, FL 33436
(407) 732-4424

Will confirm attendance and degree by phone or mail. Inquiry must include student's name, social security number. Employers may obtain transcripts upon written request accompanied by a $2.00 fee and a signed release from the student. Requests should be sent to: Registrar's Office.

A school of philosophy, religion and theology, with an enrollment of 119. Highest level of offering: master's
ACCREDITATIONS: SACS THEOL

Standing Rock College

HC1 Box 4
Fort Yates, ND 58538
(701) 854-3861 Ext. 215

Will confirm attendance and degree by phone or mail. Inquiry must include student's name, date of birth, years attended. Employers may obtain transcripts upon written request accompanied by a $2.00 fee and a signed release from the student.

A multiprogram two-year institution, with an enrollment of 261. Highest level of offering: one year but less than four years.
ACCREDITATIONS: NH

Stanford University

Stanford, CA 94305
(415) 723-2041 or 723-2086

Will confirm attendance and degree by phone or mail. Inquiry must include student's name, date of birth, years attended. Employers may obtain transcripts upon written request accompanied by a $4.00 fee and a signed release from the student.

A doctoral-level institution with a medical school, with an enrollment of 15,320. Highest level of offering: doctorate.
ACCREDITATIONS: WC APCP BUS ENG LAW MED MIDWF PTA COPSY PAST

Stanly Community College

Route 4 Box 55
Albemarle, NC 28001
(704) 982-0121 Ext. 137

Will confirm attendance and degree by phone or mail. Inquiry must include student's name, social security number. Employers may obtain transcripts upon written request accompanied by a signed release from the student. Requests should be sent to: Registrar's Office.

A multiprogram two-year institution, with an enrollment of 1,350. Highest level of offering: one year but less than four years
ACCREDITATIONS: SC RSTH RSTHT

Stark Technical College

6200 Frank Avenue North West
Canton, OH 44720
(216) 494-6170

Will confirm attendance and degree by mail. Inquiry must include student's name, social security number, years attended, release. Employers may obtain transcripts upon written request accompanied by a $2.00 fee and a signed release from the student.

A multiprogram two-year institution, with an enrollment of 3,400. Highest level of offering: one year but less than four years.
ACCREDITATIONS: NH ENGT MAC MLTAD MRT PTAA RSTHT

Starr King School for The Ministry

2441 Le Conte Avenue
Berkeley, CA 94709
(510) 845-6232

Will confirm attendance and degree by phone or mail. Inquiry must include student's name. Employers may obtain transcripts upon written request by student accompanied by a $2.00 fee.

A school of philosophy, religion and theology, with an enrollment of 51. Highest level of offering: master's.
ACCREDITATIONS: THEOL

State Center Community College District Systems Office

1101 East University Avenue
Fresno, CA 93741
(209) 442-4600

Will confirm attendance and degree by mail. Inquiry must include student's name, date of birth, social security number, years attended, release. Employers may obtain transcripts upon written request accompanied by a $2.00 fee and a signed release from the student.

A two-year institution with an enrollment of 18,000.

State Community College at East St. Louis

601 James R Thompson Boulevard
East Saint Louis, IL 62201
(618) 583-2500

Will confirm attendance and degree by phone or mail. Inquiry must include student's name, social security number. Requests should be directed to: Admissions & Records Office. Employers may obtain transcripts upon written request accompanied by a $2.00 fee and a signed release from the student.

A multiprogram two-year institution, with an enrollment of 1,375. Highest level of offering: one year but less than four years.
ACCREDITATIONS: NH

State Fair Community College

3201 West 16th
Sedalia, MO 65301
(816) 826-7100 Ext. 291
Fax (816) 827-4701

Will confirm attendance and degree by phone or mail. Inquiry must include student's name, social security number. Employers may obtain transcripts upon written request accompanied by a $2.00 fee and a signed release from the student.

A multiprogram two-year institution, with an enrollment of 2,421. Highest level of offering: two years but less than four years.
ACCREDITATIONS: NCA RSTHT

State Technical Institute at Knoxville

PO Box 22990
Knoxville, TN 37933-0990
(615) 694-6632
Fax (615) 694-6435

Will confirm attendance and degree by phone, fax or mail. Inquiry must include student's name, social security number. Employers may obtain transcripts upon written request accompanied by a signed release from the student.

A multiprogram two-year institution, with an enrollment of 5,000. Highest level of offering: one year but less than four years.
ACCREDITATIONS: SC ENGT

State Technical Institute at Memphis

5983 Macon Cove
Memphis, TN 38134
(901) 377-4193

Will confirm attendance and degree by phone or mail. Inquiry must include student's name, social security number. Employers may obtain transcripts upon written request accompanied by a signed release from the student.

A multiprogram two-year institution, with an enrollment of 8,852. Highest level of offering: one year but less than four years.
ACCREDITATIONS: SC ENGT

State University College of Technology

Delhi, NY 13753
(607) 746-4251

Will confirm attendance and degree by mail. Inquiry must include student's name, date of birth, social security number, years attended. Employers may obtain transcripts upon written request accompanied by a $5.00 fee and a signed release from the student.

State University of New York at Albany

1400 Washington Avenue
Albany, NY 12222
(518) 442-5530

Will confirm attendance and degree by phone or mail. Inquiry must include student's name, social security number, years attended. Employers may obtain transcripts upon written request accompanied by a $5.00 fee and a signed release from the student.

A doctoral-level institution with no medical school, with an enrollment of 15,938. Highest level of offering: doctorate.
ACCREDITATIONS: M BUS CLPSY COPSY LIB NY SW

State University of New York at Albany

State University Plaza
Albany, NY 12222
(518) 442-3300

Will confirm attendance and degree by phone or mail. Inquiry must include student's name, social security number, years attended. Employers may obtain transcripts upon written request accompanied by a $5.00 fee and a signed release from the student.
ACCREDITATIONS: M NY

State University of New York at Binghamton

Vestal Parkway East
Binghamton, NY 13901
(607) 777-6092
Fax (607) 777-6515

Will confirm attendance and degree by phone, fax or mail. Inquiry must include student's name, social security number. Employers may obtain transcripts upon written request accompanied by a $5.00 fee and a signed release from the student.

A doctoral-level institution with no medical school, with an enrollment of 11,964. Highest level of offering: doctorate.
ACCREDITATIONS: M CLPSY ENGT NUR NY

State University of New York at Brockport

Brockport, NY 14420
(716) 395-2211 Ext. 2531

Will confirm attendance and degree by phone or mail. Inquiry must include student's name, social security number, years attended. Employers may obtain transcripts upon written request accompanied by a $5.00 fee and a signed release from the student.

A comprehensive institution with no medical school, with an enrollment of 9,222. Highest level of offering: beyond master's but less than doctorate.
ACCREDITATIONS: M CHM DANCE NUR NY SW

State University of New York at Buffalo

1300 Elmwood Avenue
Buffalo, NY 14222
(716) 878-4811
Fax (716) 878-3159

Will confirm attendance and degree by phone or mail. Inquiry must include student's name, social security number. Employers may obtain transcripts upon written request accompanied by a $5.00 fee and a signed release from the student.

A comprehensive institution with no medical school, with an enrollment of 11,548. Highest level of offering: beyond master's but less than doctorate.
ACCREDITATIONS: M DIET ENGT NY SP SW TED CHM ACS

State University of New York at Buffalo Main Campus

Hayes B Annex
Dept. Records & Registration
3435 Main Street
Buffalo, NY 14214
(716) 831-3627

Will confirm attendance and degree by phone or mail. Inquiry must include student's name, social security number, years attended. Employers may obtain transcripts upon written request accompanied by a $3.00 fee and a signed release from the student.

Highest level of offering: doctorate.
ACCREDITATIONS: ENGT IPSY

State University of New York at Buffalo Main Campus

Hayes B, Records & Registration
3435 Main Street
Buffalo, NY 14214
(716) 831-2382
Fax (716) 831-2022

Will confirm attendance and degree by phone or mail. Inquiry must include student's name, social security number. Employers may obtain transcripts upon written request accompanied by a $5.00 fee and a signed release from the student.

A doctoral-level institution with no medical school, with an enrollment of 22,953. Highest level of offering: doctorate.
ACCREDITATIONS: M ANEST ARCH ART AUD BUS CLPSY COPSY ENG LAW LIB NY IPSY MICB MUS NMT SP SW

State University of New York at Cortland

PO Box 2000
Cortland, NY 13045
(607) 753-4701

Will confirm attendance and degree by phone or mail. Inquiry must include student's name, maiden name, date of birth, social security number, years attended. Employers may obtain transcripts upon written request accompanied by a $5.00 fee and a signed release from the student.

A comprehensive institution with no medical school, with an enrollment of 6,430. Highest level of offering: beyond master's but less than doctorate.
ACCREDITATIONS: M NYSBR

State University of New York at Farmingdale

Melville Road
Famingdale, NY 11735
(516) 420-2124

Will confirm attendance and degree by phone or mail. Inquiry must include student's name, social security number, years attended. Employers may obtain transcripts upon written request accompanied by a $5.00 fee and a signed release from the student.

A multiprogram two-year institution, with an enrollment of 12,987. Highest level of offering: one year but less than four years
ACCREDITATIONS: M ADNUR EH ENGT FUSER NY

State University of New York at Fredonia

Fredonia, NY 14063
(716) 673-3171

Will confirm attendance and degree by phone or mail. Inquiry must include student's name, social security number, years attended. Employers may obtain transcripts upon written request accompanied by a $5.00 fee and a signed release from the student.

A comprehensive institution with no medical school, with an enrollment of 4,985. Highest level of offering: beyond master's but less than doctorate.
ACCREDITATIONS: M ART MUS NY

State University of New York at Geneseo

Geneseo, NY 14454
(716) 245-5566
Fax (716) 245-5005

Will confirm attendance and degree by phone or mail. Inquiry must include student's name, social security number, years attended. Employers may obtain transcripts upon written request accompanied by a $5.00 fee and a signed release from the student.

A comprehensive institution with no medical school, with an enrollment of 5,282. Highest level of offering: master's.
ACCREDITATIONS: M AUD NY SP

State University of New York at New Paltz

New Paltz, NY 12561
(914) 257-2420

Will confirm degree by mail. Inquiry must include student's name, social security number. Requests should be directed to: Records & Registration Office. Employers may obtain transcripts upon written request accompanied by a $5.00 fee and a signed release from the student.

A comprehensive institution with no medical school, with an enrollment of 8,500. Highest level of offering: beyond master's but less than doctorate.
ACCREDITATIONS: M MUS NY

State University of New York at Old Westbury

Box 410
Old Westbury, NY 11568
(516) 876-3055

Will confirm attendance and degree by phone or mail. Inquiry must include student's name, social security number, years attended. Employers may obtain transcripts upon written request accompanied by a $5.00 fee and a signed release from the student.

A general baccalaureate institution, with an enrollment of 4,000. Highest level of offering: four or five year baccalaureate.
ACCREDITATIONS: M NY

State University of New York at Oneonta

Ravine Parkway
Oneonta, NY 13820
(607) 431-2531

Will confirm attendance and degree by phone or mail. Inquiry must include student's name, social security number, years attended. Employers may obtain transcripts upon written request accompanied by a $5.00 fee and a signed release from the student.

A comprehensive institution with no medical school, with an enrollment of 5,884. Highest level of offering: beyond master's but less than doctorate.
ACCREDITATIONS: M NY

State University of New York at Oswego

Oswego, NY 13126
(315) 341-2171

Will confirm attendance and degree by phone or mail. Inquiry must include student's name, social security number, years attended. Employers may obtain transcripts upon written request accompanied by a $5.00 fee and a signed release from the student.

A comprehensive institution with no medical school, with an enrollment of 8,000. Highest level of offering: beyond master's but less than doctorate.
ACCREDITATIONS: M MUS NY

State University of New York at Plattsburgh

Plattsburgh, NY 12901
(518) 564-2100
Fax (518) 564-3932

Will confirm attendance and degree by phone, fax or mail. Inquiry must include student's name, social security number, years attended. Employers may obtain transcripts upon written request accompanied by a $5.00 fee and a signed release from the student.

A comprehensive institution with no medical school, with an enrollment of 6,344. Highest level of offering: beyond master's but less than doctorate.
ACCREDITATIONS: M NUR NY

State University of New York at Potsdam

Pierrepont Avenue
Potsdam, NY 13676
(315) 267-2154

Will confirm attendance and degree by phone or mail. Inquiry must include student's name, social security number, years attended. Employers may obtain transcripts upon written request accompanied by a $3.00 fee and a signed release from the student.

A comprehensive institution with no medical school, with an enrollment of 4,416. Highest level of offering: master's.
ACCREDITATIONS: M MUS NY

State University of New York at Purchase

735 Anderson Hill Road
Purchase, NY 10577
(914) 251-6360

Will confirm attendance and degree by phone or mail. Inquiry must include student's name, social security number. Employers may obtain transcripts upon written request accompanied by a $5.00 fee and a signed release from the student.

A general baccalaureate institution, with an enrollment of 3,865. Highest level of offering: master's.
ACCREDITATIONS: M NY

State University of New York at Stony Brook Main Campus

Stony Brook, NY 11794
(516) 632-6885

Will confirm attendance and degree by phone or mail. Inquiry must include student's name, social security number, years attended. Employers may obtain transcripts upon written request accompanied by a $5.00 fee and a signed release from the student.

A doctoral-level institution with no medical school, with an enrollment of 16,377. Highest level of offering: doctorate.
ACCREDITATIONS: M CLPSY ENG IPSY NY

State University of New York College of Agriculture

Box 97 Knapp Hall
Cobleskill, NY 12043
(518) 234-5521

Will confirm attendance and degree by phone or mail. Inquiry must include student's name, social security number. Employers may obtain transcripts upon written request accompanied by a $5.00 fee and a signed release from the student.

A multiprogram two-year institution, with an enrollment of 2,734. Highest level of offering: up to four years.
ACCREDITATIONS: M HT NY

State University of New York College of Environmental Science & Forestry

Syracuse, NY 13210
(315) 470-6655
Fax (315) 470-6933

Will confirm attendance and degree by phone, fax or mail. Inquiry must include student's name, date of birth, social security number. Employers may obtain transcripts upon written request accompanied by a $5.00 fee and a signed release from the student. Requests should be directed to: Registrar's Office.

A comprehensive institution with no medical school, with an enrollment of 1,750. Highest level of offering: doctorate.
ACCREDITATIONS: M ENGT FOR LSAR NY

State University of New York College of Optometry

100 East 24th Street
New York, NY 10010
(212) 420-5100

Will confirm attendance and degree by phone or mail. Inquiry must include student's name, social security number, years attended, release. Employers may obtain transcripts upon written request accompanied by a $5.00 fee and a signed release from the student.

A health institution, with an enrollment of 248. Highest level of offering: doctorate.
ACCREDITATIONS: M NY OPT OPTR

State University of New York College of Technology

Canton, NY 13617
(315) 386-7042
Fax (315) 386-7930

Will confirm attendance and degree by phone or mail. Inquiry must include student's name, social security number, years attended. Employers may obtain transcripts upon written request accompanied by a $5.00 fee and a signed release from the student.

A multiprogram two-year institution, with an enrollment of 2,326. Highest level of offering: one year but less than four years.
ACCREDITATIONS: M ADNUR ADVET ENGT FUSER MLTAD NY

State University of New York College of Technology at Utica–Rome

Marcy Campus, PO Box 3050
Utica, NY 13504-3050
(315) 792-7262
Fax (315) 792-7802

Will confirm attendance and degree by phone or mail. Inquiry must include student's name, social security number, years attended. Employers may obtain transcripts upon written request accompanied by a $5.00 fee and a signed release from the student.

A comprehensive institution with no medical school, with an enrollment of 2,189. Highest level of offering: master's.
ACCREDITATIONS: M ENGT MRA NUR NY

State University of New York Downstate Medical Center

450 Clarkson Avenue
Box 60R
Brooklyn, NY 11203
(718) 270-1876

Will confirm attendance and degree by phone or mail. Inquiry must include student's name, social security number, years attended. Employers may obtain transcripts upon written request accompanied by a $5.00 fee and a signed release from the student.

A medical school, with an enrollment of 1,631. Highest level of offering: doctorate.
ACCREDITATIONS: M DMS MED MIDWF MRA NUR NY OT PTA

State University of New York Empire State College

2 Union Avenue
Saratoga Springs, NY 12866
(518) 587-2100 Ext. 209
Fax (518) 587-5404

Will confirm attendance and degree by phone or mail. Inquiry must include student's name, social security number, years attended. Employers may obtain transcripts upon written request accompanied by a $5.00 fee and a signed release from the student.

A general baccalaureate institution, with an enrollment of 6,322. Highest level of offering: master's.
ACCREDITATIONS: M NY

State University of New York Health Science Center

155 Elizabeth Blackwell
Syracuse, NY 13210
(315) 464-5540
Fax (315) 464-8823

Will confirm attendance and degree by phone or mail. Inquiry must include student's name, years attended. Employers may obtain transcripts upon written request accompanied by a $5.00 fee and a signed release from the student.

State University of New York Health Science Center at Brooklyn

450Clarkson Avenue, Box 60 R
Brooklyn, NY 11203
(718) 270-1875

Will confirm attendance and degree by phone or mail. Inquiry must include student's name, social security number, years attended. Employers may obtain transcripts upon written request accompanied by a $5.00 fee and a signed release from the student.

A medical school, with an enrollment of 1,586. Highest level of offering: doctorate.
ACCREDITATIONS: M DMS MED MIDWF MRA NUR NY OT PTA

A medical school, with an enrollment of 1,051. Highest level of offering: doctorate
ACCREDITATIONS: M BBT CYTO IPSY MED MT NY PERF PTA RAD RSTH NMT RTT

State University of New York Health Sciences Center at Buffalo

3435 Main Street
Buffalo, NY 14214
(716) 831-3627

Will confirm attendance and degree by phone or mail. Inquiry must include student's name, social security number, years attended. Employers may obtain transcripts upon written request accompanied by a $5.00 fee and a signed release from the student.

A medical school, with an enrollment of 3,207. Highest level of offering: doctorate.
ACCREDITATIONS: DA DENT MED MT NUR NY OT PHAR PTA

State University of New York Maritime College

Fort Schuyler
Bronx, NY 10465
(212) 409-7265
Fax (212) 409-7392

Will confirm attendance and degree by phone or mail. Inquiry must include student's name, years attended. Employers may obtain transcripts upon written request accompanied by a $5.00 fee and a signed release from the student.

A general baccalaureate institution, with an enrollment of 640. Highest level of offering: master's.
ACCREDITATIONS: M ENG NY

State University of New York Upstate Medical Center

(See State University of New York-Health Science Center.)

Stephen F. Austin State University

PO Box 13050–1936 North Street
Nacogdoches, TX 75962
(409) 568-2501

Will confirm attendance and degree by phone or mail. Inquiry must include student's name, social security number, years attended. Employers may obtain transcripts upon written request accompanied by a $2.00 fee and a signed release from the student. Attn: Registrar's Office.

A comprehensive institution with no medical school, with an enrollment of 12,549. Highest level of offering: doctorate.
ACCREDITATIONS: SC BUS FOR MUS NUR SW TED THEA FIDER

Stephens College

Columbia, MO 65215
(314) 442-2211
Fax (314) 876-7248

Will confirm attendance and degree by phone or mail. Inquiry must include student's name, social security number, years attended. Employers may obtain transcripts upon written request accompanied by a $2.00 fee and a signed release from the student.

A general baccalaureate institution, with an enrollment of 1,094. Highest level of offering: four or five year baccalaureate.
ACCREDITATIONS: NH MRA MUS THEA

Sterling College

Main Street
Craftsbury Common, VT 05827
(802) 586-7711 Ext. 20

Will confirm attendance and degree by phone or mail. Inquiry must include student's name, social security number, years attended. Employers may obtain transcripts upon written request accompanied by a $3.00 fee and a signed release from the student.

A two-year institution newly admitted to NCES, with an enrollment of 83. Highest level of offering: one year but less than four years.
ACCREDITATIONS: EV

Sterling College

Sterling, KS 67579
(316) 278-2173
Fax (316) 278-2775

Will confirm attendance and degree by phone or mail. Inquiry must include student's name, social security number, years attended. Employers may obtain transcripts upon written request accompanied by a $2.00 fee and a signed release from the student.

A general baccalaureate institution, with an enrollment of 450. Highest level of offering: four or five year baccalaureate.
ACCREDITATIONS: NCA TED

Stetson University

Box 8298–421 North Woodland Boulevard
Deland, FL 32720
(904) 822-7140 Ext. 375

Will confirm attendance and degree by phone or mail. Inquiry must include student's name, social security number, years attended. Employers may obtain transcripts upon written request accompanied by a $2.00 fee and a signed release from the student.

A comprehensive institution with no medical school, with an enrollment of 2,739. Highest level of offering: beyond master's but less than doctorate.
ACCREDITATIONS: SC LAW MUS

Stevens Institute of Technology

Castle Point Station
Hoboken, NJ 07030
(201) 216-5210
Fax (201) 216-8341

Will confirm attendance and degree by phone, fax or mail. Inquiry must include student's name, social security number, years attended. Employers may obtain transcripts upon written request accompanied by a $3.00 fee and a signed release from the student.

An engineering school, with an enrollment of 3,105. Highest level of offering: doctorate.
ACCREDITATIONS: M ENG

Stillman College

PO Drawer 1430
Tuscaloosa, AL 35403
(205) 349-4240
Fax (205) 349-4240

Will confirm attendance and degree by mail. Inquiry must include student's name, social security number. Employers may obtain transcripts upon written request accompanied by a $4.00 fee and a signed release from the student.

A general baccalaureate institution, with an enrollment of 731. Highest level of offering: four or five year baccalaureate.
ACCREDITATIONS: SC

Stockton State College

Student Records D 121
Pomona, NJ 08240
(609) 652-1776

Will confirm attendance and degree by mail. Inquiry must include student's name, social security number, years attended. Employers may obtain transcripts upon written request accompanied by a signed release from the student.

A general baccalaureate institution, with an enrollment of 4,750. Highest level of offering: four or five year baccalaureate.
ACCREDITATIONS: M NUR SW

Stonehill College

Washington Street
North Easton, MA 02357
(508) 238-1081

Will confirm attendance and degree by phone or mail. Inquiry must include student's name, years attended. Employers may obtain transcripts upon written request accompanied by a $2.00 fee and a signed release from the student.

A general baccalaureate institution, with an enrollment of 1,954. Highest level of offering: four or five year baccalaureate.
ACCREDITATIONS: EH TED

Stratton College

1300 North Jackson Street
Milwaukee, WI 53202
(414) 276-5200 Ext. 6

Will confirm attendance and degree by phone or mail. Inquiry must include student's name, social security number, years attended. Employers may obtain transcripts upon written request accompanied by a signed release from the student.

A single program two-year institution, with an enrollment of 572. Highest level of offering: one year but less than four years.
ACCREDITATIONS: JRCB

Strayer College

3045 Columbia Pike
Arlington, VA 22204-4338
(703) 892-5100

Will confirm attendance and degree by phone or mail. Inquiry must include student's name, social security number, years attended. Employers may obtain transcripts upon written request accompanied by a $5.00 fee and a signed release from the student.

A business school, with an enrollment of 4,283. Highest level of offering: four or five year baccalaureate.
ACCREDITATIONS: M SRCB

Sue Bennett College

101 College Street
London, KY 40741
(606) 864-2238

Will confirm attendance and degree by mail. Inquiry must include student's name, social security number, years attended. Employers may obtain transcripts upon written request accompanied by a $5.00 fee and a signed release from the student.

A multiprogram two-year institution, with an enrollment of 502. Highest level of offering: one year but less than four years.
ACCREDITATIONS: SC

Suffolk County Community College Eastern Campus

Speonk Riverhead Road
Riverhead, NY 11901
(516) 548-2501
Fax (516) 548-6244

Will confirm attendance and degree by mail. Inquiry must include student's name, social security number. Employers may obtain transcripts upon written request accompanied by a $5.00 fee and a signed release from the student.

A multiprogram two-year institution, with an enrollment of 1,964. Highest level of offering: one year but less than four years.
ACCREDITATIONS: M NY

Suffolk County Community College Selden Campus

533 College Road
Selden, NY 11784
(516) 451-4110

Will confirm attendance by mail. Inquiry must include student's name, social security number, years attended, release. Employers may obtain transcripts upon written request accompanied by a $5.00 fee and a signed release from the student.

A multiprogram two-year institution, with an enrollment of 12,542. Highest level of offering: one year but less than four years.
ACCREDITATIONS: M ADNUR DA NY PTAA

Suffolk County Community College Western Campus

Crooked Hill Road
Brentwood, NY 11717
(516) 434-6782

Will confirm attendance and degree by mail. Inquiry must include student's name, social security number. Employers may obtain transcripts upon written request accompanied by a $5.00 fee and a signed release from the student.

A multiprogram two-year institution, with an enrollment of 5,109. Highest level of offering: one year but less than four years.
ACCREDITATIONS: M ADNUR NY

Suffolk University

8 Ashburton Place
Boston, MA 02108
(617) 723-8430
Fax (617) 573-8703

Will confirm attendance and degree by phone or mail. Inquiry must include student's name, social security number, years attended, release. Employers may obtain transcripts upon written request accompanied by a $2.00 fee and a signed release from the student. Direct inquiries to Registrar's Office.

A comprehensive institution with no medical school, with an enrollment of 6,124. Highest level of offering: doctorate.
ACCREDITATIONS: EH LAW

Sul Ross State University

Alpine, TX 79832
(915) 837-8011

Will confirm attendance and degree by phone or mail. Inquiry must include student's name, date of birth, social security number, years attended. Employers may obtain transcripts upon written request accompanied by a $3.00 fee and a signed release from the student.

A comprehensive institution with no medical school, with an enrollment of 1,8660. Highest level of offering: beyond master's but less than doctorate.
ACCREDITATIONS: SC ADVET

Sullivan County Community College

Registrar's Office
Loch Sheldrake, NY 12759
(914) 434-5750 Ext. 302

Will confirm attendance and degree by mail. Inquiry must include student's name, social security number, release. Employers may obtain transcripts upon written request accompanied by a $3.00 fee and a signed release from the student.

A multiprogram two-year institution, with an enrollment of 1,656. Highest level of offering: one year but less than four years.
ACCREDITATIONS: M NY

Sullivan College

PO Box 33 - 308
Louisville, KY 40232
(502) 456-6504 Ext. 301
Fax (502) 454-4880

Will confirm attendance and degree by mail. Inquiry must include student's name, date of birth, social security number. Employers may obtain transcripts upon written request accompanied by a $5.00 fee and a signed release from the student.

A multiprogram four-year institution, with an enrollment of 1,713. Highest level of offering: baccalaureate.
ACCREDITATIONS: SACS JRCB

Sumter Area Technical College

506 N Guignard Drive
Sumter, SC 29150
(803) 778-1961 Ext. 246
Fax (803) 773-4859

Will confirm attendance and degree by phone or mail. Inquiry must include student's name, social security number. Employers may obtain transcripts upon written request accompanied by a $2.00 fee and a signed release from the student.

A multiprogram two-year institution, with an enrollment of 1,850. Highest level of offering: one year but less than four years.
ACCREDITATIONS: SC ENGT

Suomi College

601 Quincy Street
Hancock, MI 49930
(906) 482-5300 or 487-7272
Fax (906) 487-7300

Will confirm attendance and degree by mail. Inquiry must include student's name. Employers may obtain transcripts upon written request accompanied by a $3.00 fee and a signed release from the student.

A multiprogram two-year institution, with an enrollment of 598. Highest level of offering: two years but less than four years.
ACCREDITATIONS: NCA

Surry Community College

PO Box 304
Dobson, NC 27017
(919) 386-8121
Fax (919) 386-8951

Will confirm attendance and degree by phone or mail. Inquiry must include student's name, social security number, years attended. Employers may obtain transcripts upon written request accompanied by a $2.00 fee and a signed release from the student.

A multiprogram two-year institution, with an enrollment of 2,632. Highest level of offering: one year but less than four years.
ACCREDITATIONS: SC

Susquehanna University

Selinsgrove, PA 17870
(717) 374-0101

Will confirm attendance and degree by phone or mail. Inquiry must include student's name, maiden name, years attended. Employers may obtain transcripts upon written request accompanied by a $2.00 fee and a signed release from the student.

A general baccalaureate institution, with an enrollment of 1,789. Highest level of offering: four or five year baccalaureate.
ACCREDITATIONS: M MUS ACS NCATE

Swain School of Design

(See University of Massachusetts at Darmouth)

Swarthmore College

Swarthmore, PA 19081
(215) 328-8298

Will confirm attendance and degree by phone or mail. Inquiry must include student's name, date of birth, years attended. Employers may obtain transcripts upon written request accompanied by a $5.00 fee and a signed release from the student.

A general baccalaureate institution, with an enrollment of 1,326. Highest level of offering: master's.
ACCREDITATIONS: M ENG

Sweet Briar College

Sweet Briar, VA 24595
(804) 381-6179

Will confirm attendance and degree by phone or mail. Inquiry must include student's name, social security number, years attended. Requests should be directed to: Registrar's Office. Employers may obtain transcripts upon written request accompanied by a $5.00 fee and a signed release from the student.

A general baccalaureate institution, with an enrollment of 564. Highest level of offering: four or five year baccalaureate.
ACCREDITATIONS: SC

Syracuse University Central Records

Room 109, Transcripts Dept.
Steele Hall
Syracuse, NY 13244-1120
(315) 443-1870 Ext. 2422

Will confirm attendance and degree by phone or mail. Inquiry must include student's name, date of birth, social security number, years attended. Employers may obtain transcripts upon written request by student, accompanied by a $3.00 fee.

A doctoral-level institution with no medical school, with an enrollment of 21,044. Highest level of offering: doctorate.

ACCREDITATIONS: M ARCH ART AUD BUS CLPSY DIET ENG FIDER JOUR LAW NY TED LIB MUS NUR SP SW

Sysorex Institute

Attn: Personnel
335 E. Middlefield Rd.
Mountainview, CA 94043
(415) 967-2200

Will confirm attendance and degree by mail. Inquiry must include student's name, years attended, release. Employers may obtain transcripts upon written request accompanied by a signed release from the student.

A two-year institution newly admitted to NCES, with an enrollment of 8. Highest level of offering: one year but less than four years.

ACCREDITATIONS: WJ

T

Tabor College

400 South Jefferson
Hillsboro, KS 67063
(316) 947-3121 Ext. 262

Will confirm attendance and degree by phone or mail. Inquiry must include student's name, social security number, years attended. Employers may obtain transcripts upon written request accompanied by a $2.00 fee and a signed release from the student.

A general baccalaureate institution, with an enrollment of 414. Highest level of offering: four or five year baccalaureate.

ACCREDITATIONS: NH MUS SW

Tacoma Community College

5900 South 12th Street
Tacoma, WA 98465
(206) 566-5036

Will confirm attendance and degree by mail. Inquiry must include student's name, date of birth, social security number, years attended. Employers may obtain transcripts upon written request accompanied by a $2.00 fee and a signed release from the student.

A multiprogram two-year institution, with an enrollment of 4,010. Highest level of offering: one year but less than four years.

ACCREDITATIONS: NW ADNUR MRT RAD RSTH RSTHT

Tad Technical Institute

(Formerly ITT Technical Institute)
7910 Troost Ave, East 103rd Street
Kansas City, MO 64131
(816) 361-5640

Will confirm attendance and degree by mail. Inquiry must include student's name, social security number, years attended, release. Requests should be directed to: Director fo Education. Employers may obtain transcripts upon written request accompanied by a $3.00 fee and a signed release from the student.

A two-year institution newly admitted to NCES, with an enrollment of 120. Highest level of offering: one year but less than four years.

ACCREDITATIONS: NATTS

Taft College

Attn: Registrar
29 Emmons Park Drive
Taft, CA 93268
(805) 763-4282 Ext. 256
Fax (805) 763-1038

Will confirm attendance and degree by phone, fax or mail. Inquiry must include student's name, social security number, date of birth, years attended. Employers may obtain transcripts upon written request accompanied by a $1.00 fee and a signed release from the student.

A multiprogram two-year institution, with an enrollment of 1,000. Highest level of offering: one year but less than four years.

ACCREDITATIONS: WJ

Talladega College

627 West Battle Street
Talladega, AL 35160
(205) 362-0206 Ext. 219

Will confirm attendance and degree by phone or mail. Inquiry must include student's name, years attended. Employers may obtain transcripts upon written request accompanied by a $5.00 fee and a signed release from the student.

A general baccalaureate institution, with an enrollment of 615. Highest level of offering: four or five year baccalaureate.

ACCREDITATIONS: SC SW

Tallahassee Community College

444 Appleyard Drive
Tallahassee, FL 32304-2895
(904) 922-8110 Ext. 210
Fax (904) 488-2203

Will confirm attendance and degree by phone, fax or mail. Inquiry must include student's name, social security number. Employers may obtain transcripts upon written request accompanied by a signed release from the student.

A multiprogram two-year institution, with an enrollment of 9,000. Highest level of offering: one year but less than four years.

ACCREDITATIONS: SC DH RAD RSTH

Talmudic College of Florida

4014 Chase Avenue
Miami Beach, FL 33140
(305) 534-7050
Fax (305) 534-7050

Will confirm attendance and degree by phone, fax or mail. For fax inquiries call first. Inquiry must include student's name, social security number. Employers may obtain transcripts upon written request accompanied by a signed release from the student.

A school of philosophy, religion and theology, with an enrollment of 75. Highest level of offering: first professional degree.

ACCREDITATIONS: RABN

Talmudical Academy of New Jersey

PO Box 7
Adelphia, NJ 07710
(908) 431-1600

Will confirm attendance and degree by mail. Inquiry must include student's name, social security number, address. Employers may obtain transcripts upon written request accompanied by a signed release from the student.

A school of philosophy, religion and theology, with an enrollment of 44. Highest level of offering: first professional degree.

ACCREDITATIONS: RABN

Talmudical Institute of Upstate New York

769 Park Avenue
Rochester, NY 14607
(716) 473-2810

Will confirm attendance and degree by phone or mail. Inquiry must include student's name, social security number. Employers may obtain transcripts upon written request accompanied by a signed release from the student.

A specialized non-degree granting institution, with an enrollment of 23. Highest level of offering: undergraduate non-degree granting.

ACCREDITATIONS: RABN

Talmudical Seminary Oholei Torah

667 Eastern Parkway
Brooklyn, NY 11213
(718) 774-5050

Will confirm attendance and degree by mail. Inquiry must include student's name, social security number. Employers may obtain transcripts upon written request accompanied by a signed release from the student.

A specialized non-degree granting institution, with an enrollment of 180. Highest level of offering: graduate non-degree granting.

ACCREDITATIONS: RABN

Talmudical Yeshiva of Philadelphia

6063 Drexel Road
Philadelphia, PA 19131
(215) 477-1000
Fax (215) 477-5605

Will confirm attendance and degree by phone or mail. Inquiry must include student's name, social security number. Employers may obtain transcripts upon written request accompanied by a signed release from the student.

A school of philosophy, religion and theology, with an enrollment of 81. Highest level of offering: beyond master's but less than doctorate.
ACCREDITATIONS: RABN

Tampa College

3319 West Hillsborough Avenue
Tampa, FL 33614
(813) 879-6000 Ext. 45

Will confirm attendance and degree by phone or mail. Inquiry must include student's name, social security number, years attended. Employers may obtain transcripts upon written request accompanied by a $3.00 fee and a signed release from the student.

A business school, with an enrollment of 1,200. Highest level of offering: four or five year baccalaureate.
ACCREDITATIONS: SRCB

Tampa College of Lakeland

(Formerly Lakeland College of Business)
1200 US Hwy 98 South
Lakeland, FL 33801
(813) 686-1444
Fax (813) 688-9881

Will confirm attendance and degree by mail. Inquiry must include student's name, social security number, years attended. Employers may obtain transcripts upon written request accompanied by a $3.00 fee and a signed release from the student.

A multiprogram four-year institution with an enrollment of 800. Highest level of offering: four years.
ACCREDITATIONS: JRCB

Tanana Valley Community College

c/o University of Alaska
Fairbanks, AK 99775-0060
(907) 474-7521

Will confirm attendance and degree by phone or mail. Inquiry must include student's name, social security number. Requests should be directed to: Admissions & Records Office. Employers may obtain transcripts upon written request by student accompanied by a $3.00 fee and a signed release from the student.

Tarkio College

13th & McMary
Tarkio, MO 64491
(816) 736-4131 Ext. 241
Fax (816) 736-4586

Will confirm attendance and degree by phone or mail. Inquiry must include student's name, social security number. Employers may obtain transcripts upon written request accompanied by a $4.00 fee and a signed release from the student.

A general baccalaureate institution, with an enrollment of 620. Highest level of offering: four or five year baccalaureate.
ACCREDITATIONS: NH

Tarleton State University

Tarleton Station–Box T2003
Stephenville, TX 76402
(817) 968-9122

Will confirm attendance and degree by mail. Inquiry must include student's name, social security number, years attended. Employers may obtain transcripts upon written request accompanied by a $3.00 fee and a signed release from the student.

A comprehensive institution with no medical school, with an enrollment of 5,901. Highest level of offering: master's.
ACCREDITATIONS: SC MT SW TED

Tarrant County Junior College

1500 Houston Street
Fort Worth, TX 76102-6598
(817) 877-9232
Fax (817) 877-9295

Will confirm attendance and degree by phone or mail. Inquiry must include student's name, date of birth, social security number. Requests should be directed to: Admissions & Records Office. Employers may obtain transcripts upon written request accompanied by a $3.00 fee and a signed release from the student. Direct inquiries to Admission and Records.

A multiprogram two-year institution, with an enrollment of 26,822. Highest level of offering: two years but less than four years.
ACCREDITATIONS: SC ADNUR DA DH MLTAD MRT PTAA RAD RSTH SURGT

Taylor Business Institute

1 Penn Plaza
New York, NY 10119
(212) 643-2020
Fax (212) 947-9793

Will confirm attendance and degree by mail or fax. Inquiry must include student's name, date of birth, social security number, years attended, release. Employers may obtain transcripts upon written request accompanied by a $4.00 fee and a signed release from the student. Requests should be directed to: Registrar's Office.

A single program two-year institution, with an enrollment of 470. Highest level of offering: one year but less than four years.
ACCREDITATIONS: NY JRCB

Taylor University

500 W. Reade Ave.
Upland, IN 46989-1001
(317) 998-5330
Fax (317) 998-4910

Will confirm attendance and degree by phone, fax or mail. Inquiry must include student's name, years attended. Employers may obtain transcripts upon written request accompanied by a $4.00 fee and a signed release from the student. Requests should be directed to: Registrar's Office.

A general baccalaureate institution, with an enrollment of 1,700. Highest level of offering: four or five year baccalaureate.
ACCREDITATIONS: NH MUS SW TED

Taylor University–Fort Wayne

1025 West Rudisill Boulevard
Fort Wayne, IN 46807
(219) 456-2111 Ext. 211
Fax (219) 745-2001

Will confirm attendance and degree by phone, fax or mail. Inquiry must include student's name and years attended. Employers may obtain transcripts upon written request accompanied by a $2.00 fee and a signed release from the student. Requests should be directed to: Registrar's Office.

A school of philosophy, religion and theology, with an enrollment of 400. Highest level of offering: four or five year baccalaureate.
ACCREDITATIONS: NH BI

Technical Career Institutes

320 West 31st Street
New York, NY 10001
(212) 594-4000 Ext. 239
Fax (212) 629-3937

Will confirm attendance and degree by mail or fax. Inquiry must include student's name, date of birth, social security number, years attended, program attended. Employers may obtain transcripts upon written request accompanied by a $3.00 fee and a signed release from the student.

A single program two-year institution, with an enrollment of 1,904. Highest level of offering: one year but less than four years.
ACCREDITATIONS: NY ENGT NATTS

Technical College of Alamance

(See Alamance Community College.)

Technical College of the Low Country

100 South Ribaut Road
Beaufort, SC 29902
(803) 525-8210

Will confirm attendance and degree by phone or mail. Inquiry must include student's name, social security number, years attended. Employers may obtain transcripts upon written request accompanied by a $2.00 fee and a signed release from the student.

A multiprogram two-year institution, with an enrollment of 1,280. Highest level of offering: one year but less than four years.
ACCREDITATIONS: SC

Technical Trades Institute

2315 East Pikes Peak
Colorado Springs, CO 80909
(719) 632-7626

Will confirm attendance and degree by phone or mail. Inquiry must include student's name, social security number, years attended. Employers may obtain transcripts upon written request accompanied by a $2.00 fee and a signed release from the student.

A two-year institution newly admitted to NCES. Highest level of offering: one year but less than four years.
ACCREDITATIONS: NATTS

Teikyo Marycrest University

1607 West 12th Street
Davenport, IA 52804
(319) 326-9216
Fax (319) 326-9250

Will confirm attendance and degree by phone or mail. Inquiry must include student's name, social security number. Requests should be directed to Registrar's Office. Employers may obtain transcripts upon written request accompanied by a $4.00 fee and a signed release from the student.

A general baccalaureate institution, with an ebrollment of 1,453. Highest level of offering: master's.
ACCREDITATIONS: NCA NUR SW

Teikyo Post University

800 Country Club Road
PO Box 2540
Watonbury, CT 06723-2540

Will confirm attendance and degree by phone or mail. Inquiry must include student's name, social security number., years attended, release Employers may obtain transcripts upon written request accompanied by a $4.00 fee and a signed release from the student. Requests should be directed to Records Office.

A multiprogram two-year institution, with an ebrollment of 1,800. Highest level of offering: four year baccalaureate.
ACCREDITATIONS: NCA NUR SW

Telshe Yeshiva–Chicago

3535 West Foster
Chicago, IL 60625
(312) 463-7738

Will confirm attendance and degree by mail. Inquiry must include student's name, social security number, release, self addressed stamped envelope. Requests should be directed to: Records Office. Employers may obtain transcripts upon written request accompanied by a signed release from the student.

A specialized non-degree granting institution, with an enrollment of 67. Highest level of offering: master's.
ACCREDITATIONS: RABN

Temple Junior College

2600 South 1st Street
Temple, TX 76504-7435
(817) 773-9961 Ext. 212
Fax (817) 773-5265

Will confirm attendance and degree by phone or mail. Inquiry must include student's name, social security number, years attended. Requests should be directed to: Admissions Office. Employers may obtain transcripts upon written request accompanied by a $3.00 fee and a signed release from the student.

A multiprogram two-year institution, with an enrollment of 2,500. Highest level of offering: one year but less than four years.
ACCREDITATIONS: SC MLTAD MRT RSTH

Temple University

Brood & Montgomery Avenue
Philadelphia, PA 19122
(215) 787-1131

Will confirm attendance and degree by phone or mail. Inquiry must include student's name, social security number, years attended. Employers may obtain transcripts upon written request accompanied by a $3.00 fee and a signed release from the student.

A doctoral-level institution with a medical school, with an enrollment of 33,347. Highest level of offering: doctorate.
ACCREDITATIONS: M ARCH ART AUD BUS CLPSY COPSY DENT DH ENGT HSA CHE IPSY TED JOUR LAW MED MICB MRA MT MUS NMT NUR OT PHAR PTA RAD SCPSY SP SW DANCE

Tennessee Institute of Electronics

3203 Tazewell Pike
Knoxville, TN 37918
(615) 688-9422

Will confirm attendance and degree by phone or mail. Inquiry must include student's name, social security number, years attended, self addressed stamped envelope. Employers may obtain transcripts upon written request accompanied by a signed release from the student.

A single program two-year institution, with an enrollment of 150. Highest level of offering: one year but less than four years.
ACCREDITATIONS: NATTS

Tennessee State University

3500 John Merritt Boulevard
Nashville, TN 37209-1561
(615) 320-3420

Will confirm attendance and degree by phone or mail. Inquiry must include student's name, date of birth, social security number, years attended. Employers may obtain transcripts upon written request accompanied by a $1.00 fee and a signed release from the student.

A comprehensive institution with no medical school, with an enrollment of 7,038. Highest level of offering: doctorate.
ACCREDITATIONS: SC ADNUR ENG MRA MUS NUR SW TED SP

Tennessee Technological University

PO Box 5097
Cookeville, TN 38505
(615) 372-3317
Fax (615) 372-3898

Will confirm attendance and degree by phone, fax or mail. Inquiry must include student's name, date of birth, social security number, years attended. Employers may obtain transcripts upon written request accompanied by a signed release from the student. Requests should be directed to: Records Office.

A comprehensive institution with no medical school, with an enrollment of 7,494. Highest level of offering: doctorate.
ACCREDITATIONS: SC BUS ENG MUS NUR TED

Tennessee Temple University

Chattanooga, TN 37404
(615) 493-4215
Fax (615) 493-4497

Will confirm attendance and degree by phone or mail. Inquiry must include student's name, social security number, years attended, self addressed stamped envelope. Employers may obtain transcripts upon written request accompanied by a signed release from the student.

A general baccalaureate institution, with an enrollment of 1,200. Highest level of offering: master's.
ACCREDITATIONS: BI

Tennessee Wesleyan College

College Street
PO Box 40
Athens, TN 37371-0040
(615) 745-7504

Will confirm attendance and degree by phone or mail. Inquiry must include student's name, date of birth, social security number, years attended. Employers may obtain transcripts upon written request accompanied by a $2.00 fee and a signed release from the student.

A general baccalaureate institution, with an enrollment of 615. Highest level of offering: four or five year baccalaureate.
ACCREDITATIONS: SC

Terra Technical College

2830 Napoleon Road
Fremont, OH 43420
(419) 334-8400 Ext. 333
Fax (419) 334-3667

Will confirm attendance and degree by phone, fax or mail. Inquiry must include student's name, social security number. Employers may obtain transcripts upon written request accompanied by a $2.00 fee and a signed release from the student.

A multiprogram two-year institution, with an enrollment of 2,600. Highest level of offering: one year but less than four years.
ACCREDITATIONS: NH

Texarkana College

2500 North Robison Road
Texarkana, TX 75501
(903) 838-4541 Ext. 350
Fax (903) 832-5030

Will confirm attendance and degree by phone, fax or mail. Inquiry must include student's name, social security number, years attended. Employers may obtain transcripts upon written request accompanied by a $2.00 fee and a signed release from the student.

A multiprogram two-year institution, with an enrollment of 3,618. Highest level of offering: one year but less than four years.
ACCREDITATIONS: SC ADNUR

Texas A & M University Main Campus

College Station, TX 77843-0100
(409) 845-1003
Fax (409) 845-0727

Will confirm attendance and degree by phone, fax or mail. Inquiry must include student's name, date of birth, social security number, years attended. Employers may obtain transcripts upon written request accompanied by a $5.00 fee and a signed release from the student. Requests should be directed to: Records Office.

A doctoral-level institution with a medical school, with an enrollment of 41,000. Highest level of offering: doctorate.
ACCREDITATIONS: SC ARCH BUS COPSY DIETI ENG ENGT FOR IPSY JOUR LSAR MED TED BUSA VET

Texas Arts and Industry University

Santa Gertrudis
Campus Box 105
Kingsville, TX 78363
(512) 595-2811

Will confirm attendance and degree by phone or mail. Inquiry must include student's name, date of birth, social security number, years attended. Employers may obtain transcripts upon written request accompanied by a $2.00 fee and a signed release from the student. Requests should be directed to: Registrar's Office.

A comprehensive institution with no medical school, with an enrollment of 5,818. Highest level of offering: doctorate.
ACCREDITATIONS: SC ENG MUS TED

Texas Chiropractic College

5912 Spencer Highway
Pasadena, TX 77505
(713) 487-1170 Ext. 254 or 284

Will confirm attendance and degree by phone or mail. Inquiry must include student's name, social security number, years attended. Employers may obtain transcripts upon written request accompanied by a $5.00 fee and a signed release from the student.

A health institution, with an enrollment of 392. Highest level of offering: first professional degree.
ACCREDITATIONS: SC CHIRO

Texas Christian University

Box 32912
Fort Worth, TX 76129
(817) 921-7825

Will confirm attendance and degree by phone or mail. Inquiry must include student's name, date of birth, social security number, years attended. Requests should be directed to: Registrar's Office. Employers may obtain transcripts upon written request accompanied by a $2.00 fee and a signed release from the student.

A comprehensive institution with no medical school, with an enrollment of 6,747. Highest level of offering: doctorate.
ACCREDITATIONS: SC BUS DIET FIDER JOUR MUS NUR SW TED THEOL

Texas College

Office of Registrar/Director of Admissions
2404 North Grand Avenue
Tyler, TX 75702
(214) 593-8311 Ext. 272
Fax (903) 592-2342

Will confirm attendance and degree by phone or mail. Inquiry must include student's name, date of birth, social security number, years attended. Requests should be directed to: Office of the Registrar. Employers may obtain transcripts upon written request accompanied by a $3.00 fee and a signed release from the student.

A general baccalaureate institution, with an enrollment of 573. Highest level of offering: four or five year baccalaureate.
ACCREDITATIONS: SACS

Texas College of Osteopathic Medicine

3500 Camp Bowie Boulevard
Fort Worth, TX 76107
(817) 735-2201

Will confirm attendance and degree by phone or mail. Inquiry must include student's name, years attended. Employers may obtain transcripts upon written request accompanied by a $2.00 fee and a signed release from the student.

A medical school, with an enrollment of 378. Highest level of offering: first professional degree.
ACCREDITATIONS: OSTEO

Texas Lutheran College

1000 West Court Street
Seguin, TX 78155
(512) 372-8000
Fax (512) 372-8096

Will confirm attendance and degree by fax or mail. Inquiry must include student's name, date of birth, social security number, years attended. Employers may obtain transcripts upon written request accompanied by a $3.00 fee and a signed release from the student.

A general baccalaureate institution, with an enrollment of 1,357. Highest level of offering: four or five year baccalaureate.
ACCREDITATIONS: SC SW

Texas Southern University

3100 Cleburne
Houston, TX 77004
(713) 527-7011
Fax (713) 639-1878

Will confirm attendance and degree by phone, fax or mail. Inquiry must include student's name, date of birth, social security number, years attended. Employers may obtain transcripts upon written request accompanied by a $1.00 fee and a signed release from the student.

A comprehensive institution with no medical school, with an enrollment of 10,000. Highest level of offering: doctorate.
ACCREDITATIONS: SC BUS LAW PHAR RSTH SW TED

Texas Southmost College

83 Fort Brown St
Brownsville, TX 78520
(512) 544-8254
Fax (512) 544-8832

Will confirm attendance and degree by phone, fax or mail. Inquiry must include student's name, date of birth, social security number, years attended. Employers may obtain transcripts upon written request accompanied by a $1.00 fee and a signed release from the student.

A multiprogram two-year institution, with an enrollment of 5,714. Highest level of offering: one year but less than four years.
ACCREDITATIONS: SC ADNUR MLTAD RAD RSTH RSTHT

Texas State Technical Institute–Amarillo Campus

PO Box 11197
Amarillo, TX 79111
(806) 335-2316 Ext. 268

Will confirm attendance and degree by mail. Inquiry must include student's name, social security number, years attended. Requests should be directed to: Admissions Office. Employers may obtain transcripts upon written request accompanied by a $2.00 fee and a signed release from the student.

A multiprogram two-year institution, with an enrollment of 1,118. Highest level of offering: one year but less than four years.
ACCREDITATIONS: SC FIDER

Texas State Technical Institute–Rio Grande Campus at Harlingen

PO Box 2628
Harlingen, TX 78550-3697
(512) 425-0665
Fax (512) 425-0796

Will confirm attendance and degree by mail or fax. Inquiry must include student's name, date of birth, social security number, years attended. Requests should be directed to: Records Office. Employers may obtain transcripts upon written request accompanied by a $2.00 fee and a signed release from the student.

A multiprogram two-year institution, with an enrollment of 2,359. Highest level of offering: one year but less than four years.
ACCREDITATIONS: SC

Texas State Technical Institute–Sweetwater Campus

Route Three, Box 18
Sweetwater, TX 79556
(915) 235-7300 Ext. 377
Fax (915) 235-7416

Will confirm attendance and degree by phone, fax or mail. Inquiry must include student's name, social security number, years attended. Requests should be directed to: Admissions & Records Office. Employers may obtain transcripts upon written request accompanied by a $2.00 fee and a signed release from the student

A multiprogram two-year institution, with an enrollment of 750. Highest level of offering: one year but less than four years.
ACCREDITATIONS: SC

Texas State Technical College

3801 Campus Drive
Waco, TX 76705
(817) 799-3611 Ext. 2360 or
(817) 867-4816

Will confirm attendance and degree by phone or mail. Inquiry must include student's name, social security number, years attended. Employers may obtain transcripts upon written request accompanied by a $1.00 fee and a signed release from the student. Requests should be directed to: Admissions/Records.

A multiprogram two-year institution with an enrollment of 4,609. Highest level of offering: one year but less than four years.

ACCREDITATIONS: SC

Texas Tech University Health Science Center

Office of Student Services
3601 4th Street
Lubbock, TX 79430
(806) 743-2300

Will confirm attendance and degree by phone or mail. Inquiry must include student's name, social security number, years attended, release. Requests should be directed to: Records Office. Employers may obtain transcripts upon written request accompanied by a $2.00 fee and a signed release from the student.

A bachelor's or higher institution newly admitted to NCES, with an enrollment of 902. Highest level of offering: doctorate.
ACCREDITATIONS: EMT MED PTA

Texas Tech University

Registrar's Office
PO Box 45015
Lubbock, TX 79409-5015
(806) 742-3652

Will confirm attendance and degree by phone or mail. Inquiry must include student's name, date of birth, social security number, years attended. Employers may obtain transcripts upon written request accompanied by a $2.00 fee and a signed release from the student. Requests should be directed to: Admissions Office.

A doctoral-level institution with no medical school, with an enrollment of 24,707. Highest level of offering: doctorate.

ACCREDITATIONS: SC ARCH ART AUD BUS CLPSY COPSY ENG ENGT FIDER IPSY BUSA JOUR TED LAW LSAR MFCD MUS NUR SP SW

Texas Wesleyan University

1201 Wesleyan
Fort Worth, TX 76105-1536
(817) 531-4414
Fax (817) 531-4425

Will confirm attendance and degree by phone or mail. Inquiry must include student's name, date of birth, social security number, years attended. Employers may obtain transcripts upon written request accompanied by a $2.00 fee and a signed release from the student.

A general baccalaureate institution, with an enrollment of 1,629. Highest level of offering: master's.
ACCREDITATIONS: SC MUS TED

Texas Woman's University

Box 22909 T W U Station
Denton, TX 76204
(800) 338-5255
Fax (817) 898-3198

Will confirm attendance and degree by phone, fax or mail. Inquiry must include student's name, date of birth, social security number, years attended. Employers may obtain transcripts upon written request accompanied by a $2.00 fee and a signed release from the student.

A doctoral-level institution with no medical school, with an enrollment of 8,259. Highest level of offering: doctorate.
ACCREDITATIONS: SC DH DIET DIETI FIDER LIB MRA MUS NUR OT PTA SW TED

Thaddeus Stevens State School of Technology

750 E King Street
Lancaster, PA 17602-3198
(717) 299-7796
Fax (717) 396-7186

Will confirm attendance by mail or fax. Inquiry must include student's name, years attended, release. Requests should be directed to: Registrar's Office. Employers may obtain transcripts upon written request accompanied by a signed release from the student.

A two-year institution newly admitted to NCES, with an enrollment of 510. Highest level of offering: one year but less than four years.
ACCREDITATIONS: M

Thames Valley State Technical College

574 New London Turnpike
Norwich, CT 06360
(203) 886-0177
Fax (203) 886-4960

Will confirm attendance and degree by phone, fax or mail. Inquiry must include student's name, date of birth, social security number, years attended. Employers may obtain transcripts upon written request accompanied by a signed release from the student. Requests should be directed to: Registrar's Office.

A multiprogram two-year institution, with an enrollment of 1,402. Highest level of offering: one year but less than four years.
ACCREDITATIONS: EV ENGT

The American College

270 Bryn Mawr Avenue
Bryn Mawr, PA 19010
(215) 526-1448

Will confirm attendance and degree by phone or mail. Inquiry must include student's name. Requests should be directed to: Registrar's Office. Employers may obtain transcripts upon written request accompanied by a $5.00 fee and a signed release from the student.

A single program two-year institution, with an enrollment of 1,875. Highest level of offering: unergraduate non-degree granting.
ACCREDITATIONS: M

The Berkeley College of Business

44 Riffle Camp Road
West Paterson, NJ 07424
(201) 278-5400 Ext. 24
Fax (201) 278-2242

Will confirm attendance and degree by fax or mail. Inquiry must include student's name, years attended, release, self addressed, stamped envelope. Employers may obtain transcripts upon written request accompanied by a $2.00 fee and a signed release from the student.

A multiprogram two-year institution, with an enrollment of 715. Highest level of offering: two years.
ACCREDITATIONS: M JRCB

The Berkeley School

West Red Oak Lane
White Plains, NY 10604
(914) 694-8440 Ext. 51

Will confirm attendance and degree by phone or mail. Inquiry must include student's name, years attended, self addressed stamped envelope. Employers may obtain transcripts upon written request accompanied by a $2.00 fee and a signed release from the student. Requests should be directed to: Placement Office.

A single program two-year institution, with an enrollment of 723. Highest level of offering: one year but less than four years.
ACCREDITATIONS: M NY JRCB

The College of Law–University of San Fernando Valley

(See University of LaVerne College of Law.)

The College of West Virginia

(Formerly Beckley College)
PO Box AG
Beckley, WV 25802-2830
(304) 253-7351 Ext. 35
Fax (304) 253-0789

Will confirm attendance and degree by phone or mail. Inquiry must include student's name, date of birth, social security number, years attended. Employers may obtain transcripts upon written request accompanied by a $3.00 fee and a signed release from the student.

A multi program four-year institution, with an enrollment of 1,700. Highest level of offering: one year but less than four years.
ACCREDITATIONS: NCA

The Defiance College

701 North Clinton
Defiance, OH 43512
(419) 783-2357

Will confirm attendance and degree by phone or mail. Inquiry must include student's name, date of birth, social security number, years attended. Employers may obtain transcripts upon written request accompanied by a $3.00 fee and a signed release from the student.

A general baccalaureate institution, with an enrollment of 975. Highest level of offering: master's.
ACCREDITATIONS: NH SW

The Delaware Law School of Widener University

(See Widener University School of Law.)

The General Theological Seminary

175 9th Avenue
New York, NY 10011
(212) 243-5150 Ext. 276
Fax (212) 727-3907

Will confirm attendance and degree by phone, fax or mail. Inquiry must include student's name, social security number, years attended, self addressed stamped envelope. Employers may obtain transcripts upon written request accompanied by a $4.00 fee and a signed release from the student.

A school of philosophy, religion and theology, with an enrollment of 110. Highest level of offering: doctorate.
ACCREDITATIONS: M NY THEOL

The Hartford Graduate Center

275 Windsor Street
Hartford, CT 06120
(203) 548-2426

Will confirm attendance and degree by phone or mail. Inquiry must include student's name, date of birth, social security number, years attended, degree. Employers may obtain transcripts upon written request accompanied by a signed release from the student.

A business school, with an enrollment of 2,500. Highest level of offering: master's.
ACCREDITATIONS: EH

The Juilliard School

Lincoln Center
New York, NY 10023
(212) 799-5000
Fax (212) 724-0263

Will confirm attendance and degree by mail or fax. Inquiry must include student's name, social security number, years attended, release. Employers may obtain transcripts upon written request accompanied by a $5.00 fee and a signed release from the student.

A visual and performing arts school, with an enrollment of 800. Highest level of offering: doctorate.
ACCREDITATIONS: M NY

The Loop College

(See Harold Washington College.)

The Luthern School of Theology at Chicago

1100 East 55 Street
Chicago, IL 60615
(312) 753-0700

Will confirm attendance and degree by mail. Inquiry must include student's name, social security number, years attended, release. Employers may obtain transcripts upon written request accompanied by a $2.00 fee and a signed release from the student.

A school of philosophy, religion and theology, with an enrollment of 401. Highest level of offering: doctorate.
ACCREDITATIONS: THEOL

The Master's College

(Formerly Los Angeles Master's College)
PO Box 878
Newhall, CA 91322-0878
(805) 259-3540 Ext. 317
Fax (805) 254-6232

Will confirm attendance and degree by phone or mail. Inquiry must include student's name, social security number. Employers may obtain transcripts upon written request accompanied by a $3.00 fee and a signed release from the student. Requests should be directed to: Placement Office.

A general baccalaureate institution, with an enrollment of 815. Highest level of offering: four or five year baccalaureate.
ACCREDITATIONS: WC

The Medical College of Pennsylvania

3300 Henry Avenue
Philadelphia, PA 19129
(215) 842-7015
Fax (215) 849-1380 or 843-1766

Will confirm attendance and degree by phone, fax or mail. Inquiry must include student's name, date of birth, social security number. Employers may obtain transcripts upon written request accompanied by a $2.00 fee and a signed release from the student.

A medical school, with an enrollment of 544. Highest level of offering: doctorate.
ACCREDITATIONS: M ANEST IPSY MED MT RAD

The Oklahoma College of Osteopathic Medicine and Surgery

1111 West 17th Street
Tulsa, OK 74107
(918) 582-1972
Fax (918) 582-6316

Will confirm attendance and degree by mail or fax. Inquiry must include student's name, date of birth, social security number, years attended, release, self addressed stamped envelope. Requests should be directed to: Records Office. Only students may obtain transcripts.

A medical school, with an enrollment of 264. Highest level of offering: first professional degree.
ACCREDITATIONS: OSTEO

The Stevens–Henager College of Business

2168 Washington Blvd.
Agden, UT 84401
(801) 394-7791

Will confirm attendance and degree by mail. Inquiry must include student's name, maiden name, date of birth, social security number, years attended. Employers may obtain transcripts upon written request accompanied by a $2.00 fee and a signed release from the student.

A multiprogram two-year institution, with an enrollment of 150. Highest level of offering: one year but less than four years.
ACCREDITATIONS: JRCB

The University of Alabama

PO Box 870134
Tuscaloosa, AL 35487
(205) 348-4886
Fax (205) 348-9046

Will confirm attendance and degree by phone, fax or mail. Inquiry must include student's name, date of birth, social security number, years attended. Employers may obtain transcripts upon written request accompanied by a $3.00 fee and a signed release from the student.

A doctoral-level institution with no medical school, with an enrollment of 18,716. Highest level of offering: doctorate.
ACCREDITATIONS: SC AUD BUS CLPSY DIET ENG ENGT FIDER JOUR LAW LIB MUS NUR SP SW TED BUSA

The University of Maryland University College

University Boulevard at Adelphi Road
College Park, MD 20742-1668
(301) 985-7268
Fax (301) 985-7364

Will confirm attendance and degree by phone, fax or mail. Inquiry must include student's name, date of birth, social security number, years attended. Employers may obtain transcripts upon written request accompanied by a signed release from the student. There is a $3.00 fee for certified copy.

A general baccalaureate institution, with an enrollment of 1,250. Highest level of offering: master's.

ACCREDITATIONS: M MFCD

The University of Sarasota

950 South Tamiami Trail
Sarasota, FL 34236
(813) 355-2906
Fax (813) 351-1765

Will confirm attendance by mail or fax. Inquiry must include student's name. Employers may obtain transcripts upon written request by student accompanied by a $4.00 fee.

A school of education, with and enrollment of 227. Highest level of offering: doctorate.

The University of the Arts

Broad & Pine St.
Philadelphia, PA 19102
(215) 875-4848
Fax (215) 875-5467

Will confirm attendance and degree by phone or mail. Inquiry must include student's name, social security number. Employers may obtain transcripts upon written request accompanied by a $5.00 fee and a signed release from the student.

A visual and performing arts school, with an enrollment of 1,400. Highest level of offering: master's

ACCREDITATIONS: M ART MUS

The University of the State of New York Regents College Degree

1450 Western Avenue
Albany, NY 12203
(518) 474-3703

Will confirm attendance and degree by phone or mail. Inquiry must include student's name, social security number, years attended. Employers may obtain transcripts upon written request accompanied by a $7.00 fee and a signed release from the student.

A general baccalaureate institution, with an enrollment of 17,546. Highest level of offering: four or five year baccalaureate.

ACCREDITATIONS: M ADNUR NUR NY

The Wood School

8 East 40th Street
New York, NY 10016
(212) 686-9040 Ext. 36
Fax (212) 686-9171

Will confirm attendance and degree by mail. Inquiry must include student's name, maiden name, date of birth, social security number, years attended, self addressed stamped envelope. Employers may obtain transcripts upon written request accompanied by a signed release from the student. Requests should be directed to: Records Office.

A single program two-year institution, with an enrollment of 451. Highest level of offering: one year but less than four years.

ACCREDITATIONS: NY

The Wright Institute

2728 Durant Avenue
Berkeley, CA 94704
(510) 841-9230
Fax (510) 549-2591

Will confirm attendance and degree by phone or mail. Inquiry must include student's name, date of birth, social security number, SASE. Requests should be directed to: Records Office. Employers may obtain transcripts upon written request accompanied by a $2.00 fee and a signed release from the student.

A specialized school, with an enrollment of 200. Highest level of offering: doctorate.

ACCREDITATIONS: WC APA/P

Thiel College

75 College Ave.
Greenville, PA 16125
(412) 588-7700 Ext. 2110
Fax (412) 589-2021

Will confirm attendance and degree by phone, fax or mail. Inquiry must include student's name, years attended. Requests should be directed to: Records Office. Employers may obtain transcripts upon written request accompanied by a $2.00 fee and a signed release from the student.

A general baccalaureate institution, with an enrollment of 875. Highest level of offering: four or five year baccalaureate.

ACCREDITATIONS: M RSTHT

Thomas A. Edison College

101 West State Street
Trenton, NJ 08608-1176
(609) 984-1182
Fax (609) 777-0477

Will confirm attendance and degree by phone, fax or mail. Inquiry must include student's name, date of birth, social security number, years attended. Employers may obtain transcripts upon written request accompanied by a signed release from the student. Requests should be directed to: Registrar's Office.

A general baccalaureate institution, with an enrollment of 7,200. Highest level of offering: four or five year baccalaureate.

ACCREDITATIONS: M

Thomas College

1501 Millpond Road
Thomasville, GA 31792
(912) 226-1621 Ext. 20

Will confirm attendance and degree by phone or mail. Inquiry must include student's name, social security number, years attended. Employers may obtain transcripts upon written request accompanied by a $3.00 fee and a signed release from the student.

A multiprogram two-year institution, with an enrollment of 391. Highest level of offering: one year but less than four years.

ACCREDITATIONS: SC

Thomas College

180 West River Road
Waterville, ME 04901-5097
(207) 873-0771 Ext. 245

Will confirm attendance and degree by phone or mail. Inquiry must include student's name, social security number. Employers may obtain transcripts upon written request accompanied by a $3.00 fee and a signed release from the student.

A business school, with an enrollment of 1,100. Highest level of offering: master's.

ACCREDITATIONS: EH

Thomas College

1501 Millpond Road
Thomasville, GA 31792
(912) 226-1621 Ext. 20

Will confirm attendance and degree by phone or mail. Inquiry must include student's name, social security number, years attended. Employers may obtain transcripts upon written request accompanied by a $3.00 fee and a signed release from the student.

A multiprogram four-year institution, with an enrollment of 360. Highest level of offering: four years.

ACCREDITATIONS: SACS

Thomas Jefferson Medical College

1015 Walnut Street
Room 622 Curtis Bldg.
Philadelphia, PA 19107-5099
(215) 955-6748

Will confirm attendance and degree by phone or mail. Inquiry must include student's name, years attended. Employers may obtain transcripts upon written request accompanied by a $2.00 fee and a signed release from the student. Direct inquiries to (215) 955-8982 for Graduate or (215) 955-8893 for Allied Health Sciences.

A medical school, with an enrollment of 880. Highest level of offering: doctorate.

ACCREDITATIONS: M CYTO DH MED MT NUR RAD IPSY PTA

Thomas M. Cooley Law School

PO Box 13038
Lansing, MI 48901
(517) 371-5140 Ext. 294
Fax (517) 334-5716

Will confirm attendance and degree by phone, fax or mail. Inquiry must include student's name. Employers may obtain transcripts upon written request accompanied by a $3.00 fee and a signed release from the student.

A law school, with an enrollment of 1,523. Highest level of offering: first professional degree.

ACCREDITATIONS: LAW

Thomas More College

Crestview Hills, KY 41017
(606) 344-3380
Fax (606) 344-3345

Will confirm attendance and degree by fax or mail. Inquiry must include student's name, social security number, years attended, self addressed stamped envelope. Employers may obtain transcripts upon written request accompanied by a $3.00 fee and a signed release from the student.

A general baccalaureate institution, with an enrollment of 1,200. Highest level of offering: four or five year baccalaureate.

ACCREDITATIONS: SC NUR SW

Thomas Nelson Community College

PO Box 9407
Hampton, VA 23670
(804) 825-2842
Fax (804) 825-2763

Will confirm attendance and degree by phone, fax or mail. Inquiry must include student's name, social security number, years attended. Employers may obtain transcripts upon written request accompanied by a signed release from the student. Requests should be directed to: Records Office.

A multiprogram two-year institution, with an enrollment of 8,000. Highest level of offering: one year but less than four years.

ACCREDITATIONS: SC MLTAD

Thornton Community College

(See South Suburban College)

Three Rivers Community College

Three Rivers Boulevard
Poplar Bluff, MO 63901
(314) 686-4101
Fax (314) 686-0435

Will confirm attendance and degree by phone or mail. Inquiry must include student's name, date of birth, social security number, years attended. Employers may obtain transcripts upon written request accompanied by a $2.00 fee and a signed release from the student. Requests should be directed to: Registrar.

A multiprogram two-year institution, with an enrollment of 3,000. Highest level of offering: one year but less than four years.

ACCREDITATIONS: NH ADNUR MLTAD

Tidewater Community College

Route 135
Portsmouth, VA 23703
(804) 484-2121

Will confirm attendance and degree by mail. Inquiry must include student's name, social security number, release. Employers may obtain transcripts upon written request accompanied by a signed release from the student. Requests should be directed to: Admissions & Records.

A multiprogram two-year institution, with an enrollment of 18,136. Highest level of offering: one year but less than four years.

ACCREDITATIONS: SC ADNUR MRT PTAA RAD RSTH RSTHT

Tiffin University

155 Miami Street
Tiffin, OH 44883
(419) 447-6442 Ext. 216

Will confirm attendance and degree by phone or mail. Inquiry must include student's name, date of birth, social security number, years attended. Employers may obtain transcripts upon written request accompanied by a $2.00 fee and a signed release from the student.

A specialized school, with an enrollment of 1,029. Highest level of offering: four or five year baccalaureate.

ACCREDITATIONS: NH SRCB

Tift College

c/o Mercer University
1400 Coleman Ave.
Macon, GA 31207
(912) 752-2680

Will confirm attendance and degree by phone or mail. Inquiry must include student's name, date of birth, social security number, years attended. Employers may obtain transcripts upon written request accompanied by a $2.00 fee and a signed release from the student.

Tobe–Coburn School For Fashion Careers

8 East 40th Street
New York, NY 10016
(212) 460-9600

Will confirm attendance and degree by mail. Inquiry must include student's name, social security number, years attended, release, self addressed stamped envelope. Employers may obtain transcripts upon written request accompanied by a $5.00 fee and a signed release from the student. Requests should be directed to: Registrar's Office.

A single program two-year institution, with an enrollment of 521. Highest level of offering: one year but less than four years.

ACCREDITATIONS: NY NATTS

Toccoa Falls College

PO Box 800896
Toccoa Falls, GA 30598
(404) 886-6831 Ext. 5330
Fax (404) 886-6412

Will confirm attendance and degree by phone, fax or mail. Inquiry must include student's name, social security number, years attended, release. Requests should be directed to: Registrar's Office. Employers may obtain transcripts upon written request accompanied by a $2.00 fee and a signed release from the student.

A school of philosophy, religion and theology, with an enrollment of 800. Highest level of offering: four or five year baccalaureate.

ACCREDITATIONS: SC BI

Tomlinson College

PO Box 3030
Cleveland, TN 37320-3030
(615) 476-3271 Ext. 42

Will confirm attendance and degree by phone or mail. Inquiry must include student's name, date of birth, years attended. Employers may obtain transcripts upon written request accompanied by a $2.00 fee and a signed release from the student.

A multiprogram two-year institution, with an enrollment of 228. Highest level of offering: one year but less than four years.

ACCREDITATIONS: SC

Tompkins–Cortland Community College

170 North Street
PO Box 139
Dryden, NY 13053
(607) 844-8211 Ext. 303
Fax (607) 844-9665

Will confirm attendance and degree by phone, fax or mail. Inquiry must include student's name, date of birth, social security number, years attended. Employers may obtain transcripts upon written request accompanied by a $4.00 fee and a signed release from the student.

A multiprogram two-year institution, with an enrollment of 2,803. Highest level of offering: one year but less than four years.

ACCREDITATIONS: M ADNUR NY

Torah Academy for Girls

(Formerly Long Island Seminary of Jewish Studies for Women)
444 Beach 6th Street
Far Rockaway, NY 11691
(718) 471-8444 Ext. 12

Will confirm attendance and degree by mail. Inquiry must include student's name, date of birth, social security number, years attended. Employers may obtain transcripts upon written request accompanied by a signed release from the student. Attn: Registrar's Office.

A specialized non-degree granting institution. Highest level of offering: undergraduate non-degree granting.

Torah Temimah Talmudical Seminary

555 Ocean Parkway
Brooklyn, NY 11218
(718) 438-9860

Will confirm attendance and degree by mail. Inquiry must include student's name, date of birth, social security number, years attended, release. Employers may obtain transcripts upon written request accompanied by a $2.00 fee and a signed release from the student. Requests should be directed to: Registrar's Office.

A bachelor's or higher institution newly admitted to NCES, with an enrollment of 101. Highest level of offering: undergraduate non-degree granting.

ACCREDITATIONS: RABN

Tougaloo College

500 County Line Road
Tougaloo, MS 39174
(601) 977-7765

Will confirm attendance and degree by phone or mail. Inquiry must include student's name, date of birth, social security number, years attended. Requests should be directed to: Student Enrollment Management Center. Only students may obtain transcripts.

A general baccalaureate institution, with an enrollment of 837. Highest level of offering: four or five year baccalaureate.
ACCREDITATIONS: SC

Touro College

844 6th Avenue
New York, NY 10001
(212) 447-0700

Will confirm attendance and degree by phone or mail. Inquiry must include student's name, date of birth, social security number, years attended. Employers may obtain transcripts upon written request accompanied by a $10.00 fee and a signed release from the student. Requests should be directed to: Office of Registrar.

A general baccalaureate institution, with an enrollment of 8,000. Highest level of offering: master's.
ACCREDITATIONS: M APCP LAW MRA NY

Towson State University

Towson, MD 21204
(301) 830-2700
Fax (301) 830-3443

Will confirm attendance and degree by phone, fax or mail. Inquiry must include student's name, date of birth, social security number, years attended. Employers may obtain transcripts upon written request accompanied by a signed release from the student.

A comprehensive institution with no medical school, with an enrollment of 15,000. Highest level of offering: beyond master's but less than doctorate.
ACCREDITATIONS: M DANCE MUS NUR OT TED

Tracey–Warner School

401 North Broad Street
Philadelphia, PA 19108
(215) 574-0402

Will confirm attendance and degree by mail. Inquiry must include student's name, social security number, years attended, SASE. Employers may obtain transcripts upon written request accompanied by a signed release from the student.

A single program two-year institution, with an enrollment of 94. Highest level of offering: one year but less than four years.
ACCREDITATIONS: NATTS

Transylvania University

300 North Broadway
Lexington, KY 40508
(606) 233-8116
Fax (606) 233-8797

Will confirm attendance and degree by phone, fax or mail. Inquiry must include student's name, social security number, years attended. Employers may obtain transcripts upon written request accompanied by a $2.00 fee and a signed release from the student.

A general baccalaureate institution, with an enrollment of 1,076. Highest level of offering: four or five year baccalaureate.
ACCREDITATIONS: SC

Treasure Valley Community College

650 College Boulevard
Ontario, OR 97914
(503) 889-6493 Ext. 234

Will confirm attendance and degree by phone or mail. Inquiry must include student's name, date of birth, social security number, years attended. Employers may obtain transcripts upon written request accompanied by a $2.00 fee and a signed release from the student.

A multiprogram two-year institution, with an enrollment of 2,800. Highest level of offering: one year but less than four years.
ACCREDITATIONS: NW

Trenholm State Technical College

1225 Air Base Boulevard
Montgomery, AL 36108
(205) 832-9000 Ext. 35
Fax (205) 832-9777

Will confirm attendance and degree by phone, fax or mail. Inquiry must include student's name, date of birth, social security number, years attended. Employers may obtain transcripts upon written request accompanied by a $2.00 fee and a signed release from the student.

A two-year institution newly admitted to NCES, with an erollment of 800. Highest level of offering: one year but less than four years.
ACCREDITATIONS: SV PNUR

Trenton Junior College

(See North Central Missouri College)

Trenton State College

Cn 4700
Trenton, NJ 08650-4700
(609) 771-2141
Fax (609) 530-7784

Will confirm attendance and degree by mail or fax. Inquiry must include student's name, social security number, years attended. Employers may obtain transcripts upon written request accompanied by a $5.00 fee and a signed release from the student. Requests should be directed to: Records.

A comprehensive institution with no medical school, with an enrollment of 7,000. Highest level of offering: beyond master's but less than doctorate.
ACCREDITATIONS: M ENGT FIDER MUS NUR TED

Trevecca Nazarene College

333 Murfreesboro Road
Nashville, TN 37210
(615) 248-1267
Fax (615) 248-7728

Will confirm attendance and degree by phone or mail. Inquiry must include student's name, social security number, years attended. Employers may obtain transcripts upon written request accompanied by a $2.00 fee, student's social security number and a signed release from the student.

A general baccalaureate institution, with an enrollment of 1,591. Highest level of offering: master's.
ACCREDITATIONS: SC APCP MAC MUS

Tri–Cities State Technical Institute

(See Northeast State Technical Community College)

Tri–County Community College

PO Box 40
Murphy, NC 28906
(704) 837-6810
Fax (704) 837-3266

Will confirm attendance and degree by phone or mail. Inquiry must include student's name, date of birth, social security number, years attended. Employers may obtain transcripts upon written request accompanied by a signed release from the student.

A multiprogram two-year institution, with an enrollment of 724. Highest level of offering: one year but less than four years.
ACCREDITATIONS: SC

Tri–County Technical College

PO Box 587
Pendleton, SC 29670
(803) 646-8361 Ext. 192

Will confirm attendance and degree by phone or mail. Inquiry must include student's name, date of birth, social security number, years attended. Employers may obtain transcripts upon written request accompanied by a $1.00 fee and a signed release from the student. Requests should be directed to: Student Records.

A multiprogram two-year institution, with an enrollment of 3,019. Highest level of offering: one year but less than four years.
ACCREDITATIONS: SACS ADVET ENGT MLTAD

Tri–State University

PO Box 307
Angola, IN 46703
(219) 665-4241

Will confirm attendance and degree by phone or mail. Inquiry must include student's name, date of birth, social security number, years attended. Employers may obtain transcripts upon written request accompanied by a $3.00 fee and a signed release from the student.

A general baccalaureate institution, with an enrollment of 965. Highest level of offering: four or five year baccalaureate.
ACCREDITATIONS: NH ENG ENGT

Triangle Tech, Erie School

2000 Liberty Street
Erie, PA 16502
(814) 453-6016

Will confirm attendance and degree by mail. Inquiry must include student's name, social security number, years attended, release, self addressed stamped envelope. Employers may obtain transcripts upon written request accompanied by a $2.00 fee and a signed release from the student.

A single program two-year institution, with an enrollment of 210. Highest level of offering: one year but less than four years.
ACCREDITATIONS: NATTS

Triangle Tech, Greensburg Center

600 Blank School Road
Greensburg, PA 15601
(412) 832-1050
Fax (412) 834-0325

Will confirm attendance and degree by phone or mail. Inquiry must include student's name, social security number, years attended. Employers may obtain transcripts upon written request accompanied by a signed release from the student.

A multi-program two-year institution, with an enrollment of 200. Highest level of offering: one year but less than four years.
ACCREDITATIONS: ACTTS/CCA

Triangle Tech

1940 Perrysville Ave
Pittsburgh, PA 15214
(412) 359-1000 Ext. 197
Fax (412) 359-1012

Will confirm attendance and degree by phone, fax or mail. Inquiry must include student's name, date of birth, social security number, years attended. Employers may obtain transcripts upon written request accompanied by a $2.00 fee and a signed release from the student. Requests should be directed to: Academic Affairs Office.

A single program two-year institution, with an enrollment of 306. Highest level of offering: one year but less than four years.
ACCREDITATIONS: NATTS

Trident Technical College

PO Box 10367
Charleston, SC 29411
(803) 572-6324

Will confirm attendance and degree by phone or mail. Inquiry must include student's name, social security number, years attended, release. Employers may obtain transcripts upon written request accompanied by a $1.00 fee and a signed release from the student. Requests should be directed to: Admissions & Records Office.

A multiprogram two-year institution, with an enrollment of 6,400. Highest level of offering: one year but less than four years.
ACCREDITATIONS: SC DT ENGT MLTAD RAD

Trinidad State Junior College

600 Prospect Street
Trinidad, CO 81082
(719) 846-5621
Fax (719) 846-5667

Will confirm attendance and degree by phone, fax or mail. Inquiry must include student's name, date of birth, social security number, years attended. Requests should be directed to: Student Services. Employers may obtain transcripts upon written request accompanied by a $1.00 fee and a signed release from the student.

A multiprogram two-year institution, with an enrollment of 1,700. Highest level of offering: one year but less than four years.
ACCREDITATIONS: NH

Trinity Bible College

50 6th Avenue South
Ellendale, ND 58436
(701) 349-3621 Ext. 2034

Will confirm attendance and degree by phone or mail. Inquiry must include student's name, date of birth, social security number, years attended. Employers may obtain transcripts upon written request accompanied by a $3.00 fee and a signed release from the student.

A school of philosophy, religion and theology, with an enrollment of 420. Highest level of offering: four or five year baccalaureate.
ACCREDITATIONS: BI

Trinity Christian College

6601 West College Drive
Palos Heights, IL 60463
(708) 597-3000 Ext. 361
Fax (708) 385-5665

Will confirm attendance and degree by phone, fax or mail. Inquiry must include student's name. Employers may obtain transcripts upon written request accompanied by a $2.00 fee and a signed release from the student.

A general baccalaureate institution, with an enrollment of 468. Highest level of offering: four or five year baccalaureate.
ACCREDITATIONS: NH

Trinity College

125 Mich Avenue North East
Washington, DC 20017
(202) 939-5032

Will confirm attendance and degree by phone or mail. Inquiry must include student's name, social security number, years attended. Employers may obtain transcripts upon written request by student accompanied by a $5.00 fee and a signed release from the student. Requests should be directed to: Registrar's Office.

A general baccalaureate institution, with an enrollment of 838. Highest level of offering: master's.
ACCREDITATIONS: M

Trinity College

2077 Half Day Road
Deerfield, IL 60015
(312) 948-8980 Ext. 212

Will confirm attendance and degree by phone or mail. Inquiry must include student's name, years attended. Requests should be directed to: Records Office. Employers may obtain transcripts upon written request accompanied by a $2.00 fee and a signed release from the student.

A general baccalaureate institution, with an enrollment of 592. Highest level of offering: four or five year baccalaureate.
ACCREDITATIONS: NH

Trinity College

300 Summit Street
Hartford, CT 06106
(203) 297-2118
Fax (203) 297-2257

Will confirm attendance and degree by phone or mail. Inquiry must include student's name, years attended. Employers may obtain transcripts upon written request accompanied by a $2.00 fee and a signed release from the student.

A comprehensive institution with no medical school, with an enrollment of 2,169. Highest level of offering: master's.
ACCREDITATIONS: EH

Trinity College

208 Colchester Avenue
Burlington, VT 05401
(802) 658-0337 Ext. 247
Fax (802) 658-5446

Will confirm attendance and degree by phone, fax or mail. Inquiry must include student's name, date of birth, social security number. Employers may obtain transcripts upon written request accompanied by a $5.00 fee and a signed release from the student.

A general baccalaureate institution, with an enrollment of 1,100. Highest level of offering: four or five year baccalaureate, master's in education.
ACCREDITATIONS: EH SW

Trinity Community College

(Formerly Henderson County Junior College)
500 South Praireville
Athens, TX 75751
(903) 675-6221

Will confirm attendance and degree by phone or mail. Inquiry must include student's name, date of birth, social security number, years attended. Employers may obtain transcripts upon written request accompanied by a $2.00 fee and a signed release from the student.

A multiprogram two-year institution, with an enrollment of 3,795. Highest level of offering: one year but less than four years.
ACCREDITATIONS: SC

Trinity Episcopal School For Ministry

311 Eleventh Street
Ambridge, PA 15003
(412) 266-3838

Will confirm attendance and degree by phone or mail. Inquiry must include student's name. Employers may obtain transcripts upon written request accompanied by a signed release from the student.

A bachelor's or higher institution newly admitted to NCES, with an enrollment of 125. Highest level of offering: first professional degree.
ACCREDITATIONS: THEOL

Trinity Evangelical Divinity School

2065 Half Day Road
Deerfield, IL 60015
(708) 945-8800

Will confirm attendance and degree by mail. Inquiry must include student's name, date of birth, years attended. Requests should be directed to: Records Department. Employers may obtain transcripts upon written request accompanied by a $2.00 fee and a signed release from the student.

A school of philosophy, religion and theology, with an enrollment of 971. Highest level of offering: doctorate.
ACCREDITATIONS: NH THEOL

Trinity Lutheran Seminary

2199 East Main Street
Columbus, OH 43209-2334
(614) 235-4136
Fax (614) 238-0263

Will confirm attendance and degree by phone or mail. Inquiry must include student's name, date of birth. Employers may obtain transcripts upon written request accompanied by a signed release from the student. Requests should be directed to: Registrar's Office.

A school of philosophy, religion and theology, with an enrollment of 247. Highest level of offering: master's.

ACCREDITATIONS: NH THEOL

Trinity University

Box 96–715 Stadium Drive
San Antonio, TX 78284
(512) 736-7201
Fax (512) 736-7696

Will confirm attendance and degree by phone, fax or mail. Inquiry must include student's name, date of birth, social security number, years attended. Employers may obtain transcripts upon written request accompanied by a $2.00 fee and a signed release from the student. Requests should be directed to: Registrar's Office.

A comprehensive institution with no medical school, with an enrollment of 2,573. Highest level of offering: master's.

ACCREDITATIONS: SC ENG HSA TED

Trinity Valley Community College

500 South Praireville
Athens, TX 75751
(903) 675-6211 Ext. 6221

Will confirm attendance and degree by phone or mail. Inquiry must include student's name, date of birth, social security number, years attended. Employers may obtain transcripts upon written request accompanied by a $2.00 fee and a signed release from the student.

A multiprogram two-year institution, with an enrollment of 4,753. Highest level of offering: one year but less than four years.

ACCREDITATIONS: SC

Triton College

Director of Registration & Records
2000 5th Avenue, R-205
River Grove, IL 60171
(708) 456-0300 Ext. 815
Fax (708) 456-0049

Will confirm attendance and degree by phone or mail. Inquiry must include student's name, address, social security number, release. Requests should be directed to: Office of Admissions & Records. Employers may obtain transcripts upon written request accompanied by a $3.00 fee and a signed release from the student.

A multiprogram two-year institution, with an enrollment of 20,000. Highest level of offering: two year associate degree.

ACCREDITATIONS: NH ADNUR DA DT MAC MLTAD NMT PNUR RAD RSTH SURGT

Trocaire College

110 Red Jacket Parkway
Buffalo, NY 14220
(716) 826-1200 Ext. 224

Will confirm attendance and degree by phone or mail. Inquiry must include student's name, social security number, years attended. Employers may obtain transcripts upon written request accompanied by a $2.00 fee and a signed release from the student.

A multiprogram two-year institution, with an enrollment of 1,163. Highest level of offering: one year but less than four years.

ACCREDITATIONS: M ADNUR NY RAD

Troy State University at Dothan

PO Box 8368
Dothan, AL 36304
(205) 983-6556 Ext. 221
Fax (205) 983-6322

Will confirm attendance and degree by phone or mail. Inquiry must include student's name, social security number. Employers may obtain transcripts upon written request accompanied by a $3.00 fee and a signed release from the student. Requests should be directed to: Registrar's Office.

A comprehensive institution with no medical school, with an enrollment of 2,100. Highest level of offering: beyond master's but less than doctorate.

ACCREDITATIONS: SC

Troy State University at Montgomery

PO Drawer 4419
Montgomery, AL 36195-5701
(205) 241-9511

Will confirm attendance and degree by phone or mail. Inquiry must include student's name, social security number. Employers may obtain transcripts upon written request accompanied by a $4.00 fee and a signed release from the student. Requests should be directed to: Transcript Clerk.

A comprehensive institution with no medical school, with an enrollment of 2,834. Highest level of offering: beyond master's but less than doctorate.

ACCREDITATIONS: SC ADNUR

Troy State University Main Campus

University Avenue
Troy, AL 36082
(205) 670-3000 Ext. 3164

Will confirm attendance and degree by phone or mail. Inquiry must include student's name, date of birth, social security number. Employers may obtain transcripts upon written request accompanied by a $3.00 fee and a signed release from the student. Requests should be directed to: Records Office.

A comprehensive institution with no medical school, with an enrollment of 5,309. Highest level of offering: beyond master's but less than doctorate.

ACCREDITATIONS: SC NUR TED

Truckee Meadows Community College

7000 Dandini Boulevard
Reno, NV 89512
(702) 673-7040
Fax (702) 673-7108

Will confirm attendance and degree by mail or fax. Inquiry must include student's name, social security number, release. Requests should be directed to: Admissions Office. Employers may obtain transcripts upon written request accompanied by a $2.00 fee and a signed release from the student.

A multiprogram two-year institution, with an enrollment of 10,000. Highest level of offering: one year but less than four years.

ACCREDITATIONS: NW DA RAD

Truett McConnell College

Cleveland, GA 30528
(404) 865-2137
Fax (404) 865-7566

Will confirm attendance and degree by phone or mail. Inquiry must include student's name, social security number, years attended. Requests should be directed to: Registrar's Office. Employers may obtain transcripts upon written request accompanied by a $2.00 fee and a signed release from the student.

A multiprogram two-year institution, with an enrollment of 1,700. Highest level of offering: two years but less than four years.

ACCREDITATIONS: SC MUS

Truman College

1145 West Wilson Avenue
Chicago, IL 60640
(312) 878-1700

Will confirm attendance and degree by mail. Inquiry must include student's name, date of birth, social security number, years attended, release. Employers may obtain transcripts upon written request accompanied by a signed release from the student. Requests should be directed to: Registrar's Office.

A multiprogram two-year institution, with an enrollment of 11,151. Highest level of offering: one year but less than four years.

ACCREDITATIONS: NH MRT

Tufts University

Ballon Hall
Medford, MA 02155
(617) 381-3267

Will confirm attendance and degree by phone or mail. Inquiry must include student's name, years attended, social security number. Employers may obtain transcripts upon written request accompanied by a $2.00 fee and a signed release from the student. Requests should be directed to: Registrar's Office.

A doctoral-level institution with a medical school, with an enrollment of 8,000. Highest level of offering: doctorate.

ACCREDITATIONS: EH DENT ENG MED OT VET

Tulane University of Louisiana

110 Gibson Hall
New Orleans, LA 70118
(504) 865-5231

Will confirm attendance and degree by phone or mail. Inquiry must include student's name, date of birth, social security number. Employers may obtain transcripts upon written request accompanied by a $3.00 fee and a signed release from the student. Requests should be directed to: Registrar's Office.

A doctoral-level institution with a medical school, with an enrollment of 11,516. Highest level of offering: doctorate.
ACCREDITATIONS: SC ARCH ART BUS ENG HSA IPSY LAW MED MUS PH SW

Tulsa Junior College

3727 East Apache
Tulsa, OK 74115
(918) 834-5071
Fax (918) 834-5071 Ext. 351

Will confirm attendance and degree by mail or fax. Inquiry must include student's name, social security number, release. Employers may obtain transcripts upon written request accompanied by a signed release from the student. Requests should be directed to: Northeast Campus, Registrar's Office.

A multiprogram two-year institution, with an enrollment of 21,000. Highest level of offering: one year but less than four years.
ACCREDITATIONS: NH ADNUR MAC MLTAD PTAA RAD RSTH RSTHT

Tunxis Community College

Registrar's Office
Farmington, CT 06032
(203) 677-7701

Will confirm attendance and degree by phone or mail. Inquiry must include student's name, date of birth, social security number, years attended. Employers may obtain transcripts upon written request accompanied by a signed release from the student.

A multiprogram two-year institution, with an enrollment of 3,043. Highest level of offering: one year but less than four years.
ACCREDITATIONS: EH DA DH

Turtle Mountain Community College

Box 340
Belcourt, ND 58316
(701) 477-5605
Fax (701) 477-5028

Will confirm attendance and degree by mail or fax. Inquiry must include student's name, date of birth, social security number. Employers may obtain transcripts upon written request accompanied by a $1.00 fee and a signed release from the student. Requests should be directed to: Registrar's Office.

A two-year institution with an enrollment of 449. Highest level of offering: one year but less than four years.
ACCREDITATIONS: NH

Turkey Meadows Community College

(Formerly Old College)
7000 Dandini Blvd.
Reno, NV 89512
(702) 673-7040

Will confirm attendance and degree by phone. Inquiry must include student's name, social security number, years attended. Employers may obtain transcripts upon written request accompanied by a $2.00 fee and a signed release from the student.

A bachelor's or higher institution newly admitted to NCES, with an enrollment of 9,930. Highest level of offering: doctorate.
ACCREDITATIONS: NW

Tusculum College

PO Box 5050
Greeneville, TN 37743
(615) 636-7300 Ext. 311
Fax (615) 638-5181

Will confirm attendance and degree by phone, fax or mail. Inquiry must include student's name, date of birth, social security number. Employers may obtain transcripts upon written request accompanied by a $2.00 fee and a signed release from the student. Requests should be directed to: Registrar's Office.

A general baccalaureate institution, with an enrollment of 850. Highest level of offering: master's.
ACCREDITATIONS: SC

Tuskegee University

Tuskegee Institute, AL 36088
(205) 727-8011

Will confirm attendance and degree by phone or mail. Inquiry must include student's name, date of birth, social security number. Employers may obtain transcripts upon written request accompanied by a $2.00 fee and a signed release from the student. Requests should be directed to: Registrar's Office.

A comprehensive institution with a medical school, with an enrollment of 3,275. Highest level of offering: master's
ACCREDITATIONS: SC ARCH DIET ENG MT NUR OT RAD SW VET

Tyler Junior College

PO Box 9020
Tyler, TX 75711
(903) 510-2404
Fax (903) 510-2634

Will confirm attendance and degree by phone, fax or mail. Inquiry must include student's name, social security number. Employers may obtain transcripts upon written request accompanied by a $1.00 fee and a signed release from the student. Requests should be directed to: Registrar's Office.

A multiprogram two-year institution, with an enrollment of 8,000. Highest level of offering: two years but less than four years.
ACCREDITATIONS: SC DH MLTAD RAD RSTH RSTHT

U

Ulster County Community College

Stone Ridge, NY 12484
(914) 687-5075

Will confirm attendance and degree by phone or mail. Inquiry must include student's name, social security number. Requests should be directed to: Registrar's Office. Employers may obtain transcripts upon written request accompanied by a $2.00 fee and a signed release from the student.

A multiprogram two-year institution, with an enrollment of 2,900. Highest level of offering: one year but less than four years.
ACCREDITATIONS: M NY

Umpqua Community College

PO Box 967
Roseburg, OR 97470
(503) 440-4604

Will confirm attendance and degree by phone or mail. Inquiry must include student's name, social security number, years attended. Employers may obtain transcripts upon written request accompanied by a $2.00 fee and a signed release from the student. Requests should be directed to: Admissions Office.

A multiprogram two-year institution, with an enrollment of 1,394. Highest level of offering: one year but less than four years.
ACCREDITATIONS: NW

Union College

3800 South 48th Street
Lincoln, NE 68506
(402) 486-2509
Fax (402) 486-2895

Will confirm attendance and degree by phone, fax or mail. Inquiry must include student's name, social security number, years attended. Employers may obtain transcripts upon written request accompanied by a $2.00 fee and a signed release from the student. Requests should be directed to: Registrar's Office.

A general baccalaureate institution, with an enrollment of 620. Highest level of offering: four or five year baccalaureate.
ACCREDITATIONS: NCA NUR SW TED

Union College

310 College Street
Barbourville, KY 40906
(606) 546-4151 Ext. 207

Will confirm attendance and degree by phone or mail. Inquiry must include student's name, date of birth, social security number, years attended. Employers may obtain transcripts upon written request accompanied by a $3.00 fee and a signed release from the student.

A school of education, with an enrollment of 1,050. Highest level of offering: beyond master's but less than doctorate.
ACCREDITATIONS: SC

Union College

Whitaker House
Schenectady, NY 12308
(518) 370-6109

Will confirm attendance and degree by phone or mail. Inquiry must include student's name, years attended. Employers may obtain transcripts upon written request accompanied by a $2.00 fee and a signed release from the student. Requests should be directed to: Registrar's Office.

A comprehensive institution with no medical school, with an enrollment of 3,288. Highest level of offering: doctorate.

ACCREDITATIONS: M ENG HSA NY

Union County College

1033 Springfield Avenue
Cranford, NJ 07016
(201) 709-7134
Fax (908) 709-0527

Will confirm attendance and degree by mail. Inquiry must include student's name, social security number, release, years attended. Employers may obtain transcripts upon written request accompanied by a $4.00 fee and a signed release from the student.

A multiprogram two-year institution, with an enrollment of 10,000. Highest level of offering: one year but less than four years.

ACCREDITATIONS: M DA DH DT MAC MLTAD MRT PTAA RSTH

Union for Experimenting Colleges and Universities

440 E. McMellon
Cincinnati, OH 45206-1947
(513) 861-6400

Will confirm attendance and degree by phone or mail. Inquiry must include student's name, social security number. Employers may obtain transcripts upon written request accompanied by a $5.00 fee and a signed release from the student. Requests should be directed to: Registrar's Office.

A doctoral-level institution with no medical school, with an enrollment of 592. Highest level of offering: doctorate.

ACCREDITATIONS: NH

Union Theological Seminary in Virginia

Attn: Registrar's Office
3401 Brook Road
Richmond, VA 23227
(804) 355-0671 Ext. 233

Will confirm attendance and degree by phone or mail. Inquiry must include student's name, social security number. Employers may obtain transcripts upon written request accompanied by a $3.00 fee and a signed release from the student.

A school of philosophy, religion and theology, with an enrollment of 257. Highest level of offering: doctorate.

ACCREDITATIONS: SC THEOL

Union Theological Seminary

3041 Broadway
New York, NY 10027
(212) 280-1555

Will confirm attendance and degree by phone or mail. Inquiry must include student's name, years attended. Employers may obtain transcripts upon written request accompanied by a $2.00 fee and a signed release from the student. Requests should be directed to: Registrar's Office.

A school of philosophy, religion and theology, with an enrollment of 400. Highest level of offering: doctorate.

ACCREDITATIONS: M NY THEOL

Union University

Highway 45 By Pass-North
Jackson, TN 38305
(901) 668-1818 Ext. 305

Will confirm attendance and degree by phone or mail. Inquiry must include student's name, social security number, years attended. Employers may obtain transcripts upon written request accompanied by a $1.00 fee and a signed release from the student. Requests should be directed to: Registrar's Office.

A general baccalaureate institution, with an enrollment of 2,211. Highest level of offering: master's.

ACCREDITATIONS: SC ADNUR MUS NUR

United Education & Software

(Formerly National Technical Schools)
456 W. Martin Luther King
Los Angeles, CA 90037
(213) 234-9061
Fax (213) 234-9061 or 233-8433

Will confirm attendance and degree by mail or fax. Inquiry must include student's name, social security number, years attended, release. Requests should be directed to: Education Department. Employers may obtain transcripts upon written request accompanied by a signed release from the student.

A two-year institution newly admitted to NCES, with an enrollment of 700. Highest level of offering: one year but less than four years.

ACCREDITATIONS: NATTS

United Electronics Institute of Florida

Attn: Registrar
3924 Coconut Palm Drive
Tampa, FL 33619
(813) 626-2999 Ext. 74

Will confirm attendance and degree by mail. Inquiry must include student's name, social security number, release. Employers may obtain transcripts upon written request accompanied by a $3.00 fee and a signed release from the student.

A single program two-year institution, with an enrollment of 600. Highest level of offering: one year but less than four years.

ACCREDITATIONS: NATTS

United States International University

10455 Pomerado Road
San Diego, CA 92131
(619) 693-4541

Will confirm attendance and degree by phone or mail. Inquiry must include student's name, date of birth. Employers may obtain transcripts upon written request accompanied by a $4.00 fee and a signed release from the student. Requests should be directed to: Registrar's Office.

A doctoral-level institution with no medical school, with an enrollment of 2,539. Highest level of offering: doctorate.

ACCREDITATIONS: WC DANCE

United States Sports Academy

One Academy Drive
Daphne, AL 36526
(205) 626-3303 Ext. 124

Will confirm attendance and degree by phone or mail. Inquiry must include student's name, social security number. Only students may obtain transcripts. $5.00 fee.

A bachelor's or higher institution newly admitted to NCES, with an enrollment of 174. Highest level of offering: master's.

ACCREDITATIONS: SC

United Talmudical Academy of Monsey

206 Viola Road
PO Box 188
Monsey, NY 10952
(914) 425-6758

Will confirm attendance and degree by phone or mail. Inquiry must include student's name. Employers may obtain transcripts upon written request accompanied by a signed release from the student.

A specialized non-degree granting institution, with an enrollment of 669. Highest level of offering: graduate non-degree granting.

ACCREDITATIONS: 3IC RABN

United Theological Seminary

3000 Fifth Street North West
New Brighton, MN 55112
(612) 633-4311

Will confirm attendance and degree by mail. Inquiry must include student's name, social security number, years attended. Employers may obtain transcripts upon written request accompanied by a $3.00 fee and a signed release from the student.

A school of philosophy, religion and theology, with an enrollment of 250. Highest level of offering: doctorate.

ACCREDITATIONS: NCA ATS

United Theological Seminary

1810 Harvard Boulevard
Dayton, OH 45406
(513) 278-5817 Ext. 159

Will confirm attendance and degree by phone or mail. Inquiry must include student's name. Employers may obtain transcripts upon written request accompanied by a $2.00 fee and a signed release from the student.

A school of philosophy, religion and theology, with an enrollment of 524. Highest level of offering: doctorate.
ACCREDITATIONS: NH THEOL

United Wesleyan College

1414 East Cedar Street
Allentown, PA 18103
(215) 439-8709

Will confirm attendance and degree by phone or mail. Inquiry must include student's name, social security number, years attended. Employers may obtain transcripts upon written request accompanied by a $2.00 fee and a signed release from the student. Requests should be directed to: Registrar's Office.

A school of philosophy, religion and theology, with an enrollment of 223. Highest level of offering: four or five year baccalaureate.
ACCREDITATIONS: M BI

Unity College

R R S78 Box 1
Unity, ME 04988
(207) 948-3131 Ext. 244
Fax (207) 948-5626

Will confirm attendance and degree by phone or mail. Inquiry must include student's name. Employers may obtain transcripts upon written request accompanied by a $5.00 fee and a signed release from the student.

A general baccalaureate institution, with an enrollment of 420. Highest level of offering: four or five year baccalaureate.
ACCREDITATIONS: EH

University of Akron Central Office

302 East Buchtel Avenue
Akron, OH 44325
(216) 972-7111
Fax (216) 972-6097

Will confirm attendance and degree by phone (9:00a.m. -11:00a.m. and 2:00p.m.-4:00p.m. Central time), or mail. Inquiry must include student's name, date of birth, social security number, years attended. Employers may obtain transcripts upon written request accompanied by a $4.00 fee and a signed release from the student.

University of Akron Main Campus

PO Box 2230
Akron, OH 44309-2230
(216) 972-7834
Fax (216) 972-6097

Will confirm attendance and degree by phone, fax or mail. Inquiry must include student's name, date of birth, social security number, years attended. Employers may obtain transcripts upon written request accompanied by a $4.00 fee and a signed release from the student.

A doctoral-level institution with no medical school, with an enrollment of 26,644. Highest level of offering: doctorate.
ACCREDITATIONS: NH ART AUD BUS DIET ENG ENGT LAW MUS NUR RSTH SP SW TED

University of Akron Wayne General and Technical College

c/o University of Akron, Office of Registrar
PO Box 2230
Akron, OH 44309-2230
(216) 972-7834
Fax (216) 972-6097

Records are held at Main Campus at the above address. Will confirm attendance and degree by phone, fax or mail. Inquiry must include student's name, social security number. Employers may obtain transcripts upon written request accompanied by a $4.00 fee and a signed release from the student.

A multiprogram two-year institution, with an enrollment of 28,241. Highest level of offering: one year but less than four years.
ACCREDITATIONS: NH

University of Alabama at Birmingham

University Center
Birmingham, AL 35294
(205) 934-8222

Will confirm attendance and degree by phone or mail. Inquiry must include student's name, date of birth, social security number, years attended. Employers may obtain transcripts upon written request accompanied by a $3.00 fee and a signed release from the student.

A doctoral-level institution with a medical school, with an enrollment of 15,508.
ACCREDITATIONS: SC ANEST BBT BUS CYTO DA DENT DH DT ENG DIETI HSA TED BUSA IPSY MAC MED MLTAD MRA MRT MT NMT NUR OPT OT PH PTA PTAA RAD RSTH RTT SURGA SW

University of Alabama in Huntsville

116 University Center
Huntsville, AL 35899
(205) 895-6750
Fax (205) 895-6073

Will confirm attendance and degree by phone or mail. Inquiry must include student's name, date of birth, social security number. Employers may obtain transcripts upon written request accompanied by a signed release from the student. Requests should be directed to: Records Office.

A comprehensive research institution with no medical school, with an enrollment of 8,700. Highest level of offering: doctorate.
ACCREDITATIONS: SACS EMT ENG NUR ACS NASM AACSB

University of Alabama in Tuscaloosa

Records Office
Box 870134
Tuscaloosa, AL 35487-0134
(205) 348-4886

Will confirm attendance and degree by phone or mail. Inquiry must include student's name, social security number. Employers may obtain transcripts upon written request accompanied by a $3.00 fee and a signed release from the student. Requests should be directed to: Records Office.

University of Alaska Anchorage

3211 Providence Drive
Anchorage, AK 99508
(907) 786-4829
Fax (907) 786-1465

Will confirm attendance and degree by phone, fax or mail. Inquiry must include student's name, social security number, years attended, release. Employers may obtain transcripts upon written request by student accompanied by a $4.00 fee (if faxed, send original with fee.) and a signed release from the student. Requests should be directed to: Student Records Office.

A comprehensive institution with no medical school, with an enrollment of 20,000. Highest level of offering: master's.
ACCREDITATIONS: NW NUR SW

University of Alaska Fairbanks Kuskokwim Campus

Box 368
Fairbanks, AK 99559
(907) 543-4562

Will confirm attendance and degree by phone or mail. Inquiry must include student's name, date of birth, social security number, years attended. Employers may obtain transcripts upon written request accompanied by a $3.00 fee and a signed release from the student.

A multiprogram two-year institution, with an enrollment of 325. Highest level of offering: One year but less than four years.
ACCREDITATIONS: NW ENG MUS SW JOUR

University of Alaska Fairbanks

Suite 102 Signers Hall
Fairbanks, AK 99775
(907) 474-7821

Will confirm attendance and degree by phone or mail. Inquiry must include student's name, date of birth, social security number, year graduated. Employers may obtain transcripts upon written request accompanied by a $3.00 fee and a signed release from the student. Requests should be directed to: Records Department.

A comprehensive institution with no medical school, with an enrollment of 6,927. Highest level of offering: doctorate.
ACCREDITATIONS: NW ENG MUS SW JOUR

University of Alaska Southeast

11120 Glacier Highway
Juneau, AK 99801
(907) 789-4561

Will confirm attendance and degree by phone or mail. Inquiry must include student's name, social security number. Employers may obtain transcripts upon written request accompanied by a $5.00 fee and a signed release from the student.

A general baccalaureate institution, with an enrollment of 2,500 Highest level of offering: beyond master's but less than doctorate.

ACCREDITATIONS: NW

University of Alaska Southeast Sitka Campus

(Formerly Islands Community College)
1332 Seward Avenue
Sitka, AK 99835
(907) 747-6653

Will confirm attendance and degree by phone or mail. Inquiry must include student's name, date of birth, social security number, years attended. Employers may obtain transcripts upon written request accompanied by a $2.00 fee and a signed release from the student.

A general baccalaureate institution, with an enrollment of 1,400. Highest level of offering: one year but less than four years.

ACCREDITATIONS: NW

University of Albuquerque

Student Service Center
Albuquerque, NM 87131
(505) 277-2916 or 277-4214

Records are maintained by the University of New Mexico. Contact the above address for information. Will confirm attendance and degree by phone or mail. Inquiry must include student's name, social security number, years attended. Employers may obtain transcripts upon written request accompanied by a $3.00 fee and a signed release from the student. Requests should be directed to: Records Office–Room 250.

A general baccalaureate institution, with an enrollment of 1,181. Highest level of offering: four or five year baccalaureate.

ACCREDITATIONS: NH ADNUR RAD RSTH

University of Arizona

3rd Admissions Bldg., 305
Tucson, AZ 85721
(602) 621-3393

Will confirm attendance and degree by phone or mail. Inquiry must include student's name, date of birth, social security number. Employers may obtain transcripts upon written request accompanied by a $3.00 fee and a signed release from the student. Requests should be directed to: Student Records Office.

A doctoral-level institution with a medical school, with an enrollment of 36,271. Highest level of offering: doctorate.

ACCREDITATIONS: NH ARCH AUD BUS CLPSY DIETI ENG FOR IPSY JOUR LAW LIB TED LSAR MED MT MUS NMT NUR PHAR RTT SCPSY SP DANCE

University of Arkansas

Room 222, Administration Bldg.
Fayetteville, AR 72701
(501) 575-5451

Will confirm attendance and degree by phone or mail. Inquiry must include student's name, social security number, years attended. Employers may obtain transcripts upon written request accompanied by a $3.00 fee and a signed release from the student. Requests should be directed to: Registrar's Office.

A doctoral-level institution with no medical school, with an enrollment of 14,882. Highest level of offering: doctorate.

ACCREDITATIONS: NH ADNUR ARCH BUS CLPSY ENG JOUR LAW LSAR MUS SP TED

University of Arkansas at Little Rock

2801 South University
Little Rock, AR 72204-1099
(501) 569-3110

Will confirm attendance and degree by mail. Inquiry must include student's name, student ID number, release. Employers may obtain transcripts upon written request accompanied by a $3.00 fee and a signed release from the student. Requests should be directed to: Registrar's Office.

A comprehensive institution with no medical school, with an enrollment of 11,700. Highest level of offering: master's.

ACCREDITATIONS: NH ADNUR AUD BUS JOUR LAW MUS SW TED ENGT

University of Arkansas at Monticello

PO Box 3598
Monticello, AR 71655
(501) 460-1035

Will confirm attendance and degree by mail. Inquiry must include student's name, social security number, years attended, release. Employers may obtain transcripts upon written request accompanied by a $2.00 fee and a signed release from the student. Requests should be directed to: Registrar's Office.

A general baccalaureate institution, with an enrollment of 2,265. Highest level of offering: master's.

ACCREDITATIONS: NH ADNUR FOR TED

University of Arkansas at Pine Bluff

PO Box 17
Pine Bluff, AR 71601
(501) 541-6544

Will confirm attendance and degree by phone or mail. Inquiry must include student's name, years attended, social securtiy number. Employers may obtain transcripts upon written request accompanied by a $2.00 fee and a signed release from the student.

A general baccalaureate institution, with an enrollment of 3,409. Highest level of offering: four or five year baccalaureate.

ACCREDITATIONS: NH MUS NUR TED

University of Arkansas for Medical Sciences

4301 West Markham
Slot 601
Little Rock, AR 72205
(501) 686-5000

Will confirm attendance and degree by phone or mail. Inquiry must include student's name, social security number. Requests should be directed to: Registrar of Graduate School. Employers may obtain transcripts upon written request accompanied by a $1.00 fee and a signed release from the student.

A medical school, with an enrollment of 1,356. Highest level of offering: doctorate.

ACCREDITATIONS: NH CYTO DH DIETI IPSY MED MT NUR PHAR RAD RSTH SP SURGT

University of Arts

Broad and Pine
Philadelphia, PA 19102
(215) 875-4848

Will confirm attendance and degree by phone or mail. Inquiry must include student's name, social security number. Employers may obtain transcripts upon written request accompanied by a $5.00 fee and a signed release from the student. Requests should be directed to: Registrar's Office.

A visual and performing arts school, with an enrollment of 1,527. Highest level of offering: master's.

ACCREDITATIONS: M ART

University of Baltimore

1420 North Charles Street
Baltimore, MD 21201-1126
(301) 625-3333

Will confirm attendance and degree by phone or mail. Inquiry must include student's name, date of birth, social security number, years attended. Employers may obtain transcripts upon written request accompanied by a $3.00 fee and a signed release from the student. Requests should be directed to: Registrar's Office.

A comprehensive institution with no medical school, with an enrollment of 5,178. Highest level of offering: master's.

ACCREDITATIONS: M BUS LAW

University of Bridgeport

Rennell Hall
Bridgeport, CT 06601
(203) 576-4155
Fax (203) 576-4653

Will confirm attendance and degree by phone, fax or mail. Inquiry must include student's name, social security number, years attended. Employers may obtain transcripts upon written request accompanied by a $5.00 fee and a signed release from the student. Requests should be directed to: Office of the Registrar.

A comprehensive institution with no medical school, with an enrollment of 3,904. Highest level of offering: doctorate.

ACCREDITATIONS: EH ADNUR ART BUS DH ENG LAW MFCD MUS

University of California–Berkeley

123 Sproul Hall
Berkeley, CA 94720
(510) 642-1883
Fax (510) 643-9201

Will confirm attendance and degree by phone or mail. Inquiry must include student's name, date of birth, social security number, years attended. Direct inquiries to: Office of the Registrar, Verifications Unit, 123 Sproul Hall, Berkley, CA 94720. Employers may obtain transcripts upon written request accompanied by a $3.00 fee (for 5-10 day turnaround or $8.00 for 24 hour turnaround) and a signed release from the student. Requests should be directed to: Office of the Registrar, Records Division, 128 Sproul Hall, Berkley, CA 94720. .

A doctoral-level institution with no medical school, with an enrollment of 31,007. Highest level of offering: doctorate.

ACCREDITATIONS: WC ARCH BUS CLPSY DIETI ENG FOR HSA JOUR LAW OPTR LIB LSAR DIET OPT PH SCPSY SW

University of California–Davis

Office of Registrar
Room 124, Mrak Hall
Davis, CA 95616-8692
(916) 752-2973

Will confirm attendance and degree by phone or mail. Inquiry must include student's name, date of birth, social security number, years attended. Employers may obtain transcripts upon written request accompanied by a $4.00 fee and a signed release from the student.

A doctoral-level institution with a medical school, with an enrollment of 23,500. Highest level of offering: doctorate.

ACCREDITATIONS: WC APCP ENG IPSY LAW LSAR MED MT NMT VET

University of California–Irvine

Irvine, CA 92717
(714) 856-6124
Fax (714) 856-7896

Will confirm attendance and degree by mail. Inquiry must include student's name, date of birth, social security number, years attended. Employers may obtain transcripts upon written request accompanied by a $3.00 fee and a signed release from the student. Check payable to Regents of U.C.

A doctoral-level institution with a medical school, with an enrollment of 18,000. Highest level of offering: doctorate.

ACCREDITATIONS: WC ENG IPSY MED MT

University of California–Los Angeles

405 Hilgard Avenue
Los Angeles, CA 90024
(213) 825-4671
Fax (213) 206-1728

Will confirm attendance and degree by phone, fax or mail. Inquiry must include student's name, date of birth, social security number, years attended. Employers may obtain transcripts upon written request accompanied by a $4.00 fee and a signed release from the student. Requests should be directed to: Registrar's Office.

A doctoral-level institution with a medical school, with an enrollment of 34,501. Highest level of offering: doctorate.

ACCREDITATIONS: WC ANEST ARCH BUS CLPSY DENT ENG FIDER HSA IPSY LAW LIB MED MICB MRA MT NUR PH RSTH SW DANCE

University of California–Riverside

Riverside, CA 92521
(714) 787-3401
Fax (714) 787-7368

Will confirm attendance and degree by phone or mail. Inquiry must include student's name, social security number. Employers may obtain transcripts upon written request accompanied by a $3.00 fee and a signed release from the student. Requests should be directed to: Registrar's Office.

A doctoral-level institution with no medical school, with an enrollment of 8,890. Highest level of offering: doctorate.

ACCREDITATIONS: WC

University of California–San Diego

La Jolla, CA 92093
(619) 534-3150

Will confirm attendance and degree by phone or mail. Inquiry must include student's name, date of birth, social security number, release. Employers may obtain transcripts upon written request accompanied by a $3.00 fee and a signed release from the student. Requests should be directed to: Registrar's Office.

A doctoral-level institution with a medical school, with an enrollment of 14,295. Highest level of offering: doctorate.

ACCREDITATIONS: WC EMT ENG MED MIDWF RTT

University of California–San Francisco

Registrar and Admissions Office
500 Parnassus Ave., MU200
San Francisco, CA 94143-0244
(415) 476-8280
Fax (415) 476-9690

Will confirm attendance and degree by mail. Inquiry must include student's name, social security number, years attended. Employers may obtain transcripts upon written request accompanied by a $3.00 fee and a signed release from the student. Requests should be directed to: Registrar's Office.

A health sciences university, with an enrollment of 3,632. Highest level of offering: advanced professional degree.

ACCREDITATIONS: WC CYTO DENT DH DIETI IPSY MED MIDWF NMT NUR PHAR PTA PAST

University of California–Santa Barbara

1117 Cheadle Hall
Santa Barbara, CA 93106
(805) 893-7214

Will confirm attendance and degree by phone or mail. Inquiry must include student's name, date of birth, social security number. Employers may obtain transcripts upon written request accompanied by a $3.00 fee and a signed release from the student. Requests should be directed to: Registrar's Office.

A doctoral-level institution with no medical school, with an enrollment of 18,000. Highest level of offering: doctorate.

ACCREDITATIONS: WC AUD COPSY DANCE ENG SP

University of California–Santa Cruz

Santa Cruz, CA 95064
(408) 459-4412

Will confirm attendance and degree by mail. Inquiry must include student's name, social security number, years attended. Requests should be directed to: Registrar's Office. Employers may obtain transcripts upon written request accompanied by a $10.00 fee and a signed release from the student. Requests should be directed to: Transcripts Office.

A doctoral-level institution with no medical school, with an enrollment of 9,784. Highest level of offering: doctorate.

ACCREDITATIONS: WC

University of California Hastings College of Law

200 Mcallister Street, Room 208
San Francisco, CA 94102
(415) 565-4613

Will confirm attendance and degree by mail. Inquiry must include student's name, social security number, years attended. Employers may obtain transcripts upon written request accompanied by a $5.00 fee and a signed release from the student. Requests should be directed to: Records Office.

A law school, with an enrollment of 1,370. Highest level of offering: first professional degree.

ACCREDITATIONS: LAW

University of Central Arkansas

201 Donaghey
Conway, AR 72035-0001
(501) 450-3127
Fax (501) 450-5734

Will confirm attendance and degree by phone, fax or mail. Inquiry must include student's name, social security number. Employers may obtain transcripts upon written request accompanied by a $3.00 fee and a signed release from the student. Requests should be directed to: Registrar's Office.

A comprehensive institution with no medical school, with an enrollment of 8,500. Highest level of offering: beyond master's but less than doctorate.

ACCREDITATIONS: NH BUS MUS NUR OT PTA TED

University of Central Florida

PO Box 25000
Orlando, FL 32816
(407) 275-2531

Will confirm attendance and degree by phone or mail. Inquiry must include student's name, social security number, years attended. Employers may obtain transcripts upon written request accompanied by a signed release from the student. Requests should be directed to: Records Office.

A comprehensive institution with no medical school, with an enrollment of 20,000. Highest level of offering: doctorate.

ACCREDITATIONS: SC BUS ENG ENGT MRA MT MUS NUR RAD RSTH SW

University of Central Oklahoma

(Formerly Central State University)
100 North University Drive
Edmond, OK 73060-0151
(405) 341-2980 Ext. 2331
Fax (405) 341-4964

Will confirm attendance and degree by phone, fax or mail. Inquiry must include student's name, date of birth, social security number, years attended. Requests should be direct to: Academic Records. Employers may obtain transcripts upon written request accompanied by a $3.00 fee and a signed release from the student. Requests should be directed to: Academic Records.

A comprehensive institution with no medical school, with an enrollment of 14,327. Highest level of offering: master's.

ACCREDITATIONS: NCA FUSER NUR TED NCATE

University of Central Texas

(Formerly American Technological University)
PO Box 1416
Killeen, TX 76540-1416
(817) 526-8262

Will confirm attendance and degree by phone or mail. Inquiry must include student's name, social security number, years attended. Employer may obtain transcripts upon written request accompanied by a $2.00 fee and a signed release from the student. Requests should be directed to: Registrar's Office. A comprehensive institution with no medical school, with and enrollment of 600. Highest level of offering: master's.

ACCREDITATIONS: SC

University of Charleston

2300 MacCorkle Avenue South East
Charleston, WV 25304
(304) 357-4740

Will confirm attendance and degree by phone or mail. Inquiry must include student's name, social security number, years attended. Employers may obtain transcripts upon written request accompanied by a $4.00 fee and a signed release from the student. Requests should be directed to: Registrar's Office.

A general baccalaureate institution, with an enrollment of 1,500. Highest level of offering: master's.

ACCREDITATIONS: NH ADNUR RAD RSTH

University of Chicago

5801 South Ellis Avenue
Chicago, IL 60637
(312) 702-7891

Will confirm attendance and degree by phone or mail. Inquiry must include student's name, date of birth, social security number. Employers may obtain transcripts upon written request accompanied by a $5.00 fee and a signed release from the student. Requests should be directed to: Registrar's Office.

A doctoral-level institution with a medical school, with an enrollment of 9,287. Highest level of offering: doctorate.

ACCREDITATIONS: NH BUS CYTO HSA HT LAW LIB MED RSTH SW THEOL BUSA

University of Cincinnati Clermont General and Technical College

725 College Drive
Batavia, OH 45103
(513) 732-5200

Will confirm attendance and degree by mail. Inquiry must include student's name, social security number, years attended. Employers may obtain transcripts upon written request accompanied by a $4.00 fee and a signed release from the student. Requests should be directed to: Student Records.

A multiprogram two-year institution, with an enrollment of 1,206. Highest level of offering: one year but less than four years.

ACCREDITATIONS: NH

University of Cincinnati Main Campus

103 Beecher Hall
Cincinnati, OH 45221-0060
(513) 556-9912

Will confirm attendance and degree by phone or mail. Inquiry must include student's name, date of birth, social security number, years attended. Employers may obtain transcripts upon written request accompanied by a $4.00 fee and a signed release from the student. Requests should be directed to: Student Records.

A doctoral-level institution with a medical school, with an enrollment of 30,830. Highest level of offering: doctorate.

ACCREDITATIONS: NH ARCH ART AUD BBT BUS CLPSY DIETI ENG ENGT FIDER IPSY TED LAW MED MT MUS NMT NUR PHAR RAD SCPSY SP SW

University of Cincinnati Raymond Walters College

9555 Plainfield Road
Blue Ash, OH 45236
(513) 745-5600

Will confirm attendance and degree by phone or mail. Inquiry must include student's name, social security number, years attended. Employers may obtain transcripts upon written request accompanied by a $4.00 fee and a signed release from the student.

A multiprogram two-year institution, with an enrollment of 4,000. Highest level of offering: one year but less than four years.

ACCREDITATIONS: NH ADNUR ADVET DH RTT

University of Colorado at Boulder

Transcript Request
Campus Box 68
Boulder, CO 80309-0068
(303) 492-6907

Will confirm attendance and degree by mail. Inquiry must include student's name, date of birth, social security number, years attended, release. Direct inquiries to: Academic Records. Employers may obtain transcripts upon written request accompanied by a signed release from the student. Requests should be directed to: Transcript Department.

A doctoral-level institution with no medical school, with an enrollment of 22,299. Highest level of offering: doctorate.

ACCREDITATIONS: NH AUD BUS CLPSY ENG JOUR LAW MUS PHAR SP TED

University of Colorado at Colorado Springs

Austin Bluffs Parkway–PO Box 7150
Colorado Springs, CO 80933-7150
(719) 593-3361 Ext. 387

Will confirm attendance and degree by phone or mail. Inquiry must include student's name, social security number. Requests should be directed to: Records Office. Employers may obtain transcripts upon written request accompanied by a signed release from the student.

A comprehensive institution with no medical school, with an enrollment of 5,800. Highest level of offering: doctorate

ACCREDITATIONS: BUS NH ENG TED

University of Colorado at Denver

PO Box 173364
Campus Box 167
Denver, CO 80217-3364
(303) 556-2388
Fax (303) 556-4838

Will confirm attendance and degree by phone or mail. Inquiry must include student's name, social security number. Employers may obtain transcripts upon written request accompanied by a signed release from the student. Requests should be directed to: Records Department.

A comprehensive institution with no medical school, with an enrollment of 10,790. Highest level of offering: doctorate.

ACCREDITATIONS: NH ARCH ENG LSAR MUS TED

University of Colorado Health Sciences Center

Student Admissions and Records
Box A054–4200 East 9th Avenue
Denver, CO 80262
(303) 270-7676
Fax (303) 270-5969

Will confirm attendance and degree by phone or mail. Inquiry must include student's name, social security number. Employers may obtain transcripts upon written request accompanied by a signed release from the student.

A medical center, with an enrollment of 2,092. Highest level of offering: doctorate.

ACCREDITATIONS: NH APCP DENT DH HSA IPSY MED MIDWF MT NUR PTA CHPM PAST

University of Connecticut School of Medicine

Registrar's Office
263 Farmington Avenue
Farmington, CT 06030-1905
(203) 679-2153

Will confirm attendance and degree by phone or mail. Inquiry must include student's name. Employers may obtain transcripts upon written request accompanied by a signed release from the student.

A medical school, with an enrollment of 345. Highest level of offering: first professional degree.

ACCREDITATIONS: DENT MED MICB IPSY

University of Connecticut

233 Glenbrook Road–Wilber Cross
Bldg.–Room 153
Storrs, CT 06269-4077
(203) 486-3327

Will confirm attendance and degree by phone or mail. Inquiry must include student's name, social security number. Employers may obtain transcripts upon written request accompanied by a $3.00 fee and a signed release from the student. Requests should be directed to: Registrar's Offic, U77T.

A doctoral-level institution with a medical school, and an enrollment of 22,976. Highest level of offering: doctorate.

ACCREDITATIONS: EH ART AUD BUS CHPM CLPSY CYTO DIET ENG ENGT LAW MFCD TED MUS NUR PHAR PTA SP SW BUSA

University of Dallas

1845 East Northgate Drive
Irving, TX 75061-4799
(214) 721-5221

Will confirm attendance and degree by phone or mail. Inquiry must include student's name, social security number. Employers may obtain transcripts upon written request accompanied by a $2.00 fee and a signed release from the student.

A comprehensive institution with no medical school, with an enrollment of 2,466. Highest level of offering: doctorate.

ACCREDITATIONS: SC

University of Dayton

300 College Park
Dayton, OH 45469
(513) 229-4141
Fax (513) 229-4545

Will confirm attendance and degree by phone or mail. Inquiry must include student's name, social security number, years attended. Employers may obtain transcripts upon written request accompanied by a $2.00 fee and a signed release from the student.

A comprehensive institution with no medical school, with an enrollment of 10,693. Highest level of offering: doctorate.

ACCREDITATIONS: NH BUS ENG ENGT LAW MUS SW TED

University of Delaware

Newark, DE 19716
(302) 831-2131

Will confirm attendance and degree by phone or mail. Inquiry must include student's name, social security number. Employers may obtain transcripts upon written request accompanied by a $4.00 fee and a signed release from the student. Requests should be directed to: Records & Transcripts Office.

A doctoral-level institution with no medical school, with an enrollment of 17,562. Highest level of offering: doctorate.

ACCREDITATIONS: M BUS CLPSY DIET ENG ENGT IPSY MT MUS NUR PTA THEA BUSA

University of Denver

University Park
2199 S. University Blvd.
Denver, CO 80208
(303) 871-2000

Will confirm attendance and degree by mail. Inquiry must include student's name, years attended, release. Employers may obtain transcripts upon written request accompanied by a $3.00 fee and a signed release from the student. Requests should be directed to: Registrar's Office–Room 106.

A doctoral-level institution with no medical school, with an enrollment of 8,019. Highest level of offering: doctorate.

ACCREDITATIONS: NH ART AUD BUS CLPSY LAW MUS NUR SP SW

University of Denver College of Law

7039 E. 18th Ave.
Denver, CO 80220
(303) 871-6132

Will confirm attendance and degree by phone or mail. Inquiry must include student's name, years attended. Employers may obtain transcripts upon written request by student accompanied by a $2.00 fee and a signed release from the student.

A doctoral-level institution with no medical school, with an enrollment of 1,000. Highest level of offering: doctorate.

ACCREDITATIONS: NH ART AUD BUS CLPSY LAW MUS NUR SP SW

University of Detroit Mercy–McNichols Campus

4001 West McNichols Road
Detroit, MI 48221
(313) 927-1313
Fax (313) 993-1285

Will confirm attendance and degree by phone or mail. Inquiry must include student's name, date of birth, years attended. Employers may obtain transcripts upon written request accompanied by a $3.00 fee and a signed release from the student.

A doctoral-level institution with a dental school, with an enrollment of 7,888. Highest level of offering: doctorate.

ACCREDITATIONS: NH ANEST ARCH BUS DENT DH ENG LAW NMT SW NUR PSY

University of Detroit Mercy–Outer Drive Campus

(Formerly Mercy College of Detroit)
8200 West Outer Drive
Detroit, MI 48219
(313) 993-6160

Will confirm attendance and degree by phone or mail. Inquiry must include student's name, social security number, years attended. Employers may obtain transcripts upon written request accompanied by a $2.00 fee and a signed release from the student. Requests should be directed to: Registrar's Office.

A general baccalaureate institution, with an enrollment of 2,445. Highest level of offering: master's.

ACCREDITATIONS: NH ANEST APCP DIET MLTAD MRA MRT MT NUR RSTH SW

University of Dubuque

Attn: Registrar
2000 University Avenue
Dubuque, IA 52001
(319) 589-3178
Fax (319) 556-8633

Will confirm attendance and degree by phone. Inquiry must include student's name, social security number, years attended. Employers may obtain transcripts upon written request accompanied by a $5.00 fee and a signed release from the student.

A general baccalaureate institution, with an enrollment of 1,200. Highest level of offering: master's.

ACCREDITATIONS: NH NUR SW THEOL

University of Evansville

1800 Lincoln Avenue
Evansville, IN 47722
(812) 479-2267

Will confirm attendance and degree by phone or mail. Inquiry must include student's name, social security number. Employers may obtain transcripts upon written request accompanied by a $1.00 fee and a signed release from the student.

A comprehensive institution with no medical school, with an enrollment of 3,300. Highest level of offering: master's.

ACCREDITATIONS: NH ADNUR ENG MUS NUR PTA PTAA TED

University of Florida

Office of Registrar
222 Criser Hall
Gainesville, FL 32611-2051
(904) 392-1374 Ext. 229
Fax (904) 392-3987

Will confirm attendance and degree by phone or mail. Request may be made via fax. Response will not be faxed. Inquiry must include student's name, date of birth, social security number, years attended. Employers may obtain transcripts upon written request accompanied by a signed release from the student. Requests should be directed to: Attn: Transcripts.

A doctoral-level institution with a medical school, with an enrollment of 35,496. Highest level of offering: doctorate.

ACCREDITATIONS: SC ANEST APCP ARCH AUD BUS CLPSY COPSY DENT DIET DIETI ENG TED VET BUSA FIDER FOR HSA IPSY JOUR LAW LSAR MED MT MUS NUR OT PHAR PTA SP MIDWF OMA

University of Georgia

Office of Registrar
105 Academic Building
Athens, GA 30602
(404) 542-4040

Will confirm attendance and degree by phone or mail. Inquiry must include student's name, social security number. Employers may obtain transcripts upon written request by student accompanied by a $2.00 fee and a signed release from the student.

A doctoral-level institution with a medical school, with an enrollment of 25,253. Highest level of offering: doctorate.

ACCREDITATIONS: SC ART AUD BUS CLPSY COPSY ENG FIDER FOR JOUR LAW LSAR TED VET MUS PHAR SCPSY SP SW THEA

University of Hartford

200 Bloomfield Avenue
West Hartford, CT 06117
(203) 243-4134

Will confirm attendance and degree by phone or mail. Inquiry must include student's name, date of birth, social security number, years attended. Employers may obtain transcripts upon written request accompanied by a $3.00 fee and a signed release from the student. Requests should be directed to: Verification Department.

A comprehensive institution with no medical school, with an enrollment of 7,611. Highest level of offering: doctorate.

ACCREDITATIONS: EH ART ENG ENGT MT MUS NUR RSTH TED

University of Hawaii at Hilo

Hilo, HI 96720-4091
(808) 933-3322

Will confirm attendance and degree by phone or mail. Inquiry must include student's name, date of birth, social security number, years attended. Employers may obtain transcripts upon written request accompanied by a $1.00 fee and a signed release from the student.

University of Hawaii at Hilo has programs in the baccalaureate degree level, a professional certification in education. Enrollment: 2,600.

ACCREDITATIONS: WC

University of Hawaii at Manoa

Office of Admissions & Records
2530 Dole Street, C200
Honolulu, HI 96822
(808) 956-4445

Will confirm attendance and degree by phone or mail. Inquiry must include student's name, date of birth, social security number, years attended. Employers may obtain transcripts upon written request accompanied by a $3.00 fee and a signed release from the student.

A doctoral-level institution with a medical school, with an enrollment of 20,000. Highest level of offering: doctorate.

ACCREDITATIONS: WC ARCH BUS CLPSY DH ENG JOUR LAW LIB ADNUR MED MT MUS NUR PH SW DANCE

University of Hawaii – West Oahu

96-043 Ala Ike
Pearl City, HI 96782
(808) 456-5921
Fax (808) 456-5208

Will confirm attendance and degree by phone or mail. Inquiry must include student's name, social security number. Employers may obtain transcripts upon written request by student accompanied by a $1.00 fee and a signed release from the student. Requests should be directed to: Registrar's Office.

A general baccalaureate institution, with an enrollment of 700. Highest level of offering: four or five year baccalaureate.

ACCREDITATIONS: WC

University of Health Sciences–Chicago Medical School

Registrar's Office
3333 Greenbay Road
North Chicago, IL 60064
(708) 578-3229

Will confirm attendance and degree by phone or mail. Inquiry must include student's name, social security number, years attended. Employers may obtain transcripts upon written request accompanied by a $3.00 fee and a signed release from the student.

A medical school, with an enrollment of 650. Highest level of offering: doctorate.

ACCREDITATIONS: NH CLPSY MED MT PTA PAST

University of Health Sciences–College of Osteopathic Medicine

2105 Independence Boulevard
Kansas City, MO 64124
(816) 221-9698
Fax (816) 283-2303

Will confirm attendance and degree by phone, fax or mail. Inquiry must include student's name, social security number, years attended, release. Employers may obtain transcripts upon written request accompanied by a $5.00 fee and a signed release from the student.

A medical school, with an enrollment of 515. Highest level of offering: first professional degree.

ACCREDITATIONS: OSTEO

University of Houston–Academic Records

4800 Calhoun
Houston, TX 77004
(713) 749-2937

Will confirm attendance and degree by phone or mail. Inquiry must include student's name, social security number. Employers may obtain transcripts upon written request accompanied by a $ 5.00 fee and a signed release from the student.

A doctoral-level institution with no medical school, with an enrollment of 31,095. Highest level of offering: doctorate.

ACCREDITATIONS: SC ARCH BUS CLPSY ENG ENGT LAW MUS OPT PHAR BUSA SP SW TED

University of Houston–Clear Lake

Office of the Registrar - Box 13
2700 Bay Area Boulevard
Houston, TX 77058
(713) 283-2525
Fax (713) 283-2534

Will confirm attendance and degree by phone or mail. Inquiry must include student's name, social security number. Employers may obtain transcripts upon written request accompanied by a signed release from the student. Requests should be directed to: Registrar's Office.

A comprehensive institution with no medical school, with an enrollment of 6,392. Highest level of offering: master's.

ACCREDITATIONS: SC BUS HSA MFCD TED

University of Houston–Victoria

2506 E. Red River
Victoria, TX 77901
(512) 576-3151 Ext. 222

Will confirm attendance and degree by phone or mail. Inquiry must include student's name, social security number. Employers may obtain transcripts upon written request accompanied by a $3.00 fee and a signed release from the student.

A school of education, with an enrollment of 1,191. Highest level of offering: master's.

ACCREDITATIONS: SC

University of Houston Downtown

One Main Street
Houston, TX 77002
(713) 221-8020

Will confirm attendance and degree by phone or mail. Inquiry must include student's name, date of birth, social security number. Employers may obtain transcripts upon written request accompanied by a $3.00 fee and a signed release from the student. Requests should be directed to: Records Department.

A business school, with an enrollment of 7,000. Highest level of offering: four or five year baccalaureate.

ACCREDITATIONS: SC ENGT

University of Idaho

Moscow, ID 83843
(208) 885-6731
Fax (208) 885-5752

Will confirm attendance and degree by phone, fax or mail. Inquiry must include student's name, social security number. Employers may obtain transcripts upon written request by student accompanied by a $2.00 fee and a signed release from the student. Requests should be directed to: Registrar's Office.

A doctoral-level institution with no medical school, with an enrollment of 8,970. Highest level of offering: doctorate.

ACCREDITATIONS: NW ARCH DIET ENG FOR LAW LSAR MUS TED

University of Illinois at Chicago

PO Box 5220
Chicago, IL 60680
(312) 996-4384

Will confirm attendance and degree by phone or mail. Inquiry must include student's name, social security number, years attended, release. Employers may obtain transcripts upon written request accompanied by a $2.00 fee and a signed release from the student.

A doctoral-level institution with a medical school, with an enrollment of 24,067. Highest level of offering: doctorate.

ACCREDITATIONS: NH ARCH ART BBT BUS CLPSY DIET DENT PTA ENG MED MRA MT NUR OT PH PHAR SW MIDWF

University of Illinois Champaign Urbana Campus

10 H.A.B.
506 South Wright Street
Urbana, IL 61801
(217) 333-0210
Fax (217) 333-3100

Will confirm attendance and degree by phone, fax or mail. Inquiry must include student's name, social security number or date of birth, years attended. Requests should be directed to: Admissions & Records. Employers may obtain transcripts upon written request accompanied by a $2.00 fee and a signed release from the student.

A doctoral-level institution with a medical school, with an enrollment of 36,139. Highest level of offering: doctorate.

ACCREDITATIONS: NH ARCH ART AUD BUS CHE CLPSY ENG FOR IPSY JOUR LAW TED VET BUSA LIB LSAR MUS SP SW DANCE

University of Indianapolis

1400 East Hanna Avenue
Indianapolis, IN 46227
(317) 788-3368 Ext. 3220

Will confirm attendance and degree by phone or mail. Inquiry must include student's name, date of birth, social security number. Employers may obtain transcripts upon written request by student accompanied by a $2.00 fee and a signed release from the student.

A comprehensive institution with no medical school, with an enrollment of 3,233. Highest level of offering: master's

ACCREDITATIONS: NH ADNUR MUS PRA TED

University of Iowa

Jessup Hall–Room 1
Iowa City, IA 52242
(319) 335-0230

Will confirm attendance and degree by phone. Inquiry must include student's name, social security number, years attended. Employers may obtain transcripts upon written request accompanied by a $3.00 fee and a signed release from the student. Requests should be directed to: Registrar's Office.

A doctoral-level institution with a medical school, with an enrollment of 30,798. Highest level of offering: doctorate.

ACCREDITATIONS: NH APCP AUD BUS CLPSY COPSY DENT DH DIETI ENG HSA PAST JOUR LAW LIB MED MT MUS NMT NUR PHAR PTA RAD RTT IPSY TED SP SW

University of Judaism

15600 Mulholland Dr
Los Angeles, CA 90077
(310) 476-9777 Ext. 296
Fax (310) 471-1278

Will confirm attendance and degree by phone or mail. Inquiry must include student's name, years attended. Employers may obtain transcripts upon written request accompanied by a $4.00 fee and a signed release from the student.

A specialized school, with an enrollment of 160. Highest level of offering: beyond master's but less than doctorate.

ACCREDITATIONS: WC

University of Kansas–Lawrence

122 Strong Hall
Lawrence, KS 66045
(913) 864-4422

Will confirm attendance and degree by phone or mail. Inquiry must include student's name, date of birth, social security number, years attended. Employers may obtain transcripts upon written request accompanied by a $3.00 fee and a signed release from the student. Requests should be directed to: Registrar's Office.

A doctoral-level institution with no medical school, with an enrollment of 29,000. Highest level of offering: doctorate.

ACCREDITATIONS: NH ARCH ART AUD BUS CLPSY COPSY ENG TED JOUR LAW MUS OT PHAR SCPSY SP SW THEA

University of Kansas Medical Center

39th & Rainbow Boulevard
Kansas City, KS 66103
(913) 588-7055

Will confirm attendance and degree by mail. Inquiry must include student's full name, social security number, years attended. Employers may obtain transcripts upon written request accompanied by a $3.00 fee and a signed release from the student.

A medical school, with an enrollment of 2,400. Highest level of offering: doctorate.

ACCREDITATIONS: NH ANEST CYTO DIETI MED MRA MT NMT NUR PTA RAD RSTH RTT SP

University of Kentucky-Lexington

Room 10 Funhouser Bldg.
Lexington, KY 40506-0054
(606) 257-3671
Fax (606) 257-7160

Will confirm attendance and degree by phone or fax. Inquiry must include student's name, date of birth, social security number. Employers may obtain transcripts upon written request accompanied by a $4.00 fee and a signed release from the student.

A doctoral-level institution with a medical school, with an enrollment of 20,637. Highest level of offering: doctorate.

ACCREDITATIONS: SC APCP ARCH RAD BUS CLPSY DENT DIET DIETI ENG FIDER TED JOUR LAW LIB LSAR MED MT MUS NMT NUR PHAR PTA RTT SW MIDWF FOR PAST

University of La Verne College of Law

(Formerly The College of Law University of San Fernando Valley)
5445 Balboa Blvd.
Encino, CA 91316
(818) 981-4529
Fax (818) 789-1557

Will confirm attendance and degree by phone or mail. Inquiry must include student's name, years attended. Employers may obtain transcripts upon written request accompanied by a $4.00 fee and a signed release from the student. Requests should be directed to the Registrar's Office.

A law school, with an enrollment of 260. Highest level of offering: first professional degree.

University of La Verne

1950 3rd Street
La Verne, CA 91750
(714) 593-3511 Ext. 4001

Will confirm attendance and degree by phone or mail. Inquiry must include student's name, social security number. Employers may obtain transcripts upon written request accompanied by a $5.00 fee and a signed release from the student.

A comprehensive institution with no medical school, with an enrollment of 6,900. Highest level of offering: doctorate.

ACCREDITATIONS: WC

University of Louisville

2211 South Brook
Louisville, KY 40292
(502) 588-6522

Will confirm attendance and degree by phone or mail. Inquiry must include student's name, social security number, years attended. Employers may obtain transcripts upon written request accompanied by a $4.00 fee and a signed release from the student. Requests should be directed to: Student Records & Transcript Office.

A doctoral-level institution with a medical school, with an enrollment of 23,000. Highest level of offering: doctorate.

ACCREDITATIONS: SACS TED AUD BUS CLPSY CYTO DA DENT DH ENG LAW PAST MED MT MUS NMT RAD RSTH SP PTA SW

University of Lowell

1 University Avenue
Lowell, MA 01854
(508) 934-4000 Ext. 2550

Will confirm attendance and degree by phone. Inquiry must include student's name, social security number, years attended. Employers may obtain transcripts upon written request accompanied by a $1.00 fee and a signed release from the student.

A comprehensive institution with no medical school, with an enrollment of 10,308. Highest level of offering: doctorate.

ACCREDITATIONS: EH ENG ENGT MT MUS NUR PTA TED

University of Maine at Augusta

University Heights
Augusta, ME 04330
(207) 621-3000 Ext. 3146

Will confirm attendance and degree by phone or mail. Inquiry must include student's name, date of birth. Employers may obtain transcripts upon written request accompanied by a $3.00 fee and a signed release from the student.

A multiprogram two-year institution, with an enrollment of 4,500. Highest level of offering: four or five year baccalaureate.

ACCREDITATIONS: EH ADNUR MLTAD

University of Maine at Farmington

86 Main Street
Farmington, ME 04938
(207) 778-7000

Will confirm attendance and degree by mail. Inquiry must include student's name, social security number. Employers may obtain transcripts upon written request accompanied by a $3.00 fee and a signed release from the student.

A school of education, with an enrollment of 2,140. Highest level of offering: four or five year baccalaureate.

ACCREDITATIONS: EH TED

University of Maine at Fort Kent

Pleasant Street
Fort Kent, ME 04743
(207) 834-3162
Fax (207) 834-3144

Will confirm attendance and degree by phone or mail. Inquiry must include student's name, social security number. Employers may obtain transcripts upon written request accompanied by a $2.00 fee and a signed release from the student.

A general baccalaureate institution, with an enrollment of 661. Highest level of offering: four or five year baccalaureate.

ACCREDITATIONS: EH

University of Maine at Machias

9 O'Brian Avenue
Machias, ME 04654
(207) 255-3313
Fax (207) 255-4864

Will confirm attendance and degree by mail or fax. Inquiry must include student's name, social security number, release. Employers may obtain transcripts upon written request accompanied by a $2.00 fee and a signed release from the student.

A general baccalaureate institution, with an enrollment of 834. Highest level of offering: four or five year baccalaureate.

ACCREDITATIONS: EH

University of Maine at Orono

Wingate Hall
Orono, ME 04469
(207) 581-1290
Fax (207) 581-1314

Will confirm attendance and degree by phone, fax or mail. Inquiry must include student's name, social security number, years attended. Employers may obtain transcripts upon written request accompanied by a $3.00 fee and a signed release from the student. Requests should be directed to: Registrar's Office.

A comprehensive institution with no medical school, with an enrollment of 13,282. Highest level of offering: doctorate.

ACCREDITATIONS: EH ADVET ART BUS CLPSY DA DH ENG ENGT FOR IPSY MUS TED SW

University of Maine at Presque Isle

181 Maine Street
Presque Isle, ME 04769-2888
(207) 764-0311 Ext. 240

Will confirm attendance and degree by phone or mail. Inquiry must include student's name, social security number. Employers may obtain transcripts upon written request accompanied by a $2.00 fee and a signed release from the student.

A general baccalaureate institution, with an enrollment of 1,512. Highest level of offering: four or five year baccalaureate.

ACCREDITATIONS: EH MLTAD

University of Mary Hardin–Baylor

U M H–B Station 10th & College
Belton, TX 76513
(817) 939-4508
Fax (817) 939-4535

Will confirm attendance and degree by phone, fax or mail. Inquiry must include student's name, social security number. Employers may obtain transcripts upon written request accompanied by a $3.00 fee and a signed release from the student.

A general baccalaureate institution, with an enrollment of 1,732. Highest level of offering: master's.

ACCREDITATIONS: SC NUR

University of Mary

7500 University Drive
Bismarck, ND 58504
(701) 255-7500 Ext. 410

Will confirm attendance by phone or mail. Inquiry must include student's name, maiden name, social security number, years attended, release. Employers may obtain transcripts upon written request accompanied by a $2.00 fee and a signed release from the student. Requests should be directed to: Registrar's Office.

A general baccalaureate institution, with an enrollment of 1,431. Highest level of offering: master's.

ACCREDITATIONS: NH NUR SW

University of Maryland–Eastern Shore

Princess Anne, MD 21853
(301) 651-2200 Ext. 6410

Will confirm attendance and degree by phone or mail. Inquiry must include student's name, date of birth, social security number, years attended, self addressed stamped envelope. Requests should be directed to: Administrative Office. Employers may obtain transcripts upon written request accompanied by a $2.00 fee and a signed release from the student.

A general baccalaureate institution, with an enrollment of 2,300. Highest level of offering: doctorate.

ACCREDITATIONS: M PTA

University of Maryland Baltimore County Campus

Catonsville, MD 21228
(301) 455-3727
Fax (301) 455-1094

Will confirm attendance and degree by phone, fax or mail. Inquiry must include student's name, social security number. Employers may obtain transcripts upon written request accompanied by a signed release from the student.

A comprehensive institution with no medical school, with an enrollment of 8,153. Highest level of offering: doctorate.

ACCREDITATIONS: M

University of Maryland at Baltimore Professional Schools

621 West Lombard Street, Room 326
Baltimore, MD 21201
(410) 328-7480
Fax (410) 328-4053

Will confirm attendance and degree by phone or mail. Inquiry must include student's name, social security number. Employers may obtain transcripts upon written request accompanied by a $3.00 fee and a signed release from the student.

An upper division professional school, with an enrollment of 4,982. Highest level of offering: doctorate.

ACCREDITATIONS: MSA/CHE DENT DH LAW MED MT NUR PHAR PTA SW

University of Maryland College Park Campus

NORT Administrative Bldg.–Room 1101
College Park, MD 20742
(301) 314-8240
Fax (301) 314-9568   *Records 314-8257*

Will confirm attendance and degree by phone, fax or mail. Inquiry must include student's name, social security number. Employers may obtain transcripts upon written request accompanied by a $2.00 fee and a signed release from the student. Requests should be directed to: Records Office.

A doctoral-level institution with no medical school, with an enrollment of 35,000. Highest level of offering: doctorate.

ACCREDITATIONS: M ARCH AUD BUS CLPSY COPSY ENG JOUR LIB FIDER IPSY MUS SCPSY SP TED DANCE

University of Massachusetts at Amherst

Graduate Records Office
534 Goodell
Amherst, MA 01003
(413) 545-0024
Fax (413) 545-3754

Will confirm attendance and degree by phone, fax or mail. Inquiry must include student's name, social security number, years attended. Requests should be directed to: 534 Goodell. Employers may obtain transcripts upon written request accompanied by a $3.00 fee and a signed release from the student.

A doctoral-level institution with no medical school, with an enrollment of 27,162. Highest level of offering: doctorate.
ACCREDITATIONS: EH ART AUD BUS CLPSY COPSY ENG FIDER FOR HSA IPSY LSAR TED MUS NUR PH SP

University of Massachusetts at Boston

100 Morrissey Blvd.
Harbor Campus
Boston, MA 02125
(617) 287-6200
Fax (617) 265-7173

Will confirm attendance and degree by phone, fax or mail. Inquiry must include student's name, social security number. Employers may obtain transcripts upon written request accompanied by a $2.00 fee and a signed release from the student.

A general baccalaureate institution, with an enrollment of 11,711. Highest level of offering: doctorate.
ACCREDITATIONS: EH NUR

University of Massachusetts College of Public & Community Services

100 Morrissey Blvd.
Boston, MA 02115
(617) 287-6200

Will confirm attendance and degree by phone or mail. Inquiry must include student's name, social security number. Employers may obtain transcripts upon written request accompanied by a $2.00 fee and a signed release from the student.

University of Massachusetts Dartmouth

(Formerly Southeastern Massachusetts University)
Old Westport Road
North Dartmouth, MA 02747
(617) 999-8615
Fax (617) 999-8901

Will confirm attendance and degree by phone or mail. Inquiry must include student's name, social security number, years attended. Employers may obtain transcripts upon written request accompanied by a $2.00 fee and a signed release from the student. Requests should be directed to: Registrar's Office.

A comprehensive institution with no medical school, with an enrollment of 7,125. Highest level of offering: master's.
ACCREDITATIONS: EH ART ENG ENGT MT NUR

University of Massachusetts Dartmouth

(Formerly Swain School of Design)
Old Westport Road
North Dartmouth, MA 02747
(508) 999-8000

Records are held at the above address. Will confirm attendance and degree by phone or mail. Inquiry must include student's name, social security number, date of birth, years attended. Employers may obtain transcripts upon written request accompanied by a $2.00 fee and a signed release from the student.

A visual and performing arts school, with an enrollment of 5,680. Highest level of offering: four or five year baccalaureate..
ACCREDITATIONS: ART

University of Massachusetts Medical School at Worcester

55 Lake Avenue North
Worcester, MA 01655
(508) 856-2267
Fax (508) 856-1899

Will confirm attendance and degree by phone, fax or mail. Inquiry must include student's name, self addressed stamped envelope. Employers may obtain transcripts upon written request accompanied by a signed release from the student.

A medical school, with an enrollment of 416. Highest level of offering: master's.
ACCREDITATIONS: MED PAST

University of Medicine and Dentistry of New Jersey

Robert Wood Johnson Medical School
401 Haddon Ave
Camden, NJ 08103
(609) 757-7859

Will confirm attendance and degree by mail. Inquiry must include student's name, social security number, years attended, release. Employers may obtain transcripts upon written request by student accompanied by a $2.00 fee.

A medical school, with an enrollment of 148. Highest level of offering: doctorate.
ACCREDITATIONS: M CYTO DA DENT DH DIETI MED MT IPSY OSTEO RAD MIDWF

University of Medicine and Dentistry of New Jersey

Robert Wood Johnson Medical School
675 Hoes Lane
Pascataway, NJ 08854-5635
(908) 463-4565

Will confirm attendance and degree by phone or mail. Inquiry must include student's name, social security number, years attended. Employers may obtain transcripts upon written request by student accompanied by a $3.00 fee and a signed release from the student. Requests should be directed to: Registrar's Office.

A medical school, with an enrollment of 600. Highest level of offering: doctorate.
ACCREDITATIONS: M CYTO DA DENT DH DIETI MED MT IPSY OSTEO RAD MIDWF

University of Miami

PO Box 248026
Coral Gables, FL 33124-4627
(305) 284-5455
Fax (305) 284-3144

Will confirm attendance and degree by mail or fax. Inquiry must include student's name, maiden name, social security number or date of birth, years attended. Employers may obtain transcripts upon written request accompanied by a $5.00 fee and a signed release from the student. Requests should be directed to: Office of Enrollment Services.

A doctoral-level institution with a medical school, with an enrollment of 13,708. Highest level of offering: doctorate.
ACCREDITATIONS: SC ARCH BUS CHPM CLPSY CYTO ENG LAW MED MUS NMT NUR TED PTA RAD RTT MIDWF BUSA

University of Michigan–Ann Arbor

LSA Bldg. Room 1524
Ann Arbor, MI 48109-1382
(313) 764-1575
Fax (313) 764-5556

Will confirm attendance and degree by phone or mail. Inquiry must include student's name, social security number. Employers may obtain transcripts upon written request accompanied by a $4.00 fee and a signed release from the student. Requests should be directed to: Registrar's Office.

A doctoral-level institution with a medical school, with an enrollment of 36,338. Highest level of offering: doctorate.
ACCREDITATIONS: NH ANEST ARCH ART AUD BUS CLPSY DENT DH ENG FOR PAST HSA PTA TED LAW LIB LSAR MED MICB MT MUS NUR PH PHAR SCPSY SP SW DANCE

University of Michigan–Flint

Flint, MI 48502
(313) 762-3344
Fax (313) 762-3346

Will confirm attendance and degree by phone or mail. Inquiry must include student's name, social security number, years attended. Employers may obtain transcripts upon written request accompanied by a $2.00 fee and a signed release from the student. Requests should be directed to: Registrar's Office.

A general baccalaureate institution, with an enrollment of 6,500. Highest level of offering: master's.
ACCREDITATIONS: NH BUS MUS TED PTA

University of Michigan-Dearborn

4901 Evergreen Road
Dearborn, MI 48128-1491
(313) 593-5210

Will confirm attendance and degree by phone or mail. Inquiry must include student's name, social security number. Employers may obtain transcripts upon written request accompanied by a $4.00 fee and a signed release from the student. Requests should be directed to: Registrar's Office.

A comprehensive institution with no medical school, with an enrollment of 7,600. Highest level of offering: master's.
ACCREDITATIONS: NH ENG TED

University of Minnesota–Crookston

Highway 2 & 75
Crookston, MN 56716
(218) 281-6510 Ext. 346

Will confirm attendance and degree by phone or mail. Inquiry must include student's name, social security number. Employers may obtain transcripts upon written request accompanied by a $3.00 fee and a signed release from the student. Requests should be directed to: Records Office.

A multiprogram two-year institution, with an enrollment of 1,288. Highest level of offering: one year but less than two years.
ACCREDITATIONS: NH

University of Minnesota at Duluth

10 University Drive
Duluth, MN 55812
(218) 726-7500

Will confirm attendance and degree by mail. Inquiry must include student's name, date of birth, social security number. Employers may obtain transcripts upon written request accompanied by a $2.00 fee and a signed release from the student. Requests should be directed to: Registrar's Office.

A comprehensive institution with no medical school, with an enrollment of 7,800. Highest level of offering: beyond master's but less than doctorate.
ACCREDITATIONS: NH DH MEDB MUS SP SW TED

University of Minnesota at Morris

Morris, MN 56267
(612) 589-2211 Ext. 6030

Will confirm attendance and degree by phone or mail. Inquiry must include student's name, social security number. Employers may obtain transcripts upon written request accompanied by a $3.00 fee and a signed release from the student. Requests should be directed to: Records Office.

A general baccalaureate institution, with an enrollment of 1,920. Highest level of offering: four or five year baccalaureate.
ACCREDITATIONS: NH TED

University of Minnesota at Minneapolis Saint Paul

231 Pillsbury Drive South East–155
Williamson Hall
Minneapolis, MN 55455
(612) 625-5333

Will confirm attendance and degree by phone or mail. Inquiry must include student's name, date of birth, social security number. Employers may obtain transcripts upon written request accompanied by a $3.00 fee and a signed release from the student. Requests should be directed to: Transcripts Department.

A doctoral-level institution with a medical school, with an enrollment of 62,266.
ACCREDITATIONS: NH ARCH AUD BUS CLPSY COPSY DENT DH DIET DIETI PAST ENG FIDER TED FOR FUSER HSA IPSY JOUR LAW VET LSAR MED MT MUS NUR OT PH PHAR PTA RAD RTT SCPSY SP SW DANCE MIDWF THEA

University of Minnesota Technical College

c/o University of Minnesota at
Minneapolis Saint Paul
231 Pillsbury Drive South East –155
Williamson Hall
Minneapolis, MN 55455
(612) 625-5333

Records are held at the above address. Will confirm attendance and degree by phone or mail. Inquiry must include student's name, social security number. Employers may obtain transcripts upon written request accompanied by a $3.00 fee and a signed release from the student. Requests should be directed to: Records Office.

A multiprogram two-year institution, with an enrollment of 1,120. Highest level of offering: one year but less than four years.
ACCREDITATIONS: NH ADVET

University of Mississippi Main Campus

Records Office
University, MS 38677
(601) 232-7226
Fax (601) 232-5869

Will confirm attendance and degree by phone or mail. Inquiry must include student's name, date of birth, social security number, years attended. Employers may obtain transcripts upon written request accompanied by a $4.00 fee and a signed release from the student.

A doctoral-level institution with no medical school, with an enrollment of 11,033. Highest level of offering: doctorate.
ACCREDITATIONS: SC ART AUD BUS CLPSY ENG JOUR LAW TED MUS PHAR SP SW BUSA

University of Mississippi Medical Center

2500 North State Street
Jackson, MS 39216
(601) 984-1080

Will confirm attendance and degree by phone or mail. Inquiry must include student's name, social security number, years attended. Requests should be directed to: Division of Student Services & Records. Employers may obtain transcripts upon written request accompanied by a $1.00 fee and a signed release from the student.

A medical school, with an enrollment of 1,737. Highest level of offering: doctorate.
ACCREDITATIONS: ANEST CYTO DENT DH IPSY MED MRA MT NMT NUR PTA PAST

University of Missouri–Columbia

130 Jesse Hall
Columbia, MO 65211
(314) 882-8252

Will confirm attendance and degree by phone or mail. Inquiry must include student's name, social security number, years attended. Employers may obtain transcripts upon written request accompanied by a signed release from the student. Requests should be directed to: Transcripts Department.

A doctoral-level institution with a medical school, with an enrollment of 22,546. Highest level of offering: doctorate.
ACCREDITATIONS: NH BBT BUS CLPSY COPSY CYTO DIET FIDER FOR HSA HT ENG TED VET BUSA IPSY JOUR LAW LIB MED MT MUS NMT NUR OT PTA RAD RSTH SP SW

University of Missouri–Kansas City

4825 Troost
Student Services Bldg.
Kansas City, MO 64110
(816) 276-1123
Fax (816) 276-1717

Will confirm attendance and degree by phone, fax or mail. Inquiry must include student's name, social security number, years attended. Employers may obtain transcripts upon written request accompanied by a signed release from the student. Requests should be directed to: Records Office.

A doctoral-level institution with a medical school, with an enrollment of 11,464. Highest level of offering: doctorate.
ACCREDITATIONS: NH BUS DENT DH COPSY LAW MED MUS NUR PHAR TED THEA

University of Missouri–Rolla

103 Parker Hall
Rolla, MO 65401
(314) 341-4170

Will confirm attendance and degree by phone or mail. Inquiry must include student's name, date of birth, social security number. Employers may obtain transcripts upon written request accompanied by a $4.00 fee and a signed release from the student. Requests should be directed to: Registrar's Office.

An engineering school, with an enrollment of 5,177. Highest level of offering: doctorate.

ACCREDITATIONS: NH ENG

University of Missouri–Saint Louis

8001 Natural Bridge Road
Saint Louis, MO 63121
(314) 553-5546

Will confirm attendance and degree by phone or mail. Inquiry must include student's name, social security number. Employers may obtain transcripts upon written request accompanied by a signed release from the student.

A comprehensive institution with no medical school, with an enrollment of 11,596. Highest level of offering: doctorate.

ACCREDITATIONS: NH BUS CLPSY NUR OPT SW TED

University of Montana

Missoula, MT 59812
(406) 243-2995

Will confirm attendance and degree by mail. Inquiry must include student's name, social security number. Employers may obtain transcripts upon written request accompanied by a $2.00 fee and a signed release from the student. Requests should be directed to: Registrar's Office.

A comprehensive institution with no medical school, with an enrollment of 9,679. Highest level of offering: doctorate.

ACCREDITATIONS: NW AUD BUS CLPSY FOR JOUR LAW MUS PHAR PTA SP TED THEA SW

University of Montevallo

Station 6040–Palmer Hall
Montevallo, AL 35115
(205) 665-6040
Fax (205) 665-6063

Will confirm attendance and degree by phone or mail. Inquiry must include student's name, social security number, years attended. Requests should be directed to: Records Office. Employers may obtain transcripts upon written request accompanied by a $2.00 fee and a signed release from the student.

A comprehensive institution with no medical school, with an enrollment of 2,782. Highest level of offering: beyond master's but less than doctorate.

ACCREDITATIONS: SC AUD MUS SP SW TED

University of Nebraska–Lincoln

107 Administrative Bldg.
Lincoln, NE 68588-0416
(402) 472-3684
Fax (402) 472-8220

Will confirm attendance and degree by phone or mail. $10.00 fee for fax response. Inquiry must include student's name, social security number. Employers may obtain transcripts upon written request accompanied by a $3.00 fee and a signed release from the student. $13.00 fee for faxing transcript. Requests should be directed to: Records Office.

A doctoral-level institution with no medical school, with an enrollment of 24,228. Highest level of offering: doctorate.

ACCREDITATIONS: NH ADVET ARCH AUD BUS CLPSY COPSY DENT DH DIETI ENG FIDER JOUR LAW MUS SCPSY SP BUSA TED

University of Nebraska at Omaha

60th and Dodge Street
Omaha, NE 68182
(402) 554-2314
Fax (402) 554-3472

Will confirm attendance and degree by phone, fax or mail. Inquiry must include student's name, date of birth, social security number. Employers may obtain transcripts upon written request accompanied by a $3.00 fee and a signed release from the student. Requests should be directed to: Registrar's Office.

A comprehensive institution with no medical school, with an enrollment of 16,000. Highest level of offering: beyond master's but less than doctorate.

ACCREDITATIONS: NH BUS ENG ENGT MUS SW TED SP

University of Nebraska Medical Center

600 S. 42nd Street
Omaha, NE 68198-4230
(402) 559-7391

Will confirm attendance and degree by phone or mail. Inquiry must include student's name. Employers may obtain transcripts upon written request accompanied by a $3.00 fee and a signed release from the student. Requests should be directed to: Student Records.

A medical school, with an enrollment of 2,495. Highest level of offering: doctorate.

ACCREDITATIONS: NH ADNUR APCP DIETI IPSY MED MT NMT NUR PHAR PTA RAD RTT

University of Nevada–Las Vegas

4505 South Maryland Parkway
Las Vegas, NV 89154
(702) 739-3011

Will confirm attendance and degree by phone or mail. Inquiry must include student's name, date of birth, social security number, years attended. Requests should be directed to: Registrar's Office. Employers may obtain transcripts upon written request accompanied by a $2.00 fee and a signed release from the student.

A comprehensive institution with no medical school, with an enrollment of 18,000. Highest level of offering: doctorate.

ACCREDITATIONS: NW ADNUR ENGT CHM MUS NMT NUR RAD SW TED

University of Nevada–Reno

Reno, NV 89557-0002
(702) 784-6865
Fax (702) 784-4283

Will confirm attendance and degree by fax or mail. Inquiry must include student's name, date of birth, social security number, years attended, release, self addressed stamped envelope. Requests should be directed to: Admission & Records Office. Employers may obtain transcripts upon written request accompanied by a $2.00 fee and a signed release from the student.

A doctoral-level institution with a medical school, with an enrollment of 11,714. Highest level of offering: doctorate.

ACCREDITATIONS: NW BUS CLPSY ENG ENGT JOUR MED MT MUS NUR SW TED

University of New England

11 Hills Beach Road
Biddeford, ME 04005
(207) 283-0171 Ext. 473
Fax (207) 282-6379

Will confirm attendance and degree by phone, fax or mail. Inquiry must include student's name, social security number. Requests should be directed to: Registrar's Office. Employers may obtain transcripts upon written request accompanied by a $2.00 fee and a signed release from the student.

A general baccalaureate institution, with an enrollment of 923. Highest level of offering: first professional degree.

ACCREDITATIONS: EH OSTEO PTA

University of New Hampshire Keene State College

229 Main Street
Keene, NH 03431
(603) 358-2321
Fax (603) 358-2257

Will confirm attendance and degree by phone or mail. Inquiry must include student's name, social security number, years attended. Employers may obtain transcripts upon written request accompanied by a $2.00 fee and a signed release from the student. Requests should be directed to: Registrar's Office.

A general baccalaureate institution, with an enrollment of 3,512. Highest level of offering: master's.

ACCREDITATIONS: EH TED

University of New Hampshire Plymouth State College

Plymouth, NH 03264-1600
(603) 535-5000 Ext. 2346

Will confirm attendance and degree by phone or mail. Inquiry must include student's name, social security number. Requests should be directed to: Registrar's Office. Employers may obtain transcripts upon written request by student accompanied by a $3.00 fee and a signed release from the student.

A general baccalaureate institution, with an enrollment of 4,249. Highest level of offering: master's.
ACCREDITATIONS: EH TED

University of New Hampshire

7 Garrison Avenue
Durham, NH 03824
(603) 862-1502

Will confirm attendance and degree by phone or mail. Inquiry must include student's name, date of birth, social security number, years attended. Employers may obtain transcripts upon written request by student accompanied by a $3.00 fee and a signed release from the student. Requests should be directed to: Registrar's Office.

A doctoral-level institution with no medical school, with an enrollment of 11,000. Highest level of offering: doctorate.
ACCREDITATIONS: EH ENG ENGT FOR MUS NUR OT SW TED

University of New Hampshire

220 Hackett Hill Road
Manchester, NH 03102
(603) 668-0700 Ext. 236
Fax (603) 623-2745

Will confirm attendance and degree by phone or mail. Inquiry must include student's name, social security number. Employers may obtain transcripts upon written request accompanied by a $3.00 fee and a signed release from the student.

A general baccalaureate institution, with an enrollment of 365. Highest level of offering: Four or five year baccalaureate.
ACCREDITATIONS: EH

University of New Haven

Registrar's Office
West Haven, CT 06516
(203) 932-7301

Will confirm attendance and degree by phone or mail. Inquiry must include student's name, social security number. Employers may obtain transcripts upon written request accompanied by a $4.00 fee and a signed release from the student.

A comprehensive institution with no medical school, with an enrollment of 7,044. Highest level of offering: doctorate.
ACCREDITATIONS: EH ENG DIET

University of New Mexico Central Office

Student Services Center
Attn: Records, Room 250
Albuquerque, NM 87131
(505) 277-2916

Will confirm attendance and degree by phone or mail. Inquiry must include student's name, date of birth, social security number, years attended. Employers may obtain transcripts upon written request accompanied by a $3.00 fee and a signed release from the student.

A doctoral-level institution with a medical school, with an enrollment of 23,687. Highest level of offering: doctorate.
ACCREDITATIONS: NH AUD BUS CLPSY COPSY DA DH ENG IPSY JOUR LAW ARCH TED MED MT MUS NMT NUR PHAR PTA RAD SP DANCE THEA

University of New Mexico Gallup Branch

200 College Road
Albuquerque, NM 87301
(505) 863-7522
Fax (505) 863-7532

Will confirm attendance and degree by phone or mail. Inquiry must include student's name, date of birth, social security number, years attended. Employers may obtain transcripts upon written request accompanied by a $3.00 fee and a signed release from the student.

A multiprogram two-year institution, with an enrollment of 2,500. Highest level of offering: two years but less than four years.
ACCREDITATIONS: NH MLTAD

University of New Orleans

Lake Front
New Orleans, LA 70148
(504) 286-6216
Fax (504) 286-6217

Will confirm degree by phone or mail. Inquiry must include student's name, date of birth, social security number. Employers may obtain transcripts upon written request accompanied by a $5.00 fee and a signed release from the student.

A comprehensive institution with no medical school, with an enrollment of 16,356. Highest level of offering: doctorate.
ACCREDITATIONS: SC BUS ENG MUS TED BUSA

University of North Alabama

Box 5044
Florence, AL 35632
(205) 760-4316

Will confirm attendance and degree by phone or mail. Inquiry must include student's name, date of birth, years attended. Employers may obtain transcripts upon written request accompanied by a $3.00 fee and a signed release from the student.

A comprehensive institution with no medical school, with an enrollment of 5,197. Highest level of offering: beyond master's but less than doctorate.
ACCREDITATIONS: SC NUR SW TED

University of North Carolina at Asheville

1 University Heights
Asheville, NC 28804
(704) 251-6575

Will confirm attendance and degree by phone or mail. Inquiry must include student's name, date of birth, social security number., dates attended Employers may obtain transcripts upon written request accompanied by a $2.00 fee and a signed release from the student.

A general baccalaureate institution, with an enrollment of 3,200. Highest level of offering: master's.
ACCREDITATIONS: SC

University of North Carolina at Chapel Hill

Hanes Hall CB 2100
Chapel Hill, NC 27599-2100
(919) 962-3954

Will confirm attendance and degree by phone or mail. Inquiry must include student's name, social security number. Employers may obtain transcripts upon written request accompanied by a $5.00 fee and a signed release from the student. Direct inquiries to: Office of the University Registrar.

A doctoral-level institution with a medical school, with an enrollment of 21,652. Highest level of offering: doctorate.
ACCREDITATIONS: SC BUS CLPSY COPSY CYTO DA DENT DH ENG HSA IPSY JOUR TED LAW LIB MED MICB MT NUR OT PH PHAR PTA RAD SCPSY SW

University of North Carolina at Charlotte

Charlotte, NC 28223
(704) 547-2287
Fax (704) 547-2144

Will confirm attendance and degree by phone, fax or mail. Inquiry must include student's name, social security number. Employers may obtain transcripts upon written request accompanied by a $3.00 fee and a signed release from the student.

A comprehensive institution with no medical school, with an enrollment of 13,500. Highest level of offering: beyond master's but less than doctorate.
ACCREDITATIONS: SC ARCH BUS CHM ENG ENGT NUR

University of North Carolina at Greensboro

1000 Spring Garden Street
Greensboro, NC 27412
(919) 334-5946

Will confirm attendance and degree by phone or mail. Inquiry must include student's name, social security number. Employers may obtain transcripts upon written request accompanied by a $5.00 fee and a signed release from the student.

A doctoral-level institution with no medical school, with an enrollment of 11,579. Highest level of offering: doctorate.
ACCREDITATIONS: SC BUS CLPSY LIB MUS NUR SW TED

University of North Carolina at Wilmington

Office of the Registrar
601 South College Road
Wilmington, NC 28403
(919) 395-3125

Will confirm attendance and degree by mail. Inquiry must include student's name, social security number. Employers may obtain transcripts upon written request accompanied by a $2.00 fee and a signed release from the student. Direct inquiries to: Office of the Registrar

A general baccalaureate institution, with an enrollment of 8,133. Highest level of offering: master's.
ACCREDITATIONS: NURS MT SC TED

University of North Dakota Lake Region

(Formerly Lake Region Community College)
Devils Lake, ND 58301
(701) 662-8683 Ext. 340
Fax (701) 662-8688

Will confirm attendance and degree by phone, fax or mail. Inquiry must include student's name, date of birth, social security number. Employers may obtain transcripts upon written request accompanied by a signed release from the student.

A multiprogram two-year institution, with an enrollment of 810. Highest level of offering: one year but less than four years.
ACCREDITATIONS: NH

University of North Dakota Main Campus

Box 8095 University Station
Grand Forks, ND 58202
(701) 777-2711
Fax (701) 777-2696

Will confirm attendance and degree by phone, fax or mail. Inquiry must include student's name, social security number, years attended. Employers may obtain transcripts upon written request accompanied by a signed release from the student.

A doctoral-level institution with a medical school, with an enrollment of 11,060. Highest level of offering: doctorate.
ACCREDITATIONS: NH APCP ART BUS CLPSY CYTO DIET ENG HT JOUR LAW MED TED MT MUS NUR OT PTA SP SW

University of North Dakota Williston Branch

Box 1326
Williston, ND 58802-1320
(701) 774-4210

Will confirm attendance and degree by phone or mail. Inquiry must include student's name, date of birth, social security number, years attended. Employers may obtain transcripts upon written request accompanied by a signed release from the student.

A multiprogram two-year institution, with an enrollment of 833. Highest level of offering: two years but less than four years.
ACCREDITATIONS: NCA

University of North Florida

4567 St Johns Bluff Road South
Jacksonville, FL 32216
(904) 646-2620

Will confirm attendance and degree by phone or mail. Inquiry must include student's name, social security number. Employers may obtain transcripts upon written request accompanied by a signed release from the student.

A comprehensive institution with no medical school, with an enrollment of 8,000. Highest level of offering: master's.
ACCREDITATIONS: SC BUS NUR

University of Northern Colorado

Carter Hall 3002
Greeley, CO 80639
(303) 351-2231

Will confirm attendance and degree by phone or mail. Inquiry must include student's name, date of birth, social security number, years attended. Employers may obtain transcripts upon written request accompanied by a $3.00 fee and a signed release from the student.

A doctoral-level institution with no medical school, with an enrollment of 9,287. Highest level of offering: doctorate.
ACCREDITATIONS: NH AUD MUS NUR SCPSY SP TED

University of Northern Iowa

1222 West 27th Street
Cedar Falls, IA 50614
(319) 273-2241

Will confirm attendance and degree by phone or mail. Inquiry must include student's name, social security number. Employers may obtain transcripts upon written request accompanied by a $3.00 fee and a signed release from the student.

A comprehensive institution with no medical school, with an enrollment of 12,090. Highest level of offering: doctorate.
ACCREDITATIONS: NH ART MUS SP SW TED

University of Notre Dame

Main Bldg.–Room 215
Notre Dame, IN 46556
(219) 239-7043
Fax (219) 239-5872

Will confirm attendance and degree by phone, fax or mail. Inquiry must include student's name, social security number, years attended. Employers may obtain transcripts upon written request accompanied by a $2.00 fee and a signed release from the student.

A doctoral-level institution with no medical school, with an enrollment of 10,000. Highest level of offering: doctorate.
ACCREDITATIONS: NH ARCH ART BUS COPSY ENG LAW MUS THEOL BUSA

University of Oklahoma Health Sciences Center

PO Box 26901–Basic Science Education Bldg. Room 200
Oklahoma City, OK 73190
(405) 271-2359
Fax (405) 271-2480

Will confirm attendance and degree by phone, fax or mail. Inquiry must include student's name, social security number, years attended. Requests should be directed to: Admissions & Records Department. Only students may obtain transcripts.

A medical school, with an enrollment of 2,555. Highest level of offering: doctorate.
ACCREDITATIONS: NH APCP AUD CYTO DENT DH DIET IPSY MED MT NMT NUR OT PH PHAR PTA RAD RTT SP DMS

University of Oklahoma Norman Campus

1000 Asp Avenue
Norman, OK 73019
(405) 325-2012

Will confirm attendance and degree by phone or mail. Inquiry must include student's name, social security number, years attended. Employers may obtain transcripts upon written request accompanied by a $3.00 fee and a signed release from the student.

A doctoral-level institution with no medical school, with an enrollment of 21,365. Highest level of offering: doctorate.
ACCREDITATIONS: NH ARCH BUS ENG JOUR LAW LIB MUS SW TED BUSA

University of Oregon

Eugene, OR 97403
(503) 346-3111

Will confirm attendance and degree by phone or mail. Inquiry must include student's name, social security number, years attended. Employers may obtain transcripts upon written request accompanied by a $2.00 fee for copy, $5.00 for certified copy and a signed release from the student.

A doctoral-level institution with no medical school, with an enrollment of 16,200. Highest level of offering: doctorate.
ACCREDITATIONS: NW ARCH BUS CLPSY COPSY FIDER JOUR LAW LSAR MUS TED

University of Osteopathic Medicine and Health Sciences

3200 Grand Avenue
Des Moines, IA 50312
(515) 271-1461

Will confirm attendance and degree by phone or mail. Inquiry must include student's name. Employers may obtain transcripts upon written request accompanied by a $2.00 fee and a signed release from the student.

A medical school, with an enrollment of 1,300. Highest level of offering: first professional degree.
ACCREDITATIONS: NH APCP OSTEO POD

University of Pennsylvania

Franklin Bldg.–3451 Walnut Street
Room 221
Philadelphia, PA 19104
(215) 898-1561

Will confirm attendance and degree by phone or mail. Inquiry must include student's name, social security number, years attended, campus. Employers may obtain transcripts upon written request accompanied by a $3.00 fee and a signed release from the student.

A doctoral-level institution with a medical school, with an enrollment of 22,065. Highest level of offering: doctorate.
ACCREDITATIONS: M ARCH BUS CLPSY CYTO DENT DH ENG HSA HT LAW VET MED NUR SW MIDWF PSPSY

University of Phoenix

4615 East Elwood
Phoenix, AZ 85040
(602) 921-5332
Fax (602) 894-1758

Will confirm attendance and degree by phone, fax or mail. Inquiry must include student's name, social security number. Employers may obtain transcripts upon written request accompanied by a $3.00 fee and a signed release from the student.

A business school, with an enrollment of 6,669. Highest level of offering: master's.
ACCREDITATIONS: NH

University of Pittsburgh Bradford Campus

300 Campus Drive
Bradford, PA 16701
(814) 362-7600

Will confirm attendance and degree by phone or mail. Inquiry must include student's name, social security number. Employers may obtain transcripts upon written request accompanied by a $2.00 fee and a signed release from the student.

A general baccalaureate institution, with an enrollment of 1,100. Highest level of offering: four or five year baccalaureate.
ACCREDITATIONS: M

University of Pittsburgh Greensburg Campus

1150 Mt Pleasant Rd
Greensburg, PA 15601
(412) 836-9900

Will confirm attendance and degree by mail. Inquiry must include student's name, social security number. Employers may obtain transcripts upon written request accompanied by a $2.00 fee and a signed release from the student.

A multiprogram four-year institution, with an enrollment of 1,471. Highest level of offering: baccalaureate.
ACCREDITATIONS: M

University of Pittsburgh Johnstown Campus

Registrar's Office
Johnstown, PA 15904
(814) 269-7055

Will confirm attendance and degree by phone or mail. Inquiry must include student's name, social security number, years attended. Employers may obtain transcripts upon written request accompanied by a $2.00 fee and a signed release from the student.

A general baccalaureate institution, with an enrollment of 3,161. Highest level of offering: four or five year baccalaureate.
ACCREDITATIONS: M ANEST ENGT RSTH

University of Pittsburgh Main Campus

G-3 Thackerey Hall
Pittsburgh, PA 15260
(412) 624-7660

Will confirm attendance and degree by phone or mail. Inquiry must include student's name, social security number, years attended. Employers may obtain transcripts upon written request accompanied by a $2.00 fee and a signed release from the student.

A doctoral-level institution with a medical school, with an enrollment of 29,197. Highest level of offering: doctorate.
ACCREDITATIONS: M AUD BUS CLPSY DA DENT DH DIET ENG HSA TED LAW LIB MED MRA MT NUR PH PHAR PTA SP SW

University of Pittsburgh Titusville Campus

PO Box 287
Titusville, PA 16354
(814) 827-2702

Will confirm attendance and degree by phone or mail. Inquiry must include student's name, social security number. Employers may obtain transcripts upon written request accompanied by a $2.00 fee and a signed release from the student.

A single program two-year institution, with an enrollment of 350 Highest level of offering: one year but less than four years.
ACCREDITATIONS: M

University of Portland

5000 North Willamette Boulevard
Portland, OR 97203-5798
(503) 283-7321

Will confirm attendance and degree by phone or mail. Inquiry must include student's name, date of birth, social security number, years attended. Employers may obtain transcripts upon original written and signed request by student accompanied by a $3.00 fee.

A comprehensive institution with no medical school, with an enrollment of 3,000. Highest level of offering: master's.
ACCREDITATIONS: NW BUS ENG NUR TED

University of Puget Sound

Registrar's Office
1500 North Warner
Tacoma, WA 98416-0012
(206) 756-3160

Will confirm attendance and degree by phone or mail. Inquiry must include student's name, social security number, date last attended, release. Employers may obtain transcripts upon written request by student accompanied by a $2.00 fee and a signed release from the student.

A comprehensive institution with no medical school, with an enrollment of 3,943. Highest level of offering: master's.
ACCREDITATIONS: CHM NW LAW MUS OT PTA TED

University of Redlands

PO Box 3080
Redlands, CA 92373-0999
(714) 793-2121 Ext. 3232

Will confirm attendance and degree by phone or mail. Inquiry must include student's name, social security number. Employers may obtain transcripts upon written request accompanied by a signed release from the student. Fee ranges from $5.00 to $ 8.00.

A business school, with an enrollment of 2,643. Highest level of offering: master's.
ACCREDITATIONS: WC MUS

University of Rhode Island

Office of Registrar
Administration Bldg.
Kingston, RI 02881
(401) 792-2835

Will confirm attendance and degree by phone or mail. Inquiry must include student's name, date of birth, social security number, years attended. Employers may obtain transcripts upon written request accompanied by a $2.00 fee and a signed release from the student.

A doctoral-level institution with no medical school, with an enrollment of 13,616. Highest level of offering: doctorate.
ACCREDITATIONS: EH BUS CLPSY DH ENG LIB MUS NUR PHAR SCPSY TED

University of Richmond

Registrar's Office
Richmond, VA 23173
(804) 289-8639

Will confirm attendance and degree by phone or mail. Inquiry must include student's name, social security number, years attended. Employers may obtain transcripts upon written request accompanied by a $2.00 fee and a signed release from the student.

A comprehensive institution with no medical school, with an enrollment of 4,909. Highest level of offering: master's.
ACCREDITATIONS: SC BUS CHM LAW MUS

University of Rio Grande

Rio Grande, OH 45674
(614) 245-5353 Ext. 369
Fax (614) 245-9220

Will confirm attendance and degree by phone or mail. Inquiry must include student's name, social security number. Employers may obtain transcripts upon written request accompanied by a $2.00 fee and a signed release from the student.

A general baccalaureate institution, with an enrollment of 2,000. Highest level of offering: four or five year baccalaureate.
ACCREDITATIONS: NH MUS TED

University of Rochester

River Campus
Administration Bldg.
Rochester, NY 14627-0038
(716) 275-5131

Will confirm attendance and degree by phone or mail. Inquiry must include student's name, social security number, years attended. Employers may obtain transcripts upon written request accompanied by a $2.00 fee and a signed release from the student.

A doctoral-level institution with a medical school, with an enrollment of 8,559. Highest level of offering: doctorate.
ACCREDITATIONS: M BUS CHPM CLPSY ENG IPSY MED MICB MUS NUR NY PAST

University of Saint Mary of the Lake

(Formerly Saint Mary of the Lake Seminary)
Mundelein, IL 60060
(708) 566-6401 Ext. 55

Will confirm attendance and degree by mail. Inquiry must include student's name, social security number, years attended. Employers may obtain transcripts upon written request by student accompanied by a $2.00 fee and a signed release from the student.

A school of philosophy, religion and theology, with an enrollment of 205. Highest level of offering: doctorate.
ACCREDITATIONS: THEOL

University of Saint Thomas

Attn: Registrar
3800 Montrose Blvd
Houston, TX 77006
(713) 522-7911

Will confirm attendance and degree by phone or mail. Inquiry must include student's name, social security number, years attended. Employers may obtain transcripts upon written request accompanied by a $2.00 fee and a signed release from the student.

A comprehensive institution with no medical school, with an enrollment of 2,029. Highest level of offering: doctorate.
ACCREDITATIONS: SC NUR

University of San Diego

Registrar's Office
Founders, Room 113
Alcala Park
San Diego, CA 92110
(619) 260-4557

Will confirm attendance and degree by mail. Inquiry must include student's name, social security number. Employers may obtain transcripts upon written request accompanied by a $1.00 fee and a signed release from the student.

A comprehensive institution with no medical school, with an enrollment of 6,000. Highest level of offering: doctorate.
ACCREDITATIONS: WC BUS LAW NUR

University of San Francisco

Ignition Heights
2130 Fulton Street
San Francisco, CA 94117-1080
(415) 666-6886 Ext. 6316

Will confirm attendance and degree by phone or mail. Inquiry must include student's name, social security number, years attended. Employers may obtain transcripts upon written request accompanied by a $3.00 fee and a signed release from the student.

A comprehensive institution with no medical school, with an enrollment of 6,564. Highest level of offering: doctorate.
ACCREDITATIONS: WC BUS LAW NUR

University of Santa Clara

Santa Clara, CA 95053
(408) 554-6910

Will confirm attendance and degree by phone or mail. Inquiry must include student's name, social security number, years attended. Employers may obtain transcripts upon written request accompanied by a $2.50 fee and a signed release from the student.

A comprehensive institution with no medical school, with an enrollment of 7,453.

Highest level of offering: doctorate.
ACCREDITATIONS: WC BUS ENG LAW MUS

University of Science and Arts of Oklahoma

PO Box 82345
Chickasha, OK 73018-0001
(405) 224-3140 Ext. 204

Will confirm attendance and degree by phone or mail. Inquiry must include student's name, social security number. Employers may obtain transcripts upon written request accompanied by a $1.00 fee and a signed release from the student.

A general baccalaureate institution, with an enrollment of 1,451. Highest level of offering: four or five year baccalaureate.
ACCREDITATIONS: NH MUS TED

University of Scranton

Registrar's Office
Scranton, PA 18510
(717) 941-7720

Will confirm attendance and degree by phone or mail. Inquiry must include student's name, social security number, years attended. Employers may obtain transcripts upon written request accompanied by a $4.00 fee and a signed release from the student.

A comprehensive institution with no medical school, with an enrollment of 4,684. Highest level of offering: master's.
ACCREDITATIONS: M PTA TED

University of South Alabama

Registrar's Office
165 Administration Bldg.
Mobile, AL 36688
(205) 460-6251

Will confirm attendance and degree by phone or mail. Inquiry must include student's name, social security number. Employers may obtain transcripts upon written request accompanied by a $3.00 fee and a signed release from the student.

A comprehensive institution with a medical school, with an enrollment of 12,158. Highest level of offering: doctorate.
ACCREDITATIONS: SACS AUD BUS CYTO ENG MED MT MUS NUR PTA RAD TED RSTH SP

University of South Carolina–Coastal Carolina College

PO Box 1954
Conway, SC 29526
(803) 347-3161

Will confirm attendance and degree by phone or mail. Inquiry must include student's name, social security number. Employers may obtain transcripts upon written request accompanied by a $5.00 fee and a signed release from the student. Transcript requests should be directed to USC at Columbia, Records Office, Columbia, SC 29208.

A general baccalaureate institution, with an enrollment of 2,627. Highest level of offering: four or five year baccalaureate.
ACCREDITATIONS: SC ADNUR

University of South Carolina at Aiken

171 University Parkway
Aiken, SC 29801
(803) 648-6851 Ext. 3441, 3432 or 3435
Fax (803) 641-3362

Will confirm attendance and degree by phone or mail. Inquiry must include student's name, social security number, years attended. Requests should be directed to: Records Department. Employers may obtain transcripts upon written request accompanied by a $5.00 fee and a signed release from the student. Transcript requests should be directed to USC at Columbia, Records Office, Columbia, SC 29208.

A general baccalaureate institution, with an enrollment of 2,450. Highest level of offering: four or five year baccalaureate.
ACCREDITATIONS: SC ADNUR

University of South Carolina at Beaufort

800 Carteret St.
Beaufort, SC 29902
(803) 524-7112
Fax (803) 777-6349

Will confirm attendance and degree by phone or mail. Inquiry must include student's name, date of birth, social security number, years attended. Requests should be directed to: Records Department.

Employers may obtain transcripts upon written request accompanied by a $5.00 fee and a signed release from the student. Transcript requests should be directed to USC at Columbia, Records Office, Columbia, SC 29208.

A multiprogram two-year institution, with an enrollment of 842. Highest level of offering: one year but less than four years.
ACCREDITATIONS: SC

University of South Carolina at Columbia

Records Office of Registrar
Columbia, SC 29208
(803) 777-3871
Fax (803) 777-6349

Will confirm attendance and degree by phone, fax or mail. Inquiry must include student's name, social security number. Requests should be directed to: Student Records Office. Employers may obtain transcripts upon written request accompanied by a $5.00 fee and a signed release from the student.

A doctoral-level institution with a medical and law school, with an enrollment of 23,301. Highest level of offering: doctorate.
ACCREDITATIONS: SC AUD BUS CLPSY ENG JOUR LAW LIB MED MUS NUR TED PH PHAR SCPSY SP SW

University of South Carolina at Lancaster

PO Box 889
Lancaster, SC 29720
(803) 285-7471 Ext. 12
Fax (803) 286-9819

Will confirm attendance and degree by phone or mail. Inquiry must include student's name, social security number. Requests should be directed to: Records Department. Employers may obtain transcripts upon written request accompanied by a $5.00 fee and a signed release from the student. Transcript requests should be directed to USC at Columbia, Records Office, Columbia, SC 29208.

A multiprogram two-year institution, with an enrollment of 847. Highest level of offering: one year but less than four years.
ACCREDITATIONS: SC

University of South Carolina at Salkehatchie

PO Box 617
Allendale, SC 29810
(803) 584-3446

Will confirm attendance and degree by phone or mail. Inquiry must include student's name, social security number, years attended. Requests should be directed to: Records Department. Employers may obtain transcripts upon written request accompanied by a $5.00 fee and a signed release from the student. Transcript requests should be directed to USC at Columbia, Records Office, Columbia, SC 29208.

A multiprogram two-year institution, with an enrollment of 721. Highest level of offering: one year but less than four years.
ACCREDITATIONS: SC

University of South Carolina at Spartanburg

800 University Way
Spartanburg, SC 29303
(803) 599-2000

Will confirm attendance and degree by phone or mail. Inquiry must include student's name, date of birth, social security number, years attended. Requests should be directed to: Records Office. Employers may obtain transcripts upon written request accompanied by a $5.00 fee and a signed release from the student. Transcript requests should be directed to USC at Columbia, Records Office, Columbia, SC 29208.

A general baccalaureate institution, with an enrollment of 3,550. Highest level of offering: four or five year baccalaureate.
ACCREDITATIONS: SC ADNUR NUR

University of South Carolina at Sumter

200 Miller Road
Sumter, SC 29150-9990
(803) 775-6341
Fax (803) 775-2180

Will confirm attendance and degree by mail or fax. Inquiry must include student's name, social security number. Requests should be directed to: Records Department. Employers may obtain transcripts upon written request accompanied by a $5.00 fee and a signed release from the student. Transcript requests should be directed to USC at Columbia, Records Office, Columbia, SC 29208.

A multiprogram two-year institution, with an enrollment of 1,665 Highest level of offering: one year but less than four years.
ACCREDITATIONS: SC

University of South Carolina at Union

PO Drawer 729
Union, SC 29379
(803) 427-3681 Ext. 7

Will confirm attendance and degree by phone or mail. Inquiry must include student's name, social security number. Requests should be directed to: Records Department. Employers may obtain transcripts upon written request accompanied by a $5.00 fee and a signed release from the student. Transcript requests should be directed to USC at Columbia, Records Office, Columbia, SC 29208.

A multiprogram two-year institution, with an enrollment of 350. Highest level of offering: one year but less than four years.
ACCREDITATIONS: SAC SC

University of South Dakota

414 East Clark
Vermillion, SD 57069
(605) 677-5301
Fax (605) 677-5073

Will confirm degree by phone or mail. Inquiry must include student's name, social security number, years attended. Employers may obtain transcripts upon written request accompanied by a $2.00 fee and a signed release from the student. Requests should be directed to: Registrar's Office.

A doctoral-level institution with a medical school, with an enrollment of 7,051. Highest level of offering: doctorate.
ACCREDITATIONS: NH ADNUR ART BUS CLPSY DH LAW MED MUS SP SW TED

University of South Florida

4202 East Fowler Avenue
Tampa, FL 33620
(813) 974-2000

Will confirm attendance and degree by phone or mail. Inquiry must include student's name, social security number. Employers may obtain transcripts upon written request accompanied by a signed release from the student.

A doctoral-level institution with a medical school, with an enrollment of 31,638. Highest level of offering: doctorate.
ACCREDITATIONS: SC AUD BUS CLPSY ENG IPSY JOUR LIB MED NUR SP SW BUSA

University of Southern California

University Park
Transcript Office
Los Angeles, CA 90089-0912
(213) 743-1516

Will confirm attendance and degree by phone or mail. Inquiry must include student's name, date of birth, social security number. Requests should be directed to: Verification Department. Employers may obtain transcripts upon written request accompanied by a $2.00 fee and a signed release from the student.

A doctoral-level institution with a medical school, with an enrollment of 30,373. Highest level of offering: doctorate.
ACCREDITATIONS: WC APCP ARCH BUS CLPSY DENT DH DIETI ENG HSA IPSY JOUR TED LAW LIB MED MFCD MUS NMT OT PHAR PTA SW MIDWF

University of Southern Colorado

2200 Bonforte Boulevard
Pueblo, CO 81001
(303) 549-2261

Will confirm attendance and degree by phone or mail. Inquiry must include student's name, social security number. Employers may obtain transcripts upon written request accompanied by a signed release from the student. Requests should be directed to: Records Office.

A general baccalaureate institution, with an enrollment of 4,802. Highest level of offering: master's.
ACCREDITATIONS: NH ADNUR ENGT MUS NUR SW TED

University of Southern Indiana

8600 University Boulevard
Evansville, IN 47712
(812) 464-1763
Fax (812) 464-1960

Will confirm attendance and degree by phone, fax or mail. Inquiry must include student's name, social security number. Employers may obtain transcripts upon written request accompanied by a signed release from the student.

A general baccalaureate institution, with an enrollment of 7,021.
ACCREDITATIONS: NH DA DH DT ENGT RAD RSTH TED

University of Southern Maine

37 College Avenue
Gorham, ME 04038
(207) 780-5230
Fax (207) 780-5517

Will confirm attendance and degree by mail. Inquiry must include student's name, social security number, years attended. Employers may obtain transcripts upon written request accompanied by a signed release from the student. Fee is $3.00.

A comprehensive institution with no medical school, with an enrollment of 10,540. Highest level of offering: master's and juris doctorate.

ACCREDITATIONS: EH ART LAW MUS NUR SW TED

University of Southern Mississippi

Admissions & Records
Southern Station Box 5006
Hattiesburg, MS 39406
(601) 266-5396
Fax (601) 266-5816

Will confirm attendance and degree by phone or mail. Inquiry must include student's name, date of birth, social security number, years attended. Employers may obtain transcripts upon written request accompanied by a $1.00 fee per copy, $2.00 for certified copy and a signed release from the student.

A doctoral-level institution with no medical school, with an enrollment of 13,250. Highest level of offering: doctorate.

ACCREDITATIONS: SC AUD ART BUS CLPSY COPSY DIET ENGT LIB MT MUS NUR SCPSY TED BUSA SP SW DANCE THEA

University of Southwestern Louisiana

PO Box 41208
Lafayette, LA 70504
(318) 231-6000 Ext. 6295

Will confirm attendance and degree by phone or mail. Inquiry must include student's name, social security number, years attended. Requests should be directed to: Transcript Clerk. Employers may obtain transcripts upon written request accompanied by a $1.00 fee and a signed release from the student.

A comprehensive institution with no medical school, with an enrollment of 15,515. Highest level of offering: doctorate.

ACCREDITATIONS: SC ARCH ENG MRA MUS NUR SP TED

University of Steubenville

Registrar's Office
Fransciscon Way
Steubenville, OH 43952
(614) 283-6207
Fax (614) 283-6472

Will confirm attendance and degree by phone, fax or mail. Inquiry must include student's name, social security number. Employers may obtain transcripts upon written request accompanied by a $2.00 fee and a signed release from the student.

A general baccalaureate institution, with an enrollment of 1,700. Highest level of offering: master's.

ACCREDITATIONS: NCA NUR

University of Tampa

401 West Kennedy Boulevard
Tampa, FL 33606
(813) 253-6251

Will confirm attendance and degree by phone or mail. Inquiry must include student's name, social security number, years attended. Employers may obtain transcripts upon written request accompanied by a $5.00 fee and a signed release from the student.

A general baccalaureate institution, with an enrollment of 2,047. Highest level of offering: master's.

ACCREDITATIONS: SC MUS

University of Tennessee–Memphis

119 Randolph Hall
800 Madison Ave.
Memphis, TN 38163
(901) 528-5563

Will confirm attendance and degree by mail. Inquiry must include student's name, social security number, years attended. Employers may obtain transcripts upon written request accompanied by a signed release from the student. Direct inquiries to: Office of Registrar, 119 Randolph Hall.

A health science center school, with an enrollment of 1,850. Highest level of offering: doctorate.

ACCREDITATIONS: SC BBT CYTO DENT DH DIETI HT IPSY MED MRA MT NUR PHAR PTA SW

University of Tennessee at Chattanooga

615 McCallie Avenue
Chattanooga, TN 37403
(615) 755-4416

Will confirm attendance and degree by phone or mail. Inquiry must include student's name, social security number, years attended. Employers may obtain transcripts upon written request accompanied by a $2.00 fee and a signed release from the student.

A comprehensive institution with no medical school, with an enrollment of 7,464. Highest level of offering: master's.

ACCREDITATIONS: SC BUS ENG MUS NUR SW TED

University of Tennessee at Knoxville

Student Services
Knoxville, TN 37996
(615) 974-2101

Will confirm attendance and degree by phone or mail. Inquiry must include student's name, social security number, years attended. Employers may obtain transcripts upon written request accompanied by a signed release from the student.

A doctoral-level institution with a medical school at Memphis, TN, with an enrollment of 26,158. Highest level of offering: doctorate.

ACCREDITATIONS: SC ANEST ARCH ART AUD BUS CHE CLPSY COPSY CYTO DIET BUSA ENG TED VET FIDER FOR JOUR LAW LIB MT MUS NMT NUR RAD SP SW

University of Tennessee at Martin

Admissions Bldg.–Room 103
Martin, TN 38238
(901) 587-7050

Will confirm attendance and degree by phone or mail. Inquiry must include student's name, social security number, years attended. Requests should be directed to: Registrar's Office. Employers may obtain transcripts upon written request accompanied by a signed release from the student.

A comprehensive institution with no medical school, with an enrollment of 5,366. Highest level of offering: master's.

ACCREDITATIONS: SC ADNUR ENGT MUS SW TED

University of Texas at Arlington

PO Box 19088
Arlington, TX 76019
(817) 273-3719

Will confirm attendance and degree by phone or mail. Inquiry must include student's name, social security number. Requests should be directed to: Records Office. Employers may obtain transcripts upon written request accompanied by a $3.00 fee and a signed release from the student.

A comprehensive institution with no medical school, with an enrollment of 23,397. Highest level of offering: doctorate.

ACCREDITATIONS: SC ARCH BUS ENG FIDER MUS NUR SW BUSA

University of Texas at Austin

Attn: Transcripts
Main Bldg.–Room 1
Austin, TX 78712
(512) 471-7701

Will confirm attendance and degree by phone or mail. Inquiry must include student's name, social security number, years attended. Employers may obtain transcripts upon written request accompanied by a $5.00 fee and a signed release from the student.

A doctoral-level institution with no medical school, with an enrollment of 47,973. Highest level of offering: doctorate.

ACCREDITATIONS: SC ARCH AUD BUS CLPSY COPSY DIET ENG FIDER IPSY JOUR LAW TED LIB MUS NUR PHAR SCPSY SP SW THEA

University of Texas at Dallas

PO Box 830688
Richardson, TX 75083-0688
(214) 690-2341
Fax (214) 690-2599

Will confirm attendance and degree by phone, fax or mail. Inquiry must include student's name, social security number. Employers may obtain transcripts upon written request accompanied by a $5.00 fee and a signed release from the student.

A doctoral-level institution with no medical school, with an enrollment of 8,800. Highest level of offering: doctorate.
ACCREDITATIONS: SC AUD SP

University of Texas at El Paso

El Paso, TX 79968-0599
(915) 747-5544

Will confirm attendance and degree by phone or mail. Inquiry must include student's name, social security number, years attended. Employers may obtain transcripts upon written request accompanied by a $2.00 fee and a signed release from the student.

A comprehensive institution with no medical school, with an enrollment of 15,322. Highest level of offering: doctorate.
ACCREDITATIONS: SC ENG MT MUS NUR TED

University of Texas at San Antonio

Office of Admissions
6900 N. Loop 1604 West
San Antonio, TX 78249-0616
(512) 691-4530

Will confirm attendance and degree by phone or mail. Inquiry must include student's name, social security number, years attended. Employers may obtain transcripts upon written request accompanied by a $4.00 fee and a signed release from the student.

A comprehensive institution with no medical school, with an enrollment of 15,600 Highest level of offering: master's.
ACCREDITATIONS: SC ART BUS MUS PTA

University of Texas at Tyler

3900 University Boulevard
Tyler, TX 75701
(903) 566-7190

Will confirm attendance and degree by phone or mail. Inquiry must include student's name, social security number. Employers may obtain transcripts upon written request accompanied by a $2.00 fee and a signed release from the student.

A comprehensive institution with no medical school, with an enrollment of 3,670. Highest level of offering: master's.
ACCREDITATIONS: SC MT NUR

University of Texas Health Science Center at Houston

Registrar's Office
PO Box 20036
1100 Hodcombe Bldg. Suite 533
Houston, TX 77225
(713) 792-7444
Fax (713) 794-5701

Will confirm attendance and degree by phone or mail. Inquiry must include student's name, years attended. Employers may obtain transcripts upon written request accompanied by a $2.50 fee and a signed release from the student.

A health science centerl school, with an enrollment of 3,125. Highest level of offering: doctorate.
ACCREDITATIONS: SC ANEST BBT CYTO DA DENT DH DIET HT MED MT NUR PH RAD PERF

University of Texas Health Science Center at San Antonio

7703 Floyd Curl Drive
San Antonio, TX 78284-7702
(512) 567-2621
Fax (512) 567-2685

Will confirm attendance and degree by mail. Inquiry must include student's name, social security number, years attended. Employers may obtain transcripts upon written request accompanied by a $2.00 fee and a signed release from the student.

A health sciences center, with an enrollment of 2,362. Highest level of offering: doctorate.
ACCREDITATIONS: SC BBT CYTO DA DENT DH DT HT IPSY MED MT NUR OT EMT

University of Texas Medical Branch at Galveston

Old Red Room 1.212
Galveston, TX 77555-1305
(409) 722-1215

Will confirm attendance and degree by phone or mail. Inquiry must include student's name, social security number. Employers may obtain transcripts upon written request accompanied by a signed release from the student.

A medical school, with an enrollment of 1,678. Highest level of offering: first professional degree.
ACCREDITATIONS: SACS APCP BBT CYTO MED MICB MRA MT NUR OT PTA RSTH RTT

University of Texas of the Permian Basin

4901 East University
Odessa, TX 79762
(915) 367-2138
Fax (915) 367-2115

Will confirm attendance and degree by phone or mail. Inquiry must include student's name, social security number. Employers may obtain transcripts upon written request accompanied by a $3.00 fee and a signed release from the student.

A comprehensive institution with no medical school, with an enrollment of 2,100. Highest level of offering: master's.
ACCREDITATIONS: SC

University of Texas Southwestern Medical Center

5323 Harry Hines Boulevard
Dallas, TX 75235-9096
(214) 688-2671
Fax (214) 688-3289

Will confirm attendance and degree by phone, fax or mail. Inquiry must include student's name, social security number. Employers may obtain transcripts upon written request accompanied by a signed release from the student.

A medical school, with an enrollment of 1,479. Highest level of offering: doctorate.
ACCREDITATIONS: SC APCP BBT DIET IPSY MED MT PTA

University of the District of Columbia

4200 Connecticut Avenue North West
Bldg. 39 Room A09
Washington, DC 20008
(202) 282-3200

Will confirm attendance and degree by phone or mail. Inquiry must include student's name, social security number, years attended. Employers may obtain transcripts upon written request accompanied by a $2.00 fee and a signed release from the student.

A comprehensive institution with no medical school, with an enrollment of 12,832. Highest level of offering: master's.
ACCREDITATIONS: M ADNUR ENG ENGT FUSER NUR RAD RSTH SP SW

University of the Ozarks

415 College Avenue
Clarksville, AR 72830
(501) 754-3839
Fax (501) 754-3839

Will confirm attendance and degree by fax or mail. Inquiry must include student's name, release. Employers may obtain transcripts upon written request accompanied by a $2.00 fee and a signed release from the student.

A general baccalaureate institution, with an enrollment of 625. Highest level of offering: four or five year baccalaureate.
ACCREDITATIONS: NH TED

University of the Pacific

3601 Pacific Avenue
Stockton, CA 95211
(209) 946-2135
Fax (209) 946-2689

Will confirm attendance and degree by mail. Inquiry must include student's name, social security number, years attended. Employers may obtain transcripts upon written request accompanied by a signed release from the student.

A doctoral-level institution with a dental school, with an enrollment of 5,500. Highest level of offering: doctorate.
ACCREDITATIONS: WC ART BUS DENT ENG LAW MUS PHAR SP TED

University of the South

Sewanee, TN 37375
(615) 598-1314
Fax (615) 598-1145

Will confirm attendance and degree by phone or mail. Inquiry must include student's name, years attended. Employers may obtain transcripts upon written request accompanied by a signed release from the student.

A liberal arts undergraduate institution, with an enrollment of 1,100 and a graduate school of theology with an enrollment of 75. Highest level of offering: doctorate of ministry.

ACCREDITATIONS: SC THEOL

University of Toledo

2801 West Bancroft
Toledo, OH 43606
(419) 537-2701
Fax (419) 537-4940

Will confirm attendance and degree by phone, fax or mail. Inquiry must include student's name, date of birth, social security number. Employers may obtain transcripts upon written request accompanied by a $4.00 fee and a signed release from the student.

A doctoral-level institution with no medical school, with an enrollment of 21,039. Highest level of offering: doctorate.

ACCREDITATIONS: NH ADNUR BUS CLPSY ENG ENGT LAW MAC MUS NUR PHAR RSTH RSTHT TED PTA SW

University of Tulsa

600 South College
Tulsa, OK 74104
(918) 631-2253

Will confirm attendance and degree by phone or mail. Inquiry must include student's name, social security number, years attended. Employers may obtain transcripts upon written request accompanied by a $2.00 fee and a signed release from the student.

A comprehensive institution with no medical school, with an enrollment of 4,318. Highest level of offering: doctorate.

ACCREDITATIONS: NH BUS ENG LAW MUS NUR TED

University of Utah

Room 250, Student Services Bldg.
Salt Lake City, UT 84112
(801) 581-8965
Fax (801) 585-3034

Will confirm attendance and degree by phone or mail. Inquiry must include student's name, date of birth, social security number, years attended. Employers may obtain transcripts upon written request accompanied by a $2.00 fee and a signed release from the student.

A doctoral-level institution with a medical school, with an enrollment of 24,568. Highest level of offering: doctorate.

ACCREDITATIONS: NW APCP ARCH AUD BUS CHPM CLPSY COPSY ENG IPSY JOUR LAW TED BUSA MED MICB MT MUS NUR PHAR PTA RAD RTT SCPSY SP SW MIDWF

University of Vermont and State Agricultural College

360 Waterman Bldg.
Office of Registrar
Attn: Academic Transcript
Burlington, VT 05405
(802) 656-2045
Fax (807) 656-8230

Will confirm attendance and degree by phone, fax or mail. Inquiry must include student's name, social security number, years attended. Employers may obtain transcripts upon written request accompanied by a $5.00 fee and a signed release from the student.

A doctoral-level institution with a medical school, with an enrollment of 11,338. Highest level of offering: doctorate.

ACCREDITATIONS: EH ADNUR CLPSY CYTO DH ENG FOR MED MT MUS NMT TED NUR PTA RAD RTT SP SW

University of Virginia Clinch Valley College

Wise, VA 24293
(703) 328-0116
Fax (703) 328-0115

Will confirm attendance and degree by phone or mail. Inquiry must include student's name, social security number. Employers may obtain transcripts upon written request accompanied by a signed release from the student.

A general baccalaureate institution, with an enrollment of 1,594. Highest level of offering: four or five year baccalaureate.

ACCREDITATIONS: SC

University of Virginia Main Campus

PO Box 9009
Charlottesville, VA 22906
(804) 924-4122

Will confirm attendance and degree by mail. Inquiry must include student's name, social security number, years attended, release. Employers may obtain transcripts upon written request accompanied by a $3.00 fee and a signed release from the student.

A doctoral-level institution with a medical school, with an enrollment of 17,910. Highest level of offering: doctorate.

ACCREDITATIONS: SC ARCH AUD BUS DIETI ENG IPSY LAW LSAR MED MT NMT TED BUSA CLPSY PAST PSPSY NUR RAD RTT SP

University of Washington

1400 North East Campus Park Way
Seattle, WA 98195
(206) 543-8580
Fax (206) 685-3660

Will confirm attendance and degree by phone, fax or mail. Inquiry must include student's name, date of birth, social security number, years attended. Employers may obtain transcripts upon written request accompanied by a $3.00 fee and a signed release from the student. Requests should be directed to: Registrar's Office.

A doctoral-level institution with a medical school, with an enrollment of 33,238. Highest level of offering: doctorate.

ACCREDITATIONS: NW APCP ARCH ART AUD BUS CLPSY CYTO DENT ENG FOR HSA IPSY JOUR LAW LIB LSAR MED MICB MT MUS NUR OT PH PHAR PTA RTT SP SW TED BUSA

University of West Florida

11000 University Parkway
Pensacola, FL 32514-5750
(904) 474-2244

Will confirm attendance and degree by phone or mail. Inquiry must include student's name, social security number. Requests should be directed to: Office of Records and Registration. Employers may obtain transcripts upon written request accompanied by a signed release from the student.

A comprehensive institution with no medical school, with an enrollment of 8,000. Highest level of offering: master's.

ACCREDITATIONS: SC MUS NUR SW

University of West Los Angeles–Law School

12201 Washington Place
Los Angeles, CA 90066
(213) 313-1011
Fax (213) 313-2124

Will confirm attendance and degree by fax or mail. Inquiry must include student's name, social security number, years attended, release. Employers may obtain transcripts upon written request accompanied by a $3.00 fee and a signed release from the student.

A law school, with an enrollment of 375. Highest level of offering: first professional degree.

ACCREDITATIONS: WC

University of Wisconsin–Eau Claire

Schofield 130
Eau Claire, WI 54702
(715) 836-4524
Fax (715) 836-2380

Will confirm attendance and degree by phone, fax or mail. Inquiry must include student's name, social security number. Requests should be directed to: Registrar's Office. Employers may obtain transcripts upon written request accompanied by a signed release from the student.

A comprehensive institution with no medical school, with an enrollment of 10,245. Highest level of offering: beyond master's but less than doctorate.

ACCREDITATIONS: NH BUS JOUR MUS NUR SP SW

University of Wisconsin–Green Bay

2420 Nicolet Drive
Green Bay, WI 54311-7001
(414) 465-2055

Will confirm attendance and degree by phone or mail. Inquiry must include student's name, social security number. Employers may obtain transcripts upon written request accompanied by a $3.00 fee and a signed release from the student. Requests should be directed to: Registrar's Office.

A comprehensive institution with no medical school, with an enrollment of 4,876. Highest level of offering: master's.

ACCREDITATIONS: NH MUS

University of Wisconsin–La Crosse

1725 State Street
La Crosse, WI 54601
(608) 785-8000 Ext. 8576

Will confirm attendance and degree by phone or mail. Inquiry must include student's name, social security number. Employers may obtain transcripts upon written request accompanied by a $3.00 fee and a signed release from the student. Requests should be directed to: Records and Registration.

A comprehensive institution with no medical school, with an enrollment of 9,109. Highest level of offering: master's.

ACCREDITATIONS: NH BUS MUS PTA SW TED

University of Wisconsin–Madison

750 University Avenue
Madison, WI 53706
(608) 262-3811

Will confirm attendance and degree by mail. Inquiry must include student's name, social security number, years attended. Employers may obtain transcripts upon written request accompanied by a signed release from the student.

A doctoral-level institution with a medical school, with an enrollment of 44,218. Highest level of offering: doctorate.

ACCREDITATIONS: NH APCP AUD BUS CLPSY CYTO DIET DIETI ENG FIDER FOR HSA VET IPSY JOUR LAW LIB LSAR MED MT MUS NUR OT PHAR PTA RAD RTT SP SW DANCE

University of Wisconsin–Milwaukee

PO Box 729
Milwaukee, WI 53201
(414) 229-4538 (Undergraduate)
(414) 229-4984 (Graduate)
Fax (414) 229-6940

Will confirm attendance and degree by phone or mail. Inquiry must include student's name, social security number, years attended. Employers may obtain transcripts upon written request accompanied by a $3.00 fee and a signed release from the student.

A doctoral-level institution with no medical school, with an enrollment of 24,857. Highest level of offering: doctorate.

ACCREDITATIONS: NH ARCH BUS CLPSY ENG LIB MRA MUS NUR OT SP SW TED

University of Wisconsin–Oshkosh

800 Algoma Boulevard
Oshkosh, WI 54901
(414) 424-0325
Fax (414) 424-7317

Will confirm attendance and degree by phone, fax or mail. Inquiry must include student's name, social security number. Employers may obtain transcripts upon written request accompanied by a $3.00 fee and a signed release from the student.

A comprehensive institution with no medical school, with an enrollment of 10,800. Highest level of offering: master's.

ACCREDITATIONS: NH BUS JOUR MUS NUR SW TED

University of Wisconsin–Parkside

Box 2000
Kenosha, WI 53141
(414) 595-2284

Will confirm attendance and degree by phone or mail. Inquiry must include student's name, date of birth, social security number, years attended. Employers may obtain transcripts upon written request accompanied by a $3.00 fee and a signed release from the student. Requests should be directed to: Student Records Office.

A general baccalaureate institution, with an enrollment of 5,544. Highest level of offering: master's.

ACCREDITATIONS: NCA

University of Wisconsin–Platteville

1 University Plaza
Platteville, WI 53818
(608) 342-1321

Will confirm attendance and degree by phone or mail. Inquiry must include student's name, social security number. Employers may obtain transcripts upon written request accompanied by a signed release from the student. Requests should be directed to: Registrar's Office.

A comprehensive institution with no medical school, with an enrollment of 5,433. Highest level of offering: master's.

ACCREDITATIONS: NH ENG

University of Wisconsin–River Falls

River Falls, WI 54022
(715) 425-3342

Will confirm attendance and degree by phone or mail. Inquiry must include student's name, date of birth, social security number. Employers may obtain transcripts upon written request accompanied by a $2.00 fee and a signed release from the student. Requests should be directed to: Registrar's Office.

A comprehensive institution with no medical school, with an enrollment of 5,236. Highest level of offering: master's.

ACCREDITATIONS: NH JOUR TED

University of Wisconsin–Stevens Point

Stevens Point, WI 54481
(715) 346-4301

Will confirm attendance and degree by mail. Inquiry must include student's name, social security number. Requests should be directed to: Record & Registrar's Office. Employers may obtain transcripts upon written request accompanied by a $4.00 fee and a signed release from the student.

A comprehensive institution with no medical school, with an enrollment of 8,800. Highest level of offering: master's.

ACCREDITATIONS: NH AUD DANCE FOR MUS SP

University of Wisconsin–Stout

109 Bowman Hall
Menomonie, WI 54751
(715) 232-2121

Will confirm attendance and degree by phone or mail. Inquiry must include student's name, social security number, self addressed stamped envelope. Employers may obtain transcripts upon written request accompanied by a signed release from the student. Requests should be directed to: Record & Registrar' Office.

A comprehensive institution with no medical school, with an enrollment of 6,961. Highest level of offering: beyond master's but less than doctorate.

ACCREDITATIONS: NH MFCD TED

University of Wisconsin–Superior

1800 Grand
Superior, WI 54880
(715) 394-8228

Will confirm attendance and degree by phone or mail. Inquiry must include student's name, social security number, years attended. Employers may obtain transcripts upon written request accompanied by a $3.00 fee and a signed release from the student. Requests should be directed to: Registrar's Office.

A comprehensive institution with no medical school, with an enrollment of 2,200. Highest level of offering: beyond master's but less than doctorate.

ACCREDITATIONS: NH MUS SW

University of Wisconsin–Whitewater

Registrar's Office
Attn: Transcripts
Whitewater, WI 53190
(414) 472-1213

Will confirm attendance and degree by phone or mail. Inquiry must include student's name, social security number. Employers may obtain transcripts upon written request accompanied by a $3.00 fee and a signed release from the student. Requests should be directed to: Transcript Office.

A comprehensive institution with no medical school, with an enrollment of 10,737. Highest level of offering: master's.

ACCREDITATIONS: NH BUS MUS SP SW TED

University of Wisconsin

60 Petterson 750 University Avenue
Madison, WI 53706
(608) 262-3722

Will confirm attendance and degree by phone or mail. Inquiry must include student's name, social security number, self addressed stamped envelope. Employers may obtain transcripts upon written request accompanied by a signed release from the student. Requests should be directed to: Transcript Department.

A multiprogram two-year institution, with an enrollment of 43,000. Highest level of offering: one year but less than four years.

ACCREDITATIONS: NH

University of Wyoming

Box 3964 University Station
Laramie, WY 82071
(307) 766-5725

Will confirm attendance and degree by phone or mail. Inquiry must include student's name, date of birth, social security number, years attended. Employers may obtain transcripts upon written request accompanied by a $3.00 fee and a signed release from the student.

A doctoral-level institution with no medical school, with an enrollment of 12,000. Highest level of offering: doctorate.

ACCREDITATIONS: NH AUD BUS CLPSY ENG LAW MT MUS NUR PHAR SP SW TED

Upper Iowa University

PO Box 1857
Fayette, IA 52142
(319) 425-5268
Fax (319) 425-5271

Will confirm attendance and degree by phone, fax or mail. Inquiry must include student's name, date of birth. Employers may obtain transcripts upon written request accompanied by a $2.00 fee and a signed release from the student. Requests should be directed to: Registrar's Office.

A general baccalaureate institution, with an enrollment of 2,100. Highest level of offering: four or five year baccalaureate.

ACCREDITATIONS: NH

Upsala College

345 Prospect Street
East Orange, NJ 07019
(201) 266-7000

Will confirm attendance and degree by phone or mail. Inquiry must include student's name, social security number, years attended. Employers may obtain transcripts upon written request accompanied by a $5.00 fee and a signed release from the student. Requests should be directed to: Registrar's Office.

A general baccalaureate institution, with an enrollment of 1,822. Highest level of offering: master's.

ACCREDITATIONS: M SW

Urbana University

College Way
Urbana, OH 43078
(513) 652-1301 Ext. 353
Fax (513) 652-3835

Will confirm attendance and degree by phone or mail. Inquiry must include student's name, date of birth, social security number. Employers may obtain transcripts upon written request accompanied by a $3.00 fee and a signed release from the student.

A general baccalaureate, with an enrollment of 950. Highest level of offering: four or five year baccalaureate.

ACCREDITATIONS: NH

Ursinus College

Main Street
Collegeville, PA 19426
(215) 489-4111 Ext. 2225

Will confirm attendance and degree by phone or mail. Inquiry must include student's name. Employers may obtain transcripts upon written request accompanied by a $2.00 fee and a signed release from the student. Requests should be directed to: Registrar's Office.

A general baccalaureate institution, with an enrollment of 2,136. Highest level of offering: four or five year baccalaureate.

ACCREDITATIONS: M

Ursuline College

2550 Lander Road
Pepper Pike, OH 44124
(216) 449-4200 Ext. 256
Fax (216) 449-3180

Will confirm attendance and degree by phone or mail. Inquiry must include student's name, social security number. Employers may obtain transcripts upon written request accompanied by a $2.00 fee and a signed release from the student.

A general baccalaureate institution, with an enrollment of 1,583. Highest level of offering: master's.

ACCREDITATIONS: NH NUR

Utah State University

Logan, UT 84322-1600
(801) 750-3988

Will confirm attendance and degree by phone or mail. Inquiry must include student's name, social security number, years attended. Employers may obtain transcripts upon written request accompanied by a $3.00 fee and a signed release from the student. Requests should be directed to: Records Office.

A doctoral-level institution with no medical school, with an enrollment of 14,426. Highest level of offering: doctorate.

ACCREDITATIONS: NW ADNUR AUD BUS DIET ENG FOR LSAR MUS PSPSY SP SW TED

Utah Technical College at Provo

(See Utah Valley Community College)

Utah Technical College at Salt Lake City

(See Salt Lake Community College.)

Utah Valley Community College

(Formerly Utah Technical College at Provo)
1200 South 800th West
Orem, UT 84058
(801) 222-8000 Ext. 8493

Will confirm attendance and degree by phone or mail. Inquiry must include student's name, social security number, years attended. Employers may obtain transcripts upon written request accompanied by a $2.00 fee and a signed release from the student.

A multiprogram two-year institution, with an enrollment of 5,821. Highest level of offering: one year but less than four years.

ACCREDITATIONS: NW DA

Utica College of Syracuse University

Burrstone Road
Utica, NY 13502
(315) 792-3195
Fax (315) 792-3292

Will confirm attendance and degree by phone or mail. Inquiry must include student's name, date of birth, social security number. Employers may obtain transcripts upon written request accompanied by a $3.00 fee and a signed release from the student.

A general baccalaureate institution, with an enrollment of 2,352. Highest level of offering: four or five year baccalaureate.

ACCREDITATIONS: M MT NY OT SURGT

Utica Junior College

(See Hinds Community College, Utica Campus)

Utica School of Commerce

201 Bleecker Street
Utica, NY 13501
(315) 733-2307
Fax (315) 733-9281

Will confirm attendance and degree by phone or mail. Inquiry must include student's name, social security number, years attended. Employers may obtain transcripts upon written request accompanied by a signed release from the student.

A single program two-year institution, with an enrollment of 600. Highest level of offering: one year but less than four years.

ACCREDITATIONS: NY

V

Valdosta State College

Valdosta, GA 31698
(912) 333-5727

Will confirm attendance and degree by mail. Inquiry must include student's name, social security number, signed release. Employers may obtain transcripts upon written request accompanied by a $2.00 fee and a signed release from the student. Requests should be directed to: Registrar's Office.

A comprehensive institution with no medical school, with an enrollment of 7,200. Highest level of offering: beyond master's but less than doctorate.

ACCREDITATIONS: SC BUS MUS NUR TED

V

Valencia Community College

East Campus
701 N. Econlockhatchee Trail
Orlando, FL 32825
or
West Campus
1800 S. Kirkman Rd
Orlando, FL 32811
(407) 299-5000 Ext. 1320

Will confirm attendance and degree by phone or mail. Inquiry must include student's name, social security number. Employers may obtain transcripts upon written request accompanied by a signed release from the student.

A multiprogram two-year institution, with an enrollment of 21,000. Highest level of offering: one year but less than four years.
ACCREDITATIONS: SC ADNUR DH MLTAD RSTH

Valley City State University

101 College Street
Valley City, ND 58072
(701) 845-7297
Fax (701) 845-7245

Will confirm attendance and degree by phone, fax or mail. Inquiry must include student's name, social security number. Employers may obtain transcripts upon written request accompanied by a $2.00 fee and a signed release from the student.

A general baccalaureate institution, with an enrollment of 1,083. Highest level of offering: four or five year baccalaureate
ACCREDITATIONS: NH TED

Valley Forge Christian College

1401 Charlestown Road
Phoenixville, PA 19460
(215) 935-0450 Ext. 223

Will confirm attendance and degree by phone or mail. Inquiry must include student's name, social security number, years attended. Employers may obtain transcripts upon written request accompanied by a $2.00 fee and a signed release from the student.

A school of religion and theology, with an enrollment of 500. Highest level of offering: four or five year baccalaureate.
ACCREDITATIONS: BI

Valley Forge Military Junior College

1001 Eagle Road
Wayne, PA 19087
(215) 688-3153 or 688-1800 Ext. 239
Fax (215) 688-0829

Will confirm attendance and degree by phone, fax or mail. Inquiry must include student's name. Employers may obtain transcripts upon written request accompanied by a $3.00 fee and a signed release from the student. Requests should be directed to: Registrar.

A multiprogram two-year institution, with an enrollment of 220. Highest level of offering: two years but less than four years.
ACCREDITATIONS: M

Valparaiso University

Valparaiso, IN 46383
(219) 464-5212
Fax (219) 464-5381

Will confirm attendance and degree by phone, fax or mail. Inquiry must include student's name, date of birth, social security number, years attended. Employers may obtain transcripts upon written request accompanied by a signed release from the student. Requests should be directed to: Registrar's Office.

A comprehensive institution with no medical school, with an enrollment of 3,958. Highest level of offering: master's.
ACCREDITATIONS: NH ENG LAW MUS NUR SW TED

Vance–Granville Community College

PO Box 917
Henderson, NC 27536
(919) 492-2061 Ext. 265
Fax (919) 430-0460

Will confirm attendance and degree by phone or mail. Inquiry must include student's name, social security number. Requests should be directed to: Registrar's Office. Employers may obtain transcripts upon written request accompanied by a $1.00 fee and a signed release from the student.

A multiprogram two-year institution, with an enrollment of 2,000. Highest level of offering: two years but less than four years.
ACCREDITATIONS: SC R

Vanderbilt University

242 Alexander Hall
Nashville, TN 37240
(615) 322-7701
Fax (615) 343-7709
(Include company phone & address)

Will confirm attendance and degree by phone, fax or mail. Inquiry must include student's name, maiden name, field of study, social security number. Employers may obtain transcripts upon written request accompanied by a $2.00 fee and a signed release from the student. $5.00 for fax response. Requests should be directed to: Registrar's Office.

A doctoral-level institution with a medical school, with an enrollment of 9,046. Highest level of offering: doctorate.
ACCREDITATIONS: SC AUD BBT BUS CLPSY DIETI ENG IPSY LAW LIB PSPSY MED TED MT THEOL NMT NUR RSTH RTT SP DMS PERF

Vandercook College of Music

3209 S Michigan Avenue
Chicago, IL 60616
(312) 225-6288

Will confirm attendance and degree by phone or mail. Inquiry must include student's name, social security number, years attended. Employers may obtain transcripts upon written request accompanied by a $3.00 fee and a signed release from the student.

A school of education, with an enrollment of 170. Highest level of offering: master's.
ACCREDITATIONS: NH MUS

Vassar College

Raymond Avenue
Poughkeepsie, NY 12601
(914) 437-7000 Ext. 5270

Will confirm attendance and degree by phone or mail. Inquiry must include student's name, date of birth. Employers may obtain transcripts upon written request accompanied by a $2.00 fee and a signed release from the student. Requests should be directed to: Registrar's Office.

A general baccalaureate institution, with an enrollment of 2,258. Highest level of offering: master's.
ACCREDITATIONS: M NY

Vennard College

University Park, IA 52595
(515) 673-8391 Ext. 211

Will confirm attendance and degree by phone or mail. Inquiry must include student's name, social security number. Employers may obtain transcripts upon written request accompanied by a $2.00 fee and a signed release from the student.

A school of philosophy, religion and theology, with an enrollment of 201. Highest level of offering: four or five year baccalaureate.
ACCREDITATIONS: BI

Ventura College

4667 Telegraph Road
Ventura, CA 93003
(805) 654-6456
Fax (805) 654-6466

Will confirm attendance and degree by phone or mail. Inquiry must include student's name, date of birth, social security number, years attended, release. Requests should be directed to: Admissions & Records. Employers may obtain transcripts upon written request accompanied by a $3.00 fee and a signed release from the student.

A multiprogram two-year institution, with an enrollment of 10,725. Highest level of offering: one year but less than four years.
ACCREDITATIONS: WJ RSTH

Vermont College of Norwich University

College Street
Montpelier, VT 05602
(802) 828-8725
Fax (802) 889-8855

Will confirm attendance and degree by phone or mail. Inquiry must include student's name, date of birth, social security number. Employers may obtain transcripts upon written request accompanied by a $4.00 fee and a signed release from the student. Requests should be directed to: Registrar's Office.

A multiprogram four-year institution, with an enrollment of 1,500. Highest level of offering: master's.
ACCREDITATIONS: ADNUR MLTAD NUR

Vermont Law School

PO Box 96
South Royalton, VT 05068
(802) 763-8303 Ext. 2265

Will confirm attendance and degree by phone or mail. Inquiry must include student's name. Employers may obtain transcripts upon written request accompanied by a $2.00 fee and a signed release from the student.

A law school, with an enrollment of 510. Highest level of offering: first professional degree.

ACCREDITATIONS: EH LAW

Vermont Technical College

Randolph Center, VT 05061
(802) 728-3391 Ext. 302
Fax (802) 728-3321

Will confirm attendance and degree by phone, fax or mail. Inquiry must include student's name, social security number. Requests should be directed to: Records Office. Employers may obtain transcripts upon written request accompanied by a $5.00 fee and a signed release from the student.

A multiprogram two-year institution, with an enrollment of 755. Highest level of offering: two years but less than four years.

ACCREDITATIONS: EV ENGT ABET

Vernon Regional Junior College

4400 College Drive
Vernon, TX 76384
(817) 552-6291 Ext. 204
Fax (817) 553-3902

Will confirm attendance and degree by phone, fax or mail. Inquiry must include student's name, social security number. Employers may obtain transcripts upon written request accompanied by a $1.00 fee and a signed release from the student. Requests should be directed to: Office of Admissions and Records.

A multiprogram two-year institution, with an enrollment of 1,849. Highest level of offering: one year but less than four years.

ACCREDITATIONS: SC PNE

Victor Valley College

18422 Bear Valley Road
Victorville, CA 92392-9699
(619) 245-4271
Fax (245) 9745

Will confirm attendance and degree by mail or fax. Inquiry must include student's name, social security number, years attended, release. Employers may obtain transcripts upon written request accompanied by a $2.00 fee and a signed release from the student.

A multiprogram two-year institution, with an enrollment of 6,000. Highest level of offering: one year but less than four years.

ACCREDITATIONS: WJ ADNUR RSTH

Victoria College

2200 East Red River
Victoria, TX 77901
(512) 572-6411
Fax (512) 572-3850

Will confirm attendance and degree by phone, fax or mail. Inquiry must include student's name, date of birth, social security number, years attended. Employers may obtain transcripts upon written request accompanied by a $2.00 fee and a signed release from the student.

A multiprogram two-year institution, with an enrollment of 3,500. Highest level of offering: one year but less than four years.

ACCREDITATIONS: SC ADNUR RSTHT SURGT MLTAD

Villa Julie College

Green Spring Valley Road
Stevenson, MD 21153
(301) 486-7000 Ext. 2207

Will confirm attendance and degree by phone or mail. Inquiry must include student's name, years attended, social security number. Requests should be directed to: Registrar's Office. Employers may obtain transcripts upon written request accompanied by a $2.00 fee and a signed release from the student.

A multiprogram four-year baccalaureate institution, with an enrollment of 1,459. Highest level of offering: four or five year baccalaureate.

ACCREDITATIONS: M MLTAD

Villa Maria College of Buffalo

240 Pine Ridge Road
Buffalo, NY 14225-3999
(716) 871-7614

Will confirm attendance and degree by phone or mail. Inquiry must include student's name, social security number. Requests should be directed to: Registrar's Office. Employers may obtain transcripts upon written request accompanied by a $2.00 fee and a signed release from the student.

A multiprogram two-year institution, with an enrollment of 586. Highest level of offering: one year but less than four years.

ACCREDITATIONS: M NY

Villa Maria College

(See Gannon University)

Villanova University

Villanova, PA 19085
(215) 645-4030

Will confirm attendance and degree by phone or mail. Inquiry must include student's name, date of birth, social security number, years attended. Employers may obtain transcripts upon written request accompanied by a $2.00 fee and a signed release from the student. Requests should be directed to: Registrar's Office.

A comprehensive institution with no medical school, with an enrollment of 11,665. Highest level of offering: doctorate.

ACCREDITATIONS: M BUS ENG LAW NUR BUSA

Vincennes University

1002 North 1st Street
Vincennes, IN 47591
(812) 885-4220
Fax (812) 885-5868

Will confirm attendance and degree by phone, fax or mail. Inquiry must include student's name, social security number, years attended. Requests should be directed to: Records Department. Employers may obtain transcripts upon written request accompanied by a signed release from the student.

A multiprogram two-year institution, with an enrollment of 8,032. Highest level of offering: one year but less than four years.

ACCREDITATIONS: NH ADNUR FUSER PNUR PTAA RSTH THEA

Virginia Commonwealth University

PO Box 2520–827 West Franklin Street
Richmond, VA 23284
(804) 367-1349

Will confirm attendance and degree by phone or mail. Inquiry must include student's name, social security number, years attended. Employers may obtain transcripts upon written request accompanied by a signed release from the student. Requests should be directed to: Certification Office.

A doctoral-level institution with a medical school, with an enrollment of 21,600. Highest level of offering: doctorate.

ACCREDITATIONS: SC ANEST ART BUS CLPSY COPSY DENT DH DIETI BUSA PAST FIDER IPSY HSA TED JOUR MED MICB MRA MT MUS NMT NUR OT PHAR PTA RAD RTT SW

Virginia Highlands Community College

PO Box 828
Abingdon, VA 24210
(703) 628-6094 Ext. 261
Fax (703) 628-7576

Will confirm attendance and degree by phone, fax or mail. Inquiry must include student's name, social security number. Employers may obtain transcripts upon written request accompanied by a signed release from the student.

A multiprogram two-year institution, with an enrollment of 2,150. Highest level of offering: one year but less than four years.

ACCREDITATIONS: SC ADNUR

Virginia Intermont College

Bristol, VA 24201
(703) 669-6101 Ext. 246
Fax (703) 669-5763

Will confirm attendance and degree by phone or mail. Inquiry must include student's name, social security number, years attended. Employers may obtain transcripts upon written request accompanied by a $2.00 fee and a signed release from the student.

A general baccalaureate institution, with an enrollment of 517. Highest level of offering: four or five year baccalaureate.

ACCREDITATIONS: SC SW

Virginia Marti College of Fashion and Art

PO Box 580
Lakewood, OH 44107
(216) 221-8584
Fax (216) 221-2311

Will confirm attendance and degree by phone, fax or mail. Inquiry must include student's name, social security number, years attended. Requests should be directed to: Registrar's Office. Employers may obtain transcripts upon written request accompanied by a $5.00 fee and a signed release from the student.

A two-year institution newly admitted to NCES, with an enrollment of 167. Highest level of offering: one year but less than four years.

ACCREDITATIONS: NATTS

Virginia Military Institute

Lexington, VA 24450
(703) 463-6213
Fax (703) 464-7169

Will confirm attendance and degree by phone, fax or mail. Inquiry must include student's name, social security number, years attended. Employers may obtain transcripts upon written request accompanied by a $3.00 fee and a signed release from the student. Requests should be directed to: Registrar's Office.

A general baccalaureate institution, with an enrollment of 1,300. Highest level of offering: four year baccalaureate.

ACCREDITATIONS: SC ENG

Virginia Polytechnic Institute and State University

248 Burruss Hall
Blacksburg, VA 24061
(703) 231-5611
Fax (703) 231-9139

Will confirm attendance and degree by phone, fax or mail. Inquiry must include student's name, social security number. Requests should be directed to: Records Office. Employers may obtain transcripts upon written request accompanied by a signed release from the student.

A doctoral-level institution with no medical school, with an enrollment of 23,303. Highest level of offering: doctorate.

ACCREDITATIONS: SC ARCH BUS CLPSY DIET ENG VET FOR LSAR MFCD TED BUSA THEA

Virginia State University

PO Box 9217
Petersburg, VA 23806
(804) 524-5986

Will confirm attendance and degree by phone or mail. Inquiry must include student's name, social security number, years attended. Employers may obtain transcripts upon written request accompanied by a $2.00 fee and a signed release from the student. Requests should be directed to: Registrar's Office.

A comprehensive institution with no medical school, with an enrollment of 4,108. Highest level of offering: master's.

ACCREDITATIONS: SC MUS SW TED

Virginia Union University

1500 North Lombardy Street
Richmond, VA 23220
(804) 257-5845

Will confirm attendance and degree by phone or mail. Inquiry must include student's name, social security number, years attended. Employers may obtain transcripts upon written request accompanied by a $3.00 fee and a signed release from the student.

A general baccalaureate institution, with an enrollment of 1,298. Highest level of offering: first professional degree.

ACCREDITATIONS: SC SW THEOL

Virginia Wesleyan College

Wesleyan Drive
Norfolk, VA 23502-5599
(804) 455-3352
Fax (804) 466-8526

Will confirm attendance and degree by phone, fax or mail. Inquiry must include student's name, social security number. Employers may obtain transcripts upon written request accompanied by a $3.00 fee and a signed release from the student. Requests should be directed to: Registrar's Office.

A general baccalaureate institution, with an enrollment of 1,440. Highest level of offering: four or five year baccalaureate.

ACCREDITATIONS: SC

Virginia Western Community College

3095 Colonial Avenue
Roanoke, VA 24038
(703) 857-7238

Will confirm attendance and degree by phone or mail. Inquiry must include student's name, social security number., release Employers may obtain transcripts upon written request accompanied by a signed release from the student.

A multiprogram two-year institution, with an enrollment of 12,389. Highest level of offering: one year but less than four years.

ACCREDITATIONS: SC ADNUR DA DH RAD

Vista College

Teralta District Admissions
333 E. 8th St.
Oakland, CA 94606
(510) 841-8431

Will confirm attendance and degree by mail. Inquiry must include student's name, social security number, years attended, release. Requests should be directed to: Registrar's Office. Employers may obtain transcripts upon written request accompanied by a $1.00 fee and a signed release from the student.

A single program two-year institution, with an enrollment of 5,500. Highest level of offering: one year but less than four years.

ACCREDITATIONS: WJ

Viterbo College

Registrar's Office
815 South 9th
La Crosse, WI 54601
(608) 791-0040 Ext. 411

Will confirm attendance and degree by phone or mail. Inquiry must include student's name, social security number. Employers may obtain transcripts upon written request accompanied by a $3.00 fee and a signed release from the student.

A general baccalaureate institution, with an enrollment of 1,074. Highest level of offering: four or five year baccalaureate.

ACCREDITATIONS: NH DIET MRA MUS NUR TED

Volunteer State Community College

Attn: Admissions and Records
Nashville Pike
Gallatin, TN 37066
(615) 452-8600 Ext. 461
Fax (615) 452-8600 Ext 645

Will confirm attendance and degree by phone, fax or mail. Inquiry must include student's name, social security number. Employers may obtain transcripts upon written request accompanied by a signed release from the student.

A multiprogram two-year institution, with an enrollment of 4,721. Highest level of offering: one year but less than four years.

ACCREDITATIONS: SC DA EMT RADMRT PTAA RSTHT

Voorhees College

Denmark, SC 29042
(803) 793-3351 Ext. 7309

Will confirm attendance and degree by phone or mail. Inquiry must include student's name, social security number, years attended. Employers may obtain transcripts upon written request accompanied by a $2.00 fee and a signed release from the student. Requests should be directed to: Admissions & Records Department.

A general baccalaureate institution, with an enrollment of 501. Highest level of offering: four or five year baccalaureate.

ACCREDITATIONS: SC

W

Wabash College

301 West Wabash
Crawfordsville, IN 47933
(317) 362-1400 Ext. 245

Will confirm attendance and degree by phone or mail. Inquiry must include student's name, years attended. Employers may obtain transcripts upon written request accompanied by a $1.00 fee and a signed release from the student.

A general baccalaureate institution, with an enrollment of 786. Highest level of offering: four or five year baccalaureate.

ACCREDITATIONS: NH

Wadhams Hall Seminary and College

RR4-Box 80
Ogdensburg, NY 13669
(315) 393-4231
Fax (315) 393-4249

Will confirm attendance and degree by phone or mail. Inquiry must include student's name, social security number. Employers may obtain transcripts upon written request accompanied by a $3.00 fee and a signed release from the student.

A specialized school, with an enrollment of 64. Highest level of offering: four year baccalaureate.

ACCREDITATIONS: M NY

Wagner College

631 Howard Avenue
Staten Island, NY 10301
(718) 390-3207

Will confirm attendance and degree by mail. Inquiry must include student's name, social security number, years attended. Employers may obtain transcripts upon written request accompanied by a $5.00 fee and a signed release from the student. Requests should be directed to: Registrar's Office.

A comprehensive institution with no medical school, with an enrollment of 1,521. Highest level of offering: master's.

ACCREDITATIONS: M NMT NUR NY

Wake Forest University

PO Box 7207-Reynold Station
Winston–Salem, NC 27109
(919) 759-5206
Fax (919) 759-6074

Will confirm attendance and degree by phone, fax or mail. Inquiry must include student's name, social security number, years attended. Employers may obtain transcripts upon written request accompanied by a $2.00 fee and a signed release from the student. Requests should be directed to: Registrar's Office.

A comprehensive institution with a medical school, with an enrollment of 5,373. Highest level of offering: doctorate.

ACCREDITATIONS: SC ANEST APCP BUS LAW MED MT BUSA

Wake Technical Community College

9101 Fayetteville Road
Raleigh, NC 27603
(919) 772-7500 Ext. 166

Will confirm attendance and degree by phone or mail. Inquiry must include student's name, social security number, years attended, field of study. Employers may obtain transcripts upon written request accompanied by a signed release from the student. Requests should be directed to: Registrar's Office.

A multiprogram two-year institution, with an enrollment of 6,500. Highest level of offering: two years but less than four years.

ACCREDITATIONS: SACS ENGT RAD

Waldorf College

Forest City, IA 50436
(515) 582-8139
Fax (515) 582-8111

Will confirm attendance and degree by phone, fax or mail. Inquiry must include student's name, years attended. Employers may obtain transcripts upon written request accompanied by a $5.00 fee and a signed release from the student. Requests should be directed to: Registrar's Office.

A multiprogram two-year institution, with an enrollment of 500. Highest level of offering: one year but less than four years.

ACCREDITATIONS: NH

Walker College

1411 Indiana Avenue
Jasper, AL 35501
(205) 387-0511

Will confirm attendance and degree by phone or mail. Inquiry must include student's name, date of birth, social security number. Employers may obtain transcripts upon written request accompanied by a $3.00 fee and a signed release from the student.

A multiprogram two-year institution, with an enrollment of 915. Highest level of offering: one year but less than four years.

ACCREDITATIONS: SC ADNUR

Walker State Technical College

PO Drawer K
Sumiton, AL 35148
(205) 648-3271 Ext. 26

Will confirm attendance and degree by phone or mail. Inquiry must include student's name, social security number. Requests should be directed to: Paul Issacs. Employers may obtain transcripts upon written request by student accompanied by a $2.00 fee.

A two-year institution with an enrollment of 1,400. Highest level of offering: one year but less than four years.

ACCREDITATIONS: SV SACS

Walla Walla College

College Place, WA 99324
(509) 527-2811

Will confirm attendance and degree by phone or mail. Inquiry must include student's name, social security number, years attended. Employers may obtain transcripts upon written request accompanied by a $2.50 fee and a signed release from the student. Requests should be directed to: Academic Records.

A general baccalaureate institution, with an enrollment of 1,585. Highest level of offering: master's.

ACCREDITATIONS: NW ENG MUS NUR SW

Walla Walla Community College

500 Tausick Way
Walla Walla, WA 99362
(509) 527-4283
Fax (509) 527-4480

Will confirm attendance and degree by phone, fax or mail. Inquiry must include student's name, date of birth, social security number. Employers may obtain transcripts upon written request accompanied by a $2.50 fee and a signed release from the student. Requests should be directed to: Admissions Office.

A multiprogram two-year institution, with an enrollment of 3,357. Highest level of offering: one year but less than four years.

ACCREDITATIONS: NW ADNUR

Wallace State Community College at Dothan

Dothan, AL 36303
(205) 983-3521 Ext. 231
Fax (205) 983-4255

Will confirm attendance and degree by phone, fax or mail. Inquiry must include student's name, social security number, years attended. Employers may obtain transcripts upon written request accompanied by a $2.00 fee and a signed release from the student.

A multiprogram two-year institution, with an enrollment of 3,805. Highest level of offering: one year but less than four years.

ACCREDITATIONS: SC ADNUR MLTAD RSTH

Walsh College of Accountancy and Business Administration

PO Box 7006
Troy, MI 48007
(313) 689-8282 Ext. 207
Fax (313) 689-9066

Will confirm attendance and degree by phone, fax or mail. Inquiry must include student's name, social security number. Employers may obtain transcripts upon written request accompanied by a $2.00 fee and a signed release from the student.

A business school, with an enrollment of 3,000. Highest level of offering: master's.

ACCREDITATIONS: NH

Walsh College

2020 Easton Street North West
Canton, OH 44720
(216) 499-7090 Ext. 191

Will confirm attendance and degree by phone or mail. Inquiry must include student's name, social security number, years attended. Employers may obtain transcripts upon written request accompanied by a $2.00 fee and a signed release from the student.

A general baccalaureate institution, with an enrollment of 1,225. Highest level of offering: master's.

ACCREDITATIONS: NH ADNUR

Walters State Community College

500 South Davy Crockett Parkway
Morristown, TN 37813-6899
(615) 587-9722 Ext. 237 or 585-0828

Will confirm attendance and degree by phone or mail. Inquiry must include student's name, social security number, release. Employers may obtain transcripts upon written request accompanied by a signed release from the student. Requests should be directed to: Record & Admissions Office.

A multiprogram two-year institution, with an enrollment of 4,220. Highest level of offering: one year but less than four years.

ACCREDITATIONS: SC ADNUR ENGT

Wang Boston Institute of Graduate Studies

c/o Boston University
Corporate Education Center
72 Tyng Rd
Tyngsboro, MA 01879
(508) 649-9731

Records are maintained at the above location. Will confirm attendance and degree by mail or phone. Inquiry must include student's name, social security number. Employers may obtain transcripts upon written request accompanied by a $2.00 fee and a signed release from the student.

Warner Pacific College

2219 South East 68th Avenue
Portland, OR 97215
(503) 775-4366 Ext. 611

Will confirm attendance and degree by phone or mail. Inquiry must include student's name. Employers may obtain transcripts upon written request accompanied by a $3.00 fee and a signed release from the student.

A general baccalaureate institution, with an enrollment of 570. Highest level of offering: master's.

ACCREDITATIONS: NW

Warner Southern College

5301 Highway 27 South
Lake Wales, FL 33853
(813) 638-1426 Ext. 204

Will confirm attendance and degree by phone or mail. Inquiry must include student's name, social security number. Employers may obtain transcripts upon written request accompanied by a $2.00 fee and a signed release from the student. Requests should be directed to: Registrar's Office.

A general baccalaureate institution, with an enrollment of 429. Highest level of offering: four or five year baccalaureate.

ACCREDITATIONS: SC

Warren Wilson College

701 Warren Wilson Road
Swannanoa, NC 28778
(704) 298-3325 Ext. 253

Will confirm attendance and degree by phone or mail. Inquiry must include student's name, social security number. Employers may obtain transcripts upon written request accompanied by a $3.00 fee and a signed release from the student. Requests should be directed to: Registrar's Office.

A general baccalaureate institution, with an enrollment of 496. Highest level of offering: master's.

ACCREDITATIONS: SC SW

Wartburg College

PO Box 1003
Waverly, IA 50677
(319) 352-8272
Fax (319) 352-8514

Will confirm attendance and degree by phone or mail. Inquiry must include student's name, date of birth, social security number, years attended. Employers may obtain transcripts upon written request accompanied by a $4.00 fee and a signed release from the student. Requests should be directed to: Registrar's Office.

A general baccalaureate institution, with an enrollment of 1,155. Highest level of offering: four or five year baccalaureate.

ACCREDITATIONS: NH MUS SW

Wartburg Theological Seminary

333 Wartburg Place
Dubuque, IA 52003
(319) 589-0211

Will confirm attendance and degree by phone or mail. Inquiry must include student's name, date of birth. Employers may obtain transcripts upon written request accompanied by a $2.00 fee and a signed release from the student.

A school of religion and theology, with an enrollment of 223. Highest level of offering: master's.

ACCREDITATIONS: NH THEOL

Washburn University of Topeka

1700 College–Morgan Hall–Room 114
Topeka, KS 66621
(913) 231-1010 Ext. 1574

Will confirm attendance and degree by phone or mail. Inquiry must include student's name, social security number. Employers may obtain transcripts upon written request accompanied by a $1.00 fee and a signed release from the student. Requests should be directed to: Registrar's Office.

A general baccalaureate institution, with an enrollment of 6,600. Highest level of offering: juris doctorate.

ACCREDITATIONS: NH LAW MUS NUR SW TED RAD PTAA

Washington and Jefferson College

Washington, PA 15301
(412) 222-4400

Will confirm attendance and degree by mail. Inquiry must include student's name, social security number, years attended. Requests should be directed to: Registrar's Office. Employers may obtain transcripts upon written request accompanied by a $2.00 fee and a signed release from the student.

A general baccalaureate institution, with an enrollment of 1,227. Highest level of offering: four or five year baccalaureate.

ACCREDITATIONS: M

Washington and Lee University

Lexington, VA 24450
(703) 463-8455

Will confirm attendance and degree by phone or mail. Inquiry must include student's name. Employers may obtain transcripts upon written request accompanied by a signed release from the student. Requests should be directed to: Registrar's Office.

A general baccalaureate institution, with an enrollment of 2,0005. Highest level of offering: first professional degree.

ACCREDITATIONS: SC BUS JOUR LAW

Washington Bible College

6511 Princess Garden Pkwy
Lanham, MD 20706
(301) 552-1400 Ext. 214
Fax (301) 552-2775

Will confirm attendance and degree by phone or mail. Inquiry must include student's name, date of birth, social security number. Employers may obtain transcripts upon written request accompanied by a $3.00 fee and a signed release from the student.

A school of religion and theology, with an enrollment of 470. Highest level of offering: master's.

ACCREDITATIONS: BI

Washington College

Chestertown, MD 21620
(301) 778-2800 Ext. 215

Will confirm attendance and degree by phone or mail. Inquiry must include student's name. Employers may obtain transcripts upon written request accompanied by a $2.00 fee and a signed release from the student. Requests should be directed to: Registrar's Office.

A general baccalaureate institution, with an enrollment of 865. Highest level of offering: master's.

ACCREDITATIONS: M

Washington State Community College District 17 District Office

North 2000 Greene Street
Spokane, WA 99207
(509) 533-7012

Will confirm attendance and degree by phone or mail. Inquiry must include student's name, social security number. Employers may obtain transcripts upon written request accompanied by a signed release from the student. Requests should be directed to: Administrative Office.

Washington State Community College

710 Colegate Drive
Marietta, OH 45750
(614) 374-8716 Ext. 608

Will confirm attendance and degree by phone or mail. Inquiry must include student's name, social security number, years attended. Employers may obtain transcripts upon written request accompanied by a $1.00 fee and a signed release from the student.

A multiprogram two-year institution, with an enrollment of 2,098. Highest level of offering: one year but less than four years.
ACCREDITATIONS: NH MLTAD

Washington State University

Pullman, WA 99164-1035
(509) 335-5511

Will confirm attendance and degree by phone or mail. Inquiry must include student's name, date of birth, social security number, years attended. Employers may obtain transcripts upon written request by student accompanied by a $3.00 fee. Requests should be directed to: Registrar's Office.

A doctoral-level institution with a medical school, with an enrollment of 16,484. Highest level of offering: doctorate.
ACCREDITATIONS: NW ARCH BUS CLPSY DIET ENG FIDER FOR LSAR MUS NUR PHAR TED VET SP BUSA

Washington Theological Union

9001 New Hampshire Avenue
Silver Spring, MD 20903
(301) 439-0551
Fax (301) 445-4929

Will confirm attendance and degree by phone or mail. Inquiry must include student's name, date of birth, social security number. Employers may obtain transcripts upon written request by student accompanied by a $5.00 fee.

A school of philosophy, religion and theology, with an enrollment of 167. Highest level of offering: master's.
ACCREDITATIONS: M THEOL

Washington University

1 Brookings Drive–Campus Box 1143
Saint Louis, MO 63130
(314) 935-5000

Will confirm attendance and degree by mail. Inquiry must include student's name, social security number, years attended. Employers may obtain transcripts upon written request accompanied by a $4.00 fee and a signed release from the student.

A doctoral-level institution with a medical school, with an enrollment of 10,610. Highest level of offering: doctorate.
ACCREDITATIONS: NH ANEST ARCH ART AUD BUS CLPSY DENT ENG HSA LAW MED TED MICB MUS OT PTA RAD RTT SW

Washtenaw Community College

PO Box D1
Ann Arbor, MI 48106
(313) 973-3548

Will confirm attendance and degree by phone or mail. Inquiry must include student's name, social security number, years attended. Employers may obtain transcripts upon written request accompanied by a $2.00 fee and a signed release from the student. Requests should be directed to: Registrar's Office.

A multiprogram two-year institution, with an enrollment of 10,115. Highest level of offering: one year but less than four years.
ACCREDITATIONS: NH DA RAD RSTH

Waterbury State Technical College

750 Chase Parkway
Waterbury, CT 06708
(203) 575-8091

Will confirm attendance and degree by phone or mail. Inquiry must include student's name, date of birth, social security number, years attended. Employers may obtain transcripts upon written request accompanied by a signed release from the student.

A multiprogram two-year institution, with an enrollment of 1,801. Highest level of offering: one year but less than four years.
ACCREDITATIONS: EV ENGT

Watterson College

4400 Breckinridge Lane
Louisville, KY 40218
(502) 491-5000 Ext. 302

Will confirm attendance and degree by phone or mail. Inquiry must include student's name, social security number, years attended, self addressed stamped envelope. Employers may obtain transcripts upon written request accompanied by a $3.00 fee and a signed release from the student.

A multiprogram two-year institution, with an enrollment of 380. Highest level of offering: one year but less than four years.
ACCREDITATIONS: SC JRCB MAC

Waubonsee Community College

Route 47 at Harter Road
Sugar Grove, IL 60554
(708) 466-4811 Ext. 373
Fax (708) 466-4964

Will confirm attendance and degree by phone, fax or mail. Inquiry must include student's name, social security number. Requests should be directed to: Records Office. Employers may obtain transcripts upon written request accompanied by a signed release from the student.

A multiprogram two-year institution, with an enrollment of 7,402. Highest level of offering: one year but less than four years.
ACCREDITATIONS: NH

Waukesha County Technical Institute

800 Main Street
Pewaukee, WI 53072
(414) 691-5264
Fax (414) 691-5593

Will confirm attendance and degree by phone, fax or mail. Inquiry must include student's name, social security number, years attended, self addressed stamped envelope. Employers may obtain transcripts upon written request accompanied by a $2.00 fee and a signed release from the student. Requests should be directed to: Registrar's Office.

A multiprogram two-year institution, with an enrollment of 4,813. Highest level of offering: one year but less than four years.
ACCREDITATIONS: NH ADNUR MAC PNUR SURGT

Waukesha County Technical College

800 Main Street
Pewaukee, WI 53072
(414) 691-5264

Will confirm attendance and degree by phone or mail. Inquiry must include student's name, social security number, years attended, self addressed stamped envelope. Employers may obtain transcripts upon written request accompanied by a $2.00 fee and a signed release from the student. Requests should be directed to: Student Records Department.

A multiprogram two-year institution, with an enrollment of 4,813. Highest level of offering: one year but less than four years.
ACCREDITATIONS: NH ADNUR MAC PNUR SURGT

Waycross College

2001 Francis Street
Waycross, GA 31501
(912) 285-6133
Fax (912) 287-4909

Will confirm attendance and degree by phone, fax or mail. Inquiry must include student's name, date of birth, social security number. Employers may obtain transcripts upon written request accompanied by a $1.00 fee and a signed release from the student.

A multiprogram two-year institution, with an enrollment of 623. Highest level of offering: one year but less than four years.
ACCREDITATIONS: SC

Wayland Baptist University

1900 West 7th Street
Plainview, TX 79072
(806) 296-5521 Ext. 4706

Will confirm attendance and degree by phone or mail. Inquiry must include student's name, date of birth, social security number, years attended. Employers may obtain transcripts upon written request accompanied by a $3.00 fee and a signed release from the student.

A general baccalaureate institution, with an enrollment of 2,707. Highest level of offering: master's.
ACCREDITATIONS: SC

Wayne Community College

Caller Box Number 8002
Goldsboro, NC 27533-8002
(919) 735-5151 Ext. 238
Fax (919) 736-3204

Will confirm attendance and degree by phone, fax or mail. Inquiry must include student's name, social security number. Employers may obtain transcripts upon written request accompanied by a $1.00 fee and a signed release from the student.

A multiprogram two-year institution, with an enrollment of 2,003. Highest level of offering: one year but less than four years.
ACCREDITATIONS: SC DA DH

Wayne County Community College

801 West Fort Street
Detroit, MI 48226
(313) 496-2656

Will confirm attendance by phone or mail and degree by mail. Inquiry must include student's name, date of birth, social security number, years attended. Employers may obtain transcripts upon written request accompanied by a $3.00 fee and a signed release from the student.

A multiprogram two-year institution, with an enrollment of 12,505. Highest level of offering: one year but less than four years.
ACCREDITATIONS: NH ADVET DA DH

Wayne State College

200 East 10th Street
Wayne, NE 68787
(402) 375-7000 Ext. 7239

Will confirm attendance and degree by phone or mail. Inquiry must include student's name, date of birth, social security number, years attended. Employers may obtain transcripts upon written request accompanied by a $2.00 fee and a signed release from the student.

A comprehensive institution with no medical school, with an enrollment of 3,900. Highest level of offering: beyond master's but less than doctorate.
ACCREDITATIONS: NH TED

Wayne State University

Detroit, MI 48202
(313) 577-3531

Will confirm attendance and degree by phone or mail. Inquiry must include student's name, date of birth, social security number, years attended. Employers may obtain transcripts upon written request accompanied by a $2.00 fee and a signed release from the student. Requests should be directed to: Central Records.

A doctoral-level institution with a medical school, with an enrollment of 29,070. Highest level of offering: doctorate.
ACCREDITATIONS: NH ANEST AUD BUS CLPSY CYTO DIET ENG MED FUSER LAW MT MUS NUR OT PHAR PTA RTT SP SW TED

Waynesburg College

Waynesburg, PA 15370
(412) 852-3252

Will confirm attendance and degree by phone or mail. Inquiry must include student's name, date of birth, years attended. Employers may obtain transcripts upon written request accompanied by a signed release from the student. Requests should be directed to: Registrar's Office.

A general baccalaureate institution, with an enrollment of 1,000. Highest level of offering: master's.
ACCREDITATIONS: M

Weatherford College

308 East Park Avenue
Weatherford, TX 76086
(817) 594-5471 Ext. 242
Fax (817) 594-0627

Will confirm attendance and degree by phone or mail. Inquiry must include student's name, social security number, years attended. Employers may obtain transcripts upon written request accompanied by a $4.00 fee and a signed release from the student.

A multiprogram two-year institution, with an enrollment of 1,997. Highest level of offering: one year but less than four years.
ACCREDITATIONS: SC

Webb Institute of Naval Architecture

Crescent Beach Road
Glen Cove, NY 11542
(516) 671-2213
Fax (516) 674-9838

Will confirm attendance and degree by phone, fax or mail. Inquiry must include student's name, years attended. Employers may obtain transcripts upon written request accompanied by a $3.00 fee and a signed release from the student.

An engineering school, with an enrollment of 87. Highest level of offering: four or five year baccalaureate.
ACCREDITATIONS: M ENG NY

Webber College

PO Box 96
Babson Park, FL 33827
(813) 638-1431 Ext. 213

Will confirm attendance and degree by phone or mail. Inquiry must include student's name, date of birth, social security number, years attended. Employers may obtain transcripts upon written request accompanied by a $3.00 fee and a signed release from the student. Attn: Registrar's Office.

A single program two-year institution, with an enrollment of 353. Highest level of offering: master's.
ACCREDITATIONS: SC

Weber State College

Attn: Records Office
3750 Harrison Boulevard
Ogden, UT 84408-1020
(801) 626-6751

Will confirm attendance and degree by mail. Inquiry must include student's name, social security number, date of birth, years attended. Employers may obtain transcripts upon written request accompanied by a signed release from the student. Attn: Records Office.

A general baccalaureate institution, with an enrollment of 10,130. Highest level of offering: master's.
ACCREDITATIONS: NW ADNUR DH ENGT MLTAD MT MUS PNUR RAD RSTH RSTHT RTT TED SW DMS

Webster University

470 East Lockwood
Saint Louis, MO 63119-3194
(314) 968-7450

Will confirm attendance and degree by mail. Inquiry must include student's name, date of birth, social security number, years attended, release. Employers may obtain transcripts upon written request accompanied by a $2.00 fee and a signed release from the student.

A comprehensive institution with no medical school, with an enrollment of 10,175. Highest level of offering: doctorate.
ACCREDITATIONS: NH MUS

Wellesley College

Wellesley, MA 02181
(617) 446-2307
Fax (617) 431-7046

Will confirm attendance and degree by phone or mail. Inquiry must include student's name, years attended. Employers may obtain transcripts upon written request accompanied by a $2.00 fee and a signed release from the student. Requests should be directed to: Registrar's Office.

A general baccalaureate institution, with an enrollment of 2,297. Highest level of offering: four baccalaureate.
ACCREDITATIONS: EH

Wells College

Aurora, NY 13026
(315) 364-3215
Fax (315) 364-3227

Will confirm attendance and degree by phone, fax or mail. Inquiry must include student's name, date of birth, social security number, years attended. Employers may obtain transcripts upon written request accompanied by a $5.00 fee and a signed release from the student.

A general baccalaureate institution, with an enrollment of 475. Highest level of offering: four or five year baccalaureate.
ACCREDITATIONS: M NY

Wenatchee Valley College

1300 Fifth Street
Wenatchee, WA 98801
(509) 662-1651 Ext. 2136

Will confirm attendance and degree by phone or mail. Inquiry must include student's name, social security number, years attended. Employers may obtain transcripts upon written request accompanied by a signed release from the student.

A multiprogram two-year institution, with an enrollment of 2,059. Highest level of offering: one year but less than four years.
ACCREDITATIONS: NW MLTAD RAD

Wentworth Institute of Technology

550 Huntington Avenue
Boston, MA 02115
(617) 442-9010 Ext. 394
Fax (617) 442-2852

Will confirm attendance and degree by phone or mail. Inquiry must include student's name, social security number, years attended. Employers may obtain transcripts upon written request accompanied by a $1.00 fee and a signed release from the student.

A multiprogram two-year institution, with an enrollment of 3,500. Highest level of offering: four or five year baccalaureate.
ACCREDITATIONS: EH ENGT FIDER ABET NEASAC

Wentworth Military Academy

18th and Washington
Lexington, MO 64067
(816) 259-2221 Ext. 244

Will confirm attendance and degree by phone or mail. Inquiry must include student's name, date of birth, years attended, self addressed stamped envelope. Employers may obtain transcripts upon written request accompanied by a $2.00 fee and a signed release from the student.

A multiprogram two-year institution, with an enrollment of 98. Highest level of offering: one year but less than four years.
ACCREDITATIONS: NAC

Wesley College

PO Box 70
Florence, MS 39073
(601) 845-2265 Ext. 14

Will confirm attendance and degree by phone or mail. Inquiry must include student's name, date of birth, social security number, years attended. Employers may obtain transcripts upon written request accompanied by a $5.00 fee and a signed release from the student.

A school of philosophy, religion and theology, with an enrollment of 81. Highest level of offering: four or five year baccalaureate.
ACCREDITATIONS: BI

Wesley College

Dover, DE 19901
(302) 736-2434

Will confirm attendance and degree by phone or mail. Inquiry must include student's name, date of birth, years attended. Employers may obtain transcripts upon written request accompanied by a $2.00 fee and a signed release from the student. Requests should be directed to: Registrar's Office.

A multiprogram two-year institution, with an enrollment of 1,472. Highest level of offering: four or five year baccalaureate.
ACCREDITATIONS: ADNUR MT

Wesley Theological Seminary

4500 Mass Avenue North West
Washington, DC 20016
(202) 885-8650

Will confirm attendance and degree by phone or mail. Inquiry must include student's name, social security number, date of birth. Employers may obtain transcripts upon written request by student accompanied by a $3.00 fee. Attn: Registrar's Office.

A school of philosophy, religion and theology, with an enrollment of 510. Highest level of offering: doctorate.
ACCREDITATIONS: M THEOL

Wesleyan College

4760 Forsyth Road
Macon, GA 31297
(912) 477-1110 Ext. 217

Will confirm attendance and degree by phone or mail. Inquiry must include student's name, maiden name, social security number, years attended. Employers may obtain transcripts upon written request accompanied by a $2.00 fee and a signed release from the student.

A general baccalaureate institution, with an enrollment of 500. Highest level of offering: four or five year baccalaureate.
ACCREDITATIONS: SC MUS

Wesleyan University

Middletown, CT 06457
(203) 344-7933

Will confirm attendance and degree by phone or mail. Inquiry must include student's name, date of birth, social security number years attended. Employers may obtain transcripts upon written request accompanied by a $5.00 fee and a signed release from the student. Attn: Registrar's Office.

A comprehensive institution with no medical school, with an enrollment of 3,331. Highest level of offering: doctorate.
ACCREDITATIONS: EH

West Chester University of Pennsylvania

E. O. Bull Center, Room 155
West Chester, PA 19383
(215) 436-3541

Will confirm attendance and degree by phone or mail. Inquiry must include student's name, date of birth, social security number, years attended. Employers may obtain transcripts upon written request accompanied by a $3.00 fee and a signed release from the student.

A comprehensive institution with no medical school, with an enrollment of 13,000. Highest level of offering: master's.
ACCREDITATIONS: M MUS NUR RSTH RSTHT SW TED

West Coast Christian College

6901 North Maple Avenue
Fresno, CA 93710
(209) 299-7201
Fax (209) 299-0932

Will confirm attendance and degree by phone or mail. Inquiry must include student's name, date of birth, social security number, years attended. Employers may obtain transcripts upon written request accompanied by a $4.00 fee and a signed release from the student.

A school of philosophy, religion and theology, with an enrollment of 150. Highest level of offering: four or five year baccalaureate.
ACCREDITATIONS: WJ BI

West Coast University Central Office

440 Shatto Place
Los Angeles, CA 90020
(213) 487-4433 Ext. 266
Fax (213) 380-4362

Will confirm attendance and degree by phone, fax or mail. Inquiry must include student's name, date of birth, social security number, years attended. Employers may obtain transcripts upon written request accompanied by a $3.00 fee and a signed release from the student.

A comprehensive institution with no medical school, with an enrollment of 641. Highest level of offering: master's.
ACCREDITATIONS: WC ENG

West Coast University Orange County Center

440 Shatto Place
Los Angeles, CA 90020
(714) 953-2700 or (800) 248-4928

Records are held at the above address. Will confirm attendance and degree by phone, fax or mail. Inquiry must include student's name, date of birth, social security number, years attended. Employers may obtain transcripts upon written request accompanied by a $3.00 fee and a signed release from the student. Requests should be sent to: West Coast University, LA Center, 440 Shatto Place, Los Angeles, CA 90020-1765,

A business school. Highest level of offering: master's.

West Georgia College

Carrollton, GA 30118
(404) 836-6438

Will confirm attendance and degree by phone or mail. Inquiry must include student's name, social security number, self addressed stamped envelope. Employers may obtain transcripts upon written request accompanied by a $1.00 fee and a signed release from the student.

A comprehensive institution with no medical school, with an enrollment of 7,252. Highest level of offering: beyond master's but less than doctorate.

ACCREDITATIONS: SC ADNUR BUS MUS TED

West Hills College

300 Cherry Lane
Coalinga, CA 93210
(209) 935-0801 Ext. 217
Fax (209) 935-5655

Will confirm attendance and degree by phone, fax or mail. Inquiry must include student's name, date of birth, social security number, years attended. Employers may obtain transcripts upon written request accompanied by a $2.00 fee and a signed release from the student.

A multiprogram two-year institution, with an enrollment of 2,947. Highest level of offering: one year but less than four years.

ACCREDITATIONS: WJ

West Liberty State College

West Liberty, WV 26074
(304) 336-8007
Fax (304) 336-8285

Will confirm attendance and degree by phone, fax or mail. Inquiry must include student's name, date of birth, social security number, years attended. Employers may obtain transcripts upon written request accompanied by a $3.00 fee and a signed release from the student.

A general baccalaureate institution, with an enrollment of 2,465. Highest level of offering: four or five year baccalaureate.

ACCREDITATIONS: NH DH MT MUS TED

West Los Angeles College

Admissions & Records
4800 Freshman Drive
Culver City, CA 90230
(310) 287-4550

Will confirm attendance and degree by mail. Inquiry must include student's name, date of birth, social security number, release. Employers may obtain transcripts upon written request accompanied by a $1.00 fee and a signed release from the student.

A multiprogram two-year institution, with an enrollment of 8,500. Highest level of offering: one year but less than four years.

ACCREDITATIONS: WJ DH

West Shore Community College

3000 North Stiles
Scottville, MI 49454
(616) 845-6211 Ext. 125

Will confirm attendance and degree by phone or mail. Inquiry must include student's name, social security number, years attended. Employers may obtain transcripts upon written request accompanied by a $2.00 fee and a signed release from the student.

A multiprogram two-year institution, with an enrollment of 1,300. Highest level of offering: one year but less than four years.

ACCREDITATIONS: NH

West Side Institute of Technology

9801 Walford Avenue
Cleveland, OH 44102
(216) 651-1656 Ext. 22

Will confirm attendance and degree by phone or mail. Inquiry must include student's name, years attended, self addressed stamped envelope. Employers may obtain transcripts upon written request accompanied by a $1.00 fee and a signed release from the student.

A single program two-year institution, with an enrollment of 350. Highest level of offering: one year but less than four years.

ACCREDITATIONS: NATTS

West Suburban College of Nursing

Erie at Austin
Oak Park, IL 60302
(708) 383-6200 Ext. 6443

Will confirm attendance and degree by phone or mail. Inquiry must include student's name, date of birth, social security number, years attended. Only students may obtain transcripts.

A bachelor's or higher institution newly admitted to NCES, with an enrollment of 72. Highest level of offering: one year but less than four years.

ACCREDITATIONS: NH

West Texas State University

Box WT 877
Canyon, TX 79016
(806) 656-2022

Will confirm attendance and degree by phone or mail. Inquiry must include student's name, social security number, years attended. Requests should be directed to: Registrar's Office. Employers may obtain transcripts upon written request accompanied by a $3.00 fee and a signed release from the student.

A comprehensive institution with no medical school, with an enrollment of 6,474. Highest level of offering: beyond master's but less than doctorate.

ACCREDITATIONS: SC MUS NUR SW TED

West Valley College

14000 Fruitvale Avenue
Saratoga, CA 95070
(408) 867-2200 Ext. 3321

Will confirm attendance and degree by phone or mail. Inquiry must include student's name, social security number, self addressed stamped envelope. Employers may obtain transcripts upon written request accompanied by a $3.00 fee and a signed release from the student. Requests should be directed to: Admissions & Records Office.

A multiprogram two-year institution, with an enrollment of 13,907. Highest level of offering: one year but less than four years.

ACCREDITATIONS: WJ MAC

West Valley Joint Community College

3000 Mission College Boulevard
Santa Clara, CA 95054
(408) 988-2200 Ext. 1680

Will confirm attendance and degree by phone or mail. Inquiry must include student's name, date of birth, social security number, years attended. Employers may obtain transcripts upon written request accompanied by a $3.00 fee and a signed release from the student.

West Virginia Graduate College

PO Box 1003
Institute, WV 25112
(304) 766-1905

Will confirm attendance and degree by phone or mail. Inquiry must include student's name, social security number. Requests should be directed to: Record & Admissions Office. Employers may obtain transcripts upon written request accompanied by a $4.00 fee and a signed release from the student.

A school of education, with an enrollment of 3,043. Highest level of offering: beyond master's but less than doctorate.

ACCREDITATIONS: NH TED

West Virginia Institute of Technology

Fayette Pike
Montgomery, WV 25136
(304) 442-3113
Fax (304) 442-3059

Will confirm attendance and degree by phone, fax or mail. Inquiry must include student's name, date of birth, social security number. Employers may obtain transcripts upon written request accompanied by a signed release from the student.

A general baccalaureate institution, with an enrollment of 3,210. Highest level of offering: master's.

ACCREDITATIONS: NH DH ENG ENGT TED

West Virginia Northern Community College

College Square
Wheeling, WV 26003
(304) 233-5900 Ext. 260

Will confirm attendance and degree by phone or mail. Inquiry must include student's name, date of birth, social security number, years attended. Employers may obtain transcripts upon written request accompanied by a $3.00 fee and a signed release from the student.

A multiprogram two-year institution, with an enrollment of 3,000. Highest level of offering: one year but less than four years.
ACCREDITATIONS: NH ADNUR MLTAD RSTH SURGT

West Virginia School of Osteopathic Medicine

400 North Lee Street
Lewisburg, WV 24901
(304) 647-6230
Fax (304) 645-4859

Will confirm attendance and degree by phone or mail. Inquiry must include student's name, date of birth, social security number, years attended. Employers may obtain transcripts upon written request accompanied by a $3.00 fee and a signed release from the student.

A medical school, with an enrollment of 235. Highest level of offering: first professional degree.
ACCREDITATIONS: OSTEO

West Virginia State College

PO Box 1000
Institute, WV 25112
(304) 766-3137

Will confirm attendance and degree by phone or mail. Inquiry must include student's name, date of birth, social security number, years attended. Employers may obtain transcripts upon written request accompanied by a $3.00 fee and a signed release from the student.

A general baccalaureate institution, with an enrollment of 4,295. Highest level of offering: four or five year baccalaureate.
ACCREDITATIONS: NH NMT SW TED

West Virginia University

Admissions & Records
PO Box 6009
Morgantown, WV 26506-6009
(304) 293-2121
Fax (304) 293-3080

Will confirm attendance and degree by phone, fax or mail. Inquiry must include student's name, date of birth, social security number, years attended. Employers may obtain transcripts upon written request accompanied by a $3.00 fee and a signed release from the student. Requests should be directed to: Admissions & Records Office.

A doctoral-level institution with a medical school, with an enrollment of 20,000. Highest level of offering: doctorate.
ACCREDITATIONS: NH ART AUD BUS CLPSY DENT DH DIETI ENG FOR IPSY JOUR TED LAW LSAR MED MT MUS NMT NUR PHAR PTA RAD RTT SP SW

West Virginia University at Parkersburg

(Formerly Parkersburg Commnity College)
Route 5, Box 167a
Parkersburg, WV 26101
(304) 424-8220

Will confirm attendance and degree by phone or mail. Inquiry must include student's name, date of birth, social security number, years attended. Employers may obtain transcripts upon written request accompanied by a $3.00 fee and a signed release from the student. Requests should be directed to: Admissions Office.

A multi-program institution, with an enrollment of 3,500. Highest level of offering: bachelor's.
ACCREDITATIONS: NH ADNUR

West Virginia Wesleyan College

Buckhannon, WV 26201
(304) 473-8470
Fax (304) 473-8187

Will confirm attendance and degree by phone or mail. Inquiry must include student's name, date of birth, social security number, years attended. Employers may obtain transcripts upon written request accompanied by a $3.00 fee and a signed release from the student. Requests should be directed to: Registrar's Office.

A general baccalaureate institution, with an enrollment of 1,651. Highest level of offering: master's.
ACCREDITATIONS: NH MUS NUR

Westark Community College

PO Box 3649
Fort Smith, AR 72913
(501) 785-7100

Will confirm attendance and degree by phone or mail. Inquiry must include student's name, date of birth, social security number, years attended. Employers may obtain transcripts upon written request accompanied by a $1.00 fee and a signed release from the student. Requests should be directed to: Registrar's Office.

A multiprogram two-year institution, with an enrollment of 5,137. Highest level of offering: one year but less than four years.
ACCREDITATIONS: NH ADNUR SURGT

Westbrook College

716 Stevens Avenue
Portland, ME 04103
(207) 797-7261 Ext. 208

Will confirm attendance and degree by phone or mail. Inquiry must include student's name, date of birth, social security number, years attended. Employers may obtain transcripts upon written request accompanied by a $2.00 fee and a signed release from the student.

A multiprogram two-year institution, with an enrollment of 600. Highest level of offering: four or five year baccalaureate.
ACCREDITATIONS: EH ADNUR DH MAC NUR

Westchester Business Institute

325 Central Ave.
White Plains, NY 10606
(914) 948-4442

Will confirm attendance and degree by mail. Inquiry must include student's name, social security number, years attended, release. Employers may obtain transcripts upon written request accompanied by a $5.00 fee and a signed release from the student.

A multi-program two-year institution, with an enrollment of 925. Highest level of offering: one year but less than four years.
ACCREDITATIONS: NY

Westchester Community College

75 Grasslands Road
Valhalla, NY 10595
(914) 285-6810

Will confirm attendance and degree by phone or mail. Inquiry must include student's name, date of birth, social security number, years attended. Employers may obtain transcripts upon written request accompanied by a $3.00 fee and a signed release from the student.

A multiprogram two-year institution, with an enrollment of 10,000. Highest level of offering: one year but less than four years.
ACCREDITATIONS: M NY RAD RSTH

Western Baptist College

5000 Deer Park Drive South East
Salem, OR 97301
(503) 375-7014
Fax (503) 585-4316

Will confirm attendance and degree by phone or mail. Inquiry must include student's name, years attended, self addressed stamped envelope. Employers may obtain transcripts upon written request accompanied by a $5.00 fee and a signed release from the student.

A general baccalaureate institution, with an enrollment of 400. Highest level of offering: four or five year baccalaureate.
ACCREDITATIONS: NW BI

Western Bible College

(See Colorado Christian University)

Western Carolina University

Cullowhee, NC 28723
(704) 227-7216

Will confirm attendance and degree by phone or mail. Inquiry must include student's name, date of birth, social security number, release. Employers may obtain transcripts upon written request accompanied by a signed release from the student. Requests should be sent to: Attn: Registrar's Office.

A comprehensive institution with no medical school, with an enrollment of 4,746. Highest level of offering: beyond master's but less than doctorate.
ACCREDITATIONS: SC BUS MRA MT MUS NUR SW TED ENGT

Western Connecticut State University

181 White Street
Danbury, CT 06810
(203) 797-4227

Will confirm attendance and degree by phone or mail. Inquiry must include student's name, date of birth, social security number, years attended. Employers may obtain transcripts upon written request accompanied by a $3.00 fee and a signed release from the student. Requests should be sent to: Attn: Registrar's Office.

A comprehensive institution with no medical school, with an enrollment of 5,778. Highest level of offering: beyond master's but less than doctorate.
ACCREDITATIONS: EH NUR TED SW

Western Conservative Baptist Seminary

5511 South East Hawthorne Boulevard
Portland, OR 97215
(503) 233-8561 Ext. 411

Will confirm attendance and degree by phone or mail. Inquiry must include student's name, date of birth, social security number, years attended. Requests should be directed to: Registrar's Office. Employers may obtain transcripts upon written request accompanied by a signed release from the student.

A school of philosophy, religion and theology, with an enrollment of 462. Highest level of offering: doctorate.
ACCREDITATIONS: NW

Western Evangelical Seminary

4200 South East Jennings Avenue
Portland, OR 97267
(503) 654-5466
Fax (503) 654-5469

Will confirm attendance and degree by phone or mail. Inquiry must include student's name, social security number, years attended. Employers may obtain transcripts upon written request accompanied by a $5.00 fee and a signed release from the student.

A school of philosophy, religion and theology, with an enrollment of 170. Highest level of offering: master's.
ACCREDITATIONS: ATS NW

Western Illinois University

900 West Adams Street
Macomb, IL 61455
(309) 298-3150
Fax (309) 298-2400

Will confirm attendance and degree by phone or mail. Inquiry must include student's name, date of birth, social security number. Employers may obtain transcripts upon written request accompanied by a signed release from the student. Attn: Sherman Hall, Room 110.

A comprehensive institution with no medical school, with an enrollment of 13,500. Highest level of offering: beyond master's but less than doctorate.
ACCREDITATIONS: NH AUD BUS MUS SP TED

Western International University

9215 North Black Canyon Highway
Phoenix, AZ 85021
(602) 943-2311
Fax (602) 371-8637

Will confirm attendance and degree by phone or mail. Inquiry must include student's name, date of birth, social security number. Employers may obtain transcripts upon written request by student accompanied by a $5.00 fee and a signed release from the student.

A law school, with an enrollment of 4,499. Highest level of offering: master's.
ACCREDITATIONS: NH

Western Iowa Tech Community College

PO Box 265
Sioux City, IA 51102
(712) 274-6400
Fax (712) 274-6238

Will confirm attendance and degree by phone, fax or mail. Inquiry must include student's name, social security number. Employers may obtain transcripts upon written request accompanied by a $1.00 fee and a signed release from the student.

A multiprogram two-year institution, with an enrollment of 1,574. Highest level of offering: one year but less than four years.
ACCREDITATIONS: NH DA SURGT

Western Kentucky University

(Formerly Bowling Green Junior College of Business)
Bowling Green, KY 42101
(502) 745-5450
Fax (502) 745-5387

Will confirm attendance and degree by phone, fax or mail. Inquiry must include student's name, date of birth, social security number, years attended. Employers may obtain transcripts upon written request accompanied by a $2.00 fee and a signed release from the student. Requests should be directed to: Registrar's Office.

A comprehensive institution with no medical school, with an enrollment of 14,821. Highest level of offering: beyond master's but less than doctorate.
ACCREDITATIONS: SC ADNUR BUS DH ENGT JOUR MRT MUS NUR SW TED

Western Maryland College

2 College Hill
Westminster, MD 21157-4390
(301) 848-7000 Ext. 215

Will confirm attendance and degree by phone or mail. Inquiry must include student's name, social security number, years attended. Employers may obtain transcripts upon written request accompanied by a $3.00 fee and a signed release from the student.

A comprehensive institution with no medical school, with an enrollment of 1,585. Highest level of offering: master's.
ACCREDITATIONS: M MUS SW

Western Michigan University

Kalamazoo, MI 49008
(616) 387-4323

Will confirm attendance and degree by phone or mail. Inquiry must include student's name, date of birth, social security number, years attended. Employers may obtain transcripts upon written request accompanied by a $3.00 fee and a signed release from the student. Requests should be directed to: Academic Records Department.

A doctoral-level institution with no medical school, with an enrollment of 26,362. Highest level of offering: doctorate.
ACCREDITATIONS: NH APCP ART AUD BUS DANCE ENG OT SP SW TED MUS

Western Montana College

Registrar's Office
710 S. Atlantic
Dillon, MT 59725-3598
(406) 683-7371

Will confirm degree and attendance by phone or mail. Inquiry must include student's name, social security number or date of birth, years attended, self addressed stamped envelope. Employers may obtain transcripts upon written request accompanied by a $2.00 fee and a signed release from the student.

A school of education, with an enrollment of 992. Highest level of offering: one year but less than four.
ACCREDITATIONS: NW

Western Nevada Community College

2201 West Nye Lane
Carson City, NV 89703
(702) 887-3000

Will confirm attendance and degree by phone or mail. Inquiry must include student's name, date of birth, social security number. Employers may obtain transcripts upon written request accompanied by a $2.00 fee and a signed release from the student.

A multiprogram two-year institution, with an enrollment of 5,071. Highest level of offering: one year but less than four years.
ACCREDITATIONS: NW

Western New England College

1215 Wilbraham Road
Springfield, MA 01119
(413) 782-3111 Ext. 261

Will confirm attendance and degree by phone or mail. Inquiry must include student's name, social security number. Employers may obtain transcripts upon written request accompanied by a $2.00 fee and a signed release from the student.

A comprehensive institution with no medical school, with an enrollment of 5,140. Highest level of offering: master's.
ACCREDITATIONS: EH ENG LAW SW

Western New Mexico University

PO Box 680
Silver City, NM 88062
(505) 538-6118
Fax (505) 538-6155

Will confirm attendance and degree by phone or mail. Inquiry must include student's name, social security number. Employers may obtain transcripts upon written request accompanied by a $2.00 fee and a signed release from the student. Requests should be directed to: Registrar's Office.

A comprehensive institution with no medical school, with an enrollment of 1,840. Highest level of offering: master's.

ACCREDITATIONS: NH

Western Oklahoma State College

2801 North Main Street
Altus, OK 73521
(405) 477-2000 Ext. 213
Fax (405) 521-6154

Will confirm attendance and degree by phone, fax or mail. Inquiry must include student's name, date of birth, social security number, years attended. Requests should be directed to: Admissions Office. Employers may obtain transcripts upon written request accompanied by a $2.00 fee and a signed release from the student.

A multiprogram two-year institution, with an enrollment of 2,003. Highest level of offering: one year but less than four years.

ACCREDITATIONS: NCA

Western Oregon State College

345 North Monmouth Avenue
Monmouth, OR 97361
(503) 838-8182
Fax (503) 838-8141

Will confirm attendance and degree by phone or mail. Inquiry must include student's name, date of birth, social security number, years attended. Requests should be directed to: Registrar's Office. Employers may obtain transcripts upon written request accompanied by a $5.00 fee and a signed release from the student.

A liberal arts college, with an enrollment of 3,840. Highest level of offering: Four or five year baccalaureate.

ACCREDITATIONS: NW MUS TED

Western Piedmont Community College

1001 Burkemont Avenue
Morganton, NC 28655
(704) 438-6041

Will confirm attendance and degree by phone or mail. Inquiry must include student's name, social security number, release. Requests should be directed to: Student Services. Employers may obtain transcripts upon written request accompanied by a signed release from the student.

A multiprogram two-year institution, with an enrollment of 2,540. Highest level of offering: two years but less than four years.

ACCREDITATIONS: SC ADNUR DA MAC MLTAD

Western State College of Colorado

Gunnison, CO 81231
(303) 943-2047
Fax (303) 943-7069

Will confirm attendance and degree by phone, fax or mail. Inquiry must include student's name, social security number. Employers may obtain transcripts upon written request by student accompanied by a $2.00 fee. Requests should be directed to: Registrar's Office.

A comprehensive institution with no medical school, with an enrollment of 2,508. Highest level of offering: bachelor's.

ACCREDITATIONS: NH MUS TED

Western State University College of Law of Orange County

1111 North State College Boulevard
Fullerton, CA 92631
(714) 738-1000
Fax (714) 525-2786

Will confirm attendance and degree by mail. Inquiry must include student's name, social security number, release. Employers may obtain transcripts upon written request accompanied by a $3.00 fee and a signed release from the student. Requests should be directed to: Records Office.

A law school, with an enrollment of 1,370. Highest level of offering: first professional degree.

ACCREDITATIONS: WC

Western State University College of Law of San Diego

2121 San Diego Avenue
San Diego, CA 92110
(619) 297-9700

Will confirm attendance and degree by mail. Inquiry must include student's name, date of birth, social security number, release. Requests should be directed to: Registrar's Office. Employers may obtain transcripts upon written request accompanied by a $3.00 fee and a signed release from the student.

A law school, with an enrollment of 550. Highest level of offering: first professional degree.

ACCREDITATIONS: WC

Western States Chiropractic College

2900 North East 132nd Avenue
Portland, OR 97230
(503) 256-3180 Ext. 334

Will confirm attendance and degree by phone or mail. Inquiry must include student's name. Employers may obtain transcripts upon written request accompanied by a $5.00 fee and a signed release from the student. Requests should be directed to: Registrar's Office.

A health institution, with an enrollment of 428. Highest level of offering: first professional degree.

ACCREDITATIONS: NW CHIRO

Western Technical Community College Area

1601 East 27th Street, North East
Scottsbluff, NE 69361
(308) 635-3606
Fax (308) 635-6100

Will confirm attendance and degree by phone, fax or mail. Inquiry must include student's name, date of birth, social security number. Employers may obtain transcripts upon written request accompanied by a signed release from the student.

A multiprogram two-year institution, with an enrollment of 2,000. Highest level of offering: one year but less than four years.

ACCREDITATIONS: NH PNUR

Western Texas College

Snyder, TX 79549
(915) 573-8511 Ext. 214

Will confirm attendance and degree by phone or mail. Inquiry must include student's name, social security number. Employers may obtain transcripts upon written request accompanied by a $2.00 fee and a signed release from the student. Requests should be directed to: Registrar's Office.

A multiprogram two-year institution, with an enrollment of 1,319. Highest level of offering: one year but less than four years.

ACCREDITATIONS: SC

Western Theological Seminary

86 East 12th Street
Holland, MI 49423
(616) 392-8555 Ext. 20

Will confirm attendance and degree by phone or mail. Inquiry must include student's name. Requests should be directed to: Registrar's Office. Employers may obtain transcripts upon written request accompanied by a $2.00 fee and a signed release from the student.

A school of religion and theology, with an enrollment of 177. Highest level of offering: doctorate.

ACCREDITATIONS: ATS

Western Washington University

516 High Street
Bellingham, WA 98225
(206) 676-3430
Fax (206) 647-7327

Will confirm attendance and degree by phone or mail. Inquiry must include student's name, social security number, years attended. Employers may obtain transcripts upon written request accompanied by a $3.00 fee and a signed release from the student.

A comprehensive institution with no medical school, with an enrollment of 9,600. Highest level of offering: beyond master's but less than doctorate.

ACCREDITATIONS: NW AUD MUS NUR SP TED

Western Wisconsin Technical College

6th and Vine
La Crosse, WI 54601
(608) 785-9149

Will confirm attendance and degree by phone or mail. Inquiry must include student's name, social security number. Employers may obtain transcripts upon written request accompanied by a $3.00 fee and a signed release from the student. Requests should be directed to: Registrar's Office.

A multiprogram two-year institution, with an enrollment of 4,432. Highest level of offering: one year but less than four years.

ACCREDITATIONS: NH ADNUR DA EEG MAC MLTAD MRT PNUR RAD RSTHT SURGT

Western Wyoming Community College

PO Box 428
Rock Springs, WY 82902
(307) 382-1637
Fax (307) 382-1624

Will confirm attendance and degree by phone, fax or mail. Inquiry must include student's name, social security number. Employers may obtain transcripts upon written request accompanied by a $1.00 fee and a signed release from the student. Requests should be directed to: Record & Admissions Office.

A multiprogram two-year institution, with an enrollment of 2,400. Highest level of offering: one year but less than four years.

ACCREDITATIONS: NH MLTAD RAD RSTHT

Westfield State College

Western Avenue
Westfield, MA 01086
(413) 568-3311 Ext. 240
Fax (413) 562-3613

Will confirm attendance and degree by phone, fax or mail. Inquiry must include student's name, social security number, years attended. Employers may obtain transcripts upon written request accompanied by a $1.00 fee and a signed release from the student. Requests should be directed to: Registrar's Office.

A comprehensive institution with no medical school, with an enrollment of 5,130. Highest level of offering: beyond master's but less than doctorate.

ACCREDITATIONS: EH TED

Westmar College

10002 3rd Avenue South East
Le Mars, IA 51031
(712) 546-2008

Will confirm attendance and degree by phone or mail. Inquiry must include student's name, social security number. Requests should be directed to: Registrar's Office. Employers may obtain transcripts upon written request accompanied by a $3.00 fee and a signed release from the student.

A general baccalaureate institution, with an enrollment of 530. Highest level of offering: four or five year baccalaureate.

ACCREDITATIONS: NH

Westminster Choir College

Hamilton Avenue and Walnut Lane
Princeton, NJ 08540
(609) 921-7100 Ext. 295

Will confirm attendance and degree by phone or mail. Inquiry must include student's name, years attended. Requests should be directed to: Registrar's Office. Employers may obtain transcripts upon written request accompanied by a $3.00 fee and a signed release from the student.

A visual and performing arts school, with an enrollment of 350. Highest level of offering: master's.

ACCREDITATIONS: M MUS

Westminster College of Salt Lake City

1840 South 1300 East
Salt Lake City, UT 84105
(801) 484-4100
Fax (801) 466-6916

Will confirm attendance and degree by phone, fax or mail. Inquiry must include student's name, social security number. Requests should be directed to: Registrar's Office. Employers may obtain transcripts upon written request accompanied by a $2.00 fee and a signed release from the student.

A general baccalaureate institution, with an enrollment of 2,000. Highest level of offering: master's.

ACCREDITATIONS: NW NUR

Westminster College

501 Westminster Ave.
Fulton, MO 65251
(314) 642-3361 Ext. 213
Fax (314) 642-2176

Will confirm attendance and degree by phone, fax or mail. Inquiry must include student's name, years attended. Employers may obtain transcripts upon written request accompanied by a $2.00 fee and a signed release from the student. Requests should be directed to: Registrar's Office.

A general baccalaureate institution, with an enrollment of 705. Highest level of offering: four or five year baccalaureate.

ACCREDITATIONS: NCA

Westminster College

New Wilmington, PA 16172
(412) 946-7136

Will confirm attendance and degree by phone or mail. Inquiry must include student's name, years attended. Employers may obtain transcripts upon written request accompanied by a $2.00 fee and a signed release from the student. Requests should be directed to: Registrar's Office.

A general baccalaureate institution, with an enrollment of 1,645. Highest level of offering: master's.

ACCREDITATIONS: M MUS

Westminster Theological Seminary in California

1725 Bear Valley Parkway
Escondido, CA 92027
(619) 480-8474
Fax (619) 480-0252

Will confirm attendance and degree by phone or mail. Inquiry must include student's name and social security number. Employers may obtain transcripts upon written request by thestudent accompanied by a $1.00 fee. Requests should be sent to: Attn: Registrar's Office.

A master's or higher institution newly admitted to NCES, with an enrollment of 160. Highest level of offering: doctorate.

ACCREDITATIONS: WC

Westminster Theological Seminary

PO Box 27009
Chestnut Hill
Philadelphia, PA 19118
(215) 887-5511 Ext. 3809

Will confirm attendance and degree by phone or mail. Inquiry must include student's name. Employers may obtain transcripts upon written request accompanied by a $2.00 fee and a signed release from the student.

A school of philosophy, religion and theology, with an enrollment of 500. Highest level of offering: doctorate.

ACCREDITATIONS: M THEOL

Westmont College

955 La Paz Road
Santa Barbara, CA 93108
(805) 565-6060
Fax (805) 565-6234

Will confirm attendance and degree by phone, fax or mail. Inquiry must include student's name, years attended. Employers may obtain transcripts upon written request accompanied by a $4.00 fee and a signed release from the student. Requests should be directed to: Student Records Office.

A general baccalaureate institution, with an enrollment of 1,208. Highest level of offering: four or five year baccalaureate.

ACCREDITATIONS: WC

Westmoreland County Community College

Youngwood, PA 15697
(412) 925-4069
Fax (412) 925-1150

Will confirm attendance and degree by phone or mail. Inquiry must include student's name, social security number, years attended. Employers may obtain transcripts upon written request accompanied by a signed release from the student. Requests should be directed to: Records Office.

A multiprogram two-year institution, with an enrollment of 6,000. Highest level of offering: one year but less than four years.

ACCREDITATIONS: M PNUR

Weston School of Theology

3 Phillips Place
Cambridge, MA 02138
(617) 492-1960 Ext. 104

Will confirm attendance and degree by phone or mail. Inquiry must include student's name, date of birth, social security number, years attended. Employers may obtain transcripts upon written request accompanied by a $3.00 fee and a signed release from the student. Requests should be directed to: Registrar's Office.

A bachelor's or higher institution newly admitted to NCES, with an enrollment of 212. Highest level of offering: doctorate.
ACCREDITATIONS: THEOL

Wharton County Junior College

911 Boling Highway
Wharton, TX 77488
(409) 532-4560 Ext. 229

Will confirm attendance and degree by phone or mail. Inquiry must include student's name, date of birth, social security number, years attended. Employers may obtain transcripts upon written request accompanied by a signed release from the student. Requests should be directed to: Registrar's Office.

A multiprogram two-year institution, with an enrollment of 2,527. Highest level of offering: one year but less than four years.
ACCREDITATIONS: SC DH MRT RAD

Whatcom Community College

237 West Kellogg Road
Bellingham, WA 98226
(206) 676-2170
Fax (206) 676-2171

Will confirm attendance and degree by phone, fax or mail. Inquiry must include student's name, social security number. Employers may obtain transcripts upon written request accompanied by a signed release from the student. Requests should be directed to: Registrar's Office.

A multiprogram two-year institution, with an enrollment of 2,500. Highest level of offering: one year but less than four years.
ACCREDITATIONS: NW

Wheaton College

501 E. College Ave.
Wheaton, IL 60187
(708) 752-5045
Fax (708) 752-5245

Will confirm attendance and degree by phone or mail. Inquiry must include student's name, maiden name, social security number, years attended. Employers may obtain transcripts upon written request accompanied by a signed release from the student. Requests should be directed to: Registrar's Office.

A comprehensive institution with no medical school, with an enrollment of 2,520. Highest level of offering: master's.
ACCREDITATIONS: NCA

Wheaton College

Norton, MA 02766
(508) 285-7722 Ext. 247

Will confirm attendance and degree by phone or mail. Inquiry must include student's name, date of birth, social security number. Employers may obtain transcripts upon written request accompanied by a $2.00 fee and a signed release from the student. Requests should be directed to: Registrar's Office.

A general baccalaureate institution, with an enrollment of 1,105. Highest level of offering: four or five year baccalaureate.
ACCREDITATIONS: EH

Wheeling Jesuit College

316 Washington Avenue
Wheeling, WV 26003
(304) 243-2238
Fax (304) 243-2243

Will confirm attendance and degree by phone, fax or mail. Inquiry must include student's name, social security number. Employers may obtain transcripts upon written request by student. Requests should be directed to: Registrar's Office.

A general baccalaureate institution, with an enrollment of 1,088. Highest level of offering: master's
ACCREDITATIONS: NH MT NMT NUR RSTH

Wheelock College

200 The Riverway
Boston, MA 02215
(617) 734-5200 Ext. 135

Will confirm attendance and degree by phone or mail. Inquiry must include student's name, social security number. Requests should be directed to: Registrar's Office. Employers may obtain transcripts upon written request accompanied by a $2.00 fee and a signed release from the student.

A school of education, with an enrollment of 671. Highest level of offering: beyond master's but less than doctorate.
ACCREDITATIONS: EH TED SW

White Pines College

40 Chester Street
Chester, NH 03036
(603) 887-4401

Will confirm attendance and degree by mail or phone. Inquiry must include student's name, year graduated, release. Employers may obtain transcripts upon written request accompanied by a $3.00 fee and a signed release from the student. Requests should be sent to: Attn: Dean's Office.

A multiprogram two-year institution, with an enrollment of 63. Highest level of offering: one year but less than four years.
ACCREDITATIONS: EH

White Water Technical Institute

(See Indiana Vocational Technical College)

Whitman College

345 Boyer Avenue
Walla Walla, WA 99362
(509) 527-5179
Fax (509) 527-5859

Will confirm attendance and degree by phone, fax or mail. Inquiry must include student's name, years attended. Employers may obtain transcripts upon written request accompanied by a $2.00 fee and a signed release from the student.

A general baccalaureate institution, with an enrollment of 1,239. Highest level of offering: four or five year baccalaureate.
ACCREDITATIONS: NW MUS

Whittier College

PO Box 634
Whittier, CA 90608
(310) 907-4200 Ext. 241
Fax (310) 698-4067

Will confirm attendance and degree by phone, fax or mail. Inquiry must include student's name, years attended. Employers may obtain transcripts upon written request accompanied by a $3.00 fee and a signed release from the student.

A comprehensive institution with no medical school, with an enrollment of 1,000. Highest level of offering: doctorate.
ACCREDITATIONS: WC LAW SW

Whitworth College

Registrar's Office
Spokane, WA 99251-0002
(509) 466-3201
Fax (509) 466-3773

Will confirm attendance and degree by mail or fax. Inquiry must include student's name, date of birth, years attended, release. Employers may obtain transcripts upon written request accompanied by a $5.00 fee and a signed release from the student. Requests should be directed to: Registrar's Office.

A comprehensive institution with no medical school, with an enrollment of 1,764. Highest level of offering: master's.
ACCREDITATIONS: NW MUS NUR TED

Wichita State University

PO Box 58
Wichita, KS 67208
(316) 689-3055
Fax (316) 689-3795

Will confirm attendance and degree by phone or mail ($3.00 fee for written confirmation). Inquiry must include student's name, date of birth, social security number. Employers may obtain transcripts upon written request accompanied by a $3.00 fee and a signed release from the student. Requests should be directed to: Registrar's Office.

A comprehensive institution with no medical school, with an enrollment of 17,419. Highest level of offering: doctorate.
ACCREDITATIONS: NH APCP AUD BUS DH ENG ENGT MT MUS NUR PTA RSTH TED RSTHT SP SW DANCE

Widener University of Law

(Formerly Brandywine College of Widener University)
Box 7474
Wilmington, Delaware, DE 19803
(302) 478-3000 Ext. 2175

Will confirm attendance and degree by phone or mail. Inquiry must include student's name, social security number, years attended. Employers may obtain transcripts upon written request accompanied by a $2.00 fee and a signed release from the student.

A multiprogram two-year institution, with an enrollment of 737. Highest level of offering: one year but less than four years.
ACCREDITATIONS: M

Widener University School of Law

(Formerly The Deleware Law School of Widener)
PO Box 7474
Wilmington, DE 19803
(302) 477-2151
Fax (302) 477-2282

Will confirm attendance and degree by phone, fax or mail. Inquiry must include student's name, social security number, years attended. Employers may obtain transcripts upon written request accompanied by a $2.00 fee and a signed release from the student.

A baccalaureate or higher institution, with an enrollment of 885. Highest level of offering: doctorate.
ACCREDITATIONS: LAW

Widener University Pennsylvania Campus

Office of Registrar
Chester, PA 19013
(215) 499-4140

Will confirm attendance and degree by phone or mail. Inquiry must include student's name, social security number. Employers may obtain transcripts upon written request accompanied by a $2.00 fee and a signed release from the student. Requests should be directed to: Registrar's Office.

A comprehensive institution with no medical school, with an enrollment of 5,665. Highest level of offering: doctorate.
ACCREDITATIONS: M ENG HSA NUR SW

Wilberforce University

Wilberforce, OH 45384
(513) 376-2911 Ext. 735

Will confirm attendance and degree by phone or mail. Inquiry must include student's name, date of birth, social security number, years attended. Employers may obtain transcripts upon written request accompanied by a $2.00 fee and a signed release from the student. Requests should be directed to: Registrar's Office.

A general baccalaureate institution, with an enrollment of 700. Highest level of offering: four or five year baccalaureate.
ACCREDITATIONS: NH

Wiley College

711 Wiley Avenue
Marshall, TX 75670
(214) 938-8341 Ext. 222

Will confirm attendance and degree by phone or mail. Inquiry must include student's name, years attended. Requests should be directed to: Records Office. Employers may obtain transcripts upon written request accompanied by a $2.00 fee and a signed release from the student.

A general baccalaureate institution, with an enrollment of 546. Highest level of offering: four or five year baccalaureate.
ACCREDITATIONS: SC

Wilkes Community College

PO Box 120
Wilkesboro, NC 28697
(919) 651-8637
Fax (919) 651-8749

Will confirm attendance and degree by phone, fax or mail. Inquiry must include student's name, social security number, years attended. Employers may obtain transcripts upon written request accompanied by a signed release from the student.

A multiprogram two-year institution, with an enrollment of 2,600. Highest level of offering: one year but less than four years.
ACCREDITATIONS: SC

Wilkes University

PO Box 111
Wilkes-Barre, PA 18766
(717) 824-4651 Ext. 4850
Fax (717) 823-9470

Will confirm attendance and degree by phone or mail. Inquiry must include student's name, social security number, years attended. Requests should be directed to: Registrar's Office. Employers may obtain transcripts upon written request accompanied by a $2.00 fee and a signed release from the student.

A comprehensive institution with no medical school, with an enrollment of 2,731. Highest level of offering: master's.
ACCREDITATIONS: M ENG NUR

Willamette University

900 State Street
Salem, OR 97301
(503) 370-6206

Will confirm attendance and degree by phone or mail. Inquiry must include student's name, date of birth, social security number, years attended. Employers may obtain transcripts upon written request accompanied by a $2.00 fee and a signed release from the student.

A general baccalaureate institution, with an enrollment of 2,00. Highest level of offering: master's.
ACCREDITATIONS: NW LAW MUS

William Carey College

498 Tuscan Ave.
Hattiesburg, MS 39401-5499
(601) 582-6194

Will confirm attendance and degree by phone or mail. Inquiry must include student's name, social security number. Employers may obtain transcripts upon written request accompanied by a signed release from the student.

A comprehensive institution with no medical school, with an enrollment of 1,746. Highest level of offering: beyond master's but less than doctorate.
ACCREDITATIONS: SC MT MUS NUR

William Jewell College

Liberty, MO 64068
(816) 781-7700 Ext. 5129

Will confirm attendance and degree by phone or mail. Inquiry must include student's name, social security number, years attended. Employers may obtain transcripts upon written request accompanied by a $2.00 fee and a signed release from the student.

A general baccalaureate institution, with an enrollment of 1,991. Highest level of offering: four or five year baccalaureate.
ACCREDITATIONS: NH MUS NUR

William Mitchell College of Law

875 Summit Avenue
Saint Paul, MN 55105
(612) 290-6328
Fax (612) 290-6414

Will confirm attendance and degree by phone or mail. Inquiry must include student's name, social security number, years attended. Employers may obtain transcripts upon written request accompanied by a $3.00 fee and a signed release from the student.

A law school, with an enrollment of 1,170. Offering: first professional degree, juris doctorate and master's of laws in tax.
ACCREDITATIONS: LAW

William Paterson College

300 Pompton Road
Wayne, NJ 07470
(201) 595-2305

Will confirm attendance and degree by mail. Inquiry must include student's name, social security number, date of birth, years attended. Employers may obtain transcripts upon written request accompanied by a $2.00 fee and a signed release from the student. Requests should be directed to: Records Office.

A comprehensive institution with no medical school, with an enrollment of 10,033. Highest level of offering: master's.
ACCREDITATIONS: M MUS NUR SP TED

William Penn College

Registrar's Office
Oskaloosa, IA 52577
(515) 673-1001 Ext. 2082
Fax (515) 673-1082

Will confirm attendance and degree by phone or mail. Inquiry must include student's name, social security number. Employers may obtain transcripts upon written request accompanied by a $2.00 fee and a signed release from the student. Requests should be directed to: Registrar's Office.

A general baccalaureate institution, with an enrollment of 720. Highest level of offering: four or five year baccalaureate.
ACCREDITATIONS: NH TED

William Rainey Harper College

1200 W. Algonquin Road
Palatine, IL 60067-7398
(708) 397-3000 Ext. 2500

Will confirm attendance and degree by phone or mail. Inquiry must include student's name, social security number, years attended. Employers may obtain transcripts upon written request accompanied by a $2.00 fee and a signed release from the student.

A multiprogram two-year institution, with an enrollment of 26,000. Highest level of offering: one year but less than four years.
ACCREDITATIONS: NH ADNUR DH MAC MUS

William Tyndale College

35700 W. 12 Mile
Farmington Hills, MI 48331
(313) 553-7200
Fax (313) 553-5963

Will confirm attendance and degree by mail. Inquiry must include student's name, social security number, years attended, year graduated. Employers may obtain transcripts upon written request accompanied by a $3.00 fee and a signed release from the student. Requests should be directed to: Records Office.

A school of psychology, philosophy, religion and theology, with an enrollment of 302. Highest level of offering: four or five year baccalaureate.
ACCREDITATIONS: NCA

William Woods College

Fulton, MO 65251
(314) 642-2251 Ext. 248

Will confirm attendance and degree by phone or mail. Inquiry must include student's name, years attended. Employers may obtain transcripts upon written request accompanied by a $5.00 fee and a signed release from the student.

A general baccalaureate institution, with an enrollment of 781. Highest level of offering: four or five year baccalaureate.
ACCREDITATIONS: NH TED

Williams College

PO Box 696
Williamstown, MA 01267
(413) 597-4286
Fax (413) 597-4158

Will confirm attendance and degree by phone, fax or mail. Inquiry must include student's name, date of birth, social security number, years attended. Employers may obtain transcripts upon written request accompanied by a signed release from the student. Requests should be sent to: Attn: Registrar's Office.

A general baccalaureate institution, with an enrollment of 2,012. Highest level of offering: master's.
ACCREDITATIONS: EH

Williamsburg Technical College

601 Lane Road
Kingstree, SC 29556
(803) 354-7423
Fax (803) 354-7269

Will confirm attendance and degree by mail. Inquiry must include student's name, date of birth, social security number, years attended. Employers may obtain transcripts upon written request accompanied by a signed release from the student. Requests should be directed to: Registrar's Office.

A multiprogram two-year institution, with an enrollment of 500. Highest level of offering: associate degree.
ACCREDITATIONS: SC

Williamson Free School of Mechanical Trades

106 S. Middletown Road, Rt. 352
Media, PA 19063
(215) 566-1776
Fax (215) 566-6502

Will confirm attendance and degree by phone or mail. Inquiry must include student's name, years attended. Employers may obtain transcripts upon written request accompanied by a $5.00 fee and a signed release from the student.

A two-year institution, with an enrollment of 220. Highest level of offering: one year but less than four years.
ACCREDITATIONS: NATTS

Williamsport Area Community College

(See Pennsylvania College of Technology)

Willmar Community College

PO Box 797
Willmar, MN 56201
(612) 231-6613
Fax (612) 231-6602

Will confirm enrollment and dates of attendance by phone, fax or mail. Inquiry must include student's name, social security number, years attended. Employers may obtain transcripts upon written request accompanied by a signed release from the student.

A multiprogram two-year institution, with an enrollment of 1,350. Highest level of offering: one year but less than four years.
ACCREDITATIONS: NCA

Wilmington College

251 Ludovic Street
Pyle Center Box 1286
Wilmington, OH 45177-2499
(513) 382-6661 Ext. 214
Fax (513) 382-7077

Will confirm attendance and degree by phone, fax or mail. Inquiry must include student's name, years attended. Requests should be directed to: Academic Records Office. Employers may obtain transcripts upon written request accompanied by a $2.00 fee and a signed release from the student.

A general baccalaureate institution, with an enrollment of 1,8002. Highest level of offering: four or five year baccalaureate.
ACCREDITATIONS: NCA

Wilmington College

320 Dupont Highway
New Castle, DE 19720
(302) 328-9401 Ext. 108

Will confirm attendance and degree by phone or mail. Inquiry must include student's name, social security number. Employers may obtain transcripts upon written request accompanied by a $3.00 fee and a signed release from the student.

A general baccalaureate institution, with an enrollment of 1,600. Highest level of offering: master's.
ACCREDITATIONS: M

Wilson College

Chambersburg, PA 17201
(717) 264-4141 Ext. 355
Fax (717) 264-1578

Will confirm attendance and degree by phone or mail. Inquiry must include student's name, years attended. Employers may obtain transcripts upon written request accompanied by a $3.00 fee and a signed release from the student. Requests should be sent to: Attn: Office of the Registrar.

A general baccalaureate institution, with an enrollment of 700. Highest level of offering: four or five year baccalaureate.
ACCREDITATIONS: M ADVET

Wilson County Technical College

PO Box 4305–902 Herring Avenue
Wilson, NC 27893
(919) 291-1195 Ext. 283

Will confirm attendance and degree by phone or mail. Inquiry must include student's name, social security number, years attended, field studied. Employers may obtain transcripts upon written request accompanied by a signed release from the student.

A multiprogram two-year institution, with an enrollment of 1.370. Highest level of offering: one year but less than four years
ACCREDITATIONS: SC

Windward Community College

45-720 Keaahala Road
Kaneohe, HI 96744
(808) 235-7432
Fax (808) 247-5362

Will confirm attendance and degree by phone, fax or mail. Inquiry must include student's name, social security number. Employers may obtain transcripts upon written request accompanied by a $1.00 fee and a signed release from the student. Requests should be directed to: Admissions Office.

A multiprogram two-year institution, with an enrollment of 1,750. Highest level of offering: one year but less than four years.
ACCREDITATIONS: WJ

Wingate College

Wingate, NC 28174
(704) 233-8128

Will confirm attendance and degree by phone or mail. Inquiry must include student's name, social security number, years attended. Employers may obtain transcripts upon written request accompanied by a $2.00 fee and a signed release from the student. Requests should be sent to: Attn: Registrar's Office.

A general baccalaureate institution, with an enrollment of 1,700. Highest level of offering: four or five year baccalaureate.
ACCREDITATIONS: SC MAC MUS

Winona State University

Winona, MN 55987
(507) 457-5030

Will confirm attendance and degree by phone or mail. Inquiry must include student's name, social security number. Employers may obtain transcripts upon written request accompanied by a signed release from the student.

A comprehensive institution with no medical school, with an enrollment of 7,650. Highest level of offering: beyond master's but less than doctorate.
ACCREDITATIONS: NH MUS NUR TED SW CHM

Winston–Salem State University

Winston-Salem, NC 27110
(919) 750-3330

Will confirm attendance and degree by phone or mail. Inquiry must include student's name, social security number, years attended. Employers may obtain transcripts upon written request accompanied by a $2.00 fee and a signed release from the student. Requests should be sent to: Attn: Registrar's Office.

A general baccalaureate institution, with an enrollment of 2,443. Highest level of offering: four or five year baccalaureate.
ACCREDITATIONS: SC MT MUS NUR TED

Winthrop College

101 A Tillman Bldg.–Oakland Avenue
Rock Hill, SC 29733
(803) 323-2195
Fax (803) 323-2855

Will confirm attendance and degree by mail. Inquiry must include student's name, social security number, years attended. Employers may obtain transcripts upon written request accompanied by a $2.00 fee and a signed release from the student.

A comprehensive institution with no medical school, with an enrollment of 5,018. Highest level of offering: beyond master's but less than doctorate.
ACCREDITATIONS: SC ART BUS FIDER MUS SW TED

Wisconsin Conservatory of Music

1584 North Prospect Avenue
Milwaukee, WI 53202
(414) 276-5760

Will confirm attendance and degree by phone or mail. Inquiry must include student's name, social security number, years attended. Employers may obtain transcripts upon written request accompanied by a $3.00 fee and a signed release from the student.

A music school, with an enrollment of 1,800. Highest level of offering: master's.
ACCREDITATIONS: MUS

Wisconsin Indianhead Technical College in Superior

Attn: Educational Services
600 N. 21st Street
Superior, WI 54880
(715) 394-6677

Will confirm attendance and degree by phone or mail. Inquiry must include student's name, social security number, years attended, request. Employers may obtain transcripts upon written request accompanied by a signed release from the student.

A multiprogram two-year institution, with an enrollment of 860. Highest level of offering: two years but less than four years.
ACCREDITATIONS: NH

Wisconsin Indianhead Technical Institute in Ashland

2100 Beaser Ave
Ashland, WI 54806
(715) 682-4591

Will confirm attendance and degree by phone or mail. Inquiry must include student's name, social security number. Employers may obtain transcripts upon written request accompanied by a signed release from the student.

A multiprogram two-year institution, with an enrollment of 250. Highest level of offering: one year but less than four years.
ACCREDITATIONS: NCA

Wisconsin Indianhead Technical Institute in New Richmond

1019 South Knowlef
New Richmond, WI 54017
(715) 246-6561

Will confirm attendance and degree by phone or mail. Inquiry must include student's name, social security number, address. Employers may obtain transcripts upon written request accompanied by a $1.00 fee and a signed release from the student.

A multiprogram two-year institution, with an enrollment of 1,000. Highest level of offering: one year but less than four years.
ACCREDITATIONS: NH

Wisconsin Indianhead Technical Institute in Rice Lake

Attn: Student Services
1900 College Drive
Rice Lake, WI 54868
(715) 234-7082

Will confirm attendance and degree by phone or mail. Inquiry must include student's name, social security number, years attended, request. Employers may obtain transcripts upon written request accompanied by a $1.00 fee and a signed release from the student.

A multiprogram two-year institution, with an enrollment of 600. Highest level of offering: one year but less than four years.
ACCREDITATIONS: NH

Wisconsin Lutheran College

8800 West Bluemond Road
Milwaukee, WI 53226
(414) 774-8620 Ext. 17
Fax (414) 774-7560

Will confirm attendance and degree by phone, fax or mail. Inquiry must include student's name, social security number. Employers may obtain transcripts upon written request accompanied by a $2.00 fee and a signed release from the student.

A general baccalaureate institution, with an enrollment of 300. Highest level of offering: baccalaureate.
ACCREDITATIONS: NCA

Wisconsin School of Electronics

1227 North Sherman Avenue
Madison, WI 53704
(608) 249-6611
Fax (608) 249-8593

Will confirm attendance and degree by phone or mail. Inquiry must include student's name, years attended. Employers may obtain transcripts upon written request accompanied by a signed release from the student. Requests should be sent to: Attn: Registrar's Office.

A single program two-year institution, with an enrollment of 421. Highest level of offering: one year but less than four years.
ACCREDITATIONS: NATTS

Wisconsin School of Professional Psychology

9120 W. Hampton Ave., Suite 212
Milwaukee, WI 53225
(414) 464-9777

Will confirm attendance and degree by phone or mail. Inquiry must include student's name, date of birth. Employers may obtain transcripts upon written request accompanied by a $3.00 fee and a signed release from the student.

A bachelor's or higher institution newly admitted to NCES, with an enrollment of 70. Highest level of offering: doctorate.

ACCREDITATIONS: NH

Wittenberg University

PO Box 720
Springfield, OH 45501
(513) 327-6131
Fax (513) 327-6340

Will confirm attendance and degree by phone or mail. Inquiry must include student's name, social security number, years attended. Employers may obtain transcripts upon written request accompanied by a $2.00 fee and a signed release from the student. Requests should be sent to: Attn: Registrar's Office.

A general baccalaureate institution, with an enrollment of 2,183. Highest level of offering: four year baccalaureate.

ACCREDITATIONS: NH MUS RAD TED

Wofford College

429 North Church Street
Spartanburg, SC 29303-3663
(803) 597-4030

Will confirm attendance and degree by mail. Inquiry must include student's name, years attended. Employers may obtain transcripts upon written request by student accompanied by a $2.00 fee.

A general baccalaureate institution, with an enrollment of 1,100. Highest level of offering: four or five year baccalaureate.

ACCREDITATIONS: SC

Wood Junior College

R R 2 Box C
Mathiston, MS 39752
(601) 263-8128 Ext. 22
Fax (601) 263-4964

Will confirm attendance and degree by phone or mail. Inquiry must include student's name, social security number, years attended. Employers may obtain transcripts upon written request accompanied by a $2.00 fee and a signed release from the student.

A multiprogram two-year institution, with an enrollment of 550. Highest level of offering: two year associate degree.

ACCREDITATIONS: SACS

Woodbury University

PO Box 7846 Burbank
Los Angeles, CA 91510-7846
(818) 767-0888 Ext. 271
Fax (818) 504-9320

Will confirm attendance and degree by phone, fax or mail. Inquiry must include student's name, date of birth, social security number, years attended. Employers may obtain transcripts upon written request accompanied by a $5.00 fee and a signed release from the student.

A multiprogram insitution, with an enrollment of 950. Highest level of offering: master's.

ACCREDITATIONS: WC FIDER

Wor–Wic Tech Community College

30 Wesley Drive
Salisbury, MD 21801
(301) 749-8181

Will confirm attendance and degree by phone or mail. Inquiry must include student's name, years attended. Employers may obtain transcripts upon written request accompanied by a $1.00 fee and a signed release from the student.

A multiprogram two-year institution, with an enrollment of 1,247. Highest level of offering: one year but less than four years.

ACCREDITATIONS: M RAD

Worcester Junior College

c/o Nichols College
Dudley, MA 01571-5000

Will confirm attendance and degree by phone or mail. Inquiry must include student's name, social security number. Employers may obtain transcripts upon written request accompanied by a $10.00 fee and a signed release from the student.

Worcester Polytechnic Institute

100 Institute Road
Worcester, MA 01609
(508) 831-5202

Will confirm attendance and degree by phone or mail. Inquiry must include student's name, date of birth, social security number, years attended. Employers may obtain transcripts upon written request accompanied by a $2.00 fee and a signed release from the student. Requests should be sent to: Attn: Registrar's Office.

An engineering school, with an enrollment of 3,812. Highest level of offering: doctorate.

ACCREDITATIONS: EH ENG

Worcester State College

486 Chandler Street
Worcester, MA 01602
(617) 793-8035

Will confirm attendance and degree by phone or mail. Inquiry must include student's name, social security number, years attended. Employers may obtain transcripts upon written request accompanied by a $1.00 fee and a signed release from the student.

A comprehensive institution with no medical school, with an enrollment of 7,062. Highest level of offering: beyond master's but less than doctorate.

ACCREDITATIONS: EH AUD NMT NUR TED

World College West

101 South San Antonio Road
Petaluma, CA 94952
(707) 765-4500

Will confirm attendance and degree by phone or mail. Inquiry must include student's name, social security number, years attended. Requests should be directed to: Records Office. Employers may obtain transcripts upon written request accompanied by a $10.00 fee and a signed release from the student.

A general baccalaureate institution, with an enrollment of 120. Highest level of offering: four or five year baccalaureate.

ACCREDITATIONS: WC

Worthington Community College

1450 Collegeway
Worthington, MN 56187
(507) 372-2107 Ext. 203
Fax (507) 372-5801

Will confirm attendance and degree by phone, fax or mail. Inquiry must include student's name, social security number. Employers may obtain transcripts upon written request accompanied by a signed release from the student.

A multiprogram two-year institution, with an enrollment of 639. Highest level of offering: one year but less than four years.

ACCREDITATIONS: NH

Wright State University Lake Campus

7600 State Route 703
Celina, OH 45822
(419) 586-2365 Ext. 224

Will confirm attendance and degree by phone or mail. Inquiry must include student's name, social security number. Employers may obtain transcripts upon written request accompanied by a $3.00 fee and a signed release from the student.

A multiprogram two-year institution, with an enrollment of 868. Highest level of offering: one year but less than four years.

ACCREDITATIONS: NH

Wright State University Main Campus

Colonel Glenn Highway
Dayton, OH 45435
(513) 873-2451
Fax (513) 873-3301

Will confirm attendance and degree by phone, fax or mail. Inquiry must include student's name, social security number. Employers may obtain transcripts upon written request accompanied by a $3.00 fee and a signed release from the student.

A comprehensive institution with a medical school, with an enrollment of 17,000. Highest level of offering: doctorate.

ACCREDITATIONS: NH BUS CLPSY ENG IPSY MED MT MUS NUR SW TED

Wright State University Lake Campus

7600 State Route 703
Celina, OH 45822
(419) 586-2365 Ext. 224

Will confirm attendance and degree by phone or mail. Inquiry must include student's name, social security number. Requests should be directed to: Registrar's Office. Employers may obtain transcripts upon written request accompanied by a $3.00 fee and a signed release from the student.

A multiprogram two-year institution, with an enrollment of 800 Highest level of offering: one year but less than four years.
ACCREDITATIONS: NH

Wytheville Community College

1000 East Main Street
Wytheville, VA 24382
(703) 228-5541 Ext. 216
Fax (703) 228-6506

Will confirm attendance and degree by phone or mail. Inquiry must include student's name, social security number. Employers may obtain transcripts upon written request accompanied by a signed release from the student. Requests should be directed to: Record & Admissions Office.

A multiprogram two-year institution, with an enrollment of 1,584. Highest level of offering: one year but less than four years.
ACCREDITATIONS: SC ADNUR DA MLTAD

Xavier University of Louisiana

7325 Palmetto Street
New Orleans, LA 70125
(504) 486-7411 Ext. 7583

Will confirm attendance and degree by phone or mail. Inquiry must include student's name, social security number, years attended. Employers may obtain transcripts upon written request accompanied by a $2.00 fee and a signed release from the student.

A general baccalaureate institution, with an enrollment of 3,100. Highest level of offering: ph.d.
ACCREDITATIONS: SACS MUS PHAR

Xavier University

3800 Victory Parkway
Cincinnati, OH 45207
(513) 745-3941
Fax (513) 745-2969

Will confirm attendance and degree by phone or mail. Inquiry must include student's name, social security number, date of birth, years attended. Employers may obtain transcripts upon written request accompanied by a $5.00 fee and a signed release from the student.

A comprehensive institution with no medical school, with an enrollment of 6,785. Highest level of offering: master's.
ACCREDITATIONS: NCA HSA NUR RAD SW

Yakima Valley Community College

PO Box 1647
Yakima, WA 98907
(509) 575-2372
Fax (509) 575-2461

Will confirm attendance and degree by phone, fax or mail. Inquiry must include student's name, date of birth, social security number, years attended. Employers may obtain transcripts upon written request accompanied by a $1.00 fee, or a $2.00 fee for a faxed transcript, and a signed release from the student.

A multiprogram two-year institution, with an enrollment of 3,426. Highest level of offering: two years but less than four years.
ACCREDITATIONS: NW ADNUR DH PNUR RAD

Yale University

Yale Station Box 1504A
New Haven, CT 06520
(203) 432-2750 or 430-2777

Will confirm attendance and degree by phone or mail. Inquiry must include student's name, social security number, years attended. Employers may obtain transcripts upon written request accompanied by a $3.00 fee and a signed release from the student.

A doctoral-level institution with a medical school, with an enrollment of 10,749. Highest level of offering: doctorate.
ACCREDITATIONS: EH APCP ARCH CLPSY ENG FOR HSA IPSY LAW MED MUS NUR THEOL PH MIDWF

Yankton College

PO Box 133
Yankton, SD 57078
(605) 665-3661

Will confirm attendance and degree by phone or mail. Inquiry must include student's name, date of birth, social security number, years attended. Employers may obtain transcripts upon written request accompanied by a $5.00 fee and a signed release from the student. Requests should be addressed to: Attn: Records Services

A general baccalaureate institution. Highest level of offering: four or five year baccalaureate.
ACCREDITATIONS: MUS

Yavapai College

1100 East Sheldon Street
Prescott, AZ 86301
(602) 445-7300 Ext. 2150

Will confirm attendance and degree by phone or mail. Inquiry must include student's name, social security number, years attended. Employers may obtain transcripts upon written request by student accompanied by a $2.00 fee.

A multiprogram two-year institution, with an enrollment of 3,500. Highest level of offering: one year but less than four years.
ACCREDITATIONS: NH ADNUR

YDI Schools

c/o Main Maritime Academy
Student Records Office
Castine, Maine 04420
(207) 326-4311

Will confirm attendance and degree by phone or mail. Inquiry must include student's name. Employers may obtain transcripts upon written request accompanied by a $2.50 fee and a signed release from the student. Requests should be directed to Registrar's Office.

A two-year institution newly admitted to NCES. Highest level of offering: one year but less than four years.
ACCREDITATIONS: EV NHSC

Yeshiva Beth Hillel of Krasna

1366 42nd Street
Brooklyn, NY 11219
(718) 438-3535

Will confirm attendance and degree by mail. Inquiry must include student's name, social security number, years attended, release. Employers may obtain transcripts upon written request accompanied by a signed release from the student.

A specialized non-degree granting institution, with an enrollment of 25. Highest level of offering: undergraduate non-degree granting.
ACCREDITATIONS: RABN

Yeshiva Bnei Torah

737 Elvira Avenue
Far Rockaway, NY 11691
(718) 337-6419 or 327-9307

Will confirm attendance and degree by mail. Inquiry must include student's name, social security number. Employers may obtain transcripts upon written request accompanied by a signed release from the student.

A specialized non-degree granting institution, with an enrollment of 26. Highest level of offering: graduate non-degree granting.
ACCREDITATIONS: RABN

Yeshiva Chofetz Chaim Radun

24 Highview Road
Suffern, NY 10901
(914) 357-9821

Will confirm attendance and degree by mail. Inquiry must include student's name, social security number. Employers may obtain transcripts upon written request accompanied by a signed release from the student.

A specialized non-degree granting institution, with an enrollment of 37. Highest level of offering: undergraduate non-degree granting.

ACCREDITATIONS: 3IC

Yeshiva Derech Chaim

1573 39th Street
Brooklyn, NY 11218
(718) 438-3070 or 435-9285

Will confirm attendance and degree by mail. Inquiry must include student's name, social security number. Employers may obtain transcripts upon written request accompanied by a signed release from the student.

A bachelor's or higher institution newly admitted to NCES, with an enrollment of 150. Highest level of offering: first professional degree.

ACCREDITATIONS: RABN

Yeshiva Karlin Stolin

1818 54th Street
Brooklyn, NY 11204
(718) 232-7800
Fax (718) 331-4833

Will confirm attendance and degree by mail. Inquiry must include student's name, social security number, release. Employers may obtain transcripts upon written request accompanied by a signed release from the student.

A school of philosophy, religion and theology, with an enrollment of 84. Highest level of offering: first professional degree.

ACCREDITATIONS: RABN

Yeshiva of Nitra Rabbinical College

194 Division Avenue
Brooklyn, NY 11211
(718) 384-5460

Will confirm attendance and degree by mail. Inquiry must include student's name, date of birth, release. Employers may obtain transcripts upon written request accompanied by a signed release from the student.

A specialized non-degree granting institution, with an enrollment of 180. Highest level of offering: graduate non-degree granting.

ACCREDITATIONS: RABN

Yeshiva Ohel Shmuel

165 Haines Road
Bedford Hills, NY 10507
(914) 241-2700
Fax (914) 666-0280

Will confirm attendance and degree by mail or fax. Inquiry must include student's name, social security number, years attended. Employers may obtain transcripts upon written request accompanied by . signed release from the student

A specialized non-degree granting institution, with an enrollment of 38. Highest level of offering: four or five year baccalaureate.

ACCREDITATIONS: RABN

Yeshiva Ohr Elchonon Chabad/West Coast Talmudical Seminary

7215 Waring Avenue
Los Angeles, CA 90046
(213) 937-3763

Will confirm attendance and degree by mail. Inquiry must include student's name, years attended. Requests should be directed to: Administrative Assistant. Employers may obtain transcripts upon written request accompanied by a signed release from the student.

A bachelor's or higher institution newly admitted to NCES, with an enrollment of 48. Highest level of offering: four or five year baccalaureate.

ACCREDITATIONS: RABN

Yeshiva Shaar Hatorah

83-96 117th Street
Kew Gardens, NY 11418
(718) 846-1940

Will confirm attendance and degree by phone or mail. Inquiry must include student's name, years attended. Employers may obtain transcripts upon written request accompanied by a signed release from the student.

A specialized non-degree granting institution, with an enrollment of 100. Highest level of offering: undergraduate non-degree granting.

ACCREDITATIONS: RABN

Yeshiva Toras Chaim Talmudical Seminary

1400 Quitman Street
Denver, CO 80204
(303) 629-8200
Fax (303) 623-5949

Will confirm attendance and degree by mail. Inquiry must include student's name, social security number, release. Employers may obtain transcripts upon written request accompanied by a signed release from the student.

A school of philosophy, religion and theology, with an enrollment of 22. Highest level of offering: first professional degree.

ACCREDITATIONS: RABN

Yeshiva University of Los Angeles

9760 West Pico Boulevard
Los Angeles, CA 90035
(213) 553-4478 Ext. 264

Will confirm attendance and degree by phone or mail. Inquiry must include student's name, social security number. Requests should be directed to: Student Records. Employers may obtain transcripts with a signed release from the student.

A specialized non-degree granting institution, with an enrollment of 74. Highest level of offering: four or five year baccalaureate.

Yeshiva University

500 West 185th Street
New York, NY 10033
(212) 960-5400

Will confirm attendance and degree by mail. Inquiry must include student's name, date of birth, social security number, years attended, release. Employers may obtain transcripts upon written request accompanied by a $8.00 fee and a signed release from the student.

A doctoral-level institution with a medical school, with an enrollment of 5,000. Highest level of offering: doctorate.

ACCREDITATIONS: M CLPSY LAW MED NY SW

Yeshivat Mikdash Melech

1326 Ocean Parkway
Brooklyn, NY 11230
(718) 339-1090 Ext. 1126

Will confirm attendance and degree by phone or mail. Inquiry must include student's name, date of birth, social security number, years attended. Employers may obtain transcripts upon written request accompanied by a signed release from the student.

A specialized non-degree granting institution, with an enrollment of 29. Highest level of offering: undergraduate non-degree granting.

ACCREDITATIONS: RABN

Yeshivath Beth Moshe

930 Hickory Street
Scranton, PA 18505
(717) 346-1747

Will confirm attendance and degree by phone or mail. Inquiry must include student's name, social security number, years attended. Employers may obtain transcripts upon written request accompanied by a signed release from the student.

A school of philosophy, religion and theology, with an enrollment of 85. Highest level of offering: master's.

ACCREDITATIONS: RABN

Yeshivath Viznitz

PO Box 446
Monsey, NY 10952
(914) 356-1010

Will confirm attendance and degree by mail. Inquiry must include student's name, date of birth, social security number, years attended, release. Employers may obtain transcripts upon written request accompanied by a signed release from the student.

A specialized non-degree granting institution, with an enrollment of 295. Highest level of offering: graduate non-degree granting.

ACCREDITATIONS: RABN

Yeshivath Zichron Moshe

PO Box 580
South Fallsburg, NY 12779
(914) 434-5240
Fax (914) 434-1009

Will confirm attendance and degree by mail. Inquiry must include student's name, date of birth, social security number, years attended, release. Employers may obtain transcripts upon written request accompanied by a signed release from the student.

A specialized institution, with an enrollment of 119.
ACCREDITATIONS: RABN

York College of Pennsylvania

Country Club Road
York, PA 17405-7199
(717) 846-7788 Ext. 233

Will confirm attendance and degree by phone or mail. Inquiry must include student's name, date of birth, social security number, years attended, self addressed stamped envelope. Requests should be directed to: Registrar's Office. Employers may obtain transcripts upon written request accompanied by a $3.00 fee and a signed release from the student.

A general baccalaureate institution, with an enrollment of 5,000. Highest level of offering: master's.
ACCREDITATIONS: M MRA NUR RSTH RSTHT

York College

9th & Kiplinger Avenue
York, NE 68467-2699
(402) 362-4441 Ext. 203

Will confirm attendance and degree by phone or mail. Inquiry must include student's name, years attended, self addressed stamped envelope. Employers may obtain transcripts upon written request accompanied by a $5.00 fee and a signed release from the student.

A multiprogram two-year institution, with an enrollment of 395. Highest level of offering: one year but less than four years.
ACCREDITATIONS: NCA

York Technical College

452 S. Anderson Rd.
Rock Hill, SC 29730
(803) 327-8002
Fax (803) 327-8059

Will confirm attendance and degree by mail or fax. Inquiry must include student's name, date of birth, social security number, years attended, release. Employers may obtain transcripts upon written request accompanied by a signed release from the student. Requests should be directed to: Student Records.

A multiprogram two-year institution, with an enrollment of 2,563. Highest level of offering: one year but less than four years.
ACCREDITATIONS: SC DA ENGT MLTAD

Young Harris College

College Street
Young Harris, GA 30582
(404) 379-3111 Ext. 125

Will confirm attendance and degree by phone or mail. Inquiry must include student's name, date of birth, social security number, years attended. Requests should be directed to: Registrar's Office. Employers may obtain transcripts upon written request accompanied by a $2.00 fee and a signed release from the student.

A multiprogram two-year institution, with an enrollment of 482 Highest level of offering: one year but less than four years.
ACCREDITATIONS: SC

Youngstown College of Business and Professional Drafting
(See ITT Technical Institute)

Youngstown State University

410 Wick Avenue
Youngstown, OH 44555
(216) 742-3182
Fax (216) 742-1408

Will confirm attendance and degree by phone, fax or mail. Inquiry must include student's name, date of birth, social security number, years attended. Requests should be directed to: Records Department. Employers may obtain transcripts upon written request accompanied by a $5.00 fee and a signed release from the student.

A comprehensive institution with no medical school, with an enrollment of 15,000. Highest level of offering: master's.
ACCREDITATIONS: NH ADNUR DH ENG ENGT MLTAD MUS NUR RSTH RSTHT TED

Yuba College

2088 North Beale Road
Marysville, CA 95901
(916) 741-6700
Fax (916) 741-3541

Will confirm attendance and degree by mail. Inquiry must include student's name, date of birth, social security number, years attended, release. Requests should be directed to: Admissions Office. Employers may obtain transcripts upon written request accompanied by a $3.00 fee and a signed release from the student.

A multiprogram two-year institution, with an enrollment of 11,000. Highest level of offering: two years but less than four years.
ACCREDITATIONS: WJ ADVET RAD

BLANK PAGE

GUIDE TO BACKGROUND INVESTIGATIONS